2001

University of St. Francis Library

3 0301 00210216 4

W9-DDD-245

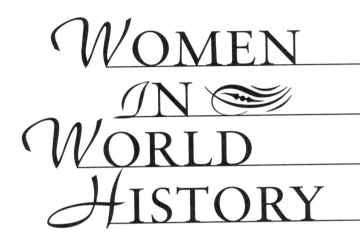

# WOMEN IN WORLD HISTORY

## A Biographical Encyclopedia

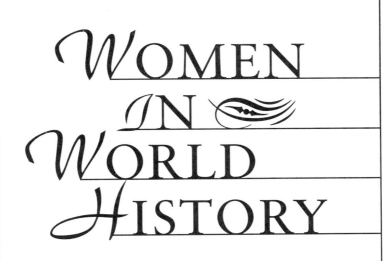

# Women in World History

## A Biographical Encyclopedia

VOLUME
**14**
Schu-Sui

Anne Commire, Editor
Deborah Klezmer, Associate Editor

**YORKIN PUBLICATIONS**

**GALE GROUP**

★

**THOMSON LEARNING**

*Detroit • New York • San Diego • San Francisco*
*Boston • New Haven, Conn. • Waterville, Maine*
*London • Munich*

LIBRARY
UNIVERSITY OF ST. FRANCIS
JOLIET, ILLINOIS

# Yorkin Publications

Anne Commire, *Editor*
Deborah Klezmer, *Associate Editor*
Barbara Morgan, *Assistant Editor*

Eileen O'Pasek, Gail Schermer, Patricia Coombs, James Fox,
Catherine Cappelli, Karen Rikkers, *Editorial Assistants*
Karen Walker, *Assistant for Genealogical Charts*

Special acknowledgment is due to Peg Yorkin who made this project possible.

Thanks also to Karin and John Haag, Bob Schermer, and to
the Gale Group staff, in particular Dedria Bryfonski, Linda Hubbard, John Schmittroth, Cynthia Baldwin,
Tracey Rowens, Randy Bassett, Christine O'Bryan, Rebecca Parks, and especially Sharon Malinowski.

## The Gale Group

Sharon Malinowski, *Senior Editor*
Rebecca Parks, *Editor*
Laura Brandau, *Assistant Editor*
Linda S. Hubbard, *Managing Editor*

Margaret A. Chamberlain, *Permissions Specialist*
Mary K. Grimes, *Image Cataloger*

Mary Beth Trimper, *Production Director*
Evi Seoud, *Assistant Production Manager*

Cynthia Baldwin, *Product Design Manager*
Tracey Rowens, *Cover and Page Designer*
Michael Logusz, *Graphic Artist*

Barbara Yarrow, *Graphic Services Manager*
Randy Bassett, *Image Database Supervisor*
Dan Newell, *Imaging Specialist*
Christine O'Bryan, *Graphics Desktop Publisher*
Dan Bono and Ryan Cartmill, *Technical Support*

While every effort has been made to ensure the reliability of the information presented in this publication, Yorkin Publications and the Gale Group do not guarantee the accuracy of the data contained herein. No payment for listing was accepted, and inclusion in the publication of any organization, agency, institution, publication, service, or individual does not imply endorsement of the editors or publishers. Errors brought to the attention of the publishers and verified to the satisfaction of the publishers will be corrected in future editions.

This publication is a creative work fully protected by all applicable copyright laws, as well as by misappropriation, trade secret, unfair competition, and other applicable laws. The authors and editors of this work have added value to the underlying factual material herein through one or more of the following: unique and original selection, coordination, expression, arrangement, and classification of the information.

Copyright © 2002
Yorkin Publications
Waterford, CT

All rights reserved including the right of reproduction in whole or in part in any form.
All rights to this publication will be vigorously defended.

Gale Group, Inc.
27500 Drake Road
Farmington Hills, MI 48331-3535

Gale Group and Design is a trademark used herein under license.

Library of Congress Catalog Card Number 99-24692
A CIP record is available from the British Library

ISBN 0-7876-4073-5
Printed in the United States of America.

**Library of Congress Cataloging-in-Publication Data**

Women in world history : a biographical encyclopedia / Anne Commire, editor, Deborah Klezmer, associate editor.
    p. cm.
    Includes bibliographical references and index.
    ISBN 0-7876-3736-X (set). — ISBN 0-7876-4069-7 (v. 10). —
    ISBN 0-7876-4070-0 (v. 11) — ISBN 0-7876-4071-9 (v. 12) — ISBN 0-7876-4072-7 (v. 13) — ISBN 0-7876-4073-5 (v. 14)
        1. Women—History Encyclopedias. 2. Women—Biography Encyclopedias.
    I. Commire, Anne. II. Klezmer, Deborah.
        HQ1115.W6 1999
        920.72'03—DC21                                                                                              99-24692

10 9 8 7 6 5 4 3 2 1

R
920.7203
W872
v. 14

**Schuch, Clara Bohm** (1879–1936).
*See Bohm-Schuch, Clara.*

## Schulenburg, Ehrengard Melusina von der (1667–1743)

*Duchess of Kendal and influential paramour of George I. Name variations: Ehrengard Melusine von der Schulemburg; Ermengarde Melusina von der Schulenburg, baroness Schulenburg; duchess of Munster; known as Melusine. Born in 1667; died in 1743 (some sources cite 1746); daughter of Gustavus Adolphus, Baron Schulenburg; had liaison (maîtresse en titre) with George I, king of England; children: (with George I) three daughters: Anna Louise (b. 1682); Petronilla Melusina, baroness of Aldborough (b. around 1693); Margaret Gertrude of Schulenburg (b. 1703).*

Ehrengard Melusina von der Schulenburg, known as Melusine, came to Great Britain in 1714 as the paramour of its newly crowned king, George I, the first in a succession of Hanoverian monarchs who would rule England after the Glorious Revolution of 1688. Described by wits of the day as "the maypole" because she was tall and slim, Schulenburg was notoriously unpopular with the British public, who despised her quest for titles and money. Despite being an object of ridicule to courtiers vying for power and influence in early 18th-century England, she was also a necessary and useful ally to those hoping to curry favor with the king.

George I had many mistresses, but Schulenburg is generally considered to have been his favorite. They had three daughters together, though George could never acknowledge their paternity without jeopardizing the terms of his divorce from his wife *Sophia Dorothea of Brunswick-Celle, who remained a virtual captive in Hanover. Even Sir Robert Walpole, later England's first prime minister, regarded Schulenburg as the unofficial queen. While providing George with the stability of a domestic life, Schulenburg still managed to look out for her own future and that of her daughters by parlaying her influence with the king into titles. Her position as the king's mistress made her a formidable presence in England's royal court: she damaged Secretary of State Charles Townsend's authority as well as that of his ally Walpole when, in response to her request for a title, they could muster only an Irish peerage, making her duchess of Munster. On the other hand, she granted their political rivals Charles Spencer and Lord James Stanhope important access to the king as a reward for their successful scheme to make her duchess of Kendal—a much more prominent and noble title.

The fortunes of the British court in the early 18th century were hardly stable, however, and after Schulenburg became involved in the failed speculations of the South Sea Company, she quickly learned to work with those who could save her reputation. The South Sea scandal erased Spencer's and Stanhope's influence in court, so Schulenburg switched her allegiance to Townsend and Walpole. Their efforts to minimize her role in the company's demise earned them her gratitude, and she worked on their behalf to establish a stable administration. Towards the end of George's reign, Schulenburg's position in the royal court was so ingrained that she was not threatened by his dalliance with the much younger **Anne Brent**, who posed no risk to her standing. George's death on June 11, 1727, brought on a period of intense grieving for Schulenburg. According to one account, she thought that George returned to her as a bird she tamed with crumbs. Ehrengard Melusina von der Schulenburg remained in England until her death in 1743.

**SOURCES:**
Carlton, Charles. *Royal Mistresses*. London: Routledge, 1990.

**Bonnie Burns**, Ph.D.,
Cambridge, Massachusetts

## Schüler, Else Lasker (1869–1945).
*See Lasker-Schüler, Else.*

# Schultz, Sigrid (1893–1980)

*American journalist and author. Name variations: (pseudonym) John Dickson. Born Sigrid Lillian Schultz in Chicago, Illinois, on January 5, 1893; died in Westport, Connecticut, on May 14, 1980; daughter of Herman Schultz (a portrait painter) and Hedwig (Jaskewitz) Schultz; attended the Lycée Racine in Paris; graduated from the Sorbonne in Paris, 1914; studied international law at Berlin University; never married; no children.*

*Witnessed the rise of the Nazi party (1920s–1930s); despite threats and intimidation, remained in Berlin in early years of World War II (1939–41), reporting on the Nazi regime; conducted interviews with Hermann Goering and Adolf Hitler; under an assumed name, filed stories that exposed concentration camps, the persecution of Jews, and other Nazi brutalities; wrote* Germany Will Try It Again *(1944).*

Sigrid Schultz was born in Chicago during the 1893 World's Fair, the daughter of **Hedwig Jaskewitz Schultz** and Herman Schultz, a Norwegian-American artist who had been commissioned to paint an official portrait of Chicago mayor Carter H. Harrison, Jr., in honor of the event. Sigrid attended school in Chicago until 1911, when she accompanied her family to Europe after her father was invited to paint William II, the king of Wurttemberg. The Schultzes remained in Europe while Herman continued to paint portraits of diplomats, royals, society beauties, and the wealthy. Sigrid, who spoke five languages fluently, attended the Lycée Racine in Paris and graduated from the Sorbonne in 1914. That year, she traveled with her family to Germany and witnessed Kaiser Wilhelm II's authorization of his nation's entrance into World War I, sending his army into Belgium en route to France. By virtue of their American citizenship, the Schultzes maintained their neutral status until the United States entered the war in 1917. Declared enemy aliens at that time, they were required to report daily to the German police. Work was scarce and food was scarcer. Schultz, who was studying international law at Berlin University, was energetic and versatile in helping her parents. She earned money by acting as an interpreter for the mayor of Baghdad, a fellow classmate who spoke no German, attending classes with him and translating the material into French.

After the war ended, Schultz found employment in 1919 at the Berlin office of the *Chicago Tribune*, working for Richard Henry Little, the *Tribune*'s Berlin correspondent. Little originally hired her as his assistant and secretary, but when he was asked by the newspaper's publisher, Robert R. McCormick, to obtain the German version of the inconclusive 1916 Battle of Jutland (the anti-Anglo McCormick mistrusted the English version of events), Schultz took it upon herself to help. Ignoring a policy that women were not allowed to enter by the front door, she marched into the German Navy office and disarmed authorities with her wit and charm. Her defiance worked, and the Navy granted Little an interview. Schultz would continue to pursue stories doggedly until she earned the notice, and finally the respect, of editors at the *Tribune*. Her earliest exclusive was an interview with Friedrich Ebert, the first president of the new Weimar Republic. When she heard that Ebert had been admitted to a private clinic, she managed to be admitted as a patient as well. Most reporters believed the hospital stay was for a routine procedure; Schultz broke the story that Ebert was dying from a ruptured appendix, and secured her reputation as a "newspaperman," a term she preferred throughout her life.

Elected a member of the board of directors of Berlin's Foreign Press Club in 1924, the first woman journalist so honored, Schultz was named bureau chief of the *Tribune*'s Berlin office in 1925. Five years earlier, she had witnessed the Kapp *putsch*, one of the initial stirrings of the Nazi movement, and she was one of the first foreign correspondents to warn readers about the Nazi threat. When she met Adolf Hitler in 1930, she was immediately aware of, and repelled by, his charismatic power. "As was his habit," she wrote, "Hitler grabbed my hand in both of his hands and tried to look soulfully into my eyes, which made me shudder, and Hitler sensed it." Her early understanding of the dire threat posed both by the nascent Nazi Party and Hitler himself stood in marked contrast to the opinions of a number of other intelligent, seasoned observers, among them her fellow Berlin journalist *Dorothy Thompson, who after interviewing him in 1931 would write of Hitler as "a man of startling insignificance."

Schultz's uncanny ability to predict the political climate in Berlin, both before and during the war, was due in part to her talents as a host, a job for which her cosmopolitan upbringing suited her perfectly. Petite and blonde, impeccably dressed, fluent in the languages of diplomacy and a gourmet cook besides, Schultz attracted some of the most influential leaders of the day to her parties, where she listened attentively to their boasting. (International business and artistic luminaries also attended her fêtes, among them the

irascible *Katherine Anne Porter, who apparently did not like her.) One of Schultz's more infamous guests was Hermann Goering, who later became Hitler's second-in-command. Goering, whom she described as a Nazi with table manners, proved to be a dangerous source of information. In 1935, he developed a plan to entrap foreign correspondents by giving them false military reports; as soon as the reports were in the journalists' possession, he would arrest them and put them on trial for espionage. But Schultz and other correspondents were forewarned of the scheme. While she was at work one day, her mother called to tell her that a man had just delivered an unmarked envelope to her home; Schultz rushed home and burned the envelope. Minutes later, the same man came to arrest her, writes **Julia Edwards**, but Schultz "told him not to bother, she had destroyed the evidence." She later confronted Goering at a luncheon honoring him and his new bride **Emmy Sonnemann (Goering)**, making it clear that she would not be intimidated. Said Goering: "You'll never learn to show proper respect for state authorities. I sup-

pose that is one of the characteristics of people from that crime-ridden city of Chicago."

In August 1939, Schultz reported what she considered to be her greatest story, the non-aggression pact between Soviet Russia and the Nazis, an alliance that shocked the world and paved the way for World War II. She was also one of the first to learn of the German invasion of Poland on September 1 of that year. She called William Shirer, CBS correspondent in Berlin, and said only two words: "It happened." Soon after, Britain declared war on Germany. For the next several years, Schultz remained in Berlin, contending with censorship and intimidation but still writing factual and controversial articles for the *Tribune*. Some of these, including the 1938–39 series "The Truth About Nazi Germany," were published under the pseudonym "John Dickson" because the information contained therein was so enraging to the Nazis. Schultz would often cross the border into Denmark or Norway to file uncensored dispatches, a risky undertaking that could have led to her arrest as a spy.

Sigrid
Schultz

As early as 1935, Schultz and some others reported on the existence of concentration camps, which at the time held more opponents of the regime and those deemed "misfits" by the Nazis than they did Jews. From then on through 1941, she reported on the Nazis' systematic and increasing aggression towards Jews, their dismantling of basic civil freedoms, and the blindly conciliatory attitude of some world leaders towards Hitler and his followers. "Schultz, of course, took care not to editorialize in the news columns," writes Edwards. Instead, she reported only facts and "succeeded in revealing," said Schultz, "a great number of terrible crimes the Nazis were committing." In 1940, she had been wounded by shrapnel from British bombs while traveling to the studio of the Mutual Broadcasting System where she worked as a radio newscaster. Her wounds did not stop her from going on the air, but the following year she contracted typhus. After returning to the United States, she wrote *Germany Will Try It Again*, a stern warning against what she feared was a growing attitude of sentimentality on the part of Americans toward Germany. "Wherever I went," wrote Schultz, "I was impressed by the number of well-meaning people who had been won to the German thesis that this War could have been avoided if 'we had been kinder to the Germans' after the last War." She tried to warn Americans of the existence of concentration camps and the plight of the Jews.

In 1943, Schultz returned to Europe as a war correspondent with the 1st and 3rd Armies and the Air Power Press Camp for the *Chicago Tribune*. In this capacity, she reported on the liberation of the concentration camps and the dental identification of the remains of Hitler, who with his mistress *Eva Braun had committed suicide in an underground bunker in April 1945. She also covered the Nuremberg war crimes trials, where her erstwhile party guest Goering was among those Nazis sentenced to death. (He committed suicide before he could be hanged.) Years later, when she was interviewed by the oral history library of the American Jewish Committee, she acknowledged that she had helped numerous Jews escape the Holocaust. Sigrid Schultz predicted the reunification of Germany and hoped that it would not be carried out under a militaristic regime. Honored with a copper plaque by the Overseas Press Club in 1969, she died in her home in Westport, Connecticut, on May 14, 1980.

**SOURCES:**
Belford, Barbara. *Brilliant Bylines*. NY: Columbia University Press, 1986.

Edwards, Julia. *Women of the World: The Great Foreign Correspondents*. NY: Houghton Mifflin, 1988, pp. 59–72.

Rothe, Anne, ed. *Current Biography 1944*. NY: H.W. Wilson, 1944.

**Bonnie Burns**, Ph.D.,
Cambridge, Massachusetts

# Schulze-Boysen, Libertas

## (1913–1942)

*German anti-Nazi activist, author, and actress who was a member of the "Red Orchestra" resistance circle. Name variations: Libertas Haas-Heye. Born Libertas Haas-Heye in Paris, France, on November 20, 1913; executed along with her husband on December 22, 1942; daughter of Professor Otto Haas-Heye (an architect) and Countess Thora Eulenburg; married Harro Schulze-Boysen (1909–1942), in 1936.*

Libertas Schulze-Boysen was born in Paris in 1913, the daughter of Professor Otto Haas-Heye, an architect, and Countess **Thora Eulenburg**, who was descended from a family with close ties to the Prussian court. Surrounded by aristocrats and members of the German leisure class, Libertas grew up in a luxurious environment on her father's family estate, Liebenberg. Intellectually adventurous and free-spirited, she was educated at exclusive private schools in Germany and Switzerland. She then worked from 1933 through 1935 in Berlin for the press department of Metro-Goldwyn-Mayer. In 1935, Schulze-Boysen became a freelance journalist, working first for the *National-Zeitung* of Essen. She later was employed by a cultural film organization closely associated with the Ministry of Popular Enlightenment and Propaganda of Joseph Goebbels. In 1936, Libertas married Harro Schulze-Boysen, who like herself came from a privileged family. Harro was concerned with social justice as well as with political and intellectual freedom. In 1933, as a member of a "conservative-revolutionary" circle, he had been arrested and tortured by the Nazis. After his release, he vowed to do all in his power to help end the Nazi dictatorship.

The opportunity for this came during World War II, when the Schulze-Boysens became leading members of the "Red Orchestra" spy organization that relayed crucial information from the Air Ministry to the Soviet Union. Libertas assisted her husband in his underground activities, including writing articles for the clandestine newspaper *Die Innere Front* and preparing pamphlets and flyers for distribution. With the help of several hundred anti-Nazis, this paper was distributed at immense risk in many of Germany's cities. Nazi intelligence, after immense effort, uncovered the large "Red Orchestra" network. Harro was arrested on August 30, 1942, Libertas a few days later on September 3. Both were taken to Prinz-Albrecht-Strasse 8, Berlin Gestapo headquarters, where they were interrogated and tortured. The Schulze-Boysens were sentenced to death and executed at Plötzensee prison on December 22, 1942. *Elisabeth Schumacher** was also killed that day.

**SOURCES:**

Biernat, Karl Heinz, and Luise Kraushaar. *Die Schulze-Boysen-Harnack-Organisation im antifaschistischen Kampf.* Berlin: Dietz, 1970.

Gollwitzer, Helmut, Käthe Kuhn, and Reinhold Schneider, eds. *Dying We Live: The Final Messages and Records of the Resistance.* NY: Pantheon, 1956.

Kraushaar, Luise. *Deutsche Widerstandskämpfer 1933–1945: Biographien und Briefe.* 2 vols. Berlin: Dietz, 1970.

Perrault, Gilles. *The Red Orchestra.* NY: Schocken, 1989.

Rürup, Reinhard. *Topographie der Terrors. Gestapo, SS und Reichssicherheitshauptamt auf dem "Prinz-Albrecht-Gelände": Eine Dokumentation.* 7th ed. Berlin: Verlag Willmuth Arenhövel, 1989.

**John Haag**, Associate Professor of History, University of Georgia, Athens, Georgia

# Schumacher, Elisabeth (1904–1942)

*German artist and anti-Nazi activist who was a member of the "Red Orchestra" resistance circle.*

*Born Elisabeth Hohenemser on April 28, 1904, in Darmstadt, Germany; executed along with her husband on December 22, 1942, at Berlin's Plötzensee prison; daughter of a prominent engineer; spent her childhood in Meiningen; married Kurt Schumacher (1905–42).*

Born in 1904 into a comfortable environment (her father was a prominent engineer) in Darmstadt, Elisabeth Schumacher spent her childhood in Meiningen. She completed her artistic training in Offenbach am Main, then moved to Berlin to work as a teacher of applied arts. There, she met Kurt Schumacher, a serious, gifted young sculptor who shared her socialist views.

Strongly anti-Nazi from the first days of the Hitler regime, and inspired by the underground work of Harro Schulze-Boysen and later *Libertas Schulze-Boysen*, the Schumachers created a clandestine organization impenetrable by spies or provocateurs. Their determination to fight against the regime was only strengthened in 1937, when Kurt's revered teacher, the master sculptor Ludwig Gies, was forced to quit the Prussian Academy of Arts. In protest, Kurt also severed his ties with what had become a subservient, almost Nazified, organization.

The start of World War II deepened the Schumachers' resolve to help bring about the destruction of the dictatorship. Their work for the

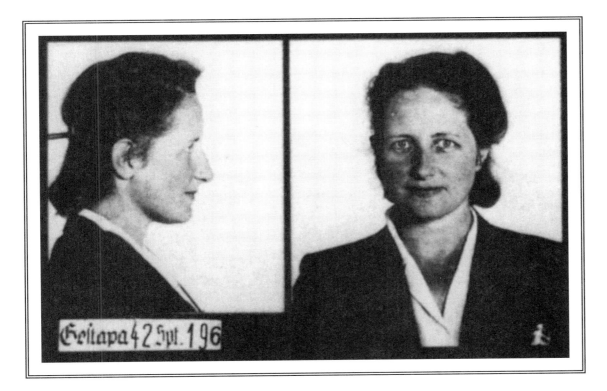

*Gestapo photograph of Elisabeth Schumacher, 1942.*

Berlin Communist underground now included providing materials for the "Red Orchestra" spy network led by their old friends the Schulze-Boysens and others, including Arvid and *Mildred Harnack. Elisabeth was able to provide important material from her job at the Reich Center for Labor Protection, while Kurt was involved in the task of sending illegal bulletins to soldiers at the front. Their increasingly dangerous existence reached its climax in August 1942 when they provided shelter for Albert Hössler, who had been trained in the Soviet Union to expand the activities of the Berlin organization. This was the Schumachers' last act of defiance of any consequence, for that September both were arrested when the "Red Orchestra" organization was smashed by the Gestapo. Sentenced to death, they were executed on the same day, December 22, 1942, at Berlin's Plötzensee prison, along with Harro and Libertas Schulze-Boysen, Arvid Harnack, and six other anti-Nazis. (Mildred Harnack would be executed the following year.)

In their fury, the Nazis destroyed most of Kurt Schumacher's sculpture, regarding it as "un-German" and symptomatic of the "Cultural Bolshevism" of the despised Weimar Republic. What did survive were some of his prison notes, hidden away in a secret recess of his cell in Plötzensee prison, which were discovered in 1946. One of his notes to his "brave Elisabeth," never received by her and dated November 30, 1942, ends with: "We very much wished to spare the German people from these terrible sufferings. Our small band fought with decency and courage."

**SOURCES:**

Arakelian, Avo. *Spuren der Ästhetik des Widerstands: Berliner Kunststudenten im Widerstand 1933–1945.* Berlin: Hochschule der Künste Berlin, 1984.

Biernat, Karl Heinz, and Luise Kraushaar. *Die Schulze-Boysen-Harnack-Organisation im antifaschistischen Kampf.* Berlin: Dietz, 1970.

Coppi, Hans. "Red Orchestra," in Wolfgang Benz and Walter H. Pehle, eds., *Encyclopedia of German Resistance to the Nazi Movement.* Translated by Lance W. Garmer. NY: Continuum, 1997, pp. 223–226.

———, Jürgen Danyel, and Johannes Tuchel, eds. *Die Rote Kapelle im Widerstand gegen Nationalsozialismus.* Berlin: Edition Hentrich, 1994.

Gostomski, Victor von, and Walter Loch. *Der Tod von Plötzensee: Erinnerungen, Ereignisse, Dokumente, 1942–1944.* Frankfurt am Main: bLoch, 1993.

Kraushaar, Luise, *et al. Deutsche Widerstandskämpfer 1933–1945: Biographien und Briefe.* 2 vols. Berlin: Dietz, 1970.

*Kunst zu Berlin 1648–1987. Staatliche Museen zu Berlin, Ausstellung im Alten Museum vom 10. Juni bis 25. Oktober 1987.* Berlin: Henschelverlag, 1987.

Perk, Willy, and Willi Desch. *Ehrenbuch der Opfer von Berlin-Plötzensee.* Berlin: Verlag Das Europäische Buch, 1974.

Rürup, Reinhard. *Topographie des Terrors: Gestapo, SS und Reichssicherheitshauptamt auf dem "Prinz-Albrecht-Gelände": Eine Dokumentation.* 7th ed. Berlin: Verlag Willmuth Arenhövel, 1989.

Wickert, Christl. *Frauen gegen die Diktatur—Widerstand und Verfolgung im nationalsozialistischen Deutschland.* Berlin: Edition Hentrich, 1995.

**John Haag,** Associate Professor of History, University of Georgia, Athens, Georgia

# Schumann, Clara (1819–1896)

*Famous German concert pianist, composer and music teacher, wife of the composer Robert Schumann, whose innovations in performance during a 60-year career helped to shape the standard modern-day piano repertory. Name variations: Clara Wieck. Born Clara Josephine Wieck in Leipzig, Germany, on September 13, 1819; died at Frankfurt am Main on May 20, 1896; daughter of Friedrich Wieck (a music teacher) and Marianne (Tromlitz) Wieck (a well-known singer); received only a few months of general education, then education in music from her father, and languages; married Robert Schumann (the composer), on September 12, 1840; children: Marie (b. 1841); Elise (b. 1843); Julie (b. 1845); Emil (1846–1847); Ludwig (b. 1848); Ferdinand (b. 1849); Eugenie (b. 1851); Felix (b. 1854).*

*Made performance debut at age nine (1828); during an extended tour in Austria, awarded the honorary position of chamber musician (K.k. Kammervirtuosin), generally reserved for established performers, in Vienna (1837); after marriage to Robert Schumann and despite the births of eight children, traveled to Russia, Denmark, France, and England to perform the music of Liszt, Rubinstein, Chopin, Schumann, and Brahms; appointed principal piano teacher at the Hoch Conservatory in Frankfurt (1878); made last public appearance (1891).*

During the 19th century, no pianist dominated the concert stage for a longer period than Clara Schumann. From her first public performance in 1828 until her 60th-year jubilee in 1888, Schumann's artistry continued to grow. On stage, she became a towering figure in the musical world, introducing some of the finest works of her day while also shaping what is now recognized as the standard piano repertoire; off stage, her teaching influenced generations of young performers.

Clara Josephine Wieck was born in Leipzig, Germany, on September 13, 1819, the oldest child in a musical family. Her father Friedrich Wieck supported the family through teaching music, operating a musical lending library, and handling the rental, sales and repair of pianos; her mother **Marianne Tromlitz** was a singer who performed frequently in the Leipzig Gewandhaus, and had also grown up in a musical family. Clara's great-grandfather, Johann George Tromlitz, had been a widely known flutist, teacher, and flute maker; her grandfather, George Christian Tromlitz, was a cantor. Clara had three brothers and a half-sister, Marie. Four months after her youngest brother's birth in January 1824, her mother requested a legal separation. Marianne was permitted to keep her young daughter with her until Clara's fifth birthday, when she was required by law to return her to her father. A year after the divorce, Marianne married Adolf Bargiel, a piano teacher and close family friend.

Although Schumann remained close to her mother, her father was the dominant figure in her life. Clara initially appeared to be a disappointment, as she did not speak until she was past four and was assumed to be hard of hearing. Despite this slow start, she proved to be an intelligent child, and Wieck, a brilliant, creative teacher whose methods continue to hold interest for piano pedagogues, wanted to use her musical gifts to validate his pedagogical approach. Schumann's general education was limited to a few months in a primary school, with eight additional months at a larger institute. She also studied languages in preparation for an international concert career. Most of the time, her days were devoted to studying the piano, with lessons also in theory, harmony, counterpoint, composition, singing, score reading and violin.

Wieck had definite ideas about the upbringing of female musicians, and he did not want his daughter performing the "feminine arts"; all his piano pupils were advised against sewing, knitting, or crocheting. Clara's domestic duties were kept as light as her study schedule was heavy. But Wieck also believed in addressing the needs of the whole pupil, and saw to it that she took long daily walks in the fresh air.

When Clara was nine, her father remarried, and her stepmother proved to be kind and loving. By that time, Schumann was an acknowledged child prodigy, who had played for Paganini and Goethe. In preparing her for a career, her father never doubted her ability or viewed her gender as a drawback.

Leipzig was a center for music, visited by many of Europe's leading musicians. Clara was still only nine when she met Robert Schumann at the home of friends. He was 18, and asked to study with Herr Wieck after hearing Clara play. About two years later, in October 1830, he

moved into the Wieck household as a boarder, and saw Clara daily. By 1833, when Clara was 14, she knew she was in love with him. When she was 15, Robert was briefly engaged to another of Wieck's pupils, **Ernestine von Fricken**, but this relationship was soon broken off. During the years 1832 to 1835, Robert Schumann composed some of his greatest works.

In 1832, Clara began a seven-month performance tour that included a lengthy stay in Paris. On April 28, 1833, she played part of a Schumann symphony, a first in the Leipzig Gewandhaus. She made tours of northern Germany in 1835, at age 16, and Leipzig also had an exceptional musical season that year, with visits by both Mendelssohn and Chopin. This was also the year that Robert first kissed her. When her father discovered their growing love, he was furious and forbade them to meet, fearing that marriage might end a brilliant career.

> $\mathcal{C}$lara Schumann . . . was the leading woman pianist of her age and was acknowledged as the peer of Liszt, Thalberg, and Anton Rubinstein.
>
> —Nancy B. Reich

In 1837, Clara Wieck won great acclaim for her appearance at the Royal Opera House in Berlin. Robert meanwhile did not give up his suit, and met her in secret. On October 15, 1837, Clara set off on a tour of Austria, where she risked playing new music by Liszt, Schumann, and Beethoven. In Vienna, her appearance was such a sensation that she was awarded the honorary position of chamber musician (*K.k. Kammervirtuosin*), generally reserved for much older performers.

As Herr Wieck continued to reject Robert's requests to marry his daughter, the couple finally decided to go to court for permission to marry without his consent. The lawsuit opened in July 1839. Although the court attempted to reconcile the parties, Wieck would have none of it and poured slander after slander on Robert's head; he also appropriated Clara's savings and refused her access to her personal belongings. In early 1840, the lawsuit was still unsettled, and Clara was under great strain when she began a new series of concerts. The court finally sanctioned the marriage on August 1 of that year, and the couple married on September 12, the day before the bride's 21st birthday. Severed from her father, Clara Schumann now faced combining marriage with a concert career, and although she continued to appear in concerts around Leipzig, her longer tours became increasingly rare.

The next few years were devoted mainly to Robert's compositions and to a growing family. Clara Schumann gave birth to eight children— **Marie Schumann** (b. 1841), **Elise Schumann** (b. 1843), **Julie Schumann** (b. 1845), Emil (1846–1847), Ludwig (b. 1848), Ferdinand (b. 1849), **Eugenie Schumann** (b. 1851) and Felix (b. 1854). In a marriage which combined two careers with so many children, it was inevitable that some conflicts would arise. Since Robert could not support his large family by composing, Clara performed to help meet their expenses. She had never intended to give up her performing career, but travel now meant finding care for the young children, as Robert, who hated being separated from his wife, traveled with her. During their 14-year marriage, while she managed to perform on innumerable concert stages, he was composing some of the world's most beautiful music. Over time it became clear, however, that he was not well. In 1854, Robert was hospitalized after attempting suicide, and he died in 1856 without regaining his mental health.

To support her family, Clara Schumann went back to extended touring, eager now to bring Robert's music to the world. Time and again her children were dispersed to the homes of devoted friends, boarding schools, pensions, and grandparents, while tours could mean missing birthdays, confirmations, and sometimes even Christmas. Fortunately her relationship with her mother continued to be close, and she was reconciled by this time with her father. Professionally, however, her life was complicated by the fact that concert managers and agents did not exist in the mid-19th century. Apart from being prepared to perform, Schumann was responsible for scheduling her concerts, renting the hall, providing light and heat, renting and tuning pianos, arranging for newspaper advertising, and printing the tickets and programs. Under these conditions, she played over 1,300 public programs in England and Europe throughout her long career.

Economies of time and money may have been behind some of Clara Schumann's most lasting innovations in the concert hall. Finding an orchestra, another of the tasks required of a performer, sometimes proved daunting, so she dispensed with the custom. She became one of the first soloists to play concerts without supporting artists and soon considered it preferable. There were also times, however, when she performed with some of Europe's great orchestras, and she also enjoyed playing with chamber groups and for sonata and lieder recitals. She also began to play by memory rather than reading from music during concerts, which was then unusual. Over time, her repertoire improved, with the dropping of flashy display pieces in favor of works by Mozart, Beethoven, Chopin, Mendelssohn, Schumann, and Brahms. Although these composers represent the standard repertoire today, in Schumann's era some were "modern," representing the avant-garde.

Schumann's children all assisted their mother, considering her "the greatest thing [they] possessed in all the world." Marie and Elise took over many household and musical tasks; Julie married at 23 and died of tuberculosis at 27, but Elise did not leave home for marriage until she was 34, and Eugenie remained until 40. Marie never left her mother. The lives of the sons were sadder: Ludwig was confined to an asylum in 1870; Felix, like Julie, died of tuberculosis; Ferdinand died in 1891, addicted to morphine due to chronic back pain, after which his mother assumed the financial support of his six children.

Clara Schumann wrote her first music while still a child, but as she grew older she found less time and energy for composing. After her marriage, she usually performed her husband's works rather than her own. Through her concerts, his compositions attained a much wider audience than they might otherwise have found. But Robert, the musical public, and reviewers all took Clara's compositions seriously. Although she was self-confident as a performer, she seemed less certain of her original works, and often needed Robert's encouragement to finish them. At the same time, she bridled if he attempted to change or revise a piece. Her insecurity is evident in an inscription to her husband on one of her creations which reads, "To my beloved husband, on 8 June 1853, a weak attempt from his old Clara."

In her late 40s, Schumann began to suffer from neuralgia and rheumatism, and she later grew deaf. Despite these infirmities, she continued to perform; her last public appearance would be in March 1891. In 1878, she embarked on a second career, becoming the full-time principal piano teacher at the Hoch Conservatory in Frankfurt; musicians from around the world flocked to study with her. Wrote Clement Harris, a Schumann student: "I am proud to be a Schumann-scholar now. I never would have dreamed how difficult it would be to get accepted to her class. Everyone in my generation is trying for it." Like her father, Clara Schumann was an excellent teacher; she mothered her students and followed their careers with great interest. Leonard Borwick, *Nathalie Janotha, *Ilona Eibenschütz, and *Adelina de Lara

Clara
Schumann

were among her outstanding students, and even today there are performers who trace their musical pedagogy back to her ways of training.

When Clara Schumann died on May 20, 1896, at age 77, she had dominated the concert stage for much of the 19th century. Despite the loss of her husband and four of her children, and despite her own illness and pain, she had met the challenges of supporting her large family, changed the style of performance on the concert stage, and won the respect of some of the century's greatest composers, including Felix Mendelssohn, Johannes Brahms, and her tragic, beloved husband.

**SOURCES:**

Brook, Donald. "Clara Schumann," in *Masters of the Keyboard*. London: Rockliff, 1947, pp. 81–95.

Burton, Anna. "Robert Schumann and Clara Wieck: a Creative Partnership," in *Music & Letters*. Vol. 69, no. 2. April 1988, pp. 211–227.

Chissell, Joan. *Clara Schumann: A Dedicated Spirit. A Study of her Life and Work*. NY: Taplinger, 1983.

———. *Schumann*. London: J.M. Dent, 1967.

Dubal, David. "Clara Schumann née Wieck," in *The Art of the Piano*. NY: Summit, 1989, pp. 236–238.

Harding, Bertita. *Concerto: The Story of Clara Schumann*. London: Harrap, 1962.

May, Florence. *The Girlhood of Clara Schumann: Clara Wieck and Her Time*. London: Edward Arnold, 1912.

Reich, Nancy B. *Clara Schumann: The Artist and the Woman*. Ithaca, NY: Cornell University Press, 1985.

———. "Clara Schumann," in *Women Making Music: The Western Art Tradition, 1150–1950*. Edited by Jane Bowers and Judith Tick. Chicago, IL: University of Illinois Press, 1986, pp. 249–281.

"Schumann, Clara Josephine (née Wieck)," in *International Encyclopedia of Women Composers*. 2nd ed. Edited by Aaron I. Cohen. Vol. II. NY: Books and Music USA, pp. 626–627.

**SUGGESTED READING:**

Nauhaus, Gerd, ed. *Marriage Diaries of Robert and Clara Schumann*. Trans. by Peter Ostwald. Northeastern University Press, 1993.

**John Haag**, Associate Professor of History,
University of Georgia, Athens, Georgia

# Schumann, Elisabeth (1885–1952)

*German soprano. Born in Merseburg, Thuringia, Germany, on June 13, 1885; died in New York on April 23, 1952; studied with Natalie Hänisch in Dresden, Marie Dietrich in Berlin, and Alma Schadow in Hamburg; married Karl Alwin (a conductor).*

*Debuted at the Hamburg Opera as the Shepherd in* Tannhäuser *(1909); made Metropolitan Opera debut (1914); was a principal member of the Vienna State Opera (1919–38); made Covent Garden debut (1924); lived in the United States and taught at the Curtis Institute of Music (from 1938); became an American citizen (1944).*

Possessed of a "a clear and high soprano of pure quality and agreeable timbre, a voice possessing the bloom of youth," Elisabeth Schumann became a highly popular opera singer from her debut in Hamburg in 1909. She had been born into a musical family in Thuringia, Germany, in 1885, to parents who recognized her talents and saw to it that she received sound training from childhood. She was also a descendant of \*Henriette Sontag, who had been the first solo soprano in Beethoven's *Missa Solemnis* and his Ninth Symphony.

After achieving immediate success in all of Europe's major opera houses, Schumann made her American debut at the Metropolitan Opera in New York City in November 1914. She won high praise for her interpretation of Sophie in *Der Rosenkavalier*, which would go on to become one of her best-known roles, as well as for her acting ability. During the remainder of the season she spent at the Met, Schumann performed as Papagena, Gretel, the first flower maiden in *Parsifal*, and Musetta. She then returned to the Hamburg Opera, performing there until 1919, when composer Richard Strauss engaged her to sing at the Vienna Opera. Her career soared both in Vienna and on the frequent tours she took with the company, and she became acclaimed particularly for the clarity and beauty with which she sang in Mozart's operas. She also became known as a supreme Lieder singer, and in 1921 traveled back to the U.S. with Strauss to perform many of his Lieder on tour.

*Elisabeth Schumann*

Schumann made her London debut (again as Sophie in *Der Rosenkavalier*) in 1924 at Covent Garden; her appearance there two years later, singing Mozart, was considered one of the season's highlights. In the 1920s and early 1930s, while still performing at the Vienna Opera, she was a featured singer at the Munich festival and appeared four times at the Salzburg festival. Her reputation as a Lieder singer and as a stellar performer of Mozart's operas continued to grow, and she made frequent guest appearances on the best European opera stages and also toured South America. Schumann's characterizations of Despina, Susanna, Zerlina, and Blonchen were considered especially memorable. In 1931, she performed again in New York, giving a concert recital at Town Hall that prompted music critic Olin Downes to write that "she recreated [Schubert's] spirit" while singing his songs. In the mid-1930s, on a return trip to the U.S., she performed at the White House before some 300 guests as well as President Franklin Delano Roosevelt and first lady *Eleanor Roosevelt.

Schumann was a revered citizen of Vienna, and had been granted one of the city's highest tributes when she was made an honorary member of the Vienna State Opera and the Vienna Philharmonic. However, her husband Karl Alwin, the conductor, was Jewish, and after the Nazi Anschluss of Austria in March 1938 they fled Vienna for America. She gave up her opera career in mid-stream, and that year joined the faculty of the Curtis Institute of Music in Philadelphia. Schumann devoted the rest of her life to teaching and singing Lieder, becoming an American citizen in 1944. At her death in New York in 1952, she left a valuable legacy in her influence on American singers and a series of recordings for the Victor label, including many Lieder.

**SOURCES:**

Ewen, David, ed. *Living Musicians.* NY: H.W. Wilson, 1940.

Puritz, E. *The Teaching of Elisabeth Schumann.* London, 1956.

Schumann, Elisabeth. *German Song.* London, 1948.

Whelbourn, Hubert. *Standard Book of Celebrated Musicians Past and Present.* Garden City, NY: Garden City, 1937.

**John Haag,**
Athens, Georgia

# Schumann-Heink, Ernestine

## (1861–1936)

*Czech-born contralto. Name variations: Tini Rössler, Rossler, or Roessler; Ernestine Heink; Madame Schumann Heink. Born Ernestine Rössler in Lieben near Prague, Bohemia (now Czechoslovakia), on June 15,* *1861; died on November 17, 1936, in Hollywood, California; eldest of four children of Hans Rössler (a lieutenant in the Austrian army) and Charlotte (Goldman) Rössler; educated at an Ursuline convent in Prague; studied with Marietta von Leclair in Graz, and Karl Krebs, Franz Wüllner and G.B. Lamperti; married Ernst Heink (secretary to the Dresden Royal Opera), in 1882 (divorced 1893); married Paul Schumann (an actor and stage manager), in 1893 (died 1904); married William Rapp, Jr. (her secretary), in May 1905 (divorced 1914); children: (first marriage) August, Charlotte, Henry, and Hans; (second marriage) Ferdinand, Marie, and George Washington (her only American-born child).*

*Made debut under name Tini Rössler, in Dresden (1878); performed in a London production of* Der Ring des Nibelungen *under Gustav Mahler (1892); made Bayreuth debut, in* Der Ring des Nibelungen *(1896); debuted at Covent Garden (1897), Berlin Opera (1898), Chicago Opera (1898), Metropolitan Opera (1899); created the role of Klytemnestra in* Elektra *in Dresden (1909); also performed in musical comedy, films, and radio.*

Ernestine Schumann-Heink was born Ernestine Rössler in Lieben near Prague, Bohemia (now Czechoslovakia), in 1861, the eldest of four children of Hans Rössler, a lieutenant in the Austrian army, and **Charlotte Goldman Rössler.** Ernestine grew up poor on army posts, moving from barracks to barracks, while periodically attending Roman Catholic convent schools. In Graz, when ex-prima donna **Marietta von Leclair** heard her sing, she offered to give lessons, and, at age 15, Ernestine gave her first public performance, as the contralto soloist in Beethoven's Ninth Symphony. She never learned to read music, however. **Marie Wilt** of the Vienna Opera was so impressed by the young girl that she arranged an audition in Vienna. But a broken-hearted Schumann-Heink failed to impress and was told to go home and become a dressmaker; she was too poor, they said, and too homely. Then, *Amalie Materna arranged an audition in Dresden which was successful, and Schumann-Heink began to sing a number of small parts at the Dresden Royal Opera. In 1882, when she married Ernst Heink, a secretary at the opera, both were dismissed, for she had not obtained permission to marry a member of the management. Instead, she procured a position at Hamburg, and during this time had three children in three years. Night after night, she sang small parts, sometimes giving 22 performances in a month for little pay. As well, Heink walked out of their marriage, leaving her with his debts and pregnant with their fourth child. (They would divorce in 1892.)

Schumann-Heink placed her children with her parents and tried to accelerate her career. Her chance came in 1889, when the principal contralto at Hamburg, **Marie Goetze**, had a quarrel with the director and refused to go on as Carmen. Despite no rehearsal and an improvised costume, Schumann-Heink replaced her and was a sensation. Appearances throughout Europe soon followed.

In 1893, she married Paul Schumann, an actor and stage manager, and reclaimed her chil-

dren. At last happy domestically, she had three more children; her husband, who was extremely supportive, was helpful to her career. In 1896, Schumann-Heink was coached by *Cosima Wagner** at Bayreuth and participated in five complete *Ring* cycles. She returned to the Hamburg Opera where most of her roles were now major ones. Soon she was in the United States debuting at the Metropolitan Opera in New York. Schumann-Heink made a great deal of money appearing in a comic opera called *Love's Lottery*, and after it closed in 1903 decided to move to the United States. Following her beloved second husband's

*Ernestine Schumann-Heink at an American bond rally.*

death in 1904, she married her business manager, William Rapp, Jr., brought her children to America, and began a 40,000-mile concert tour in the U.S., becoming a great favorite on the opera and concert stage. (She separated from Rapp in 1911 and divorced him in 1914.) When World War I broke out, her oldest son August joined the German navy and was lost in a submarine; three of her other sons enlisted with the American forces, while son Hans died of pneumonia in 1915. Schumann-Heink turned her home into a servicemen's canteen and made endless appearances on behalf of the troops.

Ernestine Schumann-Heink made her first radio appearance in 1926. Forced by the stock-market crash of 1929 to accept more commercial engagements as she supported a small army of relatives, she entered vaudeville and radio, and appeared in the motion picture *Here's to Romance* (1935). She worked in entertainment until her death from leukemia in 1936. Schumann-Heink's first recordings were made in 1903, and she continued a long association with Victor until 1931. Some of these records give a notion of her great operatic abilities. She was equally successful as a commercial singer, and many feel her recordings of "Stille Nacht" ("Silent Night") have never been surpassed.

**SUGGESTED READING:**

Lawton, M. *Schumann-Heink: The Last of the Titans.* New York, 1928.

**John Haag**, Associate Professor of History, University of Georgia, Athens, Georgia

# Schurmann, Anna Maria van

(1607–1678).

*See van Schurmann, Anna Maria.*

# Schurz, Margarethe Meyer

(1833–1876)

*German-born American who inspired the kindergarten movement in the U.S. Born Margarethe Meyer on August 27, 1833, in Hamburg, Germany; died in New York City on March 15, 1876, of complications after the birth of her fifth child; daughter of Heinrich Meyer (a merchant-manufacturer); married Carl Schurz (1829–1906, an army officer and politician), on July 6, 1852; children: Agathe Schurz (b. 1853); Marianne Schurz; Carl Lincoln Schurz; Herbert Schurz; and a daughter who died in infancy.*

Born on August 27, 1833, Margarethe Meyer grew up in Hamburg, Germany, with her older sister and two older brothers. Her parents passed on their interest in education, music and liberal political thought to their daughter. At age 16, Margarethe attended lectures by the founder of kindergarten philosophy, Friedrich Froebel, and became a disciple of this educational approach. Other adherents to the kindergarten movement (the German *kindergarten* translates to "children's garden") were her sister **Bertha Ronge** and brother-in-law Johann Ronge, whom she joined in England during 1852. There, she assisted in the administration of their kindergarten school—the first in England.

Soon after her arrival, she met Carl Schurz, a German expatriate expelled for taking part in the 1848–49 German revolution. They were married in July 1852 and left England for America that fall, eventually settling in Watertown, Wisconsin. In a back room of their home, Margarethe Schurz opened what is often regarded as the first kindergarten in the United States. Following the theories of Froebel, she provided creative play opportunities for her first daughter **Agathe Schurz** and several other children in a structured German-language environment designed to allow them to teach themselves.

This kindergarten was short-lived, however, as the family moved again in the spring of 1857, and from that time forward Schurz had few opportunities to continue her own educational work. Her contribution to the movement came largely through her association with *Elizabeth Palmer Peabody (1804–1894) whom she met in Boston, Massachusetts, during 1859. Peabody shared Schurz's interest in education for young children, but had not yet heard of Froebel's philosophy. Drawing on Schurz's knowledge and support, as well as on a trip to Europe for additional training, Peabody founded her own kindergarten school in Boston in 1860, thereby giving rise to the kindergarten movement in the United States.

Although Schurz remained committed to the concept of and need for educational opportunities for small children, her husband's career as a Civil War general (1862–65), U.S. senator from Missouri (1869–75), and editor of the New York *Evening Post* (1881–83) would lead to several relocations. During the war, she supported his efforts by providing him with secretarial assistance, caring for their children, and even reading to President Abraham Lincoln a letter of her husband's which she carried from Union lines. Though her husband thrived in his adopted country, Schurz missed Germany and crossed the Atlantic four times to assuage her homesickness, the last trip being in the winter of 1875. A year later, she died at the family's home in New York City, age 42, as a result of complications from the birth of their fifth child.

**SOURCES:**

Griffin, Lynne, and Kelly McCann. *The Book of Women.* Holbrook, MA: Bob Adams, 1992.

James, Edward T., ed. *Notable American Women, 1607–1950.* Cambridge, MA: Belknap Press of Harvard University, 1971.

Read, Phyllis J., and Bernard L. Witlieb. *The Book of Women's Firsts.* NY: Random House, 1992.

**Sally Cole-Misch,** freelance writer, Bloomfield Hills, Michigan

# Schütte-Lihotzky, Margarete

## (1897–2000)

*First Austrian woman to become a professional architect, who made important contributions to municipal planning and was particularly known for her labor-saving "Frankfurt kitchen" of the 1920s. Name variations: Margaret Shutte-Lihotzky or Schuette-Lihotzky; Margarethe Lihotzky; Grete Lihotzky; Grete Schütte-Lihotzky. Born Margarete Lihotzky in Vienna, Austria, on January 23, 1897; died in Vienna on January 18, 2000; daughter of Erwin Lihotzky and Julie (Bode) Lihotzky; had sister Adele; married Wilhelm Schütte (1900–1968, an architect), in 1927; no children.*

Margarete Schütte-Lihotzky, known as Grete, was born in Vienna in 1897, the daughter of Erwin Lihotzky and **Julie Bode Lihotzky**. Erwin, of Slavic origins, came from the province of Bukovina; Julie was descended from a Swabian family that had its roots in Germany's province of Hanover. Both sides of the family produced individuals of note, including a famous art historian in Berlin and a mayor of the city of Czernovitz in Bukovina. Intellectually, the Lihotzkys were steeped in the freethinking liberalism of the Viennese middle class in the decades before 1914. Grete's father, although an official of the monarchy, was critical of the hereditary principle of government on which Habsburg rule was based, and he and Julie raised their daughters Grete and **Adele** with an emphasis on moral choice. Throughout her life, Grete Schütte-Lihotzky would harbor a deep-seated sense of social responsibility, even when faced with life-threatening decisions.

During World War I, Schütte-Lihotzky took up the study of architecture at Vienna's Akademie für angewandte Kunst (Academy of Applied Arts). Brilliant and enthusiastic, she caught the attention of two of the school's most progressive artist-teachers, Oskar Strnad and Heinrich Tessenow, and simply ignored the atti-

tude of her renowned professor Josef Hoffmann, whose dismissive stance was summed up in his remark: *"Frauen heiraten sowieso"* ("In any case, women get married"). It was Strnad who stimulated her reformist instincts by suggesting that she visit the dwellings of Vienna's working class, where people lived in conditions of overcrowding and squalor, often with nine or more in one airless room. Calling the elegant designs for jewelry, furniture and household furnishings produced at Josef Hoffmann's Wiener Werkstätte (Vienna Workshops) "applied arts for the upper ten thousand," she rejected his philosophy as "reactionary." Instead, even while a student, she focused her energies on designing simple and affordable dwellings and interiors for working-class and white-collar families, rather than for the wealthy few. In 1917, her design for a modern kitchen won her the Max Mauthner Prize, followed two years later by the Lobmeyr Prize.

In 1923, Schütte-Lihotzky was awarded her architecture diploma from the Academy of Applied Arts, thus gaining the distinction of being Austria's first woman architect. She began working for the noted architect Adolf Loos, with whom she shared an aversion toward emphasizing "stylishness" or "smart elements" as part of architectural designs and plans. Such talk, she believed, revealed nothing more than an elitist attitude toward the pressing social requirements of the day. These needs were immense indeed in post-1918 Vienna, which as a result of defeat in war and subsequent inflation and social chaos had become a metropolis of supplicants; as many as 90,000 were homeless. Consequently, in 1923 Schütte-Lihotzky became a member of the Austrian Social Democratic Workers' Party (SDAP). By this time, although the rest of Austria was conservative and German-nationalistic in its political allegiances, the SDAP had gained control of the Vienna municipal government. In "Red Vienna," an ambitious program of social reforms was underway, starting in the early 1920s, that would last until the Social Democrats were bloodily suppressed in a civil war in February 1934.

Most impressive of the reforms was a large-scale program of public housing. Schütte-Lihotzky participated in these changes, helping to design the Winarsky-Hof, a pioneering housing project comprising 840 apartments, 40 units of which she, Strnad, and several other architects helped plan as models for the future. She also was involved in the Austrian *Siedlerbewegung*, attempts to empower workers and white-collar employees to purchase and live in their own homes in the outskirts of large cities. For her innovative work, she was awarded the Bronze Medal of the City of Vienna in 1922 and the Silver Medal in 1923. In early 1926, Schütte-Lihotzky accepted a job offer from Ernst May, who was in charge of public building projects for the German city of Frankfurt am Main. Among the many facets of her work in Frankfurt, she became interested in designing a modern, rationally conceived kitchen. Working with simple and inexpensive materials and a limited space of less than seven square meters (2.9 m. x 1.9 m.), she designed a kitchen that was practical and time-saving.

Although many of her ideas were based on years of experience, much of Schütte-Lihotzky's inspiration came from the 1921 German edition of American author **Christine Frederick**'s *The New Housekeeping: Efficiency Studies in Home Management*. Frederick's book, inspired by contemporary principles of scientific management, became the bible of household rationalization, domestic efficiency, and kitchen reform in the 1920s. In her foreword to the German edition, translator **Irene Witte** noted that Frederick was the first woman "to transfer the principles of scientific management, which had until then only been introduced into the factory, workshop, or office, into the home." Schütte-Lihotzky was able to transform Frederick's ideas into a practical reality that would benefit the working people of Frankfurt am Main. Her kitchen design was immensely successful from the start, and in Frankfurt am Main alone over 10,000 would be installed in the next few years.

In 1927, Grete married the architect Wilhelm Schütte, with whom she would share a productive partnership of more than a decade. She lived with her husband in one room with a Frankfurt kitchen attached, noting: "No children and a small flat, those are very favorable conditions, and also a man who from the beginning agrees to share the work, sometimes shopping or throwing a couple of eggs into the frying pan." Grete, who suffered from tuberculosis throughout her life, was advised against having children, though she endured two miscarriages.

In 1927, the Frankfurt Spring Fair further validated the importance of Schütte-Lihotzky's innovative kitchen design. "The New Apartment and Its Interior Fittings," an exhibition designed and realized by her, was held in the main exhibition hall. Attached to it was a special show, "The Modern Household," sponsored by the Frankfurt housewives' association. Its goal was to bring together women, architects, and industry, all striving for more modern and rational interior designs

and conveniences. Of particular interest to many professionals at the show was the kitchen of a *Mitropa* railroad dining car, an example of the economy of movement that could be made possible through modern design. The entire kitchen was the same size as Schütte-Lihotzky's Frankfurt kitchen, and when used in an actual situation, it enabled the staff to prepare meals and drinks for over 400 passengers over a 15-hour train journey, with no change of personnel.

But in 1930, as the reverberations of the previous year's stock-market crash continued, Schütte-Lihotzky fell victim to a growing global campaign to pressure working women out of their jobs. Although May had argued that his Frankfurt program would collapse without her, she was dismissed, the pretext being that she had a working husband. The Utopian vision of the Frankfurt housing project had virtually collapsed as a result of draconian cuts in its budget. Indeed, the overall situation in Germany and Austria, rapidly descending into economic despair at the onset of the world depression, and with ominous clouds of fascism on the horizon, was grim. That year, when May accepted an offer to design and build housing projects in new industrial cities for the Soviet government, which was then involved

Margarete Schütte-Lihotzky

in its first Five Year Plan to rapidly industrialize and modernize the USSR, Grete and Wilhelm became part of his team.

During these busy years, Schütte-Lihotzky had become more attracted to the militancy she believed was the essence of the Communist movement. In the summer of 1927, after bloody riots in Vienna had demonstrated to her that the SDAP leadership was unwilling to risk a revolution in Austria, she submitted her resignation, convinced that socialism could never be achieved in Central Europe if a similar lack of resolve continued to characterize the party's course of action. She chose, however, not to join the minuscule and ineffective Austrian Communist Party (KPÖ) at this time.

Despite the difficult living conditions Grete and Wilhelm encountered in the Soviet Union, Grete designed schools, kindergartens and public-housing developments. The fact that fascist regimes seized power in Germany and Austria in 1933 and 1934, easily eradicating the achievements of the Social Democratic movements in those nations, only strengthened her beliefs in a more militant form of socialism. Even the start of the Great Terror initiated by Joseph Stalin, which would devastate the USSR and cause the deaths of countless Soviet citizens, did not discourage Schütte-Lihotzky, whose work in the design and construction of projects in Magnitogorsk and other newly created industrial centers consumed her energy. By 1936, however, it was becoming only too apparent to both Grete and Wilhelm that official paranoia over alleged foreign spies and domestic "wreckers" had made it impossible for them to continue their work in the USSR. After much difficulty, both were able to leave Moscow voluntarily in early August 1937—only weeks before the remaining members of the Ernst May group were arrested and expelled from the country. For the next months, Grete and Wilhelm lived as insecure refugees from Nazism, first in Paris, then in London. Austria was annexed by Nazi Germany in March 1938, and several of Grete's colleagues either were arrested or had to flee. Work on French children's clinics and schools gave her a sense of purpose in an otherwise terrible time.

In 1938, Grete and Wilhelm were invited to fill positions at the Turkish Academy of Fine Arts in Istanbul. A sizable colony of German refugees from Nazism had settled in Turkey in the 1930s, and the young republic was moving rapidly toward economic, social, and cultural modernization. It was in 1939, while she was in Turkey, that Schütte-Lihotzky finally decided to

join the KPÖ. Founded in 1918 as one of the first Communist parties outside Soviet Russia, the Austrian Communist movement had always existed as a small sect in the shadow of the large and successful Social Democrats. By 1933, however, the failure of the SDAP to maintain itself as a viable alternative to Austro-Fascism had strengthened immensely the appeal of Communism to Austrians, both those at home and those living in exile like Schütte-Lihotzky. Being a Communist was largely a theoretical matter for an exiled Austrian architect living in Turkey, at least until 1940; then her party superiors confronted her with the need to send an agent to Vienna. This dangerous assignment was to assist in the rebuilding of an underground network gravely weakened by several years of Nazi infiltration and persecution. She accepted.

Grete and another underground agent, the engineer Herbert Eichholzer, arrived in Vienna in the last days of December 1940. Although the Soviet Union and Nazi Germany were technically allies and at peace, she knew only too well that the Hitler regime's relentless war against Marxists and socialists had not stopped. Many of her colleagues had been arrested, and some had lost their lives in Nazi prisons and concentration camps. The Gestapo and other Nazi intelligence branches had become past masters at ferreting out "subversives," and in this instance their expertise was revealed. On January 22, 1941, after only 25 days' stay in Vienna, Schütte-Lihotzky's luck ran out. She and another member of the underground, Erwin Puschmann, having been betrayed by a Nazi agent in their midst, were arrested by the Gestapo in Vienna's Café Viktoria. Both were taken to the dreaded Vienna headquarters of the Gestapo, in the Hotel Metropol on the Morzinplatz.

After harsh interrogations, she was found guilty of "preparation for high treason" and "treasonous assistance to the enemy" and sentenced by the Nazi Volksgerichtshof (People's Court) to 15 years at hard labor. Nazi officials remained largely ignorant of Schütte-Lihotzky's important role in the organization, as a result giving her a "mild" sentence. Almost all of her ill-fated colleagues in the resistance network were sentenced to death and executed. She was taken to the notorious Nazi penitentiary at Aichach, Bavaria, where she managed to survive for four years before being liberated in the spring of 1945.

When Schütte-Lihotzky arrived back in Vienna that April, she found the beautiful city profoundly disfigured from years of bombings and the final, meaningless defense of its Nazi rulers. Still, she looked forward to many active years in which she would be able to contribute to Austria's physical and moral reconstruction. This was not to be. Schütte-Lihotzky had rejoined the KPÖ upon her return to Vienna, and by 1947, with the Cold War in full bloom, to be a Communist in Austria was legal but virtually guaranteed professional, and personal, marginalization. Austria's Social Democrats were deeply hostile to Soviet Communism, which since the 1930s had meant Stalinism and oppression. Schütte-Lihotzky was effectively blacklisted. As a result of this unofficial but highly effective *Berufsverbot* (professional boycott), she would receive only two commissions in Vienna—the design of two municipal kindergartens—for the remainder of her career. As well, her marriage ended in 1950. Despite disappointments, Grete kept busy in the postwar decades. She was president and a key member of the Austrian Federation of Democratic Women, served on the board of the Austrian organization of victims of Nazism and Fascism, and was active in the Austrian Peace Council. She also ran an anti-fascist film distribution organization for a number of years. Although professionally frustrated in Austria, she carried out a number of successful kindergarten projects in Sofia, Bulgaria (1945–46), and made extended trips as a consultant and lecturer to several nations, including the People's Republic of China, Cuba, and the German Democratic Republic.

As the Cold War began to be viewed as history, Schütte-Lihotzky gained the public recognition and respect she had long been denied. In 1980, she received the City of Vienna Prize for Architecture. Special documentary programs dedicated to her life were screened on Austrian television in 1984 and 1987. In 1985, a German publisher released her memoirs of the Nazi years, a book that so impressed a growing number of admirers it would appear in a second edition in Vienna in 1994. To a younger generation of architects and planners, her work in kitchen design and town planning became known again when a book on the Frankfurt kitchen appeared in 1992. She was now universally recognized and revered as the Grand Old Lady of Austrian architecture and municipal planning. But Grete remained as stubbornly independent as ever; in 1988, she had refused to accept an important decoration from Austria's Minister of Instruction as long as Kurt Waldheim, the Austrian president burdened with a shady Nazi past, remained in office.

For her 100th birthday in 1997, she was awarded the coveted Ehrenring der Stadt Wien (Ring of Honor of the City of Vienna). In Vien-

na's 21st district, a new public-housing structure on the Donaufelderstrasse was named the "Margarete-Schütte-Lihotzky-Hof," a cluster of buildings officially designated as being "by women, for women." On that same evening, Frankfurt's German Architecture Museum opened an exhibition on Schütte-Lihotzky's now-classic Frankfurt kitchen. "I have become a persona grata," she remarked. Grete Schütte-Lihotzky—known by Austrians simply as *"die Schütte"*—died in Vienna only a few days short of her 103rd birthday, on January 18, 2000.

**SOURCES:**

Achleitner, Friedrich. "Laudatio zum Festakt für Margarete Schütte-Lihotzky anlässlich ihres 90. Geburtstages am 23. Jänner 1987," in *Bauforum*. Vol. 20, no. 119, 1987, pp. 8–9.

Beddow, Roy Manfred. "Visionary Planning in Frankfurt am Main, 1925–1933," M. Pl. thesis, Queen's University at Kingston, Ontario, 1992.

Chiu, Ch. S. *Frauen im Schatten*. Vienna: Verlag Jugend & Volk, 1994.

Collins, Christiane C. "Concerned Planning and Design: The Urban Experiment of Germany in the 1920s," in Frank D. Hirschbach *et al.*, eds., *Germany in the Twenties—The Artist as Social Critic: A Collection of Essays*. NY: Holmes & Meier, 1980, pp. 30–47.

Dawson, Layla. "Margarete Schütte-Lihotzky 1897–2000," in *The Architectural Review*. Vol. 207, no. 1237. March 2000, p. 23.

———. "Radicalism Begins at Home," in *Building Design*. February 28, 1997, p. 12.

Dokumentationsarchiv des österreichischen Widerstandes, Vienna, file 2569.

"Ehrenring der Stadt Wien für Margarete Schütte-Lihotzky," in *Rathauskorrespondenz* [Vienna]. January 21, 2000, p. 106.

Eicher, Jürgen. "Ungebrochene Lebenslust: Zum 100. Geburtstag von Margarete Schütte-Lihotzky," in *Deutsche Bauzeitung*. Vol. 131, no. 3. March 1997, p. 20.

"Im Widerstand für Österreich: Margarete Schütte-Lihotzky (1897–2000)," in *Dokumentationsarchiv des österreichischen Widerstandes Mitteilungen*. No. 146. April 2000, p. 4.

Jung, Karin Carmen, and Dietrich Worbs. "Die Einrichtung einer besseren menschlicheren Welt . . . !," in *Bauwelt*. Vol. 83, no. 4. January 24, 1992, p. 153.

———. "Soziale Architektur: Margarete Schütte-Lihotzky zum 100. Geburtstag," in *Bauwelt*. Vol. 88, no. 4. January 24, 1997, p. 136.

Krausse, Joachim. "La Cucina di Francoforte," in *Domus: Monthly Review of Architecture, Interiors, Design Art*. No. 695. June 1988, pp. 66–73, XXI–XXII.

Lihotzky, Grete. "Rationalization in the Household," in Anton Kaes, Martin Jay, and Edward Dimendberg, eds., *The Weimar Republic Sourcebook*. Berkeley, CA: University of California Press, 1994, pp. 462–465.

"Margarete Schütte-Lihotzky," in *Deutsche Bauzeitung*. Vol. 134, no. 3. March 2000, p. 8.

Noever, Peter, and Renate Allmayer-Beck, eds. *Margarete Schütte-Lihotzky: soziale Architektur, Zeitzeugin eines Jahrhunderts.* 2nd ed. Vienna: Verlag Böhlau, 1996.

Nolan, Mary. "'Housework Made Easy': The Taylorized Housewife in Weimar Germany's Rationalized Economy," in *Feminist Studies.* Vol. 16, no. 3. Fall 1990, pp. 549–577.

Reininghaus, Alexandra. "Porträt einer Zeitzeugin: Die Architektin Grete Schütte-Lihotzky," in *Du.* No. 532. June 1985, pp. 41, 118.

Schütte-Lihotzky, Margarete. *Erinnerungen aus dem Widerstand: Das kämpferische Leben einer Architektin von 1938–1945.* Edited by Irene Nierhaus. Vienna: Promedia, 1994.

———. *Die Frankfurter Küche von Margarete Schütte-Lihotzky.* Edited by Peter Noever. Berlin: Ernst & Sohn, 1992.

Sohn, Susanne. "Eine aussergewöhnliche Frau: Zum 90. Geburtstag von Margarete Schütte-Lihotzky," in *Volksstimme* [Vienna]. January 18, 1987.

Stock, Wolfgang Jean. "Eine Architektin mit aufrechtem Gang," in *Werk, Bauen + Wohnen.* No. 3. March 2000, p. 3.

———. "Einhundert Jahre jung: Zum Geburtstag der Wiener Architektin Margarete Schütte-Lihotzky," in *Baumeister.* Vol. 94, no. 1. January 1997, p. 6.

Tabor, Jan. "Pionierin der Baukunst und des Widerstandes," in *Der Kurier* [Vienna]. January 21, 1987.

Wang, Wilfried. "Built Progress: The Contribution of Margarete Schütte-Lihotzky," in *Harvard Design Magazine.* Summer 1997, pp. 14–16.

"Wohnhausanlage wird nach Schütte-Lihotzky benannt," in *Rathauskorrespondenz* [Vienna]. January 23, 1997, p. 120.

**RELATED MEDIA:**

"Das neue Frankfurt, part 2: Die Frankfurter Küche," shown on WDR-Westdeutscher Rundfunk, Cologne, 1985.

**John Haag**, Associate Professor of History,
University of Georgia, Athens, Georgia

## Schütz-Zell, Katherine (c. 1497–1562).

*See Zell, Katharina Schütz.*

## Schützin, Katherina (c. 1497–1562).

*See Zell, Katharina Schütz.*

## Schuylenburg, Helga Maria (b. 1910).

*See Löwenstein, Helga Maria zu.*

# Schuyler, Catherine Van Rensselaer (1734–1803)

*American patriot and wife of a Revolutionary War general. Name variations: Kitty Van Rensselaer. Born Catherine Van Rensselaer on November 4, 1734, in Claverack, New York; died of a stroke on March 7, 1803, in Albany, New York; daughter of Johannes Van Rensselaer (an army officer) and Engeltie (Livingston) Van Rensselaer; married her distant cousin Philip Schuyler (a Revolutionary War general), on September 7, 1755; children: Angelica Schuyler (b. 1756); Eliza-*beth Schuyler Hamilton (1757–1854); **Margaret Schuyler** (b. 1758); John Bradstreet Schuyler (b. 1765); Philip Jeremiah Schuyler (b. 1768); Rensselaer Schuyler (b. 1773); **Cornelia Schuyler** (b. 1775); Catherine Van Rensselaer Schuyler (b. 1781).*

Catherine Van Rensselaer, the first of six children of **Engeltie Van Rensselaer** and Johannes Van Rensselaer, was born into a distinguished Dutch family on November 4, 1734, in Claverack, upstate New York. Her father, an officer in the British Army and later a defender of the American struggle for independence, passed on to Catherine a strong dedication to their country. She was well educated in comparison with other women in America during the mid-18th century, and known as "delicate but perfect in form and feature." At age 20, she married a distant cousin, Philip John Schuyler, who was then a captain serving in the French and Indian War.

Together, the Schuylers represented two of New York's most prominent landholding families, but this did not automatically establish the couple's fortune. Catherine had her first two children while they were living with her mother-in-law in Albany, and she nursed the wounded when Philip's army was defeated at Ticonderoga during 1757. Several years later, she oversaw the early construction of "the Pastures," their own mansion just outside Albany, during her husband's absence. When Philip came into his inheritance, they used their now extensive landholdings to establish what would become the town of Schuylerville, complete with saw and grist mills, fields of flax and wheat, and a country house. Catherine was responsible for much of the town's development, including sharing with her husband the tasks of settling artisans and tenant farmers there.

In 1775, Philip was appointed by General George Washington as one of the four major-generals who would serve the Americans during the Revolutionary War. During the conflict, Catherine's patriotism and daring were on prominent display as British forces threatened the area around the Schuyler lands. At great danger, she traveled to their summer residence from Albany, replying to those who pleaded with her to turn back, "The General's wife must not be afraid." Once there, she burned her husband's extensive wheat fields to prevent the British from harvesting them. Her bold example convinced other area farmers to destroy their own crops.

Philip's election to Congress necessitated a move to Philadelphia, which was followed in the winter of 1779–80 by the family's relocation to New Jersey where he served as Washington's military adviser. Over the years, Catherine gave birth to a total of eight children, and followed her husband in his pursuit of a political career. Her daughter Betsey (*Elizabeth Schuyler Hamilton) married Alexander Hamilton at the Schuyler family home in 1780, three years before the end of the war. Following 48 years of happy married life, Catherine died of a stroke in 1803.

**SOURCES:**

James, Edward T., ed. *Notable American Women, 1607–1950.* Cambridge, MA: The Belknap Press of Harvard University, 1971.

**Sally Cole-Misch**, freelance writer, Bloomfield Hills, Michigan

# Schuyler, Louisa Lee (1837–1926)

*American reformer. Born on October 26, 1837, in New York City; died on October 10, 1926, in Highland Falls, New York; daughter of George Lee Schuyler (an engineer, lawyer, and grandson of Revolutionary War general Philip Schuyler and Catherine Van Rensselaer Schuyler) and Eliza Hamilton Schuyler (great-granddaughter of Philip Schuyler and Catherine Van Rensselaer Schuyler and granddaughter of Elizabeth Schuyler Hamilton and Alexander Hamilton); educated privately; never married.*

Born in New York City on October 26, 1837, Louisa Lee Schuyler enjoyed wealth and a distinguished lineage. Her father George Lee Schuyler, an engineer and lawyer, was the grandson of *Catherine Van Rensselaer Schuyler and Revolutionary War general Philip Schuyler; her mother Eliza Hamilton Schuyler was the great-granddaughter of the same Catherine and Philip Schuyler and granddaughter of *Elizabeth Schuyler Hamilton and Alexander Hamilton, the famous American statesman. Louisa spent most of her young life with her older brother and younger sister in the care of private tutors at the Hamilton family estate on the Hudson River near Dobbs Ferry, New York.

Schuyler got her first taste of charitable work through her parents' support of the Children's Aid Society of New York. She became involved in the organization in her early 20s, as a volunteer sewing instructor to immigrant children. She turned her efforts in a different direction when she became involved with another of her parents' pet projects, the Woman's Central Association of Relief, in 1861. In conjunction with the U.S. Sanitary Commission, the organization provided regional support to the Union cause during the Civil War. As chair of the group's committee of correspondence, Schuyler organized and managed a network of local groups that provided food, clothing and medical supplies to Civil War army camps and hospitals. She became widely known for her efficient leadership as well as for her ability to inspire others. She believed that the volunteers would do what was needed as long as she provided the necessary information and direction.

Establishing a lifelong pattern in which a sudden burst of energy would give way to extreme exhaustion, Schuyler collapsed when the end of the Civil War dissolved the association. She spent the following six years in convalescence in Europe and Egypt, then returned to the United States in 1871 and refocused her efforts on helping those in need. Following the same strategy she had in the war, she organized her neighbors and other prominent New York City women into a visiting committee to local jails and hospitals. In 1872, she created the State Charities Aid Association (SCAA) to formalize these citizen groups. Through frequent visits to jails, hospitals, schools and asylums, the SCAA analyzed each site's need for administrative or program improvements and educated the public about these needs. The group's efforts resulted in passage of a variety of legislative reforms to improve conditions in these facilities.

Schuyler devoted her personal efforts within the organization to improving the nursing profession and care for the mentally ill. In May 1873, she established a professional training school for nurses at Bellevue Hospital, the first of its size to maintain such high standards. In 1884, she initiated a large campaign to move the mentally ill from county poorhouses to state hospitals. New York State passed such legislation in 1890, followed in 1892 by a law providing separate accommodations and treatment for epileptics. Schuyler was instrumental in the passage of this latter legislation as well.

By 1907, Schuyler's success in improving social welfare was well known, and she was asked to become a charter trustee in the Russell Sage Foundation, founded by *Margaret Olivia Sage. Her focus shifted to the prevention of blindness in children, and she worked with several organizations—including the SCAA, the American Medical Association, and the New York Association for the Blind—to create the National Committee (later renamed Society) for the Prevention of Blindness in 1915. Schuyler's decades of reform led Columbia University to bestow an honorary Doctorate of Laws on her in 1915, only the second woman to receive such an honor. She was also awarded a medal in 1923 from the Theodore Roosevelt Memorial Association.

Schuyler's charitable work was more significant in the precedent it set for upper-class philanthropy than for its actual accomplishments. She demonstrated the need for women of social standing to take on leadership roles in bringing about reform. While many of society's elite had confined their charitable work to financial gifts, Schuyler endeavored to encourage hands-on organization of the middle classes to promote change, even though she herself played a minimal role in the day-to-day happenings of her own institutions.

In 1921, Schuyler's health deteriorated due to an illness that caused virtual blindness and paralysis on one side. She spent her final years writing magazine articles and letters on social welfare issues. She died on October 10, 1926, at the country estate of J.P. Morgan in Highland Falls, New York.

**SOURCES:**

James, Edward T., ed. *Notable American Women, 1607–1950*. Cambridge, MA: The Belknap Press of Harvard University, 1971.

McHenry, Robert, ed. *Famous American Women*. NY: Dover, 1980.

**Sally Cole-Misch**, freelance writer, Bloomfield Hills, Michigan

# Schuyler, Philippa Duke

## (1931–1967)

*African-American pianist and composer whose well-known compositions include "Manhattan Nocturne" (1943), "Rhapsody of Youth" (1948), and "Nile Fantasy" (1965). Name variations: Felipa Monterro y Schuyler; Felipa Monterro. Born in 1931 in Harlem, New York; died on May 9, 1967, in a helicopter crash in Vietnam; daughter of Josephine "Jody" Cogdell Schuyler (an artist and writer who used maiden name Josephine Cogdell) and George Schuyler (a journalist); privately educated in New York.*

*Selected writings:* Adventures in Black and White *(1960);* Who Killed the Congo? *(1962);* Jungle Saints *(1963); (with Josephine Cogdell)* Kingdom of Dreams *(1966); a fifth book,* Good Men Die, *was published posthumously (1968).*

Philippa Schuyler was born in Harlem in 1931 to interracial parents who were convinced that their differing racial backgrounds would produce an extraordinary child. **Josephine Cogdell**, a white writer, and George Schuyler, a prominent African-American journalist, encouraged and directed Philippa's life from an early

age. As a child, she received acclaim for her music from audiences of all races; once she became an adult, however, she felt she did not fit in on either side of America's racially divided society. Indeed, despite Schuyler's gift in music and her impressively high IQ (tested at 185 by New York University and others), America in the 1950s was not ready for an adult interracial artist. Schuyler left the United States and toured throughout Europe, Africa and Asia, but was never able to feel at home anywhere.

Philippa Duke Schuyler was the product of parents who planned to make her an example of the excellence that could be attained through a mulatto race as a solution to America's troubled race problem. Their high expectations were evident even in her name, "Philippa," referring to Philip of Macedonia and Philip Schuyler, the Revolutionary War general, and she did not disappoint. Schuyler's childhood was spent under the watchful eye of her mother, who served as her business manager, best friend, and director. Educated by private tutors, she was isolated from other children, and her diet was strictly controlled by Josephine. Throughout her life, Schuyler would maintain a regimented diet which did not permit artificial products such as sodas, nor alcohol, sugar, meat, cooked foods and most fats. Philippa was reading and writing at age two, composing music at age four, and performing Mozart in front of audiences at age five.

By age ten, Schuyler was nationally recognized and celebrated as the brightest young composer in America. She was invited to become a member of the National Association of American Composers and Conductors, and won several prizes for her compositions and performances. Biographical articles on her appeared in the *New York Herald Tribune*, *The New Yorker*, *Look*, *Time*, and her father's employer, the *Pittsburgh Courier*, due in large part to his visibility as a journalist and his active campaigning on her behalf.

In 1946, Schuyler made her debut as a composer and pianist with the Philharmonic Symphony Orchestra in New York City, before an audience of 12,000. As a young pianist, her reviews by both black and white critics were uniformly exceptional. Her compositions, although the efforts of a young mind, were also judged to be extraordinary. Composing seemed to come as naturally to Schuyler as seeing and hearing. She would visit a toy shop with her mother and then sit down to write "The Toy Maker's Ball," with the clacking of tiny mechanical figures beating steadily in the background.

Despite Schuyler's success as a child prodigy, her appeal to white America faded as soon as she entered young adulthood. She was no longer an intriguing phenomenon, and soon her mother could book only concerts backed by African-American organizations. Schuyler became aware for the first time of the racial prejudice from which she had been shielded throughout her childhood. "It was a ruthless shock to me that, at first, made the walls of my self-confidence crumble," she wrote. "It horrified, humiliated me."

Schuyler's response to American racism was to flee the country for Latin America, where mixed races were more prevalent. Never again would she settle permanently in the United States, choosing instead a voluntary exile of traveling and performing in more than 80 countries in Latin America, Asia, Africa and Europe. In Haiti, she played at the inauguration of three successive presidents. In Africa, she performed for such notables as Haile Selassie of Ethiopia, King George of Toro, King Kalonji of the Baluba tribe, at Independence Day celebrations for Patrice Lumumba and Joseph Kasavubu of the Congo and President Kwame Nkrumah of Ghana, and for Albert Schweitzer in his isolated leper colony in Lamberéné. But despite her tremendous international success, she was never invited to play before an American of note.

Schuyler's performances before distinguished audiences around the world failed to heal the deep wounds inflicted by America's rejection, and neither could they restore to her a stable sense of identity. She wrote bitterly of the isolation she felt: "I'm a beauty but I'm half colored, so I'm not to be accepted anyplace. I'm always destined to be an outsider, never, never part of anything. I hate my country and no one wants me in any other. I am emotionally part of nothing. . . . And that will always be my destiny."

As her concert schedule decreased in the early 1960s, Schuyler supplemented her limited performing income by writing about her travels. She published more than 100 newspaper and magazine articles in the United States and Europe, and was one of the few black writers to be syndicated by United Press International, the large newswire company. She also published four nonfiction books: *Adventures in Black and White* (a biography, 1960); *Who Killed the Congo?* (a summary of the Belgian Congo's fight for independence, 1962); *Jungle Saints* (a tribute to African missionaries, 1963); and *Kingdom of Dreams* (a quixotic study of scientific dream interpretation written with her mother, 1966). All her books tend to be provocative. An intrepid

traveler and a quick-sketch artist of landscapes and people, she reported on the political scenes of the day. In Saigon, she visited an overcrowded and undermanned city hospital where the bug-ridden wards stank in the sweltering heat and patients might share a bed with a corpse for an entire day or more. In Africa, she saw the rioting in Leopoldville (now Kinshasa). From her hotel window, she watched as the severed heads of rival tribesmen were paraded through the street on the spears of the victors. In Buenos Aires, caught in the midst of an uprising against the Peronistas, with revolution raging in the streets, she heard machine gun and mortar fire, saw bombs exploding, and passed dead bodies in the gutters.

Schuyler's most dramatic move in her quest for identity came in 1962 when she reinvented herself as "Felipa Monterro y Schuyler" in the hopes of re-entering the American music community as a Spanish musician. With this new persona, Schuyler tried to erase all the aspects of her life which had troubled her in the past, including her African-American ethnicity and her status as a former child prodigy. By the end of 1963, Schuyler had dropped "y Schuyler" to further cement a European identity and invented a whole new past for herself. Writing from Belgium to the American John Birch Society offering to join their lecture circuit on such topics as "The Red Menace in Africa," she described herself as a social worker, born and educated in Europe but working in Africa with the missionaries. She was so convincing that the society took her on as a lecturer, and she made a substantial sum on tours.

But the crowning objective of the Monterro gambit was to break into white America as a classical pianist. Both Schuyler and her mother hoped that if Monterro could establish a solid reputation in Europe, she could re-enter the American concert scene as a white and be able to perform for audiences thus far denied Philippa Schuyler. In April 1963, Felipa Monterro debuted in Switzerland. Her reviews, however, were mediocre, although the critics were impressed with her technical prowess. They seemed to be confused by the sudden appearance from nowhere of such an accomplished pianist.

Philippa Schuyler died on Tuesday, May 9, 1967, in a helicopter crash in Vietnam. She had gone there as a correspondent for William Loeb's *Manchester Union Leader* to perform for the troops, and in her unofficial capacity as lay missionary—evacuating young children, nuns, and priests from Hué to Da Nang. She was on her last "mission of mercy" when the helicopter in which she was riding crashed yards from shore. Schuyler was 35 years old. Ironically, she had visited a clairvoyant several days before and been told that on Tuesday, May 9, "her malefic period would be over and that she would emerge from the mouth of the Dragon." In her last letter home to her mother, she had written: "God, I can't wait to emerge from the Dragon's mouth."

**SOURCES:**

Bailey, Brooke. *The Remarkable Lives of 100 Women Artists.* Holbrook, MA: Bob Adams, 1994.

Smith, Jessie Carney, ed. *Notable Black American Women.* Detroit, MI: Gale Research, 1992.

**SUGGESTED READING:**

Talalay, Kathryn. *Composition in Black and White: The Life of Philippa Schuyler.* NY: Oxford University Press, 1995.

**Sally Cole-Misch,** freelance writer,
Bloomfield Hills, Michigan

## Schwartz, Betty Robinson (1911–1997).

See Robinson, Betty.

## Schwarz, Vera (1888–1964)

*Austrian soprano who was noted for her performances, with Richard Tauber, in the operettas of Franz Lehár. Born in Agram (now Zagreb, capital of Croatia) on July 10, 1888; died in Vienna, Austria, on December 4, 1964.*

Vera Schwarz was born in Agram in 1888, a child of the Austro-Hungarian Empire, an enormous medieval entity which encompassed much of Central Europe until the end of World War I. This ancient realm was multicultural and multilingual, bound together by economics and the German language. It was quite common for singers born in such outposts as the area which was once Yugoslavia to make their way to Vienna, the glorious Habsburg capital, and from there to international stardom. Like so many with talent, Vera Schwarz was drawn to Vienna where she studied before debuting at the Theater an der Wien in 1908. Soon she was singing Rosalinde in *Die Fledermaus* as well as other leading roles. From Vienna, she went to Hamburg and Berlin. In 1927, Schwarz sang *Der Zarewitsch* with Richard Tauber, marking the beginning of many Lehár operettas in which the couple would star. Because she was Jewish, Schwarz left for the United States in 1938 as the Nazi threat loomed ever larger over Europe; after the death of the Habsburg monarchy, Hitler's troops were poised to gobble up one by one the tiny countries that had replaced it. She remained in America for a decade before returning to Vienna in 1948 to teach.

**John Haag,**
Athens, Georgia

## Schwarzenbach, Annemarie (1908–1942).

*See Maillart, Ella for sidebar.*

## Schwarzhaupt, Elisabeth (1901–1986)

*German judge and politician who became the first woman in Germany to serve in a government Cabinet post. Born in Frankfurt am Main, Germany, on January 7, 1901; died in Frankfurt am Main on October 29, 1986; daughter of Wilhelm Schwarzhaupt and Frieda (Emmerich) Schwarzhaupt; never married.*

*Served as a member of the Christian Democratic Union and of West Germany's Bundestag (1953–69); was instrumental in drafting reform legislation aimed at gender equality (article 3 of the Basic Law).*

In 1961, Elisabeth Schwarzhaupt became the first female Cabinet minister of the Federal Republic of Germany. Born in the traditionally democratic city of Frankfurt am Main in 1901, Schwarzhaupt grew up in a cultured and liberal middle-class milieu. Her father Wilhelm Schwarzhaupt, who often discussed political issues with his daughter, was Frankfurt's superintendent of schools and had been active before World War I in the National Liberal Party. After 1918, he served as a delegate of the moderately liberal Deutsche Volkspartei (DVP, or German People's Party) to the Prussian Landtag (state legislature). Her mother **Frieda Emmerich Schwarzhaupt** also had a considerable influence on her, emphasizing the crucial connections between politics and morality. Schwarzhaupt had originally planned on a career in journalism, but in compliance with her parents' wishes she studied law, hoping to be a juvenile court judge. In 1930, she passed her examination as an assessor (assistant judge). As the Nazi Party grew to national prominence in the early 1930s, Schwarzhaupt took a strong stand against it, sometimes attending DVP meetings with her father where heated arguments broke out.

Shortly before Adolf Hitler came to power in 1933, Schwarzhaupt published a brochure censuring the Nazis, particularly for their stated intention of keeping women in an inferior status in their new social order, and defended her views in a public meeting near Frankfurt that was packed with Nazis. Schwarzhaupt had just begun her career, having obtained a limited-term civil-service position as a judge, first in Frankfurt and then in Düsseldorf. Her professional hopes were shattered when the nascent Nazi regime did not renew her contract. Her personal life was affected by the emergence of the Third Reich as well, for her fiancé, who was of Jewish origins, was forced to emigrate. After living at home with her parents and writing a legal dissertation, in 1934 Schwarzhaupt began working in Berlin as a legal advisor to the Reichsbund der Kleinrentner (Reich Association of Pensioners), which represented the interests of small investors and pensioners. This position, which would last until 1936, gave her insights into the plight of the aged whose savings had been destroyed in previous years by inflation.

In 1936, Schwarzhaupt became legal counsel to the central administrative board of the German Evangelical (Lutheran) Church. By this time, the church was deeply divided by internal struggles between pro-Nazi elements and those who for varying reasons wished to halt Nazi encroachments on the church. In subtle ways, Schwarzhaupt took the side of those who opposed National Socialist influences in the church, particularly by standing up for the persecuted vicars of the oppositional wing, the Confessing Church (Bekennende Kirche). Having gained the trust of important church leaders, in 1941 Schwarzhaupt was named superior church councilor. After Germany's defeat in 1945, she became a member of the church's constitutional committee. In 1947, she took on the responsibility of legal expert for the church's office of external relations, working under the renowned anti-Nazi hero Martin Niemöller.

In 1953, Schwarzhaupt overcame her reservations about joining the Christian Democratic Union (CDU), the governing conservative party headed by Konrad Adenauer. She had long wondered how a political party calling itself "Christian" might translate the ethical and moral teachings of the churches into daily reality. Yielding to pressure from various CDU members, she became a successful candidate for the Bundestag, holding a seat there from 1953 through 1969. Her most important work was done in the parliamentary committee on legal affairs, where all questions pertaining to the reform of family law were referred to her. She promoted improvements in the legal position of married women as well as the entrenchment of the principle of gender equality in the Basic Law of the Federal Republic (Grundgesetz), through her work on drafting article 3 of the Basic Law.

In 1961, in what has been described as the "uprising of the CDU Amazons," a number of CDU women members of the Bundestag petitioned Adenauer, pointedly reminding him of an earlier promise—now conveniently forgotten, they feared—to appoint a woman to his Cabinet. When Adenauer formed the Federal Republic's fourth government in the fall of 1962, he designated Schwarzhaupt as the first woman government minister in German history. Although she was sworn in as Minister of Health on November 14, 1961, her ministry did not then exist. Not until January 29, 1962, was the Ministry of Health officially established and given responsibility in all questions involving public health. After taking office, Schwarzhaupt embarked on an intensive program of study, not only attending numerous conferences, but also reading books and reports in order to become thoroughly familiar with the concerns of her ministry. One of her first projects was to authorize ongoing research into the "diseases of civilization," particularly heart and circulatory diseases and cancer.

As West Germany's chief health official, Schwarzhaupt investigated the dangers to the national well being from pollution of air and water, as well as the threats posed by noise, radiation, the purity of medications and food, and the problem of illegal drugs. Growing signs of major pollution in German streams and rivers

*Elisabeth Schwarzhaupt was honored with a German postage stamp in 1997.*

brought forth such measures as the launching of a research vessel on the Rhine in 1964, and the construction of water-purification facilities on other at-risk rivers. The problem of cigarette smoking also came to her attention; in this instance, she was convinced that education rather than legislation should be the preferred strategy. Serving as Health Minister until 1966, Schwarzhaupt remained realistic, even critical, about how much change her appointment truly signified, conceding that in many ways she had been chosen as a token woman by Adenauer and his inner circle. During her tenure, she became a veritable magnet for women's grievances (*Klagemauer für Frauen*) in the Federal Republic.

After retiring from the Health Ministry in 1966 and from the Bundestag in 1969, Schwarzhaupt assumed honorary positions in which she was still able to exert influence, if only on an informal basis. In 1966, she was awarded the Federal Republic's Grand Cross of the Order of Merit. Schwarzhaupt died in her home city of Frankfurt am Main on October 29, 1986. In her honor, a 100 pfennig postage stamp was added to the definitive series "Women in German History" and issued on October 16, 1997.

**SOURCES:**

"Bis zur Bahre," in *Der Spiegel*. Vol. 15, no. 48. November 22, 1961, pp. 29–30.

"Dr. Elisabeth Schwarzhaupt, Germany's First Woman Cabinet Minister," in *The Times* [London]. October 31, 1986, p. 24.

Elisabeth Schwarzhaupt Nachlass, Bundesarchiv Koblenz.

Reinicke, Dietrich, and Elisabeth Schwarzhaupt. *Die Gleichberechtigung von Mann und Frau nach dem Gesetz vom 18. Juni 1957.* Stuttgart: W. Kohlhammer, 1957.

Salentin, Ursula. *Elisabeth Schwarzhaupt, erste Ministerin der Bundesrepublik: Ein demokratischer Lebensweg.* Freiburg im Breisgau: Herder, 1986.

Schwarzhaupt, Elisabeth. *Gottfried Keller und die sozialen und volkserzieherischen Probleme seiner Zeit.* Inaugural-Dissertation, Universität Frankfurt am Main, 1929.

———. "Lebensbericht," in *Abgeordtnete des Deutschen Bundestages: Aufzeichnungen und Erinnerungen.* Vol. 2. Boppard am Rhein: Verlag Harald Boldt, 1983.

"Schwarzhaupt, Elisabeth (1901–86)," in Dieter K. Buse and Juergen C. Doerr, eds. *Modern Germany: An Encyclopedia of History, People, and Culture, 1871–1990.* Vol. 2. NY: Garland, 1998, pp. 902–903.

**John Haag**, Associate Professor of History, University of Georgia, Athens, Georgia

# Schwarzkopf, Elisabeth (1915—)

*German soprano, one of the great singers of the post-1945 era, who was acclaimed for her performances of Mozart and Richard Strauss and achieved equal fame in the recital hall as a Lieder singer. Name variations: Elisabeth Legge-Schwarzkopf. Born on December 9, 1915, in Jarotschin near Posen, Germany (now Jarocin near Poznán, Poland); daughter of Friedrich Schwarzkopf and Elisabeth (Fröhling) Schwarzkopf; studied at the Hochschule für Musik in Berlin, 1934–38; studied with Maria Ivogün; married Walter Legge (1906–1979, a record producer), in 1953.*

One of the most glamorous sopranos in opera, Elisabeth Schwarzkopf enjoyed an extraordinary career that spanned four decades. She was born in 1915, during World War I, in an area of Germany that would become part of Poland after 1918. An only child, she grew up a stable middle-class family that was rich in cultural traditions. Both her mother Elisabeth and her father Friedrich, a secondary-school teacher, valued the German traditions of *Kultur*, which meant books and music.

Because Friedrich taught the classics in a number of different schools, the Schwarzkopfs moved to a new town every several years, though this did not shake the family's essential solidity. Elisabeth was given every opportunity to develop her artistic talents from an early age, and her mother strongly believed in her daughter's future success. The Schwarzkopfs, however, had little extra money to spare, and did not even own a phonograph. Neither could they afford to attend opera performances. Elisabeth would be 19 "before she heard decent singing," her husband Walter Legge later noted. But music was never far away from young Elisabeth in her formative years. She began with piano lessons at age seven, and by ten she was learning to play the viola and organ. Schwarzkopf participated in a number of stage performances at her school, and by age 12 she was thinking of music as a career.

In 1934, Schwarzkopf began to study at Hochschule für Musik, Berlin's foremost music academy, where her pure, sweet singing voice, proficiency on the piano, organ and viola, and considerable knowledge of music theory had made her a strong candidate for admission. Schwarzkopf's first voice instructor, **Lula Mysz-Gmeiner**, was a noted opera and Lieder singer who claimed that both Johannes Brahms and Hugo Wolf had accompanied her in recitals of their own Lieder. Unfortunately, Mysz-Gmeiner proved to be "despotic to the point of blindness," and even worse was convinced that her new pupil, although vocally well equipped as a soprano, could in fact be turned into a contralto like herself. Perhaps Mysz-Gmeiner saw in Schwarzkopf a familiar echo of her own youth, but whatever the reason, she attempted for over a year to transform one voice into another—something that could easily do permanent damage to a singer's vocal instrument.

Schwarzkopf convinced her strong-willed mother that she was making no progress under Mysz-Gmeiner and was actually in danger of harming her voice. In turn, Schwarzkopf's mother sought out Dr. Fritz Stein, director of the Hochschule, to demand a different instructor. Stein, who was initially indignant, finally agreed to a change, and some time later, after tactful measures had been taken to minimize embarrassment to Mysz-Gmeiner, Elisabeth began voice studies with Dr. Heinrich Egonolf; he concurred that she was no mezzo, expressing confidence that she had a great future as a coloratura soprano.

The events that engulfed Germany starting in the early 1930s did not pass Schwarzkopf by. Her father, an anti-Nazi Social Democrat, lost his position as a gymnasium principal for his refusal either to join the Nazi Party or denounce his Jewish colleagues; Schwarzkopf chose the path of accommodation. Perhaps having been taught a grim lesson by her father's fate, in 1935 she joined the Hochschule's National Socialist German Student League (Nationalsozialistischer Deutscher Studentenbund, or NSDStB), rapidly rising to the level of a *Führerin*. The previous year, even before becoming an NSDStB member, Schwarzkopf had been a beneficiary of that organization's wealth and power, having been awarded a grant to finance a short trip to England during the Easter holidays in order to improve her knowledge of English. Doubtless realizing the value it would have for her career, the ambitious young artist took the final steps to join the Nazi Party in 1940. According to documentation discovered in the Berlin Document Center and the U.S. National Archives in the early 1980s by Austrian historian Oliver Rathkolb, Schwarzkopf applied to join the Nazi Party on January 26, 1940. Accepted on March 1, she was thereupon issued membership card NSDAP No. 7548960.

When the details of her wartime membership in the Nazi Party came to light in *The New York Times* in March 1983, Schwarzkopf admitted to having been a member, but suggested that "everyone" at that time associated with Berlin's Städtische Oper had been as well: "We thought nothing of it. We just did it." In a letter published in the *Times* on April 3, 1983, Schwarzkopf wrote from her home in Zurich that her father had urged her to join the Nazi Party, because "nothing was more important to

him than my singing." Becoming an NSDAP member, she wrote, was "akin to joining a union, and exactly for the same reason: to have a job." The letter ended with, "Although it was never in my repertory, I cannot help quoting Tosca: 'Vissi d'arte . . .' ['I lived for art']." It is highly unlikely that her actions will ever be completely understood, and they continue to provide fodder for her biographers and others attempting to understand the tangled relationship between the arts, individual artists, and totalitarian states in modern times.

In April 1938, soon after graduating from the Hochschule, Schwarzkopf passed an audition at the Städtische Oper (Municipal Opera) of Berlin. Within days of being hired as a probationary junior soprano, she made her opera debut on April 17, 1938, in a new production of Wagner's *Parsifal* in the short but important role of Second Flower Maiden (First Group) in Act II. Even in this supposed temple of the arts, Nazi racial politics intruded: she had to sign several documents stating she came from a family of "pure Aryan" origins, including parents and grandparents, and had never in any way been connected with the Jewish religion. In her first season at the Städtische Oper, Schwarzkopf gave 19 performances in 28 weeks, somewhat below the average.

During her next season at the Municipal Opera, 1938–39, Schwarzkopf's career progressed rapidly; she added 16 parts to her growing repertory, of which the first important one was Frasquita in the trio of Gypsies in Bizet's *Carmen*. Her second important role that season was Musetta in Puccini's *La Bohème*. Among the minor roles she mastered was that of Pepa in d'Albert's *Tiefland*, one of Adolf Hitler's favorite operas (after Wagner's work). The task of learning so many parts was made considerably easier by the fact that in the Third Reich foreign operas were customarily presented in German, not only for the ease of audience comprehension but also because of the new sense of national pride in all aspects of German *Kultur*.

Despite the incalculable suffering unleashed by its aggressions during World War II, Nazi Germany maintained a veneer of civilized life, which included the preservation of "high" culture. Operas and concerts continued to be scheduled despite the war, and such events as the 150th anniversary of Mozart's death in 1941 were celebrated with much pomp and circumstance by various organs of the vast Nazi propaganda machine. Despite food rationing and air raids, musical life continued, largely due to Pro-

LIBRARY
UNIVERSITY OF ST. FRANCIS
JOLIET, ILLINOIS

paganda Minister Joseph Goebbels' belief that a key element in assuring a German victory was keeping civilian morale high. Schwarzkopf and other rising artists benefited from these policies, since it kept them from having to work in war-related industries or, if they were male, serve at the front. From 1940 through 1942, she continued to appear on stage at the Städtische Oper despite the dangers and burdens of normal living created by air raids and what was becoming a total war.

In September 1940, *Maria Ivogün was in the audience when Schwarzkopf appeared in the role of Zerbinetta in Richard Strauss' *Ariadne auf Naxos*. Ivogün, the most famous portrayer of Zerbinetta since *Selma Kurz, was astounded by Schwarzkopf's singing, which revealed star quality and "great talent but no knowledge of technique at all." She agreed to take Schwarzkopf on as a special pupil, provided she was willing to let her voice be "taken apart and rebuilt, note by note, in the right way." Schwarzkopf's lessons with Ivogün, crucial to her emergence as one of the great singers of the 20th century, were funded by the Reichstheaterkammer (Reich Theater Chamber), the Nazi state's monopoly overseeing all aspects of the German stage. Schwarzkopf also received valuable coaching in the Lieder repertory from Ivogün's husband, the renowned accompanist Michael Raucheisen. With her enhanced vocal qualities and growing professional self-confidence, Schwarzkopf blossomed; she graduated from second-soprano roles to starring ones, in operas and operettas, including Adele in Johann Strauss, Jr.'s *Die Fledermaus*.

Accompanied by Raucheisen, Schwarzkopf began giving Lieder recitals in Berlin's Beethoven Saal in May 1942, the beginning of what would become one of the great careers of Lieder singing. By early 1943, her career was flourishing. In March and April, she presented further Lieder recitals, and on April 23 appeared in Bach's *St. Matthew Passion*. But Schwarzkopf was confronted with a major crisis when she received a diagnosis of tuberculosis, brought on, she believed, from having spent too many hours in cold, damp air-raid shelters during the ever-increasing Allied bombing raids on Berlin. At this time, Schwarzkopf also received the good news that she had been accepted as a member of the Vienna State Opera, whose leading conductor Karl Böhm had been impressed by her talent.

After spending a year at a clinic situated high on the Czech side of the Tatra Mountains, in the town of Tatranská Polianka, Schwarzkopf was released fully cured and moved to Vienna to resume her singing career in April 1944. Her illness had been fortunate in some ways, sparing her from the ever-increasing dangers of almost daily bombing raids on Berlin and, to a lesser extent, on Vienna. From April through June 1944, Schwarzkopf appeared in leading roles in several operas, including Mozart's *Entführung aus dem Serail* (Abduction from the Seraglio), Puccini's *La Bohème*, and Weber's *Der Freischütz*. In late summer, Goebbels decreed that all German theaters be closed so that their staffs could be mobilized for the hopeless "total war" campaign he continued to preach to the citizens of the Reich. Schwarzkopf found herself temporarily unemployed, but was able to give a Lieder recital in Vienna's venerable Musikvereinsaal on December 12 of that year.

In mid-April 1945, Soviet troops captured Vienna, but the demise of Nazi inhumanity did not immediately benefit the city's inhabitants. For several weeks, Soviet forces were allowed to rape and pillage. These acts of retribution were justified by Soviet commanders as an appropriate response to the bestial behavior of German soldiers during their occupation of the USSR. Schwarzkopf and her mother had prudently fled Vienna at the time of its surrender, and would live in Attersee near Salzburg for the next few months until the situation became more stable. Once the initial period of violence ceased, however, Soviet occupation authorities were solicitous in assisting Austrians in the restoration of cultural life, so that opera performances took place as early as May 1, 1945, even before the war had officially ended.

In late 1945, Schwarzkopf returned to Vienna in an American jeep. There, she performed under a cloud of uncertainty about her future, singing at the Theater an der Wien and the Volksoper, both temporary stages for the State Opera ensemble whose theater had been destroyed in a bombing raid that March. Along with a sizable number of other musicians, many of them well established in their careers, she sought ways to clear herself of the taint of Nazi sympathies. To accomplish this process of "de-Nazification," Allied occupation authorities required that individuals fill out an extensive *Fragebogen* (questionnaire) detailing one's political activities during the Nazi dictatorship. In Schwarzkopf's case, she filled out *Fragebogen* on four separate occasions, two in July 1945, one that October, and one on May 3, 1946. In the first three documents, she denied having ever been a member of the Nazi Party. Only on the fourth form did she admit that she joined the Nazi Party "in 1940 or 1941," but she maintained that she had not been allocated a

*Elisabeth Schwarzkopf*

party number. In early June 1946, the Austrian State Theater Administration ordered Schwarzkopf's deportation to Germany. An administrative error on the part of the Vienna police, however, prevented the directive from being carried out, and by the end of that year her case, and those of many other artists who had been Nazi Party members, including the gifted Austrian conductor Herbert von Karajan, had lapsed into bureaucratic inactivity. Officially, Schwarzkopf was declared de-Nazified in February 1947, at which point she was free to resume her career.

Now an Austrian citizen and having recently performed at the Salzburg Festival, Schwarzkopf traveled to London as a member of Vienna State Opera company. This would be her great breakthrough.

On March 3, 1946, British record producer Walter Legge had heard Schwarzkopf singing the role of Rosina in Rossini's *The Barber of Seville.* He heard, he said, "a brilliant, fresh voice shot with laughter, not large but admirably projected, with enchanting high pianissimi." Legge also admired Schwarzkopf's "hair-raising agility" as Constanze in Mozart's *Entführung,* and soon he was determined to bring perfection Schwarzkopf's voice, whose true nature he was convinced was that of a lyric soprano. At his urging, she began singing roles appropriate to her new voice, including Agathe in *Der Freitschütz* and the Countess in Mozart's *Le nozze di Figaro* (The Marriage of Figaro). Soon, a strong professional and personal alliance was forged; they would marry in 1953.

Behind Legge's often caustic manner and uncompromising artistic standards was a man who cherished all aspects of music. He was also—unusual for his time and place—an unabashed Germanophile, profoundly attracted to the language, music and traditions of German-speaking Central Europe. The partnership between Schwarzkopf and Legge, who wielded great power in the musical world as artistic director of EMI Records, was an alliance of intellectual equals who both sought perfection. Journalists would sometimes describe Schwarzkopf as being no more than a Trilby to Legge's Svengali, but in truth he (and von Karajan, under whose direction she would perform in memorable concerts as well as make a large number of superb recordings) challenged Schwarzkopf to fulfill her artistic potential. Legge and Schwarzkopf spent countless hours learning new repertory, particularly the Lieder that both loved so profoundly. "Legge turned Schwarzkopf, an uncommonly good soprano, into a great singer," wrote Irving Kolodin. Thanks both to Schwarzkopf's unceasing study and Legge's superb coaching, her voice reached its full maturity, best described by critic Andrew Porter as "a lustrous, powerful lyric soprano, full-toned, warm and flexible."

The upward trajectory of her career continued in 1948 when she joined London's newly formed Covent Garden Opera Company, remaining with it for five seasons and singing her many roles in English. In December of that year, she was invited to sing at Milan's fabled La Scala, and was so successful with Italian audiences that she continued to perform there on a regular basis until 1963. Countless Italian music lovers were enthusiastic about Schwarzkopf, including conductor Arturo Toscanini, who became acquainted with her talent through the 1947 von Karajan recording of Brahms' *German Requiem.* Toscanini found himself captivated by Schwarzkopf's singing of "Ihr nun habt Traurigkeit," feeling it to be something close to perfection (in his unique mix of Italian and English, Toscanini had exclaimed when he first heard the recording, "*Molte bene.* I never had the soprano so good"). In 1951, Schwarzkopf was the only non-Italian singer chosen to perform in Verdi's *Requiem* as part of the celebrations to commemorate the 50th anniversary of the composer's death.

Although Elisabeth Schwarzkopf would reign supreme as a Lieder singer as well as in a select number of roles in Mozart and Richard Strauss operas, she was in actuality an artist with a remarkably broad repertory which included the French roles of Marguerite and Mélisande, Iole in Handel's *Hercules,* and Marenka (sung in English) in Smetana's *The Bartered Bride.* In September 1951, she originated the role of Anne Trulove in Igor Stravinsky's witty opera *The Rake's Progress,* which premiered before a gala audience in Venice's Teatro Fenice. Only the superb musicality of Schwarzkopf and other members of the cast prevented a disaster, because Stravinsky had no experience as an opera conductor (deputy conductor Ferdinand Leitner provided the singers crucial cues from behind the composer's back). In 1953, Schwarzkopf participated in another world premiere, this time of Carl Orff's *Trionfo d'Afrodite* at La Scala. Although she rarely performed works of contemporary music, the ones she chose were of high quality, including Michael Tippett's powerful anti-Nazi oratorio *A Child of Our Time.*

Besides von Karajan, with whom she had a productive collaboration until the mid-1960s, Schwarzkopf enjoyed working with some of the finest conductors and Lieder accompanists of her day. From the late 1940s until his death in 1954, legendary German conductor Wilhelm Furtwängler chose Schwarzkopf to appear in many of the operas he conducted at the Salzburg Festival. These included Mozart operas which were recorded and still constitute a benchmark for these works. In 1951, Furtwängler also chose Schwarzkopf to sing in the Beethoven Ninth Symphony performance he conducted at the first postwar Bayreuth Festival, the recording of which has become a classic. In August 1953, Furtwängler accompanied Schwarzkopf in an unforgettable evening of Hugo Wolf Lieder, the recording of which also has been acclaimed by several generations of music critics. In the 1930s, Legge had singlehandedly helped to place Wolf's Lieder in the pantheon of great vocal music with his series of Hugo Wolf Society subscription 78 rpm recordings. In the 1950s, through both recitals and recordings, Schwarzkopf and Legge together continued the process of further securing Wolf's position in music history as one of the last giants among Romantic composers.

Legge once explained the essence of Schwarzkopf's success by pointing to Italian baritone Titta Ruffo. Ruffo, who sang in at least 100 operas, once said that if he had the choice of starting his career again, he would have restricted himself to five or six parts, so as to polish each of these in every detail, thus guaranteeing his dominance in these roles. "He was a wise man," noted Legge. By the mid-1950s, Schwarzkopf had come to see the wisdom of the Ruffo-Legge strategy. The six parts she chose to concentrate on for the next 15 years, the culmination of her career, were three Mozart heroines (Fiordiligi, Donna Elvira, and the Countess Almaviva), two Richard Strauss roles (the Marschallin in *Der Rosenkavalier* and the Countess in *Capriccio*), and Alice in Verdi's *Falstaff*. She also became a past master singing in several operetta classics, particularly *Die Fledermaus* and Franz Lehár's *Die lustige witwe* (The Merry Widow). In the superbly cast and finely engineered recordings of these works produced by her husband for EMI (marketed in the U.S. starting in 1953 under the Angel label), Schwarzkopf's artistry is preserved. In the 1950s and 1960s, she recorded works that remain classics more than a generation later: Richard Strauss' *Vier letzte Lieder* (Four Last Songs), which exists in three different but all superb Schwarzkopf versions, as well as works she recorded but never performed in public, including Humperdinck's *Hänsel und Gretel*, Carl Orff's *Die Kluge* (The Clever Woman), and William Walton's *Troilus and Cressida*.

Schwarzkopf made her American debut in 1953 with a Lieder recital at New York's Town Hall. Picketers on the street denouncing her as a Nazi sympathizer did not dampen the response she received inside from devotees of German music. Her American operatic debut took place in 1955 with the San Francisco Opera, whose conductor Kurt Herbert Adler had fled Nazism. Schwarzkopf sang there to great success for ten years. Her first appearance in San Francisco, on September 20, 1955, as the Marschallin in *Der Rosenkavalier*, was an overwhelming triumph. Only in 1964 did Schwarzkopf finally receive an invitation to sing at New York's Metropolitan Opera, appearing on October 13, 1964, as the Marschallin. Her relationship with this company was not always perfect, and she last sang there in 1966. By the end of the 1960s, it was clear that Schwarzkopf's career was entering its final phase. She now had to conserve her vocal resources, appearing in fewer operas each year, concentrating instead on less-strenuous Lieder recitals. Her last opera performance in America took place in Carnegie Hall on April 27, 1972. Her last opera appearance was in Brussels in 1972 as the Marschallin—a role that had become uniquely hers. In 1975, she made a farewell recital tour of the United States.

In Europe, Elisabeth Schwarzkopf continued to concertize through the 1970s, despite her declining vocal resources. She gave what would be her last Liederabend in Zurich, Switzerland, on March 19, 1979. Three days later, her husband died, having suffered a severe heart attack a week before. Schwarzkopf decided at this point to end her singing career. Walter Legge's last wishes were fulfilled: his ashes were put to rest near the grave of Hugo Wolf in Vienna's Zentralfriedhof (Central Cemetery). Determined to work despite her loss, Schwarzkopf flew to San Francisco in June 1979 to give master classes. For the next decade, she remained active in various musical activities, including directing a production of *Der Rosenkavalier* in Brussels in May 1981. She also served as a judge on panels, and took on a small number of gifted young singers as students.

As the 20th century neared its end, Schwarzkopf had little choice but to slow down. By then in her 80s, she could point with pride to such awards as the Federal Republic of Germany's Grosses Bundesverdienstkreuz (Large Cross of Achievement) as well as its coveted Pour le Mérite (an order first founded in 1740 by Prussian sovereign Frederick the Great). From Great Britain, a nation that grew to respect and love her, she had received an honorary doctorate in music from Cambridge University (1977) and the rank of Dame Commander of the British Empire (DBE), awarded by Queen *Elizabeth II (1992). As the critic Robert Jacobson wrote during her final American tour, and as the finest of her recordings illustrate, Schwarzkopf had "set an exalted standard of accomplishment in so many ways and in so many areas that our opera and concert lives are likely never to be quite the same."

**SOURCES:**

*L'Avant Scène: Opéra* [Paris]. Autumn 1983 (special issue dedicated to Elisabeth Schwarzkopf).

Berlin Document Center: personal file of Elisabeth Schwarzkopf.

Blyth, Alan. "Opera into Song," in *The Opera Quarterly*. Vol. 11, no. 3, 1995, pp. 31–38.

Breuer, Gustl. "When Marschallins Meet," in *Opera News*. Vol. 46, no. 3. September 1981, pp. 37–38.

Cassidy, Claudia. "Sorceress," in *Opera News*. Vol. 39, no. 22. May 1975, p. 13–14.

Christiansen, Rupert. *Prima Donna: A History*. NY: Penguin, 1986.

Corvetto, Anibal. "Schwarzkopf as Tenor," in *Opera*. Vol. 46, no. 8. August 1995, p. 901.

Croan, Robert, and Peter G. Davis. "Elisabeth Schwarzkopf: Point-Counterpoint," in *Opera News*. Vol. 60, no. 6. December 9, 1995, pp. 32–33, 70–71.

Dusek, Peter, and Volkmar Parschalk, eds. *Nicht nur Tenore: Das Beste aus der Opernwerkstatt*. 2 vols. Vienna: Verlag Jugend und Volk, 1986.

"Frankfurter Mozart-Medaille für Elisabeth Schwarzkopf," in *Mitteilungen der Internationalen Stiftung Mozarteum*. Vol. 31, no. 1–4, 1983, p. 110.

Gavoty, Bernard. *Elisabeth Schwarzkopf*. Geneva: Verlag R. Kister, 1958.

Greenfield, Edward. "Elisabeth Schwarzkopf," in *The Gramophone*. October 1976; November 1976; December 1985.

Honig, Joel. "Seasons of Schwarzkopf," in *Opera News*. Vol. 61, no. 2. August 1996, pp. 40–41, 52.

Hughes, Allen. "Walter Legge, Record Producer," in *The New York Times Biographical Service*. March 1979, p. 342.

Jacobson, Robert. "Viewpoint," in *Opera News*. Vol. 39, no. 22. May 1975, p. 4.

Jacobson, Robert M. *Reverberations: Interviews with the World's Leading Musicians*. NY: Morrow, 1974.

Jefferson, Alan. *Elisabeth Schwarzkopf*. Boston, MA: Northeastern University Press, 1996.

———. "Elisabeth Schwarzkopf in Vienna," in *Richard Strauss-Blätter*. No. 34. December 1995, pp. 111–120.

Kater, Michael H. *The Twisted Muse: Musicians and their Music in the Third Reich*. Oxford, UK: Oxford University Press, 1997.

Koestenbaum, Wayne. "Listening to Schwarzkopf: The Reich and the Soprano," in *The New Yorker*. Vol. 72, no. 24–25. August 26–September 2, 1996, pp. 160–163.

Legge, Walter. "Her Master's Voice," in *Opera News*. Vol. 39, no. 22. May 1975, pp. 8–12.

Levi, Erik. *Music in the Third Reich*. NY: St. Martin's, 1994.

Moore, Gerald. *Am I Too Loud?* NY: Macmillan, 1962.

———. *Farewell Recital*. London: Hamish Hamilton, 1978.

Mordden, Ethan. *Demented: The World of the Opera Diva*. NY: Simon & Schuster, 1990.

Porter, Andrew. *Music of Three Seasons, 1974–1977*. NY: Farrar Straus & Giroux, 1978.

Prieberg, Fred K. *Musik im NS-Staat*. Frankfurt am Main: Fischer Taschenbuch, 1982.

Rathkolb, Oliver. *Führertreu und gottbegnadet: Künstlereliten im Dritten Reich*. Vienna: Österreichischer Bundesverlag Gesellschaft m.b.H., 1991.

———. "Zur Entnazifizierung von Musikern nach 1945," in *Österreichische Musikzeitschrift*. Vol. 51, no. 2–3, 1996, pp. 135–137.

Sanders, Alan. *Walter Legge: A Discography*. Westport, CT: Greenwood Press, 1984.

———, ed. *Walter Legge: Words and Music*. London: Routledge, 1998.

———, and J.B. Steane. *Elisabeth Schwarzkopf: A Career on Record*. Portland, OR: Amadeus, 1995.

Schwarzkopf, Elisabeth. "Elisabeth Schwarzkopf and the Nazi Party," in *The New York Times*. April 3, 1983, section 4, p. 14E.

———. *On and Off the Record: A Memoir of Walter Legge*. 2nd ed. London: Faber, 1988.

"Schwarzkopf at 75 Looks to Music's Future," in *The New York Times*. December 25, 1990, section I, p. 16.

Shirakawa, Sam H. *The Devil's Music Master: The Controversial Life and Career of Wilhelm Furtwängler*. Oxford, UK: Oxford University Press, 1992.

Soria, Dorle J., *et al.* "Fanatic for Quality," in *Opera News*. Vol. 44, no. 2. August 1979, pp. 9–14, 18.

Steane, J.B. *The Grand Tradition: Seventy Years of Singing on Record*. 2nd ed. Portland, OR: Amadeus, 1993.

———. *Singers of the Century*. Vol. 1. Portland, OR: Amadeus, 1996.

Steane, John Barry. *Voices, Singers & Critics*. Portland, OR: Amadeus, 1992.

Stearns, David Patrick. "The Schwarzkopf File," in *Opera News*. Vol. 60, no. 6. December 9, 1995, pp. 28–30.

Tagliabue, John. "Germans Explore Ties of Musicians to Nazis," in *The New York Times*. March 17, 1983, p. C17.

**RELATED MEDIA:**

Caillat, Gérald. "Elisabeth Schwarzkopf: A Self-Portrait" (videocassette), Ideale Audience-EMI Classics, 1995.

Strauss, Richard. "Der Rosenkavalier" (videocassette of complete opera), recorded in 1962.

**John Haag,**
Associate Professor of History,
University of Georgia, Athens, Georgia

# Schwarzwald, Eugenie (1872–1940)

*Austrian educational reformer, salonnière, and philanthropist whose private school for girls in Vienna encouraged intellectual independence. Name variations: Eugenia Schwarzwald; Genia Schwarzwald; "Fraudoktor" Schwarzwald. Born Eugenie Nussbaum in Polupanowka near Czernowitz, Galicia, Austria (now Chernovtsy, Ukraine), on July 4, 1872; died in exile in Zurich, Switzerland, on August 7, 1940; daughter of Leo Nussbaum and Esther Nussbaum; had three siblings; married Hermann ("Hemme") Schwarzwald; no children.*

Eugenie Schwarzwald, who would initiate an educational revolution in Vienna, was born Eugenie Nussbaum in 1872, not in the capital of the multinational Habsburg Empire but in Polupanowka, a small, nondescript town in the forested region of the Austrian province of Galicia. She grew up in an assimilated German-speaking Jewish family who lived in relative affluence, her father being the administrator of one of the rural estates in the region. A bright student, Genia had little interest in preparing for the conventional career of a woman of the period, namely becoming a schoolteacher. Instead, she was determined to achieve a higher education, and therefore moved to Switzerland, where in 1895 she enrolled at the University of Zurich, an institution that had pioneered in women's education since 1865. After studying literature and philosophy, Genia was awarded a doctorate in 1900. That same year, as one of the first women in Austria-Hungary to earn a Ph.D., she moved to Vienna, where, in December, she married a brilliant Czernowitz-born economist named Hermann Schwarzwald, known as Hemme.

Restless and brimming over with ideas for reform, in 1901 Genia Schwarzwald purchased a girls' lyceum located on Vienna's Franziskanerplatz from educational pioneer **Eleonore Jeiteles** (1841–1918), who had been a school director since the early 1870s. In 1888, Jeiteles, a well-known feminist, had inaugurated a girls' lyceum that soon gained an excellent reputation among the solid Viennese middle class. It was this school, which opened on September 15, 1901, that Schwarzwald would quickly transform into a unique experiment in education. By the end of her first year, she had enrolled 181 girls.

After the second year, Schwarzwald moved the lyceum to a location on the Wallnerstrasse in Vienna's exclusive First District. Here, she modernized the curriculum and hired first-class teachers. Interested in the latest educational innovations, she was inspired by the writings of such contemporary school reformers as Italy's *Maria Montessori. Much of Schwarzwald's energy went into persuading officials at the Ministry of Instruction that her school was adhering to their directives, which more often than not were infuriatingly Byzantine in their bureaucratic complexity. Because of the imperial Austrian ability to ignore rules, the Schwarzwald-Schule was able to educate many hundreds of girls for more than a decade with only a certificate of provisional authorization (*provisorische Genehmigung*). Not until 1912 did her school finally receive its full statute of approval as a Mädchen-Reform-Gymnasium (Modern Girls' Secondary School). From this point on, all graduates of the Schwarzwald School were fully qualified to enter any of the universities of the Habsburg Empire.

Although women had been admitted to institutions of higher education in Austria-Hun-

gary since the late 1890s, there remained significant obstacles to full equality in the Habsburg lands. Traditional prejudices about female *cerebrale Minderwertigkeit* (intellectual inferiority) were deeply embedded. Austrian aristocrats looked down on intellectual pursuits, preferring instead to lead lives of leisure. Schwarzwald on the other hand embodied the ideals of Austria's middle class, many of them Jewish, who valued achievement and wanted to make their mark on the world, hopefully by improving it. Schwarzwald believed that a better world would be possible only if women were given the opportunity to live up to their full intellectual potentials, particularly if they could enter those professions that were solely accessible with higher educational credentials. Her primary goal was to prepare young women successfully for the difficult entrance examinations for Austrian universities. This she accomplished, often providing full tuition to girls whose families were poor or, after 1918, had lost their wealth as the result of war and raging inflation.

*Eugenie Schwarzwald*

The start of World War I in the summer of 1914 shocked Schwarzwald as much as it did any other Austrian. She not only met the new challenges faced by her school, however, but in 1915 set up soup kitchens for an increasingly impoverished middle class, as well as a volunteer social service for the hundreds of thousands of Russian prisoners of war in Austrian captivity who were generally despised and neglected. As part of her program *Wiener Kinder auf's Land* (Viennese Kids into the Fresh Air), Schwarzwald organized camps in which the children of Austrian soldiers who had died in the war were given the opportunity to spend time in the countryside, where along with recreational activities they were provided with plentiful food.

As the war dragged on, in 1917 she organized a chain of co-op restaurants where struggling Viennese families could eat a simple, nourishing lunch for a modest sum. By 1919, when the situation in Vienna had become desperate, more than a dozen of these restaurants were flourishing. Nor were the elderly forgotten. Her program *Jugend hilft Alter* (Youth Helps the Aged), known popularly as "Genia's *Greisenhilfe*" (Assistance to the Ancients), rendered practical assistance to the very old of Vienna who had been made destitute by the war. Schwarzwald mobilized middle-class teenagers of the city, who then scoured their neighborhoods to track down the elderly who were often too proud to register for free meals, and for whom they also provided basic homemaking services.

These Viennese programs were so successful that by 1923, when Germany found itself convulsed by inflation, Schwarzwald went to Berlin to organize a mass-nourishment program called the *Österreichische Freundeshilfe für Deutschland* (Austrian Friends' Assistance for Germany). Given use of Berlin's former imperial palace, she quickly established a canteen designed to alleviate the misery of the student population. It soon was known simply as the *Schlossküche* (Palace Kitchen) by both the local population and the world press which reported extensively on its remarkable achievement. One of the poor students who ate there was the young Helmuth von Moltke, an aristocrat who would later be a key figure in the unsuccessful 1944 plot to assassinate Adolf Hitler. To help finance these schemes, Schwarzwald became involved in several for-profit enterprises, including a Viennese taxi service and a commercial vegetable farm.

The growing reputation of her girls' school made it possible for Schwarzwald to preside over a brilliant salon at her home. Peter Drucker, who was close to her circle as a young man, writes that the salon became the talk of Central Europe. "It flourished because Genia understood that a salon is performing art, just like opera and ballet . . . [Her salon] was unrehearsed, spontaneous, free-form, flexible, and fast." Regularly appearing at the Schwarzwald salon was a staggering array of writers of the interwar decades, including *Karin Michaëlis, Rainer Maria Rilke, Arno Holz, Robert Musil, Bertolt Brecht, Karl Kraus, Elias Canetti, Jakob Wassermann, Carl Zuckmayer, Gottfried Benn, and Egon Friedell. Musicians were well represented, including Arnold Schoenberg, Egon Wellesz, Adolf Busch, Rudolf Serkin, **Lotte Leonard, Greta Kraus**, and Max Rostal. From the United States, regular guests at the salon included *Dorothy Thompson, Sinclair Lewis, and Edgar Ansel Mowrer. Architecture was represented by Adolf Loos, painting by Oskar Kokoschka. There was also the photographer Bill Brandt, the legal scholar (and author of the Austrian Republic's constitution) Hans Kelsen, and the young actress *Helene Weigel. Many of those who participated in the salon came to believe that it was unique. Kokoschka would refer to it in later years as "a spiritual center in the form of an open house."

The Schwarzwald School's teachers were chosen not only for their intellectual abilities, but for their teaching skills. Although Genia had stopped teaching classes early in her school's existence, she retained a strong interest in what went on in its classrooms, and occasionally would substitute for an absent instructor. As well, Kokoschka, Schoenberg, and Wellesz intermittently taught there. On one occasion, Schwarzwald attempted to point out to the Minister of Instruction that although Oskar Kokoschka lacked the formal educational credentials needed to be an officially certified teacher, the artist had excelled at teaching classes at her school and was a creative genius. Even so, the bureaucrat replied, "geniuses are not anticipated in the curriculum."

Schwarzwald was convinced that education was more than classroom experiences and should take place on a 12-month basis. To make possible her ideal of *Sommerpädagogik* (summertime pedagogy), in the 1920s she purchased a dilapidated hotel, the Hotel Seeblick, on the breathtaking Grundlsee, one of western Austria's most beautiful lakes. By the 1930s, she could boast of having made possible a university education for many hundreds of young women, some of whom would leave their mark on the arts and other aspects of European life. Among her graduates, Helene Weigel went on to become one of the great actresses of the century, *Hilde Spiel became a distinguished author in both Austria and the United Kingdom, and *Marie Langer became a psychoanalyst who in the final years of her life was a champion of the Sandinista revolution in Nicaragua. Others, such as Alice Herdan-Zuckmayer, Elisabeth Neumann, and Emmy Wellesz, not only married men who were distinguished in various fields, but were able to have significant careers of their own. At least one graduate of the Schwarzwald School, Freya Deichmann (von Moltke), was able to pass on Schwarzwald's cosmopolitan and liberal teachings to her husband. Deichmann married Helmuth von Moltke, whose consuming hatred of Nazism brought him into the ill-fated plot to kill Hitler. By the 1930s, Schwarzwald students referred to themselves as "Genia's children" or "*die Schwarzwaldkinder*," or even "*die Kinderschar von Fraudoktor.*"

In 1928, Austria's Minister of Instruction publicly declared that Schwarzwald deserved most of the credit for the educational progress that Austria had made in recent years. Her reputation remained high even though, being Jewish and identified with the liberal Weltanschauung of the pre-1914 Habsburg realm, she and her way of life were in many ways relics from the past. As late as early 1930, however, her immense prestige enabled her to virtually dictate the terms of a labor dispute that, had it not been mediated by her, would have cost tens of thousands of industrial workers their livelihoods. But Schwarzwald's world was doomed by the rise of dictatorships in Central Europe. Hitler's Third Reich was anathema to everything she stood for, and many of her students had to flee for their lives when the Nazis came to power in Germany in 1933. Schwarzwald was in Copenhagen for a lecture and scheduled cancer surgery when Hitler's troops occupied Austria in March 1938. She never returned to Vienna. Helmuth von Moltke was able to assist Hermann Schwarzwald in leaving Austria.

The Schwarzwalds went into exile in Switzerland, where they found themselves impoverished and in rapidly worsening health. The Nazis shut down Genia's school on September 15, 1938, 37 years to the day of its opening. Her beloved Hemme died in Zurich on August 17, 1939. Genia Schwarzwald died in the same city almost a year later, on August 7, 1940. On July 13, less than a month before her death, Genia had written her good friend Karin Michaëlis to inform her of her intention of "dying in as correct a fashion as I have lived."

The Schwarzwalds, and Genia's remarkable school, have been immortalized in a number of books. These include Karl Kraus' *Die letzten Tage der Menschheit* (The Last Days of Mankind), where they surface as the Schwarzgelbers. Genia appears as Diotima in Robert Musil's *Der Mann ohne Eigenschaften* (The Man Without Qualities). Characters based on her are included in many other books of the period, including Felix Dörmann's *Jazz*, a novel about inflation-era Vienna. Hans Deichmann, brother of Freya von Moltke and author of one of the most informative books about Eugenie Schwarzwald, once made a list of the most important insights he had gained from her. They were: to listen, to be open, to be patient, and not to become a victim of one's own prejudices.

**SOURCES:**

Anderson, Harriet. *Utopian Feminism: Women's Movements in fin-de-siecle Vienna.* New Haven, CT: Yale University Press, 1992.

Deichmann, Hans. *Leben mit provisorischer Genehmigung; Leben, Werk und Exil von Dr. Eugenie Schwarzwald (1872–1940). Eine Chronik.* Berlin: Guthmann-Peterson, 1988.

Drucker, Peter F. *Adventures of a Bystander: Memoirs.* New ed. NY: HarperCollins, 1991.

Dukes, Eva. "The Last 5th R. G. and Bits and Pieces from Schwarzwaldschule" (unpublished manuscript dated 1988), copy in the research library of the U.S. Holocaust Memorial Museum, Washington, D.C.

Ende, Amelia von. "Literary Vienna," in *The Bookman.* Vol. 38. October 1913, pp. 141–155.

Freund, René. *Land der Träumer—Zwischen Grösse und Grössenwahn: Verkannte Österreicher und ihre Utopien.* Vienna: Picus, 1996.

Geber, Eva, *et al. Die Frauen Wiens: Ein Stadtbuch für Fanny, Frances und Francesca.* Vienna: AUF-edition/Verlag der Apfel, 1992.

Göllner, Renate. "Mädchenbildung um Neunzehnhundert: Eugenie Schwarzwald und ihre Schulen," Ph.D. dissertation, University of Vienna, 1986.

Herdan-Zuckmayer, Alice. *Genies sind im Lehrplan nicht vorgesehen.* Frankfurt am Main: Fischer Taschenbuch, 1991.

Keintzel, Brigitta. "Eugenie Schwarzwald (geb. Nussbaum)," in Ilse Korotin, ed., *Gelehrte Frauen: Frauenbiographien vom 10. bis zum 20. Jahrhundert.* Vienna: Bundesministerium für Unterricht und kulturelle Angelegenheiten, 1996, pp. 238–241.

Kosta, Barbara. "Unruly Daughters and Modernity: Irmgard Keun's *Gilgi—eine von uns*," in *The German Quarterly.* Vol. 68, no. 3. Summer 1995, pp. 271–286.

Langer, Marie, with Enrique Guinsberg and Jaime del Palacio. *From Vienna to Managua: Journey of a Psychoanalyst.* Translated by Margaret Hooks. London: Free Association Books, 1989.

Moltke, Helmuth James von. *Letters to Freya 1939–1945.* Edited and translated by Beate Ruhm von Oppen. NY: Alfred A. Knopf, 1990.

Sachs, Harvey. "Der Ordinäre," in *The New Yorker.* Vol. 66, no. 16. June 4, 1990.

Scheu, Friedrich. *Ein Band der Freundschaft: Schwarz-wald-Kreis und Entstehung der Vereinigung Sozialistischer Mittelschüler.* Vienna: Böhlau, 1985.

Schiferer, Beatrix. *Vorbilder: kreative Frauen in Wien, 1750–1950.* Vienna: Verband Wiener Volksbildung, 1994.

Schwarzwald, Eugenie. "Bernard Shaw, der Freund der Frauen," in *Breslauer Zeitung.* February 12, 1928.

———. "Besuch in einem Kindergefängnis," in *Hannoversches Tageblatt.* August 18, 1929.

———. "Das glückliche Mädchen von Morgen," in *Der Querschnitt.* Vol. 12, 1932, pp. 235–237.

———. "Jonas Lie, ein moderner Charakter," in *Neue Freie Presse* [Vienna]. November 8, 1933.

———. "Karin Michaëlis," in *Basler Nachrichten.* March 19–20, 1932.

———. "Der Redner Kokoschka," in *Neue Freie Presse* [Vienna]. January 20, 1926.

Soden, Kristine von, and Maruta Schmidt, eds. *Neue Frauen: Die zwanziger Jahre.* Berlin: Elefanten Presse, 1988.

Streibel, Robert, ed. *Eugenie Schwarzwald und ihr Kreis.* Vienna: Picus, 1996.

Voelker, Klaus. *Ich verreise auf einige Zeit: Sadie Leviton-Schauspielerin, Emigrantin, Freundin von Helene Weigel und Bertolt Brecht.* Berlin: Transit-Buchverlag, 1999.

**RELATED MEDIA:**

"MerkMal: Die Wiener Reformpädagogin Eugenie Schwarzwald" (radio program), Deutschlandradio Berlin, December 11, 1995.

**John Haag**, Associate Professor of History, University of Georgia, Athens, Georgia

## Schweitzer, Lucille (1902–1999).

*See Lortel, Lucille.*

## Schweitzer, Nicole Henriot (b. 1925).

*See Henriot-Schweitzer, Nicole.*

# Schwimmer, Rosika (1877–1948)

*Hungarian peace activist, feminist, writer, first woman diplomat and advocate of world government, who came to prominence through her successful organization of suffrage and feminist groups and her influential opposition to the First World War. Born in Budapest, Hungary, on September 11, 1877; died of bronchial pneumonia in New York on August 3, 1948; daughter of Max B. Schwimmer (an experimental farmer and agricultural produce dealer) and Bertha (Katscher) Schwimmer; received eight years of formal schooling and a six-month commercial course; married (husband's name unknown), on January 16, 1911 (divorced January 4, 1913); no children.*

*Worked as a bookkeeper and office worker (from 1891); began organizing women in the struggle for improved working conditions as well as their political, educational and social rights (1892); founded the Hungarian Feminist Association (1904) which would*

*be instrumental in winning the vote for Hungarian women (1920); devoted herself to the cause of international peace (1914–20), traveled throughout Europe and North America to promote the cause of neutral mediation and organize women in an attempt to stop the hostilities; appointed Hungary's ambassador to Switzerland, the first woman in history to be given a diplomatic post (1918); forced to flee to Vienna because of revolution and counter-revolution in Hungary (1920) and seek refuge in U.S. (1921); unpopular with many because of her uncompromising pacifism, was denied American citizenship and spent the rest of her life in U.S. as a stateless person, working for the cause of world government; was nominated for the Nobel Peace Prize (1948) but died before the recipient was selected.*

*Selected writings: Tisza Tales (1928); (with Lola Maverick Lloyd) Chaos, War or a New World Order? (1937); Union Now for Peace or War? The Danger in the Plan of Clarence Streit (1939).*

Between May and August 1915, following The Hague Congress where women of all nations gathered to stop the worst war the world had ever endured, Rosika Schwimmer and *Chrystal Macmillan took the message of peace to all of the neutral countries. Traveling near the western front, Schwimmer wrote to a friend that it was "heartrending" to see hundreds of soldiers with "empty resigned faces go towards an unwanted death." Unable to persuade the neutrals to agree to a peace conference, Schwimmer was unusually pessimistic in a letter to another friend: "National ambitions and selfishness hold back these people. . . . Each one wants something. . . . [O]f the belligerents *not one would oppose* a neutral conference. But on the part of the neutrals there are conflicting interests which stand in the way of the first step. . . . In the meantime, the world perishes."

Rosika Schwimmer was born into a middle-class Jewish household in Budapest, Hungary, in 1877, the oldest of three children of **Bertha Katscher Schwimmer** and Max B. Schwimmer. Max was an experimental farmer who grew seed corn and dealt in agricultural produce and horses. Rosika grew up in the provincial cities of Temesvár (now Timisoara, Rumania) and Szabadka (now Subotica, Yugoslavia). Prone to illness as a child, she had only eight years of formal schooling, supplemented by private tutoring in foreign languages and music and a six-month commercial course. At age 18, because of her father's business losses, she had to find employment as an office worker.

*Opposite page*
*Rosika*
*Schwimmer*

The first of the three well-defined periods of Schwimmer's life started in 1897 when her family returned to Budapest. She immediately began to write, to lecture, and to organize. It might be said that reform was in her blood: her uncle Leopold Katscher founded the Hungarian Peace Society. Another uncle, Major Edler Lederer, held a high rank in the Austro-Hungarian army but was an outspoken opponent of warlike militarism. For the next 17 years, Schwimmer's efforts were concentrated on mobilizing all classes of Hungarian women in the struggle for their political, economic, educational, and social rights.

In 1897, at age 20, she joined the National Association of Women Office Workers and soon became its president, holding that office until 1912. In 1903, Schwimmer founded the first Hungarian Association of Working Women, and the following year she helped set up the Hungarian Council of Women, organizations which appealed, respectively, to socialist and conservative memberships. Also in 1904, she established the Hungarian Feminist Association. Unique among such societies for its inclusion of men as well as women, this group promoted feminism and supported trade unionism, land reform, suffrage and pacifism. Schwimmer's frequent European lecture tours and outstanding organizational ability ensured that the vote for Hungarian women was won in 1920, only 16 years after she founded the association.

By 1913, Schwimmer was a well-known figure in the international suffrage movement. During that year, she organized the seventh and largest congress of the International Women's Suffrage Association (IWSA) in Budapest. The congress attracted 3,000 participants from all over the world.

The period of the First World War and its immediate aftermath, 1914–20, marks the second phase in Schwimmer's life. When the war began in 1914, Rosika was 36 years old. A respected editor, writer, lecturer, and organizer who knew nine languages, she had just been asked to take up the job of International Press Secretary at the International Woman Suffrage Alliance Headquarters in London. She was hired by the American leader of the organization, *Carrie Chapman Catt, to help win favorable publicity for the issues of women's suffrage and equal rights. The English press had, thus far, been considerably more interested in the broken windows and civil disobedience practiced by the more extreme suffragists.

As **Anne Wiltsher,** in her study of the feminist peace campaigners of the First World War,

has observed, Schwimmer "had the kind of wit, eloquence and extrovert personality needed to make an effective publicist." In great demand as a speaker, she could win men over to the cause with her sly humor. "No one was neutral about Rosika Schwimmer," writes Wiltsher. "A human dynamo with a forceful personality and tireless energy, she was somebody you either loved or hated—frequently people did both at different times." Among the middle class and respectable members of the British branch of the IWSA, Rosika must certainly have seemed exotic. She smoked, enjoyed a glass of wine, and wore vividly colored, loose-fitting dresses, without either corset or brassiere. Wisely, given the social conventions of the day, she kept secret the fact that she was also a divorcee—married in 1911, she had divorced two years later and never made reference to it.

The applicant seems to be a woman of superior character and intelligence, obviously more than ordinarily desirable as a citizen of the United States. Surely it cannot show lack of attachment to the principles of the Constitution that she thinks it can be improved.

—Justice Oliver Wendell Holmes' dissenting opinion in Schwimmer's citizenship case, 1929

From the moment she received news of the assassination of Austria's Franz Ferdinand and his wife *Sophie Chotek in June 1914, Schwimmer sensed that the outcome would be war with Serbia and total European involvement. On July 9, she met with British prime minister David Lloyd George at 11 Downing Street and warned him of what she foresaw, but he dismissed her fears as alarmist.

On August 4, a great women's peace rally was held at the Kingsway Hall in London. It attracted 2,000 women, with hundreds turned away. At 11 o'clock that night, war was declared. After witnessing the "war fever" celebrations in the streets, desolate and unable to sleep, Schwimmer composed an "Open Letter" addressed to "All Men, Women and Organizations who want to stop the international massacre at the earliest possible moment." She urged U.S. president Woodrow Wilson to intervene and mediate without delay: "As all the combating nations are resolved 'to conquer or be killed to the last man' waiting for the call to mediation is equal to waiting until the absolute destruction of one or other of the belligerent nations is accomplished." She refuted the arguments of those who said intervention must only be made at the right moment,

arguing that such delay was appropriate only in the case of ordinary wars: "But what is going on today is not merely a war, but the breakdown of a world—the earthquake of civilization."

Finding her home country on the "wrong" side of the war, Schwimmer resigned from her paid position at the IWSA and decided to focus her efforts on securing mediation by neutral nations. As an "enemy alien," she was now under official surveillance and had her movements restricted. Without paid employment and having widely circulated the Open Letter at her own expense, Schwimmer was forced to sell her jewelry and even her typewriter to support herself. Convinced that President Wilson could be "a great force for peace," she made the first of several wartime journeys to America on August 25, 1914. This visit was to establish the pattern of Schwimmer's life for the rest of the war: using the vast network of suffrage organizations throughout Europe as a base, she traveled tirelessly, promoting the establishment of a neutral body that would mediate between the belligerents. She met with Wilson shortly after her arrival but was unable to convince him of the wisdom of immediate intervention.

In the United States, many women were already more liberated than their European sisters; their skirts were shorter, they had abandoned cumbersome hats and corsets, and some could already vote in state elections. Promoting both peace and suffrage, Schwimmer set out on the first of many speaking tours to rally American support, traveling to 60 cities and speaking to as many as six different audiences a day in a fifteen-month crusade. Unlike in Britain and the other belligerent nations, where women were being forced to choose between patriotism and their work for peace, women in America were able to unite against the war.

Continuing grim news from the front during Schwimmer's American peace campaign seems to have changed her personality; it was especially evident in her speaking style. Previously known for her engaging wit and humor, she now spoke "as if the pain that millions . . . now endure had suddenly acquired a voice that through her spoke its own desperate language." An observer of a speech she gave in Stockholm just before The Hague Congress recorded that Schwimmer was "greatly changed" from the woman who had spoken so confidently about suffrage in the same hall four years earlier: "She gave the impression of one who has suffered, who has lived in the very center of recent events, who has seen ideals topple. . . . [I]t was not merely her wonderful eloquence that held us all; it was the consciousness that her intense feeling of indignation . . . was . . . out of her innermost soul."

One of Schwimmer's most remarkable wartime achievements occurred at the meeting of the Women's International Congress in The Hague in April 1915. That the meeting took place at all, she said, was "one of the greatest things that women ever achieved." Although the British government withdrew the passports of its nationals, 1,136 delegates from 12 nations attended, those at war as well as the neutrals. Schwimmer was determined that the meeting produce practical results, and, largely because of her efforts, it became the first international meeting to attempt to draw up the principles of a peace settlement. Among many far-sighted recommendations, it called for the establishment of a permanent international body, with women included in its membership, that would settle international disputes, a body which Schwimmer called "a continuous conference of neutrals." Her passionate oratory, as well as bringing the conference to its feet several times, convinced the

women present to support her proposal to send envoys to the leaders of both the neutral and belligerent countries and to report back to a women's international peace party.

Schwimmer and 11 other delegates spent the summer lobbying the leaders of 14 nations and although success often seemed close at hand, first in Sweden and then in the United States, they did not obtain the international intervention they were seeking. In the autumn of 1915, Schwimmer, one of the few women who still believed that the plan could and must be made to work, persuaded the automobile magnate Henry Ford to support an unofficial neutral conference in Sweden, sending delegates from America in a "peace ship."

Like all of the pacifist initiatives of the time, especially those organized by women, the peace crusade, funded by Ford but organized and led by Schwimmer, was subject to intense criticism and ridicule in the press. Deterred by this vehement opposition, many well-known feminist pacifists refused to participate and there were almost as

*Rosika Schwimmer, with Henry Ford.*

many journalists as delegates among the 168 Americans who set sail on December 4, 1915.

The dramatic winter voyage almost overshadowed the peace conference which took place in Stockholm in February 1916. There the Americans were joined by unofficial delegations of women and men from five neutral European countries—Holland, Switzerland, Sweden, Norway and Denmark. However, Ford's fame and financial support proved a mixed blessing; his business associates were hostile, and attacks on Schwimmer's role and reputation intensified. Exhausted and discouraged, she resigned as Ford's organizer in March 1916. Schwimmer then collapsed with heart trouble and was unable to work for three months. Although Ford continued to provide some support until the United States entered the war in February 1917, the initiative achieved no more successes. In June 1916, Schwimmer and some other former members of the Ford group organized the International Committee for Immediate Mediation which sent private missions to Russia, Germany, and England.

Although Schwimmer's intensive efforts for peace through neutral mediation did not have the direct result of ending the war, she achieved remarkable success in publicizing and winning support for the cause, and her work at winning over public opinion in the neutral countries may well have contributed to keeping those nations from joining the hostilities.

With the end of the war in November 1918, the Austro-Hungarian Empire was dissolved and Hungary became a democratic republic. The new prime minister, Michael Károlyi, appointed Schwimmer as Hungary's ambassador to Switzerland, the first time in history that a woman had been named to a diplomatic post. The appointment lasted only four months; political turmoil at home forced Schwimmer to return to Hungary where she soon found herself forbidden to leave the country by the new Communist regime which she refused to serve.

The delegates to the Women's International Congress, held in Zurich in May 1919, sent a telegram to their absent colleague which read: "We recognize in you one of the most passionate champions of the cause of peace and join you in wishes for the better time we are all working for." The fall of Béla Kun's dictatorship in August 1919 brought physical danger for Schwimmer, as a "white terror" swept the country, and its supporters sought to punish all who had cooperated with either Károlyi or Kun. Aware that her pacifist and feminist activities would do nothing to endear her to the new conservative Hungarian government under Miklós Horthy, Schwimmer escaped to Vienna in 1920 and sought refuge in the United States in 1921.

The third stage of Schwimmer's life began with her arrival in America. Schwimmer once again immediately encountered the personal animosity which had dogged her Peace Ship initiative. One ultra-nationalist publication called her a German spy who had impeded American military preparedness and had kept the United States out of the conflict for two years. Other equally ill-informed sources called her a Bolshevik and a Jewish agent. Jewish groups attacked her as the cause of Henry Ford's anti-Semitism, and pacifist and feminist groups, fearing that their causes would suffer by association, abandoned her. Effectively blacklisted, she was unable to find work to support herself and had to depend on the support of her sister **Franciska** and her closest friend in America, **Lola Maverick Lloyd**.

The vicious public attacks upon Schwimmer's character and motives certainly contributed to her failure to obtain American citizenship. In 1924, groups such as the American Legion urged the government to reject her application because of her "un-American utterances and unpatriotic character." She appealed a District Court rejection to the Supreme Court but was rejected there also in a six-to-three decision in May 1929. Justice Oliver Wendell Holmes, in his dissenting opinion, eloquently supported the woman who had refused to promise to bear arms in defense of the Constitution of the United States. Referring to Schwimmer's sincere belief that war would disappear and that the world would unite in peaceful leagues, he argued that the "notion that the applicant's optimistic anticipations would make her a worse citizen is sufficiently answered by her examination which seems to me a better argument for her admission than any that I can offer. Some of her answers may excite popular prejudice, but if there is any principle of the Constitution that more imperatively calls for attachment than any other it is the principle of free thought." Although Schwimmer won a libel suit against one of her leading detractors in 1929 and the Supreme Court ruling was later reversed, she never again sought citizenship and remained a stateless person until she died.

Rather than adhering to any single state, Schwimmer devoted the last two decades of her life to the cause of world government. She was convinced that the League of Nations, and the United Nations which succeeded it, lacked sufficient authority to ensure continuing world peace. During the Second World War, she supported the establishment of an unofficial provisional world government, similar in structure to the neutral conferences she had organized during the First World War. The dropping of the first atomic bomb on Hiroshima in 1945 lent added momentum to her campaign for world government.

In 1948, Schwimmer, now 71, was nominated for the Nobel Peace Prize by 33 members of Parliament from Britain, Sweden, France, Italy, and Hungary, but she died before the recipient was selected. Only weeks before her death from bronchial pneumonia she sent a message to the Seneca Falls Centennial Celebration of the 1848 Women's Rights Convention which she was too ill to attend. Her statement conveyed the creed by which she lived and from which she had never wavered, despite unremitting attacks from her enemies and desertion by many of her friends. She wrote that she wanted to remember the radical suffragists' pledge to abolish war if they were granted political power:

> I really believed in this pledge of ours, not because I thought that women were superior to men but because, having been isolated from public affairs, I believed we were less conditioned to corruption, less perverted by narrow nationalism and protected from the militarization to which men were subjected.

Claiming that women had "descended" to aiding the First and Second World Wars, Schwimmer concluded with the hope that:

> women will retrace their steps from the many paths and blind alleys to which they have strayed in imitation of the social, political and economic morass of what we once called the "man made world," and that they will remember that we sought equality for our half of the human race, not at the lowest, but at the highest level of human aspirations.

**SOURCES AND SUGGESTED READING:**

Bussey, Gertrude, and Margaret Tims. *Women's International League for Peace and Freedom, 1915–1965: A Record of Fifty Years' Work*. London: George Allen & Unwin, 1965.

Moorehead, Caroline. *Troublesome People. Enemies of War: 1916–1986*. London: Hamish Hamilton, 1987.

Wiltsher, Anne. *Most Dangerous Women: Feminist Peace Campaigners of the Great War*. London: Pandora, 1985.

Wynner, Edith. "Rosika Schwimmer," in *Biographical Dictionary of Modern Peace Leaders*. Edited by Harold Josephson. Westport, CT: Greenwood Press, 1985, pp. 862–865.

———. "Rosika Schwimmer," in *Dictionary of American Biography*. NY: Scribner, 1964, pp. 724–728.

———. *Rosika Schwimmer, World Patriot*. London: Odhams, 1947.

**(Dr.) Kathleen Garay**,
Acting Director of Women's Studies,
McMaster University, Hamilton, Canada

## Scotland, queen of.

*See Margaret (fl. 1000s).*
*See Gruoch (fl. 1020–1054).*
*See Elflaed (fl. 1030).*
*See Ingebiorge (fl. 1045–1068).*
*See Margaret, St. (c. 1046–1093).*
*See Matilda of Northumberland (c. 1074–1131).*
*See Ethelreda (fl. 1090).*
*See Sybilla (d. 1122).*
*See Matilda (d. 1130?).*
*See Joan (1210–1238).*
*See Ermengarde of Beaumont (d. 1234).*
*See Mary de Coucy (c. 1220–c. 1260).*
*See Margaret (1240–1275).*
*See Margaret, Maid of Norway (c. 1283–1290).*
*See Isabella of Mar (d. 1296).*
*See Yolande de Dreux (d. 1323).*
*See Elizabeth de Burgh (d. 1327).*
*See Joan of the Tower (1321–1362).*
*See Drummond, Margaret (d. 1375).*
*See Ross, Euphemia (d. 1387).*
*See Drummond, Annabella (1350–1401).*
*See Beaufort, Joan (c. 1410–1445).*
*See Mary of Guelders (1433–1463).*
*See Margaret of Denmark (1456–1486).*
*See Tudor, Margaret (1489–1541).*
*See Mary of Guise (1515–1560).*
*See Mary Stuart (1542–1587).*
*See Anne of Denmark (1574–1619).*
*See Mary II (1662–1694).*
*See Anne (1665–1714).*

## Scots, queen of.

*See Scotland, queen of.*

# Scott, Ann London (1929–1975)

*American feminist. Born Claire Ann London on July 29, 1929, in Seattle, Washington; died of cancer in Baltimore, Maryland, on February 17, 1975; daughter of Claire Chester London and Daniel Edwin London (a hotel manager); graduated from Dominican Convent School; attended Stanford University, 1947–49; University of Washington, B.A., 1954, Ph.D., 1968; married Paul de Witt Tufts (a musician), in 1951 (divorced); married Gerd Stern (a poet), in 1956 (divorced 1961); married Thomas Jefferson Scott (an artist), in 1969; children: (second marriage) son Jared London (b. 1957).*

Born on July 29, 1929, Ann London Scott spent her childhood in San Francisco, where her father was manager of the luxurious St. Francis hotel. She was an excellent student and graduated from one of the city's top high schools, Dominican Convent School. In 1947, Scott received a scholarship to Stanford University, but she transferred to the University of Washington in 1949, after failing to combine the rigors of study with an active San Francisco social life. In Washington, she renewed her lifelong interest in poetry and developed a community of friends in the art world. She graduated with a bachelor's degree in 1954.

After two failed marriages and the birth of her son, Scott returned to the University of Washington in the fall of 1961 to pursue a doctorate in literature—a decision enthusiastically supported by her parents, who were concerned about her bohemian lifestyle. Her dissertation focused on Shakespeare's use of language, and her poetry was published in several well-known journals. Before she had completed her doctorate, Scott moved to Buffalo, New York, in 1965 to accept a teaching position at the State University of New York (SUNY) there. She earned her doctorate in 1968.

Scott perceived her failure to make tenure at SUNY-Buffalo as a case of sex discrimination, since male professors with fewer credentials were achieving that milestone. With the support of her third husband, artist Thomas Jefferson Scott, she began a sex discrimination study at the university which led her from the academic arena to the world of politics. Scott had founded the Buffalo chapter of the National Organization for Women (NOW), and received encouragement from that group in her conflict with SUNY. In 1970, she was elected to NOW's national board of directors, and became its Federal Contract Compliance Officer. As such, she lobbied congressional representatives and national organizations to include women in affirmative-action guidelines for all firms holding federal contracts, first at the Department of Labor and then for all radio and television stations holding Federal Communications Commission licenses. After her success in these areas, she became NOW's vice president for legislation and worked for passage of the 1972 Equal Employment Opportunity Act Amendment and the Equal Rights Amendment.

Scott's ability to network with and persuade others won her the support and admiration of those with whom she worked and lobbied. She was invited to serve on the national boards of Common Cause and the Leadership Conference on Civil Rights and, in 1974, became the American Association for Higher Education's associate director. She developed cancer that same year, however, and died in 1975 in Baltimore, Maryland.

SOURCES:

Sicherman, Barbara, and Carol Hurd Green, eds. *Notable American Women: The Modern Period*. Cambridge, MA: The Belknap Press of Harvard University, 1980.

**Sally Cole-Misch**, freelance writer, Bloomfield Hills, Michigan

## Scott, Anne (1651–1731)

*Countess of Buccleuch. Name variations: also seen as Duchess of Buccleuch. Born on February 11, 1651; died on February 6, 1731; daughter of Francis Scott (1626–1651), 2nd earl of Buccleuch; married James Crofts Scott, duke of Monmouth (1649–1685, illegitimate son of Charles II, king of England, and \*Lucy Walter), on April 20, 1663 (executed); children: Charles Scott (b. 1672), earl of Doncaster; James Scott (b. 1674), earl of Dalkeith; Henry Scott, 1st earl of Deloriane. James Crofts Scott, who always claimed his parents were married, took his wife's name upon marriage.*

## Scott, Barbara Ann (1928—)

*Canadian figure skater who won the North American, European, and World championships and a gold medal at the 1948 Olympic Games. Born on May 9, 1928, in Ottawa, Ontario, Canada; daughter of Clyde Scott (military secretary to Canada's Minister of Defense) and Mary Scott; attended the Ottawa Normal Model School until age nine and received private tutoring; married Tommy King (a press agent), on September 17, 1953; no children.*

*Began skating at age of six; was Canadian Junior Ladies' champion (1939), Canadian Senior Women's champion (1944–48), North American champion (1945–48), European and World champion (1947–48); at 19, won Ladies' Figure Skating gold medal at Olympic Games, St. Moritz, Switzerland (February 6, 1948); was the first Canadian woman to win the Lou Marsh Trophy as best Canadian athlete (1945, 1947, 1948); was a professional skater (1949–54); published autobiography, Skate With Me (1950); upon retirement, began training horses and was rated among the top equestrians in the U.S.; made an Officer of the Order of Canada (1991); inducted into the International Women's Sports Hall of Fame (1997).*

In the first half of the 20th century, Canadian women had not achieved celebrity when it came to the world of sports. All that changed on February 6, 1948, when a 5'3", 105-pound dynamo named Barbara Ann Scott captured the women's Olympic figure skating championship in St. Moritz, Switzerland. "From one end of Canada to the other there is great rejoicing," ca-

*Barbara Ann Scott*

bled Prime Minister William Lyon Mackenzie King to 19-year-old Scott, who had made a clean sweep of the highest titles in her sport, the Olympic, European, and World championships.

Born on May 9, 1928, in Ottawa, Ontario, Barbara Ann Scott grew up during the Great Depression, but appears to have enjoyed a privileged upbringing. As a youngster, she excelled in swimming, golf, and horse riding, but skating became her passion. Having received her first pair of skates as a Christmas present at age six, she began serious training three years later, already intent on becoming the world's greatest figure skater. To accommodate their determined daughter, the Scotts rescheduled her life to include private academic tutoring and long hours at the rink at Ottawa's Minto Club. Scott's father Clyde, a disabled veteran of World War I who worked in the Division of Veterans' Affairs, had considerable impact on his daughter's early life. He encouraged her natural athletic abilities, while instilling in her perseverance and self-reliance. "The main lessons my father taught me were those of sportsmanship and of self-help," said Scott. Her mother **Mary Scott** also did her part, keeping her daughter grounded. "I told her that her ambition was fine, but if she ever displayed temperament, her skating was finished," said Mary.

*To learn to skate well . . . [y]ou must like the quiet concentration of long practice sessions on a gloomy, shadowy old rink when no one speaks and the only sounds are the grind of a skate on a rough bit of surface.*

—**Barbara Ann Scott**

At age ten, Scott became the youngest skater ever to win first place for passing eight tests in basic school figures, the standard ice routines which are judged by tracings left on the ice. Her high standing in the tests spurred her to enter the Canadian Junior Ladies' championship in Ottawa the following year, which she won on the strength of her precise execution of figures. Following her win, she was taken to tea by Olympic champion *Sonja Henie.

By now, Scott's courage and grace were becoming evident, and reporters vied for interviews. Once, several arrived at her house for a 6:30 PM mini-press conference, only to find the skater tucked in bed. Before turning out the light, she recounted her "normal" day, which included music lessons, school work, and seven hours of skating. "Good skating takes up much of your life," she told the media, adding that she was determined to keep "busy" and not "fritter" her life away.

In 1940, skating with early symptoms of measles, Scott reached fifth place in the North American championship competition, and a year later she was runner-up in the Canadian Senior Ladies' championship. But that year, Clyde Scott died suddenly, and Mary and Barbara were left not only emotionally bereft but somewhat strapped for money. The loss only made Barbara more determined, and she managed to keep up her full-day training schedule. She finally won the Canadian Senior Ladies' championship in 1944, then defended her title successfully in 1945. That March, she also won the North American Figure Skating title in New York, beating out U.S. champion **Gretchen Merrill** and six other contenders. "It was the spectacular display of youthful skating exuberance by Miss Scott which carried her to victory," wrote Harry Cross in the *New York Herald Tribune*. "Little Miss Scott performed three graceful loop jumps in swift succession and went into the air freely in Salchow and Lutz leaps, varying her display with dizzy spins, all skated with a fast, perfectly balanced pace . . . and graceful repose." For her effort, Canada presented her with the Lou Marsh Memorial Trophy as the country's outstanding athlete of 1945, an award never before given to a woman. She would receive the trophy again in 1947 and 1948.

The year 1947 marked Scott's debut into international competition. That February, she won the Women's European Figure Skating championship at Davos Platz, Switzerland, and two weeks later, in Stockholm, she bested Merrill once more to become the first Canadian woman to win the Women's World Figure Skating championship. Following her European and World victories, she sailed home on the *Queen Elizabeth* and was greeted on arrival with more exuberance than was given the British royal family in 1939. She received keys to six Canadian cities, life memberships in six skating clubs and two flying clubs, a number of Canadian medals, and the key to the prestigious Men's Press Club in Toronto (which she later wore for luck while competing in the Olympics). Another gift, a canary-colored Buick convertible presented to her by the mayor of Ottawa, her hometown, became a source of controversy. By accepting such an expensive present, Scott found her amateur status threatened, as was her dream of competing in the Olympics. Following a protest from Avery Brundage, chair of the U.S. Olympic Committee (USOC), and the ensuing debate among sports columnists and even members of the Canadian Parliament, she returned the car. (After she won the Olympic medal, Ottawa's mayor again presented her with the car, now painted blue.)

In the summer of 1947, Scott embarked upon a grueling training schedule with coach Sheldon Galbraith to prepare for Olympic competition, devoting seven or more hours a day to executing figures and perfecting her routine. By her estimate, over the years she had put in a total of 20,000 hours of practice. For her final round of training, she arrived early in St. Moritz, hoping to acclimatize to the high altitude well in advance of the Winter Games.

When the competition finally got under way, Scott, wearing number 13 which she considered lucky, was called upon to execute her school figures on a succession of warm days, which made for watery ice conditions. Despite the poor ice and the encroachment of eager press photographers, she made no errors, maintaining a concentration which her fellow skaters admired and reporters extolled. The free-skating portion of the Olympic program proved equally as challenging as the figures. Without Zamboni machines to groom the ice, the surface was so full of holes and ruts from a preceding hockey game that Scott was forced to mentally revise her program while waiting her turn to perform. Nevertheless, dressed in a white fur-trimmed outfit, she turned in a flawless performance described by one reporter as "a dazzling exhibition of grace and beauty that left her rivals nowhere." Scott shared the Olympic podium with **Eva Pawlik** of Austria and ❧➤ **Jeanette Altwegg** of Great Britain, the silver and bronze medalists, respectively.

Following her Olympic win, Scott received a new round of honors and awards, including an audience with Princess *Elizabeth (II) at Buckingham Palace and a commemorative doll fashioned in her image by American doll designer Bernard Lipfert and manufactured by the Reliable Toy Company. The doll, the first ever in the image of an athlete, was provided with a new costume each year, in the same manner as the later Barbie doll, and is now a collectors' item.

On June 1, 1948, Barbara Ann Scott turned professional, announcing that a portion of her earnings would be given to the newly formed St. Lawrence Foundation, a "charitable organization for crippled and underprivileged children." During her early professional career, Scott skated at the Roxy Theater in New York, and performed an exhibition tour of Canada. Between 1949 and 1954, she performed with the Ice Capades and the Hollywood Ice Revue, keeping up an arduous schedule of constant travel. "I hate living out of a suitcase," she told reporters. "Some time I want to marry and have children,

and I believe that should be organized economically, tidily, and exactly, like Olympic skating or anything else."

Scott retired from skating in 1955 to marry press agent Tommy King, whom she met when he was working for the Hollywood Ice Revue. The couple moved to Chicago, where King became an executive with the Merchandise Mart and Scott pursued various sports and business activities, including the Barbara Ann Scott Beauty Salon, located in a Chicago suburb. In her mid-40s, she became a top equestrian, winning some 64 ribbons and 21 first places in 1966 alone. She also golfed and flew her own plane, having received her pilot's license in 1947.

Known as "Canada's Sweetheart," Barbara Ann Scott remains the only Canadian woman ever to win an Olympic gold medal in figure skating and is still connected to the skating world, serving as a judge at professional competitions. In 1991, she was made an Officer of the Order of Canada, and in 1997 she was inducted into the International Women's Sports Hall of Fame.

**SOURCES:**

*Current Biography 1948*. NY: H.W. Wilson, 1948.

Lamparski, Richard. *Whatever Became of . . . ?* 2nd series. NY: Crown, 1968.

Moore, Cay. *She Skated Into Our Hearts*. Toronto, Canada: McClelland & Stewart, 1948.

Scott, Barbara Ann. *Skate With Me*. NY: Doubleday, 1950.

**SUGGESTED READING:**

Prentice, Alison, *et al. Canadian Women: A History*. Toronto, Canada: Harcourt Brace Jovanovich, 1988.

## Scott, Blanche (c. 1885–1970)

*First American woman to fly an airplane. Name variations: Blanche Stuart Scott. Born in Rochester, New York, around 1885; died on January 12, 1970, in Rochester, New York; attended Fort Edward College, New York.*

Born around 1885, Blanche Scott had several "firsts" in her remarkable life. In 1910, she drove from New York to San Francisco in a car, only the second woman to do so. (The first had been *Alice Huyler Ramsey in 1909.) On September 2 of that same year she took the first solo airplane flight by a woman, albeit by accident when a sudden wind lifted her training plane above the runway. Flying became her life's passion, and in 1912 Scott made her first flight across the country, a 69-day trip. Soon after, she joined a flying exhibition team as the "tomboy of the air" and earned as much as $5,000 a week for her daredevil dives and other stunts. Barnstorming was a popular form of entertainment

❧➤
***Jeanette Altwegg.*** *See Albright, Tenley for sidebar.*

in the early 1900s, and she continued on the team until 1916.

Scott switched careers to screenwriting and radio broadcasting in the 1920s, but stayed involved in the continuing development of airplanes. She was invited to fly in a U.S. Air Force Shooting Star jet fighter in 1948, becoming the first woman to fly in a jet. She also served as a consultant to the Air Force Museum at Wright-Patterson Air Force Base in Ohio. On the 50th anniversary of her first flight, Scott was honored by the Antique Airplane Association. She died in Rochester, New York, in 1970.

**SOURCES:**
Read, Phyllis J., and Bernard L. Witlieb. *The Book of Women's Firsts*. NY: Random House, 1992.

**Sally Cole-Misch**, freelance writer,
Bloomfield Hills, Michigan

## Scott, Caroline Lavinia (1832–1892).

*See Harrison, Caroline Scott.*

# Scott, Charlotte Angas (1858–1931)

*English mathematician and educator. Born Charlotte Angas Scott on June 8, 1858, in Lincoln, England; died on November 8, 1931, in Cambridge, England; daughter of Caleb Scott (an educator and minister) and Eliza Ann Exley Scott; received private primary and secondary education; Girton College of Cambridge University, honors degree, 1880; University of London, B.S., 1882, D.Sc., 1885.*

Charlotte Angas Scott was born in 1858 in Lincoln, England. Her parents instilled in her a love of learning through a private education, and she entered Girton College of Cambridge University in 1876. Even though women could not receive Cambridge degrees, they could take final examinations on an informal basis. Scott finished in eighth place in the mathematics tests in 1880, the highest score recorded for a woman. However, her score was not included at commencement, and she was not allowed to attend the ceremony, although she received an honors degree from Girton. Scott lectured in math at Girton from 1880 to 1884 while studying at the University of London. She earned a B.S. in 1882 and a D.Sc. in 1885.

Soon after she graduated, Scott became the only woman of six faculty members at the newly formed Bryn Mawr College in Pennsylvania. She created the undergraduate and graduate mathematics programs and was known for her ability to make her subject understandable and exciting. She wrote *An Introductory Account of Cer-tain Modern Ideas in Plane Analytical Geometry* (1894), which became the standard textbook for colleges in the United States and Europe, and *Cartesian Plane Geometry Part I: Analytical Cones* (1907). She was also editor of the American version of *Arithmetic for Schools*. These texts stood as the primary learning references for an entire generation of students.

Scott was active in the mathematics field outside of Bryn Mawr, including membership in the New York Mathematical Society, which became the American Mathematical Society in 1894. Scott was the only woman to serve on its board of directors. She served as its vice president in 1906 and contributed 30 articles and papers to the society's journal as well as to other publications in the United States, Britain and Europe. She also contributed to the creation of the College Entrance Examination Board in 1901, and served as its chief examiner in mathematics from 1902 to 1903.

Before Scott retired in 1924 from Bryn Mawr College, she received the first endowed chair in 1909. In 1922, 140 members of the American Mathematical Society and former students returned to the college to honor Scott for her lifetime of achievements in mathematics and education. She returned to England in 1925 and died six years later in Cambridge.

**SOURCES:**
James, Edward T., ed. *Notable American Women, 1607–1950*. Cambridge, MA: The Belknap Press of Harvard University, 1971.
Ogilvie, Marilyn Bailey. *Women in Science: Antiquity through the Nineteenth Century*. Cambridge, MA: MIT Press, 1986.
Osen, Lynn M. *Women in Mathematics*. Cambridge, MA: MIT Press, 1974.
Read, Phyllis J., and Bernard L. Witlieb. *The Book of Women's Firsts*. NY: Random House, 1992.

**Sally Cole-Misch**, freelance writer,
Bloomfield Hills, Michigan

# Scott, Elizabeth Whitworth (1898–1972)

*British architect. Born in England in 1898; died in England in 1972; attended private school in Bournemouth, England, and received her degree from the Architectural Association School in 1924.*

Elizabeth Whitworth Scott followed her grandfather, Victorian architect Sir Gilbert Scott, into the field of architecture in the early 20th century. Just four years after her graduation from the Architectural Association School in 1924, her design for the Shakespeare Memorial Theatre at

Stratford-upon-Avon was chosen from 22 proposals. This building became her claim to fame although she also worked in Welwyn Garden City, Cheltenham and London, and designed extensions to Cambridge's Newnham College.

**Sally Cole-Misch**, freelance writer, Bloomfield Hills, Michigan

# Scott, Esther Mae (1893–1979)

*African-American blues singer and musician. Name variations: Mother Scott. Born on March 25, 1893, in Bovina, Mississippi; died of a stroke in Washington, D.C., on October 16, 1979; daughter of Henry S. Erves and Mary Liza Erves (both sharecroppers); had occasional schooling at Clover Valley Baptist School.*

Esther Mae Scott was the seventh child born to Mississippi sharecroppers Henry and **Mary Erves**, on March 25, 1893. She and her 13 siblings lived with their parents on a plantation as sharecroppers, and Scott became part of the family farming workforce at age five. She was not paid for her labor until she was nine, when she received 25 cents a day. Schooling was limited to a few weeks in the winter when crops were not being harvested. Life's basic needs—food, clothing and shelter—were scarce, and the family searched the woods for berries and any other fruits or vegetables.

Music was an integral part of Scott's work day. She later told Ward Silver of *Great Speckled Bird* magazine:

> The average Negro from Mississippi and other slave counties knew how to sing because singing is something to raise your ego up enough to help you solve the task you got to do. And singing looked like it'd make the day shorter for you.

She learned how to play the guitar at age eight, and picked up the mandolin, banjo and piano from friends and family.

Scott used these skills when she left home at 14 to join a vaudeville group, W.S. Wolcott's Rabbit Foot Minstrels. She toured the South for a dollar a day to sing, dance, play guitar, and promote a hair product, Jack Rabbit and Bentone Liniment. The liniment, a hoax, was bought primarily by other blacks, but Scott felt the paycheck was vital for her family and took the money home to them. She also created her own songs, added blues to her repertoire, and learned how to perform before an audience.

After two years, Scott left the show to become a maid and nurse for a wealthy family in Vicksburg, Mississippi. She stayed with them for 27 years before being let go in 1938 when the family moved into a hotel during the Depression. Through these years, she had followed the music scene and had met several blues artists, including Leadbelly and *Bessie Smith. For the next 20 years, Scott was the maid and nurse for Merty Landau Shoemaker, who lived in Baltimore, Maryland, and was the cousin of her former employer.

In 1958, Scott moved to Washington, D.C., where she revived her performing career. Joining St. Stephen and the Incarnation Episcopal Church, she became an integral part of its singing programs. She soon expanded her performances to nightclubs, as blues and folk music made a comeback in the late 1950s and early 1960s, as well as festivals and civil-rights demonstrations. Scott joined the musicians' union and was paid union wages for other work on radio and television, but usually performed church-related work for free.

Scott's reputation grew with her nightclub performances, and soon she was appearing before audiences of a much larger size. She appeared at bicentennial celebrations in Baltimore and Westminster, Maryland, and at the Smithsonian Folk Festival in Washington, D.C. (all 1976). She performed on the Mall at the Smithsonian Festival of American Folklife (1978), at Washington's National Cathedral, at Rutgers University, and to an audience of 72,000 in the Pocono Mountains. In 1971, she recorded her only album, *Moma Ain't Nobody's Fool*, the title of which reflected her nickname in the blues world: "Mother Scott."

Failing health limited Scott's performing in her later years, as she suffered from glaucoma, diabetes, and high blood pressure, and had difficulty walking. Despite having never learned to read music, she wrote verses to new songs up until shortly before her death of a stroke in Washington, D.C., on October 16, 1979. She was 86.

**SOURCES:**

Bailey, Brooke. *The Remarkable Lives of 100 Women Artists*. Holbrook, MA: Bob Adams, 1994.

Smith, Jessie Carney, ed. *Notable Black American Women*. Detroit, MI: Gale Research, 1992.

**Sally Cole-Misch**, freelance writer, Bloomfield Hills, Michigan

# Scott, Hazel (1920–1981)

*African-American musician, singer and actress. Born on June 11, 1920, in Port-of-Spain, Trinidad; died on October 2, 1981; daughter of a college professor and Alma Long Scott (a pianist and saxophonist); attend-*

*ed Juilliard School of Music; married Adam Clayton Powell, Jr. (the Baptist pastor and U.S. congressional representative), in 1945 (divorced October 1956); children: Adam Clayton Powell III.*

*Made her debut playing the piano at age three in Trinidad and at five in the U.S. at Town Hall, New York; played piano and trumpet with her mother's American Creolians Orchestra when she was 14, and was featured on her own national radio program at 16; appeared on Broadway (1938 and 1942); recorded more than a dozen records.*

*Filmography:* Something to Shout About *(1943);* I Dood It *(1943);* Tropicana *(1943);* The Heat's On *(1943);* Broadway Rhythm *(1944);* Rhapsody in Blue *(1945).*

Child prodigy Hazel Scott developed a diversified career as a singer and pianist in concerts, nightclubs, on Broadway, and in radio, films and television that lasted more than 50 of her 61 years. By combining jazz and classical music, she created a unique sound that reflected her early musical training. Scott was born on June 11, 1920, in Port-of-Spain, Trinidad. Her college professor father encouraged a love of learning, and her pianist-saxophonist mother **Alma Long Scott** recognized her daughter's exceptional piano skills while she was still a toddler. At age three, she made her professional debut in Trinidad. The family moved to the United States in 1924, and, one year later, Scott made her American debut at Town Hall in New York. By the time she was eight, Scott was invited to study at the prestigious Juilliard School of Music on a six-year scholarship. This was the first time in history the school admitted someone before the age of 16.

Scott's mother, who was active in the New York musical community, joined *Lil Hardin Armstrong's all-female swing band, the Harlem Harlicans. A year later, Alma formed her own all-women band, the American Creolians Orchestra, and Hazel joined the group when she was 14 to play piano and trumpet. This experience gave Scott additional training in performing before an audience and, in 1936 and 1937, she was featured on her own radio program. By now, Scott had developed a showy style in performing a combination of classics and jazz music, and made her Broadway debut the same year with the Count Basie Orchestra. This was followed in 1938 by a piano performance in the Broadway musical *Sing Out the News*, and six years of performances in top New York City clubs.

Returning to the theater, Scott performed in the Broadway show *Priorities of 1942*. She then joined the show's national tour, which effectively established her popularity across the country. This opportunity led to four film roles in 1943: *Something to Shout About, I Dood It, Tropicana*, and *The Heat's On*. She also appeared in *Broadway Rhythm* (1944) and *Rhapsody in Blue* (1945). A Carnegie Hall recital also came in 1945, as well as a major social event, her marriage to Baptist pastor and newly elected U.S. congressional representative Adam Clayton Powell, Jr. The couple would have one son, Adam Clayton Powell III, before divorcing in October 1956.

Scott's career continued to flourish, particularly in the nightclub setting. She was the first African-American woman to have her own television show, in the late 1940s and early 1950s, but producers canceled it after the House Un-American Activities Committee accused Scott of being a communist sympathizer. She released a statement denying any involvement in communist activities, but in those McCarthyite times the accusation alone was enough to cause a decline in her popularity.

Scott left the United States in 1962 and lived in France and Switzerland for the next five years. When she returned, she again hit the nightclub circuit along the East Coast and appeared in several television programs in the 1970s. Honored for her life's work as a pianist and performer, she was inducted into the Black Filmmakers Hall of Fame in 1978. Scott died on October 2, 1981, in New York.

**SOURCES:**

Kernfeld, Barry, ed. *The New Grove Dictionary of Jazz.* NY: St. Martin's Press, 1994.

Smith, Jessie Carney, ed. *Notable Black American Women.* Detroit, MI: Gale Research, 1992.

**Sally Cole-Misch**, freelance writer, Bloomfield Hills, Michigan

## Scott, Lady John (1810–1900).

*See Spottiswoode, Alicia Ann.*

## Scott, Margaret (1809–1873).

*See Gatty, Margaret.*

# Scott, Margaret (1875–1938)

*British golfer. Name variations: Lady Margaret Scott; Lady Hamilton Russell. Born in 1875 in Wiltshire, England; died in 1938; daughter of the earl of Eldon; married Lord Hamilton Russell.*

Born into a titled British family in 1875, Margaret Scott grew up playing golf with her three brothers on the grounds of their home in

SCOTT, MARTHA

Wiltshire, England. The game of golf, which had been played since the mid-1400s, became increasingly popular with the upper classes throughout the second half of the 19th century, but, as with many male-dominated pursuits, women who played it were considered somewhat disreputable. In Britain, women's golf courses typically were separate from those on which men played, and of a lower quality. Some women had nonetheless competed in golf tournaments since the 1500s, and in 1893 the Ladies' Golf Union was formed. Scott won the British Ladies' championship during each of the union's first three years (1893–95), and the fact that she was a member of the aristocracy removed much of the stigma from women playing the game. She retired from competing in 1895, and later married, taking the name Lady Hamilton Russell. She died in 1938.

**SOURCES:**
Elliott, Len, and Barbara Kelly. *Who's Who in Golf.* New Rochelle, NY: Arlington House, 1976.
Uglow, Jennifer S., comp. and ed. *The International Dictionary of Women's Biography.* NY: Continuum, 1982.

**Catherine Dybiec Holm**, M.S.,
Cook, Minnesota

# Scott, Martha (1914—)

*American actress who originated the role of Emily Webb in* Our Town. *Born Martha Ellen Scott on September 22, 1914, in Jamesport, Missouri; daughter of Walter Scott (a farmer and maintenance engineer) and Letha (McKinley) Scott; attended Westport High School, Kansas City, Missouri; University of Michigan, B.A., 1934; married Carleton Alsop (a radio and film producer), on September 16, 1940 (divorced 1946); married Mel Powell (a composer, pianist, and educator), in 1946; children: (first marriage) one son; (second marriage) two daughters.*

*Selected theater: made Broadway debut as Emily Webb in* Our Town *(Henry Miller's Theater, 1938); appeared as The Girl in* Foreigners *(Belasco Theater, 1939), Mara in* The Willow and I *(Windsor Theater, 1942), Kate in* Soldier's Wife *(John Golden Theater, 1944); succeeded \*Margaret Sullavan as Sally in* The Voice of the Turtle *(Morosco Theater, 1945); appeared as Connie Frazier in* It Takes Two *(Biltmore Theater, 1947), Margaret in* Design for a Stained Glass Window *(Mansfield Theater, 1950); succeeded \*Sarah Churchill as Nancy Willard in* Gramercy Ghost *(Morosco, 1951); appeared as Sylvia in* The Number *(Biltmore, 1951), Ellen Turner in the revival of* The Male Animal *(NY City Center, Music Box Theater, and tour, 1952–53), Mrs. Pennypacker in* The Remarkable Mr. Pennypacker *(Coronet Theater, 1953), Mary Reese in*

Cloud 7 *(John Golden Theater, 1958), Lucy Greer in* A Distant Bell *(Eugene O'Neill Theater, 1960), Nina in* The Tumbler *(Helen Hayes Theater, 1960), Fanny Lowe in* The 49th Cousin *(Ambassador Theater, 1960), Lillian Hudson in* Future Perfect *(Cape Playhouse, Dennis, MA, 1961); toured in stock as Mary in* The Complaisant Lover *(1962); appeared as Mattie Martin in* Open Book *(Pasadena Playhouse, 1963); toured as Pamela Pew-Pickett in* Tchin-Tchin *(1963); succeeded \*Maureen O'Sullivan as Edith in* Never Too Late *(Playhouse Theater, 1964); replaced Irene Dailey as Nettie Cleary in* The Subject was Roses *(Royale Theater and tour, 1964); appeared as Mrs. Antrobus in revival of* The Skin of Our Teeth *(Eisenhower Theater, JFK Center, Washington, D.C., and Mark Hellinger Theater, NY, 1975).*

*Selected filmography:* Our Town *(1940);* The Howards of Virginia *(1940);* Cheers for Miss Bishop *(1941);* They Dare Not Love *(1941);* One Foot in Heaven *(1941);* Hi Diddle Diddle *(1943); (cameo)* Stage Door Canteen *(1943);* In Old Oklahoma *(1943);* So Well Remembered *(1947);* Strange Bargain *(1949);* When I Grow Up *(1951);* The Desperate Hours *(1955);* The Ten Commandments *(1956);* Sayonara *(1957);* 18 and Anxious *(1957);* Ben-Hur *(1959);* Charlotte's Web *(1973);* Airport 1975 *(1974);* The Turning Point *(1977); (co-prod. only)* First Monday in October *(1981);* Doin' Time on Planet Earth *(1988).*

In one of the theater's true Cinderella stories, actress Martha Scott had only a few years of stock under her belt before landing the role of Emily Webb in the Broadway production of *Our Town* (1938). The Thornton Wilder play won a Pulitzer Prize and went on to become one of America's most famous and often-produced classics. In 1940, Scott reprised her role in the film version, earning an Oscar nomination for Best Actress.

Scott was born in 1914 in Jamesport, Missouri, and graduated from the University of Michigan in 1934. That year, she joined the Globe Theater at the Chicago World's Fair, appearing in abbreviated versions of Shakespearean plays, before moving on to stock companies in Detroit, Lansing, and Kalamazoo, Michigan. Following her breakthrough role in *Our Town*, she continued to appear on Broadway as well as in stock, combining her stage career with films and television. A solid, skillful actress, she made her mark in supporting roles and frequently succeeded or replaced the original star during a Broadway run or on tour. In 1969, the actress joined 30 of her colleagues to organize the Plumstead Playhouse, which produced revivals of classic American plays, and of which she served as director. The Playhouse's inaugural production was a revival of *Our Town*.

Scott appeared on a number of radio serials during the 1930s, and from 1950 on was regularly seen on television. She was narrator and host on the daytime series "Modern Romances" (1954–57) and was seen on such popular series as "Omnibus," "Robert Montgomery Presents," "The F.B.I.," and "Ironside." She also had a recurring role as Bob Newhart's mother on "The Bob Newhart Show."

Scott was married to radio-film producer Carleton Alsop, with whom she had a son, and later to composer, pianist, and educator Mel Powell, with whom she had two daughters. Her last film appearance was in *Doin' Time on Planet Earth* (1988).

**SOURCES:**

Katz, Ephraim. *The Film Encyclopedia*. NY: Harper-Collins, 1994.

McGill, Raymond, ed. *Notable Names in the American Theatre*. Clifton, NJ: James T. White, 1976.

**Barbara Morgan**,
Melrose, Massachusetts

*Martha Scott in* Cheers for Miss Bishop.

## Scott, Mother (1893–1979).

*See Scott, Esther Mae.*

## Scott, Rose (1847–1925)

*Australian feminist. Born in Glendon, near Singleton, New South Wales, Australia, on October 15, 1847; died on April 21, 1925; fifth of eight children of Sarah Anne (Rusden) Scott (a linguist and scholar) and Helenus Scott (a police magistrate in Maitland); educated at home by her mother; never married; children: adopted the son of her deceased sister.*

Rose Scott was born in 1847 in Glendon, near Singleton, New South Wales, Australia, and raised in a family that believed fervently in education for boys. While her brothers were packed off to private schools, she was educated at home by her mother. In 1879, upon the death of her father, Scott inherited £500 per annum which she used to care for her ailing mother. Following the death of a beloved sister, Gertie, a year later, Rose adopted Gertie's son and set up home in Woollahra, Sydney, where she became something of a celebrity. In 1891, she founded the Womanhood Suffrage League and became its secretary.

Initially, Scott worked with **Dora Montefiore**, a Marxist, and *****Vida Goldstein**. Although she refused to join a political party, Scott lobbied heavily for protective legislation: she demanded shorter hours for shop assistants, worked to raise the age of consent for girls to marry from 14 to 16, and pushed to criminalize the seduction of women under the promise of marriage. To exact such changes, she often went head to head with those feminists who supported labor.

Following the death of her mother in 1896, Scott became president of the women's committee for the Prisoners' Aid Association and soon called for a separate women's prison. In 1901, she organized the League for Political Education, of which she later became president (1910). In 1902, she was elected foundation president of the Women's Political and Educational League, campaigning for a widow's rights to share in her husband's estates and for the removal of gender barriers in the legal profession. She adamantly opposed a bill to regulate prostitution, a bill designed, in her words, to "supply clean women for profligate men."

An ardent pacifist, Scott condemned the British for the Boer War in 1900, was president of the Peace Society for many years, and decried Australia's involvement in World War I. In 1903, she did, however, champion the release of **Ethel Herringe**, who had been convicted of shooting her employer. They had had an affair, and when the employer learned she was pregnant, he not only fired her but would have nothing to do with her. In jail, Herringe gave birth to twins who were taken from her, and Scott became even more vociferous.

Rose Scott retired from public life in 1922. Though women had obtained the vote, she was disillusioned with the way she perceived them using their newfound power. She was particularly disturbed that women joined existing parties rather than formulating their own. To her, the flappers of the 1920s had become sexual playthings for men. When Rose Scott died in 1925, she left money in her will for the establishment of the Rose Scott Memorial Prize in International Law at the University of Sydney.

## Scott, Sarah (1723–1795)

*English novelist. Born Sarah Robinson in 1723 in West Layton, Hutton Magna, Yorkshire; died on November 30, 1795, in Catton, near Norwich; daughter of Matthew Robinson (a Yorkshire landowner) and Elizabeth Drake Robinson (a Cambridge heiress); sister of Elizabeth Montagu (1720–1800); married George Lewis Scott, in 1751 or 1752 (separated).*

*Selected writings:* The History of Cornelia *(1750);* A Journey Through Every Stage in Life *(1754);* Agreeable Ugliness, or the Triumph of the Graces *(1754);* Description of Millenium Hall *(1762);* Sir George Ellison *(1766);* The Test of Filial Duty *(1772).*

Sarah Scott was born in 1723, the younger sister of celebrated writer and beauty *****Elizabeth Montagu**. The sisters resembled each other so much, like two peas in a pod, that the family referred to Sarah as "The Pea." Around 1751, Sarah married George Lewis Scott, a mathematician who had served as a tutor to the future King George III, but they separated shortly thereafter, apparently due to incompatible personalities. Scott's need for an income turned out to be the start of her literary career, and she successfully sold her work, writing six novels as well as several historical and biographical works. Her fiction, all of which was published anonymously, covered topics including female independence and clandestine marriage.

After Scott left her marriage, she and her close friend Lady **Barbara Montagu** (to whom she was not related) set up an unusual haven for unattached women. Between 1754 and 1756,

**Clodia.** See
Fulvia for sidebar.

they ran a community at Bath Easton where single women could live while teaching poor children who otherwise lacked the means to obtain education. Scott's best-known novel, the utopian *Description of Millenium Hall* (1762), uses the backdrop of the female community for its plot, and features a man impressed with the group's commitment to rational pursuits. While the community at Bath Easton ended in 1756, Scott and Montagu continued living together until Montagu's death nine years later.

In addition to her novels, Scott also published a biography of Gustavus I Vasa (r. 1523–1560), king of Sweden (1761), a history of the House of Mecklenburg (1762), and *Life of Théodore Agrippa d'Aubigné* (1772). After apparently living quietly for a number of years, she died in 1795 in Catton, near Norwich, leaving instructions that all her papers and notes be burned.

**SOURCES:**

Buck, Claire, ed. *The Bloomsbury Guide to Women's Literature.* NY: Prentice Hall, 1992.

*The Concise Dictionary of National Biography.* Oxford: Oxford University Press, 1992.

Shattock, Joanne. *The Oxford Guide to British Women Writers.* Oxford: Oxford University Press, 1993.

**Catherine Dybiec Holm**, M.S.,
Cook, Minnesota

# Scribonia (c. 75 BCE–after 16 CE)

*Roman noblewoman and wife of Augustus Caesar. Name variations: Sempronia. Born around 75 BCE; died after 16 CE; younger sister of L. Scribonius Libo; married (probably) Cn. Lentulus Marcellinus (consul), in 56 BCE; married Cornelius Scipio; married Octavian (63 BCE–14 CE), who after their marriage became Augustus Caesar, emperor of Rome (r. 27 BCE–14 CE), in 40 BCE; children: (second marriage) Cornelia (who married Paullus Aemilius Lepidus, a consul in 34 BCE); (third marriage) Julia (39 BCE–14 CE).*

Scribonia's ancestors were of the second tier of the Roman political elite, for none had advanced beyond the status of praetor. Scribonia was married (probably no more than) three times. Her first husband was (probably) Cn. Lentulus Marcellinus, consul in 56. Her second spouse is even less certain, but is also said to have reached the consulship. Apparently he was a Cornelius Scipio (perhaps the consul suffect of 35 BCE), for Scribonia gave birth to their daughter *Cornelia, who would one day marry Paullus Aemilius Lepidus, who was a consul in 34 BCE.

Scribonia's third husband was Octavian, who long after their marriage became Augustus Caesar. They married in 40 BCE, at the time of

the rebellion Octavian was facing in Italy (the Perusine War, 41–40). Octavian, whose first wife was Clodia, was around 12 years younger than Scribonia (he was born in 63, she was born around 75 BCE), and the marriage was purely political. Her attractiveness lay entirely in her brother L. Scribonius Libo, who was the father-in-law and a supporter of the still-powerful Sextus Pompey. Sextus, the son of Julius Caesar's famous rival Pompey the Great, was at the time a force to be reckoned with in a world still unsettled after Caesar's assassination (44 BCE), and through Scribonia, Octavian was seeking potential allies against a possible break with Marc Antony (a break which eventually came, but not in 40).

Although in 39 BCE Octavian and Scribonia produced a daughter *Julia (his only offspring), theirs was not a happy marriage. Within months of Julia's birth, Octavian divorced Scribonia (giving as his reason his inability to put up with her nagging) so as to quickly remarry *Livia Drusilla, to whom he would stay married until his death in 14 CE. In fact, most thought Octavian married Livia far too hastily, for when they wed she was still pregnant by the husband whom Octavian had encouraged her to abandon in his own favor. Thus discarded by the future emperor, Scribonia also was forced to part with Julia, who would be raised with strictness by Augustus and Livia.

It is uncertain whether Scribonia remarried after the divorce from Octavian, but it is unlikely. When Julia fell into disgrace and was exiled in 2 BCE, Scribonia voluntarily followed her daughter into exile, first to Pandateria and then to Rhegium (4 CE). Scribonia and Julia lived together until Julia died of malnutrition in 14. Thereafter, Scribonia lived at least into 16, but it is not known how long into the imperial era she survived.

**William S. Greenwalt**
Associate Professor of Classical History,
Santa Clara University, Santa Clara, California

# Scripps, Ellen Browning

## (1836–1932)

*English-born American newspaper publisher and philanthropist. Born on October 18, 1836, in London, England; died in her sleep on August 3, 1932, in La Jolla, California; daughter of James Mogg Scripps and Ellen Mary Scripps; graduated from Knox College in 1859; never married; no children.*

The energetic and eclectic Ellen Browning Scripps started her life in London, England, on October 18, 1836. Her mother died when Scripps was five, and three years later her father moved his six children to farmland he owned in Illinois. Scripps developed an interest in literature early in life, through reading books from her father's large library to her many younger brothers and sisters (her father remarried and had five more children). When she got older, she had the rare opportunity for a woman of her time to attend college. She enrolled in the two-year course of the Female Department at Knox College, graduating in 1859, and then spent several years teaching. With the advent of the Civil War, Scripps involved herself in war-relief efforts, working for the U.S. Sanitary Commission and the Freedmen's Association.

In 1867, Scripps began what was to become an involved career in journalism. She assisted an older brother, James E. Scripps, in his management of a Detroit newspaper by serving as a proofreader and investing her meager savings in the venture. In 1873, James launched a new newspaper, the *Detroit Evening News*, and Scripps served as proofreader, copyreader, and front-page feature writer. Her column, "Matters and Things," was aimed at a large audience and included items of special interest to women. Scripps' presence also helped to smooth occasional rifts between her brother and other family members, a number of whom were also employed at the paper.

In 1878, Scripps provided financial backing for her younger half-brother, Edward Scripps, to begin a newspaper of his own, the *Penny Press*, in Cleveland, Ohio; for a time, she worked at the new paper as well as the *Detroit Evening News*. While she eventually cut down on her work duties, Scripps continued to reinvest in the newspaper ventures and helped Edward lay the basis for what would become the Scripps-Howard conglomerate of papers. Eventually, she had holdings in 16 daily newspapers across the country, greatly multiplying her income.

When Edward moved to California, Scripps followed him and eventually built her own home in La Jolla. Aided by investments in local real estate, her income increased over 40 times in the first 30 years of the 20th century, and she chose to manage the money herself rather than entrust it to lawyers. She donated much of her money to causes she considered worthy, and her generosity made her a major philanthropic figure. Although she worked in the newspaper business, Scripps also had a keen interest in science and established institutions geared towards research; her donations reflected her eclectic interests. With her brother Edward, she spearheaded the establishment of the Marine Biological Association of San Diego, which later became the Scripps Institution

of Oceanography. She also funded the Scripps Memorial Hospital in her new hometown of La Jolla, later known as the Scripps Clinic and Research Foundation, dedicated to the study of metabolism. Torrey Pines Park and the San Diego Zoo also received substantial funding from Scripps. Education received a similar boost from her wealth, with her largest contribution involving the founding, in 1926, of Scripps College for Women, one of the Claremont Colleges, in Claremont, California. Scripps wrote the school's mission statement, which speaks of the need for a college "to develop in its students the ability to think clearly and independently, and the ability to live confidently, courageously and hopefully." Although she was in her 90s when Scripps opened, she contributed over $1.5 million to the college (which she called her "new adventure") during the remainder of her life, and left it a generous provision after she died. Her alma mater Knox College likewise received a $100,000 gift.

Ellen Scripps refrained from accepting high-level posts in organizations (the exception being her directorship of the National Recreation Association from 1917 on), but she was not politically inactive. She opposed the wave of deportations of alleged communist agitators (1919–20) which occurred under Attorney General A. Mitchell Palmer, and demanded freedom for political prisoners as a member of the Amnesty League. She was also an opponent of the death penalty. Scripps died at the age of 96 in her home in La Jolla on August 3, 1932. Scripps College remains a well-respected liberal arts college for women, with just over 1,000 students.

**SOURCES:**
James, Edward T., ed. *Notable American Women, 1607–1950*. Cambridge, MA: The Belknap Press of Harvard University, 1971.

McHenry, Robert, ed. *Famous American Women*. NY: Dover, 1980.

**Catherine Dybiec Holm**, M.S.,
Cook, Minnesota

# Scrivener, Christiane (1925—)

*French economist and politician. Born on September 1, 1925; graduated from Lycée de Grenoble; graduated from Harvard Business School; married Pierre Scrivener, in 1944; children: one son (died).*

Born in 1925, Christiane Scrivener earned a diploma from the Lycée de Grenoble in France before graduating from Harvard Business School. From 1958 to 1976, she served as the director of various business and governmental agencies dedicated to international technical cooperation. A member of the Union for French Democracy (UFD), she became directly involved in politics in 1976, when she started a two-year term as junior minister for consumer affairs. Between 1979 and 1988, Scrivener served as a member of the European Parliament, and in January 1989 was named a commissioner of the European Community (EC). In this role she oversaw tax issues, and in January 1993 her responsibilities expanded to include the oversight of consumer affairs. She stepped down as commissioner in 1995, and the following year became a mediator with the Society General. Her service to the greater European community earned her prestigious commendations from such countries as Belgium and Luxemburg, and she was named an officer of the Legion of Honor in 1995.

**Catherine Dybiec Holm**, M.S.,
Cook, Minnesota

*Ida
Scudder*

## Scudder, Ida (1870–1960)

*American physician and missionary who founded the Christian Medical College and Hospital in Vellore,*

*South India.* Born Ida Sophia Scudder on December 9, 1870, in Ranipet, Madras Presidency, India; died in Kodaikanal, India, on May 24, 1960; sixth child and only daughter of John Scudder II (a medical missionary of the Reformed Church and himself the son of a medical missionary in India) and Sophia Weld Scudder (a missionary of the Reformed Church); attended Northfield Seminary in Massachusetts; Woman's Medical College of Pennsylvania and Cornell Medical College; never married; lived with Gertrude Dodd, from 1916 until Dodd's death in 1944.

Ida Scudder was born in 1870, in Ranipet, Madras Presidency, India. In 1878, her family returned briefly to the United States following a cholera epidemic and settled in Creston, Nebraska, for four years. Her father John Scudder II returned to India in 1882, and when her mother **Sophia Weld Scudder** followed in 1883 Ida went to Chicago to live with her uncle, the Reverend Henry Martyn Scudder. In 1887, when her uncle went as a missionary to Japan, Scudder enrolled at Dwight Moody's Northfield Seminary.

Scudder journeyed to the family's new post of Tindivanam, India, in 1890. Although she had originally rebelled against the family business of missionary work, her return to India to help her ill mother began a process of acceptance and inspiration. During one traumatic night of her stay, Scudder's life changed dramatically. Three women were about to give birth, but their husbands would not allow a male to attend them. So instead of seeking the help of the more experienced John Scudder, they enlisted Ida, despite her protests concerning her lack of training. All three women died of the kinds of complications that Ida knew could have been prevented by a physician. She vowed then to get a medical degree, so that she could work in India as a much-needed female physician.

Returning to America, she began study at the Woman's Medical College of Pennsylvania in Philadelphia in 1895. She transferred to Cornell Medical College for her final year, receiving her M.D. in 1899. In 1900, she went back to Vellore and began a lifelong service as a medical missionary. Scudder's father, with whom she hoped to work as an intern, died within five months of her return. Instead of despairing about the case load she faced and the prejudices and distrust of those who doubted her ability as a woman doctor, she remained in Vellore and began training others to help her in the work. In 1902, she opened the Mary Taber Schell Hospital, which also provided a central locale for much-needed medical care and for the training of nurses. While continuing to make medical rounds in the outlying rural areas, Scudder would remain the only surgeon at the hospital for 22 years.

In 1909, the hospital's nurses-training program was expanded into a regular school of nursing. In 1916, she was joined in India by her friend **Gertrude Dodd**, an unofficial, self-supporting missionary of the Reformed Church. Two years later, with Dodd's assistance, Scudder founded the Union Mission Medical School for Women in Vellore, which provided formal and certified medical education. Dodd continued to give generously, supporting students at the medical college where she also served as bursar and registrar. In 1938, when new governmental regulations threatened to close the school unless it obtained a university affiliation, Scudder began the process of obtaining certification, traveling to the United States in 1941 in search of funding. She returned to India following Gertrude Dodd's death in Florida in 1944. In 1950, the Christian Medical College (as it was renamed) became officially affiliated with the University of Madras, thereby protecting it from closure and providing continued educational opportunities for women and men. With this accomplishment, Scudder retired but remained near Vellore. She died, age 90, on May 24, 1960, at her home near Kodaikanal.

Scudder's medical work in India was particularly significant in that it provided educational opportunities for women and increased the accessibility of medical care to women in the area. Although Scudder's efforts to save the medical college from closure included converting it into a co-educational institution, causing condemnation from *Lucy Peabody and other supporters of women's education, her work remains significant. By providing for the education of locals in medical techniques, she assured the continuance of health care in the area around Vellore and released it from reliance on itinerant doctors and the presence of missionaries from foreign countries.

**SOURCES:**

Sicherman, Barbara, and Carol Hurd Green, eds. *Notable American Women: The Modern Period*. Cambridge, MA: The Belknap Press of Harvard University, 1980.

Wilson, Dorothy Clarke. *Dr. Ida: The Story of Dr. Ida Scudder of Vellore*. NY: McGraw-Hill, 1959.

**SUGGESTED READING:**

Jeffery, Mary Pauline. *Ida S. Scudder of Vellore: The Life Story of Ida Sophia Scudder*. Mysore City, India: Wesley Press, 1951.

**COLLECTIONS:**

Scudder's papers are held by the Schlesinger Library of Radcliffe College, including a transcription of an oral history project by the Medical College of Pennsylvania on women in medicine; some additional papers are located at the Christian Medical College and Hospital in Vellore, India.

**Amanda Carson Banks**,
Vanderbilt Divinity School,
Nashville, Tennessee

# Scudder, Janet (1869–1940)

*American sculptor who created a genre of garden sculptures and fountains that became highly popular in the United States. Name variations: Netta Deweze Frazee Scudder. Born Netta Deweze Frazee Scudder (also wrongly seen as Netta Dewee Frazer Scudder) on October 27, 1869, in Terre Haute, Indiana; died of lobar pneumonia on June 9, 1940, in Rockport, Massachusetts; daughter of William Hollingshead Scudder (a confectioner) and Mary (Sparks) Scudder; studied drawing at Rose Polytechnic Institute and Colarossi Academy; studied anatomy, drawing, and modeling at Cincinnati Academy of Art.*

Born in Terre Haute, Indiana, in 1869, Janet Scudder was born Netta Deweze Frazee Scudder, the third daughter and one of seven children of confectioner William Hollingshead Scudder and **Mary Sparks Scudder**. In what she would later describe as a "sad and dismal" childhood, her mother died when Scudder was five, and her father's remarriage was to a woman with whom she did not get along. A self-described roughneck, Scudder "could skin a cat, hang by my toes. . . . As for skating on ice in moonlight, no one could outdistance me." Her independent streak was reinforced by the loss of several more family members; her grandmother, who was credited with inspiring Scudder's first artistic awakening, died a few years after her mother had, and her father and favorite brother died before she turned 21.

Although not particularly interested in Longfellow's poetry when she was a child, Scudder was drawn to the illustrations she found in two volumes of his works. "[S]he became enchanted by the pictures," notes Charlotte Streifer Rubinstein, "and copied a Viking in full armor hundreds of times on scraps of old, used envelopes. When the house caught fire, she was seen lugging the two heavy volumes down the burning steps."

In addition to attending Terre Haute public schools, Scudder began advancing her talents in Saturday drawing classes at Rose Polytechnic Institute. The director there recognized Scudder's passion for art and convinced her impoverished father to find the money to send her to the Cincinnati Academy of Art, which she began attending at age 18. During her time in Cincinnati, where she changed her name from the unwieldy "Netta Deweze" to "Janet," she studied anatomy, drawing, and modeling. With encouragement from the sculptor Louis Rebisso, Scudder considered a career as a woodcarver, and she contributed to her tuition with sales of her carved wooden mantlepieces. After finishing her academy training, she moved to Chicago to live with her eldest brother. There, she found a job as a woodcarver in a factory. The union, however, did not permit women to become members, and she was forced out of the job, despite her adeptness as a carver.

There were others, though, who were willing to hire a woman with Scudder's abilities. Chicagoans were busily preparing for the World's Columbian Exposition of 1893, among them sculptor Lorado Taft and his chief architect. When told by Lorado to hire some women to help with sculptures for a display in front of the Horticulture Building, his architect reportedly replied that he would hire "anyone who could do the work . . . white rabbits if they will help out." Scudder became one of a group of women, known as Taft's "white rabbits," who assisted him in enlarging sculptures from scaled models. Several in the

*Janet Scudder*

group would emerge as leading women sculptors, including ***Bessie Potter Vonnoh**, **Enid Yandell**, **Julia Bracken**, and **Caroline Brooks**. Also among Taft's assistants was his sister, painter **Zulime Taft**; it would not be long before she and Scudder became traveling companions.

The exposition proved to be an important event in Scudder's life. In part thanks to Lorado, she was commissioned to create her own statues for the exposition's Illinois and Indiana buildings. Perhaps of even more consequence for her future, she observed Frederick MacMonnies supervising the installation of a monumental fountain in the Court of Honor; though she was too shy to approach him at the time, Scudder decided that she had to study with him. Following the exposition, she traveled with Zulime to Paris in late 1893 with a letter of introduction to MacMonnies. Initially rebuffed by him, she knocked on the door of his studio and was persuasive enough that she became one of his life drawing and modeling students. She was soon one of his assistants.

Her work with MacMonnies also provided instruction in modeling in low relief, an art which Scudder would later employ in her medallion work. Their professional relationship was cut prematurely short, however, by the jealousy of another MacMonnies assistant, who erroneously reported to Scudder that MacMonnies was unhappy with her work. Without waiting to discuss the matter with him, Scudder left for New York in 1894. Years later, she learned that the story had been completely false, and that MacMonnies, who in fact regarded Scudder as his finest assistant, had been both hurt and puzzled by her abrupt departure.

In New York, Scudder lived in poverty until a wealthy fellow art student, **Matilda Brownell**, saw to it that her father used his influence to get Scudder a commission designing the New York Bar Association's seal. From that job came others, and she designed architectural ornaments, portrait medallions, and funeral monuments. By 1896, she was earning enough of a living to return to Paris. Through MacMonnies, the Luxembourg Museum purchased some of her medallions.

A trip to Italy in the late 1890s laid the groundwork for a turning point in Scudder's artistic efforts. There, she viewed Donatello's cherubs as well as decorative statues located in the gardens of Roman villas. These works influenced her decision to create decorative sculptures, lighthearted in nature, which were designed to elicit pleasure and amusement. On her return to Paris, she used a street urchin as the model for one of her most famous works, *Frog*

*Fountain* (1901). This bronze statue featured a small boy playing in water which was shot from the mouths of three frogs. In 1899, Scudder returned to New York where her *Frog Fountain* earned the notice of prominent American architect Stanford White, who bought the statue and advised Scudder to make only four copies. The Metropolitan Museum of Art acquired one of these copies, and commissions for statuary for the gardens of the Rockefellers, Pratts, McCormicks and other millionaires followed.

Scudder returned to Paris in 1909. Her success continued with an honorable mention in the Paris Salon of 1911 for her *Young Diana*, and in 1913 she had a solo exhibition in New York. In her only architectural creation, she designed an Italian villa for a friend in Maine. The home she bought at Ville d'Avray outside Paris in 1913 provided her with a garden in which she could properly view her works in progress.

Concerned with women's rights, Scudder participated in the art committee of the National American Woman Suffrage Association (NAWSA). She designed a sculpture of a woman (dancer *Irene Castle was the model) intended for a victory fountain in Washington, D.C., to pay tribute to the suffrage movement. This work, however, was never installed.

During World War I, she returned to New York to help organize the Lafayette Fund, which raised money to aid French soldiers. Scudder also continued doing her own work and in 1915 exhibited ten pieces at the Panama-Pacific Exposition in San Francisco, where she won a silver medal. When the United States entered the war, she returned overseas, working first with the YMCA (she turned her house in Ville d'Avray over to the organization) and later with the Red Cross. For her efforts in wartime, the French government made Scudder a Chevalier of the Legion of Honor in 1925. The same year, her autobiography, *Modeling My Life*, was published.

After the war, she lived for the next 20 years at Ville d'Avray. Her friend *Mabel Dodge Luhan described Scudder as "tall and stooped a little . . . rather sentimental and very generous." Her whimsical garden works, for which she is most remembered, set a standard for a style of sculpture that became highly popular in the United States. Scudder's later works took on a more serious tone, and she developed an interest in painting which led to a New York exhibition in 1933. After World War II broke out, she returned to America and soon died of lobar pneumonia in Rockport, Massachusetts, in 1940, at age 70.

**SOURCES:**
Bailey, Brooke. *The Remarkable Lives of 100 Women Artists.* Holbrook, MA: Bob Adams, 1994.
James, Edward T., ed. *Notable American Women, 1607–1950.* Cambridge, MA: The Belknap Press of Harvard University Press, 1971.
McHenry, Robert, ed. *Famous American Women.* NY: Dover, 1980.
Rubinstein, Charlotte Streifer. *American Women Artists from Early Indian Times to the Present.* Avon, 1982.
**SUGGESTED READING:**
Scudder, Janet. *Modeling My Life*, 1925.

**David Paul Clarke**, freelance writer, Bethesda, Maryland

# Scudder, Vida (1861–1954)

*American educator and social reformer. Name variations: Vida Dutton Scudder. Born Julia Davida Scudder on December 15, 1861, in Madura, India; died on October 9, 1954, in Wellesley, Massachusetts; only child of David Coit Scudder (a Congregationalist missionary) and Harriet Louisa (Dutton) Scudder; Smith College, A.B., 1884; graduate work, Oxford University, 1884–85; Smith College, A.M., 1889; lived with Florence Converse (1871–1967, a writer), from 1919 to 1954; no children.*

*Was an instructor (1887–92), assistant professor (1892–1910), full professor (1910–28), all at Wellesley College; founded the College Settlements Association (1889); became a member for life of the Society for the Companions of the Holy Cross (1889); founded Denison House (1892); was active in the Boston Women's Trade Union (1903–12); was a founding member, Episcopal Church Socialist League (1911); founded the Church League for Industrial Democracy (1919); involved with the Fellowship of Reconciliation and the Women's International League for Peace and Freedom (1920s–30s).*

*Selected writings: The Life of the Spirit in the Modern English Poets (1895); Social Ideals in English Letters (1898); A Listener in Babel (1903); The Disciple of a Saint (1907); Socialism and Character (1912); The Franciscan Adventure (1931); On Journey (1937). Also contributed to the* Atlantic Monthly *and several religious periodicals.*

Vida Dutton Scudder was many things: novelist, scholar, teacher, settlement-house pioneer, friend of labor, pacifist, and Christian Socialist. She was passionate and intelligent, and as varied as her interests seem now, her guiding principle was that of bringing joy and wisdom to those around her. This she did during her almost 93 years.

Vida was born in 1861 in India where her father David Coit Scudder, a young Congregationalist minister, was engaged in missionary work. A few months after her birth, he drowned, and Vida and her mother **Harriet Dutton Scudder** came home to America, settling in the home of Harriet's parents in Auburndale, Massachusetts. Descended from old New England families on both sides, Vida enjoyed an indulged childhood among well-to-do and well-accomplished relatives. She and her mother spent much of her youth in Europe where Harriet instilled in her daughter a lifelong appreciation for art and natural beauty. Settling in Boston, Harriet enrolled Vida in Miss Sanger's school. Vida did well there and went on to be part of the first class to graduate from the recently opened Girls' Latin School in 1880. She then attended Smith College where her intellectual life was as stimulating as the company there. Upon graduation, Scudder, her close friend **Clara French**, and their mothers traveled to England where the young women attended Oxford College. There, Scudder was introduced to the work of John Ruskin and became increasingly aware that with her privileged status came an obligation to help those not so privileged.

Not yet sure of her life's direction, Scudder took a position in the English department at Wellesley College in 1887. At the same time, she

*Vida Scudder*

began working on a master's degree at Smith which she completed in 1889. By then, Scudder and several other graduates from women's colleges had formed the College Settlements Association (CSA). The first CSA house opened in New York City in 1889. Three years later, Scudder took a leave of absence from teaching to oversee the opening of Denison House in Boston. Along with her good friend **Helena Stuart Dudley**, who would follow fellow Wellesley professor *Emily Greene Balch as head resident, Scudder was joined in those early years at Denison House by **Florence Converse** (1871–1967). Converse, ten years younger than Scudder, had first met her as a Wellesley undergraduate. Upon her graduation in 1893, Converse entered into a passionate, fulfilling relationship with her former teacher. Their partnership would last more than 60 years, ending only with Scudder's death in 1954.

During the 1890s, Denison House became a center of labor activities in Boston with John and *Mary Kenney O'Sullivan, local labor leaders, as frequent guests. Scudder became interested in labor issues and even served briefly as a delegate to the Boston Central Labor Union. At the same time, she continued her religious quest. By 1889, she had joined the Episcopal Church and was also active in the Christian Socialist movement, worshipping at the Church of the Carpenter in Boston. However, Scudder paid a personal price for her growing radicalism. Both her mother and her superiors at Wellesley disapproved, and in 1901 she had a breakdown. She spent two years in Europe, resting, traveling, and writing a semi-fictional account of settlement-house life, *A Listener in Babel* (1903). Scudder returned to Boston in 1903 with a renewed sense of purpose. She participated in the formation of the Boston Women's Trade Union League (WTUL) and started Italian literature courses at Denison House, responding to the changing demographics of that previously Irish working-class neighborhood. She also continued her association with the Christian Socialist movement. She officially joined the Socialist Party in 1911, the same year that she founded the Episcopal Church Socialist League. In 1912, Scudder published *Socialism and Character*, her attempt to make clear the link between Marxism and Christianity.

Also in 1912, Scudder was an outspoken supporter of the striking textile workers in Lawrence, Massachusetts. This strike of radical, immigrant women was not sanctioned by the WTUL and its membership was divided over the issue. Scudder joined fellow WTUL members Mary Kenney O'Sullivan and *Elizabeth Glendower Evans in support of the strike, contrary to WTUL policy. Chastised by the Wellesley administration for her actions in Lawrence and dismayed by the political divisions within the WTUL and even within her beloved Denison House, Scudder withdrew into academic life. She built a house in Wellesley, where she and her mother moved in 1912. In 1919, they were joined by Florence Converse and her mother, and, two years later, Helena Dudley moved in as well.

Following World War I, Scudder became a pacifist. Retiring from Wellesley in 1928 after 40 years of teaching, she was able to concentrate on the work which established her as a Franciscan scholar, *The Franciscan Adventure* (1931). A fervent Christian Socialist, the 85-year-old Scudder spoke before the annual conference on Christian Social Thinking in 1945 on "Anglican Thought on Property." She died suddenly in her Wellesley home in 1954, from choking on a piece of food. Florence Converse, her beloved companion of 60 years, was by her side.

**SOURCES:**
Corcoran, Sister Catherine Theresa. *Vida Dutton Scudder: The Progressive Years.* Ann Arbor, Michigan: UMI, 1974.

Scudder, Vida Dutton. *On Journey.* NY: E.P. Dutton, 1937.

**COLLECTIONS:**
Vida Scudder Papers, Sophia Smith Collection, Smith College, and Wellesley College Archives, Wellesley College.

**Kathleen Banks Nutter**,
Manuscripts Processor at the Sophia Smith Collection,
Smith College, Northampton, Massachusetts

# Scudéry, Madeleine de (1607–1701)

*French novelist and poet. Name variations: Madeleine de Scudery or Scuderi. Born on November 15, 1607, in Le Hâvre, France; died on June 2, 1701, in Paris; daughter of Georges de Scudéry (an army captain) and Madeleine de Martel de Goutimesnil; never married; no children.*

*Orphaned (1613); was a member of Hôtel de Rambouillet (1637); had first novel published (1641); began Samedi salon (1653); suffered onset of deafness (1666); awarded prize by Académie Française (1671); had last work published (1692).*

*Selected writings:* Ibrahim, ou l'Illustre Bassa *(Ibrahim, or the Illustrious Bassa, 1641);* Les Femmes illustres ou Les Harangues héroiques *(Illustrious Women or Heroic Speeches, 1642);* Artamène ou Le Grand Cyrus *(Artamenes or the Grand Cyrus, 1649);* Clélie, Histoire romaine *(Clelia, a Romance, 1654);* Celinte *(1661);* Mathilde d'Aguilar *(1667);* La Promenade de Versailles *(1669);* Discours de la Gloire *(Discourse on Glory, 1671);* Conversations sur divers sujets *(Conversations on Diverse Subjects, 1680);* Conversations nouvelles sur divers sujets *(New Conversations on Diverse Subjects, 1684);* Conversations morales *(Moral Conversations, 1686);* Nouvelles conversations de morale *(New Moral Conversations, 1688);* Entretiens de Morale *(Treatise on Morality, 1692).*

Although she is no longer well known, the French writer Madeleine de Scudéry was perhaps the most widely read novelist of 17th-century France. Her writings, admired and imitated in her time, appeared in numerous editions and foreign language translations across Europe in the 17th and 18th centuries. She was renowned for her classical learning and sharp wit, even though her works were usually published under her brother's name. Scudéry counted among her friends and supporters members of Europe's highest elite, including King Louis XIV of France, his prime minister Cardinal Mazarin, and Queen *Christina of Sweden. For years, Scudéry was one of the leading hostesses of the French salons, and was a founding member of the aristocratic movement known as preciosity.

Yet Madeleine de Scudéry was not born into an aristocratic family, which makes her later renown even more remarkable. She was the daughter of Georges de Scudéry, a soldier from Provence, and **Madeleine de Martel de Goutimesnil**, who came from a lower-middle-class family of Le Hâvre. Born on November 15, 1607, in the port town of Le Hâvre on the western coast of France, Madeleine de Scudéry was one of five children, but only she and her older brother Georges survived infancy.

> One can call Mademoiselle de Scudéry the Muse of our Century.
>
> —Abbé de Pure

Her father served as captain of the port of Le Hâvre, a poorly paid position which apparently led him to turn to piracy to make ends meet. He was arrested and imprisoned for a short while and did not survive long after his release. He died in 1613, still a young man, leaving his family little to live on. But this was not the only tragedy Madeleine and Georges had to face as children; later that same year, their mother died as well. The Scudéry children—Georges age twelve, Madeleine only six—were left orphaned and penniless.

The story of Georges and Madeleine de Scudéry might have ended there; poor orphans in 17th-century Europe had few options, and usually turned to begging or prostitution to survive.

But the young Scudérys were much more fortunate: an uncle took them in and raised them as his own in his country manor near Rouen. He was a French courtier with a comfortable living who gave both children an exceptional education, providing the foundation for their later literary careers. Madeleine was especially drawn to her studies. She had an insatiable curiosity about the world, which led her to pursue not only the skills considered proper for a girl—singing, writing, drawing, dancing, and painting—but also the areas of knowledge usually reserved for boys. With her uncle's encouragement, Madeleine studied literature, poetry, and modern languages, including Spanish and Italian. She also spent time on the sciences of agriculture, gardening, cooking, and medicine, and played the lute. Her vast reading in contemporary novels, world history, and art would be put to use later when she wrote her popular historical romances.

Georges was likewise an apt pupil, but he was more interested in pursuing a military career. He spent ten years as a soldier, gaining some renown and a comfortable living, and then abandoned the military and turned to literary pursuits. Around 1630, he was in Paris, heart of the French social and intellectual world. His literary talents and the excellent education he had received in Rouen, combined with his claims that the Scudérys were a noble family, eased his entrance into elite circles. In 1635, his first play, *Le Prince Deguisé* (*The Disguised Prince*) opened and met with immediate success, which he followed with several more equally acclaimed plays.

Madeleine remained in Rouen until their uncle's death in 1637; she then moved to Paris to live with Georges. By this time he was an established literary figure in Paris, and his celebrity paved the way for his sister's introduction into Parisian society. Madeleine found herself at home in the cultivated environment of 17th-century French salon life, where aristocratic writers and poets would meet in the home of a noblewoman to discuss philosophy, art, and literature. (*See Salonnières.*) Much has been written about the French salons of this time, in which the hostess and guests refined the rules of proper behavior, elegant manners, and sophistication in the art of conversation. In this atmosphere Madeleine flourished, meeting some of the period's most important writers and developing numerous lifelong friendships. In particular, she is associated with the most famous salon of the period, Marquise ◄❧ **Catherine de Rambouillet**'s Hôtel Rambouillet.

Descriptions of the Hôtel and its members reveal a world of luxury, where Catherine,

❧► 
**Catherine de Rambouillet.** *See Salonnières.*

Madeleine, Georges, and others spent hours in conversation, games, dinners, and other amusements. Enjoying oneself and others was the primary purpose of the Hôtel; to be accepted as a member, one had to be well educated, witty, imaginative, and entertaining, whether through writing verses or extemporizing on a philosophical topic. Each member of the Hôtel used a name chosen from ancient literature instead of their given name; Madeleine was known as *Sappho, after the Greek poet. Even years after the Hôtel's salon ended, its members referred to themselves and others by these names.

It was while she was a member of the Hôtel that Madeleine's first novel, *Ibrahim ou l'Illustre Bassa* (*Ibrahim, or the Illustrious Bassa*), was published in 1641. Although it was signed by her brother Georges, Madeleine's authorship was openly known, at least among her acquaintances. This was true for most of her later works as well; her books were published under her brother's name or anonymously. Nevertheless, she became widely respected as a writer.

Madeleine's reasons for not using her own name can only be guessed at, as she does not reveal her motivations directly in her correspondence. Several factors probably played a role. First, her brother was a respected writer while she was unknown beyond her circle, so perhaps using his name early in her career was a simple means of finding an already established audience. After she had achieved renown on her own, she had other, more personal reasons for her anonymity. Throughout her life, Madeleine believed that she came from an old, noble family which had suffered a terrible downfall. This was not the case; the Scudéry name was indeed several centuries old, but it was not aristocratic. But Madeleine believed it was, and as one of her friends remarked, she always spoke of the misfortunes of her family as if she were speaking of the fall of the Roman Empire. She consistently referred to herself in her correspondence as a noblewoman and tried to mold her public image around this pretension. While it was necessary for a lady to be well educated and witty, it was considered improper for her to publish books, since she would be thought of only as a "woman of letters" rather than a lady of rank.

Lastly, Madeleine's works show that she was keenly aware of the widespread prejudice against women venturing into male terrain, such as writing. Perhaps using Georges' name was a practical way to let her work be read and interpreted by the general public more objectively than it would be if readers knew the author was female.

Four volumes long, *Ibrahim* is typical of Scudéry's work and typical of the historical romances so popular among French readers in the 17th century. It is set in 16th-century Constantinople, and relates the life of its protagonist Ibrahim, also called Bassa, a young Italian soldier of great renown. He is in love with a beautiful woman, but their parents will not allow them to marry. The novel follows Ibrahim on a lengthy series of adventures and winding subplots, in which his actions are usually motivated by his desire to be with his lover again. The story ends happily when they overcome all barriers and are reunited at last.

*Ibrahim* was an immediate success with the French reading public, as all of her novels would be. It remained in print continuously for over 80 years and was translated into several languages. Readers responded to Scudéry's imaginative plots, psychological insights into characters, and vivid descriptions of foreign places. But *Ibrahim* is as much a representation of Scudéry's own culture and her salon friends as it is a historical tale set in an exotic locale. As in her later novels, Scudéry's fashionable friends appear only thinly disguised as her characters. Readers familiar with the salons easily recognized themselves and other contemporary figures in Scudéry's work in both flattering and unflattering depictions. This link to their own time generated so much interest in Scudéry's readers that catalogs identifying the characters with living people appeared after each of her novels was published.

Her first nonfiction piece, *Les Femmes illustres ou les harangues héroiques* (*Illustrious Women or Heroic Speeches*), appeared in 1642. This is Scudéry's most feminist work, her longest contribution to the ongoing intellectual debates on the nature and proper roles of women which continued throughout the 17th century. The book is constructed as a series of speeches by famous women on the natural equality between the sexes. Some scholars believe that Georges contributed to the work as well, but its subject matter, style, and feminist tone clearly reflect Madeleine's lifelong interest in advocating women's equality.

Although Madeleine was happy living in Paris and enjoyed her new status as one of its leading intellectuals, she moved to Marseille in 1644 with Georges, who had accepted the post of governor of the fortress there. She continued her voluminous correspondence with her Parisian friends during her three years' separation from them. Her letters, in which she refers to her "exile" to Marseille, reveal her boredom away from the excitement of the salons and her

longing to see her friends again. She was overjoyed when Georges resigned his position, and they returned to Paris in 1647. Perhaps to establish her financial independence from her brother, Madeleine tried to obtain a position as governess to the nieces of the king's prime minister Cardinal Jules Mazarin, but she was unsuccessful and continued living with Georges.

In 1649, Madeleine published the first volume of her masterpiece, another heroic adventure tale, *Artamène, ou Le Grand Cyrus* (*Artamenes, or the Grand Cyrus*). The remaining nine volumes appeared between 1650 and 1653. *Artamène* became a bestseller, and its admirers included some of France's greatest literary figures, such as Blaise Pascal, Honoré de Balzac, and Pierre Corneille. By 1653, Madeleine had resumed her former place in the fashionable salons of Paris. At that time, the city became the center of the civil turmoil of the early 1650s known as the Fronde, in which nobles allied to wrest power for themselves from the young king and his regents. Although some of her friends

*Madeleine de Scudéry*

and her brother were among the rebels, Madeleine remained loyal to King Louis XIV during the months of the Fronde. Louis recognized her loyalty, and one day he in turn would show his support for her writings with pensions and other royal favors. Georges de Scudéry was not so politically astute, and his support for the rebels would soon haunt him.

Madeleine progressed from participating in a salon to hosting her own in 1653, a sign of the great esteem the French aristocracy had for her. A group of prominent writers and poets began to meet at her home in an elegant section of the city every Saturday, which gave the salon its name, the *Samedi* (Saturday). The Samedi became a particularly fashionable salon, in large part due to Madeleine's reputation for her novels, learning, and artful conversation, and its members met regularly until 1659. Among the Samedis was the cultured aristocrat Paul Pellisson, a member of the French Academy. Madeleine formed a particularly intimate lifelong friendship with Pellisson, with whom she exchanged poems and affectionate letters almost daily for over three decades.

Their relationship—platonic, built on friendship and mutual esteem—represents the kind of affiliation idealized by the intellectual movement known as preciosity which Scudéry and Pellisson helped to found. Preciosity was a cultural trend among elites across Europe in the late 17th century, and grew directly out of salon life. It emphasized overly refined manners and careful cultivation of the art of conversation. It also stressed the superiority of freedom and spiritual love over passionate love, valuing tenderness and friendship over the rewards of marriage. Although few of the *précieux* who subscribed to its principles while in their elegant salon meetings treated it seriously enough to remain unmarried, some, like Madeleine, chose to follow its precepts closely. She once wrote that she had been offered three proposals of marriage, including one from Paul Pellisson, but each time she had chosen freedom and "loving friendship" (*amitié tendre*) instead.

*Préciosité* was not without its critics. Numerous 17th-century French writers mocked its exaggeration of sentimentality and morality. The playwright Molière's *Les Précieuses ridicules* (*The Ridiculous Précieuses*, 1659) has been seen by some scholars as an attack on Scudéry and her friends because he mentions *Le Grand Cyrus* in it, but it is more likely that he was mocking the excesses of *préciosité* in general, rather than her specific salon. In fact, Molière actually borrowed material from Scudéry's novels, and was friends with Paul Pellisson, Nicolas Fouquet, and others in her salon.

In 1654, Georges had to flee Paris when Louis XIV and his prime minister Cardinal Mazarin regained control of the country and ended the Fronde. Georges married ✧▶ **Marie-Madeleine du Moncel de Montinvall de Scudéry** during his exile and did not return to Paris until he had regained favor with the crown in 1660. He then wanted to move in with Madeleine again, but she refused to allow it. Her relationship with her brother was always strained, although they lived together continuously before 1654 and collaborated on numerous writing projects before that year. Her depictions of him in her novels show that although she saw some good qualities in him, he was also at times dishonest, selfish, and careless with money. In addition, friends of the two noted that he often prevented her from receiving callers or going out as she wished.

When she began to find fame for herself as a writer and *salonnière*, Madeleine sought independence from her brother's control. Georges' name disappears from her letters after she started living on her own, and he is not mentioned by her again even after his death in 1667. Although they both resided in Paris, it is not clear how often brother and sister visited one another after 1660. It is notable that after that year she chose to publish her works anonymously rather than use Georges' name as the author.

The year 1654 also saw the publication of the first of ten volumes of Madeleine's third novel, *Clélie, Histoire romaine* (*Clelia, a Romance*). Her most feminist novel, *Clélie* was widely acclaimed but faced criticism from other writers for its sentimentality and views on women's equality. In keeping with her aristocratic self-image, Madeleine was usually silent about her critics' views; but in response to the writer Gilles Boileau's condemnation of *Clélie*, she showed unusual pride and defensiveness about her work. She dismissed his ridicule by remarking that a book which had been translated into Italian, English, and German could do without the praises of a writer like him.

At the height of her fame, Scudéry was granted a lifelong pension in 1657 by her friend, royal finance minister Nicolas Fouquet; he also made Paul Pellisson his business secretary. Pellisson established a literary and artistic court for Fouquet, and brought Madeleine and the members of the Samedi to Fouquet's luxurious palaces. Thus the Samedi salon at the home of Madeleine de Scudéry ended in 1659, but only because the group had discovered a pleasanter meeting place. In 1661, Madeleine published anonymously a new novel, *Celinte*, which, following the changing trends of popular literature, was much shorter than her previous works but was still a sentimental adventure story.

That same year brought misfortune for her as well. She was deeply grieved to learn in November that Fouquet had lost favor at court and had been imprisoned along with Pellisson by order of the king. She corresponded with both men during their long years in prison, and tried to obtain better living conditions for them. Fouquet would die in prison in 1680. Pellisson was released in 1666 and was able to regain royal favor, even becoming one of King Louis' secretaries. Around the same time, Madeleine, who had never fallen from Louis' favor, was rewarded by him for her loyalty with a large pension.

Although she remained in excellent health, Madeleine, now past 60, began to suffer hearing loss which eventually would force her to communicate only in writing. She still kept up a remarkably active social life, as she would well into her 80s and 90s, although the golden age of her salon life had ended with the arrest of Fouquet and Pellisson.

She also continued to publish new books every few years. A second short novel, *Mathilde d'Aguilar*, appeared in 1667, and a collection of short stories dedicated to King Louis XIV, *La Promenade de Versailles*, was published in 1669. In 1671, Madeleine won first prize with her *Discours de la Gloire* (*Discourse on Glory*) in an essay contest sponsored by the French Academy in memory of the Academician and author Honoré de Balzac. Between 1680 and 1694, the continuing demand for Madeleine's work led her to edit and publish—though still anonymously—four volumes of conversations taken from her earlier novels, in a sense condensing her works for new readers. Her international reputation was demonstrated in 1684 when, at age 77, Madeleine was elected to the Academy of the Ricovrati of Padua, Italy.

She published six more volumes of conversations in 1686, 1688, and 1692, all dedicated to Louis XIV. Many of the fictionalized conversations on philosophical topics such as love, esteem, friendship, and morality were new, indicating that she was still actively writing in her 80s. Despite her age and deafness, Madeleine continued to receive many visitors in her Paris home and kept up a prodigious correspondence with friends across France and Europe.

In 1693, she lost her dearest friend when Paul Pellisson died after a long illness. His death brought out his critics, who spread rumors that

&⊶ **Scudéry, Marie-Madeleine du Moncel de Montinvall de (1627–1711)**

*French writer.* Name variations: Marie-Madeleine de Scudéry. Born in 1627; died in 1711; married Georges de Scudéry (brother of Madeleine de Scudéry), in 1654.

Marie-Madeleine du Moncel de Montinvall de Scudéry married Georges de Scudéry, a writer, in 1654, after he had hastily left Paris to avoid the wrath of the king for his support of the failed Fronde. Georges' sister *Madeleine de Scudéry published her hugely popular novels under his name, and it appears that Marie-Madeleine may have thought these were actually written by him when their marriage took place. After their move to Paris in 1660, she became one of the *précieux*, and assisted Georges with the novel *Almahide, ou l'esclave reine* (Almahida, or The Slave Queen, 1661–63). Now considered a better writer than her husband, Marie-Madeleine is known primarily for her letters, many of which extolled friendship.

Pellisson, a convert to Catholicism, had not been sincere in his conversion. This criticism stung Madeleine, a devout Catholic, and led her to campaign vigorously and successfully against his critics to silence the rumors. But Pellisson was not the only one of Madeleine's lifelong friends to precede her in death. She eulogized each of her friends as she learned of their passing. Although she had new friends and was by no means forgotten as a writer, she had fewer and fewer companions from her days as a leading hostess of Parisian society. By the time she died, on June 2, 1701, at the advanced age of 94, Madeleine de Scudéry was the only surviving member of the Samedi salon which had helped shape French intellectual and cultural life for years, even after its closing.

**SOURCES:**

Aronson, Nicole. *Mademoiselle de Scudéry.* Trans. by Stuart R. Aronson. Boston, MA: Twayne, 1978.

McDougall, Dorothy. *Madeleine de Scudéry, Her Romantic Life and Death.* London: Methuen, 1938.

Mongrédien, Georges. *Madeleine de Scudéry et son salon.* Paris: Éditions Tallandier, 1946.

**SUGGESTED READING:**

Backer, Dorothy. *Precious Women.* NY: Basic Books, 1974.

Hoffmann, E.T.A. "Mademoiselle de Scuderi," in *Tales.* Ed. by Victor Lange. NY: Continuum, 1982.

Mason, Amelia Gere. *The Women of the French Salons.* NY: Century, 1891.

Molière. *The Pretentious Young Ladies (Les Précieuses Ridicules).* Trans. by Herma Briffault. Woodbury, NY: Barron's Educational Series, 1959.

Scudéry, Madeleine de. *Artamenes; or, The Grand Cyrus.* Trans. by F.G. Gent. London: n.p., 1655.

**Laura York**, M.A. in History, University of California, Riverside, California

## Scudéry, Marie-Madeleine du Moncel de Montinvall de.

*See Scudéry, Madeleine de for sidebar.*

## Scurry, Briana (b. 1971).

*See Soccer: Women's World Cup, 1999.*

# Seacole, Mary Jane (c. 1805–1881)

*Jamaican adventurer, autobiographer, and doctor whose exploits led her from a boarding house in Jamaica to the battlefields of the Crimean War. Name variations: Mrs. Seacole; Mother Seacole; Aunty Seacole. Born Mary Jane Grant sometime between 1805 and 1810 in Kingston, Jamaica; died, possibly in Jamaica, on May 14, 1881; buried in North West London in St. Mary's Catholic cemetery; daughter of a Scottish soldier father and a free black mother (a boarding-house keeper and "doctress"); received no formal education; married Edwin Horatio Seacole (an English merchant), on November 10, 1836; no children.*

*Widowed (c. 1837); inherited lodging house from mother (1840s); began to rebuild lodging house after fire (1843); assisted doctor during a cholera outbreak (1850); lived and worked in Panama (early 1850s); returned to Jamaica (1853); nursed numerous patients in the yellow fever epidemic (1853); traveled to England after outbreak of the Crimean War (1854); set up her "British Hotel" in Balaclava (winter 1855); returned to England at war's end (1856); published* Wonderful Adventures of Mrs. Seacole in Many Lands *(J. Blackwood, 1857); cultivated a friendship with the Princess of Wales (1870s).*

Cholera thrived in filthy conditions and, in the 19th century, transportation and trade developments helped spread the disease. Mary Seacole's patients included American merchants and hotel keepers who paid handsomely for her services, and local boatmen and muleteers who could not afford to pay anything.

In her well-written autobiography, Seacole recalled an especially harrowing night during the cholera epidemic that swept through the Isthmus of Panama around 1850, when Seacole, known as "the yellow woman from Jamaica," was living in Cruces. Late one evening, the owner of the largest local mule team approached her to ask for her help at his *kraal* (ranch), where his drivers were succumbing to the epidemic. He promised Seacole good pay if she could save the head muleteer, who was his most valued worker. When she arrived, Seacole found:

> [The hut's] roof scarcely sheltered its wretched inmates from the searching rain; its floor was damp, rank turf, trodden by the mules' hoofs and the muleteers' feet into thick mud. Around, in dirty hammocks, and on the damp floor, were the inmates of this wretched place, male and female, the strong and the sick together, breathing air that nearly choked me, accustomed as I had grown to live in impure atmosphere; for beneath the same roof the mules, more valuable to their master than his human servants, were stabled.

Eager to escape the sights and sounds in this hovel, where the terrible disease was clearly manifest in the symptoms of diarrhea, acute vomiting, and excruciating cramps, Seacole set about doctoring the sick. She lit a fire and opened all the windows and doors to provide ventilation in the enclosed space. Two patients were already beyond her help, on the verge of death. The screams and moans of others wore away at her as she nursed. Around midnight, she escaped the hut briefly for a little quiet, but the mule-owner soon summoned her back, where she found the conditions had worsened. One patient had had a relapse, some were sinking fast, and many of the sufferers were quaking in terror of death. She brought a semblance of order to the room by placing screens around the dying men, then sat by the fire, drawing her last patient in her lap, "a poor, little, brown-faced orphan infant, scarce a year old, dying in my arms," she wrote, "and I was powerless to save it."

Examining the corpse of this infant later, Seacole performed her first and last postmortem, and believed she found some answers to her questions about the disease which helped her in treating cholera sufferers later.

In her autobiography, Seacole declined to give the date of her birth, asserting her right as a woman not to reveal her age; her maiden name is also unknown. What is known is that her Jamaican mother kept a boarding house in Kingston, Jamaica, and doctored British officers and their wives who were stationed there. Seacole, who was placed in the household of an "old lady" at a young age and raised along with the woman's grandchildren, never lost touch with her birth mother. Her early introduction to the medical arts came through observing her mother's ministrations. Seacole made patients of her dolls, and later practiced her medical skills on pets, then conducted experiments on herself. Around age 12, she was spending considerable time at her mother's house, assisting her in the care of invalid British military officers.

Though little mention is given to the trip in her autobiography, Seacole went to England as a young woman, accompanying some of her relatives. Some of her most vivid memories of that trip involved the slurs of London street boys, who poked fun at her complexion, which she merely found strange, observing that she was "only a little brown." After about a year in London, Seacole returned to Kingston, then went back to London, this time with a large store of West Indian preserves and pickles to sell, in one of her earliest entrepreneurial efforts. This time she remained in England for two years.

Visits to New Providence, Haiti, and Cuba yielded merchandise Seacole could sell back in Kingston, and she was on her way to a successful career in trade when the old lady who had raised her in Kingston became ill. Seacole nursed her until the woman died, then moved into her mother's house, where she made herself useful, according to her autobiography, "in a variety of ways." Without more detail, she also establishes that it was around this time she married Edwin H. Seacole, an English merchant, and moved with him to Black River, where the couple established a store. But Edwin was sickly and kept alive only by the nursing and attention of his wife; finally, he grew so ill that they were forced to leave Black River for her mother's home. A month after they reached Kingston, Edwin died, and Mary was never to marry again, although in her autobiography she was quick to point out that her decision was not for lack of suitors.

Upon the death of her mother, Seacole inherited the boarding house. Now middle-aged, she endured a pattern that would remain with her the rest of her life: rich one day, poor the next. In 1843, the great Kingston fire destroyed the boarding house and left Seacole destitute. But she slowly began to rebuild, and her establishment took on the character of a convalescent home. When word spread of her nursing and medical skills, invalid military men flocked there, and she became more prosperous than ever.

In 1850, Seacole had her first experience with cholera when the disease swept through Jamaica with terrible force. She had drawn on her experience of watching military doctors treat patients when she traveled to Cruces, on the Isthmus of Panama, to be with her brother. When cholera struck the town, which had no doctor, people turned to Seacole for medical help. After the worst of the epidemic passed, Seacole's reputation had earned her a considerable medical practice.

Seacole's desire, at the time, however, was to open a hotel in Cruces. At first she operated a "restaurant" but took in no lodgers. When the rainy months came to an end, she moved on to Gorgona, where she opened a dining room "some thirty feet in length." The business was a success, but Seacole grew bored. She was thinking about leaving Gorgona when a fire in town ended her enthusiasm for life in Panama. Handing the business over to her brother, she returned to Kingston in 1853.

In Jamaica, she found a yellow fever epidemic raging, which engaged her nursing efforts for eight months. A period of restlessness ensued, in which she returned to Gorgona to wind up her business affairs, then accompanied her brother to the town of Panama. From there she crossed the isthmus to Navy Bay at Colon, where she ran a store for about three months, then sailed some 70 miles to Escribanos where, according to her autobiography, she spent the only period of her life "devoted to gold seeking," at one of the stations of the New Granada Gold-Mining Company.

Meanwhile news reached Seacole of the Crimean War. Great Britain, France, Turkey, and Sardinia were engaged against Russia over the domination of southeast Europe. The conflict would last until 1856, and many of the regiments Seacole had known in Jamaica were taking part in the action. Apart from their battle injuries, soldiers in the Crimea were afflicted with cholera, diarrhea, and dysentery, and Seacole knew that her experience could make her useful. In the autumn of 1854, she made her way to London to volunteer as a nurse.

Her first application was to the War Office, which showed no interest in her desire to volunteer. She then thought of approaching *Florence Nightingale, the British nurse who championed the cause of the "professional" nurse and had already gained fame for her work in the Crimea. But Nightingale had departed for the distant battlefields, so Seacole applied to one of her associates. During the interview, she was told that the full complement of nurses had been secured and that they could not use her help. Seacole wanted to believe the woman, but "read in her face the fact, that had there been a vacancy, I should not have been chosen to fill it," and understood finally that it was because of the color of her skin.

She applied next to the managers of the Crimean Fund, and was rebuffed once more. No one seemed to accept her eagerness to serve the "sick soldiery." The repeated refusals of her offers to help only brought on more questions: "Was it possible that American prejudices against colour had some root here? Did these ladies shrink from accepting my aid because my blood flowed beneath a somewhat duskier skin than theirs?" But, writes the ebullient Seacole, "I decided that I *would* go to the Crimea; and go I did, as all the world knows," even when it meant paying her own way.

Still in England, she met a Mr. Day, who had a distant connection with her late husband. Day was bound for the Crimean port of Balaclava on shipping business, and Seacole had a plan to open a hotel there for military invalids, along the lines of the boarding house she had operated in Jamaica. The two reached a financial agreement to open a store and hotel near the British military camp, and Seacole set off for the Black Sea.

After landing at Scutari, Seacole obtained an interview with Florence Nightingale, to whom she presented a letter of introduction. Nightingale showed no reservations about putting the services of the Jamaican woman to good use. Sent to the battlefront, Seacole cared for the English, French, and Sardinian combatants, as well as for the Russians, often while under fire. She helped doctors "transfer the sick and wounded from the mules and ambulances into the transports that had to carry them to the hospitals at Scutari or Buyukere," and she lived on an ammunition ship while caring for the wounded on the sick wharf in Balaclava. To the battlefields, she carried "lint, bandages, needles, thread, and medicines," and food from her own stores. She spent much of her own limited capital on medicine for the wounded and often came to their aid without request, tending the wounded on a beach, for example, where they otherwise might suffer unattended for many hours.

Seacole's and Day's British Hotel included a store, a canteen for enlisted men, a kitchen and small mess hall for officers, as well as a medical dispensary and sick bay. The establishment provided relief from life on the front, and many soldiers went there daily for treatment as outpatients. Seacole's rules did not permit intoxicants, cards, or dice on the premises, and the fame of her medical and nurturing skills led to her being known as "Mother Seacole" among the wounded.

In 1856, following the sacking of Sebastopol, the war was suddenly ended. Seacole and Day were forced to sell their hotel and inventory at a great loss, leaving Seacole deeply in debt. She returned to England "shaken in health . . . wounded, as many others did . . . [and] found myself poor—beggared." But word of her good works had preceded her, and she soon discovered that she was held by many in high regard, and acclaimed by *The Times*, *Punch*, and the *Illustrated London News*. Subscriptions were raised to release her from bankruptcy, and the lively autobiography she wrote to raise money became a bestseller.

Dividing her time between Jamaica and London, Seacole now lived well, and even became intimately connected with the family of Queen *Victoria; in the 1870s, she was unofficial masseuse to the princess of Wales, *Alexandra of Denmark. Seacole is said to have died in Jamaica in 1881, but she was buried in St. Mary's Catholic cemetery in North West London. According to her will, she owned two houses in Kingston, and her estate was valued at today's equivalent of tens of thousands of pounds sterling.

Born black and female in the 19th century, Seacole challenged the middle-class conventions of her day, living independently while she pursued her various careers. As a businesswoman, her savvy provided the financial support that allowed for the practice of the medical arts for which she became most well known, although her skills could not protect her entirely from prejudices against color in the late British Empire. Best remembered for her medical sojourn in the Crimea, she also wrote a highly readable autobiography which may be the only record of the life and character of a Jamaican woman in the 19th century.

**SOURCES:**

Alexander, Ziggi, and Audrey Dewjee, eds. *Wonderful Adventures of Mrs. Seacole in Many Lands*. Bristol, Eng.: Falling Wall Press, 1984.

Blain, Virginia, Patricia Clements, and Isobel Grundy. *The Feminist Companion to Literature in English: Women Writers from the Middle Ages to the Present*. New Haven, CT: Yale University Press, 1990.

Craig, Christine. "Wonderful Adventures of Mrs. Seacole in Many Lands: Autobiography as Literary Genre and a Window to Character," in *Caribbean Quarterly* [Jamaica]. Vol. 30, no. 2. 1984, pp. 33–47.

Josephs, Aleric. "Mary Seacole: Jamaican Nurse and Doctress, 1805/10–1881," in *Jamaican Historical Review*. Vol. 17, 1991, pp. 48–65.

Seacole, Mary. *Wonderful Adventures of Mrs. Seacole in Many Lands*. Foreword by William L. Andrews. (The Schomburg Library of Nineteenth-Century Black Women Writers.) Reprint. NY: Oxford University Press, 1988.

Uglow, Jennifer, comp. and ed. *The Continuum Dictionary of Women's Biography*. NY: Continuum, 1989.

**SUGGESTED READING:**

Alexander, Ziggi. "Let it Lie Upon the Table: The Status of Black Women's Biography in the UK," in *Gender and History*. Vol. 2, no. 1, 1990, pp. 22–33.

**Gayle Veronica Fischer**, historian and author of several articles on dress reform movements in the United States

*Opposite page*
*E*lizabeth
*C*ochrane
*S*eaman

# Seaman, Elizabeth Cochrane

## (1864–1922)

*American pioneering investigative reporter and journalist who went around the world in 72 days. Name variations: Elizabeth Cochrane; (pseudonym) Nellie Bly. Born Elizabeth Jane Cochran (later changed to Cochrane) on May 5, 1864, at Cochran's Mills, Pennsylvania; died on January 27, 1922, in New York City; daughter of Michael Cochran (a mill owner and justice of the peace) and Mary Jane (Kennedy) Cummings Cochran (a homemaker); attended Indiana State Normal School at Indiana, Pennsylvania, 1879; married Robert Livingston Seaman, on April 5, 1895.*

*Worked as a reporter for the* Pittsburg Dispatch, *which then spelled Pittsburgh without the "h" (1885–87); was a reporter for* The New York World *(1887–96); served as reporter and columnist for the* New York Journal *(1912–22).*

*Selected writings:* Ten Days in a Mad-House *(1887),* Six Months in Mexico *(1888),* The Central Park Mystery *(1888), and* Nellie Bly's Book: Around the World in Seventy-two Days *(1890).*

Nellie Bly's record-breaking trip around the world in 1889 was deemed "a tribute to American pluck, American womanhood, and American perseverance." With four days to prepare, the 25-year-old reporter for *The New York World* set out alone to break the travel record in Jules Verne's fictional *Around the World in Eighty Days.* Her lone piece of luggage, 16" wide and 7" high, contained one silk bodice, two traveling caps, veils, slippers, toilet articles, writing materials, a dressing gown, a tennis blazer, underwear, a small flask and drinking cup, handkerchiefs, and one large jar of cold cream. Bly wore a specially made traveling dress constructed to survive three months of continual wear, along with a choice of two coats—one for warmth and one for protection from the rain. She made the trip in 72 days, 6 hours, and 10 minutes, and the press coverage of her journey made her a national celebrity. The trip around the world, however, as exciting as it was, was only one brief adventure for a woman whose public life included innovations in investigative journalism, management of a large manufacturing business, feminist activity, and acquaintance with most of the prominent personalities of her day.

Elizabeth Cochrane Seaman, known as Nellie Bly, was born Elizabeth Jane Cochran in 1864 in Cochran's Mills, western Pennsylvania. Because her father Michael was a respected gristmill owner, a successful real estate specula-

tor, and a former justice of the peace (always known as Judge Cochran), the town's name was changed from Pitts' Mills to Cochran's Mills in his honor. Michael Cochran had had ten children with his first wife. Elizabeth was the third of five born to his second wife, a former widow, Mary Jane Kennedy Cummings Cochran.

Perhaps because Elizabeth was her first daughter, **Mary Jane Cochran** dressed her conspicuously in frilly pastels and white stockings. Perhaps because of her attire, the child was nicknamed "Pink"—a name that would stick until her first newspaper editor gave her a permanent pseudonym, "Nellie Bly."

In 1870, Seaman's father died, leaving no will. The family's lovely home, the mill, and other properties were sold for less than $20,000, with Mary Jane Cochran receiving the traditional "widow's thirds." The remainder was divided among the 15 children. From the time of Michael's death, financial security eluded Elizabeth and most of her family. Many years of their lives would be taken up with economic struggles—often directed against each other.

$\mathcal{E}$nergy rightly applied and directed will accomplish anything.

—Elizabeth Seaman

Family troubles continued during much of Seaman's youth. Her mother remarried, but after five years divorced her drunken and abusive husband. Living in such a home may have influenced the girl's determination to avoid problems like her mother's. In her own life, she would be resourceful, independent, and self-supporting.

Seaman's first attempt at preparing for a career was an abortive one. As Elizabeth J. Cochrane (she had changed the spelling of her last name), she spent one term at the State Normal School at Indiana, Pennsylvania, a teacher training school. Money from her inheritance quickly ran out, so at 15 she ended her formal education. Soon, the family moved to the Pittsburgh area, and it seems that Seaman tried a variety of traditional domestic female jobs.

In 1885, she read a piece dealing with the role of women in the *Pittsburg Dispatch*'s "Quiet Observations" column. The columnist's view that a woman outside her proper sphere—home—was "a monstrosity" led Seaman to respond over the signature "Lonely Orphan Girl." Although editor George Madden found the grammar and style in the original "Orphan" letter too unfinished for publication, he advertised for the author to come forward to the newspaper

office. When Seaman appeared, she was invited to write two responses to the column. The first dealt with the need for women to work and their lack of opportunities to earn a decent living, a fair criticism of the columnist's view that most women had a man to provide for them. The second piece dealt with the controversial subject of divorce, and advised that prospective spouses be required by law to engage in full disclosure of their faults before marriage. For this column, Madden decided that "Lonely Orphan Girl" would not suffice as a pseudonym, and asked the occupants of the newsroom for suggestions. Someone yelled out "Nelly Bly," the title of a familiar Stephen Foster song. Madden hastily wrote down the name, misspelling it in the process. Thus, Elizabeth Jane Cochrane became Nellie Bly. As would be typical of all her writings, the first columns Seaman published were an original combination of firsthand experience, personal opinion, and fact. From the outset, conventional subjects, conventional style, and conventional logic were not her strong points.

After those two pieces were published, Seaman was made a permanent member of the *Dispatch* staff. Her first real assignment developed into an eight-part series on the factory girls of Pittsburgh. Although her descriptions of factory conditions provided no exposés of shocking working conditions, her interest in how the women spent their free time, and her depiction of "mashing" (picking up men), gave the stories a novel angle. Despite being assigned soon afterward to "women's news"—fashion, gardening, and recipes—Seaman used even that platform as an advocate. She argued that the women of Pittsburgh could provide appropriate leisure activities for working girls.

But Elizabeth reasoned that "women's news" held little potential for advancement as a journalist. To be taken seriously, she decided to try her hand at foreign reporting, proving that a woman could be successful in that respected field. Accompanied by her mother as a chaperon, Seaman headed for Mexico in February 1886. Her account of the trip included stories about geography, food, customs, culture, and governmental corruption. These reports appeared first in regular installments in the *Dispatch*, and two years later as a book, *Six Months in Mexico*.

After the foreign assignment, routine at the *Dispatch* held little interest for Seaman. New York, she decided, was the place for an enterprising reporter to make her reputation. With the persistence that characterized her writing and career, she talked her way into the offices of

Joseph Pulitzer's *New York World*. Her idea—that she pretend to be mad in order to investigate the treatment of the mentally ill from inside an asylum—would be the beginning of the era of the "Daring Girl Reporter." After ten days disguised as a patient at Blackwell's Island Insane Asylum for Women, Seaman was released and published her experiences in a series called "Inside the Madhouse." She described brutality toward the patients, filth, icy cold baths used as punishment, and incompetent medical care. The reaction was sensational. *The World* gave Bly her own byline, her columns were discussed all over New York, and, she would claim, the story led to reform of the conditions at the mental institution. (The series was published in 1887 as *Ten Days in a Mad-House*.)

The young reporter seemed to have found her journalistic niche and style. She followed the insane asylum series with other disclosures while she assumed diverse disguises: a maid to investigate unethical employment agencies; an unwed mother to uncover agencies that bought and sold infants; a "fallen" woman to describe a reform institution; a chorus girl dancing in helmet and tights to recount life on the wicked stage; a businessman's wife to expose a corrupt lobbyist. She also developed her own skills as an interviewer, a knack for asking the probing question without alienating her subject. Seaman interviewed women prisoners, psychic healers, and female rodeo riders in Buffalo Bill's Wild West Show. She once posed as a girl from the country to report techniques for luring such young women into prostitution. That story gave Seaman the plot line for her one and only published work of fiction, *The Mystery of Central Park* (1888). During the 1888 election year, she also did a series of political articles from a women's viewpoint, including interviews with feminist attorney *Belva Lockwood, with the wives of the presidential candidates, and with all living first ladies.

The following year, Seaman got herself arrested on a charge of grand larceny and wrote about her night of incarceration. She interviewed the wives of the president's Cabinet members, boxer John L. Sullivan, and women medical students. She described fashionable resorts and learned to ride a bicycle, which at the time was still something of a novelty. Through all these stories, Seaman helped to carve out a new and respected place for women in journalism. Articles like Seaman's not only represented a woman's point of view, they helped to sell newspapers.

Her most publicized "stunt" was, of course, her trip around the world in 1889. With her sin-

gle traveling bag, Seaman went by ship and train through England, France, and Italy, stopping off for a visit with Jules Verne. Her journey took her through the Suez Canal, to Ceylon, Singapore, Hong Kong, and Japan. She sent dispatches all along the way, describing people and sights, everything from leper colonies to exotic food to the habits of her fellow passengers. Nellie Bly seemed the embodiment of the plucky, resourceful American girl and her exploits gave rise to a marketing frenzy. There were Nellie Bly contests, games, caps, pictures, and trading cards. There was also competition, as *Cosmopolitan* tried and failed to send its own woman journalist, ☙ **Elizabeth Bisland**, to break Seaman's record. Oddly enough, after her triumphal return, a successful lecture tour, and the extremely popular *Nellie Bly's Book: Around the World in Seventy-two Days* (1890), Seaman left her job at *The New York World*.

The real cause for the break with the paper is unknown, although Seaman claimed that *The World* gave her no bonus, no salary increase, no extra compensation for the trip which had greatly increased their circulation. Whatever the reason, she signed a three-year contract with *The Family Story Paper* to write fiction, though no stories survive from this publication. During this period, Seaman seemed to be suffering from a number of illnesses, both physical and emotional.

In 1893, she returned to *The World* with a front-page interview with anarchist *Emma Goldman. Seaman was back to reporting—a night at a Salvation Army shelter, interviews with a woman accused of a triple murder, a description of respectable women who spent their days gambling, stories on police corruption. She also covered "real" news, traveling to Washington, D.C., for the march of the unemployed

☙ **Bisland, Elizabeth** (1863–1929)

*American writer.* Name variations: Bessie Bisland; Elisabeth Bisland Wetmore. Born in St. Mary Parish, Louisiana, in 1863; died in 1929; grew up in Natchez; married a man named Wetmore.

Elizabeth Bisland was associate editor of the *Cosmopolitan* magazine. Her book *A Flying Trip around the World*, an account of her 1889 trip performed in 76 days, was published in 1891. She also wrote *A Widower Indeed*, with *Rhoda Broughton*, in 1892.

**SUGGESTED READING:**

Marks, Jason. *Around the World in 72 Days: The Race between* Pulitzer's Nellie Bly and Cosmopolitan's Elizabeth Bisland. Gemittarius Press.

known as "Coxey's Army," and to Chicago where she wrote a sympathetic piece on the strike against the Pullman Railway Car Company and later did a jailhouse interview with union leader Eugene V. Debs.

During a trip to the Midwest, 31-year-old Elizabeth met and married Robert Livingston Seaman, a 70-year-old bachelor and multimillionaire. Neither seemed to adjust well to the odd marriage. Robert was set in his ways and Elizabeth disliked having any restrictions on her activities. Early in 1896, Seaman returned once more to *The World*. She covered the convention of the National American Woman Suffrage Association and interviewed suffragist *Susan B. Anthony*. She did a story on Police Commissioner Theodore Roosevelt's plan to close homeless women's shelters in police stations by spending the night in one of the shelters herself. Seaman entered into the outcry for war with Spain by threatening to lead a brigade to liberate Cuba. The latter story may have driven Robert to try to protect his impulsive wife from her own recklessness. Shortly thereafter, Seaman again left *The World*, and set off for three years in Europe with her husband. While they were abroad, Robert wrote a will leaving all his property to his wife. Because of rumors of mismanagement at one of those properties, the Iron Clad Manufacturing Company, the couple returned to the United States. There, a series of tragedies occurred over the next few years. Seaman's younger sister **Kate Cochran**, her closest sibling, died of tuberculosis in 1899. The next year, the Seamans' house in Catskill, New York, burned to the ground. Seaman's mother and her brothers and their families all moved in and out of the Seaman brownstone in New York City. In February 1904, Robert was struck by a horse and wagon while crossing the street. The next month, he collapsed and died of a heart attack.

Seaman became the president of a large manufacturing company and for the next several years managed the Iron Clad. She instituted reforms in wages and working conditions, and at one point held 25 patents in her own name. Meanwhile the company's financial department was permeated with embezzlement and corruption, and over $1 million worth of checks were forged by the company's cashiers. Ultimately, Seaman was driven into lengthy litigation and bankruptcy. Women in business were at a disadvantage in those days of an unregulated economy, she maintained. Men refused to deal honorably with a female rival and, in fact, treated a woman's financial resources as fair game. If women were to protect their financial interests,

Seaman determined, the only answer was to gain the right to vote.

While her financial troubles unfolded, Seaman went to work for *The New York Evening Journal*. She covered the Republican and Democratic presidential nominating conventions in 1912. She rode in and wrote about the 1913 suffrage parade, calling it "the greatest demonstration for women's suffrage the world has ever been called upon to view." On the day of Woodrow Wilson's inauguration, Seaman climbed up on the podium before the president arrived so she could describe the view to her readers.

The next year, she set out for Europe, in part to seek help for her financial problems. Instead, she found herself in the midst of World War I. She was the first woman and one of the first foreigners to visit the war zone between Serbia and Austria-Hungary. Mistaken for a British spy, she was arrested briefly. Seaman spent most of the war in Austria, and although the United States entered the conflict on the other side, she continued to express sympathy for Austrian interests.

After the war, Seaman returned to the front page of *The Journal* with a new mission. Her stories about broken families eventually led her into an advice column, a new forum for exposing and solving problems. She answered every letter, privately if not in print, providing information about social services, finding homes for unwanted children, arguing for birth control and against capital punishment. She devoted a great deal of time to actually arranging placement for abandoned and neglected children.

Elizabeth Seaman wrote her last column on January 9, 1922. Hospitalized with bronchopneumonia complicated by heart disease, she died on January 17. A column in *The Journal* the next day spoke of her courage and her concern for the unfortunate. "Nellie Bly," it said, "was the best reporter in America."

SOURCES:

Kroeger, Brooke. *Nellie Bly: Daredevil, Reporter, Feminist*. NY: Times Books, 1994.

Rittenhouse, Mignon. *The Amazing Nellie Bly*. Freeport, NY: Books for Libraries, 1956.

*Ross, Ishbel. *Ladies of the Press*. NY: Harper, 1936.

Weisberger, Bernard A. "Elizabeth Cochrane Seaman," in *Notable American Women, 1607–1950*. Edited by Edward T. James. Cambridge, MA: The Belknap Press of Harvard University, 1971.

JUVENILES:

Johnson, Ann Donegan. *The Value of Fairness: The Story of Nellie Bly*. La Jolla, CA: Value Communications, 1977.

Noble, Iris. *Nellie Bly: First Woman Reporter*. NY: Messner, 1956.

**Mary Welek Atwell**, Associate Professor of Criminal Justice, Radford University, Radford, Virginia

# Sears, Eleanora (1881–1968)

*American sportswoman who reputedly won 240 trophies in golf, tennis, squash, field hockey, horse racing, swimming, and distance walking. Born Eleanora Randolph Sears on September 28, 1881, in Boston, Massachusetts; died on March 26, 1968, in Palm Beach, Florida; only daughter of Frederick Richard Sears (heir to a shipping fortune) and Eleanora Randolph (Coolidge) Sears (great-granddaughter of Thomas and Martha Jefferson); never married; no children.*

*Won the national doubles tennis championship four times (1911, 1915, 1916, 1917); was one of the founders of the U.S. Women's Squash Racquets Association (1928); sponsored the U.S. Olympic figure skating team and the equestrian team; an accomplished equestrian, shocked society by riding in a men's riding habit, instead of a skirt, and astride, instead of sidesaddle.*

The Boston socialite Eleanora Sears was a champion athlete in tennis and squash and was also an accomplished horsewoman and horse breeder. Born in 1881 into an elite Boston family descended from Thomas and *Martha Jefferson, Sears grew up in luxury in Boston and Paris. Throughout her life, she would use the security of her family's social status and wealth to free herself from society's expectations for a woman; she refused to marry, said what she thought, dressed as she wanted, and participated in whatever activities appealed to her. Sears was educated at home but preferred physical activities to her studies. Her father encouraged her to exercise, allowing her to accompany him on 22-mile walks between their Boston home and the family's summer home in Pride's Crossing. He also encouraged her love of horses. She first began to rebel against the norms of behavior for a woman of her status as a teenager, usually choosing the freedom of men's breeches and shirts over constricting women's fashions.

As a young adult, she took up lawn tennis, winning numerous tournaments, as well as long-distance ocean swimming. Sears' fame as a tennis player began in 1904 when she won a tournament against the former U.S. tennis champion **Marion Jones Farquhar**. Although Sears participated in many sports, she competed most often in tennis; her appreciation of the game came from her father, who was one of the first to play tennis in America (shortly after **Mary Outerbridge** introduced the sport to the U.S. in 1874). Sears' Uncle Richard won the first American men's championship in 1881, holding the title

until 1887. Between 1904 and 1924, Sears won tournament after tournament, ranking nationally in the top twenty four times. She won the Eastern States women's singles championship from 1908 to 1910, and again in 1918. In the U.S. singles championships, Sears played every year from 1911 to 1929, becoming a finalist six times. She also played doubles tennis, winning the U.S. women's doubles competition with *Hazel Hotchkiss Wightman** in 1911 and 1915, and with *Molla Mallory** in 1916 and 1917. In the 1920s, Sears traveled frequently, often competing in tennis tournaments abroad. Most notably she was a competitor at the Wimbledon championships in London in 1922, 1923, and 1924. She also loved playing squash and quickly became a champion in that sport as well. With her typical confidence and outspokenness, Sears, resentful that there were few facilities for women to play squash, publicly demanded that the Harvard Club open its facilities to women in 1918. Her demands were met, and she went on to win the U.S. women's squash championship in 1928. This was not her first public confrontation with the limited access women had to play sports. In 1912 in Burlingame, California, Sears, riding astride and wearing men's clothes, rode onto a men's polo field during a practice, and requested to be allowed to play. She was escorted off the field. Outraged, the local Burlingame Mothers' Club asked Sears to "restrict herself to the usual feminine attire in the future." Denouncing her apparel, the club passed a public resolution: "Such unconventional trousers and clothes of the masculine sex are contrary to the hard and fast customs of our ancestors. It is immodest and wholly unbecoming a woman, having a bad effect on the sensibilities of our boys and girls." Sears paid the club no mind.

With her family background, athletic ability, good looks, and outspoken demeanor, the striking blonde-haired, blue-eyed Sears attracted media attention wherever she went. She appeared in the ballrooms of New York and Boston dressed in elegant gowns by night, but by day she rode horses at full gallop and played squash in her breeches. She usually met with disapproval from her social peers, who thought her unladylike activities and male clothing eccentric, but she enjoyed the admiration of many men and women for her athletic skills. Often she sought out media publicity; yet she always maintained that she performed in sports simply because she wanted to, not out of a desire to challenge women's confined roles or for personal fame. Her personal relationships remain obscure; her name was linked in the news media to several bachelors of Boston's elite,

*Eleanora Sears*

including, in 1911, the rumor that she was engaged to Harold Vanderbilt, yet she never publicly admitted to any love interest. Known to her friends as Eleo, she maintained a home on Beacon Hill in Boston, where she often entertained at lavish parties.

Along with tennis and squash, Sears often publicly took on wagers that challenged her physical endurance, especially in marathon walking. Her pace and stamina were remarkable. In 1912, she covered over 109 miles in 41 hours, from Burlingame to Delmonte, California. Another time she walked from Providence, Rhode Island, to Boston, a distance of 47 miles, in 10½ hours. Frequently, Sears' chauffeur followed her on her long walks; the stately woman striding purposefully along the roads of New England and California, trailed by a car, became a familiar sight. She was also something of a daredevil, riding in an early airplane in 1910 and taking a submarine voyage; she also drove an automobile, certainly one of the first women to do so. Sears' sports interests were wide-ranging, and there are few sports she did not participate in at some point in her long career. She played baseball, field hockey, football, and golf; she also enjoyed boxing, trapshooting, canoeing, racing speedboats, ice hockey, and yachting. However, her love of horses was the most enduring of her interests. Sears kept the stables at her family's summer home outside Boston filled with thoroughbreds, hunters, and jumpers. She bred and trained horses herself, and spent a few hours on horseback nearly every day. Her horses were often winners at the National Horse Show in New York's Madison Square Garden. She also bred racehorses for competition in the 1950s and 1960s. Sears supported other equestrian athletes financially, making large donations and loaning her own horses to the U.S. Olympic equestrian team for many years. She also was the major benefactor of the National Horse Show. Her love of horses and of Boston made Sears the leader in the fight to preserve the Boston mounted police when budget cuts in the late 1950s threatened to eliminate them. In 1961, her contributions were crucial in rebuilding the U.S. Olympic ice-skating team after most members of the team were killed in a plane crash, including *Laurence and *Maribel Owen.

Sears maintained her active lifestyle into her later years. She served as president of the U.S. Women's Squash Racquets Association, an organization to promote women's athletics, and continued to compete herself. In 1939, she and **Sylvia Henrotin** won the women's doubles tennis championship for women over age 45. The next year, she was a semifinalist in the U.S. women's squash tournament. She was still competing in squash championships for her age group in 1954, at age 73.

In 1963 Sears, whose career had reputedly earned her over 240 trophies, retired to Palm Beach, Florida, where she died in 1968. Following her death, she was elected to the International Tennis Hall of Fame. She was also posthumously honored as an inductee of the Horseman's Hall of Fame in 1978, and the International Women's Sports Hall of Fame (for polo, golf, and squash) in 1984.

**SOURCES:**

Garraty, John A., and Mark C. Carnes, eds. *American National Biography*. NY: Oxford University Press, 1999.

Oglesby, Carole A., ed. *Encyclopedia of Women and Sport in America*. Phoenix, AZ: Oryx, 1998.

*The New York Times* (obituary). March 27, 1968.

**Laura York**, M.A. in History,
University of California, Riverside, California

# Sears, Mary (1905–1997)

*One of the foremost American oceanographers of the 20th century. Born on July 18, 1905, in Wayland, Massachusetts; died on September 2, 1997, in Woods Hole, Massachusetts; attended the Winsor School in Boston; Radcliffe College, B.S., 1927, M.S., 1929; never married; no children.*

On October 19, 2000, the U.S. Navy launched its sixth oceanographic survey ship in the Pathfinder class, 329 feet long and designed for surveying both deep ocean and coastal waters. The first Navy oceanographic ship to be named after a woman, the USNS *Mary Sears* honors one of the premier oceanographers of the 20th century. Mary Sears began her career at a time when women were barred from sailing on research and Navy vessels, but she nonetheless became one of the guiding lights of the Woods Hole Oceanographic Institute as well as the "first oceanographer of the Navy in modern times." This description by her colleague Roger Revelle refers to Sears' wartime work with the Navy, when, as a WAVE, she organized an oceanographic unit that helped American submarines avoid detection by the enemy.

Born in Wayland, Massachusetts, in 1905, Sears was educated at the Winsor School in Boston before attending Radcliffe College in Cambridge, from which she received a bachelor's degree (1927) and master's degree (1929). In 1932, while pursuing a Ph.D. in zoology at Radcliffe, she became one of the first staff research assistants at the newly founded Woods Hole Oceanographic Institute in Cape Cod. After receiving her doctorate in 1933, she worked as a research assistant at Harvard (1933–49) and an instructor at Wellesley College (1938–43), spending her summers working at various capacities at Woods Hole before 1940, when she received a year-round position there as a staff planktonologist.

In 1943, as World War II raged, Sears was commissioned a lieutenant j.g. (junior grade) in the WAVES—the U.S. Navy's women's branch—and began working at the Navy Hydrographic Office in Washington, D.C. There she founded and became head of the small Oceanographic Unit, where research from Woods Hole was used to aid submarines and warships. Her discovery that thermoclines, areas of water subject to rapid temperature changes, could be used to hide submarines from radar was of huge importance to the war effort. The Oceanographic Unit grew until it eventually took over the entire Hydrographic Office (which had previously focused on creating navigational charts); it was then renamed the Naval Oceanographic Office. In 1946, after the war had ended, Sears received a Rask-Orsted Foundation grant which enabled her to work for a year in Copenhagen, where she was awarded the Johannes Schmidt medal for her oceanographic war work. The following year she transferred to the Naval Reserve and returned to work at Woods Hole.

Over the next several decades, Sears edited some of the most important publications in the field of oceanography, helping to found the journals *Progress in Oceanography* and *Deep-Sea Research*, the latter of which she served as editor from 1953 to 1974; she also edited *Oceanography* (1961) and, with Daniel Merriman, *Oceanography: The Past* (1980), two books that are considered benchmarks in the field. In 1959, she was chair of the First International Congress on Oceanography, held at the United Nations in New York City. She also edited the annual reports and research summaries of Woods Hole from 1962 through 1973. In 1963, Sears retired from the Naval Reserve as a commander and became a senior scientist in the biology department at Woods Hole. She retired seven years later, but remained active at the institute, continuing to compile its annual collected reprints as she had since 1959, and organizing the *Oceanographic Index* until 1976. In 1978, she was named a scientist emeritus at Woods Hole.

Mary Sears was the recipient of a number of awards over the years, including honorary doctorates from Mt. Holyoke College (1962) and the University of Massachusetts at Dartmouth (1974), and an Alumnae Recognition Award from Radcliffe College (1992). In 1985, on the occasion of her 85th birthday, *Deep-Sea Research* dedicated an issue to her. She was also a fellow of the American Association for the Advancement of Science. A longtime resident of Falmouth, Massachusetts, Sears was active in the community, serving as a member of the Falmouth Town Meeting for 35 years and of the town's school committee for over 20 years. She was also the committee chair of the Children's School of Science at Woods Hole. In 1996, she attended the retirement party for Woods Hole's

*Atlantis II* research vessel, which she had christened in the 1930s. She died the following year at age 92.

**SOURCES:**
*The Cape Cod Times*. November 17, 1999; October 20, 2000.
*The Day* [New London, CT]. September 7, 1997; September 10, 1997.

## Seaxburh (c. 627–673).

*See Sexburga.*

## Seba (fl. 10th c. BCE).

*See Sheba, queen of.*

## Sebek-neferu or Sebekneferu (fl. 1680–1674 BCE).

*See Sobek-neferu.*

## Seberg, Jean (1938–1979)

*American actress who was a star of the French New Wave. Born on November 13, 1938, in Marshalltown, Iowa; thought to have died on August 31, 1979, in Paris, France; attended public schools in Marshalltown; married François Moreuil (an attorney and filmmaker), in 1958 (divorced 1960); married Romain Gary (a novelist), in 1962 (divorced 1970); married Dennis Berry (a film director), in 1972 (separated 1978); married Ahmed Hasni, in May 1979; no children.*

*Selected filmography: Saint Joan (US, 1957); Bonjour Tristesse (US, 1958); The Mouse That Roared (UK, 1959); A Bout de Soufflé (Breathless, Fr., 1960); Let No Man Write My Epitaph (US, 1960); L'Amant de Cinq Jours (The Five Day Lover, Fr.-It., 1961); Les Grandes Personnes (Time Out for Love, Fr.-It., 1961); La Récréation (Playtime, Fr., 1961); In the French Style (US-Fr., 1963); Echappement Libre (Backfire, Fr.-It.-Sp., 1964); Lilith (US, 1964); Moment to Moment (US, 1966); A Fine Madness (US, 1966); La Ligne de Démarcation (Fr., 1966); La Route de Corinthe (Who's Got the Black Box?, Fr.-It.-Gr., 1967); Les Oiseaux vont mourir au Pérou (Birds in Peru, Fr., 1968); Pendulum (US, 1969); Paint Your Wagon (US, 1969); Airport (US, 1970); Macho Callahan (US, 1970); Kill! (Kill Kill Kill, Fr.-It.-Ger.-Sp., 1971); L'Attentat (The French Conspiracy, Fr., 1972); La Corruption de Chris Miller (The Corruption of Chris Miller, Sp., 1972); Le Chat et la Souris (Cat and Mouse, Fr., 1974); Le Grand Délire (Fr., 1975); Die Wildente (The Wild Duck, Ger.-Aus., 1976).*

Described by Gary Morris as "more icon than actress," Jean Seberg soared to fame at age 17, when director Otto Preminger selected her from thousands of teenage hopefuls to play the

Jean
Seberg

title role in the film *Saint Joan* (1957), which was shot in France. Seberg was lambasted by the critics for her portrayal of \*Joan of Arc. They were equally as critical of her second effort in Preminger's *Bonjour Tristesse* (1958). Dumped by the director, she fled back to France, reemerging in a series of French New Wave films. Seberg portrayed the quintessential young American abroad, "at once naive and rock hard, teetering between respectable ambition and wild adventure." Her personal life was scarred by four unhappy marriages and harassment from the

American government over her support of the Black Panthers. Her death in 1979, age 40, was ruled a suicide.

Born in 1938 and raised in the small town of Marshalltown, Iowa, where her father owned a local pharmacy, Jean Seberg was a senior in high school when her speech teacher arranged for her to audition for the title role in Preminger's film version of Shaw's *Saint Joan*. At the time, the director's much-publicized quest to find an unknown for the role attracted 18,000 young girls from across the nation. "I think that I got the part largely because I was the only girl who didn't audition wearing a crucifix," Seberg said later, also recalling Preminger's "special gift for inspiring terror in people." (Apparently, Preminger grew more frustrated with the inexperienced Seberg as filming went on. When the actress suffered severe leg burns during the burning-at-the-stake scene, it was jokingly rumored that the director had engineered the accident in order to be rid of her.) Upon the picture's release, Seberg's performance was declared a disaster by the critics, who called her "callow and unconvincing," an "Iowa amateur." "Shaw's Joan, against which many an actress has shattered a lance, seems to have left limpid-eyed Jean Seberg with a handful of splinters," wrote Paul V. Beckley in the *New York Herald Tribune* (June 27, 1957). Seberg was so devastated by her poor showing that she spent a month in Nice, France, wandering the beach, weeping.

Meanwhile, Preminger refused to believe that he had been wrong about his young protégé and proceeded with his plans to star her in a second film, *Bonjour Tristesse* (1958), based on the novel by **Françoise Sagan**. The director, however, continued to bully the young star, threatening this time to replace her with *Audrey Hepburn. As it turned out, the critics did not find Seberg any more convincing as a sophisticated father-obsessed teenager. The reviewer for *The New York Times* suggested "sending her back to that Iowa high school from whence she came," while William K. Zinsser of the *New York Herald Tribune* (June 16, 1958) found her "about as far from a French nymph as milk is from pernod."

In the summer of 1958, Preminger turned over the remainder of Seberg's contract, which ran until 1963, to Columbia. Under the new arrangement, she was given inconsequential roles in several films, including *The Mouse That Roared* (1959) and *Let No Man Write My Epitaph* (1960). She used her downtime to improve her acting, studying with Etienne Decroux, France's master of mime, Peyton Price, a Holly-wood acting coach, and **Alice Hermes**, a New York speech coach.

Meanwhile, in September 1958, Seberg was married to François Moreuil, a Paris lawyer with connections to the French film industry whom she had met on the French Riviera. It was through Moreuil that Seberg met Jean-Luc Godard, who enlisted her to star opposite Jean-Paul Belmondo in *Breathless* (1960). The film, Godard's first, was largely improvised and concerned a French criminal and his American mistress. According to Donald La Badie, a critic for *Show*, the movie was the perfect showcase for Seberg's limited talents. "The masklike face, the self-consciousness, the flat hesitant voice, which had theretofore hindered her, were transformed to create a remarkable portrait," he wrote. Released in the United States in 1963, the film did well on the art-house circuit, although Roger Angell, writing in *The New Yorker*, remained cautious about Seberg's talent, writing that he was "unable to decide whether she acts beautifully or not at all."

After her successful French debut, Seberg starred in a series of films in which she often recreated the same corruptible innocent that had won over audiences in *Breathless*. "Apparently, for the French, at least, I seem to express a basic melancholy, a sense of loss that says something about all young women today," she said. In 1962, Seberg made the American-language film *In the French Style* (1963), playing a Yankee variation of her New Wave persona. **Judith Crist**, in the *New York Herald Tribune* (August 19, 1963), labeled it the fifth installment of the "never-ending serial" entitled "Jean Seberg, All-American Adolescent, Learns About Love in the Hotbeds of Paris."

Seberg turned in her most solid performance to date in *Lilith* (1964), portraying a schizophrenic patient who seduces her inexperienced therapist. William Peper of the *New York World-Telegram and Sun* called the performance "skillful and eerily captivating," while *Variety* found the actress "properly vague but . . . lovely." Seberg went on to appear in international films throughout the '60s and early '70s, although her career, rather than soaring, seemed to settle onto a middle ground.

Seberg's personal life was always shaky. Divorced from Moreuil in 1960, she was married to French diplomat and writer Romain Gary from October 1963 to 1970. Her next marriage was to director Dennis Barry. Separated but not divorced from Barry, Seberg then wed Algerian-born Ahmed Hasni in 1979. Three of Seberg's husbands directed her in films: Moreuil's *La Récréation* (*Playtime*); Gary's *Kill*, and Berry's *Le Grand Délire*. Seberg was also harassed by the FBI and other governmental agencies during the 1960s for her support of the Black Panthers. As well, after becoming pregnant (by Romain Gary), she suffered a miscarriage that led to a nervous breakdown. In September 1979, just months after her marriage to Hasni, the actress was found dead in her car, nine days after she had disappeared from her Paris apartment carrying a supply of barbiturates prescribed by her physician.

**SOURCES:**

Carr, Jay. "'Journals' too sketchy on Seberg," in *The Boston Globe*. June 6, 1996.

Ginna, Robert Emmett. "On Screen: Jean Seberg," in *Horizon*. Vol. IV, no. 5. May 1962, p. 80.

Katz, Ephraim. *The Film Encyclopedia*. NY: HarperCollins, 1994.

Moritz, Charles, ed. *Current Biography 1966*. NY: H.W. Wilson, 1966.

———. *Current Biography 1979*. NY: H.W. Wilson, 1979.

Sklar, Robert. *Film: An International History of the Medium*. NY: Harry N. Abrams, n.d.

**SUGGESTED READING:**

Brodeur, Paul. "How the F.B.I. Left Jean Seberg Breathless," in *The Nation*. Vol. 262, no. 12. March 25, 1996, pp. 15–16, 18.

**Barbara Morgan**,
Melrose, Massachusetts

# Secord, Laura (1775–1868)

*Canadian hero who walked 20 miles to warn British and Canadian troops of an impending American attack, thus paving the way for an end to the War of 1812. Born on September 13, 1775, in Great Barrington, Massachusetts; died on October 17, 1868, at Chippawa (Niagara Falls), Ontario, Canada; daughter of Thomas Ingersoll and Elizabeth (Dewey) Ingersoll; married James Secord, in 1797; children: Charles, Mary, Charlotte, Harriet, Appolonia, Laura, Hannah.*

*Born in the United States but moved to Canada with parents (1795); retrieved husband from the battlefield after he was wounded at the Battle of Queenston Heights; walked 20 miles to warn British and Canadian troops of impending attack (1813); remained unrewarded and unrecognized for over 20 years after her heroic deed; received payment from Prince Edward Albert (1860) as recognition for her contribution to the war effort.*

On June 24, 1813, during the War of 1812, an American force led by Colonel Charles Boerstler planned to surprise a contingent of fewer than 50 British soldiers under Lieutenant James FitzGibbon at Beaver Dams and destroy the stock of ammunition and supplies under their guard. Instead, Boerstler and his troops were ambushed by a force of Mohawk and Caughnawaga warriors. After a number of American soldiers were killed, FitzGibbon convinced Boerstler and his entire force of almost 500 men to surrender. Although this event did not signal the end of the war, it prevented American domination of the Niagara peninsula and eventually paved the way for a peace settlement in 1814. What was not recognized for at least 20 years after the Battle of Beaver Dams was that FitzGibbon would have been unprepared and unaware of the American advance had he not been forewarned by a woman who had walked through 20 miles of forest and swampland to do her patriotic duty; her name was Laura Secord.

Laura Secord was born on September 13, 1775, in Great Barrington, Massachusetts. While she was still a child her father Thomas Ingersoll sided with the rebels during the American Revolution and fought against British troops. By the time the war was over, eight-year-old Laura was dealt a severe blow when her mother **Elizabeth Ingersoll** died. For a short time, Laura was responsible for tending to her three younger sisters until their father remarried a year later, in 1784. Unfortunately, Laura's stepmother died four years later leaving the young girl motherless yet again. Shortly thereafter, however, her father was married for the third time, to **Sarah Whiting**. Although there is no record of Secord's feelings during this time, it must have been both sad and confusing for a child to have had three different mothers by the time she was 13 years old. Nevertheless, it appears that Secord had a strong sense of duty and was prepared to deal with life's trials and tribulations.

Although Secord had spent most of her early life in America, times were difficult after the revolution. Having learned that land in Upper Canada (present-day Ontario) was available under generous circumstances, Thomas Ingersoll presented a successful petition for a township grant to Lieutenant Governor Simcoe in 1793. Two years later, the Ingersolls moved to Queenston while waiting for a survey and road to be completed in the new township, Oxford-upon-the-Thames. Her father then ran a tavern in Queenston. Little is known about Laura's activities during this time except that at some point she met and became engaged to James Secord, a merchant whose family had come to Canada during the American Revolution. Sometime in 1797, 24-year-old James and 22-year-old Laura were married. They first settled in St. David's and later moved to Queenston.

During their early years together, the couple went through some difficult financial times. James' ability to manage the financial aspects of his mercantile enterprises was relatively weak and, by 1801, he had to mortgage the family farm to pay off a large debt. In addition, Laura signed away the dower rights she had to those lands. This meant that when James died she would have no financial claim to any income from the farm. While the couple no doubt saw this as only a temporary measure, Laura's situation as a widow years later would leave her in dire financial straits, and the lost income from the farm would obviously contribute to her financial woes. Nevertheless, the Secords attempted to live comfortably on his income as a wholesaler of flour, potash and other products, and they resided with their five children in a modest clapboard house in Queenston. The house, which still stands on the northwest corner of Queen and Partition streets, has been restored and is now known as the "Laura Secord Homestead Museum."

*Thus did a young, delicate woman brave the terrors of the forest . . . to do her duty to her country, and by timely warning save much bloodshed and disaster.*

—Lieutenant James FitzGibbon

The Secords were not the only members of Laura's family who were experiencing financial difficulties. Laura's father lost his contract for the Oxford township on the grounds that he had not fulfilled his part of the agreement. Under the terms of the original grant, Thomas Ingersoll and four others had agreed to bring in a minimum of 40 families as settlers within 7 years. Each family would receive 200 acres of land for a nominal land fee and Thomas was granted 1,200 acres for his efforts. By 1805, however, none of Ingersoll's associates had materialized. Consequently, when his contract was revoked he and his family moved to Port Credit where he opened up another inn known as Government House. He lived and worked in Port Credit until he died seven years later.

The year of her father's death, 1812, was an important one for the Secords. Not only was it the height of the Napoleonic Wars between Britain and France, but the United States also declared war on Britain. Because Canada was the only British possession on the North American continent, the Americans fought for domination and most of the skirmishes took place along the international border. Although most of the in-habitants of Upper Canada were American in origin, having emigrated to Canada after the revolution, the War of 1812 strengthened the country's ties with Britain and was instrumental in creating the first sense of national community among Canadians. When war was declared, the British and Canadian forces were badly outnumbered by the Americans but were better prepared for war, due to the influence of Major-General Isaac Brock, administrator of Upper Canada. For Laura Secord and her family, the war became particularly close when Queenston was attacked by American forces on October 13, 1812. Brock was mortally wounded during the attack, and Laura's husband James, who was a sergeant in the 1st Lincoln militia, was also wounded. Nevertheless, when the Battle of Queenston Heights was over, almost 1,000 American soldiers were taken prisoner and, despite the loss of Brock, the victory helped to raise the morale of Upper Canadians and convince them that they could resist an American conquest.

Laura's concern was more immediate, however. When she heard news of the battle and of her husband's wounded state, she immediately went to his aid and helped remove him from the battlefield. Legend has it that he was about to be clubbed to death by American soldiers when Laura arrived to rescue him. While colorful, this particular version of the event has no basis in historical fact. Nevertheless, Secord's willingness to enter a battlefield demonstrates both her devotion to her husband and her outstanding courage. Eight months later, her courage and determination were to be tested even further.

After the battle, Secord moved her husband and children to St. David's where they spent the winter of 1812–13. By spring, the war had gathered momentum once again, and by April the Americans had seized Fort York (present-day Toronto) where they burned the Parliament buildings and Government House. The Americans abandoned Fort York and on May 27, 1813, their fleet captured Fort George at the mouth of the Niagara River. The British troops escaped, and eight days later Lt.-Col. John Harvey led a British and Canadian militia in a surprise attack on 3,500 invading American troops encamped near Stoney Creek. Although both sides suffered severe losses, the Americans withdrew to Fort George when two of their brigadiers were taken prisoner. Both sides now set about regrouping and planning their next moves. James FitzGibbon, a lieutenant in the British army, obtained permission to set up an outpost of about 50 soldiers at a house just outside of the settlement at Beaver Dams. This house not only served as a supply depot for weapons and ammunition but also provided an advantageous position for observing the movement of American troops. FitzGibbon was determined to stop American raiding parties from harassing Canadian settlers and capturing loyal British subjects. Learning of this new threat, the American Colonel Boerstler was ordered to capture the small British force and destroy the house. What the colonel did not know was that a woman had learned of his plans and was prepared to prevent the raid from taking place.

It is not known exactly how Laura Secord gained knowledge of Boerstler's plan. In all probability she overheard the Americans speaking about the plot when they demanded a meal at her house on June 21, 1813. Secord immediately informed her husband what she had overheard and suggested that someone warn FitzGibbon. Since James was still incapacitated from his wound, Laura decided to take the news to her half-brother Charles Ingersoll who was recovering from a fever at his home in St. David's. Hoping that he had recovered, she assumed that he would make the journey to Beaver Dams and relay the information to FitzGibbon.

When she set out for St. David's at dawn on June 22, Secord had no intention of becoming a hero. At age 38, she was slightly built, with auburn hair and delicate features. For her journey, she wore a long plain cotton print dress with orange flowers and shoes and stockings. According to popular legend, Secord supposedly took a cow with her part of the way in order to distract the American sentries and, on encountering difficulty with one sentry, milked the cow in his presence to allay suspicion. She then took the cow into the woods and left it there as she proceeded on her journey to St. David's. Although this is an image that many still hold, Canadian historians have confirmed that it was the invention of 19th-century historian William Coffin, who wrote an account of her journey in 1864. Why he felt the addition of a cow necessary is unknown, but it has endured in some popular accounts.

Secord reached St. David's within an hour and was dismayed to learn that her half-brother had not recovered sufficiently to make the journey. She resolved to continue on and take the message herself. Although Beaver Dams was only ten miles away, Secord knew that she could not take the main roads without being seen by American soldiers. Consequently, she took a circuitous route through forest and swampland.

*Laura Secord*

The distance ended up stretching to 20 miles. For the first part of the trip she was accompanied by her niece, **Elizabeth Ingersoll**. As the day wore on and the weather became warmer and more humid, Elizabeth, who had always been weak, could not continue, and Laura faced the remainder of her long trek alone.

By early evening Secord was near exhaustion but knew that she was nearing the end of her destination. Suddenly and without notice she stumbled into a group of Native Indians. Wrote Secord:

Upon advancing to the Indians, they all rose and with some yells said "Woman," which made me tremble. I cannot express the awful feeling it gave me, but I did not lose my presence of mind. I was determined to persevere. I went up to one of the chiefs, made him understand that I had great news for Capt. FitzGibbon, and that he must let me pass to his camp, or that he and his party would all be taken. The chief at first objected to let me pass, but finally consented, after some hesitation, to go with me and accompany me to FitzGibbon's station, which was at the Beaver Dam, where I had an interview with him.

FitzGibbon was undoubtedly surprised to see an exhausted woman dressed in torn and dirty clothes. Fearing a trick, he was, nonetheless, convinced of the truth of her statements and began preparations to thwart the American attack. Several years later, FitzGibbon wrote of his impressions upon seeing her: "Mrs. Secord was a person of slight and delicate frame and made this effort in weather excessively warm, and I dreaded at the time that she must suffer in health in consequence of fatigue and anxiety, she having been exposed to danger from the enemy, through whose line of communication she had to pass." Secord made similar remarks many years later, wondering "how I could have gone through so much fatigue with the fortitude to accomplish it."

She did, however, accomplish what she had determined to do and, in essence, paved the way for an end to the War of 1812. When FitzGibbon learned of the planned American attack, he took precautionary measures by enlisting the help of the Native Indian forces that had arrived two days earlier. Boerstler and his American troops arrived at night on June 23, 1813, unaware of what lay in store for them the next morning. Approaching the house where FitzGibbon was stationed, they were surprised by a force of Caughnawaga and Mohawk warriors and a three-hour battle ensued. FitzGibbon persuaded the American colonel to surrender by convincing Boerstler that a much-larger British contingent lay just beyond the trees and that he might not be able to control the "savagery" of the Native Indian forces. It was later concluded that "the Caughnawaga Indians fought the battle, the Mohawks or Six Nations got the plunder, and FitzGibbon got the credit." The latter is certainly true in regards to Laura Secord.

While the Battle of Beaver Dams was not the deciding battle of the war, it convinced the Americans that they could not venture safely outside of Fort George. By December, they evacuated the fort and left Upper Canada. Although several more battles were fought, none were clearly decisive and both sides agreed to sign the Treaty of Ghent on December 24, 1814, thus finally ending the war. Despite this auspicious sign, Secord's contribution to the war effort was not made public. Historians have pondered the reasons for this reluctance to admit her significance. **Ruth McKenzie** asserts that Laura herself chose to keep her involvement unknown, fearing that publicity might threaten the safety of her family while the war continued. **Cecilia Morgan**, however, argues that "women's contributions to the defense of the colony were either downplayed or ignored in favor of the image of the helpless Upper Canadian housewife and mother who entrusted her own and her children's safety to the gallant militia and British troops." Instead, Morgan concludes, Secord's image as "a symbol of female loyalty and patriotism" was constructed by women historians in the late 19th and early 20th centuries in an effort to link loyalism, nationalism and history. For at least seven years after the Battle of Beaver Dams, Secord's momentous journey was kept from public knowledge.

Due to the increasing financial difficulties experienced by the Secords, the first written narrative of Laura's experience was included in a petition to the governor-general in which James Secord requested a license to quarry stone in the Queenston military reserve. This request was granted and another petition submitted two years later in 1822 for a wartime pension resulted in James being granted a yearly annuity of £18. In 1828, James was appointed registrar of the Niagara district Surrogate Court and in 1833 he was promoted to judge of the same court. In this capacity, he had jurisdiction over the wills and estates of deceased persons. Two years later, he resigned his judgeship to become Collector of Customs at Chippawa, whereupon the Secords finally had an income that was comfortable. This situation did not last long, however, for two of their daughters returned home to live with Laura and James when their husbands died.

Laura's financial security was, therefore, always precarious and became even more so when James died in February 1841. At age 66, the hero of Beaver Dams was struggling to support herself, her widowed daughters and grandchildren on a meager income derived from running a private school out of her home. She also submitted two additional petitions to the governor in which she underlined her impoverished state, her lack of support since her husband's death, and her new position as head of the household. Citing her husband's pension, the governor refused her request. Secord's financial troubles continued and, hoping to draw attention to her plight, her son Charles submitted a letter to the periodical *The Church* in April 1845 which publicized Laura's walk and her service to the British crown as well as to her country. Eight years later, 78-year-old Laura submitted her own account of her adventure to the *Anglo American Magazine* which was running a series on the War of 1812. Despite these attempts, Secord continued to live on a modest income, and her contribution to the war effort was still not widely known. As Morgan concludes, Laura's attempts to publicize her story "should not be seen as attempts to create a cult for herself, but rather as part of the Upper Canadian patronage game, in which loyal service to crown and country was the way to obtain material rewards."

In 1860, Secord's efforts were finally rewarded when Albert Edward (future Edward VII of England), prince of Wales, visited Chippawa. In an address presented to the prince by the veterans of the War of 1812, Secord made sure that her name was included. Upon learning of her story, the prince sent her a gift of £100 in gold; it was the only money she ever received. While this gesture resulted in more publicity for her, through newspaper and magazine articles, Secord did not become a hero overnight. When she died on October 17, 1868, at age 93, her national fame was still 20 years away.

It was primarily due to the efforts of female historians writing in the late 1880s and 1890s that Secord's story came to be known more widely. In addition to recounting her courageous walk in local historical society publications and newspapers, several amateur historians began a campaign to erect a memorial to Secord. Their efforts were finally achieved on June 22, 1901, when the monument was unveiled at Lundy Lane. A second monument was erected on Queenston Heights in 1910 by the federal government of Canada. In 1905, the provincial government of Ontario paid tribute to Secord by commissioning a painting of her that was hung in the Parliament buildings in Toronto. Finally, Secord's name became forever etched in popular memory when Frank O'Connor chose her as the emblem for his new chain of candy stores.

Although she died 20 years before her deeds became widely known, Laura Secord inspired amateur women historians to publicize her contribution to the war effort while also emphasizing the important roles that women played in forging a national identity. Although Secord herself saw it merely as her duty, her historic walk ensured her a place in the history of Canada.

**SOURCES:**

McKenzie, Ruth. *Laura Secord: The Legend and the Lady*. Toronto: McClelland and Stewart, 1971.

Morgan, Cecilia. "'Of slender frame and delicate appearance': The placing of Laura Secord in the narratives of Canadian Loyalist history," in *Journal of the Canadian Historical Association*. NS 5 (1994), pp. 195–212.

**SUGGESTED READING:**

Currie, Emma. *The Story of Laura Secord and Canadian Reminiscences*. St. Catharines, 1913.

Curzon, Sarah. *Laura Secord, the Heroine of 1812: a drama and other poems*. Toronto, 1887.

**Margaret McIntyre**, Instructor in Women's History, Trent University, Peterborough, Ontario, Canada

# Seddon, Margaret Rhea (b. 1947).

*See Astronauts: Women in Space for sidebar.*

# Sedgwick, Anne Douglas
## (1873–1935)

*American-born novelist. Name variations: Anne de Selincourt or Sélincourt; Anne De Sélincourt. Born on March 28, 1873, in Englewood, New Jersey; died in Hampstead, England, on July 19, 1935; oldest of three daughters of George Stanley Sedgwick (an attorney) and Mary (Douglas) Sedgwick; married Basil De Sélincourt (an essayist and biographer), on December 11, 1908.*

*Selected writings:* The Dull Miss Archinard *(1898);* The Confounding of Camelia *(1899);* The Rescue *(1902);* Paths of Judgment *(1904);* The Shadow of Life *(1907);* A Fountain Sealed *(1907);* Anabel Channice *(1908);* Franklin Winslow Kane *(1910);* Tante *(1911);* The Nest *(1912);* The Encounter *(1914); (nonfiction)* A Childhood in Brittany Eighty Years Ago *(1919);* Autumn Crocuses *(American title* Christmas Roses, *1920);* The Third Window *(1920);* Adrienne Toner *(1922);* The Little French Girl *(1924);* The Old Countess *(1927);* Dark Hester *(1929);* Philip-

𝒜nne
𝒟ouglas
𝒮edgwick

pa *(1930); A Portrait in Letters (posthumous, edited by Basil De Sélincourt, 1936).*

Born in 1873 and raised primarily in the affluent New York suburb of Irvington-on-Hudson, Anne Douglas Sedgwick was educated at home by a governess. Although she was only nine when her father, an attorney, took a position as a financial agent in England and moved the family to London, her early experiences in America made lasting impressions. She spent two years during her teens in Chillicothe, Ohio, living with her grandparents whom she would later recall for the "sobriety, sweetness, tradition" of their home as well as for their "Emersonian flavor, a love of books and nature."

In England, Sedgwick later recalled, she took to the London of "Gilbert and Sullivan operas, [*Lillie] **Langtry**, buns, hansom cabs, and fogs; walks with a governess in Rotten Row, and frequent visits to the National Gallery and the Old South Kensington Museum." With her education completed by age 18, she next went to Paris where her studies in painting lasted five years. A portrait she executed of her sister was shown in the Champs de Mars Salon, and she might have continued a career as an artist were it not for her father's efforts to get her first novel published. After finding the manuscript of *The Dull Miss Archinard*, a story his daughter had written for the enjoyment of her sisters, Sedgwick's father took the book to a publisher in London. It appeared in print in 1898 and proved to be a success.

Sedgwick then turned her attention to writing, eventually producing 20 books, the vast majority of which were fictional. Often regarded as being in the tradition of Henry James and *Edith Wharton in her work, Sedgwick frequently contrasted the traits of the Americans, the English, and the French.

In December 1908, she married the essayist and biographer Basil De Sélincourt. They set up home in Oxfordshire where Sedgwick continued her writing. Her ninth novel, *Tante*, was published in 1911. This work, through the character of an internationally renowned pianist, addressed one of Sedgwick's predominant themes, what James Arnquist has summarized as "the effect of egocentric persons on the lives of those drawn to them by their apparent genius or goodness."

During World War I, both Sedgwick and her husband worked on behalf of the war effort in France, providing assistance in orphanages and caring for civilian casualties in hospitals. Returning to their home in Oxfordshire after the war, she resumed her hobbies which included working in her gardens and bird watching. Her husband conducted the village choral society in which she sang, and Sedgwick saw publication of her 1924 novel *The Little French Girl*, which became a bestseller in the United States (*Ethel Barrymore starred in the dramatized version). Novelist *Esther Forbes recalled Sedgwick sitting "serene and upright by the tea-table like a Dresden goddess. The coil of prematurely white hair, the purple eyes, the pink and white smoothness of her moulded features, lent her a statuesque quality which was sweetly dispelled by her smile and by the gentle irony of her conversation."

Beginning in the late 1920s, Sedgwick suffered from a paralytic illness. She characterized the long physical decline that followed as "slow, like being devoured by an ant." While on a final visit to the United States (1931), she was present at her induction into the National Institute of Arts and Letters. After Sedgwick's death in Hampstead in 1935, her *Portrait in Letters*, edited by her husband, was published the following year.

**SOURCES:**
James, Edward T., ed. *Notable American Women, 1607–1950.* Cambridge, MA: The Belknap Press of Harvard University, 1971.

Kunitz, Stanley J., ed. *Twentieth Century Authors.* NY: H.W. Wilson, 1942.

McHenry, Robert, ed. *Famous American Women.* NY: Dover, 1980.

# Sedgwick, Catharine (1789–1867)

*American writer of popular works in the early 19th century. Born Catharine Maria Sedgwick in Stockbridge, Massachusetts, on December 28, 1789; died near Roxbury, Massachusetts, on July 31, 1867; daughter of Theodore Sedgwick (a U.S. senator, speaker in the U.S. House of Representatives, and judge on the Supreme Court of Massachusetts) and Pamela (Dwight) Sedgwick; attended the district school in Stockbridge, and adventure schools in New York City, Boston, and Albany; never married; no children.*

Shortly before *A New England Tale* appeared in print, Catharine Sedgwick's brother Harry wrote to a relative that his sister had drafted a story that she had been persuaded "with great difficulty" to have published. "What I have now told you is of course a profound secret—We all concur in thinking that a lady should be veiled in her first appearance before the public." The tale had begun, in fact, as a religious tract. Its author, by then in her early 30s, was reluctantly induced by the enthusiasm of her four brothers to expand it into a novel, which was published anonymously in 1822. Though Harry was to become his sister's literary agent, she remained diffident. "She began a literary career as if she were biding her time while waiting for the legitimate domestic career she was never to have," wrote **Mary Kelley** in *Private Woman, Public Stage*, "and to an extent she regarded her literary endeavors as a pale substitute for what she believed should be the calling of a true woman."

"Reared in an atmosphere of high intelligence," Catharine Maria Sedgwick was born in Stockbridge, Massachusetts, on December 28, 1789. By her own admission, she received a "fragmentary" education: "there was much chance seed dropped in the fresh furrow and some of it was good seed—and some of it I may say fell on good ground." Her father was a politician and diplomat, at various times a judge on the Supreme Court of Massachusetts, speaker in the U.S. House of Representatives, and U.S. senator. At home, he spent evenings reading to his children, sometimes from Shakespeare, sometimes from Cervantes.

The success of Sedgwick's first book emboldened her brothers to encourage her in her writing, which she continued, albeit grudgingly. It had been her hope that her name would never be printed "except on my tomb." In 1827, she published *Redwood*, a two-volume novel, which was followed by *Hope Leslie* (1827), *Clarence, a Tale of our Own Times* (1830), *Le Bossu* (1832), *The Linwoods, or Sixty Years Since in America* (1835), *The Poor Rich Man, and the Rich Poor Man* (1836), and *Live and Let Live* (1838).

There were also two volumes of juvenile tales, *A Love Token for Children* and *Stories for Young Persons*. *Means and Ends, or Self-Training* contained advice to young women on education and character formation, while shorter tales that had appeared in various magazines were brought out as a collection in 1835. In 1840, Sedgwick published *Letters from Abroad to Kindred at Home*; the two volumes contained a pleasant but sketchy account of people and places she had encountered during a recent tour of Europe.

The strongest trait of Sedgwick's writings "is the amiable domesticity which runs through them," wrote one early critic. But eight years after the publication of her first book, after earning significant income from her writings, Sedgwick was still unable to consider writing a proper occupation for a woman and felt "inferior" when she had to "confess" to a bank that she had no occupation.

Sedgwick never married and lived with one or another of her brothers and their families in

*Catharine Sedgwick*

Stockbridge, considered one of the most beautiful villages of the Berkshires. Encouraged to continue with the work she refused to give herself credit for, she wrote often about the town, which gained a widespread and celebrated reputation because of the qualities described in her works.

**SOURCES:**
Kelley, Mary. *Private Woman, Public Stage*. NY: Oxford University Press, 1984.

# Sedley, Catharine (1657–1717)

*Countess of Dorchester. Name variations: Katherine Sedley; Baroness of Darlington. Born in 1657; died in 1717; only child of Sir Charles Sedley (c. 1639–1701, a writer and member of Parliament); associated with James II (1633–1701), king of England (r. 1685–1689); married Sir David Colyear, in 1696; children: (with James II) Katherine Darnley (c. 1680–1743, who married James, earl of Anglesey, and was associated with John Sheffield, duke of Buckingham); James Darnley (b. 1684); Charles Darnley.*

Catharine Sedley inherited her renowned wit from her father, Sir Charles Sedley, a playwright and member of Parliament who was also known for his stylish profligacy. As mistress to the duke of York (later James II, king of England), Catharine had three children. In 1686, she was created baroness of Darlington and countess of Dorchester. She married Sir David Colyear, 2nd baronet, in 1696.

## Sedova-Trotsky, Natalia (1882–1962).

*See Trotsky, Natalia.*

## Seefried, Irmgard (1919–1988)

*German soprano. Born on October 9, 1919, in Köngetried, a small town in Swabia (southwest Bavaria); died on November 24, 1988, in Vienna, Austria; daughter of a high school teacher; married Wolfgang Schneiderhan (a violinist and concert master), in 1948; children: Barbara Maria Schneiderhan (b. January 1950).*

Irmgard Seefried was born in 1919 in Köngetried, a small town in Swabia, and learned

*Irmgard Seefried*

piano, violin, and singing under her father's tutelage. After attending Albert Greiner's song-school in Augsburg, Germany, she spent five years studying at the Augsburg Conservatoire under Albert Mayer, then attended the State Academy of Music in Munich. Seefried joined the Aachen Opera under Herbert von Karajan (1939) and made her debut there in 1940 as a priestess in Verdi's *Aïda*. In 1943, she joined the Vienna State Opera, debuting as Eva in *Die Meistersinger* on May 2. During his 80th birthday celebration (June 1844), Richard Strauss chose her to sing the role of the Composer in *Ariadne auf Naxos*, commenting after her performance, "I never knew what a good part that could be." She also sang in London, New York, Milan, Salzburg, Edinburgh, and other cities, appearing as Micaëla in *Carmen*, Susanna in *The Marriage of Figaro*, Fiordiligi in *Così Fan Tutte*, Octavian, Cleopatra, Marie, and Blanche. A superb musical talent with a broad repertoire ranging from Mozart to contemporary music, Seefried gave the world premieres of a number of pieces. She was also admired as a Lieder singer.

**David Paul Clarke,** freelance writer,
Bethesda, Maryland

## Seeger, Peggy (b. 1935).

*See Crawford, Ruth for sidebar.*

## Seeger, Ruth Crawford (1901–1953).

*See Crawford, Ruth.*

## Seeley, Blossom (1891–1974)

*American actress and singer. Name variations: Blossom Fields. Born in San Pueblo, California, on July 16, 1891; died in New York City in April 1974; married Joseph Kane (divorced); married Rube Marquand (a baseball player, divorced); married Benny Fields (a singer), in 1921 (died 1959); no children.*

A petite, blonde bundle of energy with a voice that was easily heard in the third balcony, Blossom Seeley began her stage career singing between acts at the San Francisco Repertory Theater. Stage star Lew Fields discovered her there and brought her to Broadway in 1914 to co-star with him and his partner Joe Weber (Weber and Fields) in *The Hen-Pecks*. She subsequently appeared with Al Jolson in *Whirl of Society*, and with *Marion Davies in the Irving Berlin musical *Stop! Look! Listen!* Seeley reached her zenith, however, on the vaudeville circuit, where she received top billing and popularized such songs as "The Japanese Sandman," "Smiles,"

"Way Down Yonder in New Orleans," and "California, Here I Come."

Beginning in 1921, Seeley formed an act with her third husband, singer Benny Fields, who had enjoyed little success before Seeley came along. The couple performed throughout the 1920s, although there was little doubt that Seeley was the truly talented one of the pair. In 1934, Fields went out on his own, and Seeley predicted that her husband would now become the star of the family. But he had little success as a solo act and soon faded into obscurity.

The couple had been out of the limelight for a number of years when Paramount filmed *Somebody Loves Me* (1952), a musical based on their lives, starring *Betty Hutton** and Ralph Meeker. The film sparked renewed interest in Seeley and Fields, who had an opportunity to reprise their routine on television and in such clubs as the famed Coconut Grove. They even cut a new album, *Two a Day at the Palace*. Seeley never formally retired, even after the death of her husband in 1959. She was at work on her memoirs in 1968 when she broke her hip in a fall and was taken to a Manhattan nursing home. She remained there until her death in 1974.

SOURCES:

Lamparski, Richard. *Whatever Became of . . . ?* 4th series. NY: Crown, 1973.

**Barbara Morgan**,
Melrose, Massachusetts

## Seelye, Emma E. (1841–1898).

*See Edmonds, Emma.*

# Seghers, Anna (1900–1983)

*German writer, leading literary figure in exile during the Nazi years and one of the most significant writers in Communist East Germany, whose career extended from the Weimar era to the 1970s. Name variations: Netty Reiling; Netty Radvanyi or Radványi. Pronunciation: AH-na SAYG-hers. Born Netti Reiling in Mainz, Germany, on November 19, 1900; died in East Berlin on June 1, 1983: daughter of Isidor Reiling (an art dealer); attended the universities of Heidelberg and Cologne; Ph.D. in the History of Art, Heidelberg, 1924; married László Radványi, in 1925; children: Peter (b. 1926); Ruth (b. 1928).*

*Entered University of Heidelberg (1919); won Kleist prize (1928); joined Communist Party (1928); fled Germany after Hitler came to power (1933); fled France (1940); arrived in Mexico (1941); returned to Germany (1947); won Büchner prize (1947); served as chair of East German Writers' Union (1950–1977);*

Blossom
Seeley

*given honorary doctorate, University of Mainz (1977); awarded honorary citizenship by the city of Mainz (1981).*

*Major works:* Aufstand der Fischer von St. Barbara *(The Revolt of the Fishermen of Santa Barbara, 1928);* Die Gefährten *(The Comrades, 1932);* Der Weg durch den Februar *(1935);* Das Siebte Kreuz *(The Seventh Cross, 1942);* The Excursion of the Dead Girls *(1946);* Transit *(1948);* The Dead Stay Young *(1949);* The Decision *(1959);* Trust *(1968);* Crossing *(1971);* Encounter While Travelling *(1972);* Peculiar Meetings *(1973).*

Anna Seghers stands as a notable literary figure whose life and work were closely tied to the turmoil in her native Germany. She began her writing in the 1920s, emerged as one of the most productive and successful German writers in exile during the Nazi era, and then returned to postwar Germany to play an important role in the cultural life of East Germany. She was a committed Communist who saw the need for writers to involve themselves in creating a new society. At the same time, she sometimes found her literary interests taking her in directions that led Marxist critics to question her ideological orthodoxy.

Germany in the 20th century went through tumultuous changes that affected every one of its inhabitants. Defeated in World War I, imperial Germany was transformed into the unstable Weimar Republic in the years from 1919 to 1933. Communist efforts to take power failed on several occasions during the first postwar years, and they left the German population bitterly divided between those who favored such radical change from the Left and those who opposed it. The onset of the Great Depression in 1929 set the stage for Adolf Hitler and his Nazi Party to come to power in 1933. The Nazis identified Communists and Jews as criminals and traitors within the German population, responsible for all of the nation's agonies starting with the defeat in World War I. From the onset of the Nazi era, large numbers of Germans were imprisoned or forced into exile.

The defeat of Nazi Germany in World War II brought the country under foreign military occupation—with the United States, Britain, and France controlling northern, western, and southern Germany, while the Soviet Union occupied the eastern region. The victorious wartime alliance broke down rapidly after 1945, the western zones of occupation were united into a new West German state in 1949, while the Soviet zone of occupation was transformed into a Communist state, the German Democratic Republic. The Communist revolution that had failed after World War I thus succeeded in the Soviet zone under Russian direction.

*She* does not write in order to describe, but in order, by describing, to change things.

—Martin Kane

The division of Germany, and the consequent need for Germans on both sides of the dividing line to choose between a Communist and a non-Communist future, sharpened with the passage of time. An initial revolt against Communist authorities took place in East Germany in June 1953. The physical division of Germany and the final barrier to East Germans wishing to come to the West was completed in August 1961 with the erection of the Berlin Wall. Relations between the two Germanies remained strongly hostile until the early 1970s.

German history deeply affected many German writers. In traditional Marxist ideology, literature is a tool to be used in bringing Communist governments to power and in the construction of a Communist society. Thus, writers and artists like Seghers who belonged to Communist parties such as the German one founded in 1919 were expected to implant a Marxist view of history and society into their work. An issue for such representatives of the world of cultural creation was the degree to which the complexities and possibilities of their fields of work had to be subordinated to politics: were they first of all teachers helping to bring this new political order to power? After the creation of an East German state, such figures of the cultural world had to react to a harsh and often intolerant government that threatened to punish those who did not support the existing system with sufficient zeal.

The future Anna Seghers was born Netty Reiling in Mainz on November 19, 1900. She was the daughter of a distinguished middle-class Jewish family; her father was an antique dealer and curator of the art collection of the Mainz Cathedral. During a secure childhood in the years before World War I, Seghers spent holidays in Holland and Belgium, and her mother introduced her to classic German literature. A shy and quiet child, she was apparently the contented product of a bourgeois environment. Nonetheless, in an interview published in 1967, she recalled her childhood concerns for the poor and the politically repressed.

She followed the customary German student career of attending several universities, beginning her studies in art history and Chinese culture at Heidelberg, moving to Cologne, then returning to Heidelberg to complete her doctorate. Her dissertation topic was Judaism in the works of Rembrandt. Scholars who have analyzed her literary career have suggested that elements of Chinese culture as well as the artistic techniques of Rembrandt can be found reflected in her work.

The universities of Weimar Germany were gathering points for refugees from the failed Communist revolutions of Eastern Europe. It seems likely that this was the environment in which the young woman's political interests became intertwined with Marxist ideology. Her links to Eastern Europe became personal in 1925 when she married a Hungarian sociologist, László Radványi. She had two children in the space of the next three years as she turned her interests to literature, enjoying a spectacular early success when her first novella, *The Revolt of the Fishermen of Santa Barbara*, won the prestigious Kleist Prize in 1928. By that time Netty Reiling had taken the pen name of Anna

Seghers (a minor artist who was a contemporary of Rembrandt), which she would use for the remainder of her life.

Seghers' political allegiance became a permanent influence on her work by the early 1930s. She had joined the Communist Party in 1928 and made the first of her many visits to the Soviet Union at the start of the 1930s. Her first major novel, *The Comrades* (1932), expressed her political sympathies clearly for the first time. With a multitude of characters and five separate plots, it describes revolutionary activity in a dozen different countries in the decade following World War II.

Although the details are uncertain, Seghers apparently was arrested and confined for a brief time following the Nazi rise to power in 1933, then left for exile in Paris. Like many other German authors, she discovered that her books could no longer be published or circulated in her own country. Unlike many other refugees from Nazi Germany who were stunned into silence by their expulsion, however, Seghers maintained a high level of literary productivity, writing six novels and other works between 1933 and 1947. She immersed herself in the European political scene of the '30s, visiting Austria after the repression of the 1934 workers' uprising there and going to Spain during the first year of that country's Civil War.

Although her work throughout the 1930s was grounded in sympathy for the working class and Marxist ideals, she nonetheless found herself at odds with Marxist literary critics. In a notable exchange with Georg Lukács, Seghers agreed that literature was a political weapon. Nonetheless, she expressed her objections to rules that restricted literary technique to a sterile realism. Throughout much of her career, Seghers was to arouse the concerns of more orthodox Marxists by her interest in individual psychology and her failure to present simple, heroic characters who could symbolize Communist revolution and the construction of a Marxist society.

Two of her most highly regarded works of literature came out of the tumultuous atmosphere of Europe in the 1930s. Between 1938 and 1940, she wrote her most famous novel, *The Seventh Cross*. First published in an English translation in 1942, it was set in her native Rhineland and recounted the fate of seven escapees from a Nazi concentration camp. Without direct experience of life in Nazi Germany, Seghers drew on the stories painted for her by fellow refugees. By showing how one fugitive was ultimately able to evade recapture, Seghers

presented a panoramic picture of German society under Nazism.

A basic theme of the novel was the transitory nature of Nazism and the inevitable future triumph of the healthy proletarian elements in German life. Critics have noted the Christian symbolism of the crosses on which the recaptured escapees were hung to die in this work by a committed Communist. Some of the critical acclaim for the book derives from its picture of Georg Heisler, the fugitive whose successful escape symbolized the futility of Hitler's dictatorship. He is a flawed and complex figure. By contrast, Ernst Wallau, the model Communist in the book, who is recaptured and murdered by the Nazi authorities at the concentration camp, appears only as a secondary character. The book was acclaimed by critics and became the basis for a memorable U.S. film starring Spencer Tracy as Heisler.

In 1940, Seghers and her family fled the German invasion of France. With her husband in an internment camp, she and her children tried unsuccessfully to escape from Paris for the safety of the south, but they were overtaken by the invaders and forced to return for a stay in Paris under German occupation. They reached

*Anna Seghers*

unoccupied France several months later. While in Paris, she took the daring step of speaking to young soldiers in the army of occupation to understand their feelings as Germans serving a Nazi government.

The entire family managed to secure passage out of Europe. By a circuitous route through the islands of the Caribbean and the United States, Seghers, her husband, and their children made their way to Mexico in 1941. She recalled the grueling experience while writing a friend, "I feel as though I had been dead for a year." The four of them spent the next six years in Mexico.

The novel *Transit* (1948) was a work that came directly out of Seghers' personal experiences in making this perilous passage. It considers, in a manner that critics have compared with Franz Kafka's *The Trial* and *The Castle*, the psychological pain of desperate individuals confronting an uncaring bureaucracy. Like *The Seventh Cross* and its Christian symbolism, *Transit*'s evocation of existential despair takes Seghers far from the narrow pattern followed by many of her fellow Marxist writers. Critic Martin Kane has suggested that her unwavering Marxist commitment throughout the 1930s may have crumbled temporarily in the face of the Hitler-Stalin Pact of 1939 and the unbroken string of political and military successes Germany's Nazi government was achieving.

The exiled author received a stream of tragic news while in Mexico. Her mother died in a Nazi concentration camp; her native city of Mainz was badly damaged by Allied bombing. She herself was almost fatally injured when an automobile struck her in Mexico City. Nonetheless, her literary and political energies continued to express themselves. She wrote a highly regarded novella, *The Excursion of the Dead Girls*, during 1943 and 1944 that was set in her native Mainz, again containing autobiographical elements. Told from the perspective of a narrator in Mexico, it recounts the diverse fates of a group of German schoolgirls and their teacher as some of them become Nazis and others the victims of the Nazis in later life.

Anna Seghers and her husband returned to Germany in April 1947. She was, as one critic has written, one of a group of returning writers and artists who were "convinced that their work would have a vital role to play in the creation of a new socialist society." Her most respected novel, *The Seventh Cross*, was published in German in East Berlin, and she enjoyed a period of acclaim in both the Communist and non-Communist zones of Germany. She also received the prestigious West German literary Büchner prize in Darmstadt. In short order, however, her commitment to the creation of a Communist state in the Soviet zone of occupation and her open criticism of West Germany's rearmament and orientation toward the United States tied her future life and work to East Germany.

Critic Kane has described her literary career from the late 1940s to the close of the 1960s as one dominated by "unswerving commitment" to the East German state, a "taking up of cudgels on behalf of the new society in the making." In this endeavor, she seemingly followed the maxim that public misgivings about the difficulties of building a Communist society would provide ammunition to anti-Communist forces which she had spent her career opposing. As her biographer Lowell Bangerter put it, the price she paid was to sacrifice "the humanism that informs her best early narratives."

Her first major work published in East Germany was another panoramic study of German life. She had begun to write *The Dead Stay Young* while in Mexico. This was the first of a trilogy of novels containing an examination of Germany from the close of World War I to the 1950s. In it, she used individual characters to personify the deep political divisions and conflicts.

In 1959, she published the second volume, *The Decision*, which became the object of intense criticism in West Germany and which stands as the most controversial of her writings. An influential West German review of the book accused her of "intellectual capitulation." Containing 80 main characters, it contrasts life in East and West Germany as the two societies grew apart in the years from 1947 to 1953. Her characters are presented as representatives of their social classes, and the book's educational purpose is to show the differences between East and West in a way that stresses the moral and political superiority of the Communist part of Germany. English critic Peter Hutchinson saw it as a typical product of East German didactic literature: Seghers made her characters crude representative figures drawn from East and West German society, and she constantly interjected her voice as author into the narrative to make sure readers drew the proper conclusions from the story.

As head of the Writers' Union and as one of East Germany's most famous authors, Seghers was the object of sharp criticism in West Germany for her excessive devotion to a brutal political regime. In a noted example, she decided to remain silent while one of her publishers, Walter

Janka, was tried in 1957 and sentenced to five years in prison on a trumped-up charge of conspiring against the East German state. Similarly, when West German writers called upon her to condemn the building of the wall separating East and West Berlin in 1961, she gave no reply. By 1962, a proposal to publish *The Seventh Cross* for the first time in West Germany aroused protests in the literary community there.

Seghers' direct statements on political issues pointed in the same direction. As she said in the early 1970s, one must give up smaller freedoms in order to reach a larger freedom. Overall, she personified the committed literary figure who sees herself as a teacher helping to create a new society. Bangerter has described her literary goal by noting: "Seghers compels the reader to choose between the evils of the past and the optimistic promises of a specific kind of future." Other Western literary critics have noted how her work is characterized by the personification of virtue in East Germany and its citizens and the personification of evil and aggression in West Germany.

Her novel *Trust*, published in 1968, was a continuation of the historical depiction of the split in West and East Germany. It has been criticized for being even more didactic than *The Decision* and displaying her complete surrender to the requirements of socialist realism. It deals with such controversial issues as the accusations that Jewish doctors in the Kremlin tried to poison Communist leaders in 1952 and the East German workers' revolt of 1953. Even though the book points up the insensitivity of the political system, Seghers nonetheless calls on the individual citizen to endure it in the interest of building a Communist society. By the late 1960s, some East German writers had moved beyond the stilted techniques the book employs, but Seghers continued to write in a style that had been established 20 years earlier.

Within this picture of a politically committed artist, there were some hints of a writer chafing under excessive political control. In early 1956 at the East German Fourth Writers' Congress, for example, she joined with a number of her colleagues in criticizing the supervision political authorities exercised over their work. Moreover, her work was sometimes criticized in East Germany as insufficiently orthodox in both its techniques and themes.

By the early 1970s, as relations between the two Germanies improved, there was public discussion in West Germany of honoring her as a distinguished citizen of Mainz, her birthplace. Protests deferred the awarding of the honor at that time, but she received an honorary degree from the University of Mainz in 1977. In 1981, Seghers received the accolade of being named a distinguished citizen of her home city in the Rhineland.

The changing political climate of the 1970s may have encouraged her to widen her literary scope. She was by this time a conservative luminary on the East German cultural scene with other writers moving ahead far more rapidly in using novel techniques. In the novella *Crossing*, she introduced the theme of a love story, an element that had been conspicuously missing from her earlier writing. Two years later in the short story "Encounter While Travelling" (1972), she produced an uncharacteristically romantic work picturing a fictional meeting of three great literary figures: Franz Kafka, Nikolai Gogol, and E.T.A. Hoffmann. Other works produced at this time took up the techniques of science fiction. In 1977, after a tenure of 25 years, she gave up her position as head of the Writers' Congress.

Anna Seghers died of unspecified causes in Berlin on June 1, 1983. Controversy over her political positions and her literary work continues. The memoirs of Walter Janka, which were published in 1989, reopened the question of her willingness to subordinate all to the needs of the East German state. On the other hand, recent gatherings of scholars in reunified Germany have led to a reexamination of her political views and her literary orthodoxy. Some of her newly discovered, unpublished work reflects a critical view of government actions in East Germany in the 1950s. New views of her published writing have led some critics to emphasize her use of devices like a Latin American setting as a shield against the political pressures of Communist orthodoxy. Thus they suggest that the position she expressed in her debate with Lukács in the late 1930s on the autonomy of literature can be found as an influence on her writing even in the period after 1949.

**SOURCES:**

Bangerter, Lowell A. *The Bourgeois Proletarian; A Study of Anna Seghers.* Bonn: Bouvier Verlag Herbert Grundmann, 1980.

Hutchinson, Peter. *Literary Presentations of Divided Germany: The Development of a Central Theme in East German Fiction, 1945–1970.* Cambridge, Eng.: Cambridge University Press, 1977.

Kane, Martin, ed. *Socialism and the Literary Imagination: Essays on East German Writers.* NY: Berg, 1991.

**SUGGESTED READING:**

Demetz, Peter. *After the Fires: Recent Writing in the Germanies, Austria, and Switzerland.* San Diego, CA: Harcourt Brace Jovanovich, 1986.

LaBahn, Kathleen J. *Anna Segher's Exile Literature: The Mexican Years (1941–1947)*. NY: Peter Lang, 1986.

Reid, J.H. *Writing Without Taboos: The New East German Literature*. NY: Berg, 1990.

Williams, Rhys W., Stephen Parker, and Colin Riordan, eds. *German Writers and the Cold War, 1945–1961*. Manchester, Eng.: Manchester University Press, 1992.

**RELATED MEDIA:**

*The Revolt of the Fishermen*, filmed in Moscow by Erwin Piscator, 1934.

*The Seventh Cross* (film), starring Spencer Tracy, *Signe Hasso, *Jessica Tandy, Hume Cronyn, and *Agnes Moorehead, directed by Fred Zinnemann, with a screenplay by *Helen Deutsch and costumes by *Irene, MGM, 1944.

Neil Heyman, Professor of History,
San Diego State University,
San Diego, California

## Segovia, duchess of.

See Dampierre, Emmanuela del (b. 1913).

## Segrave, Anne (d. around 1377)

*Abbess of Barking. Died around 1377; daughter of John Segrave, 3rd baron Segrave (also seen as 4th baron Segrave), and *Margaret, Duchess of Norfolk (c. 1320–1400); sister of *Elizabeth Segrave (1338–1399).*

## Segrave, Christian (c. 1250–?).

See Christian de Plessetis.

## Segrave, Elizabeth (1338–1399)

*English noblewoman. Name variations: Elizabeth Seagrave; Elizabeth Mowbray. Born in 1338; died in 1399 (Burke's Peerage says died in 1375); daughter of John Segrave, 3rd baron Segrave (also seen as 4th baron Segrave), and *Margaret, Duchess of Norfolk (c. 1320–1400); sister of *Anne Segrave; married John Mowbray (1340–1368), 4th baron Mowbray, in 1353 (slain near Constantinople, on the way to the Holy Land, on October 9, 1368); children: John Mowbray, earl of Nottingham; Thomas Mowbray (c. 1362–1399), 1st duke of Norfolk; Margaret Mowbray (fl. 1380).*

## Segrave, Margaret (c. 1280–?)

*Baroness Ferrers of Groby. Name variations: Margaret Ferrers. Born around 1280; daughter of John Segrave (1256–1325), 2nd baron Segrave, and *Christian de Plessetis; married William Ferrers, 1st baron Ferrers of Groby (d. 1325); children: *Anne Ferrers (d. 1342); Henry Ferrers, 2nd baron Ferrers of Groby (d. 1343).*

## Segrave, Margaret (c. 1320–1400).

See Margaret, duchess of Norfolk.

## Seibert, Florence B. (1897–1991)

*American biochemist who developed the skin test for tuberculosis. Born Florence Barbara Seibert on October 6, 1897, in Easton, Pennsylvania; died on August 23, 1991; daughter of George Peter Seibert and Barbara (Memmert) Seibert; Goucher College, A.B. and LL.D.; University of Chicago, Sc.D.; Yale University, Ph.D.*

For her work in developing a reliable skin test for tuberculosis, once the leading cause of death in America, Florence Seibert earned distinction as one of the country's greatest biochemists. Writing shortly after this accomplishment, **Edna Yost** noted, "The tuberculin Florence Seibert 'discovered' can be depended upon to give identical tests because she found the way to isolate pure tuberculin from its impurities. It took her ten years to do it. But that is not bad when you stop to consider that many others had been attempting over a sixty-year period to do it." Among the honors Seibert received for her work were a Guggenheim Fellowship (1937), the Trudeau Gold Medal from the National Tuberculosis Association (1938), the Garvan Gold Medal from the American Chemical Society (1942), several honorary degrees, and induction into the Women's Hall of Fame (1990).

She was born in 1897 in Easton, Pennsylvania, and had two siblings, an older brother Russell and a sister **Mabel Seibert**. Both Russell and three-year-old Florence were victims of the polio epidemic which swept through Easton. Their parents, George and **Barbara Seibert**, helped them to learn to walk with braces, which were later discarded, and relocated the family so that Florence and Russell would be nearer to school. "Because I was disabled," noted Seibert, "I stuck to things harder"; she also replaced activities which were out of her reach, like going to dances, with study. On the night that she graduated from Easton High School, she received a scholarship to Goucher College in Baltimore, Maryland. But her father was concerned about her enduring the physical challenges of a college campus, so that September he accompanied her there; he left within a week. George had quickly realized that she was at home in her new environment. "I learned . . . that I was not an invalid but could stand on my own two feet with a chance to make a contribution to the world."

Telling her teachers, "I'm going to Johns Hopkins and become a doctor," Seibert ignored those friends and faculty members who advised her against what they considered a difficult pursuit for a woman, particularly a woman with a disability. She took pre-med courses, despite knowing that her family did not have the means to put her on the path to Johns Hopkins, but changed direction upon an invitation from **Jessie Minor** (who had been her chemistry teacher) to work at the Hammersley Paper Mill Company's chemistry lab. Following Seibert's graduation in 1918, the two women worked there on behalf of the war effort, affording Seibert an opportunity to raise funds for graduate study. The two also collaborated on three papers which were printed in technical journals.

With the help of fellowships, Seibert received her Ph.D. from Yale in 1923. Her graduate work focused on creating a method for removing contaminants from distilled water. At the time, noted **Kathleen McLaughlin**, "triple-distilled water was used as a solvent for intravenous injections, but fever frequently followed such treatment. Few physicians believed that the triple-distilled water could be to blame until Dr. Seibert analyzed the water and found bacteria or bacterial products enough to induce the fever." Finding that the bacterial products were transmitted in the steam, Seibert adapted the apparatus used for distillation by "inserting a new loop, or baffle," an advancement which made possible contaminant-free water with no more than a single distillation.

A Porter Fellowship brought Seibert to the University of Chicago, where she took a position as instructor in pathology and assistant in the Sprague Memorial Institute. An award which she received at the University of Chicago, where she continued the work begun at Yale, provided the funds for her to purchase a car designed to enable her to drive with her stronger foot.

In her department was Esmond R. Long, a grant recipient from the National Tuberculosis Association, to whom Seibert served as assistant. Invited to join Long in his research, in 1924 Seibert began the work with tuberculosis for which she would be famous. Long's goal at the time, noted Yost, was to "ascertain first the chemical nature of the specific substance in raw tuberculin which gave a positive skin reaction in the tuberculous individual, and then to produce a tuberculin of such a state of purity that when any doctor anywhere injected it into a human being, he could know that whatever happened was an exact scientific result with a definite significance." Prior to Seibert's work, no tuberculin had been developed which was free of impuri-

ties. Consequently, depending on how high the test dose was in impurities, a tubercular individual might test negative for tuberculosis, making skin tests unreliable.

It was Seibert who managed to determine that pure tuberculin was a protein. Purifying this protein, however, was daunting work which took her years. The pure tuberculin which she isolated was a Purified Protein Derivative (PPD) of the tubercle bacillus. Seibert continued her work in Chicago, where she eventually became associate professor in biochemistry (1928), before following Long to the University of Pennsylvania's Henry Phipps Institute. In Pennsylvania, she was promoted from assistant to associate professor in 1937. That year, she received a Guggenheim Fellowship which made possible a year's study in Uppsala, Sweden, where she worked with the Nobel Prize-winning Swedish professor The (Theodor) Svedberg and his pupil Arne Tiselius. The latter had developed equipment which used an electrical field to separate molecules in a process known as electrophoresis. A grant from the Carnegie Foundation made it possible for the Henry Phipps Institute to procure Tiselius' new apparatus, and Seibert continued her work with the PPD upon her return. Having become an in-

Florence B. Seibert

ternational authority on the bacillus responsible for tuberculosis, she prepared the National Standard for Tuberculins in 1939, and by 1941 the skin test was ready for use.

But hesitancies on the part of the medical establishment were compounded by delays due to the outbreak of the Second World War, and it would be another several years before this test received approval for widespread use. Seibert met resistance when she testified before the World Health Organization in 1952, later remarking: "They thought that if they didn't have a big man there arguing for the test, they could push [out] this method." At 4'9", and less than 100 pounds, Seibert was hardly a big man. Disabled from her childhood experience with polio, she once remarked that she remembered her physical limitations only when approaching a full-length mirror: "That's the only time I ever remember it. And even in my forties I'm still brought up with a jolt every time I get in front of a mirror and see myself coming."

Among the 20th century's most eminent biochemists, Seibert retired eight years before the skin test developed from her work became the standard in 1966. In Florida, she and her sister Mabel, who had served as her laboratory assistant for years, worked voluntarily on cancer research. Seibert was inducted into the Women's Hall of Fame in 1990, a year before her death at age 93.

**SOURCES:**

Bailey, Brooke. *The Remarkable Lives of 100 Women Healers and Scientists.* Holbrook, MA: Bob Adams, 1994.

Block, Maxine, ed. *Current Biography 1942.* NY: H.W. Wilson, 1942.

Weatherford, Doris. *American Women's History.* NY: Prentice Hall, 1994.

Yost, Edna. *American Women of Science.* Philadelphia, PA: Frederick A. Stokes, 1943.

# Seidel, Amalie (1876–1952)

*Austrian Social Democratic leader who served as a parliamentary delegate (1919–34) and was imprisoned for her beliefs by three different regimes (in 1893, 1934, and 1944). Name variations: Amalie Rausnitz; known as Ly, short for the "Lysistrata of the women workers." Born Amalie Ryba in Vienna, Austria, on February 21, 1876; died in Vienna on May 11, 1952; daughter of Jakob Ryba and Anna (Stach) Ryba; married Richard Seidel, in 1895 (divorced); married Sigmund Rausnitz, in 1934 (died 1942); children: daughters Emma and Olga; one son.*

Amalie Seidel, one of the most effective orators and organizers among the leadership of the Austrian Social Democratic Workers Party (Sozialdemokratische Arbeiterpartei Österreichs, or SDAP), was born in Vienna in 1876, the daughter of Jakob and **Anna Stach Ryba**. At the time of her birth, the laissez-faire credo of industrial capitalism that prevailed in Austria had created inhumane working and living conditions for millions. The plight of women workers was particularly brutal, given the fact that they found themselves subjected to countless incidents of sexual harassment. For men, too, the situation in factories, mills, and workshops was one of unceasing toil in often dangerous and unhealthy conditions for pathetic wages. Seidel was born into an impoverished working-class family; her father, a locksmith and mechanic, was unable to earn a living wage despite long hours of labor. Furthermore, her mother gave birth to such a large number of children—17—that it proved impossible to feed, clothe, or properly care for them. Suffering from malnutrition and living in substandard housing, only Amalie and three other Ryba infants would survive to adulthood.

From her earliest years, Seidel sewed at home to earn a few kreuzer to help support the family. By the time she entered her teens, after eight years of primary education, her schooling ended, and she had no choice but to begin work in a local textile factory, earning a pittance for long hours. Determined to improve her circumstances, in 1892 Seidel became a member of the workers' educational organization (Arbeitebildungsverein) in the Gumpendorf district of Vienna. Although the repressive laws of Austria forbade women from being involved in any form of political organization or engaging in any form of political activity, the appearance of many local Arbeiterbildungsvereine throughout the Habsburg monarchy during these years gave workers, both men and women, the opportunity to expand their educational horizons as well as to develop a political and class consciousness.

At an October 1893 meeting of working women at which *Anna Boschek and Adelheid Dworschak (later *Adelheid Popp) addressed the assembled audience, Seidel made one of her first appearances as an orator. She not only condemned the harsh nature of industrial capitalism, but also demanded for women their full rights as citizens, namely the right to vote:

> Starting at age fourteen we have to work in factories, and our labor creates the wealth of our exploiters. If we are mature enough to be exploited at age fourteen, we should certainly be ready and able at the age of twenty to defend our own interests. In any case, we should

be able to defend them better than they have been upheld to date by the gentlemen who are currently sitting in our Parliament.

Because of this and other speeches in which she criticized the social order and demanded full political rights for women, she was arrested and placed on trial. By this time, the Vienna police regarded her as a dangerous agitator and social radical due to her leadership of the May 1893 strike of 700 female factory workers, the first successful strike of organized women workers in the nation's history. Among the women's achievements were a significant raise in wages and a lowering of the daily hours of labor to ten. A particularly sweet victory in the strike was that the women would henceforth be able to celebrate their Tag der Arbeit (Day of Labor), annually on May 1, as a holiday with full pay. Found guilty on several charges by a biased court, Seidel was sentenced to three weeks in jail. To humiliate her and break her spirit, she had to serve her time in a cell with 12 other women who were common criminals. Not surprisingly, this repressive measure backfired, serving to only strengthen Seidel's will to continue her efforts on behalf of fellow workers, who began to refer to her simply as the "Lysistrata of women workers," or even as their "Ly."

Seidel's enthusiasm and courage brought her to the attention of the SDAP founder and leader, Victor Adler. He praised her for her oratorical skills, but cautioned her to become better acquainted with history, philosophy, and the writings of Karl Marx. During her imprisonment in February 1894, she used much of her time to read books borrowed from Adler's extensive personal library.

In 1895, Amalie married Richard Seidel, an engineer. The birth of three children over the next few years changed her priorities significantly, and she concentrated on being a wife and mother. By 1900, however, she had reentered the hectic world of Social Democratic politics. Particularly in her Viennese neighborhood of Margareten, she invested hours in party work, including organizing meetings for women who were seeking additional education as well as organizing women for strikes and collective bargaining. In 1903, she was elected to the important post of chair of the SDAP national women's conference (Frauenreichskonferenz), a position she would hold until 1932. At this time, she also became chair of the important Social Democratic consumers' cooperative (Konsumgenossenschaft).

In November 1918, after more than four years of the terrible privations of World War I,

the Habsburg Empire of Austria-Hungary dissolved and the small, impoverished German-speaking remnant was proclaimed the Republic of Austria. One of the first reforms that came after the shattering political changes of 1918 was the achievement of women's suffrage. Highly respected both by her colleagues in her Viennese neighborhood and by the (male) SDAP party leadership, in 1918–19 Seidel was chosen to run for several important posts, namely that of membership in the Vienna City Council (Gemeinderat) and delegate to the constituent National Assembly. In both instances, she won the seat. Seidel would serve on the council until 1920. She would also serve as a Social Democratic delegate throughout the history of the increasingly troubled Austrian republic, without an interruption, being reelected many times from March 1919 through February 1934.

The immense demands placed on Seidel took their toll on her private life. Her marriage eroded over the years, and she had little time to spend with her three children, who increasingly felt ignored by their mother. As her family life crumbled, Seidel invested even more time into her party activities. These difficulties paled before the political and economic upheavals of the early 1930s, when the world Depression hit Austria. Austrian Social Democracy was at a loss when Nazism appeared in the streets, demanding that the old order make way for a Third Reich based on blood and "healthy" national instincts. A domestic form of fascism arose in Austria, somewhat less violent than Hitler's but every bit as anti-Socialist. In February 1934, Austria's Social Democratic movement was bloodily suppressed and a "Christian-Social" dictatorship proclaimed. For the second time in her life, Seidel was imprisoned because of her political beliefs. After serving six weeks, she was freed on March 30, 1934, when the police could not make a case of active subversion on her part. But despite her age and poor health, she was made to pay a fine of 500 Austrian schillings at the time of her release.

In 1934, having divorced her husband Richard, Seidel married Sigmund Rausnitz, a friend of many years. Both Sigmund and Richard were imprisoned that year in Wöllersdorf, an Austrian concentration camp for political prisoners. Rausnitz was particularly at risk because he was of Jewish ancestry, and this was one of the reasons Seidel married him, believing that his being married to an "Aryan" might help protect him from further persecutions. This idea proved to be illusory once Nazi Germany annexed Austria in March 1938. Facing deportation to the death camps of the east, Sigmund Rausnitz and his sister committed suicide on April 22, 1942. Seidel was devastated. In August 1944, she was arrested by Vienna's Gestapo as part of a general roundup of anti-Nazis in the aftermath of the failed plot to assassinate Adolf Hitler on July 20, 1944. Fortunately, Seidel's state of health convinced her captors at the jail of Vienna's Municipal Court (Landesgericht) that she was not a significant enemy of the regime, and she was released after ten days' imprisonment.

Seidel survived these terrors to witness the liberation of her beloved city of Vienna from Nazism in the spring of 1945. Although her health was shattered and would never be restored, she retained her faith in socialism. She died in Vienna on May 11, 1952.

**SOURCES:**

Arbeitsgemeinschaft "Biografisches Lexikon der österreichischen Frau," Institut für Wissenschaft und Kunst, Vienna, biographical file: Seidel, Amalie, geb. Ryba.

Pawlik, Gabriele. "Amalie Seidel: Die Lysistrate der Arbeiterinnen," in Edith Prost, ed., *Die Partei hat mich nie enttäuscht . . .": Österreichische Sozialdemokratinnen.* Vienna: Verlag für Gesellschaftskritik, 1989, pp. 223–252.

Seidel, Amalie. "Die ersten Arbeiterinnenstreiks," in *Käthe Leichter, ed., Handbuch der Frauenarbeit in Österreich.* Vienna: Kammer für Arbeiter und Angestellte für Wien, 1930.

Seitz, Emma. "Amalie Seidel," in Norbert Leser, ed., *Werk und Widerhall: Grosse Gestalten des österreichischen Sozialismus.* Vienna: Verlag der Wiener Volksbuchhandlung, 1964, pp. 374–380.

Sporrer, Maria, and Herbert Steiner, eds. *Rosa Jochmann: Zeitzeugin.* 3rd ed. Vienna: Europaverlag, 1987.

Weinzierl, Erika. *Emanzipation?: Österreichische Frauen im 20. Jahrhundert.* Vienna: Verlag Jugend & Volk, 1975.

**John Haag**, Associate Professor of History, University of Georgia, Athens, Georgia

## Seidel, Ina (1885–1974)

*German poet and novelist. Born in 1885 in Halle an der Saale, Germany; died in 1974; married Heinrich Wolfgang Seidel (a writer), in 1907.*

*Selected writings:* Gedichte *(Poems, 1914);* Neben der Trommel her *(Next to the Trumpet, 1915);* Weltinnigkeit *(World Inwardness, 1918);* Das Haus zum Monde *(The House at the Moon, 1916);* Das Labyrinth *(The Labyrinth, 1921);* Das Wunschkind *(The Wish Child, 1930);* Der vergrabene Schatz *(The Buried Treasure, 1955);* Das unverwesliche Erbe *(The Incorruptible Inheritance, 1958);* Michaela: Aufzeichnungen des Jürgen Brook *(Michaela: Notebooks of Jürgen Brook, 1959);* Vor Tau und Tag: Geschicte einer Kindheit *(Before Dew and Day: Story of a Childhood, 1962);* Die alte Dame und der Schmetterling *(The Old Woman and the Butterfly, 1964);* Frau und Wort *(Woman and Word, 1965);* Lebensbericht 1885–1923 *(Life Story 1885–1923, 1970).*

Ina Seidel was born in 1885 in Halle an der Saale, Germany; her mother's stepfather was the historical novelist Georg Ebers. Ina, a devout Protestant who immersed herself in literature, married Heinrich Wolfgang Seidel, another author, in 1907. After the birth of their first child, she nearly died. During her months of convalescence, she grew spiritually and turned to writing poetry. In 1914, she published *Gedichte* (Poems), followed by *Neben der Trommel her* (Next to the Trumpet) in 1915, and *Weltinnigkeit* (World Inwardness) in 1918.

Seidel's first novel, *Das Haus zum Monde* (The House at the Moon, 1916), was followed five years later by the powerful *Das Labyrinth* (The Labyrinth, 1921), in which she traced the psychic development of an enigmatic character, George Forster. Seidel's *Das Wunschkind* (The Wish Child, 1930), the story of a widowed mother who saves her child only to lose him in the Prussian wars of liberation, was considered one of the great novels of its generation.

During World War II, Seidel's Romantic nationalism and "apolitical" attitudes made it impossible for her to perceive the evils of National Socialism, but her works, based on a spirit of cultural conservatism and the restoration of traditional values, remained popular in postwar West Germany. She published shorter prose, *Der vergrabene Schatz* (The Buried Treasure, 1955) and *Die alte Dame und der Schmetterling* (The Old Woman and the Butterfly, 1964), as well as a collection of poetry in 1957. She followed this volume with the novels *Das unverwesliche Erbe* (The Incorruptible Inheritance, 1958) and *Michaela: Aufzeichnungen des Jürgen Brook* (Michaela: Notebooks of Jürgen Brook, 1959), which deals with the guilt of middle-class German Christians who had supported Hitler's Third Reich. She also wrote a volume of essays, *Frau und Wort* (Woman and Word, 1965) and such autobiographical works as *Vor Tau und Tag: Geschicte einer Kindheit* (Before Dew and Day: Story of a Childhood, 1962) and *Lebensbericht 1885–1923* (Life Story 1885–1923, 1970).

**SOURCES:**

Buck, Claire, ed. *The Bloomsbury Guide to Women's Literature.* NY: Prentice Hall, 1992.

*Columbia Dictionary of Modern European Literature.* NY: Columbia University Press, 1980.

Seidel, Ina. *Dichter, Volkstum und Sprache: Ausgewählte Vorträge und Aufsätze.* Stuttgart: Deutsche Verlagsanstalt, 1934.

———. *Luise, Königin von Preussen: Ein Bericht über ihr Leben.* Königstein and Leipzig: Eiserne Hammer, 1934.

**David Paul Clarke**, freelance writer, Bethesda, Maryland

## Seidman, Esther (1945–1995).

*See Rome, Esther.*

## Sei Shōnagon (c. 965–?)

*Japanese author of the literary masterpiece* **Makura no sōshi** *(The Pillow Book). Name variations: Sei Shonagaon. Pronunciation: SAY SHOW-nah-gohn. Born possibly in Kiyohara around 965, possibly in Kyoto, Japan; circumstances of her death are not known; great-granddaughter of Kiyohara Fukayabu (paternal great-grandfather, a poet of distinction); daughter of Kiyohara Motosuke (father, a noted scholar and poet of some repute); perhaps married Tachibana no Norimitsu (a minor court official); perhaps married Fujiwara no Muneyo (a minor court official); sometimes mentioned that she was married to, or had a relationship with, Fujiwara no Sanekata (a minor court official); children: (with Tachibana no Norimitsu) possibly a son, Norinaga; (with Fujiwara no Muneyo) possibly a daughter,* **Koma no Myōbu.**

*Became lady-in-waiting at court of Empress Sadako (early 990s); likely served until the empress' death (1001); wrote* Makura no sōshi *during that time.*

One of the most renowned prose writers in the history of Japanese literature, Sei Shōnagon was the author of *Makura no sōshi* (*The Pillow Book*), a masterpiece of world literature. A compilation of her own tastes, insights, and prejudices, the book derives its immense charm from the author's own irascible and irrepressible personality. From Shōnagon's detailed observations, we learn much about the daily lives of members of Japan's upper class in the 10th and 11th centuries.

Ironically, for a literary figure of her stature, little is known about Sei Shōnagon, apart from what can be gleaned from *Makura no sōshi*. Neither her birth date nor the date of her death is certain, and almost all biographical information about her is speculation. In fact, her true name is not known; Sei Shōnagon is the only name attributed to the author of *Makura no sōshi*. At some point, she was probably married to a man holding the position of *shōnagon* (minor counselor) in the imperial palace, since court ladies were generally called by the titles of their husband or nearest male relative.

Sei Shōnagon was born around 965 into the Kiyohara clan, which was low in official rank but illustrious in literary circles. Kiyohara Fukayabu, thought to have been her paternal great-grandfather, was a poet laureate of the Japanese imperial court. Kiyohara Motosuke, the man considered to be her father, whether natural or adopted, worked for the government as a provincial governor, but was better known as a scholar and a poet.

As was common for a woman of the Japanese upper class in her era, Shōnagon has been romantically linked to several men. It is possible that she was briefly married to a government official, Tachibana no Norimitsu; there is a tradition that at the age of 17, she had their son, Norinaga. The tradition holds that Shōnagon considered her husband dull—too unrefined to share her aesthetic sensibilities. Her name has also been linked (as wife or lover) to Fujiwara Nobuyoshi, Fujiwara no Muneyo (with whom she was said to have had a daughter, **Koma no Myōbu**), and Fujiwara no Sanekata. These last two men were both minor court officials and provincial governors.

> *When I make myself imagine what it is like to be one of those women who live at home, faithfully serving their husbands . . . I am filled with scorn.*
>
> —Sei Shōnagon

Shōnagon's domestic arrangements, however, were apparently of little concern to her; her life centered on her career at the Japanese imperial court. According to official records, Shōnagon arrived at court in 994, when she began serving as lady-in-waiting to Empress *Sadako (r. 976–1001). Despite having been a mature, experienced woman, likely nearing age 30, Shōnagon was apparently self-conscious, and thought herself unattractive and awkward in comparison with other court ladies. Initially, she tried to stay behind the curtains, observing the courtiers and their wives. But Shōnagon took pride in serving the brilliant empress and gratefully received her favors. Having impressed Sadako, who eventually succeeded in coaxing her out from behind the curtains, Shōnagon wrote *Makura no sōshi* on paper (a rare and valuable commodity) given to her by the empress.

During her service at court, Shōnagon developed a reputation for wit and erudition. From her own accounts, she comes across as a clever conversationalist with a pleasant voice. Scholars have concluded that Shōnagon's renowned erudition was probably no greater than that of most people in her circle. Most striking to her contemporaries, however, was her uncanny capacity to quote an appropriate line of poetry or reference to history on the spur of the moment in conversation. While these qualities were valued in men, it was less clear that they were thought appropriate for women. Shōnagon's rival in court, *Murasaki Shikibu, author of *Genji monogatari* (*The Tale of Genji*), castigated Shōnagon and predicted her doom. "Sei Shōnagon has the most extraordinary air of self-satisfaction. Someone who makes such an effort to be different from others is bound to fall in peoples' esteem. . . . She is a gifted woman. . . . Yet, if one gives free rein to one's emotions even under the most inappropriate circumstances, if one has to sample each interesting thing that comes along, people are bound to regard one as frivolous." Indeed, Murasaki would appear to have been not far from the mark, for tradition has it that after leaving court (most likely following the death of the empress), Shōnagon retired to a suburb of the capital, became a Buddhist nun, and died in poverty. It is also possible, however, that this legend was the invention of Buddhist moralists who were critical of what they perceived to be Shōnagon's promiscuity and her concern with worldly things.

*Makura no sōshi*—part diary, part essay, part miscellany—is, however, a lasting tribute to Shōnagon. The title was probably a generic term used to describe a type of informal book of notes which both men and women composed as they retired to their rooms in the evening and which they kept near their sleeping place. This typically Japanese literary genre was the precursor of *zuihitsu* (occasional writings, random notes) which has lasted to modern times. The combination of observation and reflection served as a model for later works which have included some of the most valued writings in Japanese literature. For the irrepressible Shōnagon, who appeared to record spontaneously and effortlessly her impressions of the world while jotting down whatever thoughts passed through her mind, it was an ideal form.

Randomly organized, *Makura no sōshi* contains more than 300 essays—some short, some long. There are eyewitness sketches of her contemporaries, imagined scenes, casual musings on social customs and etiquette, reflections on esthetics, as well as lists of her own likes and dislikes. Shōnagon's essays reflect powers of keen observation and delicate sensibility. The images she evokes are incisive, as she describes a shivering lady who imprudently quarreled herself out of a warm bed on a cold night or an insensitive lover who dons his trousers and buckles his belt in too business-like fashion. Shōnagon was a master of social satire, as illustrated in this observation: "A preacher ought to be good looking. For if we are properly to understand his worthy sentiments, we must keep our eyes on him while he speaks; should we look away, we might forget to listen. Accordingly, an ugly preacher may well be the source of sin." Shōnagon's poetic prose has extraordinary beauty and evocative power. Her images of icicles gleaming in the moonlight, the innocent charm of a child eating strawberries, or a desolate, windswept autumn garden remain in the mind. Japanese schoolchildren are still introduced to Shōnagon's writing as a model of linguistic purity.

Shōnagon's life at court was both physically and socially circumscribed; court ladies spent virtually all of their time indoors, most often behind screens and curtains which hid them from view. Shōnagon's compelling descriptions of nature were drawn, more likely, from imagination than direct experience. As was the case with her peers, Shōnagon was intolerant and callous toward people of the lower classes. She claimed to be revolted by the uncouth habits of carpenters and itinerant nuns, and she appears to have been without empathy when she laughed at an illiterate man whose house had burned down. Shōnagon's conversations, as was the case with the other women and men of the court, centered around critical judgments. She could be merciless as she ridiculed those who failed to achieve her demanding, refined standards, but she also cast her critical eye inward and laughed at herself. She was candid about her shortcomings, particularly with respect to her appearance and temperament, and her self-indictments make her lambasting of others somehow more acceptable.

Shōnagon's social criticism is most piercing, and amusing, in her discussion of romance. Under the heading "Things Apparently Distant Yet Really Near," Shōnagon listed "the relations between men and women." Love affairs at court were conducted according to elegant, prescribed ritual, with a strong aesthetic sense of how the woman and man should comport themselves. Some of the most entertaining passages of *Makura no sōshi* depict lovers' trysts and partings. With little privacy and enormous amounts of leisure, amorous adventure was the chief topic of court gossip. Whether drawing on her own experience or that of others in her list of "Shameful Things," Shōnagon observed: "A man's heart is a shameful thing. When he is with a woman whom he finds tiresome and distasteful he does not show that he dislikes her, but makes her believe she can count on him." Admirably, Shōnagon's writing about men is free from the whining, querulous tone that often characterized other women's writings of her time. Rather, Shōnagon shows herself to be a comic artist. In her list of "Hateful Things," she included: "A man with whom one is having an affair keeps singing the praises of some woman he used to know. Even if it is a thing of the past, this can be very annoying. How much more so if he is still seeing the woman!" Her comic rendering of affairs of the heart is in marked contrast to the consistently tragic portrayal of romance found in the Japanese literature of the time.

Following the death of Empress Sadako, Shōnagon left court service. In a brilliant piece of satire on society's expectations, perhaps anticipating her eventual solitary retirement, she wrote: "When a woman lives alone, her house should be extremely dilapidated, the mud wall should be falling to pieces, and if there is a pond, it should be overgrown with water-plants. It is not essential that the garden be covered with sage-brush, but weeds should be growing through the sand in patches, for this gives the place a poignantly desolate look." Sei Shōnagon was by no means a typical Japanese woman of the 10th century. At court, she had a measure of autonomy not permitted other Japanese women. It appears that Shōnagon no longer wrote after leaving court. Perhaps she lacked paper, perhaps she lost the social contact which stimulated her writing, or perhaps she lost the autonomy which had made her book possible.

SOURCES:

Morris, Ivan. *The World of the Shining Prince: Court Life in Ancient Japan*. NY: Penguin, 1964.

SUGGESTED READING:

*The Pillow Book of Sei Shōnagon*. Translated and edited by Ivan Morris. Vols. 1 and 2. NY: Columbia University Press, 1967.

Linda L. Johnson, Professor of History,<br>Concordia College, Moorhead, Minnesota

# Seizinger, Katja (1972—)

*German skier. Pronunciation: KAHT-yah SIGHTS-in-ger. Born in Datteln, West Germany, on May 10, 1972; lives in Eberbach, Germany.*

*Compiled six medals at the World Junior championships (1989 and 1990), including a gold in the Super G and a silver in the downhill in Zinal, Switzerland (1990); won a gold medal in the Super G at the World championships in Morioka, Japan (1993); had a World Cup giant slalom victory in Kloevsjoe, Sweden (1993); took the bronze medal in the Albertville Olympics in the Super G, and finished 4th in the*

*downhill and 8th in the giant slalom (1992); won Olympic gold medal in the downhill at Lillehammer (1994); won the downhill World Cup titles (1992, 1993); won two giant slaloms, in Maribor and Kvitfjell, and tallied two third-place finishes (1995–96); won overall title in World Cup (1995–96); won gold medals in the downhill and the combined at Nagano Olympics (1998).*

Alpine skier Katja Seizinger was born in 1972 and grew up in the industrial Ruhr of northern Germany; her father was a steel executive. While most German skiers hone their skills in the mountains of Bavaria, Seizinger learned to ski in the Savoy region of France, near Albertville, where her family vacationed. In 1992, the site was the home of the Winter Olympics, and Seizinger won a bronze medal in the Super G.

Seizinger went on to win the downhill World Cup titles in 1992, 1993, and 1994 and the Super G title in 1993, 1994, and 1995. She also placed first in the Super G in the 1993 World championships held in Morioka, Japan. In 1994, in Lillehammer, she took the Olympic gold medal in the downhill with a time of 1:35.93. One of her major competitors, *Picabo Street, came in second for the silver.

Seizinger placed first overall in the 1996 World Cup and also led on the 1997–98 World Cup tour going into the 1998 Nagano Olympics, having won four downhills and four Super G's. Clearly the favorite, she finished a surprising 6th in the Super G in Nagano, while Street placed first. Less surprisingly, a few days later Seizinger took the gold medal in the downhill with a time of 1:28.89, becoming the first skier, man or woman, to win consecutive downhill golds in the Olympics. Sweden's defending Olympic champion *Pernilla Wiberg placed second; France's Florence Masnada came in third. Two days later, Seizinger took her second gold medal in the women's combined, becoming only the second woman in Olympic history to win three Alpine gold medals. *Vreni Schneider of Switzerland had been the first. During the event, Wiberg fell on her first trip down the course, making way for a German sweep: Seizinger with the gold, Martina Ertl with the silver, *Hilde Gerg with the bronze. Katja Seizinger is also an avid equestrian, tennis player, and parachutist.

# Sekulić, Isadora (1877–1958)

*Serbian short-story writer, novelist, and critic. Name variations: Isidora Sekulic. Born in 1877 in Mošorin,*

*Bačka; died in 1958; trained to be a teacher; held Ph.D. from a German university.*

*Selected writings: Saputnici (Fellow Travelers, 1913); Pisma iz Norveške (Letters from Norway, 1914); Djakon Bogorodičinecrkve (The Deacon of the Church of Our Lad, 1919); Kronika palanačkog groblja (The Chronicle of a Provincial Graveyard, 1940); Njegošu knjiga duboke odanosti (A Book of Deep Homage to Njegoš, 1951); Mir I nemir (Peace and Unrest, 1957); Govor I jezik (Speech and Language, 1956).*

Isadora Sekulić was born in Mošorin, Bačka, but traveled extensively throughout Norway, France, and England. Through her travels, she broadened her cultural awareness and perfected her knowledge of several foreign languages. She trained to be a teacher and received a Ph.D. from a German university.

Sekulić's lyrical *Saputnici* (Fellow Travelers, 1913) established her reputation as a fresh voice in Serbian literature. For her second work, *Pisma iz Norveške* (Letters from Norway, 1914), she was criticized by one critic for her seeming indifference to the fate of Serbia. But her third book, the novella *Djakon Bogorodičin-ecrkve* (The Deacon of the Church of Our Lad, 1919), demonstrated her identification with Serbian Orthodox tradition. That affiliation can be seen in her later works as well, such as *Kronika palanačkog groblja* (The Chronicle of a Provincial Graveyard, 1940). As a critic, Sekulić was best known for *Njegošu knjiga duboke odanosti* (A Book of Deep Homage to Njegoš, 1951) and *Mir I nemir* (Peace and Unrest, 1957), while *Govor I jezik* (Speech and Language, 1956) deals with the challenges of translating Yugoslav literature into Western European languages.

**David Paul Clarke**, freelance writer, Bethesda, Maryland

## Selassie, Menen (1899–1962).

*See Menen.*

## Selassie, Tsahai Haile (1919–1942).

*See Tsahai Haile Selassie.*

# Selbert, Elisabeth (1896–1986)

*German Social Democratic activist and attorney who played a crucial role in expanding and defending the legal rights of women in the German Federal Republic after World War II. Born Elisabeth Rhode in Kassel, Germany, on September 22, 1896; died in Kassel on June 9, 1986; daughter of Georg Rhode and Eva Elisabeth Rhode; had one sister; graduated from the University of Göttingen; married Adam Selbert, in 1920; children: sons Gerhart and Herbert.*

Elisabeth Selbert was born into modest circumstances in Kassel, Germany, in 1896; her father, a minor civil servant, worked as a guard in the municipal youth detention center. Although Selbert was an excellent student and wished to become a teacher, the family's inadequate income did not allow for the schooling this required. After working briefly as a journalist, in 1916 she found steady employment in the telegraph office of the local post office. Four years later, Elisabeth married Adam Selbert, a printer who was a member of the Social Democratic Party (Sozialdemokratische Partei Deutschlands, or SPD).

Supported by her husband, Selbert became politically active in the SPD in the early 1920s, even though much of her time went into raising the couple's two sons. She often spoke out in SPD meetings, and was involved in election campaigns, frequently appearing on the platform with noted national candidates, including senior SPD leader Philipp Scheidemann. Believing that she could accomplish much more if she upgraded her educational credentials, in 1926 Selbert was able to earn an Abitur, the school-leaving certificate needed to qualify for university matriculation. She then enrolled at the University of Marburg. But she was unable to find an advisor for her law thesis at Marburg, so transferred to the University of Göttingen where she successfully completed her studies.

In March 1933, Selbert ran unsuccessfully for a Reichstag seat on the SPD ticket. Within weeks, the Nazi seizure of power resulted in her husband Adam losing his civil-service position and being imprisoned for a period of time in a concentration camp. In December 1934, Selbert became one of the last women admitted to the bar in Nazi Germany, before women were excluded from the legal profession. Because her husband was unable to find permanent employment, Selbert became her family's chief breadwinner over the next decade. Like most Social Democrats during the Nazi period, she avoided active opposition to the dictatorship, convinced that to do so would only bring death, suffering and martyrdom to herself and her family and not advance the cause of humanity. The Selberts' philosophy of *"Stillhalten und Abwarten"* (keeping quiet and biding one's time) lasted 12 years, until the spring of 1945.

After 1945, Selbert achieved a rapid political ascent, from city representative in Kassel, to a member of the Hesse constitutional state assembly, to deputy of the Hesse Parliament, in which she served continuously from 1946 through 1958. She rose quickly as well in the ranks of her party, serving on the SPD federal executive. Probably the high point of her career came in 1948, when she was chosen to serve on the Parliamentary Council (Parlamentarischer Rat), an American-initiated institution designed to move the Western sectors of occupied Germany toward sovereign status. Along with **Frieda Nadig** (SPD), *****Helene Weber** (CDU) and **Helene Wessel** (Zentrum), Selbert was one of the only four women members of the Parliamentary Council, the other 61 members all being male. In many ways, these women can be fairly characterized as the "Founding Mothers of Postwar German Democracy."

During sessions of the Parliamentary Council, Selbert championed the cause of full equality for women. After the body had rejected the principle "Men and women have equal rights," which she had formulated and the SPD had proposed, she mobilized public opinion. Spurred by much of the media and an aroused populace, the politicians looked reality squarely in the eye and relented, accepting Article 3.2 which stated the legal equality of the sexes. This principle would be anchored in the Basic Law (*Grundgesetz*) of the Federal Republic of Germany when it was born in the fall of 1949. In order to ensure the legal consequences of this principle, Selbert had a measure passed (Article 7) whereby all conflicting laws and restrictions would have to be revised by April 1953. Other issues that Selbert addressed included the legal equality of illegitimate children, judiciary rules, particularly the independence of judges, and the basis for the Federal Constitutional Court (*Bundesverfassungsgericht*).

Elisabeth Selbert died in her home city of Kassel on June 9, 1986. She has been honored in Germany in many ways, including a street named after her in Berlin's Neukölln district, and a 120 pfennig postage stamp issued on November 6, 1987. An Elisabeth Selbert Prize to honor those in science and journalism whose work reflects Selbert's ideals has been awarded annually since 1983.

**SOURCES:**

Asendorf, Manfred, and Rolf von Bockel, eds. *Demokratische Wege: Deutsche Lebensläufe aus fünf Jahrhunderten.* Stuttgart: Metzler, 1997.

Böttger, Barbara. *Das Recht auf Gleichheit und Differenz: Elisabeth Selbert und der Kampf der Frauen um Art. 3.2 Grundgesetz.* Münster: Westfälisches Dampfboot, 1990.

Dertinger, Antje. *Die bessere Hälfte kämpft um ihr Recht: Der Anspruch der Frauen auf Erwerb und

andere Selbstverständlichkeiten.* Cologne: Bund-Verlag, 1980.

———. *Elisabeth Selbert: Eine Kurzbiographie.* Wiesbaden: Bevollmächtigter der Hessischen Landesregierung für Frauenangelegenheiten, 1986.

Drummer, Heike, and Jutta Zwilling. *Ein Glücksfall für die Demokratie: Elisabeth Selbert (1896–1986), die grosse Anwältin der Gleichberechtigung.* Frankfurt am Main: Eichborn, 1999.

Huber, Antje, ed. *Verdient die Nachtigall Lob, wenn sie singt? Die Sozialdemokratinnen.* Stuttgart: Seewald, 1984.

Moeller, Robert G. "Reconstructing the Family in Reconstruction Germany: Women and Social Policy in the Federal Republic, 1949–1955," in *Feminist Studies.* Vol. 15, no. 1. Spring 1989, pp. 137–169.

Mühlhausen, Walter. "Selbert, Elisabeth (1896–1986)," in Dieter K. Buse and Juergen C. Doerr, eds., *Modern Germany: An Encyclopedia of History, People, and Culture, 1871–1990.* Vol. 2. NY: Garland, 1998, pp. 911–912.

**John Haag**, Associate Professor of History, University of Georgia, Athens, Georgia

*German postage stamp issued in honor of Elisabeth Selbert in 1987.*

# Selena (1971–1995)

*Mexican-American singer, known as the queen of Tejano, who was murdered before her 24th birthday. Name variations: Selena Quintanilla-Pérez. Born Selena Quintanilla in Lake Jackson, south of Houston,*

*Texas, on April 16, 1971; died of a gunshot wound in Corpus Christi, Texas, on March 31, 1995; youngest of three children, two girls and a boy, of Marcela Quintanilla and Abraham Quintanilla, Jr.; married Chris Pérez (a guitar player), in 1992.*

Known as the queen of Tejano, Mexican-American singer Selena was on the verge of a crossover to mainstream music when she was shot to death outside a motel in Corpus Christi, Texas, by **Yolanda Saldivar**. At the time of her death on March 31, 1995, two weeks shy of her 24th birthday and two days before her third wedding anniversary, Selena was not only a rising star, but a role model to a generation of young Hispanics who worshiped her. Hundreds of teenagers gathered at the scene of the shooting; thousands attended memorial services. At the Bayfront Plaza Convention Center in Corpus Christi, hour after hour 50,000 mourners from Canada and California, Guatemala and Mexico streamed slowly past her casket which was encircled by thousands of long-stemmed white roses. Her death spawned a Hollywood biopic, a cable movie, several books (one of which topped *The New York Times* bestseller list for several weeks), and thousands of articles. Five of her albums landed on Billboard's Top 200 chart, and the posthumous release of her half-English, half-Spanish album *Dreaming of You* made her one of the fastest-selling artists in music history.

Selena Quintanilla was born in 1971 in the factory town of Lake Jackson, Texas. When she was six, her father was laid off from his job as a shipping clerk at Dow Chemical and opened a Tex-Mex restaurant. Abraham Quintanilla had always loved music; in his youth, he had been the vocalist for a South Texas band called Los Dinos ("The Boys"). Recognizing talent in his young daughter—"Her timing, her pitch were perfect," he said, "I could see it from day one"—he organized a family band, with her brother Abraham III on bass and her sister **Suzette** on drums. They began performing at the restaurant. But when the Texas oil industry went belly up, so did small businesses throughout the state: the Quintanillas lost their restaurant, home, possessions, and jobs.

The family moved to Corpus Christi and began eking out a living in the music business, singing at weddings and road-house dance halls and traveling in the family van to venues throughout the back country of South Texas. When Selena was eight, she recorded her first song in Spanish, and when she was nine, the family started a Tex-Mex band, Selena y Los

Dinos. Most of her teen years were spent on the road with the group, making it impossible for her to attend school. She received her high school diploma through the mail.

Eventually, the family band moved up to ballrooms and began cutting albums for a small regional label. Selena's breakthrough came in 1987, when she won in the categories of best female vocalist and performer of the year at the Tejano Music Awards. In 1989, she and the band, which now included her husband Chris Pérez, signed with EMI, the powerful record company.

By age 19, Selena was the center of the Tejano music industry. Tejano, which literally means Texan, is a blend of pop tunes, the rhythms of Colombian *cumbia*, and German polkas—an urbanized version of Tex-Mex (called *conjunto*). Tejano arrived in Texas with the Czech and German settlers of the 19th century and flourished in the cantinas of the Mexican working class. Its danceable beat is propelled by the accordion—the heart of the Tejano sound—and the *bajo sexto* guitar. With a microphone in hand, Selena was as exotic as the music itself. Clad in a signature bustier, tight Spandex pants, and heels, she sang and strutted across the stage, exuding a combination of earthy sensuality and innate sweetness, "a **Madonna** without the controversy," noted a *Time* correspondent. Ironically, Selena could barely speak a word of Spanish; rather, she spoke English with a Texas twang. In the beginning, she memorized the lyrics of each song, most of them written out phonetically for her by her brother Abraham. In 1990, she finally began taking Spanish lessons.

Each of Selena's next six albums grew in sales. At 21, she was a millionaire, drawing crowds as large as 20,000 at the Pasadena, Texas, fairgrounds. In 1994, 60,000 came to hear her in Houston. By then, she had sold more than 1.5 million records in the U.S. and Mexico, and her recording *Selena Live* had just won a Grammy for best Mexican-American album. Moreover, she had finished filming a scene in the movie *Don Juan DeMarco* with Johnny Depp; her song "Fotos y Recuerdos" (Photographs and Memories) was number four on the Billboard Latin charts; her single from the 1994 album *Amor Prohibido* (Forbidden Love) had sold 400,000 copies and had just been nominated for another Grammy; and she had just signed a $5 million record contract with SBK Records.

With all of her success, Selena, a devout Catholic, still lived with her close-knit family in three adjoining houses in the same lower-middle-

Selena

class neighborhood of Corpus Christi where she grew up. (At the time of her death, she and Chris were designing a ten-bedroom house on ten acres of land in town.) Fans loved her because she was unpretentious and accessible. "She was one of us," said one of her Corpus Christi admirers.

"I'd see her at Wal-Mart or Kmart without makeup, like she didn't have all that money."

Selena's assailant was Yolanda Saldivar, who had once run Selena's fan club and was then managing two of the singer's boutiques, Selena, Etc., which had opened in Corpus Christi and San Antonio. A 32-year-old registered nurse, Saldivar was suspected by the family of embezzling funds, and Selena had been given the unpleasant task of confronting her. Saldivar had called Selena, claiming she had papers to prove her innocence and begging her to meet alone to discuss the matter, preferably at Saldivar's room at the Corpus Christi Days Inn. Shot once in the back with a .38-caliber revolver, Selena staggered to the lobby of the motel for help, then collapsed and later died at Memorial Medical Center. Saldivar was arrested after a nine-hour standoff, during which she sat in a pickup truck in the motel parking lot, a gun to her head and a cellular phone in her hand to confer with police.

At Saldivar's trial in October 1995, her attorney pointed a finger at Abraham Quintanilla as the indirect cause of Selena's death, arguing that he was a controlling force over the singer and was fiercely jealous of her relationship with Saldivar whom he had threatened physically and falsely accused of embezzlement. Further, he claimed that Saldivar was distraught and had intended to kill herself, but when she gestured to the singer to close the door to the room, her gun accidentally discharged (despite the fact that Selena had been shot in the back). Selena's father denied the accusations on the witness stand, but was angered and hurt by them. The trial was also difficult for her mother **Marcela Quintanilla** who at one point was hospitalized with chest pains. At the end of the two-week ordeal, it took the jury of six women and six men just two-and-a-half hours to find Saldivar guilty of first-degree murder. She was given a life sentence. In a jailhouse interview in 1995, Saldivar said she had been fighting with Selena over a "secret," that she could not reveal. Her family said the "secret" was Selena's "diary" and produced a page from the alleged journal written in Spanish. Selena's friends never saw the diary and doubted that she would write one in Spanish, a language she was just learning.

In the months following Selena's death, Abraham Quintanilla continued to market his daughter persistently, sometimes alienating music-industry insiders and journalists in the process. While many questioned Quintanilla's intentions, however, others saw a man merely trying to cope. "I personally see Abraham as burying himself in his work, being so busy that he doesn't have time to think about his loss," said Rick Garcia, a record producer. Abraham oversaw the singer's two boutiques, as well as her posthumous album *Dreaming of You*, which sold 175,000 copies on the first day of its release, an all-time record for a female artist. He also signed the deal for the biographical film *Selena* (1997), which after some on-again, off-again negotiations was written and directed by Gregory Nava. Quintanilla co-produced and served as an on-the-set advisor for the film, which drew thousands to its open auditions in San Antonio. Casting directors finally selected actress **Jennifer Lopez** for the role, which initially upset many of Selena's fans. The movie opened in March 1997 to mixed reviews but did well at the box office, supported predominantly by Latino audiences across the country.

While Selena's death devastated her family and those closest to her, it also had a lingering impact on the millions of young Hispanic women who saw something of themselves in her. "Across the nation, Hispanic girls have a 38 percent drop in self-esteem from elementary school to high school," wrote **Alisa Valdes**. "Selena—a strong, smart, talented, beautiful, successful Mexican-American woman—gave them permission to like themselves." **Lizett Padilla**, the 23-year-old Guatemalan-American actress who played Selena in the cable television movie *The Selena Murder Trial*, expressed her own strong bond with the singer. "You could tell that she was a nice person, someone you would like to have as a friend. Portraying her just exactly the way she was, that's my dream and my challenge. I just want to honor her."

**SOURCES:**

"Before Her Time," in *People Weekly*. April 17, 1995, pp. 48–53.

Carr, Jay. "Actors rise above stilted script for 'Selena,'" in *Boston Globe*. March 21, 1997.

Carroll, Ginny, and John Leland. "The Other Murder Trial," in *Newsweek*. October 16, 1995, p. 75.

Chanko, Kenneth M. "Selena's song," in *Boston Sunday Globe*. March 16, 1997.

"Death of a Rising Star," in *Time*. April 10, 1995, p. 91.

Dominguez, Robert. "Latino audiences love 'Selena,'" in *The Day* [New London, CT]. March 29, 1997.

Farley, Christopher John. "Old Rock, New Life," in *Time*. July 10, 1995, pp. 57–58.

Jerome, Richard. "Resolution," in *People Weekly*. November 6, 1995, pp. 49–51.

Kantrowitz, Barbara. "Memories of Selena," in *People Weekly*. April 1, 1996, pp. 110–112.

Leland, John. "Born on the Border," in *Newsweek*. October 23, 1995, p. 80.

Morthland, John. "Selena's Story," in *TV Guide*. December 7, 1996, pp. 29–36.

Sanz, Cynthia, and Betty Cortina. "After Selena," in *People Weekly*. July 10, 1995, pp. 36–44.

Tarradell, Mario. "Selena's Music," in *The Day* [New London, CT]. July 21, 1995.

Valdes, Alisa. "Remembering Selena," in *The Day* [New London, CT]. April 11, 1995, p. B1.

# Sell, Janie (b. 1941).

*See Andrews Sisters for sidebar.*

# Sellick, Phyllis (1911—)

*English pianist.* Born in Newburg Park, Essex, England, on June 16, 1911; married Cyril Smith (a pianist), in 1937.

Born in 1911, Phyllis Sellick studied at the Royal Academy of Music in London and then with Isidor Philipp in Paris. She married Cyril Smith in 1937 and often appeared with him in works for two pianos written by British composers Ralph Vaughan Williams and Lennox Berkeley. In 1938, she gave the world premiere of Michael Tippett's First Piano Sonata. Sellick and Smith continued their duo-piano partnership even after he suffered a stroke that cost him the use of one of his hands; from that point on, they performed piano music arranged—or in some instances composed—for three hands. Sellick began teaching at the Royal College of Music in 1964 and was initiated into the Order of the British Empire in 1971.

**John Haag,**
Athens, Georgia

# Sellwood, Emily (1813–1896).

*See Tennyson, Emily.*

# Selove, Fay (b. 1926).

*See Ajzenberg-Selove, Fay.*

# Selva, Blanche (1884–1942)

*French pianist.* Born in Brive, France, on January 29, 1884; died in Saint-Armand, France, on December 3, 1942.

Blanche Selva studied at the Paris Conservatory, making her debut in 1897. In 1904, at age 20, she stunned musical Paris by performing the entire keyboard output of Johann Sebastian Bach in 17 recitals. Selva taught at the Schola Cantorum in Paris from 1901 through 1922, as well as at the Strasbourg and Prague and Barcelona conservatories. She was also a highly regarded scholar who wrote several books, perhaps the most important being *La Sonate* (1913). As a pianist, Selva brought many works of the modern French school to the public, including the premiere of Isaac Albeniz's *Iberia*. Vincent D'Indy dedicated his Sonata, Op. 63, to Selva, which she premiered in 1908, and Albert Roussel dedicated his Suite for Piano, Op. 14, to her.

**John Haag,**
Athens, Georgia

# Selznick, Irene Mayer (1910–1990)

*American theater producer.* Name variations: Irene Mayer. Born Irene Gladys Mayer on April 2, 1910, in Brookline, Massachusetts; died in 1990; youngest of two daughters of Louis B. Mayer (the movie producer) and Margaret (Shenberg) Mayer; attended public schools in Brookline, Massachusetts; attended Hollywood School for Girls, Hollywood, California; married David O. Selznick (the movie producer), on April 29, 1930 (divorced 1948); children: Jeffrey Selznick (b. 1932); Daniel Mayer Selznick (b. 1936).

The daughter of a powerful movie mogul and the wife of another, Irene Mayer Selznick made her own mid-life debut into show business as a theatrical producer, bringing to the Broadway stage *A Streetcar Named Desire* (1947) and *The Chalk Garden* (1955), among others. Born Irene Gladys Mayer in 1910 in Brookline, Massachusetts, she was the youngest of two daughters of Louis B. Mayer and **Margaret Shenberg Mayer**. Selznick spent her first ten years in Massachusetts, where her father began his movie career as a theater owner and film distributor. After he moved into film production and formed his own company, the Mayers moved to Hollywood.

*Irene Mayer Selznick*

"There was nothing spartan about our lives, but strictness prevailed," Selznick wrote in her memoir *A Private View* (1983), describing her decidedly conservative Jewish upbringing. In 1926, she began dating one of her father's bright and ambitious new assistants, David O. Selznick, whom she married in April 1930.

Over the next 17 years, David rose to become one of Hollywood's greatest movie-makers, producing such films as *A Star is Born*, *Rebecca*, and his crowning achievement *Gone With the Wind*. In addition to his obsession with work, he partied, gambled excessively, and took drugs to keep functioning beyond the point of exhaustion. During that time, Selznick raised their two boys, ran several fully staffed houses, and generally oversaw their lavish and frantic lifestyle. "If I hadn't been so accommodating and efficient, it might have served David better in the long run," Selznick wrote. "But it wasn't his fault. I didn't feel imposed on. I was Privileged! *This* was exactly what I wanted to do: be fully used; grow, learn; have his dreams come true. This was not unselfishness, it just happened to be the limit of my ambition. I was not only old-school, I was old-country."

In 1945, following an intensive round of psychoanalysis and her husband's continued gambling and drug use, Selznick left her marriage, moving to New York. Attracted to producing, and having the right contacts, she cut her teeth on *Heartsong*, a new play by Arthur Laurents, even investing her own money in the project. The play failed in tryouts but proved to Selznick that producing plays, however difficult, might be easier than life with David.

Selznick's second project, Tennessee Williams' masterpiece *A Streetcar Named Desire*, opened on December 3, 1947, and ran for 855 performances. Directed by Elia Kazan and starring *Jessica Tandy, Marlon Brando, *Kim Hunter and Karl Malden, the play also won every major honor, including the Pulitzer Prize, the Donaldson Award, and the New York Drama Critics' Award. Selznick, now on sure footing, went on to produce *Bell, Book and Candle* (1950), *Flight into Egypt* (1952), *The Chalk Garden* (with Irving Schneider, 1955), and *The Complaisant Lover* (in association with H.M. Tennent, Donald Albery and F.E.S. Plays, 1961). After turning down John Osborne's *Look Back in Anger* and ◀ Shelagh Delaney's *A Taste of Honey*, she decided that it was time to retire from the theater. "Now I wanted options and, luckily, I could afford them," she wrote. "Once

again I was quitting while I was ahead, and with my reputation intact."

Selznick spent her later years in a sprawling home ("Imspond") two miles from the Connecticut border, sharing her life with a man whose name she may have revealed only to her former husband. Her friendship with David endured until his death in 1965. She died in 1990, age 80.

**SOURCES:**

McGill, Raymond D., ed. *Notable Names in the American Theatre*. Clifton, NJ: James T. White, 1976.

Selznick, Irene Mayer. *A Private View*. NY: Alfred A. Knopf, 1983.

Wilmeth, Don B., and Tice L. Miller, eds. *Cambridge Guide to American Theatre*. Cambridge, Eng.: Cambridge University Press, 1993.

**Barbara Morgan**,
Melrose, Massachusetts

# Sembrich, Marcella (1858–1935)

*Polish-born American lyric soprano. Name variations: Marcella Sembrich-Kochanska. Born Praxede Marcelline Kochanska (also seen as Prakseda Marcelina Kochanska, while some sources cite Kadanska) in Wisniewczyk, Galicia (part of Austrian Poland), on February 15, 1858; died in New York on January 11, 1935; one of 13 children of Casimir Kochanski (a teacher and instrumentalist) and Juliana (Sembrich) Kochanska; studied with Wilhelm Stengel at the Lemberg (Lvov) Conservatory, with Viktor Rokitansky in Vienna, and with G.B. Lamperti in Milan; married Wilhelm Stengel (a piano teacher and later her manager), on May 5, 1877 (died 1917); children: sons Marcel (died in infancy) and William Marcel, and two stepsons.*

*Debuted in Athens as Elvira in Bellini's I puritani (1877), Covent Garden as Lucia (1880), Metropolitan Opera as Lucia (1883); was department head at the Curtis Institute of Music in Philadelphia and at the Juilliard School in New York.*

Ranked with operatic sopranos *Adelina Patti, *Nellie Melba, and *Christine Nilsson, Marcella Sembrich was not only a brilliant singer, but excelled at the piano and violin as well. At a benefit concert in New York in 1884, she amazed the audience by singing a selection from Giovanni Paisiello's *Il barbiere di Siviglia*, playing a movement from a concerto by Charles-Auguste de Bériot on the violin, and, as an encore, performing a mazurka by Frédéric Chopin on the piano. Following her retirement from the stage in 1924, she taught in the vocal departments of the Juilliard School in New York and

◀
**Delaney, Shelagh.** See Littlewood, Joan for sidebar.

the Curtis Institute in Philadelphia, teaching several of her successors, including **Sophie Braslau**, *****Alma Gluck**, and *****Maria Jeritza**.

Sembrich, one of 13 children, was born Praxede Marcelline Kochanska in 1858, in a part of Austrian Poland then known as Wisniewczyk, Galicia, the daughter of Casimir Kochanski and **Juliana Sembrich Kochanska**. Casimir, a talented musician in his own right, provided for his large family by giving music lessons and occasionally performing. He instructed Marcella on the piano when she was four, and she added violin lessons at six. She also played in the family quartet and copied music for long hours, which caused her to develop vision problems later in life. When Casimir took the position of village organist in Bolechów and moved the family there, Sembrich, under the patronage of one of the townspeople, began studying piano with Wilhelm Stengel at the conservatory at Lemberg. She also began working on harmony with Charles Mikuli and sang in the conservatory chorus.

At age 16, Sembrich was recommended to Julius Epstein in Vienna, for whom she auditioned on the violin and also sang. Recognizing that Marcella had a beautiful voice, Epstein sent her to the great singer *****Mathilde Marchesi** for further evaluation. Marchesi confirmed his observations and Sembrich began voice lessons with Victor Rokitansky at the Vienna Conservatory. While in Vienna, she had the opportunity to play and sing for Franz Liszt who encouraged her by telling her that her voice was her greatest gift. She was further inspired by a performance of Adelina Patti, to whom she would later be compared.

In 1875, Sembrich went to Milan to study with Giovanni Lamperti and his father Francesco. On May 5, 1877, she married her former teacher, Wilhelm Stengel, a widower with two sons, who also became her manager. After a honeymoon in Athens, she made her operatic debut there in June, singing Elvira in *I puritani*. At the end of her engagement, which included performances in *Lucia di Lammermoor* and *Dinorah*, she returned to Vienna to work on her German repertoire with Richard Lewy and to study dramatic interpretation with the actress **Marie Seebach**.

Marcella adopted the professional name of Sembrich (her mother's maiden name) for her German debut at the Saxon Royal Opera in Dresden in 1878, singing the role of Lucia. Her success was such that she stayed in Dresden for two years, after which she signed a five-year contract with the Royal Italian Opera in London, making her debut at Covent Garden on June 12, 1880, again as Lucia. Sembrich subsequently performed in Scandinavia, France, Spain, Austria, and Russia, where she appeared at the Winter Palace of Tsar Alexander II in St. Petersburg. In 1881, she shared a command performance at Buckingham Palace with her idol Adelina Patti.

Sembrich made her American debut singing *Lucia di Lammermoor* at the Metropolitan Opera in New York during its premiere season in October 1883. That year, she appeared in 55 performances there, singing 11 different roles. The Metropolitan, however, failed to make money during that first season and brought in Leopold Damrosch, who ushered in a long stretch of Wagnerian operas. Sembrich's florid Italian style did not lend itself to the German master, and she returned to Europe, performing in Austria, Germany, France, Russia and Scandinavia. During these years, she and her husband made their home in Dresden, where Sembrich gave birth to two sons: Marcel, who died in infancy, and William Marcel.

Sembrich returned to New York in 1897, reappearing with the Metropolitan on November 30, 1898, as Rosina in *The Barber of Seville*. She remained at the Met for the next ten years, until her retirement in 1908. During that time, she became known for her temperament as well as for her bel canto style of beautiful sustained tones. During one widely publicized incident, she stormed offstage during a Chicago performance when she was upstaged by *****Fritzi Scheff** in *The Magic Flute*; in another, she refused to continue with a performance of *La Traviata* when she was informed that special guest Prince Henry of Prussia had left the premises with his entourage. Despite her occasional outbursts, the singer received $1,000 per performance at the height of her career. To keep her voice in peak condition, she adhered to a strict regimen that included five-mile walks and long periods of silence. She was said to be so sensitive about a cast in one of her eyes that all of her portraits were done in profile.

*Marcella Sembrich*

Sembrich chose her roles carefully. She undertook few Wagnerian roles, realizing that hers was not the voice for Wagner. Instead, she sang Susanna, Zerlina, Lucia, and Rosina, Queen of the Night, Gilda, Violetta, and Mimi. She was a favorite not only with audiences but also with fellow singers: Patti, Nilsson, Melba, *Emma Albani, *Etelka Gerster, and *Emma Calvé were devoted friends on stage and off. Sembrich sang in Columbia's Grand Opera Series of recordings made in 1903, a historic enterprise. She later recorded extensively for Victor Talking Machine, a popular and profitable series.

Following her retirement from the Metropolitan, Sembrich embarked on a concert career which lasted until 1917. Appearing on stage in Paris gowns and paste copies of her famous jewels, she performed a broad repertoire that included Brahms, Schumann, and the French and Italian composers, as well as the moderns Debussy and Ravel. After her husband's death in 1917, Sembrich stopped performing, devoting herself instead to teaching. Although she spent much of her time in New York, and built a summer retreat on Lake George at Bolton, New York, she never became an American citizen. She died from emphysema and heart disease in 1935 and was buried in the Stengel family mausoleum in Dresden.

SOURCES:

Arnim, G. *Marcella Sembrich und Herr Prof. Julius Hey.* Leipzig, 1898.

James, Edward T., ed. *Notable American Women, 1607–1950.* Cambridge, MA: The Belknap Press of Harvard University, 1971.

Owen, H.G. *A Recollection of Marcella Sembrich.* New York, 1950.

Warrack, John, and Ewan West. *Oxford Dictionary of Opera.* Oxford: Oxford University Press, 1992.

**Barbara Morgan**,<br>Melrose, Massachusetts

# Semenova, Ekaterina (1786–1849)

*Russian actress. Born in 1786; died in 1849; studied at St. Petersburg Theater School; married Prince Ivan Gagarin, in 1826.*

Born in 1786, Ekaterina Semenova made her stage debut at age 17 after studying with the Russian actor Dmitrevsky at the St. Petersburg Theater School. In later life, she would be coached by the poet Gnedich and by playwright and theater director Prince Sharkovsky. An extremely beautiful woman, Semenova was known for her powerful voice and impassioned acting, particularly in classics by Shakespeare, Racine, Schiller, and Ozerov. In the early 1800s, when

celebrated French actress *Marguerite J. Georges (Mlle George) drew raves for her performances in Russia, Semenova became distraught from jealousy. Their rivalry became the source of much publicity, and in 1820, feeling she had been pushed from the pinnacle of success, Semenova briefly retired. Two years later, she returned to acting, and in 1823 was widely praised for her performance in *Phèdre*. She went into semi-retirement, confining herself to roles in private theaters in St. Petersburg and Moscow, after her marriage to Prince Ivan Gagarin in 1826. Semenova was lauded in several of Pushkin's poems.

SOURCES:

Uglow, Jennifer S., comp. and ed. *The International Dictionary of Women's Biography.* NY: Continuum, 1982.

**Gloria Cooksey**, freelance writer,<br>Sacramento, California

# Semiramide (fl. 8th c. BCE).

*See Sammuramat.*

# Semiramis (fl. 8th c. BCE).

*See Sammuramat.*

# Semiramis of the North.

*See Margaret I of Denmark (1353–1412).*

# Semple, Ellen Churchill
## (1863–1932)

*American geographer and educator. Born on January 8, 1863, in Louisville, Kentucky; died on May 8, 1932, in West Palm Beach, Florida; daughter of Alexander Bonner Semple (a merchant) and Emerine (Price) Semple; Vassar College, B.A., 1882, M.A., 1891; studied at the University of Leipzig, 1891–92, 1895.*

*Founded Semple Collegiate School for Girls (1893); published* Influences of Geographical Environment on the Basis of Ratzel's System of Anthropo-geography *(1911); received the Cullum Medal of the American Geographical Society (1914); served as president of the Association of American Geographers (1921); received an honorary LL.D. degree from the University of Kentucky (1923), and the gold medal of the Geographic Society of Chicago (1932).*

*Selected writings:* American History and Its Geographic Conditions *(1903);* Influences of Geographic Environment on the Basis of Ratzel's System of Anthropo-geography *(1911);* The Geography of the Mediterranean Region: Its Relation to Ancient History *(1931).*

Born in 1863 in Louisville, Kentucky, Ellen Churchill Semple was the youngest of five siblings. Her father Alexander Semple, a merchant, died when she was 12 years old, but her mother **Emerine Price Semple** saw to it that her children were well educated, and Ellen received her early schooling from private tutors. In emulation of an older sister, she then enrolled at Vassar College, from which she graduated in 1882 as valedictorian of her class. Semple taught school in her hometown of Louisville for the next several years, while expanding her education through wide-ranging reading of history and economics.

Around 1887, while traveling with her mother in Europe, Semple was exposed for the first time to Friedrich Ratzel's theories of anthropogeography—the effect of the physical environment on human societies. Quickly enamored with his teachings, she continued her studies with renewed vigor upon her return home. In 1891, she completed a written examination from Vassar and received a master's degree. Not long after, armed with her degree, Semple traveled to Germany to study with Ratzel at the University of Leipzig. The school did not admit women students, but she was permitted to audit his classes (segregated by seating from the male students) and soon became one of his best students. His theories, particularly that human societies in similar environments will develop in similar patterns, would be a major influence on her thinking. Semple and Ratzel also developed a close friendship, and she spent much time with his family.

Following her return to the United States, in 1893 Semple and one of her sisters founded Semple Collegiate School for Girls in Louisville. She taught history there until 1895, when she revisited Leipzig to engage in further study. By 1897, she had published her first scholarly article, "The Influence of the Appalachian Barrier upon Colonial History," in the *Journal of School Geography*.

Semple did anthropogeographic research in 1901, traveling by horseback in the backwoods of Kentucky and frequently staying with local inhabitants. The publication that June in *Geographical Journal* of her observations and theories, "The Anglo-Saxons of the Kentucky Mountains," was well received and earned her a scholarly reputation. She was thereafter invited to read her writings at the Geographical Congress in Washington, D.C., and before the Royal Geographical Society in London. Semple's first book-length manuscript, *American History and Its Geographic Conditions*, was published in 1903. In that work, which was occasionally adopted as a college textbook, she presented her ideas concerning the correlation between U.S. expansion and the geographical environment of North America. In 1911, she documented her

studies in Leipzig in her most significant work, *Influences of Geographic Environment, on the Basis of Ratzel's System of Anthropo-Geography*. Semple developed the volume partly at the urging of Ratzel and partly to incorporate her own interpretations on the topics, and the result was far more than simply a description of her mentor's theories.

The following year, Semple toured the world for 18 months, visiting Japan, Mongolia, Greece, England, and the Mediterranean. This latter country would provide the basis for her last book, the fruit of 20 years' research, *The Geography of the Mediterranean: Its Relation to Ancient History*, published in 1931. Semple also taught at a number of major universities. In 1905 and 1912, she conducted a summer course at Oxford University, and from 1906 to 1924 she taught alternate years at the University of Chicago. She also taught at Wellesley College in 1914–15, at the University of Colorado in 1916, and at Columbia University in 1918. Three years later, she accepted a post as lecturer at Clark University in Worcester, Massachusetts. She remained at Clark until 1932, from 1923 as a professor of anthropogeography. As well, in the aftermath of World War I, Semple consulted for "The Inquiry," a mission convened to prepare for the peace talks at Versailles.

Semple's work was fundamental in establishing geography as a field of university study in the 20th century. The main gist of her theories—the "deterministic" approach, or the idea that societies cannot help but be shaped by their surroundings in a certain way—was replaced in her own lifetime by the "antideterministic" school of geographical thought, which holds rather that humankind can respond to environment in any number of ways, but her publications and scholarly methods helped to turn the field into a serious academic discipline. Semple received the Cullum Medal of the American Geographical Society in 1914, and in 1921 she was the first woman to be elected president of the Association of American Geographers. The University of Kentucky gave her an honorary LL.D. degree in 1923, and she received the gold medal of the Geographic Society of Chicago in 1932.

Semple, who was an asthmatic, suffered a severe heart attack in 1929, but continued to teach and completed her last book two years later. She died in West Palm Beach, Florida, of sepsis caused by a lung abscess, on May 8, 1932.

**SOURCES:**

Bailey, Brooke. *The Remarkable Lives of 100 Women Healers and Scientists.* Holbrook, MA: Bob Adams, 1994.

James, Edward T., ed. *Notable American Women, 1607–1950*. Cambridge, MA: The Belknap Press of Harvard University, 1971.

McHenry, Robert, ed. *Famous American Women*. NY: Dover, 1980.

Ogilvie, Marilyn Bailey. *Women in Science: Antiquity through the Nineteenth Century*. Cambridge, MA: MIT Press, 1986.

Read, Phyllis J., and Bernard L. Witlieb. *The Book of Women's Firsts*. NY: Random House, 1992.

**Gloria Cooksey**, freelance writer,
Sacramento, California

## Semple, Letitia Tyler (1821–1907).

*See Tyler, Letitia for sidebar.*

## Semple McPherson, Aimee (1890–1944).

*See McPherson, Aimee Semple.*

## Sempronia (c. 168 BCE–?).

*See Cornelia for sidebar.*

## Sempronia (fl. 2nd–1st c. BCE)

*Roman noblewoman. Flourished between the 1st and 2nd centuries BCE; married Marcus Fulvius Bambalio; children: Fulvia (c. 85/80–40 BCE).*

There is some confusion between this Sempronia, the mother of *Fulvia, and the Sempronia in the entry below. Though absolute certainty is impossible, they seem to be two different women. The name was quite common, and women of their class would have been politically active. Only Erich Gruen really comes down on the issue. In his book *The Last Generation of the Roman Republic*, Gruen lists them as separate women.

## Sempronia (fl. 2nd–1st c. BCE)

*Roman noblewoman, thought to have been the first woman in history to appear in a Roman court, who played a role in the political upheaval of the times when she supported the Catiline. Flourished between the 2nd and 1st century BCE; daughter of Gaius Sempronius Tuditanus; granddaughter of Gaius Sempronius Tuditanus (who had served as consul—the highest political office in the Roman Republic—in 129 BCE and had written one of the earliest works on Roman law); married Decimus Junius Brutus, a Roman consul (r. 77 BCE); married D. Junius Silanus, a Roman consul (r. 62 BCE); children: (first marriage) mother or stepmother of Decimus Junius Brutus Albinus.*

A member of a noble plebeian family, Sempronia was probably the daughter of Gaius Sem-

pronius Tuditanus who reached the consulship (Rome's highest annually elected office) in 129. The Senate gave Sempronius Tuditanus the judicial authority associated with the agrarian commission established in 133 by his kinsman, Tiberius Sempronius Gracchus. This commission had been established to redistribute public land to the Roman poor, both to make them eligible again to serve in the Roman army (at the time, military service required the possession of land) and to get them out of Rome, where they were generally unemployed and willing to sell their collective vote at election time to the highest political bidder. Thus, perhaps somewhat naively, Tiberius Gracchus intended both to strengthen the Roman army and to lessen political corruption by his reform. The public land to be redistributed, however, had long been leased at well below market rates by Rome's richest citizens, including many among the political elite. As resistance to the reform grew among those in possession of the land, so did Tiberius Gracchus' hardball tactics in an effort to ensure its passage. Political passions eventually ignited and Tiberius Gracchus was murdered, thus sparking what would amount to four generations of civil war. Whether he sided with the political backlash against the redistribution of land, or whether he realized that it would be dangerous to assume the political legacy of his martyred relative, Tuditanus refused to exercise the authority granted by the Senate. This effectively incapacitated the land commission for several years and outraged the champions of Rome's poor. Regardless, during his consulship Tuditanus went to Illyria where he successfully campaigned, thereby earning a triumph.

Born into a prominent family at a time of acute unrest, Sempronia remained near the political epicenter of the crisis-wrecked Republic for her entire life. Her husband Decimus Junius Brutus was much older than she was and had been married before their union. He held the consulship in 77, in the wake of the notorious dictatorship of Lucius Cornelius Sulla, again a highly volatile period in Roman history. Sempronia was either the mother or stepmother of Decimus Junius Brutus Albinus, who began his career as an adherent of Julius Caesar. This son or stepson served with distinction under Caesar both during the conquest of Transalpine Gaul and during Caesar's war against Gaius Pompeius Magnus which followed, winning major naval victories for Caesar in 56 and 49. So highly regarded was Brutus Albinus that Caesar elevated him to the post of governor in Gaul where he suppressed a native rebellion in 46. Nevertheless, like many others Brutus Albinus grew fearful of Caesar's emerging imperiousness and was among those who participated in Caesar's assassination (44) even though the dictator had intended that Brutus Albinus would serve as consul in 42. (Brutus Albinus is not to be confused with Marcus Junius Brutus, the leader of Caesar's assassins.) Brutus Albinus became ensnared in the civil wars that burst forth anew after Caesar's death, and eventually was himself murdered by Marc Antony in Gaul in 43.

Politics, however, was not merely a masculine prerogative in Sempronia's family. Sempronia's most nefarious flirtation with public affairs came during the 60s BCE when she appears to have favored the cause of Lucius Sergius Catilina, known as Catiline. Catiline was the scion of a down-and-out patrician house whose lack of wealth threatened to deny him the rapid political rise he thought was due his station. Early in his career he had been in the service of Sulla and was involved with that dictator's proscriptions, but Catiline's most notorious deportment began with his election to the office of praetor in 68. After serving in Rome, Catiline was made the pro-praetor of Africa for two years where he was so flagrant in extorting money from the locals (many provincial officials involved themselves in such activities, but with less greed and more discretion) that he was criminally indicted upon his return home. With a legal cloud hanging over his head, Catiline was unable to fulfill his dream of running for the consulship for both 65 and 64. Eventually he was acquitted, but many thought only through bribery. Rumor also had it that he had plotted with political radicals against those who were frustrating his ascent. His reputation besmirched, the final straw for Catiline came when he was defeated in his run for the consulship of 63 by Marcus Tullius Cicero. Humiliated by the preferment of a political newcomer, Catiline attempted to reposition himself as the champion of the poor and of those who had lost property in the civil conflicts since the time of Tiberius Gracchus. This constituency had legitimate grievances and was in need of a respectable promoter. Catiline, however, was not that man, and was again defeated when he ran for the consulship of 62. Obtaining Rome's highest office legitimately appeared hopeless: Catiline resigned himself to conspiracy and armed insurrection. His plans, however, were discovered by Cicero in November 63, and all came to nought when Catiline died in battle the following January.

The historian Sallust testifies that Sempronia was an adherent of Catiline and that at least once, when her husband was away from Rome, she allowed him and his co-conspirators to use her house close to the forum for their plotting. She is also accused of agitating among slaves on Catiline's behalf, of having fires set throughout Rome, of seducing men to Catiline's cause, and of murdering others who could not be so won over. Sallust further alleges that she committed other unnamed crimes; that although she prostituted herself, she lived so extravagantly that she amassed huge debts; that she was so passionate about sex that she approached men on the issue as much as they did her; that she thought of nothing more infrequently than modesty and chastity; that she knew more about the playing of the lyre and of dancing than a proper woman should; that she broke promises and repudiated debts; and that in all of these things, as she got older, she went from bad to worse. Despite his unflattering portrait of Sempronia, Sallust admits that she was fortunate in her birth, her beauty, her marriage, and her children. The historian also concedes that she was well educated, wrote good poetry, had a keen wit, made good conversation, had considerable charm, and that she was a woman of daring who threw herself into the causes she supported.

In fact, the two faces of Sempronia presented by Sallust are not at all difficult to reconcile, once one understands that Sallust was a supporter of the Caesar who fell victim to the assassination plot in which Brutus Albinus was a prominent member, and that Sallust wrote his account of the Catilinarian conspiracy after Caesar's murder. Thus, Sallust's characterization of Sempronia has to be read with Brutus Albinus' most notorious act in mind. That Sempronia was a well-educated model of her gender and station should be assumed. That she was fairly liberated in her manners should also be taken for granted, although Sallust's litany of her vices cannot be taken at face value, for it is difficult to see how she could have been favored in her husband and her children if she wallowed in dissipation. It was not uncommon for both men and women of Sempronia's generation and class to engage in extramarital affairs, and these occasionally provided rivals with salacious fodder for political attacks. Open licentiousness, however, was rare among the political class, for a base reputation in a candidate (or his wife, or mother) adversely affected one at the polls, as, indeed, it did Catiline himself. Regardless, since members of Sempronia's family had a track record of concern for Rome's poor, it is probably true she was attracted to Catiline at least when he began to champion the downtrodden. That she canvassed on his behalf is also not unlikely, for, even though women could not hold public office, those of Sempronia's status during the late Republic were thoroughly political creatures and helped to promote the ideologies and interests of their family's faction. How long Catiline retained Sempronia's support, however, is another matter, for it is one thing to be politically concerned and active, and another to abet armed rebellion. Since Sempronia's son or stepson remained a political force for 20 years after Catiline's conspiracy, it is likely that she had severed her ties with Catiline by the time his "crusade" devolved into open treason.

**William Greenwalt,**
Associate Professor of Classical History,
Santa Clara University, Santa Clara, California

## Sempronia (c. 75 BCE–after 16 CE).

*See Scribonia.*

## Senena (fl. 1200s)

*Lady of Lleyn. Flourished around the 1200s; married Gruffydd, Lord of Lleyn (son of Llywelyn the Great [1173–1240], Ruler of All Wales); children: five, including Llywelyn III the Last, prince of Wales.*

## Senesch, Hannah (1921–1944).

*See Senesh, Hannah.*

## Senesh, Hannah (1921–1944)

*Israel's national hero who undertook a parachute mission to help rescue Jews in her native Hungary and was captured, tortured, and executed by the Nazis. Name variations: Anna ("Anikó") Szenes (1921–39); Chana Szenes (1939–44); or Hannah Senesh or Senesch. Born Anna Szenes in Budapest, Hungary, on July 17, 1921; executed in Budapest on November 7, 1944; buried in Israel's Cemetery of Heroes; daughter of Katalin, Katherine, or Kató (Salzberger) Szenes and Béla (r.n. Schlesinger) Szenes (a writer); never married; no children.*

*Became a Zionist (1938); moved to Eretz Israel (1939); attended Agricultural School in Nahalal (1939–41); joined Sedot Yam ([Sdot-Yam], Fields of the Sea) kibbutz (1941–44); parachuted into Yugoslavia (March 13, 1944); captured by Germans and Hungarians (June 1944); stood trial for treason (October 1944).*

Hannah Senesh was born Anna Szenes, and called Anikó, in Budapest, Hungary, on July 17, 1921. Her father Béla Szenes, a well-known humorist and patron of the cultural world of café society, had written novels, poems, and a col-

umn under the name "The Coalman" for the Sunday magazine section of *Pesti Hirlap*, but was best known for his plays: eight of them had been enormous hits at the Comedy Theater of Budapest. In May 1927, six years after Hannah's birth, he died of heart failure in his sleep. He was 33. Her mother ✥➤ **Katalin Szenes** never remarried, but kept a comfortable home for Hannah and her brother Gyuri (George) who was a year older. At age seven, Hannah began writing and won a number of school prizes for her poems and translations. From age 13 on, she kept a fairly regular diary.

From the end of World War I, anti-Semitism had been on the rise in Hungary, and anti-Jewish legislation, including the *numerus clausus* which restricted the number of Jews attending Hungarian universities, was frequently put forth for parliamentary consideration. Because of the climate of the times and a desire to assimilate into Hungarian society, Béla had changed his name from the Jewish Schlesinger to the more Hungarian Szenes. The family did not, however, convert to Christianity; Jewish high holidays were still observed.

In May 1937, while attending Bármadas, a private Protestant school for girls, 16-year-old Hannah had her first serious bout with the growing anti-Semitism. Because of her high academic ranking (she was an outstanding student who would graduate *summa cum laude*) and her famous father, she had felt welcomed there, until she was elected secretary of the school's literary society by her class, the 7th form. Those in the 8th form met secretly in protest and resurrected an old rule: officers of school societies must be Protestant. Unaware, Hannah arrived for her first meeting and was told there would be a new election. She was mortified. "It is so hard to find a way out of this without humiliation or false pride, that won't be seen as a retreat, or be considered pushy," she wrote in her diary. "One has to be so careful with every move, because each fault becomes stereotyped."

From then on, Senesh felt apart from others. Not only did she withdraw from the literary society, but at 17 she became a Zionist, joining the movement that was advocating a Jewish state in Palestine. Hungary was no longer a welcoming home; Eretz Israel (the land of Israel) beckoned. Determined to be a prime candidate for emigration, Senesh studied Hebrew and agriculture and applied to agricultural school in Nahalal, near Haifa. It was 1939, the eve of World War II, and European borders were closing rapidly. That September, as Hitler's minions marched into Poland, the 18-year-old Senesh left Budapest for

Jewish Palestine, sad to leave behind her closest friend and ally, her mother Katalin. Hannah would later learn that Gyuri, who was attending textile school in Lyons, France, had also become a Zionist and planned to follow her as soon as he completed his studies.

Arriving in Haifa, Senesh took the bus to Nahalal, a *moshav* (cooperative) settlement of less than a 1,000 people, where she entered the Agricultural School for Girls. Founded in 1926 and supported by the Women's International Zionist Organization (WIZO) and the Canadian Hadassah, the agricultural school was run by **Chana Meisel**, a pioneer in training women in agriculture. About 150 girls studied there in a two-year program. Senesh quickly convinced her roommates—one from Bulgaria, one from Poland—to speak only in Hebrew, the better to learn the language of their new country. Working for months in the orchards, dairy, and chicken coop, Senesh found she still needed an outlet for her restless mind and began to tutor other students in chemistry. She would later write a play, *The Violin*, set in a girls' agricultural school.

Senesh worked hard, studied hard, and seemed to make a deep impression on all who came in contact with her. The young girl with light brown hair and blue eyes was remarkably self-assured. Her major weakness was an ineptitude with dishcloth and broom. Though she believed in physical labor, Senesh found herself locked in inward debate. Maybe her mother was right; maybe she should have enrolled in the Hebrew University. Maybe it was wrong not to use her natural talents. But pioneers cultivated the land, didn't they? Throughout her diaries, she argued with herself time after time.

Two years later, having completed the agricultural course, Senesh joined with others to found kibbutz Sedot Yam (Fields of the Sea) near the Roman ruins of the port of Caesarea on the Mediterranean seashore, between Haifa and Tel Aviv. Senesh was put in charge of the food supplies, but again something felt wrong to her. "I can't rid myself of the thought that I'm wasting years that should be spent learning, developing further," she wrote in her diary. "If I could become a real expert at something, I would help the kibbutz and find greater satisfaction for myself at the same time. . . . But that's a lie—another voice says. I am learning all the time—gaining experience of life." Senesh spent her entire four years in Israel in communal living, yet she always felt lonely, separate, and apart.

And the world outside kept intruding. When Hungary joined the German-Italian Axis

### Szenes, Katalin (b. 1899)

***Mother of Hannah Senesh.*** *Name variations: Catherine, Kató, Catalin Szenes; Katalin Senesh. Born Katalin Salzberger, the third of four daughters, in 1899; married Béla (r.n. Schlesinger) Szenes (a writer); children: Hannah Senesh (1921–1944); Gyuri (George, b. 1920).*

In 1945, after a hair-raising flight from a Nazi death march and a successful search for the grave of her daughter, Katalin Szenes narrowly made it through the now-closing borders of the new occupier of Hungary, the Russians. Landing in Palestine by way of Rumania, she began searching for her son and was advised to seek out the Jewish Agency in Jerusalem. David Ben-Gurion, at that time the head of the agency, was in a meeting when she arrived. A note was sent in and Ben-Gurion rose: "The mother of Hannah Senesh is outside," he said. "I must greet this lady." Eventually reunited with her son, Katalin Szenes lived at Kibbutz Maagan on the Sea of Galilee for a time, then worked in a nursery until her retirement.

in 1940, her father's books had been banned, depriving her mother of her income from royalties. Now letters from her mother rarely reached her. Germany's invasion of France, the fall of Paris, and the deportation of Jews in the free zone in 1942 had hastened Gyuri's departure from France. With false papers, he had made his way to Palestine by way of Spain, but, unknown to Hannah, had been intercepted by the Spanish.

"Sometimes I feel like one who has been sent . . . to perform a mission," wrote Senesh in her diary. "What this mission is, is not clear to me." She resolved to go to Hungary, bring her mother out, and organize youth emigration to Palestine. The years of confusion evaporated the instant she made her decision; the task seemed clear. She soon learned of a Haganah mission, backed by British intelligence, to drop commandos into Central Europe; they were looking for people who spoke Hungarian and were familiar with the other Central European countries—Slovakia, Yugoslavia, Rumania. The British intent was to rescue Allied airmen shot down over Central Europe; the Haganah hoped to also rescue Jews. Senesh volunteered for military service.

Her friends urged her not to go. They were convinced that a 22-year-old girl, formerly from a comfortable home in Hungary, could not withstand interrogation by the Gestapo. They warned her that she'd be a liability on the mission, the only woman among 30 Jewish commandos, parachuting into dangerous territory for the RAF. While living on the kibbutz, she began attending monthlong seminars in Haifa. As the training continued throughout 1943, Senesh's loneliness persisted, this time with her fellow soldiers. Emphasis was on weaponry, physical fitness, discipline, teamwork, patrols, marches, ambushes, infiltration, searches, and guerrilla tactics.

On the last day of January 1944, Gyuri arrived in Palestine, having spent nine months in a Spanish prison. Their reunion was brief, as Hannah, with basic training completed, left two days later for more intensive training under the British in Cairo, Egypt. There, the Jewish commandos practiced parachute jumps and learned the tricks of espionage: they studied Morse code, deconstructed and reconstructed wireless transmitters, translated ciphers, and forged documents. They were versed in what type of torture to expect if caught and how to give misinformation. Hannah Senesh was now a radio officer under British command, wearing the uniform of the British army.

*Blessed is the match consumed in kindling flame.*

—Hannah Senesh

There was disagreement between the Haganah and British Intelligence as to where to execute the drop. Hungary, though still with the Axis, was beginning to pull away from Germany, but the country had no support group to welcome paratroopers, whereas Yugoslavia had a strong partisan force. Yugoslavia was a better choice for Britain's interests but far more dangerous for Jews; most of the Jews of Yugoslavia had been liquidated. To Hannah's distress, the British won the argument. The commandos would enter Central Europe by way of Yugoslavia. Meanwhile, the British and Haganah agreed to get her mother Katalin out of Hungary.

With four other members, Senesh left Egypt in early March for the liberated town of Bari in southern Italy. On the night of March 13, 1944, they flew out from Brindisi and headed for Yugoslavia. That night "she was fearless," wrote her fellow commando Reuven Dafne. But the winds were strong and, on her jump, she drifted hundreds of yards off course, landing in a giant pine. After cutting herself loose, she was greeted by partisans, who were awed that the British had sent such a young girl to help. Her five-member group was escorted to a permanent partisan hideout. As far as the Yugoslavian partisans knew, the English-speaking commandos were British subjects on a British mission. For safety,

Hannah and her compatriots were to hide their nationality and their language.

On March 19, six days after their drop, they heard over the wireless that Germany had taken over Hungary with "friendly" troops. The mission's crafted plans, founded on the ease of entering Hungary, were now useless. To the group's surprise, the usually stoical Senesh broke down in tears. They assured her that, by now, her mother was probably out, but that was not the reason for her tears. "What are the Nazis going to do to the one million Jews there?" she asked. "While we're just sitting here, doing nothing."

Her fears would be more than realized. Hungary had been the only nation left in Central Europe where Jews were still permitted to mingle with Aryans. The country had become a haven for Jewish refugees from France, Poland, and Czechoslovakia. While Senesh sat helplessly across the border, Adolf Eichmann arrived in Budapest to liquidate Hungary's Jews. Wrote Katalin: "All the humiliating, discriminatory, annihilating laws it had taken the Nazis years to institute in other countries were put into effect and enforced in Hungary with fantastic speed." By April, all the Jews in the provinces were forced into detention camps; in May, deportations to Auschwitz began, and 12,000 Hungarian Jews were murdered each day. By July, a German representative would declare that the Hungarian countryside was free of its 437,402 Jews. They could now direct their attention to Budapest and the other cities.

During this time, Senesh and her fellow commandos pursued sabotage operations, blowing up trains, ambushing small patrols and rescuing shot-down American pilots. Wrote Dafne:

> A great number of people—partisans and civilians—were fascinated by Hannah, the young British officer smart in her army uniform, pistol strapped to her waist. . . . They had heard about her before our arrival, and she became something of a legend. When she encountered members of the high command she aroused their respect, and although the Yugoslavs had taken women into the army on an equal footing, and partisan women marched into battle alongside the men, there was a special, mysterious quality about Hannah which excited their wonder and respect.

Though her orders were to stay with the partisans in Yugoslavia, Senesh was determined to enter Hungary. She became obsessed, convinced their work was useless. The commandos tried to convince her that going into Hungary was a suicide mission; one small group could do very little. She disagreed. One small group, she

said, could boost morale. One small Jewish group might give Hungary's Jews the spark to defend themselves. She finally induced them to join her, and the Jewish commandos headed for the border, uniting with other partisans in acts of sabotage along the way.

They arrived at the border the first week in June. Not yet comfortable with the arrangements for entering Hungary, Dafne wanted to wait a little longer. Senesh's patience had run out. Against all warnings, she convinced three refugees fleeing Hungary to reverse course and return with her to

Budapest. As she left, she handed Dafne a poem, then marched down the road with one last flung "Shalom." Furious at a soldier writing poems instead of studying maps on such an occasion, Dafne threw the crumpled paper away unread. The following morning, regretful, he traversed the area and found the poem:

> Blessed is the match consumed
>    in kindling flame.
> Blessed is the flame that burns
>    in the secret fastness of the heart.
> Blessed is the heart with strength to stop
>    its beating for honor's sake.
> Blessed is the match consumed
>    in kindling flame.

That night, wrote biographer Peter Hay, Senesh and the three others "set out for the Yugoslav-Hungarian border, carrying on their shoulders the sum total of the Allied rescue effort at that moment to save the Jews of Hungary." The next morning, June 9, just across the border, two of them went into a village and were stopped by Germans; one panicked, pulled out a gun, and shot himself. In a short time, Senesh found herself surrounded by 200 Germans; she only had time to stash the wireless and jettison anything that would tip her identity. But they found a headset on the one who had already been captured. Since Senesh had insisted on bringing the wireless, she admitted the headset was hers to save her comrade.

As they were taken by train to Budapest to the military prison on Horthy Miklós Boulevard, Senesh left on a seat a seemingly innocuous book of French lyric poetry. By disposing of it, she could no longer divulge the code words under interrogation by the Hungarians, for they were located throughout the book. "She suffered dreadful tortures, and she didn't want to talk about them," wrote Yoel Palgi, another commando who landed in the same jail:

> The tooth missing from her mouth testified to this. I heard from others how they had tied her; how they had whipped her palms and the soles of her feet; bound her and forced her to sit motionless for hours on end; beat her all over the body until she was black and blue. They asked her one thing, only one thing: what is your radio code.

She never gave them the code or the names of her colleagues, but, convinced that her mother was now safely in Eretz Israel, she admitted who she was.

But Katalin was not in Israel. She was still in Budapest. On June 17, she was packing to move to the obligatory ghetto when a detective arrived from the state police and demanded that she accompany him to the military barracks on Horthy Miklós Boulevard. There, the Hungarian police interrogated a puzzled Katalin as to her daughter's whereabouts and why Hannah had gone to Palestine. Then four men dragged in her daughter. The young woman, barely recognizable, blurted out, "Forgive me, mother!" When Katalin was told to convince her daughter to talk, she refused; she assumed Hannah was withholding information for good reason.

Released, Katalin returned home. A few hours later, she was picked up by the Gestapo and taken to Polizeigefängnis, the German jail, interviewed once again, and put into a cell. Hannah was given three hours to divulge the cipher or her mother would die. For the first time, Senesh wavered. If she told of the book, others would die. If she didn't, her mother, who had not volunteered for this mission, would die. But Senesh "knew suddenly with brilliant clarity," wrote Hay, "that her mother would gladly die rather than see her daughter betray the cause." Once more, Hannah refused to talk.

After more days, more interrogations, a prisoner trusted by the Gestapo whispered to Katalin to look out her window; across the courtyard, her daughter waved from a high narrow window. Morning after morning, they signaled each other. When the same prisoner set up a rendezvous in a bathroom, mother and daughter were alone together for the first time in five years. By now Hannah had won the hardened prison matrons over to her side. With the Allied victories, Hungarians were beginning to change allegiances. Taken out of isolation and put in a cell with others, Senesh promptly added daily exercises and lectures about life in Palestine to her cellmates' routine. Rules were relaxed; mother and daughter met more often. For Hannah, the German interrogations continued, lasting for hours in an attempt to trip her up. But she had not told them she spoke German. Thus, while they translated into Hungarian, she had time to deliberate before answering.

On September 10th, as the increasingly victorious Allies grew closer, soldiers arrived and took Senesh away. Katalin was transported to an internment camp at Kistarcsa two days later. Soon released, she learned that her daughter had been taken to another prison, on Conti Street, to stand trial for treason, and she set out to find a defense attorney. On October 14th, the attorney assured her that there was nothing to worry about: Hannah would get a few years in prison which would quickly be nullified when the war was over, and it would be over soon, for even now the city was being bombarded by the Allies. But on October 15, the extremist right wing of Hungary staged a coup, forcing out the more humanitarian elements of the Hungarian government. Within hours, Eichmann was back and a new batch of anti-Jewish laws were put into effect. Hannah's trial was set for October 28th.

Senesh pleaded not guilty at the trial. She told the judges that she would never betray her country; that they, and other leaders, had betrayed their country by handing it to the Germans. She also warned the Hungarian magistrates that those responsible would pay at war's end. Her speech had a chilling effect on the court. Though she was found guilty, the judges were locked in a dilemma as to the harshness of the sentence. On the one hand, the Allies would arrive any day, and they did not want to have to explain her death. On the other, they were fearful of the Germans who expected the death sentence. So the judges announced that they were postponing the sentencing for eight more days, then fled the country.

That day, as Hannah and her mother passed in the corridor, both were relieved. By the time her sentence was announced, the Allies might be in Budapest. But without Katalin's knowledge, a death sentence was proclaimed and carried out, thought to be an illegal one-man verdict by Captain Julian Simon, the Hungarian judge advocate. On November 7, Hannah Senesh was executed for treason. Eyewitnesses say she resisted the blindfold and faced the firing squad with courage. After the war, Simon found his way to Argentina. When asked at age 74 about the execution of Hannah Senesh, he replied: "If I were to start my life over, I would have chosen again to become a military judge and would have sentenced her to death again." He seemed particularly put out that Senesh had not asked for a pardon, for he said they had given her the chance. Her pride infuriated her accusers.

The story of Hannah Senesh filtered through Hungary and Eretz Israel and into history. Her writings and diaries were preserved and eventually published with the help of Yoel Palgi. When Katalin searched for her grave, a Christian gardener named János Nyíri remembered that she was buried in the martyrs' section of the cemetery in Rákoskeresztúr; he knew, he said, because he had taken it upon himself to bury her there. Her body was disinterred, and Hannah Senesh was enshrined with full military honors overlooking Jerusalem atop Mt. Zion, near the tomb of Zionist leader Theodor Herzl, in Israel's Cemetery for Heroes.

The difference between Hannah Senesh and a million others, notes Peter Hay, is that she acted on her convictions:

> No matter what difficulties were put in her way, no matter what others were doing or not doing, no matter what difference her going would ultimately make. When she felt she had to act, she acted. . . . She understood the symbolic value of her gesture. . . . In a world that has not been kind to armed Jews or to self-willed women, . . . the symbol of a young woman dangling alone from a parachute in the dark night of Europe, while the British who sent her would not bomb the railway lines to Auschwitz, is disturbing.

**SOURCES:**

Cohn, Marta. *Hannah Senesh: Her Life and Diary*. NY: Schocken, 1973 (originally published by Hakibbutz Hameuchad, 1966).

Hay, Peter. *Ordinary Heroes: The Life and Death of Chana Szenes, Israel's National Heroine*. NY: Paragon House, 1989.

**SUGGESTED READING:**

Bar-Zohar, Michael, ed. *Lionhearts: Heroes of Israel*. Warner, 1998.

Masters, Antony. *The Summer That Bled: A Biography of Hannah Senesh*. London: Michael Joseph, 1972.

Palgi, Yoel. ". . . *és jött a fergeteg*" ("*And there came a great wind*"). Tel Aviv: Alexander, 1946.

Syrkin, Marie. *Blessed is the Match*. Philadelphia, PA: Jewish Publications Society of America, 1947.

**RELATED MEDIA:**

*Hannah's War* (148 min), produced by Golan-Globus for the Cannon Group, starring **Ellen Burstyn**, **Maruschka Detmers**, and Anthony Andrews, 1988.

## Senesh, Katalin (b. 1899).

*See Senesh, Hannah for sidebar on Katalin Szenes.*

## September, Anna (1921–1995).

*See Manner, Eeva-Liisa.*

# September, Dulcie (1935–1988)

*South African activist. Born Dulcie Evonne September in 1935 in Cape Town, South Africa; died on March 29, 1988, in Paris; never married; no children.*

Dulcie September was an educator and long-time member of the African National Congress (ANC) whose murder in 1988 shocked both France and South Africa. Born in 1935 and raised in the suburbs of Cape Town, she attended public schools and then Battswood Teacher Training College. She became a teacher in the mid-1950s, at a time when the white South African government had just imposed racial apartheid on the education system. September first became politically involved when she saw how poorly black and mixed-race children were being educated in comparison to white children. She joined the Unity Movement but left when she became dissatisfied with its passive approach to political change for racial equality. She then became a member of the National Liberation Front (NLF) of South Africa. Her covert political activities for the NLF led to her arrest in October 1963; she served a five-year prison term for sabotage and inciting political violence, although she always denied being a supporter of any kind of violence. Banned from teaching after her release, September left to study in London in 1974, where she also worked for the Anti-Apartheid Movement.

Returning to South Africa, September joined the African National Congress, serving first in the ANC headquarters in Lusaka. Her friendly but serious demeanor, her education, and her deep commitment to ending racial injustice led the ANC in 1984 to name her Chief Representative to France, Luxemburg, and Switzerland. She established an ANC office in Paris, where she was subjected to harassment and death threats from supporters of the apartheid government. In 1987, the death threats increased, and although she reported them to the French authorities, saying she believed she was being watched, she was not given police protection. On the morning of March 29, 1988, September was shot five times from behind as she opened the ANC office. She died instantly. No murderer has ever been identified, although many have suspected the Pretoria apartheid government of South Africa of the crime. September's death caused shock and outrage in her homeland and in France. She is now considered a martyr by opponents of apartheid. In 1998, on the tenth anniversary of her death, she was honored in Paris by the naming of a city plaza Dulcie September Square.

**SOURCES:**
Busby, Margaret, ed. *Daughters of Africa: An International Anthology*. NY: Pantheon, 1992.
Obituary, in *Time*. Vol. 131, no. 38. April 11, 1988.

**Laura York**, M.A. in History,
University of California, Riverside, California

## Septimia Zenobia (r. 267–272).

*See Zenobia.*

## Seraïdari, Elly (b. 1899).

*See Nelly.*

# Serao, Matilde (1856–1927)

*Italian journalist and fiction writer who commented extensively on the role of women in the newly unified Italian state.* Name variations: *(pseudonyms) Chiqui-*

ta, Paolo Spada, *and* Gibus. Pronunciation: Ma-TILL-day Ser-OW. *Born on February 26, 1856, in Patras, Greece; died of a heart attack on July 25, 1927, in Naples, Italy; daughter of Francesco Saverio Serao (an exiled Neapolitan journalist) and Paolina Bonelly Serao (a Greek noblewoman); attended Scuola normale (Normal School) in Naples, 1870–73; married Edoardo Scarfoglio, in February 1885 (separated 1902); children: (first marriage) four sons; (with Giuseppe Natale, a Neapolitan lawyer) daughter Eleonora (b. 1904).*

*Returned to Italy from Greece with her mother (1860); worked at state telegraph agency (1874–77); began work as journalist (1876); published first short stories (1878); began friendship with Eleonora Duse (1879); published first novel and moved to Rome to work as a journalist (1881); became editor of Roman newspaper (1882); founded* Corriere di Roma *with Scarfoglio (1885); returned to Naples (1887); founded literary weekly review,* La Settimana *(1902); founded her own newspaper,* Il Giorno *(1904); protested granting of women's suffrage in local Italian elections (1925); lost Nobel Prize in literature to Grazia Deledda (1926); visited by Benito Mussolini (1927).*

*Major works: (fiction)* Cuore infermo *(The Sick Heart, 1881),* Fantasia *(Fantasy, 1882),* La conquista di Roma *(The Conquest of Rome, 1885),* Vita e avventure di Riccardo Joanna *(The Life and Adventures of Riccardo Joanna, 1887),* Il paese di Cuccagna *(The Land of Cockaigne, 1891),* Suor Giovanna della Croce *(Sister Joan of the Holy Cross, 1901),* Il delitto di via Chiatamone *(The Crime of Via Chiatamone, 1908),* La mano tagliata *(The Severed Hand, 1912),* Ella non rispose *(Souls Divided, 1914),* Mors tua *(The Harvest, 1926); (nonfiction)* Il ventre di Napoli *(The Belly of Naples, 1884).*

Matilde Serao, a journalist, novelist, and short-story writer, began her career in the newly founded Italian state of the late 19th century and continued her work into the mid-1920s. Prolific both as a journalist and a fiction writer, she spent almost 50 years in newspaper work, founding four newspapers. She also published almost 40 volumes of fiction, including 30 novels and 100 short stories.

With the exception of a stay in Rome in the 1880s, Serao spent most of her life in the southern Italian metropolis of Naples. She achieved sufficient eminence to become, as **Lucienne Kroha** notes, one of Italy's "best-known public figures," despite the limits placed on women in southern Italy. She was, writes **Alba Amoia**, "Italy's first woman journalist and the prototype of the versatile contemporary woman journalist."

Serao's work, both fiction and nonfiction, features vivid portrayals of Italian society at all levels, but her writing was particularly impassioned when it focused on urban problems, such as those demonstrated in her home city of Naples. Her work also displayed a deep, complex interest in the role of Italian women. She crusaded against the poverty in which they found themselves, especially those in the South. Notes **Laura Salsini**, "Serao uncovers a subterranean, woman-centered world seldom examined by earlier or even contemporary authors."

Serao's fiction is notable for the variety of styles she employed, ranging from realism to romance to Gothic melodrama. Students of her work agree that the fundamental stylistic development in her fiction took place around the turn of the century. Having hitherto written penetrating novels about Italian society in a mainly realistic style, she now shifted to what some consider Gothic, melodramatic potboilers such as *Il delitto di via Chiatamone* (*The Crime of Via Chiatamone*, 1908) and *La mano tagliatta* (*The Severed Hand*, 1912). Anthony Gisolfi has vehemently maintained that Serao's style declined as she came to focus her literary energies on the topic of women in love. **Nancy Harrowitz**, on the other hand, has defended the continuing subtlety that Serao brought to her later writings.

Serao was born in Patras, Greece, on February 26, 1856, the daughter of **Pauline Bonelly Serao** and Francesco Serao, a Neapolitan journalist and Italian patriot. Following the failed Italian revolutions of 1848, Francesco had gone into exile due to his opposition to the ruling Bourbon dynasty in Naples, and he was unable to return during the politically repressive years before the creation of a united Italy. Her mother was a Greek noblewoman. Mother and daughter returned to Italy in 1860 and settled in Naples. They were joined only later by Serao's father. Due to Francesco's indolent ways, the young girl grew up in an atmosphere marked by poverty. Her mother took on the task of supporting the family by giving English and French language lessons in the Serao home.

Matilde showed early signs that she would not fit into the pattern of a future retiring Italian housewife. She refused to learn household tasks like sewing and knitting, and, in her words, grew up "more like a boy." Although at first she resisted learning to read, nonetheless, she soon absorbed a deep literary culture from her mother. Pauline was frequently ill, and while Matilde

tended her mother, the older woman taught the girl to speak French and English. She also taught Matilde to read, using an illustrated edition of Shakespeare, and saw to it that she obtained a secondary education.

Mathilde began attending Scuola normale (Normal School) in Naples in 1870, graduating in 1873 with a teaching degree. Instead of entering that profession, she immediately went to work in the local telegraph office. Teaching and work in a community's telegraph office were typical of the limited and underpaid occupations available for educated young women in post-Unification Italy. In the years from 1874 through 1877, Serao turned her energies in a more unconventional direction: she cultivated skills as a freelance journalist. Her first article appeared in the *Giornale di Napoli* in 1876, and, within a year, she left the telegraph office for good. Subsequently, the death of her mother from tuberculosis in 1879 and the continuing indolence of her father made Matilde the sole provider for her family. These years also saw the beginning of her lifelong friendship with the Italian actress *Eleonora Duse.

*M*atilde *S*erao

In 1881, like so many other talented Italians from the provinces, she made her way to Rome where she found full-time employment as an editor for a prominent Roman newspaper, *Capitan Fracassa*. Ironically, it had been her success as a novelist—her book *Cuore infermo* had been published that year—that brought her this opportunity. She spoke with mixed feelings about the need to leave her home city where one found "too much beauty, too much poetry, too much sea, too much Vesuvius, too much love." Her father accompanied her as she took up residence in the recently united country's capital, and she continued to provide for his needs, including his prolonged vacations.

Serao thrived in the competitive, masculine environment of Roman journalism. One of her fellow contributors to *Capitan Fracassa* was her husband-to-be, Edoardo Scarfoglio, another a Neapolitan journalist who had been drawn to the capital. Her contract required a massive productivity: 2,000 lines of print per month. She provided this with a wide-ranging set of topics, from literary criticism and interior decorating to European international affairs. To disguise her large role in the newspaper's pages, she wrote under a variety of pseudonyms including Chiquita and Paolo Spada. In testimony to her rising stature, she published her first editorial for *Capitan Fracassa* on the newspaper's front page within a few months of her arrival.

Much of her writing focused on life in her native city of Naples, and Serao wrote with the avowed purpose of pushing the national government to address urban problems of unemployment, poor schools, and municipal corruption. The historic but dilapidated and disease-ridden city was struck by a cholera epidemic in 1884, leading Serao to write a series of nine impassioned articles which Amoia has called "descriptions as powerful as Goya engravings." That same year, she and Scarfoglio were married. The union produced four children, all of them boys.

Serao and her husband founded their own newspaper, the *Corriere di Roma*, in 1885. Serao's talents were overshadowed by her husband's insistence on using the publication to settle scores with his literary rivals. Not surprisingly, *Corriere di Roma* closed after only two years of operation. The two changed the scene of their activities in 1887 when Serao, along with her husband, returned to Naples.

In Serao's native city, the couple became the coeditors of two newspapers, *Corriere di Napoli*, which soon failed, and then, in 1892, the more successful *Il Mattino*. *Il Mattino* gained a large following and published the work of such noted authors as Gabriele D'Annunzio. While working at *Corriere di Napoli*, Serao had obtained a colorful pen name, "Gibus." It referred to the top hat worn by Parisian dandies and declared her intention to write—at least at times—about high society. She also founded a literary review, *La Settimana*, but despite a distinguished list of contributors, including D'Annunzio and Benedetto Croce, it lasted only from 1902 to 1904. According to Amoia, Serao was bored by a weekly publication that offered none of the excitement of daily journalism.

Serao's marriage floundered in the face of Scarfoglio's continuing acts of adultery. In one incident, a former lover of his killed herself on the family's doorstep. There were also political issues that divided the two: she clung to a conservative mixture of monarchism and pacifism, while he was a flamboyant speaker for colonial-

ism and warmongering. The two were legally separated in 1902. Now independent as a journalist, Serao founded her own newspaper, *Il Giorno*, in 1904, becoming the first Italian woman with such an achievement to her credit. She would direct it until her death 23 years later. Meanwhile, her personal life took a new turn when she established a household with Giuseppe Natale, a Neapolitan lawyer with whom she had a daughter. She named the child Eleonora after her longtime friend Eleonora Duse, who became the infant's godmother.

*Il Giorno* served as a challenge to *Il Mattino*, which remained under the control of Scarfoglio. With her usual energy, Serao took on numerous journalistic duties including writing horoscopes and giving advice to the lovelorn. *Il Giorno* offered a variety of political messages, reflecting the complexity of Serao's own views on the issues confronting Italy. While taking a stand in favor of monarchism, she also espoused the causes of workers on strike, and *Il Giorno* was an early and consistent opponent of the Fascist movement that developed under Benito Mussolini after World War I.

A notable feature of Serao's career as a journalist, dating from the mid-1870s, was her firm opposition to women's suffrage and divorce as well as her call for an educational system that excluded women at its highest levels. She claimed that Italian women first needed to seek a more elevated and dignified position in their society before calling for the vote. Only then could they exercise the franchise free of male pressure. As for divorce, Serao contended that it would degrade women who took such an option, placing them in a vulnerable position within a male-dominated society. Amoia has suggested that Serao was crucially influenced in these views by her lifelong acquaintance with the precarious position of women in Neapolitan society.

Serao drew directly on her own experiences when she began to write fiction, and critics have emphasized the relatively high quality of her work written in the 1880s. She began with *Fantasia*, in which she followed the lives and tangled love affairs of two Italian women from their years in boarding school through adulthood. *Fantasia* was a popular and commercial success, and it signaled the start of a career in fiction in which Serao was to have steady recognition from the reading public.

In two short stories produced in the middle of the decade—"Telegrafi dello stati" and "Scuola normale femminile"—she used the state telegraph office and the women's teachers' college, where she had worked and studied, as settings, and considered how women of middle-class background could earn a living in contemporary Italy. She stressed the poverty and uncertainty in the lives of such women, as well as their vulnerability to abuse from men in positions of authority.

She then went on to center her fiction for a time in the world of the transplanted provincial, a prominent 19th-century literary theme. Her years in Rome gave rise to two of her most important novels, both reflecting her own experience as a Neapolitan newcomer in the urban capital. In *La conquista di Roma* (1885), her hero Francesco Sangiorgio is a deputy to the Italian Parliament from a small, impoverished community in southern Italy. With telling psychological insight Serao traces her hero's confrontation with the bustling social and political scene in Rome. In the end, she sends him home as a man who has abandoned his political career in disillusionment. Two years later, she continued to explore this theme in *Vita e avventura di Riccardo Joanna*. Here her protagonist was, like Serao herself, an ambitious provincial journalist drawn to the Italian capital. Riccardo Joanna builds up a successful newspaper of his own, but, like Sangiorgio, he is defeated by the demands of Roman life.

Serao's most lasting achievement as a novelist, the one she considered her masterpiece, is *Il paese di Cuccagna* (1891). Here she set her story in her home city of Naples, and she examined how a variety of characters, from all levels of Neapolitan life, become enmeshed in the city's weekly lottery. Combining vivid scenes such as the city's many religious spectacles with the pathological behavior of her protagonists, Serao presented a picture of numerous pathetic losers and a handful of winners in this frantic effort to obtain instant wealth. A decade later, Serao addressed a special social dilemma in her novel *Suor Giovanna della Croce*. Here she castigated the national government for its insensitivity in forcing the closure of monasteries and nunneries containing only tiny religious communities. Her central figure is a poverty-stricken former nun, Sister Giovanna, thrown into a cruel, modern world after a cloistered existence that has left her with none of the tools of survival.

By the start of the 20th century, Serao's novels were being translated into French and English, and she achieved a considerable reputation in the Parisian literary community. She also had readers all over the Continent. But her fiction was increasingly dominated by Gothic and melodramatic elements. Many critics believe the quality of her writing diminished with this new turn toward what Kroha calls "novels of passion." At the same time, however, many themes from her earlier works remained in evidence. One of these was a negative view of heterosexual relations and marriage. She had throughout her imaginative writing also explored the close emotional tie that can develop between two women. A common device she employed was to present two very different female characters, and, even in the presence of a male protagonist, to center her attention on the relationship between the women. While intensely interested in the personal lives of Italian women, Serao also gave much of her energy to a critical examination of the conditions of working women and the injustice of their position in a conservative, male-dominated society.

> *H*er visual and creative acuity . . . has been compared to a walking microscope that focuses on the tiniest aspects of people and objects.
>
> —Alba Amoia

Serao strongly opposed Italy's entry into World War I, and she spent the last years of her career as a journalist confronting Benito Mussolini's Fascist movement. Despite her long-standing political conservatism, she became a vocal anti-Fascist and maintained her stance even after Mussolini came to power in 1922. Her newspaper was the target for raids by Mussolini's thugs in December 1922, and it suffered harassment as well due to the system of censorship instituted by his Fascist government. True to her established principles, she objected when Italian women were permitted to vote in local elections in 1925.

A candidate for the Nobel Prize in Literature in 1926, Serao may have lost out to *Grazia Deledda because of her outspoken political opinions. The Italian government evidently refused to support Serao, especially since her most recent novel, *Mors tua* (*The Harvest*), was critical of World War I. Nonetheless, her personal and professional role in Italian life remained impressive enough for Mussolini to visit Serao at the close of her life in a vain effort to obtain her support for fascism.

Matilde Serao died of a heart attack on July 25, 1927, while working at her writing desk at her newspaper. A final tribute to her eminence came in the form of a spectacular funeral in her home city of Naples. Years earlier, when she was only 22, she had written to a friend: "I write everywhere, and about everything, with singular audacity: I fight my corner, pushing and shoving; I am possessed with a burning desire to succeed." Serao, notes Laura Salsini, was part of a "pioneering group of women authors giving voice to female experiences" at the turn of the century. Her mingling of literary styles allowed her to "express her vision of the rich panorama of female experiences, experiences that bind together her heroines in sorrow and joy, oppression and fulfillment."

**SOURCES:**

Amoia, Alba. *20th Century Italian Women Writers: The Feminine Experience*. Carbondale, IL: Southern Illinois University Press, 1996.

Arkin, Marian, and Barbara Schollar, eds. *Longman Anthology of World Literature by Women*. NY: Longman, 1989.

Baranski, Zygmunt G., and Shirley W. Vinall, eds. *Women and Italy: Essays on Gender, Culture and History*. NY: St. Martin's, 1991.

Bondanella, Peter, and Julia Conway Bondanella, eds. *Dictionary of Italian Literature*. Westport, CT: Greenwood Press, 1996.

Gisolfi, Anthony M. *The Essential Matilde Serao*. NY: Las Americas, 1968.

Harrowitz, Nancy A. *Antisemitism, Misogyny, & the Logic of Cultural Difference: Cesare Lombroso & Matilde Serao*. Lincoln, NE: University of Nebraska Press, 1994.

Kroha, Lucienne. *The Woman Writer in Late-Nineteenth Century Italy: Gender and the Formation of Literary Identity*. Lewiston, NY: Edward Mellen Press, 1992.

Russell, Rinaldina, ed. *Italian Women Writers: A Bio-Bibliographical Sourcebook*. Westport, CT: Greenwood Press, 1994.

Salsini, Laura A. *Gendered Genres: Female Experiences and Narrative Patterns in the Works of Matilde Serao*. Rutherford, NJ: Fairleigh Dickinson University Press, 1999.

Wood, Sharon. *Italian Women's Writing, 1860–1994*. London: Athlone, 1995.

**SUGGESTED READING:**

Russell, Rinaldina, ed. *The Feminist Encyclopedia of Italian Literature*. Westport, CT: Greenwood Press, 1997.

Weaver, William. *Duse: A Biography*. London: Thames and Hudson, 1984.

**Neil M. Heyman**, Professor of History,
San Diego State University,
San Diego, California

## Serbia, queen of.

See Nikola, Helene Knez (1765–1842).
See Nathalia Keshko (1859–1941).
See Draga (1867–1903).

## Serebryakova, Zinaida (1884–1967)

*Russian painter. Name variations: Sinaida Serebryakova. Born Zinaida Lanceray in Neskuchnoe, near Kharkov, Russia, in 1884; died in Paris, France, in 1967; daughter of Yevgeny also seen as Evgeny Lanceray (a celebrated sculptor); her mother's maiden name was Benois; married Boris Serebryakov (a railroad engineer), in 1905 (died 1919); children: four.*

*Selected works: Self-Portrait at the Dressing Table (1909); Portrait of a Student (1909); Mid-day and Harvest; At Dinner (1914); Bleaching Linen (1917); The House of Cards (1919); Ballerina in the Dressing Room; Snowflakes from Tchaikovsky's Ballet "The Nutcracker."*

Zinaida Serebryakova was born in Neskuchnoe, Russia, in 1884. Her family was deeply involved in the arts: her father Evgeny Lanceray was an internationally recognized sculptor; her brother Nikolai Lanceray was a talented architect; and another brother, Evgeny Lanceray, was a painter and graphic artist and a leading member of the World of Art group. Her mother was a Benois, a family known in cultural circles for raising talented musicians, architects, artists, and actors. Her maternal grandfather, Nikolai Benois, was also an architect; while her maternal uncles Nikolai and Alexander Benois, both well-known artists, were also members of the World of Art.

After the death of her father in 1886, two-year-old Serebryakova and her mother joined the Benois household. Though she was not a sociable child, Zinaida showed artistic talent at an early age when she spent a month at Princess Tenisheva's school at Talashkino, headed by Ilya Repin, in 1901. She then traveled to Italy to study the paintings of the Venetian masters. When she returned to Russia, she came under the tutelage of artist Osip Braz. In 1905, Serebryakova's studies in Paris at the Académie de la Grande Chaumière led her to the paintings of Watteau, Fragonard, and the Impressionists, including Degas, Renoir, and Monet.

By the time Zinaida returned to Russia in 1906, she had become a mature, talented artist, and she decided to join the World of Art group led by Sergei Diaghilev. The group believed in the concept of national art, encompassing not only Russian folk art traditions but also architecture and other indigenous art forms of Russia. The group recognized the importance of Western influence on Russian art and believed that artists must be knowledgeable about both art history and contemporary worldwide art. The concept of beauty and harmony was also important to them. Embracing the group's ideals, Serebryakova emphasized style over naturalistic depictions in her work, and her choice of painting Russian contemporary life and environment was unique to her.

One of her most successful paintings, *Self-Portrait at the Dressing Table*, was shown at the Union of Russian Artists exhibition in St. Petersburg in 1910. The realism, joy, and originality of the painting reflected her happy home life with Boris Serebryakov, a railroad engineer whom she had married in 1905. She also often depicted their children in her paintings, as in *At Dinner* (1914), which was considered harmonious and cheerful, yet unsentimental. Zinaida's nudes of that period were also critically admired.

Serebryakova's belief in national art was reflected in her series of "peasant" paintings, such as *Mid-day* and *Harvest*, which show peasant women working the land and at rest after labor. In these she was inspired by the Russian artist Venetsianov, who used peasant life to depict the harmony in nature. Other paintings of Serebryakova's, such as *Bleaching Linen* (1917), were admired for their rhythmic composition and simple, bold forms.

Her uncle Alexander, though reluctant to praise his own niece, claimed that Serebryakova was one of the most remarkable Russian artists of the time. In 1917, she was nominated for the title of Academician of Art and would have been the first woman to receive such an honor had she been elected. The Russian Revolution intervened, however, and the election meeting was never held.

In 1918, a fire destroyed Serebryakova's home and most of her paintings. A year later, her husband died of typhus. With four children and a sick mother to support, Serebryakova was obliged to move from her beloved Neskuchnoe to Petrograd (St. Petersburg). Her family lived in great poverty, and Serebryakova was forced to sell her paintings for low prices to buy food and clothing. In *The House of Cards* (1919), writes **M.N. Yablonskaya**, she "again depicts her children, but now they wear worn and wearied expressions. Clarity has turned to unease, peacefulness to uncertainty. Rather than looking out of the picture as they do in earlier works their attention is centred on the ephemeral house of cards."

Serebryakova tried to recapture her ideals of grace and beauty with her depictions of ballet, using children, including her daughter **Tatyana**, as models. These works (*Ballerina in the Dressing Room* and *Snowflakes from Tchaikovsky's Ballet "The Nutcracker"*) were done in a different medium: pastels on cardboard. She used them like crayons, with some shading and retouching.

In 1924, Serebryakova moved to Paris to execute a mural she had been commissioned to

Zinaida Serebryakova

paint there. Political situations did not permit her to return to Russia, and she was exiled for the remainder of her life. She was never happy in Paris, feeling that the French did not understand her simple Russian art. Wrote her daughter: "Mother felt keenly the separation from her homeland. She experienced great difficulties because of poverty, illness and approaching old age. Despite all this she preserved her interest in national art and did not alter her position. She was true to herself to the end of her days." Serebryakova traveled to Brittany, Algeria, and Morocco, and her most respected works of that period portray Brittany peasants. Although she was strongly opposed to the abstract art form that dominated the art world at the time, the World of Art movement, ironically, had helped pave the way for the emergence of avant-garde and modern art by breaking with convention. In 1966, the Soviet government officially recognized Zinaida Serebryakova's contribution to Russian art and organized a sizable touring exhibit of her work. She died in Paris the following year.

**SOURCES:**

*The Twilight of the Tsars: Russian Art at the Turn of the Century. Hayward Gallery, London 7 March 1991.* London: South Bank Centre, 1991.

Yablonskaya, M.N. *Women Artists of Russia's New Age, 1900–1935*. Edited by Anthony Parton. NY: Rizzoli International, 1990.

**Ruth Savitz**, freelance writer, Philadelphia, Pennsylvania

## Serena (d. 410).

*See Placidia, Galla for sidebar.*

## Serena, Amalie (1794–1870).

*See Amalie of Saxony.*

## Sereno, El (1880–1961).

*See Sarfatti, Margherita.*

## Sergeant, Adeline (1851–1904)

*British novelist.* Born Emily Frances Adeline Sergeant on July 4, 1851, in Derbyshire, England; died on December 4, 1904; attended a school in Weston-Super-Mare, Laleham School in Clapham, and Queen's College, London; never married; no children.

*Selected writings:* Poems *(1866);* Dicky and His Friends *(1879);* Una's Crusade *(1880);* Jacobi's Wife *(1882);* Beyond Recall *(1883);* An Open Foe *(1884);* Seventy Times Seven *(1888);* Esther Denison *(1889);* The Story of a Penitent Soul *(1892);* The Idol Maker *(1897);* The Story of Phil Enderby *(1898);* This Body of Death *(1901);* Roads to Rome *(1901).*

While she is now little read or known, Adeline Sergeant achieved a fair measure of success in her lifetime with the more than 90 novels she wrote at a rapid clip (8 of them were produced in the same year). The daughter of a Methodist missionary father and a mother who wrote inspirational verse, Sergeant was born in Derbyshire, England, in 1851, and later attended Queen's College in London. She apparently spent much of her life searching for spiritual fulfillment, leaving the Methodist Church for the Anglican Church while not yet 20, and in her 30s professing agnosticism and joining the Fabian Society. In 1893, Sergeant returned to the Anglican Church, this time associating with the High Church faction, but six years later settled on Catholicism; this transition is detailed in her *Roads to Rome* (1901).

Sergeant began her writing career early, publishing *Poems* in 1866, while she was still in her teens. After leaving college she worked for ten years as a governess, while continuing to write and publishing several novels. In 1882, two years after she stopped working as a governess, Sergeant traveled to Egypt. There she wrote *Jacobi's Wife* (1882), which was awarded a prize by the *People's Friend* of Dundee, Scotland. She began contributing regularly to the journal, and lived in Dundee from 1885 to 1887. That year she moved to London, where she was involved in social work and reform movements while continuing to publish a steady stream of novels. Many of these centered on contemporary middle-class households, and her work is read today mostly for its sociological value. Sergeant left 14 unpublished works at the time of her death in 1904.

**SOURCES:**
*The Concise Dictionary of National Biography.* Oxford: Oxford University Press, 1992.
Kunitz, Stanley J., and Howard Haycraft, eds. *British Authors of the Nineteenth Century.* NY: H.W. Wilson, 1936.

**Gloria Cooksey**, freelance writer, Sacramento, California

## Sert, Misia (1872–1950)

*Russian-born pianist and patron of the arts during the Belle Époque.* Name variations: Misia Godebska Sert. Born Marie Sophie Olga Zenaide Godebska on March 30, 1872, in St. Petersburg, Russia; died on October 15, 1950; daughter of Cyprien Quentin Godebski (a Polish sculptor) and Eugénie Sophie Léopoldine Servais Godebska (a Frenchwoman); married Thadée Natanson, on April 25, 1893; married Alfred Edwards, on February 24, 1905 (divorced 1909); married José-María Sert (a Spanish painter), on September 2, 1920 (divorced December 28, 1927).

Misia Sert was born on March 30, 1872, in St. Petersburg, Russia, a birth that resulted in the death of her French mother **Eugénie Sophie Léopoldine Servais**. Misia's father, Polish sculptor Cyprien Quentin Godebski, was too preoccupied with his own affairs, both artistic and amorous, to provide attention or guidance for the child. Misia consequently spent most of her early years with her mother's family, but also with her father in Russia. At a tender age, she showed great musical ability and for years intended to become a concert pianist. Spoiled, independent, artistic, and temperamental, she spent eight years at convent school in Paris, from 1882 to 1890. Then she ran away to London and later back to Paris, supporting herself by teaching piano lessons. Misia gave her first public concert in 1892.

On April 25, 1893, she married Thadée Natanson, son of a wealthy banking family. They moved in European artistic and intellectual circles, and he founded *La Revue Blanche*, which became one of the main journals of Belle Époque culture. Misia befriended and patronized many of the great artists and writers of the time. Beautiful and vivacious, she modeled for Auguste

Renoir, Henri Toulouse-Latrec, Edouard Vuillard and Pierre Bonnard, and appears in a number of their paintings. Stéphane Mallarmé wrote poetry for her.

After separating from Natanson, she first became the mistress of Alfred Edwards, an extremely wealthy investor and newspaper baron, and then wed him on February 24, 1905. He showered money on her, and Misia became one of the chief patrons of the arts in Western Europe. Edwards later left her for an actress, **Genevieve Lantelme**, and Misia divorced him on February 24, 1909.

The settlement with Edwards left her well off, but Misia was lonely and less independent than her unbridled life would suggest. She entered a liaison with Spanish painter José-María Sert. When Edwards died unexpectedly on March 10, 1914, his will left Misia nothing. Nonetheless her life was full. Russian ballet impresario Sergei Diaghilev, composers Igor Stravinsky and Claude Debussey, and writer Marcel Proust were part of her circle. *Gabrielle "Coco" Chanel** was her friend and sometimes rival. Misia married José-María Sert on September 2, 1920. His career flourished, with commissions flowing in from across Europe and the Americas. Driven by his powerful sensuality, he threw over Misia for a young Russian, **Roussada Mdivani**. They divorced on December 28, 1927.

When Mdivani died in the late 1930s, José-María returned to Misia. She suffered a heart attack in 1939, her eyesight began to fail, and she endured the German occupation of France. José-María left his Paris apartment and its antiques to her when he died in 1945. Misia Sert lived until October 15, 1950, her health failing and her many years as one of Paris' cultural elite a memory.

**SOURCES:**
Gold, Arthur, and Robert Fizdale. *Misia: The Life of Misia Sert*. NY: Alfred A. Knopf, 1980.

Sert, Misia Godebska. *Misia and the Muses: The Memoirs of Misia Sert*. NY: J. Day, 1953.

**Kendall W. Brown**, Professor of History, Brigham Young University, Provo, Utah

# Servilia I (fl. 100 BCE)

*Roman noblewoman. Name variations: Servilia the Elder. Flourished around 100 BCE; daughter of Q. Servilius Caepio and *Livia (fl. 100 BCE); sister of *Servilia II (c. 100–after 42 BCE); half-sister of *Portia (fl. 80 BCE) and Cato the Younger; married L. Licinius Lucullus (a consul).*

# Servilia II (c. 100–after 42 BCE)

*Roman noblewoman and mother of Brutus. Name variations: Servilia the Younger. Born around 100; died after 42 BCE; daughter of Q. Servilius Caepio and Livia (fl. 100 BCE); sister of Servilia I; half-sister of Portia (fl. 80 BCE) and Cato the Younger; married M. Junius Brutus (died 77 BCE); married D. Junius Silanus (a consul); children: (first marriage) M. Junius Brutus (the famous assassin of Julius Caesar); (second marriage) three daughters (all named Junia), Junia (who married M. Aemilius Lepidus); Junia (who married P. Servilius Isauricus); Junia (who married C. Cassius Longinus, better known as Cassius, another assassin of Julius Caesar).*

Servilia II's distant ancestor, Servilius Ahala, initially brought fame to their family when he assassinated Spurius Maelius, a would-be tyrant of Rome, in 439 BCE. However, Servilia's direct line thereafter fell into political obscurity until the generation of her father, Q. Servilius Caepio. He rose through the ranks of the Roman magistracies, obtaining the office of praetor in 91. Despite promise, he died in 90 (fighting in the Roman Social War) before winning the consulship, Rome's highest annually

*Misia Sert*

elected office. At the beginning of his career, Servilius was a political ally of M. Livius Drusus, whose sister *Livia (Servilia's mother) he married before the end of the second century. This marriage produced three children: a son, Q. Servilius Caepio, and two daughters, *Servilia I and Servilia II. Servilia I married L. Licinius Lucullus, a prominent conservative who won the consulship in 74. The younger Servilia, with whom we are primarily concerned, was born about 100. Thus, she was very young when Servilius divorced Livia (before 96), a split which indicated a political rift between Servilius and Livius. Servilia was about ten when her father and maternal uncle broke into open political animosity, for in 91 Livius (then a tribune) championed a radical legislative agenda which incited widespread rioting in Rome and led to his assassination. As an adult, Servilia straddled the political chasm defined by her father and uncle. A political creature by nature and breeding, and ambitious to oversee the complete political rehabilitation of her paternal line, Servilia worked tirelessly behind the scenes to weave a web of influence which she intended would establish her as the arbiter of Roman politics.

Servilia married twice. Her first marriage was to M. Junius Brutus (tribune in 83) and was consummated (c. 80) when Rome was under the dictatorship of Sulla. After the death of Sulla, when M. Aemilius Lepidus rebelled against the constitution which Sulla had imposed on the Republic, Servilia's husband served as a legate for the rebel's cause. After this uprising was smashed, Brutus surrendered to Pompey the Great at Mutina (77). Initially promising Brutus safe conduct back to Rome, Pompey broke his word and had Servilia's husband executed for his part in the rebellion. Before his death, however, the elder Brutus and Servilia produced a son, another M. Junius Brutus—the famous assassin of Julius Caesar.

Servilia's second husband, D. Junius Silanus, achieved the consulship in 62 with a colleague named L. Licinius Murena. Although his success was won thanks to widespread electoral bribery, and the famous Cato the Younger prosecuted Murena for his part in the corruption, Cato refused similarly to attack Silanus thanks to the latter's marriage to Servilia, Cato's half-sister. (After her divorce from Servilius Caepio, Servilia's mother had married M. Portius Cato and given birth to the younger Cato and a daughter, *Portia [fl. 80 BCE].) Servilia's staunchly conservative half-brother dominated the Optimate (Senatorial) faction of Roman politics from around 63 until his death in 46 and, as such, long

reigned as Julius Caesar's political arch-rival. Caesar was the leader of the Populares (Peoples) faction. Servilia and Cato mostly remained on good terms with each other throughout their lives, although this was often difficult for Cato, since, by the time he was establishing himself in the political arena, Servilia had become Caesar's mistress (more of which below).

With her second husband, Servilia gave birth to three daughters, all named *Junia. The oldest of these married M. Aemilius Lepidus, the son of the rebel for whom Servilia's first husband had died. This son-in-law of hers reached the consulship in 46 under Caesar's patronage and eventually became a member of the Second Triumvirate with Marc Antony and Octavian (later Caesar Augustus). The second Junia married P. Servilius Isauricus, who initially was a supporter of Cato but who became a Caesarian and served with Caesar as consul in 48. Later, this Servilius became a partisan of Octavian, for which he was rewarded with a second consulship (41). Servilia's third daughter married C. Cassius Longinus—with Brutus, one of the most renowned assassins of Caesar. Thus, through her daughters' marriages, Servilia maintained firm contacts with the two factions which defined the political extremes of the last generation of the Roman Republic.

During her heyday between the dictatorships of Sulla and Caesar, Servilia reigned as a Roman princess in all but name. Well connected and active behind the scenes, she established herself as a political broker with the appropriate contacts to attempt a reconciliation of Rome's feuding factions. These she attempted to manipulate (without much thought to political principle) so as to bolster the political clout of her family. Certainly the most intriguing relationship with political ramifications which Servilia maintained throughout her long and active career was that which she established with Julius Caesar, whose mistress she was from at latest 63 (in which year, at the time of the Catiline Conspiracy, she was sending Caesar love notes while he was on the Senate floor battling Cato for his political life) until his death in 44 (at the hands of her son, whose father some suspected was really Caesar). An indication of Servilia's intimacy with Caesar came in the youthful betrothal of her son Brutus to his daughter *Julia (d. 54 BCE). However this union might have altered the future, it never took place, for in order to cement the political alliance (the "First Triumvirate") which catapulted him into the first rank of Roman politics, Caesar altered his plans and gave Julia to Pompey (59).

Although this switch pleased Servilia not at all—she had raised Brutus to hate this same Pompey who now stole his intended bride—the move was entirely political, and it did not lead Servilia to sever her personal relationship with Caesar. (It did create a rift between Brutus and Caesar, however.) In fact, Servilia seems to have been the Roman love of Caesar's life, although both knew other "acquaintances" and neither seriously contemplated marriage with the other. Two episodes prove the depth of his affection for Servilia: in 59 (possibly in partial compensation for the changed marriage plans) Caesar gave her a huge, flawless pearl worth over 60,000 (gold) aurea—which by modern-day standards is the equivalent of millions of dollars—and in 48, after the death of Pompey, he allowed her to acquire much of her enemy's property at auction at a fraction of its true worth, a privilege he denied all others, even those as close to him as Marc Antony.

The year 48 saw Caesar victorious over Pompey in a civil war, and it also saw a temporary reconciliation between Caesar and Brutus, who in the conflict (along with his uncle Cato) had reluctantly supported Pompey. Caesar thereafter favored Brutus' rapid advancement as a personal protégé. Thus it must have come as something of a shock to both Caesar and Servilia when Brutus married *Portia (c. 70–43 BCE), the daughter of Cato, in 45 BCE. This union seems to have been precipitated by Brutus' guilt, for in 46 Cato had committed suicide rather than submit to Caesar's political domination—a path not taken by Brutus when he had reconciled with his mother's lover. Portia was an ardent supporter of her father's republicanism, and she seems to have played a large role in turning Brutus against Caesar once again. As such, Servilia and Portia became rivals, but in the contest for Brutus' political soul, Portia and the memory of Cato prevailed. One can only imagine what went through Servilia's mind when she learned that Brutus had played a leading role in the murder of Caesar in 44 BCE.

What *is* known is that Servilia did not abandon her son's interests after Caesar's assassination, probably because, despite what he had done, he represented the continuation of the political influence she had worked so hard to win for her line. In June 44, Servilia presided over the family conference at Antium at which the assassins of Caesar contemplated how they should plot their political futures in light of the growing unpopularity of their act. There Servilia promised to use her connections with the Caesarian faction in order to affect some mutually satisfactory reconciliation. For this goal did she labor, especially after Brutus left Italy for the East to raise money

and men for the military showdown looming with the Second Triumvirate (comprised of the Caesarians, Marc Antony, Lepidus, and Octavian). Despite tireless diplomatic efforts, Servilia failed. When it became apparent that Brutus would face his rivals in battle, she turned her attention to raising money for Brutus' cause, having some success in this field with the immensely wealthy, Atticus. Regardless, all of her efforts failed when Brutus died fighting in northern Greece, at Philippi, in 42. After this catastrophe, Servilia received the ashes of her son. Thereafter, nothing is known of her fate.

**William S. Greenwalt,**
Associate Professor of Classical History,
Santa Clara University, Santa Clara, California

# Sessions, Kate O. (1857–1940)

*American horticulturist. Born Kate Olivia Sessions on November 8, 1857, in San Francisco, California; died of bronchial pneumonia on March 24, 1940, in La Jolla, California; daughter of Josiah Sessions (a horse breeder) and Harriet (Parker) Sessions; University of California at Berkeley, Ph.B. in chemistry, 1881.*

*Created Balboa Park in San Diego, California (1892); became co-founder (1909), officer, and member of the board, San Diego Floral Association (1909–30s); was the first woman to receive the Meyer Medal from the American Genetic Association (1939).*

Kate O. Sessions was born in San Francisco, California, in 1857, the daughter of a prosperous horse breeder. When she was ten years old the family moved to rural Oakland, across the bay from San Francisco, where they lived on a farm and Sessions attended the local public schools. She also spent time examining the flowers in the garden her mother grew and the wildflowers she saw when she rode her pony in the hills around Oakland.

After graduating from high school in 1876, Sessions visited Hawaii, and was greatly taken by the beauty of the plants that grew on the island. The following year, she enrolled at the University of California at Berkeley, graduating in 1881 with a degree in chemistry. She then went to work as a substitute teacher in the primary grades in Oakland. In 1883, Sessions relocated to San Diego, where she took a position as an instructor and vice-principal at Russ High School (later San Diego High School). Two years later, she opened a nursery in the town of Coronado, with an office and retail outlet in San Diego. In 1892, she leased a 30-acre parcel of land from the San Diego municipal government to cultivate plants for her nursery. Under a stipulation in the

Kate O. Sessions

lease, she agreed to develop the land, in part by planting 100 trees every year; these 30 acres would become the city's Balboa Park. Sessions maintained her nursery operation continuously throughout the rest of her life, but she relocated the business periodically. In 1903, she moved the nursery to San Diego's Mission Hills neighborhood, and in 1909 she closed her retail operation in San Diego. Between 1927 and 1930, she operated the nursery in Pacific Beach, where she had lived since 1922. From 1915 to 1918, Sessions also worked as the supervisor of agriculture for the San Diego school district, providing instruction in gardening to the district's grade-school students as part of her duties. In 1939, she was employed as an instructor for the University of California Extension program.

Sessions traveled in Europe and Hawaii, collecting particularly striking, drought-resistant plant specimens that she subsequently introduced into the urban environment. She is credited with bringing numerous plants to Southern California, including the popular palm tree and assorted varieties of poppies, shrubs, eucalyptus, juniper, oak, and vines. It was reported that nearly every turn-of-the-century homeowner in rapidly expanding San Diego sought her advice and bought her plants. She also maintained a close friendship and professional relationship with naturalist *Alice Eastwood, who worked at the California Academy of Sciences. Sessions was responsible for establishing the Arbor Day observance in the city of San Diego, and contributed scores of articles to *California Gardener* magazine and other local publications. From 1909 until the 1930s, she served as an officer and board member of the San Diego Floral Association, which she was instrumental in founding. In 1935, the organizers of the California-Pacific International Exposition honored her with "K.O. Sessions Day" as part of the festival. Four years later, she became the first woman to receive the Meyer Medal of the American Genetic Association, for her work introducing non-native plants to the area.

Sessions, who as a young woman was often described as exceedingly beautiful, was usually photographed looking properly feminine, but as a general rule she tended to wear rough old clothes and men's boots, the better to grub in the dirt with. After her death on March 24, 1940, in La Jolla, California, an elementary school and a park were named in her honor in the city of San Diego, where the varieties of plants she introduced continue to grow.

**SOURCES:**

James, Edward T., ed. *Notable American Women, 1607–1950*. Cambridge, MA: The Belknap Press of Harvard University, 1971.

Norwood, Vera. *Made from This Earth: American Women and Nature*. Chapel Hill, NC: University of North Carolina Press, 1993.

Read, Phyllis J., and Bernard L. Witlieb. *The Book of Women's Firsts*. NY: Random House, 1992.

**Gloria Cooksey**, freelance writer,
Sacramento, California

# Seton, Elizabeth Ann (1774–1821)

*Catholic convert and founder of the American Sisters of Charity who was the first person born in the U.S.* *to be canonized a saint by the Roman Catholic Church. Name variations: Elizabeth Bayley Seton; Mother Seton; Saint Elizabeth Ann Seton. Born Elizabeth Ann Bayley in New York City on August 28, 1774; died of tuberculosis at Emmitsburg, Maryland, on January 4, 1821; daughter of Richard Bayley (a prominent physician) and Catherine (Charlton) Bayley; attended Mama Pompelion's academy for girls in New York, where she learned French and piano; married William Magee Seton, on January 25, 1794 (died 1803); children: Anna Maria Seton (b. 1795); William Seton (b. 1796); Richard Bayley Seton (b. 1798); Catherine Josephine Seton (b. 1800); Rebecca Seton (b. 1802).*

*Helped found the Society for the Relief of Poor Widows with Small Children (1797); following the death of husband, received into the Catholic Church (1805); moved to Baltimore to found Catholic school for girls (1808); took first vows as Sister of Charity of Saint Joseph, received first recruits into the order, and moved school and her community to Emmitsburg, Maryland (1809); cause for canonization introduced at the Vatican (1907); declared Saint Elizabeth Ann Seton by Pope Paul VI (1975).*

In 1774, the year Elizabeth Ann Bayley was born in New York City, the American colonies were on the verge of their War of Independence. She grew up as a member of New York's elite in the newly emerging nation, descended on both sides of her family from distinguished forbears of British, French, and Dutch origin. Her father Richard Bayley was a brilliant physician and the health officer of New York City, as well as the first professor of anatomy at Columbia; her mother's father was rector of St. Andrew's Episcopal Church on Staten Island. Elizabeth herself married into a wealthy merchant family and spent her young womanhood as a rather typical, if unusually religious, New York society matron, with a deep commitment to her Episcopal faith. But she ended her life in poverty as a Roman Catholic nun, and a century and a half after her death she was canonized as the first American-born Catholic saint.

Although she was reared in a privileged milieu, Seton suffered tragedies and emotional hardships early in life. Her mother **Catherine Charlton Bayley** was frequently ill and died before Elizabeth was three years old, leaving a widowed husband with three small daughters: Elizabeth, **Mary Magdalene**, and **Kitty**. Richard Bayley's dedication to his profession often seemed to take precedence over his family's needs, and he was away from home during much of Elizabeth's childhood. Shortly after the requisite year of mourning following the death of his first wife, he married **Charlotte Barclay**, a young woman of 18, who never showed much affection toward her stepchildren.

About a year after her father's remarriage, the death of her younger sister Kitty, coupled with the loss of her mother, seemed to prompt the deep religious feelings that would be a constant factor in Seton's life. In later years, she remembered the intense yearning to join her mother and little sister in heaven that lasted throughout her childhood. Seton grew up as a lonely, solitary, and introspective child who spent much of her time taking care of her six young half-siblings, who apparently returned the deep affection that she lavished on them.

> *We must walk, and walk confidently, in the obscurity of faith.*
>
> —Elizabeth Ann Seton

As teenagers, Elizabeth and her sister Mary were packed off to live with their father's relatives for years at a time. The difficult relationship between stepmother and stepdaughters, notes biographer Joseph Dirvin, can probably be confirmed by the fact that they were sent away at an age when they would have been most helpful in a household full of small children. According to her journals written years later, the loneliness and despair during this period may have led Seton to contemplate suicide. She wrote:

> Alas, alas, alas! *Tears of blood*—My God!—horrid subversion of every good promise of God in the boldest presumption—God had created me—I was very miserable. He was too good to condemn so poor a creature made of dust, driven by misery this the wretched reasoning—Laudanum—the praise and thanks of excessive joy not to have done the horrid deed the thousand promises of Eternal gratitude.

However, at age 15 she also wrote of a beautiful May morning, of experiencing the sustaining power of her religious faith. She was in a meadow, lying under a chestnut tree, when she felt overwhelmed by a religious awakening:

> God was my Father, my all. I prayed, sang hymns, cried, laughed, talking to myself of how far He could place me above all sorrow. Then I laid still to enjoy the heavenly peace that came over my soul; and I am sure, in the two hours so enjoyed, grew ten years in the spiritual life.

Although her religious beliefs were deep and ever present, Seton led the life of a typical upper-class girl. Her formal education apparently did not go far beyond lessons in French and playing the piano at a fashionable French academy in New York, but she was intelligent and well read. She studied the Bible, knew the religious verses of Thomason and Milton, and was familiar with secular literature; later in life she expressed horror in recalling that, as a young woman, she had been enamored of the writings of Rousseau. She spent summers at her family's country house, went on picnics, and greatly enjoyed balls and dinners, but frequently felt torn between the pleasures of society and a serious spiritual life. When she returned home after a ball and wanted to think of her dance partners instead of God, she found it difficult to pray. At such times, she would reproach herself for her frivolity.

In 1794, after a year of courtship, Elizabeth married William Magee Seton. He was 25 years old, and heir to the fortunes of the Seton-Maitland Company, a thriving mercantile business; she was 19. The marriage was a close and happy one, and Elizabeth's relationship with her father also grew warmer and more intimate at this time. He seems to have found pleasure in her intelligent companionship, and made almost daily use of the boat assigned to him as the health officer of New York to row out to her house on Staten Island. Even during this period, however, Seton felt the transient nature of her happiness and peace. In the enjoyment of her husband, family, and home, she sensed the danger of losing God.

In 1797, Seton and her friend *Isabella Graham helped found the Society for the Relief of Poor Widows with Small Children, and Elizabeth served as the organization's treasurer until 1804. Around this time, she also came under the spiritual influence of Dr. John Henry Hobart, the new evangelical assistant at Trinity Church in New York City, who would later become the Episcopal bishop of New York. This began a pattern in her life of looking to male clergy for spiritual guidance, as well as a tendency on her part to influence the religious lives of those around her. One of the first to be affected was her husband, who had been religiously indifferent, but became a devoted follower of Hobart. Seton also developed deep friendships with several women who shared her spirituality and remained close throughout her life. These included **Julia Scott**, who was married to New York Secretary of State Lewis Allaire Scott, and **Catherine Dupleix**, another founder of the Society for Poor Widows. One especially close confidante was her sister-in-law **Rebecca Seton**, whom she referred to as her "soul's sister."

After a few happy and prosperous years in which her first three children were born, Seton

Elizabeth
Ann
Seton

and her family were struck by a string of terrible calamities. Her vigorous father-in-law, who had been the linchpin of his large family, suffered a bad fall from which he inexplicably never recovered, and died in the spring of 1798. Without his leadership, the family was never to be the same.

The Setons had to take on the responsibility of William's seven younger siblings, and William had to take over the family business. But the merchant trade was already being seriously damaged by the undeclared war with France of the 1790s, and he did not have the business

skills of his father. The business went into a steady decline, and by December 1800 the firm was in bankruptcy. Then Elizabeth's father, who had been fighting a yellow fever epidemic in the city, succumbed to the disease. Soon, illness struck again. Before his marriage, William had contracted tuberculosis, which afflicted several members of his family. Now, worn down by his struggles in business, he grew seriously ill with a recurrence of the disease.

Doctors recommended a trip to Italy to help William recover, and the couple set sail, along with their oldest child, **Anna Maria Seton** (nicknamed Anina), in 1803. Before they could disembark in Livorno, however, their ship was placed in quarantine because of an outbreak of yellow fever in New York prior to their departure, and the family was forced to stay in a dirty and drafty *lazaretto* (public hospital) on a canal at the outskirts of the city. Seton was enraged, fearing that the terrible conditions would kill her husband. After four weeks, the family was released into the care of associates of the Seton firm, Antonio and Fillipo Filicchi, but William died a few days afterward, in Pisa.

For three months, Seton and Anna Maria lived in Florence with the Filicchis, who introduced them to Catholicism during their time of grief. In letters home, Seton admitted that she found the rituals and symbolism of Catholicism intriguing. She liked that her hosts had a family chapel and that the devout could go to church as often as they wished. She was impressed by the beauty of the Italian churches and the intense piety of the Italian people. She found the doctrine of atonement for sins particularly consoling, but she reassured her family that she would not convert.

Seton and her daughter returned to New York, accompanied by Antonio Filicchi. Back under the influence of John Hobart, she attended St. George's Episcopal Church, but began to feel torn between Catholicism and her old religion. A month after her return, her spiritual uncertainties were intensified by the death of Rebecca, her "soul's sister," from tuberculosis. Seton had confided her religious concerns to Rebecca in her letters, and now she became tormented by the thought that her sister-in-law might have died in a false religion. She suffered constant doubts, pressured by Hobart and her Protestant friends on one hand, and by Filicchi and Catholic priests on the other. Each faction gave her reading matter to win her over, warning her of the dire consequences to her soul if she abandoned true religion; Filicchi enlisted Archbishop John Carroll of Baltimore to help convince Seton to convert, and her Methodist maid begged her not to go over to the Catholics.

On a day she felt exhausted by spiritual confusion, she went to her old church of St. George's, thinking that she would remain with the familiar faith until God gave her a clear sign to do otherwise. "If I left the house a Protestant," she wrote, "I returned to it a Catholic." During the service, as she bowed her head to receive absolution en masse in the usual manner of the Episcopal Church, she realized that she had no belief in the sacrament or in the bishop who performed it. She knew then that she had to become a Catholic. Wrote Seton: "The controversies on it I am quite incapable of deciding; and as the strictest Protestant allows salvation to a good Catholic, to the Catholics I will go and try to be a good one. May God accept my intention, and pity me."

On March 14, 1805, Seton was formally received into the Catholic Church. There is no doubt that her friends and relatives were shocked and disturbed by her decision, but some biographers of Seton may have exaggerated the social stigma attached to religion by Protestants in the early American republic. The Catholic community of that time was tiny, grown from about 30,000 in 1790, and was dominated by a few wealthy families of English origin concentrated in Maryland and Pennsylvania. There were also small congregations of French, Irish and German immigrants in the major seaboard cities. Republican attitudes on freedom of religion had caused many of the anti-Catholic laws of the colonial era to be revoked, and Catholics had obtained full political rights in Virginia, Pennsylvania, Maryland, Delaware, and Rhode Island. Many states maintained some religious restrictions on office-holding (New Hampshire required until 1877 that the governor, state senators and assemblymen be Protestant), but nativist movements that targeted Catholics were not part of the nation's social and political life until a later period.

However, the republicanism that encouraged tolerance of religious differences also encouraged suspicion of the authoritarianism, ritualism, and monarchical allegiances of the Catholic Church. Also, although America was a nation of religious pluralism, the country was overwhelmingly Protestant in its society and its culture. Hobart warned Seton that in becoming a Catholic she was joining "a corrupt and sinful communion," and her godmother, **Sarah Startin**, disinherited her, although many who had known Seton continued to be supportive. Ironically, Seton, one of the founders of the Society for Poor Widows, was now a penniless widow with a young family to feed; with the help of friends, she set up a boarding house for boys attending an Episcopal school nearby.

When it appeared that Seton was influencing young people to convert to Catholicism, the acceptance of her new religion became more problematic. In one instance, her 14-year-old sister-in-law, **Cecilia Seton**, became severely ill with tuberculosis, and Seton became terrified that she would die as Rebecca had done, outside the Catholic faith. When Cecilia announced that she was converting to Catholicism, her family reacted with horror. They forbade Seton to see the girl, and threatened to send Cecilia to the West Indies to remove her from her sister-in-law's influence. Cecilia became a Catholic nonetheless, and Seton was eventually reconciled with the family, but the incident lost her support for her boarding house. Others who followed her into Catholicism included her close friend Catherine Dupleix, who was converted in 1812, and her sister-in-law **Harriet Seton**, who later converted and followed Elizabeth to Maryland.

For several years Seton scraped by, living off the generosity of friends. Then the Reverend William Dubourg, of the French order of the Society of St. Sulpice, invited her to Baltimore to open a Catholic school for girls. Archbishop Carroll agreed to the plan, and, in June 1808, she moved with her five children to Baltimore. She opened the girls' school on Paca Street and began to live a convent-like existence with her daughters and a handful of female recruits; her two sons entered St. Mary's College, where Dubourg was president. Seton wrote to Cecilia, "Everything you wish to know of me is said in a few words. In the chapel at six until eight, school at nine, dine at one, school at three, chapel at six-thirty, examination of conscience and rosary, sometimes at the chapel also at three—and so goes day after day without variation."

On March 25, 1809, Seton pronounced her first vows before Archbishop Carroll. She and four sisters began appearing in public in their black religious dress. On June 21, the small community, including Cecilia and Harriet Seton, left Baltimore to establish a convent and school in a remote rural hamlet 50 miles inland. The day that the group arrived at Emmitsburg, Maryland, July 31, 1809, is celebrated by the American Sisters of Charity as the founding day of their community. The sisters were sponsored by the Sulpicians, with the Reverend Dubourg as their superior and Seton as mother superior. Their new site was apparently the choice of another supporting sponsor, a wealthy and eccentric convert named Samuel Cooper. The first home of the sisters was a nearly uninhabitable stone farmhouse, where they slept on mattresses on the floor and the snow blew in through the cracks in the walls during winter. A priest was seldom available, and the sisters had to walk two miles to Mount St. Mary's to attend Sunday Mass. Nearly everyone became ill. Mother Seton's son William was staying at the Mount when he became so ill that she believed he was

going to die and sewed him a burial shroud. William recovered, but then Harriet Seton died suddenly; she was buried in the shroud that had been intended for her nephew.

In February 1810, the community moved to a better site, then known as St. Joseph's and now called the White House. But ill health continued, and Cecilia died later that year. In 1812, the worst blow came when Seton's oldest daughter Anina died at the age of 16. Anina had been her mother's constant companion, and had happily joined her mother in the life of a Catholic sister. Seton became so grief-stricken at this loss that friends feared she would go insane. "After Nina was taken I was so often expecting to lose my senses," she said, "and my head was so disordered" that if it were not for "daily duties always before me I did not know much of what I did or what I left undone." Still, despite all the hardship, the life of the community was not always sad. Elizabeth wrote in a letter:

> You will hear a thousand reports of non-sense about our community which I beg you not to mind. The truth is that we have the best ingredients of happiness—order, peace, and solitude. . . . [T]ake a look at our black gowns and demure looks, which, however, hide a set of as lively, merry hearts as ever met together.

The continuing order of the community was not yet settled. Mother Seton had to battle her male superiors for a say in the writing of the constitution and the community rule. Dubourg wanted to establish the sisters under the rule of the French Sisters of Charity, but Seton believed that important modifications needed to be made to accommodate the order to American conditions. For example, the French order concentrated on caring for the sick, but the need in America was for schools for Catholics. In France, the sisters were under the patronage of the wealthy and were required to teach girls who were generally poor. In America, the sisters had to be self-supporting and therefore needed to take in wealthy student boarders in order to finance their work. Not least, Mother Seton was concerned about how her own children, and her responsibility to them, would be treated under the new rule.

Most of all, Seton believed that the sisters had a right to participate in the decisions that would determine the life of their community. In this she faced a problem common to sisterhoods through the centuries. Though the authority of the male clergy over them was not questioned, the sisters felt a duty to uphold the spirit and purpose of their communities. In early 19th-century America, the problem was compounded by a Catholic clergy that was primarily French in origin and perspective.

Further difficulties arose when a new superior, Sulpician John Baptist David, made plans to write the rules himself, obtain the approval of his fellow Sulpicians, and then submit them to the sisters. David also intended to replace Seton as mother superior with his own recruit, **Rose White**. Archbishop Carroll urged Seton to be compliant, but she told him, "if any [regulations] are proposed to us without going through the necessary discussion and approbation, I can never give the example of accepting them."

The issues were resolved after the appointment of a new Sulpician superior, John Dubois, in 1811. Dubois favored a rule making the American sisters independent of the French, and Archbishop Carroll followed his lead. At a time when Catholic ecclesiastical authority in America was only vaguely defined, the archbishop was bound to favor a policy guaranteed to increase his own authority. The constitutions, modified from the French rule, gave the community the name of Sisters of Charity of St. Joseph's, and identified its members as daughters of St. Vincent de Paul, founder of the original Sisters of Charity in France in 1633. Education of all female children was emphasized; Seton was allowed to continue as mother superior and keep her children with her; and enforcement or further changes of the rules required the approval of three clergy members: the archbishop, the Sulpician superior in Maryland, and the Sulpician superior residing in Emmitsburg.

Before Seton's death in 1821, a community of Sisters of Charity had been established in Philadelphia in 1812, and another in New York City in 1817. By 1900, the American Sisters of Charity were in communities from Cincinnati to Halifax, Nova Scotia, and had missions in China, Korea, and Bermuda. They numbered 5,000 and represented 12% of the 40,000 Catholic sisters in America at the turn of the century. In the 20th century, this population would nearly triple by the 1960s, when the number of sisters began to decline.

The immigration of the 19th century vastly expanded the small numbers of American Catholics of Seton's day. Without the labor of sisterhoods such as hers, the building of the institutional Catholic Church in America would have been impossible. By 1900, Catholicism was the single largest religious denomination in the United States (one in six Americans by then were Catholic), and the Church had established thousands of schools, hospitals, orphanages and missions. This huge institutional structure was almost entirely dependent on the services of Catholic sisters.

Even before her death, friends and confidants of Mother Seton called attention to her unusual piety, devotion and spirituality; Archbishop Carroll was already saying that she was a saint. At the time she died, her confessor Father Bruté instructed everyone who knew her to save all her writing and correspondence. In 1907, her cause for canonization was introduced to the Vatican, and 12 volumes of her diaries, letters, prayer books and other material were submitted for study as authenticated writings, in place of living witnesses to her sanctity. In 1936, the Vatican declared that her cause could be formally introduced. In 1959, her spirituality was declared "heroic," and she was given the title of venerable. In 1963, Seton was beatified and called blessed after two miraculous cures were credited to her intercession. Another cure in 1963 was studied by the Holy See, which finally declared it truly miraculous. On December 12, 1974, Pope Paul VI decreed her Saint Elizabeth Ann Seton. The first American-born saint, she was canonized on September 14, 1975, at St. Peter's Basilica in Rome.

**SOURCES:**

Dirvin, Joseph I. *Mrs. Seton: Foundress of the American Sisters of Charity*. NY: Farrar, Straus and Giroux, 1975.

Dolan, Jay P. *The American Catholic Experience: A History from Colonial Times to the Present*. NY: Image Books, 1985.

*Elizabeth Seton: Selected Writings*. Edited by Ellin Kelly and Annabelle Melville. NY: Paulist Press, 1987.

Jarvis, William. *Mother Seton's Sisters of Charity*. Columbia University, 1984.

Melville, Annabelle M. "Seton, Elizabeth Ann Bayley," in *Notable American Women, 1607–1950*. Cambridge, MA: Belknap Press of Harvard University, 1971.

**SUGGESTED READING:**

Ewens, Mary. *The Role of the Nun in Nineteenth Century America*. NY: Arno Press, 1978.

Laverty, Sister Rose Maria, S.C. *Loom of Many Threads: Sisters of Charity*, 1958.

Melville, Annabelle M. *Elizabeth Bayley Seton, 1774–1821*. NY: Scribner, 1951.

Ruether, Rosemary Radford, and Rosemary Skinner Keller. *Women and Religion in America: The Nineteenth Century*. San Francisco, CA: Harper and Row, 1981.

Thompson, Margaret Susan. "Discovering Foremothers: Sisters, Society, and the American Catholic Experience," in *U.S. Catholic Historian*. Vol. 5, 1986, pp. 273–290.

**COLLECTIONS:**

Elizabeth Seton Papers, Archives of St. Joseph's Provincial House, Emmitsburg, Maryland; letters of Elizabeth Seton, manuscripts, Archives of the Archdiocese of Baltimore; letters of Carroll and Elizabeth Seton,

Archives of Georgetown University, Special Collections Division.

**Elizabeth Milliken**, Ph.D. in American History, Cornell University, Ithaca, New York

# Seton, Grace Gallatin (1872–1959)

*American feminist, suffragist, explorer, and writer who established the Biblioteca Femina. Name variations: Grace Seton-Thompson. Born on January 28, 1872, in Sacramento, California; died of a heart attack on March 19, 1959, in Palm Beach, Florida; daughter of Albert Gallatin and Clemenzie (Rhodes) Gallatin; graduated from Packer Collegiate Institute, Brooklyn, New York (1892); married Ernest Thompson Seton (the naturalist and writer), in 1896 (divorced 1935); children: Ann Seton, known as Anya Seton (a writer, 1904–1990).*

*Participated in the organization of the Camp Fire Girls (1912); served as president of the Connecticut Woman Suffrage Association (1910–20); served as president of the National League of American Pen Women (1926–28 and 1930–32); established the Biblioteca Femina, a collection of books and pamphlets by women writers throughout the world (1930s).*

*Selected writings:* A Woman Tenderfoot *(1900);* Nimrod's Wife *(1907);* A Woman Tenderfoot in Egypt *(1923);* Chinese Lanterns *(1924);* Yes, Lady Saheb *(1925);* Magic Waters *(1933);* Poison Arrows *(1938); (poetry)* The Singing Traveler *(1947).*

In 1872, in Sacramento, California, Grace Gallatin Seton entered the world as "one of those people," she wrote, "who were born believing in suffrage." Her life of writing, adventure, and feminist pursuits would include travels around the world as well as the organization of her Biblioteca Femina, a collection of women's writing from around the world.

Grace was the daughter of Albert and **Clemenzie Gallatin**. After their divorce in 1881, nine-year-old Grace was the only one of the Gallatins' three children to remain with her mother. Clemenzie eventually remarried, and they relocated to New York where Grace was enrolled at Brooklyn's Packer Collegiate Institute. Her father and siblings were largely absent from her life until a close relationship developed with her sister in the years to come. Subsequent to her graduation (1892), she took instruction in printing and bookmaking. Grace was only 17 when she joined the campaign for women's suffrage, and in the years 1910 to 1920 she would go on to become first vice-president and then president of the Connecticut Woman Suffrage Association.

In 1894, Grace encountered the writer and naturalist Ernest Thompson Seton while she was traveling in Europe, and they married two years later in Manhattan. To accommodate her enjoyment of city living and his desire for country life, the couple wintered in New York and summered in the country. She contributed to his efforts by providing editorial and design assistance on his books. Grace impressed her husband on their camping trips together, with Ernest calling her "a dead shot with the rifle" and noting that she "met all kinds of danger with unflinching nerve." So much did she appreciate the outdoors that Grace would later participate in the founding of the Camp Fire Girls.

Grace Seton's first book, *A Woman Tenderfoot*, appeared in 1900. In detailing her horseback journey in the Rockies, she made recommendations for women's clothing which would allow for freedom of movement while achieving a desired aesthetic. Four years later, following a miscarriage, she had her first and only child. With neither the skills nor the inclination for homemaking, she employed servants to run the house and governesses to rear young Ann (**Anya Seton**), who was later to follow in her parents' footsteps as a writer.

In France during the First World War, Seton contributed to the war effort by putting together a motor unit of women who provided supplies to soldiers, work which earned her decoration by the French government. After war's end, her own career as a writer, lecturer, feminist, and suffragist took her in a different direction from her husband (after several years of separation, they would divorce in 1935). From 1926 to 1928, and again from 1930 to 1932, she served as president of the National League of American Pen Women. Seton's position with the National Council of Women as chair of letters (1933 to 1938) led her to organize an assembly of women writers over whom she presided at Chicago's International Congress of Women during 1933. This work gave rise to what is considered Seton's most significant contribution, her Biblioteca Femina, which included 2,000 volumes and 100 pamphlets written by women from all over the world. This collection, containing many works unavailable in libraries, increased recognition for women writers and was eventually donated to the library of Northwestern University.

Seton traveled extensively in the 1920s and 1930s, striking out for locations around the globe, including Egypt, Japan, China, and India. From donkey rides in the Libyan desert to a safari by elephant in Vietnam, Seton sought out

adventure and wrote about it in a series of books which provided historical perspectives on the countries she traveled in, as well as assessments of women's status in these regions.

While Seton's writings tended to be apolitical, she participated as a Republican in political causes, including working for equality for women within the Republican National Committee and campaigning for Herbert Hoover and Thomas E. Dewey. She held office in numerous organizations and was a member of many social clubs, with her name often appearing in the society pages. As her later years brought increased interest in Eastern religions, the 1940s found her visiting the ashrams of the spiritual leader Yogananda; her poems in *The Singing Traveler*, published in 1947, reflect Eastern influences. Following a varied and productive career, she died in 1959 in Palm Beach, Florida.

**SOURCES:**
Sicherman, Barbara, and Carol Hurd Green, eds. *Notable American Women: The Modern Period.* Cambridge, MA: The Belknap Press of Harvard University, 1980.

## Seton, Mother (1774–1821).
*See Seton, Elizabeth Ann.*

## Seton-Thompson, Grace (1872–1959).
*See Seton, Grace Gallatin.*

## Setsuko Chichibu (1909–1995).
*See Chichibu, Setsuko.*

## Severa, Marina
*Roman noblewoman. First wife of Valentinian I, Roman emperor (r. 364–375); children: Gratian. Valentinian's second wife was \*Justina (fl. 350–370).*

## Severance, Caroline M.
### (1820–1914)
*American suffragist, abolitionist, and club founder. Born Caroline Maria Seymour on January 12, 1820, in Canandaigua, New York; died on November 10, 1914, in Los Angeles, California; eldest of five children of Orson Seymour (a banker) and Caroline (Clark) Seymour; attended Upham Female Seminary and Miss Almira Bennett's Boarding School in Owasco Lake, New York; graduated from the female seminary of Mrs. Elizabeth (Stryker) Ricord in Geneva, New York, in 1835; also briefly attended the Auburn Female Seminary; married Theodoric Cordenio Severance (a banker), in 1840; children: Orson Seymour Severance (1841–1841); James Seymour Severance (b. 1842); Julia Long Severance (b. 1844); Mark Sibley Severance (1846); Pierre Clarke Severance (1849).*

*Founded the American Equal Rights Association with Susan B. Anthony (1866); founded the American Woman Suffrage Association with Lucy Stone and others (1869); established the New England Woman's Club (1868) and the Friday Morning Club in Los Angeles (1891); acknowledged as the first woman to register to vote under California's new woman suffrage law (1911).*

Caroline M. Severance was born in 1820 in Canandaigua, New York, and spent her youth in nearby Auburn after her father's death in 1824. There, her guardian and paternal uncle, James S. Seymour, a devout, conservative Presbyterian, held sway. After attending several private girls' schools, she graduated with honors from the Female Seminary of Geneva in 1835. In 1840, she married banker Theodoric C. Severance. The couple moved to Cleveland, where they had five children, the first of whom died in infancy.

Severance and her husband were active in liberal causes and founded the Independent Christian Church, which was against slavery. Her interest in women's suffrage grew as she attended women's rights conventions in Ohio and New York, and in 1853 she presided over the first meeting of the Ohio Women's Right's Association. The following year, Severance presented a memorial to the Ohio legislature asking for property rights for women.

In 1855, the family moved to Boston, where Severance continued her involvement in intellectual, religious, and reformist activities. She presented a paper, "Humanity, a Definition and a Plea," to the Parker Fraternity Lecture Course, becoming the first woman to speak in the course. From 1856 until the Civil War broke out, Severance spoke on abolitionism to audiences in Massachusetts and Rhode Island. In 1866, she and \***Susan B. Anthony** founded the American Equal Rights Association, and in 1869, Severance joined \***Lucy Stone** in organizing the American Woman Suffrage Association. She was also a founder of the Moral Education Association of Boston in 1873 and served as its first president.

Following a move to Los Angeles in 1875, she and her husband founded the city's first Unitarian congregation, and she began a women's club in 1885 that later became the Los Angeles Women's Club. During that same year, she organized the Los Angeles Free Kindergarten Association, which advocated making kindergarten part of the Los Angeles school system. In 1891, Severance organized her third women's club, the Friday Morning Club, which, like the others, advocated for civic reform.

Severance remained active after her husband's death in 1892, serving as president of the Los Angeles County Woman Suffrage League from 1900 to 1904. She became the first woman to register to vote under California's new woman suffrage law in 1911, and died three years later, age 94.

**SOURCES:**

*Eminent Women of the Age.* Hartford, CT: S.M. Betts, 1868.

James, Edward T., ed. *Notable American Women, 1607–1950.* Cambridge, MA: The Belknap Press of Harvard University, 1971.

McHenry, Robert, ed. *Famous American Women.* NY: Dover, 1980.

**Deborah Conn**, freelance writer, Falls Church, Virginia

# Séverine (1855–1929)

*French writer and lecturer, in her time the most famous female journalist in the world, who was the first French woman to run a newspaper and to earn a living as a regularly featured columnist in major newspapers. Name variations: Caroline Rémy or Remy; Caroline Rémy Guebhard; Mme. Adrien Guebhard or Guébhard; Severine. Pronunciation: say-VREEN. Born Caroline Rémy on April 27, 1855, in Paris, France; died at Pierrefonds (Oise) of uremia on April 24, 1929, and was buried there in the village cemetery; daughter of Marie-Joseph-Onésime Rémy (a civil servant) and Mlle Villiaume-Geniès; educated at home and at the Biré (Neuilly) and Bessières (Paris) boarding schools; married Antoine-Henri Montrobert in 1871 (divorced c. 1885); married Dr. Adrien Guebhard, in 1885 (died 1924); children: (first marriage) two sons, Louis-Georges-Auguste Montrobert (b. 1872); (with Guebhard) Roland Guebhard (1880–1926).*

*Fled Paris with her parents during the Commune and married to escape from home (1871); had a son with Adrien Guebhard and met Jules Vallès (1880); tried to commit suicide (1881); launched* Le Cri du Peuple *with Vallès and began to write (1883); married Guebhard (1885); directed* Le Cri du Peuple *(1885–88); descended into a mine to report on a disaster (1890); interviewed Pope Leo XIII (1892); raised money for unfortunates (1894–96); came under severe personal attack during the Lebaudy Affair (1896); covered the Dreyfus Affair for* La Fronde *(1898–99); became converted to political rights for women (1900); was especially active in peace and women's causes (1912–14); advocated a negotiated peace (1916–18); spoke in honor of the Russian Revolution (1917); spoke at a women's reception for President Wilson, and joined* l'Humanité *(1919); joined and then left the Communist Party (1921–23); gave her last speech, at a*

*Opposite page*

*Caroline M. Severance*

*rally protesting death sentences for Sacco and Vanzetti (1927); published her last article (1929).*

*Writings (collected articles published in Paris unless otherwise noted):* Pages rouges *(H. Simonis Empris, 1893);* Notes d'une frondeuse *(H. Simonis Empris, 1894);* Pages mystiques *(H. Simonis Empris, 1895);* En marche *(H. Simonis Empris, 1896);* Affaire Dreyfus—Vers la lumière—Impressions vécues *(P.-V. Stock, 1900);* Sainte-Hélène, pièce en deux actes, en prose *(V. Giard & E. Brière, 1904), a two-act play;* Sac-à-Tout *(1906), a children's story; with Ferdinand Buisson, Victor Bérard, and Paul Painlevé,* Pour l'Arménie indépendente *(Ligue des Droits de l'Homme et du Citoyen, 1920);* Line, 1855–1867 *(G. Crès, 1921), an autobiography of her childhood; with Comtesse de Noailles, J.-G. Frazer, and Paul-Louis Couchoud,* Quatre Témoignages sur Anatole France *(La Charité-sur-Loire: A. Delayance, 1924);* Choix du papiers, annotés par Évelyne Le Garrec *(Éditions Tierce, 1982).*

*Selected important collaborations:* Le Cri du Peuple *(1883–88);* Le Gaulois *(1888–92, 1897);* Le Gil Blas *(1888–92);* Le Figaro *(1890–94, 1895);* l'Éclair *(1890–93, 1894–1901);* La Presse *(1890–91);* Le Journal *(1892–1901);* l'Écho de Paris *(1892–96);* Le Matin *(1892–94);* La Libre Parole *(1893–96);* La Fronde *(1897–1901);* Le Figaro *(1901–03);* Le Gil Blas *(1903–05, 1911–14);* Le Petit Parisien *(1906–07);* l'Intransigeant *(1909–14);* l'Oeuvre *(1909–11);* Le Matin *(1911–14?);* Excelsior *(1912–13);* Le Bonnet Rouge *(1913–14);* Le Journal *(1914–15);* La Guerre Sociale *(1915);* La Victoire *(1916);* La Vie Féminine *(1916–19);* Le Journal du Peuple *(1917–22);* La Verité *(1917–18);* Le Populaire du Centre *(1917);* l'Humanité *(1919–22);* Le Journal du Peuple *(1917–22);* l'Humanité *(1919–22);* La France de Nice *(?–?);* Le Petit Provençal *(?–?);* l'Ère Nouvelle *(1922–25);* Paris-Soir *(1923–?);* La Volonté *(1925–28);* La Fronde *(1926–27);* Le Cri des Peuples *(1928–29).*

Jean Lorraine snidely dubbed her "Our Lady of the Tear in the Eye." And a fellow journalist who disliked her once mockingly (but not inaptly) caricatured her approach to their profession: "Séverine is always for the unfortunates against society, for the washouts against the winners, for the thieves against the policeman, for the cat against the naughty children, for the mice against the cat, for the crumb of bread against the mice." Indeed, heart-wrenching descriptions of misery and moving denunciations of injustice were core staples of the fare she served up to her readers in the more than 6,000 articles she wrote over a span of 46 years. She was no mere "sob sister," however; her utter sincerity, fiery

courage, high intelligence, and formidable writing skill won her an uncontested right to be numbered among the greatest journalists of her time. Moreover, she attained a place no woman before her had reached in the thoroughly suffocating, masculine world of *la grande presse.*

Suffocation was the leitmotif of Caroline Rémy's childhood and youth until she providentially met the revolutionary socialist journalist and novelist Jules Vallès (1832–1885). Nothing in her early life would have predicted her destiny. She was born on April 27, 1855, in Paris. Her father, Marie-Joseph-Onésime Rémy (1819–1881), from Lorraine, made a modest career in the Paris Prefecture of Police as chief of the bureau overseeing wet-nurses and then as inspector of insane asylums. Honest and hardworking, he and his wife, formerly **Mlle Villiaume-Geniès** (1822–1913), from a well-regarded Parisian family, were archetypical specimens of Victorian respectability. They had no fortunes to fall back upon and thus were captives of the status conferred by a position in Napoleon III's bureaucracy. Late in life, Caroline, their only child, described them in her autobiographical novel, *Line (1855–1867),* as "well-beloved jailers"; she felt herself to be "made of their flesh" but not "of their race."

Not until her mature years did she appreciate her parents' plight, remembering especially how hard her father worked and understanding how strong were the forces binding them to a monotonous routine of work and professional social obligations. They loved her, no doubt, but it was her maternal grandmother (d. 1867) and a peasant nurse who brought light into a tightly disciplined life bereft of siblings or playmates. Of her grandmother, she wrote, "She taught me . . . kindness. She had it in the blood toward people, toward animals, toward plants, toward everything which suffering can touch . . . toward the wicked." That lesson reached deep into her soul.

Caroline learned to read even before being sent at age eight to the Biré boarding school in Neuilly. She spent two dull years there, followed by even more dreary years at the Bessières school in Paris. She received a sound education in geography, arithmetic, Latin, classical French literature, Victor Hugo (whom she worshipped), and sewing, while secretly devouring the latest works. The theater, her parents' sole diversion, led her to dream of an acting career. Her father quashed it: "I would prefer to see you dead!" He gave her two choices, virtually the only ones available to respectable young ladies outside the walls of a convent, namely, schoolteaching or marriage. The classroom

Séverine

spelled monotony. Then, to her parents' mortification, in 1870 she compromised the second choice by secretly writing love letters to a boy. They packed her off to a penitentiary convent but released her when they discovered she had written the letters for a cousin. Presently, the outbreak of the Franco-Prussian War (1870–71) effectively ended her girlhood.

During the siege of Paris (September 1870–January 1871), she rolled bandages and cared for the wounded. She never forgot the sight of a student near her on the street whose brains splashed onto his briefcase when he was struck by a shell fragment. Her experiences left her with a permanent revulsion against war. The revolt of the Paris Commune (March–May 1871) impressed her also, for when her family fled the city she found the Communard fighters at the gates to be brave, good-natured fellows, not the monsters of murder and lust imagined by her parents.

The year 1871 dealt her one final shock: marriage. Sixteen and desperate to escape, she agreed two months after their introduction to marry a charming gas company employee in his late 20s, Antoine-Henri Montrobert. Her wedding night, October 26, was a disaster, in effect a rape of a pitifully naïve girl. Montrobert revealed himself as a hypercritical bully who treated her (as the law allowed him to do) as his property. Nine months later, on July 28, 1872, she had a son, Louis-Georges-Auguste Montrobert. She gave him to a nurse, returned to her parents, and obtained a separation which granted Montrobert custody of their child.

*I* shall remain, according to the verse of the poet, "The voice which says Misery! the mouth which says No!"

—Séverine

Forced now to earn a living, for six years she gave piano lessons and did embroidery while sometimes acting in amateur productions. In 1878, she became a reader-companion to a Madame Guebhard in Neuilly, where she met her son, Adrien (1849–1924), later a distinguished archaeologist and anthropologist. Love blossomed. To avoid publicity, in late 1879 or early 1880 she went to Brussels with the Guebhards to bear a son, Roland. While there, she met Jules Vallès, a Communard now in exile, at the home of her physician, a Dr. Sénerie. She was not impressed, but Vallès was.

In 1880, the exiled Communards were granted amnesty. Vallès returned to Paris and in late October called on Caroline to ask her to act in a charity benefit. She complied and then, becoming fascinated with this famous rebel, novelist, and journalist, agreed to become his apprentice. Her parents, appalled, forbade it. Desperate, she tried to commit suicide by shooting herself in the chest. To Vallès, she wrote, "I die of what makes you live: revolt and hatred. . . . I die from having been but a woman while there burns in me a virile and ardent ideal [*pensée*]." Miraculously, she recovered in two months. If she had

subconsciously intended to extort her parents' consent, she succeeded. (Her father died later that year.) Her direction in life set, she advanced from Vallès' apprentice to editorial assistant to collaborator. Gossip to the contrary, she was his worshipful disciple, not his mistress.

On October 28, 1883, the first issue of *Le Cri du Peuple* rolled out, principally financed by Adrien Guebhard. A month later, on November 23, Caroline's first article appeared, signed "Séverin"; but on December 15 she adopted the feminine form, "Séverine." She began her first weekly column on February 15, 1884, devoting it to arts and letters, a staple for the rest of her career. Writes Claude Bellanger, the *Cri* was "the first of the socialist dailies to acquire an important audience in the working world." Vallès opened his paper to all shades of socialist opinion. Séverine warmly embraced his eclectic, tolerant approach. A socialist she was and would remain, but she had no truck with technical social analysis, historical exposition, or the exegesis of dogma popular among the rising Marxists. Rather, factual descriptions of real people and situations comprised the bedrock for any generalizations she chose to erect. Nor did she theorize about the future; the Revolution, when it destroys the bourgeois fortress, will usher in the reign of equality and justice. In the meantime, expose inequality and injustice and work to eradicate them: that is task enough.

Séverine and Adrien nursed Vallès, a tubercular diabetic, during his last year. At his death (February 14, 1885), he left her in charge of the *Cri* and with the text of an unfinished novel, *l'Insurgé* (1886), which she prepared for publication. Vallès' influence on her can hardly be overstated. She confessed she habitually asked herself, "What would Vallès have done or thought?" A year after his death, she wrote: "He was certainly, indeed, the tutor of my mind, the creator of conviction. The little I know, the little I want, it is to him I owe it. He drew me out of the mud of the bourgeoisie, he took the trouble to fashion and to mold my soul in his own image, he made the sort of doll that I was into a sincere and simple creature, he gave me a heart of a citizenness and the brain of a citizen" (*Le Cri du Peuple*, February 15, 1886).

Séverine was now the first French woman— possibly the world's first—to direct an important newspaper. Vallès had taught her journalism, and she loved it, finding it a "peculiar malady" in which the roar of the rotary presses becomes "the most beautiful music" and the smell of printer's ink a "perfume" beyond compare. Problems with the staff and a public airing of her personal life, however, finally led her to resign after three years (August 29, 1888). She tired of trying to conciliate all brands of socialism in the face of the Marxist faction led by their "pope," Jules Guesde (1854–1922). Her sympathy toward the anarchists, whose notoriety peaked between the mid-'80s and mid-'90s, particularly offended them, as did the presence of Georges de Labruyère (b. Poidebard) on the staff.

After passage of the divorce law in 1884, Séverine had divorced Montrobert and on December 2, 1885, married Adrien Guebhard, now a research professor on the Faculty of Medicine at the University of Paris. But soon thereafter she hired Labruyère away from l'Echo de Paris to enliven her paper. The same age as she, a good journalist and popular novelist, and by contemporary accounts "a strapping blade," he had a murky past, having been a soldier who reportedly abandoned a wife and three children, and was rumored to be an informant for the Sûreté Générale. They began a liaison which lasted until his death in 1920. Meanwhile, by 1888, she separated from Adrien, who went off to study geology in the Alps but still sent her 500 francs a month. They corresponded regularly, especially because of their son, whose custody he retained.

Meanwhile, Guesde's faction withdrew from the Cri in 1887 to found a short-lived rival, La Voie du Peuple. They denounced Labruyère as a police spy and tarred Séverine by repeating steamy details of their affair which had first appeared in l'Echo de Paris. She refused to cave in. Still, the struggle at the Cri took its toll.

By the time she resigned, she had begun earning extra money by writing for Le Gaulois (as "Renée") and Le Gil Blas (as "Jacqueline"), fashionable major papers whose directors coveted her talents. From 1888 until 1900, Séverine was at the peak of her popularity and earning power, "a unique figure in the annals of the French press," writes André Billy. She contributed weekly columns to a number of major papers, usually several at once (seven in 1892, six in 1893–94), with an original for each, and sometimes contracted for special assignments with other papers. This immense labor paid her 3–4,000 francs a month, five times the pay of members of Parliament. She leased a fine apartment, supported her mother (to 1913) and, not infrequently, Labruyère, and bought a mansion ("Les Trois Marches") on the outskirts of Pierrefonds near the forest of Compiègne, a residence which *Marguerite Durand later would pur-

chase from her heirs and convert for a time into a retreat for women journalists.

Séverine would write for any paper, whatever its coloration, providing she could choose her subjects and freely express her opinions. Vallès, she said, had taught her the merit of preaching to the world at large, not just to the converted. Such was her talent and reputation that publishers were willing to suffer her anarchist-tinged socialism in order to have her on board. This mutual forbearance explains why she appeared not just in left-wing papers but in the royalist Le Gaulois, conservative society papers like Le Figaro, mass-circulation giants like Le Journal or l'Echo de Paris, and Édouard Drumont's rabidly anti-Semitic La Libre Parole. Her subjects were as diverse as her outlets, although she infused them all with a reforming message, even when writing literary or art criticism. She would never let her readers forget: "Each paving stone of our streets is a heart of a wretch over whom passes—spirited, pretty, dressed up—the retinue of the rich." She wrote against the exploitation of children, the abuse of women, and (to a scandalized public) in favor of a right to abortion; against vivisection, cruelty to animals, and blood-sports (especially bullfighting); against the oppression visited on Native Americans, Armenians, Bulgarians, and Algerian Arabs; against maltreatment of soldiers in disease-ridden barracks and transports. Despite critics who accused her of publicity-seeking, in the "Carnet de Séverine," a regular feature from July 1894 to May 1896, she described needy cases and raised huge contributions; female "visitors" checked out the stories, and the funds were carefully controlled. It has been said that, especially because of the "Carnet," she was, save for the actress *Sarah Bernhardt, probably the best-known woman in France in the 1890s.

As a reporter, she won notice for her walk through the smoking ruins of the Opéra-Comique in 1887. In 1890, she became the first woman reporter to descend into a mine when she reported on an explosion at St.-Étienne which cost 150 lives; two days later, it exploded again. Her greatest coup came when she, a nonpracticing Catholic, obtained an exclusive interview with Pope Leo XIII (r. 1878–1903) on July 31, 1892 (in Le Figaro, August 4), in which, among other things, she elicited a condemnation of rising anti-Semitism, causing a commotion. Later, on September 28 in Le Journal, she described disguising herself as a worker in a sugar mill to report on the terrible conditions causing a strike. And in May 1897 her visit to the scene of the horrific Charity Bazaar fire, which incinerated over 100 society women, resulted in gruesome depictions which set a standard for realistic reportage.

In politics, she would neither support nor condemn General Georges Boulanger (1837–1891), behind whom gathered a motley protest movement (1886–89), threatening the Third Republic (1870–1940) with populist military rule or a monarchist restoration. Her failure to denounce Boulanger led the Possibilist Socialists at the *Cri* to resign. (Meanwhile, Labruyère left to help found the Boulangist *Le Cocarde*, whose title she suggested.) In her opinion, Boulangism was the product of widespread disgust over the politicians' corruption and failure to address social questions, a sentiment she shared. Boulanger, she thought, was a decent fellow, but shallow. When his movement collapsed, she predictably defended him against his persecutors. His suicide on the grave of his mistress struck her not as ridiculously theatrical but as a testimony to love; she dedicated *Notes d'une frondeuse* (1894) to "The Memory of Two Lovers." It was she, too, who fingered Mermeix (Gustave Téry) as the author of the exposé of Boulangism's inner workings, *Les Coulisses de boulangisme* (1890).

As for anarchism, she admired the courage and free spirit of its advocates. When bomb-throwing and assassinations ensued, she would not praise these acts directly but wrote of their causes in the vast swamps of desperation-breeding slums which cried out to be eradicated. Amidst the uproar, hers was an unpopular position.

Ultimately, it appears she found herself paying for this stance. Combined with the Max Lebaudy affair and her ongoing involvement with the erratic Labruyère, it caused her to lose contracts; by 1897, she was down to 1,200 francs per month. In 1891, Labruyère had been sentenced to 13 months in prison (overturned on appeal) for aiding, on Séverine's advice, the escape from France of one Alexandref Padlewski, the nihilist assassin of a Russian intelligence paymaster, General Seliverstoff. Later, in 1893, Labruyère fought a duel in defense of Séverine's honor over an article she wrote in 1885. It was the Max Lebaudy affair in 1895–96, however, that caused Séverine the most trouble. She had raised an outcry over protracted sick leaves given by the army to this dissolute heir to a vast sugar fortune. When he suddenly died of typhoid fever on December 24, 1895, criticism rained down on her. She retorted that debauchery on his numerous leaves had fatally undermined his constitution. Then, on January 11,

1896, Labruyère was arrested for allegedly having tried to extort funds from Lebaudy via another journalist. The famed polemicist Henri de Rochefort (1831–1913) rushed to attack Séverine, who maintained that Labruyère had been framed by the journalist in an attempt to bribe him to get her to drop the Lebaudy affair. Rochefort and others dragged her private life through the press again, and again she fought back. Labruyère was acquitted in March 1896 for lack of evidence, but, on April 25, a fatigued Séverine resigned from *La Libre Parole*, citing doctors' orders.

She continued at *l'Eclair* and *Le Journal* until 1901, but her association with Marguerite Durand's *La Fronde* and the treason case against Captain Alfred Dreyfus occupied center stage. She had known Durand—her first close female friend—since the Boulanger days. Durand needed her for her daring enterprise, the world's first daily entirely written and produced by women. Séverine bargained hard (business was business) but came aboard and appeared in the first issue, December 9, 1897. Coincidentally, the Dreyfus Affair was now exploding after lying dormant since the wealthy Jewish captain's conviction in December 1894. (The Dreyfus Affair began in 1894 when Captain Alfred Dreyfus, the highest-ranking Jewish officer in the French army, was convicted of passing military secrets to the Germans. The possibility that Dreyfus had been convicted by army officials who deliberately used falsified evidence created a deep split in the French population. The "Affair," as it came to be known in France, ended with the exoneration of Dreyfus, but not before France had almost come to civil war.)

Séverine was at *La Libre Parole* in 1894 when it broke the news of the army's arrest of Dreyfus. She disliked "the Jewish Spirit," which she equated with exploitive capitalism and arrogance, and thought Jews often invited persecution, although she deplored violence against them or any minority. Like virtually everyone, she had rejoiced at Dreyfus' conviction. She ignored subsequent attempts to interest her in the case, but the army's rapid trial and acquittal of Major Esterhazy (the real author of the incriminating *bordereau*) followed by Émile Zola's denunciation of this farce in his letter "J'accuse!" on January 13, 1898, led her to grasp the issues and demand the truth (January 15). Through the main phase of the Affair (1898–99), she was a prominent member of the band of journalists who fought to get Dreyfus a fair retrial. She experienced, as she put it, "the immense ecstacy of confronting the cries for death and the brutal violence of imbeciles." She was threatened with assassination (June 3, 1898) and carried a pistol for defense. Victor Basch, a colleague, described her as "the great comfort of the little Dreyfusard army. She had in the midst of anguish the heroism of the smile."

The Dreyfus Affair was probably her finest hour, for she fought for justice while conquering her own anti-Semitism as she came to appreciate its malignant power even in a nation as enlightened as France. Her articles, many republished in *Vers la lumière* (1900), remain valuable troves for historians, notably for the Rennes trial (August–September 1899), which convicted Dreyfus again before he was pardoned (September 19) by an embarrassed government.

Séverine's support of Dreyfus, when added to her trouble over anarchism, Lebaudy, and Labruyère, alienated many readers. After 1900, she was much less in vogue than she had been in the 1890s. Probably sensing *La Fronde*'s coming financial failure, she left it in late 1901, although she remained friends with Durand. Her efforts became somewhat scattered; she wrote a play, *Sainte-Helène* (1904), and a children's story, *Sac-à-Tout* (1906), and in 1905–08 she seems to have experienced bouts of depression. Still, she was hardly unemployed. From 1900 to the First World War (1914–18), she appeared at one time or another in 29 newspapers and periodicals, including some of the largest, as usual treating all manner of subjects. Also, a series of lectures on the Dreyfus Affair in Brussels in October and November 1899 opened an auxiliary career. She became a fine lecturer and spoke frequently in France, Belgium, and Switzerland on such disparate subjects as Vallès, vivisection, poverty, world peace, the Armenian massacres, women writers, and feminism.

She came to feminism surprisingly late. In 1885 and 1893, she declined calls to run symbolically for Parliament, professing disdain for universal suffrage ("a wormy apple") and politicians: to be a deputy "is to be a zero, a zero that is always suspect and often harmful." Women have a healing and consoling mission, "the power to inspire, but not the creative force." She cherished her utter independence, would join no organizations (save for the League of the Rights of Man and of Citizen, formed during the Affair), and, besides, intensely disliked "unladylike" behavior. It was the Fifth International Congress on the Condition and Rights of Women (1900), organized by Durand, which finally converted her fully to political action and the vote for women, lacking which, she now ad-

mitted, their economic and social condition—which she had long deplored—could not be remedied. It was one of her virtues that she never feared admitting an error or changing her mind. In 1912–14, she was a leader in the fight for the vote. In 1912, she went with *Hubertine Auclert and Durand and 20 others to the Chamber of Deputies to demand it. On May 20, 1914, in a speech to the National League for the Vote for Women, she proposed a federation of all women's suffrage groups; and on May 26 she chaired a meeting of the French League for the Rights of Women, containing delegates from 18 associations, which passed a resolution creating such a federation. Furthermore, she initiated the Condorcet demonstration in Paris on July 5, 1914, when some 6,000 women marched for the vote, the largest such event in France to date.

Séverine linked feminism to pacifism. She strongly supported the prewar peace movement inspired by *Bertha von Suttner. The outbreak of war in 1914 appeared to her an unmitigated tragedy. It also affected her personally, as both her sons served at the front and invasions forced her to abandon Pierrefonds for Sauges (Haut-Loire) in 1914 and Savigny-sur-Orge (Seine-et-Oise) in 1918. Her pacifism relegated her to small, left-wing papers. She railed against the lying propaganda and the rigid, often stupid, censorship which cut swaths through her articles, and wrote of suffering soldiers, civilian heroism, and humanitarian work by women. She spoke, too, making a great address (November 28, 1915) at the Trocadero in honor of the heroic English nurse *Edith Cavell, and another at a demonstration on April 1, 1917, hailing the Russian Revolution. From January 1916 until the government shut it down in July 1917, she joined a study group of about 20 intellectuals devoted to ferreting out the truth about the origins and conduct of the war. Through the last two years of the war, she advocated a negotiated peace to save what could be saved and thus was labeled a "defeatist." Her article "Prayer to the Unnamed," i.e., to peace (January 1, 1917, in *Le Journal du Peuple*), became a fixture in postwar secondary school textbooks. She ardently championed former premier Joseph Caillaux, who sought a negotiated peace but was prosecuted for treasonous communication with the Germans. She also defended fellow pacifists like Charles Rappaport and **Lucie Colliard** and courageously testified (with Durand) on March 26, 1918, at *Hélène Brion's trial for sedition.

When the war ended, she felt no joy, only relief. At a women's reception for President Woodrow Wilson on January 25, 1919, she spoke in support of his projected League of Nations. Fearing that the war had terribly distorted people's thinking, she ridiculed the rising cult of the Unknown Soldier, charging that it was only sanctifying future butcheries: "Since the people need a religion, they offer a new idol to the fervent." Instead, wounded soldiers, widows, and orphans, victims of a war fought to enrich capitalist profiteers, should be given better treatment.

Revolted by what the capitalist world had wrought, she seized upon the Russian Revolution, currently in its most idealistic phase, as humanity's new hope. In an uncharacteristic act, she joined the Socialist Party (and the staff of l'Humanité) in 1919 and on January 12, 1921, joined the Communist Party when it split from the Socialists. She even wrote (November 5, 1922) that she looked "toward Moscow as one consults the pole star, in order not to deviate from the right path." Two months after this effusion, however, she was excommunicated for refusing Moscow's order to resign from the League of the Rights of Man and of Citizen. "I am not made for discipline," she wrote in 1925, "and all compulsion rouses in me immediate insubordination." Still, she never repudiated the Soviet Union, although she did express regret that it remained a dictatorship.

Through the 1920s, she faithfully reflected mainstream leftist views. She warmly supported the League of Nations, criticized any stern treatment of Germany as likely to plant seeds of war, and deplored the rise of dictatorships in Eastern Europe. Benito Mussolini's movement, which confused so many in the '20s and '30s, deceived her not at all: "Fascism is not only the enemy of our liberties—it is war!" (La Volonté, November 28, 1925).

Her personal life had settled down without losing its unorthodox flavor. Her relations with Labruyère became episodic after the late 1890s and remained stormy. They often lived apart, for he was a difficult man. He died in 1920. The ever-forgiving Adrien then returned to spend his last years with her, dying on May 28, 1924. She admired him—"my best friend"; they simply had different temperaments, she explained. Sadly, their son, Roland, probably embittered by his mother's abandonment of him as a child, sued over the inheritance. He died in 1926, but his widow continued the suit.

Séverine worked until the end. She joined the briefly revived La Fronde in 1926–27, and in 1927 she and Durand had the satisfaction of being the first women invited to the Association of Journalists (la Maison des journalistes),

where they spoke. She made her last speech at a huge rally on July 23, 1927, at the Cirque de Paris protesting the impending execution in the United States of the anarchists Sacco and Vanzetti. The ovation for her went on for ten minutes. In 1928, she joined her grandson-in-law Bernard Lacache's new Le Cri des Peuples, which boasted a roster of big names—H.G. Wells, G.B. Shaw, Albert Einstein, Henri Barbusse, and Stefan Zweig. Her last article, decrying King Alexander's establishment of a dictatorship in Yugoslavia, appeared in the Cri on February 10, 1929.

During 1928 her health declined. In February 1929, she began to hemorrhage and suffer from uremia. She rallied in March but died at "Les Trois Marches" on April 24. Her last words were, "Always you must work. Always you must tell the truth." Some 2,000 people, many in official delegations, followed her casket to the Pierrefonds cemetery after civil rites. Her epitaph reads, "I have always struggled for Peace, Justice, and Fraternity." In Paris, a park along the boulevard Mortier in the 20th arrondissement was named for her.

Séverine was an attractive, stylish woman to the end of her life, with reddish-blonde hair—until it suddenly turned prematurely white following a hysterectomy on March 16, 1899—violet blue eyes, dark eyebrows, thick lips, strongly defined features, and a fine figure. Given her upbringing, one can well imagine her remaining the decorative "doll" she described herself as being. Beneath that pleasing exterior, however, brewed a volcano of energy and will. She made her way against all odds in a man's world to the highest reaches of her profession. By chance, she met Jules Vallès. To him, she owed her life, she believed. It is hard to disagree. An anarchist in spirit, he taught her to love independence. She once defined anarchism: "The core of the doctrine is, in a word, to leave to each the independence of his temperament, his character, his judgment." He also taught her to heed the compassion whose first stirrings had been awakened by her grandmother. In temperament, she was sentimental and romantic, a daughter of Victor Hugo and *George Sand. Critics complained that her sensibility overrode her reason. She paid them no heed. In 1887, she had stated her credo: "With the poor always, despite their errors, despite their faults, despite their crimes!" For 46 years, through thousands of articles and speeches, she remained true to her vision of her mission: "The voice which says Misery! the mouth which says No!"

SOURCES:

Braude, Beatrice. "Séverine: An Ambivalent Feminist," in *The Feminist Art Journal*. Vol. 2, 1973, pp. 14–15.

———. "Séverine, 'écrivain de combat,'" in *Nineteenth Century French Studies*. Vol. 4, 1976, pp. 404–412.

Delfau, Mireille. "Séverine journaliste: Une héritière méconnue de la Commune," in *Les Écrivains français devant la Guerre de 1870 et devant la Commune: Colloque, novembre 1970*. Paris: Librairie Armand Colin, 1972, pp. 164–172.

Le Garrec, Évelyne. *Séverine, une rebelle (1855–1929)*. Paris: Éditions du Seuil, 1982.

Offen, Karen. "Séverine," in *An Encyclopedia of Continental Women Writers*. Edited by Katherine M. Wilson. NY: Garland, 1991.

Rafferty, Frances. "Madame Séverine (1855–1929)." Ph.D. diss., University of Notre Dame, 1974. University Microfilms 75–01866.

———. "Madame Séverine: Crusading Journalist of the Third Republic," in *Contemporary French Civilization*. Vol. 1, 1977, pp. 185–201.

Séverine. *Choix de papiers, annotés par Évelyne Le Garrec*. Paris: Éditions Tierce, 1982.

SUGGESTED READING:

Bellanger, Claude, *et al. Histoire générale de la presse française*. 3 vols. Paris: Presses Universitaires de France, 1969–72.

Billy, André. *Les Écrivains de combat*. Paris: Les Oeuvres représentatives, 1935.

———. *l'Époque 1900*. Paris: J. Tallandier, 1951.

Bonnefon, Jean de. *La Corbeille des roses, ou les dames de lettres*. Paris: Société d'éditions de Bouville, 1909.

Braude, Beatrice. "Séverine, the Independent." Ph.D. diss., City University of New York, 1971. University Microfilms 72–5069.

Bredin, Jean-Denis. *The Affair: The Case of Alfred Dreyfus*. Trans. Jeffrey Mehlman. NY: George Brazillier, 1986.

Brogan, Denis W. *The Development of Modern France, 1870–1939*. London: Hamish Hamilton, 1967.

Cazes, Albert. "Une Princesse du journalisme: Séverine (1855–1929)," in *La Grande Revue*. June 1930, pp. 361–385; July 1930, pp. 105–124.

Guerlac, Othon. *Trois Apôtres: Drumont, Rochefort, Séverine*. Paris: Alcan-Lévy, 1896.

Kleeblatt, Norman L., ed. *The Dreyfus Affair: Art, Truth, and Justice*. Berkeley, CA: University of California Press, 1987.

Lacache, Bernard. *Séverine*. Paris: Gallimard, 1930.

Lecigne, Chanoine C. *Madame Séverine*. Arras: Suer-Charruey, 1902.

Néré, Jacques. *Le Boulangisme et la presse*. Paris: A. Colin, 1964.

Salomon, Michel. *Études et portraits littéraires*. Paris: Librairie Plon, 1896.

Seager, Frederic H. *The Boulanger Affair: Political Crossroads of France, 1886–1889*. Ithaca, NY: Cornell University Press, 1969.

Vallès, Jules. *Correspondance avec Séverine*. Préface et notes de Lucien Scheler. Paris: Les Éditions français réunis, 1972.

Wright, Gordon. *France in Modern Times*. 4th ed. NY: W.W. Norton, 1987.

COLLECTIONS:

In Paris: Bibliothèque Marguerite Durand; microfilms of the newspapers for which she wrote are available through the Association pour la conservation et reproduction photographique de la presse (ACRPP).

**David S. Newhall**,
Professor Emeritus of History, Centre College,
author of *Clemenceau: A Life at War* (Edwin Mellen, 1991)

## Sevier, Clara Driscoll (1881–1945).

*See Driscoll, Clara.*

## Sévigné, Marie de (1626–1696)

*French aristocrat and landowner best known for the lively series of letters which she wrote to her daughter over the course of more than 20 years. Name variations: Marie Rabutin-Chantal; Marie de Rabutin Chantal; Madame de Sévigné; Marquise de Sevigne. Born in Paris, France, on February 5, 1626; died on April 17, 1696, at Les Rochers, Provence; only child of Celse-Bénigne de Rabutin-Chantal (1596–1627) and Marie de Coulanges (1603–1633); granddaughter of \*Jeanne Françoise de Chantal (1572–1641); married Henri, Marquis de Sévigné (1623–1651), on August 4, 1644; children: Françoise-Marguerite, future countess de Grignan (1646–1705); Charles (March 12, 1648–March 26, 1713).*

*Born into the French aristocracy but orphaned at age seven; raised by her extended family and given a good education; age 18, married a noble (1644); after husband was killed in a duel (1651), raised her children and administered her estates while maintaining her independence; became deeply attached to her daughter and wrote to her whenever the two were separated after the daughter's marriage (1670).*

*Selected writings: (edited by Roger Duchêne) Correspondance de Mme de Sévigné (Paris, 1972–78). Madame de Sévigné's letters are her main claim to fame; witty, dramatic, poetic, and boldly descriptive, they provide a unique perspective on the high politics of the reign of the magnificent Sun King, while they are also rich in the details of everyday life, revealing the feelings of a mother far away from the daughter she loves.*

"M. de Langlée has given \***Mme de Montespan** a dress of gold on gold, all embroidered with gold, all edged with gold, and on top of that a sort of gold pile stitched with gold, mixed with a certain gold, which makes the most divine stuff ever imagined. The fairies have secretly woven this work; no living hands could have devised it." Marie de Sévigné's prose glitters like the sheen of the dress she describes, and her style is as light and nimble as those magical weavers.

On her father's side, Marie's forebears were distinguished Burgundian nobility, the men with a reputation for wit and swordplay and the women known for their piety; her paternal grandmother, *Jeanne de Chantal, had become a nun after she was widowed and was to be declared a saint in 1767. On the Coulanges side, the family was bourgeois rather than noble and had only recently become wealthy. Celse-Bénigne de Rabutin married **Marie de Coulanges** in 1623 but because of his involvement in a dueling scandal the following year, his properties were confiscated and he was sentenced to death. Probably protected by his high rank, Sévigné's father escaped and returned to Paris after a few months. A son who was born in 1624 did not survive the year; a daughter died at birth in 1625. Marie Rabutin-Chantal (later Sévigné), the couple's third child, "a survivor, blessed with a robust constitution, with a happy nature, with a touch of genius" according to **Frances Mossiker**, one of her biographers, was born on February 5, 1626.

*I* have never known a love so strong, so tender, so delicious as that you harbor for me. I sometimes think how that love . . . has always been the one thing in the world for which I longed most passionately.

—Madame de Sévigné to her daughter

Marie was only 18 months old when her father was killed. Involved in another illegal duel, he had left Paris to fight against the English; accounts of his gallant death report that he had three horses killed under him before he fell in battle. The little girl was orphaned in 1633, at the age of seven, when her mother suddenly died. She was cared for by her maternal grandparents for four years and, following their deaths, by her uncle; she was raised with her cousin, Philippe-Emmanuel de Coulanges whom she called "little Coulanges," her lifelong friend.

The girl received an excellent education, as befitted her aristocratic birth: she studied Italian and Spanish and was later to read works in these languages for pleasure. An avid reader from her youth, she was not an intellectual, but she knew some Latin and was able to hold her own in the company of scholars. She learned singing and dancing, skills essential for one destined to move in court circles, but, thanks to her bourgeois relatives, she also acquired a sound business sense and an appreciation for the virtues of thrift and self-restraint.

Few observers called Sévigné a great beauty, given the exacting standards of the day. Even one of her greatest friends, Countess *Marie-

**Madeleine de La Fayette**, observed in her famous "pen-portrait" that there were "imperfections." However, the countess concluded that "when one listens to you to talk, one loses sight of the fact that your features are not entirely regular; one credits you with a flawless beauty." Apart from the brilliance and wit of her conversation, Marie had the particular gifts of empathy, loyalty and kindness, gifts which were to turn her admirers, both male and female, into devoted friends.

On August 3, 1644, at age 18, she was married to a Breton noble, Henri, Marquis de Sévigné. The marquis, although he was from a family with a lineage as noble as Marie's, had reached the age of 21 without securing either a position at court or a military commission. He was good looking, hot tempered, and seems not to have been in love with his wife. The couple honeymooned at Les Rochers, the groom's romantic château in Brittany, and the new bride soon found herself frequently left alone there while her husband pursued his affairs and courted his mistresses in Paris. It was also cheaper to maintain the household in Brittany; her new husband was such a spendthrift that Marie's relatives insisted on the legal separation of her estates so that they could not be sold to cover his debts. Mme de Sévigné never forgot the humiliation of that turbulent time; she observed more than 40 years later: "The state of matrimony is a dangerous disease: far better to take to drink in my opinion."

**Françoise-Marguerite de Sévigné** (later countess de Grignan), the couple's first child, and the one who was always to hold first place in her mother's heart, was born in Paris on October 10, 1646; their son Charles was born 18 months later, on March 12, 1648. Her errant husband boasted of his romantic conquests to his wife's cousin, Roger, Count de Bussy-Rabutin. As Bussy tells it, in his scandalous and vindictive *An Amorous History of the Gauls*, he sprang to his cousin's defense: "were she not your wife, she's the one whom you would seek as your mistress." When Sévigné spurned Bussy's own offer to become her lover, he criticized "the frigidity of her nature" and, while he did not accuse her of taking other lovers, suggested that "if one judges by intent rather than action, that's another story." Bussy also observed that "for a lady of quality, her humor is a bit too broad, her manner a bit too free. . . . [S]he will condone and even encourage the most risqué topics of conversation, as long as they are veiled in innuendo." Marie was 28 when her husband was killed in a dispute with another man over his latest mistress. He died on Marie's birthday, February 5, 1651. She was understating the case when she recollected, in a letter written in 1671, "I have been unfortunate when it comes to husbands."

Understandably, Sévigné later remembered the year of her widowhood as "calm and happy enough, a blessedly uneventful year, free of notoriety, out of the public eye." She turned to her family for support and advice. Her uncle, the Abbé de Coulanges, whom she called "Bien Bon" (very, very good), established himself as her financial manager; "he was my father and benefactor to whom I owed all the serenity and peace of mind that made my life so sweet."

She was not to stay out of the public eye for long. As a young, attractive, accomplished and wealthy widow, she was soon the center of attention and the subject of many "pen portraits," descriptive prose pieces which were the fashion of the day. Her friend, the novelist *Madeleine de Scudéry, praised her physical charms, her skills in conversation, her voice, which was "sweet, well-modulated, pleasant to the ear." Scudéry observed that she "writes like she talks . . . that is to say, in the most delightful, most scintillating manner possible to imagine." On her return to Paris, Mme de Sévigné frequented the famous salon of ❦▶ Mme de Rambouillet, known for its gatherings of intellectuals and brilliant conversation. Women played leading roles in establishing new standards of civility and culture in Paris and the movement was to influence the whole of Europe. Sévigné was one of the so-called *précieuses*, satirized by Molière in his comedy *Les Précieuses ridicules*. His witty portrayal is clear indication that the male intellectuals were being made to feel somewhat insecure by the "ridiculous female pedants."

Sévigné's falling-out with her cousin Bussy dates from 1658. She had promised him a loan for a military campaign but, probably on the advice of Bien Bon, withdrew the offer. It was then that he composed his negative pen portrait, later integrated into his full-length novel, *An Amorous History of the Gauls*, published in 1665. Bussy's account details all her physical and moral defects, from eyes of different colors to her frigidity and fawning admiration for royalty. Mme de Sévigné was not alone in her displeasure; because of the book's unflattering description of the court of Louis XIV, Bussy was imprisoned for a year and then exiled to his Burgundian estates for the rest of his life. He seems to have genuinely regretted his depiction of his cousin; as well as sending her his repeated apologies in his letters, he expressed public regret

❦▶ **Grignan, Françoise-Marguerite de Sévigné, Countess de** (1646–1705)

*French intellectual. Name variations: Francoise de Sevigne. Born on October 10, 1646; died on August 16, 1705; 1646; daughter of Marie de Sévigné (1626–1696) and Henri, Marquis de Sévigné (1623–1651); educated at Sainte-Marie at Nantes; married François Adhémar de Monteil de Grignan, count de Grignan, in 1668; children: one son and a number of daughters, including Pauline de Simiane.*

As a disciple of the French philosopher René Descartes, Françoise-Marguerite de Sévigné, Countess de Grignan, became known as a *femme philosophe*. She lived with her husband in Provence, and corresponded a great deal with her mother *Marie de Sévigné, who was renowned as a woman of letters—the primary scholarly medium of the time. However, at Françoise's request, after her death her letters to her mother were burned by her daughter, **Pauline de Simiane**. De Simiane also feared that her mother's remaining correspondence could inspire gossip about the family. So a young cousin burned what was left, and only some fragments of Françoise's letters to her husband and to her uncle, Roger, Count de Bussy-Rabutin, remain.

**Catherine Hundleby,** M.A. Philosophy, University of Guelph, Ontario, Canada

▶❦
***Rambouillet, Mme de.*** *See Salonnières.*

when his collected letters were published in 1697, calling Mme de Sévigné "the prettiest woman in France, my close relative whom I have always loved, whose friendship for me I could never doubt. It is a stain on my life."

Some 1,100 of Sévigné's letters survive. While she enjoyed a wide and varied correspondence with friends and relatives, the great bulk of the letters which have been preserved were to her daughter. The nature of that relationship: intense, emotional, perhaps, at times, obsessive, has been the subject of speculation and theorizing in the 300 years since her death. Readers of the letters have suggested that the passionate affection which Sévigné felt for her daughter may have been the outcome of her repressed sexuality. While her letters show her to have been flirtatious, and she certainly never lacked admirers, there is no evidence that she indulged in a single affair. Although Mossiker has called her an *allumeuse* (a lighter of fires), Sévigné wanted to maintain her independence, to continue to make her own decisions and to advance the interests of her children, especially her daughter. In the 20th century, *Virginia Woolf, in *The Death of the Moth*, called the mother's feeling "a passion that was twisted and morbid," a judgment that seems unduly harsh, when close mother-daughter relationships are now celebrated and, perhaps, more common.

Françoise made her court debut in 1663 at the age of 17, dancing in a ballet with the king. In the years that followed, there were rumors that the lascivious King Louis would be adding her to his lengthening list of mistresses, but she may have already been showing signs of that aloof, reserved nature which was later to make her relations with her mother so complex. Whatever the reason, the king's glances wandered in other directions. Although she was educated, witty and, according to some, even more beautiful than her mother, Françoise was still unmarried at 21, an advanced age for an eligible and aristocratic woman. Count de Bussy, not always reliable in his judgment of character, observed that "hers is an intelligence tinged with bitterness. . . . She will make as many enemies for herself as her mother has made friends." Negotiations were started and abandoned with several potential suitors; Françoise might have been looking for something more than a "suitable" match.

Finally, in January 1669, Sévigné completed the arrangements for her daughter's marriage to François Adhémar de Monteil de Grignan, count de Grignan. The groom was from a noble family with an ancient lineage in Provence, the warm and exotic province of southern France, and he possessed extensive lands. The 37-year-old count had been married twice before, but both wives had died. Not handsome, but tall and graceful, the count was clearly acceptable to Françoise. Sévigné may well have put aside her sound financial instincts in the effort to please her daughter; she must have discovered during the course of negotiations that the count was a man of extravagant habits and that most of his annual revenues went towards paying off his debts. However, she liked her new son-in-law and cheerfully set about leasing a Paris house large enough to accommodate both households, clearly expecting to keep her daughter close at hand. The count's appointment as lieutenant-governor of Provence in November 1669 came as a surprise; an even greater surprise was her daughter's subsequent announcement that she planned to move to the far-off south to be with her husband. A miscarriage and another pregnancy delayed the departure, but on February 4, 1671, Françoise left Paris to live in Provence. It was with this separation that Sévigné's brilliant series of letters to her daughter commenced.

The devoted, passionate tone was established immediately: the mother wrote on February 9: "you would rather write and tell me how you feel about me than tell me so, face to face. . . . I think constantly of you. It is what the devout call an 'habitual thought'—the way one should think of God, if one were devout. Nothing can distract me from my thought of you." The following week's letter was full of yearning: "Oh, my darling, how I wish I could see you, if only for a moment, to hear your voice, to embrace you, just to see you pass by, if nothing more. . . . This separation racks my heart and soul—I feel it as if it were a physical pain."

When she was not lamenting and longing, Mme de Sévigné was soon advising and instructing. We have only one side of the dialogue; the letters from Françoise have not survived, but we see and hear her through her mother's letters. Sévigné worked at changing her daughter's haughty manner: "I see you making your curtsies, fulfilling your official duties. You are doing very well, I assure you, but try, my child, to accommodate yourself a little more to what is not really bad, to be tolerant of mediocrity, to be grateful for that which is not totally ridiculous." She was continually fearful of her daughter's repeated pregnancies, enquiring as to whether she had had her periods, advising the couple not only to sleep in separate beds but also to have someone else sleep in the room, and warning that she would not come to visit if her daughter were pregnant again. Another oft-repeated refrain was her advice to the couple to economize and live less extravagantly: "without a little substance—everything is difficult, everything is bitter. I pity those who bring on their own ruin. . . . I die of fear when I think of all the mouths you have to feed," yet at the same time the mother, who lived vicariously in the splendors of her daughter, recounted: "You picture it to me with an air of grandeur and a magnificence with which I am enchanted."

Deeply as she missed her daughter, Sévigné lived a full and eventful life, whether she was in the bustling city of Paris or at Les Rochers, her isolated château in rocky Brittany, and she vividly presented all of it for the delight of her absent daughter. Acutely interested in fashion, when she first saw the new short and curly hairstyle at court she dismissed it as "ridiculous." Within a few days the new style was "charming," and she told her daughter, "I will have a doll's hair dressed in this fashion and send it to you." While she was never more than on the fringes of the court circle, Sévigné was well connected, and her famous letter written in April 1671 reads like the account of an eyewitness. She tells her daughter of the king's visit to his cousin, the

Marie de Sévigné

Prince de Condé, at Chantilly during which Vatel, the prince's famous chef, killed himself. Recounting the dramatic tale, she uses the present tense and reports the exact words of the participants: "At four o'clock in the morning, Vatel is pacing from place to place. Everyone is asleep." Wrongly believing that there will be no more fish delivered—"'Is that all there is?' 'Yes, Monsieur'"—and that he will be disgraced, he:

> places his sword against the door and runs it through his heart—although not until the third try, the first two wounds not being mor-

tal. He falls dead. The shipments of seafood come in from all directions. They look for Vatel to distribute it. They go to his room. They try to open the door; they burst it open; they find him drowned in his own blood.

While life in Brittany may have lacked Paris' level of drama, it was not without grandeur and magnificence of its own. In the summer of 1671, for example, the governor of Brittany invited Sévigné to dinner. The event, a meal for 28, while not on the scale of dinners at the royal court, was impressive:

> These are sumptuous repasts: the platters of roast are carried away from the table looking as if they have never been touched. And as for the pyramids of fruit, the doors are not high enough to accommodate them! Our forefathers did not foresee such monstrosities; they built doors scarcely over head-height. . . . One of these pyramids . . . composed of twenty pieces of porcelain, toppled as it came through a door—with a crash so loud as to drown out the violins, the oboes and the trumpets!

But after the celebrations, Sévigné was always glad to return to the tranquility of Les Rochers, observing that she "dies of hunger" at such events and longs to eat and return to her walks: "I have a happy nature which adjusts to and finds amusement in everything"; "I am convinced that most of our ills come from keeping our rumps glued to the seat of a chair."

Sévigné's letters show her to be a woman of tremendous vitality and resilience, finding delight in her surroundings, whether amidst the unprecedented splendor of the court at Versailles or the tree-lined *alleés* of her Brittany estate. She was blessed with energy and good health and was particularly fond of walking, a habit which doubtless assisted her in maintaining her vitality far longer than was customary in the 17th century. While the separation from her daughter, broken by Sévigné's visits to Provence and her daughter's visits to Paris, never ceased to trouble and sadden her, often the longed-for periods of reunion were not the idyllic times for which she pined. It was almost as if the realities of daily life together could not match the memories of the past nor the dreams of the future. After her daughter stayed with her in Paris for 15 months during 1674 and 1675, Sévigné wrote: "If I sometimes get my feelings hurt, it is I who am in the wrong. . . . There are people who wanted to make me think that the exorbitancy of my love embarrassed you, that my eagerness to know and fulfil your every wish annoyed you."

One of Sévigné's few periods of ill health commenced when she entered her 50s; the symp-

toms suggest that they were connected with menopause. She experienced swollen hands which made writing difficult and suffered from irregular bleeding. Her cousin Bussy sent advice from Burgundy; he claimed to have learned from a doctor "that hale and hearty women like you, who have been widowed early and who repress their natural instincts, are subject to the vapors." His solution was to suggest that she take a lover, and he expressed his regret that he was too far away to benefit from his own advice. But even the unaccustomed ailments did not dull her wit and humor; instructed to "take the cure" at the famous hot springs of Vichy, she wrote to her daughter in May 1676: "Today I started my showers. They provide a fairly good rehearsal for purgatory. One goes completely naked into a small subterranean chamber where there is a pipe of hot water controlled by a woman who directs the flow to whatever part of the body you wish. To go there with not so much as a fig leaf on is a rather humiliating experience." Humiliating or not, the results were positive: "The irregularities are regular again, and it is primarily to make this 'adieu' final and to ensure a final cleansing that I have been sent here, and I believe it was the right thing."

Sometimes Sévigné's humor verged on the macabre. In Paris during July 1676, she was among the crowd which witnessed the execution procession of the infamous \***Marie de Brinvilliers**, a young woman who had practiced the art of poisoning in the charity hospitals before setting to work on her brothers, father, husband and others who had earned her disfavor. As Sévigné reported to her daughter: "La Brinvilliers has gone up in smoke. . . . Her poor little body was tossed, after the execution, into a raging fire, and her ashes scattered to the winds. So that, now, we shall all be inhaling her! And with such evil spirits in the air, who knows what poisonous humor may overcome us?"

The famous description of the dress of gold comes, fittingly, in a letter Sévigné wrote after her first visit to the already fabled new royal Palace of Versailles in July 1676. However, the sight of such wonders could not make up for her daughter's absence, and yet when they spent periods of time together they squabbled incessantly over money, the respective states of one another's health, and particularly about Françoise's repeated pregnancies. In a letter written in the spring of 1678 when her daughter was but a few steps away, sharing her house in Paris, Sévigné reveals how difficult the relationship had become: "I fear your outbursts. I cannot bear them; they leave me dumbstruck and devastated.

If you think me a stupid woman you are right. Face to face with you, I always am—obsessed with you as I am." One of the few surviving letters written by Françoise dates from this period; writing to her husband in Provence she tells him how much she misses him and their children: "Oh, my God, will there never come a year when I can go to join my husband without having to desert my Mother? . . . But if I must choose between you, I will not hesitate to follow my very dear Count whom I love and embrace with all my heart."

As soon as they were apart, the two women became the most devoted correspondents once again, and Sévigné clung once more to the "lifeline" of her daughter's letters. She was reluctant to leave Paris to attend to her Brittany estates because of the increased distance from her daughter in the south; she did not journey there to attend her son's wedding in February 1684. While she loved her son, enjoyed his company, and was generous in her financial support, her love for him had none of the obsessive passion which she felt for her daughter. When she finally made the visit in September 1684, she reported rather smugly to Françoise concerning her new daughter-in-law that she was "given to only moments of gaiety because she suffers from the vapors. She changes her expression a hundred times a day without finding one that is becoming to her. Her health is extremely delicate. She practically never takes a walk. She is always cold. By nine o'clock she has faded away completely. . . . One would never guess that this house has a mistress other than me."

By the early 1680s, with Sévigné in her late 50s and her daughter in her late 30s, the tone of the letters, and the nature of the relationship they reflect, begins to change. While she does not cease to worry and to give unsolicited advice, mostly on financial matters, there is a new confidence and serenity and fewer references to quarrels and misunderstandings: "You are all in all to me," she wrote in September 1684, "and never has a mother been so well loved by a well-loved daughter as I by you. Oh, my darling, how once you veiled such boundless treasures from me." Reflecting her calmer state of mind, Sévigné reported that her "health is perfect. . . . I am free of the vapors. I think they came over me only because I was apprehensive about them; now that I scorn them, they have gone off to frighten some other silly soul."

Despite her advancing age, she was clearly still considered a desirable woman. In the summer of 1685, when Sévigné was 59, she received a proposal of marriage from the duke de Luynes, a widower of 65. Such a marriage would have brought her a title and a position at court as well as financial security; she had left herself with only a meager income since making a generous settlement to her son upon his marriage. But she appears not to have given the offer serious consideration; she refused to take "another master" after 30 years of independence. Only the previous year, still adjusting to the presence of a new daughter-in-law, she had written with a sense of pride: "I feel strongly that my seal should read simply Madame de Sévigné. Nothing more is necessary. No one will confuse me with anyone else during my lifetime, and that's enough."

While she would never call herself "devout" and frequently expressed the wish to be closer to God, the later letters show Sévigné increasingly referring to the will of "Providence" and expressing her resignation to its dictates: "Whoever tried to deprive me of my belief in Providence would deprive me of my only comfort. . . . I need to believe that it is the Creator of the Universe who disposes of our lives. When it is with Him that I must take issue, I no longer take issue with any other, and so I can submit." While she was always a woman who could relish the quiet delights of the country as well as the lavish excesses of the town, the later letters seem to show Sévigné increasingly treasuring her periods of contemplation in the solitude of the countryside.

One of Sévigné's letters of June 1689 paints a picture of her life at Les Rochers for her daughter: she records rising at eight, hearing Mass, picking orange blossoms, having lunch, doing needlework and reading until five in the afternoon—she or her son, when he is at home, usually read aloud to the others. She then leaves the château to walk in the forests with a servant, taking a selection of books, including a devotional work and a history book; "I daydream a bit about God and about His Providence." She returns when she hears the bell for supper at eight and there is often more reading aloud before bed; "We live so well-regulated a life, that it is almost impossible not to keep well." When a correspondent from Paris affectionately called her "old," both Sévigné and her daughter were clearly shocked at the word: "I admit that I was astonished, because I am, as yet, conscious of no deterioration which might remind me of it. . . . [I]t is only when I think about it, that I realize my age." She survived the harsh Breton winter and wrote in May that she had never felt so well, attributing her state to the regular life and "gentle and healthful exercise." Drinking a little white wine and receiving a letter from her daughter by every courier, "I ask myself what has become of all those ridiculous little ailments of mine."

Sévigné's letters were full of the coming of spring in 1690; she uses a lively, teasing tone in April: "What color do you think the trees have been for the last week? Answer me! You will say 'green.' Not so! They are red! There are little buds, all ready to open up, which are truly red, but then they all unfurl and make a little leaf, and since they do not come out all at once, the effect is a lovely mixture of red and green." In a subsequent letter, she herself becomes the embodiment of the season: "I have managed so well that spring is here in all its beauty! Everything is green. It was no easy task to see to it that all those buds unfurled, that the red all turned to green. When I finished with all those elms, I had to go on to the beeches, then to the oaks. . . . It is my great leisure I have to thank for this opportunity and, in truth, my dear bonne, it has been the most delightful experience imaginable."

Such *joie de vivre* hardly accords with the picture of Sévigné presented by **Harriet Ray Allentuch**, whose biography describes her "brooding" in later years and writes of "a passion insatiable, demanding, and never-satisfied; illness, disappointed hopes, the spectacle of death and ruin all around her." There was, of course, some diminution in Sévigné's exuberant vitality towards the end. The year 1693 was especially difficult: her cousin and lifelong correspondent, Bussy, died as did her two closest friends, **Mme de Lavardin** and Mme de La Fayette. Hail damaged the crops, there was famine and disease in Paris, and Sévigné fled to Provence. There she found her daughter weak, and Françoise soon became extremely ill with severe premenopausal bleeding and a deteriorating liver condition. Perhaps with a premonition that this would be the last of her many journeys, Sévigné wrote in February 1695: "I will die without any cash on hand, but without any debt as well. That is all I ask of God, and that suffices for a Christian."

Nursed, and no doubt lectured, by her devoted mother, Françoise was too weak even to attend the wedding of her only son in November 1695, although the ceremony took place in the chapel at Grignan. Sévigné's weariness is evident in a letter to a relative in January 1696: "As for me, I am no longer good for anything. I have played my role in life, and had I been consulted, I would never have chosen so long a life. . . . But we are fortunate that it is the will of God by which this, as all other things in this world, is decided; everything is better left in His hands than ours." The following month brought her 70th birthday and at the end of the next month, on March 29, 1696, Sévigné wrote her last letter. It was, appropriately enough, an expression of sadness to her cousin Coulanges over the death of the young son of old friends.

On April 6, 1696, Sévigné fell ill with a fever and took to her bed. She received the Last Anointing of the Church on April 11 and died on April 17. The precise cause of her death is unknown. Even more puzzling is the absence of her beloved daughter, not only from the funeral but, according to all the evidence, from her mother's sickbed before her death. Through the centuries, there have been rumors that there had been a quarrel and that the stubborn Françoise had refused to attend her dying mother. Mossiker, on the other hand, suggests that the mother finally gave up the daughter she loved more than anything in the world in the attempt to prepare her soul for death.

It is clear that Sévigné had felt the pull of Jansenism, that austere, self-denying form of the Catholic religion, for most of her life, and that she had long realized that her passionate affection for her daughter stood between, or perhaps stood in the place of her feelings towards God. As long ago as 1671, she reported that the saintly old Jansenist of Port Royal, Arnauld d'Andilly, had reprimanded her: "[H]e told me that I was very foolish not to give thought to my salvation; that I was an outright pagan, that I had set you up as an idol in my heart, and that sort of idolatry was as dangerous as any other kind, even though it might not seem sinful to me." She had often lamented her own overly intellectual and insufficiently devout approach to religion and her later letters show her more prone to reflection and contemplation of spiritual things in her beloved woods. But if Sévigné had banned her daughter from her sickbed, she could surely not have kept her away from her funeral.

It seems more likely that the daughter, whose health had appeared to be improving under her mother's devoted care, suffered a relapse and was physically unable to be with her mother at the end. We can certainly imagine Sévigné, with her last remaining strength, insisting that her daughter not be called and that she, who had known so little sickness, would soon recover. Even at the last, she would have put her daughter's health before any other consideration. Sixteen years earlier, she had made her wishes clear: "I pray that Providence will not reverse the natural order of things which made me your mother and brought me into the world long before you. . . . I should be the first to go."

The life of Mme de Sévigné cannot be ranked among the most exciting and eventful lives, even of her time and place. France in the 17th century was a beacon for all the world; its culture and refinement were models to be emulated, and its most powerful citizens lived lives that seem more crammed with happenings and somehow perhaps more significant than our own. In such exalted company, Sévigné's doings are of only secondary rank: she only occasionally spoke to the king; she was not invited to all of the most fashionable events; she experienced some of the most important happenings of the day only at second hand or not at all. And yet, we have the pleasure of knowing this warm and witty woman more intimately than we know any other woman of her century or of almost any other period. In her sparkling letters, and especially in those to her daughter, she reveals her innermost thoughts and the reader is able to experience the scenes which Mme de Sévigné first evoked for her beloved daughter's eyes. When, at age 70, her voice falls silent, we feel that we have lost a friend.

**SOURCES AND SUGGESTED READING:**

Allentuch, Harriet Ray. *Madame de Sévigné: A Portrait in Letters*. Baltimore, MD: Johns Hopkins Press, 1963.

Duchâtelet, Roger, ed. *Correspondance de Mme de Sévigné*. Paris: Fayard, 1972–78.

Mossiker, Frances. *Madame de Sévigné: A Life and Letters*. NY: Alfred A. Knopf, 1983.

Ojala, Jeanne A., and William T. Ojala. *Madame de Sévigné: A Seventeenth-Century Life*. NY: Berg/St. Martin's Press, 1990.

Williams, Charles G.S. *Madame de Sévigné*. Boston, MA: Twayne, 1981.

Thackeray, Miss (Lady *Anne Isabella Ritchie). *Madame de Sévigné*. Philadelphia, PA: J.B. Lippincott, 1881.

(Dr.) Kathy Garay,
Acting Director of the Women's Studies Programme,
McMaster University, Hamilton, Ontario, Canada

# Sewall, Lucy Ellen (1837–1890)

*American physician and feminist. Born in April 1837 in Roxbury, Massachusetts; died on February 13, 1890; elder of two daughters of Samuel Edmund Sewall and Louisa Maria (Winslow) Sewall; graduated from New England Female Medical College, 1862; never married; no children.*

Lucy Ellen Sewall was one of the first women to become a medical doctor in the United States. She was born in Roxbury, Massachusetts, in 1837 and grew up in a prominent, liberal New England family. Her mother **Louisa Winslow Sewall**, who came from a family of well-off Quakers in Portland, Maine, was an abolitionist. Her father Samuel E. Sewall, who

served in the Massachusetts Senate, was also an active abolitionist as well as a firm advocate of women's rights. In 1850, when Lucy was 13, her mother died; her father would marry his sister-in-law, **Harriet Winslow List**, in 1857.

After meeting Dr. *Marie Zakrzewska, who became the chair of obstetrics at the New England Hospital for Women, Sewall decided to pursue a medical career. She enrolled in the New England Female Medical College in Boston in 1859, graduated in 1862, and then studied for a year in London and Paris. Upon her return in 1863, she became resident physician of the New England Hospital for Women and Children. She spent much of her time with poor women and was well respected for her work in obstetrics. In 1869, she resigned her residency to become one of two attending physicians at the hospital and devote more time to her private practice. In 1881, Sewall and a group of seven other women physicians offered Harvard University $50,000 to provide medical study for women. The university declined the offer.

Sewall suffered from poor health most of her life, and she died of a heart condition in 1890 at age 52. In 1892, a new maternity building at the New England Hospital for Women and Children was dedicated to Sewall and her father, who had been a director and trustee of the institution.

**SOURCES:**

James, Edward T., ed. *Notable American Women, 1607–1950*. Cambridge, MA: The Belknap Press of Harvard University, 1971.

**Deborah Conn**, freelance writer,
Falls Church, Virginia

# Sewall, May Wright (1844–1920)

*American educator, suffragist, club founder, writer, and pacifist. Born May Eliza Wright on May 27, 1844, in Greenfield, Wisconsin; died of kidney disease on July 23, 1920, in Indianapolis, Indiana; second daughter and youngest of four children of Philander Montague Wright and Mary Weeks (Brackett) Wright; Northwestern Female College, Mistress of Science, 1866, Master of Arts, 1871; married Edwin W. Thompson (a mathematics teacher), in 1872 (died 1875); married Theodore Lovett Sewall (an educator), in 1880 (died 1895); no children.*

*Co-founded Indianapolis Equal Suffrage Society (1878); co-founded the Girls' Classical School of Indianapolis (1882); helped found the Western Association of Collegiate Alumnae (1883); served as chair of the executive committee of the National Women Suffrage Association (1882–1890); helped establish the*

*National Council of Women and the International Council of Women (1888); founded the General Federation of Women's Clubs (1889); headed the World Congress of Representative Women (1893).*

*Selected writings:* Women, World War, and Permanent Peace *(1915);* Neither Dead Nor Sleeping *(1920).*

May Wright Sewall was born in 1844 in Greenfield, Wisconsin, where her father Philander Montague Wright, of old New England stock like his wife **Mary Brackett Wright**, had brought the family to start a farm. A gifted child, May was reputedly reading Milton before she was ten. After being tutored at home by her father, who had previously worked as a schoolteacher, she attended academies in Wauwatosa and Bloomington, Wisconsin. Sewall then taught school in Waukesha to earn money for college before enrolling in Northwestern Female College (now part of Northwestern University) in Evanston, Illinois. She graduated in 1866 with a Mistress of Science degree and taught school in Mississippi, Michigan, and Indiana while also pursuing graduate work at Northwestern Female College, from which she received a Master of Arts degree in 1871.

The following year, Sewall married Edwin W. Thompson, and both began working in Indianapolis at what later became Shortridge High School, she as a teacher of German and English literature and he as a mathematics teacher. She continued teaching there after her husband's death in 1875. That same year, she became an early member of the Indianapolis Woman's Club (for which she would design a clubhouse, the Propylaeum, built in 1891). Already a strong proponent of women's suffrage, in 1878 she joined with *Zerelda G. Wallace to found the Indianapolis Equal Suffrage Society. Sewall became secretary of the organization, which served as an alternative to the local branch of the American Woman Suffrage Association (AWSA), founded by *Lucy Stone. In 1880, she married Harvard-educated Theodore Lovett Sewall, who ran a boys' school in Indianapolis, and stopped teaching. The following year, Sewall became deeply involved in the push for a suffrage amendment in Indiana, which would fail by a narrow margin in 1883. She and her husband meanwhile, in 1882, had founded the Girls' Classical School of Indianapolis. Sewall would serve as administrator of the school, which quickly became prominent in the area, for 25 years. After 1889, she would be assisted in running the school by her husband Theodore, who closed his own school in order to join her that year.

Even as she began running her new school in 1882, Sewall also became chair of the executive committee of the National Woman Suffrage Association (NWSA), *Susan B. Anthony's and *Elizabeth Cady Stanton's rival to the AWSA. She would hold this position for the next eight years, often testifying to Congress in the struggle for suffrage. In 1887, a meeting of the Indianapolis Equal Suffrage led to the organization of an Indiana branch of the NWSA, of which Sewall served as chair of the executive committee for two years. In 1888, she co-organized, with *Frances Willard, and attended an international women's assembly in Washington, D.C., marking the 40th anniversary of the first women's rights convention in Seneca Falls, New York. At the assembly was born the National Council of Women, intended as an umbrella organization for all stripes of women's groups in the country, for which Sewall served as initial recording secretary. The creation of the National Council of Women was followed a year later, again by Sewall and Willard, by that of the International Council of Women, of which she was an active member. Also in 1889, she traveled to Paris as a delegate of the NWSA and the National Council of Women to the International Congress of Women, sponsored by the French government in connection with the Exposition Universelle. Speaking in French, Sewall delivered one of the principal addresses at the congress, and won high praise for her eloquence.

By this time she had become a prominent lecturer on higher education for women and equality before the law. Sewall delivered addresses at most of the suffrage conventions across the United States, and also wrote a number of articles and chapters for books promoting suffrage and education. For several years, she edited a women's column in the *Indianapolis Times.* She put her ideas into practice at her girls' school, where the curriculum included the novelty (some considered it a dangerous practice for girls) of physical education as well as a deep grounding in mathematics and ancient and modern languages. Her students were encouraged to believe that all fields of knowledge were both open to them and worthy of their attention. Sewall also instituted dress reform at the school, no small matter in an era when longtime corset use could seriously impair health. As well, in 1883 she became a founder of the Indianapolis Art Association and its art school, which would later become the John Herron Art Institute. On the national level, she was active in the Association of Collegiate Alumnae and was a founder

(1883) and twice president of the Western Association of Collegiate Alumnae (1886, 1888–89), both forerunners of the American Association of University Women.

In 1892–93, Sewall traveled abroad to kindle interest in and recruit speakers for the World's Congress of Representative Women, planned to coincide with the Columbian Exposition in Chicago in 1893. She presided over the congress, at which 300-plus women from numerous countries read papers on all facets of women's issues. Her husband died in 1895, but Sewall continued running her school and actively pursuing suffrage and social improvements for women. She was an organizer of an Indianapolis "Ramabai Circle," dedicated to raising funds for *Pandita Ramabai's efforts to educate young widows in India, and remained active in the General Federation of Women's Clubs, of which she had been a founder in 1889. Sewall served as president of the National Council of Women from 1897 to 1899, and as president of the International Council of Women from 1899 to 1904. In 1900, she was appointed a U.S. representative to the Paris Exposition by President William McKinley. During the last 15 years of her life, she was an active member of the American Peace Society. In 1915, she published *Women, World War, and Permanent Peace* and also presided over the International Conference of Women Workers to Promote Permanent Peace at the Panama Pacific Exposition in San Francisco. That December, she accompanied *Rosika Schwimmer on the "Peace Ship" (*Oscar II*), funded by Henry Ford in an attempt to end the war in Europe.

After closing her school in 1907, Sewall had moved to Cambridge, Massachusetts, and later to Eliot, Maine. Despite having for years attended the Unitarian Church with her husband, she turned to spiritualism after his death, apparently seeking contact with him. Her book *Neither Dead Nor Sleeping*, published in the last year of her life, described her experiences with psychic phenomena. Once described as "powerful, dominant, and queenly in personality," able to inspire both "tender and loyal friendships and vivid aversions," Sewall died in Indianapolis in 1920, age 76.

SOURCES:
*Dictionary of American Biography.* 20 vols. NY: Scribner, 1935, p. 610.

Eagle, Mary Kavanaugh Oldham. *The Congress of Women Held in the Woman's Building, World's Columbian Exposition.* Chicago, IL: International, 1895, pp. 771–775.

Gates, Susa Young. *The Relief Society Magazine.* September 1920, pp. 499–501.

James, Edward T., ed. *Notable American Women, 1607–1950.* Cambridge, MA: The Belknap Press of Harvard University, 1971, pp. 269–271.

Logan, Mrs. John A. *The Part Taken by Women in American History.* Wilmington, DE: Perry-Nalle, 1912, pp. 580–581.

McHenry, Robert, ed. *Famous American Women.* NY: Dover, 1980.

**Harriet Horne Arrington**, freelance biographer, Salt Lake City, Utah

# Seward, Anna (1742–1809)

*English poet. Name variations: "Swan of Lichfield"; Benvolio. Born in Eyam, Derbyshire, England, on December 12, 1742; died at the Bishop's Palace, in Lichfield, Staffordshire, on March 25, 1809; elder of two surviving daughters of Thomas Seward (rector of Eyam and later canon of Lichfield and Salisbury) and Elizabeth Hunter Seward (whose father had been headmaster of Lichfield Grammar School and the teacher of Dr. Samuel Johnson); never married; no children.*

Anna Seward was born in 1742 in Eyam, Derbyshire, England, and grew up in the household of an aspiring writer. Her father co-edited the works of Beaumont and Fletcher, mingled with the literati, and encouraged his daughter's bookish ways. Seward began to write in her mid-30s and was a frequent contributor to the *Gentlemen's Magazine*. Having never married, she remained at home to care for her father after her mother's death in 1780. When her only sister died in 1764, Seward's affection turned to Honoria Sneyd (who later became the second wife of Richard Lovell Edgeworth and stepmother of *Maria Edgeworth). Seward also made many forays to London to visit a wide circle of writer friends. Toward the end of the 18th century, she was a well-known figure at literary salons.

It was Anna Seward who supplied Boswell with details about the early years of Dr. Samuel Johnson, who had been a student of her father's. Her dislike for Johnson was well known when she parodied his letters in the *Gentlemen's Magazine* under the signature Benvolio. In 1782, she published her poetical novel *Louisa*, a work in which she took great pride. Her poem "Llangollen Vale," published in 1796, describes a visit she made to Lady Eleanor Butler and Sarah Ponsonby, the *Ladies of Llangollen.

Upon her death in 1809, Seward bequeathed her poetical works to Sir Walter Scott, who had them published with a memoir in three volumes in 1810. Though Scott declined to market her 12-volume manuscript of letters which she had meticulously revised for publication, the letters were printed by Archibald Constable in six volumes in 1811. Biographies of Seward include E.V. Lucas' *A Swan and Her Friends* (1907), **Margaret Ashmun**'s *The Singing Swan* (1931), and H. Pearson's *The Swan of Lichfield* (1936).

# Sewell, Anna (1820–1878)

*English writer whose sole published work,* **Black Beauty,** *became both a bestselling children's classic and a rallying cry for 19th-century organizations which campaigned for the humane treatment of animals. Pronunciation: SUE-uhl. Born on March 30, 1820, in Yarmouth, Norfolk, England; died in Old Catton, near Norwich, England, on April 25, 1878; daughter of Isaac Sewell (a bank manager) and Mary Wright Sewell (a writer); had one brother; educated at home with books purchased from her mother's earnings as a writer and at a day school near Stoke Newington; never married.*

*Moved to Dalston, where she was given horse-riding lessons (1822); moved to Stoke Newington, where she eventually injured an ankle while running during a rainstorm (1832); moved to Brighton (1836); moved to Wick and began teaching a class in biology to workingmen (1848); received hydrotherapy treatments in Germany (1846 and 1856); moved to Old Catton (1867); began writing* Black Beauty *(1871); completed manuscript for* Black Beauty *and was paid £20 for the story (1877); published* Black Beauty *during Christmas season (1877); favorable reviews appeared (January 1878); 30,000 copies sold at time of her death (1878).*

*Selected writings:* Black Beauty: The Autobiography of a Horse *(Jarrold, 1877, published in America as* Black Beauty: His Grooms and Companions, *J.F. Murphy, 1891); other editions include those illustrated by Cecil Aldin (Jarrold, 1912); Katharine Pyle (Dodd, 1923); Alice B. Woodward (Bell, 1931); Rowland Wheelwright (Harrap, 1932); John Beer (Dodd, 1941); Fritz Eichenberg (Grosset, 1945); Wesley Dennis (World, 1946); (illustrated and adapted) Paul Brown (Scribner, 1952); Lionel Edwards (Ward, Lock, 1954); Charles Mozley (F. Watts, 1959); Charlotte Hough (Penguin, 1968); Victor Ambrus (Brockhampton, 1973).*

The life of the English writer Anna Sewell, the author of *Black Beauty*, was filled with paradoxes. Despite the fact that the novel would become a classic, it was her only published work and would appear in print only three months before her death. While she intended the book to be read mainly by workers who cared for horses, *Black Beauty* became both a timeless children's story and a rallying point for the British and American Societies for the Prevention of Cruelty to Animals. And although *Black Beauty* sold more than 30 million copies, becoming one of the most enduring popular literary works from the 19th century, Sewell's name was absent when her country's major biographical reference work, *Dictionary of National Biography*, was published.

Sewell was born in London in 1820, the daughter of Isaac Sewell and ❦➤ **Mary Wright Sewell**, both strict Quakers. Her family was forced to move frequently because of repeated economic troubles. At the time of Anna's birth, her father was closing out a failing business. Before her brother Philip was born two years later, another business venture had failed. Forced to declare bankruptcy, the family sold much of their furniture, including a tea set which had been a wedding gift from Mary Sewell's parents.

After a search that lasted several weeks in 1822, friends helped the family locate a small house at Dalston. The Sewells would stay there for ten years. Anna saw very little of her father, who left for work at eight in the morning and returned home at about eight at night. Between mother and daughter, however, a close bond emerged, so much so that Mary, on her daughter's ninth birthday, wrote, "Anna Sewell has this day completed her ninth year, and is in many respects a delight and comfort to her mother."

To help her family financially, Mary Sewell began to write, producing the first in a series of books for children, *Walks with Mamma*. With her earnings, she purchased books for her children's education at home. Setting high standards for their learning, she also took Anna and her brother on natural history outings and on visits to the British Museum. After reading that horseback riding contributed to both good character and good health, she arranged for her daughter to be given riding lessons.

In 1832, the family moved to Stoke Newington, where they remodeled a small house which they named "Palatine Cottage." Set in the middle of an ornamental garden with a goldfish pond, Palatine Cottage also was surrounded by sufficient land for the family to keep cows—hoping to sell the milk to neighbors—as well as ducks, hens, pigs, rabbits and bees. The family worked together to milk the cows and churn butter. There was, Sewell wrote, "no idea of degradation belonging to the work . . . and time passed most pleasantly."

For Sewell, the four-year stay at Stoke Newington, with the animals that she loved, reinforced the teachings of her family's Quaker religion regarding the care of animals. Although Mary left Quakerism during these years for a more evangelical Protestantism, the family observed Quaker rules against hunting, believing in "a tender consideration . . . for the creatures of God." In an indirect way, Stoke Newington also made it possible for Sewell to attend a nearby day school. To this point, Sewell's education had been in the form of tutoring from her mother three times a week. The topics were reading, writing, and natural history, but Sewell also read works by Wordsworth, Shakespeare and Tennyson. She especially liked Alfred, Lord Tennyson's poem "In Memoriam."

When Mary Sewell's brother arrived at Stoke Newington for an extended visit, she was unable to continue her tutoring and arranged to have Anna enrolled in a day school located about a mile away. The school gave Sewell the companionship of girls her age, even though their clothes differed from her own Quaker dress. It also introduced her to subjects, such as French and mathematics, that Mary Sewell had not emphasized. Anna, who loved to do watercolors and sketches, also received her first professional art instruction. Although her mother considered painting materials to be an extravagance, one of Sewell's favorite pastimes as an adult would be painting landscapes.

An accident Sewell suffered during the years at Stoke Newington would have a major effect on her life. Attempting to run in a downpour while on her way home from school, she slipped and fell on a steeply sloping section of the road, injuring an ankle. Thinking the injury to be only a sprain, Mary decided not to consult a doctor. When she finally took her daughter to physicians, the injury was apparently worsened by the medical treatment they prescribed, including bleeding. For Sewell, only 14 years old at the time, it was the beginning of what her mother called a life of "constant frustration."

From 1836 to 1845, the family lived at Brighton, where Sewell's father finally obtained secure and well-paying employment as branch bank manager for the London and County Joint Stock bank. The family began to think that the doctors' treatments were helping, and Anna resumed a moderately active life, going out with friends and taking a few steps at a time. Sewell also began to learn to play the piano, and both mother and daughter worked to help the poor in the Brighton workhouse.

## Sewell, Mary Wright (1797–1884)

*English author. Born Mary Wright in England in 1797; died in 1884; daughter of John Wright (a Quaker); married Isaac Sewell (a bank manager), in 1819; children: *Anna Sewell (1820–1878, a writer); Philip Sewell (b. 1822).*

Mary Wright Sewell was born in 1797, the daughter of John Wright, a Quaker. She was a governess at an Essex school before marrying Isaac Sewell (a bank manager) in 1819. In 1835, she joined the Church of England. Sewell, who had an abiding interest in philanthropy, was also the author of verses and stories of a moral nature, including her poem collections *Stories in Verse* (1861) and *Poems and Ballads* (1886).

From 1845 through 1858, the Sewells moved on to three other houses, at Lancing, Haywards Heath, and Chichester. Sewell's condition appeared to improve for a time, and the family purchased a pony and trap for her. It was her duty to drive her father to the train station in the morning and pick him up there after work in the evening. She showed pride in her skills as a driver, training the pony to respond to verbal signals and avoiding use of the whip. On one occasion she was overheard to say, "Now thee must go a little faster—thee would be sorry for us to be late at the station." Having become accustomed to animals at Palatine Cottage, Sewell showed an interest in the kind of care the hired hands were giving her pony. She made it a habit to visit the stable regularly, watching the pony eat oats in the mornings and evenings and inspecting the straw to make certain that it was clean.

While at Lancing, Sewell's condition worsened. She was able to walk with a crutch, but physicians were unable to diagnose the condition with any precision. Her mother was increasingly becoming her chief nurse. Hydrotherapy treatments during two trips to Germany by Sewell and her mother—to Marienbad in 1846 and to Boppard in 1856—appeared to be beneficial. Sewell began standing and walking for longer periods.

At this time her mother began to write a variety of verses and ballads, some of which became bestsellers. Among these were her 1862 book *Thy Poor Brother* and two ballads, including "Mother's Last Words." Sewell, who helped her mother prepare the manuscripts, also wrote a number of verses and short stories, none of which were published. While Anna and Mary were becoming constant companions, the traditional roles of mother and daughter were somewhat reversed.

Sewell, who had been confined indoors so much of her adult life, had become the more organized and responsible of the two, a fact that led her mother to nickname her "My nannie."

In 1858, the family moved to Wick, staying for six years in a house that they named "Blue Lodge." Here Mary increased her pace of writing, but Anna's health appeared to worsen. Although by now she was able to stand for only a few seconds at a time, she was often seen looking out of a window which overlooked a garden. In a letter written to a friend in late 1858, Mary Sewell referred to her daughter as "quite lame" but "very active according to her own measure."

At Wick, mother and daughter established a temperance society and an educational institute for workers who took a pledge not to drink. Sewell, who taught biology, sometimes would drive her pony and cart alone into the village at night, frequently making her way under difficult weather conditions. By the last year at Wick, however, she was unable to help her mother with an active schedule which included visiting women in the local workhouse, writing letters for them, and arranging for girls who had run away from home to return to their families.

*If* we see cruelty or wrong that we have the power to stop, and do nothing, we make ourselves sharers in the guilt.

—Anna Sewell

In addition to the problem with her ankle, Sewell apparently also suffered from other undiagnosed ailments during the last 20 years of her life, although some writers have wondered whether her symptoms, such as an occasional shortness of breath, might have been the result of her relatively confined lifestyle. Life in 19th-century England was seldom pleasant for unmarried women—or "spinsters," in Victorian terms. *Florence Nightingale was reported to have said that for unmarried women, there was no tyranny "like the petty grinding tyranny of a Good English Family."

The family moved to Bath in 1864 and finally to Old Catton. There, Sewell discovered that her pony did not like the streets, which were paved with small round pebbles, and was amused that the pony insisted on finding its own way around the edge of the road. Eventually, at age 54, Sewell became so weak that her family gave up her cart and pony.

*Black Beauty* was written during these years at Old Catton, when Sewell was in her 50s. By now she was confined largely to sitting at home, often on the family sofa. She kept a journal, written in the pages of an old account book and covering the years 1870–77. "I am quite poorly in pain," she reportedly wrote in an early entry. In the midst of journal entries which described the activities of her family, such as comments on her mother's continuing work as a Sunday School teacher, she wrote a brief running commentary indicating her progress in writing *Black Beauty*.

In 1871, she noted, "I am writing the life of a horse"; in December 1876, she added, "I am getting on with my little book, *Black Beauty*. I have for six years been confined to the house, and to my sofa, and have from time to time, as I was able, been writing what I think will turn out a little book, its special aim being to induce kindness, sympathy, and an understanding treatment of horses . . . I am anxious, if I can, to present the true condition [of cabmen], and their great difficulties, in a correct and telling manner."

Sewell conceded that she had been influenced by a friend who told her about the Anglican theologian Horace Bushnell, who had written a book about animals. She wrote that he had "helped me feel it was worth a great effort to try to bring the thoughts of men more in harmony with the purpose of God on this subject." She also admitted being influenced by people with whom she had talked about horses. Although confined to her house, she told of a cabman who stopped by her window for a chat and bemoaned the necessity of working on Sunday. He recalled driving a woman on a Sunday who, when she paid him, also gave him a pamphlet which described Sunday work as sinful. "Now m'am," the cabman told Sewell, "I call that hypocrisy—don't you?"

After Sewell wrote pages in pencil, they were recopied by her mother. When the book was completed, Mary Sewell asked Jarrolds, her publisher in London, to read "this little thing of my daughter's." Jarrolds offered £20 for the rights to the book, and Sewell accepted the proposal on the advice of her mother, who told her that new authors could not reasonably expect to be paid more.

Considering that it was apparently written in fits and starts, and when Sewell's health allowed, *Black Beauty* was remarkably seamless. Presented as the "autobiography of a horse," with Sewell as the translator from "the original equine," *Black Beauty* traces the life of a gelding with "racing blood" in his veins who is alternately mistreated or lovingly cared for, as he is

*From the movie* Black Beauty, *starring Mark Lester.*

sold from one owner to another. The narrative opens with an idyllic life for the four-year-old horse, who is at first owned by a kindly Squire Gordon, whose wife, after considering and rejecting names such as "Blackbird" and "Ebony," settles on the name "Black Beauty." Among the grooming staff, the favorite of Black Beauty is a cheerful 14-year-old, Joe Green.

Sold when the Gordon family moves for health reasons, Black Beauty suffers under the control of a coachman who applies the hated bearing rein, which forces the horse's neck back into an unnaturally high position, makes it difficult to see from the side, and cuts off the horse's wind. When the coachman, in a drunken state, drives Black Beauty recklessly, the horse, who has a loose shoe, is injured (this section of the book becomes an occasion for comments on the evils of drink).

Goodhearted and malevolent owners follow: among them, a kindly owner whose groom feeds the oats provided for the horses to his pet rabbits instead; a London cabman who treats Black Beauty well and helps the horse navigate the confusing and congested streets of London; a corn dealer who overworks his horses nearly to death, using them to pull wagons overloaded with grain; and a master who raises horses for racing at English fairs. The novel ends when Black Beauty is bought by Joe Green, his beloved caretaker from his time with the Gordons.

The novel has a number of sharply drawn portraits of horses and ponies, and at least some of them seem to reflect Sewell's own experiences. These included Merrylegs, who appears to be based on Sewell's own pony. Other horses may be composites or inventions, such as Ginger, a Chestnut mare driven vicious by human mistreatment, including a brutal "breaking-in." Ginger reappears, very late in the novel, as a broken-down horse with a slumbering gait, a frequent cough, and legs that have been swollen from overwork. While intended as a morality tale on the human mistreatment of animals, and especially horses, the book includes many details about the feeding and general care of horses, including common horse ailments.

The novel, with its portrayal of cities as congested and unpleasant, reflected Sewell's own views of what large cities became after the Industrial Revolution; it also reflected her belief, common in Victorian England, that human society was properly a hierarchy, and that the lower classes served the upper classes, just as horses served human beings. Its central message, however, was Sewell's belief: "We call them dumb animals, and so they are, for they cannot tell us how they feel, but they do not suffer less because they have no words." Her motivation was "to show what gentle and devoted friends horses can be"; the book appears to be an act of gratitude for animals, which had enriched her life and made it possible for her to be mobile.

The early printings of *Black Beauty* contained the dedication, "To my dear and honoured MOTHER whose life no less than her pen was devoted to the welfare of others, this little book is affectionately DEDICATED." In fact,

when Sewell died in April 1878, some three months after the publication of her novel, her mother, noticing that most carriages in the funeral procession used bearing reins on their horses, walked down the line of vehicles and requested that the offensive reins be removed.

It is estimated that by the time of Sewell's death, some 30,000 copies had been printed. By 1890, an estimated 216,000 copies had been sold, and the words "Recommended by the British SPCA" were appearing in editions in her native country. By 1894, the popularity of the book caused Jarrolds to produce several editions of the book at different price levels, ranging from a paper edition for a shilling, a school cloth edition for one and sixpence, and a literary edition with "cloth elegant binding" for two shillings.

While one British publication noted that "it would be difficult to conceive of a book more admirably suited to the purpose" of the Royal Society for the Prevention of Cruelty to Animals, the British society was not the first organization to embrace *Black Beauty*. George Angell, the founder of the Massachusetts Society for the Prevention of Cruelty to Animals, the American Humane Education Association, and the magazine *Our Dumb Animals*, recognized the importance of the book for his movement very early. A supporter sent a copy to him in February 1880. He concluded that the book might be as much of a "boost" for his movement as *Harriet Beecher Stowe*'s *Uncle Tom's Cabin* had been for abolitionism.

Within two weeks of receiving a copy of the book, Angell had begun soliciting funds for an American edition, planning to print, initially, 10,000 copies, with the eventual goal of distributing 100,000 copies. It would be a pirated edition, printed without copyright permission, a fact that Angell justified with the statement that the author had "died unmarried after the publication of the book; that her mother, a widow, died soon after"; that the author had received a "mere 20 pounds" from the original British publisher; that there was no American copyright; and that his organization could undersell and underprice any other American publisher. The goal was to place a copy of *Black Beauty* in every American home, an important step in the progress "not only of the American, but of the world's, humanity and civilization."

*Black Beauty* played a role in the gradual abolition of the bearing rein, as organizations for the humane treatment of animals began to campaign, on both sides of the Atlantic, against its use and against the abuse of horses used for heavy labor, particularly in mining work. *Black*

*Beauty* also became a 20th-century phenomenon. Of the British novelists of the 19th century, only the books of Charles Dickens proved more popular a century later. One writer has calculated that *Black Beauty* is the sixth most popular work in the English language. The book has been translated into French, Italian, Hindustani, and Japanese, among other languages. An Italian edition was produced in Boston, and a Spanish edition appeared in New York City. Three motion picture versions have appeared, with Sewell's family receiving a modest payment for the first one, which was made in 1921.

Anna Sewell succeeded in convincing many of her readers of the importance of "kindness, sympathy, and an understanding treatment of animals." However, while her book has certainly stood the test of time, notes one writer: "The book has lived; the author has been forgotten."

**SOURCES:**

Baker, Margaret J. *Anna Sewell and Black Beauty*. New York, London, and Toronto, 1956.

Bayly, Mrs. (*sic*). *The Life and Letters of Mrs. Sewell*. London: Nisbet, 1889.

Chitty, Susan. *The Woman Who Wrote* Black Beauty: *The Life of Anna Sewell*. London: Hodder & Stoughton, 1971.

Starrett, Vincent. "Anna Sewell," in *Buried Caesars: Essays in Literary Appreciation*. Freeport, NY: Books for Libraries Press, reprint 1968, pp. 204–223.

**SUGGESTED READING:**

Montgomery, Elizabeth R. *The Story behind Great Books*. NY: Dodd, Mead, 1946.

Showalter, Elaine. *A Literature of Their Own: British Women Novelists from Bronte to Lessing*. Princeton, NJ: Princeton University Press, 1999.

**COLLECTIONS:**

Anna Sewell left almost nothing in the way of papers; an autobiography, essentially part of a long letter written by Sewell's mother to her grandchildren, is included at the beginning of Mrs. Bayly's book; a family friend, Mrs. Bayly has also been the main source of information regarding Sewell's journal and some of her correspondence.

**RELATED MEDIA:**

*Black Beauty* (films), Vitagraph, 1921, Monogram Pictures, 1933, Twentieth Century-Fox, 1946.

*Black Beauty* (film), starring Mark Lester, Tigon British Film Productions and Chilton Film & Television Enterprises, 1971.

*Courage of Black Beauty* (film), Alco Pictures, 1957.

*Your Obedient Servant* (film), adaptation of *Black Beauty*, Thomas A. Edison, 1917.

**Niles Holt**, Professor of History,
Illinois State University,
Normal, Illinois

# Sewell, Edna (1881–1967)

*American advocate for farm women. Born Edna Belle Scott in Ambia, Indiana, on August 1, 1881; died in Lafayette, Indiana, in 1967; daughter of Clinton Scott (a farmer) and Emma (Albaugh) Scott; married Charles W. Sewell, in 1897 (died 1933); children: Greta Geneive Sewell (b. 1900); Gerald Scott Sewell (1904–1945).*

*Organized and helped direct first home improvement tours ever conducted in the U.S.; was instrumental in prompting the American Farm Bureau Federation (AFBF) to welcome women as members; served as board member of the Indiana Farm Bureau; headed Associated Women of the AFBF (1934–50).*

Edna Sewell was born in 1881 in Ambia, Indiana, into a farm family. She attended a one-room elementary school and graduated from high school in Oxford, the county seat. In 1897, she married Charles W. Sewell, a local farmer, and the couple had two children, **Greta Geneive Sewell** in 1900 and Gerald Scott Sewell in 1903.

The family moved to Otterbein, Indiana, in 1906. Two years later, Sewell presented a paper, "The Woman in the Home and Community," while addressing the Benton County Farmers' Institute, which was followed by similar engagements in surrounding counties. In 1913, she started a farmers' social club, which later became a local chapter of the American Farm Bureau Federation (AFBF). Sewell's efforts to help farm women led to an offer from Purdue University to organize the first home improvement tours ever conducted in the United States. The tours demonstrated new and more efficient ways for American farm wives to care for their families and homes. Sewell was assistant leader of Home Demonstration Agents at Purdue for a year, and in 1920 she helped to develop a home economics course in conjunction with the Indiana State Fair.

A speech by Sewell at the second annual meeting of the fledgling AFBF led to a resolution by the organization to welcome women as members. In 1921, U.S. Secretary of Agriculture Henry C. Wallace invited Sewell to join six others as Indiana's delegates to the National Agriculture Conference convened by President Warren Harding. That year she also became a second vice president, head of the women's department, and a member of the board of the Indiana Farm Bureau. In 1927, she directed the newly established Home and Community Department of the AFBF, which in 1934, the year after her husband's death, became the Associated Women of the AFBF. Sewell served as its head until she retired in 1950.

Sewell was a frequent speaker at meetings and conferences throughout the country, and in

1947 and 1950 she was the federation's delegate to the Associated Country Women of the World conference in Europe. She also served as a consultant on rural health to the American Medical Association, receiving a citation for distinguished service. Other honors came her way as well, including distinguished service awards from the University of Wisconsin (1933) and the AFBF (1950). Sewell died of kidney failure in 1967 at a nursing home in Lafayette, Indiana.

**SOURCES:**
Read, Phyllis J., and Bernard L. Witlieb. *The Book of Women's Firsts.* NY: Random House, 1992.
Sicherman, Barbara, and Carol Hurd Green, eds. *Notable American Women: The Modern Period.* Cambridge, MA: The Belknap Press of Harvard University, 1980.

**Deborah Conn**, freelance writer,
Falls Church, Virginia

# Sewell, Elizabeth Missing

## (1815–1906)

*British novelist and children's writer. Born on February 19, 1815, in Newport, Isle of Wight; died on August 17, 1906, in Bonchurch, Isle of Wight; daughter of Thomas Sewell (a solicitor) and Jane (Edwards) Sewell; educated in Newport and Bath; never married; no children.*

*Selected writings:* Stories, Illustrative of the Lord's Prayer *(1840)*; Amy Herbert *(1844)*; Laneton Parsonage *(1846–48)*; Margaret Percival *(1847)*; The Experience of Life *(1852)*; Katharine Ashton *(1854)*; Ursula *(1858)*; Thoughts for Holy Week *(1857)*; A History of the Early Church *(1861)*; Principles of Education *(1865)*; Autobiography *(1907)*.

Elizabeth Sewell was born in 1815 in Newport, Isle of Wight, one of 12 children of **Jane Edwards Sewell** and solicitor Thomas Sewell. Elizabeth, who attended a day school in Newport and went to boarding school in Bath, was strongly influenced by a brother, William Sewell (1804–1874), who was a leading figure in the Oxford Movement that emphasized the catholic (not Roman Catholic) heritage of the Church of England and objected to the undue influence of the state in church affairs. Another brother was the first premier of New Zealand; another the warden of New College.

Sewell's first book, *Stories, Illustrative of the Lord's Prayer*, was published in 1840. When her father died, she and her siblings contributed a portion of their earnings to help clear the family debt, and Sewell dedicated herself to the care of her younger brothers and sisters. Because of

this, she never married, and many of her works express the theme of the duty and rewards in the life of a single woman. She wrote the three-part *Laneton Parsonage* (1846–48) to teach children about the use of the Catechism. When John Henry Newman, one of the leaders of the Oxford Movement, converted to Roman Catholicism, she wrote the anti-Catholic novel *Margaret Percival* (1847). Though her novels *Amy Herbert* (1844), written for young girls, and *Katharine Ashton* (1854) stress moral and religious duty, she wrote about her own childhood in her most popular book, *The Experience of Life* (1852). Sewell also wrote travel books, devotional works, and school textbooks.

In 1866, she established the St. Boniface School for girls at Ventnor. The school was based on her liberal views on women's education, which she discussed in *Principles of Education* (1865). Sewell died, age 91, in Bonchurch, Isle of Wight, in 1906.

**SOURCES:**
Buck, Claire, ed. *The Bloomsbury Guide to Women's Literature.* NY: Prentice Hall, 1992.
Shattock, Joanne. *The Oxford Guide to British Women Writers.* NY: Oxford University Press, 1993.

**SUGGESTED READING:**
Sewell, Eleanor M., ed. *The Autobiography of Elizabeth M. Sewell*, 1907.

**Deborah Conn**, freelance writer,
Falls Church, Virginia

# Sewell, Mary Wright (1797–1884).

*See Sewell, Anna for sidebar.*

# Sexburga (c. 627–673)

*Queen of Wessex. Name variations: Seaxburg; Seaxburh; Sexburh. Born around 627; died in 673; married Kenwealh, also seen as Coinwalch or Cenwalh, king of West Saxons or Wessex (r. 643–672).*

Sexburga, who succeeded her husband Cenwalh after his death, reigned as queen of Wessex from 672 to 673. She was said to have been a "woman of courage," and of a "subtle and extensive genius," but she was deposed because her nobles refused to obey the orders of a woman.

# Sexburga (d. around 699)

*Queen of Kent, second abbess of Ely, and saint. Name variations: Saint Sexburga; Sexburga of East Anglia. Born in East Anglia; died around 699; daughter of Saewara and Anna, king of East Anglia (r. 635–654); sister of Elthelthrith (630–679) and ***With-***

*burga*; half-sister of *\*Ethelburga (d. 665); married Earconbert also known as Ercombert, king of Kent (r. 640–664), around 640; children: Egbert, king of Kent (r. 664–673); Hlothere, king of Kent (r. 673–685); Earcongota; \*Ermenilda (who married Wulfhere, king of Mercia).*

Saint Sexburga was born in East Anglia, the daughter of **Saewara** and Anna, king of East Anglia (r. 635–654). Around 640, she married Earconbert, of Kent, who is said by the Venerable Bede to have been the first English king to order the destruction of idols throughout his realm. He also ordered everyone to observe Lenten fasts. Sexburga founded a monastery for nuns in Isle of Sheppey and became its abbess. Around 679, on the death of her sister *\*Elthelthrith*, the first abbess of Ely, Sexburga succeeded her. Her tenure ran for around 20 years, until her own death around 699. Sexburga's feast day is July 6.

# Sexton, Anne (1928–1974)

*Major modern American poet who was one of the chief architects of the confessional school of poetry before her death by suicide. Name variations: Anne Gray Harvey. Born Anne Gray Harvey on November 9, 1928, in Newton, Massachusetts; committed suicide on October 4, 1974; daughter of Ralph Churchill Harvey and Mary Gray (Staples) Harvey (both of whom were descended from prominent New England families, in Massachusetts and Maine, respectively); attended a Wellesley public school prior to being sent to Rogers Hall, a boarding school for girls in Lowell, Massachusetts, until, at age 19, she went to the Garland Finishing School for Women in Boston; married Alfred Muller Sexton II; children: Linda Gray Sexton (b. July 21, 1953); Joyce Ladd Sexton (b. August 4, 1955).*

*Awards:* Poetry's Levinson Prize for All My Pretty Ones (1962); traveling fellowship of the American Academy of Arts and Letters (1963); elected a fellow of the Royal Society of Literature (1965); travel grant from the Congress of Cultural Freedom (1965); Pulitzer Prize for Poetry for Live or Die (1967); honorary Phi Beta Kappa from Harvard (1968) and from Radcliffe (1969); Guggenheim fellowship (1969); honorary Litt.D. from Tufts University (1970) and Fairfield University (1972); Crashaw Chair in Literature at Colgate University (1972); honorary Litt.D. from Regis College (1973); served on Pulitzer Prize jury (1973).

*Selected works:* To Bedlam and Part Way Back (Boston: Houghton Mifflin, 1960); "Dancing the Jig," in New World Writing (Vol. 16, 1960); "Classroom at Boston University," in Harvard Advocate (Vol. 145, November 1961); "On 'Some Foreign Letters,'" in Poet's Choice (ed. by Paul Engle and Joseph Langland, NY: Dial, 1962); All My Pretty Ones (Boston: Houghton Mifflin, 1962); "The Last Believer," in Vogue (Vol. 15, November 1963); (with Maxine Kumin) Eggs of Things (NY: Putnam, 1963); (with Kumin) More Eggs of Things (NY: Putnam, 1964); Selected Poems (London: Oxford University Press, 1964); "The Barfly Ought to Sing," in Triquarterly (Vol. 7, Fall 1966); Live or Die (Boston: Houghton Mifflin, 1966); (foreword) Aliki Barnstone's The Real Tin Flower: Poems About the World at Nine (NY: Collier-Cromwell, 1968); Poems by Thomas Kinsella, Douglas Livingstone and Anne Sexton (London: Oxford University Press, 1968); Love Poems (Boston: Houghton Mifflin, 1969); (with Kumin) Joey and the Birthday Present (NY: McGraw-Hill, 1971); Transformations (Boston: Houghton Mifflin, 1971); "The Letting down of the Hair," in The Atlantic Monthly (March 1972); The Book of Folly (Boston: Houghton Mifflin, 1972, includes unpublished story "The Ballet of the Buffoon"); "The Freak Show," in American Poetry Review (Vol. 2, no. 3, May–June 1973); "A Small Journal" ("All God's Children Need Radios"), in Ms. (November 1973); The Death Notebooks (Boston: Houghton Mifflin, 1974); The Awful Rowing Toward God (Boston: Houghton Mifflin, 1975); (ed. by Linda Gray Sexton) 45 Mercy Street (Boston: Houghton Mifflin, 1975); (with Kumin) The Wizard's Tears (NY: McGraw-Hill, 1975); (ed. by Linda Gray Sexton and Lois Ames) Anne Sexton: A Self-Portrait in Letters (Boston: Houghton Mifflin, 1977); Words for Dr. Y.: Uncollected Poems with Three Stories (Boston: Houghton Mifflin, 1978, includes "The Ghost," "The Vampire," "The Bat or To Remember, To Remember"); "Journal of a Living Experiment," in Journal of a Living Experiment: A Documentary History of the First Ten Years of Teachers and Writers Collaborative (ed. by Phillip Lobate, pp. 44–75, NY: Teachers and Writers Collaborative, 1979); The Complete Poems (Boston: Houghton Mifflin, 1981); (ed. by Steven E. Colburn) No Evil Star: Selected Essays, Interviews and Prose (Ann Arbor: University of Michigan Press, 1985); (ed. by Diane Wood Middlebrook and Diana Hume George) Selected Poems of Anne Sexton (Boston: Houghton Mifflin, 1988).

One of the most important English-speaking poets of the mid-20th century and a founding mother of the variously celebrated and maligned confessional school of poetry, American writer

Anne Sexton was, above all, a woman of contradictions. Having reached the pinnacle of poetry both artistically and professionally quite young in her career, she nevertheless succumbed to the demons of despair when she took her own life after numerous failed attempts. Poet and housewife, public performer and private agoraphobic, Sexton lived a bifurcated life: she was at once a disciplined, methodical, incisive poet who honed her craft and shrewdly marketed herself, and a disorganized, helpless, and needy woman who was propped up and sustained by the caretaking efforts of family and friends. It is no wonder that she spent the better portion of her 46 years tortured by life and flirting with death, branded, as she was from the onset of adulthood, by the mystery and the mischief of mental illness.

*Surely the words will continue, for that's what's left that's true.*

—Anne Sexton

The youngest of three daughters, Sexton was born Anne Gray Harvey, into an affluent household on November 9, 1928, in Newton, Massachusetts, a suburb of Boston. Her father Ralph Churchill Harvey, who was born on February 7, 1900, went from being a well-heeled drummer to owning a thriving wool business. Unlike his stodgy banker-father before him, Ralph nurtured a taste for the pleasures of a lavish social life, an ambition his socialite wife apparently shared, according to biographer **Diane Middlebrook**. Her father's cavalier attitude and fondness for the good life did not soften his parenting style, however, at least as Sexton remembered it. In therapy, she recalled his asking her to leave the table because he was disgusted with her acne, and insisting that the girls be dressed up and presentable at all times. Ralph Harvey showed no signs of the mental instability exhibited by his father, who suffered a breakdown following the collapse of a banking venture in Puerto Rico, or his sister, **Frances Harvey**, who committed suicide at age 69, ironically, one year after her famous niece's own suicide.

Anne's mother **Mary Staples Harvey**, born March 14, 1901, was the only child of the aristocratic Dingley-Staples family. She was descended from a long line of notable New England journalists and politicians, and her father Arthur Gray Staples, a writer, was the editor and publisher of the *Lewiston Evening Journal*. Mary Harvey evidently inherited her father's penchant for writing, and he saw to it that she was well educated, first at a private boarding school and then at Wellesley College. Father and daughter enjoyed a close relationship, reading together and listening to Red Sox games on the radio, and she displeased him when she met and married Ralph Harvey two years into college. Mary did not complete college, but she did write poetry, an occupation that later placed her in competition with her poet daughter.

Despite fond memories of childhood summers on Squirrel Island, Maine, in the company of the maternal side of the family, Sexton did not have a happy childhood. Close to neither mother nor father, she also shared little in common with her older sisters: **Jane Harvey** (b. 1923) and **Blanche Harvey** (b. 1925). As adults, both chafed at Sexton's airing of private family matters in public, as well as her depiction of an unhappy childhood. Interestingly, however, both the eldest Jane and the youngest Anne would commit suicide by middle age. The children were reared in a strictly regulated household under the close supervision of a nanny-nurse who saw to it that the Harvey girls were the well-groomed and well-behaved children demanded by their father. With her brash behavior and careless appearance, Sexton apparently took exception to this expectation, and as a result, she was often banned from the family dining room and required to take her meals in the kitchen. Her defiance was an early indication that she had an "attitude" and a matching style all her own.

The Harvey girls attended Brown Elementary School and Wellesley Congregational Church, although the family was not in the least religious. The parents apparently adored each other, yet remained distant from the children who competed for their attention. Their time spent on Squirrel Island was the happiest for Sexton, and it was during these summers that she delighted in playing her favorite role as actress on the family-made stage. Perhaps it was here that she first developed her sense of the dramatic and those theatrics that would later render her public poetry readings so moving and memorable. In those years, Sexton was most fond of her maternal great-aunt **Anna Ladd Dingley**, who led an unusually unconventional life for a woman of her time, working as a journalist and traveling around Europe. Sexton's namesake and very likely her first love, "Nana," as Anne called her, moved into the Harvey household when Anne was 11 and her mother Mary was away nursing her own father Arthur Gray Staples. After her grandfather's death in April 1940, childhood summers at Squirrel Island regretfully came to an end for Anne.

But the wool business in the Depression era was booming, and Ralph Harvey built a lavish

Anne
Sexton

home for his family in Weston, another Boston suburb. The easy wealth led to squandering and excess, and both parents took up drinking as a main occupation until Ralph admitted himself to a treatment center. By 1950, he would stop drinking altogether, but not before his company showed

signs of his neglect. These years also made their mark on Sexton, who remembered her father as having been a mean drunk who mistreated her.

She was also having problems at school—she skipped a grade, only to have to repeat another one, and shortly after her grandfather's death she had to be hospitalized for constipation. It was advised at this time that Sexton should undergo psychological counseling—perhaps a sign of things to come—but the family failed to heed the advice. During this time, Nana came to be a friend and mother-replacement for Anne, their relationship solidified by Nana's continual presence after joining the household. But her close companionship with Nana, who served as a key stabilizing factor in her life, would deteriorate owing to two simultaneous developments—Anne's activities outside the home in her teenage years, and Nana's mental decline after she lost her hearing (c. 1941). Yet another event prefiguring things to come in Sexton's own life occurred when her beloved Nana had to be hospitalized and treated with electroshock therapy (c. 1943). Anne's "loss" of Nana came at a time when her father's drinking was at its worst, and just as his own father suffered yet another breakdown. She also felt guilty for having separated herself from Nana in her quest to have an identity outside the household, and this twin pain of loss and guilt returned to plague Sexton in later life.

Nevertheless, a blossoming and rebellious Sexton galloped through her teens and took up the pastimes of smoking, drinking, and flirting. She was tall, slim, elegant, and crazy about boys, which is reportedly what prompted her anxious parents to send her off to boarding school. At Rogers Hall in Lowell, Massachusetts, Anne continued her minor study in boys, while participating in school activities, including plays, basketball, and cheerleading. She also wrote "Cinquains" for the school literary magazine, and her poetry became a point of contention between her and her mother who laid claim to the title of family poet. Mary Harvey's skepticism (and perhaps her jealousy) put an end to Anne's writing for a decade, when Mary had her daughter's poems examined for authenticity. Where boys were concerned, however, Sexton's spirits were not dampened. Several infatuations, one steady boyfriend, and an engagement later, Anne met and eloped with Alfred Muller Sexton II, whom she called Kayo, while she was attending the Garland Finishing School in Boston. She was 19 at the time of their elopement to Sunbury, North Carolina, which occurred at the suggestion of her mother when it was thought that Anne might already be pregnant.

Sexton's parents might well have been relieved that their somewhat loose and uncontrollable daughter was finally settling down, but Kayo's parents were disappointed, especially after he quit medical school and the distasteful financial dependence that came with it. The young couple lived, unhappily, between the homes of both families until they got their own apartment. Kayo worked in the family wool business while Anne took on odd jobs, including selling lingerie. She got on well with her sister-in-law, **Joan Sexton**, and the two did some modeling work; Anne had the svelte figure and dramatic features of a model, but her acne was problematic. More problematic was her relationship with **Billie Sexton**, her mother-in-law, who viewed Anne as lazy and self-indulgent. Indeed, Anne was not adapting well to the constraints of married life, and for a time she had a romance with a Harvard surgeon and friend of Kayo's. Just as Mary Harvey had taken matters in hand by persuading Anne to elope, here, too, she took control by arranging for Anne to see a therapist, Dr. **Martha Brunner-Orne**, and Anne gave the surgeon up. This early infidelity, however, was a sign of things to come, as Sexton's 25-year marriage was peppered with similar romances and affairs.

In 1950, Kayo enlisted in the Naval Reserves, leaving Anne behind with a job in a bookstore and a struggle with her need for romance and adventure. A reunion with Kayo left her pregnant with their first child, and she joined him for a time at his base in San Francisco. Returning home to Weston, buoyed by an apparently recovered Nana living nearby, Anne awaited the birth of **Linda Gray Sexton** which came on July 21, 1953. With the help of Mary Harvey, the Sextons purchased their first home after Kayo returned to civilian life and a salesman's job for his father-in-law's wool company. By the time of her second child's birth on August 4, 1955 (**Joyce Ladd Sexton**), Anne was 27 and showing signs of the mental illness that would shadow her for the next 19 years. Her beloved Nana had died the previous year, and Anne suffered from severe postpartum depression after Joy's birth. Kayo's frequent business trips left her alternately melancholy and crazed, and Linda Gray Sexton, in *Searching for Mercy Street*, claims that her mother was physically abusive to her during these times. Depression, especially in Kayo's absence, was exacerbated by the agoraphobia that Anne suffered, a condition which persisted throughout her life. Her terror of being in places outside the home, unless they were routine and familiar, oddly contrasted with the public life, such as readings and teaching, that came later with her success as a poet. On the homefront during the children's younger years, it was Billie who accommodated Sexton's neurosis by chauffeuring the children, shopping for their clothes, and running household errands. Increasingly, as her poetry pulled her into public places, she used alcohol to anaesthetize and prepare herself. Throughout her life, however, her inability to function normally and in a caretaker's role, particularly in Kayo's absences, established a lifelong pattern of family intervention. Kayo's father helped finance her therapy, first with Dr. Brunner-Orne and later with Brunner-Orne's son Dr. Martin Orne. She began treatment with Martin Orne in 1956, after the first of what would prove to be a series of suicide attempts and subsequent hospitalizations (some lasting months at a time), and it was he who prompted her to resume writing poetry. During these early years of marriage, Sexton's illness rendered her unfit to cope with the children, so Joy lived with Kayo's mother Billie while Linda was shunted off to live with Anne's sister Blanche and husband. Linda remembered this period as a terrifying one, both because of the extensive separation from her mother and the physical and emotional abuse she suffered at the hands of her exacting uncle. Joy evidently fared better under the nurturing eye of Billie whom she came to see as her "second mother."

Although Sexton experienced brief periods of recovery, stimulated in large part by her avid interest in writing the poetry which Orne advised for therapeutic reasons, she and the household never returned to—if indeed it ever had been in—a "normal" state. The children were eventually returned to her care, but Kayo's absences and Anne's inability to deal with her daughters and daily wifely duties was a prescription for family disaster. "I was trying my damndest to lead a conventional life, for that was how I was brought up," observed Sexton. "But one can't build little white picket fences to keep nightmares out." She was diagnosed with everything from insomnia to anorexia and rage to suicidal impulses; moreover, quite possibly, writes Middlebrook, "biochemical imbalances . . . intensified the underlying psychological vulnerabilities that were the primary focus of her therapy." But whatever the origin or precipitating factors, whether post-partum depression or the alleged lack of her mother's attention and love, Sexton suffered from a mental illness from which she could periodically escape through her poetry, but from which she could never finally recover.

Her renewed interest in poetry stimulated her interest in returning to school, an enterprise Mary Harvey refused to support because she was already underwriting a good portion of Anne's medical expenses. But by 1958 Sexton

found other ways to educate herself, through reading books of psychology and participating in poetry workshops where she had the good fortune to work with the likes of such experienced mentors as John Holmes, W.D. Snodgrass, and Robert Lowell. Over time, Sexton educated herself, and what began as a form of therapy quickly turned into her main preoccupation, her art, and her life. While she battled her emotional demons, she grew as a poet. Experiences that would have been painful for a well-adjusted individual, such as her mother's breast cancer surgery and, two years later, her death on March 10, 1959, followed hard by her father's death due to a stroke three months later, were exacerbated by Sexton's emotional illness. The family learned to accommodate her growing absorption in writing; and the invariable relapses and their constancy, combined with the invaluable assistance of Kayo's mother in managing the home, enabled the little-educated, middle-class wife and mother of two to develop into a first-rate poet. For a time at least, the healthy blend of treatment, medication, and poetry gave Sexton's life meaning and kept her alive. But it was not without regret that she placed her art before her "female" duties: "I realize with guilt, that I am a woman, that it should be my husband, or my home—not writing. But it is not—I love the children but am not feminine enough to be all lost in their care." Sexton might not have judged herself so harshly (nor been judged so harshly by society) had she been living with today's more enlightened standards, but this was the 1950s when a woman's place was in the home and the domestic sphere was no place for a poet.

In the poetry workshops, Sexton formed invaluable relationships, and chief among these was her relationship with lifelong friend and fellow poet **Maxine Kumin**, whom she met at the poetry seminar directed by John Holmes at Boston University that both attended in 1957. Radcliffe-educated Kumin, according to Middlebrook, was the first to recognize Sexton's talent and potential as a poet. They shared their poetry and looked after their children together; they participated in workshops and talked daily on the telephone critiquing each other's work and supporting one another, and they collaborated on children's stories. In 1958, Sexton also had the good fortune of meeting and working with poet W.D. Snodgrass at the Antioch Writers' Conference, thanks to the scholarship she earned with her promising work. She then continued studying under Robert Lowell at Boston University, and it was there that she befriended the then little-known ***Sylvia Plath**, whose fate as unhappy housewife and confessional poet infatuated with death would be curiously similar to Sexton's. But it was the combined influence of Kumin and Snodgrass that was most influential in Sexton's early development as a confessional writer who transformed autobiographical experiences into art. With their help, she found a first-person voice and a form appropriate to her imagination, which was fueled by her ceaseless wrestling match with the devil of madness. Other mentors and advisers followed in this early period, such as the poet (and later her lover) James Wright, with whom she sustained an extensive correspondence, and George Starbuck, another short-term lover, who spent long hours with her and Plath at the Ritz Bar talking poetry.

Even as Sexton's poetry saved her, it also robbed her of domestic contentment, particularly as her husband Kayo's disapproval of her activity and her new bohemian friends mounted. Linda recalled the trepidation caused by the frequent eruptions between her parents that often began with too many drinks before dinner and ended in Anne being beaten by a furious and frustrated Kayo. Theirs was evidently a co-dependent and mutually abusive relationship—although her abuse came from her quick tongue, and his from his fast fists—but Anne's ongoing therapy and Kayo's short-term treatment failed to alter the dynamics between them. Anne needed Kayo who labored under the strain of performing the domestic duties that Anne neglected; and Kayo apparently needed her, for he ultimately resigned himself to Anne's ambitions and infidelities.

The year 1959 brought yet another loss when Anne's father-in-law was killed in a car accident. Shortly thereafter, a pregnant Anne convinced Kayo that she should get an abortion, as, very likely, he was not the child's father. Her "professional" relationship with mentor James Wright also turned personal, and at one point Sexton managed to spend several days with him at a workshop in Montauk, Long Island. Once again, the children were left in the care of her in-laws, Billie and Joan. On another occasion, and owing to yet another recognition of her talent, Sexton left home to attend the prestigious Bread Loaf Writers Conference as a Robert Frost fellow. An emergency surgery to remove her appendix and an ovary later that year did not dampen her enthusiasm or slow her progress—she was well on the way to meet her destiny as poet "extraordinaire."

Between the workshops and the breakdowns, the suicide attempts (or pseudo-suicide attempts), the domestic conflict and the affairs, Sexton was working hard at crafting her poetry and sculpting a new and timeless identity. *To Bedlam and Part Way Back* was published in 1960. It took little more than two years to write and was largely based on her experience in a mental institution. This first volume of poetry, which was nominated for a National Book Award, found both an audience and favor among critics, despite the newness of the confessional mode and the cynicism with which some viewed it. Perhaps Sexton herself best answered such cynicism when she exclaimed: "The difference between confession and poetry? is after all, art."

A writer with a decidedly female voice and consciousness, writing in a period of pre-feminism and eschewing such labels, Sexton nevertheless understood how the constraints of gender interfered with art. She connected her poetry to her marginalized position as a woman and a housewife, even though she refused to take a political position on the matter. Perhaps her illness, rebellion against convention, and numerous infidelities were a passive-aggressive response to such limitations. In any event, tellingly, of the four up-and-coming female poets of her day—Maxine Kumin, *Adrienne Rich, Sylvia Plath, and Sexton—it was Sexton, writes Middlebrook, who tapped the limitations "women felt in conforming to prevailing feminine stereotypes." In this way, Sexton, the non-feminist, ironically modeled herself after her own mother, whom she berated for being distant and self-absorbed.

Within two years, Sexton followed the success of her first book with another success, *All My Pretty Ones*, in 1962. The "mature artist" by 1962, she continued to use her poetry to tussle with the unorthodox themes of "mental illness, sexual love, and spiritual anguish," writes Middlebrook, reaching a wide and appreciative audience as a result. Her second volume won *Poetry*'s Levinson Prize the year it appeared, and the following year it won the coveted National Book Award. Another relapse and hospitalization came sometime after the book appeared in print, but, like Humpty Dumpty, Sexton continued to work and continued to pull herself back together with the help of her psychotherapist, steadfast family, and a cadre of colleagues and friends. While pursuing her vocation as a poet, she embarked on another career, that of teaching poetry in workshops, first at Harvard University in 1961 and then at Radcliffe College. Along with her friend Maxine Kumin, she was also awarded one of the first poetry scholarships for Independent Study at Radcliffe Institute, an experimental program for married, educated women. In addition to these achievements, Sexton received the first traveling fellowship of the American Academy of Arts and Letters. In her second year under scholarship at the institute, Sexton met and befriended another budding American housewife-writer, *Tillie Olsen. By 1962, then, Sexton was well on her way to establishing herself among the new literary elite, an activity that brought financial as well as public rewards which boosted Sexton's self-esteem. Her success and the corresponding ebullience that it brought carried her through her most extended period of recovery, from about 1963 to 1967—a gift paradoxically earned by her mental illness.

Traveling was always a challenge for the agoraphobic Sexton. But loath to turn down the honor associated with the first travel fellowship, she agreed to accept it, only to share it with **Sandy Robart**, a friend and neighbor who accompanied her—as friends often did—on her trip to Europe. The report of her friend and fellow poet Sylvia Plath's death on February 12, 1963, did not deter Sexton from undertaking the trip, but she did write the poem "Wanting To Die." In it, she expresses her kinship with Plath and foreshadows the enigmatic death-desire that linked them: "But suicides have a special language,/ Like carpenters they want to know *which* tools./ They never ask *why build*."

Her upbeat spirits during the trip notwithstanding, Sexton's planned 12-month tour was cut short by a weather-change in Venice, punctuated by a brief affair in Rome, and she returned home. By November, Sexton was again suicidal. She was readmitted to the hospital, and this time the twin addictions to alcohol and sleeping drugs were added to her death-addiction. A short-term recovery was soon followed, however, by a far-reaching setback when Orne took a position at the University of Pennsylvania after seven years as Sexton's therapist. In the remaining years of her life, Sexton found several stand-ins, including her friend, the psychiatrist **Ann Wilder**, who lived in San Francisco, followed by several other nearby professionals, but she never found as satisfactory a replacement. Her relationships with Wilder, and later, with an official psychiatrist, complicated matters when they turned romantic and sexual. Nevertheless, while her mental health declined and her alcoholism worsened, Sexton plodded on.

Under the "professional" care of the doctor who conducted an unethical affair with Sexton while she was in therapy, and for which she paid—Anne continued writing and garnering accolades. Her *Selected Poems* was published in

London in 1964, and the following year saw her elected to the Royal Society of Literature. She was also reworking a play, *Mercy Street*, that was originally underwritten by a Ford Foundation grant and produced at the Charles Playhouse in Boston in 1963. The play, a pet project of Sexton's, housed many of the ghosts, either real or imagined, of Sexton's past, including a father-daughter relationship bordering on incest and a great-aunt gone mad for having witnessed it. Her work on the play, which was eventually successfully produced off-Broadway, gave Sexton an opportunity to work in the theater for which she seemed to have a flair, as the theatrics she employed in her numerous public readings demonstrated. By the 1970s, she had raised her reading fees to a whopping $1,000 and distinguished herself by not being a stuffy or prosaic poetry reader; instead, she was "dressed to the nines" and ever the performance artist with an entourage always in tow.

On the homefront, the children had grown, and in an unhealthy role-reversal Anne became overly involved with, and more dependent on, them, particularly on Linda, her eldest. In *Searching for Mercy Street*, Linda relates the emotional demands that her mother placed upon her, which occasionally veered toward sexual abuse. In one instance, Linda had to cut her vacation at riding camp short to return home and care for Anne who was unable to be alone; her therapist was away on vacation at the time, and on these occasions, writes Middlebrook, "Sexton caused her family great distress by insisting on the priority . . . of her needs." In late adolescence Linda felt it necessary to extricate herself from her needy and unbalanced mother, an effort that brought pain as well as difficulty to Anne.

Her mental illness, though kept in check, was never far away, but neither were the tributes earned by her work. Another relapse and suicide attempt in July 1966 was followed by yet another award—a grant from the Congress of Cultural Freedom, which she used to treat Kayo to a trip to Africa and Europe. That same year also saw the publication of her fourth volume of poetry, *Live or Die,* which went on to win the Pulitzer Prize for Poetry the following year as well as the Shelley Memorial Prize. But 1966 closed on a down-turn for Sexton when she fell and broke her hip the same day she turned 38 years old. A nine-month convalescence followed, during which time she was cared for by a nurse and admirer of Sexton's poetry, **Joan Smith**. By this time Sexton had other hired help as well, including **Jean Moulton**, her secretary, and a housekeeper, **Mary LaCrosse**. She had also contracted the services of a literary agent to help manage the demand for public performances and to market her play. Despite the fact that the novel she had begun never materialized, her professional life as usual was on a roll, while her private life faltered.

The next eight years were, similarly, alternately productive and problematic. By 1967, she was earning a steady salary as a lecturer at Boston University, a position that ultimately became a full professorship on the strength of her work and accomplishments. Her reputation was solidified by the Pulitzer, and her popularity grew with an increased demand for her to "perform" her readings; and perform them she did with her legendary cigarette, husky voice, long legs, and carefully timed dramatic pauses. She was invited to do a reading of her poetry at the International Poetry Festival of London (1967), along with such renowned poets as W.H. Auden and John Berryman. Indeed, over the seven years remaining of her life, the acclaim and honors accorded Sexton accrued, and her work-pace and output never wavered, regardless of her trance-like fugue episodes, the depression and breakdowns, the desperate affairs and emotional setbacks, and the persistent agoraphobia and eventual estrangement from her husband and daughters. Harvard honored her with a Phi Beta Kappa (1968), as did Radcliffe (1969). In 1968, she performed in a touring rock group that adapted her poetry, and she returned to her own origins as a writer when she started offering poetry workshops at McLean Hospital, a mental institution. In this venture, she was assisted by **Lois Ames**, a psychiatric social worker whom she started seeing professionally, and in whose care she remained until her death. Her fifth book, *Love Poems*, appeared in 1969, after the contents had first been published individually in magazines. The poems elicited attention and some negative criticism because of their sexual explicitness, particularly relating to her affairs with married men. Shrewdly marketed, however, it came out on Valentine's Day and sold 4,000 copies in the first month. The same year, she worked on the American Place Theater production of her play *Mercy Street*, accepted a Guggenheim fellowship, and led poetry workshops at Oberlin College. Then came a spate of honorary doctorates, from Tufts University, Fairfield University, and Regis College, along with a Crashaw Chair in Literature at Colgate University. The year 1970 saw another suicide attempt, but 1971 saw yet another volume of poetry, *Transformations*, which was an adaptation of the fairy tales of the Brothers Grimm and inspired by daughter Linda's fond-

ness for them. Besides *Love Poems*, it was one of her most popular books, despite its witch-narrator and dark, ribald tone. In 1973, it was adapted and produced as an opera by the Minnesota Opera Company.

Sexton's health continued to fluctuate: her weight ballooned as a result of the thorazine she took and a broken hip, and her neediness increased, especially after the "official" psychiatrist ended their affair for the last time. The year 1971 saw another suicide attempt and, six months later, a repeat stay at Westwood Lodge. But her enthusiasm for work and infidelities did not flag. Between her writing, workshops, public appearances, and flings with men (usually admirers, poets and/or academics), she provided individual tutorials to fledgling poets. But she was increasingly estranged from her daughters who were building a "normal" life away from her, and dissatisfied with Kayo who adopted a posture of emotional and physical distance, despite the periodic rages that spurred physical abuse and frightened Sexton. By 1972, Sexton felt compelled to end her nearly 25-year relationship with Kayo, but despite the hired help she did not find her primary caregiver so easy to replace. She lived alternately with the Kumins and devoted neighbors, Loring and **Louise Conent**—who also helped to care for Joy and to support Linda, now at Harvard—as well as with other committed friends. Ultimately, however, even though Sexton was considered a warm and attentive friend, virtually everyone tired of the demands that her emotional instability placed upon them. She reignited a final, hopeful romance with Philip Legler, a married man and an academic, and the relationship seemed to spur a rebirth of sorts in Sexton, especially when they started plotting to run away together. But his obligations to his family ultimately overrode his passion for Anne. News of this sent Sexton into a tailspin that included several overdose attempts, requiring yet another hospitalization, this time at the Human Resource Institute of Boston.

Sexton worked manically until about 1973, publishing *The Book of Folly* in 1972, and two years later, just months before her death, *The Death Notebooks*. By 1973, the writing slowed, while her loneliness and alcohol intake increased, a sure-fire prescription for despair, especially for Sexton who lived with despair like an ever-present roommate. The therapists and caregivers came and went, and the family stayed away. On October 4, 1974, Anne Sexton killed herself by sealing the garage door and running the engine of her 1967 red Cougar; the exhaust fumes finished the job that the overdose of prescription pills never quite did. Her daughter Linda, whom she made her literary executor, graduated from Harvard and became a writer; Joy earned a nursing degree at Simmons College; and Kayo remarried and moved back into the home he had shared with Sexton.

Posthumous publications included *The Awful Rowing Toward God* (1975), *45 Mercy Street* (1976), *Words for Dr. Y.* (1978), and *The Complete Poems* (1981). In all, in her short but dazzling and industrious career, Anne Sexton produced ten volumes of poetry and one play, and prior to the 1990s, Houghton Mifflin reportedly had sold one-half million of her volumes. Sexton left ample evidence of her life behind, including journals, mementoes, scrapbooks and correspondence. None of these artifacts, however, nor the accounts of those who worked with her and loved her, could finally or fully explain the emotional illness that plagued her life and certified her suicide. But she did leave her poetry, a testament to the preeminence of the art born of her illness, and as she herself said: "Surely the words will continue, for that's what's left that's true."

**SOURCES:**

King Barnard Hall, Caroline. *Anne Sexton*. Boston, MA: Twayne, 1989.

Middlebrook, Diane Wood. *Anne Sexton: A Biography*. Boston, MA: Houghton Mifflin, 1991.

Sexton, Anne. *Collected Poems*. Boston, MA: Houghton Mifflin, 1981.

———. *No Evil Star*. Edited by Steven E. Colburn. Ann Arbor, MI: University of Michigan Press, 1985.

———. *A Self-Portrait in Letters*. Edited by Linda Gray Sexton and Lois Ames. Boston, MA: Houghton Mifflin, 1977.

Sexton, Linda. *Searching for Mercy Street*. Boston, MA: Little, Brown, 1994.

**COLLECTIONS:**

Anne Sexton's papers are housed in the Harry Ransom Humanities Research Center at the University of Texas at Austin.

**Kathleen Waites Lamm**,
Associate Professor of English and Women's Studies,
Nova Southeastern University,
Fort Lauderdale, Florida

# Seyfert, Gabriele (c. 1948—).

*See Fleming, Peggy for sidebar.*

# Seyler, Athene (1889–1990)

*British comedic actress of stage and film. Born in London, England, on May 31, 1889; died in 1990; daughter of Clarence H. Seyler and Clara (Thies) Seyler; attended Coombe Hill School, King's Langley, and Bedford College; studied at the Academy of Dramatic Art; married James Bury Sterndale-Bennett (died); married Nicholas Hannen.*

English actress Athene Seyler had a long and successful stage career, after making her debut at the Kingsway Theatre on February 11, 1909, as Pamela Grey in *The Truants*. Her other stage roles included Rosalind in *As You Like It* (St. James Theatre, 1920), Polly in *Kind Hearts and Coronets* (Lyric, Hammersmith, 1920), Gabrielle in *The Coming of Gabrielle* (St. James, 1923), Beatrice in *Much Ado About Nothing* (Strand, 1924), Hermia in *A Midsummer Night's Dream* (Drury Lane, 1924), Miss Moffatt in *The Corn is Green* (Duchess, 1939), Madame Ranevska in *The Cherry Orchard* (New, 1941), Fanny Farrelly in *Watch on the Rhine* (Aldwych, 1942), Veta Louise Simmons in *Harvey* (Prince of Wales, 1949), and Amy Beringer in *First Person Singular* (Duke of York, 1952).

Her films include *This Freedom* (1922), *The Perfect Lady* (1932), *The Citadel* (1938), *Quiet Wedding* (1940), *Dear Octopus* (1943), *Nicholas Nickleby* (1947), *Queen of Spades* (1948), *Young Wives' Tale* (1951), *Pickwick Papers* (1953), *Yield to the Night* (1956), *Campbell's Kingdom* (1958), *The Inn of the Sixth Happiness* as Mrs. Lawson (1958), *Make Mine Mink* (1959), and *Nurse on Wheels* (1963). Seyler also directed for the stage and authored (with Stephen Haggard) *The Craft of Comedy* (1944). Elected president of the Royal Academy of Dramatic Art (1950) and the Theatrical Ladies Guild (1950), she received the CBE in 1959.

# Seymour, Arabella (1575–1615).

*See Stuart, Arabella.*

# Seymour, Catherine (c. 1540–1568).

*See Grey, Catherine.*

# Seymour, Elizabeth (d. 1776).

*See Percy, Elizabeth.*

# Seymour, Frances (d. 1674).

*See Stuart, Arabella for sidebar on Frances Devereux.*

# Seymour, Frances (d. 1679)

*Countess of Holderness. Died in 1679; interred on January 5, 1680, in Westminster Abbey, London; daughter of *Frances Devereux (d. 1674) and William Seymour (1587–1660), 2nd duke of Somerset (r. 1660–1660); married Richard Molyneux, 2nd viscount Molyneux; married Thomas Wriothesly (1607–1667), 5th earl of Southampton (r. 1624–1667); married Conyers Darcy, 2nd earl of Holderness, in 1676; stepchildren: *Rachel Russell (1636–1723).*

# Seymour, Frances Thynne

## (1699–1754)

*English poet and countess of Hertford. Name variations: Frances Thynne; duchess of Somerset. Born on May 10, 1699, in Longleat, Warminster, Wiltshire, England; died on July 7, 1754, at Percy Lodge, Iver, Buckinghamshire, England; interred in Westminster Abbey; daughter of Honorable Henry Thynne and Grace Strode Thynne; married Algernon Seymour (b. 1684), Baron Percy, earl of Hertford and later 7th duke of Somerset, on March 1, 1715; children: *Elizabeth Percy (1716–1776), duchess of Northumberland; George Seymour (b. 1725), Lord Beauchamp.*

An English noblewoman, Frances Seymour, countess of Hertford, was a patron of letters and a poet herself. She was born in 1699 and raised at the palace of Longleat until her father, heir to Viscount Weymouth, died in 1708; she then moved with her mother **Grace Strode Thynne** to Leweston. Frances received a thorough education in history, languages, and literature. In 1715, her mother agreed to Frances' marriage to Algernon Seymour, earl of Hertford and the heir to the duke of Somerset. Despite the 15-year difference in their ages, the couple were very happy, as their voluminous surviving correspondence reveals. Frances Seymour had two children, dividing her time between the Hertford estate at Marlborough and their London home.

In 1723, her husband was named to the House of Peers, and she was appointed Lady of the Bedchamber to the princess of Wales, later Queen *Caroline of Ansbach**, a position she would hold until 1737. Her duties required considerable time at the royal court, where she became an intimate of the queen and other noblewomen who shared her literary interests. Her first known verses were written about 1723, and throughout her life she would often exchange verses with her correspondents. In 1725, she allowed some to be printed, though anonymously, in the poetry collection *A New Miscellany*. Despite the praise her poems received, Seymour always considered writing only a pastime and resisted publication. Often her poems imitate the style of well-known contemporary writers, or are written as odes to literary figures or friends. She had a close relationship with *Elizabeth Singer Rowe**, a religious Dissenter whom the Thynnes had protected, and whose poetry Seymour patronized and had published. In 1744, her only son died; in 1750 her husband, duke of Somerset since 1748, died as well. Deeply moved by their deaths, Seymour sought consolation in religious devotion. After 1744, Seymour's letters and verses were devoted more to pious themes, reflecting the influence of Rowe and of another correspondent, the Methodist leader *Selina Hastings**, countess of Huntingdon. Frances Seymour retired from public life after 1750 but continued to compose religious verses until her death at age 55.

**SOURCES:**

Buck, Claire. *The Bloomsbury Guide to Women's Literature*. NY: Prentice Hall, 1992.

Hughes, Helen Sard. *The Gentle Hertford: Her Life and Letters*. NY: Macmillan, 1940.

**Laura York**, M.A. in History,
University of California, Riverside, California

## Seymour, Georgiana (d. 1884).

*See Norton, Caroline for sidebar.*

## Seymour, Jane (c. 1509–1537).

*See Six Wives of Henry VIII.*

# Seymour, Jane (d. 1679)

*English noblewoman. Name variations: Lady Jane Seymour; Lady Clifford. Died on November 23, 1679; daughter of *Frances Devereux (d. 1674) and William Seymour (1587–1660), 2nd duke of Somerset (r. 1660–1660); married Charles Boyle, 2nd Lord Clifford, on May 7, 1661; children: Mary Boyle (1671–1709, who married James Douglas, 2nd duke of Queensbury); Charles Boyle, 3rd earl of Cork.*

## Seymour, Jane (d. 1884).

*See Sheridan, Jane Georgina.*

## Seymour, Margaret (d. 1550).

*See Wentworth, Margaret.*

## Seymour, Marjory (d. 1550).

*See Wentworth, Margaret.*

# Seymour, Mary (d. 1673)

*Countess of Winchelsea. Name variations: Countess of Winchilsea. Died before April 10, 1673; daughter of *Frances Devereux (d. 1674) and William Seymour (1587–1660), 2nd duke of Somerset (r. 1660–1660); became first wife of Heneage Finch, 3rd earl of Winchelsea (r. 1639–1689), before 1653. Heneage Finch was also married to Diana Willoughby, Catherine Norcliffe (d. 1679), and Elizabeth Ayres (d. 1745).*

# Seymour, Mary F. (1846–1893)

*American entrepreneur and journalist. Born Mary Foot Seymour in Aurora, Illinois, in 1846; died in*

*New York, New York, on March 21, 1893; daughter of Ephraim Sanford Seymour (a lawyer and writer) and Rosette (Bestor) Seymour; educated in private schools in Wilbraham, Massachusetts, and Somerville, New Jersey, and completed her education at the Twelfth Street School in New York City.*

*Established the Union School of Stenography in New York City (1879), and ultimately three other firms; launched the bimonthly* Business Women's Journal *(1889), which later became the* American Woman's Journal.

Mary F. Seymour was born in Aurora, Illinois, in 1846, the daughter of Ephraim Sanford Seymour, a lawyer and writer, and **Rosette Bestor Seymour**. Following Ephraim's death in a gold-mining town in Nevada City, California, in 1851, Rosette relocated to Wilbraham, Massachusetts, with her four children, to be near her married sister. The family later moved to Jersey City, New Jersey. Mary attended private schools in Wilbraham and Somerville, New Jersey, and graduated from the Twelfth Street School in New York City in 1864.

Seymour wrote verse and stories for children and was briefly a grade-school teacher in New York City and Jersey City. She suffered from poor health, however, and during periods of enforced rest, learned shorthand, and later became a court stenographer. When Remington's first efficient typewriters came on the market in the late 1870s, Seymour realized that there would be a demand for typists (or type-writers as stenographers were then called) and started the Union School of Stenography in New York City in 1879. The enterprise was a success, and she soon expanded her business to four schools, a company that employed 25 stenographers, and an employment bureau, the Union Stenographic and Typewriting Association.

In January 1889, Seymour launched a bimonthly publication, the *Business Women's Journal*, which included stories of successful women, news of women's organizations, and tips of the trade. That same year, she organized the Mary F. Seymour Publishing Company to produce the journal. The enterprise sold stock, and its officers were all women, including *May Wright Sewall, Isabella Beecher Hooker, *Frances E. Willard, and Lady Henry Somerset (*Isabella Somerset). In October 1892, Seymour introduced the *American Women's Journal*, which incorporated the *Business Women's Journal*, in an effort to reach a wider audience.

Seymour became an advocate of woman suffrage and used her skills to support various women's groups, including the International Council of Women in Washington, D.C., in 1888, and the First Triennial Council of the National Council of Women in 1891. In 1893, age 47, she died of pneumonia at her home in New York. The *American Women's Journal* lasted only three years after her death.

**SOURCES:**

Bird, Caroline. *Enterprising Women.* NY: New American Library, 1976.
James, Edward T., ed. *Notable American Women, 1607–1950.* Cambridge, MA: The Belknap Press of Harvard University, 1971.
Read, Phyllis J., and Bernard L. Witlieb. *The Book of Women's Firsts.* NY: Random House, 1992.

**Deborah Conn**, freelance writer, Falls Church, Virginia

# Seyrig, Delphine (1932–1990)

*Lebanese-born French stage and screen actress. Born on April 10, 1932, in Beirut, Lebanon; died on October 15, 1990, in Paris, France; children: one son.*

*Selected filmography:* Pull My Daisy *(US, 1958);* L'Année dernière à Marienbad *(Last Year at Marienbad, 1961);* Muriel *(1963);* La Musica *(1966);* Accident *(UK, 1967);* Baisers volés *(Stolen Kisses, 1968);* Mister Freedom *(1969);* La Voie Lactée *(The Milky Way, 1969);* La Rouge aux Lèvres *(Daughters of Darkness, Fr.-US, 1971);* Peau d'Ane *(Donkey Skin, 1971);* Le Journal d'un Suicide *(1972);* La Charme discret de la Bourgeoisie *(The Discreet Charm of the Bourgeoisie, 1972);* The Day of the Jackal *(UK-Fr., 1973);* A Doll's House *(UK, 1973);* The Black Windmill *(UK, 1974);* Eulallie quitte les Champs *(The Star, the Orphan and the Butcher, 1974);* Aloise *(1974);* India Song *(1975);* Jeanne Dielman 23 Quai de Commerce 1080 Bruxelles *(1975);* Caro Michele *(It., 1976);* Der letzte Schrei *(Ger., 1977);* Baxter—Vera Baxter *(1977);* Repérages *(Faces of Love, Switz., Fr., 1979);* Le Chemin perdu *(Switz.-Fr., 1979);* Chère Inconnu *(I Sent a Letter to My Love, 1980);* Fresh Orlando *(Ger., 1981);* Le Grain de Sable *(1983);* Dorian Grey in Spiegel der Boulevardprese *(Dorian Grey in the Mirror of the Popular Press, 1983);* Les Années 80 *(Golden Eighties, 1986);* Seven Women Seven Sins *(Ger.-Fr.-US-Aus.-Belg., 1987);* Johanna d'Arc of Mongolia *(Joan of Arc of Mongolia, Ger., 1989);* Window Shopping *(released posthumously, 1994).*

Born in 1932 in Beirut, Lebanon, to French Alsatian parents, actress Delphine Seyrig built her reputation on the Paris stage before arriving in America in 1956. In New York, she studied at the

*Hooker, Isabella Beecher. See Stowe, Harriet Beecher for sidebar.*

Actors Studio, performed on television, and appeared in the underground 16mm film *Pull My Daisy* (1958), written by Jack Kerouac. Returning to France, she made her professional film debut in 1961, portraying a complex role in *Last Year at Marienbad*, an early feature film of the experimental director Alain Resnais. The largely plotless and highly ambiguous movie not only won the grand prize at the 1961 Venice Festival, but advanced Seyrig's reputation considerably. Throughout of 1960s and 1970s, she played major and minor roles in international films of note, including Luis Buñuel's *The Discreet Charm of the Bourgeoisie*, a surrealist fable which won the Academy Award for Best Foreign Film of 1972.

A dedicated feminist, Seyrig also appeared in the films of a number of women directors, notably *Marguerite Duras' *India Song* and **Chantal Akerman**'s *Jeanne Dielman* (both 1975). In the late 1970s, Seyrig directed her own major film, *Soi belle et tais-toi* (1977), as well as a number of experimental videotaped shorts. The actress made her last appearance in *Window Shop-*

*Bianca Maria Sforza*

*ping*, which was released posthumously in 1994, four years after her death from lung disease.

**Barbara Morgan,**<br>Melrose, Massachusetts

## Sforza, Angela (fl. 1500s)

*Milanese noblewoman. Flourished in the 1500s; daughter of Carlo Sforza (b. 1461) and *Bianca Simonetta Sforza; married Ercole di Sigismondo d'Este; children: Sigismondo d'Este (d. 1579).*

## Sforza, Anna (1473–1497)

*Duchess of Ferrara. Name variations: Anna d'Este. Born in 1473; died in 1497; daughter of *Bona of Savoy (c. 1450–c. 1505) and Galeazzo Maria Sforza (1444–1476), 5th duke of Milan (r. 1466–1476); married Alfonso I d'Este (1476–1534), 3rd duke of Ferrara and Modena, in 1491; no children. Alfonso I's second wife was *Lucrezia Borgia (1480–1519).*

## Sforza, Battista (1446–1472)

*Duchess of Urbino. Born in 1446; died in 1472; daughter of Allesandro Sforza (1409–1473), lord of Pesaro and Cottignola, and *Costanza Sforza; married Federigo Montefeltro (1422–1482), 1st duke of Urbino; children: Giovanna Montefeltro (who married Giovanni della Rovere); Guidobaldo (1472–1508, who married *Elisabetta Montefeltro [d. 1526]); *Elisabetta Montefeltro (who married Roberto Malatesta). Federigo's first wife was Gentile Brancaleone.*

## Sforza, Beatrice (1427–1497).
See Este, Beatrice d'.

## Sforza, Bianca Maria (1423–1470).
See Visconti, Bianca Maria.

## Sforza, Bianca Maria (1472–1510)

*Holy Roman empress. Born on April 5, 1472, in Milan; died on December 31, 1510, in Innsbruck; daughter of *Bona of Savoy (c. 1450–c. 1505), duchess of Milan, and Galeazzo Maria Sforza (1444–1476), 5th duke of Milan (r. 1466–1476); half-sister of *Caterina Sforza (c. 1462–1509); became second wife of Maximilian I (1459–1519), Holy Roman emperor (r. 1493–1519), in 1494; stepchildren: *Margaret of Austria (1480–1530). Maximilian was first married to *Mary of Burgundy (1457–1482).*

In 1494, Charles VIII of France invaded Italy. Having defeated Charles in the Burgundian

Wars just the year before, Maximilian I was not willing to see the French king establish his power in Italy. Accordingly, Maximilian joined an anti-French league along with Spain, the pope, Milan and Venice, but poverty kept him from offering effective help. As part of the alliance, and as a means of getting financial aid, Maximilian married Bianca Maria Sforza in 1494. Bianca Maria's uncle, Ludovico il Moro, was the ruler of the wealthy city of Milan whose funds permitted Maximilian to undertake a small expedition to Italy in 1496. The marriage was a failure from the beginning. Maximilian found Bianca Maria "nervous, capricious, indulgent, sickly, and gloomy," and his neglect of her made these traits worse. Eventually, he all but confined her to her quarters in the palace at Innsbruck.

**SOURCES:**

White, Arthur. "Maximilian I," in *Historic World Leaders.* Edited by Anne Commire. Detroit, MI: Gale Research.

# Sforza, Bianca Simonetta

*Milanese noblewoman. Married Charles also known as Carlo Sforza; children: \*Ippolita Sforza (who married Alessandro Bentivoglio); \*Angela Sforza (who married Ercole di Sigismondo d'Este).*

# Sforza, Bona (1493–1557)

*Queen of Poland and duchess of Bari. Name variations: Bona of Poland. Born in January 1493 (some sources cite 1494) in Milan, Italy; died on November 19, 1557 (some sources cite 1558), at Bari, Italy; daughter of Giangaleazzo or Gian Galeazzo Sforza, duke of Milan (r. 1476–1479), and Isabella of Naples (1470–1524); became second wife of Zygmunt I Stary also known as Sigismund I the Elder (1467–1548), king of Poland (r. 1506–1548), in December 1517; children: Zygmunt August also known as Sigismund II Augustus (1520–1572), king of Poland (r. 1548–1572); \*Isabella of Poland (1519–1559, who married John Zapolya, king of Hungary [r. 1526–1540]); Zofia also known as Sophia (who married Henry, duke of Brunswick); \*Catherine Jagello (1525–1583, who married John III, king of Sweden); \*Anna Jagello (1523–1596, who married Stephen Bathory, king of Poland-Lithuania). Sigismund I the Elder's first wife was \*Barbara Zapolya (mother of \*Hedwig of Poland who married Joachim II of Brandenburg).*

Bona Sforza was born in Milan in 1493, the second child of Gian Galeazzo Sforza, duke of Milan and head of one of Italy's most powerful families, and the Spanish princess ✥➤ **Isabella of Naples**. Bona was three years old when her father died in 1496. A struggle for the succession ensued between partisans of Bona's brother, six-year-old Francesco Sforza (d. 1511), and her uncle Ludovico il Moro (Sforza). Ludovico soon triumphed, taking control of Milan and forcing out Bona, her mother, and her siblings. Francesco was made a prisoner of Ludovico's allies in France, where he died in 1511. In compensation for her losses, Ludovico gave Isabella the small duchy of Bari. Although Isabella spent the rest of her life struggling to retain Bari from other enemies, she managed to create there a court well known for its Renaissance writers, artists, and poets. Raised in this intellectual climate, Bona absorbed the Renaissance values of scholarship and humanism, along with her mother's strong political ambition.

Isabella sought a marriage for Bona which would allow her to regain the political power taken from her by Ludovico Sforza. As Bona's younger sister had died in 1501 and her brother was a prisoner in France, Bona was her mother's only hope for recapturing her lost power. Marriage negotiations with the new duke of Milan, Ludovico's son, ended when Isabella learned how weak his control on Milan was. Isabella then looked farther afield for her daughter's husband, turning to negotiations with the ruling house of Poland. The kingdom of Poland in the 16th century encompassed much of Eastern Europe, and claimed Lithuania and western Russia as well, making it an important player in European politics. Its king Sigismund I was recently widowed and seeking new political alliances in Italy. Isabella believed that a powerful ally such as Sigismund could help her regain Milan.

In 1517, the negotiations were concluded, and 24-year-old Bona was married by proxy to 52-year-old Sigismund in an elaborate ceremony at Naples. She departed for Poland in February 1518, finally meeting her new husband in April in Krakow. There a second wedding was celebrated, followed by Bona's coronation. Polish chroniclers of the events described Bona as highly learned and beautiful, with blonde hair and very dark eyes. Sigismund fell in love with his young wife, who quickly became a major influence in his reign.

The king was an intellectual and moderate ruler, well liked by his subjects for his efforts to bring peace and economic prosperity to Poland. Despite their age difference, the new royal couple shared similar interests. He was vitally fasci-

➔✥ *Isabella of Naples. See Este, Beatrice d' and Isabella d' for sidebar.*

nated with the Italian Renaissance culture in which Bona had been raised. They also came to share a passionate determination to preserve the royal dynasty and enhance the crown's power after the births of their five children, including four daughters and the future king of Poland.

Like most queens, Bona presided over the social aspects of court life—receiving guests, planning banquets and other events, supervising the daily management of the royal residences. Her most lasting contributions to Polish culture were her efforts to introduce the Renaissance of her native Italy to her adopted land. With Sigismund's encouragement, Bona brought Italian writers, painters, architects, and musicians to her court. Her architects designed castles and palaces, and redesigned existing ones in the new Renaissance style. She also established art studios and workshops for the foreign artists to teach their crafts.

In addition, Bona was unusually active for a queen politically and economically. In 1524, her mother Isabella died, leaving Bona the contested duchy of Bari. There were several contenders for its possession, primarily Francesco Sforza (d. 1535), son of *Beatrice d'Este and her mother's old enemy Ludovico Sforza. Although Bona was the rightful heir, her claim was weakened politically by her absence from Italy and by the fact that she was part of a culture which usually favored male heirs over female heirs. Unwilling to relinquish her rights to Bari despite her distance from it, Bona spent many years alternately fighting and negotiating with Bari's would-be ruler until Francesco, duke of Milan (r. 1521–1535), died.

Bona then turned her attention back to Poland, becoming involved in the political struggles emerging between the crown, aristocracy, and landholding gentry. She supported Sigismund's desire to strengthen royal power and centralize authority in the king. She contributed to this effort by promoting her followers to key positions at the royal court, materially rewarding their support of the king at the expense of the old nobility, who found themselves losing offices traditionally held by their families. In doing so, she helped create a new magnate class loyal to and dependent on royal favor.

She also challenged Polish tradition to ensure that her family would continue to rule for generations to come. Poland's Sejm (Parliament) had traditionally elected new monarchs on the old king's death; hoping to avoid the possibility that her son Sigismund (II) Augustus would not be chosen, Bona arranged for his early coronation in 1530, while her husband still reigned. This af-

front to Poland's aristocracy, combined with her other political maneuvers, earned the queen the animosity of the old noble and gentry classes, who traditionally opposed any increase in royal power or centralization of royal authority. In 1537, this animosity erupted in armed opposition to the king and queen, forcing them to reverse some of their reforms in favor of the gentry.

Bona was also active economically. Recognizing the king's dependence on Parliament to vote him funds for state administration, she sought to increase crown revenues, hoping to make the king independent of Parliament by giving him alternate sources of funds. She introduced Italian crops and invested her wealth in revitalizing Polish industry and commerce. Bona also established a considerable personal fortune for herself in Poland by using its collapsing feudal system of land tenure to her advantage. She incorporated old fiefs into her personal domain, eventually collecting the revenues from 15 towns and over 160 villages. After her death, her son incorporated these holdings into the royal domain.

In 1548, King Sigismund died at age 82. To Bona's satisfaction, her 28-year-old son Sigismund Augustus succeeded to the throne peacefully. But soon her relationship with her son soured, a fact which became obvious when his new wife, Polish-born ❧➤ Barbara Radziwell, died in 1551. (Sigismund had also been married to ❧➤ Elizabeth of Habsburg who died in 1545.) It was known that Bona had opposed the marriage because she had hoped to find a royal bride in France or Italy for her son. Public opinion accused Bona of poisoning the young queen (who actually died of cancer), but despite the lack of evidence, Sigismund Augustus refused to defend his mother against the rumors. Soon Bona began to consider returning to Italy and to her duchy of Bari, which she had not visited since she had left Italy in 1518.

It was 1556 before the dowager queen of Poland arrived in Bari, leaving Poland over the protests of her daughters. Now about 64 years old, she was received with great honor by her subjects. For the next two years, Bona established a Renaissance court which echoed that of her mother Isabella. She patronized artists and musicians, funded building projects, and contributed to religious foundations in her duchy. In November 1558, Bona died. She was buried in a magnificent tomb in the cathedral of San Nicolo di Bari.

SOURCES:
Masellis, Vito. *Storia di Bari*. Trani: Vecchi, 1960.
*La Regina Bona Sforza Tra Puglia e Polonia*. Conference papers. Warsaw: Polish Academy of Science, 1987.

**Laura York**, M.A. in History, University of California, Riverside, California

### ❧▶ Barbara Radziwell (1520–1551)

*Queen of Poland. Name variations: Radziwill. Born in 1520; died in 1551; sister of Nicholas the Black Radziwell and cousin of Nicholas the Red Radziwell, both princes of Lithuania; married the last of the Gasztolds (died); became second wife of Zygmunt August also known as Sigismund II Augustus, king of Poland (r. 1548–1572).*

On \***Bona Sforza**'s urging, her son Sigismund II Augustus had married Princess \***Elizabeth of Habsburg** (1543), the daughter of Emperor Ferdinand I. Within one year, the marriage had fallen apart, Elizabeth had failed to produce an heir, and Bona was dissatisfied with her new daughter-in-law. In the second year of the marriage, Sigismund and Elizabeth separated but did not divorce. When the young princess died in 1545, some speculated that Bona had put an end to the marriage with poison.

Two years later, Sigismund secretly eloped with Barbara Radziwell, the widowed daughter of a Lithuanian *Hetman* ("general"). This second marriage came as a shock to both Bona Sforza and the Polish Sejm (Parliament). Fearing that Sigismund's Lithuanian in-laws might influence his decisions in Polish matters, the Sejm immediately demanded an annulment. Sigismund refused. But when the union failed to produce an heir over the next four years, the marriage's end had a similar ring: the untimely death of Barbara Radziwell. Although the Lithuanian princess' death was shrouded in mystery and intrigue, many observers concluded that Queen Bona had poisoned yet another daughter-in-law. (In actuality, Barbara died from cancer.) The death of his second wife devastated Sigismund, and he never forgave his subjects' intrusion into his love "for the beautiful Barbara." He then married \***Catherine of Habsburg**, sister of his first wife Elizabeth of Habsburg.

### ❧▶ Elizabeth of Habsburg (d. 1545)

*Queen of Poland. Name variations: Élisabeth d'Autriche; Archduchess Elisabeth or Archduchess Elizabeth. Died in 1545; daughter of Ferdinand I, Holy Roman emperor (r. 1556–1564), and \*Anna of Bohemia and Hungary (1503–1547); sister of Maximilian II, Holy Roman emperor (r. 1564–1576), \*Joanna of Austria (1546–1578), \*Catherine of Habsburg (1533–1572), \*Anna of Brunswick (1528–1590), \*Eleonora of Austria (1534–1594), and others; married Zygmunt August also known as Sigismund II Augustus (1520–1572), king of Poland (r. 1548–1572); no children.*

## Sforza, Cammilla

*Milanese noblewoman. Name variations: Camilla or Cammilla Marzano. Married Costanzo Sforza (1447–1483). Costanzo had an illegitimate son Giovanni Sforza (1466–1510), lord of Pessaro.*

## Sforza, Caterina (c. 1462–1509)

**Countess of Forlì and the "most famous virago of the Renaissance" who conducted military operations and defended besieged fortresses in 15th-century Italy.** *Name variations: Caterine Sforza; Catherine Sforza, countess of Forli and Imola or Imolo; Caterina de Medici; Caterina Sforza Riario. Born Caterina Sforza in late 1462 or early 1463 in Milan, Italy; died in Florence, Italy, in 1509; illegitimate daughter of Galeazzo Maria Sforza (1444–1476), duke of Milan, and Lucrezia Landriani (wife of Giampietro Landriani); married Girolamo Riario, in 1477 (died 1488); began liaison with Giacomo Feo, in 1489 (died 1495); married Giovanni de Medici, in 1497 (died 1498); children: (first marriage) Bianca Riario (b. 1478), Ottaviano Riario (b. 1479), Cesare Riario (b. between 1480 and 1482), Giovanni Livio Riario (b. 1484), Galeazzo Riario (b. 1485), Francesco Sforza Riario (b. 1487), and a daughter who died in infancy; (liaison with Feo) Bernardino, later called Carlo (b. 1490); (second marriage) Ludovico, later called Giovanni delle Bande Nere (1498–1526).*

*Lived with birth mother until 1466, when she was transferred together with siblings to father's household; betrothed at age ten to Girolamo Riario; married at age 14 and moved to Rome (1477); became countess of Forlì (1481), and thereafter lived primarily in Forlì and Imola; had first bout of quartan fever (1482); during papal succession (1484), rode into Rome and seized the Castel Sant'Angelo; acted as judge against assassination conspiracy and imposed severe punishments (1487); husband Girolamo Riario assassinated (1488); successfully held the fortress of Ravaldino during revolt of Forlì after assassination, even when children were threatened (1488); served as regent for oldest son, ruling Imola and Forlì (1488–1500); exacted bloody retribution after assassination of lover Giacomo Feo in Forlì (1495); negotiated with Niccolò Machiavelli, envoy of Florence (1499); defended Ravaldino in Forlì against Cesare Borgia (1499–1500); captured and imprisoned in Rome (1500–01); retired to Florence (1501–09).*

Caterina Sforza was a strong, vibrant woman, often described as a "Renaissance virago," who wielded sex, the sword, and diplomacy to secure her power. She lived in Italy in the late 15th and early 16th centuries, a time of conspiracy and intrigue. City-states, republics and kingdoms pitted themselves against one another; popes ruled like kings; assassinations by blade, poison, and garrote were common; and blood and vengeance were more prevalent than mercy and forgiveness. Yet it was also the Italy of Leonardo da Vinci, Michelangelo, and the humanists, and of Savonarola as well as Machiavelli.

The Sforzas rose to prominence as *condottieri*, or captains of bands of mercenaries, and the Sforza women were no strangers to warfare. One of Caterina's ancestors, Muzio Attendolo, was the first to adopt the nickname of "Sforza." When he was imprisoned in the early 15th century, his sister *Margaret of Attenduli donned armor and rescued him—a decade before *Joan of Arc appeared on the battlefield in France. Like these women, Caterina Sforza wore armor and played a military role, but she was no rescuer or saint; Sforza fought for her own purposes.

$\mathcal{S}$he commanded enormous respect and was even feared by the soldiers for her insistence on iron discipline, cruelly enforced.

—Ernst Breisach

Caterina was very like her grandfather, Francesco Sforza (1401–1466), who seized power as the duke of Milan in the mid-15th century. He was the ideal Renaissance soldier: tall, handsome, athletic, a capable warrior and a skilled strategist. His oldest son, Galeazzo Maria, was a wild youth with a strain of cruelty in his nature. While still a teenager, he began a long affair with *Lucrezia Landriani, his best friend's wife. She gave birth to four illegitimate children: Carlo in 1461 and Caterina in late 1462, followed by *Chiara Sforza and Alessandro. Galeazzo Maria acknowledged the children, and when he became duke upon his father's death in 1466, he brought them into his own household. In 1468, the duke married 19-year-old *Bona of Savoy, who seems to have been a loving stepmother to Caterina and her siblings. Bona's son, Gian Galeazzo Sforza, was the designated heir, but the other children were part of the extended family.

Caterina enjoyed the typical Renaissance childhood of a young girl of noble family in 15th-century Italy. She learned to read and write, was educated in religious matters, and was important primarily as a tool of diplomacy: noble daughters, even illegitimate ones, were quite useful in making politically advantageous marital ties with other families. When Caterina was ten years old, she was betrothed to 29-year-old Girolamo Riario, a rather crude and lusty character of humble family origins, who was propelled to prominence when his uncle became Pope Sixtus IV.

Sixtus had been known as a gentle scholar prior to his election. Afterwards, as historian Will Durant noted in *The Renaissance,* he underwent "one of the strangest transformations in papal history," presiding over a Rome that was "a hotbed of intrigues, a battleground of ever-warring powerful nobles, a place of the ready and murderous dagger" which "did not readily tolerate a saintly pope." It was Sixtus who appointed Torquemada as head of the Spanish Inquisition. Sixtus also ensured that his relatives prospered. Otherwise, Girolamo Riario would not have been a suitable match for Caterina.

Galeazzo Maria Sforza of Milan had earlier been forced to cede the city of Imola to Sixtus IV. Located in the region of north-central Italy known as Romagna, Imola was important because of its location on a major road connecting other significant cities. The concession and the betrothal helped consolidate an alliance between the Sforza of Milan and the new pope, while improving Caterina's future prospects. A year after the betrothal, in late 1473, the pope granted Girolamo control of Imola. A few months later, Girolamo's status was further elevated when his brother, the cardinal of San Sisto, died and left him a great inheritance. Girolamo became the pope's "right-hand man," an important advisor of increasing influence and power.

Meanwhile, Caterina continued her education. There is little evidence that she excelled in the humanistic disciplines of oratory or music, but her physical skills in dancing, games, and riding horses were impressive. From a young age, Caterina Sforza was a woman of action and not words.

On the day after Christmas 1476, Caterina Sforza lost her father to assassins' knives. Since the duke's legal heir, Caterina's half-brother, was still an infant, a struggle for power ensued, with the late duke's brother, Ludovico il Moro (Sforza), eager to assume control. Caterina's stepmother Bona of Savoy wrote to the pope to encourage an early marriage between Caterina and Girolamo; the groom was unable to attend the ceremony, so the two were wedded by proxy in early 1477. In late April, Girolamo

Caterina
Sforza

sent an escort to take 14-year-old Caterina to Imola. She arrived on May 1, stopping to dress in fine brocades and expensive jewels before entering the town. Sforza was met with songs, flowers, and the keys to the city; it was a friendly greeting that would stand in stark contrast to the way she would be forced to leave in later years. Two weeks later, she proceeded to Rome, where she was finally met by her husband. She was blessed by the pope and treated to gifts of jewels and sumptuous banquets in honor of her marriage.

Though Caterina was pleased by the faded grandeur of Rome, her feelings about her new husband were not recorded. Girolamo was a brash and vindictive young man, redeemed by rare moments of charm, whose dominant characteristic was ambition. He was often gone from Rome for extended periods, leaving Caterina to her own devices. She was occupied partly by nearly continuous pregnancies; she had nine children in 20 years, the first seven with Riario. Her first child was a daughter **Bianca Riario**, born in the spring of 1478; sons followed in August 1479 (Ottaviano) and August 1480 (Cesare).

When Girolamo Riario was awarded Imola by the pope, he gained the responsibility for defending the city. The Papal States of central Italy were under the political control of the pope, but the upheavals of the previous century had allowed some areas to gain relative independence. Fifteenth-century popes like Sixtus IV invested a great deal of effort in regaining control of the region, and did not flinch from employing deception and open violence to achieve their ends. Among Girolamo's chief enemies was the Medici family, who ruled Florence and threatened the security of the Papal States. Girolamo was behind a botched assassination attempt against Lorenzo de Medici in April 1478; it is uncertain whether the pope had condoned the conspiracy. Girolamo had his eye on several cities in Romagna, but gained only one in addition to Imola: Forlì, which he was awarded in 1480 at the expense of its former rulers, the Ordelaffi family. The justification for the takeover was to bring the city under direct papal rule.

While Girolamo was trying to expand his personal empire, Caterina pursued a fairly traditional life as a young Roman wife. She engaged in half-hearted attempts to gather priests and scholars to her court in the humanistic tradition. However, she was far more strongly drawn to physical pursuits, and was passionate about "the chase"—riding out with her hunting dogs on parties to hunt deer and boar. This pleasant life was disrupted when Girolamo decided to move the family to his possessions in Romagna in July 1481. As the new count and countess of Forlì, Girolamo and Caterina entered the city to a wild celebration. Although she was five months' pregnant, Caterina rode in on horseback beside her husband. She was 18 years old, blonde, and, by the standards of the day, strikingly beautiful.

Caterina's sheer physical presence, which she enhanced with displays of wealth, impressed the people of Forlì. She continued to pursue her passion for the hunt, despite her pregnancy.

However, Girolamo seems to have made little effort to gain popular support, and had few dealings with his public. Then in late 1481, when the couple made a brief visit to Venice, they were horrified to learn of an Ordelaffi plot to assassinate them upon their return. Though the plot was thwarted, Girolamo and Caterina lived thereafter with the suspicion that their own people were ready to betray them in favor of the Ordelaffi. Girolamo has been described as the "cruel and rapacious" "despot of Forlì"; it seems his natural tendencies to viciousness were only aggravated by his increasing paranoia.

Caterina insisted on returning to Rome in late 1481, when she was eight months' pregnant; she had a second daughter a few days after the long journey, but the child survived only briefly. Then in late 1482, she was beset by quartan fever, a form of malaria that would plague her for the rest of her life. Caterina's independence and self-reliance were tempered during this period of loss and isolation, for Girolamo was away at a war that erupted between the Papal States and Venice on one side, and Ferrara, assisted by Milan, Naples, and Florence, on the other. The war ended without much change of territory, but Girolamo was hailed as a hero for victories that in fact were the work of *condottiere* Roberto Malatesta.

Girolamo and Caterina returned to Imola and Forlì in mid-1483 to defend their territories against new incursions by the Ordelaffi, backed by Venice. Caterina began to take a personal interest in military affairs, participating directly in the control of their soldiers, and insisting "on iron discipline cruelly enforced." A new assassination plot was discovered, further alienating Caterina and Girolamo from the people of Forlì. They left for Rome, leaving the town's governor the chore of rounding up and executing the conspirators.

Back in Rome, Caterina became a frequent companion of her husband's uncle, the pope. Rumors began to circulate that the relationship was more than merely familial, though this seems unlikely. At the same time, Girolamo continued to polish his reputation as a military figure, carrying out sieges and attempting seizures of territory in his uncle's name.

The death of Sixtus IV on August 12, 1484, threw all Girolamo's ambitions to the wind. Riots and disorder seized Rome; mobs attacked the property of the pope's relatives and looted with abandon. The day of the pope's death, Caterina was with her husband and children, encamped near the site of a siege. Girolamo beat a hasty retreat towards Rome, but was ordered by the cardinals of the church to remain outside the city. The election of a new pope was underway, and everyone hoped to sway the vote to their own benefit. While Girolamo was barred from marching through the streets of Rome in a show of military force, his wife was not so constrained.

Civil war seemed likely and Rome was in chaos. Caterina Sforza leapt into action to try to retain the power and prestige of her family. She mounted a horse, despite being seven months' pregnant, and rode with a companion straight through Rome to the Castel Sant'Angelo. Declaring that she was claiming the fortress in order to secure it for the pope's legal successor, she chased out many of the occupants, closed and barricaded the gates, and bullied the soldiers into obedience. Ernst Breisach wrote that they "considered her cruel and fierce but obeyed her grudgingly." This achievement is more astonishing in view of Caterina's unsoldierly appearance: she stormed the castle wearing a tan satin dress, a plumed velvet hat, and a man's belt with a curved sword and bag of gold ducats.

Despite Caterina's grand gesture, Girolamo was not rewarded by the cardinals of the Church. He was allowed to retain Imola and Forlì, but agreed to return the Castel Sant'Angelo to them. At first, Caterina was reluctant to accede to her husband's wishes, seeing his bargain as a failure, and she had additional soldiers smuggled into the fortress. But she could not hold out alone and accepted a safe conduct to her husband's side. With the pope dead, they had no base of power in Rome, and retreated once more to Forlì. The new pope, Innocent VIII, was satisfied to leave them in peace in their Romagnol holdings. Now eight months' pregnant, Caterina rode back to Forlì with her husband, and gave birth there to a son in late October.

Caterina and Girolamo lived a relatively peaceful life for a few years. Although they were now on the margins of power, they still had some influence; Girolamo's nephew, Cardinal Raffaello Riario, had become an important person in the Church, and assisted them. Another source of support was Caterina's uncle, Ludovico il Moro, who ruled Milan. The brother of Caterina's deceased father, Ludovico acted as regent for her young half-brother from 1481 to 1494. Ludovico was known as an intelligent and cultured man. Though clever and devious, he was also generous and merciful; he seems to have had little of the cruelty that sometimes marked his brother and his niece Caterina. In 1482, Ludovico brought Leonardo da Vinci to Milan, where the artist worked until 1499. Da Vinci designed costumes for Ludovico's pretty young wife, *Beatrice d'Este, painted portraits of the family (now lost), and created his most ambitious work: a portrayal of the last supper of Christ to decorate the wall of the refectory of Ludovico's favorite church, the Santa Maria delle Grazie.

While da Vinci painted in Milan, Caterina and Girolamo lived quietly in Forlì. They were still regarded as outsiders by the people, but for a time there were no active revolts or conspiracies against them. They hired workers to complete the fortress of Ravaldino and to work on other family properties. Caterina became increasingly reluctant to sit on the sidelines while her husband governed; financial worries and provincial boredoms led to quarrels. An outbreak of plague in Forlì in April 1486 caused new financial strains, as the Riario hired medical attendants to care for rich and poor alike. By late fall 1486, Caterina had been forced to pawn most of her jewelry.

The Riario moved from Forlì to Imola in the spring of 1487. Caterina enjoyed a brief visit to her family in Milan, but was recalled when Girolamo became seriously ill. His ailment left him greatly weakened, and Caterina took over many of his duties—and began to plan the best course to follow if Girolamo should die. It was clear that whatever happened, retaining control of the fortress of Ravaldino in Forlì would be critical. An obstinate *castellan* (keeper of the castle) was refusing to allow her admittance until old debts were settled; in August, through a combination of conspiracy and assassination, Caterina regained control of Ravaldino, and installed Tommaso Feo as castellan. During these events, the remarkable Caterina rode on horseback from Imola to Forlì and then back, and gave birth to her seventh child the day after her return.

Less than a month later, in September 1487, Caterina rode back to Forlì once more to deal with a new conspiracy. Girolamo invested her as judge, and the punishment she invoked was harsh. Six people were executed and quartered; their heads were placed on poles at the gates of the town, and other body parts were prominently mounted in various parts of Forlì.

Caterina's vengeance did not deter further conspiracies. On April 14, 1488, Girolamo was stabbed to death in a dining hall of the palace. Awakened with the news, Caterina rushed to barricade herself and her children in her apartments and had the forethought to send a messenger to Milan first for help. By morning, a mob had gathered outside the palace, calling for the reinstatement of the Ordelaffi. They broke into the palace and took Caterina and her children prisoner. The palace was ransacked and Girolamo's corpse was mutilated in the town square.

Those in the fortress of Ravaldino remained loyal to the Riario, and Caterina was dragged out to order their surrender. Feo refused, as did the castellan of Schiavonia, a smaller fortress. Feo stated that he would give up Ravaldino only if Caterina were permitted to meet with him personally, in the fortress. After much argument, the conspirators agreed. While they held Caterina's children and her mother and sister as hostages, Caterina was allowed to enter Ravaldino—which she then refused to leave.

The story of Caterina's defiant defense of Ravaldino has been repeated in many works of history. There are several versions of a famous scene where the rebel citizens threatened to kill her children if she did not surrender. Some historians, such as Durant, write that "she told them from the ramparts that she had another child in her womb, and could easily conceive more." Others, including Machiavelli, enliven the story by claiming that she raised her skirts to reveal her genitals and shouted down that the people were fools; didn't they realize she could simply make more children? It appears that Caterina did claim (falsely) to be pregnant, and implied that she could always have more children. Feo threatened that if the children were harmed, he would bombard the town, and reminded them that Caterina's uncle Ludovico, duke of Milan, would exact vengeance as well. Later the children were dragged before the fortress, crying, and Feo ordered his cannons to fire a few warning shots; this proved sufficient to cause the revolutionaries to retreat.

Caterina ordered Feo to take potshots at the homes of her enemies. Both she and the Ordelaffi hoped for outside assistance, but it was slow in coming. Ultimately, Caterina's supporters arrived first: nearly 2,000 soldiers from Bologna and more than 6,000 from Milan. The Forlìvesi braced for pillage, but Caterina prevented it; she had no interest in ruling a ruined city. The main conspirators left town, and the Forlìvesi, sensing that the key to survival was to appease Caterina, began to shout for her and her oldest son, Ottaviano. Caterina's children were brought to her, and the whole town wept with joy at the reunion. Caterina, only 25 years old, was now the ruler of Forlì and Imola, in fact if not in law.

Her rule was harsh. She hired brutal captains to carry out her vengeance for her husband's assassination. Dozens of people were jailed, and several were hanged, then dismembered. The sight of blood and severed human limbs in the piazza inspired the townspeople to restore most of what had been looted from the Riario palace. Later, Caterina received a pledge of loyalty from the town accepting her as regent for her son. During the spring and summer of 1488, she secured her power, with the support of Cardinal Raffaello Riario and the duke of Milan. Their backing helped procure a papal bull granting her the legal right to govern until her son Ottaviano reached maturity.

The young widow was, by all accounts, an exceptionally handsome woman—but one in a precarious position. As historian **Christiane Klapisch-Zuber** notes in *Women, Family and Ritual in Renaissance Italy*, any woman living alone in Renaissance Italy was suspect. "An unmarried woman was considered incapable of living alone or in the absence of masculine protection without falling into sin. . . . [S]ecular society did not set much store by [the widow's] chances of remaining chaste." Widows were in an extremely difficult position, as any impropriety could compromise both their father's and their late husband's families, and they were expected to seek the protection of a man's household. Widows who chose to live chastely could move in with their husband's relatives and keep their children. A widow who preferred to return to her birth family or to remarry had to leave her children behind with their father's family, and was generally regarded as a "cruel mother," as much for reclaiming her dowry as for leaving her children—even though young widows were usually pressured by their birth families to regain their dowries and remarry, forming new political alliances. The "good mother," in Renaissance Italy, was the widow who renounced the pleasures of marriage and dedicated herself to her children—under the supervision of the late husband's family, to be sure.

Only a few wealthy widows, like Caterina Sforza, could choose to live independently. Outwardly, she was the "good mother," rejecting many opportunities for remarriage in order to remain Ottaviano's regent, thus securing his inheritance. Yet if she refused either to remarry or to give up her children, she also refused to live in celibacy. Sforza was healthy, young, attractive, and wealthy; she wanted to keep her family, her power, and still fulfill her personal needs. She wanted to have it all when no woman could expect so much; queens like *Elizabeth I and saints like Joan paid the price of chastity for their power, while other women traded independence for the security and social acceptability of marriage. Caterina Sforza refused to play either madonna or wife, so it is not surprising she was later labeled a whore. Even so, it was her political choices, rather than her social ones, that would eventually lead to her downfall.

During the summer of 1489, Caterina made a surprising liaison with the scion of her former enemies, 29-year old Antonio Maria Ordelaffi. The two spent weeks together in a country house, heedless of the scandal. Cardinal Raffaello Riario expressed his shock, and the pope considered giving Forlì to one of his own sons, since Caterina was leading "a disorderly life." The cardinal arranged for Ordelaffi to be sent to Venice, much against his will. Caterina was left alone to endure another extended bout of quartan fever in the fall of 1489.

During the next several years, Caterina faced continual challenges from obstinate captains and castellans, many of whom she owed money. The Feo family became increasingly important, as Tommaso Feo had been a loyal servant during the assassination crisis. Then in late 1489, Caterina began a six-year association with Tommaso's younger brother, 19-year-old Giacomo Feo. In August 1490, she attempted to secure her power by imprisoning Tommaso, who had gained too much influence, and replacing him as castellan of Ravaldino with Giacomo. Through intrigue and deception, she gained tighter control of her fortresses in Imola as well. She felt secure enough to begin flaunting convention; her relationship with Giacomo, which was kept hidden during the early months, became increasingly open. It was hard to maintain secrecy when Caterina had a son, Bernardino, in 1491. Giacomo Feo continued to gain power, becoming commander-in-chief of Caterina's troops and her constant escort and advisor.

Caterina's people began to resent Giacomo's influence, and saw him as a threat to the rightful heir, Ottaviano. A conspiracy to assassinate Giacomo was discovered in September 1491, and four men were imprisoned. But on the whole things were peaceful, and Caterina once again enjoyed hunts, parties, and dances. She also pursued her longtime interest in alchemy. Caterina maintained a massive book of prescriptions with many formulas for preserving beauty, inducing abortion, healing common ailments, and so forth. Recipes for poisons were also written into her book.

In 1492, Rodrigo Borgia became Pope Alexander VI, initiating the reign of the Borgias. This seemed at first to be a favorable development for Caterina, since Alexander VI was Ottaviano's godfather. However, Rodrigo had fathered a number of children of his own, including Cesare Borgia and *Lucrezia Borgia, whom he publicly acknowledged. He recognized early on that Cesare had the "iron and gall" required for success in Italian politics, and did a great deal to advance his power. Tall, blond, clever and handsome, Cesare Borgia embodied the ideal of Italian Renaissance. His strength and physical prowess were the stuff of legends; he once reportedly decapitated a bull in a single stroke. Cesare has been compared to Girolamo Riario; both were close relatives of a pope, and acted as that pope's leading general in the field. In many ways, however, Cesare Borgia was like Caterina herself: far more a person of action than of books and words. Ironically, it was Cesare Borgia who would bring Caterina Sforza's power to an abrupt end.

In late 1494, Caterina's half-brother, the legal heir to the Duchy of Milan, died, and her uncle Ludovico il Moro was finally awarded the title. In that same year, he agreed to accept assistance from the French against his enemies in Italy. When he did so, other Italians invited in the Spanish. France and Spain then vied for dominance in Italy for the next 15 years. Caterina Sforza attempted to remain neutral during the power struggles of the late 15th century, sometimes favoring the pope and his ally, Naples, and at other times allying herself with her uncle in Milan and the French. While armies moved back and forth in Romagna, Caterina did her best to preserve her property from pillage, switching allegiance when necessary. She even brought back Tommaso Feo as governor of Imola, then of Forlì.

Caterina and Giacomo Feo's relationship became increasingly turbulent, yet she seemed more and more dependent on him. He attempted to impose restrictions upon her, insisting, for example, that she could not enter her own fortresses without him. Observers of the time noted that heated battles occurred when Giacomo dictated new rules, but Caterina invariably complied, apparently from fear of losing her lover.

Giacomo Feo's arrogance extended not just to Caterina, but to her people as well. They regarded him as a base-born upstart; resentment mounted against him, and in August 1495 his fate was sealed. He was returning from a day of picnicking with Caterina, her children and guests when he was fatally stabbed and then mutilated. Caterina's vengeance was immediate and severe; Tommaso Feo was her main instrument.

For a brief time, she suspected her two oldest sons of being connected with the assassination. Her late husband's illegitimate son, Scipio, remained by her side, but was then imprisoned for 18 months when he criticized the brutality of her retribution. The Ghetti family, which had staged the assassination, was decimated: some members, including a woman, were thrown into a spiked well and left to die; a child's throat was slit; one man was quartered while still alive. Dozens of people suffered torture and execution, including 20 children. This episode turned the people of Forlì permanently against Caterina Sforza, especially since many of them saw Giacomo's death as a desirable thing.

In 1496, a year after Giacomo's murder, Caterina fell in love with another somewhat younger man: Giovanni de Medici of Florence. His family background assured him of plush quarters in the fortress during his visit, and he was soon moved to rooms adjacent to Caterina's own. One observer of the time noted that the Forlìvesi jested that Caterina must be afraid of a cold bed, but because Giovanni de Medici was of noble birth, the affair was seen as tolerable compared to her scandalous tie to the commoner Giacomo Feo. But if the people of Forlì were willing to tolerate the widow's dalliance with the handsome Giovanni, her peers were not. The relationship was seen in political terms as solidifying Caterina's inclination towards Florence, and her uncle was displeased. Publicly, of course, Caterina denied that Giovanni was more than a friend and business associate. This pose was difficult to sustain when in August 1497 she was noticeably pregnant. In September, Caterina and Giovanni were secretly married. Her power rested on the pope's investiture of her son Ottaviano as the Riario heir of Forlì and Imola, and her marriage into another family could jeopardize that inheritance.

During the same period, Caterina developed a correspondence with Girolamo Savonarola of Florence, a noted spiritual figure of the day; the artists Botticelli and Michelangelo were among his devotees. Savonarola was more the medieval saint than "Renaissance man"; under him, Florence held the "bonfires of the vanities," purging itself of sin. This grim and righteous man was an unlikely mentor for Sforza. He offered her political advice, suggesting that justice, good works, and faith in God were the best course.

More concerned with security than with justice, Caterina set about reinforcing her fortresses. However, during this pregnancy—her last—she refrained from galloping out on the sort of personal inspections she might have made earlier, and in April 1498 gave birth to a son. The child, Ludovico (later called Giovanni delle Bande Nere), would one day be a national hero. At the time, she was forced to keep the birth, like her marriage, as far from public eyes as possible.

Caterina did her best to turn her oldest son Ottaviano into at least as good a military figure as she herself had been, but it was a fruitless endeavor. Ottaviano was a fat man on his way to true obesity; he was also indolent and unconcerned with affairs of leadership. While Caterina astutely engaged in diplomatic maneuvers during the period of the Pisan War, Ottaviano played at being an equestrian.

The summer of 1498 brought new disasters. Waves of epidemics spread because of the heat, and Giovanni de Medici would be among the victims. Caterina had spent much of the summer traversing her territory with the captain of her forces, overseeing military campaigns. She was called from the field when Giovanni, who had been sent to a spa to recover from his illness, died suddenly. This time there were no conspirators against whom to vent her anguish; she returned to the battlefields, resumed her activities, and before long found a new lover, Ottaviano Manfredi. Refined, attractive, young, and bright, he was well suited to the dynamic and vibrant Caterina, and even became a close friend of her oldest son. Unfortunately, Manfredi suffered the unlucky fate of so many of Caterina's mates: in April 1499, he was gruesomely murdered by rivals of his family. Caterina had lost four lovers in 11 years. A month later, she found a new companion in Giovanni di Casale, an emissary sent by her uncle.

In the final year of the 15th century, there was peace for neither Italy nor Caterina Sforza. Both she and her uncle in Milan found themselves the targets of a new alliance between the pope and France. While France, once Milan's ally, turned invader and forced Ludovico il Moro out of Milan, Caterina was set upon by the pope and the forces of Cesare Borgia.

She began to negotiate to gain the support of Florence against her enemies. They sent her a special envoy, Niccolò Machiavelli, who was just beginning his long career in Florence. Later a famous diplomat and writer, Machiavelli was on his first diplomatic mission with this visit to Caterina Sforza. He was told to appease her without promising military protection. When she realized his purpose, she suggested he return to Florence and get new instructions; otherwise, there would be no agreements. "She proved too subtle for him," writes Durant, "and he came back empty-handed, chastened." She was less successful in her negotiations with Lorenzo de Medici over his brother Giovanni's estate; their disputes became openly hostile when it came to the future of the son she had borne Giovanni.

In 1499, Alexander VI set out to seize direct control of key towns in the Papal States. He declared that Caterina Sforza had usurped the rights to Imola and Forlì from the Church, and called her a tyrant who would be forcibly removed if she refused to resign. She bargained and pleaded. Many say that she poisoned the letters she sent the pope. But she refused to give up her possessions.

In late 1499, Cesare Borgia, only in his early 20s, led an army of 15,000 into Romagna. The city of Imola surrendered to his proxy without a fight, although the fortress held out for a time. The fall of Imola disheartened the Forlìvesi, who had no stomach for an extended siege and little loyalty to Caterina. Forlì surrendered to Cesare himself. Relieved at being spared a battle, the citizens staged a celebration in his honor. They soon regretted their easy capitulation when Cesare's French troops began pillaging and raping as if they were conquerors.

Caterina could have simply retreated to Florence, where she had citizenship, and waited for the next papal succession. After all, "fleeing to fight another day" was the course her own uncle had chosen. Characteristically, she refused to give up so easily; she immured herself within the citadel with her garrison, as she had done 12 years earlier when Girolamo was murdered. Borgia offered her safe passage if she would surrender, and promised to settle her on a small estate; reportedly, she did not deign to answer. Instead, she walked the battlements dressed in plate armor.

Caterina was supported by a few dozen people: some Sforza relatives from fallen Milan, her lover Giovanni di Casale, and Scipio, her late husband's illegitimate son. She commanded about 900 soldiers, mostly unreliable mercenaries—hardly a match for Borgia's impressive army. But they had the advantage of defending a heavily fortified position, and when Cesare's artillery opened fire on December 28, Ravaldino answered with its own barrage. Several days of artillery exchange ensued, during which Caterina managed to sneak in a few reinforcements. Finally, Borgia staged an assault. By January 11, 1500, serious breaches had been made in the walls of Ravaldino and Borgia's soldiers were able to enter the fortress. The castellan lured one group of soldiers into a tower, then shut them in and set out ammunition that had been stored there. Caterina and her men retreated to the main tower. Protected by a cuirass (leather breastplate), Caterina ordered a counterattack and took part in the fighting. But Borgia's army was too strong; many of Caterina's soldiers surrendered or were taken prisoner, including her lover and the castellan, while Caterina fought her way back to the tower. Soon afterwards, she was captured by a French captain and handed over as a prisoner to Cesare Borgia. It is widely reported that he raped her after her capture.

Eventually Caterina Sforza was taken to Rome, but she stubbornly refused to sign away her legal rights to Forlì and Imola. She attempted to escape from the Belvedere Palace, where she was being held, and as a result ended up in a prison cell in Sant'Angelo—the very fortress she had captured 16 years before. After a year and a half, she was finally released to a nunnery. The intercession of the French, and their guarantee of her freedom if she signed away her territories, together with the detrimental effects of a long imprisonment, where she feared poison in every meal, finally persuaded her to concede. The effect of imprisonment reputedly turned her hair white.

Despite her obstinance in defending Forlì, Caterina had made contingency plans. During the siege, she sent what was left of her jewels and other valuables, along with her children, to Florence to wait out the course of events. In the summer of 1501, she herself was allowed to retire to Florence, to spend the rest of her life in powerless seclusion. Her son Ottaviano was a disappointment; he eventually became a bishop and lived in obscurity. Her other children made respectable marriages; her son Cesare became archbishop of Pisa; and finally, she was left with only her youngest, Giovanni de Medici. A child after her own heart, he was interested in riding, fencing and swimming. She concentrated on his training from the time he was ten, in 1507, until her death two years later at the age of 46. She appears to have died from a liver ailment combined with peritonitis and pleurisy.

Down through the centuries, Caterina Sforza has been held up as an example. She was an extraordinary woman whose life could not be neatly categorized according to Renaissance standards; thus she was praised by some, excoriated by others. Her ability to survive as a ruler was admired, though her harsh methods were abhorred—more for being imposed by a woman than as inappropriate techniques of political control.

In his *Discourses*, Niccolò Machiavelli tells the story of Caterina Sforza's defiance of the assassins who murdered her husband in 1488; he was impressed by the clever stratagem by which she regained control of the fortress. He also used Sforza as an example in his most famous book *The Prince*. In his discussion of the merits of fortresses in helping rulers retain power, Machiavelli notes that in his time, they were generally not very useful—except in the case of Caterina Sforza, countess of Forlì. Her fortress, he says, enabled her to retain power during the insurrection after her husband's death; "yet the fortresses were later of little avail even to her, when Cesare Borgia attacked her, and her hostile people united with a foreigner." He suggests that "it would have been more secure for her, both early and late, not to have been hated by the people than to have had fortresses."

Caterina Sforza has been described by historians as a despot and tyrant, as one who governed with "all-too-masculine force" rather than with wisdom. The same qualities that were praised in Cesare Borgia were despised in Sforza. In *Women of the Renaissance*, **Margaret L. King** points out that, like Joan of Arc, the Renaissance woman who donned armor was not revered, but reviled; "she was hated because she did what men did, and triumphantly."

**SOURCES:**

Bradbury, Jim. *The Medieval Siege*. Woodbridge: Boydell, 1992.

Collison-Morley, L. *The Story of the Sforzas*. NY: Dutton, 1934.

King, Margaret L. *Women of the Renaissance*. Chicago, IL: University of Chicago Press, 1991.

**SUGGESTED READING:**

Breisach, Ernst. *Caterina Sforza: A Renaissance Virago*. Chicago, IL: University of Chicago Press, 1967.

**Reina Pennington**, Ph.D. Candidate in Military and Women's History, University of South Carolina, Columbia, South Carolina

## Sforza, Chiara (b. around 1464)

*Milanese noblewoman. Born around 1464; illegitimate daughter of Galeazzo Maria Sforza (1444–1476), duke of Milan, and *Lucrezia Landriani (wife of Giampietro Landriani); sister of *Caterina Sforza (c. 1462–1509).*

## Sforza, Christierna (1521–1590).

*See Christina of Denmark.*

## Sforza, Costanza (fl. 1445)

*Noblewoman of Pesaro. Name variations: Constanza or Costanza Varano. Flourished around 1445; married* Allesandro Sforza (1409–1473), lord of Pesaro and Cottignola; children: *Battista Sforza (1446–1472); Costanza Sforza (1447–1483); Allesandro also had an illegitimate daughter, *Ginevra Sforza (d. 1507).*

## Sforza, Ginevra (d. 1507)

*Noblewoman of Pesaro. Name variations: Ginevra Bentivoglio. Died in 1507; illegitimate daughter of Allesandro Sforza (1409–1473), lord of Pesaro and Cottignola; married Sante Bentivoglio; married Giovanni Bentivoglio.*

## Sforza, Ginevra Tiepolo

*Noblewoman of Pesaro. Born Ginevra Tiepolo; became third wife of Giovanni Sforza (1466–1510), lord of Pesaro. His first wife was *Maddalena Sforza (1472–1490); his second wife was *Lucrezia Borgia.*

## Sforza, Ippolita (1446–1484).

*See Ippolita.*

## Sforza, Ippolita

*Milanese noblewoman. Name variations: Ippolita Bentivoglio. Daughter of Carlo Sforza (b. 1461) and *Bianca Simonetta Sforza; married Allesandro Bentivoglio.*

## Sforza, Isabella (1470–1524).

*See Este, Beatrice d' and Isabella d' for sidebar on Isabella of Naples.*

## Sforza, Maddalena (1472–1490)

*Noblewoman of Pesaro. Name variations: Maddalena Gonzaga. Born in 1472; died in 1490; daughter of *Margaret of Bavaria (1445–1479) and Frederigo also known as Federico Gonzaga (1441–1484), 3rd marquis of Mantua (r. 1478–1484); sister of *Elisabetta Montefeltro (1471–1526); first wife of Giovanni Sforza (1466–1510), lord of Pesaro. Giovanni's second wife was *Lucrezia Borgia; his third *Ginevra Tiepolo Sforza.*

## Sforza, Margherita (1375–?).

*See Margaret of Attenduli.*

## Sforza, Polissena

*Ferrarese noblewoman. Name variations: Polissena Malatesta. Second wife of Sigismondo Pandolfo*

*Malatesta (1417–1486). His first wife was *Ginevra d'Este (1414–1440).*

## Sforza, Seraphina (1434–1478)

*Italian Catholic saint. Born in Urbino, Italy, in 1434; died in 1478; daughter of Guido Sforza, count of Montefeltro, and Catherine Colonna (d. around 1440); married Allesandro Sforza (1409–1473), lord of Pesaro and Cottignola, in 1448; entered Franciscan order around 1457.*

Seraphina Sforza was born into an aristocratic Italian family in 1434. Her father Guido Sforza was a count, and her mother *Catherine Colonna** was the niece of Pope Martin V. Orphaned at an early age, Seraphina was raised in Rome at the Colonna Palace.

The widower Allesandro Sforza, duke of Pesaro, treated Seraphina with respect at the time of their marriage in 1448. He even left her in charge of his realm when he was away at war in 1456, and Seraphina apparently did an excellent job of managing her husband's business. Nonetheless, after he started an affair with **Pacifica**, a doctor's wife, he did everything in his power to make Seraphina's life miserable. He humiliated her in public, beat her, tried to strangle her, and on several occasions attempted to poison her. Because of one such attempt, she was left half-paralyzed for the rest of her life.

Thereafter, Allesandro had Seraphina kept captive in the convent of the Poor Clares in Pesaro, and guards were positioned to keep anyone from coming to her aid. He even brought a judge with him to stand outside her cell while he tried to make her admit to adultery, but Seraphina refused to speak. A year and a half later, she chose to take vows in the order of St. Francis. She eventually was made abbess and lived a praiseworthy life counseling her sisters in the religious community until her death in 1478.

**Ruth Savitz**, freelance writer,
Philadelphia, Pennsylvania

## Shaarawi, Huda (1879–1947)

*Egyptian political activist who led demonstrations against British colonial rule; worked to end marriage for underage girls, the institution of the harem, and the wearing of the veil; became prominent in the Wafd political party; and founded the Egyptian Feminist Union, the country's preeminent voice for women for many decades. Name variations: Sh'arawi; Hoda Charaoui. Born Nur al-Huda Sultan on her father's estate near the town of Minya (Minia), Egypt, in 1879;*

*died in Cairo in 1947; daughter of Sultan Pasha (a wealthy landowner who eventually became president of Egypt's Chamber of Deputies) and Iqbal Hanim (a Turco-Circassian); tutored at home, becoming fluent in several languages; married Ali Shaarawi (a cousin many years her senior), in 1892; children: daughter Bathna (b. 1903); son Muhammad (b. 1905).*

*Married at age 13 (1892); after 15 months of marriage, returned to live with her mother for the next seven years (c. 1894); traveled with husband to Paris, and witnessed the freedom of European women (c. 1901); founded the Intellectual Association of Egyptian Women (1914); demonstrated with other women against British rule (1919); elected president of the Wafdist Women's Central Committee (1920); as founder and president of the Egyptian Feminist Union, led a delegation to the International Alliance of Women in Rome and stopped wearing her veil (1923); founded Club of the Women's Union (1925); awarded the Nishan al-Kamal, Egypt's highest state decoration (1945).*

*Selected publications:* Harem Years: The Memoirs of an Egyptian Feminist, 1879–1924 *(The Feminist Press, 1987).*

Following World War I, women around the globe sought greater political and economic freedom. As they organized to alter the status quo, certain common issues emerged, including the right to vote, the necessity for guarantees of equal treatment under their country's laws, and their need to be socially and politically informed. In Egypt, the struggle for these rights was launched by the most sophisticated, privileged women in the nation, and led by Huda Shaarawi. But the women of Egypt had other obstacles to surmount: polygamy, the rigid seclusion of harem life, and exclusion from public involvement.

Huda Shaarawi was born Nur al-Huda Sultan on her parents' estate near the Egyptian town of Minya in 1879. Her father was Sultan Pasha, an immensely wealthy landowner. A provincial administrator who owned a substantial library, he had a deep love for Arabic poetry and later became president of Egypt's Chamber of Deputies. Huda was the first child of her father's second wife **Iqbal Hanim**, a Circassian who came from a mountainous area of Turkey. Turco-Circassians formed a large part of Egypt's ruling class and men like Huda's father favored Circassian women, who were often slaves, as wives and concubines. Iqbal Hanim was never a slave, but had come to Egypt as a child, and maintained close relationships with her Turco-Circassian relatives. Huda and her brother,

Umar Sultan, lived with their mother in the same harem as did their father's first wife and children. Relationships in this extended family were peaceful, and Huda had a great love for **Umm Kabira,** or "Big Mother."

Early in the 19th century, from 1805 to 1849, Egypt had been ruled by Muhammed Ali, who changed his country from a province of the Ottoman Empire to a semi-autonomous state, modernizing the army, expanding the country's health services, and beginning a secular education system for males which would be extended to females in the 1870s. Muhammed Ali also began the cultivation of cotton, which supplied the textile mills of England, and instituted an extensive railway and carriage system. In 1869, two decades after the end of his rule, the opening of Egypt's Suez Canal linked Great Britain to its Indian Empire, and Cairo became a world city with an opera, fabulous mansions, and a rich cultural life.

*In moments of danger, when women emerge by their side, men utter no protest. Yet . . . men refuse to see the capabilities of women.*

—**Huda Shaarawi**

While the Egypt in which Huda grew up looked to the future, it also clung to the past. For one thing, polygamy was still a widespread practice. The seclusion of women was not a tenet of Islam, but it was a social convention that had become connected with economic standing—only the wealthy could afford to set aside a portion of the house solely for women and children—and the harem where Huda passed her childhood was a sign of her family's status. Since the honor of the family rested on the sexual purity of its women, that purity must be guarded by eunuchs, or castrated males, and the support of the harem's many inhabitants could thus be a considerable drain on a man's wealth.

Veiling was common in and out of the harems, and the practice was followed by all women, whether Muslim, Jewish, or Christian. While poor women frequently worked outside the home, either with or without their husbands, wealthy women rarely stirred from within the harem's walls. On the rare occasion when one did, accompanied either by eunuchs or a male family member, she took the harem's seclusion with her by covering herself with the veil. Fully practicable only by the elite, the harem and the veil, and their attendant isolation, thus became status symbols in themselves.

Huda spent her early childhood in happy prosperity, playing with her brother, Umar Sul-

tan, and the siblings of her father's first wife. Although her father was frequently away due to his political duties, he made time for his children and indulged them with chocolates, and her maternal grandmother and uncles often came from Turkey to spend the warm Egyptian winters with the family. Sometimes Huda went with her mother to visit **Amina Hanim Afrandi,** wife of khedive (viceroy of the sultan) Muhammad Taufiq, at the palace, and sometimes there were friends of the family who came to call.

When Huda was five, her father died, and he was greatly mourned by his two wives and children. Life continued in the harem, where Huda learned to play the piano well and became fluent in Arabic, Turkish, and French; she also read the books in her father's library, and memorized parts of the Koran, which was considered a rare feat for a girl. From Anbar, an Abyssinian slave, and Matta, the gardener, she learned a great deal about horticulture. In the late afternoons, a servant, Said Agha, took the children on outings, to take part in feasts and street celebrations where they enjoyed buying sweetmeats from vendors' carts.

After the age of nine, the life of Muslim girls in the harem grew more confined. Gradually, Huda was allowed to leave the seclusion of the harem less often, and her contact with members of the opposite sex was restricted to male relatives. When she was 13, she learned that she was to be married to her cousin Ali Shaarawi, a much older man with a concubine and children twice her age, whom she thought of as a father or older brother. Upon learning the news, she cried for three hours.

By 1892, recognition in Egypt of the difficulties polygamy presented for families, and especially for women, was fairly widespread. In an attempt to protect her daughter, Iqbal Hanim asked Ali Shaarawi to sign a document promising to have no further relations with the mother of his children and never to take another wife. Though he refused, even the document's existence showed that changes in the country were already under way. Iqbal told Huda, "Accept things as they are for the moment, my daughter, and, God willing, in the future he will agree to these conditions."

The wedding celebration lasted three days, with much music and gaiety, and Huda reveled in the festivities. Soon afterward, however, she was forbidden by her husband to play the piano or visit relatives, and became depressed; then a loud argument occurred between Ali and her mother about his slave concubine. After 15 months of marriage, Ali returned to live with the mother of his children, and the young bride returned to her mother.

Although the refusal of Huda Shaarawi to live with her husband was unusual, her life was happy for the next seven years. She studied Arabic literature, piano, and poetry, and attended concerts at the Khedival Opera House. Spending summers by the seaside in Alexandria, she enjoyed the experience of shopping for herself, rare for a woman of the harem, and even convinced her mother to join her. She also began to attend the salon of **Eugénie Le Brun** (Rushdi), a Frenchwoman who had married Husain Rushdi Pasha. With Mme Rushdi, Shaarawi perfected her French, and she explored such topics as the wearing of the veil, which many viewed as an impediment to their advancement, with women who attended the salon.

After seven years, Shaarawi went back to her husband. He took her to Paris, where she discovered a new world in which women moved about freely in the streets. Upon her return to Egypt, she gave birth to a daughter **Bathna** (1903) and a son Muhammad (1905). Bathna was a sickly child, and Shaarawi and her mother took the children to Turkey for three months, unescorted by her husband. Back in Egypt, she made another dear friend, **Marguerite Clement**, from France, who suggested giving lectures to Egyptian women. It was a radical proposal because public gatherings of women were unheard of, but Shaarawi convinced Princess **Ain al-Hayat** to sponsor the event, which was held at Cairo's new university and was a great success.

Among these wealthy Egyptian women, discussion increased about ways to improve the lot of their countrywomen. When Shaarawi proposed a school for women and a dispensary, Princess Ain al-Hayat was especially enthusiastic about the dispensary, and the women set about raising money in a variety of ways. Through private donations, lavish fundraising, and a scheme for collecting stamp revenues, enough money was found to rent a modest building on Shariah Baramuni, in the impoverished Muhammad Ali neighborhood of Cairo, where several Egyptian and European doctors volunteered their medical services. Shaarawi also felt the need to encourage women in intellectual pursuits, and in April 1914 the Intellectual Association of Egyptian Women was established, a precursor of the powerful women's organization that was to play an important role in the country's struggle for independence.

At the end of World War I, Egypt was still under British colonial rule. As resistance to the

Huda Shaarawi

British increased, Egypt's upper-class women, who had slowly overcome many restrictions of the harem, used the impetus of the national struggle to bring the harem system to an end. When the first appeals for independence were denied, the Egyptians formed the Wafd Party in protest against foreign domination, with Huda Shaarawi's husband as party treasurer. In their common struggle against colonialism, the couple now grew closer, as Ali kept his wife informed of all his decisions in the event that he might be killed. On March 16, 1919, she was part of a group of women who assembled in protest, carrying placards which read "Down with Oppressors and Tyrants" and "Down with Occupation." The procession was soon surrounded by British troops, and when a soldier pointed a gun at Shaarawi, she defiantly taunted, "Let me die so Egypt shall have an *Edith Cavell," referring to the English nurse executed as a spy by the Germans during the recent war. The troops hesitated to fire on the women, and Shaarawi and the others stood their ground for three hours. When they made their way back to their carriages, they left the colonial British badly shaken.

By April, when many Egyptians had been killed or imprisoned for defying colonial rule, a more violent demonstration of women occurred. This time the troops struck out with bayonets and fired on houses, and **Shafiaq bint Muhammad** became the first woman killed by a British bullet. As women of all classes joined in the political fray, some took part in the strikes that were organized to paralyze the country, stationing themselves in government doorways to urge workers to stay away. In this atmosphere of growing protest, Huda Shaarawi and other women demanded the resignation of the government. Egypt's prime minister Husain Rushdi, husband of Shaarawi's late friend Eugénie Le Brun, responded to the demand by announcing, "The women want my resignation," and he quit his office that day.

By 1920, Egyptian women decided to form their own political body, the Wafdist Women's Central Committee, and Huda Shaarawi was elected its president. A rift developed between the men and women of the Wafd movement after male leaders, returning from a meeting in London with the British government about an independence proposal, made the terms known to a number of male organizations but ignored the women's committee. In a letter written December 12, 1920, Shaarawi summed up the women's outrage: "We criticized the delegates from the Wafd for disregarding our rights and our very existence by neglecting to solicit our views," then demanded an apology, which the women received.

When Saad Zaghlul, the leader of the independence movement, returned to Egypt, Shaarawi was caught between the position of her husband, who opposed Zaghlul, and her own position as president of the women's party, although she managed to negotiate between the two. In January 1922, after Zaghlul had been deported by the British, the women resorted to more militant tactics, passing resolutions that demanded the end of martial law and voting for an economic boycott against the British. Since women inherit money and property under Islamic law, these moves had considerable force, and the boycott proved to be effective. By 1922, with many leading Egyptians imprisoned or deported, women had become the glue holding the Wafd movement together.

In February 1922, Ali Shaarawi died, but Huda continued her role in the independence struggle. Egypt became a constitutional monarchy the following year, although it would remain under some British control until the last British troops were finally withdrawn in 1957. According to the first Egyptian constitution, "All Egyptians are equal before the law. They enjoy equally civil and political rights and are equally charged with public duties and responsibilities without distinction of race, language, or religion." Unfortunately, the wording in 1923 made no provision for women's right to vote. That year, Huda Shaarawi founded the Egyptian Feminist Union and was elected its first president, then led a delegation to the International Alliance of Women, held in Rome. On her return home, she arrived in Cairo unveiled, and never donned the veil again. Disappointed that women's rights were treated as secondary to independence, she eventually broke with the Wafd Party and resigned. The issue by then, however, was not feminism, but nationalism, because she believed that the Wafd movement was continuously compromising the rights of all Egyptians.

In 1925, Shaarawi helped start the Club of the Women's Union. A cultural center with imposing headquarters in the heart of Cairo, the organization raised funds for the support of a clinic and dispensary, craft workshops, and child-care facilities, as well as the publication of two journals dedicated to women's issues. By this time, it was Shaarawi's view that women must enter the workplace in order to gain the financial independence essential for equality. Believing also that there should be no more 13-year-old brides, she worked to establish a minimum age for marriage, limit the easy access that men had to divorce, and restrict the practice of polygamy, as well as to increase women's access to education. In the 1930s, with many more women by then in the Egyptian work force, Shaarawi pressured the labor office to hire a woman inspector to investigate women's working conditions, and encouraged a step-up in the campaign for women's suffrage. She also worked on behalf of Palestinian women who lost their homes during the establishment of Israel, and in 1944 she became the first president of the newly founded Arab Feminist Union. In 1945, two years before her death, her lifelong activism for the rights and independence of all Egyptians, but especially women, was acknowledged when she was awarded the Nishan al-Kamal, Egypt's highest state decoration, for services to her country.

Today, as is the case in every nation, all contradictions in Egyptian society concerning the status of women have still not been erased, but the work of Huda Shaarawi is widely recognized for bringing permanent changes in the status of women in Egypt and to the entire Muslim world. (*See also Egyptian Feminism.*)

**SOURCES**:

Baron, Beth. "Unveiling in Early Twentieth-Century Egypt: Practical and Symbolic Considerations," in *Middle Eastern Studies*. Vol. 25, no. 3. July 1989, pp. 370–386.

Croutier, Alev Lytel. *Harem: The World Behind the Veil.* NY: Abbeville Press, 1989.

Eliraz, Giora. "Egyptian Intellectuals and Women's Emancipation, 1919–1939," in *Asian and African Studies*. Vol. 16, no. 1. March 1982, pp. 95–120.

Hatem, Mervat. "Through Each Other's Eyes: Egyptian, Levantine-Egyptian, and European Women's Images of Themselves and of Each Other (1862–1920)," in *Women's Studies International Forum*. Vol. 12, no. 2, 1989, pp. 183–198.

Hourani, Albert. *Arabic Thought in the Liberal Age.* Cambridge: Cambridge University Press, 1983.

Marsot, Afaf Lutfi al-Sayyid. *Egypt in the Reign of Muhammed Ali.* Cambridge: Cambridge University Press, 1984.

Peirce, Leslie P. *The Imperial Harem. Women and Sovereignty in the Ottoman Empire.* NY: Oxford University Press, 1993.

Schölch, Alexander. *Egypt for the Egyptians! The Socio-Political Crisis in Egypt, 1878–1882.* London, 1981.

Shaarawi, Huda. *Harem Years: The Memoirs of an Egyptian Feminist, 1879–1924.* Trans. and edited by Margot Badran. NY: The Feminist Press, 1987.

**Karin Loewen Haag,** freelance writer, Athens, Georgia

# Shabazz, Betty (1936–1997)

*African-American civil-rights and education activist. Name variations: Betty Sanders; Sister Betty X. Born on May 28, 1936, in Detroit, Michigan; died on June 23, 1997, in New York, New York; attended Tuskegee Institute; received R.N. from Brooklyn State Hospital School of Nursing; earned master's degree in public health administration from Jersey City State College; received Ph.D. in education administration from University of Massachusetts; married Malcolm Little known as Malcolm X also known as Malik El-Shabazz (1925–1965, the Black Muslim leader), in 1958; children: six daughters, Attallah Shabazz; Qubilah Shabazz; Makaak Shabazz; Malikah Shabazz; Gamilah Shabazz; Ilayasah Shabazz.*

*Served as director of department of communications and public relations at Medgar Evers College and led the school's office of institutional advancement.*

Betty Shabazz was a dedicated human-rights activist who came to national attention when her husband, Black Muslim leader Malcolm X, was assassinated while preaching in 1965. Shabazz, who was in the audience with her four children and pregnant with twins when the shots rang out, bent over to shield the children with her body. She not only raised the six children on her own and continued with her husband's civil-rights and political work, but also went on to become a dedicated leader on educational issues. Throughout her life, Betty Shabazz worked tirelessly to unite politically active black women. She "was so much more than Malcolm's widow," said **Myrlie Evers-Williams**.

Born in Detroit, Michigan, in 1936, she was raised in a sheltered, middle-class, Methodist environment by her adoptive parents. Betty attended her father's alma mater, Tuskegee Institute in Alabama, where she had her first encounter with racism. Her parents were unable to acknowledge the problem and thought Betty was somehow to blame.

Betty moved to New York in the 1950s and continued her study of nursing at Brooklyn State Hospital. While she was still a student, a friend invited her to hear Malcolm X speak at an Islamic temple, and they were later introduced. Shabazz and Malcolm discussed the causes and effects of the racism she had encountered in Alabama; she became deeply interested in the issue, as well as in the Nation of Islam, and began to teach women's classes at Islamic Temple 7. Shabazz helped type and correct papers for Malcolm, and he helped plan discussion topics for her classes. Following Islamic principles, they never dated in the conventual sense but met only when chaperoned or with a group. After Shabazz finished nursing school, Malcolm proposed over the telephone while on a speaking engagement in Detroit. Although her parents were not in favor of the marriage because Malcolm was not a Methodist, they were married in 1958. Around the time of the wedding, Shabazz converted to Islam.

As Malcolm became more prominent as a civic leader, the couple spent much time apart. In 1963, after he broke with the Nation of Islam and their separatist policies to pursue his ideas of global unity, they were subjected to much hostility, including harassing telephone calls. Two years later, Malcolm was murdered at the Audubon Ballroom in New York City. For three weeks after his death, Shabazz was unable to sleep. She was then invited to make a Hajj, or spiritual journey, to Mecca in her husband's place, and she credited that pilgrimage with helping her to sort things out. She returned home to Mount Vernon, New York, to raise her daughters alone, learning to remain calm and cheerful for their sake.

Shabazz reared the children according to Malcolm's principles, believing that it was the parents' duty to teach children about their heritage and cultural traditions. The girls received a well-rounded education, learning Arabic, French, and ballet. She also thought it important that her daughters broaden their scope and took them on trips to Africa, the Middle East, and the West Indies. Remarkably, she also found time to continue her own education, receiving a master's degree in public health administration from Jersey City State College and going on to earn a Ph.D. in education from the University of Massachusetts at Amherst.

In 1976, Shabazz became associate professor of health education at Medgar Evers College in Brooklyn. She soon became director of the department of communications and public relations and head of the school's office of institutional advancement. By then a national figure as an educator and civil-rights activist and deeply revered in the black community, Shabazz made speaking appearances throughout the United States. She always tried to spread Malcolm's message of unity and advancement of blacks, and was a champion of black women in their struggle against oppression.

For many years, Shabazz believed that Nation of Islam leader Louis Farrakhan was responsible for the assassination of her husband, in retaliation for Malcolm's split from the Nation of Islam. In turn, her adult daughter **Qubilah Shabazz** was accused of plotting Farrakhan's death in what many believed was a set-up by a government informer (she did not go to trial). Betty Shabazz eventually reconciled with Farrakhan, in part due to his support of Qubilah during that time, and even spoke at his Million Man March. In 1997, Qubilah's 12-year-old son Malcolm, whom Shabazz had been caring for, set fire to her apartment in Yonkers, New York, perhaps in a bid to get himself sent home to his mother in Texas. During the blaze, Shabazz suffered third-degree burns over 80% of her body. Shortly afterwards, she died in a New York City hospital. While her daughters and friends including *Maya Angelou, Evers-Williams, and *Coretta Scott King mourned her untimely death and celebrated her life, New York congressional representative Charles Rangel said: "Her husband was harassed and hounded and finally assassinated in front of her and her children. She could have gone into permanent mourning and the world would have understood. But she returned to school, received her Ph.D., educated her children and picked up her husband's mantle."

**SOURCES:**
*Contemporary Black Biography.* Detroit, MI: Gale Research.

*People Weekly.* December 30, 1997, p. 183.

Smith, Jessie Carney, ed. *Notable Black American Women, Book II.* Detroit, MI: Gale Research, 1998.

*Time.* June 16, 1997, pp. 48–49.

**SUGGESTED READING:**
Brown, Jamie Foster, ed. *Betty Shabazz: A Sisterfriends' Tribute in Words and Pictures.* NY: Simon & Schuster, 1998.

**Ruth Savitz,** freelance writer,
Philadelphia, Pennsylvania

## Shackleton, Mary (1758–1826).
*See Leadbetter, Mary.*

## Shadd, Mary Ann (1823–1893).
*See Cary, Mary Ann Shadd.*

# Shafer, Helen Almira (1839–1894)

*American educator and college president. Born on September 23, 1839, in Newark, New Jersey; died on January 20, 1894, in Wellesley, Massachusetts; graduated from Oberlin College, 1863; never married.*

*Taught in New Jersey; taught mathematics at St. Louis High School under William Torrey Harris; offered chair in mathematics at newly founded Wellesley College (1877); succeeded Alice Freeman Palmer as president of Wellesley (1888–94).*

Helen Almira Shafer was born in Newark, New Jersey in 1839 and spent the early years of her life there until her father, a Congregational minister, moved the family to Oberlin, Ohio. She graduated from Oberlin College in 1863, where she had been an outstanding student. Shafer spent two years teaching in New Jersey and then moved to St. Louis High School to teach mathematics.

By 1877, Shafer had established her reputation as a gifted teacher, attracting the attention of her talented contemporary William Torrey Harris, then the superintendent of St. Louis schools and later the U.S. commissioner of education. She was offered the chair of mathematics at Wellesley College in Massachusetts, then only two years old. Working hard to build her department from scratch—and establish the highest possible standards—Shafer was recognized for the intellectual rigor and unqualified success of her teaching methods. It was said that Wellesley mathematics students outperformed their male counterparts at Harvard.

In 1888, Shafer succeeded *Alice Freeman Palmer as president of Wellesley. Judicious, practical and well liked, Shafer worked to reorganize and broaden the college's curriculum. She introduced the elective system that continued to characterize Wellesley long after her tenure ended.

She also established a psychological laboratory, the first in a women's college and one of the earliest in any college, in 1891. In 1892, she recommended to the trustees that alumnae be represented on the Wellesley board.

As well, she presided over a liberalization of the college's social life, restoring some sororities and overseeing the introduction of the college periodicals, the old *Courant* (1888), the *Prelude* (1889), and the first senior annual, the *Legenda of 1889*. What has been described as the "old boarding-school type of discipline" was relaxed in favor of greater independence for students. As former student **Caroline Williamson Montgomery** noted in a memorial sketch of Shafer: "Again and again have Wellesley students said, 'She treats us like women, and knows that we are reasoning beings.'"

A quiet and dignified woman with a keen sense of humor, completely dedicated to her chosen profession, Shafer spent the last ten years of her life quietly battling tuberculosis. Her health forced her to spend the winter of 1890–91 in the milder climate of Thomasville, Georgia, but she returned to Wellesley as soon as she could. Popular with students and faculty, she was made an honorary member of the class of 1891. Shafer died in January 1894, the only Wellesley president to die while in office. In 1902, her portrait, painted by Kenyon Cox, was presented to the college by the Alumnae Association.

**SOURCES:**

Converse, Florence. *Wellesley College: A Chronicle of the Years 1875–1938*. Wellesley, MA: Hathaway House Bookshop, 1939.

McHenry, Robert, ed. *Famous American Women*. NY: Dover, 1980.

**Paula Morris**, D.Phil.,
Brooklyn, New York

# Shafik, Doria (1908–1975)

*Leading Egyptian feminist and founder of the Bint al-Nil Union, which fought for women's right to vote (granted in 1956 largely as a result of her hunger strike), who was condemned for protesting Nasser's dictatorial powers and isolated politically for almost 20 years. Name variations: Durriyah or Dori'a Shafiq; Doria Chafik. Born Doria Chafik in Tanta, Gabiyya, on December 14, 1908; committed suicide in Cairo, Egypt, on September 20, 1975; daughter of Ahmad Chafik Sulaiman Effendi (a civil engineer) and Ratiba Nasif Qassabi Bey (a member of a prominent family); attended Notre Dame des Apôtres; privately tutored for the French baccalauréat, passed in 1929; attended the Sorbonne in Paris, 1930–32, returned to obtain a doctorate, 1936–39; married Nour Ragai (an Egypt-*

*ian lawyer), in 1937; children: daughters Aziza (b. 1942) and Jihan (b. 1944).*

*Was second in her country in baccalauréat examinations (1929); began work as the inspector for French languages in secondary schools throughout Egypt (1942); founded Bint al-Nil Union, first as a magazine, then as political organization (1948); organized the closing of the Egyptian Parliament by women (1951); organized the storming of Barclay's Bank that led to the final downfall of British colonial rule (1952); went on first hunger strike for women's right to vote (1954); women's suffrage granted in the new constitution (1956); placed under house arrest for protesting dictatorial powers of Nasser government (1957); lived final years in seclusion until committing suicide (1975).*

The title of *bey* at the end of the name of **Ratiba Nasif Qassabi Bey** indicates the prominence of her family. According to Islamic custom, however, because Ratiba's mother produced no male heirs, she lost control over her share of her family's inheritance at the time she was widowed, and the daughter was left with no wealth of her own. Except for this circumstance, the marriage of Ratiba to Ahmad Chafik would probably never have taken place. He was a civil engineer for the government, and of middle-class background, lower in social standing than his wife. But their union proved a happy one, producing six children. The third of these, and second daughter, was Doria Shafik, born on December 14, 1908, in Tanta, Gabiyya, Egypt.

Doria's earliest years were spent in Mansura, where her father worked as an engineer. She then went to live in Tanta with her maternal grandmother, so that she could attend Notre Dame des Apôtres, a prominent French mission school. When Doria was 13, her mother died in childbirth, a searing experience which she recounted in her memoirs:

> The loss of my mother left a wound so large that it marked the whole of my life. As an outlet for my despair and desolation I concentrated all my energy into reading and studying. The result was that I progressed so rapidly that I found myself in the same class as my sister.

Following her mother's death, Doria left Notre Dame des Apôtres to live in Alexandria with her father and siblings. The city had no girls' secondary school and Ahmad Chafik could not afford to send his daughter to boarding school, but because he recognized her exceptional academic talents he hired private tutors to prepare her for the examination for the highly respected French baccalauréat high-school degree.

The examination was set for June 1929. Looking for moral support during the grueling test period, Doria wanted to sit near a friend whose last name was "Soriatis," and since the seating was alphabetical, she altered the spelling of her last name from "Chafik" to "Shafik," which she kept the rest of her life. She need not have worried about her test performance, however; her score was the second-highest in the nation.

*The true meaning of the women's movement is the complete cooperation between men and women, not the continuous struggle between the two.*

—Doria Shafik

The dream of the promising young student was to study philosophy at the Sorbonne in Paris. When her father could not afford such a great expense, Doria wrote to one of Egypt's best-known feminist leaders, *Huda Shaarawi, for help. Shaarawi invited the young girl to Cairo to discuss her future, and Shafik later wrote about this meeting (emphasis Shafik):

> She spoke to me about the causes which led her towards the path of "Feminism." She related the unhappiness she had experienced within the harem—when, newly married, she was almost a prisoner in her own home. For the first time I realized that this lady—rich, beautiful, having everything—*had suffered*; that there must be some "values" beyond the material ones. . . . I left the palace with a great quietness of the Soul. . . . *convinced that nothing really worthwhile can be accomplished without suffering.*

The encounter was to influence the course of Shafik's life. By the 1920s, Egypt's internal struggle for the emancipation of women was a well-established movement. European colonialization of Egypt in the 19th century, first by the French and then the English, caused many Egyptians to question the tenets of their traditional culture, and many believed that their backwardness in social outlook had cost them their independence. Leaders among both men and women advocated legal reforms to improve the status of women, arguing for the abolition of such practices as female seclusion in the harem, arranged marriages, and the wearing of the veil. Many intellectuals believed that a radical social transformation would be required to save the nation. Doria Shafik was 11 years old at the time of the Revolution of 1919, when Egyptians rose up against British colonial rule, and many of its women were brought into the mainstream of political life. They had cut telephone lines, disrupt-

ed rail service, stormed jails, and held large demonstrations; hundreds died in the struggle. In 1922, the British had granted Egypt limited sovereignty, although the country remained under strong British influence. A few years later, when a new constitution was drafted, women were not given the right to vote, despite their heroic contributions. But a shift toward an expanded political role for women was under way, and feminists like Huda Shaarawi were eager for bright young women like Doria Shafik to join their ranks.

Shaarawi arranged for the financial assistance that allowed Shafik to begin her studies at the Sorbonne in 1930, at age 16. Her European experience differed from that of the previous generation of Egyptian feminists who came largely from the ranks of the rich and enjoyed unprecedented access to hotels, restaurants, shops, and theaters during their brief stays. The women of Shafik's generation discovered European life as students, in a world made up of crowded classrooms and cafés. But the contrast between the freedom of Paris and the restrictions on their return to Egypt could be equally profound. In the summer of 1932, Doria Shafik returned to a culture from which she now felt estranged. Two years as a teacher at a girls' lyceé in Alexandria did not alleviate her alienation, partly because of the social pressures put on her to marry.

In 1936, Shafik returned to Paris to obtain her doctorate and met Nour al-Din Ragai, a cousin and friend in her childhood who was also studying on scholarship. The two reestablished their relationship and were married in 1937. After completing their doctorates, they returned to Cairo in 1939, just before the outbreak of World War II.

Shafik applied to teach at the University of Cairo, but her application was refused by the dean of the faculty of arts on the grounds that "her beauty and modern style" were not suited for the instruction of young men. She then took a job with the Ministry of Education, as the inspector for French languages in secondary schools throughout Egypt. In 1942, she gave birth to a daughter, **Aziza**, and in 1944 her second daughter, **Jihan**, was born.

Still feeling thwarted professionally, Shafik decided to pursue another career. Initially, she was offered the position of editor-in-chief of a new magazine founded by **Princess Chewikar**, the ex-wife of King Fuad I. Shafik ultimately rejected the job because the journal was published in French, the language of Egypt's elite, rather than in Arabic, the language of the masses. In

1948, Shafik launched her own journal, *Bint al-Nil* (Daughter of the Nile), to champion women's rights. The magazine carried a column entitled "Let Bint al-Nil Solve Your Problems," which soon drove Shafik to realize that such a case-by-case approach to women's issues was woefully inadequate: "Women should have an equal say in the laws that ultimately affect them and their children. The only solution . . . [is] to build up a Feminist Union to demand political rights for women."

Several events helped shape Shafik's new direction. One was the death of Huda Shaarawi in 1947, which signaled a generational change in the Egyptian feminist movement. Another was her firsthand view of the struggle of Palestinian women fighting Israel to keep their homeland. Wrote Shafik:

> In Palestine I was fascinated by the role women play, not only in social life but also in political life as well. You find each woman beside the man struggling for the nation. And when circumstances required or conditions became difficult, she would stick to him like the Arab villages stick to the mountains of the nation. The Palestinian woman gives every visitor the idea that there is a real feminist movement in Palestine and this movement has its weight and value in the life of the country.

Eager to implement Palestinian women's level of involvement in Egypt's political life, Shafik moved to expand *Bint al-Nil* into a political movement as well as a magazine. Past organizations like the Egyptian Feminist Union and Mabarra had concentrated on social welfare issues like education and improved health care, functioning as charities rather than as political entities, and in Shafik's eyes, they had outlived their purpose. She wanted to shape the appeal of Bint al-Nil to middle-class professional women who found their careers hindered by law and social custom. This emerging class in a more urban Egypt required a new political direction. The nascent Bint al-Nil Union thus declared three objectives: 1) to establish constitutional and parliamentary rights for all women; 2) to promote literacy programs, health and social services, and small industries to aid women; and 3) to arouse public awareness of the conditions of women and children.

The Bint al-Nil Union was essentially declaring war on the status quo. Organized locally at first, it was soon making its voice heard at the national level. On February 19, 1951, a thousand women made an assault on the Egyptian Parliament, forcing the gates, overpowering the guards, and entering the chambers with cries of

Doria Shafik

"Down with Parliament without women" and "Women's place is next to yours." They occupied the chambers for three hours. As an instigator of this demonstration, Doria Shafik was ordered to appear in court. When the case came to trial, hundreds of Bint al-Nil supporters converged on the courtroom, the judge adjourned the hearing indefinitely, and the Bint al-Nil union was spurred to new growth.

Coinciding with the birth of Bint al-Nil was a resurgence of Egyptian nationalism. Resentment of British colonialism had been growing since the end of World War II. Egypt's Suez Canal was the most prominent geographical link to India, the crown jewel of the British Empire. But India had achieved independence from the British in 1947 and many felt that Egypt should do the same, especially as it was becoming obvious that the British Empire was rapidly disintegrating.

Like the feminists in the Revolution of 1919, Shafik grasped the link between Egyptian nationalism and the liberation of women within the country. As Bint al-Nil grew, she decided that the Union should be used to form its own all-woman military unit. Some 200 young women had received training when it was decided that the unit should be used to close down Barclay's

Bank, a symbol of British colonialism. On January 26, 1952, a group of Bint al-Nil's paramilitary forces surrounded the entrances of Barclay's and prevented employees from entering. The event sparked a mob action, the bank was attacked and burned and soon other parts of Cairo were in flames.

The attack proved a foretaste of events to come. After months of demonstrations, Gamal Abdel Nasser seized control of Egypt on July 23, 1952. Briefly, the new government seemed to offer the opportunity Doria Shafik and the Bint al-Nil Union had been waiting for. That year, she put up her name as a candidate for the general elections, effectively challenging the law denying women the right to vote. When she was hospitalized for an appendectomy, hundreds of women came to the clinic where she received surgery, bringing long lists of names petitioning the government to allow Shafik to run for public office. After the Minister of the Interior returned Shafik's letter of candidacy, more demonstrations erupted, but they had no impact on the new government.

Feminist issues, in fact, were not on Nasser's agenda. When the Constitutional Assembly was formed in March 1954, there was no mention of any role for women. Wrote Shafik (emphasis Shafik):

> I felt women's rights were in danger. Lacking women, the Assembly might adopt a constitution in which women's rights were not guaranteed. . . . *I decided to play the last card. I decided to go on a hunger strike to death for "women's full political rights."*

She prepared a statement in French, English, and Arabic that was sent to eminent personalities, members of the government, and the national and international press. Joined by 14 other women, Shafik went on a hunger strike that drew national and international attention, and the government gave the appearance of acceding to her demands. But it was not until the adoption of the Egyptian Constitution in 1956 that women were actually allowed to vote, and then only after they obtained individual government permission, a burden not placed on male voters.

Although Shafik won the battle, she did not win the war. President Nasser, who was far more interested in establishing Egypt's preeminence in the Middle East than in women's issues, was also intolerant of dissent, no matter how moderate. A leader like Doria Shafik, who could inspire women to invade Parliament, occupy banks, and engage in hunger strikes, was a serious potential threat. As his government slowly began to quash dissent from every quarter, larger state-controlled systems were put in charge of political parties and feminist unions. Many who disagreed with the new government had already been arrested and imprisoned when Doria Shafik made her final public appearance.

On February 6, 1957, Shafik entered the Indian Embassy in Cairo after announcing to the government and the media that she was undertaking a second hunger strike to protest "the onset of dictatorship that is leading Egypt into bankruptcy and chaos." Nasser struck swiftly, placing her under house arrest (later lifted). Her name was banned forever in the media, and the Bint al-Nil Union was closed. Soon, all surviving women's associations were denouncing Doria Shafik as a traitor.

For the next 18 years, Shafik lived in self-imposed seclusion. During this time, she wrote three manuscripts about her life. Shunned for an ideology deemed too "Western," she was confined to political isolation and paralysis until September 20, 1975, when her name resurfaced with the announcement of her death. She had leapt from the sixth floor of her apartment building.

Doria Shafik's vision of equality for women went unshared by many Egyptians who viewed feminism as a Western ideology espoused by traitors to the Nasser regime. Removed from the rhetoric of her time, however, it is clear that Shafik was a nationalist who loved her country, and a moderate who advocated a balance between Islamic teaching and feminist reform. Her fault, if it can be labeled as such, was a burning determination that women should be treated equally. (*See also Egyptian Feminism.*)

**SOURCES:**

Badran, Margot. "Independent Women: More Than a Century of Feminism in Egypt," in *Arab Women: Old Boundaries, New Frontiers.* Edited by Judith E. Tucker. Bloomington, IN: Indiana University Press, 1993, pp. 129–148.

"Doria Shafik," in *The Times* [London]. September 23, 1975, p. 17.

Hatem, Mervat. "Through Each Other's Eyes: Egyptian, Levantine-Egyptian and European Women's Images of Themselves and of Each Other (1862–1920)," in *Women's Studies International Forum.* Vol. 12, no. 2, 1989, pp. 183–198.

Khater, Akran, and Cynthia Nelson. "Al-Harakah al-Nissaiyah: The Women's Movement and Political Participation in Modern Egypt," in *Women's Studies International Forum.* Vol. 11, no. 5, 1988, pp. 465–483.

Masuad, Samar F. "The Development of Women's Movements in the Muslim World," in *Hamdard Islamicus.* Vol. VIII, no. 1, 1986, pp. 81–86.

Nelson, Cynthia. "Biography and Women's History, On Interpreting Doria Shafik," in *Women in Middle*

*Eastern History*. Edited by Nikki R. Keddie and Beth Baron. New Haven, CT: Yale University Press, 1991, pp. 310–334.

———. "The Voices of Doria Shafik: Feminist Consciousness in Egypt, 1940–1960," in *Expanding the Boundaries of Women's History*. Edited by Cheryl Johnson-Odim and Margaret Strobel. Bloomington, IN: Indiana University Press, 1992, pp. 158–172.

**Karin Loewen Haag**, freelance writer, Athens, Georgia

## Shafiq, Dori'a or Durriyah (1908–1975).

*See Shafik, Doria.*

## Shaftesbury, countess of.

*See Lamb, Emily (d. 1869).*

## Shaginian, Marietta (1888–1982)

*Russian poet, author, dramatist, and literary critic who was one of the most prolific, versatile and best-known women authors of the Soviet era. Name variations: Marietta Shaginyan; Marietta Sergeyevna Shaginyan; Mariètta Sergeevna Shaginián; (pseudonym) Jim [Dzhim] Dollar; "Re." Born Marietta Sergeevna Shaginian in Moscow, Russia, on March 21, 1888; died in Moscow on her 94th birthday on March 21, 1982; daughter of a physician; educated in Moscow and Germany; married Y.S. Khachatryants (Ia. S. Khachatriants); children: one daughter.*

*Selected writings:* Orientalia *(1913);* Two Moralities *(1914);* Journey to Weimar *(1914);* Svoya sudva *(One's Own Fate, 1923);* Peremena *(The Change, 1923);* Adventures of a Society Lady *(1923);* Mess-Mend, ili Ianki v Petrograde *(Mess-Mend, Yankees in Petrograd, 1925);* KiK: Roman-kompleks *(KiK: Novel-complex, 1929);* Gidrotsentral *(Hydrocentral, 1931);* Chelovek i vremia *(Man and Time, 1980). Wrote about 70 other books, including biographical studies of William Blake, Vladimir Lenin, Goethe, Sergei Rachmaninoff, and Taras Shevchenko; awarded the Lenin Prize (1972).*

One of the most prolific women writers in Russian literary history, Marietta Shaginian was born in 1888 and grew up in Moscow under privileged circumstances. Both her parents were of Armenian ancestry, but they were Russified intellectuals who played an active part in the cultural life of Moscow and an influential role in her life. Her father, a prominent physician who lectured at Moscow University, was a convinced atheist and ardent admirer of classic Russian authors, particularly Alexander Pushkin, as well as of the great German writer Johann Wolfgang von Goethe. From her gifted mother, she acquired

what would be a lifelong appreciation of music. An alert, inquisitive student, Shaginian attended Moscow's Rzhevskaia Gimnazia and was an omnivorous reader from her earliest years.

The death of Shaginian's father in 1902 was a profound blow. Left financially destitute, the family was forced to return to live with maternal relatives in the town of Nakhichevan, near Rostov on the Don. At age 15, Shaginian, although suffering from the effects of progressive congenital otosclerosis which would eventually lead to a state of profound deafness, returned to Moscow intent on supporting herself by tutoring and selling her writings. Life was a struggle for Marietta and her younger sister **Lina**, as they lived together in a windowless room. But Marietta soon became a regular contributor on Moscow's artistic and literary life to both the Moscow press and a number of newspapers in the provinces, *Priazovskii krai* (The Azov Region), *Kavkaskoe slovo* (The Caucasian Word) and *Baku* (Baku). She also published her first poem in 1903. Inspired by the cultural thaw that followed the failed Revolution of 1905, Shaginian began to probe into contemporary issues of social justice, as in her "Song of the Worker," which appeared in the newly established weekly *Artisan Voice* in May 1906.

During the years just before 1914, Shaginian was at the center of the remarkably creative intellectual life of the Russian Empire during the Romanov dynasty's last years. Successfully combining her career as a journalist and poet with academic studies, she enrolled in 1908 as a student of history and philosophy in the Gere Advanced Courses for Women, a pre-revolutionary idea of a women's college, graduating with a degree in 1912. At the same time, she continued writing. In 1909, Shaginian self-published her first collection of poems, *Pervye vstrechi* (First Encounters). Although the book was stylistically derivative and attracted scant critical interest, it contained finely crafted short lyrics that reflected her confidence in her own and her nation's future.

A compulsive letter writer, Shaginian initiated correspondence with the Symbolist poets Andrei Belyi and *Zinaida Gippius. In his memoirs, Belyi described Shaginian as one of the many young "truth seekers" who were drawn to him and his circle. Gippius too was impressed by Shaginian, complimenting her initial letter for being "so intelligent and *sober*. You know, it's very important that it's sober. That's so rare nowadays." While moving in literary circles, Shaginian also became acquainted with the work of pictorial artists, including Kuzma Petrov-Vodkin, whose art was strongly influenced by the traditions of Russian icons, and about whose work Shaginian would write an essay in 1923.

For a period of several years, Shaginian was an informal member of the neo-Christian circle led by Gippius and her husband Dmitrii Merezhkovskii. She continued to write and publish poetry, often with nature as a subject, displaying a firm technique and a clarity unusual among her fellow Symbolist writers. In her second published volume of poems, *Orientalia* (1912), she found the literary renown she had been seeking. *Orientalia* went through six editions, the last in 1922, and brought delight to its readers, even though some critics noted clichés about the Mysterious East. Shaginian argued that her "racial consciousness," as an ethnic Armenian with a rich cultural heritage from the world of the Caucasus, gave her a unique ability to interpret these exotic regions to Russians. "After the sexless and incorporeal treatment of love by the Symbolists, [mine is] a lyric poetry of flesh and blood." *Orientalia* relied on images both exotic and erotic:

> Whoever you may be—come in, stranger.
> Gloomy is the evening, sweet is the scent of
>   spikenard
> The couch, laid with a golden leopard skin,
> Has long awaited you.

Shaginian's search for truth made her explore various ideas based on religious revolution. She was briefly a member of the Novosyolovtsi (New Settlers) group, but soon left it. Then, she found meaning in the doctrines advocated by Gippius and Merezhkovskii, but these ideals too proved to be unsatisfying for her. Gippius served as a role model for Shaginian for a time, and Marietta's daily letters to Zinaida, written in 1910 while her "preceptress" was living in Paris, are evidence of a strong emotional dependency on the older poet. But the relationship ended abruptly after Shaginian wrote a scathing review of Gippius' novel *Chortova kukla* (The Devil's Doll). Zinaida regarded the review, entitled "Theater of Marionettes," as tantamount to treason and ceased communicating. Despite the rupture, Shaginian continued to respect much of Gippius' work and published an analysis and defense of Gippius' poetry, *O blazhenstve imushchego* (On the Bliss of the Prosperous Man, 1912), as well as *Dve Morali* (Two Moralities, 1914), a polemical pamphlet on the "woman question" that echoed many of Gippius' thoughts.

On the eve of World War I, Shaginian's love of music brought her into contact with two of Russia's most brilliant musicians. The first was Nikolai Medtner, a composer and pianist with whose family she lived on and off during the years 1912–14. She also regarded Nikolai's brother Emilii as a philosophical mentor. Both musically and philosophically, she shared much with Nikolai. They both adored Goethe, and were convinced that musical modernism was an abomination that had to be combated. The other musician was the composer and piano virtuoso Sergei Rachmaninoff. Shaginian wrote an article on Rachmaninoff for Nikolai Medtner's journal *Trudy i dni* (Works and Days), and, using the pseudonym "Re" (the note D), she began writing Rachmaninoff in February 1912. From the start of their letter exchange, Rachmaninoff revealed more of himself to Shaginian than he would to any of his other correspondents. In his second letter (March 15, 1912), he asked her to send him texts for songs and found a number of her poems to his liking. These would be published as part of the set entitled Fourteen Songs, Op. 34 (the last of these would be the famous *Vocalise*). Their correspondence would end only as a result of Rachmaninoff's self-imposed exile from Russia soon after the Bolshevik revolution.

The fateful summer of 1914 found Shaginian in Weimar, Germany, where she planned to carry out research for a major study of Goethe. World War I broke out in early August of that year, and the Russian Empire and the German Reich became enemies. Her notes eventually became *Puteshestvie v Veimar* (Journey to Weimar), which because of war and revolution would not be published until 1923. Though Shaginian was interned for some time, she was released in neutral Switzerland. There, she first encountered Russian political exiles, members of the radical Bolshevik faction, who remained true to Marxist internationalism while the Social Democratic leadership in the combatant states embraced a policy of patriotic national defense. Once back in Russia, Shaginian returned to her various activities with undiminished energies. In 1917, she married a philologist of Armenian origins, Y.S. Khachatryants, and in the following year gave birth to her only child, a daughter. Despite motherhood, she remained remarkably productive, producing that same year a dramatic cycle of nine short plays "not for the theater" somewhat paradoxically entitled *Teatr* (Theater).

Although she considered herself a Christian and did not apply for membership in the Communist Party until 1941, Shaginian greeted the Bolshevik revolution of November 1917 with enthusiasm. In one of her last writings, published in 1981, a year before her death, she spoke of how the takeover "brought me the greatest joy I have ever experienced in my long life. It is hard to describe the feeling of joy that fell to the lot of my generation." At the time, however, the reality of the situation was much more prosaic. For one thing, Shaginian's first novel *Svoya sud'ba* (One's Own Fate), a sharp critique of the Russian intelligentsia which had been written in 1915–16, could not be brought to the attention of the reading public. The manuscript had been accepted for publication by *Vestnik Evropy* (Herald of Europe), but only the first few chapters appeared in print before the journal closed in 1918. When it was finally published in 1923, the novel, which originally celebrated Christian values of humility and self-sacrifice, had been drastically revised to emphasize atheist arguments and the importance of membership in the collectivity as a key to a healthy psyche (both versions of the novel are critiques of Sigmund Freud's then-novel concept of psychoanalysis).

In a Russia wracked by civil war and famine, Shaginian did what she could to bring about the social transformation she so ardently believed in, but on a daily basis what mattered most was finding sustenance. Shaginian and a number of other intellectuals were saved from starvation and the cold when they were invited to live in the former Yeliseyev mansion in Petrograd (formerly St. Petersburg), a luxurious 18th-century mansion which had been owned by a wealthy merchant before the revolution. At the initiative of novelist Maxim Gorky, starting in 1919 the mansion became the House of Arts, providing shelter and food not only to Shaginian but to such other noted writers as Nikolai Gumilev, Osip Mandelstam, and Mikhail Zoshchenko. During these difficult years, Shaginian also spent time in Rostov on the Don, where she taught weaving and gave lectures on raising worker productivity. Increasingly drawn to the Armenian homeland of her parents, she also served for a period as an official of the local soviet in the village of Chaltyr.

In the 1920s, Shaginian was energized by the considerable artistic freedom granted to intellectuals who supported the ideals of the Bol-

*Soviet postage stamp issued in 1988 to honor Marietta Shaginian.*

shevik revolution. Experimentation was permitted and even encouraged, the idea being that new artistic genres and approaches would serve the goals of the revolution by making its message more dramatic and easily grasped by the masses, many of whom were only now emerging from centuries of ignorance and illiteracy. Realizing that much of Russian prose was dull, even boring, Shaginian and several of her contemporaries set out to write engaging, ideological adventure novels. In 1923, Bolshevik ideologist Nikolai Bukharin had called on Soviet writers to produce works in the spirit of "Red Pinkertonism," books written in the style of Western detective novels which would entertain but also serve to educate and indoctrinate the masses in the spirit of revolutionary ideals.

For Shaginian, the result of this imperative was the innovative serialized novel *Mess-Mend, ili Ianki v Petrograde* (*Mess-Mend, Yankees in Petrograd*), which appeared in ten installments in 1924. Using the pseudonym "Jim Dollar," she created a long, complex narrative which boils down to an ongoing struggle between workers and capitalists. In the novel, the world's richest man, Jack Kressling, plots to destroy the recently established Soviet state by employing a sinister hypnotist and murderer named Grigorio Chiche. Although the enemies of the Soviet republic are rich, powerful, and ruthless, Shaginian more than matches them with Mess-Mend, a secret global organization defending the interests of the proletariat against capitalist machinations. The Mess-Mend network is led by Mike [Mick] Thingsmaster, "the All-American Bolshevik" who never grows tired of reminding his fellow proletarians that they alone are "the masters of life." Says Thingsmaster:

> Just think. No one has yet realized that we are the strongest, richest, happiest of men. It is we who make the houses in our cities, the furniture in the houses, the clothes that people wear, bread, books, cars, instruments, utensils, weapons, ships, cannons, sausages, beer, shackles, locomotives, carriages, rails—it is we who make these things and no one else.

With a plot, wrote one critic, that is "deliriously convoluted and ultimately incoherent," Shaginian's novel was entertaining and extremely popular with the Soviet reading public, which followed each installment with increasing involvement as Mike Thingsmaster and his band of enlightened, class-conscious American workers always managed to outsmart the world's evil millionaires and fascists.

Although some Soviet critics called *Mess-Mend* too unrealistic and frivolous to be of any redeeming social value, it remains a book of more than just historical interest. Literary historian **Laura Goering** has described it as "Shaginian at her best, where her imagination and storytelling prowess are given free rein, and even the ideological content is treated with a light touch." A decade later, in 1934, Shaginian fondly recalled it as her "happiest book" to date. Capitalizing on her success, in 1925 she published two "agitation-adventure novellas" as sequels to *Mess-Mend*: *Lori Lane, Metallworker* and *The International Car*. The immensely popular *Mess-Mend* was also successfully adapted for the screen.

In 1929, Shaginian published a frankly experimental novel, *KiK: Roman-kompleks* (KiK: Novel-complex), *KiK* being an abbreviation for *Koldunia i Kommunist* (The Witch and the Communist). A type of detective story, *KiK* is a montage of documents that includes letters, newspaper articles, advertisements, and telephone conversations. Added to this are four sections telling what happened when the protagonist, Comrade Lvov, disappeared, each one being a different account: a Byronic poem, a novella, a melodrama in verse, and the scenario for a documentary film. In the final episode of *KiK*, Lvov himself appears to give a literary critique of the four versions, all of which turn out to be inaccurate in their depiction of the facts of the case. According to her introduction to a 1956 edition, Shaginian wrote this literary tour de force to protest the "narrow literary specialization" of her contemporaries as well as to "pass a literacy test in all literary genres."

In 1931, Shaginian published *Gidrotsentral* (Hydrocentral), a "production novel" set in a hydroelectric station in Soviet Armenia. Taking to heart dictator Josef Stalin's exhortation to Soviet artists to participate in the first Five Year Plan, Shaginian lived at the site in Armenia for four years to study firsthand the building of Socialism through the reality of creating a massive hydroelectric power station on the Dzoraget River. When the first shacks of the station were built, Shaginian moved into a tiny room where she could "see the stars at night through the cracks in the walls." From these experiences came a complex, richly detailed novel that is generally recognized as an early form of the Socialist Realism genre which would characterize Soviet literature during the final two decades of Stalin's dictatorship. Shaginian later recalled that the characters in her novel "were based on real people whom I loved and got to know really well." The publication of *Gidrotsentral* solidified Shaginian's reputation as a reliable supporter of the regime, despite the fact that she had admitted in a 1926 autobiographical sketch that she could not join the Communist Party of the Soviet Union. "I am a believing Christian," she wrote, "and that constitutes not a passing fancy, but the essence of my personality, its roots that I cannot deny." Writing in the early 1920s, Soviet leader and literary critic Leon Trotsky observed that Shaginian viewed reality from a position that was "unrevolutionary, Asiatic, passive, Christian and non-resistant," going on to denounce her work for embodying a spirit of "fatalistic submission [and] fatalistic Christianity [and for being] anti-revolutionary in her very essence."

While remaining as productive as ever in the 1930s, writing mainly journalistic and critical essays, Shaginian also became increasingly involved in several of the important artistic controversies of the day. On several occasions, she took positions that were out of step with the official, orthodox line. In 1934, she argued against the venerated Maxim Gorky in the debate on whether the Russian language should be protected from the "contaminating influences" of other languages or dialects, speaking forcefully in favor of mutually enriching interactions between the literary language and "substandard" forms. In 1935, she was the lone voice of protest at a meeting of the Writers' Union when she disagreed with Stalinist guidelines for book reviewers. Her challenge to the new, rigid criteria used to consign books to oblivion caused considerable embarrassment to the organizers of the session. In 1936, she submitted her resignation from the Writers' Union to protest lack of material support for writers, an act that brought forth a resolution from the union's Presidium condemning her action as being both "deeply anti-social" and a "serious political mistake."

In 1936, after visiting the recently opened Lenin Museum in Moscow, Shaginian decided to investigate in detail how "the boy Volodya Ulyanov had grown into a leader." Soon, she published several articles on this subject, becoming ever more immersed in detailed research into the family origins and early years of Vladimir Ulyanov, who in time became V.I. Lenin, founder of the Soviet Union. Written as a novel but based on accurate and detailed research, including interviews with Lenin's sister ❧➤ **Marie Ulyanova** and his widow *Nadezhda Krupskaya, Shaginian's novel *Bilet po istorii, Chast' I: Sem'ia Ul'yanovykh* (Ticket to History, Part I: The Ulyanov Family) was published in Moscow in 1938. The book initially received excellent reviews, including one by Dmitri Ulyanov, Lenin's brother, published in *Izvestia* on March 24,

1938. Soon, however, a devastating assessment of the novel was issued by the Communist Party's Central Committee, which described the book as "a politically harmful, ideologically hostile work" and condemned Krupskaya for encouraging Shaginian to write it. In August 1938, the Politburo banned the publication of all books about Lenin, a ban that was not lifted until October 1956. Having survived the bloody years of Stalinism, Shaginian would then be able to see her massive research project on Lenin appear in print again, first in a journal in 1957, then in book form in 1958. When her epic tetralogy on Lenin and the Ulyanov family was completed, her accomplishments were finally recognized with a Lenin Prize awarded in 1972.

Marietta Shaginian's curiosity prompted her to investigate innumerable areas of literature and culture. One of these was the life and work of the Ukrainian national poet Taras Shevchenko (1814–1861), who was born a serf but was able to educate himself and in time became the prophet of an oppressed nation. Shaginian's book on Shevchenko, published in 1941, was an important contribution to knowledge of the great Ukrainian writer's life and impact, and took issue with a number of traditional interpretations tending to favor Russian versus Ukrainian cultural influences in his career. Not surprisingly, the book's second edition, published in 1946, was full of "corrections" that brought back many of the older prejudices, or eliminated the often bold insights of the first edition. Shaginian's 1944 doctoral dissertation, which concentrates on Shevchenko's aesthetics, remains a major source for scholars studying Shevchenko's thought.

Although she had often chosen to display signs of independence under the Stalinist dictatorship, Shaginian's published work before 1953 supported the Soviet state and its Socialist Realist aesthetic. Because of the immensity of her literary output, its quality varies considerably, and the breadth of her interests guaranteed that some of her writings would contain questionable judgments and factual errors. When an intellectual "thaw" set in after the 1953 death of Stalin, she became an easy target for some reform-minded writers, particularly since she had been awarded a Stalin Prize as recently as 1951. In a 1954 article in the literary journal *Novyi Mir* (New World), Mikhail Lifshits listed Shaginian's numerous errors and documented many of her more pompous and inane pronouncements. Although the facts presented in the article were correct, the Soviet literary establishment rose in Shaginian's defense and in

**Ulyanova, Marie.**
*See Barkova, Anna for sidebar.*

the final analysis her reputation emerged enhanced rather than diminished.

By the end of the 1950s, Shaginian was universally acknowledged by her promoters and detractors alike as the doyenne of Soviet letters, a venerable women who was not only prolific but versatile and energetic. Shaginian admitted that when writing about a subject, "the worst habit of my life" would often cause her to "jump ahead, compare things, draw parallels, extend all kinds of premature generalizations—and the more easily you succeed in this, the less clear is your conception of the subject." Even at this senior stage of her career, she endured severe criticism from the highest levels of the Communist Party and the Soviet state. During one such inquisition in the 1950s, both Shaginian and the poet *Margarita Iosifovna Aliger were the objects of "extravagant attacks" by Nikita Khrushchev, but both artists defended their work "bravely and logically while contradicting [him]."

In 1978, on the occasion of Marietta Shaginian's 90th birthday, she received the highest civilian decoration the Soviet Union could bestow, the title Hero of Socialist Labor. Deaf and now rapidly becoming blind, she continued to work during the 1970s on a final volume of her memoirs. *Chelovek i vremia (Man and Time)* is a remarkable exercise in recollection written by a handicapped author of advanced age. Covering the first 30 years of her life, the book recreated images of a Russian way of life increasingly remote to the contemporary mind and temperament. Shaginian's *Man and Time*, which has been described as a major contribution to Russian memoir literature, was written with great effort. When the eighth and last installment was published in *Novy Mir* in November 1979, on the last page in small type there were the words: "Ninety years and four months. Peredelkino-Moscow." The memoir was published as a book in 1980, and Shaginian died two years later, on her 94th birthday.

Marietta Shaginian was honored on the 100th anniversary of her birth when a 10-kopeck postage stamp was issued on April 2, 1988. In the post-Soviet era, her reputation remains under a cloud, perhaps most of all because of what David Shepherd has called "the compromising taint of sustained official recognition." Yet there are significant signs that this writer is in the first stages of being seriously studied and evaluated by scholars, and perhaps one day will again be enjoyed by a select circle of readers sensitive to the illogic of history. Goering has suggested that in Shaginian's "disarming sincerity" we have the tone of "someone who is in-variably in the ecstatic state of a person who has finally found the truth." This might serve to explain how a writer of talent could traverse the entire Soviet era "in a state of myopic oblivion," unaware of the failures and terrors all around her. As far back as 1925, the emigré poet Vladislav Khodasevich offered an explanation of Shaginian's peculiar inability to detect the massive evils that often hid behind a rhetorical screen of human advancement: "[She] had a good heart and, waving her cardboard sword, she was always rushing to defend or defeat someone, and in the end it somehow always turned out that she defeated virtue and defended the villain. But it was always done out of a good heart and with the best intentions."

**SOURCES:**

Betz, Margaret. "The Icon and Russian Modernism," in *Artforum*. Vol. 15, no. 10. Summer 1977, pp. 38–45.

Bittenek, Krystyna. "Afterword to Shaginian," in *Ararat: A Quarterly*. No. 54. Summer 1973.

Brown, Edward James. *The Proletarian Episode in Russian Literature, 1928–1932*. NY: Columbia University Press, 1953.

Christensen, Peter G. "Contextualizing Kuleshov's *Mr. West*," in *Film Criticism*. Vol. 18, no. 1. Fall 1993, pp. 3–19.

Clark, Katerina. *Petersburg: Crucible of Cultural Revolution*. Cambridge, MA: Harvard University Press, 1995.

———. *The Soviet Novel: History as Ritual*. 3rd ed. Bloomington, IN: Indiana University Press, 2000.

Davies, Mildred. "Shaginián, Marìetta Sergéevna ('Jim Dollar')," in Marina Ledkovsky, Charlotte Rosenthal and Mary Zirin, eds., *Dictionary of Russian Women Writers*. Westport, CT: Greenwood Press, 1994, pp. 568–571.

"Dr. Marietta Shaginian," in *The Times* [London]. April 6, 1982, p. 14.

Franz, Norbert. "Die russische Kriminalliteratur in den Jahren 1924 und 1925," in *Zeitschrift für slavische Philologie*. Vol. 48, no. 1, 1988, pp. 91–110.

Goering, Laura. "Marietta Shaginian," in Christine D. Tomei, ed., *Russian Women Writers*. Vol. 2. NY: Garland, 1999.

———. "'Der Mensch muss wieder ruiniert werden': Marietta Shaginian's Journey to Weimar," in *Germano-Slavica*. Vol. 7, no. 2. Fall 1993, pp. 67–81.

Kelly, Catriona. *A History of Russian Women's Writing, 1820–1992*. Oxford, UK: Clarendon Press, 1994.

Kemp-Welch, A. *Stalin and the Literary Intelligentsia, 1928–39*. NY: St. Martin's Press, 1991.

Kosachov, Natalie. "Literary and Related Art Biography by Marietta Shaginian," Ph.D. dissertation, University of Ottawa, 1973.

Luckyj, George S.N. "Shevchenko Studies One Century After the Poet's Death," in *Slavic Review*. Vol. 21, no. 4. December 1962, pp. 722–735.

———, ed. *Shevchenko and the Critics, 1861–1980*. Translations by Dolly Ferguson and Sophia Yurkevich. Toronto: University of Toronto Press, 1980.

Martyn, Barrie. *Rachmaninoff: Composer, Pianist, Conductor*. Aldershot, UK: Scolar Press, 1990.

McCauley, Karen Anne. "The Aesthetics of Production: The Russian Avant-Garde and the Rise of Socialist Realism," Ph.D. dissertation, University of California, Los Angeles, 1995.

Nathan, Robert Stuart. "Mike Thingsmaster, the All-American Bolshevik," in *The New York Times Book Review*. August 18, 1991, p. 12.

Odarecenko, Petro. "Sevcenko in Soviet Literary Criticism," in Volodymyr Mijakovs'kyj and George Y. Shevelov, eds., *Taras Sevcenko, 1814–1861: A Symposium*. s-Gravenhage: Mouton, 1962, pp. 259–302.

Roberts, Graham. *The Last Soviet Avant-Garde: OBERIU—Fact, Fiction, Metafiction*. Cambridge, UK: Cambridge University Press, 1997.

Russell, Robert. "Red Pinkertonism: An Aspect of Soviet Literature of the 1920s," in *Slavonic and East European Review*. Vol. 60, no. 3. July 1982, pp. 390–412.

Serebryakov, Konstantin. "Doyenne Authoress," translated by Peter Mann, in *Soviet Literature*. No. 9 (354), 1977, pp. 16–22.

Shaginian, Marietta. *Creative Freedom and the Soviet Artist*. London: Soviet News, 1953.

———. *Iozef Myslivechek*. 2nd rev. ed. Moscow: Mol. gvardiia, 1968.

———. *Journey Through Soviet Armenia*. Moscow: Foreign Languages Publishing House, 1954.

———. "Man and Time (From the Reminiscences)," translated by Helen Tate, in *Soviet Literature*. No. 9 (390), 1980, pp. 33–113.

———. *Mess-Mend: Yankees in Petrograd*. Translated by Samuel D. Cioran. Ann Arbor, MI: Ardis, 1987.

———. "Not a Utopia but Real Experience," translated by Peter Tempest, in *Soviet Literature*. No. 4 (397), 1981, pp. 3–28.

———. *Retracing Lenin's Steps*. Translated by Suzanne Rosenberg. Moscow: Progress, 1974.

———. "Three Looms," in Joshua Kunitz, ed. *Azure Cities: Stories of New Russia*. Translated by J.J. Robbins. NY: International, 1929, pp. 271–278.

Shepherd, David. *Beyond Metafiction: Self-Consciousness in Soviet Literature*. Oxford, UK: Clarendon Press, 1992.

———. "Canon Fodder? Problems in the Reading of a Soviet Production Novel," in Catriona Kelly, Michael Makin and David Shepherd, eds. *Discontinuous Discourses in Modern Russian Literature*. NY: St. Martin's Press, 1989, pp. 39–59.

Stephan, Halina. "*LEF* and the Development of Early Soviet Prose," in *Slavic and East European Journal*. Vol. 24, no. 4. Winter 1980, pp. 369–386.

Surkov, Alexei. "A Many-Sided Talent (For the 90th Birthday of Marietta Shaginyan)," in *Soviet Literature*. No. 4 (361), 1978, pp. 136–140.

Taubman, Jane A. "Women Poets of the Silver Age," in Toby W. Clyman and Diana Greene, eds. *Women Writers in Russian Literature*. Westport, CT: Greenwood Press, 1994, pp. 171–188.

Wiren-Garczynski, Vera von. "Marietta Shaginian: Mother of Us All," in *Ararat: A Quarterly*. Vol. 9, no. 3. Summer 1968.

**John Haag**,
Associate Professor of History,
University of Georgia, Athens, Georgia

## Shaginyan, Marietta (1888–1982).

*See Shaginian, Marietta.*

## Shagrat al-Durr (d. 1259).

*See Shajar al-Durr.*

# Shajar al-Durr (d. 1259)

*Sultana of Egypt. Name variations: Shajar al Durr; Shajarat; Shagrat al-Durr; Spray of Pearls. Died in 1259 (some sources cite 1258) in Cairo; married Najm ad Din also known as al-Salih Ayyub or Salih II Ayyub, Ayyubid sultan of Egypt, in 1240 (died 1249); married Aybak, Mamluk sultan of Egypt, in 1250; stepchildren: Turan or al-Muazzam Turanshah.*

Shajar al-Durr, one of the few women in Muslim history to have ruled as sultana, played an important role in the defeat of the Seventh Crusade. Little is known about her family background except that she was Turkish and had been a slave before her marriage. In 1240, she became the wife of Salih II Ayyub, the sultan of Egypt. In 1249, she acted as regent of Egypt while her husband was on a military campaign in Damascus. The Crusading army led by the French king Louis IX had captured the port city of Damietta in June 1249; Shajar organized the Egyptian army against the Crusaders. When Salih II died shortly after his return to Mansourah in November 1249, Shajar concealed his death by claiming he was too ill to leave his tent. In this way, she ruled alone in his name, successfully keeping his death a secret until the heir to the sultanate, her stepson Turan, returned from Syria to take power. In the spring of 1250, she and Turan organized the defense of Cairo against Louis, defeating the Crusaders and capturing the king. Louis was ransomed and had to surrender Damietta in April, after which he sailed for Palestine. Turan was then assassinated in May by Mamluk (Turkish) military officers of the Egyptian army who wanted a Mamluk sultan.

Their choice fell on Shajar, who thus became the first Mamluk (Turkish) sultan of Egypt and the first female sultan to rule in her own name. (The Mamluk period would last for two centuries.) With the strong support of the Egyptian military leaders, Shajar began to consolidate her power, issuing coins in her name. However, because she was a woman, the overlord of Egypt, the caliph of Baghdad, refused to recognize her rule as legitimate. Shajar was forced to abdicate after only a few months. The caliph sent the Mamluk soldier Aybak to take her place. Shajar, still ambitious for power, arranged to marry Aybak, and together they consolidated Mamluk rule in Egypt, making a new capital at Cairo. During their eight years of joint rule, Shajar, called sultana, promulgated laws and issued decrees; according to contemporary reports, she was a more active ruler than her husband. When Aybak tried to take a second wife in 1259, however, Shajar became jealous of his bid for more power and had him assassinated. Soon two military factions were fighting over the future of the sultanate: those who supported Shajar's continued rule, and those who wanted Aybak's son by his former wife to rule. Shajar's faction was defeated, and she was murdered at the instigation of Aybak's son. Later her bones were removed to a mosque named in her honor where they remain today.

**SOURCES:**

Jackson-Laufer, Guida M. *Women Who Ruled*. Santa Barbara, CA: ABC-CLIO, 1990.

Mernissi, Fatima. *The Forgotten Queens of Islam*. Cambridge, Eng.: Polity Press, 1993.

Waddy, Charis. *Women in Muslim History*. NY: Longman, 1980.

**Laura York**, M.A. in History,
University of California, Riverside, California

## Shakespeare, Anne (1556–1623).

*See Hathaway, Anne.*

## Shambaugh, Jessie Field (1881–1971).

*See Field, Jessie.*

## Shamiram (fl. 8th c. BCE).

*See Sammuramat.*

# Shapiro, Betty Kronman

## (1907–1989)

*International president of B'nai B'rith Women. Name variations: Rebecca Shapiro. Born Rebecca Kronman in Washington, D.C., on September 26, 1907; died of cancer in Washington, D.C., on March 18, 1989; daughter of Nathan Kronman (a grocer) and Monya "Mollie" (Bogorod) Kronman (active in numerous Jewish community organizations); attended Business High School, Washington, D.C.; attended George Washington University and Cornell University; married Michael Shapiro, on July 5, 1936 (died November 23, 1976); no children.*

*Worked as school secretary (1924–29) and office manager, Washington, D.C., branch, Hebrew Immigrant Aid Society (1929–43); served as president, National Council of Jewish Juniors, Washington, D.C., Section (1936); founded and served as officer, Service Council of the Jewish Community Center, Washington, D.C., during World War II; had over 40 years of activism with B'nai B'rith Women, including founder and member, Abram Simon Chapter, Washington, D.C. (1952–89), president, Argo Chapter, Washing-*

*ton, D.C. (1952–53), regional president, Eastern Seaboard District 5 (1955–56), co-sponsored Kronman Youth Awards for outstanding civic service (1955–65), coordinated first Inter-faith Conference (1957), was international president (1968–71), convened a conference to address urban crisis and established anti-poverty committee (1968), was founder and first chair, Public Affairs Program, and International Affairs Committee chair (1971–74), convened first Women's Plea for Soviet Jewry in Washington (1971), founded and chaired Ad-Hoc Leadership Conference on Washington, D.C., Jewish Women's Organizations (1971–75), was founder and chair, Jewish Women's Network, Washington, D.C. (1977–80).*

After Betty Shapiro's 1968 election as the international president of B'nai B'rith Women, a reporter asked how she became head of the 140,000-member Jewish women's organization. "I suppose I would be falsely modest if I said I did not have leadership qualities," she replied. "I'm more of a shirt-sleeve type, the kind of person who needs to pitch in on whatever needs doing, whether it's conferring with people at the highest level or sorting a box of rummage for my chapter's fund-raising program." Over more than 40 years of community service, her leadership qualities often put her in the spotlight. For example, at the UN Decade Conference for Women in Nairobi in 1985, the government threatened to throw the women out of their hotel. Shapiro held a press conference and mobilized a string of women lawyers. By the time the fully armed soldiers arrived, she had organized a sit-down in the hotel lobby. At 78, Betty Shapiro won the fight.

Betty Shapiro was born Rebecca Kronman in Washington, D.C., in 1907, one of four children of Nathan and **Mollie Kronman**, Russian immigrants who owned a Washington, D.C., grocery store. Mollie was active in numerous Jewish women's organizations and led efforts to establish the local Hebrew Home for the Aged and the Hebrew Sheltering Society. Betty was a leader like her mother from early childhood. She and her friends would "sit outside on the iron stoop everyday where we'd have a club," she said. "I don't remember what we did, but I was president." She was also a celebrated athlete. She coached and managed a girls' basketball team at the Jewish Community Center while she played on her own high school team. Offered a contract to play professionally, she declined. Instead, at 16, she began a secretarial career, working at Langley Junior High School in Washington, D.C., from 1924 to 1928, and in California at South Pasadena Junior High School in 1928.

Shapiro returned to Washington the following year and worked in the Washington office of the Hebrew Immigrant Aid Society (HAIS) from 1929 to 1943. During the Holocaust, her work took on new urgency as she processed applications for assistance from thousands whose visas had been refused. Although not trained as a lawyer, she often presented cases to review boards at the departments of State and Justice, managing to save a number of people. In addition, she was an active volunteer during World War II, visiting wounded soldiers for the National Council of Jewish Juniors. As a co-founder of the Service Council of the Jewish Community Center, she helped organize recreational activities and other functions for the men and women flooding Washington every month to take wartime government jobs. In 1943, she joined B'nai B'rith Women and began volunteering in the organization's veterans' service program.

Throughout the 1950s, Shapiro held increasingly visible positions in B'nai B'rith Women. She was elected president of the Argo Chapter in Washington, D.C., in 1952, and of the entire Eastern Seaboard in 1955. In 1957, she convened the organization's first inter-faith conference. In 1958, she participated in a ten-day inspection tour of Radio Free Europe installations in Munich and Lisbon, the only representative from a Jewish organization on the tour.

Of all her activism for B'nai B'rith Women, she considered founding the organization's Public Affairs Program her greatest accomplishment. She created a liaison between B'nai B'rith Women and the government, and placed members in the forefront of policy making. Many credit Shapiro with transforming B'nai B'rith Women (now called Jewish Women International) from a social service organization to a political advocacy group. As the organization's international president from 1968 to 1971, she urged its involvement in political action. In 1968, she convened a conference of 40 women's organizations to develop strategies for addressing urban poverty and violence. She was also a vocal advocate for civil rights even after riots in Washington, D.C., destroyed her husband's business. A strong supporter of the Equal Rights Amendment and an advocate of abortion rights, she encouraged B'nai B'rith Women to endorse a feminist platform, and went as the group's representative to feminist conferences in Nairobi, Copenhagen, and Houston.

Shapiro also fought to expose and eradicate anti-Semitism in the feminist movement. At the first National Woman's Conference in Houston, Texas in 1977, she organized an ad hoc Jewish Women's Caucus. Under her leadership, the caucus waged a successful fight to prevent a clause in the conference's final statement equating Zionism with racism. Less than a year before her death from cancer, Shapiro was inducted into the District of Columbia Commission on Women's Hall of Fame.

**SOURCES:**

Chaiet, Joyce. Oral History with Betty Shapiro. *The Jewish Historical Society of Greater Washington Oral History Project, Volume Three.* Partially funded by a grant from the Humanities Council of Washington, D.C.

Colp, Judith. "Betty Shapiro: A Woman of Vision and a Trooper in the Trenches," in *Washington Jewish Week.* September 1, 1988.

Ohliger, Gloria. "How Things Look on Top of the Table," in *The Washington Daily News.* March 19, 1968.

Shapiro, Betty K. "We Saw So Much to Make Us Proud," in *B'nai B'rith Women's World.* February 1959.

**SUGGESTED READING:**

Fishman, Sylvia Barack. *A Breath of Life: Feminism in the American Jewish Community.* Hanover, NH: Brandeis University Press, 1995.

**COLLECTIONS:**

Betty K. Shapiro Collection, Jewish Historical Society of Greater Washington, Lillian and Albert Small Jewish Museum, Washington, D.C.; Betty K. Shapiro Collection, B'nai B'rith Women National Headquarters, Washington, D.C.

**RELATED MEDIA:**

*Southwest Remembered* (audiotape), Washington, DC: Lamont Productions, 1980.

**Denise D. Meringolo,** Curator,
Jewish Historical Society of Greater Washington,
Washington, D.C.

# Shaposhnikova, Natalia (1961—)

*Soviet gymnast. Name variations: Natalya. Born on June 24, 1961.*

In 1980, in the U.S.-boycotted Moscow Olympics, Natalia Shaposhnikova won gold medals for her performance in the horse vault and the team all-around, and bronze medals for the balance beam. She also tied with East Germany's **Maxi Gnauck** for a bronze medal in the floor exercise.

# Sharaff, Irene (1910–1993)

*American costume designer. Pronunciation: SHAR-eff. Born in Boston, Massachusetts, in 1910; died in New York City on August 16, 1993; studied at the New York School of Fine and Applied Arts, the Art Students League, New York City, and the Grande Chaumière in Paris; never married; no children.*

*Selected filmography:* Girl Crazy *(1943);* Meet Me in St. Louis *(1944);* Yolanda and the Thief *(1945);* The Dark Mirror *(1946);* The Best Years of Our Lives *(1946);* The Secret Life of Walter Mitty *(1947);* A Song Is Born *(1948);* An American in Paris *(1951);* Call Me Madam *(1953);* A Star Is Born *(1954);* Brigadoon *(1954);* Guys and Dolls *(1955);* The King and I *(1956);* Les Girls *(1957);* Porgy and Bess *(1959);* Can-Can *(1960);* West Side Story *(1961);* Flower Drum Song *(1961);* Cleopatra *(1963);* The Sandpiper *(1965);* Who's Afraid of Virginia Woolf? *(1966);* The Taming of the Shrew *(1967);* Funny Girl *(1968);* Hello Dolly! *(1969);* The Great White Hope *(1970);* The Other Side of Midnight *(1977);* Mommie Dearest *(1981).*

Over the course of her 50-year career, costume designer Irene Sharaff worked on some of America's most significant musicals, often producing costumes for the stage and film productions of the same work, such as *Flower Drum Song, Funny Girl, West Side Story,* and *The King and I.* She also designed for non-musicals, among them the films *The Sandpiper* (1955), *The Great White Hope* (1970), and *Mommie Dearest* (1981). Known for her stylish creations and her use of color, Sharaff also worked in television, ballet, nightclubs and fashion illustration.

Sharaff was born in Boston, Massachusetts, in 1910, and originally wanted to become a painter. She was trained at New York's School of Fine and Applied Arts and the Art Students League, and also attended the Grande Chaumière in Paris. She began her career as an assistant to *Aline Bernstein, at the Civic Repertory Theater Company in New York, and many of her earliest shows included scenery as well as costumes. She first gained recognition for her sets and costumes for *Eva Le Gallienne's 1932 production of *Alice in Wonderland,* then went on to design scenery and costumes for the Ballets Russes de Monte Carlo. By the mid-1930s, Sharaff was designing major Broadway plays, including *As Thousands Cheer, Lady in the Dark, On Your Toes,* and *A Tree Grows in Brooklyn.* She launched her Hollywood career with the musical *Girl Crazy* in 1944 and worked steadily in films from then on, designing for both

*Irene Sharaff (right), with Olivia de Haviland.*

the stage and movies simultaneously. During her lifetime, she was nominated for sixteen Academy Awards, winning five. She won her first for her scenery and costumes in the ballet sequence in *An American in Paris* (1951). That same year, she created the sumptuous oriental costumes for the stage production of *The King and I*, for which she not only won a Tony, but set a trend in fashion and interior decorating that lasted for several years. In 1956, the designer won an Oscar for her work on the film version of *The King and I*. She also won for *West Side Story* (1961), *Cleopatra* (1963), and *Who's Afraid of Virginia Woolf?* (1966).

Sharaff's remarkable color sense came from her art background. She claimed that she saw everything in blocks of color, "rather like painting a picture." She elaborated in an interview: "If I have a leitmotif, a logo, I suspect it is associated with the colors I prefer—reds, pinks, oranges—and with a certain cut which seems to reappear in many of the shows and films I've worked on." Although she dressed many stars and celebrities, Sharaff believed that true style was a very rare thing. "The only theater people I can think of who have it are *Audrey Hepburn and Betty Bacall," she said in a 1967 interview. "The one who had it to the greatest degree was *Gertie Lawrence. She could make a sackcloth tied with a belt look stylish." Sharaff, who made her home in New York, suffered from emphysema toward the end of her life, and died at the age of 83, of congestive heart failure.

**SOURCES:**
Katz, Ephraim. *The Film Encyclopedia*. NY: Harper-Collins, 1994.

Leese, Elizabeth. *Costume Design in the Movies*. NY: Dover, 1991.

"Obituary," in *The Day* [New London, CT]. August 17, 1993.

Wilmeth, Don B., and Tice L. Miller, eds. *Cambridge Guide to American Theater*. NY: Cambridge University Press, 1993.

**Barbara Morgan,**
Melrose, Massachusetts

## Sharelli (fl. 1275 BCE).

*See Akhat-milki.*

# Shariyya (b. around 815)

*Arabian singer, one of the best known of her time, who is famous in Arabian history and folklore. Born in Basra (now Iraq) around 815.*

One has only to possess a superficial knowledge of Arabian history to recognize how valued "songstresses" were. The film stars of their era, they commanded the highest respect and salaries, and wealthy, powerful men vied to have them in their courts and homes. Shariyya, one of the most famous Arabian singers, was born in Basra (now Iraq) around 815. Her father, who may have been from the Banu Sama ibn Lu'ai tribe, would not recognize his illegitimate daughter. Her mother was a slave. In some versions of her life story, Shariyya was stolen from her parents, sold into slavery, and taught the art of singing by a woman who later sold her in Baghdad. In other versions, the woman who sold her was her mother who came from the Banu Zuhra tribe. Whatever the truth, Shariyya must have shown exceptional talent at age seven because Ishaq al-Mausili and Ibrahim ibn al-Mahdi, the two most significant musicians of that period, attended the auction and attempted to purchase her. (This is an indication of just how valuable a commodity a potential songstress could be, for few other females were so sought after.) Finally, Ibrahim ibn al-Mahdi bought the young girl, freed her, and married her so that she could not be taken from him. Some said this was a marriage in name only.

Caliph al-Mutasim offered 70,000 dinars for Shariyya, but Ibrahim refused the money. When Ibrahim died, Shariyya learned that she had not legally been married to him, and so her status as a slave had not actually changed. She was then sold to a succession of caliphs—al-Mutasim (r. 833–842), al-Watiq (r. 842–847), al-Mutawakki (r. 847–862), al-Muntasir (r. 861–862), al-Mustain (r. 862–866), Al-Mutazz (r. 866–869), and al Mutamid (r. 870–892). Throughout her career, Shariyya grew more famous and more powerful. During the caliphate of al-Mutawakki, a great rivalry developed between Shariyya and *Oraib, another famous songstress. Oraib represented the classical Arabian tradition, while Shariyya was famous for singing in the more romantic Persian style. Both women sang before devoted fans who cheered one or the other wildly.

Shariyya set Caliph al-Mutamid's poems to music, for which she was richly rewarded. By this time, when she was over 60, she had established a singing school, and she also sold several of the slaves she had personally trained to him. Shariyya performed during a brilliant epoch in Arab culture, occupying one of its most prominent places and consequently has been celebrated for centuries. Few, if any, European prima donnas enjoyed the loyalty and prestige singers like Shariyya and Oraib commanded during their lifetimes.

**John Haag,**
Athens, Georgia

# Sharp, Katharine Lucinda

## (1865–1914)

*American librarian who advanced the teaching of librarianship in the late 19th and early 20th centuries.* Name variations: K.L.S. Born on May 21, 1865, in Elgin, Illinois; daughter of John William Sharp and Phebe (Thompson) Sharp; died in Saranac Lake, New York, on June 1, 1914; Northwestern University, Evanston, Illinois, Ph.B., 1885, Ph.M., 1889; New York State Library School, B.L.S., 1892, M.L.S., 1907.

*Established libraries in Wheaton, Illinois, and Xenia, Ohio (early 1890s); served as head of the Armour Institute of Technology's department of library economy; transferred the Armour Institute's library school to the University of Illinois and created the Illinois State Library School (1897); published* Illinois Libraries *(1906–08).*

Born an only child in Elgin, Illinois, in 1865, Katharine Lucinda Sharp was only seven when her mother died in 1872. She was then raised by relatives of Elgin and Dundee, and enrolled at Elgin Academy before attending Northwestern University in Evanston at age 16. Her father had remarried, and in 1881, her half-brother, with whom she would have a close relationship throughout her life, was born. Sharp played an active role in school affairs and went on from her undergraduate work to receive her Ph.M. in 1889. The late 1880s found her teaching Latin, French, and German at Elgin Academy, but she soon knew that a teaching career was not to her liking. In 1888, she accepted a position as assistant librarian at the newly established Scoville Institute (Oak Park, Illinois), where her interest in library work was sparked.

Sharp began studies in 1890 at the New York State Library School (NYSLS) which was then under the directorship of Melvil Dewey. While pursuing her studies there, she proved an especially adept librarian and supervised the initial organization of the Adams Memorial Library in Wheaton, Illinois, and the Xenia, Ohio, public library. Sharp received a Bachelor of Library Science degree (B.L.S.) from NYSLS in 1892 and after graduation was selected to create the school's comparative library exhibit for the Chicago World's Fair (1893). The exhibit proved a great success, and the attention it brought helped Sharp secure an appointment as the librarian and head of the department of library economy of Chicago's new Armour Institute of Technology in December 1893. The program she began there was only the fourth library school in the country.

Sharp trained 41 librarians during her four years at Armour. She was elected to the council of the American Library Association (1895), directed a summer school for librarians offered by the Wisconsin Library Association (1895 and 1896), and became active in promoting the establishment of public libraries in Illinois through collaborative programs involving the State Teachers' Association and the State Federation of Women's Clubs. Such pursuits earned her yet more notice in the library profession, and she soon received offers from both the University of Wisconsin and the University of Illinois to move the Armour Institute's library program to their schools, where the program could enjoy more substantial financial backing. Armour's administration did not oppose the move, and in 1897 Sharp transferred the institute's entire library-studies program, including students, some faculty, and equipment, to the University of Illinois. There it became the Illinois State Library School.

At the University of Illinois, Sharp began to lobby for changing the school's requirements for the B.L.S., which at the time demanded two years' previous college study for admission into the two-year library-study program. In 1903, three years' prior college education became required, followed by Sharp's goal of four years in 1911. While working to improve library training, she applied herself to expanding enrollment, and the number of students in the program reached 75 in 1900. Known as demanding and inflexible, she was nonetheless a measurably effective and admired teacher who trained prominent librarians including **Mary Eileen Ahern, Margaret Mann, Cornelia Marvin,** and *****Alice S. Tyler.** Though the term "projects" was not yet in use, her students conducted projects and engaged in both group discussions and seminars. Sharp (called K.L.S. by students) also took her classes on field trips, including week-long junkets to inspect Chicago's fine libraries.

During Sharp's tenure at the University of Illinois, there were no library-science textbooks available for use, and the extensive notes from which she taught were written down verbatim by her students. Her influence in the field was to continue long after her retirement, and it is likely that many of her class notes were incorporated into the first library-science textbooks—three of the first seven of which were authored by Sharp's students Margaret Mann and F.K.W. Drury—which began to appear in the mid-1920s. While meeting her obligations as a teacher, librarian, and administrator, Sharp also continued her own studies, receiving the degree of Master of Library Science (M.L.S.) from the

New York State Library School in 1907 for what is considered the most significant of her published works, the 800-page *Illinois Libraries*, a history of all the state's libraries.

The death of both her father and half-brother, in addition to her own weak health, led Sharp to resign from her position with the Illinois Library School in 1907. In recognition of her contributions to the study of library science, the University of Illinois awarded her an honorary M.L.S.

During her retirement, Sharp lived with Melvil Dewey and his first wife **Annie Godfrey Dewey** (1849–1922) at the Lake Placid Club in upstate New York. Shortly after her 49th birthday, she received severe injuries in an automobile accident and died on June 1, 1914, in Saranac Lake, New York. She was buried in Dundee, Illinois. A memorial plaque by Lorado Taft for the University of Illinois alumni was inscribed: "Nobility of character and grace of person were united with intellectual vigor and scholarly attainments. She inspired her students and associates with sound standards of librarianship and ideals of service."

**SOURCES:**

Danton, Emily Miller, ed. *Pioneering Leaders in Librarianship*. Boston, MA: Gregg Press, 1972.

James, Edward T., ed. *Notable American Women, 1607–1950*. Cambridge, MA: The Belknap Press of Harvard University, 1971.

# Sharp, Margery (1905–1991)

*British author who wrote the "Miss Bianca" children's books. Born on January 25, 1905, in Malta; died on March 14, 1991, in London, England; third daughter of J.H. Sharp; Bedford College of London University, B.A., 1929; married Major Geoffrey L. Castle, in 1938 (died 1990).*

*Selected works: (plays)* Meeting at Night *(1938),* Lady in Waiting *(1941),* The Foolish Gentlewoman *(1949); (adult novels)* Rhododendron Pie *(1930),* Fanfare for Tin Trumpets *(1932),* The Nymph and the Nobleman *(1932),* Flowering Thorn *(1934),* Sophie Cassmajor *(1934),* Four Gardens *(1935),* Nutmeg Tree *(1937),* Harlequin House *(1939),* Stone of Chastity *(1940),* Cluny Brown *(1944),* Britannia Mews *(1946),* Lise Lillywhite *(1951),* The Gipsy in the Parlour *(1954),* The Tigress in the Hearth *(1955),* Eye of Love *(1957),* Martha in Paris *(1962),* Martha, Eric, and George *(1964),* The Sun in Scorpio *(1965),* In Pious Memory *(1967),* Rosa *(1970),* The Innocents *(1971),* The Last Chapel Picnic, and Other Stories *(1973),* The Faithful Servants *(1975),* Summer Visits *(1977); (children's books)* The Rescuers *(1959),* Melisande *(1960),* Something Light *(1960),* Miss Bianca *(1962),* The Turret *(1963),* Lost at the Fair *(1965),* Miss Bianca in the Salt Mines *(1966),* Miss Bianca in the Orient *(1970),* Miss Bianca in the Antarctic *(1970),* Miss Bianca and the Bridesmaid *(1972),* The Magical Cockatoo *(1974),* The Children Next Door *(1974),* Bernard the Brave *(1976),* Bernard into Battle *(1978).*

Margery Sharp, who was born in 1905 to British parents living on the island of Malta, was sent to England to attend Streatham Hill High School; she went on to receive a degree in French from Bedford College, University of London, in 1929. Sharp began her career as a writer early in life, publishing several poetic works during her high school years. She also traveled extensively while still young, and in 1929 was selected as a member of the first British University women's debating team to visit the United States.

After returning from America and completing her undergraduate studies, Sharp devoted

*Margery Sharp*

her time to writing. Her first novel, *Rhododendron Pie*, was published in 1930. She also tried her hand as a playwright, and several of her works were produced in London during the 1930s and 1940s. Her 1937 novel *The Nutmeg Tree* was a bestseller, and in 1948 the book was made into a movie, *Julia Misbehaves*, starring *Greer Garson and Walter Pidgeon. Sharp married Geoffrey L. Castle, a major in the British army, in 1938, and during World War II served as a teacher for the Armed Forces Education Program. This briefly preempted her career, but she resumed writing before the war's end and in 1944 published *Cluny Brown*. Ernst Lubitsch subsequently directed a successful film version of this comic novel, starring Charles Boyer and *Jennifer Jones as the orphan Cluny. Sharp's Victorian-era melodrama *Britannia Mews* (1946), with a screenplay by Ring Lardner, Jr., was filmed as *Forbidden Street* in 1949 and starred *Maureen O'Hara, *Sybil Thorndike, and Dana Andrews. Later, her short story "The Tenant" would be adapted for the screen as *The Notorious Landlady* (1962), starring *Kim Novak and Jack Lemmon. From the 1930s on, Sharp published numerous novels for adult readers, many of which were serialized in leading British and American literary magazines, including *Harper's Bazaar*, *Punch*, and the *Saturday Evening Post*, during the 1940s and 1950s.

Although she had met with success as a writer of fiction for adults, Sharp would find her true vocation as a writer of children's books, beginning with *The Rescuers* (1959), which introduced the elegant and refined white mouse named Miss Bianca. Well educated and a writer of dramatic poetry, Miss Bianca is the pet of an ambassador's son; in this first book, she is described thus:

> There were the most fantastic rumors about her: for instance, that she lived in a Porcelain Pagoda; that she fed exclusively on cream cheese from a silver bonbon dish; that she wore a silver chain around her neck, and on Sundays a gold one. She was also said to be extremely beautiful, but affected to the last degree.

In *The Rescuers*, Miss Bianca descends from her rarefied heights to join the Mouse Prisoners' Aid Society, which works to comfort prisoners and free wrongly imprisoned humans. Illustrated by Garth Williams, the book was published as an adult novel but quickly proved a major success as a children's book. After its publication, Sharp concentrated on creating further fictional works for children, including seven more books featuring Miss Bianca and her faithful friend Bernard

the pantry mouse. Considered among the best were *Miss Bianca: A Fantasy* (1962), *Miss Bianca in the Salt Mines* (1966), and *Miss Bianca in the Antarctic* (1970). New installments of the Miss Bianca tale met with less-than-ecstatic responses during the 1970s. Nevertheless, Miss Bianca's popularity among the reading public was mostly unaffected, and the series was translated into numerous languages, including Norwegian, Hebrew, and Portuguese. Sharp published two non-series children's books, *The Children Next Door* and *The Magical Cockatoo*, in 1974, but these were met with such a lack of enthusiasm that she returned to the mice rescuers for her final works, *Bernard the Brave* (1976) and *Bernard into Battle* (1978), which focused on Miss Bianca's long-suffering admirer.

The "Miss Bianca" series received a tremendous boost when Walt Disney Productions released its popular animated adaptation of *The Rescuers*, featuring the voices of Bob Newhart, *Geraldine Page, and *Eva Gabor as Miss Bianca, in 1977. Nonetheless, Sharp did not publish again after 1978. She suffered a mild stroke in 1986, and her husband died in 1990. That same year Disney produced *The Rescuers Down Under*, an animated sequel to the earlier film, sparking public interest that led to the reprinting of the "Miss Bianca" series in paperback. Margery Sharp died in March 1991.

**SOURCES:**

*Children's Literature Review*. Vol. 27. Detroit, MI: Gale Research, 1992.

Commire, Anne, ed. *Something About the Author*. Vol. 29. Detroit, MI: Gale Research, 1982.

Kunitz, Stanley J., and Howard Haycraft, eds. *Twentieth Century Authors*. NY: H.W. Wilson, 1942.

Overmyer, Elizabeth C. "Margery Sharp," in *Dictionary of Literary Biography*, Vol. 161: *British Children's Writers Since 1960*. Edited by Caroline C. Hunt. Detroit, MI: Gale Research, 1996.

**Grant Eldridge**, freelance writer, Pontiac, Michigan

# Shattuck, Lydia (1822–1889)

*American naturalist, botanist, and educator. Born Lydia White Shattuck on June 10, 1822, in East Landaff, New Hampshire; died on November 2, 1889, in South Hadley, Massachusetts; daughter of Timothy Shattuck (a farmer) and Betsy (Fletcher) Shattuck; graduated from Mt. Holyoke Seminary in 1851; never married; no children.*

Lydia Shattuck was born in 1822 on a farm in rural New Hampshire near the Franconia Mountains. Her father was a farmer whose ancestors had arrived in New England in 1642, and her mother was a woman of artistic sensibility who encouraged Shattuck's love of wild flowers. Both parents were supportive of her desire to obtain an education and become an independent woman.

Shattuck completed her secondary education and started working as a teacher at a district school at the age of 15. For the next 11 years, she taught and pursued her education at more advanced schools in New Hampshire and Vermont. Shattuck enrolled at Mt. Holyoke Seminary in South Hadley, Massachusetts, in 1848, and soon became a student and follower of the school's founder, *Mary Lyon, who was then in very poor health. Under Lyon's tutelage, Shattuck expanded her love of wild flowers into a consuming interest in botany. She also maintained a working knowledge of chemistry, physics, physiology, and astronomy. Shattuck graduated from Mt. Holyoke with honors in 1851, and remained on campus to become an instructor.

She quickly became one of the most highly regarded teachers at Mt. Holyoke, and her reputation was sufficient to gain her selection by Louis Agassiz as one of the initial 50 students at the Anderson School of Natural History at Penikese Island, off Woods Hole, Massachusetts, in 1873. While on Penikese Island, Shattuck obtained knowledge in the new field of marine biology and developed professional contacts among her scientific colleagues. In later years, she was a member of the Woods Hole Biological Laboratory Corporation.

After returning to Mt. Holyoke, Shattuck was instrumental in the creation of the school's herbarium and botanical gardens—she personally collected many of the specimens held by these collections. She traveled extensively in her capacity as a botanist, visiting Canada, Europe, the western United States, and Hawaii in search of new and rare plants. Aside from the establishment of botanical collections, her primary contribution to the field of botany was as a classifier of plant species. Although she did not publish any notable scholarly works, she corresponded regularly with the leading naturalists of the day, including Asa Gray, an early proponent of Charles Darwin's theory of natural selection. While she was a religious woman who believed that the beauty of the natural world was evidence of divine providence, she nonetheless was persuaded by Darwin's new theory, which was causing a worldwide uproar, and shared it at the school. Through her teaching activities, Shattuck also wielded considerable influence within the scientific community. She inspired her students to note the beauty of nature even while examining it in a scientific manner.

Mt. Holyoke Seminary became Mt. Holyoke College in 1888, and the following year Shattuck retired as professor emeritus. She continued to live on campus as her health rapidly failed, and she died there on November 2, 1889. Following her death, Mt. Holyoke named its newly constructed chemistry and physics building in her honor. A later physics building, built in the 1950s to replace the first one, was also named after her.

**SOURCES:**
James, Edward T., ed. *Notable American Women, 1607–1950.* Cambridge, MA: The Belknap Press of Harvard University, 1971.

**Grant Eldridge**, freelance writer,
Pontiac, Michigan

# Shavelson, Clara Lemlich (1888–1982).

*See Lemlich, Clara.*

# Shaver, Dorothy (1897–1959)

*American business executive who was president of Lord & Taylor for many years.* Born on July 29, 1897, in Center Point, Arkansas; died on June 28, 1959, in Hudson, New York; daughter of James D. Shaver (a lawyer) and Sallie (Borden) Shaver; attended the University of Arkansas for two years; attended the University of Chicago for one year; never married; no children.

Began working at Lord & Taylor (1924); served as general consultant to the Office of the Quartermaster General (1942–45); became president of Lord & Taylor stores (1945); voted outstanding woman in business by the Associated Press (1946, 1947); received the American Woman's Association award for feminist achievement (1950); recognized for "outstanding support of American design" by the Society of New York Dress Designers (1953).

Dorothy Shaver was born in the small town of Center Point, Arkansas, in 1897. Her family soon moved a short distance to the larger town of Mena, where she completed her primary and secondary education. In 1915, James Shaver enrolled his daughter in the University of Arkansas in a move designed to foil a romance of which he did not approve. After two years there, Shaver transferred to the University of Chicago, joining her sister **Elsie Shaver**, who was studying art in that city. When Elsie earned $600 for illustrating a catalog for Marshall Field & Company, the sisters decided to move to New York City to seek their fortune.

Upon reaching New York, Shaver was impressed by the commercial success of Kewpie dolls, the cherubic creations of entrepreneur *Rose O'Neill which were then a national craze. Dorothy encouraged her sister, who made dolls for her own amusement, to design a family of dolls for retail sale. Elsie duly produced the dolls, called the "Little Shavers," and Dorothy undertook to market them. Her efforts soon succeeded when a distant cousin, Wallace Reyburn, who worked for the Lord & Taylor department store and its owner, Associated Dry Goods Corporation, agreed to sell the Little Shavers at Lord & Taylor. Reyburn also provided Shaver with marketing, production, and distribution advice. The Shaver sisters successfully produced and sold their dolls for four years. In 1924, Elsie tired of the operation, and Shaver joined the staff of Lord & Taylor.

Shaver's first post at Lord & Taylor was in the store's comparison shopping bureau, where she checked prices in competing stores to insure that Lord & Taylor's own pricing was in line with the wider market. Within two months, she became the director of the bureau. In 1925, she was named the head of interior decoration and fashion, and in this post established a bureau of fashion advisors to work directly with clothing designers and producers. This innovative arrangement insured that Lord & Taylor's product lines met customer needs and desires; it is now a standard feature among fashion retailers.

In recognition of her contributions to Lord & Taylor, Shaver was named to the store's board of directors in 1927, while barely 30. The following year, she increased Lord & Taylor's public visibility and profitability by importing modern decorative artworks from Europe for display and sale in the store. The exhibit, which included objects by Picasso, Braque, and Utrillo, was the first of its kind in the United States, and proved hugely influential in home decoration. Shaver became a vice-president of Lord & Taylor in 1931 and remained an innovative force in retail administration. She inspired and oversaw the store's window displays, which consistently met with public and critical approval, created the unique "Bird Cage" lunchroom and men's soup bar in the store, instituted the first clothing department solely for teenagers, and played a pivotal role in the creation of Lord & Taylor's branch store network. The success of her efforts is shown by the fact that Lord & Taylor was able to pay dividends to its shareholders every year from 1931 to 1943 (save for the Depression year of 1933), while parent company Associated Dry Goods paid no dividends at all in that same period.

Shaver's success helped concentrate attention on American fashion and played a role in making New York City an international fashion center. At a time when most people looked to Europe for fashion, she championed American designers, including *Claire McCardell, Lilly Daché, swimsuit innovator *Rose Marie Reid, *Pauline Trigère, Clare Potter, and William Pahlmann. In 1938, Shaver was instrumental in the creation of the annual Lord & Taylor American Design Awards.

During World War II, Shaver served as a general consultant to the Office of the Quartermaster General, advising on the purchase of merchandise and women's uniforms. She was also active in the American Red Cross and sat on the board of the American Women's Volunteer Services throughout the war.

Shaver was elected president of Lord & Taylor in 1945. Her salary was $110,000, at the time the largest ever paid to an American woman, and both this and her presidency drew much public attention and even a few letters containing marriage proposals. It was also pointed out by *Life* magazine that male executives in similar positions received three times her salary. Under her direction, the store's sales rose from $30 million to $100 million by 1959. Shaver was voted the outstanding woman in business by the Associated Press in 1946 and 1947, received the American Woman's Association's award for feminist achievement in 1950, and was presented with the first award for outstanding support of American design by the New York Dress Designers Society in 1953. A fellow of the Metropolitan Museum of Art, she also played an important role in founding that institution's Costume Department. Shaver suffered a mild stroke in 1959, and was still recovering when she suffered a second, more severe stroke, after which she had to be hospitalized. She died later that year following a third stroke. In 1976, the first "outstanding individual whose creative mind has brought new beauty and deeper understanding to our lives" received the Dorothy Shaver Rose Award, an annual commemoration from Lord & Taylor of Shaver's contribution to American fashion and design.

**SOURCES:**
Rothe, Anna, ed. *Current Biography 1946*. NY: H.W. Wilson, 1946.
Sicherman, Barbara, and Carol Hurd Green, eds. *Notable American Women: The Modern Period*. Cambridge, MA: The Belknap Press of Harvard University, 1980.

**Grant Eldridge**, freelance writer, Pontiac, Michigan

# Shaw, Anna Howard (1847–1919)

*American social reformer, physician, and Methodist cleric whose lecture tours did much to promote women's suffrage throughout the U.S. Born Anna Howard Shaw on February 14, 1847, in Newcastle-upon-Tyne, England; died on July 2, 1919, of pneumonia at her home in Moylan, Pennsylvania; daughter of Thomas Shaw and Nicolas (Stott) Shaw; attended high school in Big Rapids, Michigan; attended Albion College, Michigan, from fall of 1873 until 1876; graduated with a degree in divinity from the School of Theology, Boston University, 1878; Boston University, M.D., 1886.*

*Licensed to preach in the Methodist Episcopal Church (1871); became minister of the Wesleyan Methodist Church in East Dennis, Massachusetts (1878); ordained a clergywoman in the Methodist Protestant Church (1880); resigned pastorate (1885) to become, first, a freelance lecturer for suffrage and then a national lecturer for the Women's Christian Temperance Union; became vice-president of the National American Woman Suffrage Association (1892) and served as president (1904–15); began tenure as chair of the Woman's Committee of the Council of National Defense (1917); embarked on final lecture tour for the League to Enforce Peace (1919).*

She was only 5' tall and rather stout. Her hair, worn in a pompadour, was prematurely white, but "her black eyes sparkled and her smile won an audience immediately," wrote an admirer in an early edition of the *Dictionary of American Biography*. Anna Howard Shaw was a physician, social reformer, and Methodist cleric who spread the message of suffrage across the United States and won credibility for the movement at a crucial time through her extraordinary public-speaking skills. Shaw gave over 10,000 speeches during her career and was praised by suffragist *Carrie Chapman Catt as "the greatest orator among women the world has ever known." Part of Shaw's success lay in her ability to combine new ideas with old values. She affirmed Christianity, patriotism and motherhood, yet she passionately supported the right of women to vote and to speak from the pulpit and lecture platform. Her entire career was a demonstration that women could be dynamic, forceful speakers and clear thinkers.

Shaw was born on St. Valentine's Day in 1847 in Newcastle-upon-Tyne, England. She was the sixth child of Thomas Shaw and **Nicolas Stott Shaw**. Thomas proudly identified himself as a descendant of the "fighting Shaws of Scot-

land," but turned his own hand to the less rambunctious occupation of painting wallpaper. He has been described by subsequent historians as everything from "irresponsible" to "restless, visionary and idealistic." Never satisfied with life as it was, he was always moving on to another place, hoping it would be better. Thomas moved his family across the Atlantic to Massachusetts and eventually to a log cabin in the Michigan wilderness, 100 miles from the nearest railroad station, while he pursued a variety of impractical business schemes. For Shaw's mother, the move was one last defeating blow, and she suffered a nervous breakdown.

Despite the outrage which Shaw felt at her father's treatment of his family, she inherited a trait of his that would prove invaluable: her life-long conviction that humans could make the world a better place. She recalled that her father had not only given refuge to a runaway slave but enlisted in the army during the Civil War, even though he was too old to be drafted. She also inherited her father's love of reading and an interest in issues that challenged the human mind. "Our modest library . . . contained several histories of Greece and Rome," she writes, "which must have been good ones, for years later, when I entered college, I passed my examination in ancient history with no other preparation than this reading. There were also a few arithmetics and algebras . . . and the inevitable copy of *Uncle Tom's Cabin*, whose pages I had freely moistened with my tears. . . . It soon became known among our neighbors . . . that we had books and that father liked to read aloud, and men walked ten miles or more to spend the night with us and listen to his reading."

Thomas Shaw's long absences from home provided his daughter with confidence to survive extreme physical and psychological hardships. Anna assumed responsibility for the family's well-being by taking over many of the chores normally reserved for the men of the household. She dug the well, collected and carried home the sap, cleared the land, plowed the fields, and assisted in the gathering of the family's food supply. She often helped her younger brother Harry to catch fish: "We had no hooks or lines but Harry took wires from our hoop-skirts and made snares at the ends of poles. My part of this work was to stand on a log and frighten the fish out of their holes by making horrible sounds which I did with impassioned earnestness."

By the time she was 13, Shaw had resolved to follow a path which deviated from the role of wife and mother expected of most women. "For some reason," she writes, "I wanted to preach, to talk to people, to tell them things. Just why, just what I did not yet know—but I had begun to preach in the silent woods, to stand up on stumps and address the unresponsive trees, to feel the stir of aspiration within me." She rejected a proposal of marriage from an awkward young man dressed in a flannel shirt and trousers made of flour-bags, and, after a short time teaching school, moved to Big Rapids, Michigan, to begin high school. She was 23 years old.

> $\mathcal{O}$pponents of woman suffrage are not merely opponents of woman suffrage; they are opponents of democracy.
>
> —Anna Howard Shaw

Her teachers encouraged Shaw to develop her speaking and debating skills; equally important, life in Big Rapids exposed her to two visiting ministers in the Universalist Church, *Mary Livermore and Marianna Thompson. The Universalists, followers of a liberal Protestant tradition similar to Unitarianism, had been ordaining women as ministers for some time. Shaw's motivations in deciding to become a cleric are not entirely clear, but she was impressed by Livermore and Thompson. Hearing of Shaw's interest, a local Methodist leader, Dr. Peck, invited her to preach at a Methodist gathering. It was a compliment to Shaw but also a way to ease the chronic shortage of preachers in a rapidly growing frontier area. She worked for hours preparing the sermon which she delivered before a large audience gathered, in part, to hear a woman preacher. As she started to preach, she trembled so badly that the kerosene in a lamp at her elbow shook in its globe. Though her family strongly denounced her unconventional behavior, Peck was sufficiently impressed to use Shaw to fill local pulpits. In 1871, she was officially licensed as a preacher in the Methodist Episcopal Church.

Encouraged by a high-school counselor, Lucy Foot, Shaw entered Albion College in the fall of 1873. While there, she was able to support herself by preaching in neighboring towns and by lecturing on behalf of the temperance campaign, a movement which advocated restrictions on the sale and consumption of alcohol. These engagements taught her a great deal about the difficult and unexpected situations which crop up on the lecture circuit, particularly for a woman. She describes in vivid detail one occasion on which she was scheduled to preach at a lumber camp. After vainly trying to find some means of regular transportation, she reluctantly accepted a ride in a two-seated wagon with a rather suspicious looking driver. On an impulse, she had packed a revolver in her bag, and it was this impulse which saved her life. During the long overnight journey through a dense forest, Shaw's worst fears were confirmed. Her driver had no intention of delivering her to her destination but instead planned to keep her captive in the wilderness.

> I felt my hair rise on my scalp with the horror of the moment, which seemed worse than any nightmare a woman could experience. But the man was conquered by the knowledge of the willing, waiting weapon just behind him. He laid his whip savagely on the backs of the horses and they responded with a leap which almost knocked me out of the wagon. . . . That morning I preached in my friend's pulpit as I had promised to do, and the rough building was packed to its doors with lumbermen. . . . My driver of the night before, who was one of their number, had told his pals of his experience, and the whole camp had poured into town to see the woman minister who carried a revolver.

In February 1876, Shaw pressed on with her plans to become a minister by entering the School of Theology at Boston University. She later described the decision as "stepping off a solid plank and into space." Not only was she one of the first women to attend the university, but her selection of the divinity program made her even more of a curiosity. Shaw was subjected to discriminatory remarks by faculty members who opposed the opening of the school to women. Though she also experienced some hostility from fellow students, she does not dwell on these incidents in her autobiography. Readers get the impression that she was more sorely afflicted by institutional policies which either ignored or excluded women. Men were able to take advantage of group food plans and low-cost housing not available to women. Also, the area was glutted with theological students willing to preach in local pulpits. Congregations were reluctant to hire a woman when so many men were competing for available positions. When she did receive an invitation to preach, Shaw was never sure whether she was to be paid for her services in compliments or cash. In the wilderness of Michigan, there had been wolves at the door at night; in Boston, they could be heard even at high noon.

One result of her precarious existence was her inability to climb the three flights of stairs to her classrooms without stopping for rest once or twice. On one of these occasions, she was discovered by a Mrs. Barrett, superintendent of the

*Opposite page*
*A*nna
*H*oward
*S*haw

Women's Foreign Missionary Society which had offices in the same building. Sympathetic to her plight, Barrett arranged for Shaw to receive $3.50 a week from an anonymous benefactor, on condition that she devote herself full-time to completing her theological degree.

Upon graduation from the School of Theology in 1878, Shaw secured a job as the pastor of a Wesleyan Methodist Church in East Dennis, Massachusetts. A year later, in an address entitled "Women in the Ministry," she outlined the basis for her position that God intended women to preach. She pointed out that women such as *Miriam the Prophet and *Deborah the judge had public ministries in ancient Israel. Also, Jesus did not relegate women to inferior positions. In other speeches, she displayed impressive skills as a Biblical scholar, arguing from her knowledge of the Greek language and ancient history that Paul's command that "women keep silent in church" was addressed only to the women of his day who were creating disturbances by interrupting the preacher.

At East Dennis, Shaw carried out a full line of pastoral duties. She visited the sick, conducted funerals and weddings, counseled, preached and took on all the necessary administrative tasks. Yet as she was only licensed and not ordained, she could not administer the Protestant sacraments of baptism and the Lord's Supper to her congregation. Along with **Anna Oliver**, another Boston University graduate, Shaw applied for ordination in the Methodist Episcopal Church in 1880.

As a preliminary step, Shaw and Oliver were examined by a candidate's board and pronounced fit for ordination. When the matter was raised at the New England Conference of the Methodist Episcopal Church, however, the presiding bishop summarily declared that there was no place for women in ministry. Oliver decided to fight the decision but Shaw felt differently, claiming, "I am no better and stronger than a man, and it is all a man can do to fight the world, the flesh and the Devil, without fighting the church as well."

An acquaintance suggested that Shaw take her request to the Methodist Protestant Church, a branch of the Methodist family formed in 1830 by people who wanted a greater role for lay members in the governance of the church. Shaw agreed to this plan and her name was put before the Annual Conference in Tarrytown, New York. The debate which ensued was furious, intense, and at times comical. The leader of the opposition raced up and down the aisle of

the church quoting the Bible to prove his case against women ministers. How could a woman obey her husband and at the same time preach to him? How could a woman minister obey the Bible which says that "an elder shall be the husband of one wife"? Would not a woman become a financial burden on the church if she could not find a congregation to employ her? Despite the heated feelings on both sides, the conference voted by a large majority to ordain Shaw.

The service was set for the evening of October 12, 1880, in this same Tarrytown church. Those who opposed Shaw's ordination took consolation in the fact that a substantial collection would be reaped from the large crowd that would gather that evening. They were not disappointed. The occasion, detailed in Shaw's autobiography as one of great beauty and dignity, was punctuated by a moment of humor when Shaw was asked to promise, as part of her vows, that she would not chew tobacco.

On return to her congregation, Shaw settled once again into the routine of parish life. She found her work challenging and to her liking, but she kept one eye on wider horizons by keeping in touch with friends in Boston. Encouraged by her brother James, who was a physician, she eventually decided to alleviate some of her restless energy by enrolling in a course leading to a medical degree from Boston University. She also worked as a paramedic and social worker in the slums of South Boston. In 1886, Shaw would become one of the first women in the United States to hold both a medical and a theological degree.

Shaw's exposure to the desperate plight of the prostitutes of South Boston, as well as to the interests of her friends, rekindled her desire to become more actively involved in social reform. She made a radical decision in 1885 to resign her pastorate and began a career of lecturing on temperance and suffrage, first in a freelance capacity and then for the Redpath Lecture Bureau. At a revival meeting conducted by evangelist Dwight Moody, Shaw met *Frances Willard who persuaded her to lecture for the Women's Christian Temperance Union and to head their suffrage division. Shaw's career took another turn in 1888 when *Susan B. Anthony heard her preach at the International Council of Women. Two years later, Shaw began lecturing for Anthony's National American Woman Suffrage Association (NAWSA). In 1892, she became vice-president of the organization and served as president from 1904 until 1915.

Shaw became nationally known as a superb speaker, and it was in this role that she made her greatest contribution to the suffrage movement. Since her speeches were almost always extemporaneous, historians have been forced to reconstruct most of them from newspaper accounts and notes taken by those in her audiences. Her speaking style was dynamic, animated, and enthusiastic. She conveyed her points in a plain, direct manner complemented by an array of humorous and stimulating anecdotes. She had unusual physical stamina which she attributed to her battle to survive in the Michigan wilderness. Her autobiography describes all-night journeys through blizzards to get to lectures and one attempt to silence her by burning down the hall in which she was speaking. Above all, as a speaker Shaw never lost sight of the cherished beliefs and values of her audiences as she crisscrossed the country.

The empathy which Shaw established with her listeners was based on her sensitivity to their religious and patriotic sentiments. Unlike many other suffrage leaders who were outspoken in their opposition to Christianity, Shaw based her entire argument for suffrage on Christian principles, albeit liberal ones. She claimed that God was an active force in human civilization, leading nations through a process of evolution which would, one day, result in the establishment of God's kingdom on earth. America had reached a high level in this process with its democratic form of government, but a troublesome inconsistency persisted. America was not a true republic because women could not vote. It was instead an oligarchy based on sex which was a violation of God's will for the nation.

In keeping with 19th-century stereotypes about the nature of women, Shaw also argued that women should vote because the voice of God could be heard particularly in their abundant moral visions. America would be improved by women's political participation because women were more peace-loving and were more willing to devote themselves to lives of service in order to create a moral and just society. And Shaw made it plain to her listeners that the Bible affirmed such activities.

Shaw's leadership as president of NAWSA was a matter of some controversy and several attempts were made to oust her from the office. To her credit, she presided over a period of growth in the organization's budget and membership, and she did much to build up local groups. She had little aptitude, however, for administrative work and inherited a poorly coordinated organization which even lacked a national headquarters until 1909. Also, Shaw found it difficult to deal with the militant tactics of the next generation of suffragists. In 1915, she resigned her position, though she continued to lecture for NAWSA until she was persuaded to chair the Woman's Committee of the Council of National Defense in 1917. This was a body established to coordinate the war efforts of American women during World War I. Shaw supported the war only reluctantly, and she used her position to underscore her belief that the ballot for women would mean fewer violent conflicts. Women, in her view, were especially sensitive to the costs of war. Her management of the Woman's Committee was effective, and in May 1919 she received the nation's Distinguished Service Medal.

Shaw's pacifist tendencies led her in 1918 to join the League to Enforce Peace, and, the following year, she agreed to accompany ex-president William Howard Taft on a lecture tour in May and June to advocate the League of Nations. She lectured as many as five times a day and the grueling schedule finally took its toll. Anna Howard Shaw collapsed in Springfield, Illinois, and died of pneumonia several weeks later at her home in Pennsylvania.

**SOURCES AND SUGGESTED READING:**

Brown, Earl Kent. "Archetypes and Stereotypes: Church Women in the Nineteenth Century," in *Religion in Life*. Vol. 43. Autumn 1974, pp. 325–336.

Linkugel, Wil A., and Martha Solomon. *Anna Howard Shaw: Suffrage Orator and Social Reformer*. Great American Orators, no. 10. Westport, CT: Greenwood Press, 1991.

McGovern, James R. "Anna Howard Shaw: New Approaches to Feminism," in *Journal of Social History*. Vol. 3. Winter 1969–70, pp. 135–153.

Pellauer, Mary D. *Toward a Tradition of Feminist Theology: The Religious and Social Thought of *Elizabeth Cady Stanton, Susan B. Anthony and Anna Howard Shaw*. NY: Carlson, 1991.

Shaw, Anna Howard. *The Story of a Pioneer*. NY: Harper & Brothers, 1915.

Spencer, Ralph W. "Anna Howard Shaw," in *Methodist History*. Vol. 13, 1974–75, pp. 33–51.

Stanton, Elizabeth Cady, Susan B. Anthony, *Matilda Joslyn Gage, and *Ida Husted Harper, eds. *History of Woman Suffrage*. 6 vols. NY: Fowler and Wells, 1881–1922.

**COLLECTIONS:**

Correspondence in the Schlesinger Library, Radcliffe College, Cambridge, Massachusetts.

**Barbara J. MacHaffie**,
Associate Professor of History and Religion,
Marietta College, Marietta, Ohio

## Shaw, Elizabeth (fl. 1500s)

*Mistress of James V. Flourished in the 1500s; mistress of James V (1512–1542), king of Scotland (r. 1513–1542); children: (with James V) James Stewart (b. around 1529), abbot of Kelso and Melrose.*

## Shaw, Elizabeth (1920–1992)

*Irish illustrator, cartoonist, travel writer, author, and autobiographer. Name variations: Elizabeth Shaw-Graetz. Born in Belfast, Northern Ireland, in 1920; died in 1992; married Rene Graetz, in 1946.*

Born in Belfast, Northern Ireland, in 1920, Elizabeth Shaw attended the Chelsea Art School in London, England, where her teachers included Henry Moore and Graham Sutherland. During World War II, she distinguished herself as an illustrator and cartoonist, contributing to such publications as *Our Time* and *Lilliput*. After moving to Germany in 1946, Shaw married Swiss-born Rene Graetz. They learned German and sought to establish a Communist society in Berlin. Shaw and Graetz attended the founding meetings of the United Nations Educational, Scientific, and Cultural Organization (UNESCO) in Paris, France. During the McCarthy era of virulent anti-Communism in mid-1950s America, their friends included a number of American and British dissidents.

Although establishing her reputation with caricatures of East Berlin's intelligentsia, Shaw devoted two decades to collaborating with **Bertha Waterstradt** on the production of *Das Magazin*, which published the work of women writers and artists. During this time, she also wrote and illustrated children's books, earning international acclaim for her illustrations for a collection of Bertolt Brecht's verse for children. Shaw's career included exhibitions of her work by the British Arts Council in Coventry and in Belfast, and receipt of the *Kathe Kollwitz Prize in 1981. Later, Shaw parlayed her many journeys, especially throughout Ireland, into several travel books. She completed her autobiography, *Irish Berlin*, which was published in German in 1990. She died two years later.

**SOURCES:**

Newman, Kate, comp. *Dictionary of Ulster Biography*. Belfast: Queen's University of Belfast, 1993.

**Grant Eldridge**, freelance writer,
Pontiac, Michigan

## Shaw, Flora (1852–1929)

*British journalist and staunch advocate of imperialism whose articles played a vital role in educating both the public and politicians about the British Empire. Name variations: Lady Lugard; Dame Flora Shaw. Born Flora Louise Shaw in December 1852 in Kimmage, Ireland; died in Abinger, England, on January 25, 1929; daughter of George Shaw (a general) and Marie (de Fontaine) Shaw; married Sir Frederick Lugard, on June 11, 1902.*

*Wrote children's books in effort to support herself and siblings (1874–85); published* Castle Blair *(1877); began writing short stories and articles for a variety of journals and newspapers; developed attitudes about imperialism while researching unfinished history of England; became colonial editor for* The Times *(1893); implicated in scandal over Jameson Raid (1895); was joint founder of War Refugee Committee during World War I; made Dame of the British Empire (1918).*

*Selected publications:* Castle Blair *(1877);* Hector *(1883);* A Sea Change *(1885);* Colonial Chiswick's Campaign *(1886);* The Story of Australia *(1898);* A Tropical Dependency *(1905).*

The last two decades of the 19th century saw a voracious European declaration of formal empire around the world. In 1885, at the height of the so-called Colonial Scramble, the European powers involved convened the Congress of Berlin in order to set ground rules and legitimize their conquest of the rest of the globe. By 1889,

Flora
Shaw

European concern about the continuation of the slave trade in the newly acquired African colonies peaked and led to calls for a new international meeting to draft plans to make good on earlier promises to eradicate slavery. The Brussels Conference, convened in November 1889, primarily concerned itself with enforcing the superficial anti-slavery statements made by participants at the earlier Berlin Congress and attempted to create a concrete and detailed program to eliminate the slave trade in the African interior. Public interest in the Brussels meeting was particularly high, leading to heavy coverage by the European press. Among the crowd of journalists covering the Brussels Conference was a lone woman, Flora Shaw, who was soon to become a potent and learned force in imperial politics.

Even as a child Flora Shaw was no stranger to imperialism. Her grandfather, Sir Frederick Shaw, was a prominent figure in Irish politics and represented Dublin in the British Parliament. Flora's father George Shaw, a second son who stood to inherit neither wealth nor title, made a career for himself in the army, eventually rising to the rank of general. While serving with the British forces in Mauritius, he met and married **Marie de Fontaine**, the youngest daughter of the last French colonial governor. Marie's already precarious health was further weakened when she had 14 children in quick succession. Her third child, born in December 1852, was christened Flora Louise after Marie's mother.

Each year, from May to October, the Shaw children lived at their grandfather's estate at Kimmage, near Dublin. On these visits, Sir Frederick instilled in his grandchildren the sense of duty and responsibility inherent in noblesse oblige. In 1861, when Flora was nine years old, her father was promoted and made commandant of the army garrison at Woolwich, outside of London. Along with a spacious new house, the commandant and his children had access to the soldiers' extensive library. Flora quickly availed herself of the opportunity to supplement the meager education which, in true Victorian fashion, she and her sisters received at home under the tutelage of their mother and governess.

Within a few years of the move to Woolwich, her mother had become an invalid requiring constant care, a task which fell to Flora and her older sister **Mimi Shaw**. Increasingly burdened with maintaining the household and caring for the growing brood of children, the young Flora soon fell ill and was sent to France to recuperate with relatives. Returning in 1869, having perfected her French while abroad, Flora entered her first season as a debutante. This exposure to the balls and parties hosted by her upper-class neighbors proved to be short-lived. When Mimi married and left home the following year, the entire burden of educating and caring for ten younger siblings, as well as nursing her invalid mother, was passed on to Flora. The constant heavy lifting and strenuous exercise involved resulted in a permanent spinal injury which was to cause years of pain later in her life.

Deprived of maternal advice after Marie's death in late autumn of 1870, Shaw was continually forced to stretch her resources in order to maintain the household on the fixed allowance that her father provided. Her own financial difficulties soon led her to explore ways in which she could help her poorer neighbors, most of whom worked in a nearby carriage factory. Shaw's solution to their mutual difficulties was to open a co-op which bought and sold goods at greatly reduced prices. Her household duties and management of the co-op continued until her father remarried in August 1872, finally freeing her to visit friends and rediscover the joys of European travel.

When her sister Mimi's husband went bankrupt two years later, Flora, anxious to help, began thinking about writing for a living. Encouraged by the author John Ruskin, whom she had befriended just prior to her mother's death, Shaw began working on a series of children's stories. Her first effort, the semi-autobiographical *Castle Blair* (1877), received universally favorable reviews. Although it was popular enough to go through eight editions, Shaw made little money from this novel since her inexperience led her to sign a bad contract and surrender her copyright for a pittance. Shaw's newfound notoriety soon led, however, to an invitation to write for *Aunt Judy's Magazine* (established by *Margaret Gatty) where, over the next several years, she published an increasing number of short stories and longer serialized pieces. Some of these works were later reissued as novels, providing her with the opportunity to hone her writing skills and supplement the small allowance which she received from her father.

In 1881, Shaw took over housekeeping duties for her friend Colonel Charles Brackenbury and his wife at their home in Waltham Abbey. While living with the Brackenburys, she met a social worker who exposed her to the problems of urban poverty and prostitution which plagued Victorian England. Like many other women of her day, Shaw was appalled by the plight of the poor and resolved to make a differ-

ence. By the spring of 1883, however, she felt compelled to withdraw from established social-reform campaigns since she lacked the necessary religious convictions. Convinced that her time was better spent influencing popular opinion and educating the general public about the plight of urban workers, Flora zealously resumed her literary career.

While vacationing with friends in Surrey during the spring of 1883, the 31-year-old Shaw fell in love with the surrounding countryside and rented several rooms in the town of Abinger. She quickly established a close friendship with her neighbor, George Meredith, who introduced her to a wider literary circle which included Robert Louis Stevenson. While in Abinger, she continued to write short stories and began extensive research for a planned history of England from *Elizabeth I through the reign of *Victoria. As a result, Shaw became transformed into an ardent and enthusiastic supporter of the British Empire and its potential future. At the same time, however, she came to fear the inevitable decline of empires predicted by historian Edward Gibbon and worried that the slums and urban decay that had arisen as the result of the industrial revolution were the early signs of this decline. Shaw concluded that the only solution was continued imperial expansion which would both renew the imperial economy and relieve congestion at home by fostering emigration. Her enthusiasm for imperialism soon superseded her interest in both history and social reform, leading her to read everything pertaining to the colonies that she could lay her hands on.

> *S*he has got imperialism in place of ordinary human feelings or religion or sympathy or chivalry.
>
> —*Mary Kingsley

Eager to see some of the areas which she had been reading about, Shaw traveled with friends to the British possession of Gibraltar in the fall of 1886. Knowing that her finances would be strained by the trip, George Meredith introduced her to the editor of the prestigious *Pall Mall Gazette* who offered her the chance to submit freelance articles for publication. Instead of producing typical travel essays, Shaw conducted extensive interviews with Zebehr Pasha, a Sudanese political figure and slave trader who had been imprisoned in Gibraltar by the British after the death of General Charles George Gordon. Her articles, which were sympathetic to Zebehr's cause and his demands for a trial to determine his status, were published to great public acclaim in June 1887. Shaw followed these with a longer and fuller account of Zebehr's life which was published in the *Contemporary Review* later that fall. Before the last segment appeared, Zebehr Pasha was released and sent to Cairo, a fact which he later attributed to her intervention. Shaw had found her vocation and spent the next 15 years as an increasingly powerful, popular and influential journalist.

While in Gibraltar, Shaw also traveled to Morocco and began studying its politics and history. Although mostly interested in the need for reforms and the elimination from European consulates of corrupt officials who sold their protection to native merchants, Shaw quickly became an expert in the political intricacies created by the European colonial presence. When rumors of the sultan's death surfaced in the fall of 1887, the British public's interest in the Moroccan problem was renewed. Shaw cemented her reputation as a journalist by providing a largely ignorant public with detailed and informed accounts of the situation. As the result of her work in Morocco, other newspapers began expressing an interest in hiring her and the editorial board of the *Pall Mall Gazette* asked her to begin submitting book reviews and regular articles for its monthly magazine.

Shaw returned to England the following winter to prepare for a trip to Egypt in the company of longtime family friends. Prior to her departure, she was commissioned by the editor of the *Manchester Guardian* to write regular pieces for his readers. Consequently, when Shaw arrived in Cairo in December 1888, she was a fully accredited reporter for two established and influential British newspapers. In addition to playing tourist and being entertained by a grateful Zebehr Pasha, Shaw also made use of letters of introduction to gain access to people in government and official circles. Not content with this new circle of contacts, Shaw also met and befriended Moberly Bell, the local correspondent for *The Times*, who placed his extensive network of sources at her disposal. She used these contacts to greatly enhance her knowledge of the tense political situation in Egypt, all of which Shaw faithfully transmitted to her readers in England. In the midst of these efforts to improve her journalistic abilities, she also took the time to improve her language skills (which already included fluent French and a working knowledge of Italian and Spanish) by adding Arabic to her repertoire. These skills enhanced her ability to conduct both interviews and primary research in preparation for her many articles on colonialism.

In April 1889, Shaw returned to England and began churning out a series of reviews and daily articles for both the *Pall Mall Gazette* and the *Manchester Guardian*. Building on her reputation as a colonial reporter, she started writing on an even wider variety of subjects ranging from the use of heavy guns by the military to the essays of Ralph Waldo Emerson. Although the topics of her many articles often touched on widely disparate issues, she never wrote an article without first conducting extensive background research. As a result, Shaw soon became a well-known figure at the Colonial Office and was recognized as an authority on colonial and international political problems.

Professional recognition of her abilities and connections soon followed. In November 1889, Shaw was sent by the *Manchester Guardian* to cover the Brussels Anti-Slavery Conference. She was quite pleased by this public acknowledgement of her work and worth, an extremely rare occurrence for Victorian women. Due to her growing stature both as a journalist and a colonial expert, she was increasingly drawn into official social circles where she met such figures as Rudyard Kipling and befriended both Sir George Goldie and Cecil Rhodes.

When the Brussels Conference ended, Shaw returned to Abinger in time for Christmas. Already tired from overwork and her ever-present spinal problems, she soon began facing financial difficulties when she agreed to pay her sister **Alice**'s art school tuition. Shortly thereafter, Mimi and her children returned from France and moved in with Flora, placing an even greater strain on the latter's meager financial resources. The final straw came in early February when her old friend Charles Brackenbury became ill and came to Abinger to be nursed back to health. Shaw was devastated when he died later that spring.

Characteristically, it took the prospect of new work to take her mind off these problems. In March 1890, Moberly Bell left Egypt to take over as assistant manager of *The Times*. After being approached for advice on how to revive the flagging reputation of the newspaper, Shaw urged Bell to begin publishing regular articles on colonial subjects. He agreed and offered her the chance to join the regular staff of *The Times*. This new position not only meant more money and prestige, it also provided Shaw with the opportunity to reach and educate a larger and more influential audience about the benefits of empire.

By the end of 1891, however, the combination of too many commitments and a long illness forced Shaw to relinquish her position on the permanent staff of the *Manchester Guardian*. Her doctors insisted that her convalescence, which was already slowed by her exhaustion from overwork, could only be completed by a long vacation, something which Shaw's altered finances could ill afford. Convinced that she would be an even more valuable colonial reporter after acquiring firsthand experience with the empire, Moberly Bell proposed a solution to her financial dilemma and offered to send her on a working holiday to South Africa as special correspondent for *The Times*. Shaw gratefully accepted Bell's offer and left for Cape Town in April 1892, traveling without maid or companion to lend her countenance. While in South Africa, she traveled extensively in the interior and began immersing herself in the intricacies of Anglo-Boer politics and disputes. Convinced that the future of South Africa lay in cooperation between the Boers, who were descendants of Dutch setters, and the newly arrived British immigrants, Shaw began publicly advocating conciliatory measures on both sides. Her increasingly vocal calls for Anglo-Boer cooperation soon led her into renewed contact with Cecil Rhodes, who was then prime minister of Cape Colony. Impressed by his ideas about colonial development and his vision of Africa, Shaw soon became one of Rhodes' most enthusiastic supporters both privately and in print.

Flora's published letters from South Africa were so popular with *The Times*' readers that Bell asked her to continue her duties as special correspondent in Australia. Before leaving the Cape, Shaw set up a series of local contacts, a process which she repeated everywhere that she traveled, thereby enabling her to remain well informed about colonial affairs even after her eventual return to London. On arrival in Australia, she quickly plunged into the intricacies of antipodean politics and economics for the benefit of her readers in the metropole. The continued popularity of Shaw's articles and letters in *The Times* soon led to new orders to return home by way of Canada where she was to continue gathering information and establishing contacts for later use in her work. As Bell had hoped, on her return to England in June 1893 Shaw was able to use the extensive firsthand experience with the empire acquired on her world travels to inject new life and detail into her many colonial articles, to the delight of both her readers and her editors.

While in Australia, Shaw had learned of her father's death. Since none of the Shaw children had a good relationship with their stepmother, Flora resolved to secure her sisters' independence by supporting them financially after her return to England. For the next eight years,

Shaw was to share her home with her sisters Alice, **Marie** and **Lulu**. As if this were not enough for her already overburdened finances, Flora also periodically supported her sisters Mimi, **Thomasina** and their children. As her financial burdens increased, Shaw requested and received a raise from *The Times* on condition that she cease her work for other newspapers. Along with her raise, she was given new responsibilities and was made colonial editor, a position she was to hold for the next seven years. As colonial editor, she appointed all correspondents, organized their work, wrote lead articles for the paper, and controlled some of the flow of information on which politicians and other public figures based their decisions about matters of imperial policy.

Throughout the winter of 1894, Shaw wrote consistently sympathetic articles in support of Rhodes and the British settlers in the autonomous Boer Republics who were agitating for full political rights. The Jameson Raid in December 1895 almost proved her undoing. L.S. Jameson, a close friend and associate of Rhodes, had simply tired of waiting for a planned uprising of British settlers against the Boers and acted on his own. When news of the raid reached her in London, Shaw printed a forged telegram sent to her by contacts in Johannesburg which made it appear as if Jameson and his invaders had been invited into the Transvaal to protect revolting British settlers. When the full details about the Raid became known, both Shaw's reputation and that of *The Times* were in jeopardy. Because she had printed the forged telegram, which was used in good faith to justify the Raid, and had been in close contact with both Rhodes and Joseph Chamberlain, the British colonial secretary, many imperial critics thought that Shaw was the go-between in a Colonial Office plot to engineer an incident which would result in full-scale British intervention. Moreover, since Shaw was a prominent member of *The Times*' staff, the newspaper's credibility as an impartial reporter of events was also called into question. Early efforts at damage control proved futile. Against Shaw's advice, Rhodes refused to reveal the extent of his role in the Raid and was eventually called to London to testify before a Parliamentary Committee investigating the situation in South Africa. Shaw herself was twice called to testify before the committee. Each time, she was careful to say that she had acted as a private citizen when encouraging Rhodes' ventures and steadfastly refused to implicate *The Times* in the Raid. In the end, the investigating committee was forced to reluctantly accept Shaw's explanation that her contacts with Rhodes and Chamberlain were merely part of her job as a journalist rather than evidence of participation in a sinister government plot. Shaw's testimony went a long way toward restoring her damaged reputation and many later congratulated her for her calm, cool performance on the stand.

Shaw emerged from the enquiry exhausted and soon returned to work in order to forget the whole ordeal. The discovery of gold in the Klondike in 1898 renewed British interest in Canada. Consequently, she was sent to the Yukon by *The Times* to record her impressions of the goldfields. What she found was a near total lack of sanitation, high mortality, rampant disease and corrupt local officials, all of which she dutifully reported to her readers. When her account finally appeared in the Canadian press, it caused an uproar and led to a full-scale government investigation. Once public scrutiny of the Klondike goldfields had begun, Shaw moved on and traveled throughout the rest of Canada, greatly increasing her knowledge of Canadian politics and history.

By mid-November 1898, she was back at work in London. In addition to her regular articles in *The Times*, which increasingly focused on the events leading to the 1899 outbreak of the Boer War, Shaw published *The Story of Australia*. In the spring of 1899, she also wrote and edited the articles on imperialism for the new edition of the *Encyclopedia Britannica* which was being sponsored by *The Times*. These articles were followed in early 1900 by several introductory chapters which she wrote for *The Times History of the South African War*. Despite Shaw's seeming success, the turn of the century found her increasingly unhappy with both her private life and her position at *The Times*. According to some biographers, Shaw had fallen in love with Sir George Goldie several years previously. When he failed to propose after the death of his first wife, she was devastated and reportedly suffered a nervous breakdown. Her relationship with her chief editor, who had never forgiven her for compromising the reputation of *The Times* during the Jameson Raid scandal, had become equally problematic. On the advice of her doctors, who worried that her health might be immutably ruined unless she avoided further stress, the 48-year-old Shaw resigned from the permanent staff of *The Times* in early September 1900.

Shaw's retirement, which proved to be short lived, was marked by a steady stream of visitors to her home in Abinger. Among them was Sir Frederick Lugard whom she had first met in 1893 when she reviewed one of his books for *The Times*. Shaw soon discovered that they had a great deal in common and maintained a regular correspondence with him over the ensuing years. Their friendship took on new depths when Lugard, home on extended leave in 1901 from his post as governor of Northern Nigeria, asked Shaw to marry him in Madeira the following spring. After announcing their engagement, Flora, who had become increasingly concerned and upset about the continuation of the Boer War and the atrocities committed by both sides, decided to travel to South Africa in order to gain firsthand knowledge of events. Recommissioned as a special correspondent for *The Times*, she set sail for South Africa in early December 1901, accompanied for the first time by a maid as a concession to her future husband. As always, her detailed accounts of events in war-torn South Africa were eagerly awaited by a British public hungry for news.

Shaw returned to England in March 1902 to begin preparing for her wedding. Within a few months, she set sail for Madeira in order to await Lugard's arrival. They were married on June 11 and after a brief honeymoon set out for Nigeria where Flora spent most of her time reading and entertaining. Shortly after her arrival at her husband's post, Shaw contracted a severe case of malaria and was forced to return to England by the end of the year. Although she periodically considered rejoining Lugard in Africa, her health never improved enough to make that possible. Instead, she busied herself with her first social season as Lady Lugard and began writing a history of Nigeria from antiquity through the period of British administration. Published in 1905, the extensively researched and erudite *A Tropical Dependency* was well received by critics who hailed it as the definitive work on British policy in Nigeria.

Sir Frederick returned to England on leave in May 1905. Although she was very proud of her husband's achievements, Shaw was not above using her own extensive contacts in the Colonial Office to try and influence his career. Despite an earlier favorable response to her suggestion that Lugard be given six months of leave for each six-month period that he spent in Nigeria, when Lord Elgin took over the Colonial Office in 1906 he flatly refused to sanction such an arrangement. Upset by the prospect of another separation and worried about his wife's health, Sir Frederick resigned from his post and briefly retired to Abinger in September 1906. This arrangement was not to last since he was simply too good an administrator to keep at home. Although his primary interest was in Africa, Lugard readily accepted the governorship of Hong Kong which the Colonial Office offered him in the spring of 1907. Shaw accompanied him to his new post and briefly assumed the duties expected of a governor's wife. The Chinese climate and Shaw's busy schedule, which included endless social functions and language lessons, took an inevitable toll on her health. Over the next several years, she spent more time in England recuperating from operations and recurrent illnesses than she spent in Hong Kong with her husband.

In early 1912, the Colonial Office asked Lugard to return to Africa to oversee the consolidation of Northern and Southern Nigeria under a single governorship, a move which he had long advocated. After consulting with Flora, whose declining health necessitated her permanent relocation to England, he accepted on condition that he be given more frequent leave to spend with his wife in England. Shaw, who maintained homes in both London and Abinger, filled the time between his visits with a growing interest in domestic politics. She was particularly interested in the question of Irish home rule and publicly supported the Ulster Protestants who feared that Irish independence would make them a minority in a united Catholic Ireland. Convinced that civil war was imminent, Shaw began making contingency plans for the evacuation of women and children.

When World War I broke out, Shaw set aside her concerns about Ireland and transformed her plans for evacuating Irish children into a campaign to evacuate Belgian refugees instead. As a founding member of the War Refugee Committee, she was involved in all stages of planning the evacuation, including fundraising, publicity and the arrangement of transportation and accommodation. Although her efforts were very successful, rising tensions stemming from her tendency to bypass official channels forced Shaw to withdraw from the War Refugee Committee's daily operations. Her commitment to the cause did not diminish, however, and she continued to work behind the scenes as a member of the organization's executive committee. When the war finally ended, Shaw turned her attention to arranging the repatriation of refugees who had fled to England. As a reward for her ceaseless wartime efforts, she was created a Dame of the British Empire in 1918.

When Sir Frederick's governorship of united Nigeria expired the following year, the Lugards retired to their home in Abinger. Shaw occupied her time with writing occasional articles for the *Manchester Guardian* and reviews for *The Times Literary Supplement*, and helped her husband with his book *The Dual Mandate*. Her primary occupation, however, was agriculture. When the war broke out, growing food was depicted as an act of patriotism. Shaw took part zealously and soon became an accomplished farmer. In 1921, she started a hamper trade which sold and delivered the produce from her prizewinning farm. Despite its popularity, the hamper trade proved to be an unprofitable business, and within a few years Shaw was forced to divest herself of all but a market garden which she retained until her death.

Although she traveled to Geneva with Sir Frederick for the 1923 League of Nations Mandates Commission, which was to decide the fate of the captured German colonies, by 1925 Shaw's traveling days were over. While eagerly working on several articles with her husband for the *Cambridge History of the British Empire*, Shaw suffered a serious heart attack in September 1927 which left her bedridden for the better part of a year. Her brief recovery after Lugard was made a baron in the 1928 New Year's Honors List proved to be illusory. Within a few weeks, she had suffered a relapse and died peacefully in her sleep on January 25, 1929.

Despite her many unusual accomplishments, Flora Shaw proved unable to escape from typical Victorian notions that women and their contributions were less important than men. Convinced that her own life was unworthy of being recorded, she spent her final days working on a biography of her husband, leaving it to future chroniclers to piece together the enormity of her own impact on British public opinion and imperial affairs.

**SOURCES:**
Bell, E. Moberly. *Flora Shaw (Lady Lugard, DBE)*. London: Constable, 1947.
Callaway, Helen, and Dorothy O. Helly. "Crusader for Empire: Flora Shaw-Lady Lugard," in *Western Women and Imperialism*. Nupur Chaudhuri and Margaret Strobel, eds. Bloomington, IN: Indiana University Press, 1992, pp. 79–97.
Cumpston, Mary. "The Contribution to Ideas of Empire of Flora Shaw, Lady Lugard," in *Australian Journal of Politics and History*. Vol. 1. May 1959, pp. 64–75.
Perham, Margary. *Lugard*. 2 vols. London: Collins, 1956.

**SUGGESTED READING:**
Callaway, Helen. *Gender, Culture and Empire: European Women in Colonial Nigeria*. Bloomington, IN: Indiana University Press, 1991.
Lewis, Jane. *Women in England 1870–1950: Sexual Divisions and Social Change*. Bloomington, IN: Indiana University Press, 1984.
Strobel, Margaret. *European Women and the Second British Empire*. Bloomington, IN: Indiana University Press, 1991.

Trollope, Joanna. *Britannia's Daughters: Women of the British Empire*. London: Hutchinson, 1983.

Woods, Oliver, and James Bishop. *The Story of The Times*. London: Michael Joseph, 1983.

**COLLECTIONS:**

Correspondence and papers located in *The Times* Archives, London; Rhodes House Library, Oxford University; Lugard papers, Bodleian Library, Oxford University.

**Kenneth J. Orosz**, Ph.D. Candidate
in European History,
Binghamton University,
Binghamton, New York

# Shaw, Mary G. (1854–1929)

*American actress, lecturer, and women's suffrage leader. Born on January 25, 1854, in Boston, Massachusetts; died of heart disease in New York City on May 18, 1929; daughter of Levi W. Shaw (a carpenter and builder) and Margaret (Keating) Shaw; graduated from Girls' High and Normal School in Boston, in 1871; married twice; second marriage to the Duc de Brissac (divorced); children: (first marriage) Arthur Shaw (an actor).*

Mary G. Shaw taught in Boston until her voice gave out from overuse in the classroom. She then turned to acting, joining the Boston Museum stock company in 1879. In the 1880s, her dramatic talent attracted the attention of *Helena Modjeska with whom she played for several seasons, and where she attained distinction by the power and intelligence of her acting. Shaw soon became recognized as one of the leading dramatic actresses of her time, and from 1890 to 1910 appeared in many notable New York productions. She was one of the first actresses to present Henrik Ibsen on the American stage, when she created a profound impression with her portrayal of Mrs. Alving in *Ghosts*. Throughout her life, Shaw gave much of her time to the cause of women's suffrage with brilliant lectures throughout the country. In 1909, she had starred in *Elizabeth Robins' play *Votes for Women* at Wallack's Theater in New York. Mary Shaw died in 1929 while on tour with *Eva Le Gallienne's Civic Repertory Company production of *The Cradle Song*.

# Shaw, Nance Langhorne (1879–1964).

See Astor, Nancy Witcher.

# Shaw, Patricia Hearst (b. 1954).

See Hearst, Millicent for sidebar on Patricia Campbell Hearst.

# Shaw, Pauline Agassiz (1841–1917)

*Swiss-American philanthropist and advocate of early childhood education. Born Pauline Agassiz on February 6, 1841, in Neuchâtel, Switzerland; died of bronchial pneumonia on February 10, 1917, in Jamaica Plain, Massachusetts; daughter of Louis Agassiz (the naturalist) and Cécile (Braun) Agassiz; stepdaughter of Elizabeth Cary Agassiz; educated at her stepmother's school for girls in Boston; married Quincy Adams Shaw (a businessman), on November 13, 1860 (died 1908); children: Louis Agassiz; Pauline; Marian; Quincy Adams; Robert Gould.*

The daughter of renowned paleontologist and geologist Louis Agassiz, Pauline Agassiz was born in Neuchâtel, Switzerland, in 1841. Her father traveled to America to lecture at Harvard University in 1846, and he was still there two years later when her German-born mother **Cécile Braun Agassiz** died of tuberculosis. Pauline, as well as her older brother Alexander and older sister **Ida Agassiz**, was looked after by relatives until 1850, when Louis Agassiz married ***Elizabeth Cary Agassiz** and the children traveled to live with them in Cambridge, Massachusetts. The household in which Pauline grew up was frequented by members of Harvard's vibrant intellectual community, and she was educated at the school for girls that Elizabeth Cary Agassiz began running in their home in 1855. Louis Agassiz taught there, as did a number of his fellow professors at Harvard, and the school quickly gained an excellent reputation; among Pauline's classmates was ***Clover Adams**.

At age 19, Pauline married Quincy Adams Shaw, a wealthy Harvard graduate who had traveled through the Rockies with Francis Parkman (her sister Ida married Parkman). Quincy's mining investments with Pauline's brother would soon begin earning him one of the largest fortunes in Boston. This wealth enabled them and their five children to live in great style on an estate in what is now the Jamaica Plain section of Boston, with a view of Jamaica Pond, and allowed Pauline Shaw, long enamored of children's education, to devote herself to philanthropy in that field. Early childhood schooling was then something of a novelty: although the first English-language kindergarten in America had been opened by *Elizabeth Peabody in Boston in 1860 amid some excitement, the idea of such a school had not caught on widely with the general public. With the money to back up her strong belief in the importance of early education, in 1877 Shaw opened two kindergartens in Boston. Within six years she was supporting financially and overseeing the general activities of 31 kindergartens scattered throughout the Boston area, a number of them housed within the public schools. In 1888, 14 of her schools were accepted into Boston's public school system, beginning the city's commitment to public kindergarten.

Involvement with the children of working-class parents had led Shaw to concern for their parents as well. One year after she had begun supporting her first kindergartens, she began organizing day nurseries for working mothers, and by the 1890s these day nurseries were full-fledged community centers. Located in poor areas of the city usually underserved by local government (and in an era all but devoid of public welfare programs), these "neighborhood houses" provided libraries, vocational training, health information, citizenship classes, and recreational facilities. In 1881, she also founded an industrial training school in the North End of Boston where public school children were taught manual arts, which seven years later led to her founding a training school for teachers of manual arts. In all her projects Shaw sought to eliminate racial distinctions and open doors for the poor and for immigrants. In 1901, she founded the Civic Service House in the North End, intended to provide civic training for immigrants. Impressed with the project, Frank Parsons, a Boston University professor, set up a school within the house to teach local workers English, industrial economics, and history. With Shaw's assent and funding, Parsons later organized the Vocation Bureau at the Civic Service House to provide guidance for Boston students considering career options. The Vocational Bureau continued assisting students for years, and also sparked a major educational innovation when the idea was championed by Harvard University's education department and public schools began regularly employing guidance counselors for students.

Shaw became a proponent of women's suffrage around the end of the 19th century, quietly contributing substantial sums to the cause if not actually marching in parades. Believing that achieving the vote would be important not only in itself but as a way to get women involved in civic causes, in 1901 she founded the Boston Equal Suffrage Association for Good Government, serving as its president for the rest of her life. The association's executive secretary, whose tireless lobbying for suffrage she funded, was *Maud Wood Park. She also gave generous amounts to suffrage campaigns both in her home state and in other states, and helped keep afloat the *Woman's Journal*, the weekly suffrage paper published by ✥➤ Alice Stone Blackwell (sister of *Lucy Stone).

The beginning of World War I in 1914 reinforced Shaw's commitment to the cause of world peace, and she remained a staunch supporter of peace and suffrage organizations until her death on February 10, 1917. She had encouraged her children to follow her example of philanthropy, once noting in a letter to them simply, "I had too much." She used much of her wealth to improve the world around her and ameliorate the sufferings of those less fortunate, quietly and without a desire for applause or for the projects she funded to be named after her. In fall 2000, Pauline Agassiz Shaw was inducted into the Women's Hall of Fame in Seneca Falls, New York, as a day-care pioneer.

**SOURCES:**

James, Edward T., ed. *Notable American Women, 1607–1950*. Cambridge, MA: The Belknap Press of Harvard University, 1971.

**Ginger Strand**, Ph.D., New York City

## Shazar, Rachel (1888–1975).

*See Katznelson-Shazar, Rachel.*

# Shearer, Moira (1926—)

*Scottish-born British ballerina whose success as a dancer and actress in films tends to overshadow her achievements in ballet. Name variations: Mrs. Ludovic Kennedy. Born Moira Shearer King on January 17, 1926, in Dunfermline, Fifeshire, Scotland; daughter of Harold Charles King (a civil engineer) and Margaret Crawford (Reid) Shearer; married Ludovic Kennedy (a writer and lecturer), in 1950.*

*Entered the International Ballet Company (1941), and danced as the Fairy of Song Birds in* Aurora's Wedding *and the Guardian Swallow in* Planetomania; *danced with the Vic-Wells Ballet in the Pas de deux in* Orpheus and Eurydice, *and became soloist (1942), dancing such roles as the Serving Maid in* The Gods Go a-Begging, *the Pas de deux in* Les Patineurs, *the Nightingale in* The Birds, *Pride in* The Quest, *Pas de trois and Rendezvous pas de deux in* Promenade *(all 1943), the Polka in* Façade, The Butterfly *in* Le Festin d'araignée, *the Young Girl in* Spectre de la rose, Chiarina *in* Le Carnaval, *and A Lover in* Miracle in the Gorbals *(all 1944), Odile in* Swan Lake, Mlle Théodore *in* The Prospect Before Us, Lover *in* The Wanderer, Countess Kitty *in* Les Sirèns, *and the Dancer in* The Rake's Progress *(all 1945); earned rank of ballerina (1946); appeared on stage and in film (1948–62); retired from dancing (1954), except for a*

**Blackwell, Alice Stone.** *See Stone, Lucy for sidebar.*

*single television appearance in Gillian Lynne's* A Simple Man, *choreographed for the Northern Ballet Theater (1987).*

*Films:* The Red Shoes *(1948);* Tales of Hoffmann *(1951);* The Story of Three Loves *(1953);* The Man Who Loved Redheads *(1954),* Peeping Tom *(1960),* Black Tights *(1962).*

*Stage: appeared as Titania in Shakespeare's* A Midsummer Night's Dream *(Edinburgh Festival, 1954), and as Sally Bowles in Christopher Isherwood's* I Am a Camera *(Bournemouth, 1955); appeared in title role in* Major Barbara *(London, 1956); performed for an entire season with the Bristol Old Vic (1955–56).*

Moira Shearer was born on January 17, 1926, in Dunfermline, Fifeshire, Scotland, the daughter of Harold Charles King, a civil engineer, and **Margaret Reid Shearer**, who had a great love of dance. As a child, she lived in Ndola, Northern Rhodesia, where her father had a position for several years. There, Moira studied dance under **Ethel Lacey**, who had been a pupil of the celebrated Enrico Cecchetti. Shearer became even more connected with the Russian Imperial Ballet tradition after returning to England in 1936, where she continued her ballet training under **Nadine Legat**, and much later took lessons from the legendary *****Tamara Karsavina.**

In 1940, age 14, Shearer was accepted into the ballet school of *****Ninette de Valois** that had been established as a training center for the newly founded Sadler's Wells Ballet. One year later, she became a member of the International Ballet under **Mona Inglesby**, a company noted for its experimental work which introduced ballet into such plays as *Twelfth Night* and *Everyman*. It was with this group that Shearer made her debut at the Alhambra Theater, Glasgow, on May 10, 1941. Her London debut, still with the International Ballet, took place a few months later at the Lyric Theater on August 26. Shearer appeared with the International Ballet as the Fairy of Song Birds in *Aurora's Wedding* and the Guardian Swallow in *Planetomania*, then with the Vic-Wells Ballet in the Pas de deux in *Orpheus and Eurydice*.

In April 1942, Shearer joined the Sadler's Wells Ballet Company where the brilliant choreographer Frederick Ashton was devising new and exciting productions for the company's stars Robert Helpmann and *****Margot Fonteyn.** There Shearer, along with fellow newcomer *****Beryl Grey**, was soon dancing such roles as the Serving Maid in *The Gods Go a-Begging*, the Pas de deux in *Les Patineurs*, the Nightingale in *The Birds*, Pride in *The Quest* (her first critical success), the Pas de trois in *Promenade*, the Rendezvous pas de deux in the same ballet (1943), the Polka in *Façade*, The Butterfly in *Le Festin d'araignée*, the Young Girl in *Spectre de la rose*, Chiarina in *Le Carnaval*, A Lover in *Miracle in the Gorbals* (1944), Odile in *Swan Lake*, Mlle. Théodore in *The Prospect Before Us*, Lover in *The Wanderer*, Countess Kitty in *Les Sirèns*, and the Dancer in *The Rake's Progress* (1945).

Throughout the bombing of London during World War II, the Sadler's Wells Company continued to perform both in London and on tour in the provinces. Beginning in 1943, Ashton began to choreograph for other dancers in the company besides Helpmann and Fonteyn, and it was Grey and Shearer who attracted his attention.

Immediately after Germany's capitulation in 1945, the Sadler's Wells went on tour to France and Belgium and before the end of the year toured Germany, with Shearer dancing her first major roles in *The Nutcracker* and in *Spectre de la Rose*. In February 1946, Covent Garden Opera House reopened, and Sadler's Wells settled there permanently; the following month, Shearer danced her first full-length classical role, as Princess Aurora in *The Sleeping Beauty*. By the end of the 1946 season, still barely 20, she had attained the status of ballerina, was dancing the lead in *Les Sylphides*, and was one of three dancers of that distinction alternating in the starring role of Aurora in *The Sleeping Beauty*.

In 1947, Léonide Massine cast Shearer as the Can-Can dancer opposite him when he staged *La Boutique Fantasque* for the Sadler's Wells, and cast her again for his ballet *Mam'zelle Angot*. The turning point in Shearer's career occurred that year when British film producer J. Arthur Rank offered her the starring role in his Technicolor version of *The Red Shoes*, a story inspired by Hans Christian Andersen's folk tale of enchanted red shoes that drove the wearer to dance until she died. At first, the 22-year-old Shearer was reluctant to do a motion picture, but with the encouragement of de Valois she finally accepted the role. The film was an enormous success wherever it was shown, running for months in New York City, enthralling audiences everywhere, and making Shearer an internationally famous film star before she had reached her peak as a dancer.

An astonishing beauty with rich red hair, blue eyes, a lovely face, a slight but perfect figure, and a delicate manner, Shearer was the first and only ballerina to become a movie star. While ballets had been previously filmed and other

Moira
Shearer

dancers had appeared in movies before (most notably *Vera Zorina), she paved the way for other ballet performers (*Zizi Jeanmaire, Collette Marchand, Rudolph Nureyev, Mikhail Baryshnikov) to extend their careers by pursuing acting parts on the screen. Despite her initial success, however, Shearer's films were limited in number. Apart from *The Red Shoes* (1948), they include *Tales of Hoffmann* (1951), *The Story of Three Loves* (1953), *The Man Who Loved Redheads* (1954), the controversial *Peeping Tom* (1960), and *Black Tights* (1962).

Shearer soon found that her success in *The Red Shoes* caused problems with her peers and dance critics who suggested that she was no longer serious about her work in ballet. Stung by the criticism, she always maintained that she had gone into *The Red Shoes* under pressure and that she fully preferred dancing to screen acting. Fortunately, she was able to follow her success on the screen by dancing the title role in *Giselle* at the Edinburgh Festival (1948), a performance that was a great success.

> [T]he recognition that Shearer was somehow "unclassifiable" . . . goes far to explain her undiminished appeal across the decades.
>
> —Adrienne McLean

The tearing of a ligament by Margot Fonteyn on the opening night of Ashton's *Don Juan* in 1948 caused the part to be given to someone else, but when the new full-length Ashton ballet *Cinderella* opened on Christmas Eve, the title role intended for Fonteyn was given to Shearer. Critics soon regarded her as the equal of Fonteyn in the purity of her classic style. That same year, coached by Tamara Karsavina, she made her debut in the title role in *Giselle*.

In October 1949, the Sadler's Wells Ballet made its first appearance at the Metropolitan Opera House in New York, and then toured the eastern United States and Canada with Shearer alternating with Fonteyn in the principal roles. Everywhere she enchanted audiences and won high plaudits from the critics. Upon returning to England in 1950, Shearer married Ludovic Kennedy, a former lieutenant in the Royal Navy, who was by then a college librarian, writer, and lecturer.

In the few years remaining to her dancing career, Shearer appeared at the Metropolitan Opera House again in 1950 and 1954 (the latter followed by a nine-week tour of the United States and Canada), and in between performed in Paris with Roland Petit's Ballets de Paris, dancing the role of Carmen. When Balanchine staged his *Ballet Imperial* for Sadler's Wells in 1950, he is said to have preferred Shearer to Fonteyn in the production.

As a dancer, Shearer was noted for her technical brilliance, her keen intelligence, her sharp polish, her grace and charm, her seeming weightlessness on the stage, and for her sheer physical beauty. On the other hand, she was faulted for a certain coldness and reserve in her performance, and there is no question that Fonteyn had a greater emotional depth of the kind necessary to the great classical roles. Never-

theless, Shearer always maintained that her favorite roles were precisely those of the great ballet classics—Giselle, the Young Girl in *Spectre de la Rose*, and the dual role of Odette-Odile in *Swan Lake*—and in time, despite her perceived limitations, she became the only serious rival to Fonteyn on the London ballet scene. The question over which of the two was to be regarded as the greater dancer, however, was not to be resolved; in 1954, still only in her 20s, Shearer retired from dancing. Then, instead of pursuing her film career, she chose to go on the stage. Once again, her appearances were not numerous, and she starred in only a few productions: as Titania in Shakespeare's *A Midsummer Night's Dream* (Edinburgh Festival, 1954), as Sally Bowles in Christopher Isherwood's *I Am a Camera* (Bournemouth, 1955), and in the title role in *Major Barbara* by George Bernard Shaw (London, 1956). In 1955, she performed for an entire season with the Bristol Old Vic, the provincial training company for the Old Vic in London, appearing most notably as Ondine in the play of that name. In 1956, barely 30, Shearer gave up her performing career to devote herself to her family and private life save for the two films in the early 1960s and a single television appearance dancing in **Gillian Lynne**'s *A Simple Man* choreographed for the Northern Ballet Theater in 1987.

In her later years, Shearer became a member of the General Advisory Council of the British Broadcasting Corporation (BBC) and in the 1970s served as director of Border Television. In 1986, she published a book on George Balanchine. Despite the brevity of her career, Shearer has remained a revered figure from the Golden Age of British ballet, and through her films, which preserve the record of her style, she has continued to exert an influence over ballet.

**SOURCES:**
Franks, A.H. *Approach to the Ballet.* New York, 1948.
Gibbons, M. *The Red Shoes Ballet.* New York, 1948.
"Moira Shearer," in *Current Biography.* NY: H.W. Wilson, 1950.
Music Collection, Free Library of Philadelphia.

**SUGGESTED READING:**
Clarke, Mary. *The Sadler's Wells Ballet.* London, 1955.
Shearer, Moira. *Balletmaster: A Dancer's View of George Balanchine.* London, 1986.
Vaughn, David. *Frederick Ashton and his Ballets.* New York, 1977.

**Robert H. Hewsen**, Professor of History, Rowan University, Glassboro, New Jersey

# Shearer, Norma (1900–1983)

*Canadian-born actress who was one of the major stars of 1930s Hollywood. Born Edith Norma Shearer*

*on August 10, 1900, in Montreal, Canada; died at the Motion Picture Country Home on June 12, 1983; daughter of Andrew Shearer and Edith Mary (Fisher) Shearer; educated in the public schools of Montreal; married Irving G. Thalberg (the film producer), in 1928 (died 1936); married Martin Arrouge (a ski instructor), in 1942 (died August 8, 1999); children: (first marriage) Irving Thalberg; **Katharine Thalberg**.*

*Selected filmography:* The Flapper *(1920);* The Restless Sex *(1920);* Way Down East *(1920);* The Stealers *(1920);* The Sign on the Door *(1921);* Channing of the Northwest *(1922);* The Bootleggers *(1922);* The Man Who Paid *(1922);* The Devil's Partner *(1923);* A Clouded Name *(1923);* The Wanters *(1923);* Pleasure Mad *(1923);* Lucretia Lombard *(1923);* Man and Wife *(1923);* Broadway after Dark *(1924);* Trail of the Law *(1924);* Blue Water *(1924);* The Wolf Man *(1924);* Empty Hands *(1924);* Broken Barriers *(1924);* He Who Gets Slapped *(1924);* The Snob *(1924);* Married Flirts *(1924);* Lady of the Night *(1925);* Waking Up the Town *(1925);* Pretty Ladies *(1925);* A Slave of Fashion *(1925);* Excuse Me *(1925);* The Tower of Lies *(1925);* His Secretary *(1925);* The Devil's Circus *(1926);* The Waning Sex *(1926);* Upstage *(1926);* The Demi-Bride *(1927);* After Midnight *(1927);* The Student Prince *(1927);* The Latest From Paris *(1928);* The Actress *(1928);* A Lady of Chance *(1928);* The Trial of Mary Dugan *(1929);* The Last of Mrs. Cheyney *(1929);* The Hollywood Revue of 1929 *(1929);* Their Own Desire *(1929);* The Divorcee *(1930);* Let Us Be Gay *(1930);* The Stolen Jools *(comedy short, 1931);* Strangers May Kiss *(1931);* A Free Soul *(1931);* Private Lives *(1931);* Strange Interlude *(1932);* Smilin' Through *(1932);* Riptide *(1934);* The Barretts of Wimpole Street *(1934);* Romeo and Juliet *(1936);* Marie Antoinette *(1938);* Idiot's Delight *(1939);* The Women *(1939);* Escape *(1940);* We Were Dancing *(1942);* Her Cardboard Lover *(1942).*

After acquiring the unofficial title of "First lady of MGM" with her marriage to studio head Irving Thalberg in 1928, Norma Shearer reached stardom under her husband's artful supervision. "His handling of her career was a tri-

Norma Shearer

umph," wrote David Shipman. Shearer, who was nominated for five Academy Awards and won the coveted trophy as Best Actress for her performance in *The Divorcee* (1930), continued her reign at MGM for several years after Thalberg's death in 1936.

She was born Edith Norma Shearer in 1900 in Montreal, Canada, the daughter of **Edith Fisher Shearer** and Andrew Shearer, a businessman. Attending public schools in Montreal, she enjoyed skating, swimming, and skiing, and also studied the piano. But when her husband's enterprise failed, Edith packed up her two daughters, Norma and **Athole Shearer**, and took them to New York, hoping to find work for them in show business. After failing an audition with Florenz Ziegfeld, who told her she would never make it because she was too short and had fat legs and a cast in one eye, Shearer modeled and worked as a film extra until she signed on with agent Edward Small; he got her a small role (fourth billing) as a minister's daughter in the silent movie *The Stealers* (1920).

Thalberg, then at Universal (though he would eventually transform MGM), saw her performance and set out to hire the young actress. But the Shearers, unable to find work in Hollywood, had gone back East. It was not until 1923, when he was about to join forces with Louis B. Mayer in the MGM studio, that Thalberg tracked her down. At that time, Shearer signed a five-year contract with the fledgling MGM and embarked on her debut film for that studio, *Pleasure Mad* (1923), which was marketed as "A Story of Today and the Mad Lust for Pleasure among the Bright Lights and Gilded Cafés." Shearer was then loaned out for several pictures before returning to Metro to play Consuelo, the bare-back rider, in *He Who Gets Slapped* (1924), opposite Lon Chaney. By 1925, the actress had made her mark in silent pictures and had also captured the heart of Thalberg, known as "the boy wonder," who began grooming her for stardom.

Shearer was savvy, and might indeed have made it big in the movies without Thalberg's assistance. Although she was not beautiful by Hollywood standards, or the most talented actress available, she was possessed with a driving ambition, great insight into the nature of filmmaking, and a canny ability to see where she fit in. She wisely resisted typecasting, and with Thalberg's help was able to balance her roles, doing both drama and comedy. Her husband was also able to surround her with the best writers, directors, and promoters. After their marriage, Shearer starred in some of MGM's finest movies, including the five for which she received Oscar nominations: *Their Own Desire* (1929), *A Free Soul* (1931), as *\*Elizabeth Barrett Browning* in *The Barretts of Wimpole Street* (1934), as Juliet in *Romeo and Juliet* (1936), and the title role of *\*Marie Antoinette* (1938). Following Thalberg's death in 1936, she played leading roles in two of the studio's best pictures of the decade (both 1939): the movie version of Robert E. Sherwood's Pulitzer Prize-winning *Idiot's Delight*, with Clark Gable, and *\*Clare Booth Luce*'s *The Women*, co-starring *\*Joan Crawford*, *\*Rosalind Russell*, and *\*Joan Fontaine*, among others, and featuring a screenplay by *\*Anita Loos* and *\*Jane Murfin*. Without Thalberg's guidance, however, Shearer turned down the starring roles in *Gone With the Wind* and *Mrs. Miniver*, appearing instead in the back-to-back flops *We Were Dancing* and *Her Cardboard Lover* (both 1940). "On those two, nobody but myself was trying to do me in," she said. In 1942, she married ski instructor Martin Arrouge, 20 years her junior, and retired from the screen. The couple continued to live in the house Shearer had shared with Thalberg until they moved to a new home in West Hollywood in 1960. The actress was blind for many years before her death from bronchial pneumonia in 1983.

**SOURCES:**

Katz, Ephraim. *The Film Encyclopedia*. NY: HarperCollins, 1994.

Lamparski, Richard. *Whatever Became of . . . ?* 1st & 2nd series. NY: Crown, 1967.

Shipman, David. *The Great Movie Stars: The Golden Years*. Boston, MA: Little, Brown, 1995.

**Barbara Morgan**,
Melrose, Massachusetts

# Sheba, Queen of (fl. 10th c. BCE)

*Queen of Axum in Ethiopia and Sheba in southern Arabia who is known in the Jewish, Christian, and Islamic traditions as peer and lover of Solomon, king of Israel, and maternal ancestor of Ethiopia's royal dynasty.* Name variations: Balkama; Balkis, Bilkas, or Bilkis; Balqis or Bilqis; Makeda; Nicaula; Panther in the Blossom; Queen of the South (Eteye of Azeb); Saba, Sabbe, or Seba; Sibyl or Sibylla.

*The earliest mention of the queen comes from the Old Testament where she undertakes a diplomatic trading mission to King Solomon in Israel from the territories she ruled in modern-day Ethiopia and Yemen. From the Biblical source, legends of the queen developed in Jewish, Christian, and Islamic literature. She was said to have been the lover of Solomon, and Ethiopians claim her as the ancestor of their royal line.*

*In the West, she is associated with the legend of the True Cross upon which Jesus was crucified.*

The enigmatic queen of an uncertain land called Sheba is mentioned only twice in the Old Testament. According to I Kings 10 and 2 Chronicles 9, rumors of the wealth and wisdom of Solomon, king of the ancient Hebrews, had reached the distant land of Sheba, and so the queen traveled to Jerusalem to meet him. She arrived in the magnificent capital with "a large retinue of camels laden with spices, gold in great quantities, and precious stones." But interested in more than Solomon's riches, the queen of Sheba was drawn to the king because of his reputation for wisdom. She tested Solomon by posing subtle and puzzling questions; "not one of them was too abstruse for the king to answer." The queen was overawed, "there was no more spirit left in her." She said to Solomon, "Your wisdom and your prosperity go far beyond the report which I had of them. Happy are your wives, happy these courtiers of yours who wait on you every day and hear your wisdom! Blessed be the Lord your God who has delighted in you and set you on the throne of Israel." The two monarchs then exchanged gifts. The queen gave Solomon gold, jewels, spices, and a precious wood called almug. In exchange, "King Solomon gave the queen of Sheba all she desired, whatever she asked, in addition to all that he gave her of his royal bounty." She then departed and returned to her native land.

Although the queen of Sheba disappears from the Biblical narrative at this point, it is by no means the last history hears of her. Legends of this elusive queen developed and flourished in the Jewish, Islamic, and Christian traditions and in the national histories of Africa and Arabia. Yet the historical identity of the queen is a puzzle, and the location of Sheba mentioned in I Kings and 2 Chronicles is uncertain. Sheba, Seba, Saba, and the Sabeans or Sebeans are mentioned in a variety of contexts in the Old Testament which uses variant spellings for what appears to be the same location. The terms are all associated with great wealth and a faraway land; however, the precise location of this territory is not evident from Biblical sources.

There are several men named Sheba mentioned in the Bible who may have been the eponym for the home of the famous queen. Genesis identifies Sheba as a descendant of Noah's son Ham (Gn 10.7), and again in a later verse as the offspring, not of Ham, but of his brother Shem (Gn 10.28). Abraham and his wife *Ketu-

rah also had a grandson named Sheba who was the forefather of a tribe in northern Arabia (Gn 25.3). Another later Sheba, who was a near contemporary of Solomon, led the northern tribes of Israel in rebellion, challenging the suzerainty of David, king of Israel and Solomon's predecessor (I Sm 19–20; 1 Kgs 12).

Of these several choices, the most likely namesake of the queen of Sheba's homeland is the grandson of Noah (through either Ham or Shem) whose descendants, called Sabeans, established themselves as traders in southern Arabia and on the eastern coast of Ethiopia. The Jewish historian Josephus (b. 37/8 CE), although vague on the location of Sheba, confirms its location by placing it roughly in Egypt or Ethiopia. Archaeological research indicates that the Sabeans may have been associated with northern and southern tribes of the Arabian peninsula, occupying the portion of southwest Arabia which is today known as Yemen with a sphere of influence extending to the far north. The Old Testament records several accounts of the Israelites obtaining gold, frankincense, sweet cane, spices, gems, and other precious goods from the Sabeans who acted as middlemen for commercial exchanges between Israel and Africa, India, and lands farther east. The archaeological record supports this view, indicating that the Sabeans excelled in moving trade in precious goods between India, Africa, and the Fertile Crescent. There is other evidence that in the first millennium BCE the Sabeans colonized the adjacent Ethiopian coasts, especially the areas around Eritrea and Tigre which once comprised the kingdom of Axum. For example: (1) Geez, the ancient language of Axum, is related to Semitic languages spoken in Arabia, (2) Judaism flourished in both Ethiopia and southern Arabia in the 10th century BCE, and (3) the Habasha tribe after which Abyssinia (an earlier name for Ethiopia) was named, originated in Yemen. In many respects, then, this area in southern Arabia matches the Biblical description of Sheba, but there are some discrepancies between the archaeological evidence and the written sources. For instance, although the land occupied by the Sabeans was certainly rich enough to satisfy the Biblical description of the land of the queen, it did not attain its wealth until several centuries after Solomon and the queen were reputed to have lived (c. 992–952 BCE).

This queen, who remains mysterious and unnamed in the Bible, is better known from other sources. In southern Arabia and Africa, she is called Bilkis. In the Tigray region of northern Ethiopia, the queen of Sheba is Eteye of

Azeb, or Queen of the South. The Yemenites call her Balkama, and the Quran refers to her as Balkis. Josephus called her Nicaula after Herodotus' reference to the queen widows of Egypt by that name. Throughout Ethiopia, the queen of Sheba is Makeda the Beautiful, Panther in the Blossom.

It is largely the tantalizing suggestion made in the cryptic phrase, "King Solomon gave the Queen of Sheba all she desired," that has given rise to the lore of the queen of Sheba. What was it that the wealthy queen could have wanted from Solomon besides the gifts he had already bestowed? One tradition answers: his love. Snatches of the story of how the queen obtained that love are preserved in textual fragments from Syria, Armenia, Palestine, Egypt, Arabia Felix, and Ethiopia.

The Ethiopian constitution, ratified in 1955, contains an article which enshrines the ancient claim that Makeda is the maternal ancestor of the royal line and that the kings are descendants of Solomon and the queen of Sheba. The Ethiopian tradition alleges that while the queen was in Jerusalem she and Solomon produced an heir, and that the Ethiopian kings up through Haile Selassie descended from Solomon. In the late 13th century (CE), a scribe named Yishak claimed that he and six of his companions had translated into Geez, the ancestral language of Ethiopia, an ancient Arabic text originally written in Coptic (Egyptian). They called the work *Kebre Negast*, or *The Glory of the Kings* (1270). It is a pastiche of local and regional legends and oral traditions inspired by the Old and New Testaments, various apocryphal works, and Jewish and Islamic sources. The intent of the *Kebre Negast* was to set apart the Ethiopians as a chosen people, a new Israel, and to defend the ascendancy of the emperor Yekuno Amlak of the Shoan dynasty who claimed legitimacy because of his Solomonic ancestry. Yekuno Amlak argued successfully that in him the rightful kings, progeny of the queen of Sheba and Solomon, and scions of the root of Jesse, were restored to the Ethiopian throne (1270).

According to the *Kebre Negast*, in the 10th century BCE a powerful queen named Makeda ruled over the prosperous kingdoms of Axum in Ethiopia and Sheba in southern Arabia. (Some versions of the story claim that Sheba or Saba was not in Arabia at all but on the African side of the Red Sea near Axum.) According to the time-honored law of this land, the royal sovereign had to be both female and virgin. Makeda was such a sovereign. She lived in Axum of the Blue Hills and ruled her territory in peace and prosperity. She was young, loved, rich, learned, wise, and beautiful, but not happy. The reason for her discontent was that she had a "hideous deformity." Because her mother saw a prancing goat while pregnant with the queen, Makeda's right foot was hoofed and hairy. The young Makeda chose to remain virgin and to accept the throne rather than marry, thinking that because of her strange foot she would never attract a suitable partner.

Hope of reversing the malformation came to Makeda, however, when her fleet-master returned from a trading voyage and brought her word of the magnificent King Solomon whose wealth was surpassed only by his wisdom. Rumor had it that when Solomon was young his God, Yahweh, agreed to give him what he most desired, and he asked for knowledge. Not only was Solomon learned, but he was skilled in the magic arts and reputed to know the language of birds and animals and to have skill in exorcising evil spirits. The queen of Sheba thought that a man with these talents would be able to transform her abnormal limb to its healthy state. She determined to travel to Jerusalem to test all aspects of her fleet-master's story. She concocted several riddles for Solomon to solve, collected a quantity of precious, marvelous goods she hoped would rival the riches of Solomon, and resolved to seek his aid with her very private problem of the foot. Some versions of the story omit reference to Makeda's strange foot and claim that she, young and inexperienced in ruling, went to Jerusalem expressly to learn the art of statecraft from the king of Israel.

Makeda set out for Jerusalem, stopping on the way at Sheba, the secondary capital of her domain. When she reached Solomon's kingdom, she was greeted with singular honor, partially because of her beauty and wealth, partially because, according to Jewish legend, Moses had ruled over Axum for 40 years after he and his people fled Egypt, and partially because Solomon was fascinated by the stories of her peculiar foot and longed to see it for himself. For this reason, he devised a plan to trick Makeda. He had one of his artisans lay a floor of glass over the marble pavement in the reception room of the palace and ordered that water be pumped in between the marble and the glass accompanied by colored, free-swimming fish so as to create the illusion that the hard surface was a pool of water. When Solomon first granted audience to Makeda, he sat at the far end of his reception room and bade her approach him. To do this, she would have to take off her sandals and walk across what appeared to be the pool of water;

*Evelyn Brent appeared as the Queen of Sheba in a 1928 film.*

and although the queen was hesitant to remove her shoes and reveal her hoofed foot, she hoped that it would be submerged in the water and hidden from sight. She lifted her skirts to keep them dry, stepped out onto the glassed surface, and instinctively, thinking she was stepping into water, leapt onto a piece of timber laying nearby. Just as Makeda was about to cry out in shame because she had unthinkingly exposed her misshapen limb, her right foot was transformed on contact with the wood and became as straight and beautiful as the left. The potent, healing timber upon which she had leapt was a portion of

the Tree of Knowledge from which Adam and *Eve ate the forbidden fruit in the Garden of Eden. Some versions of the story omit the reference to the miraculous wood and claim that Solomon concocted a salve made of lime and arsenic which cured the queen's malady.

The two monarchs found much to admire in each other. Both were young, beautiful, and rich, but more significantly, they suited each other in their cunning. They spent many hours together, each posing riddles for the other. Solomon asked Makeda which is the best, first love or last. The queen correctly answered that the best love is that which is both first and last. She, in turn, tested the king by presenting him with several children all dressed alike and asking him to distinguish the boys from the girls. Solomon threw balls in the air; the boys caught them, the girls stooped to collect the balls from the ground. Solomon had his answer as, according to the king, "Kneeling identifies the female sex." Makeda accompanied Solomon as he adjudicated legal cases in court and marveled at his insight. He educated her on the history of his people and their God. She told him of her land of Axum, founded by the Ethiops in the time of Abraham.

*King Solomon gave the Queen of Sheba all she desired, whatever she asked, in addition to all that he gave her of his royal bounty.*

—1 Kings 10.13

The friendship grew into passion. One night Solomon came to Makeda's quarters, serenaded her, then asked for her love. The queen, despite her desires, replied that the law of Axum and Sheba required that she remain a virgin. Solomon, wily as ever, agreed that he would not press her unless she came willingly into the sleeping chamber which adjoined her own quarters where he would spend the night. Makeda agreed, not knowing that Solomon had instructed his stewards to lace her food with thirst-inducing spices and to empty the jug of water that rested beside her bed. The queen awoke in the night, needing water. Seeing that her jug was empty, she crept into the chamber where Solomon was sleeping in order to drink from the jug by his bed. The king, of course, was not asleep, and when Makeda entered the chamber he arose and held the queen to her promise.

Another version of the story reveals Solomon as even more devious. The king compelled the queen of Sheba to promise that in exchange for her virginity she would vow to take nothing from Jerusalem that belonged to him. Makeda agreed. On the night of the seduction, Solomon fed the queen paprika, onion seed, and garlic so that she would awake in the night parched. While she slept, the king's stewards wrote the words "Property of Solomon" on Makeda's water jug. She woke late at night and gulped down the water by her bed, only to find out too late that she had taken something that belonged to Solomon, and so she was compelled to repay him with the gift of her body.

The queen soon prepared to return to Africa. With her, she took a great deal from the land of Israel. She was pregnant with Solomon's child and laden with riches beyond imagination given to her by the king. Among the treasures was a ring which, according to the Talmud (a Jewish holy book), God originally gave to Adam in Eden. When the first humans were expelled from the Garden, the jewel studded-ring flew from Adam's finger and lodged under one of the pillars of Yahweh's throne until God sent it to Solomon through the Archangel Gabriel. Most significant of all, Makeda had adopted a new deity, Yahweh, the God of Israel. She was determined to supplant the pagan deities of her own territories with the worship of the one God of Israel. The queen of Sheba also promised Solomon that, although their son would not rule Israel after him, he would be the king of Axum and Sheba. She intended to reverse the ancient tradition of her kingdom. It would no longer be governed by virgin-queens, but by kings.

Sheba called her son Menelik (also spelled Menelek, Menilek, or Menyelek), meaning "Other-Self." His state name was Walda-Tabbib (Son of the Wise Man). The boy was not only adored by his mother, but he was accepted by his people. They agreed to alter the time-honored law and be ruled by kings. As for Makeda's other innovations, the people of Axum and Sheba were not so receptive. They did not accept their queen's new God of Israel, and she wisely did not force them, but worshipped Yahweh privately and raised her son to do so.

When Menelik grew to adolescence, his mother decided to send him to Jerusalem to become acquainted with his father and his father's kingdom on the firm condition that he would return to Axum and not be persuaded to remain in Jerusalem and accept the crown of Israel. So that Solomon would recognize his son, Makeda gave him the ring Solomon had given her when she departed Jerusalem. Menelik had heard his father's praises sung by Makeda his entire life, but when he reached Jerusalem the boy found the king of Israel much changed. The energy and keen intellect which had once been his most precious assets had become his bane. After Makeda left Jerusalem, Solomon became bored with his wives, so added hundreds more from pagan lands. In frenetic and meaningless activity, he moved from one building plan to another, consuming his people's taxes to increase the magnificence of his palaces and the magnitude of his foreign conquests. The king had become dissipated and cruel; he neglected those duties in the law courts which once brought him such fame and pleasure, but most shocking of all, Solomon was no longer diligent in his worship of Yahweh.

He slept through morning sacrifice because he was too sodden with wine from the previous night's indulgence. Nevertheless, despite his decline, Solomon was still a remarkable man, and he and his young son spent many pleasurable hours and days together.

After several months, but too soon for his father's liking, Menelik decided it was time to return to his own land. Solomon prepared an elaborate ceremony to publicly proclaim his son king of the Ethiops. The boy was anointed with holy oil and admonished that, as king, he and his people must worship none but Yahweh. When he vowed to obey the God of Israel, however, Menelik had no idea of the turn that promise would take.

Azariah, son of the high priest of Jerusalem, watched the young Ethiopian king with interest. He and the other temple priests had become discouraged and then disgusted with Solomon's indifference toward, and neglect of, his religious obligations. Azariah saw in Menelik a chance to rejuvenate the ancient faith and a king who could honor Yahweh in a manner befitting His glory. He resolved to steal the Ark of the Covenant which contained the stone tablets inscribed with the Ten Commandments that Yahweh had delivered to his people through the patriarch, Moses. The priest's reasoning was that the ark could not be moved unless God gave his blessing to the theft. Azariah would make the effort to remove the ark, and if Yahweh disapproved, He would strike the young priest down; Azariah decided it was worth the risk. He had his artisans fashion a duplicate ark, and the evening before Menelik's departure from Jerusalem, Azariah, during the process of performing sacrifices, had the duplicate ark brought into the Temple and placed where the Ark of the Covenant was kept. "Lady Zion," the genuine ark containing the Ten Commandments, was smuggled out of the Temple and placed with the goods that Menelik was taking with him back to Axum. An Arabic variant of the story claims that it was not the high priest but Menelik himself who stole the ark. In any case, "Lady Zion" and the power of Yahweh left Jerusalem with the young king of the Ethiops, escorted by an entourage of Hebrew priests. Accompanied by the power of the Lord, Menelik and his party traversed the desert at an unprecedented speed and reached Sheba within a few days. They crossed over the Red Sea to Africa, levitated through the air by the power of the ark.

Back in Jerusalem, on the eve of Menelik's departure, Solomon was troubled in his sleep by a dream that the glory of Israel had departed to another land. The vision was confirmed when those temple priests who were not privy to the theft soon discovered the ruse. Solomon assembled his troops and pursued Menelik's party, but was unable to overtake it.

The ark arrived safely in Axum. Makeda was at first scandalized that her son had acquiesced to robbing his father of the God of Israel, but when Menelik explained to her that Solomon had married foreign wives and dabbled in the worship of the pagan gods Bel, Moloch, Sobku and Hathor, the queen of Sheba accepted the ark and resolved that her son would be as a second David and that her land would be as a second Israel, strong and prosperous, righteous in the Lord God of the Hebrews.

A wholly different tradition about the queen of Sheba is recorded in the Islamic holy book, the Quran. According to this story, the queen (Balkis) did not travel to Solomon for a medical cure, riches, or answers to riddles; she was summoned. Solomon, the mighty king of Israel, had the ability to commune with birds and beasts (according to Jewish chronicles this power came to Solomon through his magical ring in which was embedded a mandrake root). The king called before him all those over whom Allah had given him dominion: "jinn [a type of demon] and men and birds" but the king was angry because he saw that the hoopoe bird was absent. The hoopoe soon made his appearance and explained that he had been flying over the width and breadth of the land doing the work of God by seeking to know if there were nations which prospered although they did not worship Allah. He found such a place called Sheba: "I found a woman ruling . . . and she has a mighty throne. I have found her and her people doing obeisance to the sun rather than to Allah. Satan has made their works seem fair to them and has turned them aside from the way and they are not rightly guided."

Solomon immediately sent the hoopoe to Sheba with a letter demanding that the queen surrender herself and her lands to him and to the service of Allah. Hoping to avoid conflict, she sent a gift to Solomon, but the king replied to her messenger, "Will ye add riches to me, though what Allah has given me is better than what he has given you?" He threatened to invade Sheba if the queen herself did not come to him. Balkis obeyed; she prepared to travel to Jerusalem, but Solomon wanted more still. Once again, he gathered his assembled functionaries, asking, "Ye chiefs, which of you can bring me her throne before [she] comes to me in submission?" In this passage, the throne, which is silver and 30 cubits high, symbolizes material wealth and ephemeral, earthly dominion which contrasts adversely to the riches and power possible to those who submit to Allah. Ifrit, an aggressive and crafty jinn, offered to bring the throne of Queen Balkis to Solomon by force, but the wise king favored the plan of one of his scholars who agreed to transfer the throne mystically from Axum to Israel by tapping the spiritual power inherent in the holy book. "Within the twinkling of an eye," it was done.

Balkis traveled to Jerusalem, and on her arrival Solomon asked her to look at the throne which had been lifted from her own land to his in order to see if she would recognize it, although it had been magically transformed. Balkis recognized the throne and understood that Solomon was not only richer than she but surpassed her in wisdom and strength due to the power of his God; because of this she tentatively agreed to convert to Islam. As recorded in the *Kebre Negast*, Balkis was asked to approach the king in the reception room of his palace. She entered, saw the floor which she thought was a lake, lifted her skirts to keep them dry, thus exposing her legs. When Solomon explained that the floor was not water but "smooth with slabs of glass" the queen was ashamed that she had behaved in so undignified a manner and exposed what a lady should keep hidden. Once more Solomon, backed by the power of Allah, had gotten the better of the mighty Balkis who had spent a lifetime devoted to pagan gods. Now her conversion was complete; the queen of Sheba agreed whole-heartedly to "submit, with Solomon, to the Lord of the Worlds."

The legend of the queen of Sheba has also had a long and full life in the Christian tradition. Jesus named her as one of the just who will rise up to condemn unbelievers at the end of time, implicitly identifying himself with Solomon and the Queen of the South with the Church, his beloved spouse: "The Queen of the South will appear at the Judgment when this generation is on trial and ensure its condemnation, for she came from the ends of the earth to hear the wisdom of Solomon" (Mt 12.42 and Lk 11.31). Like in the Quran, the queen willingly submitted to Solomon and his God, and so she is worthy to judge those who do not readily yield to Christ—the new Solomon.

For medieval Christians, the queen of Sheba became a symbol of prudent submission and a bridge between the dispensation of the Jews and the "more perfect" epoch of Christianity. The 6th century bishop Gregory of Tours wrote a biography of St. *Monegunde in which he praised her by comparing the holy woman to "the wise queen who came to hear the wisdom of Solomon." In the 7th century, Isidore of Seville cast the queen of Shebaas a metaphor of the church of the Gentiles seeking Christ. In high medieval romance literature, Makeda takes her place beside two other queens, *Helena (c. 255–329), mother of Constantine the Great, and *Bertha (d. 783), mother of the great Frankish Christian emperor, Charlemagne. This trio of women all assisted powerful men in extending Christianity to the "heathen." Incidentally, popular legend imputed to Bertha a webbed foot. The 14th-century *Mirror of Human Salvation* portrays the queen of Sheba as the pagan potentate who bowed to the superior power of the God of Abraham—a metaphor of conversion to Christianity.

Christian tradition has made much of the incident of the queen and the magical log which, in the African story, cured Makeda's limb, but, in the West, Makeda had a webbed rather than a hoofed foot. According to the *Legenda Aurea* (*Golden Legend*), a widely known collection of miracle stories recorded by Jacobus de Voragine in the mid-13th century, the cross upon which Jesus was crucified was made from the same wood upon which the queen of Sheba leapt in the court of Solomon. According to the myth, Adam's son, Seth, plucked a branch of Eden's Tree of Knowledge and planted it in the mouth of his dead father. This branch grew out of the "Old Adam" and awaited the arrival of the "New Adam": Jesus, who would give the human race a second chance, a second beginning. (Jewish legend holds that the Ten Commandments were carved with a sliver from that same wood.) Solomon cut down the famous tree to use it in the construction of his palace, the Domus Saltus. However, when the workers tried to fit the log in place, it became too long or too short, even when it had been cut to specifications. The wood clearly did not wish to become a beam in the Domus Saltus, and so Solomon had it placed over a brook called Kedron (or Kidron) to serve as a bridge.

When the queen paid her visit to Solomon, she refused to tread upon the bridge because, through the power of grace, she sensed it was sacred. Instead, the humble and wise monarch lifted her skirts and waded across the stream. As she did so, the waters transformed her webbed foot into a perfect human limb. The queen then made a prophecy about the wooden bridge saying, "The Savior of all the world will be hanged thereon, by whom the realm of the Jews shall be defaced and cease." Solomon, terrified by Makeda's prediction, had the bridge destroyed and threw the wood into a pond which instantly began to exhibit miraculous powers of healing. When the time came for Jesus' crucifixion, the enlivened beam rose from the bottom of the pool and floated to Jerusalem. Syrian and Arabic sources do not speak of a bridge, but rather they indicate that the wood was set in an inner room of the temple and that Makeda placed a silver ring upon it in gratitude for her cure. Each successive king of Israel imitated Makeda's donation, and it was these silver rings which the high priests used to pay Judas Iscariot for his betrayal of Jesus.

Dozens of versions of the story of the bridge exist in a variety of vernacular languages and artistic representations. Piero della Francesca's fresco (1452–66) in Arezzo, Italy, portraying Makeda at the bridge is one of the most famous treatments of this subject. The queen is modest and reserved, yet regal and confident in her prophecy of the future. The legend of the bridge links Makeda to the aforementioned Helena, who miraculously discovered the True Cross of Christ in the early 4th century. From medieval clerics such as Petrus Comestor (d. 1178), to secular Renaissance figures such as Thomas Malory in *Le Morte d'Arthur* (1470), Christian writers highlighted the queen's role in the history of the cross.

Because Makeda instinctively recognized that the log bridge had played and would continue to play a central role in salvation history, medieval authors fashioned her as one of the Sibyls (pagan prophets with foreknowledge of Jesus and his mission); hence, medieval literature refers to her as Sibyl or Sibylla. In the 16th century, the queen was brought to the service of a variety of anti-Semitic and apocalyptic texts in which she is "The Thirteenth Sibyl" because she foresaw the Crucifixion and the end of the "evils" of the unbelieving heathens and Jews. One 15th-century collection of woodcuts called *The Book of the Rood*, which was inspired by Thomas Malory's work, has Solomon torturing Queen Sibyl because her prophecy was so unflattering to the Jews. She is tied to a stake with her deformed foot well forward and very much in view.

Along with the motif of the bridge, the queen of Sheba's webbed foot has, over the centuries, piqued a great deal of interest—inspiring artists, writers and folklorists. For most commentators, the deformed foot is a symbol of the queen's imperfection before her conversion. A mosaic in the cathedral of Otranto, produced by a monk called Pantaleone in 1165, represents the web-footed Makeda as a siren juxtaposed to a mermaid: both classical figures of dangerous se-

duction and eroticism. The theme is repeated in a myriad of Western representations from a 12th-century sculpture in Dijon, France, to 15th-century Bohemian woodcuts. There is a tradition in Western culture which associates bird-footedness with lust. The Jerusalem Bible argues that feet are often metaphors for sexual organs. The deformed foot (which is by no means restricted to the queen of Sheba in Western lore—it echoes in the story of Cinderella) represents fearful secrets, hidden under women's dresses, that are foul and disgusting, but still irresistible. Fulgentius (d. 533) wrote that bird-bodied sirens of classical myth have "hen like feet" because "lust scatters all that it possesses." Before her conversion, Makeda was dangerous, not just because she was pagan, but also because she was alluring, powerful, and autonomous: the virgin queen. By the time Makeda left Jerusalem, she had changed; she had been tamed—no longer web-footed, no longer pagan, no longer virgin, no longer queen. She had abdicated her throne to Solomon's child whom she carried in her womb.

In medieval romance, web-footedness is a sign of deviancy. Mythological harpies and she-monsters have misshapen limbs, especially hoofed, cloven, or bird feet. Satan and his minions are traditionally portrayed with hoofed or bird-like, clawed feet. Reformation writers Edmund Spenser, Martin Luther, and Philip Melanchthon caricatured the Catholic Church as a creature with misshapen limbs. Spenser says of the personified Church, "And eke her feet most monstrous were in sight." In several ways, then, misshapen bird feet are temptations to sin. They are metonyms of lust, paganism, and heresy.

In addition to parenting the line of Ethiopian kings, the queen of Sheba's love affair with Solomon has fertilized centuries of Western and Eastern art, music, and literature. Ethiopian, Jewish, and European Christian sources all consider Solomon's love poetry, recorded in the *Song of Songs*, to have been composed for Makeda. For this reason, she is often black-skinned in artistic representations because in the *Song of Solomon* the beloved says, "I am black, and comely" (Song 1.5). Medieval artists frequently pictured the queen as a Moor. This is true, for example, of an enamel plaque on the altar of Nicholas of Verdun (1181) and a stained-glass window in the church of St. Thomas at Strasbourg (c. 1280). By the Renaissance, however, the queen was no longer portrayed with what was at the time considered an unflattering black skin; rather, artists subtly alluded to her exotic, African origins. For instance, illustrations in the 15th-century *Hours of*

*Catherine of Cleves* pictures a Moorish lady-in-waiting beside the queen, and in Piero della Francesca's fresco one of the queen's maids is African, identifiable more by her headdress than her color. Representations of the queen meeting Solomon have been a favorite design for bridal trousseau chests. The modern poets W.B. Yeats and Robert Browning capitalized on the brief and romantic encounter between the two magnificent, exotic monarchs. In *Solomon to Sheba*, Yeats plays off the tradition that Solomon composed his songs for Makeda: "Sang Solomon to Sheba,/ And kissed her dusky face. . . . Sang Solomon to Sheba,/ And kissed her Arab eyes."

The variety of aspects of the queen of Sheba's tale which has provided grist for artistic representation is astonishing. She is paralleled with Balaam's ass in several medieval texts and in the portal sculptures at Chartres Cathedral (1230). In the Old Testament, Balaam's she-donkey was able to perceive the presence of the angel of the Lord when her master, Balaam, was not (Nm 22.22–35). In the same way, Sheba recognized that the wooden bridge would become Christ's cross when Solomon considered the log a worthless piece of unusable timber. This pairing of the lowly ass and the hoof-footed woman makes sense when we consider that in each story there is a reversal of roles. The ass, foolish and humble, proves to be clairvoyant, and the submissive queen, who cannot outwit Solomon, is superior to him in spiritual wisdom.

The queen is also represented, in a variety of contexts, exchanging riddles with Solomon. A 17th-century Dutch theme park called Old Labyrinth featured automata of Solomon and Sheba quizzing each other. Myriad riddle books, written from the middle ages on, contain riddles ascribed to Solomon and Sheba.

The image of the mighty queen in submission to an even mightier king and the possibilities for creating elaborate court spectacle particularly appealed to Renaissance artists. Hans Holbein represented Henry VIII as a Solomon accepting obedience from the queen of Sheba, who was meant to symbolize the pope. Tintoretto and Veronese both portrayed Makeda as the grateful supplicant of a mighty king. Veronese's *The Queen of Sheba Before Solomon* depicts a regal, mildly disdaining Solomon, strikingly like the youthful Charles Emanuel to whom the painting was dedicated on his accession to the dukedom of Savoy in 1580. It was not unusual for the Renaissance artist to flatter his patron by featuring him as a type of Solomon, accepting the resigned adoration of the queen—young and beautiful, but clearly less po-

tent than he. The Flemish painter Lucas de Here produced a similar version of the subject in which the Solomon is a portrait of Philip II of Spain. The queen of Sheba is also memorialized in music. Handel and Goldmark both wrote operas and minuets about her adventurers.

The exotic, beautiful, clairvoyant Queen of the South, tantalizingly obscure in the first source to mention her, has cast her shadow over 2,000 years of history and all seven continents. Each time her story is told, it takes on the coloring of the culture which tells it. In the Jewish holy books, the queen is Jewish. In the Quran, she becomes Muslim. In the Christian legends, she is a Christian at heart a thousand years before Christ. For Ethiopians, Makeda is the mother of the royal line. The present-day religious movement of Rastafarians counts Sheba among its most important saints. The queen of Sheba has attracted such diverse devotees because she presents so many possibilities. She combines qualities that are glorious and praiseworthy, though dangerous in combination. She is the exemplary woman, but she also has properties of the ideal man: power, cunning, and autonomy. Yet, in every version of the queen's story, her perfection is somehow blemished. In the Quran and Old Testament, the queen is physically flawless, but ultimately she cannot match the great Solomon: "There was no more spirit left in her." In the Ethiopian and Christian legends, Makeda bests King Solomon, but her perfection is marred because she has the foot of an animal. Under the veneer of flawlessness lies a lust that even this model woman cannot control. Perhaps this larger-than-life Queen of the South has been a favorite of legend weavers because she was not quite ideal.

**SOURCES:**
Bernard, Carlo, and Pierluig De Vex. *L'opera complete del Tintoretto*. Milan: Russell Editor, 1970.
Coke, Richard. *Veronese*. London: Jupiter Books, 1980.
Lightbown, Ronald. *Piero della Francesca*. NY: Abbeville Press, 1992.
Marcus, Harold G. *A History of Ethiopia*. Berkeley, CA: University of California Press, 1994.
Pankhurst, E.S., and R.K.P. Pankhurst. "Special Issue on the Queen of Sheba," in *Ethiopian Observer*. Vol. I, no. 6, 1957, pp. 178–204.
Warner, Marina. *From the Beast to the Blonde: On Fairy Tales and Their Tellers*. NY: Farrar, Straus and Giroux, 1994.
Wheeler, Post. *The Golden Legend of Ethiopia: The Love-Story of Makeda Virgin Queen of Axum and Sheba and Solomon the Great King*. NY: D. Appleton-Century, 1936.

**SUGGESTED READING:**
Budge, E.A. Wallis. *The Queen of Sheba and Her Only Son Menyelek*. Oxford: Oxford University Press, 1892.

Clapp, Nicholas. *Sheba: Through the Desert in Search of the Legendary Queen.* NY: Houghton Mifflin, 2001.

Devisse, Jean. *The Image of the Black in Western Art, II from the Early Christian Era to the "Age of Discovery."* Cambridge: Cambridge University Press, 1979.

Hess, Robert T. *The Modernization of Autocracy.* Ithaca, NY: Cornell University Press, 1970.

Serrano, Miguel. *The Visits of the Queen of Sheba.* London: Routledge & Kegan Paul, 1972.

Talmud. Steinsaltz Edition. NY: Random House, 1989.

**Martha Rampton**, Assistant Professor of History,
Pacific University, Forest Grove, Oregon

# Sheehan, Patty (1956—)

*American golfer. Born Patty Sheehan in Middlebury, Vermont, on October 27, 1956; daughter of a ski coach; attended San Jose State.*

*Was Nevada State Amateur (1975–78) and California State Amateur (1978–79); won several LPGA tournaments, including Mazda Japan Classic (1981), Orlando Lady, Safeco, and Inamori classics (1982), Corning, Henredon, and Inamori classics, and LPGA championship (1983), Elizabeth Arden, McDonald's, and Henredon classics, and LPGA championship (1984), Safeco Classic (1990); won the U.S. Open (1992).*

Though Patty Sheehan excelled as a golfer, she began her sports career as a skier. Her father, a ski instructor at Middlebury College, coached the U.S. Olympic team in 1956. Thus, it was no surprise that 13-year-old Patty Sheehan was rated the best skier in her age class in the nation. After the family moved to Nevada, however, Sheehan took up golf. For four years in a row, she won the Nevada State Amateur title (1975–78). She also won the California Amateur from 1978 to 1980 and was the national college champion. In 1980, Sheehan played on the Curtis Cup team, winning all four of her matches.

In 1981, she turned pro and was named LPGA Rookie of the Year. The following year, she had 18 top-10 finishes and 3 wins, until her powers seemed to fail her. Though she was diagnosed with pneumonia and was also suffering from arthritis in both hands, she was named Player of the Year in 1983, winning the Corning Classic, the Henredon Classic, the Inamori Classic, and the LPGA championship. The next year, Sheehan won the *Elizabeth Arden Classic, the LPGA championship, and the McDonald's Kids' Classic. She was awarded a bonus of $500,000 for winning two of three LPGA events. Combined with her first prize earnings, that bonus gave her the largest award ever achieved by a professional golfer to that date.

At the 1992 U.S. Open, Sheehan birdied the final two holes, then took on **Juli Inkster** in an 18-hole playoff. Sheehan's win ended a minor drought and impressively dispelled her U.S. Open jinx. A three-time runner-up, in 1990 she had squandered a nine-stroke lead to lose by one to **Betsy King**. Three years before, in sudden-death play at the Nabisco-*Dinah Shore Open, King had holed a bunker shot to take another win over Sheehan.

**SOURCES:**

Markel, Robert, Nancy Brooks, and Susan Markel. *For the Record: Women in Sports.* NY: World Almanac, 1985.

**Karin Loewen Haag**,
Athens, Georgia

# Sheehy-Skeffington, Hanna (1877–1946)

*Irish reformer whose feminist and nationalist aspirations were often in conflict, though she pursued both with dedication and courage. Name variations: Johanna Mary Sheehy; Hanna Sheehy; Mrs. Sheehy-Skeffington. Born Johanna Sheehy on May 24, 1877, in County Cork, Ireland; died in Dublin, Ireland, on April 20, 1946; daughter of David Sheehy (a member of the Irish Parliamentary Party) and Elizabeth (McCoy) Sheehy; attended Dominican Convent, Dublin; Royal University of Ireland, B.A., 1899, M.A., 1902; married Frank Sheehy-Skeffington, in 1903 (died 1916); children: Owen (b. 1909).*

*Co-founded Irish Women's Franchise League (1908); helped establish The Irish Citizen (1912); imprisoned as a suffragist (1912 and 1913); husband killed in Easter Rising (1916); made lecture tour of U.S. (1916–18); met with President Wilson (1918); imprisoned in Liverpool, Dublin, and Holloway (1918); served as judge during War of Independence (1919–21); made lecture tour of U.S. and Canada (1922–23); visited League of Nations (1923); attended Women's International League for Peace and Freedom Conference in Prague (1929); journeyed to Moscow (1930); imprisoned in Armagh (1933); made lecture tour to U.S. and Canada (1933–34); established Women's Social and Political League (1937); toured U.S. (1937–38); was a candidate in general election (1943).*

*Selected publications: "British Militarism in Ireland as I have known it," in Democracy in Ireland Since 1913 (NY: Donnelly Press, 1917); Impressions of Sinn Fein In America (Dublin: Davis Publishing, 1919); Ireland—Present and Future (NY: Donnelly Press, 1919). As a journalist, published hundreds of articles.*

When Hanna Sheehy-Skeffington was growing up in the late 19th century, the sentiment of nationalism overshadowed much else in Ireland. Nationalists, constitutional and revolutionary, were looking for Irish independence. The constitutional nationalists, the Irish Parliamentary Party, sat in the British Parliament and hoped for a Home Rule Bill to be enacted which would grant Ireland dominion status. The various revolutionary nationalist groups were planning a rebellion which would result in an Irish Republic. At the same time, the demand for women's suffrage was also being heard and many women were not willing to wait for the national problem to be solved until they had the vote.

Sheehy's father, uncle and grandfather were active participants in the Irish nationalist cause and were connected with constitutional and revolutionary nationalist organizations. Her father was a member of the Irish Parliamentary Party and the Sheehy household, No. 2 Belvedere Place in Rathmines, Dublin, served as a meeting place for many of Dublin's nationalists and intellectuals. Her mother was a strong woman who firmly believed all her children should be treated equally.

𝒩ow that the first stone has been thrown by suffragists in Ireland, light is being admitted into more than mere government quarters, and the cobwebs are being cleared away from more than one male intellect.

—Hanna Sheehy-Skeffington

Hanna Sheehy was born in County Cork in 1877 and moved to Dublin as a young girl. She was the eldest of six children, four girls and two boys. One of her earliest memories was of going to visit her uncle, a priest, Eugene Sheehy, in Kilmainham Jail for revolutionary activities. Hanna was educated with her sisters at the Dominican Convent in Eccles Street, Dublin. She was quite religious in her youth and even considered becoming a nun, however this side of her personality was to disappear as she entered her 20s and became critical of a church which she saw as oppressive to women and controlling education. In the year before she attended university, she suffered from tuberculosis and visited the European continent in order to recover.

Sheehy attended university in Dublin, studied foreign languages, received a B.A. in 1899 and an M.A. in 1902. Like others in this first generation of female university students, Sheehy became very interested in feminism. She campaigned for female students to attend the same lectures as male students and was a founder member of the Irish Women's Graduates Association in 1902. She met her future husband Frank Skeffington during her student days, and they found that their common interest in feminism, socialism, nationalism, and the literary world brought them together.

They married in 1903, took each others' names, and thus became the Sheehy-Skeffingtons. She worked as a teacher and he as a registrar at University College in Dublin. He had to resign his position in 1904 after being censured for speaking out against restrictions imposed upon women. Thereafter, he worked as a freelance journalist. When their son Owen was born in 1909, they demonstrated their opinion of the Catholic Church, and created a minor scandal, by not having him baptized.

The Sheehy-Skeffingtons and their good friends James and *Margaret Cousins were disillusioned with the existing women's suffrage societies in Ireland. They believed the older societies, such as the Irish Women's Suffrage and Local Government Association and the Irish Women's Suffrage Society, were ineffective. In their years of existence, these societies had made little advance, especially in the realm of national politics. Their methods were mild and their drawing-room tactics were peaceful. The two couples decided to form a militant suffrage society suitable to the different political situation of Ireland. Therefore, in 1908, the Irish Women's Franchise League (IWFL), a non-political, non-denominational, militant organization, was established. It had branches throughout the country, and it had both Protestant and Catholic women as members, thus contradicting the common belief that it was a Dublin-based Protestant organization. By 1913, it had over 800 members and had to move into larger headquarters.

Nationalist organizations, including nationalist women's organizations such as Cumann na mBan, accused the suffrage movement in Ireland as being part of the British suffrage movement. Sheehy-Skeffington declared that this was far from the case. It had associations with suffragists from all over the world (particularly the United States) and took a very independent line on policy and tactics. Among Sheehy-Skeffington's papers are letters from an admirer in the Isle of Man, a French feminist, and correspondence with American suffragists. Suffragists came to Ireland on lecture tours from Norway, Australia, South Africa, the U.S., as well as from Great Britain. These accusations were difficult for Sheehy-Skeffington since she regarded herself as both a feminist and a nationalist. While there were

Hanna Sheehy-Skeffington

many connections with English suffrage societies and while some Irish suffragists underwent training and imprisonment in England, she argued that the IWFL was very much an Irish organization. This conviction was evident when an English organization, the Women's Social and Political Union (WSPU), tried to set up a branch in Ireland. A correspondence took place between Sheehy-Skeffington and *Christabel Pankhurst of the WSPU in which Sheehy-Skeffington firmly told Pankhurst that there was no place for a branch of the English organization in Ireland.

The IWFL shared the same meeting room in Dublin, the Antient Concert Rooms, as the Irish Socialist Party. This is of interest since Sheehy-Skeffington was always strongly inclined towards socialism and was very much impressed by and often quoted the Irish socialist James Connolly (who would die in the 1916 Rebellion). She frequently repeated his declaration that while the working class were slaves, women were the slaves of slaves.

Sheehy-Skeffington met weekly with other members of the IWFL. They made their strategy known to their followers, and the Irish public in general, through meetings, public lectures, tours throughout Ireland, and in the pages of their weekly newspaper, *The Irish Citizen*, which was established in 1912. Followed by its title, the paper always displayed the slogan, "For Men and Women Equality, The Rights of Citizenship, For Men and Women Equality, The Duties of Citizenship," expressing the dual political and feminist concerns of the IWFL. It was not only important for women to have the vote as women, but also as citizens. Sheehy-Skeffington was a regular contributor to the columns of the *Citizen* and, for a time, its editor.

What singled out the IWFL from other suffrage societies in Ireland was its adaptation of militant tactics. Members disrupted political meetings, petitioned Irish and British politicians, threw ink in mail boxes, and smashed windows. They heckled Winston Churchill on a visit to Belfast and harassed Prime Minister Herbert Asquith. John Redmond, the leader of the Irish Parliamentary Party, was frequently a victim of their attacks. Their militancy usually followed failed women's suffrage amendments to the Home Rule Bill or other doomed suffrage legislation in the British Parliament. Militant action was not without consequence, and, after the women smashed glass or carried out some other destructive act, they were tried and imprisoned.

In 1912, on the eve of imprisonment to serve a month's sentence for breaking 19 windows in government buildings in Dublin, Sheehy-Skeffington acknowledged:

> The novelty of Irishwomen resorting to violence on their own behalf is, I admit, startling to their countrymen who have been accustomed to accept their services (up to and including prison, flogging at the cart-tail, death by torture) in furtherance of the cause of male liberties. There is an element of unwomanly selfishness in the idea of women fighting for themselves repellent to the average man.

She was among those Irish suffragists whose relatives had been in prison for the nationalist cause; therefore, respectability and imprisonment were not necessarily seen by them as incompatible. Her father and uncle had been imprisoned for their beliefs. Indeed, her father had been in prison six times in connection with Home Rule and had undergone hunger strikes. It is interesting that while she often compared the imprisonment of suffragists to the imprisonment of nationalists, the nationalists saw the militancy of the suffragists as a major distraction and considered it unpatriotic.

While in prison, she continued to write articles and book reviews for the *Citizen*. She went on a hunger strike 92 hours before she was released in sympathy with two other suffragists who had received long-term sentences and hard labor. She wrote of the hunger strike: "At first one misses the break of meal time in prison, and does not if one is wise let one's thoughts dwell upon dainties. In novels one skips allusions to food hurriedly." She was imprisoned again in 1913 and went on another hunger strike.

When World War I began in the summer of 1914, the IWFL continued to campaign for women's suffrage, unlike some other British and Irish suffrage organizations which decided to back the war effort. The war was not seen as an issue which should detract from the cause. Sheehy-Skeffington and her husband were very much opposed to the conflict. It was an English war, they were pacifists, and they were socialists. They campaigned against conscription in Ireland and spoke out against the war effort which led to short-term imprisonment for Frank and put them both permanently on the English authorities' blacklist.

The struggle for women's suffrage went into the background, but never died, when the nationalist struggle took a major place in Sheehy-Skeffington's attention in 1916. On Easter Monday, revolutionaries took over the General Post Office in Dublin, as well as other key locations. They issued a Proclamation which stated, among other things, that men and women would have equal rights in the new Irish republic. Frank Sheehy-Skeffington was killed on the third day of the Rising. As a pacifist, he had gone out on the wartorn streets of Dublin and organized a Citizen's Defense Force to prevent looting. He was arrested and shot that day without trial by the English Captain Colthurst. There was no legitimate reason for his execution, and Sheehy-Skeffington demanded a court-martial. She did not believe justice was done when Colthurst got a slap on the wrist and was sent to a mental hospital for a period.

It is evident in her writings that, through this incident, Sheehy-Skeffington became convinced that she needed to draw worldwide attention to her husband's murder and to the executions of the revolutionaries when the Rising was suppressed. She argued that their deaths were another manifestation of what she called "British Militarism in Ireland." This became the title of a pamphlet she wrote and of lectures she gave on the topic.

The country most likely to listen, be sympathetic, and, perhaps, exert some pressure on the English was the United States. Though the English refused to give her a passport, she managed to cross the Atlantic with her son, despite them, at the end of 1916. Sponsored by the American organization Friends For Irish Freedom, she raised money for the nationalist organization Sinn Fein. Her tour was not popular with everyone, especially after April 1917 when the Americans joined the British in the war. Some meeting halls refused to let her lecture, and she was briefly arrested in San Francisco. Even so, she attracted large crowds at over 250 venues, including Carnegie Hall in New York and Faneuil Hall in Boston. At the Dreamland Rink in San Francisco, 8,000 came to hear her. The high point of her visit was a meeting with President Woodrow Wilson in January 1918, three days after he had drawn up his Fourteen Points for World Peace and a day after Congress had passed the Federal Amendment for women's suffrage in the United States. She presented the president with a petition from the Irish nationalist women's organization Cumann na mBan, which asked that he support Ireland's bid for freedom.

On her return from the U.S. in July 1918, she was held by British authorities for a period in Liverpool. Managing to elude them, she traveled to Dublin where she was rearrested and sent to the women's prison in Holloway (London) after beginning a hunger strike. When she continued the strike and got progressively weaker, she was released under the Cat and Mouse Act, which had first been introduced in 1913 to deal with hunger-striking suffragists.

The war ended in November 1918, and in December there was a general election. Qualified women over 30 in Great Britain and Ireland were enfranchised under the Representation of the Peoples Act and could thus vote in the election. (All women over 21 in Ireland would be enfranchised after 1921.) Elected Irish nationalist MPs (members of Parliament) refused to sit at Westminster and formed their own parliament, the Dáil, in Dublin in January 1919. Thus, the Irish War of Independence officially began, as the illegal Irish parliament refused to listen to England and obey its authority. Sheehy-Skeffington served as a judge in the courts set up by the First Dáil. Her nephew has written about the paradox of Sheehy-Skeffington being a pacifist and at the same time serving in illegal courts which gave orders for executions. He concludes that both she and her husband "came to interpret pacifism in a minimalist manner, as requiring their own personal abstention from violence but not precluding alliance with violent rebels in a civil capacity." The war dragged on for a year and a half and ended, after much bloodshed, with the production of the Anglo-Irish Treaty in the summer of 1921.

Ireland was promptly torn apart between those who supported and those who opposed the treaty. It partitioned Ireland into the Irish Free State which was comprised of 26 counties, and the six Northern counties which remained as part of the United Kingdom. It also stated that members of the Dáil had to swear an oath of allegiance to the British monarch. There were other parts of the treaty that were also repugnant to some Irish nationalists, including the stipulation that the British would keep the Irish ports. Sheehy-Skeffington sided with the Anti-Treatyites, also known as the Republicans, who opposed the new Irish Free State and who would only be satisfied with an all-Ireland Republic. According to R.M. Fox who met Sheehy-Skeffington just after the treaty was signed: "From no one did I get such a clear impression of implacability, of irreconcilable opposition to anything less than complete national independence."

Civil war broke out between the Republicans and the Free Staters. Sheehy-Skeffington went to the U.S. and Canada, this time to raise money for the families of Irish Republican prisoners. She visited over 25 states and raised $120,000. She also visited the League of Nations as a delegate of the "Republican" government when the Free State applied for membership in 1923. She continued to support the idea of an Irish Republic after the Republicans lost the civil war in 1923, and she was active on committees that campaigned for the release of Republican prisoners. She also wrote for the Republican newspaper, *An Poblacht*, and supported the Irish Republican Army.

However, life had to go on after the disappointment of the Anglo-Irish Treaty and the futile civil war, and Sheehy-Skeffington continued to play an active role in Irish life. In the years between the wars, she worked as a journalist writing for diverse newspapers, both national and international. She was a well-known book re-viewer and drama and film critic. She also con-tinued to teach French and German. However, work conditions were not always good, and her health, which was never great, continued to de-teriorate. The world of radio beckoned to her, and she made a number of successful broadcasts discussing various aspects of Irish life. She was particularly concerned about the growing cen-sorship in the 1930s and wrote articles and chaired talks on the subject.

She made two more trips to the U.S. (1934–35, 1937), lecturing about the position of women in Ireland, the 1916 Rebellion, her fore-bodings concerning fascism in Italy and Ger-many, and her thoughts on Communism in the Soviet Union. When she returned home, she made lecture tours about her American experi-ences, fascinating Irish people with stories about life in the United States.

Her travel was not confined to the new world. In 1929, she attended a conference of the Women's International League of Peace and Free-dom in Prague and became the group's vice-presi-dent. Having been denied a passport to attend its first meeting at The Hague during WWI, she found this trip to be particularly fulfilling. In 1930, Sheehy-Skeffington went to the Soviet Union as a delegate of the Friends of the Soviet Union and attended a conference in Moscow. She also visited Leningrad. It would seem that she was one of the many world observers who were duped by Stalin and accepted the window-dressing of Stalinism. She went away duly convinced, prais-ing the position of women in the Soviet Union. As she crossed the border into Northern Ireland in 1933 which was now part of the United King-dom, she was arrested, since the government of Northern Ireland deemed her to be politically un-desirable. She was imprisoned for a month.

The position of women remained a passion-ate interest for Sheehy-Skeffington. Even though they now had the vote, their position was most certainly not one of equality. As the new Irish state took on an identity of its own, it was very much imbued with a Catholic ethos. Sheehy-Skeffington's writings of the 1920s and 1930s reflect her concerns. She protested about the de-plorable conditions of women teachers and the lack of equal pay; she condemned the elimina-tion of women from juries in 1927, and fought against the marriage ban which refused to let women have careers in civil service or education after they married.

In 1937, she had reason to renew some of the zeal she had demonstrated in the early pre-suffrage days. The prime minister of Ireland, Ea-monn de Valera, brought out a new constitution which, with some amendments, remains Ire-land's constitution. The charter conveyed that women's sphere was in the home and asserted that women should never feel the need to go out to work. Moreover, no law should be enacted to allow the breakup of a marriage. Abortion was, and still is, out of the question. Before it was passed, Sheehy-Skeffington endeavored to publi-cize what women's position would be like under the new constitution. She was fighting a lost cause, and the women of Ireland were largely in-different to her pleas.

Sheehy-Skeffington and others became con-vinced that there was a need for a women's party, since none of the main political parties were representing their interests. Thus the Women's Social and Political League was formed, a year later to be known as the Women's Social and Progressive League (WSPL). Sheehy-Skeffington was its chair for six years and was backed by the organization in 1943 as a candi-date in the general election. The League also supported three other independent candidates, none of whom won. When asked the question, "Will women not vote for women?," Sheehy-Skeffington replied, "Women, the average and sub-average, still have that inferiority complex, just as there were negro-slaves who were op-posed to emancipation." However, she felt that their very candidature was a victory: "The chal-lenge to the party-system has at least been made by the independent women: their election cam-paign has set the public thinking."

Hanna Sheehy-Skeffington died in 1946 at the age of 69. The themes of nationalism and feminism were woven through her life as she witnessed the transition to Irish freedom and the enfranchisement of women. Though all the ex-pectations she had for both did not become a re-ality, she lived to see them happen, and she also served to keep the women's movement alive in Ireland in the 1920s and 1930s. Her life embod-ied the conflicts many active politicized women experience. She had campaigned for what she believed was good for the nation and what was good for Irish women. Not everyone agreed that these were necessarily the same thing. However, just as she was not inhibited by the British mili-tary after they murdered her husband, and went to the United States to plead her case, so too, in independent Ireland, she was not inhibited by the repressive Catholic State and spoke out for the rights of women in a nation which largely es-chewed them.

**SOURCES:**

Cruise O'Brien, Conor. "Twentieth Century Witness," in *The Atlantic Monthly*. Vol. 273. no. 1. January 1994, pp. 49–72.

Fox, R.M. *Rebel Irish Women*. Dublin: Talbot Press, 1935.

Levenson, Leah, and Jerry Naderstad. *Hanna Sheehy Skeffington: A Pioneering Irish Feminist*. Syracuse, NY: Syracuse University Press, 1986.

Luddy, Maria. *Hanna Sheehy-Skeffington*. Dublin: Irish Historical Association, 1995.

Mooney, Joanne E. "Varieties of Irish Republican Womanhood: San Francisco Lectures during their United States Tours, 1916–1925," unpublished master's thesis, San Jose State University, 1991.

Murphy, Cliona. *The Women's Suffrage Movement and Irish Society in the Early Twentieth Century*. Philadelphia, PA: Temple University Press, 1989.

Sheehy-Skeffington, Hanna. "British Militarism As I Have Known It," in *Democracy in Ireland Since 1913*. NY: Donnelly Press, 1917, pp. 21–34.

———. *Impressions of Sinn Fein in America*. Dublin: Davis, 1917.

———. "An Irish Pacifist," in *We Did Not Fight*. Edited by Julian Bell. London: Cobden Sanderson, 1935, pp. 339–353.

———. "Reminiscences of an Irish Suffragette," in *Votes for Women: Irish Women's Struggle for the Vote*. Edited by Andree Sheehy-Skeffington, *et al.* Dublin: Andree D. Sheehy-Skeffington and Rosemary Owens, 1975.

——— (Hanna Sheehy), "Women and the University Question," in *New Ireland Review*. Vol. 17. May–August 1902, pp. 148–151.

———. "Women in Politics," in *The Bell*. Vol. 7. November 1943, pp. 143–148.

———. "The Women's Movement-Ireland," in *Irish Review*. July 1912, pp. 225–227.

Ward, Margaret. *In Their Own Voice: Women and Irish Nationalism*. Dublin: Attic Press, 1995.

———. *Unmanageable Revolutionaries: Women and Irish Nationalism*. Kerry: Brandon, 1983.

**COLLECTIONS:**

The Hanna Sheehy-Skeffington papers are in the National Library, Dublin, Ireland.

**Cliona Murphy**, Professor of History, California State University, Bakersfield, and author of *The Women's Suffrage Movement and Irish Society in the Early Twentieth Century*

# Shelby, Juliet (1902–1984).

*See Minter, Mary Miles.*

# Sheldon, Mary Downing (1850–1898).

*See Barnes, Mary Downing.*

# Sheldon, Susannah.

*See Witchcraft Trials in Salem Village.*

# Shelest, Alla (1919—)

*Soviet ballerina.* Born in Russia in 1919; studied at the Leningrad Ballet.

Alla Shelest began her studies at the Leningrad Ballet in 1927, graduating ten years later. Her first prominent role was that of the Girl-Swan in \***Agrippina Vaganova**'s *Swan Lake* with the Kirov company in 1938–39. Shelest appeared as Zarema in *The Fountain of Bakhchisary*, Nikia in *La Bayadère*, Juliet in *Romeo and Juliet*, Myrtha in *Giselle*, the Lilac Fairy and Aurora in *The Sleeping Beauty*, Yekaterina in *The Stone Flower*, Bird-Girl in *Shurale*, and the Tsar-Maiden in *The Humpbacked Horse*. During the 1960s, her appearances at the Kirov became less frequent, and she turned to coaching young dancers in the company.

# Shelley, Harriet (1795–1816).

*See Shelley, Mary for sidebar on Harriet Westbrook.*

# Shelley, Mary (1797–1851)

*Romantic author of* Frankenstein *and other texts who is as notable for her influence on her lover and husband Percy Bysshe Shelley as for her own writings.* Name variations: Mary Godwin Shelley; Mary Wollstonecraft Shelley. Born Mary Wollstonecraft Godwin on August 30, 1797, in London, England; died in Chester Square, London, on February 1, 1851; daughter of William Godwin (a political philosopher) and Mary Wollstonecraft (1759–1797, author of A Vindication of the Rights of Woman); married Percy Bysshe Shelley (the poet), in 1816; children: William (died young); Clara (died young); Percy.

Eloped with Percy Bysshe Shelley (1814); wrote Frankenstein (1816–17); lost two of her children and her husband in quick succession (by 1822); edited Shelley's works for posthumous publication; published The Last Man (1826), and Rambles in Germany and Italy (1844), shortly before succumbing to a brain tumor and eventual death (1851).

Selected writings: Frankenstein (1817); History of a Six Weeks' Tour (1817); Matilda (1820); Proserpine (1820); Midas (1820); Valperga (1823); Posthumous Poems of Percy Bysshe Shelley (1824); The Last Man (1826); The Fortunes of Perkin Warbeck (1830); Lives of the Most Eminent Literary and Scientific Men of Italy, Spain and Portugal (1835); Lodore (1835); Rambles in Germany and Italy (1844).

Mary Wollstonecraft Godwin Shelley entered a world in the throes of change. She was born in 1797, eight years after the storming of the Bastille initiated the French Revolution, which wholly altered the political and social landscape of Europe. Child of \***Mary Wollstonecraft** and William Godwin, thinkers whose ideas inspired and were inspired by the spirit of the age, she would live to participate in a literary revolution as radical as its political counterpart: Romanticism. With Lord Byron, John Keats, and her lover and husband Percy Bysshe Shelley, she became a major figure in the "second generation" of Romantics. Before she died of a brain tumor in 1851, Mary Shelley produced six novels, including *Frankenstein*, as well as biographies, travel books, essays, reviews and poems. As the only major figure of the second generation to have survived into the Victorian age, she is further responsible for consolidating their reputation. Ironically, owing in large part to her own critical efforts, she has been overshadowed by her male counterparts, especially her husband. Only recently have we come to recognize her for her own formidable accomplishments.

"Thou child of love and light," Percy Shelley called her, referring to her remarkable parentage. The sole product of a brief union between Godwin and Wollstonecraft, she was raised with a sense of destiny. Her birth was portended by tempests and the appearance of a comet in the skies over London. When Mary was ten days old, her mother died from complications associated with her birth. This left Mary and her half-sister ◄ **Fanny Imlay** in the sole care of Godwin, who, until his affair with Wollstonecraft, had been free of emotional ties. One of the most influential philosophers of his day, Godwin advanced radical theories for which he gained a loyal following of disciples, including the young Percy Shelley. In his enormously popular *An Enquiry Concerning Political Justice* (1793), Godwin argued against the interference of government and other institutions in human affairs. He held that reason alone can lead humans to moral action and to justice: "It is to the improvement of reason . . . that we are to look for the improvement of our social condition."

In his private life, Godwin had sought to embody the liberal principles he espoused, shunning political positions and earning a living by his writings. He freely shared what little wealth he possessed and expected others to do the same when he was in need. He expected people not only to share property but lovers as well. He had entered into an affair—his first romantic liaison—with Wollstonecraft, who at the time claimed to be married to Gilbert Imlay. In fact, she was Imlay's scorned lover and the mother of his child, Fanny Imlay. Despite their shared philosophical belief in marriage as a confining institution, Godwin and Wollstonecraft married once they learned she was pregnant. After his wife's death, Godwin published *Memoirs of the*

*Author of A Vindication of the Rights of Woman*, scandalizing the reading public with its revelations of Wollstonecraft's previous affairs. Their daughter's own romantic life would be shaped by their paradoxical example.

In death, Mary Wollstonecraft exerted perhaps more power over her daughter than she might have in life. Her grave in St. Pancras cemetery became a sacred spot of spiritual and intellectual pilgrimage to the young Mary. As a child, she learned to write her name by tracing the inscription on her mother's tombstone. Emily Sunstein argues, "Mary learned her mother's history in more intimate detail than if Wollstonecraft had lived, and worshiped her both as rational intellectual and romantic heroine who had defied injustice, custom, and prudence." In both her life and her art, Mary sought to realize Wollstonecraft's ideals. In *A Vindication of the Rights of Man* (1790), Wollstonecraft defended the principles of the French Revolution against Edmund Burke's attack in *Reflections on the Revolution in France*. She tersely dismissed his "wild declamation" and reminded him: "There are rights which men inherit at their birth, as rational creatures, who were raised above the brute creation by their improvable faculties; and that, in receiving these, not from their forefathers but, from God, prescription can never undermine natural rights."

More influential for Mary was Wollstonecraft's *A Vindication of the Rights of Woman* (1792), which extended her defense of human rights specifically to women. In this, one of the earliest feminist tracts, she examined the social system which limited women by encouraging them to nurture certain vanities and frivolities and preventing them from developing either their minds or their moral capacities. Marriage, she noted, cast women as property and doomed them to a childlike status. Essentially, she attempted to apply the broad strokes and ideals of the French Revolution to women and argued vehemently for their civil rights, most particularly their right to an education. Her reward for this exhaustive and well-reasoned social study is best characterized by the scurrilous remarks of Horace Walpole who referred to its author as "a hyena in petticoats."

Wollstonecraft's vision of a class of women liberated from oppressive social conditions was not lost on her daughter, however. Nor was it lost on the generation of poets and thinkers that followed. Admired and romanticized by Percy Shelley, Byron, Edward John Trelawny, and others, her writing drew some of the most notable English Romantics to her daughter and heir to her

**Imlay, Fanny.**
See
*Wollstonecraft,
Mary* for sidebar.

Mary
Shelley

ideas. Moreover, Mary Wollstonecraft's commitment to both human and women's rights became the mantra that guided Mary Shelley's own life.

Besides a keen sense of social justice, Mary Shelley inherited a sharp mind and nurtured a rich imagination. In the absence of her mother and a system of education for females, her father took a strong hand in guiding her education. He doted on his precocious and gifted daughter, and she, in turn, grew attached to him. She developed an eagerness to please him that followed her well into her adult years and frequently worked to her own disadvantage. Godwin's decision to marry **Mary Jane Vial**, then known as Mrs. Clairmont, shattered young Mary's insular world and distinctive claim to her father's guidance and affections.

Vial brought two children into the marriage, Charles and Jane Clairmont (later known as ❧ **Claire Clairmont**). Godwin's expanding household (further enlarged by the birth of William), not only punctured the harmony between Mary and her father, but placed a wedge between Mary and her stepmother. Mary viewed the new Mrs. Godwin, a practical-minded, domestic woman, as a poor replacement for her mother. In some ways, Mary never recovered from the displacement she suffered upon Vial's taking up of her wifely duties.

*If I have never written to vindicate the Rights of women, I have ever befriended women when oppressed. . . . I do not say aloud—behold my generosity & greatness of mind—for in truth it is simple justice.*

—Mary Shelley

Nevertheless, Mary continued to nurture her love of books and learning. In 1808, at age ten, she published her first juvenilia. While she thrived on the intellectual and literary stimulation of her father's circle, which included Samuel Taylor Coleridge, her unhappiness at home did not abate. The family sent her to a boarding school for a time during this turbulent pre-adolescent period and, eventually, to a family friend in Scotland. Besides meeting her first significant like-minded friend, **Isabel Baxter** (**Robinson**), Mary found herself in an adventurous and exotic setting conducive to her imaginative yearnings. A turning point in her life, this sojourn in Scotland set the stage for her concern with the occult and the mystical that figure so prominently in her classic first novel, *Frankenstein*. In her introduction to *Frankenstein*, she characterizes the land and its effect on her:

> . . . my habitual residence was on the blank and dreary northern shores of the Tay, near Dundee. Blank and dreary on retrospection . . . they were not so to me then. They were the eyry of freedom, and the pleasant region where unheeded I could commune with the creatures of my fancy.

Returning to London in the spring of 1814, the 17-year-old Mary met her father's new disciple and her future lover, the 21-year-old poet Percy Bysshe Shelley. Heir to his grandfather's fortune, Percy promised Mary financial support.

Though married to ❧ **Harriet Westbrook**, he immediately attracted Mary with his radical beliefs and sensitive genius. She had praised *Queen Mab*, a poem celebrating republican government, with extensive notes on atheism, free love, and vegetarianism. For his part, Percy was drawn by her remarkable parentage: according to Sunstein, "she fulfilled his ideal of the daughter of Wollstonecraft, his goddess of freedom and love, sired by Godwin, his lawgiver." In his eyes, her delicate beauty was matched by her intelligence. Describing her to Jefferson Hogg, he gushed, "*Then*, how deeply did I not feel my inferiority, how willingly confess myself far surpassed in originality, in genuine elevation & magnificence of the intellectual nature." During their courtship, the pair took long walks in St. Pancras cemetery and may even have consummated their affair behind her mother's gravestone.

Percy and Mary believed that their affair embodied the ideas of her famous parents. Consequently, they were shocked to learn of Godwin's disapprobation. He forbade that Mary see Percy, and almost succeeded in convincing her to leave Percy to his wife, who claimed to be pregnant with their second child. Percy, however, according to Mary's stepsister Jane, "declared unless she joined him as Partner of his Life—he would destroy himself." Mary agreed to run away with him and, with Jane along as translator, the lovers fled for France and embarked on a European trek which would give rise in 1817 to her travel book, *History of a Six Weeks' Tour*.

As Mary herself noted, "It was acting a novel, being an incarnate romance." Their flight and their subsequent life together was Romanticism writ large: their acts embodied the intensity, enthusiasm and rebellion characteristic of the spirit of the age. Ironically, while they maintained that they were living out Godwin's philosophy, Godwin excommunicated his daughter on her return to London (though this did not prevent him from accepting Percy's money). She sought solace from her mother's memory, reading for hours at her grave.

In their life together, the lovers persisted in fulfilling their shared radical ideals. They established an ambitious work schedule, writing and studying in the mornings, engaging in some form of exercise in the afternoons, and then reading aloud in the evenings. Mary kept careful (but incomplete) records that attest to the formidable scope of their studies, from literature and philosophy to history and science. To prepare for their extensive European travels, Mary studied languages—she would master five: Latin, Greek,

French, Italian and Spanish—and took great pleasure in reading texts in their original languages and in the country of their origin. Despite her self-deprecating remarks to the contrary, Mary and Percy were intellectual equals, providing each other with the support essential for imaginative achievement. Some speculate that without Mary's encouragement Percy might have pursued philosophy rather than poetry.

"Our house is very political as well as poetical," Mary told a friend. Both were determined republicans, perceiving England's postwar policies as a threat to individual freedoms. Against the threat of Napoleon, the British government had suspended *habeas corpus* and routinely jailed those who published works critical of its rule. The Peterloo massacre—in which government forces killed 11 demonstrators for parliamentary reform—convinced her that England was taking a turn toward despotism and distanced her from her native land, leading her eventually to embrace exile in Italy. A committed republican, she saw hope for Europe in revolutionary movements in Spain, Italy, and, later, Greece.

Personally, as well as intellectually, they committed themselves to liberal principles drawn from Mary's ideas and from Percy's own works. While Mary persistently defended their cohabitation, she could not commit herself entirely to the ideal of free love. Percy had greater success in converting her stepsister Jane, who changed her name to the more elegant Claire, with whom he sustained an intimate friendship. Because of this, their côterie was unfairly and repeatedly labeled the "League of Incest."

As a result of Claire's dogged pursuit of Lord Byron, wildly famous as much for his poetic as his sexual daring, Mary and Percy entered into a period that fused literary triumph and personal tragedy. Though the two male poets have been linked ever since, it was originally Mary, not Percy, whom Byron wanted to see, owing to her remarkable heritage. She became his favorite and their friendship became the stuff of legend—immortalized to this day in popular novels and films—for their association gave rise to *Frankenstein*.

In 1816, the group agreed to summer in Switzerland, renting neighboring houses. Along with Byron's physician, John Polidori, they gathered at the fireplace one stormy evening to read ghost stories. At evening's end, Byron launched a challenge: each would write a ghost story. Although Byron intended that he and Mary would publish a tale together, Mary produced the outline of her own novel, leaving Polidori to write "The Vampyre," based on Byron's idea.

### ❧▸ Clairmont, Claire (1798–1879)

*Stepsister of Mary Shelley. Born Clara Mary Jane Clairmont in 1798; died in 1879; daughter of Mary Jane Vial and an unknown father; stepdaughter of William Godwin; stepsister of Mary Shelley (1797–1851); children: (with Lord Byron) daughter Allegra (1817–1822).*

The daughter of an unknown father and **Mary Jane Vial** (William Godwin's second wife), 18-year-old Claire Clairmont was briefly Lord Byron's mistress in Switzerland in 1816; she had their daughter **Allegra** in 1817. Though Byron refused to see her, Claire relentlessly continued her pursuit, a fatal attraction, and there was a great deal of contention between the couple as to who would bring up the child. Byron won out and installed Allegra in a convent at Bagnacavallo, 12 miles from Ravenna, Italy, where she caught typhus and died on April 19, 1822. Byron was frantic, and Claire never completely recovered. Except for a four-year sojourn alone as a governess in Russia, Clairmont lived with *Mary Shelley periodically throughout the rest of her life, despite Mary's recurrent longing for "absentia Clariae." Though she was celebrated in Percy Shelley's poem "To Constantia Singing," Clairmont wrote in 1829: "I have trodden life alone, without a guide and without a companion and before I depart for ever I would willingly leave with another, what my tongue has never yet ventured to tell. I would willingly think that my memory may not be lost in oblivion as my life has been."

**SUGGESTED READING:**

Stocking, Marion Kingston, ed. *The Clairmont Correspondence: Letters of Claire Clairmont, Charles Clairmont, and Fanny Imlay Godwin.* Vol. I, 1808–1834, Vol. II, 1835–1879. Baltimore, MD: Johns Hopkins University Press, 1996.

### ❧▸ Westbrook, Harriet (1795–1816)

*Wife of Percy Shelley. Name variations: Harriet Shelley. Born Harriet Westbrook in 1795; drowned herself in the Serpentine River in November 1816; daughter of a retired tavern keeper; married Percy Bysshe Shelley (the poet), in August 1811; children: daughter Ianthe Shelley (b. 1813); Charles Shelley (b. 1814).*

The marriage of Harriet and Percy Shelley was always irregular. The poet had a preference for threesomes. First he set out to encourage a ménage that included his wife and schoolteacher **Elizabeth Hitchener**. He then promoted a three-way relationship with a friend from Oxford, Thomas Jefferson Hogg. Harriet resisted. Abandoned by Percy Shelley, Westbrook committed suicide when she discovered she was carrying the child of another man.

Returning to England, Mary Shelley composed her famous story of Dr. Frankenstein and his monster when she was just 18. Her feat is all the more remarkable when viewed against the conditions of its composition. Feminist critics, such as **Ellen Moers**, have erroneously argued that Mary Shelley's tale of revivification owes its origins to fears of childbirth sparked by the death of her prematurely born first child (the oft-mentioned death of her son William did not occur until after she had completed the novel). Such readings diminish the enduring lesson of *Frankenstein*: man's Promethean daring and overreaching presents us with an irreducible paradox, for it is at once the source of human creation and the origin of disaster. Critics further diminish the impact of a series of events that transformed Mary and Percy's relationship from a novel of "incarnate romance" to a tragedy of epic proportions.

In quick succession, Mary learned that her half-sister Fanny had committed suicide by taking laudanum and that Percy's wife Harriet had drowned herself. Percy fought for custody of his children, marrying Mary to improve his chances. While the marriage restored Mary's favor, it did nothing to help Percy's case. Instead, Percy's dogged defense of his principles only added fuel to the League of Incest charges, and he lost his fight. Byron's break with Claire, who eventually had their illegitimate daughter **Allegra**, only added to Mary's worries, for she and her husband were forced to mediate between the two over custody. Adding to this indignity were rumors that Percy had fathered the child.

Mary was thus surprised when *Frankenstein* became a phenomenal success. Sir Walter Scott praised the novel's "supernatural" fiction and the author's "original genius." Owing to its anonymous publication (which Mary had rightly thought would improve its chances for publication), the novel was initially believed to have been written by Percy. He did assist Mary in revisions and added a preface, but the novel's conception and composition were her own. Once she admitted her authorship, *Frankenstein*'s popularity only increased.

To recover from the crises that had marked its composition and to restore Percy Shelley's ailing health, the Shelleys moved to Italy in 1818 with their two children, Clara, who turned one during the trip, and William, who was three. When baby Clara died of dysentery, Mary was plunged into despair and took refuge in her work. She had begun research for the historical novel that would become *Valperga*, while Percy was experiencing his *annus mirabilis*, composing his poetic drama, *Prometheus Unbound*, and *The Cenci*. Both were fighting against the thought that Clara's death was punishment for making Harriet suffer, when William suddenly and unexpectedly died. Mary's inconsolable grief and guilt would drive an irretrievable wedge in her relationship with Percy. At 22, she felt that she should "have died" with her son "on the 7th of June."

Withdrawing into herself, incapable of seeking consolation from Percy, who desperately needed her comfort, both emotional and physical, she again turned to work as an outlet, beginning *Matilda*. This story of a girl's incestuous involvement with her father can be seen as Mary's attempt to release her guilt at having betrayed her own father by eloping with Percy.

At the end of 1819, Mary gave birth to her sole surviving child, Percy Florence Shelley, and by 1820 had poured herself into the composition of *Matilda* while continuing her research for *Valperga*. Her coldness toward her husband meant that he sought love, in an ideal, Platonic sense, elsewhere, first with **Emilia Viviani** and then with **Jane Williams**, wife of their close friend Edward Williams. Mary appears to have silently tolerated these relationships, believing their own union to be transcendent and everlasting. The events of the coming year were to prove her wrong.

By 1822, the Shelleys had moved with Byron to Pisa, where Mary continued her studies and Percy composed *Hellas* and *The Triumph of Life*. He also developed a passion for boating, having purchased a yacht christened *Don Juan* by Byron. Their relationship with Byron soon soured, for Claire learned that their daughter Allegra had died of typhus in the convent school Byron had chosen for her. Another tragedy soon followed: Mary miscarried three months into another pregnancy, hemorrhaging so badly that Percy saved her from bleeding to death only by placing her in a tub of ice. She was still recovering when she learned Percy had died: his ship capsized during a storm. The bodies of the poet and his companion on the trip, Edward Williams, later came ashore at Leghorn, where they were burned, owing to quarantine regulations.

Byron best described Mary during this ordeal: "Terror impressed on her brow, a desperate sort of courage seemed to give her energy. . . . I have seen nothing in tragedy on the stage so powerful, or so affecting." After Percy's death, Mary saw her life as the remaining chapter of an epic tragedy, believing that she would die at 36 as her mother had (Wollstonecraft had actually died at 38). Instead, as Sunstein contends, until her death at age 54, "she remained remarkably productive, enduringly resilient, and true to herself."

Percy Shelley's premature death, which Mary had often presaged, left her guilty and emotionally devastated. Moreover, despite her legal claim to his grandfather's estate—through marriage and his surviving son Percy Florence—Sir Timothy, Percy Shelley's father, stood in the way. Virtually destitute at 24 with a two-year-old child in her care and her father constantly clamoring for more of the promised Shelley money, Mary sold Percy Bysshe's legacy to his father for a small allowance. She was also forced to leave Italy, the country she had come to call home.

Despite the numerous emotional setbacks and relentless financial concerns, Mary persisted in educating herself—in other languages, literature, and philosophy—and was determined, like her mother before her, to live by her pen. In addition to her own writing, Mary mapped out how she would bring Percy's genius to the world in the form of a biography and new editions of his poems. Although Sir Timothy continued to impede her, particularly with the biography, she succeeded. She edited Percy's works for a posthumous collection that would bring him the readership both she and he felt he had deserved in life. This enormous task was, in her mind, her greatest achievement. Contemporary editors of Percy Shelley's works owe much to her careful compilations of his original manuscripts: 26 workbooks in addition to numerous separate sheets of paper.

In some ways, this most difficult period of her life—the post-Percy Shelley era—was also her most productive. Deprived of his protection from the world, as well as his tutelage, she negotiated through an oftentimes hostile world—rumors about her and Percy abounded and British society had never forgiven their elopement and liaison—and wrote some of her most ambitious works, including *The Last Man*. A novel of science fiction like *Frankenstein*, it looks to the 21st century and the end of the human race. Its dark vision and republican leanings found an unsympathetic audience.

Biographers of Mary Shelley have noted her political conservatism as she moved into middle age and as England entered the Victorian era. An

*From the movie* Frankenstein Meets the Wolfman, *one of the many films using Mary Shelley's creation.*

established woman of letters, she nevertheless struggled for acceptance in a prudish and unforgiving British society. No longer the young, carefree radical, she grew less sure that revolution could answer contemporary social and political inequities. She also questioned its high cost. Her priorities changed as the post-Romantic world did. Ever anxious for the health and welfare of her surviving son Percy Florence Shelley, she concerned herself with his future. Moreover, regardless of her differences with Godwin and his wife, she was a dutiful daughter who continued to help support her aging parents.

True to her maternal legacy, however, Mary Shelley's most steadfast quality was her attentiveness to social injustice and, in particular, the oppression of women. Like Wollstonecraft, who had helped a sister **Eliza Wollstonecraft** escape from a possibly abusive husband, Mary frequently came to the aid of other women in distress: examples include her stepsister Claire, who shared her home periodically throughout her life; Jane Williams and her children whom Mary lived with, loved, and helped support (after both husbands drowned) until Jane married Jeff Hogg; **Gee Paul**, divorced by her husband for having an affair, and for whom Mary negotiated visiting privileges with her children; and childhood friend Isabel Baxter Robinson who later had a child out of wedlock and applied to Mary for protection. (Sunstein recounts how Mary arranged for her to escape from the country, escorted by a transvestite friend, **Mary Diana Dods**, posing as her husband.)

By 1830, Mary's publications saw her listed in the *Athenaeum* "at the top of its second rank of leading English authors" like Coleridge, Wordsworth and her own Percy Shelley. But Mary persisted in shunning any publicity. Fearful of prompting the ire of Percy's father on whom her son's future depended, and gun-shy of the kind of scandal elicited by her early years with Percy, Mary kept a low profile. She toured the continent and visited her beloved Italy, where she spent her famous youth, only once before dying of a brain tumor in Chester Square, England, in 1851 at the age of 53.

Mary Shelley left behind a rich legacy and resource in her notes and journals documenting not only her own life and work, but her husband's. Her novels, travel books, biographical essays and political writings are now receiving the critical attention and study they deserve.

**SOURCES:**
Godwin, William. *An Enquiry Concerning Political Justice.* London: Penguin, 1976.

Philip, Mark. *Godwin's Political Justice.* Ithaca, NY: Cornell University Press, 1986.

St. Clair, William. *The Godwins and the Shelleys: A Biography of a Family.* NY: W.W. Norton, 1989.

Shelley, Mary Wollstonecraft. *Frankenstein.* Ed. by Johanna M. Smith. Boston, MA: Bedford Books, 1992.

Sunstein, Emily. *Mary Shelley: Romance and Reality.* Baltimore, MD: Johns Hopkins University Press, 1989.

Wollstonecraft, Mary. *A Wollstonecraft Anthology.* Ed. by Janet Todd. NY: Columbia University Press, 1990.

**SUGGESTED READING:**
*The Journals of Mary Shelley 1814–1844.* Ed. by Paula R. Feldman and Diana Scott-Kilvert. 2 vols. Oxford: Clarendon Press, 1987.

*The Letters of Mary Wollstonecraft Shelley.* Ed. by Betty T. Bennett. 3 vols. Baltimore, MD: Johns Hopkins University Press, 1980, 1983, 1988.

**COLLECTIONS:**
Papers of Mary Shelley and her family, owned by Lord Abinger, are on deposit at the Bodleian Library, Oxford.

**RELATED MEDIA:**
*Frankenstein* (film), starring Colin Clive, **Mae Clarke**, and Boris Karloff, directed by James Whale, produced by Universal, 1931.

*Gothic*, starring Gabriel Byrne, Julian Sands, and **Natasha Richardson**, directed by Ken Russell, 1986.

*Haunted Summer*, starring Phillip Anglim, **Laura Dern**, and Eric Stoltz, directed by Ivan Passer, produced by Martin Poll and the Cannon Group, 1988 (based on the novel by **Anne Edwards**, the movie centered around Godwin, Shelley, Byron, and Clairmont during that 1816 summer in Switzerland).

**Kate Waites Lamm**, Associate Professor, and **Suzanne Ferriss**, Assistant Professor, in the Liberal Arts department of Nova University, Fort Lauderdale, Florida

# Shepard, Helen Miller (1868–1938)

*American philanthropist. Name variations: Helen Miller Gould. Born Helen Miller Gould in New York City on June 20, 1868; died in 1938; eldest daughter of Jay Gould (1836–1892, the financier) and Helen Day (Miller) Gould; briefly attended New York Law University; married Finley Johnson Shepard (1867–1942, an executive of the Missouri Pacific Railway), on January 22, 1913; children: Olivia Margaret; Finley Fay; Helen Anna.*

Helen Miller Shepard was born Helen Miller Gould in New York City in 1868, the eldest daughter of financier Jay Gould and **Helen Day Miller Gould**. From 1892, when she inherited part of the family fortune, Shepard was known for her charity. Besides large donations, she gave her personal services to various movements for public and social welfare. She contributed $100,000 to the victims of the St. Louis cyclone in 1896, and funded a library and the Hall of Fame building at New York University, as well as the naval branch of the Brooklyn YMCA. She also gave generously to Rutgers, Vassar, and Mt. Holyoke Colleges, and financed the Woody Crest, a home for crippled children.

Shepard's most important work seems to have been for U.S. soldiers during the Spanish-American War. At the outbreak of the conflict in 1898, among other things, she contributed $100,000 to the U.S. government for relief of soldiers at Camp Wycoff (also seen as Wikoff), Long Island. On December 5, 1898, General Joseph Wheeler, with the help of Congressional Representative Stallings, introduced a bill in the U.S. House of Representatives that provided recognition of her benevolence; a medal was presented by President William McKinley.

## Shepard, Mary (1909–2000).

*See Travers, P.L. for sidebar.*

# Shephard, Gillian (1940—)

*British politician. Born Gillian Watts on January 22, 1940; daughter of Reginald Watts (a cattle farmer) and Bertha Watts; attended North Walsham High School for Girls; St. Hilda's College, Oxford, M.A., 1961; married Thomas Shephard, in 1975; children: two stepsons.*

Raised in a rural area of eastern England, where her father had a small livestock business, Gillian Shephard was educated at the local girls' school, and on the basis of her performance there won a state scholarship to St. Hilda's College at Oxford. After studying modern languages, she graduated with an M.A. in 1961 and began to teach. Two years later, she became a civil servant, working as an education officer and schools inspector until 1975. That year she married Thomas Shephard, who was raising two young sons after the death of his first wife, and left paid employment to care for them. A member of the Conservative Party, Shephard was elected to the Norfolk County Council (in West Norfolk) in 1977, and became vice chair of the council's social services committee. She later became chair of that committee and of the committees on museums, on personnel, and on education. In 1981, she was appointed deputy leader of the council, and also began serving as chair of the West Norfolk and Wisbech Health Authority, the local branch of the National Health Service. She gave up that position in 1985, when she became chair

of the Norwich Health Authority. Shephard relinquished both this post and her deputy leadership of the Norfolk County Council in 1987, when she was elected to Parliament.

During her first years in Parliament, Shephard was a member of the Select Committee on Social Services, and in 1989 was appointed under-secretary of state in the Department of Social Security. The following year, she was named minister of state at the Treasury, and in 1991 took on the additional position of deputy chair of the Conservative Party. In 1992, she joined the Cabinet as secretary of state for unemployment. Shephard left that post in 1993, when she became minister of agriculture, food and fisheries; a year later, she was appointed secretary of state for education. The scope of this post was widened the following year, when she was named secretary of state for education and employment. In 1997, growing electoral discontent with the policies of Conservative Prime Minister *Margaret Thatcher* and her successor John Major led to a sweeping defeat at the polls for the Conservative Party (which received its slimmest percentage of the vote since 1832). Many Conservatives lost their seats in Parliament, but Shephard won reelection, and as the Labour Party took control of Parliament under Prime Minister Tony Blair, she was named shadow (opposition party) leader of the House of Commons. From 1998 to 1999, she was shadow secretary of state for the environment, transport, and the regions (meaning that she was the Conservative Party's official voice for responding to policies set by the actual secretary of state for those departments). While still a member of Parliament, in 2000 Shephard published *Shephard's Watch: Illusions of Power in British Politics*, an examination of the workings of government and political parties in Britain.

**SOURCES:**
Drost, Harry. *What's What and Who's Who in Europe.* NY: Simon & Schuster, 1995.
*Who's Who 1999.* NY: St. Martin's Press, 1999.

**Ginger Strand**, Ph.D., New York City

# Shepherd, Dolly (d. 1983)

*British parachutist and balloonist. Born in England; died in 1983.*

Known as Britain's "Parachute Queen," Dolly Shepherd was waiting tables at "Ally Pally" in London's Great Hall when celebrated parachutist and balloonist Captain Auguste Gaudron turned up at one of her tables. Purportedly, before

Gaudron finished dining, he had convinced the 17-year-old to take to the skies. Shepherd made her first jump from a gas-filled balloon after only 30 minutes of training. According to another version of the story, however, she was attending a London performance of Buffalo Bill Cody's Wild West show in 1903 when she was plucked from the audience by Buffalo Bill himself. She helped him out with a stunt he usually performed with his wife, and in gratitude Cody introduced her to a balloonist. However she got started, Shepherd soon joined a troupe of parachutists which toured Britain performing daredevil jumps before enthralled onlookers. Jumping from hot-air balloons 1,000 feet in the sky and sailing to earth with only a rudimentary wood-and-canvas parachute, she saw some of her fellow parachutists killed in accidents and was herself injured several times. In 1912, a woman with whom she was performing discovered too late that her parachute was faulty, and both jumped with only Shepherd's parachute to protect them. Shepherd ended up badly hurt, perhaps paralyzed, but with the aid of unorthodox treatment was able to walk, and jump, again. Unnerved, however, she finally quit parachuting, and during World War I worked as a driver and mechanic in France. Shepherd chronicled her adventures in the 1997 book *When the 'Chute Went Up: Adventures of a Pioneer Lady Parachutist* (written with Peter Hearn and **Molly Sedgwick**).

**SOURCES:**
"Books," in *This England*. Autumn 1997.

**SUGGESTED READING:**
Cadogan, Mary. *Women With Wings: Female Flyers in Fact and Fiction*. Chicago, IL: Academy, 1993.

# Shepherd, Mary (c. 1780–1847)

*Scottish philosopher. Name variations: Lady Mary Shepherd; Lady Mary Primrose. Born Mary Primrose around 1780; died on January 7, 1847; second daughter of Neil Primrose, 3rd earl of Rosebery; married Henry John Shepherd, on April 11, 1808 (died January 7, 1847).*

*Selected works: An Essay on the Relation of Cause and Effect, Controverting the Doctrine of Mr. Hume, Concerning the Nature of that Relation (1824); Essays on the Perception of an External Universe and Other Subjects Connected with the Doctrine of Causation (1827); essays critical of the views of John Fearn in Parriana (1829); a response to Fearn in Fraser's Magazine (1832); possibly another book.*

Little is known about Lady Mary Shepherd, born around 1780, the daughter of the 3rd earl

of Rosebery, Neil Primrose. In 1808, she married Henry John Shepherd, son of the Rt. Honorable Sir Samuel Shepherd, exchequer of Scotland from 1819 to 1830. Shepherd wrote two, possibly three, books. Both *An Essay on the Relation of Cause and Effect* and *Essays on the Perception of an External Universe* were published many years after her marriage, in 1827 and 1829. Shepherd took a particular interest in the philosopher David Hume, and often addressed her arguments against the views of the contemporary Scottish philosophers. She was particularly concerned with the skepticism of Hume, and its implication of atheism. Shepherd also published a set of criticisms of the views of the retired naval officer turned philosopher John Fearn, in a collection called *Parriana*. His reply and her response were published together in *Fraser's Magazine* in 1832.

**SOURCES:**
Atherton, Margaret. *Women Philosophers of the Early Modern Period*. Indianapolis, IN: Hackett, 1994.
Kersey, Ethel M. *Women Philosophers: A Bio-critical Source Book*. NY: Greenwood Press, 1989.

**Catherine Hundleby**, M.A. Philosophy, University of Guelph, Guelph, Ontario, Canada

# Shepitko, Larissa (1939–1979)

*Soviet filmmaker. Name variations: Larisa Shepitko or Shepit'ko. Born in 1939 in Armtervosk, eastern Ukraine; died on July 2, 1979, in an automobile accident outside Moscow; educated at the VGIK state film school; married Elem Klimov (a film director); children: one son.*

*Selected films: Znoi (Heat, 1963); Krylya (Wings, 1966); Ty i ya (You and I, 1971); Voskhozdenie (The Ascent, 1977).*

Larissa Shepitko was an acclaimed Soviet film director whose career was cut short by an early death. Born in the eastern Ukraine in 1939, she enrolled in the VGIK state film school in Moscow at the age of 16. Although her beauty inspired suggestions that she try a career in front of the camera, she stayed true to her determination to direct, and studied with famous director Alexander Dovzhenko.

Shepitko's two student shorts, *The Blind Cook* (1961) and *Living Water* (1962), were well received, and her first feature, *Znoi* (Heat, 1963), was made when she was 22. The film portrayed the harsh conditions and struggles on a state-owned communal farm in what is now Kyrgyzstan in a style that was both lyrical and realistic, and earned her immediate respect as a director. Like all her films, it was gorgeously shot and included a striking musical score, testifying to Shepitko's interest in both music and painting. *Znoi* was produced on a treeless location in temperatures that reached 120 degrees, so hot the film stock melted in the camera. When Shepitko came down with jaundice during the shoot and was too weak to walk, she was so determined to continue working that she had herself carried on a stretcher to various scenes.

The forced retirement of Soviet premier Nikita Khrushchev in 1964 interrupted the trend of greater freedom in the arts, and Shepitko's fearless commentary on modern Soviet society in her later films became suspect. Her 1966 film *Krylya* (Wings) received guarded praise from the Soviet press. The magazine *Iskusstvo Kino* (October 1966) dedicated 20 illustrated pages to the movie, finding in it "much of importance and (in the right sense of the word) edification." *Krylya* focused on the personal struggles of a woman who had been a celebrated fighter pilot during World War II as she adjusts to the more traditional role again expected of a woman in post-war Soviet society. The film earned Shepitko notice as "one of the important filmmakers of the Soviet new wave," and while some Soviet critics worried that it was a critique of wartime heroism, some American critics saw in it an implied condemnation of a society that expected a heroic combat veteran to return to the restricted life traditionally deemed best for women.

Shepitko next began work on *Radina electichestva* (The Homeland of Electricity), a film about poverty during the era of the Russian Civil War, but authorities put an end to the production in 1968. (Later completed, it would be released in 1987 as one of two short films collectively titled *The Beginning of an Unknown Century*.) In 1971, she completed *Ty i ya* (You and I), the story of a middle-aged doctor undergoing a personal crisis and her first film shot in color. The film's structure required viewers to reconstruct chronology and various story lines, and reminded some critics of films by French New Wave directors. (Shepitko's work earned her frequent comparisons to that of Alain Resnais as well as the early films of *Leni Riefenstahl.) Again, Communist authorities disapproved of her brazen exposing of contemporary society's ills, particularly in her depiction of the alienation of the Russian intelligentsia. They also found fault in her unconventional narrative techniques.

In 1977, Shepitko released what would prove to be her last film, *Voskhozdenie* (The Ascent), which follows a small group of soldiers struggling to survive in German-occupied Byelorussia in 1942. Shepitko was hailed for her "masculine" ability to depict the gritty horrors of war, and the film—stunningly shot in black and white—won a Golden Bear at that year's Berlin Film Festival. Although her films were unofficially suppressed in the Soviet Union, Shepitko received international attention. Considered a "breakthrough" director, she was offered the opportunity to direct in Hollywood, which she postponed until she could improve her English. She never got the chance, however, for in 1979, while scouting locations for her next film, *Farewell*, Shepitko was killed along with four members of her crew in an auto accident near Moscow. The film was made after her death by her husband Elem Klimov, who in 1981 also released the short photomontage *Larissa*.

SOURCES:

Attwood, Lynne, ed. *Red Women of the Silver Screen.* London: Pandora, 1993.

Foster, Gwendolyn A., ed. *Women Film Directors: An International Bio-critical Dictionary.* Westport, CT: Greenwood Press, 1995.

Katz, Ephraim. *The Film Encyclopedia.* 3rd ed. NY: HarperCollins, 1998.

Wakeman, John, ed. *World Film Directors.* NY: H.W. Wilson, 1988.

**Ginger Strand**, Ph.D.,
New York City

# Sheppard, Kate (1847–1934)

*British-born suffragist who was a key figure in gaining enfranchisement for women in New Zealand. Name variations: Mrs. K.W. Sheppard. Born Catherine Wilson Malcolm in 1847 in Liverpool, England; died in 1934 in Christchurch, New Zealand; daughter of Andrew Wilson Malcolm (a lawyer) and Jemima Crawford (Souter) Malcolm; married Walter Sheppard, in 1870 (died 1915); married William Lovell-Smith, in 1925; children: (first marriage) Douglas (1880–1910).*

Born in 1847 in England, Kate Sheppard was 21 when she moved with her widowed mother and siblings from Liverpool to Christchurch, New Zealand, where one of her older sisters already lived. In 1870, she married Walter Sheppard, with whom she would have one son, and soon became involved in the Women's Christian Temperance Union (WCTU).

In 1885, American feminist **Mary Leavitt** visited New Zealand, and Sheppard began to dedicate herself to the cause of equality and suffrage for women. As president of the New Zealand WCTU, in 1886 she founded the Franchise Department, devoted to the enfranchisement of women, which she believed would not only help women achieve equality but also help society at large by adding women's voices to debates on social and economic policy. She wrote articles and pamphlets, organized countless meetings with women in small towns throughout New Zealand, and lobbied widely with politicians and other public figures. From 1891 to 1894, she edited the women's page of the *Prohibitionist*, the twice-monthly magazine of the temperance movement, advocating for temperance and women's suffrage. When the Canterbury Women's Institute, which would largely coordinate the various groups working towards suffrage, was founded in 1892, Sheppard became head of its Economics Department and de facto head of the institute's push for suffrage. First one, then a second, and then a third petition for enfranchisement for women—the last reportedly signed by one out of every four grown women in the country—were submitted to the New Zealand Parliament. The bill passed in the Lower House in September 1893. Prime Minister Richard John Seddon was adamantly set against suffrage, but his attempts to ensure that the bill would be defeated in the Upper House backfired, causing two councilors to change their votes at the last minute; it passed with a margin of two votes. The enfranchisement of Maori women was then added to the bill, and on September 19, 1893, Sheppard received a telegraph from Prime Minister Seddon that the bill had been signed into law. New Zealand had become the world's first nation to grant all its majority-age female citizens the right to vote. When general elections were held two months later, some 90,000 women voted.

Sheppard continued advocating for improvement of women's condition. Upon its founding in 1896, she became president of the National Council of Women, which quickly became New Zealand's most respected and widely known women's group, and maintained a busy schedule as a public speaker, writer, and lobbyist. She traveled overseas several times to meet with suffragists in other countries. Among her greatest concerns were health and social reforms, divorce and separation rights, equal pay,

and economic independence. In 1896, she wrote and proposed to Parliament a "common fund" bill to mandate that a married woman with children who did not work outside the home would receive, by law, a set portion of her husband's earnings, to be used for home and family expenses, as just compensation for the work she did inside the home. The bill did not pass. From 1898 through 1903, Sheppard edited *White Ribbon*, a monthly women's newspaper, but she began experiencing poor health and (perhaps longstanding) marital difficulties. After suffering a nervous breakdown, in 1903 Sheppard moved to England with her husband.

The move did not, apparently, heal the rift in their relations, and in 1905 she returned to New Zealand, where she lived with William and **Jennie Lovell-Smith**. Walter Sheppard would die in 1915, and in 1925, after Jennie Lovell-Smith died, Sheppard and William Lovell-Smith would be married. Kate Sheppard lived fairly quietly in these years, although she became involved again with the National Council of Women after World War I, advocating both equality and world peace. She was all but forgotten in the decades after her death in 1934. Only with the rise of feminist scholarship towards the end of the 20th century did her achievements and ideas begin to be recognized and written about. A street in New Zealand is now named in her honor.

**SOURCES:**

Hyman, Prue. *Biographical Dictionary of Women Economists*. Draft, 1998.

Waring, Marilyn J. "How the Vote Was Won: The Centenary of World Women's Suffrage, in New Zealand," in *Ms.* January–February 1993, pp. 16–17.

**SUGGESTED READING:**

Devaliant, Judith. *Kate Sheppard—A Biography*. Penguin, 1992.

**Ginger Strand**, Ph.D.,
New York City

# Sheremetskaia, Natalia (1880–1952)

*Russian empress for one day. Name variations: Sheremetskaya; Nathalie Brasova; Countess Brassovna; Natasha. Born on June 27, 1880; died in an automobile accident in September 1952; daughter of Serge Scheremetersky; married Mamontov; married Wulfert; married Michael Aleksandrovich Romanov (1878–1918, son of Alexander III, tsar of Russia, and \*Marie Feodorovna), grand duke Thronfolger, in July 1912; children: George M. (1910–1931, died in an automobile accident).*

Natalia Sheremetskaia was technically married to the tsar of Russia for a few hours. When her brother-in-law Nicholas II abdicated in 1917, her husband Michael, son of Alexander III, became Michael II. But Michael had no interest in becoming the tsar in the middle of a revolution and abdicated within hours. A beautiful Russian divorcée and nonroyal, Natalia created a scandal when she married Michael in 1912. Their life and letters are contained in Rosemary and Donald Crawford's *Michael and Natasha: The Life and Love of Michael II, the Last of the Romanov Tsars* (Scribner, 1997).

## Sheridan, Caroline Elizabeth
(1808–1877).

*See Norton, Caroline.*

## Sheridan, Caroline Henrietta Callander (1779–1851).

*See Norton, Caroline for sidebar.*

## Sheridan, Clare (1885–1970)

*English sculptor, journalist, and travel writer. Name variations: Clare Frewen Sheridan. Born Clare Consuelo Frewen on September 9, 1885, in London, England; died in 1970 in Brede, England; daughter of Moreton Frewen and Clara (Jerome) Frewen; niece of Jennie Jerome Churchill (1854–1921); married Wilfred Sheridan, on October 10, 1910 (died 1915); children: Margaret (b. 1911); Elizabeth (1912–1913); Richard (1915–1936).*

Born into the English upper classes in 1885, Clare Frewen Sheridan spent her early years in London and at the family home in Sussex. Her father Moreton Frewen inherited little wealth and struggled for years to make his fortune through cattle-ranching, gold mining, and other schemes in the United States and Africa, but left the family dependent on their wealthy relatives for support. Her mother **Clara Jerome Frewen** came from New York's social elite and was the sister of Lady *Jennie Jerome Churchill. Clare was tutored in London, Ireland, Paris, and Germany, but made little progress in her studies except in foreign languages. Her family's financial problems made it difficult for her to find a suitor, but Clare, sensitive and intelligent, decided she wanted to be a writer anyway. She became the protégée of Rudyard Kipling and Henry James who encouraged her ambitions, but she considered her first novel a failure and burnt it. In 1910, she married Wilfred Sheridan, with whom she had fallen in love several years earlier. He came from a respectable but poor Irish family; their decision to marry caused a rift between Clare and her parents, who had demanded that she marry a wealthy aristocrat in order to support them. The newlyweds moved outside London; Clare had two daughters in 1911 and 1912, but the younger died of tuberculosis in 1913.

Sheridan wanted a memorial stone erected over her daughter's grave, and resolved to design it herself. She entered a technical school to study sculpture and found that expressing herself in clay helped her through her grief. However, the next year Wilfred joined the British army fighting in World War I. Sheridan gave birth to a son in September 1915, one week before her husband was killed in action. With little income and two children, she left her children in her parents' care and set up a studio in London, launching a career as a professional sculptor. At first she sold only decorative pottery, but soon her connections to the London elite led to commissions for portrait busts in marble and bronze. By 1920, she was well established in London, and a one-woman exhibition of her work was planned for the fall. That summer, Sheridan traveled secretly to Moscow, on the invitation of a Russian ambassador to England. She was lodged at the Kremlin where she modeled busts of the Bolshevik leaders Vladimir Lenin and Leon Trotsky as well as other Russian political figures. On her return home in 1921, she was surprised to find that London society and many in her own family branded her a traitor for living with England's enemies in Communist Russia. There was great media interest in her experiences, however, and she soon published a memoir, *Mayfair to Moscow*. She moved to New York to set up a studio and brought her children over from England. Clare became friends with the editor of the *New York World* newspaper, and went to Mexico to write articles for the paper on life there. Her exploits and her quick, impressionistic writing style made Clare Sheridan well known in the U.S.; at the invitation of movie producer Samuel Goldwyn, she went to Hollywood, where she became a close friend of Charlie Chaplin. When it was falsely reported in the press that they were engaged, Sheridan had little choice but to return to New York.

In 1922, she went to England as correspondent on European affairs for the *New York World*. Over the next two years, she would interview top political figures during a key period in the emergence of the new Europe in the aftermath of World War I, including Kemal Ataturk, founder of Turkey, Irish nationalist leaders, and the kings of Rumania and Bulgaria. At Benito Mussolini's invitation, she went to Rome where she was able to interview him at length. Her articles on these meetings were considered major scoops in the American press. She returned to Europe in 1923 as permanent correspondent from Germany for the *World* but continued to travel across Europe as events unfolded. It was the combination of her unique status as a female journalist, her remarkable beauty, her family connection to Winston Churchill, and her lack of public political commitments which gave Sheridan access to people most male journalists were not allowed to meet in a period of international hostility. The Soviet ambassador to London then offered her a visa to visit southern Rus-

sia, which she quickly accepted. She and her brother Oswald Frewen took his motorcycle across southern Europe to the Ukraine and Crimea in 1924. Clare fell in love with the country and declared herself a Communist. She nonetheless hoped to settle with her children in Constantinople, yet after only one year there they left for Algiers when it was rumored Clare was a spy for the Communists. From 1927 to 1931, they lived in Bikstra in the Sahara, Sheridan producing several novels as well as travel books on her experiences in Europe and Russia, and continuing to sculpt as well. Always restless,

*Clare Sheridan*

Sheridan moved back to England again, where she met and sculpted a bust of Mohandas Gandhi. In 1936, after the sudden death of her son, Sheridan moved briefly to an art colony in the American Rockies, finding consolation in sculpting once again. She rejoined her family in Sussex at the outbreak of war in 1939, and in 1946, after the war's end, left for Italy. There she converted to Catholicism, then moved to Galway in Ireland. The depth of her spiritual feeling is revealed in her Irish sculptures, mostly large-scale religious works in wood or stone, often portraying madonnas, still on display in Galway churches. She received few commissions in Ireland, and left in 1952 to return to her house in Bikstra. There she wrote her final book, the autobiographical *To the Four Winds*.

In 1959, Sheridan returned for the last time to England and settled in Brede Village, Sussex. She remained there until her death at age 84 in 1970. A posthumous exhibition of Clare Sheridan's works was shown at the Rye Art Gallery in Sussex in 1971.

**SOURCES:**

Leslie, Anita. *Cousin Clare: The Tempestuous Career of Clare Sheridan*. London: Hutchinson, 1976.

Sheridan, Clare. *To the Four Winds*. London: A. Deutsch, 1957.

**Laura York**, M.A. in History, University of California, Riverside, California

## Sheridan, Dinah (1920—)

*English actress who starred in the comedy classic* **Genevieve.** *Born Dinah Nadyejda Mec on September 17, 1920, in Hampstead, England; daughter of James Mec and* **Lisa Mec** *(both photographers); attended Sherrards Wood School; trained at the Italia Conti school; married Jimmy Hanley (an actor), on May 8, 1942 (divorced 1952); married Sir John Davis (an executive at Rank), in 1954 (divorced 1965); married Jack Merivale (an actor), in 1986 (died 1990); married Aubrey Ison, in 1992; children: (first marriage) Jeremy Hanley (b. 1945, a member of Parliament),* **Jenny Hanley** *(b. 1947, a model and actress), another daughter who died at birth; (second marriage) three stepchildren.*

*Selected filmography:* Irish and Proud of It *(1936);* Landslide *(1937);* Behind Your Back *(1937);* Full Speed Ahead *(1939);* Salute John Citizen *(1942);* Get Cracking *(1943);* For You Alone *(1944);* 29 Acacia Avenue *(1945);* Murder in Reverse *(1945);* The Hills of Donegal *(1947);* Calling Paul Temple *(1948);* The Huggetts Abroad *(1949);* The Story of Shirley Yorke *(1949);* Dark Secret *(1949);* No Trace *(1950);* Blackout *(1950);* Paul Temple's Triumph *(1950);* Where No Vultures Fly *(1951);* The Sound Barrier *(1952);* Appointment in London *(1950);* The Gilbert and Sullivan Story *(1953);* Genevieve *(1953);* The Railway Children *(1971);* The Mirror Crack'd *(1980).*

Born in England in 1920 to a German mother and a Russian father, Dinah Sheridan made her London stage debut at the age of 12 and soon thereafter joined a tour of *Peter Pan*, playing Wendy to *Elsa Lanchester's Peter and Charles Laughton's Captain Hook. She continued acting in theater throughout her teens, and made her first film, *Irish and Proud of It* (1936), when she was 16. Over the next three years she appeared in six more films, briefly interrupting her career at the beginning of World War II to work as an ambulance driver. In 1942, she married actor Jimmy Hanley, with whom she would have two surviving children before they divorced in 1952. While Sheridan continued appearing in films regularly, including *Get Cracking* (1943) with George Formby, a former music-hall performer who was then the most popular comedian in Britain, she never quite made it to stardom in those years.

In 1953, Sheridan filmed her 23rd movie. None of the four stars had been the producers' initial choice; she had gotten her role only after **Claire Bloom** declined it. Nonetheless, *Genevieve* was a huge hit, catapulting Sheridan to "overnight" success. Also starring *Kay Kendall, Kenneth More and John Gregson, the story about two couples racing cross country in vintage cars proved one of the most successful films of the year, and is still considered a classic example of British comedy. However, the following year Sheridan married for a second time, to executive John Davis, and at his insistence retired from the screen at the height of her popularity. While the marriage was not successful, it lasted until 1965. (During the divorce proceedings, the judge cut short her successful petition on grounds of cruelty by saying he didn't want to hear the "disgraceful details.") She promptly returned to the stage and to movies, and in 1972 played the mother in the perennially popular film adaptation of *Edith Nesbit's *The Railway Children*. Sheridan, who had two subsequent successful marriages, made her last onscreen appearance in 1980, in the *Agatha Christie mystery *The Mirror Crack'd*, with *Elizabeth Taylor, Rock Hudson, and *Kim Novak.

## Sheridan, Elizabeth Ann (1754–1792).

*See Linley, Elizabeth.*

## Sheridan, Frances (1724–1766)

*Irish novelist and dramatist. Born Frances Chamberlaine in Dublin, Ireland, in 1724; died in Blois, France, on September 26, 1766; youngest of five children of Philip Chamberlaine (an Irish cleric) and Anastasia Whyte; married Thomas Sheridan (a well-known actor-manager), in 1747; children: three sons, including Richard Brinsley Sheridan (1751–1816, Irish dramatist and parliamentary orator), and three daughters, including writers \*Alicia Lefanu (1753–1817) and \*Elizabeth Lefanu (1758–1837).*

Frances Sheridan was born Frances Chamberlaine in Dublin in 1724, the youngest of five children of Philip Chamberlaine, a cleric, and **Anastasia Whyte**, who died shortly after her birth. Frances was raised by a father who did not believe women should be taught how to write, though he reluctantly allowed her to learn how to read. Then, her older brothers took her in hand and secretly taught her writing, Latin, and botany. By age 15, Frances had written a romance and two sermons. She met and married actor-manager Thomas Sheridan and raised six children, including the famous Irish playwright Richard Brinsley Sheridan.

At the urging of her friend Samuel Richardson, Frances Sheridan published the highly successful *Memoirs of Miss Sidney Biddulph* in 1761. She also wrote the play *The Discovery*, which starred her husband and David Garrick and later become a stock piece for Garrick. *The Dupe*, starring \*Kitty Clive in the 1763–64 season at Drury Lane, was less successful. When financial problems forced the Sheridans to move to Blois, France, Frances continued to write, including the novel *A Trip to Bath*, completed one year before her sudden death in 1766. The book, finally published in 1902, was discovered to contain an antecedent to her son's famous character Mrs. Malaprop in his play *The Rivals*. An Oriental tale, *Nourjahad*, was also published posthumously. Frances Sheridan's memoirs were printed by her novelist granddaughter \*Alicia Lefanu (c. 1795–c. 1826) in London in 1824.

## Sheridan, Helen Selina (1807–1867).

See Blackwood, Helen Selina.

## Sheridan, Jane Georgina (d. 1884).

See Norton, Caroline for sidebar on Georgiana Seymour.

## Sheridan, Margaret (1889–1958)

*Irish soprano who had leading roles at La Scala and Covent Garden and was particularly acclaimed for her singing of Puccini's operatic heroines. Name variations: Margaret Burke Sheridan; Margaret Burke-Sheridan. Born Margaret Burke Sheridan on October 15, 1889, in Castlebar, County Mayo, Ireland; died in Dublin on April 16, 1958; daughter of John Burke Sheridan (a postmaster) and Mary Ellen (Cooley) Burke Sheridan; educated at Convent of Mercy, Castlebar; Dominican Convent, Eccles Street, Dublin; and Royal Academy of Music, London, 1909–11; studied in Rome with Alfredo Martino, 1916–18; never married; no children.*

Early in 1918, a young Irish singer, quite unknown in Italy, made her first appearance on the operatic stage, at Rome's Constanzi Opera House. The route by which she had arrived there was as romantic as the plots of the operas in which she was to sing. While practicing at the window of her room in the Quirinale Hotel, just across the street from the Opera House, Margaret Sheridan had been overheard by its director, **Emma Carelli**. When the soprano playing Mimi in a forthcoming production of *La Bohème* suddenly fell ill, Carelli remembered that voice, and sent a message to summon its owner. Inexperienced as she was, Sheridan was able to convince the director of her ability to sing the role and, with only four days to spare, the two worked together frantically to prepare for the first performance. On February 3, Margherita Sheridan, as she was billed, made her debut in what was to be her most celebrated role, before an audience which included the king of Italy and Margaret's patron and friend, inventor Giuglielmo Marconi. Described by both critics and public as "*una Mimi deliziosa*," Sheridan won admiration for both her voice and her acting: she was, according to *Il Messaggero*, "a young artist blessed with a wonderful voice who gave an unforgettable performance." Another critic particularly praised her performance in the final act, "which she rendered with emotive sweetness of voice."

Margaret Sheridan's triumph on that evening marked the opening of a short but glittering career which brought her from the obscurity of a small town in the west of Ireland to the leading opera houses of the world. Born Margaret Burke Sheridan in Castlebar, County Mayo, 29 years before, she was the youngest child of John Burke Sheridan, the local postmaster, and **Mary Ellen Burke Sheridan**. The family was a long-established and prominent one in the area, and Margaret's early life was both emotionally and financially secure. A lively, warmhearted and attractive child, she was her father's favorite, and friends noted her "lovely, fair and fresh coloring" and the "regal pose to her head."

At the age of four, Margaret was sent to the local Convent of Mercy school, where music was an important part of the curriculum. There, she began to learn singing and basic musical theory, and her promise as a singer quickly became apparent. When she was just five, however, her previously stable life was disrupted by the death of her mother. The tragedy left a void at home which was filled with family quarrels, intensified by her father's increased dependence on alcohol and later his poor health. In 1901, he died following a short illness, leaving his youngest daughter and son in the care of his friend, the local parish priest, Reverend Patrick Lyons. The family home was sold, and, with virtually all her links with the past destroyed, Sheridan left Castlebar for the Dominican Convent at Eccles Street in Dublin, where she was to spend the next seven years of her life.

Margaret was fortunate in that Eccles Street, one of the leading girls' schools in Ireland at that time, had a high reputation for musical education. Mother **Clement Burke**, who taught music and singing, quickly discovered her new student's outstanding talent, and became a major influence on Margaret's life and career. Another source of encouragement was Dr. Vincent O'Brien, conductor of the Eccles Street choir, who in 1908 arranged for her first solo public appearance at Dublin's Rotunda Rooms, on a bill which starred O'Brien's most famous pupil, John McCormack. In the same year, she won the gold medal in the mezzo-soprano section at the annual Feis Ceoil competition, and her success opened up a new range of opportunities in the Dublin musical world. The critics were united in their approval, praising her "divinely sweet" voice, her power, phrasing and enunciation, but it was clear that she deserved further training. In May 1909, she left for London, where she was to study at the Royal Academy of Music under William Shakespeare.

Sheridan's talent quickly won recognition at the Academy, and one of her fellow students later recalled "the amazing colour and beauty of tone she possessed." In order to supplement the bursary which financed her studies, she performed at private drawing-room concerts, while also taking further classes from the famous singing teacher **Olga Lynn** and embarking on her first serious love affair, with an Irish MP, Richard Hazelton.

Increasingly, Margaret saw opera rather than the concert stage as her favorite medium, but was unsuccessful in obtaining a contract to sing at the Royal Opera House, Covent Garden. The outbreak of war in 1914 dealt a further, and apparently decisive, blow to her operatic ambitions. While singing at a reception given by **Lady Howard de Walden**, however, her voice attracted the admiration of the Italian-Irish inventor Giuglielmo Marconi, who persuaded her to accompany him to Italy for further study. The choice, as she told a schoolfriend, was "between love and ambition and . . . her advisers had prevailed upon her to leave love and follow ambition." In 1916, therefore, leaving Hazelton behind, she sailed with Marconi for Italy.

In Rome, Sheridan was fortunate in meeting the composer Francesco Tosti, who introduced her to the noted operatic coach Alfredo Martino. Martino's judgment was that her voice "had strong potential, but mainly because of faulty training, she had developed several bad habits, one of which was straining in the upper register." He agreed to take her on as a pupil, and with his help, Margaret worked to develop and correct her vocal technique, to raise her voice from mezzo to full soprano, and to master the operas in which she hoped to sing, and which she heard at the city's Constanzi Opera House. In early 1918, she had the chance to appear there when Carelli suddenly appointed her to sing Mimi in Puccini's *La Bohème*. Although Martino disapproved, believing that she was not yet ready for operatic roles, Sheridan went on to make her triumphant debut on February 3, 1918. Initially engaged for just one night, she sang Mimi in six further performances during that season, while continuing her studies with Martino.

In the following year, 1919, Sheridan fulfilled her long-standing ambition to sing at Covent Garden, appearing there in *La Bohème*, *Madama Butterfly*, and in the Covent Garden premiere of Mascagni's *Iris*. She was extremely nervous about her first London performance, in which she was to follow *Nellie Melba, and at which most of her Irish and English supporters were to be present, but the occasion, on May 27, was another resounding success. On July 8, Margaret appeared in the demanding title role of *Iris*, and once again, critics and audience were unanimous in their praise.

Sheridan's London season was to be important for more than professional reasons, since it brought her into contact for the first time with Colonel Eustace Blois, an administrator at Covent Garden. Handsome, humorous and cultivated, Blois shared with Margaret not only a love of music but also memories of Ireland, where he had spent many summers during his boyhood. The two developed a friendship which over the next few years grew into a love affair, despite the fact that Blois was married and that everything in Sheridan's devoutly Catholic convent upbringing was opposed to such a relationship. Other strains included their frequent separations because of work, and the discretion which they had to exercise at all times. Nevertheless, the relationship was to be the most important of Sheridan's life, and was to last for more than a decade.

Margaret's achievements in London enhanced her reputation in Italy. Returning there at the end of the season, she settled in Milan, declaring, to those who were skeptical, that a foreigner could sing Italian opera, and that as an Irishwoman she had the passion, the strength and the sensitivity required. When she appeared in December 1919 at the Dal Verme opera house in *Madama Butterfly*, the newspaper *Corriere della Sera* noted her nationality, but admitted that "either by luck or instinct she sings as an Italian . . . only the colour of her lower notes revealed her different origin." Among those who came to see her were the conductor Arturo Toscanini and Puccini himself, who praised what he regarded as her totally new interpretation of the role he had written, and the "dramatic intensity and childlike appeal" which she brought to it.

Margaret was to become one of the supreme exponents of Puccini's work, as the composer himself recognized. "He spoke of her," according to the conductor Bellezza, "as a great hope for the future, both for the opera world in general and for his own works in particular," and regarded her as the definitive Butterfly. He also chose and personally coached her for the part of Manon in a new performance of *Manon Lescaut*, first given in Rimini in 1923, and after his death in the following year, she took part in a number of commemorative events held throughout Italy.

As a singer and as an actress, Sheridan had managed to win over the notoriously critical Milanese audience. In 1922, following a successful season at the San Carlo theater in Naples, she was invited to join the company at Milan's premier opera house, La Scala, under its director, the autocratic Toscanini. Margaret described him as "the greatest dictator ever known in the world of opera," but admitted his huge influence within it, in promoting advances in technique and a much greater realism in performance, and in the demands which he made on his singers.

"In future, he decided, Manon must look like Manon. He acted as a sort of Svengali. He compelled us to do things. He educated us. He made us read and study in detail the period of the opera we were rehearsing."

Margaret was to make her La Scala debut in the revival of Catalani's *La Wally* and, following a well-received short season in Naples, the production opened at La Scala on April 6, 1922. Physically, Sheridan's qualifications for the part of the beautiful young heroine were immediately apparent; her first aria proved that vocally, too, she was perfectly suited to the part, and worthy of the traditions of La Scala. As one member of the audience on that night later recalled, "Margherita sang throughout the piece with freshness, an air of effortless ease, a dramatic power, a charm that took the whole theater by storm. She had a terrific ovation."

In the following year, Sheridan returned to La Scala for the world premiere of Respighi's *Belfagor*. While the opera had mixed notices, her performance won plaudits from audience and critics. In the 1923–24 season, she received further praise for her performance in Primo Riccitelli's comic opera *I compagnacci*, and as Maddalena in *Andrea Chenier*. However, this would be her final appearance on the stage at La Scala. Her disappearance was due not to any decline in her vocal abilities, but rather to her worsening relations with Toscanini. Their disagreements were partly professional, with Toscanini regarding Sheridan as temperamental and self-willed and believing that her active social life interfered with her work. There were also profound political differences: Toscanini was a convinced and outspoken anti-fascist, while Margaret, if not positively a supporter of Mussolini, displayed no antipathy towards him, and certainly numbered many fascists among her friends and admirers. Toscanini was particularly irritated by an interview she gave to a fascist newspaper, in which, as a foreigner, she expressed her gratitude to the regime for allowing her the privilege of working in Italy.

By 1924, therefore, Sheridan's career at the center of Italian opera was at an end. However, she had little difficulty in finding work elsewhere. In late 1924, she sang Maddalena in *Andrea Chenier* at Bologna, moving on to further engagements in Genoa and Modena, and then to London, where Blois was by now managing director of Covent Garden. Engaged as one of the stars of the 1925 International Season, Margaret appeared in *Madama Butterfly* and in *Andrea Chenier*, with the tenor Giacomo Lauri-Volpi. As in 1919, her performances attracted large audiences and won almost unanimous admiration, with the *Daily Telegraph* remarking on the psychological depth apparent in her singing of Butterfly, and on "her voice of loveliest most velvety character."

After a number of appearances in Italy, Sheridan returned to Covent Garden for the 1926 season, for which luminaries such as Melba, Feodor Chaliapin, Lauritz Melchior, and the conductor Bruno Walter had also been engaged. Once more, she had great success in *Bohème*, and as Lauretta in *Gianni Schicci*. With Blois' encouragement, she also signed her first recording contract, and in the following year made a number of records, of operatic arias and of Irish songs, for HMV. In 1929–30, she was one of the artists performing on the first complete recording of *Butterfly*, opposite the Australian tenor Lionelo Cecil. However, her recording career would be a troubled one, plagued by her restlessness and perfectionism, which led to repeated delays and cancellations. Indeed, between 1930 and 1944, she would make no recordings at all.

As was now her practice, Sheridan returned to Italy for the winter of 1926–27, but a planned return to La Scala, as Dolly in the world premiere of Wolf-Ferrari's *Sly*, had to be canceled because of ongoing nose and throat problems. These also prevented her appearance at Covent Garden in the 1927 season, but she was sufficiently recovered by the following year to sing Mimi and to appear, in the secondary but more sympathetic part of Liu, in Puccini's *Turandot*, with *Eva Turner in the eponymous role. Sheridan continued to suffer from throat infections, and her first performance at Covent Garden in 1929 had to be canceled at short notice. A few weeks later, however, she scored "a notable triumph," according to *The Daily Telegraph*, in the title role of *Manon Lescaut*, in which she was partnered by the great tenor Pertile. As one critic recorded, "last night Margaret Sheridan and Signor Pertile gave their duets in superb style, each artist in splendid voice and blending their singing most effectively."

Although nobody yet knew it, Sheridan's operatic career was drawing inexorably to an end. Her performance as Mimi at Covent Garden in 1929 was her last appearance in this role. In February 1930, she performed for the last time in Italy, when, with Pertile, she sang *Gianni Schicchi* at a gala performance in Turin. Returning to London in May, she appeared, with Gigli, in *Andrea Chenier*, as well as in performances of *Butterfly* and *Otello*, and it was as Desdemona

that she made her last appearance on the operatic stage, at Covent Garden, on June 16, 1930.

The next few years were to be dogged by continued disappointments. Her health continued to be poor, necessitating a number of operations, and as offers of work diminished, so did her income. In addition, the strains on her relationship with Blois intensified. Knowing that marriage was impossible, since Blois had no intention of seeking a divorce from his wife, and dogged by religious scruples, Sheridan eventually ended the affair. She was deeply unhappy, and her sense of loss was compounded by Blois' death not long afterwards.

With her confidence at such a low ebb, the prospect of a comeback was daunting, and the three years of inactivity had weakened her voice. Because her early training had been curtailed, she lacked the technique to make good this decline, and therapy at voice clinics in Salzburg and in London failed to resolve her problems, which were as much psychological as physical. According to E. Herbert-Caesari, who treated

*Margaret Sheridan*

her for a number of years, "a devastating emotional upheaval had obviously shattered all faith in herself and her will to return to public performance." In 1939, at age 50, "her voice," he noted, "was as sound as a bell. . . . The quality was truly exquisite and more than ever evident as a result of her technical studies. If only certain inhibitions could have been uprooted and mental readjustments crystallised there was nothing whatever to prevent her returning to her well-loved opera stage. The desire was now there, but not the full will."

Despite her long absences from Ireland, "Maggie from Mayo," as she liked to call herself, had always maintained her links with her home country. During the late 1930s, she spent a number of holidays there, and in 1940, with Europe at war and her own career showing no sign of revival, she made the decision to live permanently in Dublin. The move, however, was almost certainly a retrograde one in professional terms. In 1944, she did take part in a recording of Irish songs and arias for HMV, which showed that her voice, though demonstrating signs of strain, was still rich and as expressive as ever. Nevertheless, she steadfastly resisted all offers of public engagements. Her declared ambition to teach came to nothing, and she repeatedly refused invitations to return to Italy where more opportunities would certainly have been available. With no prospect of singing professionally again, she led an aimless and financially precarious existence, a flamboyant and instantly recognizable, if somewhat pathetic, figure in the insular and unsophisticated Dublin of those years.

In 1950, however, Sheridan visited the United States for the first time, in response to an invitation from the American National Arts Foundation to serve on a committee which was to search for promising singers. In New York, she met Emerson and **Ruth Axe**, millionaire art patrons who were to become her closest American friends. During the final years of her life, she returned frequently to New York on foundation business, and for a taste of the luxury and excitement which Dublin could not provide. In 1956–57, while on her final visit there, she complained of feeling unwell. Tests showed that she had cancer, and she insisted on returning to Dublin, where she died on April 16, 1958. Tributes came from her friends, such as President Sean O'Kelly and the leading Irish actor Michael MacLiammoir, and from the Italian ambassador and former colleagues, both at home and abroad. **Gloria Davy** and *Ebe Stignani were among the artists who sang excerpts from Verdi's *Requiem* at her funeral mass, but most appropriate of all

was the tribute paid at Dublin's Gaiety Theatre on the evening following her death, when the cast and audience, at the opening performance of *Manon Lescaut*, stood in silent remembrance of one of the greatest Manons of them all, "Margherita Sheridan, Prima Donna."

SOURCES:
Chambers, Anne. *Adorable Diva: Margaret Burke Sheridan, Irish Prima-Donna, 1889–1958.* Dublin: Wolfhound Press, 1989.
Sadie, Stanley, ed. *The New Grove Dictionary of Opera.* London: Macmillan Press, 1992.
Smith, Gus. *Irish stars of the opera.* Dublin: Madison, 1994.

Rosemary Raughter,
freelance writer in women's history,
Dublin, Ireland

## Sheridan, Mrs. Richard Brinsley
(1754–1792).

*See Linley, Elizabeth.*

# Sherif, Carolyn Wood (1922–1982)

*American social psychologist who, with her husband, pioneered research methods, particularly in the study of the psychology of women.* Name variations: Carolyn Wood. Born Carolyn Wood on June 26, 1922, in Loogootee, Indiana; died of cancer in 1982; graduated from West Lafayette High School, 1940; Purdue University, B.S. with highest honors, 1943; State University of Iowa, M.A., 1944; attended Columbia University; University of Texas, Ph.D., 1961; married Muzafer Sherif (a social psychologist), in 1945; children: Sue (b. 1947); Joan (b. 1950); Ann (b. 1955).

Born in Loogootee, Indiana, in 1922, Carolyn Wood Sherif was the youngest of three children in a family which promoted academic excellence. While many girls at the time received little encouragement in aspiring to a professional career, Carolyn's parents applauded her ambitions to enter Purdue University after her high school graduation in 1940. She rejected her father's wishes that she pursue the field of home economics, opting instead to enter an experimental program for women science majors which provided a historical and humanist perspective on the study of science. Although it offered little in the way of psychology, the program's interdisciplinary approach profoundly influenced her later research in that field.

Carolyn's outstanding academic record upon her graduation in 1943 won her a place in the master's program at the State University of Iowa. There, she began reading the works of acclaimed Turkish social psychologist Muzafer

Sherif, then a professor at Princeton University, and became a great admirer of his research. After completing her master's degree, she moved to Princeton, New Jersey, where she found a job with a Gallup subsidiary. The research—conducted primarily for commercial purposes such as data collection on upcoming films—did not satisfy her professional ambitions, and an unwanted romantic advance by the research director cemented her plans to return to graduate school. She received an assistantship with Muzafer Sherif at Princeton, but had to commute to Columbia University in New York City for her doctoral courses because Princeton did not accept women students. This assistantship with Muzafer was the beginning of a long relationship that would encompass both their professional and their personal lives. The two were married in 1945.

For the next 16 years, Carolyn Sherif was an unrecognized, essential part of Muzafer's research, and often co-wrote articles with him in addition to raising their three daughters. The climate of the times resulted in academia's failure to recognize her contributions to her famous husband's findings on intergroup relations, and her role in their work, despite her credits as co-author, was largely ignored. She did not hold any academic positions of her own during these years, but moved with Muzafer to Yale and to the University of Oklahoma, collaborating on his research there. In 1958, she renewed her doctoral studies, at the University of Texas, and the following year finally earned an official position, as a research associate at the Institute of Group Relations at the University of Oklahoma.

Sherif's years as a research associate were tremendously productive, and it was during this time that she published, in conjunction with her husband, some of her most influential books: *Intergroup Conflict and Cooperation: The Robbers Cave Experiment* (1961, which for over 20 years remained one of the most cited studies in the field), *Reference Groups: Exploration into Conformity and Deviation of Adolescents* (1964); *Problems of Youth* (1965), and *Attitude and Attitude Change* (1965). In the course of their research, the Sherifs argued that human behavior needed to be studied in the context of the environment in which the behavior occurred, taking into account setting, the presence of other individuals, and cultural values and norms. Their incorporation of what previously had been regarded as peripheral factors into the study of social behavior was unique in its interdisciplinary approach. Sherif's research into attitudes within the framework of the self-system in *Attitude and Attitude Change* is considered her most important contribution to the field of social psychology. She proposed that the understanding of the "self" was necessary to any study on attitudes and behavior, although this idea did not become fully accepted until the late 1970s.

Four years after completing her doctoral thesis in 1961, Sherif accepted a position as a visiting faculty member in the psychology department at Penn State University; her husband became a visiting faculty member in the sociology department. She graduated from "visiting faculty" to a tenure-track position the following year, but her promotion to full professor was slow in coming. Despite her impressive research credentials, Sherif might have remained only an associate professor had the women's movement not raised awareness about gender inequality within the university system. She earned a full professorship at Penn State in 1970, and a few years later, after the U.S. Department of Health, Education, and Welfare began investigating the university for alleged discriminatory salary practices, began earning as much as a man with her credentials would have received. Sherif credited the women's movement with leading to improvements within academia—"I know I did not become a better social psychologist between 1969 and 1972," she once noted, "but I surely was treated as a better one"—and devoted much of her research in the 1970s to the study of the psychology of women. In her famous study "Bias in Psychology," published as a chapter in *The Prism of Sex* (1979), she argued that the field of psychology had reinforced myths about the inferiority of women by setting up narrowly focused studies designed to support the prejudices of the male-dominated establishment. She applied her findings on intergroup relations to her study of gender identity in her noted paper, "Needed Concepts in the Study of Gender Identity." A consulting editor of *Psychology of Women Quarterly* from its founding in 1977, she also was a key figure in the creation of both a course on women and psychology and a women's studies program at Penn State.

Well-deserved honors finally started coming Sherif's way in the mid-1970s, beginning with her election as a fellow in the American Psychological Association in 1976. The association greatly benefited from her service on a variety of committees and her leadership of the Division on the Psychology of Women. She was also honored by the national honor societies Psi Chi and Sigma Xi, acting as the national lecturer for the latter from 1981 until her untimely death from cancer in 1982. At the time, she had been appointed editor of the *Journal of Social Issues*, and was slated to receive the American Psychological Foundation's Award for Distinguished Contributions to Education in Psychology (it was awarded posthumously). After her death, the Division on the Psychology of Women sponsored the Carolyn Wood Sherif Award as the highest honor given for research and teaching on the psychology of women.

**SOURCES:**

Bailey, Brooke. *The Remarkable Lives of 100 Women Healers and Scientists*. Holbrook, MA: Bob Adams, 1994.

O'Connell, Agnes N., and Nancy Felipe Russo, eds. *Women in Psychology: A Bio-Bibliographic Sourcebook*. NY: Greenwood Press, 1990.

**Ginger Strand**, Ph.D.,
New York City

## Sherman, Mary Belle (1862–1935)

*American clubwoman who lobbied on behalf of the national-parks movement. Born Mary Belle King on December 11, 1862, in Albion, New York; died of cerebral thrombosis on January 15, 1935; daughter of Rufus King and Sarah Electa (Whitney) King; educated at St. Xavier's Academy and Park Institute in Chicago; married John Dickinson Sherman, on February 10, 1887 (died 1926); children: John King.*

*Selected writings:* Parliamentary Law at a Glance *(1901, later retitled* Parliamentary Law and Rules of Procedure).*

Born in 1862 in Albion, New York, Mary Belle King was educated in Rochester, New York, and Chicago. At age 25, she married newspaper editor John Dickinson Sherman. The couple had one son, John, whose upbringing was Sherman's primary occupation during his early years. Encouraged to become a member of the Chicago Woman's Club by her mother-in-law **Louise Dickinson Sherman**, she became increasingly active in this group and other clubs, serving as recording secretary for the Chicago Woman's Club and the General Federation of Women's Clubs. After a parliamentary-law study group met at her home and piqued her interest, Sherman became enough of an expert on the subject to write a handbook entitled *Parliamentary Law at a Glance* (1901) and to serve as an instructor in the field at the John Marshall Law School in Chicago. She also acted as parliamentarian for the Illinois Federation of Women's Clubs.

Sherman ascended to the position of vice-president of the General Federation of Women's Clubs in 1908, but an illness contracted while on a tour of women's clubs in the Panama Canal Zone severely crippled her effectiveness. She retreated to the family's vacation home in Estes Park, Colorado, to recuperate. She became convinced of the salutary nature of the wilderness, and thereafter dedicated herself to the conservation of land for national parks. She sufficiently regained her strength to become the chair of the conservation department of the General Federation in 1914 and began lobbying for the formation of the National Park Service. This goal was accomplished in 1916, and she was responsible for the creation of a number of park areas in the Grand Canyon and in parts of the Rocky Mountains. Known as the "National Park Lady," Sherman was an advocate of nature study at the elementary-school level and pushed for the planting of trees along highways.

From 1924 to 1928, Sherman served as president of the General Federation of Women's Clubs. She was also appointed vice-president of the American Forestry Association and a trustee of the National Park Service, in addition to holding a number of other advisory positions. Several months after being struck by a bus, she died of cerebral thrombosis in 1935.

**SOURCES:**

James, Edward T., ed. *Notable American Women, 1607–1950*. Cambridge, MA: The Belknap Press of Harvard University, 1971.

**Ginger Strand**, Ph.D.,
New York City

## Sherwin, Belle (1868–1955)

*American suffragist and civic leader. Born on March 25, 1868, in Cleveland, Ohio; died of bronchopneumonia on July 9, 1955; daughter of Henry Alden Sherwin (an industrialist) and Mary Frances (Smith) Sherwin; educated in public schools in Cleveland; attended St. Margaret's School in Waterbury, Connecticut; Wellesley College, B.S., 1890; conducted graduate work at Oxford University, 1894–95; never married; no children.*

Belle Sherwin, who after the ratification of the 19th Amendment would serve as the second president of the League of Women Voters, was born in 1868 in Cleveland, Ohio. The daughter of **Mary Smith Sherwin** and Henry Alden Sherwin, founder of the Sherwin-Williams Paint Company, she was fortunate to inherit sufficient wealth to make her financially independent, allowing her to pursue causes important to her, as well as strong organizational skills, the desire to work hard, and a clear moral vision. She was educated in the Cleveland public schools and at the private St. Margaret's School in Waterbury, Connecticut. She then attended Wellesley College, where the educational ethos and belief in useful women fostered by *Alice Freeman Palmer, the school's president, had a lasting impact on her life. Particularly influenced by her classes in history and economics, Sherwin received her B.S. in 1890. She would sustain a long relationship with Wellesley, donating many financial gifts and serving as a trustee and then trustee emerita from 1918 to 1952.

After attending Oxford University for graduate study in history (1894–95), Sherwin tried her hand at teaching, but soon returned to Cleveland to begin a career in social and civic work. After organizing English-language classes for the city's Italian immigrants, Sherwin set up the Cleveland Consumers' League in 1900. She would head its investigations into industrial conditions for several years. In 1902, after the creation of the Cleveland Visiting Nurses' Association, she became a member of its board, chairing the committee on recruitment and training of nurses and facilitating its eventual attachment to the city's official public health system. Organized and energetic, Sherwin proved a natural leader.

In 1910, while suffragist *Maud Wood Park was visiting Cleveland to drum up support for women's suffrage, Sherwin joined the College Equal Suffrage League, although she remained more involved with her civic work than with the fight for the vote for the next several years. In 1916, middle- and upper-class women of the city were suddenly divided into factions by the founding of a local branch of the National Association Opposed to Woman Suffrage. In response to the disruptions to Cleveland society caused by the introduction of this group—the diametric opposite of the country's largest suffrage organization, the National American Woman Suffrage Association (NAWSA)—Sherwin founded the Women's City Club as a place for both sides to meet and debate the issue without viciousness. The suffrage question was temporarily transferred to the back burner nationwide the following year, when the United States entered World War I. Because of her administrative experience and reputation, Sherwin was named chair of the Women's Committee of the Ohio branch of the United States Council of National Defense. In this capacity, she supervised and integrated the efforts of some 60 women's organizations involved with social welfare programs, conservation of food, and industrial recruitment.

After the war, Sherwin focused her energies on women's suffrage, becoming president of the Cleveland Suffrage Association in 1919. The 19th

Amendment, granting women the right to vote, was already wending its way through Congress and the states by this time, and Sherwin became an enthusiastic proponent of NAWSA president *Carrie Chapman Catt's idea for a successor organization to NAWSA aimed at educating enfranchised women on their new civic rights and responsibilities. With the ratification of the amendment in 1920, NAWSA, having achieved its aim, was transformed into the National League of Women Voters (NLWV), with Maud Wood Park as president. As vice-president, Sherwin took charge of the department organized to educate and train women in the performance of their civic duties. Despite the materials the department created and distributed on citizenship and on the mechanics of politics and voting, in the first two national elections after women were permitted to vote, far fewer exercised this right than Sherwin or many others had hoped.

In 1924, Sherwin was elected president of the NLWV, and moved to Washington, D.C. Aiming to change the poor turnout of those previous elections and create informed, educated women voters, she consolidated the far-flung programs and committees of the NLWV at its D.C. headquarters. An excellent spotter of talent who expected those around her to work as hard as she did, Sherwin described the organization as "a university without walls . . . whose members enter to learn and remain to shape the curriculum." Over the decade that she served as president, the NLWV became known for the even-handed accuracy of its research and evolved into the non-partisan educational organization that it remains today. She was admired for her intelligence and diplomacy, and for the way in which she united the various factions of the group into an authoritative organization respected for its balance and objectivity.

Succeeded as president of the NLWV in 1934 by *Marguerite Milton Wells, Sherwin accepted an appointment to the Consumers' Advisory Board of the National Recovery Administration, President Franklin Roosevelt's program to combat the Depression. She also served on the Federal Advisory Committee of the U.S. Employment Service. Sherwin left Washington in 1942 to return to Cleveland, where she remained active in civic life until her death of bronchopneumonia in 1955.

SOURCES:

Sicherman, Barbara, and Carol Hurd Green, eds. *Notable American Women: The Modern Period.* Cambridge, MA: The Belknap Press of Harvard University, 1980.

**Ginger Strand**, Ph.D., New York City

## Sherwood, Mrs. John (1826–1903).

See Sherwood, Mary Elizabeth.

## Sherwood, Josephine (1886–1957).

See Hull, Josephine.

# Sherwood, Katharine Margaret
## (1841–1914)

*American journalist, poet and civic leader. Name variations: Kate Brownlee; Kate Brownlee Sherwood. Born Katharine Margaret Brownlee on September 24, 1841, in Poland, Ohio; died after suffering a stroke on February 15, 1914; daughter of James Brownlee (a Scottish immigrant and judge) and Rebecca (Mullen) Brownlee; educated at Poland Union Seminary; married Isaac Ruth Sherwood (a journalist who later served in Congress), in 1859; children: Lenore and James.*

*Published two volumes of poetry,* Camp-Fire, Memorial-Day, and Other Poems *(1885) and* Dream of Ages: A Poem of Columbia *(1893); served as first president of the Ohio Newspaper Women's Association (1902).*

Katharine Margaret Brownlee was born in 1841 in Poland, Ohio, and educated at the local seminary. At age 18, she married Isaac Ruth Sherwood, a journalist who would later serve as a congressional representative from Toledo. During the Civil War, while he worked his way up to the rank of brigadier general in the Union Army, Katharine—better known as Kate—took over her husband's duties with the *Williams County Gazette* in Bryan, Ohio. There she edited and served as manager of the paper, following the events and battles of the Civil War that would mark her, like so many of her generation, for the rest of her life. Isaac returned to journalism after the war, and from 1875 to about 1885 Sherwood helped him edit the *Toledo Journal*. In 1883, she was one of the founders of the Woman's Relief Corps (WRC), an auxiliary of the Grand Army of the Republic, the organization for veterans of the Union Army. Founded over ten years before the United Daughters of the Confederacy, the WRC, of which Sherwood later served as national president, provided charity for poor Northern veterans, worked for legislation to provide pensions for nurses who had served during the Civil War, and within 25 years grew to include over 100,000 members.

Sherwood's first collection of poetry, much of which previously had appeared in various newspapers, was published in 1885. *Camp-Fire, Memorial-Day, and Other Poems* focused primarily on the Civil War and its aftermath, with such poems as "Christmas at the Soldiers' Orphans' Home" and "Thomas at Chickamauga." Called "the poetess of the Congressional Circle," Sherwood became widely known for these poems and the ones included in her second book, *Dream of Ages: A Poem of Columbia*. This work, published in 1893, was a wide-ranging, allegoric history of America, celebrating patriotism (as did so many of her poems) while also recalling the strife between Native Americans and white settlers, North and South, and slaves and masters. None of her poems have retained an audience, but they clearly struck a chord with readers of the day.

Sherwood meanwhile continued her career as a journalist, working as a Washington correspondent for a newspaper syndicate, serving as editor of the women's department of the *National Tribune*, a Washington, D.C., newspaper that focused on issues of interest to Union Army veterans and their families, and writing satires on politics for the *New York Sun*. In 1902, she became the first president of the Ohio Newspaper Women's Association. She was also deeply involved in civic causes, particularly in regards to education, children's welfare, and the inculcation of patriotism in schools and public life. Sherwood belonged to a number of women's clubs (she had served as the first president of the Canton, Ohio, branch of the Sorosis Club in 1893), and was a proponent of women's suffrage. She suffered a stroke in Washington, D.C., where her husband was serving in Congress, in January 1914, and a second stroke three weeks later. After her death on February 15, 1914, the *Toledo News-Bee* noted in her obituary: "No other woman has occupied so important a place in Toledo's public life."

**SOURCES:**

James, Edward T., ed. *Notable American Women, 1607–1950.* Cambridge, MA: The Belknap Press of Harvard University, 1971.

Willard, Frances E., and Mary A. Livermore, eds. *A Woman of the Century,* 1893.

**Ginger Strand**, Ph.D.,
New York City

# Sherwood, Mary (1856–1935)

*American doctor and public health advocate. Born on March 31, 1856, in Ballston Spa, New York; died of a coronary occlusion on May 24, 1935, in Baltimore, Maryland; daughter of Thomas Burr Sherwood (a lawyer and farmer) and Mary Frances (Beattie) Sherwood; educated at the State Normal School in Al-*

bany, New York; Vassar College, A.B., 1883; University of Zurich, M.D., 1890.

Mary Sherwood was born in 1856 in Ballston Spa, New York, into an academic family which included her father Thomas Burr Sherwood, who gave up a law career for farming; her sister **Margaret Pollock Sherwood**, later an English literature professor at Wellesley College; and her brother Sidney Sherwood, who would become an associate professor of economics at Johns Hopkins University. Sherwood advanced from the State Normal School in Albany to Vassar College, where she earned an A.B. degree in 1883 and a post as a chemistry assistant until 1885. A teaching position in geometry and astronomy at Packer Collegiate Institute in Brooklyn, New York, ended the following year, when she decided to embark on a career in medicine.

Although *Elizabeth Blackwell had become the first woman to graduate from medical school in America over 30 years earlier, many American medical schools still refused to accept women students. Sherwood traveled to Switzerland to attend the University of Zurich, where women had been permitted to study for decades. Among the courses she took was one in bacteriology, then so new a field that few courses were taught on it anywhere in the world. After four years at the University of Zurich, she earned her M.D. degree in 1890. Her thesis was published in a German medical journal.

Sherwood returned to the United States and joined her brother Sidney in Baltimore. The recently established Johns Hopkins Hospital there declined to accept her for a residency because she was a woman, but several male doctors at the hospital were glad to have her work in their wards. In 1892, Dr. *Lilian Welsh, with whom she had studied in Zurich and forged what would be a lifelong friendship, joined her in Baltimore, and the two opened an office together. It was Sherwood's "unbounded optimism and a kind of characteristic obstinacy," Welsh would later comment, that saw them through the rocky first years of the practice when patients were still suspicious of two women doctors. In addition to their private practice, Sherwood and Welsh took charge of the Evening Dispensary for Working Women and Girls of Baltimore, a charitable clinic, in 1893. The clinic provided other female physicians with much-needed experience, and also highlighted the need for better health care for women and children; over the 17 years she was involved with the clinic before it closed in 1910, this need would become an increasing concern for Sherwood.

In 1894, she accepted an appointment as medical director of the Bryn Mawr School for girls in Baltimore, and her professional relationship with Welsh continued as the latter assumed a similar position at the Woman's College of Baltimore (later Goucher College). Bryn Mawr was ahead of its time in offering medical care to its students and Sherwood (whose predecessor had been Dr. *Kate Campbell Hurd-Mead) headed up the efforts to treat and prevent disease. Her expertise in detecting the beginning stages of contagious diseases prompted the Baltimore Public School Board to retain both Sherwood and Welsh to examine teachers about to be hired to work in the public schools; she would maintain these examinations until 1923, when they were transferred to the purview of the Baltimore City Health Department. While also continuing to work at Bryn Mawr, in 1919 Sherwood became the first director of the Baltimore City Health Department's Bureau of Child Welfare. She organized the work of this new bureau and remained its director until 1924. In that capacity, she also became the first woman in the city to head a municipal bureau.

Sherwood attended to women's political as well as physical health. Perhaps remembering her own struggle to earn a medical education, she was active in the fight to open up Johns Hopkins' graduate schools to women students as a member of the Baltimore Association for the Promotion of the University Education of Women. She also advocated for women's suffrage before the passage of the 19th Amendment in 1920; 14 years before that, she had served as *Susan B. Anthony's physician while the ailing activist was in town for a convention. A member of numerous Baltimore government boards and the first chair of the obstetrical section of the American Child Health Association, Sherwood eased up on some of her many obligations in the later years of her life, but continued to work for the Bryn Mawr School until her death in 1935.

**SOURCES:**

James, Edward T., ed. *Notable American Women, 1607–1950*. Cambridge, MA: The Belknap Press of Harvard University, 1971.

**Ginger Strand**, Ph.D.,
New York City

# Sherwood, Mary Elizabeth

## (1826–1903)

*American author and etiquette expert. Born Mary Elizabeth Wilson in Keene, New Hampshire, on October 27, 1826; died of heart disease in New York City on September 12, 1903; daughter of James Wilson (a lawyer and politician) and Mary Lord (Richardson) Wilson; educated at George B. Emerson's school in Boston; married John Sherwood (a lawyer), on November 12, 1851 (died 1895); children: James Wilson (died in childhood); Samuel (b. 1853); Arthur Murray (b. 1856); John Philip (died 1883).*

*Selected writings:* The Sarcasm of Destiny *(1878);* A Transplanted Rose *(1882);* Manners and Social Usages *(1884);* Sweet-Brier *(1889);* The Art of Entertaining *(1892);* Poems by M.E.W.S. *(1892);* An Epistle to Posterity—Being Rambling Recollections of Many Years of My Life *(memoirs, 1897);* Here & There & Everywhere *(memoirs, 1898).*

Born in 1826 into a well-respected family in Keene, New Hampshire, Mary Elizabeth Sherwood was the first child of **Mary Richardson Wilson** and James Wilson, a lawyer who would later follow in the footsteps of his father and become a member of Congress. She grew up very much enamored of the finer things in life, a trait implicitly encouraged during her education at George B. Emerson's boarding school for girls in Boston. A journey west with her father in 1842, to rough settlements in what would become the states of Wisconsin and Iowa, was not to her liking, but she found her métier five years later, when her father was elected to Congress and moved the family to Washington, D.C. Her mother died shortly thereafter, and Sherwood served as hostess for her father until 1850, greatly enjoying the social scene in the capital.

Mary brought her passion for society life into her marriage when she wed lawyer John Sherwood in 1851. The couple settled in Manhattan and Sherwood became part of New York society, attending *Anne C.L. Botta's literary salon, traveling in style to fashionable places, and working on such charitable causes as fund raising for the restoration of Mount Vernon, George and *Martha Washington's home. She also had four sons, one of whom died young, and occasionally wrote short stories and poems that were published in various periodicals. During the Civil War, Sherwood was among those wealthy women who raised money for the Sanitary Commission by organizing the Metropolitan Fair in 1864. By the 1870s, however, the expense of a society lifestyle forced her to begin an active writing career to supplement her husband's income.

Sherwood began publishing pieces on etiquette, as well as short stories, in such respected magazines as *Frank Leslie's Weekly* and *Appleton's Journal*, though her first novel, *The Sar-*

*casm of Destiny*, received little attention when it appeared in 1878. Her second effort, *A Transplanted Rose* (1882), proved quite popular with its story of a girl from the West adapting herself to fit New York society. In 1884, she turned from novels to publish her most popular work, *Manners and Social Usages*. Guidebooks to manners were increasingly popular in the 19th century, as more and more of the "nouveau riche" entered society without the training in this area that would have been provided by a wealthy upbringing. Sherwood's *Guide* gave tips on everything from using a fork correctly to cultivating human kindness (she thought it incumbent upon those endowed with wealth to deal benignantly with their inferiors), and went through a number of reprintings. *Sweet-Brier*, her third novel, was published in 1889.

A breadwinner herself, Sherwood was cautiously supportive of greater opportunities for women in education and the workplace. However, her views were largely traditional, and in her etiquette guides as well as her novels she championed the natural and highest calling of women as their becoming, in her words, "domestic women, good wives and mothers." Her first concern was "good society," which she continued to pursue even after her husband had to sell their home and its contents in 1890. She had been traveling abroad at the time, and upon her return they began living in hotels. Sherwood published a book of poetry and another social guide, *The Art of Entertaining*, in 1892, while her husband gradually faded into what was probably depression. He died in 1895, broken both physically and mentally. Sherwood, who had not given up her jewels to help with the family's economic situation, continued to live in hotels and to cultivate her upper-class acquaintances. She suffered badly from rheumatism but faithfully made the social rounds, and published two volumes of memoirs detailing the people she had met in her travels (among them Charles Dickens and Daniel Webster), *An Epistle to Posterity* (1897) and *Here & There & Everywhere* (1898). Described by playwright Robert E. Sherwood, her grandson, as "a very gaudy old lady until the end," she died in New York City in 1903.

**SOURCES:**

Edgerly, Lois Stiles, ed. *Give Her This Day: A Daybook of Women's Words.* Gardiner, ME: Tilbury House, 1990.

James, Edward T., ed. *Notable American Women, 1607–1950.* Cambridge, MA: The Belknap Press of Harvard University, 1971.

**Ginger Strand**, Ph.D.,
New York City

# Sherwood, Mary Martha

## (1775–1851)

*British children's author. Born Mary Martha Butt on May 6, 1775, in Stanford, England; died on September 20, 1851, in London; daughter of Dr. George Butt (chaplain to George III) and Martha Sherwood; educated at Reading Abbey; married Henry Sherwood, in 1803; children: five, including Sophia Kelly; adopted three more.*

*Author of hundreds of stories and morality tales for children, including* Henry and His Bearer *(1815),* The Indian Pilgrim *(1818), and* The History of the Fairchild Family *(1818); a selection of her stories appeared as* The Juvenile Library *(1880) after her death.*

Mary Martha Sherwood was born in Stanford, England, in 1775, the daughter of rector George Butt, chaplain to King George III. Mary was not the only member of the family destined for literary popularity, for her sister **Lucy Lyttleton Cameron** (1781–1858) would also have a prolific career writing for children, penning the novels *The History of Margaret Whyte* (1798) and *The Two Lambs* (1821). At Reading Abbey, Mary received a classical education and started to write while still in school. Her first popular success came in 1802 with her story *Susan Gray*, a morality tale aimed at bolstering religion among the poor.

In 1803, Mary married her cousin Henry Sherwood, an army officer. When he was posted to India, she left their young daughter in England and joined him. Sherwood wrote many children's stories in India while also doing charitable work for soldiers' orphans, three of whom she adopted and raised with her own five children. The family later returned to England, where her career took off with the publication of *Henry and His Bearer*, a morality tale for children that proved to be wildly successful. Rivaling *Harriet Beecher Stowe*'s later American classic *Uncle Tom's Cabin* in its popularity, the 1815 tale was translated into many languages and went through nearly 100 editions.

Sherwood's most famous book was *The History of the Fairchild Family* (1818), the title-page of which described it as "a child's manual . . . calculated to show the importance and effects of religious education." The book, while highly moralistic, also contained some fairly gruesome and thrilling scenes that were appealing to children, and it went through 14 editions before Sherwood published a sequel in 1842. A third part appeared in 1847, and it is believed that by that time the book had been read by the vast majority of middle-class children in England. It would continue to be reprinted in various editions for the next 50-odd years.

In addition to her numerous other didactic works for children, Sherwood studied Hebrew and wrote a dictionary to the prophetic books of the Bible which was never published. She also kept a journal for her entire life, which her daughter **Sophia Kelly** used after Sherwood's death in 1851 to write the biography *Life of Mrs. Sherwood* (1854). Kelly had also collaborated on some of Sherwood's later stories, and published a novel of her own, *The Anchoret of Montserrat*.

**SOURCES:**

*The Concise Dictionary of National Biography*. Oxford: Oxford University Press, 1992.

Drabble, Margaret, ed. *The Oxford Companion to English Literature*. 5th ed. NY: Oxford University Press, 1985.

Shattock, Joanne. *The Oxford Guide to British Women Writers*. Oxford: Oxford University Press, 1993.

**Ginger Strand**, Ph.D.,
New York City

## Shestov, Xenia (1560–1631).

*See Martha the Nun.*

## She-Wolf of France.

*See Isabella of France (1296–1358).*

# Shigeko (1925–1961)

*Japanese princess. Born in 1925; died in 1961; eldest daughter of *Nagako (1903–2000) and Hirohito (1901–1989), emperor of Japan (r. 1924–1989); married Prince Morihiro (son of Prince Higashikunim, the first postwar prime minister); children: one son.*

## Shikibu, Murasaki (c. 973–c. 1015).

*See Murasaki Shikibu.*

# Shiley, Jean (1911–1998)

*American high jumper who won a gold medal in the 1932 Olympics. Name variations: Jean Newhouse. Born in Harrisburg, Pennsylvania, on November 20, 1911; died on March 11, 1998, in Los Angeles, California; graduated from Temple University, 1933.*

*Competed in Olympics, placing 4th in high jump (1928); won national titles (1929, 1930, and 1931); won the gold medal in the high jump in the Los Angeles Olympics (1932), beating favorite Babe Didrikson Zaharias.*

Born in Pennsylvania in 1911, Jean Shiley was fortunate to attend Haverford Township

**Catherwood, Ethel.** *See Balas, Iolanda for sidebar.*

High School, where, unlike most schools of the time, female and male students had equal opportunities in all areas including sports. Funds for transportation, uniforms, coaches, and all other expenses for girls' and boys' sports were split evenly, and girls competed in hockey, basketball, track and field, tennis, swimming, golf, and other sports. Boys had 12 football games a season; girls had 12 hockey games. Shiley played on the basketball team, whose coach **Ethel David** had two rules—no athlete could play unless her grades were up to par, and no poor sportsmanship was tolerated.

During the 1927–28 season, **Dora Lurie**, a sportswriter for the *Philadelphia Inquirer*, covered one of Haverford Township High's basketball games. Impressed by Shiley's ability to jump as high as 4'10", Lurie encouraged her to try out for the high jump in the Olympics. She also set up an appointment for Shiley with Lawson Robertson, a track coach at the University of Pennsylvania who served as an Olympic coach. To Shiley's surprise, Robertson agreed to train her. Not a member of any club or sponsoring or-

*Jean Shiley*

ganization, she had to pay her own entry fee at the Olympic trials in Newark, New Jersey, where she made the team for the 1928 Olympics in Amsterdam.

While some members of her family disapproved of her choosing to go to Europe unchaperoned at age 16, others bought Shiley clothes and gave her a huge send-off. Once on board ship bound for the Netherlands, the teenager was dazzled by the elegant surroundings, especially the dining room's elaborate table settings. She soon made friends on board, including the "black gang" in the ship's furnace room and Jack Kelly, an Olympic hopeful who would later have a daughter named *Grace Kelly. The athletes continued living on the ship after their arrival in Amsterdam, which Shiley found much more enjoyable than did some others who considered the commute to the Games tiresome. Her participation in the high-jump competition, however, came and went in a blur. Canadian **Ethel Catherwood** took the gold medal, while Shiley came in fourth.

Returning to high school, she graduated the following year and was awarded a scholastic scholarship to Temple University in Philadelphia. But the school did not have competitive sports for women, and so the only way Shiley could compete was in national meets. Practicing was difficult. At home she had had the high-school field and the corn field across the street, while in Philadelphia there was only the Meadowbrook Club, a men's club operated by Wanamaker's department store. Women were not allowed inside. She had to stand outside and beg to see the coach, Lew Speeler. Nonetheless, the club agreed to let her practice and to pay her way to meets. She won national titles in 1929, 1930, and 1931, setting the American indoor record for the high jump in 1929 and 1930.

When Shiley left for the Olympic trials in Evanston, Illinois, in 1932, she had only a train ticket and five dollars, for the Olympic Committee paid for athletes' expenses in Evanston. Despite intense heat (temperatures went as high as 105°), Shiley tied *Babe Didrikson Zaharias in the high-jump trials and headed for the Olympic Games in Los Angeles as captain of the American track-and-field team. By that time, Zaharias was a celebrity to the press and the American public; Shiley was a cipher. The two staged what has been called the "greatest one-on-one duel in Olympic history." Zaharias won the javelin and then the hurdle, and was poised to take the high jump. Shiley and Zaharias matched each other jump for jump, both clearing 5'5" to set a world record. In the jumpoff for the gold medal, each made 5'5¾", but the "western roll" that Zaharias was accustomed to using—diving head first over the bar—was not, some thought, according to the rules. These specified that athletes take off with one foot, land on the other, and never let their shoulders precede their body across the bar. Shiley was encouraged by other athletes to cite Zaharias for a foul, but she refused; she liked her talented competitor. Eventually, however, the "western roll" was ruled illegal, placing Zaharias second, with a silver medal, while Shiley was awarded the gold. Members of the press corps were indignant: the Babe had been robbed.

Shiley had hopes of attending medical school after she graduated with a degree in physical education and history from Temple University in 1933, but the Depression was at its height, and she simply did not have the money. Jobs were scarce, so she taught swimming and worked part-time as a lifeguard to make ends meet. Shiley considered herself fortunate when she landed a WPA job teaching typing. In 1936, she went to see Dan Ferris of the U.S. Olympic Committee about trying out for that year's Olympics. He maintained that by teaching swimming for money she had violated her amateur status, thus making her ineligible for Olympic competition. The fact that she was a track-and-field star, not a swimmer, was irrelevant. The decision was final. Shiley was inducted into the USA Track & Field (USATF) Hall of Fame in 1993, nearly 60 years later. She died in 1998.

**SOURCES:**
Carlson, Lewis H., and John J. Fogarty. *Tales of Gold.* Chicago, IL: Contemporary Books, 1987.

**Karin L. Haag**, freelance writer, Athens, Georgia

# Shinn, Millicent Washburn
## (1858–1940)

*American psychologist and author who published one of the few systematic observations of infant development available in English at the end of the 19th century. Born in Niles, California, on April 15, 1858; died of heart disease in Niles on August 13, 1940; daughter of James Shinn and Lucy Ellen (Clark) Shinn; graduated from Oakland (CA) High School, 1874; University of California, A.B., 1880, Ph.D., 1898.*

The daughter of a farmer and orchard-tree nursery owner, Millicent Washburn Shinn was born on a ranch in Niles, California, in 1858. Some of her earliest influences were family members: her brother Charles Howard Shinn later became an established writer and key figure in the early Western conservation movement, while her cousin Edmund Clark Sanford was a prominent psychologist. Shinn also found a helpful mentor in one of her teachers at Oakland (California) High School, poet Edward Rowland Sill. Both in high school and in college at the University of California, Shinn received encouragement and advice from Sill in her literary career. She earned her A.B. in 1880, and took on the editorship of the *Overland Monthly* publication in 1883, contributing poems and stories.

Although she retained her position as editor of *Overland* until 1894, Shinn had a more important project in the works. In 1890, her brother's wife gave birth to a daughter, and Shinn began keeping a journal of the infant's mental and physical development. Her jottings and research were published as *Notes on the Development of a Child* in 1893. At the same time, she enrolled at the University of California as a graduate student, and in 1898 became the first woman to receive a Ph.D. there. Her work on infant development was recognized in her field as one of the few systematic observations available in English, and she further popularized her views by writing several articles and a book, *The Biography of a Baby* (1900). Shinn became quite well known for her psychological work, but after *Biography* she retired to her family ranch and lived a quiet life. She died of heart disease in 1940.

**SOURCES:**

James, Edward T., ed. *Notable American Women, 1607–1950*. Cambridge, MA: The Belknap Press of Harvard University, 1971.

**Ginger Strand**, Ph.D.,
New York City

# Shipley, Ruth B. (1885–1966)

*First woman to head a division of the U.S. Department of State. Born Ruth Bielaski in Montgomery County, Maryland, on April 20, 1885; died in Washington, D.C., on November 3, 1966; daughter of Alexander Bielaski (a Methodist minister) and Roselle Woodward (Israel) Bielaski; married Frederick William van Dorn Shipley, in 1909 (died 1919); children: Frederick William.*

Born in Maryland in 1885, Ruth B. Shipley spent her childhood at her grandfather's Maryland farm and her family's home in Washington, D.C., attending high school in Washington. She got her first job at age 18, as a clerk in the U.S. Patent Office. She remained in that post until she resigned and moved to the Panama Canal Zone with her new husband, Frederick Shipley, in 1909.

They returned to Washington in 1914, when her husband's illness made it necessary for Shipley to support the family, which now included their son. With the help of her brother A. Bruce Bielaski, who was then head of the FBI, Ruth found a job as a clerk in the Department of State. What started as a temporary position became a 41-year career during which she became one of the highest-paid women in government. Her rise through the ranks began with her appointment as special assistant to Assistant Secretary A. Adee, followed by a position as assistant to the chief of the Office of Coordination and Review, **Margaret M. Hanna**. Shipley proved so successful in these jobs that she became the first permanent chief of the Passport Division, directly in charge of 70 employees, in 1928. Her annual $4,000 salary ranked her as one of the most highly compensated women on the government's payroll, and she was the first woman to head a major division of the Department of State.

Despite her high-profile position, Shipley did not relish the publicity or Washington's glittering social scene, but worked quietly and efficiently at improvements in her division. In the course of her career, her office grew significantly as she weathered the international upheaval of World War II. She was responsible for monitoring Americans' international travel when the Neutrality Acts of the 1930s severely curtailed travel in war zones. For security reasons, after the U.S. declared war on the Axis powers in 1939, all American passports were invalidated, and Shipley oversaw the international replacement process. Few citizens were permitted to travel to Axis countries, and Shipley, although she had no authority to do so, banned Japanese-Americans from fishing off the Pacific Coast without passports. (That effectively cut off the livelihoods of Japanese immigrants who fished commercially, for they were not yet allowed to become naturalized citizens in that era.) Responding to press questions of heavy-handedness at the Passport Division during the war, President Franklin D. Roosevelt noted with respect, "Mrs. Shipley is a wonderful ogre." After the war, Shipley found her role expanded even further as she began supervising visas and immigration, in addition to her responsibilities with passports and American travel. With millions of files under her care, she earned the respect of Congress both for her ability to manage such vast amounts of information and because her agency was one of the few to turn a profit.

One of Shipley's most controversial actions occurred in 1950, when she contributed to the drafting of the McCarran Internal Security Act, which aimed to deny passports to suspected Communists. As a staunch anti-Communist, she used her power to restrict the travel of many leftist figures, whether they were admitted Communists or not. Under her direction, Paul and *Eslanda Robeson, Linus Pauling, Arthur Miller, Rockwell Kent, *Elizabeth Gurley Flynn, Leo Szilard, W.E.B. Du Bois, and Herbert Aptheker had their applications for passports rejected with the vague explanation that their travel was "prejudicial to the interests of the United States."

In the first years of the McCarran Act, Shipley's control was absolute, as there was not even an appeals process until the mid-1950s. When pressed for an explanation about why a particular passport application had been rejected, she rarely gave one, or, if she did, stated reasons that were highly political, such as her assertion that physicist Martin Kamen had not been forthright in his testimony before the House Un-American Activities Committee. Shipley's role in the Mc-

Carthyism of the Cold War era drew harsh criticism from liberal America, and the power of her position was gradually dismantled during the later 1950s and the 1960s. The ability of the chief of the passport division arbitrarily to deny passports was denied with a federal appeals court's decision to install a review process in the 1950s, and in 1964, in *Aptheker* v. *Secretary of State*, the Supreme Court forced the department to offer due process to passport applicants.

By this point, Shipley had long since retired, having refused Secretary of State John Foster Dulles' request that she remain in her post. At her retirement in 1955, she was honored by the State Department with the Distinguished Service Award. She died 11 years later in Washington, D.C.

**SOURCES:**

Garraty, John A., ed. *American National Biography.* Vol. 19. NY: Oxford University Press, 1999.

———, and Mark C. Carnes, eds. *Dictionary of American Biography.* Supplement 8. NY: Scribner, 1988.

Read, Phyllis J., and Bernard L. Witlieb. *The Book of Women's Firsts.* NY: Random House, 1992.

Rothe, Anna, ed. *Current Biography 1947.* NY: H.W. Wilson, 1947.

**Ginger Strand**, Ph.D.,
New York City

# Shipman, Nell (1892–1970)

*Canadian-born actress and filmmaker. Name variations: Helen Foster Barham. Born Helen Foster Barham in October 1892 in Victoria, British Columbia, Canada; died in January 1970 in Cabazon, California; married Ernest Shipman (a writer), in 1911 (divorced 1920); married Charles Ayers (an artist), in 1925 (divorced 1934); children: (first marriage) Barry Shipman (b. 1912); (second marriage) twins Daphne and Charles (b. 1926).*

*Wrote, produced, and starred in numerous films, including* God's Country and the Woman *(1916),* Baree, Son of Kazan *(1918),* Back to God's Country *(1919),* Something New *(1920),* A Boy, a Bear and a Dog *(1921),* The Girl from God's Country *(1921),* The Grub Stake *(1922),* The Light on Lookout *(1923),* Trail of the North Wind *(1923);* The Golden Yukon *(1927); wrote screenplay for what became* Wings in the Dark *(1935); also wrote novels, including* Get the Woman *(1930), and an autobiography,* The Silent Screen and My Talking Heart *(1987).*

Nell Shipman, born in 1892 in British Columbia, Canada, left home at a young age to pursue an acting career in vaudeville. In 1912, she and her husband Ernest Shipman moved to

Southern California. Within two years, Shipman had established herself as a writer for the early film industry's major studios, including Vitagraph, Selig and Universal. Along with other women film pioneers like *Mary Pickford and *Frances Marion, she was able to assume a position of power and freedom that would be denied to women once the Hollywood studio system became entrenched in the 1920s.

Nell Shipman

In addition to writing scenarios, Shipman gained popularity as a film star in 1916 with the release of *God's Country and the Woman,* a wildlife adventure film which she also produced and directed. In it, the young heroine is terrorized by the same villain who had raped her mother years before, and she is rescued from his clutches by her husband and a pack of dogs (which eat him). It was a huge success, and earned Shipman the nickname "The Girl from God's Country." Like most of Shipman's other works, *God's Country and the Woman* featured the relationship between a strong heroine and the natural world, portraying humans as part of a larger order. The movie also featured the classic Shipman triangle in which the heroine is threatened sexually by a villain who is subsequently killed by a good man with whom she is united.

Much of the film's appeal stemmed from its dazzling winter snow scenes that captured the excitement of the wilderness; Shipman always preferred to shoot on location, even after constructed studio sets came into fashion as inexpensive substitutes. To further authenticate her movies' settings, she kept a menagerie of nearly 200 animals that she raised and trained, and they starred with her (with credits) in her subsequent "God's Country" films. Very often a Shipman heroine has a dog to thank for protecting her virtue, as in the film *Baree, Son of Kazan* (1918). Shipman relied heavily on melodramatic plots, the beauty of the north country wilderness, and the appeal of her animals to sell her films to audiences.

Having earlier rejected a seven-year contract offered by Samuel Goldwyn (a decision she later regarded with some regret), in 1920 she formed her own production company, Nell Shipman Productions, divorcing her husband at the same time. Priest Lake, Idaho, became the new home for her collection of animals and a small cast and crew, where she produced movies along the same lines as her Hollywood pictures. (An area of Priest Lake State Park is now called Nell Shipman Point, in honor of the first filmmaker to shoot in Idaho.) She wrote the screenplay for, starred in, co-directed and trained the animals for the company's 1921 release *The Girl from God's Country*, which was shot on location over a six-month period. Several other films followed, but the lack of a major distributor forced an end to the independent company in 1925, when Shipman donated her animals to the San Diego Zoo and married artist Charles Ayers. Some critics have cited her failure to evolve the plots and characters of her movies along with the changing tastes of her audience as a reason for the company's demise.

Shipman scaled back her involvement with the movies after this point, although she continued to write prolifically. She began penning films for the "talkies," in addition to the novels *Get the Woman* (1930) and the autobiographical *Abandoned Trails*. Her last feature film release was *The Golden Yukon* (1927). A script she wrote for a movie she had hoped to produce was later filmed as *Wings in the Dark* (1935), starring *Myrna Loy as a stunt pilot and Cary Grant as a blind ex-aviator. Shipman died in 1970. Her autobiography, *The Silent Screen and My Talking Heart* (1987), is a fascinating account of the early days of Hollywood, a world in which women briefly were as successful and powerful as men.

**SOURCES:**
Acker, Ally. *Reel Women: Pioneers of the Cinema 1896 to the Present*. NY: Continuum, 1991.
Rainey, Buck. *Sweethearts of the Sage*. Jefferson, NC: McFarland, 1992.
Unterburger, Amy L., ed. *Women Filmmakers & Their Films*. Detroit, MI: St. James Press, 1998.

**Ginger Strand**, Ph.D.,
New York City

# Shippen, Peggy (1760–1804)

*Second wife of Benedict Arnold, who lived most of her life amid the enmity caused by his treason.* Name variations: Margaret Shippen Arnold; Peggy Shippen Arnold; Mrs. Benedict Arnold; Margaret Shippen. Born Margaret Shippen in 1760 in Philadelphia, Pennsylvania; died on August 24, 1804, in Epping, Essex, England; youngest of five children of Edward Shippen (a judge); became second wife of Benedict Arnold (1741–1801, military governor of Pennsylvania who defected to the British in 1780), on April 8, 1779; children: Edward Shippen Arnold; James Robertson Arnold; **Sophia Arnold**; George Arnold; William Fitch Arnold. Benedict Arnold was first married to **Margaret Mansfield** who died in 1775.

The second wife of Benedict Arnold, the most infamous traitor in American history, Peggy Shippen was aware of her husband's treasonous activities during the Revolutionary War and may have even aided the "villainous perfidy" which culminated in the delivery of West Point, America's most crucial fortification at the time, to the British. In the aftermath of her husband's transgressions, Shippen proved to be a strong, resourceful woman. "Arnold had the power to act, to defy the stresses of business and the dangers of the battlefield; but Peggy had the power to endure," wrote Milton Lomask. "He could not cope with failure and disgrace. She could—and did."

Shippen was a young, golden-haired Philadelphia socialite in June 1778, when Benedict Arnold, a 37-year-old widower and war hero, became the military governor of Pennsylvania and established his headquarters in the city. During the British occupation of the city, Shippen had enjoyed the attention of a number of handsome young officers, and she probably met Arnold at yet another social event. Although she was 19 years Arnold's junior, the two fell in love and married on April 8, 1779. They took up residence in his magnificent country house, "Mt. Pleasant," located on the banks of the Schuylkill, where they lived quite lavishly, far above their means. It may have been Arnold's accumulating debt that led him to take advantage of his authority.

In May 1779, shortly after the marriage, the radical Pennsylvania Council accused Arnold of having utilized his military office for private gain. While awaiting a court-martial that he had demanded in order to clear his name, Arnold began his treasonous correspondence with Sir Henry Clinton, the British commander-in-chief in America, in which he revealed crucial military secrets, including troop movement, disposition of supplies, and the route and strength of the French forces. In the summer of 1780, after being cleared by the court of most of the charges against him, Arnold, by his own request, was appointed by General George Washington to command West Point, where he continued his deceitful plot. Within four months, he had seriously weakened the garrison and depleted its provisions, all the while reassuring Washington that a

Peggy
Shippen

British attack could not succeed. On September 21, Arnold arranged to surrender West Point to Major John André, British adjutant-general and chief of spies. The plan was thwarted, however, when André was captured by American troops two days later while carrying incriminating papers in Arnold's own hand, which were subsequently turned over to General Washington. However, by the time Washington traveled to the Arnold home, Arnold had heard of André's capture and made an escape, leaving Shippen behind with the couple's infant son.

Other than her knowledge of her husband's subversive activities, it is difficult to determine Shippen's involvement in the plot. A story was circulated at the time that she confessed to a friend that she had persuaded her husband to betray his country, but there is nothing but hearsay to support that theory. Some believe, however, that her ambitions were such that she may indeed have influenced him, thinking he would be lavishly rewarded by the British. Whatever her degree of involvement, when Washington and his aides arrived at West Point, they found her seemingly in a state of madness, clutching her child to her and muttering incoherently. "General Arnold will never return: he is gone: he is gone forever; *there, there, there,*" she said pointing to the ceiling, "the spirits have carried [him] up there." The next day, when Shippen appeared to have calmed down, Washington gave her the choice of joining her husband in British-held New York, or returning home to Philadelphia. She chose to go to Philadelphia, but the local authorities would not let her stay. In November, she joined her husband in New York, where he had received from Henry Clinton the British military rating of brigadier general and was commanding a Loyalist legion. The Arnolds resided there until December 1781, when they sailed for England, taking along their young family, which now included a second son born in New York. In England, Shippen was presented at court, the king pronouncing her "the most beautiful woman he had ever seen."

Over the next few years, during which time Shippen gave birth to several more children, the couple slowly slipped into obscurity. After 1782, Arnold had no military post and no job. The family lived in a series of leased houses in moderately fashionable neighborhoods, and Shippen devoted herself to her children. She also was attentive to Arnold's three sons by his first wife, and to his only surviving sister, **Hannah Arnold**. In 1785, Arnold left his wife and children in England and sailed to St. John in the Canadian province of New Brunswick. There he purchased property and started a merchandising enterprise. He also fathered an illegitimate son (John Sage), a transgression for which his wife apparently forgave him, for she joined him in New Brunswick in 1787. A year later, she attended a family reunion in Philadelphia, where some old friends and even some relatives snubbed her on the street. "How difficult it is," she wrote to her sister in the summer of 1790, shortly after returning to St. John, "to know what will contribute to our happiness in this life. I had hopes that by paying my beloved friends a last visit, I should insure to myself some portion of it, but I find it far otherwise."

Shippen also faced an increasingly difficult time in New Brunswick, where her husband was widely disliked. In 1791, the animosity toward him turned violent when a mob burned an effigy labeled "traitor" on the front lawn of their home. A few weeks later, the Arnolds sold their property and household goods and prepared to sail back to England. Arnold applied for a military post but nothing was forthcoming, so he returned to his old trade on the high seas. He later served for two years as a volunteer officer under General Charles Grey, who commanded the British land forces in the West Indies. At home, Shippen dealt with the couple's mounting financial problems and some serious crises involving the children. In the spring of 1800, their only daughter Sophia had a paralytic stroke that left her a semi-invalid. A month later, their son Edward died in India, where he was serving as an officer in the British engineers.

By January 1801, Arnold's health began to fail. His death on June 14 of that year left Shippen in a "despairing state," as she confessed in a letter to her father. Despite her grief, she moved into a smaller home and over the next few years attempted to pay off her husband's debts and to educate her children. Her own health took a turn for the worse in November 1803, when she was diagnosed with "a cancer." A year before her death, she wrote a letter to her stepsons: "To you I have rendered an essential service; I have rescued your Father's memory from disrespect, by paying all his just debts; and his Children will now never have the mortification of being reproached with his speculations having injured anybody beyond his own family. . . . I have not even a tea-spoon, a towel, or a bottle of wine that I have not paid for."

Peggy Shippen died on August 24, 1804, at the age of 44. Her children went on to lead respectable and successful lives, a tribute to her strength and fortitude. "As a devoted wife and mother," wrote Lomask, "faithful to her bargains and gallant under strains, the lovely Mrs. Benedict Arnold had made a good ending to an ill-starred life."

**SOURCES:**
Flexner, James Thomas. "Benedict Arnold: How the Traitor Was Unmasked," in *American Heritage*. Vol. XVIII, no. 6. October 1967.
Lomask, Milton. "Benedict Arnold: The Aftermath of Treason," in *American Heritage*. Vol. XVIII, no. 6. October 1967.

**Barbara Morgan**,
Melrose, Massachusetts


## Shirley, Anne (1917–1993).

*See Montgomery, Lucy Maud for sidebar.*

## Shirley, Selina (1707–1791).

*See Hastings, Selina.*


# Shiubhlaigh, Maire Nic (1884–1958)

*Irish actress and founder member of the Irish National Theatre Society (1903). Born Mary Elizabeth Walker in Dublin, Ireland, in 1884 (some sources cite 1888); died in Drogheda, County Louth, Ireland, on September 9, 1958; daughter of Matthew Walker (a printer and newsagent) and Marian (Doherty) Walker; married Eamon Price (a major-general), in 1928.*

For Maire Nic Shiubhlaigh and many of her contemporaries, their involvement in the theater began in the myriad political and cultural clubs which existed in Dublin at the turn of the 20th century. Her father's printing firm typeset a considerable amount of the literature and propaganda for Irish nationalist organizations, and the family home was a meeting point for many of those involved in the movement. Her brother Frank was also in the theater, as were two of their sisters, Ann and Gypsy, who acted under the stage names ❧▶ **Eileen O'Doherty** and **Betty King**. Maire was the first actor to use the Irish form of her name for stage purposes. She joined ***Maud Gonne**'s Inghinidhe na hEireann (Daughters of Ireland) which was such a valuable launching ground for other theatrical careers, notably that of ***Sara Allgood**. The Inghinidhe drama group was directed by Frank and Willie Fay who were to have a major influence on Nic Shiubhlaigh's career. By 1902, the future of the Irish Literary Theatre, which had been established by Yeats, Edward Martyn, and ***Augusta Gregory**, was uncertain, and in the spring of that year the Fay brothers agreed to stage *Deirdre* by George Russell (Æ) and *Kathleen Ni Houlihan* by Yeats and Lady Gregory. Maire played the roles of the Mother in *Deirdre* and Delia Cahill in *Kathleen Ni Houlihan*. In the latter, she took over the title role from Maud Gonne with great success, later paying tribute to the power and beauty of Gonne's Kathleen in her memoirs.

After the success of these performances, the idea of making the group more permanent was considered, and in February 1903 Yeats, Lady Gregory, and the Fays set up the Irish National Theatre Society. Maire Nic Shiubhlaigh, a founder member, was on the management committee. In March, the society gave the first performances of Yeats' *The Hour Glass* and Lady Gregory's *Twenty-Five*; Maire played leading roles in both. In May, the company visited London for the first time, and critic A.B. Walkley commented on Maire's "strange, wan disquieting beauty." Over the next two years, she created roles in two more Yeats plays, *The King's Threshold* (1903) and *The Shadowy Waters* (1904), and in two plays of John Millington Synge, *In the Shadow of the Glen* (in which she introduced the role of Nora Burke) and *Riders to the Sea*. Thomas Keohler, another founder member, thought that she made a major contribution to Yeats' early dramatic work: "She represented something of his first early dreams of the dramatic beauty and imagination which have never been realised." Nic Shiubhlaigh, like other actresses trained by Frank Fay, had a beau-

❧▶ **O'Doherty, Eileen** (b. 1891)
*Irish actress. Born Anna Walker in Dublin, Ireland, in September 1891; daughter of Marian (Doherty) Walker and Matthew Walker; sister of *Maire Nic Shiubhlaigh; educated in Dublin and studied for the stage under W.G. and F.J. Fay.*

In 1905, Eileen O'Doherty made her stage debut with the Irish National Theatre Society at the Abbey Theatre, Dublin, as the child in *The Hour Glass*. During her career, she worked regularly at the Abbey and at the Court Theatre in London, appearing as Babsy in *The Shewing-up of Blanco Posnet*, the Old Woman in *Deirdre*, Bridget Twomey in *Harvest*, Mary Kate in *The Eloquent Dempsey*, Mrs. Desmond in *The Cross Roads*, Mrs. Pender in *The Casting Out of Martin Whelan*, Maura Morrissey in *Birthright*, Margaret in *The Piedish*, Nerine in *The Rogueries of Scapin*, Miss Joyce in *Hyacinth Halvey*, Mary Brien in *The Mineral Workers*, Maria Donnelly in *Family Failing*, Mrs. Keegan in *The Supplanter*, Kate Moran in *Crusaders*, and Mrs. Geoghegan in *The White Headed Boy*. O'Doherty also toured in England, Scotland, and the United States.

tiful speaking voice which reminded the writer Padraic Colum of "bird calls on a still day."

In 1904, ***Annie Horniman**, a wealthy Englishwoman who admired Yeats' work, offered to provide a permanent home for the society, and in December 1904 the Abbey Theatre gave its first performances. But serious disagreements emerged over the following year when Horniman offered a grant to enable the actors to turn professional. The nationalist core of the company, many of whom had belonged to Inghinidhe na hEireann and other nationalist groups, felt it was a betrayal of their original ideals to accept salaries from Horniman. Nic Shiubhlaigh, who had a job at the Dun Emer Industries run by Yeats' sisters *Elizabeth and *Lily Yeats, was uncertain whether to accept the Horniman offer. Yeats and Lady Gregory were anxious to retain her at the Abbey, but she finally decided to follow the Fays who were setting up their own company, the Theatre of Ireland, which became a formidable rival to the Abbey for a while. Maire was its leading actress, but the company would disband in 1912. In 1910, she returned to the Abbey at Lady Gregory's invitation, and in 1911 she toured England and the United States with the company. On her return to Ireland, she became increasingly involved with various amateur dramatic groups, including William Pearse's Leinster Stage Society, the drama group at Patrick Pearse's school, St. Enda's, and the Irish Theatre of Joseph Plunkett and Thomas Mc-

Donagh. All four men would be executed after the 1916 Easter Rising.

In 1914, as political events moved to a crisis in Ireland with the passing of the Home Rule Bill, she joined the nationalist Cumann na mBan (the Women's League) and did concert work for the organization. At Easter 1916 when the Irish republican rebellion broke out in Dublin, she joined one of the rebel garrisons but managed to leave before it surrendered. In later years, Nic Shiubhlaigh continued to work for various amateur dramatic groups around Ireland and also did some radio broadcasts of the early Abbey plays. She married Eamon Price, a senior officer in the Irish army, in 1928. In 1955, she published a valuable and illuminating book of memoirs, *The Splendid Years*, which brought the first decade of the century to vivid life. She declared that she had never regretted her long involvement with amateur drama and in fact dedicated the book "To All Other Dramatic Societies." Maire Nic Shiubhlaigh died in September 1958. Her husband had died some years before, and she had moved to County Meath to be near her sister Gypsy. Yeats' father, the artist J.B. Yeats, painted two exquisite portraits of her; one is in the National Gallery of Ireland and the other hangs in the Abbey Theatre.

**SOURCES:**

Hogan, Robert, and James Kilroy. *The Abbey Theatre: The Years of Synge 1905–1909.* NJ: Humanities Press, 1978.

———. *Laying the Foundations 1902–1904.* NJ: Humanities Press, 1976.

Shiubhlaigh, Maire Nic. *The Splendid Years.* Dublin: James Duffy, 1955.

Tracey, Alice, "Maire Nic Shiubhlaigh of the Abbey Theatre," in *Carloviana* [Carlow]. Vol.1, no. 11. December 1962.

**Deirdre McMahon**,
lecturer in history at Mary Immaculate College,
University of Limerick, Limerick, Ireland

## Shizuka Gozen (fl. 12th c.)

*Legendary beauty who was the lover of Minamoto no Yoshitsune.* Pronunciation: She-zoo-kah Goe-zen. *Flourished in the later 12th century; no other details are known.*

Shizuka Gozen is one of the great, tragic, romantic heroines of Japanese history. While she is likely to have lived, her story is a romantic legend, written in numerous works of medieval fiction which chronicle the Minamoto-Taira War (1180–1185). Said to have been a spectacular beauty, and the best dancer in the country, Shizuka was the mistress of Minamoto no

Yoshitsune, a brilliant warrior. When Minamoto no Yoritomo turned against Yoshitsune, his younger brother, Yoshitsune fled, accompanied by Shizuka. She could not keep up, however, and so was seized by warriors loyal to Yoritomo and taken to his headquarters. Yoritomo forced the beautiful Shizuka, against her will, to dance for him. As she danced, she sang songs that attested to both her love for Yoshitsune and his military skill. She went so far as to gloat that Yoshitsune had successfully evaded his enemies. While she thus taunted her captor, her dance was so beautiful that Yoritomo swallowed the insults and spared her life. Not long thereafter, she gave birth to Yoshitsune's son. The child was killed, and Shizuka became a Buddhist nun.

**SOURCES:**

Benton, Margaret Fukazawa. "*Hōjo Masako: The Dowager Shōgun," in *Heroic with Grace: Legendary Women of Japan.* Edited by Chieko Mulhern. Armonk, NY: M.E. Sharpe, 1991.

**Linda L. Johnson**, Professor of History,
Concordia College, Moorhead, Minnesota

## Shochat, Manya (1878–1961)

*Jewish socialist and revolutionary who founded the first kibbutz in Israel.* Name variations: Mania Shochat; Manya Wilbushevitz; Manya Shochat-Vilbushevich. *Born in 1878 in Lososna, Russia; died in 1961; married Yisrael Shochat, in 1908; children: Geda and Anna.*

*Helped settle Eretz Israel, the area of Palestine that would eventually become the state of Israel; was instrumental in arming Jews to protect them from Arab aggression; founded kibbutz (collective farm) movement; campaigned for the Zionist cause and worked to improve Arab-Jewish relations.*

Manya Shochat was born on her father's estate in Lososna, Russia, in 1878 into a family of ten children. Her wealthy grandfather, a supplier to the Russian army, had abandoned Jewish traditions and customs to become more accepted in the landowning class. Shochat's father, however, clung to Judaism, and made sure his children received a Jewish education. As a young teenager, Shochat became aware of the hard conditions faced by laborers and fully committed herself, despite her own privileged background, to bringing about change through labor movements.

At age 15, Shochat ran away from home and worked in a Polish factory until she was retrieved by the police. Undeterred, she convinced her brother, Gedaliah, to let her work in his carpentry shop in Minsk. There she earnestly devoted herself to the cause of the worker, visiting factories and advocating the education of laborers as a means to transform them into activists. She also established ties with the Jewish community, having had little contact with Jews in Lososna.

Shochat's association with the Bundists made the most sense initially, as the Jewish socialist labor group seemed a happy alliance of her twin interests in labor reform and the Jewish people. Their demands were simple: the right to form labor unions, the right to free speech, and the right to strike. However, the Bundists were primarily interested in orchestrating mass demonstrations of Jewish workers rather than educating them and attending to their needs individually, and neither did they favor Jewish emigration to Palestine. Several of Shochat's brothers had emigrated to Eretz Israel, a part of Palestine that was home to many Jewish settlers, and Shochat soon aligned herself more with the Poale Zion Party (Workers of Zion), from which sprung the Labor Zionist movement.

Her activities did not escape the notice of governmental authorities, who arrested her in 1899 for inciting the workers. Shochat's year-long stay in prison only made her more determined to accomplish her goal of organizing Jewish workers, but there were forces at work equally set on crushing the movement. Anti-Semitic sentiment in Russia had occasionally erupted into "pogroms," or organized massacres of Jews, since 1881, and in 1903 one occurred in Kishinev in which 47 were killed and hundreds more injured. The slaughter only served to further fuel the Zionist movement. It also inspired Shochat to conspire with others to murder the man they considered responsible for much of the killing: Count Vyacheslav Konstantinovich Plehve, minister of the interior. An informer revealed the assassination plot before it could be carried out, however, and Shochat fled the country for Eretz Israel, arriving on January 2, 1904.

Shochat continued her fight for workers' rights in her new country. After traveling around the territory for several months, she found that many Jews lived in conditions of terrible poverty, unable to find jobs, while wealthy Jewish farmers hired Arabs to work their land for low wages. The plight of the starving Jews inspired Shochat in her campaign for collective farms run by the Jewish workers themselves. This, she felt, was the only way for Israel to truly become a Jewish nation. In the course of stirring up support for her idea, she met and married Yisrael Shochat, who joined with her to launch the idea of collective farming.

In 1907, Shochat traveled to Europe and the United States to gain financial support for the collective farms and to study Communist settlements. She faced skepticism from Zionist supporters, but nonetheless the first collective farm, or kibbutz, was established in Sejera that year. Its 18 members shared the work equally, an equality that extended to the 6 female members who farmed alongside the men. They also stood watch against aggression from hostile Circassian neighbors, and this need for guards became as integral to the idea of a successful collective as did the farming. To this end, a Jewish armed force known as Hashomer was organized in 1909, the first of its kind. The goal of Hashomer, in which Manya and Yisrael were central figures, was purely protective rather than for the purposes of war, as its members hoped to co-exist peacefully with their Arab neighbors.

Hashomer decided to send the Shochats to Turkey so that they might become better acquainted with Turkish law in the mediation of disputes with the surrounding Arabs. In 1913,

*Israeli postage stamp issued in honor of Manya Shochat.*

they returned to Eretz Israel, but the war between Turkey and the Balkans—the latter from which most of the Jews in Palestine derived—caused Turkish authorities who ruled Palestine to look on the Jewish settlements with hostility. Turkish agents demanded that the settlements hand over their weapons, orders which members of Hashomer defied by hiding their arsenals. In 1914, Turkish authorities arrested Shochat, accusing her of hiding weapons. Both she and Yisrael were deported to Turkey, where they remained for three years.

The Shochats finally returned to Eretz Israel in 1919, and Manya continued her efforts to arm Hashomer. In the face of increasing Arab violence and pogroms in Jerusalem, the leaders of Hashomer decided that a broader-based defense network was necessary. On June 13, 1920, the secretive, intimate framework of Hashomer expanded into the Haganah. As a member of this group, Shochat assisted in all aspects of the construction of a rudimentary army, including the smuggling of weapons and illegal Jewish immigrants into Eretz Israel; the establishment of the first arms factory (it fronted as a factory for the repair of farm equipment); the birth of an infant air force (gliders used for surveillance); and the direction of the first military academy. Under her leadership, most of the Jewish settlements had the protection of Haganah units by 1927.

Despite the constant tension between the Arabs and the Jews, Shochat still hoped for a peaceful resolution to the conflict. Even though the Zionists expended much of their energy in acquiring land for future settlements, Shochat believed that this goal should not be accomplished at the cost of dispossessing Arabs. To this end, she pushed for the establishment of the Jewish-Arab League, a joint association of Arabs and Jews, in 1931. Throughout her life, she worked for good relations with the Arabs. She supported education for Arabs and shared facilities (such as hospitals) for Arabs and Jews, and encouraged contact between the two groups so that they could learn about each other.

During World War II, Shochat turned her attention to the enormous influx of Jewish refugees fleeing the European Holocaust. She campaigned for better conditions for the refugees, as many lived in squalid conditions in transit camps. Often living among the refugees in the camps, she exhausted her weakening physical resources in providing relief to the starving and distressed. Her energies were divided further by the Israeli War for Independence in 1947, efforts which were rewarded by the official declaration of the Israeli state on May 14, 1948. Israel's independence spurred Shochat on in her work towards the betterment of Arab-Jewish relations. However, her health began to fail, and she developed severe eye problems that caused her great pain for the remainder of her life. She died in 1961.

**SOURCES:**

Ben-Zvi, Rachel Yanait. *Before Golda: Manya Shochat.* Biblio Press, 1989.

**Ruth Savitz**, freelance writer, Philadelphia, Pennsylvania

# Shoemaker, Carolyn (1929—)

*American astronomer. Born on June 24, 1929, in Gallup, New Mexico; Chico State College in California, B.A., M.A.; Northern Arizona University, Ph.D., 1990; married Eugene Shoemaker (1928–1997, a geologist and astronomer), on August 18, 1951; children: three.*

*With her husband and David Levy, discovered the Shoemaker-Levy 9 comet (1993); holds the world record for number of comets—32—discovered by a living astronomer (as of 2001).*

Astronomer Carolyn Shoemaker, who has discovered over 800 asteroids and 32 comets—more than any living astronomer, and only 5 fewer than the all-time record set in the 19th century—did not even begin working as an astronomer until middle age. Born in 1929, she married Eugene Shoemaker, a geologist and astronomer, in 1951, and left her job as a teacher the following year to raise their family. While Eugene worked with the U.S. Geological Service (USGS) and NASA and pioneered the field of planetary science, Carolyn raised their three children. When the children were grown, she joined him as a unpaid partner in tracking comets for his work as head of the astrogeology department of the USGS. In 1980, she became a visiting scientist there. The pair averaged three discoveries a year, with Carolyn making additional discoveries that made her the world record-holder for comet finds. (Eugene discovered 29.) Her self-taught skill at scanning telescopic photographs of the night sky is credited with her high number of comet discoveries.

In 1993 the Shoemakers, together with astronomer-writer David Levy, discovered the Shoemaker-Levy 9 comet, one of the most celebrated comet discoveries of the 20th century. The comet was actually a string of at least 21 pieces on a collision course with the planet Jupiter. The resulting impact in 1994 released a force equal to 10,000 times the energy stored in the Earth's Cold War stash of nuclear weapons, creating fiery holes in Jupiter's atmosphere equal to the size of Texas in a six-day barrage of mammoth shock waves and vast clouds of debris. The spectacular celestial phenomenon was the first that scientists had the opportunity to observe in this solar system. On the basis of this and other finds, Shoemaker was awarded the NASA Exceptional Scientific Achievement Medal in 1996.

On July 18, 1997, Shoemaker and her husband were conducting research on impact crater geology in Alice Springs, Australia, when an automobile accident killed Eugene and critically injured Carolyn. After hearing that his remains would be cremated, a former graduate student of Eugene's, planetary scientist **Carolyn C. Porco**, suggested fulfilling his desire to travel to the moon by sending his ashes there. Shoemaker was touched, and NASA embraced the idea wholeheartedly. In 1998, she watched as his ashes, contained in a capsule etched with a photograph of the Hale-Bopp Comet and a quotation from *Romeo and Juliet*, in honor of their love for each other, were launched to the moon on the Lunar Prospector.

Since 1989 a research professor of astronomy at Northern Arizona University, which granted her a doctorate in 1990, Shoemaker also serves on the staff of the Lowell Observatory in Flagstaff, Arizona. Her remarkable achievements in astronomy led to her being named a Fellow of the American Academy of Arts and Sciences.

**SOURCES:**

Levy, David H. "Comet Hunters, Night Watchmen of the Heavens," in *Smithsonian*. Vol. 23, no. 3. June 1992.

———. *Shoemaker by Levy: The Man Who Made an Impact*. NJ: Princeton University Press, 2000.

"Out of this World," in *People Weekly*. July 18, 1994.

*Time*. May 23, 1994, p. 57.

**Ginger Strand**, Ph.D.,
New York City

## Shōken Kōtaigō (1850–1914).

*See Haruko.*

## Shonagon, Sei (c. 965–?).

*See Sei Shonagon.*

# Shore, Dinah (1917–1994)

*Popular American singer and television personality. Born Frances Rose Shore on March 1, 1917, in Winchester, Tennessee; died of ovarian cancer on February 24, 1994, in Beverly Hills, California; elder of two daughters of Samuel Shore and Anna Shore; attended Vanderbilt University; married George Montgomery (an actor), in 1943 (divorced 1962); married Maurice Smith (a businessman), in 1963 (divorced 1964); children: (first marriage)* **Melissa Montgomery** *(b. 1948); John David (adopted, 1954).*

*Pursued a singing career on radio (from 1930s), becoming one of the country's most popular entertainers throughout radio's Golden Age; though an effort to expand her talents to musical films (1940s) was mainly unsuccessful, her transition to television (1950s) resulted in a 40-year, Emmy Award-winning career as a variety and talk show host; also known nationally as an accomplished golfer and promoter of the sport.*

*Filmography:* Thank Your Lucky Stars *(1943);* Up in Arms *(1944);* Follow the Boys *(1944);* Belle of the Yukon *(1944); (voice only)* Make Mine Music *(1946);* Till the Clouds Roll By *(1946);* Fun and Fancy Free *(1947);* Aaron Slick from Punkin Crick *(1952); (cameo only)* Oh, God! *(1977);* Health *(1979).*

*Television:* "The Dinah Shore Chevy Show" *(1951–61);* "Dinah Shore Specials" *(1964–65 and 1969);* "Dinah's Place" *(1970–74);* "Dinah!" *(1976);* "A Conversation with Dinah" *(1990–92).*

The birthday celebration at a Beverly Hills restaurant one March night in 1994 was a quiet affair, despite a guest list that included some of Hollywood's best-known celebrities and power brokers. A birthday cake had been placed at the head of the table, its single candle left burning in front of the empty seat of honor which would have been occupied by Dinah Shore, who had passed away just a week before. She had been a best friend not only to those present but to the millions of Americans she had entertained during a remarkable 50-year career.

Although Shore had harbored a childhood dream of becoming famous, she kept it to herself during those years growing up in Winchester, Tennessee, a small town just outside of Nashville. She had been plain Frances Rose Shore back then. Born in 1917, she was the elder of two daughters of Samuel and **Anna Shore**. Samuel owned the only department store in Winchester, the first of what would become a modest chain of stores throughout greater Nashville, and would often provide free entertainment for his customers by standing little Fanny Rose up on the counter and making her sing "America the Beautiful." The Shores were one of a handful of Jewish families living in and around Nashville, and some said that Fanny Rose's singing ability came from a granduncle who had been a cantor. Shore would often point to the Sunday evening gospel services to which she was taken by an African-American nanny as one of her earliest musical influences.

Whatever the source of her show-business inclinations, it was plain to everyone that Dinah felt entirely at home in front of an audience when, at age four, she appeared in a local production called "A Tom Thumb Wedding" as a Japanese girl, bundled into a kimono and with an ornamental comb stuck in her hair. When the comb fell out during a particularly deep bow to the boy playing her husband, Dinah ran across the stage after it, provoking peals of delighted audience laughter. "I didn't mind," she once remembered. "I said to myself, 'Gee, they're laughing *with* me.'" Later, Shore found an outlet for her talents by becoming a cheerleader at Hume-Fogg High School, where her warm personality and good humor placed her consistently in the "most popular" category. During her high school years, she sang at local charity affairs and school programs, still keeping her dream of a show-business career to herself and, in fact, announcing she wanted to be a social worker when she was accepted at Vanderbilt University in 1934. Even so, she found work singing with Nashville dance bands on weekends and was thrilled when Nashville's WSM offered her a part-time job on one of its musical programs. Even better, New York's prestigious WNEW offered her a two-week contract, at five dollars a week, to sing on the station during her summer vacation. She had auditioned for them by performing one of her favorite songs, *Dinah*. "That Dinah girl," with her silky combination of Southern sweetheart and blues-struck lover, proved a popular attraction with WNEW's audience, as did another young singer just starting out on the station, Frank Sinatra, who dubbed her "the Dixie Flyer." Encouraged, little Fanny Rose from Tennessee moved to New York City the next year and began auditioning as Dinah Shore.

## $\mathcal{B}$e sure to have a dream.

—Dinah Shore

It seemed at first as if her decision might have been hasty. She was turned down as a vocalist by both Tommy Dorsey and Benny Goodman, and she could find only sporadic employment in radio, despite the response she had received a year earlier. She was not yet well known enough to be offered nightclub dates, and even Shore would admit that she wasn't the most graceful of dancers and wouldn't do credit to any chorus line. It was the recording studio that came to her rescue after two years of struggle. Shore won recording contracts with both NBC and RCA as a "sustaining artist," meaning she was paid noth-

ing for her actual recording work but would be paid royalties on any of her records that sold more than a certain number of copies. She found additional employment cutting audition disks of new songs for music publishers. Finally, in 1939, she appeared on her first album as a "girl" singer with a long-forgotten group called "The Chamber Music Society of Lower Basin Street" and, more important, had her first hit single, "Yes, My Darling Daughter." But it was one of her low-paying audition disks that propelled Shore into the medium that would make her childhood dream come true, radio.

One of her audition disks had been "Havana for a Night," done as a test recording for Xavier Cugat's band not long after arriving in New York. Late in 1939, as *Variety*'s music editor Bernie Woods once recalled, Eddie Cantor was looking for a female vocalist for his new radio show. Woods brought the talent scout Cantor had hired to a record shop on Seventh Avenue and played the Cugat record for him. "At first, the only ones aware of [Shore's] great talent were the music publishers . . . and trade paper men," Woods recalled. "But word slowly got around about her and she got better and better jobs." Cantor agreed to audition this new young vocalist from Tennessee, and in 1940 Shore had her first job on national network radio. Cantor's audience was immediately taken with Shore's style. "Dinah made it big because she was . . . a class act," Woods wrote in his memoirs. "She handled herself well and avoided the pitfalls that tripped up so many female vocal aspirants of the time. She persistently rejected jobs that did not appear to further her career." One of those jobs was an eager offer from Tommy Dorsey, who had turned her down only a few years before, but Dinah, sensing that her future lay in radio and in recording, turned the tables and refused Dorsey's proposal. As if to prove her right, her 1942 recording of "Blues in the Night" quickly sold a million copies.

Cantor moved his show to California in 1941, and Shore soon found herself in the company of film stars and movie moguls. She was particularly taken with a dashing young actor named George Montgomery, whom she had first seen in the 1941 Western *The Cowboy and the Blonde*. Although Montgomery had enlisted in the Army by the time Shore arrived in Los Angeles, most of his time was served doing domestic duty and the opportunity soon arose for the two of them to meet. "I saw him, I wanted him," Dinah once said. "I despaired of him, but I finally married him." The nuptials were performed in Las Vegas on December 5, 1941, portrayed in

fan magazines as a fairy-tale union of two of Hollywood's most beautiful people. The picture seemed even more perfect when a daughter Melissa was born to the couple in 1948. During the '40s, Shore tried her hand at filmmaking, appearing in a series of bland studio musicals and

quickly discovering that no one considered her particularly photogenic or glamorous enough for the big screen. She fell back on her radio and record work, hosting her own radio show sponsored by General Foods in 1943, and entertaining troops at training camps around the country and in Europe during World War II. After the war, Shore returned to her busy radio schedule, although a new medium was by now attracting everyone's attention.

Shore's neighborly, girl-next-door demeanor may not have been suited for movies, but it was perfectly matched for the more intimate television screen. The spontaneity of early television especially appealed to her. "Live TV has that little element of human fallibility," Shore once said. "If you make a mistake, you can use that ol' hambone and capitalize on it." After several appearances on variety shows hosted by friends she had made in radio—*Kate Smith, Perry Como, and *Patti Page, among them—Shore was offered her own show, to be sponsored by General Motors. "The Dinah Shore Chevy Show" premiered on NBC in 1951, and no Sunday night was complete unless Shore sang the show's theme song, "See the USA in your Chevrolet," and blew her audience her trademark goodnight kiss.

Although Shore and Montgomery adopted a son, John David, in 1954, Shore had time for little else but her show during its ten-year run, winning two Emmy Awards along the way. By the late 1950s, the strains on her family life began to show. "I've always lived for whatever I'm doing at the moment," Shore once said. "When I work, I love every minute of it. That's probably why I didn't realize how much time my career took away from my family." The truth came as a hard blow when, after 22 years together, Shore and Montgomery were divorced in 1962, a year after "The Chevy Show" had ended. Although little was said publicly by either of them about the reasons for their separation, she and Montgomery managed to remain close friends after their divorce. Montgomery even made sure to point out, when asked about Shore's success, that "she projects just what she is—a simple, good woman."

After her divorce, Shore temporarily gave up television and retired to Palm Springs with her two children, where she took up tennis and was often seen playing doubles with her partner, a businessman named Maurice Smith, whom she married that same year. Little more than a year later, however, she and Smith were divorced—again, with little publicity or comment from either partner. Shore would remain single for the rest of her life, with her divorce from Smith marking the beginning of her most prolific period. In addition to a series of popular television specials during the mid-1960s, Shore made her debut in the world of professional golf. Colgate, one of the sponsors of her TV specials, had plans to extend its visibility into professional sports by

sponsoring a major golf tournament on the Ladies Professional Golf Association (LPGA) tour and proposed using Shore as the tournament's celebrity host. Shore had been enjoying the sport ever since her move to Palm Springs in the 1950s, and her acceptance of Colgate's suggestion led to the Dinah Shore Classic, which soon became a major televised event on the tour. Shore's trim figure, in pleated golf skirt and sun visor, remained a fixture of the sport for some 30 years, and the Dinah Shore Classic over which she presided each year is still an important stop on the LPGA professional tour.

Shore managed to combine her active show-business career with a rich social life, counting some of the nation's most influential people among her close friends. Her dinner parties were known for an eclectic mix of guests, ranging on any given evening from *Esther Williams and *Rosemary Clooney to Joe Namath and famed agent Irving Lazar. Although a loyal Democrat throughout her life, Shore often entertained Ronald and *Nancy Reagan in Palm Springs and accepted invitations to White House affairs after the couple moved to Washington. "Whenever you saw her, she was happy and upbeat," remembers Lee Minelli, the widow of director Vincente Minelli. "We used to kid her and say: 'Here comes Miss Sunshine.' But we meant it." Shore meant it, too. "I know I'm gushy," she once told an interviewer. "I guess it's a carryover from my cheerleader days."

By the early 1970s, television's pervasive influence had grown beyond the evening hours. Advertisers were quick to realize the potential of daytime TV, and especially the waiting audience for the format which became so ubiquitous, the daytime talk show. Shore's homespun style and spontaneous humor were a perfect match. "Dinah's Place" premiered in 1970, the first in a string of such shows stretching over the next 20 years, earning Shore three more Emmy Awards. Among her guests on "Dinah's Place" during 1971 was actor Burt Reynolds, then at the height of his film career and, at 38, nearly 20 years Shore's junior. "I felt a pull on my heart immediately," Reynolds later remembered, and shocked the audience by asking Shore on the air if she would go to Palm Springs with him that weekend. The ensuing four-year-long affair was a public one, especially attracting attention when the two began living together in Shore's Palm Springs home, but ended badly when Reynolds left Shore for actress Sally Fields in 1976. "If I have any class," Reynolds now admits, "it came from Dinah. In terms of preparing for the rest of my life, I was so damn lucky to have been with her." Characteristically, Shore kept her anguish to herself and never spoke publicly about the affair. Lee Minelli says simply, "He was the love of her life."

Despite a certain amount of negative publicity surrounding her affair with Reynolds, Shore's popularity never wavered. In addition to her television work, she published the first of three cookbooks, *Someone's in the Kitchen with Dinah*; gracefully assumed the role of grandmother when her daughter married and started her own family; and proudly attended her son's graduation from college when he earned a degree in forestry. In 1990, at 73 years of age, Shore was still energetically hosting a talk show, "Conversation with Dinah," on cable TV's Nashville Network and regularly playing golf and tennis. But in 1993, she confided to her friend **Angie Dickinson** that she had been having trouble with stomach pains and was consulting a doctor. The diagnosis was ovarian cancer. "Even after she told us about her illness," Dickinson says, "she felt she would get well." Only her closest friends knew of Shore's situation until it became evident later that year that there was little hope of recovery. Shore died peacefully at home in Palm Springs on February 24, 1994, with George Montgomery and her two children at her bedside. Her death came just one week shy of her 77th birthday.

With her passing, some of the sunshine seemed to go out of American show business. Despite her success, Shore never seemed to forget that she was just Fanny Rose from Tennessee, the hometown girl with a dream who always blew her national audience a big kiss after entertaining them with songs, stories, and easy, front-porch conversation. She was Hollywood's "greatest and only angel," as Burt Reynolds sadly commented, speaking for millions by adding, "Dinah was the most wonderful friend I ever had."

SOURCES:

Anderson, Nancy. "Look Who's Back," in *Good Housekeeping*. Vol. 210, no. 1. January 1990.

Goodman, Mark, and Doris Bacon. "No One Finah," in *People Weekly*. Vol. 41, no. 10. March 21, 1994.

Reynolds, Burt. *My Life*. NY: Hyperion, 1994.

Woods, Bernie. *When the Music Stopped: The Big Band Era Remembered*. NY: Barricade, 1994.

**Norman Powers**, writer-producer,
Chelsea Lane Productions,
New York, New York

# Shore, Henrietta (1880–1963)

*Canadian-born American painter. Born in 1880 in Toronto, Canada; died in 1963 in Carmel, California; studied at the Art Students League in New York City and at Heatherley's Art School in London.*

Born into a large family in Toronto, Canada, in 1880, painter Henrietta Shore first studied art under **Laura Muntz** in Toronto. As a young woman, she began spending part of each year in New York City, studying at the Art Students League. There, she was taught by William Merrit Chase and, after 1902, by Robert Henri, who proved a lasting influence as she developed a modernist style of abstracted realism. Shore's tendency to paint closeup studies of objects with attention to vibrant color and fluid lines, rather than detail, drew comparisons with her contemporary *Georgia O'Keeffe; for a time, Shore would be considered by many the superior painter of the two. In 1913, she moved to the West Coast where she quickly made a name for herself as an innovator in West Coast art. Only two years later, she won a silver medal at the Panama-Pacific Exposition in San Diego, and this plus her role in establishing the Los Angeles Society of Modern Artists cemented her reputation. In 1918, Shore and **Helena Dunlap** were given a two-woman exhibition at the Los Angeles County Museum.

Shore returned to New York City in 1921, and shortly thereafter a retrospective of her work was held at the Worcester Art Museum in Massachusetts. She was honored as one of 25 representatives of American art in Paris in 1924, and in 1925 was a founding member of the New York Society of Women Artists, led by *Marguerite Thompson Zorach. Her time in New York City produced such semi-abstract works as *Source* and *The unfolding of life*, although as the decade progressed, she turned more and more to simplified landscapes of rock formations, shells and desert plants. One such study inspired modernist photographer Edward Weston, a close friend, to duplicate her work in his photography. The result created quite a stir in the American photographic community.

Shore began living in the art colony at Carmel, California, in 1930. She taught art and painted throughout the decade, although opportunities for her to exhibit fell off sharply after 1933. While she was commissioned to paint six public murals in California by the Treasury Relief Art Project in 1936 (one series of which can still be seen at the Santa Cruz Post Office), her art declined in popularity during the Depression, and she was soon living in poverty. Shore was committed to an asylum for a time near the end of the 1950s, and died in 1963 in Carmel.

SOURCES:

Bailey, Brooke. *The Remarkable Lives of 100 Women Artists*. Holbrook, MA: Bob Adams, 1994.

Dunford, Penny. *A Biographical Dictionary of Women Artists in Europe and America Since 1850*. Philadelphia, PA: University of Pennsylvania Press, 1989.

**Ginger Strand**, Ph.D.,
New York City

## Shore, Jane (c. 1445–c. 1527)

*Legendary mistress of Edward IV, king of England. Born Jane Wainstead around 1445; died around 1527; daughter of Thomas Wainstead (a London mercer); married William Shore (a goldsmith); mistress of the marquis of Dorset, Lord Hastings, and Edward IV.*

Born around 1445, Jane Wainstead married while still a girl. As the wife of a prosperous goldsmith in Lombard Street, she and her husband William Shore were often at court on business. There, she met King Edward IV and was his mistress by the mid-1470s. Shore used her influence with the king to petition the pope for an annulment of her marriage on the grounds of impotence. The outcome has not been recorded. "For many he had, but her he loved," wrote Sir Thomas More. More claimed that she had a ready wit, was of a friendly nature, and used her considerable influence with the king for the common good.

Edward's brother, Richard III, had a different view. On the death of Edward IV in 1483, Richard (who had sired seven illegitimate children himself), accused Shore of witchcraft and had her hauled before the bishop of London's court for harlotry. Her penance was to forfeit all her material possessions (to Richard, of course) and to walk the streets of London barefoot, wearing a white sheet and carrying a lighted candle. Jane Shore died around 1527, probably in her early 80s, "lean, withered, and dried up, nothing left but shrivelled skin and bone," noted one chronicler. The agonizing details of her death in a ditch by starvation have not been verified, though the old ballad of "Jane Shore" gives precise details of the circumstances.

**RELATED MEDIA:**

*Richard III* (film), starring Laurence Olivier and directed by Olivier; the non-speaking role of Jane Shore was played by *Pamela Brown, 1955.

## Short, Elizabeth (1925–1947)

*American murder victim known as "The Black Dahlia." Name variations: The Black Dahlia. Born in Medford, Massachusetts, in 1925; daughter of Phoebe Short; murdered in Los Angeles, California, on January 15, 1947.*

On January 15, 1947, in an L.A. suburb, a nude body was spotted amid the refuse of a vacant lot by a passerby; the corpse had been severely mutilated, hacked in two at the waist, and the initials "B.D." carved deeply into one thigh. There was reason to believe that most of the mutilation had taken place while the victim was still alive. Checking for prints, the FBI came up with the name of Elizabeth Short, a 22-year-old from Medford, Massachusetts, who had a police record caused by a one-time arrest for juvenile delinquency: she had been charged with drinking while underage.

In a swirl of publicity, Elizabeth Short's mother was brought to L.A. Though **Phoebe Short** was unable to give a positive identification because the body was so disfigured, she did produce a recent letter from her daughter, mailed from San Diego. The inquiries began there.

The dual investigations of press and FBI to uncover the events leading up to the death of Elizabeth Short revealed the following: she was born in Medford. Her parents had separated when she was six and her father had moved to California, taking one of the family's five children with him. Phoebe Short had a difficult time working, feeding, and attending to four children on her own. As a result, in 1942, Elizabeth left home at 17 and took a job as a waitress in Miami. She soon fell in love with a young soldier, but the country was at war, and he was killed in battle. It was said that Short found solace in drink and other men. While drinking with soldiers in a café in Miami, she was arrested for being underage, given a rail ticket to Medford by the authorities, and told to return home. Instead, she exited the train early and found another waitressing job in another town. Again she fell in love; this time with Army Air Force Major Matt M. Gordon, Jr., and in 1944 Short went back home to await her soldier's return. On August 22, 1946, she received a telegram from Gordon's mother: the Air Force major had been killed in action.

The following day, Short set out for California in search of a movie career, joining the Hollywood casting lines for work as an extra. She was said to be beautiful. To contrast her milk-white complexion and raven hair, she began to dress in black, including her dress, stockings, and underwear; she even wore a jet black ring. Someone nicknamed her the Black Dahlia, and the name stuck. When movie work grew harder to find, Short moved to San Diego and took another waitressing job. Reputedly, she also continued drinking and continued to be seen with an assortment of men.

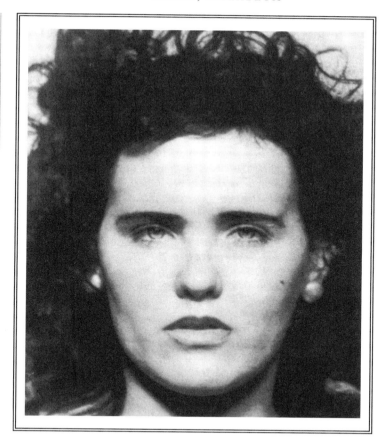

The slaying of Elizabeth Short, a.k.a. The Black Dahlia, is one of the most famous unsolved crimes in American history. There were no clues that led to the killer. Weeks after the murder someone anonymously sent a few of Short's belongings to an L.A. newspaper: her birth certificate, address book, and Social Security card. Aside from that, the police followed up on hundreds of phony leads. Many men and one woman confessed to the crime, but they could not match the gory details of the slaying known only by the police. In lieu of a serious suspect, the press held Elizabeth Short's reputation accountable.

Author James Ellroy, whose mother **Jean Hilliker Ellroy** was murdered in 1958 under similar unsolved circumstances, published *The Black Dahlia* in 1987. In 1995, **Janice Knowlton** published *Daddy Was the Black Dahlia Killer*, in which she pointed the finger at her father George Knowlton, who had dated Short. As well, John Gilmore, whose father was an officer with the Los Angeles Police Department (LAPD) at the time of the murder, claims in his *Severed: The True Story of the Black Dahlia Murder* (1998) that the LAPD's chief suspect was Jack Wilson, a reclusive burglar, alcoholic, and possi-

*Elizabeth*
*Short*

*Opposite page*
*Jane*
*Shore*

ble serial killer. Wilson, however, died in a hotel fire in the 1980s, just days before his pending arrest. Gilmore also contends that Wilson might have been responsible for the slaying of socialite **Georgette Bauerdorf**, who was murdered only months before Elizabeth Short. According to Larry Harnisch, a *Los Angeles Times* reporter who is working on a book about the murder, Short was killed by L.A. surgeon Walter Alonzo Bayley, whose daughter knew Short's sister, and whom he says may have been suffering from problems with alcohol and the early symptoms of Alzheimer's disease. With the increasing passage of time and the deaths of so many putative suspects, it seems likely that the mystery of who killed Elizabeth Short will endure.

**SUGGESTED READING:**

Ellroy, James. *The Black Dahlia*, 1985.

Gilmore, John. *Severed: The True Story of the Black Dahlia Murder*. Los Angeles, CA: Amok, 1998.

## Shorter, Mrs. Clement (1866–1918).

*See Sigerson, Dora.*

## Shorter, Dora (1866–1918).

*See Sigerson, Dora.*

## Shoshi, Empress (fl. 990–1010).

*See Murasaki Shikibu for sidebar.*

# Shouse, Kay (1896–1994)

*American philanthropist responsible for Wolf Trap. Name variations: Mrs. Jouett Shouse; Catherine Filene Shouse. Born Catherine Filene in 1896 in Boston, Massachusetts; died in Naples, Florida, in December 1994; daughter of A. Lincoln Filene (a Boston philanthropist and department store owner) and Therese Filene; Wheaton College, B.A., 1918; Harvard University, M.Ed., 1923; became second wife of Jouett Shouse (a former Kansas congressional representative, newspaper publisher, and assistant secretary of the U.S. Treasury), on December 2, 1932. Jouett Shouse was first married to Marion Edwards Shouse; they had two children.*

Called "the most extraordinary woman I have ever known" by opera great *\*Beverly Sills*, Kay Shouse was born in 1896 in Boston, where her father A. Lincoln Filene built upon the family fortune by establishing Federated Department Stores. She attended Wheaton College in Massachusetts, and while there set up a series of conferences among students and deans from women's colleges for the promotion and study of employment opportunities for women. Graduating in 1918, she joined the U.S. Employment Service as an assistant to the head of the women's division.

Two years later, she published *Careers for Women* (rev. ed. 1932), marking the start of an eventful decade that would also see her receive the first master's degree in education awarded to a woman by Harvard University (1923). Appointed by President Calvin Coolidge as chair of the first federal prison for women, Shouse focused on rehabilitation and created a job-training program for inmates. She was also actively involved in the Democratic Party, serving on the Democratic National Committee as the first woman delegate from Massachusetts and in 1922 co-founding the Women's National Democratic Club with *\*Florence Jaffray Harriman*.

In 1930, Shouse bought about 56 acres of land in Fairfax County, Virginia, in an area near the stream commonly known as Wolf Trap Creek, to which she would add a little over 100 acres more in the next three decades. She married Jouett Shouse, a former Democratic congressional representative and newspaper publisher, in 1932, and a few years later began organizing chamber music concerts for a local Washington, D.C., museum. The couple lived primarily in the Georgetown section of D.C., but spent much time at their Wolf Trap Farm, where Shouse raised farm animals and late in the 1930s began breeding dogs. She organized the army's General Clay Fund for German youth after World War II, and in 1956, after the ill-fated Hungarian Revolution, she organized and raised half a million dollars for the Washington Hungarian Relief Fund. In 1958, President Dwight D. Eisenhower appointed her to the board of trustees of the newly created National Cultural Center—later the John F. Kennedy Center for the Performing Arts—on which she would serve until 1980, when she became an honorary board member.

Shouse is perhaps best known for Wolf Trap Farm Park, the only national park for the performing arts in America. Searching for some way to preserve her land in Virginia, in 1965 she donated 100 acres of the farm, as well as money for construction of an amphitheater, to the National Park Service on condition the park be used for the promotion of the performing arts. The donation was accepted by Congress the following year, and in 1971 Wolf Trap Farm Park opened to the public. It is now a world-renowned arts center both for performing and for education in the arts. Shouse remained actively involved in managing Wolf Trap until near the end of her long life.

Shouse's contributions to education and dedication to philanthropy won her numerous national and international honors over the years. Among these were the Commander's Cross of Merit from Germany (1954), being made a Dame Commander of the British Empire by Queen *Elizabeth II (1976), the Presidential Medal of Freedom, America's highest civilian award (1977), being made an Officier dans l'Order des Arts et des Lettres, France's highest civilian award (1985), the Medal of Honor from Austria, and the National Medal of the Arts (1992). She was also the recipient of over a dozen honorary doctorates, and the Catherine Filene Shouse Career Center at Hood College was named in her honor, as was Wheaton College's Filene Center for Work and Learning. She died in 1994.

## Showa empress.
*See Nagako (1903–2000).*

## Shrewsbury, countess of.
*See Stafford, Catherine (d. 1476).*
*See Hastings, Anne (d. after 1506).*
*See Talbot, Elizabeth (1518–1608).*
*See Stuart, Arabella for sidebar on Mary Talbot (d. 1632).*

## Shrimpton, Jean (1942—)
*British fashion model. Born in 1942 in High Wycombe, England; married Michael Cox (a photographer), in 1979; children: son Thaddeus (b. 1979).*

With her kohl-lined eyes, long legs and what photographer Cecil Beaton called "Pekingese features," Jean Shrimpton was seen as the epitome of a new type of woman of the 1960s: bold, hip and sexually free. She appeared on the covers of numerous fashion magazines, most prominently *Vogue*, and was featured on the cover of *Newsweek* in May 1965 (at which time she was making the unheard-of sum of $60 per hour). The following November, she attended the very proper Melbourne Gold Cup Derby in Australia wearing a skirt that stopped eight centimeters above her knees. As shocking as the briefness of her skirt—some consider it the debut of the miniskirt—was her failure to wear hat, gloves or stockings. The outfit was reported, condemned, and illustrated with photographs on the front pages of newspapers throughout the world. Shrimpton was one of the top models of the mid-'60s, along with **Veruschka, Penelope Tree,** and the preternaturally thin *Twiggy, who soon eclipsed her as the reigning fashion symbol of the era. As her modeling career tapered off towards the end of the decade, Shrimpton made

one poorly received movie, then turned to photography. She published *Jean Shrimpton: An Autobiography*, in 1990, and is now the owner and manager of a 17th-century inn in remote Cornwall, England.

**SOURCES:**
Martin, Jean, ed. *Who's Who of Women in the Twentieth Century.* Crescent Books, 1995.
*People Weekly.* August 1999.

**SUGGESTED READING:**
Stoddard, Chris, and Angie Dickinson. *Swingin' Chicks of the '60s.* CEDCO Publishing, 2000.

Ginger Strand, Ph.D., New York City

## Shriver, Eunice Kennedy (1921—)
*American pioneer in advocacy for the mentally and physically challenged, president for many years of the Joseph Kennedy Foundation, and a founder and organizer of the Special Olympics. Name variations: Eunice Kennedy. Born Eunice Mary Kennedy in Brookline, Massachusetts, on July 10, 1921; daughter of Joseph Patrick Kennedy (financier, diplomat, and head of several government commissions) and Rose (Fitzgerald) Kennedy; granted a bachelor's degree in sociology from Stanford University, 1943; married (Robert) Sargent Shriver, in 1953; children: Robert Sargent Shriver III (b. 1954, an investor and film producer); Maria Owings Shriver (b. 1955, an NBC correspondent who married actor Arnold Schwarzenegger); Timothy Perry Shriver (b. 1959, CEO of the Special Olympics); Mark Kennedy Shriver (b. 1963, a Maryland legislator and telephone executive); Anthony Paul Kennedy Shriver (b. 1965, a mental-retardation activist and president of a drug-delivery company).*

*Worked in the U.S. State Department (1943–45); became foundation director of the Joseph P. Kennedy, Jr., Foundation for the care and research of the disabled (1957); campaigned for her brother John F. Kennedy for the presidency of the U.S. (1960); during Kennedy's presidency, became advocate for the developmentally challenged (1962); instituted private day camp for the retarded (1963); joined others in establishing the Special Olympic Summer Games (1968); retired as president of the organization (1988).*

A young girl in a wheelchair races toward the finish line, her arms pushing furiously at the wheels. Born with cerebral palsy, she lives with the double burden of being both mentally and physically challenged. To her left, another competitor is gaining on her, but the sound of the cheering crowd encourages her toward the finish line, and suddenly she is over it. Like every other competitor who finishes the event, she receives a hug, but in this international competition she is also the winner of the gold medal.

More than 80 nations now send athletes to compete in the annual Special Olympics, begun in 1968. In nearly every community in the United States, there is a program to sponsor disabled athletes. Official summer sports include aquatics, athletics, basketball, bowling, horseback riding, gymnastics, roller skating, soccer, softball, and volleyball. Official winter sports include alpine skiing, cross-country skiing, figure skating, speedskating, and floor hockey. Thanks to the attitudes of support and competition encouraged by the Special Olympics, thousands of people cross new frontiers of achievement, acquire new skills, gain confidence and make lifelong friends every year. No single person is more responsible for the aims and achievements of its programs than Eunice Kennedy Shriver.

In 1921, Eunice Mary Kennedy was born in Brookline, Massachusetts, into one of America's more remarkable families. Her father Joseph P. Kennedy had amassed one of the country's largest fortunes; her mother *Rose Fitzgerald

Eunice Kennedy Shriver, with her brother John F. Kennedy.

Kennedy was the central figure in the family's life. Both parents were Boston Irish, the children of immigrants who came to America when the Irish took the lowest paying jobs and often lived in slums. But Eunice's maternal grandfather John F. Fitzgerald had become mayor of Boston, and her parents had prospered more than anyone might have imagined. Eunice's brothers and sisters included Joseph Kennedy, Jr., John Fitzgerald Kennedy, *Rosemary Kennedy, *Kathleen Kennedy, ❧➤ Patricia Kennedy Lawford, Robert F. Kennedy, ❧➤ Jean Kennedy Smith, and Edward "Ted" Kennedy. Rose was a strict but loving mother, and Joseph was frequently away, although he took charge of the children when Rose took vacations from the large clan. Both parents invested a great deal of time in raising their brood, and both expected the children to be successful. Theirs was an extremely close family who enjoyed sailing, horseback riding, conversation, and each other.

When Eunice was five, the family moved to New York. That same year, her father purchased a summer home in Hyannis Port, Massachusetts, which became the center of happy childhood memories. During the 1930s, while many suffered through the economic throes of the Great Depression, the Kennedy family did not, largely because Joseph Kennedy took most of his investments out of the stock market before the crash in 1929. In 1932, the family's horizons were widened when Joseph Kennedy worked for the presidential campaign of Franklin D. Roosevelt. After Roosevelt's election, Kennedy served in his administration as chair of the new Securities and Exchange Commission, the Maritime Commission, and as U.S. ambassador to Great Britain. Life was exciting for the family who moved first to Washington and then to London, then grew more intense after the Germans began to bombard London in 1940, and the Kennedys moved to the country.

Many would envy the life of Eunice Kennedy, as the daughter of wealthy and prominent parents. But life with the Kennedys was not without trials. Eunice's older sister Rosemary, born during the 1918 flu pandemic, was developmentally challenged. The Kennedys took an unusual step for the era when they refused to institutionalize their daughter. At a time when public opinion sanctioned sending such a child away, to be considered dead by all but the closest family members, Joseph Kennedy posed the question, "What can they do for her that her family can't do better?" For as long as Eunice could remember, Rosemary was part of the family. She looked much like her mother Rose, but she developed

slowly. At meals, someone would cut her meat, which she could not do, but she went sailing, and she loved to sing when her mother played the piano. Joseph Kennedy grew increasingly upset about her, however, as he became aware of how little she would ever progress.

After the U.S. entered World War II, the entire family returned to the States. Eunice attended Stanford University and obtained a bachelor's degree in sociology in 1943, then worked in Washington for the State Department from 1943 to 1945. After a brief period at the Department of Justice, she was assigned as a social worker to the Federal Penitentiary for Women in Alderson, West Virginia.

After 1941, her sister Rosemary showed serious signs of deterioration. No longer the contented girl who loved dressing up and having ribbons put in her hair, she grew withdrawn and irritable. She was taken to numerous specialists, one of whom suggested to her father that she undergo a surgical lobotomy. In an era before tranquilizers, the risky operation involved cutting into the lobes of the brain to eliminate the girl's aggressive behavior, while leaving her mental functions relatively intact.

*Rosemary was different. My mother was told she would catch up, but she never did.*
—Eunice Kennedy Shriver

With what he assumed to be his daughter's best interests at heart, but without telling anyone else in the family, Joseph Kennedy decided to have the lobotomy performed. The surgery, however, was botched, leaving Rosemary in a zombie-like state. Eventually, Rosemary was permanently institutionalized, and Joe Kennedy remained tormented by what he had done to his daughter.

On August 12, 1944, tragedy struck again when the oldest son, Joseph Kennedy, Jr., then a pilot stationed in England, was killed on a bombing mission. Four years later, on May 13, 1948, Eunice's sister Kathleen died in a plane crash in Europe. In 1946, Joseph created the Joseph Kennedy, Jr., Foundation in memory of his son, supplying it with more than $1 million a year in funding. When Joe Kennedy asked his daughter Eunice to determine how the foundation's money could best be spent, she began to travel the country visiting institutions for the developmentally challenged. In one place after another, what she found was appalling: adults and children crowded into bleak buildings, treated in many cases like criminals, tied to chairs, reeking of urine, and spending their lives with nothing to

Lawford, Patricia Kennedy. See Kennedy, Rose Fitzgerald for sidebar.

Smith, Jean Kennedy. See Kennedy, Rose Fitzgerald for sidebar.

do. Most of the care she found was in stark contrast to the treatment Rosemary had received at home, or even in the Catholic institution where she was looked after lovingly by nuns.

For Eunice Kennedy, the next few years were personally and professionally fulfilling as she set about establishing the goals of the Kennedy Foundation. One was to fund research dedicated to mental retardation, a topic that was still rarely discussed in public and that received virtually no attention in the country's medical schools. In 1953, she married Robert Sargent Shriver, and the birth of five children—Robert, Maria, Timothy, Mark, and Anthony—followed in quick succession. Despite the pleasures and demands of her own family, Eunice Kennedy Shriver became director of the Kennedy Foundation in 1957. When her brother John F. Kennedy decided to run for the presidency, the Shrivers became valuable workers in the campaign organization leading up to Kennedy's election in 1960.

In the White House, President Kennedy asked his sister to prepare a report on the physical education of the mentally challenged to be presented to a panel he had organized. Eunice Shriver, however, decided to do a great deal

*Danny Szeles (left) and Chris Burke at the Special Olympics, Central Michigan University, 1995.*

more. Taking the position that if the president's family could be open about the issue of mental disability, all Americans would be encouraged to do the same, Shriver decided to tell Rosemary's story. Under Eunice's supervision, David Gelman wrote an article for *The Saturday Evening Post*, in which she passed along information from specialists. When the piece appeared, the openness of the Kennedy clan about what long had been seen by many families as a matter of private shame became a dramatic step in changing American attitudes. In 1962, convinced of the value of publicity, Shriver took a further step when she and Sargent persuaded the public service Advertising Council to devise newspaper and magazine ads which targeted the issue.

Remembering how Rosemary had loved sailing, swimming, and camping, Shriver was distressed to discover that no camps existed for the mentally challenged. In June 1963, she and her husband began a five-week day camp in their own spacious backyard in Rockville, Maryland. One hundred volunteers were recruited, one for each day camper, and Shriver was particularly impressed to see how much the skills of the campers improved, especially in team sports.

From 1963 to 1968, Shriver endured the public and personal tragedies of the assassinations of her brothers John and Robert Kennedy as well as the ongoing institutionalization of Rosemary. By this time, Eunice had begun to think about establishing some kind of sporting event for the developmentally challenged. Then, in 1968, **Anne McGlone** and representatives of the Chicago Park District approached the Kennedy Foundation with the idea of funding a national event organized along Olympic lines for developmentally challenged children. With Eunice Shriver's enthusiastic support, the first Special Olympic Summer Games were launched on July 20, 1968, at Soldier's Field in Chicago. The event was such a success that a nonprofit corporation was established to sponsor future events.

Under Shriver's vigorous leadership, the organization known informally as the Special Olympics grew explosively. An elaborate system was set up to channel athletes through a network of local and regional competitions to reach the national level of annual competition. The program eventually encompassed 25,000 areas and districts, then grew to include an international competition with athletes participating from more than 80 countries. In addition, more than one million athletes in 156 countries participate in local Special Olympics programs.

The Special Olympics differed in some ways from the regular Olympics. For one thing, medals were not awarded to countries, and national anthems were never played; it was the effort and achievement of the individual participants that was honored. For another, "huggers" were assigned to wait across the finish line for every athlete, ready to congratulate them no matter what their time or score.

Many have been amazed by what Special Olympians have achieved. For example, some teams began to compete successfully against their non-disabled peers. A new competition called Unified Sports had to be established for the challenges between the disabled and the non-disabled, and the latter had to learn never to take the ability of their competitors for granted. Unsurprised by this development, Eunice Kennedy Shriver believed in keeping the stakes of the competition high. As she said:

> Let us not be satisfied with a game that *looks* like soccer; an event that is *almost* like the high jump; a race that could *pass* for a 400-meter relay. . . . The bedrock principle on which our program rests is this: for the great majority of the mentally [challenged], Special Olympics is the mainstream.

To guarantee the ongoing financial support of the Special Olympics, Shriver sought corporate sponsors like McDonald's, Nike, Coca Cola, and IBM. Sports celebrities and movie stars were asked to contribute their time, and, with this amalgam of money and glitz, the events began to attract outstanding media attention—attention that the developmentally challenged had long deserved. Eunice's daughter **Maria Shriver**, by then well known as a television commentator, entreated her husband Arnold Schwarzenegger to coach body building, and other members of the Kennedy clan showed up regularly at Special Olympics fundraisers and events. Queen *Noor al-Hussein of Jordan, singer John Denver, and actor Christopher Reeve have taken part, and regular Olympic coaches have donated their time to the training of the athletes. Eunice's son Bobby produced a television special for the ABC network that gained the event more publicity, and since 1968 more than half a million individuals from around the world have been participants. At the Alaska Games in March 2001, over 10,000 athletes competed.

Eunice Kennedy Shriver retired as president of the Special Olympics organization in 1988, at age 67. In 1993, the civil rights of a long-ignored and overlooked segment of the American population were finally established with the passage of the Americans with Disabilities Act. Without

Eunice Kennedy Shriver's campaigns to bring the issues of the developmentally challenged out of the closet and onto the playing fields, it is possible that the legislation would still be waiting to be passed. On a more individual level, her work can be seen in the determination that continues to drive Special Olympians across the finish line.

**SOURCES:**
Birmingham, Stephen. "The Kennedy Women: America's Seven Wonders," in *Harper's Bazaar*. Vol. 113, no. 3227. October 1980, pp. 20, 24, 29–30.
Brown, Fern G. *Special Olympics*. NY: Franklin Watts, 1992.
Davis, John H. *The Kennedys: Dynasty and Disaster, 1848–1983*. NY: McGraw-Hill, 1984.
Dietl, Dick. "Special Olympics, Special Lady," in *Journal of Rehabilitation*. Vol. 49, no. 2. April-May-June 1983, pp. 9, 13–14.
Goodyear, Sara Jane. "1,000 Retarded Kids Compete in Chicago Special Olympics," in *Chicago Tribune*. Section 1A. July 21, 1968, p. 4.
Moss, Desda. "Disabled's Champion Steps Back," in *USA Today*. April 11, 1990, p. 2A.
Rainie, Harrison, and Katia Hetter. "The Most Lasting Kennedy Legacy," in *U.S. News and World Report*. November 15, 1993, pp. 44–47.
Shriver, Eunice Kennedy. "Hope for Retarded Children," in *The Saturday Evening Post*. Vol. 235, no. 33. September 22, 1962, pp. 71–75.
———, Civia Tamarkin, and Steve Dale. "Eunice Shriver's Olympian Friends," in *People Weekly*. Vol. 28, no. 7. August 17, 1987, pp. 30–33.

**SUGGESTED READING:**
Leamer, Laurence. *The Kennedy Women*. Villard, 1994.

**Karin Loewen Haag,**
freelance writer,
Athens, Georgia

# Shtern, Lina (1878–1968)

*Russian physiologist noted for her discovery of the hematoencephalic barrier and other major scientific discoveries. Name variations: Lina Solomonovna Shtern; Lina Solomonovna Stern; Lina Salomonowna Schtern; Lina Sterna. Born on August 26, 1878, in Liepaja (Libava), Latvia, Russia; died in Moscow on March 7, 1968; educated at the University of Geneva.*

*Was a professor at the University of Geneva; returned to Russia (1925), and became a major figure in Soviet medical research; was the first woman admitted to the USSR Academy of Sciences; survived the anti-Semitic purges of the late Stalin era; lived to an advanced age as the most illustrious woman scientist of the USSR.*

Born into a prosperous Jewish family in Russian Latvia in 1878, Lina Shtern received a medical education in Switzerland and, upon graduation from the University of Geneva in 1904, was invited to join the department of physiology at that institution. She quickly won international recognition for her research in the area of oxidation enzymes and in 1917 was appointed a professor in the biochemistry department of the University of Geneva. Able to speak all of the major European languages, she was a well-known and highly respected scientist not only in Switzerland but in much of Europe as well. Shtern was also prosperous, due in part to her work as a consultant to a number of pharmaceutical firms. In 1925, impressed with the potential for fundamental social changes in the newborn Soviet Union, she moved to Moscow. There she became head of the sub-department of physiology of the Second Moscow Medical Institute, a post she would hold until 1949. In 1929, Shtern became director of the Institute of Physiology of the USSR Academy of Sciences, a position that also lasted until 1949.

Lina Shtern investigated many physiological systems during her long scientific career, but her most important work took place in the period between 1915 and 1935. During this time, she studied the special physiological mechanism in the central nervous system which ensures constancy of the internal medium of the brain and which protects it from harmful external influences, primarily from substances contained in the blood that may damage the brain's nervous tissue. She called this mechanism the "hematoencephalic barrier," that is, a barrier between the blood and the brain tissue, and this term has since become established in medicine and biology. Shtern subsequently extended the principle of barrier mechanisms, based on the permeability of blood capillaries, to all the organs of the body, and it was given the name "histohematic barrier," a term also used in contemporary physiology.

By the mid-1930s, Lina Shtern had become one of the most respected scientists in the Soviet Union. She also gained recognition abroad, being chosen in 1932 as a member of the German Academy of Natural Sciences. In 1934, she was named Honored Scientist of the Russian Soviet Federal Republic. Besides her research and administrative duties, she served as editor of the *Bulletin of Experimental Biology and Medicine*. In 1935, her 543-page monograph on the hematoencephalic barrier was published, and she was the dedicatee of *Problems of Biology and Medicine*; this massive *Festschrift* in her honor was a volume of more than 700 pages of articles written by eminent scientists from around the globe. She became a member of the Communist Party of the Soviet Union in 1938. The following year, Shtern was the first woman to be named an Academician (full member) of the USSR Academy of Sciences.

During World War II, she concentrated on solving problems of immediate concern to the armed forces, particularly the treatment of wounded military personnel. Her wartime research included important discoveries in the treatment of shock, including a novel method of injecting a solution of potassium phosphate directly into the brain. For her wartime innovations, Shtern was awarded a Stalin Prize in 1943. Outspoken and fearless, Shtern hated injustice wherever she encountered it. In 1943, she wrote Joseph Stalin a letter protesting the ousting of Jews from Soviet scientific and state institutions.

After World War II, Stalin's growing paranoia led him to single out Soviet Jews as enemies of his regime, labeling them "rootless cosmopolitans" and "agents of Zionism." Despite her international scientific reputation, Shtern was not exempt from this wave of persecution. She was at great risk, not only for her blunt criticism of Soviet acts of anti-Semitism but also for having been a member of the wartime Jewish Antifascist Committee created to draw sympathy for the USSR's heroic struggle against Nazi invaders. Many Jewish leaders were murdered or thrown into the Gulag labor camps during this time. In 1949, Shtern was removed from her several positions, and in 1952 she and a large number of other Soviet Jews were placed on trial on trumped-up charges of being American-Zionist agents and other fantastic offenses. In July 1952, she was sentenced to a term of life imprisonment. Shtern spent almost three years imprisoned at Moscow's notorious Lubianka, as well as a short time at Lefortovo prison, which she later described as "hell." She was released in 1954 and rehabilitated with full restoration of her honors, including becoming head of the USSR Academy of Science's physiology laboratory. She had outlived dictator Stalin and was able to witness a full renewal of her status as a major scientific pioneer, which was reflected in the publication of a number of laudatory books and articles demonstrating her many achievements. Lina Shtern died in Moscow on March 7, 1968.

SOURCES:

Kagan, Solomon R. *Jewish Medicine*. Boston, MA: Medico-Historical Press, 1952.

Knight, Amy. *Beria: Stalin's First Lieutenant*. Princeton, NJ: Princeton University Press, 1993.

Kommoss, Rudolf. *Juden hinter Stalin: Die jüdische Vormachtstellung in der Sowjetunion, auf Grund amtlicher Sowjetquellen dargestellt*. 3rd–4th rev. ed. Berlin: Nibelungen-Verlag, 1944.

Kostyrchenko, Gennadii. *Out of the Red Shadows: Anti-Semitism in Stalin's Russia*. Amherst, NY: Prometheus, 1995.

"Lina & the Brain," in *Time*. Vol. 49, no. 9. March 3, 1947, p. 45.

Pinkus, Benjamin, and Jonathan Frankel. *The Soviet Government and the Jews, 1948–1967: A Documented Study*. Cambridge: Cambridge University Press, 1984.

Podolsky, Edward. *Red Miracle: The Story of Soviet Medicine*. NY: Beechhurst, 1947.

Rapoport, Louis. *Stalin's War Against the Jews: The Doctors' Plot and the Soviet Solution*. NY: Free Press, 1990.

Rapoport, Yakov. *The Doctors' Plot of 1953*. Cambridge, MA: Harvard University Press, 1991.

Richthofen, Bolko Freiherr von. "Judentum und bolschewistische 'Kulturpolitik,'" in *Forschungen zur Judenfrage*. Vol. 8. Hamburg: Hanseatische Verlagsanstalt, 1943, pp. 134–162.

Rosin, Iakov Anan'evich, V.B. Malkin, and Oleg Georgievich Gazenko. *Lina Solomonovna Shtern, 1878–1968*. Moscow: "Nauka," 1987.

Smirnova, N.V., S. Ia. Rapoport, and S.R. Zubkova. *Lina Solomonovna Shtern*. Moscow: Akademiia Nauk SSSR, 1960.

Turkevich, John, *et al. Soviet Men of Science: Academicians and Corresponding Members of the Academy of Sciences of the USSR*. Princeton, NJ: D. Van Nostrand, 1963.

Vaksberg, Arkady. *Stalin Against the Jews*. Translated by Antonina W. Bouis. NY: Alfred A. Knopf, 1994.

**John Haag**, Associate Professor History,
University of Georgia, Athens, Georgia

## Shub, Esther (1894–1959)

*Soviet film editor and director who was one of the first to use montage editing to create compilation films. Name variations: Esfir Shub. Born Esfir Ilyianichna Shub on March 3, 1894, in Chernigovsky district, Ukraine; died on September 21, 1959, in Moscow; attended the Institute for Women's Higher Education in Moscow.*

*Filmography as director, screenwriter and editor:* The Fall of the Romanov Dynasty *(1927);* The Great Road *(1927);* The Russia of Nicholas II and Leo Tolstoy *(1928);* Today *(1930);* Komsomol *(1932);* Moscow Builds the Metro *(1934);* Land of the Soviets *(1937);* Spain *(1939);* Twenty Years of Soviet Cinema *(with Vsevolod Pudovkin, 1940);* Fascism Will Be Defeated *(1941);* Native Land *(1942);* The Trial in Smolensk *(1946);* Across the Araks *(1947).*

Born in the Ukraine in 1894, Esther Shub attended the Institute for Women's Higher Education in Moscow. After working in the experimental theaters of poet Vladimir Mayakovsky and her friend Vsevolod Meyerhold, she began a career as a film editor. Shub edited more than 200 films, mostly foreign films that needed to be recut and retitled for Soviet audiences to comply with censorship guidelines. In the course of her work, she became interested in the intellectual possibilities of film editing, splicing together pre-existing footage to create an entirely different result. This style of editing, known as montage, was pioneered by husband-and-wife collaborators Dziga Vertov and *Elizaveta Svilova, and was also being explored by Shub's colleague Sergei Eisenstein.

Shub became so skilled in montage editing that, against the wishes of the Goskino film company for which she worked, she virtually created the compilation method of documentary filmmaking; Mayakovsky would call her "the pride of our cinematography." In 1927, she made her first and most famous compilation film by cutting together old footage from newsreels, filmed war reports, and even home movies of the Russian royal family, having scoured every available source for documentary material. *The Fall of the Romanov Dynasty* dealt with the early years of the Russian Revolution, from 1912 to 1917, and was extremely well received. That same year Shub made *The Great Road* (1927), in honor of the 1917 October Revolution. Her technique influenced Eisenstein, and she visited the set and advised the director during production of his classic film *October: Ten Days that Shook the World* (1928).

Shub considered Vertov her teacher, although she disagreed with his conviction that film should not be scripted. The pair also differed on the issue of authenticity, as Shub believed a documentary could include both staged and real-life footage. Despite their differences, Vertov recognized Shub's genius, calling her "one of the most significant figures in Soviet documentary film of the silent era."

When movies began to use sound, Shub temporarily abandoned her compilation method to create an ultrarealistic style, predating *cinema verité* by 30 years. In her film *Komsomol* (1932), she purposely integrated the making of the film with the film itself, on screen. Microphones and cameras were clearly visible in some instances, and shots of people stumbling, stuttering or looking directly into the camera were also included to replace the illusion of reality with reality itself. Shub also completed a script for a film to be called "Women" (1933–34), which was to explore the ways in which women's roles had changed since the Revolution, although the movie was never made. She oversaw a workshop in photomontage for a class taught by Eisenstein at the VGIK film school in Moscow from 1933 to 1935, the year she received the title of Honored Artist of the Republic, and edited several other documentaries in the last years of the 1930s. Among these was *Spain* (1939), a compilation of newsreels and frontline film of the Spanish Civil War. The following year she co-directed, with Vsevolod Pudovkin, *Twenty Years of Soviet Cinema*. She became chief editor of the *News of the Day* serial at the Central Studio for Documentary Film in Moscow in 1942, and made her last film, *Across the Araks*, in 1947, 12 years before her death in Moscow. Shub's autobiography, *My Life—Cinema*, which contains extensive commentary on filmmaking techniques, was published in Russia in 1972.

**SOURCES:**

Acker, Ally. *Reel Women: Pioneers of the Cinema 1896 to the Present*. NY: Continuum, 1991.

Attwood, Lynne, ed. *Red Women on the Silver Screen*. London: Pandora, 1993.

Foster, Gwendolyn A., ed. *Women Film Directors: An International Bio-Critical Dictionary*. Westport, CT: Greenwood Press, 1995.

Katz, Ephraim. *The Film Encyclopedia*. 3rd ed. NY: HarperCollins, 1998.

Lyon, Christopher, ed. *The International Dictionary of Films and Filmmakers*, Vol. II: *Directors/Filmmakers*. Chicago, IL: St. James Press, 1984.

Uglow, Jennifer S., ed. *The International Dictionary of Women's Biography*. NY: Continuum, 1982.

**Ginger Strand**, Ph.D.,
New York City

## Shuhua Ling (1904–1990).

*See Ling Shuhua.*

## Shōtoku, Empress (718–770).

*See Kōken-Shōtoku.*

## Siberia, princess of (1805–1863).

*See Volkonskaya, Maria.*

## Sibirskii, N. (1876–1921).

*See Samoilova, Konkordiya.*

## Sibley, Antoinette (b. 1939).

*See Fonteyn, Margot for sidebar.*

## Sibyl or Sibylla (fl. 10th c. BCE).

*See Sheba, Queen of.*

## Sibylla.

*Variant of Sybilla.*

## Sibylla (1160–1190)

*Queen of Jerusalem. Name variations: Sibyl, Sybil, or Sybilla. Born in 1160 in Jerusalem; died in 1190 in Jerusalem; daughter of Almaric I, king of Jerusalem (r. 1162–1174), and Agnes of Courtenay (1136–1186); sister of Baldwin IV, king of Jerusalem (r. 1174–1183); married William of Montferrat, count of Jaffa and regent of Jerusalem, in 1176 (died 1180); married Guy of Lusignan, later king of Jerusalem (r. 1186–1192), in 1180; children: (first marriage) Bald-win V (b. 1179), king of Jerusalem (r. 1185–1186); (second marriage) two daughters, names unknown, who both died in 1190.*

A princess of the Latin Crusader kingdom of Jerusalem, Sibylla was born in 1160, the daughter of King Almaric I and *\*Agnes of Courtenay*. Sibylla married a Frankish noble, William of Montferrat, count of Jaffa, in 1176; their only child Baldwin (V) was born in 1179, two months after Count William died of malaria. She then married her lover, Guy of Lusignan, in 1180, despite her brother King Baldwin IV's disapproval of their adulterous relationship and of Guy himself. The couple had two daughters, names unknown.

Dying of leprosy, Baldwin IV reluctantly appointed Guy regent of Jerusalem, but Guy's ineptitude led Baldwin IV to banish him from the kingdom and name Sibylla's infant son Baldwin as his heir. King Baldwin IV died in 1185; his young grandson, Baldwin V, survived him less than a year. The two claimants for the crown were then Sibylla, as Almaric's only surviving child from his first marriage, and her half-sister *\*Isabella I of Jerusalem*, daughter of his second marriage to *\*Maria Comnena*. Sibylla was crowned queen by popular acclaim in 1186, but her new subjects refused to accept the corrupt and imprudent Guy as their king. Sibylla had him crowned anyway.

In 1187, Jerusalem was attacked by Saladin, the Muslim sultan of Egypt and Syria, who hoped to reconquer the holy city and drive out the Christian rulers. In the course of the war, the Christian army was defeated by Saladin's superior forces and Guy of Lusignan was taken prisoner. Sibylla surrendered Jerusalem after a siege in October 1187, effectively ending the Crusader kingdom which had lasted almost a century. Her pleas to Saladin to release her husband succeeded in 1188; Guy continued making war against Saladin with the army of the Third Crusade under the English king Richard I. The former queen remained politically active and hoped the Crusade would reestablish her hereditary right to rule Jerusalem, but in 1190 she died unexpectedly in an epidemic, as did her two daughters.

Sibylla's death left the Christian claim to the throne of Jerusalem empty; Guy of Lusignan tried unsuccessfully to claim it. Eventually King Richard I sold Guy control of Cyprus, where he died in 1194.

**SOURCES:**

Jackson-Laufer, Guida. *Women Who Ruled*. Santa Barbara, CA: ABC-CLIO, 1990.

Runciman, Steven. *A History of the Crusades*, vol. 2. Cambridge: Cambridge University Press, 1987.

**Laura York**, M.A. in History,
University of California, Riverside, California

## Sibylla of Armenia (fl. 1200s)

*Countess of Tripoli. Flourished in the 1200s; married Bohemund VI, prince of Antioch (r. 1251–1268), count of Tripoli (r. 1251–1275); children: \*Lucia, countess of Tripoli (r. 1288–1289); Bohemund VII (d. 1287), prince of Antioch and count of Tripoli (r. 1275–1287).*

## Sibylle du Faubourg Saint-Germain, La (1772–1843).

See Lenormand, Marie Anne Adélaïde.

## Sibylle Elizabeth of Wurttemberg (1584–1606)

*Electress of Saxony. Born on April 10, 1584; died on January 20, 1606; daughter of \*Sibylle of Anhalt (1564–1614) and Frederick, duke of Wurttemberg-Mompelga; sister of Louis Frederick (b. 1586), duke of Wurttemberg; married John George I, elector of Saxony, on September 16, 1604.*

## Sibylle of Anhalt (1564–1614)

*Duchess of Wurttemberg-Mompelga. Born on September 20, 1564; died on November 16, 1614; daughter of Joachim Ernst (b. 1536), prince of Anhalt, and Agnes of Barby (1540–1569); sister of \*Elizabeth of Anhalt (1563–1607); married Frederick, duke of Wurttemberg-Mompelga, on May 22, 1581; children: \*Sibylle Elizabeth of Wurttemberg (1584–1606); Louis Frederick (b. 1586), duke of Wurttemberg.*

## Sibylle of Brunswick-Luneburg (1584–1652)

*Duchess of Brunswick-Dannenberg. Born on June 3, 1584; died on August 5, 1652; daughter of \*Dorothy of Denmark (1546–1617) and William the Younger, duke of Luneburg; married Julius Ernst, duke of Brunswick-Dannenberg, on December 18, 1617.*

## Sibylle of Burgundy (1065–1102)

*Duchess of Burgundy. Name variations: Sibylle de Bourgogne. Born in 1065; died on March 23, 1102; daughter of William I, count of Burgundy, and Etienette de Longwy; sister of \*Gisela of Burgundy (fl. 1100s); married Eudes I the Red (1058–1103), duke of Burgundy (r. 1079–1103), in 1080; children: Helie also known as Ela (b. 1080); Florine of Burgundy (b. 1083); Hugh II (b. 1085), duke of Burgundy (r. 1102–1143); Henry of Burgundy (b. 1087), a priest.*

## Sibylle of Burgundy (1126–1150)

*Queen of Sicily. Name variations: Sibylle de Bourgogne. Born in 1126; died on September 19, 1150; daughter of Hugh II (b. 1085), duke of Burgundy (r. 1102–1143), and \*Mathilde de Mayenne; became third wife of Roger II, king of Sicily (r. 1103–1154), duke of Apulia (r. 1128–1154), in 1149. Roger II's first wife was \*Beatrice of Rethel; his second was \*Elvira (d. 1135).*

## Sichelgaita of Salerno (1040–1090)

*Duchess of Apulia. Born in 1040 in Salerno; died in 1090 in Normandy; daughter of the duke of Salerno; sister of Gisulf II, Lombard prince of Salerno; second wife of Robert Guiscard (d. 1085), a Frankish noble, duke of Apulia and Calabria, count of Sicily (r. 1057–1085); children: Roger Gorsa or Borsa, duke of Apulia and Calabria (r. 1085–1111); Helena (betrothed to Constantine, son of the emperor Michael VII); Matilda (who married Raymond Berengar II, count of Barcelona); Mabel (who married William of Grandmesnil); \*Emma (who married Odo, the marquis); and others.*

Sichelgaita of Salerno was a princess of Lombardy and the hereditary duchess of Apulia in southern Italy. She was the second wife of the Frankish noble Robert Guiscard (his first wife was \*Aubrey of Buonalbergo) and became his most valuable ally in the constant wars in which he engaged. She is described in chronicles, most notably those of Byzantium's \*Anna Comnena, as Amazonian, a tall woman, strong and muscular. Anna's chronicle tells of the Battle of Durazzo, in which Robert led an army of Normans against the Byzantines. Sichelgaita rode beside her warrior husband, dressed from head to toe in armor, urging on their troops. According to Anna, Sichelgaita even ordered some retreating Normans to return to the fight, chasing after them with a spear until she managed to herd them back into the battle. As they aged, Robert and Sichelgaita returned to Normandy and became actively involved in the politics of the Frankish kingdom.

**SOURCES:**

LaBarge, Margaret. *A Small Sound of the Trumpet: Women in Medieval Life*. Boston: Beacon Press, 1986.

**Laura York**, M.A. in History,
University of California, Riverside, California

## Sicily, queen of.

## Sicily, regent of.

# Siddal, Elizabeth (1829–1862)

*English painter, writer, and artist's model who was the face of the Pre-Raphaelite movement.* Name variations: Elizabeth Rossetti; Mrs. Dante Gabriel Rossetti. Born Elizabeth Eleanor Siddal on July 25, 1829, in Holborn, England; died on February 11, 1862, in London; daughter of Charles Siddal and Elizabeth (Evans) Siddal; married Dante Gabriel Rossetti (the painter and poet), on May 23, 1860; children: one daughter (stillborn).

For nearly 150 years, Elizabeth Siddal has been a familiar figure to many who may not know her name. A model for the Pre-Raphaelite Brotherhood of mid-19th century painters, Siddal was also a painter in her own right. She grew up in a working-class family in London, and with her sisters was apprenticed to a dressmaker around 1840. She was modestly educated, but her parents discouraged her interest in literature, and she received no academic artistic training. By age 20, she was supporting herself as a dressmaker.

In 1849, she met Walter Deverall, an artist associated with the Pre-Raphaelite artists' frater-nity. Deverall was struck by Siddal's beauty, especially her dark red hair, and asked her to model for one of his paintings. Elizabeth's serious approach to art and outgoing personality made her an accepted member of the Brotherhood, who referred to her affectionately as "Miss Sid." She can be identified in many paintings and drawings by Holman Hunt, John Everett Millais, for whom she posed for his famous *Ophelia*, and Dante Gabriel Rossetti, who painted her numerous times, most often as Dante's beloved *Beatrice (Portinari). By 1852, she was working regularly with Rossetti, who was the first to encourage her own artistic interests.

Soon Siddal became his pupil as well as his model; as her studies progressed, she stopped modeling professionally for other artists. Rossetti's support was crucial to her development as a painter, since she could not afford formal schooling, a studio, or the art materials he provided. At this time she was still working as a dressmaker and designer, and living with her parents. Her relationship with Rossetti deepened; his sister, the poet *Christina Rossetti, wrote, "He feeds upon her face by day and night." Rossetti painted Siddal so often that her face came to signify the Pre-Raphaelite movement. She was credited by his contemporaries with having inspired the young artist to a higher level of accomplishment, and Rossetti himself portrays her centrality to his own success in a poem when he triumphs: "They that would look on her must come to me." By 1854, they were regularly traveling together, leading their friends to assume, wrongly, that they were engaged. In fact, although they were in love, there was no official engagement until 1860.

In 1855, Siddal met the wealthy and respected art critic John Ruskin, Rossetti's friend and supporter. Ruskin became a faithful, generous patron and friend to Elizabeth. He purchased many of her drawings, provided her with an annual allowance, and introduced her to other potential patrons. Ruskin's financial support improved Siddal's life dramatically, leaving her free to travel on the Continent and pursue her intellectual and artistic talents. Most of her subjects were drawn from Romantic poetry and literature. Her first public showing came in 1857, when some of her watercolors were included in an exhibition of Pre-Raphaelite work. The success of this first show encouraged Siddal to continue painting. She adopted the Pre-Raphaelite focus on chivalry and other medieval themes, and developed a personal style which, though it reflects her lack of formal training, is deeply romantic and intensely colorful.

Elizabeth Siddal

After an extended trip to France in 1855–56, she returned to London. Rossetti continued to waver on the issue of marriage, promising to marry her and then finding reasons to wait. Frustrated, Siddal broke off the relationship in 1857. She spent some of the next several years with her family, but most of the time she was living in Sheffield, attending classes at the School of Art. Around 1859, her health began to fail; apparently she had become addicted to laudanum, an opiate then widely prescribed as a sedative in England. Early in 1860, she reconciled with Rossetti, and in May they finally mar-

ried, settling in London. Siddal continued painting throughout her marriage, and also secretly composed poetry that was discovered by Rossetti after her death.

In 1861, she gave birth to a stillborn girl, an experience which further damaged her health and led to a deep depression. This depression only worsened her addiction to laudanum, and on February 10, 1862, she suffered an overdose of the drug. Elizabeth Siddal died the next day at age 32. Her death was ruled an accident, although there were rumors that it had been a suicide. Rossetti made the grand gesture of burying with her the only copy of all the poems he had written for her, including the beginnings of his sonnet cycle *The House of Life*. Seven years later, with the support of his friends, he changed his mind. Siddal was exhumed and the poems retrieved and published, securing his fame and her reputation not as a painter and poet in her own right, but as Rossetti's "muse." More recently, Siddal and the small number of works she completed have been rediscovered by art historians, who are restoring her to her rightful place in the history of the Pre-Raphaelite movement.

**SOURCES:**

Marsh, Jan. *Elizabeth Siddal 1829–1862: Pre-Raphaelite Artist*. Sheffield: The Ruskin Gallery, 1991.

Nochlin, Linda. "By a Woman Painted: Artists in the 19th Century," in *Ms*. July 1974, pp. 73–74.

Yeldham, Charlotte. *Women Artists in Nineteenth Century England and France*. NY: Garland, 1984.

**Laura York**, M.A. in History, University of California, Riverside, California

## Siddons, Mrs.

See Siddons, Sarah (1755–1831).
See Siddons, Harriet (1783–1844).

## Siddons, Harriet (1783–1844)

*British actress. Name variations: Mrs. Siddons. Born Harriet Murray in 1783; died in 1844; daughter of Charles Murray; married Henry Siddons (b. 1774, an actor and the son of *Sarah Siddons).*

A Shakespearean actress of note, and the wife of actor Henry Siddons, Harriet Siddons was seen regularly at London's Covent Garden between 1798 and 1805. From 1805 to 1809, the actress performed at Drury Lane, at which time she appeared with the popular actor Robert William Elliston (1774–1831), playing Juliet to his Romeo. After 1809, Siddons assisted her husband Henry, who managed the Edinburgh Theater until his death in 1815.

## Siddons, Sarah (1755–1831)

*Tragic actress who, by the dramatic power of her performances and the moral rectitude of her private life, helped to raise the status of the theater in Britain. Name variations: Sarah Kemble; Mrs. Siddons. Born Sarah Kemble on July 5, 1755, in Brecon, Powys, England; died on June 8, 1831, in London; eldest child of Roger Kemble (an actor-manager) and Sarah "Sally" (Ward) Kemble; sister of actors John Philip Kemble (1757–1823), Stephen Kemble (1758–1822), Charles Kemble (1775–1854), and *Eliza Kemble (1761–1836, known as Mrs. Whitlock); aunt of Fanny Kemble (1809–1893); educated by her mother and at Thornloe House, Worcester; married William Siddons, on November 26, 1773 (died March 11, 1808); children: Henry Siddons (b. October 4, 1774); Sarah Martha Siddons, known as Sally (b. November 5, 1775); Maria Siddons (b. July 1, 1779); Frances Emilia Siddons (b. April 1781 and died in infancy); Eliza Ann Siddons (June 2, 1782–1788); George John Siddons (b. December 1785); Cecilia Siddons (b. July 25, 1794).*

*First extant playbill containing Siddon's name (February 12, 1767); lived at Guy's Cliffe, Warwick (1771–73); gave moving performance of Venice Preserved (1774); endured London debut failure (December 29, 1775); joined the Theater Royal, Bath (1778); began lifelong friendship with Thomas Lawrence (c. 1780); made triumphant return to Drury Lane (October 10, 1783); befriended the Galindos (1802); moved to Covent Garden (1803); gave farewell performance as Lady Macbeth (June 22, 1812).*

*Theater: some of her most popular roles were Isabella in* Isabella *by Southerne, Euphrasia in* The Grecian Daughter *by Murphy, Jane in ***Jane Shore*** by Rowe, Calista in* The Fair Penitent *by Rowe, Belvidera in* Venice Preserved *by Otway, Isabella in* Measure for Measure *by Shakespeare, Constance in* King John *by Shakespeare, Zara in* The Mourning Bride *by Congreve, Lady Macbeth in* Macbeth *by Shakespeare, Volumnia in* Coriolanus *by Shakespeare, Mrs. Haller in* The Stranger *by Kotzebue.*

The newspapers on the morning of October 11, 1783, contained rave notices concerning Drury Lane's new tragic actress—Mrs. Siddons. As the eponymous heroine in Thomas Southerne's play *Isabella*, she had swept London theatergoers off their feet. She had shown herself to be in possession of that ability so prized by audiences in an age dedicated to "sensibility"— namely the ability to make men weep openly and women fall into hysterics or faint clean away with the force of their emotions. Her earliest biographer James Boaden must have thought he was paying her a great compliment when he stated that "literally the greater part of the spectators were too ill to use their hands in her applause." By the end of the season, nine months later, she had given 80 major performances (at least 5 of which had been attended by King George III and Queen *Charlotte of Mecklenburg-Strelitz) and earned in all about £1,800 at a time when a provincial actress would have considered herself very fortunate to have made £300 in the same period. She was fêted by London society and invited to give private readings at Buckingham House, the London residence of the king and queen. Many years later, she told Boaden, "One could not appear in the presence of the Queen except in a Dress, not elsewhere worn, called a Saque . . . in which costume I felt not at my ease" yet the queen "expressed herself surprised . . . that I had conducted myself as if I had been used to a court."

Sarah Siddons belonged to a theatrical family. Her grandfather, John Ward, was the manager of a group of strolling actors who worked an area of Western England which stretched from Lancashire to Gloucestershire. Unlike many bands of players at the time, John Ward's company was renowned for its high moral standards. Ward had come under the influence of the preacher John Wesley, who founded Methodism and insisted on strict rules of conduct both from his family and his work force. He was not pleased when his daughter, Sally (**Sarah Ward Kemble**), fell in love with one of his actors as he had hoped that his children would marry outside the profession. But when Sally and Roger Kemble eloped in 1763 he is said to have remarked, "Well, my dear child, you have not disobeyed me; the devil himself could not make an actor of your husband."

Sally's husband had not become an actor until he was about 30 years old. Born in Hereford in 1721, he was raised a Roman Catholic and educated at a local seminary of good reputation. It is possible that for many years he was a barber. His father-in-law's early scruples must have been overcome, for when John Ward retired he left the company to the Kembles. They were an excellent team. Roger was handsome, polite and gentle in his dealings with others. Sally adhered to her father's belief in respectability and was a strict disciplinarian. She must have been a remarkable woman. As well as acting and helping to manage a company constantly on the move, she gave birth to 12 children between 1755 and 1777. Eight of them reached adulthood; six of these took up acting.

Roger and Sally's first child was born on July 5, 1755, almost definitely in Brecon (though Siddons' sister **Anne Kemble**, who was born nine years later, says it was "Denbigh, not Brecon"). It seems that the rest of the company had already moved on to Llandrindod Wells. The baby was called Sarah after her mother. Not a great deal is known about her early childhood. The Kembles appear to have been reasonably well off so presumably there were servants to help care for the children as the company moved from town to town and both mother and father were engaged in the promotion, rehearsal, and presentation of plays. Certainly whenever they remained long enough in one place some schooling was arranged for them and, as they became older, the boys attended various Catholic boarding schools and colleges. The girls were brought up Protestants like their mother.

In her memoirs, *Hester Lynch Piozzi wrote a story which she claimed Siddons, her friend for many years, had told her. As a child, Sarah read many stories about Reynard the Fox. On seeing the animal for the first time, chained in an inn yard, "she immediately went upstairs changed her Ribbons hasted down again,— & her father found her a quarter of an hour afterwards curtsying respectfully before the Kennel door— What's ys for? said he. I am begging *Mr Reynard* replied Mrs Siddons—to *play me no Trick* while we remain in the Town."

Thomas Campbell, whose biography of Siddons was published only three years after her death, told another story which he said was related to him by his subject. One night Sarah took her prayer book to bed with her, intending to leave it open at the prayer for fine weather because the next day, as long as it was dry, her mother was taking her to an outdoor party at which she was to wear a particularly becoming new pink dress. On waking at dawn, she found that rain "was pelting at the windows" and that she had inadvertently had the prayer book open at the page containing the prayer for rain. She corrected her mistake, went to sleep again and on reawakening found that "the morning was as pink and beautiful as the dress she was to wear."

It is certain that Siddons first appeared on the stage at a very early age. Thomas Holcroft, an actor with the company, speaks of her being promoted "as a juvenile prodigy" and being encouraged by her mother to "repeat the Fable of the Boys and the Frogs" at a family benefit performance. There is a playbill in existence for February 12, 1767, which shows that the 12-year-old Sarah was appearing in Worcester as the young princess *Elizabeth Stuart in a play entitled *Charles the First*. Her ten-year-old brother John and her eight-year-old sister Fanny were also part of the cast, so it seems reasonable to assume that Sarah was already a seasoned performer.

However, Siddons also spent some of her time in Worcester at school, apparently somewhat to the disconcertion of the other pupils. She attended Thornloe House, a private school for "young ladies." One such young lady, writing home to her mother, described how she had quizzed the newcomer, "as indeed, dear Mama, you have advised me to do, to avoid the possibility of becoming intimate with an unsuitable or ungenteel acquaintance." It is arguably to Siddons' credit that she readily admitted her parentage "without blush or confusion," but the shocked interlocutor "thought it best to make a curtsy and return to the other young ladies."

*Sarah's public hauteur resulted both from her being an intensely private person and from an acute consciousness of carrying the burden of her profession.*

—Sandra Richards

By the time Sarah was 17, she was in love with a member of the company who had been with them for a number of years. He was more than ten years older. At the same time, she was being courted by a certain Mr. Evans Squire of Pennant. As the possessor of £300 a year, he was a more attractive suitor in the eyes of her parents than an impecunious supporting actor, but Siddons refused him and on November 26, 1773, she married her actor—William Siddons (in his biography of Sarah's brother, *John Philip Kemble*, Herschel Baker calls him Henry). By now she was 19 and had spent the intervening time at Guy's Cliffe, Warwick, in the household of a rich widow, Lady **Mary Greatheed**. She seems to have been more of a companion than a servant and to have used to the full the opportunity afforded her of learning how to behave in the company of well-bred society. William had remained with the Kembles' band of strolling players and a month after their marriage "Mrs Siddons" was billed to perform in Wolverhampton.

The following year, the Siddonses struck out on their own and joined another company led by two actors called Crump and Chamberlain. At a performance of *Venice Preserved*, Sarah's representation of Belvidera so moved the ladies in Lord Bruce's party that, as he told William on meeting him in the street next day, "they had wept so excessively that they were unpresentable in the morning, and were confined to their rooms with headaches." The Honorable **Henrietta Boyle**, Lord Bruce's stepdaughter, became Sarah's patron and lifelong friend. She immediately set about providing her with a more expensive wardrobe than Sarah could have afforded herself. Lord Bruce recommended her to David Garrick, the manager of the theater in Drury Lane, London.

Then, as now, it was the dream of every English actress to work in London. But Garrick had the reputation of his company to consider. He contacted two or three of his "talent scouts," asking their opinions of Siddons' ability, and it was not until the end of December 1775 that she joined Drury Lane. Garrick had acted just in time—his rivals at Covent Garden had already begun negotiating for her services. By now she had two children. The eldest was just over a year old and the second had been born prematurely, Sarah having gone into labor during a performance in Gloucester.

Siddons made her London debut as Portia in *The Merchant of Venice* on December 29. Though it was one of her favorite roles, she must have been feeling far from her best. She was still weak from childbirth, with two babies to care for, and had not arrived in London until mid-December. As far as is known, it was her first visit to the capital, and she may have been totally unprepared for the scale both of the city and the theater. Her opening night was a failure. Naturally timid, she was completely overcome by nervousness. Her movements were uncertain, and her voice vacillated between hoarseness and inaudibility. She had a catastrophic season and her contract was not renewed for the following year. Throughout her life, Siddons remained bitter about her experience. She felt that Garrick, while seeming to favor her, had merely been using her to taunt his three established leading ladies who, in time-honored fashion, were temperamental and jealous of the young upstart actress.

For the next six years, Siddons worked the provinces and added three more daughters to her family. By now most major cities had a theater, and the Siddonses, although far from rich, were able to earn a reasonable living. In the autumn of 1778, Sarah was invited to join the theater company at Bath. This was, in its way, promotion. Because of Bath's reputation as a social center, it was considered to have the country's leading provincial theater. The manager, John Palmer, also leased a theater in Bristol, and Siddons was engaged to perform in both places. It was hard work, especially between the middle of March and the end of May 1779. Siddons has described her schedule during those ten weeks, while in the last stages of her third pregnancy: "After the Rehearsal at Bath on a Monday morning, I had to go and act at Bristol in the evening of the same day, and reaching Bath again after a drive of twelve miles, long after midnight, I was obliged to represent some fatigueing part there on the Tuesday evening." Wednesdays and Fridays she was back in Bristol. Thursdays and Saturdays she appeared in Bath. Only a month later, on July 1, her second daughter was born.

It was all worth it, however, for it was during those years that Sarah Siddons built up her

Sarah
Siddons

reputation as a tragic actress. Most of Palmer's repertoire was comedy, for that was what the audiences wanted, but Thursday night was "Tragedy Night." This was in the somewhat vain hope of attracting the more seriously minded among the population of Bath, as the rest were all at the weekly Cotillion Ball in the Assembly Rooms. Siddons, by the sheer force of her performances, changed all that and, as Boaden wrote, "The Thursday nights, from a vacuum, soon became a plenum." By July 1780, she was being invited back to Drury Lane (Garrick had retired at the end of Sarah's previous season there), and she was finally persuaded to return in September 1782.

As has already been noted, Sarah's return was a triumph and she was to remain the undeposed Queen of Tragedy until her retirement in 1812. She maintained that if a part were "in nature" then she was sure that she could play it. "In nature" to Siddons meant "possessing credible human emotions." She would then set about heightening these emotions by the force of her dramatic presentation. She brought to her acting an unprecedented dignity of bearing which ennobled the characters she played. Furthermore, she was a conscientious student and never stopped developing a part. Her interpretations of Isabella in *Measure for Measure*, Volumnia in *Coriolanus*, and Lady Macbeth in *Macbeth* are considered to have been particularly fine, and Sarah chose to portray Lady Macbeth in her farewell performance on July 22, 1812.

She was to remain at Drury Lane until 1802 when the money problems which had dogged her for many years finally forced her to leave. Although her own brother, John Philip Kemble, had been actor-manager there since 1788, the finances of the theater were in the hands of Richard Brinsley Sheridan, the politician, dramatist, and entrepreneur. He was charming and persuasive in manner but an incompetent and unscrupulous businessman. Tired of fighting for payment, Sarah and John left together, and, a year later, joined the rival company at Covent Garden where John became part owner. Sarah had been in the habit of touring the provinces during the three months' closure of Drury Lane every summer, and she spent the whole of her year away from London on an extended tour, mainly in Ireland.

Garrick had done much to tame the unruly behavior of London audiences, but Siddons still received her share of hostility mixed with all the adulation. At Drury Lane in October 1784, she was subjected to "the degradation of hissing and hooting and all the humiliating circumstances of public scorn," as she herself expressed it, when falsely accused of refusing to perform at a fellow actor's benefit night while in Ireland. She also suffered a whole season of anti-social behavior following the rebuilding of Covent Garden after it had burned down in September 1808. Riots were organized in protest against the higher prices. They became known as the O.P. (Old Price) Riots and were noisy, often violent affairs. Boaden has described "an efficient O.P. Rioter" preparing for a night at the theater with "his watchman's rattle, or dustman's bell, or post-boy's horn, or French-horn, or trombone, with a white night-cap in his pocket—his placards of a dozen feet in length wound about his body, and his bludgeon for close action with the enemy." Passive protestors stood with their backs to the stage; active ones performed the "O.P. dance"—a rhythmic foot-stamping and stick-banging as accompaniment to the roaring of "O.P.! O.P.! O.P.!"

During her career, Siddons had her portrait painted many times. Engravings were sometimes made of these portraits to be sold cheaply, a form of publicity similar to today's posters of celebrities from the pop world. Two of the most famous of these were both produced in the mid-1780s—Thomas Gainsborough's portrait of her as a society lady and *The Tragic Muse* by Sir Joshua Reynolds. The artist with whom she was to be most associated, some say with whom she was in love, was Thomas Lawrence. He was born in 1769 and she may have first met him while staying at his father's inn in Devizes. He was a child prodigy and before the age of 13 he had made several drawings of her. He began to draw and paint her again in the late 1790s. At the same time, he was drawing Sarah's two eldest daughters, **Sally** and **Maria Siddons**. His complicated love affair with both girls and its tragic consequences can be read in Oswald G. Knapp's *An Artist's Love Story*. He never married and Sarah never lost touch with him. Her niece, *****Fanny Kemble**, reports overhearing her say to her brother: "Charles, when I die, I wish to be carried to my grave by you and Lawrence." It was not to be, for Thomas died before her, on January 7, 1830.

Compared with many actresses of the period, Siddons was a model of respectability yet she did not entirely avoid scandal during her lifetime. There were whisperings about the nature of her relationship with Lawrence and more than whisperings about the Galindos. **Catherine Galindo** at first encouraged her husband's friendship with Sarah in the hope of furthering her own acting career, but later became jealous and in 1809 published an open "Letter to Mrs Siddons" in which she accused the actress of ruining her marriage. Sarah maintained a dignified silence throughout the furor which followed. As she wrote to her nephew, "It would be lowering myself, to enter the lists with persons, the indecency of whose characters is become so notorious." It was her moral integrity in private as much as her dramatic prowess in public which helped to raise the status of the British actress in the late 18th and early 19th centuries.

Although Sarah was the family's main provider, everything she earned legally belonged to her husband. Biographers' opinions about William and his relationship with Sarah are divided. As Sarah's star rose so William's declined, and he became fully employed in managing her appearances, her finances, and in caring for the children who continued to be born at regular intervals until 1785. In 1788, Siddons suffered a miscarriage; that same year, her daughter Eliza Ann died. Her last child **Cecilia Siddons** was born in 1794. There are witnesses to suggest that William was greedy for money, driving hard bargains with Sarah's employers and keeping her constantly at work. But there are others to testify that he was a pleasant companion, fond of his family, and making sure that Sarah had a generous allowance from her earnings. There is no reason why a second-rate actor should turn into a brilliant administrator, and he probably did the best he could in a job that was beyond his capabilities and not really to his taste. Gradually the couple seem to have drifted apart, though there was never any formal separation. By 1801, William was in ill health and living permanently in Bath. He died in 1808, four years before Siddons retired from the stage. She wrote a friend: "May those to whom I am dear remember *me* when *I* am gone as *I* now remember *him*, forgetting and forgiving all my errors, and recollecting only my quietness of spirit and singleness of heart."

Throughout her career, Siddons talked and wrote of the joys of retirement. She envisaged a quiet cottage in the country and frequently maintained that she only worked to support her family and to ensure them all financial security. Yet after she had attained her projected goal—£10,000—in 1876, she continued to act for another 26 years. It would seem, then, that she was tied to the theater by bonds far stronger than those of money. Even when officially retired, she returned occasionally for benefit performances. For example, in the autumn of 1815, she fulfilled a ten-night engagement in Edinburgh on behalf of the family of her son Henry, who had died of tuberculosis at the early age of 40. In succeeding years, she continued to give play readings in her own home and died, according to her sister Fanny, "peaceably and without suffering" at the age of 76.

SOURCES:

Baker, Herschel. *John Philip Kemble: The Actor in His Theater*. NY: Greenwood Press, 1942.

Manvell, Roger. *Sarah Siddons: Portrait of an Actress*. London: Heinemann, 1970.

Richards, Sandra. *The Rise of the English Actress*. London: Macmillan, 1993.

SUGGESTED READING:

French, Yvonne. *Mrs Siddons: Tragic Actress*. London: Derek Verschayle, 1954.

Knapp, Oswald G. *An Artist's Love Story: Told in the Letters of Sir Thomas Lawrence, Mrs. Siddons and her Daughters*. London: George Allen, 1905.

**Barbara Evans**,
Research Associate in Women's Studies,
Nene College, Northampton, England

# Sidney, Dorothy (1617–1684)

*Countess of Sunderland who was celebrated in poetry. Name variations: Lady Dorothy Sidney; Lady Dorothy Spencer; Lady Sunderland; Sacharissa. Born in 1617 in Scion House in England; baptized on October 5, 1617, in Isleworth, Middlesex; died in 1684 and buried on February 25 at Brington; eldest of eight daughters of Robert Sidney, 2nd earl of Leicester, and* **Dorothy Percy** *(daughter of the 9th earl of Northumberland); sister of Lady* **Lucy Sidney**; *married Henry, 3rd Lord Spencer (later created earl of Sunderland), on July 11, 1639 (killed in battle, 1643); married Robert Smythe (a Kentish gentleman), in July 1652; children: (first marriage)* **Dorothy Spencer** *(who married George, Viscount Halifax); Robert Spencer; Henry Spencer; Penelope Spencer (died young).*

Lady Dorothy Sidney was celebrated as "Sacharissa" in poems of Edmund Waller, though Edmund Lodge in his eponymous *Portraits* irritably points out that Waller "raised his own fame without rendering justice to hers." Surrounded by suitors before age 16, Sidney spurned them all, including Waller, whom it is said was so severely afflicted by the disappointment that he left the country. In reality, he remained home and took another wife. "The mind that can pour forth its griefs in song will find no great difficulty in recalling a desperate solution," sniffed Lodge.

In 1639, Sidney married Henry, 3rd Lord Spencer, who was soon after created earl of Sunderland. The marriage was brief. After serving 12 months in the army of Charles I, Sunderland was pierced by a cannon ball at the battle of Newbury on September 20,

$\mathcal{D}$orothy
$\mathcal{S}$idney

1643. Soon after, Lady Sunderland gave birth to a daughter. She then retired to their estate in Brington, in Northamptonshire, where she lived for several years and was the benefactor of harassed clergy and Royalists. In 1652, she remarried. Lady Dorothy Sidney died in 1684 and was buried on February 25 at Brington.

**SOURCES:**

Lodge, Edmund. *Lodge's Portraits of Illustrious Personages of Great Britain.* Vol. VI. London: William Smith, n.d.

## Sidney, Margaret (1844–1924).

*See Lothrop, Harriet.*

## Sidney, Mary (1561–1621).

*See Herbert, Mary.*

# Sidney, Sylvia (1910–1999)

*American actress. Born Sophia Kosow on August 8, 1910, in the Bronx, New York; died of throat cancer on July 1, 1999; studied acting at the Theater Guild School; married Bennett Cerf (a publisher), in 1935 (divorced 1936); married Luther Adler (an actor), in 1938 (divorced 1947); married Carlton Alsop (a publicist), in 1947 (divorced 1950); children: Jacob Adler (deceased).*

*Selected theater: made stage debut in* The Challenge of Youth *(1926); appeared in* The Squall *(1927),* Broadway Lights *(1927),* Gods of the Lightning *(1928),* To Quito and Back *(1937),* Pygmalion *(1939),* The Gentle People *(1939),* Angel Street *(1941),* The Fourposter *(1951),* A Very Special Baby *(1956),* Auntie Mame *(1958), and* Enter Laughing *(1963).*

*Selected filmography:* Broadway Nights *(cameo, 1927);* Thru Different Eyes *(1929);* City Streets *(1931);* Confessions of a Co-Ed *(1931);* An American Tragedy *(1931);* Street Scene *(1931);* Ladies of the Big House *(1931);* The Miracle Man *(1932);* Merrily We Go to Hell *(1932);* Make Me a Star *(cameo, 1932);* Madame Butterfly *(1932);* Pick Up *(1933);* Jennie Gerhardt *(1933);* Good Dame *(1934);* Thirty Day Princess *(1934);* Behold My Wife *(1935);* Accent on Youth *(1935);* Mary Burns—Fugitive *(1935);* The Trail of the Lonesome Pine *(1936);* Fury *(1936);* Sabotage *(A Woman Alone, UK, 1936);* You Only Live Once *(1937);* Dead End *(1937);* You and Me *(1938);* One Third of a Nation *(1939);* The Wagons Roll at Night *(1941);* Blood on the Sun *(1945);* The Searching Wind *(1946);* Mr. Ace *(1946);* Love from a Stranger *(1947);* Les Misérables *(1952);* Violent Saturday *(1955);* Behind the High Wall *(1956);* Summer Wishes, Winter Dreams *(1973);* God Told Me So *(1976);* I Never Promised You a Rose Garden *(1977);* Damien: Omen II *(1978);* Hammett *(1982);* L'assassino dei poliziotti *(Cop Killers or Corrupt, It., 1983);* Beetlejuice *(1988);* Used People *(1992).*

Born Sophia Kosow in 1910 in the Bronx, New York, the daughter of Russian Jewish immigrants, Sylvia Sidney decided at age 11 to become an actress, then set out to make it happen. She studied dancing and elocution as a child, and left high school at 15 to join the Theater Guild School, where she was she was known as something of a maverick. She made her professional stage debut in Washington at age 16, in *The Challenge of Youth*, then took over the lead in the New York production of *The Squall*. Her first screen effort, as a screaming witness in the courtroom drama *Thru Different Eyes* (1929), brought her to the attention of studio heads at Paramount. By 1931, she had signed a contract and was on her way to becoming one of the studio's brightest stars.

Small, dark, and waiflike in appearance, Sidney exuded vulnerability, which the studio exploited in the 1930s by invariably casting her as the downtrodden girl of the working class. "Her heart-shaped face and trembling petal lips invited sympathy, and her sad eyes expressed the silent cry of a suffering generation," writes Ephraim Katz, explaining Sidney's popularity during the Depression. She played a sweet young girl whose boyfriend becomes involved in racketeering in *City Streets* (1931); an unmarried mother in *Confessions of a Co-Ed* and again in *An American Tragedy* (both 1931); a prisoner in *Ladies of the Big House* (1932); a fugitive from the police in *Mary Burns—Fugitive* (1935); the girlfriend of a fugitive in *Fury* (1936); and the sister of a criminal living in the slums in *Dead End* (1937). Occasionally, the actress was allowed to try her hand at lighter fare, such as her dual role opposite Cary Grant in *Thirty Day Princess* (1934), and her portrayal of a secretary who is pursued by her boss in *Accent on Youth* (1935). By the early 1940s, Sidney was growing tired of being typecast as a victim and began returning more and more to the stage. She played character roles in three films during the 1950s, then for the most part retired from movies. "I didn't leave Hollywood because of anybody but myself," she said later. "I just got disgusted with myself. I didn't know who I was, as an actress or a person."

During the 1950s and 1960s, Sidney busied herself with stage and television appearances, and published a book on needlepoint that was said to be one of the best on the subject. She made a film comeback in 1973, playing **Joanne Woodward**'s doomed mother in *Summer Wishes,*

*Winter Dreams,* for which she was nominated for an Academy Award for Best Supporting Actress. In 1986, she received a Golden Globe and was nominated for an Emmy for her portrayal of the compassionate grandmother of an AIDS patient in the television movie "An Early Frost."

Sidney was tough and sharp-witted, much the opposite of her 1930s screen image. She also had a reputation for being somewhat difficult to work with; her battles with the late Josef von Sternberg, who directed her on the screen, were legendary. Sidney also had a series of tumultuous marriages: her first and shortest to publisher Bennett Cerf (1935–36), a second to actor Luther Adler (1938–47), and a third to publicist Carlton Alsop (1947–1950). The actress had one son, Jacob Adler, who died in the mid-1980s of ALS, or Lou Gehrig's disease. From the time of his diagnosis, Sidney became an active volunteer for the ALS Foundation.

In her later years, Sidney lived alone in Connecticut with her two Pekingese. She continued to work, making her last film appearances in *Beetlejuice* (1988) and *Used People* (1992). In

*From the movie
Dead End,
starring Sylvia
Sidney and Joel
McCrea.*

1990, she was given the Life Achievement award by the Film Society of Lincoln Center. She died nine years later, at age 88.

**SOURCES:**

Anderson, Polly. "Obituaries," in *The Day* [New London, CT]. July 2, 1999.

Katz, Ephraim. *The Film Encyclopedia.* NY: HarperCollins, 1994.

Lamparski, Richard. *Whatever Became of . . . ?* 3rd Series. NY: Crown, 1970.

Shipman, David. *The Great Movie Stars: The Golden Years.* Boston, MA: Little, Brown, 1995.

**Barbara Morgan**,
Melrose, Massachusetts

# Siebert, Muriel (c. 1932—)

*American financial company executive and New York State banking commissioner who was the first woman to own a seat on the New York Stock Exchange. Born around 1932 in Cleveland, Ohio; daughter of Irwin J. Siebert (a dentist) and Margaret Eunice (Roseman) Siebert; attended Western Reserve University (now Case Western Reserve University), 1949–52; never married; no children.*

While vacationing in New York City during college, Cleveland-born Muriel Siebert visited the New York Stock Exchange and decided she would like to work there. Dropping out of college after the death of her father from cancer and moving to New York in 1954, she claimed to have a college degree and was hired as a securities analyst. Although she was assigned the industries of movies and airlines because they were, at the time, considered unimportant, Siebert quickly proved to be an excellent analyst, and forged important ties with corporate clients. She advanced rapidly on Wall Street, changing firms whenever her salary increases did not match those of her male colleagues; at times, she would discover that her co-workers were being paid 50 to 100% more than she was. Made a partner at a brokerage firm for the first time in 1960, within several years she was earning enough to consider going into business for herself.

In 1967, Siebert decided to buy a seat on the New York Stock Exchange, which had been exclusively male since its founding in 1792. Members who had promised to support her backed down at the last minute, there was hostility among some of the 1,300-odd men at the exchange, and Siebert's longtime bank would not lend her the purchase price. She secured a loan for the $445,000 from another bank, reported her lack of a college degree on her seat application, and on December 28, 1967, became the first woman member of the New York Stock Exchange. She later recalled the governor of the exchange asking, "And how many others are there behind you?" (As it turned out, she would remain the only woman member for the next ten years.) Muriel Siebert & Co., Inc. was highly successful, performing research for corporations and buying and selling financial analyses of stocks. When the Securities and Exchange Commission deregulated brokers' commissions in 1975, Siebert's company was the first to offer discounts to individual buyers. Traditionalists on Wall Street were further shocked when the company began advertising its discount brokerage heavily, but Siebert's business soared, and both discounted commissions and advertising are standard with many firms today.

Two years later, Siebert was appointed New York State banking commissioner by Governor Hugh Carey. The first woman so appointed, she put her company in a blind trust and began supervising the management of the $400 billion in assets in state banks. Savings institutions were going into bankruptcy throughout the country during that era, but Siebert worked hard and successfully to prevent the failure of struggling New York credit unions, savings banks, and savings and loans associations, using state funds to ensure solvency when necessary, and none failed during her five-year term. She also helped to restructure regulations on foreign banks, bringing the state over $100 billion in funds from foreign countries. Although she won praise from the banking industry for her performance as banking commissioner, by 1982 Siebert was looking for a new challenge. After running unsuccessfully for nomination to the Senate in the Republican primary, she returned to the chair and presidency of Muriel Siebert & Co.

The firm had suffered some business losses in her absence, but Siebert rejected buyout proposals and by 1985 had so improved the company's performance she herself was able to buy out two failed competitors. That year she became a founding member of the National Women's Forum, a networking organization for successful professional women. In 1990, she created the Siebert Philanthropic Program, which diverts some of her company's new securities profits to charities chosen by the issuers; over $2 million had been donated within the decade. She also founded the Women's Entrepreneurial Fund, which issues loans at no interest to women with small businesses. Now with offices in New York City, Los Angeles, and Boca Raton, Muriel Siebert & Co. went public in 1996. Siebert herself, often cited as one of the top role models for women in business, lectures frequently on college campuses and to youth groups. She also advocates tirelessly throughout the country for women running for political office, whether Republican or Democrat, noting, "Until 50 percent of the politicians are female we just need to support good women." The recipient of numerous honorary doctorates as well as the Women's Equity Action League Award (1978) and the Women's Hall of Fame's inaugural *Emily Warren Roebling Award (1984), she lives in suitable style on Manhattan's Upper East Side.

**SOURCES:**

*Contemporary Newsmakers.* 1987 Cumulation. Detroit, MI: Gale Research, 1988.

*The Day* [New London, CT]. May 21, 1995, pp. E1–E2.

Gilbert, Lynn, and Gaylen Moore. *Particular Passions.* NY: Clarkson N. Potter, 1981.

Martin, Jean, ed. *Who's Who of Women in the Twentieth Century.* Crescent Books, 1995.

Read, Phyllis J., and Bernard L. Witlieb. *The Book of Women's Firsts.* NY: Random House, 1992.

**Ginger Strand**, Ph.D.,
New York City

# Siege Warfare and Women

## (8th c.–17th c.)

*An overview of women's participation in sieges during some of pre-18th-century Europe's major wars.*

Since the time of Troy, women have been direct participants in siege warfare, both as besiegers and, more commonly, as defenders. Some, like *Joan of Arc, played an important symbolic role in rallying military forces. As fortresses became more numerous, siege warfare became more common. Throughout the Middle Ages, in Europe in particular, women were expected to play their part in time of siege. High-ranking families often had scattered holdings, and while a male head-of-household was traveling, his wife, mother, or daughter was expected to "hold down the fort"—often quite literally. Men—and sometimes, women—might also be gone for months or years on Crusade or fighting in dynastic wars, where they might be imprisoned; again, women often took an active role in maintaining and defending the family's properties.

Women who found themselves besieged by an enemy were usually offered the option of surrender and safe conduct. Many chose to fight, despite the often severe consequences of defeat. A well-supplied castle or fortress could hold out against an enemy for long periods, hoping that allies might arrive to lift the siege or that the besieger might simply grow weary of enduring the food shortages, exposure to weather, and spread of disease that beset armies encamped for any length of time.

Women both defended and conducted sieges in the early centuries of the Middle Ages. Before the 12th century, many queens and queen-regents were directly involved in military action, including *Ethelburg (fl. 722), *Ethelflaed, Lady of the Mercians, **Adelaide of Susa**, *Emma of Burgundy, and *Emma of Italy (fl. 948–990). The armies of the abbess *Matilda of Quedlinburg were instrumental in preserving the papacy in Italy during this period.

Queens become less prominent in the mid-to-late Middle Ages, when inheritance laws increasingly began to restrict women's access to power. However, the military responsibilities of noblewomen increased, as there were frequent conflicts over territory. *Emma of Norfolk (d. 1100) held Norwich castle in the absence of her husband during the rebellion against William the Conqueror in 1075. *Sichelgaita of Salerno fought by the side of her husband, the famous conqueror Robert Guiscard, in many sieges in the southern Mediterranean. In 1129–1130, ❧▸ **Agnes of Saarbrucken** defended the city of Spires against Bavarian and Saxon forces when her husband Frederick II, duke of Swabia, left her in charge. She held out for the better part of a year; finally, with no hope of relief, she was forced to surrender to King Lothar.

Women were often caught up in the civil and religious wars of the time. Englishwoman ❧▸ **Nicolaa de la Haye**, the hereditary castellan of Lincoln, held the castle during the rebellion against King John in 1216; he later appointed her sheriff. Many women, like *Guirande de Lavaur, were involved in the French battles of Simon de Montfort against the Cathars. In the 14th century, the brutal wars between Robert Bruce of Scotland and the English, and civil war in England between the loyalists and the Lancastrians, occasioned a number of sieges that placed women like Lady Badlesmere (❧▸ **Margaret de Clare**), *Isabella of Buchan and *Agnes Dunbar in military roles. ❧▸ **Katharine Grandison**, countess of Salisbury, defended the castle of

❧▸
*See sidebar on the following page*

❧▸
*See sidebars on the following page*

❧▸ **Agnes of Saarbrucken** (fl. 1130)

**Duchess of Swabia.** *Name variations: Agnes von Saarbrücken. Flourished around 1130; daughter of Frederick, count of Saarbrucken; became second wife of Frederick II (c. 1090–1147), duke of Swabia (r. 1105–1147), around 1130 or 1135. Frederick's first wife was *Judith of Bavaria, mother of Frederick I Barbarossa.*

### Haye, Nicolaa de la (1160–1218)

*Sheriff of Lincolnshire. Born in 1160 in Lincolnshire, England; died in 1218 in Lincolnshire; heiress of the de la Haye barony and hereditary castellan of Lincoln; lived during the reigns of Richard I and King John; married Gerard de Camville.*

An English noblewoman, Nicolaa de la Haye inherited substantial wealth and property from her father, including the post of castellan (constable of a castle) of Lincoln. Several times, she had to defend her castle and estates against her enemies, most notably when the castle was placed under siege during the rebellion of the English barons against King John in 1216. Despite a breach in the walls, her forces captured half the knights in the rebel army and won a virtually bloodless victory. Nicolaa's high rank and popularity led her to be chosen sheriff of Lincoln, a position she held until her death in 1218.

Laura York, M.A. in History,
University of California, Riverside, California

### Clare, Margaret de (fl. 1280–1322)

*English noblewoman thought to be Lady Badlesmere. Name variations: Margaret de Clare; Margaret de Badlesmere; Marguerite de Clere; Lady Badlesmere. Flourished between 1280 and 1322; daughter of Thomas de Clare, lord of Thomond, and Juliane Fitzgerald; married Gilbert de Umphraville, in 1289; married Bartholomew Badlesmere (d. 1322), Lord Badlesmere, in 1312; children: \*Elizabeth Badlesmere (fl. 1315–1342); Sir Giles Badlesmere; \*Maud Badlesmere (d. 1366, who married John de Vere, 7th earl of Oxford).*

In September 1321, at the outbreak of civil war in England between the loyalists and the Lancastrians, King Edward II sent his queen \*Isabella of France (1296–1358) to the castle of Lord Badlesmere at Leeds, Kent. Lady Badlesmere had been left to guard the castle and told to admit no one, so she would not permit the queen, who was accompanied by armed troops, to enter. Fighting ensued and some of the queen's attendants were killed. In mid-October, King Edward opened siege on the castle, and it soon fell. Many members of the castle garrison were executed, including Lord Badlesmere who was hanged at Canterbury in 1322. Lady Badlesmere and her children were sent to the Tower of London, and their subsequent fate is unknown. The lady's name is not given, but she is thought to be Margaret de Clare, wife of Bartholomew de Badlesmere.

### Grandison, Katharine (fl. 1305–1340)

*Countess of Salisbury. Flourished between 1305 and 1340; married William Montacute (1301–1343), 1st earl of Salisbury; children: Philippa Montacute (who married Robert Mortimer, 2nd earl of March); William de Montacute, 2nd earl of Salisbury (d. 1361, who married \*Joan of Kent); John.*

Wark in Northumberland against the Scots for several months in 1341; the siege was eventually raised by the arrival of Edward III's troops. In 1395, \*Margaret Keith, Lady Lindsay, successfully defended the Scottish castle of Fyvie against her nephew, Robert Keith.

The Hundred Years War between the French and English from the mid-14th to the mid-15th centuries offers a number of examples of women involved in war. Two women were prominently immersed in the battles for the succession to the duchy of Brittany in the mid-14th century: \*Jeanne de Penthièvre and \*Jeanne de Montfort. And in 1428, the English besieged Orléans on the bank of the Loire, and unwittingly provided the opportunity for Joan of Arc to become the best-known figure in the history of siege warfare.

Even women of relatively un-noble origins might find themselves cast as military leaders and fighters. \*Margaret Paston of mid-15th century England was among these, and is perhaps one of the best examples of how women in her position routinely functioned as military auxiliaries. Italian women, particularly of the Sforza family, were especially prominent in the 15th century. \*Margaret of Attenduli (Sforza) defended Tricarico against siege and rescued her brother from imprisonment. In the 16th century, \*Caterina Sforza fought against Cesare Borgia and negotiated with Machiavelli. The Sforza also fought against women; Francesco Sforza faced a determined corps of women, commanded by Camilla Rodolfi, who defended Vigevano against his siege.

The religious wars of the 16th century in France involved many women in siege warfare in such places as Metz, Poitiers, La Rochelle, Aubigny, Cahors, and Lille. Other instances in the 16th century include Kristina Gyllenstierna during the siege of Stockholm in 1520; Améliane du Puget in the siege of Marseilles in 1524; Marie Fourreé de Poix in the siege of Saint-Riquier in 1535; \*Marguerite Delaye, who lost an arm in the siege of Montélimar in 1569;

Kenau and **Amaron Hasselaar**, sisters in the siege of Haarlem in 1573; *Madeleine de Saint-Nectaire who defended Miremont from Henry IV's forces in 1575; and others.

The English civil wars of the 17th century, from 1642 to 1651, were characterized by numerous sieges of small strongholds, and provide a number of examples of women defenders of besieged castles. Among the Royalists were ✥▸ **Charlotte Stanley**, countess of Derby; Lady **Mary Winter** who refused to surrender Lidney House to Parliamentary forces; Lady *Blanche Arundel, who defended Wardour Castle for the royalists; and Lady ✥▸ **Mary Bankes**, who held Corfe Castle. On the Parliamentarian side, *Lady Brilliana Harley held Brampton Bryan Castle against the king for more than six months.

In addition to high-ranking women (and their women servants and attendants) who defended their castles, urban women of the lower classes sometimes found themselves besieged as well. The women of Gloucester and London were praised for their assistance during the sieges of the civil wars; the women of Lyme became famous for helping to repel the Royalists in 1643. In any siege, women naturally participated in defensive actions; examples include Marseilles and Pavia in 1425, Siena in 1552–53, Leucate in 1637, and Estagel in 1639. Women were injured or killed while carrying water or hanging out laundry in besieged cities and castles; they also helped build defensive entrenchments, acted as lookouts, cast bullets from lead, and threw rocks and boiling water from the battlements. Many women also fought. In Italy, 30 women of Mugello kept numerous armed men at bay in 1352; in Siena in 1554, three women's battalions uniformed in red and violet taffeta fought on the city walls.

Siege warfare continued to involve women as it was practiced on an increasingly brutal scale in the 17th century. As larger cities were fortified

## ✥▸ Stanley, Charlotte (1599–1664)

*French Huguenot and Royalist heroine during the English Civil Wars. Name variations: Charlotte de la Trémoille; countess of Derby. Born Charlotte de la Trémoille in 1599; died in 1664; daughter of Duc de Thouars; granddaughter of William the Silent (1533–1584), prince of Orange; married James Stanley, 7th earl of Derby (known as Lord Strange until 1642).*

Seven years older than her husband James Stanley, Charlotte Stanley, countess of Derby, was said to have been a better soldier. In 1643, she was left in charge of Lathom House, a formidable fortress. She refused to surrender the stronghold to local Parliamentary forces, which began a bombardment of Lathom. When Parliamentarians attempted to cut off her water supply, she sent out a party and successfully stole their largest gun. After holding out for three months from February to May, despite her neighbor's pleas to surrender, she was relieved by Royalist forces and withdrew with her husband to the Isle of Man. In December 1645, the Parliamentarians laid siege on Lathom once more and, without the fortitude of Charlotte Stanley, the fortress surrendered. In 1651, James, known as the "Martyred Earl," joined forces with Charles II at Worcester and was captured and executed. Charlotte Stanley was notorious in 17th-century England. A Parliamentarian saying went: "Three women ruined the Kingdom: *Eve, the Queen [*Henrietta Maria], and the countess of Derby."

## ✥▸ Bankes, Mary (d. 1661)

*British royalist. Name variations: Lady Mary Bankes. Birth date unknown; died in 1661; daughter of Ralph Hawtrey of Ruislip; married Sir John Bankes (a prosecutor and later chief justice of the Court of Common Pleas); children: daughters (names unknown).*

During the English Civil Wars of the 17th century, Lady Mary Bankes was a Royalist who held Dorset's Corfe Castle while her husband stayed with the king Charles I in London. When she began to fear that Parliamentarian forces would attack her fortress, she stored many provisions and locked the gates to prevent surprise attacks. In 1643, the local Parliamentary Committee demanded that Lady Bankes turn over the four remaining guns of the castle to them, which she eventually did. However, she refused to surrender the castle, and on June 23, 1643, the first siege began. A force of some 600, led by Sir Walter Earle, attacked her with two siege engines. During the final assault, Lady Bankes personally defended the upper ward of the castle with only five soldiers, her daughters, and her women attendants. By heaving stones and red-hot embers down on the men attempting to climb ladders, Lady Bankes and her small force prevented a breach in the castle's defenses. The report of an approaching Royalist relief force ended the first siege of Corfe. Lady Bankes was besieged again in 1645 after her husband's death; this time a traitor apparently gave the enemy entry to the castle. Bankes and her children were permitted to depart without injury.

and attacked, and firearms were introduced, women appear to be frequently active as defenders, particularly during the period of the Thirty Years' War. For example, the Spanish women of San Mateo are reported to have been especially energetic in shooting at their besiegers.

Women's participation in siege warfare was widespread and varied for centuries throughout Europe. Women provided an important force that supplemented, and sometimes substituted for, the trained military forces of the time.

**SOURCES:**

Barrow, G.W.S. *Feudal Britain: The Completion of the Medieval Kingdoms, 1066–1314.* London: Arnold, 1956.

Bennett, H.S. *The Pastons and their England.* Cambridge: Cambridge University Press, 1932.

Bingham, Caroline. *The Crowned Lions: The Early Plantagenet Kings.* London: David & Charles, 1978.

Blashfield, Jean F. *Hellraisers, Heroines, and Holy Women.* NY: Superlative House, 1981.

Butler, Pierce. *Women of Mediaeval France.* Vol. 5. Philadelphia, PA: Barrie, 1907.

Collison-Morley, L. *The Story of the Sforzas.* NY: Dutton, 1934.

Comnena, Anna. *The Alexiad of Anna Comnena.* Trans. by E.R.A. Sewter. NY: Penguin, 1969.

Echols, Anne, and Marty Williams. *An Annotated Index of Medieval Women.* NY: Markus Wiener, 1992.

Fell, Christine, Cecily Clark, and Elizabeth Williams. *Women in Anglo-Saxon England and the Impact of 1066.* Colonnade, 1984.

Fittis, Robert Scott. *Heroines of Scotland.* London: Alexander Gardner, 1889.

Froissart, Jean. *The Chronicle of Froissart.* NY: AMS, 1967.

Fryde, Natalie. *The Tyranny and Fall of Edward II, 1321–1326.* Cambridge: Cambridge University Press, 1979.

Gribble, Francis. *Women in War.* NY: Dutton, 1917.

Haskell, Ann S. "The Paston Women on Marriage in Fifteenth-Century England," in *Viator.* Vol. 4, 1973, pp. 459–471.

Jones, Michael. *The Creation of Brittany: A Late Medieval State.* London: Hambledon, 1988.

———. *Ducal Brittany, 1364–1399.* Oxford: Oxford University Press, 1970.

Kendall, Paul Murray. *The Yorkist Age: Daily Life during the Wars of the Roses.* NY: Norton, 1962.

Marks, Claude. *Pilgrims, Heretics, and Lovers: A Medieval Journey.* NY: Macmillan, 1975.

Melegari, Vezio. *The Great Military Sieges.* Trans. by Rizzoli Editore. NY: Crowell, 1972.

Norwich, John Julius. *The Kingdom in the Sun: 1130–1194.* NY: Harper, 1970.

Powicke, Sir Maurice. *The Thirteenth Century.* 2nd ed. Oxford: Oxford University Press, 1991.

Tallett, Frank. *War and Society in Early-Modern Europe, 1495–1715.* London: Routledge, 1992.

Vann, Richard T. "Women in Preindustrial Capitalism," in *Becoming Visible: Women in European History.* Eds. Bridenthal, Renate and Claudia Koonz. Boston, MA: Houghton Mifflin, 1977, pp. 192–216.

Wakefield, Walter L. *Heresy, Crusade and Inquisition in Southern France 1100–1250.* London: Allen & Unwin, 1974.

**SUGGESTED READING:**

Fraser, Antonia. *The Warrior Queens.* NY: Knopf, 1989.

———. *The Weaker Vessel: Woman's Lot in 17th-century England.* London: Weidenfeld, 1984.

Hacker, Barton C. "Women and Military Institutions in Early Modern Europe: a Reconnaissance," in *Signs: Journal of Women in Culture and Society.* Vol. 6, no. 4, 1981, pp. 643–671.

Marshall, Rosalind K. *Virgins and Viragos: A History of Women in Scotland from 1080 to 1980.* Chicago, IL: Academy Chicago, 1983.

McLaughlin, Megan. "The woman warrior: gender, warfare and society in medieval Europe," in *Women's Studies.* Vol. 17, 1990, pp. 193–209.

Plowden, Alison. *Women All on Fire: The Women of the English Civil War.* London: Sutton, 1998.

Stafford, Pauline. *Queens, Concubines, and Dowagers: The King's Wife in the Early Middle Ages.* Athens, GA: University of Georgia Press, 1983.

Reina Pennington, Ph.D. Candidate
in Military and Women's History,
University of South Carolina,
Columbia, South Carolina

# Siems, Margarethe (1879–1952)

*German soprano. Born on December 30, 1879, in Breslau (now Wroclaw), Poland; died on April 13, 1952, in Dresden; studied with Aglaja von Orgéni and *Pauline Viardot.*

*Made debut in Prague as Marguerite in* Les Huguenots *(1902); joined the Prague Opera (1902) and the Dresden Court Opera (1908); was the leading dramatic coloratura soprano in Dresden (1908–20); created roles of Chrysothemis in* Elektra *(1909) and of the Marshallin in* Der Rosenkavalier *(1911), both in Dresden; created the role of Zerbinetta in* Ariadne auf Naxos *in Stuttgart (1912); made Covent Garden debut (1913); taught at the Berlin Conservatory and then in Dresden and Breslau.*

Shortly after Margarethe Siems debuted at the Prague Opera, the brilliant soprano **Irene Abendroth** retired. Siems, who took over many of the older soprano's roles, remained at Prague for 11 years. Richard Strauss cast her as Chrysothemis in his new opera *Elektra* in 1909, and in 1911 she became the first Marshallin in

*Margarethe Siems*

*Der Rosenkavalier* which also premiered in Dresden. She not only fulfilled the composer's vocal requirements but also responded to Max Reinhardt's stage direction, and the Marshallin would become her most famous role. Her voice, rather than her acting ability, accounted for her fame. After appearing in many European opera houses, Siems retired to teach.

**John Haag**,
Athens, Georgia

# Sieveking, Amalie (1794–1859)

*German humanitarian, charity worker, and educator who played an important role in making philanthropic activities more available to German Lutheran women. Born Amalie Wilhelmine Sieveking in Hamburg, Germany, on July 25, 1794; died in Hamburg on April 1, 1859; had three brothers; never married.*

Born a patrician's daughter in 1794 in Hamburg, Amalie Sieveking was orphaned at an early age, her mother dying when she was four and her father when she was fifteen, in 1809. Because her father's fortune had been eroded by the French occupation and the end of a once-prosperous trade with Great Britain, Amalie and her three brothers were separated and sent to board in the homes of relatives and friends. Her own school lessons—but not her brothers'—were discontinued. Later, in her adult years, when she had become a proselytizer for women's entrance into public charity, she made much of the disparity in educational opportunities for women and men. Sieveking discovered her own talent as a teacher in the household where she lived, and instituted a series of six-year instructional programs for girls which she continued throughout her life. In 1813, she opened her first school with six pupils. Her graduates would serve as a major source of her public influence, because her former pupils were dedicated disciples and ardent correspondents.

In the "moral diary" (*Sonntagsunterhaltungen* or Sunday Conversations) Amalie Sieveking kept during her early 20s, she wrote of the personal turmoil and self-examination of this period of her life. In one passage, she wrote defiantly, "If not a happy wife and mother, then founder of an order of Sisters of Charity!" The desire to do charitable work found little support in the Lutheran culture Sieveking grew up in. Martin Luther had left little room for the development of women's service in his new church, except for wives of the clergy. Although for a time intrigued by the Roman Catholic Sisters of Charity, Sieveking became skeptical when she

scrutinized the statutes of the Bavarian order: "The yoke is too slavish, the chains too restrictive. The free spirit would be struck dead by the multiplicity of little legalisms."

Two events in Hamburg propelled Sieveking from speculation to action. The first was a campaign launched by the local press in 1830 to identify and publicize the failures of municipal poor relief in the city. The second was the devastating cholera epidemic of 1831. During the outbreak, Sieveking volunteered as a nurse at the plague hospital, but no one followed her example.

On May 23, 1832, joined by 12 other women, she founded the Weiblicher Verein für Armen- und Krankenpflege (Female Association for the Care of the Poor and Sick). This society was not meant to be comprised of full-time professional workers, but of women who gave their talents and their spare time to Christian charity and social welfare work. The aim of her group as envisioned by Sieveking was to visit the households of impoverished invalids and their families in accordance with recommendations from the public administration, and to provide practical and material help as well as spiritual guidance.

*Postage stamp issued by the Federal Republic of Germany to honor Amalie Sieveking, 1955.*

The statutes of the association recognized that the numbers of clients the group could expect to serve and the nature of its commitment would necessarily depend both on the number of members recruited and the financial resources at its disposal. No woman was to consider membership unless she could expect to devote herself to at least one and preferably two house calls each week, and to at least one meeting each week with other members of the association to assess the results of their visits. Sieveking's idea lit a flame that grew slowly but steadily over the next decades. From its original 12 members in 1832, the society expanded to include 53 during its first decade, 70 by the late 1840s, and 85 by the time of Sieveking's death in 1859. As the membership grew, the caseload expanded from an original 85 families to 256. Funded by voluntary contributions, the expendable income of the association increased from 1,332 banco marks the first year to 47,000 in 1859.

In 1841, during a visit to Bremen, Sieveking carried her message outside of Hamburg. Over the next years, organizations similar to hers were founded in many other German cities. Primarily conservative, Sieveking espoused an idea of the "emancipation of women" that looked back to a simpler, essentially rural and patriarchal social order. In her public speeches, she cajoled fathers and husbands to allow the women of their households to engage in charitable activities; she never questioned their authority to do so. She also accepted the oppression of the poor as an unalterable condition of society. Although her concepts of female emancipation would differ radically from those of a later generation, Sieveking displayed a high degree of idealism, energy, and practical organizational talent. In many ways, she was a prophet of Christian stewardship long before the term was invented. Amalie Sieveking died in Hamburg on April 1, 1859. A postage stamp of the Federal Republic of Germany was issued in her honor on November 15, 1955.

SOURCES:
Beckmann, Hanna. *Evangelische Frauen in bahnbrechender Liebestätigkeit im 19. Jahrhundert.* Berlin: F.A. Herbig, 1927.

Evans, Richard J. *Death in Hamburg: Society and Politics in the Cholera Years, 1830–1910.* Oxford: Clarendon Press, 1987.

Garland, Mary. *The Oxford Companion to German Literature.* Oxford: Oxford University Press, 1997.

Gewin, Everard. *Pietistische Portretten.* Utrecht: H. de Vroede, 1922.

Herbst, Wilhelm. *Amalie Sieveking: Dienerin Jesu an Armen und Kranken.* 2nd rev. ed. Giessen and Basel: Brunnen, 1964.

Herzel, Catherine. *Heroes of the Church.* Edited by Gustav K. Wiencke. Philadelphia, PA: Lutheran Church Press, 1971.

Jenssen, Christian. *Licht der Liebe: Lebenswege deutscher Frauen.* Hamburg: Verlag Broschek, 1938.

Kuessner, Theodor. *Die Erweckungsbewegung in Hamburg im Spiegel der Briefe, Tagebücher und theologischen Schriften Amalie Sievekings.* Hamburg: F. Wittig, 1986.

Poel, Emma. *Life of Amelia Wilhelmina Sieveking.* Edited by Catherine Winkworth. London: Longman, Roberts & Green, 1863.

Prelinger, Catherine M. *Charity, Challenge, and Change: Religious Dimensions of the Mid-Nineteenth Century Women's Movement in Germany.* NY: Greenwood Press, 1987.

———. "Prelude to Consciousness: Amalie Sieveking and the Female Association for the Care of the Poor and the Sick," in John C. Fout, ed., *German Women in the Nineteenth Century: A Social History.* NY: Holmes & Meier, 1984, pp. 118–132.

**John Haag,** Associate Professor of History, University of Georgia, Athens, Georgia

## Sigbrit or Sigbritt, Mother
**(fl. 1507–1523).**
*See Willums, Sigbrit.*

## Sigerson, Dora (1866–1918)

*Irish poet and novelist. Name variations: Dora Sigerson Shorter; Mrs. Clement Shorter. Born in Dublin, Ireland, on August 16, 1866; died on January 16, 1918, in Buckinghamshire, England; eldest daughter of George Sigerson (a scholar, surgeon, and writer) and Hester (Varian) Sigerson (a poet and novelist); educated at home; sister of **Hester Sigerson Piatt** (a writer); married Clement King Shorter (editor of the* Illustrated London News*), in July 1895.*

"Her very absence from Ireland has made her . . . more Irish than if she had never left it," wrote Douglas Hyde of Dora Sigerson. At the time of her marriage to Clement Shorter, editor of the *Illustrated London News*, Sigerson moved from her precious Dublin to London where she remained homesick for the rest of her life. During the Easter Rising in Ireland in 1916, she worked tirelessly for her imprisoned compatriots and strained her health in the process.

The daughter of writers, George and *Hester Sigerson, Dora grew up more interested in art and sculpting than in poetry. With the encouragement of her two great Catholic friends, *Katharine Tynan and *Louise Imogen Guiney, Sigerson published *Verses* (1894), *The Fairy Changeling and Other Poems* (1897), *My Lady's Slipper and Other Poems* (1899), *Ballads and Poems* (1899), *The Father Confessor* (1900), and *The Woman Who Went to Hell and Other Poems* (1901). Tynan once wrote that Sigerson looked like the "Greek Hermes: she wore her hair short and it was in masses. She had a beautiful brow, very fine gray eyes, a warm pale color, and vivid red lips." A sculpted memorial of Irish patriots, rendered by Sigerson, stands in the Dublin cemetery where she was brought home to rest.

## Sigerson, Hester (d. 1898)

*Irish novelist and poet. Born Hester Varian in Cork, Ireland; birth date unknown; died in 1898; daughter of Amos Varian of Cork; married Dr. George Sigerson (a writer and historian), in 1861; children: *Dora Sigerson (1866–1918); Hester Sigerson Piatt (a poet).*

Hester Sigerson was a frequent contributor to *The Boston Pilot*, *The Gael*, and *Irish Fireside*. Her one novel *A Ruined Race* was published by Sheed and Ward in 1889.

## Signoret, Simone (1921–1985)

*Academy-award winning French actress and social activist who appeared in a number of film classics during her 40-year career. Born Simone Henriette Charlotte Kaminker on March 25, 1921, in Wiesbaden, Germany; died on September 30, 1985, in Normandy, France; daughter of André Kaminker and Georgette (Signoret) Kaminker; married Yves Allegret (a director), in 1948 (divorced 1949); married Yves Montand (a singer-actor), in 1950; children: (with Allegret) Catherine Allegret (an actress, b. 1947).*

*Moved to Paris with her family while still a child; eventually forced to work as a typist to support family when the Nazis invaded Paris and her Jewish father fled to London; after several years working as an extra in films, was given her first leading role (1947), beginning her career as a versatile and accomplished character actress of the French screen; won international recognition; received Academy Award as Best Actress for* Room at the Top *(1958); published two volumes of memoirs and a novel.*

*Filmography:* Le Prince Charmant *(1942);* Les Visiteurs du Soir *(1942);* La Bôite aux Rêves *(1945);* Les Démons de l'Aube *(1947);* Back Streets of Paris *(UK, 1947);* Fantômas *(1947);* Against the Wind *(UK, 1948);* L'Impasse de Deux Anges *(1948);* Dedée d'Anvers *(1948);* Swiss Tour *(Switz., 1949);* Manèges *(1950);* La Ronde *(1950);* Le Traqué *(1950);* Ombre et Lumiére *(1951);* Casque d'Or *(1952);* Thérèse Raquin *(1953);* Les Diaboliques *(1955);* La Mort en le Jardin *(1956);* Les Sorcières de Salem *(The Crucible, 1957);* Room at the Top *(1958);* Adua e le Campagne *(Ital.,* 1960); Le Mauvais Coups *(1961);* Term of Trial *(UK, 1962);* Le Jour et l'Heure *(1963);* Dragées au Poivre *(1963);* Ship of Fools *(US, 1964);* Paris Brûle-t-il? *("Is Paris Burning?," 1966);* The Deadly Affair *(UK, 1967);* Games *(US, 1967);* The Sea Gull *(US-UK, 1968);* L'Armée des Ombres *(1969);* L'Americain *(1969);* Le Chat *(1970);* La Veuve Couderc *(1970);* Rude Journée pour la Reine *(1973);* Défense de Savoir *(1974);* La Chair de l'orchidée *(1974);* Police Python 357 *(1976);* La Vie devant soi *(Madame Rosa, 1977);* Une Femme dangereuse *(1978);* Judith Therpauve *(1978);* L'Adolescente *(1980);* Chére inconnu *(1980);* L'Étoile du Nord *(1982);* Guy de Maupassant *(1982); (narration only)* Des Terroristes à la retraite *(1983).*

They were an odd pair and it was an odd meeting place for a first date that March night in 1941. He was a political revolutionary from a wealthy, conservative Swiss family; she was the daughter of a Jewish father and worked as a secretary for a Paris newspaper well known as a mouthpiece for the occupying Germans; and the place chosen for their meeting was the Left Bank's Café de Flore, that bastion of anti-Nazi, anti-fascist intellectuals and artists on the Boulevard Saint-Germain, as yet untouched by the occupation forces roaming the capital. For Claude Jaeger, the evening marked the beginning of his work as an elusive leader of the Resistance movement; for Simone Kaminker, stepping into the Flore that evening was the start of a career in which politics and art would be inextricably bound. "By opening that door," she later said, after adopting her mother's maiden name and becoming Simone Signoret, "I was entering a world that would change the rest of my life."

So momentous was that entry that Signoret would always consider it as important a date as the day of her birth on March 25, 1921, in Wiesbaden, Germany, where her father was stationed as part of the victorious French forces posted in Germany after that country's defeat in World War I. André Kaminker, the son of Jewish immigrants from Poland who had settled in France during the previous century, kept his ancestry carefully hidden even from his own daughter. "I don't know very much about my father," Signoret once said, "except that he was born in France, that he had fought for France, and that being French was enormously important for him." André's eagerness to be perceived as French, and never as a Jew, left Simone with little sense of her heritage and, she later said, led to feelings of separation and an anxiety-ridden desire for acceptance. Simone's mother **Georgette Signoret** continually criticized her husband for betraying his heritage and for flaunting the privileges of a victorious army amid the devastation and misery of a ruined Germany. From Georgette, who came from a working-class family, Simone absorbed something of a social conscience, remembering how her mother would engage her in philosophical discussions, even as a child. Simone was an only child until her family moved back to France and settled in the middle-class Paris suburb of Neuilly, where two brothers—Alain and Jean-Pierre—were born within a year of each other.

Although Simone harbored a young girl's fantasies of becoming a famous actress, it seemed her future would be dedicated to more serious pursuits. She studied philosophy in secondary school, helped form a student magazine dedicated to philosophical issues called "The Hyphen," and met a young philosophy professor named Jean-Paul Sartre, who had come to teach at the boys' school across the street. During his daughter's school years, André found work as a translator and interpreter and was disturbed by the content of a speech carried live by French radio that he was assigned to translate. It was Adolf Hitler's Nuremberg speech of 1934, the first major policy statement by the Nazi leader. Not long after, André nervously sent his wife and children to Vannes, in the French countryside, and left France for London, where he served as a translator for the BBC and remained for the duration of the war. Cut off from Paris by the German invasion of 1939, Simone spent the first year of the war helping her mother feed and billet the German soldiers passing through on their way to the capital who winked knowingly at Georgette's claim that the family name was a Breton one. Georgette and her two sons finally returned to Neuilly during the winter of 1940 while Simone finished her education at the Vannes lycée, taking her baccalauréate (the French equivalent of a bachelor's degree) in philosophy.

Georgette's struggle to raise three children on her meager income as a seamstress forced Simone to find work in occupied Paris as a secretary for a collaborationist newspaper, *Les Nouveaux Temps*, which was owned by the father of a school friend. It was at this point that she met Claude Jaeger and walked into the Café de Flore that March night. There, while German troops roamed the city, she met intellectuals and artists who, like herself, turned their disaffections and anxieties into philosophical tracts, poetry, painting, plays, and films. She renewed her acquaintance with Sartre, just then codifying his thinking into what would be called Existentialism, struck up a friendship with *Simone de Beau-

voir, and met such luminaries of the French art world as Picasso, Giacometti, and Soutine. She heard the rebellious talk of Communists, Italian anti-fascists, Spanish republicans, and fearful Jews. Although her relationship with Jaeger soon ended, and Simone never actively joined the French Resistance, the political activism that would mark her later life was first nurtured by the relationships formed at the Flore, many of which lasted for the rest of her days. As the first sign of her new direction, she quit her job at *Les Nouveaux Temps*, telling her employer that she was leaving "because you see, monsieur, you'll all end up being shot." (An accurate prediction, as it turned out: the editor of the paper was executed for treason after the war.) An apartment she shared with Yves Allegret, a young film director she met at the Flore, was an active message center for Resistance activities; and Signoret once discovered that a suitcase she had been asked to deliver for a friend contained ammunition bound for Resistance fighters just outside Paris. "I did not perform a single heroic act," Signoret admitted, "but I did no harm, which in itself is not so bad."

It was because of the Flore, too, that her film career was launched. Among the café's habitues were filmmakers such as screenwriter Jacques Prévert, Marcel Carné, Robert Bresson, and the Allegret brothers, Yves and Marc, all of whom began offering her work as an extra in their productions. Fearing that the German-controlled Vichy government would never grant her a work permit under the name Kaminker, Simone adopted Georgette's maiden name and began studying acting, although her teacher declared she could only be a comic actress because of a minor speech impediment which changed her sibilants to a "ch"—the "Signoret sound" which would later be imitated by thousands of French young women.

Despite the German occupation, the French film industry remained relatively unaffected for much of the war and turned out 120 films in the period, some of them still considered classics of French cinema—like Bresson's *Les Anges de Péchés* (*Angels of the Streets*) and Carné's *Les Enfants du Paradis* (*Children of Paradise*), starring *Arletty. Signoret learned her craft in small roles for these and other directors, such as Sacha Guitry, Abel Gance, and Henri-Georges Clouzot. Carné cast her in her first significant, although non-speaking, role in 1942's *Les Visiteurs du Soir* (released in subtitled English as *The Devil's Envoys*), while Signoret made her first stage appearance the same year as "a woman of the people of Thebes" in a modest

Simone
Signoret

production by a tiny repertory company in Paris. By war's end, Simone's craft had matured to the point where even a small role could be burnished to perfection in her care. Typical of such parts was her performance in Yves Allegret's *Démons de l'Aube* (*Demons of Dawn*), in which she was given only one scene as a barmaid attempting to excite the passion of a simple-minded village boy with a kiss. "A classic scene, apparently without much scope for variation," a crew member remembered many years later, "which is why on the set, we all suddenly had a sense of revelation.

She was born for the cinema, there were no two ways about it. Her performance was like a second birth." The metaphor was an apt one, for Signoret was at the time pregnant with Allegret's child—a girl, Catherine, born just before the film's release in 1947. The couple's relationship had begun during the war, but it was not until after Catherine's birth that Simone and Yves were married, in 1948.

*I haven't done all I would have liked to do, but I've never done anything I didn't want to.*

—Simone Signoret

*Démons de l'Aube* marked Simone's acceptance as a serious actress, bolstered by her performance as a hard-hearted streetwalker changed by the power of love in 1948's *Dédée d'Anvers*, also directed by Allegret, and in that same year's *Impasse des Deux Anges*. "Simone Signoret has finally found the part she was looking for," *Paris-Presse* told its readers, "which immediately raises her up with the first rank of French screen actresses." *Le Figaro* was particularly impressed with her ability to silently communicate emotion. "Her silences are as important as her words," the newspaper said. "She acts with her mouth, her eyes, and her skin." Audiences fell in love with the character of Dédée, and were particularly struck by Signoret's dazzling, almost regal beauty and smoldering sensuality, "glowing like a greengage," as one reviewer put it. But Signoret was more concerned with developing a convincing character and went to great lengths with makeup and wardrobe to help her with the transition. "It's almost chemical, the way you turn into that other person," she once observed. "I forget that I'm Signoret." Filmgoers were so attached to Dédée that Simone's work as the manipulative, greedy Dora in 1950's *Manèges* (also directed by Allegret) brought howls of protest, even after Signoret defended herself by claiming that it was a film's message as a whole that was important to her, not merely her own character. "I can easily play a Gestapo informer in an anti-fascist film," she said, "but I can't play a model mother or a proud mistress in a fascist film." Among Signoret's other films during the immediate postwar period were the first of many pictures dealing with wartime heroism, 1948's *Against The Wind*, a British film in which Signoret played a French Resistance fighter aided by British paratroopers.

After working in twelve films in less than eight years and establishing herself as a leading actress of the French screen, Signoret retired to the south of France during the summer of 1949, taking Catherine and Allegret's son from a previous marriage with her. It was during her stay at a luxurious hotel in St. Paul-de-Vences, not far from Nice, that Signoret's life took another turn, as significant as the night nine years before when she had walked into the Café de Flore. She met and fell in love with Yves Montand, a nightclub and cabaret performer about to become the most popular entertainer in France. Montand had come to the same hotel to recover from a two-year affair with singer *Edith Piaf, and often recalled his first sight of Simone Signoret in August 1949, standing "formidably blond, in a sundrenched courtyard . . . surrounded by hovering doves. I approached softly, trying not to disturb the doves." The next four days was a swirl of *l'amour fou*. "We had been struck by lightning," Signoret said, "and something indiscreet and irreversible happened." Yves Allegret was surprised to find Simone waiting on the road near the hotel with the children on the day he came to join her, and was forced to accept Signoret's declaration that she had fallen in love with another man and wanted a divorce. Leaving her daughter with Allegret, Signoret moved in with Montand at his flat in Neuilly. The two became inseparable, Simone forsaking her film work, not to mention Catherine, to accompany Montand on tour. "If Yves cannot live without singing," she declared, "I cannot live without him."

Although Signoret's acting career was on hold, her social activism was not. With the Cold War now firmly dividing East and West, both she and Montand were among the first to sign the so-called Stockholm Petition in 1950, which called on the world's nations to stop the testing and development of atomic weapons and which was suspected by political conservatives of being inspired by the Soviet Union. The two were also prominent in protests against France's bleak colonial war in Indochina, soon to be inherited by the United States, and were known to be sympathetic to the Communist Party, especially after neither of them denied an accusation published in *Le Figaro* that they were, in fact, party members. Signoret claimed in later years that neither she nor Montand had ever actually joined the party and had ignored *Le Figaro*'s report only to avoid lending it legitimacy by responding to it. Nonetheless, their left-leaning proclivities along with the notoriety of their relationship now began to affect their careers, especially outside France. Although both Signoret and Montand had earlier signed contracts with American producers—Signoret with Howard Hughes' RKO Pictures and Montand with Warner Bros.—the politically conservative atmosphere that now gripped Hollywood during the years of the McCarthy hearings denied them any hopes of traveling to the United States. Both contracts were quietly allowed to expire.

In December 1950, Signoret and Montand were formally married. Catherine was brought to live with her mother and stepfather in an old bookshop on Paris' Île de la Cité, near the Pont Neuf. Simone returned to films with one of her most radiant performances, in Max Ophuls' *La Ronde*, a witty, risqué comedy of manners set in 19th-century Vienna, and in Jacques Becker's *Casque d'Or* (*The Golden Helmet*), appreciated much more 30 years later than when first released in 1952. Becker's dark tale of underworld treachery and murder in turn-of-the-century France, in which Signoret appeared as a gangland mistress with the aggressively blonde coiffure from which the picture took its name, met with modest success elsewhere in Europe but was a failure in France, where it was not shown again for ten years after its short-lived opening in Paris. Simone announced after the film's demise that she was leaving the screen for good and retiring to the country home in Normandy that she and Montand had just purchased. But little more than a year later, her performance in Maurice Carné's 1953 version of *Thérèse Racquin*, in which she played Zola's passionate, doomed heroine, was received to great acclaim and was credited with helping the film to win the Golden Lion at that year's Venice Biennale. Carnè's picture was followed by the classic suspense thriller, Henri-Georges Clouzot's *Diabolique*, which starred Signoret and *Vera Clouzot as the mistress and spouse, respectively, of the bullying headmaster of a boys' school. The film is still much admired for its famous concluding plot twist and the scene in which the two women collude in the husband's bathtub drowning and then carry the body downstairs in a wicker basket. As with *Casque d'Or*, the movie has fared better in retrospect than it did at the time of its release. The shoot itself was far from a pleasant experience for Simone, who constantly battled with the imperious Clouzot and his loyal wife Vera. To make matters worse, Signoret was at the same time in rehearsal for a French stage version of Arthur Miller's *The Crucible*, in which she had the role of the saintly ✥➤ Elizabeth Proctor. "I went straight from a murderess to a New England Puritan without any transition," she said, "and the next day I would be a murderess again . . . when the director, his wife, and I were no longer on speaking terms." She derived some consolation from the fact that Montand was playing opposite her as John Proctor when the play opened in December 1954, and that her old friend Sartre was working on a film version (released in 1957 as *Les Sorcières de Salem*) which was to be shot in what was then East Germany. Miller, whose play was widely interpreted as a condemnation of McCarthy's "red-baiting," was unable to attend the opening, having been questioned about his ties to suspected Communists by McCarthy's congressional committee and denied a passport to travel outside the United States.

As if Signoret's willingness to shoot a picture in East Berlin weren't enough to confirm her critics' accusations of Communist sympathies, Montand's acceptance of a concert tour through Eastern Europe finished the job. A further crisis arrived when, only a few months after Montand agreed to the tour, the Soviet Union invaded Hungary to repress growing anti-Communist sentiment and the right-wing clamor against Signoret and Montand increased precipitously in volume. "For Montand and me," Simone later recalled, "November of 1956 was the most absurd, the most awful, the saddest and most instructive month of our . . . years together." Montand turned to Sartre for advice, but Sartre could only offer the unhelpful opinion, "If you go, you support the Russians. If you stay, you support the fascists." In the end, Montand decided to honor his contract by claiming he was traveling behind the Iron Curtain as an emissary of peace to prevent further brutalities by Moscow. Signoret remained very much in the background during the tour, although she and Montand politely demanded an explanation for the invasion from Nikita Khrushchev during a much-reported dinner at the Kremlin, during which Khrushchev claimed his army had been invited to enter Hungary by "Hungarians afraid of the fascists."

In the swirl of ideological accusation and recrimination, Signoret's career seemed to grind to a halt. She was caught between her political detractors, who considered her a dangerous leftist, and young French directors like François Truffaut, Louis Malle and their New Wave comrades, who avoided her as an icon of the old régime they were seeking to undermine with their brash new style of filmmaking. "The future belongs to very young girls and pretty young woman," Signoret lamented, even though she was only in her 40s at the time. A further blow was struck in 1958 when her younger brother, Alain, a promising director in his own right, drowned while shooting a documentary about the French fishing industry.

It was an offer of work in a British film that helped her recover from her brother's death and, at the same time, resuscitate her career. *Room at the Top*, shot in 1958, brought with it interna-

◄✥
***Proctor, Elizabeth.*** *See Witchcraft Trials in Salem Village.*

tional acclaim and an end to Signoret's screen reputation as a hard-hearted mistress or a streetwalker. Her portrayal of Alice Aisgill, the vulnerable French housewife who indulges in an ill-fated affair with a younger man in a dreary Yorkshire industrial town, is generally considered to mark the peak of her career. *Room at the Top* was one of the top-grossing pictures of the late 1950s in nearly every Western country except, ironically, France, where film audiences were perhaps less fascinated with stories of adulterous *amours*. The film was released just as Signoret was traveling to America (on a restricted visa) with Montand, who had been signed for a one-man Broadway show. By the time they arrived in New York, Signoret's fame had grown to such proportions that she feared she might overshadow her husband whom, she worried, "people might take for an actress' husband." But Montand's Broadway debut was equally acclaimed, making the two of them the darlings of the international jet set and sending the couple to a newly liberalized Hollywood, which handed Signoret its Best Actress award for *Room at the Top* and offered Montand a contract for two pictures, one of which was George Cukor's *Let's Make Love*. The scandalous publicity surrounding Montand's brief affair with co-star *Marilyn Monroe* hit the trade press in the middle of shooting, but Signoret knew her marriage to Montand was strong enough to survive the incident, although she was less sure about Monroe's marriage to Arthur Miller. Maintaining a calm demeanor amid the furor, she answered one reporter's question by inquiring politely, "You know many men, do you, who would have stayed indifferent while having Marilyn Monroe in their arms?" Many years later, she wrote, "[Monroe] will never know how much I didn't hate her, and how I understand the story, which only concerned the four of us." Besides, there was much to otherwise occupy her attention at the time, chiefly the news that she had won the Best Actress award from both the British Film Association and the Cannes Film Festival for her work in *Room at the Top*.

Signoret worked nearly continually during the tumultuous 1960s, gracefully accepting roles as middle-aged housewives or heroic Resistance fighters in pictures such as 1961's *Les Mauvaises Coupes* (released in the U.S. as *Naked Autumn*), another older woman-younger man story set against the German occupation of France; 1962's *Le Jour et l'heure* (*The Day and the Hour*), about a bourgeois housewife who smuggles an American flyer to safety during the war; and in Stanley Kramer's 1965 production of

*Katherine Anne Porter*'s novel *Ship of Fools*, in which she appeared as the Contessa opposite José Ferrer and *Vivien Leigh*. She returned to the Paris stage as the greedy Regina in a French version of *Lillian Hellman*'s *The Little Foxes* (which Simone had translated into French), and in London as Lady Macbeth opposite Alec Guiness. All were roles for mature women. "After you're forty—come on, let's say forty-five," Signoret pointed out, "you can take one of two routes. Either you cling to parts that keep you looking thirty-five or thirty-six as long as possible, or you can be like everybody else and quietly accept the idea that forty-five puts you on the road to forty-six, not forty-four."

Although earlier in the decade Signoret had signed a petition against the continued French occupation of Algeria, she realized she was too old to become involved in the 1968 student riots that swept France in May of that year and kept her distance, spending much of that spring and summer in Sweden shooting Sidney Lumet's adaptation of *The Sea Gull*, in which she played Irina. Nonetheless, both she and Montand appeared in two ideologically opinionated films by Costa-Gavras (portraying in one the parents of a character played by Catherine, in her first film role), and lent their support to a workers' hunger strike at a Renault factory—although when the resulting riots ended in the shooting death of one of the protestors, Signoret once again had to defend herself against charges of misplaced sympathies. She denied her actions were politically inspired, saying she preferred the term "social activism," and pointed out that she had never joined any formal party or engaged in militant activities.

Signoret entered what friends kindly called her "mature period" with her appearance in 1970's *Le Chat* (*The Cat*), a marital drama in which she and the great French actor Jean Gabin appeared as an argumentative older couple. Audiences were shocked at Simone's puffy face, limping gait, and excess weight, while film magazines gossiped that she had become too cynical to maintain her former good looks. Fans were convinced Signoret's career was over when she published the first of two volumes of memoirs in 1976, which sold well even though certain reviewers claimed she hadn't written it herself. (Signoret sued one magazine for libel and won.) *Adieu Volodia*, a novel based on her imaginings about her father's life as a Jew in Paris before World War I, appeared in the early 1980s. "As soon as I stop acting," she told her readers, "I feel the urge to write. When you're writing a book, what is exciting is being your own director . . . and best of all, your own producer."

Her willingness to use her age as a catalyst for her acting produced a stunning performance in 1977's *La Vie devant soi* (released with English subtitles as *Madame Rosa*), her riveting portrayal of an aging Holocaust survivor who also happens to be the good-hearted madam of a brothel. As careful with her wardrobe and makeup at 56 as she had been at 18, Simone wore a gaudy flowered housedress several sizes too small to make her look grossly obese and, more subtly, had a concentration camp number borrowed from her makeup artist (an actual survivor of the camps) inked onto her arm. The number is never seen in the film, covered by wardrobe, but Signoret's meticulous attention to characterization demanded it be placed there.

In 1980, Signoret was admitted to a Paris hospital for what was publicized as a gallbladder operation, but which many friends privately believed was the first sign of cancer. Her eyesight, too, began to suffer, although she continued working. Her last film was 1982's *Guy de Maupassant*, in which she played the French writer's mother. By the time she worked on what would be her last role, the 1985 television drama "The Music Hall," she was virtually blind, although no one could tell when the cameras rolled and she became the loud, boisterous elderly patron of a German music palace in 1935. "When I hear the clapper board," she told an interviewer, "it's like seeing." After filming was completed, Signoret returned with Montand to their beloved Normandy, where her cancer worsened. "Don't come too early," she told a friend who telephoned to ask if he might drop in for a visit, "or you'll find me very tired. If you come at an early hour, you can take a nap in my beautiful garden." On September 30, 1985, with Montand and Catherine at her side, Signoret quietly passed away.

Simone Signoret's admirable career successfully merged the introspection of an intellectual, the social concern of an activist, and the passion of an artist to produce a body of work respected as much for its commitment and professionalism as for its quality. In her personal life, too, Signoret never lost her honesty or her dignity as a woman, mother, and wife in the midst of the entertainment industry's glitter and artificiality. Her last words reported by Montand indicate she had finally come to terms with the dislocations and anxieties of her childhood. "I am," she is said to have murmured, "at peace."

**SOURCES:**

Darrach, Brad. "Yves Montand: The Most Seductive of Frenchmen Looks Ahead to New Conquests," in *People Weekly*. Vol. 29, no. 19. May 16, 1988.

David, Catherine. *Simone Signoret*. Translated from the French by Sally Sampson. London: Bloomsbury, 1992.

Josselin, Jean-François. *Simone: deux ou trois choses que je sais d'elle*. Paris: Grasset, 1995.

Signoret, Simone. *Le lendemain, elle était souriante . . .* Paris: Seuil, 1979.

**Norman Powers**, writer-producer,
Chelsea Lane Productions,
New York, New York

# Sigolena of Albi (fl. 7th c.)

*French deaconess and saint. Flourished in the 7th century in Albi, France.*

One of the early female saints, Sigolena of Albi is known because an anonymous admirer, probably a monk or nun over whom she had held office, wrote of her life. This biography tells of young Sigolena's marriage against her will: her parents forced her to marry but she wanted to dedicate herself to serving God. She even supposedly offered to give her husband everything she owned if he would agree to dissolve the union and let her leave. She was still married to him when he died, but her widowhood finally gave her an opportunity to live as she wished; she founded a monastery and became its leader, and was consecrated as a deaconess.

That office was highly controversial and had even been forbidden by the Church in the 6th century, though several women besides Sigolena are found to have held the office in the 7th century. A deaconess was defined as a widowed woman who took a nun's vows and devoted herself to prayer, abstinence, and charitable work. However, she was also blessed with an authority similar to that of a priest—she could administer the sacraments and give benediction to a congregation. Hence the controversy over the legitimacy of the office, since the Church wavered on the question of women's sanctity and their ability to exercise authority over the souls of men. Sigolena served as deaconess for many years, and was canonized shortly after her death.

**SOURCES:**

Dunbar, Agnes. *Dictionary of Saintly Women, vol. I*. London: G. Bell, 1904.

Klapisch-Zuber, Christiane, ed. *A History of Women in the West, vol. II: Silences of the Middle Ages*. Cambridge: Belknap-Harvard, 1992.

**Laura York**, M.A. in History,
University of California, Riverside, California

# Sigourney, Lydia H. (1791–1865)

*American author and poet. Pronunciation: Sig-ER-nee. Born Lydia Howard Huntley on September 1,*

*1791, in Norwich, Connecticut; died on June 10, 1865, in Hartford, Connecticut; only child of Ezekiel Huntley (a gardener) and Zerviah or Sophia (Wentworth) Huntley; educated in Norwich and Hartford; married Charles Sigourney (a hardware merchant), on June 16, 1819 (died 1854); children: Mary (b. 1827); Andrew (b. 1831); and three others (stillborn); stepchildren: three.*

*Selected works: Moral Pieces, in Prose and Verse (1815); The Square Table (anonymously, 1819); Sketch of Connecticut, Forty Years Since (anonymously, 1824); Evening Readings in History (anonymously, 1833); The Farmer and the Soldier (1833); Letters to Young Ladies (1833); Tales and Essays for Children (1835); Letters to Mothers (1839); \*Pocahontas, and Other Poems (1841); Pleasant Memories of Pleasant Lands (1842); The Voice of Flowers (1846); The Weeping Willow (1847); Olive Leaves (1852); Past Meridian (1854); The Daily Counsellor (1859); The Man of Uz, and Other Poems (1862); Letters of Life (1866).*

Known as "the sweet singer of Hartford," Lydia H. Sigourney was the one of the best-known poets (together with \*Frances Osgood and ◀❧ Elizabeth Oakes Smith) publishing in the early-to-mid-19th century. She was a highly prolific writer whose vast popularity influenced other women writers of her day, but whose importance did not survive into the 20th century. Largely forgotten, her work is considered by contemporary critics as overly affected, morally pious, and sentimental.

Born in Norwich, Connecticut, in 1791, the only child of Ezekiel and **Zerviah Wentworth Huntley**, Lydia was surrounded by people who encouraged her love for reading and writing. Her father worked as a gardener for **Madame Lathrop**, the widow of Dr. Daniel Lathrop and the daughter of the Hon. Joseph Talcott, governor of Connecticut. The elderly Mrs. Lathrop was so fond of Sigourney that she often asked her to read aloud from the Bible and from Edward Young's *Night Thoughts*. Lydia's mother

encouraged her to read \***Ann Radcliffe**'s *The Mysteries of Udolpho*, and prodded her to write a novel of her own.

Present at Mrs. Lathrop's death, Sigourney was apparently so grief-stricken that her parents sent her to Hartford to stay with the Wadsworths, relatives of the deceased. There she received further instruction from the wealthy Daniel Wadsworth and spent a few months attending local female seminaries. For three years beginning in 1811, Lydia and a friend, **Nancy Maria Hyde**, ran their own school for young ladies. Wadsworth, however, eventually asked her to teach in a school he had opened for the education of his daughter's friends; she continued to teach while launching a writing career, which rapidly assumed center stage. In 1815, she published her first book, *Moral Pieces, in Prose and Verse*, based upon material previously prepared for her students. With subscriptions secured by Wadsworth, she used the profits of the book to support her aging parents. The following year, her work appeared in periodicals such as the *North American Review*.

Upon her marriage in 1819 to Charles Sigourney, a Hartford hardware entrepreneur and widower with three children of his own, Sigourney relinquished her teaching position. Moreover, her husband demanded that Sigourney publish her work anonymously, deeming it unseemly for a woman to garner public attention. Although she devoted much time to decorating the home he built for her and raising their children, Sigourney was also active in charitable work and philanthropy, contributing regularly to at least 20 periodicals to raise funds for favored causes.

Sigourney emerged from anonymity when her husband's business prospects declined and they were forced to sell their large home. She began to publish prolifically, particularly in magazines and journals after 1832. In 1833, she produced her most famous book, *Letters to Young Ladies*, and within a year had published eight more volumes. Now the family breadwinner, Sigourney became a dominant presence in American magazines of the mid-19th century. Estimates of her work include thousands of magazine articles and poems in nearly 300 different publications, most of which were compiled and republished in book form. By 1850, Sigourney had achieved a popularity in both America and Europe equal to that of famed poets Henry Wadsworth Longfellow and William Cullen Bryant. Several American magazine publishers, including *Godey's Lady's Book*, *Ladies' Com-*

*Lydia H. Sigourney*

❧▶
**Smith, Elizabeth Oakes.** *See* Anthony, Susan B. for sidebar.

*panion*, and *Graham's Magazine*, competed for her name on the title pages of their publications.

At least part of Sigourney's popularity lay in her business acumen and methods of aggressive self-promotion. She cultivated the acquaintance of influential literary, social, and political figures on both sides of the Atlantic through unsolicited correspondence and visits to illustrious figures' homes, often leaving copies of her work with them. She had a habit of exaggerating the most casual of acquaintances into unsupported intimacy for the purposes of greater fame and increased sales.

Sigourney's writing was always highly personal, for she drew upon her own interpretations of historical events, her own conversations and thoughts, and even aspects of daily housework for inspiration. Her work was highly patriotic, moralistic, religious, and consistently pious (temperance was a frequent theme). Sigourney's most frequent topic, and one with which she would have much experience, was the death of children. Three of her own were stillborn, and a son, Andrew, died of consumption at age 19. However, her poems were optimistic, often ending with the image of the child's spirit ascending to heaven.

Although contemporary critics fault Sigourney's work for its sentimentality, likening it to greeting-card verse, women writers of Sigourney's time were relegated to the sphere of the sentimental for their subject matter. Further, Sigourney's fulfillment of the American dream as a poor girl who had grown famous appealed to her female readership's hopes and dreams for themselves. Although much of her fame derived from the unsophisticated literary tastes of her readers, she became popular precisely because she was able to put their thoughts into words, and she practiced the lessons that her poems taught: sobriety, thrift, patience, and virtue.

Sigourney completed her autobiography, *Letters of Life*, shortly before her death on June 10, 1865. Published in 1866, its scant mention of her husband may imply the unhappiness that permeated their marriage. By this time, her popularity was very much in decline, due mainly to the changing tastes of her audience. Although she failed to achieve literary immortality and outlived her own fame, she was an immensely popular poet who became a role model for similarly industrious women of her day.

**SOURCES:**

Baym, Nina. "The Rise of the Woman Author," in *Columbia Literary History of the United States*. NY: Columbia University Press, 1988, pp. 296–298.

Bowles, Dorothy A. "Lydia H. Sigourney," in *Dictionary of Literary Biography*, Vol. 73: *American Magazine Journalists, 1741–1850*. Detroit, MI: Gale Research, 1988.

Gay, Carol. "Lydia Huntley Sigourney," in *Dictionary of Literary Biography*, Vol. 42: *American Writers for Children Before 1900*. Detroit, MI: Gale Research, 1985.

James, Edward T., ed. *Notable American Women, 1607–1950*. Cambridge, MA: The Belknap Press of Harvard University, 1971.

McHenry, Robert, ed. *Famous American Women*. NY: Dover, 1980.

**Howard Gofstein**, freelance writer, Detroit, Michigan

## Sigrid the Haughty (d. before 1013)

*Queen of Denmark. Born in Sweden; died before 1013; daughter of Tosti-Skogul; married Eric VI the Victorious, king of Sweden; became second wife of Sven or Sweyn I Forkbeard, king of Denmark (r. 985–1014), king of England (r. 1014), around 996 (divorced); children: (first marriage) Olof or Olaf Skötkonung or Skötkonung, king of Sweden (r. 994–1022); Holmfrid Ericsdottir (who married Svein, earl of Ladir); (second marriage) Svantoslava; \*Estrith (fl. 1017–1032). Sigrid the Haughty also had a liaison with Vissavald, prince of Kiev; Sweyn's first wife was \*Gunhilda of Poland (d. around 1015).*

## Sigurana, Caterina (fl. 1543)

*Italian heroine. Name variations: Catherine. Flourished around 1543.*

In 1543, aided by Khair ad-din Barbarossa and his Muslim Turks, Francis I, king of France, began a two-month siege of Nice; the defenders of Nice refused various offers to surrender. A huge attack was mounted against the city on August 15, the city wall was breached, and a Turkish standard-bearer was able to plant his flag. At this point, Caterina Sigurana, a washerwoman, attacked the Turk and stole the standard. Her achievement spurred her fellow defenders to renewed efforts, and Nice continued to hold against its attackers. Though the city was surrendered on August 23, the castle was not taken and the besiegers withdrew in early September. Caterina Sigurana has been remembered ever since as a hero of the city.

## Sigurdsen, Gertrud (1923—)

*Swedish politician. Born on January 11, 1923 (one source cites 1928), in Nävekvarn, Sweden; children: two sons.*

Gertrude Sigurdsen began her 40-year career in Swedish politics in 1949, as Secretary for the Confederation of Trade Unions—a position she held for 15 years before becoming Information Secretary of the Information Division in 1964. Five years later, in 1969, she was elected as a Social Democrat to Parliament, where she served as Minister for Internal Development Assistance from 1973 to 1976 and was a member of the Parliament Standing Committee on Foreign Affairs until 1982. Focusing attention on public health issues, she became Minister for Public Health and Medical Services in 1982, and served as Minister for Health and Social Affairs from 1985 until her retirement in 1989.

**Howard Gofstein**, freelance writer,
Detroit, Michigan

# Sikakane, Joyce Nomafa (1943—)

*South African journalist and anti-apartheid activist. Name variations: Joyce Sikhakane. Born Joyce Nomafa Sikakane in 1943 in Soweto, South Africa; daughter of Amelia Nxumalo and Jonathan Sikakane; attended Orlando High School; married Kenneth Rankin (a physician); children: Nkosinathi; Nomzamo; Samora; Vikela.*

Joyce
Sikakane

*Worked as a reporter for the* World, *Johannesburg (1960–68); was a freelance reporter for the* Rand Daily Mail *and a staff reporter with the* Post *and the* Drum *(1968); became the first African female staff reporter at the* Rand Daily Mail *(1968); detained under Terrorism Act (May 12, 1969); charged under Suppression of Communism Act (December 1, 1969); released with banning orders (September 14, 1970); went into exile in Zambia (July 1973); family reunited and married Kenneth Rankin.*

Before she leaves for work every morning, a mother locks her young children in a room from which all sharp objects have been removed. There they remain, with a plate of food and a chamberpot, until she returns in the evening. Incidents such as this were part of the daily lives of the citizens of Soweto. Soweto township in the Republic of South Africa, writes one historian, was "a bastard child born out of circumstances following the dispossession of the African people and the discovery of gold in the Witwatersrand."

In Soweto township in 1943, in a four-room house located in Orlando, a second girl was born to the Sikakane household. Her parents named her Joyce; her grandfather named her Nomafa (inheritance). Her mother **Amelia Nxumalo** stayed home with the children, knowing that this was the only way they would get good care. When the children were old enough, they were sent to church schools in a futile attempt to shield them from the government-mandated "Bantu" education system, which aimed to make black children subservient to whites and fit only for manual labor.

After finishing high school, Sikakane, like many of her classmates, refused on principle to attend the apartheid government's tribal colleges. Instead, she pursued her interest in writing and in 1960 began reporting for the *World*, a newspaper run by whites that catered to the black population of Johannesburg. Sikakane's job description was listed with the authorities as that of a filing clerk, since the law forbade African women from doing such skilled work as reporting.

In 1968, dissatisfied with the sensationalistic stories that she was expected to file at the *World*, Sikakane applied to the *Rand Daily Mail* for a position. Reluctant to hire an African woman as a reporter, the paper took her on as a freelancer. She also fell in love and became engaged to a Scottish doctor, Kenneth Rankin, but their mixed-race relationship was illegal in South Africa. Rankin returned to Scotland; Sikakane prepared to join him. Meanwhile, she built a name for herself at the *Rand Daily Mail*, reporting extensively on the impact of apartheid in the townships. She continued to demand that the paper put her on its staff. "Because the *Mail* was taking a long time in deciding on my job prospects," she wrote, "I staged a demonstration by walking out and taking a full-time job with *Post* and *Drum*. . . . As I was now in great demand, I wanted to prove a point to the *Mail* that as an intelligent black woman journalist I was a force to be reckoned with." The *Rand Daily Mail* gave in to her demands, and Joyce Sikakane became their first female African staff reporter.

Her triumph was short-lived. Less than a year later, at 2 AM on May 12, 1969, the police appeared at Amelia Nxumalo's door. They searched the house and placed Sikakane under detention. Brought to Pretoria Central Prison, she was kept alone in a dank, windowless cell and interrogated numerous times, once for three days straight, about her activities on behalf of the outlawed African National Congress (ANC). As she wrote, "[W]hat we had been doing was something that would not, in any other country, be considered 'terroristic': we were involved with the welfare of political prisoners, helping to make arrangements for families of prisoners to visit their husbands or parents." On December 1, 1969, after more than six months in prison, Sikakane was among 21 activists, including **Winnie Madikizela-Mandela**, **Martha Dhlamini**, **Thokozile Mngoma** and **Rita Ndzanga**, charged on 21 counts under the Suppression of Communism Act. The trial, a farce, did more to expose the state's brutality than prove a case against the accused. One witness for the prosecution was fellow activist **Shanthie Naidoo**, whom Sikakane and the others had been told had volunteered to testify against them. Brought from her jail cell to the courtroom, Naidoo said on the witness stand that she had been threatened with the arrest of her entire family to force her to testify, and then cited her friendship with Sikakane and Madikizela-Mandela in declining to give evidence. "I will not be able to live with my conscience if I do," she said. (She subsequently spent four months in solitary confinement.) On February 16, 1970, all charges against the activists were withdrawn. With relatives singing in celebration, Sikakane and the others began to leave the courtroom. The police promptly re-detained them before they had a chance to leave the building.

Sikakane spent another six months in prison, separated from the general convict population but able to hear the sounds of guards beating women prisoners with *sjamboks* and the hymns men prisoners sang before one of their number was hanged. Along with the other activists, she was finally released in September, after 17 months in prison. They were then served with banning orders, which were used by the apartheid government to restrict the movement and activities of "political agitators." As a banned person, in effect a non-person, Sikakane returned to Soweto, itself a non-place, jokingly called "so-where-to" by the people who lived there.

Unable to find permanent employment, and with the threat of another government crackdown in the air, Sikakane decided in 1973 to leave South Africa for Zambia and the exiled branch of the ANC. Once beyond the borders of the apartheid state, she finally was able to marry. Together with Rankin and their four children, Sikakane lived in Scotland and then in Zimbabwe, writing and campaigning, continuing to fight against the injustices of apartheid that she had witnessed in her birthplace of Soweto. Her autobiographical *A Window on Soweto* was published in 1977.

**SOURCES:**

Sikakane, Joyce. *A Window on Soweto*. London: International Defence and Aid Fund, 1977.

**SUGGESTED READING:**

Busby, Margaret, ed. *Daughters of Africa*. London: Jonathan Cape, 1992.

Mandela, Winnie. *Part of My Soul Went with Him*. Edited by Anne Benjamin, adapted by Mary Benson. Reinbek bei Hamburg: Rowohlt Taschenbuch Verlag GmbH, 1984.

Berrian, Brenda, ed. *Bibliography of African Women Writers and Journalists*. Boulder, CO: Lynne Reinner, 1985.

**Muhonjia Khaminwa**, freelance writer, Cambridge, Massachusetts

# Silang, Gabriela (1731–1763)

*Leader of a revolt in the Ilocos region of the Philippines in 1763 aimed at establishing a government to replace the Spanish colonial government.* Name variations: Josefa Gabriela Silang. Born Maria Josefa Gabriela Silang on March 19, 1731, in the village of Caniogan, town of Santa, Ilocos Sur, in the Spanish-colonized Philippines; executed by hanging on September 20, 1763, in the town of Vigan, Ilocos Sur; parents unknown except that her father was an Ilocano peasant and her mother was an Itneg, two ethno-linguistic groups in the Ilocos region of the northern Philippines; obtained the equivalent of elementary schooling in the convent school of her town; married a rich widower around 1751 (died); married Diego Silang (leader of the Ilocano or Ilokano revolution), around 1757 (assassinated May 28, 1763); no children.

*Separated from her pagan mother in early childhood, and reared as a Christian by the town's parish priest; first marriage arranged by her father (c. 1751); after she was widowed, married Diego Silang (c. 1757); British seized Philippines from the Spanish (1762); after Diego's assassination, assumed leadership of the rebellion against Spanish colonial rule until her defeat (1763).*

In a public square in Makati, metropolitan Manila, stands a monument of Gabriela Silang on horseback. Her story, celebrated in poetry and song, has inspired other women of the Philippines to leadership in revolutionary movements, including "Santa" in the province of Leyte in 1862, and the image of a widow as leader found its modern counterpart in the career of *Corazon Aquino, elected the country's first woman president in 1986. In the modern Philippines, there is also an umbrella organization, involved in women's rights and other political causes ranging from the ouster of foreign military bases to opposition to nuclear power plants, named in honor of the 18th-century Gabriela.

$\mathcal{G}$abriela Silang's passion for justice drove her to continue the armed struggle begun by her husband. She infused the struggle with the brilliance and serenity of a woman warrior.

—Lilia Quindoza Santiago, Filipino poet

Despite all this, in a society influenced by Christian values resulting from more than 300 years of Spanish colonial rule, women in Philippine society have long been considered secondary to men. Even Gabriela, living at a time when society constricted her development into a fully rounded person, was overshadowed by her husband. Her achievement in becoming a revolutionary leader is therefore all the more worthy of the praise she has been accorded.

At the time of Gabriela Silang's birth in the town of Santa in the Ilocos region, the Philippines had been under Spanish colonial rule for almost 200 years. Santa was a suburb of Vigan, the principal maritime town of northern Philippines, and both were strategic colonial outposts at the mouth of the Abra River. In turn, the river was the gateway to the Cordilleras, the mountain ranges inhabited by the Itnegs (also called Tinguians) and other pagan tribes of northern Philippines. Between the upland agricultural communities and the lowland towns and cities there was considerable exchange of goods, and the coastal maritime towns in par-

ticular were the hubs of commerce with the outside world, where Chinese merchants brought in porcelain, silk and other luxuries to exchange for products brought by the Spanish from Mexico and Spain. Even before the arrival of the Spanish conquistadors, Vigan had been visited by Chinese, Indian and Arab traders. Gold dust, hand-woven cotton cloth, beeswax, resin, rice wine, and rice cakes were among the goods shipped from there to Manila, the major Spanish metropolis and capital in the Philippines. When natural disasters such as flooding and typhoons prevented commerce with the capital, Vigan was at times the rival of Manila, its prosperity visible in the concentration of big old stone houses with tiled roofs owned by settlers of foreign extraction.

The marriage of Gabriela's parents also suggests that there was more to the interaction between upland and lowland communities than the exchange of goods. Little is actually known about Gabriela's early life, except that her father was Christian and her mother remained pagan, and that Gabriela stayed in her mother's village at some time in her youth, when she developed a liking for the tribespeople. The cross-cultural marriage of her parents could also suggest that the Christianized citizens of Philippine towns in the 18th century did not emulate the Spanish pretensions of racial superiority towards other pagan ethnic groups, but we might also surmise that cultural differences played a part in the parents' separation. Gabriela lived in two worlds, staying in her mother's village and later staying with her father, who had ambitions for his daughter: she would marry a rich man.

She acquired the equivalent of an elementary school education in the church convent, where Father Tomas Millan, the town's parish priest, considered her an adopted daughter. Legend has it that when she once saw a poor woman in the churchyard, she handed over a priceless pendant as an act of charity, indicating the values of charity and philanthropy developed under the church's influence.

At age 20, Gabriela was betrothed by her father to a rich widower. He died shortly after their marriage, and Gabriela became a wealthy young widow, attracting many suitors, including Diego Silang, an educated man of means in Vigan who became her second husband. The coupled remained childless, but lived happily for five years. In this period, Diego became the trusted messenger of Father Millan, Gabriela's foster father, delivering confidential reports and bringing back letters from Manila. He made

Gabriela
Silang

contacts and friendships, and had many conversations with a Spanish lawyer, Santiago Orendain. Their friendship would later become crucial in Diego's negotiations with the British, when events beyond the Philippines began to affect their lives.

During the Seven Years' War then being waged in Europe, colonies of the various European powers were drawn at times into the fray. Spain, because it was allied with France, was subject to attack by the British, and in 1762 British warships sailed from their ports in India to oust the Spaniards from their colonial outpost at Manila. The government in Manila, caught by surprise, immediately handed over the city to the invaders, and the archbishop of Manila was made governor-general. Elsewhere in the Philippine archipelago, however, the Spaniards continued to resist, and further pacification proved less easy. To soften Spanish resistance, the British began to promise reforms to the colonized natives, sowing seeds of revolt throughout the Philippine territory. After the conquest of Manila, the Silangs were among those who viewed the arrival of the British as an opportunity to gain independence for their people.

As Diego was drawn into inciting rebellion, the spirit of charity and philanthropy sown in Gabriela's childhood found fruition in her close collaboration with her husband in the cause against oppression. In their country, the *principales* were the class of prosperous native elites who worked for the Spaniards as administrators and tax collectors, wielding tremendous political and economic power, able to exploit the people by collecting taxes over and above those decreed by the Spaniards. When the Silangs raised the slogan "wrest power from the *principales* and restore it to the people," they were setting out to overturn the social pyramid by attacking the class to which they themselves belonged. At first it was only the people of the towns who rallied behind the banner of the revolt, but the Silangs also hoped to broaden their power base by attracting a combined force of the inland Tinguian warriors and Ilocanos. Meanwhile, the Silangs had organized a force, armed with all sorts of weapons, that joined in a march and defeated the Spanish in a decisive battle at the town of Cabugao; soon afterward, the Spanish were ousted from Vigan. Under British protection, Diego Silang assumed the position of captain-general and local governor in Vigan. On December 14, 1762, he proclaimed the independence of the Ilocos region and established a government of the people.

Both the ousted Spanish functionaries and members of the elite were naturally aghast at the changes Diego had instituted, overturning practices that had allowed them to enrich themselves at the expense of the poor by practicing exactions and illegal usury. His actions also freed common men from the hated feudal practices of *corvée*, or unpaid labor, and the paying of tribute, requiring instead that the *principales* pay for the maintenance and upkeep of the government. In return, he promised to allow the elite to live normal lives provided that they did not openly defy the government, although the priests of some towns were put under house arrest at the convent in Bantay town.

The offended church functionaries and elites were soon allied in planning the Silangs' assassination. Two friends of Diego, Miguel Vicos and Pedro Becbec, were hired to carry out the plot. On May 28, 1763, on the pretext of showing a summary of the tax collection, they gained entry into the Silang house, past unsuspecting guards. According to the account of an Augustinian priest, Fray Vivar, Diego had just come out of a room when Vicos "took out his *trabuco* [blunderbuss], discharged all its contents, and Silang fell dead." The fallen body was stabbed several times before the assassins made their escape, while a group of the elites distracted the Silang forces by creating confusion in the town.

Gabriela, having escaped assassination, swore to avenge the death of her husband. Rallying troops under the leadership of Nicolas Cariño and other trusted aides of Diego, she withdrew to Pidigan, Abra, her mother's town, in search of support from Tinguian mountain warriors. Eventually, she was able to organize a force that made a dramatic surprise attack against Becbec and his followers in the town of Santa, putting her enemies to flight. Then she joined with Cariño's forces in the town of Cabugao, where a fortress for the revolutionary army was established.

The Spaniards soon had a force of 6,000 organized for a counterattack. In a battle employing firearms and bows and arrows, both sides fought with daring, but the Tinguian mountain warriors, unaccustomed to fighting in the plains, were scattered by the firefight, Cariño was hit by musketfire, and the revolutionary army had to retreat to the hills of Abra. On July 11, 1763, the Spaniards marched in victory back into Vigan.

Gabriela reorganized a Tinguian force of 2,000 men, combined with the remnants of Cariño's defeated force, and headed toward Vigan, but the military advance did not remain secret for long. Her former foster parent, Father Millan, now governor of Vigan, commanded 300 archers to attack the flanks of Gabriela's troops while his main force waited in the town square. In the suburb of Bantay, Gabriela's army set fire to the houses of the town's elites and *principales* before advancing on the walled town. Although the image of Gabriela entering Vigan on horseback at the head of her army is a romantically vivid and lasting image, the attack was in fact the perfect setup for an ambush. While enemy archers rained arrows on her army's flanks, her forces were hit from the front by cannon balls and musket fire, and the terrified Tinguian warriors retreated in panic. Scattered and demoralized, the survivors fled back to their camp in Abra.

Gabriela had no time to regroup her troops. On September 20, 1763, a Spanish force, led by Manuel Arza y Urrutia, pushed into the Abra hinterlands in search of her camp, offering rewards to other warrior tribes in the Cordilleras. After a prolonged pursuit through the mountains, Gabriela and 90 of her followers were captured. She was returned to Vigan, where she suffered humiliation and psychological torture, forced to witness the flogging of hundreds of her suspected followers and the hanging of 90 more, before she herself climbed the scaffold to her execution. Her period of leadership had been brief, but her martyrdom and courage made her a lasting example to women of the Philippines.

**SOURCES:**

Ancheta, Herminia M., and Michaela Gonzales. *Filipino Women in Nation Building.* Quezon City: Phoenix, 1984, pp. 248–249.

De los Reyes, J.P. "A Heroine of Ilocandia," in *Chronicle Magazine.* Vol. 18, no. 26. September 28, 1963.

Pagador, Flaviano R. "Maria Josefa Gabriela Silang, the Great Ilocano Heroine," in *Ilocos Review.* Vol. 2, no. 2, 1970.

Routledge, David. *Diego Silang and the Origins of Philippine Nationalism.* Quezon City: Philippine Center for Advanced Studies, 1979.

Simbulan, Clemente. "Women Patriots of Yesterday," in *Filipina.* Vol. 1, no. 22. November 1944.

Zaide, Gregorio. *Great Filipinos in History.* Manila: Verde Bookstore, 1970, pp. 594–597.

**Jaime B. Veneracion**,
chair of the Department of History,
University of the Philippines,
Diliman, Quezon City, Philippines

## Silanpää, Miina (1866–1952).

*See Sillanpää, Miina.*

## Silesia, duchess of.

*See Hedwig of Silesia (1174–1243).*
*See Anna of Bohemia (fl. 1230s).*

## Silinga, Annie (1910–1983)

*Member of the African National Congress, organizer of the first Federation of South African Women's conference, and lifelong opponent of pass laws. Pronunciation: See-LEE-nga (nasal "ng" as in "gong"). Born in 1910 in the Transkei, South Africa; died in Langa, South Africa, in 1983; married; children.*

*Moved with husband to Cape Town, Somerset West (1937); joined the Langa branch of the ANC, arrested during Defiance Campaign (1952); was part of group that planned the first Federation of South African Women's conference in Cape Town (1953);* *led women of the Western Cape in anti pass-law protests (1954); arrested for refusing to carry a pass (1955); deported to Namaqualand, returned to Cape Town and was arrested again, one of 156 activists arrested and charged with treason (1956); released after charges were dropped (1957); elected president of the Cape Town ANC Women's League (1958); arrested after Sharpeville and Langa massacres (1960).*

For over six months in 1952, the African National Congress (ANC) and the South African Indian Congress organized a campaign of civil disobedience against the National Party government of South Africa. They mobilized the people to challenge the laws that segregated public spaces in South Africa according to race. Although she had just joined the Langa branch of the ANC, Annie Silinga was one of the many participants arrested during the Defiance Campaign. Together with her six-month-old baby, she served two weeks in jail. Undeterred, Silinga devoted the rest of her life to resisting apartheid, especially the application of pass laws to women. Her determination served as an example to many others who followed her in the struggle.

*I used to sit and think, and worry, about what would happen to my children under apartheid if I should die—that gave me the strength to fight.*

—Annie Silinga

Silinga became interested in politics after attending meetings in the township of Langa, Cape Town, where she lived. She first moved to Cape Town from the Transkei in 1937 when she was 27 years old. Her childhood had been happy, during a time of plenty, before overpopulation led to soil erosion and overgrazing of the land. Teenage girls of her generation spent their days helping maintain the family compound and looking after the younger children. The Transkei was part of the reserves, the 13% of land where the majority non-white population was allowed to live. By 1937, conditions had deteriorated to the point where Silinga was desperate to move. Her "babies," she said, "had been dying in the Transkei." When her husband found work in the Cape, Silinga joined him, hoping for better medical facilities.

For the first time, they could live together as a family. At his previous job in the mines of Johannesburg, accommodation was not provided for the families of the mine-workers and regulations forbade women from staying there for extended periods. In the Cape, Silinga and her husband had five children and together led what she described as a traditional life. The family moved into the new African township of Langa after

World War II. It was here that Silinga attended meetings at which measures to improve conditions for the community were discussed. Out of concern for the future of her children, she decided to join the African National Congress.

The white-supremacist National Party had come into power in 1948, largely on the vote of white farmers. Determined to preserve "white power," they set about increasing apartheid policies. Through the 1950s, the National Party passed legislation codifying the Bantustan policy whereby Africans were increasingly restricted to the reserves. The Abolition of Pass Laws and Co-ordination of Documents Act (1952), in true doublespeak, actually strengthened the government's ability to control the movement of Africans in and out of the urban centers. As well, the pass system was extended to include women. The Group Areas Act (1950), the Suppression of Communism Act (1950), and the Bantu Education Act (1953) sought to further segregate the different races, suppress opposition to the government policies, and, through the schools, restrict the opportunities African youth had to acquire a meaningful education.

The government's determination to issue passes to women sparked a decade of marches, petitions, and demonstrations by South African women. Annie Silinga led such a protest in the Western Cape in 1954. Alarmed by the resistance, the government delayed issuing passes until 1956. Even then, women continued to protest: burning passes, refusing to register, and holding mass demonstrations.

In 1953, Silinga, by then a member of the ANC Women's League (ANCWL), was part of the core group that organized the first meeting of the Federation of South African Women (FSAW), to harness the outrage of women against the pass-law issue. The group was led by Ray Alexander, communist and trade unionist, and included **Gladys Smith** of the Cape Housewives' League, **Katie White** of the Women's Food Committee, and **Dora Tamanda** of the ANCWL and the Communist Party of South Africa. At the first conference, held in Johannesburg in April 1954,

*Annie*
*Silinga*

delegates pledged to build a multiracial organization that would both advocate for women's rights and fight against the apartheid government. During the conference, a National Executive Committee was elected to coordinate the direction the organization would take. Silinga was one of those elected to the NEC.

The following year, Silinga was arrested for refusing to register for a pass. Under the Group Areas Act, the Cape Town region had been declared a "Colored" zone where only individuals of mixed African and European ancestry could live. Despite having lived in the region since 1937, Silinga was deported to Namaqualand in the Transkei in February 1956. She was taken there under police escort, but ever defiant she returned to her home in Langa as soon as she could. Arrested again, she was later released. Through the years, Silinga continued to defy attempts to remove her from the Cape. She never registered for a pass and always returned home to Langa.

"You have tampered with the women; you have struck a rock." This battle cry was unleashed on August 9, 1956, when 20,000 women organized by the FSAW marched on the prime minister's office in Pretoria to protest the issuing of passes. Unable to see Prime Minister Strijdom, they left piles of signed protest letters outside his office. That day was extremely important in the history of South Africa.

The anti-pass demonstrations were part of a campaign of mass civil disobedience launched by the Congress Alliance in the early 1950s. The Alliance was a grouping of various anti-apartheid organizations, including the ANC, the South African Indian Congress, and the Congress of Democrats. In late 1956, the government cracked down on the Alliance, arresting 156 leaders and charging them with treason and conspiring to overthrow the state. Silinga was arrested along with Oliver Tambo and Nelson Mandela, future leader of the independent Republic of South Africa, and such FSAW leaders as *Lilian Ngoyi and *Helen Joseph.

Mandela in his autobiography recalls that by making the arrests, the government had unknowingly convened the "largest and longest unbanned meeting of the Congress Alliance in years." After a couple of weeks, the accused were released on bail. The initial phase of the Treason Trial lasted until December 1957 when the state dropped charges against 61 of the defendants. Silinga was one of those released.

Annie Silinga continued her activism. She was elected president of the Cape Town ANCWL in 1958. Two years later, she was one of those arrested after the police massacred Africans during demonstrations protesting the pass-laws in Sharpeville and Langa townships. Again she was released without being charged. That same year, the white government banned the ANC as an illegal organization.

Silinga lived in Langa until her death in 1983. At that time, she was being cared for by her children. Without a pass, she could not receive her pension and other benefits that would have helped in her old age. She was proud to have opposed the humiliation of the pass despite these costs. Shortly before she died, she told an interviewer: "I should like to live in a South Africa where black, white, and colored women can all work and live together without trouble. Even now we must try and stand together." Seven years later, the ANC was unbanned.

**SOURCES:**

Lipman, Beata. *We Make Freedom: Women in South Africa.* Boston, MA: Pandora Press, 1984.

Van Vuuren, Nancy. *Women Against Apartheid: The Fight for Freedom in South Africa, 1920–1975.* Palo Alto, CA: R&E Research Associates, 1979.

Walker, Cheryl. *Women and Resistance in South Africa.* NY: Monthly Review Press, 1982, 1991.

**SUGGESTED READING:**

Lapchick, Richard E., and Stephanie Urdang. *Oppression and Resistance: The Struggle of Women in Southern Africa.* Westport, CT: Greenwood Press, 1982.

Mandela, Nelson Rolihlahla. *Long Walk to Freedom: The Autobiography of Nelson Mandela.* MA: Little, Brown.

**Muhonjia Khaminwa**, writer, Cambridge, Massachusetts

# Silkwood, Karen (1946–1974)

*American anti-nuclear activist and lab technician who—possibly armed with information that proved tampering in quality control at the Kerr-McGee plutonium plant in Oklahoma City—was killed while driving to meet a reporter from* The New York Times. *Born Karen Gay Silkwood on February 19, 1946, in Longview, Texas; died in a car accident on her way to Oklahoma City, Oklahoma, on November 13, 1974; daughter of William Silkwood (a paint contractor); attended Lamar College in Beaumont; married Bill Meadows, in 1966 (divorced 1972); children: three.*

*Interested in science, had taken lab technician courses before applying to work in Kerr-McGee's Cimarron nuclear facility in Oklahoma City (1972); became suspicious of a poor plant safety record of 17 contamination incidents involving 77 employees, all the more so after she was contaminated (1974); determined to prove the need for better safeguards for workers, gathered information to deliver to David Burnham, a reporter; killed in an auto accident (1974); no trace of the information she was carrying was ever found.*

Karen Silkwood was born in 1946 in Longview and grew up in Nederland, in the heart of the Texas petrochemical region halfway between Port Arthur and Beaumont, where the hum of oil refineries broke the stillness. At night, their bright lights and tall torches lit the sky. The petrochemical industry had long supported the Silkwood family both directly and indirectly. Her grandfather was employed in one of the first oil refineries in the area, joining the Oil, Chemical, and Atomic Workers (OCAW) union. Karen's father was a paint contractor and her mother worked in a bank. Like their neighbors, the Silkwoods were moderately prosperous. The eldest of three girls, Silkwood had an ordinary childhood, happy and secure. She rode her bike, played with dolls, and enjoyed tennis. A member of Future Homemakers of America, Silkwood played flute in the band and was on the volleyball team.

*[I]f something was wrong, [Silkwood] was not going to stand by and ignore it.*

—Karen Miller Patterson

But Karen Silkwood also excelled in science at a time when science was considered a field for men. She especially loved chemistry. A good student, she was a member of the National Honor Society and one of 22 honor graduates in the class of 1964. Classmates at the local high school remembered a well-rounded individual who stuck by her principles. Noted her friend **Karen Miller Patterson**:

> As I remember Karen, she was the kind of person who, if something was wrong, was not going to stand by and ignore it. She was not afraid to stick her neck out. When she went into anything, she put everything into it and she stayed with it. It was like that in the band, in sports—even down to batting a volleyball around in my driveway at night. She was intensely loyal. She'd stick up for her friends.

After graduating from high school, Silkwood attended Lamar College in Beaumont on a scholarship from the Business Professional Women's Club. She spent the first summer after her freshman year at her grandmother's in Kilgore, Texas, where she met Bill Matthews; the two eloped after a whirlwind courtship.

Married life proved difficult. Matthews worked in the oil fields, which meant constant moves throughout Texas and Oklahoma. As well, three children were born in quick succession, and financial difficulties eventually led to bankruptcy. After several years, Silkwood left her husband, taking the children with her; she supported the family by working in hospitals. When Matthews filed for divorce and decided to remarry, Silkwood realized single motherhood was too great a burden for her to manage successfully. She offered Matthews and his new wife custody of the children, explaining to her parents and friends that they would provide a more stable environment. In 1972, Karen Silkwood moved to Oklahoma City to work in a laboratory at the Cimarron facility of Kerr-McGee.

She was enthusiastic about her new position. As a producer of fuel rods used in nuclear fission reactors, Kerr-McGee was on the frontlines of modern technology. Having taken high school and college courses in advanced chemistry, trigonometry, physics, zoology, and radiology, Silkwood felt her scientific skills could be used in the laboratory. She had always been extremely conscientious and meticulous, qualities which this work demanded. Not long after she began working at the Cimarron river plant, Silkwood joined the Oil, Chemical, and Atomic Workers Union, probably because her grandfather had once been a member. When the union went on strike in 1972, she walked the picket line. After nine weeks, she returned to work when the strike proved unsuccessful.

Over the next two years, Silkwood established a new life in Oklahoma. She fell in love and became involved with Drew Stephens, a fellow laboratory analyst, though he was married at the time. After a few months, Stephens left his wife and filed for divorce. A sports car enthusiast, he taught Silkwood to drive in rallies and competitions; she turned out to be an excellent driver and won several trophies. The couple enjoyed collecting records, especially rock, as well as country and western. Union activities were another shared interest. Silkwood was elected as one of three governing committee members of the OCAW local in the spring of 1974. Her expanded union activities were to change the focus of her life and eventually lead to her death.

Silkwood's first sense that things were not as they should be at the Kerr-McGee facility occurred in May 1974: a co-worker fainted on the job. When health officers tried to revive the worker with smelling salts and then brought in a faulty oxygen tank, Silkwood was outraged. She began to complain, convinced that better procedures should be in place in a facility that manufactured nuclear rods. That summer, Silkwood and her co-workers noticed a production speedup and a rapid turnover of employees. Between January and October 1974, 99 of 287 workers, or 35% of the workforce, left the facility. Kerr-McGee was requiring its employees to put in 12-hour days and giving them little notice when they were changed from day to night shifts. A high turnover rate, long hours, and continual shift changes inevitably led to a precipitous decline in safety standards. Silkwood was well aware of the dangers of the plutonium handled at the plant. One of the most toxic substances on earth, plutonium is 20,000 times more lethal than cobra venom; minuscule amounts can poison and kill. Dissatisfied with working conditions in the Cimarron river facility, Silkwood began to document safety procedures at the plant.

In its four years of operation, the Kerr-McGee plant had accrued a dismal safety record; 77 employees had been involved in 17 contamination incidents. One occurrence had been a threat to public health, when an employee left the plant "hot" and went to eat at a restaurant in Crescent. In another incident, seven workers received levels of airborne plutonium above those sanctioned by the Atomic Energy Commission (AEC). In January 1974, an employee had had "a small portion of skin excised to remove plutonium in a wound." Kerr-McGee was careless in handling nuclear waste as well. Because of storage in improper containers, nuclear waste seeped out of drums onto a flatbed truck, leaking onto the axle, tires, and ground on more than one occasion. Although no one had documented Kerr-McGee's approach to the handling of nuclear waste, the company's sloppy record was already well known before Karen Silkwood began a close scrutiny of plant safety procedures.

Silkwood was working the 4 AM shift in the Emission Spectrography Laboratory on the night of July 31–August 1, 1974, when radioactive material was found on air-sample filter papers in the room in which she was stationed. A urine sample collected from her showed nuclear contamination. Kerr-McGee's past safety record combined with Silkwood's personal experience transformed the lab technician into a zealot. She began to carry a notebook with her everywhere, openly documenting safety conditions in the plant. During this same period, her personal life began to disintegrate. Stephens, who had quit his job at Kerr-McGee because of poor working conditions, became concerned about Silkwood, whose weight dropped from 112 pounds to 94 in four months. She slept less and less, and began to rely increasingly on sleeping pills and tranquilizers. Placidyl, Parest, and Quaalude were all prescribed for the nervous insomniac.

Stephens watched as Silkwood took prescription drugs in increasing quantities while her obsession with safety at the Cimarron river plant grew. Said Stephens:

> I felt it was consuming everything she had, mentally and physically. She just lived it, couldn't let it go and relax, particularly in the last month she was alive. I never accepted it. The good times that we'd had together were being lost to what happened at the plant. I didn't think it was good for either of us, especially for Karen on the basis of the physical considerations. I told her this. She said, "They need me."

Karen Silkwood's fears about the dangers of nuclear power flew in the face of conventional wisdom at the time. When atomic bombs were dropped on Japan to end World War II, Americans were awestruck by this new source of energy. Clearly it could kill, but in the right hands, most reasoned, nuclear power could greatly benefit humankind. A deluded public developed a naive outlook toward nuclear power and weapons. Thousands of bomb shelters were constructed throughout the country when Americans learned that the Soviet Union had developed its own nuclear weapons. If they could survive the initial blast, many believed, it would be a simple

*Poster distributed by Supporters of Silkwood.*

task to re-emerge from their shelters to rebuild. Little attention was paid to the fact that plutonium retains its radioactivity for 250,000 years. Nuclear contamination could affect life on earth far longer than anyone imagined. Silkwood would challenge conventional wisdom, warning of the dark side of nuclear energy.

By the fall of 1974, she was locked into a fierce battle with the management of Kerr-McGee, and the OCAW union contract was coming up for renewal on December 1. There had already been a bitter battle waged between the OCAW and Kerr-McGee at its New Mexico uranium mines the year before, culminating in a six-month strike. On October 16, Kerr-McGee gave its employees the opportunity to determine whether or not the OCAW would continue to represent them. If the union were decertified, company managers believed that labor relations would improve. It was precisely during this time that Silkwood arrived at union headquarters in Washington, D.C., with allegations that health and safety conditions at the Cimarron plant imperiled the workers, and that quality-control information had been falsified. Officials in Washington were alarmed by these allegations. A member of the Washington staff, Steve Wodka, recalled, "The consequences here were very deep and very grave, not only for the people in the plant, but for the entire atomic industry and the welfare of the country. If badly made pins were placed into the reactor without deficiencies being caught, there could be an incident exposing thousands of people to radiation."

When the vote was taken in mid-October, the OCAW won the right to represent Kerr-McGee employees, 80 to 61. Silkwood continued taking notes on the job. At this point, she was regarded as a threat by the Kerr-McGee management, a troublemaker who could cost the corporation dearly. After four days off at the beginning of November, Silkwood checked in at the Metallography Lab on November 5 at 1:20 PM. She worked in a glovebox, a sealed box in which radioactive materials are handled, until 6:30 that evening. When she inspected her hands on monitoring instruments, she discovered she was contaminated. An analysis of her coveralls determined that Silkwood had up to 20,000 disintegrations per minute; the Kerr-McGee limit was 500 disintegrations per minute. Silkwood was taken to a shower to be decontaminated, which required scrubbing three times with a mixture of Tide and Clorox. Urine and fecal samples were taken and left on a rack outside the shower, but they were unattended for an hour. When the levels of radiation on her person were shown to be safe again, she returned to work until 1 AM.

Silkwood reported to the plant for a contract negotiating meeting before 8 AM the following morning. When a check with a monitor revealed contamination, she returned for three more scrubbings of Tide and Clorox which burned her skin. Fecal and urine samples showed extremely high levels of radiation. Silkwood brought in new samples on November 7 for additional testing. When these proved heavily contaminated, inspectors from Kerr-McGee swarmed her apartment, which also showed high concentrations of radiation. The highest levels were in the bathroom and kitchen, but clothes, cosmetics, personal effects, carpet, appliances, kitchen cabinets, and the ventilation system were all removed for burial. Extremely distraught, Silkwood had no explanation for the contamination. Drew Stephens was checked for radiation, but he had none on his person or in his home. Said Stephens:

> She was hysterical over the telephone. When she got [to my house], she was a crying, shaking nervous wreck, wondering where all the people had gone. It's the kind of thing where you go back to the apartment and you wonder if it all really happened. There was nobody there, compared to 20 people and this whole splendid show going on when she left. She was convinced at that point that she was going to die of plutonium contamination. She just sat and shook.

Soon after, charges surfaced that Silkwood had contaminated herself, or that the union had adulterated urine and fecal samples given to the AEC.

The final six days of Karen Silkwood's life were spent in consultation with officials trying to determine the extent of contamination she had suffered. She worked on November 13, 1974, reporting in for the 8 AM shift. At 6 PM, she made arrangements to meet with David Burnham, a reporter from *The New York Times*, at a Holiday Inn on the northwest edge of Oklahoma City. While Silkwood was driving at 50 to 55 mph on Highway 74, on a straight stretch of desolate road, her 1973 Honda went onto the shoulder and over the edge of a culvert, slamming into a southern wall. She died instantly; she was 28.

When Karen Silkwood's body was found, there were no notebooks or manila folders, though friends were certain she had taken specific information to her meeting with *The New York Times'* reporter. Her death was ruled an accident: the highway patrol determined she had fallen asleep at the wheel, and an autopsy showed a small amount of methaqualone in her body which could have impaired her reactions. Silkwood had been understandably anxious and sleep deprived, everyone knew that, but some were not willing to accept this version of her death. An examination of the auto supported their theory that she had been bumped from behind and forced off the road, causing the fatal crash. Bill Silkwood, Karen's father, was immediately suspicious and ordered an autopsy, and the family took Kerr-McGee to court asking for $10 million in damages. The case dragged on for years before finally being settled out of court.

Karen Silkwood did not die quietly. Magazine articles, books, television shows, and a movie explored her life. In the months and years after her car went off the road, she became a symbol of all that was wrong with the nuclear-power industry. Health and safety rules were found to be wanting, and Kerr-McGee was forced to close the Cimarron river plant a year after her death. The death of Karen Silkwood ended America's naivete about nuclear weapons and nuclear power, long before Chernobyl. Protests against nuclear power plants were followed by protests against the use of nuclear weapons. It remains her legacy.

*From the movie Silkwood, starring Kurt Russell, Meryl Streep, and Cher.*

**SOURCES:**

"Editorials. The Real Stuff?" in *The Nation*. Vol. 238, no. 1. January 14, 1984, pp. 3–4.

"Karen Silkwood," in *Contemporary Heroes and Heroines*. Ray B. Browne, ed. NY: Gale Research, 1990, pp. 376–379.

"Karen Silkwood," in *The Progressive*. Vol. 43. April 1979, p. 9.

"Karen Silkwood: From Activist to Protest Symbol," in *The New York Times Biographical Service*. May 1979, p. 705.

Keerdoja, Eileen, and Lucy Howard. "The Silkwood Case," in *Newsweek*. Vol. 92, no. 15. October 9, 1978, p. 26.

Kohn, Howard. *Who Killed Karen Silkwood?* NY: Summit Books, 1981.

Nocera, Joseph. "Brief Reviews: The Killing of Karen Silkwood," in *The New Republic*. May 16, 1981, pp. 39–40.

Phillips, B.J. "The Case of Karen Silkwood," in *Ms*. Vol. 3, no. 10. April 1975, pp. 59–66.

"Poisoned by Plutonium," in *Time*. Vol. 113, no. 12. March 19, 1979, p. 35.

Raloff, Janet. "Silkwood—The Legal Fallout," in *Science News*. Vol. 125, no. 5. February 5, 1984, pp. 74–75, 79.

Rashke, Richard. *The Killing of Karen Silkwood: The Story Behind the Kerr-McGee Plutonium Case*. NY: Houghton Mifflin, 1981.

"Silkwood Case Laid to Rest," in *Science News*. Vol. 130, no. 9. August 30, 1986, p. 134.

"Silkwood: End of the Fantasy Road," in *National Review*. Vol. 36, no. 1. January 27, 1984, pp. 20–21.

"The Silkwood Mystery," in *Time*. Vol. 105, no. 3. January 20, 1975, pp. 47–48.

Starr, Mark, and Nancy Cooper. "Silkwood: No Easy Answers," in *Newsweek*. Vol. 102, no. 26. December 26, 1983, p. 23.

Stein, Jeffrey. "Karen Silkwood: The Deepening Mystery," in *The Progressive*. Vol. 45. January 1981, pp. 14–21.

Williams, Dennis A., and Pamela Ellis Simons. "Silkwood 'Vindicated,'" in *Newsweek*. Vol. 93, no. 22. May 28, 1979, p. 40.

**RELATED MEDIA:**

*Silkwood* (128 min. film), starring **Meryl Streep**, Kurt Russell, and **Cher** (nominated for an Oscar for Best Actress), screenplay by **Nora Ephron** and **Alice Arlen**, directed by Mike Nichols, released by 20th Century-Fox in 1983.

**Karin Loewen Haag**,
freelance writer,
Athens, Georgia

# Sill, Anna Peck (1816–1889)

*American educator who founded Rockford Female Seminary (later Rockford College)*. Born Anna Peck Sill on August 9, 1816, in Burlington, New York; died of pneumonia on June 18, 1889, in Rockford, Illinois; daughter of Abel Sill (a farmer) and Hepsibah (Peck) Sill; attended Miss Phipps' Union Seminary, Albion, New York; never married; no children.

Anna Peck Sill, the youngest of ten children, was born in 1816 in Burlington, New York, the daughter of Abel Sill and **Hepsibah Peck Sill**. Her father had come to that frontier area from Lyme, Connecticut, more than 25 years earlier and established a farm. Her mother was the daughter of a prominent New York judge, Jedediah Peck, who was responsible for the creation of free rural schools in New York by writing a bill and actively pursuing its enactment; he had also fought to eliminate that state's policy of imprisoning debtors. An educated woman, Hepsibah Sill strongly influenced her daughter's own development.

From age four, Anna Sill walked two miles daily to a local school, while at home she acquired such traditional domestic skills as spinning and weaving. Having undergone a religious conversion in her mid-teens, Sill possessed deep religious convictions throughout her life. Although inspired to become a foreign missionary, she decided that her calling lay more in providing education to the "wild Northwest."

Sill left Burlington at age 20 to become a teacher at the district school in Barre, New York, where she supplemented her weekly $2 income by spinning and weaving. In 1837, she left Barre to study at Miss Phipps' Union Seminary in Albion, New York, where she also became a teacher the following year. In 1843, she accepted a position directing a seminary in Warsaw, New York, which she held for three years before becoming head of the female department of the Cary Collegiate Institute in Oakfield, New York. Five years later, in 1849, the Rockford, Illinois, community invited her to open a private girls' school there.

Classes at the Rockford Female Seminary began in July 1849 with 60 students. The first building of the new seminary, supported by $6,000 in local donations, was erected in 1852—the same year Sill was confirmed as its principal. The seminary's overflowing enrollment led to the decision to build another structure, and during a visit to New York and New England, Sill solicited funds sufficient to begin construction of the second building, named Linden Hall.

Anchoring her educational philosophy in the belief that education should be a tool of religion, Sill sought to establish the Rockford Female Seminary as an exemplar of Christian values and of service to the community. Opposed to coeducation and the presence of women in public life, Sill also held rigid views regarding appropriate behavior for women. Patterning the school after

*Mary Lyon's Mt. Holyoke Seminary, Sill emphasized Biblical and classical studies. She also exerted authoritarian control over the institution and employed a rote instructional style with a demanding student workload. Sensitive, however, to growing criticism of her methods, Sill adapted to shifting educational needs by instituting administrative changes in the mid-1850s. The emergence of female schools with more secular curricula, such as Vassar, Wellesley, and Smith, further influenced Sill to seek the elevation of Rockford Female Seminary to collegiate status, and in 1882 the seminary began to grant degrees. Although Sill's desire to see physical improvements to the institution was not fulfilled before her retirement in 1884, her successor, **Martha Hillard MacLeish,** continued efforts in building renovations as well as the raising of faculty standards. Anna Peck Sill lived in Linden Hall as principal emerita until her death from pneumonia in 1889. Three years later, Rockford Female Seminary was renamed Rockford College.

**SOURCES:**

James, Edward T., ed. *Notable American Women, 1607–1950.* Cambridge, MA: The Belknap Press of Harvard University, 1971.

McHenry, Robert, ed. *Famous American Women.* NY: Dover, 1980.

**Howard Gofstein**, freelance writer,
Detroit, Michigan

## Sillanpää, Miina (1866–1952)

*Finnish political figure, journalist, and activist. Name variations: Miina Sillanpaa; Miina Silanpaa. Born in 1866; died in 1952.*

Miina Sillanpää, considered one of the most important politicians in early 20th-century Finland, began her 40-year career in Parliament in 1907 while the country was still under Russian control. Following World War I, she edited *Working Women*, a trade union periodical, while simultaneously performing her duties as a Helsinki city councillor. As Finland's first woman member of Parliament, Sillanpää served as Minister of Social Affairs for two years beginning in 1926, and chaired the Social Democratic Women's League in 1931. She became Speaker of Parliament in 1936, a position she held until her retirement in 1947. Sillanpää devoted much of her time and energy to improving social conditions, especially for working women with children. Active in the co-operative movement, from 1945 until 1952 she chaired the Ensi Kotien Liito, a group of homes for single mothers. In 1968, a bronze sculpture

designed by Aimo Tukianinen and entitled "The Torch" was dedicated in Tokoinranta, Finland, to Sillanpää's memory.

**Howard Gofstein**, freelance writer,
Detroit, Michigan

*Miina
Sillanpää*

## Sills, Beverly (1929—)

*American coloratura soprano, director of the New York City Opera, and chair of Lincoln Center, New York, who gained wide recognition for her superb handling of classic "bel canto" roles and her strong dramatic instincts. Name variations: (nickname) "Bubbles." Born Belle Miriam Silverman on May 25, 1929, in Brooklyn, New York, one of three children of Morris Silverman and Sonia Silverman; married Peter B. Greenough, on September 17, 1956; children: Meredith Greenough (b. 1959); Peter Greenough (b. 1961); stepchildren: three from husband's previous marriage.*

*Began singing on radio at age three (1932); began formal vocal studies at age seven (1936); made her op-*

eratic debut in Philadelphia as Frasquita in Carmen *(1947), followed by several years of touring with small repertory companies before appearing with the New York City Opera (1955); sang with New York City Opera (1955–70); debuted in Vienna as Queen of the Night in* Die Zauberflöte *(1967); debuted at Teatro alla Scale (1969), Covent Garden (1970); sang at most of the world's great opera houses before her formal debut at the New York Metropolitan Opera (1975); became general director of the New York City Opera (1979), rescuing it from financial insolvency and building its artistic reputation during her eight-year term; retired from the stage (1980); named chair of New York's Lincoln Center (1994); began hosting "Live From Lincoln Center" television series.*

One day in 1982 the general director of the New York City Opera paid a visit to the New Jersey warehouse where most of the sets for the company's productions were stored. The purpose of the visit was to take an inventory of what was available for the financially troubled company's upcoming season, but for Beverly Sills it was one of the most powerful experiences of her professional life. Stacked against the cobwebbed walls were the collected memories of her career as America's best-known operatic performer, some of the sets still bearing notes she'd attached to them during rehearsals for her most famous roles, and every scratch and dent recalling the triumphs of her reign as the prima donna of the company she was now desperately trying to save from financial ruin. Even though she had not sung professionally for two years, the realization that she was no longer America's favorite opera singer finally settled in. "For the first time in more than twenty-five years," she later wrote of that warehouse visit, "I was sure no one would be shouting 'Brava, diva!'"

See sidebar on p. 338

Opera had been Beverly Sills' life since childhood. Her earliest memories were of the arias of *Lily Pons and *Amelita Galli-Curci floating through her family's Brooklyn home. Both her parents came from cultured Eastern European backgrounds; **Sonia Silverman**, whom everyone called Shirley, had immigrated with her parents from Russia in 1917, while Sills' father Morris Silverman was from a prominent Rumanian family. Although Morris' job as an assistant manager for the Metropolitan Life Insurance Company in New York was not high paying, the Silvermans made sure that Beverly (born Belle Miriam Silverman in 1929) and her two brothers had the best that careful economies could buy. Her mother took her to her first opera at the age of eight—Delibes' *Lakmé*, sung

by Shirley's idol, Lily Pons, at the old Metropolitan on 39th Street in Manhattan. "Someday," Shirley told her daughter, "you're going to sit at a table with a Frenchman on one side and an Italian on the other, and you're going to be able to converse with them." Belle could, indeed, rattle off phrases in French by the time she was five, as well as sing most of the major arias she heard on her mother's opera records.

It was, in fact, "Caro nome" from Verdi's *Rigoletto* that brought her first paying job at the age of seven on the Major Bowes Amateur Hour, one of the nation's most popular radio shows of the day. She sang the aria for the Major himself at her audition, and when she performed it on the air shortly afterward, the studio audience's response sent the Major's "applause meter" spinning. It was her first appearance using the name Beverly Sills, suggested by a family friend who convinced her parents that a Jewish name would be a disadvantage in the show-business world. Sills became a regular on the show for the next three years, a skeptical Morris making sure the $65 she received every week went into a special savings account for Beverly's education. It was Major Bowes who saw to it that Sills was chosen to record the country's first commercial jingle, for Rinso laundry soap ("Rinso white, Rinso white, happy little washday song," Beverly trilled); and it was the Major who suggested to Shirley that formal singing lessons might be in order. While both mother and daughter were eager to follow the Major's advice, Beverly's father had no enthusiasm for such an outlandish idea. "My father wouldn't even acknowledge my dream," Sills says. "Singing simply wasn't a respectable profession."

Nonetheless, Shirley defied her husband by taking Beverly to audition for the woman who would become Sills' mentor and second mother for the next 34 years. ◄ **Estelle Liebling** was the last surviving pupil of legendary vocal teacher *Mathilde Marchesi** and, even better to Shirley's way of thinking, had taught Galli-Curci herself. But there was some confusion when mother and daughter arrived at Liebling's studio in midtown Manhattan. Liebling assumed it was Shirley, not Beverly, who had come to audition. "I don't teach little girls," she sniffed. "I don't even *know* any little girls." But Sills' rendition of Arditi's *Il Bacio*, which Liebling had taught many years before to Galli-Curci, persuaded Liebling to offer Beverly a 15-minute lesson every Saturday morning. Soon, the lessons expanded to 30 minutes, then to twice a week. Liebling, like Shirley, insisted that Beverly's future lay well beyond her native Brooklyn. "You're going to be a cultured woman," she

sternly told her young pupil, and would often invite Sills to her elegant dinner parties attended by many of New York's cultural elite.

Liebling took great pains to develop Sills' talent as a coloratura soprano, in the manner of *Maria Callas and, before her, Beverly's beloved Lily Pons. Sills was given precise lessons in French, since a coloratura's accent and diction must be flawless and able to withstand the soaring vocal embellishments that are a trademark of the *bel canto* style. Leibling also worked tireless-

**Liebling, Estelle** (1880–1970)

*American soprano and vocal teacher. Born in 1880; died in 1970; studied with \*Mathilde Marchesi and Selma Nicklass-Kempner.*

Estelle Liebling appeared with a number of European and American opera companies, including a stint with the Metropolitan Opera (1903–04). She also toured with John Philip Sousa's band, performing at over 1,600 concerts. By 1930, she had retired from touring and begun teaching. At one time affiliated with the Curtis Institute, she was also the longtime singing teacher of opera great \*Beverly Sills.

ly to develop Sills' dramatic skills, with Liebling calling out "Text! Text! Text!" whenever she felt Beverly was merely singing the composer's music rather than paying attention to the meaning of the librettist's words. So profound was Liebling's influence on every aspect of Sills' life that "Miss Liebling" or "Estelle" were much too informal addresses for Beverly to use. Liebling was simply "Teacher." "Three-quarters of who I am came from my family," Sills says. "The other 25 per cent came from Miss Liebling."

After eight years of rigorous training, Liebling decided that Sills was ready for her first public appearances, and convinced her friend, the producer J.J. Shubert, to send Beverly out on a Gilbert and Sullivan tour of Shubert theaters in the East and Midwest in 1944. It was to be the first of many road tours with small repertory companies which Sills would undertake. Shubert, who liked to call her "the youngest prima donna in captivity," cast Beverly in the title role of *Patience*—a role Sills especially enjoyed for its comic opportunities. A second Shubert tour followed later that year, this time offering her singing roles in such operettas as *The Merry Widow* and *Countess Maritza*. Between these two tours, Sills graduated from New York's Children's Professional School and, much to her father's dismay, refused to accept a college scholarship to study law. Also that year, New York's opera lovers took note of the inaugural season of the New York City Opera, which Mayor Fiorello La Guardia promised would be "opera for the people."

In 1947, Liebling packed Sills off to Philadelphia to study *bel canto* with the artistic director of that city's Civic Opera, Guiseppi Bamboscheck, who gave her her first classic opera role in the company's production of Bizet's *Carmen* in 1947, in which Beverly sang Frasquita. Although it was a small role, Sills could now say with conviction that she was an opera singer.

Unfortunately, the collective arms of the opera world did not seem to be opening wide to receive her. Instead, Sills earned her living by singing at resorts in New York's Catskill Mountains; at a private and discreet men's club in a New York City brownstone, in which a platform containing herself and a piano were wheeled from table to table, and in which the tips were routinely $100 bills; and on a cruise ship sailing between New York and Buenos Aires, on which she gave two concerts in each direction.

She had nearly turned down the cruise, for Morris, Sills was told, had fallen ill with tuberculosis. Urged by both her parents to accept the job, she discovered on her return some weeks later that Morris had died of lung cancer four days before the ship arrived in New York. He was only 53, and his death plunged the family into despair and, almost as bad, financial embarrassments, for Morris' will took more than a year to probate. With her two brothers away at school, Beverly and her mother were forced to move into a one-bedroom apartment in Manhattan. But her training continued, for Shirley would never allow her daughter's career to suffer.

Under Liebling's careful hand, Sills began building a repertoire of classic French roles—Massenet's *Manon* and *Thaïs*, Charpentier's *Louise*, and Offenbach's *Tales of Hoffmann*, among them—and refined her understanding of them with a two-month study program at the Paris Opèra arranged by Liebling. On Sills' return from Paris, Liebling urged her to accept the role of Violetta for a touring-company production of *La Traviata*, which left New York in September 1951 and played 63 consecutive performances before the cast was given a night off. Despite the grueling schedule, the tour sharpened Sills' acting abilities and gave her a thorough understanding of the role she would sing more than a hundred times in her career.

While she was now singing strictly opera, Sills' dream of becoming a diva seemed as far away as ever. A season with the San Francisco Opera in 1953 appeared to be going well for her, in which she made her debut singing Helen of Troy in Boito's *Mefistofele* and went on to sing Doña Elvira in Mozart's *Don Giovanni*. But the season ended abruptly when Sills' natural exuberance got her in trouble with the company's artistic director at the time, Kurt Adler, who had cast her as one of the eight Valkyries in Wagner's *Die Walküre*. As she and her sister goddesses were making their somber exit, Sills' horned helmet fell from her head and clattered to the stage; but instead of maintaining the inscrutable demeanor natural to a Valkyrie, Beverly ran to pick up the derelict headpiece and clapped it back on, much to the amusement and delight of the audience. Adler, fuming backstage, accused her of being drunk, while Sills proved with a sharp "Drop dead!" that she was nothing of the kind, and her employment with the company ended forthwith. She would not sing again in San Francisco for 18 years, on which occasion Adler left the offending helmet in her dressing room, filled with flowers and a note saying "Welcome home."

Throughout the early 1950s, Liebling had sent Sills to audition for the struggling young New York City Opera (NYCO), the company that had had its first season when Beverly was graduating from high school in 1944. By 1954, Sills had auditioned no less than seven times for the NYCO's director, Dr. Joseph Rosenstock, always taking care to dress modestly and sing her most comfortable *bel canto* roles from Donizetti, Rossini, and Bellini. When Rosenstock called her back an eighth time, Sills persuaded Liebling to find out why the man kept listening to her but never gave her a job. Rosenstock, Beverly learned, loved her voice but felt she had no "personality." Frustrated and angry at such treatment, Sills showed up for her eighth audition dressed in black mesh stockings, spiked heels, and a revealing blouse, with her hair hanging loose down her back. Since she had by now sung everything in her repertoire for Rosenstock, she launched into "La mamma morta" from *Andrea Chénier*, written for heavy-voiced, dramatic sopranos and hardly appropriate for a coloratura soprano. "I knew it was the wrong thing for me to sing, but I was *very* angry and I wanted him to know it," Sills remembers. "Believe me, he *knew* it." Rosenstock hired her for the company's 1955 fall season.

The City Opera at the time was housed in an old Shriners' temple on Manhattan's 55th Street, a venue never designed for grand opera. Although Mayor La Guardia's promise of "an opera company for the people" had been strictly followed by offering inexpensive seats (the most expensive ones costing two dollars), the result was also inexpensively mounted productions and short seasons—merely a week in the fall, and three weeks in the spring—and a chronically depleted treasury. Nonetheless, the company had boldly decided to mount Strauss' *Die Fledermaus*, and Rosenstock chose Sills to sing Rosalinda. Shirley made all of her daughter's costumes for the role, while adding a five-dollar white fox stole found at the Ritz Thrift Shop around the corner from the theater. Sills' perfor-

mance, in which she stressed the comic proportions of the part, was the first that attracted widespread attention, after nearly 15 years of professional singing. *The New York Times* wrote that the City Opera had added "an accomplished singer to its roster" and told its readers that the production as a whole was "the best musical you can see in this city on or off Broadway." Rosalinda was the beginning of Sills' 25-year relationship with the City Opera, and of her long-awaited dream of opera stardom.

> *D*on't think you're like every other girl in school, because you're not.
>
> —Estelle Liebling to Beverly Sills, 1936

Sills toured with the company between its fall and spring seasons and, at a party given by the Cleveland Press Club, met the club's president, Peter Greenough. Greenough was the son of a wealthy Massachusetts family who owned the *Cleveland Plain Dealer*. At the time of their meeting, Greenough was in the midst of a lengthy and acrimonious divorce proceeding. He and Sills were immediately attracted to one another, although their courtship could not be described as being of operatic proportions, with several missed dates and unanswered phone calls before the relationship became serious and culminated in their marriage, in Estelle Liebling's studio, on September 17, 1956. The two remained devoted to one another, but the early years of the marriage were not without problems—from Greenough's conservative New England family, who disliked the fact he'd married a Jew, and from Sills' family, who disliked the fact she'd married a Gentile. Adding to the worry was the tension between Sills and Greenough's three daughters from his first marriage, who suddenly found themselves with a Jewish opera diva from Brooklyn for a stepmother. Both Beverly and her husband were ostracized for years by their friends and families, and it is a testament to the strength of their marriage that it survived.

Fresh from her triumphant debut season with the City Opera in New York, Sills saw her status among her peers rise again with her stunning performance in Montemezzi's notoriously difficult *The Love of Three Kings*, in which she sang the role of Fiora. Her old friend from the Philadelphia Civic Opera, Bamboscheck, had frantically called her on January 1, 1956, little more than a week before the opera's opening on the 9th, to say that his Fiora had fallen ill. "I didn't know anyone stupid enough to try it," he later said, "or smart enough to learn it." Although Montemezzi's work is essentially a long tone poem, with none of the characteristic arias and duets of standard opera, Sills learned the part by listening to recordings nearly constantly over a four-day period, then embarking on four days of hurried rehearsals before the production opened to critical acclaim. But it was the 1958 New York City Opera season that finally put Beverly Sills at the pinnacle of American opera.

Julius Rudel had assumed the directorship of the NYCO after Joseph Rosenstock's retirement in 1956, although the company's board of directors nearly closed the company down that year for lack of money before Sills prevailed on them to try one more year with reduced salaries and production staff. Rudel gave Sills the title role in Douglas Moore's modern opera, The Ballad Of Baby Doe, which would anchor the company's "All American Opera" season of 1958. The role was her biggest challenge, both musically and dramatically. "Baby's got a lot to sing," Sills has noted, "and her hardest aria comes at the very end. To sing the part, you need to sustain a high energy level all the way through." Then, too, the character of Baby Doe is hardly a sympathetic one. She is the "other woman" of Moore's opera, for whom a wealthy silver miner in 19th-century America abandons his wife and children. Sills knew that it would take all the dramatic technique she had learned from "Teacher" to keep the audience on her side. Keep them she did, all the way to the opera's tragic conclusion and Baby Doe's dying aria before the mouth of the silver mine in which her lover has just perished. New York's Herald Tribune was so enthralled with her performance that it placed a review on its front page, an unusual step for a mass-readership daily journal; and the rest of the opera press was equally rapturous. Baby Doe convinced Beverly, who had been thinking of retiring to a quiet life as Mrs. Peter Greenough, that her 25 years of work had finally paid off.

But events, as it happened, nearly proved otherwise. Sills became pregnant shortly after Baby Doe's premiere, and was forced into temporary retirement in mid-1959 to give birth to a daughter, Meredith, in August; and to a son—Peter, nicknamed Bucky—born in June 1961. Within a six-week period, Sills and her husband were told that Meredith suffered from total deafness, while Peter was severely autistic and would need to spend the rest of his life in an institution. "I was overwhelmed by the children's handicaps," Sills has said. "My behavior changed. I would not leave the house. I stayed home and got terribly domestic." Months of de-pression passed before she agreed to Peter's suggestion that she resume studying with Estelle Liebling. It was not until 1962 that she felt able to face the public and resume performing for the City Opera in New York, and it was opera that would complete her recovery.

In 1966, the City Opera moved into its new home at Lincoln Center and marked the occasion by opening the season that year with a production of Handel's Guilio Cesare. Although Rudel had gone outside the company to find his Cleopatra, Sills insisted that the role should be given to her—even threatening to quit the company if Rudel wouldn't agree. After much maneuvering and negotiating, Sills sang the role she had instinctively felt would re-launch her career, and brought the entire house to its feet with the aria which closes the work's second act, "Se pieta." "It was a joyous, healing experience for me," she remembers. "All those hours and years . . . of rehearsing and performing were my escape from being Beverly Sills." As if in confirmation, she was invited for the first time to sing at the world's greatest opera houses—La Scala in 1969, where her performance as Pamira in Rossini's Le Siège de Corinthe led Italian critics to call her "the new Callas"; at Covent Garden and Berlin's Deutsche Opera in 1970; and, finally, in 1975, a triumphant debut at the Metropolitan in a reprise of her Pamira. (She had already sung at a Met-sponsored outdoor concert production of Don Giovanni in 1966.) The nearly unanimous praise for her cited her "full-toned, perfectly poised, firmly centered" technique, even when she took on the more difficult bel canto roles, including all three of "Donizetti's queens"—Elizabeth in Roberto Devereaux, Anne in Anna Bolena, and Mary in Maria Stuarta. At her formal retirement in 1980, she was among the world's best-known, most accessible opera singers whose reputation reached throughout the entertainment industry and the nation's cultural life. Among those in attendance at her final appearance for the New York City Opera on the night of October 27, 1980, were *Dinah Shore, *Mary Martin, Carol Burnett, Burt Reynolds, Walter Cronkite, and a host of opera luminaries such as Renata Scotto, Placido Domingo, Sherrill Milnes, and *Leontyne Price. Even more satisfying for Sills, the gala event raised more than $1 million for the opera company she now headed.

Appointed the general director of the New York City Opera in 1979, Sills assumed the position fulltime the morning after her farewell, descending from a flower-strewn stage to the subterranean administrative offices below the plaza of Lincoln Center. Her transition from diva to director was not without its skeptics, but Sills felt well prepared for her new role. "I had been in the theater for fifty years," she says, "and at *this* theater from the very opening night. What I didn't know, I learned." But even Beverly admitted that she probably wouldn't have taken the job if she had known the extent of the NYCO's debt in 1980—a monumental $5 million. "I was not prepared for the complexities of the financial state," she now admits. "And I could not reveal the true financial picture because no one puts money into a bankrupt organization. I had to keep the giggly, bubbly look that everyone expected from me." Sills knew better than anyone that it cost well over $100,000 to mount just one production at Lincoln Center in 1980, to say nothing of the competition from the better-known and better-endowed Metropolitan with which her company shared Lincoln Center. But she tackled the job with all the concentration and discipline with which she had prepared for her most difficult roles, deciding to set her sights on popularizing opera by going for a mass audience and a bigger box office instead of the more traditional, but smaller, audience of devotées who favored the Met for "serious" opera. With no money to hire an advertising agency, she designed the company's ads herself (one of them, for *Faust*, bearing the line, "Feel like hell? Come see Faust!"). She personally devised cost breakdowns for all the company's productions and saw to it that they were strictly followed; introduced new works by composers known more for their Broadway appeal, like Stephen Sondheim's *Sweeney Todd*; and, to the horror of opera lovers everywhere, installed "supertitles," allowing audiences to read line-by-line English translations of a work's lyrics projected over the proscenium. She traveled tirelessly across the country on fund-raising expeditions, calling on some of her husband's wealthy business friends for help. In 1983 alone, Sills raised more than $9 million. When the warehouse in which the company's sets and costumes were stored burned to the ground in 1985, she managed to raise $5 million in four months to rebuild the company, which opened its 1986 season on schedule. In 1988, when she decided to step down, the New York City Opera was financially healthy and rated as one of the country's best repertory companies.

There were other honors along the way—honorary doctorates from Harvard and from New York University; the President's Medal of Freedom, awarded by Jimmy Carter in 1980; and her chair of the March of Dimes' Mother's March on Birth Defects, for which she has raised

millions of dollars. In 1994, Sills was named chair of Lincoln Center, responsible for fund-raising and policy-making, bringing new challenges which she accepted, at age 66, without hesitation. "I only know that I've always tried to go a step past wherever people expected me to end up," Beverly Sills said at the time. "I'm not about to change now."

**SOURCES:**

Brady, Kathleen. "The Executive Superstar of the Opera," in *Working Woman*. Vol. 12. June 1987.

Jellinek, George. "Arias" (sound recording review), in *Opera News*. Vol. 60, no. 3. September 1995.

Sills, Beverly, with Lawrence Linderman. *Beverly: An Autobiography*. NY: Bantam, 1987.

Slonimsky, Nicolas, ed. *Baker's Biographical Dictionary of Musicians*. 8th ed. NY: Schirmer, 1992.

**Norman Powers**, writer-producer,
Chelsea Lane Productions,
New York

## Silva, Maria Helena Vieira da (b. 1908).

*See Vieira da Silva, Maria Elena.*

# Silver, Joan Micklin (1935—)

*American film producer, screenwriter, and director. Born Joan Micklin on May 24, 1935, in Omaha, Nebraska; daughter of Russian-Jewish immigrants Maurice David Micklin (a businessman) and Doris (Shoshone) Micklin; Sarah Lawrence College, B.A., 1956; married Raphael D. Silver (b. 1930, a real estate entrepreneur), on June 28, 1956; children:* **Dina Silver** *(a producer);* Marisa Silver *(a director);* **Claudia Silver** *(a director).*

*Selected filmography: (writer)* Limbo *(also known as* Chained to Yesterday *and* Women in Limbo, *1972); (director and writer)* Hester Street *(1975); (director and writer for television)* Bernice Bobs Her Hair *(1976); (director)* Between the Lines *(1977); (producer)* On the Yard *(1979); (director and writer)* Head Over Heels *(1979, re-released as* Chilly Scenes of Winter, *1982); (director for television)* How to Be a Perfect Person in Just Three Days *(1983); (director for television)* Finnegan Begin Again *(1985); (director)* Crossing Delancey *(1988); (director)* Loverboy *(1990); (director of Segment 2 for television)* Prison Stories: Women on the Inside *(1991); (director for television)* Big Girls Don't Cry . . . They Get Even *(also known as* Stepkids, *1992); (director for television)* A Private Matter *(1992); (director for television)* In the Presence of Mine Enemies *(1997); (director for television)* Invisible Child *(1999); (director)* A Fish in the Bathtub *(1999).*

Although Joan Micklin Silver's directorial debut in 1975's *Hester Street* garnered a mixed critical reception, audiences loved the film and turned the self-financed venture into a multimillion-dollar sleeper. Silver defied moviemaking convention with this gritty, unsentimental, black-and-white chronicle of Jewish immigrant life on the Lower East Side of New York at the turn of the 20th century. Prevailing against the industry's widespread sexism, she has directed a body of work that explores individual relationships, frequently within the context of ethnicity and the clash of cultures.

Joan Micklin was born to Russian-Jewish immigrant parents on May 24, 1935, in Omaha, Nebraska. She grew up on movies, going to double features several times a week. In 1956, a few weeks after her graduation from Sarah Lawrence College as a student of literature and music, she married Harvard-educated real estate entrepreneur Raphael Silver, whose father was a Cleveland, Ohio, rabbi. The couple settled in Cleveland, where Silver wrote for community theater, taught music to disturbed children, and gave birth to three daughters: Dina, Marisa, and Claudia. The family moved to New York City in 1967, and she contributed to the *Village Voice* and scripted short educational pieces for the *Encyclopaedia Britannica* while trying to interest Hollywood in one of her screenplays.

Silver's first foray into feature films was her 1972 co-authorship with **Linda Gottlieb** (who would produce *Dirty Dancing* in 1987) of *Limbo*, a story about the wives of men being held as prisoners-of-war in Vietnam. Universal Studios bought the property but then rewrote the film and gave it to director Mark Robson, whose directorial vision Silver did not share. After this disappointing experience, Silver realized that the only way to preserve the integrity of her artistic vision was to become a director herself.

She then wrote and directed several educational and documentary shorts for the Learning Corporation of America, hoping to land directorial opportunities in mainstream feature filmmaking. Her short work, *The Immigrant Experience* (which documents the 1907 arrival in America of a Polish Catholic family and is generally considered the precursor of *Hester Street*), elicited a favorable critical response and won several awards, but it failed to establish Silver as a promising writer or director. Frustrated by the film industry's widespread sexism, Silver and her husband formed Midwest Film Productions, which enabled her to create her own filmmaking opportunities. Raphael took time off from his successful real-estate ventures to raise money for what would be his wife's first feature, *Hester Street*.

Silver based *Hester Street* on the 1896 novella *Yekl* by Abraham Cahan, a storyteller who chronicled Jewish immigrant life in New York City. Drawing upon a universal theme, the clash between old and new traditions, the film features the slick young immigrant Jake (Steven Keats) striving to shed his Old World traditions by adopting those of his progressive new home. After his tedious sweatshop job, he spends his evenings at a dancing academy and begins an affair with the decidedly progressive and pennywise Mamie (**Dorrie Kavanaugh**), a Polish-Jewish immigrant with dreams of starting her own dancing academy. Jake's timid and pious wife Gitl (**Carol Kane**, who earned an Oscar nomination for her performance) also arrives in America with their son, only to further remind Jake of the Old World conventions he seeks to escape. Gitl eventually divorces Jake and shrewdly ends up with Mamie's nest egg. Growing ever stronger and more independent, she begins her own romance with Bernstein, the cerebral and scholarly boarder (Mel Howard) whose values more closely resemble her own. Distributors initially dismissed *Hester Street* as an "ethnic oddity," but after its strong receptions at the Dallas and Cannes Film Festivals, the film became the surprise hit of the season, turning the modest $370,000 venture into a $5-million property that was released in 20 other countries.

Still ignored by the major film studios, Silver turned to public television in 1976 with *Bernice Bobs Her Hair*, a 45-minute film which she wrote and directed, based on a story by F. Scott Fitzgerald. The Silvers also had to use the profits from *Hester Street* to finance their 1977 project *Between the Lines*, a film in which the characters nostalgically long for the 1960s. The movie, which features John Heard and **Lindsay Crouse**, unknown actors at the time, elicited a generally favorable reaction from critics. Silver then began work on filming *Chilly Scenes of Winter*, based on a novel by **Ann Beattie**, in which the characters again lament the onset of the 1970s. Released in 1979 by distributors as *Head Over Heels* to a disappointing reception, it was re-released under its original title in 1982, minus the puzzlingly happy ending. Although the film garnered a more generous critical response, it burdened Silver with the label of spokesperson for her generation.

Several of Silver's films are romantic comedies in which she simply transcends the genre. In a 1985 work for television, *Finnegan Begin Again*, directed by Silver, a 65-year-old award-winning journalist (Robert Preston) who writes an increasingly bitter advice column for the lovelorn while caring for his sickly wife, embarks upon a relationship with a vibrant middle-aged teacher (**Mary Tyler Moore**) who is involved in a comfortable but unsatisfactory affair with a married man. Returning to the clash between old-fashioned and modern traditions, Silver's 1988 *Crossing Delancey* concerns a young Jewish professional whose grandmother hopes to marry her off via a marriage broker. Hampered by a desire to distance herself from the Old World of her Jewish origins, the main character (**Amy Irving**) must also distinguish between her romantic notions and reality before she can fall in love. And in 1990, Silver created *Loverboy* in which Patrick Dempsey in the title role of a paid escort to frustrated married women discovers how romance can enrich even the most shallow of his relationships. Comparing Silver's work in the genre of romantic comedy to that of Woody Allen, Richard Lippe and Rob Edelman suggest that her films, "while utilizing the structural strengths and comic potentials of the generic formulas, are offering a contemporary vision of the tensions underpinning heterosexual relations, and . . . predominately respond to these tensions in a progressive manner." However, unlike Allen, "Silver is much less sentimental and precious about her characters."

During the 1980s, Silver also renewed her activities in theater, developing and directing the musical revue *Maybe I'm Doing It Wrong*, based on the work of songwriter Randy Newman, and the feminist revue *A . . . My Name Is Alice*, with **Julianne Boyd**, which featured songs and short sketches by several contributors. According to Ally Acker, as a feminist, Silver prefers to express her philosophy subtly in her work rather than by creating films that present women only in powerful and successful positions. Her own success as a director, however, has enabled her to hire other women to work on the production crews of her films. And she has encouraged her own daughters to enter the profession—all three are either directors or producers—the most prominent of whom is director **Marisa Silver**, whose films include *Old Enough, Permanent Record, Vital Signs,* and *He Said She Said*.

**SOURCES:**

Acker, Ally. *Reel Women.* NY: Continuum, 1991.

Edelman, Rob, and Richard Lippe, in *Women Filmmakers and Their Films.* Edited by Gwendolyn A. Foster and Katrien Jacobs. Detroit; MI: St. James Press, 1998.

Foster, Gwendolyn A. *Women Film Directors: An International Bio-critical Film Dictionary.* Westport, CT: Greenwood Press, 1995.

Wakeman, John, ed. *World Film Directors, Volume II, 1945–1985.* NY: H.W. Wilson, 1988.

**Howard Gofstein**, freelance writer,
Detroit, Michigan

# Silvia Sommerlath (1943—)

*Queen of Sweden. Name variations: Queen Silvia. Born Silvia Renate Sommerlath on December 23, 1943, in Heidelberg, Baden-Wurttemberg, Germany; daughter of Alice Soares de Toledo and Walter Sommerlath; graduated from the Munich School of Interpreting, 1969; married Carl XVI Gustavus, also known as Charles XVI Gustavus (1946–1973), king of Sweden (r. 1973—), on June 19, 1976, at Storkyrkan Cathedral, Stockholm; children: Victoria (b. 1977); Carl Philip (b. 1979); \*Madeleine (b. 1982).*

Silvia Renate Sommerlath was born the only daughter of **Alice Soares de Toledo** and Walter Sommerlath, a German industrialist, at the height of World War II on December 23, 1943. Her Brazilian mother had fled to Heidelberg, Germany, to escape Allied bombings in Berlin, and the family stayed there until the end of the war. With Germany in ruins, Walter realized that his best hope for prosperity lay in Brazil, where a job awaited him as branch manager for a Swedish firm. Two years passed before Allied authorities granted him permission to leave Germany. When they did, the Sommerlaths moved into a large pink and white villa in Brazil. Rather than becoming swept up in the splendor of their surroundings, however, the Sommerlaths raised their children modestly. Four-year-old Silvia attended a strict private school supplemented by home-based instruction in languages and sewing. Her father demanded absolute obedience and forbade her to play with boys. She also seldom saw her female friends.

Silvia's restricted lifestyle continued with the Sommerlath family's return to Heidelberg in 1957. She struggled with the German language, although she was fluent in Portuguese, Spanish, and English. Her new, exclusive private school was attended only by children of the upper class and was surrounded by walls that were 13 feet high. Silvia remained there for eight months until the family moved again, this time to Düsseldorf, where she attended Luisenschule, another extremely conservative school. Her harsh upbringing, in comparison to those of her classmates, began to make her feel like an outcast. Her mother would not allow her to venture out socially unless one of her brothers chaperoned.

After she passed her final exams at Luisenschule, Silvia enrolled in an interpreters' school founded by Professor Paul Schmit, the man who had translated the words of German dictator Adolf Hitler into several languages. Silvia studied under Schmit for four years and then found a

*Silvia Sommerlath, with Carl XVI Gustaf.*

$300-a-month position with the Argentinean Embassy. This was followed by a position as an interpreter for a Spanish firm at international conventions. In 1972, she was chosen as chief hostess of the Munich Olympics, surpassing 1,500 other candidates for the honor. It was there, on March 16, 1972, that she met His Royal Highness Prince Carl Gustav of Sweden (Carl XVI Gustavus).

The young prince had lost his invitation to a reception hosted by the president of the German Olympic Committee. Upon hearing that the prince had been denied admission by the head usher, the president of the committee asked Silvia to serve as Carl Gustav's official escort for the evening. Although Silvia was romantically involved with a 36-year-old financial consultant at the time, a second meeting between the couple occurred a year later at a party, and their courtship began. Silvia was 32 when her engagement to Carl Gustav, now king, was officially announced in March 1976. The couple married on June 19, 1976, at the Storkyrkan Cathedral—making Silvia the 25th queen of Sweden. It was the first royal wedding in Sweden since Gustavus IV Adolphus' marriage to *Frederica Dorothea of Baden in 1797. The wedding was widely attended, although the union was slighted by *Elizabeth II of England, who sent only the duke and duchess of Gloucester as her representatives. More than five million people watched the nuptials on television.

Silvia proved to be a capable manager, increasing efficiency and working behind the scenes to prepare the royal residence for state events. Despite the king's vast personal fortune and an annual stipend of approximately $2 million, the couple chose not to live as opulently as other European royalty. Silvia introduced new economy measures to the castle to ensure that nothing would be wasted, and likewise disposed of excess ceremony attached to her station, such as curtsying at court.

The new casual style of the Swedish monarchy perfectly suited Silvia, who still enjoyed department store sales and was frequently seen cycling with her children, wearing sweatpants and sporting a ponytail. While keeping up with world events, Silvia filled her days with visits to hospitals and foster homes, and with delegations of her constituents. A believer in gender equality, she encouraged her husband to support legislation to change the laws of monarchical succession from the first son to the first child, making her daughter, Princess *Victoria, heir to the Swedish throne. Parliament adopted the measure in 1979.

Silvia used her position as representative of Sweden to advocate on behalf of children. The challenges facing disabled and disadvantaged youngsters became her special cause, and she devoted much energy to supporting research on children and handicaps through the Royal Wedding Fund and Queen Silvia's Jubilee Fund. Her efforts garnered her the "Deutsche Kulturpreis" in 1990. At the international level, Silvia took part in the First World Congress against Commercial Sexual Exploitation of Children, held in Stockholm 1996. As the 20th century came to a close, she established the World Childhood Foundation, dedicated to improving the quality of life of the world's children. Other causes that benefited from her dedication included the Mentor Foundation, active in the fight against drug abuse, and the Silvia Home in Drottningholm, instrumental in the training of personnel in the treatment of the insane. During the 1990s, she received honorary degrees from Åbo University in Finland, the Karolinska Institute in Stockholm, the University of Linköping and Göteborg University, as well as the Chancellor's Medal from the University of Massachusetts.

**SOURCES:**
Boulay, Laure, and Françoise Jaudel. *There are Still Kings: The Ten Royal Families of Europe.* NY: Clarkson Potter, 1981.

**Howard Gofstein**, freelance writer, Detroit, Michigan

## Simburg, Wyomia Tyus (b. 1945).

*See Tyus, Wyomia.*

## Simcox, Edith (1844–1901)

*British journalist, labor activist, and social reformer. Name variations: (pseudonym) H. Lawrenny. Born on August 21, 1844; died on September 15, 1901; daughter of Jemima Haslope and George Price Simcox (a merchant).*

*Selected writings:* Natural Law: An Essay in Ethics *(1877);* Episodes in the Lives of Men, Women and Lovers *(1882);* Primitive Civilizations *(1894).*

Perhaps best remembered as one of novelist George Eliot's (*Mary Anne Evans) most ardent admirers, Edith Simcox earned esteem for her own substantial contributions to economic theory and social reform in England. Simcox, who was born into a prosperous middle-class Victorian family in 1844, possessed the same intellectual potential as her two brothers; unlike them, however, she was unable to attend Oxford, which did not admit women as degree candidates until 1920. Although her formal education extended no further than grammar school, she was a self-educated woman who learned several languages and was particularly well read in literature and philosophy. The magnitude of her knowledge is evinced by the sweeping array of subjects about which she wrote articles for leading Victorian periodicals. As well, for more than 25 years, she contributed reviews under the pseudonym "H. Lawrenny" on literature and economics to the distinguished journal *The Academy.* Founded in 1869 by a group of young university liberals, it boasted a prestigious roster of writers and editors, including Matthew Arnold, George Saintsbury, and Walter Pater.

Particularly influenced by her reading of philosophers Jeremy Bentham, John Stuart Mill, and August Comte, Simcox developed her own socialist ideas, which formed the basis of her work on behalf of women and laborers. According to James Diedrick, "Simcox's major writings might be seen as both extending and modifying (especially in terms of class and gender) Mill's arguments on political economy, ethics, and the women's question."

Simcox first met Eliot shortly after her glowing and insightful review of *Middlemarch* appeared in *The Academy* in 1872. Eliot resided in London and hosted many important intellectuals and writers of the day at her Sunday gatherings, and Simcox was a frequent visitor until the author's death in 1880. Although Simcox's beliefs were well established by the time she met Eliot, she referred to Eliot as her "idol" and attributed all her subsequent accomplishments to Eliot's influence. While Eliot was receptive to Simcox's friendship and welcomed her into her home, Diedrick notes that Eliot was uncomfortable with her fervent professions of devotion. Two years after Eliot's death, Simcox published *Episodes in the Lives of Men, Women, and Lovers*, comprising 11 loosely connected fables that obliquely explore her love for Eliot in fictional terms.

Unlike other Victorian feminists who were frequently concerned primarily with suffragist issues, Simcox involved herself in the trade-union movement through her acquaintance with *Emma Paterson, who had been secretary of the Women's Suffrage Association (1872–73) and had founded the Women's Protective and Provident League (1874). They formed the Shirt and Collar Makers' Union on July 1, 1875, and were admitted to the eighth annual Trade Union Congress, which met in Glasgow in October 1875, becoming the first women delegates. At that meeting, Simcox called for the improvement of factory inspections, reduced work hours, and parliamentary representation of the working class. That same year Simcox partnered with **Mary Hamilton** in creating a cooperative shirt-making workshop, Hamilton and Company, which provided women with useful employment under humane conditions. Throughout her life, Simcox was active in organizing workers, speaking at union meetings, and representing English trade unions at labor conferences.

Simcox took her plans for reform to the schools upon her overwhelming election to the London School Board as the Radical candidate in 1879. During her successful three-year term, she visited classrooms and spoke with teachers, worked with the board to set and enforce school policies, and observed the boards of other schools throughout England—all of which earned her high praise from other members of the school board.

Simcox's major writings were scholarly in nature. Her 1877 *Natural Law: An Essay in Ethics* attempted to identify the "laws" that underlie human relations in order to contribute to a "science" of society in accordance with her rationalist beliefs. "Revealing all of the major influences on her thinking," writes Diedrick, "*Natural Law* is an amalgam of Spinozan ethics, Comtean Positivism, and Utilitarianism—all leavened by a sympathetic awareness of human frailty inspired by Eliot's novels." In 1894, after an enormous amount of research, she published *Primitive Civilizations; or, Outlines of the History of Ownership in Archaic Communities*, which delineates the history of property, concluding that modern English society fell short of precedents set by older civilizations like Egypt and Babylonia concerning the distribution of wealth, power, and status. She also examined the treatment of women in various civilizations, as Diedrick notes, "particularly . . . how social expectations and legal structures shape the lives of women and mothers." Simcox determined that women had been accorded a greater position in non-Western societies than they had in English society.

By the time *Primitive Civilizations* was published, Simcox's career as an activist and writer was drawing to a close. Although she still supported trade unions, she was becoming dismayed by internal petty political squabbles, and was no longer writing on a regular basis. Suffering from recurrent respiratory problems and failing eyesight, Simcox died on September 15, 1901. Although she had hoped to be buried at Highgate Cemetery near her beloved George Eliot, she was buried with her mother, with whom she had lived most of her life, at Aspley Guise near Bedford.

**SOURCES:**

Diedrick, James. "Edith Jemima Simcox," in *Dictionary of Literary Biography*, Vol. 190: *British Reform Writers, 1832–1914*. Detroit, MI: Gale Research, 1998, pp. 289–297.

Shattock, Joanne. *The Oxford Guide to British Women Writers*. NY: Oxford University Press, 1993.

Simcox, Edith Jemima. *A Monument to the Memory of George Eliot: Edith Jemima Simcox's Autobiography of a Shirtmaker*. Edited by Constance M. Fulmer and Margaret E. Barfield. NY: Garland, 1998.

**Howard Gofstein**, freelance writer, Detroit, Michigan

## Simeoni, Sara (1953—)

*Italian high jumper.* Born in Italy on April 19, 1953.

Won a silver medal in the high jump at the Montreal Olympics (1976); won a gold medal in the high jump at the Moscow Olympics (1980); won the bronze medal in the European championships (1982); won the silver medal at the Los Angeles Olympics (1984).

As a child, Sara Simeoni dreamed of being a ballet star, but she kept growing. At age 12, told that she was too tall and her feet were too big for ballet, she switched to high jumping, realizing one half of her wish. In Italy and elsewhere, she became a star. She set a best-on-record performance in the high jump on August 4, 1978, in Brescia, Italy, with a jump of 6'7". In the 1980 Olympic Games in Moscow, she beat out competitor *Rosemarie Ackermann for the gold medal with a jump of 6'5½", breaking the Olympic record. After that, she was plagued with injuries. She came out of retirement four years later, when her battle with *Ulrike Meyfarth was the highlight of the 1984 Olympics in Los Angeles. After Simeoni took the silver at 6'6¾", she laughed, kissed a startled photographer, and went back into retirement.

## Simionato, Giulietta (1916—)

*Italian mezzo-soprano.* Born on May 12, 1916, in Forlì, Italy; daughter of Felice Simionato (director of the local prison) and Giovanna (Truddaiu) Simionato; studied in Rovigo with Locatello and in Milan with Palumbo; grew up on the island of Sardinia.

Won first place in a bel canto competition in Florence (1933); sang in premiere of Pizzetti's Orsèolo (1933); debuted at Teatro alla Scala (1936); debuted at Edinburgh Festival (1947), Covent Garden (1956), Metropolitan Opera (1959); retired (1966).

Raised on the island of Sardinia, where she received her earliest voice lessons from nuns at the convent school she attended, Giulietta Simionato initially sang only "for the Madonna," at the insistence of her highly religious mother. **Giovanna Truddaiu Simionato** vetoed the suggestion that her daughter receive further vocal training, but, after her death when Giulietta was 15, the family moved to a town near Padua, where Giulietta began her vocal training in earnest. She sang publicly in provincial cities twice before she was 20, and in 1933 beat over 385 other competitors to win a bel canto contest in Florence. Three years later, she made her debut in Milan at the venerable Teatro alla Scala, singing Beppe in L'Amico Fritz.

Simionato continued to sing secondary roles at La Scala for the next eight years, finally growing so frustrated with her stagnant career that she struck out on her own. For three years, she performed throughout Italy in such leading roles as Carmen, and in 1947 she appeared at the Edinburgh Festival. That same year she was invited back to La Scala, savoring her vindication with a performance of the title role in Mignon. She would remain a star in Milan for the rest of her career, particularly acclaimed for her roles in such operas as Anna Bolena, Il Barbiere di Siviglia, La Favorita and I Capuleti ed i Montecchi. One of the most beloved opera stars of the 1950s, Simionato also performed internationally, singing to wide praise in Salzburg, London, Vienna, Mexico City, Paris, Madrid, Geneva and Rio de Janeiro, among other cities. She sang for the first time in the United States in 1954, in a production of Bellini's Norma with *Maria Callas at the Chicago Lyric Opera. Five years later, Simionato made her debut at the Metropolitan Opera in New York City, winning paeans from the critics for the role of Azucena in Il Trovatore. She would continue to perform at the Met until her retirement. Simionato also gave frequent concert performances and solo recitals and made a number of recordings, which were highly popular despite the fact that some believe they do not show her voice to the best advantage. A longtime resident of Rome, she bemoaned the "dissonance" of modern music, and had become a symbol of an older era in opera by the time she left the stage in 1966.

Giulietta Simionato

**SOURCES:**
Moritz, Charles, ed. Current Biography Yearbook. NY: H.W. Wilson, 1960.

## Simkhovitch, Mary (1867–1951)

*American social reformer.* Born Mary Melinda Kingsbury on September 8, 1867, in Chestnut Hill, Massachusetts; died on November 15, 1951, in New York City; daughter of Isaac Franklin Kingsbury and

*Laura (Holmes) Kingsbury; Boston University, B.A., 1890, elected to Phi Beta Kappa; graduate study at Harvard Annex (later Radcliffe College), University of Berlin, and Columbia University; married Vladimir Gregorievitch Simkhovitch (an economics professor), in January 1899; children: Stephen (b. 1902); Helena (b. 1904).*

*Selected writings:* The City Worker's World *(1917);* Neighborhood: My Story of Greenwich House *(1938);* Group Life *(1940);* Here is God's Plenty *(1949).*

A key figure in the settlement house movement during the first half of the 20th century, Mary Simkhovitch founded the Association of Neighborhood Workers in 1901. The following year, she established Greenwich House, which under her 45 years of guidance became a primary influence in the settlement house movement.

Born on September 8, 1867, in the affluent Chestnut Hill suburb of Boston, Mary Melinda Kingsbury graduated from Newton High School in Newton, Massachusetts, in 1886. She chose to attend nearby Boston University, where she became a member of the Phi Beta Kappa honor society and graduated with a B.A. in 1890. During her college years, as the leader of a group for teenaged girls at St. Augustine's Episcopal Church, she first encountered "slum" life, which galvanized her interest in housing reform. Carroll Smith-Rosenberg notes that this experience taught Simkhovitch an elemental principle of social reform: "Before any help can be given the situation must be felt, realized and understood at first hand," she wrote. "Only that which is lived can be understood and translated to others."

After graduating from college, Simkhovitch taught high school Latin in Somerville, Massachusetts, for two years, before resigning due to her lack of patience with grading papers and instructing remedial students. In 1892, she began graduate work at the all-female Harvard Annex (later Radcliffe College), where she studied medieval history, philosophy, and sociology. Then, with the help of a scholarship from the Women's Educational and Industrial Union, she went to the University of Berlin, escorted by her mother. While in Berlin, she met Vladimir Gregorievitch Simkhovitch, whom she would marry in 1899; between academic terms, she also visited Italy, Paris, and London, where she remained to attend the International Socialist Trade Union Congress. Although she did further graduate work in sociology, economics, and history at Columbia University upon her return to America, she was anxious to apply her education to prac-

tical issues related to urban life and industrialization. She left school in 1897 to live at the College Settlement House on New York City's Lower East Side, where she was a mentor to the teenaged *Eleanor Roosevelt, then a volunteer teacher at the house. Wanting to experience the changing face of urban America firsthand, Simkhovitch became head resident and learned Yiddish so she could communicate with the area's Jewish immigrants.

After a year, she accepted a position of chief resident at the Friendly Aid House. Her experience there differed markedly from that of the nonsectarian College Settlement House, which not only had been bolder in its approach to solving housing and other community-based problems, but had encouraged a cooperative spirit with the neighborhood residents. Because the Friendly Aid House was church-supported, it considered the project a charity and emphasized religious inculcation; it was also more restrictive in its policies. This prompted Simkhovitch in 1901 to found a settlement house that would incorporate the values and methods she considered most important. Under Simkhovitch's direction, Greenwich House became a premiere settlement within the movement and was responsible for numerous important studies on such social issues as slum housing, unemployment, racism, and immigrant groups. Simkhovitch encouraged broader social reform and envisioned the settlement as an impetus for unity within the community. Donations from local philanthropists enabled Simkhovitch to create the Greenwich Village Cultural Association, which then established Greenwich House as a center of cultural activity in the neighborhood. She created neighborhood meeting places, theater programs, and recreational undertakings to bring the community together in cultural and social pursuits. The settlement had the support of such prominent figures as John Dewey, Eleanor Roosevelt, Jacob Riis, and Felix Adler, and later residents included writer *Zona Gale and social reformer *Frances Perkins. In a biographical excerpt in *Women of Valor*, Simkhovitch discusses her utilization of various national and local governmental programs to accommodate Greenwich House's weekly attendance which had doubled to nearly 10,000 people during the height of the Great Depression.

Simkhovitch worked alongside other social reformers and settlement house leaders, becoming active within the housing-reform movement and the Outdoor Recreation League. Her prominence in the movement became such that she was elected president of the National Federation of Settlements in 1917. Although deeply involved with all activities of Greenwich House, Simkhovitch also maintained a rigorous schedule of activities beyond its borders. She was instrumental in the 1907 founding of the Committee on the Congestion of Population, having witnessed all the evils associated with overcrowded housing. Active in politics, Simkhovitch served on the Mayor's Public Recreation Commission in 1911, on the executive board of the National Consumers' League starting in 1917, and was a member of the New York City Recreation Committee in 1925. Mayor Fiorello La Guardia recognized her effectiveness as an advocate and administrator by appointing her vice chair of the New York City Housing Authority in 1934.

On the national level, Simkhovitch spoke on behalf of Theodore Roosevelt in the 1912 presidential campaign and championed the cause of women's suffrage. Her lifelong efforts in public housing reform attracted her to the New Deal policies of Franklin D. Roosevelt. Successful in adding a provision for the first federally funded low-income public housing to the National Industrial Recovery Act of 1933, she achieved another legislative victory in her drafting of the public housing bill that became the Wagner-Steagall Housing Act of 1937.

Although Simkhovitch continued her active involvement in the New York City Housing Authority, in 1946 she retired from the directorship of Greenwich House, where she died on November 15, 1951.

SOURCES:

Block, Maxine, ed. *Current Biography 1943*. NY: H.W. Wilson, 1943.

McHenry, Robert, ed. *Famous American Women*. NY: Dover, 1980.

Sicherman, Barbara, and Carol Hurd Green, eds. *Notable American Women: The Modern Period*. Cambridge, MA: The Belknap Press of Harvard University, 1980.

Sternsher, Bernard, and Judith Sealander, eds. *Women of Valor*. Chicago, IL: Ivan R. Dee, 1990.

Stroup, Herbert. *Social Welfare Pioneers*. Chicago, IL: Nelson-Hall, 1986.

**Howard Gofstein**, freelance writer, Detroit, Michigan

## Simkins, Modjeska (b. 1899).

*See Clark, Septima for sidebar.*

## Simmern, Anne (1616–1684).

*See Gonzaga, Anne de.*

## Simmern, duchess of.

*See Marie of Brandenburg-Kulmbach (1519–1567).*

## Simmern, Elizabeth (1618–1680).

*See Elizabeth of Bohemia.*

## Simmons, Gertrude (1876–1938).

*See Bonnin, Gertrude Simmons.*

# Simmons, Jean (1929—)

*English actress. Born Jean Merilyn Simmons on January 31, 1929, in Crouch Hill, London, England; youngest of four children of Charles Simmons (a physical education teacher) and Winifred Ada (Loveland) Simmons; attended Orange Hill School for Girls; married Stewart Granger (an actor), on December 20, 1950 (divorced 1960); married Richard Brooks (a director), on November 1, 1960 (divorced 1977); children: (first marriage) Tracy Granger; (second marriage) Kate Brooks.*

*Selected filmography:* Give Us the Moon (UK, 1944); Mr. Emmanuel (UK, 1944); Kiss the Bride Goodbye (UK, 1944); Meet Sexton Blake (UK, 1944); The Way to the Stars (Johnny in the Clouds, UK, 1945); Caesar and Cleopatra (UK, 1945); Great Expectations (UK, 1946); Hungry Hill (UK, 1946); Black Narcissus (UK, 1947); Uncle Silas (The Inheritance, UK, 1947); The Woman in the Hall (UK, 1947); Hamlet (UK, 1946); The Blue Lagoon (UK, 1949); Adam and Evelyne (Adam and Evelyn, UK, 1949); So Long at the Fair (UK, 1950); Cage of Gold (UK, 1950); Trio (UK, 1950); The Clouded Yellow (UK, 1950); Androcles and the Lion (1953); Angel Face (1953); Young Bess (1953); Affair With a Stranger (1953); The Robe (1953); The Actress (1953); She Couldn't Say No (1954); The Egyptian (1954); A Bullet Is Waiting (1954); Desiree (1954); Footsteps in the Fog (UK, 1955); Guys and Dolls (1955); Hilda Crane (1956); This Could Be the Night (1957); Until They Sail (1957); The Big Country (1958); Home Before Dark (1958); This Earth Is Mine (1959); Elmer Gantry (1960); Spartacus (1960); The Grass Is Greener (UK, 1960); All the Way Home (1963); Life at the Top (UK, 1965); Mister Buddwing (1966); Divorce American Style (1967); Rough Night in Jericho (1967); The Happy Ending (1969); Say Hello to Yesterday (UK, 1971); Mr. Sycamore (1975); Dominique (UK, 1978); Yellow Pages (Going Undercover, UK, 1985); The Dawning (1988).

The youngest of four children, Jean Simmons was born in 1929 in Crouch Hill, London, England, and spent her childhood in the Golders Green section of that city until the outbreak of World War II in 1939, when she and her siblings, along with many other London children, were evacuated to Somerset. She returned to the city at age 14, when she began lessons at the Aida Foster School of Dancing. It was there that she was spotted by a movie talent scout who asked her to audition for the role of *Margaret Lockwood's sister in the film *Give Us the Moon* (1944). Director Val Guest selected Simmons over 200 hopefuls, launching her movie career. Over the next two years, she played minor film roles while continuing her dance studies. At age 16, she was selected to play the young Estella in *Great Expectations*, a role that caught the attention of Laurence Olivier, who chose her to play Ophelia in his 1948 screen production of *Hamlet*.

Although inexperienced in Shakespeare, and guided line by line in the role by Olivier, Simmons turned in a remarkable performance. "Jean Simmons is extraordinarily enchanting and touching as Ophelia," wrote Howard Barnes. "Starting at a low pitch she builds to the famous mad scene with authority and eloquence." The reviewer for *Time*, while admitting that Simmons lacked experience, remarked on her "oblique, in-

dividual beauty" and "trained dancer's continuous grace," adding that "she is the only person in the picture who gives every one of her lines the bloom of poetry and the immediacy of ordinary life." For her performance, Simmons won the Best Actress prize at the Venice Festival and a nomination for an Academy Award. Olivier also offered Simmons a chance to work with the Old Vic Company, which she declined in favor of a role in *Blue Lagoon* (1949), the drawing point being its location shots in the South Pacific. (Actress **Brooke Shields** fared little better in a remake of the film in 1980.)

In 1950, Simmons arrived in the United States on the arm of actor Stewart Granger, whom she married quietly on December 20, after his divorce from actress **Elspeth March**. It became necessary for Simmons to legally dissolve her contract with Howard Hughes before making her American film debut in *Androcles and the Lion* (1953); the complicated court battle lasted a year. The actress also made three other films in 1953—*The Actress*, *Young Bess* (in which she portrayed a youthful Queen *Elizabeth I), and *The Robe*—all considered to be among her best. They were followed by the historical dramas *The Egyptian* and *Desiree* (both 1954), in which Simmons played Desiree Clary (*Désirée) to Marlon Brando's Napoleon. She appeared opposite Brando once more in *Guys and Dolls* (1955), playing his love interest Sarah Brown in a musical role that was unlike anything she had done before. "She is surprisingly appealing in a part with almost no potential, and her Havana dance is a high point of the picture," wrote Stephen Sondheim in *Films in Review* (December 1955).

In June 1956, the Grangers became U.S. citizens, and Simmons gave birth to a daughter Tracy. The marriage ended in 1960, with charges of "outrageous cruelty" from the actress, who was now romantically involved with director Richard Brooks. Granger likened the split to a child breaking away from a parent: "The trouble with me is that I did everything for Jean in our marriage. I taught her how to read, how to talk, how to walk, how to carry herself. I taught her art, literature, current events. She was such a child. Our entire relationship was like Pygmalion." As for Simmons, she relinquished the Arizona Ranch on which the couple had lived, but got custody of Tracy. Soon after the divorce, Simmons married Brooks, who also provided her sensitive direction in *Elmer Gantry* (1960), one of the actress' most memorable films.

For the most part, Simmons was off the screen for three years following *Elmer Gantry*,

*Jean Simmons*

during which time she and Brooks welcomed a daughter Kate. She made her return in *All the Way Home* (1963), in the role of a wife who loses her beloved husband in an automobile accident. "She is irresistibly heart-tearing," reported Bosley Crowther. Alvin Marill concurred, writing in *Films in Review* (February 1972) that none of Simmons' seven films after *All the Way Home* even warrant discussion. The actress, however, did receive a second Oscar nomination for *The Happy Ending* (1969), also directed by Brooks, in which she plays a wife who turns to alcohol and men after her 15-year marriage comes apart.

Taking a respite from movies in the early 1970s, Simmons toured for two years in the musical *A Little Night Music*, after which she returned to work in occasional film and television. The actress divorced Brooks in 1977, but not before crediting him with helping her mature. "I had nothing but filmmaking and an over-protected life until I met him. He helped me realize that there was more to life than standing in front of a camera. And he taught me not to be afraid of accepting myself as being human and vulnerable."

**SOURCES:**

Katz, Ephraim. *The Film Encyclopedia*. NY: Harper-Collins, 1994.

Marill, Alvin H. "Jean Simmons," in *Films in Review*. February 1962.

Rothe, Anna, ed. *Current Biography 1952*. NY: H.W. Wilson, 1952.

**Barbara Morgan**,
Melrose, Massachusetts

## Simms, Ruth Hanna McCormick
(1880–1944).

*See McCormick, Ruth Hanna.*

## Simon, Jennifer Jones (b. 1919).

*See Jones, Jennifer.*

## Simon, Kate (1912–1990)

*Polish-born American autobiographer and travel writer. Born Kaila Grobsmith on December 5, 1912, in Warsaw, Poland; died of cancer on February 4, 1990, in Manhattan, New York; daughter of Jacob Grobsmith (a shoemaker) and Lina Babica (a corsetiere); Hunter College, B.A., 1935; lived with Stanley F. Goldman (a physician, d. 1942); married Robert Simon (a publisher), in 1947 (divorced 1960); children: daughter Alexandra (d. 1954).*

*Selected writings:* New York Places and Pleasures: An Uncommon Guidebook *(1959);* Italy: the Places in Between *(1970, 1984);* England's Green and Pleasant Land *(1974);* Fifth Avenue: A Very Social History *(1978);* Bronx Primitive: Portraits in a Child-hood *(1982);* A Wider World: Portraits in an Adolescence *(1986);* A Renaissance Tapestry: The Gonzaga of Mantua *(1988);* Etchings in an Hour Glass *(1990).*

Widely praised for her lively and entertaining prose, Kate Simon established her literary reputation as a travel writer with the 1959 publication of her successful *New York Places and Pleasures*, and went on to write similar guides for such cities as Mexico, Paris, London, and Italy. The recipient of awards from the National Book Critics Circle and the English Speaking Union, Simon was considered a master of the genre. J.H. Plumb of *The New York Times Book Review* wrote that she had made "one of the dullest forms of literature a brilliant work of art."

Born on December 5, 1912, Kate Simon lived in a Warsaw, Poland, ghetto before immigrating to the United States with her mother and younger brother. They settled with her father—who had left Poland when Kate was four—in the Tremont section of the Bronx. Simon did not get along with her overbearing father, clashing over his desire to see her become a concert pianist. Although she exhibited a talent for the instrument, she rebelled by refusing to practice and he countered with a threat to end her high school career with one year of secretarial training. Simon was saved from that fate by a letter from her principal indicating that the gifted student belonged in the academically challenging environment of James Monroe High School. Much of her free time, however, was devoted to caring for her younger brother and sister—a responsibility she recalled with some bitterness in her 1982 memoir of her early childhood, *Bronx Primitive: Portraits in a Childhood*.

Simon left her intolerable home situation and supported herself by teaching piano and English. The teenager found work as a nanny for an eccentric and radical couple, who introduced her to the exhilarating world of culture. Simon chronicled this time of struggle and discovery in her 1986 memoir *A Wider World: Portraits in an Adolescence*. She became an English major at Hunter College and adopted a bohemian lifestyle. While still in college, she began living with Stanley F. Goldman, a medical doctor (some sources indicate that they eventually married), with whom she had a child, Alexandra. Goldman died in 1942, the victim of several brain tumors, and 12 years later daughter Alexandra—in the throes of a similar illness—committed suicide.

In 1947, Kate married publisher Robert Simon, and began working in the editorial field for a number of publications, including *The New Republic, The Nation, Publishers Weekly,* and the Book-of-the-Month Club. Her second marriage provided her with the financial security to travel and from that point on she earned wide acclaim for lively, discerning, and highly perceptive travel writing. Her first book, *New York Places and Pleasures: An Uncommon Guidebook*, written in 1959 from an insider's perspective on the city, was a huge success. It attained bestseller status and went through several revisions after the first edition. She also wrote *Italy: the Places in Between* (1970 and 1984); *England's Green and Pleasant Land* (1974); *Fifth Avenue: A Very Social History* (1978); and *A Renaissance Tapestry: The Gonzaga of Mantua* (1988). The National Book Critics Circle, the English Speaking Union and Hunter College bestowed awards upon Simon for her writing.

At the time of her death from cancer in 1990, Simon was scheduled to begin teaching a writing course at Hunter College, and had recently submitted to Harper & Row a third autobiographical manuscript, *Etchings in an Hour Glass*, which dealt with her college years, two marriages, and most recent travels.

*Kate Simon*

**SOURCES:**
Andrews, Deborah, ed. *The Annual Obituary 1990.* Chicago, IL: St. James Press, 1991.
Flint, Peter B. *The New York Times* (obituary). February 5, 1990.
Garraty, John A., ed. *American National Biography.* NY: Oxford University Press, 1999.
Ryan, Bryan, ed. *Major 20th-Century Writers.* Vol. 4. Detroit, MI: Gale Research, 1991.

**Howard Gofstein**, freelance writer,
Detroit, Michigan

## Simon, Simone (1910—)

*French actress.* Born on April 23, 1910, in Béthune, France; attended schools in Berlin, Budapest, and Turin; never married; no children.

*Selected filmography:* Le Chanteur inconnu *(Fr., 1931);* Mam'zelle Nitouche *(Fr., 1931);* Tire-au-Flanc *(Fr., 1933);* Le Lac aux Dames *(Fr., 1934);* Les Yeux noirs *(Dark Eyes, Fr., 1935);* Les Beaux Jours *(Fr., 1935);* Girls' Dormitory *(US, 1936);* Ladies in Love *(US, 1936);* Seventh Heaven *(US, 1937);* Love and Hisses *(US, 1937);* Josette *(US, 1938);* La Bête humaine *(The Human Beast, Fr., 1938);* All That Money Can Buy *(1941);* Cat People

*(1942)*; Tahiti Honey *(1943)*; The Curse of the Cat People *(1944)*; Mademoiselle Fifi *(1944)*; Pétrus *(Fr., 1946)*; Temptation Harbor *(UK, 1947)*; Donne senza Nome *(Women Without Names, It., 1950)*; La Ronde *(Fr., 1950)*; Olivia *(Pit of Loneliness, Fr., 1951)*; La Plaisir *(House of Pleasure, Fr., 1952)*; Double Destin *(Fr., 1955)*; The Extra Day *(UK, 1956)*; La Femme en Bleu *(1973)*.

Although it was once rumored that actress Simone Simon was the love child of *Marion Davies and William Randolph Hearst, she was in fact born in 1910 in Béthune, France, to a French engineer father and an Italian mother. After living in a number of European locales as a child, Simon and her family settled in Paris when she was in her teens. There, she worked briefly as a fashion designer and model before she was discovered in a Paris café by Russian director Victor Tourjansky, who offered her a part in his forthcoming Paris-location movie, *Le Chanteur inconnu* (1931). Audiences were enchanted by Simon, with her petite stature and kittenish quality. After roles in several additional French films, among them *Mam'zelle Nitouche* (1931), *Le Lac aux Dames* (1934), and *Les Beaux Jours* (1935), Simone came to the attention of 20th Century-Fox, which brought her to America billed as "Europe's Sweetheart."

It was not an easy transition for Simone, who for the next two years had a running battle with the studio over the roles they selected for her and their efforts to give her a sleeker, more glamorous appearance. From the studio's point of view, she was temperamental and uncooperative. Fox replaced her with *Claudette Colbert in *Under Two Flags* (1936), intended as her American debut, relegating her to a small role in *Girls' Dormitory* (1936) instead. She subsequently appeared in *Seventh Heaven* (1937), *Love and Hisses* (1937), and *Josette* (1938), gaining quite a following. Despite her growing popularity, however, she returned to France.

Following her glowing performance in Claude Renoir's *La Bête humaine* (The Human Beast, 1938), she was invited back to Hollywood. Her second visit proved to be more productive. The best of her second round of American films, *Cat People* (1942), was praised by *Pauline Kael as revolutionary in the horror movie genre for its artful use of suggestion, sound effect, and camera angles; *Cat People* and its sequel *Curse of the Cat People* (1943) are now considered classics. During the early 1940s, in addition to her film work, Simon made a few vaudeville appearances and starred in the ill-fated musical *Three After Three*, which closed before making it to Broadway.

Simone
Simon

At the end of World War II, Simon once again returned to France. She continued to make French, English, and European movies throughout the mid-1950s, then was not seen on the screen again until 1973, when she appeared in *La Femme en Bleu*. She did make an appearance on the Paris stage in 1966, in *La Courte Paille* opposite Jean Meyer. The actress never married, although her relationship with a wealthy married Frenchman was the talk of Paris for many years.

SOURCES:

Halliwell, Leslie. *Halliwell's Film Guide*. NY: Scribner, 1983.

Katz, Ephraim. *The Film Encyclopedia*. NY: Harper-Collins, 1994.

Lamparski, Richard. *Whatever Became of . . .?* 2nd series. NY: Crown, 1967.

**Barbara Morgan**,
Melrose, Massachusetts

# Simone, Nina (1933—)

*African-American singer, songwriter, and pianist.*
*Born Eunice Kathleen Waymon on February 21,*

1933, in Tryon, North Carolina; daughter of John Divan Waymon (a day laborer) and Mary Kate Irvin (a minister); graduated as valedictorian of an Asheville, North Carolina, boarding school; attended the Juilliard School in New York; married Donald Ross, in 1958 (divorced 1959); married Andy Stroud, in 1961 (divorced 1970); children: Lisa Celeste Stroud (b. 1961).

Named by the Radio Disc Jockeys as Most Promising Singer of the Year (1960); was the first woman to receive Jazz Cultural Award; honored by Jazz at Home Club as Woman of the Year (1966); designated by the National Association of Television and Radio Announcers as Female Jazz Singer of the Year (1967).

Selected discography: Little Girl Blue (Bethlehem, 1958); Nina Simone & Her Friends (Bethlehem, 1959); The Amazing Nina Simone (Colpix, 1959); Nina Simone at Town Hall (Colpix, 1960); At Newport (Colpix, 1961); Forbidden Fruit (Colpix, 1961); At the Village Gate (Colpix, 1962); Sings Ellington (Colpix, 1962); Nina's Choice (Colpix, 1963); At Carnegie Hall (Colpix, 1963); Broadway-Blues-Ballads (Philips, 1964); Folksy Nina (Colpix, 1964); In Concert (Philips, 1964); I Put a Spell on You (Philips, 1965); Let It All Out (Philips, 1966); Pastel Blues (Philips, 1966); Wild Is the Wind (Philips, 1966); With Strings (Colpix, 1966); High Priestess of Soul (Philips, 1967); Silk & Soul (RCA, 1967); Sings the Blues (RCA, 1967); 'Nuff Said (RCA, 1968); The Best of Nina Simone (Philips, 1969); And Piano! (RCA, 1969); To Love Somebody (RCA, 1969); Black Gold (RCA, 1970); The Best of Nina Simone (RCA, 1971); Here Comes the Sun (RCA, 1971); Gifted & Black (Canyon, 1971); Emergency Ward! (RCA, 1972); Live at Berkeley (Stroud, 1973); It Is Finished (RCA, 1974); Lamentations (Versatile, 1977); Black Soul (RCA, 1977); Pure Gold (RCA, 1978); Baltimore (CTI, 1978); Cry Before I Go (Manhattan, 1985); Nina's Back (VPI, 1985); Don't Let Me Be Misunderstood (Mercury, 1988); The Best of Nina Simone (RCA, 1989); The Blues (Novus, 1991); The Best of the Colpix Years (Roulette, 1992); A Single Woman (Elektra, 1993); Point of No Return (soundtrack; RCA, 1993); The Essentials (RCA, 1993); The Essentials, Vol. 2 (RCA, 1993); Feeling Good (Mercury, 1994); After Hours (Verve, 1995); The Colpix Years (Rhino, 1996); Sings Nina (Verve, 1996); Saga of the Good Life and Hard Times (RCA, 1997).

Perhaps one of the most difficult singers to categorize, Nina Simone has recorded comfortably in many genres—from soul and jazz to gospel and popular music. Called the "High Priestess of Soul" by many of her admirers, Simone indicated in a 1997 interview with Brantley Bardin that she prefers to be remembered as "a diva from beginning to end who never compromised in what she felt."

Nina Simone was born Eunice Kathleen Waymon on February 21, 1933. She was the sixth of eight children born to John Divine Waymon and **Mary Kate Waymon**, who raised the children in an environment of music. She began playing piano by ear at the age of three, recalling in her autobiography, I Put a Spell on You: "Everybody played music. There was never any formal training; we learned to play the same way we learned to walk, it was that natural." Simone's substantial gift for music caused many to think of her as a prodigy; by the age of six, she was the regular pianist at the family's church. When the family was unable to afford piano lessons, a woman for whom Simone's mother worked paid for formal lessons with **Muriel Massinovitch**, who passed on her appreciation of Bach to her pupil. By the time Simone was in her senior year of high school, she had earned a one-year scholarship to the Juilliard School of Music in New York City. Intending to become the first black concert pianist, Simone had hoped her study at Juilliard might propel her into an opening at the prestigious Curtis Institute in Philadelphia. Her dreams ended when the institute rejected her application. Disappointed and convinced that racism was to blame, Simone stayed in Philadelphia for a while teaching piano. However, when she learned that one of her less-talented students had secured a summer job playing piano in Atlantic City, New Jersey, and was earning twice as much as she was earning, she left Philadelphia for Atlantic City herself. She took a job playing in a nightclub in 1954 and changed her name to Nina Simone (choosing "Nina" after a childhood nickname, and "Simone" after the actress *Simone Signoret).

Simone's career as a singer began serendipitously when the nightclub owner informed her that playing the piano wasn't enough, that she was required to sing as well. As she performed, she began to blend the genres that had influenced her into a fresh synthesis of music. "I knew hundreds of popular songs and dozens of classical pieces," she wrote in her autobiography, "so what I did was combine them: I arrived prepared with classical pieces, hymns and gospel songs and improvised on those, occasionally slipping in a part from a popular tune." Her increasing popularity prompted a move to more upscale dinner clubs, and in 1957 New York's Bethlehem Records signed her to cut an album.

After the album's release the following year as *Little Girl Blue*, Simone signed a contract in which she unknowingly relinquished all her rights—a mistake that cost her more than $1 million. It would be the first of many troubled relationships with her record labels. The success of the album's first single—a version of George and Ira Gershwin's "I Loves You, Porgy"—established her reputation, however, and became a Top 20 hit. It also prepared the way for her first concert at New York's Town Hall. Her popularity was such that she was soon touring throughout America and Europe.

Although Simone occasionally composed her own music, she found the most success by recording songs of other singers. Audiences loved her vocal interpretations, and her record label capitalized on the power of her performance by releasing several live albums. John S. Wilson of *The New York Times* hailed Simone as a unique and gifted interpreter who made each song her own: "[By] the time she has finished turning a song this way and that way, poking experimentally into unexpected crannies she finds in it, or suddenly leaping on it and whaling the daylights out of it, the song has lost most of

Nina Simone

its original colorization and has become, one might say, 'Simonized.'" The early 1960s saw the release of at least nine albums, half of which were live; as the decade wore on, she released another seven in a three-year period.

Simone rejected the label "jazz singer" as a way to describe her, and even thought of it as a racial epithet because she believed it was a label the white community used for black musicians. In the early 1960s, Simone's feelings of racial oppression merged with the influential friendship of civil-rights activist and playwright *Lorraine Hansberry. Simone's songs soon began to combine political aspects of the civil-rights movement, causing some to label her a protest singer, another term she dismissed. Inspired, however, by the bombing of a Baptist church in Birmingham, Alabama, which killed four black girls, ◄ Denise McNair, ◄ Cynthia Wesley, ◄ Addie Mae Collins, and ◄ Carol Robertson, and the assassination of civil-rights leader Medgar Evers in Mississippi, Simone wrote "Mississippi Goddam," which became an anthem of sorts for the civil-rights movement. The song won her the admiration of such black artists and leaders as Stokely Carmichael, *Miriam Makeba, Langston Hughes, and James Baldwin. For the rest of the decade Simone was regarded as the true singer of the civil-rights movement, with songs like "Sunday in Savannah," "Backlash Blues," and a ballad declared by the Congress of Racial Equality (CORE) to be the black national anthem, "To Be Young, Gifted, and Black." She received accolades as the "Most Promising Singer of the Year" in 1960, "Woman of the Year" by the Jazz at Home Club in 1966, and "Female Jazz Singer of the Year" by the National Association of Television and Radio Announcers in 1967.

Despite her professional success, the 1960s were a time of personal struggle for Simone. Following the deaths of Martin Luther King, Jr., Malcolm X, Lorraine Hansberry, and Langston Hughes, she believed the civil-rights movement had ended and felt pessimistic about the United States, believing it could probably never abolish racism. As an artist, she was disturbed by disrespectful audiences and angry over pirated recordings and the inadequate compensation she received for her work. Moreover, the Internal Revenue Service, accusing her of tax evasion, had begun to pursue her. After a divorce from her second husband, her manager Andy Stroud, in 1970, she began what would be a 15-year exile from the United States, residing variously in Switzerland, Liberia, Barbados, France, and England. Although she had released nine albums in the late 1960s and early 1970s with the RCA

label, Simone recorded little after leaving America with the exception of the critically acclaimed *Baltimore* album in 1978. In an attempt to revive her career, she went to London where a man who had promised to help her instead assaulted and abandoned her. She unsuccessfully attempted suicide, awaking gratefully the following morning in a London hospital with renewed hope for her future.

In 1985, Simone ended her self-imposed exile and returned to the United States. She performed in several concerts and recorded the album *Nina's Back*. Two years later, an advertising agency in England chose a 1958 Simone song, "My Baby Just Cares for Me," for a Chanel perfume commercial. The song was re-released in Europe in 1987 and became a hit. Simone settled in Bouc-Bel-Air in the south of France in 1991. That same year, she published her autobiography, *I Put a Spell on You*, to positive reviews. In 1993, Simone signed to the Elektra label and recorded her first album for a major studio in nearly 20 years, *A Single Woman*, which met with mixed reviews. Simone was also featured on the soundtrack of the movie *Point of No Return* that year.

Simone gained some unwanted press in 1995, however, when the media reported that she had shot a teenaged boy. Apparently, while gardening in her backyard, she had been disturbed by the noise of two boys swimming next door. After they ignored two requests by Simone to be quiet, she shot a buckshot rifle over the hedge in their direction. One of the teenagers suffered slight injuries, and she was ordered to pay a fine of $4,600 plus damages to his family. Placed on probation for 18 months, Simone also received psychological counseling. That same year, she was also given a two-month suspended sentence, plus a $5,000 fine, for causing and fleeing a 1993 automobile accident in which two motorcyclists had been injured in Aix-en-Provence, France.

During the late 1990s, Simone's career enjoyed a surge with the release of anthology collections of her work by Verve, Rhino, and RCA. In an assessment of Simone's work in *All Music Guide to Jazz*, Richie Unterberger, who considers the recordings she made for Philips in the mid-1960s to be her best, captures the artist's essence: "Simone's moody-yet-elegant vocals are like no one else's, presenting a fiercely independent soul who harbors enormous (if somewhat hard-bitten) tenderness."

**SOURCES:**

*Details.* January 1997, p. 66.

Igus, Toyomi, ed. *Book of Black Heroes: Great Women in the Struggle.* Just Us Books, 1991.

❦►
*Denise McNair,*
*Cynthia Wesley,*
*Addie Mae*
*Collins, and*
*Carol*
*Robertson. See*
*Davis, Angela for*
*sidebar.*

*Newsweek.* September–October 1995.

Phelps, Shirelle, ed. *Contemporary Black Biography.* Vol. 15. Detroit, MI: Gale Research, 1997.

Simone, Nina, with Stephen Cleary. *I Put a Spell on You* (autobiography), 1991.

Smith, Jessie Carney, ed. *Notable Black American Women.* Detroit, MI: Gale Research, 1992.

*Time.* October 2, 1995.

Unterberger, Richie. *All Music Guide to Jazz.* Edited by Michael Erlewine, *et al.* San Francisco, CA: Miller Freeman, 1996.

**Howard Gofstein**, freelance writer, Detroit, Michigan

## Simonetta, Bianca.

*See Sforza, Bianca Simonetta.*

# Simonovich-Efimova, Nina

## (1877–1948)

*Russian artist and puppet maker. Name variations: Nina Efimova Simonovich or Simonovicha. Born Nina Yakovlevna Simonovicha in 1877 in St. Petersburg, Russia; died in 1948; daughter of Yakov Mironovich Simonovich (a pediatrician) and Adelaida Semyonovna Bergman (a kindergarten advocate); attended high school in St. Petersburg; studied painting with O. Shmerling, and in the Paris studios of Delécluze, Eugene Carrière, and Henri Matisse; married Ivan Efimov (a sculptor), in 1906; children: at least one son, Adrian.*

Born into a wealthy and cultured Russian family in 1877, Nina Simonovich-Efimova grew up among progressive musicians, teachers, and artists, including her father Yakov Mironovich Simonovich, a pediatrician, her mother **Adelaida Semyonovna Bergman**, who in 1866 had organized Russia's first kindergarten, her aunt **Valentina Serova**, a composer, and her cousin Valentin Serov (1865–1911), a famous painter. Serov was instrumental in Simonovich-Efimova's artistic development through encouraging her in art classes and critiquing her early work. After graduating from a St. Petersburg high school in 1896, she taught for two years in Tbilisi while studying painting at O. Shmerling's studio. Her experiences during this time finally convinced her to dedicate herself entirely to art, and she picked up an added interest in puppet and shadow theater—a field in which she would be particularly innovative.

Simonovich-Efimova honed her drawing skills in Paris, studying at Delécluze's studio, but her first love was painting. Serov again lent a hand in her training by suggesting she attend the Stroganov Institute and, later, by directing her back to Paris to apprentice in the studio of Sym-

bolist painter Eugene Carrière. She gained valuable insight into the styles of Impressionist painters such as Van Gogh and Toulouse-Lautrec, and returned to Russia for further instruction from Serov, joining the Moscow School of Painting, Sculpture and Architecture where he taught. Her cousin's influence diminished somewhat after her marriage to sculptor Ivan Efimov in 1906, but he remained the primary motivator in her early career.

Another sojourn to Paris in 1908 resulted in her enrollment in Henri Matisse's studio. Her paintings at this time were traditional in composition and bore a strong use of color, which also played a major role in her easel paintings of Russian peasants during the years 1911 to 1915. Simonovich-Efimova was particularly drawn to the demanding art of silhouettes, and during the late 1920s she would also take up portrait painting, completing a number of unusual works in this genre.

Simonovich-Efimova found her true calling after she and her husband opened their first puppet theater in 1918. Through the Theater of Marionettes, Petrushkas and Shadows, she devoted the rest of her career to developing the art form of puppetry. "In the years of the Revolution," she wrote, "my artistic interests turned in another direction, to the puppet theatre. . . . I felt that the theatre was what the people very much needed at that stormy period. They looked at it with great hungry eyes. Theatre then was like bread." Introducing a dynamic combination of culture and elegance to her puppet shows, she succeeded in creating puppets detailed and vivid enough to communicate high drama. The innovative rod-puppets that Simonovich-Efimova built forever changed Russian puppet theater. The figures had rods attached to their joints, which allowed them to move more gracefully than had their predecessors. The range of expression allowed by Simonovich-Efimova's puppets drew hordes of spectators and critical raves to the more than 1,500 puppet theater performances she and Efimov organized between 1918 and 1936. Many of these they wrote themselves; they also staged several of Shakespeare's plays, with *Macbeth* considered the standout production. The Theatre of Marionettes attracted the participation of other artists excited by the symbolism inherent in puppetry, including *Liubov Popova, *Alexandra Exter (who created marionettes in the theater's earliest years), Vladimir Favorsky, and Pavel Florensky.

Puppetry was, in many ways, Simonovich-Efimova's response to what she considered to be the chasm between the left and right wings of the Russian art world. She was a member of the Four Arts Society, which aimed to synthesize painting, architecture, graphic design and sculpture—a union she achieved with her puppets. Unfortunately, the rise of Stalin's preferred style of Socialist Realism resulted in the decline in popularity and approval of her highly symbolic art form before her death in 1948. While she created a wide range of art, including puppets, paintings, graphics, theater designs, and sculpture, nearly 3,000 in all, only in the last decades of the 20th century did her work begin receiving attention from art historians.

**SOURCES:**
Yablonskaya, M.N. *Women Artists of Russia's New Age*. Edited by Anthony Parton. London: Thames & Hudson, 1990.

**Lisa C. Groshong**, freelance writer, Columbia, Missouri

## Simons, Frieda Hennock (1904–1960).

*See Hennock, Frieda B.*

# Simpson, Adele (1903–1995)

*American fashion designer. Born Adele Smithline on December 8, 1903, in New York City; died on August 23, 1995, in Greenwich, Connecticut; fifth daughter of Latvian immigrants; studied design at Pratt Institute; married Wesley Simpson (a textile executive), in 1927 (died 1976); children: Joan and Jeffrey.*

Born in New York City on December 8, 1903, Adele Simpson performed in vaudeville as a child, billed as "Babe Adele Smithline, the Petite Nightingale." Her true calling, however, would be behind the scenes, dressing celebrities as well as an entire generation of upper-middle-class American women in her meticulously constructed ready-to-wear fashions. Simpson studied design at Pratt Institute in Brooklyn, New York, then began working in the early 1920s as a dress designer at Ben Gershel's Seventh Avenue design house, which made ready-to-wear dresses. Seventh Avenue was the center of New York's clothing world, and Simpson enjoyed a meteoric rise to fame, becoming the city's highest paid designer by the time she turned 21 and replacing her older sister Anna as head designer at Gershel's.

In 1928, Simpson moved on to another of New York's Seventh Avenue houses, Mary Lee Fashions, where she began designing a line of clothing under her own label. She won a Coty American Fashion Critics award for her designs in 1947. (She was also one of the first designers, after *Claire McCardell, to market separates, although that innovation would not catch on for years with women accustomed to buying a full outfit.) In 1949, she purchased Mary Lee Fashions and renamed it Adele Simpson. There, from her office decorated entirely in pink and white, she created the Adele Simpson line, featuring classically cut suits and matching jacket and dress ensembles. (As did many American designers, she regularly traveled to Paris to view, and crib from, the new haute-couture and ready-to-wear collections.) Her conservative, ladylike clothes particularly appealed to her middle-aged clientele, who clamored for the simple, wearable fabrics and designs. The outfits, which were often color-coordinated and praised for being "safe," were reasonably priced and available in the most fashionable stores of the day, including B. Altman, Saks Fifth Avenue, and Bonwit Teller. Simpson eschewed trends in favor of a classic look that weathered the radical fashion trends of the 1960s and 1970s. She was so popular that first ladies *Lady Bird Johnson and *Pat Nixon both considered her their favorite designer, and she provided them with dresses for several state occasions. (*Jacqueline Kennedy, however, had quite different taste in clothing.)

Despite the high-profile celebrities who wore her designs, Simpson claimed, "I don't make clothes for a woman to make an entrance in. She has to live in them," and this low-key style proved enormously successful. By 1973, the company was turning more than a million yards of fabric into Adele Simpson clothes, grossing $6 million yearly. Simpson herself lived in style, inhabiting a seven-story townhouse on Manhattan's East Side. The house featured an entire apartment devoted to Simpson's collection of fabric and memorabilia, including costumes and dolls from all over the world. She called it her "Simpsonian Institute."

Upon her retirement in 1985, Simpson turned her company over to her daughter **Joan Raines** and son-in-law Richard Raines. Six years later, they sold it to a clothing company from Lowell, Massachusetts, which before her death in 1995, at age 91, dropped the Adele Simpson line and filed for bankruptcy.

**SOURCES:**
*Biography News*. Vol. 2, no. 2. March–April 1975. Detroit, MI: Gale Research, 1975.
*Current Biography*. October 1995. NY: H.W. Wilson, 1995.
*Newsweek*. September 1995.
*The New York Times* (obituary). August 24, 1995, p. D21.
*Time*. September 4, 1995, p. 23.

**Lisa C. Groshong**, freelance writer, Columbia, Missouri

## Simpson, Edna Oakes (1891–1984)

*American congressional representative (January 3, 1959–January 3, 1961). Born on October 26, 1891, in Carrollton, Greene County, Illinois; died on May 15, 1984, in Alton, Illinois; married Sidney E. Simpson (a congressional representative, died 1958).*

Edna Oakes Simpson was in her late 60s when her husband Sidney Simpson died in November 1958, during his eighth term as a Republican U.S. congressional representative from Illinois. He had been up for reelection barely a week later, and the Republican committee from Illinois' 20th Congressional District chose Edna Simpson to run in her husband's place. She did not make any public appearances in support of her campaign, but nonetheless swept past the Democratic challenger at the polls and was elected to the House of Representatives later that month.

Simpson served a single term, from January 1959 to January 1961, during which she did not make a single speech on the House floor. She served on the Committee on Interior and Insular Affairs and on the Committee on House Administration. During her term she proposed to include full railroad retirement benefits, in addition to veterans' benefits, for eligible retirees as an amendment to the Railroad Retirement Act. Declining to seek reelection, Simpson left Washington in 1961 to return to her hometown of Carrollton, Illinois, where she lived the rest of her life. She died in May 1984.

**SOURCES:**

Office of the Historian. *Women in Congress, 1917–1990.* Commission on the Bicentenary of the U.S. House of Representatives, 1991.

**Lisa C. Groshong**, freelance writer,
Columbia, Missouri

## Simpson, Elspeth (1738–1791).

*See Buchan, Elspeth.*

## Simpson, Helen (1897–1940)

*Australian-born British writer now best known for her detective novels. Born Helen de Guerry Simpson on December 1, 1897, in Sydney, Australia; died during the German bombing of London on October 14, 1940; daughter of Edward Percy Simpson (a solicitor) and Anne (de Lauret) Simpson; attended Sacred Heart Convent and Abbotsleigh, both in Australia; studied in France; studied music at Oxford; married Denys (or Denis) John Browne, in 1927; children: daughter Clemence.*

*Selected writings:* Pan in Pimlico: A Fantasy in One Act *(1924);* The Baseless Fabric *(1925);* Acquittal *(1925);* Cups, Wands, and Swords *(1927);* Mumbud-

*Edna Oakes Simpson*

get *(1928); (with Clemence Dane)* Enter Sir John *(1928);* The Desolate House *(1929); (with Dane)* Printer's Devil *(1930);* 'Vantage Striker *(1931);* Boomerang *(1932); (with Dane)* Re-Enter Sir John *(1932);* The Woman on the Beast: Viewed From Three Angles *(1933);* The Spanish Marriage *(1933);* Henry VIII *(biography, 1934);* Saraband for Dead Lovers *(1935);* The Female Felon *(1935);* Under Capricorn *(1937); (with Dane)* A Woman Among Wild Men: Mary Kingsley *(biography, 1938);* Maid No More *(1940).*

Helen Simpson was born in Sydney, Australia, on December 1, 1897, of aristocratic French lineage. After attending schools in New South Wales, she left Australia at age 16 to pursue further education in Europe. During World War I, from 1914 to 1918, Simpson worked as a decoder, unscrambling secret messages for the British Admiralty. She went on to study music at Oxford University, where she was one of the earliest women undergraduates. Her acquaintance at Oxford with fellow mystery writer *Dorothy L. Sayers and others led her to become a charter member of the Detection Club. Simpson produced a wide range of work during her lifetime, including plays, novels, translations from the French, histories, biographies, and even recipe books. Her claim to fame, however, rests in her five mystery or detective novels, three of which were written in collaboration with *Clemence Dane.

Simpson had already published a number of works, including seven plays, a book of poetry, and a book of short stories, prior to her collaboration with Dane. Her first novel, *Acquittal* (1925), was allegedly written in only 21 days, to win a bet. More of a psychological study than a crime novel, it begins with the heroine's acquittal on a charge of murdering her husband and ends with her having to choose between two suitors, one of whom unquestioningly accepts her innocence; the other, less convinced, does not care.

Simpson's literary collaboration with Dane began with *Enter Sir John*, published in 1928. The protagonist of this mystery and the two that followed, *Printer's Devil* (1930) and *Re-Enter Sir John* (1932), is an actor-manager of an English theater, probably the product of Dane's background as a playwright. Like a number of fictional English detectives, Sir John is an amateur at solving crimes who first tries his hand at it while attempting to overturn the murder conviction of a young actress named Martella; in the course of the novel, he both uncovers the real criminal and falls in love with Martella. All three of the Simpson-Dane novels feature a fully realized world of the theater in which recurring characters, complex from the start, develop further in each story. They also share a dark view of human personality, highlighting the possibilities of mental dissociation, something approaching split personality, not only in the criminals but, to a lesser yet still significant degree, in Sir John and Martella.

Between the second and third installments of the Sir John series, Simpson wrote 'Vantage Striker', which stands as evidence that she was responsible for the darker strains in their collaborative work. Written in the politically charged atmosphere of England in 1931, the novel features two main characters who become suspects when the British prime minister is murdered. The novel was less frivolous than Simpson's work with Dane, but its close association with the tense politics of 1930s England has caused it to become somewhat dated with the passage of time.

Although she never lived permanently in Australia after moving to England, Simpson used an Australian setting for two of her most famous works of fiction: *Boomerang* (1932) and *Under Capricorn* (1937). The former, a saga covering four generations of a family of French descent, not unlike Simpson's own family, won the James Tait Black Memorial Prize. *Under Capricorn*, the story of an Irish ex-convict's marriage to an aristocratic Irish woman, set in Simpson's homeland of New South Wales, was filmed by Alfred Hitchcock in 1949, with *Ingrid Bergman and Michael Wilding in the lead roles. Her 1935 novel *Saraband for Dead Lovers* would also be filmed, in 1948 (released in the U.S. as simply *Saraband*), starring Stewart Granger, *Joan Greenwood, and *Flora Robson.

Among the other books Simpson wrote were a translation from the French of *Heartsease and Honesty, being the Pastimes of the Sieur de Grammont, Steward to the Duc de Richelieu in Touraine* (1935), a book of recipes for cold food, and (with Dane) a biography of the intrepid Victorian traveler *Mary Kingsley, *A Woman Among Wild Men* (1938). She also worked as a radio broadcaster, and in 1938 ran unsuccessfully as a Liberal candidate on the Isle of Wight. In October 1940, during World War II, Simpson died unexpectedly of shock brought on after German bombers attacked the London hospital in which she was recuperating from an operation. She was 42.

**SOURCES:**

Hayne, Barrie. "Helen Simpson," in *Dictionary of Literary Biography*, Vol. 77: *British Mystery Writers, 1920–1939*. Edited by Bernard Benstock and Thomas F. Staley. Detroit, MI: Gale Research, 1989.

Kunitz, Stanley J., and Howard Haycraft, eds. *Twentieth Century Authors*. NY: H.W. Wilson, 1942.

Reilly, John M., ed. *Twentieth-Century Crime and Mystery Writers*. NY: St. Martin's Press, 1980.

Wilde, William H., Joy Hooton, and Barry Andrews. *The Oxford Companion to Australian Literature*. Melbourne, Australia: Oxford University Press, 1985.

**Lisa C. Groshong**, freelance writer, Columbia, Missouri

# Simpson, Mary Michael (1925—)

*American priest and psychotherapist. Born on December 1, 1925, in Evansville, Indiana; daughter of Link Wilson Simpson and Mary Garrett (Price) Simpson; Texas Women's University, B.A., B.S., 1946; graduated from New York Training School for Deaconesses, 1949; graduated from Westchester Institute Training in Psychoanalysis and Psychotherapy, 1976.*

*First American nun to be ordained an Episcopal priest (1977); first woman to become a canon in the American Episcopal Church (1977); first ordained woman invited to preach at Britain's Westminster Abbey (1978).*

Born in 1925 in Evansville, Indiana, Mary Michael Simpson graduated from Texas

Women's University in 1946 and from the New York Training School for Deaconesses in 1949. She began her long and distinguished career with the Episcopal Church as a missionary at the Holy Cross Mission in Bolahun, Liberia, on the west coast of Africa, in 1950. Upon her return to the United States in 1952, Simpson worked at Margaret Hall School, a girls' school run by the Episcopal Order of St. Anne in Versailles, Kentucky, serving as academic head from 1958 to 1961. A member of the Order of St. Helena (an offshoot of the Order of St. Anne), she then served as the sister in charge of the Convent of St. Helena mission in Liberia (1962–67) and as director of novices there (1968–74).

Simpson returned to the United States in 1974 to become a pastoral counselor on the staff of the Cathedral of St. John the Divine in New York City. She supplemented her counseling skills through training at the Westchester Institute Training in Psychoanalysis and Psychotherapy, from which she graduated in 1976. Two years earlier she had opened her own private practice as a psychoanalyst, adding on a directorship of the Cathedral Counseling Service in 1975.

In 1976, the Episcopal General Convention agreed to open the priesthood to women. Only months later, in January 1977, Simpson became the first American nun to be ordained an Episcopal priest. (Several other women were ordained shortly thereafter.) While she received considerable support, there were some who felt that the convention had erred in its decision, and a number of people—including two sisters in her order—declined to receive communion from a woman. That year Simpson added to her duties at the Cathedral of St. John the Divine by becoming a canon there, the first woman canon (assistant to the dean) in the American Episcopal Church. In 1978, she was invited to preach at London's venerable Westminster Abbey, becoming the first ordained woman to preach there. Her invitation, from one of Westminster Abbey's canons, was part of a tour designed to boost support for the ordination of women in the Church of England. Simpson retired from the Cathedral of St. John the Divine in 1987, becoming an honorary canon, although she has since served as a pastor at several churches in the New York City area. A contributing author of *Yes to Women Priests* (1978), she is also the author of *The Ordination of Women in the American Episcopal Church: The Present Situation* (1981).

**SOURCES:**
Read, Phyllis J., and Bernard L. Witlieb. *The Book of Women's Firsts*. NY: Random House, 1992.

*Who's Who in Religion.* 4th ed. Wilmette, IL: Marquis Who's Who, 1992.

**Lisa C. Groshong**, freelance writer, Columbia, Missouri

# Simpson, Valerie (1946—)

*African-American songwriter, performer, and record producer who, with her husband, became the writing team of Ashford and Simpson. Born in the Bronx, New York, on August 26, 1946; sister of Ray Simpson, lead vocalist for the Village People; studied music at Chatham Square School; married Nickolas Ashford (a songwriter), in 1974.*

In 1964, fresh out of high school, Valerie Simpson teamed up with Nickolas Ashford and began writing songs. With the success of the Ray Charles recording of their "Let's Go Get Stoned" (1966), they signed on with Berry Gordy's Motown organization and wrote a series of hits for other performers, including Marvin Gaye and **Tammi Terrell**'s romantic duets "Ain't No Mountain High Enough" and "You're All I Need to Get By" and ❧➤ **Diana Ross**' "Reach Out and Touch (Somebody's Hand)," which set Ross' solo career in motion after her break with \***The Supremes**. During this time, Simpson also made two impressive solo albums, *Exposed!* (1971) and *Valerie Simpson* (1972), which are often overlooked because they did not sell well.

The pair launched their own performing career—as Nick & Valerie—in 1973 (a year before their marriage), with the albums *Keep It Comin'* (Motown) and *Gimme Something Real* (Warner Bros.). Their first breakthrough success was in 1977 with the gold album *Send It*, which included the Top Ten R&B hit "Don't Cost You Nothing." It was followed by another gold-seller, *Is It Still Good to Ya?*, considered their best album of the 1970s. Yet a third gold album, *Stay Free* (1978), contained the single "Found a Cure," another song making the pop Top 40. Their biggest album hit of all time was *Solid* in 1984.

Meantime, the couple continued to tour and create hits for such clients as Diana Ross, **Gladys Knight** and the Pips, and **Whitney Houston**, for whom they wrote "I'm Every Woman," which was included on the soundtrack of *The Bodyguard* in 1993.

**Barbara Morgan**, Melrose, Massachusetts

# Simpson, Wallis Warfield (1895–1986).

*See Windsor, Wallis Warfield, duchess of.*

❧
*Ross, Diana.*
*See*
*Supremes, The.*

## Sims, Naomi (1948—)

*Entrepreneur who was the first major African-American fashion model. Born on March 30, 1948, in Oxford, Mississippi; graduated from Westinghouse High School in Pittsburgh; studied briefly at New York's Fashion Institute of Technology; married Michael Findlay (an art dealer); children: John Phillip.*

*Was the first African-American woman featured on the covers of major fashion magazines (late 1960s); founded the Naomi Sims Collection (1973); founded Naomi Sims Beauty Products (1985).*

Naomi Sims was born on March 30, 1949, in Oxford, Mississippi. Her early childhood was marked by chaos and abandonment, as her father left the family when she was an infant, her mother suffered a nervous breakdown, and Sims and her sisters were separated after being sent to live with various relatives. Sims was raised by loving foster parents, but continued to battle the usual adolescent insecurities, which were magnified by a height (5'10" by the time she was 13) that would one day propel her to the pinnacle of modeling. The insecurity remained for years, but her self-reliance helped to transform her from a gangling adolescent into a striking teenager.

After graduating from Westinghouse High School in Pittsburgh, Sims moved to New York City to study at the Fashion Institute of Technology. During college, she began modeling for a fashion illustrator at the rate of $6 per hour. Her modeling career received a boost after she boldly approached top fashion photographer Gosta Peterson, who hired her at a rate of $60 per hour. Finding the double demands of a growing modeling career and college studies too taxing, Sims left school to focus on her work.

Despite the tenfold increase in her modeling fees, she nonetheless went through weeks of unemployment, living on borrowed money from the modeling agency that was representing her. Sims therefore eagerly accepted a *New York Times* assignment that placed her on the cover of its *Fashion of the Times* supplement—the first for a black model. That cover photograph was to change the fashion industry and the national perception of beauty. Never before had a woman of such deep, rich color been used to exemplify beauty. Fashion designer Halston understood the significance of the exposure of Sims: "She was the great ambassador for all black people. . . . She broke down all the social barriers." Indeed, Sims became the first black model published on the covers and in the pages of such Anglo-American bastions of fashion as *Vogue, Ladies' Home Journal, Life,* and *Cos-*

*mopolitan.* She won such honors as the Model of the Year Award in 1969 and 1970, and earned a spot on the International Best-Dressed List for several years in the 1970s. *Ladies' Home Journal* named her one of its Women of Achievement in 1970; she received the key to the city of Cleveland, Ohio, in 1971; and the governor of Illinois proclaimed September 20, 1973, Naomi Sims Day.

Despite her tremendous success, Sims found modeling both shallow and boring. She left the profession while still a youthful 24, and turned her attention to establishing herself as an entrepreneur. Dissatisfied with the quality of wigs available to African-American women, Sims started a wig company in 1973. Its cornerstone product used a synthetic fiber called Kanekalon Presselle, which she invented and patented, that closely approximated the texture of black women's hair. The wigs in the Naomi Sims Collection became enormously popular and propelled her to higher levels of financial success.

In 1985, Sims formed another thriving company, Naomi Sims Beauty Products, with wares exclusively formulated for African-American women, sold throughout the United States and in the Bahamas. She served as chair of the board, and her continued business achievements brought more recognition, including an invitation to be executive-in-residence at the School of Business Administration of Georgetown University in Washington, D.C. Sims also wrote several books, all published by Doubleday, including *All About Health and Beauty for the Black Woman* (1975), *How to Be a Top Model* (1979), *All about Hair Care for the Black Woman* (1982), and *All about Success for the Black Woman* (1983). Married and the mother of one son, she has lectured on such subjects as sickle-cell anemia, education, and drug abuse, and served on the board of directors of the Northside Center Child Development in Harlem, New York.

**SOURCES:**
*Essence.* January 1986, p. 41.
*Ladies' Home Journal.* November 1968, p. 114.
*People.* August 22, 1977, pp. 14–19.
Smith, Jessie Carney, ed. *Notable Black American Women.* Detroit, MI: Gale Research, 1992.

**Lisa C. Groshong**, freelance writer, Columbia, Missouri

## Sinaida.

*Variant of Zinaida.*

## Sinclair, Catherine (fl. 1475)

*Duchess of Albany. Flourished around 1475; daughter of *Elizabeth Douglas (d. before 1451) and William*

Sinclair, earl of Orkney and Caithness; married Alexander Stewart (c. 1454–1485), 1st duke of Albany, around 1475 (divorced due to propinquity of blood in 1477); children: Alexander (b. around 1477), bishop of Moray; Margaret Stewart (d. after July 5, 1542, who married Patrick Hamilton of Kincavil); Andrew. Alexander's second wife was *Anne de la Tour (d. 1512).

# Sinclair, Catherine (1800–1864)

*Scottish novelist and children's writer. Born on April 17, 1800, in Edinburgh, Scotland; died on August 6, 1864, in London, England; daughter of Sir John Sinclair (a politician and agriculturist) and Diana (Macdonald) Sinclair; never married; no children.*

*Selected writings:* Charlie Seymour; or, The Good Aunt and the Bad Aunt (1832); Modern Accomplishments, or the March of Intellect (1836); Modern Society: or, The March of Intellect (1837); Hill and Valley, or Hours in England and Wales (1838); Holiday House: A Series of Tales (1839); Scotland and the Scotch; or, the Western Circuit (1840); Shetland and the Shetlanders; or, The Northern Circuit (1840); Modern Flirtations; or, A Month at Harrowgate (1841); Scotch Courtiers and the Court (1842); Jane Bouverie; or, Prosperity and Adversity (1846); The Lives of the Caesars; or, the Juvenile Plutarch (1847); The Journey of Life (1847); The Business of Life (1848); Sir Edward Graham; or, Railway Speculators (1849); Lord and Lady Harcourt; or, Country Hospitalities (1850); The Kaleidoscope of Anecdotes and Aphorisms (1851); Beatrice; or, The Unknown Relatives (1852); Popish Legends or Bible Truths (1852); The Priest and the Curate; or, The Two Diaries (1853); Lady Mary Pierrepoint (1853); Frank Vansittart; or, The Model Schoolboys (1853); The Cabman's Holiday: A Tale (1855); Cross Purposes, a Novel (1855); Modern Superstition (1857); Letters (1861–1864).

Catherine Sinclair was a prolific and popular writer whose early children's book *Holiday House: A Series of Tales* (1839), marked a turning point in the history of children's literature. Those who objected to whimsy and imaginative literature for children (and there were many in that era) had difficulty finding fault with a book that was highly moral and instructive, and at the same time allowed children the right to be young and boisterous and make mistakes.

Born in 1800 in Edinburgh, Scotland, Sinclair was the fourth daughter of **Diana Macdonald Sinclair** and Sir John Sinclair, a politician and the president of the Board of Agriculture. At age 14, she became her father's secretary; she

held that position for the next 21 years, until his death in 1835. She never married, devoting her life to her father, her writing, and acts of charity.

Sinclair was both an enthusiastic Protestant and a writer with a vivid and lively imagination. These nearly conflicting elements helped in the creation of novels that gained her an enduring reputation despite the moral tone of her work. Nearly all of her books were written for young people, with a special emphasis on attracting them to the right path rather than forcing them to it. The majority of her works stress the pitfalls of growing up and the dangers faced by young people—especially young women—as they prepare to enter the adult world. Her attention to detail is highlighted in her several guidebooks, including *Shetland and the Shetlanders* and *Scotland and the Scotch* (both 1840), which are steeped in the history and folklore of the regions.

Many of Sinclair's tendencies as a writer are found in her first book, *Charlie Seymour; or, The Good Aunt and the Bad Aunt* (1832), which was written, as were many of her early books, for her niece **Diana Boyle** and nephew George Frederick Boyle. Sinclair did not publish another book before her father's death in 1835; soon thereafter, however, she produced two lengthy but well-received novels, *Modern Accomplishments, or the March of the Intellect* (1836) and its conclusion, *Modern Society: or, The March of Intellect* (1837). Aimed at young women on the brink of maturity, these books endeavored to show the reader the bad results of making shallow choices and presented the Christian way of life as highly desirable.

Sinclair's most important literary contribution, *Holiday House* (1839), is the written version of a series of tales she had told her niece and nephew, featuring three children whose natural goodness cannot be quashed by the adversities of life. In the midst of their adventures, Sinclair placed the "Nonsensical Story of Giants and Fairies," in which Master No-book is tempted from home by the fairy Do-nothing and saved by the fairy Teach-all from the giant Snap-em-up who devours lazy, fat, selfish children. Although heavily moral, the collection is hailed as one of the first books for children intended chiefly for pleasure, and it is groundbreaking in not condemning children for their natural inclinations for play or to get into mischief. While most books of the times polarized children as good or bad, obedient or disobedient, Sinclair created stories in which children were allowed to laugh and play and experience life.

A devout Christian, Sinclair was strongly anti-Catholic and used her writing to expose "papists" as dishonest and deceitful. *Popish Legends or Bible Truths* (1852), *Modern Superstition* (1857), and the scathing *Beatrice* (1852) make it abundantly clear that she was horrified by what she considered the Catholic Church's ability to use the stories of saints' lives, attractive to children's imaginations, as a tool for mind control. She saw in the bland and boring stories given to children by strict Protestants the annihilation of the "right" Protestant way of life; hence her interest in writing literature that appealed to childish fancy while retaining its ability to "improve" the reader.

Sinclair's other works are primarily concerned with the teaching of children, especially young girls, and on setting them on the right path to heaven. *Jane Bouverie* (1846), *Modern Flirtations* (1841), *Lord and Lady Harcourt; or, Country Hospitalities* (1850), and, in some respects, *Beatrice* all perform this function. Among her books aimed at boys were *Charlie Seymour* and *Frank Vansittart; or, The Model Schoolboys* (1853). She also wrote a number of unabashed religious tracts, for example *The Journey of Life* (1847) and *The Business of Life* (1848), which are not stories so much as conversations and advice for living. Sinclair's final and most popular projects were her *Letters* (1861–64) for children. These books, in which certain words were replaced with pictures, were extremely popular, selling some 100,000 copies each.

In addition to her writing, Sinclair also devoted her energy to philanthropy, providing money to build seats for pedestrians along well-traveled roads, establish drinking fountains around Edinburgh, where she lived all her life, found soup kitchens, and fund a mission station. She died while staying with one of her brothers in Kensington, England, on August 6, 1864.

**SOURCES:**

Buck, Claire, ed. *The Bloomsbury Guide to Women's Literature.* NY: Prentice Hall, 1992.

*The Concise Dictionary of National Biography.* Oxford: Oxford University Press, 1992.

John, Judith Gero. "Catherine Sinclair," in *Dictionary of Literary Biography*, Vol. 163: *British Children's Writers, 1800–1880.* Edited by Megan Khorana. Detroit, MI: Gale Research, 1996.

Kunitz, Stanley J., and Howard Haycraft, eds. *British Authors of the Nineteenth Century.* NY: H.W. Wilson, 1936.

Shattock, Joanne. *The Oxford Guide to British Women Writers.* Oxford: Oxford University Press, 1993.

**Lisa C. Groshong**, freelance writer, Columbia, Missouri

## Sinclair, Eleanor (d. 1518)

*Countess of Atholl. Died in 1518; daughter of William Sinclair, earl of Orkney and Caithness; married John Stewart also known as John of Balveny (c. 1440–1512), 1st earl of Atholl; children: Anne Stewart (fl. 1515). John Stewart was first married to \*Margaret Douglas (b. around 1427), the "Fair Maid of Galloway."*

## Sinclair, May (1863–1946)

*Influential English novelist, critic, suffragist, and philosopher of the early 20th century, whose novel* The Divine Fire *was the sensation of 1904. Name variations: (pseudonym) Julian Sinclair. Born Mary Amelia St. Clair Sinclair in Rock Ferry, Cheshire, England, in 1863; died in Aylesbury, Buckinghamshire, England, on November 14, 1946; sixth child and only daughter of William Sinclair (a shipowner) and Amelia (Hind) Sinclair; educated by tutors, self-taught, and spent one year at Cheltenham Ladies' College (1881–82); never married; no children.*

*Selected writings: (novels)* The Divine Fire *(1904),* Mr. and Mrs. Nevill Tyson *(1898),* The Helpmate *(1907),* The Creators *(1910),* The Belfry *(1916),* The Tree of Heaven *(1917),* Mary Olivier: A Life *(1919),* Life and Death of Harriet Frean *(1922),* The Allinghams *(1927); (biography)* The Three Brontës *(1912), as well as a fictionalized version of their lives, entitled* The Three Sisters *(1914); (autobiography)* A Journal of Impressions in Belgium *(1915); also published a number of collections of short stories, including* Uncanny Stories *(1923) and* The Intercessor and Other Stories *(1931).*

May Sinclair was a famous English novelist between 1904 and 1930, whose reputation has now evaporated. Chronologically she holds a place in English women's literature after George Eliot (\***Mary Anne Evans**) and before \***Virginia Woolf**, and she is one of the authors who created a transitional literature between Victorianism and Modernism. Prolific and energetic, she wrote 24 novels in all, using several distinct styles: early works on philosophical idealism, a "middle period" series advocating social reform, and a later group bringing the insights of Freudian psychology to a wide popular audience. She pioneered in "stream of consciousness" writing and, like her contemporary Samuel Butler and her successor D.H. Lawrence, specialized in depictions of the intense, suppressed emotionality of English family life. She was also a poet, critic, and essayist, befriended many of the great literary modernists, including Ezra Pound and T.S. Eliot, and helped them in their early struggles for publication and recognition.

May Sinclair

Sinclair was born in 1863 in Cheshire, just across the River Mersey from the port of Liverpool. Her Scottish father and Irish mother had five sons before May, but were an incompatible couple. **Amelia Hind Sinclair** was puritanical; William Sinclair was a heavy drinker and womanizer. He had inherited a shipping business but in 1870, when May was seven, he went bankrupt. The family broke up, never to reunite, and from then on May lived in a succession of different parts of England with her mother, suddenly forced into genteel poverty. She was always secretive about her early years and biographers have found it difficult to unravel the details. Several have inferred its outline from her later novel *Mary Olivier*, however, which appears to be strongly autobiographical. It implies that she was involved in a prolonged love-hate relationship with her mother and that, thirsty for the formal education that had been granted to her brothers but denied her, retreated into books and learning.

We do know that at the age of 18 she was sent to Cheltenham Ladies' College, a pioneering boarding school for girls, where she made a highly favorable impression on the principal, *Dorothea Beale. Her first published work was a school essay on Descartes that Beale published in the college's magazine, which shows incredible maturity and insight for a largely self-taught teenager. After just one year Sinclair left school but her friendship with Beale persisted in a long and profound correspondence. Beale was alarmed to find Sinclair losing her conventional Christian faith but introduced her to the writings of T.H. Green, whose Anglicized version of German philosophical idealism filled part of the religious void in her life, as it did for many of her spiritually restless contemporaries. Beale remained an influential figure and tried to discourage Sinclair from writing fiction, which she regarded as a frivolous alternative to straight philosophy. Sinclair was strong enough to go ahead with her fiction in any event but never lost interest in its philosophical underpinnings and wrote two full-scale philosophical studies, *A Defence of Idealism* (1917) and *The New Idealism* (1922), much later in life.

*If* the isolation and the battles with her mother in her early life left her outwardly timid, they also left her with an unyielding core, with a tendency to question and challenge authority, and with great sensitivity to any incursions on the freedom and integrity of the individual.

—Hrisey D. Zegger

Sinclair spent the next 18 years (1882–1901) nursing her sick mother whose death in 1901 finally enabled her to concentrate on her own literary career. All her brothers were heavy drinkers and all died prematurely, as did her estranged father, leading her to expect that her heredity probably condemned her too to a premature grave. In any event, she lived to be 83. During the 1880s and 1890s, chronically impoverished, she published several translations from German, in which she was fluent, on subjects as diverse as church history and army reform. She also wrote and published a book of poetry, *Nakiketas*, a poetical rendering of her philosophical quest, under a male pseudonym, "Julian Sinclair." Her first novel, *Audrey Craven* (1897), coincided with a move to London after more than a decade in secluded coastal Devonshire. It too was a fictional vindication of her idealistic philosophy. With letters of encouragement from two of the great novelists of her day, Henry James and George Gissing, Sinclair then began work on *The Divine Fire*. Its publication in 1904 transformed her overnight from a struggling, almost anonymous figure into a novelist famous throughout the English-speaking world.

*The Divine Fire* also bears the imprint of Green's philosophy, which emphasized the im-portance of self-realization and of being true to one's self in the face of all obstacles. It tells the story of a Cockney poet who overcomes a series of adversities, including low social class and being disowned by his father, in pursuit of a career in literature. His inner reward is the knowledge that he has been true to himself; his outer reward is the hand in marriage of Lucia, the heroine, whom he wins from an opportunistic rival. The novel's popularity in England was outstripped by the acclaim it received in New York. Sinclair's American publisher, Henry Holt, invited her to tour America and promote it. On this visit, she met President Theodore Roosevelt in the White House and stayed with novelist *Sarah Orne Jewett. She also attended Mark Twain's 70th birthday party. He found her so impenetrably shy and silent that at the end of dinner he thanked her for "a remarkably interesting silence." From then on, she visited America regularly and remained a favorite of American readers until the 1930s.

Despite her reticence, Sinclair gradually became an important figure on the British literary scene, not only as a writer but as a critic of fiction and poetry. Like her contemporaries H.G. Wells and Samuel Butler, and like her juniors James Joyce and D.H. Lawrence, she was in revolt against what she thought of as the stifling conventions of Victorian middle-class life. She was sympathetically interested in daring literary experiments, opposed censorship, and was among the first critics to see real genius in the poetry of Ezra Pound and T.S. Eliot. She acclaimed Eliot's "Love Song of J. Alfred Prufrock" at a time when it was slighted by most other critics, and she protested in public against the suppression of Lawrence's novel *The Rainbow* in 1915. She became a London literary host, encouraging and welcoming writers from her own and younger generations to her house in St. John's Wood. Among them were many of the prominent English writers of the years 1900 to 1930, including H.G. Wells, John Galsworthy, Bertrand Russell, Hugh Walpole, *Rebecca West, and the spiritualist *Evelyn Underhill, and such visiting Americans as Upton Sinclair, Ezra Pound, and Sinclair Lewis. She never served alcohol, however, remembering her father's and her brothers' fatal drunkenness.

Her own writing continued to explore the psychological burden of family life. In *The Helpmate* (1907), a censorious Victorian bride discovers that her husband had had a sexual affair before meeting her. She punishes him by trying to "uplift" him to a form of perpetual chastity but the husband regards sex as a physiological drive he cannot deny, and he eventually reacts by having another affair. His bitter comment: "It's as simple as hunger and thirst: and if there's no clean water you drink dirty water." The reconciliation scene at the end, where the wife yields to his demands, was shocking for its time; its message was that spiritual love needs the support of sexual love and that the Victorian ideal of the sexless helpmeet was destructive.

*The Helpmate*, and other successors to *The Divine Fire*, began to address themes of social injustice. It was a jarringly "realistic" view of family life by comparison with her earlier works. A later novel, *The Combined Maze* (1913), explored the economic forces pressing down on lower middle- and upper-working class families and stifling their aspirations. A social and political reform particularly close to Sinclair's heart was votes for women. She became an advocate of female suffrage, contributed regularly to the journal *Votes for Women*, and wrote a treatise on the philosophy of feminism. She even marched on behalf of suffrage in a London parade and later conveyed her experiences into *The Tree of Heaven* (1917), a pro-suffrage novel. At the same time, she was dismayed by the increasingly violent tactics used by some of the militant suffragists led by *Emmeline and *Christabel Pankhurst, which included arson fires and campaigns of smashing London shop windows in the years 1910 to 1912. Her characters Mrs. Blathwaite and her daughter Angela are thinly disguised versions of the Pankhursts and her heroine, Dorothy, condemns their bullying intolerance.

Sinclair also pioneered in the use of "stream of consciousness" narration, particularly to invoke the feelings of young children as they come to apprehend the world. She reacted enthusiastically to the works of Sigmund Freud, sharing his view of the psychological struggle and repression that takes place as a child is socialized into the world, and the psychosexual drama of parent-child relationships. She befriended Ernest Jones, the pioneer of English psychoanalysis who was also Freud's first English translator, and contributed funds for establishing the first psychoanalytic clinic in London. Her novel *The Three Sisters* (1914) is an early fictional treatment of suppressed sexuality and intergenerational sexual rivalry. Some critics (especially the men) found it embarrassingly frank in its insistence on women's sexuality and its denial of the Victorian ideals of saintly self-sacrifice in women. Her postwar novel *Anne Severn and the Fieldings* (1922) pursued Freud's themes of sublimation and hysteria, showing how energy that cannot be used sexually is diverted into the constructive work of civilization or, if something goes wrong, into hysteria.

In 1914, the outbreak of the First World War interrupted Sinclair's literary and philosophical work. Although she was now 51, she volunteered to serve in an ambulance brigade with the British Expeditionary Force in Belgium. She had expected to be terrified by the carnage of battle but, oddly, found her role exciting and even pleasurable; she said seeing the war was a way of "touching Reality at its highest point in a secure and effortless consummation." Independent-minded, and far older than most members of the force, however, she soon proved unsuited to the work and her commander, Dr. Hector Munro, urged her to return to Britain where she could put her considerable talents to work as a fund raiser. Her few weeks in Belgium did, however, give her a taste of the war's reality and prevented her from the romanticization of the conflict which remained common to Britons on the "home front." Nevertheless, she did think the war worth fighting and shared the spirit of war-glorification of most of her contemporaries—a theme evident in the last sections of *The Tree of Heaven*. She published her Belgium journals and donated the royalties to the ambulance service. *Tasker Jevons* (1916) was another element of her contribution to the war effort, a novel about a successful writer who saves his failing reputation by acting heroically as an ambulance volunteer in the war. She modeled the character of Jevons on her friend and literary rival Arnold Bennett.

In the postwar years Sinclair continued to publish prolifically. *Mary Olivier* (1919), a fictional rendering of her childhood in impressionistic or "imagist" style, is now regarded by many critics, especially feminists, as her masterpiece. Unlike her wartime books, it was self-consciously artistic, with the stream of consciousness method more highly developed than ever before, and comparable to that of *Dorothy Richardson's *Pilgrimage*, which she had praised in an enthusiastic review. Some of it was written in the second person singular: "When you smelled mignonette you thought of Mamma and Mark and the sumach tree, and Papa standing on the steps, and the queer laugh that came out of his beard. When it rained you were naughty and unhappy because you couldn't go out of doors." It contained an attack on Victorian religiosity as shallow and punitive, and built up a powerful indictment of parents' stifling of their children's ambitions. Its heroine, Mary, struggles against the constraints of convention and propriety to become a real individual, a struggle played out in a symbolic interaction of light and darkness.

Although Mary spends 20 years nursing her mother and is forced to renounce her lover, she begins to succeed as a writer (as had Sinclair herself) and to feel she is true to her real self.

Throughout the 1920s, Sinclair was one of the established figures of English literature, widely admired, much published, and a regular press pundit. In 1931, however, after a last burst of creativity and the publication of four novels in four years, she was forced to stop writing because of the onset of Parkinson's disease. She moved from London to Bierton, near Aylesbury, Buckinghamshire, where she lived with her housekeeper and companion **Florence Bartrop**, who had joined her in 1919. The last 15 years of her life were a disappointing anticlimax after her three decades of eminence. By then, such philosophers as Bertrand Russell and Wittgenstein were eclipsing the memory and reputation of her mentor T.H. Green, while a new literary generation, notably Virginia Woolf and the Bloomsbury Group, was pushing further the literary methods she had helped to develop. Sinclair lived through the Second World War and died quietly in 1946 at Bierton.

Her works were all out of print by the 1960s but her reputation did enjoy a minor revival during the new feminist movement of the 1970s and 1980s, where she was acclaimed for her psychological insight into gender issues. As critic Jean Radford wrote in 1980, introducing a new edition of Sinclair's *Mary Olivier*, that novel "contains one of the most sustained and concentrated portraits of a mother-daughter relationship in fiction. . . . In nineteenth century fiction there is a curious silence about the mother-daughter relationship. In a surprising number of texts the mother is dead, usually in childbirth, but fictionally 'killed off' as an active agent in her daughter's characterization. In *Mary Olivier* the reverse is true; father, brothers, lovers fall away, one by one, leaving the two women confronting each other in a symbolic return to the mother-child relation." Her eclipse is not entirely surprising. She was one of several daring innovators of her era but was always conventional enough to attract a big and admiring audience. Much of her work can still be read with pleasure, but more as a historical curiosity than as great literature in its own right.

**SOURCES:**

Boll, Theophilus E.M. *Miss May Sinclair: Novelist.* Rutherford, NJ: Fairleigh Dickinson University Press, 1973.

Ford, Ford Madox. *Return to Yesterday.* London: Gollancz, 1931.

Kaplan, Sydney. *Feminine Consciousness in the Modern British Novel.* Urbana, IL: University of Illinois Press, 1975.

Sinclair, May. *The Divine Fire.* NY: Henry Holt, 1904.

———. *Mary Olivier: A Life.* Originally published 1919, reprint NY: Virago, 1980.

Tynan, Katharine. *The Middle Years.* London: Constable, 1916.

Zegger, Hrisey D. *May Sinclair.* Boston: Twayne, 1976.

**COLLECTIONS:**

Sinclair Papers, University of Pennsylvania.

**Patrick Allitt**, Professor of History,
Emory University, Atlanta, Georgia

## Singa.

*See Njinga.*

## Singer, Elizabeth (1674–1737).

*See Rowe, Elizabeth Singer.*

# Singer, Winnaretta (1865–1943)

*American-born artist, musician, and patron of the arts who established the Fondation Singer-Polignac.* Name variations: *Princess Edmond de Polignac; Princesse de Polignac; Princess Winnie; Princess de Scey-Montbéliard. Born Winnaretta Eugénie Singer on January 8, 1865, in Yonkers, New York; died of a heart attack on November 26, 1943, in London, England; daughter of Isaac Merritt Singer (millionaire creator of the Singer sewing-machine) and Isabelle Eugénie Boyer Singer of Paris, France; educated at home by governesses; married Prince Louis de Scey-Montbéliard, on July 27, 1887, in Paris (civil divorce, March 1891, marriage annulled, February 1892, in Rome); married Prince Edmond de Polignac, on December 15, 1893, in Paris (died in Paris, August 8, 1901); no children.*

*Moved with family to Paris, France (1866); moved to England (1870); father died (July 23, 1875); returned to Paris (1878); studied art in studio of Félix Barrias; exhibited paintings in Salon in Paris (1885–90); bought palace in Venice (December 1894); translated Thoreau's* Walden, *published in* La Renaissance latine *(December 1903–January 1904); established Polignac Prize in the Royal Society of Literature, London (1911); created Fondation Singer-Polignac (March 25, 1928).*

Winnaretta Singer was a talented musician and an accomplished artist, a patron of avant-garde culture, and presided over one of the most illustrious salons in Paris. She was wealthy, independent-minded, reserved, and urbane. She collected Impressionist paintings before they were publicly acclaimed, commissioned works by modern composers, such as Eric Satie and Igor Stravinsky, and developed friendships with Marcel Proust, Jean Cocteau, and her neighbor in

Paris, the poet ***Anna de Noailles**. Her generous financial subsidies ensured the success of Sergei Diaghilev's Ballets Russes in Europe. A lesbian, Singer contracted two marriages, her concession to prevailing social convention. In time, her "inner circle" was largely comprised of homosexuals who shared her cultural interests and adhered to a discreet code of behavior.

Isaac Merritt Singer was a self-made millionaire and father of 22 children, 6 of whom were born in wedlock. Gregarious and socially ambitious, Singer left the United States in 1861 to avoid being conscripted into the army during the Civil War and to escape his latest mistress. In France, he mingled easily with French society and met his future wife, 20-year-old Isabelle Eugénie Boyer. In 1863, they moved to America and married. Their son, Mortimer, was born six weeks later, followed by Winnaretta Eugénie in 1865, three more sons and another daughter. Singer acknowledged all his children by his several mistresses; each went by the name Singer and was provided for in his will.

Winnaretta was two years old when the Singers returned to France in 1866. Music was already an important part of the Singer household, and Isaac Singer's riches provided a cultured environment for his children. However, in 1870, at the outbreak of the Franco-Prussian War, the Singers fled France and settled in London and then in Torbay in Devon where Isaac built a large, elegant mansion. In July 1875, when Winnaretta was ten, her father died. After three years, **Isabelle Singer** decided to return to her native Paris, the cultural and social center of Europe. Soon after arriving in France in 1878, she married a Luxemburg noble, Vicomte d'Estenburg and Duc de Camposelice. The new duchess was beautiful, and when Frédéric Bartholdi was sculpting his Statue of Liberty during the 1880s, he modeled the head of the famous statue on her facial features. Isabelle's salon soon attracted a cultured elite who enjoyed the lavish weekly musical events that spurred Winnaretta's own interest in music.

Winnaretta did not approve of her mother's marriage, and their relations were often strained. In contrast to Isabelle, there was "something slightly intimidating" about Winnaretta; her reserved demeanor added to her air of aggressiveness, which masked a shyness that was not readily apparent. In Paris, Winnaretta developed an interest in art and studied with the formalistic Félix Barrias. But she much preferred the unconventional works of the Impressionists Manet, Sisley, and Monet, whose paintings were rejected and ridiculed by the artistic arbiters and critics of Paris. Their unorthodox techniques provided a "different way of looking at life" for Singer. Having no need to earn a living, she could follow her own artistic inclinations and develop her talents as she wished. In 1885, she exhibited a full-length self-portrait at the prestigious Salon in Paris, and several canvases were shown in the next few years. The Louvre asked her to prepare their catalogue in English for the museum, attesting to her fluency in French and English and to her artistic acumen.

Art remained a lifelong interest, but music came to occupy the center of her cultural pursuits. Musicians and painters attended her mother's salon, and in 1880, she met Gabriel Fauré for whom she later served as patron for over a decade. In 1882, Winnaretta accompanied her mother to the Bayreuth Festival in Germany, which became for her an "annual pilgrimage" to hear the music of Wagner.

As an unmarried young woman, Singer was socially restricted; to be fully integrated into so-

Winnaretta Singer

ciety, she needed a suitable marriage. Her mother was determined to see her children marry into "the top ranks of French society," and Isabelle chose Prince Louis de Scey-Montbéliard, the third son of an old aristocratic family, as Winnaretta's prospective husband. Their marriage in July 1887 freed Winnaretta from her mother's "custodianship" and allowed her to establish her own house and control her fortune. Unfortunately, the prince's "idea about the nature of their marriage differed from hers"; their conjugal incompatibility led to a separation shortly thereafter and to a civil divorce in March 1891. The marriage was officially annulled by the Roman Curia in February 1892. Winnaretta's lesbian leanings were known before she married, but her husband had not taken this seriously despite his wife's insistence on "a marriage of convenience," a marriage in name only.

*She possessed a certain timeless quality: she could mix with all types of people but felt most at ease with forward-looking artists whatever their age.*

—Michael de Cossart

As a result of her failed marriage, writes Michael de Cossart, "Winnaretta would never again put herself in a position in which she might find herself dominated in any way by another human being." However, she had benefited from her alliance with a noble family; she had acquired a title and social status. Invited to the illustrious salons of the time, she met many of the cultural and intellectual elite of Europe. Her sexual orientation was not a secret, but Singer was discreet and never approved of homosexual displays in public. The more mature, wiser Winnaretta also "had acquired an incisiveness of mind and a directness of approach which . . . were considered too aggressive" at times and intimidated even those who knew her well.

Indeed, she was most comfortable with homosexuals, both men and women, and formed close friendships with "the great or notorious" if they shared common interests. The laissez-faire attitude of French society towards sexual preferences contributed to the relaxed civility found in the salon culture. And Singer's salon became one of the most refined and popular gatherings in Paris. In 1890, she bought a large mansion on the avenue Henri-Martin (home of the Fondation Singer-Polignac today) and began to reconstruct it in the 18th-century French classical style. Her friend, Comte Robert de Montesquiou, who was known for his exquisite taste in objets d'art and decor, helped decorate the Grand Salon and huge music room that con-

tained an organ. They also shared an interest in music. Montesquiou had suggested to Fauré that he compose a musical score for the poet Paul Verlaine's *Claire de lune*; the first performance was given in a special concert in Singer's house. Works by Vincent d'Indy, Ernest Chausson, and Emmanuel Chabrier also debuted there. Singer became close friends with Chabrier and Ignacy Paderewski and with the painter John Singer Sargent (no relation to her) who painted a full-length portrait of Singer entitled the *Princess de Scey-Montbéliard*. Sargent was also responsible for introducing Winnaretta to the beauty and cultural pleasures of Venice where she later bought a handsome villa on the Grand Canal.

By 1892, Singer had achieved a position in Parisian society and was considered the "guiding spirit behind an increasingly avant-garde salon." In addition, she had begun to commission works from modern composers she favored, such as Fauré and Chabrier. She also learned not to interfere with their creativity, but to allow them to develop their own ideas. Although she had attained acceptance in society, her money alone would not admit her to "the more stimulating circles of French society," Montesquiou told her. Moreover, she was a "divorced" woman which was an awkward position. He urged her to remarry, and he had a prospect in mind.

The ideal husband for Singer would be Prince Edmond de Polignac, a close friend of Montesquiou. The prince was from one of the oldest aristocratic families in Europe, a composer, "a musician and dilettante with exquisite taste." Grandson of *Marie Antoinette*'s favorite, *Yolande Martine de Polignac*, and great-uncle to the future Prince Ranier of Monaco, Prince Edmond had both royal and social connections; and Winnaretta had the wealth to ensure them an elegant lifestyle. Moreover, he was a well-known homosexual, which allowed Singer to pursue her own sexual orientation. She was 28 years old when she married the 59-year-old prince in December 1893, at the Chapelle des Carmes in Paris with only family members present. Montesquiou felt slighted and never forgave them; Cossart suggests that because Montesquiou was homosexual, his presence would have called unnecessary attention to "the unconventional marriage" of the couple.

In spite of their unusual alliance, a "deep sympathy and mutual respect" developed between them. Their love of music, art, and literature provided the basis for a "tender and happy" marriage. The prince, who was bilingual like Singer, introduced her to Henry James and the painter James Whistler. They collected paintings by the Impressionists and several Old Masters. Annual art exhibitions were held at Singer's house, and she and the prince were welcome in the salons of productive artists who were associated with a more bohemian lifestyle. The prince was a composer whose work had been praised by Wagner, and Singer had his works played at her evening musical events. Handel and Bach (her favorite composers) were also often featured. The princess' salon had the reputation of being one of four "academic" salons in Paris, "a forum for ideas on anything connected with civilization," from art to politics. Her guests were an eclectic mix of writers, composers, and social figures: the refined Marcel Proust, the flamboyant Oscar Wilde and his lover "the beautiful Lord Alfred Douglas," the couturiere *Coco Chanel, Maurice Ravel, and Claude Debussy. In 1894, Singer bought a 15th-century mansion in Venice, presented it to her husband and renamed it the Palazzo Polignac. As in her Paris residence, music and cultural gatherings made it a social center for the arts.

In the latter years of the 19th century, the Belle Époque was "becoming less beautiful, less integral as an age." Notes Cossart, Singer and her circle of friends became aware that homosexuality was under attack as "the wasting disease of degeneracy infecting the pleasantly intellectual spirit," especially among the more strait-laced English. Oscar Wilde was imprisoned in Reading Goal in England in 1895, condemned for exhibiting "an unmanly style of life and way of thinking." On his release, Singer again entertained him in her home and appeared with him in public. She and Prince Edmond, however, escaped criticism for they closely guarded their private life, and their marriage was "an acknowledgment that society's most sacred convention—appearances—must be respected." If their salon was perceived "as being per se immoral" by a few Parisians, it was almost universally agreed that "Winnaretta ran what was the most important music salon in Paris." Music lovers and friends were attracted to the refined decorum of the Polignacs' salon where were heard the premier performances of future great composers who recognized the value of their host by dedicating their works to her. Singer was also responsible for introducing the dancer *Isadora Duncan to her guests; Prince Edmond was charmed by her performance, but Singer found Duncan's technique and style "not really serious enough." Her brother (Paris) Eugene Singer was also impressed and carried on a passionate affair with

Isadora; they had a son Patrick (b. 1910), who would drown in the River Seine with Patrick's half-sister Deirdre and a governess in 1913.

Prince Edmond died in 1901, leaving Singer "disoriented" and restless. She spent increasingly long periods away from Paris, mixing with an international elite throughout Europe. In an age of growing nationalism, the princess was convinced that "National consciousness was a barrier to intellectual development," and thought of herself as a "citizen of the world." During the Edwardian era, she bought a house in London (1908) which became a cultural mecca for London high society. And although shy she embarked on a series of relationships with women. However, she avoided associating with the uninhibited, assertive women of that world, such as *Gertrude Stein, *Natalie Clifford Barney, and Princess Violette Murat. On the other hand, Singer enjoyed male company, and her salon attracted intelligent, creative individuals, such as Cocteau, Proust, Diaghilev, José-Maria Sert, Thomas Mann, Pablo Picasso, Winston Churchill, and Raymond Poincaré (future president of France), each able to appreciate and contribute to the wide-ranging conversation.

Around 1906, Singer had met the Russian impresario Diaghilev at a dinner party given by the Grand Duke Paul of Russia. Through her salon, Diaghilev met potential backers who followed Singer's example of generous support for more than two decades. She thought him to be a genius, and she was the major financial contributor to the successful season of the Ballets Russes in 1908, which introduced Nijinsky, Ida Rubenstein, and *Anna Pavlova to Paris audiences. At the same time, she was a patron of young artists, Sert, *Romaine Brooks, and Jacques-Emile Blanche. Encouraging and supporting young talent never interfered with her own intellectual pursuits. At age 50, she began to teach herself ancient Greek so she could read Plato and Aristotle in the original. In a short time, she had mastered the language and delighted in discussing the classics and philosophy with Henri Bergson and the British diplomat Sir Ronald Storrs. Her studies led to an interest in Greek and Roman coins which she collected. And she continued to collect art which graced her several residences. In 1911, Singer provided a large sum of money to the Royal Society of Literature in London for an annual prize to be awarded to an author chosen by the members; the Polignac Prize was established as a tribute to Prince Edmond.

When World War I began in 1914, Singer remained apolitical, but was pleased that her

Rubenstein, Ida. See Brooks, Romaine for sidebar.

friend Poincaré was president of France. In her opinion, "governments, any government, were not held in high regard concerning competence." Nor did the women's suffrage movement receive her support; she was more concerned with the social role of women than with obtaining political rights for them. Singer remained in Paris during the war, even as the Germans came within sight of Paris. She gave substantial sums of money to *Marie Curie to pursue her work on radium, which would benefit wounded French soldiers, and raised funds for the army and navy through charities and art exhibitions. Money was also dispensed among Russian artists, such as Stravinsky and Diaghilev, who were cut off from their resources after the Russian Revolution. To save the Ballets Russes company, Singer contacted her relative, Prince Pierre de Polignac, the son-in-law of the prince of Monaco; Pierre and his wife **Charlotte** became patrons and agreed to help obtain a contract with the Monte Carlo Opera.

During the war, the princess maintained her salon and continued her patronage of avant-garde artists. She bristled when their public performances met with raucous laughter and catcalls. Cocteau's ballet *Parade*, with music by Satie, elicited such a reaction, as did the latter's Greek drama set to music (*Socrate*) where "boos and titters" greeted the performance. Singer was his patron and "became known as the fairy-godmother to his disciples." She appreciated the modern, the daring, and frequented parties attended by the Dadaists, by Picasso, Cocteau, André Breton, and Paul Claudel. She tried to foster the reputation of the poet Paul Valéry who attended her salon and occasionally gave lectures there. Not every talented artist fit into Singer's refined salon atmosphere; the young composer Maxime Jacob, for example, "was not sufficiently attuned to sophisticated life to qualify for entry into the inner circle of friends."

By the mid-1920s, the heyday of the grand salons was passing, writes Cossart, but not at Singer's where "all aspects of civilized life . . . without much attention to the social standing of the participants" continued to flourish. By the end of the decade her "inner circle" was comprised of homosexuals. Among them was *Violet Trefusis, Singer's lover for ten years, and Violet's husband Denys who was knowledgeable about music. However, Singer and her friends had little contact with groups such as Gertrude Stein's; Picasso had introduced Stein to the princess during the war, but Stein "was not European enough," and too masculine for Winnaretta. Her antipathy is evident in her re-

fusal to even meet the American composer Virgil Thomson who was a friend of Stein.

If Paris was changing, so was Venice. Millionaires and American *nouveaux riches* brought "decay and decline" to the Old World culture center, epitomized by the professional American party arranger *Elsa Maxwell who served "the uninspired rich." Still, Singer enjoyed the plethora of parties, balls, and dinners given by the newer arrivals in Venice; the English Cunards, Victor, Edward, and the eccentric *Nancy Cunard, Lady ◄ Diana Duff Cooper and her husband Alfred were among Singer's acquaintances.

The princess was socially and physically active, but as friends and relatives her own age (63) were dying, she began to think about properly disposing of her riches. In 1926, in Venice, her friend Maurice Paléologue suggested she create "a foundation which could foster and endow artistic and scientific projects," and fund activities at the Collège de France. Singer thus became the college's "second protector"—after King Francis I. Her friend Raymond Poincaré became the first president of the Fondation Singer-Polignac which was "authorized by special legislation on 25 March 1928 and confirmed as an independent body under Swiss law as the Institut Singer-Polignac on 22 December 1934." Thinking of her own mortality, Singer decided in the spring of 1927 to visit the United States which she had not seen since she was two years old. The French referred to her American origins at times, a country that was foreign to her. Violet and Denys Trefusis accompanied her on the trip to Washington, D.C., where they met the "taciturn" President Calvin Coolidge, and on a tour of the Southern states. Finding "little intellectual stimulation in the plutocratic circles" she encountered in America, they left for Cuba. As she told reporters, she had not been to America for over sixty years, and "it would probably have to wait another sixty before she returned." Moreover, as she had always known, Paris was "the only place she ever regarded as home."

She knew, too, that her patronage of the arts was essential if new works were to be encouraged and performed. Singer continued to subsidize the Ballets Russes and provided financial backing for Stravinsky's *Oedipus Rex*. After a preview at her house, the public performance in 1927 failed to impress the audience or the critics. As *Janet Flanner, who wrote for *The New Yorker* magazine, noted, "The Latin was sung, with Italian pronunciation, to the French audience by Russians." Diaghilev's death in 1929 "marked the end of an artistic era" and "the end

*Cooper, Diana Duff.* See Bagnold, Enid for sidebar.

of a period of Winnaretta's life." Pure music—opera, chamber, and orchestral music—interested her more, and led to closer ties with *Nadia Boulanger and her students. The princess further commissioned Nicolas Nabokov's *Job*, Stravinsky's *Persephone*, and a symphony by Kurt Weill. In 1933, her friends arranged a special concert of all the music that composers had dedicated to her, a tribute "to her contributions to the music world." She also had kept in touch with literary friends, Ezra Pound who shared her interest in music, the poet Léon-Paul Fargue whom she admired for his compassionate nature, and Jean Cocteau who insisted Winnaretta resembled Dante in Giotto's portrait of him. Addicted to opium, Cocteau displayed erratic behavior that made him a difficult friend. After the death of Anna de Noailles, Singer became close friends with *Colette, both being "naturally witty, clever and down to earth."

Singer's place in *le grand monde* of Paris was secure; she was equally in demand socially in England where she served as a link to civilized Europe, a woman of unquestioned taste. At a party at Lady (**Sibyl**) Colefax's house, Singer was not impressed with the music (*Mad Dogs and Englishmen* and other "popular" fare) enjoyed by several of the English guests, including King Edward VIII and his American paramour, Mrs. Wallis Simpson (*Wallis Warfield, duchess of Windsor). The latter lacked "sophistication" according to Singer who "could put on a cold, forbidding look of detachment," notes Cossart, when she found herself among those "who were less than civilized by [her] standards."

In Paris, Singer continued to support the arts. She provided a monthly allowance to the pianist *Clara Haskil, helped fund the career of **Renata Borgatti**, also a pianist, and financed the founding of the Nadia Boulanger Orchestra. In the late 1930s, the princess began suffering from angina and made out a final will to dispose of her remaining property. She left a legacy to many who had benefited from her largesse over the years, and she discharged the debt owed by the Duc d'Ayen, allowing him to purchase his family's château at Maintenon. Paintings and objets d'art were bequeathed to the Louvre Museum. Houses, books, furniture, and money were to be distributed among her heirs, and bequests were made to composers, musicians, and artists.

The Fondation Singer-Polignac was already actively supporting the arts. In addition, laboratories were established at the Collège de France, and over the years conferences on natural history, hormonal research, and astro-physics were held. Archaeological expeditions to Greece were funded, and money was provided for the restoration of the Hagia Sophia in Istanbul. A ship named *Winnaretta Singer* was given to the Institut Oceanographique for use in underwater studies, and a mobile lab was purchased for the Institut Pasteur in Dakar, Senegal. Singer also gave to charities and causes; she financed construction of Salvation Army hostels and the renovation of working-class housing in Paris.

On September 3, 1939, an era and a way of life abruptly ended when Britain and France declared war on Nazi Germany. Singer had gone to England to bury her brother Franklin in the family vault in Torquay. Her family persuaded her to stay in England as the war escalated, and she rented a small apartment in London. When France fell to the German onslaught in June 1940, Singer realized she was now a refugee and that "her world had collapsed." Fearful and unwell, she was cut off from her sources of income from Singer shares. She worried about her Paris house, but the German officials in Paris mistakenly assumed she was in a neutral South American country and did not confiscate her property. Always hoping to return to Paris and her friends, she occupied her time by painting, attending concerts, galleries and museums, and socializing. By the autumn of 1943, her attacks of angina intensified. On November 24, she gave a dinner party, went to a luncheon the next day and spent the evening with friends. At 2:00 AM on the 26th, Singer suffered a heart attack and died without seeing her beloved Paris again. A requiem mass was celebrated on December 1, and the Princess de Polignac was buried beside Prince Edmond in Torquay.

**SOURCES:**

Cossart, Michael de. *The Food of Love: Princesse Edmond de Polignac (1865–1943) and Her Salon.* London: Hamish Hamilton, 1978.

Haight, Mary Ellen Jordan. *Paris Portraits, Renoir to Chanel: Walks on the Right Bank.* Salt Lake City, UT: Peregrine Smith, 1991.

Mignot-Ogliastri, Claude. *Anna de Noailles, Une Amie de la Princesse Edmond de Polignac.* Méridiens Klincksieck, 1987.

**SUGGESTED READING:**

Cossart, Michael de. "Princesse Edmond de Polignac: Patron and Artist," in *Apollo.* Vol. CII, no. 162. August 1975.

Gavoty, Bernard [Clarendon]. "À la Memoire de la Princesse de Polignac," in *Le Figaro.* December 9, 1965.

Hall, Richard. "Princesse Winnie," in *Opera News.* Vol. 3–4, nos. 9–10, 1969–70.

Haslach, Linda Allison. "Entre Nous: Vocal Music from the Salon of Winnaretta Singer, the Princesse Édmond de Polignac." D.M.A. thesis, School of Music, University of Maryland, College Park, 1999.

Polignac, Winnaretta, Princesse Edmond de. "Memoirs," in *Horizon*. Vol. XII, no. 68. August 1945.

**Jeanne A. Ojala**,
Professor Emerita, Department of History,
University of Utah, Salt Lake City, Utah

### Singleton, Anne (1887–1948).

*See Benedict, Ruth.*

### Singleton, Mary (1724–1789).

*See Brooke, Frances.*

## Singleton, Penny (1908—)

*American actress best known for her portrayal of Blondie. Name variations: Dorothy McNulty. Born Mariana Dorothy McNulty on September 15, 1908, in Philadelphia, Pennsylvania; attended Columbia University; married Lawrence Singleton (a dentist), in 1937 (divorced 1939); married Bob Sparks (a film producer), in 1941; children: two daughters.*

*Selected theater:* Good News *(1928);* Follow Through *(1929);* Walk a Little Faster *(1932);* Hey Nonny, Nonny *(1932); replaced Ruby Keeler in* No No, Nanette *(1971).*

*Selected filmography: (as Dorothy McNulty)* Good News *(1930),* Love in the Rough *(1930),* After the Thin Man *(1936),* Vogues of 1938 *(1937),* Sea Racketeers *(1937); (as Penny Singleton)* Swing Your Lady *(1938),* Racket Busters *(1938),* Boy Meets Girl *(1938),* Secrets of an Actress *(1938),* The Mad Miss Manton *(1938),* Hard to Get *(1938),* Blondie *(1938), 28 "Blondie" episodes (1938–1950),* Go West Young Lady *(1941),* Footlight Glamour *(1943),* Young Widow *(1946),* The Best Man *(1964),* Jetsons: The Movie *(voice only, 1990).*

Penny Singleton is best remembered for her portrayal of Blondie, the long-suffering wife of bumbling Dagwood Bumstead and the mother of Baby Dumpling and Cookie, all characters based on the popular comic strip *Blondie* by Chic Young. The initial movie of *Blondie* (1938), a low-budget programmer, was an unexpected hit and spawned a series of sequels, a long-running radio show, and two short-lived television sitcoms (1957 and 1968). When her stint as Blondie ended, Singleton became a union activist for the American Guild of Variety Artists (AGVA).

A niece of former Postmaster General James Farley, Singleton was born Mariana Dorothy McNulty in Philadelphia, Pennsylvania, in 1908. After attending Columbia University, she launched her show-business career as a singer and dancer, appearing in several Broadway musicals before making her way to Hollywood. Her only notable films before Blondie were *Good News* (1930), in which she reprised her stage role, and *After the Thin Man* (1936), in which she also played a dancer. She married Dr. Lawrence Singleton, a dentist, and also published a book of children's verse.

Singleton was not the first choice for Blondie, but took over the role when actress **Shirley Deane** became ill. Sequels to the original movie, which co-starred Arthur Lake as Dagwood, began in 1939 with *Blondie Meets the Boss* and appeared at the rate of several per year until 1943, when the studio pulled the plug. Public outcry, however, forced them to reinstate the series in 1945 (*Leave It to Blondie*), and it endured until 1950 (*Beware of Blondie*). When "Blondie" debuted on radio in 1939 (with Singleton and Lake reprising their movie roles), it was panned as "silly" by *Variety*. "It is impossible to predict anything but a minimum audience to a minimum engagement," they added. Defying the critics, the show lasted for eight years. In

*Penny Singleton, with Arthur Lake.*

the meantime, Singleton divorced her husband and married movie producer Robert Sparks, who produced some of the Blondie films.

Although Singleton made several other feature films (*Go West Young Lady*, *Swing Your Partner*, and *Young Widows*), she was pretty much saddled with Blondie for her entire film career. When the films and radio series ended, she briefly, but quite successfully, appeared in nightclubs, including a stint as a headliner at the Thunderbird Hotel in Las Vegas. She was not involved in either of the Blondie television series, the first of which starred **Pamela Britton** and the second, **Patricia Harty**.

Union activities eventually drew Singleton's interest away from performing. She served two terms as president of AGVA in the 1950s, but began battling union officials over some of their policies during the early 1960s. In 1962, she testified before a House committee on union activities, accusing AGVA of creating "sweetheart contracts" which forced women working in strip bars to mingle with the customers, thus encouraging prostitution. Suspended from the union for her stand, she later sued members of the executive board, demanding that they account for treasury money. Singleton's suit and a countersuit by the union were settled out of court and the actress was reinstated as a member. In 1966, as vice president and executive secretary of the union, she organized the first strike of the Rockettes against Radio City Music Hall, which lasted for 27 days. Singleton returned briefly to the New York stage in 1971, replacing *Ruby Keeler in *No No, Nanette*. She was also the voice of Jane Jetson for the popular Hanna-Barbera cartoons and for the feature film *Jetsons: The Movie* (1990).

**SOURCES:**

Katz, Ephraim. *The Film Encyclopedia*. NY: HarperCollins, 1994.

Lamparski, Richard. *Whatever Became of . . . ?* 2nd series. NY: Crown, 1967.

McNeil, Alex. *Total Television*. NY: Penguin Books, 1996.

**Barbara Morgan**,
Melrose, Massachusetts

# Sintenis, Renée (1888–1965)

*German sculptor and engraver whose sculptures of young animals and children were extremely popular in pre-Nazi Germany but were removed from museums as "degenerate art" during the Third Reich. Name variations: Renee Sintenis. Born Renate Alice Sintenis in Glatz, Silesia, on March 20, 1888; died in Berlin on April 22, 1965; daughter of Bernhard Sintenis; married Emil Rudolf Weiss (a painter and printmaker, 1875–1942); no children.*

*Received many honors, including being the first sculptor to be elected to the Prussian Academy of the Arts; after World War II, taught at the Academy for the Graphic Arts.*

Descended from French Huguenots who had sought religious freedom in Prussia two centuries earlier, Renée Sintenis was born in Silesia in 1888, the first year of the reign of Kaiser Wilhelm II. As the daughter of a highly successful attorney, she grew up in an atmosphere of affluent security in the picturesque town of Neuruppin in the Mark Brandenburg, a district of Prussia renowned for the beauty of its lakes and forests and for its contribution to the arts. It was also the birthplace of novelist Theodor Fontane and architect Karl Friedrich Schinkel. From her earliest years, Sintenis loved the presence of animals, many of which were her pets in her family's large yard. She revealed artistic talent at a young age, drawing constantly, and was first exposed to a systematic study of art at the Stuttgart Academy from 1902 to 1905. Her father disapproved of her artistic inclinations, insisting that she prepare herself for a secretarial career, but after temporarily bowing to his wishes by briefly working in his law office, she finally broke with her family to resume her art studies. From 1908 to 1912, she was enrolled at Berlin's Kunstgewerbeschule (School of Applied Arts), where she studied drawing and painting under the noted Leo von König (1871–1944). At the same time, Sintenis also studied sculpture with Wilhelm Haverkamp (1864–1929) and became acquainted with the sculptor Georg Kolbe, for whom she also modeled.

By 1913, when several of Sintenis' sculptures of dancing women and women's portraits were exhibited in the Freie Berlin Secession, she was starting to show unmistakable signs of artistic maturity and a singular style. Her early sculptures are characterized by smooth surfaces and stylized forms. By 1915–16, she was producing sculptures of animals, including young horses, calves, goats, and donkeys. In 1915, she celebrated the first solo exhibit of her work, the most outstanding being her animal study of a foal. Although she received encouragement and technical advice from August Gaul, a noted contemporary sculptor of animals, Sintenis' style was uniquely her own from the start of her career, and it would never be difficult for art lovers and collectors to identify a work by Sintenis. She never used models for her studies, relying entirely on her own imagination.

Stylistically, Renée Sintenis was able to create a blend of impressionist and expressionist values, strongly rooted in naturalism. Her animal studies, most of which would be cast in bronze, reflected her fascination with animals, but it was not their structure that most interested her. Rather, Sintenis' goal was always to capture the foal, the dog, the ram in motion. Instinctively, she chose to portray the animal as not yet grown, still gamboling on a meadow, unsure and without the coordination found in the adult state. Most of her sculptures are rough in surface, small animal figures in which windblown manes are very often a distinguishing mark. Although her animal studies constitute Sintenis' most remarkable work, she also created a number of impressive self-portraits. Her graphic works, which succeed in loose outline in capturing sketched motion, also continue to impress collectors and art historians alike.

In December 1917, Sintenis married the painter and printmaker Emil Rudolf Weiss, who made many portraits of her and with whom she would collaborate on a number of book projects. A crucial development in her career was Sintenis' friendship with the poet Rainer Maria Rilke (1875–1926), which began in 1915. Through Rilke, she was able to establish contacts with most of the leading writers and artists of Berlin, greatly enhancing interest in her work by an affluent elite able to purchase it. Of equal importance was her professional relationship with the Berlin art dealer and gallery owner Alfred Flechtheim. Flechtheim, who featured the works of both Sintenis and her husband in his gallery, was a master of publicity and marketing. He recommended to his Paris business partner Daniel-Henri Kahnweiler that he too feature Sintenis' sculptures in his own gallery; Flechtheim told his French colleague, "*Die Dinger sind ganz entzückend und der Name der Künstlerin absolut undeutsch.*" ("The things are totally enchanting and the artist's name is absolutely not a German one.") Quickly, the charm and delicacy of her small bronzes became the talk of Berlin, then Germany, then Europe. For Flechtheim, "the things" were commodities to sell, and this is what he did brilliantly, convincing affluent clients of their value as embellishments to a smart modern apartment.

By the mid-1920s, Sintenis was once again moving into new artistic terrain. This time, she began depicting humans in motion, particularly athletes. From this highly creative period of her career come several of her most striking bronzes, including her superbly caught portrait of the great Finnish Olympic runner of the period, Paavo Nurmi. For her 1926 bronze of *The Runner Nurmi* (National Gallery, Berlin), Sintenis

was awarded the Olympia Prize in 1932. Soon after its creation, a copy of *The Runner Nurmi* was purchased by the French government and placed in the Rodin Museum in Paris. This was one of the first pieces of German sculpture bought by France after World War I, and was considered at the time to be a significant gesture of reconciliation between the two bitter enemies.

Other sports-inspired works of this period included *The Boxer* (1925, Niedersächsisches Landesmuseum, Hannover), *The Football Player* (1927, Kunsthalle, Bremen), and *The Polo Player* (1929, National Gallery, Berlin). She also created a number of portrait busts, including ones depicting André Gide, Joachim Ringelnatz, and Ernst Toller. In 1932, she created the first of several small bear figurines, the "Berlin bear" being the traditional heraldic symbol of the city. Her Berlin bear became immensely popular with the public, and after World War II copies of it were often used for various prizes, including (starting in 1951) as the prize figurine of the Berlin Film Festival. On his 1963 visit to West Berlin, U.S. president John F. Kennedy was presented with a copy of Sintenis' bronze Berlin bear.

In 1931, Sintenis became the first woman sculptor to be elected to the Prussian Academy of Arts. She and her husband were now at the height of their fame, enjoying a prosperity that contrasted markedly with the economic depression of the early 1930s. Sintenis moved in liberal circles, and both she and Weiss were outspoken anti-Nazis at a time when the Hitler phenomenon was rapidly gaining strength. Sintenis was regarded by the Nazis as one of a large number of "un-German" artists and intellectuals, not so much for her art, but rather for her friends, colleagues, and acquaintances. Starting with her dealer Alfred Flechtheim, who was Jewish and strongly linked to modern trends in art, many of the people in her and her husband's circle were Jews, leftists, liberals, and creative personalities in conflict with the conservative ideals the Nazis claimed they wished to uphold. Furthermore, Sintenis was known to have close ties to Berlin's "Eldorado," its gay and lesbian community, and was alleged by some to be a lesbian herself.

The Nazi takeover in 1933 brought a cultural as well as a political upheaval in Germany. Jews, liberals and artistic radicals were removed from German intellectual and cultural life. Sintenis' husband was involuntarily pensioned off from his professorship at the School of Applied Arts. After she refused to resign voluntarily from the Prussian Academy of Arts, in February 1934 she was expelled on "racial grounds" from what was now a thoroughly purged institution. The Nazi cultural bureaucracy had heard rumors that Sintenis was of partially Jewish ancestry, although convincing documentation was never found, but mere suspicions were sufficient to warrant her expulsion. Fortunately, Sintenis had been immensely popular before 1933, and the Nazis generally ignored rather than targeted her. Despite their expulsions, the couple continued to be productive. Flechtheim fled Germany in 1933, but his successor Alex Vömel continued to act as Sintenis' agent.

Although her situation was unclear and could always worsen, she was even able to exhibit on several occasions during the Nazi years. More important, she continued to find buyers for her creations on the private art market. Cautiously, she was even able to criticize the underlying assumptions of Nazi-inspired art, as when she indicated in an April 1936 newspaper interview that she would continue to present her artistic vision in a small, human format rather than on a monumental (i.e., Nazi and fascist) scale. By the late 1930s, the Nazi regime had

classified Sintenis' work as "degenerate art" (en-tartete Kunst), causing eight of her pieces to be removed from public museums and galleries. Privately held works by her were, however, not confiscated from private collections, and thus these survived the Third Reich.

World War II was a catastrophe for the world, and Renée Sintenis was in no way spared. Many of her Jewish and other friends had already fled Germany, but a number of German-Jewish artists died in the Holocaust. In 1942, her husband died. The Allied bombing of Berlin destroyed much of the world she had known. On May 1, 1945, one of the very last days of fighting in Berlin, her studio was destroyed. All that she was able to save from it was a treasured item, a small painting by Henri Rousseau.

In 1945, Germany had been freed of the Nazi dictatorship, but it was a nation in ruins. Sintenis was determined to make a contribution to the reconstruction of Germany, and despite the fact that she did not have a studio for a number of years, she began once again to sculpt. In

Renée Sintenis

1947, she also resumed teaching at the Academy of Applied Arts, becoming a full professor there in 1955. Various honors she received over the next years included membership in the coveted knight's branch Order of the Pour le Mérite (1952), and in 1953 she was awarded the Federal Cross for Achievement (Bundesverdienstkreuz) of the Federal Republic of Germany.

Renée Sintenis died in Berlin on April 22, 1965. After her death, that city honored the artist by naming the Renée-Sintenis-Platz in her honor, a small and *gemütlich* site situated off the Friedrich-Wilhelm-Platz. Since 1948, the Berlin municipal government has awarded the Renée-Sintenis-Prize to outstanding sculptors. At the time of her death, many young Germans had not heard of Sintenis. In recent years, her sculptures have been rediscovered, and her reputation as an artist has risen significantly as her life and work are placed in the context of her times.

In the United States, a number of Sintenis' works are held by major museums, including two lithographs from late in her career (1951), *Girl Seated* and *Profile of a Woman*, both in the collection of the National Gallery of Art, Washington, D.C. Perhaps one of Renée Sintenis' "all-time hits" is her *Bronze Donkey*, which is located at the Farnsworth entrance of the Detroit Institute of Arts. The only work in the museum that visitors are encouraged to touch, the 30-inch donkey has been a favorite with generations of museumgoers in Detroit, particularly young visitors, and over many years has been rubbed to a satiny gold finish.

**SOURCES:**

*Ausstellung von Skulpturen, Zeichnungen und graphischen Werken von Renée Sintenis.* Düsseldorf: Galerie Vömel, 1978.

Barron, Stephanie. *German Expressionist Sculpture.* Chicago, IL: University of Chicago Press, 1983.

Becher, Johannes Robert. *Auf andere Art so grosse Hoffnung.* Berlin and Weimar: Aufbau-Verlag, 1969.

Behne, Adolf. "Mensch und Kreatur," in *Aufbau* [Berlin]. Vol. 4, no. 3. March 1948, pp. 247–248.

Berger, U. "Renée Sintenis," in *Weltkunst.* Vol. 54, no. 5, 1984, pp. 518–519.

Buhlmann, Britta. *Renée Sintenis: Werkmonographie der Skulpturen.* Darmstadt: Wissenschaftliche Buchgesellschaft, 1987.

Bushart, Magdalena. "Der Formsinn des Weibes: Bildhauerinnen in den zwanziger und dreissiger Jahren," in *Profession ohne Tradition: 125 Jahre Verein der Berliner Künstlerinnen.* Berlin: Kupfergraben, 1992, pp. 135–150.

*Eldorado: Homosexuelle Frauen und Männer in Berlin, 1850–1950: Geschichte, Alltag und Kultur.* 2nd rev. ed. Berlin: Edition Hentrich, 1992.

Giedion-Welcker, Carola. *Contemporary Sculpture.* NY: Wittenborn, 1955.

Hagelstange, Rudolf, Carl Georg Heise, and Paul Appel. *Renée Sintenis.* Berlin: Aufbau-Verlag, 1947.

Heukenkamp, Ursula, ed. *Unterm Notdach: Nachkriegsliteratur in Berlin 1945–1949.* Berlin: Erich Schmidt, 1996.

Jacobi, Fritz. "'Die Tiere fordern nichts von mir': Zu Leben und Werk von Renée Sintenis, 1888–1965," in *Museums-Journal.* Vol. 9, no. 2. April 1995, pp. 36–37.

Jürgs, Britta. *Wie eine Nilbraut, die man in die Wellen wirft: Portraits expressionistischer Künstlerinnen und Schriftstellerinnen.* Grambin: Aviva, 1998.

Kiel, Hanna. *Renée Sintenis.* Reprint ed. Berlin: Rembrandt, 1956.

Kolberg, Gerhard, ed. *Die Expressionisten: Vom Aufbruch bis zur Verfemung.* Ostfildern-Ruit: G. Hatje, 1996.

*Kunst in Berlin 1648–1987: Staatliche Museen zu Berlin, Ausstellung im Alten Museum vom 10. Juni bis 25. Oktober 1987.* Berlin: Henschelverlag, 1987.

Longus. *Hirtengeschichten von Daphnis und Chloe.* Hamburg: Hauswedell, 1935.

Meskimmon, Marsha. *The Art of Reflection: Women Artists' Self-Portraiture in the Twentieth Century.* NY: Columbia University Press, 1996.

———, and Shearer West, eds. *Visions of the "Neue Frau": Woman and the Visual Arts in Weimar Germany.* Aldershot: Scolar Press, 1995.

"Renee Sintenis, 77, Known For Animal Sculpture, Dies," in *The New York Times.* April 24, 1965, p. 29.

Ringelnatz, Joachim. *Tiere.* Berlin: Karl H. Henssel, 1949.

Rochard, Patricia. *Der Traum von einer neuen Welt: Berlin 1910–1933.* Mainz: P. von Zabern, 1989.

Roh, Franz. *German Art in the 20th Century.* Translated by Catherine Hutter and edited by Julia Phelps. Greenwich, CT: New York Graphic Society, 1968.

Sintenis, Renée. *Tiere: 20 Zeichnungen.* Berlin: Gebrüder Mann, 1947.

**John Haag**, Associate Professor History, University of Georgia, Athens, Georgia

# Sipilä, Helvi (1915—)

*Finnish lawyer and international advocate for women's rights. Name variations: Helvi Sipila. Born Helvi Linnea Sipilä on May 5, 1915, in Helsinki, Finland; daughter of Vilho Sipilä and Sanni Maukola; attended the University of Helsinki; married Sauli Sipilä, in 1939; children: one daughter and three sons.*

Born in 1915 in Helsinki, the capital of Finland, Helvi Sipilä later attended the University of Helsinki, then worked as an acting judge in Finland's rural districts from 1941 to 1942. The following year, she served as secretary of Finland's Ministry of Supply before opening her own law office in 1943. Sipilä was only the second woman in Finland with a private practice, and her professional status merited her ascendancy to the presidency of the International Federation of Women Lawyers in 1954.

Sipilä continued her government service during the 1950s through her work on government committees related to children's social benefits, citizenship education, marriage legislation, and international development. While she maintained her law practice, her interest in advancing the status of women and children spurred her to take on a number of leadership roles in Finnish and international organizations throughout the following years, including chief commissioner of the Finnish Girl Guides (1952–69), which overlapped with her membership in the World Committee of the World Association of Girl Guides and Girl Scouts (1957–66); chair of the Finnish Refugee Council (1965–72), of which she remains a member; member of the Finnish delegation to the United Nations General Assembly (1966–72); member of the Council of the Human Rights Institute in Strasbourg (from 1969); and vice-president of the International Council of Women (from 1970). A Finnish representative to the United Nations (UN) Commission on the Status of Women from 1960 to 1968 and from 1971 to 1972 (the year she closed her law office to devote her full attention to international affairs), Sipilä became Assistant Secretary-General for Social Development and Humanitarian Affairs at the UN in 1973. She was the first woman to hold that post.

When the UN proclaimed 1975 to be International Women's Year, Sipilä became the project's Secretary General. She also served as Secretary General for the UN World Conference in Mexico City that year; 20 years later, in 1995, she would give a speech at the opening ceremony of the 4th World Congress on Women in Beijing. Sipilä retired from the UN in 1980, although she remained active over the following decades in the Finnish commission of the UN Development Fund for Women (UNIFEM). In 1981, she became the first woman to run for president of Finland. Sipilä was the recipient of numerous accolades for her work on behalf of women, including some 12 honorary doctorates, the Commander of Finland's White Rose (1977), the Great Cross of Finland's Lion (1989), the inaugural Helvi Sipilä Award from the U.S. Committee for UNIFEM (1999), and the International Bar Association's first lifetime achievement award for women, the Outstanding International Women's Award (2001).

**SOURCES:**

*The Bermuda Sun.* February 2, 2001.

*The International Who's Who.* 55th ed. London: Europa, 1991.

Kinnear, Karen L. *Women in the Third World: A Reference Handbook.* Santa Barbara, CA: ABC-CLIO, 1997.

Uglow, Jennifer S., comp. and ed. *The International Dictionary of Women's Biography.* NY: Continuum, 1982.

**Lisa C. Groshong**, freelance writer, Columbia, Missouri

# Sipprell, Clara (1885–1975)

*Canadian-born photographer.* Born Clara Estelle Sipprell in Tillsonburg, Canada, in 1885; died in Bennington, Vermont, in 1975.

Born to a widowed mother in 1885, noted 20th-century photographer Clara Sipprell spent her early years in Canada, moving to Buffalo, New York, when she was ten. She left school in 1904, to assist her brother Frank in his photographic studio, and later became his partner in the enterprise. In Buffalo, Sipprell exhibited her early work in the Buffalo Camera Club's annual exhibitions from 1910 to 1914.

In 1915, Sipprell established her own studio in New York's Greenwich Village, and during the decades of the 1920s and 1930s, she reached the height of her career. Her work appeared in numerous magazines, including *American Magazine of Art, American Girl, Mentor,* and *Revue du vrai et du beau.* During this period, she exhibited at the second and third National Salon of Pictorial Photography at the Albright Art Gallery in Buffalo (1921 and 1922), the International Salon of the Pictorial Photographers of America in New York City, and at various locations in Europe, where she traveled extensively.

Sipprell's work, which included portraits, still lifes, landscapes, and cityscapes, was distinguished by its softly focused images and natural lighting. Many prominent people sat before her camera, including King Gustav V of Sweden, poet Robert Frost, author *Pearl S. Buck, pianist Sergei Rachmaninoff, and photographer Alfred Stieglitz. In her portraits, Sipprell sought to create a mood and milieu complementary to the subject.

Sipprell spent her summers in Vermont, first in Thetford, then in Manchester, where she moved permanently in the 1960s. The photographer, who never married, died there in 1975. After her death, her work was rediscovered and catalogued in *The Photo-Pictorialists of Buffalo.* A major exhibition followed at the Albright-Knox Art Gallery in Buffalo in 1981. Another major retrospective, *Clara Sipprell: Pictorial Photographer,* was held in 1990, at the Amon Center Museum in Fort Worth, Texas, followed by a tour.

**SOURCES:**

Rosenblum, Naomi. *A History of Women Photographers.* NY: Abbeville Press, 1994.

**SUGGESTED READING:**

McCabe, Mary Kennedy. *Clara Sipprell: Pictorial Photographer.* Fort Worth, TX: Amon Carter Museum.

# Sirani, Elizabetta (1638–1665)

*Italian painter. Name variations: Elisabeth Sirani. Born in Bologna, Italy, in 1638; died in August 1665; daughter of Gian Andrea Sirani (1610–1670, an artist); never married; no children.*

Praised as *"la gloria del sesso donnesco"* by Carlo Cesare Malvasia, a 17th-century biographer of Bolognese artists, Elizabetta Sirani created some 170 works, including paintings, drawings, and etchings, before her untimely and suspicious death at the age of 27. Consciously modeling her style on that of Guido Reni (1575–1642), the most influential Bolognese painter of the time, Sirani was known for her incredible speed, once completing a Madonna and Child portrait for an out-of-town visitor in time for it to dry and be taken home with him. Sirani's artistic association with Reni, in whose tomb she was buried, and the ease with which she dashed off her pictures, made her a local celebrity and something of a tourist attraction.

The artist was born in 1638, the daughter of Gian Andrea Sirani, a Bolognese artist who also worked in the style of Reni. It was Malvasia, however, rather than Sirani's father, who discovered her gifts and encouraged her to paint. She turned professional at age 17 and by 1662 had about 90 works to her credit. She finished another 80 or so before her death, working mostly for private patrons, although she also had some public commissions, including a large *Baptism* for the chapel of a Bolognese church.

As **Ann Sutherland Harris** and **Linda Nochlin** point out, Sirani's mastery of Reni's technique and idiom was quite extraordinary, particularly since the young artist received no personal instruction from either Reni or her father:

> She emulated Reni's elevated sentimentality, his avoidance of any true psychological drama, his preference for subjects with static figures, and above all his intention to create beautiful images rather than to move the spectator deeply or make strong moral statements.

They go on to note that Sirani also mastered many of Reni's techniques, and even surpassed him on some occasions. "Her drapery forms tend to be more sculptural, more angular, and more complex than his," they write, "her tonal range is darker, her colors deeper and richer than his were after 1630; her facial expressions are less bland, more particular." In composition, as well, Sirani moved away from Reni, using her own designs. The brush-and-wash technique of her drawings was also an individual invention, unlike any standard drawing methods of the time.

Of Sirani's impressive output, much of which has yet to be studied and evaluated, three paintings—*Judith Triumphant* (1658), *The Penitent Magdalene in the Wilderness* (1660), and *Porcia Wounding her Thigh* (1664)—are representative. Sutherland and Nochlin believe that the latter two paintings alone set a standard of quality that equals that of Reni's best works. The last work, which takes its subject from the story of *Portia in Plutarch's Life of Brutus, is unique in its representation of the courage and heroism of a woman, a point of view seldom seen in the visual arts of the time. Painted in the year before her death, it is also one of the artist's most beautifully executed works. Notable among Sirani's etchings are *St. Eustace Kneeling before a Crucifix* (1656) and *The Beheading of St. John* (1657).

The sudden death of the artist in her prime immediately aroused suspicion that she had been poisoned. Her maid became the primary suspect after admitting to putting a packet of what she believed to be sugar and cinnamon into her mistress' soup after receiving it from an unidentified woman. After a hasty trial, conducted unfairly according to Malvasia, the maid was exiled. An autopsy did reveal that Sirani had holes in her stomach, although they may indeed have been ulcers, then impossible to diagnose. Whatever the cause, Sirani's early death begs the question of how she would have evolved as an artist had she lived longer. Sutherland and Nochlin believe that she would have developed a more forceful personal style and point to her later works as "stronger technically, better drawn, more firmly constructed." They cite *Madonna and Child*, completed in the last year of her life, as "beautifully composed" and expressing more genuine feeling than Reni ever conveyed.

**SOURCES:**

*Harrap's Illustrated Dictionary of Art & Artists.* Kent, Eng.: Harrap's Reference, 1990.

Harris, Ann Sutherland, and Linda Nochlin. *Women Artists: 1550–1950.* L.A. County Museum of Art: Knopf, 1976.

**Barbara Morgan**,
Melrose, Massachusetts

# Sirikit (1932—)

*Queen and regent of Thailand. Name variations: Princess Mom Rajawongse Sirikit Kitiyakara or Mom Rajawong Sirikit Kitiyakara; Sirikit Kitiyakara. Born in Bangkok, Thailand, on August 12, 1932; daughter of Prince Chandaburi Suranath (Nakkhatra Mongkol Kitiyakara), a diplomat, and Mom Luang Bua (Snidwongse) Kitiyakara; educated at St. Francis Xavier*

*Opposite page*
*Sirikit*

*School in Bangkok, later at schools in France, Denmark, England, and Switzerland; married Bhumibol Adulyadej also known as King Rama IX, on April 28, 1950; children: Princess Ubol Ratana (b. 1951); Prince Ma Ha Vajiralongkorn (b. 1952); Crown Princess Sirindhorn (b. 1955); Princess Chulabhorn (b. 1957).*

*Crowned queen of Thailand (1950); acted as regent (1956); active in Thai Red Cross and public health issues; promoted Thai cottage industries by establishing (1976) the Foundation for the Promotion of Supplementary Occupations and Related Techniques.*

Queen Sirikit has been an untiring advocate for the well-being of the people of Thailand, whether it be their access to adequate health care or promotion of their livelihoods. Born a princess as the daughter of Prince Chandaburi Saranath and **Mom Luang Bua Kitiyakara** on August 12, 1932, she was educated at a French Catholic school in Bangkok until her father's work in the diplomatic service moved the family to Europe. There she studied in France, Denmark and England, learning to speak both French and English fluently.

While pursuing her studies in Lausanne, Switzerland, Sirikit became reacquainted with Bhumibol Adulyadej, another Thai student and a distant cousin. Bhumibol had succeeded unexpectedly to the Thai throne in June 1946 after his elder brother was found shot to death in the royal palace. Feeling that he needed more preparation before becoming head of state, Bhumibol postponed his coronation and went to Switzerland to study political science. In the summer of 1949, he announced his engagement to Sirikit, and on April 28, 1950, they were married in Bangkok in a brief Buddhist ceremony, much simpler than those usually held for royal weddings. Bhumibol was crowned King Rama IX on May 5 of that year, and Sirikit was crowned queen. The couple spent another year in Switzerland before returning to Bangkok to settle in the royal palace. Between 1951 and 1957, Sirikit had four children, three girls and one boy, and devoted as much time as she could to overseeing their upbringing.

Much admired by the public for her beauty, warmth, and grace, Queen Sirikit made the promotion of cottage industries her special project, especially the production and export of handwoven Thai silk. She encouraged rural people to practice their traditional crafts, obtaining markets for their products, and, in cases where traditional knowledge had been lost, sending instructors to help the people rediscover lost art forms

and craft techniques. The Foundation for the Promotion of Supplementary Occupations and Related Techniques (SUPPORT), which she founded in 1976, created a chain of shops to sell native crafts, gave rural women training in indigenous arts, and provided training and materials to establish artists' cooperatives.

Sirikit also had great interest in the health of the Thai people, participating regularly in fund raising for the Red Cross. On August 12, 1956, she became president of the Thai Red Cross, and in 1959, after the death of the executive vice-president, took over those duties as well. She worked to improve the public health system; organized aid for refugees, orphans, wounded soldiers and flood victims; and visited leper colonies and village health centers in remote areas of the country where the royal family had never been before. She also campaigned for a vaccination program that was credited with saving the nation's poultry industry.

In 1956, the king, who in Thai tradition also serves as a Buddhist priest, took a sabbatical from his governmental responsibilities, from October 22 to December 7, in order to fulfill his religious duties. He named Sirikit to rule in his place. At the conclusion of her brief tenure, she was granted by the government the title of Somdech Phraborom Rajininath, a high honor, in recognition of the excellence with which she had fulfilled the office of regent.

The royal couple wanted to know firsthand the conditions and needs of the people throughout Thailand. They also subscribed to the philosophy that part of royal responsibility is to bring together other countries and improve world relationships. To this end they promoted assimilation of foreigners, especially refugees, into Thai culture and made several tours of state to foreign countries around the world. In 1959 and 1960, they visited Vietnam, Burma (now Myanmar), and Indonesia, and in June 1960 took a six-month tour of the West, beginning in the United States where Bhumibol had been born.

Queen Sirikit made the conservation of Thailand's forests a high priority. As a member of the World Wildlife Fund, she promoted the afforestation of one of Thailand's most arid regions and worked to protect wildlife habitats, particularly those of endangered species. In recognition of her efforts, in 1986 the chair of the board of directors for the World Wildlife Fund named her an outstanding protector of the environment.

In 1979, the brilliant and popular Princess **Sirindhorn**, Sirikit's second daughter and third child, received from the National Assembly the special dynastic title of Ma Ha Chakri, naming her crown princess because her brother, Prince Ma Ha Vajiralongkorn, was uninterested in the monarchy, and her elder sister, Princess **Ubol Ratana**, an MIT graduate, had renounced her title and married a U.S. citizen. This historic event was followed in the early 1980s by the Thai Parliament's revising the succession laws to permit a female monarch for the first time. (Sirikit's last-born child, Princess **Chulabhorn**, a gifted scientist with a doctorate in organic chemistry, received the coveted Einstein Gold Medal in 1986 and set up the Chulabhorn Research Institute to promote scientific research in Thailand.)

In 1985, exhausted by her hectic schedule, Queen Sirikit retired from public life for several years. She returned after some needed rest to accompany her husband on the diplomatic circuit, visiting many foreign countries in both the East and the West. Sirikit's popularity is evident in the many buildings and centers named after her, including the large convention center in Bangkok. Her birthday is a national holiday set aside to honor mothers.

Sirikit also received several prestigious honors from outside Thailand's borders in recognition of her humanitarian efforts. Several United Nations organizations honored her with awards, including the Food and Agriculture Organization which bestowed on her the Ceres Medal for her work among rural Thai women in 1979. The United Nations Educational, Scientific, and Cultural Organization (UNESCO) likewise honored her with the Borobudur Gold Medal in 1992 for her efforts to preserve Thailand's cultural heritage, and both UNICEF and UNIFEM recognized her efforts on behalf of Thai women that same year. The Royal College of Physicians in Great Britain awarded her an honorary fellowship for her "deep concern for the health and welfare of the people of Thailand," the highest honor conferred by the 470-year old institution, in 1988. Her part in helping homeless refugees earned her the Center for Migration Studies Immigration and Refugees Policy Award two years later, and in 1991 she became the first foreigner to receive the International Humanitarian Award from the Friends of the Capital Children's Museum of Washington, D.C., for her work in providing children in remote areas with educational opportunities.

While speaking of her active involvement in the monarchy and the many responsibilities she has shouldered during her life, Queen Sirikit said of Thai women: "they never had the feeling of being inferior to their menfolk." She became proof of that as an indispensable and visible part of her husband's public life with an active interest in the continuing changes taking place in her beloved Thailand.

**SOURCES:**

*Current Biography 1960.* NY: H.W. Wilson, 1960.

Jackson, Guida M. *Women Who Ruled.* Santa Barbara, CA: ABC-CLIO, 1990.

**Malinda Mayer**, writer and editor, Falmouth, Massachusetts

## Sirimavo (1916–2000).

*See Bandaranaike, Sirimavo.*

## Sirota, Beate (1923—)

*Austrian-born American opera impresario who wrote women's equality into the Japanese constitution. Name variations: Beate Sirota Gordon. Born on October 25, 1923, in Vienna, Austria; daughter of Leo Sirota (a concert pianist) and Augustine (Horenstein) Sirota; married Joseph Gordon, on January 15, 1948; children: Nicole (b. 1954); Geoffrey (b. 1958).*

A long-time leader in Japanese-American cultural relations, Beate Sirota is also well known as the woman who wrote women's equality into the Japanese constitution. She was born in 1923 in Vienna, the daughter of **Augustine Horenstein Sirota** and Leo Sirota, the renowned Russian-born pianist. Concerned about the increasingly vocal conservatism and anti-Semitism of Austria, Leo accepted the invitation of the Japanese government to move to Japan to teach at the imperial music academy. Beate grew up in Japan and moved to the United States in 1939 to attend Mills College in northern California. Fluent in Japanese, German, Russian, French, Spanish, and English, she found work as a translator of Japanese radio broadcasts for the Office of War Information in San Francisco during World War II. She was also given her own radio show in which she produced propaganda to be broadcast to Japan. In 1942, she graduated from Mills with a degree in languages, and took a position in New York as a fact-checker for *Time* magazine. Following the Japanese surrender in 1945, Sirota returned immediately to Japan, where after much effort she located her parents, alive but very ill. In order to stay in Tokyo to care for them, Sirota got a job working in the Government Section of General Headquarters, the American occupation government division charged with developing a new, liberal Japanese government. She was the only civilian woman working for the division.

In February 1946, the 22-year-old Sirota was assigned to the Civil Rights Commission during the secret drafting of the new constitution. The 25 members of the Government Section were given only nine days to prepare a complete draft; Sirota researched existing democratic constitutions for ideas. She was then assigned to write the articles on women's rights because of her intimate knowledge of the inferior status of Japanese women. She hoped to make guarantees of women's and children's rights explicit, recognizing that future governments could easily amend vague statements. Long secret negotiations followed with representatives of the defeated administration; her draft proposals on gender equality were strongly opposed by Japanese officials. "Their main target," writes **Susan J. Pharr**, "was Article 24, guaranteeing the equality of women in family life, which was seen to threaten the basis of male domination and female subordination in the family." However, although most of her articles on women's and child social welfare were eliminated, to her deep disappointment (she was said to have wept), her fundamental statements of gender equality in legal status, marriage, divorce, and property rights, and her article on academic freedom, were finally accepted. Sirota also acted as translator during these meetings. The new constitution was promulgated as the work of the Japanese on November 3, 1946. By then, 39 Japanese women had been voted into the Diet and, though they had had no input in the nascent constitution, they had strongly supported it. Sirota's vital role in establishing Japanese women's legal equality remained secret for many years.

In 1947, Sirota left Japan for New York, where her parents and fiancé, Lt. Joseph Gordon, also an expert on Japan, were already waiting. Sirota and Gordon married in 1948. Sirota was working as a translator when she became an interpreter in 1952 for a Japanese cultural exchange program, specifically *Fusaye Ichikawa, Japan's leading suffragist. This opportunity, combined with Sirota's upbringing in music and the arts, led to a new career promoting traditional and modern Japanese artists abroad. In addition to caring for her two children, Sirota began writing on Japanese traditional arts and then worked at the Japan Society. In the 1950s and 1960s, she arranged for troupes of dancers to perform at schools and acted as a liaison for Asian artists hoping for exposure in America. In 1960, she began her long association with the Asia Society, becoming director of its performing arts program in 1970. She retired from the Asia Society in 1993, but has remained active in promoting Asian-American cultural relations as an arts consultant from her home in New York, as well as an editor of the *International Encyclopedia of Dance*. In 1998, Beate Sirota was recognized for her long years of dedication to promoting Japanese culture abroad with a decoration by the Japanese government. More recently, she was awarded the John D. Rockefeller III Award for her outstanding contribution to the modern Asian arts.

**SOURCES:**

Gordon, Beate Sirota. *The Only Woman in the Room: A Memoir*. Tokyo: Kodansha, 1997.

Pharr, Susan J. "The Politics of Women's Rights," in *Democratizing Japan*. Edited by Robert E. Ward and Sakamoto Yoshikazu. Honolulu: University of Hawaii Press, 1987, pp. 221–252.

**Laura York**, M.A. in History,
University of California, Riverside, California

## Sisi, empress.

*See Elizabeth of Bavaria (1837–1898).*

## Sisk, Mildred Gillars (1900–1988).

*See Gillars, Mildred E.*

## Sissi, empress.

*See Elizabeth of Bavaria (1837–1898).*

## Sisulu, Albertina (1918—)

*South African anti-apartheid activist and African National Congress (ANC) official, who is called the "mother of the nation" for her role in the struggle against apartheid. Name variations: Nontsikelelo Albertina Sisulu; Mama Sisulu. Born on October 21, 1918, in the district of Tsomo, Transkei, South Africa; daughter of Benjamin Boniliawe and Nonani Thethiwe; certified as a nurse; married Walter Sisulu (an anti-apartheid activist and ANC official), on July 17, 1944; children: daughters Nonkululeko, Lindiwe, and Beryl (adopted); sons Max, Mlungisi, Zwelakhe, Jonqumzi (adopted), Gerald (adopted), and Samuel (adopted).*

Nontsikelelo Albertina Sisulu—better known as Albertina Sisulu—was born among the Xhosa people in the district of Tsomo, Transkei, South Africa, in 1918. At that time, South Africa operated under apartheid, a policy institutionalizing strict racial segregation as well as political and economic discrimination against South Africa's nonwhite majority. "Because I grew up in a rural area where I rarely saw a white face and I had nothing whatever to do with the government, I thought we were independent," Sisulu told **Diana E.H. Russell**. Orphaned in youth, Sisulu was frustrated in her ambition to become a teacher by the need to support her younger siblings. She later finished grade school and trained

as a nurse, which required less schooling than did a teaching degree. She began learning about the injustice of apartheid only when she started working in the black hospital in Johannesburg and was required to be under the supervision of white nurses, even when she held seniority over them. She would work as a nurse in Johannesburg from 1944 to 1981.

Albertina met her future husband, Walter Sisulu, in Johannesburg in the early 1940s. Through their courtship, she became politically active herself, attending with him the founding discussions of the Youth League, which would transform the moderate African National Congress (ANC) into a militant nationalist resistance movement. They married in 1944. Serving as best man at their wedding was Nelson Mandela, another ANC leader who later would be imprisoned on the infamous Robben Island for decades, along with Walter. Anton Lembede, chair of the Youth League at the time, warned Sisulu, "You are marrying a man who is already married to the nation."

In 1949, as the movement geared up for the anti-apartheid resistance campaigns, Walter became the ANC's first full-time general secretary. For this, he gave up his income-earning job, and Albertina assumed the task of chief family breadwinner. Over the next 15 years Walter was imprisoned eight times, banned, placed under house arrest, tried twice for treason, and finally, in 1964, incarcerated for life in prison on Robben Island with Mandela and six other ANC leaders. Through these harrowing years, Sisulu had five children and adopted her deceased sister-in-law's two children as well (two more adopted children would later join the family), supporting them all on her earnings as a nurse.

Although she long stood in the shadow of her husband's activism, Sisulu became an important South African political figure in her own right. She joined the ANC's Women's League in the 1940s, serving as deputy president from 1954 to 1963. Also in 1954, she helped form the multiracial Federation of South African Women (FSAW), of which she would later become president in 1980, after the death of *Lillian Ngoyi. With FSAW, Sisulu led huge demonstrations against the extension to women of the hated pass laws and against the introduction of the infamous Bantu education system. Her opposition to women's passes brought her first jail sentence in 1958, with **Winnie Madikizela-Mandela** and others.

By the 1960s, the women's movement, like the ANC (which had been outlawed in 1960), was being crushed by shootings, arrests, trials and bans. In 1963, with Walter underground in the sabotage campaign of Umkhonto we Sizwe ("Spear of the Nation," the ANC's organization for armed struggle), Sisulu was held for three months in solitary confinement under the new 90-day detention law designed to crush opponents without bringing them to trial. Seventeen years of continuous bans followed, including ten years during which she was subject to dusk-to-dawn house arrest. Her livelihood was saved by the intercession of the Johannesburg Nursing Association, which demanded that she be permitted to keep working, and by financial assistance from the International Defence and Aid Fund for Southern Africa. By the early 1980s, after the 1976 Soweto uprising, the women's movement, like the ANC, began to reemerge as the government grappled with massive unrest and attempted cautious reforms.

Sisulu was arrested again in 1983 and sentenced to four years' imprisonment for leading ANC songs, distributing its literature, and displaying its black, green, and gold flag. She managed to get freedom pending appeal and suspension of half the sentence. Meanwhile, also in 1983 Sisulu had helped found the United Democratic Front (UDF), incorporating hundreds of anti-apartheid groups, and was elected one of its three co-presidents while in her jail cell. The UDF's purpose was to oppose a new government-inspired constitution that claimed to provide for non-white power-sharing—with coloreds and Indians only, not with blacks—that was immediately recognized as a sham. As the government responded with increasing violence to peaceful protests, Sisulu and other UDF leaders were arrested and charged, ironically, with fomenting violent revolution. The case was dismissed for lack of credible evidence.

Many of Sisulu's children followed in their parents' footsteps, including Max, the eldest, who at age 17, in 1963, was arrested and held in solitary confinement with his mother. Another son, Mlungisi, was arrested after a national protest in 1984. Zwelakhe, Sisulu's youngest son, became a prominent journalist, but was detained for more than eight months in 1981 and prohibited from practicing journalism or participating in union activities. He traveled to the United States in 1985 to study at Harvard University and upon returning to South Africa was detained again. In addition, Sisulu's oldest daughter, **Lindiwe Sisulu**, was jailed and tortured in 1976. She also left South Africa, but worked for the ANC abroad.

Despite the persecution, there was evidence that reform was on the way. In 1989, champion

Albertina Sisulu

of apartheid President P.W. Botha was replaced as party leader by the more flexible F.W. de Klerk who became president in September. Along with a group of anti-apartheid activists, Sisulu traveled to the United States that year to meet with President George Bush, using the first passport granted to her by the South African government. She was also the first South African black nationalist leader to meet with a U.S. president. De Klerk lifted all restrictions placed on Albertina on October 14, 1989. Walter gained his freedom from Robben Island the following day, and Mandela was released shortly thereafter to assume a key leadership role in the dismantling of apartheid in 1990 and 1991. With the ANC no longer considered an "illegal" organization, Albertina helped resurrect the ANC Women's League to mobilize black South African women, while Walter served as deputy president of the ANC. As the ANC Women's League's deputy president, Sisulu proposed that South African women should participate in shaping a Woman's Charter to be included in an ANC proposal on gender rights for the new constitution. On February 1, 1991, President de Klerk repealed the remaining legislative pillars of apartheid in South Africa.

Sisulu left the presidency of the UDF and became the president of the World Peace Council in Johannesburg in 1992. When free democratic elections were held in South Africa for the first time in 1994, Sisulu—revered as the "mother of the nation" for her sacrifices in the cause of freedom—was elected a member of Parliament.

**SOURCES:**

*Crisis.* Vol. 101, no. 4. May–June 1994, p. 2.

*Encyclopedia of World Biography.* 2nd ed. Detroit, MI: Gale Research, 1998.

*Maclean's.* Vol. 107, no. 18. May 2, 1994, p. 28.

Russell, Diana E.H. *Lives of Courage: Women for a New South Africa.* NY: Basic, 1989.

*Who's Who in the World.* 15th ed. New Providence, NJ: Marquis Who's Who, 1998.

Williams, Gwyneth, and Brian Hackland. *The Dictionary of Contemporary Politics of Southern Africa.* NY: Macmillan, 1988.

**Lisa C. Groshong**, freelance writer, Columbia, Missouri

## Sitha (1218–1275).

*See Zita of Lucca.*

## Siti binti Saad (c. 1880–1950).

*See Saad, Siti binti.*

## Sitoe, Aline (c. 1920–1944).

*See Aline Sitoe.*

## Sitwell, Edith (1887–1964)

*Major 20th-century British poet, awarded the title of "Dame" in recognition of her literary achievements, who was co-creator, with Sir William Walton, of the groundbreaking music and poetry "entertainment" entitled* Facade. *Pronunciation: SIT-well. Born Edith Louisa Sitwell on September 7, 1887, in Scarborough, England; died on December 9, 1964, in Keat's Grove, Hampstead, England; first and only daughter of Sir George Reresby Sitwell (a British aristocrat) and Lady Ida (Denison) Sitwell (daughter of a wealthy father and aristocratic mother); had two brothers, Osbert and Sacheverell Sitwell; never married; no children.*

*Educated by nurses, tutors, and governesses, including Helen Rootham who became her governess (1904); with Rootham, left her family home to live in London (1913); published her first collection of poems,* The Mother and Other Poems *(1915); was introduced to Bloomsbury circle members (1916); served as editor of* Wheels *(1916–21); participated in failed first performance of* Fanfare *at home of brother Osbert*

*(1922); published* Bucolic Comedies *(1923); began annual trips to Paris (1923); scored success with public performance of* Fanfare *(1926); met Pavel Tchelitchew in Paris (1927); published* I Live Under a Black Sun *(1937); published* Street Song *(1942); published* The Shadow of Cain, *generally considered her best work of poetry (1947); visited New York and Hollywood (1948); participated in unsuccessful project to produce motion-picture script from her* Fanfare *for Elizabeth (1948); named Dame Commander of the Order of the British Empire (1948); published* Collected Poems *(1954); converted to the Roman Catholic Church (1955); read her poetry at London "memorial concert" in observance of 75th birthday (1962).*

*Selected poetry:* Facade *(1922);* Bucolic Comedies *(1923);* The Sleeping Beauty *(1924);* Rustic Elegies *(1927);* Street Songs *(1942);* The Shadow of Cain *(1947).*

*Selected prose:* Aspects of Modern Poetry *(1934);* Victoria of England *(1936);* I Live Under a Black Sun *(1937);* Fanfare for Elizabeth *(1946);* The Queen and the Hive *(1962);* Taken Care Of *(published posthumously, 1965).*

"I was unpopular with my parents from the moment of my birth," Dame Edith Sitwell wrote in her memoirs. "I was in disgrace for being female, and worse, as I grew older, it was obvious that I was not going to conform to my father's standard of beauty."

Raised in a household where she never received tenderness "from either parent," Sitwell experienced, throughout her early years, what she described as "the incipient anguish of the poet I was to become." Despite a childhood that she believed was an "unqualified hell," Sitwell used her memories to fashion a successful, and ultimately eminent, career as a poet.

Although convinced that she was "peculiar looking," she forced herself into the public eye, eventually becoming a major figure in 20th-century British poetry. Her achievements were given special recognition in 1948, when Queen \***Elizabeth II** awarded her the title of "Dame Commander of the Order of the British Empire."

Despite her dark memories, Sitwell had been born into privilege; her family was proud of its aristocratic roots. Her father's family could trace its aristocratic lineage back to the time of the Plantagenet kings, when the family had been awarded a baronetcy as a reward for a special reception held for the Prince of Wales. The family's large estate near Chesterfield, England, named Renishaw, is thought to be the model for the mansion portrayed in D.H. Lawrence's novel *Lady Chatterley's Lover.*

Sitwell's father, who ascended to the baronetcy at age two, was often described as eccentric. Introverted and scholarly, he spent much of his time at his hobbies of history and landscaping. Sitwell's mother Lady **Ida Sitwell** was unhappy in the marriage. Only 17 years old when her marriage was arranged by parents, she attempted to run away within days of the ceremony. Her parents promptly forced her to return to the Sitwell estate. Sitwell remembered that her mother's physical beauty was greater than any portrait revealed, but she also remembered that her mother was bored from long stays at the country homes owned by the family. She often stayed in bed all day, reading and, eventually, drinking heavily. Sitwell also recalled that her mother believed she had married beneath her—her family line had been earls—and sometimes told Sitwell, "I am better born than you."

Sitwell later wrote that both parents were "strangers" who knew nothing of what was "in my heart." They favored her two younger brothers, Osbert and Sacheverell. As adults, her brothers recalled that their mother constantly criticized Edith in public. Sitwell later realized that, as the first-born child, she had been conceived before her unhappy mother was ready for motherhood. "No wonder," she later wrote, that "my mother hated me throughout my childhood and youth." In her memoirs, published posthumously, she wrote, "I now feel only pity for my mother, a poor young creature, married against her will into a kind of slave-bondage."

But she also realized that her parents would have preferred that their first-born be a boy. When her brother Osbert was born, Sitwell attempted to run away from home. "When I was born," she later reminisced, "my mother would have liked to have turned me into a doll. It was a great disappointment to them that I was not a boy. If I had been Chinese I should have been exposed on the mountain with my feet bound."

Sitwell's tense relationship with her parents was made worse by their constant concern over her "unconventional" appearance. They were not worried by Sitwell's increasingly "elongated" face, since that had been a Sitwell family trait for many generations. But they were convinced that she suffered from curvature of the spine and that her nose had a "crooked bridge." A specialist who was consulted about the first problem decided that Sitwell should be strapped between two iron frames when she went to sleep.

Although they were told that nothing could be done to change her nose, her parents often called attention to the "defective nose" in public. When the family sat for a joint portrait done by the painter John Singer Sargent, Sitwell recalled being "white with fury" that on this occasion her father uncharacteristically tried to hold her "tenderly." She was just as angry when her father mentioned the crookedness of her nose to the painter. Her pain over such treatment lingered into her adult life: as an adult, she was amused to realize that Sargent had painted her with a "normal" nose and had given a crooked, "aquiline" nose to her father.

A precocious child, Edith Sitwell found creative ways to rebel. When the four-year-old was asked by a family friend what she wanted to become when she grew up, she replied, "a genius." At that age, she was already able to read the fairy tales of the Brothers Grimm and Hans Christian Andersen. Told that she must memorize the poem "The Boy Stood on the Burning Deck," she instead scandalized her parents by memorizing parts of Alexander Pope's *The Rape of the Lock.*

> *No other poet of our time has written so many lines which delight the imagination and give us a sense of magical freedom.*
>
> —Edwin Muir

She sought to escape her parents' judgments by seeking solace in nature and spending time with her grandmothers, **Lady Londesborough** and **Lady Sitwell**, who considered her a "dear child" and had much more favorable attitudes toward her than her parents. She also was given personal attention by a Londesborough aunt who worried over the "fits of fright" that Sitwell exhibited. While staying with Lady Londesborough, she was even allowed to visit the grave of Algernon Charles Swinburne, whose poems fascinated her but were anathema to her parents.

When she spent time at Renishaw and at Woods End, the smaller, "dark" house near Scarborough that the family often occupied, the young Edith was fascinated by the surrounding areas and gardens. The grounds were a source of inspiration for her later poems, particularly the gardens at Renishaw, which she remembered as "huge and dreamlike." The Yorkshire coast also impressed her for its "tides, the wild rush of waves, that sweep inward, so that it seemed the sound of one's own blood."

Her education was sporadic. Nurses and governesses sometimes found her to be as exasperating as her parents believed her to be. For a while, she was sent to classes in art or given special tutors in art. When **Helen Rootham** became her governess in 1904, Helen discovered that Sitwell had special interests in music and poetry. Rootham encouraged her to study the poetry of Alexander Pope and Swinburne, and she arranged for a music tutor to teach Sitwell the music of Chopin. Sitwell gave to Rootham much of the credit for the fact that she became a poet.

It was the beginning of a lifelong, if sometimes tense, friendship between the two, in which Helen would often function as "protector" for the inexperienced and vulnerable Edith. But Rootham, who urged Sitwell to attend more parties in order to improve her social skills, often tried to take advantage of Sitwell's social connections. An aspiring singer, Rootham would often introduce Sitwell at parties as "Miss Sitwell, who is to play for me." Sitwell would be banished to wait in the servants' quarters by unknowing hostesses or hosts.

Yet Sitwell's independence and feistiness, which led her mother to call her a "very violent child," would not let her keep silent in such situations. On one occasion, she overheard a hostess expressing the wish to be invited to the lavish parties of Lady Londesborough. As Sitwell left the party with Rootham, she told the hostess, with malicious satisfaction, "I must see that my aunt invites you."

Sitwell later concluded that the motivation for much of her poetry was her own, inner rebellion against the lifestyles of her parents. She became a poet, she wrote, despite her background, and not because of it. "I was subjected," she wrote, "to a devoted, loving, peering, inquisitive, interfering, stultifying, middle-class suffocation." It left her determined that she would not "become like everyone else." When she was told by left-wing writers that she had not had enough "proletarian experiences" to produce good poetry, she replied that her unhappy childhood had given her a special sympathy for the dispossessed. She disliked the snobbish attitudes of many of her parents' friends, and she had particular sympathy for her parents' servants who reached retirement age and then seemed, like her, to be unwanted and lonely.

In 1913, when Sitwell was 25, she was allowed to move to London with Rootham. Although Sitwell had a much smaller trust fund than her brothers, Rootham was able to find an affordable, if small, apartment in the Bayswater section. Edith supplemented her income by working at the Chelsea Pension Office. When

asked at parties why she lived where she did, she usually replied, "Because I have not much money." When she had extra money, she often spent it on fashionable clothes, saying that she was going to "dress as stylishly as possible" to cover a "lack of beauty."

The year after she moved to London, Sitwell's mother became involved in a financial scandal. It was the first time Sitwell felt sympathy for her mother. Lady Ida had become embroiled in debt far beyond her means to pay, and while Sitwell's father agreed to pay off many of the debts, he refused to recognize debts Lady Ida had incurred through an American, Julian Osgood Field. Field had agreed to give money to Lady Ida in return for social introductions to prominent British families. Instead, he obtained money for her by borrowing, in her name. In 1915, when Sitwell's father was in France on military duty, her mother was found liable for the debt and sentenced to a "period of detention" in a British prison.

As Sitwell became acquainted with many of the literary luminaries of Britain, her apartment in Bayswater was visited by a variety of individuals who were prominent in the arts or literature, such as the photographer Cecil Beaton and members of the Bloomsbury circle of literary writers, including the writers Aldous Huxley and *Virginia Woolf. Sitwell, who did not like competition from other women "in the same line of work," made a poor initial impression on Woolf. Woolf described Sitwell as being a very tall young woman who wore a "perpetually puzzled expression" and "a high silk headdress covering her hair, so that it is not known if she has any."

During her early years at Bayswater, Sitwell was able to have her first poems accepted for publication. One of them had been published in a British newspaper in 1913, but her emergence as a poet really dates from 1915 when her first book of poetry, *The Mother and Other Poems*, was published.

From 1916 through 1921, Sitwell was editor of the literary annual *Wheels*, and she used the magazine to recognize new talent. For much of her adult life, she would "adopt" talented younger writers as her protégés. *Wheels* was the first publication to give major recognition to the British poet Wilfred Owen, killed in action in 1918, whose wartime poems later became the inspiration for the composer Benjamin Britten's *War Requiem*.

Most of the contributors to *Wheels*, including Sitwell herself, opposed the prevailing school

Edith
Sitwell

of "Georgian poets," led by Edwin Marsh and Sir John Squire. Sitwell believed that the "Georgian poets" had overdone the trend, dating from the time of the 18th-century poet William Wordsworth, of attempting to bring the "language of ordinary speech into poetry." Their rhymes, and their subject matter, seemed too conventional and predictable to her. Starting with her book of poems entitled *Bucolic Comedies* (1923), Sitwell tried to portray the world as "one image of wonder mirrored by another image of wonder." She emphasized that the world is viewed through our senses, in a process she termed "sense transfusion." She experimented with language and rhythm in poetry, using first the "language" of one of the human senses, and then the "language" of another one of the human senses. Often, the images she used were drawn from fairy tales, mythology, history, and even nursery rhymes.

One of the contributors to *Wheels*, the Chilean poet and painter Alvaro Guevara, became a personal friend, frequently escorting Sitwell to concerts and exhibitions. While Sitwell apparently hoped for more than friendship, the bisexual Guevara preferred another contributor to *Wheels*, *Nancy Cunard. Sitwell's relationship with Guevara set a pattern for many of the men in her life, a number of them homosexual or bisexual. Finding herself unattractive to men who interested her, she apparently made a virtue out of necessity when she declared, "Artists should not marry."

Sitwell's relationship with the Russian émigré painter Pavel Tchelitchew, who lived in Paris, followed a similar pattern. In 1923, Sitwell and Rootham began to make annual visits to Paris; in 1932, they settled there, partly to be closer to Rootham's sister and partly because Sitwell believed that there would be fewer distractions to her work. In Paris, Sitwell became a regular guest at parties given by the Americans *Gertrude Stein and her companion *Alice B. Toklas. At these functions, Stein generally sat with the male guests, while Toklas entertained the women. Paying Sitwell what she considered the ultimate compliment—that she had "the mind of a man"—Stein invited Sitwell to sit next to her at these parties. She was the only other woman so honored. In turn, Sitwell secured invitations for Stein to speak at Oxford and Cambridge.

Stein told a friend, "I have an Englishwoman for Pavel to paint." But she did not vouch for Tchelitchew's character. Introducing the two of them, Stein commented, "If I have presented Pavel to you, it is your responsibility. His character is not my affair." Tchelitchew had already noticed Sitwell at a party, where he had been fascinated by her looks and had declared that she had the "most beautiful nose that any woman ever had." He produced several paintings of her over the course of their friendship.

Sitwell became Tchelitchew's patron, introducing him to prominent and wealthy families who might buy his art. She found him "the most generous man I have ever known," while Tchelitchew responded, "I have no real friend but you." For many years, they conducted a voluminous correspondence. Sitwell may have been in love with Tchelitchew, and, since she had grown up in protected surroundings and was living with another woman who was her protector, she did not give a second thought to the succession of men who lived with him. She preferred not to talk about the possibility that Tchelitchew was homosexual—a topic she called "squiggly things."

But her friendship with Tchelitchew ended only when he showed her one of his paintings at the New York Museum of Modern Art in 1948. Not knowing what to say, she remained silent, a response he took to be a great insult. When Tchelitchew later explained his alienation from Sitwell by commenting that she was "not feminine enough," a friend noted that he really meant "not passive enough."

The early 1920s brought all three Sitwells to the attention of the British literary establishment, although not all of the publicity was favorable. The cause of the attention was *Facade*, a musical and poetic "entertainment" that Edith Sitwell and her two brothers presented in 1922. *Facade* combined the music of the composer and friend William Walton with poems written by Edith Sitwell. She admitted that she did it as "kind of a dare. Willie gave me certain rhythms and said, 'There you are, Edith. See what you can do with that.'" The first production, presented in the home of her brother Osbert, was a disaster. While Sitwell intended her poems to be witty "gaiety"—the audience was "meant to laugh," she wrote—the production totally confused the audience. Sitwell read her poems while sitting behind a painted curtain, speaking through a kind of megaphone called a "Segerphone." Often, her voice could not be heard above the music.

In terms of Sitwell's development as a poet, *Facade* was a bold experiment, allowing her to deemphasize the "end rhymes" of poetry and to emphasize, instead, the "assonant" and "dissonant" sounds of the English language in a sophisticated way. It would take three performances of *Facade* until audiences would begin to appreciate the work's merits, however. A more polished performance, given at the Aeolian Theater in 1923, was no more successful than the first. "Brickbats are flying," said Sitwell, using her favorite phrase to describe times of trouble. Virginia Woolf wrote that she had heard that the "Sitwells are reciting what seems to be shear nonsense through a megaphone." One critic summarized *Facade* as "the drivel they paid to hear."

A strong enmity developed between all three Sitwells and the writer and playwright Noel Coward, who parodied *Facade* and the Sitwell family in a sketch entitled "The Swiss Family Whittlebot." In an obvious reference to Edith Sitwell, he wrote that "Hernia (Whittlebot) is preparing for the publication of her new book, 'Gilded Sluts and Garbage.'"

By the time of the third performance of *Facade*, in 1926, the merits of the work were being recognized, although it would be some time before the work reached its current status as a landmark in poetry and music. Basking in their new fame, Edith Sitwell and her brothers assumed the role, during the 1920s, of the *enfants terrible* of British literary circles. They placed an advertisement in a London newspaper announcing that "Miss Edith Sitwell and Mr. Osbert Sitwell have much pleasure in announcing a general amnesty [for all those who had offended them]. This does not apply to habitual offenders." When a reviewer implied that they had reached literary prominence through energy and self-assurance rather than because of any literary talent, all three Sitwells successfully sued the writer for libel.

During the 1930s, Edith Sitwell's reputation as a poet continued to grow. Virginia Woolf now found her "magestical" and "monumental." Fellow poet William Butler Yeats became a champion of her poetry, and it was partly because of his advocacy for her work that she was awarded the Royal Society for Literature Medal for Poetry.

Although Sitwell still seemed shy and vulnerable, the feistiness she had displayed as a child would not let her remain silent in the face of attack. She used one of her prose works, *Aspects of Modern Poetry* (1934), to attack her critics, including Wyndham Lewis, a former friend. The book's misuse of quotations, however, left her open to charges of distorting her opponents' words.

Increasingly, she turned to prose writing to supplement her income. Her book *Bath*, published in 1932, was a history of the city of Bath. She published a variety of historical books, in which she placed more emphasis on helping her reader to "live" the period than in attempting to create objective historical scholarship. These works included *Alexander Pope* in 1930 and *Victoria of England* in 1936. Her book *I Live Under a Black Sun*, which appeared in 1937, concerned the life of Jonathan Swift, while her *Fanfare for Elizabeth* (1946) dealt with the life of Queen *Elizabeth I.

Rootham, who was diagnosed with cancer in 1930, died in 1938. After World War II began in 1939, Sitwell left Paris and returned to live with her two brothers at Renishaw while their

parents were living elsewhere. Sitwell found the quiet atmosphere of the large estate ideal for her work, and during the next ten years her productivity matched the prolific writing pace she had achieved during the 1920s.

By the time of the 1940s, Sitwell had gained the reputation of being the major woman poet in Britain in the first half of the century. During the war years, the adjective "woman" was dropped, and she came to be considered one of the major British poets of the century. Her book of poems entitled *Street Songs* (1942) was about people who endured against impossible hardships—a topic appropriate for wartime Britain. At the war's end, she had been horrified by the atomic bomb. Her book of poems entitled *The Shadow of Cain* (1947) described a division of matter in the universe into warring particles, a not-so-veiled reference to the bomb.

Increasingly, she was asked to give public readings of her poetry, to audiences which included Queen *Elizabeth (Bowes-Lyon) and the princesses Elizabeth (II) and *Margaret Rose. Her wartime readings became legendary. During one poetry reading in 1944, air raid sirens began to sound, but she refused to move, and gave special emphasis to a line from one of her poems which described "rain falling in a field of blood." The audience, transfixed, remained motionless as well. One observer called it "a magnificent performance worthy of a British admiral . . . dictating orders from the bridge in the middle of a naval engagement."

In 1948, her stature in British literature was recognized by Queen Elizabeth II, who bestowed on her the title of "Dame Commander of the Order of the British Empire." Asked by a bystander at one of her lectures why she called herself "Dame," Sitwell replied, with typically caustic wit, "I don't. The Queen of England does." Four universities in Britain awarded her honorary degrees: Oxford, Durham, Leeds, and Sheffield.

In 1948, Sitwell crossed the Atlantic. The trip was primarily a U.S. lecture tour, and she used it as an opportunity to attack her critics from foreign soil. "No one," she noted, "realizes what a tough old demon they've got to deal with." She was charmed by her reception. "How much I do like Americans—anyone who doesn't must be mad," she wrote a friend. In New York City, she was honored at a book party which included playwright Tennessee Williams, writer Gore Vidal, American poet *Marianne Moore, and British poets W.H. Auden and Stephen Spender. Yet she found New York City to be overwhelming. "Everyone appeared to be young," she marveled. "It was not possible to imagine that a people so alive could be old." When a listener at one of her lectures told her, "I have read one of your books," she replied, with playful sarcasm, "Don't spoil me."

The purpose of a trip to Hollywood was to work on a screenplay for a motion-picture version of her *Fanfare for Elizabeth*. "It would be nice," she declared, "to have some money for once." The script was never completed. The reason, she told friends, was that Hollywood screenwriters wanted the motion picture to open with a pillow fight, followed by the first appearance of *Anne Boleyn—clothed only in a towel.

Because she met a number of stars she admired, Sitwell did not consider her Hollywood stay to be a waste of time. "I must say," she wrote, "that I couldn't have enjoyed Hollywood more." Among those she met were *Mary Pickford, *Ethel Barrymore, Harpo Marx, *Marilyn Monroe, and the director George Cukor. Sitwell took a strong dislike only to the columnist *Hedda Hopper. When Hopper, in one of her newspaper columns, referred to Sitwell as a "little old lady," Sitwell retaliated by telling almost everyone she met that there was a rabies epidemic in Hollywood, caused, she added, by the fact that Hopper had bitten a local dog.

The next few years were a time of sadness. The poet Dylan Thomas, whose work she had championed, died in 1953. Her brother Osbert was diagnosed with Parkinson's disease. Religious references had always been part of her poetry, and in the post-World-War-II years her poems often reasserted the goodness of God against the background of the horrors of a violent world. When a listener at one of her poetry readings criticized her for not dealing with the "dignity of man" in her poetry, she replied that she thought themes such as the dignity of Christ were more important. It did not surprise friends that in 1955 she converted from the Anglican to the Roman Catholic faith. The priest who received her into the Church seemed to indicate, however, that she did not seem completely orthodox in her beliefs: he called her a "very eccentric Catholic."

Sitwell remained in demand for poetry readings throughout the 1950s, including an appearance at the Edinburgh Festival of 1959. She had become more assertive in dealing with audiences. When members of one audience complained they could not hear, she replied, "Get a hearing aid." On another occasion, she responded with, "I am not going to ruin my voice to please you." Asked to lower the papers in her hand so that audience members could see her better, she quipped, "You won't like what you see."

Her last work of poetry was *The Outcasts* (1962). Her last prose publication was *The Queen and the Hive*, which also appeared in 1962. The same year, she was lionized at a special "celebration concert" in London to mark her 75th birthday; the program combined music with her poetry, some of which she read. A short time before, her old enemy Noel Coward had visited her, and they had reconciled.

Sitwell's last 18 months were filled with illness, but she resolved that she would go on an around-the-world tour by ship in 1964. By the time the ship reached Bermuda, she had to be taken off by stretcher and flown back to London. Her remaining months were spent in a small cottage not far from where the poet John Keats had lived. She died on December 9, 1964.

Her gravestone is engraved with lines from one of her poems:

> The past and present are one—
> Accordant and discordant, youth and age
> And death and birth. For out of one came all—
> From all comes one.

**SOURCES:**
Bradford, Sarah, Honor Clerk, Jonathan Fryer, Robin Gibson, and John Pearson. *The Sitwells and the Arts of the 1920s and 1930s.* Austin, TX: University of Texas Press, 1996.
Glendinning, Victoria. *Edith Sitwell: A Unicorn among Lions.* NY: Alfred Knopf, 1981.
Lehmann, John. *A Nest of Tigers: The Sitwells in Their Times.* Boston, MA: Little, Brown, 1968.
Salter, Elizabeth. *Edith Sitwell.* London: Oresko Books, 1979.
Sitwell, Edith. *Taken Care Of: The Autobiography of Edith Sitwell.* NY: Atheneum, 1965.

**SUGGESTED READING:**
Salter, Elizabeth. *The Last Years of a Rebel: A Memoir of Edith Sitwell.* London: Hutchinson, 1967.
Villa, Jose Garcia, ed. *A Celebration for Edith Sitwell.* NY: New Directions, 1948.

**COLLECTIONS:**
Many of Sitwell's papers, including correspondence and notebooks, were purchased by, and are housed in, the Humanities Research Center of the University of Texas at Austin. Other letters are held by the libraries of the University of Sussex and of the University of Durham, England. Her letters to Pavel Tchelitchew, held at Yale University, were made available in the year 2000.

**Niles Holt**, Professor of History,
Illinois State University,
Normal, Illinois

# Sivali (d. 93 CE)

*Queen of Ceylon. Died in 93 CE; daughter of Āmandagāmani Abhaya, ruler of Ceylon (modern-day Sri Lanka); sister of Cūlābhaya.*

According to the *Mahāvamsa* (a chronicle of the history of Sri Lanka written by a Buddhist monk named Mahānāma in the 4th century), Sivali was one of a line of pious rulers of the Vijaya dynasty whose capital was at Anuradhapura. In antiquity, Sri Lanka was for the most part politically unified but free neither from raids originating in India nor from domestic rebellion. Sivali's grandfather, Mahādāthikamahānāga, inherited the throne upon the death of his childless brother, Bhātikābhaya. Both knew long and relatively peaceful reigns, of 12 and 28 years respectively, throughout which they manifested their piety (especially by patronizing the Buddhist monasteries within their kingdom) and attained reputations as great builders. Sivali's father Āmandagāmani Abhaya ruled for almost ten years and was similarly inclined. However, his younger brother, Kanirajānutissa, murdered him and usurped the throne. This act generated political unrest which was not entirely doused when Cūlābhaya (Āmandagāmani Abhaya's son and Sivali's brother) ascended the throne after his uncle had reigned for three years. Cūlābhaya's reign, however, itself lasted only a year and his death inaugurated a dynastic civil war. For a short time, Sivali's faction held sway, and she was recognized as queen. Nonetheless, her reign too was brief. After only four months, Sivali's cousin, Ilanāga (who was probably the son of Kanirajānutissa), dethroned Sivali and had her executed. Thereafter, although the authority of Ilanāga was contested, the royal line proceeded from him until the Vijaya dynasty was overthrown and replaced by that of the Lambakanna (127 CE).

**William S. Greenwalt**, Associate Professor of Classical History, Santa Clara University, Santa Clara, California

# Six Wives of Henry VIII

*English queens whose marriage to, and in some cases deaths at the hands of, Henry VIII led to the founding of the Church of England and one of the most widely known epochs in the British monarchy.*

*Catherine of Aragon (1485–1536). Spanish princess, renowned for her piety, dignity, and strength of character, who was queen of England and wife of Henry VIII for 24 years.* Name variations: Katherine or Catharine; (Spanish) Catalina. Born on December 16, 1485, in Spain; died of cancer on January 7, 1536, in Kimbolton, England; daughter of Isabella I (1451–1504), queen of Castile, and Ferdinand II, king of Aragon (r. 1479–1516); sister of Juana la Loca (1479–1555); married Arthur, prince of Wales, in 1501 (died 1502); became first wife of Henry VIII (1491–1547), king of England (r. 1509–1547), in 1509; children: Mary I (1516–1558, queen of England); and a number who were stillborn.

Educated at Spanish royal court; betrothed to Arthur, prince of Wales (1489); widowed (1502), lived in seclusion and poverty for the following eight years; acted as regent for Henry VIII (1513); confronted Henry VIII in court and appealed divorce proceedings to Rome (1529); banished from court (1531); divorced from Henry VIII by Archbishop Cranmer (1533).

*Boleyn, Anne (c. 1507–1536). English queen who precipitated the English Reformation and gave birth to England's most famous queen, Elizabeth I.* Name variations: Nan Bullen. Pronunciation: Bow-lin. Born in 1507 (some sources cite 1501) somewhere in England; executed on May 19, 1536, in London; daughter of Thomas Boleyn (a diplomat-courtier) and Elizabeth Howard (d. 1538); married Henry VIII (1491–1547), king of England (r. 1509–1547), in 1533; children: Elizabeth I (1533–1603), queen of England (r. 1558–1603). (See also Boleyn, Anne.)

Educated at royal courts in the Netherlands and France; appointed lady-in-waiting to Queen Catherine of Aragon (1526); became object of Henry VIII's affection (1527); became Henry's mistress (1532); crowned queen of England (1533); miscarried male child (January 1536); accused of adultery and treason, beheaded (May 19, 1536).

*Seymour, Jane (c. 1509–1537). Third wife of Henry VIII who gave birth to the king's only male heir, Edward VI.* Pronunciation: See-more. Born around 1509 (some sources cite 1506) in England; died from puerperal fever at Hampton Court on October 24, 1537; daughter of Sir John Seymour (a courtier) and Margaret Wentworth (d. 1550); married Henry VIII (1491–1547), king of England (r. 1509–1547), in 1536; children: Edward VI (1537–1553), king of England (r. 1547–1553).

Lady-in-waiting for queens Catherine of Aragon and Anne Boleyn; began to receive the attentions of Henry VIII (1535); died after giving birth to Henry VIII's only male heir (1537).

*Anne of Cleves (1515–1557). German royal, who was briefly married to Henry VIII and lived the rest of her life in England as the king's "good sister."* Born on September 22, 1515, in Cleves, Germany; died of cancer on July 16, 1557, in England; daughter of John III, duke of Cleves, and Maria of Julich-Berg; married Henry VIII (1491–1547), king of England (r. 1509–1547), in January 1540 (divorced July 1540); lived the rest of her life in England as Henry's "good sister."

*Howard, Catherine (1520/22–1542). Young, head-strong woman who captured the heart of the aging Henry VIII and became his fifth wife.* Born between 1520 and 1522 in Lambeth, England; beheaded for adultery and treason on February 13, 1542, in the Tower of London; interred at Chapel Royal, Tower of London; daughter of Lord Edmund Howard and Joyce Culpeper; first cousin of Anne Boleyn (1507–1536); married Henry VIII (1491–1547), king of England (r. 1509–1547), on July 28, 1540; began adulterous relationship with Thomas Culpeper, 1541.

*Parr, Catherine (1512–1548). Sixth wife of Henry VIII, whose tact and intelligence enabled her to act as regent and nursemaid for the ailing king.* Name variations: Katherine Parr. Born in 1512 in England; died of puerperal fever on September 5, 1548, after giving birth to a girl; daughter of Sir Thomas Parr of Kendal and Maud Greene Parr (1495–1529); married Edward Borough, in 1529 (died 1532); married John Neville (1493–1543), 3rd Lord Latimer, in 1533; married Henry VIII (1491–1547), king of England (r. 1509–1547), in 1543 (died 1547); married Thomas Seymour (brother of Jane Seymour), Lord Admiral of England, in March 1547; children (fourth marriage) Mary Seymour (August 29 or 30, 1548–September 5, 1548; an 18th-century historian claimed that she grew to adulthood and married Sir Edward Bushell).

Widowed twice before marrying Henry VIII (1543); acted as regent (1544); wrote and published religious treatise (1545); argued with Henry over religious issues and was almost convicted of heresy (1546); Henry VIII died (January 1547); published second religious treatise (1547). Selected publications: Prayers and Meditations (1545); Lamentations of a Sinner (1547).

Henry VIII is one of England's most famous kings. Much of his reputation and fame rests upon the fact that he chose not one, but six women, to be his wife over the course of his 38-year reign. Of these six wives, he divorced two, two more were executed by his command, and one outlived him. All of his wives, save perhaps Catherine Howard, displayed intelligence, dignity, and perseverance during their marriage to the irascible and headstrong Henry.

## Catherine of Aragon

Ironically, the first of the king's wives was not originally destined to marry him. A royal princess from one of the most powerful monarchies in Europe, Catherine of Aragon first came to England as the bride of Henry VIII's older brother Arthur, prince of Wales. She was born on December 16, 1485, the youngest daughter of the two reigning Spanish monarchs, *Isabella I of Castile and Ferdinand II of Aragon. In her early years, Catherine was strongly influenced by her mother who cultivated in the young girl a sense of dignity and pride in her status as a true royal princess. Isabella made sure that Catherine and her three elder sisters—*Isabella of Asturias (1471–1498), *Juana la Loca (1479–1555), and ◀ Maria of Castile (1482–1517)—were given a proper Renaissance education. The future queen of England learned to read and write Latin as well as law, music, dancing, and drawing. From her mother, she also learned that marriage was a lifetime commitment and that, while both partners had an obligation to support one another, it was a wife's duty to submit to her husband's will. Catherine's formative years instilled in her a deep sense of piety and chastity.

Early modern marriages among the royal houses of Europe were almost always dependent upon political relations between the respective countries of the bride and groom-to-be. By the end of the 15th century, Spain was constantly hostile towards France and thus, when time came to arrange for the marriage of his youngest daughter, Ferdinand looked towards England. Negotiations for a marriage between Princess Catherine and Henry VII's eldest son Arthur were finalized in March 1489, when Catherine was only four years old. For much of her childhood, therefore, Catherine grew up with a sense that her destiny was in England.

In October 1501, her fate was about to be realized when she arrived in England. In appearance, the 16-year-old princess had reddish-gold hair, a fair complexion and an oval face. She was small in stature and, while not fat, was rather plump. Her fiance, 15-year-old Arthur, was well educated although small and under-developed for his age. Catherine was warmly greeted from the moment she arrived in England. Pageants and grand spectacles saluted her wherever she went. On November 14, 1501, two days after she had entered the city of London, Catherine of Aragon married Prince Arthur at St. Paul's Cathedral. Arthur's younger brother, ten-year-old Henry, was on hand to lead the princess up the aisle and participate in the wedding festivities.

Within a few weeks, it became clear to Catherine that all was not well; her marriage had yet to be consummated. Although this could become a problem, it did not worry either her parents or her father-in-law who argued that since they were both young, consummation could

---

*Maria of Castile (1482–1517).* See Isabella I for sidebar.

*Opposite page* Catherine of Aragon

wait. Thus, Catherine followed her husband to spend the winter in Ludlow Castle on the border of Wales. Unfortunately, Arthur, whose health had always been frail, fell ill in March and died of tuberculosis shortly thereafter on April 2. Seventeen-year-old Catherine of Aragon was a widow after only five months of marriage. While the news was devastating, both parties decided that the best solution to the problem of the Anglo-Spanish marriage alliance was to betroth Arthur's widow to his younger brother Henry, who was now heir to the English throne. Consequently, on June 23, 1503, another marriage treaty between Spain and England was signed.

For Catherine, however, this turn of events was not an occasion for mirth. Henry VII, a stern and unloving man, sent her off to Durham House in London where she was kept in virtual isolation for the next six years. She knew little English and, as a foreigner in a strange land, these were unhappy years for the princess. Since her father Ferdinand delayed sending over the remaining half of her dowry, Henry VII refused to supply her household with sufficient funds. Many of Catherine's staff, including her Spanish confessor and her favorite lady-in-waiting, left her impoverished household to return to Spain. Isolated and lonely, Catherine turned to religion as a comforting solace. During these years, she also suffered from several illnesses, most of which were probably caused by depression. Finally, on April 21, 1509, Henry VII died. Two months later, Catherine of Aragon married the new King Henry VIII on June 11.

Her 18-year-old husband was tall, fair-haired and very handsome. Young King Henry VIII was an energetic, well-educated and athletic monarch who enjoyed music, dancing, and hunting. He was also deeply in love with his wife. The 23-year-old Catherine was still very pretty and was noted for her long, thick auburn hair and beautiful complexion. With a new and vigorous young king, the English royal court was revitalized. Tournaments, parties, and pageants celebrated both the coronation of the new king as well as his recent marriage. Soon after their marriage, Catherine became pregnant but later gave birth to a still-born girl. Although the king was disappointed, he knew that they were both young and that there was still time to beget a male heir.

Henry's devotion to and trust of his queen was readily apparent in 1513 when he declared Catherine regent while he went on campaign against France. She governed the country well in his absence. The Scots, as traditional allies of

France, attempted to invade England while King Henry was on the Continent but were horribly defeated at the Battle of Flodden on September 9, 1513. As proof of her governing abilities, Catherine sent the blood-stained coat of the slain Scottish King James IV to Henry in France, declaring that she had kept her promise of defending England against its enemies. Nor did she neglect her wifely duties. Affectionate letters were exchanged between them, and Catherine sent over several shirts that she had sewn herself.

The early years of their marriage were happy ones. Catherine accompanied Henry to every public function while he wore her initials on his sleeve at tournaments and affectionately called himself "Sir Loyal Heart." During these years, Catherine was often pregnant but suffered either miscarriages or stillbirths. On February 18, 1516, she gave birth to her only surviving child; a girl, Mary (later *Mary I). Although Henry was disappointed, he was still optimistic about the future birth of a male heir to the throne.

By 1516, however, Catherine was becoming quite stout and the age difference between them was becoming more noticeable. Nonetheless, she remained a popular queen and was well known for her religious piety as well as her patronage of scholars. In addition, she maintained an important influence with the king. On May 1, 1517, hundreds of Londoners rioted against what they believed was undue economic dominance by foreigners. King Henry was not a monarch who tolerated disobedience, however, and, as a result, many of the rioters were executed. When 400, many of them women and children, still remained in detention, Queen Catherine successfully pleaded for their release and pardon.

While the king continued to hope for a male heir, he did not remain entirely faithful to his wife. Early modern husbands were not well known for their fidelity and Henry VIII had at least two mistresses during his marriage to Catherine of Aragon. In 1519, when Catherine gave birth to another stillborn daughter, Henry's mistress, ◄ Elizabeth Blount, gave birth to a son. Two years later, he was dallying with ◄ Mary Boleyn. By the 1520s, Henry was

becoming increasingly concerned that he would have no male heir to succeed him. Like many other 16th-century parents, the king believed that his failure to beget a male heir was a sign of God's punishment. In spite of his efforts to please God, which included going on pilgrimages and praying several times a day, by 1525 Henry was convinced that his wife was unable to provide him with a son. One year later, he decided that his marriage to Catherine must be dissolved.

The justification for God's anger he found in the Old Testament commandment that a man must not marry his brother's widow. Although Catherine swore that her marriage to Arthur had never been consummated, Henry was convinced that because they had ignored the commandment, God was preventing them from producing a male heir. Thus, Henry's decision to dissolve his marriage was based upon his own theological arguments. By 1527, however, all of his attention was focused on a young woman who soon overtook Catherine's place in the king's heart.

## Anne Boleyn

The date of Anne Boleyn's birth was never recorded, although it is assumed that she was born in either 1501 or 1507. She was one of three daughters of Thomas Boleyn and ◄ Elizabeth Howard. By the reign of Henry VIII, the Boleyn family had risen in both wealth and status. Anne spent her formative years at the royal courts in the Netherlands and France. During her seven years in France, she learned how to speak French fluently as well as sing, dance, play musical instruments and dress stylishly; she was also exposed to reformed religious ideas. Growing up with royal children provided Anne with a sense of dignity and self-worth. At the courts of *Margaret of Austria (1480–1530) in the Netherlands and *Louise of Savoy in France, Anne was also exposed to competent, intelligent, and influential female role models.

In 1521, Anne returned to England. Her father, in the meantime, was busily arranging the marriages of his children. Negotiations for a marriage between Anne and the son and heir of Sir Piers Butler, earl of Ormond, had broken off by 1523. Anne was relieved because she had formed a romantic attachment to Lord Henry Percy, heir to the earldom of Northumberland. Henry VIII's chief minister, Cardinal Wolsey, however, soon discovered their love affair and forced Percy to give up the relationship. Although Anne's reaction to the loss of her beloved is unrecorded, doubtless she learned that aristocratic marriages were more a matter of satisfying

*Howard, Elizabeth.* See Boleyn, Anne (separate entry in Vol. 2) for sidebar.

*Mary Boleyn.* See Boleyn, Anne (separate entry in Vol. 2) for sidebar.

◄ **Elizabeth Blount** (c. 1502–c. 1540)

*Mistress of Henry VIII. Name variations: Bessie Blount; Lady Talboys. Born around 1502; died around 1540; daughter of John Blount; married Gilbert Talboys, Lord Talboys of Kyme; children: (with Henry VIII) Henry Fitzroy, duke of Richmond.*

one's family's ambitions and the interests of the crown than of love.

By the time she was appointed as a lady-in-waiting to Queen Catherine in December 1526, Anne Boleyn had matured into a captivating and intelligent young woman. Yet she was not a beauty by contemporary standards. Instead of the customary blonde hair and blue eyes, 20-year-old Anne had lustrous, thick dark brown hair, black eyes and an elegant, long neck. It was her charm, energy and intelligence which captured the 36-year-old king's attention when they first met in May 1527. Henry fell deeply in love with her almost instantly and, as a result, became even more convinced that his first marriage must be dissolved.

For Catherine of Aragon the appearance of a new young woman who had caught the king's eye was nothing new. Unfortunately, by 1527, she was in a very insecure position: she had not produced a male heir and, at age 42, was past child-bearing age. More important, Anne Boleyn refused to become Henry's mistress. Although she was in love with the king, she determined not to become his concubine. Consequently, for the next five years she sustained Henry's passion by denying him full sexual relations. Finally, unknown to Catherine, Henry had convened a secret tribunal in May 1527 to determine the legality of his first marriage. Although attempts were made to maintain the secrecy of the proceedings, word leaked out. The "King's Great Matter," as the divorce came to be known, was now public and international news.

In June, Henry confronted Catherine asserting that their marriage was not lawful and that he must separate from her. Catherine burst into tears, insisting that her marriage to Arthur had never been consummated. The king remained unmoved. Catherine, though upset, was determined to fight for the survival of her marriage. She managed to smuggle out a letter to her nephew, Holy Roman Emperor Charles V, who responded by giving her his full support. For Henry, this was a serious blow to his plans. In May 1527, Charles' imperial troops had sacked the city of Rome and kidnapped Pope Clement VII. Consequently, Clement was unwilling to slander the emperor's aunt by granting Henry's request for a divorce.

By the early months of 1529, Henry was even more anxious to have his marriage annulled. In May, the papal legate Cardinal Campeggio convened a tribunal to enquire into the king's marriage. On June 21, in full view of the entire court, Catherine made a final desper-ate plea to save her marriage. Kneeling down before the king, she said:

> Sir, I beseech you for all the love that hath been between us, let me have justice and right, take of me some pity and compassion, for I am a poor women, and a stranger, born out of your dominion. I take God and all the world to witness that I have been to you a true, humble and obedient wife.

She repeated publicly that her marriage to Arthur had not been consummated. Since Henry's entire case was built around the Biblical injunction against marrying his brother's wife, this was an unfortunate admission. Finally, Catherine asked that the case be tried in Rome in front of the pope. Finished, she rose up and curtsied to her husband. As she slowly moved out of the court, she was called, three times, to return. She replied to her nervous assistant, however, that she would not tarry in a court so prejudiced against her.

The proceedings continued, although by July it was clear that Campeggio was unwilling to make a decision. In an effort to buy time, Campeggio prorogued the court but it never met again. Henry, outraged by this turn of events, turned his wrath upon Cardinal Wolsey whom he stripped of all offices and lands. Wolsey died a year later, a broken man.

Contemporaries blamed Anne Boleyn for Wolsey's fate, though it was the cardinal's failure to secure a quick divorce for the king that led to his demise. Wolsey's fall from grace was noted by the king's new chief minister, Thomas Cromwell, who recognized that the king's desire for a divorce did not prevent him from turning his back on loyal servants.

After 1529, the king was forced to look for new methods to obtain the divorce. Led by Cromwell, steps were taken to deviate power away from the papacy and into the king's hands; thus began the English Reformation. In 1531, Henry VIII was declared Supreme Head of the Church of England. A year later, the clergy surrendered their legal autonomy to the king. Henceforth, all future clerical legislation required royal assent.

By the summer of 1531, it was evident that Queen Catherine was no longer the king's consort. In August, she was ordered to move away from court while Henry sent various delegations of clerics and nobles who tried to persuade her to have the case settled in England. Catherine steadfastly refused, declaring that the authority to dissolve lawful marriages lay with the pope, not King Henry.

Anne Boleyn's star, in the meantime, was rapidly rising. She was given separate apartments close to the king and now appeared openly at his side on formal occasions. Anne's triumph, however, was not shared by the majority of Henry's subjects. Catherine of Aragon was still a popular queen and, even though she was placed in virtual seclusion, the people of England refused to forget her. Anne was openly referred to as "the King's whore." Nonetheless, in September 1532, she was created Lady Marquess of Pembroke and was given lands and manors in Wales and Middlesex. More significantly, in October Anne accompanied Henry to Calais where they visited the French king, Francis I. It was also sometime during this visit that Anne and Henry finally became lovers. By December, she was pregnant and on January 25, 1533, they were secretly married.

Four months later, the king publicly announced his marriage to Anne Boleyn, and Thomas Cranmer, the new archbishop of Canterbury, decreed that the king's marriage to Catherine of Aragon was invalid. Catherine was asked to give up the title of queen and, as widow of Prince Arthur, to take the title of dowager princess of Wales instead. Thus, in a stroke, the king attempted to erase the past 24 years of their marriage. Defiant, Catherine refused to give up her title. In July, Pope Clement finally came to her aid by condemning the king's marriage to Anne. By this point, however, his words were meaningless since Anne Boleyn had already been crowned queen of England on June 1.

At her coronation, Queen Anne was five months pregnant. On September 7, 1533, she gave birth, not to the king's long-awaited male heir, but to a girl, whom they named Elizabeth (later *Elizabeth I). Although both Henry and Anne were disappointed, they were still confident that Anne would bear a son. And, in the early months of 1534, Henry was hopeful once more when Anne was again pregnant. Hope turned to despair when she miscarried in late June. From this point on, Henry's feelings for his wife began to wane, and by September it was widely rumored that the king had taken a mistress.

Despite these events, Anne remained optimistic about her future, especially when she became pregnant once more in autumn 1535. Her confidence was shattered when she prematurely delivered a male child in January 1536. This event led to her tragic and rapid downfall. Not only was the child premature, but it is likely that it was also deformed. This had devastating consequences. Early modern society believed that the birth of a deformed child was a sign of God's punishment on the parents for committing sexual sins. More significantly, it was believed that witches, due to their excessive lust and deviant sexual acts, gave birth to deformed children. These popular beliefs provided a convenient excuse for a sovereign who wanted to rid himself of an unwanted wife. By 1536, Henry had already set his sights on another young woman at court, Jane Seymour. In addition, Catherine of Aragon had died on January 7, at age 50. Thus, Henry was rid of his first wife and was determined to eliminate the second. These events combined to ensure the swift and inevitable fall of Anne Boleyn.

By mid-March, Henry was publicly flirting with Seymour at court. On April 30, several arrests were made. Five men, one of whom was her brother, were accused of having had sexual relations with Queen Anne. Anne, realizing that her time was short, confronted Henry with three-year-old Elizabeth in her arms proclaiming her innocence. The king was unmoved. On May 2, Anne Boleyn was taken by barge to the Tower of London. In a strange twist of fate, she was housed in the same apartments she had stayed in before her triumphant coronation just three short years before. She was charged with inciting, through witchcraft, the accused men to have sex with her. She was also charged of afflicting the king with bodily harm and of conspiring to kill him. Few people at court, including members of her family, remained loyal to her once they knew she had fallen out of Henry's favor. A new star, in the form of Jane Seymour, was in ascendance.

Anne Boleyn's trial took place on May 15, 1536. She confronted her 26 male judges in a calm and composed manner. Although she denied all of the charges, they declared her guilty. Her uncle, the duke of Norfolk, sentenced her to death. Two days later, Henry VIII divorced her. On the same day, the five men who had been accused of being her lovers, including her brother, were executed on Tower Hill. On May 18, when Anne was told that she was to be beheaded, she greeted the news with, "I have heard say the executioner was very good, and I have a little neck," then put her hands around her neck and laughed. The following morning, 29-year-old Anne Boleyn was executed in front of a large crowd. Twenty-four hours later, Henry VIII was formally betrothed to Jane Seymour.

## Jane Seymour

The young woman who had captured the king's affections as early as 1535 was the opposite of Anne Boleyn in both appearance and personality. Jane Seymour was born into an aristocratic family that had slowly risen in wealth and status. Her father Sir John Seymour had been knighted by Henry VII in 1497 and later served under Henry VIII as a gentleman of the bedchamber. Her mother *Margaret Wentworth was descended from Edward III and thus Jane could claim royal blood in her family tree. Jane, the eldest of three surviving daughters and three sons, was probably born in 1509.

Like Anne Boleyn, Jane Seymour was in her mid-20s when she caught the king's eye, though little is known of her education or upbringing. She was at court from an early age serving as lady-in-waiting to both queens Catherine and Anne. Of her appearance, it is clear from contemporary portraits that she exhibited some of the 16th-century ideals of beauty; fair hair, a pure white complexion, high forehead and an oval-shaped face. Although she had none of Anne Boleyn's dark and sensuous beauty, Jane's charm of character outweighed any defects of appearance and, significantly, was much more to the king's liking. Her personal motto, "Bound to Obey and Serve," neatly sums up Jane Seymour's personality. Virtuous, calm and good-natured, she was everything a 16th-century Englishwoman was supposed to be. Henry VIII and Jane Seymour were married on May 30, 1536. For the next month, celebrations were held throughout London as the king showed off his new queen.

Although she was not to become as heavily involved in state affairs as her predecessor, Jane was responsible for reconciling the king with his eldest daughter. Mary (I) steadfastly refused to accede to the belief that Henry's marriage to her mother Catherine of Aragon had been invalid. Unfortunately, as he grew older, Henry VIII became less patient with anyone who disobeyed his wishes, and he was prepared to send Mary to the Tower in order to obtain her obedience. Finally, she capitulated and agreed to all of the king's demands. On June 14, 1536, Mary wrote a letter to her father begging his forgiveness and, with Jane's encouragement, the king agreed to reinstate her. From this point on, Mary was a frequent visitor at court.

As the royal couple traveled throughout the realm that summer, the new queen's good and virtuous reputation spread quickly. It was obvious that she was beloved by both her husband and the English people. The same could not be said about the king who, during the last few years, had forcibly dissolved the majority of English monasteries while swallowing up their

abundant wealth. The displaced monks and nuns were left to live as beggars and many people believed that the king had gone too far with his religious reforms. Resentment was greatest in the northern and eastern counties and by September 1536 a rebellion, known as the Pilgrimage of Grace, had broken out. The queen, who was a conservative in religion, had some sympathy with the rebels. Consequently, she attempted to plead with the king for leniency. In full view of the court, Jane fell upon her knees in front of Henry and begged him to restore some of the smaller monasteries. Henry, visibly angry, ordered his wife to get up and not to meddle in his affairs, pointedly referring to the fate of "the late Queen" (Anne).

In spite of this small spat, their marriage was a happy one. The king's affection for his third wife only increased in intensity when she informed him in January 1537 that she was pregnant. Four months later, the happy news was announced officially. Throughout that spring and summer, the king was cheerful and

Jane
Seymour

content. By late September, Jane took to her chamber and on October 12, after two days' labor, she gave birth to a son. At age 46, and after almost 30 years of matrimony, Henry VIII's dream had finally come true—he now had a male heir to succeed him. Although it was later rumored that the baby was delivered by Caesarean section, this was not possible since Jane would never have survived the operation. Throughout the country English people celebrated the royal birth by lighting bonfires and ringing bells. On October 18, 1537, baby Edward (IV) was officially proclaimed prince of Wales. While the child appeared to flourish, his mother did not. Jane Seymour fell ill with puerperal fever and, at age 28, died 12 days after the birth of her son, on October 24.

Henry VIII, though grief-stricken, began searching for a new bride less than one month after the death of his third wife. In this instance, he instructed his ministers to look abroad for a suitable candidate. As always, a royal marriage was closely tied to international affairs. In June 1538, Charles V and Francis I signed a treaty binding them to friendship, effectively leaving Henry VIII in political isolation. In addition, Pope Paul III reissued the Bull of Excommunication against Henry. Consequently, Henry's chief minister, Thomas Cromwell, suggested a union with one of the Protestant German families in order to secure an alliance against Charles V. By 1539, English envoys were being sent to Cleves to determine if Anne, the eldest daughter of the duke of Cleves, would be a suitable match for the king.

## Anne of Cleves

Anne of Cleves was born on September 22, 1515, and was the second of four children born to Duke John III and *Maria of Julich-Berg. Her upbringing was strict. Anne was only educated to read and write in her own language, and she could neither sing nor play an instrument. In appearance, she looked older than her 24 years. Tall and thin, she was not a typical Renaissance beauty. A contemporary French ambassador described her as "of middling beauty, with a determined and resolute countenance." Henry, however, was determined to learn more and sent the artist Hans Holbein to paint her portrait.

The result was not displeasing to the king and on October 4, 1539, a marriage treaty was signed. It was agreed that Anne would travel by land, rather than water, to Calais. She reached the French port on December 11 and, after several delays caused by inclement weather, finally arrived in England on December 27. Henry, increasingly impatient to see his new bride, visited her in secret and in disguise at Canterbury. Unfortunately, he was distressed by what he saw. Anne's plain looks and solemn demeanor were definitely not what he had expected. He returned to speak to her, this time without a disguise, but he remained unimpressed. He later remarked to Cromwell, "I like her not."

Though Anne of Cleves was not beautiful by contemporary standards, she was not ugly either. It is likely that Henry was not sexually attracted to her and, as a result, was unenthusiastic about his upcoming marriage. He even hoped for a way out. It was rumored that Anne had once made a premarital contract with the son of the duke of Lorraine. Unfortunately for Henry, his council found no evidence to support the claim. Resolved to his fate, and seeing the necessity of keeping Emperor Charles V at bay, 48-year-old Henry VIII married 25-year-old Anne of Cleves on January 6, 1540.

Anne had no idea of the king's feelings towards her. Due to her strict upbringing, she was

*Anne of Cleves*

never told the "facts of life" and, as a result, was unaware that her marriage had not yet been consummated. From the wedding night on, the king complained that he could not bring himself to engage in sexual relations with his new wife. Outwardly, however, the royal court was happy. A queen's household was established once more, and Henry behaved courteously towards his bride in public. In late February 1540, Anne of Cleves finally learned how and why her marriage had not been consummated. Although she was worried, she waited patiently and hopefully for the king to change his mind.

Unfortunately, time was not on her side. A combination of political, religious, and emotional developments contributed to the failure of the king's fourth marriage. Internationally, the alliance between France and the Holy Roman Empire was becoming strained and both sides were making friendly overtures towards England. The alliance with Protestant Germany was, therefore, no longer as advantageous as it had been. Religiously, there was a strong Catholic faction at court headed by the powerful and ruthless duke of Norfolk. Finally, by April 1540, Henry had fallen passionately in love with one of Anne's ladies-in-waiting, Catherine Howard, and wanted to marry her.

## Catherine Howard

Catherine Howard, a first cousin to Anne Boleyn, was the daughter of Lord Edmund Howard and **Joyce Culpeper**. She was probably born sometime between 1520 or 1522. Although no authentic portrait of her survives, contemporaries described her as small in stature, not beautiful but pretty and exceptionally vivacious. Unlike the king's fourth wife, Catherine Howard exuded sex appeal and was appealing to men. She was brought up in an impoverished household and, after her mother died, was sent to live with her step-grandmother *Agnes Tylney, duchess of Norfolk. During her time there, she had two romantic liaisons, one of which was sexual. Catherine's education was haphazard at best and she remained headstrong and immature.

When she came to court to serve in Anne of Cleves' household, she fell in love with one of the king's courtiers, Thomas Culpeper. Despite this, her fortune changed when the king set his sights on her. Once the king's intentions became known, Catherine's family supported the infatuation and coached the young girl on how to behave with Henry. Events moved rapidly. Cromwell, whom the king blamed for his disastrous marriage to Anne of Cleves, was arrested

on June 10, 1540. Accused of high treason and heresy, he was sentenced to death without a trial.

Meanwhile, Anne of Cleves had no idea that the king wanted to divorce her. Over the past few months, she was slowly learning to speak English, and it was clear that the people were coming to love and respect her. Nonetheless, the king's mind was made up. On July 9, 1540, Parliament granted the king a divorce. Anne of Cleves submitted to Henry's will without protest and was duly rewarded with a substantial settlement of lands and money. Henceforth, she was to be regarded as the King's "good sister."

While it is uncertain how Anne felt about this turn of events, it is clear that she was shrewd enough to know that it was not in her best interests to cross the king of England. After the king's marriage to Catherine Howard on July 28, Anne of Cleves continued to visit the royal court. In all likelihood, she probably enjoyed her new position. She maintained an honorable place at court as first lady after the queen and the royal daugh-

*Catherine Howard*

ters. Author **Antonia Fraser** has concluded that like a rich widow, Anne "had a household, a large income and property, untrammelled by any need to bow before any male authority except that of the English King." It is quite possible that Anne of Cleves was one of the happiest, and the luckiest, of the six wives of Henry VIII.

It was clear that Henry was head-over-heels in love with his new young wife. A contemporary observed that the king was "so amorous of her that he cannot treat her well enough, and caresses her more than he did the others." During the first months of their marriage, he showered her with jewels, clothing, and gifts. Catherine, as an impressionable and pleasure-loving young woman, accepted the king's attentions gratefully. As a newlywed couple, they made an interesting sight. Henry VIII was nearly 50 years old and was by now very fat. He had varicose ulcerations on his legs which caused him pain and did not improve either his moods or his temper. His bride, on the other hand, was small, young and slender. Their marriage, however, appeared to be a success.

Anne of Cleves continued to visit the court, and on New Year's Eve 1541 she and Catherine Howard danced together while Henry retired early to bed. By the spring, Catherine took a step which ultimately led to her downfall. She resurrected her relationship with Thomas Culpeper. For several months, her affair went undetected. By late autumn, while she and the king were on a tour of the northern counties, an informant told Archbishop Cranmer of her past behavior. Although divulging secrets was not unusual in royal courts, it is likely that a faction in the palace, fearful that the reactionary religious party was gaining too much influence, betrayed Catherine.

Her fall was swift. By November, her lovers were interrogated and tortured. Henry was outraged and threatened to kill Catherine himself. It was up to Archbishop Cranmer, however, to wrest a confession out of her. When he confronted her, she collapsed and told him everything. He reported, "I found her in such lamentation and heaviness, as I never saw no creature, so that it would have pitied any man's heart in the world, to have looked upon her." Henry VIII, however, was not a man who held much pity for his wives and Catherine was arrested on November 12, 1541, and was taken to Syon Abbey. According to legend, before she left Hampton Court, Catherine Howard attempted to plead with Henry but was dragged away, screaming, by her attendants. The gallery is said to be haunted by a woman clad in white whose screams vanish with her.

By December, most members of the Howard family were sent to the Tower of London and by February 1542 Catherine was also transferred there. Although she had never confessed to her adultery with Culpeper (which was grounds for treason), she was condemned to die on February 11, 1542, under an Act of Attainder. Two days later, she was executed on the same block and in the same place as her cousin Anne Boleyn. She was not yet 21.

After the death of Catherine Howard, the king was once again looking for a new wife. This time, however, there was no young lady waiting to take over as queen, such as the situation had been when the king married Anne Boleyn and Jane Seymour. Some members of the English court secretly hoped that Henry might reconcile with Anne of Cleves, though this was not something the king himself envisioned. As always, international politics played a role in Henry VIII's marital affairs and in July 1542 the short-lived peace between the Holy Roman Empire and France was waning. Henry, adhering to England's traditional enmity with France, chose to side with the emperor thus ruling out any chance for a French bride. By early 1543, it appeared that he had already made his choice. The king was becoming close to a widow named Catherine Parr.

## Catherine Parr

Catherine Parr was probably born in 1512 and was the eldest child of Sir Thomas Parr of Kendal and *Maud Greene Parr. The Parrs were a wealthy aristocratic family who had connections to the royal lineage, and Catherine's mother had served as a lady-in-waiting for Catherine of Aragon. In 1517, her father died leaving her mother to care for her three children. Moving away from London and the royal court, Catherine was brought up on the family estates in Northamptonshire. Her education was typical of aristocratic young women, though she did not learn Latin until much later on in life. Nonetheless, she developed a deep and abiding love of learning.

When Henry VIII first cast his eyes upon Catherine Parr, she was already a widow from two previous marriages. Her first marriage took place in 1529 when she was just 17 years old. She was married to a young aristocrat, Edward Borough, whose father served in the household of Anne Boleyn. Three years later, he died leaving Catherine a widow at age 20. Since it was difficult for any woman, wealthy or poor, to survive economically on her own, Catherine married for the second time in 1533. This time, her husband was much older. John Neville, Lord Latimer, at age 40, was 20 years older than his young bride. Nonetheless, Catherine's second marriage appeared to be a happy and successful one. She was responsible for a large household in Yorkshire as well as bringing up her husband's daughter from a previous marriage.

During the last years of her husband's life, Catherine spent more time in London where she developed connections with the royal court. Her sister, *Anne Parr, was lady-in-waiting to Queen Catherine Howard, and Catherine Parr soon engaged in what became a lasting friendship with Princess Mary. It was during this period that Catherine also became interested in the more evangelical aspects of the reformed religion. In February 1543, just two weeks before the death of her husband, King Henry presented several gifts to Catherine. While she was pleased by the king's attention, she soon faced a personal dilemma. She had fallen in love with Thomas Seymour, brother of the late Queen Jane, and now had to decide between duty to her family or love. She chose duty. In a letter to Thomas, she explained: "As truly as God is my God, my mind was fully bent to marry you before any man I know. Howbeit, God withstood my will . . . and made me renounce utterly mine own will, and to follow his will most willingly."

Four and a half months later, Catherine Parr married King Henry VIII on July 12, 1543. The 31-year-old queen had light auburn hair and was the tallest of Henry's six wives. She enjoyed dancing and dressing well. In one year, for example, she ordered 47 new pairs of shoes. Catherine Parr was also fond of music and animals. During her years as queen of England, she lived up to her motto: "To be useful in all I do." Her love of learning blossomed under Henry's patronage and in 1545 she wrote and published a short manual of religious exercises entitled *Prayers and Meditations.*

As always with royal marriages, the new queen's family rose quickly in status. Catherine's sister, her cousin and her stepdaughter soon joined her household while her brother was created earl of Essex. She was greatly admired by everyone and, more important, developed an excellent relationship with all three of her royal stepchildren. Princess Mary remained in Queen Catherine's household until the death of Henry VIII. Nearly everyone approved of the new queen. The Lord Chancellor described her as "a woman, in my judgment, for certain virtue, wisdom and gentleness, most meet for His Highness. And sure I am that his Majesty never had a

KATHARINE PARRE

*Catherine Parr*

wife more agreeable to his heart than she is." The only person who appeared to hold less enthusiasm for the royal marriage was Anne of Cleves who believed, wrongly, that she would be reconciled with the king. This was an unrealistic hope, for Catherine's 51-year-old husband was content with his new wife. To prove his trust in her, Henry declared Queen Catherine regent to rule in his name when he went on campaign in France in July 1544. Affectionate letters were exchanged between the royal couple until Henry returned in October.

For much of her marriage, Catherine acted as nurse to Henry VIII who still suffered from leg pains. Household records confirm that she attempted to ease his pain with various herbal remedies and soothing massages. The last years of Henry's reign were dominated by a struggle for power between the two most important factions at court: the Seymours and the Howards. Both represented differing aspects of the religious atmosphere during the king's remaining years. The Seymours adhered to more evangelical and, for Henry, more subversive views, while the Howards were closely akin to the king's own "Catholic" religious preferences. Henry, who had never been a tolerant man, became less so in his declining years and an increasing persecution of heretics characterized the remaining time of his reign.

Catherine Parr was a pious woman whose religious tendencies differed from those of her husband. This is readily apparent in her second religious treatise, *The Lamentation of a Sinner*, which, significantly, was not published until after Henry's death in 1547. The work was strongly anti-papal and advocated a personal study of the Bible. Although she usually kept her religious opinions to herself during her marriage, on several occasions she argued with Henry about religion. No woman since Anne Boleyn was ever allowed to contradict the king, and in July 1546 Henry began taking steps to remove Catherine by charging her with heresy. Fortunately, Catherine became aware of the king's intentions and, using all of her tact and intelligence, managed to have the charges dropped. Taking refuge in traditional sexual stereotypes, she told Henry that she would no longer discuss religious matters with him because, as a woman, she was subject to his will. In a masterful display of discretion, she also asserted that the only reason she had argued with him was in an effort to get his mind off the pain in his legs. Her arguments were persuasive, and the king, giving her "very tender assurances of constant love," was once again reconciled with his queen.

From this point on, Henry VIII's health began to deteriorate, and Catherine spent more and more of her time nursing her ailing husband. In December, the queen and the princesses Mary and Elizabeth left London to spend Christmas at Greenwich. Catherine never saw her husband again. Henry VIII died on January 28, 1547, at the age of 55. The Seymours quickly seized power and Edward Seymour, duke of Somerset and Lord Protector of England, took over the guardianship of young King Edward VI.

Thirty-six-year-old Catherine Parr was once again a widow. This time, however, as queen dowager, she was still first lady of England until Edward married. Shortly after King Henry's death, she rekindled her relationship with Thomas Seymour, who was now Lord Admiral. Though the exact date of their marriage is unknown, it is likely that it took place sometime in March 1547. Eight months later, Catherine Parr was pregnant with her first child.

During Catherine's marriage to Seymour, Princess Elizabeth came to live in their house-hold. Catherine and Elizabeth had developed a deep and abiding friendship which, unfortunately, became threatened when Catherine's husband began flirting with the young princess. Although her love for Elizabeth was strong, Catherine sent her away. While contemporaries believed that Catherine took this step out of jealousy, it is more likely that her decision was based on a deep concern for the princess' reputation and safety. Despite this incident, Catherine's marriage to Seymour was a happy one. On August 30, she gave birth to a girl whom they named Mary. Unfortunately, like many other women in the 16th century, Catherine did not survive the birth. She soon fell ill with puerperal fever and died on September 5, 1548, at age 36. Her infant daughter died on the same day.

In 1547, the only surviving wife of King Henry VIII was Anne of Cleves. Beset by money problems, she lived through the short reign and death of Edward VI and spent the last years of her life under the reign of her close friend Queen Mary I. She never lived to see the coronation of Elizabeth and died on July 16, 1557, at age 42.

**SOURCES:**

Baldwin-Smith, Lacy. *A Tudor Tragedy: The Life and Times of Catherine Howard*. London: Jonathan Cape, 1961.

Fraser, Antonia. *The Wives of Henry VIII*. Harmondsworth: Penguin, 1992.

Ives, E.W. *Anne Boleyn*. Oxford: Basil Blackwell, 1986.

Martiensson, Anthony. *Queen Catherine Parr*. London: Secker and Warburg, 1973.

Mattingly, Garrett. *Catherine of Aragon*. NY: Vintage, 1960.

Paul, J.E. *Catherine of Aragon and Her Friends*. London: Burns and Cates, 1966.

Warnicke, Retha. *The Rise and Fall of Anne Boleyn*. Cambridge: Cambridge University Press, 1989.

Weir, Alison. *The Six Wives of Henry VIII*. London: Bodley Head, 1991.

**SUGGESTED READING:**

Loades, David. *Mary Tudor: A Life*. Oxford: Oxford University Press, 1989.

Neale, John E. *Queen Elizabeth I*. London: Jonathan Cape, 1961.

Ridley, Jasper. *Henry VIII*. London: Constable, 1984.

Scarisbrick, J.J. *Henry VIII*. Berkeley, CA: University of California Press, 1968.

**RELATED MEDIA:**

*Anne of the Thousand Days* (146 min. film), starring Richard Burton and **Genevieve Bujold**, directed by Charles Jarrott, 1969.

*Henry VIII and His Six Wives* (125 min. film), starring Keith Mitchell, **Frances Cuka**, and **Charlotte Rampling**, directed by Waris Hussein, 1972.

*The Life of King Henry VIII* (play) by William Shakespeare.

*The Private Life of Henry VIII* (96 min. film), starring Charles Laughton, **Binnie Barnes**, *****Elsa Lanchester**, and *****Merle Oberon**, directed by Alexander Korda, 1933.

"Six Wives of Henry VIII," 6-part BBC series (9 hrs.), starring **Annette Crosbie** as Catherine of Aragon, **Dorothy Tutin** as Anne Boleyn, **Ann Stallybrass** as Jane Seymour, **Elvi Hale** as Anne of Cleves, **Angela Pleasance** as Catherine Howard, **Rosalie Crutchley** as Catherine Parr, and Keith Mitchell as Henry VIII.

**Margaret McIntyre**,
Instructor in Women's History,
Trent University, Peterborough, Ontario, Canada

## Skandhalaki, Ivi (c. 1907–c. 1991).

*See Melissanthi.*

## Skarbek, Krystina (1915–1952).

*See Granville, Christine.*

## Skavronska, Marta (1684–1727).

*See Catherine I.*

## Skavronsky, Catherine (1684–1727).

*See Catherine I.*

## Skeffington, Hanna Sheehy (1877–1946).

*See Sheehy-Skeffington, Hanna.*

## Skillman, Hope (c. 1908–1981).

*See Schary, Hope Skillman.*

## Skinner, Constance Lindsay
(1877–1939)

*Canadian-born American author and historian. Born Constance Annie Skinner on December 7, 1877, in Quesnel, British Columbia, Canada; died from arteriosclerosis and coronary occlusion on March 27, 1939, in New York City; daughter of Robert James Skinner (an agent for the Hudson's Bay Company) and Annie (Lindsay) Skinner; educated in private schools in Vancouver and California; never married.*

*Selected writings:* David *(play, 1910);* Good Morning, Rosamund! *(play, 1917);* Pioneers of the Old Southwest *(1919);* Adventurers of Oregon *(1920);* Adventures in the Wilderness *(with C. Wissler and W.C.H. Wood, 1925);* Silent Scot, Frontier Scout *(1925);* Becky Landers, Frontier Warrior *(1926);* White Leader *(1926);* Roselle of the North *(1927);* Tiger Who Walks Alone *(1927);* Andy Breaks Trail *(1928);* Ranch of the Golden Flowers *(1928);* The Search Relentless *(1928);* Red Willows *(1929);* Red Man's Luck *(1930);* Songs of the Coast Dwellers *(1930);* Debby Barnes, Trader *(1932);* Beaver, Kings and Cabins *(1933);* Rob Roy, the Frontier Twins *(1934).*

Constance Lindsay Skinner was born in rural British Columbia, Canada, in 1877, the daughter of Robert James Skinner and **Annie Lindsay Skinner**. Robert was a British agent for the Hudson's Bay Company, so she grew up among pioneers of the Western frontier at a Canadian Northwest fur-trading post near the Peace River. Skinner was educated at home until the age of 14, when her family moved to Vancouver and enrolled her in private schools. She also began publishing short stories in Vancouver newspapers. Two years later, she moved to an aunt's house in California because of frail health. She would live in the United States for the rest of her life, although her memories of her frontier upbringing and exposure to local Indians strongly influenced her and her writing.

Upon moving to California, Skinner began working as a journalist for newspapers there, soon taking as her middle name the maiden name of her mother, who was descended from Scottish poet Lady *Anne Lindsay. She became a music and theater critic while also covering fires and murders for such papers as the *San Francisco Examiner* and the *Los Angeles Times*. (She also became friendly with actress *Helena Modjeska after interviewing her, and lived for a summer at Modjeska's house in La Jolla.) In 1910, a play she wrote called *David* was produced at the Forest Theater in Carmel, California. Skinner later spent three years in Chicago, writing for the *Chicago American*, before moving to New

*Constance Lindsay Skinner*

York City. There she found work writing poetry and essays for *Bookman*, the *North American Review*, *Poetry*, and other magazines, garnering poetry prizes from both *Poetry* and London's *Bookman*. After her second play, *Good Morning, Rosamund!*, was produced in Manhattan in 1917, she wrote in *Bookman* that her plays, which espoused patriotic themes, helped "Americanize our non-reading amusement-seekers of foreign birth and foreign ideas."

Skinner's reputation as a historical writer grew when she was asked to contribute to the 50-volume Yale University "Chronicles of America" series, for which she wrote *Pioneers of the Old Southwest* (1919) and *Adventurers of Oregon* (1920). Later, she collaborated with Clark Wissler and William C.H. Wood on *Adventures in the Wilderness* (1925), published by the Yale "Pageant of America" series. Although Skinner's historical works received praise for being readable and lively, some were criticized for falling short of historical accuracy. "The effort to maintain a swiftly moving narrative has betrayed the author into sacrificing clarity," wrote a critic in the September 1920 *Mississippi Valley Historical Review*.

Undaunted by the criticism, Skinner produced a popular series of historical adventure tales for children, all based on frontier life, drawn from the experiences of her own childhood; among these were *Silent Scot, Frontier Scout* (1925), *Becky Landers, Frontier Warrior* (1926), *Ranch of the Golden Flowers* (1928), and *Debby Barnes, Trader* (1932). Of Skinner's children's books, librarian and critic *Anne Carroll Moore wrote that Skinner was "essentially a poet and historian whose childhood remains vivid and whose understanding and appreciation of primal people—the Indians, the voyagers, the coureurs-de-bois—is instinctive and secure."

In 1930, Skinner published a well-received collection of poetry, *Songs of the Coast Dwellers*, that drew on legends of the Squamish Indians of British Columbia. Her history of the fur trade in North America, *Beaver, Kings and Cabins*, was published three years later. In 1935, Skinner began editing a series of historical books for Farrar & Rinehart, designed to highlight the importance of America's major rivers and the roles they had played in the country's history. The series grew out of an idea she had had for documenting the historical importance of rivers throughout the world; in its focus on America, she said, she hoped the books would "kindle imagination and . . . reveal American folk to one another." The series proved quite popular and

eventually included over forty volumes, but Skinner herself lived to see only six published. She was unable to finish her own book on the Missouri River before she died in New York City on March 27, 1939, surrounded by frontier artifacts in her Park Avenue apartment. One year later, the annual Constance Lindsay Skinner Award, a bronze plaque awarded to a woman who has made "an outstanding contribution to the world of books," was established by the Women's National Book Association.

SOURCES:

James, Edward T., ed. *Notable American Women, 1607–1950*. Cambridge, MA: The Belknap Press of Harvard University, 1971.

Kunitz, Stanley J., and Howard Haycraft, eds. *Twentieth Century Authors*. NY: H.W. Wilson, 1942.

McHenry, Robert, ed. *Famous American Women*. NY: Dover, 1980.

**Lisa C. Groshong**, freelance writer,
Columbia, Missouri

# Skinner, Cornelia Otis (1901–1979)

*American stage actress and author. Born on May 30, 1901, in Chicago, Illinois; died on July 9, 1979, in New York City; daughter of Otis Skinner (a stage actor) and Maud (Durbin) Skinner (an actress); attended the Baldwin School in Bryn Mawr; attended Bryn Mawr College; studied with Émile Dehelly; studied theater at the Jacques Copeau School in Paris; married Alden Sanford Blodget, in October 1928; children: son Otis; stepchildren: two.*

*Selected writings:* Tiny Garments *(1932);* Excuse It, Please *(1936);* Dithers and Jitters *(1938);* Soap Behind the Ears *(1941); (with Emily Kimbrough)* Our Hearts Were Young and Gay *(1942);* Nuts in May *(1950);* Bottoms Up! *(1955);* The Ape in Me *(1959);* Elegant Wits and Grand Horizontals *(1962);* Madame Sarah *(1966);* The Life of Lindsay and Crouse *(1976).*

Born in Chicago on May 30, 1901, Cornelia Otis Skinner seemed destined for an acting career. Her father Otis Skinner earned renown in American theater during the late 19th and early 20th centuries, particularly for his performance in *Kismet*, and her mother **Maud Durbin Skinner** was for a time the leading lady in his company. Even though Maud stopped performing to devote herself to the family, she and Cornelia joined Otis on several of his tours, and both parents fostered a love of the theater in their daughter. The Skinners settled in Bryn Mawr, Pennsylvania, when Cornelia turned five. Otis was frequently away on tour, but Cornelia grew up treasuring his affectionate letters and weekends home.

Already interested in the theater, Skinner did not relish her studies at the Baldwin School in Bryn Mawr, an apathy that extended into her brief college career at Bryn Mawr College. After leaving during her sophomore year, at age 19 she traveled to Europe with her mother. There she studied acting in Paris under the private tutelage of Émile Dehelly and at the Jacques Copeau School.

In August 1921, Skinner made her first professional stage appearance in Buffalo, New York, performing a small part in *Blood and Sand* with her father in the starring role. A month later, she moved with the show to the Empire Theater on Broadway. Throughout the 1920s, Skinner appeared in several plays, while also fostering a writing talent that first blossomed in 1925 with *Captain Fury*, a play written for her father.

Skinner found her niche in writing monologue-driven character sketches in which she also performed. These one-woman shows were memorable for their wit as well as her satiric yet sympathetic portraits of human nature. Transforming into new characters often with no more than the aid of a prop, she toured the United States and eventually England. Among her productions were *The Wives of Henry VIII* (first performed in 1931), *The Empress *Eugénie* (1932), *The Loves of Charles II* (1933), and *The Mansions on the Hudson*. Another audience favorite was her adaptation of *Margaret Ayer Barnes'* novel *Edna, His Wife* (1937), which required Skinner to portray three generations of women. She recreated her love of turn-of-the-century Paris in the grand production of the musical revue *Paris '90* in 1952, another solo show in which she commanded 14 different roles.

Skinner did not neglect ensemble acting in her career, although critical recognition in this area did not come until her starring role in George Bernard Shaw's *Candida* in 1935. Other much-acclaimed performances included her 1944 portrayal of the wife of an American diplomat in *The Searching Wind* by *Lillian Hellman*, and her depiction of the ex-wife of a playboy in the comedy *The Pleasure of His Company* (1958), which Skinner co-wrote with Samuel Taylor.

In a multifaceted career, Skinner also had success with her several humorous, lighthearted books based on her own experiences, starting with *Tiny Garments* in 1932. In 1942, she and **Emily Kimbrough** were co-authors of the best-selling *Our Hearts Were Young and Gay*, a chronicle of a trip they had taken together. Two years after its publication, the story became a movie starring *Diana Lynn*, and in 1948 *Jean

**Kerr** adapted the work for the stage. Skinner's later books earned her critical recognition as a serious author, with **Rose MacMurray** writing in the *Washington Post* of *Elegant Wits and Grand Horizontals* (1962): "As we read Mrs. Skinner's lively prose, we are compelled by her headlong narrative, beguiled by her humor, and likely to forget that we are in the presence of genuine scholarship." Her last book, *The Life of Lindsay and Crouse*, appeared in 1976. She was also a longtime contributor of essays and light verse to magazines, including *Vogue*, *The New Yorker*, and *Harper's Bazaar*, and many of Skinner's writings appeared in published collections of her work over the course of three decades. She also wrote scripts for the radio series "William and Mary" and narrated for radio and television programs, including the NBC-TV show "Debutante '62." The day after her death of a cerebral hemorrhage in her home on July 9, 1979, *The New York Times* remembered Skinner as "one of the favorite stage personalities of devoted audiences for more than thirty-five years because

*Cornelia
Otis
Skinner*

of her ability to provoke laughter that was balm for her barbs."

**SOURCES:**

Herbert, Ian, ed. *Who's Who in the Theatre.* Detroit, MI: Gale Research, 1977.

Moritz, Charles, ed. *Current Biography 1964.* NY: H.W. Wilson, 1964.

Robinson, Alice M., *et al.*, eds. *Notable Women in the American Theatre.* CT: Greenwood Press, 1989.

**Kimberly A. Burton**, B.A., M.I.S.,
Ann Arbor, Michigan

# Skinner, Mollie (1876–1955)

*Australian novelist. Name variations: (pseudonym) R.E. Leake. Born in Perth, Western Australia, in 1876; died in 1955; educated in England.*

*Selected writings:* Letters of a V.A.D. *(1918);* The Boy in the Bush *(1924);* Black Swans *(1925);* Men Are We *(1927);* Tucker Sees India *(1937);* WX—Corporal Smith: A Romance of the A.I.F. in Libya *(1941);* Where Skies Are Blue *(1946);* The Fifth Sparrow *(autobiography, 1972).*

Although she was educated in England, novelist Mollie Skinner was born in 1876 in Western Australia, and spent most of her life there. Her first careers were in nursing and journalism; a Quaker, she also spent some time working among the poor in London. Working in India during World War I provided background material for her first novel, *Letters of a V.A.D.*, published in 1918 under the pseudonym R.E. Leake. In 1922, Skinner met English novelist D.H. Lawrence, with whom she collaborated on her most famous book, *The Boy in the Bush* (1924). Sixty years later, this chronicle of rural immigrant life in 1880s Australia was made into an Australian television series. Skinner's later works include *Black Swans* (1925), a 19th-century romance; a collection of stories focusing on Aborigines, *Men Are We* (1927); *Tucker Sees India* (1937); *WX—Corporal Smith: A Romance of the A.I.F. in Libya* (1941); and *Where Skies Are Blue* (1946). Her autobiography, *The Fifth Sparrow*, was published in 1972, 17 years after her death.

**SOURCES:**

Buck, Claire, ed. *The Bloomsbury Guide to Women's Literature.* NY: Prentice Hall, 1992.

Wilde, William H., Joy Hooten, and Barry Andrews. *The Oxford Companion to Australian Literature.* Melbourne, Australia: Oxford University Press, 1985.

**Kimberly A. Burton**, B.A., M.I.S.,
Ann Arbor, Michigan

# Sklodowska, Manya or Marie (1867–1934).

*See Curie, Marie.*

# Skoblikova, Lydia (1939—)

*Soviet speedskater who was the first athlete to win four gold medals in a Winter Olympics. Name variations: Lidija. Born in Zlatoust, Chelyabinsk, Soviet Union, on March 8, 1939.*

*Won six Olympic gold medals: in the 500 meters (1964), 1,000 meters (1964), 1,500 meters (1960 and 1964), and 3,000 meters (1960 and 1964); won gold medals in the World championship in the 500, 1,000, 1,500, and 3,000-meters (1963); won women's all-around World championship once more (1964).*

When Lydia Skoblikova competed in the 1960 Squaw Valley Winter Olympics, she won a gold medal in the 3,000 meters and another in the 1,500 meters, in which she set a world record of 2:52.2. Her teammate **Klara Guseva** took the 1,000 meters, in which Skoblikova placed 4th. In 1963, Skoblikova swept the World championship in the 500, 1,000, 1,500, and 3,000 meters, winning a gold medal in each event. In 1964, she was World champion for a second time.

When the 1964 Winter Olympics arrived in Innsbruck, the 24-year-old Siberian schoolteacher ruled the ice oval. Every day, for four days, she won a gold medal, the first four-gold medal performance in the Winter Games. In three events, she broke Olympic records, skating the 500 meters in 45 seconds flat, the 1,000 meters in 1:33.2, and the 1,500 meters in 2:22.6. Skating conditions prevented her from setting a fourth record in the 3,000 meters; the ice was slushy and there were puddles on the course. Even so, her performance outshone her competitors, and Skoblikova crossed the finish line a full 3.6 seconds ahead of second place **Pil-Hwa Han** of North Korea and **Valentina Stenina**, who tied for the silver. Shortly after, Skoblikova was appointed to full membership in the Communist Party by Soviet Premier Nikita Khrushchev. At her final Olympic competition in the 1968 Grenoble Winter Games, Skoblikova's reign had ended. She finished 11th in the 1,500 meters. Few athletes have so dominated a single sport, however, as this Russian schoolteacher.

**SOURCES:**

Markel, Robert, Nancy Brooks, and Susan Markel. *For the Record. Women in Sports.* NY: World Almanac, 1985.

Woolum, Janet. *Outstanding Women Athletes.* Phoenix, AZ: The Oryx Press, 1992.

**Karin Loewen Haag**,
Athens, Georgia

# Skovoronski, Marta (1684–1727).

*See Catherine I.*

---

# Skram, Amalie (1846–1905)

*Norwegian author who is regarded as one of the leading Nordic naturalist writers of her time. Name variations: Bertha Skram. Born Bertha Amalie Alver in Bergen, Norway, in 1846; died in Copenhagen, Denmark, on March 13, 1905; eldest of five surviving children of Mons Monsen Alver and Ingeborg Lovise (Sivertsen) Alver (descendants of farmers and laborers); married Bernt Ulrik August Müller (a ship's captain), in 1864 (divorced 1882); married Erik Skram (a Danish writer), on April 3, 1884 (separated 1890, divorced 1900); children: (first marriage) two sons, Jakob and Ludvig; (second marriage) one daughter, Johanne Skram.*

*Published first story (1882), which was followed by her breakthrough as a writer of novels (1885); married Erik Skram, who brought her to Copenhagen (1884); remained in Copenhagen the last five years of her life (1900–05).*

*Selected works: "Madam Höiers Leiefolk" ("Mrs. Höier's Renters," 1882); Constance Ring (1885); "Karens Jul" ("Karen's Christmas," 1885); Bön og anfägtelse (Prayer and Temptation, 1885); Knut Tandberg (1886); Hellemyrsfolket (tr. The People of Hellemyr, 1887–98); Lucie (1888); Fjäldmennesker (Mountain People, 1889); Bornefortallinger (children's stories, 1890); "In Asiam profectus est" (1890); Fru Ines (Mrs. Ines, 1891); Forraadt (tr. Betrayed, 1892); Agnete (1893); Professor Hieronimus (1895); Paa Sct. Jörgen (At Saint Jorgen's Hospital, 1895); Sommer (Summer, 1899); Julehelg (Christmas Celebration, 1900); Mennesker (People, 1902–05); "Ruskvejr" ("Rough Weather," 1979).*

Amalie Skram, born Bertha Amalie Alver in 1846 in Bergen, Norway, grew up in a family of nine children; her mother **Ingeborg Sivertsen Alver** had had all nine in the course of thirteen years. Only five of them, Amalie and four younger brothers, grew to adulthood, and her mother survived them all. Amalie was an unusually bright and pretty child who blossomed into a woman of surpassing beauty. At school, she was well liked and admired for her scholastic ability as well as for her lovely brown eyes and shining braids, long enough to form a cushion where she sat. With her Spanish looks went a hot, impulsive temper and considerable mood swings.

School was the place where Amalie could be most herself. At home, her mother's strict Lutheran views and constant demands for her daughter's domestic services tied her to the trivialities of everyday cares and petty concerns. Occasionally, she would rebel and, instead of going home

after school, follow in the wake of alcoholics and street people as they wandered through the slums of Bergen. Skram would arrive home late to cold food and scoldings, but she would forget about those the next time she felt herself irresistibly drawn to watch and observe the most abject population of her hometown.

Because of her gender, Amalie was barred from entering the city's high school, but the girls' school from which she graduated furnished her with a reasonably good basic education, especially in languages. Skram had finished her schooling when her father Mons Monsen Alver went bankrupt due to unsuccessful speculations in shipping and herring. Having lost the grocery story with which he had supported his family, he subsequently emigrated to America, leaving his wife and children in near poverty. Skram's biographers have theorized that her subsequent engagement to a ship's captain, Bernt Ulrik August Müller, ten years her senior, was engineered by her mother as a means of getting her daughter financially settled. It is a fact that the new bride

*Norwegian postage stamp issued in 1996 to honor Amalie Skram.*

was entirely ignorant of the matrimonial duties owed her spouse, and she faulted her mother for having neither offered advice nor invited questions in the matter of wifely responsibilities. As the skipper's mate, Amalie was expected to accompany her husband on his voyages to Mexico, the West Indies, South America, and Australia, and somewhat to her surprise, she found life on a sailing ship much to her liking. It suited her high spirits and energetic pursuit of knowledge, and soon her husband would brag that she was as good a seafarer as any. As a wife in the captain's cabin, she experienced greater difficulties of adaptation. She had grown up in a divisive home and bore the imprint of her mother's pietistic teachings of sin and guilt. On their wedding night, she had found Müller's sexual advances disgusting, and she appears to have refused them on other occasions to the extent to which it was possible, given their confined space and the walls of listening ears.

*𝒩ot a single kind or laudatory word, neither privately nor publicly, not one, not one. Only invectives and vulgarities.*

**—Amalie Skram, on the reception of her novel *Constance Ring***

After 12 years spent either in the captain's quarters or separated due to Amalie's pregnancies and the births of their two sons, Müller turned his back on the sea and bought a mill outside Bergen. For about a year, the couple, along with eight-year-old Jakob and ten-year-old Ludvig, lived a life of great diversity albeit little genuine happiness. The beautiful wife filled her life with parties and amateur theatricals, and wrote articles and literary reviews for Norwegian newspapers. Eventually, however, the increasingly strained relationship was brought to a crisis. Amalie suffered a nervous breakdown and was placed at the Gaustad asylum. Though she recovered after a couple of months, she refused to return to her husband. Instead, she demanded a separation and spent the next three years living with first one then another of her brothers. Her divorce was granted in 1882.

The sorrow and disappointment she had suffered in the breakdown of her marriage were to some extent mitigated by the feeling of liberation that accompanied her divorce. But with that came a certain bitterness at the realization that "the world will trample on a garden that has no surrounding fence." She possessed youth, beauty, and talent, but she was also a divorcée and a one-time patient at an asylum; in sum, she was an easy target for criticism. To avoid it, she isolated

herself to the extent to which she could bear the boredom of the small provincial town of Fredrikshald. She cooked and kept house for her brother and her sons and wrote newspaper articles and reviews promoting contemporary psychological and naturalistic works. She especially commended such authors as Henrik Ibsen and the Danish I.P. Jakobsen who refused to write of the world as a better place than it is and instead faced the indignities of humanity. In her opinion, they were the true agents of progress. "It is a writer's task to raise the consciousness of his readers," she noted. "It is his responsibility to break away from old patterns of thinking and behavior and thereby lay the groundwork for a better society." She endorsed Ibsen's observations that women's inferior condition in society was caused by deficiencies in their upbringing, by husbands treating their wives as things or servants, and by women's toleration of those inequities.

Skram's outspokenness and general boldness added to her unconventional social position; it also put a severe strain on her relationship with her conservative and puritanical brother, who as an inhabitant of a small provincial town had an image to uphold. It was therefore a relief to both of them when Amalie and her two sons left Fredrikshald in the summer of 1881 to move in with her brother Wilhelm Alver who was a school principal in Kristiania (Oslo). Here, she breathed more freely, sharing the air with artists and scientists and exchanging ideas with writers, painters, and women who fought for emancipation. Here, too, however, her impulsive nature and beautiful eyes invited slander, gossip, and even a caricature in a story titled "Modern Ladies." Critics of the literary left were divided in their attack or support of the piece, and Amalie felt deeply betrayed by the latter. Pressing financial concerns were added to her troubles when her brother died in 1883 and left her without means for subsistence.

A year earlier, she had met the Danish writer and journalist Erik Skram at an anniversary celebration for the great Norwegian poet Björnstjerne Björnson, Amalie's friend and mentor. Erik had fallen in love with the bright and lovely Norwegian writer and during the following year kept up an avid correspondence not only attesting to his love but initiating and encouraging discussions of literary, political, and moral issues. His courting won her heart, and they were married on April 3, 1884; from that time on, she considered herself Danish. As a writer for left-wing publications, Erik made little money, but he was a first-rate journalist and, according to his memoirs, content to give up his own novel writing to function as inspiration and mentor to his wife's greater talents. He became an unbending taskmaster, demanding total honesty and seriousness in everything she wrote based on his conviction that those were the qualities that would distinguish her work. He was able to furnish significant suggestions pertaining to style and taste as well. Amalie Skram's strength lay in her precise reproduction of the pungent, earthy speech of the laborers and farmers in the country around Bergen, but occasionally she would exceed the boundaries of decorum and good taste.

Erik Skram became an invaluable guide for his wife's literary career. He encouraged her to move from sketches and short stories to longer works, and as a journalist he protected her from attacks by Norwegian critics, especially after her first novel had been returned from the publisher upon acquaintance with its contents. Erik also supplied her with a home where she could shine among their friends with her sparkling intellect and domestic grace and abilities.

Even so, Amalie Skram found it difficult to sustain a balance between the roles of artist and wife. This became further complicated with the birth of a daughter in the middle of writing her major work, the tetralogy *The People from Hellemyr*. To get the solitude she needed, she would have to leave home periodically, which in turn would make her feel guilty and vulnerable to the disapproval of society. She was close to a nervous breakdown when her husband joined her doctor's entreaties that she seek help from the prominent psychiatrist Knud Pontoppidan. She agreed to spend a week or two at his hospital (Saint George in Copenhagen) but once there found herself declared insane and detained against her will. Erik obeyed Pontoppidan's injunctions against visitors and did not attempt to see his wife, even after she managed to smuggle out a note imploring him to come. She was eventually transferred to a hospital for the incurably insane but released because the doctor in charge found no evidence of insanity. On her return to the world, she was in a state of mental and bodily exhaustion from which she never fully recovered. She nonetheless found the strength to write two volumes about her stay in the psychiatric ward (*Professor Hieronimus* and *At Saint George*), so scathing in their criticism of hospital conditions that Pontoppidan found it necessary to resign from his post as head physician. Skram refused to see her husband ever again, and they were divorced in 1900. The remaining five years of her life she spent in Copenhagen with her daughter **Johanne Skram**.

They were difficult years. Her health was precarious and her finances no less so. Monetary worries made concentrated writing arduous even after she was granted a writer's stipend from the Danish government. "The Danes recognized her power and her importance as an artist by granting her a stipend," writes Theodore Jorgenson. "From Norway she received nothing but the execrations of the horrified upholders of social canons. Her art, however, continued to be thoroughly Norwegian." Skram died on March 13, 1905. She felt she could no longer write and in her despair may have committed suicide; her daughter suggests as much. Skram had wanted a quiet funeral without benefit of either clergy or flowers. "Let the living receive flowers, but spare the dead," reads her last will and testament. "This outrageous luxury of huge amounts of flowers in the middle of winter, at exorbitant prices, thrown into the grave to rot for the benefit of none. Think of how many hungry children could eat their fill for that money." But Denmark wanted to honor its adopted daughter and staged an elaborate memorial service. The great hall in the Students' House in Copenhagen was transformed into a hall of sorrows with black draperies and masses of flowers and wreaths. Denmark's most prominent poets and composers wrote texts and music for the occasion, and many of her friends participated, as did many of Copenhagen's cultural elite. Now the words were spoken which she had longed to hear, about her brilliance and tender heart, about the progressive work she had done at the expense of personal happiness, about the flowers she had been given too late.

These men and women in the great hall rued their failure to understand and support Skram and her works. Later generations have shown greater appreciation of her skillful handling of points of view, her precise and bold descriptions, courageous choice of themes, and undaunted explorations of the human condition. It is not difficult, however, to understand the feelings of shock and dismay that Skram's works elicited, especially in her Norwegian contemporaries: she was a woman treating the subject matter of the French naturalists, a combination no one so far had dared to visit upon the pietistic, conservative, and provincial Norwegian society of the late 1800s.

Amalie Skram's first short story "Mrs. Höier's Renters" deals with the death of baby twins whose family has been evicted one cold November night. Their father, a laborer with a wooden leg, is a brutal drunkard, dreaded and feared by his wife who has borne eight children in six years, the twins only a couple of days prior to the eviction. One child begs, another steals, and two are lame. It is a tale of hunger, cold, dirt, misshapen limbs, brutality, alcoholism, and crime. The story ends the morning after the eviction. The mother has given the babies alcohol mixed with water; she herself has drunk it straight. The twins do not wake up the next morning, and when the mother does, she finds the police have arrived to take her to jail. She is condemned to three years of forced labor, given only the meager consolation that she "would have a roof over her head for the duration." The critics' allegation that Skram had read too much Emile Zola was ironic in that she had read none; the story, she maintained, was based entirely on an experience of her own. She wrote it to show the conditions of the destitute in Norway, as she herself had observed them as a child, and to demonstrate the failure of social institutions and individual charity.

In her ensuing four novels, Skram explores the relationship between husband and wife, a theme as controversial in Norway of the 1880s as that of social inequities. It was also the foremost literary issue of the time. Flaubert, Maupassant and Daudet in France, Tolstoy in Russia, and Ibsen and Björnson in Norway were writing novels, stories and plays about marriage, divorce and adultery. *Constance Ring*, which is based on Skram's experiences in her first marriage, denigrates the depravity characteristic of men's bachelorhood, marriage as an institution for the support of women, and the double standards of morality. The "new" element in the work is the treatment of the main character's unsatisfied emotional and sexual longings, the nature of which she herself does not understand. Constance is "cold" and remains cold. If she "had been given twenty men, they would all have played her false," Skram wrote. Constance's early difficulties, as she attempts to respond to her first husband's advances, are caused by her too-close attachment to her mother and her adherence to her mother's teachings connecting sex with shame and guilt. This and later novels precede Freud's thesis regarding the significance of a girl's relationship with her mother as it influences her relationship to sex and her attempts at self-realization. As a contribution to the general literary debate, the novel invited discussion of the necessity for changes in the way women were brought to consider their sexuality. They must be taught about their erotic drives and taught to be wives, one critic maintained. That, in turn, would make their husbands better men. Skram agreed, adding that she had discussed the topic of sexuality with numerous women and concluded that as far as erotic fulfillment went, women could be divided into two groups. One group, the happier, were the more sensual. They were progeny of women who for generations had accepted their sexual drives. They had no sexual problems, no matter whom they married. The other kind never experienced sexual fulfillment; they were the more numerous. "They are so embarrassed," Skram writes in a letter from 1885, "so sure that they are the exception, the abnormal ones, and they are so relieved, so happy when they hear that others feel the same way."

Yet Skram did not believe that inherited attitudes and upbringing alone resulted in frigidity. Some men, too, were to blame. Their general behavior and brutishness would necessarily have an adverse effect on women and make them resist their advances. With sexual fulfillment, she noted, a woman could change and in the process raise her husband above the level his bestial nature had destined him to sink.

Given those allegations, it is understandable that the publication of *Constance Ring* proved, as one critic put it, to be the "most laborious birth of any book in Norway." The editor of a major publishing house had accepted the novel for publication but rejected it after a first reading, finding its descriptions of marriage too extreme. Norwegian newspapers started a campaign against the book prior even to its publication by a small Kristiania press.

Skram's subsequent books about marital disharmony deal with problems experienced by both wives and husbands. *Betrayed*, for example, is not only the story of a sexually experienced man taking advantage of an inexperienced young woman. It dramatizes the mutual destruction of two people who have internalized the morality and rules of behavior of their contemporaries. Living is shown to be a painful activity for men as well as for women.

The series of marriage novels was interrupted by the first volume in Skram's major work *The People of Hellemyr*. It tells about four generations of farmers, their family ambitions, and their feelings of inferiority and decay. Demoralizing poverty, sickness and death exceed their physical, mental, and spiritual resources and they succumb to alcohol and despair. Again, the detailed descriptions of physical and spiritual poverty invited mostly censure, although some critics conceded that Amalie Skram was a good storyteller, albeit of the photographic type. One of the major Oslo newspapers did admit that the undisguised venom directed at Skram's book was directed as much against the prevailing fashion of literary Realism and Naturalism as practiced by Zola and Tolstoy. Skram's imitations, the conservative press asserted, account for the graphic details of, for example, a birth scene or a deathbed. The living conditions she described were beyond imagining by her critics. They did not recognize the farmers, laborers, and sailors of the first two volumes and refused to acknowledge the veracity of characterizations and settings, especially because they were created by a "lady." The fact that the individual situations Skram generated were unforgettable and true indicators of her talent added to their distress.

To her great sorrow, Skram could not finish the fourth volume, which she worked on during the last months of her life. That notwithstanding, the famous Danish critic Georg Brandes pronounced *The People of Hellemyr* the first great Norwegian novel, placing Skram among the foremost writers of her time. "It makes one watch," Brandes marveled, "not a woman's exquisite embroidery but the weaving of the three Nornes."

**SOURCES:**

Bjerkelund, Ragni. *Amalie Skram: Dansk Borger, Norsk Forfatter.* Oslo: Aschehough, 1988.

Engelstad, Irene. *Sammenbrudd og gjennombrudd.* Oslo: Pax Forlag, 1984.

Jorgenson, Theodore. *History of Norwegian Literature.* NY: Macmillan, 1933.

Koltzow, Liv. *Den unge Amalie Skram.* Oslo: Gyldendal Norsk Forlag, 1992.

**Inga Wiehl,** a native of Denmark, teaches at Yakima Valley Community College, Yakima, Washington

# Skrine, Agnes (c. 1865–1955)

*Irish poet, novelist and reviewer. Name variations: Agnes Higginson Skrine; Nesta Skrine; (pseudonym) Moira O'Neill. Born Agnes (Nesta) Shakespeare Higginson at Springmount, Cushendun, County Antrim, Ireland, around 1865; died at Ferns, County Wexford, Ireland, on January 22, 1955; daughter of Charles Henry Higginson and Mary Higginson; educated at home; married Walter Clarmont Skrine, on June 5, 1895; children: three sons, two daughters, including Molly Keane (1904–1996).*

*Selected writings:* An Easter Vacation *(Lawrence & Bullen, 1893; E.P. Dutton, 1894);* The Elf Errant *(Lawrence & Bullen, 1893; E.P. Dutton, 1894);* Songs of the Glens of Antrim *(Blackwood, 1901);* More Songs of the Glens of Antrim *(Blackwood, 1921);* Collected Poems of Moira O'Neill *(Blackwood, 1933).*

Agnes Skrine, known in her youth as Nesta Higginson, was born in Springmount, Cushendun, around 1865. She came from a close-knit family (her parents were first cousins) and grew up in the beautiful Glens of Antrim in northeast Ireland. After her marriage, she would spend little time there, but their hold on her imagination would be evident in her preface to her *Collected Poems* (1933): "These songs of the Glens of Antrim were written by a Glenswoman in the dialect of the Glens and chiefly for the pleasure of other Glens-people." Skrine published two novels while still single. The first, *An Easter Vacation*, was issued in London in 1893 and then in New York the following year. The Poet Laureate John Masefield would describe it as "a happy and witty book, containing one of the best studies known to me of a high spirited, finely natured boy." Another novel, *The Elf Errant*, was published in New York in 1894.

In 1895, Agnes married Walter Clarmont Skrine, an Englishman whose family had ranching interests in Canada. They spent some time in Canada and the second section of her *Collected Poems*, entitled "Songs from North-West Canada," tells of the time she spent there. She and her husband returned to Ireland and bought an estate in County Kildare, not far from Dublin. Their daughter, the novelist *\*Molly Keane*, claimed that her parents' marriage was extremely happy: "she gave up everything for my father. She absolutely adored him." In 1901, Skrine published a collection of poems *Songs of the Glens of Antrim* which had considerable success. Masefield described them as "poignant poems about her homeland, a few miles of the Irish coast, glen, moorland, mountain, and the sea, long-loved and made more intensely precious by exile." Of the *Songs*, "Corrymeela," "Waters of the Moyle," "Loughareema," and "Gold of Ballytearim" were singled out for special praise, and a number of the poems were set to music by Hamilton Harty and Charles Villiers Stanford. Stanford's musical setting of "Loughareema" achieved great popularity and was a signature piece of the singer Alexander Plunket Greene. Under the pseudonym Moira O'Neill, Skrine wrote regularly for many years for the Edinburgh-based *Blackwood's Magazine* which was regarded as one of the most prestigious literary journals of the day. One of the most interesting aspects of her work was that although she came from an Anglo-Irish Big House background (which was the *mise-en-scène* of many of her daughter's novels), she wrote popular dialect poems about country people. Her scholarship, as was noted by *The Times* after her death, was of the Victorian age: "The inadequacy of the cliché that Victorian scholarship and the intense appreciation of the arts which so often accompanied it were alone made possible by Victorian leisure is well illustrated by her literary career."

Her poem "The Solitary Life" has an auto-biographical tinge, especially when she writes, "Till I forget the world, almost forget myself." Keane confirmed this aspect of her mother's character. She "never really shared her literary and musical interests with us . . . and was practically a recluse. She was certainly a social recluse: she wasn't at all interested in the social life around her." She also never mixed in the literary world which her daughter thought would have suited her well, particularly since the Irish Literary Revival was at its height when she and her husband returned to Ireland. Skrine devoted her time to her family, writing, music and gardening. She was also religious, and every morning the family assembled for prayers.

During the Irish War of Independence (1919–21), when the family home was burned down, Skrine was much more affected than her husband. The Skrines moved to County Wexford in southeast Ireland, where Agnes and Walter were to spend the rest of their lives. Keane's career as a novelist and playwright, which took off in the late 1920s, was viewed with some ambivalence by her mother. "She was so terribly conscientious in her heart and mind that she didn't really approve of what I was doing." Skrine took particular exception when Molly based characters in her writings on members of the family. Walter died in June 1930. Agnes survived him by 25 years and died at the age of 90 in 1955. In his *Dictionary of Irish Literature*, Robert Hogan described her as "a pallid Irish version of Burns" but acknowledged the quality of some of her poems, especially "Corrymeela" and "Marriage." An obituary written in *The Times* after her death noted that while her output was not large, the quality was of a high order and possessed "an exquisite sense of the value and music of words."

**SOURCES:**

Hogan, Robert. *Dictionary of Irish Literature*. Vol. 2. Westport, CT: Greenwood Press, 1996.

Quinn, John, ed. "Molly Keane," in *A Portrait of the Artist as a Young Girl*. London: Methuen. 1986.

*The Times* (London). January 25, 29, 1955; February 3, 7, 10, 1955.

**Deirdre McMahon**, lecturer in history at Mary Immaculate College, University of Limerick, Limerick, Ireland

## Skrine, Mary Nesta (1904–1996).

*See Keane, Molly.*

## Skuratova, Maria (d. 1605).

*See Maria Skuratova.*

## Slagle, Eleanor Clarke (1871–1942)

*American leader in occupational therapy. Born Ella May Clarke on October 13, 1871, in Hobart, New York; died of a coronary thrombosis on September 18, 1942, in Philipse Manor, New York; daughter of John Clarke (a sheriff) and Emmaline J. (Davenport) Clarke; attended Claverack College in Columbia County, New York; married Robert E. Slagle (divorced); no children.*

Born Ella May Clarke in 1871, the daughter of a former Civil War officer, Eleanor Slagle grew up in New York State. She attended Claverack College for a short time before moving to Chicago and marrying Robert E. Slagle, whom she later divorced. It was not until she was in her late 30s that Eleanor Slagle became involved in social welfare, caring for the mentally ill at *Jane Addams' Hull House in Chicago. In 1908, Slagle was among the first to take a course in "Invalid Occupation" at what would later become the school of social work at the University of Chicago.

Her interest in occupational therapy was greatly influenced by psychiatrist Adolf Meyer, who became the first director of the Henry Phipps Psychiatric Clinic at the John Hopkins Hospital in Baltimore. In 1913, Meyer asked Slagle to organize the clinic's occupational therapy program. Her career took off quickly. By 1915, she was the director of Chicago's Henry B. Favill School of Occupations, which specialized in the training of occupational therapy aides.

In 1918, Slagle became the Illinois Department of Public Welfare's superintendent of occupational therapy. While serving in this position, she organized a therapy program for Illinois mental hospitals. She proved so successful in this task that she became director of occupational therapy for the New York State Hospital Commission four years later, and spent the rest of her career with the commission. Under Slagle's leadership, occupational therapy for the mentally ill at the state hospital level expanded greatly. She was responsible for increasing the number of therapy classes for patients, hiring higher qualified therapists, and originating ward classes and occupational centers. In ten years, her effective leadership had introduced nearly 70,000 patients in New York's state mental hospital system to occupational therapy programs. Slagle's accomplishments became the model for institutions throughout the United States, and her guidance was frequently sought in the development of similar programs across the nation.

Eleanor Slagle was active in improving the professional practice through the organization she helped found in 1917, the National Society for the Promotion of Occupational Therapy. Later renamed the American Occupational Therapy Association, it advocated minimum training standards and registration for occupational therapists. Slagle also envisioned the association as an informational contact for institutions desiring to set up occupational therapy programs. Besides holding prominent positions in professional occupational therapy associations, she also encouraged influential civic groups to help meet the rehabilitative needs of the mentally ill through therapy.

Having served as secretary, vice president, president, and finally executive secretary, Slagle retired from her post at the American Occupational Therapy Association in 1937. During her retirement dinner, *Eleanor Roosevelt paid tribute to the renowned occupational therapist, and Slagle's old mentor, Dr. Adolph Meyer, referred to her as "the personification of occupational therapy." She died on September 18, 1942, in Philipse Manor, New York, having suffered from arteriosclerosis for the last ten years of her life.

**SOURCES:**

James, Edward T., ed. *Notable American Women, 1607–1950*. Cambridge, MA: The Belknap Press of Harvard University, 1971.

**Kimberly A. Burton**, B.A, M.I.S.,
Ann Arbor, Michigan

## Slaney, Mary Decker (1958—)

*American track-and-field middle-distance runner.*
*Name variations: Mary Decker. Born Mary Teresa Decker on August 4, 1958, in Bunnvale, New Jersey; one of four children of John Decker (a New Jersey tool-and-die maker) and Jacqueline Decker; married Ron Tabb (a marathoner), in 1981 (divorced 1983); married Richard Slaney (a British discus thrower), in 1985; children: Ashley Lynn (b. 1986).*

Although she has never won an Olympic medal and her career has been plagued with medical problems, Mary Decker Slaney is recognized as one of the great female runners. Born in 1958 in New Jersey, Slaney moved with her family to Huntington Beach, California, in 1969. There, at age 11, she entered a children's cross-country race. Her easy win and the pressure of competition convinced her to keep running. At first competing without a coach or formal instruction, Slaney continued winning races for her age group, including a statewide meet. Her natural ability was then developed under the guidance of

the coach of a local girls' track club; within two years, she was breaking speed records. In 1971, she set a world record for her age group in the 800-meter race. Her desire to win led her to compete in seven races in one week, including a marathon; the effort put her in the hospital for an emergency appendectomy. Nevertheless, Slaney continued to push herself, training two and a half hours a day in two workouts. In 1972, she qualified for the U.S. Olympic track team, but at age 13 she was too young to compete.

Recognized nationally by age 14, when she was able to compete in open races unrestricted by age group, Slaney began her career in international competition when she was chosen to join the American Amateur Athletic Union's track team in 1973. On a tour of the Soviet Union, Africa, and Western Europe, she repeatedly surprised spectators with victories over older runners. She won in the 800 meters in Minsk, beating an Olympic medalist, and by the end of 1974 held three world records for middle-distance races. She was, however, the subject of an international incident when a Soviet runner shoved her off the track during the 4x800 relay in the USSR. Enraged, Slaney threw a baton at her opponent—twice. Both teams were disqualified and Slaney admonished, but she did not suffer in popularity. "Little Mary Decker," as the press had dubbed her (she was less than 100 pounds and about 5' tall in 1974), was a favorite with spectators and reporters. Her six-inch growth spurt in 1975, coupled with an intensive training regimen, led to the first of the many debilitating injuries she would suffer in her career. Shin splints and stress fractures were treated with physical therapy, acupuncture, and anti-inflammatory drugs, to no avail; Slaney had to give up her dream of competing in the Olympic Games of 1976.

She graduated from high school in 1976 and moved to Boulder, Colorado, to enroll at the University of Colorado on a track scholarship, despite ongoing problems with stress fractures. In 1977, she successfully underwent surgery for a condition known as compartment syndrome, caused when her calf muscles grew too large for the surrounding sheaths, and was soon running without pain for the first time in two years. After competing in meets in Australia, she beat her own indoor world record for 1,000 yards at the U.S. Olympic Invitation in Los Angeles. She then left college in 1978 to train full-time under the guidance of Olympic medalist Dick Quax. However, afflicted with tendinitis, Slaney could compete in only a few events.

She then moved to Eugene, Oregon, and her career began to take off again. In January 1980, she set new world records in New Zealand and in the U.S. for the mile and 1,500-meter races respectively, then went on to break the world record for the 880-yard event and the U.S. record for the 800-meter event at the San Diego Invitational track meet in February. She qualified for the 1980 Summer Olympics in Moscow but did not compete due to the U.S. boycott, competing in several international track meets that summer instead. Surgery to mend a torn Achilles tendon followed by a second shin-muscle operation kept her out of training and competition for an entire frustrating year. As had happened before and would happen again, Slaney's physical injuries were followed by an impressive comeback. In European meets in late 1981, she ran the 10,000 meters for the first time and beat the previous record by an astonishing 42 seconds. In September 1981, Mary married Ron Tabb, a champion marathoner; they would separate less than two years later.

The year 1982 was arguably her single best year, as she set five world records in indoor and outdoor races, including a 4:18 mile. She was named female athlete of the year by the Associated Press, as well as Jesse Owens International Amateur Athlete of the Year, the first woman to be so honored. Stress fractures of the ankle continued to plague Slaney in 1983, but they did not prevent her from winning against Olympic medalists at the World Track and Field championship in Helsinki. That year she also received the Amateur Sportswoman of the Year award from the Women's Sports Foundation and was named Sportswoman of the Year by *Sports Illustrated*. She became a spokeswoman for Nike shoes in the early 1980s, and accepted contracts with Eastman Kodak and Timex as well. By 1984, she held every American distance record from 800 to 10,000 meters.

Mary Decker Slaney was a sure bet for the gold medal going into the 1984 Los Angeles Olympics. Forced to choose between the 1,500- and 3,000-meter races because the events overlapped on the schedule, she chose the 3,000. But one of her fans was a South African runner from Bloemfontein named ❧ **Zola Budd**, who had trained by racing barefoot on the farm where she grew up. By 1983, Budd was number one in the world in the 5,000 meters (setting an unofficial record five seconds faster than Slaney's), but South Africa was banned from the Olympics because of its policy of apartheid. Finding a loophole and a paternal grandfather who had been a British citizen, Budd moved to England and began preparing for the Olympics as an English citizen (granted in two weeks' time). But the young girl, who only wanted to run, was now enveloped in a swirl of controversy and animosity. Animosity because she displaced British runners; controversy because she became a lightning rod for her country's racist policies. On her arrival in Los Angeles, Budd also learned that her South African citizenship had been revoked. Her solace: that she would be running against her idol, Slaney. On that fateful day which was to damage both their lives, each woman approached the starting line burdened with pressures.

Just past the mid-point of the 3,000-meter race, in one of the most famous collisions in the history of sports, Slaney became entangled with Budd, lost her balance, and pulled a hip muscle. Unable to rise, she was carried off the field. It had been her last chance for a gold medal. Sadly, Budd, who came in seventh, had to endure the continual booing of the spectators as she continued around the oval; Rumania's **Maricica Puica** won. As to who was at fault, theories abound. After the race, an inconsolable Slaney blamed Budd and refused to accept an apology; though Budd was initially disqualified, she was reinstated upon judicial review of the videotape. Shortly thereafter, she married, retired from competition and returned to Bloemfontein. In a 1994 interview for *People Weekly*, Slaney maintains that Budd moved to take the lead. "I let her, and then she cut across too soon. Even though I had people telling me she did it intentionally, I never thought she did. I don't hate her. I hated the fact that it was an opportunity for me that got messed up." Mary went from celebrity to outcast when the press caught her after the race berating the weeping Budd for tripping her. Although Slaney later said she regretted the outburst and did not believe Budd had deliberately tried to trip her, her popularity had suffered greatly.

After recovering from her hip injury, Slaney made another comeback in 1985, setting a world record in the indoor 2,000 meters. A

❧▶ **Budd, Zola** (1966—)
*South African world-champion runner. Name variations: Zola Budd Pieterse. Born in 1966 in Bloemfontein, Orange Free State, South Africa; married Michael Pieterse (a businessman); children: daughter Lisa.*

Following the disastrous 1984 Olympics, Zola Budd returned to South Africa to marry and raise a family. In 1992, when the IOC readmitted South Africa to the Olympics, Budd was on the country's first integrated team.

Mary
Decker
Slaney
(right)

month later, she set another world record for the mile, defeating both Budd and Puica. That year, Mary married British discus champion Richard Slaney. In 1986, she gave birth to a daughter, and was back in training a week later. Although she qualified for the 3,000-meter run in the 1988 Olympics in Seoul, she did not medal. Because of the misadventure at the L.A. Olympics, Slaney had consistently set fast paces off the block so that she could avoid running with the pack, a habit that brought her in 10th. She failed to qualify for the 1992 Olympic Games.

As determined as ever, Decker, age 37, qualified in the 1996 Olympic trials for the 5,000-meter event, but was eliminated in the first round of competition. Scandal followed in 1997 when it was learned that the International Amateur Athletic Federation had suspended her for testing positive for excessive testosterone levels during the 1996 Olympic trials. Slaney maintained that she had never taken performance-enhancing drugs, and filed suit against the IAAF for a lost competition season and damage to her reputation. She was supported by the USA Track and Field federation. However, the IAAF refused to relent and although she was allowed to compete again, the records she earned after June 1996 were discounted; in 1999, she was stripped of the 1997 medal she earned in the 1,500-meter event at the World Indoor championships.

Mary Decker Slaney still holds five American records from the 800-meter to the 3,000-meter event. Living with her husband in Eugene, Oregon, she is now a master's runner, competing in road races and track meets across the United States.

**SOURCES:**

"Going the Distance," in *People Weekly*. October 17, 1994.

Jacobs, Linda. *Mary Decker: Speed Records and Spaghetti*. St. Paul, MN: EMC Corp., 1975.

Markel, Robert. *The Women's Sports Encyclopedia*. NY: Henry Holt, 1997.

Moritz, Charles, ed. "Mary Decker," in *Current Biography Yearbook 1983*. NY: H.W. Wilson, 1984.

Newman, Matthew. *Mary Decker Slaney*. Mankato, MN: Crestwood House, 1986.

Woolum, Janet. *Outstanding Women Athletes: Who They Are and How They Influenced Sports in America*. Phoenix, AZ: Oryx, 1992.

**Laura York**, M.A. in History,
University of California, Riverside, California

## Slavenska, Mia (b. 1916)

*Yugoslavian-born ballerina, choreographer, and teacher. Name variations: Mia Corak. Born Mia Slavenski-Brod in Yugoslavia in 1916 (one source cites 1914); studied for seven years at the Royal Academy of Music, Zagreb; had dance training in Zagreb, Vienna, Paris (under Bronislava Nijinska), and New York (under Vincenzo Celli); also studied modern dance with Harald Kreutzberg and Mary Wigmore; married Kurt Neumann, in 1946; children: at least one daughter, Maria.*

A child prodigy, Mia Slavenska debuted at the Zagreb National Opera House at age five, in 1921, and stayed on to become a soloist in 1931 and prima ballerina in 1933. That year she joined *\*Bronislava Nijinska*'s short-lived Théâtre de la Danse in Paris, receiving wild ac-

claim from Parisian audiences during her season there. In 1936, Slavenska appeared in the movie *La Mort du Cygne* (released in America as *Ballerina*), considered one of the few classic movies about dance. Two years later, she became a lead dancer with the legendary Ballets Russes, and from July to September 1938 dazzled London audiences both with her artistry and her beauty (Slavenska was known for her red-gold hair and pale skin). Among the ballets the company performed in that season were *Les Sylphides*, *Gaite Parisienne*, *Les Elfes*, *Carnevale* and *Giselle*, in which Slavenska danced the title role.

Shortly before the start of World War II, the Ballets Russes visited America, where Slavenska chose to remain. Forming her own Slavenska Ballet Variante in Hollywood, she toured the U.S., South America, and Canada from 1944 to 1952. During these years, she also married Kurt Neumann and became an American citizen. While continuing to tour with her own troupe, in the immediate postwar years Slavenska made guest appearances with the London Festival Ballet, the Ballets Russes, and Ballet Theatre. In 1952, with English dancer Frederic Franklin, she formed the Slavenska-Franklin Ballet, which the following year toured throughout America and Canada. They also performed in Japan, the first foreign ballet group to do so since *\*Anna Pavlova*'s. The company's best-known production was an adaptation of Tennessee Williams' *A Streetcar Named Desire*, choreographed by *\*Valerie Bettis*, in which Slavenska danced the role of Blanche to high praise. From 1955 to 1956, she was prima ballerina with the Metropolitan Opera Ballet, while also working with regional companies and at the Jacob's Pillow Dance Festival. Slavenska retired from dancing at the close of the 1950s, and began a long teaching career both in New York City and in California, where she lived with her husband near Los Angeles. Along with Frederic Franklin, Irina Baronova, **Raven Wilkinson, Nini Theilade**, Marc Platt and **Moscelyne Larkin**, among others, in June 2000 she attended a celebration and reunion of the Ballets Russes in New Orleans.

## Slenczynska, Ruth (1925—)

*American pianist. Name variations: Ruth Slenczynski. Born in Sacramento, California, on January 15, 1925; daughter of Josef Slenczynski (a violinist and once head of the Warsaw Conservatory).*

Ruth Slenczynska's talents were evident at an early age, but her ambitious violinist father subjected her to a regime of extreme severity.

**Baronova, Irina.** *See Toumanova, Tamara for sidebar.*

She played in public in Berlin at age six, and performed a concerto in Paris five years later. Hailed as one of the great musical prodigies of the age, she studied with *Marguerite Long, Artur Schnabel, Alfred Cortot and Egon Petri. Sergei Rachmaninoff showed an interest in her future. By her mid-teen years, her career disintegrated, as the psychological toll of exploitation and mental abuse began to make itself felt in emotionally flat and mechanical performances. Slenczynska withdrew from her musical career to put her life in order; after more than a decade of therapy and confidence-building, she resumed public performances, to mostly positive reviews. In later years, she taught at the University of Southern Illinois, occasionally giving recitals. She published an account of her struggles, *Forbidden Childhood* (Doubleday), in 1957, and four years later published a guide to piano practice, *Music at Your Fingertips*.

**SOURCES:**

Pincherle, Marc. *The World of the Virtuoso*. Translated by Lucile H. Brockway. NY: W.W. Norton, 1963.

Slenczynska, Ruth. *Forbidden Childhood*. Garden City, NY: Doubleday, 1957.

**John Haag**,
Athens, Georgia

## Slesinger, Tess (1905–1945)

*American novelist and short-story writer. Born in New York City in 1905; died in 1945; daughter of middle-class Jewish immigrant parents; attended the Ethical Culture School; studied at Swarthmore College, 1923–25; attended Columbia School of Journalism, taking* Dorothy Scarborough's *course in the short story, B.Litt., 1927; married Herbert Solow (a leftist activist and writer), in 1928; married Frank Davis (a film producer and writer), in 1936; children: two.*

After receiving a degree from Columbia, Tess Slesinger worked as an assistant fashion editor on the New York *Herald Tribune* in 1926, then became assistant on the New York *Evening Post Literary Review*. By the 1930s, she had co-founded *The Menorah Journal* with her first husband, had written enough short stories for a collection, *Time: The Present* (1935), had published her novel *The Unpossessed* (1934), and was marching in protests and speaking on the inequities of economics and race. With most of her writing well received, Slesinger had become something of a literary celebrity; her strength was in tragicomedy.

In 1935, the writer was invited to Hollywood to work on the screen adaptation of *Pearl S. Buck's *The Good Earth* (1937), with

Talbot Jennings, **Claudine West**, and an uncredited *Frances Marion. That same year, Slesinger wrote *The Bride Wore Red* (1937) for director *Dorothy Arzner. With her second husband, Frank Davis, Slesinger also wrote the screen adaptation of *Betty Smith's *A Tree Grows in Brooklyn* (1945), which was nominated for an Academy Award. Once in Hollywood, Slesinger's literary output slowed down considerably, but her activism continued. She helped establish the Screenwriters Guild.

## Slessor, Mary (1848–1915)

*Scottish Presbyterian missionary to West Africa. Name variations: Mary Mitchell Slessor. Born Mary Mitchell Slessor in December 1848 in Gilcomston, near Aberdeen, Scotland; died of swamp fever on January 13, 1915, in Use, the Calabar, Nigeria; daughter of Robert Slessor (a shoemaker) and Mary Slessor (a weaver and textile factory worker); attended public schools until age 14, when she entered the factories of Dundee; never married; children: a number officially and unofficially adopted.*

*Awards and honors: named honorary associate of the Hospital Order of St. John of Jerusalem in England.*

*Ruth Slenczynska*

*Moved from Gilcomston to Dundee, Scotland (1859); left school to join her mother in the textile factories, beginning to work a full factory schedule (1862); inspired by the reports of David Livingstone in the* Missionary Record, *a church publication, began to educate herself (1866); offered her services to the Foreign Missions Board of the Scottish Presbyterian Church (1875), setting sail for the Calabar, West Africa (August 1876); served in the Calabar Mission Field, an area of Nigeria that included Duke Town, Old Town, Creek Town, and Okoyong and far into the interior of Nigeria to Enyong Creek (1876–1915).*

*Mary*
*Slessor*
**(seated)**

Having heard stories of the Scottish Presbyterian Church's mission in Calabar since her childhood, Mary Mitchell Slessor began a process of introspection after hearing the reports of David Livingstone's death in 1874. This culminated with her offering her services to the Foreign Missions Board of the Presbyterian Church in 1875. Sailing for Calabar the following year, she began her mission in Duke Town, Old Town, and Creek Town along the Calabar River in Nigeria. Slessor quick-

ly established relations and soon held an honored, if difficult, role, among the Igbo and Okoyong tribes. In June 1879, she was sent home for health reasons, remaining there for 18 months.

While in Scotland, Slessor became determined to move farther into the forests of the Calabar, insistent that this is where her true work lay. She returned to Duke Town in 1880 and journeyed into the interior, setting up mission outstations in Qua, Akim, and Ikot Ansa. While she worked as a teacher and nurse, primary among her goals was the eventual elimination of the murder of twin children, who were regarded as elements of witchcraft to the area tribes. To this end, she would rescue twins, often bringing them into her home and raising them as her own.

Slessor was again invalided home to Scotland in May 1883, returning to Africa in October 1885. Three years later, the Mission Board assented to her wishes and allowed her to move farther into the interior. She established a station at Ekenge and began work with members of the Okoyong, moving about an extended area while

serving as a nurse, teacher, and arbitrator among the local tribes. In late 1890, she came down from the bush into Duke Town to recover from a serious bout with swamp fever, and became engaged to fellow missionary Charles Morrison. Sent home to Scotland in January 1891 on medical leave, she returned to Africa in February 1892, arriving in Duke Town shortly before Morrison was permanently invalided home. He eventually resigned from the mission and moved to America where he died.

While the mission board supported Slessor's drive to work with tribes in the interior, they were unable to find and support missionary assistance for her. In 1898, worn down and severely ill, she returned to Edinburgh as an invalid, taking with her four of her adopted daughters. Concerned about the safety of her other children and the condition of her missionary area, she returned to Africa in December 1898, while still ill. Leaving her adopted daughter **Jean** and other pupils behind to run the schools she had already established at Ekenge, Ifako, and other stations, Slessor continued her drive inland, in 1902 moving to Itu to work with the Aro and in 1903 even farther inland along the Enyong Creek. Although successful in establishing schools and drawing the attention of local colonial agents, she was again invalided home in the spring of 1907, taking with her her adopted son Daniel. Returning in October 1907, Slessor began work to establish a long-hoped-for project, a women's settlement in the area. In 1908, she succeeded with the establishment of one at Use, where she remained, administering to the women of the area. It was at Use that she died of swamp fever on January 13, 1915.

**SOURCES:**

Buchan, James. *The Expendable Mary Slessor*. Edinburgh: Saint Andrew Press, 1980.

Deen, Edith. *Great Woman of the Christian Faith*. NY: Harper and Brothers, 1959.

**SUGGESTED READING:**

Syme, Ronald. *Nigerian Pioneer: The Story of Mary Slessor*. NY: Morrow, 1964.

**COLLECTIONS:**

Some papers relating to Mary Slessor's mission in Calabar are located in the Papers of the United Presbyterian Foreign Missions' Board, Church of Scotland Library, Edinburgh; other personal papers, including letters, are located at the Dundee Central Library and the Edinburgh University Library.

**Amanda Carson Banks**,
Vanderbilt Divinity School,
Nashville, Tennessee

# Slocum, Frances (1773–1847)

*American woman abducted and raised by Native Americans. Name variations: Maconaqua; Ma-conaquah. Born on March 4, 1773, in Warwick, Rhode Island; died of pneumonia on March 9, 1847, in Indiana; daughter of Jonathan Slocum (a farmer) and Ruth (Tripp) Slocum; married a Delaware tribesman, in 1791 (divorced); married Shepancanah (a Miami chief), around 1794 (died 1832); children: daughters Kekesequa (b. 1800) and Ozahshinqua (b. 1809); two sons who died in childhood.*

Frances Slocum was born in Warwick, Rhode Island, in 1773, the third daughter among ten children of Quaker farmers Jonathan Slocum and **Ruth Tripp Slocum**. On her father's side, she was descended from one of the country's first English settlers. During the Revolutionary War, when Frances was four years old, her family moved to the Wyoming Valley, settling in what is now Wilkes-Barre, Pennsylvania. They were among a number of settlers, most of them pro-independence, who farmed lands spread out around the so-called Forty Fort. As the war went on, the Patriots in the area forced out those settlers who remained loyal to the king. A number of these Tory settlers banded together with other Tories and local tribes, and in the summer after the Slocums arrived this group attacked the valley, killing settlers and laying waste to farms and settlements. The settlers fled to Forty Fort, where, outnumbered two or three to one (sources vary) by the attackers, they fought desperately and were overwhelmed on July 3, 1778. Some two-thirds of the several hundred settlers were gruesomely killed by Native Americans and Tories in what is now known as the Wyoming Massacre, but the Slocum family, perhaps because of their friendship with local Indians, was spared. While most of the other survivors immediately left the valley, the Slocums, devout Quakers, remained. That November, however, one of the Slocum sons (without telling his parents) joined a punitory expedition against the Indians who had taken part in the massacre. In retaliation, a small group of Delaware tribesmen attacked the Slocums' home and captured a neighbor and five-year-old Frances.

A few weeks later, Jonathan Slocum was murdered. The neighbor who had been abducted with Frances managed to return home some years later, reporting that the little girl was still alive. At the end of the Revolutionary War, her brothers began searching for her, visiting Indian villages from Pennsylvania all the way west to Detroit without luck. Before her death in 1807, Ruth Slocum, who never got over the loss of her daughter, asked her remaining children to keep looking for Frances. Their search would last 59 years.

Slocum had spent the first night after her abduction near Abraham Creek in what is now Frances Slocum State Park in Pennsylvania. She was then taken to a village near Niagara Falls, where she was adopted by a Delaware couple whose daughter had recently died. Now called Weletawash, she lived with her new family on the Detroit River for a time before they moved to the Miami Indian town of Kekionga (now Fort Wayne, Indiana). Gradually she forgot how to speak English, and forgot the first name she had been given at birth. When she was about 19 years old, she was briefly married to a Delaware man, but the marriage ended when he decided to move farther west and she chose to stay in Indiana with her family.

Around 1794, Slocum married a Miami named Shepancanah and took the name of Maconaqua ("Little Bear"). The couple had four children, daughters **Kekesequa** and **Ozahshinqua** and two sons who died in childhood, and later moved near Indiana's Mississinewa River. Her husband eventually went deaf, forcing him to give up his position as war chief in their village. The family then relocated to a small settlement a few miles up the river which became known as Deaf Man's Village. Although her home became increasingly surrounded by white settlers, Slocum's heritage was not recognized by them, and she and her family lived peacefully, with her daughters remaining close by after their marriages. After her husband's death in 1832, Slocum, well respected within the Native American community, continued to manage their sizable farm on her own, raising cattle and some 100 horses.

In January 1835, George Ewing, a traveling fur trader who spoke the Miami language, noticed the lightness of Slocum's skin. Now elderly by the standards of the day, wanting to tell her story and assuming that the members of her birth family were dead (she had always feared they would take her away if they found her), Slocum told him of her background. She revealed what she remembered, including her father's name, that she had lived on the Susquehanna River in Pennsylvania, and that her family had been Quakers. She requested that he not repeat her story until after she was dead, but a little while later Ewing sent a letter to the postmaster in Lancaster, Pennsylvania, seeking any Slocums in the area. His letter was published in a local paper in March 1837, and the story reached Joseph Slocum, one of her younger brothers, who notified another brother and a sister. That September, the siblings traveled to Slocum's village in Indiana, meeting her again after over half a century. The reunion, facilitated by two interpreters, was an uncomfortable one; Slocum initially did not believe their claim of blood ties, and thought they were trying to steal her land. (By this time, white settlers were already notorious for their greed for land.) Finally convinced of their sincerity, Slocum shared a meal with her siblings, but she refused to return East with them, wanting to remain near her daughters and grandchildren. As her story spread among white settlers, they began calling her "the White Rose of the Miamis."

In 1840, when the Miami agreed to relinquish the last of their land in Indiana, Slocum sought help from her white family members. They successfully petitioned Congress to allow her to remain on the land that had been granted to her daughters under an earlier treaty. (While it was Slocum's land, the government in Washington did not consider her a Native American, although it did consider her daughters Native Americans, and thus had conducted that previous treaty with them.) In 1846, then in her early 70s, she invited her nephew George Slocum and his family to join her and help run the farm. Slocum died of pneumonia the following year, and was buried beside her husband and two sons. A monument erected over her grave by some of her many descendants in 1900 was later relocated along the Mississinewa River, where it stands to this day, near Indiana's Frances Slocum State Park.

**SOURCES:**

Griffin, Lynne, and Kelly McCann. *The Book of Women: 300 Notable Women History Passed By*. Holbrook, MA: Bob Adams, 1992.

James, Edward T., ed. *Notable American Women, 1607–1950*. Cambridge, MA: The Belknap Press of Harvard University, 1971.

**Kimberly A. Burton**, B.A., M.I.S.,
Ann Arbor, Michigan

# Slosson, Annie Trumbull

## (1838–1926)

*American entomologist. Born in 1838 in Stonington, Connecticut; died in 1926; daughter of Gurdon Trumbull and Sarah Trumbull; educated in Hartford, Connecticut; married Edward Slosson, in 1867.*

Annie Trumbull Slosson, for whom a number of insect species are named, made her mark as an entomologist with a collection of unusual insects which she gathered at her homes in Florida and New Hampshire. Slosson's studies did not contribute any new theories to science, but she presented many then-unknown specimens to specialists for analysis. She also wrote descriptions of the physical characteristics and habits of insects she collected, and published several stories about natural history intended for lay readers.

SOURCES:

Ogilvie, Marilyn Bailey. *Women in Science: Antiquity Through the Nineteenth Century.* Cambridge, MA: MIT Press, 1993.

**Kimberly A. Burton**, B.A., M.I.S.,
Ann Arbor, Michigan

# Slowe, Lucy Diggs (1885–1937)

*Educator who was the first African-American woman dean of Howard University. Born on July 4, 1885, in Berryville, Virginia; died of kidney disease on October 21, 1937, in Washington, D.C.; daughter of Henry Slowe and Fannie (Porter) Slowe; graduated from Howard University, 1908; Columbia University, M.A. in English, 1915.*

Lucy Diggs Slowe was born on July 4, 1885, in Berryville, Virginia, the youngest of Henry and **Fannie Porter Slowe**'s seven children. By the time she was six years old, both of her parents had died, and she was raised thereafter by a paternal aunt in Lexington, Virginia. When she was 13, the family moved to Baltimore, Maryland, where she attended public schools and graduated at the top of her class in 1904. She then became a scholarship student at Howard University in Washington, D.C., where she was one of the founders of Alpha Kappa Alpha Sorority, the first Greek-letter organization for black women.

After graduating from Howard in 1908, Slowe taught English at her alma mater, Baltimore Colored High School. In 1915, she earned a master's degree in English from Columbia University and began teaching at a Washington, D.C., high school. When the District of Columbia's first junior high school for black children was established in 1919, Slowe was appointed principal. In this position, she instituted an integrated in-service course for junior high school teachers, which was conducted by Columbia University. Three years later, in 1922, Slowe was appointed dean of women at Howard University, the first black woman to achieve that position. She also served as a professor of English and education.

Throughout her professional career, Slowe was active in the struggle to elevate black women to a level of equality with whites and black men, and she sought to make the most of her role as women's dean. Deans of women at black colleges traditionally had functioned more as chaperons or guardians of morality than as educators, but as an administrator and educator, Slowe was far more concerned with developing black woman culturally and preparing them for leadership roles than with enforcing strict rules. She commented in *The Education of Negro Women and Girls* that "when a college woman cannot be trusted to go shopping without a chaperon, she is not likely to develop powers of leadership."

Slowe was also concerned that black women students were not benefiting from a new national movement in higher education that focused on broadening the "whole" student by integrating career guidance, health services, athletics, and cultural activities into the academic experience. She took steps to expose her students to the fine arts, by instituting a cultural series, and to refinement, by organizing women's social functions.

Slowe's mission to improve conditions for her students was also achieved through her active participation in organizations that promoted the advancement of black women. In 1923, she became the first president of the National Association of College Women (NACW), an organization of black women college graduates of accredited liberal arts colleges and universities. Its mission was three-fold: to raise the standards in the colleges where black women were educated; to improve conditions for black women faculty; and to encourage advanced scholarship among women. Another priority of the NACW was to influence the presidents of black colleges to appoint well-trained deans of women. In 1929, she organized the National Association of Deans of Women and Advisors to Girls in Negro Schools, which became independent of the NACW in 1935 as the number of women advisors and deans of black colleges grew. With *Mary McLeod Bethune, Slowe helped found the National Council of Negro Women and served as the organization's first executive secretary. She served on the advisory board of the National Youth Administration, and was an active member of the National Association of Deans of Women, the Women's International League for Peace and Freedom, and the YWCA.

An accomplished tennis player, Slowe won 17 cups in an era when few blacks competed with whites in that sport. She sang contralto in the St. Francis Catholic Church and in the Madison Street Presbyterian Church in Baltimore. During the last 15 years of Slowe's life, **Mary Burrill**, a recognized Washington, D.C., public school teacher and playwright, was her partner and housemate. Still active as dean of women at

Howard, Lucy Diggs Slowe died of kidney disease in October 1937. A stained-glass window in Howard University's chapel commemorates her lasting influence, and a dormitory is named her memory.

**SOURCES:**

James, Edward T., ed. *Notable American Women, 1607–1950.* Cambridge, MA: The Belknap Press of Harvard University, 1971.

Smith, Jessie Carney, ed. *Notable Black American Women.* Detroit, MI: Gale Research, 1992.

**Kimberly A. Burton**, B.A., M.I.S.,
Ann Arbor, Michigan

## Slutskaya, Vera (1874–1917)

*Russian revolutionary leader who played an important role in the Bolshevik Party from 1902 until her death a few days after the Bolshevik Revolution.*
*Name variations: Vera Slutskaia; Vera Kliment'evna Slutskaia. Born Berta Bronislavovna Slutskaya in Minsk on September 17, 1874; killed in action in Tsarskoe Selo (now Pushkin), on November 12, 1917.*

Born into a family of merchants, Vera Slutskaya was a dentist by profession but joined the Russian revolutionary movement in 1898. For a brief period, 1901–02, she was a member of the Bund, a Jewish revolutionary organization. In 1902, however, she joined the Bolshevik faction of the Russian Social Democratic Labor Party (RSDLP), later known at the Communist Party. A participant in the revolution of 1905–07 in Minsk and St. Petersburg, Slutskaya was a member of the military organization of the RSDLP. She served as a delegate to the fifth congress of the RSDLP in 1907, and was later assigned to carry out party work in St. Petersburg.

From 1909 to 1912, Slutskaya lived in exile in Germany and Switzerland. In 1913, she resumed party work in St. Petersburg, and was arrested several times by the tsarist police. The following year, she was exiled to the Caucasus. After the overthrow of tsarism in early 1917, she became a member of the St. Petersburg (now named Petrograd) committee of the Bolsheviks. An excellent orator and agitator, Slutskaya was a party organizer among poor women as well as secretary of the party's Vasileostrovskii Island district committee. During this turbulent time, she was a delegate to the sixth congress of the RSDLP. She also took part in the armed uprising in Petrograd during the October revolution of 1917.

When Vladimir Ilyich Lenin took the podium on November 7, 1917, to announce the dawn of Soviet rule in Russia, Slutskaya was in the audience along with \***Alexandra Kollontai**,

\***Nadezhda Krupskaya**, \***Elena Stasova** and other Bolshevik women. As the delegates stood to sing the socialist anthem "The Internationale," American journalist John Reed noticed that Kollontai had tears in her eyes. Leaving the hall after the meeting, \***Konkordiya Samoilova** ran into Slutskaya. "Isn't it true, Vera," Samoilova beamed, "that even if all of us have to die, it will have been worth it just to live through this evening?" "Yes, of course," Slutskaya agreed immediately. This encounter stuck in Samoilova's memory, because less than a week later, on November 12, 1917, Vera Slutskaya was killed in a skirmish with anti-Bolshevik forces near Tsarskoe Selo while she was involved in transporting medicine to Red Guard units.

**SOURCES:**

Clements, Barbara Evans. *Bolshevik Women.* Cambridge, UK: Cambridge University Press, 1997.

Karpetskaia, N.D. "Vovlechenie Trudiashchikhsia Zhenshchin Petrograda v Revoliutsionnoe Dvizhenie (Mart-Iiul' 1917 g.)" [The Involvement of the Toiling Women of Petrograd in the Revolutionary Movement (March–July 1917)], in *Vestnik Leningradskogo Universiteta.* No. 8, 1966, pp. 45–53.

Mierau, Fritz, ed. *Links! Links! Links! Eine Chronik in Vers und Plakat.* Berlin: Rütten & Loening, 1970.

Rips, Samuil Matusovich and Tat'iana Vasil'evna Kushtevskaia. *Vera: Stranitsy Zhizni V.K. Slutskoi.* Moscow: Izd-vo polit. lit-ry, 1991.

**John Haag**, Associate Professor History,
University of Georgia, Athens, Georgia

## Slye, Maud (1869–1954)

*American pathologist who was one of the first scientists to demonstrate that cancer is inheritable. Born Maud Caroline Slye on February 8, 1869 (some sources erroneously cite 1879), in Minneapolis, Minnesota; died of a heart attack on September 17, 1954, in Chicago, Illinois; daughter of Florence Alden (Wheeler) Slye and James Alvin Slye (a lawyer and writer); attended the University of Chicago; Brown University, B.A., 1899; never married; no children.*

Likened to an American \***Marie Curie**, pathologist Maud Slye was among the first scientists to demonstrate that cancer is inheritable. She was born in Minneapolis in 1869, the second child of James Slye, a lawyer, and **Florence Wheeler Slye**, who were educated and of respectable standing but far from wealthy. Her mother hoped Maud would spend her life in the arts, as a painter or a writer—her father wrote on the side—but she chose to pursue biology, acting on her love of nature. When the family moved to Iowa, the Slye children attended public schools in Des Moines and Marshalltown. After Maud graduated from high school in 1886, she worked briefly as a stenographer before entering the University of Chicago, reportedly with only $40 to her name. She took a full load of courses while working as a secretary to the university's president, which resulted in a nervous break-down after three years. She then spent some time recovering her health with relatives in Woods Hole, Massachusetts, before completing her un-dergraduate studies at Brown University, where she received a B.A. in 1899.

For six years, Slye taught pedagogy and psy-chology at Rhode Island State Normal School. In 1908, she accepted the invitation of an old ac-quaintance and professor at Woods Hole Marine Biological Laboratory to be his graduate assis-tant in the biology department at the University of Chicago. After briefly studying mice with ner-vous disorders, she became interested in the in-heritance of cancer. Most scientists at the time believed that cancer was spread through a virus, although some had suggested, with little hard evidence, that heredity might be a key factor in the development of the disease. Her supervisor was a proponent of the contagion theory, but Slye nonetheless began performing breeding ex-periments with her mice to research the heredity hypothesis. She used her own small income to fund these investigations, and is said sometimes to have sacrificed meals in favor of spending her money on feed for the lab mice.

In 1911, the well-endowed Sprague Memor-ial Institute was set up at the University of Chicago, and upon joining its staff that year Slye was provided with better facilities and substan-tially more money to conduct her research. Two years later, she presented her first paper to the American Society for Cancer Research, based on studies involving 5,000 mice. In the paper, she theorized that heredity played an important role in susceptibility to cancer and refuted the idea that cancer was a contagious disease. She was appointed director of the Cancer Laboratory at the University of Chicago in 1919, and by 1926 had been promoted to associate professor of pathology, which she remained until her retire-ment in 1944. In those years, Slye bred, cared for and kept family records on more than 150,000 mice, tracking those which developed cancer and those which did not. A strong propo-nent of keeping similar records on the human population in America (and, presumably, pre-venting human breeding when necessary), she firmly believed that such a registry could wipe out cancer. She kept an immaculately clean labo-ratory and took special care of her mice to pre-

Maud Slye

vent them from contracting other diseases that might skew her results or destroy the popula-tion. Her concern for the mice made her so fear-ful of leaving them in someone else's care that she did not take a vacation in 26 years.

Slye originally theorized that a single reces-sive gene was responsible for susceptibility to cancer, but she also recognized that gene suscep-tibility alone could not lead to the development of the disease in a mouse or a human being. The single-gene theory had been debunked by 1936, so Slye revised her original theory to suggest that two genetic factors were responsible—one to de-termine the type of cancer and the other to deter-mine its location. And although future research proved even her revised theory to be oversimpli-fied to the point of error, Slye's careful, compre-hensive studies helped establish the role played by heredity in determining an individual's sus-ceptibility to cancer.

Slye's contributions to cancer research were recognized with a number of honors, including a medal from the American Medical Association (1914), the Ricketts Prize from the University of Chicago (1915), an award from the American Radiological Society (1922), and an honorary doctorate of science from Brown University

(1937). She also published two volumes of poetry, *Songs and Solaces* (1934) and *I in the Wind* (1936). Maud Slye died of a heart attack in Chicago in 1954.

**SOURCES:**

Bailey, Brooke. *The Remarkable Lives of 100 Women Healers and Scientists.* Holbrook, MA: Bob Adams, 1994.

Block, Maxine, ed. *Current Biography 1940.* NY: H.W. Wilson, 1940.

Sicherman, Barbara, and Carol Hurd Green, eds. *Notable American Women: The Modern Period.* Cambridge, MA: The Belknap Press of Harvard University, 1980.

**Kimberly A. Burton**, B.A, M.I.S.,
Ann Arbor, Michigan

# Smart, Elizabeth (1913–1986)

*Canadian-born novelist and poet. Born on December 27, 1913, in Ottawa, Ontario, Canada; died of a heart attack on March 4, 1986, in London, England; daughter of Russel Smart (a patent lawyer) and Emma Louise Parr; graduated from Hatfield Hall in Canada; attended King's College in England; never married; children: (with poet George Barker) Georgina, Christopher, Sebastian, Rose.*

*Selected writings:* By Grand Central Station I Sat Down and Wept *(1945);* A Bonus *(1977);* The Assumption of the Rogues and Rascals *(1978);* Ten Poems *(1981);* Eleven Poems *(1982);* In the Meantime *(1984);* Necessary Secrets: The Journals of Elizabeth Smart *(1986);* Juvenilia: Early Writings of Elizabeth Smart *(1987);* Autobiographies *(1987).*

Born in 1913 in Ottawa, Ontario, Canada, Elizabeth Smart was the third child of Russel Smart, a patent attorney, and **Emma "Louie" Smart**, who highly valued their place in the social circle of Ottawa diplomatic and political life. Her mother would not permit her to attend college after she finished her studies at the private Hatfield Hall, so Smart and her sister instead spent a year in England. There she fulfilled her role as a debutante by studying music and violated it by attending King's College. On her return to Ottawa, she decided to pursue writing rather than music and wrote society notes and editorials for the *Ottawa Journal* before departing for the more literary environment of New York City. After she submitted some poems to Lawrence Durrell, Smart received an introduction to poet George Barker, with whom she would have four children and live with on and off for many years, despite the fact that he remained married to another woman.

Smart returned to Canada in 1940, living at Pender Harbour in British Columbia, where the first of her children with Barker was born in August 1941. During her stay at Pender Harbour, Smart wrote *By Grand Central Station I Sat Down and Wept* (1945), a lyrical novel in first person with a loosely autobiographical plot. The story of a passionate wartime affair which meets with social and legal repression, it depicts the impossibility of love in a brutalized world and the tragic predicament of a woman who views herself as condemned always to wait for a man over whose actions she can have no control.

Three decades would pass between this first novel and her second publication. During World War II, Smart lived with Barker in Washington, D.C., working at the British Army Office and then at the Information Office of the British Embassy. In 1943, expecting her second child, she arranged a transfer from Washington to London. Though she was dismissed from her job on arrival because of her pregnancy, she resolved to stay in England and over the next 20 years supported herself and her children with a variety of jobs in journalism, including writing for fashion magazines and doing advertising copywriting.

In 1966, Smart retired to a cottage in Flixton, north Suffolk. There she devoted herself to gardening, to raising two grandchildren, and, as evidenced by her journals during this period, to a long struggle with writer's block. *A Bonus*, a collection of poems published in 1977, reveals the preoccupations of Smart's life. It is an uneven book, reflecting its author's disdain for literary fashion and her ability to capture in an image or an epigram the wisdom and violence of her struggle. The great traditional theme of the garden dominates the book, its fertility and rampant energy moving the poet to meditations on her characteristic concerns of pain, futility, love, and death.

Smart's second novel, *The Assumption of the Rogues and Rascals*, was published in 1978. Employing a first-person narrator who sporadically observes her world and reflects upon it, this novel comments much more sharply upon the position of women in modern society than had Smart's earlier works. The novel as a whole presents its narrator's episodic discovery of her own strength and command of the "eccentric genes" necessary for writing. *Ten Poems* (1981) and *Eleven Poems* (1982) followed.

Published in 1984, *In the Meantime* is a varied collection of works—poems, an autobiographical sketch of childhood, a 1979 extract from her journals, and a biographical narrative, written in 1939, about Smart's lifelong sense of being haunted and determined by her obsessively protective mother. This story, "Dig a Grave and Let Us Bury Our Mother," is considered one of her most powerful works, and has been compared to *Djuna Barnes' novel *Nightwood* both in theme and style. Among the poems collected in *In the Meantime* is a sequence concerned with another aspect of Smart's last years, her return to Canada as a recipient of a Senior Arts Grant from the Canada Council in 1982. Living first in Toronto and then taking up an appointment as writer-in-residence at the University of Alberta in Edmonton, Smart sought understanding from a new generation of readers. She then returned to England, where she died in London on March 4, 1986, shortly after the publication of her journals as *Necessary Secrets*, which reveals the autobiographical basis of most of her works.

**SOURCES:**

Buck, Claire, ed. *The Bloomsbury Guide to Women's Literature.* NY: Prentice Hall, 1992.

Sullivan, Rosemary. *By Heart: The Life of Elizabeth Smart.* Flamingo, 1991.

Weir, Lorraine. "Elizabeth Smart," in *Dictionary of Literary Biography*, Vol. 88: *Canadian Writers, 1920–1959.* Second Series. Edited by W.H. New. Detroit, MI: Gale Research, 1989.

**Kimberly A. Burton**, B.A., M.I.S.,
Ann Arbor, Michigan

## Smeal, Eleanor (1939—)

*President of the Feminist Majority, and former president of the National Organization for Women (NOW), who led the national ERA campaign, discovered the gender gap in voting, and spearheaded feminist drives for more than a quarter of a century.* Name variations: Ellie. Born Eleanor Cutri on July 30, 1939, in Ashtabula, Ohio, but raised in Erie, Pennsylvania; daughter of Peter Cutri (a home builder, developer, and owner of a General Insurance agency) and Josephine Cutri (both first generation Italian-Americans); graduated Phi Beta Kappa from Duke University, 1961; awarded master's degree in political science and public administration from the University of Florida, 1963; completed work in 1971 for a doctoral degree, including a dissertation, except for footnotes and formal presentation, on "Attitudes of Women Toward Political Candidates"; married Charles Smeal, in 1963; children: Tod (b. 1964, a Ph.D. in molecular biology), Lori (b. 1968, a lawyer).

Awards: honorary doctor of law degree from Duke University (1991).

Lived in Ashtabula and Cleveland, Ohio (1939–49), Erie, Pennsylvania (1949–84) and Melbourne and West Palm Beach, Florida (1950s–66); moved to Pittsburgh (1967) because of husband's work; through books read while bedridden for a year because of back problems and complications after birth of her daughter, experienced feminist awakening (1969); joined National Organization for Women (1970); founded the South Hills Chapter of NOW (1971) and served as its president (1971–73); was a founder and member of the board of the South Hills NOW Day Nursery School (1972–77); became Pennsylvania NOW state coordinator and president (1972–75); served as NOW national board member (1973–75); served as member of the Bylaws, Budget, Financial Development and Conference Implementation Committees (1973–75); served as chair of the NOW national board (1975–77); served as president of NOW (1977–82, 1985–87); with Peg Yorkin, cofounded the Fund for the Feminist Majority and Feminist Majority Foundation (1987), and served as president (1987—).

Known throughout the nation as a leading advocate for women's rights, Eleanor ("Ellie") Smeal appears frequently on television and radio, testifies before Congressional committees on a wide variety of women's issues, and speaks to diverse audiences nationwide on a broad range of feminist topics. She has played a leading role in both national and state campaigns to win women's rights legislation and in a number of landmark state and federal court cases for women's rights.

The development of a feminist consciousness was the result of small awakenings. Smeal remembers keeping score for her father's boys' baseball team and realizing years later how much she had yearned to play instead; she remembers making Phi Beta Kappa at Duke University and being dissuaded from attending law school; she remembers spending a year bedridden after the birth of her second child and mulling over reasons why there was no disability insurance for homemakers; she remembers going to a bridge party one night to discover that every young suburban matron in the room was on tranquilizers except her.

One of the modern architects of the drive for women's equality, Smeal is known as both a political strategist and a grassroots organizer. In 1980, she was the first to identify the "gender gap"—the difference in the way women and men vote—and popularized its usage in the analysis of polling data and election returns to enhance women's voting clout. Willing to make waves, Smeal called for the women's movement, despite much controversy both in the media and the movement itself, to return to the streets in the mid-1980s to dramatize popular support for abortion rights. When many said it could not be done, she led the first national abortion-rights march in Washington, D.C., of over 100,000, and ten marches in cities across the nation.

In 1987, Smeal co-founded and became president of the Fund for the Feminist Majority and Feminist Majority Foundation. *Peg Yorkin, chair of the board of the Feminist Majority, gave the foundation $10 million, the largest single financial contribution to a feminist organization in history. The Fund for the Feminist Majority sponsors the "Feminization of Power Campaign," the largest state and national campaign to focus on recruiting record numbers of feminists to run for public office. Smeal toured the nation encouraging women to run for office from 1987 to 1992 and promoted the idea that women must flood the political tickets. Unless more women run, "Women would not have equality with men in Congress until the year 2333," she warned. She also promoted the passage of gender-balance laws requiring governors and mayors to appoint equal numbers of women and men to boards and commissions.

> $\mathcal{W}$e are determined to change the face of American politics until women are not only equal, but until there is justice in our society.
> —Eleanor Smeal

The Feminist Majority Foundation specializes in education and research projects aimed at empowering women. Smeal co-authored, with Foundation staff, *Empowering Women* reports in business, medicine and philanthropy, and works to break the glass ceiling barring women's advancement into leadership. Moreover, as the Foundation president, she spearheaded the largest public education campaign on the need for RU-486 or Mifepristone (the French abortion pill) and new contraceptive development. Smeal traveled to France and Germany to meet with scientists and pharmaceutical executives to win release of the chemical compound, which she believed, if widely available, would reframe the abortion debate. (While RU-486 was approved by the FDA in September 2000 and was hailed by women's and family-planning organizations, it was immediately subject to condemnation from anti-abortion groups. As well, some Republicans have successfully pushed for local laws that require the offices of doctors who prescribe it to meet the same physical standards as abortion clinics: number of rooms, width of hallways, number of employees, etc., to discourage distribution.)

Smeal, as president of the Feminist Majority Foundation, also co-authored and co-produced two award-winning 30-minute videos, *Abortion Denied: Shattering Young Women's Lives*, about the devastating impact of parental consent and notification laws, and *Abortion For Survival*, a documentary on abortion as a global public health issue.

Perhaps best known for her leadership in the National Organization for Women (NOW), Smeal served longer than any other president of NOW (three terms), from 1975 to 1982, and from 1985 to 1987. Under her guidance, NOW became the preeminent feminist organization in the nation. She directed a total administrative and ideological restructuring of the organization, taking it from a very small membership base to a mass membership base, and from a catalytic approach to political action.

Smeal's work at the grassroots level in Pennsylvania helped to spearhead the drive to integrate Little League baseball, to pass and then to enforce the Pennsylvania State Equal Rights Amendment, and to litigate numerous sex discrimination in employment lawsuits. With two small children of her own, she helped found a full-time day nursery school (7 AM–6 PM) which provided quality child care and promoted the teaching of democracy and the scientific method. Although Smeal's dream of having a feminist group meeting on every neighborhood block was not realized, she worked to found some 54 Pennsylvania NOW chapters statewide and advocated the formation of multiple NOW units in big cities, small towns, and suburban communities.

During the period from 1977 to 1982, membership in NOW increased six-fold and NOW's annual budget increased from $500,000 to over $10 million. During that same period, Smeal led the nationwide campaign for ratification of the Equal Rights Amendment and also spearheaded the drive for NOW to form political action committees (PACs). The number of NOW PACs at all levels—local, state, and national—increased during that time from 0 to 81.

Smeal was the first housewife to be elected president of NOW. She introduced the first Homemakers' Bill of Rights into Congress and fought to make Social Security benefits more equitable for homemakers and employed women. During her first term as NOW president, Smeal helped navigate passage of the federal Pregnancy Discrimination Act and to stop the Human Life Amendment, as well as to win a congressional extension for ratification of the Equal Rights Amendment.

Her reelection as president of NOW in July 1985 was characterized by the *Washing-*

*E*leanor
*S*meal

*ton Post* as "an important milestone in the feminist movement's continuing debate over its tactics and direction." Smeal had promised to go back to the streets to demonstrate the movement's political power and popular support.

Believing one must know one's opposition, Smeal led efforts to track anti-feminist extremists. She initiated an aggressive legal strategy to stop violence against clinics and health-care workers which was victorious before the Supreme Court in the *NOW* v. *Scheidler* case.

This work to counter anti-abortion extremists continues to date; the Feminist Majority Foundation's Clinic Defense project is the largest such effort in the nation.

Smeal has appeared on all network news shows including the "Today Show," "Good Morning America," and "Crossfire," as well as many of the best-known national TV shows such as the "Phil Donahue Show." Her leadership has been acknowledged by a variety of well-known publications. The *World Almanac* for 1983 chose her as the fourth most influential women in the United States; she was named by *Time* magazine as one of the 50 Faces for America's Futures in its August 6, 1979, cover story; and she was featured as one of the six most influential Washington lobbyists in *U.S. News and World Report*. In 1995, Smeal noted: "Before the late 1960s, women were just 3% of law students and 8% of medical students. Now, we're 40% of both. . . . In the 1960s, women were in only 20% of all job categories, mostly in those predominantly filled by women, such as secretaries, teachers, and nurses. . . . Now, we account for 25 to 30% of *all* professions. On the surface, this may seem a minor improvement. But given where we were just three decades ago, it's more like an explosion."

**SOURCES:**

*Carabillo, Toni, Judith Meuli, and June Csida. *The Feminist Chronicles, 1953–1993*. Los Angeles, CA: Women's Graphics, 1993.

*NOW Times.* 1977–1994.

Koeppel, Barbara. "The Progressive Interview: Eleanor Smeal," in *The Progressive*. November 1995, pp. 32–34.

Smeal, Eleanor. *Why and How Women Will Elect the Next President*. NY: Harper and Row, 1984.

**SUGGESTED READING:**

Davis, Flora. *Moving the Mountain, The Women's Movement in America Since 1960*. NY: Simon & Schuster, 1991.

**COLLECTIONS:**

Schlesinger Library, NOW papers, especially 1977–82.

**RELATED MEDIA:**

*NOW's 20th Anniversary* (2 hr. video), with over 100 celebrities, Peg Yorkin Productions, 1986.

**Toni Carabillo**,
author of *The Feminist Chronicles, 1953–1993*
(Women's Graphics, Los Angeles, 1993)

# Smedley, Agnes (1892–1950)

*American author, foreign correspondent, and leading defender of the People's Republic of China. Born Agnes Smedley on February 23, 1892, in Campground, Missouri; died of pneumonia in a nursing home, following a partial gastrectomy, in Oxford, England, on May 6, 1950; buried in China; daughter of Charles H. Smedley (an itinerant laborer) and Sarah (Ralls) Smedley (a washerwoman); attended Tempe Normal School (Arizona), 1911–12, San Diego Normal School, 1913–14, summer school, University of California, 1915, evening session, New York University, 1917; graduate work, University of Berlin, 1926; married Ernest George Brundin, on August 14, 1912 (divorced 1916); common-law marriage with Virendranath Chattopadhyaya, 1921–25; no children.*

*Family moved to various mining settlements in southeastern Colorado (1904); worked as part-time laborer before adolescence; became rural schoolteacher, Raton, New Mexico (1908–10); taught typing, San Diego Normal School Intermediate School (1914–16); was an activist for India liberation in New York (1917–20) and Berlin (1920–28); served as correspondent for Frankfurter Zeitung (1928–32), and for Manchester Guardian (1938–41); was a freelance journalist.*

*Selected writings:* Daughter of Earth *(Coward-McCann, 1929);* Chinese Destinies: Sketches of Present-Day China *(Vanguard, 1933);* China's Red Army Marches *(Vanguard, 1934);* China Fights Back: An American Woman with the Eighth Route Army *(Vanguard, 1938);* Battle Hymn of China *(Knopf, 1943);* The Great Road: The Life and Times of Chu Teh *(Monthly Review, 1956); (eds. Jan and Steve MacKinnon)* Portraits of Chinese Women in Revolution *(Feminist Press, 1976).*

On the western edge of Beijing, in an area know as Baboshan, a small marble monument bears the inscription: "In memory of Agnes Smedley, American revolutionary writer and friend of the Chinese people." Here, in the National Revolutionary Martyrs Memorial Park, lie the ashes of a foreign journalist who used all her talents to aid the Chinese Communist armies in their fight against Nationalist and Japanese forces. Indeed, it is in China that Agnes Smedley is best remembered.

There is far more, of course, to the life of Agnes Smedley. In her 58 years, she had been country schoolteacher, birth-control pioneer, crusader for the freedom of India, feminist activist, and novelist. Yet, during the 1930s, Smedley won fame by her crusade to publicize the suffering produced by the Japanese invasion and to make the cause of Chinese Communists known to the outside world. She sustained the longest tour in 1930s China of any foreign journalist, man or woman. State Department-hand John Paton Davies recalled Smedley wearing "a slumped fatigue cap pulled down to her ears over her lank bobbed hair, a wrinkled cotton

Agnes
Smedley

tunic and trousers, neatly wound cotton puttees, and cloth shoes."

As a war correspondent, Smedley shared the life of the troops—on foot, horseback, or (because of a back injury) on a stretcher. In September 1937, for an entire week, she lay flat on her back just outside of Xian in an old-style compound that just happened to be the headquarters of the Eighth Route Army.

Even then, though she tried in every way to share the privation of the troops, she always felt privileged. She wrote in 1938:

I will always have food though these men hunger. I will have clothing and a warm bed though they freeze. They will fight and many of them will die on frozen battlefields. I will be an onlooker. I watched them blend with the darkness of the street; they still sang. And I hungered for the spark of vision that would enable me to see into their minds and hearts and picture their convictions about the great struggle for which they gave more than their lives.

Agnes Smedley was born on February 23, 1892, in a windswept two-room cabin in Campground, Missouri. Her father Charles H. Smedley did odd jobs and possessed only a third-grade education. Her mother **Sarah Ralls Smedley** had only slight schooling; Sarah worked in the homes of others in exchange for food.

In 1904, the Smedley family moved to Trinidad, Colorado, where, Agnes later said, "Rockefeller's Colorado Fuel and Iron company owned everything but the air." The Smedleys lived in a tent on the Purgatory River; Charles hired himself out, hauling sand and bricks at three dollars a day. Soon, however, the river bed was flooded, and the family lost its meager possessions. Charles began similar work in Tercio, Colorado, while Sarah briefly ran the Tin Can Boarding House in Trinidad. Frequently drunk, Charles often abandoned his family. Sarah felt forced to become a washerwoman at $1.30 a day. The family moved frequently—from Trinidad to Delagua back to Trinidad again to Tercio.

The five Smedley children attended school irregularly, Agnes never finishing grade school. "I was in my early twenties before I learned who Shakespeare was," she later recalled, "and in my forties before I read his plays." Wrote Smedley:

> I fought boys with jimson weeds and rocks. Nothing could make a lady out of me. When I was nine my mother put me out to work washing dishes and caring for squawling babies.

Beginning at age 14, Agnes labored as a domestic, rolled cigars in a tobacco store, and aided her mother at the washboards. Early in 1908, she started teaching at a primary school in Raton, New Mexico, but the death of her mother of a ruptured appendix in February 1910 left her responsible for a household of four. After entrusting her siblings to others, she set out on her own. She recalled:

> I resented my mother's suffering and refused to follow in her footsteps. . . . It seemed that men could go anywhere, do anything, discover new worlds, but that women could only trail behind or sit at home having babies. Such a fate I rejected. . . . For years, I wandered from one job to another—stenographer, waitress, tobacco stripper, book agent, or just plain starveling.

In September 1911, she was admitted as a special student at the Normal School in Tempe, Arizona, where she was editor-in-chief of the student newspaper and supported herself as a domestic and restaurant dishwasher. On campus, she sported a gun and dagger and went by her Indian name of Ayahoo. (She had Native American blood on her father's side.)

At Tempe, Smedley met a young civil engineer, Ernest George Brundin, whom she married impulsively. Never desiring children, she had two abortions. In 1913, she entered San Diego Normal School, and within a year taught typing in its intermediate branch. In June 1916, the Brundins moved to Fresno, where Agnes briefly worked for the *Fresno Morning Republic*, but by the fall she returned alone to San Diego, her marriage in shambles. She had just resumed her post as typing instructor when Normal's president fired her for membership in the Socialist Party.

Moving to New York City, Smedley immediately became active in Socialist circles. Representing the People's Council for Peace and Democracy, a radical group opposed to the United States' entry in World War I, she preached the antiwar gospel outside factories. She also became a disciple of Lajpat Rai, founder of the India Home Rule League of America.

In 1918, Smedley was twice jailed, first in March and then in October, for violating the federal espionage act. Charges included seeking to incite rebellion against the British in India, thereby weakening America's major wartime ally, and passing herself off as a diplomat. She was also accused of illegally disseminating birth-control information. At one point she was held for six months in New York's famous Tombs prison, spending time in solitary confinement and becoming a celebrity among the city's liberal-left community. Released on bail early in December 1918, she wrote for the Socialist *Call* and ran the daily operations of the *Birth Control Review*. Dedicated as ever to the cause of India, she served as executive secretary of the newly organized Friends of Freedom for India, directed its India News Service, testified before a Senate committee, and arranged a major rally.

Always the rebel, Smedley left the United States in December 1920 without a passport, her indictment still pending. Serving as a stewardess on a Polish-American freighter, she jumped ship at Danzig and made her way to Berlin, then the center of the India nationalist movement in Europe. Originally, she sought to represent the India movement of America at a meeting in Moscow, but she soon became engrossed in a number of other projects—writing for radical American journals, teaching English at the University of Berlin, briefly attending graduate courses at the university, and fostering Germany's first state birth-control clinic. As noted by her biographers, the MacKinnons, Smedley's Berlin life centered on "shabby rooming houses in the company of impoverished students, penny-pinching landladies, and furtive revolutionary nationalists."

Soon after arriving in Berlin, Smedley became the common-law wife of Indian revolutionary Virendranath ("Viren" or "Chatto") Chattopadhyaya, who was nearly 20 years her senior. Her relationship with the high-caste cultivated Chatto was stormy to say the least, and she later recalled that it had such "endless difficulties" that:

> My desire to live ebbed and I lay ill for nearly three years. For whole days I remained in a coma, unable to move or speak, longing only for oblivion. . . . More than death I feared insanity, and the terror of this possibility haunted my very dreams. Once I attempted suicide, but succeeded only in injuring myself.

In 1923, Smedley wrote a friend, "I am wasting my life and know it, and yet there is no other way open to me. I am 31 years of age and still an ignorant, uncultured, undeveloped animal." When in 1925 she broke off with Chatto, she would never again play the role of a spouse, though she would subsequently have many lovers. Chatto later emigrated to Leningrad, married a Russian, and died in a labor camp sometime between 1938 and 1941.

At the suggestion of anarchists *Emma Goldman and Alexander Berkman, Smedley underwent psychoanalysis. Eventually her case study became the kernel of a semi-autobiographical novel, *Daughter of the Earth* (1929). The book described one Mary Rogers, who spent her childhood on a barren farm, "with a dissipated, half-Indian father, a weary drudge of a mother, and an ever-increasing brood of younger brothers and sisters." She wrote, "We belonged to the class who have nothing and from whom everything is always taken away." In this work, certain events and geographical data were changed.

In November 1928, Smedley left Germany for China, a land she saw as the focal point of the coming showdown between Asian nationalists and European imperialists. Initially, she had sought to write for the Indian press and to serve as a liaison between Indian and Chinese students. Arriving in Shanghai early in May 1929, she attempted to make contact with the Sikh community but found it bitterly factionalized. Her association ended when she returned home one day to find the severed head of a Sikh in her wastebasket.

Smedley's career was still unsettled. Until 1932 she was a special correspondent for the *Frankfurter Zeitung*, Germany's most influential newspaper, but for several years afterwards all work was freelance. From July 1933 to April 1934, she lived in the Soviet Union, receiving treatment for a heart condition at a Soviet sana-

torium in Kisolodsk in the Caucasus. Returning to New York in mid-September to find work as a foreign correspondent, she met with failure, and in October she went back to China.

Lack of permanent employment did not keep Smedley from writing. From 1932 to 1934, together with American Harold Isaacs, she published an English-language weekly *China Forum*. In 1933, her *Chinese Destinies*, a collection of old and new articles, was published. As her narrative was laden with stereotypes of lean and unselfish Communists fighting fat and grasping landlords, it failed to serve as effective journalism. Her *China's Red Army Marches* (1934) was equally partisan if a bit more concrete in data. It described the Red Army campaigns of 1927 and 1931 against the Guomindang in terms of dynamic guerrillas defeating depraved Fascist-led mercenaries.

Throughout her decade in China, Smedley remained the quintessential activist. In 1930, together with Lu Xun, then China's most gifted writer, and with Mao Dun, professor at Shanghai University, she helped organize the League of Left Wing Writers. She also aided in founding the China League for Civil Rights, a group that was dissolved after Guomindang assassins killed

*Postage stamp issued by People's Republic of China in honor of Agnes Smedley in 1985.*

***Song Qingling.***
*See Song Sisters.*

***He Zizhen.*** *See Jiang Qing for sidebar.*

its general secretary. In early 1936, she worked with ◀❀ Song Qingling, widow of revered head of state Dr. Sun Yat-sen, to establish the National Salvation Association, a group that sought joint Communist-Guomindang defense against the Japanese. Yet Smedley soon broke with Qingling over seed money allocated to an English-language journal, and the rupture always remained a bitter one.

In the early '30s, no other Western reporter had the access to the leadership of Chinese Communist Party (CCP) possessed by Agnes Smedley. In Shanghai, she attended party meetings, indeed was an integral, though ill-disciplined, part of the Comintern apparatus in China. At one point, Red Army commander Zhou Jianbing (Chou Chien-ping) clandestinely convalesced at her home. Smedley's radical activities did not endear her to Chiang Kai-shek's ruling Guomindang Party, which was quick to attack both her politics and morals. Because of tight surveillance from Shanghai's Guomindang and British police, she had to change her address frequently.

In fact, at one point, Smedley's closeness to CCP leaders hurt her with the Communists. When party chair Mao Zedong sought to establish initial contact with the Western press, he invited Edgar Snow, not Smedley, to his Yenan headquarters. Mao correctly saw Smedley as an out-and-out CCP partisan with limited access to the Western press, whereas Snow's articles had appeared in such journals as the *Saturday Evening Post* and the *New York Herald-Tribune*. Privately, Smedley burned with envy.

In the summer of 1936, Smedley set out for Xian, doing so at the request of Red Army commander Liu Ding. She was the only Western journalist present during the bizarre incident of December 1936, involving the capture and brief imprisonment of Chiang Kai-shek by warlord Zhang Xueliang (Chang Hsueh-liang). During the crisis, she served as a liaison with Communist forces, who were very much part of the negotiations with Chiang. Every night, she spoke from a local radio station, broadcasts that made Smedley an international figure but permanently stamped her as a Communist apologist. For example, on January 8, 1937, the *New York Herald-Tribune* carried her picture on the front page. The headline read, "American Woman Recruits Reds for Revolt in Northwest China"; the story hinted that she had been involved in dark intrigues against the Nationalist government. The Associated Press referred to her as "the one-time American farm girl who may become a virtual 'white empress' over yellow-skinned mil-

lions." Earl Browder, secretary-general of the American Communist Party, felt forced to deny that Smedley represented either the American or Chinese Communist Party. The New York *Daily Worker*, which always followed the Soviet stance, scolded Smedley for criticizing Chiang, whom it portrayed as leading an all-China coalition against Japan.

Finally in January 1937, Smedley received what she had long desired: an official invitation to visit Communist army headquarters in the mountain citadel of Yenan. During her half-year's stay, she directed a rat-extermination campaign, and—much to the chagrin of Yenan's women—taught square dancing to the troops. Her advocacy of free love further alienated the females within the camp. So did her reprimanding of young officials for being afraid of their wives. Mao's wife, ◀❀ He Zizhen, threatened to kill her but withdrew when Smedley reputedly flattened her with a single punch. Late in August, already *persona non grata*, Smedley fell off a horse, injuring her back. A month later, she left Yenan.

During her stay, she had sought to join the CCP but was rejected, an act that—in the words of the MacKinnons—was "a devastating blow from which Smedley never recovered." It was her unbridled individualism, noted her two biographers, that caused her rejection. As she herself said in 1943 about another Communist Party, the American one, "I never believed that I myself was especially wise, but I could not become a mere instrument in the hands of men who believed that they held the one and only key to truth."

Though always enthusiastic about the CCP, Smedley detested its leader, Mao Zedong, perhaps seeing him as responsible for her rebuff. She wrote in the 1940s:

> I saw Mao on many occasions in Yenan, either in the cave where he worked or elsewhere. I found him physically repulsive. It was difficult to meet his eye and he would answer my questions in a roundabout, impersonal way. There were times when he would not answer them at all, and [thus gave] me the impression that he had not heard them.

In July 1937, Smedley joined the Communist forces on the battlefront against the Japanese. These months were the happiest of her life, and in her book *China Fights Back: An American Woman with the Eighth Route Army* (1938), she ably shared her enthusiasm. Though chaotically organized and going so far as to boast that CCP troops were "sexual ascetics," it contained accurate combat reporting.

In January 1938, acting on instructions from the leading CCP general, Zhu De (Chu Teh), whom she greatly admired, Smedley went to China's provisional capital at Hankou. Here she became a publicist for Dr. Robert K.S. Lim's Chinese Red Cross Medical Corps. Though lacking all tact, she was able to extract contributions from American and British embassies, the Standard Oil Company, and such Guomindang officials as Foreign Minister T.V. Song. She even wrote a chapter on hospitals for a book edited by *Song Meiling, commonly known as Madame Chiang Kai-shek. Though she was out of sympathy with Chiang and the Songs, Smedley knew her effort would help injured troops. Extremely dedicated, she would transport wounded soldiers to hospitals at her own expense.

British journalist *Freda Utley, a close friend in Hankou during this time, offers the following description of Smedley:

> No picture of Agnes can do her justice. A high, broad forehead, with soft brown hair falling over her right temple, candid pale blue eyes which could wrinkle up in laughter, or look upon the world with passionate pity or fierce and scornful anger. She was one of the few people of whom one could truly say that her character had given beauty to her face, which was both boyish and feminine, rugged and yet attractive.

In November 1938, after Hankou fell to the Japanese, Smedley joined the New Fourth Army, a Communist guerrilla force. Until April 1940, she journeyed in the hills north and south of the Yangtze River, visiting resistance units under both Communist and Guomindang leadership. During her travels, she fostered medical centers and delousing stations, secured supplies from the Red Cross, and lectured on international affairs to peasants and army recruits. By now she was special China correspondent for the *Manchester Guardian*, and her articles appeared as well in such journals as the *China Weekly Review*, the *Nation, Asia*, and even *Vogue*.

In the summer of 1941, Smedley experienced malaria and malnutrition. That September, her gallbladder was removed in Hong Kong. She had reached the high point of her journalistic career, though she paid heavily for it in failing health. Her days in China were over.

Late in December 1941, she returned to the United States. While living in Ojai, California, she wrote *Battle Hymn of China* (1943), an extensive firsthand account. Preaching unity among all Chinese factions, she muted her attacks on the Guomindang. At the same time, she was so anti-Japanese that she accepted the verac-

ity of the Tanaka Memorial, a so-called Japanese blueprint for world conquest, long exposed as a forgery. For political reasons, she ignored the bitterness between the CCP and its foes and hid the strong personal loneliness she felt upon leaving Hankou. Similarly, in public, she was ardently pro-Soviet, for she was unwilling to criticize a major ally of China. In reality, according to the MacKinnons, "Stalinism repulsed her."

One of the few spiritually great people I have ever met.

—Freda Utley

As a writer, lecturer, and broadcaster, Smedley met with tremendous popularity in the years 1943–44. She even lectured to a special army training school at Harvard. Much of the time, she lived at Yaddo, a retreat for creative artists near Saratoga Springs, New York. But her fate was being sealed. She became more overtly pro-CCP, in the process attacking Guomindang leaders. For example, in 1943, she accused Song Meiling of living according to a standard "totally out of harmony with the bitter lives of the soldiers and common people of China." Publisher Henry R. Luce, she claimed, was following a "Guomindang line." Such rhetoric was bound to create enemies, and she in turn was subject to bitter attack from Representative Walter Judd (Rep.-Minn.), China editor J.B. Powell, and author Lin Yutang.

By 1944, Smedley was under investigation by the Federal Bureau of Investigation, and within two years she had made the FBI's special Security Watch List, those people subject to "custodial detention" in times of national emergency. Soon the FBI was accusing her of being a Soviet agent. By 1949, FBI observation was so severe that she sometimes hid in the trunk of a car when leaving her new residence in Sneeden's Landing, New York.

As the Cold War emerged, Smedley's popularity collapsed. During the Chinese civil war, she called the Communists the popular choice of the Chinese people and denounced the presence of U.S. Marine and naval forces in China. Still no Stalinist, she supported Marshal Tito's independent Yugoslav brand of Communism. In February 1949, a 33,000-word report issued from General Douglas MacArthur's Tokyo headquarters identified Smedley as a secret agent of the Soviet Union. She denounced the accusation as "despicable lies" and threatened to institute legal proceedings. Secretary of the Army Kenneth C. Royall publicly admitted that there was no evidence against her and apologized. Even after her death, however, Major General Charles A. Willoughby, MacArthur's chief of intelligence, repeated the accusation in his book *Shanghai Conspiracy: The Sorge Spy Ring* (1952), writing outright, "Smedley set up a spy ring in Peiping and Tientsin." In 1964, the leading authority on the subject, historian Chalmers Johnson, denied any espionage activities on Smedley's part though he did find her aiding masterspy Richard Sorge, a journalist who had been her lover, in establishing contacts in Beijing.

In 1949, Smedley moved to Wimbledon, England, where she found the cost of living cheaper. Suffering from heart trouble and insomnia, she hoped to complete her biography of Zhu De, published posthumously in 1956, while awaiting a visa to China.

Freda Utley, a former Communist who ended up a bitter foe of Stalin and Mao, found Smedley "a tragic figure, doomed to destruction by her virtues, her courage, her compassion for human suffering, her integrity and her romanticism." Although falsely accused of being a Soviet agent, Smedley was, if anything, a genuine anarchist. Captain Frank Dorn, U.S. military attaché to Hankou in 1938, accurately referred to "this intense, unhappy woman" as "a radical with a great heart," one who "refused to submit to any form of discipline and distrusted all political leaders."

Less than two weeks before she died, she wrote a friend:

> I am not a Christian and therefore wish no kind of religious rites over my body—absolutely none. I have had but one loyalty, one faith, and that was to the liberation of the poor and the oppressed, and within that framework, to the Chinese revolution as it has now materialized. . . . As my heart and spirit have found no rest in any land on earth except China, I wish my ashes to live with the Chinese revolutionary dead.

On May 6, 1950, Agnes Smedley died of pneumonia following a partial gastrectomy. Her request for burial in China was granted.

**SOURCES:**

MacKinnon, Jan, and Steve MacKinnon. "Introduction" to Agnes Smedley's *Portraits of Chinese Women in Revolution*. Old Westbury, NY: Feminist Press, 1976.

MacKinnon, Janice R., and Stephen R. MacKinnon. *Agnes Smedley: The Life and Times of an American Radical*. Berkeley, CA: University of California Press, 1988.

**SUGGESTED READING:**

Johnson, Chalmers. *An Instance of Treason: Ozaki Hotsumi and the Sorge Spy Ring*. Stanford, CA: 1964.

Shewmaker, Kenneth E. *Americans and Chinese Communists, 1927–1945: A Persuading Encounter*. Ithaca, NY: Cornell University Press, 1971.

Utley, Freda. *Odyssey of a Liberal: Memoirs*. Washington, DC: Washington National Press, 1970.

**COLLECTIONS:**

The papers of Agnes Smedley are located in the Hayden Library, Arizona State University, Tempe.

**Justus D. Doenecke**, Professor of History, New College, University of South Florida, Sarasota, Florida

# Smedley, Menella Bute

## (c. 1820–1877)

*English poet and novelist. Name variations: (pseudonym) S.M. Born around 1820 in Great Marlow, Buckinghamshire, England; died on May 25, 1877, in London, England; daughter of Edward Smedley (an encyclopedia editor, poet, and cleric) and Mary (Hume) Smedley; sister of writer Frank Smedley; educated at home by her father; never married; no children.*

*Selected writings:* The Maiden Aunt *(1848);* The Story of a Family *(1851);* The Use of Sunshine, a Christmas Tale *(1852);* Nina: A Tale for the Twilight *(1853);* Lays and Ballads from English History *(1856);* The Story of Queen Isabel, and Other Verses *(1863);* Twice Lost *(1863);* Linnet's Trial *(1864);* A Mere Story *(1865);* The Colville Family *(1867);* Poems *(1868); (with Mrs. E.A. Hart)* Poems Written for a Child *(1868);* Child-Nature *(1869);* Child-World *(1869);* Other Folks' Lives *(1869);* Two Dramatic Poems *(1874);* Silver Wings and Golden Scales *(1877).*

Born in Great Marlow, Buckinghamshire, England, Menella Bute Smedley was the daughter of Edward Smedley, a cleric, writer, and tutor, and **Mary Hume Smedley**. Sources differ about Menella's exact year of birth, which is estimated between 1815 and 1820; during childhood, her fragile health necessitated her living away from her parents for several years, presumably with relatives. The oldest of five children, she was later educated at home, receiving a thorough grounding in the classics—a rare privilege for a girl of the time—that served her well in her writing career. The family lived in London until her father's failing health caused him to retire and move with his family to Dulwich. Smedley assumed her father's professional responsibilities as his health continued to deteriorate.

Literary interests were endemic to the Smedley family, providing influences that helped shape Menella's writing career. Her father was an encyclopedia editor whose only volume of poems was published posthumously, while her brother Frank Smedley is best known for his popular boys' novel *Frank Farleigh*. More directly, Smedley's Aunt Hart, who wrote children's literature, encouraged her first efforts at writing, which were published under the pseudonym "S.M." Smedley, who never married, lived a productive life as a writer of poetry, novels, stories, and plays and as a philanthropist devoted to the education and training of poor children. Several of her books are geared toward children, such as *Poems Written for a Child* (1868), *Child-World* (1869), and *Silver Wings and Golden Scales* (1877).

Smedley's literary themes demonstrate her interest in English history, myths and fairy tales, Irish culture, women's roles in society, religious faith, death, and, enduringly, Italian independence (she wrote a number of poems extolling Garibaldi). One of her early novels, *Nina: A Tale for the Twilight* (1853), revolves around abducted girls, valiant Christian soldiers, seraglios, ruffians, and political intrigues involving monarchical succession. She explored similar story lines in *Lays and Ballads from English History* (1856), which methodically traces English monarchical history reign by reign in a series of poems. Christianity and the patriotic concept of England as the world's greatest nation undergirds the history, as does the celebration of British values.

The title poem of *The Story of Queen Isabel, and Other Verses* (1863) features a long narrative stylistically similar to the lays and ballads of the 1856 volume. Notable in this collection is Smedley's increasingly vocal criticism of the restrictive roles and inequities imposed on women by society, a standard romanticized through the medieval courtly love tradition and legitimized by Christian precepts. She was unwilling to address the connections between religion and women's traditional place in society, however, and the promotion of Christian values so central to her writing frequently borders on didacticism. A typical Victorian daughter in her devotion to her curate father and his mission, Smedley channeled her Christian beliefs into practical, rather than literary, modes of reform, by participating in charity work. Nevertheless, her work, while promoting Christian values, also depicts strong heroines who are loyal and courageous and do not hesitate to confront life-threatening events in defense of their convictions. The novels *Twice Lost* (1863) and *Linnet's Trial* (1864), and the tale "A Very Woman" (1849), for example, feature heroines who are drawn in terms of strength, loyalty, and intellectual vigor rather than feminine fragility.

Smedley's later poetry includes *Poems Written for A Child*, co-authored with **Mrs. E.A. Hart**, and the collection *Poems* (both 1868); the latter includes a five-act drama titled *Lady Grace*. She died in 1877.

**SOURCES:**

Kunitz, Stanley J., and Howard Haycraft, eds. *British Authors of the Nineteenth Century*. NY: H.W. Wilson, 1936.

Logan, Deborah A. "Menella Bute Smedley," in *Dictionary of Literary Biography*, Vol. 199: *Victorian Women Poets*. Edited by William B. Thesing. Detroit, MI: Gale Research, 1999.

Shattock, Joanne. *The Oxford Guide to British Women Writers*. NY: Oxford University Press, 1993.

**Kimberly A. Burton**, B.A., M.I.S.,
Ann Arbor, Michigan

# Smendzianka, Regina (1924—)

*Polish pianist. Born in 1924.*

Regina Smendzianka studied with Zbigniew Drzewiecki (1890–1971) in Warsaw. Besides carrying on an important concert career, she has also done significant work as a teacher. Her notable recordings include a superb performance of the Sonata No. 2 by Polish composer *Grazyna Bacewicz. She has also recorded Bacewicz's piano *Etudes*.

**John Haag**,
Athens, Georgia

# Smith, Abby and Julia

*Sisters and lifelong social and political reformers who refused to pay taxes unless they could vote and in consequence had their livestock seized.*

*Smith, Abby (1797–1878). Name variations: Abba. Born Abby Hadassah Smith on June 1, 1797, in Glastonbury, Connecticut; died in the same house in which she had been born on July 23, 1878; fifth daughter of Zephaniah Hollister Smith (a cleric turned lawyer) and Hannah Hadassah Hickok Smith (an astronomer, mathematician, translator and linguist); primarily educated at home by parents, supplemented by short stays at various schools and private tutoring; never married; no children.*

*Smith, Julia (1792–1886). Born Julia Evelina Smith on May 27, 1792, in Glastonbury, Connecticut; died in Hartford, Connecticut, on March 6, 1886; fourth daughter of Zephaniah Hollister Smith (a cleric turned lawyer) and Hannah Hadassah Hickok Smith (an astronomer, mathematician, translator and linguist); primarily educated at home by parents, supplemented by short stays at various schools and private tutoring; married Amos Parker, on April 9, 1879; no children.*

*Family moved back to Glastonbury (1795); both sisters lived at home with parents and three other sisters, learning and teaching; first mention of charitable work among free blacks (1819); Julia taught at Troy Female Seminary (1823) and returned home (1824); family joined Hartford Anti-Slavery Society, hosted abolitionists, distributed literature, initiated petitions (1830s–1860s); father died (1836); both became interested in Millerism (early 1840s); mother died (1850); Julia, with Abby's aid, translated the Bible five times (1847–1855); third sister, Laurilla, died (1857); second sister, Cyrinthia, died (1864); unfairly taxed by town of Glastonbury (1869); traveled together to the Connecticut Woman's Suffrage Association in Hartford (1869); first sister, Hancy Zephina, died (1871); Julia tried to register to vote and was refused (1873); both refused to pay taxes (1873); Abby spoke before town meeting (1873); both began to speak in public on suffrage (1873–78); both bought back seven Alderney cows seized for auction, garnered national attention (1874); Julia spoke at Worcester Convention for Woman's Suffrage (1874); Abby addressed a crowd outside town meeting from a wagon after having been refused a voice inside the building (1874), and spoke before the Woman Suffrage Committee of the Connecticut State Legislature (1874); both fought town's attempt to auction off Smith land (1874); Julia spoke at the National Woman Suffrage Association (1876); both bought back cows seized for auction twice more (1876); both won court appeal and regained land (1876); Bible translation published (1876); Julia addressed the Congressional Committee on Privileges and Elections (1878); auction of the contents of the Smith house by Julia's husband (1884). Publications by Julia:* The Holy Bible: Containing the Old and New Testaments; Translated Literally From the Original Tongues *(Hartford, 1876);* Abby Smith and Her Cows, With A Report of the Law Case Decided Contrary to Law *(Hartford, 1877).*

Abby and Julia Smith were the two youngest children of a remarkable family who lived in a small Connecticut farm town in the 19th century. The five daughters, along with their accomplished mother and father, formed what an observer called "a constellation of superior stars in an atmosphere of purity and intelligence," a household comprised largely of women whose words and deeds defy historical generalizations about male and female relationships, female education and capacity, and even the nature of reform movements such as abolition and woman suffrage.

The life histories of the Smith parents go a long way toward explaining how Julia, Abby, and their sisters made names for themselves and

their family, first in their small town and later in the entire nation. The father of this clan, Zephaniah Hollister Smith (1759–1836), was born on a farm in the Eastbury section of Glastonbury, Connecticut. In 1778, at age 20, he entered Yale College to study for the ministry and graduated four years later in spite of the hardships of the American Revolution, including food shortages and direct attack by the British. Zephaniah began his career as minister at the Congregational Church of Newtown, Connecticut, and at age 27 allied himself with a woman as spiritually and intellectually questing as himself.

**Hannah Hadassah Hickok** (1767–1850) was only 18 when she married, but she was already more educated and accomplished than most people twice her age. The only child of parents who believed in education for girls, Hannah grew up in South Britain, Connecticut. Her father David Hickok had been educated at Yale College and her mother **Abigail Johnson Hickok** was a prosperous and talented weaver. David Hickok farmed and taught local children, and his own daughter was his star pupil. A venturesome spirit with a fine mind, young Hannah learned astronomy and mathematics, creating her own almanac when such books were rare. She also built her own clock, developing a facility for mechanics that would stay with her throughout her life. An expert equestrian, Hannah, alone or with a female cousin, would ride to towns 80 or even 100 miles away to visit relatives. Perhaps Hannah's greatest gift was for languages, and she remained a poet and translator (from Italian and French) all of her life. Her diary does not tell us how she came to meet the young minister from Newtown, but they married on May 31, 1786, and almost immediately began a family.

In 1795, the young couple and their three little girls moved back to Zephaniah's hometown of Glastonbury five years after he gave up the ministry. After a brief period as a merchant, he became a lawyer, and Hannah gave birth to the last two of her brood. The Smith parents endowed each girl with an impressively elaborate appellation. **Hancy Zephina Smith** (1787–1871) combined both parents' first names, **Cyrinthia Sacretia Smith** (1788–1864) reflected the couple's knowledge of Latin and Greek, and **Laurilla Aleroyla Smith** (1789–1857) fulfilled her designation by becoming the "artistic one." Julia Evelina Smith (1792–1886) was named after *Fanny Burney's eponymous heroine, described as "well educated and accustomed to good company; she has a natural love of virtue and a mind that might adorn any station however exalted."

*Julia (left) and Abby Smith.*

Abby Hadassah Smith (1797–1878), the youngest, was the only sister with an "ordinary" Biblical name. The five girls and their parents lived together in the same house all of their lives—none of the sisters married except Julia, who wed after the last of her siblings died.

Though a distant relative maintained that as young women the Smith sisters made a pact not to marry, no evidence of this exists. In a newspaper interview given by Julia and Abby late in their lives, the sisters recalled that "their father had imbibed a prejudice against marriage laws, and a distrust of man's chivalry, while discharging his duties as a lawyer."

The family lived a quiet life, farming and learning. Their proximity to Hartford allowed a cosmopolitan escape from their rural simplicity. Zephaniah practiced law and served in the State Legislature and as justice of the peace. The five girls were extremely well educated, mostly at home by both their parents, where they pursued the same course of study mastered by young men preparing for Harvard or Yale. During short stints at schools including the Litchfield Academy, the Smith girls studied geography, grammar, composition, English literature, arithmetic, moral and natural philosophy, Biblical history, science, music and drawing. Tutors who visited the family to teach Latin and other subjects were soon succeeded by the older girls, who took on the task of instructing the younger ones. In order to improve their daughters' French, the Smith parents boarded out Julia and Abby with a refugee family from Haiti who had settled in New Haven. The plan worked. Both sisters gained in proficiency, which Julia maintained by keeping her diary in French for 32 years.

*Abby Smith and her cows are marching on like John Brown's soul.*

—Isabella Beecher Hooker

But even in this unusual company of intellectual achievers, Julia's commitment to the life of the mind stands out. Family stories relate how she persisted in studying Latin, though plagued by boys, and how, when her father failed to bring her a coveted Latin grammar, the 14-year-old rode to Hartford on horseback to fetch it herself. Whether or not these stories are apocryphal, they present a consistent view of Julia's character and her role in the family as "the scholar." As is often true in large families, each child marked out a position for herself: The oldest sister, Zephina, was musical, Laurilla painted, Cyrinthia proved an outstanding needlewoman, and Abby was the quiet, domestic one.

Even more than education, religion deeply influenced the personalities and lives of the Smith family. Many 19th-century Americans made the worship of a Christian God a central part of their lives, but, as might be expected, the Smiths' religious allegiance was even more intense and particular. Almost immediately upon his graduation from Yale, Zephaniah discovered the ideas of Scottish theologian Robert Sandeman, who claimed that knowledge of God, and hence salvation, could be achieved only by an intellectual apprehension of the Bible. Remarkably intolerant even for the time, the Sandemanians (or "Glasites") did not last long, perhaps because of their insistence on complete discipline and a return to early Church practices, such as "love feasts" and foot-washing. Perhaps they most horrified mercantile New England by their insistence on the literal interpretation of the Biblical injunction not "to lay up treasures upon earth," but rather to give all possessions to the poor and live by faith alone.

To Sandemanians, with their emphasis on individual experience, ministers were superfluous or dangerous. This attitude keenly affected Zephaniah and motivated him to abandon the ministry, the "preaching for pay," which decision triggered the family's move back to Glastonbury. Though none of the Smiths ever became an "official" disciple, the Sandemanian philosophy exerted a significant influence on the family's religious life, most obviously in their gradual spurning of the church and clergy and their conviction that faith led to action.

In 1823, at age 30, Julia Smith left home to join her sister Laurilla as a teacher at the Troy Female Seminary, run by *Emma Willard, in upstate New York. Julia instructed girls in French, Latin and arithmetic, while studying Euclidean geometry, which she speedily discovered she despised. She stayed only ten months, the presence of her beloved sister not sufficient to compensate for homesickness. Plagued by frequent headaches and sore throats, Julia returned to Glastonbury to resume her studious family life. In 1836, the domestic tranquillity was shattered by Zephaniah's death from a fall. The Smith women felt keenly the loss of their male protector and "public voice."

As young girls, and then as young women, the Smith sisters enjoyed active social lives, both within their home circle and with the local young people. But their lives were more profoundly shaped by work that came increasingly to occupy their time—charitable work, especially projects that brought them in contact with the small free black population of Glastonbury. Beginning in 1819, mentions of teaching and visiting these families appear in Julia's diary. Philanthropic efforts were part of many Northern middle-class women's lives; benevolent societies abounded in 19th-century America, driven usually by conservative impulses to safeguard the social order. But, as many scholars point out, such "traditional" activities often had radical implications, taking middle-class women out of their homes and exposing them to society's inequities. That was the effect charity work had on the Smith household. Early in the 1830s, the Smith sisters, led by their mother, became abolitionists.

Many respectable people were abolitionists by the Civil War, but such folk were considered dangerous and radical in the 1830s. Driven by their own day-to-day experience of the lives led by free blacks and by a religious faith that demanded social action, the Smith family, never having seen a slave, joined the Hartford County Anti-Slavery Society. They hosted meetings at their house, and Julia distributed an anti-slavery newspaper, *The Charter Oak*. Hannah and her daughters faithfully attended state conventions and meetings and entertained abolitionists in their home. It does not seem that the Smith family suffered censure from the town for their renegade stand, perhaps because of the family's prominence, perhaps because of their reputation for eccentricity. Regardless, it was a courageous stand to take.

Historians of the abolitionist movement have assembled a collection of characteristics of the early abolitionists, and at first glance the Smith clan seems to possess all of them. They were rural New Englanders, born between 1790 and 1810, well educated and troubled by spiritual discontent. But the Smiths were different in at least one important aspect. In contrast to many Northern abolitionists whose social imaginations were limited, the Smiths did not work for abolition only within their own social stratum. They did not hold themselves aloof from personal contact with blacks, nor did they believe them inferior. In their work, they constantly crossed color and class lines, taking anti-slavery petitions and newspapers to the workers in the mill and welcoming black leaders. During the winter of 1842, Julia recorded that she attended "the fair of the people of color" in Hartford.

Unlike many more moderate anti-slavers of this period, the Smiths followed famed abolition leader William Lloyd Garrison, for whom they literally provided a platform when mainstream churches in Hartford rebuffed him, in calling for immediate emancipation rather than colonization or other "halfway measures." The Smith women worked not just for slaves' freedom; their concern extended to the plight of "oppressed people of color," free blacks who daily lived with the burden of prejudice.

One of the chief strategies in the war against slavery was to present petitions to Congress, the petition being a traditional venue for the politically voiceless, especially women. Hannah Smith authored some of the earliest of the petitions that flooded Congress, prompting Southern congressmen to institute the notorious "Gag Rule," which prevented them being read. Outraged by what he considered an unconstitutional abuse of free speech, Representative John Quincy Adams read them anyway, to the fury of his colleagues and the growing approval of Northern Americans. The congressional reaction to women's petitions played a large part in convincing Northerners that the "Slave Power" was a threat to liberty. The Smiths sent numerous petitions, protesting not only slavery itself, but also the expansion of slavery into Western lands, the slave trade and colonization. Belying the stereotype of naive, female "do-gooders," the Smith petitions display the women's sophisticated understanding of abolitionist movements in England, Bermuda, and the Caribbean, as well as their facility with legal language, the latter due to Julia's study of law, which she mastered to such an extent that after her father's death she performed legal services for her neighbors.

Though the Smith family had lived outside of conventional church affiliations for decades, Julia's and Abby's major break came in the early 1840s when the sisters became involved in Millerism, the millennialist movement that would grow into the Seventh Day Adventist Church. A Vermont farmer, William Miller, claimed that the world would end in 1844, based on calculations made with Biblical information. Though Julia never admitted her involvement with Millerism, evidence exists that the Smith sisters took this prophecy quite seriously. On the last day of 1842, Julia Smith ended her diary after 32 years, expecting 1843 (the year Miller originally set as the planet's last) to usher in the Second Coming of Christ. Memoirs written by friends after the sisters' deaths state that at this time the sisters renounced the world, as many did, letting their plants die and preparing accession robes. However, on the appointed day, thousands of people gathered in groups to await their Savior, only to suffer the "Great Disappointment" at the coming of a new dawn.

Whether or not the stories about the Smith sisters' accession robes are true, there is no doubt that the "Great Disappointment" inspired Julia Smith's greatest work. When the end of the world came and went, Miller blamed his miscalculations on his reliance on Bible interpreters and "authorities." Julia compared her King James version with the Hebrew Bible and "saw by the margin that the text had not been given literally, and it was the literal meaning we were seeking." Thus, Julia, aided by Abby and a pious friend, **Emily Moseley**, began her unprecedented accomplishment—a literal translation of the Holy Bible, from the "Original Tongues." For eight years (1847–1855) Julia worked, learning Hebrew to add to her knowledge of Latin and Greek, often so immersed in her effort she did not hear the dinner bell. Moseley and the other Smith sisters met with her weekly to discuss her findings and to read from the small, hand-bound folios that eventually contained 10,000 pages. Abby was particularly committed to the task, often referring to the work as "our" Bible.

By 1855, Julia had translated the work not only once (the only single person in the world to have done so, for Bible translations were and are generally done by committee) but five times, working from Latin, Greek and Hebrew, each time striving to approach the original meaning. Her insistence on translating not for style but as closely as possible to the original renders the wording of this singular document somewhat wooden and decidedly odd. Julia Smith's version of Genesis 1:3 reads: "And God will say there shall be light, and there shall be light. And God will see the light that it is good, and God will separate between the light and between the darkness. And God will call to the light day, and to the darkness he called night: and the evening shall be, and the morning shall be one day."

Julia's mixing of the future with the past tense in the Old Testament, while peculiar to the ear, gives a surprising immediacy to the text. As she explains, "It seems that the original Hebrew had no regard to time and that the Bible speaks for all ages." For Julia, regularizing the tenses risked meddling with the sacred word. The awkwardness of her prose stems from her reluctance to sacrifice grammatical precision for the niceties of correspondence and translation. She thought that "the promiscuous use of the tense" signaled the reader not to depend on the word itself but to discover the hidden meaning, quoting St. Paul's contention that the "letter kills, but the Spirit gives life." Reflecting the Sandemanian emphasis on Bible reading, Julia believed that words were not an end in themselves but rather a channel through which God could communicate beyond language. Julia's Bible has also been called the "Feminist Bible," but it is important to note that it is not feminist in language or intent. Though she did prefer "Jehovah" to "Lord" or "God," and translated "*Eve" to mean "life," she made none of the inclusive modifications advocated by modern feminist Bible scholars.

In the midst of this activity, death began to affect the busy household of women. Hannah

died at age 83 on December 27, 1850. Seven years later, Laurilla died, and every seven years after that another Smith sister would be "freed by the Redeemer." By 1869, the remaining Smiths were old women. Cyrinthia had died in 1864, leaving 82-year-old Zephina, 78-year-old Julia and 72-year-old Abby. But the Smith women were not destined to pass out of life peacefully; on the contrary, in the years between 1869 and 1878, Julia and Abby achieved national fame.

The catalyst to this remarkable occurrence was their discovery that they, and two other single women, were being taxed at a higher rate than the men of their town. Julia protested to the tax collector, but to no avail. Spurred by their sense of injustice, Julia and Abby attended the first convention of the Connecticut Woman Suffrage Association in Hartford. The two elderly ladies listened to speeches by ◀❧ Isabella Beecher Hooker, *Elizabeth Cady Stanton, *Susan B. Anthony, their old colleague William Lloyd Garrison, and *Julia Ward Howe. The Smith sisters returned home resolved to work for woman suffrage, and henceforth presented their dispute as one of suffrage rather than mere unfairness. Their cry became: "Taxation Without Representation!"

Over the next nine years, the Smith sisters engaged in legal skirmishes with the town fathers of Glastonbury, conflicts detailed in *Abby Smith and Her Cows*, a small chapbook compiled by Julia in 1877. Their public activity was only temporarily stayed by Zephina's death in 1871. The local press embraced the story of the two old ladies and their fight for justice, and Julia and Abby kept the story and the flames alive by frequent letters and interviews. The town selectmen reacted to the negative press by trying to ignore the women, to the extent of not recording their words or their presence in town-meeting minutes. But the sisters were not deterred. When refused a voice in the meeting hall, they mounted a wagon outside the building and spoke. At the beginning of their struggle, though angry, they paid their taxes. Only after the town refused to allow them to register to vote in 1873 did Julia and Abby escalate their resistance and decide not to pay the annual tax.

On New Year's Day, 1874, the town took action against them, and this time the story made the front page of newspapers all across New England. The tax collector confiscated seven Alderney cows, beloved by the sisters as pets, and held them for auction. Sympathy for the sisters exploded across the region and then the nation. The names of the seven cows—Jessie, Daisy, Proxy, Minnie, Bessie, Whitey, and Lily—

❧▶

*Hooker, Isabella Beecher.* See *Stowe, Harriet Beecher for sidebar.*

became household words; prominent suffragists, like Stanton, Garrison and *Lucy Stone, publicly and privately supported the sisters; newspapers published poetic tributes and compared the incident to the Boston Tea Party, dubbing Abby "Sam Adams redivivus." At the auction, the sisters were able to buy back their property, in effect paying their taxes.

Over the next five years, the cows would see the auction block twice more, and the town, desperate and abashed, would resort to more and more devious methods to quell the rebellious sisters. They seized and auctioned off a valuable piece of land, an action which Julia and Abby fought in court, eventually proving it illegal in the State Supreme Court. Meanwhile, the sisters became increasingly active in the cause of suffrage, precipitating a shift in the family dynamics. Though both sisters were in demand at conventions and meetings, Abby, "the quiet, domestic one," became the public speaker of the family. A "Defense Fund" was established, and hair from the cows' tails was made into bouquets and sold to help defray legal costs.

The Smith sisters' suffrage message was as simple and as radical as their abolitionist credo—legal rights belonged to all, regardless of race or sex, and women were as fit as men (or fitter) to be citizens. Their suffrage speeches belie historical generalizations that suffragism was entirely a white, middle-class movement. At the Worcester Convention for Woman's Suffrage, Julia related that one of the town's arguments against giving women the vote was that it would "let in all the Catholic women and other good for nothing working women. We say 'do right and let the heavens fall,' leave the consequences to God." Indeed, Abby and Julia believed poor women needed the vote all the more to combat male physical cruelty and drunkenness.

Before they were done, both sisters would address the Connecticut State Legislature and the Congressional Committee on Privileges and Elections. They became elder stateswomen to a new generation of suffragists, symbols of the Revolution to the nation, and their battles served as potent reminders to a public celebrating a century of freedom. Julia and Abby undoubtedly knew they made good copy and responded with their characteristic intelligence and good humor, naming their new calves Martha Washington and Abigail Adams and two cows Taxey and Votey. Julia spoke of them during a speech at the National Woman Suffrage Association in Washington, D.C.: "It is something a little peculiar that Taxey is very obtru-

sive; why, I can scarcely step out of doors without being confronted by her, while Votey is quiet and shy, but she is growing more docile and domesticated every day, and it is my opinion that in a very short time, wherever you find Taxey there Votey will be also."

In 1855, Julia had been motivated to translate the Bible by religious rather than social concerns, but in 1875 her decision to publish her work resulted directly from suffragism and the battle with Glastonbury—"We thought it might help our cause to have it known that a woman could do more than any man has ever done." In a revelatory aside, she also disclosed that she wanted to be known as something more than Abby Smith's sister. A thousand copies, published with the sisters' own money, rolled off the presses in 1876. It was a women's project throughout—typeset by women (perhaps the first book thus set), proofread by a woman, and sold by female canvassers. It was quickly dubbed the "Alderney Edition," after the livestock that inspired its public appearance. In 1898, leading suffragists Elizabeth Cady Stanton, Lucy Stone, **Frances Ellen Burr**, and *Matilda Joslyn Gage published a commentary called *The Woman's Bible*, using Julia's translations as their ultimate Scriptural authority.

The Smith sisters traveled and spoke frequently until Abby's death on July 23, 1878, at age 81. The battle with Glastonbury ceased, and though the Smiths had won some legal points, no women could vote, and Julia was still liable for tax. Though Julia continued to speak on behalf of suffrage, she was slowed not only by age but her own personal circumstances. In 1879, at age 86, she married Amos Parker, an elderly lawyer from New Hampshire. Sadly, the marriage did not go well, and the last years of Julia's life were taken up by lawsuits brought by relatives who felt robbed of their expectations upon her marriage. Many of Julia's friends and neighbors sided with the relatives, suspecting that Julia had fallen under the influence of Parker, who, they surmised, had only married her to pass on her estate to his children. Their fears must have seemed realized when, under his orders in 1884, the contents of the Smith family's Glastonbury home were auctioned off.

In 1884, age 92, Julia gave a talk at the Connecticut State Suffrage Association to a delighted audience. In November 1885, she broke her hip, and she died on March 6, 1886. But trouble did not end with her death. Her will, which left everything to Parker, was contested by a neighbor who bore witness to another will that cut off Parker. In the end, Amos Parker prevailed and received Julia's estate, perhaps against her wishes. But Julia Smith, true to form, had the last word—she is buried under her father's name, in the Glastonbury cemetery, in proper family order, between Laurilla and Abby.

At the end of their lives, so many of the goals for which Julia and Abby fought remained unfulfilled—women still did not have the vote in America; as they feared, abolition of slavery did not uproot racial prejudice; and Julia's Bible remained a freak curiosity. But if the "Spirit gives life," these two women stand as exemplars of faith in action, and it is unlikely that they mourned lives devoted to spiritual enlightenment and social justice. Surely, even by their own stringent standards, they had, as Julia Smith translated: "contested earnestly the good contest . . . completed the course . . . and kept the faith."

**SOURCES:**

Housley, Kathleen L. *The Letter Kills But the Spirit Gives Life: The Smiths—Abolitionists, Suffragists, Bible Translators.* Glastonbury, CT: Historical Society of Glastonbury, 1993 (provides the most lively, readable and complete account of the Smith family to date; contact the Glastonbury Historical Society to obtain a copy).

Shaw, Susan J. *A Religious History of Julia Evelina Smith's Translation of the Holy Bible: Doing More Than Any Man Has Ever Done.* San Francisco, CA: Mellen Research Press, 1993.

Smith, Julia Evelina. *Abby Smith and Her Cows, With A Report of the Law Case Decided Contrary to Law.* NY: Arno Press, 1972 (contains a collection of newspaper clippings and a trial transcript).

Speare, Elizabeth G. "Abby, Julia, and the Cows," in *American Heritage.* June 1957, Vol. VIII, no. 4, pp. 54–57, 96.

Stern, Madeline B. "The First Feminist Bible: The 'Alderney' Edition, 1876," in *Quarterly Journal of the Library of Congress.* Vol. XXXIV, no. 1, 1977, pp. 23–31.

**COLLECTIONS:**

Historical Society of Glastonbury owns most of their papers.

**RELATED MEDIA:**

"Abby, Julia and the Seven Pet Cows," teleplay broadcast on "Telephone Time," CBS, January 7, 1958, starring *Judith Anderson.

**Catherine A. Allgor,**
Assistant Professor of History,
Simmons College, Boston, Massachusetts

# Smith, Ada (1894–1984)

*African-American jazz singer and celebrated Parisian club owner. Name variations: Bricktop; Brickie. Born Beatrice Queen Victoria Louise Virginia Smith in Alderson, West Virginia, on August 14, 1894; died in New York on January 31, 1984; third daughter and youngest of five children of Hattie (Thompson) Smith and Thomas Smith; married Peter Ducongé (a saxophonist), in 1929 (separated 1933, never divorced).*

Paris in the early 20th century was the place of choice for those who loved good times and good music. People came from all over the world to enjoy life in this lively city and many of them were African-American entertainers. One such was Ada Smith, also known as Bricktop. She began dancing and singing as a child in Chicago where her mother moved after her father's death in 1898. **Hattie Smith,** who had been born into slavery around 1861, ran rooming houses and worked as a maid. Ada played Harry in *Uncle Tom's Cabin* at Chicago's Haymarket Theater when she was four or five years old. At age 14, she was in the chorus at the Pekin Theater, the first theater of consequence in Chicago to devote its playbill to black drama.

By age 16, she was touring with the Theater Owners' Booking Association (TOBA). Barron Williams, owner of Barron's Exclusive Club in New York City, gave Smith the name Bricktop because of her flaming red hair and freckles. By age 20, she had traveled throughout the United States and moved on to Europe. In 1924, she opened her own club on Rue Pigalle in Paris which she called Chez Bricktop. Celebrities flocked there. Evelyn Waugh, John Steinbeck, *Josephine Baker, and Ernest Hemingway were only a few of her regular patrons. Another was the prince of Wales who eventually became King Edward VIII until he gave up the throne to marry the woman he loved, Mrs. Wallis Simpson (*Wallis Warfield, duchess of Windsor). Smith taught His Royal Highness how to do the dance called the Blackbottom. In 1929, she married the saxophonist Peter Ducongé, and the two settled into an estate in Bougival, outside Paris. She then opened a new, better, and bigger Bricktop in 1931, hiring on her constant companion and friend *Mabel Mercer to be her assistant. That same year, Smith opened another café in Biarritz for the summer season. Cole Porter arrived in Paris with the song "Miss Otis regrets, she's unable to lunch today." There is some dispute as to whether it was written for Bricktop or their mutual friend *Elsa Maxwell, but Smith performed it regularly to the delight of her oft-requesting audience.

When war threatened, Smith left Paris in October 1939, with the help of the duchess of Windsor and *Elsie de Wolfe; Smith was one of the last American entertainers to leave France. Returning to New York, she headed straight for Harlem. "Across the pond things are different. Negroes were as welcome in my place as any of the ritziest white people. I made no distinction. In America it's far different and one finds himself at wit's end to keep clear of ugly or embarrassing situations." Despite the segregated clubs,

Smith became a well-known host in café society. With other nightclub operators, she opened the Brittwood on 140th Street in 1940. Though at first successful, she never quite regained her Paris popularity. In 1943, she moved to Mexico City where she stayed for six years.

After the war, Smith returned to Paris (1949). But "the Paris Smith returned to was vastly different from the pre-war days," writes **Juanita Karpf** in *Notable Black American Women.* "Parisians had begun to reflect some of the distinctly American attitudes towards blacks—an attitude Smith believes was imported and perpetuated by white American soldiers." Ada Smith persevered and the new Bricktop opened in May 1950. "Her opening night," wrote *\*Janet Flanner, "was an extraordinary, chic jam of people." But by Christmas business was off, and the club was eventually closed.

Smith left for Rome in 1951 and opened a club on the Via Veneto. Having converted to Catholicism in 1943, she became involved in Italian charities, raising money for the housing of war orphans. She also became close friends with Bishop Fulton J. Sheen. After retiring, Smith returned to the United States in 1964. In 1970, she released her only recording ("So Long, Baby"). In 1973, she made a documentary, *Honeybaby, Honeybaby!* A decade later, she published her autobiography, *Bricktop.* When she was 89, Mayor Ed Koch gave her New York City's seal and a certificate of appreciation for her "extraordinary talent and indomitable spirit." Ada Smith died in her sleep on January 31, 1984, and was buried in Woodlawn Cemetery in the Bronx.

**SOURCES:**

Sadie, Stanley, ed. *New Grove Dictionary of Music and Musicians.* 20 vols. NY: Macmillan, 1980.

Smith, Jessie Carney, ed. *Notable Black American Women.* Detroit, MI: Gale Research, 1992.

**SUGGESTED READING:**

Bricktop [Ada Smith Ducongé], with James Haskins. *Bricktop.* NY: Athenaeum, 1983.

**COLLECTIONS:**

Personal papers housed in the Schomburg Center for Research in Black Culture, New York City.

**John Haag**,
Athens, Georgia

## Smith, Alexis (1921–1993)

*Canadian-born actress. Born Gladys Smith on June 8, 1921, in Penticton, British Columbia, Canada; died on June 9, 1993, in Los Angeles, California; attended Los Angeles City College; married Craig Stevens (an actor), in 1944; no children.*

*Selected filmography:* The Lady with Red Hair *(1940);* Steel Against the Sky *(1941);* Dive Bomber *(1941);* Gentleman Jim *(1942);* The Constant Nymph *(1943);* The Adventures of Mark Twain *(1944);* The Doughgirls *(1944);* The Horn Blows at Midnight *(1945);* Conflict *(1945);* Rhapsody in Blue *(1945);* San Antonio *(1945);* Of Human Bondage *(1946);* Night and Day *(1946);* Stallion Road *(1947);* The Two Mrs. Carrolls *(1947);* The Woman in White *(1948);* The Decision of Christopher Blake *(1948);* Whiplash *(1948);* South of St. Louis *(1949);* Any Number Can Play *(1949);* One Last Fling *(1949);* Montana *(1950);* Undercover Girl *(1950);* Here Comes the Groom *(1951);* The Turning Point *(1952);* Split Second *(1953);* The Sleeping Tiger *(UK, 1954);* The Eternal Sea *(1955);* Beau James *(1957);* This Happy Feeling *(1958);* The Young Philadelphians *(1959);* \*Jacqueline Susann's Once Is Not Enough *(1975);* The Little Girl Who Lives Down the Lane *(Can., 1977);* Casey's Shadow *(1978);* La Truite *(The Trout, Fr., 1982);* Tough Guys *(1986).*

A statuesque beauty who played leads or second leads in Hollywood movies of the 1940s and 1950s, Alexis Smith retired from films in 1959, then made a stunning Broadway comeback in Stephen Sondheim's hit musical *Follies* (1971), for which she won a Tony Award as Best Actress. With her career reignited, she worked almost up until her death from cancer in 1993. The actress' long-time marriage to actor Craig Stevens was one of Hollywood's more enduring relationships.

Smith was born in 1921 in Penticton, British Columbia, Canada, and gained some of her early acting experience in summer stock. She was a student at Los Angeles City College when a Warner Bros. talent scout spotted her in a school production and arranged for a screen test. As a result, Smith signed a long-term contract with the studio and throughout the '40s and '50s, appeared in such movies as *Dive Bomber* (1941), *Doughgirls* (1944), and *The Woman in White* (1948). Usually playing pretty, resourceful, and slightly remote characters, she appeared with some of Hollywood's most popular leading men, including Errol Flynn (*San Antonio*, 1945), Cary Grant (*Night and Day*, 1946), Ronald Reagan (*Stallion Road*, 1947), and Clark Gable (*Any Number Can Play*, 1949). Smith left films after appearing in *The Young Philadelphians* (1959).

Following a 16-year hiatus, she opened in *Follies*, a musical centering around a bittersweet reunion of aging showgirls in a Broadway theater scheduled for demolition. Smith provided one of the evening's highlights with her rendition of "Could I Leave You?," as much a tirade as a song, leveled against her philandering husband. Following her triumph in *Follies*, Smith appeared in several movies and on Broadway in *The Women*, *Summer Brave*, and the musical *Platinum*, in which she played a fading movie star who attempts a comeback as a rock singer. Although Smith received good reviews, the show closed prematurely. The actress also had a recurring role in the television series "Dallas" (1984), and in 1988 was in the short-lived television drama "Hothouse."

**SOURCES:**

Katz, Ephraim. *The Film Encyclopedia*. NY: Harper-Collins, 1994.

"Obituaries," in *The Day* [New London, CT]. June 10, 1993.

**Barbara Morgan**,
Melrose, Massachusetts

## Smith, Alys Pearsall (1866–1951).

*See Berenson, Mary for sidebar on Alys Smith Russell.*

# Smith, Amanda Berry (1837–1915)

*Slave-born Protestant evangelist and missionary. Born Amanda Berry on January 23, 1837, in Long Green, Maryland; died of a paralytic stroke in Sebring, Florida, on February 24, 1915; daughter of Samuel Berry and Miriam Matthews, slaves on adjoining farms; married Calvin Devine, in September 1854; married James Smith, in 1863; children: (first marriage) name unknown (died in infancy) and Mazie; (second marriage): Nell, Thomas Henry, and Will.*

*Began career as itinerant evangelist in Holiness circles (1869); traveled to England to preach (1878) and left to become missionary to India (1879); worked as missionary in West Africa (1882–89); traveled to Great Britain before returning to the U.S. and settling in the Chicago area; began work on establishment of orphanage for African-American children (1895); opened Amanda Smith Orphan's Home for Colored Children (1899); moved to Florida (1912).*

Amanda Berry Smith was born into bondage in Long Green, Maryland, in 1837, the daughter of slaves living on adjoining farms. Her father Samuel Berry earned the money to purchase his freedom by working late into the night, making brooms and husk mats to sell at a local market. Buying the freedom of his wife **Miriam Matthews** and their five children proved to be much harder, however, and it was only because of a promise made on her deathbed by the mistress of Miriam Matthews that they were finally freed.

The family lived as "freedmen" in Maryland for a short time, then took jobs on the farm of John Lowe in Pennsylvania. Sam Berry's house became a regular stop for runaway slaves on the Underground Railroad, and Amanda Smith's recollections of her girlhood are filled with stories of courage and fear as the family hid runaways between the bed ropes and mattresses and watched in horror as the bloodhounds attacked fugitives near their home.

Amanda was educated primarily by her parents, who could both read and write. She did attend school briefly when she was eight and again when she was thirteen, but she taught herself how to read by cutting out large letters from a newspaper and asking her mother to arrange them in words on a windowsill. Throughout her life, she was an avid reader of the Bible and religious literature, and as a mother she would work with great determination for the education of her daughter **Mazie Devine** and her adopted African son Bob in the face of grave financial obstacles.

When Amanda was 13, she became a domestic servant in a small town near York, Pennsylvania. One night she attended a revival meeting in a local Methodist church. While she was seated at the back because she was the only African-American present, a white woman in the audience invited Smith to repent her sins and accept Jesus as savior. "I went home and resolved I would be the Lord's and live for him," wrote Smith. Amanda and her parents joined a Methodist church, but when she attended her class meeting, the small support group for prayer and study in the Methodist tradition, she was required to wait until the prayers of the white members were ended before she could speak. As a result, she would be late in arriving at her employers' to serve Sunday dinner. Pressure from her employers and a study of books which were critical of Christianity temporarily cooled her religious passion.

Amanda continued to earn her living as a live-in servant in families in eastern Pennsylvania and the Baltimore area. In 1854, she married her first husband Calvin Devine, who soon proved to be a heavy drinker, although "in many things he was good." Her first child died in infancy, and in 1855 she fell dangerously ill. Near death, she had a vision, first of an angel standing at the foot of her bed, telling her to "go back," and then of herself preaching at a large camp meeting. Although it would be some time before she found inner peace, the vision and her recovery rekindled her dedication to Christianity.

By the start of the Civil War, Amanda had a daughter Mazie. Her husband enlisted in the

Union army, was sent to the South, and was never heard from again. In a desperate financial plight, Amanda moved to Philadelphia and did laundry, ironing, cleaning and cooking, boarding the child out with a succession of families. In 1863, it was primarily the promise of a stable home, and a chance to begin her evangelistic work, that moved Amanda to marry James Smith, a deacon in the African Methodist Episcopal Church. The opportunity for financial security proved false when James lost interest in becoming a licensed preacher, reducing his chances of an adequate income for the family. The marriage was not a happy one, and the family was in constant need.

In 1865, they moved to New York City, where James took a job at Leland's Hotel. Their material circumstances were not much improved, and loneliness drove Amanda to join women's societies for the wives of master masons. She continued to take in washing and ironing and hired herself out as a maid; at times, conditions were so spartan that an ironing board served as her bed. When James accepted a better job as a coachman in New Utrecht, New York, Amanda did not go with him, refusing to be uprooted again. Another reason was religion. By this time, her spiritual life was also being renewed.

An acquaintance in New York had told her about the experience of sanctification, a key concept in an important Protestant movement in America known as the Holiness movement. Sanctification involved much more than simply the forgiveness of sins based on a person's belief in Jesus. A sanctified Christian was so closely directed by God that she or he rarely sinned intentionally; if ordinary conversion were like God's moonlight, sanctification was like his sunlight, permeating all the dark corners of the heart. This was, in Smith's words, "the pearl of greatest price—the blessing of a clean heart." Smith claimed to have such an experience in September 1868, while listening to the preaching of John Inskip at the Green Street Church in New York City.

During her second marriage, Smith gave birth to three children, all of whom died at a young age. After the death of her husband in 1869, she was poised to begin her career as an evangelist with the particular message that the complete Christian was the sanctified Christian. She resolved to work "in God's vineyard," as he directed. She continued to support herself as a cook and cleaning woman, as well as taking in mending and laundry, but she rejected positions as a live-in domestic servant because they would require her to work on Sundays. She passed out

tracts about sanctification in the street, spoke privately to people about the experience in their homes, addressed small prayer groups and sang in African-American and white Methodist churches in Brooklyn and Harlem, gradually widening her audiences until she was also speaking at revivals.

Smith once referred to herself as a "speckled bird" among her people, indicating that she was regarded as an oddity, and even a threat. The public view of her was partly due to her modest circumstances and her plain Quaker style of dress, but it was also due to her message and the fact that she was a woman. The doctrine of sanctification was controversial, contested by many Christian leaders who doubted the reality of such an experience, declaring that it was extreme arrogance to even consider the possibility of existing in such a sinless partnership with God.

> *I* have been bought twice and set free twice, and so I feel I have a good right to shout.
>
> —Amanda Berry Smith

Until 1869, Smith's evangelism was confined to the area around New York City. In November of that year, she claims, she was called directly by God while sitting in church one Sunday. She had a vision of the word "Go" in the front of a church and then distinctly heard the word "preach." Although she was virtually penniless, she moved to Salem, New Jersey, where she remained until June 1870, launching a decade of service as an itinerant preacher throughout the northeastern United States. She was in particular demand at Holiness camp meetings. Throughout her travels, Smith believed that God put the seal of approval on her labors by providing money when it was needed, and a rich harvest of souls.

In front of her audiences, Smith would sometimes merely describe her experience of sanctification and sing a beloved hymn; at other times, however, her "exhortations" based on texts from the Bible caused consternation, by coming very close to formal preaching. Over the years she found many churches closed to her because she was a female evangelist, and once she began traveling widely she often had to contend with protests in local newspapers.

In 1872, Smith felt called to attend the general conference of the African Methodist Episcopal Church in Nashville, despite the fact that she was discouraged by men in her denomination who feared she represented a faction within the church which supported the ordination of women. The ordination issue was never raised, but Smith felt the rebuff of the church's leaders and their well-dressed wives. In her autobiography she writes, "I give this little story in detail, to show that even with my own people, . . . I have not always met with the pleasantest things. But I still have not backslidden, nor felt led to leave the church." Nevertheless, her presence and reputation kept alive the question of the role of women in the church. In 1884, her influence helped to persuade the church to license women as evangelists, and in 1890, it helped to create the position of deaconess for women committed to social work.

The A.M.E. conference was forced to acknowledge Smith's influence, not only because of her work in its own churches, but because of the following she built up among white audiences, especially at camp meetings. Racism, however, was clearly another obstacle in her work. Because she was an African-American, there were many restaurants and hotels where she could not stop when traveling, and she was sometimes insulted by members of the white congregations to whom she preached. After she became well known, she was sometimes asked if she would not prefer to be white, to which she would reply, "No, we who are the royal black are very well satisfied with His gift to us in this substantial color. I, for one, praise Him for what He has given me, although at times it is very inconvenient." When her crusade eventually took her to Egypt, the beauty and the strength of the black men and women she saw reinforced her pride in her race, as did her realization that God had chosen Egypt as the hiding place for the infant Jesus and the home of Moses.

In 1878, Smith overcame her fear of the sea and sailed for England to visit the great Holiness gathering at Keswick. On board the *Ohio*, she raised many eyebrows as a black woman traveling without an escort, but she struck up a friendship with Quakers, who were accustomed to female preachers and encouraged her to hold services for the passengers.

Smith toured England as an itinerant preacher, speaking outdoors, in public halls and in Baptist and Methodist churches, her expenses for the journey met by friends. Her sincerity and fervor, accompanied by a rich contralto voice, won her wide acclaim, even from those who had never heard a woman formally address an audience. During the tour she met missionary **Lucy Drake**, who persuaded Smith to accompany her back to India. After visiting Paris and Rome, they arrived in Bombay in November 1879. Two months later, Smith began a tour of the mission stations and churches in India, advocating the doctrine of sanctification and encouraging abstinence from alcohol. Temperance became an important theme of her overseas work after she witnessed the extensive importation of alcohol into India and Africa by European merchants.

In Smith's *Autobiography*, she recalls a service in which she gave her views on the famous passage in I Corinthians 14, in which the apostle Paul directed that "women keep silent in the churches." In the only time she chooses to address this issue directly, she explains her belief that Paul meant in this case for women and men to keep silent while another was speaking, so as to preserve the good order of the Christian community. The evangelist was convinced that God had kept the promise he made through the ancient prophet Joel, who wrote that the spirit of God would someday descend upon both the sons *and* daughters of Israel.

In 1881, Smith was back in the U.S. when she set sail again, making a brief stopover in England before heading for Monrovia to begin a new chapter in her evangelical endeavors. As a child she had heard her parents speak of Africa, and she had read a newspaper which featured scenes from native villages; years later, however, while attending a mission day at a Holiness camp meeting, she had been struck by the realization that none of its programs were directed toward the continent of Africa. At first she resolved to prepare her daughter to pursue this crusade, but Mazie did not share her mother's evangelical zeal, and it was not until 1881 that Smith herself could act on her concerns.

Beginning in Monrovia, she conducted tours of the kind she had started in India, but this time between bouts of fever. She worked closely with local church leaders, including the Methodist bishops. She remained in West Africa for eight years, primarily in Liberia and Sierra Leone.

In 1890, Smith returned to the U.S., and after a brief period of itinerant preaching she settled into a Chicago suburb to write her *Autobiography*. Although suffering from chronic rheumatism, she also purchased land there to establish an orphanage for African-American children. The institution languished, however, because of a perpetual lack of funding, and was eventually destroyed by fire.

For a brief period in her life, when she lived in Philadelphia, Smith had owned property; in 1912, she gratefully accepted the offer of a house in Sebring, Florida, to which she could retire. It was there that she died, in 1915, of a stroke.

SOURCES AND SUGGESTED READING:

Cadbury, M.H. *The Life of Amanda Smith*. Birmingham, England: 1916.

Smith, Amanda Berry. *An Autobiography; The Story of the Lord's Dealings with Mrs. Amanda Smith the Colored Evangelist*. With an introduction by Jualynne E. Dodson. NY: Oxford University Press, 1988.

"Smith, Amanda Berry," in *Notable American Women 1607–1950: A Biographical Dictionary*. Vol. 3. Edited by Edward T. James. Cambridge, MA: The Belknap Press of Harvard University, 1971.

Taylor, Marshall William. *The Life, Travels, Labors and Helpers of Mrs. Amanda Smith; the Famous Negro Missionary Evangelist*. Cincinnati, OH: printed by Cranston & Stowe for the author, c. 1886.

**Barbara J. MacHaffie**,
Associate Professor of History and Religion,
Marietta College, Marietta, Ohio

## Smith, Barbara Leigh (1827–1891).

*See Bodichon, Barbara.*

## Smith, Bathsheba (1822–1910)

*General president of the Relief Society of the Church of Jesus Christ of Latter-day Saints. Born Bathsheba Wilson Bigler on May 3, 1822, in Shinnston, Harrison County, Virginia (which became part of West Virginia after the Civil War); died in 1910; seventh of eight children of Mark Bigler and Susannah (Ogden) Bigler; married George A. Smith, on July 26, 1841 (died 1875); children: George A. Smith, Jr. (b. July 7, 1842, killed in an Indian raid in southern Utah on November 2, 1860); Bathsheba Smith, known as Kate (b. August 14, 1844, who married Clarence Merrill); John Smith (b. March, 1847, and died the same day).*

The seventh of eight children, Bathsheba Smith was born on May 3, 1822, on her parents' 300-acre plantation in Shinnston, Harrison County, Virginia. Her father Mark Bigler was of Pennsylvania Dutch descent and her mother **Susannah Ogden Bigler** had been raised in Maryland, the Ogden family having provided one of Maryland's early governors. Bathsheba became an accomplished equestrian as she grew up, and acquired management skills from her father through accompanying him on his plantation inspections.

In August 1837, at age 15, she met George A. Smith, an elder of the recently founded Church of Jesus Christ of Latter-day Saints (commonly known as the Mormon Church), who was traveling through the region on an ecclesiastical mission. Their nearly four-year courtship was interrupted by his frequent travels (including a two-year mission to England), but he nonetheless found time, as he noted in his journal, to accept invitations to 17 turkey dinners at the Bigler

home. During this time, Bathsheba and her family moved from Virginia to Nauvoo, Illinois, which had been settled in 1839 by Joseph Smith, founder of the Mormon Church, and 5,000 of his followers. There she and George were married on July 26, 1841; his wedding gifts to her included Staffordshire china acquired during his trip to England and art materials, for she had begun studying painting with a British portrait artist who had settled in Nauvoo.

The couple's first child, George, was born in 1842 (five years later, a second son would die soon after his premature birth), the same year that Smith became a charter member of the Nauvoo Female Relief Society. Religious and charitable, she blessed the sick and washed and anointed women prior to childbirth, in accordance with Joseph Smith's instructions. She also painted portraits of her husband and parents, as well as two leading officials in Nauvoo. Her second child, daughter Bathsheba—called Kate to distinguish her from her mother—was born in August 1844. Less than a month before that, however, the long-simmering distrust with which local non-Mormons viewed the Mormons of Nauvoo had escalated into the arrest and murder by a mob of Joseph Smith. The church was in turmoil, and Bathsheba and George aligned themselves with the large faction headed by Brigham Young. In 1846, Young led many of the Nauvoo Mormons, including George Smith, westward, where they settled the following year in what would become Salt Lake City, Utah. George then returned east to escort Bathsheba and their children to the new settlement. She made the trek with a single trunk, packed with art supplies, the portraits she had painted, and the tools with which to make the lace she was acclaimed for.

The family arrived in the Salt Lake Valley in 1849. Smith soon proved to be a natural pacesetter in the frontier community, her position enhanced after her husband was elected leader of the Utah Territorial legislature at its inception in 1850, and reelected at each session thereafter until his death in 1875. She held the position of treasurer of the local Relief Society, and for several years served as president of the 17th Ward Relief Society. At a meeting of Salt Lake City women in early 1870, Smith proposed "that we demand of the Governor the right of franchise." The motion was presented by the women's committee to Acting Governor S.A. Mann on February 12, 1870. His subsequent signature to the bill made women in Utah the first in the nation to exercise the right to vote. (The territory of Wyoming had also passed legislation to allow women to vote, but Utah voters cast their ballots earlier in the season.) After Brigham Young organized the churchwide Retrenchment Society, Smith was selected as one of its three women leaders. In 1882, she was elected to the board of directors of Deseret Hospital, a major source of medical care in the isolated community. The hospital had three staff physicians—all women—could accommodate 40 to 50 patients, and sponsored midwifery classes and a nursing school. In October 1888, Smith became the second counselor of the national Relief Society, with **Zina D.H. Young** named general president. The Relief Society actively supported the formation of the National Council of Women at that group's initial meeting in Washington, D.C., in 1889, and was part of the ensuing International Council of Women.

In 1893, Zina Young was chosen to take charge of the woman's department of the Salt Lake Temple, with Smith as her first assistant and **Minnie J. Snow** as her second assistant. Eleven years later, after Young's death, Smith became general president of the Relief Society. As president, she particularly stressed advances in education and health services, sponsoring nursing and midwifery classes, supporting home industry, and introducing "mothers' classes," with lessons on marriage, prenatal care, child rearing, and home improvement. The Relief Society also remained active in national and international women's organizations. With support from Lorenzo Snow, president of the Mormon Church, Smith coordinated local women's organizations to raise funds for a building to house their groups. These efforts were successful, leading to the erection of a building with offices for the Relief Society, the Young Woman's Mutual Improvement Association (an outgrowth of the Retrenchment Society), and the Primary Organization for children. (Included in the building by Mormon leaders were offices for the presiding bishopric, for which reason those leaders named it the "Bishop's building.") The building was dedicated in January 1910. Later that year, still president of the Relief Society, Smith died after a brief illness. Called "a master of organization, but never imperious" whose favorite farewell to friends was "peace be unto thee, peace unto this house," she was granted a funeral service in the Mormon Tabernacle, the first woman to be so honored.

**SOURCES:**

*Biographical Record of Salt Lake City & Vicinity.* Salt Lake City, 1910, pp. 168–169.

Ludlow, Daniel, ed. *Encyclopedia of Mormonism.* Vol. 3. NY: Macmillan, 1992, pp. 1320–1321.

Peterson, Janet, and LaRene Gaunt. *Elect Ladies.* Salt Lake City, UT: Deseret, 1990, pp. 61–76.

Tingey, Martha H. "A Tribute of Love," in *Young Woman's Journal.* Vol. 37. July 1925, pp. 419–421.

Whitney, Orson F. *History of Utah.* Vol. 4. Salt Lake City, UT: George Q. Cannon, 1898–1904, p. 578.

*Woman's Exponent.* August–September 1910, p. 12.

**Harriet Horne Arrington**, freelance biographer, Salt Lake City, Utah

# Smith, Bessie (1894–1937)

*African-American vocalist and "Empress of the Blues" who was one of America's greatest jazz singers. Born on April 15, 1894 (some sources cite 1895) in Chattanooga, Tennessee; died in Clarksdale, Mississippi, on September 26 (some sources cite the 27th), 1937, from injuries suffered in an automobile accident while touring; one of seven children of William Smith (a part-time Baptist minister) and Laura Smith; married Earl Love (died c. 1920); married John "Jack" Gee (a Philadelphia night watchman), on June 7, 1923 (estranged at time of her death); children: (second marriage) one adopted son, Jack Gee, Jr.*

*After minimal schooling, began singing for traveling shows in segregated venues throughout the South before moving to Philadelphia (1920); made first recordings (1923) and quickly became the best-known blues performer (1920s); career declined during the Depression, due in part to changing musical tastes.*

On a day in 1970, workers arrived at Mount Lawn Cemetery, near Philadelphia, to erect the headstone for a grave that had lain unmarked for 33 years, even though the funeral for the deceased had attracted some 7,000 mourners back in 1937. The gravestone was somber and restrained, two qualities which could never have been applied to Bessie Smith, the Empress of the Blues.

Hardly anyone except poor Southern blacks had heard of "the blues" when Smith was born to a poverty-stricken family in Chattanooga, Tennessee, in 1894. Because no government regulation at the time considered it necessary to record the births of African-American children, Smith's birth date of April 15 can only be inferred from a marriage certificate she filled out 30 years later; and Smith was notorious for shortening her age by a year or two when she felt like it. She was one of seven children born to **Laura Smith** and William Smith, a part-time preacher, in what Bessie described as a "little ramshackle cabin" not far from the Tennessee River. William died when Bessie was still a baby; she was only eight when Laura passed away, leaving the eldest daughter **Viola** in charge of the family. Little is known about Smith's childhood, except that she sometimes sang and danced for spare change on Chattanooga's Ninth Street, and that she is unlikely to have received more than a rudimentary education.

Economic opportunities for rural southern blacks in early 20th-century America were limited to sharecropping or other menial labor, or in the thriving traveling shows that provided the only source of entertainment and amusement in an otherwise bleak existence. (Many of the traveling shows were actually owned by white theatrical producers from the North.) With their roots in the minstrel shows and vaudeville of the late 19th century, these traveling shows would play one or two nights in small storefronts or tents before moving on to the next town; and it was in one of these shows that Smith's older brother Clarence had been appearing for some months as a dancer when he suggested she audition, too. Hired on as a chorus girl, Smith was soon challenging the popularity of the most famous black performer of the day, *Ma Rainey, who would come to be known as "The Mother of the Blues." The blues, with roots in the traditional ballads and work chants of black slaves, was relatively unknown by white audiences outside the South when Smith began touring.

Blues lovers have long cherished the story that Ma Rainey and her husband kidnapped Smith from her home in Chattanooga and forced her onto the show circuit, giving her a firsthand education in the blues. But there appears to be no truth to the yarn. Bessie's sister-in-law, Maude Smith—Clarence's wife—traveled on the road with Smith during the 1920s and, as an elderly woman, recalled for biographer Chris Albertson that "Bessie and Ma Rainey sat down and had a good laugh about how people was making up stories of Ma taking Bessie from her home. Ma never taught Bessie how to sing." What is known is that Smith, by 1912, was earning ten dollars a week on producer Irwin C. Miller's circuit. "She was a natural born singer, even then," Miller said many years later, although he admitted that he had Smith fired from his show, the motto of which was a Ziegfeld Follies-inspired "Glorifying the Brownskin Girl," because Smith's skin color was too dark.

Smith seemed genuinely unaware of her talent, but audiences all along the circuits she traveled caught on quickly. By the time she arrived at Atlanta's famous "81" theater, they were throwing money on the stage after her rendition of "Weary Blues," and guffawing and whistling through the bawdy lyrics of Smith's earthy numbers about the passion and frustration of love. The "81" became Smith's home base for several years

before she headed north in 1918 to play Baltimore, with the nation's largest black population outside of Washington, D.C. At some time during this period, she married the son of a prominent Georgia family, Earl Love, about whom little is known save that he had died by 1920.

Smith ventured farther north during 1921 and 1922, playing Philadelphia and Atlantic City, New Jersey, the newly discovered playground of the Roaring '20s with its demand for jazz, blues, and the black musicians who knew them best. By this time, record companies were beginning to realize the potential for so-called "race records," especially after "Crazy Blues," the first known blues vocal to be recorded, sold 100,000 copies in 1920. It was sung by *Mamie Smith (no relation to Bessie), a vaudeville artist from Ohio, who also has the distinction of being the first black female vocalist ever to be recorded.

Bessie Smith's first approaches to record companies were not successful; one of them even turned her down because she didn't sound "black" enough. But the growing audiences that crammed every theater she played provided evidence much to the contrary. By 1923, Smith was filling the house in Philadelphia in a revue called How Come? which included five blues numbers in its score, and would have traveled with the show to her New York City debut if she hadn't had a fight with the show's writer and gotten herself fired before the show left Philadelphia. She quickly found work at Horan's cabaret, where a handsome young man named John Gee shyly asked her for a date. Jack Gee was a night guard in Philadelphia, and had been following Smith ever since Atlantic City; her affection for him only increased when, on their first time out together, Jack was shot during an argument and ended up in the hospital. Smith visited him every day, moved in with him when he was released, and officially became Mrs. Jack Gee in June 1923.

By then, Smith had her first recording contract, with Columbia Records, for which she auditioned in February. One story has it that Columbia's director of "race records," Frank Walker, remembered hearing her in a club in Selma, Alabama, some years earlier and sent his "race record judge"—a songwriter and pianist named Clarence Williams—to Philadelphia to bring her into the studio. Another version is that Williams himself had been promoting Smith for some time before setting her up with Columbia; and yet another tale is that a record-store owner in Philadelphia suggested to Williams that Smith try out for Columbia. The correct story will never be known, but everyone remembered how

Jack Gee pawned his nightwatchman's uniform to buy Smith a dress for the recording date, although Frank Walker was not impressed when Smith walked into the studio. "She looked like anything *but* a singer," he once recalled. "She looked about seventeen, tall and fat, and scared to death—just awful!"

*Her* shortness of range, in singing the blues, was no handicap. In terms of what she was saying, and how, she had all the range she needed.

—Henry Pleasants

Recording studios in those days were simple affairs—a small room with one wall covered by a curtain, through which poked a large metal tube with a wide opening. The sounds that traveled down the tube were scratched directly onto a rotating wax disc, from which a metal master was made and from which copies could be struck. If a mistake were made, a new disc had to be loaded for another take. Smith went through several takes of "T'Ain't Nobody's Business If I Do" and "Down Hearted Blues" before the session was called off without a usable recording. Things went better the next day, with the first of Smith's now-treasured Columbia recordings successfully captured—another version of "Down Hearted Blues" as well as "Gulf Coast Blues," which Clarence Williams had written for Smith. Williams persuaded Smith to take him on as her manager, signing a contract for her with Columbia for $125 per successfully recorded song. But Jack Gee, who had plans for managing Smith himself, became suspicious of Williams, and discovered that Williams was actually pocketing half of Smith's recording fee for himself. The scene which followed was typical of Smith's turbulent life and career; she and Gee stormed into Williams' office and beat him until Williams agreed to tear up the contract. Frank Walker hastily arranged a new contract directly with Columbia Records, guaranteeing Smith $1,500 in the next 12 months for a set number of recordings. Bessie and Jack were delighted, although neither thought to question Walker about the contract's provision that no royalties would be paid, for Walker well knew that that was where the real money lay. Considering Walker a model of generosity, Smith named him her manager. Columbia's faith in Bessie Smith was confirmed when "Down Hearted Blues" sold nearly 800,000 copies on its release in June 1923. For the next several years, Smith's Columbia recordings would outsell those of any other blues performer and, some said, keep Columbia Records afloat in its early years.

The eager public which snapped up her records also paid top dollar to see Smith live at the scores of theaters she played throughout the Northeast, the Midwest, and the South. When Smith arrived in Birmingham, Alabama, with her touring show, newspaper reports claimed that "streets were blocked, hundreds and hundreds and hundreds were unable to gain entrance to the performance" which, one paper said, "left the house in riot." Parallels have been drawn between Smith's shows and religious revival meetings. Guitarist Danny Barker, who often played with Smith as a young man, called attention to her Baptist upbringing and noted that "you would recognize a similarity between what she was doing and what those preachers and evangelists [from the South] did. . . . She could bring about mass hysteria"; and Ralph Ellison claimed that "within the . . . Negro community, she was a priestess." More simply, audiences identified with Smith and the songs she sang; knew all about the pain of a cheating lover in "Down Hearted Blues," the loneliness for home in "Gulf Coast Blues," or the joys of free-wheeling passion in "I'm Wild About That Thing," one of Smith's gleefully erotic songs which she never failed to sing with suggestive abandon.

It was a tribute to Smith's extraordinary gifts that she built a respectable following among whites, too, who were at first startled by her florid costumes, enormous plumed headpieces, and clanking costume jewelry before discovering her talent for music, comedy, and seductive dancing. Because audiences were strictly segregated, Smith frequently had to play the same show twice, and she has often been criticized for agreeing to play to whites-only audiences. But she sang the same songs and gave the same performance to both groups; it was the music that mattered to her and to her audiences, for both of whom the term "civil rights" was far in the future. Then, too, white audiences could afford to pay more for their seats, and Smith was always glad to oblige, never deluding herself about how cultured whites viewed her. "You should've seen them ofays lookin' at me like I was some kind of singin' monkey," she once told friends after singing at an all-white party in Manhattan—a party from which she exited drunk, after consuming six or seven straight whiskeys and knocking her hostess to the floor, growling obscenities. Among her Northern white admirers was journalist Carl Van Vechten, who would become the music editor of *The New York Times*. He described a 1925 performance he attended in Newark, New Jersey, in which Smith "wore a crimson satin robe, sweeping up from her trim ankles, and embroidered in multi-colored sequins in designs. Walking slowly to the footlights . . . she began her strange, rhythmic rites in a voice full of shouting and moaning and praying and suffering."

Smith herself seemed unimpressed with her own impact, outside of the fact that she was making more money for one week's performance than she had seen in all her years as a child in Chattanooga. She was, in fact, often insecure about her talent and refused to appear on the same bill with anyone else who sang blues. Her

only major competition in the early 1920s was *Ethel Waters, who recalled being allowed to play the same bill in Atlanta with Smith as long as she, Ethel, stayed away from blues. But the audience would have none of it, forcing the management into an argument with Smith in which she complained of "these Northern bitches" (Waters was from Pennsylvania) invading her territory. It was only when the show had closed that Smith told Waters, "You ain't so bad. It's only that I never dreamed that anyone would be able to do this to me in my own territory and with my own people. And you damn well know," Smith

Bessie
Smith

made sure to add with her usual salty vocabulary, "you can't sing worth a f——."

She needn't have worried. The Roaring '20s was Smith's time. She toured, sang, and recorded tirelessly, her volatile temper and sharp tongue the fear of many, who were always sure to call her "Miss Bessie." She would take on anyone, man or woman, white or black, with flying fists and screaming voice if she felt she had been wronged; she drank liberally, making sure she was always supplied with a small bottle of corn liquor for her purse; and often made up a death in the family when a particularly diligent bout of drinking left her too ill to sing. At the same time, she was profligate with the considerable amounts of money she was being paid (by 1924, up to $2,000 a week), sending sums back home to her family in Tennessee, bailing friends out of jail, buying meals for down-and-out friends and expensive suits for Jack, who had promptly quit his job as a watchman when the money started rolling in. Although Jack never became Smith's manager, he often passed himself off as such and made sure that the one-sheets announcing Smith's appearances always said "Jack Gee Presents Bessie Smith." Smith preferred to leave her business affairs to her brother Clarence, and her recording affairs to Frank Walker who, she said, was the only white man she trusted.

In 1925, at the height of her career, Smith was traveling from city to city in her own, 72'-long railroad car with her first *Harlem Frolics* vaudeville show, the car being large enough to carry the entire cast, their costumes, props, tents for the more rural venues, along with a kitchen and bathrooms with hot and cold running water. The year was notable for two other events: her recording of "St. Louis Blues," with a 24-year-old Louis Armstrong on cornet, still considered the definitive version of W.C. Handy's song; and her first appearance in Chattanooga since leaving home nearly 15 years before. The house was packed all three nights, but the visit was marred when Smith was stabbed in the side by a man whom she had beaten at a party for harassing one of her chorus girls. Although she spent a night in the hospital, she walked out under her own steam the next morning and was back on stage that night.

As the decade wore on, however, problems arose—first in Smith's personal life, and then in her career. She and Jack, often separated by her busy touring schedule, both engaged in a series of affairs which frequently ended in mutual accusations and physical assaults—on each other and on each other's paramours. The last straw for Jack was the night he caught Smith dallying

with one of her chorus girls, for he had been unaware until then of her bisexual tendencies. Smith managed to make it up with him and buckled down to a strenuous, sober work schedule; and, intent on creating a family atmosphere, brought her entire family—nine sisters, in-laws, nephews and nieces—from Chattanooga to Philadelphia, installing them in two houses she bought for them. In 1926, she and Jack adopted the six-year-old brother of one of her chorines, whom they named Jack, Jr. Smith showered gifts and motherly attention on "Snooks" while she was in town and left him to the care of her relatives when she was on the road. All seemed calm and domestic—until, that is, Smith grew restless again. **Ruby Walker**, Jack Gee's niece, was a lead chorus girl in many of Smith's shows during the '20s, and remembered that her aunt could never last for more than a month or two before looking for some fun. "She would go out for two or three weeks, ball, and then be ready to keep quiet for a month or two," Walker said. "But she could never last much longer than that." Smith for a time adopted the strategy of having her drinks served to her in the ladies' room of whatever saloon she found herself in, on the theory that Jack couldn't reach her there; but her husband would be waiting for her when she emerged, and a fistfight would inevitably ensue. There were arguments over the quantities of money Smith attempted to keep away from Jack by depositing them in her sister Viola's bank account, and disputes over the fact that Smith could easily go through $16,000 in three months with her liberality. But it was the $3,000 she gave to Jack to put together a new show that blew the marriage apart.

The show, a revue called *Steamboat Days*, was scheduled to go on the road in 1928—and Jack did, indeed, organize costumes, playing dates, and theaters. But when the show reached Indianapolis, Smith discovered that he had also taken some of the money and invested it in a show starring the woman with whom he had been carrying on a passionate affair for some months, **Gertrude Saunders**, another of Irving Miller's "brownskinned beauties." The fight that resulted, in Jack's hotel room in Columbus, Ohio, left both Smith and Jack bruised and bleeding, to say nothing of the room itself, in which hardly a stick of furniture was left intact. Smith accosted Saunders at least twice when their paths crossed on the tour circuit in the coming months, by which time she and Jack had permanently separated.

By 1929, the course of Smith's career began a downward spiral. Ironically, it was the year that Columbia released the song which is most closely identified with her, "Nobody Knows You When You're Down and Out." Smith was certainly down by mid-1929, lonely and depressed after the breakup with Jack. "I'd find her crying," said her sister-in-law, Maude Smith. "She would sit up in bed, unable to sleep, and she said she was lonesome." More ominous was that, by 1929, the blues craze seemed to have run its course. Swing music was just around the corner, and many of the record companies which optimistically sprang to life to exploit the blues trend had gone out of business; Columbia was virtually the only record company left still releasing blues songs. Smith, too much of a superstar to be immediately affected, nonetheless recorded four popular, non-blues numbers and, as if trying to find a new outlet for her talents, starred in a short, 17-minute film, *St. Louis Blues*, based on Handy's song, in which she played a wronged woman left to drown her sorrows in gin. When the opportunity to appear on Broadway in an all-black musical, *Pansy*, came her way, Smith agreed to sign on—her only appearance in a Broadway theater. It was a disastrous production that closed after three performances, and only lasted that long because of Smith's singing and dancing. With public tastes turning away from vaudeville and toward radio and films, it was an especially hard time for black performers, already marginalized in a shrinking industry. Then, in October 1929, came the stock-market crash.

While Smith continued to tour and record during the early years of the Depression, bookings became harder to find and her once prodigious salaries disappeared. The Theater Owners Booking Association (TOBA), which managed the only black theater circuit and which had been Smith's lifeblood, began to crumble from dwindling audiences and spiraling rents. It eventually collapsed in the mid-1930s. Even Columbia Records felt the pinch, signing no new artists and cutting back on its repertory. In November 1931, Smith was told her contract would not be renewed. In her nine years with Columbia, Smith had earned a total of some $28,500, but now there was precious little of it left. Although she enjoyed a successful tour with a show called *Moanin' Low*, she told friends on her return to Philadelphia that there was "a lot of worry out there," and that she didn't think things would ever be the same again.

Even worse for her, Bessie discovered that Jack, now living with Gertrude Saunders, had placed their adopted son in an orphanage. After Smith's death, "Snooks" would spend much of his adolescence moving from one institution to another and fall into a number of illegal activi-

ties before being revealed in the media in the 1960s as "Bessie Smith's long-lost son."

Things seemed to brighten by 1935, by which time Smith had begun a relationship with an old friend from her early days, Richard Morgan. Morgan had made a comfortable living as a bootlegger during Prohibition, which had been repealed in 1933, and now lived the leisurely and respectable life of a millionaire. He helped support Smith financially and emotionally during the tough times and knew enough to keep his distance when she was in one of her "ballin'" periods. It even seemed that Smith was being rediscovered after four hard years, especially when she began to modify her repertoire to include numbers in the new musical style, swing. She resumed recording for Columbia, under the guidance of John Hammond, a wealthy New Yorker related to the Vanderbilts who would go on to build the careers of such stars as *Billie Holiday—who, as it turned out, Smith replaced in 1936 at a Manhattan jazz club when Holiday fell ill. As a new generation discovered Smith, she found herself in demand again, soon appearing at The Famous Door, one of Manhattan's earliest and most popular 52nd Street clubs. "New York Sees Bessie Smith, Wonders Where She's Been," went one headline, though Smith had never stopped working and had been playing to full houses in the South all along.

In September 1937, Smith agreed to appear in a touring show called Broadway Rastus, which was to open in Memphis and then travel throughout the South during the autumn and early winter. Smith took Richard Morgan with her, letting him drive the old Packard in which she now traveled—a far cry from the railroad car days. Reviews were favorable in Memphis, and Smith and Morgan were in an optimistic mood on the night of September 26, when they decided to drive ahead of the rest of the company to the tour's next stop in Mississippi. During the early morning hours of September 26, on a lonely stretch of Route 61 near Clarksdale, Mississippi, the Packard collided with the rear of a trailer truck. Although Morgan, who was driving, received only cuts and bruises, Smith—riding in the passenger seat, the side of the car which slammed into the body of the truck—was severely injured, with a crushed ribcage, a nearly severed right arm, and serious head injuries. She was pronounced dead on arrival at the nearest hospital, the cause of death listed as shock, internal injuries, and loss of blood.

For many years after, it was claimed that Smith died because white hospitals refused to admit her and too much time had passed before a black hospital could be found. The story gained wide credence after John Hammond published an article making the claim in Down Beat—an article which Hammond, more than 30 years later, confessed to biographer Albertson had been based on hearsay. (Edward Albee's 1960 play, The Death of Bessie Smith, is, in turn, based largely on Hammond's article.) The press tended to ignore the white doctor who arrived at the accident scene and the black ambulance driver who took Smith to the hospital in Clarksdale, both of whom repeatedly claimed that Smith got the best care available on a deserted country road before being taken straight to the blacks-only G.T. Thomas Hospital. Some months later, the emergency-room doctor who treated her claimed that even if she had arrived only moments after the crash, there was little that could have been done to save her. Nonetheless, Hammond's version is still perpetuated, as if Smith's manner of dying were more important than anything she did in life.

The story gained renewed currency in the media coverage surrounding the small ceremony that unveiled Smith's headstone in 1970, with John Hammond in attendance representing Columbia Records, which had paid for half the costs of the stone. Absent from the proceedings was the donor of the other half—*Janis Joplin, who chose not to attend, it was said, for fear of stealing attention from Smith herself. "She showed me the air, and taught me how to fill it," Joplin once said of Smith. Joplin, who would die of a drug overdose two months after the ceremony, had often publicly acknowledged the importance of Smith's work in her own career, as have Billie Holiday, *Dinah Washington, Bonnie Raitt, and a host of other blues and pop singers whose debt to Bessie Smith justifies the words carved on her gravestone:

The Greatest Blues Singer in the World
Will Never Stop Singing.

SOURCES:

Albertson, Chris. Bessie. NY: Stein and Day, 1972.

Carr, Ian, Digby Fairweather, and Brian Priestley. Jazz: The Essential Companion. London: Grafton Books, 1988.

Feinstein, Elaine. Bessie Smith. NY: Viking, 1985.

Martin, Flo. "The Complete Recordings. 3 vols." (sound recording review), in American Music. Vol. 11, no. 3. Fall 1993.

Marvin, Thomas F. "'Preachin' the Blues': Bessie Smith's Secular Religion and Alice Walker's 'The Color Purple,'" in African American Review. Vol. 28, no. 3. Fall 1994.

Moore, Carman. Somebody's Angel Child. NY: Thomas Y. Crowell, 1969.

Pleasants, Henry. *The Great American Popular Singers.* NY: Simon and Schuster, 1974.

**SUGGESTED READING:**

*Davis, Angela Y. *Blues Legacies and Black Feminism: Gertrude "Ma" Rainey, Bessie Smith, and Billie Holiday.* NY: Pantheon, 1998.

**Norman Powers**, writer-producer,
Chelsea Lane Productions,
New York, New York

# Smith, Betty (1896–1972)

*American novelist and playwright. Born Elisabeth Keogh on December 15, 1896 (one source cites 1904), in Brooklyn, New York; died on January 17, 1972; daughter of John Keogh and Catherine (Wehner) Keogh; attended the University of Michigan, 1927–30; attended Yale University Drama School, 1930–34; married George H.E. Smith, in June 1924 (divorced 1938); married Joseph Piper Jones (a journalist), in 1943 (divorced 1951); married Robert Finch, in June 1957 (died 1959); children: (first marriage) Nancy, Mary.*

*Selected writings: (novels)* A Tree Grows in Brooklyn *(1943),* Tomorrow Will Be Better *(1948),* Maggie-Now *(1958),* Joy in the Morning *(1963); (plays)* Folk Stuff *(1935),* His Last Skirmish *(1937),* Naked Angel *(1937),* Popecastle Inn *(1937),* Saints Get Together *(1937),* Trees of His Father *(1937),* Vine Leaves *(1937),* The Professor Roars *(1938),* Western Night *(1938),* Darkness at the Window *(1938),* Murder in the Snow *(1938),* Silvered Rope *(1938),* Youth Takes Over; or, When A Man's Sixteen *(1939),* Lawyer Lincoln *(1939),* Mannequins' Maid *(1939),* They Released Barabbas *(1939),* A Night in the Country *(1939),* Near Closing Time *(1939),* Package for Ponsonby *(1939),* Western Ghost Town *(1939),* Bayou Harlequinade *(1940),* Fun After Supper *(1940),* Heroes Just Happen *(1940),* Room for a King *(1940),* Summer Comes to the Diamond O *(1940),* To Jenny With Love *(1941),* Boy Abe *(1944),* A Tree Grows in Brooklyn *(musical, with George Abbott, 1951),* Durham Station *(1961).*

When *A Tree Grows in Brooklyn* was published in 1943, critics of the day readily assumed that the story of a young girl growing up in a Brooklyn tenement during the early 1900s was

*From the movie A Tree Grows in Brooklyn, starring Peggy Ann Garner, Dorothy McGuire, Joan Blondell, and Ted Donaldson.*

largely an autobiographical account of first-time novelist Betty Smith's own childhood. Smith herself was born Elisabeth Keogh on December 15, 1896, in the Williamsburg section of Brooklyn, New York. After leaving school at the age of 14 with only an eighth-grade education, she worked first in a factory and in retail before moving on to clerical jobs in New York City. She married George Smith in 1924, had two daughters, and moved to the Midwest, where her husband attended law school at the University of Michigan. They divorced in 1938.

When her daughters were old enough to go to school during the day, Smith enrolled at the University of Michigan as a "special student" and took courses in writing. She eventually wrote articles for the *Detroit Free Press* and the NEA syndicate. When Smith's one-act plays won her the University of Michigan's prestigious Avery Hopwood Award, she decided to focus her attention on playwriting and enrolled at the Yale University School of Drama. At Yale, Smith earned the Rockefeller Fellowship in Playwriting and the Rockefeller Dramatists' Guild Playwriting Fellowship. During the 1930s and early 1940s, she wrote over 70 one-act plays (all of them either produced or published), and was involved in the theater in a variety of ways, including acting in a few plays, working as a playreader, and a brief stint as a radio performer. By this time, she had made her home in Chapel Hill, North Carolina.

Although she was a seasoned playwright for nearly a decade, *A Tree Grows in Brooklyn* was Smith's first novel. The book was an instant success with critics and readers alike. Smith commented, "One night . . . I, an obscure writer living quietly and on modest means in a small Southern town, went to bed as usual. I woke up the next morning to be informed that I had become a celebrity." The nostalgic *A Tree Grows in Brooklyn* was noted for both its heart-warming tone and its grimly realistic nature. Smith's young heroine, Francie Nolan, became a national figure. Two years after it was published, Elia Kazan directed a hugely popular movie version of the book for 20th Century-Fox, starring *Dorothy McGuire, *Joan Blondell, and *Peggy Ann Garner as Francie, that won Garner a special Academy Award and has since gone on to become a classic. Smith had tried to sell the book to Hollywood studios for $5,000 before its publication, but was refused. Its exceptional popularity quickly changed producers' minds and led to offers up to $50,000. Smith held out for $55,000. Despite the similarities between *A Tree Grows in Brooklyn*'s fictional Francie Nolan and Smith's Brooklyn upbringing, Smith claimed that her

own childhood had not been nearly as grim as Francie's and that she held no bitter memories. *A Tree Grows in Brooklyn* had sold some six million copies by the early 1970s, was translated into 16 languages, and was required reading for millions of American schoolchildren.

Smith's next two novels, *Tomorrow Will Be Better* (1948) and *Maggie-Now* (1958), were also set in Brooklyn, but achieved far less success. Still, *Maggie-Now* won the Sir Walter Raleigh award for fiction in 1958. Her last novel, the autobiographical *Joy in the Morning* (1963), was set in Michigan; she had lost her connection to Brooklyn, she admitted, and could no longer honestly set a story there. A member of the Authors League and the Dramatists Guild, Smith served as a faculty member at the University of North Carolina, Chapel Hill, in 1945–46, and continued writing plays. In 1951, she collaborated with George Abbott on a musical version of *A Tree Grows in Brooklyn*. She died in 1972.

**SOURCES:**

Block, Maxine, ed. *Current Biography 1943.* NY: H.W. Wilson, 1943.

Commire, Anne, ed. *Something About the Author.* Vol. 6. Detroit, MI: Gale Research, 1974.

Gunton, Sharon, ed. *Contemporary Literary Criticism.* Vol. 19. Detroit, MI: Gale Research, 1981.

**Kimberly A. Burton**, B.A., M.I.S., Ann Arbor, Michigan

# Smith, Bill (1886–1975)

*Australian jockey. Name variations: Wilhelmina Smith. Born in 1886 in Australia; died near Cairns, Australia, in 1975.*

Horse racing was long considered a sport exclusively for men; only in the 1970s did women begin breaking in to that closed world, and it was not until 1974 that the Australian Jockey Club officially recognized women jockeys. Over 70 years before that, however, Bill Smith was known in North Queensland, Australia, for his skill with riding racehorses. He was said to have been small and slightly built, as is necessary for a jockey, but spoke harshly and swore constantly, and was considered eccentric for refusing to change clothes with the other jockeys before and after a race. Sixteen-year-old Smith won Australia's St. Leger Quest Derby in 1902 and the Jockey Club Derby the following year. In 1909–10, he won the Victorian Oaks Derby. He spent the last several years of his life reclusively, and in 1975, the year after women jockeys were allowed to race in Australia, he died and was discovered to have been a woman. It is not known why she continued to live as a man long after her racing days were over. She was buried under the name of Wilhelmina Smith.

**SOURCES:**

Radi, Heather, ed. *200 Australian Women: A Redress Anthology.* NSW, Australia: Women's Redress Press, 1988.

**Kimberly A. Burton**, B.A., M.I.S.,
Ann Arbor, Michigan

## Smith, Charlotte (1749–1806)

*English novelist and poet. Name variations: Charlotte Turner Smith. Born Charlotte Turner in London, England, on May 4, 1749; died in Tilford, near Farnham, Surrey, on October 28, 1806; eldest daughter of Nicholas Turner of Stoke House, Surrey, and Anna (Towers) Turner; sister of Catherine Ann Dorset (c. 1750–c. 1817, a noted writer of children's books); married Benjamin Smith, in 1765; children: 12, one of whom, Lionel Smith (1778–1842), rose to the rank of lieutenant-general in the army and was governor of the Windward and Leeward Islands (1833–39).*

Charlotte Smith, born in 1749 in London, was three years old when her mother **Anna Towers Turner** died. Brought up by her aunt, Charlotte was sent to mediocre schools until she was 12. Four years later, her father Nicholas Turner arranged her marriage to Benjamin Smith, son of a merchant who was a director of the East India Company. The newlyweds lived at first with Benjamin's father, who was impressed with Charlotte's business acumen and his son's lack thereof, and wanted the young couple to remain with him. But in 1774 Charlotte and her husband moved to Hampshire. Though the marriage was unhappy, the couple would have 12 children. In 1776, Charlotte's father-in-law died, leaving his estate to his grandchildren. The will was so complicated, however, that Charlotte spent years in litigation. Six years later, the feckless Benjamin was imprisoned for debt. After sharing her husband's confinement for several months, Charlotte determined to leave the prison and make a living as a writer.

Smith's first publication was *Elegiac Sonnets and other Essays* (1784), dedicated to her friend, poet William Hayley, and printed at her own expense. To escape creditors, she and her family lived in a tumble-down château near Dieppe for some months, where she composed a translation of Prévost's *Manon Lescaut* (1785) and *The Romance of Real Life* (1786), borrowed from *Les Causes Célébres* (French criminal trials).

On her return to England, Smith and her husband agreed to an amicable separation. From then on, she devoted herself to novel writing and financially assisting her children and her husband until his death in Berwick jail in 1806. Her chief works are *Emmeline, or the Orphan of the Castle* (1788), *Ethelinde* (1789), *Celestina* (1791), *Desmond* (1792), *The Old Manor House* (1793), *The Young Philosopher* (1798), and *Conversations introducing Poetry* (1804). Charlotte Smith died at Tilford, near Farnham, Surrey, on October 28, 1806. A memoir of her by her sister **Catherine Ann Dorset** was included in Walter Scott's *Miscellaneous Prose Works* (1829).

**SUGGESTED READING:**

Curran, Stuart, ed. *The Poems of Charlotte Smith.* NY: Oxford University Press, 1993.

Hilbish, F.M.A. *Charlotte Smith: Poet and Novelist,* 1941.

## Smith, Chloethiel Woodard (1910–1992)

*American architect and city planner. Name variations: often incorrectly spelled Cloethiel. Born on February 2, 1910, in Peoria, Illinois; died on December 30, 1992, in Washington, D.C.; daughter of Oliver Ernest Woodard and Coy Blanche (Johnson) Woodard; University of Oregon, Bachelor of Architecture, with honors, 1932; Washington University, Master of Architecture in city planning, 1933; married Bromley Keables Smith, on April 5, 1940; children: Bromley Keables Smith; Susanne Woodard Smith.*

*Became partner in Keyes, Smith, Satterlee & Lethbridge (1951–56); became partner of Satterlee & Smith (1956–63); founded Chloethiel Woodard Smith & Associated Architects (1963).*

Born in Peoria, Illinois, in 1910, Chloethiel Woodard Smith was only 12 when she decided to be an architect, simply because she found it fun to see buildings constructed. That childhood decision endured, and she enjoyed a successful lifelong architectural career. In 1932, she graduated with a bachelor's degree in architecture from the University of Oregon, then went on to earn a master's of architecture in city planning the following year at Washington University.

In 1951, Smith entered into partnership with Arthur H. Keyes, Jr., Nicholas Satterlee, and Francis Lethbridge to form Keyes, Smith, Satterlee & Lethbridge. Five years later, she and Satterlee established a partnership, Satterlee & Smith, which operated until 1963 when Smith established her own architectural firm in Washington, D.C. Her projects ranged from the U.S. Chancery and ambassador's residence in Asunción, Paraguay, to Crown Towers in New Haven, Connecticut. However, she became especially well known for her urban renewal work and community planning projects on the waterfront in Washington, D.C., La Clede Town in St. Louis, Missouri, and a complex of townhouses in Reston, Virginia.

Smith preferred to give her multi-family housing complexes a sense of the past, complete with a main street, and to keep things on a small scale with an abundance of open space. Her designs were sensitive to the needs of families with children as well as commercial enterprise. Although her work was deemed "banal" and "overly cute" by some critics, as noted in *Women in Architecture*, her success was undeniable. Described by **Barbaralee Diamonstein** as "a constructor of environments that are thoughtful solutions to human need," Smith consistently delivered tradition-based architecture throughout her career. Elected to the College of Fellows of the American Institute of Architects in 1960 and considered one of the nation's most successful woman architects, Smith was also honored by her alma mater in 1982 with the University of Oregon Distinguished Service Award.

**SOURCES:**

Diamonstein, Barbaralee. *Open Secrets: Ninety-four Women in Touch with Our Time.* NY: Viking, 1970.

Torre, Susana, ed. *Women in American Architecture: A Historic and Contemporary Perspective.* NY: Whitney Library of Design, 1977.

**Kimberly A. Burton**, B.A., M.I.S.,
Ann Arbor, Michigan

## Smith, Clara (1894–1935)

*African-American blues singer, known as the Queen of the Moaners. Born in Spartanburg, South Carolina, in 1894; died on February 21, 1935, in Detroit, Michigan; married Charles Wesley (a baseball manager), in 1926.*

Like those of many blues singers, Clara Smith's early years are obscure. She was born in Spartanburg, South Carolina, in 1894, and endured poverty and discrimination. Smith began her singing career in Southern vaudeville and eventually became a popular performer on the Theater Owners' Booking Association (TOBA) circuit. By 1923, she was in Harlem and a year later had her own club, the Clara Smith Theatrical Club. From 1925 to 1928, she recorded mostly for Columbia. Her throbbing, moaning voice was backed by such prominent jazz artists as Louis Armstrong on the cornet, Coleman Hawkins on the sax, Don Redman on the clarinet, and James P. Johnson on the piano. Clara, who recorded two duets with *Bessie Smith, pre-

ferred suffering, tragic heroines for her subject, such as the ones featured in "Every Woman's Blues" and "Awful Moaning Blues." She recorded over 125 songs in her career, with her last recording session in 1932. Three years later, she died of a heart attack at age 41 in Detroit, Michigan. Among early female blues singers, notes Roger Kinkle, she was "probably only surpassed by Bessie Smith and *Ma Rainey."

**SOURCES:**

Herzhaft, Gérard. *Encyclopedia of the Blues.* Translated by Brigitte Debord. Fayetteville, AR: University of Arkansas Press, 1992.

Kinkle, Roger D. *The Complete Encyclopedia of Popular Music and Jazz: 1900–1950.* Vol III. Arlington House, 1974.

Santelli, Robert. *The Big Book of Blues: A Biographical Encyclopedia.* NY: Penguin, 1993.

Smith, Jessie Carney, ed. *Notable Black American Women.* Detroit, MI: Gale Research, 1992.

**John Haag**,
Athens, Georgia

## Smith, Dodie (1896–1990)

*English playwright and novelist who is best remembered for her play* **Dear Octopus** *and her children's book* **The Hundred and One Dalmations.** *Name variations: (pseudonyms) C.L. Anthony, Charles Henry Percy. Born Dorothy Gladys Smith on May 3, 1896, in Whitefield, Lancashire, England; died on November 24, 1990; daughter of Ernest Walter Smith and Ella (Furber) Smith; attended Manchester School and St. Paul's Girls' School, London; studied stage acting at the Royal Academy of Dramatic Art, London; married Alec Macbeth Beesley (her business manager), in 1939 (died 1987).*

*Selected writings (as Dodie Smith, unless otherwise indicated):*

*Plays:* British Talent *(as C.L. Anthony, 1924);* Autumn Crocus *(as C.L. Anthony, 1931);* Service *(as C.L. Anthony, 1932);* Touch Wood *(as C.L. Anthony, 1934);* Call It a Day *(1935);* Bonnet Over the Windmill *(1937);* Dear Octopus *(and co-director, 1938);* Lovers and Friends *(1943);* Letter from Paris *(1952);* I Capture the Castle *(1952);* These People, Those Books *(1958);* Amateur Means Lover *(1961).*

*Screenplays:* Schoolgirl Rebels *(as Charles Henry Percy, 1915);* The Uninvited *(adaptation, with Frank Partos, 1944);* Darling, How Could You! *(adaptation, with Lesser Samuels, 1951).*

*Novels:* I Capture the Castle *(1948);* The New Moon with the Old *(1963);* The Town in Bloom *(1965);* It Ends with Revelations *(1967);* A Tale of Two Families *(1970);* The Girl from the Candle-lit Bath *(1978).*

*For children:* The Hundred and One Dalmatians *(1956);* The Starlight Barking: More about the Hundred and One Dalmatians *(1967);* The Midnight Kittens *(1978).*

*Autobiographies:* Look Back with Love: A Manchester Childhood *(1974);* Look Back with Mixed Feelings *(1978);* Look Back with Astonishment *(1979);* Look Back with Gratitude *(1985).*

A popular English playwright noted for her humorous insights into ordinary lives, Dodie Smith is probably best remembered as the author of *The Hundred and One Dalmatians*, made perpetually famous by Walt Disney Productions' animated and live-action film adaptations.

Born Dorothy Gladys Smith in 1896 and initially nicknamed "Dodo," which evolved into "Dodie," she grew up surrounded by artistic relatives who influenced her future career. Her father Ernest Smith died when she was a baby, and her mother **Ella Furber Smith** raised her in her maternal grandparents' home in Old Trafford, Manchester. Both her mother and grandmother wrote and composed in a house that reverberated with the sounds of musical instruments. Through assisting her uncle, an amateur actor, with his lines, Smith became interested in the theater, especially the art of playwriting. Although she had written her first play by the age of nine, she initially wanted to act.

When her mother remarried in 1910, Smith moved to London, where she attended St. Paul's Girls' School and later the Royal Academy of Dramatic Art (RADA). While at the academy, she received slightly more than £3 for the screenplay *Schoolgirl Rebels*, which she sold to a silent film company. She also performed with other students and eventually joined the Portsmouth Repertory Theater, which took her to France to entertain the troops during World War I. Smith left her relatively unsuccessful acting career in 1923 to work for Heal & Son furniture store, where she remained for eight years, first as a buyer and then as a department head.

Although Smith's first one-act play, *British Talent*, was performed in 1924 at the Three Arts

*From the movie* One Hundred and One Dalmatians *(1961).*

Club, an amateur theater in London, she produced no other plays for several years. However, in 1931 her writing career brightened when she sold *Autumn Crocus*, a romantic comedy written under the pseudonym C.L. Anthony. Critically successful, the play was Smith's breakthrough work, and within two years she had achieved an astonishing popularity. Similar success followed with two other plays written under the C.L. Anthony pseudonym, *Service* and *Touch Wood*. In 1935, Smith's *Call It a Day* was the first play written under her real name and proved to be the most financially rewarding. It ran for almost 200 performances in New York and more than 500 performances in London, which allowed Smith to concentrate solely on her writing. Despite the failure of her 1937 play, *Bonnet Over the Windmill*, to achieve major success, Smith returned in 1938 with *Dear Octopus*, which became the best known of all her plays. The first production starred famed actors Dame *Marie Tempest and John Gielgud.

In 1939, Smith married her longtime friend and colleague from Heal's, Alec Beesley. During World War II, they sailed, with their pets and Rolls-Royce in tow, to the United States, where they remained until the 1950s. While living in Los Angeles, she wrote the 1943 play *Lovers and Friends* as well as film scripts. In 1948, homesick for England, Smith published her first novel, *I Capture the Castle*, a bestseller about an adolescent girl's first experiences with love and maturity in a decrepit castle. Six years later, Smith adapted this work for the stage, where it met with audience approval but critical ambivalence.

Smith returned to England in 1953 and, in addition to her other writing, began to write several stories for children. She penned *The Hundred and One Dalmatians* in 1956, a popular book made even more so when Walt Disney Productions adapted it as an animated film in 1961. Walt Disney Studio's live-action version, *101 Dalmations* (1996), and its live-action sequel, *102 Dalmations* (2000), both starring **Glenn Close** as Cruella De Vil, continue to add to the book's success. A dog lover who owned several pet Dalmatians, Smith continued the canine caper in 1967 with a lesser-known sequel, *The Starlight Barking: More about the Hundred and One Dalmatians*. She made felines her main characters in 1978 with *The Midnight Kittens*.

Smith died in 1990, having devoted the last years of her life to working on a four-volume autobiography that spanned from childhood to her sojourn in the United States: *Look Back with Love: A Manchester Childhood* (1974), *Look Back with Mixed Feelings* (1978), *Look Back with Astonishment* (1979), and *Look Back with Gratitude* (1985). Not always a fervent favorite with critics, Smith once addressed that issue in an interview with *Contemporary Authors*. "I consider myself a lightweight author," she quipped, "but God knows I approach my work with as much seriousness as if it were Holy Writ."

**SOURCES:**
Buck, Claire, ed. *The Bloomsbury Guide to Women's Literature*. NY: Prentice Hall, 1992.
*Contemporary Authors*. New Rev. Series. Vol. 37. Detroit, MI: Gale Research, 1992.
Shattock, Joanne. *The Oxford Guide to British Women Writers*. Oxford: Oxford University Press, 1993.

**SUGGESTED READING:**
Grove, Valerie. *Dear Dodie: The Life of Dodie Smith*. London: Pimlico, 1997.

**RELATED MEDIA:**
*Autumn Crocus* (70 min. film), starring Ivor Novello and *Fay Compton, produced in England by Basil Dean, 1934.
*Call It a Day* (89 min. film), starring *Olivia de Haviland, Ian Hunter, **Anita Louise**, *Frieda Inescort, and *Bonita Granville, directed by Archie Mayo, Warner Bros., 1937.
*Dear Octopus* (78 min. film), adapted from Smith's stage play by **Esther McCracken**, starring *Margaret Lockwood, Michael Wilding, and *Celia Johnson, directed by Harold French, produced by Gainsborough-EFI in England, 1945 (released in America under the title *The Randolph Family*).
*The Hundred and One Dalmatians* was filmed by Walt Disney Productions as *One Hundred and One Dalmatians*, 1961, and revived in 1996 with a live-action film starring Jeff Daniels, Glenn Close, and *Joan Plowright, and with a sequel in 2000 starring Glenn Close and Gèrard Depardieu entitled *102 Dalmatians*.
*Looking Forward* (76 min. film), based on the play *Service*, starring Lionel Barrymore, Lewis Stone, and **Benita Hume**, directed by Clarence Brown, screenplay by *Bess Meredyth and H.M. Harwood, Metro-Goldwyn-Mayer, 1933.

**Kimberly A. Burton**, B.A., M.I.S.,
Ann Arbor, Michigan

## Smith, Edith Blackwell (1871–1920).

*See Holden, Edith B.*

# Smith, Eliza Roxey Snow
## (1804–1887)

*American poet and influential member of the early Mormon Church. Name variations: Eliza Roxey Snow; middle name sometimes spelled "Roxcy" or "Roxcey." Born Eliza Roxey Snow on January 21, 1804, in Becket, Berkshire County, Massachusetts; died on December 5, 1887, in Salt Lake City, Utah; daughter of Oliver Snow III (a farmer) and Rosetta Leonora (Pettibone)*

*Snow; sister of Lorenzo Snow (president of the Mormon Church, 1898–1901); attended grammar school in Mantua, Ohio; became a plural wife of Joseph Smith (1805–1844, founder of the Church of Jesus Christ of Latter-day Saints), in June 1842 (died June 1844); became a plural wife of Brigham Young (1801–1877, leader of the Church of Jesus Christ of Latter-day Saints), in June 1849; no children.*

Eliza Roxey Snow Smith was born in 1804, the second of seven children of deeply religious parents who were both descended from early Puritan settlers. Two years after her birth, the family moved from Massachusetts to a farm in Mantua, Ohio, where they quickly grew prosperous. When Eliza was still young, they left the Baptist Church for the Campbellite (or Reformed Baptist) Church. Eliza received her formal and domestic education at a local school and excelled in weaving; she also took her Bible studies very seriously. During her teen years, she began writing poetry, some of which was published in local journals, including the Ravenna *Courier* and the *Ohio Star.*

In 1831, Joseph Smith, founder of the newly established Mormon Church, visited the Snows' home. Joseph, as well as his views on religion, made a marked impression on Eliza and her family. Many Campbellites in Ohio converted to Mormonism around this time, and in 1835 Eliza's mother and sister did so as well. Shortly thereafter, Eliza accompanied them to the Mormon settlement in Kirtland, Ohio, and that April she was baptized into the church by Joseph Smith. Her brother Lorenzo Snow converted the following year; many years later, he would become president of the church. Toward the end of 1836, Eliza moved from her parents' home in Mantua to Joseph Smith's home in Kirtland, where she served as a governess to his children and a companion to his wife *Emma Hale Smith. Contributions she made from her family's considerable funds helped erect the Mormon temple in Kirtland; she also conducted a school for girls. With many other Mormons from Kirtland, a few years later she moved to Jackson County, Missouri, which Joseph Smith thought would be fertile ground for his church. Locals were suspicious, however, and in the face of persecution the Mormons fled to Illinois, to recently secured land on the Mississippi. Here, in a town they named Nauvoo, the church enjoyed a measure of security and attracted thousands of new followers.

In 1841, Joseph Smith quietly introduced the concept of polygamy into the Mormon religion, although he would not offer it as a public "revelation" for over a year. In a secret ceremo-

ny that June, Eliza became one of his plural wives. (Some have estimated that he eventually had some 50 wives.) Intelligent and well educated for the time and place, Eliza Smith became an important member of Nauvoo society, and played a crucial part in establishing the role of women in the Mormon Church. She was a founding member of the charitable Women's Relief Society in 1842, and pioneered "temple work" that became part of the religion's permanent tradition. As word of the practice of polygamy spread, however, it gave further ammunition to the church's detractors. Smith was one of several women who publicly denied that they were involved in plural marriages, although this did nothing to quiet the controversy. Emma Hale Smith, as well, did not take kindly to the practice, despite a revelation through Joseph instructing her to welcome "all those that have been given unto" her husband. One story, perhaps apocryphal, has Emma attacking a pregnant Eliza in 1844 with sufficient force to cause her to miscarry. In June of that year, Joseph was arrested and jailed in nearby Carthage after ordering the destruction of the printing presses of a local newspaper that had charged him with adultery. On June 27, a mob broke into the jail and murdered both Joseph and his brother.

While the church became riven with factionalism in the aftermath of Joseph's death, Smith went to live in the family home of Brigham Young, who had inherited the position of church leader. In 1846–47, she was one of the thousands of Mormons who traveled west with him from Nauvoo to the Salt Lake Valley, where they settled. In 1849, she became one of Young's many plural wives. Six years later, he appointed her president of the Endowment House, where church work was carried out before the temples were built. Having continued to work with the Women's Relief Society in Utah, in 1866 she became the society's general president. In this post she directed the development of hygiene classes, a women's newspaper, numerous charitable projects, and cooperative stores that sold homemade Mormon goods. In 1882, she also oversaw the opening of the Deseret Hospital for women, the frontier community's first hospital, which was staffed with three women physicians. Smith traveled throughout Utah in connection with these projects, and remained president of the Relief Society until her death.

In 1869, Brigham Young gave Smith charge of the newly formed Young Ladies' Retrenchment Association, a group organized to fight a decline in societal behavior. Under her guidance, it evolved into the Young Ladies' Mutual Improvement Association, one of the main women's organizations in the church. In 1878, she organized and directed a meeting in defense of polygamy that was attended by 15,000 Mormon women. Smith was a dedicated advocate of the practice, and staunchly refuted critics of Mormonism who used it as an example of the subjugation of women by the church, pointing out that the territory had granted women the right to vote in 1870. In 1880, she was named president of Mormon women's organizations throughout the world. As well, she never gave up writing. Her work includes *Poems, Religious, Historical and Political* (1856 and 1877) and *Biography and Family Record of Lorenzo Snow* (1884), the life story of her brother, whom she had accompanied to Palestine on a missionary tour in 1872. She also wrote a number of hymns, the best known being "O My Father, Thou That Dwellest." Called the "mother of Mormonism," she died in Salt Lake City in December 1887.

**SOURCES:**

James, Edward T., ed. *Notable American Women, 1607–1950.* Cambridge, MA: The Belknap Press of Harvard University, 1971.

McHenry, Robert, ed. *Famous American Women.* NY: Dover, 1980.

**Kimberly A. Burton**, B.A, M.I.S.,
Ann Arbor, Michigan

## Smith, Elizabeth "Betsy" (1750–1815).

*See Adams, Abigail for sidebar.*

## Smith, Elizabeth Oakes (1806–1893).

*See Anthony, Susan B. for sidebar.*

## Smith, Elizabeth Quincy (1721–1775).

*See Adams, Abigail for sidebar.*

## Smith, Emily James (1865–1944).

*See Putnam, Emily James.*

# Smith, Emma Hale (1804–1879)

*Wife of Joseph Smith, founder of the Church of Jesus Christ of Latter-day Saints, who was one of her husband's earliest converts but later broke with the church over the doctrine of polygamy.* Name variations: *Emma Hale Smith Bidamon. Born Emma Hale on July 10, 1804, in Harmony, Pennsylvania; died on April 20, 1879, in Nauvoo, Illinois; daughter of Isaac Hale (a farmer) and Elizabeth (Lewis) Hale; briefly attended public school; married Joseph Smith (1805–1844, founder of the Church of Jesus Christ of Latter-day Saints), on January 18, 1827, in South Bainbridge, Pennsylvania; married Major Lewis Crum Bidamon in April 1847 in Nauvoo, Illinois; children:*

*(first marriage) Alvin (died young); Thaddeus (died young); Louisa (died young); Joseph Smith III (b. 1832, later president of the Reorganized Church of Jesus Christ of Latter-Day Saints); Frederick; Alexander; Don Carlos (died young); another son (died young); David; (adopted twins) Joseph Murdock (died young) and Julia Murdock.*

Emma Hale Smith was born in 1804 into a large farming family near the Susquehanna River in Harmony, Pennsylvania, where her parents Isaac and **Elizabeth Lewis Hale**, originally from Vermont, had been the among the first white settlers. While her education was somewhat sketchy owing to the place and time, she attended grammar school in the area and grew up canoeing and horseback riding. Described as dignified and beautiful, with "enormous hazel eyes," she was still living in her parents' house when Joseph Smith came to board there in 1825 while he worked for a local landowner. Although Isaac Hale was none too impressed with his boarder, Emma was. Isaac twice turned down Joseph's request for her hand in marriage, and in January 1827 Emma and Joseph eloped and were married in South Bainbridge, New York.

The couple lived first with Joseph's parents, Joseph and **Lucy Mack Smith**, in Manchester, New York, and it was there, on September 22, 1827, that Joseph finally received from the angel Moroni the gold plates on which the *Book of Mormon* was inscribed. Emma and Joseph moved several times in the next few years as he sought privacy and safety for his translation of the plates. She served as his first copyist in the translation, with Joseph on one side of a curtain reading from the plates with the seer stones, the Urim and Thumim, and translating the plates from the "reformed Egyptian" in which they were written, while on the other side of the curtain Emma wrote down what he said. He never allowed her to see the plates themselves, although she was permitted to touch them while they were covered with wrappings. This apparently became somewhat of a sore spot for her after the first publication of the *Book of Mormon* in March 1830, which contained sworn testimony from 11 people who claimed to have seen the "reformed Egyptian" written on the plates. Within two months of the publication, over 40 people acknowledged Smith as an apostle of Jesus Christ and the elder of this new church. Emma was baptized into the church in June, and a month later Joseph had a revelation in which she was designated the "Elect Lady," whose calling was to support her husband and exhort the church.

By this time Joseph had already been arrested once (for "setting the country in an uproar"), the first of many such arrests and attempts to keep him quiet. In January 1831, due to growing local hostility, the Smiths moved with the church to Kirtland, Ohio. Three months later, Emma gave birth to twins who died soon after, and adopted the twins of a friend who had died in childbirth. She would give birth to seven more children, only four of whom survived to adulthood. Life in Kirtland was not easy, for though converts flocked to Joseph's church, many non-Mormons in the area were deeply suspicious. Emma once watched him being tarred and feathered by a mob. To support the family, she took in boarders. Among these were some of the men who built Kirtland's first Mormon temple, completed in 1836; around the same time, Emma published a hymnal which she had been charged by one of Joseph's revelations with preparing. Following the economic panic of 1837 and large-scale local hostility, in 1838 the Smiths and the Mormon colony moved to Far West, Missouri, near Independence, where a large colony of Mormons had already been established. Joseph was arrested later that year, and early in the winter of 1839 the colony was hounded out of Missouri. Emma walked across the frozen Missouri River with her four young children and one of her husband's manuscripts (*Holy Scriptures, Translated and Corrected by the Spirit of Revelation*) safely hidden in her clothes.

In Illinois, the Mormons settled in Commerce, which they renamed Nauvoo and which quickly attracted converts and new settlers. It was granted a charter in 1840, as a result of politicians trying to win the 15,000-strong Mormon vote, and within five years would be the most populous city in the state. Economic and religious institutions were also founded, primary among them the Mormon Temple, completed in 1843. The year before that, the Female Relief Society had been founded with 20 members and a mission to uphold community morals and provide charity. Emma was elected the first president of the society, which grew to over 1,100 members by the end of the year; although its activities were suspended for a time after 1844, it is now the largest women's organization in the Mormon Church. Persecution by non-Mormons continued, however, and in addition, Emma had discovered that Joseph, having received (but not publicized) a revelation about the "order of Jacob"—plural marriage—had begun taking additional "wives." (Among the first of these 50 or more women was *Eliza Roxey Snow Smith**, in 1841.) Emma's protests and distress were to no avail, and in 1843 he showed her a revelation charging her to "receive all those that have been given unto my servant Joseph" or else go against the law of God.

While the subject was not bandied about, word of the possible practice of polygamy spread and led to increased anti-Mormon sentiment. In 1844, after much religious and social unrest, Joseph Smith and his brother Hyrum yielded to the threatening forces of the Illinois militia and were imprisoned in Carthage, Illinois. On June 27, 1844, while they were awaiting trial, the militia, with faces blackened for disguise, attacked the jail and lynched them. Emma Smith obtained the body of her husband and buried it secretly to prevent his grave from being ravaged by the mobs. (Many years later, she replaced it with a more open and stately resting place.) Joseph Smith's position at the head of the church was filled by Brigham Young, with whom Emma entered into a protracted battle over her late husband's property. Young saw most of it as the inheritance of the church, while she was concerned with providing for her children (the last of whom was born five months after Joseph's death). When Young led a majority of the Nauvoo Mormons to religious freedom in Utah in 1847, Emma chose to remain in Nauvoo with her children and a remnant of the Mormon colony. While her difficulties with Young played a large part in this decision, the main sticking point seems to have been polygamy, which Young endorsed and Emma still abhorred. (In 1852, Young published what was presented as Joseph Smith's revelation on plural marriage.)

She remained an otherwise devout Mormon, however, and continued to raise her children in the faith of their father. She remarried at the end of 1847 to Major Lewis Crum Bidamon, with whom she lived happily despite the fact that he was not a Mormon, and cared for Joseph Smith's mother Lucy Mack Smith until her death in 1856. In 1860, her eldest son **Joseph Smith III** became president of what would come to be called the Reorganized Church of Jesus Christ of Latter-Day Saints; his son would later succeed him. That the Reorganized Church resisted the practice of polygamy was primarily due to Emma's refusal to accept this as a policy dictated by Joseph and her insight that such practices would only alienate the church more from the surrounding community and society. She remained active in the Reorganized Church until her death in 1879.

**SOURCES:**

Fischer, Norma J. *Portrait of a Prophet's Wife: Emma Hale Smith*. Salt Lake City, UT: Silver Leaf Press, 1992.

**SUGGESTED READING:**

Newell, Linda King. *Mormon Enigma: Emma Hale Smith, Prophet's Wife, "Elect Lady," Polygamy's Foe, 1804–1879.* Garden City, NY: Doubleday, 1984.

**COLLECTIONS:**

Papers relating to Emma Hale Smith, including some letters, are located at the archives of the Reorganized Church of Jesus Christ of Latter-Day Saints in Independence, Missouri.

**Amanda Carson Banks**,
Vanderbilt Divinity School,
Nashville, Tennessee

# Smith, Erminnie A. Platt

## (1836–1886)

*American ethnologist. Born Ermina Adele Platt on April 26, 1836, in Marcellus, New York; died of heart disease and a cerebral embolism on June 9, 1886; daughter of Joseph Platt (a farmer and Presbyterian deacon) and Ermina (Dodge) Platt; graduated from Troy Female Seminary in New York, 1853; studied at universities in Strassburg and Heidelberg, Germany, and attended the School of Mines in Freiburg, Germany; married Simeon H. Smith (a lumber dealer), in 1855; children: Simeon, Willard, Carlton, and Eugene.*

*Was the first woman to practice in the field of ethnology; was the first woman elected a fellow of the New York Academy of Sciences (1885); was the first woman to hold an office (secretary of the anthropology section) in the American Association for the Advancement of Science; became a member of the London Scientific Society.*

Erminnie (originally Ermina) A. Platt Smith was the ninth of ten children born to **Ermina Dodge Platt** and Joseph Platt, a successful farmer and Presbyterian deacon. Her mother died when Erminnie was only two years old, and her father became a tremendous influence upon her life. His rock-collecting hobby stimulated her interest in geology and other sciences. In 1853, she graduated from *Emma Willard's Troy Female Seminary in New York, where she excelled in the study of languages. Two years later, she married wealthy Chicago lumber dealer Simeon H. Smith. During this time, Erminnie Smith's interest in geology led her to museum work as she classified and labeled mineral specimens destined for European institutions.

In 1866, the Smiths moved from Chicago to Jersey City, New Jersey, where Simeon later served as the city's finance commissioner. The mother of four sons, Erminnie spent their early years at home, but when the family moved temporarily to Germany for the boys' schooling, she took the opportunity to continue her own education as well. She studied crystallography and German literature at Strassburg and Heidelberg, and in Freiburg took a two-year course in mineralogy at the School of Mines.

Upon her return to the United States in the mid-1870s, Smith created a small mineralogical museum in her home and visited other homes to conduct a series of lectures on geological and cultural subjects. In 1876, this project blossomed into the Aesthetic Society, a group of women who met regularly to discuss science, literature, and the arts. The society often attracted as many as 500 people to witness demonstrations of new inventions, such as the phonograph, or to hear such prominent figures as Matthew Arnold speak. She further popularized science by directing programs for Sorosis, the women's club in New York City. In recognition of her work to promote scientific endeavors, she was elected into the American Association for the Advancement of Science.

Through her widespread promotion of science, Smith learned of the emerging field of anthropology and took special interest in Native American ethnology. Raised near the Onondaga reservation in New York, Smith focused her studies on the Iroquois Nation, and spent most of her time among the Tuscarora tribe, which bestowed upon her the name of "Beautiful Flower." From 1880 to 1885, she devoted her summers to traveling to reservations in New York and Canada under the auspices of the Smithsonian Institution's Bureau of American Ethnology, which partially funded her work. Smith also received the expert advice of longtime Iroquois researcher Lewis Henry Morgan. She compiled an Iroquois dictionary of more than 15,000 words and recorded a collection of legends, which was published in 1883 by the Bureau of American Ethnology as *Myths of the Iroquois.*

The first woman to engage in ethnographic field research, Smith dedicated the rest of her life to its study. Through her pioneering efforts, the training of native informants became a standard technique in field research as a method of collecting information of greater accuracy. Each year she read papers on her Iroquois research at the annual meetings of the American Association for the Advancement of Science, and in 1885 she was elected secretary of the association's anthropology division, the first woman to hold an officer position. She was also the first woman to become a fellow of the New York Academy of Sciences, and held a similar position in the London Scientific Society. In 1886, at age 50, Erminnie A. Platt Smith died of heart disease and a cerebral embolism.

**SOURCES:**

James, Edward T., ed. *Notable American Women, 1607–1950*. Cambridge, MA: The Belknap Press of Harvard University, 1971.

Read, Phyllis J., and Bernard L. Witlieb. *The Book of Women's Firsts*. NY: Random House, 1992.

**Kimberly A. Burton**, B.A., M.I.S.,
Ann Arbor, Michigan

## Smith, Francie Larrieu (b. 1952).

*See Larrieu, Francie.*

## Smith, Hannah Whitall (1832–1911).

*See Thomas, M. Carey for sidebar.*

# Smith, Hazel Brannon (1914–1994)

*White Southern newspaper owner and editor, one of the few journalists in her region to oppose racism during early desegregation efforts, who was the first woman editor to win a Pulitzer Prize. Name variations: Hazel Brannon. Born on February 4, 1914, in Gadsden, Alabama; died on May 14, 1994, in Cleveland, Tennessee; daughter of Doc Boad Brannon (an electrical contractor) and Georgia Parthenia Brannon; graduated from high school in Gadsden; University of Alabama, B.A. in journalism, 1935; married Walter Dyer Smith, in 1950; no children.*

*Following high school graduation, became a reporter and then advertising representative for the Etowah Observor (1930–32); was managing editor of the University of Alabama student newspaper, Crimson-White (1932–33); purchased her first newspaper in Mississippi, the Durant News (1936); bought the Lexington Advertiser (1943), and later owned papers in towns of Flora and Jackson; campaigned editorially against corruption in her local Holmes County, and against racist economic, political and legal policies in the county and state, which made her a target of financial and personal harassment; honored for her editorial writing by the National Federation of Press Women (1948, 1955); received award of the Mississippi Association of Teachers in Colored Schools (1948); named an "admired southern integrationist" by Ebony magazine (1954); received the Herrick Award of the National Editorial Association (1956); received Fund for the Republic citation and Mississippi Press Association Convention commendation (1957); 27th Annual Matrix Table at Marquette University, sponsored by Theta Sigma Phi (1958); granted Elijah Lovejoy Award from Southern Illinois University (1960) and Golden Quill Editorial Award from International Conference of Weekly Newspaper Editors (1963); awarded Pulitzer Prize for editorial writing (1964); was the subject of the television movie "A Passion for Justice: The Hazel Brannon Smith Story," starring Jane Seymour in the title role (1994).*

When Hazel Brannon Smith was awarded the Pulitzer Prize for editorial writing in 1964, she noted that she had never intended to be a leader in the fight for integration in Mississippi, but that the segregationist White Citizens Council had thrust her into the role. "I believe in obeying the law," she said, "and they were set on disobeying it."

Born Hazel Brannon on February 4, 1914, in the upcountry Alabama town of Gadsden, she was the first child of Doc Boad Brannon, an electrical contractor, and **Georgia Parthenia Brannon**; eventually, she would have four sisters and brothers. Too young to go to college when she finished high school at age 16, Hazel went to work at the *Etowah Observor*, writing "personals," short items on church suppers, weddings, teas, and other social events involving families in the area, for which she was paid five cents an inch.

The editor liked her work so much that he assigned her to front-page news, then changed her duties again after a banker observed that she was "wasted on news and ought to sell advertising." Her success at ad sales led the paper to put her on salary instead of commission to save itself money; she also kept the paper's books. After two years at the *Observor*, Smith knew what she wanted: her own newspaper.

In 1932, at age 18, she entered the University of Alabama and became managing editor of the school newspaper in her freshman year. She maintained good grades and also enjoyed an active social life that included her selection as a beauty queen of the Delta Zeta sorority. Taking to heart the counsel of her favorite professor, who encouraged his bright students to remain in the South, she reached the conviction that "the South is my home and my love, and I don't ever expect to leave it."

After graduating in 1935, Smith began looking around for an economically troubled newspaper to buy. Over in Holmes County, Mississippi, the *Durant News* looked like a good prospect, since it had had three editors in 13 months, and Hazel was able to make the purchase with a $3,000 loan. Townspeople in that region of flatlands and hills began to make bets on how long she would last, with no one wagering even six months. In a short time, however, the paper's circulation of 600 had risen to 1,400.

Mississippi newspaper editor Hodding Carter, who met Smith soon after she bought the

*News*, once described Holmes County as combining an "arrogant feudalism" with "provincial suspicion, racial and religious bigotry and [a] predilection for violence." It was into this environment that Smith, at age 21, brought her dedication to observance of the law and her enthusiasm for reporting the truth.

*My* interest has been to print the truth and protect and defend the freedom of all Mississippians.

—Hazel Brannon Smith

Working the long hard hours typical of most small-newspaper owners, she honed her publishing skills while also learning the printing trade. In addition to covering the routine local news of births, deaths, marriages, arrests and local government activity, she wrote a regular editorial column, "Through Hazel Eyes," which called attention to issues people sometimes preferred to ignore. One favored establishing a public health clinic to treat venereal disease, a subject rarely discussed in public at the time. While seeing the son of a well-known family, Hazel was told by her date, "Ladies just don't talk about venereal disease," to which she replied, "Well, I ain't no lady. I'm a newspaper woman."

In four years, advertising sales and outside printing jobs had paid for the Durant paper. In 1943, Brannon bought the *Lexington Advertiser*, which paid for itself in three years. She later bought small papers in Flora and another nearby town, all of which were printed on the press in Lexington.

Smith had the small-town publisher's belief in community and the importance of a newspaper in supporting a good quality of life for local residents. In one instance, when a firm was proposing to build a factory in Lexington, she flew north to inspect the company and its executives, and returned to persuade her readers to vote for the bond issue that would finance the plant.

In the early years of her ownership, her editorials dealt often with the misuse of public power and called for human respect and dignity for all persons, including African-Americans; she campaigned through her column against gambling and liquor interests and corrupt local politicians. In 1946, her editorial coverage led to the indictments of 64 public officials for their misdoings. That same year, when five white men were indicted for the whipping death of a black man, Smith printed an interview with the victim's widow. While the five defendants were not convicted, Hazel was cited for contempt of court for interviewing a witness. She was given a 15-day

jail sentence, a $50 fine, and an admonition from the judge: "I realize you are putting on a great campaign for law and order, but if you read history, you will see that the only Perfect Being did not make much of a hit with His reform." The jail sentence was remanded to a two-year suspension "under good behavior," which the young editor appealed to the state supreme court, where the ruling was eventually in her favor.

In 1948, Smith was honored with the top award of the National Federation of Press Women for her editorial condemning a jury which had acquitted an alleged bootlegger who later killed another man in an auto crash. That same year, she received a certificate of merit from the Mississippi Association of Teachers in Colored Schools.

A year later, with her business in small newspapers solidly established, 35-year-old Hazel decided to take a break by going on a world cruise. On board ship, she met the ship's purser, Walter Dyer Smith, from Philadelphia. Hazel and Smitty fell in love and were married in 1950.

More a pragmatist than an idealist, Hazel Brannon Smith was elected twice as a Mississippi delegate to the Democratic National Convention along with states' rights politicians. In press circles, she said, "A crusading editor is one who goes out and looks for the wrongs of the world. I just try to take care of things as they come up. I try to make them a little better." In fact, however, attempts to make things better in Holmes County would lead her directly into the crusade for civil rights that was soon to dominate her region.

From 1951 to 1954, Smith turned her attention to political and legal corruption in Holmes County. Her outspoken editorial campaigns were aimed particularly against Sheriff Richard F. Byrd whose connections to special interests made him indifferent to local illegalities. Smith's writings earned her enemies among some of the more wealthy and powerful local citizens.

In 1954, following the handing down by the U.S. Supreme Court of its famed *Brown* v. *Board of Education* decision, which heralded the end of officially accepted racial discrimination in public schools, Smith was visited in her office by a leading Lexington citizen. He brought news of plans by local white residents to organize against the ordered desegregation, and was there to test whether the group could count on Smith's "cooperation." Made aware of the intention of the newly formed White Citizens Council to intimidate blacks, she challenged him. "[I]t's not a good thing for anyone to be a little scared," said Smith. "People can't live under fear, and it will end up with all of us scared, and it will be a big scare. What you're proposing to do is take away the freedom of all the people in this community."

A factor in the "big scare" that subsequently consumed Holmes County was Smith's coverage of Sheriff Byrd's controversial shooting of Henry Randle, an African-American who apparently had done no wrong. In her editorial reprimand, she wrote:

> [T]he laws in America are for everyone—rich and poor, strong and weak, black and white. The vast majority of Holmes County people are not rednecks who look with favor on the abuse of people because their skins are black. [Byrd] has violated every concept of justice, decency and right. He is not fit to occupy office.

When Byrd sued Smith for libel, she was found guilty by the county court which assigned an award of $10,000 in damages. Smith appealed the verdict, while the campaign to intimidate her into silence broadened; her refusal to condemn federal and state officials for any moderate or supportive positions on integration had by that time incurred the wrath of many whites found throughout Holmes County. Later in the year, she reported the shooting and wounding of a black schoolteacher who had complained to a white man about the damage he did to her yard while turning his car around. Smith was approached by members of the White Citizens Council and others who tried to get her to kill the story, but she refused. The trespasser was never arrested, but both the teacher, a 20-year veteran, and her husband were fired from their jobs. Meanwhile, the White Citizens Council condemned Smith for favoring integration and criticized her acceptance of national awards which they alleged were sponsored by "Communist-infiltrated organizations."

In 1962, she would write:

> Worrying unduly about the so-called 'communist menace' in Mississippi is something like a minister orating on the sins of the people in Timbuktu when his own congregation sits uneasily in skid row. There are many things we fear more than communism in Mississippi—and chief among them is a fascist-type home grown organization which already is more of a threat to freedom-loving people in Mississippi than the communists will ever be. We refer specifically to the White Citizens' Councils of Mississippi which too often in too many cases have adopted and followed methods that would make a communist green with envy.

In November 1955, after Byrd's libel decision against Smith was reversed by the Mississippi supreme court, she told *Time* magazine, "I don't regard this as a personal victory, but rather as a victory for the people's right to know." The editorial that had generated the suit meanwhile brought Smith more awards, including the highest honor of the National Federation of Press Women for the second time. The National Editorial Association presented her with its Herrick Award "for editorial writing, embracing the highest type of American principles and ideals," and in 1957, the Fund for the Republic recognized Smith as "an American whose actions have made an unusual contribution to advancing the principles of freedom and justice and the Bill of Rights." At the Mississippi Press Association convention that year, a unanimous vote commended "Mrs. Hazel Smith, editor of the *Lexington Advertiser* and the *Durant News* for her epochal fight in the interest of freedom of the press."

But the repercussions for her actions had barely begun. In January 1956, Holmes County hospital trustees, who were dominated by members of the White Citizens Council, arranged for the firing of Walter Smith from his position as hospital administrator, although the medical staff asked unanimously for his reinstatement. One trustee stated on the record that it was not a move against Smitty himself but because "his wife [had] become a controversial person." The following day, Smitty became a newspaperman and, according to Hazel, "a damn good one."

When legal intimidation did not deter Smith's position, the White Citizens Council organized an advertising boycott. Although most merchants held out for some three years, and Smith discovered that many who did not agree with her positions were supporters of a free press, advertising in her papers eventually dropped 50%. Vandalism at their home and a bombing at one of the newspaper offices were also used against the Smiths, as well as hate handbills, gossip and name-calling. In one widely told account that is also a telling example of the tenor of the times, the Smiths were "rumored" to have entertained Dr. **Arenia Mallory**, the president of the all-black Saints Junior College in Lexington. Hazel was urged to print a denial of this, which she vehemently refused to do. During this period, Smith became the printer for the *Mississippi Free Press*, a civil-rights newspaper, and sat on a local advisory committee of the Civil Rights Commission.

Dissatisfied with the ineffectiveness of its threats, the White Citizens Council founded a rival newspaper in 1958, subsidized by wealthy council members. Lack of advertising was by this time draining Smith's papers financially, although readership continued at previous levels. Increased national recognition, through the honor of a Matrix Table bestowed by Marquette University's Theta Sigma Phi, merely increased the financial stress.

In 1960, a cross was burned on the Smiths' lawn, signifying the sentiments of local groups against her. Rather than be browbeaten, according to Hodding Carter, "Hazel herself descended upon them as the cross burned and . . . removed the license tag from their car so that proof of ownership . . . could be made." That year, Smith was honored with the Elijah Lovejoy Award "for demonstrating the ability to perform under great stress . . . her role as editor of the community's newspapers so effectively as to win the approval and support, in growing numbers, of the right thinking people of her town and county."

In 1961, in spite of their severe financial losses, the Smiths built a modern printing plant in Lexington where all their papers were printed, including the *Mississippi Free Press*, arousing further threats and defamation. In December, the Smiths and others, including civil-rights leader Medgar Evers, were observed meeting in the Jackson offices of the *Free Press* by segregationists. Unable to verify their suspicions because an evergreen tree protruding from the trunk of the Smiths' car obscured its license plate, the snoopers nevertheless signed an affidavit concerning their observations. The White Citizens Council distributed their findings to news media, legislators and white citizens of Holmes County. A state senator announced that although Hazel Brannon Smith was no longer respected but "shrewd and scheming," she would not be prosecuted. He failed to mention the crime she might have committed. The following spring, the state legislature passed a "reprisal law" regarding publication of official business proceedings of Holmes County towns; a state representative went on record as saying that he understood the law "concerned a woman editor who has been writing things which don't go along with the feelings in the community," but otherwise the insinuations remained vague.

Smith meanwhile continued to call attention to racial injustices. On May 16, 1963, her editorial took a Holmes County deputy sheriff to task for arresting a 58-year-old African-American farmer, Hartman Turnbow, on the charge of firebombing his own home. The only testimony at the preliminary hearing had come from the deputy, and that testimony had included hearsay evidence. For this commentary, Smith received the Golden Quill Editorial Award from the International Conference of Weekly Newspaper Editors.

In 1964, Smith became the first woman to win a Pulitzer Prize for editorial writing; her column on the firebombing had been among the entries she had submitted. The Pulitzer committee noted Smith's "steadfast adherence to her editorial duty in the face of great pressure and opposition," and *Newsweek* magazine reported that "[s]everal Southerners were not particularly happy over the selection."

In the summer of 1964, which has become known as Freedom Summer in civil-rights history, hundreds of college students and other civil-rights workers came south to Mississippi to join a campaign for registering African-American citizens to vote. In the city of Jackson, both the morning and afternoon papers were owned by the Hederman family, vigorous opponents of desegregation. Smith's *Northside Reporter* was the only newspaper to give alternative views of the registration campaign. That summer, the offices of the *Reporter* were bombed.

Prior to her targeting by racists, Smith had had a debt-free, profitable business in Holmes County, and the goodwill of her community. By 1965, after ten years of an advertising boycott, she was $100,000 in debt and had mortgaged her property to keep the papers going. Her staff had shrunk from fifteen to five. To raise funds, she went on the lecture circuit, receiving from $300 to $1,000 per speech. Help also came from the Hazel Brannon Smith Fund established at the *Columbia Journalism Review* of the University of Missouri, and at Saints Junior College in Lexington, Smith was presented with $2,852 on Editor's Appreciation Day, while the school's President Mallory offered "just a suggestion" that African-Americans might give their business only to area merchants who advertised in Smith's paper.

Through the following years of change in civil-rights laws and society's behavior and attitudes, Hazel Brannon Smith continued to publish the *Lexington Advertiser*. Her husband died in 1982, and Smith finally felt forced to sell the *Advertiser* in 1985 due to her own ill health and financial strain. Treated eventually for Alzheimer's disease, she moved to Cleveland, Tennessee, in 1988, to be cared for by her niece. On April 17, 1994, a television movie about her career, titled "A Passion for Justice: The Hazel Brannon Smith Story" and starring **Jane Seymour**, was broadcast by the ABC network. The program received criticism from family members because Smith, who had recently been diagnosed with cancer and was financially destitute, received none of the show's proceeds. She died a few weeks later, on May 14, and was buried in her hometown of Gadsden, Alabama.

Her legacy to journalistic and civil-rights history might best be summed up by her comments upon receiving the Pulitzer Prize:

> All we have done here is try to meet honestly the issues as they arose. We did not ask for, nor run from this fight. . . . But we have given it all we have, . . . years of our lives, loss of financial security and a big mortgage. We would do the same thing over, if necessary.

**SOURCES:**

"Appreciation Day," in *Newsweek*. December 13, 1965, p. 70.

Carter, Hodding. "Woman Editor's War on Bigots," in *First Person Rural*. Garden City, NY: Doubleday, 1963 (first published in *St. Louis* [Missouri] *Post Dispatch*, November 26, 1961).

Casey, Maura. "Pulitzer winner Hazel B. Smith: penniless heroine," in *The Day* [New London, CT]. June 5, 1994.

"Former Lexington editor dies in local nursing home," in *Cleveland* [Tennessee] *Daily Banner*. May 16, 1994.

Harris, T. George. "The 11-year siege of Mississippi's lady editor," in *Look*. November 16, 1965.

"The Last Word," in *Time*. November 21, 1955, p. 75.

Morrison, Minion K.C. *Black Political Mobilization: Leadership, Power, and Mass Behavior*. SUNY Series in Afro-American Studies. Albany, NY: State University of New York Press, 1987.

Obituary. *Cleveland* [Tennessee] *Daily Banner*. May 16, 1994.

Obituary. *Los Angeles Times*. May 16, 1994, Sec. A.

"Prize and Prejudice," in *Newsweek*. May 18, 1964, p. 76.

Sallis, Charles, and J.Q. Adams. "Desegregation in Jackson, Mississippi," in *Southern Businessmen and Desegregation*. Edited by Elizabeth Jacoway and David R. Colburn. Baton Rouge, LA: Louisiana State University Press, 1982.

Smith, Hazel Brannon. "Arrest of Bombing Victim is Grave Disservice," in *Pulitzer Prize Editorials: America's Best Editorial Writing, 1917–1979*. Edited by David W. Sloan. Ames, IA: Iowa State University Press, 1980 (first published in *Lexington Advertiser*. May 16, 1963).

**SUGGESTED READING:**

Beasley, Maurine Hoffman. *Taking Their Place: A Documentary History of Women and Journalism*. Washington, DC: American University Press in cooperation with the Women's Institute for Freedom of the Press, 1993.

Belford, Barbara. *Brilliant Bylines: A Biographical Anthology of Notable Newspaperwomen in America*. NY: Columbia University Press, 1986.

Braden, Maria. *She Said What?: Interviews with Women Newspaper Columnists*. Lexington, KY: University of Kentucky Press, 1993.

Carter, Hodding. "Their Words were Bullets: The Southern Press," in *War, Reconstruction and Peace*. Mercer University Lamar Memorial Lectures, no. 12. Athens, GA: University of Georgia Press, 1969.

Hardy, Gayle J. *American Women Civil Rights Activists: Biobibliographies of 68 Leaders, 1825–1992*. Jefferson, NC: McFarland, 1993.

Marzolf, Marion. *Up from the Footnote: A History of Women Journalists*. NY: Hastings House, 1977.

Schlipp, Madelon Golden and Sharon M. Murphy. *Great Women of the Press*. Carbondale, IL: Southern Illinois University Press, 1983.

Streitmatter, Rodger. *Raising Her Voice: African-American Women Journalists who Changed History*. Lexington, KY: University Press of Kentucky, 1994.

**RELATED MEDIA:**

"A Passion for Justice: The Hazel Brannon Smith Story" (television movie), starring Jane Seymour, produced by Mitch Engel and Edgar J. Scherick Associates, directed by James Keach, first aired on ABC on April 17, 1994.

**Margaret L. Meggs**,
independent scholar
on women's and disability issues,
Havre, Montana

## Smith, Jean Kennedy (1928—).

*See Kennedy, Rose Fitzgerald for sidebar.*

# Smith, Jessie Willcox (1863–1935)

*American painter and highly successful illustrator. Born Jessie Willcox Smith on September 8, 1863, in Philadelphia, Pennsylvania; died on May 3, 1935, in Philadelphia; buried in Woodland Cemetery, Philadelphia; youngest of four children, two girls and two boys, of Charles Henry Smith (an investment broker) and Katherine DeWitt (Willcox) Smith; attended the School of Design for Women (later Moore College of Art), Philadelphia, 1885; attended the Pennsylvania Academy of the Fine Arts, 1885–88; studied under Howard Pyle at the Drexel Institute of Arts and Sciences, 1894; never married; no children.*

*Awards, honors: Bronze Medal, Charleston Exposition (1902); Mary Smith prize of the Pennsylvania Academy of the Fine Arts (1903); silver medal, St. Louis Exposition (1904); Beck prize of the Philadelphia Water Color Club (1911); silver medal for water colors, Panama-Pacific Exposition (1915).*

*Began career teaching kindergarten for a year; after early training did several drawings for* St. Nicholas *magazine, but it was during her study with Pyle that she received her first book commissions; went on to illustrate such classics as* Little Women *and* A Child's Garden of Verses; *did advertisements and illustrations for periodicals, including* Ladies' Home Journal, Collier's, Scribner's, Harper's *and* Good Housekeeping, *for which she did covers.*

*Selected books illustrated: Henry Wadsworth Longfellow,* Evangeline *(illustrated with Violet Oakley, Houghton, 1897); Mary P. Smith,* Young Puritans in

Captivity *(Little, Brown, 1899); Louisa May Alcott,* An Old-Fashioned Girl *(Little, Brown, 1902); Mabel Humphrey,* The Book of the Child *(illustrated with Elizabeth Shippen Green, F.A. Stokes, 1903);* **Frances Hodgson Burnett,** In the Closed Room *(McClure, Phillips, 1904); Robert Louis Stevenson,* A Child's Garden of Verses *(Scribner, 1905); Helen Whitney,* The Bed-Time Book *(Duffield, 1907); Aileen C. Higgins,* Dream Blocks *(Duffield, 1908); Carolyn Wells,* The Seven Ages of Childhood *(Moffat, Yard, 1909); (Jessie Willcox Smith, comp.)* A Child's Book of Old Verses *(Duffield, 1910); Betty Sage,* Rhymes of Real Children *(Duffield, 1910); (Penrhyn Coussens, comp.)* A Child's Book of Stories *(Duffield, 1911); Angela M. Keyes,* The Five Senses *(Moffat, Yard);* Dickens' Children: Ten Drawings by Jessie Willcox Smith *(Scribner, 1912); Clement C. Moore,* 'Twas the Night Before Christmas *(Houghton, 1912);* The Jessie Willcox Smith Mother Goose *(Dodd, 1914); Alcott,* Little Women *(Little, Brown, 1915); Priscilla Underwood,* When Christmas Comes Around *(Duffield, 1915); Charles Kingsley,* The Water Babies *(Dodd, 1916); Mary Stewart,* The Way to Wonderland *(Dodd, 1917);* The Little Mother Goose *(Dodd, 1918); George MacDonald,* At the Back of the North Wind *(McKay, 1919); (Ada and Eleanor Skinner, comps.)* A Child's Book of Modern Stories *(Duffield, 1920); MacDonald,* The Princess and the Goblin *(McKay, 1920);* **Johanna Spyri,** Heidi *(McKay, 1922); (Ada and Eleanor Skinner, comps.)* A Little Child's Book of Stories *(Duffield, 1922); Nora A. Smith,* Boys and Girls of Bookland *(Cosmopolitan, 1923); (Ada and Eleanor Skinner, comps.)* A Very Little Child's Book of Stories *(Duffield, 1923); Samuel Crothers,* The Children of Dickens *(Scribner, 1925); (Ada and Eleanor Skinner, comps.)* A Child's Book of Country Stories *(Duffield, 1925); (Jessie Willcox Smith, comp.)* A Portfolio of Real Children *(Duffield). Also illustrator of "Beauty and the Beast" and "Goldilocks," and with Elizabeth Shippen Green illustrated a calendar, "The Child" (1903).*

One of the most popular and financially successful women artists of the Victorian era, and certainly one of the most prolific, Jessie Willcox Smith created illustrations for over 200 *Good Housekeeping* magazine covers as well as for numerous children's books, including Charles Kingsley's classic *The Water Babies.* Particularly acclaimed for her images of children, each individualized with a distinctive personality, she brought a new standard of realism to the art of illustration. Smith, a stately but shy woman who never married, spent her entire life in the Philadelphia area, living for many years in

a communal home with two other well-known women artists, *Elizabeth Shippen Green and *Violet Oakley.

Jessie Willcox Smith was born in Philadelphia on September 8, 1863, the youngest of the four children of Charles and **Katherine Willcox Smith.** Her father, an investment broker, had moved the family to Philadelphia from New York before she was born, and although the Smiths were not listed on Philadelphia's social register, Jessie and her siblings were raised to conform to the strict social standards of the day. Smith was educated at private schools in Philadelphia until the age of 17, during which there was no outward sign of her artistic talents. "The margins of my schoolbooks were perfectly clean and unsullied with any virgin attempts at drawing," she said later.

Smith was sent to finish her education in Cincinnati where she began training for a career as a kindergarten teacher, a safe and acceptable career choice for a woman of her day and one her parents encouraged. Her plans were waylaid, however, when she was asked to accompany a female cousin who was planning to give drawing lessons to a young professor. "I went along as chaperone," she explained, "it was in the day of chaperones." When her cousin asked the young man to begin by drawing a lamp that was in the room, Smith also took up a pencil to keep him company. She finished her sketch in a few swift lines, while the professor labored intensely, and went back to reading the book she had brought along. On the strength of that first drawing, Smith's talent was revealed, and she was thereafter encouraged by her friends to give up teaching and go to art school.

Returning to her family home in Philadelphia in 1885, Smith enrolled at the School of Design for Women. There she studied portraiture under William Sartain, one of the few classes she enjoyed. In the fall of that year, she transferred to the Pennsylvania Academy of the Fine Arts, where she was taught by the controversial Thomas Eakins, among others. "Only the most tenacious student could subject herself to the rigorous demands of Eakins' teaching, which made no allowances for the 'frailties' of women," reported one observer. Smith later called Eakins a brilliant artist but a "madman." (Fanatical about anatomical studies, he was eventually asked to leave the academy for removing a loincloth from a male model during a women's life class.) While never complaining about Eakins' teaching methods, Smith did note that her fellow students at the academy were a glum and self-

*Opposite page*

*Jessie Willcox Smith*

absorbed lot, suffering continually from what she termed "academy slump."

In 1888, while still attending the academy, Smith participated in the first public showing of her work, displaying a painting at the 58th Annual Academy Exhibition. In June of that year, after completing her course of study, she secured her first assignment as a freelance artist, painting Japanese figures on place cards for a business executive who was hosting a dinner party in conjunction with a performance of *The Mikado*. Later that year, her first illustration appeared in *St. Nicholas*, a magazine for children, and soon afterwards she secured a full-time position illustrating advertisements and borders for editorials for *Ladies' Home Journal*. It was her hope to earn enough money to finance a move out of her parents' house into her own home, which she was able to do around 1896. Although advantageously located in the center of town, within walking distance to her job, it was a very modest two-room apartment, making space a serious problem.

In 1894, Smith joined Howard Pyle's inaugural class in illustration at Drexel Institute, which met on Sunday afternoon when she did not have to work. Pyle's influence on her was profound; he was not only her teacher but mentored her early career. Smith subsequently attended the informal classes he conducted at a grist mill at Brandywine, and she was also one of the few promising students he accepted without tuition when he started his own school in Wilmington, Delaware, in 1900. From the beginning, Pyle changed Smith's view of illustrating, encouraging her to abandon some of the constraints of her academy education. "At the Academy, we had to think about compositions as an abstract thing," she said, "whether we needed a spot here or a break over here to balance, and there was nothing to get hold of. With Mr. Pyle it was absolutely changed. There was your story, and you knew your characters, and you imagined what they were doing, and in consequence you were bound to get the right composition because you lived these things. . . . It was simply that he was always mentally projected into his subject."

Through Pyle, who customarily gave work he didn't have time to complete to his most talented students, Smith received her first commission, illustrations for a book about Native Americans. Pyle also recruited Smith, and her fellow student Violet Oakley, to create illustrations for the Houghton Mifflin edition of Longfellow's *Evangeline* (1897). In the preface to the text, Pyle discussed his students' illustra-

tions. "I do not know whether the world will find an equivalent pleasure to my own in the pictures that illustrate this book," he wrote, "for there is a singular delight in beholding the lucid thoughts of a pupil growing into form and color; the teacher enjoys a singular pleasure in beholding his instruction growing into a definite shape. Nevertheless, I venture to think that the drawings possess both grace and beauty."

Along with Oakley, Smith also met Elizabeth Shippen Green at Drexel. The three women became close friends and ultimately established a home and studio together, first in an apartment in the city, then at the Red Rose Inn, a remodeled colonial inn at Villanova, outside Philadelphia. There they were joined by several of their parents and another friend, **Henrietta Cozens**, who took over the housekeeping and gardening chores. In 1905, following both Green's engagement to a young Philadelphia architect and the sale of the inn, Smith, Oakley, and Cozens moved to Hill Farm, in nearby Chestnut Hill. The women named their new home "Cogslea," a combination of the first letters of their last names and the old English word *lea*, meaning meadow. The artists were described in the press as "that group of very clever young women . . . [who] live out their daily artistic lives under one roof in the gentle camaraderie of some old world 'school.'"

Smith received national recognition in 1902, winning a bronze medal for paintings exhibited at the Charleston (South Carolina) Exposition. Her first commercial success was "The Child," a calendar self-published in collaboration with Elizabeth Shippen Green. The success of the calendar, reissued as *The Book of the Child* (1903), led Smith to a commission for her first children's book, *Rhymes for Real Children* (1903). From then on, she had more commissions than she could handle, leading her artist friends to dub her "the mint." Some of her most lucrative commissions came through advertisements and illustrations for various magazines, including *Ladies' Home Journal, Collier's, Scribner's, Century, Harper's*, and *Good Housekeeping*, the latter of which paid her $1,800 per cover. She also produced advertisements for Ivory and Cuticura soaps, Kodak, Campbell Soup, Fleischmann's Yeast, and Cream of Wheat.

Although magazine and advertisement commissions paid the rent, Smith derived the most satisfaction from her illustrations for children's books. Her early work in this area included illustrations for Robert Louis Stevenson's *A Child's Garden of Verses* (1914), \***Louisa May Alcott**'s *Little Women* (1915); **Priscilla Under-**wood's *When Christmas Comes Around* (1915), and Kingsley's *Water Babies* (1916), which, according to Richard Dalby, is "one of the most perfect combinations of pictures and prose in the Golden Age of book illustration." Smith's illustrated children's books had great appeal for adults as well. While making a gift of one of her works to a young child who posed for her, Smith included the following note: "To Pierre— With the understanding that if he finds this book too young for his advanced years—he shall give [it] to his father."

In 1914, needing more space and privacy, Smith moved into her own house ("Cogskill"), which she had built on property adjacent to Cogslea. Henrietta Cozens, as well as Smith's brother and an aunt, **Mrs. Roswell Weston**, also moved into the new house, helping to fill some of its 16 rooms. Like Cogslea, Smith's new residence boasted an exquisite garden, an ideal place for her young models to run and play freely. "I would watch and study them, and try to get them to take unconsciously the positions that I happened to be wanting for a picture," she said, explaining her process. Smith eschewed professional child models, calling them "an abomination and a travesty on childhood. All the models I have ever had for my illustrations are just the adorable children of my kind friends, who would lend them to me for a little while." When more formal poses were necessary, Smith would hold a child's attention by telling fairy stories, using all the animation she could muster while continuing to keep focused on her painting. "Alas the resplendent Cinderella sometimes stops halfway down the stairs, slipper and all, while I am considering the subtle curve in the outline of the listener's charming, enthralled little face." Smith continued to illustrate children's books until 1925, when she began to concentrate more on portraits and magazine covers. She worked for *Good Housekeeping* until 1933. Her later book illustrations included **Nora A. Smith**'s *Boys and Girls of Bookland* (1923) and several anthologies by **Ada** and **Eleanor Skinner**.

Smith, a tall, handsome woman with dark hair and fair skin, never married, although in her middle years she annually hosted a Swiss businessman who came to the United States to visit. Reportedly, each year he proposed marriage, and each year she refused. She truly loved and delighted in children and, throughout her career, financially supported some 11 of them, including the daughter and two sons of her invalid sister. Her generosity also extended to other causes; she frequently donated posters to orphanages and charities.

In 1933, although suffering from a variety of ailments, Smith embarked on her first trip to Europe, accompanied by a nurse and a niece of Henrietta Cozens. The trip proved to be a struggle for the ailing artist, who had deteriorated markedly by the time of her return. Smith died in her sleep on May 3, 1935, and was buried in Woodland Cemetery, in the city of her birth. In 1936, the Pennsylvania Academy of the Fine Arts mounted a memorial exhibit of Smith's work. The catalog contained a tribute from Smith's longtime friend **Edith Emerson**, who praised the artist for her generosity and kindness. Art critic **Rilla Evelyn Jackman** perhaps best summed up Smith's contribution to American illustration: "In the peculiar place which Miss Smith holds in the art world she is quite as worthy of our interest as are many of the artists who paint easel pictures for our great exhibitions or murals for our public buildings," she wrote. "In fact, she, more than most of them, is bringing art to the people. We are proud of the eagle, and fond of the warbler, but even for them we would not give up the robin and the bluebird."

**SOURCES:**

Bailey, Brooke. *The Remarkable Lives of 100 Women Artists*. Holbrook, MA: Bob Adams, 1994.

Commire, Anne, ed. *Something about the Author*. Vol. 21. Detroit, MI: Gale Research, 1980.

Dalby, Richard. *The Golden Age of Children's Book Illustration*. NY: Gallery Books, 1991.

James, Edward T., ed. *Notable American Women, 1607–1950*. Cambridge, MA: The Belknap Press of Harvard University, 1971.

McHenry, Robert, ed. *Famous American Women*. NY: Dover, 1980.

Rubinstein, Charlotte Streifer. *American Women Artists*. Boston, MA: G.K. Hall, 1982.

Schnessel, Michael S. *Jessie Willcox Smith*. NY: Thomas Y. Crowell.

**SUGGESTED READING:**

Carter, Alice A. *The Red Rose Girls: An Uncommon Story of Art and Love*. NY: Abrams, 2000.

**Barbara Morgan**,
Melrose, Massachusetts

## Smith, Julia (1792–1886).

*See joint entry under Smith, Abby and Julia.*

## Smith, Julia Frances (1911–1989)

*American composer. Born Julia Frances Smith in Denton, Texas, on January 25, 1911; died in New York City on April 27, 1989; one of seven children of Julia (Miller) Smith (a piano teacher) and James Willis Smith (a professor of mathematics); North Texas State College, B.A.; New York University, M.A., 1933; married Oscar Vielehr (an engineer), on April 23, 1938.*

*Applied for a composition fellowship at Juilliard to study with Rubin Goldmark; began teaching at Hamlin School in New Jersey; member of the Orchestrette Classique, an all-women's orchestra, for which she composed several works; composed Cynthia Parker which premiered (1939), the first of several operas; became a leader in having women's compositions performed; wrote a book on Aaron Copland (1955), and* Directory of American Women Composers *(1970); one of five women composers honored by the National Council of Women of the U.S. (1963); premiered the opera* Daisy *based on the life of Juliette Gordon Low (1973) which was performed more than 30 times in the next six years.*

Julia Frances Smith was born in Denton, Texas, in 1911, one of seven children of **Julia Miller Smith**, a piano teacher, and James Willis Smith, a professor of mathematics. She received her A.B. from North Texas State College where she composed the school's alma mater, and her M.A. from New York University in 1933.

When Smith applied for a fellowship to study composition at Juilliard in 1933, Rubin Goldmark, her future teacher, told her, "I have decided not to waste any more of Juilliard's money on fellowships for women. . . . All you gifted women composers come to New York, study a few years, then go back home, get married, have children, and that is the last that one ever hears of them as composers. Men will starve to become and remain composers but your sex has proved time again that you simply can't face the rigors of life alone." A spirited Texan, Smith replied, "*This* one can; Von Mickwitz, Friedberg, and George Wedge believe in me, why can't you?" Goldmark weakened, saying, "If you turn out like most of my women students, this will be the last fellowship I will ever extend to a woman."

Smith, who composed six operas as well as many other works, proved her point. Her first opera, *Cynthia Parker*, premiered in 1939 in New York, launching her career as a composer. Hollywood was even interested in filming it, but Smith refused to change the ending in order to ensure box-office success. Other operas followed, including *Daisy*, based on the life of *Juliette Gordon Low, which was performed 30 times in the six years after it was written. Smith also wrote works for piano, voice, organ, chamber groups, chorus, and orchestra.

Interested in the piano pieces of Aaron Copland, she wrote a book about them which appeared in 1955. She also worked to ensure that the compositions of other women composers were heard. In this effort, she wrote *Directory of American Women Composers*, published in 1970. The following year, she sent a letter to the National Endowment for the Arts (NEA), pointing out that no woman had ever received an outright grant in music, despite the fact that over 600 women composers were working at the time. Sizable grants for women from the NEA began in 1974. Despite her work as an author and activist, Smith's efforts as a composer continued. She proved in her long and successful career that women could endure in the musical world.

**SOURCES:**

Cohen, Aaron I. *International Encyclopedia of Women Composers*. 2 vols. NY: Books & Music (USA), 1987.

**John Haag**, Professor of History, University of Georgia, Athens, Georgia

## Smith, Kate (1907–1986)

*American singer who was a symbol of U.S. optimism and patriotism throughout the mid-20th century. Born Kathryn Elizabeth Smith in Greenville, Virginia, on May 1, 1907; died in Raleigh, North Carolina, on June 17, 1986, of complications from diabetes; daughter of William and Charlotte Smith; had one sister, Helena; educated in local schools; never married; no children.*

*Began singing and dancing in childhood at church socials and, during World War I, in army camps in and around Washington, D.C.; appeared in first vaudeville musical (1926) and embarked on a 50-year singing career on stage, in films, and on network radio and television; a tireless campaigner for charity causes, was also an outspoken proponent of American virtues, symbolized by many recordings and renditions of Irving Berlin's "God Bless America"; forced to retire because of health problems (mid-1970s); made few public appearances thereafter.*

Americans from coast to coast were huddled around their radio sets one winter's night in 1943, during the bleakest period of World War II. They weren't listening to war news; rather, they had tuned in to a war-bond variety show hosted by a strong-voiced woman whose songs, chatter, and cheery encouragement meant more to them than anything even President Franklin Roosevelt could say. On that single broadcast on CBS radio, Kate Smith would raise more money for the war effort than any other performer throughout the war years. Her voice was as familiar to Americans as the ample figure and wide-open face that beamed out at them from phonograph album covers, from magazines and newspapers and, if they were lucky, from the stage of a nearby theater or auditorium. She attracted a daily radio audience of some 25 million, singing in a powerful, resonant voice or sharing plain advice on meeting life's problems head-on; she had everything from racehorses to flowers to bombers named after her; and her many performances of "God Bless America" were so stirring in their patriotism that many mistook it for the new national anthem. Even President Roosevelt wasn't immune, choosing to introduce her to the king and queen of England in 1939 by saying, "Your Majesties, this is Kate Smith. This is America."

By her own definition "just a plain, simple woman," Smith carried a nation through 50 years of depression, war, and social upheaval with her unflagging optimism and a voice that conductor Leopold Stokowski once told her was a gift from God. But Smith's parents must have wondered if their daughter even had a voice for the first few years after her birth in Virginia in the spring of 1907. William and **Charlotte Smith** did not hear a peep out of little Kathryn Elizabeth for nearly four years; but she finally began singing and talking at the same time, as if both were equally natural to her.

"For as long as I can remember," she once wrote, "my greatest desire in life and my most complete happiness has been to sing," although she had no formal musical education and was unable to read music. She pointed to her family's church singing every Sunday as an early influence, along with the experience of singing for a visiting group of French World War I heroes, to which they responded with great enthusiasm and affection. A third factor, Smith said, was the Charleston, the dance that was all the rage in the early 1920s, when she had reached her teens. By then, she was singing and dancing in church socials and for groups of World War I veterans, and would always bring down the house with the dance that had become a symbol of the roaring '20s. The stage became her home, and applause her sweetest music. "The crowd cheers, applauds, stamps its feet, yells friendly greeting," she said. "My heart fills to bursting. They like me! They know me!"

The audience's affection may have had a tinge of surprise, too, for at first glance, Smith did not appear to be the type to break into an energetic dance routine. By the time she was 20, Smith had assumed the physique described in those days as "strapping," generous in girth and robust in proportion. But during her early career, she would be known as much for her light-footed hoofing as for her singing, and she was talented enough at both for Broadway producer Abe Erlanger to notice her in a Washington vaudeville revue in 1925—a job she had taken after dropping out of the nursing school in which her parents had insisted she enroll after high school. He offered her a part in his upcoming Broadway show, *Honeymoon Lane*, playing a character called Tiny Little, a slapstick role trading on her ample figure that earned her many laughs but little attention as a serious singer. Nevertheless, she stuck it out and even toured with the production before recording several songs from the show for Columbia Records, which were the first of some 3,000 records she would make over the next 50 years.

Similar parts in other vaudeville shows followed which, although small, caused enough stir for Warner Bros. to make a short film, *Kate Smith: Songbird of the South*, at its Manhattan studios in 1929. Such shorts were the music videos of the day, used as filler between full-length features in movie theaters. In her first film, Smith sang "Carolina Moon" to such effect that Warner's advertised the Vitaphone release with the slogan, "If a Vitaphone act could take encores, you'd have to play this one all night." But Smith's next stage appearance nearly drove her from the business. She played opposite Bert Lahr in George White's *Flying High* and was subjected to Lahr's constant, ad-libbed, on-stage jabs and jokes about her weight, in which he encouraged the entire cast to take part. Lahr, soon to become familiar to millions as the Cowardly Lion in MGM's *The Wizard of Oz*, refused Smith's pleas to stop making fun of her, even on the night when Kate knew her grandparents would be in the audience. In later years, a more repentant Lahr claimed that Smith's inexperience on stage had been stealing his laughs, but what Smith was really stealing from him was the show. The critics praised her more than they did Lahr, although even the best of them couldn't resist mentioning her formidable physique. "Kate Smith is sitting on top of the world; nothing else would bear the weight," was a typical comment. Despite the $450 a week White was paying her, Smith was preparing to quit the show, and the stage. "There was no getting away from the fact," she later said, "that those who remembered me at all thought of me as a fat girl first and, second, as a singer." But one night, someone walked into her dressing room who saw things the other way around.

At the time, Ted Collins was a recording executive with Columbia Records, and what he saw on stage was a vocal artist with immense potential. Collins took matters in hand, getting

Lahr and the rest of the cast to stick to the script, and proposing to become Smith's manager when the show closed. It was the beginning of a professional friendship that would last for 40 years and turn Kate Smith into a national institution.

> *I* have a hunch that microphone will become quite a pal of yours, Kathryn.
>
> —Manager Ted Collins, after Kate Smith's first radio show, 1931

Collins knew that Smith's future was in radio and records, not in the theater. By 1931, she had the first of many recording contracts with Columbia; had been introduced to national radio audiences on Rudy Vallee's "Fleischmann's Hour," the most popular show on the air at the time; and by spring of that year, had her own show on CBS three times a week, on the first of which Smith introduced what would become her theme song, "When the Moon Comes Over the Mountain." Smith herself had written the lyrics as a poem, which Collins had musician friends set to music. The first show—the first, in fact, of over 15,000 radio broadcasts—went out nationwide over CBS on April 26, and Smith later confessed to a bad case of nerves waiting for the network connection light to turn green. She wasn't even sure how to begin the show, so Collins suggested just a simple hello. Thus was born another of Smith's trademarks, the "Hello, everybody! This is Kate Smith!" which opened every show from then on, along with her equally simple "Thanks for listenin'!" at the end. The program became so popular that CBS expanded it to five days a week, until it went off the air two years later when Smith's contract ran out. By then, she was earning $3,000 a week. All the while, she kept up a nearly constant recording schedule, played a host of charity fundraisers, did several more one-reelers for Warner's, and appeared in her first feature film for Paramount, *The Big Broadcast*, in which Bing Crosby, perhaps with tongue in cheek, referred to her as "America's greatest singer." Her segment of the film was shot on a New York soundstage to accommodate her radio schedule, but when her program went off the air, Paramount offered her a starring role in a film to be shot in Hollywood. Smith found herself heading West for the first time in her life.

Originally calling it *Moon Song*, Paramount decided to rename the picture *Hello, Everybody!* to capitalize on Smith's radio success. The studio again accommodated Smith's radio schedule (she was still doing guest spots, even though her own show was off the air) by building a studio especially for her on the lot, and made sure she wined and dined with the stars. But Smith was not impressed. "There is . . . a lack of sincerity," she would later write of movie people. "Friendship, or what passes for it, is bestowed lightly on anyone in a position of importance." At a dinner given especially in her honor, attended by the likes of Clark Gable and Randolph Scott, Smith found herself mentally looking for the exit and "wishing for an apple, a glass of milk, and a good book." Deciding that Hollywood was not the milieu for a hometown girl, Smith finished the picture but asked Collins to get her out of her contract for future films—the only time in her professional life she broke such an agreement.

Back in New York, Collins swiftly got her a one-week's engagement at the Palace on Broadway, headlined as *Kate Smith and her Swanee Revue*, which went on the road after its Broadway run as one of the last great touring vaudeville shows. Now Smith was in her element, spending much of 1932 and 1933 trooping from town to town, meeting everyday Americans—rather than self-centered Hollywood stars—and reveling in the magic of the road; a magic, she said, that had nothing to do with bright lights, fancy parties, and artificial frivolity, but with "sharing things with old friends and making new ones; of work well done, and the reward of applause, which is like no other music." The tour crisscrossed the country for months, giving Smith her first real experience of the country whose virtues she would propound so eagerly in the coming years. She went on sleigh rides in Minneapolis, played golf in Texas, and went deep-sea fishing off the coast of California.

By the time the tour ended late in 1933, Smith and Ted Collins had formed a management company, Kated, Inc., to manage her own career and those of other vaudeville artists. The two partners split the proceeds down the middle, and the arrangement would earn both of them a prosperous return—an estimated $50 million for Smith alone during her career. Collins had lined up a radio schedule that would keep Smith on the air nearly constantly for the next 20 years. Renewing her contract with CBS, she went back on the air in 1934 with "The Kate Smith Matinee Hour," followed by "Kate Smith's All-Star Revue" in 1935 and "Kate Smith's Coffee Time" later the same year, sponsored by the Atlantic and Pacific Tea Company (better known as A&P) which reported a 25% increase in coffee sales. "Coffee Time" was Smith's first show to use a live studio audience, along with another innovation thought up by Collins—a segment of the show he called "Command Performance,"

which honored acts of heroism by real people and rewarded them with cash prizes. The response, and the number of entries for the awards, grew to such proportions that the segment had to be phased out and the fund Smith had set up for the prizes turned over to the Red Cross. During each "Coffee Time," Smith would also interview sports stars, military heroes and other personalities.

In addition to her radio shows, Smith continued a tireless round of charity appearances, raising money for everything from cancer research to tree-planting schemes. Although some critics saw these appearances as nothing but free publicity for her, Smith paid them no mind. Depression-era Americans loved their Kate, and relied on her to lift their spirits with a song and a cheerful word of advice. "I like to feel that I'm making people a little happier, especially people who are ill or in trouble," she said, and purposefully selected a repertoire of uplifting, sentimental songs that would be enjoyable and understandable to the widest possible audience. In 1938, on a show dedicated to the Armistice that had ended World War I 20 years before, Smith introduced the song that became hers and hers alone—"God Bless America." Collins had gone to Irving Berlin for something to mark Armistice Day, and Berlin produced the stirring paean evoking American majesty and might that Smith would sing on 65 consecutive shows and perform scores of times in numerous recorded versions until her retirement. The song earned millions in royalties, which both Smith and Berlin donated to the Girl and Boy Scouts of America; and when Berlin's original manuscript of the song was discovered in Las Vegas in 1990, the Kate Smith God Bless America Foundation put it up for auction, using the $295,000 it brought to good purpose for its many charitable activities.

In the same year that "God Bless America" swept the nation, Ted Collins introduced yet another innovation for Smith—a show on which she never sang at all. "Kate Smith Speaks" began as a 15-minute chat show during which Smith dispensed her own brand of homespun wisdom, offered her favorite recipes as well as ways to deal with "excess avoirdupois," and pronounced her opinions on a number of issues. With Hitler about to invade Poland and throw Europe into chaos, she spoke out against the cruelty of war; she mustered support for a new series of child-labor laws then under consideration in Washington; and she urged women to step outside the home and get involved in government affairs "so that they may use whatever influence they have in their community to work toward better health conditions, greater education, and other improvements which relate directly to youth and to the home." "Kate Smith Speaks" was on the air every day for 13 years, and became as much a part of the day as the lunchtime soup and sandwich.

During World War II, it seemed as if Smith were everywhere but on the front lines. She raised some $600 million for the war effort through bond drives, entertained the troops in training camps around the nation, sent them off with a hearty wave from the docks, and cheered them up when they were sent home, injured, to hospitals. She and Ted Collins went wherever the Defense Department wanted them, often paying their own way, and broadcast "The Kate Smith Hour" live from any location. Her most popular records were issued during the war, from "White Cliffs of Dover" to "When You Wish Upon a Star." She was called "radio's Statue of Liberty," and it seemed only natural that she should be awarded the Patriotic Service Cross when the war was over. Around 1952, Smith was voted in a Gallup poll one of the three most popular women in the world, sharing the honor with *Eleanor Roosevelt and Queen *Elizabeth II.

The 1950s brought a new entertainment medium, and Smith did not miss a beat, appearing on NBC-TV's "The Kate Smith Hour" in 1950 in addition to keeping her radio commitments. By 1952, she was on radio or television a total of ten hours a week, rehearsing the rest of the time and continuing her charity appearances—a schedule grueling enough that doctors warned her she risked a stroke if she continued, especially since her "excess avoirdupois" now reached well over 200 pounds. Heeding their advice, she and Collins decided to take 1954 off. Smith spent the time recuperating at Camp Sunshine, the home she had built on a small island in New York's Lake Placid, while Collins rested at his own newly built place on the mainland. Both could be seen zipping around the lake in Smith's speedboat, *Sunshine I.* The hiatus stretched into the next year when Collins had a near-fatal heart attack and Smith vowed to stay at his side.

Kate
Smith

She returned to the air in 1956 with a revival of "The Kate Smith Hour," this time on ABC, and a radio show once a week for Mutual that began in 1958. In 1960, she left ABC for CBS, where she and Collins mounted "The Kate Smith Show" on Monday nights at 7:30. But the show was canceled after only one season, leaving Smith with no television presence at all, outside of guest appearances. As usual, Collins had an idea.

The sold-out Carnegie Hall concert of November 1962, backed by Skitch Henderson's orchestra, is still talked about in pop music circles. It was as if America were discovering Kate Smith all over again. "Her voice has lost none of its robust resonance," wrote critic John Wilson. "Her delivery was easy and effortless, her tone mellow and smooth, and she can still belt out a powerhouse climax." Offers started pouring in, for films, television, and personal appearances. Smith accepted as many as she could, even appearing once with a full-leg cast after a fall that fractured her ankle. But the revival of her career was cut short when Ted Collins suffered another heart attack in May 1964 and died. Devastated by the loss, Smith announced she was taking six months off and went into seclusion at Camp Sunshine. "He was my manager, my partner, my devoted friend," Smith said of him. "Unselfishness and loyalty were deeply ingrained in this kindly, outgoing, laughing, generous man."

For the next two years, little would be heard from her. Health problems began to appear, starting with double pneumonia shortly after Collins' death. This was followed by another fall later that same year and, eventually, news that she had been stricken with the diabetes that had plagued her father. Smith took comfort from close friends and family, and from the spirituality that had always been the foundation of her natural optimism. She embraced the Catholic faith in 1965 and would remain a devoted adherent for the rest of her life. Her private meeting with Pope Paul VI at the Vatican in 1966 was, she said, the high point of her life, as well as the only time she ever left her beloved United States. By 1967, she felt sufficiently restored to tell an interviewer, "It's no good to stop. If you have it in you to keep going, keep moving on, then that's what you've got to do." Smith had decided it was time to move on.

That year, she re-emerged with a reissue of many of her bestselling records, then with personal appearances on television and on the stage. In 1969, she starred in her own nationally syndicated television special, and sang "God Bless America" to a crowd of 350,000 gathered in Washington in 1970 for "Honor America Day." Her final TV special in 1973 was another syndicated show carried by 160 stations, "Kate Smith Presents Remembrances . . . and Rock," which numbered among its guests *The Supremes; and among her final recordings that year was a version of "Smile" that she recorded with rock pianist Doctor John. But her most unexpected new audience was the Philadelphia Flyers hockey team which, suffering through a discouraging season, substituted the national anthem with one of Smith's rousing versions of "God Bless America." They found themselves in the Stanley Cup playoffs that year, and actually won the Cup the next year, with Smith cheering them on from the bleachers.

During the nation's bicentennial year, Smith was admitted to a New York hospital for a respiratory illness, but unexpectedly lapsed into a diabetic coma from which she emerged with her eyesight impaired and her mental abilities reduced. Declared legally incompetent in 1979, Smith was moved to Raleigh, North Carolina, where she lived as an invalid with her sister. Still, she summoned enough strength to travel to Los Angeles in the spring of 1982 to receive a special Emmy Award for her contributions to television. In the fall of that year, she went to the White House to receive the nation's highest civilian award, the Medal of Freedom, from President Ronald Reagan. "Kate always sang from the heart," he said, "and so we always listened with our hearts."

Kate Smith died in June 1986 and was buried in her beloved town of Lake Placid. It seemed as if one of the best parts of America had passed away with her, but Smith wouldn't have stood for the mournful postmortems. "I guess my creed is to get as much good, clean, wholesome fun out of life as you can," she once wrote, and that is exactly what she did.

**SOURCES:**

Pitts, Michael. *Kate Smith: A Bio-Bibliography.* NY: Greenwood Press, 1988.

Slonimsky, Nicholas, ed. *Baker's Biographical Dictionary of Musicians.* 8th ed. NY: Schirmer Books, 1992.

Smith, Kate. *Living Life in a Great Big Way.* NY: Blue Ribbon Books, 1938.

**Norman Powers**, writer-producer,
Chelsea Lane Productions,
New York

# Smith, Lillian (1897–1966)

*American writer, civil-rights activist, and devoted Southerner who dedicated her life to educating Americans about the evils of prejudice broadly defined and to pressing white Southerners to recognize that segre-*

*gation harmed them also. Born Lillian Eugenia Smith on December 12, 1897, in Jasper, Florida, a small community near the Georgia border; died of cancer in Emory Hospital, Atlanta, Georgia, on September 28, 1966; buried on Old Steamer Mountain, Georgia; daughter of Annie (Hester) Smith and Calvin Warren Smith (a merchant and later children's camp administrator); attended Piedmont College, 1916; Peabody Conservatory, 1917–20; Columbia University Teachers College, 1927–28; longtime companion of Paula Snelling, 1930–66.*

*Awards: Honor Roll of Race Relations, Schomburg Collection of New York Public Library (1942); Page One Award, Newspaper Guild of New York (1944); \*Constance Lindsay Skinner Award, Women's National Book Association (1945); Southern Authors Award, Special Citation National Book Award Committee; honorary Doctorate of Humane Letters, Howard University, and honorary Doctor of Letters, Oberlin College (1950); Georgia Writers Award (1955); Sidney Hillman Prize (1962); Queen Esther Scroll of Women's Division of the American Jewish Congress (1965); Charles S. Johnson Award of Fisk University (1966).*

*Family moved to Rabun County, Georgia (1915); helped her father run the Laurel Falls Hotel on Old Steamer Mountain; served as director of music, Virginia School in Huzhou (Huchow), a Methodist academy for wealthy Chinese girls in Zhejiang (Chekiang or Che-chiang) Province (1922–25); returned home to take over Laurel Falls Camp when father's health failed (1925); directed camp (1925–48); elected president, Macon Writers Club (1935); founded, with Paula Snelling, Pseudopodia (1936), name changed to North Georgia Review (1937) and to The South Today (1942); traveled the South with Snelling as Rosenwald Fund fellows to investigate racial and class divisions in education and employment; served as member of the Rosenwald Scholarship Committee (1942–44); was an active member of the board of the Southern Conference of Human Welfare (1942–44); Strange Fruit banned in Boston (1944); joined the boards of the NAACP, the ACLU, and CORE (mid-1940s); joined the Chicago Defender as weekly columnist (1948); learned of breast cancer (1954); teenage arsonists set fire to her home on Old Steamer Mountain, destroying library, manuscripts and correspondence; wrote Now is the Time to urge the South to comply with Brown v. Board of Education (1955); hospitalized for recurrence of cancer (1955); elected vice-chair, ACLU (1956); actively supported Montgomery Bus Boycott and the Montgomery Improvement Association; became advisor to Student Nonvio-*

*lent Coordinating Committee (1960); was traveling with Martin Luther King, Jr., when he was arrested for driving with an expired license in Atlanta (1960); re-hospitalized for cancer (1962); actively worked with students challenging segregation, writing Our Faces, Our Worlds (1963) and advising Southern Students Organizing Committee; hospitalized twice for lung cancer (1964); defended Julian Bond's right to be seated in the Georgia Legislature (1965).*

*Selected writings: (editor) South Today (1936–45); Strange Fruit (1944); Killers of the Dream (1949, rev. 1962); The Journey (1954); Now Is the Time (1955); One Hour (1959); Memory of a Large Christmas (1961); "The Ordeal of Southern Women," in Redbook (May 1961); "A Strange Kind of Love," in Saturday Review (October 20, 1962); Our Faces, Our Worlds (1963); "The Day It Happens to Each of Us," in McCall's (November 1964); "Old Dream, New Killers," in Atlanta Constitution (January 14, 1966).*

On February 29, 1944, Lillian Smith's first novel *Strange Fruit* was published and created an immediate sensation. Set in a fictional town in southern Georgia, *Strange Fruit* tells of white Tracy Deen's love for black Nonnie Anderson and Deen's reluctance to confront the town's racial customs to marry the woman he loves. When Anderson becomes pregnant with Deen's child, Deen pays his employee Henry to marry Anderson and to claim the child as his own. Later when Deen is killed, Henry is unjustly accused of Deen's murder and is lynched by an enraged white mob.

Smith used this plot to tell a story "about the 'strange fruit' of our racist culture and show how that 'strange fruit'—Tracy, his sister, his mother, and Nonnie of course and all the *people* came out of our twisted way of life." She wanted to underscore the "restricting, rigid frame of segregation" and how that damaged "the children who grow up in it, who are forced to bind their feeling, their love and their fear, their hate and their dreams to this pattern."

By mid-May, *Strange Fruit* reached the top of *The New York Times'* bestseller list and reviewers began to give the novel serious attention. On May 20, responding to a complaint from a man who bought the novel for his daughter and who objected to the one-time use of a common four-letter verb describing intercourse, the Boston police labeled *Strange Fruit* obscene and banned sales. The literary scholar Bernard De Voto objected and immediately purchased the book in front of the Boston police to test the ban. He was arrested and the obscenity trial began.

Overnight, Lillian Smith became a literary sensation and, much to her dismay, the public began to treat *Strange Fruit* as a risqué romantic novel rather than a passionate indictment of Southern prejudice. "They aren't considering the racial problems laid bare in the book; nor the hypocrisy of the church; nor the strains in the family life; they are focusing entirely on the dirt," Smith complained to her friend Frank Taylor.

While sales continued to increase, the ban in Boston held firm and the postmaster of the United States tried to keep the book from being distributed through the mails. This mail ban held until *Eleanor Roosevelt, a friend of Smith's, interceded with Franklin Roosevelt who overruled his postal director. The novel continued to sell very well, and Smith later adapted it for Canadian and Broadway theater companies. The controversy catapulted her into national prominence as a writer and as a passionate opponent of segregation and racial and sexual prejudice.

*There is a problem facing each of us, black and white, but it is not the "Negro problem." It is the problem, for Negroes, of finding some way to live with white people. It is the problem, for whites, of learning to live with themselves.*

—Lillian Smith

In many ways, Smith's stark description of the innate hostility of prejudice was autobiographical. Born near the end of the 19th century, the eighth of ten children in a wealthy, loving middle-class family, Smith initially encountered little public intolerance. Indeed, as a young girl, she studied music, attended the local symphony and theater, read voraciously, and generally experienced the comfort associated with a white, privileged female childhood.

Yet as **Anne Loveland** recounts, Smith's childhood was also filled with contradictions and rejections. She was born Lillian Eugenia Smith on December 12, 1897, in Jasper, Florida, a small community near the Georgia border, the daughter of **Annie Hester Smith** and Calvin Warren Smith. Lillian's father, a successful merchant and civic leader, was active in town politics and served as a steward in the Methodist Church across the street from the Smith household. Yet family discussions of God centered on damnation as much as redemption; and Smith struggled to reconcile loving Aunt Chloe, the black woman who worked for her family, with what she later labeled in an essay on her childhood entitled "Growing Into Freedom," as "the bleak rituals of keeping the Negro in his place."

Gradually, the young Smith understood that sex was a key rationale for this racial division. Recalling her parents' emphasis on segregation in *Killers of the Dream*, Smith wrote that they saw the policy as the "only logical expression of the lessons on sex and white superiority and God. Not only Negroes but everything dark, dangerous, evil must be pushed to the rim of one's life. Signs put over doors in the world outside and over minds seemed natural enough to children like us, for signs had already been put over forbidden areas of our body."

Family crises added to this anxiety. In 1911, Smith's brother Dewitt died from typhoid and four years later her father lost his business; the family was forced to make their summer home in rural Clayton, Georgia, their primary residence. Smith had just completed high school when the family moved, and she did not find the transition from a small Florida city to a rural Georgia town an easy one. She tried to pursue her studies by attending Piedmont College in nearby Demorest, but after one year (1915–16) was forced to return home to help her parents run the Laurel Falls Hotel they had made from their residence. She spent the next year teaching school during the day and cooking and cleaning for her family during the evenings and summer vacations.

These financial difficulties did not dissuade Smith from pursuing a music career, however, and she spent three poverty-stricken years in Baltimore studying at the Peabody Conservatory. There she often lived on coffee and chocolate bars, walked several miles to class, and supported herself by offering music lessons to the YWCA and the Police Athletic League and working as an accompanist for classes held for American Can Company and Bethlehem Steel Works employees. This experience introduced Smith to a new side of prejudice, "slums, poverty, factories—much I had known nothing about." Smith also fell in love with a man who at first kept his marriage a secret from her. Dejected, she eventually broke off the relationship and, after realizing that her interest in music exceeded her talent, she left the Conservatory and returned home in 1921.

But Smith did not stay in Georgia long. When the Virginia School in Huzhou, China, a Methodist-affiliated academy for upper-class Chinese girls, invited Smith to join its faculty as head of its music department, she eagerly accepted the offer. Here, for the first time, Smith lived in a woman-only community and observed what women could achieve when they were able to set their own agenda. Yet this experience was not an entirely pleasant one. As *Jo Ann Robinson recalled, Smith's encounter with "Western imperialism and indigenous politics quickened her awareness of the destructiveness of divisions based upon race and class."

By summer 1925, Calvin Smith's health deteriorated to the point where he could no longer manage Laurel Falls, the summer camp he had converted from the hotel in 1920; Smith unhappily yielded to family pressures and left China to take over management of the camp. While she had spent a few summers employed at Laurel Falls, she had never planned to make that her life's work. She objected to her father's blatant patriotic pageants and emphasis on sporting competition, never enjoyed horseback riding and the other physical activities the camp offered, and disapproved of its "over-emotionalized atmosphere."

But once she assumed responsibility, she began to reshape the camp in her own interests. She fired most of the counselors, hired new women whose areas of expertise reflected her own concerns, and replaced many sports with artistic and dramatic programs. When her father's health allowed her a brief respite, she

Lillian Smith

spent the fall of 1927 attending Columbia University's Teachers College where she took courses in psychology, history and education. The following summer, she incorporated her new academic expertise into programs which encouraged campers to explore their own emotions and confront the psychological and social forces which influenced their lives. In 1929, Smith decided that she might as well buy the camp from her father and have the control over camp finances that she had over camp activities. Her father agreed and Smith ran Laurel Falls every summer until 1948, when she decided to close the camp and concentrate on writing.

Laurel Falls played a more important role in Smith's life than a mere financial one. It was there that Smith met **Paula Snelling**, a trim athletic woman Calvin Smith had hired as an equestrian counselor in 1921, and with whom Smith would develop a full lifelong partnership. When Calvin Smith died of cancer in April 1930 and Annie Hester Smith decided to spend the winter with her sons in Florida, Smith began to spend the winters with Snelling in Snelling's Macon apartment. Over the next five winters, with Snelling's encouragement, Smith began to write and to become an active member of the Macon arts community. She became such an integral part of the Macon literary scene that her peers elected her president of the Macon Writers Club in the early winter of 1935.

That summer, Snelling was almost killed in a horseback riding accident, and the Smith-Snelling relationship took a new turn. As Snelling recuperated from her trampling, she moved into Smith's cabin on Old Steamer Mountain, and Smith assumed financial responsibility for herself, Snelling, and Smith's invalid mother. That Christmas, tragedy struck again when they learned that a 19-year-old woman who had been one of their favorite campers had committed suicide. Grappling with depression and winters of isolation, and missing the intellectual stimulation of Macon, Smith and Snelling decided to begin a literary magazine dedicated to publishing Southern writers and essayists. Smith assumed responsibility for fiction while Snelling edited essays and book reviews.

In 1936, *Pseudopodia* (renamed *North Georgia Review* in 1937 and *The South Today* in 1942) appeared. It was the first Southern publication owned by whites which published writings by Southern blacks. Noted for its unflinching assault on racial prejudice, segregation, and racial violence, the magazine soon expanded and began to allow women writers more space to ad-

dress issues associated with gender and class discrimination. The magazine grew in influence and reached a circulation high of 10,000 before Smith ceased its publication in 1945 in order to concentrate on her own writing.

Smith did not confine her commitment to attacking segregation to the pages of her journal. She began to study psychology, history, religion, and anthropology intensively as part of a life-long quest to understand the causes and consequences of prejudice. And she began to open her home to the writers whose articles she published, the artists and thinkers she admired, and writers whose works she studied. This led to the first social biracial gatherings in Clayton. The Rosenwald Fund recognized the two women's commitment and awarded them two-year fellowships which they used to travel the South and investigate the social and economic consequences of segregation. Smith's travels increased her visibility, and the Southern Conference for Human Welfare (SCHW) asked her to join its board. She agreed and served until 1944, when she resigned because she believed the SCHW was not doing enough to abolish segregation and promote integration. Throughout the 1940s, while running Laurel Falls, editing her literary journal, and speaking out against Jim Crow policies, Smith continued to work on her own writing. By 1944, she finished her most controversial novel, the aforementioned *Strange Fruit*, and achieved national fame.

Smith's study of psychology and her readings of Freud convinced her that prejudice was learned at an early age and that bold persistent efforts must be made to counteract the innate biases the white-dominated educational, political and religious institutions had on children and their parents. She dedicated most of her energy in the late '40s to writing *Killers of the Dream*, her most passionate attack on the pernicious effects of Southern racial custom. When it became apparent that she could not run Laurel Falls and meet her publisher's deadline, she opted to close the camp and devote all her time to writing. *Killers*, a series of essays which clearly revealed Smith's linking of gender roles with racial violence and segregated custom and which argued that a rigidly enforced fear of female and black sexuality were the underpinnings of white racism, appeared in 1949 to mixed reviews and disappointing sales.

Not content to limit her time to writing, Smith also joined the boards of the NAACP, CORE, ACLU and other national civil-rights organizations in the mid-'40s. She traveled the country speaking out against the poll tax, segregated school systems, and the misuse of Christianity to justify Jim Crow practices. At home, she attacked white moderates who counseled patience and who argued that segregation should be dismantled gradually. She campaigned against Dixiecrats and in support of "true liberals" who wanted immediate integration.

By the 1950s, financial hardship returned, her health declined, and her interest in religion took a different turn. Struggling against breast cancer (which would be detected in 1954), the "rabid" fear promoted by Joseph McCarthy's anti-Communism, and the "smothering" she believed her Southern critics imposed on her work, Smith tried to balance her personal quest for strength with her professional interest in cultural mores. She began to study the writings of Paul Tillich, Rollo May, Mohandas Gandhi, and Pierre Teilhard de Chardin.

This quest led to Smith's third publication *The Journey*, a collection of autobiographical essays which Snelling later defined as "the epiphanies which were hers as she sought to find and define the meanings of life." Indeed, in a posthumous collection of Smith's speeches and essays, *The Winner Names the Age*, Snelling argued that *The Journey* is the clearest description of Smith's conviction and cited the following quote as the perfect distillation of Smith's belief:

> To believe in something not yet proved and to underwrite it with our lives: it is the only way we can leave the future open. . . . To find the point where hypothesis and fact meet; the delicate equilibrium between dream and reality; . . . the hour when faith in the future becomes knowledge of the past; to lay down one's power for others in need; to shake off the old ordeal and get ready for the new; to question, knowing that never can the full answer be found; to accept uncertainties quietly, even our incomplete knowledge of God: this is what man's journey is about, I think.

After recuperating from breast cancer surgery, Smith threw herself into urging the South to comply with the *Brown* v. *Board of Education* decision. Two white teenagers responded by setting her home on fire, destroying in the process manuscripts, her library, and over 10,000 letters she had saved. Undaunted, as white resistance increased, Smith decided to write another plea for racial tolerance, *Now Is the Time* (1955).

When the black citizens of Montgomery, Alabama, began to boycott the segregated city bus system in December 1955, following the arrest of *Rosa Parks, Smith, a long-time student of Mohandas Gandhi, was ecstatic and, despite a recurrence of cancer, raised money and spoke out whenever possible on the virtue of their actions. Escalating white violence had convinced her that while litigation was important, nonviolent resistance was crucial to successful implementation of integration. Thrilled by the leadership exhibited by Martin Luther King, Jr., and other civil-rights leaders, Smith urged whites and blacks to join forces in nonviolent protest against racial prejudice. Her support of King developed into friendship. Indeed, when King was arrested for driving with an expired license in the summer of 1960, he had attracted the attention of a police officer because a white woman was sitting next to him as he drove through a white Atlanta suburb. Smith was that woman, and King was driving her from his house to Emory Hospital where she was to have another cancer operation the following morning.

Smith, delighted by the actions of black students who peacefully demanded service in the Greensboro (N.C.) Woolworth's, also eagerly supported student sit-ins. This led the Student-Nonviolent Coordinating Committee (SNCC) to invite Smith to address its 1960 regional conference and to look to her for moral, political, and financial support. However, as the civil-rights movement became more diverse in its strategy and as some SNCC members began to argue against nonviolent resistance, Smith became troubled by the division and began to investigate the split within the movement. *Our Faces, Our Words* (1964) chronicled the frustrations and aspirations of these new leaders.

By 1965, her 16-year struggle with cancer kept Smith at home and her activism was limited to writing speeches to be delivered by colleagues and to publishing occasional articles urging the end of Jim Crow, cautioning civil-rights activists against allying the movement to the developing anti-Vietnam movement, and pleading for the recognition that prejudice and stereotyping harmed the bigot as much as the bigot's target. Lillian Smith died on September 26, 1966, at Emory Hospital where she had been treated for yet another occurrence of cancer, now in the lungs. She was buried on Old Steamer Mountain, Georgia.

**SOURCES:**

Gladney, Margaret Rose, ed. *How Am I To Be Heard?: Letters of Lillian Smith*. Chapel Hill, NC: University of North Carolina, 1993.

Loveland, Anne C. *Lillian Smith: A Southerner Confronting the South*. Baton Rouge, LA, 1986.

Robinson, Jo Ann. "Lillian Smith: Reflections on Race and Sex," in *Southern Exposure*. No. 4, 1977, pp. 43–48.

Smith, Lillian. *The Winner Names the Age.* Edited by Michelle Cliff. Preface by Paula Snelling. New York, 1978.

Sullivan, Margaret. "Lillian Smith: The Public Image and the Personal Vision," in *Mad River Review.* Vol. 2. Summer 1967, pp. 3–21.

**SUGGESTED READING:**

Durr, Virginia. *Outside the Magic Circle.* Tuscaloosa, AL, 1985.

Kneebone, John T. *Southern Liberal Journalists and the Issue of Race, 1920–1944.* Chapel Hill, NC, 1985.

Miller, Kathleen Atkinson. "Out of the Chrysalis: Lillian Smith and the Transformation of the South," Ph.D. dissertation, Emory University, 1984.

White, Helen, and Redding S. Sugg, Jr., eds. *From the Mountain: An Anthology of the Magazine Successively Titled Pseudopodia, the North Georgia Review, and South Today.* Memphis, TN, 1972.

**COLLECTIONS:**

Correspondence, papers and manuscripts relating to *Pseudopodia, et al.* located in the Rare Books and Manuscripts Department, University of Florida Libraries.

Correspondence, papers and memorabilia which survived the 1955 fire, or which were written after that date, located in the Hargrett Rare Books and Manuscript Library, University of Georgia.

**Allida M. Black**,
Visiting Assistant Professor of History and American Studies,
Penn State University, Harrisburg, Pennsylvania

# Smith, Mabel (1924–1972)

*African-American blues singer. Name variations: Big Maybelle. Born Mabel Louise Smith on May 1, 1924, in Jackson, Tennessee; died on January 23, 1972, in Cleveland, Ohio.*

One of the few women blues singers after 1950, "Big Maybelle" Smith joined the ranks of **Koko Taylor** and \***Willie Mae (Big Mama) Thornton** in keeping the jazz form alive. She was born Mabel Louise Smith in 1924 in Memphis, Tennessee, and developed her powerful vocal style singing in church, accompanying herself on the piano. After winning first prize in a Memphis talent show in 1932, she traveled the country with a number of bands before hooking up with Tiny Bradshaw in 1947. Life on the road was difficult for the singer, whose encounters with segregation and sexual harassment led to a drug problem. From 1947 on, in addition to touring, Smith recorded for King, Okeh, Savoy and Rojac, with several of her songs landing on the rhythm-and-blues charts. She also appeared in *Jazz on a Summer Day*, a film about the 1959 Newport Jazz Festival. During the 1960s, Smith performed regularly at the Harlem Savoy, but complications from diabetes kept her from public appearances after 1967. She died of the disease in 1972.

**SOURCES:**

Clarke, Donald, ed. *The Penguin Encyclopedia of Popular Music.* NY: Viking, 1989.

Cohn, Lawrence. *Nothing But the Blues.* NY: Abbeville, 1993.

**Barbara Morgan**,
Melrose, Massachusetts

# Smith, Mamie (1883–1946)

*African-American blues recording artist and actress whose 1920 recording of "Crazy Blues" began the post-World War I craze for blues. Born Mamie Robinson Smith on May 26, 1883, in Cincinnati, Ohio; died on October 30, 1946, in New York City; married William "Smitty" Smith, in 1912; married Sam Gardner, in 1920; married a third time in 1929.*

Called the "Queen of the Blues," Mamie Smith recorded the first blues songs and influenced the style of many African-American singers who followed. She also enjoyed a career as an actress in film and on the vaudeville stage. Facts about her family and early life are obscure; she left her home in Cincinnati in 1893 to join a touring dance troupe, the Four Dancing Mitchells, and by 1912 was appearing as part of Tutt's Smart Set dance company. Her marriage to a singer William "Smitty" Smith that year soon ended. After 1913, Smith worked in nightclubs in Harlem, New York, as a dancer, vaudeville performer, and vocalist. Tall and beautiful, with an expressive contralto voice, Smith wore lavish costumes of sequined, velvet gowns on stage and was a very popular performer in Harlem by the late 1910s, during the early Harlem Renaissance. Her nightclub shows included trapeze acts, comedy, songs, and dancing. In 1918, she appeared at the Lincoln Theater in the musical *Maid in Harlem*. The musical's producer, Perry Bradford, a major New York composer and songwriter, was trying to find a record label to record black artists. Columbia turned him down, as did Victor Records after allowing Bradford's protégé and stage star Mamie Smith to make a test record of his pop tune "That Thing Called Love." When the record was bootlegged and became popular in New York, Bradford was finally able to convince the skeptical managers of Okeh Records (part of the General Phonograph Corporation) that blacks would buy records made by black singers. He encouraged them to record blues songs with Smith.

Thus in early 1920, at age 36, Smith made the first commercial recordings by a black woman, performing Bradford's pop tunes "That Thing Called Love" and "You Can't Keep a

Good Man Down." The record's success led Okeh Records to bring Smith back to record "Crazy Blues" and "It's Right Here for You" in August. The first commercial blues record made, "Crazy Blues" was enormously successful nationwide, selling over 75,000 copies in its first month of release and over one million copies in its first year. Its success set off a recording boom in what were termed "race records" by record companies, which sought to record female vocalists with styles similar to Smith, now nationally known. This opened the way for many of the now-classic blues, jazz, and popular singers, such as *Bessie Smith (no relation), to get their start in commercial recording, and made blues a standard part of American music. Smith considered herself a vaudeville and jazz performer rather than a blues singer, but she continued making blues records throughout the 1920s with her band, the Jazz Hounds. After leaving Okeh Records in 1923, she signed with Ajax Records in 1924, Victor in 1926, and Okeh again, recording for them from 1929 to 1931. She was at the height of her fame in the 1920s and 1930s while based in New York, earning up to $3,000 for an appearance. Crowds lined up at theaters for tickets to hear Mamie Smith. She was a wealthy woman who owed three New York mansions, with a new electric player piano in every room. Smith was in much demand in New York and toured the United States widely before the effects of the Depression greatly reduced her audience. Between 1932 and 1934, she toured in the musical *Yelping Hounds*, and in 1936 she was performing in Europe. She also appeared in several movies, including *Paradise in Harlem* (1939), *Sunday Sinners* (1940), and *Murder on Lenox Avenue* (1941). Smith was married two more times, about 1920 and in 1929, but information about her second and third husbands is sketchy.

Despite the high fees she earned, Smith was constantly in debt due to her extravagant lifestyle; when she fell ill in 1944, age 61, she had few resources and was living in an Eighth Avenue boarding house. Severely arthritic, she entered Harlem Hospital that year and died there in 1946, bankrupt. She was buried in the Frederick Douglass Memorial Park Cemetery on Staten Island. In 1964, a memorial concert was held in New York to raise funds for her re-interment under a headstone dedicated by her fans of Iserlohn, Germany, to the "first lady of the blues."

**SOURCES:**
Carr, Ian, Digby Fairweather, and Brian Priestley. *Jazz: The Essential Companion*. London: Grafton, 1988.

Harrison, Daphne Duval. *Black Pearls: Blues Queens of the 1920's*. New Brunswick, NJ: Rutgers University Press, 1988.

Herzhaft, Gérard. *Encyclopedia of the Blues*. Trans. by Brigitte Debord. Fayetteville: University of Arkansas Press, 1992.

Smith, Jessie Carney, ed. *Notable Black American Women*. Detroit, MI: Gale Research, 1992.

Tirro, Frank. *Jazz: A History*. NY: W.W. Norton, 1993.

**Laura York**, M.A. in History,
University of California, Riverside, California

## Smith, Margaret (b. 1942).

See Court, Margaret Smith.

## Smith, Margaret Bayard (1778–1844).

See Eaton, Peggy for sidebar.

# Smith, Margaret Chase

## (1897–1995)

*U.S. congressional representative and four-term senator, known as the "conscience of the Senate," who was the first senator to publicly oppose Joseph McCarthy and the first woman candidate for a major party nomination for the U.S. presidency. Born Margaret Madeline Chase on December 14, 1897, in Skowhegan, Maine; died of a stroke in Skowhegan on May 29, 1995; daughter of George Emery Chase (a barber) and Carrie Matilda (Murray) Chase (of Scottish and French-Canadian background and a member of the Daughters of the American Revolution); attended elementary and high school in Skowhegan, graduating from Skowhegan High School in 1916; married Clyde Harold Smith, on May 14, 1930 (died 1940); no children.*

*Raised entirely in Skowhegan, Maine, where she completed high school; worked briefly as a teacher, then had a series of positions in local businesses and for the Skowhegan* Independent Reporter; *active in local Republican politics, especially following her marriage to Clyde Smith; served as her husband's secretary during his two terms in the U.S. House of Representatives; elected to House of Representatives to succeed her husband (1940), and for three more terms; elected to the U.S. Senate (1948), and for three more terms, becoming the first woman to serve more than two Senate terms; specialized in issues related to the armed forces and defense, as well as labor; was noted for an "independent" voting record, often supporting Democratic as well as Republican measures in Congress; elected to the Senate by the widest margins in Maine's history; became the first woman candidate for a major party's presidential nomination (1964); served in the Senate until her retirement (1973). Held many honorary college degrees and was the recipient of numerous awards, including the Freedom Award for Americanism from the Freedoms Foundation (1950), the Veterans of Foreign Wars medal for Amer-*

*icanism (1954), and the Distinguished Service Award on National Defense from the Reserve Officers Association (1955); was voted "Woman of the Year" several times and rated by the Gallop Poll three times as one of the ten most admired women in the world.*

*Writings: (collection of speeches, with William C. Lewis, Jr.) Declaration of Conscience (1972).*

As the woman with the longest service in the history of the U.S. Senate, and the first woman candidate for the presidential nomination of one of the two major parties, Margaret Chase Smith carved a unique position in the history of American politics. Known as a "Woman of Courage"—the title of her major biography—and an "independent" Republican unafraid to oppose or support ideas of either party, Senator Smith was respected as an effective practicing politician as well as a pioneer for women in 20th-century American politics. Her story also reveals some of the major issues of the political climate of the United States in the pre- and post-World War II eras.

Margaret Madeline Chase was born into the cold climate of Maine on December 14, 1897, in the small community of Skowhegan, which was to be her lifelong home. Her immediate family was not prosperous during her childhood. Her great-grandfather had owned land south of Skowhegan, and her grandfather, John Wesley Chase, was a Civil War veteran and Methodist minister. Her father George Chase suffered from severe headaches which limited his prospects and achievements; he ran a small local barbershop. Her mother **Carrie Murray Chase** was of Scotch and French-Canadian descent, and with her father's Irish-English ancestry, Margaret's ethnic heritage mirrored that of Maine as a whole. Margaret was the eldest of six children, two of whom died in childhood; a brother Wilbur remained in Skowhegan, as did one sister Laura, while another sister Evelyn lived in Chevy Chase, Maryland, near Margaret's home while she served in Congress.

As a small girl, Margaret would wander into her father's barber shop, located near the family home, and listen to the talk of the community among her father's customers. The living was sparse, and Smith remembered the struggle to keep the family together. "Mother always got my clothes too big so I could grow into them," she said. And, "Mother always felt that if she kept us busy we'd be the better for it." The children were involved in as many activities as the family could support, with Margaret being interested in a number of things, including basketball and playing the piano. The family also took reg-

ular summer excursions in the outdoors. They would picnic and occasionally be able to afford a night at nearby lake resorts. These outings, and the general attitude of remaining positive and pulling together as a family, were critical experiences for the young Margaret.

During young girlhood, Smith also developed patterns of independence and hard work which were obvious in her later political career, and important to her success. At only 13, she began to supplement the family income by working at the Green Brothers' five-and-ten, where her mother also worked from time to time. Smith pursued a commercial course in high school, and was known as a hardworking student, respected by her teachers and classmates. When Smith was at the height of her career, her former English teacher, **Dorothy Elliott**, noted, "At seventeen she was the same person she is today. Her essential qualities have matured. They haven't changed." Graduating from high school, she was a confident and competent young woman, sensitized to the conditions of working people through her own experiences and the experiences of her family.

In the years following, Smith pursued a variety of commercial positions. She worked briefly as a teacher in a one-room school, but decided that type of work was not for her. Subsequently, she was employed as a switchboard operator for the local telephone company, and later an executive with the commercial department. Although she had wanted to attend a college or professional school, she was financially unable to do so. In 1919, she began work as a circulation manager of a weekly newspaper, the Skowhegan *Independent Reporter;* she also worked in the advertising and editorial departments. From 1928 to 1930, she was office manager of a woolen mill in Skowhegan and also treasurer of the New England Waste Process Company in Fairfield, Maine. By 1928, recognized as a promising professional woman in her area, she was serving as president of the Maine Federation of Business and Professional Women's Clubs. These years introduced her to many key business and professional leaders of her community. Indeed, her work at the newspaper led to her marriage, in 1930, to Clyde Harold Smith.

Clyde Smith was one of the preeminent politicians and leaders of his community. Seeking office 48 times, he was never once defeated. "Mostly we went campaigning," Margaret once said of her courtship. "Anyone who ever spent any time with him ended up going campaigning." A Skowhegan businessman and co-owner of the *Independent Reporter*, Clyde was prominent in state as well as local politics. He was a hard-fighting, daring politician whose career culminated with election to the U.S. House of Representatives in 1936. Prior to this election, Margaret shared his campaigning in Maine, and also served as Republican State Committee-woman. During her husband's two terms in the House, Smith worked as his secretary and assistant, further developing her own political skills and reputation. Thus, it was really her marriage to Clyde Smith that led to her career in politics, a common pattern for women who served in U.S. political office in the mid-20th century.

In 1940, Clyde suffered a second, stronger heart attack—an earlier one having occurred in 1937—and decided he should not seek re-election; he persuaded Margaret to pursue the House seat in his stead. Shortly after this plan was announced publicly, he died. Margaret Chase Smith thus faced her first major campaign for national office on her own. The odds against her were tremendous. By 1940, there had been a number of women in Congress, but most of these were appointed to fill unexpired terms (usually of their husbands) rather than being elected in their own right. Many in the U.S. still believed that politics

Margaret
Chase
Smith

was too "dirty" a profession for women, or that women lacked the necessary competencies to serve well in public office.

At this time, Smith drew upon her skills, her stamina, and her own personal network in Maine as well as her husband's. She faced, and won, four elections in a seven-month period in 1940: a special primary for candidates for Clyde Smith's seat, a runoff primary election, a special election to the unexpired term in May, and the regularly scheduled general election in November. She was swept to victory by impressive margins in all of these contests, and in 1941 was seated as one of only 7 women among the 435 members of the House. She set out to carve a position for herself in this body, and to promote the interests of the working people she considered her primary constituents.

*As an American, I condemn a Republican "Fascist" just as much as I condemn a Democrat "Communist." I condemn a Democrat "Fascist" just as much as I condemn a Republican "Communist." They are equally dangerous to you and me and to our country. As an American, I want to see our nation recapture the strength and unity it once had when we fought the enemy instead of ourselves.*

—Margaret Chase Smith, "Declaration of Conscience" (June 1, 1950)

Although she was denied her first choice of committee assignment, the House Labor Committee, she used her assignment on the House Military Affairs Committee (later the Armed Services Committee) to inform herself on defense matters, which would be an important area of her expertise over the subsequent years, and to see that Maine got its share of federal industrial contracts. This, in turn, served the working constituency to which she was most loyal. She also became known as the "Mother of the Waves," because she waged a long and early struggle for women's rights within the military, and introduced the legislation which first allowed WAVES (Woman Accepted for Volunteer Emergence Service) to serve in hospitals and offices overseas during World War II. In 1944, she also led a fight against the Tabor Amendment, which would have cut in half the funds for community services and harmed the interests of many children whose parents were busily engaged in the war effort. She later supported the European Recovery Plan after World War II, developing a reputation for understanding foreign policy as well as defense-

related issues. On these issues, she at times opposed members of her own party and was criticized by them, developing the image of an "independent" Republican. "I don't really vote against my party that often," she once said, "but I've gotten the reputation of being a liberal because I cast those votes on some very dramatic issues." However, her voting record in the House reveals that she did vote against the majority of her party about one-third of the time.

While serving in the House, Smith developed a quiet, dignified image that was to persist throughout her career. She became recognizable by the fresh rose she wore or placed on her desk each day. Respected for her grasp of military and foreign policy issues, very important at this time, she was also considered unusual for focusing on issues not usually pursued by women. She served her district skillfully, but was also seen as a national stateswoman. Aware of the value of publicity, she used it well in her own behalf as well as for the betterment of the Republican Party, which was very much a minority party during the 1940s.

Encouraged by her success in the House and the national reputation she was developing, Margaret Chase Smith in 1947 made another major leap in her political career, with the decision to seek the Republican nomination for the U.S. Senate seat being vacated by popular Maine Senator Wallace H. White. Odds against her success in this campaign were even greater than in her House races; by this time, six women had served in the U.S. Senate, but none had initially won a regular election. She announced her candidacy very early, hoping to overcome her lack of financial backing. Two popular Republican former governors of Maine were formidable opponents in the primary campaign, and her candidacy was also opposed by many major corporations in the state. She organized and conducted an impressive grass-roots campaign to offset these initial disadvantages, and won both the primary and general elections in 1948 by landslides. Her margin of victory in the general election was the greatest in Maine's history and clearly established Smith as a formidable campaigner.

Spanning four terms, her Senate service continued many of the policy interests and the hardworking style of her House years. One of the most dramatic moments occurred in her first major speech, in 1950. Smith issued a ringing "Declaration of Conscience" in which she expressed alarm at the activities of fellow Republican Senator Joseph McCarthy. In the preceding years, McCarthy had been conducting a well-publicized series of investigations into alleged Communist activities of numerous prominent Americans. Many senators were privately appalled at the "witch-hunting" aspects of these proceedings, and the damage they were doing to individuals. However, no senators had had the courage to publicly oppose McCarthy's actions. Lawmakers feared attack on the Senate floor and worried that they too might be added to the list of Communist sympathizers. It was not a minor concern. Two Republican senators who had incurred McCarthy's wrath had been defeated in subsequent elections, having been charged with Communist leanings. As well, some victory-starved Republicans, including senior senator Robert Taft, were encouraging McCarthy, while opposition from the Democrats was dismissed as partisan politics. At this time, Smith was only a freshman senator; freshmen senators did not make waves, much less speeches in their first few months in office. But Smith approached six other Republicans for backing and returned home to write a speech. On June 1, with rumors of what was to come and a crowded gallery, with most of the senators at their desks and Joseph McCarthy sitting directly behind her, she took the floor. "I would like to speak briefly and simply about a serious national condition," she began:

> The United States Senate has long enjoyed worldwide respect as the greatest deliberative body in the world. But recently that deliberative character has too often been debased to a forum of hate and character assassination, sheltered by the shield of congressional immunity. It is ironic that we senators can in debate in the Senate impute to any American who is not a senator any conduct unworthy or unbecoming an American—and without that nonsenator American having any legal redress against us. Yet if we say the same thing in the Senate about our colleagues, we can be stopped on grounds of being out of order.
>
> I speak as a Republican. I speak as a woman. I speak as a United States Senator. I speak as an American. I think it is high time that we remember that we have sworn to uphold and defend the Constitution. I think it is high time that we remember that the Constitution as amended speaks not only of freedom of speech but also of trial by jury, not trial by accusation. Those of us who shout the loudest about Americanism in making character assassinations are all too frequently those who by our own words and acts ignore some of the basic principles of Americanism:
>
> > The right to criticize,
> > The right to hold unpopular belief,
> > The right to protest,
> > The right to independent thought. . . .

> I don't want to see the Republican Party ride to political victory on the four horsemen of calumny—fear, ignorance, bigotry, and smear.

At this point, "Republican senators began walking out in droves," wrote *Margaret Truman in *Women of Courage*. "Soon, almost the only Republicans on the floor were the six senators who had pledged to support her Declaration of Conscience. The departing Republicans were joined, I regret to report, by a number of Democrats. But Senator McCarthy did not move from his seat. He sat there, glowering ominously at Senator Smith's back." McCarthy would later denounce Smith as a friend of Communists and persuade an oil-rich native of Maine to run against her in the Republican primary. Though McCarthy knew his crony might not win, he was hoping a tough primary would deplete her treasure chest for the election campaign and ensure her defeat. But Smith was a canny politician, who spent little on her campaigns. Already prominent as a woman in the Senate, Smith became even better known after her stand. Reaction was generally positive, enhancing her reputation with all but the staunch supporters of McCarthy.

In the Senate, Smith continued to develop her expertise on national defense, security, and foreign policy. Traveling abroad, she became known as a key voice for these issues during the Cold War era. She also continued to support some of Democratic President Franklin Delano Roosevelt's New Deal legislation, such as extension of Social Security, federal aid to education, and civil-rights laws. Her backing of these measures continued her reputation as an independent Republican.

In 1952, Smith was widely mentioned as a potential vice-presidential candidate. Asked by a radio announcer what she would do if she woke up one morning in the White House, she replied, "I'd go straight to Mrs. Truman and apologize. Then I'd go home." She served on the Senate Republican Policy Committee—despite her independent voting record—and the Appropriations, Armed Services, Space, and Rules committees. Her toughest re-election challenge was surmounted in 1954, when she defeated a protégé of Senator McCarthy's by a margin of five-to-one, setting yet another record for the total number of votes in a contested primary. She won re-election two more times, in 1960 and 1966, and served longer in the Senate than any other woman.

Smith's Senate performance is well represented by an incident that occurred in 1963, when she cast what she called "a very troubled vote" against the Limited Test Ban Treaty nego-tiated by the Kennedy Administration. Despite her desire for peace, she viewed the world, as her biographer Frank Graham, Jr., puts it, "more with the eyes of a general than with those of a diplomat. America's security preoccupied her." Thus, fearing that the treaty might adversely affect the nation's security, she reluctantly opposed it. She had illustrated, once again, her fierce independence in Congress.

In 1964, Margaret Chase Smith announced her candidacy for the presidency of the United States, the first woman to seek the nomination of one of the two major parties. The Republican primary contests were dominated by the candidacy of the eventual nominee, conservative Senator Barry Goldwater of Arizona, and those of his more liberal opponents, such as governors William Scranton (Pennsylvania), Nelson Rockefeller (New York), and George Romney (Michigan). Justifying her candidacy, Smith pointed out that she actually had more national government experience than any of the other contenders, particularly in the foreign policy area, which was true. Nonetheless, her opponents maintained that her candidacy would "confuse" the results of the important New Hampshire primary. Smith's best primary showing was in Illinois, where she polled 23% of the popular vote. Probably reflecting the climate against women seeking major office at the time, however, she received the votes of very few delegates at the Republican National convention. Her candidacy was nonetheless important, establishing the right of well-qualified women to run for any office in the country.

Smith continued her Senate service through the tumultuous years of the 1960s. She persisted in her advocacy of strong foreign and defense policies, the championing of the rights of women (particularly in the military), and her support of critical domestic policies of vital interest to working Americans. Her reputation for hard work, integrity of position, and independence characterized her Senate service until her retirement from public life in 1972, at age 75. Her outstanding political service, her expertise in policy areas often dominated by men, and her pioneering in both senatorial and presidential politics ensure her lasting contribution to American history. "Throughout her career in Congress, Margaret Chase Smith had her own highly personal style," wrote Truman. "She tended to be taciturn, like most down-easters. She never ran off at the mouth and she was not especially fond of people who had this tendency. She preferred to work behind the scenes, on the com-

mittees where the real business of Congress is done, and let others do the orating on the House or Senate floor. When she made a speech, it was to say something important."

**SOURCES:**
Barber, James David, and Barbara Kellerman, eds. *Women Leaders in American Politics*. Englewood Cliffs, NJ: Prentice-Hall, 1986.

Graham, Frank, Jr. *Margaret Chase Smith: Woman of Courage*. NY: John Day, 1964.

"Margaret Chase Smith, senator 24 years, dies," in *Boston Globe*. May 30, 1995.

Smith, Margaret Chase with William A. Lewis, Jr. *Declaration of Conscience*. Garden City, NY: Doubleday, 1964.

"Straight Shooter," in *People Weekly*. June 12, 1965.

Truman, Margaret. *Women of Courage*. NY: Morrow, 1976.

**SUGGESTED READING:**
Wallace, Patricia Ward. *The Politics of Conscience: A Biography of Margaret Chase Smith*. Praeger, 1995.

**Jacqueline DeLaat**,
McCoy Professor of Political Science and Leadership,
Marietta College, Ohio

# Smith, Mary Ellen (1861–1933)

*Canadian legislator and social reformer. Name variations: Mary Ellen Spear. Born on October 11, 1861, in Devonshire, England; died on May 3, 1933, in Vancouver, British Columbia, Canada; married.*

*First woman elected to the British Columbia Legislative Assembly (1918–28); first woman in the British Empire appointed as a Minister (1921); first woman to serve as Acting Speaker of the Legislature (1928).*

A native of England, Mary Ellen Smith was born in Devonshire, England, in 1861, and immigrated to Canada with her husband in the early 1890s. Residing originally in Nanaimo, British Columbia, they eventually settled in Vancouver, where she became active in several women's organizations, including the National Council of Women, Women's Canadian Club, Imperial Order Daughters of the Empire (IODE), the Red Cross of British Columbia, and the Vancouver Women's Liberal Association.

Smith's husband, a Liberal member of the British Columbia legislature, died in office in 1917, and Smith was elected to his seat in 1918, becoming the first woman in the British Empire to do so. Faithful to her campaign slogan of "women and children first," Smith supported the Minimum Wage Act for Women and Girls in 1918. Although she initially ran for her husband's seat as an Independent, she won subsequent elections by sizable majorities in 1920 and 1924 as a member of the Liberal Party.

In March 1921, Smith became the first woman in the British Empire to be appointed Minister without Portfolio. However, she resigned the office that November to continue her political career as a legislator. Throughout her ten years in office, Smith worked to improve the conditions of women and children and to ensure their rights under the law.

In addition to her legislative duties, Smith was a sought-after speaker both within and outside of Canada. She was especially popular in Europe where she represented the government in promoting immigration to Canada. In 1928, she served briefly as the Acting Speaker of the Legislature, another first for women in the British Empire, and in 1929 she represented Canada at the International Labour Conference in Geneva, Switzerland. Smith died in Vancouver, British Columbia, on May 3, 1933.

**Martha Jones**, M.L.S.,
Natick, Massachusetts

## Smith, Mary Pearsall (1864–1944).

*See Berenson, Mary.*

## Smith, Melanie (b. 1949).

*See Taylor, Melanie Smith.*

## Smith, Mother (1904–1994).

*See Smith, Willie Mae Ford.*

## Smith, Naomi Gwladys Royde-.

*See Macaulay, Rose for sidebar on Naomi Royde-Smith.*

## Smith, Nora Archibald (c. 1859–1934).

*See Wiggin, Kate Douglas for sidebar.*

## Smith, Pauline (1882–1959)

*South African-born writer. Born in Oudtshoorn, South Africa, in 1882; died in 1959; daughter of British parents; educated in Britain.*

*Selected writings: (short stories) The Little Karoo (1925); (novel) The Beadle (1926); also wrote children's stories.*

The daughter of British parents who had emigrated to South Africa, Pauline Smith was born there in Oudtshoorn in 1882 but left the country at age 12 to attend school in Britain. Her father's death prevented Smith from returning to South Africa except for rare visits. She also endured poor health and a limited income while living mostly in Dorset, on England's south coast.

Among the literary acquaintances Smith made in England was novelist Arnold Bennett,

who became her mentor, encouraging her to write about her South African heritage and introducing her to the works of French and Russian realist writers. In 1925, Smith published her first collection of short stories, *The Little Karoo*. The book focused on the conflicts between rich and poor in rural South Africa during the last years of the 19th and the early part of the 20th centuries. Her novel *The Beadle* (1926) also dealt with social problems among the Afrikaans-speaking community of her childhood, including issues of racial conflict. Though the book somewhat idealized the patriarchal community, it also questioned its subordination of women and black South Africans.

When Bennett died in 1931, Smith became increasingly consumed by self-doubt and greatly missed his support. She published a tribute to him, *A.B. '. . . a minor marginal note'* (1933), then a collection of children's stories, *Platkops Children* (1935), but, discouraged by her failing health and the spread of fascism in Europe, and disheartened at the prospect of an apartheid system in South Africa, she was unable to complete her next novel. Smith died in 1959, leaving behind several unpublished works, including a South African journal (1913–14) and letters to writers Frank Swinnerton and *Sarah Millin.

**SOURCES:**

Buck, Claire, ed. *The Bloomsbury Guide to Women's Literature.* NY: Prentice Hall, 1992.

**Elizabeth Shostak**, freelance writer,
Cambridge, Massachusetts

## Smith, Robyn (1942—)

*American jockey who was the first woman to win a stakes race. Name variations: Melody Dawn Miller; Caroline Smith; Robyn Caroline Smith; Robyn Astaire. Born Melody Dawn Miller in San Francisco, California, on August 14, 1942; daughter of Constance Miller; married Fred Astaire (the actor and dancer), in 1980 (died 1987).*

Robyn Smith, the most famous woman jockey in the United States during the 1970s, has been reluctant to divulge details about her past. Rather, she constructed a personal history which included being the daughter of a wealthy lumberman, losing her parents when she was quite young, growing up in Hawaii, graduating from Stanford University, and signing a movie contract with MGM Studios, in order to hide the reality of a troubled family life. Reliable information shows that Smith was born in San Francisco, California, on August 14, 1942, one of five children of **Constance Miller**, who named her Melody Dawn. "It was a very painful delivery," said Miller. "She weighed nine pounds, six ounces. I almost lost my life giving birth to her." From early infancy, Smith's family life was chaotic. The headstrong, prickly Constance Miller married four times and moved often. When Smith was still quite young, her mother's health failed, and the household was temporarily scattered. Smith was placed for adoption by the Oregon Protective Society in the home of prosperous lumberman Orville L. Smith and his wife. She was there for some time. "They had a shyster lawyer put through these bogus adoption papers," claimed Miller, "and there was money exchanged between the Smiths and the Protective Society. They thought they could buy her soul." Angry at this placement, Constance (then known as Constance Palm) brought a court action with the help of Catholic Charities in 1947 to have the adoption set aside. This action was denied by a Morrow County court before that decision was overturned by the state supreme court. Justice George Rossman ordered that Smith be returned to her mother and then placed in a foster home through Catholic Charities; his reasoning was that children should be put in homes of the same religious background. It became a landmark case in the state of Oregon.

The victory was hollow for Constance. Catholic Charities was intent on keeping mother and daughter separated. "If anyone ever got a raw deal, it was this mother," Miller wrote Bill Mulflur, sports editor of the *Oregon Journal*. "These holier-than-thou Catholics go to Mass every morning and then talk about their neighbors all week long. What hypocrisy!" Smith spent portions of the following years in and out of foster homes, and was again separated from her family during high school. (For one seven-year period, mother and daughter did not meet.) Because of a severe asthma condition that required hospitalization, Smith did not graduate from high school until 1961, when she was 19. By then, she was living with five other foster girls in the home of Frank and Hazel Kucero. But Smith had kept in touch with the Orville Smith family; after completing school she avoided her own family (she would eventually cease contact with her mother and siblings) and moved to Seattle to be with the Smiths, beginning to call herself Caroline Smith. She did not remain long with them, however, and eventually enrolled in the acting workshop at Columbia Pictures in Hollywood.

During this period, according to Smith, she dated a man who had a horse under the tutelage of Bruce Headley, a trainer at Santa Anita. Through this contact, she obtained a job galloping Headley's horses. "Thank God it was dark those mornings and nobody really saw what I looked like on a horse," said Smith. "After I'd been working for Bruce for about four months, he got his first look at me galloping a colt one morning. 'You don't know too much about working a horse, do you?' he said. I admitted I didn't, but he stuck with me and I gradually learned what I was doing."

Then *Kathy Kusner made headlines when she went to court in Maryland and won the right to ride in races, and Smith set out to become a professional jockey. She faced many obstacles. While most jockeys start training in childhood, Smith had only begun developing the reflexes and skills needed to be an expert rider when she was in her 20s. Her physical size (5'7" and 125 lbs.) was also a strike against her, since most jockeys are only 5' tall. And even though she received her jockey's license in 1969—track officials felt a female jockey would attract spectators—Smith quickly discovered that gender prejudice in the male-dominated arena of horseracing would hinder her entry into the races, even after she proved herself.

On April 5, 1969, Smith rode in her first race at Golden Gate Park near San Francisco. She finished second. She went on to ride in 40 races on the California country fair circuit. Owners were leery of placing her on their mounts, so Smith left the West Coast for the New York area, hoping for an opportunity. "I decided that if I was going to make it in racing," she said, "it was going to be first cabin or not at all." She finally got her break when the owner of the horse Exotic Bird agreed to let her race at the prestigious Aqueduct track in Queens on December 5, 1969. Exotic Bird had not demonstrated remarkable speed in the past, but Smith managed a fifth-place finish in a close race.

Her accomplishment did not result in well-deserved recognition from owners and trainers, who continued to shun her as a jockey. While most experienced male jockeys race more than 1,000 times in a year, Smith raced less than 100, mostly on mediocre horses. "The better Robyn gets, the more jealous others get," said noted jockey Eddie Arcaro. In the early 1970s, she proved her skill and tenacity by winning 18–20% of her races against horses with better records. Along with her races, she won the admiration of Alfred Gwynne Vanderbilt, who owned a top stable and was chair of the New York Racing Association. She became a regular rider for him. On March 1, 1973, she was the first woman jockey to win a stakes race, riding North Sea to victory in the $27,450 Paumanok Handicap at the Aqueduct.

**Sports Illustrated**

JULY 31, 1972   60 CENTS

SENSATION IN SILKS

JOCKEY ROBYN SMITH

Robyn Smith

Although she was racing at the most presti-gious tracks by 1975, Smith chose to retire that year. In 1980, she married acting legend Fred Astaire, 42 years her senior, who, as the owner of several champions, shared her love for horse racing. They settled down in Beverly Hills, where she continued to live after Astaire's death in 1987.

**SOURCES:**

Haney, Lynn. *The Lady is a Jock*. NY: Dodd, Mead, 1973.
Moritz, Charles, ed. *Current Biography 1976*. NY: H.W. Wilson, 1976.

Sherrow, Victoria. *Encyclopedia of Women and Sports.* Santa Barbara, CA: ABC-CLIO, 1996.

**SUGGESTED READING:**

Brown, Fern G. *Racing Against the Odds: Robyn C. Smith.* Raintree Editions of Children's Press, 1976.

**Elizabeth Shostak**, freelance writer, Cambridge, Massachusetts

## Smith, Ruby Doris (1942–1967).

*See Robinson, Ruby Doris Smith.*

## Smith, Samantha (1972–1985)

*American peace advocate. Born in 1972; died in a plane crash in Auburn, Maine, on August 25, 1985; daughter of Arthur Smith and Jane Smith; attended Manchester Elementary School, Manchester, Maine.*

Samantha Smith was a bright and attractive ten-year-old in 1982, when a classroom discussion about the threat of nuclear war prompted her to write a letter to then Soviet leader Yuri V. Andropov expressing her fears and concerns. "I have been worrying about Russia and the United States getting into a nuclear war," she began. "Are you going to vote to have a war or not? If you aren't please tell me how you are going to help to not have a war. . . . I would like to know why you want to conquer the world or at least our country." Samantha closed with a youthful plea for peace. "God made the world for us to live together in peace and not to fight."

Samantha had almost forgotten about the letter when, in April 1983, a reporter from United Press International called her school and said he had seen the letter in *Pravda*, the official state newspaper of the Soviet Union, and wondered whether Samantha had written it. Samantha went home that afternoon and wrote another letter to the Soviet ambassador in Washington, asking if he could explain what was going on. On April 25, she received a 500-word letter from Andropov himself, in which he likened Samantha to Becky Thatcher in Mark Twain's novel *Tom Sawyer*, calling her "courageous and honest." He went on to assure her that he was doing everything he could to prevent war, and ended the letter with an invitation to Samantha and her parents to visit the Soviet Union that summer, as guests of the country.

As the Smiths planned their journey, the media went into high gear. Journalists for *Time*, *Newsweek*, and *People*, as well as for the Soviet press, all showed up at the Smith household, and Samantha traveled to New York for interviews with Ted Koppel and **Jane Pauley**, and to California for an appearance with Johnny Carson. By July 23, 1983, when the family left to visit the Soviet Union, 11-year-old Samantha Smith was a national celebrity.

The Smiths' two-week tour was carefully monitored, and centered on Soviet schoolchildren. Samantha visited Moscow and Leningrad, and also traveled to the Artek Pioneer Camp near the Black Sea, where she spent a few days with the "Young Pioneers," a youth group similar to the Girl Scouts and Boy Scouts in the United States. She met *\*Valentina Tereshkova*, the first woman in space, and had lunch with the U.S. ambassador. The only thing missing from the itinerary was an interview with Andropov, who was reportedly too busy with matters of state to meet with her.

While most Americans viewed Samantha's trip as a diplomatic coup, some believed that the entire affair had been overblown. Others questioned Soviet intentions; *US News and World Report* ran an editorial entitled, "Samantha Smith—Pawn in Propaganda War." Samantha's father

*Postage stamp issued by the USSR in honor of Samantha Smith, 1985.*

Arthur addressed some of the concerns about propaganda. "I suppose there might be something in that," he said. "At the same time, it doesn't take too much to realize they have a lot to lose too. You can't hide the economic conditions of a country, even from the back seat of a limousine."

Samantha's homecoming was marked with a huge parade and a ceremony presenting her with the key to Manchester. The young celebrity now balanced schoolwork, sports, and leisure time with television appearances, speeches, and travel. She wrote a book entitled *Journey to the Soviet Union*, and traveled with her mother **Jane Smith** to the Children's International Symposium in Kobe, Japan, where she proposed that U.S. and Soviet leaders exchange granddaughters for several weeks every year. "A president wouldn't want to send a bomb to a country his granddaughter would be visiting," she said in a speech.

During the 1984 election year, with her father now acting as her manager, Samantha hosted a special on the Disney Channel to educate children about politics and the presidential candidates, and in 1985, she was cast as Robert Wagner's daughter in the television series "Lime Street." In August of that year, flying home with her father from filming in England, her plane crashed and exploded during a rainstorm in Auburn, Maine. Everyone aboard, including six other passengers and the crew, was killed.

The funeral for Samantha Smith and her father was attended by hundreds, although the U.S. government did not sent a representative. Vladimir Kulagir, first secretary for cultural affairs from the Soviet embassy in Washington, spoke at the ceremony, calling Samantha a symbol of peace and friendship between the United States and the Soviet Union. "Samantha was like a small but very powerful and brilliant beam of sunshine which penetrated the thunderstorm clouds which envelop between our two countries," he said. "The best message and memory to Arthur and Samantha would be if we continue what they started and reach over borders with goodwill, friendship and love."

Samantha's influence did not end with her death. The Soviet government issued a stamp in her honor and named a flower and a diamond after her. In her home state of Maine, a life-size statue of Smith was erected in front of the State Library in Augusta, which depicts her releasing a dove. Beside her is a bear, a symbol of both the Soviet Union and Maine. In October 1985, Samantha's mother established the Samantha Smith Foundation, dedicated to encouraging peace and friendship between children of all countries. The foundation sponsored several conferences and exchange programs between the United States and the Soviet Union. One of the tributes to the young ambassador came from a poem printed in *Pravda*, "The child has died, but she had time enough to shake the minds and souls of people."

**SOURCES:**

Bush, Maribeth. "Samantha Smith," on Can Do! web page, 1997–2001.

Malvasi, Meg Greene. "Samantha Smith: America's Youngest Ambassador," in *History for Children*. Suite101.com, 1996–2001.

"Obituary Notice," in *Contemporary Newsmakers*, 1985.

**SUGGESTED READING:**

Galicich, Anne. *Samantha Smith: A Journey for Peace*. Minneapolis, MN: Dillon, 1987.

**Barbara Morgan**,
Melrose, Massachusetts

## Smith, Sarah (1832–1911).

*See Stretton, Hesba.*

## Smith, Scottie Fitzgerald (1921–1986).

*See Fitzgerald, Zelda for sidebar on Frances Scott Fitzgerald.*

## Smith, Sheila Kaye- (1887–1956).

*See Kaye-Smith, Sheila.*

# Smith, Sophia (1796–1870)

*American philanthropist who became the first woman to found and endow a women's college when she founded Smith College in Northampton, Massachusetts. Born in Hatfield, Massachusetts, on August 27, 1796; died in Hatfield on June 12, 1870; one of seven children and eldest of four daughters of Joseph Smith (a farmer and Revolutionary War soldier) and Lois (White) Smith; niece of Oliver Smith (founder of Smith charities in Northampton); attended a local school and spent one term at a school in Hartford, Connecticut; never married; no children.*

Though she herself had been denied an education, Sophia Smith used her considerable fortune to endow Smith College, chartered in 1871, thereby ensuring that future generations of young women would have the opportunity for higher learning. Born in 1796, the daughter of a prosperous farmer in Hatfield, Massachusetts, Smith received some rudimentary schooling in her town and in nearby Hadley and attended a school in Hartford, Connecticut, for one term. She spent the rest of her uneventful life in Hatfield with her family. Described as "shy, plain, . . . and, as she grew older, increasingly suspicious and melancholy," she became even more reclusive after losing her hearing at age 40. When her father Joseph Smith died in 1836, he bequeathed a large estate to Sophia and her three surviving siblings, Austin, Joseph, and **Harriet Smith**. Austin was an exceptionally cheap man who charged his sisters a fee each time they used the family's carriage and greatly resented the fact that his taxes helped to pay for the town's school. At some point he left Hatfield for New York City, where his business acumen and parsimonious living greatly increased his own and the family fortune. Meanwhile, back in Massachusetts, Joseph and Harriet died, and Sophia continued to live as frugally as she had when Austin was there.

When Sophia was 65, Austin died, leaving a plethora of unnotarized wills. Because these were all invalid, Sophia Smith inherited everything. She promptly built herself a mansion, the finest house in town, and furnished it in high style and luxury. (Despite her deafness and solitude—she lived with only a maid—one of these luxuries was a grand piano.) After living there for several years, she determined to put the rest of her money to good charitable use. Smith consulted the Reverend John Morton Greene, pastor of the Hatfield Congregational Church.

*Sophia Smith*

Greene was an advocate of women's education, and strongly advised Smith to donate funds to Amherst College, his alma mater, and to Mt. Holyoke Female Seminary, where his wife **Louisa Dickinson** had studied. Smith decided to use her inheritance to establish an institution for the care of the deaf instead. However, when the Clarke School for the Deaf opened in Northampton in 1868, it eliminated the need for a similar institution.

Greene again suggested that she donate her fortune to Mt. Holyoke, whose founder *Mary Lyon had been distantly related to Smith, and she again declined. Finally, he suggested that she become "to all time a Benefactress" by endowing a women's college that would bear her name. This idea suited her, and she asked Greene to work on plans for such a college, which it was decided would be located in nearby Northampton. Sophia Smith died in Hatfield on June 12, 1870, following a stroke. In her will she left a generous bequest to the Andover Theological Seminary in Andover, Massachusetts, as well as smaller gifts to a variety of missionary organizations. The bulk of her wealth, over $393,000, was left to Smith College, making her the first woman in America to found and endow a women's college. She wrote in her will: "It is my opinion that by the higher and more Christian education of women . . . their weight of influence in reforming the evils of society will be greatly increased; as teachers, as writers, as mothers, as members of society, their power for good will be incalculably enlarged." The college opened in 1875, with 14 students, and went on to become one of the most prestigious women's colleges in the nation. Sophia Smith was inducted into the Women's Hall of Fame at Seneca Falls, New York, in the autumn of 2000.

**SOURCES:**

James, Edward T., ed. *Notable American Women, 1607–1950.* Cambridge, MA: The Belknap Press of Harvard University, 1971.

Kendall, Elaine. "Founders Five," in *American Heritage.* February 1975.

McHenry, Robert, ed. *Famous American Women.* NY: Dover, 1980.

Read, Phyllis J., and Bernard L. Witlieb. *The Book of Women's Firsts.* NY: Random House, 1992.

**Elizabeth Shostak**, freelance writer, Cambridge, Massachusetts

# Smith, Stevie (1902–1971)

*British novelist, book reviewer, short-story writer, and "poet of frozen anguish." Name variations: Florence Margaret Smith; Peggy Smith. Born Florence Margaret Smith in Hull, Yorkshire, England, on Septem-*

*ber 20, 1902; died of a brain tumor in Ashburton, Devonshire, England, on March 7, 1971; second daughter of Charles Ward Smith and Ethel (Spear) Smith; never married; no children.*

*Father deserted family (1903); moved to London suburb of Palmers Green (1906); enrolled in private school, Palmers Green High School and Kindergarten (1907); enrolled in North London Collegiate School for Girls (1917); worked as secretary for London publishing firm (1923–53); began writing poetry (1924); had six poems published in* New Statesman *(1935); published* Novel on Yellow Paper *(1936); attempted suicide (1953); received the Cholmondeley Award for Poetry (1966); awarded the Gold Medal for Poetry by Queen Elizabeth II (1969).*

*Selected writings:* Novel on Yellow Paper *(London: Cape, 1936; NY: Morris, 1937);* A Good Time Was Had By All *(London & Toronto: Cape, 1937);* Over the Frontier *(London: Cape, 1938);* Tender Only to One *(London: Cape, 1938);* Mother, What Is Man? *(London & Toronto: Cape, 1942);* The Holiday *(London: Chapman & Hall, 1949);* Harold's Leap *(London: Chapman & Hall, 1950);* Not Waving but Drowning *(London: Deutsch, 1957); (illustrated by Smith)* Some Are More Human Than Others: Sketchbook *(London: Gaberbocchus, 1958); (illustrated and with an introduction by Smith)* Cats in Colour *(London: Batsford, 1959; NY: Viking, 1960);* Selected Poems *(London: Longmans, Green, 1962; Norfolk, CT: New Directions, 1964);* The Frog Prince and Other Poems *(London: Longmans, Green, 1966);* The Best Beast *(NY: Knopf, 1969); (edited)* The Poet's Garden *(NY: Viking, 1970); (edited)* The Batsford Book of Children's Verse *(London: Batsford, 1970);* Scorpion and Other Poems *(London: Longman, 1972);* The Collected Poems of Stevie Smith *(London: Allen Lane, 1975; NY: Oxford University Press, 1976); (edited by Jack Barbera and William McBrien)* Me Again: Uncollected Writings of Stevie Smith *(London: Virago, 1981; NY: Farrar, Straus & Giroux, 1982).*

A few months before Stevie Smith tried to commit suicide, she wrote her famous poem about a dead man who says to a living acquaintance who stood on the shore while he drowned, "I was much too far out all my life/ And not waving but drowning." In these two poignant lines, Smith sums up her own condition, the unconventional Victorian, the prim and proper eccentric, the lonely woman who longed for public recognition yet resented any intrusion into her private commonplace life. She was an anomaly as a human being, a poet who achieved her lofty literary goal and a woman to whom "being alive is like being in

enemy territory." In her world, Stevie Smith saw herself, too, as "not waving but drowning."

Stevie Smith has been described as "one of the most musical British poets of the century"; she has also been labeled "an airhead and an egghead" and a misanthrope. In the 1960s, Smith was a literary celebrity, a kind of cult figure among youthful radicals. Conservative, reclusive, and frugal, she endured loneliness and disappointment, labored at her boring job as a secretary for 30 years, and "suffered from her ambivalence toward [religious] faith." As "one of the most consistent and most elusive of poets," Stevie Smith is currently the most anthologized British female poet. If her private life was prosaic and regimented, her poetry allowed her to soar above the dour reality of her daily existence.

Florence Margaret Smith, then known as Peggy, was born in 1902 into a middle-class family in Hull, Yorkshire. Her mother **Ethel Spear Smith** was the daughter of a successful engineer, a "frail romantic," who married the handsome Charles Ward Smith, a man "with a taste for drink and wanderlust." He was employed by his family's coal-exporting business, but he longed for adventure, to go to sea. In 1906, when Smith was four years old, Charles abandoned his wife and two daughters and went to sea. Although he and Ethel never divorced, Charles rarely contacted his family and never provided them any financial support. Throughout her life, Stevie Smith resented his "defection" which made her wary of men and their sense of commitment. Ethel, her sister **Margaret Spear**, and the girls moved from Hull to London; with a small legacy from Ethel's father, they took up residence in the London suburb of Palmers Green. Stevie lived in the house at 1 Avondale Road—what she called "a house of female habitation"—for the rest of her life.

In London, Stevie and her sister **Molly** (born in 1901) attended private schools. At age five, Stevie contracted tubercular peritonitis and spent time in a convalescent home. She was an average student; she received a prize for literature in high school but no scholarship for a university education. Molly graduated from the university and became a teacher, while Stevie took a six-month secretarial course in London. Smith's lack of academic achievement was a source of shame which she tried to remedy by becoming a voracious reader. She devoured the classics and read D.H. Lawrence, Aldous Huxley, Oscar Wilde, *Virginia Woolf, and French criticism, but consciously avoided reading contemporary poetry: "one will get the lines crossed and begin writing their poems and they will begin writing one's own," she stated. Stevie *would* be a writer, a poet, and she would be original, uninfluenced by other modern poets. The demure female Smith household was religious, members of the Anglican Church. Smith eventually regarded herself as an "Anglican agnostic"; she was not certain God existed, but He "made humankind less lonely in the universe." And that included Stevie.

## Who and what is Stevie Smith?

## Is she woman?

## Is she myth?

—Ogden Nash

In February 1919, Ethel Smith died; Charles showed up at his wife's funeral, displaying uncharacteristic grief; the next year, he remarried. His second wife called him "Tootles" which elicited Smith to remark, "if he can inspire someone to call him Tootles, there must be things about him I don't see." Stevie never reconciled with her father and found she was just "too busy" to attend his funeral 30 years later. Stevie's Aunt Margaret became the center of her life, her greatest love on whom she could always depend. Molly was teaching in Suffolk, and when she converted to Roman Catholicism in 1928, Stevie was disturbed, but it made her give serious consideration to religion which is amply demonstrated in her writing.

While Molly had a university degree and a career, Stevie had to settle for work as a secretary; in 1923, she became private secretary to Sir Neville Pearson, chair of a publishing firm in London. During slack periods in her often undemanding, humdrum work, Smith began writing poems. Having read almost a book a day for years, she had broadened her horizons and her knowledge of literature and style. However, it would be 11 years before she had anything published, and it would be a novel, not poetry. In the meantime, she toiled at her "demeaning" job, lived with her maiden aunt in the dull London suburb, and dreamed of entering the exalted ranks of the British literary set.

Love and men did not figure prominently in Smith's personal life, but she did have two brief, unsatisfactory love affairs before rejecting the idea of marriage. On a trip to Germany in 1931, she met Karl Eckinger, a handsome Swiss-German graduate student whom she had known in London. He was a great admirer of all things German, but Stevie was not, and this led to their break up. In Berlin, she stayed with Jewish friends and was shaken when she saw a swastika painted on their doorpost. The Nazis were already a frightful presence, and Smith began to despise Germany, an attitude she held for the rest of her life. Stevie has been accused of being anti-Semitic because of remarks that appeared in her *Novel on Yellow Paper*. She did think Jews "weren't really English" and were "pushy," a view not uncommon in England at the time.

A year later, Smith met her second handsome lover, Eric Armitage, with whom she was physically, but not emotionally, compatible. They became informally engaged, but Eric expected to acquire a conventional wife, a role that a nascent poet could never accept. As Smith expressed it, "Marriage, I think/ For women/ Is the best of opiates./ It kills the thoughts" (from *Me Again*, 1981). She came to regard men in general as "tomcats" though she had several male friends during her lifetime. Moreover, she had a negative reaction to children: "Thank heaven they aren't mine." She had a similar attitude towards cats. Smith was not a modern feminist, but she was aware of and had experienced the consequences of a male-dominated world. She wanted men to be fair, kind, and supportive; however, in truth, she found them "generally inadequate, unfeeling, and destructive." Her irresponsible father and her lovers only served to reinforce her beliefs.

The first poems Smith submitted to a literary agent were rejected for their "dubious literary quality," their "ugliness" and "snobbishness." Her first success came in 1935, when David Garnett published six of her poems in the *New Statesman*. When she approached the firm of Chatto and Windus about publishing a book of verse, they suggested she first write a novel. She did; in six weeks, Smith completed *Novel on Yellow Paper* (typed on yellow office paper, hence the name). However, it was turned down as "too quixotic, not structured enough, and without commercial possibilities." Stevie persevered, and the manuscript was finally accepted by Jonathan Cape; it was widely reviewed and well received. The heroine of the novel, Pompey Casmilus, a fictional version of Stevie Smith, also appears in the sequel, *Over the Frontier* (1938). Pompey lived with a maiden aunt in a suburb of London, had a boring job and unsatisfactory relationships. Critics recognized the novels as autobiographical, and the same was true of her first book of poetry, *A Good Time Was Had by All*, published by Cape in 1938.

Stevie enthusiastically embraced her sudden fame and became a member of the London liter-

Stevie
Smith

ary scene. A curious change in her behavior at this time has been associated with her newly acknowledged talent; she began to dress like an adolescent schoolgirl (she was 36), to talk baby talk, and to act mischievously. In literary circles it was said she "wanted to be spoiled," to be "fawned over and doted upon like a precious child." This peculiar behavior became more pronounced with time; it would appear that this child-like persona permeates her writing, too. One critic noted that her work "has the air of an odd, only, lonely child."

It is not surprising that death was a recurring theme in Smith's writing. The rise of fascism in Europe in the 1930s, and the coming of World War II in 1939, had a profound effect on her. She saw "war and aggression as immature male games," but instead of withdrawing into a safe protective shell during the war years, Stevie became an air-raid warden and fire watcher in London. After working all day, she went home to have dinner with her aunt, then back to London to report on fires from the intense German bombing which destroyed many parts of the city. It was dangerous, exhausting work, but despite the awful conditions she continued to write.

Though Stevie was "not a natural novelist," she began her last novel, *The Holiday*, which was published in 1949 after seven years of rewriting and revisions. Again, her heroine, Celia, is "a Stevie reincarnation," but the novel was not successful. Her only book of poetry to appear during the war years was *Mother, What is Man?* (1942) which, as usual, dealt with "her explorations of her fears of both death and life." Smith also joined PEN, the international writers' organization that was active in bringing writers and editors out of German-occupied areas of Europe.

Wartime inflation forced Stevie to supplement her regular salary. She began to review books and tried to obtain a position with the British Broadcasting Corporation (BBC). Her employer discouraged her from seeking work at the BBC, saying she didn't speak clearly and had a lisp; he most likely didn't want to lose a valuable employee who would be hard to replace due to the wartime labor shortage. Smith had hoped she might read her prose and poetry on the Overseas Program at the BBC which was run by the British novelist George Orwell, author of *Animal Farm* (1945) and *Nineteen Eighty-Four* (1949). It is believed that Smith and Orwell had an affair, although he was married at the time. They shared conservative, anti-Communist views, but Orwell did nothing to help Smith become a reader on the program. She was angry and exacted her revenge in her novel *The Holiday*, where Orwell is satirized in the character of Basil Tate with an intimation of homosexuality. After the war, Stevie's short stories similarly alienated friends who were objects of her cynical, sarcastic view of human relations. She also began to give public readings of her poetry in her distinctive sing-song voice, both for the money and the public acclaim it brought. By 1949, she was reading her work on BBC broadcasts.

In the 1950s, Stevie Smith was no longer fashionable. *Harold's Leap* (1950) sold poorly even for a book of verse. She wanted to quit her secretarial job and go into editing; it is indicative of the times that the publishing firm for which she worked did not think to offer this published writer an editorial position. In addition to working full-time and reviewing books, Stevie was caring for her Aunt Margaret who was almost immobile. Moreover, she could not get any of her writings published, she had a painful knee injury, and she had tax problems. In April 1953, Smith wrote "Not Waving but Drowning," a solemn, muted cry of desperation. Three months later, she slashed her wrists in an unsuccessful suicide attempt as she sat at her desk in her office. In another poem, "The Old Sweet Dove of Wiveton," she writes of the lonely "dove of peace" who sits in its nest "Murmuring solitary/ Crying for pain, Crying most melancholy/ Again and again."

After Stevie retired from the publishing firm, she became a full-time writer, and with the publication of *Not Waving but Drowning* in 1957, she once again gained public recognition. Her work fit into the "French theater of the absurd" which was currently in vogue. Books of her drawings (*Some Are More Human Than Others*, 1958, and *Cats in Colour*, 1959) brought greater awareness of her creativity. *Cats* is uncharacteristically humorous: "Cats are like children," Stevie wrote, "more interesting when observed, and most adorable when they are someone else's." The BBC produced her radio play, *A Turn Outside*, in 1959, and she frequently appeared on radio programs which increased her audience.

The early 1960s were dominated by health problems, an operation on her knee and removal of a benign breast tumor. But the decade also brought Smith the critical acclaim she craved. *Selected Poems* (1962) and inclusion in *Penguin Modern Poets 8* (1966) brought her an offer to undertake a poetry tour in the United States; she declined, citing her diminished energy. Her poems now appeared in leading American periodicals, including *The New Yorker, The New York Review of Books*, and *The Atlantic Monthly*, and were translated into French and German. When *The Frog Prince and Other Poems* appeared in 1966, Stevie was called "the most original poet writing in English today." The poems mainly deal with man's relationship to God and with death: "For those who suffer, death is freedom," she declared. And death was "a lover to be embraced most gladly." If God were dead, as many claimed in the postwar period, death was the only god there was. Sanford Sternlicht notes Smith "wanted to believe" in God, in Christianity: "She allowed God his maleness but feminized Him too. He could rule her universe, but it had better be through love." But Stevie did not accept the Christian doctrine of heaven and hell—"Hell is humanity," she decided (like Jean-Paul Sartre's "Hell is other people"). She rejected the idea of an afterlife and eternal damnation, the Biblical account of Creation, and that "scripture was divinely inspired." However, as she told her friend **Kay Dick**, she was "a backslider as a non-believer." Smith's ambivalence towards God is clearly stated in her poem "God the Eater": "There is a god in whom I do not believe/ Yet to this god my love stretches,/ This god whom I do not believe in is/ My whole life, my life and I am his."

In 1966, Stevie Smith received the Cholmondeley Award for Poetry, a recognition of her achievements by fellow writers. Two years later, *The Best Beast* was issued, and, in November 1969, Stevie was awarded the Queen's Gold Medal for Poetry. Queen *Elizabeth II* personally made the formal presentation of the award during a private audience. For this momentous occasion, Smith bought a hat at a rummage sale at her church; at Buckingham Palace, she met with the queen for 20 minutes.

Aunt Margaret with whom Stevie had lived in the "house of female habitation" since 1906, did not live to see her niece receive the Gold Medal; she died in March 1968, at the age of 96. Smith continued to live, alone, in "the Victorian relic" that she called "her fortress and her cave." She would neither move nor renovate the house on Avondale Road. Stevie continued to give poetry readings, to write poetry, and to review books. In April 1970, she fell, cracked three ribs and injured her knee. That November, she went to stay with her sister Molly, who had had a stroke in 1969, in Devonshire. By early January 1970, Stevie was seriously ill; she was told that she had an inoperable malignant brain tumor. She died in Ashburton Hospital in March 1971, at age 68. As early as 1937, Stevie had envisioned an end to existence, to her own life; she had determined that "When I have had enough/ I will arise/ And go unto my Father/ And I will say to Him:/ Father, I have had enough."

According to Sternlicht, "Stevie Smith . . . was a wounded she-devil savaging male privilege, and a gay, witty woman enjoying her gender role in a patriarchal society while spoofing it." Her poetry continued to attract new readers for she spoke to human concerns in simple, basic, non-academic language. *The Collected Poems of Stevie Smith* was published in 1975, and a few years later Virago Press republished her novels. *Stevie*, a play about her life by Hugh Whitemore, was staged successfully in London in 1977, and the next year a film version was produced, star-

ring *Glenda Jackson* who had met and liked Stevie and had read her poetry publicly.

Like *Emily Dickinson*, Stevie Smith "created her own circumscribed world, one whole and coherent, if slightly tilted." In this slightly skewed world of her construction, wrote Sternlicht, "animals are always good and people seldom . . . angels try to understand humans instead of vice versa . . . men are insufficient and women never learn the fact . . . and loneliness is the steady companion." In her three novels and nine volumes of poetry, she speaks intensely of human anxieties and fears, but her readers come to realize that "Stevie's not drowning but waving."

**SOURCES:**
*Dictionary of Literary Biography*, Vol. 20: *British Poets, 1914–1945*. Edited by Donald E. Stanford. Detroit, MI: Gale Research, 1983.
*In Search of Stevie Smith*. Edited and with an introduction by Sanford Sternlicht. Syracuse, NY: Syracuse University Press, 1991.
Sternlicht, Sanford. *Stevie Smith*. Boston: Twayne, 1990.

**SUGGESTED READING:**
Barbera, Jack, and William McBrien. *Stevie: A Biography of Stevie Smith*. London: Heinemann, 1985.
———, and Helen Bajan. *Stevie Smith: A Bibliography*. Westport, CT: Meckler, 1987.
Dick, Kay. *Ivy and Stevie: *Ivy Compton-Burnett and Stevie Smith*. London: Duckworth, 1971, Allison and Busby, 1983.
Rankin, Arthur. *The Poetry of Stevie Smith: Little Girl Lost*. Gerrards Cross, Buckinghamshire: Colin Smythe, 1985.
Spalding, Frances. *Stevie Smith: A Biography*. NY: W.W. Norton, 1989.

**RELATED MEDIA:**
*Stevie: A Play from the Life and Work of Stevie Smith* by Hugh Whitemore, produced in London (1977).
*Stevie* (102 min. film), starring Glenda Jackson, **Mona Washburne**, Alec McCowen, and Trevor Howard, based on the play by Hugh Whitemore, produced in England by Bowen-First Artists, 1978.

**Jeanne A. Ojala**,
Visiting Scholar, Department of History,
University of Minnesota, Minneapolis, Minnesota;
Professor Emerita, Department of History,
University of Utah, Salt Lake City, Utah

# Smith, Trixie (1895–1943)

*American blues singer whose recordings with Louis Armstrong are particularly remembered. Born in Atlanta, Georgia, in 1895; died in New York City on September 21, 1943.*

Trixie Smith was born in 1895 in Atlanta, Georgia, and studied at Selma University before she decided to focus on singing. In 1915, she left the South for New York where she appeared in numerous vaudeville shows and eventually became a featured vocalist. When blues became the rage in the 1920s, Smith began recording on the Black Swan label. In 1922, she entered a blues contest in New York and won first place with "Trixie's Blues," also recorded by Black Swan. Smith is particularly remembered for "Railroad Blues" and "The World Is Jazz Crazy and So Am I" which featured Louis Armstrong on cornet. In the 1920s, blues singers named Smith predominated: *Bessie Smith, *Clara Smith, and *Mamie Smith were all performing at the same time as Trixie Smith. But by 1926, Smith's recording career was effectively over, even though she recorded for Decca in the late 1930s. She continued to work on stage in cabaret revues, musical shows, and theatrical productions until her death in 1943.

**SOURCES:**

Santelli, Robert. *The Big Book of Blues: A Biographical Encyclopedia*. NY: Penguin, 1993.

**John Haag**,
Athens, Georgia

## Smith, Virginia Dodd (1911—)

**American congressional representative (1975–1991).**
*Born Virginia Dodd in Randolph, Fremont County, Iowa, on June 30, 1911; graduated from University of Nebraska, Lincoln, in 1936; married a Nebraska wheat farmer.*

*Virginia Dodd Smith*

U.S. congressional representative Virginia Dodd Smith, a Republican from Nebraska, was active in legislation and policies that served the agricultural and ranching interests of her state. Born in Iowa in 1911, Smith grew up there and graduated from Shenandoah (Iowa) High School. She attended the University of Nebraska in Lincoln, graduating in 1936 with a B.A. in education, married a Nebraska wheat farmer, and became active in local and regional affairs.

Smith chaired the women's bureau of the American Farm Bureau Federation from 1955 to 1974, and was active in the American Country Life Association. From 1950 to 1960, she was a member of the U.S. Department of Agriculture's Home Economics Research Advisory Committee, and she was active in the Nebraska Republican Party, serving as a delegate to the Republican National conventions from 1956 to 1972. In 1960, Smith was appointed a delegate to the White House Conference on Children and Youth. She served on the U.S. Department of Health, Education, and Welfare's Clearinghouse on Rural Education and Small Schools Advisory Board from 1972 to 1974. In 1973, Smith served on the U.S. Department of Commerce's Census Advisory Committee on Agricultural Statistics. Smith won election as a representative from Nebraska to the 94th Congress in 1975, and was reelected to seven succeeding terms. She was not a candidate for reelection in 1990 and retired in 1991.

During her first congressional term, Smith served on the Education and Labor Committee, and on the Committee on Interior and Insular Affairs. In her second term, she joined the Committee on Appropriations. She became the ranking Republican member of the Subcommittee on Rural Development, Agriculture and Related Agencies, and worked assiduously to promote the interests of farmers and ranchers.

**SOURCES:**

Office of the Historian. *Women In Congress, 1917–1990.* Commission on the Bicentenary of the U.S. House of Representatives, 1991.

**Elizabeth Shostak**, freelance writer, Cambridge, Massachusetts

## Smith, Virginia Thrall (1836–1903)

**American social worker.** *Born Tryphena Virginia Thrall in Bloomfield, Connecticut, on August 16, 1836; died in Hartford, Connecticut, on January 3, 1903; daughter of Hiram Thrall (a businessman and surveyor) and Melissa (Griswold) Thrall; educated at the Suffield (Connecticut) Institute, the Hartford Female Seminary, and Mt. Holyoke Seminary; married William Brown Smith (a businessman), on December*

31, 1857 (died 1897); children: Oliver Cotton Smith (b. 1859); Edward Carrington Smith (b. 1861); **Lucy Virginia Smith** (b. 1865); **Kate Richardson Smith** (b. 1867); William Brown Smith (b. 1871); Thomas Hammond Smith (b. 1874).

Chosen as administrative head of Hartford City Mission (1876); instrumental in establishing kindergartens in Connecticut public schools; appointed to State Board of Charities (1882); became director of Connecticut Children's Aid Society (1892); established Home for Incurables (1898), later named the Newington Hospital for Crippled Children.

A pioneer in the field of child care in Connecticut, Virginia Thrall Smith enjoyed a comfortable early life. She was one of six children born to Hiram Thrall, a businessman, and **Melissa Griswold Thrall**. Virginia—who had been christened Tryphena Virginia—attended the Suffield (Connecticut) Institute, the Hartford Female Seminary, and, from 1856 to 1857, Mt. Holyoke Seminary. On December 31, 1857, she married William Brown Smith, a businessman, and settled with him in Hartford. They had six children, three of whom died of diphtheria in infancy.

Smith was active in church and social affairs, giving readings at small social gatherings and playing the organ at church events. She also wrote stories for local newspapers. In 1876, she became the head of the Hartford City Mission, an organization sponsored by the city's six Congregational churches which provided food and clothing to the needy. Smith quickly expanded the mission's activities, starting a loan fund and a women's sewing class as well as a singing school for girls and a boys' club. In 1878, she established a volunteer group of 33 charitable visitors, and in 1879 began a program that sent city children to the countryside for summer vacations. Two years later, Smith set up a laundry and a cooking school, a girls' sewing school, and a kindergarten. The kindergarten program was so successful that, by 1885, Connecticut authorized the establishment of public kindergartens throughout the state.

In 1882, Smith was appointed to the State Board of Charities, which gave her the opportunity to devote her energies to children's welfare. Disturbed by the housing of poor children in almshouses with senile, insane, or criminal adults, she pushed for legislation to establish temporary county children's homes; this was enacted in 1883. Smith also established, within the City Mission, a program that placed unwanted children in adoptive homes. Though many professionals respected her approach, local officials

resented Smith's interference in affairs that they had administered themselves. When one of the babies Smith placed in an adoptive home died in 1892, these officials used the death to suggest that Smith was guilty of "baby farming" and of making Hartford a dumping ground for indigents from other states. Though several defended her, including John Hooker, husband of suffragist ❧▶ **Isabella Beecher Hooker**, Smith's reputation was damaged, and she resigned her position at the City Mission.

The women's branch of the Hartford City Mission reorganized as the Children's Aid Society and continued Smith's work. In 1892, **Mrs. Francis Bacon** and others organized the Connecticut Children's Aid Society, of which Smith served as director and paid secretary until her death. Smith's last major achievement in child care came in 1898, when she opened the Home for Incurables to provide care for handicapped children who could not be adopted. The institution later became the Newington Hospital for Crippled Children. Smith, who had been widowed in 1897, died in Hartford in 1903.

**SOURCES:**
James, Edward T., ed. *Notable American Women, 1607–1950*. Cambridge, MA: The Belknap Press of Harvard University, 1971.

**Elizabeth Shostak**, freelance writer, Cambridge, Massachusetts

**Hooker, Isabella Beecher.** See Stowe, Harriet Beecher for sidebar.

# Smith, Willie Mae Ford
## (1904–1994)

*Legendary African-American gospel singer who was featured in the documentary* Say Amen, Somebody. *Name variations: Mother Smith. Born in Rolling Fort, Mississippi, on June 23, 1904 (some sources cite 1906); died in St. Louis, Missouri, in 1994; daughter of Clarence Ford (a railroad brakeman) and Mary (Williams) Ford (a restaurant owner); attended school until eighth grade; married James Peter Smith (owner of a small business), in 1924 (died 1950); children: Willie James Smith; **Jacquelyn Smith Jackson**; (adopted) Bertha Smith.*

*Debuted with sisters in Ford Sisters quartet (1922); performed with Ford Sisters at National Baptist Convention (1924); established and became director of the National Convention of Gospel Choirs and Choruses Soloists Bureau (1932); toured extensively throughout the U.S. (1930s–1940s); sang with Mahalia Jackson at Easter Sunrise Service, Hollywood Bowl, California (late 1940s); ordained as a minister in the Lively Stone Apostolic Church, St. Louis, Missouri (mid-1950s); served for 17 years as director of the Education Department of the National Baptist*

*Convention; featured in documentary film* Say Amen, Somebody *(1982); received National Endowment for the Arts Heritage Award as outstanding American folk artist (1988).*

An inspiration for several generations of American gospel singers, Willie Mae Ford Smith, known as Mother Smith, was born on June 23, 1904, in Rolling Fort, Mississippi. She was one of 14 children born to Clarence Ford, a railroad brakeman, and **Mary Williams Ford**. Willie Mae's maternal grandmother, who sometimes cared for the children, had been a slave, and Smith remembered her "singing, clapping, and doing the 'Rock Daniel,' her name for the holy dance." When Willie Mae was 12, the family moved to St. Louis, Missouri, which was to remain Smith's lifelong home. Here, Mary Ford opened a restaurant where Willie Mae sometimes worked. Clarence and Mary were devout Baptists, and passed on strict religious teachings to their children.

Willie Mae received little formal schooling or musical education, but began singing with her sisters **Mary, Emma**, and **Geneva** as the Ford Sisters quartet in 1922. They performed at the 1924 National Baptist Convention, but their style was considered too exuberant and dramatic to be much in demand at the time. In the following years, the sisters married and the quartet broke up, but they encouraged Willie Mae to launch a solo career.

In 1924, Willie Mae married James Peter Smith, a small businessman with whom she would have two children, Willie James Smith and Jacquelyn Smith Jackson. During the 1930s, Willie Mae was often on the road. She met gospel pioneers Thomas A. Dorsey and **Sallie Martin** in 1932, and joined their gospel movement. In 1936, she organized the Soloists Bureau of the National Convention of Gospel Choirs and Choruses for Dorsey, and for several years taught new generations of gospel singers. Her performance of "If You Just Keep Still," which she composed in 1937, was considered the standard for solo gospel singing.

Smith left the Baptist Church in 1939, when she was called to evangelical work in the Church of God Apostolic. She was ordained a minister in the Lively Stone Apostolic Church in St. Louis in the mid-1950s. During the 1940s and 1950s, Smith made concert appearances and performed at church revivals, pioneering a style that used small introductory sermons and song text explication—an approach that conservative church members found disturbingly close to the blues, but that others emulated. Smith knew and worked with the top gospel singers of the time,

including Dorsey and Martin, **Roberta Martin**, and *****Mahalia Jackson**. Among her most noted protégés are **Bertha Smith**, whom Willie Mae and her husband had adopted in the 1930s, **Myrtle Scott, Martha Bass**, the O'Neal Twins, **Edna Gallman Cooke**, and Brother Joe May. Though Smith did not record during her early career, many of her followers recorded verbatim versions of her arrangements.

Late in her career, Smith made some recordings of her songs. These include "I Believe I'll Run On" and "Going on With the Spirit" on the Nashboro Label, and "I Am Bound for Canaan Land" (Savoy SL 14739). In 1982, Smith was featured in the esteemed documentary film *Say Amen, Somebody*. She received a Heritage Award from the National Endowment for the Arts in 1988 as an outstanding American folk artist. Smith, who was widowed in 1950, died in St. Louis in 1994.

**SOURCES:**
Smith, Jessie Carney, ed. *Notable Black American Women*. Detroit, MI: Gale Research, 1992.
*Time* (obituary). February 14, 1994.

**Elizabeth Shostak**, freelance writer, Cambridge, Massachusetts

# Smith, Zilpha Drew (1851–1926)

*American social worker. Born on January 25, 1851 (Smith gave her birth date as 1852, but town records cite 1851), in Pembroke, Massachusetts; died on October 12, 1926, in Boston, Massachusetts; daughter of Silvanus Smith (a carpenter) and Judith Winsor (McLauthlin) Smith; graduated from the Girls' High and Normal School in Boston, 1868.*

*Became registrar of Associated Charities of Boston (1879) and served as general secretary (1886–1903); served as associate director, Boston School for Social Workers (1904–18).*

Social worker Zilpha Drew Smith did much to professionalize charity work at the end of the 19th century. Born in Pembroke, Massachusetts, in 1851, she grew up in East Boston. Her parents Silvanus and **Judith McLauthlin Smith** were descendants of *Mayflower* pilgrims, and they endowed their six children with a strong commitment to social causes such as abolition, temperance, education, women's suffrage and religious tolerance. The Smith ideal also emphasized the importance of hard work and wholesome family relationships, values that Zilpha went on to promote in her social-work career.

After graduating from the Girls' High and Normal School in Boston in 1868, Smith worked briefly as a telegrapher before accepting a job revising the Suffolk County probate court index. In 1879, she became registrar of the Associated Charities of Boston, a newly established organization that consolidated the city's various social-welfare groups. In this position, Smith managed the confidential investigation of all charity cases among the groups, and emphasized "friendly visiting" to promote more personal relationships between charity workers and their recipients. Under Smith's leadership, the Associated Charities became one of the country's most successful organizations of its kind. The association used both paid and volunteer agents and allotted responsibility by district. In addition, training classes were set up for district administrators as well as for what were increasingly being called case workers. Smith also established discussion groups for workers through which they could learn from each other and boost morale. Social work professionals from other regions, among them *Mary E. Richmond of Baltimore, who became a close friend, often visited Boston to observe Smith's innovations. Smith was also active in the National Conference of Charities and Correction, and lectured at the New York School of Philanthropy. One of her lectures was used as the basis of Richmond's 1917 textbook *Social Diagnosis*.

In 1903, Smith resigned her position as general secretary of Associated Charities, which she had held since 1886. Thereafter, she devoted her attention to the training of social-work professionals. She became associate director of the new Boston School for Social Workers, which set a milestone in the development of the social-work field by requiring a full year's academic training. At the Boston School, Smith developed special problem classes that used case records to illustrate professional techniques. Smith retired in 1918, and became a member of the Massachusetts Society of Mayflower Descendants in 1924. She died in Boston in 1926.

**SOURCES:**

James, Edward T., ed. *Notable American Women, 1607–1950*. Cambridge, MA: The Belknap Press of Harvard University, 1971.

McHenry, Robert, ed. *Famous American Women*. NY: Dover, 1980.

**Elizabeth Shostak**, freelance writer,
Cambridge, Massachusetts

## Smith Court, Margaret (b. 1942).

*See Court, Margaret Smith.*

## Smith-Robinson, Ruby Doris
(1942–1967).

*See Robinson, Ruby Doris Smith.*

## Smithson, Harriet Constance
(1800–1854)

*Irish actress.* Name variations: Henrietta Constance Smithson; Madame Berlioz. Born in Ennis, Ireland, in 1800; died on March 3, 1854; daughter of a theatrical manager; married Hector Berlioz (the composer), in October 1833 (separated 1840).

Debuted at Crow Street Theatre in Dublin as Lady Teazle (1815); appeared at London's Drury Lane Theatre as Letitia Hardy (1818); appeared in Paris (1828, 1832).

Irish actress Harriet Constance Smithson, the daughter of a theatrical manager, was born in Ennis in 1800. She made her stage debut at the Crow Street Theater, Dublin, in 1815 as Lady Teazle in Sheridan's *The School for Scandal* (one source reports the role as Albina Mandeville in Reynolds' *Will*), and appeared as Letitia Hardy at the Drury Lane Theater in London in 1818. For several years, Smithson performed at provincial theaters, and made successful appearances in Boulogne and Calais in 1824. In 1828 and 1832, Smithson and the eminent Shakespearean actor William Macready performed in Paris, where her talents were greatly admired. She played such roles as *Jane Shore, Desdemona, Juliet, and Ophelia, causing a sensation and attracting the attention of several admirers. Among these was the composer Hector Berlioz, whom Smithson married in 1833. By then, however, her popularity had waned, and she was in financial straits. Berlioz continued to support her even after their separation in 1840. Smithson died on March 3, 1854.

**Elizabeth Shostak**, freelance writer,
Cambridge, Massachusetts

## Smithson, Henrietta Constance
(1800–1854).

*See Smithson, Harriet Constance.*

## Smyth, Ethel (1858–1944)

*British composer whose six operas and many orchestral and choral works differ greatly from other British compositions of the period, and who now ranks among the top 20th-century composers.* Name variations: Dame Ethel Smyth. Born Ethel Mary Smyth in Marylebone, England, on April 22, 1858; died in Woking, England, on May 9, 1944; daughter of a major-general in the British army; educated by governesses at home and at Putney before undertaking serious study of music at the Conservatory in Leipzig; never married; no children.

*Began formal music training with Alexander Ewing (1875); began study at the Conservatory in Leipzig (1877); studied orchestration with Heinrich von Herzogenberg, the Austrian composer (1878); orchestral work "Serenade" given its first major performance at the Crystal Palace (1890); first of six operas, Fantasio, performed at Weimar (1898);* Der Wald *produced at Covent Garden (1902);* The Wreckers *produced (1906); participated in the women's suffrage movement and served a jail term for her activities (1910–13); honored with title Dame of the British Empire (1922).*

*Major works—operas:* Fantasio *(1892–94);* Der Wald *(1899–1901);* The Wreckers *(1903–04);* The Boatswain's Mate *(1913–14);* Fete Galante *(1923);* Entente Cordiale *(1925); Soli, Chorus, and Orchestra* Mass in D *(1891).*

*Chorus and orchestra:* Hey Nonny No *(1911);* Sleepless Dreams *(1912);* A Spring Canticle *(1926);* The Prison *(1930).*

*Chamber music: String Quintet, Op. 1 (1884); Sonata for Cello and Piano, Op. 5 (1887); Sonata for Violin and Piano (1887); String Quartet (1902–12); Trios for Violin, Oboe, and Piano (1927).*

*Organ: "Five Short Chorale Preludes" (1913); "Prelude on a Traditional Irish Melody" (1939).*

From an early age, Ethel Smyth demonstrated a directness and force of will that people around her learned to either admire or loathe. Although her family was not musical, she was influenced early by a governess who had studied at the Leipzig Conservatory, and at age nine she wrote in her diary that her ambition was "to be made a Peeress in my own right because of music." Despite the fact that her formal training in music did not begin until she was 17, it was a goal she would live to achieve.

Unlike many English composers of her era who chose pastoral themes, Smyth produced highly charged music of astonishing breadth and power. Her six operas and numerous symphonic and orchestral pieces are turbulent but melodious and masterful works. In her forthright way, she was also an outspoken suffragist who went to jail for demonstrating for women's right to vote, and the author of ten books whose well-written portraits of public figures of her day made them bestsellers.

Ethel Mary Smyth was born in Marylebone, England, on April 22, 1858, the fourth of eight children. Her father was a military man who served as a major-general in the Bengal Army, then returned from India after the mutiny and led a quiet, prosperous life. Her mother managed the large Victorian household, where the children were educated by governesses. Later, Ethel attended school at Putney where she studied music, drawing, French, German, astronomy, chemistry, literature, and "how to darn stockings."

Smyth's formal musical training began with Alexander Ewing. Two years later, in the summer of 1877, she was 19 when she overheard her parents making plans for her coming-out season of balls and beaux. Determined to have none of it, she decided on a course of action:

> I quite deliberately adopted the methods used years afterwards in political warfare by other women, who, having plumbed the depths of masculine prejudice, came to see that this was the only road to victory. I not only unfurled the red flag, but determined to make life at home so intolerable that they would have to let me go, for their sakes. Towards the end I struck altogether, refused to go to church, refused to sing at our dinner-parties, refused to go out riding, refused to speak to anyone, and one day father's boot all but penetrated a panel of my locked bedroom door . . . [until] there was nothing for it but to capitulate.

That autumn, Ethel Smyth departed for Leipzig, to study music composition.

In Victorian England, music was considered the highest feminine accomplishment, but acceptable only so long as it was performed in the privacy of one's home; public performance remained a purely male domain. England's Royal Conservatory admitted women, but there was a tacit understanding that they were there to pursue careers in teaching. The study of composition was acceptable as long as a woman confined herself to lilting melodies suitable to gracing the drawing room. Smyth was out for something different.

In Leipzig, through her friend **Elisabeth von Herzogenberg**, Smyth was drawn into the musical circle of \*Clara Schumann and Johannes Brahms. As a student, she met Edvard Grieg, Antonin Dvorak, and Peter Tchaikovsky, but after a year she quit the conservatory in disgust because she could get no one to teach her orchestration. After Tchaikovsky advised her to study orchestration on her own, she engaged the Austrian composer Heinrich von Herzogenberg to teach her.

Always comfortable with expressing her opinions, Smyth occasionally found her relations with some of the world's best-known composers less than cordial. Once, in the presence of

*Ethel Smyth*

Edvard Grieg, who had not been introduced to her, she was criticizing the compositions of Franz Liszt when Grieg demanded, "What the devil does a two-penny-halfpenny whippersnapper like you mean by talking like this of your betters?" Through further discussion, however, Grieg gained enough respect for her opinions to apologize for his outburst.

Smyth began composing in the late 1870s, when she was in her 20s, but by the mid-1880s, few of her works had been heard in public performance. On the rare occasion that her compositions reached an audience, critics typically found the works "deficient in the feminine charm that might have been expected of a woman composer." In despair, Smyth wrote to the violinist Joseph Joachim that her gender was being held against her. Joachim wrote to reassure her, "If your creative instinct is genuine it will not perish on that account, which reflection should console us both." And to be fair, there were contemporary male British composers, like Frederich Delius, who had an equally difficult time obtaining performances of their work.

In 1890, Smyth's circumstances began to improve. Her *Serenade*, an orchestral work in four movements, was played at a Crystal Palace concert. The following year, she composed her Mass in D which was presented by the Royal Choral Society at the Royal Albert Hall on January 18, 1893, under the direction of Sir Joseph Barnaby. Greater successes followed. In 1898, her first opera, *Fantasio*, premiered in Weimar, Germany. A second opera, *Der Wald*, was produced in Berlin and Covent Garden in 1902, and in New York in 1903.

Smyth had a gift for vocal composition and for large works, and in an era when Richard Wagner's revolutionary operas dominated the musical world, it is perhaps not surprising that she increasingly directed her talents toward opera. Between 1892 and 1925, Smyth wrote six operas, all of which reached the stage, an extraordinary feat for any composer.

One work she struggled to sell was *The Wreckers*, inspired by a visit to the Scilly Isles off the southwestern coast of England. On the island of Tresco, Smyth had visited a cave near the sea with a freshwater lake full of blind fish, known as the Piper's Hole. The lake, cave, and a boat chained "like Charon's ferry" made a deep impression on her, and became the inspiration for her story. The opera is set in a coastal village in Cornwall where the inhabitants earn a living by plundering shipwrecks, using false beacons to lure ships onto the rocks and their crews to certain death. Mark and Thirza are a star-crossed couple who are caught by the Wreckers while trying to thwart these nefarious activities. Chained together in a sea cave, they are left to be drowned by the incoming tide. "For five years," according to the conductor Sir Thomas Beecham, "Ethel Smyth, wearing mannish tweeds and an assertively cocked felt hat, had been striding around Europe, cigar in mouth, trying to sell her opera *The Wreckers* to timorous or stubborn impresarios." Finally, in 1906, she succeeded.

*Somerville, Edith.* See joint entry under Somerville and Ross.

Beecham also reported on a backstage visit after a matinee performance of *The Wreckers* by King Edward VIII. According to the conductor, the monarch "was very gracious and he almost kissed Ethel. He certainly shook me by the hand. I don't think he actually succeeded in kissing Ethel. No man within my recollection ever has succeeded or did succeed in kissing Ethel." While she allowed few liberties with men, Smyth's most important personal relationship was with Harry Brewster, her companion and lover. When Brewster died in 1908, she "felt like a rudderless ship aimlessly drifting hither and thither."

Women were also central to Smyth's emotional life, as both friends and lovers, and she knew some of the most illustrious women of the era. Among her friends and supporters, some of whom provided the generous subsidies that allowed her music to reach the public, were *Vita Sackville-West, *Virginia Woolf, Empress *Eugenie of France, the British feminist leader *Emmeline Pankhurst, ↞ Edith Somerville, and Vernon Lee (*Violet Paget). Wrote Smyth:

> [A]ll my life, even when after years had brought me the seemingly unattainable, I have found in women's affection a peculiar understanding, mothering quality that is a thing apart. Perhaps too I had a foreknowledge of the difficulties that in a world arranged by man for man's convenience beset the woman who leaves the traditional path to compete for bread and butter, honours and emoluments. . . . The people who helped me most at difficult moments of my musical career . . . have been members of my own sex.

It was such close associations which probably made her involvement with the British suffrage movement inevitable. In the world of the arts, where she found no rules—only chances to be given or withheld—it was her experience that the chances were far more frequently withheld from women than from men. She was particularly infuriated, for instance, by the fact that women were excluded from performing in the leading orchestras. Women in music were subject to the double burden of having no political or public voice, and no strong musical traditions to nourish them. In her writings she often described the system of male dominance at work in the music world as "The Inner Circle," "The Male Machine," or "The Gang." In one particularly telling description of her situation, she wrote:

> Year in and year out, composers of the Inner Circle, generally University men attached to our musical institutions, produced one choral work after another—not infrequently deadly dull affairs—which . . . automatically went the round of our Festivals and Choral

Societies. . . . Was it likely, then, that the Faculty would see any merit in a work written on such different lines—written too by a woman who had actually gone off to Germany to learn her trade?

In 1910, Smyth stepped away from her work as a composer, which by then was flourishing, to work for the suffragist movement as a member of the Women's Social and Political Union (WSPU). Friends like the critic Frank Howes and Thomas Beecham were rankled, feeling that Smyth was too talented to be wasting her time on politics. Smyth's response was to apply music to politics by composing "March of the Women," with words written by *Cicely Hamilton, which became the "Marseillaise" of the suffrage movement. As demonstrations grew, "March of the Women" was heard increasingly in the streets throughout Britain, although it was rarely sung. Women preferred to shout the lyrics.

As demonstrations grew more heated, Emmeline Pankhurst asked for volunteers to smash the windows in the homes of politicians who opposed women having the vote. Smyth rose to the challenge by marching to the home of a Cabinet minister, "Lulu" Harcourt, where she gave Pankhurst a demonstration of how to break a window with a rock, and was promptly arrested. Beecham wrote of visiting her during her two-months' confinement in Holloway Prison:

I went to see her several times. But on this particular occasion when I arrived, the warden of the prison, who was a very amiable fellow, was bubbling with laughter. He said, "Come into the quadrangle." There were the ladies, a dozen ladies, marching up and down, singing hard. He pointed up to a window where Ethel appeared; she was leaning out, conducting with a toothbrush, also with immense vigor, and joining in the chorus of her own song.

Smyth was still in her 50s when she began to go deaf after 1913; by the end of her long life, she could not hear at all. Frustrated by composing, she turned to writing, penning many brilliant portraits of notable people of the day, including Johannes Brahms, Queen *Victoria, Emmeline Pankhurst, Violet Paget, and Maurice Baring. Smyth could be vividly opinionated in writing about fellow composers, and showed her admiration in particular for the conductor Sir Henry Wood, as the first to start "mixed bathing in the sea of music and so successful was the innovation that many orchestras followed suit." She was unusually frank for the time about her own life and personal relations, and she continued to campaign for more equitable treatment in the music world, a position that she ultimately

felt paid off. She wrote ten books in all, and became a bestselling author.

The whole English attitude toward women in art is ludicrous and uncivilized. There is no sex in art. How you play the violin, paint, or compose, is what matters.
—Ethel Smyth

In 1922, Smyth's childhood dream came true when she was honored for music with the title of Dame of the British Empire. Almost a decade later, Smyth was 73 when she became friends with the writer Virginia Woolf, who was many years her junior. Smyth was mesmerized by Woolf, who was somewhat taken aback at first by the older woman's fervor. (Despite Smyth's deafness, or perhaps because of it, contemporaries often found her to be "exhausting and obstinate, especially where, first, her own music, and second, women's rights were concerned.") Nevertheless, the two became friends, having a great deal in common, especially their writing. Although there were times when Smyth's force of character strained the relationship, many have felt that no one has described Ethel Smyth better than Woolf. In her private diary, an entry dated February 2, 1931, gives Woolf's picture of the composer at a rehearsal of her final work, *The Prison*, written for orchestra and chorus:

She stood at the piano in the window, in her battered felt, in her jersey and short skirt conducting with a pencil. There was a drop at the end of her nose. . . . She sang now and then; and once, taking the bass, made a cat squalling sound—but everything she does with such forthrightness, directness, that there is nothing ridiculous. She loses all self-consciousness completely. She seems vitalized; all energized. . . . What if she should be a great composer? This fantastic idea is to her the merest commonplace: it is the fabric of her being. As she conducts, she hears music like Beethoven's. As she strides and turns and wheels about to us perched mute on chairs she thinks this is about the most important event now taking place in London. And perhaps it is.

Smyth lived until 1944, when she died at age 86. In the late 20th century, as her powerful music was increasingly performed to new audiences, her genius was rediscovered. Ethel Smyth changed the pervading view of women in music. "She was a stubborn, indomitable, unconquerable creature," said Beecham. "Nothing could tame her, nothing could daunt her, and to her last day she preserved these remarkable qualities." In her willfully forthright manner, Smyth affirmed this view shortly before her death, when she told a companion, "I think I shall die soon, and I intend to die standing up."

**SOURCES:**

Abromeit, Kathleen A. "Ethel Smyth, 'The Wreckers,' and Sir Thomas Beecham," in *The Musical Quarterly*. Vol. 73, no. 2, 1989, pp. 196–211.

Beecham, Sir Thomas. "Dame Ethel Smyth (1858–1944)," in *The Musical Times*. Vol. 99, no. 1385. July 1958, pp. 363–365.

Bernstein, Jane A. "'Shout, Shout, Up with your Song!' Dame Ethel Smyth and the Changing Role of the British Composer," in *Women Making Music: The Western Art Tradition, 1150–1950*. Edited by Jane Bowers and Judith Tick. Chicago, IL: University of Illinois Press, 1985, pp. 304–324.

Dale, Kathleen. "Dame Ethel Smyth," in *Music and Letters*. Vol. 25, no. 4. October 1944, pp. 191–194.

———. "Ethel Smyth's Prentice Work," in *Music and Letters*. Vol. 30, no. 4. October 1949, pp. 329–336.

Smyth, Ethel. *The Memoirs of Ethel Smyth*. NY: Viking, 1987.

Wood, Elizabeth. "Lesbian Fugue: Ethel Smyth's Contrapuntal Arts," in *Musicology and Difference*. Edited by Ruth A. Solie. Berkeley, CA: University of California Press, 1993, pp. 164–183.

———. "Women, Music, and Ethel Smyth: A Pathway in the Politics of Music," in *The Massachusetts Review: Woman: The Arts*, 1983, pp. 125–139.

**John Haag**, Associate Professor,
University of Georgia, Athens, Georgia

## Smythe, Emily Anne (c. 1845–1887)

*English relief worker and author.* Name variations: *Viscountess Strangford. Born Emily Anne Beaufort around 1845; died at sea in 1887; daughter of Sir Francis Beaufort (1774–1857, a rear admiral and hydrographer); married Percy Ellen Frederick William Smythe, 8th viscount Strangford of Ireland, in 1862.*

Active in relief work, Emily Anne Smythe was born Emily Anne Beaufort around 1845, the daughter of Sir Francis Beaufort, a rear admiral and hydrographer. In 1862, she married Percy Smythe, 8th viscount Strangford of Ireland. In 1875, she organized a fund for the relief of the Bulgarian peasants, and in 1877, during the war in Turkey, she established and supervised a hospital for Turkish soldiers. Her writings include *Egyptian Sepulchres and Syrian Shrines* (1861) and a work about the eastern shores of the Adriatic. As a descendent of the Beauforts of the Crusades, Smythe was the recipient of the Order of the Holy Sepulchre, which she received from the patriarch of Jerusalem. She died at sea in 1887.

## Smythe, Maria Anne (1756–1837).

*See Fitzherbert, Maria Anne.*

## Smythe, Pat (1928–1996)

*English horsewoman and show jumper.* Name variations: *Patricia Smythe. Born near Richmond-upon-Thames, England, in 1928; died in 1996; married Sam Koechlin (a Swiss lawyer), in 1963; children: two daughters.*

*Won Prince of Wales Cup for England as member of Nations Cup Team (1952); won bronze medal and was first female show jumping team member at Stockholm Olympic Games (1956); won European Ladies' championship (1957, 1961–1963); won British Jumping Derby (1962).*

English horsewoman Pat Smythe was born in East Anglia in 1928 and grew up riding ponies in Richmond Park near London. After her father died, the family moved to Gloucestershire, and she was evacuated during the World War II bombings. As a child, Smythe helped to run her mother's guest house and made deliveries with a pony and trap; she also worked on local farms and schooled horses. When she was 14, Smythe got her first horse, Finality, with which she competed at her initial International Show at White City in 1946. Her performance was so impressive that Harry Llewellyn, head of the British show jumping team, invited her to join the team for their first tour abroad. At the Horse of the Year Show in 1950, Smythe tied for first place with Llewellyn in a famous jump-off.

Smythe went on to win several White City and Harringay Horse of the Year Shows, and competed in European and North American tours. In 1950 in Paris, she set a European record height of 6'10⅞" for women jumpers. In 1952, Smythe became the first female rider on a Nations Cup Team, and won the Prince of Wales Cup for England. During a ten-year stretch starting that year, she was victorious in a record eight British Show Jumping championships, an accomplishment for which she was made an Officer of the British Empire (OBE). Smythe also won the European Ladies' championship in show jumping four times. In 1956, she became the first female member of an Olympic show jumping team, and won a bronze medal for England at the Stockholm Games. Smythe also won the British Jumping Derby in 1962. After the 1960 Rome Olympics, Smythe retired. She married Swiss lawyer Sam Koechlin in 1963 and had two daughters. After the end of her jumping career, Smythe continued to train horses and published several children's books along with her 1992 autobiography *Jumping Life's Fences*.

**Elizabeth Shostak**, freelance writer,
Cambridge, Massachusetts

## Snell, Hannah (1723–1792)

*English soldier. Born on April 23, 1723, in Worcester, England; died in Bethlehem Hospital on February 8,*

*1792; the daughter of a hosier; married James Summs (a sailor); children: one.*

The daughter of a hosier, Hannah Snell was born in 1723 in Worcester, England. She was orphaned at age 17 and went to live with her sister in London. While still quite young, she met and married James Summs, a sailor, who abused her and then abandoned her when she was pregnant with their first child. Determined to find him, Snell left her baby with her sister and, disguised as a man, joined the infantry regiment battling the supporters of Charles Edward Stuart (1720–1788), known as Bonnie Prince Charlie. Snell got into trouble with her sergeant, and after being punished with a flogging she deserted and headed south.

In Portsmouth, using her brother-in-law's name of James Gray, she joined the crew of the sloop *Swallow* which accompanied Edward Boscawen's fleet of 30 to the East Indies in 1747. During the assault on the French garrison at Pondicherry in August 1748, in which the British lost a third of its land force of 6,000 and the French lost 250, Snell was badly injured in the groin, but succeeded in removing the bullet herself, so that the surgeon would not learn her gender. After recovering, she served on the *Tartar* and the *Eltham*, distinguishing herself in action.

Upon her return to Europe, Snell discovered that her husband was dead, thus ending her mission. Receiving a government pension for her service, she retired from soldiering and wrote a somewhat exaggerated account of her adventures under the title *The Female Soldier, or the Surprising Adventures of Hannah Snell* (1750). She also gave exhibitions on the London stage, dressed in full military regalia. With the money she earned from her autobiography and her performances, she was able to open an inn which she called the Female Warrior. By one account, Snell was married a second and third time before her death in Bethlehem, a notorious hospital for the insane from which the word *bedlam* derives, on February 8, 1792.

**Barbara Morgan**,
Melrose, Massachusetts

## Snitkina, Anna (1846–1918).

*See Dostoevsky, Anna.*

## Snow, Eliza Roxey (1804–1887).

*See Smith, Eliza Roxey.*

## Snow, Helen Foster (1907–1997)

*American activist and writer. Name variations: (pseudonym) Nym Wales. Born in Cedar, Utah, on Septem-*

*ber 21, 1907; died in Guilford, Connecticut, in January 1997; daughter of John Moody (a lawyer) and Hanna (Davis) Foster (a teacher); attended University of Utah, 1925–27, and Yenching University and Tsinghua University, Peking, 1934–35; married Edgar Snow (d. 1972, an author, foreign correspondent, and photographer), on December 25, 1932 (divorced 1949).*

*Was a foreign correspondent and activist in China (1931–38); was active in establishing Chinese Industrial ("Gung Ho") Cooperatives in Shanghai (1938).*

*Selected writings, all published under pseudonym Nym Wales except as noted:* Inside Red China *(1939); (with* **Kim San**) Song of Ariran: The Life Story of an Asian Revolutionary *(1941);* The Chinese Labor Movement *(1945);* Red Dust: Autobiographies of Chinese Communists *(1952);* Notes on the Beginnings of the Industrial Cooperatives in China *(1958);* Notes on the Chinese Student Movement, 1935–36 *(1959);* My Yenan Notebooks *(1961, reprinted as* An American Experience in Yenan, *1973); (memoir under Helen Foster Snow)* My China Years *(1984).*

Writer and activist Helen Foster Snow became best known for her role in the founding of the Chinese Industrial Cooperatives in the late

*H*annah *S*nell

1930s. She was also a prolific author and a genealogist. Snow was born in Cedar, Utah, on September 21, 1907, the daughter of John Moody Davis, a lawyer, and **Hannah Davis Foster**, a schoolteacher. She attended the University of Utah from 1925 to 1927 and began her professional life as a string correspondent for the Scripps-Canfield League of Newspapers in Seattle, Washington, in 1931. That same year, the prospect of a secretarial job through her father's mining connections drew her to China, where she would remain for almost a decade. At that time, China was in the midst of political and social upheaval, as Communists and Fascists vied for power. Politically naive on her arrival, Snow soon found herself sympathizing with and actively supporting Communist activities.

In 1932, Helen married foreign correspondent, writer, and photographer Edgar Snow, whom she had met in China. Though Edgar preferred to remain outside of politics, he helped Snow and Rewi Alley organize the Chinese Industrial Cooperatives in Shanghai around 1938. These organizations, known as "Gung Ho" cooperatives, spread throughout China by the late 1950s. Snow has been credited with creating the concept, which she believed offered a viable way for emerging nations to produce goods and compete economically.

Conversant in French, Spanish, Italian, and various Chinese dialects, Snow traveled extensively throughout Asia, Indonesia, and Europe. After returning to the United States from China, she became active in several organizations, including the National Society of Literature and the Arts, the Association for Asian Studies, the U.S.-China People's Friendship Association, and the Committee of Concerned Asian Scholars. During the World War II years, Snow worked as a book reviewer for the *Saturday Review of Literature*. She served as vice-chair of the board of directors of the American Committee in Aid of Chinese Industrial Cooperatives from 1941 to 1952, and was a sponsor of the American Committee for Spanish Freedom in 1943, during the Spanish Civil War. She was also a board member of the Committee for a Democratic Far Eastern Policy from 1945 to 1956 and was a co-founder of the Congress of American Women in 1945.

Under the pseudonym Nym Wales, Snow wrote a number of books about China, including *Inside Red China* (1939), *China Builds for Democracy: A Story of Cooperative Industry* (1941), *The Chinese Labor Movement* (1945), *Red Dust: Autobiographies of Chinese Communists* (1952), *Notes on the Beginnings of the In-* *dustrial Cooperatives in China* (1958), and *Notes on the Chinese Student Movement, 1935–36* (1959). Snow also published several books under her own name, including her memoir, *My China Years* (1984), as well as works on genealogy and contributed to numerous books and anthologies. Her books on China have remained important records of the country's history during the pre-revolutionary years.

In 1978, Snow, who had divorced in 1949, returned to China to work with a television crew on a documentary program. She was awarded an honorary Doctor of Letters from St. Mary's of the Woods College in Indiana in 1981. That year, Snow was also nominated for the Nobel Peace Prize. She died in Guilford, Connecticut, in January 1997.

**SOURCES:**

*Contemporary Authors New Revisions Series*. Vol. 46. Detroit, MI: Gale Research, 1995.

Fadool, Cynthia R., ed. *Contemporary Authors*. Vols. 57–60. Detroit, MI: Gale Research, 1976.

"Obituary," in *The Day* [New London, CT]. January 14, 1997.

**Elizabeth Shostak**, freelance writer, Cambridge, Massachusetts

## Snow, Lady (1912–1981).

*See Johnson, Pamela Hansford.*

# Snow, Valaida (c. 1903–1956)

*African-American singer, dancer, and musician, best known of the early female jazz horn players and called the "Queen of the Trumpet," who entertained audiences in North America, Europe and Asia from the '20s to the '50s. Name variations: Valaida Edwards. Pronunciation: Vah-LAY-da. Born in Chattanooga, Tennessee, on June 2, sometime between 1903 and 1909; died in New York City on May 30, 1956, of a cerebral hemorrhage; father was in show business and mother was a versatile musician and music teacher; married Ananias Berry, in 1934; married Earle Edwards, in 1943; no children.*

*Was performing professionally by age three or four; made her Broadway debut in Chocolate Dandies (1924); toured the Far East with the band of drummer Jack Carter (1926–28); toured Europe, Russia, and the Middle East (1929); co-starred with Ethel Waters as a bandleader and trumpet soloist in Rhapsody in Black (1931); cut her first record, with the Washboard Rhythm Kings (1932); led a group that included Earl Hines at the Grand Terrace Ballroom in Chicago (1933); appeared in London in the musical Blackbirds (1934); moved to Los Angeles, where she began to ap-*

*pear in movies, including* Take It from Me, Irresistible You, *and the French film* L'Alibi *(1935); taken prisoner by the Nazis while working in Copenhagen (1941); freed from a concentration camp in a prisoner exchange after 18 months and returned to New York (1943); made her performance comeback, including an appearance at the Apollo Theater (1943); moved back to Los Angeles (1945); played Town Hall in New York (1949); played New York's Palace Theater (1956).*

*Selected discography:* Hot Snow: Valaida Snow, Queen of the Trumpet, Sings and Swings *(Foremothers, Vol. 2. Rosetta Records, RR 1305);* Swing is the Thing *(World-EMI, SH 354);* Jazz Women: A Feminist Retrospective *(Stash Records, ST-109);* Women in Jazz: Swingtime to Modern *(Stash Records, ST-113);* Forty Years of Women In Jazz *(Jass Records, Jass CD 9/10).*

Onstage at the Orpheum, the singer would have her audience enthralled. With her flair for performance, and her supple voice, she would give a lively rendition of "My Heart Belongs To Daddy," in which she would tease, plead and, most of all, swing. After finishing the final verse, she would reach into a pocket hidden in the folds of her full skirt, pull out a trumpet, and launch into a "hot" solo, while the crowd went wild.

So went the desription of trumpet player **Clora Bryant**, as she regaled attendees at an International Women's Brass Conference with a sampling of what it was like to watch Valaida Snow mesmerize an audience. Snow gave these ingenious demonstrations of her multiple talents in the Los Angeles jazz clubs where she played in the 1940s. According to liner notes written by pianist *Mary Lou Williams for Forty Years of Women In Jazz*, "Valaida was a great show woman who could walk out and grab the audience," dancing, singing, and playing trumpet, all on the same tune. A female musician playing a brass instrument usually associated with men, she had earned her fame during the Depression, when a woman who worked was often despised for stealing a job from a man. Snow's ability to combine several skills for the price of one not only provided diverting entertainment for her fans during difficult times, but no doubt served as a form of employment insurance.

Born into a musical family in Chattanooga, Tennessee, in the early 1900s, Valaida Snow was performing by the age of three or four. Her father was in show business, but it was her mother, a versatile musician and music teacher who had studied at the all-black Howard University, who groomed her children for musical careers. Snow had three sisters—**Alvaida, Lavaida,** and **Hattie**—who sang;

*Valaida Snow*

Valaida also learned to play cello, guitar, accordion, harp, saxophone, clarinet, bass violin, banjo, and mandolin. But the trumpet was the instrument that captured her imagination; it has been said that she studied for a time with one of the great female trumpet players of the 1920s, **Dyer Jones.**

In 1920, Snow could be heard playing at the entertainment spots in Philadelphia and Atlantic City. In 1922, she reached New York, where she danced, sang, and played both violin and trumpet in Barron Wilkin's Harlem Cabaret. The 1920s saw a boom in black musical theater, and in 1923, Snow appeared in a musical with vocalist and band leader *Blanche Calloway,* an older sister of Cab Calloway, and in Will Masten's revue *Follow Me.* The following year, Snow made her Broadway debut, playing the role of Manda in *Chocolate Dandies,* a musical by the black composing team of Eubie Blake and Noble Sissle, with a cast that included the legendary *Josephine Baker.*

In 1926, Snow toured in England, then traveled to Shanghai, where she danced, sang and played trumpet as a specialty act in drummer Jack Carter's band. She stayed in China until 1928, recognized by then as an international celebrity (eventually she would speak seven languages and enjoy fame on three continents). After a brief return to the States, she traveled to Paris to play in Lew Leslie's *Blackbirds*, a popular black musical that was often revamped and gave a start to a number of African-American performers, including vocalists *Nina Mae Mc-Kinney and ◄☙ Florence Mills.

**Mills, Florence.**
*See Women of the Harlem Renaissance.*

Snow toured Russia, the Middle East and Europe before returning again to the U.S., where she co-starred with *Ethel Waters in another Lew Leslie extravaganza, *Rhapsody in Black*, in 1931. At one point in the program, she served as band leader, directing Pike Davis' Continental Orchestra; she also performed a stunning trumpet solo on George Gershwin's "Rhapsody in Blue." On October 5, 1932, she played her first recording date with the Washboard Rhythm Kings, a group that included clarinet and saxophone player Ben Smith. In the course of her career she would record more than 50 songs, mostly on European labels.

In 1933, Snow played in Chicago at the Grand Terrace Ballroom with the orchestra of the great jazz pianist Earl "Fatha" Hines, and later toured with the band for a year. Hines had been a fan of Snow's since the late '20s, and was especially fond of a dance number in which she stepped in and out of several pairs of shoes, doing the steps appropriate to each type of footwear, from ballet to clog dancing to soft shoe.

*I* always liked her trumpet playing. She was hitting high C just like Louis Armstrong.

—Mary Lou Williams

Any consideration of Snow's career must include reference to the historical difficulties faced by women who played brass instruments, such as trumpet. **Hattie Gossett** and **Caroline Johnson**, in their article "jazzwomen: they're mostly singers and piano players only a horn player or two hardly any drummers," traced the origins of such discrimination against women who played the "power instruments" in jazz to both African and European origins. Snow has sometimes been criticized for perpetuating the myth of the female musician as a novelty, but had she concentrated solely on playing her trumpet, it is unlikely that she could have attained even a fraction of her success. Despite the "novelty" aspect of her performances, her musicianship on the trumpet was highly acclaimed by the great jazz musicians of her time, including one whose influence

touched trumpet players from that era to decades beyond, Louis Armstrong.

Although popular with black audiences in the U.S., Snow, like many African-American performers, found greater opportunities to perform and record abroad. She traveled to Europe six times during her career, sometimes staying for extended intervals, and became known there as "Queen of the Trumpet" and "Little Louis." She also played in Shanghai, Hong Kong, Beijing (Peking), Burma (now Myanmar), Tokyo, Bombay and Cairo, performing the first live jazz ever heard in some of these locations. In *Black Women in American Bands and Orchestras*, **D. Antoinette Handy** suggested that Snow may have been as important an American "jazz ambassador" as the musicians Coleman Hawkins, Fats Waller, Bill Coleman, and Benny Carter who were traditionally awarded this title.

While starring in Lew Leslie's *Blackbirds of 1934* in England, Snow married Ananias Berry, her partner in some of the song and dance acts. (The marriage would later end.) That same year, she became one of the first artists to play the Apollo Theater in New York, only a month after it opened, with a group called The Twelve Syncopators. In 1935, she moved to Los Angeles and appeared in the film *Take It from Me*, then returned to New York the following year to headline again at the Apollo.

Also in 1936, Snow returned to Europe, where she appeared in Paris with Maurice Chevalier, the popular French singer and film star, and made the first of two French films, a mystery entitled *L'Alibi*. For the next five years, she remained based in Sweden and France, recording more than 40 records in London, Stockholm, and Copenhagen, often performing the vocals as well as trumpet solos. In 1939, she made her second French movie, *Piéges*, before heeding the warning to depart along with other Americans because of the impending invasion by the Nazis. In 1941, Snow was performing in Copenhagen when leaflets dropped from airplanes filled the streets, announcing that Denmark was now claimed by Germany. She was captured by Nazis at bayonet point as she tried to leave the country. All her possessions, including clothing, jewelry and a golden trumpet given to her at a command performance before Queen *Wilhelmina of the Netherlands, were confiscated, and she was interned in the Wester-Faengle concentration camp. In the brutal encampment, Snow was reduced to near starvation on a diet that included little more than potatoes. In 1956, Harrison Smith reported in an article for *Record*

*Research* that "prisoners were given 15 lashes by whip each week." Snow once received a severe gash on her head for using her own body to protect a young girl who was being severely beaten.

She remained a prisoner of war for 18 months and would certainly have died had she not been released in a prisoner exchange. Most likely, she was chosen for this liberation because someone with the power to make such a decision was a fan. She returned to New York by ship in 1943, weak and in ill health, only to find that her mother had died after hearing a rumor that her daughter had been killed overseas.

That year, Snow married Earle Edwards, a former performer who supported her in regaining her physical and mental health. When she began to perform again, Edwards became her new manager. She fronted the Sunset Royal Band for a road show, touring military bases stateside and playing another engagement at the Apollo.

In 1944, Snow performed in the movie *Irresistible You*. The following year, she was settled in Los Angeles, where she became popular on the local theater circuit, played many of the Central Avenue venues that were home to a burgeoning black jazz scene in the 1940s, and was heard at the Orpheum by the younger Clora Bryant. Sometimes Snow performed with her sister Lavaida, a successful vocalist. In 1945, Valaida played in a show with Los Angeles trombonist and arranger *Melba Liston, who recalled the sad feeling the brilliant trumpet player evoked: "She was so talented, so beautiful, and so sweet. But she was so unhappy. She was like hurt all the time." According to others who had known Snow before the war, she never fully recovered from the horrors she had witnessed and experienced in the concentration camp.

Snow continued to tour the U.S. and Canada. In 1949, she starred in a Town Hall concert in New York, billed as a "dramatic contralto" and backed by an all-male choir, singing spirituals and songs by Harold Arlen and George Gershwin. In the early 1950s, she made several recordings, including a group of tunes with the orchestra of tenor sax player, arranger and composer Jimmy Mundy. Her last engagement was at New York's Palace Theater, where she performed a heavy schedule of three shows daily. At the close of the engagement, she suffered a stroke. Snow was in bed for three weeks before she was taken to a hospital, where she died of a cerebral hemorrhage on May 30, 1956. Her exact age was not known, but she was under 60.

**SOURCES:**

Bogle, Donald. *Brown Sugar: Eighty Years of America's Black Female Superstars.* NY: Da Capo, 1980.

Bryant, Clora. "The History of Women in Jazz" lecture, given at the International Women's Brass Conference, St. Louis, Missouri, May 31, 1993.

Chilton, John. *Who's Who of Jazz: Storyville to Swing Street.* Time-Life Records Special Edition, 1978.

Dahl, Linda. *Stormy Weather: The Music and Lives of a Century of Jazzwomen.* NY: Limelight, 1989.

Driggs, Frank. *Women in Jazz.* NY: Stash Records, 1977.

Gossett, Hattie, and Caroline Johnson. "jazzwomen: they're mostly singers and piano players only a horn player or two hardly any drummers," in *Heresies.* Vol. 3, no. 2, issue 10, 1980.

Handy, D. Antoinette. *Black Women in American Bands and Orchestras.* Metuchen, NJ: Scarecrow, 1981.

Leder, Jan. *Women in Jazz: A Discography of Instrumentalists, 1913–1968.* Westport, CT: Greenwood Press, 1985.

Peretti, Burton W. *The Creation of Jazz.* Urbana, IL: University of Illinois Press, 1992.

Placksin, Sally. *Jazzwomen, 1900 to the Present.* London: Pluto Press, 1985 (also published as *American Women in Jazz*, Wideview, 1982).

Reed, Tom. *The Black Music History of Los Angeles—Its Roots.* Los Angeles, CA: Black Accent on LA Press, 1992.

Reitz, Rosetta. Liner notes from *Hot Snow: Valaida Snow, Queen of the Trumpet, Sings and Swings.* Rosetta Records, RR-1305.

Smith, Harrison. "Valaida's Gone," in *Record Research.* Vol. 2, no. 12. July–August, 1956.

Williams, Mary Lou. Liner notes from *Forty Years of Women in Jazz.* Jass Records, Jass CD 9/10.

**SUGGESTED READING:**

Cliff, Michelle. "A Woman Who Plays Trumpet is Deported" (fiction based on Snow's life) in *Bodies of Water.* NY: Dutton, 1990.

**Sherrie Tucker**,
freelance writer and jazz disk jockey
in San Francisco Bay Area, California

# Snyder, Alice D. (1887–1943)

*American educator. Born Alice Dorothea Snyder on October 29, 1887, in Middletown, Connecticut; died of a heart attack on February 17, 1943, at her Vassar College campus apartment; daughter of Peter Miles Snyder (a minister) and Grace Evelyn (Bliss) Snyder (a pianist and mathematics teacher); sister of Franklyn Bliss Snyder (president of Northwestern University) and Edward Douglas Snyder (professor of English at Haverford College); graduated from high school in Rockford, Illinois, 1905; Vassar College, A.B., 1909, A.M., 1911; University of Michigan, Ph.D. in English and philosophy, 1915; never married; no children.*

Born in 1887 in Middletown, Connecticut, Alice D. Snyder grew up in a highly educated family. Her mother **Grace Bliss Snyder** was an 1877 Vassar College graduate, pianist, and mathematics teacher. Her father Peter Miles Snyder graduated from Williams College in 1874 and traveled abroad before entering the seminary. Although ill health impeded much of Snyder's early schooling, the family house was filled with conversation and books, and her parents encouraged Alice and her two brothers to write parodies and poems.

The family relocated to Burlington, Vermont, and then Rockford, Illinois, where Snyder graduated from high school in 1905. Having selected her mother's alma mater, Snyder earned an A.B. from Vassar in 1909. Offered a fellowship in English, she remained at Vassar to complete her A.M. degree in 1911 while also acting as an assistant in English at Rockford College. With her master's degree in hand, she became an instructor in English at Vassar in 1912. In 1914, she became an assistant in rhetoric at the University of Michigan, where she received her doctorate in both English and philosophy a year later.

Snyder returned to Vassar's English department and developed a reputation as a caring and inspiring teacher. She contributed substantially to the scholarship on Samuel Taylor Coleridge, the basis of her doctoral dissertation, and revived critical interest in his nonfiction writings. Over the years, she authored several books on Coleridge and 17 articles, obtaining previously unpublished manuscript material from his great-grandson. Snyder also helped to develop educational policy at Vassar and served on the College Entrance Examination Board committee.

In addition to active participation in the Modern Language Association and the Modern Humanities Research Association, Snyder was an advocate of larger contemporary social issues, such as women's suffrage, the Better Housing League, the Teachers' Union, the American Labor Party, and the National Council for American-Soviet Friendship. In 1943, at age 55, Snyder died of a heart attack at her Vassar campus apartment. She was buried in Watertown, New York.

**SOURCES:**
James, Edward T., ed. *Notable American Women, 1607–1950*. Cambridge, MA: The Belknap Press of Harvard University, 1971.

**Lisa Frick**, freelance writer,
Columbia, Missouri

# Snyder, Ruth (1893–1928)

*American murderer. Born Ruth Brown in New York in 1893; executed on January 12, 1928, in New York's Sing Sing Prison; daughter of Josephine Brown; educated through the eighth grade; married Albert Snyder (an art editor for* Motor Boating *magazine), in 1915 (murdered in 1927); children: Lorraine Snyder (b. 1918).*

On the night of January 12, 1928, Ruth Snyder, a Long Island housewife, was electrocuted at New York's Sing Sing prison for the murder of her husband Albert Snyder. Following her to the death chamber was (Henry) Judd Gray, her lover and accomplice. The executions were the climax of one of the most sensational murder cases of the 1920s, made more so by the intense media war between New York's tabloid newspapers. The battle for exclusivity went down to the wire and reached new heights in poor taste. So eager was the New York *Daily News* to scoop the *Mirror* one last time that they smuggled a reporter into the execution with an unauthorized camera tied to his ankle. The picture he snapped of Snyder strapped in the electric chair, as the lethal current surged through her body, appeared the next day on the front page of the *Daily News*, under the one-word headline, "Dead!" The illicit photograph is still considered the most remarkable, albeit repulsive, exclusive in the history of criminal photojournalism.

Snyder's background hardly portended the way in which she would die. Born Ruth Brown in Manhattan in 1893, the daughter of working-class Scandinavians, she left school after the eighth grade and went to work at the telephone company while taking a business course in the evenings. Hoping more for an early marriage than a successful career, she took a secretarial job with *Motor Boating* magazine, where she met Albert Snyder, a handsome art editor 13 years her senior who became the first man she seriously dated. She married him after a few short months. The couple began life together in Brooklyn, where their daughter **Lorraine Snyder** was born in 1918. Then, with Albert's promotions and salary increases, they moved to a larger apartment in the Bronx, and finally to an eight-room house on Long Island. Outwardly, Snyder enjoyed all the trappings of a successful marriage, but the union was troubled at the core. While Snyder was gregarious and fun-loving, her husband was gloomy and ill-tempered. She adored children and would have liked more; he had not wanted children in the first place and resented the fact that his only child was a girl. Albert also frequently compared Snyder to his first and more "serious" fiancée, who had died before they could marry. According to Ruth's mother **Josephine Brown**, the marriage was so unhappy that she had advised her daughter to seek a divorce.

Snyder ignored her mother's suggestion and opted for adultery. Her lover Judd Gray, a corset

*Ruth Snyder on
the stand.*

and brassiere salesman, was a married man with a daughter who also had several other mistresses around the country. The couple conducted their secret affair for 18 months before the murder, frequently trysting at the Waldorf while tiny Lorraine spent the afternoon riding up and down the elevators. Although it was never determined just who initiated the murder plot, the deed was carried out in the early morning hours of March 20, 1927, after Snyder and her husband had returned from a party. (The motive was said to be several insurance policies worth close to $100,000 which Snyder had taken out on her husband without his knowledge.) While Albert slept, Judd Gray, fortified by a bottle of liquor, entered the bedroom and attempted to kill Albert by striking him on the head with a five-pound sash weight. The first blow, however, only awakened Albert, who began fighting back. Unable to continue, Gray called out, "Help me, Momsie," and Snyder entered the room and finished the job, crushing her husband's skull. The pair then chloroformed and strangled Albert with picture wire before she called the police. When the authorities arrived, Snyder said she had been burglarized at the hands of a swarthy intruder who struck her on the head and left her bound and gagged. Under intense interrogation, however, she broke down and confessed, saying that it was all Gray's idea. Gray, who was later arrested at a hotel in Syracuse, also confessed, blaming everything on Snyder.

Legions of reporters were assigned to the case, generating hundreds of thousands of words and almost as many photographs. Every sordid detail of the affair was recounted. In the sexist climate of the times, Snyder was particularly vilified by the press, who dubbed her the "fiend wife," the "faithless wife," the "marble woman," and "Ruthless Ruth, the Viking Ice Matron of Queens' Village." The slightly more conservative New York *Post* deemed her a "hard-faced woman," no doubt "oversexed," and most certainly out for "power and authority." The *Mirror* went so far as to hire Dr. Edgar Beall, a well-known phrenologist, to study photographs of Snyder and prepare an analysis. Beall, after examining Snyder's image feature by feature, determined that her face revealed "the character of a shallow-brained pleasure-seeker, accustomed to unlimited self-indulgence, which at last ends in an orgy of murderous passion and lust, seemingly without a parallel in the criminal history of modern times." Other celebrity reporters hopped on the pseudoscientific bandwagon; *Natacha Rambova drew her conclusions after observing Snyder for one hour in the courtroom: "There is lacking in her character that real thing, selflessness. She apparently doesn't possess it and never will. Her fault is that she has no heart." In a highly acclaimed article, playwright Willard Mack declared, "If Ruth Snyder is a woman, then by God you must find some other name for my mother, wife or sister."

By contrast, Judd Gray was portrayed as a "model citizen," a "regular fellow" in the clutches of an "evil temptress." "All facts now adduced point to a love-mad man completely in the sway of the woman whose will was steel," wrote the *Herald Tribune*. "She dominated him, police said, and forced her will upon him, even when he desired to back out on some of her proposals." In the courtroom, Gray's lawyer reiterated the domination theory. "That woman," he told the jury and the hordes of eager reporters, "like a poisonous snake, drew Judd Gray into her glistening coils, and there was no escape." With Snyder cast as a source of evil, "as *Eve in league with Satan," writes **Ann Jones**, her attorney had difficulty making her case. As one *Post* reporter described it: "He was a knight fighting a battle of terrific odds for a golden damsel disguised as a blonde, fattish and ice-hard housewife." Blocked by the judge from saying much on the stand, Snyder later wrote her story for the *Mirror* while awaiting execution on death row; it was "an erratic jumble of painful remembering, rage, religious platitudes, and grief," notes Jones. In it, Snyder claimed that as her affair with Gray proceeded, he began to blackmail her, threatening to tell her husband if she broke it off. Fearing that she might lose her daughter in a showdown, she did what he told her. She said the insurance policies and the murder were all his idea and that she tried to talk him out of it. On the night of the murder, she had set out a bottle of bootleg whiskey as he demanded, but instead of taking it and leaving the house, he stayed and was hiding when she and Albert returned from their party. After Albert went to sleep, she tried to convince Gray to leave, but he went upstairs and, while she was in the bathroom, committed the murder.

In the end, the jury found both Snyder and Gray guilty of murder, and at a sentencing on May 9, 1927, both were condemned to death in the electric chair. Snyder's hysterical reaction to the sentencing was reported by the *Mirror* as "the immemorial device of her sex to wring pity from male hearts," while Gray was praised as finding "enough of traditional manhood in him to take his medicine without whining." The press and the public also eagerly supported Snyder's execution, even though a woman had not been put to death in the electric chair in New York since *Martha Place** became the first in March 1899. When Governor Al Smith denied her application for clemency, *The New York Times* applauded the decision in an editorial: "Equal suffrage has put women in a new position. If they are equal with men before the law, they must pay the same penalties as men for transgressing it."

In her last interview for the *Mirror*, Snyder said that if she could live over again, she would opt for a "straight life." "I wish a lot of women who may be sinning could come here and see what I have done for myself through sinning," she ran on, "and maybe they would do some of the thinking I have done for months and they would be satisfied with their homes and would stop wishing for things they should try to get along without when they can't have them."

**SOURCES:**

Jones, Ann. "She Had to Die!," in *American Heritage*. October–November 1980.

Nash, Jay Robert. *Look For The Woman.* NY: M. Evans, 1981.

**Barbara Morgan**,
Melrose, Massachusetts

## Soaemias, Julia (d. 222).

See Julia Maesa for sidebar.

## Soames, Lady (b. 1922).

See Churchill, Clementine for sidebar on Churchill, Mary.

## Soares, Manuel (1892–1958).

See Lisboa, Irene.

## Sobakin, Marta (d. 1571)

*Russian empress for less than one month.* Died on November 13, 1571; daughter of Vassili Sobakin; became third wife of Ivan IV the Terrible (1530–1584), tsar of Russia (r. 1533–1584), on October 28, 1571.

## Sobek-neferu (fl. 1680–1674 BCE)

*Female pharaoh who was the last ruler of ancient Egypt's 12th Dynasty and co-builder of the famous Labyrinth.* Name variations: Nefrusobek; Scemiophris; Sebek-neferu; Sebekneferu; Sebeknefru; Sobekneferu. Flourished around 1680 to 1674 BCE; daughter of Amenemhet III (a pharaoh); sister of Amenemhet IV.

The daughter of Amenemhet III, pharaoh of Egypt's 12th Dynasty, Sobek-neferu succeeded her brother, Amenemhet IV, to the throne as a full-fledged monarch. She was the first female known to carry a complete set of kingly titles and is portrayed in sculpture wearing the kingly *nemes* headdress and a male kilt over her own dress. Like a dutiful heir, Sobek-neferu finished her father's great temple next to his pyramid at Hawara. This structure was so large and complex it became known as one of the Seven Wonders of the ancient world: the Labyrinth. The female pharaoh also constructed other temples throughout Egypt during her reign. She may have not married, as no heirs of hers are known.

That the government did not collapse at the end of her reign and that she was recorded on official king lists centuries later, shows that she was accepted and succeeded in her role. She should not be regarded as an illegitimate usurper as has sometimes been suggested.

**Barbara S. Lesko**,
Department of Egyptology, Brown University,
Providence, Rhode Island

## Sobieski, Clementina (1702–1735)

*Polish princess.* Name variations: Mary, Marie, or Maria Sobieska; Clementine or Clementina Sobiewski; Clementina Sobieska; Maria Clementina Stewart or Stuart. Born Marie Casimir Clementina on July 18, 1702, in Silesia; died of scurvy on January 18, 1735, at the Apostolic Palace, Rome; interred in St. Peter's Basilica, Vatican; daughter of Prince James Sobieski (son of John III, king of Poland, and Marie Casimir) and Hedwig Wittelsbach; married Prince James Francis Edward Stuart (1688–1766), duke of Cornwall, known as the Old Pretender, on September 1, 1719; children: Charles Edward Stuart (1720–1788), known as Bonnie Prince Charlie, the Young Pretender; Henry Stuart (1725–1807), cardinal of York.

Born in 1702, Clementina Sobieski was descended from the ruling houses of Poland and the Holy Roman Empire; she was the daughter of Prince James Sobieski (son of John III, king of Poland, and \*Marie Casimir) and \*Hedwig Wittelsbach. She was raised at her parents' court at Ohlau, in her mother's native province of Silesia. In 1718, Clementina's parents agreed to a marriage for her with the English prince James Edward Stuart (later known as the Old Pretender). Stuart, the exiled son of \*Mary of Modena and the deposed Catholic king James II, was struggling to win back the throne; marriage to the wealthy Sobieski princess would bring a large dowry which he badly needed. However, the English king George I hoped to stop the marriage and persuaded the Holy Roman emperor to have Clementina and her party arrested as they passed through Austria on the way to her fiancé in Italy. Clementina was imprisoned for several months near Innsbruck. When diplomacy failed to free her, the princess resorted in April 1719 to a desperate plan of escape in which she fled her castle prison dressed in a maid's clothes. She and her party hurried through Austria to the Papal States, where she and James Stuart were married on September 1. The pope, a strong proponent of the Stuart claim to England, gave the couple the Palazzo Muti in Rome and paid their expenses. The Stuart supporters, known as Jacobites, were overjoyed with the birth of Clementina's first child, the new Stuart prince Charles Edward Stuart, known as Bonnie Prince Charlie, in December 1720.

By 1722, however, Clementina's marriage had begun to fail under the stress of their exiled, uncertain position, the tedium of court life, and the couple's personality conflicts. James Stuart was 14 years her senior, somber and concerned only with the military efforts needed to try to secure his throne. He had little time to devote to his young wife, who suffered from homesickness and loneliness. In response, Clementina turned more and more to her religious devotions. Domestic quarrels erupted over their son's education and James Stuart's toleration of Protestant courtiers at their court. In November 1725, believing that her husband was an adulterer and that she had enemies in their household, Clementina left the Palazzo Muti and entered a convent. She remained there for two years. Her actions caused a major scandal across Europe, and served to weaken the Stuart cause abroad.

*Clementina Sobieski*

In 1727, she was reunited with her husband and sons, and settled in Bologna. She refused to participate in social activities, however, spending her time in prayer and working among the poor. The Stuarts returned to Rome in 1730. Clementina's strenuous efforts to help the unfortunate and her ascetic lifestyle combined with long periods of fasting to destroy her health. The so-called queen of England died of scurvy in January 1735, at age 32. The pope ordered a state funeral and had her buried at St. Peter's in Rome. In her will, Clementina left little to her sons and husband. The majority of her immense Sobieski wealth in money and jewels was given to the Catholic Church in Rome. Some of her priceless bequests may still be seen in the Sobieski Room at the Vatican.

**SOURCES:**

Kybett, Susan M. *Bonnie Prince Charlie*. NY: Dodd, Mead, 1988.

McLynn, Frank. *Charles Edward Stuart: A Tragedy in Many Acts*. London: Routledge, 1988.

**Laura York**, M.A. in History, University of California, Riverside, California

## Sobieski, Cunigunde (fl. 1690s).

*See Cunigunde Sobieska.*

## Sobieski, Marie (1702–1735).

*See Sobieski, Clementina.*

## Sobieski, Teresa.

*See Cunigunde Sobieska.*

# Soccer: Women's World Cup, 1999

*U.S. Women's National Soccer Team (1982–2001). Established by the National Collegiate Athletic Association (NCAA), in 1982, as the first national women's soccer team to compete internationally; coached by Anson Dorrance until 1994, when Tony DiCicco took over; winner of two World Cups (1991 and 1999); winner of Olympic gold medal (1996); team voted Female Athletes of the Year by AP member newspapers and broadcast outlets (1999); winner of Olympic silver medal (2000).*

*1999 World Cup roster: (defenders) Lorrie Fair, Christie Pearce, Carla Overbeck (and co-captain), Tiffany Roberts, Joy Fawcett, Brandi Chastain, Sara Whalen, Kate Sobrero; (forwards) Shannon MacMillan, Mia Hamm, Tiffeny Milbrett, Cindy Parlow, Kristine Lilly, Danielle Fotopoulos; (midfielders) Michelle Akers, Julie Foudy (and co-captain), Tisha Venturini; (goalkeepers) Briana Scurry, Tracy Ducar, and Saskia Webber.*

Featured players:

*Akers, Michelle (1966—). Midfielder. Name varia-tions: Michelle Akers-Stahl. Born on February 6, 1966, in Santa Clara, California; attended the Univer-sity of South Florida, Orlando; married.*

Won (individual) Hermann Trophy (1988); won Team gold medal, World championships (1991 and 1999); won bronze medal, World championships (1995); won gold medal, Olympic Games, in Atlanta, Georgia (1996); named Female Soccer Athlete of the Year (1990 and 1991); was a founding player of the Women's United Soccer Association (WUSA); pub-lished (with Gregg Lewis) The Game and the Glory: An Autobiography (Zondervan, 2000).

*Chastain, Brandi (1968—). Defender. Born Brandi Denise Chastain on July 21, 1968, in San Jose, Cali-fornia; graduated from Santa Clara University; mar-ried Jerry Smith (a soccer coach at Santa Clara Univer-sity); children: stepson Cameron.*

Won Team gold medal, World championships (1991 and 1999); won gold medal, Olympic Games (1996); won silver medal, Olympic Games (2000);

*was a founding member of the Women's United Soc-cer Association (WUSA); signed with the Bay Area CyberRays (2001).*

*Fawcett, Joy (1968—). Defender. Born Joy Biefeld on February 8, 1968, in Inglewood, California; one of nine children of Terry and Beverly Biefeld; attended the University of California, Berkeley; married Walter Fawcett (a software engineer); children: two daugh-ters, Katelyn Rose (b. May 17, 1994) and Carli (b. May 21, 1997).*

Was chosen Female Soccer Athlete of the Year (1988); won Team gold medal, World championships (1991 and 1999); won gold medal, Olympic Games (1996); won silver medal, Olympic Games (2000); was a founding member of the Women's United Soccer Associ-ation (WUSA); signed with the San Diego Spirit (2001).

*Foudy, Julie (1971—). Midfielder and co-captain. Born on January 23, 1971, in Mission Viejo, Califor-nia; graduated from Stanford University, 1993; mar-ried Ian Sawyers.*

Won Team gold medal, World championships (1991 and 1999); bronze medal, World champi-

*U.S. Women's National Soccer Team, 1999.*

onships (1995); won gold medal, Olympic Games (1996); won silver medal, Olympic Games (2000); was a founding member of the Women's United Soccer Association (WUSA); signed with the San Diego Spirit (2001).

**Hamm, Mia (1972—). Forward and first scorer in the world—male or female—to achieve 108 goals.** Born Mariel Margaret Hamm on March 17, 1972, in Selma, Alabama; one of six children of William Hamm (a pilot in the U.S. Air Force) and Stephanie Hamm (a ballerina); attended Notre Dame High School, Wichita Falls, Texas; graduated from Lake Braddock Secondary School, Burke, Virginia; graduated from the University of North Carolina, 1994; married Christiaan Corey (a Marine Corps pilot), on December 17, 1994 (separated).

Became leading scorer in the world, man or woman, with 108 goals; was a member of the U.S. national team (1987–99); was four-time member of the NCAA women's soccer championship team (1989–93); named ACC tournament MVP (1989 and 1992); named ACC Player of the Year (1990, 1992, and 1993); won two World Cup championships (1991 and 1999); set NCAA single-season scoring record of 59 goals, 33 assists for 92 points (1992); was National Player of the Year (1992–94); received the Mary Garber Award as ACC Female Athlete of the Year (1993 and 1994); named U.S. Soccer Female Athlete of the Year (1993–98); received the Honda Broderick Cup as Most Outstanding Female Athlete in all college sports (1994); was named MVP of the U.S. Cup (1995); won gold medal, Olympic Games (1996); led U.S. national team in scoring with 9 goals, 18 assists for 27 points in 23 games (1996); won silver medal, Olympic Games (2000); was a founding member of the Women's United Soccer Association (WUSA); signed with the Washington Freedom (2001).

**Lilly, Kristine (1971—). Forward.** Born on July 22, 1971, in Wilton, Connecticut; graduated from the University of North Carolina.

Won Team gold medal, World championships (1991 and 1999); won Hermann Trophy (1991); named Female Soccer Athlete of the Year (1993); won bronze medal, World championships (1995); won gold medal, Olympic Games (1996); won silver medal, Olympic Games (2000); was a founding member of the Women's United Soccer Association (WUSA); signed with the Boston Breakers (2001).

**Overbeck, Carla (1969—). Defender and co-captain.** Born Carla Werden on May 9, 1969, in Pasadena, California; attended the University of North Carolina; married Greg Overbeck (a restaurateur); children: one son Jackson (b. August 14, 1997).

Won Team gold medal, World championships (1991 and 1999); won bronze medal, World championships (1995); won gold medal, Olympic Games (1996); won silver medal, Olympic Games (2000); was a founding member of the Women's United Soccer Association (WUSA); signed with the Carolina Courage (2001).

**Scurry, Briana (1971—). Goalkeeper.** Born Briana Collette Scurry on September 7, 1971, in Minneapolis, Minnesota; attended the University of Massachusetts.

Won Team gold medal, World championships (1991 and 1999); won bronze medal, World championships (1995); won gold medal, Olympic Games (1996); won silver medal, Olympic Games (2000); was a founding member of the Women's United Soccer Association (WUSA); signed with the Atlanta Beat (2001).

"For three weeks during the summer," noted Barry Wilner in December 1999, "the Women's World Cup was a sporting phenomenon. What was expected to be a nice little soccer tournament turned into The Associated Press Story of the Year, a success beyond even what its participants imagined possible." How had women's soccer in America emerged from obscurity into a national sensation? The success of the sport in the States had a great deal to do with an exceptional team, the members of which captured the public's imagination with their competitive spirit, celebrity potential, and undisputed ability to deliver the goods on the field.

The history of the U.S. Women's National Soccer Team began in 1972—ten years before the team was actually established—with the passage of Title IX, the government mandate requiring school sports programs to treat male and female athletes equally. The resulting expansion of women's athletic programs in high schools and colleges fortuitously coincided with an interest in soccer, a sport already well established in European countries but slow to gain a foothold in the United States. Over the next decade, the schools, as well as numerous suburban youth soccer leagues across the country, produced a bumper crop of outstanding young women players, many of whom went on to play on college teams. By 1982, interest was such that the National Collegiate Athletic Association (NCAA) began a collegiate national championship women's soccer tournament, and that same year the first U.S. women's team was selected to compete in the international arena. Under head coach Anson Dorrance (also the women's soccer coach at the University of North Carolina), and captained by **April Heinrichs**, the initial team included such players as Michelle Akers, Mia Hamm, **Carin Jennings Gabarra**, Kristine Lilly, Julie Foudy, and Joy Fawcett, names known only to soccer insiders at the time. The Americans played their first match, a 1–0 loss to Italy, in August 1985, with little fanfare. "We all had a vision for the future," says Heinrichs, who went on to become the women's coach at the University of Virginia and with the U.S. U-16 team. "I didn't think it would become this great, this dominant, this wonderful, but, boy, looking back, it was wonderful."

The national team played its first World Cup match on November 17, 1991, and subsequently won the tournament in the finals against China. "When we started the team, we never thought there would be a World Cup," remarked midfielder Julie Foudy. "It was always a mystical thing. And now we're holding it." **Lauren Gregg**, the assistant coach of the national team, regarded the '91 tournament as a showcase of the team's uniquely American style of play: "risk oriented, attacking, playing in a way to make a difference. We were a country that in the eyes of the world shouldn't be winning a World Cup. We upped the ante for the rest of the countries."

But the World Cup victory went virtually unheralded in the United States; some newspapers didn't even note the win. The national team continued to practice and play with little press or recognition until 1994, when the hype surrounding that year's men's World Cup, coupled with the recognition of women's soccer as a medal event in the Olympics, brought the team some well-deserved attention. Magazines began to carry features on some of the players and, lured by the status of the team as an Olympic medal favorite, corporate sponsors began popping up. For the first time, the women were put on salary (hardly comparable to their male counterparts, but a start), and a new training facility in Orlando, Florida, became a priority. With heightened visibility, however, came new challenges. The Olympic decision impacted other countries as well, and they too were giving women's soccer more attention. There were new professional leagues in Sweden, Norway, and Germany, and the competition for the upcoming World Cup promised to be fierce.

Some problems arose within the team's ranks when Coach Dorrance surprised everyone with the announcement that he was stepping down, and team stalwart Michelle Akers, battling Chronic Fatigue and Immune Dysfunction Syndrome (CFIDS), was often unable to play.

Under new head coach Tony DiCicco, however, the year leading up to the World Cup was a surprisingly good one for the team, and they looked strong going into the 1995 tournament. The players progressed to the semifinal match-up against Norway, their arch rivals since the 1991 Cup finals. The Norwegians played a rough physical game, putting the United States on the defensive at the onset. Ten minutes into the competition, Norway made the first goal, then kept the U.S. at bay for the rest of the game. Michelle Akers, who was playing hurt and managed to get off only one shot, remarked of the devastating defeat: "It's like having your guts kicked out of you."

To prepare for the upcoming summer Olympics, the team regrouped in Orlando during January 1996 and dedicated themselves to the goal of winning a gold medal. They bonded as a team like never before—living, practicing, and even socializing together. The first match of the Olympics (held in Orlando not far from the training center on July 21, 1996) was attended by an unprecedented 25,000 fans who watched the Americans beat Denmark 3–0, despite a temperature on the field of 100 degrees. The team continued to battle its way to the finals, winning over Sweden 2–1, and then advancing over Norway in a breathtaking 2–1 victory in overtime. Another record crowd turned out to watch them triumph 2–1 over a superb Chinese team, although as *Time* magazine's Bill Saporito pointed out, few television viewers saw them win the gold medal because NBC scuttled the game in favor of the diving competition.

The Olympic victory turned the national spotlight on the team, bringing lucrative endorsement deals to several players as well as requests for interviews and personal appearances. Posters of superstar Mia Hamm and her selection as one of *People* magazine's Most Beautiful People of the Year gave rise to what was termed, in '90s parlance, the "babe" factor, a distraction that was further fueled by Julie Foudy's photograph in a swimsuit issue of *Sports Illustrated* and Brandi Chastain's appearance in *Gear* magazine clad only in cleats and a strategically placed soccer ball. The latter raised some eyebrows, but the team's predominant image was a wholesome, positive one, especially for young female soccer hopefuls, many of whom had never before had strong role models in the sports world. Noted Akers in reference to the team's high profile:

> Now little girls all over the U.S. and the world put on their uniforms and lace up their cleats with the example and opportuni-

ty of the U.S. National Team to inspire and encourage them to chase their dreams on the soccer filed—and beyond. This realization alone is an incredible and wonderful achievement for all of us who have battled and won the right to pursue our potential as soccer players and people.

When it came time to plan for the 1999 Women's World Cup, **Marla Messing,** CEO of the Women's World Cup Organizing Committee, convinced the male-dominated International Federation of Football Associations (FIFA) that the women's team was equal in drawing power to the men's. Thus, the 32 matches of the tournament were staged in large stadiums in major cities across the country and were also televised on ABC, ESPN, and ESPN2. Even the advertising had a gender-equity theme, like the Nike spot featuring Mia Hamm and Michael Jordan in an "anything-you-can-do-I-can-do-better" face-off. "We have established a world-class, world-caliber, stand alone event for women like none other," Messing boasted. Indeed, the tournament proved to be all that and more, generating the sale of some 650,000 tickets—75,000 for the opening game alone, the largest number ever for a women's sporting event. And the women's team didn't disappoint the promoters or the fans. From their first win over Denmark (3–0) to their quarterfinal squeak by Germany (3–2), the excitement generated by the U.S. team eventually drew over 90,000 fans, including President Bill Clinton, to Pasadena's Rose Bowl on July 10, 1999, to witness the final play-off game against a formidable Chinese team.

The event was as taut a defensive battle as anyone could imagine, resulting in 120 minutes of scoreless play, including two overtime periods. During the last breathless minutes of overtime, the Chinese almost stole the match, but **Fan Yunjie**'s header off a corner kick was mercifully cleared off the line by Kristine Lilly. The game then went to a penalty-kick shoot-off— much dreaded by players and determined as much by luck as by skill. Americans Carla Overbeck and Joy Fawcett made their first two penalty shots, as did **Xie Huilin** and **Qui Haiyan** of China. **Liu Ying,** however, was stopped by a tremendous save by American goalkeeper Briana Scurry, which cleared the way for Kristine Lilly to land her shot and tip the score to 3–2. **Zhang Ouying** then made the fourth penalty kick, as did Mia Hamm. **Sue Wen** also connected, tying up the score. Then Brandi Chastain slammed the ball into the left corner of the goal to win the match 5–4 and clinch America's place in soccer

history. While Chastain joyfully fell to her knees, pumped her fists in the air, and stripped off her jersey to reveal her black sports bra, her teammates flooded the field to hoist the World Cup and receive their gold medals. "The last five games have been for all of America to jump on our backs," said **Tiffeny Milbrett.** "This was for us. That's why we wanted it so bad. We had come from so far and done so much. We want to be able to go out right." Commenting on a win that was watched with awe around the world, Kristine Lilly noted: "This moment is more than a game. It's about female athletes. It's about sport. It's about everything. I don't think we can sustain this level of attention. But I think people caught on to us. They attached themselves to us and I don't think they're going to let go." Lilly's remark would prove to be prophetic.

The response to the U.S. Women's National Soccer Team proved just how far the world had come since the days of Pierre de Coubertin, founder of the modern Olympics, who wrote in 1937, "Let women do all the sports they wish— but not in public." Yet members of the team were not content to rest on their World Cup and Olympic successes. To advance their sport, they supported the founding of a professional American women's soccer league, an enterprise that would cost millions of dollars. By the crowds drawn to their matches around the world, as well as the newly proven television appeal of women's soccer, the team demonstrated that women's professional soccer in America had the potential to draw the kind of support required to sustain a new league. In April 2001, hailed as the premiere international professional women's league, the Women's United Soccer Association (WUSA) made its debut appearance in a match between the Washington Freedom, Mia Hamm's team, and the Bay Area CyberRays, Brandi Chastain's team, at RKF Stadium in Washington, D.C. In an indication that the future of American women's professional soccer looks bright, start-up costs for the league ran to $64 million dollars. Two years before the league's first game, Mia Hamm was already looking ahead of its inception: "I hope it can succeed on its own. . . . What we don't want is just for it to be around for a couple of years. We want it to endure the test of time and be around for my kids to play in."

Among the standouts of the history-making 1999 World Cup victory were names that would not be soon forgotten: Michelle Akers, Brandi Chastain, Joy Fawcett, Julie Foudy, Mia Hamm, Kristine Lilly, Carla Overbeck, and Briana Scurry.

## Michelle Akers

An original member of the U.S. national team, midfielder Michelle Akers scored the first goal in the squad's history in 1985. In career scoring, she was just five goals behind Mia Hamm in the spring of 1999, even though she had played 32 fewer matches. Hamm called her the best goal scorer ever to play the game: "Not only does she have a shot that is probably measurably harder than anyone else's in the world . . . but her sophistication in finishing is remarkable. Michelle scores goals through power and finesse and from all different angles."

A four-time All-American at the University of Southern Florida, in 1988 Akers received the first Hermann Trophy, given to the nation's top college player. She almost took the 1991 World Cup single-handedly, scoring ten goals in six matches, including the winner in the final with Norway. In 1995, she went down with head and knee injuries in the opener, and the team subsequently lost the cup.

Distinguished by her thick mane of curly blonde hair and knees that bear the scars of at least 12 operations, Akers became a symbol of triumph over adversity as the nation watched her play the highest caliber of soccer while battling Chronic Fatigue and Immune Dysfunction Syndrome (CFIDS). "It's just a pain in the butt to live with, there's no other way to put it," said a 33-year-old Akers who was diagnosed with CFIDS in 1993 and had to alter her game to conserve energy. "You get these migraines that are unbearable, you can't sleep, you're dizzy all the time and your short-term memory is shot." For her to keep playing, Akers' will often had to override warning symptoms from her body. At the 1996 Olympic semifinals against Norway, with every muscle in her body on fire, she saved the day by landing a penalty kick that tied the score 1–1 just 14 minutes before the end of the match. (**Shannon MacMillan** went on to score the game-winning point in overtime.) After the penalty kick, Akers was ousted off the field by the U.S. trainers, who immediately hooked her up to an IV. The effort cost her a year (1997) on the sidelines.

Although up and running for World Cup '99, Akers was never sure if she'd be able to play until just before a game, and once in the game she never knew how long she would hold out: "I have to make sure I stay strong enough to make it to the next game. I always have to worry if I'm going to run out of gas. And it can happen without any warning." She played the full opener against Denmark (and scored a goal), but only made it through the first half in the game against Nigeria before coach DiCicco took her out. In the final play-off game against China, Akers made the most of what would be her last World Cup, spearheading a China-breaking defense with a recklessness that forced her out of the game near the end of regulation play and would cost her the post-game celebrations and appearances. She once remarked: "I need to play with wild abandon every once in a while or it wouldn't be me."

A shoulder injury combined with the CFIDS kept Akers from joining her team for their silver-medal-winning run at the Olympics in 2000. That year, her autobiography, written with Gregg Lewis, appeared as *The Game and the Glory: An Autobiography*. To build back her strength with hopes of playing in the Women's United Soccer Association (WUSA) during 2002, Akers took a year off in 2001, spending time in physical therapy and running her non-profit organization for kids, Soccer Outreach International. Akers helped to increase awareness about CFIDS by testifying before Congress in May 1996. "If you saw me today," she said, "you would see a healthy, physically fit, elite athlete. But I'm not. I am sick. Some days it is all I can do to get through the day. . . . I have learned to accept CFIDS as an opportunity to make a difference. I have turned this weakness into a strength . . . and even though it is still raging inside me, I refuse to be beaten by it. I will overcome. And I will show others how to overcome."

## Brandi Chastain

Noted for her diligence, versatility, and phenomenal kick, Brandi Chastain emerged as the hero of the 1999 World Cup tournament. After committing a huge gaffe in the game against Germany, when she scored in her own net, Chastain set things right by slamming in the fifth and decisive penalty kick in the spectacular play-off game against China. The winning goal prompted her to tear off her jersey (revealing a black Nike sports bra) in a gesture that, despite some controversy, would live on in the national consciousness as symbolic of the historic victory. Remarked Skip Wollenberg in July 1999: "Brandi Chastain may have created the best-known new undie since the Wonderbra when she doffed her jersey after delivering the winning kick at the Women's World Cup. Nike, which makes the soccer team's sports bras, is now trying to figure out how to convert that moment of marketing magic into new sales." For her part, Chastain later chalked the moment up to temporary insanity: "I thought, My God, this is the greatest moment of my life on the soccer field! I just lost my head." Her stunning pose—sans uniform—in *Gear* magazine also captured more than a little attention. "Hey, I ran my ass off for this body," she noted. "I'm proud of it."

Chastain played forward on the 1991 World championship team, then was not called up again until the 1996 Olympics, at which time she switched to the backfield. When the team shifted formations in 1998, she moved to midfield, displaying again her ability to play a variety of positions. Her strong kicking skills prompted coach Tony DiCicco to remark: "You can't tell if she's right- or left-footed, which is very rare." Chastain practices with a vengeance and is also a consummate student of the game. "If there's a game on TV, she's in front of it," said DiCicco.

A native Californian, Chastain is married to Jerry Smith, head coach at Santa Clara University. During her down time, she serves as an assistant women's soccer coach at Santa Clara. Chastain's off-field activities, which have included several appearances on late-night television, have not interfered with her seriousness about soccer and the reputation of the women's national team. "People will keep this in their memory a long time," she noted, referring to America's recapturing of the World Cup. "The lasting impression will be that 20 people on the field gave their all. Not only for themselves but for their country."

## Joy Fawcett

Joy Fawcett, along with teammate Carla Overbeck, redefined the term "soccer mom." Within three months of giving birth to each of her daughters, Fawcett returned to the field, keeping her girls with her on the road and while training in Florida. A veteran of the women's national team since 1987, she started and played every minute of every match of World Cup '95 and the '96 Olympics. At the Olympics, Fawcett assisted on Tiffeny Milbrett's gold medal-clinching goal against China. A three-time All-American at the University of California, Berkeley, Fawcett also holds the school's all-time scoring record with 55 goals and 23 assists. In 1993, she was hired as UCLA's first women's soccer coach, a position she held until 1998.

Her husband Walter, a software engineer in Orange County, California, visits the family at least once a month. "It's crazy," remarked teammate Kristine Lilly who watches Fawcett's balancing act with something like awe. "After practice, we get to kick back and relax a little, but Joy is off running around with the kids. I don't know where she gets the energy from." Fawcett, though, thinks nothing of combining soccer with raising a family: "I have eight brothers and sisters, so seeing my mom raise all of us and run a day-care center at the same time, well, I've got some catching up to do." Since 1998, both Fawcett and Overbeck, the only other mother on the team, have received a little help from the U.S. Soccer Federation which agreed to pay $750 a week for a nanny; still, the commitments of a soccer career and family life call for a good balancing act. Coach Tony DiCicco was initially worried that the arrangement might affect Fawcett's stamina, but she remained a stalwart of the team. A founding player of the WUSA, Fawcett began her play for the league on the San Diego Spirit. At age five, her daughter Katey was ready to start playing in a kiddies soccer league and was already bragging about her kick.

## Julie Foudy

By all accounts, U.S. team midfielder and co-captain Julie Foudy ("Loudy") is the team loudmouth. "She's very vocal and directive on the field," noted teammate Carla Overbeck. "Her competitive spirit is unbelievable, and she makes sure we keep our heads in the game." Just 17 when she joined the national team in 1988, Foudy made her presence felt immediately. "Oh, she was little Miss Prom Queen right from the start," remarked Akers. "She didn't miss a step, and nothing intimidates her. She has the most exuberant personality of anyone I've ever met, and she's dynamic on and off the field."

A California native, Foudy was a two-time all American at Mission Viejo High School in California and a four-time All-American at Stanford University. Graduating with a degree in biology in 1993, where she was accepted into medical school but delayed enrollment for the 1996 Olympics, Foudy started and played every match at the 1991 Women's World Cup. She missed the 1995 championships, however, because she was on her honeymoon. At the 1996 Olympics, she assisted on Shannon MacMillan's spectacular sudden-death overtime goal in the 2–1 win over Norway, which Mia Hamm called "the most important pass ever for women's soccer in the United States."

In 1998, Foudy was hired by ESPN as an in-studio analyst for the men's World Cup. "She studied her butt off for that, learning all she could about the players and the teams," said Kristine Lilly, who wasn't surprised by Foudy's foray into television. "When she's committed to something, she'll do it to the best of her abilities." Foudy received excellent reviews for her commentary.

A well-built 5'6" brunette with a radiant smile, Foudy was also tapped by *Sports Illustrated* for their swimsuit issue, although the shoot was a wholesome frolic on the beach with her husband Ian. Then it was right back to barking out orders to teammates (part of her job as midfielder—soccer's equivalent to a quarterback). "If I was quiet," she said, "people would think something was wrong." Foudy was a founding player of the WUSA, beginning her participation in the league on the San Diego Spirit.

## Mia Hamm

The star forward of the U.S. World Cup Women's Soccer Team and the number one goal scorer ever, man or woman, Mia Hamm served as a driving force behind the growing popularity of women's soccer in America during the 1990s. Following the gold-medal win of the Women's Soccer Team at the 1996 Olympics, the fresh-faced 27-year-old became one of the most recognized athletes in the nation and a role model to thousands of young schoolgirls who dreamed of glory on the soccer field. "I think she's the best player in the world, absolutely," remarked long-time teammate Julie Foudy. "In the women's game, when you find a fast player they're usually not as sharp technically because they've always been able to kick the ball and outrun everybody. That's what makes Mia so tough, she's fast and she has great technical ability." But Hamm has not always had the same ease with her star status as she does on the field. "I'm just another player trying to fill my role on this talented team," she said in a 1998 interview in *Scholastic Coach & Athletic Director*. "Since I score goals, I get more attention. But ask anyone on the team and they will tell you how important our defenders, midfielders, and goalkeepers are to our success."

A self-described "military brat" as the daughter of an Air Force colonel, Hamm grew up in Florence, Italy, and in American cities in Alabama, California, Texas, and Virginia, following her father's postings. Constantly on the move, she found stability on the soccer field during her young life. Although she played on a few all-girl teams while growing up, primarily she played with the boys. "It was either play with the boys or not play at all," she writes in her 1999 book *Go for the Goal*. "Most important, playing with boys really helped me become competitive and develop that combative spirit I have today." As a kid, Hamm played other sports too, trying to keep up with her older brother Garrett, a Thai-American orphan whom the Hamms adopted when he was eight. Mia was five when Garrett joined the fami-

ly, and the two became best pals almost immediately. She would later recall: "He let me hang out with him and his friends and play football, soccer and basketball with them." Garrett's own dreams of a professional baseball career were dashed when he was diagnosed with aplastic anemia at 16, but he remained a constant source of inspiration to his little sister.

At 14, Hamm played in a U.S. Soccer Federation women's tournament in New Orleans, Louisiana, where she met Anson Dorrance, then coach of the women's team at the University of North Carolina and of the U.S. women's national team. He was so impressed with her explosive speed and athletic ability that he recruited her on the spot, making her the youngest player ever to make the national team. Dorrance was later quoted in *Newsweek* (June 21, 1999) as remarking: "this little girl took off like she was shot out of a cannon. I thought, 'Oh my God.' I couldn't believe the athleticism." Dorrance also steered Hamm to the University of North Carolina, where he served as her coach. With Hamm's parents in Italy during her college years, she found a father figure in Dorrance and became close to his family. "Even as a freshman, Mia had unbelievable talent," said Dorrance. "If she had never practiced a lick, she'd still have been one of college soccer's all-time great players."

But Hamm did practice, developing a masterful dribble—executed equally well with either foot—incredible focus, and, of course, her remarkable ability to slam the ball into the net to make the goal. "A great finisher can analyze in a split second what the goalie is doing, what surface of the foot to use, and then put the ball in exactly the right spot," she said. "It's an ability to slow down time. You don't actually shoot any faster than any other players do, but you process a lot more information in the same time." A relentless competitor, she developed a reputation for pushing herself to an almost super-human capacity.

Hamm played on four straight NCAA championship teams, was named All-American three times, and became the NCAA's all-time scorer. In 1991, she took a year off from college to help the national team win the first-ever Women's World championship held in China, a victory that was barely noted in American newspapers. She then returned to school, graduating in 1994 with a degree in political science and an armful of athletic awards, including the Mary Garber Award as ACC Female Athlete of the Year and the Honda Broderick Cup given to the most outstanding female athlete in collegiate sports. Soon after graduating, she married

Christiaan Corey, a Marine Corps pilot and fellow Chapel Hill student.

There was little time to enjoy married life, however, as another World Cup tournament was on the horizon. The hype surrounding the 1994 men's World Cup, coupled with the addition of women's soccer as an Olympic-medal event, brought a rush of attention to the women's soccer team. A new training center was established in Florida, and team members were put on salary for the first time, thus allowing them to focus entirely on World Cup practice. They faced new challenges when Coach Dorrance left to focus on his collegiate team, and Tony DiCicco took his place. In addition, the team was up against the promise of stiff competition in defense of the Cup. "Anyone of the teams could beat us this year," Hamm cautioned at the time. "We're all basically equal in talent." The remark would prove to be prophetic. The U.S. was ultimately overcome in the semifinals by their arch rivals Norway, who kept them at bay by establishing a 1–0 lead in the first half of the game which they never relinquished. The tournament saw Hamm fight for her team not only from her regular position but also as goalkeeper, which she played for several minutes in their second game, against Denmark, when Briana Scurry was ejected on a controversial hand-ball infraction and the team had already used up its allotment of three substitutions.

If anything, the loss of the World Cup energized Hamm, who set the determined tone for the team as they entered the 1996 Olympic Games in Atlanta. Spraining her ankle in the opening round against Sweden, she rose above the pain to help the U.S. to victory over Norway in the semifinal, paving the way for the final confrontation with China. A record 76,000 fans filled the stadium to witness the match-up, including Hamm's family and brother Garrett, who was now very ill. Hamm performed several crucial passes to push the Americans ahead 2–1, until her ankle finally gave out just before the end of the game. Her teammates kept China at bay for the remaining 60 seconds, and they had the gold. Hamm ignored the pain while sprinting to the field to join her teammates. Summing up the leaping, screaming, and hugging that followed, she noted: "We went bananas."

Hailed as the hero of the game, Hamm was now the darling of the sports world. Her celebrity status grew daily with a flood of endorsement offers that included Nike and Gatorade. There were endless requests for interviews and photo sessions. A crowd of adoring fans dogged her for autographs, and she made a television commercial with fellow North Carolina alum Michael Jordan. But the notoriety made her cringe. "It's weird getting attention," she said. "I'm not this perfect person." In May 1997, she was named one of *People* magazine's 50 Most Beautiful People, an honor about which her teammates proudly teased her without mercy.

While Hamm was adjusting to life in the spotlight, her brother was waiting for a bone-marrow transplant, his only hope for survival. Hamm used her new-found celebrity to help in the search for a compatible marrow donor for him, a quest complicated by Garrett's Thai-Anglo background and lack of biological siblings. She used every public appearance, speaking engagement, and soccer clinic to distribute flyers explaining the importance of bone-marrow screening and describing the process. Garrett finally received a transplant in February 1997 but died from complications the following April, leaving behind a wife and small son. His death was a devastating blow for Hamm.

To be with her family, she missed the first two games of the Olympic Victory Tour in April 1997. Knowing that her brother would have wanted her to get back out on the field, she joined the team for the third game of the tour in Milwaukee: "To focus mentally after that ordeal was one of the biggest challenges I've faced, and I must admit I really struggled to cope with my emotions and concentrate on soccer, but my teammates were remarkable in their caring for me and my family. There's no way I could have come back without their support and love, and I will always be grateful." To carry on her brother's name, she established The Mia Hamm Foundation, which raises funds and makes charitable grants to organizations dedicated to battling bone-marrow diseases.

While some might have thought that the Olympic gold-medal performance of 1996 would be hard to surpass, Hamm and the U.S. Women's Team went on to victory in the 1999 Women's World Cup—a win of epic proportions both for the team and for women's soccer in America—which the players felt eclipsed any of their previous successes. Over a three-week period in late June and July 1999, the tournament was played in seven different venues across the U.S. and became one of the most spectacular sporting events in recent years. "The crowd was absolutely unbelievable," said Hamm of the record 79,000 fans who turned out at Giants Stadium in East Rutherford, New Jersey, to watch the first game. She booted in the first goal 17 minutes into the

Mia
Hamm

first half, but it was team chemistry that won the game and propelled them through five subsequent wins to a final match-up with their old nemesis, China. The play-off game—before a record crowd of over 90,000 at the Rose Bowl in Pasadena, California, and an unprecedented number of television viewers as well—resulted in 120 minutes of scoreless soccer, including two 15-minute sudden death overtime periods. In the end, everything would boil down to a penalty-kick shoot-out to determine the winner. After scoring kicks by Carla Overbeck, Joy Fawcett,

Kristine Lilly, Hamm, and Brandi Chastain, and a spectacular save by goalkeeper Briana Scurry who prevented China's **Liu Ying** from scoring on the third penalty kick, the United States won 5–4, securing their second World Cup triumph. After the team swarmed onto the field to join Chastain, the victory celebration began—initiated by a lap with Old Glory around the arena and the gold-medal ceremony—and then went on for days. After a whirlwind of parades and personal appearances, Hamm and her teammates were back in camp preparing for the U.S. Cup in early October and the 2000 Olympics (where the team would take the silver medal).

Hamm's dream of a professional women's soccer league came to fruition in 2001, when she played for the Washington Freedom, one of eight teams of the fledgling Women's United Soccer Association (WUSA). For the league to succeed, it was clear that Hamm (voted "the most appealing female athlete" in a Burns Sports and Celebrities poll of ad executives) would need to put aside her dislike of personal publicity to take an active, visible part in promoting the WUSA. While recognizable faces play an enormous role in sports, "[f]or new leagues, stars are even more vital," wrote **Rachel Alexander** in the *Washington Post* (April 11, 2001). "Fans need a point of entry." Having once told a reporter to "get a life" when asked how it felt to make her record-breaking 108th international goal (against Brazil in 1999), Hamm may never have warmed to the spotlight, but, as *Billie Jean King** noted, Hamm's goal of advancing soccer would likely require her to bear the burdens of fame. "It is very, very important to her," said Hamm's agent David Bober, "to make [the league] work."

When not on the field or training, Hamm serves as a volunteer coach for the University of North Carolina women's soccer team. She enjoys working with young people and is also active with City Block Soccer, an inner-city soccer league which she was involved in as a child, and Nike's P.L.A.Y. (Participate in the Lives of American Youth). For relaxation, she plays golf, reads, or just kicks back and watches television. Although known as shy and serious in demeanor, she shows other traits to her teammates, prompting Foudy to remark: "I think Mia's dream is to direct 'Saturday Night Live.' She's like this closet comic. We're constantly acting out skits. She has this dry sense of humor, and she does these nutty impersonations. Unfortunately, she doesn't let people see that side of her."

In addition to soccer, Hamm is devoted to the work of her foundation, which was estab-lished with the support of Nike, Mattel, and Gatorade. Along with supporting bone-marrow research, the foundation's mission is to empower young female athletes. Hamm's brother Garrett is with her every time she steps onto a field. In her deal with Nike, the shoe company agreed to inscribe his initials, GJH, on the bottom of every pair of her signature shoes, the Nike Air Zoom M9 ("M9" standing for Mia and her number 9). "I've been blessed by so many things," she noted, "but I would give them all up to have him back."

## Kristine Lilly

Since her first appearance with the national team against China in 1987, forward Kristine Lilly made more appearances for her country than any other soccer player in history, male or female. Raised in Wilton, Connecticut, where she returns each summer to run the Kristine Lilly Soccer Academy, she led Wilton High School to three state titles. At North Carolina University, Lilly was a four-time All-American and won four NCAA titles (1989–92).

Known for her work ethic and drive, Lilly is described as "the epitome of consistency" by teammates Overbeck, Foudy, and Akers. "She's my favorite player in the world," adds Akers. "She has it all. She's got the winner mentality. She's extremely skillful with both feet. Tactically, she knows the game as well as anyone. When I talk to young kids, I tell them to watch Lil."

Lilly, who is never far away from her beloved golden retriever Molson, is known as a compassionate friend to her teammates. A big New York Jets fan, she was particularly pleased that their home stadium in New Jersey's Meadowlands was selected as one of the venues for the 1999 World Cup.

## Carla Overbeck

Like her teammate Joy Fawcett, co-captain and defender Carla Overbeck combines motherhood with the demands of her career. Her young son Jackson accompanied her at camp and on the road, and her husband Greg, a restaurateur in Chapel Hill, North Carolina, visits the two for a few days every couple weeks. "It's really tough being without my family," he admitted. "But Carla has worked so hard and sacrificed everything to be on this team, and I totally support what she's doing." Although Jackson, who along with Joy Fawcett's two girls is in the care of a nanny when she is practicing or playing, seems to be thriving, Overbeck does have moments of doubt. "Now Jackson associates his father with the telephone," she says. "The other day my cell phone rang when Greg was with us, and Jackson still said, 'Daddy.'"

Overbeck attended Richardson High School in Dallas but didn't play soccer until she was at the University of North Carolina, where she won four NCAA titles. She made her first appearance with the national team in June 1988 and was one of two players to start and play every minute of both the World Cup '95 and the '96 Olympics (fellow mom Joy Fawcett was the other). From August 4, 1993, to August 1, 1996, Overbeck played 63 consecutive matches for the U.S., a record for any U.S. National Team member, male or female. She was a founding player of the WUSA who began her play with the league as a member of the Carolina Courage. When not playing or training, she serves as the assistant women's soccer coach at Duke University.

While to her teammates Overbeck is a calming influence—"You could make a horrible play, and she's right there telling you to forget about it," said Kristine Lilly—such calmness does not extend to her opponents: "If you're a forward shooting down the tube at her," said Akers, "you'd better strap on your shinguards 'cause she's not gonna let you get by easy. She's hard back there. And she's totally committed to winning. That motivates the rest of the team to do the same."

## Briana Scurry

"I knew that was going to be the one," said goalkeeper Briana Scurry following her remarkable block of **Liu Ying**'s shot at the goal during the penalty-kick shoot-off that determined the winner of the U.S.-China play-off for the 1999 World Cup. "She just didn't look like she wanted to be there. She didn't have that confidence. You could see it in the way she walked up there." Scurry, who hadn't faced a penalty kicker in four years, took full advantage of her observations, staring Ying down with her formidable scowl, then taking a dive left to swat away the oncoming ball. Her job done, she didn't even watch teammate Chastain's winning drive into the net, afraid she might jinx it. Only when the screaming crowd of 90,000 rose to their feet did the joy register in a smile. Even in the middle of celebrating the victory, Scurry was already thinking about which of her teammates she might not see again. "I'll probably have post-excitement syndrome," she said about the days ahead. "Be totally depressed for the next three months."

The U.S. team's only African-American starter, Scurry earned the title of shutout queen while at the University of Massachusetts, where she racked up 37 shutouts in 65 starts. She

joined the U.S. national team in 1984 and during her first season recorded 7 shutouts in 12 starts. Although she suffered a back injury in an auto accident in 1995, she was back in goal for the World Cup as well as for the Olympics in 1996 and 2000. A founding player of the WUSA, Scurry began her contribution to the league as a member of the Atlanta Beat.

Described by Mia Hamm as "cat-quick" and having nerves of steel, Scurry regards courage as one of the most important traits of goal keeping. "Many aspects of the position require that you stick your head into places most people wouldn't dare," she noted. "Sometimes you get kicked in places any sane person definitely wouldn't want to get kicked in, but that's just part of the job."

**SOURCES:**

Alexander, Rachel. "Hamm in a New League of Her Own," in *The Washington Post*. April 11, 2001, p. A01.

Christopher, Matt. *On the Field with . . . Mia Hamm*. Boston, MA: Little, Brown, 1998.

French, Scott. "The Fantasticks!" in *The FIFA WWC '99 Official Program*. Pindar Press, 1999.

Guise, Joe. "Showstoppers," in *The FIFA WWC '99 Official Program*. Pindar Press, 1999.

Hamm, Mia, with Aaron Heifetz. *Go for the Goal*. NY: HarperCollins, 1999.

Heifetz, Aaron. "Overture: Grand entrance for women's soccer," in *The FIFA WWC '99 Official Program*. Pindar Press, 1999.

Markel, Robert, ed. *The Women's Sports Encyclopedia*. NY: Henry Holt, 1997.

Mazzola, Gregg, and J. Brett Whitesell. "Person to Person," in *Scholastic Coach & Athletic Director*. Vol. 66, no. 5. December 1998, pp. 44–53.

McDowell, Dimity, and Grant Wahl. "The Home Team," in *Sports Illustrated for Women*. Summer 1999.

Murphy, Melissa. "Inkster, Hamm honored by Women's Sports Foundation," in *The Day* [New London, CT]. November 19, 1999.

Powers, John. "Atop the World," in *Boston Sunday Globe*. July 11, 1999.

———. "Scurry's saving grace there when it counted," in *Boston Sunday Globe*. July 11, 1999.

———. "This group is history," in *The Boston Globe*. July 12, 1999.

Saporito, Bill. "Crazy for the Cup," in *Time*. Vol. 153, no. 25. June 28, 1999, pp. 62–63.

———. "Flat-out Fantastic: The New Dream Team," in *Time*. Vol. 154, no. 3. July 19, 1999, pp. 60–67.

Springer, Shira. "They have world at their feet," in *The Boston Globe*. July 11, 1999.

Starr, Mark. "Keeping Her Own Score," in *Newsweek*. June 21, 1999.

Sullivan, Robert. "Goodbye to Heroin Chic. Now It's Sexy to Be Strong," in *Time*. Vol. 154, no. 3. July 19, 1999, p. 62.

Tresniowski, Alex, with Fran Brennan, Grace Lim, and Joseph V. Tirella. "Getting Their Kicks," in *People Weekly*. Vol. 51, no. 25. July 5, 1999, pp. 171–173.

Wilner, Barry. "It's Double the Pleasure for U.S. Women," in *The Day* [New London, CT]. December 25, 1999, p. C1.

Wollenberg, Skip. "Women's Soccer Team Latest Hot Property for Madison Avenue Wizards to Market," in *The Day* [New London, CT]. July 14, 1999, p. C4.

Wyllie, John Philip. "The First Lady of Soccer," in *Soccer Digest*. Vol. 21, no. 6. March 1999, pp. 16–21.

**SUGGESTED READING:**

Longman, Jere. *The Girls of Summer: The U.S. Women's Soccer Team and How It Changed the World.* HarperCollins, 2000.

**Barbara Morgan**,
Melrose, Massachusetts

# Söderbaum, Kristina (1912—)

*Swedish star of German films during the Nazi era.*
*Name variations: Kristina Soderbaum or Soederbaum.*
*Born in Djursholm-Stockholm, Sweden, on September 5, 1912 (one source cites 1909); daughter of Henrik Söderbaum; married Veit Harlan (a director); children: sons, Caspar and Kristian.*

Born in 1912 in a suburb of Stockholm, Sweden, Kristina Söderbaum wished to be an actress as a young girl, but her father, a chemistry professor who also served as president of the committee that awarded the Nobel Prizes, did not approve of her going on stage, or worse, appearing in films. In 1930, she moved to Berlin to study art history. Not until her father's death did she seriously attempt a film career. Remaining in Germany, in 1936 Söderbaum made her film debut in *Onkel Bräsig*, a patriotic drama that would be quickly forgotten. Although she displayed skill, was attractive, and had learned to speak German (almost) without an accent, Söderbaum had a career that seemed to be going nowhere until 1938, when director Veit Harlan came across some of her photographs in studio files.

Harlan had become one of Nazi Germany's leading film directors by the late 1930s, both because he enjoyed the protection of Joseph Goebbels, the regime's powerful Minister of Propaganda and Public Enlightenment, and also because he was ideologically loyal to Nazism and gifted at turning out, on schedule, one successful film after another. Harlan chose Söderbaum to play the leading role in *Jugend* (Youth), the story of a tragic love which ends when the unhappy heroine drowns herself. The public loved Söderbaum's acting in *Jugend*, turning her into a star virtually overnight. As well, Harlan and Söderbaum got married. Before 1938 was over, Harlan had directed another film with Söderbaum in the lead, the mystery *Verwehte Spuren* (Covered Tracks). She played a woman in Paris who investigates the cause of her mother's disappearance, only to discover that her body had been hidden

because she had died of the plague. With a first-rate script by *Thea von Harbou, *Verwehte Spuren* too was successful, and Söderbaum's reputation soared.

In 1939, on the eve of World War II, Söderbaum appeared in a patriotic epic set in the past, *Das unsterbliche Herz* (The Immortal Heart). Acting alongside Heinrich George and Paul Wegener, two of the great stars of the German stage, Söderbaum was more than able to hold her own. The film was popular with German audiences, and even received praise from *The New York Times* when it was shown in Manhattan in October 1939, only weeks after Nazi Germany's conquest of Poland. Another 1939 film starring Söderbaum was *Die Reise nach Tilsit* (The Journey to Tilsit), based on a story by Hermann Sudermann (1857–1928). More than the previous films she had starred in, this one was strongly influenced by Nazi and German ideology. Söderbaum found herself perfectly cast as Elske, the blonde, demure young wife of an arrogant young husband who betrays her with a lustful, promiscuous and provocatively clad Polish woman named Madlyn (played by **Anna Dammann**). *Die Reise nach Tilsit* is typical of Goebbels' propaganda, including the idea that city folk are corrupt, and that only in pure rural types like Elske do "German" (i.e., Nazi) ideals instinctively continue to flourish.

Söderbaum's appearance in the next film in her career, *Jud Süss* (1940), was to haunt her for the rest of her life. A highly polished work of anti-Semitism, *Jud Süss* was based on a novel by the German-Jewish writer Lion Feuchtwanger published before the Nazis came to power. Although fiction, Feuchtwanger's book was based on an actual historical episode in the 18th century in which a Jewish financier was convicted of having bankrupted the state treasury and executed. The Nazis distorted the story to use it as a framework for anti-Semitic propaganda. The role of Dorothea Sturm, the pure German girl who is raped by the Jewish villain Joseph Süss Oppenheimer (Jud Süss), did not even exist in the Feuchtwanger novel, but was inserted by Harlan who very likely did so with the encouragement of Goebbels. When Söderbaum found out that the actress **Viktoria von Ballasko** was being considered for the role of Dorothea, she moved decisively to secure it for herself. After being attacked by Jud Süss, Dorothea can no longer live in a state of dishonor and drowns herself. Since Söderbaum had already played the role of a young woman who drowns herself some years before, and would do so again in the future, some Germans pinned on her the nick-

*Opposite page*
$\mathcal{K}$ristina
$\mathcal{S}$öderbaum

name *Reichswasserleiche* (Reich Water Corpse). Although it was released in 1940, before the start of the Holocaust and mass murder of European Jewry, *Jud Süss* was nevertheless an important component of the Nazi regime's increasingly radical policies against Jews who lived under their rule, and was designed to strengthen public approval and support of these measures.

After *Jud Süss*, Söderbaum appeared in several more large-budget films. In *Die goldene Stadt* (1942, The Golden City), only the second film to be made in color by a German studio, she appears as Anna, a German country girl whose dream is to see Prague, the "golden city." However, like it did for her mother before her, contact with the city brings only tragedy. Having been seduced by a cousin and now pregnant, Anna is rejected by all, including her father. Going to the swamp that had once been her mother's grave, she drowns herself. Metaphorically, Anna's fate was deserved, because she had abandoned her rural homeland and become infected with the evil spirit of the city of Prague.

In 1943, Söderbaum starred in *Immensee*, based on the classic novel by Theodor Storm (1817–1888). As Elisabeth, the ideal Aryan woman with blue eyes and blonde hair whose life is the embodiment of "Germanic fidelity" (*Deutsche Treue*), she marries a man to forget her unrequited love for a young musician, and then learns to love and respect her husband. Again shot in color, this film celebrated the sanctity of marriage (the Nazi regime often proclaimed the primacy of "family values"). The beauty of the stark north German landscape created an idyllic mood that must have been in dramatic contrast to the lives of most Germans in 1943, when it became clear that the Reich might lose the war. Söderbaum even appeared briefly in a nude swimming scene in the film, but its intent was not erotic but rather to emphasize the racially beneficial aspects of the outdoor life. Söderbaum ended 1943 by filming *Opfergang* (Sacrifice), in which, not surprisingly, she dies at the end.

The last film in which Kristina Söderbaum would appear in Nazi Germany was the patriotic epic *Kolberg* (1945). By the time this film was shot, in 1944, it was clear to all that the Third Reich was doomed. Nevertheless, Goebbels spent vast amounts of money and engaged a large number of troops as extras so as to create a Hollywood-style extravaganza. The film was set in the Napoleonic era and based on an actual historical event, except for the fact that the actual Kolberg, unlike the one of Goebbels' fantasy, did surrender at the end. The theme of *Kolberg*

was "no surrender." As Maria Werner, another 100% Aryan woman, Söderbaum displays courage and tenacity, refusing even to think of surrendering although she becomes the sole survivor of her family. At the end, she is presented as an exemplar of Nazi virtue when the mayor of the town tells her, "Yes, Maria, you have given everything you had. But not in vain. . . . [W]hen someone takes upon himself so much suffering, then he is truly a beautiful person. You are noble, Maria; you have done your duty; you were not afraid to die."

After World War II, Harlan was accused of having collaborated with the Nazi regime and stood trial for the first time in the spring of 1949, a proceeding that ended in an acquittal. Söderbaum, as a Swedish citizen, could have continued with her career during this period, and did in fact receive offers of work in her native Sweden, as well as in Italy and even in Germany. She refused these, however, until her husband was cleared of all charges and could thus resume his career as well. Two more trials of Harlan followed, ending in April 1950, when he was again acquitted. At this point, the couple resumed their joint career, but the world had changed and success largely managed to elude them. From 1951 to 1958, Söderbaum starred in seven more films, often receiving good reviews for her acting, which some critics believed had grown more nuanced and subtle with the passage of time. But the films themselves were generally not deemed wholly successful, either as art or commerce. Kristina Söderbaum made one final screen appearance, in Hans Jürgen Syberberg's *Karl May* (1974). After her husband's death in 1964, she devoted much of her time to photography. Her memoirs were first published in 1983.

**SOURCES:**

Kreimeier, Klaus. *The Ufa Story: A History of Germany's Greatest Film Company, 1918–1945.* Berkeley, CA: University of California Press, 1999.

Lowry, Stephen. *Pathos und Politik: Ideologie in Spielfilmen des Nationalsozialismus.* Tübingen: Niemeyer, 1991.

Nagl-Exner, Marianne. *Venezianischer Bilderbogen: Ein kleiner lyrischer Begleiter.* Augsburg: Augsburger Druck- und Verlagshaus, 1979.

Rentschler, Eric. *The Ministry of Illusion: Nazi Cinema and Its Afterlife.* Cambridge, MA: Harvard University Press, 1996.

Romani, Cinzia. *Tainted Goddesses: Female Film Stars of the Third Reich.* Translated by Robert Connolly. NY: Sarpedon, 1992.

Sanders-Brahms, Helma. "Zarah," in Hans Günther Pflaum, ed., *Jahrbuch Film 81/82.* Munich: Hanser, 1981, pp. 165–172.

Schulte-Sasse, Linda. *Entertaining the Third Reich: Illusions of Wholeness in Nazi Cinema.* Durham, NC: Duke University Press, 1996.

Söderbaum, Kristina. *Nichts bleibt immer so: Erinnerungen.* Rev. ed. Munich: Herbig, 1992.

Vincendeau, Ginette. *Encyclopedia of European Cinema.* NY: Facts on File, 1995.

Welch, David. *Propaganda and the Nazi Cinema 1933–1945.* Oxford, UK: Clarendon Press, 1983.

Zentner, Christian, and Friedemann Bedürftig, eds. *The Encyclopedia of the Third Reich.* Translated and edited by Amy Hackett. 2 vols. NY: Collier Macmillan, 1991.

**John Haag**, Associate Professor of History, University of Georgia, Athens, Georgia

# Södergran, Edith (1892–1923)

*Finnish poet, whose work went relatively unrecognized in her lifetime, now acknowledged as a germinal poet and a major liberating force for Scandinavian poetry. Born in St. Petersburg, Russia, on April 4, 1892; died at Raivola on Midsummer Day (June 24), 1923; daughter of Matts Södergran and Helena (Holmroos) Södergran; never married; no children.*

*Spent her life in Raivola, Finland, with her mother as companion; attended the girls' division of the German Hauptschule in St. Petersburg where she began to write poetry (1902–09); was a recurring patient at sanatoriums, treated for tuberculosis (1909–14); published four politically and stylistically controversial collections of poetry as well as a book of aphorisms; some of her poems translated into German by \*Nelly Sachs.*

*Selected works: Dikter (Poems, 1916); Septemberlyran (The September Lyre, 1918); Rosenaltaret (The Rose Altar, 1919); Brokiga iakttagelser (Manifold Observations, 1919); Framtidens skugga (The Shadow of the Future, 1920).*

Though Edith Södergran lived in Finland, close to the Russian border, her major works are in Swedish, which was the language spoken at her home. Her father's family had lived in the Swedish-speaking coastal region of western Finland since the beginning of the 18th century, and her mother was also a Swedish-speaking Finn, daughter of ironmaster Gabriel Holmroos. Matts Södergran and **Helena Holmroos Södergran** had met in St. Petersburg, Russia, where Matts was employed by Alfred Nobel, and their only child Edith was born there on April 4, 1892. Shortly afterwards, the family moved to Raivola, a village just inside the Finnish border, where Holmroos had purchased a house for them. It had a Russian quality to it, with its brightly painted balconies, verandas, and windows, and a large garden slanting towards a lake. Edith would climb the tall maples or place ladders against adjoining wooden buildings to ascend to the rooftops. From up there, she would observe the cats walking about in the courtyard or run after one in an attempt to stroke it. Cats were important to her throughout her life and, along with her mother, became her only steady companions.

Södergran was deeply attached to her mother with whom she shared a love of literature. To develop that interest and to provide a good liberal arts education, Helena enrolled Edith in a prestigious German school in St. Petersburg and moved with her daughter into the city for each term. Edith was a student there from the time she was ten until she turned sixteen, and she acquired a well-rounded education that stressed modern languages and literature. Trips to concerts, theaters, and museums were part of the curriculum as well; all lessons and conversations were in German, which remained Södergran's "best" language despite her choice of Swedish for her poetry.

Between January 1907 and the summer of 1909—when she was between 14 and 16 years old—Södergran wrote around 200 poems, 20 in Swedish, 5 in French, and 1 in Russian; all the rest were in German and heavily influenced by the German Romantic poet Heinrich Heine. They express a profound love of nature and a great yearning for a kindred soul with whom she might share this love. She had a severe schoolgirl crush on her French teacher, Henri Cottier, and felt intimately connected to two of her fellow students. A recurrent theme in her poetry is that of death with which the young poet was already familiar. Her father's health had been declining, and in May 1906 he had been diagnosed with tuberculosis. A year later, he was declared incurable at the sanatorium of Nummela, and he returned to Raivola to spend his last summer there. Possibly Edith contracted tuberculosis from her father; certainly, her visit to him at the sanatorium had filled her with a dread of disease, "a fear without bounds, a dreadful horror of death, a fear of this illness, this slow conscious death," as she wrote in a letter to her doctor several years later. Accompanying that fear was a keenly felt confusion about her identity and direction in life. She expresses her sentiment in a poem from 1908:

I do not know to whom to bring my songs
I do not know in whose language to write.
. . .
I curse loneliness
And look in the wide world
For a heart
And look into people's eyes.
And seek a human soul

That could understand me
Yet their eyes are so foreign to me
They look upon other things.

In that same year, she caught a severe cold, and on New Year's Day of 1909, she learned the devastating news that she was suffering from the early stages of tuberculosis.

Södergran was sent to the sanatorium she knew and dreaded, spending five extended periods at Nummela between 1909 and 1911. Her biographers have surmised that her neglected exterior and eccentric manners displayed there were a camouflage for her horror of illness. They describe her as "ugly, dirty, and oily"; she would answer questions rudely and take to the rooftops when it was time for her doctor's visit. As a countermeasure to such aloofness, she tried to initiate an affair with a junior staff member, and she improved her Swedish by extensive reading in Swedish and Finnish classics and in animated conversations with fellow Finland-Swedish patients. Her goal was to leave the sanatorium to enter a women's college where she could study literature and philosophy.

She is a very great poet . . . one of our Byzantines, brave and loving as your Emily Brontë. It is a pity that such a rare bird should be buried for the world in a grave over which the war has passed several times.

—Gunnar Ekelöf

Instead, she and her mother set off for the sanatorium at Davos in Switzerland, the setting for Thomas Mann's *The Magic Mountain*. The Södergrans stayed at a nearby hotel while Edith received treatment from a doctor whose special interest in the psychological effects of tuberculosis made him particularly suited for her case. Edith took a deep liking to Dr. Muralt whom she thought "powerful and ingenuous" and in whose care she appeared "calm, distinguished and reserved," a far cry from the eccentric girl at Nummela. She never forgot him, and when she died at Raivola a dozen years later, his photograph was still on her bedside table. Partially due to his calming influence, Södergran read extensively at Davos. She discovered English writers and Walt Whitman, whose *Leaves of Grass* would be an influence on her later poetry. Anticipating a trip to Milan and Florence, she began learning Italian and reading Dante, whose *Inferno* she thought a representation of the sanatorium: "No one speaks, but everyone screams, tears are not tears and all sorrows are without strength." Yet from her window she could see mountain meadows, green forests, and white

Alpine peaks: promises of a future life she could still hope would be hers.

The Södergran women returned to Finland in late May 1913 to spend the summer at Raivola. Their days there were punctuated by seven trips to Nummela for "insufflation" treatments: filling Edith's lungs with nitrogen gas. The winter spent again at Davos provided little change in her deteriorating physical condition, and the outbreak of World War I in the summer of 1914 prevented further trips. The war also ended Edith's secret relationship with a Finnish doctor 16 years her senior, who was drafted for a military hospital. One last stay at Nummela was terminated by Södergran's running away. She was determined to concentrate on her poetry.

To that end, she approached the publishing house of Holger Schildt, who agreed to print her poems provided she would demand no royalties. Södergran accepted, and *Dikter (Poems)* appeared at Christmas of 1916 to mixed reviews. Drawing on inspiration from Whitman, Rimbaud, Max Dauthendey, and *Else Lasker-Schüler**, and heavily influenced by Södergran's childhood reading of fairy tales, the poems were too audacious, too "morbid," too "formless," too incomprehensible for their time and place. Only one critic called the book a cause for "rejoicing," because it not only introduced a "new name" into Scandinavian poetry, but also pointed in a direction not seen before.

Södergran was crushed by the criticism of her work and wrote little the following year, 1917. Other factors of physical and political nature contributed to the slender output. In March, she convinced her mother to make a trip with her to St. Petersburg so they might see for themselves the changes wrought in the aftermath of the abdication of the Russian tsar Nicholas II. The Bolshevik Revolution terrified and delighted her. Inspired by her reading of Friedrich Nietzsche, she saw in the upheavals a new stage in the development of the world. Despite an attack of pulmonary bleeding brought on by the exertions of the journey, she was determined to be a part of events. So she participated vicariously through a focused reading of not only Nietzsche but the futuristic Russian poets, Aleksandr Blok, Andrey Bely, Konstantin Balmont, Igor Severyanin and Vladimir Mayakovsky.

This literary and political focus and concentration gave her the strength to go to Helsinki in the fall of 1917 to make the acquaintance of "literary personalities." They were puzzled and intrigued by her presence, describing her as "mysterious and as if marked by fate," pale and unhealthy in appearance, but "avid for conversation," someone to whom experiencing the "fantastic" and thinking the "impossible" were second nature. They felt unable to help her, however. Södergran was too "extraordinary, too highly charged with her solitary exaltation for her contact with [them] to be even a little fruitful." She, in turn, found her colleagues "starchy, reserved, impersonal."

She returned to Raivola to face the outbreak of civil war in Finland. Her village was located just inside a Red zone and therefore subject to frequent attacks by White saboteurs cutting the lines of supply. When the White army captured Raivola, war had penetrated the rural environs, and the Södergrans were caught. Native speakers of neither Russian nor Finnish, they could not be sure of safety or economic survival, as the fall of the Russian tsar had lost them their Russian and Ukrainian securities. Understandably, Edith Södergran's excitement at witnessing the creation of a new world was tempered with fear of its destruction. *Septemberlyran (The September Lyre)*, which was accepted for publication in November 1918, expresses her ambivalence. The poems reflect her horror at the devastation of war but are suffused with hope that a man-god would emerge to herald the higher stage of development resulting from war's divinely induced upheavals. "The World is Bathing in Blood" exemplifies her sentiment.

> The world is bathing in blood because God had
> to live.
> In order that his glory may persist, all others
> must perish . . . .
> God wants to create anew. He wants to reform
> the world to a clearer sign. . . .
> What it is he creates no one knows. But it moves
> like a dread over half-awake senses.

This troubling ambivalence led to severe misgivings about the contents of her poems and their reception. To soften the anticipated critical response, she wrote a letter to her publisher asking if critics of the "provincial press and the broad public" could be kept away from the book. Perhaps unwisely, as a second step she went public with her sentiments. She published a "preface" to the poems in a Helsinki newspaper before the critics had submitted their reviews. Her book, she wrote, was only for those few individuals "who stand nearest the frontier of the future." Only they would understand how she herself was sacrificing "every atom" of her strength for the "great cause." She exhorted individuals to "place themselves in the service of the future," hoping she would not be alone with "that greatness which [she had] to bring." Expectedly, the male establishment thought her a megalomaniac, a "Nietzsche-crazed" woman; someone, indeed, who had been "infected by the same intellectual disease which in the political field is called Bolshevism." Readers and critics alike showed little understanding of her efforts to assimilate the political crisis with that of her own disease-ridden body and articulate her resulting, and highly subjective, understanding in poetry. Her desire to bring her readers into contact with the cosmic forces with which she communicated was perceived as a sign of hysteria.

Yet some fellow writers jumped to the poet's defense, and a literary feud developed in the press. A young Helsinki poet and critic, **Hagar Olsson**, wrote admiringly of the poems, which she found "pure" and "glowing," but regretfully of the damage the poet had done her own cause by publishing "explanations." Olsson considered those an act of self-aggrandizement, even propaganda. A flurry of letters ensued. In a final exchange, Olsson called Södergran a poet who had "consecrated herself to the role of mere instrument and medium. . . . This human being bears the earnestness of death with her . . . and her soul, at least in blessed moments, is as empty and pure as a Stradivarius waiting for the master's touch."

Södergran had responded to Olsson's first public letter of defense with a private one explaining how her publisher had deleted some of the best poems from the collection, which had thereby lost its "weight." Her publication in *Dagens Press* had been an attempt to avert the attacks she knew would be launched. She concluded her letter with an appeal to Olsson for friendship: "Could we reach a hand to one another? . . . Could there be a godlike relationship between us, so that all barriers between us would fall? . . . Are you the sea of fire I will plunge into? . . . [Y]ou ought to be worthy of the highest form of friendship, which Nietzsche advised his followers against on grounds of prudence." Olsson's additional contributions to the feud astonished and delighted Edith Södergran, who thought she had finally found a companion, a "sister" in whom she could confide.

But she would be disappointed. Hagar Olsson's career as a publicist and socialist literary critic allowed considerably less time for friendship and sisterly exchange than Södergran craved. Yet Olsson realized she was her friend's link with the world and responded to Edith's frequent letters and requests for visits as she could. In February 1919, she spent some time at Raivola at Södergran's specific command. Ols-

*Edith Södergran*

son had been issued an ultimatum: either she come, or Edith would break with her forever. Likely, Olsson's guilt at not having been able to fully honor her friend's demands accounts for the delay in her publishing Södergran's letters. It took her 25 years after the poet's death before Olsson could face the material and edit it. The letters, published in 1955 as *Ediths brev (Edith's Letters)*, are painful reading as they reveal the rather one-sided nature of the relationship between the two women, but they are helpful to an understanding of the writer's emotional and intellectual development.

The "sister" segment of Södergran's third collection of poems, *Rosenaltaret (The Rose Altar)*, alternately celebrates and grieves her find of a "sister." The imagery of "Spring Mystery" conveys the miraculous nature of the encounter. "My sister/ you come like a spring wind over our valleys . . . / The violets in the shadow breathe sweet fulfillment/ I will take you to the sweetest corner of the woods:/ there we shall confess to each other how we saw God." In contrast, the fear of loss and betrayal indigenous to a friendship of such intensity surfaces in "I Believe in My Sister," despite its title. "My sister . . ./ Has she betrayed me?/ Does she carry a dagger at her bosom—the light-footed one?" The collection, which appeared in the spring of 1919, received modest attention in the press despite one reviewer's opinion that it was among "the strongest poetry written in Swedish during recent times." Another called Södergran an "expressionist" who "measures the uttermost boundaries of woe and jubilation."

In the summer of 1919, Olsson made a second visit to Raivola. She was horrified at the conditions of poverty in the Södergran household where scant money was obtained from the sale of household effects and furniture. Nonetheless, Södergran was at work on another collection of poetry. In subsequent letters to Olsson, she describes herself during the fall of that year as suffused with an "infernal electricity" almost "impossible to endure." This highly charged emotional state was partly due to her struggle between two irreconcilable poles of longing and desire. She had departed from her reliance on Nietzsche, who represented her sensual and sexual yearnings, and embraced the nature mysticism of the Swiss anthroposophist Rudolf Steiner, which drew her to Christ and God.

Edith Södergran had always felt contained in nature, and now she demanded that nature "answer her thought." As a spiritual guide, Steiner offered her "the experience of the divine nature of reality," as her biographer Gunnar Tideström puts it. Her reading of Steiner occupied considerable time during the remaining years of her life, as did her activities in pursuit of money. Her letters to Olsson tell of her plans to write reviews for *Dagens Press*, to do translations and even to photograph the soldiers in the village. A Norwegian writer came to her aid temporarily by suggesting that half the fee for a translation of one of her books be given to an "ill or aged writer." The thousand marks were awarded to Södergran.

*Framtidens skugga (The Shadow of the Future)*, which would be Södergran's last collection of poems, appeared in November 1920. Again allegations of megalomania and madness greeted the publication. Readers mistook her highly charged images of grandeur for representations of her own importance and power; they failed to hear in the voice of the poet that of a human being who attempts to surrender her body and free herself from earthly concerns and material wants, even as she is racked with desire. "I am quite broken by forcing myself to Christianity," she wrote to Olsson. "I am hungry as a wolf for Dionysus. . . . May one dance with Christ, or is the dance the devil's sole property?"

An attack of Spanish influenza in the winter of 1920 left her further exhausted, and to that physical setback was added an intellectual defeat. A volume of German translations of Finnish-Swedish poetry which she had prepared and sent to the Rowohlt publishing firm in the fall of 1922 was rejected by the German publisher on the grounds that times were unfavorable for poetry. Hagar Olsson then dispatched to Raivola her friend and protégé Elmer Diktonius, a writer of the Helsinki avant-garde. He arranged for Södergran to write poems and articles for a new magazine, *Ultra*, intended to announce contemporary literature in the North. At his instigation, and supported by Olsson, Södergran wrote a translation of Igor Severyanin's poem "Overture" for the second issue of the magazine and new poems of her own for subsequent issues. The payment she received took her through the winter, but when *Ultra* was discontinued after five issues, she lost both an avenue for her literary creations and a much-needed source of income.

"Nothing shimmers, nothing glistens anymore," she wrote to Olsson shortly before Christmas of 1922. She worried that her mother and her friend had plans of sending her to the dreaded sanatorium again. But it did not come to that. Hagar Olsson was on the Riviera when she learned the news of Södergran's death in March 1923; the immediate cause was heart failure. Edith Södergran was buried in the yard of the Russian church.

Two years later, in 1925, Elmer Diktonius edited a collection of Södergran's poems titled *Landet som icke är (The Land Which Is Not)*. It included the *Ultra* poems as well as some previously published and unpublished work. In the 1930s, a monument was erected on her grave by the Finland-Swedish Authors' Union. At the ceremony, Diktonius read his poem in Södergran's memory and the aging Helena Södergran spoke, as he reported, "in words she cast out in bursts [like] scenes in some classic tragedy." The site became the destination of pilgrimages for Finland-Swedish and Swedish poets until the Winter War of 1939–40 destroyed the church, the grave, and the Södergran home.

In 1960, when Edith Södergran had been generally acknowledged as a major liberating force for Scandinavian poetry and her reputation was growing throughout and beyond all of Scandinavia, the same Authors' Union received permission from Soviet authorities to erect a monument in a new Culture Park. The theme of the ceremony was Finnish-Soviet friendship, a political tribute. Thirteen years later, on the 50th anniversary of Södergran's death, a second, more literary ceremony was held at the same site. On that occasion, her poems were read in four tongues: Swedish, Finnish, Russian, and French. The new monument is located several hundred yards from the actual grave, a fitting reminder that in death as in life, Edith Södergran remains a poet off center.

**SOURCES:**

Lindner, Sven, ed. *Edith Södergran: Triumf att finnas till.* Stockholm: Albert Bonniers, 1975.

McDuff, David, trans. *Complete Poems: Edith Södergran.* Newcastle upon Tyne: Bloodaxe, 1984.

Schoolfield, George C. *Edith Södergran: Modernist Poet in Finland.* Westport, CT: Greenwood Press, 1984.

Tideström, Gunnar. *Edith Södergran.* Stockholm: Albert Bonniers, 1960.

Inga Wiehl, native of Denmark,
teaches at Yakima Valley Community College,
Yakima, Washington

## Sodermanland, duchess of.

*See Marie Pavlovna (1890–1958).*

## Söderström, Elisabeth (1927—)

*Swedish soprano. Name variations: Elizabeth Soderstrom or Soederstroem. Born on May 7, 1927, in Stockholm, Sweden; studied with Andrejeva von Skilodz at the Royal Academy of Music and Opera School in Stockholm; married Sverker Olow, in 1950; children: three sons.*

*Debuted at Stockholm (1947), Glyndebourne (1957), Metropolitan Opera (1959), Covent Garden (1960); sang in premiere of Argento's The Aspern Papers in Dallas (1988); became artistic director of the Drottningholm Court Theater (1990).*

At the Royal Opera in Stockholm, Elisabeth Söderström was part of a tightly knit ensemble which included **Kerstin Meyer, Nicolai Gedda** and *****Birgit Nilsson.** Though neither large nor conventionally beautiful, her essentially lyric-soprano voice had a quick vibrato and silver purity, qualities that made her singing memorable. Söderström was a fascinating singing actress who was daring enough to perform the music of living composers. Among the modern roles she performed were the Governess in *The Turn of the Screw*, Jenny in Richard Rodney Bennett's *The Mines of Sulphur*, Daisie Doody in Blomdahl's *Aniara*, Elisabeth Zimmer in Henze's *Elegy for Young Lovers*, and the aging prima donna in Argento's *The Aspern Papers*. Her diversified career meant that Söderström did not

always receive the international fame which she was due. Her recording career began late and does not capture her great vocal abilities.

**SUGGESTED READING:**

Söderström, Elisabeth. *In My Own Key* (autobiography), 1979.

John Haag,
Athens, Georgia

## Sofia.

*Variant of Sophia or Sophie.*

## Sofia Magdalena (1746–1813).

*See Sophia of Denmark.*

## Sofia of Spain (b. 1938).

*See Sophia of Greece.*

## Sofie.

*Variant of Sophia or Sophie.*

## Sofronova, Antonina (1892–1966)

*Russian artist best remembered for her urban landscapes. Name variations: Antonina Fedorovna; Antonina Fyodorovna Sofronova. Born in 1892 in Droskovo in Orel Province, Russia; daughter of a doctor; graduated from the Girls' Commercial College in Kiev, 1909; studied art at the School of Feodor Rerberg in Moscow, 1910; studied under Ilya Mashkov, 1913.*

Born in 1892 in Droskovo, a village in Orel Province, Russian artist Antonina Sofronova is best remembered for her cityscapes. Sofronova graduated from the Girls' Commercial College in Kiev in 1909 and moved to Moscow the following year to study art at the School of Feodor Rerberg. In 1913, she began studying under Ilya Mashkov, where she stayed until the Revolution. In 1914, the "Knave of Diamonds" exhibition included her work among those of French painters Georges Braque and André Derain, Russian painters Petr Konchalovsky, Aristarkh Lentulov, Kazimir Malevich, Ilya Mashkov, and Alexei Morgunov, and Spanish painter Pablo Picasso. Her paintings were also featured at the "World of Art" exhibition in 1917.

During the 1910s, Sofronova focused on figurative paintings, but by the end of the decade, her style was of a more Expressionist nature, focusing on the abstract and other subjective graphic explorations into the areas of form and color. Her *Portrait of My Daughter* (1919) provides a glimpse into a new approach to art by yielding attention to color and spatial arrangement. During the 1920s, she taught with Mikhail Sokolov at the State Art Studios in Tver.

Her work from this time included Expressionist landscapes and Cubist portraits.

For a brief period Sofronova turned to the graphic designs of production art, aligning herself with Constructivism, a movement that originated in the Soviet Union and is characterized by abstract geometric design. Her later work, however, shows that her foray into Constructivism was merely a phase and not representative of her own philosophy of art.

Sofronova went on to become an artist of the urban landscape, and cities show up as a recurrent theme in her works. She grew to see profound similarities between urban and rural subjects, recognizing not only likeness of form but an inherent organic sameness in which one emerged from the other and could easily return to it. From 1924 to 1925, she completed watercolors and ink drawings titled *Moscow Street Types*. In this series, she juxtaposed the city's down-and-out, the homeless and drunk, with such rural images as sunflowers. By the end of the 1920s, she was still working on Moscow cityscapes, producing a series of paintings noted for their unique use of color and evocative tone. According to **M.N. Yablonskaya**, Sofronova's work during this period reveals the influence of French painter Maurice Utrillo, whose "quiet and nostalgic cityscapes" of Paris had been exhibited in Moscow in 1928.

In 1929, Russian artists influenced by the Impressionist trends came together to form "Group 13" (the number of artists in its first exhibition). The group's goal was to communicate their impressions of nature with immediacy, and they considered their study sketches and watercolors complete works of art. Intrigued by their approach, Sofronova participated in the group's 1931 exhibition, which would be its last because of negative reviews generated by the changing attitude toward art under the Communist system. The Soviet government labeled as "formalist" any work that did not take a realistic approach or lacked what it considered social or political value. Sofronova herself was criticized, and she rarely showed her work in public after a restrictive decree issued by the government abolished all official art groups in 1932. Two years later, Socialist Realism was declared to be the only avenue of expression appropriate for artists in the Soviet Union. Sofronova continued painting but eventually retreated to isolation, dying in 1966.

**SOURCES:**
Yablonskaya, M.N. *Women Artists of Russia's New Age, 1900–1935*. Edited by Anthony Parton. NY: Rizzoli International, 1990.

**Lisa Frick**, freelance writer,
Columbia, Missouri

# Sohier, Elizabeth Putnam

## (1847–1926)

*American advocate for libraries. Born in 1847; died in 1926.*

Elizabeth Putnam Sohier spent her lifetime working for the cause of libraries, recognizing the importance of the institutions in educating the masses. In an era when public libraries were practically nonexistent, Sohier believed that every town should have library service and persuaded the Massachusetts legislature to establish the Free Public Library Commission in 1890. It was the first state agency of its kind in the nation, charged with establishing libraries across the state. Sohier was appointed to the board and served as its secretary until her death 36 years later, faithfully attending every meeting. In its first 14 years, the commission helped form more than 100 libraries, thanks to Sohier's efforts. She had acquaintances in nearly every region of the state and used these contacts to convince important players to join her cause. The governor of Massachusetts once called her the "ablest" politician in the state. Although she herself possessed tremendous clout, she opposed women's suffrage.

A *Mayflower* descendant and member of the Mayflower Society, Sohier also was active in the Woman's Education Association, which furnished traveling libraries, lent picture collections, and published lists of new books for libraries. She also helped found the Library Art Club, which offered traveling collections of pictures, and the Massachusetts Library Aid Association, which handled donations she and her friends made to the library cause. To encourage child literacy, Sohier started a program of awarding certificates to children who read a certain number of books. She also worked for library programs to help immigrants become literate. When the United States became involved in World War I, she persuaded the commission to provide library service for the soldiers. Sohier died in 1926, leaving $1,000 to the Woman's Education Association, $5,000 to the library commission, and $10,000 to the Beverly Public Library, where she had served as a trustee for 30 years.

**SOURCES:**
Danton, Emily Miller, ed. *Pioneering Leaders in Librarianship*. Boston, MA: Gregg Press, 1972.

**Lisa Frick**, freelance writer,
Columbia, Missouri

# Soissons, countess of.

*See Mancini, Olympia (c. 1639–1708).*

## Soissons, queen of.

See Fredegund (c. 547–597).

## Sojourner Truth (c. 1797–1883).

See Truth, Sojourner.

## Sokolova, Lydia (1896–1974)

*English dancer who performed with Sergei Diaghilev's Ballet Russe, the company with which her name is always associated.* Name variations: Hilda Munnings; stage name at first Hilda Munningsova, then Lydia Sokolova; Mrs. Nicholas Kremnev. Born Hilda Munnings in Wanstead, Essex, England, on March 4, 1896; died at Sevenoaks, England, on February 5, 1974; received her early training at Steadman's Academy in London; studied under Anna Pavlova and other Russian dancers; married Nicholas Kremnev (a dancer), in 1917; children: daughter, **Natasha Kremnev** (b. 1917).

Made debut in the pantomime Alice in Wonderland *(1910); toured the U.S. with Mikhail Mordkin's Imperial Russian Ballet (1911–12); toured Germany and Austria-Hungary with the Theodore Kosloff Company (1912–13); danced with the Ballet Russe of Sergei Diaghilev (1913–29), appearing as The Polovetsian Maid in* Polovetsian Dances *from* Prince Igor, *in* Les Sylphides, *and as a nymph in* L'Après-midi d'un Faune *(1913–14), as Papillon in* Le Carnaval *and in* Le Soleil de Nuit *(1915), in* Las Meninas *(1916), as Ta-Hor in* Cléopatre, *as a bacchante in* Narcisse, *as Kikimora in* Contes Russes, *as the Apple Woman in* Til Eulenspiegel *(1917), as the Tarantella dancer in* La Boutique Fantasque, *in the finale of* Le Tricorne *(1919), as the Chosen Virgin in* Le Sacre du Printemps, *as Death in* Le Chant du Rossignol, *as the Miller's Wife in* Le Tricorne, *in a character pas de deux in* Le Astuzie Femminili *(1920), as La Bouffonne in* Chout, *as the Cherry Blossom fairy and Red Riding Hood in* The Sleeping Princess *(1921); was a principal dancer in the London revue* You'd be Surprised *(1923); appeared as Chloe in* Daphnis and Chloe, *as Chanson dansée in* Les Biches, *as the sorceress in* Night on Bald Mountain, *as Perlouse in* Le Train Bleu, *and as a principle dancer in* Les Sylphides *(1924); appeared as a muse in* Zéphire et Flore, *as The Friend in* Les Matelots, *as a soloist in* Polovetsian Dances *(1926), as the Nurse in* Romeo and Juliet, *as a goddess in* Triumph of Neptune *(1926), as a dancer in* Le Bal *(1929); retired (1929); reemerged to perform with the Woizikowsky Company (1935), and in the Ivor Novello musical* Crest of the Wave *(1937); choreographed* Russki-Plasski *for the Ballet de la Jeunesse Anglaise (1939); retired again; returned as the Marquise Silvestra in* The Good-Humoured Ladies *(1962).*

Born Hilda Munnings in Wanstead, Essex, England, on March 4, 1896, Lydia Sokolova is best known for being the first British dancer to be offered a permanent contract with the Ballet Russe, the celebrated Russian company of Sergei Diaghilev. Though self-deprecating as a dancer, she was by most accounts better than she believed herself to be and was highly regarded as one of the best character dancers with the Diaghilev company.

Although she was related to Sir Alfred Munnings, the British painter of horses and once president of the Royal Academy, there was little in Hilda Munnings' background to suggest that her future would involve an artistic career. As a young girl, she studied piano and reached the point of passing serious examinations when she began taking dance lessons at Steadman's Academy in Great Windmill Street. After about a year of exposure to classical ballet, she made her

*Lydia Sokolova*

debut in the corps de ballet of a production of the Christmas pantomime *Alice in Wonderland* at the Savoy Theater in London in 1910. Soon after, she saw *Anna Pavlova (1881–1931) dancing with Mikhail Mordkin (1881–1944) at the Palace Theater in 1911. At first her parents were unable to understand her excitement over Pavlova and the fact that she was spending her lunch money on repeated matinee tickets to see her idol, but at her pleading they went to see Pavlova for themselves. After watching her perform, they agreed to support their daughter's goal of becoming a professional dancer. Hilda's father wrote to Mordkin to arrange for dance lessons with him at the then high sum of five guineas an hour (worth about $25 at that time).

*I* never have been and never could be a classical ballerina, but the fun I had taking such different roles by choreographers of such varied genius, was more rewarding . . . than all the laurels and fortunes of Pavlova.

—Lydia Sokolova

Soon after Hilda began her lessons, however, Mordkin and Pavlova quarreled, and Pavlova broke with him. Most of Mordkin's dancers, the majority of them Polish, took his side in the dispute and, under his management, formed a company of their own, grandiosely titled The All-Star Imperial Russian Ballet. They went into rehearsal at once. Fortunately, the company was made up of some of the finest dancers then appearing outside of Russia, including besides Mordkin and his wife **Bronislava Pozhitskaya**, such performers as Kühn, Morosa, Schmoltz, **Ekaterina Gelzer** and **Julia Sedova**, and was able to secure a tour of the United States. When one of the six English dancers whom Mordkin had hired to flesh out his ensemble took sick ten days prior to departure, Mordkin replaced her with the 15-year-old Hilda Munnings.

The company, which sailed on the *President Lincoln* in 1911, was immediately dogged by misfortune. After a successful though short engagement at the Metropolitan Opera House in New York, during which they performed *Swan Lake, Giselle, Copéllia*, and *Russian Wedding and Grands Divertissements*, the company set out on tour. Jealousies among the dancers over billing and over who was the prima ballerina plagued the tour, and one by one the dancers dropped out. By the time the company returned to New York, there was hardly anyone but the English girls left in the cast. At this point, the Moscow-born dancer Alexandre Volinine

(1882–1955), who had previously arrived in America on a ballet tour sponsored by the impresario Charles Frohman, took it upon himself to form a second company with the six English girls. *Lydia Lopokova, also in America with Frohman, joined somewhat later as a soloist. The second company fared no better than the first and ended with the cast being stranded in New Orleans. Eventually, Hilda succeeded in returning to England after having danced in 120 towns in seven months and often giving two performances in a single day in two different localities.

Upon her return to London in 1912, Hilda immediately secured a position with Theodore Kosloff's family troupe, performing with Kosloff himself at the London Coliseum and then on tour in Germany and Austria-Hungary. In April of the following year, she was accepted into Diaghilev's company, the Ballet Russe. Here she found her professional home, remaining with the company until Diaghilev's death in 1929, leaving it only occasionally to perform in various London productions (1914–15) and some outside productions of Léonide Massine's company (1922–23).

The quarter century between 1890 and the First World War was of overwhelming importance both in the history of Western civilization and in the emergence of the modern world, the era that saw the coming of the automobile, aircraft, motion picture, and radio, the triumph of the electric light, phonograph, and telephone; the era that produced the major works of Einstein, Freud, Shaw, Proust, and a host of other authors; the era that gave us Picasso in art, Stravinsky in music, and innovators in every field of human endeavor. The role of the great transformer in dance at this time belongs to Sergei Diaghilev (1872–1929), who, while neither a dancer nor a choreographer himself, had an uncanny gift for recognizing new and exciting talents and with exquisite taste and extravagant flair developed a new world of classical ballet for the new 20th century. Patronized by the imperial family, Diaghilev brought Russian ballet to the Western world—not the traditional ballet of the Bolshoi and Marinsky theaters but a fresh, exciting ballet that explored fresh ground in choreography, music and theatrical presentation. Founded in Paris in 1909, his Ballet Russe from the beginning gathered together the most innovative choreographers: Michel Fokine, Léonide Massine, Vaslav Nijinsky, his sister *Bronislava Nijinska, and a very young George Balanchine; the newest dancers: Anna Pavlova, *Tamara Karsavina, Gelzer, Mordkin, Adolph Bolm and, again, Nijinsky and his sister; the most contemporary composers: Rimsky-Korsakoff, Ravel, Debussy, Milhaud, Poulenc, Richard Strauss and the then avant-garde Igor Stravinsky and Sergei Prokofiev; and young and exciting scenery and costume designers drawn from the broader world of art: Picasso, Utrillo, Braque, Miro, Matisse, and especially Leon Bakst. Together these artists dazzled first Paris and then all of Europe with their lavish productions of such exotic new ballets as *The Firebird, Les Sylphides, Schéhérazade, Petrouchka, Spectre de la Rose,* and *Le Sacre du Printemps,* which created a riot in the theater at its first performance in Paris in 1913. It was into this brilliant, glittering and exotic new world of 20th-century ballet that the not quite 17-year-old English girl Hilda Munnings walked when she joined the Diaghilev company in Monte Carlo in April 1913.

Under the aegis of Diaghilev, Hilda was at first dubbed Hilda Munningsova, but in 1915 he personally rechristened her Lydia Sokolova in honor of the Russian dancer **Anna Sokolova** whom he much admired. This would be her professional name for the rest of her career. Diaghilev was difficult to work with, restless, moody, ever seeking novelty. Since most of the company consisted of Russians who spoke no English, the newly baptized Lydia Sokolova was forced to learn at least some Russian while she absorbed the myriad other lessons, techniques and impressions nearly overwhelming her on every side. Sokolova had already taken lessons from Pavlova, Ivan Custine, and Alexandre Shiryaev, and now came under the discipline of the great Enrico Cecchetti. Following the advice of Shiryaev, she learned everything that she could from her Russian colleagues. Shiryaev had a particularly important influence on Sokolova's career, because it was he who urged her to concentrate on character parts which were to become her great forte.

Above all, Sokolova trained under Léonide Massine, who dominated the choreography of the Ballet Russe from 1917 until he was supplanted by Nijinska in the '20s, to the extent that in time she became known as a Massine dancer. Massine emphasized character dancing, and, struck by Sokolova's strength, endurance and striking stage personality, choreographed several major parts for her and assigned her the most difficult roles, the most important of which was that of the Chosen Virgin in his staging of *Le Sacre du Printemps* (1920). Previously Massine had created the role of the Tarantella dancer for her in *La Boutique Fantasque* and the Miller's Wife in *Le Tricorne* (both in 1919), and

later he would create for her the roles of Death in *Le Chant du Rossignol* (1920), the Tarentella dancer in *Le Astuzie Femminili* (both in 1920), and The Friend in *Les Matelots* (1925).

After the death of Diaghilev in 1929, his company broke up, and at 33 Sokolova's career as a dancer came virtually though not entirely to an end. She devoted the rest of her active years to teaching, arranging, and later to assisting the Royal Academy of Dancing. In 1935, she came out of retirement to appear in London as the leading dancer with the company of Leon Woizikowsky, an old colleague from her Diaghilev days, and in 1939 again in London she choreographed *Russki-Plasski* for **Lydia Kyasht's** Ballet de la Jeunesse Anglaise. In 1942, she choreographed *The Silver Birch.* She also gave lectures and wrote occasional articles on the Diaghilev years, but she is best remembered for her sober account of life with the Ballet Russe in her memoir *Dancing for Diaghilev.* In 1962, she agreed to appear in a revival of the ballet *The Good-Humoured Ladies,* taking the pantomime role of the Marquise Silvestra.

Lydia Sokolova may not have been a great ballerina but she was certainly a great character dancer whose gifted interpretations made her one of the perennial and most important ornaments of the Ballet Russe. Though her pirouettes en point may have been less than impressive, she learned marvelous control from Pavlova, the Dalcroze method of Eurythmics from Nijinsky, and was blessed with technical brilliance, excellent timing, and a great comic sense. Her elevation, learned from her Russian colleagues, was also excellent, and her vigorous and forceful style enabled her to take on the most demanding roles originally devised by Bronislava Nijinska for herself. Lydia Sokolova died at Sevenoaks, Kent, on February 5, 1974, at age 78.

**SOURCES:**
Anderson, John. *Dance.* New York, 1974.
Music Collection, Free Library of Philadelphia.
Sokolova, Lydia. *Dancing for Diaghilev.* Edited by Richard Buckle. London, 1960.

**SUGGESTED READING:**
Buckle, Richard. *In the Wake of Diaghilev.* New York, 1983.
Garafola, Lynn. *Diaghilev's Ballet Russes.* New York, 1989.

**Robert H. Hewsen,** Professor of History, Rowan University, Glassboro, New Jersey

# Sokolow, Anna (1910–2000)

*American choreographer and teacher who was an innovator in the field of modern dance and introduced modern dance to Mexico and Israel. Born on February 9, 1910, in Hartford, Connecticut; died on March*

*29, 2000, at her home in Manhattan; daughter of Samuel Sokolow and Sara (Cohen) Sokolow; never married; no children.*

*Studied dance with Martha Graham and choreography with Louis Horst at the Neighborhood Playhouse; was a dancer with Graham's first company, the Graham Dance Company (1929–37); assisted Horst in dance composition classes; formed her own company, the Dance Unit (1933); studied ballet with Margaret Curtis at the Metropolitan Opera House (1938); taught at Herbert Berghof acting studio, the American National Theater and Academy, and the Juilliard School, in addition to numerous universities, including Ohio State University, University of Utah, City College, and New York University.*

Anna Sokolow, who enjoyed a lengthy and prodigious international career that changed the course of modern dance, was born in 1910, in Hartford, Connecticut, to Polish immigrants. She spent her childhood in New York City where, after her father Samuel's death, her mother **Sara Cohen Sokolow** worked in the garment industry and became an early member of the International Ladies' Garment Workers Union. Sokolow became interested in dance after observing a settlement house class and, against her mother's wishes, began to take lessons herself. She studied with Bird Larson at the Emanuel Sisterhood Settlement until the age of ten, when she was sent to study with **Blanche Talmud** at the Neighborhood Playhouse. By her mid-teens she was a student in classes at the Neighborhood Playhouse. It was there that *Martha Graham and Louis Horst (Graham's musical director and the first teacher of modern dance choreography in the United States) were exploring their theories of modern dance. A student of the Children's Professional Company at the Neighborhood Playhouse, Sokolow studied with Graham and Horst and became Horst's assistant.

In 1929, at age 19, Sokolow joined the Graham Dance Company, where she performed many important solo roles. At the same time, she also danced with the Workers Dance League, which sponsored her own company, the Dance Unit. Her work in the 1930s focused primarily on social issues related to the Depression. In 1934, she toured the Soviet Union with the Dance Unit but met with resistance on the part of the classically trained Russians, who preferred ballet. Sokolow and the Dance Unit made their Broadway debut in 1937 at the Guild House, in a concert sponsored by the *New Masses*. Sokolow left Graham's company in 1938 to study ballet with **Margaret Curtis** at the Metro-

politan Opera House. A year later, she assisted with choreography for the WPA Federal Theater Project's *Sing for Your Supper*, which enjoyed a successful run in New York City.

Attracting critical attention by this time, Sokolow accepted an invitation to take her company to Mexico City for a six-week engagement, after which she agreed to stay on and teach at the Mexico City Opera and Ballet. Finding Mexican audiences more receptive to the dramatic elements in her work than the Russians, Sokolow formed the first modern-dance group in Mexico and began to weave Mexican themes into her work. She stayed in Mexico for a year and afterwards returned regularly for the next several years to train dancers. In the early 1950s, Sokolow received another international invitation, sponsored by the American Fund for Israel Institutions, to teach at the Inbal Theater Dance Company, a Yemenite dance group in Israel. As in Mexico, her unique talents led to bigger projects and repeated visits to Israel. In 1962, she founded the Lyric Theater there, largely as the result of her teaching, choreographing, and written proposals to the government. This company pioneered the development of several other modern-dance groups in Israel. Sokolow was acknowledged as the founder of modern dance in both Israel and Mexico.

Anna Sokolow's distinguished work for the Broadway stage included the choreography for the 1947 musical *Street Scene*, with a libretto by Kurt Weill, based on the 1929 Pulitzer Prize-winning play by Elmer Rice. She also choreographed Marc Blitzstein's *Regina*, Tennessee Williams' *Camino Real*, and Leonard Bernstein's *Candide*, plus the Public Theater's original off-Broadway production of the rock musical *Hair* in 1967. In her 1961 piece *Dreams*, Sokolow delved for subject matter into the subconscious and its unleashed demons of the dream world as she reflected upon the victims of Nazi horrors. Her most significant and abiding work, however, is 1955's *Rooms*, with a jazz score by Kenyon Hopkins, which deals with the crushing loneliness that individuals can endure. Critics recognized that in the universality of its theme, Sokolow had created a masterpiece. In the late 1950s, *Rooms* was presented on national television.

Despite the tendency of critics to recognize Sokolow solely for her socially significant choreography, she did not so limit herself. Her dramatic, comedic, and lyric work includes a vast array of expression beyond her frequent theme of alienation, and such notable companies as the Joffrey Ballet, Ballet Rambert, José Limon Company, and others include her works in their repertoire. Her talent was officially recognized by several honorary degrees and prestigious awards, including an American Dancer Award (1938); a *Dance Magazine* award (1961); senior Fulbright scholarships to Japan (1966) and England (1975); the Creative Arts Medal from Brandeis University and the Tarbut Medal from the America-Israel Cultural Foundation (both 1974); the Aztec Eagle—the highest Mexican civilian honor given to a foreigner (1988); and the Samuel E. Scripps Lifetime Achievement Award (1991). In 1998, Sokolow was inducted into the C.V. Whitney Hall of Fame at the National Museum of Dance. She died at the age of 90 at her home in New York City on March 29, 2000.

### SOURCES:

*Current Biography 1969*. NY: H.W. Wilson, 1969.

Uglow, Jennifer, ed. *International Dictionary of Women's Biography*. NY: Continuum, 1989.

Warren, Larry. *Anna Sokolow: The Rebellious Spirit*. Harwood Academic, 1991.

**Lisa Frick**, freelance writer,
Columbia, Missouri

## Solano, Solita (1888–1975)

*American novelist, journalist, editor, and translator. Born Sarah Wilkinson in Troy, New York, in 1888; died in Orgeval, France, on November 22, 1975; daughter of Almadus Wilkinson (a lawyer); attended *Emma Willard's School in Troy, New York, and Sacred Heart Convent; married Oliver Filley, in 1904 (marriage annulled, 1913); no children.*

*Lived in the Philippines (1904–08); tried stage career, New York (1908); had career as journalist in Boston and New York (1914–20); met Janet Flanner (winter 1918–19); was on assignment for* National Geographic *magazine in Europe (1921–22); settled in Paris (fall 1922); met Nancy Cunard (fall 1924); was secretary to George I. Gurdjieff, Russian mystic (1932); was a reporter for* Detroit Athletic Club News *(1932); returned to U.S. (October 1939); returned to France (1952, 1954–75).*

*Selected writings: "Paris between the Wars: An Unpublished Memoir," in* The Quarterly Journal of the Library of Congress *(vol. 34, 1977, pp. 308–314);* The Uncertain Feast *(NY: Putnam, 1924);* The Happy Failure *(NY: Putnam, 1925);* This Way Up *(NY: Putnam, 1927);* Statue in a Field *(Paris?, 1934); "Nancy Cunard: Brave Poet, Indomitable Rebel," in* Nancy Cunard: Brave Poet, Indomitable Rebel, 1896–1965 *(edited by Hugh Ford, Philadelphia: Chilton, 1968).*

Solita Solano was strong-willed, independent, and exotic-looking. She rebelled against her puritanical, patriarchical middle-class family, loved women and travel, and lived much of her adult life in Paris, France. Her ambition was to become a writer, but her novels "had the honor of not pleasing most critics."

Solano was born in Troy, New York, in 1888 and christened Sarah Wilkinson, but "she hated her Anglo-Saxon birth name with its upstate associations," and adopted the name of a fictitious Spanish grandmother. Her childhood was not happy; her father disapproved of her literary ambitions and locked up his library to prevent her from reading his books. Solano felt she was ugly and less favored than her younger brothers. In 1934, she expressed this in a poem: "Is this a daughter?/ . . . Can't you act like your brother?/ . . . No one asks you to be beautiful/ No one wants you with a brain/ A damnable thing for a woman." Moreover, formal education did not appeal to her; sent to a convent school "for more discipline," Solano lied, stole, and read forbidden books.

When her father died in 1903, Solano's portion of the estate was entrusted to her two younger brothers to administer. And she was forbidden to marry without the consent of her mother or brothers (or their heirs) or she would forfeit her inheritance. In 1904, she eloped with Oliver Filley, an engineer with the Bureau of Public Works in the Philippines. During the next four years, Solano "surveyed land, plotted maps" and helped construct roads in the Philippines; she also learned three Malay languages, was prominent in the social life of Manila, and traveled to China and Japan. The marriage failed, and Solano escaped by climbing out of a bedroom window during the night. In 1913, the marriage was annulled, but she still had lost any claim to her inheritance.

Back in the States, Solita tried to become an actor in New York, but soon realized she had no real talent. She then moved to Boston where she worked for several years as a reporter, feature editor, drama critic, and editor for the Boston *Traveler*, and later for the Boston *Journal*. Success in journalism did not, however, satisfy her desire to "write truly great fiction." In late 1918, she went to New York to work for the *Tribune* and began writing short stories based on her experiences in the Philippines. And she met and fell in love with *Janet Flanner. Solano became, claims one historian, "the first great—and in many ways undiminished—love of Janet's life."

Flanner adored Solano who was "worldly and elegant and lovely," spoke Spanish and Italian fluently, had published short stories, and was an admired journalist. According to **Brenda Wineapple**, Solano wanted "beauty and passion and rapture" in her life, and to "defy time's laws for love and loveliness." With Flanner, Solano fulfilled her desire.

Solita went to Greece and Constantinople on assignment for *National Geographic* in 1921, accompanied by Flanner who had left her husband (they later divorced). After finishing Solano's travel assignments in Europe, the women decided to settle in Paris (in 1922) where they hoped to become part of French life, not just live on the margins as so many expatriates did. They settled into the Hôtel Bonaparte on the Left Bank (in 1977, Solita wrote a short memoir of the 16 years they lived there) and spent each afternoon and early evening working on their novels. Both women disliked domesticity and never set up regular housekeeping. Among their many famous acquaintances in Paris were James Joyce, F. Scott Fitzgerald, Ernest Hemingway (whose "male histrionics," they thought, were "childish"), *Natalie Clifford Barney, and *Gertrude Stein; women played a major role in their lives, especially the wealthy English owner of the Hours Press, *Nancy Cunard. The three women became "a fixed triangle," and as Solita noted, they "survived all the spring quarrels and the sea changes of forty-two years of modern female fidelity." Solano had achieved the sexual and economic freedom she had sought by defying social convention and living by her own rules.

However, Solita was less successful in her literary career; she published three novels between 1924 and 1927, none of which sold well, and returned to journalism. The novels all dealt with "a fundamental ugliness and decay in the hearts and minds of modern human beings," and with "the failures of human relationships." Solano now turned to writing articles about Paris for the *Detroit Athletic Club News* as Flanner (under the pen name Genêt) did for *The New Yorker*. During the 1930s, fascism was threatening to destabilize Europe, and Solano regretted that even Paris was changing. A friend introduced her to the charismatic Russian mystic George Gurdjieff, who had founded a spiritual community at Fontainebleau-Avon. At first, Solano was not impressed, but she was seeking "something otherworldly and romantic" and finally became one of his disciples, serving as Gurdjieff's secretary for five years.

In September 1939, France and England went to war with Germany, and on October 15, Solano and Flanner sailed from Bordeaux to America. They took up residence in a hotel in New York, but Solano was depressed. Leaving France had been difficult, and Flanner had a new lover. Solita knew that she was "about to lose Janet." To aid the war effort, Solano joined the American Women's Volunteer Services which trained women to serve in war-related jobs. However, she felt she had lost direction. She no longer had the urge to write, and she felt "homeless" and wanted "an entirely new life." Solano had a new companion, **Elizabeth Jenks Clark**, known as Lib, but she still remained in touch with Flanner and helped manage her finances. Solano loved Paris where she and Flanner had been happy together, but how could she return "to those scenes where all is so changed, so lonely, where all my heart, in pieces now, will ever be."

In the early 1950s, Solano and two friends bought a house in Orgeval, outside of Paris. Flanner had also returned to France after the war, and Solano again was involved in editing Flanner's "Letters from Paris" for *The New Yorker*. Solano now led a quiet, more sedentary life, pursuing her interest in etymology and occasionally doing editing work. In 1966, John C. Broderick, chief of the Manuscripts Division of the Library of Congress, contacted Janet Flanner and, later, Solano about donating their papers to the Library. Flanner did not want to undertake the task, but agreed to make their papers available. Solano spent the last decade of her life collecting and organizing the private and professional documents that comprise the Flanner-Solano Papers in the Library of Congress. Broderick describes this as Solano's "memorial."

By the early 1970s, Solita acknowledged that she was "being erased" from Janet's life. But the "fixed triangle" that had bound Solano, Flanner, and Cunard together in "modern female fidelity" is preserved in the collections of their papers.

**SOURCES:**
Chisholm, Anne. *Nancy Cunard: A Biography*. NY: Alfred A. Knopf, 1979.
*Dictionary of Literary Biography*, Vol. 4: *American Writers in Paris, 1920–1939*. Edited by Karen Lane Rood. Detroit, MI: Gale Research, 1980.
Wineapple, Brenda. *Genêt: A Biography of Janet Flanner*. NY: Ticknor & Fields, 1989.

**COLLECTIONS:**
The Flanner-Solano Papers are located in the Library of Congress.

**Jeanne A. Ojala**,
Visiting Scholar, Department of History,
University of Minnesota, Minneapolis, Minnesota;
Professor Emerita, Department of History,
University of Utah, Salt Lake City, Utah

# Solms, princess de.

*See Rute, Mme de (1831–1902).*

# Solms, Thérèse de (1840–1907).

*See Blanc, Marie-Thérèse.*

# Solntseva, Yulia (1901–1989)

*Russian actress and director. Name variations: Iuliia Ippolitovna Solntseva; Yuliya Solntseva. Born on August 7, 1901, in Moscow, Russia; died in October 1989; studied philosophy at Moscow University; graduated from the State Institute of Music and Drama in Moscow; married Aleksandr Dovzhenko, in 1927 (died 1956).*

*Filmography (as actress): Aelita (1924); Cigarette-Girl from Mosselprom (1924); Earth/Soil (1930).*

*Filmography (as director): Shchors (1939); Liberation (1940); Bucovina-Ukrainian Land (1940); The Battle for Our Soviet Ukraine (Ukraine in Flames, 1943); Victory in the Ukraine and the Expulsion of the Germans from the Boundaries of the Ukrainian Soviet Earth (1945); Life in Bloom (1948); Egor Bulytchev and Others (1953); Unwilling Inspectors (Reluctant Inspectors, 1955); Poem of the Sea (Poem of an Inland Sea, 1958); Story of the Turbulent Years (The Flaming Years or Chronicle of Flaming Years, 1961); The Enchanted Desna (1965); The Unforgettable (Ukraine in Flames, 1968); The Golden Gate (1969); Such High Mountains (1974); The World in Three Dimensions (1979).*

Born in Moscow in 1901, Yulia Solntseva was considered one of the most beautiful actresses of the Soviet Union's post-Revolution years. According to **Oksana Bulgakova** in Lynne Attwood's *Red Women on the Silver Screen*, the melodramas in which these beautiful actresses starred did not disappear after the Revolution, rather they "underwent their own socialist revolution" and became vehicles for revealing social evils or Western decadence. Solntseva gained fame in 1924 when she performed the title role of the barely dressed Martian princess in Yakov Protazanov's science-fiction melodrama *Aelita*, and as the cigarette girl in Yuri Zhelyabuzhsky's *Cigarette-Girl from Mosselprom*. Her role in the latter, that of a beauty who becomes a film actress and falls in love with a cinematographer, suggests Rob Edelman, was a re-enactment of her own relationship with director Aleksandr Dovzhenko, whom she married in 1927. She made her final appearance on screen in Dovzhenko's *Earth/Soil* in 1930.

*Earth/Soil* was the beginning of a lifelong collaboration between the two as co-directors of several films. Edelman believes that the entire body of Solntseva's work bears the influ-

ence, if not the outright imprint, of Dovzhenko, who with Sergei Eisenstein and Vsevolod Pudovkin, was a genius of Russian filmmaking. Solntseva's most notable early works are documentaries that focus on the Ukraine and the beginnings of World War II. In 1940, she was the sole director of the documentary *Bucovina-Ukrainian Land*, which followed the movement of the Russian army into the Western Ukraine and Byelorussia after Germany invaded Poland. She then collaborated with Yakov Avdeyenko on the 1943 film *The Battle for Our Soviet Ukraine*, and with Dovzhenko on the 1945 *Victory in the Ukraine and the Expulsion of the Germans from the Boundaries of the Ukrainian Soviet Earth*. Edelman posits that even in these films, the images of serenity contrasted with the devastation of war "clearly are reflective of Dovzhenko's aesthetic."

When Dovzhenko died of a heart attack in 1956, he had been working on *Poem of an Inland Sea*, the first part of a trilogy about a Ukrainian village. Solntseva committed herself to its completion, and the work eventually received the Lenin Prize. She further dedicated herself to finishing and filming all of Dovzhenko's unrealized work, sublimating her own creative perspective to it. Although critics tend to assess Solntseva's work in terms of her husband's aesthetic vision, Edelman acknowledges that in the early 1950s, prior to Dovzhenko's death, Solntseva did turn to eminent theater companies in Russia to film short plays that they had produced. She also created *The Golden Gate*, a 1969 film about her relationship with the director, and in 1974, she made a film in which Dovzhenko did not figure—*Such High Mountains*, which focused on education. Film critics propose that this body of independent work provides insight into what Solntseva might have consistently produced had she not relied so heavily on her husband's artistic inspiration. "At the very least," concludes a contributor to *Women Film Directors*, Solntseva ought to be remembered as a "co-creator" of her husband's films, "and a woman who never received the credit due her for her considerable contribution to the art of Soviet cinema." Named an Honored Artist of the Republic in 1935, she died in 1989.

**SOURCES:**

Attwood, Lynn. *Red Women on the Silver Screen: Soviet Women and Cinema from the Beginning to the End of the Communist Era*. London: Pandora, 1993, pp. 145, 151–152.

Edelman, Rob. "Yulia Solntseva," in *Women Filmmakers and Their Films*. Edited by Amy Unterburger. Detroit, MI: St. James Press, 1998.

Katz, Ephraim. *The Film Encyclopedia.* NY: Harper-Collins, 1994.

*Women Film Directors: An International Bio-critical Dictionary.* Edited by Gwendolyn A. Foster. Westport, CT: Greenwood Press, 1995.

**Lisa Frick**, freelance writer,
Columbia, Missouri

# Solomon, Hannah Greenebaum

## (1858–1942)

*American welfare worker and community activist. Born on January 14, 1858, in Chicago, Illinois; died on December 7, 1942, in Chicago; fourth of ten children of Michael Greenebaum and Sarah (Spiegel) Greenebaum; attended public schools; studied piano with Carl Wolfsohn; married Henry Solomon, on May 14, 1879 (died 1913); children: Herbert, Helen, and Frank.*

*Was one of the first Jewish members of the Chicago Woman's Club (1877); participated in the founding of the National Council of Jewish Women and became its first president (1890–1905); co-founded the Illinois Federation of Women's Clubs (1896); was a founding member of Women's City Club (1910). Author of A Sheaf of Leaves (1911) and Fabric of My Life (1946).*

Hannah
Greenebaum
Solomon

Born in Chicago, Illinois, in 1858, Hannah Greenebaum Solomon was the fourth of ten children born to Michael and **Sarah Greenebaum,** who had immigrated to the United States from the German Palatinate a decade earlier. A successful hardware merchant, her father was also an influential person within the local Jewish community. Her parents belonged to Chicago's first Reform Judaic congregation and Hannah attended Temple school for her early education. After completing her secondary studies at West Division (Chicago's only public high school) in 1873, she studied piano with Carl Wolfsohn, and took an interest in the local arts scene.

Solomon maintained an active involvement in Jewish social and cultural organizations, which introduced her to many of Chicago's influential women. In 1877, she and her sister **Henriette Frank** became the first Jewish members of the Chicago Woman's Club (CWC). Although she reduced her community activity following her 1879 marriage to merchant Henry Solomon and the births of her three children, Hannah returned to public life in 1890 to help prepare for the World's Columbian Exposition to be held in Chicago in 1893.

Solomon was recruited to organize a national Jewish Women's Congress (JWC) to participate in the Parliament of Religions for the Exposition. Uniting Jewish women from across the United States for the first time, she urged them to continue their organization beyond the end of the fair, thus creating the permanent National Council of Jewish Women (NCJW). Solomon was elected the organization's first president and, under her leadership, more than 50 local chapters were established within 6 years. Together with *Susan B. Anthony and *May Wright Sewall, she also represented the National Council of Women at the convention of the International Council of Women in Berlin in 1904. Upon her retirement as president in 1905, the group named her honorary president for life.

Active in the formation of the Illinois Federation of Women's Clubs (IFWC) in 1896, Solomon also participated in numerous local community service projects, including provision of aid and assistance to Russian Jews and other immigrants to Chicago throughout the 1890s. Solomon conducted a survey of the needs and facilities available to Chicago immigrants in 1896, and used funds raised by the Chicago chapter of the NCJW to establish the Bureau of Personal Service, which provided legal and other support to recent arrivals. Because of the close proximity of the Jewish community to Hull House, Solomon also had the opportunity to work with *Jane Addams on behalf of the community's children. As well, she was instrumental in creating the first Cook County Juvenile Court in 1899.

After retiring from the NCJW presidency in 1905, Solomon began her affiliation with the Illinois Industrial School for Girls, which was renamed the Park Ridge School for Girls in 1907. She was instrumental in relocating the school to improved facilities. Solomon continued her activities in other areas of community service, founding the Women's City Club (WCC) in 1910 to promote social welfare and improved public health. She was named chair of the new club's committee investigating Chicago's waste disposal system.

In 1911, Solomon published *A Sheaf of Leaves,* a collection of her speeches. She remained active in community service until the early 1920s, then she retired to travel and further explore her interest in music and the arts. She died on December 7, 1942, in Chicago. Her autobiography, *Fabric of My Life*, was published posthumously in 1946.

**SOURCES:**

James, Edward T., ed. *Notable American Women, 1607–1950.* Cambridge, MA: The Belknap Press of Harvard University, 1971.

McHenry, Robert, ed. *Famous American Women.* NY: Dover, 1980.

**Grant Eldridge**, freelance writer,
Pontiac, Michigan

# Solomonia

*Grand princess of Moscow. Name variations: Salome Saburova. Daughter of Yuri Saborov; became first wife of Vasili also known as Basil III Ivanovich (1479–1534), grand prince of Moscow (r. 1505–1534), on September 4, 1505 (divorced in 1526); no children. Following her divorce, Solomonia was sent to a convent.*

## Solov'era, Poliksena (1867–1924).

*See Teffi, N.A. for sidebar.*

# Somer, Hilde (1922–1979)

*Austrian pianist known for her performances of modern works and her innovative concert techniques. Born in Vienna, Austria, on February 11, 1922; died in Freeport, the Bahamas, on December 24, 1979.*

Hilde Somer was born in Vienna in 1922 and studied with her mother, a talented musician. Her family fled the Nazis in 1938 and, once settled in the United States, Somer continued her musical education with Rudolf Serkin at the Curtis Institute of Music in Philadelphia. She also took private lessons from Claudio Arrau. Specializing in modern piano music, Somer succeeded brilliantly with the largely neglected Latin American repertoire. She brought such extraordinary compositions as Juan José Castro's *Sonatina española* to the attention of the musical public. She also commissioned a number of piano concertos from contemporary composers, including John Corigliano, Jr. (1968) and Antonio Tauriello (1968), and made several acclaimed recordings of music by the Argentinean composer Alberto Ginastera (1973). In 1978, always eager to experiment with new concepts in music, she performed a "Spatial Concerto" by Henry Brant. Intrigued by the music of the Russian composer Aleksandr Scriabin, Somer once gave a "light works" recital at Lincoln Center's Alice Tully Hall in New York City that used colored images projected on a screen to create a psychedelic effect, in keeping with the composer's theories of a new artistic synthesis of sounds and colors.

**John Haag**,
Athens, Georgia

## Somers, Ann (1932–1983).

*See Gorham, Kathleen.*

## Somers, Jane (b. 1919).

*See Lessing, Doris.*

# Somerset, Anne (1631–1662)

*English noblewoman. Name variations: Anne Howard. Born in October 1631 at Raglan Castle; died in 1662; daughter of Edward Somerset, 2nd marquess of Worcester, and* **Elizabeth Dormer** *(d. 1635); sister of* **\*Elizabeth Somerset**; *married Henry Howard (1628–1683), 6th duke of Norfolk (r. 1667–1683), in 1652; children: Henry Howard (1655–1701), 7th duke of Norfolk (r. 1683–1701); Thomas Howard;* **Elizabeth Howard** *(d. 1732, who married George Gordon, 1st duke of Gordon). Henry Howard, 6th duke of Norfolk, was also married to* **Jane Bickerton***.*

## Somerset, Blanche (1583–1649).

*See Arundel, Blanche.*

## Somerset, countess of.

*See Beaufort, Joan (c. 1410–1445) for sidebar on Margaret Holland (1385–1429).*

*See Beaufort, Margaret (1443–1509) for sidebar on Beauchamp, Margaret (d. 1482).*

*See Howard, Frances (1593–1632).*

## Somerset, duchess of.

*See Beauchamp, Eleanor (1408–1468).*

*See Stuart, Arabella for sidebar on Frances Devereux (d. 1674).*

*See Percy, Elizabeth (1667–1722).*

*See Seymour, Frances Thynne (1669–1754).*

*See Norton, Caroline for sidebar on Georgiana Seymour (d. 1884).*

# Somerset, Elizabeth (fl. 1650)

*Baroness Powys. Name variations: Elizabeth Herbert; Lady Elizabeth Somerset. Flourished around 1650; daughter of* **Elizabeth Dormer** *(d. 1635) and Edward Somerset, 2nd marquess of Worcester; sister of* **\*Anne Somerset** *(1631–1662); married William Herbert (1617–1696), 1st marquis of Powis, 3rd baron Powis or Powys; children:* **Mary Herbert** *(who married Sir George Maxwell);* **Frances Herbert** *(who married*

*Lord Seaforth); **Anne Herbert** (who married Viscount Carrington); William Herbert, 1st marquis of Powis or Powys; ***Lucy Herbert** (1669–1744); ***Winifred Maxwell** (1672–1749).*

## Somerset, Henrietta (1669–1715)

*Countess of Suffolk. Name variations: Lady Henrietta Somerset; Henrietta Howard. Born in 1669; died on August 2, 1715; daughter of Henry Somerset, 1st duke of Beaufort, and **Mary Capell** (1630–1714); married Henry Horatio O'Brien (1670–1690), Lord O'Brien, on June 24, 1686 (died of smallpox); married Henry Howard (1670–1718), 6th earl of Suffolk (r. 1709–1718), in April 1705; children: (first marriage) Henry O'Brien (b. 1688), 8th earl of Thomond; Elizabeth O'Brien (1689–1689); **Mary O'Brien** (d. 1716); Margaret O'Brien. Henry Howard was also married to Auberie Anne Penelope O'Brien (1668–1703), Lady Walden.*

## Somerset, Henrietta (d. 1726)

*Duchess of Grafton. Name variations: Lady Henrietta Somerset. Died in 1726; daughter of **Rebecca Child** (d. 1712) and Charles Somerset, marquess of Worcester; married Charles Fitzroy (1683–1757), 2nd duke of Grafton (r. 1690–1757); children: Charles Henry Fitzroy (b. 1714), earl of Euston; George Fitzroy, earl of Euston (b. 1715); Augustus Fitzroy (b. 1716); Charles Fitzroy (b. 1718); **Caroline Fitzroy** (d. 1784, who married William Stanhope, 2nd earl of Harrington); ***Isabel Fitzroy** (1726–1782); **Harriet Fitzroy** (d. 1735).*

## Somerset, Lady Henry (1851–1921).

See Somerset, Isabella.

## Somerset, Isabella (1851–1921)

*British philanthropist and temperance leader. Name variations: Lady Henry Somerset; Isabel Somerset; Isabella Caroline Cocks. Born Isabella Caroline Cocks in London, England, on August 3, 1851; died on March 12, 1921; eldest daughter of Charles Somers Cocks (1819–1883), viscount Eastnor and 3rd earl of Somers, and Virginia Pattle (d. 1910); sister of Adeline Cocks (later the duchess of Bedford); married Lord Henry Richard Charles Somerset, on February 6, 1872 (divorced 1878); children: Henry Charles Somers Augustus Somerset (1874–1945).*

*President of British Women's Temperance Association (1890–1903); founded home for inebriate women (1895); president of World's Women's Christian Temperance Union (1898–1906).*

A member of the British nobility, Isabella Somerset was born in London in 1851, the daughter of Charles Somers Cocks, 3rd earl of Somers, and **Virginia Pattle**, whose father was a Bengal civil servant. Isabella was raised with wealth and privilege, enhanced by the friendship her father, a court attendant and member of the House of Lords, maintained with Queen *Victoria. On February 6, 1872, Isabella married Lord Henry Somerset (second son of the 8th duke of Beaufort), who was comptroller of Queen Victoria's household (1874–79) and a member of Parliament for Monmouthshire (1871–80). Four years after the birth of their son, they were divorced, and Isabella retained custody of their child.

Following the death of her father in 1883, Isabella Somerset inherited a large estate in the country at Eastnor, where she lived in a castle, and another large tract in the city tenanted by over 125,000 people. Although she could have lived her life in oblivious splendor, she felt responsible for the welfare of her tenants and devoted much of her time and income to helping them.

Inspired by her father, who had been a scholar, Somerset set to studying the causes of poverty and crime and concluded that the evil underlying much of it was in the traffic in liquor. She took the pledge of total abstinence, and encouraged some of her tenants to do the same, thereby starting a temperance society. In 1895, she founded Duxhurst, a home for inebriate women near Reigate, which was the first institution of its kind in England to treat the women as patients rather than as criminals. She also visited the homes of her tenants, giving Bible readings in their kitchens, and invited mothers to the castle to instruct them in child rearing.

As word of her work spread, Somerset was often asked to speak to groups outside her own domain and began traveling on behalf of her temperance work. In South Wales, she spoke to miners and their families, holding meetings in tents and halls and going into the pits during the midday breaks. In 1890, she became president of the British Women's Temperance Association, a position she held until 1903. Her travels took her to America to attend the World's Women's Christian Temperance Union, of which she served as president from 1898 until 1906.

While in America, she met and became close friends with *Frances E. Willard, the Union's founder and the leader of the National Prohibition Party. Upon her return to England, Somerset attempted to implement some of the methods she had witnessed in the American temperance movement, but with little success. At the end of her presidency of the World's Women's Christian Temperance Union, she devoted the remainder of her life to helping patients at Duxhurst, until her death on March 12, 1921.

SOURCES:

Davis, H.W.C., and J.R.H. Weaver, eds. *The Dictionary of National Biography, 1912–1921.* Oxford University Press.

*Woman: Her Position, Influence, and Achievement throughout the Civilized World.* Springfield, MA: King-Richardson, 1902.

**Malinda Mayer**, writer and editor, Falmouth, Massachusetts

## Somerville, Edith (1858–1949).

*See joint entry under Somerville and Ross.*

# Somerville, Mary Fairfax

## (1780–1872)

*Scottish mathematical physicist and scientific popularizer. Born Mary Fairfax on December 26, 1780, in Jedburgh, Scotland; died on November 29, 1872, in Naples, Italy; interred in the English cemetery in Naples; daughter of Margaret (Chartres) Fairfax (sister-in-law of Dr. Thomas Somerville who wrote* My Own Life and Times*) and William George Fairfax (a vice-admiral); educated by self-study as well as boarding school; married Samuel Greig (a Russian consular agent), in 1804 (died 1807); married her maternal cousin William Somerville (a doctor and inspector of the army medical board), in 1812 (died 1860); children: (first marriage) Woronzow Greig (1805–1865), William Greig (1806–1814); (second marriage) Margaret Farquhar Somerville (1813–1822), Thomas Somerville (1814–1815), Martha Chartres Somerville (b. 1815), Mary Charlotte Somerville (b. 1817).*

*Enrolled at Miss Primrose's Academy for Girls, Musselburgh, Scotland (1789); moved to Edinburgh (1793); moved to London (1805); death of husband (1807), returned to Scotland; awarded silver medal by editors of* Mathematical Repository *magazine (1811); moved to London (1815); experimented with magnetism (1825); submitted paper to the Royal Society (1826); elected to the Royal Astronomical Society and awarded royal pension (1835); moved to Italy (1838); elected member of the American Geographical and Statistical Society (1857); elected member of the American Philosophical Society (1869); Victoria Gold Medal awarded by the Royal Geographical Society (1869); elected to the Italian Geographical Society (1869).*

*Selected publications:* Mechanism of the Heavens *(London: John Murray, 1831);* On the Connection of the Physical Sciences *(London: John Murray, 1834);* Physical Geography *(London: John Murray, 1848);* On Molecular and Microscopic Science *(London: John Murray, 1869).*

In December 1780, **Margaret Chartres Fairfax** was returning from London after bidding farewell to her husband William Fairfax, a Scottish vice-admiral, who was departing on a long sea voyage. When she reached Jedburgh, Scotland, and the house of her sister, Margaret went into labor on the day after Christmas; it was here that Mary Somerville was born.

Mary Somerville grew up in Burntisland, Scotland, a quaint coastal village where licensed beggars, or gaberlunzie men, wore blue coats and still went from door to door. During her father's long absences, the family lived frugally. The Fairfax house stood near the shore, and its garden ran down to the water. Somerville spent many hours exploring the rugged seacoast and observing nature. She wrote:

> I never cared for dolls, and had no one to play with me. I amused myself in the garden,

*Mary Fairfax Somerville*

which was much frequented by birds. I knew most of them, their flight and their habits. . . . We fed the birds when the ground was covered with snow, and opened our windows at breakfast-time to let in the robins, who would hop on the table to pick up crumbs. The quantity of song birds was very great, for the farmers and gardeners were less cruel and avaricious than they are now—though poorer.

Upon his return from sea, William was shocked to discover that his daughter, although nine years of age, could neither read nor write proficiently. The family resolved to send Mary to Miss Primrose's Academy for Girls in Musselburgh. It was a period of her life which Somerville remembered less than fondly. The clothing she was forced to wear struck her as strange. "I was enclosed in stiff stays with a steel busk in front, while above my frock, bands drew my shoulders back till the shoulder blades met. Then a steel rod, with a semi-circle which went under my chin, was clasped to the steel busk in my stays. In this constrained state I and most of the younger girls, had to prepare our lessons."

If the clothing at Miss Primrose's was less than satisfactory, Mary Somerville found the curriculum equally so. Contemporary education for women consisted chiefly of developing minimal literacy skills, in order that they might read the Bible and keep household accounts. "The chief thing I had to do was to learn by heart a page of Johnson's dictionary," she wrote, "not only to spell the words, give their parts of speech and meaning, but as an exercise of memory to remember their order of succession."

After she completed a year at Miss Primrose's Academy, Somerville's full-time education came to an end. She returned to Burntisland, and spent much of her days reading. Mary's mother, a conventional if easy-going woman, did not object. However, soon after her return Aunt Janet came to live with them. Somerville observed: "My mother did not prevent me from reading, but my aunt Janet . . . greatly disapproved of my conduct. She was an old maid who could be very agreeable and witty, but she had all the prejudices of the time with regard to women's duties."

Following her aunt's advice, Somerville was sent to the village school to learn the practical skill of needlework. This educational pattern continued when Mary and her mother moved to Edinburgh when Somerville was 13. There she attend a school which taught cooking, dancing, drawing, and painting, along with the basics of penmanship and arithmetic. It was in the Scottish capital that Somerville first studied the piano, beginning a lifelong passion.

During the summer, Mary and her mother visited her relatives and future in-laws in Jedburgh. The experience was a germinal one. Wrote Somerville:

> For the first time in my life I met my uncle, Dr. Somerville, a friend who approved of my thirst for knowledge. During long walks with him . . . I had the courage to tell him that I had been trying to learn Latin, but I feared it was in vain: for my brother and other boys, superior to me in talent, and with every assistance, spent years in learning it. He assured me, on the contrary that in ancient times many women—some of them of the highest rank in England—had been very elegant scholars, and that he would read Virgil with me if I would come to his study for an hour or two every morning before breakfast which I gladly did.

With Dr. Somerville's encouragement Mary taught herself Latin and read Caesar's *Commentaries*, as well as enough Greek to get through portions of Xenophon and Herodotus. Another source of reading material was ladies' fashion magazines, which contained riddles, puzzles, and basic mathematical problems. It was in one such magazine that Mary Somerville first discovered algebra. Fascinated by this new mathematical system, she persuaded her brother's tutor, Mr. Gaw, to purchase some books on the subject for her. Thus, Mary Somerville obtained a copy of Bonnycastle's *Algebra* and a copy of Euclid's *Elements*. When discovered by her father reading these texts, she was forbidden to pursue her studies. Her family feared the negative effect that rigorous study would have upon her health. Nevertheless, she secretly continued to read.

In 1804, Mary married Samuel Greig, a captain in the Russian Navy. The couple transferred their residence to London, where Greig was appointed Russian consul and commissioner of the Navy. Her new husband had little sympathy for her intellectual pursuits, and for a time her education ended, save for lessons in French. In the two years following their marriage, Somerville gave birth to two sons. By the third year of their marriage, however, Samuel Greig died prematurely. Somerville found herself financially independent, and free for the first time from the control of parents and husband.

A widow, she returned to Scotland, settled in Edinburgh, and resumed her education, reading Isaac Newton's *Principia Mathematica*, and studying physical astronomy and mathematics. Although her female relatives objected to her scientific interests, she nevertheless found support among the Edinburgh scientific community. John Playfair, the mathematician and geologist, happily assisted her, and she corresponded frequently with William Wallace, one of Playfair's protégés. At the time, Wallace was a contributor to *Mathematical Repository* and to *Ladies' Diary*. Both magazines offered prizes for solutions of mathematical problems. In 1811, Mary Somerville won a silver medal for her solution to a problem on Diaphantine equations published in *Mathematical Repository*.

After 15 years abroad in the army medical corps, Mary's cousin, William Somerville, returned to Scotland in 1811. In 1812, the couple married and William became head of Scottish military hospitals. William shared Mary's interests. As a classical scholar himself, he was unfailingly supportive of his wife's efforts to secure an education.

With the encouragement of her husband and the advice of William Wallace, Mary Somerville purchased a library of recent mathematical texts from France. She was fortunate, for at the time English mathematicians were largely unfamiliar with new mathematical theories emanating from France. Scotland, however, enjoyed a historical relationship with France which predated the Union of the Crowns. Thus, the Scots were much more open to French ideas. The library which Mary purchased in 1813 included 15 French works published between 1795 and 1813. "I could hardly believe that I possessed such a treasure," she wrote.

In 1815, William was ordered to London. Accompanied by her husband, Mary was able to attend lectures there at the Royal Institution, including those given by Sir Humphrey Davy. Introduced by mutual friends, the Somervilles soon began to frequent scientific circles. Many were charmed by Mary's intellect and obvious interest in science.

After a brief trip to the Continent, the Somervilles settled in Hanover Square, a district of London where many scientists resided, and where various scientific societies made their home. During the 1820s, Mary acquired a number of scientific friends, prominent among them John Herschel, *Caroline Herschel, Charles Babbage, William Whewell, and George Peacock. Thus while women were barred from British universities, Somerville managed to serve an apprenticeship under some of the most talented scientists of the day. She also made the acquaintance ✎➤ Lady Byron and her daughter, *Ada Byron Lovelace.

Mary Somerville began her scientific career in 1825, undertaking experiments in magnetism.

She focused the sun's rays on a sewing needle. After prolonged exposure, the needle appeared to be magnetized by the sun's violet rays. The experiment was the subject of her first scientific paper, submitted to the Royal Society in 1826. Sir John Herschel was much impressed, and his opinion was shared by the Society. Somerville's theory was accepted, and held to be valid for several years until further research negated it.

In 1827, Somerville received a request from a Scottish friend, Lord Brougham, to write a popular version of Pierre de Laplace's *Celestial Mechanics* for the Society for the Diffusion of Useful Knowledge. His hope was to make the French work accessible to English audiences. A writer was needed with a grasp of scientific methodology, but who could communicate the contents of the book without recourse to technical language and abstract mathematical symbols.

Uncertain of her abilities, Mary Somerville accepted Lord Brougham's offer. Her acceptance, however, was conditional. She stipulated that should she fail, the manuscript would be destroyed. In addition, Somerville went to great lengths to conceal the project from all but her immediate family. She wrote of the experience:

> I rose early and made such arrangements with regards to my children and family affairs that I had time to write afterwards; not, however, without many interruptions. . . . At Chelsea I was always supposed to be at home, and as my friends and acquaintants came so far out of their way on purpose to see me, it would have been unkind and ungenerous not to receive them. Nevertheless, I was sometimes annoyed when in the midst of a difficult problem someone would enter and say, I have come to spend a few hours with you. However, I learnt by habit to leave a subject and resume it again at once. . . . Frequently I hid my papers as soon as the bell announced a visitor lest anyone should discover my secret.

*Mechanism of the Heavens* was published in 1831, and became an instant success. The book was far more than just a translation of Laplace's work, for it also contained Somerville's own theories. At Cambridge, Somerville's translation was adopted as a core text in mathematics by Whewell and Peacock.

*On the Connection of the Physical Sciences*, Somerville's second book, was published in 1834. It proved to be an even greater success than her first. Her thesis dealt with the interrelation of the sciences, and Mary's choice of material greatly influenced the contemporary definition of the physical sciences. The book was translated into French, Italian, and Swedish.

*Byron, Lady.* See Lovelace, Ada Byron for sidebar on Anne Milbanke. ◀✿

In 1835, Mary Somerville and Caroline Herschel were elected as the first female members of the Royal Astronomical Society. Somerville was also elected to the Société de Physique et d'Histoire Naturelle de Genève, the Royal Irish Academy, and the Bristol Philosophical and Literary Society. A pension of £200 was awarded by the British crown, and Somerville's publisher, John Murray, commissioned a portrait of her which now hangs in the National Portrait Gallery of Scotland.

By 1838, William's health was beginning to falter, and the family moved to the warmer climate of Italy. There Mary spent the remaining 34 years of her life, principally in Florence, Rome, and Naples. Isolated as she was from the centers of scientific research, she nonetheless managed to produce *Physical Geography*, in 1848. It was her third and most successful work. Widely praised by scientists, including Alexander Humboldt, the text was used in universities for the next 50 years.

William Somerville died in 1860. He had been his wife's constant companion, supporter, and assistant for over 45 years. In 1865, Woronzow Greig, their son, also died. Mary was increasingly alone. At the suggestion of her daughter **Martha Somerville**, Somerville began to work on her last book, *On Molecular and Microscopic Science*, which explored the realm of the molecular composition of matter and the microscopic structure of plant life. By the time of its publication, she was 89.

Between 1840 and 1857, Mary Somerville had been honored with memberships in no less than 11 Italian scientific societies. In 1857 and 1869, she was made a member of the American Geographical and Statistical Society and the American Philosophical Society, respectively. The Royal Geographical Society conferred the Victoria Gold Medal upon her in 1869, and she also became a member of its Italian counterpart, the Italian Geographical Society.

Throughout her life, Mary Somerville had remained a vocal advocate for women's education. At the request of John Stuart Mill, she was the first to sign his parliamentary petition supporting women's suffrage. She noted, "Age has not abated my zeal for the emancipation of my sex from the unreasonable prejudice too prevalent in Great Britain against a literary and scientific education for women." Somerville found the situation in the United States equally disturbing. While American law had granted suffrage to the newly emancipated male slaves, of which she approved, the law still refused to grant it, as she

wrote, "to the most highly educated women of the Republic."

At age 92, in 1872, Mary Somerville died peacefully in her sleep. At the time of her death, she had been rewriting an essay on quaternions. Somerville was granted her fondest wish—to grow old without any impairment of her mental faculties. Shortly before her death, she wrote poignantly:

> The short time I have to live naturally occupies my thoughts. In the blessed hope of meeting again with my beloved children, and those who were and are dear to me on earth, I think of death with composure and perfect confidence in the mercy of God. . . . We are told of the infinite glories of that state (heaven), and I believe in them, though it is incomprehensible to us; but as I do comprehend, in some degree at least, the exquisite loveliness of the visible world, I confess I shall be sorry to leave it. I shall regret the sky, the sea, with all the changes of their beautiful colouring; the earth, with its verdure and the flowers: but far more shall I grieve to leave animals who have followed our steps affectionately for years, without knowing for certainty their ultimate fate, though I firmly believe that the living principle is never extinguished.

Upon her death, Mary Somerville willed her library to Ladies' College at Hitchin, now Girton College, Cambridge. In 1879, Oxford University created Somerville College in her honor. As well, the Mary Somerville scholarship for women in mathematics was established at Oxford.

No aspect of mathematics was beyond Mary Somerville's grasp. However, her overriding passion for all aspects of science permeates her work. She saw in science a beauty and logic which were a parallel of the natural world. One can only speculate about the results had Somerville received an education earlier in life. Certainly her most productive years as a scientist were severely undercut by lack of opportunity. Like so many contemporary women, Mary Somerville was largely excluded from the traditional scientific world.

Her writings were comprehensive and comprehensible, yet authoritative enough to be relied upon by professional scientists. Her early difficulties in acquiring an education encouraged Somerville to write accessibly about science, free of complex formulas and jargon. Her democratic attitude toward scientific writing was her greatest asset, and her ability to popularize science earned her unparalleled popularity, as well as a reputation for thoroughness of intellect and depth of understanding.

**SOURCES:**

Alic, Margaret. *Hypatia's Heritage*. London: Women's Press, 1986.

Eves, Howard. *In Mathematical Circles*. Boston, MA: Prindle, Weber and Schmidt, 1969.

Mozan, H.J. *Women in Science*. Cambridge, MA: MIT Press, 1974.

Patterson, Elizabeth C. *Mary Somerville and the Cultivation of Science, 1815–1840*. Dordrecht, Holland: Martinus Nijhoff, 1983.

Somerville, Martha. *Personal Recollections of Mary Somerville*. Boston, MA: Roberts Brothers, 1874 (during the last few years of her life, Mary Somerville noted down some memoirs which were published by her daughter Martha).

Tabor, Margaret E. *Pioneer Women*. London: Sheldon Press, 1933.

**SUGGESTED READING:**

Patterson, Elizabeth C. *Mary Somerville, 1780–1872*. Oxford: Oxford University Press, 1979.

**Hugh A. Stewart**, M.A.,
University of Guelph,
Guelph, Ontario, Canada

# Somerville, Nellie Nugent

## (1863–1952)

*American suffragist and state legislator. Born Eleanor White Nugent on September 25, 1863, near Greenville, Mississippi; died of cancer on July 28, 1952, in Ruleville, Mississippi; daughter of William Lewis Nugent and Eleanor Fulkerson (Smith) Nugent; attended Whitworth College in Brookhaven, Mississippi; Martha Washington College in Abingdon, Virginia, A.B., 1880; married Robert Somerville (a civil engineer) in 1885 (died 1925); children: Robert Nugent Somerville (b. 1886); Abram Douglas Somerville (b. 1889); Eleanor Somerville (b. 1891); Lucy Somerville Howorth (1895–1997).*

*Named corresponding secretary of the Mississippi Women's Christian Temperance Union (1894); became chair of the Mississippi Woman Suffrage Association (1897); elected vice-president of the National American Woman Suffrage Association (1915); was the first woman elected to the Mississippi state legislature (1923–27); served as a delegate from Mississippi to the national convention of the Democratic Party (1925).*

Nellie Nugent Somerville was born Eleanor White Nugent in 1863 near Greenville, Mississippi, on a plantation that belonged to her maternal grandmother, **S. Myra Cox Smith**. Her father William Lewis Nugent was then in the Confederate Army. Two years previous, Union forces had shot Nellie's grandfather and burned the family home in Greenville. Nellie was two years old when her mother died, and she went to live with her grandmother. After his second wife died, William married a third time, to **Aimee Webb**, and Nellie returned to live with them in Jackson, Mississippi, in 1870. William prospered there as a member of the bar, and Nellie enjoyed a life of privilege as the daughter of one of the wealthiest men in the state.

She attended Whitworth College, a finishing school in Brookhaven, Mississippi, but her intellectual capabilities soon exceeded the school's resources and she transferred to Martha Washington College, from which she graduated in 1880. Nellie augmented her formal education by reading extensively in the areas of political theory, theology, history, and public affairs. After completing college, she turned down an offer to study law as a member of her father's firm, opting instead to return to her grandmother's home and tutor the children of a Greenville banker. She married civil engineer Robert Somerville in 1885 and had four children, one of whom, **Lucy Somerville Howorth**, became a noted Mississippi jurist.

Despite family obligations, Somerville formed a relationship with national suffragist leader *Carrie Chapman Catt in the early 1890s, and became an outspoken advocate of women's suffrage. She was also influenced by *Frances Willard and the temperance movement, and in 1894 took a leadership role in the Mississippi chapter of the Women's Christian Temperance Union as corresponding secretary. Somerville then founded the Mississippi branch of the Woman Suffrage Association in 1897, taking on the difficult task of building the suffrage movement in a state notorious for its conservative politics. Through efficient organization and intelligence, she advocated public health and occupational safety programs in addition to the right to vote. Her activities on behalf of women's suffrage secured her the position of vice-president of the National American Woman Suffrage Association (NAWSA) in 1915.

Somerville's social reform and women's rights work led her to develop an increasing interest in politics, and in 1923 she became the first woman elected to the Mississippi state legislature. Her image as a genteel Southern woman deflected much of the hostility accorded to women in the public arena, but she proved to be anything but gentle and demure while in office. She became a powerful figure in Mississippi's Democratic Party with a reputation for being stern, argumentative, and effective. She used her considerable influence to reform the state mental hospital, and was named as a delegate to the National Democratic Convention in 1925. Somerville's radicalism, engendered by her stand on women's suffrage, did not extend to other areas, however. She opposed pacifism and the federal child labor amendment, while supporting a poll tax (aimed at excluding African-Americans from the voting booths). She was also an outspoken proponent of states' rights by the late 1940s.

Following her husband's death in 1925, Somerville became a speculator in real estate and soon amassed a considerable fortune. Although no longer active in political or women's rights activities after finishing her term in the Mississippi legislature in 1927, Somerville continued to be in demand as a public speaker and writer, and retained an interest in real-estate speculation. She died of cancer on July 28, 1952, in Ruleville, Mississippi.

**SOURCES:**

Sicherman, Barbara, and Carol Hurd Green, eds. *Notable American Women: The Modern Period.* Cambridge, MA: The Belknap Press of Harvard University, 1980.

**Grant Eldridge**, freelance writer,
Pontiac, Michigan

# Somerville and Ross

*Cousins and collaborators who in their novels and other writings chronicled the declining fortunes of their class, the Anglo-Irish gentry, in the decades before Irish independence.*

*Somerville, E. (1858–1949). Name variations: Edith Somerville. Born Edith Œnone Somerville on May 2, 1858, in Corfu, Greece; died in Castletownshend, County Cork, Ireland, on October 8, 1949; eldest daughter of Thomas Henry Somerville and Adelaide (Coghill) Somerville; educated at home by governesses and then at art schools in London, Düsseldorf and Paris; never married; no children.*

*Awards: Doctor of Letters, Trinity College, Dublin (1932); elected to Irish Academy of Letters (1933); Gregory Gold Medal, Irish Academy of Letters (1941).*

*Spent most of life at family home in Castletownshend, County Cork; studied art (1870s–1880s); met cousin Violet Martin (1886) and began a literary collaboration; published their first novel (1889) and between then and Martin's death (1915) published ten books and numerous articles in British and Irish periodicals; continued the collaboration after Martin's death with the help of spiritualism and seances and wrote 14 other books; had exhibitions of her paintings and also had a horse-coping business (1920s–1930s).*

*Ross, Martin (1862–1915). Name variations: Violet Martin. Born Violet Florence Martin on June 11, 1862, at Ross House, Oughterard, County Galway,*

*Ireland; died on December 21, 1915, in Cork, Ireland; youngest child and fifth daughter of James Martin and Anna Selina (Fox) Martin; educated at home and briefly at Alexandra College, Dublin; never married; no children.*

*Spent early years at Ross; after father's death (1872), family moved to Dublin and also spent some time in England; first met cousin Edith Somerville (1886); returned to Ross (1888) but stayed frequently at Edith's family home in Castletownshend; after mother's death (1906), lived there permanently; health deteriorated following a serious accident (1898); died from a brain tumor (1915).*

*Selected publications:* Through Connemara in a Governess Cart *(1893, new ed., Virago, 1990);* In The Vine Country *(1893, new ed., Virago, 1991);* The Real Charlotte *(1894, new ed., A&A Farmar, 1999);* Some Experiences of an Irish R.M. *(1899) and* Further Experiences of an Irish R.M. *(1908, republished in one volume by J.M. Dent, 1991);* In Mr Knox's Country *(Longmans Greene, 1915);* Irish Memories *(Longmans Greene, 1917);* Mount Music *(Longmans Greene, 1919);* Wheeltracks *(Longmans Greene, 1923);* The Big House of Inver *(1925, new ed., A&A Farmar, 1999);* The States through Irish Eyes *(Houghton Mifflin, 1930).*

The writing team of Somerville and Ross was comprised of cousins Edith Somerville and Violet Martin, who wrote under the name of Martin Ross. Violet Martin's family had been established in Ireland since the 12th century and became one of the largest landowners in County Galway, in the western province of Connacht. The family home was Ross House, on Ross Lake, near Oughterard, north of Galway city, where Violet was born in 1862. The family had been Catholic but her great-grandfather joined the (Anglican) Church of Ireland when he married in the 1770s. The family's financial fortunes declined after the Irish famine of the 1840s when her father James Martin incurred serious debts trying to help his starving tenants. He died in 1872 when Violet was ten. She was aware that it marked the end of an era: "With his death a curtain fell for ever on the old life at Ross, the stage darkened, and the keening of the tenants as they followed his coffin . . . was the last music of the piece." His death coincided with the beginning of the political extinction of the Anglo-Irish gentry class to which the Martins belonged. From the 1870s onwards, with the expansion of the electorate there was a growing movement towards Home Rule, Irish self-government, to which Violet Martin and her family were opposed.

After James Martin's death, Ross House was shut and his widow **Anna Fox Martin**, with her daughters Violet and **Selina Martin**, moved to Dublin. Violet started keeping a diary in 1875 which detailed her activities in Dublin. Her only education was from a governess who came three days a week but she did lessons by herself and learned French and Greek. She was also a keen churchgoer and attended weekly Bible study meetings, as well as visiting asylums and orphanages. Despite all this activity, she wrote in the preface to her 1879 diary: "The chronicle of a wasted time." In 1882, she visited London for the first time and stayed with her eldest brother Robert and his wife. Robert Martin was a journalist and writer of some prominence and he introduced his sister to literary and theater circles in London. In January 1886, Anna Martin and her daughters went to stay in the picturesque west Cork village of Castletownshend on the southern Atlantic coast. The village was dominated by three families who had intermarried over many generations and produced numerous soldiers, sailors and administrators for the service of the British Empire: the Somervilles who lived at Drishane House, the Coghills who lived at Glen Barrahane, and the Townshends who lived at The Castle. Anna Martin and **Adelaide Coghill Somerville** of Drishane were cousins, but Violet had not met any of her Somerville relations until she went to Castletownshend in 1886.

The Somervilles had come to Ireland in the 1690s, and eight generations had lived at Drishane, a large damp house which was periodically infested with rats and other vermin. Edith Somerville, who was four years older than Violet Martin, was born in 1858 at Corfu in Greece where her father was serving with the British army. She had five brothers and a sister to whom she was devoted. She was educated by governesses at home but briefly attended a course of lectures at Alexandra College in Dublin. A talented artist, she had studied at art school in Düsseldorf and Paris in the early 1880s. By the mid-1880s, her illustrations were being published in several London journals, and her family provided her with a coach-house as a studio. Her closest friend had been her cousin **Ethel Coghill** but Ethel's marriage in 1880 had come as a shock, "an aggravated nightmare" Edith called it, and they were never as close again. After the "wasted time" in Dublin, Violet found life at Castletownshend with her Somerville and Coghill cousins exhilarating: there were large family meals, picnics, tennis, boating, riding, choir practice, cards, painting and spiritualism. Edith was absent from Castletownshend for most of the spring of 1886, and it was after her re-

turn that the friendship between her and Violet deepened. She always called her "Martin" to distinguish her from another Violet in the family. In summer 1886, Violet was attempting to write some articles when it was suggested that Edith might do the illustrations. They collaborated on an article on palmistry which was published in *The Graphic* in October 1886. Violet stayed on at Drishane when her mother returned to Dublin but rejoined her in December 1886. The frustration caused by these separations between the cousins intensified in the years ahead.

When she rejoined Edith at Drishane in August 1887, they discussed the possibility of a literary collaboration and soon started writing *An Irish Cousin*. For both women, money was initially the main reason as they were financially dependent on their families. By the 1880s, the agricultural depression and land agitation in Ireland which culminated in the Land War resulted in reduced rental incomes for both the Martins and the Somervilles. "Spinster" sisters like Edith and Violet were expected to be unpaid housekeepers and companions, maintaining the house until their brothers came back from London or imperial service. Their families expressed some disapproval about their literary activities, as Edith recalled in *Irish Memories* (1917). "When not actually reviled, we were treated with much the same disapproving sufferance that is shown to an outside dog that sneaks into the house on a wet day." Their novel was nicknamed "The Shocker" by the rest of the family.

*All our writing was done in casual scrapes. We had no consideration for ourselves and still less did anyone else show us.*
—**Edith Somerville**

Edith also described their method of collaboration which has intrigued many scholars of their work. "Our work was done conversationally. One or other—not infrequently both simultaneously—would state a proposition. This would be argued, combated perhaps, approved or modified; it would then be written down by the (wholly fortuitous) holder of the pen, would be scratched out, scribbled on again." Sections of some books were written when they were apart. They would then send each other what they had written; they also read chapters to their families and took careful note of their reactions. Both were assiduous eavesdroppers and always wrote down interesting or amusing conversations they heard in their daily lives. Subjects noted in one of their commonplace books included Hunting,

Dogs, Letters, Trains, Horses, Racing, Beggars, Abuse and Exclamations, Blessings and Commendations, Drink and Fighting, and the Supernatural. In her critical study of Somerville and Ross, **Hilary Robinson** has observed that "it is a mystery why their collaboration worked so well, and how they managed to produce together work superior to anything either of them produced independently. They shared tastes, distastes and a fine sense of the ridiculous; theirs was a common inheritance and environment; somehow they were catalysts for each other and the result was literature." Violet's sense of mood and atmosphere was darker than Edith who was better at light humor. She always regarded Violet as the greater writer but resented any analysis of their collaboration which she regarded as a divine gift.

In summer 1888, their work on *An Irish Cousin* was interrupted when the Martin family returned to Ross. The return was forced on them by the fraud of their land agent who had embezzled large sums of the estate rents. Anna Martin agreed to live at Ross and look after the estate while Robert remained in London. But times had changed since their departure in the early 1870s. The house was in poor condition and the Land War had caused political tensions which meant that the family was not treated with the same deference as before. Since money was so short, Violet herself did a lot of the physical clearing-up. She managed to get away to Drishane for two months from October to December 1888, and while there she and Edith learned that *An Irish Cousin* had been accepted for publication. When it was released in September 1889, it received good reviews and was into a second printing by the following month. This led to commissions from other publishers and from magazines.

In summer 1890, they toured Connemara in the west of Ireland for a travelogue for the *Lady's Pictorial*. This was later published as *Through Connemara in a Governess Cart* (1893), a book Robinson considers the weakest of their travel books. But the travelogue was successful, and in 1891 they received a commission from the *Lady's Pictorial* to write another, this time about the vineyards of Bordeaux, which was published as *In the Vine Country* (1893). They also completed their second novel, *Naboth's Vineyard*, which was published in 1891. This was despite continuing disruptions at Ross. There were more pleasant distractions for Edith in 1891 when she and her brother Aylmer founded the West Carbery Hunt which absorbed increasing amounts of her time and especially money over the following years. Violet, a keen equestrian, also liked to hunt.

In February 1893, Somerville and Ross finished their third novel, *The Real Charlotte*, which is considered to be their best work. They themselves recognized its quality, although Edith's family thought it vulgar. Several of the characters were in fact drawn from members of their families, and Lady Dysart was based on Edith's mother Adelaide. The novel, as Hilary Robinson has written, is a detailed picture of Anglo-Irish Protestant society at the end of the 19th century. It is set in the town of Lismoyle where the heroine, the beautiful, headstrong Francie Fitzpatrick, is disapproved of by the Lismoyle women but admired by the men. Francie's fate is sealed by the jealousy of Charlotte Mullen who loves her husband Lambert. The book was well reviewed in May 1894 when it was published, and it earned them much needed money, most of which went on the upkeep of either Ross or Drishane and hunting.

With the death of Edith's mother in 1895, followed by that of her father in 1898, she effectively became the mistress and manager of Drishane as all her brothers were away. She and Violet had acquired a literary agent, J.B. Pinker, who urged them to consider writing about a subject close to their hearts, hunting. They started writing several short stories in summer 1898 and the first three of what became the "Irish R.M." series were published in the *Badminton Magazine* the following autumn. The stories were soon bought for book form by Longmans and were published as *Some Experiences of an Irish R.M.* in 1899. The narrator, Major Yates, is the Irish R.M. (the initials stand for Resident Magistrate) but as an Englishman is frequently bewildered by the eccentric events and personalities which he encounters in Ireland. As with *The Real Charlotte*, Somerville and Ross borrowed from real life. Major Yates' house strikingly resembled Ross, while the servants, especially Mrs. Cadogan, resembled the cook at Drishane. The book was an enormous success, and by December 1899 the first edition of 3,000 copies had sold out.

Although Somerville and Ross were writing at the time of the Irish Literary Revival, they tended to avoid the literary world. They were acquainted, though not impressed, with some of its luminaries. Edith had met Oscar Wilde in 1888 and considered him "a great fat oily beast." When W.B. Yeats praised *The Real Charlotte*, Violet privately thought he looked like "a starved R.C. [Roman Catholic] curate—in seedy black clothes. He is egregiously the poet, murmurs ends of verse to himself with a wild eye." Violet loathed Yeats' great love ***Maud Gonne** because of her nationalist beliefs. She remained on good terms with *Augusta Gregory although she never took up Gregory's offer to write a play for the Abbey Theater in Dublin. For her part, Edith was less than pleased when one of her cousins, Charlotte Payne-Townshend, married George Bernard Shaw whom she described as less than a gentleman and a cad to boot, although she later changed her opinion.

Their agent was pressing them to write a further series of R.M. stories, but the only books which appeared over the next seven years were two collections of previously published stories, *All on the Irish Shore* (1903) and *Some Irish Yesterdays* (1906). Ross and Drishane respectively were absorbing a lot of their attention, and Violet was also coping with the aftermath of a serious hunting accident in November 1898 which permanently damaged her health. Her brother Robert died in 1905, followed by her mother in 1906, after which she moved to Drishane permanently. In 1908, a new series of R.M. stories was finally published, *Further Experiences of an Irish R.M.*, and sold well. But despite its success, money continued to be a problem. Edith had to give up the West Carbery Hunt because of the expense, while the dairy farm which she set up with her sister Hildegarde Somerville failed after a few years. She and Violet wrote only two more books after 1908, *Dan Russel the Fox* (1911) and *In Mr Knox's Country* (1915), the final collection of R.M. stories.

When the First World War broke out in 1914, there were fears of a German invasion, as Castletownshend faced the western approaches of the Atlantic. In May 1915, some of the bodies from the *Lusitania* sinking were washed up in the village harbor. Violet became ill in September 1915 with severe headaches, but it was not until she went into a nursing home in Cork that a brain tumor was diagnosed. She gradually went into a coma and died on December 21, 1915. Edith was so shattered she could not bear to attend the funeral. The Somervilles and the Coghills had always been interested in spiritualism and Edith's interest had increased considerably after her parents' deaths. Seances were regularly held at Drishane, and the family used a local medium, Jem Barlow. Following Violet's death, Edith tried to desperately to contact her spirit, and at a seance in June 1916 she finally believed she had made contact through automatic writing. From now until her death, she consulted Violet's spirit regularly not just about writing but about everyday problems. Because she firmly believed that their collaboration continued through these seances, she wanted the

subsequent books to be published under the joint authorship of Somerville and Ross. Her publishers, however, were reluctant to endorse this practice, as it attracted ridicule, and after *Mount Music* (1919) her writings were published under her name alone.

In 1917, Somerville published *Irish Memories* which was in its fourth reprint by January 1918. As her biographer Maurice Collis writes, the book was about Violet whom Edith portrayed as a saint. The chapter "When First She Came" was an idyllic account of the year Violet arrived at Castletownshend. However, Edith did not describe her death, nor did she refer to the seances. The book ends: "I will try no more. Withered leaves, blowing in through the open window before a September gale, are falling on the page. Our summers are ended. Vanity of vanities." Edith had always regarded Violet as the greater writer, and this sentence indicates that Edith did not intend to write any more novels. But she changed her mind and in 1919 published *Mount Music*. Its publication coincided with an important new friendship with composer *Ethel Smyth. She and Edith were the same age, and Smyth was just getting over the death of her lover Henry Brewster the previous year. Smyth was impressed with Edith's paintings and arranged an exhibition in London. Over the next few years Somerville paid regular visits to London and became acquainted with many in Smyth's literary and artistic circle. Smyth tried to expand Edith's literary tastes but soon realized that Edith mostly liked what she knew. At the beginning of 1920, she and Smyth spent a three-month holiday in Sicily. However, there were undercurrents of sexual tension and misunderstanding in their friendship. Smyth was bisexual and wanted a physical relationship; Somerville, although her latent lesbianism seems obvious with hindsight, did not want sexual relations and made this clear to Smyth who accepted it reluctantly.

Edith's family had come out of the First World War unscathed, but within months of the war's end the Irish War of Independence started and Cork was one of the most disturbed areas of the country. Politically, Somerville was out of sympathy with the Irish rebels but she greatly disapproved of the actions of the British forces and described herself as "half rebel and Miss-Facing-both-ways." She approved the settlement which ended the war and gave Ireland independence in 1921 but this was followed by a year-long civil war which in many ways was even worse than the earlier troubles. Cork was once more a major area of fighting. In 1923, after the war, Somerville visited London again for another exhibition of her paintings. *Wheeltracks*, a collection of articles, was also published and both were successful. After this, she started work on a new novel, *The Big House of Inver*, which was the most important of her post-Violet fiction. In fact, the novel was inspired by a letter which Violet had written to Edith in 1912 about a visit to Tyrone House in County Galway, the home of the aristocratic St. George family who were living in dilapidated squalor. *The Big House of Inver* describes the story of the Prendeville family between 1739 and 1912, "one of those minor dynasties," Somerville wrote, "that, in Ireland, have risen, and ruled, and rioted and have at last crashed in ruins." The central character is Sibby, the illegitimate daughter of the Big House. Since Edith had never actually seen Tyrone House, Violet's old home Ross was the model for the Big House.

Although the novel sold 10,000 copies, money remained a problem as most of Somerville's earnings went into the upkeep of Drishane. In February 1929, she visited America for the first time and went on a lecture tour; there was also a successful exhibition of her paintings. Her account of her American visit, *The States through Irish Eyes,* was rather thin and perfunctory. In 1932, she published a biography of her (and Violet's) great-grandfather Charles Kendal Bushe who had been lord chief justice of Ireland. The research proved difficult, and she summoned his spirit in several seances to get the required information. But neither this nor the American book sold well and financial troubles loomed once more. However, with the help of her trusted groom, Michael Hurley, she started a horse-coping business which was successful and which led to another American visit in 1936. Edith's brother Boyle, who had served with distinction in the Royal Navy, had retired to Castletownshend, and they worked together on a family history which was eventually published privately in 1940. However, in March 1936, Boyle was murdered by the IRA because he had been giving references to local men who wanted to join the Royal Navy. For Edith, who had survived the Troubles and the civil war, his murder was a bitter blow not eased by the fact that the murderers were never found.

With the outbreak of the Second World War in 1939, life became very difficult for Edith as the income from her books and horses evaporated. She had relied on her brother Cameron's pension to help with the upkeep of Drishane, but this disappeared with his death in January 1942. Her nephew Desmond Somerville was now the owner of Drishane, but he was serving with the British army and did not return to Ireland until after the war. With Desmond's return in 1946, she and her sister Hildegarde moved to another house in the village, Tally Ho. It was a smaller, more convenient house for two old women, but Edith hated leaving Drishane. In 1947, a collection of articles and reminiscences, *Happy Days*, was published, and the following year, to her great satisfaction, Oxford University Press included *The Real Charlotte* in its "World's Classics" series. On May 2, 1948, she celebrated her 90th birthday, but she hated her physical feebleness and confided to her diary: "Never thought that I would have to end a good active hardworking life dying like a worn out old horse in a corner of a field." This was the last entry. Edith Somerville died on October 8, 1949, and was buried next to Violet Martin in the local graveyard.

**SOURCES:**
Collis, Maurice. *Somerville and Ross: A Biography.* London: Faber and Faber, 1968.

Cronin, John. *Somerville and Ross.* Lewisburg, PA: Bucknell University Press, 1972.

Cummins, Geraldine Dorothy. *Dr E.Œ Somerville.* London: Andrew Dakers, 1952.

Kreilkamp, Vera. *The Anglo-Irish Novel and the Big House.* Syracuse, NY: Syracuse University Press, 1998.

McCormack, W.J. *Ascendancy and Tradition in Anglo-Irish Literature from 1789 to 1939.* Oxford: Clarendon Press, 1985.

Robinson, Hilary. *Somerville and Ross: A Critical Appreciation.* Dublin and NY: Gill & Macmillan/ St. Martin's Press, 1980.

**SUGGESTED READING:**
*The Selected Letters of Somerville and Ross.* Edited by Gifford Lewis with a foreword by *Molly Keane. London: Faber & Faber, 1989.

**COLLECTIONS:**

The journals, correspondence and papers of Somerville and Ross are located in the Berg Collection, New York Public Library.

**RELATED MEDIA:**

"The Irish R.M.," drama series based on the R.M. stories, starring Peter Bowles, Bryan Murray, **Anna Manahan**, and Niall Tóibín, Little Bird Productions with Channel Four and RTE, 1982–85.

**Deirdre McMahon**,
lecturer in history at Mary Immaculate College,
University of Limerick, Limerick, Ireland

# Somogi, Judith (1937–1988)

*American choral and orchestra conductor. Born on May 13, 1937, in Brooklyn, New York; died of cancer on March 23, 1988, in Rockville Center, Long Island, New York; daughter of Louis Somogi (a Hungarian) and Antonina Somogi (a Sicilian); Juilliard School of Music in New York, M.M. degree, 1961; never married; no children.*

*Was assistant conductor to Thomas Schippers and Leopold Stokowski before becoming conductor in*

*New York (1974) and principal conductor of the Frankfurt Opera (1982).*

Judith Somogi was one of only a handful of professional female orchestra conductors. "Conducting," she once said, "is something you learn by doing." It was a skill many women never learned, because they were not allowed on the podium, although that began to change in the 1920s and 1930s. Somogi was born in 1937 and grew up on Long Island, where she performed as a church organist and then choir director. She attended the Juilliard School of Music in New York, studying violin, organ, and piano, and completing her M.M. degree in 1961. She then attended the Berkshire Music Center in Tanglewood, Massachusetts.

Somogi supported herself as a piano teacher, then joined the New York City Opera in 1966 as a rehearsal pianist. For the next eight years, she performed a variety of tasks as pianist, coach, and chorus master, before she was finally given the opportunity to conduct. In between opera seasons, she worked as assistant conductor at the Spoleto Festival in Italy and at the American Symphony Orchestra in New York. In 1974, Somogi debuted as the first female conductor of the New York City Opera, conducting *The Mikado* and *La Traviata*. Throughout the 1970s, she appeared in San Francisco, San Diego, Los Angeles, Pittsburgh, and San Antonio conducting orchestra and operatic productions. Her European debut was in Saarbrücken in 1979. Somogi traveled frequently while pursuing her career. "When you get new luggage that you insist on carrying on the plane," she said, "you know you're traveling more." Oklahoma loomed large in her professional career as she conducted both the Tulsa Philharmonic and the Oklahoma City Orchestra. Phillips Petroleum, whose corporate headquarters is in Bartlesville, Oklahoma, sponsored a television documentary, "On Stage with Judith Somogi," which was shown on PBS.

Eventually, however, she spent more and more time in Germany where she enjoyed the varied approaches to music making. In 1981, Somogi left for West Germany, where after conducting *Madama Butterfly* she was offered the position of First Kappelmeister (principal conductor) at the Frankfurt Opera (1982). In 1984, she was the first woman to conduct in a major Italian opera house when she directed Gluck's *Orfeo ed Euridice* at the Teatro La Fenice in Venice. Somogi never returned to perform in New York. She remained at the Frankfurt Opera until administrative changes and declining

health from cancer caused her to retire in 1987 and return to Long Island, New York. Judith Somogi died at age 47, at the height of her illustrious career, after battling cancer for four years.

**SOURCES:**

Baker, Theodore, ed. *Baker's Biographical Dictionary of Musicians*. 8th ed. NY: Schirmer, 1992.

Holland, Bernard. "Judith Somogi, 47, a Conductor; Among First Women on Podium," in *The New York Times Biographical Service*. March 1988, p. 38.

Hughes, Allen. "City Opera Conductor Has Busy Baton," in *The New York Times Biographical Service*. September 1980, p. 1337.

Kupferberg, Herbert. "Conducting Herself with Style," in *American Way*. April 1981, pp. 104–108.

**Laura York**, M.A. in History,
University of California, Riverside, California

# Sondergaard, Gale (1899–1985)

*American actress who was the first woman to receive the Academy Award for Best Supporting Actress (1936), for her portrayal of Faith in* Anthony Adverse.
*Name variations: Gale Biberman. Born Edith Holm Sondergaard in Litchfield, Minnesota, on February 15, 1899; died in Woodland Hills, California, in August 1985; graduated from the University of Minneapolis, 1921; married second husband Herbert Biberman (a stage director), in 1930; children: one daughter.*

*Selected filmography:* Anthony Adverse *(1936);* Maid of Salem *(1937);* Seventh Heaven *(1937);* The Life of Emile Zola *(1937);* Lord Jeff *(1938);* Dramatic School *(1938);* Never Say Die *(1939);* Juarez *(1939);* The Cat and the Canary *(1939);* Sons of Liberty *(1939);* The Llano Kid *(1940);* The Blue Bird *(1940);* The Mark of Zorro *(1940);* The Letter *(1940);* The Black Cat *(1941);* Paris Calling *(1941);* My Favorite Blonde *(1942);* Enemy Agents Meet Ellery Queen *(1942);* A Night to Remember *(1943);* Appointment in Berlin *(1943);* Isle of Forgotten Sins *(1943);* The Strange Death of Adolf Hitler *(1943);* Spider Woman *(1944);* Follow the Boys *(1944);* Christmas Holiday *(1944);* The Invisible Man's Revenge *(1944);* Gypsy Wildcat *(1944);* The Climax *(1944);* Enter Arsene Lupin *(1944);* The Spider Woman Strikes Back *(1946);* Night in Paradise *(1946);* Anna and the King of Siam *(1946);* The Time of Their Lives *(1946);* The Road to Rio *(1947);* Pirates of Monterey *(1947);* East Side, West Side *(1949);* Slaves *(1969);* Pleasantville *(1976);* The Return of a Man Called Horse *(1976);* Echoes *(1983).*

The daughter of a professor, Gale Sondergaard was born in Litchfield, Minnesota, in 1899, and became interested in acting while she was in high school, where she also learned that she would never be ingenue material. "It's such a pity that you can't be an ordinary girl at an ordinary tea party," said one of her teachers after she had lost a coveted leading role in a school play. "But you can't be—you have something much more interesting to offer." After graduating from the University of Minnesota School of Drama, Sondergaard began her acting career with a stock company under the direction of *Jessie Bonstelle. She then made her Broadway debut replacing *Judith Anderson in the role of Nina in Eugene O'Neill's *Strange Interlude*, after which she signed a three-year contract with the Theater Guild. Sondergaard appeared in a number of plays before leaving the theater to follow her second husband, writer-director Herbert Biberman, to Hollywood. Feeling out of place in the movie capital, she was quite willing to sacrifice her career, but her husband's agent convinced her to audition for the supporting role of Faith Paleologus in *Anthony Adverse* (1936). Director Mervyn LeRoy, who was looking for an unknown, cast her. That year, the Academy of Motion Picture Arts and Sciences added Best Supporting Actress to its roster of awards, and Sondergaard became the first winner in the new category. The actress went on to supporting parts in numerous films, usually cast as an evil character. By 1940, she had gained the reputation as Hollywood's "Queen of the Heavies," although in an interview in 1971, she pointed out that she had also portrayed sympathetic characters (e.g., Madame Alfred Dreyfus in *Emile Zola*), but that moviegoers only remembered her villains. In 1946, Sondergaard received a second Academy Award nomination for her supporting role of Lady Thiang in the film adaptation of *Margaret Landon's *Anna and the King of Siam*, starring *Irene Dunne and based on the life of *Anna Leonowens.

Sondergaard's film career came to a halt when she was blacklisted following the House Un-American Activities Committee hearings (HUAC). Her husband, one of the "Hollywood Ten" who refused to give testimony to HUAC, was sent to prison. Sondergaard did not reemerge until 1965, when she appeared in the off-Broadway one-woman show *Woman*. In 1969, she returned to films, playing a small role in a project of her husband's called *Slaves*. After that, she made guest appearances on the television shows "Get Smart" and "It Takes a Thief," and had a six-month run on the soap opera "The Best of Everything." Sondergaard returned to the screen again in *Pleasantville* and *The Return of a Man Called Horse* (both 1976), and made her last film *Echoes* (1983) just two years before her death.

SOURCES:
Katz, Ephraim. *The Film Encyclopedia*. NY: Harper-Collins, 1994.
Maltin, Leonard. "FFM Interviews Gale Sondergaard," in *Film Fan Monthly*. April 1971.

**Barbara Morgan,**
Melrose, Massachusetts

## Song, Mrs. Charles Jones (c. 1869–1931).
*See Song Meiling for sidebar on Ni Guizhen.*

## Song Ching Ling (1893–1981).
*See Song Sisters for Song Qingling.*

## Song Eling (1890–1973).
*See Song Sisters for Song Ailing.*

## Song Guizhen (c. 1869–1931)
*See Song Meiling for sidebar on Ni Guizhen.*

# Song Meiling (b. 1897)

*Leading member of the most influential Chinese family of the first half of the 20th century, and wife of Generalissimo Chiang Kai-shek, who was undoubtedly the most powerful woman of her time.* Name variations: *Soong or Sung May-ling, Mayling, or Mei-ling; Madame Chiang, Madame Chiang Kai-shek or Madame Chiang Kaishek; Mme. Jiang Jieshi; Chiang Mei-ling. Pronunciation: Soong MAY-ling. Born on March 5, 1897, in Shanghai, China; youngest daughter of Charlie Jones Song (a business leader and philanthropist born Hon Chao-Shun or Jia-shu Song) and Ni Guizhen (Ni Kweitseng, daughter of a wealthy scholar family in Shanghai who believed in Christianity, also known as Song Guizhen); educated at Potwin's private school, Wesleyan College, and Wellesley College, Massachusetts; married Chiang Kai-shek (1887–1975, the nationalist leader and ruler of China, 1927–49), on December 1, 1927. (See also Song Sisters.)*

Bearing a name that can best be translated as "Beautiful Life," Song Meiling was born in Shanghai on March 5, 1897, the fourth of six children of Charlie Jones Song and ✥➤ Ni Guizhen. The American-educated Charlie was a devout Methodist who made his fortune publishing Bibles in Chinese as well as importing heavy machinery. He had secretly been a most powerful backer of the revolutionary movement of Dr. Sun Yat-Sen. Ni Guizhen stemmed from one of China's oldest and most illustrious evangelical Christian families. A native of Shanghai, she had received a Western education and was a pillar of Shanghai Methodism.

In all China, no family would be better connected. One sister of Meiling, ◀✥ Song Ailing (*see Song Sisters*), married H.H. Kung, later

China's leading banker, finance minister, and supposedly a lineal descendent of Confucius. Another, ◀❧ **Song Qingling** (*see Song Sisters*), married the founder of the Chinese republic, Sun Yat-sen. One brother, the extremely wealthy T.V. Song, became the economic wizard of the Chinese government, intermittently serving as economic minister, foreign minister, and prime minister. Two other brothers, T.L. Song and T.A. Song, were financiers.

Tutored at home until 1907, Meiling was sent to Miss **Clara Potwin**'s modest preparatory school in Summit, New Jersey. In the summer of 1908, she accompanied her sister Qingling to the Georgia hill town of Demorest. Meiling spent the eighth grade in a local school there while Qingling began studies at Wesleyan College, Macon. Bright, precocious, and occasionally sassy, Meiling soon became an unofficial student at Wesleyan; college administrators broke formal rules to permit her access to classes.

In 1912, Meiling began her freshman year at Wesleyan, but within a year transferred to the prestigious Wellesley College in Wellesley, Massachusetts, from which she graduated in 1917. Proficient in her courses and in athletics, and speaking English with a lilting Georgia accent, she was known for her inquisitive attitude, independence of thought, and rugged honesty. By then, she felt so Americanized that she confessed, "The only thing Chinese about me is my face."

Returning to Shanghai in 1917, Song Meiling became known for her drive, charm, and wit. As she was hardly acquainted with her own country, it took formal lessons to make her fluent in Chinese. She soon became one of the city's leading socialites. In the words of biographer Roby Eunson: "She had beauty and breeding and money to dress exquisitely, making her an asset to any of the endless and lavish parties held by foreigners and a few westernized Chinese." Yet, highly community-minded, she was active in the Film Censorship Board and the Young Women's Christian Association. She was the first woman and the first Chinese national to serve on the Municipal Council's child labor committee, which in 1924 issued a damning report on sweatshop conditions.

In early December 1921, Song Meiling met the nationalist general Chiang Kai-shek, whose armies controlled much of China. Though uneducated and inarticulate, Chiang was a determined and forceful military leader. Yet only on December 1, 1927, were they married. The wedding was a major social event embodying a union between China's new business elite and an equally new and

---

❧▶ **Ni Guizhen** (c. 1869–1931)

*Matriarch of the influential Song family. Name variations: Song Guizhen; Mrs. Charles Jones Song; Mme Charlie Song or Soong; Ni Kwei-tsent or Ni Kweitseng; Ni Kwei-tseng Song or Soong; Mammy Soong. Born Ni Guizhen (Ni Kwei-tseng or Ni Kweitseng) around 1869; died of cancer in 1931; daughter of Yuin San; married Charlie Jones Song (a business leader and philanthropist born Hon Chao-Shun or Jia-shu Song), in 1886; children: six, including \*Song Ailing (1890–1973); \*Song Qingling (1893–1981); \*Song Meiling (b. 1897); T.V. Song (diplomat, finance and foreign minister, who married Anna Chang); T.L. Song (Song Zeliang or Tse-liang); and T.A. Song (Song Ze-an or Tse-an).*

Ni Guizhen was a direct descendant of prime minister Wen Dinggong (Wen Ting-Kung) of the Ming dynasty who was converted to Christianity under the tutelage of the Jesuit Matthew Ricci in 1601. In the 17th century, his daughter built churches and hospitals. Ni Guizhen's mother veered from her Catholic upbringing and became a Protestant when she married Ni Guizhen's father Yuin San. In 1886, the well-educated 17-year-old Ni Guizhen married Charlie Jones Song, an American-educated Methodist minister who had a degree in theology from Vanderbilt. Charlie Song left the ministry and set up a printing house to publish Bibles while Ni Guizhen brought up their six children, sending them to McTyeire School, a Methodist school in Shanghai. She later was instrumental in sending her daughters to Wesleyan College in Macon, Georgia. A devout Christian, Ni Guizhen gave Bible readings and was known for her charity. When Chiang Kai-shek once asked Meiling, "What exactly is a Christian?" she replied, "My mother is the finished product. I am a Christian in the making."

**SOURCES:**
Deen, Edith. *Great Women of the Christian Faith*. NY: Harper, 1959.

---

ambitious military caste; it was attended by 1,300 people and made the front page of *The New York Times*. Meiling's mother Guizhen had opposed the marriage because Chiang was a Buddhist and a bigamist, sister Qingling opposed the match because she found Chiang betraying the ideals of her deceased husband, Dr. Sun. Yet sister Ailing, brother T.V., and brother-in-law H.H. Kung all supported the union, and Chiang helped fend off objections by claiming that he had made a proper divorce and would study Christianity. (Chiang was then married to ❧▶ **Chen Jieru**; his first wife was ❧▶ **Mao Fumei**.) After the wedding, he became a Methodist, becoming baptized in 1930.

American journalist **\*Helen Foster Snow** writes of the marriage: Meiling "was a hostage in the ancient Chinese tradition, a pledge of good

❧▶

*See sidebars on the following page*

### ❧▶ Chen Jieru (fl. 1920)

*Second wife of Chiang Kai-shek. Name variations: Ch'en Chieh-ju. Flourished around 1920; said to have been a prostitute; became second wife of Chiang Kai-shek (1887–1975), in November 1921 (marriage lapsed). Chiang's first wife was *Mao Fumei.*

### ❧▶ Mao Fumei (1892–?)

*First wife of Chiang Kai-shek. Name variations: Mao Fu-mei. Born in 1892; became first wife of Chiang Kai-shek, in 1909 (divorced 1921); children: Zhang Jingguo (Chiang Ching-kuo), later president of the Republic of China (Taiwan).*

At age 17, Mao Fumei entered into an arranged marriage with 14-year-old Chiang Kai-shek, whom she had never seen. They were married for 12 years. Their son, Zhang Jingguo, would be president of the Republic of China (Taiwan).

faith between families and political interests. But Chiang was a dashing and handsome officer of strong personality and boundless ambition, and there is no reason why it should not have been a love match on both sides." Qingling was caustic, saying Chiang "would have agreed to be a Holy Roller to marry Meiling. He needed her to build a dynasty." Yet later, Qingling would claim that without Meiling's guidance, Chiang's authoritarian rule "might have been much worse."

A few days after their marriage, the couple moved to Nanjing (Nanking), where Chiang was selected to head the Guomindang government. As first lady of China, Song Meiling—now known as Madame Chiang Kai-shek—organized hospitals, nursing corps, schools for orphans, rural service clubs, and recreation halls for soldiers. She served continually on government committees, made inspection tours, and frequently accompanied Chiang to the front lines, where he was first fighting warlords and then Communists. Here she changed silk and satin gowns for a slack suit, high-heeled slippers for flat walking shoes. Often she would sleep in railway stations, thatched huts, and farm houses. In October 1929, she and her husband traveled in China's northeast, the first time she really became known among the Chinese people. Notes biographer *Emily Hahn:

> She began to emerge in her own right into the public eye during the wanderings. The necessity of making speeches day after day cured her of shyness and toughened her against the fatigues of what might be called electioneering. In each city she took upon herself the job of marshaling the women and

urging them to help in a nationwide reform. She talked against the old ways of China, the incarceration of upper-class women, the menace of opium and of dirt and poverty; she begged them to develop a sense of social responsibility.

More than anyone else, Meiling was the spearhead of Chiang's "New Life Movement," an effort to unite China around an ideology combining tenets of Dr. Sun, Christian missionaries, and traditional Confucianism. By following the "four virtues" of courtesy, service, honesty, and honor, China would have a new national consciousness that would enable it to solve its "four great needs": clothing, food, housing, and transportation. Claiming "'Except a man be born again' he cannot see New Life," she called on women to cultivate their own "four virtues": chastity, appearance, speech, and work. Though New Life involved such projects as Western hygiene, the construction of sewers, improving the water supply, and attacks on superstition, the movement seemed embodied in simplistic maxims: don't spit, safety first, good roads, watch your step, keep to the right, line up here, fresh air and sunshine, swat the fly, brush your teeth, take your vitamins, love thy neighbor, stop, look and listen, better babies, and clean up, paint up, fix up.

Such details, Meiling said, were merely outward signs of far more important spiritual reforms, centering on China's "four values": propriety, justice, integrity, and conscientiousness. *Time* magazine correctly called New Life "a big dose of the castor oil of Puritanism." She once said, "Putting new wine into old bottles is not an easy task. . . . I have spent one hundred per cent of effort to get one per cent of result."

Despite such crusades, she occasionally sounded like a Social Darwinist. When, in 1935, someone told her that it was useless to speak of New Life while Chinese people lacked rice, she replied, "There is plenty of rice. But those who have it hoard it, and those who do not have it do not understand the dignity of labor. No work is too hard if one is honest."

Her personality and power remain debated to this day. Positive qualities included administrative ability, a lively sense of phrasing, quickness of mind, and unquestioned devotion to her nation. To such admirers as Henry Luce, America's most powerful publisher, she was "the brains of China," the chic, gracious, and cultured modernizer of a land in the process of being rescued from feudal despotism by Western technology, foreign investment, and the Christian religion. In Luce's *Time* magazine, Generalissimo Chiang was always the "Gissimo," Mme

Chiang "the Missimo" and indeed Luce was the greatest factor in making the couple familiar to the American public.

Mme Chiang's critics were particularly prevalent among American journalists and the lower-ranking diplomatic corps. To them, she was a woman of intense arrogance, imperious ego, and ostentatious wealth, a spoiled insincere snob wrapped in furs and bedecked with jade. Some claimed that she was the model for Milton Caniff's cartoon character "The Dragon Lady."

Though no one would deny that Meiling was a woman of great influence, the extent of her dominance is also disputed. According to American journalist John Gunther, writing in 1939, "She is probably the *second* most important and powerful personage in China," coming "immediately after the Generalissimo in influence." Writes biographer Sterling Seagrave, Chiang Kai-shek "offered her the opportunity to implement historic changes, to alter the life of China according to her will. [Meiling] saw herself as a Medici able to alter destinies." Yet historian Donald G. Gillin is far more cautious, denying that the Songs, and in particular Meiling, were the real power behind Chiang. "On the contrary," writes Gillin, "Chiang probably made such extensive use of the Songs and the Kungs in part because they lacked real power. They were peculiarly dependent upon him and, therefore, likely to remain loyal to him in a political environment where treachery and betrayal were commonplace."

As Chiang Kai-shek spoke no English, Meiling served as his interpreter and voice to the Western world, thereby possessing untold influence in crucial diplomatic negotiations. Highly conscious of the need for a positive American image of her nation, and alert to all techniques of public relations, she did all she could to enhance China's visibility. She granted interviews and wrote letters, magazine articles, and books—all designed for an American audience and all stressing her nation's rich cultural heritage and highlighting her Christian roots and U.S. education. If, arguably, she had negligible impact on fellow Chinese, she was such an asset in molding Western opinion that Chiang confessed she was worth ten divisions.

In 1936, Chiang briefly put Meiling in charge of China's air force, by making her secretary-general of the Commission on Aeronautical Affairs. The procuring system had become so shot with corruption that Chiang would trust no one but his wife to buy planes at the market price. Journalist **Frances Gunther** quipped: "Was this the face that launched a thousand airships?"

On December 12, 1936, Chiang Kai-shek was kidnapped at Xian (Sian) just as he was about to launch an anti-Communist "annihilation campaign." Warlord Zhang Xueliang (Chiang Hsueh-liang), known as "the Young Marshal," and General Yang Huzheng (Yang Hu-Cheng), who controlled much of northwestern China, sought to convince the generalissimo to cancel all such plans, join forces with the Communist guerrillas based at Yenan, and create a united front against further Japanese pene-

tration. To rescue her husband, Meiling immediately flew to Xian. As her plane was about to land, she pulled a revolver from her handbag and gave instructions to William Henry Donald, an Australian and close family adviser, to shoot her if she were attacked. Though the specific negotiations that ensued are still a matter of speculation, she gained widespread admiration for her courage. Chiang wrote in his diary:

> I was so surprised to see her that I felt as if I were in a dream. I had told T.V. more than once the day before that my wife must not come to Xian, and when she braved all danger to come to the lion's den, I was very much moved and almost wanted to cry.

Beginning in July 1937, China was involved in full-scale war with Japan. Touring the battlefront that October, Mme Chiang was almost killed when a Japanese plane strafed her car while she was visiting hospitals at the front. In 1938, she organized the evacuation of thousands of Hankou (Hankow) factory workers and their families. During the war, she led the National Refugee Children's Association, which supported 25,000 orphans, and with her sister Ailing started the Women's Advisory Committee, an effective war-relief group.

Meiling often broadcast to the United States, pleading with Americans to boycott Japanese goods and to stop supplying oil to Japan. Furthermore, her books saturated the American market. The year 1938 saw her *Messages in War and Peace*, a potpourri of speeches and articles that nonetheless revealed much of her thinking. In 1940, *This Is Our China* appeared, a series of essays that combined such matters as her religious faith, travel impressions, and tales of old dynasties with an impassioned indictment of the Japanese. A year later, her *China Shall Rise Again* was published, a condemnation of the democracies for failing to aid China and a prediction of her nation's ultimate triumph. In 1943, still another volume of speeches, *We Chinese Women*, came out.

After December 7, 1941, the day the Japanese attacked Pearl Harbor, the United States was China's full-fledged ally. In November 1942, at the invitation of American politician Wendell Willkie, Mme Chiang flew to the U.S. First, she underwent secret treatment at New York's Harkness Pavilion for urticaria (hives), a skin disease; her entourage took up the entire 12th floor. Then, for two weeks, she was the guest of Franklin D. Roosevelt at Hyde Park. The president had privately opposed the visit, fearing that she would agitate against the prevailing Europe-first strategy. At one point, she startled FDR by indicating how she would handle a major coal-mining strike then plaguing the U.S.; she drew her hand across her throat and made a gagging sound.

Addressing both houses of Congress separately in February 1943, she appealed to the U.S. to alter its wartime priorities by defeating Japan before tackling Germany. Indicting what she saw as Western apathy towards Asia, she quoted a Chinese proverb: "It takes little effort to watch the other fellow carry the load." Her speech, which had impact and was repeatedly interrupted by congressional applause, was described in *Newsweek* in the following way:

> The effect was enchanting. The lady was dark and petite. She wore a long, tight-fitting black gown, the skirt slit almost to the knee. Her smooth black hair was coiled simply at the nape of her neck. Her jewels were of priceless jade. Her slim fingers were redtipped. She wore sheer hose and frivolous high-heeled slippers.

From Washington, she toured the United States, crossing the nation by train and everywhere asking for aid. She spoke to 20,000 at New York's Madison Square Garden, 30,000 at Los Angeles' Hollywood Bowl (where a special "Madame Chiang Kai-shek March" was performed). Though arrogant towards hospital and hotel staff, she thoroughly charmed American politicians, movie stars, and business leaders. "No figure on the world stage stirs the American imagination more than hers," said *The New York Times*.

On July 4, 1943, Meiling arrived at the mountain stronghold of Chongqing (Chungking), China's temporary capital. Here she strongly championed U.S. General Claire Chennault, whose advocacy of air power—in her eyes—promised military victory without the troublesome task of reforming the corrupt Chinese army. "If we destroy fifteen Nippon [Japanese] planes each day," she said, "soon there will be none left." At the same time, she opposed the strategy of U.S. General Joseph Stilwell, commander of American and Chinese forces in Burma (now Myanmar), who was Chiang Kai-shek's chief of staff and a defender of intensive ground action. Mme Chiang sought the removal of U.S. ambassador Clarence Gauss, who reported candidly of Chinese ineptitude; banned American journalist Edgar Snow, whom she claimed was a Comintern agent; wanted Luce to fire *Time* staffer Theodore White, a critic of Guomindang rule; and banished hostile U.S. correspondent *Agnes Smedley from ever returning to China. Meiling spoke frequently against the British, accusing them of selfish over-concentra-

tion on the defense of their own island, and endorsed independence for India.

From November 22 to 26, 1943, Mme Chiang accompanied her husband to the Cairo summit meeting. Never in good health, she collapsed during the conference. Yet Roosevelt hoped to win the confidence of the couple, assuring them of China's membership in the Big Four and the postwar return of Manchuria, Taiwan, and the Pescadores islands. Said FDR later to a reporter:

> I never was able to form any opinion of Chiang in Cairo. When I thought about it later I realized all I knew is what Madame Chiang had told me about her husband and what she thought. She was always there and phrased all the answers. I got to know her, but this fellow Chiang—I could never break through to him.

Unbeknownst to Meiling, the Cairo summit marked the apex of her political career. Henceforth, the Chiangs were on a downward slope. Tormented continually by her urticaria (which led to the constant changing of her sheets) and jealous of Chiang's continued attention to his former wife Chen Jieru, in June 1944 she left China. At Chiang's farewell party for his wife, he publicly denied any infidelity. First she traveled with sister Ailing to Brazil, where H.H. Kung had many investments, then in September journeyed to New York, where she remained in seclusion at the Kung household in Riverdale. Only in July 1945, as World War II was coming to an end, did she return to Chongqing.

On November 30, 1948, she again arrived in the United States, this time to secure American military aid for Chiang's war against the Communist forces of Mao Zedong. She also wanted three billion dollars over a three-year period. With the cautious Harry S. Truman now U.S. president and with a Democratic administration wary of massive commitments in Asia, the trip was something of a flop. This time there was no White House invitation, no address to Congress. Tired and unsmiling, she was again forced to live a hermit-like existence at the Kung estate.

In January 1950, Meiling returned to Asia, this time not to China, which was under Mao's rule, but to the island fortress of Taiwan, where her husband had set up a rump government. Always caustic when she so desired, she responded to Britain's recognition of the People's Republic of China by saying, "Britain has bartered the soul of a nation for a few pieces of silver." She continued her involvement in social work, particularly orphanages, schools, and groups advancing the welfare of women. More then ever, she had to speak publicly for a husband increasingly turning senile, while engaging in a quiet rivalry with her stepson Zhang Jingguo (Chiang Ching-kuo), later president of the Republic of China (Taiwan).

August 1953 and April 1954 saw her again journeying to the U.S., the first time to arouse American enthusiasm for regaining the mainland, the second to help block the proposal to seat Mao's regime in the United Nations. In 1958, 1965, 1966, and 1970, she returned to America, the latter two times for mastectomy operations. Addressing Wellesley students in 1965, she was only a shadow of her former self, lapsing at times into incoherence:

> The intersitical periods within the seasons bring forth a plentitude in natural proliferation of brilliant or subtle colors . . . within the purfled walls.

When on April 5, 1975, Chiang died at age 87, Song Meiling (who was estranged from his successor, her stepson) settled in Lattingtown, Long Island, at the estate of her nephew, the New York financier David Kung. Since that time she has lived there or in New York City in seclusion. On March 10, 1998, she turned 100 and celebrated quietly, still in New York after 23 years.

**SOURCES:**

Eunson, Roby. *The Soong Sisters.* Franklin Watts, 1975.

Hahn, Emily. *The Soong Sisters.* NY: Doubleday, Doran, 1941.

Seagrave, Sterling. *The Soong Dynasty.* NY: Harper and Row, 1985.

**SUGGESTED READING:**

Chiang Kai-shek and Mme. Chiang Kai-shek. *General Chiang Kai-shek.* NY: Doubleday, 1937.

Chiang May-ling Soong. *China Shall Rise Again.* NY: Harper, 1941.

———. *This is Our China* (published in England as *China in Peace and War*). NY: Harper, 1940.

———. *We Chinese Women.* Clark, 1943.

Fairbank, John K. *China: A New History.* Cambridge, MA: Harvard University Press, 1992.

Spence, Jonathan D. *The Search for Modern China.* NY: W.W. Norton, 1990.

Thompson, James C., Jr. *While China Faced West: American Reformers in Nationalist China, 1928–1937.* Cambridge, MA: Harvard University Press, 1969.

**Justus D. Doenecke**, Professor of History,
New College of the University of South Florida,
Sarasota, Florida

## Song Qingling (1893–1981).

*See Song Sisters.*

# Song Sisters

*Siblings who were direct and powerful participants in the 20th-century struggle between Nationalists and Communists that changed both China and the world.*

*Song Ailing (1890–1973). Chinese financier and philanthropist who held together and expanded the Song family fortune through a half-century of revolution and war.* Name variations: *Soong Eling, Eye-ling, or Ai-ling; Sung Eling; Madame H.H. Kong or Madame H.H. Kung; Chinese name of Ailing means "pleasant mood"; Christian name was Nancy in honor of Nannie Carr, wife of Julian Carr, her father's benefactor in North Carolina.* Pronunciation: *Soong EYE-ling. Born on December 12, 1890, in Shanghai, China; died on October 20, 1973, in New York City; eldest child of Han Chiao-shun, universally known as Charlie Jones Song (a publisher of Bibles) and Ni Guizhen (Ni Kwei-tseng, known later as Song Guizhen or simply Mammy); elder sister of Song Qingling and Song Meiling; educated at Wesleyan College, Georgia, 1904–09; married Kong Xiangxi also spelled K'ung Hsiang-hsi (1880–1967), in April 1914 (in the West, he was known as H.H. Kung, and she was therefore known as Madame Kung); children: Ling-i (known is Rosamund, b. 1916); Ling-ki'an (David, b. 1917); Ling-wei (Jeannette, b. 1918); Ling-chieh (Louie, b. 1919).*

*Song Qingling (1893–1981). Pro-Communist wife of Sun Yat-sen who was elected vice chair of the People's Republic of China, awarded the Stalin International Peace Prize, was active in the international peace movement, and worked with China Welfare while continuing her lifelong commitment to assisting women and children.* Name variations: *Madame Sun Yat-sen or Sun Yatsen; Soong Ching Ling; Soong Qingling; Song Chingling or Ching-ling; Sung Chingling. Born on January 27, 1893, in Shanghai; died on May 29, 1981, in Beijing; second daughter of Han Chiao-shun, universally known as Charlie Jones Song (a publisher of Bibles) and Ni Guizhen (Ni Kwei-tseng, known later as Song Guizhen or simply Mammy); sister of Song Ailing and Song Meiling; educated at Potwin's private school in Summit, New Jersey, and at Wesleyan College, 1907–13; married Sun Yat-sen (father of the Chinese Revolution), in 1915.*

*Elected executive member of Guomindang Central Committee (1926); with sisters, gave radio broadcasts to American audience on the Anti-Japanese War in China (1940); elected vice chair of the People's Republic of China (1949); received the Stalin International Peace Prize (1951).*

*Song Meiling (b. 1897). Wife of Chiang Kai-shek whose savvy use of modern media and public relations strongly influenced American opinion in the revolutionary struggles in China from the 1930s to the 1960s.* Name variations: *Soong or Sung May-ling,*

*Mayling, or Mei-ling; Madame Chiang; Madame Chiang Kai-shek, or Chiang Kaishek; Mme. Jiang Jieshi; Chiang Mei-ling. Pronunciation: Soong MAY-ling. Born on March 5, 1897, in Shanghai, China; youngest daughter of Charlie Jones Song (a business leader and philanthropist born Hon Chao-Shun or Jia-shu Song) and Ni Guizhen (Ni Kwei-tseng, daughter of a wealthy scholar family in Shanghai who believed in Christianity, also known as Song Guizhen); educated at Potwin's private school, Wesleyan College, and Wellesley College, Massachusetts; married Chiang Kai-shek (1887–1975, the nationalist leader and ruler of China from 1927 to 1949), on December 1, 1927. (See also separate entry on Song Meiling, p. 564.)*

The eye of the political hurricane that swept away old China in 1911–12 lasted for almost half a century before subsiding to allow a new China to be established. The Song family was at the center of the maelstrom. Song Qingling married the so-called father of the revolution, Sun Yat-sen. Song Meiling married the creator of the modern Chinese state, Chiang Kai-shek. As the eldest child, Song Ailing, who married businessman H.H. Kung, "stayed home to mind the store," while brothers T.V., T.L., and T.A. Song prospered in the West, supported the Chiang Kai-shek government, and came to be arch-opponents of the eventual winners of the revolution, the Communists. Though dissimilar beliefs led the Song sisters down different paths, each exerted influence both on Chinese and international politics. By marrying men of political distinction and adhering to their own political pursuits, the three daughters played key roles in modern Chinese history.

The story begins with Charlie Song, father of the famed Song siblings. Though his background and early life were enshrouded in the legends created by his own and his children's accomplishments, the basic facts seem to be that Charlie Song came to the United States in 1878 as a boy, was educated by Methodists in North Carolina as a teenager, was ordained as a deacon in 1885, and was then sent back to Shanghai as a missionary. Somewhere along the line, he had changed his variously spelled Chinese name to Charlie Soon in North Carolina and to Charlie Song in China. He married a Chinese Christian woman named ❧➤ **Ni Guizhen** (Ni Kwei-tseng) in 1887 and set out to raise a family and earn a living.

Starting with success in the noodle manufacturing business, by 1904 Charlie Song had diversified to become a major investor in tobacco and cotton, and the primary publisher of Bibles and English-language commercial publications in east Asia. After securing his family fortune, Charlie Song poured his profits into the budding revolutionary movement against the dying Manchu regime. He would die a wealthy man in 1918.

In childhood, Ailing was known as a tomboy, smart and ebullient; Qingling was known as the intellectual, pretty and pensive; and Meiling was considered a plump child, charming and headstrong. For their early education, they all went to McTyeire, the most important foreign-style school for Chinese girls in Shanghai. In 1904, reflecting the American influence which rejected in some respects the traditional Chinese denigration of women, Charlie Song asked his friend William Burke, an American Methodist missionary in China, to accompany the 14-year-old Ailing to Wesleyan College in Macon, Georgia, for her college education. Thus it was that Ailing embarked on an American liner with the Burke family in Shanghai. But when they reached Japan, Mrs. Burke was so ill that the family was forced to remain, and Ailing sailed on alone. Despite a genuine Portuguese passport on her arrival in San Francisco, the schoolgirl was pulled aside and told that Chinese were restricted from entering America. For the next three weeks, Ailing was transferred from ship to ship until an American missionary helped solve the problem. Finally she arrived at Georgia's Wesleyan College, where she was well treated. She worked hard at her studies and exhibited a flair for drama as she played the part of the Japanese woman Cio-Cio-San in a college presentation of Puccini's opera *Madame Butterfly*. But she never forgot her experience in San Francisco. Later, in 1906, she visited the White House with her uncle, who was a Chinese imperial education commissioner, and complained to President Theodore Roosevelt of her bitter reception in San Francisco: "America is a beautiful country," she said, "but why do you call it a free country?" Roosevelt was reportedly so surprised by her straightforwardness that he could do little more than mutter an apology and turn away.

In 1907, Qingling and Meiling followed Ailing to America. Arriving with their commissioner uncle, they had no problem entering the country. They first stayed at Miss **Clara Potwin**'s private school for language improvement and then joined Ailing at Wesleyan. All six Song siblings would receive American educations at their parents' encouragement.

As the first child and eldest daughter, Ailing assumed responsibility early in life. Receiving her degree in 1909, she returned to Shanghai,

❧
*Ni Guizhen. See Song Meiling for sidebar (p. 565).*

where she took part in charity activities with her mother. With her father's influence, she soon became secretary to Dr. Sun Yat-sen, the Chinese revolutionary leader whose principles of Nationalism, Democracy and Popular Livelihood greatly appealed to many Chinese. In October 1911, soldiers mutinied in Wuhan, setting off the Chinese Revolution. Puyi, the last emperor of China, was overthrown, and the Republic of China was established with Sun Yat-sen as the provisional president. Charlie Song informed his daughters in America of the great news and sent them a republican flag. As recalled by her roommates, Qingling climbed up on a chair, ripped down the old imperial dragon flag, and put up the five-colored republican flag, shouting "Down with the dragon! Up with the flag of the Republic!" She wrote in an article for the Wesleyan student magazine:

> One of the greatest events of the twentieth century, the greatest even since Waterloo, in the opinion of many well-known educators and politicians, is the Chinese Revolution. It is a most glorious achievement. It means the emancipation of four hundred million souls from the thralldom of an absolute monarchy, which has been in existence for over four thousand years, and under whose rule "life, liberty, and the pursuit of happiness" have been denied.

However, the "glorious achievement" was not easily won. When Qingling finished her education in America and returned home in 1913, she found China in a "Second Revolution." That year, on the domestic front, Yuan Shikai, a Manchu general turned revolutionary, pushed aside the idealistic Sun to become a dictator. More seriously, on the international scene Japan was laying claim to Chinese territory. In a series of wars which coincidentally occurred every ten years (1884–85, 1894–95, and 1904–05), Japan had emulated the European imperialist nations by grabbing the provinces of Korea and Taiwan. In 1914, when Europe was embroiled in World War I (1914–18), Japan would be ready to take advantage and make further claims on Chinese territory. Yuan would die in 1916, but the Bolshevik Revolution in 1917 and the failure of the Versailles Treaty to protect China's interests would not benefit Sun Yat-sen. Indeed, Chinese anger and frustration would boil over in the May 4 Incident (1919), when university faculties and students demonstrated against Japanese plans to exploit China. This heralded the rise of Communism in China.

In 1913, along with Sun Yat-sen, the entire Song family fled to Japan as political fugitives. During their stay, Ailing met a young man named Kong Xiangxi (H.H. Kung) from one of the richest families in China. Kung had just finished his education in America at Oberlin and Yale and was working with the Chinese YMCA in Tokyo. Ailing soon married Kung, leaving her job as Sun Yat-sen's secretary to Qingling, who firmly believed in his revolution.

During that same brief exile, it was Qingling, the second daughter, who broke the mold first. Flying in the face of convention, both Chinese Confucianist and American Methodist, she fell in love with Sun Yat-sen and informed her parents of her desire to marry him. The Songs were appalled. Qingling was barely 20; Sun Yat-sen was over 50, and already married to **Lu Ssu**. Charlie Song hauled his family back to Shanghai and confined Qingling to her upstairs room. But Qingling escaped back to Japan to live with Sun Yat-sen, eventually marrying him in 1915 after he divorced Lu Ssu.

Meanwhile, Meiling had transferred from Wesleyan to Massachusetts' Wellesley College to be near her brother T.V. Song, who was studying at Harvard and could take care of her. When she heard of her parents' reaction to Qingling's marriage, Meiling feared that she might have to accept an arranged marriage on her return to China; thus, she hurriedly announced her engagement to a young Chinese student at Harvard. When her anxiety turned out to be unnecessary, she renounced the engagement. Meiling, who stayed in America the longest (1908–17), was seen as the "party girl" of the three, which meant that she was frivolous only in contrast to her sober sisters. All three sisters were educated in the prim Methodist (Victorian-era Christian) pattern. Not only did they become practicing Christians, but they became fluent in English and were better educated and more prepared for the public world than the average woman, Chinese or American.

Ailing, as the respectable Madame Kung, remained above these scandalous doings, more interested in business than politics. She and her husband lived in Shanghai and rapidly expanded their business in large Chinese cities, including Hong Kong. A shrewd entrepreneur who usually stayed away from publicity, Ailing was often said to be the mastermind of the Song family. Like her father, she produced children and money. In four consecutive years, Ailing gave birth to a girl and a boy, and a girl and a boy: Ling-i (Rosamund), in 1916; Ling-Ki'an (David), in 1917; Ling-wei (Jeannette), in 1918; and Ling-chieh (Louie), in 1919. During this decade when the revolution turned sour for Sun Yat-sen and his Nationalist

Party, known as the Guomindang, Ailing, her husband H.H. Kung, and her brother T.V. Song were successful in the financial community.

Qingling continued working as Sun Yat-sen's secretary and accompanied him on all public appearances. Though shy by nature, she was known for her strong character. After the death of Yuan Shikai, China was enveloped in the struggle of rival warlords. Qingling joined her husband in the campaigns against the warlords and encouraged women to participate in the Chinese revolution by organizing women's training schools and associations. In the 1920s, the Russians sent Michael Borodin to enlist Chinese revolutionaries into the Communist crusade against Western capitalism. Sun Yat-sen attempted to straddle the Communist versus the West rivalry. As long as Sun was alive, the Guomindang Party remained equally receptive to assistance from Russia and Western Europe and America. Unfortunately, Sun Yat-sen died in 1925, factions in the Guomindang split, and there ensued a power struggle to succeed him. His widow Qingling,

sympathetic with Guomindang leftists whom she regarded as faithful to Sun Yat-sen's principles, became a Communist, but the Kungs and the Song brothers were among the wealthy Chinese who struggled to keep the revolution anti-Communist. In the following years, Chiang Kai-shek, who attained control of the Guomindang with his military power, persecuted Guomindang leftists and Chinese Communists. In 1927, he asserted his leadership by purging the Guomindang Party of all its Communists. By so doing, Chiang committed himself irrevocably to the West to gain the economic support of the international business community to which Kungs and Songs belonged. He alienated many Chinese revolutionaries who hated their own upper class. In their minds, the Chinese upper class was not only opposed to thoroughgoing democratic reform but were also associated with the "white foreign devil" imperialists. He also alienated many Chinese patriots who wanted to resist the aggression of Japan. Therefore, while Chiang Kai-shek gained the necessary support from wealthy Chinese and rich American Christians to survive in

*Qingling, Ailing, and Meiling with orphans.*

the short term, he had fatally undermined his chance to unify the Chinese against their imperialistic neighbors, both Russia and Japan.

Next to the fall of the Manchu dynasty in 1911, Chiang Kai-shek's purge was the most crucial decision which shaped the subsequent direction of China's 20th-century revolution. It was in December of that year (1927) that Chiang Kai-shek married Song Meiling, thereby greatly enhancing his political life because of the Song family's wealth and connections in China and America. Whereas Qingling never approved of the marriage (believing that Chiang had not married her little sister out of love), Ailing was supportive. Perceiving Chiang as the future strongman of China, Ailing saw in their marriage the mutual benefits both to the Song family and to Chiang. Although Meiling was eager to marry Chiang, Ailing made it happen. Genuinely interested in securing happiness for her baby sister, she also discerned in Chiang the man who would protect the family interests from the rising Communist movement. Qingling was opposed. Not only did she dislike this match for conventional class and religious reasons (Chiang Kai-shek was already married to ◄⁕ **Chen Jieru** and came from the lower classes), she also opposed it for the same political reasons her sister favored it. While it is too much to say that he made his epochal decision to purge the Communists in order to win the hand of Meiling, there is no question that Chiang made this decision to win the support of the Kung and Song families.

❦ ►
*Chen Jieru*. See
*Song Meiling* for
*sidebar*.

As Madame Sun Yat-sen, Qingling ardently defended her husband's principles and continued her revolutionary activities. In denouncing Chiang's dictatorship and betrayal of Sun Yat-sen's principles, Qingling went to Moscow in 1927, and then to Berlin, for a four-year self-exile. Upon her return to China, she would continue to criticize Chiang publicly.

Chiang's purge almost succeeded. While it annihilated all the Russian-born and educated leaders of the Communist Party, it did not kill the Chinese-born Communists (like Mao Zedong and Zhou Enlai) who would assume leadership. Unfortunately for Chiang and the relatively few, but rich, Western-oriented and Christian Chinese, Chiang's purge served to strengthen the Communist movement. By eliminating the foreign leadership, he forced the Communists to rely on peasant support. For over seven years, Chiang's army pursued the remnant who, led by Chinese-born Mao Zedong, fled from the coasts and the cities to reach the interior. The handful of Communists who survived the epochal "Long March" (1934–35) lived to fight another day—eventually to win everything.

The more immediate problem after 1927 was posed by Japan. In 1931, Japan seized Manchuria, China's most industrial province. Declaring the creation of an independent state called Manchukuo, the Japanese placed ("restored") Puyi on the ancestral throne from which he had been deposed by Sun Yat-sen's forces in 1912, at age three. Although the United States persuaded the League of Nations to refuse to recognize Manchukuo's existence as an independent nation, Japan responded merely by withdrawing from the League and preparing for war. With the Western democracies paralyzed by the Great Depression and mesmerized by the rise of Fascism in Mussolini's Italy and Nazism in Hitler's Germany, nobody was inclined to help the beleaguered government of Chiang Kai-shek against Japan. Relations would continue to deteriorate until July 7, 1937, when Japan provoked an "incident" at the Marco Polo Bridge outside of Beijing (Peking) and declared war on China. World War II had begun in Asia.

Meiling's marriage to Chiang meant that the Song family was deeply involved in China's business and financial affairs. Both Ailing's husband Kung and her brother T.V. Song alternately served as Chiang's finance minister and, at times, premier. In 1932, Ailing accompanied her husband on an official trip to America and Europe. When she arrived in Italy, she was given a royal reception even though she held no public titles.

In 1936, two Guomindang generals held Chiang Kai-shek hostage in Xian (the Xian Incident) in an attempt to coerce him into fighting against the Japanese invaders, rather than continuing the civil war with Chinese Communists. When the pro-Japan clique in Chiang's government planned to bomb Xian and kill Chiang in order to set up their own government, the incident immediately threw China into political crisis. In a demonstration of courage and political sophistication, Meiling persuaded the generals in Nanjing to delay their attack on Xian, to which she personally flew for peace negotiations. Her efforts not only helped gain the release of her husband Chiang, but also proved instrumental in a settlement involving the formation of a United Front of all Chinese factions to fight against the Japanese invaders. The peaceful solution of the Xian Incident was hailed as a great victory. Henry Luce, then the most powerful publisher in America and a friend to Meiling and Chiang, decided to put the couple on the cover of *Time* in 1938 as "Man and Wife of the Year." In a confidential memo, Luce wrote: "The most difficult problem in Sino-American publicity concerns the Song Family. They are . . . the head and front of a pro-American policy."

The United Front was thereafter formed and for a time it united the three Song sisters as well. Discarding their political differences, they worked together for Chinese liberation from Japan. The sisters made radio broadcasts to America to appeal for justice and support for China's anti-Japanese War. Qingling also headed the China Defense League, which raised funds and solicited support all over the world. Ailing was nominated chair of the Association of Friends for Wounded Soldiers.

Meiling now stepped forward for her long day in the sun. Of course, the Kung-Song businesses were supporting the Chiang regime in order to protect and enhance their financial interests, but it was Meiling who became the stalwart ambassador to the international community. Taking advantage of her personal beauty and fervent piety, as well as her American connections with the missionary-oriented Christian churches, she became Madame Chiang Kai-shek the diplomat. She cultivated especially good relations with the American news media. In this respect she was helped by the *Time* magazine organization founded by China-born Henry Luce whose zeal for the Chiang regime was exceeded only by that of his wife *Clare Boothe Luce (whose own beauty, piety and articulateness matched Meiling's). All through the 1930s, 1940s, 1950s, and well into the 1960s, Madame Chiang Kai-shek spread the gospel that the real war was the holy war being waged between Christ and Satan. The good democratic, Christian, and capitalistic Chinese were fighting first against the wicked Japanese from 1930 to 1945 and then against godless Communism after 1945.

The year 1942 saw Meiling's return to America for medical treatment. In February 1943, she was invited to address the American Congress; she spoke of brave Chinese resistance against Japan and appealed to America for further support:

> When Japan thrust total war on China in 1937, military experts of every nation did not give China a ghost of a chance. But, when Japan failed to bring China cringing to her knees as she vaunted, the world took solace. . . . Let us not forget that during the first four and a half years of total aggression China has borne Japan's sadistic fury unaided and alone.

Her speech was repeatedly interrupted by applause. In March, her picture again appeared on the cover of *Time* as an international celebrity. She began a six-week itinerary from New York to Chicago and Los Angeles, giving speeches and attending banquets. The successful trip was arranged by Henry Luce as part of his fund-raising for United China Relief. Meiling's charm extended past Washington to the American people, and the news media popularized her in the United States and made her known throughout the world. Indeed, her success in America had a far-reaching effect on American attitudes and policies toward China.

*I* sing a song of Soongs.
—John Gunther

Soon afterward, Meiling accompanied Chiang to Cairo and attended the Cairo Conference, where territorial issues in Asia after the defeat of Japan were discussed. The Cairo summit marked both the apex of Meiling's political career and the beginning of the fall of Chiang's regime. Ailing and Meiling seemed to be standing on the wrong side of history. Although Chiang Kai-shek was on the winning side of World War II, and attended the Cairo Conference in 1943 to guarantee his Chinese government a permanent seat in the United Nations, Mao Zedong's Communist armies drove Chiang out of China in 1949, first to Tibet and then to permanent exile on the island of Taiwan. Even though the Chiangs would be able to keep Mao's government out of the United Nations for 20 more years, until the Nixon-Kissinger expeditions in 1969, they were unable to reverse the results of the revolution. The Communists who were all but exterminated in China in 1927 recovered to drive the Kungs and Songs out of China forever.

Corruption in Chiang's government had run so rampant that—despite a total sum of $3.5 billion American Lend-Lease supplies—Chiang's own soldiers starved to death on the streets of his wartime capital of Chongqing (Chungking). While China languished in poverty, the Songs kept millions of dollars in their own American accounts. In addition to the corruption, Chiang's government had lost the trust and support of the people. Meiling made a last attempt to save her husband's regime by flying to Washington in 1948 for more material support for Chiang in the civil war. Harry S. Truman's polite indifference, however, deeply disappointed her. Following this rebuff, she stayed with Ailing in New York City until after Chiang retreated to Taiwan with his Nationalist armies.

Ailing had fled China with her husband in 1947, taking most of her wealth with her; she never returned to China or even Taiwan. While in the States, she and her family worked for Chiang's regime by supporting the China Lobby and other public-relation activities. In 1967, H.H. Kung died. Though Ailing suffered from intermittent bouts with cancer from 1949 on, she endured until 1973 when she died in New York City on October 20, at age 83.

Because of their differing political beliefs, the three Song sisters took different roads in their efforts to work for China. Song Ailing, a.k.a. Madame Kung, embodied the American dream of one century and created the American nightmare of the next. She was formed to a great degree by well-meaning American Protestant Christians in the 19th century. They wanted to convert all China to the American Christian, capitalistic way of life. And as a pious, rich, and influential product of American culture, she played a crucial role in directing American foreign policy in the 20th century. This road led to three wars in Asia, initially to apparent victory but then to tragedy and ultimate disappointment. In the words of the most recent biographer of the Song Sisters, Ailing was "a woman of enormous financial accomplishment, . . . perhaps the wealthiest woman ever to put it all together with her own cunning, the broker of [Meiling]'s marriage to Chiang Kai-shek, the principal contriver of the Song family legend, and the true architect of the dynasty's rise to power."

Qingling had been isolated from the rest of her family when the Communists, led by Mao Zedong and Zhou Enlai, won her allegiance as Sun Yat-sen's widow as they destroyed the regime of Chiang Kai-shek and confiscated the Chinese property of the Kung and Song families. Qingling remained in China, leading the China Welfare League to establish new hospitals and provide relief for wartime orphans and famine refugees. When Chinese Communists established a united government in Beijing in 1949, Qingling was invited as a non-Communist to join the new government and was elected vice chair of the People's Republic of China. In 1951, she was awarded the Stalin International Peace Prize. While she was active in the international peace movement and Chinese state affairs in the 1950s, she never neglected her work with China Welfare and her lifelong devotion to assisting women and children. Qingling was one of the most respected women in China, who inspired many of her contemporaries as well as younger generations. She was made honorary president of the People's Republic of China in 1981 before she died. In accordance with her wishes, she was buried beside her parents in Shanghai.

SOURCES:

Hahn, Emily. *The Soong Sisters*. Garden City, NY: Doubleday, Doran, 1941.

Li Da. *Song Meiling and Taiwan*. Hong Kong: Wide Angle Press, 1988.

Liu Jia-quan. *Biography of Song Qingling*. China Cultural Association Press, 1988.

Seagrave, Sterling. *The Soong Dynasty*. NY: Harper, 1985.

SUGGESTED READING:

Akers, Samuel Luttrell. *The First Hundred Years of Wesleyan College*. Macon, GA, 1976.

Coble, Parks M., Jr. *The Shanghai Capitalists and the Nationalist Government: 1927–37*. Cambridge, MA: Harvard University Press, 1980.

Eunson, Roby. *The Soong Sisters*. NY: Franklin Watts, 1975.

Fairbank, John. *China: A New History*. Cambridge, MA: Belknap Press of Harvard University, 1992.

Fairbank, John King. *The United States and China*. Cambridge, MA: Harvard University Press, 1979.

Isaacs, Harold R. *The Tragedy of the Chinese Revolution*. Cambridge, MA: Harvard University Press, 1961.

Jacobs, Dan. *Borodin: Stalin's Man in China*. Cambridge, MA: Harvard University Press, 1981.

Salisbury, Harrison. *The Long March*. New York, 1985.

Sheridan, James E. *China in Disintegration*. The Free Press, 1975.

Snow, Edgar. *Red Star Over China*. 1st rev. and enlarged ed. New York, 1968.

Spence, Jonathan. *To Change China: Western Advisers in China 1620–1920*. Boston, 1969.

Sun Yat-sen. *Chinese Revolutionary*. New York, 1927.

Terrill, Ross. *Mao*. New York, 1960.

*Tuchman, Barbara. *General Stilwell and the American Experience in China: 1911–45*. New York, 1970.

Wilbur, C. Martin. *Sun Yat-sen: Frustrated Patriot*. New York, 1976.

**Liping Bu**, Ph.D. in History, Carnegie Mellon University, Pittsburgh, Pennsylvania, and **David R. Stevenson**, formerly Associate Professor of History, University of Nebraska at Kearney, Nebraska

# Sonja (1907–2000).

*See Kuczinski, Ruth.*

# Sonja (1937—)

*Queen of Norway. Name variations: Sonja Haraldsen. Born Sonja Haraldsen on July 4, 1937, in Oslo, Norway; daughter of Dagny (Ulrichsen) Haraldsen and Carl August Haraldsen (a clothing shop proprietor); studied dressmaking and tailoring at the Oslo Vocational School, 1954–55; attended the Swiss Ecole Professionelle des Jeunes Filles, a women's college in Lausanne, Switzerland; University of Oslo, B.A., 1971; studied English at Cambridge University, England; married Prince Harald of Norway, later Harald V, king of Norway (r. 1991—), on August 29, 1968; children: *Martha Oldenburg (b. 1971); crown prince Haakon Oldenburg (b. 1973).*

Sonja, queen of Norway, is now well regarded for her intelligence, elegance, and many works of goodwill. It was not always so. Born Sonja Haraldsen in Oslo in 1937, the daughter of **Dagny Ulrichsen Haraldsen** and Carl August Haraldsen, she worked as a sales clerk in her father's clothing shop. Sonja met Prince Harald (later Harald V) at an officers' ball and a romance developed. The prince's father King Olav V did not approve of the match because Sonja was a commoner. Olav had already allowed his daughter, Princess ***Ragnhild Oldenburg**, to marry a commoner, and there was concern among many Norwegians that the monarchy would become middle class. The Haraldsens decided to send their daughter to France with the hope that Sonja would change her mind about her feelings for the prince. While there, she worked as an au pair in Corrèze. However, Sonja and Prince Harald wrote to each other the entire time she was gone, and upon her return the two met in secret at every opportunity for ten years. King Olav tried to dissuade his son from marrying Sonja, but Harald was willing to renounce his right to the throne for her. After seeking advice from members of Parliament, the government, and the heads of the different political parties, King Olav announced his son's engagement to Sonja. Since her father had died in 1959, King Olav escorted Sonja down the aisle at the wedding on August 29, 1968, to show his support of the marriage.

Sonja may not have been of royal lineage, but she had the qualities necessary for the position of first lady of the kingdom. The finishing school she had attended in Lausanne, Switzerland, had prepared her for running a large household. She was fluent in both French and English, the latter of which she studied at Cambridge University in England. Since Olav's wife ***Martha of Sweden** had died in 1954, Sonja accompanied King Olav to official royal ceremonies so he could instruct her on the details of her new position. The Norwegian people immediately accepted Sonja as the crown princess, and she was well liked for her charm, grace, and expert skiing ability.

Sonja also devoted a great deal of time to charitable causes. Her calendar filled quickly with her visits to day-care centers and hospitals and her volunteer work with disabled children. In 1972, she set up the HRH Princess Märtha Louise Fund, named for her daughter, to offer aid to Norway's disabled children. Her commitment to helping children, combined with her leadership abilities, made her a natural fit for the presidency of the Norwegian Red Cross' children's aid division, a role which expanded to in-

*Sonja*

clude the vice-presidency of the larger organization in 1987.

Another cause dear to Sonja's heart was the plight of refugees. Although she functioned primarily in a fund-raising capacity, she also visited refugee camps to gain a better understanding of the difficulties unique to those in exile. The United Nations' High Commissioner for Refugees honored her work by awarding her the Nansen Medal in 1982. She used the award money, totaling $50,000, to build schools for refugees in Tanzania. Sonja became queen of Norway in 1991 upon the death of King Olav. When Harald took his oath of allegiance to the Constitution in front of the Storting (the national assembly), Sonja accompanied him. It had been 69 years since a queen (***Maud**) had last entered the national assembly.

**SOURCES:**

Laure, Boulay, and Françoise Jaudel. *There Are Still Kings: The Ten Royal Families of Europe.* NY: Crown, 1981.

**Susan J. Walton**, freelance writer, Berea, Ohio

## Sonning, Noelle (1895–1986).

*See Streatfeild, Noel.*

## Sontag, Henriette (c. 1803–1854)

*German soprano who was one of the era's stellar performers on the European and American opera and concert stages. Name variations: Henrietta Sontag; Jetterl Sontag; Countess Lauenstein; Countess de Rossi or di Rossi. Pronunciation: SUN-Tahg. Born in Coblenz (Koblenz) in the German Rhineland on January 3, probably in 1803; died of cholera on June 17, 1854, in Mexico City; daughter of Franz Sontag (a stage actor and comedian) and Franziska von Markloff Sontag (a singer and actress); attended Royal Conservatorium of Prague, 1815–1820; married Count Carlo di Rossi, in spring 1828; children: Alexander, Camillo, Marie, Luigi, Alexandrine.*

*Made debut as child actress (1807); made debut as child singer (1809); settled in Prague (1815); made debut as an opera star in Prague (1820); appeared in Vienna, Berlin, Paris, and London (1823–30); elevated to the Prussian nobility as Countess Lauenstein (1828); formally presented as Countess di Rossi, journeyed via Poland to Russia (1830); her husband named Sardinian minister to the German Confederation (1834); joined him on diplomatic assignment to Russia (1838–43); cared for her sister, Nina (1843–46); lost family fortune during European revolutions (1848); renewed career as a singer (1849); toured U.S. (1852–54); made trip to Mexico (1854).*

*Major roles and appearances: Agathe, Der Freischütz (1823); Pamina, The Magic Flute (1823); Rosina, The Barber of Seville (1823); (title role) Euryanthe (1823); Ninth Symphony of Beethoven (1824); Isabella, L'Italiana in Algeri (1825); Rosina, The Barber of Seville (1827); (title role) Semiramide (1828); Desdemonda, Othello (1828); Donna Anna, Don Giovanni (1829); (title role) Linda di Chamounix (1849); Rosina, The Barber of Seville (1849); Susanna, The Marriage of Figaro (1849); Miranda, The Tempest (1850); Zerlina, Don Giovanni (1853); Princess Isabella, Roberto il Diavolo (1853).*

The handful of women who became great opera singers of Europe during the first half of the 19th century had a unique opportunity. While the shifts in the political and economic world offered numerous chances for advancement for men, there were few comparable openings for women to obtain fame, fortune, and a degree of power. Within the musical world, however, great divas like *Giuditta Pasta and *Giulia Grisi were personalities to reckon with.

The opera stars who lived through these years saw their careers influenced and sometimes transformed by the political and economic shifts of the time. They sometimes found themselves in the midst of revolutions and endangered by marching armies. Their talents let them share in the wealth of an economically advancing society, and the revolution in transportation—with railroads and steamships taking the place of stage coaches and sailing vessels—gave them unprecedented latitude to travel. Most of this handful of remarkable women who conquered the opera world of the time were Italians. One, however, was a petite, blue-eyed German with an extraordinary soprano voice.

She was born Henriette Gertrude Walpurgis Sontag on January 3, probably in the year 1803. As Rupert Christiansen has noted, she is one of those singers who was born "in the proverbial theatrical trunk." Her parents were stage performers of varying backgrounds. Her mother **Franziska Sontag** was the daughter of a German government official; she ran off with Franz Sontag, a traveling actor, and the two formed a typical stage couple to which their daughter was soon added. Indeed, her mother delivered Henriette shortly after appearing on a stage in Coblenz.

Henriette's stage career began almost as soon as she could walk. She made her debut as an actress at the age of four, and she sang on stage for the first time at the age of six. Even at this early age, the child struck informed listeners with the beauty of her singing voice.

Meanwhile, the Sontag family suffered a number of misfortunes. Franz proved to be an unfaithful husband, and he was crippled as a result of a fall during a performance in 1810. In a further blow to the family's finances, Franziska's career was interrupted when she unexpectedly became pregnant with Henriette's sister, **Nina Sontag**.

Franziska returned to the stage to increasing acclaim and her talented young daughter took on more and more roles as a singer and actress. Franz's role in the family became more and more marginal. He abandoned his wife and daughters and died in Mainz in 1814. When Franziska accepted a contract for a series of appearances at the Ständetheater in Prague, Henriette and her sister spent some time with their mother's upper-class family in the Rhineland, then joined their mother. Henriette, now 11, was probably old enough to understand that her mother was involved in a series of romantic liaisons with local actors there. Her own strict code of morals perhaps found its origins in her discomfort with the situation.

The future opera star began her formal musical education in Prague. Up to that point, Sontag had acquired no formal training, although her talent was evident. Figures in the Prague music world, including the conductor at the Ständetheater where both mother and daughter performed, urged that she begin a serious program of study.

The authorities of the Royal Conservatorium of Prague bent the rules to allow the talented youngster to begin her studies even though, at 11, she was technically too young to enter the institution. In the next five years, notes her biographer Frank Russell, her voice "developed its inherent flexibility until it became the brilliant instrument which was without peer in the field of coloratura." Her mother, by now a renowned figure on the stages of Central Europe, served as her drama coach. Frau Sontag also drew on her own bourgeois class background to train her elder daughter for a proper role in society.

Henriette's operatic career began with dramatic suddenness in 1820 in a series of events that seem taken from a shallow novel. A distinguished tenor, Friedrich Gerstäcker, was scheduled to give a number of performances in Prague. The local soprano was taken ill, and Henriette was the only possible substitute. Once again Conservatorium authorities had to suspend their rules for her benefit: she had not yet finished her course of study, and she was technically barred from performing as a professional. The most vehement objections came from Franziska, who thought it was premature to place her daughter on an operatic stage where professional standards applied. Henriette's self-confidence—she had to be ready in only three days—and desire to take up the opportunity overcame her mother's reservations.

The young singer, still only 16, performed superbly. Her debut under such colorful circumstances intrigued the music world of Prague. The tenor she was expected to support ended up being overshadowed by Henriette's triumph, and he left the city infuriated. She followed this initial success by taking on more and more roles in Prague, all the while continuing her studies at the Conservatorium.

Sontag's career soon moved on to the wider stage of the Austrian Empire's largest city and the center of European music, Vienna. Her mother was the force behind the family's relocation: Henriette was becoming too friendly with the son of an aristocratic family in Prague, a relationship that threatened to disrupt her career without offering any hope of personal happiness. A move to Vienna opened new professional horizons while shutting the door on this romantic dilemma.

As a German singer, the young soprano faced some barriers. Italian music and Italian singers dominated. Nonetheless, her reputation as a musical prodigy preceded her, creating the chance for auditions before the giants of the musical scene. She passed with flying colors, performed brilliantly in German works by Weber and Mozart, all the while preparing to sing in Italian. It meant learning a new language and a new repertoire. Her triumph in *The Barber of Seville* made a snobbish Viennese audience forget her German features: blonde hair and blue eyes. Writes Russell: "Vienna, in one night, found a new idol." Her success was underlined when Carl Maria von Weber chose her for the first performance of his new opera, *Euryanthe*. Ludwig von Beethoven personally requested that she perform in the debut of his Ninth Symphony in May 1824. She joined three other vocal soloists in this signal event.

*She was, in truth, a living marvel.*

—Benjamin Lumley

Guarded by her mother and her own sense of morals, Sontag avoided the numerous opportunities an attractive young opera star had for an illicit liaison with a Viennese noble. She likewise remained free of a romantic link with one of the middle-aged gentlemen who governed the musical scene. Russell believes that at this time she may have begun to make the acquaintance of the young Italian diplomat Count Carlo di Rossi. Then a promising junior member of the Sardinian Legation in Vienna, Rossi was destined to have both a prominent diplomatic career and a central role in Sontag's life.

In 1825, the Sontag family moved to Berlin. Rossi had been reassigned to Berlin, and Henriette perhaps wished to follow him. In any case, she needed successes in other musical capitals besides Vienna, and there was a lively musical world in the Prussian capital, patronized by King Frederick William III.

As she had in Prague and Vienna, Sontag swiftly won over Berlin's music professionals and its audiences. She responded with a frenzy of activity. Her natural singing technique allowed her to perform more frequently than one of today's sopranos would consider, giving approximately 150 performances a year. Notes Russell, Berlin had gone "Sontag-mad." The men of the royal family, including the king, were some of her greatest admirers; army officers bribed her servants so that they could drink champagne from one of her slippers; and crowds serenaded her from the street below her apartment. Karl von Holtei, her impresario, fell madly in love with her, and it took all her tact to turn him away gracefully while maintaining their business ties.

Sontag's affections turned in a different direction: toward the aristocratic diplomat, Carlo di Rossi. A marriage between an opera singer and an aristocrat was unheard of in this era; singers became the mistresses, not the spouses, of such men. Nonetheless, the spectacular German singer saw no such limits. Her mother came from the upper ranks of bourgeois society, and her own manners were equally suited to the drawing room and to the stage. The precise development of their early relationship remains unclear, but it appears they were in love by mid-1827. In the spring of 1828, they were secretly married in Paris. An open marital tie would have meant the end of Carlo's diplomatic career.

Meanwhile, Sontag's own career moved from one success to another. She appeared in

*Henriette Sontag*

Paris in 1827, and her professional acclaim was accompanied by her welcome into the highest social circles. She found that only the royal court, centered on King Charles X, was unwilling to treat her as more than a stage performer. A return tour to Germany brought her frenzied greetings in one city after another. In the university town of Göttingen, an exuberant crowd destroyed the coach in which she had been traveling. The group's leader declared, before the police arrested him, that Sontag had sanctified the vehicle, and no lesser being should ever be allowed to ride in it.

By the last years of the 1820s, Sontag was one of the most famous women in Europe. She was in the process of amassing a substantial fortune, partly in payment for her stage appearances, partly in the form of jewels and other gifts from wealthy admirers. In short order she was off to London, the last great music center in Western Europe she had not yet conquered.

Up to this point in her career, Sontag had not encountered direct, bitter competition with other operatic sopranos. The small group of prima donnas who were her peers included such figures as the Spaniard *Maria Malibran and the Italian Giuditta Pasta, both of them now in London. In short order, Sontag found herself drawn to joint performances, either for charity or in private gatherings in aristocrat homes, with each of them. Instead of the customary friction marking the relationships among Europe's female opera stars, Sontag and Malibran, Sontag and Pasta, developed friendly ties based upon mutual admiration.

By mid-summer 1828, the vibrant German soprano found her personal life growing more complicated. She was now pregnant, and her husband's efforts to get the king of Sardinia to recognize their marriage publicly got nowhere. He was even more pained by the opposition of his own family, and he responded by breaking ties with them. Pain of a different sort came in November: in circumstances that remain unclear, Henriette suffered a fall in Paris and this in turn led to a miscarriage. Her health remained precarious for some time.

The German prima donna's equivocal position in European society soon took a turn for the better. Her old admirer Frederick William III, the king of Prussia, elevated her to the ranks of Prussia's minor nobility, naming her Countess Lauenstein. She could now be received as socially acceptable at the Prussian court. Writes Russell, "It was Frederick William's wedding gift to the Count and Countess di Rossi." A more grudging concession came from the monarch of

Sardinia, Carlo's employer. He would permit an official announcement of the marriage between Rossi and Sontag, but there was a condition. She had to bring her singing career to an end. That was something she was not yet prepared to do.

In 1830, even though she continued to pursue her singing, the Sardinian monarch relented. She and her husband were formally received at the Sardinian Legation in Paris as Count and Countess di Rossi. She briefly played the dual role of operatic diva and diplomatic hostess before embarking on her most adventurous travel so far: a tour of Russia. Her husband remained in Western Europe, busy with the diplomatic crises created as a series of revolutions spread across the Continent.

Sontag put aside Carlo's well-founded reservations and made the dangerous journey, in part through a war zone controlled by Polish rebels against Russian rule. The lucrative contract she had signed combined with her pride as a reliable performer to compel her to go.

In both Moscow and St. Petersburg, as usual, she performed to appreciative audiences. Following a farewell appearance in Hamburg, it appeared she was at the end of her career, determined to devote herself to being the spouse of a successful Italian diplomat. Her new status was sealed by a formal reception at the court of her greatest admirer among the ranks of European royalty, Frederick William III of Prussia.

In 1831, her husband received a notable promotion, being named Sardinian minister to the kingdom of Holland. The count and countess now settled in The Hague where they had their first child, a son named Alexander. Before the year was out, a second son, Camillo, had arrived. In 1834, she had her first daughter, **Marie di Rossi**. Although she had formally retired from the stage, Henriette maintained her musical routine, practicing regularly with an accompanist. Nonetheless, her life was governed by her husband's career. The count's fortunes rose and fell with the changes in the political situation in the Sardinian capital of Turin. For a time, it appeared he would be penalized by his enemies with a posting to Brazil. Luckily for the young couple, a change in the political balance in Turin brought a more desirable posting to Frankfurt as minister to the German Confederation.

The great soprano continued to perform on rare occasions. She gave a charity concert in 1836 to raise money for victims of a flood in Hungary, and she sang for her husband's diplomatic colleagues in 1838. The latter perfor-mance constituted a literal farewell; Carlo, Henriette, and their family were now off to St. Petersburg where he was to serve as Sardinian representative, with the rank of full ambassador, at the court of Tsar Nicholas I of Russia. It was a plum diplomatic assignment.

Henriette put aside her reservations—she had disliked Russia in 1830 and she was concerned about the health and comfort of her children there—and made the move. She quickly made a fast friend in the person of Tsar Nicholas' wife *Charlotte of Prussia, who had been born a Prussian princess. She also performed regularly at the request of the tsar as the star of a private opera company the Russian monarch formed in her honor. Nonetheless, one of her concerns became reality when her young son Camillo died in Russia.

At her insistence, her husband obtained a transfer from his post in St. Petersburg. In the spring of 1843, they returned to serve in Central Europe. Back in Prussia, life resumed some of its older forms: she was welcomed at court, and in June 1844, she gave birth to her last child, a daughter named **Alexandrine di Rossi**. She spent much of her time aiding her sister Nina, who had abandoned a career as a singer to enter a nunnery, then left because the physical strain of a cloistered life proved too much. The two sisters had been close companions throughout their lives, and Henriette was deeply devoted to her younger sibling.

In 1848, as in 1830, Henriette's life fell under the shadow of momentous political events. Revolution swept the Continent, starting in France in February, then moving eastward and southward to disrupt the existing order throughout Germany, Italy, and much of Eastern Europe. The former opera star turned diplomat's wife found her family's finances a chief victim of the upheaval. Her investments in industrial enterprises became worthless, and the banks in which she had deposited her fortune collapsed. Meanwhile her husband's career suffered a serious setback. The unrest had caused a crisis in Sardinia leading to slashing cutbacks in the diplomatic corps.

Fortunately, she still found herself the object of attractive proposals for renewing her singing career. To restore her family's financial prospects, she accepted an offer to appear in London. Given their social status, the Count and Countess di Rossi had to obtain permission from King Victor Emmanuel II of Sardinia for Henriette to sing professionally. When this was not forthcoming, the count ended his career as a diplomat. For the remainder of his wife's life, he would accompany Henriette on her tours with no function other than to smooth the way for her.

There were no precedents for the return of an opera singer to professional performances after such a long absence, and Sontag drew massive crowds in London from her first appearances. Some may have come out of curiosity, to see if she could live up to her legendary reputation. She was performing in the shadow of the illustrious young Swedish soprano *Jenny Lind, who had dominated the musical world of London in the last years of the 1840s. Sontag began her first performance by crossing the stage and greeting with a curtsy her husband and her four children. At the age of 45, she was still a vibrantly attractive woman, and the crowd soon cheered her continuing vocal brilliance. Writes Russell, "It was, they agreed, an incomparable voice." She had no need to fear competition, not even competition "with her own illustrious past." The director of the theater in which she appeared, impresario Benjamin Lumley, declared that she appeared to be merely 25 and possessed a voice of unchanged beauty. Her other role, as the wife of an Italian noble, also continued. She and her husband were received by the highest levels of English society, including a private audience with Queen *Victoria.

Sontag soon moved on to triumphs in Paris. Normally harsh critics like Théophile Gautier hailed her. The composer Adophe Adam wrote: "This artist unites the qualities of youth and freshness to all the talents of the experienced and finished artist. It is impossible to imagine that art or talent could reach so high." For him, she was "one of those prodigies which nature alone can create." She was soon back to equal acclaim in Germany.

The ease of travel in the age of the steamship and the railroad not only made European tours easy. It also opened the way for success across the Atlantic. Sontag soon followed in the footsteps of Jenny Lind and agreed to appear in the United States before retiring for good. Leaving her children in Germany, she arrived in New York in September 1852, assured by the musical entrepreneurs who were arranging her tour that she would be treated with greater dignity than P.T. Barnum had shown the Swedish star. At first, she was not expected to perform grand opera; instead, she was scheduled for a round of concert appearances.

She found herself greeted by cultivated and knowledgeable music lovers in New York society, but raucous crowds of admirers surrounded her hotel in scenes much like those Lind had endured. Critics found her concert performances superb. She seemed more elegant in appearance than Lind. Her voice, one critic noted, may have lost some of its beauty in the lower tones due to age, but "in the upper and middle register her organ is perfect." John Dizikes has suggested that her success in America depended less on her vocal talents and dramatic abilities than upon the American fascination with titles and aristocrats.

At this time, the noted Italian soprano *Maria Alboni was also singing in the United States. Sontag soon proved the more popular, and Alboni returned to Europe. The natural rivalry between the two stirred the young American writer *Louisa May Alcott in 1854 to write her first published short story, "The Rival Prima Donnas," about this dramatic situation.

Sontag moved on to concerts in Philadelphia and Boston. In the latter city, one member of the audience was the president-elect, Franklin Pierce. In 1853, under the wing of opera producer Max Maretzek, she was able to sing in grand opera in New York. Her tours extended during 1854 through the South with particular success in New Orleans. In April, she moved on to perform in Mexico.

Her biographer attributes her decision to make this final tour before returning to Europe to financial reasons. She continued to feel her family's danger of falling into poverty. Traveling in a country noted for its revolutions, civil wars, and poor health standards might have frightened a less confident woman. But she had not been afraid of revolution in Poland in 1830. As Russell put it, "there was steel in her character" and a deep belief in "her extraordinary luck."

Tragedy arrived quickly. Before beginning her series of concerts in Mexico City, she needed to grow acclimated to the thin air of the high plateau on which the city stood. Thus, she accepted the invitation of a wealthy Mexican who had served with her husband as a young diplomat in Vienna to stay at the family hacienda. There she was exposed to cholera, and, shortly after her arrival in Mexico City, it became evident she had contracted the disease. She died in the Mexican capital on June 17, 1854.

Henriette Sontag is relatively unknown compared to her contemporaries. As her biographer has noted, she had no Barnum to publicize her nor did she plummet from the stage in an early death like Malibran. Her career was marked by brevity, interrupted by nearly two decades of marriage and virtual retirement. Her mild and agreeable temperament made her personality less memorable than more mercurial sopranos although observers were struck by her physical beauty. Nonetheless, she presented a voice that was, according to Christiansen, "sweet, pure, and accurate, backed by what was probably the soundest technique of her era." While not a remarkable actress, she could sing, in the words of Hector Berlioz, "like the lark at heaven's gate."

**SOURCES:**

Christiansen, Rupert. *Prima Donna: A History*. London: Bodley Head, 1984.

Dizikes, John. *Opera in America: A Cultural History*. New Haven, CT: Yale University Press, 1993.

Rosenthal, Harold, and John Warrack. *The Concise Oxford Dictionary of Opera*. 2nd ed. London: Oxford University Press, 1979.

Russell, Frank. *Queen of Song: The Life of Henrietta Sontag*. NY: Exposition, 1964.

Sadie, Stanley. *The New Grove Dictionary of Music and Musicians*. Vol. 17. London: Macmillan, 1980.

**SUGGESTED READING:**

Lindenberger, Herbert. *Opera: The Extravagant Art*. Ithaca, NY: Cornell University Press, 1984.

Mordden, Ethan. *Opera Anecdotes*. NY: Oxford University Press, 1985.

Parker, Roger, ed. *The Oxford Illustrated History of Opera*. Oxford: Oxford University Press, 1994.

**Neil M. Heyman**, Professor of History,
San Diego State University,
San Diego, California

# Soong.

*See Song.*

# Soong Chingling (1893–1981).

*See Song Sisters for Song Qingling.*

# Soong Eling (1890–1973).

*See Song Sisters for Song Ailing.*

# Soong May-ling (b. 1897).

*See Song Meiling; also Song Sisters.*

# Sophia.

*Variant of Sofia and Sophie.*

# Sophia (fl. early 2nd c.)

*Saint. Name variations: Sofia; St. Wisdom. Flourished early 2nd century in Rome; married and widowed; children: daughters Pistis, Elpis and Agape. Feast day is August 1 (September 30 in the Roman Martyrology).*

In the early history of the church, Christians often substituted a pious pseudonym for the actual name of a saint or martyr. Some of the pseudonyms were Greek, some Latin, and they generally were instructive or had a mystical meaning (e.g. Pistis, meaning faith). Nothing is

known of Sophia. Her name, or pseudonym, was found on a tomb in a cemetery reserved for martyrs on the Aurelian Way; thus, it was assumed that she had died for her faith. The legend that has grown up around the names on this tomb—Sophia, **Pistis**, **Elpis** and **Agape** (Wisdom, Faith, Hope and Charity in Greek)—is almost certainly derived from an Eastern allegory about the cult of Divine Wisdom. According to the legend, Wisdom was a widowed Roman during the time of Emperor Hadrian. Her three young daughters were persecuted for their Christian beliefs: 12-year-old Faith was scourged and thrown into boiling pitch, while 10-year-old Hope and 9-year-old Charity were tossed into a furnace. When these punishments did not hurt them, they were beheaded. Wisdom died praying at their graves three days later. Greek churches were often dedicated to Saint Sophia, but the magnificent church in Istanbul, the Hagia Sophia, is not. In effect *Hagia Sophia* means Holy Wisdom, or Holy Spirit; it refers not to a woman but to the word of God.

# Sophia (c. 525–after 600)

*Empress of Byzantium and Rome. Born around 525; died after 600; daughter of Sittas and Comitona (sister of Empress Theodora); niece of Empress Theodora (c. 500–548); married Flavius Justinus or Justin II (son of Emperor Justinian I's sister, Vigilantia), emperor of Byzantium and Rome (r. 565–578); children: son Justus; daughter Arabia.*

Empress Sophia was born around 525, the daughter of Sittas and ❧ **Comitona** who was the oldest of three sisters. Comitona, ❧ **Anastasia**, and the future empress *Theodora were the daughters of Acacius, a keeper of bears at the Circus of Constantinople, and an unnamed actress-dancer. As such, the family was of lowly status but in contact with many of the most elevated members of the imperial court of the late Roman Empire. With her sisters, Comitona began a career as an "actress" (with an apparently lewd stage show). However, her prospects vastly improved after her sister Theodora caught the attention of Justinian I, whose mistress and eventual wife she became. Justinian brought Theodora and her sisters to court, where they came to enjoy a quantum leap in status, especially after Justinian became emperor in 527. It is not known whether Comitona was as attractive or as beguiling as her famous sister, but not long after Theodora's status as Justinian's wife and empress was legitimized, Comitona herself mar-

❧
***Comitona.*** *See joint entry under Anastasia and Comitona.*

❧
***Anastasia.*** *See joint entry under Anastasia and Comitona.*

ried a high official named Sittas (probably in 528). Sophia seems to have been born several years before her parents' union was officially sanctioned by church and state, but this was a time and place where unsanctioned liaisons were common, even among the mighty.

Sophia's father probably was of Gothic origin, and he began his career as a member of Justinian's bodyguard. Just prior to his marriage to Comitona, Sittas (with the famous Belisarius) commanded two plundering incursions into Armenia. Almost certainly it was the military competency demonstrated during these missions which induced Justinian to honor Sittas by allowing him to become the emperor's brother-in-law. Probably in 529, an additional indication of Justinian's favor came in Sittas' appointment as the first ever "Master of Soldiers" for Armenia. Sittas' performance in his new capacity justified Justinian's faith in his ability, for he again met with military success: so much so, in fact, that Justinian began to employ his talents against the Sasanid Persians—the Roman Empire's most powerful eastern rival. In 532, Sittas became a diplomat as well as a general, for in that year he helped to negotiate a peace with the Persians which the otherwise hard-pressed (at the time) Justinian very much desired. By 536, there existed two additional indications that Sittas' star was rapidly rising: first, he was elevated into the ranks of the prestigious patrician order (a status which Sophia would also attain, although it is not known whether she did so as a result of Sittas' success or as the result of her own rise to power), and second, he was assigned a new command, this time against the Bulgars. When he was absent from Armenia and the east, however, the Roman position there deteriorated. As a result, it was not long until Sittas was reassigned to Armenia. Before he could reestablish Rome's domination in the region, however, he was killed during a treacherous ambush planned by some whom he thought to be allies (539).

Sophia thus reached a marriageable age only after her father's death. Yet, she did so at a court where Sittas' memory was held in extreme reverence. This, plus the fact that Justinian and Theodora had no children of their own, led Sophia to develop an especially close relationship with her imperial uncle and aunt. Upon the urging of Theodora, when it came time for Sophia to marry (probably about 542), Justinian arranged for her to be given to Justin (II), the son of the emperor's sister, *Vigilantia. This union was important to Theodora for two reasons. First, it enhanced the status of Justin, whom Theodora wanted Justinian to name as

his successor in lieu of Germanus (Justinian's cousin and closest living relative, whom Theodora loathed). And second, Sophia's marriage created a second link between Justinian's family and Theodora's, thereby reinforcing Theodora's influence and helping to insulate her from political detractors. Although Theodora died (548) long before Justinian (565), her influence over him in the matter of succession was never overcome by those who preferred Germanus to Justin. Thus, when Justinian died and Justin II became an Augustus (emperor) of the Roman world, Sophia officially began her reign as an Augusta.

Justin II and Sophia had two children: a son Justus and a daughter **Arabia**. Unfortunately, Justus died before the imperial accession of his parents, leaving Justin II with no direct heir. Arabia reached adulthood and married a Baduarius, who served as a military commander under his father-in-law, especially against the Lombards. Apparently the relationship between Justin II and Baduarius was occasionally rocky. In the end, however, that did not matter. Baduarius died (probably in 576) fighting the Lombards in the vain attempt to keep them from seizing northern Italy from the eastern Empire. Thus, he predeceased Justin II and could not become his imperial successor. Baduarius and Arabia had a daughter, **Firmina**.

Although Justin II demonstrated promise when his uncle, the imperial predecessor, still lived, and although the early years of his reign generally knew the benefits of competent rule, by 574 Justin began to exhibit signs of mental illness. Thereafter, he increasingly became isolated from both his subjects and imperial affairs, and Sophia began to assert herself in the running of the empire. Sophia apparently was conventionally religious (unlike her aunt who stirred up religious controversy), so she met with little opposition over matters of the spirit. She demonstrated a strong will and an ambitious nature—qualities not unlike those which had emancipated Theodora from the sordid world of the circus and catapulted her to the heady heights of the imperial palace.

Sophia grew as her husband diminished, principally in the always contentious arena of court politics. She especially concerned herself with the problem of her husband's successor, since after 574 Justin II was decreasingly competent. Sophia's ally in the factional rivalry which developed over the succession was Tiberius (II Constantine), the commander of the Imperial Bodyguard, whom Justin II named as his caesar (junior emperor) in 574 upon the recommendation of Sophia. Tiberius was a handsome man. In fact, he was so good looking that many suspected that Sophia coveted more than his political and military insight. Fueling such suspicion was the fact that after Tiberius' promotion to caesar, Sophia refused to allow Tiberius the right to bring his wife ❧▶ **Ino-Anastasia** to live at the palace. Indeed, it is probable that Sophia maneuvered to marry Tiberius after it became clear that Justin II's health was mortally declining. However, it is more likely that the passion which drove her to Tiberius was a lust to retain imperial power and influence, rather than a physical desire for his body.

Regardless, before Justin II died Sophia became the first late Roman Augusta to be portrayed on imperial coins—a symbolic recognition of her imperial significance. This honor was appropriate since Sophia was especially engaged in the economic affairs of the empire as an advocate of debt relief. This fiscal concern for the plight of the poor was coupled with an enthusiasm for the dispensing of charity. Indeed, charity was an imperial virtue expected of emperors and empresses, but even so, Sophia was zealous in shouldering this responsibility.

Between 574 and 578 Sophia, with Tiberius at her side, dominated the imperial court and its day-to-day business. When it became clear that Justin II had little time to live, Sophia urged her decrepit husband to appoint Tiberius as a full Augustus. Justin II did as Sophia advised—and just in time, for a little more than a week after the promotion of Tiberius, Justin II died. Then, Sophia received a shock. Although she was expecting Tiberius to marry her (after the appropriate period of mourning), he did not. While continuing to honor Sophia after his accession (referring to her in public as "Mother"), Tiberius brought his wife Ino-Anastasia and two daughters to the palace, removing Sophia from its central apartment. Clearly, Tiberius had no intention of allowing Sophia to remain an empress in practice as well as in name under his watch (she did, however, retain the title of Augusta).

This "betrayal" incited Sophia to attempt to replace Tiberius on the throne with a Justinian who was the son of Justin II's one-time imperial rival, Germanus. Unfortunately for Sophia, however, Tiberius learned of her plans and nipped them in the bud. He seems to have considered the impetuous Justinian as no threat, for Sophia's would-be agent was pardoned. On the other hand, Tiberius punished Sophia as befit one with her status and past: he removed her entirely from the central court and placed her under house arrest in a residence of her own. Nonetheless, although Tiberius controlled access to Sophia, he never ceased to show her respect in public and he continued to permit her the use of the title Augusta. In fact, Tiberius seems to have truly respected Sophia's political instincts, for when his own health rapidly declined in 582, mandating the appointment of a successor, he called in Sophia to petition her advice. Sophia favored one Maurice Tiberius, and largely because of her recommendation, Tiberius soon appointed that man as his imperial heir.

Within a fortnight of this announcement, Tiberius was dead, Maurice was an Augustus, and Sophia had returned to her freedom. Little is known about Sophia during Maurice's reign, but it seems likely that her incarceration under Tiberius had taught her a lesson about the appropriate behavior expected of an aging Augusta. Apparently Sophia got along well with Maurice's wife ❧▶ **Constantina** (daughter of Tiberius and Ino-Anastasia), which would never have been the case if Sophia was perceived as interfering overmuch in imperial politics. The last we know of Sophia concerns a ceremony on Easter in 601,

---

❧▶ **Ino-Anastasia** (fl. 575–582)

*Byzantine empress. Flourished around 575 to 582; married Tiberius II Constantine, Byzantine emperor (r. 578–582); children: *Constantina (who married Maurice Tiberius [Mauritius], Byzantine emperor [r. 582–602]); another daughter.*

❧▶ **Constantina** (fl. 582–602)

*Byzantine empress. Name variations: Constantia. Flourished between 582 and 602; daughter of Tiberius II Constantine, Byzantine emperor (r. 578–582), and Ino-Anastasia; married Maurice Tiberius (Mauritius), Byzantine emperor (r. 582–602); children: nine.*

Constantina, the daughter of Emperor Tiberius II Constantine and Empress *Ino-Anastasia, was given in marriage to Maurice Tiberius, a Cappodocian who had risen in prominence in the army and assumed the throne by this union. The couple had nine children. Maurice's military reforms would play an important part in saving the empire in future years, but when he gave an unpopular order to his troops campaigning against the Avars north of the Danube, it caused a revolution. As Phocas I entered the city, Maurice Tiberius and Constantina fled with their children. Maurice was captured and ordered to watch as Phocas beheaded all of the children, including an infant. Phocas then beheaded Maurice. The fate of Constantina is unknown.

when she and Constantina presented a richly decorated crown to Maurice which thereafter graced Hagia Sophia as an imperial symbol. Thus, Sophia seems to have lived harmoniously for about 20 years at the court of her own husband's successor, once removed. Whether Sophia lived to see the imperial overthrow of Maurice by Phocas in 602 is not known, but if she did it is not likely, given her age and the length of time she had been removed from the center of politics, that there was much she could have done to prevent that coup.

**William S. Greenwalt**,
Associate Professor of Classical History,
Santa Clara University, Santa Clara, California

## Sophia (1464–1512).

*See Sophie of Poland.*

## Sophia (fl. 1500s)

*Duchess of Brunswick. Name variations: Zofia. Flourished in the 1500s; daughter of \*Bona Sforza (1493–1557) and Zygmunt I Stary also known as*

Sigismund I the Elder (1467–1548), king of Poland (r. 1506–1548); married Heinrich also known as Henry, duke of Brunswick.

## Sophia (1630–1714)

*Electress of Hanover. Name variations: Sophia or Sophie Simmern; Sophie von Hannover; Sophia Wittelsbach. Born in Wassenaer Court, The Hague, Netherlands, on October 13 or 14, 1630; died at Schloss Herrenhausen, Hanover, Germany, on June 8, 1714; interred at the Chapel of Schloss Herrenhausen; 12th child of Frederick V, king of Bohemia, and Elizabeth of Bohemia (1596–1662, the winter queen and daughter of James I, king of England); married Ernst August also known as Ernest Augustus (d. 1698), elector of Hanover and duke of Brunswick-Lüneburg, on September 30, 1658; children: George Louis, later George I (1660–1727), king of England (r. 1714–1727); Frederick (1661–1690); Maximilian (1666–1726); \*Sophie Charlotte of Hanover (1668–1705); Charles (1669–1691); Christian (1671–1703); Ernest (1674–1728), duke of York and Albany.*

Sophia was born in Wassenaer Court, The Hague, Netherlands, in 1630, the 12th child of Frederick V, king of Bohemia, and *\*Elizabeth of Bohemia* (daughter of James I, king of England). While residing after 1649 at Heidelberg with her brother Charles I, elector Palatine of the Rhine, Sophia was betrothed to George William, afterwards duke of Lüneburg-Celle. However, in 1658, she married his younger brother, Ernst August, who became elector of Brunswick-Lüneburg, or Hanover, in 1692. Sophia's married life was not happy. Her husband was unfaithful, three of her children were stillborn, and three of her six sons died in battle. (Frederick was felled at the battle of Siebenburgen and Charles died in the battle of Pristina, both fighting the Turks; Christian drowned in the Danube while fighting the French.) Other family concerns included a long-lived animosity between Sophia and her daughter-in-law *\*Sophia Dorothea of Brunswick-Celle* (1666–1726), wife of her eldest son George Louis (the future George I, king of England).

As a Stuart and a granddaughter of James I, Sophia's name had been referred to in connection with the English throne over the years. However, in 1689, when considering the Bill of Rights, Britain's House of Commons refused to place her in the line of succession. The matter was successfully set aside for the next 11 years, until 1700, when the state of succession in Eng-

*Sophia (1630–1714)*

land became more critical. The king, William III, was ill and childless; William, duke of Gloucester, the only surviving child of the princess Anne (1665–1714, future Queen *Anne), had just died. The strong Protestant feeling in the country, the threat from the Stuarts, and the hostility of France, made it crucial that all Roman Catholics be excluded from the throne. Electress Sophia was the nearest heir who was a Protestant. She had also become a widow in 1698.

Accordingly, by the Act of Settlement of 1701, the English crown settled upon "the most excellent princess Sophia, electress and duchess-dowager of Hanover" and "the heirs of her body, being Protestant," in the likelihood that there were no children of William III or Queen Anne. Sophia watched affairs in England during the reign of Anne with great interest, although her son, the elector George Louis, objected to any interference in that country, and Anne disliked all mention of her successor. An angry letter from Anne possibly hastened Sophia's death, which took place at Herrenhausen on June 8, 1714; less than two months later, Anne died, and Sophia's son, George Louis, became king of Great Britain and Ireland as George I.

## Sophia (1868–1927)

*Countess of Torby. Name variations: Countess de Torby. Born on June 1, 1868; died on September 14, 1927; daughter of Natalie Alexandrovna Pushkin (daughter of the poet Alexander Pushkin) and Nicholas of Nassau (1832–1905); married Michael Michaelovitch (grandson of Tsar Nicholas I), on Feb 26, 1891; children: *Nadejda Michaelovna (1896–1963), countess of Torby (who married George Mountbatten, 2nd marquess of Milford Haven).*

## Sophia (b. 1957)

*Rumanian princess. Name variations: Sophia Hohenzollern. Born on October 29, 1957, in Tatoi, near Athens, Greece; daughter of Michael (b. 1921), king of Rumania (r. 1927–1930, 1940–1947), and *Anne of Bourbon-Parma (b. 1923).*

## Sophia, countess of Chotek (1868–1914).

See Chotek, Sophie.

## Sophia, landgravine of Thuringia (fl. 1211).

See Elizabeth of Hungary (1201–1231) for sidebar.

## Sophia, queen of Spain (1938—).

See Sophia of Greece.

## Sophia Alekseyevna (1657–1704)

*Able and ambitious daughter of Tsar Alexis who served as regent of Russia from 1682 to 1689 for her brother Ivan V and half-brother Peter I. Name variations: Tsarevna Sophia; Regent Sophia; Susanna; Sofya Alekseevna, Aleksyeevna, Alexeevna, or Alexinova. Pronunciation: So-PHE-uh Alek-SAY-vnah. Born Sophia Alekseyevna on September 17, 1657, in Moscow, Russia; died at the Convent of Novodevichy in Moscow on July 3, 1704; daughter of Tsar Alexis I (Aleksei of Alexius) Mikhailovich Romanov (1629–1676) and Maria Miloslavskaia (1626–1669); sister of Fyodor (Theodore) III and Ivan V, both tsars; educated informally at her father's court and tutored by Simeon Polotsky and Sylvester Medvedev; never married; no children.*

The daughters of early Russian tsars traditionally lived cloistered religious lives, seldom marrying or appearing in public. But Sophia Alekseyevna, daughter of Tsar Alexis I Mikhail-

Sophia
Alekse-
yevna

ovitch, was a headstrong and ambitious woman who was continually defiant of traditional customs. When her brother Fyodor III died in 1682, her half-brother Peter (the future Peter I the Great), son of Alexis and his second wife *Natalya Naryshkina, was proclaimed tsar. Objecting to a government dominated by the Naryshkins, Sophia cunningly broke with tradition and followed the hearse, crying and publicly demonstrating her grief. Leaving the cathedral after the funeral, she made open accusations that Fyodor had been poisoned and her younger brother, the feeble-minded Ivan (V), was being passed over in the succession. Her public charges incited the *streltsy* (palace troops) to revolt and murder several members of the Naryshkin family. Sophia calmed the *streltsy* and the populace by arranging for 16-year-old Ivan to become co-ruler with their half-brother, 10-year-old Peter, with Ivan as senior tsar. With the approval of the *zemsky sobor* (national assembly), Sophia, at the age of 25, assumed the role of regent for the youthful tsars. Thus governmental power in Russia was in the hands of Sophia Alekseyevna.

Sophia was born in Moscow on September 17, 1657, the sixth child and fourth daughter of Tsar Alexis and ◄⚶ **Maria Miloslavskaia**. She was baptized in the Cathedral of Dormition by Patriarch Nikon on October 4. Little is known of Sophia's childhood and young womanhood. Because of her mother's frequent illnesses and pregnancies, Sophia's upbringing in the *terem* (women's quarters) of the Kremlin palace was guided by her Aunt **Irina Romanov**, a dour spinster whose broken betrothal to a Danish prince had left her withdrawn and bitter. Sophia's early

⚶► **Miloslavskaia, Maria** (1626–1669)

*Russian empress. Name variations: Miloslavskaya, Miloslavna, or Miloslavski. Born Maria Ilyanova Miroslavskaia in 1626; died on March 3 or 4, 1669; born into the powerful Miloslavsky family of Russian nobles; daughter of Ilya Milosavsky; became first wife of Alexis I (1629–1676), tsar of Russia (r. 1645–1676), on January 16, 1648; children: 14, including Eudoxia (died after 1706); Marpha (1652–1705, who became a nun); Dimitri (d. 1667); Alexis (1653–1670); *Sophia Alekseyevna (1657–1704); Ivan; Fyodor also known as Theodore III (1661–1682), tsar of Russia (r. 1676–1682); Theodosia (1662–1676); Marie Romanov (1663–1723); Michael (1664–1669); Catherine Romanov (1669–1718); Anna Romanov (1655–1674); John also known as Ivan V (1666–1696), tsar of Russia (r. 1682–1689). Alexis' second wife was *Natalya Narishkina.*

years were likely dominated by compulsory prayers, pious conversations, and frequent whippings. The daughters of Russian tsars were unfortunately unmarriageable to European nobles because of religious and political differences, or to Russian princes because such men, despite their nobility, were beneath the royal family's dignity. Usually the tsarevnas were doomed to both celibacy and seclusion. But the veil of obscurity was lifted when Sophia passed her tenth birthday. It became obvious that her active mind demanded more than idle gossip, needlework, antics of court dwarfs and pious conversations.

When the opportunity arose, Sophia enjoyed listening to conversations between the tsar, his heir, and intimate advisors. She was also interested in the outside world. She learned about the English Parliament from the tsar's English doctor, Samuel Collins, and about greater Russia from A.L. Ordyn-Natchokin during his palace visits. Although it was against convention for her to speak to her elders, she could, nonetheless, listen carefully and respond to their questions. She and her brother Alexis (1653–1670) were very close, and one day he proposed to their father that his tutor, Simeon Polotzky, should also tutor Sophia.

Simeon Polotzky, a Belorussian monk, was interested in Western thought and culture and was proficient in several languages. He taught Sophia geography, politics, and diplomacy. She also studied Latin, French, and Polish but loved history so much that she convinced Collins to teach her English history. It is recorded that she opposed the English Parliament's execution of Charles I and believed the Thirty Years' War was a futile endeavor. Under the tutelage of Polotsky and his protégé Sylvester Medvedev, Sophia grew to appreciate Western achievements and culture. She also came to understand that Russia's isolation should be ended by the gradual introduction of Western reform to Russia. Polotsky was impressed enough with his young pupil to dedicate his book *Crown of the Catholic Faith* to her in 1670.

Sophia's mother died on March 3, 1669, and her father remarried in 1671 to Natalya Naryshkina, who gave birth to the future Peter I on June 4, 1672. His birth accelerated the rivalry between the Miloslavsky and Naryshkin families. Natalya eased the tyrannical restrictions of the *terem* by permitting the other women and herself the privileges of attending the theater, open coach rides, public appearances and trips away from Moscow. The more relaxed rules allowed Sophia to advance her political knowledge and to make important contacts with influential politicians and military officers.

On January 30, 1676, Tsar Alexis died and was succeeded by his 14-year-old son, Fyodor III Alexivitch (r. 1676–1682). Sophia moved into a commanding position, because the sickly young tsar was devoted to her. But Sophia knew that the unavoidable struggle between the two rival families would be decided by the person who held the throne. She had the disadvantage of having two brothers in poor health, while the Naryshkins had a robust heir in Peter and the support of Artamon Matvyeev, the powerful minister of foreign affairs and guardian of Natalya Naryshkina. Compounding matters was the fragile health of Fyodor and his failure to produce heirs. Sophia realized that the real crisis would come following his death, when the choice would be made between the feeble-minded Ivan and the healthy Peter. Fyodor's reign was ruled by ambitious favorites, whose positions were made more precarious by the power struggle between the Miloslavsky and Naryshkin families. By 1682, the young tsar's health was critical and his strength ebbed from day to day. Fyodor refused to name an heir despite pressure from both families and Patriarch Joachim, a Naryshkin supporter. Sophia, who remained silent, knew that her own relatives would oppose a woman as regent or ruler. Her only confidants were Prince Vasili Golitsyn, already believed to be her lover, and Sylvester Medvedev. It has been written that Sophia set aside court etiquette and nursed her brother through his fatal illness and was also present during all the final attempts to manipulate the succession by the various factions. Fyodor died at the age of 20 on April 27, 1682.

Taking advantage of the confusion following Fyodor's death, the Naryshkins, with the support of the patriarch, the princes, and much of the Muscovite citizenry, engineered the accession of Peter. The success and rapidity of the succession created consternation in the disorganized Miloslavsky faction. Fearing exile and persecution, they placed their hopes and efforts behind Sophia. Because she knew that her family's fortunes might rest on the military's support of the traditional succession, Sophia had carefully ingratiated herself to the officers of the *streltsy* by inviting them to the Kremlin and cleverly reminding them of Ivan's inheritance rights. At the funeral it was traditional for the mother of the new tsar to be the only woman in the procession. But Sophia and all of her ladies, wearing brief veils, broke tradition and left the *terem* to walk along with Natalya and Peter behind the

hearse. When they arrived at the cathedral, Natalya angrily ignored the service and returned to the palace. Following the funeral service, Sophia boldly addressed the crowd: "Ah, here we are left all alone with nobody to protect us. My brother Ivan's rights have been passed over most unjustly . . . and it should be known to all . . . that wicked people hurried on my poor brother Fyodor's death."

The general public had doubts about the Naryshkin family's ability to govern, and they certainly disliked the prospect of a long regency for the ten-year-old Peter. But the important support for Ivan came from the *streltsy* whose dissatisfaction concerning their declining importance predated Fyodor's death. Within a week of the funeral, 19 *streltsy* regiments had declared their support for Ivan and the Miloslavsky family. On May 15, the *streltsy*, incited by Sophia's accusations, openly rebelled by attacking the palace, killing several influential members of the Naryshkin faction, and demanding that Ivan be proclaimed tsar. Natalya and Peter were not harmed. After a few days of violence, Sophia calmed the *streltsy* by showering them with gifts of money and promotions and by enlisting their support for a political compromise. By the end of May, they had proposed, and a frightened *zemski sobor* had proclaimed, a dual monarchy with Ivan V as the first and Peter I as the second tsar. In addition, at the demand of the *streltsy*, the assembly installed Sophia as regent until the youthful co-tsars were of age. Power had passed to the Miloslavsky family in general and to Sophia in particular. From 1682 to 1689, she served as the first female ruler during the imperial period of Russian history.

Sophia quickly formed her government. She appointed Prince Vasili Golitsyn as minister for foreign affairs and her uncle, Prince Ivan Miloslavsky, as treasurer. In addition, she gave the education ministry to Sylvester Medvedev and appointed Fyodor Shaklovity, an obscure civil servant, as secretary of state. Sophia had a double throne constructed for the co-tsars and a third throne, one step lower than the tsars', was built for her. She signed all decrees, her likeness appeared on all Russian coins, and her nameday, the feast of *St. Sophia, was made a national holiday. Sophia was a prudent, even-tempered woman who did not approve of coarse language and practiced an extreme piety by uncommonly large numbers of visits to religious houses and churches. Although she was stout and plain in appearance, Sophia was a sensual woman who apparently shared her favors with both Golitsyn and Shaklovity even as she assumed the regency.

While the two men should have been bitter rivals, they remained friends and loyally served Sophia until the tragic end.

Sophia, with some reservations, had appointed Prince Ivan Andreevich Khovansky as commander of the *streltsy*. Khovansky was an enthusiastic supporter of the "Old Believers," those who opposed earlier religious reforms and favored a return to the old rituals of the Eastern Orthodox Church. He made threats to the regency and appealed to the officer ranks of the *streltsy*, many of whom were in favor of the old rituals. After trying to hold a debate, which became disorderly, Sophia met with smaller groups of the *streltsy* where she defended the Orthodoxy of her father and brothers and used a combination of gifts, strong drink and money to win their loyalty. Still mistrusting Khovansky and never certain about the loyalty of the *streltsy*, Sophia suddenly moved the tsars and the court from Moscow to the nearby village of Kolomenskoe as part of the annual tour of monasteries and country estates. Moving from village to village, Sophia's court reached Vozdvizhenskoe, a short riding distance from the sacred fortress-monastery of Troitsko-Sergievsky. Khovansky, who had continued his intrigues against Sophia, was invited, along with his son, to discuss business matters. In the meantime, she accused him of treason against the church and throne, and her council found him guilty and condemned him to death. Khovansky and his son were arrested on the road to Vosdvizhenskoe and were executed on the feast day of St. Sophia.

With the Khovansky threat removed, Sophia returned to Moscow. Because the *streltsy*, most of whom had supported Khovansky, had lost their zeal for confrontation, Sophia astutely issued a pardon to all the regiments after placing Shaklovity in command. She later transferred 12 of the 19 regiments to assignments on the Russian borders. Sophia returned to her normal routine of working long hours at her desk. She drew up plans for the first land survey, imposed penalties on public brawling, encouraged the growth of publishing houses, prepared ordinances for fire safety in cities, and attacked lawlessness and brigandage in Russia. Most of her domestic programs followed traditional Russian policies such as improvement of tax assessment and collection, efforts to eradicate government graft and corruption, peasant registration laws, and placating the nobility by efforts to prevent peasants from fleeing to the borders. She endeavored to improve Russian society by signing commercial treaties with Sweden and Poland, eased taxation to encourage cottage industries, encouraged foreign artisans to settle in Russia, and increased exports in furs, iron, and textiles.

Culturally, Sophia turned away from Greco-Byzantine influences in favor of Western European forms. Golitsyn was a cultured man with Western leanings who studied Latin and maintained a large library. Together, they encouraged the study of Latin and Greek and encouraged Russian contacts with the large foreign population in Moscow. The Russian-Slavonic-Greek-Latin Academy was opened with a more secular program in 1687. In art, architecture, and literature, a distinctive style referred to as "Moscow Baroque" replaced the old Russian cultural traditions. These changes, which had begun under Tsar Alexis, were continued under Sophia's regency. In art, the new style included straight perspectives, landscapes, still life, use of light and shade and a shift from a predominantly religious art to secular themes and portrait painting. Artists like Ivan Artemievich Bezmin and Simon Ushakov rose to prominence as transitional painters commissioned by the Miloslavskys, churches, and other prominent families during the regency. Literature reflected influences from the Ukraine, Poland, and Byelorussia as the individual author's personality was permitted to filter through his style. This can be seen in the verses of Simeon Polotsky, Sylvester Medvedev, and Karion Istomin which were popular at the regency court.

The problems inherent for a regent were made worse for Sophia by conditions already in existence, and the unfortunate domestic and foreign policy choices she pursued. Like the previous Romanovs, she failed to improve the conditions of the Russian masses, reform the rapid growth of serfdom, or settle the great schism in the Russian churches which were the major sources of discontent and impending upheavals in Russian society. Instead of innovative solutions or liberal change, the regency fell back to the traditional methods of suppression and police control.

In foreign policy, Sophia overruled her advisors, and approved a permanent peace negotiated by Golitsyn with Poland in 1686. Russia received Kiev and the territory east of the Dnieper River in exchange for joining a European alliance against the Turks. Sophia enthusiastically sponsored two disastrous military campaigns led by Golitsyn in 1687 and 1689 against the Turkish-supported Crimean Tatars. Sophia's efforts to proclaim the campaigns as victories increased the unpopularity of her government with the Russian populace.

These failures overshadowed successful treaties concerning borders, religious toleration, and commerce negotiated with Denmark and Sweden in 1684. To end armed hostilities with China over the Amur River region, Sophia signed the Treaty of Nerchinsk in 1684, the first treaty China ever signed with a Western power. But because Sophia ceded much of the Amur basin to China, the treaty was criticized by her opponents and added to her unpopularity at home.

Sophia knew that her reign was temporary in nature and that one day Peter would challenge her authority. Her brother Ivan was half-witted and nearly invalid. She had procured a bride for him (*Praskovya Saltykova) in 1684 but the marriage produced four daughters and no male heir. On the strength of doubts that Ivan had the stamina to consummate a marriage, the rumor developed that Sophia had placed another youth in the bride's bed. Other rumors suggested that she would have Peter, Natalya, and other members of the Naryshkin family murdered. During the regency, Peter divided his time between the court and the village of Preobrazhenskoye where he acted out military fantasies, first with toy soldiers and later with real soldiers. He studied geometry, navigation, geography and other subjects under the tutelage of several foreign scholars and adventurers. Peter grew to resent Sophia and concluded that she would eventually move against him.

Because of his interest in the army and military campaigns, it was probably the disastrous Crimean campaigns by Golitsyn that aroused Peter's concern. The first incident between Sophia and Peter occurred on July 8, 1684, at the Feast of Our Lady of Kazan to celebrate Russia's deliverance from the Poles. Sophia had attended the ceremony annually since becoming regent, but Peter, suddenly enraged at her presence, ordered her to leave the cathedral. When she refused, he lost his temper and left the ceremonies. Two weeks later, tension was further increased when Peter refused to honor the contrived victories of Golitsyn in the Crimea. After those events, Sophia kept a special *streltsy* guard around her. Rumors of impending plots dominated discussion in Moscow.

On August 7, 1689, Sophia requested an escort of *streltsy* for a pilgrimage to the country. Peter, who was staying at Kolomenskoye Palace, was awakened at midnight by an informer warning him that the *streltsy* would soon arrive. This was untrue, but Peter hysterically fled by horseback to Troitsko-Sergievsky, the same monastery that had shielded Sophia seven years earlier. Natalya and the loyal Preobrazhenskoye Guards ar-

rived to support Peter. Sophia tried to rally the *streltsy* regiments, nobles, and the populace but her pleas for support fell on deaf ears. Peter's impassioned call for support was answered by his friends in the foreign quarter, the *streltsy*, and most of the prominent noble families. Sophia was isolated, and she and her leading supporters were arrested. Fyodor Shaklovity was cruelly tortured but refused to implement Sophia in a plot against Peter. He and many other of Sophia's advisors were executed. Prince Golitsyn was stripped of his possessions and banished into exile. Sophia, still only 32 years old, was confined in the Novodevichy convent in Moscow.

It is doubtful that Peter had as much to fear from Sophia as he thought. She and her supporters had plans to dethrone Peter in favor of Ivan but there was never evidence of any plot against his life. If Sophia intended to murder Peter, she would hardly have waited until he came of age but would have legally ended the regency earlier. Peter, who as a boy had seen his Naryshkin relatives murdered in 1682, never trusted the *streltsy* or Sophia. When another *streltsy* revolt in support of Sophia was suppressed in 1698, Peter violently tortured, executed and exiled many of the elite troops. Concluding that he was unsafe with Sophia at liberty, he forced her to take the veil on October 21, 1698. Sophia, who took the name Susannah, was permitted only limited visits from her closest relatives on feast days. She died on July 3, 1704, and was buried the following day under a white tombstone in the Church of the Immaculate Virgin of Smolensk. She had emerged from the inferior position of women in the *terem* to seize power and govern the Russian people. She had ruled with competence and success during the transitory period prior to the reign of Peter the Great.

**SOURCES:**

*Almedingen, E.M. *The Romanovs: Three Centuries of an Ill-fated Dynasty.* NY: Holt, Rinehart and Winston, 1966.

Hughes, Lindsey A.J. "'Ambitious and Daring Above Her Sex': Tsarevna Sophia Alekseevna (1657–1704) in Foreigners' Accounts," in *Oxford Slavonic Papers.* Vol. 21, 1988, pp. 65–89.

———. "Sofiya Alekseevna and the Moscow Rebellion of 1682," in *Slavonic and East European Review.* Vol. 63, 1985, pp. 518–539.

———. "Sophia Alekseevna (1657–1704)," in *Modern Encyclopedia of Russian and Soviet History.* Vol. 36, 1984, pp. 165–172.

———. "Sophia, Regent of Russia," in *History Today.* Vol. 32. July 1982, pp. 10–15.

———. *Sophia: Regent of Russia 1657–1704.* New Haven, CT: Yale University Press, 1990.

Korb, Johann Georg. *Diary of an Austrian Secretary of Legation at the Court of Tsar Peter the Great.* Edited and translated by Count MacDonnel. 2 vols. London: Frank Cass, 1968.

O'Brien, C. Bickford. *Russia Under Two Tsars, 1682–1689: The Regency of Sophia*. Berkeley, CA: University of California Press, 1952.

Schakovskoy, Z. *Precursors of Peter the Great: The Reign of Tsar Alexis, Peter the Great's Father, and the Young Peter's Struggle Against the Regent Sophia for the Mastery of Russia*. London: Jonathan Cape, 1964.

**SUGGESTED READING:**

Bergamini, John D. *The Tragic Dynasty: A History of the Romanovs*. NY: Putnam, 1969.

de Jonge, Alex. *Fire and Water: A Life of Peter the Great*. NY: Coward, McCann and Geohegan, 1980.

Graham, Stephen. *Peter the Great*. Westport, CT: Greenwood Press, 1971.

Massie, Robert K. *Peter the Great: His Life and World*. NY: Alfred A. Knopf, 1980.

Putnam, Peter Brock. *Peter, The Revolutionary Tsar*. NY: Harper and Row, 1973.

**RELATED MEDIA:**

"Peter the Great," NBC television miniseries based on Robert Massie's book, starring **Vanessa Redgrave** as Sophia.

**Phillip E. Koerper**, Professor of History, Jacksonville State University, Jacksonville, Alabama.

# Sophia Carlotte (1673–1725)

*Countess of Platen. Name variations: Sophia Charlotte of Kielmansegge. Born in 1673; died in 1725; had liaison with King George I (1660–1727), king of England (r. 1714–1727).*

# Sophia Dorothea of Brandenburg (1736–1798)

*Duchess of Wurttemberg. Name variations: Dorothea Frederica of Brandenburg-Schwedt; Princess Dorothea. Born on December 18, 1736; died on March 9, 1798; married Frederick II Eugene, duke of Wurttemberg; children: Frederick II (1754–1816), duke of Wurttemberg (r. 1797–1802), elector of Wurttemberg (r. 1802–1806), also known as Frederick I, king of Wurttemberg (r. 1797–1816); Ludwig also known as Louis Frederick Alexander (1756–1817), duke of Wurttemberg; Eugene (b. 1758), duke of Wurttemberg; \*Sophia Dorothea of Wurttemberg (1759–1828), also known as Marie Feodorovna, empress of Russia; William (b. 1761); Freiderike (1765–1785, who married Peter Frederick Louis I, duke of Oldenburg); \*Elizabeth of Wurttemberg (1767–1790); Alexander (1771–1833), duke of Wurttemberg.*

# Sophia Dorothea of Brunswick-Celle (1666–1726)

*Duchess of Ahlden and the "uncrowned queen" of England. Name variations: Sophie of Brunswick-Zell; Sophia Dorothea of Brunswick-Lüneberg or Luneberg; princess of Ahlden; electress of Hanover. Born on September 5, 1666, at Celle Castle, Germany; died on November 13, 1726, at Castle of Ahlden, Hanover, Germany; interred at Celle Church, Germany; daughter of George William, duke of Celle and Brunswick-Lüneberg, and his morganatic wife Eleanor Desmier (1639–1722); married George Louis of Hanover, later George I (1660–1727), king of England (r. 1714–1727), on November 21, 1682 (divorced 1694); associated with Philip Christopher, count von Königsmarck; children: George II (1683–1760), king of England (r. 1727–1760); Sophia Dorothea of Brunswick-Lüneburg-Hanover (1687–1757). George I also had children with Ehrengard Melusina, baroness Schulenburg.*

A princess of the ruling house of Celle in what is now northern Germany, Sophia Dorothea was the only child of Duke George William of Celle and a French noblewoman, \***Eleanor Desmier**. Her parents were not legally married when she was born in 1666; Sophia was already nine years old before her birth was retroactively legitimated by their marriage and she gained the title of princess of Celle. Intelligent and high-spirited, Sophia was educated only in the accomplishments appropriate to a noble girl, such as music, embroidery, and languages. She was fluent in German and Dutch, but used French for daily conversation and correspondence. She was too impatient for more serious study, however, and preferred games and fashion to her books.

Despite her illegitimate birth, there was no lack of prospective husbands for the little princess. She was the only heir of her wealthy parents, who spent years negotiating and weighing the benefits of various marriage alliances for her. In the end, however, Sophia was betrothed at age 15 to her first cousin George Louis of Hanover (later George I, king of England), son of her uncle Ernst August, duke of Hanover. George's parents saw the marriage as the way to unite the duchies of Celle and Hanover under one rule, increasing the power of the Hanover family.

Many biographers have written of the marriage between Sophia Dorothea and George Louis as if it were inevitably doomed, usually blaming either Sophia or George for its failure. But its fate could not have been predicted when the marriage was celebrated with much pomp and ceremony in November 1682. The two young people were quite different in temperament and barely knew one another, but this did not distinguish them from other newly married couples from princely families.

In 1683, their first child, a son, was born (later George II, king of England). Sophia and George began to spend most of their time apart after this. The relatives of George Louis, especially his mother, the electress *Sophia (1630–1714), hated and despised his wife, and this feeling was soon shared by the prince himself. George was frequently absent on military campaigns, but even when he was at court, the personality differences between the two led them to keep separate quarters. George preferred to spend his time with friends and with his several mistresses; Sophia preferred the company of her courtiers and ladies-in-waiting to that of her husband. A second child, *Sophia Dorothea of Brunswick-Lüneburg-Hanover, was born in 1687 after a brief reconciliation.

Around 1690, Sophia began a correspondence with a Swedish count, Philip von Konigsmarck, who was serving in the Hanoverian army. They became lovers in 1692, an affair which was an open secret at the Hanover court. Sophia Dorothea was warned to break off the relationship by her husband and parents, but she refused to stop seeing Philip. Many of the passionate letters Sophia and Philip exchanged have survived, showing that the two hoped to run away together but could not for lack of money. (One source claims, however, that Sophia's infidelity to her husband is not absolutely proved, contending that the letters purported to have passed between Konigsmarck and Sophia are probably forgeries.) Despite the opulence in which Sophia lived, she actually owned no wealth or property in her own name, and Philip was deeply in debt. They also wrote of their fear of arrest and imprisonment for adultery, but Sophia pressed George for a divorce anyway in the hope of someday being free to wed Philip.

As long as Philip was serving the house of Hanover, the affair was allowed to continue despite repeated warnings to both parties. But in 1694 their relationship became a matter of state concern, and George and his parents were pushed to bring a violent end to it. In that year, Count von Konigsmarck left the Hanoverian army for a position in the army of Saxony, enemy to the house of Hanover. The ducal court feared that Konigsmarck would elope with Sophia and use her as a political tool against the Hanovers. When Philip returned to Hanover to announce his resignation in July, he was assassinated at the duke's orders. Sophia, unaware of Philip's death, was arrested and soon became a virtual prisoner at the remote castle of Ahlden in the duchy of Celle. A divorce was quickly arranged in which Sophia, as the guilty party,

was forbidden to remarry. In an agreement between Sophia's father and George's father, Sophia was to be confined at Ahlden permanently by her father. She was permitted a personal income but was not allowed to see her two children. In a time when wives could be executed for adultery, it was probably the best outcome she could expect.

Sophia Dorothea remained at Ahlden the rest of her life. Although few saw her as a threat if released, it was fear of Hanover's enemies using her as a tool which kept her confined. Anti-Hanover propaganda said that she had been unjustly accused and should be freed from her harsh imprisonment. Thus Sophia Dorothea, isolated in her castle, became a rallying point for those opposed to George as duke of Hanover and (eventually) as king of England, who sought to justify war against the powerful duchy by claiming to be rescuing an innocent victim of George's cruelty.

For the most part unaware of and certainly uninvolved in these plans, Sophia Dorothea adapted to life at Ahlden. She kept her own court, held the title of duchess of Ahlden, and was allowed to receive some guests (she saw her

Sophia
Dorothea of
Brunswick-
Celle

mother often). Sophia also amassed a considerable fortune from property inherited from her father. She did not see her former husband again; nor did she ever see her children or her 17 grandchildren, although she was able to write to them. Her relationship with her son and daughter was strained, to say the least. Her daughter Sophia Dorothea of Brunswick-Lüneburg-Hanover refused Sophia's request to help her secure release from Ahlden; her son refused to speak of her, even years after the divorce when he reigned as George II of England.

Sophia Dorothea remained at Ahlden for over 40 years. Even after George I succeeded to the throne of England in 1714, he refused to honor Sophia's request for freedom. Although her few supporters referred to her as queen of England, it was her ex-husband George's favorite mistress *Ehrengard Melusina von der Schulenburg who actually fulfilled that role (he never remarried). The "uncrowned queen" of England died at the age of 60.

**SOURCES:**

Hatton, Ragnhild. *George I: Elector and King*. Cambridge, MA: Harvard University Press, 1978.

Wilkins, W.H. *The Love of an Uncrowned Queen: Sophie Dorothea, Consort of George I*. NY: Duffield, 1906.

**Laura York**, M.A. in History,
University of California, Riverside, California

## Sophia Dorothea of Brunswick-Lüneburg-Hanover (1687–1757)

*Queen of Prussia. Name variations: Sophia Guelph; Sophia Dorothea Hanover; Sophia Dorothea of England. Born on March 16 (or 26), 1687 (some sources cite 1685), in Hanover, Germany; died on June 29, 1757, in Monbijou Palace, near Berlin, Germany; buried in Potsdam, Brandenburg, Germany; daughter of George I (1660–1727), king of England (r. 1714–1727), and Sophia Dorothea of Brunswick-Celle (1666–1726); married Frederick William I (1688–1740), king of Prussia (r. 1713–1740); children: Frederick Louis (1707–1708); *Wilhelmina (1709–1758, who married Frederick of Bayreuth); Frederick William (1710–1711); Frederick II the Great (1712–1786), king of Prussia (r. 1740–1786); Charlotte Albertine (1713–1714); *Frederica Louise (1715–1784, who married Charles William, margrave of Ansbach); *Philippine Charlotte (1716–1801); Louis Charles William (1717–1719); Sophia Dorothea Maria (1719–1765); *Louisa Ulrica of Prussia (1720–1782, who married Adolphus Frederick, king of Sweden); *Anna Amalia of Prussia (1723–1787); Augustus William Hohenzollern (1722–1758); Henry (1726–1802, who married Wil-*

*helmina of Hesse-Cassel [1726–1808]); Ferdinand (1730–1813, who married Anne Elizabeth Louise, princess of Schwedt [1738–1820]).*

Sophia Dorothea of Brunswick-Lüneburg-Hanover was born in 1687 in Hanover, Germany, the daughter of George I, the future king of England, and *Sophia Dorothea of Brunswick-Celle (1666–1726). She married Frederick William I (1688–1740), king of Prussia (r. 1713–1740), and their son Frederick Hohenzollern (Frederick II the Great) was born on January 24, 1712, in Berlin. Frederick William I governed the boy's upbringing by appointing tutors and commanding them to teach only the basic skills such as reading, writing, and counting. Believing that these skills would enable Frederick to rule efficiently someday, his father strictly instructed the tutors not to teach music, the arts, literature, or philosophy. Secretly, however, Sophia Dorothea and the tutors taught these subjects to the crown prince who thus became acquainted with Enlightenment literature and philosophy; he even became an accomplished flutist. When Frederick William discovered the transgression, he dismissed the tutors and, beginning about 1728, took personal charge of his son's education.

## Sophia Dorothea of Wurttemberg (1759–1828)

*Russian empress, grand duchess, and later dowager empress who was the wife of Tsar Paul I. Name variations: Marie Feodorovna; Maria Feodorovna or Fyodorovna; Mariia Fedorovna; Sophia Dorothea of Württemberg. Born Sophia Dorothea Augusta Louisa on October 14 (o.s.) or October 25, 1759, in Stettin, Pomerania; died on November 5 (o.s.) or November 12, 1828, probably in St. Petersburg, Russia; daughter of Frederick II Eugene (b. 1732), duke of Wurttemberg (r. 1795–1797), and Sophia Dorothea of Brandenburg (1736–1798); educated at home; married Paul I (1754–1801), tsar of Russia (r. 1796–1801, who was the son of Catherine II the Great), on September 26 (o.s.) or October 7, 1776; children: Alexander I (1777–1825), tsar of Russia; Constantine (1779–1831, who married Anna Juliana of Saxe-Coburg); Alexandra Pavlovna (1783–1801); Helena Pavlovna (1784–1803, who married Frederick Louis of Mecklenburg-Schwerin); Marie Pavlovna (1786–1859, who married Charles Frederick, duke of Saxe-Weimar); Olga (1792–1795); Catherine of Russia (1788–1819, who married William I of Württemberg); Anna Pavlovna (1795–1865, who married William II, king of the Netherlands); Nicholas I*

*(1796–1855), tsar of Russia (r. 1825–1855); Michael (1798–1849), grand duke.*

In the fall of 1776, just before her 17th birthday, Sophia Dorothea of Wurttemberg, the daughter of the Prussian ruler of the German duchy of Württemberg, married Paul Petrovich (later Paul I), the only son of *Catherine II the Great of Russia. The young woman, in conformity with Russian custom, converted from Lutheranism to Orthodoxy and took the name of Marie Feodorovna. For the first 20 years of her marriage, she lived the comfortable but isolated existence of a grand duchess as her husband waited for his mother to die. After this finally happened in 1796, Sophia Dorothea spent a brief but often unhappy five years as the wife of the reigning tsar and as empress of Russia. Following Paul's assassination in 1801, Sophia Dorothea became a formidable dowager empress and a force for conservatism in Russia until her own death in 1828.

Sophia Dorothea was born in 1759 in Stettin, Pomerania, the daughter of Frederick II Eugene, duke of Wurttemberg, and *Sophia Dorothea of Brandenburg. She was brought up in a close-knit and happy family living in the town of Montbéliard close to the French frontier. Her limited home education stressed morals and manners, dancing and needlepoint. While she read fairly widely and was exposed to Rousseauian romanticism, she was not a product of the Enlightenment or wide-ranging in her interests. Because she was healthy, attractive, well mannered and of royal blood, she was considered ideal marriage material by many of the ruling houses of Europe. Indeed, in 1776 she was engaged to two men: the first was Louis, prince of Hesse-Darmstadt, who was subsequently bought off with 10,000 rubles and another bride when Catherine decided that Sophia Dorothea was the perfect mate for her son.

Paul, whose first wife *Natalie of Hesse-Darmstadt had died in childbirth, was not, however, an ideal husband. By nature, he was impatient, temperamental and suspicious, demanding absolute respect and obedience from all who were beneath him and especially from his second wife. His obsessive behavior and uncontrollable temper led many contemporaries and historians to question his mental stability. Initially, these traits did not bother Sophia Dorothea. She respected and adored her husband, had no ambitions of her own, and was content to live a life of quiet domesticity in the Russian countryside. She also fulfilled her principal function by quick-

ly producing male heirs for the Russian throne. A son Alexander was born 15 months after her marriage, followed by another son Constantine in 1779. She then had five daughters—*Alexandra Pavlovna (1783–1801), *Helena Pavlovna (1784–1803), *Marie Pavlovna (1786–1859), Olga (1792–1795), *Catherine of Russia (1788–1819), and *Anna Pavlovna (1795–1865)—all but one of whom lived to maturity, and another two sons near the end of the century. After a year-long tour of Europe with her husband in 1781–82, Sophia happily settled down to remodeling and redecorating Pavlovsk—a lovely estate 36 miles from St. Petersburg. It was there that she spent much of her time picnicking with her family, playing parlor games, and looking after the upbringing of her daughters. During the first half of their marriage, Sophia "became the single most important person in [Paul's] adult life," according to Roderick McGrew. She "provided him with a secure emotional refuge and a personal bond on which he could depend."

The difficulty in her life was not her husband but rather her domineering mother-in-law. Catherine was not on good terms with her son who, by all rights, should have held the throne she occupied. She isolated him from all state affairs, considered removing him from the line of succession, and insisted on raising his two older sons in St. Petersburg. Many in her court snubbed or insulted Paul and Sophia, and foreign dignitaries considered it politic to avoid Pavlovsk as well as Paul's other estate at Gatchina. Paul, bored by his political inactivity and restless in the country, ultimately looked for more stimulating company than his wife could provide and found it in one of her ladies-in-waiting, Catherine Nelidova. While their intense relationship was platonic, it hurt Sophia and weakened her marriage. In time, the two women formed a unique alliance and worked together to give Paul the emotional support he needed and to control his frequent public outbursts of temper.

In 1796, Catherine finally died, and Paul, to the surprise of some, took over as tsar of Russia. During his first years in office, he consulted his wife on domestic reform, put her in charge of the Society for the Education of the Daughters of the Nobility, and personally crowned her his empress. There were those in court, however, who did not like the stabilizing influence of the Sophia-Nelidova alliance or the pro-Prussian, anti-French policy which "the empress' party" advocated. In 1798, it was suggested to Paul that his often pregnant wife should avoid the possibility of further children and that she and her friends were getting much of the credit for domestic change while he was not receiving the public respect he deserved. The ever-suspicious and vengeful tsar decided to teach his totally innocent wife a lesson. He took a new mistress, **Anna Lopukhina**; installed her in a royal apartment; banished Nelidova from St. Petersburg; and removed Sophia from all affairs of state. Three years later, Paul was assassinated by military and court figures who did not like either his pro-French foreign policy or his increasingly erratic behavior at home. Sophia, who knew nothing of the plot and briefly tried to succeed her husband, became the dowager empress when her eldest son ascended to the throne as Alexander I.

She carried out her new role in a much different fashion than she had her earlier duties as grand duchess. As Paul's long-suffering wife, Sophia Dorothea had been conventional, cheerful, a bountiful mother and respectful spouse who conspicuously avoided the intrigues of Catherine's court. She was criticized only for her intellectual shallowness and dullness. As Paul's grieving widow, she assumed a different persona. She demanded the respect she was never accorded by her mother-in-law to the point of insisting that she, and not Alexander's wife *Elizabeth of Baden, should be the first lady of Russia. Sophia insulted and isolated her daughter-in-law in much the same way she had been treated by Catherine. As dowager empress and matriarch of Russia, Sophia bombarded her son with reprimands and advice and insisted that he pay homage to her at Pavlovsk on a weekly basis. Her court, laced with protocol and ceremony, became the unofficial center of St. Petersburg's society. If it lacked the sexual impropriety of Catherine's court, it also had none of the intellectual brilliance and cultural glitter of her predecessor's.

Sophia Dorothea of Wurttemberg played a more important political role in the first quarter of the 19th century than she had in the last 25 years of the 18th. She pressured Alexander to make sure none of Paul's murderers held important positions in his government. She became the center for much of the conservative opposition to Alexan-

*Sophia Matilda (1777–1848)*

der's early liberal reforms, and she worked to undermine reforming ministers such as Michael Speransky, especially if she considered them to be pro-French. In the long run, her most lasting influence was through one of her younger sons. Denied a role in the education and upbringing of Alexander and Constantine, she had reasserted her familial rights after the death of Catherine. Rather than being brought up on the ideas of the Enlightenment, as had their older brothers, Nicholas and Michael learned conservative values and military traditions at Pavlovsk. It should come as no surprise therefore that Nicholas (I), who unexpectedly succeeded Alexander in 1825, became the most reactionary tsar in modern Russian history. His mother died three years into his reign at the age of 69.

**SOURCES:**

McGrew, Roderick. *Paul I of Russia, 1754–1801.* Oxford: Clarendon, 1992.

Ragsdale, Hugh. *Tsar Paul and the Question of Madness: An Essay in History and Psychology.* Westport, CT: Greenwood Press, 1988.

> **R.C. Elwood**, Professor of History,
> Carleton University, Ottawa, Canada

# Sophia Matilda (1773–1844)

*English royal.* Name variations: *Sophia Guelph. Born Sophia Matilda on May 29, 1773 (some sources cite 1772), at Gloucester House, Grosvenor Street, London, England; died on November 29, 1844, at Ranger's House, Blackheath, Kent, England; buried at St. George's Chapel, Windsor; daughter of William Henry, 1st duke of Gloucester and Edinburgh (brother of George III, king of England), and *Maria Walpole (1736–1807).*

# Sophia Matilda (1777–1848)

*Princess royal of England.* Name variations: *Princess Sophia, Sophia Guelph. Born Sophia Matilda on November 3, 1777, at Buckingham House, London, England; died on May 27, 1848, at Kensington, London, England; daughter of George III (1738–1820), king of England (r. 1760–1820), and Charlotte of Mecklenburg-Strelitz (1744–1818); sister of George IV (1762–1821), king of England (r. 1820–1830); children: (with General Thomas Garth) Thomas Garth (b. 1800).*

Princess Sophia Matilda was born in 1777, the daughter of George III, king of England, and **Charlotte of Mecklenburg-Strelitz**. In a family plagued by scandals, Sophia had a child fathered by an unknown man—gossipmongers hatefully spread the name of her brother Ernest Augustus, the duke of Cumberland. Her father, who was having his own mental problems, had been told that his expanding daughter with the testy temperament had dropsy. The king found it miraculous when she reappeared one day, back to her former self, and maintained she had been healed by consuming beef.

## Sophia of Bavaria (fl. 1390s–1400s)

*Queen of Bohemia. Flourished between the 1390s and 1400s; daughter of John II of Munich, duke of Bavaria (r. 1375–1397) and \*Catherine of Gorizia; second wife of Wenceslas IV the Drunkard (1361–1419), duke of Luxemburg (r. 1383–1419), king of Bohemia (r. 1378–1419), and (as just Wenceslas) Holy Roman emperor (r. 1378–1400).*

## Sophia of Bayreuth (1700–1770)

*Queen of Denmark and Norway. Name variations: Sophie Magdalene of Brandenburg-Kulmbach; Sofie-Magdalene of Kulmbach-Bayreuth. Born on November 28, 1700; died on May 27, 1770, in Christianborg, near Copenhagen, Denmark; daughter of Christian Henry, margrave of Brandenburg-Kulm; married Christian VI, king of Denmark and Norway (r. 1730–1746); children: Frederick V (1723–1766), king of Denmark and Norway (r. 1746–1766); Louise (1724–1724); \*Louise of Saxe-Hilburghausen (1726–1756).*

## Sophia of Byzantium (1448–1503)

*Russian empress, niece of the last two Byzantine emperors, and second wife of Ivan III, grand prince of Moscow. Name variations: Sofia or Sophie Paleologa, Paleologue, or Paleologos; Sophia Palaeologus; Zoë or Zoe Palaeologus. Born Zoë Paleologus in Byzantium in 1448; died in Moscow on April 7, 1503; daughter of Thomas Paleologus, despot of Morea, and Catherine of Achaea (d. 1465); niece of Constantine XI (r. 1448–1453), Byzantine emperor; educated in Rome; became second wife of Ivan III the Great (1440–1505), grand prince of Moscow (r. 1462–1505), on November 12, 1472; children: Helene of Moscow (1474–1513, who married Alexander, king of Poland); Theodosia of Moscow (1475–1501); Vasili also known as Basil III (1479–1534), tsar of Russia (r. 1505–1534); Yuri (b. 1480); Dimitri of Uglitsch (b. 1481); Eudoxia of Moscow (1483–1513, who married Peter Ibragimovich, prince of Khazan); Simeon of Kaluga (b. 1487); Andrei also known as Andrew of Staritza (b. 1490).*

Sophia of Byzantium had unusual family ties. She was the niece of the last two Byzantine emperors, the ward of two popes in Rome, the wife of Grand Prince Ivan III the Great of Moscow, and the mother of his successor Basil III. She brought with her to Russia both her Byzantine and her Roman heritage, and she left her mark on Ivan's court and on the architecture of his capital.

Sophia of Byzantium was born Zoë Palaeologus in 1448, during difficult times, the daughter of Thomas Paleologus, despot of Morea, and **Catherine of Achaea**. The first half of the 15th century witnessed the overrunning of the once wealthy and highly civilized Byzantine Empire by the Ottoman Turks. In 1453, her uncle, the Byzantine emperor Constantine XI, died in a fruitless attempt to save his capital of Constantinople (now Istanbul). Seven years later, her father, who was Constantine's younger brother, was forced by the Turks to flee his principality of Morea (present-day Greece) for the Adriatic island of Corfu. When Thomas and Catherine died in 1465, Sophia and her two older brothers were taken to Rome where they became the wards of Pope Paul II. Sophia benefited from spending her teenage years in Renaissance Italy. She received an exceptional education under the direction of Cardinal Bessarion. Unlike most women of her day, she learned to speak and read several European languages. Bessarion also influenced her decision to convert from Eastern Orthodoxy to Roman Catholicism.

As both Sophia and the papacy realized, the future of the orphaned girl lay in marriage. One of those approached was Ivan III, grand prince of Muscow. From the pope's point of view such a marriage would strengthen ties with Moscow and possibly lead to a union of the Eastern and Western branches of Christendom. At the very least, the grand prince might be drawn into an alliance to stop the spread of the Muslim Turks in Europe. From Ivan's point of view, he needed more sons since his first wife \***Maria of Tver** had died in 1467 having produced only one possible heir. Moreover, the prestige of marrying the niece of the last Byzantine emperor would enhance the dignity of the Muscovite ruler. Negotiations, which lasted for three years, finally led to a Catholic marriage by proxy in Rome on June 1, 1472. A month later, Sophia was delighted to leave the restrictive life of the pope's court for the long journey to Moscow. She and her large entourage arrived on November 12 and on the same day, after accepting the Orthodox faith and the name of Sophia, she was married again in a Russian service to the 32-year-old grand prince.

Life in Moscow must have been a shock for Sophia after her very civilized upbringing in Rome. The country was landlocked and isolated, its economy was in decay after more than two centuries of Mongol domination, and education and culture were almost totally lacking. Her husband had begun the task of uniting the state, consolidating his own political powers, and slowly modernizing the economy of Muscovy. Sophia adapted surprisingly well to her new life. She did her part by importing Italian architects, artisans, masons and other specialists to rebuild in stone many of Moscow's old wooden buildings and to beautify the city. The stone walls and towers of the Kremlin were constructed during this period and an Italian armorer built a foundry in Moscow which produced the first reliable cannon for Ivan's army as well as bells for the Kremlin's churches. Sophia's court, which attracted an increasing number of foreign visitors, undoubtedly provided a whiff of Western air and a taste of the Renaissance to an otherwise backward and isolated country. Some historians have suggested that she also helped to formalize and dignify the procedures of Ivan's own court and the machinery of his government.

Sophia of Byzantium's other contribution to Muscovite history was in producing children and backing by sometimes dubious means the claim of her eldest son, Basil, to succeed her husband. Her first child *Helene of Moscow, who subsequently married the king of Poland and Lithuania and was used as an excuse for a war with Lithuania, was born in 1474. She was followed by *Theodosia of Moscow (b. 1475), Basil (b. 1479), *Eudoxia of Moscow (b. 1483), and four more sons. Succession became an issue in 1490 when Ivan's son and heir by his first wife died, perhaps poisoned on Sophia's orders, but not before producing a son of his own, Dmitri. This left two claimants to the throne but no obvious heir apparent. Ivan could choose either his grandson Dmitri, who was only six years old, or Sophia's 11-year-old son Basil. The question remained unresolved until 1497 when Ivan chose Dmitri, largely for the foreign allies his family would bring for Moscow's war with Lithuania. Sophia continued to push her own son's claims and in 1499 succeeded in having the decision reversed. Russian and later Soviet historians have long argued whether in this fight she backed or opposed Russia's aristocratic class in its own efforts to curb the steady growth of monarchial absolutism. What is obvious now is that she sought primarily to further the interests of her son and that Basil, when he finally came to power in 1505 two years after his mother's death, continued the centralizing policies of his father and contributed to the further strengthening of the Muscovite state.

**SOURCES:**

Fennell, J.L.I. *Ivan the Great of Moscow.* London: Macmillan, 1961.

Miller, David B. "Sophia (Zoe) Paleologos," in the *Modern Encyclopedia of Russian and Soviet History.* Vol. 36, 1984, pp. 172–175.

**R.C. Elwood,** Professor of History, Carleton University, Ottawa, Canada

# Sophia of Denmark (1217–1248)

*Margravine of Denmark. Name variations: Sophia Valdemarsdottir or Waldemarsdottir. Born in 1217; died on November 3, 1248; daughter of *Berengaria (1194–1221) and Valdemar also known as Waldemar II the Victorious, king of Denmark and Norway (r. 1202–1241); married John I, margrave of Brandenburg, in 1231. John I's second wife was *Jutta of Saxony.*

# Sophia of Denmark (1746–1813)

*Queen of Sweden. Name variations: Sofia Magdalena or Sophia Magdalena Oldenburg. Born on July 3, 1746; died on August 21, 1813; daughter of *Louise of England (1724–1751) and Frederick V (1723–1766), king of Denmark (r. 1746–1766); sister of Christian VII, king of Denmark (r. 1766–1808); married Gustavus III (1746–1792), king of Sweden (r. 1771–1792); children: Gustavus IV Adolphus (b. 1778), king of Sweden (r. 1792–1809); Charles Gustaf (b. 1782).*

# Sophia of Gandersheim (c. 975–1039)

*Abbess of Gandersheim. Born in 975 or 978 in Germany; died in 1039 at abbey of Gandersheim, Germany; daughter of Otto II (955–983), Holy Roman emperor (r. 983–983), king of Germany (r. 973–983), and Theophano of Byzantium (c. 955–991); sister of Otto III (980–1002), Holy Roman emperor (r. 983–1002); never married; no children.*

An imperial princess, Sophia of Gandersheim was the daughter of the powerful Holy Roman empress *Theophano of Byzantium. Like her sister *Adelaide of Quedlinburg, Sophia left the royal palaces of her parents and entered a convent as a young girl. She showed a great piety early on, and became well respected for her deep devotion to God. After some years, Sophia became abbess of the large, powerful religious establishment at Gandersheim. Under her rule, Gandersheim increased its reputation as a place of great learning and became a popular refuge for wealthy German noblewomen.

**Laura York**, M.A. in History,
University of California, Riverside, California

# Sophia of Greece (1914—)

*English royal.* Name variations: Sophia Oldenburg; Sophia of Spain. Born on June 26, 1914, in Corfu, Greece; daughter of Prince Andrew of Greece and *Alice of Battenberg (1885–1969); married Christopher Ernest, prince of Hesse-Cassel, in 1930; married George Guelph, in 1946; children: (first marriage) *Christine of Hesse-Cassel (b. 1933); (second marriage) three, including Welf and George.

# Sophia of Greece (1938—)

*Queen of Spain.* Name variations: Sophia Oldenburg; Sophie of Spain; Sofia; Sofia of Spain. Born on November 2, 1938, in Psychiko, near Athens, Greece; daughter of Fredericka (1917–1981) and Paul I (1901–1964), king of the Hellenes (r. 1947–1964); sister of Constantine II, king of Greece (r. 1964–1973); married Juan Carlos I (1938—), king of Spain (r. 1975—), on May 14, 1962; children: *Elena (b. 1963); *Cristina (b. 1965); Felipe or Philip, prince of the Asturias (b. 1968).

Sophia of Greece was born in Athens on November 2, 1938, the daughter of the future Paul I of Greece and *Fredericka. She went into exile with her parents when Nazi Germany invaded Greece during World War II and only returned following the referendum that reinstated the monarchy in 1946. Her father became king in 1947. Educated abroad and more fluent in English than in Greek, she studied archaeology, nursing, and classical music, one of her greatest passions.

In 1961, she became engaged to Juan Carlos de Borbón y Borbón (later Juan Carlos I), the son of Juan de Borbón, the pretender to the Spanish throne, despite concern that he was Catholic and she Greek Orthodox. Before their marriage in Athens on May 14, 1962, Greeks marched through the streets to protest a special tax levied to fund her dowry and wedding. The hatred towards her brother Constantine II, then king of Greece, had spilled over to Sophia. (Constantine would go into exile in 1967 and Greece would abolish the monarchy in 1974.)

The couple eventually took up residence in Spain, at least in part out of hope that Spanish

dictator Francisco Franco would announce that the monarchy was to be restored upon his death and that Juan Carlos would be his successor. In 1969, Franco finally designated Juan Carlos as his heir, and when the dictator died in 1975, Juan Carlos and Sophia became the monarchs.

Efforts by Sophia and Juan Carlos to improve relations with the Jewish and Islamic peoples, who had flourished in Spain during the Middle Ages but had been driven out by militant Catholicism, led to her receipt of the Wiesenthal Prize in 1994. She has done much to patronize and promote Spanish arts and culture, especially music. In 2000, she was honored with the Grameen Foundation USA's humanitarian award for her efforts in fighting poverty.

In 1998, Sophia returned to Greece for the first time in 17 years. (She had journeyed there in 1981 to attend her mother's funeral.) Though she and her husband were greeted by President Costis Stephanopoulos, there were no crowds, and they were not allowed to stay in the presi-

*Sophia of Greece (1938—)*

dential mansion, the royal palace of Sophia's childhood.

**SOURCES:**

Frederica, Queen of the Hellenes. *A Measure of Understanding.* London: 1982.

Kern, Robert W., ed. *Historical Dictionary of Modern Spain, 1700–1988.* NY: Greenwood Press, 1990.

Powell, Charles. *Juan Carlos of Spain.* NY: St. Martin's Press, 1996.

**Kendall W. Brown**, Professor of History, Brigham Young University, Provo, Utah

## Sophia of Kiev (fl. 1420s)

*Queen of Poland. Fourth wife of Jagiello (1377–1434), grand duke of Lithuania, who became Vladislav also known as Ladislas II (or V) Jagello, king of Poland (r. 1386–1434); children: Ladislas III or VI (1424–1444, also known as Vladislav), king of Poland (r. 1434–1444) and Hungary (r. 1440–1444); Casimir IV (1427–1492), king of Poland (r. 1447–1492). Jagiello's first wife was \*Jadwiga (1374–1399); his second wife was Anna of Cilli; his third was Elzbieta.*

## Sophia of Malines (d. 1329)

*Duchess of Guelders. Died in 1329; married Renaud, also known as Rainald or Reginald II the Black Haired (d. 1343), duke of Guelders (also known as count of Gelderland), count of Zutphen; children: Margaret of Guelders (d. 1344); Isabella of Graventhal, abbess of Graventhal; \*Matilda of Guelders (d. 1380); \*Mary of Guelders (d. 1405, who married William VI, duke of Juliers). Renaud's second wife was \*Eleanor of Woodstock (1318–1355).*

## Sophia of Mecklenburg (1508–1541)

*Duchess of Lüneburg. Born in 1508; died on June 17, 1541; daughter of \*Ursula of Brandenburg (1488–1510) and Henry III, duke of Mecklenburg; married Ernest the Pious of Zelle, duke of Lüneburg, on June 2, 1528; children: Francis Otto (b. 1530), duke of Brunswick; Henry (b. 1533), duke of Danneburg; William the Younger (b. 1535), duke of Lüneburg.*

## Sophia of Mecklenburg (1557–1631).

*See Anne of Denmark for sidebar.*

## Sophia of Mecklenburg (1758–1794)

*Princess of Denmark. Name variations: Sophia Fredericka; Sophia Frederica; Sofie Frederikke of Mecklenburg-Schwerin. Born Sophia Fredericka on August 24,* 1758; died on November 29, 1794; daughter of Louis of Mecklenburg-Schwerin and **Charlotte Sophie of Saxe-Coburg-Saalfeld** (1731–1810); married Frederick Oldenburg (1753–1805), prince of Denmark (son of Frederick V, king of Norway and Denmark, and \*Maria Juliana of Brunswick), in 1774; children: Julian Marie (1784–1784); Christian VIII (1786–1848), king of Denmark (r. 1839–1848); Juliane (1788–1850, who married William, landgrave of Hesse); \*Charlotte Oldenburg (1789–1864, who married William of Hesse-Cassel).*

## Sophia of Nassau (1824–1897)

*Grand Duchess of Saxe-Weimar. Name variations: Sophie von Nassau. Born on April 8, 1824; died on March 23, 1897; daughter of \*Anna Pavlovna (1795–1865) and William II (1792–1849), king of the Netherlands (r. 1840–1849); married Charles Alexander, grand duke of Saxe-Weimar, on October 8, 1842; children: Charles Augustus (b. 1844), grand duke of Saxe-Weimar; Marie Alexandrine of Saxe-Weimar (1849–1922, who married Henry VII, prince Reuss of Kostritz); Elizabeth Sybilla of Saxe-Weimar (1854–1908, who married John, duke of Mecklenburg-Schwerin).*

## Sophia of Nassau (1836–1913)

*Queen of Sweden. Born Sophia Wilhelmina Marianne on July 9, 1836, in Biebrich; died on December 30, 1913, in Stockholm, Sweden; daughter of William George (b. 1792), duke of Nassau, and \*Pauline of Wurttemberg (1810–1856, granddaughter of Frederick I); married Oscar II (1829–1907), king of Sweden (r. 1872–1907), on June 6, 1857; children: Gustavus V (1858–1950), king of Sweden (r. 1907–1950); Oscar Charles Augustus, count of Wisborg (1859–1953); Charles of Sweden (1861–1951, who married \*Ingeborg of Denmark); Eugene Bernadotte (1865–1947), duke of Närke.*

## Sophia of Pomerania (1498–1568)

*Queen of Denmark and Norway. Name variations: Sofie; Sophie of Pommerania. Born in 1498; died on May 13, 1568, in Keil; daughter of Bogislav also known as Boleslav X, duke of Pomerania; became second wife of Frederik or Frederick I (1471–1533), king of Denmark and Norway (r. 1523–1533), on October 9, 1518; children: Johann (1521–1580); \*Elizabeth of Denmark (1524–1586); Anna Oldenburg (d. 1535); Adolf (1526–1586, of the Holstein-Gottorp line); \*Dorothea of Denmark (1528–1575); Frederick (1532–1556), baron von Hildesheim.*

# Sophia of Spain (b. 1914).

*See Sophia of Greece.*

# Sophia of Sweden (1801–1865)

*Grand duchess of Baden. Born on May 21, 1801; died on July 6, 1865; daughter of Gustavus IV Adolphus (1778–1837), king of Sweden (r. 1792–1809), and *Frederica Dorothea of Baden (1781–1826); married Leopold (1790–1852), grand duke of Baden (r. 1830–1852), on July 25, 1819; children: eight, including *Alexandrina of Baden (1820–1904, who married Ernest II, duke of Saxe-Coburg-Saalfeld); Louis II of Baden, grand duke of Baden (b. 1824); Frederick I (1826–1907), grand duke of Baden; William of Baden (1829–1897); *Mary of Baden (1834–1899); *Cecilia of Baden (1839–1891, also known as Olga Feodorovna); Charles of Baden (b. 1832).*

# Sophia of Thuringia (fl. 1211).

*See Elizabeth of Hungary (1201–1231) for sidebar on Sophia, landgravine of Thuringia.*

# Sophia of Thuringia (1224–1284)

*German duchess and founder of landgraviate of Hesse. Name variations: Sophie von Thuringen or Thüringen. Born on March 20, 1224; died on May 29, 1284 (some sources cite 1275); daughter of St. Elizabeth of Hungary (1207–1231) and Ludwig IV of Thuringia; niece of Henry Raspe IV of Thuringia; became second wife of Henry II (1207–1248), duke of Brabant (r. 1235–1248), around 1240; children: *Elizabeth of Brabant (1243–1261); Henry I (b. 1244), landgrave of Hesse (Henry I was first male ruler of Hesse).*

Sophia of Thuringia was born in 1224, the daughter of St. *Elizabeth of Hungary (1207–1231) and Ludwig IV of Thuringia, and niece of Henry Raspe IV of Thuringia, a major landowner in Germany. She married Henry II of Brabant around 1240. When Sophia's cousin Henry of Meissen fought against Sophia and Henry over Thuringia, Meissen was triumphant. But Sophia's descendants were given Hesse as a consolation. Henry II's first wife was *Marie of Swabia (c. 1201–1235).

# Sophia of Wurttemberg (1818–1877)

*Queen of the Netherlands. Born Sophie Frederica Mathilde on June 17, 1818, in Stuttgart, Germany; died on June 3, 1877, at Het Loo, Apeldoorn; daughter of*

*Catherine of Russia (1788–1819) and William I (b. 1781), king of Wurttemberg (r. 1816–1864); became first wife of William III (1817–1890), king of the Netherlands (r. 1849–1890), on June 18, 1839; children: William Nicholas (1840–1879); Maurice (1843–1850); Alexander (1851–1884). Following the death of Sophia of Wurttemberg in 1877, William III married *Emma of Waldeck, mother of Queen *Wilhelmina, in 1879.*

# Sophia of Zahringen (fl. 12th c.)

*Saxon noblewoman. Flourished in the 12th century in Saxony; daughter of Henry the Black (d. 1126), duke of Saxony and Bavaria, and possibly *Wolfida of Saxony (c. 1075–1126); sister of *Judith of Bavaria, Welf also known as Guelph VI (d. 1191), and Henry the Proud (d. 1139), duke of Bavaria; married Bertold of Zahringen.*

A Saxon noble, Sophia of Zahringen married Bertold of Zahringen as a young woman, bringing a large dowry with her. Sophia came from a powerful German ruling family which held the duchies of Saxony and Bavaria. Her brother Henry the Proud, duke of Bavaria, was one of the most significant men in west European politics in the 12th century. Always a loyal supporter of her brother's royal claims, Sophia aided him in military and financial ways after Bertold died. Henry welcomed her assistance in his struggles against rival nobles, even putting her in command of at least one of his sieges.

**Laura York**, M.A. in History,
University of California, Riverside, California

# Sophie (fl. 1200s)

*Scandinavian royal. Flourished in the 1200s; daughter of *Richeza Eriksdottir and Niels of Werle, also known as Nicholas II von Werle; granddaughter of Erik V Klipping or Clipping, king of Denmark (r. 1259–1286); married Gerhard.*

# Sophie (1734–1782)

*French princess. Name variations: Madame Sophie. Born Sophie Elizabeth Justine; youngest daughter of Louis XV (1710–1774), king of France (r. 1715–1774), and *Marie Leczinska (1703–1768); sister of *Adelaide (1732–1800), *Louise Elizabeth (1727–1759), and *Victoire (1733–1799).*

# Sophie Amalie of Brunswick-Lüneberg (1628–1685)

*Queen of Denmark. Name variations: Sophia of Lüneburg; Sophia Amelia of Brunswick; Sophia*

*Amelia of Brunswick-Luneburg. Born on March 24, 1628, in Herzberg; died on February 20, 1685, in Copenhagen, Denmark; daughter of George Guelph (b. 1582), duke of Brunswick-Lüneburg (d. 1641) and *Anne-Eleanor of Hesse-Darmstadt (1601–1659); married Frederick III (1609–1670), king of Denmark and Norway (r. 1648–1670), on October 1, 1643; children: Ulrik Frederik Gyldenlove; Christian V (1646–1699), king of Denmark and Norway (r. 1670–1699); *Anna Sophia of Denmark (1647–1717, who married John George III of Saxony); Jørgen or George of Denmark (who married Queen *Anne of England); *Frederica Amalie (1649–1704); *Wilhelmine (1650–1706); Frederick (1651–1652); *Ulrica Eleanora of Denmark (1656–1693, who married Charles XI, king of Sweden); Dorothea (1657–1658).*

## Sophie Caroline (1737–1817)

*Margravine of Brandenburg. Born Sophie Caroline Marie on October 8, 1737; died on December 23, 1817; daughter of *Philippine Charlotte (1716–1801) and Charles, duke of Brunswick-Wolfenbüttel; married Frederick, margrave of Brandenburg, on September 20, 1759.*

## Sophie Charlotte of Hanover (1668–1705)

*Queen of Prussia who brought her Hanoverian cultural heritage to the backward Prussian court and became patron, pupil, and good friend of the great mathematician and philosopher Gottfried Wilhelm Leibniz. Name variations: Sophia Charlotte; Sophie Charlotte of Brunswick-Luneberg or Brunswick-Lüneberg; also baby-named "Figuelotte." Born Sophie Charlotte or Sophia Charlotte on October 20, 1668 (some sources cite October 12, 1662), in Schloss Iburg, near Osnabruck; died on February 1, 1705 (some sources cite January 21, 1706), in Hanover, Lower Saxony, Germany; interred at the Royal Chapel, Berlin; daughter of Ernst August, duke of Brunswick, who was elevated to elector of Hanover, and the duchess Sophia (1630–1714), electress of Hanover (granddaughter of King James I of England); sister of George I (1660–1727), king of England (r. 1714–1727); became second wife of Frederick III (1657–1713), elector of Brandenburg (r. 1688–1701), later Frederick I, king of Prussia (r. 1701–1713), on October 8, 1684; children: Frederick William I (1688–1740), king of Prussia (r. 1713–1740). Frederick's first wife was *Elizabeth Henrietta of Hesse-Cassel (1661–1683).*

Sophie Charlotte of Hanover's life was shaped by blood and deed. By blood, she had the rare good fortune to become a queen. By deed, she made herself into a patron of the arts and philosophy in the rising new state of Prussia. But, by birth, Sophie Charlotte was a typical female pawn in the royal game of European politics. She was the daughter of a duke who rose to the title of elector in the Holy Roman Empire, and of a duchess who was the granddaughter of a bona fide king.

Sophie Charlotte's father was Ernst August, duke of Brunswick, of the house of Lüneburg, a minor branch on the Hanoverian tree, until 1692, when he became its Elector of the Empire. Except for the fact that there were only a limited number of electors, ranging from seven during the Reformation to nine at a later period, this was little more than a flattering extra title. On rare occasions, however, about once in a generation, electors had the opportunity to elect a new Holy Roman emperor, making them for a brief period recipients of respect and patronage in the form of social and political perks, if not outright bribes.

Sophie Charlotte's mother, *Sophia (1630–1714, electress of Hanover), was genealogically far more important than her husband Ernst August, whom she had married in 1658, more than 30 years before his elevation to elector of Hanover. Sophia was the daughter of *Elizabeth of Bohemia (1596–1662) and the granddaughter of King James VI of Scotland, who also ruled England as James I (the same who authorized the definitive translation of the Bible into English in 1611). Sophia would live until 1714, long after her daughter's death. When Sophia died within weeks of the death of her cousin *Anne (1665–1714), who had been the queen of England since 1701 but had no immediate heir, the English throne passed to Sophia's son George Louis, the brother of Sophie Charlotte, who became George I of England. (George would be the founding father of England's House of Hanover; the royals would change this Germanic name to Windsor during World War I.)

Sophie Charlotte, born in 1668, was only 16 when she became the second wife of Crown Prince Frederick Hohenzollern (later Frederick I, king of Prussia), in 1684. Her father-in-law was Frederick William of Brandenburg, known as the "Great Elector," who had laid the foundation for the modern state of Brandenburg-Prussia during his half-century reign from 1640 to 1688.

As a young West German woman thrust into a world of East Prussian men, Sophie Charlotte did not have an easy time. She had been raised as a Hanoverian, where the arts were promoted and appreciated. Once she reached the court at Berlin, she faced a struggle to maintain her sense of civilization against the grimly practical Calvinism and militarism of the Hohenzollern family into which she had married. Her native Hanover, just across the Rhine from France, lay in the cultural shadow cast by the palace at Versailles, built just a quarter of a century earlier by King Louis XIV. The costly and splendid social activities and artistic enterprises at the new French court had provoked imitation and emulation in many other courts around Europe, and none had been more receptive to this "high culture" than Hanoverians, while few individual women had proved more receptive than Duchess Sophia and her daughter Sophie Charlotte. For Hanoverians, Prussia was beyond the pale, locked in deprivation and barbarism. For their part, the Prussians responded to this Francophilic snobbery with a loathing of Westerners in general and the females among them in particular.

The Prussian hostility toward the eager pretensions and aspirations of Sophie Charlotte was embodied in her father-in-law Frederick William. Long before she was born, the Great Elector had inherited a kingdom in an economically backward part of Germany that had been ravaged during the first half of the 17th century by the terrible Thirty Years' War. By penny-pinching and squeezing his subjects into supporting an enormous (for them) standing army, he had molded this realm into a formidable military regime. But in the creation of his new Brandenburg-Prussian state, he had forced his family and court into sacrificing elementary comforts as well as cultural adornments like music and artistic entertainment.

By the end of his long, successful life, the Great Elector had absolutely no use for the frivolity of art and music. Moreover, he had also lost a handsome, tough, and congenial first son, who died prematurely. In his twilight years, Frederick William was bitterly angry at having to settle for a wimpy second son as his successor to the throne. The young Frederick was not only physically unattractive and spiritually unmilitary, he was a sensitive soul with an artistic bent who wanted to spend money on fancy things, further exacerbating the old man's rage against intellectual and artistic people. Then the second wife of this second son arrived at his court, prepared to introduce the high culture of Hanover to the backward Prussians. The old elector disliked his daughter-in-law as much as she disliked him, and at his court Sophie Charlotte endured royal ridicule and social persecution.

In 1688, Frederick William died. That same year, Sophie Charlotte gave birth to her only son (Frederick William I), who was promptly named for his renowned grandfather, and her husband Frederick became elector of Brandenburg, the title by which he would rule for the next 13 years.

Freed from the dominating influence of her father-in-law, Sophie Charlotte turned happily to indulging her cultural tastes, and encouraged her husband in spending the hoarded savings of the new state. After years of chafing under the anger and stinginess of his embittered father, Frederick was easily persuaded. The Great Elector had left a full treasury, and Frederick was willing to plumb it. He was also susceptible to the charming and sophisticated example set by court life at Versailles. Apart from the sheer enjoyment of their access to the arts, these Francophilic new imitators used art to glorify themselves, as well as to buttress the authority and prestige of their newly emergent absolutist government. Sophie Charlotte now had virtually a free hand to "educate" the rustic Prussians. Relishing the pursuit of her own pleasures in music, philosophy, and the building of royal residences, she made herself into an intellectual and a patron of arts.

> The only book-length work [Leibniz] ever published, the famous *Theodicy* (1710), owes its origin to the many conversations between the philosopher and [Sophie Charlotte of Hanover] in the gardens of Lutzenburg in Berlin.
>
> —Olan Brent Hankins

In music, the young ruler brought the influence of her mother Sophia's Hanoverian heritage to the Berlin world, expanding the musical horizons of eastern Germans. A few years hence, the musical tradition of Hanover would flower in England through the works of George Frederick Handel; meanwhile, she was helping to lay the foundation of appreciation that would make the reception of the music of Johann Sebastian Bach universal during that same period.

It was in philosophy that Sophie Charlotte contributed most directly to the general culture of Europe, through her cultivation of a deep and lasting friendship with Gottfried Wilhelm Leibniz, the outstanding genius of the age. She also presided over religious debates among Jesuits, Protestants, and free-thinkers, preparing herself to participate in the arguments by reading the works of Pierre Bayle, the French advocate of religious toleration. She earned the recognition the English free-thinker John

Toland who dedicated his *Letters to Serena* to her. With Leibniz, she enjoyed long conversations about topics as diverse as the existence of the soul, the Roman philosophy of Lucretius, and perpetual motion machines. She also spurred him toward the publication, finally, of his *Theodicy*, the only formal work he ventured to publish in his lifetime.

For herself, Sophie Charlotte must have found her husband's patronage of architects most welcome. Near the village of Lutzenburg, the gifted architect Johann Arnold Nering built his most outstanding creation for her, the country palace she playfully called "Lustenburg" (*lust* means "pleasure" in German). Sophie Charlotte worked hard to make this showplace a "mini-Versailles," replete with the performances of ballets, operas, and comic masquerades. After her death, it would be appropriately renamed Charlottenburg.

During the first half of his reign, Frederick continued his father's policy of being the only continental ally of France, then under the rule of Louis XIV. But Louis was engaged in his first big empire-building war to extend France's frontier to the Rhine, and after the respite afforded by the Treaty of Risjwik in 1697, Frederick allowed himself to be persuaded by the embattled Habsburg emperor in Vienna to change his alliance. In 1701, Frederick was elevated by Habsburg edict from elector of Brandenburg to King Frederick I of Prussia. His authorization of this medieval promotion in rank was a maneuver to detach Prussia from its French alliance at the outset of the War of Spanish Succession (which coincided with the second half Frederick's rule). Sophie Charlotte thus became the queen of Prussia.

Sophie Charlotte's last days were dimmed by the sad realization that her son Frederick William I was turning into a crude, narrow-minded, anti-cultural clod like his namesake grandfather. Fortunately she was spared the spectacle of Frederick William's brutally repressive treatment of his own son and of his wife *Sophia Dorothea of Brunswick-Lüneburg-Hanover. (His attempt to make the youth into "a man" by squelching his artistic talents became the subject of gossip all over Europe and remains a historical scandal to this day.)

Sophie Charlotte died in 1705, at age 37, eight years before her son succeeded his father as Frederick William I. His rule would last for the next quarter-century, until 1740. It was in the reign following his that her cultural aspirations were vindicated by the intellectual and artistic accomplishments of that same tormented grandson, who came to the throne as Frederick II and became known to history as Frederick II the Great. In almost a half-century of rule, from 1740 to 1786, he performed the military feats which pushed Prussia into central European hegemony and laid the foundation for the creation during the next century of the Prussianized modern Germany by Otto von Bismarck. And while gaining prominence across Europe for his diplomacy, he resurrected the cultural concerns of his grandmother, cultivating philosophy and the arts, and won the acclaim by the French *philosophes*, especially Voltaire, as a model for Plato's "philosopher king." With his ascent, Sophie Charlotte deserves to be designated the first non-French host of the female-dominated salon culture of the European Enlightenment.

**SOURCES:**

There are no biographies of Sophie Charlotte in English; her story has to be extrapolated from the larger one of the Hohenzollern and Hanoverian families in Germany. In Frey, she is treated as a disagreeable person, but she is praised by Eulenberg as an aspiring intellectual who provides patronage for cultural events. Hankins emphasizes her inspiring and constructive influence on Leibniz.

Eulenberg, Herbert. *The Hohenzollerns.* Translated by M.M. Bozman. NY: Century, 1929.

Frey, Linda and Marsha Frey. *Frederick I: The Man and His Time.* NY: Columbia University Press, 1984.

Hankins, Olan Brent. *Leibniz as Baroque Poet.* Frankfurt: Stanford German Studies, Verlag Herbert Lang, 1973.

**David R. Stevenson**, formerly Associate Professor of History, University of Nebraska at Kearney, Nebraska

# Sophie Charlotte of Oldenburg

## (1879–1964)

*Duchess of Oldenburg. Born on February 2, 1879, in Oldenburg; died on March 29, 1964, in Westerstede, Oldenburg; daughter of Frederick Augustus, grand duke of Oldenburg, and Elizabeth Anna Hohenzollern (1857–1895); married Eitel-Frederick, prince of Prussia, on February 27, 1906 (divorced 1926); married Harald von Hedemann, on November 24, 1927.*

# Sophie Elisabeth, Duchess of Brunswick-Lüneburg.

*See Braunschweig-Lüneburg, Sophie Elisabeth (1613–1676).*

# Sophie Hedwig (1677–1735)

*Danish princess. Name variations: Sophie Hedwig Oldenburg. Born on August 28, 1677; died on March*

*13, 1735; daughter of \*Charlotte Amalia of Hesse (1650–1714) and Christian V (1646–1699), king of Norway and Denmark (r. 1670–1699).*

## Sophie Louise of Mecklenburg (1685–1735)

*Queen of Prussia. Born on May 16, 1685; died on July 29, 1735, in Grabow; became third wife of Frederick III (1657–1713), elector of Brandenburg (r. 1688–1701), later Frederick I, king of Prussia (r. 1701–1713), on November 28, 1708. Frederick's first wife was \*Elizabeth Henrietta of Hesse-Cassel; his second was \*Sophie Charlotte of Hanover.*

## Sophie of Austria (1805–1872).

*See Sophie of Bavaria.*

## Sophie of Bavaria (1805–1872)

*Archduchess of Austria. Name variations: Sophia; Sophie of Austria. Born on January 27, 1805, in Munich, Germany; died on May 28, 1872, in Vienna, Austria; daughter of Maximilian I Joseph of Bavaria, elector of Bavaria (r. 1799–1805), king of Bavaria (r. 1805–1825), and \*Caroline of Baden (1776–1841); twin sister of \*Maria of Bavaria (1805–1877); married Franz Karl also known as Francis Charles (son of Francis II, emperor of Austria); children: Franz Josef also known as Francis Joseph (1830–1916), emperor of Austria; Maximilian (1832–1867), emperor of Mexico; Karl Ludwig also known as Charles Louis (1833–1896, who married \*Maria Annunziata of Naples); Ludwig Viktor also known as Louis Victor (1842–1919).*

## Sophie of Bavaria (1847–1897).

*See Sophie of Bayern.*

## Sophie of Bayern (1847–1897)

*Duchess of Alençon. Name variations: Sophie of Bavaria; duchess of Alencon. Born on February 22, 1847; perished in the fire of the Paris charity bazaar on May 4, 1897; daughter of \*Ludovica (1808–1892) and Maximilian Joseph (1808–1888), duke of Bavaria; sister of \*Elizabeth of Bavaria (1837–1898); married Ferdinand, duke of Alençon, on September 28, 1868; children: Louise of Orleans (b. 1869, who married Alfons of Bavaria); Emanuel (b. 1872), duke of Vendôme. Sophie of Bayern was once betrothed to Ludwig II, king of Bavaria.*

## Sophie of Brandenburg (1568–1622)

*Electress of Saxony. Born on June 6, 1568; died on December 7, 1622; daughter of \*Sabine of Brandenburg-Ansbach (1529–1575) and John George (1525–1598), elector of Brandenburg (r. 1571–1598); married Christian I, elector of Saxony, on April 25, 1582; children: Christian II (b. 1583), elector of Saxony; John George (b. 1585), elector of Saxony.*

Sophie of Bavaria (1805–1872)

## Sophie of Denmark (d. 1286)

*Queen of Sweden. Name variations: Sophie Eriksdottir. Died in 1286; daughter of \*Jutta of Saxony (d. around 1267) and Erik or Eric IV Ploughpenny (1216–1250), king of Dennmark (r. 1241–1250); married Waldemar I, king of Sweden (r. 1250–1275), in 1260; children: Ingeborg (d. around 1290, who married Gerhard II, count of Plön); Eric (b. 1272); \*Ryksa (fl. 1288); Katherina; Marina (who married Rudolf, count von Diephold in 1285); Margaret, a nun.*

## Sophie of Hohenberg (1868–1914).

*See Chotek, Sophie.*

## Sophie of Holstein-Gottorp
### (1569–1634)

*Duchess of Mecklenburg.* Born on June 1, 1569; died on November 14, 1634; daughter of Adolf (1526–1586), duke of Holstein-Gottorp (r. 1544–1586), and *Christine of Hesse (1543–1604); married John V, duke of Mecklenburg, on February 17, 1588; children: Adolf Frederick I (b. 1588), duke of Mecklenburg-Schwerin.

## Sophie of Hungary (d. 1095)

*Duchess of Saxony.* Died on July 18, 1095; daughter of *Richesa of Poland (fl. 1030–1040) and Bela I, king of Hungary (r. 1060–1063); sister of St. Ladislas I (1040–1095), king of Hungary (r. 1077–1095) and Geza I, king of Hungary (r. 1074–1077); married Magnus (c. 1045–1106), duke of Saxony (r. 1072–1106), around 1071; children: *Wolfida of Saxony (c. 1075–1126); Eilica of Saxony (c. 1080–1142, who married Otto von Ballenstadt).

## Sophie of Liegnitz (1525–1546)

*First wife of the elector of Brandenburg.* Born in 1525; died on February 6, 1546; daughter of Frederick III, duke of Liegnitz; became first wife of John George (1525–1598), elector of Brandenburg (r. 1571–1598), on February 15, 1545; children: Joachim Frederick (1546–1608), elector of Brandenburg (r. 1598–1608). John George's second wife was *Sabine of Brandenburg-Ansbach (1529–1575); his third was *Elizabeth of Anhalt (1563–1607).

## Sophie of Lithuania (1370–1453)

*Princess of Moscow.* Born in 1370; died on June 15, 1453; daughter of Vitold, prince of Lithuania; married Basil I, prince of Moscow, on January 9, 1392; children: Basil II the Blind (b. 1415), prince of Moscow; *Anna of Moscow (1393–1417); Yuri (b. 1395); Ivan (b. 1396); Anastasia of Moscow (b. around 1398, who married Odellko, prince of Kiev, in 1417); Daniel (b. 1401); Vasilissa of Moscow (b. around 1403, who married Alexander of Susdal); Simeon (b. 1405); Marie of Moscow (who married Yuri, prince of Lithuania).

## Sophie of Montferrat

*Byzantine empress.* Name variations: Sophia Monteferrata; Monferrato; Empress of Nicaea. Born of Italian ancestry; became second wife of her cousin John VIII Paleologus (1391–1448), emperor of Nicaea (r. 1425–1448), then divorced. John VIII's first wife was *Anna of Moscow (1393–1417); his third was *Maria of Trebizond (d. 1439).

## Sophie of Nassau (1902–1941)

*Princess of Saxony.* Name variations: Sophie von Nassau. Born on February 14, 1902; died on May 31, 1941; daughter of *Marie-Anne of Braganza (1861–1942) and William IV (1852–1912), grand duke of Luxemburg; married Ernest Henry (b. 1896), prince of Saxony, on April 12, 1921; children: Dedo (b. 1922); Timo (b. 1923); Gero (b. 1925).

## Sophie of Poland (1464–1512)

*Margravine of Ansbach.* Name variations: Sophia or Zofia. Born on May 6, 1464; died on October 5, 1512; daughter of *Elizabeth of Hungary (c. 1430–1505) and Casimir IV Jagiellon, grand duke of Lithuania (r. 1440–1492), king of Poland (r. 1446–1492); married Frederick V of Ansbach, margrave of Ansbach, on February 14, 1479; children: Albert of Prussia (b. 1490), duke of Prussia (r. 1526–1568); George of Ansbach (b. 1484), margrave of Ansbach; Casimir (b. 1481), margrave of Brandenburg.

## Sophie of Prussia (1870–1932)

*Queen of the Hellenes.* Name variations: Sophia; Sophia Hohenzollern; queen of Greece. Born Sophie Dorothea Ulrika Alice on June 14, 1870, in Potsdam, Brandenburg, Germany; died on January 13, 1932, in Frankfurt-am-Main, Germany; buried in November 1936 in Tatoi, near Athens, Greece; third daughter of Frederick III (1831–1888), emperor of Germany (r. 1888), and *Victoria Adelaide (1840–1901, daughter of Queen *Victoria); sister of Kaiser Wilhelm II of Germany (r. 1888–1918); married Constantine I (1868–1923), king of the Hellenes (r. 1913–1917, 1920–1922), on October 27, 1889; children: George II (1890–1947), king of Greece (r. 1922–1923, 1935–1947); Alexander I (1893–1920), king of Greece (r. 1917–1920); *Helen of Greece (1896–1982, who married Carol II, king of Rumania); Paul I (1901–1964), king of Greece (r. 1947–1964); Irene (b. around 1904, who married the duke of Aosta); Catherine.

## Sophie of Russia (c. 1140–1198)

*Queen of Denmark.* Name variations: Sophie of Polotzk. Born around 1140; died on May 5, 1198; daughter of Vladimir, prince of Novgorod, and *Richizza of Poland (1116–1185); married Valdemar *also known as Waldemar I the Great (1131–1182), king of Denmark (r. 1157–1182), in 1157; children: Canute VI (1163–1202), king of Denmark (r. 1182–1202); Waldemar II the Victorious (b. 1170), king of Denmark (r. 1202–1241); Sophie (d. 1208, who married Siegfried III, count of Orlamunde, in 1181); *Richizza of Denmark (d. 1220); Margaret (a nun at Roskilde); Marie (a nun at Roskilde); *Helen of Denmark (d. 1233); *Ingeborg (c. 1176–1237/38, who married Philip II Augustus, king of France); and another daughter who married Philip of Swabia, king of the Romans.*

## Sophie of Solms-Laubach

## (1594–1651)

*Margravine of Ansbach. Born on May 15, 1594; died on May 16, 1651; daughter of John George I of Solms-Laubach; married Joachim Ernst (1583–1625), margrave of Ansbach (r. 1603–1625), on October 14, 1612; children: Albert (b. 1620), margrave of Ansbach.*

## Sophie Valdemarsdottir (d. 1241)

*Princess of Mecklenburg-Rostok. Died in 1241; daughter of *Leonor of Portugal (1211–1231) and Valdemar or Waldemar the Younger (1209–1231), king of Denmark (r. 1215–1231); married Henry Burwin III, prince of Mecklenburg-Rostok.*

## Sophonisba (c. 225–203 BCE)

*Carthaginian noblewoman who chose suicide over Roman slavery during the Second Punic War. Name variations: Sophoniba; Sophonisbe. Born around 225 BCE; committed suicide in 203 BCE; daughter of the Carthaginian Hasdrubal (son of Gisgo); married Syphax; married Masinissa.*

Sophonisba was born around 225 BCE, the beautiful daughter of the Carthaginian Hasdrubal. Hasdrubal, son of Gisgo, was a major player in the Second Punic War fought between Rome and Carthage (218–201 BCE). From 214 until 206, Hasdrubal was one of the generals who sought to keep Rome from seizing Spain from Carthage. Initially, he was successful, helping to defeat the army of the elder P. Cornelius Scipio and killing the Roman general in the process (211 BCE). However, when the Roman war effort in Spain was turned over to the elder Scipio's strategically brilliant son, P. Cornelius Scipio Africanus, the tide turned on Carthage and Hasdrubal: after the Battle of Ilipa (206 BCE), the latter fled Spain, leaving it to Rome.

With Spain lost to Carthage, Hasdrubal fled to North Africa and Syphax, a Numidian chieftain of the Masaesylii tribe, intent on fostering the waning Carthaginian war effort. Hasdrubal's mission to Syphax was of great importance for his city, for Syphax had openly rebelled against Carthage's hegemony in North Africa (c. 214 BCE) and in 206 BCE was being wooed by the younger Scipio as an ally against Carthage. Making Hasdrubal's assignment all the more critical was the fact that Masinissa (another Numidian chieftain and a rival of Syphax), who had been an ally of Carthage until the loss of Spain, was at the time defecting to the Roman cause. Any hope for a Carthaginian victory in this long and bitter conflict would be dashed if Rome could unite Numidia against Hasdrubal's city.

Hasdrubal's efforts to secure an alliance with Syphax were successful after he offered the stunning Sophonisba in marriage to the Numidian. Thus, Sophonisba's charms acquired for Carthage an ally as that city desperately mounted a last ditch effort against Rome. In the short term, Sophonisba's marriage alliance turned Numidian affairs in Carthage's favor, for Syphax was able to expel Masinissa from the latter's ancestral chiefdom. However, when Scipio Africanus invaded Africa (204 BCE), it soon became evident that no Numidian ally could save Carthage. In 203 BCE, Syphax met Scipio in the Battle of the Great Plains, to the west of Carthage, and was decisively defeated. Fleeing to his kingdom, Syphax contemplated making his peace with Rome, but was dissuaded from doing so by Sophonisba. While Scipio was otherwise engaged against Carthage, however, Masinissa and one of Scipio's lieutenants, C. Laelius, invaded Syphax's realm. Syphax was once again defeated in battle and soon thereafter captured by his enemies.

In Roman hands, Syphax was destined to be deported to Italy (where he would die in captivity in 201 BCE). Nevertheless, before Syphax met this fate Sophonisba played out her most famous moment. After Syphax's defeat, Masinissa was the first of his enemies to enter Cirta, Syphax's capital. There, Sophonisba approached Masinissa to beg his protection from the Romans. Desperate to avoid falling captive to the bitter foes her father had schooled her to hate, she threw herself before her husband's victorious rival and begged him for sanctuary. Masinissa was stunned by Sophonisba's beauty, and she, seeing the effect her physical presence was having on him, decided to alter the nature of her approach. Rather than throwing herself upon his mercy, Sophonisba began to behave seductively. Almost immediately Masinissa promised to do all he could to protect her. In fact, it is alleged that he took her as a wife virtually on the spot. Another version of the story is somewhat less fevered. In this telling, Sophonisba and Masinissa had been betrothed before her father decided to offer her to Syphax. Meeting him upon his entry into Cirta, she pleaded with him not to turn her over to her father's enemies. He promised he would not, and married her. Both versions agree that when the Roman Laelius arrived at Cirta and discovered that Masinissa was entranced by Sophonisba, he was furious and refused to acknowledge the legitimacy of their "marriage." Although he wanted to send Sophonisba (with Syphax) as a prisoner to Scipio Africanus, in the interest of diplomacy Laelius nevertheless agreed to allow Scipio to decide Sophonisba's fate.

As a result of this decision, Sophonisba remained with Masinissa when Syphax was forwarded to Scipio. Syphax, however, had his revenge. Extremely jealous and angry about Sophonisba's willingness to abandon him for his victorious rival, Syphax went out of his way to convince Scipio that she constituted a potentially dangerous influence on Masinissa. Worried by the implications of Masinissa's overly hasty appropriation of Syphax's rabidly anti-Roman, Carthaginian spouse, Scipio ordered Masinissa to quit this new marriage and to send Sophonisba to him as a legitimately won war captive. Distressed and wishing to grant Sophonisba her wish (or, in the second version, to keep his promise) that she never fall into Roman hands, Masinissa chose to disregard this command. Instead, he apologized to Sophonisba for being incapable of otherwise "saving" her, and procured for her a cup of poison. Thus offered her release from Roman captivity, Sophonisba defiantly drained the cup, preferring annihilation to slavery. In this act, she foreshadowed the fate of her native city: too proud to submit to absolute Roman dominion, Carthage would also one day opt for honorable destruction over Roman bondage.

**William S. Greenwalt,**
Associate Professor of Classical History,
Santa Clara University, Santa Clara, California

# Sorabji, Cornelia (1866–1954)

*First Indian woman to become a lawyer. Born on November 15, 1866, in Nasik, in the Bombay presidency, India; died on July 6, 1954, in London, England; fifth daughter of nine children of the Rev. Sorabji Karsedji Langrana (an ex-Zoroastrian) and Francina (also seen as Franscina); graduated from Decca College in Poona, India, in 1886; studied at Somerville College in Oxford, England; received Bachelor of Civil Law (BCL) in 1922.*

*Selected writings:* Love and Life Behind the Purdah *(1901);* Sun-Babies *(1904);* Between the Twilights *(1908);* Social Relations: England and India *(1908);* Indian Tales of the Great Ones Among Men, Women and Bird-People *(1916);* Therefore *(1924);* Susie Sorabji, A Memoir *(1932);* India Calling *(1934);* India Recalled *(1936).*

Cornelia Sorabji was born on November 15, 1866, in Nasik, in the Bombay presidency in India. Her father, a Parsi who converted to Christianity, raised Cornelia and her eight siblings with an appreciation for Indian and British culture, both of which shaped her life. Another influence was her mother's concern for the numberless Indian women repressed by cultural customs that forced them to live lives of seclusion. Both Cornelia and a younger sister, **Susie Sorabji**, picked up her reformist tendencies. While Susie went on to a career as an educational reformer, Cornelia became determined to improve the condition of India's widows, orphans and wives through the courts.

Sorabji became the first female student at Decca College in Poona. Her grades merited her ascension to the top of her class, but, when she received her degree in 1886, her gender prevented her from collecting the scholarship to a British university the school typically gave to its number-one student. The setback prevented further schooling for another two years, but she eventually made it to Somerville College at Oxford with the help of friends. Doors which had been closed to other women opened for Sorabji as she cultivated friendships with many distinguished people in the fields of law, politics, social service and literature, including *Florence Nightingale and the vice-chancellor at Oxford, Benjamin Jowett. Her studies in civil law should have been a purely academic pursuit since women were not allowed to advance to the examination, but her connections granted her special permission to take the exam in 1892. She passed, but did not actually receive her degree for another 20 years, as women were not allowed to become lawyers until 1919.

Even without the degree, Sorabji embarked on her life's work, returning to India in 1894 to become an advocate for women in the court system. As a private individual, she represented women appearing in court, but longed for official recognition as a lawyer. India proved to be as unyielding as England on this point, denying her professional standing even after she passed two exams. Sorabji did manage to achieve some notice when the Indian court system honored her request to appear in court as an adviser on behalf of women in 1904. Her legal work for hundreds of women, as well as her efforts on behalf of infant welfare and nursing, earned her the Kaisar-i-Hind gold medal in 1909.

Sorabji continued this work until she officially passed the bar in 1923, after which she started her practice as a lawyer in Calcutta. Failing eyesight necessitated a move to London at the close of the 1920s, and although she returned to India during the winters, she was more in sympathy with her adopted country than with the independence movement in her native land. During her later years, she wrote memoirs of her family (including her sister Susie, who died in 1931) and of her years as an adviser in the Indian courts. Previous to these works, she had published numerous stories, mostly about Indian women, which she geared towards a British audience. Her final work before her death in 1954 was her editing of *Queen Mary's Book for India*, a small anthology of India-oriented themes.

**SOURCES:**

Blain, Virginia, Patricia Clements, and Isobel Grundy. *The Feminist Companion to Literature in English*. New Haven, CT: Yale University Press, 1990.

Williams, E.T., and Helen M. Palmer, eds. *The Dictionary of National Biography, 1951–1960*. Oxford: Oxford University Press, 1971.

**Susan J. Walton**, freelance writer, Berea, Ohio

## Soraya (b. 1932).

*See Pahlavi, Soraya.*

## Sorgdrager, Winnie (1948—)

*Dutch politician. Born in The Hague, the Netherlands, on April 6, 1948; studied law at Groningen University; received doctorate in 1971.*

Winnie Sorgdrager's background as a public prosecutor in the regional courts of Arnhem and The Hague in the Netherlands prepared her for her role as minister of justice. She was born on April 6, 1948, in The Hague, the Netherlands, and studied at Groningen University. In 1971, the same year she passed her doctoral examinations, she began work at Twente University of Technology as an educational guidance counselor. Eight years later, she became a public prosecutor at Almelo, rising to the position of advocate-general in 1986 and procurator-general in 1993. In August 1994, she became the country's minister of justice as a Democrat in the Kok government. As such, she oversaw the court system, recommend-

ing reforms for better administration at the local level, and also proposed ways of better utilizing DNA testing in the prosecution of serious crimes and sex offenses. A few weeks before her term ended in 1998, she came under fire for her ministry's failure to halt the flow of child pornography in the country, and pledged to make the fight against child abuse her top priority.

**Susan J. Walton**, freelance writer, Berea, Ohio

## Sorel, Agnes (1422–1450)

*French beauty and mistress of King Charles VII of France. Name variations: Agnès Sorel. Born in 1422 in France; died in 1450 in France; daughter of Jean Soreau, lord of Coudun, and **Catherine de Maignelais**; never married; children: (with Charles VII, king of France)* ✥➤ *Charlotte de Brézé) (c. 1444/49–?, whose son Louis de Breze married **Diane de Poitiers**); Jeanne de France (who associated with Antoine de Bueil, count of Sancerre); Marie de Valois, also seen as Marguerite de France (who associated with Olivier Coëtivy).*

***Charlotte de Brézé.*** *See Diane de Poitiers for sidebar.*

✥➤

*Agnes Sorel*

A powerful mistress to a French king, Agnes Sorel was born into the petty French nobility. She was lady-in-waiting to *Isabelle of Lorraine, queen of Naples, when she met King Charles VII of France, soon becoming his mistress and moving to his court in Paris in 1444. Women of Agnes' birth could not reasonably hope for a legitimate place in the higher nobility or royal families; often those who were ambitious and power-hungry ended up as mistresses to kings, thereby gaining a higher status and greater wealth and power. It is not clear in Agnes' case whether she simply desired the influence that came from being the king's mistress or she was truly in love with Charles. It is clear, however, that Agnes exerted great power at the court and over Charles' actions.

She gained contradictory reputations at court and across the kingdom; some condemned her as an immoral prostitute, while others reported her to be a highly intelligent, practical, and kind woman. Eager to help her family, Agnes tried to influence Charles to raise their social status and put some of them into official positions, without too much success. King Charles did, however, grow very attached to his attractive mistress, granting her several estates which made the former lady-in-waiting a very wealthy woman in her own right. She was closely involved with the politics of the court and acted as an unofficial counselor to Charles. She held much more influence over the French court than did Charles' queen, *Marie of Anjou, whose position she more or less usurped.

Agnes Sorel was only 28 when she died suddenly and suspiciously. Poison was suspected, and may be true, considering the number of enemies the powerful and influential Agnes acquired during her six years at court. Charles seems to have truly mourned Agnes, but her murderer, if there were one, was never found.

**SUGGESTED READING:**
D'Orliac, Jehanne. *The Lady of Beauty: Agnes Sorel*. Lippincott, 1931.

**Laura York**, M.A. in History,
University of California, Riverside, California

# Sosa, Mercedes (1935—)

*Argentine folk singer and performer of working-class, populist songs who is called "The Voice of the Americas." Born on July 9, 1935, in Tucuman Province in central Argentina.*

When Mercedes Sosa sang, she took her life in her hands. During the 1970s, hundreds, even thousands, of Argentineans disappeared, often killed by right-wing death squads. Because of her lyrics, Sosa's life was in constant danger, but she continued to sing nonetheless. She was born in 1935 into a poor family, and although her grandfather was not from an Indian background, he spoke perfect Quechua. Her friends encouraged her to sing on a local radio station at age 15, and thus her career was born. It was not easy finding work as a folk singer, so Sosa often appeared at festivals and theaters in smaller towns, particularly in nearby Uruguay and Chile, before becoming well known in Buenos Aires. She often sang protest songs. By the mid-1970s, she had recorded over 16 albums and was known throughout South America. Never seeking commercial success or mimicking foreign styles, Sosa sang accompanied only by guitar and drum, wearing a poncho. During Argentina's darkest years, Mercedes Sosa did, indeed, become the voice of her people.

**SOURCES:**
Norman, Bob. "Protest Singers of Latin America: Mercedes Sosa," in *Sing Out!* Vol. 24, no. 3. July–August 1975, pp. 18–19, 27.

**John Haag**,
Athens, Georgia

# Sosipatra (fl. 4th c.)

*Ephesian philosopher. Flourished in the 4th century; born in Ephesus in Asia Minor; educated by two male guardians who were seers; married Eustathius (an orator and diplomat); after the death of Eustathius, became the consort of the philosopher Aedesius and they founded a school of philosophy together; children: (with Eustathius) three sons, including Antoninus.*

Sosipatra was a late pagan "philosopher" and wife of Eustathius, an orator and occasional diplomat. Eustathius was also a kinsman of Aedesius, a noted neo-Platonic philosopher. According to Eunapius in *Lives of Philosophers* (a work which treated pagan intellectuals about as objectively as contemporary Christian writers did their "saints" in their own *Lives*, that is, with much adoration and little concern for historical accuracy), Sosipatra was a towering pagan intellectual during an age when Christians were doing all they could to expunge paganism. Again according to Eunapius, as great a man as Eustathius was, Sosipatra's wisdom made that of her husband seem insignificant by comparison.

Sosipatra was born near Ephesus in Asia Minor. As Eunapius has it, her father was prosperous, and she lived a decorous youth until she was five, when two mysterious strangers, dressed in skins, made their way to her father's estate. There the strangers were employed by the steward to tend to the estate's vines. When the earth brought forth a bounty beyond all expectation, Sosipatra's father suspected the work of the gods. He invited his enigmatic employees to dine with him and showed them every consideration. Thus fêted, the two met Sosipatra and were captivated by her charm. They then revealed that their powers far transcended what they had so far demonstrated, and asked Sosipatra's father to surrender both her and his estate to them for four years, and also that he absent himself while they nurtured both. They promised that daughter and land would be well cared for, and that when the father returned he would scarcely recognize either. Sosipatra's father agreed, telling his servants, who remained, to do the bidding of the pair.

In the following years, these "heroes" (or maybe "demons," as Eunapius allows) initiated Sosipatra into such mysteries as even those who wanted to discover, could not. When the father returned, he was awestruck at the improvements brought to his estate and daughter—especially after the latter, without his speaking, revealed to him everything that he had done and felt while he was away. Thinking Sosipatra some sort of a goddess, the father fell before the strangers and besought their identities. They revealed that they were initiates in "Chaldean" wisdom, after which he begged them to stay on and continue their husbandry. They nodded an assent, but said nothing more. Then, Sosipatra's father fell asleep, and they gave to Sosipatra clothes adorned with magic symbols and books which they ordered her to seal in a chest. As day broke, the Chaldeans went out as if to work as usual and Sosipatra went to her father to tell him about how she had spent the night. He wished to reward the strangers richly, but they were nowhere to be found, and it was then that Sosipatra apparently understood their cryptic statement that they were about to travel to the "western ocean."

Sosipatra was by this time fully initiated into the lore of the Chaldeans, so that even though she returned to her father's charge, he went in awe of what she had become and meddled in none of her affairs. Sosipatra is said to have had no other teachers, but forever after she not only constantly quoted the works of famous poets, philosophers and sophists, she also understood them fully, even when others around her could only dimly perceive their wisdom.

She then decided to marry and chose Eustathius as the only living man somewhat worthy of herself. In her proposal to him (a stunning role reversal at the time), she predicted that they would have three children together, that all of these would know the happiness of the gods but none of them would know human success, that Eustathius would die in five years and be rewarded in the next life (with his spirit rising to the "orbit of the moon")—although his reward would not equal hers. Immediately the happy couple married and all came to pass as Sosipatra foretold.

After Eustathius died, Sosipatra lived in Pergamon (Pergamum) with Aedesius where the two founded a school. Although Aedesius was renowned and drew many students to his lectures, Sosipatra is said to have outshone him in the eyes of their students. During this period, Sosipatra is reported to have been the victim of Philometor (one of her kinsmen) who fell in love with her and resorted to magic to have her return his passion. Philometor was successful until Sosipatra, who had no need anymore for such attachments, convinced Maximus, another of her students, to counter Philometor's spell with another. The remedy worked and, although Maximus had operated in secret, Sosipatra nevertheless related to him exactly what he had done, where he had done it, and when. We are told that far from being angry at Philometor, Sosipatra actually admired him all the more after his plot to win her affections, because he had the good sense to so greatly esteem her.

Somewhat later, the same Philometor is said to have suffered a carriage accident, which Sosipatra recognized from afar as it was happening. Since she accurately described to those around her the details of the accident, she gained a reputation for having the gift of omnipresence. She died leaving three sons, only one of whom, Antoninus, is said to have been worthy of his parents. He devoted his life to studying esoteric lore and magic in Egypt, where he lived almost like a Christian hermit while doing his best to keep alive the worship of the old gods. He also is said to have had the gift of prophecy and to have foretold of the ultimate defeat of the gods he so passionately served.

Eunapius' account of Sosipatra provides us a fascinating picture of what passed for pagan philosophy in the 4th century, for clearly, the logical regimens of the past were being enveloped by esoteric learning, magical initiation and theurgy, as Christianity pressed hard upon the disappearing culture of pagans.

**William Greenwalt**,
Associate Professor of Classical History,
Santa Clara University, Santa Clara, California

# Sothern, Ann (1909–2001)

*American actress who had a popular television series and was nominated for an Oscar for her performance in* The Whales of August. *Name variations: acted under the name Harriette Lake. Born Harriette Arlene Lake on January 22, 1909, in Valley City, North Dakota; died on March 15, 2001, in Ketchum, Idaho; eldest of three daughters of Walter Lake (an actor) and Annette Yde-Lake (a concert singer); attended the University of Washington; married Roger Pryor (an actor-bandleader), on September 27, 1936 (divorced 1943); married Robert Sterling (an actor), on May 23, 1943 (divorced 1949); children: (second marriage) daughter,* Patricia Ann Sterling *(an actress).*

Selected filmography as Ann Sothern unless otherwise noted: (as Harriette Lake) The Show of Shows (1929); (as Harriette Lake) Hearts in Exile (1929); (as Harriette Lake) Doughboys (1930); (as Harriette Lake) Hold Everything (1930); (as Harriette Lake) Broadway Through a Keyhole (1933); (as Harriette Lake) Footlight Parade (1933); Let's Fall in Love (1934); Melody in Spring (1934); The Party's Over (1934); The Hell Cat (1934); Blind Date (1934); Kid Millions (1934); Folies Bergère (1935); Eight Bells (1935); Hooray for Love (1935); The Girl Friend (1935); Grand Exit (1935); You May Be Next (Panic on the Air, 1936); Hell-Ship Morgan (1936); Don't Gamble with Love (1936); My American Wife (1936); Walking on Air (1936); The Smartest Girl in Town (1936); Dangerous Number (1937); Fifty Roads to Town (1937); Ali Baba Goes to Town (1937); There Goes My Girl (1937); Super Sleuth (1937); There Goes the Groom (1937); Danger—Love at Work (1937); She's Got Everything (1938); Trade Winds (1938); Maisie (1939); *Elsa Maxwell's Hotel for Women (Hotel for Women, 1939); Fast and Furious (1939); Joe and Ethel Turp Call on the President (A Call on the President, 1939); Congo Maisie (1940); Brother Orchid (1940); Gold Rush Maisie (1940); Dulcy (1940); Lady Be Good (1941); Ringside Maisie (1941); Panama Hattie (1942); You John Jones (1942); Three Hearts for Julia (1943); Swing Shift Maisie (The Girl in Overalls, 1943); Thousands Cheer (1943); Cry Havoc (1943); Maisie Goes to Reno (You Can't Do That to Me, 1944); Up Goes Maisie (1946); Undercover Maisie (Undercover Girl, 1947); April Showers (1948); Words and Music (1948); The Judge Steps Out (Indian Summer, 1949); A Letter to Three Wives (1949); Nancy Goes to Rio (1950); Shadow on the Wall (1950); The Blue Gardenia (1953); The Best Man (1964); Lady in a Cage (1964); Sylvia (1965); Chubasco (1967); The Killing Kind (1973); The Golden Needles (1974); Crazy Mama (1975); The Manitou (1978); The Little Dragons (voice only, 1980); The Whales of August (1987).

Remembered as the wisecracking Maisie Ravier in the popular "Maisie" movie series of the 1940s, and for her portrayal of a similarly spunky character on the 1950s television series "Private Secretary," Ann Sothern was a talented actress and singer who, by most accounts, should have attained greater movie stardom than she did. Only very late in her career was she recognized by the film academy, winning an Oscar nomination in 1988 for her supporting role in *The Whales of August*, which also starred veteran actors *Bette Davis, *Lillian Gish, and Vincent Price. "She was one of those people who I think was never, ever appreciated in her own time," said Robert Osborne, a columnist for the *Hollywood Reporter*. "There was nothing she couldn't do."

The eldest of three daughters of **Annette Yde-Lake**, a concert singer, and Walter Lake, an actor who also held a variety of other jobs, Sothern was born in Valley City, North Dakota, on January 22, 1909. She was christened Harriette Lake, under which she acted until 1934. Her paternal grandfather was Simon Lake, who invented the modern submarine, and her maternal grandfather was Hans Nilson, the noted Danish concert violinist. Because of her mother's career, the family was constantly on the move, and Sothern spent her childhood in Michigan, Iowa, and Minnesota. When the Lakes divorced in 1927, Sothern lived with her father in Seattle while attending the University of Washington. After a year, however, she left school to pursue a career in the movies.

The fact that her mother was working as a vocal coach at Warner Bros. may have helped Sothern secure her first movie role, a bit in the musical revue *The Show of Shows* (1929). She appeared in two additional films at Warner Bros. before transferring to MGM. The new studio, however, had little more than brief walk-ons for Sothern, so when Florenz Ziegfeld offered her a part in the Broadway show *Smiles* (1930), she jumped at the opportunity. During the show's tryout in Boston, however, Sothern was dropped from the cast, putting her New York debut on hold. Taking the setback in stride, she secured a role in the Rodgers and Hart musical *America's Sweetheart* (1931), in which she and Jack Whiting introduced the song "I've Got Five Dollars." Characterized by one reviewer as a "lovely synthesis, one part *Ginger Rogers, one part *Ethel Merman," Sothern went on to appear on Broadway in *Everybody's Welcome* (1931), followed by a seven-month tour in the Pulitzer Prize-winning *Of Thee I Sing*. In 1933, the actress was set to replace *Lois Moran** during the Broadway run of the show when the New York theaters closed for the summer due to an unprecedented heat wave; she was once again out of work.

Sothern returned to Hollywood, where in 1934, she signed a long-term contract with Columbia. For the next three years, she played ingenues in a series of assembly-line pictures which did little to advance her career. "I'd trade a 'pretty girl' role any day in the week for that of an old hag, if the hag was a real character," she said at the time. Released by Columbia in 1936, she went over to RKO, where she was cast in a quartet of bland romantic comedies with Gene Raymond: *Walking on Air, The Smartest Girl in Town* (both 1936), *There Goes My Girl* (1937), and *She's Got Everything* (1938). Although occasionally loaned out to other studios, she was still unable to find the kind of challenging roles she desired.

Meanwhile, in September 1936, Sothern had wed actor-bandleader Roger Pryor whom she had met in 1932, while on tour in *Of Thee I Sing*. "I will never play another sweet leading role on the screen as long as I live," she said as she relinquished her lucrative contract with RKO. Free of film commitments, she traveled with Roger, sometimes performing as a vocalist with his band. But producer Walter Wanger lured Sothern back into films with the role of a dim-witted but warm-hearted stenographer in *Trade Winds* (1938), for which she received rave notices. Her performance led to the title role in *Maisie* (1939), that of a plucky Brooklyn chorus girl who Sothern viewed as a refreshing change from the romantic roles of which she had grown so tired. The first Maisie film was enormously popular and spawned nine sequels and a radio version, all of which starred Sothern. While continuing in the Maisie series, she also appeared in other films, including the musical *Lady Be Good* (1940), in which she introduced the memorable song "The Last Time I Saw Paris," which won an Oscar for Best Song of 1941.

In 1942, Sothern divorced Pryor and married MGM actor Robert Sterling, with whom she had a daughter Patricia Ann in 1944. Although she hoped to leave pictures and devote her time to being a wife and mother, the marriage deteriorated into a series of breakups and reconciliations before ending in divorce in 1949. That year, she also snagged her best dramatic

role to date in Joseph L. Mankiewicz's *A Letter to Three Wives*, with *Linda Darnell and *Jeanne Crain. She was cast in another dramatic role—a murderer—in *Shadow on the Wall* (1950), after which she contacted infectious hepatitis and was laid up for two years.

In 1952, with her movie career seemingly over, Sothern turned to television, making her dramatic debut on "Schlitz Playhouse of Stars." Hoping to bring Maisie to television as a series, but unable to procure the rights, Sothern embarked on the comedy series "Private Secretary," creating the Maisie-like character of Susie McNamara, a confirmed busybody who interfered regularly in the life of her long-suffering boss, played by Don Porter. The show was an enormous success, running for four seasons. Along with the sitcom, Sothern appeared on a color special of *Lady in the Dark* (September 1954) and launched a nightclub act which she debuted in Las Vegas and later took to the Chez Paree in Chicago. When her television series was cancelled in 1957, she moved into a new sitcom, "The Ann Sothern Show." In addition to her busy performing schedule, she was involved in a cattle ranch (run by her father), a music publishing enterprise, and a sewing center in Sun Valley, Idaho, where she had a home. "I leave the house early in the morning and I bring home the bacon late at night and the servants think I'm crazy to work so hard," she replied when asked if she was a workaholic.

In 1961, Sothern moved to New York, where she made a pilot for a television show that did not sell and was involved in another ill-fated musical. In 1964, somewhat older and heavier, she resumed her film career, playing character roles in a number of features, notable among them *Lady in a Cage* (1964). She also continued to make television appearances, including several on *Lucille Ball's popular "The Lucy Show."

In 1973, while appearing in a dinner theater production in Jacksonville, Florida, Sothern was struck by a piece of scenery, which injured a lumbar vertebra and damaged some nerves in her legs. Although told she would not walk again, the actress recovered enough to get around quite well with the use of a cane. Her career, however, was largely limited to a few B movies, including *Crazy Mama* (1975), in which she appeared with her daughter, also an actress. She recaptured her former status, however, with her role in *The Whales of August* (1987), a study of aging, for which she was nominated for an Academy Award. That year, she also recorded an album of her own musical compositions. From 1984 on, Sothern made

her home in Ketchum, Idaho, where she died on March 15, 2001, at the age of 92.

**SOURCES:**
Katz, Ephraim. *The Film Encyclopedia*. NY: HarperCollins, 1994.
"Obituary," in *Boston Globe*. March 17, 2001.
Parish, James Robert, and Michael R. Pitts. *Hollywood Songsters*. NY: Garland, 1991.

**Barbara Morgan,**
Melrose, Massachusetts

## Sothern, Mrs. E.H. (1866–1950).

*See Marlowe, Julia.*

## Sotomayor, Maria de Zayas y (1590–c. 1650).

*See Zayas y Sotomayor, María de.*

## Soubiran, Marie-Thérèse de (1834–1889).

*See Marie-Thérèse de Soubiran.*

## Soubirous, Bernadette (1844–1879).

*See Bernadette of Lourdes.*

## Souez, Ina (1903–1992)

*American soprano. Born Ina Rains on June 3, 1903, in Windsor, Colorado; died on December 7, 1992, in Santa Monica, California; studied with Florence Hinman.*

*Debuted as Mimì in Ivrea (1928); performed at Covent Garden in London (1929 and 1935); performed at Glyndebourne Festival (1934–39); performed at City Opera in New York (1945).*

Of Cherokee descent, Ina Souez was born Ina Rains in 1903 in Colorado. Her early vocal training took place under the tutelage of Canadian contralto **Florence Hinman**, who was sufficiently impressed to send the girl to Europe. Souez made a splash on the European stages in Milan, London, Paris and Rome, debuting in *Ivrea* in 1928 as Mimì. She performed at London's Covent Garden in 1929 and 1935. She also became the prima donna at the Glyndebourne Festival during the mid-to-late 1930s, later returning to the United States to perform in New York City at the City Opera in 1945. Her most acclaimed performances were her Mozartean roles as Donna Anna in *Don Giovanni* and Fiordiligi in *Così fan tutte*, the recordings of which were the first commercial ones available. After World War II, Souez joined Spike Jones' music and comedy troupe. As a member, she participated in such Jonesian clowning as warbling while wearing a large hat decorated with pigeons. Her ten-year stint with the troupe launched her into another career teaching voice in San Francisco and Los Angeles. She spent the last eight years of her life in a nursing home in Santa Monica, California, following a stroke, and died in 1992.

**SOURCES:**

*The New York Times Biographical Service.* December 10, 1992.

*Time.* December 21, 1992.

Susan J. Walton, freelance writer,<br>Berea, Ohio

## Soule, Aileen Riggin (b. 1906).

*See Riggin, Aileen.*

## Soule, Caroline White (1824–1903)

*American author and Universalist minister. Born Caroline White on September 3, 1824, in Albany, New York; died on December 6, 1903, in Glasgow, Scotland; third of six children of Nathaniel White and Elizabeth (Mèrselis) White; graduated from the Albany Female Academy, 1841; married Henry Birdsall Soule (a Unitarian Universalist minister), on August 28, 1843 (died 1852); children: five.*

*Named first president of the Women's Centenary Association (1871–80); became minister of St. Paul's Universalist Church in Glasgow (1880). Author of* Home Life *(1855),* The Pet of the Settlement *(1860), and* Wine or Water *(1862).*

Caroline White Soule was born in Albany, New York, in 1824, the third of six children of Nathaniel and **Elizabeth White**. She was baptized in the Dutch Reformed Church to which her mother belonged, but was raised as a Unitarian Universalist, her father's faith. Soule entered the Albany Female Academy at age 12 and graduated with high honors in 1841. She became principal of the female department of the Universalist-sponsored Clinton Liberal Institute in Clinton, New York, in 1842.

Caroline married Henry Birdsall Soule, a former teacher at the Clinton Liberal Institute and a Unitarian Universalist minister, on August 28, 1843, in Albany. After residing briefly in Utica, New York, where her husband's church was located, the family moved frequently throughout New England for the next several years. During this time, Caroline Soule began to write articles for publication in newspapers as a means of supplementing the family's income. Her husband retired briefly from the ministry in 1850 because of fragile health. Although he recovered sufficiently to accept the position of pastor of the Unitarian Church in Granby, Con-

necticut, in 1851, he died of smallpox the following January, leaving Caroline on her own with five young children and few possessions.

Soule took a teaching position to support her family and intensified her writing efforts. After publishing a biography of her late husband in 1852, she soon became a popular contributor to a variety of Universalist publications, including *Rose of Sharon* and *Ladies' Repository*. Financially burdened, Soule was forced to move her family in 1854 to a log cabin on the Iowa prairie, where she lived for ten years. Soule had achieved sufficient public recognition to have a collection of her moral tales, entitled *Home Life*, published by Abel Tompkins in 1855, and the following year she was named a regular correspondent for *Ladies' Repository*. In 1860, she wrote a novel based on prairie life entitled *The Pet of the Settlement*; however, with periodical writing taking up more of her time, she published her last book, *Wine or Water*, in 1862, and returned to Albany in 1864.

Soule became the assistant editor of *Ladies' Repository* in 1865 but relinquished that position in 1867 and relocated to New York City to edit her own Sunday school paper, *The Guiding Star*, for Unitarian congregations. Deeply involved in church activities, in 1869 Soule assisted with the formation of the Women's Centenary Aid Association (WCAA), a fund-raising organization benefiting the Unitarian Church. An immediate success, the WCAA reorganized in 1871 as the Woman's Centenary Association (WCA)—the first national organization of church women in the United States—and Soule was elected its initial president. Under her leadership, the WCA assisted disabled pastors, fostered home and missionary work, and facilitated educational opportunities for women interested in the ministry. A widely known and popular public speaker, Soule was also a proponent of the temperance movement and an active member of the Association for the Advancement of Women.

Soule's demanding speaking schedule and organizational commitments caused her health to deteriorate, and she took a sabbatical to the north of England and Scotland in 1875. While in the United Kingdom, Soule addressed numerous Unitarian congregations, and organized a Scottish Unitarian Universalist convention before returning to her duties in the United States. She went back to Scotland as a missionary in the employ of the WCAA in 1878, and was named minister of St. Paul's Universalist Church in Glasgow the following year. Soule was officially ordained as a Unitarian Universalist minister in

1880, and retired as president of the WCAA. She returned to the United States to work for the WCAA in 1882, after which she moved to Scotland permanently in 1886. Soule retired from the ministry in 1892 but remained active in social service and charitable activities. She died in Glasgow, Scotland, on December 6, 1903.

**SOURCES:**

James, Edward T., ed. *Notable American Women, 1607–1950*. Cambridge, MA: The Belknap Press of Harvard University, 1971.

Read, Phyllis J., and Bernard L. Witlieb. *The Book of Women's Firsts*. NY: Random House, 1992.

**Grant Eldridge**, freelance writer,
Pontiac, Michigan

## Sourdis, Isabelle de.

*See Estrée, Gabrielle d' for sidebar.*

## Southampton, countess of.

*See Villiers, Barbara.*

## Southcott, Joanna (1750–1814)

*English prophet and sectarian who believed that the Holy Spirit spoke through her and promised the imminent end of the world and Christ's Second Coming. Born in Tarford, Devonshire, England, in 1750; died in London on December 27, 1814; daughter of William Southcott and Hannah Southcott; received no formal education; never married; no children.*

*Was a domestic servant until the age of 42, then a prophet, writer inspired by the Holy Spirit, preacher, and interpreter; moved to London (1802); toured the English provinces, preaching.*

Joanna Southcott was a poor servant girl from the southwest of England who, at the age of 42, announced that God had chosen her as a messenger of his Second Coming. She began to write prophecies and published 65 books filled with them between 1801 and her death in 1814. Thousands of English men and women, rich and poor alike, followed her, and believed in 1814 that she was about to give birth to the Messiah through a miraculous Virgin Birth, and would name him Shiloh. She gave every sign of imminent maternity but died and was found to have had no more than a phantom pregnancy. She was the most famous millenarian prophet of her era and still has followers up to the present.

Her father, a tenant farmer, claimed to be descended from nobler folk and passed on to his daughter a sense of her dignity and a tendency to perceive slights from anyone who doubted her supernatural claims. The family were churchgo-ers and read the Bible regularly, giving Joanna a sense of her own sinfulness and unworthiness before God. Her remarks on her mother's death, while she was in her teens, are characteristic. "My mother's death sank deep into my heart. Since that, I may say I have been desirous to Live in the Knowledge of the Lord but to my Shame I can reproach myself I have forgot Him days without number and am an unworthy object of His loving kindness." She had a limited education, could read and write, but appears to have read few books beyond the Bible, a collection of an aunt's poems, and a history of the Turkish Empire, which seemed to her to hold clues to prophetic interpretation.

As a young servant girl, Southcott was courted by a succession of eligible young men, farmers, shopkeepers and even a young squire, but, after being tempted to accept each offer of marriage, she turned back to her intensifying religious life. Throughout her youth and early middle age, she worked first as a cook and then as an upholsterer's assistant, opening a shop of her own in 1790. Two years later, she had her first religious vision, of men and horses flying through the air and fighting one another. She also saw hosts of angels and a vision of the beautiful Holy Spirit commanding her:

> All of a sudden the Spirit entered in me with such power and fury, that my senses seemed lost; I felt as though I had power to shake the house down, and yet I felt as though I could walk in air, at the time the Spirit remained in me; but did not remember many words I said, as they were delivered with such fury that took my senses; but as soon as the Spirit had left me, I grew weak as before.

She became convinced that she was the woman described in the Biblical book of Revelation, "a woman clothed with the sun, and the moon under her feet, and upon her head a crown of twelve stars." In the following years, she also began to deliver prophecies about the prospects of the forthcoming harvest and the welfare of local dignitaries, including an Anglican bishop whose death she accurately foretold. The harvest predictions were often right too, leading some people to conclude that she was a witch, while others countered that she was blessed with divine foresight and was a protection *against* witchcraft. She certainly believed in the reality of witchcraft and although she favored the Bible over astrology she *did* believe that planets could create a good or bad influence, and that "there is a world in the moon and in that world Satan dwells."

Southcott was popular among poor people because of her outspoken denunciation of rich landowners who took advantage of popular hunger by hoarding grain until the prices rose during the economic upheavals of the French Revolutionary era. Speaking as God's mouthpiece at a time when such words risked prosecution for sedition, she declared that "my charges will come heavy against them and my judgments must be great in the land if they starve the poor in the midst of plenty." She compared "the shepherds of England" with "Ninevah, Sodom and Gomorrah." The wealth of the Anglican hierarchy, some of whom were major landowners in their own right, also set her against them.

Critics, of whom she always had many, charged that Joanna Southcott was an illiterate fraud. She countered by writing down and sealing her prophecies before witnesses, permitting them to be opened after they had been confirmed in reality. She made no claim to being their author. Rather, she said, the Spirit possessed her, and she was merely the instrument through which they were put down on paper, often in the form of doggerel verse. Her writing was awkward and ungrammatical, and eventually she switched to "dictating" the revelations of the Spirit to a more literate secretary, but she insisted that she had no control over where or when the inspiration to write would come over her. Some of these revelations praised Southcott herself, such as the verse in which she wrote:

> For on earth there's something new appears
> Since Earth's foundation plac'd I tell you here
> Such wondrous woman never was below.

In 1801, she took her savings of £100 to a printer in the Devonshire city of Exeter and asked him to print a collection of these prophecies, under the title *The Strange Effects of Faith*. The publication caused a sensation in the region and enabled her fame to spread more widely, into other parts of England. She moved the following year to London and continued her outpouring of pamphlets, books, and predictions, explaining Daniel and Revelation, denouncing atheists like Thomas Paine, and promising salvation and Heaven for all believers.

These were the years of the French Revolution and the Napoleonic Wars. Several historians who have studied Southcott's life think she may have been inspired by the dramatic political upheavals of her age. It is certainly striking that her first revelation came at the same time as the French Revolutionary terror, and that many of her invocations of Revelation had the same mood as William Blake's or those of his prophet-contemporary Richard Brothers, whom many of her own followers had admired. She was one of many contemporaries who thought that the Beast named in Revelation was none other than Napoleon, and that she was now witnessing the last days in the history of the world, preparing for the return of Jesus. She reassured the civil authorities, who suspected her of sedition, that her followers would fight in defense of England if it were invaded by France and that she was totally opposed to the French Revolution. The revolution against Satan, not against monarchy, was the one she preached, and she had no objection to a stratified society so long as the superiors recognized their duty towards the poorer sort.

She began giving to her followers, who named themselves "Johannas" or "Southcottians," papers closed with a red seal which promised that they would "inherit the Tree of Life to be made Heirs of God and joint heirs with Jesus Christ." A trade in these sealed papers soon developed which, as one historian has noted, is comparable to the medieval trade in holy relics. Many holders of them believed that they were guarantees of immortality, a point which Southcott had to discourage. "I exhorted them," she said of her followers, "to be Steadfast in the faith. Hoping if they lived to the coming of the Lord that they would be waiting like the Wise Virgins to enter in with the bridegroom . . . but if they died before the time I hoped they would come with the Lord in Glory."

> *Joanna's confusion of her identity with that of a biblical figure, the Woman of Revelation, was a reflection not only of her own neurotic sensibilities but also of the disturbed international scene, which encouraged her belief that the world had entered the last days and that all the extraordinary characters of the prophetic books must soon be making their appearance.*
>
> —James K. Hopkins

Among her critics was the poet Robert Southey who saw her as a simple-witted woman being manipulated by unscrupulous followers. He was horrified by the popular enthusiasm for Southcott and told a friend that "had she been sent to Bedlam [a lunatic asylum] ten years ago, how many hundred persons would have been preserved from this infectious and disgraceful insanity." Also critical were the Calvinist Methodist leaders who had drawn Southcott's fire for preaching about the threat of Hell rather than about God's infinite love and forgiveness, and the scornful Anglicans who denied her supernatural gifts. She had attended Methodist and Anglican services for a while in 1790s but now rejected both as unauthentic, and her followers began to build chapels of their own. Enthusiastic worship gatherings often brought together a thousand or more followers, who were buoyed by Southcott's preaching of universal salvation.

In 1804, there were rumors of a French invasion, and Joanna foresaw that "Nine parts of the Inhabitants of London will perish, as the streets will be filled with dead Bodies, French as well as English." This prophecy never came true. Shortly thereafter, she asked for a "trial" in London to quiet allegations that she was a fraud, a point about which she was always sensitive, and about which she questioned herself frequently and closely. Many of her old Exeter neighbors and friends were called to testify to her blameless life and good character, and several of the middle- and upper-class women and men in her movement also defended her claims. Among them were the aristocratic Reverend Thomas P. Foley, a wealthy widow named **Jane Townley**, and Townley's companion **Ann Underwood**. Surviving lists drawn up at the time show that two thirds of all Southcottians were women, and that the strongholds of the movement were the southwest, London, and the industrial areas of Lancashire and Yorkshire in the north of England, with domestic servants being particularly enthusiastic participants. Southcott spent long periods living with Jane Townley and Ann Underwood who acted as her secretaries and scribes and freed her from all material want.

In 1813, in her *Third Book of Wonders*, Southcott announced that she was going to give birth to "Shiloh," the "second Christ." She claimed to have known this since 1794 but only now to have fully understood that she, like *Mary the Virgin, was to give birth to the Messiah. She was then 63 years old but, showing every sign of pregnancy, went into seclusion and prepared for the great event. A prominent doctor, Joseph Adams, visited her and said that she was indeed about to give birth, and 17 of the 21 physicians who examined her came to the same conclusion. Friends said they felt the baby kicking. Wealthier followers contributed a carved and gilded crib worth £200 and other gifts to the forthcoming child. Southcott was even offered a large house by London's Green Park for the delivery. Newspaper correspondents discussed the obstetrical, religious, and moral aspects of the case while awaiting its outcome, and several impostors, posing as Joanna Southcott, tried to raise money for themselves. Rumors that she was about to give birth to an illegitimate child by one of her followers also circulated and one

day "there was a great riot . . . before Joanna's house, and they threw violently many stones and brickbats gainst the house and doors and *they*, the inhabitants, were much alarmed."

The expected date of delivery came and went, three more months passed, in which Southcott's health declined rapidly, pain forced her to take opium for relief, and she died on December 27, 1814. She had given strict instructions that no autopsy should be attempted for four days after her death, apparently believing that the child could live on inside her for that time. When an autopsy was performed it showed that the pregnancy had been delusional. The absence of the child led at once to a rumor among her closest followers that the child *had* been born secretly, or perhaps spiritually, and was even now transforming the world, an idea given added weight by the fact that the "American War" (i.e. the War of 1812) came to an end on the day of Southcott's death.

Different groups of followers began to observe different rituals, according to their own divine message, and many of her former followers saw themselves as the next prophet. "One group ended a prayer meeting by letting loose a small black pig, which they attacked with knives and sticks until they killed it. They then burned it and scattered the ashes on their heads." Another group, following Southcott's friend George Turner, believed his prediction that the world would end on January 28, 1817. They gave away or destroyed all their possessions as the great day approached, and Turner himself was so dismayed at the failure of his prophecy that he descended into madness and died five years later. These disciples of Southcott endured frequent disappointments in the following years, but sects have persisted up to the present, including the House of David in America and the Panacea Society in Bedford, England.

**SOURCES:**
Balleine, G.R. *Past Finding Out: The Tragic Story of Joanna Southcott and Her Successors.* London: S.P.C.K., 1956.
Hopkins, James K. *A Woman to Deliver Her People: Joanna Southcott and English Millenarianism in an Era of Revolution.* Austin, TX: University of Texas Press, 1982.
Thompson, E.P. *The Making of the English Working Class.* NY: Vintage, 1966.
Wright, Eugene Patrick. *A Catalogue of the Joanna Southcott Collection at the University of Texas.* Austin, TX: University of Texas Press, 1968.

**Patrick Allitt**,
Professor of History,
Emory University, Atlanta, Georgia

# Southesk, countess of.

*See Carnegie, Maud (1893–1945).*

# Southey, Caroline Anne

## (1786–1854)

*British poet and prose writer. Name variations: Caroline Bowles. Born Caroline Anne Bowles on October 7, 1786, in Lymington, Hampshire, England; died on July 20, 1854, in Lymington; only child of Captain Charles Bowles and Anne (Burrard) Bowles; married Robert Southey (the poet), in 1839 (died 1843).*

*Selected writings:* Ellen Fitzarthur *(anonymously, 1820);* The Widow's Tale *(1822);* Solitary Hours *(1826);* Tales of the Moors *(1828);* Chapters on Churchyards *(1829);* Tales of the Factories *(1833);* Selwyn in Search of a Daughter *(1835);* The Birth-Day *(1836);* Robin Hood: A Fragment *(with Robert Southey, 1847);* The Correspondence of Robert Southey with Caroline Bowles *(1881).*

Caroline Anne Bowles was born in 1786, the daughter of Captain Charles Bowles of the East India Company and **Anne Burrard Bowles**, on the family estate in Lymington, Hampshire, England. Her father retired shortly after her birth. Both of Caroline's parents died when she was a child, and she lost the majority of her inheritance through the improper dealings of one of her guardians. Her adoptive stepbrother, Colonel Bruce, provided her with an annual allowance of £150, but she soon found this to be inadequate and began writing to supplement her income.

Caroline submitted the metric tale *Ellen Fitzarthur* to poet Robert Southey in 1820, and he was sufficiently impressed to forward the work to publisher John Murray. It appeared anonymously later that year. She continued to correspond with Robert, and enjoyed further literary success with the publication of her poetry collections *The Widow's Tale* (1822) and *Solitary Hours* (1826). She also contributed a collection of stories in serial form to *Blackwood's Magazine* (1829), which was published as a book, *Chapters on Churchyards*, later the same year. Caroline exhibited an interest in the social issues of her day, publishing *Tales of the Factories*, a collection of poems on the lives of industrial workers, in 1833. She received critical praise from Henry Nelson Coleridge for her long poem, *The Birth-Day*, in 1836.

As Caroline's professional status rose, Robert took an increasing interest in her work and invited her to collaborate with him on an epic poem on the subject of Robin Hood. She proved unable to write in the meter required by the poem, however, and the project was soon abandoned. Despite the failure of their literary collaboration, the two were married soon after the death of his first wife **Edith Fricker Southey** in 1839, and they settled at Robert's home in Keswick, England. The marriage proved unhappy due to his deteriorating mental health and the rejection of Caroline by her new stepchildren, except for Robert's eldest daughter, **Edith Southey**. Caroline regarded her husband's death in 1843 with a sense of relief. He left her £2,000 in his will, a modest sum that barely covered the debts he had also left her.

Caroline Southey returned to Lymington and did not resume her writing career following her husband's death. She released what had been completed of her joint project with Robert Southey as *Robin Hood: A Fragment* in 1847. Her financial situation was eased when the crown awarded her an annual pension of £200 near the end of her life. She died at her family's home in Lymington on July 20, 1854. Her correspondence with Robert Southey was published in 1881 as *The Correspondence of Robert Southey with Caroline Bowles*.

**SOURCES:**

Blain, Virginia. *Caroline Bowles Southey, 1786–1854: The Making of a Woman Writer.* Ashgate, 1997.

Kunitz, Stanley J., ed. *British Authors of the Nineteenth Century.* NY: H.W. Wilson, 1936.

Shattock, Joanne. *The Oxford Guide to British Women Writers.* Oxford: Oxford University Press, 1993.

**Grant Eldridge**, freelance writer, Pontiac, Michigan

# Southworth, E.D.E.N. (1819–1899)

*Popular American novelist. Born Emma Dorothy Eliza Nevitte on December 26, 1819, in Washington, D.C.; died in the Georgetown district of Washington, D.C., on June 30, 1899; elder of two daughters of Charles Le Compte Nevitte and his second wife, Susannah (Wailes) Nevitte; sister of* **Frances Henshaw Baden**; *graduated from her stepfather's school, 1835; married Frederick Hamilton Southworth (an inventor), in 1840 (separated 1844); children: Richmond, Charlotte Emma.*

*Selected novels:* Retribution, a Tale of Passion; or The Vale of Shadows *(1849);* The Deserted Wife *(1849);* The Mother-in-Law; or The Isle of Rays *(1851);* Shannondale *(1851);* The Curse of Clifton; or The Widowed Bride *(1852);* The Discarded Daughter; or the Children of the Ilse: A Tale of the Chesapeake *(1852);* Virginia and Magdalene; or The Foster Sisters *(1852);* India: The Pearl of Pearl River *(1853, originally serialized as "Mark Sutherland");* The Lost Heiress *(c. 1853);* The Missing Bride; or Miriam the Avenger *(1854);* Broken Pledges, A Story of Noir et Blanc

*(1855); Vivia; or The Secret of Power (c. 1856); The Three Beauties (1858); The Hidden Hand, a Novel (1859, Part II as Capitola's Peril [c. 1907]); The Lady of the Isle; or, The Island Princess (1859); The Gipsy's Prophecy; or The Bride of an Evening (1861); Hickory Hall; or The Outcast (1861); The Broken Engagement; or Speaking the Truth for a Day (1862); Love's Labor Won (1862); The Fatal Marriage (1863); Self-Made; or Out of the Depths (1863–64); The Bridal Eve; or Rose Elmer (1864); Allworth Abbey (1865); Fair Play; or The Test of Lone Isle (1865–66, originally serialized as "Britomarte, the Man-Hater" [1868], sequel published as How He Won Her [1865–66]); The Bride of Llewellyn (1866); The Fortune Seeker; or The Bridal Day (1866); The Prince of Darkness, a Romance of the Blue Ridge (1866); The Coral Lady; or The Bronzed Beauty of Paris (1867); The Widow's Son (1867); The Bride's Fate (1869, sequel published as The Changed Brides; or Winning Her Way [1869]); The Family Doom; or The Sin of a Countess (1869, sequel published as The Maiden Widow [1870]); Cruel as the Grave (1871, sequel published as Tried for Her Life [1871]); The Lost Heir of Linlithgow (1872, sequel published as A Noble Lord [1872]); A Beautiful Fiend; or Through the Fire (1873, sequel published as Victor's Triumphs [1874]); A Husband's Devotion (1874); The Rejected Bride (1874); Reunited (1874); The Mystery of Dark Hollow (1875); "Em" (1876); The Bride's Ordeal (1877, sequel published as Her Love or Her Life [1878]); The Red Hill Tragedy (1877); A Skeleton in the Closet (1878, sequel published as Brandon Coyle's Wife [1893]); Sybil Brotherton (1879); Trail of the Serpent (1879); Why Did He Wed Her? (1884, sequel published as For Whose Sake? [1884]); A Deed Without a Name (1886, followed by sequels Dorothy Harcourt's Secret [1886], To His Fate [1886], When Love Gets Justice [c. 1886]); An Exile's Bride (1887); A Leap in the Dark (1889, sequel published as The Mysterious Marriage [1893]); Nearest and Dearest (1889, sequel published as Little Nea's Engagement [1889]); Unknown; or The Mystery of Raven Rocks (1889); For Woman's Love (1890, sequel published as An Unrequited Love [1890]); The Unloved Wife (1890, sequels published as When the Shadows Darken [n.d.] and Lilith [1890]); The Lost Lady of Lone (1890, sequel published as The Struggle of a Soul [1904]); Gloria (1891, sequel published as David Lindsay [1891]); Em's Husband (1892); Only a Girl's Heart (1893, sequel published as Gertrude Haddon [1894]); The Widows of Widowville (1894); Sweet Love's Atonement (1904, sequel published as Zenobia's Suitors [1904]); Her Mother's Secret (1910, sequels pub-*lished as Love's Bitterest Cup [1910] and When Shadows Die [1910]); The Bride's Dowry (n.d.); The Doom of Deville (n.d.); Eudora (n.d.); When Love Commands (n.d., sequel published as Fulfilling Her Destiny [n.d.]); The Initials: A Story of Modern Life (n.d.); The Three Sisters (n.d.).*

*Selected short fiction:* Old Neighborhoods and New Settlements; or Christmas Evening Legends (1853); The Wife's Victory; and Other Nouvellettes (1854); The Haunted Homestead and Other Nouvellettes, with an Autobiography of the Author (1860); (with sister, Frances Henshaw Baden) The Christmas Guest; or The Crime and the Curse (1870); (with sister) The Artist's Love (1872); (with sister) The Spectre Lover (1875); (with sister) The Fatal Secret (1877); (with sister) The Phantom Wedding; or The Fall of the House of Flint (1878).

E.D.E.N. Southworth was born Emma Dorothy Eliza Nevitte in Washington, D.C., on December 26, 1819, the elder of two daughters of Charles Le Compte Nevitte and **Susannah Wailes Nevitte**. When she was three years old, Southworth lost her father to the lingering effects of a wound he had received as a soldier in the War of 1812. Two years later, her mother married schoolmaster Joshua L. Henshaw, who had served as Daniel Webster's personal secretary. Southworth recalled her childhood as a lonely one, with its happiest moments spent exploring Maryland's Tidewater region on horseback; during those rides, she acquired an abiding interest in the area's history and folklore.

Having attended her stepfather's school, Southworth completed her secondary education in 1835 at the age of 15. She accepted a position as a schoolteacher, remaining in that capacity until 1840, when she married Frederick Hamilton Southworth, an inventor from Utica, New York. The Southworths moved to a one-room log cabin in Prairie du Chien, Wisconsin, in 1841, where Emma continued teaching until the birth of their first child in 1843. Frederick Southworth lacked the ability to secure permanent employment or adequately provide for his family, and the marriage was an unhappy one. The couple, with their son and Frederick's mother, eventually moved in with Emma's mother and her second husband. However, when Southworth became pregnant again, they were ousted from the house by her stepfather. Soon Frederick abandoned his family to seek Brazilian gold, and Emma returned to Washington to give birth to a daughter. Although Southworth never discussed her marriage directly, many of her stories featured heroines who were on the margins of society, who were abused or neglected by their spouses, or were constrained by the patriarchal culture of the 19th century.

Lacking familial support, Southworth returned to teaching to maintain her two young children, but her inadequate annual salary required her to work in a federal land office as a copyist to supplement her income. And late at night, she would write. Her first story, *The Irish Refugee*, was serialized in 1846 in the *Baltimore Sunday Visitor*. This work attracted the attention of Gamaliel Bailey, editor of the *National Era*, who began publishing Southworth's stories regularly. Her first novel, *Retribution*, appeared in both serial and book form in 1849, which subsequently increased her success as a writer and enabled her to move her family to more spacious housing in the fashionable Georgetown district of Washington. That same year, she entered into an agreement with the *Saturday Evening Post*. This lasted for eight years until ongoing criticism of her work by Henry Peterson, the *Post*'s editor, propelled her to an exclusive publishing arrangement with Robert Bonner of the *New York Ledger* in 1857.

Southworth's business relationship with Bonner, who paid her well and whom she considered a friend, would last her entire life. Although her work sold steadily, her personal life suffered. She and her children were in ill health throughout the early 1850s, which interrupted her ability to work and decreased the family's income. However, in exchange for sole serial publication rights to Southworth's work, Bonner had ensured her an income regardless of any periods of inactivity brought on by poor health. This arrangement remained in place for 30 years, during which time Southworth wrote prolifically; as the *New York Ledger* became one of the bestselling periodicals in the United States, she became one of the most popular novelists of her day.

Considering Southworth a pivotal figure in the development of the American novel, **Amy Hudock** suggests that her novels "taught the world a vision of the American woman that equaled in power and influence James Fenimore Cooper's presentation of the American man that so captured international attention." A skillful writer, Southworth deftly used the machinations of the Gothic romance style to create stories brimming with melodramatic conventions, which appealed to readers, while also developing protagonists with greater depth of character than their counterparts in typical stories of the day. In her most popular novel, *The Hidden*

**E.D.E.N.**
*Southworth*

*Hand* (1859), Southworth introduces Capitola who makes her own way in an unjust world rather than be rescued from evil circumstances by men. She shakes free from a wicked guardian who steals both her mother and her inheritance, and triumphs over the prejudices of the day through her courage and boldness. Southworth also creates the ideal male character with Ishmael, the hero of her 1863–64 serialization *Self-Made; or Out of the Depths*. Even though Ishmael is of low birth, he manages to establish himself in society through hard work and virtue. He struggles to become an esteemed lawyer so that he might pay homage to his mother, thereby dignifying all women and becoming their advocate. According to **Beatrice K. Hofstadter**, these two characters reflect society's democratization of the older class system through "the social changes that accompanied the transformation of provincial, traditional antebellum America into a dynamic, socially mobile industrial society."

Southworth was an influential writer who impacted popular culture and changed accepted notions of the day, especially that of a woman's place in the public sphere. The cause of women's suffrage was of great importance to her, as was the abolition of slavery. Southworth had traveled to England in 1859 and remained there until 1862; when she returned to the United States in the midst of the Civil War, she was a vocal supporter of the Union. "In an era when debates over human rights dominated the political and social landscape," notes Hudock, "Southworth wrote fiction celebrating strong independent women, abolition of slavery, people who transcend or ignore class distinctions, and persons who stand firm against oppression of any sort."

Southworth moved to Yonkers, New York, in 1876, where she continued to write prolifically until returning to Georgetown in 1890. A compilation of her work, published in 1877, ran to an extraordinary 42 volumes. She began to develop an interest in spiritualism and joined the Swedenborgian Church in 1883. **Mary Kelley** writes that in 1894, at the end of her long and successful career, Southworth granted an interview with the *Washington Post* in which she noted that she had written 73 books and that was enough. She died five years later in Georgetown, on June 30, 1899.

**SOURCES:**

Buck, Claire, ed. *The Bloomsbury Guide to Women's Literature.* NY: Prentice Hall, 1992.

*Columbia Literary History of the United States.* NY: Columbia University Press, 1988, pp. 292, 301–301, 469, 563–564.

Edgerly, Lois Stiles, ed. and comp. *Give Her This Day: A Daybook of Women's Words.* Gardiner, ME: Tilbury House, 1990.

Hofstadter, Beatrice K. "E.D.E.N. Southworth," in *Notable American Women, 1607–1950.* Edited by Edward T. James. Cambridge, MA: The Belknap Press of Harvard University, 1971.

Hudock, Amy. "Overview of Southworth's Writing and Her Place in Literary History" on Marshall University web site.

Kelley, Mary. *Private Woman, Public Stage: Literary Domesticity in Nineteenth-Century America.* NY: Oxford University Press, 1984, pp. 158–163.

McHenry, Robert, ed. *Famous American Women.* NY: Dover, 1980.

Weatherford, Doris. *American Women's History.* NY: Prentice-Hall, 1994.

**Grant Eldridge**, freelance writer,
Pontiac, Michigan

## Souza, Adele de (1761–1836).

*See Souza-Botelho, Adélaïde Filleul, marquise of.*

# Souza-Botelho, Adélaïde Filleul, marquise of (1761–1836)

*French aristocrat who had a son with Talleyrand, survived the Revolution to become a popular author, and was the mother of general and diplomat Charles Auguste, count of Flahaut. Name variations: Adelaide Marie Emilie Filleul, marquise of Souza Botelho; Adele de Souza; Sousa. Born Adélaïde-Marie-Émilie Filleul in Paris, France, on May 14, 1761; died on April 10, 1836; daughter of Marie lrène Catherine de Buisson de Longpré (daughter of the seigneur of Longpré, near Falaise) and a middle-class man of Falaise named Filleul (who was one of the king's secretaries); married Alexandre Sebastien de Flahaut de la Billarderie, count of Flahaut (a soldier of some reputation, who was many years her senior), on November 30, 1779; married José Maria de Souza Botelho Morão e Vasconcellos (Portuguese minister plenipotentiary in Paris), in 1802; children: (with Charles Maurice de Talleyrand) Charles Auguste (b. April 21, 1785), count of Flahaut de la Billardérie.*

*Fled France for Great Britain (1792); published first novel, Adèle de Sénange (1794); moved to Germany (1794); returned to France (1797).*

Adélaïde Filleul was born in Paris in 1761, the daughter of **Irène de Buisson de Longpré** and a wine commissioner and royal secretary named Filleul. After her mother's death, she went to live in the Louvre Palace with her older sister ❦▶ **Julie,** who in 1767 had married the marquis of Marigny, brother of ***Madame de Pompadour.** Frequenting the intellectually vibrant and amoral society of late *ancien régime* Paris, Adélaïde attracted the attention of Alexandre Sébastien de Flahaut de la Billarderie, count of Flahaut, a poor aristocrat. Julie agreed to the count's proposal of marriage to Adélaïde, and the wedding took place on November 30, 1779. She was barely 18, he 54. It was a union of convenience for both: the count appreciated having a young beauty as his companion during his forays into society, and he supported her from his royal pensions and gifts from his brother, the count of Angiviller. Adélaïde claimed the marriage was never consummated.

Her real affection she conferred instead on Charles Maurice de Talleyrand and in 1785 had a son with Talleyrand, Charles de Flahaut. No scandal resulted, and her husband, the count, publicly accepted the baby as his own. But the onset of the French Revolution in 1789 posed other challenges. The Revolutionary government stopped paying her husband's royal pensions. Aristocrats lived in fear, and the count of Flahaut had to go into hiding in Boulogne, with papers Talleyrand secured for him. In 1792, Adélaïde fled to England with her son and joined the society of émigrés at Mickleham, Surrey, described in Mme d'Arblay's (***Fanny Burney**) *Memoirs.* The following year, during the Reign of Terror, Adélaïde's husband was arrested and died at the guillotine.

Forced to live by her wits to support herself and her son, she sold off her jewels and then began writing novels. Her first, *Adèle de Sénange*, was published in London in 1794. Sentimental and somewhat autobiographical, it described a young French woman who, married to an older man, falls in love against her will with another, younger and more attractive man. It reportedly earned her 40,000 francs.

In 1795, Adélaïde moved to Germany and then, in 1797, returned to France with the protection of Talleyrand, by that time minister of foreign relations under the Directory. She tried to claim an estate in Le Mesnil-Bernard that had belonged to her mother's family, but the Revolutionary government had outlawed her as one of the émigrés, traitorous aristocrats who had left France to escape their just punishments. Her political connections sufficed, however, to have her name removed from the list of proscribed émigrés. Talleyrand provided a position for their son Charles de Flahaut in the navy's Official Records Office.

During Napoleon's reign, Adélaïde flourished. She published *Emilie et Alphonse* in 1800. Set amidst late *ancien régime* aristocratic life, it again portrayed an unhappy marriage, where family and society prevented a young couple from following their love. In 1802, despite some jealousy from Talleyrand, she married José Maria de Souza Botelho Morão e Vasconcellos, a Portuguese diplomat resident in Paris who admired her novels. This made Adélaïde the marquise of Souza-Botelho.

With no strong political convictions herself, Adélaïde had little difficulty in adapting to the new regimes. Her later novels gracefully depicted aristocratic society, especially during the Napoleonic and Bourbon Restoration periods. The most famous was *Eugène de Rothelin*, published in 1808. Like the earlier books, it emphasized the need for emotional fulfillment. Mildly moralistic, her works contained finely crafted descriptions of French aristocratic life. They include: *Eugénie et Mathilde ou Mémoires de la famille du comte de Revel* (1811), *Mademoiselle de Tournon* (1820), *La Comtesse de Fargy* (1822), and *La Duchesse de Guise* (1831). Her son Charles de Flahaut served on Napoleon's staff and became a general, peer of France, and diplomat. Adélaïde helped educate her grandson, the duke of Morny, born of Charles de Flahaut's liaison with Queen *Hortense de Beauharnais* (1783–1837). The marquise of Souza-Botelho died in 1836 in Paris. Her complete works were published in 1811–1822.

> ❧ **Julie** (fl. 1770)
> *Marquise de Marigny. Flourished around 1770; eldest daughter of Marie Irène Catherine de Buisson de Longpré (daughter of the seigneur of Longpré, near Falaise) and a wine commissioner and royal secretary named Filleul; sister of *Adélaïde Filleul, marquise of Souza-Botelho (1761–1836); married Abel François Poisson (1727–1781), marquis de Marigny (brother of *Madame de Pompadour).*

**SOURCES:**
Bearne, Catherine Mary Charlton. *Four Fascinating French Women.* NY: Brentano's, 1910.
Bernardy, Françoise. *Son of Talleyrand: The Life of Comte Charles de Flahaut, 1785–1870.* Trans. by Lucy Norton. NY: Putnam, 1956.
Maricourt, André, Baron de. *Madame de Souza et sa famille: les Marigny, les Flahaut, Auguste de Morny (1761–1836).* 2nd ed. Paris: Emile-Paul, 1907.
Poniatowski, Michel. *Talleyrand et l'ancienne France, 1754–1789.* Paris: Librairie Académique Perrin, 1988.

**Kendall W. Brown**, Professor of History, Brigham Young University, Provo, Utah

# Sowerby, Millicent (1878–1967)

*British postcard and children's book illustrator. Born in 1878, possibly in Gateshead, Colchester, England; died in 1967; daughter of John G. Sowerby (an illustrator who flourished between 1876 and 1914); sister of author Githa Sowerby.*

*Illustrated "Postcards for the Little Ones" series and children's books including* Alice in Wonderland *(1907),* A Child's Garden of Verses *(1908), and many others; illustrated many children's books written by her sister Githa Sowerby.*

Born the daughter of illustrator John G. Sowerby in 1878, Millicent Sowerby took up her father's craft to become one of the best-loved postcard artists of the Edwardian age. Many of her cards depicted *Kate Greenaway* girls or idyllic scenes from Shakespeare. Her series "Postcards for the Little Ones," which portrayed merry, wholesome children and nursery rhyme vignettes, was extremely popular; sales consistently numbered in the thousands.

Sowerby also illustrated many books for children from her studio in South Kensington, London. Her works were included in editions of *Alice in Wonderland* (1907), *A Child's Garden of Verses* (1908), *Grimm's Fairy Tales* (1909), and *Little Stories for Little People* (1910). At the same time, she started a very successful and productive partnership illustrating children's books written by her sister, **Githa Sowerby**. Millicent and Githa worked together for over 20 years, producing such books as *Children, Yesterday's Children, The Wise Book, The Merry Book*, and many other similarly cheerful stories. Millicent Sowerby continued to paint watercolors well into her 80s and enjoyed painting flowers. She died in 1967 at the age of 89.

**Ruth Savitz**, freelance writer,
Philadelphia, Pennsylvania

# Spafford, Belle Smith (1895–1982)

*Social work advocate who served as president of the Relief Society of the Church of Jesus Christ of Latter-day Saints as well as the National Council of Women and the International Council of Women. Born Marion Isabelle Sims Smith in Salt Lake City, Utah, on October 8, 1895; died of cancer on February 2, 1982, in Salt Lake City; daughter of Hester (Sims) Smith and John Gibson Smith; graduated from LDS High School, Salt Lake City, 1912, and University of Utah Normal School, 1914; attended classes in social work at Brigham Young University; married Willis Earl Spafford (district manager of an insurance company), on March 23, 1921 (died 1963); children: Mary (b. 1923); Earl (b. 1926).*

*Awards, honors: Distinguished Service Award (1951) and honorary Doctor of Humanities (1956) from Brigham Young University; honorary life membership in the Utah State Conference of Social Work; University of Utah Distinguished Alumni Award and Outstanding Woman of the Year Award from Ricks College, Idaho (both 1970); National Council of Women endowed the Belle S. Spafford Archival Research Program Fund at New York University; Belle S. Spafford Endowed Chair in Social Work established at University of Utah (1987); Brigham Young University Distinguished Achievement Award; Distinguished Service Award for the Crusade for Freedom; one of ten outstanding women from Utah cited in* Famous Mothers in American History.

*Became a member of the general board of the Relief Society (1935); served as editor of* Relief Society Magazine *(1937–45); was a counselor in the General Relief Society (1942); served as general president of the Relief Society (1945–71); was vice-president of the National Council of Women (1948–56); served as a delegate to triennial meetings of International Council of Women at Philadelphia (1947), Montreal (1957), and Washington, D.C. (1963); was chair of the U.S. delegation to the ICW triennial meetings at Helsinki (1954), Teheran (1966), and Bangkok (1969); served as president of the National Council of Women*

*(1968–70); was a member of National Advisory Committee to the White House Conference on Aging; served as vice-president of the American Mothers Committee; was the first female member of the board of governors of LDS Hospital and of the board of trustees of Brigham Young University; became an officer of the board of directors of the National Association for Practical Nurses; was a special lecturer at the School of Social Work at the University of Utah.*

Belle Smith Spafford was born in Salt Lake City, Utah, in 1895, the youngest of seven children in a family which belonged to the Church of Jesus Christ of Latter-day Saints. Her father John Gibson Smith had died a few months before her birth, but income from his business provided well for the family. Her mother **Hester Sims Smith**, of Scottish ancestry, shared with her children an enthusiasm for music, art, good books and education while training them to be frugal, studious, industrious, and independent. They were provided with music lessons and attended college—Belle graduated from the Normal School of the University of Utah in 1914. Following the practice of most members of the Church of Jesus Christ of the Latter-day Saints, they also spent some time on missions for their church.

During the influenza epidemic in 1918, Belle's brother John lost his wife in childbirth, and Belle moved to his home in Provo, Utah, to help care for his children. She also attended classes in social work at Brigham Young University, where she met Willis Earl Spafford, called Earl, who worked as a district manager at a life insurance company. They were married in 1921, and their first child, a daughter Mary, was born in 1923.

Earl encouraged Spafford to pursue her interest in social work, hiring help at home to enable her to take classes at the University of Utah; he would remain supportive of her career throughout their marriage. In 1926, the year her son Earl was born, Belle joined the Relief Society, the largest women's organization within the Mormon Church. From 1937 to 1945, she served as editor of the society's magazine. In 1945, she became the general president of the Relief Society, making her the head of an international organization comprised of some 230,000 women members.

During her presidency of the society, Spafford initiated and administered programs for numerous social service agencies, among them ones focused on unwed mothers (in Utah, Arizona, Nevada, and Idaho), adoption services, services for battered and abused children and wives, Native American foster care, and youth guidance programs. She also oversaw the construction of the Relief Society Building, the group's headquarters, which was dedicated in October 1956. For more than 20 years Spafford worked with the Department of Social Work at the University of Utah, providing staff and space for the training of its students. She helped to design the university's graduate program in social work, which included both class work and the field work that provided students with practical experience. She also helped to ensure the passage in the Utah legislature of bills providing for university education for social workers; these became the legislative formula followed by a number of other states.

The Relief Society had been a member of both the National Council of Women (NCW) and the International Council of Women (ICW) from the time these organizations were founded in Washington, D.C., in 1888. A longtime member of the NCW, which had a membership of more than 20 million women, Spafford served the council in many capacities over 42 years. From 1968 to 1970, she was president. Her roles in the Relief Society and the NCW also led to many ancillary positions, including chair of the Scholarship Committee of the National Association of Practical Nurses, membership in the National Advisory Committee to the White House Conference on Aging, delegate to the Western Regional White House Conference on Traffic safety, and membership on the board of the Women's Advisory Council of the New York World's Fair.

Although her husband, who after 27 years in life insurance had been appointed a collector for the U.S. Treasury Department, died in 1963, Spafford was actively involved with her children and grandchildren. Taking time from her many civic responsibilities, she held individual "scholar's nights" for her ten grandchildren, during which one would have dinner at her house and discuss and write about a subject of the child's choice. Spafford stepped down from the presidency of the Relief Society in 1971, after over 25 years of distinguished service. She received a number of awards in recognition of her work, including an honorary doctorate from Brigham Young University (1956) and the Outstanding Woman of the Year award (1970) from Ricks College in Idaho; she was also the first woman appointed to the board of trustees of Brigham Young University. The day she retired from the presidency of the National Council of Women, October 23, 1979, was designated "Belle Spafford Day" by the council. In her honor, the NCW also endowed a fellowship—the Belle S.

Spafford Archival Research Program Fund—at New York University. She died in Salt Lake City a little over two years later, on February 2, 1982. In 1987, the Belle S. Spafford Endowed Chair in Social Work was established at the University of Utah. The following year, the National Council of Women presented a posthumous award for her work in establishing the American Regional Council of the International Council of Women.

**Harriet Horne Arrington**,
freelance biographer,
Salt Lake City, Utah

## Spahn, Helen May (1867–1957).

See Butler, Helen May.

# Spain, Jayne (1927—)

*American businesswoman who pioneered the employment of the handicapped. Name variations: Mrs. John A. Spain. Born Jayne Baker on March 28, 1927, in San Francisco, California; elder daughter of four children of Lawrence I. Baker (a businessman) and Marguerite (Buchanan) Baker (died 1984); attended the University of California, 1944–47, and the University of Cincinnati, 1947–50; Edgecliff College in Cincinnati, L.L.D., 1969; married John Spain (b. 1923, a lawyer), on July 14, 1951; children: Jeffry Alan (b. 1953, a physician); Jon Kimberly (b. 1955, a business manager).*

*Inherited Alvey-Ferguson, manufacturer of conveyor systems; innovated program to hire and train blind employees; traveled worldwide promoting employment of handicapped, women's rights, and American business practices; appointed vice-chair of the President's Civil Service Commission by President Richard Nixon (1971); was executive professor in residence at George Washington University (1980s).*

During the mid-20th century, gravity and power conveyor systems used in stockrooms, factories, post offices, and hundreds of other applications were engineered and manufactured primarily by Alvey-Ferguson, a company in Florence, Kentucky. After World War II and during the Korean War, these systems were a growing commodity in great demand. When Jayne Baker inherited a controlling interest in Alvey-Ferguson from her family in 1950, she had already spent considerable time and energy doing volunteer work with the handicapped, so the idea of employing the physically challenged, highly innovative for its time, was natural for her. Although she received many offers to buy the company when she initially took control, she responded to naysayers by turning Alvey-Ferguson into a model of employee involvement and opportunity for handicapped workers. When she married John Spain in 1951, she informed him that he was marrying a company.

Jayne Spain's idea was to train blind workers to assemble the 450 small parts that made up a finished product. She recruited the Cincinnati Association for the Blind to work out a system for teaching assembly patterns, then learned how the system was taught so that she could teach it to others. Eventually one out of ten workers at Alvey-Ferguson was handicapped. The program was such a success that Spain began traveling throughout the country promoting the hiring of the handicapped, not as an act of charity, but because it was good business. The U.S. government invited her to attend trade shows overseas to show that American capitalism was not heartless, and in each country she learned enough of the language to teach a dozen blind nationals to do assembly work. She made well over 50 trips abroad, visiting every continent but Antarctica and dozens of countries, both capitalist and communist, promoting not only the hiring of the handicapped and capitalist business practices, but also the right of women to equal opportunities in education and hiring. In one instance, she spent six weeks in India discussing business practices and business opportunities with Indian businessmen. In 1966, Spain sold Alvey-Ferguson to Litton Industries, but she remained as Litton division president and in 1971 became a director.

In 1971, President Richard Nixon appointed her vice-chair of the President's Civil Service Commission. As one of three directors, her mission was to get more women and handicapped people into high-level government jobs, but she was also responsible for overseeing all government employees, establishing policies for hiring and firing and codes of behavior, and hearing grievance cases. In the 1980s, Spain was appointed executive professor in residence at George Washington University in Washington, D.C., where she taught business courses. She did endless charity work and was on the board of many colleges and universities. Among her offices were president of Convalescent Hospital for Children in Cincinnati, Ohio; president of the Greater Cincinnati Hospital Council; board member of Beatrice Foods; board member of Ohio National Life Insurance (later Ohio Financial Services); and senior vice-president of Gulf Oil. She was named several times to the list of the Fifty Most Influential Women in America. Spain retired from active work in December 1993.

**SOURCES:**
Bird, Caroline. *Enterprising Women*. NY: New American Library, 1976.
Diamonstein, Barbaralee. *Open Secrets*. NY: Viking Press, 1970.

**Malinda Mayer**, writer and editor,
Falmouth, Massachusetts

## Spain, queen of.

*See Isabella of Portugal (1503–1539).*
*See Elizabeth of Valois (1545–1568).*
*See Elisabeth of Habsburg for sidebar on Anne of Austria (c. 1550–1580).*
*See Anne of Austria for sidebar on Margaret of Austria (c. 1577–1611).*
*See Elizabeth Valois (1602–1644).*
*See Maria Anna of Austria (c. 1634–1696).*
*See Marie Louise d'Orleans (1662–1689).*
*See Maria Anna of Neuberg (1667–1740).*
*See Marie Louise of Savoy (1688–1714).*
*See Farnese, Elizabeth (1692–1766).*
*See Louise Elizabeth (1709–1750).*
*See Maria Barbara of Braganza (1711–1758).*
*See Maria Amalia of Saxony (1724–1760).*
*See Maria Luisa Teresa of Parma (1751–1819).*
*See Bonaparte, Julie Clary (1771–1845).*
*See Maria Josepha of Saxony (1803–1829).*
*See Isabella II for sidebar on María Christina I of Naples (1806–1878).*
*See Isabella II (1830–1904).*
*See Maria Christina of Austria (1858–1929).*
*See Maria de las Mercedes (1860–1878).*
*See Ena (1887–1969).*
*See Sophia of Greece (b. 1938).*

## Spalding, Catherine (1793–1858)

*American nun who helped to establish schools, orphanages, and a hospital on the Kentucky frontier.*
*Name variations: Mother Catherine. Born in Charles County, Maryland, on December 23, 1793; died in Louisville, Kentucky, on March 20, 1858; parents may have been Edward Spalding and Juliet (Boarman) Spalding.*

*Entered the sisterhood (1812); elected first mother superior of the Sisters of Charity of Nazareth (1813); took vows (1816); established what became St. Catherine's Academy in Lexington, Kentucky (1823); opened Presentation Academy in Louisville (1831); established St. Joseph's Hospital (1832) and St. Vincent's Orphan Asylum (1833); directed construction of convent church at Nazareth, Kentucky (1850–56).*

Catherine Spalding, known through most of her life as Mother Catherine, was a pioneer for the Catholic Church in an area of the country that was, at the time, the West. There is some ambiguity regarding her early life. She was born in Maryland, but around 1799 she moved to Kentucky, either with both parents or with her widowed mother. Shortly after this move, she and her sister Ann were orphaned, leaving them to be raised by relatives.

In December 1812, Reverend John David, later bishop, announced his intention to set up a Roman Catholic teaching sisterhood in the American frontier. This sisterhood was to serve Bishop Benedict J. Flaget's new diocese, the first to be established west of the Allegheny Mountains. David had established a seminary for the training of priests on a donated farm at St. Thomas' near Bardstown, Kentucky. It was there that Spalding, a beautiful 19-year-old, presented herself, along with two older women, to help form the sisterhood. The new novices, known as the Sisters of Charity, lived in great poverty while carrying out charitable work among the poor and sick of the area, in addition to performing domestic and farm work. Spalding, who assumed the position of mother superior in 1813, oversaw the establishment of a school in 1814. Within four years, rapid growth from the original nine students necessitated the building of a brick house to board the increasing number of pupils.

In 1819, Mother Catherine ended her second term as superior, and although Father David and the nuns wanted her to continue, she stood firmly by the rule that limited the superior to two consecutive terms. In 1823, she went to Scott County where she helped to establish what became St. Catherine's Academy in Lexington. She returned to the position of mother superior for another six-year tenure in 1824, but found the order in chaos. The nuns had moved to Nazareth, Kentucky, and begun construction on a convent and school there, but the bookkeeping was in disarray and they were heavily in debt. Mother Catherine managed to bring about order, and in July 1825 the first class graduated from Nazareth Academy. The distinguished audience to the examination included Secretary of State Henry Clay, who presented the diplomas. In 1829, the Kentucky legislature granted the sisterhood and the school legal status, and in 1826 Pope Leo XII recognized the order, granting it spiritual advantages.

Although Mother Catherine served as mother superior in Nazareth for two more six-year terms beginning in 1838 and in 1850, she devoted most of her last 30 years to charity work in Louisville, Kentucky, where she had

moved in 1831 and opened the city's first Catholic school. During a devastating cholera epidemic in 1832–33, she nursed the sick and cared for children orphaned by the disease. She was observed more than once returning to the sisters' house from a sick call with an infant in her arms, another in her apron, and a third toddling beside her clinging to her skirt. Her concern for these orphans gave rise to St. Vincent's Orphan Asylum, the most cherished of her life's works, and the first Catholic infirmary in Kentucky, which became St. Joseph's Hospital. She convinced wealthy patrons, both Catholic and Protestant, to contribute to and support these institutions. She also opened an orphan asylum at the seminary in Bardstown and directed the construction of the convent church at Nazareth.

Mother Catherine died in Louisville of bronchitis contracted in the course of her charity work. In accordance with her wishes, she was buried in the mother house cemetery at Nazareth near the grave of her friend and mentor, Bishop John David. She left behind a legacy of work with the poor and with orphans, as well as a strong order of 145 sisters in 16 convents in Kentucky, Tennessee, and Indiana.

SOURCES:
James, Edward T., ed. *Notable American Women, 1607–1950*. Cambridge, MA: The Belknap Press of Harvard University, 1971.
McHenry, Robert, ed. *Famous American Women*. NY: Dover, 1980.
Read, Phyllis J., and Bernard L. Witlieb. *The Book of Women's Firsts*. NY: Random House, 1992.

**Malinda Mayer**, writer and editor, Falmouth, Massachusetts

## Spalding, Eliza (1807–1851).

*See Whitman, Narcissa for sidebar.*

# Spark, Muriel (1918—)

*Prominent English novelist and a convert to Roman Catholicism whose works focus on moral conflicts and religious belief. Born Muriel Sarah Camberg on February 1, 1918, in Edinburgh, Scotland; daughter of Bernard (Barney) Camberg (a Jewish mechanical engineer) and Sarah (Cissy) Uezzell Camberg; attended James Gillespie's School for Girls, 1924–36; attended Heriot-Watt College, 1936; married Sydney Oswald Spark (S.O.S.), in 1937 (divorced 1942); lives with Penelope Jardine (a sculptor); children: one son, Robin Spark.*

*Moved to Rhodesia (1937); returned to England (1944); became secretary of the Poetry Society and editor of* Poetry Review *(1947); founded her own maga-*

*zine,* Forum *(1949); received prize for her short story "The Seraph and the Zambesi" (1951); baptized into Anglican Church (1953); received into Roman Catholic Church (1954); lived in Israel (1961); lived in New York (1962–66); moved to Rome (1966); awarded Order of the British Empire (1967); moved to rural Tuscany (1985); gave first television interview (1996).*

*Major works: (poetry)* The Fanfarlo and Other Verse *(1952); (novels)* The Comforters *(1957),* Memento Mori *(1959),* The Bachelors *(1960),* The Girls of Slender Means *(1963),* The Prime of Miss Jean Brodie *(1961),* The Mandelbaum Gate *(1965),* The Abbess of Crewe *(1974),* Territorial Rights *(1979),* Loitering with Intent *(1981),* The Only Problem *(1984),* A Far Cry from Kensington *(1988),* Symposium *(1990),* Reality and Dreams *(1997),* Aiding and Abetting *(2001); (nonfiction)* Mary Shelley *(1986),* Curriculum Vitae: Autobiography *(1992).*

Muriel Spark is a major English writer who first appeared on the London literary scene in the early 1950s. Although she started her career as a poet, around the age of 40 she turned the bulk of her energies to a series of complex and highly regarded novels. Starting in 1957, she produced seven novels in seven years, and her prodigious output has now reached a total of 20 novels along with children's books, short stories, and biographies. Spark's writing mixes elements of melodrama, the macabre, and satire. A central theme in her writing, however, has been her view of life as a Roman Catholic in the modern world, reflecting her adult conversion to the Catholic faith. Writes **Dorothea Walker:** "She sees Roman Catholicism, the religion she came to embrace, as underlying all truth and as the revealer of that truth." Her practice of taking novelists as her heroines in several books has given Spark the chance to explore the process of writing and the relationship between illusion and reality.

Spark's complex style set her apart from many of her contemporaries and confounded critics' efforts to characterize her work readily. Thus, Joseph Hynes has referred to her "penchant for loose ends and unresolved mysteries." Alan Bold has insisted that, while "her books do not ignore world events," nonetheless "Spark is never merely topical, for her novels are haunted by the specter of theological eternity." The richness of her body of work, including her interest in communities of women, has also opened the way for examination from new angles such as **Judy Sproxton**'s recent effort to consider Spark from a feminist perspective. Noting that "Spark is not a feminist in the sense that she asserts specific rights

for women," Sproxton sees her as a writer who has devoted substantial energy into an effort to examine women's character. She has, according to Sproxton, "depicted women in a search for a dignity and possession of mind which . . . vindicates a woman's spiritual integrity."

Spark was born Muriel Sarah Camberg in Edinburgh, Scotland, on February 1, 1918. Her religious background was mixed: her father Bernard Camberg was a Jew from Scotland, and her mother **Sarah Uezzel Camberg** was an English Presbyterian. As Spark later recalled, neither parent was particularly interested in religious affairs, but she was to make up for that with a consuming interest in her own spiritual life. Some critics trace the theme of moral responsibility in her work to Spark's awareness of her Jewish-Scottish heritage, augmented by her fervent Catholicism following her conversion in 1954.

In her recent autobiography, *Curriculum Vitae,* Spark recalled her life to 1957 with an abundance of details about her childhood and schooling, including her early interest in literature. She wrote poetry starting at the age of nine and spent her free time between the ages of ten and sixteen in the local public library. Although she came from a family "of high aspirations and slender means," the young girl had the advantage of an education at one of Scotland's stellar institutions of learning, James Gillespie's School for Girls, which she attended from 1924 to 1936. She later described herself as the school's poet and dreamer and fondly recalled the intellectual encouragement and freedom she found there. After completing school, she took business courses at Heriot-Watt College in Edinburgh and held a variety of jobs: teacher at a local private school, private tutor, and secretary in a department store.

"I longed to leave Edinburgh and see the world," Spark wrote in her autobiography; this restlessness strongly influenced her decision to marry a young schoolteacher, Sydney Spark, whom she had met at a dance. In August 1937, she left for South Africa to meet her husband-to-be in Rhodesia, where he had begun to work on a three-year teaching contract. They married in Salisbury, Southern Rhodesia, on September 3, 1937. She came to regret this as "a disastrous choice" when she became acquainted with Sydney's hidden mental problems. Only years later did she learn that another distinguished writer-to-be, *Doris Lessing, lived in Southern Rhodesia at the same time. The adult Spark lamented the fact that in her loneliness as

Muriel Spark

a 19-year-old newlywed in a remote country, she had no chance to meet such a likely intellectual companion.

Becoming pregnant, Spark rejected her husband's suggestion that she undergo an abortion.

After a difficult delivery, she gave birth to her only child, a son whom she named Robin, on July 9, 1938. The outbreak of war and her husband's enlistment brought Spark some respite from his belligerent personality, but she soon instituted divorce proceedings.

Spark became involved with a young RAF officer, Arthur Foggo, in the period after her divorce. When he was killed during a sea voyage, she found herself deeply depressed and decided to return to Britain, arriving there in early 1944. Her young son followed a few months later. Spark worked for the final portion of the wartime period in the political intelligence branch of the British Foreign Office. There she helped write broadcasts designed to undermine morale in Nazi Germany. Living in a residence for women, the Helena Club, she picked up background for her 1963 novel *The Girls of Slender Means*.

After the war, she took a job on a magazine connected with the jewelry trade but soon entered the London literary world as an editor and freelance writer. In 1947, Spark became a secretary at the Poetry Society and found herself editing the Society's magazine, *Poetry Review*. For a brief time in 1949 she had her own poetry magazine, *Forum*.

*I don't claim my novels are true . . . I claim that they are fiction, out of which a kind of truth emerges.*

—Muriel Spark

By the early 1950s, Spark was active as a literary critic. Much of her work, including a study of *Emily Brontë and an edition of *Mary Shelley's letters, was done in collaboration with Derek Stanford. A milestone in her career came in 1951 when her short story "The Seraph and the Zambesi" won an important literary contest. In 1954, she received strong encouragement, including financial support, from Macmillan, the London publisher, to try her hand at a novel. The result was *The Comforters*. Published when she was almost 40 years old, this work by an unknown novelist received an enthusiastic response from such members of the London critical establishment as Evelyn Waugh. From that time on, Spark abandoned poetry to concentrate her formidable talents on the writing of novels.

Spark wrote *The Comforters* during a period of intense emotional strain connected to her search for a religious identity. In 1953, she had been received into the Anglican Church, but within less than a year, largely under the influence of the writings of John Cardinal Newman, she went on to become a Roman Catholic. Although the spiritual and intellectual comfort of the Catholic Church proved to be a decisive attraction for her, Spark found herself disturbed by the personalities of many of the individual Catholics she encountered. As she put it in an interview given in 1961, "Good God, I used to think, if I become Catholic, will I grow like them?" Both psychotherapy and the relief she obtained following her decision to become a Catholic gave her enough emotional support to let her move on with her career. Converts to Catholicism were to play a major role in the casts of her novels.

*The Comforters* contained a complex plot with such melodramatic elements as an elderly woman who engages in diamond smuggling. Nonetheless, the work's main elements reflect the intense religious concerns within Spark's mind, elements that set the tone for much of her later writing. It is, in part, the story of a Catholic convert who finds her life dominated by hallucinatory voices that she hears. She herself is writing a novel, while the voices that come to her seem to be dictating a novel and making her a character in it. Such problems of identifying reality through the use of the human mind as well as the complexities of writing a novel were themes to which Spark would return in *Loitering with Intent*.

The Catholic characters in *The Comforters* are presented in an unfavorable light and, as Dorothea Walker notes, her portrait of one of them, Mrs. Hogg, is "one of the most savage of any of the Catholics in her work." Walker speculates that as a newly converted Catholic Spark had little tolerance for coreligionists who did not share her own zeal and idealism.

Spark's second novel, *Robinson*, appeared in 1958, and, like *The Comforters*, it contained a heroine who was a Catholic convert. *Robinson* did not enjoy the acclaim of its predecessor, but Spark soon produced a new major success the following year with the publication of *Memento Mori*. Once again she presented an eccentric take on the traditional novel. Her characters are elderly men and women, each of whom receives at least one mysterious telephone call reminding them of their impending demise. Spark explores the way in which these very different individuals, some inside a nursing home, others still living independently, respond to this jarring message. She drew much of her information about the elderly from a personal friend, **Teresa Walshe**, who worked as a nurse caring for geriatric patients. Despite the apparently macabre subject, the novel's tone reflected the author's admiration for the courage, resilience, and humor of the elderly characters she described.

The best known, most accessible, and commercially the most successful of Spark's works was *The Prime of Miss Jean Brodie*. Alan Bold finds this "arguably her masterpiece." Appearing in 1961, it was subsequently transformed into a stage play and then a movie. In the words of Norman Page, it first seems "to belong to farce or comedy of manners," but it soon moves on to become "a theological drama with tragic overtones." The story focuses on a flamboyant, charismatic teacher at a school for girls in Spark's native Edinburgh. Spark clearly drew upon her own experiences at James Gillespie's School in the 1920s and 1930s. In her autobiography, she identified one of her memorable teachers there, **Christina Kay**, as the individual who "bore within her the seeds of the future Miss Jean Brodie."

Although religion plays a significant role in the novel—as it does in all of Spark's works—the plot has no suggestion of supernatural voices. Instead, it shows how one of Miss Brodie's students, drawn to her and then offended enough to betray her, uses Brodie's pro-fascist ideas to bring about the teacher's dismissal. In what might be seen as an act of repentance, the young girl goes on to become a nun. The book manages to make Miss Brodie, despite her odious political ideas, into a complex and largely sympathetic figure. She offers unlimited personal inspiration to her young charges and imaginatively undermines the sterile school routine. Told from numerous points in time, the book is also notable for its success in ignoring the shape of normal chronology.

Spark's next major success came in 1965 with the appearance of *The Mandelbaum Gate*. She had lived in Israel for several months during 1961 to gather material for this novel. It was an emotional moment in Israel's history as the country conducted the trial of Adolf Eichmann, one of the key figures in the Holocaust. Set in the Middle East, this latest literary endeavor gave Spark an opportunity to write about Jews, Arabs, and expatriate Englishmen in a contemporary setting. The first of her works to deal with a politically charged contemporary topic, *The Mandelbaum Gate* also reflected Spark's personal background and concerns. Her heroine, Barbara Vaughan, like Spark herself, came from a mixed English Protestant and Jewish background and had converted to Roman Catholicism.

The longest and most conventional of her works, *The Mandelbaum Gate* seemed to refute her 1963 statement that she was "writing minor novels deliberately, and not major novels," since she had no desire to become a "Mrs. Tolstoy." A compulsively rapid writer—*The Prime of Miss Jean Brodie* according to Alan Bold was completed in eight weeks—Spark required a full two years to produce this lengthy book.

The title of Spark's novel symbolized the split in the Middle East, since the Mandelbaum Gate separated Israel's portion of Jerusalem from that held by Jordan. The gate allowed Spark to explore the absurdity of political hatred. It also reflected Barbara Vaughan's multiple identities: in order to visit Christian shrines in Jordan, she was compelled to hide her Jewish background from the authorities at the Jordanian border. When her Jewish identity was revealed, Vaughan found her safety jeopardized until acquaintances in the British consulate and the Arab community aided her clandestine return to Israel.

In 1967, Spark's literary achievements received official recognition when she was awarded the Order of the British Empire. By then she had relocated permanently to Italy where she now set a number of her works. Spark herself split her time between Rome and a villa in Tuscany. Her career continued with the regular appearance of major works such as *The Abbess of Crewe* in 1974. Here Spark, drawing on the events of the Watergate scandal, turned her religious interests in a new direction as she examined how a community of nuns went about choosing a new leader.

**Ruth Whittaker** has noted that this book "transcends the realistic comparison [with the Watergate scandal] and becomes a timeless parable about power and corruption." Nonetheless, here Spark engages in a wicked brand of parody. The election of the convent's new leader is corrupted by listening devices and other forms of political trickery. Reflecting the attempt by supporters of President Richard Nixon to bug the opposition's political headquarters, the book recounts how nuns raid a candidate's sewing basket to find politically useful information.

The hypocrisy of the entire community of supposedly pious nuns can be seen by the fact that the convent owns expensive real estate in London as well as grim slum property in Chicago. One widely traveled nun embodies the personality and interests of American Secretary of State Henry Kissinger. Like *The Prime of Miss Jean Brodie*, *The Abbess of Crewe* was sufficiently accessible to a broad audience to be made into the film *Nasty Habits*, starring *Glenda Jackson, in 1977.

*Loitering with Intent*, published in 1981, saw Spark return to a theme of *The Comforters*: the relationship between creativity and reality in the experiences of a novelist. Once again, writes Page, Spark has produced "a novel about the novel." The heroine, Fleur Talbot, is a novelist who is supporting herself by editing autobiographical manuscripts collected by an evil-minded aristocrat, Sir Quentin Oliver. The manuscripts are supposed to be kept secret but Oliver uses the material in them to blackmail and manipulate the individuals who have written these accounts. Reality and fiction come to imitate each other when the heroine ends the life of her novel's hero in an automobile accident; she then discovers that Oliver has died in similar fashion.

In 1985, Spark and her longtime friend, the sculptor **Penelope Jardine**, moved permanently to Tuscany. There, they set up housekeeping in a restored 14th-century church near the city of Arezzo. In 1986, Spark produced a revised version of her biography of Mary Shelley, originally written in 1951; meanwhile, she went on producing fiction. Three new novels appeared in less than a decade: *A Far Cry from Kensington* in 1988; *Symposium* in 1990; and *Reality and Dreams* in 1997. While the last two received only mixed reviews, Spark's reputation remains solid. For Alan Bold, "She is one of the most subtle stylists of her time, a master . . . of the paradox, a literary illusionist of enormous agility." As Walker noted, "In intricacy of plot, wit of dialogue, and inventiveness of character, Muriel Spark remains a gifted novelist who shows in each novel an innate originality." Norman Page has expressed an equal enthusiasm: "A Muriel Spark novel contrives to be simultaneously unmistakable and unpredictable."

In 1992, Spark produced an autobiography, *Curriculum Vitae*, tracing her life down to early 1957. Her avowed purpose was to set the record straight in the face of stories about her that seemed too favorable. True to her gritty determination to pursue truth, she took pains to note that in giving "a picture of my formation as a creative writer," she was refuting stories that showed her, falsely, in too favorable a light. In 2001, at age 83, Spark was earning strong reviews for her 21st novel, *Aiding and Abetting*, a work of fiction based on the disappearance of the 7th earl of Lucan in 1974, after he allegedly murdered the family nanny while mistaking her for his wife. Wrote Paul Gray, she "has lost none of her skill and verve in portraying flamboyantly wicked people behaving according to 'a morality devoid of ethics or civil law.'"

**SOURCES:**

Bold, Alan. *Muriel Spark*. London: Methuen, 1986.

Gray, Paul. "A Game of Rat and Louse," in *Time*. March 12, 2001.

Hosmer, Robert E., Jr. "Writing with Intent: The Artistry of Muriel Spark," in *Commonweal*. Vol. 116, no. 8. April 21, 1989, pp. 233–241.

Hynes, Joseph. *The Art of the Real: Muriel Spark's Novels*. Rutherford, NJ: Fairleigh Dickinson University Press, 1988.

Page, Norman. *Muriel Spark*. Houndmills, Basingstoke, Hampshire, England: Macmillan, 1990.

Schiff, Stephen. "Muriel Spark between the Lines: Cultural Pursuits," in *The New Yorker*. Vol. 69, no. 14. May 24, 1993, pp. 36–43.

Spark, Muriel. *Curriculum Vitae: Autobiography*. Boston, MA: Houghton Mifflin, 1992.

Sproxton, Judy. *The Women of Muriel Spark*. NY: St. Martin's Press, 1992.

Wakeman, John. *World Authors, 1950–1970*. NY: H.W. Wilson, 1975.

Walker, Dorothea. *Muriel Spark*. Boston, MA: Twayne, 1988.

Whittaker, Ruth. *The Faith and Fiction of Muriel Spark*. NY: St. Martin's Press, 1982.

**SUGGESTED READING:**

Bold, Alan, ed. *Muriel Spark: An Odd Capacity for Vision*. London: Vision Press, 1984.

Hynes, Joseph, ed. *Critical Essays on Muriel Spark*. NY: G.K. Hall, 1992.

Kemp, Peter. *Muriel Spark*. NY: Harper and Row, 1975.

Stanford, Derek. *Muriel Spark: A Biographical and Critical Study*. London: Centaur Press, 1963.

**RELATED MEDIA:**

*Nasty Habits* (92 min. British film), starring Glenda Jackson, *Melina Mercouri, *Geraldine Page, *Sandy Dennis, *Anne Jackson, Anne Meara, *Edith Evans, and Susan Penhaligon, directed by Michael Lindsay-Hogg, produced by Bowden/Brut, 1977.

*The Prime of Miss Jean Brodie* (a comedy in two acts), adapted by **Jay Presson Allen**; opened at the Helen Hayes Theater on Broadway on January 16, 1968, starring **Zoe Caldwell**, directed by Michael Langham, and produced by Robert Whitehead (the play opened in London with **Vanessa Redgrave** in the lead).

*The Prime of Miss Jean Brodie* (116 min. British film), screenplay by Jay Presson Allen; starring **Maggie Smith** (who won an Oscar for Best Actress in the role of Brodie), *Celia Johnson, Pamela Franklin, and Robert Stephens, produced by Fox, 1969.

**Neil M. Heyman**, Professor of History, San Diego State University, San Diego, California

# Speght, Rachel (1597–c. 1630)

*English polemicist and poet who wrote in support of women's spiritual equality to men. Born in London, England, in 1597; died around 1630; daughter of Reverend James Speght; married William Procter (a gentleman), in 1621; children: two.*

In 1613, Joseph Swetnam published a notorious attack on women entitled *An Araignment of Lewde, Idle, Froward and Unconstant Women*. In 1617, at age 20, Rachel Speght, the daughter of Reverend James Speght, was the first to publish a response and refutation. Her *A Mouzell for Melastomus: The Cynicall Bayter of, and Foule Mouthed Barker against Evahs*

*Sex* was dedicated to "all vertuous Ladies Honourable or Worshipfull and to all other of Hevahs sex fearing God." In it, Speght used scripture to emphasize women's traditional virtues and to establish them as men's spiritual equals. She was careful not to confuse this spiritual equality with social or political equality. The work apparently met with enough approbation that some readers accused her of publishing her father's work as her own.

In 1621, Speght published a second work, *Mortalities Memorandum, with a Dreame Prefix'd, Imaginarie in Manner, Reall in Matter.* The dedication is an allegorical poem intended to prove her detractors wrong. In this work, the central female character journeys from natural ignorance to divine knowledge, leading to full humanity and immortality, with the help of Thought, Experience, Knowledge, Industrie, and Disswasion. Except for her marriage at age 24 to William Procter in 1621 and the birth of two children, nothing is known about Speght's life after the publication of her second book.

**SOURCES:**

Buck, Claire, ed. *The Bloomsbury Guide to Women's Literature.* NY: Prentice Hall, 1992.

Shattock, Joanne. *The Oxford Guide to British Women Writers.* Oxford: Oxford University Press, 1993.

**Malinda Mayer**, writer and editor,
Falmouth, Massachusetts

# Spellman, Gladys Noon

## (1918–1988)

*U.S. congressional representative from Maryland (January 3, 1975–February 24, 1981). Born Gladys Blossom Noon in New York City on March 1, 1918; died in Rockville, Maryland, on June 19, 1988; daughter of Henry Noon and Bessie G. Noon; educated at public schools in New York City and Washington, D.C.; attended George Washington University in Washington, D.C., and the graduate school of the U.S. Department of Agriculture; married Reuben Spellman; children: Stephen, Richard, Dana, and Eric.*

Born Gladys Blossom Noon in 1918 in New York City, Gladys Spellman received her early education in New York City and Washington, D.C., before enrolling in George Washington University. Following graduate work with the U.S. Department of Agriculture, she taught in the public schools of Prince Georges County, Maryland. She initially became involved in politics through her 1962 election to the Prince Georges County Board of Commissioners, winning re-election in 1966. Her three-year term as

councilwoman-at-large, beginning in 1971, catapulted her into a bid for the Fifth District seat in the U.S. House of Representatives as a Democrat. She won election that year to the first of three terms in Congress.

Spellman focused much of her attention on the civil service during her career in Congress. She supported the training of civil servants in labor-management relations through a proposed amendment to the Intergovernmental Personnel Act of 1970, and rejected hiring and promotion restrictions of federal workers. When President Jimmy Carter proposed reforms to the civil service system in 1978, she opposed the measures, reserving special criticism for the Senior Executive Service as something which would politicize the civil service. She favored adjusted cost-of-living increases for those retired from the military and federal notification of retirees' spouses if they would not be receiving survivors' benefits. As a member of the Committee on Banking, Currency and Housing, Spellman voted for a proposal authorizing $7 billion in loan guarantees to

help pull New York City out of severe financial difficulties in 1975. Two years later, she supported the establishment of a bank to provide loans to consumer-owned cooperatives, and an extension of the federal revenue-sharing program.

On October 31, 1980, Spellman suffered a heart attack while on the campaign trail to her fourth term in office. Although only semi-conscious during the balloting four days later, she was re-elected by an overwhelming majority. Unfortunately, she proved unable to discharge her duties of office, and her seat was declared vacant on February 24, 1981. Her husband Reuben Spellman ran in nomination for her office in the special primary held in April, but finished second in a field of six. Gladys Spellman died on June 19, 1988.

**SOURCES:**
Office of the Historian. *Women In Congress, 1917–1990.* Commission on the Bicentenary of the U.S. House of Representatives, 1991.

**Malinda Mayer**, writer and editor, Falmouth, Massachusetts

# Spence, Catherine (1825–1910)

*Australian writer, journalist, reformer, and public speaker. Born Catherine Helen Spence near Melrose, Scotland, on October 31, 1825; died in Australia in 1910; fifth of eight children of David Spence (a lawyer and banker) and Helen (Brodie) Spence; completed formal schooling in Melrose at about age 14; never married.*

*Became first successful woman novelist in Australia with publication of* Clara Morison: A Tale of South Australia during the Gold Fever *(1854); was active in work with destitute children, the women's suffrage movement, and electoral reform; wrote first social studies textbook used in Australia,* The Laws We Live Under *(1880); was the first woman in Australia to run for public office (1897); statue in her memory placed in Light Square, Adelaide (1986).*

Catherine Spence was a woman of enormous talent who poured her considerable energy into supporting both political and social causes. Her work was a major catalyst in creating a more progressive environment in Australia in the late 19th century. She was born in 1825 and raised in Scotland until 1839, when her father David Spence moved the family to Australia after his failed wheat speculations bankrupted them. This financial disaster also ended Spence's hope of attending the advanced school for girls in Edinburgh as she had planned. At 17, Spence became a governess and felt great satisfaction in

having her own earnings. This desire for self-sufficiency, plus her unhappiness with the Calvinist doctrine of predestination, turned her against marriage and motherhood.

In 1854, Spence anonymously published *Clara Morison: A Tale of South Australia during the Gold Fever*, becoming the first Australian woman to publish a novel. She followed this with a second anonymous novel in 1856, *Tender and True: A Colonial Tale*. After these successes, she began writing serialized novels that appeared in newspapers under her own name, including *Mr. Hogarth's Will* (1865), *The Author's Daughter* (1867), and *Gathered In*. Her utopian novel *Handfasted* was submitted for a prize offered by the *Sydney Mail*, but was rejected as "too socialist and therefore dangerous." Spence's writings consistently offer valuable social and political insights into colonial life in the 1850s and 1860s, extending beyond the conventional domestic romances of the day. She wrote fiction for the next 30 years, producing, among other titles, *An Agnostic's Progress* (1884) and *A Week in the Future* (1889).

Spence also wrote as a journalist, anonymously or under a pen name, covering a wide range of topics. In 1878, after 30 years of publishing articles anonymously, she was appointed to the daily South Australian *Register* as a regular outside contributor, and finally obtained a byline. She became a well-known journalist and literary critic for newspapers in South Australia and Victoria and in major British reviews such as *Cornhill* and *Fortnightly*, often drawing criticism as a radical feminist. Spence wrote about a wide range of contemporary issues, and welcomed the opportunity to promote her favorite causes. Among these, the three most important to her were the plight of destitute children, election reform, and votes for women.

In 1872, Spence worked with **Caroline Emily Clark** to establish the Boarding-Out Society. Essentially a fostering program, the society placed children from the government industrial school with families and monitored their development. Spence backed up her beliefs with personal action by raising three successive families of orphaned children herself. Her work with destitute children merited her appointment to the new State Children's Council in 1887 and to the government Destitute Board ten years later. As a member of the school board in East Torrens, she argued strongly for a state-run Advanced School for Girls, which was opened in 1879. At the invitation of the government, she wrote the first social studies textbook used in

Australian schools, *The Laws We Live Under* (1880), 20 years before such a course was introduced in any of the other colonies.

Spence considered election reform to be one of the most important issues of her day. She spoke in favor of proportional representation, which she called "effective voting." As early as 1861 she published *A Plea for Pure Democracy* in support of her ideas. When asked to present a lecture for the South Australian Institute, she rejected the convention that required she write the speech and give it to a man for presentation. Instead, she insisted on reading it herself, saying that she wanted "to make it easier for any woman who felt she had something to say to stand up and say it." Her invitation to preach by the Unitarian Church, to which she was a convert, led to further speaking engagements. In 1892, she launched a campaign for effective voting by speaking on public platforms throughout South Australia, in Melbourne, Sydney, and across the United States, addressing a series of conferences at the Chicago World's Fair in 1893. In promoting this cause, she stood for election to the Federal Convention of 1897. Although she was unsuccessful, she was the first woman in Australia to run for public office.

During this time, Spence was also working hard for suffrage for women. She became vice-president of the Women's Suffrage League in 1891 and did not slow her suffrage activities after the vote was won in 1894. South Australia was the first colony to grant female suffrage, and Spence spoke about it in Great Britain and the United States, befriending like-minded women such as *Charlotte Perkins Gilman, *Susan B. Anthony, *Jane Addams, and *Millicent Garrett Fawcett, and supporting the Melbourne suffragist *Vida Goldstein, the Sydney suffragist *Rose Scott, and the feminist journalist *Alice Henry. From 1901 until her death in 1910, Spence was chair of the Co-operative Clothing Company, a shirt-making factory owned and operated exclusively by women, with both owners and workers holding stock. The year before she died, she presided at the formation of the Women's Non-Party Political Association.

When Catherine Spence died, she was mourned as "The Grand Old Woman of Australia." A statue in her memory was erected in Light Square in Adelaide in 1986. Interest in her fiction was revived a century after it was written, and *Clara Morison* appeared in three new editions after 1971.

**SOURCES:**

Buck, Claire, ed. *The Bloomsbury Guide to Women's Literature*. NY: Prentice Hall, 1992.

Radi, Heather, ed. *200 Australian Women*. NSW, Australia: Women's Redress Press, 1988.

Uglow, Jennifer, ed. *Dictionary of Women's Biography*. NY: Continuum, 1989.

**Malinda Mayer**, writer and editor, Falmouth, Massachusetts

# Spencer, Anna (1851–1931)

*American minister, reformer, lecturer, and writer. Born in Attleboro, Massachusetts, on April 17, 1851; died in New York City on February 12, 1931; third daughter and youngest of four children of Francis Warren Garlin and Nancy Mason (Carpenter) Garlin; attended public schools and a private college; married William Henry Spencer, on August 15, 1878 (died 1923); children: Fletcher Carpenter Spencer (b. 1879 and died in infancy); Lucy Spencer (b. 1884).*

*Was the first woman minister in Rhode Island; served as associate director and lecturer at New York School of Philanthropy (1903); was associate director of New York Society for Ethical Culture (1904); worked for child labor and factory inspection laws; was special lecturer at University of Wisconsin and director of the Institute of Municipal and Social Service in Milwaukee, Wisconsin (1908–11); wrote over 70 magazine articles on various aspects of social services.*

Born on April 17, 1851, Anna Spencer grew up in Providence, Rhode Island, a city and state with strong Quaker and abolitionist leanings. Her mother **Nancy Garlin**, a staunch abolitionist, supported John C. Frémont, the popular explorer and abolitionist, in his nearly successful campaign for president. Influences such as this helped shape Spencer's strong moral beliefs and her clear-eyed view of the social problems of the day. From 1869 to 1871, she taught in the Providence schools and wrote for the *Providence Daily Journal*. She soon began making public appearances, addressing social issues, many of them controversial, and earning a reputation for being a vibrant, compelling orator with an articulate expository style.

Disagreeing with the establishment over doctrinal issues, Spencer withdrew from the Union Congregational Church of Providence in 1876. During the next two years, she preached for the Free Religious Society, and in 1878 she married William Henry Spencer, a Unitarian minister 11 years her senior, who encouraged the increasingly liberal trend of her religious thinking. After her marriage, she sometimes preached in her husband's churches; in 1891, she was ordained and received her own pastorate at the Bell Street Chapel in Providence, a liberal, non-denominational group. Her ordination received some public notice since she was the first female minister in Rhode Island.

In 1902, the Spencer family moved to New York City where Spencer joined and became associate director of the Society for Ethical Culture. Based on Immanuel Kant's teachings that every person is an end in himself/herself and worthy as an individual, Ethical Culture was promoted as a religion by the society's director, Felix Adler. He believed that morality was based not on religious or philosophical dogma, but on community efforts to promote social welfare, an idea much in keeping with what Spencer had been preaching. She clashed with Adler, however, and left the movement after two years, although she continued her membership in Unitarian and other liberal religious groups throughout the remainder of her life.

Spencer's social concerns eventually became a more important focus for her life than religious organizations. Her work in Providence through the founding of the Society for Organizing Charities and her efforts to pass child labor and factory inspection laws laid the foundation for her future endeavors. As a member of the board of control of the State Home and School for Dependent Children, she went to the World's Columbian Exposition in Chicago where she spoke on the subject of "The Relation of the Church to Charities" and chaired the symposium on disadvantaged children. While in New York City, Spencer became associate director and lecturer at the School of Philanthropy, later taking teaching and administrative positions at a number of institutions, including the University of Wisconsin; the Summer School of Ethics in Madison, sponsored by the American Ethical Union; the Meadville (Pennsylvania) Theological School; the University of Chicago; and Teachers College at Columbia University.

In 1908, Spencer began writing a series of magazine articles, eventually producing over 70 of them. They appeared in scholarly journals such as *The American Journal of Sociology* and *The International Journal of Ethics*; periodicals about social work such as *Forum* and *Survey*; and popular magazines such as *Harper's* and *Ladies' Home Journal*. Her best known book, *Woman's Share in Social Culture* (1913), is a compilation of articles focusing on a variety of women's issues such as the difficulties of employed married women, the problems of unmarried and elderly women, and the subjects of prostitution, divorce, and suffrage. Her views echoed those of *Charlotte Perkins Gilman in

the belief that, rather than seek equality with men, women should evolve new ethical and social arrangements based on their female talents and insights. This train of thought continues in *The Family and Its Members* (1923) in which she attacked the concept of "free love" as a destabilizing influence on families. She also argued against the idea that women must be economically independent in order to be fully free, acknowledging the husband as the primary provider for the family. Spencer was particularly concerned about the problem of prostitution, seeing this as a result of the economic position of women, and she campaigned for programs geared to training prostitutes for socially useful occupations. As a leader in the American Purity Alliance, she helped develop it into the American Social Hygiene Association and headed its Division of Family Relations, introducing courses on the family into high schools and colleges.

Spencer was also an active participant in several social reform movements as an advocate of temperance, women's suffrage, and pacifism. She was a member of the Rhode Island Women's Christian Temperance Union as well as the national body, the Anti-Saloon League, and the Unitarian Temperance Society. She had joined the Rhode Island Woman's Suffrage Association when she was just 17, was a close friend of *Susan B. Anthony, and attended and spoke at conventions of the National Woman Suffrage Association. As a pacifist, she was on the executive committee of the National Peace and Arbitration Congress of 1907, vice-chair of the Woman's Peace Party in 1915, and president of the Woman's International League for Peace and Freedom after World War I.

Spencer succumbed to a heart attack while attending a dinner of the League of Nations Association at the age of 80. She was buried at Swan Point Cemetery in Providence.

**SOURCES:**

James, Edward T., ed. *Notable American Women, 1607–1950*. Cambridge, MA: The Belknap Press of Harvard University, 1971.

**Malinda Mayer**, writer and editor, Falmouth, Massachusetts

# Spencer, Anne (1882–1975)

*African-American poet who was a founding member of the Harlem Renaissance. Name variations: when her mother resumed her maiden name, Anne was known as Annie Bethel Scales. Born Anne Bethel Bannister in Henry County, Virginia, on February 6, 1882; died on July 27, 1975, at age 93; daughter of freed slaves Joel Cephus Bannister and Sarah Louise*

*(Scales) Bannister; graduated from the Virginia Seminary, 1899; married Edward Spencer, on May 15, 1901; children: two boys and a girl.*

A founding member of the Harlem Renaissance in the 1920s, Anne Spencer was born in 1882 in Henry County, Virginia, the daughter of former slaves Joel Cephus Bannister and **Sarah Louise Scales**. She was brought up in the home of a barber, where her mother, who had separated from her husband, had placed her for her betterment. Sarah also made sure Anne attended the Virginia Seminary in Lynchburg, giving her an opportunity to mingle with affluent blacks. Anne Spencer proved an apt student and gave the 1899 valedictory at her graduation.

Two years later, she married fellow classmate Edward Spencer and the couple settled down in Lynchburg. Beginning with "Before the Feast at Shushan," the majority of Spencer's poems were published in the 1920s and appeared in major anthologies. Strongly influenced by *Olive Schreiner, her poetry deals more with gender than with race.

The Spencer home became a salon for African-American artists, including Langston Hughes, W.E.B. Du Bois, James Weldon Johnson, and Claude McKay. Anne's garden, along with her lively mind, sparked much of the pilgrimage. The well-tended garden of flowers, which became the "soul" of her poems, is now a historical landmark. "God never planted a garden," she wrote. "But he placed a keeper there."

A civil-rights activist and feminist, Spencer helped found Lynchburg's first NAACP chapter, started a suffrage club, refused to ride segregated public transportation, and was the librarian at Dunbar High School for over 20 years so that black children would be exposed to books otherwise unavailable. Anne Spencer retired from the public eye in 1938, and became a recluse after the death of her husband in 1964. Illness caused the end of her reading and writing; it also caused her absence at the Virginia Seminary and College when they awarded her an honorary degree in 1975.

**SUGGESTED READING:**

Greene, J. Lee. *Time's Unfading Garden: Anne Spencer's Life and Poetry.* Baton Rouge, LA: Louisiana State University Press, 1977.

Smith, Jessie Carney, ed. *Notable Black American Women.* Detroit, MI: Gale Research, 1992.

**RELATED MEDIA:**

*Echoes from the Garden: The Anne Spencer Story* (documentary film), produced by the Anne Spencer Memorial Foundation, Byron Studios, 1980.

**Malinda Mayer**, writer and editor, Falmouth, Massachusetts

Anne Spencer

## Spencer, Diana (1961–1997).

*See Diana.*

## Spencer, Dorothy (1617–1684).

*See Sidney, Dorothy.*

# Spencer, Dorothy (b. 1909)

*American film editor. Born in Covington, Kentucky, on February 2, 1909.*

*Selected filmography:* Married in Hollywood *(1929);* The Case Against Mrs. Ames *(1936);* Blockade *(1938);* Trade Winds *(1939);* Stagecoach *(1939);* Foreign Correspondent *(1940);* Sundown *(1941);* To Be or Not to Be *(1942);* Heaven Can Wait *(1943);* Lifeboat *(1944);* A Tree Grows in Brooklyn *(1945);* A Royal Scandal *(1945);* Dragonwyck *(1946);* Cluny Brown *(1946);* My Darling Clementine *(1946);* The Ghost and Mrs. Muir *(1947);* That Lady in Ermine *(1948);* The Snake Pit *(1948);* Down to the Sea in Ships *(1949);* Three Came Home *(1950);* Under My Skin *(1950);* Fourteen Hours *(1951);* Decision Before

Dawn *(1951)*; Lydia Bailey *(1952)*; Man on a Tightrope *(1953)*; Night People *(1954)*; Demetrius and the Gladiators *(1954)*; Broken Lance *(1954)*; Prince of Players *(1955)*; Soldier of Fortune *(1955)*; The Left Hand of God *(1955)*; The Rains of Ranchipur *(1955)*; The Man in the Gray Flannel Suit *(1956)*; A Hatful of Rain *(1957)*; The Young Lions *(1958)*; The Journey *(1959)*; From the Terrace *(1960)*; North to Alaska *(1960)*; Wild in the Country *(1961)*; Cleopatra *(1963)*; Circus World *(1964)*; Von Ryan's Express *(1965)*; The Lost Command *(1966)*; A Guide for the Married Man *(1967)*; Valley of the Dolls *(1967)*; Daddy's Gone a-Hunting *(1969)*; Happy Birthday, Wanda June *(1971)*; Earthquake *(1974)*; The Concord—Airport '79 *(1979)*.

A film editor of extraordinary skill and longevity, Dorothy Spencer enjoyed a career that spanned five decades, and included such motion pictures as an adaptation of *Betty Smith*'s novel *A Tree Grows in Brooklyn* (1945), an adaptation of **Mary Jane Ward**'s novel *The Snake Pit* (1948), as well as *The Left Hand of God* (1955) and *A Hatful of Rain* (1957). Spencer collaborated with some of Hollywood's best directors, including John Ford, Alfred Hitchcock, Ernst Lubitsch, and Elia Kazan, and received four Academy Award nominations: for *Stagecoach* (1939), *Decision Before Dawn* (1951), *Cleopatra* (1963), and *Earthquake* (1974).

# Spencer, Elizabeth (1921—)

*American novelist and short-story writer. Born in Carrollton, Mississippi, on July 19, 1921; daughter of James L. Spencer (a farmer) and Mary J. (McCain) Spencer; Belhaven College, B.A., 1942; Vanderbilt University, M.A., 1943; married John Rusher (an educator), on September 29, 1956.*

*Selected writings:* Fire in the Morning *(1948)*; The Crooked Way *(1952)*; The Voice at the Back Door *(1956)*; The Light in the Piazza *(1960)*; Knights and Dragons *(1965)*; No Place for an Angel *(1967)*; Ship Island and Other Stories *(1968)*; The Snare *(1972)*; The Stories of Elizabeth Spencer *(1981)*; The Salt Line *(1984)*; Jack of Diamonds and Other Stories *(1988)*; The Night Travellers *(1991)*; Landscapes of the Heart *(autobiography, 1998)*.

Elizabeth Spencer is best known for her short stories and for her novel *The Light in the Piazza*, which was made into a film in 1962. She was born in 1921 in Carrollton, Mississippi, the daughter of prosperous farmers, and grew up

with stories of all kinds—the Bible, traditional stories, local history, and classic literature. While attending Belhaven College, she met writer *Eudora Welty* and formed a lifelong friendship with her. Faculty at Belhaven encouraged Spencer to pursue a graduate degree, so she went to Vanderbilt University, then the intellectual gathering place of Agrarian Luddites, who were dedicated to the preservation of the rural traditions of Southern culture and land ownership. As a student there, she met Allan Tate, Robert Penn Warren, whom she counted as a colleague, Donald Davidson, who became her mentor, and John Crowe Ransom. After college, Spencer taught English and creative writing at several schools: Northwest Mississippi Junior College in Senatobia (1943–44), Ward-Belmont in Nashville (1944–45), and for several years at the University of Mississippi. She also served a stint as a reporter for the *Nashville Tennessean* (1945 and 1946).

Spencer published her first novel, *Fire in the Morning*, in 1948. In it, she created a fictional community, Tarsus, Mississippi, that resembles the Mississippi hill country she knew as a child. The novel has an intricate, well-made plot and vivid characters, and its themes are chiefly discovery and reversal: a young man finds that the past cannot be separated from the present, that his good intentions are no assurance of good deeds and outcomes, that evil is rarely dramatic and clearly designated. Though a fire at night is the more familiar image of destruction, as the epigraph makes clear, a fire in the morning can be more devastating. Spencer's controlling metaphor is exact: burning in full sunlight, fire, like evil, takes on a stealthy ordinariness, its ambiguity and mediocrity bemusing those in its presence.

Spencer turned again to the hill country people of Mississippi for her next novel, *This Crooked Way* (1952). The story is a family chronicle taken from a brief account in *Fire in the Morning*. With her third novel, *The Voice at the Back Door* (1956), she completed what amounts to a cycle of novels that, taken together, portray the social and political circumstances of the rural South during the first half of the 20th century. In this novel, she focused upon the racial relationships in a small Mississippi town between the end of World War II and the beginning of the civil-rights upheavals of the 1960s, a time when peaceable change in the white South's treatment of blacks seemed possible. *The Voice at the Back Door* portrays a society described in rich detail, succeeding both as social criticism and as a portrait of provocative characters caught up in the business of living. The novel was widely reviewed and much praised for its penetrating insights into the motives of human action, as well as for the social realism that Spencer evokes through taut dialogue and fast-paced narrative.

In 1953, Spencer was awarded a Guggenheim fellowship and left the United States to live in Italy and write full-time. Reflective of this, her subsequent four novels are about North Americans in Europe. The first of these were *The Light in the Piazza* (1960) and *Knights and Dragons* (1965). Critics particularly praised the novella *The Light in the Piazza*, which received the first McGraw-Hill Fiction Award and also was made into a Hollywood film starring *\*Olivia de Havilland* and Rossano Brazzi. The American-in-Europe theme, as well as the book's concern with subtle motives and introspections, led to many comparisons with Henry James. Even the plot, concerning the courtship and marriage of a blushingly open and innocent American girl to an Italian, suggests a Jamesian influence. *No Place for an Angel* (1967) enlarges upon and intensifies Spencer's earlier portraits of displaced Americans who wander haphazardly in and out of foreign countries, relationships, and private dreams of success.

In *The Snare* (1972), Spencer took a different direction in her exploration of the possibilities for living in a menacing world. The threat that the main character faces is not stultifying materialism, or lotus-eating artiness, or even power hunger; it is rather her discovery within herself of an unappeasable appetite for bestiality that matches an appetite for human, civilized life. The novel's New Orleans setting serves, as does Italy in the earlier novels, as an enlarged symbol of the possibilities for life beyond the conventional margins of most Americans' lives.

Spencer also published dozens of short stories, many of which won prizes and inclusion in story anthologies. *Ship Island and Other Stories* (1968) shows her artisanship and control in the handling of the form and includes some memorable characters who are marked by mystery and vitality. Like the novels, the stories vary in setting from small Southern towns to Europe, and they show many different stylistic approaches.

Women and girls are key characters in Spencer's collections of short stories. In *Jack of Diamonds and Other Stories*, their relationships are the central theme. "Spencer is dispassionate about domestic morality but intensely curious about the things people do, the lies they live and the truths they hide. Her stories are graceful, solidly crafted and honest," observed R.Z. Shepherd in *Time*. *On the Gulf* is a collection of all the stories Spencer set in the semitropical Mississippi Gulf region. According to Robert Phillips in *Southern Review*, "Each of the girls or women in these stories is on a journey toward self-knowledge."

In 1956, Spencer married John Rusher, a native of Cornwall, England, and two years later they moved to Montreal, Canada, where she taught at Concordia University from 1976 until 1986. She returned at last to the South in 1986 when she accepted a professorship in creative writing at the University of North Carolina in Chapel Hill. Spencer retired from teaching in 1992 and concentrated on writing her autobiography, *Landscapes of the Heart*, published in 1998.

**SOURCES:**

Buck, Claire, ed. *The Bloomsbury Guide to Women's Literature*. NY: Prentice Hall, 1992.

Commire, Anne, ed. *Something About the Author*. Vol. 14. Detroit, MI: Gale Research, 1978.

*Contemporary Authors*. Vol. 65. New Rev. Series. Detroit, MI: Gale Research, 1998.

*Contemporary Literary Criticism*. Vol. 22. Detroit, MI: Gale Research, 1982.

Prenshaw, Peggy Whitman. "Elizabeth Spencer," in *Dictionary of Literary Biography*, Vol. 2: *American Novelists Since World War II*. 2nd series. Detroit, MI: Gale Research, 1978.

Zenner, Boyd. "Ungracious Living," in *The Women's Review of Books*. July 1998.

**Malinda Mayer**, writer and editor, Falmouth, Massachusetts, and **Peggy Whitman Prenshaw**

## Spencer, Georgiana (1757–1806).

*See Lamb, Caroline for sidebar on Georgiana Cavendish.*

## Spencer, Henrietta Frances (1761–1821).

*See Lamb, Caroline for sidebar.*

## Spencer, Jane (b. 1957).

*See Diana for sidebar.*

# Spencer, Lilly Martin (1822–1902)

*British-born American painter. Born Angélique Marie Martin in Exeter, England, on November 26, 1822; died in New York City on May 22, 1902; oldest of four children of Giles Marie Martin (a French teacher) and Angélique (le Petit) Martin; educated at home; attended the Academy of Design in New York City; studied painting informally with Charles Sullivan and Sala Bosworth in Marietta, Ohio, and John Insco Williams in Cincinnati, Ohio; married Benjamin Rush Spencer, in August 1844 (died 1890); children: Benjamin Martin, Angelo Paul, Charles, William Henry, Flora, Pierre, and Lilly Caroline.*

*Emigrated to the United States from Great Britain as a child (1830); had first show, in Marietta, Ohio (1841); studied in Cincinnati (beginning 1841) and became established as leading local genre artist; launched as nationally known genre artist by the American Art-Union; Truth Unveiling Falsehood declared a masterwork on its completion (1869).*

Lilly Martin Spencer was born Angélique Marie Martin in Britain on November 26, 1822, the daughter of Giles Martin and **Angélique le Petit Martin**. Spencer's parents were French utopians who emigrated to the United States with their three children in 1830. Supporting progressive causes such as abolition, the temperance movement, and women's suffrage, they intended to establish a utopian cooperative community. Although they never achieved this goal, they provided a liberal and open environment for their children.

Spencer, known by her nickname "Lilly," was educated at home, reading from the family's vast and eclectic library. Recognizing her artistic talents early, her parents sent her to the Academy of Design in New York City before she was ten, while they were living in New York. When the family moved to Marietta, Ohio, Spencer was encouraged by two local artists, Charles Sullivan and **Sala Bosworth**, who introduced her to oils. At 17, she filled the plaster walls of the family home, Tupperford Farm, with charcoal murals that included full-sized portraits of family members, a water view as seen from a public square, and domestic scenes of a boy teasing a cat, a woman kneading bread, and a child taking its first step. Spencer became a local celebrity and her home a local tourist attraction.

By the time she was 18 Spencer had produced over 50 oil paintings, including portraits, genre scenes, and scenes inspired by literature. With the help of Charles Sullivan, she held her first exhibition in 1841 to raise money for her studies. The exhibition attracted so much attention from critics that Nicholas Longworth, a wealthy art patron from Cincinnati, offered to sponsor her training in Boston and Europe. Although no one knows why Spencer refused this offer, there is speculation that it was because he mandated that she study in Europe for seven years before exhibiting again, or because she adhered to a current movement among American artists to establish a native tradition of painting without "foreign" training.

In the fall of 1841, Spencer moved to Cincinnati, Ohio, home to an active artists'

colony and a community of progressive thinkers. She studied briefly with James Beard and John Insco Williams, but soon surpassed her teachers. Her family's support was so complete that later that spring her father Giles moved to Cincinnati and taught private French lessons to help support her. By 1846, she had firmly established herself as a leading local artist of portraits and romantic and genre works.

In 1844, she married Benjamin Rush Spencer. Their marriage, like all of Spencer's life, was both happy and progressive. Early on, Benjamin realized that Lilly would be the main provider for the family, so he took on all the domestic chores commonly assigned to the wife and helped with the business side of Lilly's work, while she supported him and their large family with her painting.

Spencer exhibited wherever she could—the Cincinnati Society for the Promotion of Useful Knowledge, the Young Men's Mercantile Library, and art supply stores—but it was the art-union that finally gave her financial success and recognition. The Cincinnati and New York art-unions did much to popularize art in the mid-1800s. For five dollars, subscribers joined the union, were given an engraving of a painting by an American artist, and entered into a lottery for an original oil painting. Although obviously commercial, the art-unions generated a large number of sales and a wide audience for American artists. The works chosen for the lottery were displayed in advance and widely publicized. In 1847, Spencer exhibited at the first show of the Western Art-Union in Cincinnati, and several of her works were engraved for distribution during the next two years. In 1849, the Western Art-Union commissioned an engraving of Spencer's painting *One of Life's Happy Hours* as the first premium for its members. In the 1852 exhibition at the American Art-Union in New York City, Spencer's works brought higher prices than those of George Caleb Bingham, John James Audubon, Eastman Johnson, and William S. Mount. By the time anti-lottery legislation killed the art-unions in 1852, Spencer was firmly established as an important American artist.

The exhibitions at the Western Art-Union in Cincinnati and American Art-Union in New York led to her being commissioned to do the illustrations for the book *Women of the American Revolution* by \*Elizabeth F. Ellet. These illustrations were reproduced in *Godey's Lady's Book*, thereby receiving nationwide distribution. At this point, Spencer turned from "fancy and historical" pieces to concentrate on anecdotal, domestic scenes, many inspired by her own children. The public clamored for genre works more than for other styles, especially the sentimental and humorous anecdotal scenes Spencer produced, and she became extremely popular. Some of her more well-known paintings are *Domestic Happiness* (1849), *The Jolly Washerwoman* (1851), *Peeling Onions* (1852), *Shake Hands* (1854), *"This Little Pig Went to Market"* (1857), and *The Gossips* (1857).

In 1848 the family moved to New York City, where Spencer showed and studied at the National Academy of Design. She received commissions to illustrate books and magazines and to paint portraits. Among her subjects were *Caroline Scott Harrison, the wife of President Benjamin Harrison, the feminists *Elizabeth Cady Stanton and *Ella Wheeler Wilcox, and Robert G. Ingersoll, "the Great Agnostic." Spencer found Ingersoll's views sympathetic (as thousands of Americans did not), and painted him with his two grandchildren.

In 1858, Spencer moved her considerable family to Newark, New Jersey, but shortly afterwards rented a studio in New York City where she worked. It was there that she created *Truth Unveiling Falsehood*, finished in 1869. Acclaimed by critics as her masterpiece, it was an allegorical painting showing Truth protecting a young mother nursing her baby. Spencer turned down two offers of $20,000 for the painting, which unfortunately was lost with the passage of time.

Lilly Martin Spencer stopped exhibiting in 1876, and four years later moved to Poughkeepsie, New York, where she continued painting portraits. Her husband died in 1890, and in 1900, at age 78, she moved back to New York City, established a studio, and began to receive old friends and new commissions. She died at her easel in the spring of 1902 and was buried beside her husband in Highland, New York.

**SOURCES:**

Harris, Ann Sutherland, and Linda Nochlin. *Women Artists: 1550–1950*. L.A. County Museum of Art: Knopf, 1976.

James, Edward T., ed. *Notable American Women, 1607–1950*. Cambridge, MA: The Belknap Press of Harvard University, 1971.

McHenry, Robert, ed. *Famous American Women*. NY: Dover, 1980.

Rubinstein, Charlotte Streifer. *American Women Artists*. Boston, MA: G.K. Hall, 1982.

**Malinda Mayer**, writer and editor, Falmouth, Massachusetts

## Spencer, Sarah (b. 1955).

*See Diana for sidebar.*

## Spencer-Churchill.

*See Churchill.*

## Spencer-Churchill, Baroness (1885–1977).

*See Churchill, Clementine.*

## Spenser, Violet (d. 1910).

*See Cook, Edith Maud.*

## Speranza (c. 1821–1896).

*See Wilde, Jane.*

# Sperling, Hilde (1908—)

*German tennis star who was a greatly respected player on the international tennis circuit in the 1930s. Name variations: Hilde Krahwinkel. Born Hilde Krahwinkel in 1908; married Sven Sperling (a Danish tennis star).*

*Won the French (three times) and Swiss championships; was runner-up at Wimbledon (1931).*

Hilde Sperling had several strikes against her on the international tennis circuit. She was tall and ungainly, with an unusual style of play. Her grip was even more unusual, for an early injury to the ligaments in the fourth and fifth fingers of her right hand made it difficult for her to hold a racquet. "She is one of the best yet most hopeless looking tennis players I have ever seen," commented American champion Bill Tilden. "Her game is awkward in the extreme, limited to cramped unorthodox ground strokes without volley or smash to aid her, yet she has been the most consistent winner in women's tennis each year since 1934. She is another proof of that great tennis truth that it is where and when you hit a tennis ball, not how, that wins matches."

Sperling rose in the ranks in German tennis in the early 1930s and soon placed third behind *Cilly Aussem and **Marie Louise Horn**. Her style made her appear an easy match, but more than one player discovered this was not the case. As American star *Helen Hull Jacobs learned to her sorrow, Sperling was full of surprises. Her pace was slow but steady, gradually wearing down her opponent. She did not execute volleys or smashes in the traditional style, but her shots were well placed and her net returns excellent. Reporting on one of Jacobs' unexpected losses to Sperling, the Associate Press wrote, "The unexpected defeat of Miss Jacobs was largely the American's own fault and the result of her inability to employ her best high-powered tennis against an opponent who stood on the baseline and with a slight movement to either side or a step forward appeared to cover the whole backcourt . . . 20, 30 and even 50 stroke rallies were reeled off in the grim, rather uninteresting struggle." The struggle was dull to everyone except Sperling.

Although her height might have been a disadvantage, Sperling used it as an asset. She often had to take only three steps to her competitor's five, which eventually tired more than one player. Many on the tennis circuit adored Sperling for her humor. Once after a long championship match against Jacobs at Wimbledon, both players had blistered and swollen feet. Jacobs eventually prevailed, winning the match and the tournament. That night, she received a telegram from Sperling. "Wish I could be with you," it read, "but even my husband's shoes are too small for me tonight."

**SOURCES:**
Jacobs, Helen Hull. *Gallery of Champions.* Freeport, NY: Books for Libraries Press, 1970.

**Karin Loewen Haag,**
Athens, Georgia

# Spessivtzeva, Olga (1895–1980)

*Russian ballerina. Name variations: Olga Spessivtse-va. Born in Rostov, Russia, in 1895; died in 1980; daughter of an opera singer; graduated from the Imperial Maryinsky Theater ballet school in 1913.*

The daughter of an opera singer, Olga Spessivtzeva was born in 1895 in Rostov, Russia, and grew up in an orphanage in St. Petersburg. With her sister **Zinaida** and brother Alexander, she attended the Imperial Maryinsky Theater ballet school, later named the Kirov, where she studied under Michel Fokine and *\*Agrippina Vaganova*. Following her graduation in 1913, Spessivtzeva joined the Maryinsky Ballet and by 1918 was promoted to ballerina, dancing principal roles for the next five years in *Esmeralda, Giselle, Chopiniana (Les Sylphides), The Nutcracker, Paquita, Le Corsaire, Bayaderka, The Sleeping Beauty, The Daughter of Pharoah, Don Quixote,* and *Swan Lake.* While on a leave of absence, she also toured the United States with Sergei Diaghilev's Ballet Russe in 1916, dancing with Vaslav Nijinsky in the *Blue Bird* and *Le Spectre de la Rose.*

Reputedly the greatest Russian Romantic ballerina of her generation, Spessivtzeva rejoined the Ballet Russe in 1921, dancing Aurora in *Sleeping Beauty* (that production titled *Sleeping Princess*) with Pierre Vladimirov. In 1923, along with *\*Alexandra Danilova*, Spessivtzeva left Russia for good. She first worked with the Teatro Colón in Buenos Aires, Argentina, for one year, before joining the Paris Opéra where she remained until 1932, rising to *première danseuse étoile* in 1931. During an Australian tour with the Victor Dandré-Alexander Levitov company, the ballerina began to reveal the first signs of chronic depression. In 1943, she suffered a nervous breakdown, and was confined to a mental hospital for the next 20 years. Friends eventually pushed for her discharge, and Spessivtzeva lived out her days at *\*Alexandra Tolstoy*'s Russian settlement, the Tolstoy Farm in Rockland County, New York.

**SUGGESTED READING:**
Dolin, Anton. *The Sleeping Ballerina,* 1960.

# Spewack, Bella (1899–1990)

*Rumanian-born American playwright and screenwriter. Name variations: Bella Cohen. Born Bella Cohen in Transylvania on March 25, 1899; died in Manhattan, New York, on April 27, 1990; daughter of Adolph Cohen and Fanny (Lang) Cohen; educated at Washington Irving High School in the Bronx, New York; married Samuel Spewack, around 1922 (died 1971); no children.*

*Selected plays with Samuel Spewack:* The Solitaire Man *(1926);* Poppa *(1928);* The War Song *(1928);* Clear All Wires *(1932);* Spring Song *(1934);* Boy Meets Girl *(1935);* Leave It to Me *(1938);* Miss Swan Expects *(1939);* Woman Bites Dog *(1946);* Kiss Me Kate *(1949);* Two Blind Mice *(1949);* The Golden State *(1950);* My Three Angels *(1953);* Festival *(1955).*

*Selected filmography with Samuel Spewack:* The Nuisance *(1932);* The Secret Witness *(1932);* The Gay Bride *(1934);* The Cat and the Fiddle *(1934);* Rendezvous *(1935);* Boy Meets Girl *(1938);* Vogues of 1938 *(1938);* Three Loves Has Nancy *(1938);* My Favorite Wife *(1940);* Weekend at the Waldorf *(1945);* Kiss Me Kate *(1953);* Move Over Darling *(1963).*

As a playwright, Bella Spewack made her mark with the musical *Kiss Me Kate,* a loose adaptation of Shakespeare's *The Taming of the Shrew* which she co-wrote with her husband. First produced in 1949, the play enjoyed an initial run of over 1,000 performances on Broadway and was credited with reviving the career of its composer Cole Porter. Born Bella Cohen in Transylvania in 1899, the daughter of Adolph Cohen and **Fanny Lang Cohen**, Bella Spewack came to New York City at the age of three. In her autobiography *Streets: A Memoir of the Lower East Side,* she recounted her youth as a Jewish immigrant raised by a single mother in Manhattan. Fanny, a live-in domestic, took in sewing and eventually boarders in an attempt to make ends meet. Spewack and her two younger brothers, one of whom needed constant nursing, changed homes every year as their mother sought more affordable accommodations, but Fanny Cohen refused to allow her daughter to work in a factory because she wanted her to be a "lady." Bella finished her schooling at Washington Irving High School in the Bronx in 1917.

Spewack worked first as a journalist, starting at the socialist newspaper *The New York Call*. Her impressive writing garnered her work at other papers, including *The New York Times, The New York Herald Tribune*, and the *Evening Mail*. Her writing also caught the eye of fellow reporter Sam Spewack, whom she married around 1922. Immediately following their marriage, the pair traveled to Moscow, where they both served as foreign correspondents for *The World*. Bella achieved distinction both for the quality of the stories she sent back to the States and as one of the few female foreign correspondents at the time.

Despite her success in journalism, Spewack turned her talents to the theater upon their return to America in 1926, becoming a press agent. Although Sam continued to write for *The World*, he found time to collaborate with Bella in the creation of Broadway scripts. They utilized their experiences in Moscow to write their first hit, *Clear All Wires*, in 1932. Although supposedly a satire on Eastern European politics and American bureaucracy, it was more of a farce about a globe-trotting journalist who creates as much news as he covers. The play was later turned into the musical *Leave It to Me*, featuring tunes by Cole Porter. It also launched the career of actress \***Mary Martin** and featured a young Gene Kelly in the chorus.

The year 1932 also saw the Spewacks' first Hollywood projects, with the scripts for *The Nuisance* and *The Secret Witness*. Over the years, they wrote approximately 20 movies, many of them cinematic adaptations of their stage hits. Their Hollywood experiences spawned another successful Broadway play in 1935, *Boy Meets Girl*, poking fun at the film industry and the people involved in it.

Throughout the 1930s and 1940s, the Spewacks consistently had their productions on the Broadway stage, averaging one a year. Much of their success stemmed from their formulaic approach to writing, as they stuck to the standard, lighthearted "boy-meets-girl" kind of love stories that lifted the spirits of their post-Depression audiences. The sentiment they so ably con-veyed was linked to madcap comedy and slapstick, featuring the harassed, the scatterbrained and other cartoonish characters designed to elicit easy laughs.

But none of their plays equaled the success of their 1949 musical *Kiss Me Kate*. Although Spewack did not consider *The Taming of the Shrew* to be one of Shakespeare's best, she was sold on the project by the presence of Cole Porter, who agreed to write the songs. The play won a Tony Award. In 1953, it was made into a movie, the same year the Spewacks scored another hit on Broadway with *My Three Angels*, an adaptation of a French play about three likeable scoundrels. Their 1955 play *Festival*, however, received terrible notices and was rescued from early closure only by Bella Spewack's personal appeals from the stage after every performance. It would be their last play, although they did write the movie *Move Over Darling* in 1963.

In addition to her accomplishments on the stage and screen, Bella Spewack also achieved a degree of fame for her work as a publicist for the Girl Scouts Association prior to her marriage. She is credited with the invention of the Girl Scout Cookie, which developed into an enduring national fund-raising campaign. Bella Spewack died in Manhattan on April 27, 1990.

**SOURCES:**

Andrews, Deborah, ed. *The Annual Obituary 1990.* Chicago, IL: St. James Press, 1991.

Kunitz, Stanley J., ed. *Twentieth Century Authors.* NY: H.W. Wilson, 1942.

**Malinda Mayer**, writer and editor, Falmouth, Massachusetts

# Speyer, Ellin Prince (1849–1921)

*American philanthropist and socialite. Name variations: Mrs. John A. Lowery; Mrs. James Speyer. Born Ellin L. Prince in Lowell, Massachusetts, on October 14, 1849; died in New York City on February 23, 1921; only daughter and younger of two children of John Dynely Prince (a chemist) and Mary (Travers) Prince; educated by private tutors; married John A. Lowery, in October 1871 (died 1892); married James Speyer (1861–1941, a banker and philanthropist), on November 11, 1897; no children.*

*Was one of the founders of the United Hospital Fund (1881); helped establish the New York Skin and Cancer Hospital (1886); founded club for working girls (1883); organized girls' branch of Public School Athletic League (1906); was chair of subcommittee on unemployment among women (1915); was an advocate for animals; raised funds for the Lafayette Street Hospital for animals.*

Ellin Speyer was born Ellin Prince in 1849 in the mill town of Lowell, Massachusetts, to which her grandfather, John Dynely Prince, an expert textile printer, had emigrated in 1855. Both her parents died before she was 14 years old, and she spent her young adult years with and uncle and aunt in an environment of privilege, wealth, and social prominence. Her uncle William Riddell Travers was a wealthy New York lawyer, wit, and social leader; her aunt was the daughter of Judge Reverdy Johnson who at one time was minister to Great Britain. In later years, Speyer made good use of her position and influence to nurture her three most active interests: the availability of health care, the needs of working women, and, dearest to her heart, the welfare of animals.

Little is known about her marriage to John Lowery, although Speyer was married to him for over 20 years until his death in 1892. Her known charitable work began in 1881 when she helped to found the Hospital Saturday and Sunday Association, which later became the United Hospital Fund, and served as treasurer of its women's auxiliary. She continued her hospital work by helping to establish the New York Skin and Cancer Hospital in 1886 and by serving in the American Red Cross during two wars.

Speyer evinced a sustained concern for the needs of working women at a time when only the neediest women worked outside the home and were often badly exploited and ill used. In 1883, she founded a club for working girls, called the Irene Club, of which she served as president and treasurer for 30 years. This club was the seed from which grew a national network of societies supporting the needs of working girls. Speyer also helped to fund the New York League of Women Workers and the Working Girls Vacation Society. In 1906, she opened her home to the girls' branch of the Public School Athletic League. In 1915, Mayor John P. Mitchel appointed her chair of his subcommittee on unemployment among women. This committee provided employment in its workshops for hundreds of jobless women.

Speyer's interest in working women led her to try to help African-American women and children in particular. Her charities included St. Mary's Free Hospital for Children, the Nursery for Colored Children, and the National League on Urban Conditions among Negroes, all at a time when the specter of slavery was still very much a part of recent memory and practice.

In 1897, she married James Speyer, a banker and well-known philanthropist who be-longed to a distinguished German-Jewish family. After their marriage, she became a leading society figure known for her gracious manners and witty and intelligent conversation. She was a member of the socially exclusive Colony Club for women, a patron of the Metropolitan Opera company, and a supportive friend of artists. In 1902, Speyer and her husband gave $100,000 to the Teachers College of Columbia University to found an experimental school which was named after them.

In her middle years, Speyer began the work that meant the most to her, that of protecting and helping animals. In 1910, she founded the New York Women's League for Animals, heading the organization for the remainder of her life. Using her influence with other wealthy socialites, she raised funds for the Lafayette Street Hospital for animals, which after her death was renamed the Ellin Prince Speyer Free Hospital for Animals in her honor. She was particularly sensitive to the plight of work horses which were often mistreated. She organized the "Work Horse Parade," giving out medals for the best-cared-for horses from the New York City police, fire, and street-cleaning departments; she found homes for horses retired by the police department; and she provided special nonslip shoes for work horses to prevent them from sliding on the icy winter streets. In her will, her largest bequest was to her beloved animal hospital.

Ellin Speyer died at her home on Fifth Avenue on February 23, 1921, at age 71. Her friend, violinist Fritz Kreisler, played at her funeral at the Cathedral of St. John the Divine, after which she was buried in Sleepy Hollow Cemetery in Tarrytown, New York.

**SOURCES:**

James, Edward T., ed. *Notable American Women, 1607–1950*. Cambridge, MA: The Belknap Press of Harvard University, 1971.

**Malinda Mayer**, writer and editor, Falmouth, Massachusetts

# Speyer, Leonora (1872–1956)

*American poet and violinist. Born Leonora Von Stosch in Washington, D.C., on November 7, 1872; died in New York City on February 10, 1956; daughter of Count Ferdinand Von Stosch and Julia (Thompson) Von Stosch; married in 1893 (divorced); married Edgar Speyer (a banker), in 1902; children: (first marriage) four daughters, Enid (who married Robert Hewitt); Pamela (who married Count Hugo Moy); Leonora Speyer (d. 1987, who lived with \*Maria Donska); and Vivien.*

Concert violinist with Boston Symphony Orchestra (1890); won Pulitzer Prize for poetry for Fiddler's Farewell (1927); taught poetry at Columbia University in New York City.

Leonora Speyer played the violin from the time her "chin was firm enough to hold it." She began her career as a concert violinist at the age of 17 playing with the Boston Symphony Orchestra in 1890, and appeared later with the New York Philharmonic. When a severe bout of neuritis stopped her from playing, her friend *Amy Lowell awakened her interest in the Imagist poets, and she started writing poetry herself. Her love of writing poetry overwhelmed her interest in playing the violin. "Having played the violin since my early youth," she said, "it seemed but another expression, perhaps a more subtle one, of the same art to find myself writing, studying, deep in the metrics of musical words." *Harriet Monroe and Robert Bridges were responsible for first getting her work published, and her writings, nearly all lyrics or ballads, frequently appeared in various publications.

Speyer lived abroad for a time in London and Paris, but returned in 1915 to settle in New York City. In 1927 she won the Pulitzer Prize for poetry for her book Fiddler's Farewell. Published in 1926, it was especially noted for its wit and understanding of the feminine character. Other works include A Canopic Jar (1921), Naked Heel (1931), and Slow Wall: New and Selected Poems (1939), which appeared in a larger edition, The Slow Wall: Poems together with Nor Without Music, in 1946.

Near the end of her life, Speyer taught poetry at Columbia University. "There is no teaching a student to acquire talent," she said; "no amount of study may contrive a gift. That is God's affair. But the actual process of poetry—writing, the color and harmony of words, can be, surely must be learned. The instrument must be mastered like any other instrument."

SOURCES:

Kunitz, Stanley J., and Howard Haycraft, eds. Twentieth Century Authors. NY: H.W. Wilson, 1942.

**Malinda Mayer**, writer and editor, Falmouth, Massachusetts

# Spiel, Hilde (1911–1990)

Austrian novelist, essayist, journalist, historian, critic, and major literary figure who examined the values of her fellow Austrians with a sharp critical eye. Born Hilde Maria Spiel in Vienna, Austria, on October 19, 1911; died in Vienna on November 29, 1990; daughter of Hugo Spiel and Marie (Gutfeld) Spiel; graduated from the University of Vienna, 1936; married Peter de Mendelssohn; married Hans Flesch Edler von Brunningen; children: daughter, Christine; son, Anthony Felix.

Hilde Spiel was born in Vienna in 1911, less than three years before the outbreak of World War I, a global conflagration that would destroy the venerable Habsburg Empire. There, she grew up in middle-class comfort and security. Her parents, both Jewish, had converted to Roman Catholicism and were in love with the imperial city that boasted of the Ringstrasse, the Opera House, Grinzing, and St. Stephen's Cathedral. When she was 15, Hilde was enrolled by her liberal-minded parents in the famous progressive secondary school directed by educational reformer *Eugenie Schwarzwald. The intellectually precocious Spiel found herself exposed to some of the most original and challenging minds of the day, having as her teachers such brilliant artists as Oskar Kokoschka and Adolf Loos. Young Hilde was not merely a bookworm, however. She won a school championship in water polo and, like many young Austrians, looked forward every winter to skiing in the nearby mountains.

As a student at the University of Vienna, Spiel continued to take full advantage of a city, which, though impoverished by war and inflation, still remained intellectually exciting. Among her professors at the university were two scholars of world distinction, philosopher Moritz Schlick and psychologist Karl Bühler. At age 22, in 1933, Spiel published her first novel, Kati auf der Brücke (Cathy on the Bridge), a surprisingly mature work that won her the Julius Reich Prize that same year. Over the next few years, she enjoyed the carefree life of an unmarried young woman of the 1930s, including a trip to Italy where she had a brief affair with the novelist Alberto Moravia.

Spiel completed her studies at the university in 1936, with a dissertation, Darstellungstheorie des Films (A Theory of Representation for Films), that was in many ways prophetic of post-1945 film theory and indicated her promise. By this time, although she loved Vienna, she had decided to leave Austria. The bloody suppression of the Social Democratic Party in 1934 destroyed the last vestiges of democracy, and a reactionary pro-fascist regime showed signs of making major concessions to the growing power of the Nazi Third Reich to the north. In 1936, too, Spiel's teacher Moritz Schlick was assassinated in the University of Vienna by a student thought to be demented but very likely also attracted to Nazi ideals. Having married the writer Peter de Mendelssohn that same year, Spiel and her husband emigrated to London in October 1936. In February 1937, her maternal uncle Felix, who had volunteered as a medical orderly on the side of the Spanish Republic, was killed in the defense of Madrid during the bloody battle of Jarama.

Soon after their arrival in London, Spiel and her husband mastered English, and by 1939 she had published a novel, *Flute and Drums*, in that language. The war years were spent raising a daughter and a son, and staying alive under the constant threat of aerial bombardment. By 1946, Spiel was back in Vienna, now as a journalist wearing the uniform of a British officer. She wrote her husband describing how much she was enjoying herself in the bombed-out city, asking him, "Is that very bad of me?"

In 1963, after years of agonizing about the decision, Spiel returned to Vienna for good. Though she was fully aware of Austria's consid-

erable complicity in the crimes of the Third Reich, including the Holocaust which cost the lives of some of her relatives (a grandmother had died in the Nazis' "model ghetto," Theresienstadt), she was so drawn to the city of her birth that she felt it was where she belonged. Returning to Austria did not, however, mean that Spiel became complacent about her fellow Austrians' faults. In her writings, she continued to examine their weaknesses as well as their cultural energy and capacity for old-world charm. From this period of her life, in which Spiel became increasingly interested in the rich history of pre-1914 Austria, came her highly regarded biography of the influential salonnière *Fanny von Arnstein. Over the next decades, Spiel would become an important personality in Viennese intellectual life, regarded by many as the city's most outstanding *femme de lettres*, and indeed the reigning Grande Dame of Austrian literature. To the delight of many loyal readers, she reported on Austrian affairs, both literary and political, in elegantly written journalism that appeared in the *New Statesman* as well as in *Die Welt*.

In her sometimes critical books about Austria, Spiel angered her conservative or complacent compatriots with her portrayals of the dark side of a culture that the outside world frequently saw in terms of Strauss waltzes and *Sachertorte*. She turned down an invitation in 1988 to speak at the opening of the prestigious Salzburg Festival, because she did not want to share the podium with Austrian president Kurt Waldheim, who had been accused of concealing his activities as an officer of the German armed forces in Yugoslavia during World War II. At other times, however, she would declare her affection for the best in Austrian culture, as she did in her essay "I Love Living in Austria," in which she explained why she had returned.

In the final years of her life, Spiel battled cancer but refused to let her declining health stop the writing of her memoirs. She was able to complete both volumes of her autobiography, *Die hellen und die finsteren Zeiten: Erinnerungen 1911–1946* (The Bright and the Dark Times: Memoirs 1911–1946), which was published in 1989, and *Welche Welt ist meine Welt? Erinnerungen 1946–1989* (Which World is My World? Memoirs 1946–1989), which appeared in 1990. In early 1990, Hilde Spiel received the last of her many awards, the coveted Goethe Medal. She died in Vienna on November 29, 1990.

**SOURCES:**

Beller, Steven. "Reflecting on the Murk," in *TLS: The Times* [London] *Literary Supplement*. No. 4539. March 30–April 5, 1990, p. 340.

*Hilde Spiel*

Brinson, Charmian, *et al.*, eds. *"England? Aber wo liegt es?": Deutsche und Österreichische Emigranten in Grossbritannien 1933–1945.* Munich: Iudicium Verlag GmbH., 1996.

Davy, Richard. "Group to Plead for Detained Czechs," in *The Times* [London]. March 10, 1972, p. 7.

Fliedl, Konstanze. "Hilde Spiel's Linguistic Rights of Residence," in Edward Timms and Ritchie Robertson, eds., *Austrian Exodus: The Creative Achievements of Refugees from National Socialism.* Edinburgh: Edinburgh University Press, 1995, pp. 78–93.

Frederiksen, Elke, ed. *Women Writers of Germany, Austria, and Switzerland: An Annotated Bio-Bibliographical Guide.* NY: Greenwood Press, 1989.

"Hilde Spiel, Austrian Writer," in *The Washington Post.* December 3, 1990, p. D4.

Hildebrandt, Irma. *Hab meine Rolle nie gelernt: 15 Wiener Frauenporträts.* Munich: Eugen Diederichs, 1996.

Lorenz, Dagmar C.G., ed. *Contemporary Jewish Writing in Austria: An Anthology.* Lincoln, NE: University of Nebraska Press, 1999.

McLaughlin, Donal. "Written in Britain: Publications by German-Speaking Literary Exiles in the Nineteenth and Twentieth Century," in Panikos Panayi, ed., *Germans in Britain Since 1500.* Rio Grande, OH: Hambledon Press, 1996, pp. 95–112.

Spiel, Hilde. *The Darkened Room.* London: Methuen, 1961.

———. "Exil und Rückkehr: Hilde Spiel im Gespräch," in Hartmut Krug and Michael Nungesser, eds. *Kunst im Exil in Grossbritannien, 1933–1945.* Berlin: Verlag Frölich & Kaufmann und NGBK, 1986, pp. 289–295.

———. *Flute and Drums.* London: Hutchinson, 1939.

Strickhausen, Waltraud. *Die Erzählerin Hilde Spiel, oder, "Der weite Wurf in die Finsternis."* NY: Peter Lang, 1996.

Thomas, Gina. "A Literary Traveller between Worlds," in *The Guardian.* December 6, 1990, p. 39.

"Werwowarum," in *profil: Das unabhängige Nachrichtenmagazin Osterreichs.* Vol. 14, no. 2. January 10, 1983, p. 62.

Wiesinger-Stock, Sandra. *Hilde Spiel: Ein Leben ohne Heimat?* Vienna: Verlag für Gesellschaftskritik, 1996.

Zeller, E. "Nicht Figur geworden: Laudatio für Hilde Spiel," in *Deutsche Akademie für Sprache und Dichtung, Darmstadt, Jahrbuch 1981,* 2, 1982, pp. 63–66.

**John Haag,** Associate Professor of History, University of Georgia, Athens, Georgia

## Spira, Camilla (1906–1997).

*See Spira, Steffie for sidebar.*

## Spira, Steffie (1908–1995)

*Austrian-born German actress and author. Name variations: Steffi Spira; Steffie Spira-Ruschin. Born Steffanie Spira in Vienna, Austria, on June 2, 1908; died in Berlin, Germany, on May 10, 1995; daughter of Fritz (formerly Jacob) Spira (1881–1943) and Wilhelmine Emilie Charlotte (Lotte) Andresen Spira, known as Lotte Spira-Andresen (1883–1943); sister of*

*Camilla Spira (1906–1997); married Günter Ruschin (1904–1963, an actor), in 1931; children: son Thomas; daughter Rutta (died in 1941 as an infant).*

On November 4, 1989, East Berlin's vast Alexanderplatz was packed with close to 1 million demonstrators—the largest public rally in German history. They had gathered to show their determination to achieve full democracy in their tottering neo-Stalinist state, the German Democratic Republic (GDR). As the 15th and last speaker of the day, Steffie Spira, a revered actress whose physical persona was that of a plump elderly *oma* (grandma), addressed the crowd:

> In 1933 I went alone to a foreign country taking nothing with me. In my head however I brought along some words from Bertolt Brecht's poem *Lob der Dialektik* [In Praise of Dialectics] which say:
> "No certainty can be certain
> Those still alive can't say 'never'
> He who is aware where he stands—how can anyone stop him moving on?
> And from nothing will yet emerge: today."
>
> I wish for my great-grandchildren to grow up in schools without roll-calls and political indoctrination or that they have to wear uniforms and carry torches as they march past the Big Shots [*die hohen Leute*]. I have one more proposal: Let us transform Wandlitz [the district of East Berlin reserved for high government officials] into a retirement home [*Altersheim*]! Those among them who are over the age of sixty can remain there if they do what I will now do—relinquish my place and depart [*Abtreten*]!

With these words, Spira became one of the most popular women in the GDR, expressing along with such others as \***Bärbel Bohley** the desire of the populace for sweeping reforms and an end to the GDR regime's repressions. Five days later, the Berlin Wall ceased to exist as a dividing line between Germans.

Born into a family of actors, the sisters Steffie and ⚜▸ Camilla Spira both became actresses themselves. Their father Fritz Spira, a Vi-

⚜▸ **Spira, Camilla** (1906–1997)
*German actress. Born in Hamburg, Germany, on March 1, 1906; died in Berlin on August 25, 1997; daughter of Fritz (formerly Jacob) Spira (1881–1943) and Wilhelmine Emilie Charlotte (Lotte) Andresen Spira, an actress known as Lotte Spira-Andresen (1883–1943); sister of \*Steffie Spira (1908–1995); married; children: two sons.*

ennese-born singer and comic actor, was noted for his humor, whereas their mother **Lotte Spira-Andresen** was more interested in serious drama. The Spira marriage was a mixed one: Fritz was of Jewish ancestry and Berlin-born Lotte of Lutheran background. As well, the family's move to Berlin in 1911 resulted in their daughters' spoken German becoming a colorful "bilingual" (*zweisprachig*) mixture of Viennese and Berlin accents. As a young girl, Steffie yearned to become a dancer, and was already enrolled to begin her studies in 1924 with ***Mary Wigman** in Dresden. Unfortunately an accident, resulting from some horseplay with her high-spirited Viennese cousins, caused knee and tendon injuries so severe that they ended her dreams of a dance career. The stage now beckoned both Camilla and Steffie, and they soon found success in Berlin's theaters, Camilla becoming a singing and acting star in various operettas, including Ralph Benatzky's 1930 smash hit *Im Weissen Rössl* (White Horse Inn).

Steffie was also successful on the Berlin stage, as well as in several films. Financially, however, her situation was often precarious and, along with many other German actors, she was an active trade unionist, attempting to bring about a modicum of economic protection in a profession notorious for its lack of security. In January 1928, Steffie became part of German theater history by appearing in the small role of Hiobja in the successful premiere of Bertolt Brecht's *Mann ist Mann* (Man is Man), part of a cast that boasted such stars as Heinrich George and ***Helene Weigel**. By the early 1930s, however, Steffie's life had begun to move on a different track from that of her sister. Whereas Camilla showed scant interest in Germany's increasing turbulence, made worse by economic depression, Steffie became active in the struggle against Fascism and Nazism. Particularly among the young, despair was the prevailing mood, and the future looked grim. Growing numbers of Germans, including Steffie, believed that only a thorough social revolution would halt Adolf Hitler and his legions of brown-shirted barbarians in their tracks.

Steffie made two decisions in 1931 that would alter the course of her life. She married Günter Ruschin (1904–1963), a young actor of Jewish ancestry and an ardent Communist, and she also joined the Communist Party of Germany (Kommunistische Partei Deutschlands or KPD). From this point on, her life and art were inseparable from the struggle to transform Germany into a Marxist republic. Disdaining the world of the "bourgeois stage," she and her husband became

members of Gustav von Wangenheim's Truppe 31, an actors' collective that traveled throughout Germany to present political agitprop productions satirizing the flaws of capitalism and warning of the imminent threat of Hitlerism.

The march of Nazism could not be halted either through theater performances or the ballot box, however, and on January 30, 1933, Hitler was appointed Germany's chancellor. Ironically, on February 2, 1933, Camilla sat through the premiere of her new film *Morgenrot* (Break of Dawn), a patriotic war epic, with Hitler and other Nazi leaders in attendance, and was praised that evening as "the perfect embodiment of German womanhood." (Camilla, a stunning blonde, had "perfect Aryan" features.) Within days of Hitler's accession to power, a reign of terror against political foes of the Nazis, particularly those on the left, swept through Germany. Truppe 31 was banned as "subversive," and brown-shirted thugs broke into and smashed the artists' apartment block on the Laubenheimer Platz in Berlin-Wilmersdorf where Steffie lived with her husband and infant son Thomas. During this time, her husband was arrested and thrown into a Nazi prison cell. Fearing for her own and her infant's life, Steffie fled to Zurich, Switzerland. Only because of a clerical error was Günter Ruschin released from prison, and he was able to flee Germany and join his wife and son in their Swiss refuge. Soon, the family went into permanent exile in Paris, where along with thousands of other émigrés they struggled to survive.

Life was precarious for Steffie and Günter, and both had little choice but to find odd jobs to pay the rent. Günter began an improbable career as a textile salesman while Steffie worked as a cleaning woman for rich French families, but in her spare time she continued to appear on stage, including performances at Die Laterne (The Lantern), a cabaret founded and run by and for German-speaking exiles from Germany, Austria and Czechoslovakia. Steffie continued to develop as an artist during these years and was also able to appear in non-cabaret roles, including a major part in the October 1937 world premiere of Bertolt Brecht's topical play on the Spanish Civil War, *Die Gewehre der Frau Carrar* (Mrs. Carrar's Rifles). On May 21, 1938, she performed one of the lead roles in *99%: Bilder aus dem Dritten Reich* (99%: Pictures from the Third Reich), a selection of excerpts from another anti-fascist Brecht play that would appear in final form as *Furcht und Elend des Dritten Reiches* (Fear and Misery of the Third Reich, published in English as *The Private Life of the Master Race*).

Meanwhile, back in Nazi Germany, Camilla, no longer celebrated as "the perfect Aryan woman" because of her mixed parentage, was only able to keep her stage career alive by performing for the Nazi-approved Jüdischer Kulturbund (Jewish Culture League), which served both to maintain the morale of Germany's beleaguered Jewish community and provide the Nazi propaganda machine with evidence to convince a doubting world how truly "magnanimous" the Third Reich could be toward its "non-Aryan" subjects. Nazism took a toll on the entire Spira family. Fritz, who accepted a theater job in Poland, convinced Lotte to divorce him in order keep her own career alive in Germany. As a result, Lotte Spira-Andresen's acting career once again began to flourish, whereas her former husband sank into obscurity and poverty in Vienna, where he began to live in 1935. In November 1938, at the time of the infamous Kristallnacht pogrom, Camilla fled Nazi Germany with her husband and two sons. Although they hoped to reach the United States, that nation's doors had slammed shut, and they found themselves in Amsterdam, perilously close to the Third Reich.

The start of World War II in September 1939 resulted in "security measures" that authorized the arrest and incarceration of all German nationals in France, virtually all of whom were anti-Nazi refugees (most of them defined as being Jewish by the Third Reich) like Steffie and Günter. Husband and wife were sent to different internment camps, she first to prison in La Roquette and ultimately to a camp at Rieucros (near Mende, Departement Lozère), and he to a camp at Le Vernet. Both camps were notorious, but the greatest anxiety for the couple was being separated from their six-year-old son Thomas. A distraught Steffie did not know of his whereabouts or condition for almost a year, when she was reunited with him. In Rieucros, a camp created exclusively for women enemy aliens, Steffie played an important role in maintaining the morale of her fellow detainees by organizing plays, dramatic readings and other cultural events.

*Steffie Spira speaking at Alexanderplatz, East Berlin, November 4, 1989.*

In early 1941, the situation brightened when the Ruschins received an American visa, but in August it was withdrawn. By then, U.S. diplomatic officials had decided that their nation's security would be gravely threatened by refugees with Communist sympathies. However, Mexico's consul-general in Marseilles, Gilberto Bosques, whose government was both anti-Nazi and a friend of Spanish Republican refugees still living in France, provided the family a visa to emigrate to Mexico.

Despite the fact that Steffie was pregnant and in precarious health as a result of her many months in Rieucros, she had little choice but to cross the Pyrenees via the route established by *Lisa Fittko. In Madrid, en route to the relative safety of Portugal and embarkation to the New World, Steffie gave birth to a daughter named Rutta, who lived only a few days. Sailing from Lisbon on the freighter *Serpa Pinto* (Red Snake), the Ruschins arrived in Veracruz, Mexico, in mid-December 1941. For the next five-and-a-half years, they lived in Mexico City, where Steffie worked as a cook, cleaning woman, and nurse-companion to terminally ill patients. She and her husband also ran a lending library of German-language books which allowed them to socialize with fellow refugees but did little to put food on the table. During these years, Steffie continued to act as well as direct, becoming a member of the Heinrich Heine Club, a cultural center of German-speaking émigrés which chalked up a remarkable artistic record under unusual circumstances.

Meanwhile, as German troops swept across the Netherlands in May 1940, Camilla and her family tried to escape to England, but their train was bombed. Trapped in occupied Amsterdam, she continued to appear on stage with other Jewish actors. In May 1943, she was taken to Westerbork concentration camp, a transit facility for Dutch and other Jews destined for Auschwitz and the Final Solution. Camilla not only was able to continue to perform in Westerbork, whose commandant found her attractive, but was saved by her mother Lotte, who in Berlin managed to convince Nazi officials that her oldest daughter was not half-Jewish as they had believed, but "pure Aryan." She told them that Camilla had been born as the consequence of an affair with an Aryan lover, and that Fritz Spira had never been her biological father. The fabrication was successful, and consequently Camilla and her family were released from Westerbork in October 1943. Only weeks later, in December, Lotte died in Berlin. Fritz did not survive the year 1943 either, finding death in the Ruma concentration camp in Yugoslavia. Before the 1941 Nazi invasion of Yugoslavia, he had secured a visa for Shanghai, but was captured by the Nazis before he could escape. Camilla and her family survived the Holocaust by spending the remainder of the war in hiding in Amsterdam. In 1945, they emigrated to the United States, but being homesick they returned to Berlin in 1947.

That same year, 1947, Steffie finally succeeded in returning to Germany from Mexico with her husband and son. As much an idealistic Communist as ever, she hoped to participate in the building of a socialist society in the Soviet Occupation Zone of Germany, which became the German Democratic Republic (Deutsche Demokratische Republik or GDR) in October 1949. Starting in 1948, Steffie resumed her acting career on the stages of East Berlin, particularly the Deutsches Theater and the Volksbühne (People's Playhouse), where she became a favorite of Berlin audiences for such roles as Mutter Wolffen in Gerhart Hauptmann's *Der Biberpelz* (The Beaver Fur) and the rug merchant Frau Hassenreuther in the Bruno Besson production of Brecht's *Der gute Mensch von Sezuan* (*The Good Woman of Szechuan*). She also appeared in starring roles in a number of GDR motion pictures for the state-owned DEFA Studio, including *Schneewittchen: Ein Märchenfilm nach den Gebrüdern Grimm* (Snow White: A Fairy Tale Film Taken from the Grimm Brothers, 1961), *Die Grosse Reise der Agathe Schweigert* (Agathe Schweigert's Long Trip, 1972), and *Die Beunruhigung* (Apprehension, 1982).

Although Steffie was an active member of the all-powerful Socialist Unity Party (Sozialistische Einheitspartei Deutschlands or SED), in private she had growing doubts about the justness of its conception of socialism, particularly after the suppression of a GDR workers' uprising in June 1953, and the GDR's participation in the Soviet-led military suppression of Czechoslovakia's 1968 "Prague Spring" reform movement. The repressive atmosphere of the GDR affected her own life when Günter Ruschin lost his post as the Volksbühne's chief dramatic producer in 1959 as punishment for having presented Vladimir Mayakovsky's play *The Turkish Bath* in an anti-Stalinist version deemed subversive by SED bureaucrats. Broken in spirit, Ruschin suffered two heart attacks and died prematurely in 1963 at age 59. Another blow to Steffie's faith in the "real existing socialism" the GDR claimed to embody took place in 1984 when her son Thomas fled to the West. Years later, he recalled that although she could never support his decision, with the passage of time she was able to accept it.

For four decades, from the late 1940s to the collapse of the GDR in 1989, Camilla and Steffie Spira lived very different lives, although both were acclaimed Berlin actresses in their sectors of the divided city. Even before the erection of the Berlin Wall in 1961, they met only occasionally, and, when they did, it was rarely in a spirit that was warm or sisterly. During these years, Camilla was able to create a highly successful career for herself as an actress on the Berlin and West German stage, as well as in films and in later years on television where she was incomparable in "motherly" roles. For decades, West German soap operas relied on Camilla to be "Mutter Spira."

The world changed dramatically in 1989, not only for Germany but for the Spira sisters. On the 40th anniversary of the GDR, in October 1989, Steffie showed her bitter dissatisfaction with the regime headed by such unyielding hardliners as Erich and *Margot Honecker by displaying from her apartment window the GDR flag marked with a ribbon of mourning crepe (Trauerflor). After she gave her short but incisive speech at the mass Alexanderplatz demonstration on November 4, 1989—broadcast live over GDR television and reported throughout West Germany—she became a major celebrity. When the Berlin Wall ceased to divide Germans, the two sisters met and reconciled. Within months, they became superstars of the new, united Germany. Grande Dame Camilla and unrepentant Marxist reformer Steffie continued to disagree on many political questions, but now they did so on stage before enthusiastic audiences, or before film cameras to capture for posterity a unique moment in the troubled history of Germany.

The warmth of the two elderly sisters' feelings for each other reflected a national euphoria that began to evaporate even before the two German states were united on October 3, 1990. In September 1990, on the eve of unification, Camilla told a reporter from The New York Times that she recalled the fall of the Berlin Wall less than a year earlier as having been "very beautiful but I couldn't empathize." She continued, "I don't see why we have to be united. I have an uneasy feeling, an oppressive feeling." Steffie agreed with her sister's criticism of the speed of and need for unification, reiterating her lifelong faith in socialism by declaring "I am an internationalist. I've had such good experiences with people from many nations."

In their last years of life, the bond between the two sisters remained strong. With the publication of two books, Steffie became renowned as an author as well as an actress. Camilla remained the dignified embodiment of a now-vanished tradition of German acting. She also probed into the most painful parts of her life, which included a 1991 visit to Westerbork in which she struggled to maintain her composure. Both sisters enjoyed not only their renewed personal encounters, but also found pleasure in the their late fame. Steffie gave countless interviews to journalists and historians, while Camilla fought the infirmities of advanced age by remaining active as a woman of the stage. In her last public appearance, in March 1992, Camilla appeared at a commemorative evening to honor the achievements of Berlin's Jüdischer Kulturbund under the Nazi dictatorship, reading poems by the great German-Jewish Romantic poet Heinrich Heine. Steffie died in Berlin on May 10, 1995. Camilla died in the same city on August 25, 1997. After her death, Berlin made Steffie Spira a permanent part of its history by naming a street in her honor.

**SOURCES:**

Akademie der Künste, Berlin: Abteilung darstellende Kunst, Nachlass Steffie Spira; Nachlass Gustav von Wangenheim (Truppe 31 file).

Douer, Alisa, and Ursula Seeber, eds. Wie weit ist Wien? Lateinamerika als Exil für österreichische Schriftsteller und Künstler. Vienna: Picus, 1995.

Eisenbürger, Gert. "Steffie Spira," in Gert Eisenbürger, ed., Lebenswege: 15 Biographien zwischen Europa und Lateinamerika. Hamburg: Verlag Libertäre Assoziation, 1995, pp. 99–108.

Funke, Christoph. "Herz für das Volk: Zum Tod der Berliner Schauspielerin Steffie Spira," in Der Tagesspiegel [Berlin]. May 12, 1995.

Geissler, Cornelia. "Die Ost-West Schwestern: Camilla und Steffie Spira," in Katharina Raabe, ed. Deutsche Schwestern. Berlin: Rowohlt, 1997, pp. 378–403.

Grandjonc, Jacques, and Theresia Grundtner, eds. Zone d'ombres. Aix-en-Provence: Alinéa, 1990.

Grynberg, Anne. Les camps de la honte: Les internés juifs des camps français (1939–1944). Paris: La Découverte, 1999.

Habel, F.-B. "Zeugin des Jahrhunderts: Der Bühnen- und Filmliebling Camilla Spira wird heute 90 Jahre alt," in Neues Deutschland [Berlin]. March 1, 1996, p. 11.

Hanffstengel, Renata von, et al., eds. Mexiko, das wohltemperierte Exil. Mexico City: Instituto de Investigaciones Interculturales Germano-Mexicanas, 1995.

"Der Idee des Sozialismus treu: Am Mittwoch ist die Schauspielerin Steffie Spira gestorben," in die tageszeitung [Berlin]. May 12, 1995.

Kamm, Henry. "Evolution in Europe: Anxiety Tugs at Germany's Jews, Bitterness Sears the Die-Hard Nationalists," in The New York Times. September 25, 1990, p. A10.

Keithly, David M. The Collapse of East German Communism: The Year the Wall Came Down, 1989. Westport, CT: Praeger, 1992.

Kruger, Loren. "'Stories from the Production Line': Modernism and Modernization in the GDR Production

Play," in *Theatre Journal*. Vol. 46, no. 4. December 1994, pp. 489–505.

Lewy, Hermann. "Meister Ihres Faches: Steffi Spira," in *Theater der Zeit*. Vol. 4, no. 9. September 1949, p. 36.

Mittenzwei, Werner. *Das Leben des Bertolt Brecht oder Der Umgang mit den Welträtseln*. 2 vols. Frankfurt am Main: Suhrkamp, 1987.

———, et al., eds. *Theater in der Zeitenwende: Zur Geschichte des Dramas und des Schauspieltheaters in der Deutschen Demokratischen Republik, 1945–1968*. 2 vols. Berlin: Henschelverlag, 1972.

Philipsen, Dirk. *We Were the People: Voices from East Germany's Revolutionary Autumn of 1989*. Durham, NC: Duke University Press, 1993.

Schivelbusch, Wolfgang. *In a Cold Crater: Cultural and Intellectual Life in Berlin, 1945–1948*. Translated by Kelly Barry. Berkeley, CA: University of California Press, 1998.

Schnare, Horst. "Meister Ihres Faches: Camilla Spira," in *Theater der Zeit*. Vol. 4, no. 9. September 1949, p. 34.

Spira, Steffie. *Rote Fahne mit Trauerflor: Tagebuch-Notizen*. Freiburg im Breisgau: Kore, 1990.

———. *Trab der Schaukelpferde: Autobiographie*. Freiburg im Breisgau: Kore, 1991.

Stern, Frank. "The Return to the Disowned Home—German Jews and the Other Germany," in *New German Critique*. No. 67. Winter 1996, pp. 57–72.

Sucher, C. Bernd. "Das Lächeln der Heiteren: Zum Tode von Camilla Spira," in *Süddeutsche Zeitung*. August 28, 1997.

"Tante Courage—Steffie Spira ist gestorben," in *Frankfurter Allgemeine Zeitung*. May 13, 1995, p. 29.

Thalmann, Rita. "Jewish Women Exiled in France After 1933," in Sibylle Quack, ed. *Between Sorrow and Strength: Women Refugees of the Nazi Period*. Cambridge, UK: Cambridge University Press, 1995, pp. 51–62.

Von Hallberg, Robert. *Literary Intellectuals and the Dissolution of the State*. Chicago. IL: University of Chicago Press, 1996.

Wangenheim, Gustav von. *Da liegt der Hund begraben, und andere Stücke aus dem Repertoire der Truppe 31*. Reinbek bei Hamburg: Ernst Rowohlt, 1974.

Willett, John. *The Theatre of the Weimar Republic*. NY: Holmes & Meier, 1988.

**RELATED MEDIA:**

*Bei uns um die Gedächtniskirche rum—Berlin Cabaret: Friedrich Hollaender und das Kabarett der zwanziger Jahre* (2 CDs, Edel 0014532TLR, 1996).

Cramer, Horst, and Marlet Schaake. "*So wie es ist, bleibt es nicht: Die Geschichte von Camilla und Steffie Spira*" (film produced in 1990 for the SWR-Südwestdeutscher Rundfunk).

Menge, Marlies. "Zeugen des Jahrhunderts" (television documentary broadcast by ZDF Fernsehen, April 1993).

Schaaf, Stefan. "Exil in Mexico: Deutsche Künstler gegen Hitler" (radio documentary program broadcast by station RIAS Berlin, February 16, 1993).

**John Haag**, Professor of History, University of Georgia, Athens, Georgia

# Spiridonova, Maria (1884–1941)

*Political assassin who was a hero to the Russian peasantry and a leader of an abortive coup against the fledgling Bolshevik government in 1918. Name variations: Mariya Spiridovna or Spiridinova. Born Maria Alexandrovna Spiridonova on October 16, 1884, in the town of Tambov, Russia; shot to death by Soviet secret police in September 1941 in the Ural town of Orel; daughter of Alexander Alexandrovich (a provincial civil servant of modest means) and Alexandra Yakovlevna; never married; no children.*

*Shot a government official at the behest of the Russian Socialist Revolutionary Party (SRs, 1906); jailed until the country's political prisoners were amnestied (1917); became a leading figure of the leftist faction of the SRs, the LSRs, who first supported, then opposed the Bolshevik-led Soviet government; organized the assassination of the German ambassador to Russia, which almost resulted in the overthrow of the Bolsheviks (1918); most of the rest of her life spent in exile or in jail; shot by the Soviet police (1941).*

Maria Spiridonova was one in a series of women of late 19th- and early 20th-century Russia who devoted themselves to the revolutionary cause with a martyr-like fervor. She served as an unwavering leader for the Russian socialist movement; for her devotion, she faced the wrath of both tsarist and Soviet governments, and spent the vast majority of her adult life in captivity.

Maria Spiridonova was born in 1884, the second of four children. She entered school at the age of 11, but was forced to leave 7 years later due to poor health and "household circumstances." For a short while, she was an office worker for the provincial government.

The Russia of Spiridonova's youth was undergoing massive social and economic upheavals. Unfortunately, the country's leader, Tsar Nicholas II, was both weak and despotic—a dangerous combination—and proved unable to cope with the challenges Russia faced. In January 1905, the tensions came to a head when thousands of men and women marched on the Tsar's Winter Palace in the capital, St. Petersburg, demanding better working conditions. When the guards were unable to turn the crowd away, they panicked and began firing indiscriminately, killing hundreds. Bloody Sunday, as it has become known, sparked a year of upheavals that culminated in a series of general strikes in the fall. On October 17, 1905, the government was forced to grant Russia's first constitution—the October Manifesto.

The revolutionary tenor of the period was not confined to the capital. Strikes and demonstrations were shaking the peace of the provincial regions as well, including Maria's hometown of Tambov. On March 24, 1905, she was arrested at a youth demonstration, held in police custody for a short while, then released.

Spiridonova had been politically active since her school days, when she joined the Socialist Revolutionary Party (SRs), heirs to the populist peasant parties of the 1860s and 1870s. The SRs believed that Russia's only hope for change lay in a socialist revolution based in the countryside. SR party members also inherited some of their predecessors' penchant for terrorist acts as a way of forcing political and social action from recalcitrant governments.

The party in Tambov was outraged at the brutal quashing of peasant uprisings in their region during the 1905 revolutionary upheavals; they decided to pass a death sentence on one of the officials who led the government reprisals— General Luzhenovsky. Spiridonova volunteered to perform the assassination herself. After tracking him for days, she shot and killed him at the Borissoglebsk train station on January 16, 1906. She made no effort to escape from Luzhenovsky's Cossack guards who quickly surrounded her and beat her until she was close to death. While in custody, she was tortured and developed tuberculosis as a result of her treatment; her health remained frail for the rest of her life.

Spiridonova was put on trial in March, found guilty, and sentenced to hang. Her sentence sparked an outcry from leftists both at home and abroad, and was eventually commuted to life imprisonment. The next 11 years were spent in a series of tsarist prisons. The conditions varied, but in all the institutions the "politicals" were housed together and formed bonds of friendship and loyalty that were to last for the rest of their lives. As well, their commitment to socialism remained firm; if anything, it grew stronger while in captivity.

In March 1917, the centuries-old Romanov dynasty was overthrown and replaced by a liberal Provisional Government. One of its first acts was to order the release of all political prisoners held in tsarist jails. Once freed, Spiridonova stayed in the Far East for a few months where she was elected mayor of the town of Chita. She remained devoted to the socialist cause, however, and soon returned to the capital where she teamed up once again with her comrades in the SRs.

The situation in Petrograd, as St. Petersburg was then known, was chaotic. At the time of the establishment of the Provisional Government, a second governing body was also formed, consisting of a series of soviets (councils) representing workers, peasants and soldiers. Many socialist parties were represented, including the SRs and their main Marxist rivals, the urban-based Bolsheviks, led by Vladimir Ilyich Lenin.

One of the main issues facing Russia's leaders was the country's participation in World War I. Although the war was draining the country's resources, the Provisional Government felt that it would be best for Russia to continue to support her allies, the British and the French. The SRs and the Bolsheviks opposed this strategy, and argued that Russia should leave the war immediately. The SRs themselves were not completely certain on this issue, and in May the party split unofficially over their war policy. The so-called Right faction argued that Russia should remain in the war, while the Left SRs (LSRs) argued that they should quit fighting at once.

When Maria arrived in Petrograd, she sided with the LSRs, though she fought for months to keep the party together. Partially by virtue of her great popularity and perceived moral force as Luzhenovsky's assassin, she rose to become one of the leaders of the faction, as well as the editor

Maria Spiridonova

of the LSR journal *Our Way*. She spent much of the summer spreading revolutionary propaganda among the masses.

Throughout 1917, the LSRs and the Bolsheviks grew closer together as both parties believed that it was impossible to work with the new liberal leadership. When the Bolsheviks instigated a revolt against the Provisional Government in November, the LSRs supported them, though they did not provide any substantial assistance.

The LSRs were invited to work with the Bolsheviks following the Revolution, and the first Soviet government had 11 Bolshevik and 7 LSR commissars. Spiridonova was not appointed a commissar, but remained outside the government, speaking at workers' gatherings, attending party and soviet meetings and working on the party journal.

*Of all the opponents of the Bolsheviki I had met, Maria Spiridonova impressed me as one of the most sincere, well-poised and convincing.*

—*Emma Goldman

At approximately the same time, the split within the SRs became irreparable, and the LSRs held their first official Party Congress in November. Spiridonova's speech at the gathering, as recalled by her biographer and colleague Isaac Steinberg, summarizes the position of the LSRs in Russian politics, and helps underscore her own particular role as well: "[L]et us bear in mind the high moral principle on which [the party] was built up. . . . It is the duty of us LSRs . . . to cleanse the moral atmosphere. . . . What we are striving for is the ennoblement of the human personality in this material struggle." She also revealed her ambivalence to the Bolsheviks: "Large masses stand behind the Bolsheviks today, but that is a temporary phenomenon . . . because Bolshevism has no inner inspiration."

The LSRs worked with the Bolshevik government for a number of months and their role at this time was ambiguous. When the Bolsheviks dissolved the popularly elected Constituent Assembly in January 1918 after they failed to receive a majority of the vote, the LSRs supported them; a number of their members were also involved in the new government's notorious secret police, the Cheka. At the same time, LSRs members urged the Bolsheviks not to impose the death penalty, and did make some attempt to restrain the excesses of the Cheka. They also lobbied tirelessly on behalf of the Russian peasantry.

In any event, the Bolshevik/LSR coalition broke down quickly. The Bolsheviks, who had hoped they could simply walk away from the war, found themselves forced to negotiate with Germany for a peace treaty. Spiridonova and the LSRs virulently opposed such negotiations, and urged the Bolsheviks to break off talks with Germany. Lenin was not convinced, and the Soviets and Germans signed a peace treaty on March 3, 1918—the Treaty of Brest-Litovsk. The LSRs left the government in protest, though they did not resign from the Soviets, and therefore managed to retain some leverage over the Bolsheviks.

Perhaps the final blow was the government's emergency food policy. In the face of growing civil unrest and food shortages, the government began seizing grain from the peasantry to feed the workers in the cities. Lenin declared that the government was initiating a "war against the *kulak*" (rich peasant), although many of the poorer peasants also lost their grain in the requisitioning. As champions of the peasantry, the LSRs were strongly opposed to such heavy-handed tactics.

Despite the differences between the parties, Spiridonova tried to keep the coalition together for as long as possible. However, by June, she had become convinced that working with the Bolsheviks was no longer possible. She and the other LSR leaders then decided to take action to express their displeasure both with the Bolsheviks in general and their relations with Germany in particular. In the terrorist tradition of the party, Spiridonova organized the assassination of the German ambassador to Russia, Count Wilhelm von Mirbach, in the hopes that it would spark a revolutionary war with Germany.

On July 4, at the All-Russian Congress of Soviets, a series of LSRs members took the floor and loudly criticized the Bolsheviks. Spiridonova herself spoke that day and the next, trying to convince the Bolsheviks to change their policies. She accused the Bolsheviks of betraying the cause of the peasantry, and of being more interested in abstract theories than in the needs of the poor. The Bolsheviks were unmoved.

Consequently, on July 6, two members of the LSRs entered the German embassy in Petrograd and shot the ambassador. In the chaotic hours following the assassination, the LSRs seized the Cheka headquarters, and held its head, Felix Dzherzhinsky, hostage. However, they did not press their advantage, and the Bolsheviks counterattacked the following day, retook the Cheka headquarters and arrested many leaders of the LSRs, including Spiridonova.

At her trial, Spiridonova took full responsibility for organizing the assassination of Mirbach, although in her testimony she denied that there had been any plans to overthrow the Bolshevik government:

> I organized the assassination of Mirbach from beginning to end. . . . [T]he Central Committee never mentioned the overthrow of the Bolshevik Government. What happened was merely a result of the excitement with which the Russian Government rushed to the defense of the assassinated agents of German imperialism, and of an attempt at self-defense on the part of the Central Committee of the party which carried out the assassination.

Whatever the intentions of the LSRs, the Soviets came closer to being toppled in July 1918 than they ever had before or would be again for decades.

Spiridonova was tried on November 27 and sentenced to a year in prison. Others on the LSR Central Committee received sentences of three years, which might illustrate that the Bolsheviks were aware of her immense popularity with the Russian people. Grigorii Zinoviev, a leading Bolshevik at the time, called her a "wonderful woman" with a "heart of gold" whose imprisonment kept him awake at night.

After her release from prison, Spiridonova immediately entered the Russian underground and went to meetings with workers, peasants and soldiers, trying to provide the people with a socialist alternative to the Bolsheviks. She was rearrested on February 18, 1920, in a countrywide sweep aimed at the LSRs and sentenced to a year in a mental sanatorium. She escaped and returned to the underground, only to be arrested one final time on October 26, 1920. The rest of her life was spent in a variety of prison establishments, hospitals and remote exile towns.

In 1937, at the height of Stalin's murderous purges, Spiridonova was seized from her place of internal exile, the Ural town of Ufa, and, along with 12 other former LSRs members, accused of plots against the Bashkir Communist leadership. While they were held on these charges, however, the entire Bashkir government itself was arrested, so charges of plots against Stalin and Politburo member Klementi Voroshilov were substituted. On December 25, 1937, she was sentenced to 25 years in prison, and sent to Orel to serve her time. In September 1941, as the Germans advanced on their position, the prisoners at Orel, including Maria Spiridonova, were murdered by Soviet forces.

**SOURCES:**

Bezberezhev, S.V. "Maria Alexandrovna Spiridonova," in *Voprosy istorii.* No. 9, 1990.

Bunyan, James, ed. *Intervention, Civil War and Communism in Russia, April–December 1918: Documents and Materials.* Baltimore, MD: Johns Hopkins Press, 1936.

Conquest, Robert. *The Great Terror: A Reassessment.* Oxford: Oxford University Press, 1990.

Debo, Richard. *Revolution and Survival: The Foreign Policy of Soviet Russia, 1917–1918.* Toronto: Toronto University Press, 1979.

Goldman, Emma. *My Disillusionment in Russia.* NY: Thomas Y. Crowell, 1970.

Pipes, Richard. *The Russian Revolution.* NY: Alfred A. Knopf, 1991.

Schapiro, Leonard. *The Origin of the Communist Autocracy: Political Opposition in the Soviet State, First Phase, 1917–1922.* Cambridge, MA: Harvard University Press, 1966.

Steinberg, Isaac. *Spiridonova: Revolutionary Terrorist.* London: Methuen, 1935.

Ulam, Adam. *The Bolsheviks: The Intellectual and Political History of the Triumph of Communism in Russia.* NY: Collier, 1965.

**Susan Brazier**, freelance writer, Ottawa, Ontario, Canada

# Spivey, Victoria (1906–1976)

*African-American blues singer and songwriter whose performances set the pattern for singers today. Name variations: Victoria Regina Spivey; Vicky Spivey; Queen Victoria; occasionally recorded as Jane Lucas. Born on October 15, 1906, in Houston, Texas; died on October 3, 1976, in New York City; daughter of Grant Spivey (a musician) and Addie (Smith) Spivey (a nurse); married Reuben Floyd, in 1928 (divorced c. early 1930s); married William Adams (a dancer), in the mid-1930s (marriage ended c. 1951); married twice more.*

*Selected discography:* Woman Blues *(Bluesville, 1054);* The Blues is Life *(Folkways, FS 3541);* Basket of Blues *(Spivey, 1001);* Victoria and Her Blues *(Spivey, 1002);* Three Kings and the Queen *(Spivey, 1004);* The Queen and Her Knights *(Spivey, 1006);* Three Kings and the Queen, Vol. 3 *(Spivey, 1014);* Victoria Spivey's Recorded Legacy of the Blues, 1927–37 *(Spivey, 2001).*

One of eight children, Victoria Spivey was born in Houston, Texas, in 1906. Both her father Grant Spivey, a musician who had a string band with several of her brothers, and her mother **Addie Smith Spivey**, a nurse and amateur singer, were the children of ex-slaves. Growing up in a household filled with music, Vicky learned to play the piano as a child and often entertained at parties to make extra money. After her father was killed in an accident, these jobs became important for the family's economic survival, and while still in her early teens she and a brother played in local bordellos and music halls. In the 1920s, as the blues craze swept the country, she began working at clubs in Houston and Dallas, where she also heard such performers as *Ma Rainey, *Mamie Smith, and *Ida Cox. Another important influence in these years was bluesman Blind Lemon Jefferson, with whom she frequently performed at house parties and picnics.

Spivey then moved on to St. Louis, where in 1926 she made her first recording for the local Okeh label. "Black Snake Blues" was a hit that later became a classic, and within two years she had recorded about 38 songs for Okeh, including such hits as "Spider Web Blues," "Dirty Woman Blues," and "TB Blues." Written while she was working for the Saint Louis Music Company and recorded in 1927, "TB Blues" reflected the huge increase of tuberculosis among African-Americans in the era (as well as the popular belief that the disease was divine punishment for immoral behavior) and was one of Spivey's most well-known songs from the '20s. Many of her songs were characterized by double entendres,

*Victoria Spivey*

sly sexual references, even rollicking obscenities, while others were bitterly honest descriptions of hard lives, all sung in a somewhat nasal voice and employing what she called her "tiger moan." Jim O'Neal described her music in *Rolling Stone* as "grim tales of death, despair, cruelty, and agony, underscored by her somber piano and stark Texas blues moans." Spivey also performed in revues, including 1927's *Hits and Bits from Africana*; a fellow performer in that show was *Jackie Mabley, who would later become famous as "Moms" Mabley. As well, she performed on occasion with her sisters Addie "Sweet Pea" Spivey, Elton "Za-Zu" Spivey, and Leona Spivey.

Spivey moved to Chicago in 1930, and although the national enthusiasm for blues began to wane as the Depression took hold and swing began its rise, she continued to work regularly. She performed with such musicians as Sonny Boy Williamson, Memphis Minnie (*Lizzie Douglas), and Big Bill Broonzy in Chicago, and starred in the revue *Tan Town Topics 1933* on tour in Texas and Oklahoma. With her second husband Bill Adams, a dancer, she also appeared in the revue *Hellzapoppin*. Spivey worked colleges, dances, pavilions, and radio remotes throughout the Midwest and Southwest, as well as in vaudeville theaters and the Apollo Theater in New York City, and recorded with the Decca and Vocalion labels (sometimes using the name Jane Lucas). In the mid-1930s, she toured with Louis Armstrong. While many blues artists had faded into obscurity by then, Spivey continued performing throughout the 1940s. She retired from the stage only in 1952, when she became an organist for a church in Brooklyn.

During the late 1950s and '60s, younger white artists and audiences rediscovered the blues. Spivey was soon performing in the newly popular blues festivals and in clubs in New York City. She also set up her own recording company, Spivey, reissuing a number of her own albums and reintroducing such singers as *Alberta Hunter, *Lucille Hegamin, and Hannah Sylvester from career oblivion. Among the other artists who recorded on the Spivey label were Luther Johnson, Lucille Spann, Olive Brown, Sugar Blue, Memphis Slim, Big Joe Williams, and a young Bob Dylan (who also played on a few of her albums). A legend by the 1970s, Spivey appeared in the 1974 concert "Philadelphia Folk Festival," broadcast on PBS. She also performed on the BBC program "The Devil's Music—A History of the Blues" in 1976. Spivey died of an internal hemorrhage later that year in New York City.

SOURCES:

Harris, Sheldon. *Blues Who's Who: A Biographical Dictionary of Blues Singers.* New Rochelle, NY: Random House, 1987.

Smith, Jessie Carney, ed. *Notable Black American Women.* Detroit, MI: Gale Research, 1992.

# Spofford, Harriet Prescott

## (1835–1921)

*American author. Name variations: Harriet Elizabeth Spofford. Born Harriet Elizabeth Prescott on April 3, 1835, in Calais, Maine; died of arteriosclerosis on August 14, 1921, on Deer Island, in Amesbury, Massachusetts; daughter of Joseph Newmarch Prescott (an attorney and lumber merchant) and Sarah Jane (Bridges) Prescott; educated at schools in Newburyport, Massachusetts; attended the Pinkerton Academy, Derry, New Hampshire; married Richard S. Spofford, in 1865 (died 1888); children: one son, Richard (b. 1867, died in infancy).*

*Selected writings:* Sir Rohan's Ghost *(1860);* The Amber Gods *(1863);* Azarian: An Episode *(1864);* New England Legends *(1871);* Art Decoration Applied to Furniture *(1878);* The Servant Girl Question *(1881);* Poems *(1882);* Hester Stanley at Saint Marks *(1883);* Ballads about Authors *(1887);* A Scarlet Poppy, and Other Stories *(1894);* In Titian's Garden *(1897);* Old Madame, and Other Tragedies *(1900);* The Children of the Valley *(1901);* The Great Procession *(1902);* Old Washington *(1906);* The Fairy Changeling *(1910);* The Making of a Fortune *(1911);* A Little Book of Friends *(1916);* The Elder's People *(1920).*

Of English ancestry, Harriet Prescott Spofford was born in Calais, Maine, in 1835, the daughter of Joseph Prescott and **Sarah Bridges Prescott**. As a young teen, she and her four siblings suddenly found themselves fatherless after Joseph abandoned the family to head west in an attempt to rebuild the fortune lost by his father during the War of 1812. The family moved to Newburyport, Massachusetts, to make a new home near relatives. Here Spofford received her education, with two years spent at the Pinkerton Academy in Derry, New Hampshire.

Spofford first began to take her writing seriously at the age of 16, when an essay she wrote on the insanity of the title character in William Shakespeare's *Hamlet* won a contest she had entered. Encouraged, she began submitting short stories to Boston newspapers and weekly magazines as a way of stabilizing her family's tenuous financial state. Her new source of income was offset by the return of her father, in poor health

and impoverished, providing Spofford with an incentive to produce as much saleable writing as possible. A prolific and inventive writer who was praised for her insights into the workings of the human conscience and her love of nature, she was soon producing quantities of writing—everything from short stories and poetry to children's books, travelogues, and novels—setting a pace that would not falter throughout a career that spanned six decades.

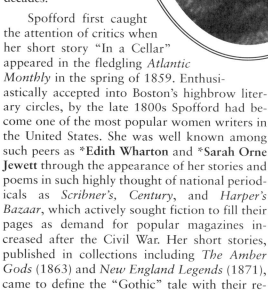

Harriet Spofford

Spofford first caught the attention of critics when her short story "In a Cellar" appeared in the fledgling *Atlantic Monthly* in the spring of 1859. Enthusiastically accepted into Boston's highbrow literary circles, by the late 1800s Spofford had become one of the most popular women writers in the United States. She was well known among such peers as *Edith Wharton and *Sarah Orne Jewett through the appearance of her stories and poems in such highly thought of national periodicals as *Scribner's, Century,* and *Harper's Bazaar,* which actively sought fiction to fill their pages as demand for popular magazines increased after the Civil War. Her short stories, published in collections including *The Amber Gods* (1863) and *New England Legends* (1871), came to define the "Gothic" tale with their reliance upon legend, mystery, and elements of mysticism and the supernatural.

In addition to her short-story collections, such as *A Scarlet Poppy, and Other Stories* (1894) and *Old Madame, and Other Tragedies* (1900), Spofford also produced the poetry collections *In Titian's Gardens* (1897), a highly praised critique of *Charlotte Brontë published as the introduction to the 1898 edition of Brontë's *Jane Eyre,* children's books that included *The Fairy Changeling* (1910), and the essay collection *A Little Book of Friends* (1916), as well as a number of novels. Her first full-length work of fiction, the anonymously published *Sir Rohan's Ghost* (1860), preceded her marriage to attorney Richard Spofford, with whom she eventually built a house in Amesbury, Massachusetts, large enough for her to entertain the literary women friends with whom she joined in rejecting the naturalism of novelist Henry James. While critical estimation of Spofford's works declined as her productivity increased in the latter decades of the 1800s, by 1900 she had turned to the familiar subject of her native New England, and her story collection *The Elder's People* (1920) did much to reclaim her literary reputation. Arteriosclerosis resulted in her death in her home on August 14, 1921.

**SOURCES:**

Buck, Claire, ed. *The Bloomsbury Guide to Women's Literature.* NY: Prentice Hall, 1992.

James, Edward T., ed. *Notable American Women, 1607–1950.* Cambridge, MA: The Belknap Press of Harvard University, 1971.

McHenry, Robert, ed. *Famous American Women.* NY: Dover, 1980.

**Pamela Shelton**, freelance writer, Avon, Connecticut

## Spotswood, Claire Myers

(1896–1983).

*See Owens, Claire Myers.*

# Spottiswoode, Alicia Ann

(1810–1900)

*Scottish poet and composer. Name variations: Lady John Scott; Alicia Ann Spottiswood. Born Alicia Ann Spottiswoode (or Spottiswood) at Lauder in Berwickshire, in 1810; died on March 13, 1900; married Lord John Scott (son of the duke of Buccleugh), in 1836 (died 1860).*

Under the name Lady John Scott, composer Alicia Ann Spottiswoode wrote the words and music for many popular Scotch songs of the 19th century. These titles include "Douglas Tender and True," "Durisdeer," "The Comin' o' the Spring," "Ettrick," and the popular "Annie Laurie."

**Catherine Dybiec Holm**, M.S., Cook, Minnesota

# Sprague, Kate Chase (1840–1899)

*American socialite. Name variations: Catherine Jane Chase; Kate Chase. Born Catherine Jane Chase on August 13, 1840, in Cincinnati, Ohio; died of a liver and kidney ailment on July 31, 1899, near Washington, D.C.; daughter of Salmon Portland Chase (a politician) and Eliza Ann (Smith) Chase; educated at Henrietta B. Haines' finishing school, New York City; studied music and languages at Lewis Heyl's seminary; married William Sprague (a politician), in 1863 (divorced 1882); children: William Sprague (b. 1865);*

*Ethel Sprague (b. 1869); Portia Sprague (b. 1872); Kitty Sprague (b. 1873).*

Born Catherine Jane Chase in 1840 in Cincinnati, Ohio, into a wealthy family, Kate Sprague was the only child of Salmon P. Chase and his second wife **Eliza Smith Chase**. His first wife, Kate's namesake, had died in childbirth. Then, Eliza died when Kate was five. Eighteen months later, she had a stepmother, then a half-sister born in 1847. Despite these upheavals, Kate enjoyed a privileged childhood and began to receive a great deal of attention from her widower father when her stepmother died in 1852. A U.S. senator since 1849, Salmon won the governorship of his home state of Ohio in 1855 and had aspirations of running for the presidency. Kate returned his devotion by leaving her finishing school at age 15 to become his official hostess. She transformed the family house into a social gathering place by redecorating, purchasing expensive furniture, and outfitting herself with a wardrobe suitable for a society hostess. She gave lavish, well-attended parties, drawing up guest lists with an eye to furthering her father's ambitions.

While Chase was unsuccessful in his bid to win his party's presidential nomination, in 1860 he was appointed secretary of the treasury under President Abraham Lincoln. The family moved to Washington, D.C., where Kate once again transformed their new home into a social gathering place. At 21 years of age, she was considered among the city's most prominent hostesses, as well as one of the most eligible young ladies of the area. In 1862, she caught the eye of William Sprague, a Rhode Island industrialist running for senator of his state. He was elected senator in 1863, the same year the couple married. President Lincoln and most of Washington society attended the Chase-Sprague wedding. The couple returned from their honeymoon to make their home with Kate Sprague's father, for whom Sprague continued to act as hostess.

Unfortunately, the marriage proved to be extremely unhappy, due in part to William's profligate ways and to Kate's disillusionment regarding her new husband's stature in political society. Sprague had been under the impression that her husband's position as former governor of the state of Rhode Island and his senatorial rank indicated he was well connected politically and socially, and was shocked to discover that Rhode Island's bluebloods and his peers in the Senate considered him to be an inferior man who had bought his way into politics. The couple quickly became the subject of gossip when Sprague went alone to Europe three years after their marriage to escape her husband's philandering and bouts of heavy drinking. Despite her father's attempts to reconcile the couple, and Sprague's efforts to find some solace by outfitting their lavish summer home at Narragansett Pier, Rhode Island, and promoting Salmon Chase's political career, life took a turn for the worse. After two more failed bids for the Democratic presidential nomination—in 1864 and 1868—Chase retired from his position as chief justice of the Supreme Court, dying in 1873. After her father's death, Sprague had no one to help her cope with her situation and took a lover, New York senator Roscoe Conkling. A national scandal ensued after Conkling was driven from her home at gunpoint by William Sprague, who had unexpectedly returned from a trip abroad to find the couple together. No longer able to show her face in the social circles that had once revered her, Sprague went to Europe, then moved to her father's home near the nation's capital; she and William were divorced in 1882.

Kate Sprague's remaining years read like a Victorian novel. Secluded in her father's home as her family wealth diminished, and becoming increasingly reclusive, she attempted to retain her luxurious lifestyle by selling off the house's furnishings. Her son committed suicide and two of her daughters left her for distant regions of the country, leaving the youngest, Kitty, who was mentally impaired, in the care of her mother. Once the family inheritance was gone, Sprague was forced to sell chickens, eggs, and dairy products door to door in the city where she had once reigned supreme as a leader of society. In 1896, several friends of her father formed a trust fund, which supported her until her death from a liver and kidney ailment three years later.

**SOURCES:**

James, Edward T., ed. *Notable American Women, 1607–1950.* Cambridge, MA: The Belknap Press of Harvard University, 1971.

**SUGGESTED READING:**

*American Heritage.* August 1956, p. 41.

**Pamela Shelton**, freelance writer,
Avon, Connecticut

# Spray of Pearls (d. 1259).

*See Shajar al-Durr.*

# Springfield, Dusty (1939–1998)

*British-born pop singer. Born Mary Isobel Catherine Bernadette O'Brien in Hampstead, England, on April 16, 1939; died of breast cancer on March 2, 1999, in Henley-on-Thames, England; sister of Tom O'Brien (a musician); never married; no children.*

*Began performing in a girl group called The Lana Sisters (1958), then joined her brother and a friend to form a group called The Springfields (1960), their release of "Silver Threads and Golden Needles" becoming an international bestseller; released first record as a solo performer, "I Only Want to Be with You" (1963) and followed it with a string of successful, folk-rock singles that brought her to the #1 position on the British charts with her hit recording of "You Don't Have to Say You Love Me" (1966); saw her career slip (1970s–1980s), but returned to the charts (late 1980s) through recording of "Do I Deserve This?" with the Pet Shop Boys; seemed destined for rediscovery, but was diagnosed with breast cancer (mid-1990s); was inducted into the Rock and Roll Hall of Fame (1998) and, just weeks before her death, was awarded the Order of the British Empire.*

When she was 16, Mary Isobel Catherine Bernadette O'Brien did an amazing thing. She was at the time a shy, plump, red-headed schoolgirl from a respectable middle-class family in suburban London, nicknamed "Dusty" for her love of playing football in the streets with her brother and his friends. But within a matter of weeks, she had transformed herself into a fetching blonde who would, during the 1960s, become the "Queen of the Mods" among young Brits infatuated with Carnaby Street, Nehru jackets, and the Beatles. "I made a conscious decision to change my appearance," Springfield once said of her transformation. "I must have hated myself so much. I realized there was a whole world out there and I wanted to be part of it." It would not be the last time she would reinvent herself during a lifetime in the mercurial world of the music industry.

Music had been a part of her life from early on. Her father, an income tax consultant, indulged an eclectic taste in music that easily encompassed Beethoven and *Ella Fitzgerald; while her Irish Catholic mother's fondness for the ballads and laments of the Old Country provided an early folk influence. Her older brother Tom, meanwhile, was a fan of jazz and Latin-American music. "I was torn between jazz and Aaron Copland," Springfield said. "My parents made me listen, without me realizing it, to all sorts of music." Her own early passion was for blues, but her first amateur performances as a teenager during the 1950s in small London clubs favored folk and selections from her brother's collection of Latin-American songs. She made her professional debut in 1958 singing as part of an all-girl trio called The Lana Sisters, a job she had found by answering a notice in a magazine. The Lana Sisters were one of many girl groups like the more successful Kaye Sisters and The Mudlarks known for novelty songs like "Seven Little Girls Sitting on a Back Seat." The Lana Sisters recorded a few such numbers and sang them on television shows that were the British equivalent of "American Bandstand," but Dusty eventually decided that wearing a blue tulle skirt or silver lamé pants was not her style. Her time as a Lana Sister proved educational, however, for she carefully studied lighting setups, microphone and stage technique and television staging; and by the time her brother Tom invited her to join a group he was forming, she was the only member of the new trio with any show-business knowledge.

Nevertheless, The Springfields—as Tom O'Brien called the folk group he created in 1960 with Dusty and a guitar-playing friend—became an international sensation with their release of "Silver Threads and Golden Needles," a folk-rock tune in which Dusty's voice held sway in harmony with the two men. Although it was never released in Britain, the song was a huge hit in the United States, where folk music was undergoing a renaissance. The Springfields were "absolutely cheerful as hell," Dusty once recalled. "In actual fact, we weren't, but we appeared to be and we didn't sing very in tune but we sang quite loudly and there was a niche for us at that time." The Springfields enjoyed considerable success during their two years together, but failed to survive when Dusty's yearning for a solo career proved too strong to resist, and she left the group in 1963 to record her first solo hit, "I Only Want to Be with You." It marked the beginning of an astonishing climb up the British charts with a string of hits that included "I Just Don't Know What to Do with Myself," "Stay Awhile" and "Little by Little." She gained a reputation for an uncanny eye for the right material and for working closely with producers and arrangers to create a sound all her own. "Her songs hinted at unspoken, desperate truths about sexuality that weren't there for discussion by little boys," one critic observed, taking note of her husky voice with its overtones of American soul. It was a comparison that pleased Springfield, who had been deeply impressed by black artists like *Dionne Warwick during a United States tour in 1962. "I have a definite and deep affinity with black musicians," she said at the time. "They put much more expression and feeling into their music than whites. I like to think that I do, too." She was also impressed with American record producer Phil Spector's "wall of sound" approach to orchestration, supporting such artists as The Ronettes, The Crystals and **Darlene Love** with a full complement of percussion, brass and strings at a time when most British groups were lucky to have an unamplified standup bass and a piano for their studio arrangements. In England, Springfield's demands on her musicians soon led to a reputation for being difficult to work with. "They'd never heard this stuff before," Dusty said. "I'm asking somebody with a standup bass to play Motown bass lines, and it was a shock."

But her innovations paid off. It took her only three years to reach the #1 spot on the British charts in 1966 with "You Don't Have to Say You Love Me," an emotional ballad about a woman's loneliness that Springfield delivered with melodramatic power. Despite her tendency toward American idioms, Dusty had first heard the song at the San Remo music festival, sung in Italian, and by a man. "I just knew that when the audience stood up in the middle of the instrumental and applauded that this was obviously the right song to do," she said of the number's attraction for her. "I just knew it was time for a big, Italian-type ballad and it was such a strong, strong tune." Backed by a lush string arrangement that built to an impressive crescendo by song's end, Springfield sang the English lyrics written for her with a poignancy and boldness unusual for a "girl singer" of the time. Her ascension to the reigning icon of Mod London was assured when she delivered the song live on Britain's wildly popular television music show "Ready, Steady, Go!," wearing a mini-skirt and knee boots and adorned with dark mascara, pale lipstick, and the bee-hive bouffant that started a fashion craze. As further proof of her influence, Springfield was named Best Female Vocalist in Britain's prestigious *New Musical Express* awards in a near consecutive run from 1964 to 1969, missing the honor only in 1968.

Almost as famous as the "Dusty Springfield sound" and the "Dusty Springfield look" was the "Dusty Springfield party," at any number of clubs and restaurants, with its trademark food fight. Springfield would use the slightest provocation—a rude waiter, a patronizing recording executive, a superior attitude from a fellow artist—to hurl whatever delicacy was at hand. "It was usually just a *vol-au-vent*," Dusty protested years later, "but it inevitably missed and hit someone else, which set everyone off. What I liked was the chaos it caused; the way things came out of people who were really quite prim." More serious notoriety came from Springfield's refusal to play to segregated audiences in South Africa during a 1964 tour, for which she was banished from the country and

<br />Dusty
<br />Springfield

her records whisked off the record-store shelves and destroyed. Although she was ostracized by older members of the British music business for the repercussions her protest caused for other artists, it only increased her popularity among younger audiences and led to her own BBC tele-

vision show in the late 1960s with an eclectic mix of guests that included *Tina Turner, Jimi Hendrix, and even Woody Allen.

Springfield's popularity in the United States rode the wave of the so-called "British invasion" of American pop, led by the Beatles and the Rolling Stones. Her first hit single, "I Only Want to Be with You," rose to the Top 20 on the American charts in 1963; "Wishin' and Hopin'" followed the next year, reaching the Top 10; and "You Don't Have to Say You Love Me" hit #4 two years later. But her American popularity was more than just chart numbers for Springfield, for she soon gained a reputation among American soul and rhythm and blues artists as an enthusiastic champion in Britain of Berry Gordy's "Motown Sound." She even promoted and hosted a BBC television special, "The Sound of Motown," introducing such acts as *Martha Reeves and The Vandellas, *The Supremes, The Ronettes, and The Temptations to English audiences. During her American tours, Springfield would often include appearances at traditionally black venues as part of a Motown tour. "I mostly hung out with the Ronettes . . . and shared a dressing room with them," Dusty once recalled. "It was, like, a hundred and four degrees in this very, very small dressing room and all our beehives were in there—three black beehives and one white one. It was collisions constantly."

*It* would have been easy to go the diva route, but there's no substance and it bores me.

—Dusty Springfield

Initially, her attachment to rhythm and blues helped Springfield survive the music industry's transition by the late 1960s to a harder-edged variety of rock music, away from the splashy colors and cheerful good fun of the previous decade. As her record sales in Britain began to slip for the first time in her career, she turned increasingly to America, signing with Atlantic Records to handle her career in the United States. The result was the album considered her best, *Dusty in Memphis*, produced and recorded in that legendary city in 1968. It was her first collection of songs in the spare "Memphis Sound" style successfully employed by black artists like **Aretha Franklin** and Percy Sledge, with its simple rhythm track and underplayed guitar lines. "I hated it at first," she later said of her experience with the album and the style. "I was someone who had come from thundering drums and Phil Spector, and I didn't understand sparseness. I didn't understand that the sparseness gave it an atmosphere." The album was a turning point for her, however. It failed to find a large audience but it saved Springfield from the variety house and cabaret circuit frequented by acts on the downward slopes of their careers. Dusty had found a new, more musically sophisticated audience, although a much smaller one than she had been used to. The trend

continued with her next album, 1969's *A Brand New Me*, in which she tried out a more melodic form of rhythm and blues centered in Philadelphia and known as "Philly Soul." Like *Dusty in Memphis*, the new album was only a modest commercial success, attracting the admiration of musical sophisticates and fellow musicians. It was, as one critic wrote, "after-hours music made by musicians for one another's sake."

*A Brand New Me* proved to be an ironic choice of title. The series of albums Dusty recorded during the 1970s was a jumble of musical styles that only confused the public and failed to find the consistent audience of her earlier years. Springfield later blamed the decline on her misplaced trust in her American managers. "After all, they had all managed the best people," she said. "I should have followed my intuition, though—my insides told me that it was wrong." Little more than ten years after taking Britain and America by storm, Springfield now found herself playing nightclubs and doing television shows in what she called her "Rent-a-Diva" period, but going nowhere professionally or musically. There followed a confused period of California living, a concept Dusty admitted had been influenced by the movies she had seen as a child in Hampstead. The reality proved otherwise. There were two more failed albums, followed by depression and alcohol and drug abuse. "California can be a dangerous place to come to alone. It's a very strange country in many ways. Out of sheer disenchantment, I was really anaesthetizing myself by taking too many tranquilizers and drinking too much. Somewhere—you never know where—I crossed the line from heavy drinking into problem drinking." Some years later, Springfield admitted she had entertained thoughts of suicide, but somehow pulled herself back. By 1978, she could tell a journalist that she had "grown up more last year than in the whole of the rest of my life put together" and offered her first album in several years as proof.

*It Begins Again* and 1979's "Living Without Your Love" were hardly commercial hits, but Dusty seemed invigorated by returning to the studio and by her first British tour in six years to promote *It Begins Again*. She delivered well-received performances at London's Drury Lane Theater and at the Royal Albert Hall and met the curiosity merited by her return from obscurity with aplomb, telling one press conference that the worst thing that could happen to her was not losing her professional standing but "to lose myself along the way, just as I nearly lost myself before trying to hang onto that part of me that is Mary O'Brien as opposed to that part of me that is Dusty Springfield." Her new self-confidence led her to explore other outlets for her music. There were several songs performed as part of film scores, notably "It Goes Like It Goes" for the Academy Award-winning *Norma Rae*; and, in a turnaround that caught the industry off-guard, her release in 1982 of the erotically charged disco album *White Heat*. It was, said *New Musical Express*, "a huge leap away from the relative security of the cabaret circuit into the dangerous currents of pop commercialism." Critics hailed the album as a triumphant comeback, although, once again, the record failed to catch on in record stores and, once again, it seemed as if Springfield's career was over.

But a second comeback lay in store when Dusty was approached in 1987 by the British techno-pop group the Pet Shop Boys, otherwise known as Neil Tennant and Chris Lowe, who wanted her to sing with them on "What Have I Done to Deserve This?," to be released as a single. "That was a watershed," said Springfield. "It just sort of plopped into my life and changed it." Tennant and Lowe, she discovered, had long been fans of the husky, sensual delivery of her Memphis and Philly soul albums of the '70s and had decided that "What Have I Done to Deserve This?" was a perfect vehicle. "What is it you want?" Springfield asked them when she arrived in a London studio in the fall of 1987 to begin work. "The sound of your voice," was the simple reply. To her amazement, the song rocketed to #2 on both the British and American charts. It was quickly followed by "Nothing Has Been Proved," written by Tennant and Lowe for the film *Scandal*, about Britain's John Profumo-**Christine Keeler** sex scandal of 1963, and released as a single and as a video, with Dusty appearing as an elegant nightclub singer. Finally, after nearly 20 years, it seemed Springfield was back in the commercial mainstream.

In 1990, she released her most successful album in 30 years, *Reputation*, produced by the Pet Shop Boys. The album's reflective lyrics touched on the impermanence of fame and the need for self-acceptance, using a variety of musical idioms from rap to Motown to ballad. The album was, as one critic said, "Dusty's songs of experience," but Springfield had no intention of making *Reputation* her swan song. By 1993, after moving back to Britain and receiving an offer of a new contract from Columbia, Dusty once again veered off in a new direction by asking that the planned new album be recorded in Nashville, where she had long ago recorded with The Springfields. *A Very Fine Love* (1995), although not a country album, drew on the impressive musical talent present in Nashville. "There are some

amazing musicians there," Springfield said after the album's release, "and though they're best known for playing country, their skills in the pop and R&B fields are equally well developed. They really enjoyed themselves on these tracks."

But the weeks working on the record were arduous ones, with Dusty frequently complaining of chest pains that obliged her to work in short bursts before fatigue took over. Returning to Britain when the album was completed, she was diagnosed with breast cancer and underwent a series of radiation treatments while the release of *A Very Fine Love* was delayed. "It was a bit dodgy for a time, but I came through it," Springfield told a reporter after she had learned her cancer was in remission. "I don't think this thing is going to get me." *A Very Fine Love* was finally released in June of 1995, earning only mediocre reviews and struggling to reach #43 on the British charts. It was, *Country Music* magazine complained, "warmed-over pop-soul" and a poor comparison to *Reputation* of five years earlier. By now, however, Dusty was immune to negative reviews. She pronounced herself pleased with *A Very Fine Love*, especially the album's last track, the honky-tonk blues number "Where Is a Woman to Go," sung by a lonely woman in "a little 'ole bar across town" facing up to the mistakes in her life. "It's very much a grown-up woman's song," Springfield said, "and it means a lot to me."

*A Very Fine Love* would prove to be her last album. Her breast cancer returned in 1996, forcing her to embark on a rigorous series of chemotherapy treatments. By early 1998, the rumors of Springfield's deteriorating condition were too prevalent to dismiss. "I am amazed at her courage," her manager told *USA Today*, "but she loves life and is not giving up yet." But by the time Dusty was awarded Britain's coveted Order of the British Empire (OBE), she was too weak to attend the ceremony at St. James's Palace in person. Only close friends knew that the cancer had by now spread to her bones and had become terminal. On March 2, 1999, ten days before she was to be inducted into the Rock 'n' Roll Hall of Fame, Dusty Springfield died peacefully at her home in Henley-on-Thames, just outside London. Over a thousand people crowded into the streets around the small Catholic church where Springfield's funeral was held on March 12, fans reaching out to touch the glass-enclosed carriage that carried her coffin. "Let youngsters like **Whitney Houston** and **Mariah Carey** sing with bravado," one writer said in eulogy of her. "Dusty Springfield, with a mere vocal wink, can still go places that aren't in the repertory of their imaginations."

Springfield once said that her great misfortune was her early success, and hinted at the challenge that lay before her during an interview in 1968, during those heady years as "Queen of the Mods." "I feel like two separate people," she said then. "When they announce me as Dusty Springfield, I stand backstage and think myself into her personality." In the end, she learned to accept both parts of herself, to give herself the love that millions of others had showered on her all her life.

**SOURCES:**
Hoerburger, Rob. "The Lives They Lived: Dusty Springfield," in *The New York Times Magazine*. January 2, 2000.
O'Brien, Lucy. *Dusty.* Rev. ed. London: Sidgewick & Jackson, 1999.

**Norman Powers**, writer-producer,
Chelsea Lane Productions,
New York, New York

# Spry, Constance (1886–1960)

*British floral designer. Born Constance Fletcher on December 5, 1886, in Derby, England; died on January 3, 1960; educated at Alexandra School and College, Dublin.*

*Began her career as a professional flower arranger (1920s); founded a school of floristry (1930s), followed by a cooking school and finishing school after World War II; served as an advisor on the decorations for numerous London weddings and galas, including the coronation of Queen Elizabeth II at Westminster Abbey (1953); lectured and published several books on flower arranging and cooking.*

The career of British designer Constance Spry, who was born in 1886 in England and raised in Ireland, in many ways prefigured that of U.S. designer **Martha Stewart** more than half a century later. During her years as head of the Woman's Staff at the Ministry of Aircraft Production during World War I, Spry first explored flower arranging as a curative for the depressing war-time atmosphere. She soon marketed her talent into a successful flower design shop, which she opened in London when she was in her 30s. Within ten years, her unique designs and savvy marketing abilities made her work so popular in London high society that she combined her love of arranging with her abilities as a teacher in founding a school of floral design during the 1930s. After World War II, Spry and several associates formed London's Cordon Bleu Cookery School, another successful venture that benefited from her expertise. Spry was active in the "Ideal Home" trends that took shape in Great Britain in the 1950s as a reaction to the devastation caused by decades of bombings and social disruption during two world wars. A finishing school for young ladies which she ran at Winkfield Place, Windsor, promoted home design and taught a variety of domestic skills to the future wives of England.

Well known not only for her teaching but as the author of 13 books on cooking and design, Spry was in demand as a lecturer and traveled throughout Great Britain, as well as to Australia, the United States, and Canada, promoting her ideas and designs. In 1953, she was honored by a request to serve as an advisor with regard to the floral decorations for the coronation of Queen *Elizabeth II at Westminster Abbey. An in-demand designer for London society, Spry continued to create settings for many royal weddings, social galas, and gatherings for the arts until her retirement. Through the Royal Gardeners' Orphan Fund, she also used her considerable influence to raise large sums of money to aid needy children throughout Great Britain.

**SOURCES:**
*Current Biography.* NY: H.W. Wilson, 1940.
Uglow, Jennifer, ed. *The International Dictionary of Women's Biography.* NY: Continuum, 1989.

**SUGGESTED READING:**
Coxhead, E. *Constance Spry,* 1975.

**Pamela Shelton**, freelance writer,
Avon, Connecticut

# Spurgeon, Caroline F.E. (1869–1942)

*English educator and authority on Chaucer and Shakespeare. Born Caroline Frances Eleanor Spurgeon in Punjab, India, in 1869; died on October 24, 1942; educated at Cheltenham College, England; Oxford University, B.A., 1899.*

Caroline F.E. Spurgeon was born in Punjab, India, in 1869. From 1901 to 1906, she was a lecturer at England's Bedford College for Women, and head of its English literature department from 1913 to 1929. From 1906 to 1913, she was a lecturer at the University of London, before becoming the first woman to hold a professorship (1913–29) there. While a visiting professor at Barnard College in New York City from 1920 to 1921, Spurgeon helped organize the International Federation of University Women and became its first president (1920–24). Her major writings include *Mysticism in English Literature* (1913), *Five Hundred Years of Chaucer Criticism and Allusion* (1920–25), *Keats's Shakespeare* (1928), and *Shakespeare's Imagery, and What It Tells Us* (1935). In 1939, ill health caused Spurgeon to move to Tucson, Arizona, where she died three years later.

**SOURCES:**
*The New York Times* (obituary). October 25, 1942, p. 44.

# Spyri, Johanna (1827–1901)

*Swiss author who changed the course of children's literature for Switzerland and the world with her book* Heidi. *Name variations: nicknamed "Hanni" and "Hanneli"; first name also spelled Joanna. Pronunciation: Spee-REE. Born Johanna Heusser on July 12, 1827, in Hirzel, Switzerland; died on July 7, 1901, in Zurich; daughter of Dr. Johann Jakob Heusser and Meta (Schweizer) Heusser; aunt of* **Emily Kempin Spyri** *(1853–1901, who was the first woman in Europe to earn a doctorate of law degree, though she was prohibited because of her gender from practicing law); married Bernhard Spyri, in 1852; children: one son, Bernhard Diethelm Spyri.*

*Selected writings:* Heidi *(1880, trans. from the German by Helen B. Dole and published as* Heidi: A Story for Children and Those That Love Children, *Ginn, 1899 [other editions illus. by* **\*Maginel Wright**, *Rand McNally, 1921;* **\*Jessie Willcox Smith**, *McKay, 1922; Gustaf Tenggren, Houghton, 1923; Dorothy Lake Gregory and Milo Winter, Rand McNally, 1925; Marguerite Davis, Ginn, 1927; Maud and Miska Petersham, Garden City, 1932; Hildegarde Woodward, Appleton-Century, 1935; Charles Mozley, F. Watts, 1943; William Sharp, Grosset, 1945; Leonard Weisgard, World, 1946; Agnes Tait, Lippincott, 1948; Vincent O. Cohen, Dutton, 1952; Jenny Thorne, Purnell, 1975; another edition with illustrations from the film starring Shirley Temple, Saalfield, 1937]);* Red-Letter Stories *(trans. from the German by Lucy Wheelock, Lothrop, 1884);* Rico and Wiseli *(trans. from the German by Louise Brooks, De Wolfe, Fiske, 1885);* Uncle Titus *(trans. from the German by L. Wheelock, Lothrop, 1886);* Grittli's Children *(trans. of* Gritlis Kinder *by L. Brooks, Cupples & Hurd, 1887);* In Safe Keeping *(trans. from the German by L. Wheelock, Blackie & Son, 1896);* Einer vom Hause Lesa *(F.A. Perthes, Gotha, Germany, 1898);* Schloss Wildenstein *(F.A. Perthes, 1900);* Aus dem Leben *(C.E. Mueller, Halle, Germany, 1902);* Dorris and Her Mountain Home *(trans. from the German by Mary E. Ireland, Presbyterian Committee, 1902);* Moni the Goat Boy, and Other Stories *(trans. of* Moni der Geissbub *by Edith F. King, Ginn, 1906);* Heimatlos *(trans. from the German by Emma Stetler Hopkins; illus. by Frederick Richardson, Ginn, 1912);* Chel: A Story of the Swiss Mountains *(trans. from the German by Helene H. Boll, Eaton & Mains, 1913);* The Rose Child *(trans. from the German by Helen B. Dole, Crowell, 1916);* What Sami Sings with the Birds *(trans. from the German by H.B. Dole, Crowell, 1917);* Little Miss Grasshopper *(trans. from the German by H.B. Dole, Crowell, 1918);* Little Curly Head: The Pet Lamb *(trans. of* Beim Weiden-Joseph *by H.B. Dole, Crowell, 1919, published as* The Pet Lamb, and Other Swiss Stories, *Dutton, 1956);* Cornelli *(trans. from the German by E.P. Stork; illus. by Maria L. Kirk, Lippincott, 1920);* Toni: The Little Wood-Carver *(trans. from the German by H.B. Dole, Crowell, 1920);* Erick and Sally *(trans. from the German by H.H. Boll, Beacon Press, 1921);* Maezli: A Story of the Swiss Valleys *(trans. from the German by E.P. Stork; illus. by M.L. Kirk, Lippincott, 1921);* Tiss: A Little Alpine Waif *(trans. from the German by H.B. Dole; illus. by George Carlson, Crowell, 1921);* Trini: The Little Strawberry Girl *(trans. from the German by H.B. Dole; illus. by G. Carlson, Crowell, 1922);* Jo: The Little Machinist *(trans. from the German by H.B. Dole, Crowell, 1923);* Vinzi: A Story of the Swiss Alps *(trans. from the German by E.P. Stork; illus. by M.L. Kirk, Lippincott, 1924);* Joerli: The Story of a Swiss Boy *(trans. of* Die Stauffermuehle *by Frances Treadway Clayton and Olga Wunderli, B.H. Sanborn, 1924;* The Little Alpine Musician *(trans. from the German by H.B. Dole, Crowell, 1924);* The New Year's Carol *(trans. from the German by Alice Howland Goodwin; illus. by Grace Edwards Wesson, Houghton, 1924);* Veronica and Other Friends *(trans. from the German by L. Brooks, Crowell, 1924);* Arthur and Squirrel *(trans. from the German by H.B. Dole, Crowell, 1925);* Children of the Alps *(trans. from the German by E.P. Stork; illus. by Margaret J. Marshall, Lippincott, 1925);* The Children's Carol *(trans. from the German by H.B. Dole, Crowell, 1925);* Francesca at Hinterwald *(trans. from the German by E.P. Stork; illus. by M.J. Marshall, Lippincott, 1925);* Eveli: The Little Singer *(trans. from the German by E.P. Stork; illus. by Blanche Greer, Lippincott, 1926);* Eveli and Beni *(trans. from the German by H.B. Dole, Crowell, 1926);* Peppino *(trans. from the German by E.P. Stork; illus. by B. Greer, Lippincott, 1926);* In the Swiss Mountains *(trans. from the German by H.B. Dole, Crowell, 1929);* Boys and Girls of the Alps *(trans. from the German by H.B. Dole, Crowell, 1929);* Renz and Margritli *(trans. from the German by H.B. Dole, Crowell, 1931).*

Johanna Spyri

Johanna Heusser Spyri grew up in a lovely and charming village nestled into the Swiss countryside and later lived as a middle-class housewife in her nation's capital, Zurich. Yet, incredibly, this somewhat ordinary Victorian-era woman altered the direction of children's literature, first for her own country, and then for the world.

She was born the fourth of sixth children to Dr. Johann Jakob Heusser and **Meta Schweizer Heusser** in the village of Hirzel on July 12, 1827. Hirzel was a romantic place to grow up. ◀❧ **Marguerite Davis**, who illustrated Johanna's most famous work *Heidi* in the 1927 American centennial edition celebrating the author's birth, described the hamlet:

> There are flowers everywhere. In the village the houses are neat and tidy, with vegetable gardens, and of course, flowers. Everything looks orderly, clean and comfortable. Just outside the village, and still higher up the mountain, is the white house that belonged to Joanna's parents. From the house, if you look down over the tops of the fir trees into the valley, you can see the great lake of Zurich, with snow-covered mountains behind it.

The Heussers' household was an extended one, including six children (Theodor, Anna, Christian, Johanna, Ega, Meta and Christel) and a maternal grandmother and two maternal aunts. This arrangement, which was not unusual for European households of the 19th century, seems to have offered Spyri a bright, happy childhood.

Certainly, the places to play surrounding the Heusser house at Hirzel stimulated her young imagination. The children amused themselves with hide-and-seek in the barn, carved their names in the tree trunks of the nearby woods, and the boys tried to capture their sisters' "castle," in reality a landmark stone which rested in the middle of the forest. Local legends abounded of fairies and gnomes who reputedly inhabited the glens and valleys about Hirzel. Johanna's childhood friend **Anna Ulrich** recalled that the future author was fascinated by the sound of the wind rustling amongst the firs. Her love for nature already had begun.

Ulrich described her friend as "lively, without being at all nervous, beaming with cheerfulness, with sparkling eyes in a narrow, florid face with regular features, scintillating with the joy of life and feeling neither cold nor heat nor weariness." More specifically, Johanna's hair was dark brown, her eyes gray-blue.

Surprisingly, given her later literary acumen, student Johanna disappointed her elders. Her teacher in the local village school called her a "dunce." She was particularly deficient in drawing, an art young girls were supposed to cultivate in that time. Before many years passed, she left the school and received private instruction from Pastor Tobler in the local rectory. There, with one of her sisters and the pastor's own daughter, she began to show promise.

Spyri early demonstrated an eagerness for poetry, and she received encouragement in this art both at the rectory and at home. Pastor Tobler featured poems as a regular part of his curriculum. One of her aunts recited ballads at home while her father made each of the children compose a weekly poem to be given to the family each Sunday evening. Often, the young Johanna composed for less interested and even less talented siblings. Her own mother lingered long at poetry and songs around the house.

A shadow of sadness entered Spyri's life at age nine. She lost her grandmother, and in the same year her mother and one of her aunts journeyed to the resort of Pfäfers "for the cure," in other words, most likely in order to receive treatment for tuberculosis. When her three older siblings traveled to the resort, she was bereft, and to cheer her Dr. Heusser temporarily sent her to stay with relatives near Zurich, located seven miles away from Hirzel. Johanna made the odyssey alone in five hours on foot. Several of her future child characters would also experience melancholy and undertake similar journeys.

Several other experiences factored into her young life. Father Heusser placed a lamb under the holiday tree one Christmas, thus inspiring the future children's story "The Pet Lamb." She also was enchanted by a harp purchased by herself and a friend on one of their excursions to Zurich and time-shared between them. In addition to dolls and a doll theatrical house, she took

---

❧▶ **Davis, Marguerite** (b. 1889)

*American illustrator of children's books. Born on February 10, 1889, in Quincy, Massachusetts; attended Vassar College and Boston Museum of Fine Arts School.*

Along with the 1927 English translation of *Johanna Spyri's Heidi*, Marguerite Davis illustrated many books in her 25-year career, including *Christina Rossetti's Sing-Song* (1924); Robert Louis Stevenson's *A Child's Garden of Verses* (1924); *Louisa May Alcott's Under the Lilacs* (1928); *Laura E. Richards' Tirra Lirra* (1932); and Elizabeth Coatsworth's *The Littles House* (1940).

---

a particular interest in illustrated books including the *Vertuch* by Goethe.

One special friend, however, was destined to last a lifetime. One of brother Theodor's chums at gymnasium (high school) frequented the Heusser household on Saturdays, a tall, slender student named Bernhard Spyri. Bernhard shared the family's love of poetry and the theater and joined them in excursions throughout the local countryside. Gradually, warmth developed between Bernhard and the "little wild creature, who never failed to give a witty and clever answer." Johanna reminded him of a "clear, bubbling mountain brook." In the words of Ulrich:

> [Bernhard] was faithful and true, a man of honor from the crown of his head to the sole of his feet; Johanna felt this even then. And he knew just as surely that the happiness of his life depended [on her]. . . . It was a childhood love, which lasted throughout life.

The two married in 1852 and settled in Zurich where Bernhard, who had studied law, became a respected town clerk. Thereafter, Johanna led a secluded life as a mother and housewife. Their first and only child, Bernhard Diethelm Spyri, was born in 1852. Unfortunately, his life was short. Some sources say he died of tuberculosis during his student years while others maintain he lasted until 1884, the same year that Johanna's husband died. Johanna's attachment to anonymity has left few details to posterity. In fact, no biography exists in the English language and most of her letters, personal papers and even original manuscripts seem to have been lost through the years either from accident or on purpose.

Before the deaths of her husband and son, however, Spyri began writing, a profession she would pursue to the end of her days. She penned her first stories in 1870, at age 43. In this year, France and the German states, neighboring nations to the north and west of Switzerland, were at war. Initially, she wrote in order to donate any proceeds to the orphans of this Franco-Prussian War. Spyri probably assisted the International Red Cross, a charity organized in Switzerland in 1864. Certainly, orphans figured prominently in her children's stories.

Her initial works were published anonymously. Her first story for adults, "A Leaf on Vrony's Grave," came out in 1871, the year the Franco-Prussian War ended. Throughout the 1870s, her writing blossomed. Her most famous work, *Heidi*, occupied several of these years and originally comprised two large stories which might properly be termed novellas—*Heidi: Her Years of Wandering and Learning* (published

anonymously, 1880) and *Heidi Makes Use of What She Has Learned* (1881, the first work published under her own name). Publishers combined these two large stories featuring the child-heroine Heidi into one book in the early 1880s. The product, known in the German language as *Heidi's Years of Apprenticeship and Travels*, was successful immediately and sold 13 editions over the next decade. Translators converted her work into English in 1884, the same year her husband and son died.

> *A* timid shyness caused her to make the urgent request not to describe her life to the public, for she did not wish to have her innermost, deepest soul laid bare to human eyes.
>
> —Anna Ulrich

The storyline in *Heidi* is familiar to most readers of children's literature. A five-year-old orphan girl, Heidi, presents a challenge for her Aunt Dete's family life at the Sesemann household in Frankfurt, Germany. Dete sends Heidi away to a mountain above the village of Dorfli in Switzerland to live with her grandfather who has become, through the years, a bitter and antisocial recluse. During the following three years, Heidi befriends the goatherd Peter and his blind grandmother and experiences the beauty of the alpine country while bringing out the latent warmth and caring of her grandfather. Dete then returns to Dorfli and convinces the grandfather that Heidi's future lies in Frankfurt where she can obtain proper schooling. Dete's motivation is to provide a friend for Dr. Sesemann's sickly and morose daughter, Klara. While in Frankfurt, Heidi touches the lives of all but becomes homesick for her mountain retreat and eventually returns to the arms of her grandfather. Longing for Heidi's companionship, Klara and the Sesemann family visit the mountain and all come together in friendship and understanding. Klara is healed.

The success of *Heidi* surprised Spyri but did not alter her desire for anonymity. Meanwhile, her stories continued. As with *Heidi*, two of her tales in German were translated into English and published as one volume, *Grittli's Children: A Story of Switzerland* in 1884. Other works followed in the 1880s and 1890s: *The Story of Rico, The Mountain Miracle, Lauri's Rescue, The Pet Lamb, Moni, the Goat Boy, Cornelli, Mäzli: a Story of the Swiss Valleys, or Castle Wonderful, Trini, the Little Strawberry Girl, Tiss, a Little Alpine Waif, Eveli, the Little Singer, The Fairy of Intra, Gay Little Herbli, Jo, the Little Machinist, Francesca in Hinterwald, Arthur* and *Squirrel, Toni the Woodcarver, The Bird's Message, Vinzi: a Story of the Swiss Alps, What Sami Sings with the Birds, The Rose Child, The New Year's Carol,* and *The Children's Carol,* are only a representative few of the over 50 stories produced by Johanna Spyri. Her last work, *The Stauffer Mill,* was published in Berlin in 1901.

Probably lamenting the recent loss of her loved ones, Spyri moved to a new home at Zeltweg 9, near the capital city's municipal theater, in 1886. Within years, she became an invalid, but kept gracing the world with her stories until her death on July 7, 1901. Johanna Spyri lives on, however, through her life's work. According to literary critic **Anne Thaxter Eaton**: "It is probable that no other book of its time, showing a background foreign to English and American young readers, had such a success or has implanted itself so firmly in youthful memories as did 'Heidi.'"

*From the movie* Heidi, *starring Jean Hersholt and Shirley Temple.*

Indeed, Spyri changed the course of children's literature. She stated that she wrote not only for children, but for those who love children. During her latter years in Zurich, Spyri as-

sociated with C.F. Meyer and other intellectuals who did not believe in "talking down" to children in stories. In this way, she managed to write works which transcended age, and time itself. According to critic **Bettina Hürlimann**, the enormity of Spyri's very success heralded a certain danger for the path of Swiss literature:

> These new tales created their effects from real life, a thing which few German books were doing at that time. Above all, religious and social questions figured in these tales and they were based on the actual experience of Johanna Spyri, who was the daughter of a country doctor. Almost everything she describes could actually have taken place. Even the rural elements played a bigger part here than in the corresponding German publications. The result was that the Swiss writers pounced on the salient features and would not let go of them. What in Johanna Spyri had been new and unique now became a general Swiss style, only a little modified or changed.

Surprisingly, no definitive volume of "collected works" exists in English nor does such a volume seemingly exist anywhere in the world.

Yet, *Heidi* and other story collections have appeared throughout the years translated into most of the major languages. Author Charles Tritten wrote two sequels to *Heidi* in English entitled *Heidi's Children* and *Heidi Grows Up* in the 1930s and both have been available in paperback as late as the 1980s.

Admirers of Johanna Spyri may locate more information from the Swiss National Tourist Office, the Swiss Institute for Juvenile Literature in Zurich, or by contacting the Heidi Museum in Hirzel, Switzerland. Travelers may enter the magic realm of Heidi from the town of Maienfeld near the Liechtenstein border and climb to Heidi's Alp from the Heidihof Hotel. Or, readers may simply enjoy the armchair romance of Johanna Spyri's enduring tales, for, as one writer noted: "They convey a message as sweet, pure and wholesome as the breeze which blows continually from the summit of her beloved Alps."

**SOURCES:**

Carpenter, Humphrey and Mari Prichard. *The Oxford Companion to Children's Literature*. Oxford University Press, 1984.

Commire, Anne. *Something about the Author*. Vol 19. Detroit, MI: Gale Research, 1980.

Hardyment, Christina. *Heidi's Alp: One Family's Search for Storybook Europe*. London: William Heinemann, 1987.

Hürlimann, Bettina. *Three Centuries of Children's Books in Europe*. NY: World, 1968.

Ulrich, Anna. *Recollections of Johanna Spyri's Childhood*. Translated by Helen B. Dole. NY: Thomas Y. Crowell, 1925.

Wilson, Katharina M., ed. *An Encyclopedia of Continental Women Writers*. Vol 2: L–Z. NY: Garland, 1991.

**SUGGESTED READING:**

Doyle, Brian, ed. *The Who's Who of Children's Literature*. London: Hugh Evelyn, 1968.

Egoff, Sheila, ed. *Thursday's Child: Trends and Patterns in Contemporary Children's Literature*. Chicago, IL: American Library Association, 1981.

Fisher, Margery. *Who's Who in Children's Books: A Treasury of the Familiar Characters of Childhood*. NY: Holt, Rinehart and Winston, 1975.

Spyri, Johanna. *The Children's Christmas Carol*. Englewood Cliffs, NJ: Prentice-Hall, 1957.

———. *Heidi*. Translated by Helen B. Dole. Illustrated Junior Library. NY: Grosset & Dunlap, 1994.

**RELATED MEDIA:**

*A Gift for Heidi* (motion picture), RKO Radio Pictures, 1962.

*Heidi* (87 min. film), starring *Shirley Temple (Black), Jean Hersholt, and Arthur Treacher, directed by Allan Dwan, 20th Century-Fox, 1937.

*Heidi* (98 min. film), starring **Elsbeth Sigmund** and Heinrich Gretler, United Artists, 1954.

*Heidi* (94 min. film), starring **Eva Maria Singhammer** and Gustav Knuth, Warner Bros.-Seven Arts, 1968.

*Heidi* (film), starring Sir Michael Redgrave, Maximilian Schell, and *Jean Simmons, first presented as a tele-

vision special on the National Broadcasting Network, November 17, 1968.

*Heidi* (musical play) by William Friedberg and Neil Simon, Samuel French, 1959.

*Heidi: The Living Legend* (motion picture), ACI Films, 1974.

*Heidi and Peter* (89 min. film), starring Heinrich Gretler, Elsbeth Sigmund, based on novel *Heidi Makes Use of What She Has Learned*, United Artists, 1955.

*Heidi's Song* (94 min. animated film), with voices of Lorne Greene, Sammy Davis, Jr. and **Margery Gray**, Hanna-Barbera, 1982.

**David L. Bullock**, Ph.D.,
author of *Allenby's War:*
*the Palestine-Arabian Campaigns, 1916–1918*
(London: the Blandford Press, 1988)

## Squier, Miriam (1836–1914).

*See Leslie, Miriam Folline Squier.*

## Squires, Helena E. (1879–1959)

*Canadian legislator who was the first woman to campaign for and win a seat in the Newfoundland House of Assembly. Name variations: Lady Helena E. Strong Squires. Born Helena E. Strong in 1879 in Little Bay Islands, Newfoundland; died in 1959 in Toronto, Canada; daughter of James Strong (a supplier to the fishing industry); attended boarding school in St. Johns, the Methodist College, and Mount Allison University; married Richard Squires (later prime minister of Newfoundland), in 1905; children: seven.*

A twin, Helena E. Strong was born in Little Bay Islands, Newfoundland, in 1879. Her family, like many families in that region, was involved in the fishing industry and owned a supply business. Helena attended a private boarding school in St. Johns and the Methodist College before training at Mount Allison University to become a teacher.

In 1905, she married Richard Squires who, with the full support of his wife, began his political career in 1909 and eventually became prime minister of Newfoundland in the 1920s and 1930s. Although Helena Squires often traveled with her husband throughout the province and abroad, she also had seven children to raise and a home to manage. Interested in improving conditions for women, she taught her domestic help the skills necessary to improve their professional positions. She was also active in charity work, instrumental in the founding of a teachers college and maternity hospital, and served as president of the Grace Hospital Auxiliary for many years.

Although she was an opponent of women's suffrage, in 1930 Squires became the first woman to campaign for and win a seat in the Newfoundland House of Assembly. That same year, her father James Strong was appointed by Richard Squires to the Legislative Council. However, the Liberal government lost public support in 1932 and a riot ensued when the House of Assembly tried to meet that April, trapping both Richard and Helena in the House during the fracas. As a result of the June election that followed, they both lost their positions. In 1949, when Newfoundland officially became a part of Canada, Helena Squires was elected the first president of the Liberal Association of Newfoundland. She died in Toronto in 1959.

**Martha Jones**, M.L.S.,
Natick, Massachusetts

## St.

*See Saint.*

## Staal, Mme de (1684–1750).

*See Staal de Launay, Madame de.*

## Staal-Delaunay, Mme de (1684–1750).

*See Staal de Launay, Madame de.*

# Staal de Launay, Madame de

## (1684–1750)

*French writer whose memoirs and letters furnish a candid view of French high society in the 18th century and the frustrations experienced by a talented woman confronting obstacles of gender and class. Name variations: Madame de Staal; Madame de Staal-Delaunay; Baronne de Staal-Delaunay; Rose Delaunay; Rose Delaunay, Baronne de Staal; Rose Staal de Launay; Marguerite Cordier de Launay. Pronunciation: ROSE der-low-NAY, bar-RON der STALL. Born Marguerite-Jeanne Cordier in Paris, France, on August 30, 1684; died on June 15, 1750, in Gennevilliers (Seine) or Sceaux (Seine); buried at the church of Sceaux; second daughter of Cordier (an artist) and Rose de Launay Cordier, known as Rose de Launay; educated in the Convent of Saint-Louis, Rouen; married Baron de Staal, in 1734 or 1735; no children.*

*Began to live at the Convent of Saint-Louis (1691); fell in love with the Marquis de Silly (c. 1700); took employment with the Duchess of Maine (1711); earned welcome notoriety for letter to Fontenelle on the Tétar affair (1713); organized the "Grand Nights of Sceaux" (1714–15); imprisoned in the Bastille as a participant in the Cellamare Conspiracy (1718–20); was in love with the Chevalier de Ménil (1719–c. 1721); death of Dacier ruined a probable marriage (1722); entered a loveless marriage to Baron de Staal (1734–35); wrote her memoirs (c. 1736–41).*

*Selected writings: Mémoires de Madame de Staal-Delaunay (numerous editions, in particular, London: 1755, 4 vols. in 2, including the comedies L'Engouement and La Mode; Paris: A. Renouard, 1821, as Oeuvres de Madame de Staal, including letters; Paris: A. Lemerre, 1877, Mathurin de Lescure, ed.; Paris: Mercure de France, 1970, Gérard Doscot, ed.); see also English translations by Selina Bathurst (London: R. Bentley, 1877) and Cora Bell (NY: Dodd, Mead, 1892); Abrégé de métaphysique, Léa Gilon, ed., 1978.*

"My experience is exactly the reverse of what is seen in novels, where the heroine, brought up as a humble shepherdess, becomes an illustrious princess. In my childhood I was treated as a person of distinction, and in the course of time I discovered that I was nobody, and that nothing in the world belonged to me." So begins, on a grim, coldly realistic note, the famed memoirs of Madame de Staal de Launay. She wrote them soon after her marriage, at age 50, ended whatever chance she still had to live a fulfilling life. Five years after her death, they were published and recognized at once as a classic of French literature.

Her father was a painter named Cordier. Her mother **Rose de Launay** Cordier, a beautiful woman, was pregnant with her second child when, for reasons unknown, she fled with him to England in 1684. She separated from Cordier and returned to Paris, where Staal de Launay was born Marguerite-Jeanne Cordier on August 30, 1684. Rose resumed using her maiden name, de Launay, as did Marguerite who also took the name Rose. Staal de Launay would be known as Rose de Launay until her marriage. She never knew her father; she wrote that when he died, a few years after her birth, she shed tears but did not know why. Meanwhile, her mother, all but destitute and with two daughters in tow, found refuge, through the intervention of friends, at the Abbey of Saint-Sauveur in Evreux, Normandy, where the prioress, **Mme de La Rochefoucauld** (sister of the author of the *Maxims*), sheltered her free of charge. Two nuns, the **Grieu sisters**, became friends with her and, wrote Staal de Launay in her memoirs, "took a violent affection for me." When the elder of the sisters was appointed abbess of the Priory of Saint-Louis at Rouen, they both left. With her mother's consent (mother and daughter were never especially close), they took the seven-year-old girl with them. From then until she was 26, the future Mme de Staal de Launay lived at the Saint-Louis convent.

The priory, she wrote, "was like a small state in which I reigned as sovereign." Four nuns and lay sisters waited on her, supported by the Grieu sisters' family allowance: "They deprived themselves of everything that I might lack nothing." She confessed her failure to acknowledge properly their sacrifices and admitted that she "acquired all the faults of the great. This has since taught me to excuse similar defects in them, and has shown me how easily we persuade ourselves that everything is made for us." Over the years, she developed a small "court" of friends. Among them were the poet Abbé Guillaume de Chaulieu; the historian Abbé René de Vertot; a learned lawyer, M. de Brunel; and several young noble women her age who came for stays: Mlle *Louise d'Épinay, Mlle de la Ferté, Mlle de Neuville, and especially Mlle de Silly, her closest friend.

Staal de Launay was intellectually precocious. She grew up among adults, was serious by nature, cultivated a rational turn of mind, and read everything in the convent's library plus whatever she could borrow. For a time, she devoured novels and tried writing some before (at

Madame de Staal de Launay

Mlle de Silly's urging) plunging into the philosophies of Descartes and Malebranche. She even wrote a brief philosophical treatise. Her education, in short, exceeded by far that of most women even of the privileged classes at the time. But what would she do for a living? In adolescence, she thought of becoming a nun but at length shrank from the finality of the vows. Not surprisingly, she became the abbess' secretary.

And marriage? She was not especially pretty, and a near-fatal bout of smallpox in her teens had left its mark. Her intellect made her somewhat bossy and didactic. But she had sufficient finesse and pleasantness to experience some innocent love affairs—more accurately, infatuations, crushes on her part—with male visitors to the convent. While sojourning at Mlle de Silly's home, she fell deeply in love with her friend's brother, a soldier ten years her senior, the Marquis de Silly. Yet what could she hope for? She had no dowry and was not of noble blood, so marriage with him was all but impossible. She saw him and corresponded with him for many years, only gradually realizing that to him she was a friend and an agreeable source of information, no more. At bottom, he was a selfish careerist who ended by committing suicide (November 19, 1727), because he had failed to reach the highest posts of the army.

> The knowledge of a truth redeems the loss of a pleasure.
>
> —Mme de Staal de Launay

In her late 20s, Staal de Launay found her life changed drastically when the abbess died. The surviving Grieu sister failed to be elected successor and hence lacked the resources to continue supporting her. Staal de Launay confronted "the abyss." Having no dowry, she could not be admitted as a full-fledged nun, even if she truly wanted to take the vows. Proudly declining financial assistance from Vertot, Silly, Brunel, and a M. de Rey (a former object of her affections), she went to Paris to pursue her only good option, namely, a position as governess-tutor in a noble household.

Her search for a job occupies a long section of her memoirs, evidently because it was at this point that she brutally encountered the prejudices of the nobility toward commoners and because she was later hired by a household where she would remain for the rest of her life. For most of a year (it would appear) many prominent people tried to help her while she stayed at the Paris Convent of the Presentation supported by friends. Her sister, **Henriette de Launay**, played a key role by putting her in touch with her own employer, the **Duchess of la Ferté**—sister of **Charlotte Eléonore de la Mothe Houdancourt**, duchess of Ventadour (1661–1744), with whom their mother had briefly held service. Staal de Launay swiftly impressed Ferté as a paragon of knowledge. To her intense discomfort the duchess proceeded to shop her around: "I was no longer in a position to have a will of my own, or to resist the will of others. . . . I found that I was to be led about like a monkey or any other animal that plays tricks at a fair." Her interlocutors sometimes simply asked her to say something clever or profound.

Certainly she had an opportunity to mingle with the elite. Through Vertot, a friend and relative of Ferté, for example, she met the anatomist Vernay, who introduced her to **Mme de Vauvray**, mistress of a salon whose frequenters included the philosophes Bernard de Fontenelle and Abbé Charles de Saint-Pierre. Despite these connections, no prospect bore fruit until Ferté took her to the Château de Sceaux, palatial residence of Louis XIV's eldest bastard son, Louis Auguste de Bourbon, duke of Maine (1670–1736), and his tiny, doll-like, but formidable wife, **Louise-Bénédicte de Bourbon** (1676–1753), duchess of Maine and granddaughter of Louis II Condé ("the Great"). The duke's factotum, Nicholas de Malézieu (1650–1727)—a poet, lawyer, and polymath, member since 1701 of the Académie Française—took great interest in her. An opening appeared in the form of service with **Mlle de Clermont**, niece of the Duchess of Maine. But Staal de Launay would have to go through Malézieu to be hired. When Malézieu spoke highly of her to the Duchess of Maine, the latter took notice and said that if she were as good as he claimed then she wanted her for herself.

Unfortunately, Ferté, by now much attached to Staal de Launay, decided *she* wanted her. Staal de Launay had long since concluded she did not want to stay with Ferté because of her volcanic temper, style of life, and the jealousies certain to be inspired among the other servants, beginning with her own sister. So she contacted Malézieu on her own. Ferté found out, waxed furious, but let her accept Malézieu's offer of employment (January 24, 1711) to begin in the spring. Ferté's pain was eased by an element of revenge, for she knew—as Staal de Launay did not—that a place as a lady's maid was coming open, and that was where, not as companion-secretary, the Duchess of Maine would most likely put her. And so it was. To Staal de Launay's intense pain and disappointment, after all the efforts on her behalf, she found herself relegated without ado to an attic alcove and the status of a common servant, superciliously ignored now by the duchess and even Malézieu himself as just another member of Sceaux's huge staff.

Staal de Launay proved utterly inept as a lady's maid and dresser, clumsy (not helped by her poor eyesight) and inexpert at sewing. She grew depressed with this "melancholic and wearisome life" riddled with petty humiliations, and even contemplated suicide. Her mistress, the absolute ruler of Sceaux, was a difficult person, imperious and willful, although (as Staal de Launay confessed in her memoirs) unexpectedly patient with her. To a surprising degree, she wanted to please this petite tyrant for whom she felt a grudging admiration and even, in time, a genuine fondness. Her memoirs are carefully nuanced. On the surface she has nothing bad to say about the woman who employed her for 39 years, but an unmistakable note of frustration and resentment runs through the lines. Interestingly, she ends her memoirs with a long passage fulsomely praising the Duke of Maine at his death—which makes the absence of a similar eulogy of her mistress all the more striking.

Several offers of employment, albeit questionable, surfaced, but on Vertot's advice she declined them. It was the Tétar (or Testart) affair which "caused me to emerge unexpectedly from the profound obscurity in which I lived." **Mlle Tétar**, with her mother's connivance, sought to escape a marriage proposed by her father, a prominent lawyer, by claiming to be tortured by a spirit (an imp) while in bed. She would secretly manipulate a spring to produce a movement which a gullible public concluded was of satanic origin. Philip Bourbon-Orléans (1674–1723), 2nd duke of Orléans (the future regent), was taken in, and his friend Fontenelle appeared to believe out of respect for him. The Duchess of Maine, who (for reasons to be explained) never missed an opportunity to make Orléans look foolish, asked Staal de Launay to write anonymously to Fontenelle and chide him tactfully for his naïveté. She wrote a wonderfully adroit, humorous letter (December 1713) which caused Fontenelle and Orléans to laugh off the whole business. Copies were made, and Staal de Launay quickly became known to *Tout Paris* as the author. As a result, the duchess suddenly, at last, realized she had a full-fledged companion-secretary at hand. Such was the position to which Staal de Launay was promoted—for life, as it turned out.

She soon acquired a coterie of her own, including Vertot, the savant Duverney, writers

Jean de Valincourt and Antoine La Motte-Houdar, Fontenelle, and even a would-be husband (the now mid-70ish Chaulieu). A marriage prospect collapsed when the fall of a ministry removed a minister who was expected to give her future husband a fine post. Despite its "variety and charm" (as she admitted), hers was no easy life, for the duchess, who hardly slept, made demands at all hours, and the other servants scorned her out of jealousy.

Her most notable role became that of co-producer, with Malézieu, of the famous "Grand Nights of Sceaux," some 16 spectacular entertainments by and for the Maines in 1714–15. With Louis XIV in his last days, the duchess was bent on showing up gloomy Versailles and winning support for her husband at court. The affairs featured songs, poems, dances, illuminations, tableaux, and plays. Staal de Launay, "the veritable soul" of the Nights, wrote much of the material, including two comedies, *L'Engouement* (Infatuation) and *La Mode* (Fashion). Beneath the light surface of these plays lay a serious theme: women's lack of education prevents them from carrying out important responsibilities—the principals in the plays are widows—as mother and head of the family. The women of the upper class (her audience) are frivolous, naïve dolls lacking wills of their own, educated only for playing social games. Hers was a female version of women's lives, writes **Léa Gilon**, not Molière's male version. Realism sets the tone, as in the memoirs. She had to be careful, however, not to offend, so the themes were handled very deftly and the plays were well applauded.

The only truly dramatic event of Staal de Launay's life came with her arrest and imprisonment in the Bastille (December 29, 1718) as a result of the Cellamare Conspiracy. She remained there until June 1720. She was involved because the Duchess of Maine was the prime mover in this clumsy plot to redeem her husband's fortunes. The outlines of the conspiracy are as follows:

Upon the death of his grandson in May 1714, Louis XIV, only a year from death himself, had decided to declare his already legitimized bastard sons (of whom the Duke of Maine, son of the *****Marquise de Montespan**, was the eldest) eligible to succeed to the throne if other branches of the royal family became extinct. Because his successor now would be his great-grandson, who was only a child (Louis XV, 1710–1774), a regency would be necessary, and in his will he named as regent his nephew, Philip Bourbon-Orléans. Once in office, Orléans persuaded the Parlement of Paris in July 1717 to set aside the edict of 1714 and, alas, remove the Duke of Maine as commander of the Household Troops and guardian of young Louis. Outraged over this insult to her husband, the duchess plotted to replace Orléans with Philip V of Spain (Louis XIV's grandson), while Maine, restored to his status, would serve as Philip's proxy at Versailles. Maine went along with his wife's shaky scheme only reluctantly.

At the duchess' command, Staal de Launay searched out legal precedents regarding legitimized princes and served as the conduit for letters between the Maines and agents dealing with the Spanish court and the Spanish ambassador to Versailles, the Prince of Cellamare. Staal de Launay had no illusions about the business, suspecting the conspiracy would fail and fatally damage the Maines. But the duchess laughed off her warnings. Staal de Launay wrote in her memoirs, "I won't explain their plot, for I never understood it," adding dryly, "and perhaps they didn't either." Probably she was ignorant of many details and, for that matter, preferred not to know. But she almost certainly knew much more than her memoirs imply or what she told her interrogators. Of all the participants, she proved to be the most courageous, faithful, and self-sacrificing.

While imprisoned, she refused to make any declaration (a condition of her release) unless she were told exactly what to talk about. She was the last of the conspirators to be freed. The Abbé (later Cardinal) Guillaume Dubois, Orléans' right-hand man, decided, because of his own ambitions and the public's sympathy for the Duke of Maine, not to try the conspirators once he obtained their confessions. The duchess, imprisoned at Dijon, gave way after three months, and the rest gradually followed suit. When told she might as well confess because the duchess had already done so, Staal de Launay cannily replied that since that was the case she saw no reason why they should examine her further. Finally, the duchess thanked her and told her to reply. She gave a declaration (February 1, 1720) about which she later wrote: "I told them only things that no one cared to know, and others that they would have preferred not to hear."

Was her stay in the Bastille disagreeable? Quite the contrary. She wrote of it (apparently ignoring her childhood), "It is the only happy time I ever spent in my life." For one, the Bastille was by no means the grim dungeon of legend. It was "a very tolerable hotel," a "prison of privileged bunglers," with facilities for only 40 to 50 inmates. They enjoyed an extraordinary freedom within the walls, the only strict control being applied to communication with the outside. Prisoners were allowed their own servants, books, writing materials, musical instruments, and pets, and the food and drink, provided at the king's expense, was abundant and rich—so rich that some asked for simpler fare. If one were still dissatisfied, meals could be sent in. Staal de Launay, attended by her maid, occupied her days with reading, card-playing, needlework, and caring for her cats, while M. de Valincourt kept her supplied with comforts and money. From August 1719, moreover, she occasionally dined at the governor's table.

A second reason was that she had found "more liberty than I had lost." In lines easily read as an acid commentary on her life at Sceaux, she wrote: "It is true that in prison one does not follow one's own will, but on the other hand, one does not obey the will of another. . . . one is exempt from subjugation, duties, and the formalities of society; and taken altogether, it is perhaps the place where one enjoys most liberty." Of her leaving, she wrote, "I felt only confused sensations; joy, if there was any, did not stand out." There was a third reason why the Bastille had not proved so disagreeable: she had fallen in love with a fellow detainee from the conspiracy, the Chevalier de Ménil. With the Marquis de Silly, he was the other great love of her life. She had been apprehensive at first, but his character, maturity (he was older than her 35 years), moderation, and persistence won out: "I beheld a liberator." They exchanged many letters, and in due course he visited her clandestinely in her "cell" (a comfortable room). They were aided by the King's Lieutenant at the prison, Major de Maisonrouge, a former cavalry captain. He became a kind of Cyrano de Bergerac, for he fell deeply in love with her. He later told her that "every time he took or gave our letters," wrote Staal de Launay, "he was plunging a dagger into his own heart." She described him as "a straight-forward soldier, full of natural good qualities, accompanied, but not disfigured, by a certain toughness and rusticity of manner." Ménil obsessed her, however.

He was released to his home in Anjou on January 5, 1720. They continued to correspond via Maisonrouge, but Staal de Launay detected a change in his tone. She grew troubled about her future while awaiting her own release. The thought of returning to a convent—maybe to Presentation—recurred, as it usually did when she was unhappy. But the duchess wanted her back. Everything now depended on Ménil. Upon her release early in June, she went to Sceaux

(June 6) but returned to Paris to visit the convent and retrieve some belongings at the Bastille. She found Maisonrouge ill and dejected. As a memento, she gave him a piece she had written. The truth about Ménil became all too clear after a couple of strained meetings. He had found another love back home. Staal de Launay was devastated: "I would sooner have expected the sky to fall from heaven, than any change to take place in the heart of the Chevalier de Ménil."

She returned to Sceaux, where life resumed its old course, although dampened by the late unpleasantness (so to speak) and a temporary separation of the Maines. When the duchess fell seriously ill, Staal de Launay felt she could not desert her. But she became deeply depressed, wanting only solitude. Valincourt tried to obtain a pension for her, but the project foundered. She came to realize what she had missed in not responding to Maisonrouge's devotion. In her memoirs, she described him as "the only man by whom I believed myself to be truly loved." She decided to resume contact with him. It was too late. She learned he had died at his provincial home, brokenhearted. His death inspired some self-examination: "I mourned him far more than I had appreciated him. . . . To meet with ingratitude"—she might have been thinking, too, of the duchess—"is always the destiny of devotion too faithful and pure." Life now seemed "without aim or object."

Staal de Launay devoted the last portion of her memoirs to her eventual marriage, in 1734 (or 1735). She experienced mixed feelings about the whole business because she had been burned so often, yet she found it hard to submerge her "passions," as she put it. Marriage would confer two advantages. It would raise her social standing, and if she married a noble she would be accepted at court and into the duchess' circle, eat at her table, ride in her carriage, and so forth. It also could make it possible for her to "procure some degree of liberty." Death was now reaping a harvest among her family and friends: her sister during her (Staal de Launay's) imprisonment and her mother soon after her release, Chaulieu, Valincourt, the Marquis de Silly, Mme de Grieu, and others. A pension finally settled on her by the Duke of Maine after her imprisonment plus bequests from dead friends provided her with resources. But plainly she wanted some confirmed status beyond her unclassifiable occupation as reader and friend to the duchess.

A projected marriage to a wealthy widower and well-known classicist, André Dacier (1651–1722), fell through on the verge of consummation when he died suddenly. She had a succession of suitors, but all suffered from various drawbacks. Retirement to a convent still beckoned. Through it all, she continually felt bound not to do something to which the duchess (who was adamantly determined to keep her) would not consent. The duke suggested that a man of position, preferably noble, be found among his many dependents. A friend of hers and the duchess knew a 50ish artillery officer in the Swiss Corps. (Maine was commander of the Swiss and Grand Master of the Artillery.) Baron Jean-Jacques de Staal was living in a new country house at Gennevilliers (about six miles northeast of Paris) with his two daughters. Staal de Launay (who was now a milk-drinker, she tells us) dreamed of a country life and found that the house "recalled the simplicity of the golden age." She described Staal as good tempered, calm, of "unstudied politeness . . . a person whose society cannot be disagreeable and is incapable of causing animation as of giving annoyance"—a delicate way of saying he was boring. He received the promotion to captain he had long coveted, and all was ready.

It now dawned on Staal de Launay that she had consented too soon. The daughters, she learned, owned the house and openly resented her. The dream of a bucolic idyll dissolved: "Human pride conceals from us the paltry circumstances which have assisted in forming our decisions even on occasions of great importance," she wrote. Notes biographer Maurice Rat, "For the cows she accepted Staal." Probably the bitterest line in her memoirs describes her wedding: "The bride, bound and adorned, was led to the altar." Staal's daughters refused to attend. In no time she was back on duty at Sceaux, where she soon found the duchess unwilling even to allow her to spend Holy Week at Gennevilliers before her husband left on duty: "I now saw that I had only tightened the chains that I had endeavored to slacken." Her social standing had improved, but she could sense that the duchess was uncomfortable with her new status: "I perceived that, unlike baptism, the sacrament of marriage does not wipe away the stain of original sin." To finish it off, her dearest friend, **Mme de Bussy**, died, and the final illness of the Duke of Maine (1736) compelled her to stay close by the duchess for a year. With a tribute to the late duke, she abruptly ended her memoirs.

The years after 1736 slid by quietly. Festivities resumed at Sceaux after a year's mourning for the duke, but less frequently and intensely than in the golden years before the Cellamare affair. Staal de Launay still read to the duchess into the wee hours, but near the end of her days she was becoming blind. Possibly to come to terms with her life and to fill the empty hours, she wrote her memoirs, probably ceasing after 1741. Sometimes she took refuge at Gennevilliers, "the land where one sleeps." Distinguished guests stayed at Sceaux, the most notable being Voltaire and *Mme du Châtelet, from 1747 to 1749, before he left for Potsdam and Frederick the Great's patronage. Staal de Launay disliked that whole interlude intensely, feeling, for some reason, a special distaste for Châtelet. In compensation, she relished the visits (since 1728) of a writer, her last great friend, the ◄❧ Marquise du Deffand (1697–1780), with whom she exchanged mordantly witty letters about the current scene at Sceaux.

❧►
*Deffand, Marquise du.*
*See Salonnières.*

Rose Staal de Launay died on June 15, 1750, aged 66, at Gennevilliers (or possibly Sceaux), writes Mathurin de Lescure, "without missing too much the life she left and without thinking too much about the other." She was buried at the church at Sceaux. In 1755, after the death of the Duchess of Maine in 1753 but while her husband still lived, her memoirs appeared and received instant acclaim.

Her life was a tale of disappointments and missed opportunities, a striking case of talent frustrated by rigid conventions confining women and commoners to inferior roles. She was highly intelligent, courageous, resilient, and cool. On the other hand, in a self-portrait Mme du Deffand suggested she write, she did not spare herself: "Launay is of medium height, thin, dry, and unpleasant [*désagréable*]. Her character and her mind are like her face; there is nothing awry, but nothing pleasing [*aucun agrément*]." Her characteristic irony tempered her strong sense of self-worth. She surely was unlucky in love, for example, but she ruefully admitted that while she wanted always to be governed by reason, she suffered greatly because reason is so often powerless against feeling. Her frustration broke through in the most striking passage in her self-portrait, where she wrote, "The love of liberty is her dominant passion: a passion which would have rendered dependence insupportable if she had not found in her servitude pleasures which have helped her to bear it." But then, reading it over, she changed its whole thrust: "The love of liberty is her dominant passion; a most unfortunate passion for one who has spent the greater part of her life in servitude; hence her state has always been unsupportable to her despite the unhoped-for pleasures she was able to find in it."

Mme de Staal de Launay's memoirs, wrote Friedrich Grimm at their appearance, have "en-

riched our literature by a work unique in its genre." By which he implied that what we know as autobiography had appeared, for memoirs previously were essentially historically oriented. She had almost nothing to say about the public events of her times save the Cellamare Conspiracy, for which she remains, even so, a very discreet, if still important, witness. She was far from being principally a memorialist of the court of Sceaux and the grandees who mingled there, as she has often been portrayed, although, again, she has justly remained a valuable source of knowledge about life in the first decades of the 18th century. Certainly her position afforded her a matchless opportunity to observe the great ones of the day—as the 19th-century master critic Sainte-Beuve remarked, "absolutely like one observes large fish in a small basin." Given what she suffered at those grandees' hands, it is remarkable that she delivered no diatribe against them. Even her treatment of the duchess is above any reproach of maliciousness. (Her correspondence, however, contains a pitiless dissection.) As W.H. Lewis remarks, "She is neither overawed by, nor contemptuous of the great; finds them, on the whole, much like other people, only a little more ridiculous."

Rather, the core interest of the memoirs (and of her correspondence) lies in the revelation of "the defeat of an intelligent, educated, spirited woman," notes Buchanan. Perhaps (probably) she wrote, as did many other women, to give her thwarted life some retrospective meaning. In so doing she took risks. Women were ridiculed for even trying to write seriously—only 5% of 18th-century French memoirs were by women—and memoirs, certainly after Staal de Launay's, by nature exposed to public view some of the most intimate details of their writers' lives, writes Susan Kinsey. Given the course of her life, one wonders why a woman so discreet preserved "the record of her most private defeats," writes **Judith Curtis**, unless her pain "had hallowed them and made them fit for display."

It is not just the content, however, which sets her memoirs apart from so many others. She was a splendid stylist with a true gift for acute observation. She is "the pupil who has become the equal of the master, La Bruyère," wrote Sainte-Beuve, recalling that 17th-century *grand maître* of unvarnished character studies. The same words appear again and again in descriptions of her style: concise, keen, incisive, marked by finesse and *le mot juste*, mordant, exquisitely ironic, elegant, effortless ("no groping around," says Sainte-Beuve), *classique*, sober, restrained, subtle, original, true to life, secretly bitter. Her writing contains an epigrammatic strain: "Anything tending to assure us of our own merits seems at least probable"; or "One has a greater aversion to the foibles from which one is exempt than to those to which one yields"; or "The heart never fails to betray the reason, whatever lessons it may have received." Examples abound. Despite innumerable opportunities to indulge in it, however, there is no sentimentality. La Bruyère and Fontenelle were the models for her age; Rousseau had yet to appear.

It is cool, unblinking observation and subtle self-revelation served by a masterful command of language and style which makes Mme de Staal de Launay one of the premier writers of classical French prose. How ironic a fate for an ironist whose life is commonly described as "failed."

**SOURCES:**

Buchanan, Michelle. "The French Editions and English Translations of the Memoires of Madame de Staal," in *Eighteenth Century Studies*. Vol. 6, no. 3, 1973, pp. 322–333.

———. "Une Ombre à la fête de Sceaux: Madame de Staal-Delaunay," in *The French Review*. Vol. 51, no. 3. Baltimore, 1978, pp. 353–360.

Curtis, Judith. "The Epistolières," in *French Women and the Age of Enlightenment*. Samia I. Spencer, ed. Bloomington, IN: Indiana University Press, 1984.

*Dictionnaire des Lettres Françaises: XVIII<sup>e</sup> siècle*. Paris: Librairie Arthème Fayard, 1951—.

Gilon, Léa. "Mme. de Staal-de Launay, dramaturge sous la Régence," in *Studies on Voltaire and the Eighteenth Century*. Vol. 192, 1980, pp. 1506–1513.

Kinsey, Susan R. "The Memorialists," in *French Women and the Age of Enlightenment*. Samia I. Spencer, ed. Bloomington, IN: Indiana University Press, 1984.

Lescure, Mathurin de. "La Baronne de Staal," in *Les Femmes philosophes*. Paris: E. Dentu, 1881, pp. 191–210.

Lewis, W.H. *The Sunset of the Splendid Century: The Life and Times of Louis Auguste de Bourbon, Duc du Maine (1670–1736)*. NY: William Sloane Associates, 1955.

*Oxford Companion to French Literature*. Sir Paul Harvey and J.E. Heseltine, eds. Oxford: The Clarendon Press, 1959.

Rat, Maurice. "Madame de Staal," in *Les Femmes de la Régence*. Paris: Berger-Levrault, 1961, pp. 129–145.

Sainte-Beuve, Charles-Augustin. *Portraits littéraires*. Vol. 3. Paris: Garnier Frères, 1862, pp. 437–452.

Staal-Delaunay, Marguerite-Jeanne Cordier, Baronne de. *Mémoires de Madame de Staal-Delaunay*. Gérard Doscot, ed. Paris: Mercure de France, 1970.

———. *Memoirs of Madame de Staal de Launay*. Selina Bathurst, tr. London: Richard Bentley & Son, 1877.

**SUGGESTED READING:**

Carette, Mme. A. Bouvet. *Madame de Staal-Delaunay*. Paris: Ollendorff, 1891.

Charvet, P.E., gen. ed. *A Literary History of France*. Vol. 2: *The Seventeenth Century*; Vol. 3: *The Eighteenth Century*. London: Ernest Benn, 1967—.

Crumpecker, Margery Ann. "Three Eighteenth Century Women Writers: Contravening Authority." City University of New York dissertation, 1998.

Deffand, Marie de Vichy-Chamrond, Marquise du. *Correspondence complète de la Marquise du Deffand*. 2 vols. Paris: H. Plon, 1865.

Gilon, Léa. "Mme. de Staal de Launay, femme de théâtre." University of Massachusetts dissertation, 1978.

Gourdin, Jean-Luc. *La Duchesse du Maine: Louise-Bénédicte de Bourbon, princesse de Condé*. Paris: Pygmalion, 1999.

Lambert, Anne-Thérèse de Marguenat de Courcelles, Marquise de. *Oeuvres complètes de Madame la Marquise de Lambert suivis de ses lettres à plusieurs personnages célèbres*. 2 vols. Paris: D'Hautel, 1813.

Staal-Delaunay, Marguerite-Jeanne Delaunay, Baronne de. *Memoirs of Madame de Staal-Delaunay*. 2 vols. Cora Bell, tr. NY: Dodd, Mead, 1892.

**David S. Newhall,**
Pottinger Distinguished Professor of History Emeritus,
Centre College, Danville, Kentucky

# Stade, Richardis von (d. 1152)

*Abbess of Bassum. Died on October 29, 1152, at Bassum Abbey, Germany; daughter of the noble family of Stade; sister of Hartwig, archbishop of Bremen; never married; no children.*

A German nun, Richardis von Stade eventually became an abbess. Born into a noble German family and sent to a convent as a child, Richardis is best known for her many years at the convents of Disibodenberg and Rupertsberg, where she served as secretary and advisor under her abbess, the great mystic *Hildegard of Bingen*. Richardis seems to have been Hildegard's closest friend and companion. Well educated and a talented writer, she translated and edited Hildegard's visionary writings and prepared them for production as manuscripts.

Although not a mystic herself, Richardis was, like Hildegard, familiar with classical literature, was fluent in Latin, and studied science, including medicine, astronomy, and anatomy. Their relationship appears to have grown more personal in their later years together at Rupertsberg. When Richardis' family arranged a position for her as abbess at the convent of Bassum, Hildegard was extremely upset; she even wrote letters to her secretary's family, urging them not to let her leave Rupertsberg, and begged Richardis not to go. But Richardis accepted the abbessy of Bassum, perhaps as a position befitting her social rank, and in so doing caused Hildegard much pain. Richardis left Rupertsberg in 1151. Unfortunately, she died after only one year as abbess of Bassum. As her brother Hartwig, the archbishop of Bremen, records, she had planned to return to Hildegard (perhaps just for a visit), but death intervened.

**SOURCES:**

Beer, Frances. *Women and Mystical Experience in the Middle Ages.* Woodbridge, England: Boydell, 1992.

**Laura York**, M.A. in History,
University of California, Riverside, California

# Staël, Germaine de (1766–1817)

*A precursor of Romanticism and modern literary criticism whose liberalism reflected 18th-century thought and made her an active adversary of Napoleon Bonaparte. Name variations: Anne Louise Germaine Necker; Madame de Stael or Staël; Baronne or Baroness de Staël von Holstein; (nickname) Minette. Born in Paris, France, on April 22, 1766; died in Paris on July 14, 1817; daughter of Jacques Necker (a financier and director general of finance for Louis XVI) and Suzanne (Curchod) Necker (a governess); cousin of ❦➤ Albertine Necker de Saussure (1766–1841); married Eric Magnus, baron de Staël von Holstein, in Paris, on January 14, 1786; secretly married John Rocca in Coppet, on October 10, 1816; children: (first marriage) Gustavine (b. July 22, 1787, died young); (with Louis, comte de Narbonne-Lara) Auguste (b. August 3, 1790) and Albert (b. Nov. 20, 1792); (with Benjamin Constant) Albertine, Duchesse de Broglie (b. June 8, 1797); (in secret with John Rocca) Louis Alphonse Rocca (b. April 7, 1812).*

*Published* Letters on the Writings and Character of Jean-Jacques Rousseau *(1788); was present at opening of Estates-General, Versailles (May 5, 1789); father resigned as French finance minister (September 3, 1790); published* Sophia, or the Secret Feelings *(October 1790); published* Reflections on Peace *(1794); published* On the Influence of the Passions *(autumn 1796); met Napoleon Bonaparte (December 6, 1797); published* On Literature *(April 1800); published* Corinne or Italy *(May 1, 1807); published* On Germany *in London (November 4, 1813); suffered a stroke in Paris (February 21, 1817).*

Germaine de Staël did not fit the stereotypical image of femininity in the 18th century. Physically unattractive and tastelessly attired, she was known for her brilliant mind and her writings, her unconventional lifestyle, and her opposition to Napoleon Bonaparte. She was the product of liberal, free-thinking Parisian salon society and the Calvinist religion. From these sources, she absorbed her liberal idealism, her sentimental romanticism, and her anti-Catholicism. Nothing was more dear to her than her adored father and the city of Paris.

Brought up in a narrowly religious household by staid, dull, emotionally inhibited parents, de Staël led an abnormally proscribed life. As chief financial officer in Louis XVI's government, her famous father, the Swiss financier Jacques Necker, was destined to play a vital role in the decade prior to and during the early years of the French Revolution. A self-made millionaire, Necker was more at ease among accountants than in Parisian society; devoid of cultural interests and social graces, he was respected only for his business acumen. Her mother ❦➤ **Suzanne Necker**, daughter of a Swiss Protestant pastor, was prudish and socially ambitious, a perfect mate for her lackluster husband.

Until she was 12, de Staël lived in a singularly adult world. Her mother supervised her education which was confined to intellectual and spiritual instruction; no physical activity was permitted, no contact with children was allowed. Suzanne Necker's salon also served as a classroom for her precocious child. Every Friday afternoon, Germaine listened to the brilliant discourse of some of the most celebrated thinkers of the Age of Enlightenment: Denis Diderot, Jean Le Rond d'Alembert, George Buffon, Melchior Grimm, and Edward Gibbon. Lessons in Latin and English and reading and copying extracts from books supplemented her weekly attendance at her mother's salon. Germaine's mind was thus assiduously cultivated at the expense of an active, playful childhood.

Germaine was not allowed to leave the house without her mother, nor did she have a friend her own age until she was 12. Intensive supervision of her every thought and action and her heavy schedule of daily lessons ended abruptly when she became seriously ill. The doctor removed Germaine from her mother's care, and ordered her to rest, to discard her corset, and to avoid mental strain. During the summer of 1779, she lived at the Necker country estate in Saint Ouen, near Paris. In this freer atmosphere, a bond of deep affection grew between daughter and father; since 1777, Jacques Necker had served as director general of finance for Louis XVI, but, at Saint Ouen, he could escape from his duties and his God-fearing wife. Germaine's unbounded adoration of her father developed into open rivalry with her mother for his affection. De Staël's biographer, J.C. Herold, stresses this hero worship and notes that "her entire life was spent in celebrating him." This anomalous attachment is evident in de Staël's diary entry of July 31, 1785: "Of all men in the world it is he whom I would have wished for a lover." Conversely, in her novel *Corinne or Italy*, she drew a savage caricature of her mother who "liked to make others' lives as drab as possible."

There is no doubt, as Herold concludes, that de Staël's "emotional involvement with her mother and father was the most decisive factor in her formation." But the repressive environment of childhood did not carry over into adulthood. After she married, Germaine had numerous lovers of whom her parents disapproved, and she infuriated them further by having illegitimate children. Indeed, her lovers were dashing and worldly and generally amoral, her equals, but never her masters. De Staël refused to be dominated, to be used as a mere paramour.

In the late 18th century, marriage among the upper classes often meant freedom for women, which greatly appealed to de Staël. Because she was one of the richest heiresses in all Europe, her parents decided that only a Protestant noble would be suitable for her. Few French nobles fit the religious requirement, and Germaine insisted that she live in France, no matter who the suitor was. After long, intricate negotiations involving the French royal family and the king of Sweden, Eric Magnus de Staël von Holstein was selected. But Eric had to be appointed as Swedish ambassador to France and made a baron before he could marry Mlle Necker. Among the conditions of the marriage contract, agreed to by Eric and signed by the French royal family, was that Germaine would never have to live in Sweden. The wedding was held in the chapel of the Swedish embassy in Paris. Germaine had no romantic illusions about marriage or about Baron de Staël, and love would be sought elsewhere. The baron had, of course, married for money, but he loved Germaine. She, free of parental constraints, intended to live without bonds of dependence or obligation. After her marriage, she had her formal presentation at court; she arrived late and split her dress while curtseying before Queen *Marie Antoinette, and in general violated court etiquette. Lacking in beauty, manners and social graces, tactless and arrogant, Germaine often defied social convention. In spite of her being witty, intelligent, and a brilliant conversationalist, Parisian society ridiculed her gauche behavior. No woman, no matter how talented, could be forgiven such bold eccentricities, and Germaine de Staël never was forgiven.

In the Swedish embassy, Germaine established her own salon, attended by a new generation of thinkers whose major interest was politics. An attentive listener and avid talker, she had the ability to analyze and criticize without inhibiting her guests. Her illustrious circle included Thomas Jefferson, the Marquis de Lafayette, and Charles Maurice de Talleyrand-Perigord. Germaine had also begun to concentrate on

## Necker de Saussure, Albertine (1766–1841)

*Swiss writer. Born in 1766; died in 1841; daughter of Horace-Bénédict de Saussure (1740–1799, the Swiss physicist and geologist); cousin of Germaine de Staël (1766–1817); married into the Necker family.*

A cousin to *Germaine de Staël by marriage and an intimate friend, Albertine Necker de Saussure was a writer who lived in Geneva, Switzerland. Her chief works were *Notice sur le caractère et les écrits de Mme de Staël* (1820) and her treatise on children's education, *L'Éducation progressive, étude du cours de la vie* (1828–32, 3 vols.). She also translated Schlegel's lectures on theater.

## Necker, Suzanne (1739–1794)

*French-Swiss essayist and salonnière. Name variations: Mme Necker. Born Suzanne Curchod in France in 1739; died in 1794; daughter of Louis Curchod (a pastor); grew up near Lausanne; married Jacques Necker (a Swiss banker and French finance minister), in 1764; children: Germaine de Staël (1766–1817).*

Daughter of a Swiss Protestant minister, Suzanne Curchod Necker was educated by her father in his pastorate near Lausanne. Following his death, she moved to Paris where she served as a "ladies' companion." She married Jacques Necker in 1764. Though Suzanne Necker was neither a Parisian nor known for her social polish, she hosted a successful salon for philosophes and encyclopaedists and was prized for her honesty and intelligence. She left behind some miscellaneous writings, published as *Mélanges extraits des manuscrits* (Various Extracts from Manuscripts, 1798) and *Nouveaux Mélanges* (Further Extracts, 1801). Necker, who was responsible for the education of her daughter *Germaine de Staël, promoted the education of women and also advocated a court of women to adjudicate petitions for legal separations.

writing; *Sophia, or The Secret Sentiments* shocked Suzanne Necker by its revelation of Germaine's excessive love for her father. Jacques Necker, who never took Germaine's, or any woman's, writing seriously, was undisturbed. He indulged his daughter in her writing, but never allowed her to have a writing desk in his house. However, Germaine acquired a portabledesk with a hinged top, which she carried with her throughout her life. Marriage, which in practice she loathed, gave her freedom to live her own life, and freedom to write. To de Staël, writers had a "mission"—to act as moral guides, to explore human conduct, as individuals and as members of society. When her *Letters on the Writings and Character of Jean-Jacques Rousseau* was published in 1788, Mme de Staël was recognized as a writer of distinction.

Pregnancy was as distasteful as marriage, and her first child, Gustavine, who died at 18 months, was cared for by household servants. De Staël was already suffering from periods of depression and loneliness, and she longed for passionate, blissful love as described by the Romantic writers of the time. To fill the void, she had a brief affair with Talleyrand, the future revolutionary and foreign minister. Through him, she met and fell in love with Comte Louis de Narbonne-Lara whose career ambitions she successfully promoted.

> *"Madame,"* Napoleon informed her, "I do not want women mixed up in politics."
>
> "You are perfectly right," Mme de Staël replied, "but in a country where their heads are cut off, it is only natural for them to want to know why."
>
> —Exchange between Napoleon Bonaparte and Madame de Staël

During the 1780s, Jacques Necker had been dismissed and reappointed as financial minister a number of times. When delegates to the Estates-General met in Versailles in May 1789, inaugurating ten years of revolution, they initially looked to Jacques to bring about urgently needed financial reform. Germaine was excited about the possibilities for political reform in France to achieve happiness through a liberal constitution and rule by an enlightened elite. She envisioned a new world in the making and saw an opportunity to influence politics through the political moderates who frequented her salon. She attended Assembly meetings, but did not participate. Unlike some feminist activists, de Staël did not campaign for the right of women to participate in public affairs, but she wanted them to have equal civil rights, freedom of religion, of speech, assembly, and the press, which would benefit everyone. When her father resigned his post in September 1790 and moved to his château at Coppet, Switzerland, she decided to stay in Paris. Relations with her parents were further strained after Germaine gave birth to a son by Narbonne. De Staël exerted influence through her political friends, contributed to their speeches and reports, and worked behind the scenes to promote their careers and her own ideas. She was responsible for Narbonne's appointment as minister of war and reportedly wrote some of his bulletins.

With the overthrow of the monarchy in August 1792, Mme de Staël's constitutional monarchist friends went into hiding. Pregnant again, and in danger herself, she hid Narbonne and others in the Swedish embassy and arranged their escape from France. When she tried to leave Paris for Switzerland, she was arrested, but after an appeal to a political acquaintance she was released. From Coppet, she continued to provide money and documents for victims of political persecution. After the birth of another son, she traveled to England to join Narbonne. Exiled French royalists in England attacked her as an adulterer and instigator of revolution, while in France leftist radicals equally condemned her for her "aristocratic" views. Leaving England in May 1793, she again went to Coppet where Narbonne was to join her, but he procrastinated. De Staël was a difficult woman, demanding and domineering, and she enervated her many lovers. She complained of his ingratitude; she had saved his life, paid his debts, and bought him a house in Switzerland. Still, he ignored her entreaties. Her dejection is poignantly iterated in her treatise *On the Influence of the Passions.* Mme de Staël laments the lot of women: the code of honor and mutual respect that binds men together does not carry over into male-female relations. And she deplored the unjust double standard of morality that vilified women who dared to defy social convention.

When Narbonne finally arrived, he resumed his liaison with a former mistress. It was then that Germaine met the brilliant intellectual Benjamin Constant. She continued to write and publish works on politics and fiction. Her *Reflections on Peace* excoriated Robespierre and the Terror and blamed the European powers for not supporting the moderates whom de Staël saw as the sole hope for establishing a liberal regime in France. By May 1795, Germaine had reopened her salon in Paris and strove to influence the course of events. She favored a republic based on ownership of property, but all people would enjoy civil rights, fair taxation, and equal justice and opportunity. Abstract equality was a chimera, a lower-class demand that would impede progress. Following an attempted coup by royalists in August, Benjamin Constant and another friend were arrested. They were released only after Germaine personally appealed to a member of the Directory government. Her efforts resulted in her expulsion from France. Kept under police surveillance at Coppet, she and Benjamin Constant continued to collaborate on political writings. Baron de Staël eventually persuaded the Directory to allow his wife to return to France, but not until May 1797

*Germaine de Staël*

❧▶

*See sidebar
on the
following page*

was she permitted to live in Paris where her (and Constant's) daughter ❧▶ **Albertine**, later duchesse de Broglie, was born in June. Mme de Staël, Constant, and several moderates founded the Club de Salm to spread their political principles, and she continued to help beleaguered friends. Through her intercession, Talleyrand was able to return from the United States and was appointed minister of foreign affairs. She lent him money and helped launch his career, but he, like so many others, failed to acknowledge his debt to her.

## ❧► Albertine (1797–1838)

*Duchesse de Broglie. Name variations: Albertine de Staël. Born Albertine Ida Gustavine de Staël in Paris, France, on June 8, 1797; died on September 22, 1838; illegitimate daughter of Germaine de Staël and Benjamin Constant; married (Achille Charles Léonce) Victor, duc de Broglie (1785–1870, French minister of the interior, 1830, and foreign affairs, 1832–34 and 1835–36), in February 1816; children: Jacques Victor Albert, duc de Broglie (b. 1821, a French politician, publicist, and historian who was ambassador to London, 1871, and premier, 1873–74 and 1877).*

Born in Paris in 1797, Albertine Ida Gustavine de Staël was the illegitimate daughter of \*Germaine de Staël and Benjamin Constant. Cherishing the causes of her grandmother \*Suzanne Necker rather than those of her mother, Albertine wrote moral and religious essays which were collected after her death under the title *Fragments sur divers sujets de religion et de morale* (1840).

In December 1797, a new chapter in her life began: de Staël met Napoleon Bonaparte. Impressed by his intelligence and ability, she hoped to draw him into her circle, even though she was intimidated by his emotional reserve and serious demeanor. However, Bonaparte disapproved of women who meddled in politics, and even of intelligent, vocal women in general. Women were to be modest and retiring, decorative accessories in polite society. The formidable, assertive de Staël was the antithesis of his feminine ideal. Napoleon became her *bête noire*, and she became an irritating thorn under his imperial crown. Members of the Directory did not approve of her either. She pestered them to refund two million francs her father had lent the French Treasury. Her political writings and activities were "troublesome" to the stability of the regime, and her friends were suspect. As punishment, she was exiled again. Why not simply imprison this outspoken woman? Because arresting her would do more harm to the regime than good.

At Coppet, Germaine kept abreast of political developments in Paris. Anticipating another change in regime, she entered Paris on the eve of the coup of 18 Brumaire (November in the Republican calendar) in 1799, which overthrew the Directory. She hoped that Bonaparte and his co-conspirators would install a moderate republic based on enlightened principles. All her hopes were dashed when Bonaparte installed his authoritarian regime, the Consulate. Mme de Staël soon had direct access to Napoleon through his brothers Joseph and Lucien who frequented her salon, and Benjamin Constant, now a member of the government. But instead of reducing Napoleon's dislike for officious females, Germaine continued to aggravate him; this mutual enmity ceased only with Napoleon's downfall. Moreover, as Germaine's literary reputation flourished, each book brought an angrier response from Bonaparte. Nothing in *On Literature* (1800) or *Delphine* (1802) was directly critical of Bonaparte, but he reacted strongly. *On Literature*, a highly original work, examines various national literatures, relating them to their social and historical contexts. In *Delphine*, Mme de Staël explores issues such as religion and marriage and divorce as they affect society, especially women. Reproached by critics as unwomanly and immoral and by Bonaparte as a direct attack on his social policies, the book caused Bonaparte to exile her from Paris, her spiritual home.

Now a widow, Germaine was unwilling to live in the provinces or with her father at Coppet, both of which she found too dull, so she set out for Germany, accompanied by Benjamin Constant and two of her children. She intended to collect material for a book on Germany, its culture and its people. She visited Frankfurt and Weimar where she met Schiller and Goethe. In Berlin, Queen \*Louise of Prussia and the nobility fêted her, and she engaged a tutor for her children. On learning of her father's death, she went to Coppet. She and Constant had a written agreement to marry, but she decided against it; she would lose her title of baronne and she was still skeptical about marriage, believing it would cost her her independence and identity.

Still forbidden to reside in France by Bonaparte, now Emperor Napoleon I, she set out for Italy. Traveling to Milan, Rome, Naples, Venice, and Florence, she met the Italian literary and artistic elite, climbed Vesuvius, and visited Pompeii. During the summer of 1805, at Coppet, she worked on her novel *Corinne*, and hosted many of the most illustrious and talented figures of that time. But Germaine missed the stimulation, the energy of Paris, and was determined to return. As a major figure in the Romantic movement in Europe, Mme de Staël had no interest in nature, or country living. For a brief time, she resided in Auxerre, then Rouen, and risked venturing into Paris for a few days. **Renée Winegarten** describes a meeting between Germaine's son Auguste and Napoleon in December 1807; the young man asked the emperor to allow his mother to return to Paris. "As long as I live she will never set foot in Paris again," he replied. "Women should stick to knitting."

Instead, Germaine wrote, and her novel *Corinne or Italy* was a great success. The heroine is an independent woman of genius, restless and unhappy, but a remarkably talented poet and actress, obviously patterned after her creator (as was Delphine). Mme de Staël praised Italian culture but lamented the lack of freedom in Italy. As king of Italy (since 1805), Napoleon interpreted the book as a criticism of French rule there. But his reaction was mild compared to actions taken when Germaine attempted to publish *On Germany* in France. Napoleon forbade publication, and the manuscript and proof pages were seized; the work was "not French," according to the minister of police. Once again the strong arm of the state prevailed—she was sent into exile from France.

Isolated from friends and society, she found solitude frightening and unnatural. The loneliness of women of genius served as a theme in several of her works. Brief sexual affairs could not compensate for the energizing urbanity of Paris. She was miserable, but that never interfered with her writing and commenting on the major issues of the day. Then she met John Rocca, an officer in the hussars, who had been wounded in the Peninsular Wars and suffered from tuberculosis. He was a devoted lover and later her husband, and father of her son Louis Alphonse Rocca (b. April 1812). From her "prison" at Coppet, Germaine, two of her children, and Rocca set out for Vienna (late May 1812). From Vienna, she traveled to Russia on the eve of Napoleon's Russian campaign (June 1812). In her *Ten Years of Exile*, she describes the exotic grandeur of Moscow as it was before Napoleon's army arrived and the Moscovites burned the city. In St. Petersburg, she met Tsar Alexander I, and they discussed plans for defeating Napoleon. Mme de Staël sailed to Stockholm to confer with her friend Jean Bernadotte, Napoleon's marshal and the effective ruler of Sweden (later king of Sweden as Charles XIV John); she had determined that he should command the allied military effort against Napoleon and eventually govern France. But Bernadotte was less resolute than Germaine, and her scheme eventually failed. After eight months in Sweden, she went to England where she was admired as a writer and staunch opponent of Napoleon. But her brusque manner, immodest necklines, and propensity for talking too much offended the English sense of propriety and provided grist for malicious gossip. During her 11-month stay, she met poets, members of Parliament, and aristocratic social reformers; she also obtained a contract with John Murray to publish *On Germany*,

one of her major works, which appeared in November 1813. While in England, Germaine continued writing as usual. She worked on *Ten Years in Exile* and began a study of the French Revolution based on her own experiences and observations. In her view, the early promise of liberal reform, a written constitution, and individual liberty had augured well for the future happiness of France, but Robespierre and the Terror had betrayed the Revolution. Political ideology had replaced religious faith, but had retained the fanaticism and intolerance which fuelled persecution and violence, now in the name of the state. Censorship and banishment were ever-present reminders to Mme de Staël that she was the object of state-sponsored harassment, because she advocated rule by a landowning elite and despised one-man rule as exemplified by Napoleon.

Napoleon was defeated by a coalition of allies in April 1814, and de Staël quickly returned to France. She accepted the restoration of the Bourbon dynasty without enthusiasm, and the allied occupation of France saddened her. However, in March 1815, Napoleon escaped from exile on Elba, and de Staël departed for Coppet. She resumed residence in Paris after Waterloo and was again welcomed at court. Needing a substantial dowry to enable her daughter Albertine to marry the indigent Victor, duc de Broglie, Mme de Staël appealed to Louis XVIII to redeem the two million francs her father had lent the Treasury in 1790. This was granted, but a similar request to Benjamin Constant to return what she had loaned him was refused. Her daughter Albertine was married in February 1816, and that autumn de Staël secretly married Rocca at Coppet. The château again became the gathering place of distinguished European intellectuals and politicians, including the social outcast Lord Byron whom she had met in England.

On her return to Paris, de Staël met with foreign diplomats to argue for reducing the number of occupation forces and the indemnity imposed on France. Suffering emotional strain from years of exile and persecution, her last pregnancy, and the effects of abusing drugs, especially opium to relieve insomnia, she had a stroke in February 1817, which left her paralyzed but able to speak. She died a few months later, age 51. Napoleon, whose ego matched that of his arch-adversary, described her as a woman of great talent and intellect, a woman whose reputation would last.

**SOURCES:**

Charvet, P.E. "Madame de Staël," in *A Literary History of France: The Nineteenth Century, 1789–1870*. NY: Barnes & Noble, 1967.

Herold, J. Christopher. *Mistress to an Age: A Life of Madame de Staël.* Indianapolis, IN: Bobbs-Merrill, 1958.

Winegarten, Renée. *Mme de Staël.* Lemington Spa: Berg, 1985.

**SUGGESTED READING:**

Gutwerth, M. *Mme de Staël, Novelist: The Emergence of the Artist as Woman.* Urbana, IL: University of Illinois Press, 1978.

Larg, David Glass. *Madame de Staël: Her Life as Revealed in Her Work, 1766–1800.* Trans. by Veronica Lucas. NY: Alfred A. Knopf, 1926.

Posgate, Helen B. *Madame de Staël.* NY: Twayne, 1968.

**Jeanne A. Ojala,** Professor Emerita, Department of History, University of Utah, Salt Lake City, Utah

## Stafford, Anne (c. 1400–1432)

*Duchess of Huntington and Exeter. Name variations: Anne Holland; Anne Mortimer; countess of March. Born around 1400; died on September 20, 1432; daughter of Edmund Stafford, 5th earl of Stafford, and \*Anne Plantagenet (1383–1438); married Edmund Mortimer, 5th earl of March, about 1415; married John Holland (1395–1447), duke of Huntington (r. 1416–1447), duke of Exeter (r. 1443–1447), before March 5, 1427; children: Henry Holland, 2nd duke of Exeter; \*Anne Holland (fl. 1440–1462). John Holland then married \*Beatrice of Portugal (d. 1439) and \*Anne Montacute (d. 1457).*

## Stafford, Anne (d. 1472)

*English noblewoman. Died around April 14, 1472; interred at Lingfield; daughter of Humphrey Stafford, 1st duke of Buckingham, and \*Anne Neville (d. 1480); married Aubrey de Vere (son of the 12th earl of Oxford), in April 1460; children: Thomas, Lord Cobham.*

## Stafford, Anne (d. 1480).

*See Beaufort, Joan for sidebar on Anne Neville.*

## Stafford, Catherine (d. 1419)

*Countess of Suffolk. Name variations: Catherine de la Pole. Died on April 8, 1419; interred at Wingfield Church, Suffolk; daughter of Hugh Stafford (c. 1344–1386), 2nd earl of Stafford (r. 1351–1386), and \*Philippa Stafford; married Michael de la Pole (1368–1415), 2nd earl of Suffolk (r. 1385–1415, who died at the siege of Harfleur); children: Michael de la Pole (c. 1395–1415, killed in battle at Agincourt), 3rd earl of Suffolk; William de la Pole (1396–1450, murdered), duke of Suffolk; John de la Pole; Alexander de la Pole; Thomas de la Pole.*

## Stafford, Catherine (d. 1476)

*Countess of Shrewsbury. Died on December 26, 1476; daughter of \*Anne Neville (d. 1480) and Humphrey Stafford, 1st duke of Buckingham, 1st earl of Stafford; married John Talbot, 3rd earl of Shrewsbury, around 1467; children: George Talbot (b. 1468), 4th earl of Shrewsbury.*

## Stafford, Catherine (fl. 1530)

*Countess of Westmoreland. Flourished around 1530; daughter of \*Eleanor Percy (d. 1530) and Edward Stafford (1478–1521), 3rd duke of Buckingham (executed on May 17, 1521); married Ralph Neville (1497–1555), 4th earl of Westmoreland (r. 1499–1555); children: Henry Neville, 5th earl of Westmoreland; Dorothy Neville (d. around 1546, who married John de Vere, 16th earl of Oxford); Margaret Neville (d. 1559, who married Henry Manners, 2nd earl of Rutland).*

## Stafford, Constance (d. 1474)

*Countess of Wiltshire. Name variations: Constance Greene. Died on March 2, 1474; daughter of Margaret Roos and Henry Green; married John Stafford, 9th earl of Wiltshire (r. 1469–1473), in 1458; children: Edward Stafford (b. 1470), 10th earl of Wiltshire.*

## Stafford, countess of.

*See Audley, Margaret (fl. 1340s).*
*See Stafford, Philippa (d. before 1386).*
*See Anne Plantagenet (1383–1438).*

## Stafford, Eleanor (d. 1530).

*See Percy, Eleanor.*

## Stafford, Elizabeth (d. 1532)

*Mistress of Henry VIII, king of England. Name variations: Countess of Essex. Died before May 11, 1532; interred at Boreham, Essex; daughter of Henry Stafford (1455–1483), 2nd duke of Buckingham (r. 1460–1483), and \*Katherine Woodville (c. 1442–1512); married Robert Fitzwalter (c. 1483–1542), earl of Essex, on July 23, 1505; children: Henry Radcliffe, 2nd earl of Sussex; George Radcliffe; Humphrey Radcliffe. Following the death of Elizabeth Stafford, Robert Fitzwalter married Margaret Stanley.*

## Stafford, Elizabeth (1494–1558)

*Duchess of Norfolk. Born in 1494; died in 1558; daughter of Edward Stafford (1478–1521), 3rd duke*

of Buckingham (executed on May 17, 1521), and *Eleanor Percy (d. 1530); married Thomas Howard (1473–1554), 3rd duke of Norfolk (r. 1524–1554), on January 8, 1512 or 1513; children: Henry Howard (1517–1547), earl of Surrey; *Mary Fitzroy (c. 1519–1557); Thomas Howard, Viscount Bindon. Thomas Howard's first wife was *Anne Howard (1475–1511).

# Stafford, Jean (1915–1979)

*Pulitzer Prize-winning American novelist, short-story writer, essayist, and journalist. Born in Covina, California, on July 1, 1915; died of cardiac arrest in White Plains, New York, on March 26, 1979; daughter of John Richard Stafford (a writer, reporter, and rancher) and Mary Ethel McKillop; attended the University of Colorado, Boulder, 1932–36 (received B.A. and M.A. degrees); studied philology at the University of Heidelberg, Germany, 1936–37; married Robert (Cal) Lowell (the poet), on April 2, 1940 (divorced 1948); married Oliver Jensen (an editor at Life magazine), on January 28, 1950 (divorced 1953); married A.J. Liebling (the writer), on April 3, 1959 (died 1963); no children.*

*Taught at Stephens College, Columbia, Missouri (1937–38); had first story published (1939); published Boston Adventure (selected for People's Book Club, 1944); awarded Guggenheim fellowship and National Institute of Arts and Letters Grant (1945); received second Guggenheim fellowship and National Press Club Award (1948); received O. Henry award for "In the Zoo" (1955); named a fellow at the Center for Advanced Studies, Wesleyan University (1964–65); awarded Rockefeller Foundation Grant (1965); taught at Columbia University (1967–68); received Pulitzer Prize for Collected Stories (1970); elected to National Academy of Arts and Letters (1970); suffered a stroke (1976).*

Jean Stafford, like St. *Teresa of Avila, lived in her own "Interior Castle" where dwelt her imaginative, creative, private self. She was ambitious, egocentric, mentally and physically fragile, socially timid, the perennial outsider who suffered from "a sense of 'dislocation' that had no cure." Stafford hated her father for his inadequacies, dismissed her mother as irrelevant, and disliked the West where she was born and brought up. It has been noted that the misfits, the irascible, the unloved and unwanted females in her fiction vividly reflect the stages of her own disordered life and of her quest for a new identity—to be an orphan free of all familial ties would have suited her just fine.

Jean Stafford was born in 1915 in Covina, California, the youngest of four children. Her father John Richard Stafford had been a newspaper reporter and a rancher, but after he squandered his inheritance, he sold their large house and land and moved the family to Colorado. Her mother **Mary Ethel Stafford** converted their new home in Boulder into a boardinghouse which embarrassed Jean, despite the fact that her mother's efforts secured college educations for all four children. Moreover, Jean resented her father's inability to provide for his family; a failure as a writer of stories and a novel about the Old West, he became bitter and reclusive. After her father died, Jean wrote to her sister **Mary Lee Stafford** that John Stafford "was completely undisciplined and completely lazy and completely self-indulgent and I can't forgive him." And she never did. Alienation from family was not all that made Stafford want to escape her surroundings. As she recalled, "the Rocky Mountains were too big to take in, too high to understand, too domineering to love." Her rejection of family and environment caused Stafford to turn inward and to writing.

At age six, Stafford wrote a poem, "Gravel, gravel on the ground," which later appeared in her book *The Mountain Lion*. She also wrote stories and produced a novel set in the British Museum. Her early writing reflects her incredible command of language; in a story, she described a man's black hair as "oleaginous." Stafford was a good student and at age 15 won the annual state high school essay contest with a story that mocked her father. Attending the University of Colorado on a scholarship was Stafford's first step towards independence and creating an individual persona. She wanted to attain respectability, but did not join a sorority. Instead, she associated with fellow students who were interested in literature and the rather bohemian campus lifestyle of the 1930s. However, despite her achievements and abilities, Stafford suffered from loneliness and insecurity. Reserved and secretive about herself, she avoided intimacy and romantic encounters.

At the university, Stafford worked as a model for life-drawing art classes, posing nude, she wrote, while she was "grimly sketched in charcoal and viscously painted in oil." By the time she was a junior, she had developed an interest in medieval languages and wrote her master's thesis on "Profane and Divine Love in English Literature in the Thirteenth Century." In four years, Stafford had earned B.A. and M.A. degrees, and she decided to become a philologist. Education, she hoped, would help her acquire wealth and culture where "no untoward noises . . . no barbaric speech, no rough manners" were allowed. This may explain Stafford's friendship with **Lucy McKee**, a rich, intelligent, sexually promiscuous young law student whose hedonistic lifestyle attracted Jean. In 1935, Lucy committed suicide. Stafford tried throughout her literary career to write about Lucy and campus life in the 1930s; "In the Snowfall" would undergo many revisions but never be completed. Like McKee, Stafford's physical and psychological health were unstable during much of her adult life, and alcohol compounded these problems.

> *Writing is a private, an almost secret enterprise carried on within the heart and mind in a room whose doors are closed.*
>
> —Jean Stafford

In a play written in 1936, which won first prize and was performed on campus, Stafford had already discovered that "You search the four corners of the earth for love and warmth, and your soul yells out in anguish. But the world is hostile eternally, even to those who make the most beautiful things." With a frightening prescience, Jean Stafford had written her own life scenario. No person or place ever lived up to her expectations, no love ever satisfied her need to belong, and she battled a hostile world, often of her own making, while writing her incomparable prose.

After earning two degrees in four years, Stafford received a fellowship to study at the University of Heidelberg in Germany, allowing her to escape from her "benighted family" and to savor the beauty of Old World culture. Germany was in the throes of Nazification, and at the university each class period ended with a "Heil Hitler," which Stafford also said. Without approving of the Nazi ideology, she admitted she was glad to have been there in that "alarming time," living in "a nation of madmen in the third stage of paranoia, believing sincerely that they are the New Messiah." Stafford attended classes for only one month before losing interest in her studies. Instead, she began working on a novel which she failed to get published, but she slowly realized that she was not attracted to a scholarly life. Heidelberg did, however, provide Stafford with material for her later short stories and with a lifelong friend, James Robert Hightower, who had a fellowship to study Chinese and became a professor at Harvard University. Their relationship was platonic and intellectual, never as intimate as Hightower would have liked. Jean was, and remained, fearful of personal involvements, even with her three husbands.

Knowing she had to earn a living, Stafford returned to the States in April 1937 and attended a writers' conference in Boulder in July. This gave her the opportunity to meet established writers and to show them some of her poems, a short story, 105 pages of a new novel, and her journal from Heidelberg. These contacts did not result in publication, but Stafford was not discouraged, and one contact changed her life: Ford Madox Ford introduced Jean to the future well-known poet, Robert (Cal) Lowell, a member of elite Boston society. He would provide Stafford with entrée into his world through marriage.

However, marriage was a distant prospect, and Jean had to find a job. It took her only one year to become disillusioned with teaching freshman English at Stephens College, a "charm school" for women as she portrayed it in her short story "Caveat Emptor." The girls were "frivolous," she wrote, and nearly all were "dumb but beautiful." As they prepared for their roles as future wives and mothers, they knitted in class and wrote term papers on the advantages of long engagements and "A Short History of Fingernail Polish." The faculty was hardly less mediocre; they were, Stafford recalled, "not evil, simply foolish and misguided. They were academicians who scorn intellectuals—and are proud of it." Stafford's complaints about her students to the administration led to her dismissal. Disenchanted with academia, she turned to her writing. In early 1938, she submitted a novel about Lucy McKee to a publisher. The manuscript was rejected; her use of stream of consciousness was "too meandering," they said, and the sex scenes were not convincing. Ford Madox Ford had advised Stafford to avoid employing autobiography in fiction. But she ignored his advice at this time and in the future. Jean Stafford wrote using her own experiences, her fears and desires, and her fantasies.

In the summer of 1938, Stafford's personal and professional lives were in complete disarray. She had two men, Hightower and Lowell, in her life, but she was afraid that "she was a frigid woman doomed to love from a distance and to betray." Moreover, she refused to abandon writing to become a wife like her mother, whom she deemed vapid. A visit to her family left her repulsed: "I hope that I will not remember how it is how ugly it is how tragic how heartbreaking." But she did remember, and the gulf between Stafford and her family was never bridged. She realized "that the price of pursuing the life of the mind was the loss of a home," of her home with her family. In the fall, Jean had a fellowship at the University of Iowa to teach and participate in the Writer's Workshop. Once again, she hated the academic atmosphere and teaching, and one night in mid-semester she boarded a bus and fled to New York, her imagined cultural nirvana. Marriage to Hightower could have solved her problem of what to do next, but Jean could not answer the question "do art and love mix?" at the time—or at any time in her life.

From New York, Stafford moved to Boston and resumed her acquaintance with Robert Lowell. After leaving a nightclub one evening in December 1938, Lowell lost control of his car and crashed; Jean suffered serious facial lacerations and internal injuries. She sued Lowell and his family for $25,000, but the lawsuit did not end their courtship. Lowell's parents never approved of Stafford; she lacked "pedigree" and was an unsuitable match for a Lowell. Indeed, Robert Lowell represented the social and cultural class that Stafford envied, but she expressed reservations about marrying a man who "scared" her and often "got savage." And even though she loved Hightower, she confessed to him that "my selfishness is so all consuming that I can't help hurting you." Stafford married Low-

Jean
Stafford

ell in New York in April 1940, thus achieving her desire to become an "insider," to belong to elite Boston society. But she was still ambivalent about marriage and about Lowell. As she wrote to Hightower, "Poor Cal! What a life he will have with me." **Ann Hulbert** questions whether Jean would have married if her novel, *Autumn Festival*, had been accepted by the Atlantic Monthly Press. The focus of the novel was the experience of a girl at the University of Heidelberg who took up with the Nazis, embracing her ancestral fatherland—not a popular subject in late 1939 as the real-life Nazis spread through Eastern Europe.

Stafford and Lowell soon left for Baton Rouge where he would pursue graduate work at Louisiana State University while Jean worked as a secretary at the *Southern Review*. She enjoyed the intellectual stimulation at the university, keeping house, and attempting a different style of writing. A short story based on her experience in the hospital after the car crash eventually became part of her first published novel, *Boston Adventure*. From reading the mystic St. Teresa of Avila, Stafford "found a deep symbolic landscape" which influenced her writing; Jean's short story "The Interior Castle" utilizes St. Teresa's belief that "our soul [is] like a castle . . . in which there are many rooms." Finally, Stafford had discovered the symbols and images that gave structure to her work.

Her marriage was a less solid structure. Lowell had become a zealous convert to Roman Catholicism which consumed his creative energies. "Impious habits" such as smoking and drinking were no longer allowed, an injunction Stafford ignored. Lowell's piety did not preclude his being physically abusive. He hit Stafford and broke her nose which required further surgeries. As she confided to Hightower, "I'm boxed up and I'm hopeless and there is no one to talk to." Reflexively she became ill, took to her bed, and began writing *Boston Adventure*.

Returning to New York in the fall of 1941, both Jean and Cal worked for a Catholic publishing house, and they had frequent contact with the New York literary crowd associated with the prestigious literary journal, the *Partisan Review*. Novelist *Caroline Gordon and her husband, the poet Allen Tate, introduced them to other well-known figures, such as Philip Rahv, Delmore Schwartz, and Robert Giroux, a young editor at Harcourt, Brace. At Cal's insistence, Jean also did Catholic volunteer work, encountering "discomfort both with faith and with the vulgarity of the physical world." But in New

York, Stafford could still withdraw into her own interior castle and produce fiction. In April 1942, she signed a contract with Harcourt, Brace, and in July, she and Cal went to live with the Tates in Monteagle, Tennessee. During the year with the Tates, Stafford worked on *Boston Adventure* while Lowell finally began writing the poetry that would make his name. The Tates and Lowell were merciless in criticizing Jean's novel, but it was creative, not malicious, criticism. As Hulbert notes, this year was Stafford's "first extensive and intensive exposure to life devoted to art."

From Monteagle, Stafford went to Yaddo, the writers' colony in Sarasota, New York. She was anxious to finish her novel, but she was not happy at Yaddo and her typical response to a stressful situation was to become ill. Stafford felt "a sense of alienation from the literary company" there whom she labeled "abject souls." She quickly abandoned Yaddo and went to join Lowell in New York. In September 1943, Lowell was to be inducted into the army; when he refused to serve, he was sentenced to a year and a day in prison. Lowell's mother **Charlotte Winslow Lowell** unfairly blamed Jean for her son's predicament. Alone again, Stafford continued to revise her novel and renewed her contacts among the local literary circles whom she described as "cut-throats . . . ambitious and bourgeois frights." But she needed these contacts for without them she felt "abandoned and uncreative." Lowell was paroled in March 1944; in prison he had become a more zealous Catholic which worried Stafford. Their marriage was severely strained already, and they had not had sex since Lowell's religious conversion. But their creative energies were enhanced, it seemed, by their proximity to one another.

Despite their personal problems, they rented a house in Connecticut and resumed their writing. Stafford's short stories were being published, and Lowell was writing poetry, which pleased Jean. *Boston Adventure* appeared in September 1944 and was an immediate success: over 200,000 copies were eventually sold. This led to a new worry—how would her literary friends react to a commercially popular work? Would substantial royalties denigrate the literary value of the novel? On the other hand, Stafford hoped the money would enable her to buy a house, a large house set in beautiful, natural surroundings, a refuge where she could settle down and develop roots. With this in mind, she often published in popular magazines rather than the more distinguished literary journals. She also took a position teaching creative writing at Queens College in Flushing, New York, in the spring of 1945. Stafford was never comfortable in front of a class, but she wanted the additional income.

That same spring, Jean received a $1,000 prize from the National Institute of Arts and Letters for *Boston Adventure* and a fellowship from the Guggenheim Foundation to work on a sequel to the novel. A few months later, she bought *her* house in the village of Darmariscotta Mills, Maine, which required extensive renovation, so Stafford and Lowell lived with Delmore Schwartz for several months. Schwartz envied Lowell's social background and created ill feelings between Stafford and Lowell. Jean was depressed, drank excessively, and suffered from insomnia, all while trying to write her second novel, *The Mountain Lion*, for which she already had a contract with Harcourt, Brace. She needed to live in a house that belonged to her. But to Lowell, the house "seemed to mean imprisonment," and he accused Stafford of trying "to stifle him" with her domesticity.

*The Mountain Lion* took only nine months to write. It is an important part of her literary output; the novel, Molly (the main character), and her own life were "inextricably and tragically connected," she told Lowell. As Stafford noted, "I was so much Molly that finally I had to write her book." The themes of the "disunity of the American identity" and the "conflict of social values that warps personal identity" were based on Jean's life experiences in the West. Like the novel, her fine short story "An Influx of Poets" is based on her and Lowell's lives during the horrendous summer of 1946, when Stafford, Lowell, and several literary friends shared the house in Maine. Lowell became physically abusive, and Jean drank, had debilitating headaches, and trouble sleeping. Moreover, Lowell openly flirted with Stafford's friend **Gertrude Buckman**, ex-wife of Delmore Schwartz. Jean lamented to her sister Mary Lee, "Being a writer and being married to a writer is a back breaking job and my back is now broken." However, Stafford never blamed Lowell for their situation. She lost her husband and her house after that terrible summer, and she thought she was losing her mind.

Stafford was hurt and felt insecure as a writer. In the fall of 1946, she signed herself into the Payne Whitney Psychiatric Clinic in New York Hospital. Again Jean was "dislocated" and sought a safe haven and a stable environment. But she was ambivalent about being "cured" of her anxieties; if her mental state were stabilized, would this destroy her creative abilities? Stafford also feared that she had "no objective existence." She wanted assurance "that I am a woman, that I am a reality and not an abstraction." Lowell had cruelly informed her that no one could love her, and Jean admitted that she had difficulty with intimacy. This was obvious when her mother died. When she joined her family in Oregon, she was again treated like the youngest child. Further, her father was boring, and her sister **Margie Stafford** told her she was fat. Jean felt unloved and unwanted. Returning East, she had to sell the house in Maine which saddened her even more.

After a year in the hospital, Stafford was uncertain about her future; she had medical bills, a broken marriage, and no home. In November 1947, she moved to an apartment in New York and began to take science courses at Columbia. To make money, she wrote articles for *Vogue* and still struggled with her novel based on Lucy McKee's suicide. Stafford needed to find a new niche, a new outlet for her creativity. Thus began a decade-long association with *The New Yorker* magazine and the acquisition of new friends. In one of her stories, "Children Are Bored on Sunday," which was largely autobiographical, Stafford dealt with "the tension between the rustic and the sophisticate, the colloquial and the refined"—her own Western self versus her Eastern persona. Old friends, such as the poet John Berryman, told her the story was weak, and she should be ashamed of herself for writing it. Moreover, *The New Yorker* was too middlebrow, too philistine for the *Partisan Review* crowd. Stafford had signed a contract in November for "In the Snowfall," her Lucy novel, but she would never finish or publish it.

In April 1948, Jean spent six weeks in the Virgin Islands to get a divorce from Lowell. Her story "A Modest Proposal" reflects her reaction to the women who "littered the terrace and the lounges of the hotels, idling through their six weeks' quarantine." When she returned to New York, Stafford continued to publish her short stories and to receive awards, a second Guggenheim and a National Press Club Award. She set out on a trip to Europe in the spring of 1949, on assignment for *The New Yorker*. She proved to be "an able reporter" and enjoyed her new role. Back in New York, she again had to confront the "demons" she faced each time she attempted to work on "In the Snowfall"—her father and Lucy McKee herself. Stafford feared that psychiatry might have dulled her "gift" for writing: "If it has, God knows what will become of me because it is the only thing in the world I have." She reluctantly set the novel aside and began work on a new novel, *The Catherine Wheel*.

While the book is stylistically one of Stafford's best pieces of writing, it is obvious that she was not fully "engaged in her material."

There is little doubt that Stafford was creative but rather neurotic, admired and successful but dissatisfied with her life. She wanted to marry, to have a real home of her own; in January 1950, she acquired a husband and a house. Oliver Jensen was an editor at *Life* magazine, Yale educated, and well-off financially. However, living at "a low pitch" quickly lost its appeal for Stafford. She drank heavily, complained about Jensen's "tedious friends," and had trouble writing. Relations with her own family were also strained. Following a family gathering in Colorado, Stafford wrote: "I am amazed that all of us did not commit suicide in our cradles." She returned to New York and entered the hospital, her escape from emotional traumas. Normal human relations seemed impossible. At the end of 1952, Stafford took up residence again in the Virgin Islands to obtain a divorce from Jensen. As with Lowell, she did not blame Jensen: "I am all you say, a liar, a breaker of promises, an alcoholic, an incompetent . . . a hypochondriac."

Personal failure was the result of her inability to be "overtly loved," she told a friend. But her literary career and reputation were still widely acclaimed. She won three O. Henry awards for her stories, and *The Catherine Wheel* sold well. In 1953, her first collection of short stories, *Children Are Bored on Sunday*, was a great success, and she had another contract for a novel. Despite her literary successes, Stafford "was terrified by the patterns of her life, . . . by the fact that she had imagined and had written much that had happened later." As Hulbert notes, "Stafford's own existence imitated her art, rather than the other way around." Although she had two to four stories published each year and would receive a Pulitzer Prize for her *Collected Stories*, Stafford fretted over what she feared most, loss of her creativity.

She needed to escape from her usual haunts, and in the summer of 1956, she went to London. Her writing had become a crushing burden, and she needed to separate herself from Lowell with whom she had remained in touch. Lowell had had a second mental breakdown, and Stafford was emotionally drained herself. In London, she socialized with writers and intellectuals, drank too much, and consulted a psychiatrist. And she met A.J. Liebling who also wrote for *The New Yorker*. He was what Stafford needed, a protector, and he admired her. After reading her work, he wrote her that "really you are a better writer than almost anybody I know." They were married in April 1959, and contentment began to take precedence over writing for Jean. She claimed she was happy for the first time in her life. But she continued to drink and to worry about how to balance marriage and writing. Conflicts soon arose over Stafford's "highbrow *PR* [*Partisan Review*] pedigree and the lowlife reporter tastes that Liebling liked to cultivate." By July 1960, they were often going their separate ways.

In a dream, Stafford conceived the idea of writing a novel about her Scottish ancestors. She traveled to the Isle of Arran in the Firth of Clyde and then to Samothrace, following her dream. Inertia overwhelmed her desire to write the story, however, though she did publish numerous articles, interviews, satirical pieces, and book reviews for *Vogue, McCall's, Esquire*, and *Mademoiselle* during the 1960s, including an article for *Horizon* on the film *The Misfits* starring *Marilyn Monroe* and Clark Gable. After a short trip to Europe in the summer of 1963, Liebling became ill and died on December 28. The next month Stafford was hospitalized with numerous, serious medical problems. In April, she had a mild heart attack. When released from the hospital, she moved into Liebling's house in East Hampton, Long Island.

Stafford maintained contact with former friends and with Lowell. He was instrumental in securing a fellowship for Jean at Wesleyan University in 1964. Here, surrounded by scholarly academics, Stafford hoped to revive her creative energies. However, she soon realized she could not write in an academic environment. Her collection *Bad Stories* appeared while she was at Wesleyan and received good reviews. She also went to Dallas, Texas, to interview **Marguerite Oswald**, mother of Lee Harvey Oswald, the assassin of President John F. Kennedy, for *McCall's* magazine. Unable to relate to "the assassin's peculiar mother," Stafford wrote an unflattering portrait of Mrs. Oswald. A year later, her only nonfiction work, *A Mother in History*, was published. This elicited a barrage of hate mail which accused Stafford of being a Jew, a Communist, a member of the right-wing John Birch Society, anti-Catholic, and having besmirched the "sacred throne of motherhood."

As she aged, Stafford became a quarrelsome curmudgeon. When her father died, she did not attend the funeral; her sisters had called her collect to inform her of his death, and Jean was furious that she had to pay the $1.75 for the call. She severed relations with her family forever. To Jean, the 1960s were too disorderly, too individualistic, too "me" centered. This was evident in a class she taught at Columbia; the students had no interest in or appreciation of classical writers, and Stafford could not relate to the current popular culture. As she remarked on the youth of the time, they "love nobody but themselves and their cry is *I* want *mine*!" The social upheavals repelled her: "Things grow grimmer and grimmer. Anger alone keeps me alive." Teaching was not her forte, but she gave invited lectures and wrote articles on the state of society, the use of incomprehensible jargon, on manners, etiquette, and the women's movement (she denied being a feminist). To avoid direct contact with the unenlightened outside world, Stafford created an alter ego, Henrietta Stackpole, who wrote letters for Jean and served as "an intermediary with a vulgar world." Stafford accepted an honorary degree from the University of Colorado in 1972, but discouraged her sister Mary Lee from attending the ceremony. Jean did, however, remain in touch with both Hightower and Lowell. In Lowell's poem "Jean Stafford, a Letter," her former husband wrote, "You have spoken so many words and well,/ being a woman and you . . . someone must still hear/ whatever I have forgotten/ or never heard, being a man." Angrily dismissing his assessment of her, she vowed she would have nothing more to do with him. But Robert Lowell was the subject of her last published story, "An Influx of Poets" (1978).

A stroke in December 1976 robbed Stafford of the ability to speak; a friend told her, "You can't speak because you find everything unspeakable. You can't talk because you see no one fit to talk to." In over forty stories and three novels, Stafford's female characters were often orphans, social misfits who suffered from culture and class "dislocation." Similarly, Stafford had become a recluse, an orphan of her own making. Before she died in March 1979, she ordered her tombstone engraved with a snowflake, the symbol of "In the Snowfall," the novel she never wrote.

**SOURCES:**

*Dictionary of Literary Biography*, Vol. 2: *American Novelists Since World War II*. Edited by Jeffrey Helterman and Richard Layman. Detroit, MI: Gale Research, 1978.

Hulbert, Ann. *The Interior Castle: The Art and Life of Jean Stafford*. NY: Alfred A. Knopf, 1992.

Walsh, Mary Ellen Williams. *Jean Stafford*. Boston, MA: Twayne, 1985.

**SUGGESTED READING:**

Goodman, Charlotte Margolis. *Jean Stafford: The Savage Heart*. Austin, TX: University of Texas Press, 1990.

Hamilton, Ian. *Robert Lowell: A Biography*. NY: Random House, 1982.

Laskin, David. *Partisans: Marriage, Politics, and Betrayal Among the New York Intellectuals*. NY: Simon and Schuster, 2000.

Roberts, David. *Jean Stafford*. Boston, MA: Little, Brown, 1988.

Straus, Dorothea. "Jean Stafford," in *Shenandoah*. Vol. 30, no. 3, 1979, pp. 85–91.

**Jeanne A. Ojala**, Professor Emerita,
Department of History, University of Utah,
Salt Lake City, Utah

# Stafford, Jo (1920—)

***Popular American singer of the 1940s and 1950s.** Born Jo Elizabeth Stafford on November 12, 1920, in Coalinga, California; daughter of Grover Cleveland Stafford (an oilman) and Anna (York) Stafford (a banjoist); married John Huddleston (divorced); married Paul Weston (an arranger-conductor), in 1952; children: (second marriage) Tim and Amy.*

Born in 1920 in Coalinga, California, where her father had come to seek his fortune in the California oil fields, singer Jo Stafford may have inherited some of her musical talent from her mother **Anna York Stafford**, who in addition to being a distant cousin of World War I hero Alvin York was also a highly acclaimed five-string banjoist. Stafford began her professional career singing in a trio with her sisters **Christina** and **Pauline**. The girls had their own weekly radio shows and also performed with David Broekman's California Melodies and with productions starring the Crockett Family of Kentucky. When marriage broke up the sister act, Stafford joined seven male singers in a group called the Pied Pipers. In 1938, the Pied Pipers were hired by Tommy Dorsey, but after only ten weeks with the band, the group split up. Stafford later joined three other singers (also called the Pied Pipers) and continued working with Dorsey for the next three years. During this time, she recorded "I'll Never Smile Again" with Frank Sinatra, who later praised her vocal technique. "She can hold notes for sixteen bars if she wants to," he said. Stafford and the Pipers left Dorsey in late 1942, after which they worked successfully on various radio shows, including "Your Hit Parade."

Stafford left the group in 1944, to go out on her own. She was immediately signed by Johnny Mercer for his radio show and to record with his newly formed Capitol Records. Before the end of World War II, Stafford was rivaling *Dinah Shore as the most popular female singer in the country, particularly with soldiers. By 1946, after making guest appearances on numerous radio shows, she launched her own radio series, "Chesterfield Supper Club."

Jo
Stafford

In 1950, Stafford began receiving international recognition with a series of tape-recorded youth programs broadcast worldwide on the Voice of America. She soon added another weekly musical show for Radio Luxemburg, then Europe's most powerful station. In 1952, she appeared at the London Palladium and toured the British Isles and the Continent for the Voice of America. That same year, she married Paul Weston, a conductor-arranger whom she had been working with since the 1940s. (Stafford had earlier been married briefly to John Huddleston, one of the Pied Pipers.) The couple had two children, Tim and Amy.

Stafford remained active during the early 1950s, recording and making regular appearances on many of the popular television variety programs and on her own series, "The Jo Stafford Show," which was launched in 1954. In the late 1950s, the singer curtailed her activities somewhat to devote more time to her children, although she continued to record and make occasional appearances on those television shows based in Hollywood, where she and her husband made their home. (Stafford also limited her television work because of her vision. "Idiot cards don't exist for people with eyesight like mine," she said.) In 1961, the family spent the summer in London, where Stafford did a series of shows for the ATV British network.

Stafford is one of the few performers to have three plaques on Hollywood's Boulevard of the Stars: for radio, television, and recordings. Her recording career culminated in a diamond award as the first recording artist to sell 25 million records. Among her best-known hits are "You Belong to Me," "Whispering Hope" (with Gordon MacRae), "Shrimp Boats," "Make Love to Me," and "Jambalaya." Her later recordings include more standards, Broadway show tunes, and some jazz. She also produced some religious albums for Corinthian and the World Library of Sacred Music.

Well known for her sense of humor, Stafford has also moonlighted as a couple of other singers, Cinderella G. Stump and Darlene Edwards (whose recordings with Jonathan Edwards—really Paul Weston—are some of the best comedy spoofs ever made). Under her first alias, Cinderella Stump, Stafford recorded "Timtayshun," a hillbilly version of the 1933 hit "Temptation," for which she tapped into her family's Southern roots. Capitol sent it out to disc jockeys saying only that Stump was a well-known singer out to have a little fun. After the recording sold 1 million copies, the record company finally revealed the singer's name, although most people did not believe it was Stafford until she performed the song live on a coast-to-coast broadcast.

The Jonathan and Darlene Edwards albums that Stafford made with her husband were an outgrowth of a party act the two performed parodying all the mediocre lounge singers and pianists they had encountered in their past travels. "At the piano, Jonathan blithely missed notes, fumbled for others, and completely misplaced still others," write Roy Hemming and David Hajdu, "usually while completely garbling the beat. Darlene, meanwhile, kept madly up with him in all respects, continually sliding into notes or wandering blithely off-key (usually exactly a quarter-tone off), holding on to notes or jumping ahead of Jonathan unpredictably, always demonstrating more gusto than musical accuracy." The initial Jonathan and Darlene Edwards album, issued in 1952, with a photograph on the cover of two left hands side-by-side on a keyboard, was such a hit that Columbia subsequently issued four more. One of the albums, *Jonathan and Darlene in Paris*, won a Grammy Award.

By the 1960s, Stafford had pretty much ended her career, although she came out of retirement in the 1970s for another Darlene Edwards album and one of Fats Waller and Duke Ellington songs. One of her last public appear-

ances was to celebrate the 25th anniversary of SHARE, a charitable organization that aids the mentally challenged with which she has been associated for many years.

**SOURCES:**
Hemming, Roy, and David Hajdu. *Discovering Great Singers of Classic Pop*. NY: Newmarket, 1991.
Kinkel, Roger. *The Complete Encyclopedia of Popular Music and Jazz 1900–1950*. New Rochelle, NY: Arlington House, 1974.

**Barbara Morgan,**
Melrose, Massachusetts

## Stafford, Margaret (d. 1396)

*Countess of Westmoreland. Name variations: Margaret Neville; Margaret de Stafford. Born before 1364; died on June 9, 1396; daughter of *Philippa Stafford (d. before 1386) and Hugh Stafford, 2nd earl of Stafford; married Ralph Neville (b. 1363), 1st earl of Westmoreland; children: John Neville (b. 1387); Ralph Neville (d. 1457); Anne Neville (who married Gilbert de Umfreville, 3rd baron of Umfreville); Margaret Neville (d. 1464, who married Richard Scrope, 3rd Lord Scrope).*

## Stafford, Mary (d. 1543).

*See Boleyn, Anne for sidebar on Mary Boleyn.*

## Stafford, Philippa (d. before 1386)

*Countess of Stafford. Name variations: Philippa Beauchamp; Philippe Beauchamp. Died before April 6, 1386; daughter of Thomas Beauchamp (b. 1313), 3rd earl of Warwick (some sources cite 11th earl of Warwick), and *Catherine Mortimer (c. 1313–1369); married Hugh Stafford, 2nd earl of Stafford, on March 1, 1350; children: Ralph Stafford, Lord Stafford; *Margaret Stafford (d. 1396, who married Ralph Neville, 1st earl of Westmoreland); Joan Stafford (d. 1442, who married Thomas Holland, 3rd earl of Kent); Thomas Stafford (c. 1368–1392), 3rd earl of Stafford; William Stafford (b. 1375); *Catherine Stafford (d. 1419, who married Michael de la Pole, 2nd earl of Suffolk); Edmund Stafford (1378–1403), 5th earl of Stafford.*

## Stagecoach Mary (c. 1832–1914).

*See Fields, Mary.*

## Stahr-Lewald, Fanny (1811–1889).

*See Lewald, Fanny.*

## Staley, Dawn (1970—)

*American athlete. Born on May 4, 1970, in Philadelphia, Pennsylvania; graduated from the University of Virginia, 1992.*

*Won numerous athletic honors throughout high school and college career; was a member of the gold medal-winning women's basketball team representing the U.S. in the Atlanta Olympics (1996); played with the American Basketball League's Philadelphia Rage (1996–97); moved to the Women's National Basketball Association (1998).*

At 5'6", Dawn Staley seemed an unlikely candidate for the U.S. women's Olympic basketball team, but her incredible high school and college basketball career proved that height is not as important as determination and talent. Born in 1970 and raised in Philadelphia, the youngest of a family of five children, Staley attended Philadelphia's Dobbins Technical High School, where she excelled in athletics, particularly basketball. Determined to be the first in her family to graduate from college, she received a scholarship to the University of Virginia, where she began her academic studies in 1988.

At Virginia, Staley continued the successful career she had begun in high school, leading her team to the National Collegiate Athletic Association (NCAA) Final Four playoffs three years in a row and becoming the most outstanding player of the playoffs in 1991. A three-time winner of the Kodak All-American award, two-time winner of the Women's Basketball Coaches' Naismith Player of the Year award, and recipient of numerous other athletic kudos, Staley also had the respect of her teammates, who elected her team captain in 1992, her senior year at the University of Virginia. At graduation, she held the NCAA career record with 454 steals and the Virginia record for career points and assists during her four years of collegiate play.

From college, it was a natural jump to the Olympic trials, and Staley made the grade. In 1992, she was a member of the R. William Jones Cup team, and from 1993 to 1995 played around the world, taking time out to participate in the 1994 Goodwill Games, where she was named Most Valuable Player after averaging 9.3 points per game. In 1996, Staley was selected to serve on the U.S. Olympic team, where her ranking as its shortest member belied her impressive points-per-game score against Korea. Staley's contributions in the area of rebounds, assists (an average of 3.5 per game) and free throws (she sank nine of ten against Brazil) enabled the United States to take home the gold. That year, Staley also gave back to the community through her establishment of the Dawn Staley Foundation which sponsored an after-school project, a scholarship program and a series of basketball clinics.

After her Olympic success, Staley entered the world of professional basketball, joining the American Basketball League's Philadelphia Rage in her hometown. She was a two-time All-Star with the league before moving to the less intensive Women's National Basketball Association (WNBA) on a three-year contract in September 1998. The WNBA's shorter schedule allowed Staley to rest her battered knees in preparation for a second Olympic run in the 2000 Games. As a leader with the Charlotte Sting, she pulled the team together for a run to the playoffs, averaging 11.5 points and 5.5 assists per game. She added to her team's strengths with her precision passing and her remarkably accurate free-throw shooting, the second-best in the league. Her play earned her the 1999 Sportsmanship Award and the American Express Small Business Entrepreneurial Spirit Award. At the 2000 Games in Sydney, Australia, the U.S. women's basketball team—including Staley, *Sheryl Swoopes, *Lisa Leslie, Natalie Williams and *Teresa Edwards—fought hard against an excellent Australian women's team in the final round, winning the gold medal with a score of 76–54. Among all-time USA Olympic competitors, Staley ranks fourth in assists, with 28. She now serves as head coach of women's basketball at Temple University, one of the youngest Division 1 head coaches in America.

**Pamela Shelton**, freelance writer,
Avon, Connecticut

## Stalin, Nadezhda (1901–1932).
*See Alliluyeva-Stalin, Nadezhda.*

## Stalin, Svetlana (b. 1926).
*See Alliluyeva, Svetlana.*

## Stammers, Kay (1914—)

*British tennis player.* Name variations: Katherine Menzies. Born on April 3, 1914, in St. Albans, Hertsfordshire, England.

Beginning her tennis career at an early age, British tennis player Kay Stammers was a junior champion at age 14 and was the first 17-year-old to compete in the Wimbledon championships (1931). Stammers went on to represent Great Britain against the United States in the Wightman Cup for five years (1934–39), beating out such players as *Helen Hull Jacobs and *Alice Marble. She also won the Surrey hard court singles championship three years in succession, from 1932 to 1934, and again in 1936. Stammers, who was known for her strong left-handed forearm drive, was the first British player to beat *Helen Newington Wills in 11 years (1935).

# Stampa, Gaspara (1523–1554)

*Italian poet. Born in 1523 in Padua, Italy; died on April 23, 1554, in Venice, possibly a suicide; daughter of Bartolomeo Stampa (a gold merchant) and Cecilia Stampa; sister of Cassandra Stampa (a singer); studied classics, history, philosophy, music, Latin, and Greek; never married; no children.*

Widely regarded as the greatest Italian woman poet, Gaspara Stampa was born in 1523 at the height of the Italian Renaissance, the daughter of **Cecilia Stampa** and Bartolomeo Stampa, a gold merchant. After Bartolomeo died in 1530, Cecilia moved her three children to Venice to live near her family. (Gaspara had a brother Baldassare and a sister **Cassandra Stampa**.) Unusual for middle-class girls, Gaspara and Cassandra received the ideal education fashionable at the time for the daughters of nobles, including training in classical languages, literature, music, art, history, and rhetoric. It is thought

Gaspara Stampa

that Cecilia, lacking the funds to give her two daughters large dowries, hoped to educate them for careers as *virtuose*, professional singers and accompanists who performed under the patronage of the Venetian elite.

The three children were exceptionally talented at music, and became renowned in Venice; their home became a center of Venetian music and literary life. Stampa sang, played music, and recited poetry for the distinguished scholars and artists who gathered at the family's home and was considered the most talented of her siblings.

She underwent a spiritual crisis in 1544 on the death of her beloved brother and withdrew from social activities. However, by 1548 she was at the height of her fame, and in that year she fell in love with Collaltino di Collalto, count of Treviso. Despite the fact that in her poems she described herself as young and inexperienced at the time, it is likely that she had, by age 26, enjoyed love affairs, although historians have debated for centuries whether she was in fact a courtesan.

Stampa's affair with Collalto, which was immortalized in the majority of her surviving poems, lasted off and on for three years. Collalto was apparently not as enamored as Stampa, and was in addition often away from Venice serving in the French army. The years of this affair mark the emergence of Stampa as a poet of considerable originality and eloquence, praising her lover but also expressing her physical passion and the emotional turmoil his inconstancy caused her. Many of her sonnets were inspired by Petrarch's poems for his beloved Laura (\*Laure de Noves), yet they are clearly expressive of Stampa's own feelings and personal experience. Her poetry circulated among the salons of Venice and brought her much admiration.

In 1550, Stampa lived for a time with Collalto, but by the end of the year the relationship had ended. After suffering from a deep depression, Stampa eventually fell in love again, with the wealthy Venetian patrician Bartolomeo Zen. Zen was a far more devoted lover than the half-hearted Collalto, and they remained together for two years. In 1553, Stampa, suffering from ill health, moved to Florence to regain her strength. In that year, her admirers arranged for the publication of three of her sonnets in an anthology of Venetian poetry.

She returned to Venice in April 1554, dying from an undiagnosed illness two weeks later. That autumn her sister Cassandra edited the first edition of Stampa's sonnets, published as *Rime d'amore* (Love Sonnets). The book was not widely distributed, and for almost two centuries Stampa's works were barely known. A descendent of Collaltino di Collalto had the poems republished in 1738 to honor his ancestor's memory, which again brought celebrity to Stampa's name. Some poems included in the collection were translated into English in 1881. Romantic writers of the 19th century republished the poems often. At the same time, lacking adequate documentation about her life, they also built up legends about Gaspara Stampa which persisted for many decades, including the legend that she had committed suicide when Collalto left her. The few facts available on her life, sensationalized, became the subject of novels and plays, portraying her as simply a tragic victim of love or a worldly courtesan rather than as an accomplished artist. Only recently has Gaspara Stampa's work been critically reexamined and republished, restoring her to her place among the poets of the Italian Renaissance.

**SOURCES:**

Bassanese, Fiora. *Gaspara Stampa*. Boston, MA: Twayne, 1982.

Warnke, Frank. *Three Women Poets: Renaissance and Baroque*. London: Associated University Presses, 1987.

**Laura York**, M.A. in History, University of California, Riverside, California

# Stanford, Jane (1828–1905)

*American philanthropist and co-founder of Stanford University. Name variations: Mrs. Leland Stanford. Born Jane Lathrop on August 25, 1828, in Albany, New York; died of a heart attack on February 28, 1905, in Honolulu, Hawaii, while on a cruise; daughter of Dyer Lathrop (a businessman) and Jane Ann (Shields) Lathrop; educated at Albany, New York, Female Academy, 1840–41; married Leland Stanford (an attorney and governor of California), in 1850 (died 1893); children: Leland Stanford, Jr. (1868–1884).*

*Moved from New York to California, following husband, who made a fortune in the mining business; after son's death, devoted the family fortune to the establishment of Stanford University; after husband's death, continued to oversee the construction of the Stanford campus.*

Descended from a member of one of the first wave of English colonists to settle New England, Jane Stanford was born in 1828 and raised in Albany, New York, where her father Dyer Lathrop was a successful businessman and her mother **Jane Shields Lathrop** raised the couple's seven children in the family's comfortable middle-class home. In 1850, at age 22, Jane married Leland Stanford, an ambitious and enterprising attorney, and they moved west to the growing community of Port Washington, Wisconsin, where Leland had begun a law practice. The couple's early years would be difficult ones that would find them often apart; in 1852, Leland's law office, including his entire law library, was destroyed in a fire. Jane returned to her family home in Albany while Leland followed his brothers to the West Coast in an effort to recoup his financial losses. A savvy businessman, he found success in the mining trade, and returned to Jane in 1855 with a fortune of over $125,000. The lure of California and its riches soon proved too strong a temptation for the Stanfords, and they moved west again to make their home in Sacramento, Leland with the intention of embarking on a political career. Elected governor of California in 1861, Leland made millions of dollars as a railroad builder over the next decade. In addition to performing her role as the wife of a successful businessman and politician, Jane Stanford was involved in various philanthropic endeavors until the birth of her first and only child, Leland, Jr., in 1868.

Leland, Jr., became the focus of the couple's life, and he received every benefit that their vast wealth could bestow. Tragically, while in Florence, Italy, during a world tour taken by the family in celebration of his anticipated first year of college, Leland, Jr., was stricken with typhoid fever and died on March 13, 1884, shortly before his 16th birthday. In dealing with their tragic loss, the bereaved parents found an outlet for their grief by remembering their son's love of learning. They determined to found a university in his honor, to be named the Leland Stanford Jr. University, and in 1885 plans were underway to build it on their 7,000-acre agricultural estate in Palo Alto; the present-day Stanford University is the result of their efforts.

The university held its initial classes in the fall of 1891, using the first buildings constructed from the couple's master plan for the university. Unfortunately, Leland Stanford, Sr., died two years later, leaving Jane Stanford to sort out a complex financial situation that included closing out her husband's business interests in addition to setting up plans for the administration of the school's $20 million endowment. Advised to close the school while funds were locked during the probate process, Stanford declined, and used her own income from her husband's estate and monies gained from the sale of her jewelry to keep the school open. In 1894, the school's existence was again threatened when the U.S. government filed a $15 million claim against the Stanford estate. Only by the considerable lobby-ing efforts of Jane Stanford was the government's claim recalled, and the school's endowment was completed in 1901 through the transference of $11 million in negotiable securities and 100,000 acres of real estate.

Under Stanford University's founding grant, Jane Stanford was given a great deal of power in determining matters regarding the planning and growth of the campus as well as in the choice of curriculum and faculty at the college. Idealizing the school as a shrine to her son and husband, Stanford began an ambitious building program that sorely tested the school's budget. While her dictates became increasingly whimsical due to her escalating reliance on spiritualism in making decisions, the efforts of the school's president to interject reasonable questions regarding fiscal restraint went unheeded. The conflict between Stanford's idealized vision and the school's ability to provide a proper education came to a head in 1900 when the 72-year-old Stanford demanded that popular economics professor and respected scholar Edward A. Ross be dismissed from his teaching position due to his overt socialist leanings. Demanding non-partisanship, Stanford stated that her decision was based on the prayer she had done concerning the matter, a justification that did not sit well with several members of the university's staff, who promptly resigned in protest. The incident made the national press, and educators from across the nation joined in condemning Stanford's decision to dismiss Ross.

Hurt by the outcry from Stanford faculty, Jane Stanford relinquished her powers under the trusteeship in 1903 and, after a world tour, revisited schools and friends in New York State and throughout New England. While on a cruise in the Pacific, she suffered a fatal heart attack; she was buried with her son and husband on the campus of Stanford University. In addition to her dedication to Stanford University, Jane Stanford is remembered for founding several kindergartens in the Palo Alto area, and for establishing an orphanage, the Children's Hospital, in Albany, New York, in memory of her parents.

SOURCES:

James, Edward T., ed. *Notable American Women, 1607–1950*. Cambridge, MA: The Belknap Press of Harvard University, 1971.

King, William C. *Woman*. Springfield, MA: King-Richardson, 1902.

**Pamela Shelton**, freelance writer,
Avon, Connecticut

# Stanford, Mrs. Leland (1828–1905).

*See Stanford, Jane.*

## Stangeland, Karin Michaëlis (1872–1950).

*See Michaëlis, Karin.*

## Stanhope, Hester (1776–1839)

*Aristocratic English traveler who pioneered Western access to remote areas of the Middle East and later settled in the region, performing humanitarian services and acquiring a reputation for wisdom and sanctity. Name variations: Lady Hester Stanhope. Born Hester Lucy Stanhope on March 12, 1776, at Chevening, Kent, England; died at Djoun, Lebanon, on June 23, 1839; daughter of Charles, Viscount Mahon, later 3rd earl Stanhope (a radical politician) and Hester Pitt, Lady Mahon (daughter of William Pitt, the Elder); received fragmentary education, mainly from governesses and her father; never married; no children.*

*Left England for good (1810); became first European woman to enter Syrian city of Palmyra (1813); settled in Lebanon in 1820s, becoming object of a romantic cult.*

In the spring of 1813 an extraordinary event occurred amidst the ancient ruins of Palmyra, deep in the Syrian desert. Accompanied by a Bedouin escort, an Englishwoman, Lady Hester Stanhope, resplendent in male Bedouin costume, arrived to receive the plaudits of the local population. Her feat was a remarkable one. Many travelers had tried but very few had succeeded in braving the rigors of the arid climate and the dangers from warring tribes to reach the capital of Queen *Zenobia, the fabled monarch, who in the 3rd century CE had defied the hegemony of Rome to carve out a desert empire. As Lady Hester approached Palmyra, her Bedouin escorts engaged in sham battles with each other and with the male Palmyrenes: symbolic contests for the favor of their charismatic guest. When she entered the town, young women stood motionless on pedestals formerly occupied by statues, and then, as Lady Hester passed, they leapt down to join in a revelry of song and dance. At Palmyra's ceremonial arch, one of them crowned her with a wreath of flowers as the local residents acclaimed her their *melika* (queen).

What this pageant signified for the Syrian inhabitants of Palmyra remains obscure, but for Stanhope it was the high point of a life which, until then, had been rich in incident but without apparent direction. In the first flush of her triumph, she wrote back to England:

> Without joking, I have been crowned Queen of the Desert under the triumphal arch at Palmyra. . . . If I please I can now go to Mecca alone; I have nothing to fear. I shall soon have as many names as Apollo. I am the sun, the star, the pearl, the lion, the light from Heaven. . . . I am quite wild about these people; and all Syria is in astonishment at my courage and success. To have spent a month with some thousand of Bedouin Arabs is no common thing.

Though, in some respects, Stanhope's later career was anticlimactic, she would continue to play an active part in the turbulent history of the Middle East. In subsequent generations, other European adventurers would follow in her footsteps, rejecting the constricting values of their homelands in a quest for fulfillment through engagement with the culture and conflicts of the Arab world. Her career thus foreshadowed that of T.E. Lawrence ("Lawrence of Arabia"), whose daring exploits alongside his Arab allies in the First World War brought him the kind of fleeting fame that Stanhope had enjoyed over 100 years before. A number of intrepid women would also follow Stanhope's lead, among them *Gertrude Bell, who reached the interior of Arabia in 1913 and who would later play a crucial role in the politics of the Middle East.

There was little in Stanhope's early life that pointed to her curious destiny, though from a young age she exhibited qualities of intelligence and independence as well as a yen for adventure. Her childhood and adolescence took place against a backdrop of convulsive events in the Americas, Europe, and the Middle East. She was born in 1776, the year of the American Declaration of Independence; she reached her teens as revolution erupted in France; and she attained maturity as the forces of Napoleon I were engaging in warfare with British-led coalitions, titanic struggles that spilled over from Europe to intersect with endemic conflict in the Middle East.

The eldest of three sisters, Hester was born into a family deeply involved in the international politics of the period. Her grandfather was William Pitt, the Elder, the powerful war minister who had helped to build Britain's North American empire and who died in 1778 grieving its impending destruction. Her bachelor uncle, the austere William Pitt, the Younger—for whom Hester retained an enduring affection and respect—served as Britain's prime minister in the darkest days of the Napoleonic Wars. Her father Charles, Earl Stanhope, was an amateur scientist who also engaged in the politics of the day but in ways that many of his contemporaries regarded as highly perverse. He became an enthusiast for the leveling principles of the French Revolution, styling himself "Citizen" Stanhope. He tried to expunge all evidence of his aristocratic lineage from the family home at Chevening, Kent, and he insisted that his children were to receive no privileges as a consequence of their birth. To acquaint Hester with the lifestyle of humble folk, he sent her, when she was 14 years old, to look after turkeys on the local common. He did, however, recognize her considerable intelligence and sought to sharpen it by engaging her in philosophical discussion. He also encouraged her passion for horses, and she became a superb rider.

Stanhope, in later life, expressed pride in her father's disregard for convention (a trait that she inherited), but she was resistant to his democratic enthusiasms. She denounced his radical friends as "a pack of dirty Jacobins." She always remained highly conscious of her highborn status and conducted herself accordingly. Though she invariably showed a genuine and well-informed concern for the problems endured by oppressed peoples, whether in England or the Middle East, it was the concern of the patrician for those she deemed her inferiors, not that of the instinctive democrat for her equals.

Her father's odd conduct completed an estrangement with his daughters which had really begun following the death of their mother **Hester Pitt** when Stanhope was only four years old. Charles quickly remarried, and his new wife showed little interest in the welfare of her stepdaughters. Hester, however, remained in the family home until her early 20s, sustained by a strong, almost maternal, affection for her three younger half-brothers, the children of her father's second marriage. After finally leaving Chevening in 1800 to live with her grandmother, Hester, with typical audacity and skillful planning, contrived the escape of the eldest son, Lord Mahon, from their father's clutches. Enlisting the aid of her uncle, Prime Minister William Pitt, she arranged for Mahon to flee to Germany, where he enrolled as a student at the University of Erlangen. Shortly afterwards, Stanhope, taking advantage of an interval of peace, began her own career as an overseas traveler, touring through France, Italy, and Germany. The resumption of war, however, obliged her to return to England, where sad news awaited her: her beloved grandmother had died while she was away.

Stanhope now faced a difficult situation. A return to Chevening was out of the question, and she had few resources of her own. Fortunately, help was at hand. William Pitt, temporarily out of office, welcomed her into his household. The following year, 1804, he was reappointed as prime minister and Stanhope in effect became his host. She was the confidante of leading politicians, soldiers, and diplomats who admired her for her wit, intelligence, and candor. Not everyone was charmed, however. Her wit was often laced with acid, and many of its victims were not disposed to forgive the source of their discomfiture. Stanhope's unconventional approach to affairs of the heart also threatened to compromise her social reputation. Innocent in themselves, her friendships with men were conducted openly and without regard for the fussy, often hypocritical, proprieties which polite society demanded as the hallmark of "virtuous" unmarried women.

> *I* have been thought mad—ridiculed and abused; but it is out of the power of man to change my way of thinking upon any subject.
>
> —Lady Hester Stanhope

Though Stanhope became the object of some malicious tongue-wagging, she was effectively shielded from too much overt criticism for as long as she enjoyed the protection and patronage of her uncle William Pitt. When he died in office in 1806, it was both a bitter personal loss for Stanhope and one that left her exposed to the recriminations of her detractors. Other tragedies would shortly follow. Stanhope had befriended a veteran soldier, General Sir John Moore, who was appointed commander of the British forces in Spain and Portugal, with Charles Stanhope, Hester's favorite half-brother, as his aide-de-camp. In January 1809, both were killed at the battle of Corunna. Legend has it that Moore died with Hester Stanhope's name on his lips.

"To have lost by one fatal blow the best and kindest of brothers, and the dearest of friends, is a misfortune so cruel, that I am convinced I can never recover," Hester wrote to a friend. After Pitt's death she had attempted to maintain a household in London; now she decided to withdraw from high society. In 1810, she embarked on a foreign tour, initially with no clear destination in mind. As it turned out, she would remain a permanent exile. Her decision to quit her native country was born in part out of a disgust with what she regarded as the hypocrisies and corruption of her social class and, more mundanely, out of financial necessity. Parliament had granted her a yearly pension of £1,200 following Pitt's death, a sum inadequate to maintain her accustomed style of living in England but one which offered the prospect of an agreeable existence in the Mediterranean world.

Stanhope was accompanied, among others, by her newly engaged physician, Dr. Charles Meryon, who would remain a loyal friend throughout nearly all of her adventures. As the niece of a former prime minister, Stanhope successfully demanded permission to travel on vessels of Britain's Royal Navy, despite the fact that the country was still at war with Napoleon. Stanhope and her companions proceeded first to Gibraltar, the British colony at the entrance to the Mediterranean, where they met Michael Bruce, a rich young Englishman, who joined Stanhope's party as it made its way across the Mediterranean. On the island of Malta, Stanhope and Michael Bruce became lovers. She announced the event in a letter to Bruce's father, a gesture which broke all convention but which was typical of her candor and lack of false modesty. In a subsequent letter, she hinted that her conduct had made a return to England impossible, even had she desired it. "I will never give an opportunity to those fair ladies who have married for a title, a house and diamonds, having previously made up their minds to be FAITHLESS WIVES, to SNEER at me," she wrote.

From Malta, Stanhope's party sailed into the territory of the Ottoman Turks, then the imperial power in the eastern Mediterranean and Arab worlds. In Athens, Stanhope met Lord Byron, the celebrated poet. Both destined to become icons of romantic cults, they took an instant dislike to each other. Stanhope insinuated that Byron was a plagiarist, and Byron condemned Stanhope as "that dangerous thing—a female wit."

After Greece, Stanhope's destination was Constantinople (now Istanbul), the capital of the Turkish Empire and a place rarely visited by Western Europeans. Despite the restrictions placed on women in that strictly Muslim society, Stanhope refused to modify her conduct. On one famous occasion, she sat on her horse, upright and unveiled, as the sultan passed before her in full procession on his way to pray at the mosque, while the local inhabitants bowed in obeisance to their secular and spiritual leader. "There is probably no other example of a European female having ridden through the streets of Constantinople in this manner," wrote Dr. Meryon, "and it may be reckoned as a proof of her courage that she did so." Certainly, Stanhope intended no disrespect by her conduct, and it was a measure of her personality that none was ever taken. She continued to travel through the sultan's dominions with his *firman* (passport) in hand, and she reciprocated his support by henceforth seeking to uphold his authority in his troubled lands.

After lingering for over a year in the vicinity of Constantinople, Stanhope and her party embarked for Egypt in October 1811. En route, they were shipwrecked off the island of Rhodes, losing nearly all their possessions and barely escaping with their lives. Undaunted, Stanhope arranged for another boat to take her to the Egyptian port of Alexandria. Her wardrobe having been lost in the shipwreck, she now adopted the traditional, loose-fitting costume of the Turkish male as her usual mode of attire. In the Egyptian capital of Cairo, she was graciously received by Mehemet Ali, the powerful local ruler, who, though nominally the viceroy of the Turkish sultan, had imperial dreams of his own. The two made a favorable impression on one other, but Stanhope would later oppose Mehemet Ali's expansionist ambitions in the region.

The Holy Land was Stanhope's next destination; and from there she ventured to the mountains of Lebanon, where she encountered the mysterious religious sect known as the Druzes. Though she did not know it at the time, it was here in this beautiful though turbulent region that she would eventually make her permanent home. Her reputation preceding her, she journeyed on to Syria, where she made a dramatic entry into Damascus, still something of a forbidden city for Europeans, or at least one where they were usually obliged to maintain a discreetly low profile. Stanhope was now becoming increasingly entranced with the Arab way of life and, against the advice of her friends, began planning the dangerous expedition to Palmyra.

Her triumph there was quickly followed by misfortune. Plague was sweeping through the region, leaving thousands dead in its wake. Though Stanhope's party prudently retreated to the coast, she fell ill with the disease, or something akin to it, and was left seriously weakened. Just before that happened, Michael Bruce had left for England. He and Stanhope would correspond for awhile, but they never saw each other again. Uncertain of her future course of action, Stanhope drifted back to Lebanon. In 1821, she accepted the invitation of a local ruler to settle at Djoun, the site of a former monastery, high in the Lebanese mountains. Despite being desperately short of money, she succeeded in constructing there a virtual fortress, adorned with a magnificent garden.

Stanhope had now deliberately removed herself from European society, but until the final months of her life she was no recluse. Nor was Djoun immune from the troubles of the region. Then as now Lebanon was a zone of conflict. The authority of the sultan was in rapid decline there, and local warlords battled to assume it. Amid the turmoil, Djoun became a place of refuge for the victims of these civil wars and the ravages of disease that accompanied them. Despite her growing distaste for European Christians, Stanhope also gave sanctuary to those of them in the area who fled to Djoun in the panic that followed the battle of Navarino in 1827, when the combined forces of Britain, France, and

Russia destroyed the Turkish fleet. Exhausted by her relief efforts on that occasion, Stanhope almost succumbed to a bout of yellow fever.

Her boldest stand was taken against the armies of the Egyptian ruler Mehement Ali, which overran Syria and Lebanon in the early 1830s. She refused to capitulate to the invader, and her home once again became a haven for the victims of war. Her efforts were not simply humanitarian. In 1837, in the twilight of her life, she supported a rebellion of her Druze neighbors against their new Egyptian overlords. Mehemet Ali complained

Hester
Stanhope

that, "she had given him more trouble than all the insurgent people of Syria and Palestine."

The extraordinary reputation that Stanhope acquired among her neighbors was heightened by a belief that she was a prophet with occult powers. This perception was obviously exaggerated, though Stanhope certainly acquired an interest in astrology, producing horoscopes for her guests. She also flirted with the idea that she would someday be crowned "Queen of Jerusalem" in company with a new messiah. Such messianic tendencies apart, she became a conscientious student of the monotheistic religions which had their fountainhead in the region of Stanhope's adopted home. She seems, ultimately, to have embraced a kind of syncretic theology which drew from Judaism, Christianity, and Islam. A sympathetic account of Stanhope's religious opinions was provided by Alphonse de Lamartine, the French poet, whose description of Stanhope in his *Souvenirs d'Orient* contributed to her becoming the object of much romantic speculation in Europe.

Stanhope's final years were not happy ones. News of her brother James' suicide in 1825 threw her into despondency and completed her sense of isolation from her native country. After that, she never again stepped outside the walls of Djoun, though she remained deeply involved in the affairs of the region. Her spirit was indomitable to the end, however. In 1837, she wrote: "My body is nothing; the heart is as full of fire as ever." In the summer of 1838, stripped of her pension and in dire poverty, she sent Meryon back to England for the last time. Her final letters to him combined fatalism and courage. "Remember! All is written: we can change nothing of our fate by lamenting and grumbling," she wrote. Lady Hester Stanhope died, destitute and probably alone, in June 1839.

### SOURCES:

Bruce, Ian. *The Nun of Lebanon: The Love Affair of Lady Hester Stanhope and Michael Bruce.* London: Collins, 1951.

Duchess of Cleveland. *The Life and Letters of Lady Hester Stanhope.* London: John Murray, 1914.

Meryon, Charles Lewis. *Memoirs of the Lady Hester Stanhope as related by Herself in Conversation with Her Physician.* London: Henry Colburn, 1846.

———. *Travels of the Lady Hester Stanhope as related by Herself in Conversation with Her Physician.* London: Henry Colburn, 1846.

Tidrick, Kathryn. *Heart-beguiling Araby.* Cambridge: Cambridge University Press, 1981.

### SUGGESTED READING:

Childs, Virginia. *Lady Hester Stanhope: Queen of the Desert.* London: Weidenfeld and Nicolson, 1990.

Haslip, Joan. *Lady Hester Stanhope: A Biography.* London: Cobden Sanderson, 1934.

### COLLECTIONS:

Correspondence, papers, and memorabilia in the Kent Record Office, Maidstone, England, and in the Forster Collection, Victoria and Albert Museum, London.

**John Sainsbury**, Associate Professor of History, Brock University, St. Catherines, Ontario, Canada

# Stanislavski, Maria Lilina

## (fl. early 1900s)

*Russian actress who was the wife of Constantin Stanislavski. Name variations: Maria Petrovna Perevostchikova; Maria Lilina Perevozchikova; Mme Stanislavsky; Maria Stanislavski or Stanislavskaya; acted under the name Maria Lilina. Born Maria Lilina Petrovna Perevostchikova; daughter of Petrov Perevostchikov (a lawyer); married Constantin Stanislavski (1863–1938, an actor, director, and teacher of acting), on July 5, 1889; children: Xenia (died in infancy); Kira Stanislavski; Igor Stanislavski.*

The daughter of a well-known lawyer, Maria Perevostchikova met Constantin Stanislavski when she made her acting debut with him in a charity performance of *Spoiled Darling* in 1888. At the time, she was a teacher at a Moscow high school for girls and was breaking all the rules of respectable female behavior by appearing on the stage. Although she attempted to hide her theatrical activities by performing under the name Maria Lilina, the alias did not prevent her from losing her job. At Stanislavski's invitation, she joined The Society of Art and Literature which he founded later that same year. She appeared on stage with him again in the society's production of Schiller's *Kabale and Liebe*. "It seems that we were in love with each other, but did not know it," Constantin wrote later in his biography *My Life In Art*, "but we were told of it by the public. We kissed each other too naturally, and our secret was an open one to the public. In this performance I played less with technique than with intuition, but it is not hard to guess who inspired us, Apollo or Hymen." She and the young Constantin were married at Liubimovka on July 5, 1889. According to his biographer Jean Benedetti, Constantin was fortunate in his marriage. "Lilina was a remarkable woman," he writes, "always supportive yet never offering blind adulation, offering criticism where needed and going her own way artistically if she had to."

The newlyweds set up housekeeping in Moscow, in an apartment at the Stanislavski family residence at Red Gates. Household duties and childrearing soon took precedence over Maria's career. In the course of the next six years, she gave birth to three children: Xenia (who died in infancy), **Kira Stanislavski**, and Igor Stanislavski. When not pregnant, Maria took to the stage whenever possible. In his biography, Constantin praises her "feeling for costume" and her "taste and inventiveness," suggesting that she may have been involved with the design elements of his productions as well. She also knew English and frequently interpreted for him.

Constantin, who believed that the theater was his destiny and that his name would go down in history, continued to pursue his passion while also fulfilling his duties to the family's textile business. This double commitment left little time for Maria and the children, a matter of contention that strained her to the point of illness. An enforced separation in 1896 (the house at Red Gates was commandeered by the German delegation who were attending the coronation of Tsar Nicholas II, and Maria and the children went to stay with relatives while Constantin remained in Moscow) did little to solve the problem. While on holiday with her husband sometime later, after he had established the renowned Moscow Art Theater, Maria wrote to her daughter Kira: "Papa writes all day and thinks about his plan. I read."

Over the years, Maria apparently came to grips with her husband's divided attention and became content to support his artistic struggles. She remained his devoted disciple and a member of the company of the Moscow Art Theater, although \*Olga Knipper-Chekova emerged as the company's leading actress. There is nothing to suggest that Maria was an extraordinarily talented actress, but is also unlikely that she would have competed with her husband for the spotlight, or that he would have willingly relinquished it to her. As Benedetti points out, however, Maria had a mind of her own. Along with the rest of the Moscow Art Theater company, she had difficulty with the Stanislavski Method of Acting as it was evolving. In 1909, during rehearsals for *Blue Bird*, she told Constantin outright that she did not find his new ideas helpful.

In later years, as Constantin became famous, Maria protected him from an eager public and helped manage his busy schedule. After 1930, he was frequently ill, but she was nonetheless shocked by his death in the late summer of 1938, shortly before the Russian edition of his *An Actor's Work on Himself: Part One* was completed. The book was released that fall, prompting Maria to write: "At three in the afternoon they sent an advance copy of his book, the labour of his life, three weeks after his death.

Why is fate so cruel? Who knows, if he had seen this book in his lifetime what a boost it might have been, what a stimulus to go on living."

While her husband was buried in the cemetery of the New Maiden Monastery along with other notable Russians, Maria slipped into obscurity. It is to be hoped that, upon her own death, she was laid to rest beside her husband, or, at the very least, in the nearby corner of the graveyard reserved for the members of the original Moscow Art company.

**SOURCES:**
Benedetti, Jean. *Stanislavski*. NY: Toutledge, 1988.
Stanislavsky, Constantin. *My Life in Art*. Trans. from the Russian by J.J. Robbins. Boston, MA: Little, Brown, 1927.

**Barbara Morgan**,
Melrose, Massachusetts

## Stankowitch, Countess of.

*See La Grange, Anna de (1825–1905).*

## Stanley, Charlotte (1599–1664).

*See Siege Warfare and Women.*

# Stanley, Kim (1925–2001)

*American actress who was nominated for three Academy Awards. Born Patricia Kimberley Reid on February 11, 1925, in Tularosa, New Mexico; died from cancer on August 20, 2001, in Santa Fe, New Mexico; daughter of J.T. Reid (a professor of philosophy) and Ann (Miller) Reid (a painter and interior decorator); attended the University of New Mexico; University of Texas, B.A. in psychology, 1945; studied acting at the Pasadena Playhouse, 1945–46; studied acting at the Actors Studio; married Bruce Franklin Hall (an actor), in 1948 (divorced); married Curt Conway (an actor-director, divorced 1956); married Alfred Ryder (an actor-director), in August 1958; children: (second marriage) a daughter and a son; (third marriage) a daughter.*

*Selected theater: New York debut as Iris in* The Dog Beneath the Skin *(Carnegie Recital Hall, 1948); title role in* Saint Joan *(Equity Library, 1949); Broadway debut as replacement for Julie Harris in the role of Elisa in* Montserrat *(Fulton Theater, 1949); appeared as Adela in* The House of Bernarda Alba *(ANTA, 1951), Anna Reeves in* The Chase *(Playhouse, 1952), Millie Owens in* Picnic *(Music Box, 1953), Georgette Thomas in* The Traveling Lady *(Playhouse, 1954, and repeated role on television); appeared as Cherie in* Bus Stop *(Music Box, 1955), Virginia in* A Clearing in the Woods *(Belasco, 1947); London debut as Maggie in* Cat on a Hot Tin Roof *(Comedy Theater, London, 1958); appeared as Sara*

*Melody in* A Touch of the Poet *(Helen Hayes, New York, 1958), Lea de Lonval in* Cheri *(Morosco, 1959), Elizabeth von Ritter in* A Far Country *(Music Box, 1961), Sue Barker in* Natural Affection *(Booth, 1963), Masha in* The Three Sisters *(Morosco, 1964, and repeated role at London's Aldwych Theater in 1965).*

*Selected filmography:* The Goddess *(1958);* Seance on a Wet Afternoon *(1964);* The Three Sisters *(1977);* Frances *(1982);* The Right Stuff *(1983).*

A product of the Actors Studio and a proponent of the psychological approach to characterization known as the Method, Kim Stanley reached the peak of her acting career in the 1950s, with such award-winning performances as Millie in *Picnic* (1953), and Cherie in *Bus Stop* (1955), and with her highly acclaimed London debut as Maggie in the Tennessee Williams play *Cat on a Hot Tin Roof* (1958). In the 1960s, the actress left the stage to teach, after which she made only occasional appearances on screen and television.

Stanley was born Patricia Kimberley Reid in 1925 in Tularosa, New Mexico, where her father was a professor at the University of New Mexico and where Stanley briefly attended college and also made her stage debut in 1942 in a production of *Thunder Rock*. She subsequently transferred to the University of Texas and graduated in 1945, with a degree in psychology. She continued her acting studies at the Pasadena Playhouse in California, leaving after a year to go to New York in search of a job. "The first producer I saw was Russel Crowse, who ordered me to go back to Texas," she told Earl Wilson in 1955. "I don't blame him. I sat everybody down and made them listen to me do Shakespeare—very badly."

Ignoring Crowse's directive, Stanley persevered, although she supported herself mainly by working as a model and a waitress. After two years, she joined the Actors Studio where she studied with Elia Kazan and Lee Strasberg. In 1948, she made her New York debut in the avant-garde production *The Dog Beneath the Skin* by W.H. Auden and Christopher Isherwood. She subsequently appeared in *him*, by e.e. cummings, and in *Yes Is For a Very Young Man*, by *Gertrude Stein. Her work in the latter play was praised by Brooks Atkinson who called her "a talented actress with temperament, craft, and, if there is any justice on Broadway, a future."

Stanley made her Broadway debut in 1949, replacing *Julie Harris as Elisa in *Montserrat*. After subsequent Broadway engagements in *The House of Bernarda Alba* and *The Chase*, Stanley was offered the role of Millie in William Inge's *Picnic*, a play that takes place in a small Kansas town. Once again, Brooks Atkinson sang her praises. "As a tom-boy sister with brains and artistic gifts, Kim Stanley gives a penetrating performance that conveys the distinction as well as the gaucheries of a disarming young lady," he wrote. Walter Kerr found her performance promising, but was put off by her nervous-tic mannerisms, "the lolling tongue, and the sing-song rhythms, cuts across and falsifies the independent vision of her performance; it also makes her seem more a cretin than a class intellectual." Kerr's comments aside, the play received the Pulitzer Prize and Stanley was awarded the Drama Critics' Award for Best Supporting Actress of the year.

Following another acclaimed performance as Georgette Thomas in *The Traveling Lady*, a role she later reprised on television, Stanley was cast in a second Inge play, *Bus Stop*, in the role of Cherie, an Ozark girl who becomes a nightclub singer. In what Brooks Atkinson termed a "glowing performance that is full of amusing detail," Stanley stopped the show each night with her parody of a chanteuse crooning "That Old Black Magic." The actress, claiming to be completely tone deaf, said she patterned her singing on that of a vocalist she once heard in a honky-tonk. For her performance in *Bus Stop*, Stanley received the Donaldson Award and the New York Drama Critics Award as Best Actress.

In January 1958, Stanley made her London debut as Maggie in *Cat on a Hot Tin Roof*. Critic Richard Buckle, in *Plays and Players*, called her performance "a triumph of subtlety and vitality. Her first-act duel with Brick is almost a monologue, and it is wonderful to watch her, obsessed by the sole idea of becoming his wife again, going at him with her drill of nervous energy, charged by love and will power, only to retreat and crumble miserably before the laconic implacability of his replies. . . . The way she switches from catty defensiveness in brushes with her brother-in-law and his wife to a consoling warmth with which to envelop the moaning Big Mama is magical too."

In addition to her stage work, Stanley appeared in five films during her career, winning Academy Award nominations for three of them: *The Goddess* (1958), *Seance on a Wet Afternoon* (1964), and *Frances* (1982), in which she played the mother of actress *Frances Farmer. She preferred television over the big screen, however, and by 1955 had appeared in some 75 different television roles. She once said that she found the medium very relaxing. "I never think anybody's

watching," she said in an interview with the *New York World-Telegram and Sun* in 1954, "until I go home to Texas, and find out they see everything." Many of Stanley's small screen roles were in dramatic specials, but she also made guest appearances on various series. In 1963, she received an Emmy for her performance in "A Cardinal Act of Mercy," an episode on "Ben Casey."

In 1959, following performances as Sara Melody in *A Touch of the Poet* and Lea de Lonval in *Cheri*, Stanley received the ANTA Award for her outstanding contribution to the art of living theater. She continued to perform through 1965, after which she began to teach drama at the College of Santa Fe, New Mexico. Her last stage appearance was as Masha in a 1964 revival of *The Three Sisters*. She died from cancer on August 20, 2001, in Santa Fe, New Mexico.

**SOURCES:**

Boardman, Gerald. *The Oxford Companion to American Theater*. NY: Oxford University Press, 1984.

Candee, Marjorie Dent, ed. *Current Biography Yearbook 1955*. NY: H.W. Wilson, 1955.

Katz, Ephraim. *The Film Encyclopedia*. NY: HarperCollins, 1994.

Morley, Sheridan. *The Great Stage Stars*. Australia: Angus & Robertson, 1986.

Wilmeth, Don B., and Tice L. Miller, eds. *Cambridge Guide to American Theater*. Cambridge: Cambridge University Press, 1993.

**Barbara Morgan**,
Melrose, Massachusetts

# Stanley, Louise (1883–1954)

*American home economist and federal administrator. Born on June 8, 1883, in Nashville, Tennessee; died of cancer on July 15, 1954, in Washington, D.C.; daughter of Gustavus Stanley and Eliza (Winston) Stanley; Peabody College at University of Nashville, A.B., 1903; University of Chicago, B.Ed., 1906; Columbia University, A.M., 1907; Yale University, Ph.D., 1911; never married; children: (adopted) one daughter.*

*Became known both academically and professionally for her efforts to improve the quality of life in American homes, particularly with regard to nutrition of the poor; was selected the first female bureau chief of the U.S. Department of Agriculture; developed diet plans, compiled data to be used in the base-year consumer price index, and encouraged the standardization of clothing sizes; directed nutritional education programs throughout Latin America.*

Born in Nashville, Tennessee, in 1883, Louise Stanley lost both her parents when she was just four years old. Stanley was intellectually gifted and, with her inheritance, pursued ad-

*Opposite page
From the movie
Seance on a Wet
Afternoon,
starring Kim
Stanley and
Richard
Attenborough.*

vanced degrees at some of the most prestigious universities in the United States, including bachelor's degrees from the University of Tennessee and the University of Chicago. Graduating from Columbia University's master's program in 1907, Stanley immediately joined the staff of the home economics department at the University of Missouri, and served as department chair from 1917 until 1923. Concurrent with her teaching duties in Missouri, the tireless Stanley entered Yale University and worked toward her Ph.D., graduating in 1911.

During the early 1900s, the growing field of home economics was considered important due to concern over the quality of life of America's households. Advances had been made in the field of nutrition, but many Americans, particularly those in rural and impoverished sections of the country, had no education in the dietary requirements that could prevent disease. In 1917, Congress passed the Smith-Hughes Act, which funded agricultural, industrial, and home economics curricula in U.S. public schools, and Stanley's continued lobbying efforts on behalf of the American Home Economics Association was instrumental in strengthening that congressional mandate. Six years later, the U.S. Department of Agriculture (USDA) formed a Bureau of Home Economics, and Stanley was selected as its first bureau chief. Leaving the University of Missouri, she moved to Washington, D.C., and developed research programs and educational initiatives reflecting her goal of improving the well-being of America's families. The four dietary plans developed under her direction were the foundation of several government welfare programs instituted during the Great Depression, as well as of European relief programs following World War II. Nationwide surveys on family income, spending, and savings made between 1938 and 1941 were used by the Bureau of Home Economics to establish a base line for the cost-of-living index that served as a yardstick of the domestic U.S. economy throughout the second half of the 20th century.

World War II found Stanley working as assistant director of the Human Nutrition and Home Economics Bureau, a branch of the Agricultural Research Administration. This position allowed her to further her interest in bringing nutrition education to families on an international scale. Families in several Latin American countries benefited from her push for nutrition surveys and educational programs, as did rural farming communities and minority populations throughout the United States; Stanley saw the latter group as lacking nutrition education be-cause of racial injustice. Leaving the bureau in 1950, she went into semi-retirement by serving as a consultant for the USDA's office of Foreign Agricultural Relations.

Stanley retired from government service in 1953, although she continued to devote her time to the cause of improving the U.S. standard of nutritional health, as well as encouraging young women to pursue professions within the field of home economics. Devoted to her students, colleagues, and to the cause of home economics education, Stanley never married, although she adopted a daughter in 1929. The year before her death in 1954, a scholarship was established in her name by the American Home Economics Association. A building at the University of Missouri also bears the name of the woman who devoted her life to making home economics valid as an academic discipline and opening pathways to careers in the home economics field to countless women.

**SOURCES:**
Read, Phyllis J., and Bernard L. Witlieb. *The Book of Women's Firsts.* NY: Random House, 1992.
Sicherman, Barbara, and Carol Hurd Green, eds. *Notable American Women: The Modern Period.* Cambridge, MA: The Belknap Press of Harvard University, 1980.

Pamela Shelton, freelance writer,<br>Avon, Connecticut

# Stanley, Margaret

*Countess of Essex. Name variations: Margaret Radcliffe. Daughter of \*Anne Hastings (c. 1487–?) and Thomas Stanley, 2nd earl of Derby; interred at St. Lawrences Pountney, London; married Robert Fitzwalter Radcliffe, earl of Essex, in 1532; children: Sir John Radcliffe.*

## Stanley, Rosalind Frances (1845–1921).

See Howard, Rosalind Frances.

# Stanley, Winifred Claire
## (1909–1996)

*American attorney and politician. Born Winifred Claire Stanley on August 14, 1909, in the Mount Hope section of the Bronx, New York; died on February 29, 1996, in Kenmore, New York; eldest of six children of John Francis Stanley and Mary (Gill) Stanley; University of Buffalo, B.A., magna cum laude, 1930, LL.B., 1933, J.D., 1933; never married.*

*Became assistant district attorney for Erie County, New York, and served a single term as New York State's Republican Representative-at-Large to the U.S. House of Representatives, the youngest female member of*

*Congress up to that point; returned from Washington, D.C., to state service in Albany, first as counsel to New York's Employee's Retirement System, then as assistant attorney general until her return to private practice.*

Born in the Bronx, New York, in 1909, the eldest of six children, Winifred Claire Stanley moved with her family to upstate New York as a young girl and attended public schools in her hometown of Buffalo. She was an outstanding and energetic student, winning numerous commendations and active in a variety of extracurricular activities. Remaining at the home of her close-knit family, she attended the University of Buffalo beginning in 1926, earning three degrees, including a law degree. Stanley was one of four women to graduate from the university's law school in 1933, and was honored with the Edward Thompson award, given to the student with the highest scholastic average over a three-year period.

Admitted to the Bar of the State of New York in 1934, Stanley practiced law in Buffalo for four years before becoming the first woman to be appointed as Erie County's assistant district attorney in 1938. In that position, she prosecuted such cases as abandonment of women and children until 1942, when she successfully ran for the U.S. House of Representatives on the Republican ticket. Her war-time platform consisted mostly of preparing the nation for peace at the end of World War II. Serving in Congress from 1943 to 1945 in an at-large seat that was eliminated following the census of 1940, Stanley was assigned to committees on patents and on civil service, and voted, along the lines of her fellow Republicans, against several of the New Deal policies endorsed by President Franklin Roosevelt; she did, however, support Roosevelt's proposal to end poll taxes. With the expected elimination of her house seat in 1945, Stanley did not attempt a second elected office. Instead, she returned to upstate New York after accepting New York Governor Thomas Dewey's offer of the position as counsel to the New York State Employee's Retirement System. She held that post from 1945 to 1955.

In 1955, Stanley returned to the office of the attorney general, this time as an assistant attorney general for the state of New York, and worked out of the state capital at Albany for the next 24 years. In 1980, she returned to the private practice of law, first in Albany and then in Kenmore, following a move to that town in 1981. Retiring in 1986, Stanley died ten years later. Active in civic, political, and social affairs throughout her life, Stanley never married, pre-

ferring to dedicate her life to her career in public service. Her youth, intelligence and success as a prosecutor came as a surprise to both her colleagues and the press early on in her career, as many were struck by her vivacity, good looks, and her wardrobe, which caused her to be chosen one of the Fashion Academy's best dressed women of 1943.

*Winifred Claire Stanley*

**SOURCES:**

*Current Biography.* NY: H.W. Wilson, 1943.

Office of the Historian. *Women in Congress, 1917–1990.* Commission on the Bicentenary of the U.S. House of Representatives, 1991.

**Pamela Shelton**, freelance writer,
Avon, Connecticut

## Stannard, Mrs. Arthur (1856–1911).

*See Winter, John Strange.*

## Stannard, Henrietta (1856–1911).

*See Winter, John Strange.*

## Stannus, Edris (1898–2001).

*See de Valois, Ninette.*

# Stanton, Elizabeth Cady

## (1815–1902)

*American women's rights activist, journalist, reformer, polemicist, and historian, co-convener of the 1848 Seneca Falls Convention, whose lifelong efforts on behalf of women's rights won her worldwide admiration. Name variations: "Cady." Born on November 12, 1815, at Johnstown, New York, 40 miles northwest of Albany; died on October 26, 1902, at home in New York City; one of 11 children, 6 of whom died before adulthood, of Daniel Cady (a prosperous lawyer who went on to become an associate justice of the New York Supreme Court for the Fourth District) and Margaret (Livingston) Cady; attended Emma Willard's Troy Female Seminary, 1831–33; married Henry Stanton (a well-known abolitionist and lawyer), on May 1, 1840; children: seven (two daughters and five sons), including Daniel Cady Stanton (b. March 1842), two more sons by 1845, and Harriot Stanton Blatch (1856–1940).*

*Attended World Anti-Slavery convention in England (June 1840), where she met the Quaker abolitionist and women's rights advocate Lucretia Mott; collaborated with Mott in calling first women's rights convention at Seneca Falls, New York (1848); teamed up with Susan B. Anthony in what would prove a lifelong friendship and women's rights partnership (1851); co-founded and edited* The Revolution, *a women's rights newspaper, with Anthony (1868–70); co-founded and led National Woman Suffrage Association (1869–90); served as president of the National American Woman Suffrage Association (1890–92); co-wrote and edited* History of Woman Suffrage *(1886); wrote* The Woman's Bible *(1895) and an autobiography,* Eighty Years and More *(1898).*

In her autobiography, *Eighty Years and More*, Elizabeth Cady Stanton told how at age 11 she tried to console her father, lost in grief over the death of his only son. As he sat before his son's casket in their front parlor, he took no notice of Elizabeth, who had climbed upon his knee and rested her head on his shoulder. At last, he burst out, "Oh, my daughter, I wish you were a boy!" She threw her arms around his neck and cried out, "I will try to be all my brother was." Stanton would endeavor throughout her father's lifetime to be an honorary son. To that end, she became skilled at horseback riding, able to take a horse across four-foot fences; she learned Greek, Latin, and philosophy. She pored over her father's law books, attended court sessions, won second place in the Johnstown Academy Greek competition, and became skilled at de-

bate. She was at the top of her class at Johnstown Academy, the only girl taking higher math and language courses.

Her father Judge Daniel Cady at first seemed proud of his daughter's accomplishments, encouraging her to read and take part in dinner-table debates with the many law clerks and guests who gathered regularly at the Cady household. As she reached young adulthood, however, and began to show interest in women's rights, young Elizabeth often found herself at loggerheads with her autocratic father.

Elizabeth's mother **Margaret Livingston Cady** was a strong-willed, independent woman who once had insisted upon including the votes of women parishioners in the election of a new pastor, even as she clung to more traditional notions of female accomplishment in the raising of her daughters. To her mother's frustration and consternation, Elizabeth preferred sitting in her father's law office to embroidery, music, dance lessons, and parlor conversation.

Even as a child, Elizabeth recognized the legal disabilities of women. In her autobiography, she told how the "cruelty of the laws" concerning women infuriated her. She decided to cut all laws unfair to women out of her father's legal books. Daniel Cady managed to dissuade her only by pointing out the futility of her gesture, explaining that laws could be changed solely in the legislature. Stanton would later credit this remark with inspiring her to a lifetime of political activism on behalf of women. She would petition and address state legislatures—and ultimately, the U.S. Congress—in favor of laws granting women wider political and legal rights.

Stanton's childhood was passed in an elegant mansion that housed the large Cady family, numerous law students, and the 12 liveried servants employed to keep such a large establishment running. Her mother would have eleven children in all—six girls and five boys. Four of the boys died in childhood, and the fifth son died shortly after graduating from Union College. It was this death that sparked Elizabeth's resolve to fill the place of a son in her father's affections.

At 15, she entered the Troy Female Seminary. Run by Miss *Emma Willard, the Troy Female Seminary was one of the premier upper-level academies for women. Though there were not as yet any colleges open to women in the United States, Emma Willard sought to emulate the curricula of men's colleges, teaching her young charges logic, physiology, and philosophy, as well as mathematics, history, rhetoric, and lan-

Elizabeth
Cady
Stanton

guage. While progressive in the matter of women's education, Willard was opposed to granting women increased political and legal rights. Though she would grow beyond Emma Willard in her pursuit of women's rights, Elizabeth Cady Stanton retained a lifelong admiration and affection for her early mentor.

Elizabeth Cady graduated in 1833. Her family wealth and social status meant that she need not work, either within the home or outside. She joined a church auxiliary, but for the most part, the years following her graduation were filled with parties, family visits, hayrides, and parlor entertainments. Stanton played the piano and guitar and took long rides on her horse. She was an avid reader who enjoyed the intellectual camaraderie of her older sister **Tryphena**'s husband, Edward Bayard.

By 1838, Elizabeth had become a frequent visitor at the home of Gerrit Smith, a first cousin on her mother's side. Gerrit and **Ann Smith** were wealthy philanthropists and ardent reformers. They supported prison reform, dress reform, and equal rights for women, among other reform movements of the 1820s and 1830s. Their most ardent interest, however, was the antislavery cause. At their home, a stop on the Underground Railroad, Elizabeth met abolitionist agents, runaway slaves, politicians, and reformers. She was awakened to the challenge of reform ideas, though her position as Judge Cady's daughter prevented her from taking an active role in any of her cousin's crusades.

> *The strongest reason why we ask for woman a voice in the government under which she lives; in the religion she is asked to believe; equality in social life, where she is the chief factor; a place in the trades and professions, where she may earn her bread, is because of her birthright to self-sovereignty; because, as an individual, she must rely on herself.*

—Elizabeth Cady Stanton

At the Smiths' home, Elizabeth met and fell in love with Henry Stanton. Ten years older than she, Henry had earlier trained for the ministry, studying at Lane Seminary in Cincinnati. Following the walkout of the "Lane Rebels," Stanton became a paid abolitionist agent, a dangerous occupation in the mid-1830s. He went on to become a member of the executive committee of the national antislavery society. Urbane, handsome, eloquent, and intelligent, Henry Stanton met his match in the high-spirited, equally intellectual Elizabeth Cady. He proposed within a month of their first meeting, and Elizabeth accepted.

Judge Cady objected to the match on the grounds of both Stanton's antislavery activity and his social inferiority. Elizabeth was forced to postpone her marriage, but on May 1, 1840, she and Henry were married in Johnstown. By mutual consent, they omitted the words "and obey" from the ceremony. On May 12, 1840, they set off for London to attend the international gathering of antislavery activists. Fellow boarders at their London establishment included the highly controversial female delegates, among these *Lucretia Mott. This charming and vivacious wife and mother of six, who was as well a Quaker minister, abolitionist, and women's rights advocate, would prove crucial to Stanton's development over the next decade. Stanton, raised in the conservative Scotch Presbyterian religion, heard Lucretia Mott preach a sermon in the Unitarian chapel in London. It marked the first time she had ever heard a woman make a public address. Filled with admiration, Stanton sought Mott's company at every available opportunity. In her autobiography, she wrote, "Mrs. Mott was to me an entire new revelation of womanhood."

On the day that the male delegates voted to exclude the female antislavery delegates from the convention's proceedings, Stanton sat beside Mott. Afterward, they walked home arm in arm, their indignation fired, talking about plans to form a society "to advocate the rights of women." It would be eight years before their plans were realized. In the meantime, after their return to America, Stanton and Mott corresponded about women's rights. For the Stantons, the next few years were busy ones. Henry Stanton studied law with Judge Cady, clerking in his office, while Elizabeth read law, philosophy, and history. She gave birth to the first of her seven children, Daniel Cady Stanton, in March 1842. By 1845, she was the mother of three sons, busy with domestic affairs. Her sole foray into the public arena was to petition and lobby for passage of the New York Married Women's Property Act of 1848, a women's rights first in the United States.

In June 1848, Henry, Elizabeth, and their three lively sons moved to a large home on two acres in Seneca Falls, New York. There, chance would bring her in contact again with Lucretia Mott and her sister, *Martha Coffin Wright, who were visiting nearby. On July 13, Stanton, Mott, Wright, their hostess Jane Hunt, and a fifth woman—Mary Ann McClintock—met and decided to hold a public conclave to discuss the position of women in society. They inserted an invitation in the *Seneca County Courier* calling all women to a "convention to discuss the social, civil, and religious condition and rights of women" to be held July 19–20.

In their attempt to set an agenda, the five women adopted the Declaration of Independence as their model. Elizabeth Cady Stanton was chosen to prepare the document, which came to be called "A Declaration of Rights and Sentiments." It called for equality in property rights, education, employment, equity at law, and the "sacred right to the elective franchise." The older women worried about the suffrage plank, but Stanton was adamant about its inclusion. Without political rights, she argued, women would continue to be powerless. More than a hundred people crowded into the Wesleyan Chapel on the day of the convention, and after a lively debate, Stanton's suffrage resolution passed.

While the Seneca Falls convention has come to be regarded as marking the formal beginning of the movement for women's rights in the United States, it would be two more years before an organized national convention on the subject would take place in Worcester, Massachusetts. This would be followed by a series of local and national conventions which Stanton, mired in domestic responsibilities, would not attend. Indeed, it was 1860 before Stanton would attend another women's rights convention. In the meantime, she continued to correspond and had begun to send anonymous articles to reform journals.

A Seneca Falls neighbor, *Amelia Bloomer, had begun publication of a temperance magazine called The Lily. In it, under the pseudonym "Sunflower," Stanton published a series of articles. Emboldened by their warm reception, Stanton was soon affixing her own initials to her magazine pieces. During the 1850s, she gave birth to four more children. Henry Stanton was elected to the New York State Senate, and with seven children and an oft-absent husband, Stanton had little time for the rapidly growing women's rights cause other than as an occasional correspondent.

In 1851, Elizabeth Cady Stanton adopted the Bloomer costume, the modified pantaloon dress popularized by her friend Amelia Bloomer. She was wearing this costume on an evening in March 1851 when she was introduced to *Susan B. Anthony. "I liked her thoroughly," Stanton would recall in her autobiography. The friendship that resulted would endure for 50 years. Anthony, unmarried, organized, fervent, and tireless, would prove the perfect counterpart to Stanton's theoretical brilliance and rhetorical prowess. Together, they would help to change the course of history.

The other continuing influence on Stanton through the early years of women's rights activity was Lucretia Mott. Mott repeatedly urged Stanton to take part in the conventions and activities that burgeoned throughout the country under the leadership of *Lucy Stone. She was less successful than Anthony, who first urged Stanton to write a speech for the 1852 meeting of the Woman's State Temperance Society and then convinced her to deliver it herself. Again at Anthony's urging, Stanton agreed to testify before the New York State Senate on behalf of an expansion of the 1848 Married Woman's Property Act in February 1854. She had 50,000 copies of her testimony printed with the intention of selling them as tracts. The logic and power of her arguments brought her repeated invitations to speak, most of which Stanton declined. In addition to the burden of domestic responsibilities, she had to contend with the infuriated opposition of her father, who believed that women's public activity was deplorable. It would be 1860, a year after her father's death, before Stanton would re-emerge as a public figure.

Stanton's seventh and last child was born in 1859. In that same year, her father died. A substantial inheritance from her father and the end of childbearing freed Elizabeth Cady Stanton from the burden of domestic responsibilities. She was able to hire domestic help, and she resumed public activity in 1860, addressing the Judiciary Committee of the New York legislature. This was followed by a contentious appearance at the Tenth National Woman's Rights convention, at which Stanton introduced ten resolutions favoring divorce. Other women's rights leaders, among them Lucy Stone, had urged Stanton not to introduce the topic of divorce, fearing that the highly controversial subject would serve to discredit what had been until then a rapidly growing national movement. Characteristically, Stanton refused to modify her views. Although Stanton's speech was widely censured and brought an outraged response from friends and foes of women's rights, she refused to drop the subject. First, last, and always, Stanton—far ahead of her time—would have the courage of her convictions.

The onset of the Civil War temporarily halted women's rights activity. With Susan B. Anthony and Lucy Stone, Stanton founded the Woman's National Loyal League, which succeeded in obtaining almost half a million signatures on a petition calling for passage of a 13th Amendment abolishing slavery. After the war, the women's rights organizers urged a merger with the antislavery society, hoping to hitch the rising star of woman suffrage sentiment to the push for increased suffrage rights for former slaves. The resulting organization, the American Equal Rights Association, split on the issue of supporting woman suffrage. The AERA leaders preferred to divide the two suffrage causes, seeing black (male) suffrage as having both more immediacy and more likelihood of ratification in the states.

Bitterly disappointed, Stanton and Anthony turned on their former allies. In 1867, they accepted money and aid from a notoriously racist Democratic politician, George Francis Train, in a Kansas campaign for woman suffrage. Train and a fellow Democrat would later finance the publication of a women's rights newspaper, The Revolution, which Stanton and Anthony edited from 1868 until its demise early in 1870. Stanton used its editorial columns to urge universal suffrage and to implore readers to reject the 14th and 15th amendments. The racist and inflammatory language of the editorials exacerbated earlier tensions over the Train alliance; the result was a split in the women's movement, culminating in the formation in 1869 of two separate woman suffrage organizations. Stanton and Anthony headed the National Woman Suffrage Association (NWSA); Lucy Stone and *Julia Ward Howe headed the American Woman Suffrage Association—an unfortunate division that would last until 1890, when the two organizations would merge to form the National American Woman Suffrage Association (NAWSA). Under Stanton and Anthony's leadership, the NWSA led an annual drive for a 16th Amendment.

By the late 1860s, Stanton was in great demand as a public speaker. She traveled and lectured throughout the United States, earning handsome fees for her speeches. During the decade of the '70s, Stanton devoted herself to writing and public speaking, often championing wildly unpopular causes with the same brilliant logic and acerbic language that guaranteed large audiences wherever she went.

The fortunes of woman suffrage and of the National Association suffered in the early 1870s following a NWSA alliance with *Victoria Woodhull, a free-love advocate and blackmailer who outraged and shocked public sensibility. Woodhull's involvement of Stanton and Anthony in the Henry Ward Beecher-*Elizabeth Tilton scandal of the mid-'70s also brought notoriety to woman suffrage organizations, and for some years the "National" association was reduced to parlor meetings in New York City. Through it all, Stanton traveled widely, her lectures organized by the New York Bureau. She had 12 prepared lectures; in addition to woman suffrage, she spoke on co-education, marriage and maternity, the subjection of women, and divorce, among other topics dear to her heart.

By 1880, Stanton had begun to spend more time in the Tenafly, New Jersey, home she had purchased. A bout with pneumonia and an omnibus accident led her to sharply curtail her traveling. At 65, she was ready for a new challenge—the writing and editing of *History of Woman Suffrage*. Anthony had come to Tenafly to help with the enormous task of assembling the papers, speeches, convention proceedings, legal documents, and biographies that would eventually run to six large volumes. In 1880, Stanton's attempt to vote in the November election was thwarted, despite her reasoned protest that she owned property, paid taxes regularly, was literate, etc.

After six months of intensive labor, in May 1881, they published the first volume of *History of Woman Suffrage*, chronicling the movement up to 1860. Stanton and Anthony had been joined in the effort by *Matilda Joslyn Gage, a wealthy suffragist from upstate New York. Now the three women immediately went to work on volume two. Stanton's daughter ⚜➤ Harriot Stanton (Blatch), who had graduated from college and was studying mathematics in France, came back to help with completion of the second volume. Immediately following its completion in May 1882, the two Stanton women sailed for France.

Returning in 1883 at Anthony's urging, Stanton began work on volume three of *History of Woman Suffrage*; in October 1886, she returned to Europe. There she remained until summoned home by Anthony in the winter of 1888. Anthony had planned an international meeting to be held in Washington for the purpose of celebrating the 40th anniversary of the Seneca Falls meeting. At the International Council of Women meeting, Stanton received a standing ovation. She went on to address a Senate hearing on suffrage, urging other women to continue their legislative efforts.

In February 1890, the National and American Woman Suffrage associations held their first joint meeting. Elizabeth Cady Stanton was elected president of the merged organizations, a position largely honorary, as immediately after the convention Stanton returned to England, where she remained for 18 months. In 1892, she was present at her last NAWSA meeting, at which she delivered what many regard as her greatest speech, "The Solitude of Self." Women, she argued with her usual eloquence, must rely upon themselves; they must be permitted independence in all things. She received a standing ovation, and 10,000 copies of the speech were made for wide distribution. She also appeared for the last time before Congress, giving the same speech before the Senate Committee on Woman Suffrage.

By now, Stanton was widowed, plagued by rheumatism, severely overweight, and ready for a more sedentary life. She continued to write speeches for Anthony, although in later years, it appeared to Stanton that her old friend had become too conservative. Nonetheless, Anthony made heroic efforts to arrange an 80th birthday celebration for Stanton. It took place at New York's Metropolitan Opera House, and it was a great success. Flowers filled the hall, and tributes to Stanton went on through an entire evening. Though she was not strong enough to deliver her own address and had to have it read for her, its stinging indictment of religious tradition and superstition showed that Stanton had not lost the power to outrage friends and critics alike.

Just two weeks later, Stanton published *The Woman's Bible*, which attacked the patriarchal

## ❧▶ Blatch, Harriot Stanton (1856–1940)

*American reformer. Born Harriot Eaton Stanton in Seneca Falls, New York, on January 20, 1856; died in Greenwich, Connecticut, on November 20, 1940; daughter of Elizabeth Cady Stanton (1815–1902, the suffragist) and Henry B. Stanton (an abolitionist, politician, and journalist); attended private schools; attended Boston School of Oratory; Vassar College, B.A., 1878, M.A., 1894; studied in Berlin and Paris; married William Henry Blatch (an English businessman), in 1882 (died 1915); children: two daughters (one died in infancy).*

Harriot Stanton Blatch's career as a reformer is hardly surprising given the political activities of her parents, reformers *Elizabeth Cady Stanton and Henry Stanton. Blatch attended private schools and graduated from Vassar in 1878, after which she spent a year at the Boston School of Oratory and two years abroad. Upon her return, she assisted her mother and *Susan B. Anthony on their book *History of Woman Suffrage*, contributing a 100-page chapter on *Lucy Stone's American Woman Suffrage Association, a rival of Stanton's and Anthony's own National Woman Suffrage Association. In 1882, Harriot married English businessman William H. Blatch, whom she had met on her European voyage. She lived in England for the next 20 years, during which time she was prominent in the reform work of the Fabian Society and also collaborated with British sociologist Charles Booth on a statistical study of English villages, for which she received her master's degree from Vassar in 1894.

After her return to the United States in 1902, the year of her mother's death, Blatch became involved with the Women's Trade Union League and the National American Woman Suffrage Association. In 1907, partly in reaction of the apathy and infighting she found in the latter organization, she founded the Equality League of Self Supporting Women. Initiating a British-style political approach that incorporated open-air meetings, parades, and poll watchers, the newly formed group was able to attract thousands of new working women to the cause of suffrage. In 1910, they changed their name to the Women's Political Union, and in 1916 merged with the Congressional Union (later the National Woman's Party) under *Alice Paul.

Following the death of her husband in 1915, Blatch spent two years in England settling his affairs before returning to the United States to become head of the speakers bureau of the wartime Food Administration and a director of the Woman's Land Army. After the war and the successful outcome of the suffrage campaign, she continued to champion women's rights and socialist causes. Opposing protective legislation for women, she worked with the National Woman's Party for a federal equal-rights amendment.

Blatch's writings include a book on the war work of European women, *Mobilizing Woman-Power* (1918), and *A Woman's Point of View* and *Roads to Peace* (both 1920). In 1922, with her brother, she published *Elizabeth Cady Stanton, as Revealed in Her Letters, Diary and Reminiscences*. Her autobiography, *Challenging Years*, written with **Alma Lutz**, a popular journalist of the day, was published in 1940. After suffering an injury in 1927, Harriot Blatch was confined to a nursing home until her death on November 20, 1940, at the age of 83.

**Barbara Morgan,**
Melrose, Massachusetts

bias of the Bible's male creators. In questioning traditional religious scholarship, Stanton stirred up a hornet's nest of angry response. Highly controversial, *The Woman's Bible* went through seven printings. At the next NAWSA convention, a resolution censuring it passed, marking the end of Stanton's association with the organized suffrage movement. She continued to write and publish articles and in 1898 published her autobiography, *Eighty Years and More*. Reporters and pundits continued to ask her opinion on matters ranging from politics to immigration.

Stanton spent her final years reading, writing, and dictating letters and articles, her mind clear, her reasoning cogent, her passion for the cause of women's rights unspent. On October 22, 1902, she dictated a letter to President Theodore Roosevelt, urging him to support a federal woman suffrage amendment. On October 25, she wrote a similar letter to the first lady, *Edith Kermit Roosevelt. The next day, October 26, 1902, Elizabeth Cady Stanton died—her intellectual vigor and her intense devotion to the cause of women with her to the last. The world mourned her passing.

### SOURCES:

DuBois, Ellen Carol, ed. *The Elizabeth Cady Stanton-Susan B. Anthony Reader: Correspondence, Writings, Speeches*. Rev. ed. Boston, MA: Northeastern University Press, 1992.

Griffith, Elisabeth. *In Her Own Right: The Life of Elizabeth Cady Stanton*. NY: Oxford University Press, 1984.

Lutz, Alma. *Created Equal: A Biography of Elizabeth Cady Stanton, 1815–1902*. NY: John Day, 1940.

Stanton, Elizabeth Cady. *Eighty Years and More: Reminiscences, 1815–1897.* NY: T. Fisher Unwin, 1898 (reprinted, NY: Schocken, 1971).

——. *The Selected Papers of Elizabeth Cady Stanton and Susan B. Anthony.* New Brunswick, NJ: Rutgers University Press, 1997.

Stanton, Theodore, and Harriot Stanton Blatch, eds. *Elizabeth Cady Stanton as Revealed in Her Letters, Diary and Reminiscences.* NY: Harper & Bros., 1922.

**SUGGESTED READING:**

Flexner, Eleanor. *Century of Struggle: The Woman's Rights Movement in the United States.* NY: Atheneum, 1970.

Gordon, Ann D., ed. *The Selected Papers of Elizabeth Cady Stanton and Susan B. Anthony: Volume One: In the School of Anti-Slavery, 1840–1866.* NJ: Rutgers University Press, 1996.

*History of Woman Suffrage* vols. 1–3. NY: Arno and the New York Times reprint, 1969, of Fowler and Wells, 1881 original.

**COLLECTIONS:**

Elizabeth Cady Stanton Collection, Library of Congress; NAWSA Collection, Library of Congress; Elizabeth Cady Stanton Papers, Schlesinger Library of Radcliffe College; Papers of Elizabeth Cady Stanton and Susan B. Anthony, microfilm edition edited by Patricia G. Holland and Ann D. Gordon.

**RELATED MEDIA:**

"One Woman, One Vote," a documentary on suffrage history available from Education Films, Inc.

**Andrea Moore Kerr**, Ph.D.,
women's historian and independent scholar, Washington, D.C.,
and author of *Lucy Stone: Speaking Out for Equality*

# Stanwood, Cordelia (1865–1958)

*American ornithologist. Born Cordelia Stanwood in 1865 in Ellsworth, Maine; died in 1958 in Maine; educated at a New England teachers' college; never married; no children.*

*Became fascinated by birds and began taking notes and photographs; published many articles in Bird Lore, attracting the attention of other ornithologists; her meticulous notes and over 900 photographs served as a major contribution to ongoing studies of North American bird life.*

Born in 1865 and raised on her family's 40-acre estate in Ellsworth, Maine, Cordelia Stanwood left home as a young woman with the intention of devoting her life to teaching children and earning a sufficient living to send money home to her parents. Unfortunately, she lacked the proper teaching credentials, and her salary was substandard; she could barely pay for the necessities. By the time she reached her late 20s, she had nonetheless saved enough money to enroll at a New England teachers' college with the hopes that a teacher's certificate would qualify her for the standard wage in her field. When Stanwood graduated, however, the job market had become saturated with younger graduates, and she was forced to take a job in Providence, Rhode Island, at even less money than she had earned before. In 1901, depressed and feeling there was no way out of her constant state of poverty, the 36-year-old Stanwood suffered a nervous collapse and was sent first to a Boston sanitarium and thence home to her parents' house in Maine.

Stanwood's occasional fits of hysteria, which served to alienate her from her father, were eventually eased by her growing fascination with the birds that lived on her parents' property. In 1906, she began taking a series of detailed notes of her observations while on walks in the woods, noting particularly bird-nesting behavior, nest building, and variations in bird song. While Stanwood's personal behavior became increasingly eccentric, her passion for observation and for recording her observations of birds in minute detail inspired the budding ornithologist to write articles on birds that were published in a variety of periodicals, including *Bird Lore*. These pieces caught the attention of several well-known professionals in the field of ornithology who began lengthy correspondences with Stanwood, requesting information on her observations that she willingly shared.

After the death of her father, Stanwood supported herself and her mother with the money made from her writing, needlework, and a small amount of farming she did on the family acreage. Using money from an inheritance left her by an aunt, Stanwood purchased a camera equipped with a tripod and a telephoto lens and learned the art of nature photography. Able to sit for hours in order to get a good photograph, Stanwood was selling her photographs to magazines and field guides by 1920. After the death of her mother when Stanwood was 67, she became totally obsessed with birds, and supported herself in a minimalist fashion by selling stationery items door to door; otherwise, all her time was spent photographing or observing birds. By 1955, Stanwood's ability to support herself through various odd jobs had diminished to the point that she was forced to move from her family's Maine home into a state-run nursing facility, where she died at the age of 93. Her family estate later became the Stanwood Wildlife Sanctuary.

**SOURCES:**

Bailey, Brooke. *The Remarkable Lives of 100 Women Healers and Scientists.* Holbrook, MA: Bob Adams, 1994.

Norwood, Vera. *Made From This Earth*. Chapel Hill, NC: University of North Carolina, 1993.

**Pamela Shelton**, freelance writer, Avon, Connecticut

# Stanwyck, Barbara (1907–1990)

*American actress who spent 55 years in front of the camera playing saucy dames.* Born Ruby Katharine Stevens at 246 Classon Avenue in Brooklyn, New York, on July 16, 1907; died on January 20, 1990, at St. John's Hospital in Santa Monica, California, of congestive heart failure and emphysema; daughter of Byron Stevens (a construction worker) and Catherine (McGee) Stevens; married Frank Fay (a song-and-dance man), on August 26, 1928 (divorced February 1936); married Robert Taylor (an actor), on May 14, 1939 (divorced February 1952); children: (adopted) son Dion Fay.

*Filmography:* Broadway Nights *(1927);* The Locked Door *(1930);* Ladies of Leisure *(1930);* Illicit *(1931);* Ten Cents a Dance *(1931);* Night Nurse *(1931);* The Miracle Woman *(1931);* Forbidden *(1932);* Shopworn *(1932);* So Big *(1932);* The Purchase Price *(1932);* The Bitter Tea of General Yen *(based on a novel by ***Grace Zaring Stone***, 1933);* Ladies They Talk About *(1933);* Baby Face *(1933);* Ever in My Heart *(1933);* Gambling Lady *(1934);* A Lost Lady *(1934);* The Secret Bride *(1935);* The Woman in Red *(1935);* Red Salute *(1935);* Annie Oakley *(1935);* A Message to Garcia *(1936);* His Brother's Wife *(1936);* Banjo on my Knee *(with dialogue by ***William Faulkner***, 1936);* The Plough and the Stars *(1937);* Interns Can't Take Money *(1937);* This Is My Affair *(1937);* Stella Dallas *(1937);* Breakfast for Two *(1937);* Always Goodbye *(1938);* The Mad Miss Minton *(1938);* Union Pacific *(1939);* Golden Boy *(1939);* Remember the Night *(1940);* The Lady Eve *(1941);* Meet John Doe *(1941);* You Belong to Me *(1941);* Ball of Fire *(1942);* The Great Man's Lady *(1942);* The Gay Sisters *(1942);* Lady of Burlesque *(1943);* Flesh and Fantasy *(1943);* Double Indemnity *(1944);* Hollywood Canteen *(1944);* Christmas in Connecticut *(1945);* My Reputation *(1946);* The Bride Wore Boots *(1946);* The Strange Love of Martha Ivers *(1946);* California *(1947);* The Two Mrs. Carrolls *(1947);* The Other Love *(1947);* Cry Wolf *(1947);* B.F.'s Daughter *(1948);* Sorry, Wrong Number *(1948);* The Lady Gambles *(1949);* East Side, West Side *(based on ***Marcia Davenport***'s novel with a screenplay by ***Isobel Lennart***, 1949);* The File on Thelma Jordan *(with a rewrite by ***Ketti Frings***, 1950);* No Man of Her Own *(1950);* The Furies *(1950);* To Please a Lady *(1950);* The Man with a Cloak *(1951);* Clash by Night *(1952);* Jeopardy *(1953);* Titanic *(1953);* All I Desire *(1953);* The Moonlighter *(1953);* Blowing Wild *(1953);* Witness to Murder *(1954);* Executive Suite *(1954);* Cattle Queen of Montana *(1955);* The Violent Men *(1955);* Escape to Burma *(1955);* There's Always Tomorrow *(1956);* The Maverick Queen *(1956);* These Wilder Years *(1956);* Crime of Passion *(1957);* Trooper Hook *(1957);* Walk on the Wild Side *(1962);* Roustabout *(1964);* The Night Walker *(1965).*

*Television:* "The Barbara Stanwyck Show" *(NBC series, 1960–61);* "The House that Wouldn't Die" *(ABC movie);* "A Taste of Evil" *(movie, 1970);* "The Letters" *(ABC movie, 1973);* "The Big Valley" *(ABC series, 1965–69);* "Dynasty II: The Colbys" *(ABC series, 1985). Also many stints on* "Lux Radio Theater."

Barbara Stanwyck, whose childhood was off-limits during celebrity interviews throughout her life, reluctantly admitted in her 80s, "All right, let's just say that 'poor' is something I understand. . . . I just wanted to survive and eat, and have a nice coat."

Born Ruby Stevens at 246 Classon Avenue in Brooklyn, New York, on July 16, 1907, Stanwyck was not quite three when her pregnant mother was knocked down by a drunk while exiting a streetcar, and hit her head against a curb. The daughter of an Irish immigrant and mother of five, Catherine Stevens died a month later. Two weeks after that, Stanwyck's father joined a work crew digging the canal in Panama and never returned. At the time of his flight, Barbara's sisters **Maud** and **Mabel** were teenagers, sister **Mildred** was eight, and brother Byron was six. After the older sisters married, the upbringing of Byron and Barbara fell to Mildred, then 14, who had become a showgirl. When Millie went on tour, she boarded the children with relatives or neighbors, or dumped them in sundry foster homes. Stanwyck had a predilection for running away, her brother Byron told Axel Madsen, but he always knew where to find her, "on the stoop on Classon Avenue, where she'd be sitting 'waiting for Mama to come home.'"

During the summers of 1916–17, approaching age ten, Stanwyck tagged along with the touring Mildred, watching from the wings and learning the routines. Lacking interest in school, she quit at 13, and took a job wrapping packages at Abraham & Straus. "The plain wrapping, not the fancy," she said. Occasionally, Millie would take her little sister to the movies to see **Pearl White** in *The Perils of Pauline*. Recalled Stanwyck:

It was not money wasted. Pearl White was my goddess and her courage, her grace and her triumphs lifted me out of this world. I read nothing good, but I read an awful lot. Here was escape! I read lurid stuff about ladies who smelled sweet and looked like flowers and were betrayed. I read about gardens and ballrooms and moonlight trysts and murders. I felt a sense of doors opening. And I began to be conscious of myself, the way I looked, the clothes I wore. I bought awful things at first, pink shirtwaist, artificial flowers, tripe.

Stanwyck signed on as a typist at the Jerome H. Remick Music Company, the next best thing to being in show business. By 15, she was performing in the back row of the chorus, pulling in $35 a week. She would remember her days as a chorus girl with fondness. That same year, she was hired for the 1922 Ziegfeld Follies, starring ◄ Gilda Gray. Moving into a cold-water flat on 46th Street with fellow chorines **Mae Clarke** and **Wanda Mansfield**, Stanwyck also worked midnights for *Texas Guinan. By 1924, she was an experienced hoofer, appearing in the *Keep Kool Revue* and *Gay Paree*, and dancing the Black Bottom in *George White's Scandals of 1926*.

It was in 1926 that Ruby Stevens changed her name to Barbara Stanwyck and landed a part in her first straight play. *The Noose* opened at the Hudson Theater on October 20, 1926, and ran nine months; the following year, Stanwyck made her film debut with *Broadway Nights*, a silent with sound effects. Her Broadway breakthrough was *Burlesque* by Arthur Hopkins and George Manker Watters, which opened on September 1, 1927, at the Plymouth Theater.

On August 26, 1928, Stanwyck married Frank Fay, a Broadway song-and-dance man whose career was also on the rise. Flush with their New York success and Stanwyck's United Artists' contract to appear in *The Locked Door*, the young hopefuls arrived in Hollywood by train in March 1929. *The Locked Door* proved an inauspicious beginning, however, since the movie was director George Fitzmaurice's first talkie, and he paid more attention to the sound equipment than to performances. Fitzmaurice, who had worked with a galaxy of gorgeous stars, kept griping that he couldn't make Stanwyck look beautiful no matter how hard he tried. "He kept arranging all kinds of drapery and tapestries behind me," she said. Finally, in that wry delivery that was to be her trademark, she told him, "They sent for me. I didn't send for them."

The 5'3" actress with the husky voice (Richard Chamberlain dubbed it "a million-dollar case of laryngitis") made her breakthrough, finally, with *Lady of Leisure*, her fourth movie,

**Gray, Gilda.** See Bow, Clara for sidebar.

in 1930. This time, director Frank Capra appreciated his leading lady. "Naive, unsophisticated, caring nothing about makeup, clothes or hairdos, this chorus girl could grab your heart and tear it to pieces," wrote Capra. "She knew nothing about camera tricks, how to 'cheat' her looks so her face could be seen, how to restrict her body movements in close shots. She just turned it on—and everything else on the stage stopped."

Stanwyck made three more movies that year, but her two-career marriage—one partner ascending, the other descending—was falling apart. The hard-drinking Fay was abusive physically as well as mentally in the face of a plummeting career; their marriage would subsequently be fodder for a movie classic. In 1931, David Selznick found the script *A Star is Born* so close to the Fay-Stanwyck alliance that he checked with his lawyers about possible litigation and was promptly presented with 20 pages of similarities. Selznick then brought in a team of writers, including *Dorothy Parker, to camouflage the story. The script remained a notorious *film à clef* and sat on the shelf for years.

Meanwhile, Stanwyck stuck with Fay, trying to get him to stop drinking and renew his career. In December 1932, she adopted a boy, Dion Fay. That same year, she made *Forbidden*, based on *Fannie Hurst's 1930 bestseller *Back Street*. The picture was Columbia's top moneymaker, but for Stanwyck the filming was a disaster. Her angry husband had returned to New York to resuscitate his waning career, while she fought a bitter court battle to get out of her Columbia contract; then a fall from a horse during shooting resulted in a dislocated tailbone. "It hurt," she said in 1984. "It still hurts." Stanwyck spent her days on the set and her nights in a hospital, in traction.

She was filming movie after movie in the 1930s: *Shopworn, So Big, The Bitter Tea of General Yen, Ladies They Talk About, Baby Face, Gambling Lady, The Secret Bride, The Woman in Red, Red Salute*, and *A Lost Lady*. (The last of these, an adaptation of *Willa Cather's 1923 novel, so outraged Cather that a codicil in her will forbade any future dramatizations of her writings.) From 1933 to 1935, Stanwyck shot five of these movies for Warner Bros., but her husband was making so much trouble for studio heads—complaining about her hours, brawling at the Brown Derby restaurant—that Warner's dropped her. That, and one more personal assault, convinced Stanwyck to file for divorce in November 1935. Six months later, the IRS garnisheed her wages for non-

Barbara
Stanwyck as
Stella Dallas.

payment of her husband's taxes. (Fay would eventually revive his career in *Mary Coyle Chase's Harvey.)

But Stanwyck was financially shrewd and secure. She was a savvy businesswoman who founded the Athena National Sorority in 1933 for young professional businesswomen. Unlike other stars who were tied by the contract system to one studio that loaned them out, Stanwyck freelanced after her Columbia court battle. She was able to pick and choose, to negotiate stronger contracts, signing one- or two-picture deals as she went, hopping from studio to studio.

In 1935, she signed with RKO to do *Annie Oakley* (directed by George Stevens), *A Message to Garcia*, and *The Bride Walks Out*. She then went to MGM for *His Brother's Wife*, co-starring Robert Taylor. Though Taylor was reputed to be gay, the two hit it off so well that he bought a ranch next to hers in Northridge.

When *A Star is Born* finally began filming in 1937, a child custody suit involving Fay and Stanwyck hit the newspapers, sending producers scrambling for another screenwriter to give their script further distance. The custody battle was an odd anomaly, since neither Fay nor Stanwyck ever devoted much attention to the young Dion. "Barbara tried to teach Dion to be tough," wrote Madsen. "As a child she had hated discipline. . . . She recited a poem she had learned by heart. . . . 'When comes the eaglet's time to fly/ No mother-softness robs him of his sky'. . . . He had to learn to be responsible for himself. He sure couldn't count on Frank Fay." (When the boy turned six, he was shipped off to boarding school. In 1946, age 14, he would be sent to Culver Military Academy in Indiana, and later claim that he did not see his mother for the next four years.)

*S*he has played five gun molls, two burlesque queens, half a dozen adulteresses and twice as many murderers. When she was good, she was very, very good. And when she was bad, she was terrific.

—Walter Matthau

Ironically, in 1937, Stanwyck was about to start filming the remake of the *Olive Higgins Prouty* novel *Stella Dallas*, to be directed by King Vidor. In this consummate movie about mother love, Stella Dallas is so successful in preparing her daughter for high society that the daughter is mortified by her low-class mother. The famous fadeout has Stanwyck standing in the rain outside an iron gate, watching through the window as her daughter marries into the upper crust. Samuel Goldwyn's 1924 silent version had starred *Mrs. Leslie Carter* and Edward G. Robinson, with a screenplay by *Frances Marion*. This time Stanwyck fought for the part, even putting up with a detested screen test. "I was spurred by the memory of the magnificent performance of the late Belle Bennett in the first movie version," she told the *Saturday Evening Post*. "Also, there was unusual stimulation in the dual nature of the part; it was like playing two different women simultaneously. Always Stella has to be shown both in her

surface commonness and in her basic fineness." Nominated for an Academy Award as Best Actress for her performance, Stanwyck lost to *Luise Rainer for *The Good Earth*.

Taylor and Stanwyck were not in love, though they enjoyed each other's company. But the Hollywood studio's morals squad was diligent. When *Photoplay* magazine ran an article by Sheilah Graham, under the pen name Kirtley Baskette, entitled "Hollywood's Unmarried Husbands and Wives"—naming Stanwyck and Taylor along with Lombard and Gable—the studio shotgunned the wedding. Stanwyck married Robert Taylor on May 14, 1939, with studio publicists in attendance. Although there was a solid gay community in Hollywood during the 1930s, homosexuality was against the law and could ruin careers at a time when drugs, drinking, and sexual promiscuity were winked at. Gays routinely went through with the nuptials known as "lavender" marriages engineered by studios to protect the stars.

Stanwyck's relationship with her lifelong publicist ❧ Helen Ferguson was long a cause for speculation. Whether or not it was sexual, it was a major relationship for nearly 30 years. Owner of the Helen Ferguson Agency, the twice-married, twice-divorced Ferguson handled all of Stanwyck's publicity, advised her on career moves, protected her, and even lived with her, off and on, for extended periods. Ferguson came into Stanwyck's life during the last days of her marriage to Fay, and acted the role of a mother hen, limiting press access to the star, sitting in on interviews, and always being there in a crisis. At one time, *Joan Crawford lived directly across the street from Stanwyck, in Brentwood, and Crawford's bisexuality notwithstanding, these two actors also became lifelong friends.

As a star, Stanwyck always had a large gay following. "When Stanwyck confronted men there was no subliminal I'm-Jane-you're-Tarzan glint," wrote Madsen. "Stanwyck was mocking and emotionally honest, and the way she related to the opposite sex was different from that of the screen's other tough ladies." But Stanwyck was also uncomfortable going outside the norm. She had problems of intimacy not just with men, but with everyone. In her later years, when a gay activist asked about her sexual preference, writes Madsen, "he was nearly thrown out of her house."

Once their stars were nicely married, the studios expected the couples to be seen doing the town two or three evenings a week—hair and gowns dutifully supplied. Stanwyck and Taylor hated the circuit, but they conformed. "I'll go to

Ciro's or the Trocadero with Bob some evening," she said. "I'll be wearing a lovely gown, and my hair all doozied up. No sooner do I get there when I think, gee, I look awful."

High-caliber Stanwyck releases dominated the year 1941. In her first light comedy, *The Lady Eve*, she co-starred with Henry Fonda, trendily decked out by costume designer *Edith Head, who also became a good friend. "Like *Bringing up Baby*," wrote *Pauline Kael 40 years later, *The Lady Eve* "is a mixture of visual and verbal slapstick, and of high artifice and pratfalls. Barbara Stanwyck keeps sticking out a sensational leg, and Henry Fonda keeps tripping over it. . . . [N]either performer has ever been funnier." The discovery of Stanwyck's comedic powers made her a prime contender for *Meet John Doe*, co-starring Gary Cooper and directed by Frank Capra. Another classic comedy, *Ball of Fire*, directed by Howard Hawks and also starring Gary Cooper, opened in December. Nominated for an Academy Award for *Ball of Fire*, Stanwyck lost to *Joan Fontaine for *Suspicion*.

Stanwyck continued making comedies, notably *Lady of Burlesque* based on *Gypsy Rose Lee*'s successful novel *The G-String Murders*, directed by William Wellman. Always the professional, always on time, Stanwyck was a far cry from some of the demanding stars of her day. Beloved by crew and cast, she championed those with less power; she was friendly with electricians, camera assistants, makeup and wardrobe crew. Cecil B. De Mille once wrote that he never worked with an actress "more cooperative, less temperamental, and a better workman. . . . [W]hen I count over those of whom my memories are unmarred by anyway unpleasant recollection of friction on the set . . . Barbara's name is the first that comes to mind."

On the set, she was known as Queen Babs. "There is the same air of cool detachment, casual assurance," wrote Frank Nugent. "She sits on the doorstep of her dressing room—knitting occasionally, or reading a book, or sipping one of the 14 cups of coffee she consumes in the course of a studio day. She looks more like a housewife listening to the radio while shelling peas than an actress about to take off into the emotional stratosphere. Then the bell rings—and it's Killer Stanwyck in the ring, knocking the audience dead." (When the fledgling actress *Marilyn Monroe was two hours late for her first scene with Stanwyck while filming the 1952 movie *Clash By Night*, Stanwyck never said a word. When Monroe proceeded to blow her lines 26 times, resulting in 26 takes, Stanwyck never said a word.)

## ❧▶ Ferguson, Helen (1901–1977)

*Hollywood press agent. Name variations: Helen Hargreaves. Born in Decatur, Illinois, on July 23, 1901; died in March 1977 in Florida; married William "Big Bill" Russell (an actor); married Robert L. Hargreaves; no children.*

One of Hollywood's best-known publicity agents, Helen Ferguson got her start playing bit parts in 13 Essanay two-reelers in Chicago; she made her stage debut in 1926. In 1930, she ditched acting for her first public relations job and eventually managed the Helen Ferguson Publicity Agency, at 321 South Beverly Drive in Los Angeles, with associate **Jewel Smith**. Among the stars they handled were *Loretta Young, Clark Gable, Henry Fonda, and *Barbara Stanwyck, with whom Ferguson was close friends for almost three decades. Ferguson died in 1977 after a lengthy illness. Her filmography as an actress includes *Miss Lulu Bett, Hungry Hearts, The Famous Mrs. Fair, Within the Law*, and *The Unknown Purple*.

Though Stanwyck was compliant, she would not hesitate to fight for others. On the 1949 shoot of *To Please a Lady* in Indiana, she requested adjoining rooms for herself and her longtime maid, **Harriett Corey**. When told that Indianapolis' best hotel would not accommodate blacks, Stanwyck suggested that MGM make reservations for her and Corey in the best "colored" hotel. MGM quickly resolved the problem with Indianapolis' best hotel.

She also championed fellow players. When *Golden Boy* began shooting on April 1, 1939, her leading man was the extremely nervous neophyte William Holden. The powers that be wanted to replace him during the first week. "My God, he's only had a week," she told Harry Cohn. "I don't know what you want. None of us can walk on water." She then coached Holden throughout the shoot. From that time on, every April 1, Holden sent her two dozen roses and a white gardenia. As they stood side-by-side as presenters at the April 1978 Academy Awards, Holden made an impromptu speech, surprising Stanwyck and delighting the audience, thanking her once again.

But Stanwyck was always generous with fellow actors. She thrilled to a good performance. In a guest column for the *Hollywood Reporter*, she chanted: "I wrote a fan letter to *Olivia de Havilland for *The Snake Pit*, to *Bette Davis for *Jezebel* and *Dark Victory*. I'll never forget Victor Mature's scene at the foot of the cross in *The Robe*. . . . I'll buy *Claire Trevor, period. And what about that *Ida Lupino? . . . I lack the words to express the last but not the least of my memories—no words are worthy of the unforgettable, the incomparable—Hell, I need only one word anyway. Here it is—*GARBO."

Having been supported by some excellent scripts, Stanwyck also had great respect for writers. "To me the words come first. If it ain't on paper, it ain't ever gonna get up on the screen." She had good reason; her writers included Preston Sturges, Frank Capra, Herman Mankiewicz, and **Viña Delmar**.

In the 1940s, however, American politics began to split the Hollywood community. Stanwyck, like her husband, was a right-wing conservative, and she and Taylor were founding members of the Motion Picture Alliance for the Preservation of American Ideals (MPAPA) against the aims of left-wing unions, guilds, and intellectuals. MPAPA members included Clark Gable, Gary Cooper, *Ayn Rand, and *Hedda Hopper. The organization stood for the if-I-can-pull-myself-up-by-the-bootstraps-so-can-you school of self-reliance. "In our special field of motion pictures," went the MPAPA premise, "we resent the growing impression that this industry is made up of, and dominated by, communists, radicals and crackpots." Put in historical perspective, Stanwyck was in the national mainstream, in step with the fearful mood that would result in the witchhunt for subversives led by Senator Joseph McCarthy. In 1946–47, Robert Taylor was to testify as a friendly witness before the House Committee on Un-American Activities (HUAC) in Hollywood and in Washington; before the Committee, Taylor named three "suspected communists": writer Lester Cole, actor Howard Da Silva, and Canadian starlet **Karen Morley**. Though Stanwyck was known to give patriotic lectures at Hollywood parties, she wisely sidestepped such public hangings. Much of the talent she had worked with and admired for years was ideologically on the other side.

Ironically, once it was decided that political conformity was essential for the nation's security, sexual conformity became part of the same outlook. "You can hardly separate homosexuals from subversives," Senator Kenneth Wherry told the *New York Post*. "Mind you, I don't say every homosexual is a subversive, and I don't say every subversive is a homosexual, but [people] of low morality are a menace to the government."

For Stanwyck, meanwhile, another career shift came in 1944, with the Raymond Chandler/Billy Wilder screenplay *Double Indemnity*. Adapted from a novel by James M.

Cain, the movie was directed by Wilder. In it, Stanwyck played an unredeeming, conniving malcontent who convinces Fred MacMurray to kill her husband to collect on his insurance; all that and in a blonde wig. Stanwyck remembered thinking, "This role is gonna finish me." Instead, the critics uniformly praised her performance. Said Stanwyck:

When I mention "atmosphere" in *Double Indemnity*—that gloomy, horrible house the Dietrichsons lived in, the slit of sunlight slicing through those heavy drapes—you could smell that death was in the air, you understood why she wanted to get out of there, no matter what. And for an actress, let me tell you the way those sets were lit, the house, Walter's apartment, those dark shadows, those slices of harsh light at strange angles—all that helped my performance.

Nominated again for Best Actress, Stanwyck lost to *Ingrid Bergman for *Gaslight*.

By 1947, the silvery streaks had arrived in her hair. While Stanwyck was shooting *B.F.'s Daughter*, the front office ordered her to dye the gray out; Stanwyck refused. The year 1948 brought *Sorry, Wrong Number*, a tour-de-force about a bedridden neurotic who hears over crossed telephone wires the arrangements for her own murder and spends the night trying to get help. Nominated for an Academy Award, Stanwyck lost to *Jane Wyman for *Johnny Belinda*, but she remained popular at the box office, making movie after movie: *To Please a Lady, The File on Thelma Jordan, The Furies*.

In 1950, Robert Taylor was in Italy on the shoot of *Quo Vadis* when their 12-year-marriage hit the rocks. Gossip drifted out of Italy about Taylor's dalliance with a 25-year-old divorcee named **Lia de Leo**, but Stanwyck put on her usual front. When Hedda Hopper called to confirm that Taylor wanted a divorce, Stanwyck drawled, "He didn't say anything about it at breakfast, but wait a minute, I'll ask him." Even so, she headed for Rome, with Helen Ferguson in tow, but it did no good. Divorce papers were filed in 1951, and from then on, she preferred the company of her friends *Joan Blondell and **Nancy Sinatra**. By 1964, Ferguson, now wheelchair-bound, had faded from her life.

In the 1950s, Stanwyck's career began to slide. "The characters she was offered were one dimensional," wrote Madsen, "usually women with guns locked in deadly battles of the sexes. Flaunting her white hair . . . , she lent her sneer and throaty laughter to wayward, evil women who, by the fade-out, were usually dead, unless they shared the reins with the one man who

*From the movie* Meet John Doe, *starring Gary Cooper and Barbara Stanwyck.*

dared stand up." She made her last movie, *The Night Walker*, in 1965, with ex-husband Taylor, who died four years later.

Television meanwhile had come calling. On September 19, 1960, "The Barbara Stanwyck Show," an NBC anthology series, made its debut; Stanwyck starred in 32 of 36 episodes and was awarded an Emmy, but the show was canceled the following year. "As I understand it from my producer, . . . they want action shows and have a theory that women don't do action.

The fact is, I'm the best action actress in the world. I can do horse drags, jump off buildings, and I've got the scars to prove it." She begged to play authentic frontier women, like *Belle Starr, *Pauline Cushman, *Poker Alice, or *Calamity Jane. She came close, playing the matriarch of a prominent ranching family in ABC's "The Big Valley" (1965–69), appearing in 105 of the 112 episodes. Before signing, she warned the producers: "I'm a tough old broad. Don't try to make me into something I'm not. If you want someone to tiptoe down the Barkley staircase in crinoline and politely ask where the cattle went, get another girl." Stanwyck enjoyed working on the show; she was less thrilled doing ABC's 1985 "Dynasty II: The Colbys." "I say the same line every week," she groused.

Stanwyck was acting her age; her stark white hair was a trademark. "The misguided ladies I've seen have made me think all the fretting, fussing, stewing, lying, and dyeing, all the tensions created by wanting to be forever young, age one faster. They look what they are—battle-scarred veterans of their lost war against time. I decided not to enlist in that war three years before I turned forty."

In 1981, she had begun to endure a string of misfortunes. On the night of October 27, when she was 74, Stanwyck was awakened in her home on Loma Vista by a flashlight in her face. Behind it stood a gun-toting robber in a ski mask, who hit her and threw her in a closet, where she lay bleeding. Afterward, Stanwyck became reclusive. She made a rare social appearance was at the 1982 Academy Awards, when she was awarded an honorary Oscar.

That same year, she ventured forth to play another matriarch; this time in the ten-hour ABC miniseries "The Thorn Birds," based on **Colleen McCullough**'s novel, for which the actress took home another Emmy. But Stanwyck suffered from chronic emphysema, and in a house-burning scene during the filming she ingested more than a whiff of smoke, causing her to end that day at St. Joseph's Hospital. The bronchial aftereffects lingered for about a year, causing four emergency trips to hospitals.

In May 1984, she was diagnosed with cataracts; on June 22, 1985, her house was gutted by fire (newspapers reported that she dashed back in to save letters from ex-husband Taylor); and the day she received the American Film Institute's Lifetime Achievement Award (April 9, 1986), she had to check herself out of St. John's Hospital in Santa Monica; in constant pain from a sprained back, she returned to the hospital the same evening. On January 20, 1990, at age 82, Barbara Stanwyck died at St. John's of congestive heart failure, complicated by emphysema. By request, her ashes were scattered over the desert in Lone Pine, California.

In 1965, while gazing out the window of a New York hotel room with another friend, Detroit newspaper columnist **Shirley Eder**, Stanwyck had commented, "You know, Shirley, I can remember when I was poor—oh so poor and so cold because my coat was too thin to give warmth. But as cold as I was, I loved being outside when the first snow fell on New York City. It was magic time for me then, and it's still magic, except now, with my feet on the radiator, I'm so nice and warm."

**SOURCES:**

Madsen, Axel. *Stanwyck*. NY: HarperCollins, 1994.

# Stapleton, Maureen (1925—)

*American actress who won an Emmy, an Oscar, and a Tony. Born Lois Maureen Stapleton in Troy, New York, on June 21, 1925; graduated from Catholic Central High School, Troy, New York; studied acting at the Herbert Berghof Acting School, New York; married Max Allentuck (a producer), in 1949 (divorced 1959); married David Rayfiel (a playwright), in May 1965 (divorced); children: (first marriage)* **Cathy Allentuck**; *Danny Allentuck.*

*Selected theater: New York debut as Sarah Tansey in* The Playboy of the Western World *(Booth Theater, October 1946); appeared as Iras in* Antony and Cleopatra *(Martin Beck Theater, November 1947), Miss Hatch in* Detective Story *(Hudson Theater, March 1949), Serafina in* The Rose Tattoo *(Martin Beck Theater, February 1951, followed by a tour); appeared as Flora in* Twenty-Seven Wagons Full of Cotton *(Playhouse Theater, April 1955), Lady Torrance in* Orpheus Descending *(Martin Beck Theater, March 1957), Ida in* The Cold Wind and the Warm *(Morosco Theater, December 1958), Carrie in* Toys in the Attic *(Hudson Theater, February 1960), Amanda Wingfield in a revival of* The Glass Menagerie *(Brooks Atkinson Theater, May 1965); had three roles in* Plaza Suite *(Plymouth Theater, February 1968); appeared as Evy Meara in* The Gingerbread Lady *(Plymouth Theater, December 1970), Georgie Elgin in* The Country Girl *(Billy Rose Theater, March 1972), Birdie in a revival of* The Little Foxes *(1981).*

*Selected filmography:* Lonelyhearts *(1959);* The Fugitive Kind *(1960);* Vu du Pont *(A View From the Bridge, Fr.-It., 1962);* Bye Bye Birdie *(1963);* Trilogy *(1969);* Airport *(1970);* Plaza Suite *(1971);* Interiors

*(1978); The Runner Stumbles (1979); Lost and Found (1979); The Fan (1981); On the Right Track (1981); Reds (1981); Johnny Dangerously (1984); Cocoon (1985); (voice only) The Cosmic Eye (1985); The Money Pit (1986); Heartburn (1986); Hello Actors Studio (doc., 1987); Sweet Lorraine (1987); Made in Heaven (1987); Nuts (1987); Doin' Time on Planet Earth (1988); Cocoon: The Return (1988); Passed Away (1992).*

Having built her reputation playing unglamourous down-to-earth character roles,

actress Maureen Stapleton has always been aware that she could not rely on her beauty to get by. "People looked at me onstage and said, 'Jesus, that broad better be able to act,'" she once remarked. And act she did, winning an Emmy, an Oscar, and a Tony in a career that has spanned almost five decades. Stapleton has always slipped easily between drama and comedy, displaying a remarkable range and impeccable control of her craft.

Born in Troy, New York, in 1925, Stapleton attended Catholic Central High School, where

*From* The Gathering, Part II, *starring Maureen Stapleton and Efrim Zimbalist, Jr.*

she performed in all the school plays. Most afternoons, when school was out, she made her way to the local cinema, staying until closing time. It was only later, after she had scraped up enough money to study with Herbert Berghof in New York City, that she realized acting was not just about glamour and money. "It was a whole new world," she told **Helen Ormsbee** of the New York *Herald Tribune* in February 1951. "In Troy I used to go to movies and dream of being a star, with money and lovely clothes. But in this new world I learned other values—integrity in acting, for instance. . . . Herbert Berghof gave us all a love of the theater."

Stapleton got some of her early experience in a summer stock company that 22 of Berghof's students started in Blauvelt, New York, in the summer of 1945. The following summer, she joined a stock company in Mount Kisco, New York, refining her skills further. Returning to New York City, she snagged a small role in *The Playboy of the Western World*, then after understudying the larger part of Pegeen Mike, she played it for a week opposite Burgess Meredith. Afterwards, she took any small roles that came her way and also became a charter member of the Actors Studio, where she studied with Robert Lewis and Lee Strasberg.

In 1951, after a lengthy audition process, Stapleton was chosen to play Serafina, the widowed Sicilian-American heroine of Tennessee Williams' play *The Rose Tattoo*. (Williams had written the role for *Anna Magnani, but she was unable to master English well enough for a Broadway production. She did play the role in the later movie.) The part, for which Stapleton mastered an Italian accent, signaled her true arrival in the theater. "Maureen Stapleton's performance is triumphant," proclaimed *The New York Times*. "The widow is unlearned and superstitious and becomes something of a harridan after her husband dies. Miss Stapleton does not evade the coarseness of the part. But neither does she miss its exaltation. For Mr. Williams has sprinkled a little stardust over the widow's shoulders and Miss Stapleton has kept the part sparkling though all the fury and tumult of the emotion." For her performance, Stapleton won a Peabody Award and a Tony as Best Actress. The role became a classic of her repertoire and was revived several times in her career.

Following appearances in *The Emperor's Clothes*, *The Crucible*, and *The Sea Gull* during the 1953–54 season, Stapleton created exquisite characterizations in two additional Tennessee Williams plays: Flora in *Twenty-Seven Wagons Full of Cotton*, which Richard Watts, Jr., of the *New York Post* called "a masterpiece of acting," and Lady Torrance, the proprietor of a dry-goods store in *Orpheus Descending*. Although the critics were not wild about the latter play, they were overwhelmingly positive about Stapleton's performance. "Her fiercely intelligent eyes always carry conviction," declared Walter Kerr, "you're sure that she does know and feel everything the author says she knows and feels."

In 1960, Stapleton appeared as Carrie in *Toys in the Attic*, the last major play by *Lillian Hellman and the winner of that year's New York Drama Critics' Circle Award. *Toys* concerns two unmarried sisters (the other played by *Anne Revere) and their brother (Jason Robards, Jr.), whose marriage tears the family apart. Stapleton, whom critics called "comic, discerning, awkward and pathetic," admitted that the part was difficult for her.

Stapleton launched her film career in 1959, winning an Oscar nomination for her first movie performance, in *Lonelyhearts* (1959), and for her work in *Airport* (1970) and *Interiors* (1978). She finally won the golden statue for her portrayal of *Emma Goldman in *Reds* (1981). Television has also proven to be a creative outlet for the actress, who won a Sullivan Award for her performance as Sadie Burke in a production of *All the King's Men* (May 1958) and an Emmy Award for her performance in *Save Me a Place at Forest Lawn* (1967).

Stapleton's earliest comedy success was in the role of the matchmaking aunt in S.N. Behrman's autobiographical play *The Cold Wind and the Warm* (1959), which she played with "uproarious, upholstered aplomb," according to Kenneth Tynan. Walter Kerr also found her delightful. "It is an expansive and honest pleasure to watch Maureen Stapleton, as matchmaker for a Jewish neighborhood and foster-mother to practically everyone in sight, turn a speculative eye on an attractive and available spinster, invent a handful of splendid lies to account for the failure of a promised suitor to show up, and, in a burst of breathless efficiency, hustle the lass off to the corner drugstore where there are prospects with every milk shake."

In 1968, Stapleton took on the challenge of three roles in Neil Simon's comedy *Plaza Suite* and in 1970 appeared as Evy Meara in his *The Gingerbread Lady*, which chronicles the demise of a once-popular singer who turns to the bottle. Critics had problems with both Stapleton's performance and Simon's play, dismissing it as a series of one-liners. Critic John Simon lauded her "timing and emphasis" but thought she was miscast. **Allene Talmey**, writing for *Vogue*, also thought Simon's plot was weak, but found Stapleton's character well drawn and brilliantly acted.

While Stapleton's career hummed along, her personal life was shaky. In an interview on Mike Wallace's *Night Beat* in 1957, she said that she had been undergoing psychiatric treatment for over two years because she felt her life was "so disorganized." In her feisty 1995 autobiography *A Hell of a Life?* (written with **Jane Scovell**), she disclosed earlier problems with alcohol and also took the blame for her two failed marriages, one to theater producer Max Allentuck, with whom she had two children, and another to playwright David Rayfiel. Although Stapleton never drank before a performance, she apparently made up for lost time after the curtain came down. In her book, she writes that her son Danny would shout at her when she started slurring her words: "Stop talking German, Mom. I hate it when you talk German!"

One of Stapleton's later stage appearances was a revival of *The Glass Menagerie* at New York's Circle in the Square in 1975. (She had first played the role in 1965.) The actress continued to make occasional films throughout the 1980s and early 1990s, including *Cocoon: The Return* (1988) and *Passed Away* (1992). Having long since made peace with her demons, Stapleton resides in Lenox, Massachusetts, and is still on the lookout for a good role.

**SOURCES:**

Katz, Ephraim. *The Film Encyclopedia*. NY: Harper-Collins, 1994.

McHugh, Clare. "Telling it Like it Was," in *People Weekly*. October 23, 1995.

Moritz, Charles, ed. *Current Biography 1959*. NY: H.W. Wilson, 1959.

Morley, Sheridan. *The Great Stage Stars*. Australia: Angus & Roberts, 1986.

Wilmeth, Don B., and Tice L. Miller, eds. *Cambridge Guide to American Theater*. Cambridge and NY: The Cambridge University Press, 1993.

**Barbara Morgan**,
Melrose, Massachusetts

# Stapleton, Ruth Carter (1929–1983)

*American faith healer. Name variations: Ruth Carter. Born Ruth Carter on August 7, 1929, in Archery, Georgia; died on September 26, 1983, in Hope Mills, North Carolina; daughter of Earl Carter and Lillian (Gordy) Carter; attended Georgia State College for Women, 1946–48; attended Methodist College and the University of North Carolina, receiving an M.A. in English; married Robert Stapleton, on November 14, 1948; children: Lynn, Scott, Patti, and Michael.*

The sister of former American president Jimmy Carter, Ruth Carter Stapleton was a popular Christian evangelist. The third of four children of Earl and **Lillian Carter**, Ruth was born in 1929 and raised on the Carter family farm in Plains, Georgia. The family belonged to the local Baptist congregation, but was not especially pious. Later in life, Stapleton would ascribe her emotional problems as an adult to her upbringing. She felt unloved by her mother, a nurse often absent from home. Her father, however, favored Stapleton over his other children and displayed an affection for her that others saw as unhealthy. After a public school education, she entered Georgia State College for Women in 1946. An average student, Ruth at the time had little interest in a higher education. She dropped out in 1948 to marry Robert Stapleton, a veterinarian, and moved to Fayetteville, North Carolina. She had four children (the last in 1959) and was, outwardly, a contented homemaker, wife, and mother of a prosperous family.

However, she secretly suffered from severe depression, which she attributed to being unprepared for the responsibilities of marriage and motherhood. She felt that she lacked a purpose in life; her depression caused her marriage to suffer, and eventually she withdrew emotionally from her family and friends. Hoping to find personal fulfillment, she resumed her education at Methodist College and the University of North Carolina, studying English, psychology, and theology. After completing a master's degree in English, she took a job teaching high school in Fayetteville. Still suffering from depression and a sense of failure, she went into psychoanalysis and also began attending Bible classes at nearby Fort Bragg. Although she left psychoanalysis after a few months, she began to find in Christian theology the inner peace she sought.

As religion gained importance in her life, she was dismissed from her teaching position for discussing the Bible in class. Shortly afterwards, she took over the Bible classes at Fort Bragg. She taught there until 1966, establishing a large following in the Fayetteville area with a dynamic preaching style that combined theology with elements of psychoanalysis. Yet she remained unfulfilled, and in 1966 her depression led her to attempt suicide. Following this trauma, she came to see the childhood roots of her emotional problems, and, as she stated, finally allowed God to heal the painful memories of her past. She became a "born again" Christian and developed a therapy of "inner healing" based on her own experience. Her marriage and her relationships with her children improved dramatically after her conversion. Hoping to help others reach the same kind of religious and emotional peace she had found, Stapleton, with her husband's aid, began preaching her message across the South. The response to her meetings—which blended self-help psychology, meditation, and prayer—was substantial, and earned her a reputation for faith healing. She was careful to maintain that she did no healing herself; all healing came from God.

In the same year as her own conversion, Stapleton was instrumental in the conversion of her older brother Jimmy, disconsolate after a lost gubernatorial race. Stapleton became involved as a campaigner in all of her brother's subsequent political races, drawing on her own wide following across the South and Midwest. Their joint celebrity led *Time* and *Newsweek* to publish interviews with Stapleton in the months prior to Carter's election as president in 1976. Carter believed his sister's celebrity and her ability to motivate her supporters were vital to his election.

In 1972, she and Robert Stapleton founded a non-profit corporation, Behold, Inc., to handle the income from her lectures, audiotapes, and books. Her popularity continued to grow during her 15 years of active preaching and made her relatively wealthy. Although she was personally a Southern Baptist, Stapleton's ministry was non-denominational and attracted Protestants and Catholics. She held workshops and spiritual healing retreats across the United States, then abroad, from Europe to Japan. Stapleton began publishing her message in 1976 with *The Gift of Inner Healing*, in which she described her own path to fulfillment. The work sold almost half a million copies, testifying to the widespread American following she enjoyed. Other works came later, such as *Experiencing Inner Healing* and *In His Footsteps*. These books offered a total therapy combining theology and psychology with prescriptions for a holistic diet and physical exercise. In 1978, she and her husband founded a retreat, Holovita Ranch, near Dallas, Texas.

In 1983, Stapleton was diagnosed with pancreatic cancer, the same disease Earl Carter had died from. She refused conventional medical care, relying instead on her belief in divine healing through prayer and meditation. She survived only a few months after the diagnosis, dying in September at age 54.

**SOURCES:**

Bourne, Peter. *Jimmy Carter*. NY: Scribner, 1997.
Stapleton, Ruth Carter. *The Gift of Inner Healing*. Waco, TX: Word, 1976.

**Laura York**, M.A. in History,
University of California, Riverside, California

# Starbuck, Mary Coffyn
## (1644/45–1717)

*American minister. Born on February 20, 1644 or 1645, in Haverhill, Massachusetts; died on November 13, 1717, in Nantucket, Massachusetts; daughter of Tristram Coffyn (a magistrate) and Dionis (Stevens) Coffyn; educated at home; married Nathaniel Starbuck (a farmer), around 1663; children: Mary, Elizabeth, Nathaniel, Jethro, Barnabas, Eunice, Priscilla, Hepzibah, Ann, and Paul.*

The seventh of nine children of a British immigrant and his wife, Mary Coffyn Starbuck was born in Haverhill, Massachusetts. The Coffyns taught Mary to both read and write, giving her a talent unusual for a young woman of her day. In 1660, when Mary was in her mid-teens, the family moved to the island of Nantucket after her father Tristram Coffyn, along with several business associates, implemented plans to purchase and colonize the tiny island off the Massachusetts coast. In this isolated community, Mary found a husband in Nathaniel Starbuck, a fellow Nantucket resident and the son of one of her father's business associates. Nathaniel and Mary had ten children, only two of whom lived to adulthood, as Nathaniel became a prosperous farmer and entered the local political arena.

Dissatisfied with both her family's religion and the Baptist leanings of her husband, Starbuck welcomed the arrival of several Society of Friends (Quaker) missionaries to the island between 1698 and 1704. Open to a religion that supported women as equal members and welcomed the ministrations of each of its members rather than a "professional" minister, she accepted their request that she host weekly religious services for family and friends. With the help of both her husband and her son, Nathaniel Starbuck Jr., and with the support of several Friends from the mainland, Starbuck was instrumental in helping the tiny island boast a substantial Quaker presence by 1710. A capable public speaker, she became Nantucket's first minister, as well as an active voice in community affairs and local politics. Together with her husband, she opened her home up for public meetings and gained a reputation as a fair adjudicator in local disputes, earning the nickname "the great Woman" for her efforts. Mary Starbuck died on the island of Nantucket in 1717 at the age of 72, her works surviving only as oral history recounting the early days of what would soon become one of the most prosperous whaling centers in North America.

SOURCES:

James, Edward T., ed. *Notable American Women, 1607–1950*. Cambridge, MA: The Belknap Press of Harvard University, 1971.

**Pamela Shelton**, freelance writer,
Avon, Connecticut

# Stark, Freya (1893–1993)

*British explorer and author who made several journeys to remote areas of the Middle East and whose knowledge of the people and the area proved invaluable to the Allied cause during World War II. Name variations: Dame Freya Stark. Born Freya Madeline Stark on January 31, 1893, in Paris, France; died on May 9, 1993, in Asolo, Italy; daughter of Robert Stark (a sculptor) and Flora Stark (an artist); educated by governesses; attended the University of London and the School of Oriental and African Studies; married Stewart Perowne, in 1947.*

*Due to travels between England and Italy, became fluent in English, Italian, German, and French; learned Arabic and made three long journeys into the interior of the Middle East; aided the Allies during World War II; continued to travel and write throughout her long life; awarded Triennial Burton Memorial Medal, Royal Asiatic Society (1934); Mungo Park Medal, Royal Scottish Geographical Society (1936); Founders Medal, Royal Geographical Society (1942); Percy Sykes Memorial Medal, Royal Central Asiatic Society (1951); Cross of the British Empire (1953); and made Dame of the British Empire (1972).*

In the country of Northwest Luristan, Freya Stark and her guide picked their way across the rough terrain. She had crossed the Persian border illegally, as her guide had no passport. After becoming separated, the two had regrouped in the area of low hills and scraggly oak trees where the Lurs tended their flocks. Stark was searching for a hoard of gold ornaments, daggers, coins, and idols said to be hidden in a cave. Soon after locating some early Muslim graves, the pair ran into a group of mounted police and were promptly delivered to the district governor in Husainabad, the capital. The governor, who was amused to find a captured Englishwoman before him, wanted to know how she had survived in a wilderness notorious for its bandits. When Stark returned to Tehran, she learned her capture by the Persian police had been quite fortunate. Murderers had been stalking her footsteps, determined to kill the woman wandering about Luristan and opening graves. Amused, Freya Stark, adventurer and explorer, planned her next foray.

Freya Madeline Stark was born in Paris on January 31, 1893, in the Montmartre studio of her parents, artists Robert and **Flora Stark**, who were first cousins. Freya's travels began at age two-and-a-half when she and her younger sister **Vera Stark** were carried across the Alps in a basket to Cortina, Italy. Her mother had grown up in Italy, while her father was from the Devonshire moors, so Freya's was a cosmopolitan upbringing. From childhood, Stark was fluent in English, Italian, German, and French. She also taught herself Latin. But her parents' marriage was not happy—her mother hated the damp cold of the moors—and in 1901, they separated. While her mother settled in Asolo, a village in the foothills of the Dolomites, her father moved to Canada.

It was in Italy that Stark had her first brush with death. In a factory run by her mother, Freya's hair was caught by machinery, with the resulting loss of part of her scalp and the mutilation of an ear. A young doctor in Turin, who had pioneered a new method of skin grafting, was credited with saving the young girl's life. That life was made more complicated by a family relationship with the factory manager, Count Mario di Roascio, whom Freya detested and who was with her during the accident. He seemed to have a strange power over her mother. When Freya grew up, the count asked for her hand in marriage. Turned down, he married her younger sister Vera, becoming a permanent family member whom Freya never accepted.

*No wonder that yours is a powerful nation. Your women do what our men are afraid to attempt.*

—District governor of Luristan to Freya Stark

Though Stark was largely educated by governesses, at age 19 she entered Bedford College in London where she remained for two years before the outbreak of World War I. She then began nurses' training at a clinic in Bologna where she was courted by a bacteriologist, Guido Ruata, nearly 20 years her senior. When Stark contracted typhoid and became desperately ill, Ruata obtained a new post, broke off their engagement, and married a woman with whom he had had a long-standing liaison. It was at this time that Stark began to think of learning Arabic and traveling to the Middle East. In 1916, she returned to Asolo for the rest of the war where she received another proposal from Gabriel de Bottinis de Ste Agnes. But by this time, Stark's sights were set on distant horizons.

First she built up a modestly profitable market-garden business, using the money for Arabic lessons. She also took a course in Arabic and Persian at the London School of Oriental and African Studies. Stark first set foot in Asia in November 1927 when she settled for the winter in Brummana in Lebanon as well as in Damascus. She returned to Lebanon in 1929 and 1931 to undertake three solo journeys—two in Luristan and one in Mazanderan, south of the Caspian Sea. Out of these travels came the book which established her name as a writer, *The Valley of the Assassins.*

In the winter of 1934–35, Stark traveled into the Arabic interior—only the fifth European woman to undertake such a journey (The others were *Gertrude Bell, *Jane Digby el Mesrab, *Hester Stanhope, and ◄ Anne Blunt.) Her style of wandering was quite different from that of previous European explorers. She was fluent in Arabic and understood local customs as well as the language. Stark preferred to travel alone if possible, though she often had one male guide. She did not travel as a wealthy European, but rather as a wayfarer dependent on the goodwill of her hosts. She was especially sensitive about European slights to locals and felt strongly that such superior attitudes destroyed communication. Stark often stayed in harems where she learned a great deal. She had, however, the advantage of also being able to fraternize with Arabic men. Her unmarried state was a great advantage in the Middle East, as many Arabic cultures venerate women who never marry.

Traveling from Mukalla on the Arabian coast, Freya Stark was soon staying in elaborately decorated multi-storied mud houses that towered over the plains of the interior. As always, she chose to go to the most isolated, inaccessible places. This journey brought another dance with death when she contracted measles and became extremely ill with a dilated heart. The good care she received at the hands of her Arab hosts as well as her rescue by the Royal Air Force (RAF) operating from Aden saved her life. After a long recovery, she began a second journey from Mukalla in the winter of 1937–38. Here she contracted dengue fever and suffered greatly. This time there was no RAF rescue and only the devoted care of her hosts restored her health. Her adventures were recorded in *The Southern Gates of Arabia* (1936) for which she received the Royal Scottish Geographical Society's Mungo Park Medal. Asked if she faced difficulties traveling alone as a woman, she replied, "No. I was sincerely out for knowledge and that is a respected thing in the East." Although the fact that she was a woman no doubt played a role in the many close relationships Stark

◆▶
***Anne Blunt.*** *See Lovelace, Ada Byron for sidebar.*

formed, her genuine love of the people in the area was probably an even greater factor.

As the 1930s drew to a close, Stark was forced to make a painful choice. Her ties to Italy were very close—she had four Italian nieces and nephews after Vera's marriage. But Fascist Italy allied itself with Hitler's Germany, so Stark had to choose between her English and Italian identities. In early 1939, she offered her services to the British Foreign Office. A month after World War II began on September 1, 1939, she was posted to Aden as an Arabist attached to the Ministry of Information. Her mother and much of her family remained in Italy, while she chose to serve Great Britain. Here she met Stewart Perowne who became a friend and whom she would later marry disastrously. Soon the war in the desert was raging as German General Erwin Rommel, the "Desert Fox," fought brilliantly in North Africa. The British feared the Germans and Italians would influence Arabs in Egypt and throughout the Middle East and form a fifth column which would destroy their tenuous hold on the area. Maintaining a grip on this petroleum-rich area was vital. Germany had few oil reserves and was intent on acquiring this critical resource. It was during this time that Freya Stark devised an effective strategy to counter German influence.

Traveling into the interior to shore up Anglo-Arab ties, Stark arrived in San'a in Yemen in February 1940 after a tortuous six-day journey by truck over what "nobody in England would call a road." As an employee of the British Ministry of Information, she presented herself to the foreign minister. She then decided her efforts must be directed to another important person in the town, the foreign minister's wife. Soon, Stark was attending tea parties where her fluent Arabic was obviously a trump card. Her ultimate goal was to show movies demonstrating Great Britain's power. This, however, was no easy task, as movies and recordings were forbidden on religious grounds as inventions by infidels. At first, Stark described the movie to the minister's wife saying she would never dream of showing it unless the woman's husband agreed. In no time at all, a projector was set up in the harem where a show of Britain's "ruling the waves" made a tremendous impression. Shortly after the women had viewed the film, Stark heard the projector whirring in another part of the house. Peeping in, she saw the minister and his colleagues deeply engrossed in the film. The Arabian women demanded more and more films which found their way to the men. The Italians and Germans were furious about this public-relations coup, which was repeated throughout the Middle East.

In Cairo, Stark used a similar technique when she launched the Brotherhood of Freedom, an organization created to fight fascism. While the group was never overtly pro-British, members met for discussions and briefings. Stark used this ever-expanding organization to spread positive rumors about Britain at a time when, in actual fact, Hitler's armies were winning everywhere. She insisted, for example, on forecasting the demise of the Nazis when the loss of Allied-

occupied Tobruk was imminent. Her instincts were rewarded, however, when the victories of El Alamein and Stalingrad proved a turning point for the Allies. In 1943, Stark was sent on a tour of the United States by the British government, which hoped she would be able to influence American politicians to oppose the creation of a Jewish state in Palestine. (While she was not anti-Semitic, she was firmly against the Zionist cause, believing that the removal of Arabs who already lived in the land would sow the seeds for violent conflict in the future.) Stark was already a well-known writer, a decorated explorer, and a

Freya Stark

respected linguist, and her efforts in the war only increased her fame.

When the war ended, Stark returned to her home in Asolo. Fortunately, her family had been well cared for by the villagers who had also done all in their power to guard her house. As always, Stark's empathy with others transcended national boundaries and temporary human conflicts. In September 1947, she married Stewart Perowne, a marriage which lasted only six months. Perowne, whose orientation was not heterosexual, saw the marriage as one of convenience between friends, while Stark wanted matrimony in the fullest sense. With the breakup of this brief alliance, she became interested in history and began visiting classical sites in Persia and the coast of Western Turkey. The books *Ionia: A Quest*, *The Lycian Shore* and *Alexander's Path* were written as a result. She then explored Roman frontiers in Asia and recorded her adventures in *Riding to the Tigris*. Although Stark was almost 70, her desire for adventure was as strong as ever.

At the age of 77, Dame Freya Stark, who had been made Dame of the British Empire for her service to England, embarked on the first of three mounted treks into the Himalayan foothills. She also ventured to the great Cambodian temples of Angkor Wat before going on to China. In 1968, she was in Afghanistan, traveling by Land Rover. Soviet Central Asia soon beckoned as well. In her 90s, Stark's trips became less arduous, and she confined herself mostly to Europe. Many of these travels led to books enabling her to live comfortably off her royalties.

Stark embarked on her final journey at age 100 on May 9, 1993. She had traveled and recorded much in her long life. Photos inevitably show a smiling, happy person who shrugged off illness and discomfort in order to explore. Her view of the world did not depend on national or geographical boundaries, which she felt were completely arbitrary. Ever open, she placed herself completely in her hosts' hands and was never betrayed by this instinct.

**SOURCES:**

Brent, Peter. *Far Arabia. Explorers of the Myth*. London: Weidenfeld & Nicolson, 1977.

"British Agent," in *Newsweek*. January 17, 1944, p. 51.

"Dame Freya Stark," in *The Times* [London]. May 11, 1993, p. 17.

Flint, Peter B. "Dame Freya Stark, Travel Writer, Is Dead at 100," in *The New York Times*. May 11, 1993.

"Freya Stark of Arabia," in *Newsweek*. November 2, 1953, pp. 92–93.

"Freya Stark's Journey," in *The New York Times*. May 12, 1993, p. A18.

Fussell, Paul. *Abroad: British Literary Traveling Between the Wars*. NY: Oxford University Press, 1980.

Geniesse, Jane Fletcher. *Passionate Nomad: The Life of Freya Stark*. NY: Random House, 1999.

Kiernan, R.H. *The Unveiling of Arabia: The Story of Arabian Travel and Discovery*. London: Harrap, 1937.

Lawton, John. "A Lifelong Journey," in *Aramco World*. Vol. 44, no. 4. July–August 1993, pp. 2–7.

Moorehead, Caroline. *Freya Stark*. NY: Penguin, 1985.

Ruthven, Malise. *Traveller Through Time: A Photographic Journey with Freya Stark*. NY: Viking, 1986.

*Sackville-West, Vita. "Stark, Freya," in *A Library of Literary Criticism*. Vol. III. Edited by Ruth Z. Tempe and Martin Tucker. NY: Frederick Ungar, pp. 178–179.

Tidrick, Kathryn. *Heart-beguiling Araby*. Cambridge: Cambridge University Press, 1981.

**John Haag**, Associate Professor of History, University of Georgia, Athens, Georgia

# Starovoitova, Galina (1946–1998)

*Russian politician, advisor to Boris Yeltsin, who was assassinated in 1998. Pronunciation: Sta-ro-VOI-to-va. Born Galina Vasil'evna in Cheliabinsk, RSFSR, on May 17, 1946; murdered in St. Petersburg, Russia, on November 20, 1998; daughter of Vasilii Stepanovich (a professor and Party organizer who held an important position in the defense industry) and Rimma Iakovlevna; Leningrad College of Military Engineering, B.A., 1966; Leningrad State University, M.A. in social psychology, 1971; Institute of Ethnography of the USSR Academy of Sciences, Ph.D. in psychology, 1980; married Grigorii Borshevskii; married Andrei Volkov (a physicist), in 1998; children: (first marriage) son, Platon Grigor'evich Borshevskii.*

*Was a member of the USSR Congress of People's Deputies (1989–91); was a member of the Russian Congress of People's Deputies (1990–93); was an advisor to Boris Yeltsin on inter-ethnic affairs (1991–92); was a member of Russian State Duma (1995–98); ran for president of the Russian Federation (1996).*

*Publications: Ethnic Groups in the Modern Soviet City (in Russian; Leningrad: Nauka, 1987), based on her Ph.D. dissertation; numerous articles and interviews in the press on the political situation in the former Soviet Union (1988–98).*

On November 20, 1998, Galina Starovoitova, a member of the Russian State Duma (Parliament), was shot dead in the hallway of her St. Petersburg apartment building. It was widely believed that Starovoitova had been the victim of a contract killing because of her history as a fierce and uncompromising fighter for democracy in Russia. The top leadership, including President Boris Yeltsin, for whom she had worked as an advisor on inter-ethnic issues, vowed to get to the bottom of her murder, noting the importance both of her commitment to the development of democracy in Russia and the need to stop the contract killings of politicians and businesspeople by organized crime and political extremists. Starovoitova was a popular public figure among the citizenry; on the day of her funeral, more than 10,000 mourners came to pay their respects as she lay in state.

Thus ended the turbulent and brief political career of a woman who is commonly described in epitaphs as courageous and noble, a person of integrity, a representative of the cream of the Russian intelligentsia. Writes Adam Michnik: "Their principle was the truth; their characteristic was straightforwardness; their method was a nonviolent way of forcing change; their spiritual climate was free from hate and thoughts of revenge." "In burying Galina Starovoitova," noted Bill Powell, "many Russians wondered whether they were also burying what she stood for: their country's flagging experiment with liberalism and democracy."

Born Galina Vasil'evna in Cheliabinsk in 1946, Starovoitova began her professional life in 1966 when, having graduated from the Leningrad Military College for Engineering with a B.A., she worked first as a laboratory assistant in a research institute. From 1968 to 1971, she worked as a sociologist at a research institute specializing in the technology of ship-building. In 1971, having graduated from Leningrad State University with an M.A. in social psychology, Starovoitova worked as a psychologist first at a factory, then at an architectural-planning organization; she also taught social psychology at two post-secondary institutions.

In 1973, Starovoitova began her Ph.D. studies at the Institute of Ethnography at the USSR Academy of Sciences. Three years later, she defended her dissertation on "Problems of ethnosociology of ethnic groups in the modern city." The study was based on material gathered on the Tatar population in Leningrad (now St. Petersburg). Starovoitova worked as a researcher at the Institute of Ethnography and at the Centre for the Study of Inter-ethnic Relations, also part of the Academy of Sciences.

Starovoitova's first political act occurred in 1968, when she signed a petition protesting the Soviet invasion of Czechoslovakia, an action for which she was interrogated by the KGB. Subsequent independent-minded activity was confined to private discussions around the kitchen table with like-minded friends—until 20 years later, when Armenia and Azerbaijan went to war over Nagorno Karabakh.

As part of her work at the Academy of Sciences, Starovoitova had conducted field work in Nagorno Karabakh, an Armenian enclave in the republic of Azerbaijan. In 1988, Nagorno Karabakh voted to secede from Azerbaijan and to join with the republic of Armenia. Times had changed since 1968; Mikhail Gorbachev's policy of *glasnost* (openness) allowed citizens to publicly air their opinions in ways that had previously been impossible or dangerous; indeed, one of the goals of *glasnost* was to win the support of the intelligentsia. Starovoitova pursued several initiatives to help solve the problem of Nagorno Karabakh. She wrote a personal letter of support to her friends and colleagues in Armenia, which was distributed widely and broadcast over Radio Liberty; and she visited the region to discuss with Armenian and Azerbaijani authorities her proposals to bring an end to the conflict, which were based on the right of Nagorno Karabakh to sovereignty. Starovoitova's life as a politician began formally in 1989, when she was elected to the USSR Congress of People's Deputies (Parliament) as a representative from Armenia.

Galina
Starovoitova

On the spectrum of political movements, Starovoitova belonged to Democratic Russia, the largest popular democratic faction. Long a leading light in the party, in February 1993 she was elected co-chair of Democratic Russia's council of representatives. Five years later, she was elected the sole chair. She was closely associated with Boris Yeltsin from the outset of her political career. After being elected to the USSR Congress of People's Deputies, Starovoitova joined the Inter-regional Group of Deputies, the most important of the reform-oriented blocs in the Congress, among whose leaders were Andrei Sakharov and Yeltsin. The Inter-regional Group called for a faster pace of economic and political reform. In 1990, Starovoitova was also elected as a representative of Leningrad to the Russian Congress of People's Deputies. Her association with Yeltsin continued—he was the chair of the Supreme Soviet (a subunit of the larger Congress), and she belonged to his closest circle of advisors.

In 1991, President Yeltsin appointed Starovoitova as his advisor on inter-ethnic affairs. The appointment was short lived, lasting only until November 4, 1992, when she was dismissed because of their differences over questions of sovereignty and territorial integrity. The former Soviet Union was composed of 15 republics, all of which became independent countries in 1991. The Russian Federation itself retained its character as a quilt of ethnic groups, typically territorially based in their own administrative units. Part of the political process since the breakup of the USSR in 1991 has been to define the relationship between the Russian national government and the ethnic groups, and to address the historical grievances of ethnic minorities within Russia. In the fall of 1992, fighting broke out on the border of the national republics (within Russia) of North Ossetia and Ingushetia over contested territory. Russian troops were sent in to stabilize the situation, and the Russian government and media adopted a predominantly pro-Ossetian stance. Starovoitova was opposed to this stance, drawing attention to the reasons behind Ingushetia's actions. She also floated the idea of redrawing the boundary, which Yeltsin did not support. Anecdotal evidence suggests that the president of North Ossetia pressured Yeltsin into dismissing Starovoitova.

Apart from the differences in inter-ethnic affairs, it appears that Starovoitova was also dismissed, as were other radical democrats in Yeltsin's Cabinet, in the course of his ongoing struggle with the Supreme Soviet during 1990–93 (the Supreme Soviet was selected from the 1,068-member Russian Congress of People's Deputies and was a 268-member bicameral body). Much of this struggle stemmed from his radical economic reform agenda. Yeltsin alternated between confrontation and conciliation with the Supreme Soviet in order to implement economic reform; one method he used to gain the support of the Supreme Soviet was to dismiss his more radical Cabinet members. Ultimately, the confrontation with the Supreme Soviet boiled down to determining the relative weight of the powers of the presidency and the legislature in ruling the country. It is clear from her own writings that Starovoitova, who had been a member of the Constitutional Assembly convened by Yeltsin in June 1993 to draft a new constitution, was highly critical of Yeltsin's efforts to concentrate power in the presidency.

After she was dismissed, Starovoitova left politics for several years and resumed her life as a researcher. She was a visiting professor at the Watson Institute for International Studies at Brown University, and a visiting professor of democracy at the Transregional Center for Democratic Studies at the New School University. Yegor Gaidar, a fellow democrat who served in Yeltsin's Cabinet, invited Starovoitova to join his Institute for the Economy in Transition in 1993. She formed an ethno-political studies laboratory and worked there until 1996.

When elections were held for the Russian State Duma in December 1993, Starovoitova did not run. Elections were held again in December 1995, and Starovoitova ran and won a seat in Leningrad. She ran for the presidency in 1996—the only female candidate—but was unable to gather the signatures necessary for a place on the ballot. She may have been planning to run again in the elections scheduled for 2000.

Starovoitova was one of the few women to hold a significant post in the Yeltsin government. Indeed, the overall percentage of women deputies declined precipitously with the advent of free elections. Under the old system, in which the Supreme Soviet was a rubber stamp and true power resided in the Politburo of the Communist Party, on average one-third of deputies at the all-union and union republic levels were women. In the 1990 elections to the Russian State Duma, the percentage of women deputies was 5%; 1993, 13.5%; 1995, 9.8%. As of 1999, of the 27 committees in the State Duma, 2 were headed by women: the Committee on Women, Family, and Youth Affairs and the Committee on Ecological Protection (among the least influential of the committees). The vice-premier of the government of Russia was a woman—**Valentina Matvienko**.

Gender stereotyping along traditional lines is quite strong in Russia. Starovoitova remarked on the difficulties that women politicians have in achieving high office. When asked in an interview for *Argumenty i fakty* if a woman could become president, she replied, "According to the results of a poll, 47% of the population would prefer a woman president, and another 22% would not be against. People believe that women are better than men—they don't drink and they don't start wars. But there is a glass ceiling that women hit." Similarly, in early 1992 there were rumors that Yeltsin would appoint Starovoitova as minister of defense. She noted that society had not matured to the point that it would accept a woman, let alone a civilian, in such a post. "Hers was a name that many Russians knew," wrote Paul Quinn-Judge after her murder, "and if she no longer held great political power, her moral power remained intact."

**SOURCES:**

*Argumenty i fakty.* No. 48. November 1998, p. 3.

Gessen, Masha. *Dead Again: The Russian Intelligentsia after Communism.* London: Verso, 1997, chapter 7.

Michnik, Adam. "A Death in St. Petersburg," in *The New York Review of Books.* Vol. 46, no. 1. January 14, 1999, pp. 4–6.

Powell, Bill. "Requiem for Reform," in *Newsweek.* December 7, 1998.

Quinn-Judge, Paul. "Russia's Gunpoint Politics," in *Time.* December 7, 1998.

Starovoitova, Galina. "What Future for Democracy," in *Perspective.* Vol. 5, no. 3. January–February 1995.

**Janet Hyer**,
Centre for Russian and East European Studies,
University of Toronto, Ontario, Canada

# Starr, Belle (1848–1889)

*Confederate sympathizer, rancher and convicted horse thief, who associated with outlaws and made an enduring name for herself as the "Bandit Queen" of the Old West. Name variations: American Bandit Queen; The Lady Desperado; Queen of the Desperadoes; Petticoated Terror of the Plains. Born Myra Maybelle (or Maebelle) Shirley on February 5, 1848, in Jasper County, Missouri; gunned down on February 3, 1889, en route to Younger's Bend; daughter of John Shirley (a horse breeder and tavern owner) and Elizabeth "Eliza" (Pennington) Shirley; married Jim Reed, on November 1, 1866 (died 1874); (possibly) married Bruce Younger, on May 15, 1880 (marriage ended after three weeks); married Sam Starr, on June 5, 1880 (died 1886); married Jim July, in 1886; children: (first marriage) Rosie Lee Reed (b. 1868, known as Pearl Starr, speculated to be the illegitimate daughter of Cole Younger); Edward "Eddie" Reed (b. 1871).*

*Charged with horse stealing (July 31, 1882); tried by "Hanging Judge" Isaac Parker and sentenced to two six-month prison terms; released for good behavior after nine months.*

In Belle Starr's day, it was unusual for a woman to wear pistols, let alone wear them over an expensive, black velvet dress, while riding sidesaddle and sporting a plumed hat. As a girl, Belle Starr dreamed of becoming a famous stage star; while she was not to appear in theaters, she did achieve legendary status, an infamous character from America's outlaw past. She grew up in the heated political atmosphere of her family's tavern, where Confederate sympathizers held passionate discussions concerning the Civil War that was underway during her teenage years. Her parents, backers of the cause these young men had fought for, were among those who offered food and protection to people like Jesse and Frank James, the Younger brothers, the Fishers and Jim Reed, who would become the first of Starr's four husbands.

To many Confederate sympathizers, robbing banks and other businesses owned by Northerners was considered a justifiable extension of the Civil War. Legend has it that Belle Starr served as a scout for the Confederates, fought Union militia, and dressed as a man to participate in robberies. In truth, her crimes may have been confined to horse stealing and harboring fugitives, but her lifestyle was so unusual for a woman of her time that she captured the imagination of writers who were hoping to entertain their 19th-century readership. The public became fascinated with her romantic name and the notion of a woman in the rough outlaw world normally reserved for men. She did, in fact, live and associate with many outlaws throughout her short life, but she considered herself a lady. Starr is said to have detested other women for the most part, especially those who condemned her behavior as shameful. Regardless of the seemingly endless myths that grew up around her, it is clear that she was extraordinary in her defiance of the social attitudes of the day.

Starr's death, still an unsolved mystery, deepened the intrigue she had inspired in life. She was gunned down two days before her 41st birthday, and several are the names of her potential killers. Her corpse was anointed with turpentine and oil of cinnamon. Her body was dressed in black velvet and laid in a pine coffin lined with black shrouding trimmed in white lace. Her arms were crossed, with one hand grasping the handle of her favorite revolver, which was later stolen from her grave.

For years, biographers have claimed to tell the "real" story of Starr's life, but in doing so they often contradicted each other, suggesting the likelihood that once so much myth is perpetuated the fictions cling like impurities to the facts. In 1997, Richard Arnott writing in *Wild West* made a comprehensive attempt to put forth what is actually known about Belle Starr from available evidence. He writes: "[F]ascinating, often fantastic, stories led to the myth and legend of Belle Starr. . . . [Her] true life was one without glamour."

Census records indicate that on February 5, 1848, Starr was born Myra Maybelle to John and **Eliza Pennington Shirley** in Jasper County, near Carthage, Missouri. Eliza, a seamstress and pianist from Kentucky who was known for her social eloquence, was closely related to the Hatfield family who later became famous for their feud with the McCoys. Belle's father, a successful breeder of fine Kentucky horses, became respected for his articulate political philosophy and gained the informal title of "Judge" Shirley. In 1856, he sold the family's land, and they relocated to Carthage where he acquired an inn and tavern on the town square. In addition to these properties, he owned a livery stable and a blacksmith shop. Arnott notes that the Shirley enterprises nearly filled a city block: "The 1860 census estimated the worth of John Shirley's holding at $10,000, a significant sum in those days. He was a respected member of the community; his library was an attraction to the intelligentsia, as were Eliza's piano and her gracious Southern manners."

Belle received her education in classical languages, music, and "the three Rs" at the Carthage Female Academy. Though she acquired training appropriate to her status, the extent to which she acquired her mother's manners is debatable. Said to have been teased for being skinny and homely, she was reported by some sources to have displayed her rage in tantrums. Starr played piano at weddings, church meetings, barn dances and her father's tavern, where she had an audience. An admirer of the outdoors, she explored the countryside with Bud, her older brother. He taught her to ride a horse with proficiency and instructed her in using a gun.

Their region was traversed by both the Confederate and Union armies. Notes Arnott: "Irregular bands of jayhawkers and 'Red Legs' laid waste to Missouri communities in support of the Union. Guerrillas and bushwhackers, led by 'Bloody Bill' Anderson and William Clarke Quantrill, retaliated with death and destruction in Kansas." Like her parents, Starr resented the encroachment of any Union actions on her family's way of life. Her brother Bud took up with the bushwhackers, to the delight of his father. Arnott speculates that Starr used her social interactions to gain information which could then be passed to her brother. Biographer S.W. Harman recounted one story in which Starr rode all night through the Missouri woods, during the war, to warn her brother that a Federal party was looking for him. Harman describes the end of her "famous 35-mile ride" when she was intercepted in Newtown County by a major in the Union Army, who then sent a detachment of cavalry to Carthage to capture her brother. According to Harman, when the officer laughed at the annoyance of the teenage girl:

> This served to anger her and she gave expression to her rage in loud and deep curses. Then she would sit at the piano and ratle [sic] off some wild selection in full keeping with her fury; the next instant she would spring to her feet, stamp the floor and berate the major and his acts with all the ability and profanity of an experienced trooper, while the tears of mortification rolled down her cheeks, her terrible passion only increased by the laughter and taunts of her captor.

Thinking his men had already captured Starr's brother, the major released Belle, who purportedly sprang to the door, rushed out and cut long switches from some cherry bushes to use as riding whips. "I'll beat them yet," she is said to have declared, as she rode off on horseback, deserting the main road, vaulting fences and leaping over ditches. The major lifted his field glass and watched her retreat, saying, "Well, I'll be damned, she's a born guerilla. If she doesn't reach Carthage ahead of my troopers, I'm a fool." According to this story, Starr reached her brother in time and then, while riding at a leisurely pace, met the cavalry as they entered Carthage, whereupon she curtsied and told them her brother had left half an hour before.

What is known for certain is that her brother was eventually killed by Federal militia. Arnott puts the date of his death in June 1864, when he was killed while climbing a fence to escape the Federal forces in Sarcoxie, Missouri. Stories would later be written about an armed 16-year-old Starr going out to take her revenge, but Arnott finds no documentation to substantiate such claims. According to many accounts, though, the effect of all she had witnessed instilled a deep hatred in her for Yankees.

By age 15, Starr is reported to have associated with men from all walks of life and developed a headstrong personality. Her independence, unusual for a girl of her day, proved attractive to many men of the border country. Much has been made

*Belle Starr posing with Blue Duck; both are wearing handcuffs.*

of her purported beauty (and that of her daughter **Pearl Starr**). At best the issue is subjective, and perhaps unimportant, but existing photographs and some less impassioned accounts suggest that it may be more accurate to describe Starr as plain, even homely. She did not necessarily blossom as

some more fanciful versions of her history have claimed. "She has been described," writes Arnott, "as 'bony, flat chested with a mean mouth; hatchet faced; gotch-tooth tart.'" Whether or not such descriptions have any basis in fact, Starr was not to want for the love of outlaws.

In 1864, near the end of the Civil War, Federal troops captured Carthage and burned the city, including the Shirley house. The family then moved to Texas, where in 1867 John Shirley acquired a farm and built a new home and boarding house near Scyene, a community in Dallas County. The new tavern became a favorite gathering place for ex-Confederates who were finding it difficult to adjust to postwar society. Names like the James brothers and the Youngers blanketed the newspapers, as such outlaws robbed banks and held up trains. Roving bands of homeless men, embittered by defeat, found their way to Texas and John Shirley's bar.

One outlaw band which sought shelter with the Shirleys brought Starr her first husband, Jim Reed, a former soldier who had arrived in Texas with the remnants of his cavalry regiment in 1866. Starr had already met Reed, reportedly the quiet and religious son of a wealthy farmer from Rich Hill, Missouri, when both were children. One popular tale of their wedding has the makings of high drama. It includes a 19- or 18-year-old Starr defying her parents by riding off with Reed and his gang, and then being wed in a ceremony on horseback performed by one of the gang members. But Arnott cites a copy of their marriage license which indicates they were married by the Reverend S.M. Williams on November 1, 1866. He believes that Reed, "not yet a wanted man," was not even an objectionable choice to Starr's parents.

Although Reed first moved in with the Shirleys, by late 1867 the couple had returned to Missouri where they resided at the Reed homestead. A daughter, Rosie Lee, was born during September 1868. Starr's affectionate name for her was Pearl, and that became the name by which she would be known.

The paternity of the child has been a source of dispute among biographers. Many claim that Pearl was the illegitimate daughter of Starr and Cole Younger. Indeed, Starr is said by some to have called her daughter Pearl Younger and to have claimed that Cole was the father. By his own account, however, Cole Younger had visited the Shirleys in 1864 but did not see Starr again until 1868, when she was already six-months' pregnant. His denial of paternity has been disbelieved by some, but Arnott notes that "a manuscript compiled by Richard Reed, younger brother of Belle's husband, supports Younger's story."

Not long after she gave birth to Pearl, Starr lost another brother, Ed. She has typically been portrayed by biographers in the next months as a young mother gallivanting through Dallas saloons and dance halls. "This has been refuted by a neighbor of the Reeds who recalled Belle and the baby living at the Reed household and attending church," writes Arnott. Meanwhile, her husband was often away from home. He took up with the Cherokee Tom Starr, a known killer who ran a successful whiskey business with his sons. Before long, Reed ran into trouble with the law for murder and for his involvement in Tom's whiskey dealings and became a fugitive. Reed and Belle took Pearl with them to California (1869), and in 1871 Belle gave birth to James Edwin, also known as Eddie or Ed. By many accounts, this was a happy time for her, until Reed's identity as a fugitive was revealed. Trying to get a step ahead of the authorities, Reed rode horseback to Texas while Belle and the children made the trip by stagecoach.

In Texas, the family settled with the help of Cole Younger on a farm near Scyene. As the wife of one of the country's most sought-after outlaws, Belle is reported to have had difficulties fitting in with the Dallas and Scyene communities, though she is said to have cultivated the acquaintance of its citizens. Problems clung to Reed, to whose crimes were added two more killings. With a reward out for his capture, he and Belle headed for Indian Territory, while their children remained in Scyene with the Shirleys.

In November 1873, Reed was one of three robbers who stole $30,000 from the family of Creek Indian Watt Grayson; they dangled Watt and his wife from a tree in order to learn the money's location. The bandits "stretched" Grayson's "neck in a noose repeatedly," writes **Grace Ernestine Ray**, "but he revealed nothing until they began to torture his wife in the same manner. Then he told them where the money was hidden." Belle was rumored by some to have taken part in the robbery while dressed as a man. But according to Arnott, "No member of the Grayson family, nor any of the hired hands who had witnessed the robbery, mentioned a woman dressed as a man, or even a slightly built man."

After seven years of eventful marriage, Reed's crimes and his affair with **Rosa McCommas** prompted Belle to leave him. She went to live with her parents in Scyene.

In August 1874, with a price on his head, Reed was killed by Deputy Sheriff John T. Morris (also seen as Jim Morris). According to one popular version of the ensuing events, Reed's body was taken to McKinney, Texas, where authorities sent for Belle to identify him. At the time, a widow's denial of her husband's identity invalidated offers of rewards. Belle is said to have looked at the body, then told Morris and other law authorities, "If you want the reward for Jim Reed, you will have to kill Jim Reed. This is not my husband." Morris did not receive the reward, and Reed's body was buried in an unmarked grave near McKinney. The veracity of this tale, however, is in doubt. According to Arnott, newspaper accounts indicate that his body was identified "by those who knew Reed." Biographer Burton Rascoe believed that Reed's body was identified by numerous witnesses and accuses Harman, among others, of perpetuating other inaccuracies: the date of Belle Starr's birth, that she was a twin, or altering the name of the major who arrested her. Apparently, a few months after Reed's death, John Morris was killed by an unknown party.

Meanwhile, Belle is said to have had problems in her community. In March 1875, a committee seeking ways to remove her, as well as the outlaws who frequented the Shirley premises, sent a letter to the governor arguing:

> For several years past the town of Scyene, Dallas County, Texas, and vicinity, has been noted as a place of resort for horse thieves, desperadoes and other bad characters—certain parties having located themselves here as a place of rendezvous for such characters, thus giving aid and comfort to thieving and marauding bands infesting all parts of the state.

They complained about James Reed, the San Antonio mail robber, "his widow being no less celebrated in such exploits than her notorious paramour," suggesting that she was in the habit of "donning often male attire" and riding hundreds of miles "to apprise outlaws of pending danger."

Starr's activities in the several years after Reed's death remain in dispute. Some note that in 1875 a Dallas grand jury indicted her for arson after she burned a store. The district judge set her bail at $2,500, which was deemed an excessive amount by a Dallas reporter. Months later, on August 12, 1875, a grand jury charged her with theft of a gelding, a serious charge in late '70s Texas. Starr was jailed. According to one story, she persuaded her jailer to elope with her, returning him to his wife shortly afterward with a card sewed into his coat which the unfortunate man failed to discover until too late. One source claims that it read, "Found to be unsatisfactory on using." Arnott questions the legitimacy of the arson incident and subsequent jailing for horse stealing. He suggests that

these are examples of writers trying "to fill in the gaps in Belle's story. . . . Such activities are not, however, reflected in court records or newspaper accounts."

The widow Starr is thought to have married Cole Younger's uncle Bruce on, according to Phillip Steele, May 15, 1880. If this marriage did take place, it was short lived. Three weeks later, she married Sam Starr, the three-quarters-Cherokee son of Tom Starr. Arnott asserts that she was likely 32 when they married, and Sam may, or may not, have been 23. "By this marriage," writes Grace Ray, "the Caucasian wife acquired a landright in the Cherokee Nation, and she and Sam established a home on an allotment on the bank of a bend in the Canadian River. This became the notorious Younger's Bend, where Belle was to be victim to cowardly violence." While one source notes that the name Younger's Bend was bestowed by Tom Starr because of his admiration for the Younger Gang, other biographers have inferred that "Younger's Bend" reflected Belle's devotion to Cole Younger. Pearl and Eddie, who had been staying with relatives, joined their mother and stepfather on the land.

There are many accounts of Belle's great love for her daughter Pearl and the friction between Belle and Eddie. Some sources describe him as a continual source of irritation to his mother. Being sent away to be raised by his grandparents for years, and having a sister who could do virtually no wrong, may have contributed to the disintegration of an already difficult relationship. Others sources, however, indicate that Belle displayed a maternal feeling for both of her children.

Younger's Bend became a shelter for criminals. "[Belle] gave comfort to Sam and his outlaw friends," continues Ray. "Jesse James and some of the Youngers also came sometimes to Younger's Bend to hide out for a time. . . . Belle, to use her own words, befriended 'brave and gallant outlaws.' A newspaper quoted her as follows: 'There are three or four jolly, good fellows on the dodge now in my section, and when they come to my home they are welcome.'" Dime novelists of the time soon had her leading outlaw gangs throughout the nation, robbing stagecoaches, trains and banks. It appears that she had ample grounds for libel suits, but it also seems that she enjoyed and even embellished the stories.

Belle and Sam were charged with horse stealing on July 31, 1882. They went to trial before "Hanging Judge" Isaac C. Parker (his gallows were dubbed "The Gates of Hell") in March. If a reporter for the *New Era* is to be believed, Belle showed "a devil-may-care expression during her entire trial." Both she and her husband were found guilty of larceny, and they were fortunate that Parker displayed an uncharacteristic leniency in sentencing: Belle to two six-month terms, and Sam to one twelve-month term, in the Detroit House of Correction. In what Ray has called "a progressive prison which conducted academic classes, and tried to reform inmates," Sam's disinterest in learning apparently earned him hard labor, and it has been written that Belle charmed herself into a position as the warden's assistant. They were both released for good behavior after they had served nine months and returned to Younger's Bend. Writes Arnott: "Belle had become plump and dowdy while in prison, but she still rode and danced gracefully. She often adorned herself in a black velvet riding habit and rode sidesaddle, carrying her six-shooter. . . . She also liked to read and play a piano she had freighted into the Bend."

According to Arnott, after the fugitive John Middleton came to Younger's Bend seeking shelter, he and the Starrs became suspects in thefts from the Seminole and Creek treasuries (1885). Middleton decided it was time to move on, and the Starrs helped him to escape. He was found dead just days after they parted company, apparently having drowned while crossing a river on a horse the Starrs had procured for him. Upon learning of his death, the Starrs also found out that the mare they had purchased for him had not been sold to them by its owner. Belle was charged with larceny. "A writ was issued for her arrest in January 1886. She surrendered to the U.S. marshal at Fort Smith and was indicted, with trial set for September."

Sam Starr also became accused of a hold-up and more than one robbery. Rather than face the law, he opted for the life of a fugitive but was still able to see Belle on visits to Younger's Bend. Their home was raided by a posse after Belle was identified by an eyewitness as one of three people responsible for a number of farm-settlement robberies during February 1886. The witness claimed that Belle had been dressed in men's attire.

In Fort Smith, Belle pleaded not guilty and made bail. While she was there, the famous picture of Belle Starr with convicted murderer Blue Duck, both in handcuffs, was taken. The photograph led many to believe that Starr and Blue Duck were lovers, and that, in Ray's words,

"Belle's employment of expert counsel [for Blue Duck] would effect commutation of his [death] sentence to life imprisonment." Arnott, however, writes of the photograph: "She did it at the request of Blue Duck's attorney, who apparently thought it would help his client in his pending appeal of a death sentence. This was the first and last time Belle saw Blue Duck." Arnott also goes on to note that the counsel which Starr is rumored to have employed for Blue Duck was in California that year.

When Starr stood trial in June, witnesses were unable to identify her, and she was discharged late in the month, only to return in three months for the larceny trial. Here, too, she was cleared. She left Forth Smith to find her husband, injured, at the home of his brother. Sam had been wounded by Indian police who had shot and killed his horse. She convinced him to turn himself in rather than risk being taken by Indian officers. While out on bail after his indictment, Sam was shot to death on December 17, 1886, by Frank West, a long-time enemy, at a Christmas party.

The deaths of two of her three husbands apparently did not make Starr shy of outlaws. "The widow Starr returned to Younger's Bend," writes Arnott, "and took Jack Spaniard, a notorious outlaw, to bed almost before Sam's body was cold." As was typical of her relationships, her time with Spaniard was forced to an end when his crimes caught up with him. He was hanged for murder.

Sam Starr's death meant that Belle's property at Younger's Bend was in jeopardy, because she was no longer married to an Indian. Her fourth marriage, however, renewed her claim to the land. She married the Creek Indian Bill July (some sources cite Jim July), the 24-year-old adopted son of Tom Starr. Bill's alias was Jim Starr, and some have written that it was Belle who requested the name change. By many accounts, her relationship with July, 14 years her junior, was a mother-son relationship and not necessarily a loving one. Her son Eddie was far from enamored with his mother's latest husband, who was little more than seven years older than he. Like his father and stepfather before him, Eddie became a horse thief.

Pearl became pregnant out of wedlock, and Belle tried to thwart the relationship between Pearl and the man responsible, attempting to force a marriage instead between Pearl and a wealthy Fort Smith liveryman. Pearl opted to have the baby rather than visit a "noted Fort Smith physician," and Belle vowed never to see the child, a promise she apparently kept in the short time she had left.

Belle had been warned by the tribal council that any further harboring of fugitives would earn her expulsion from Younger's Bend. When Edgar A. Watson approached her about renting some land, she eagerly accepted his money, unaware that he was a fugitive. Starr then learned from Watson's wife that the Florida authorities were after him for murder. Concerned with protecting her home, she tried to refund his money, but Watson refused to let her out of the deal. "In a face-to-face confrontation," writes Arnott, "she chided him with a comment that Florida authorities might be interested in his whereabouts." Watson was more than a little angry when he took back his rent money and settled on a nearby farm. He would soon be one among several individuals said to have motive for the murder of Belle Starr.

Starr and her husband July departed Younger's Bend together on February 2, 1889— he en route to Fort Smith to face Judge Parker and charges of horse stealing, and she to go shopping. In San Bois, they spent the night with friends. The next morning, February 3, July continued on to Fort Smith while Starr headed back to Younger's Bend. On the way, she stopped to see some neighbors, the Rowes, for a weekly Sunday gathering at their home. According to Arnott, Starr's son Eddie had been staying with the Rowes, and she had "had hoped to see [him]." Eddie, however, had already left. Edgar Watson was among the other guests, and Arnott records that he left shortly after Starr entered. Arnott continues: "Belle ate and chatted with her friends. She was nibbling on a piece of cornbread as she went out the door and headed for Younger's Bend. The road passed within several hundred yards of the Watson place. As Belle turned onto the river lane, a shotgun blast blew her from the saddle."

As she tried to get up from the road, she was hit with a second shot in the face and shoulder. Her horse raced back to Younger's Bend. An alarmed Pearl set out to look for her mother, who was not yet dead when Pearl found her. According to Ray, Starr's "Winchester lay nearby, but had not been fired. As shocked Pearl bent over her mother, Belle relaxed, then sank into nothingness."

It is said that neighbors, deputy marshals and Cherokee friends attended the funeral. Each member of the tribe dropped a small piece of cornbread into the casket, in a custom honoring the dead. The headstone on her grave was carved with a bell, a star, a horse, her brand, a clasped hand holding flowers, and the epitaph:

> BELLE STARR
> Born in Carthage, Missouri
> February 5, 1848
> Died February 3, 1889
> Shed not for her the bitter tear
> Nor give the heart to vain regret,
> Tis but the casket that lies here,
> The gem that filled it sparkles yet

Perhaps she was murdered by Edgar Watson. Both Starr's husband July and her son Eddie accused him. He was, in fact, arrested in connection with the murder but was later acquitted. Perhaps she was murdered by her son Eddie. According to several accounts, he had defied his mother by taking her prize horse to a barn dance. Belle, who hated his rough treatment of her horses, was allegedly enraged upon finding her abused horse and whipped Eddie viciously. Dr. Jesse Mooney, Jr., told his family that Ed had come to him with wounds from a whip all over his body. "I'm going to kill her for this," Eddie supposedly said. Perhaps she was murdered by her daughter Pearl for having stopped Pearl's marriage to the man she loved and, according to Arnott, working "to get Pearl's daughter placed in an orphanage." Or perhaps she was murdered by her husband July, whom she had reportedly caught in a relationship with a young Cherokee. Still others have been mentioned as possible suspects.

Jim July was killed by a deputy a few weeks after Starr's death. Watson was later killed in Florida. Eddie was said to have been killed in a saloon brawl in Wagoner. And Pearl was thought to have been a prostitute and bordello madam before her death in her late 50s.

As for Starr, the extent to which she caught the popular imagination cannot be overstated. Her story, apocryphal though it may be, has been portrayed in numerous fictional stories and films as well as biographies, newspaper accounts, and poetry. The fascination with this female desperado may be lasting, as may be the intersections of truth and fiction which her unusual life inspired.

**SOURCES:**

Arnott, Richard D. "Bandit Queen Belle Starr," in *Wild West*. August 1997.

Harman, S.W. *Belle Starr: The Female Desperado.* TX: Frontier Press, 1954.

Rascoe, Burton. *Belle Starr: "The Bandit Queen."* NY: Random House, 1941.

Ray, Grace Ernestine. *Wily Women of the West.* San Antonio, TX: Naylor, 1972.

Rogers, Cameron. *Gallant Ladies.* NY: Harcourt, Brace, 1928.

Steele, Phillip. *Starr Tracks: Belle and Pearl Starr.* LA: Pelican, Gretna, 1989.

**SUGGESTED READING:**

Hicks, Ed. *Belle Starr and her Pearl*, 1963.

Mooney, Charles W. *Doctor in Belle Starr Country.* Oklahoma City, OK: Century Press, 1975.

Scott, Jennette. *Belle Starr in Velvet* (as told by Pearl Starr's granddaughter).

Shackleford, William Yancy. *Belle Starr, the Bandit Queen.*

Shirley, Glenn. *Belle Starr and her Times: The Literature, the Facts, and the Legends.* Norman, OK: University of Oklahoma Press, 1982.

Winn, Robert G. *Two Starrs: Belle the Bandit Queen, Pearl, Riverfront Madame.* Fayetteville: Washington County Historical Society, 1979.

**RELATED MEDIA:**

*Belle Starr* (87 min. film), starring *\*Gene Tierney* and Randolph Scott, directed by Irving Cummings, 1941.

*Belle Starr's Daughter* (86 min. film), starring **Ruth Roman** and George Montgomery, directed by Lesley Selander, 1948.

"Belle Starr," starring *\*Elizabeth Montgomery*, directed for television by John A. Alonzo, script by James Lee Barrett, 1980.

**Susan Slosberg**,
Adjunct Professor of Public Relations,
Baruch College, The City University of New York,
New York, New York

# Starr, Eliza Allen (1824–1901)

Ellen
Gates
Starr

*American writer, lecturer on art and religion, poet, and teacher of art. Name variations: Eliza Ann Starr. Born Eliza Ann Starr on August 29, 1824, in Deerfield, Massachusetts; died on September 7, 1901, in Durand, Illinois; daughter of Oliver Starr (a dyer and farmer) and Lovina Allen Starr; aunt of \*Ellen Gates Starr (1859–1940), socialist reformer and co-founder of Hull House; educated at the Deerfield Academy, Massachusetts; studied painting under Caroline Negus Hildreth; never married; no children.*

*Wrote verse and articles on Christian art published in periodicals; works on Christian art include* Patron Saints *(1st series, 1871, 2nd series, 1881),* Pilgrims and Shrines *(2 vols., 1885) and* The Three Archangels and the Guardian Angel in Art *(1899); collected poems published as* Songs of a Lifetime *(1887); awards include Notre Dame University's Laetare Medal (1885) and medallion from Pope Leo XIII (1899).*

Eliza Ann Starr, who adopted Allen as a middle name in adulthood, was born in Deerfield, Massachusetts, in 1824, the daughter of Oliver Starr, a dyer and farmer, and **Lovina Allen Starr**. Eliza was encouraged by her parents to pursue her early interests in art and literature, and she studied painting under **Caroline Negus Hildreth**, a well-known miniature painter and wife of the historian Richard Hildreth. In 1845, Starr moved to Boston to continue her studies with Caroline Hildreth, where the seeds for her conversion to Catholicism were sown. After teaching privately in Brooklyn, Philadelphia, and Natchez, Mississippi, Starr returned to Boston and was baptized as a Catholic in 1854.

In 1856, Starr moved to Chicago, establishing her own studio and launching a career as an art teacher and lecturer on Christian art. She combined groundbreaking teaching techniques with conservative, religious art appreciation, both of which proved widely influential in the cultural life of Chicago. Adopting Hildreth's dictum "never copy," Starr was the first teacher of drawing and painting in the Midwest who worked exclusively from nature and casts. She was also one of the first Americans to use photographs and slides in her popular lectures, conducting influential talks on "The Literature of Art" in Midwestern and Eastern cities throughout the 1870s and 1880s.

A writer of verse and essays on Christian art, Starr published numerous books of art appreciation informed by her devout faith. Her best-known work, *Pilgrims and Shrines* (1885), was inspired by a European trip of 1875–77, paid for by admirers. Her collected poems were first published in 1867 and updated in 1887 as *Songs of a Lifetime*. She was honored for her service to the Catholic Church with Notre Dame University's Laetare Medal in 1885 and a medallion from Pope Leo XIII in 1899. Starr never married and was deterred from a religious vocation by persistent poor health, although she became a member of the Third Order of St. Dominic. She died at the age of 77 and was buried in Calvary Cemetery, Chicago, wearing a Dominican habit.

**SOURCES:**

James, Edward T., ed. *Notable American Women, 1607–1950.* Cambridge, MA: The Belknap Press of Harvard University, 1971.

**Paula Morris**, D.Phil.,
Brooklyn, New York

# Starr, Ellen Gates (1859–1940)

*American settlement house worker and labor supporter who co-founded Hull House. Born in Laona, Illinois, on March 19, 1859; died in Suffern, New York, on February 10, 1940; third of four children of Caleb Allen Starr and Susan (Gates) Starr; niece of *Eliza Allen Starr (1824–1901); attended Rockford (Ill.) Seminary, 1877; never married; no children.*

When one thinks of Hull House, the preeminent American settlement house which opened its doors in Chicago in 1889, one thinks of its founder *Jane Addams. Yet, alongside Addams for the first 20 years was Ellen Gates Starr. The two had met while attending Rockford Seminary during the late 1870s. Unlike her wealthier friend Addams, Starr could only afford to attend the seminary for one year before finding work as a teacher. Beginning in 1879, she taught for several years at the exclusive Miss Kirkland's School for Girls in Chicago. Meanwhile, Addams was still in search of meaningful work. In 1888, while traveling together in Europe, Addams and Starr decided to open a settlement house, patterned after London's Toynbee Hall. In 1889, using Addams' money and donations from the parents of Starr's pupils, the two bought a run-down mansion on Chicago's West Side.

During the 1890s, Hull House was the center of Chicago social and labor reform. While Jane Addams concentrated on the overall management, and labor organizers such as *Mary Kenney O'Sullivan and social reformers such as *Florence Kelley lived and worked out of the settlement, Ellen Gates Starr focused on bringing art to the impoverished immigrants of the neighbor. She organized reading clubs and art history classes as well as classes in bookbinding as an art. However, as the decade continued, Starr became increasingly involved in labor organizing, realizing the futility of art appreciation if one were hungry from lack of work at other than subsistence wages. In 1896, she participated in her first strike, assisting Chicago women textile workers. Starr joined the Women's Trade Union League in 1903 and took part in several more strikes, including a 1914 strike of Chicago waitresses during which she was arrested.

Throughout this period, Starr considered herself a Christian Socialist and by 1916, when she ran unsuccessfully for alderman, she was a member of the Socialist Party. However, she had long been in search of a deeper spiritual meaning to her life. After her intense relationship with Addams ended in the early 1890s, when Addams began what would be a 40-year partnership with **Mary Rozet Smith**, Starr spent years looking for a greater purpose. In 1920, she found that purpose when she joined the Roman Catholic Church. In 1929, after back surgery left her paralyzed from the waist down, Starr took up residence at the Convent of the Holy Child in Suffern, New York. She died shortly before her 81st birthday and was buried in the convent where she ended her spiritual quest.

**SOURCES:**

Carrell, Elizabeth Palmer Hutcheson. *Reflections in a Mirror: The Progressive Woman and the Settlement Experience.* Ann Arbor, MI: University of Michigan Press, 1981.

**COLLECTIONS:**

Ellen Gates Starr Papers, Sophia Smith Collection, Smith College.

**Kathleen Banks Nutter**, Manuscripts Processor at the Sophia Smith Collection, Smith College, Northampton, Massachusetts

# Starr, Kay (1922—)

*Popular American singer. Born Katherine LaVerne Starks on July 21, 1922, in Dougherty, Oklahoma; daughter of Harry Starks (a laborer and full-blooded Iroquois) and Annie Starks (of Irish descent).*

One of a cadre of popular female singers of the 1940s and 1950s, Kay Starr was born Katherine LaVerne Starks in 1922 in Dougherty, Oklahoma, but as a child lived in Dallas and then in Memphis. There she had her own radio show, "Starr Time," on WREC and was a featured singer on the station's popular "Saturday Night Jamboree." In 1937, she got her first major break when bandleader-violinist Joe Venuti came to Memphis and invited her to sing with his band during their three-week gig at a local hotel. After the engagement, Starr continued to perform with Venuti's group each summer for the next two years. In addition, she sang with the orchestras of Bob Crosby, Glenn Miller, and Charlie Barnet. While with Barnet, she made her first recordings, most notable among them a blues rendition of "Share Croppin' Blues," which brought her some recognition. Her tenure with Barnet came to an abrupt end, however, in 1945, when she contracted pneumonia and collapsed during an Army camp show. Upon recovery, she realized she had lost her voice. Starr preferred bed rest, treatments, and not speaking for six months to the alternative: surgery. Though her voice eventually improved, she was left with a deeper and huskier sound, a sound that would become her trademark.

Following her hiatus, Starr moved to Los Angeles, where she worked in nightclubs and recorded. In 1947, she signed a contract with Capitol, whose roster of stars at the time included *Peggy Lee, *Jo Stafford, and *Margaret Whiting. In competition with such talent, Starr experienced some difficulty in finding the right material; it was not until her cover of Russ Morgan's "So Tired," in January 1949, that she hit the top ten charts for the first time. Her performing and recording career flourished through the 1950s and encompassed such hits as "Hoop-Dee-Doo," "Bonaparte's Retreat" (her first major hit), "I'm the Lonesomest Gal in Town," "Side by Side," "Angry," "I'll Never Be Free" (with Tennessee Ernie Ford), "Changing Partners," and "Wheel of Fortune," which earned her her first gold record and was the #2 top-selling single of 1952. During the peak years of her career, Starr also recorded several theme or "concept" albums, beginning with *Movin'* (1959), an uptempo jazz album, and including *Losers, Weepers . . .* (1960), *I Cry By Night* (1962), and *Just Plain Country* (1962).

Like that of so many other popular vocalists of the era, Starr's popularity waned in the '60s with the advent of rock 'n' roll. She continued to sing in concert and nightclub venues in the United States and England, although she cut back on performances during the 1970s to devote more time to her family. In the late 1980s, she was featured in the revue *4 Girls 4*, interchangeably with *Helen O'Connell, *Rosemary Clooney, Rose Marie, and Margaret Whiting; in 1993, Starr was in London appearing with Pat Boone's *April Love Tour*. Her album *Live at Freddy's* was released in 1997.

**SOURCES:**

Kinkle, Robert D. *The Complete Encyclopedia of Popular Music and Jazz 1900–1950*. Vol. 3. New Rochelle, NY: Arlington House, 1974.

**Barbara Morgan**,
Melrose, Massachusetts

## Starr, Mae Faggs (1932–2000).

*See Faggs, Mae.*

# Stasova, Elena (1873–1966)

*Russian Bolshevik revolutionary and Communist leader. Pronunciation: Stas-O-va. Born Elena Dmitrievna Stasova into an aristocratic family in St. Petersburg, Russia, on October 15, 1873; died in Moscow on December 31, 1966; daughter of Dmitri Vasilievich Stasov (a lawyer) and Poliksena Stepanovna Stasova (a well-known feminist); niece of Nadezhda Stasova (1822–1895).*

*Taught among the poor and joined revolutionary movement (1890s); avoided capture by the police for five years; joined V.I. Lenin's group; exiled to Siberia (1913–16); did not participate in October revolution (1917); was elected secretary of Bolshevik Party Central Committee (1919); resigned post in protest (1920); worked in Germany for Comintern (1921–25); worked for MOPR (1927–37); served as editor of International Literature (1938–46); retired (1946) and was briefly imprisoned but continued to speak out on basic political issues; long honored as one of the last of the Old Bolsheviks.*

Born into an aristocratic family of dissidents on October 15, 1873, Elena Dmitrievna Stasova grew up in a time of intense political, intellectual and artistic ferment. Her father Dmitri Vasilievich Stasov was a prominent lawyer who often defended revolutionaries in court, while her mother **Poliksena Stepanovna Stasova** was one of tsarist Russia's most outspoken feminists. Elena's aunt was *Nadezhda Stasova, a pioneer feminist, and an uncle, Vladimir Stasov, was Russia's first professional art critic. Surrounded by brilliant women and men, Elena Stasova received an ex-

*Kay Starr*

cellent education at home from tutors and later at an exclusive girls' gymnasium. Her career goal early in life was to become a physician.

The turbulent political scene quickly caught Stasova's attention after her graduation. She taught classes to poor workers and in this way came in contact with a growing revolutionary movement. Appalled by the living conditions of the urban working class and seeing no hope for reform from above, by 1898 Stasova had chosen to become a professional revolutionary. Quickly revealing a strong practical bent, she was a master of the nuts and bolts of building and maintaining a professional organization. Stasova's talents were crucial in fostering the survival and growth of the illegal Social Democratic revolutionary organization. A stern disciplinarian, she regarded mushy Romanticism as dangerous to the party and, because of her impatience with incompetence and sloth, earned the party name "Comrade Absolute" (*Tovarishch Absoliut*), an alias she would bear with pride. Stasova avoided capture for five years, a remarkable record in tsarist Russia. She possessed a rock-hard sense of political morality and well-honed technical skills in revolutionary work. When functioning for the party in Tiflis, she broke with the Caucasus branch because of its emphasis on terrorism.

Stasova temporarily quit revolutionary activity to work as an elementary schoolteacher. Within a short time, however, she returned to the revolutionary movement. Arrested, she was sentenced to exile in Siberia, living there from 1913 until 1916. On hand for the collapse of tsarism in early 1917, she quickly became a jack-of-all-trades for the revived Bolshevik Party, helping to bring a moribund organization back to life. On the eve of the October 1917 Bolshevik Revolution, she found herself frozen out of the center of power by Yakov Sverdlov and others. Only in March 1919 did she return to power, when she was elected secretary of the Bolshevik Party's Central Committee. By March 1920, she had decided to resign in protest over intrigues she regarded as directed against her. Despite Stasova's superb credentials, she would never again hold a party post that wielded genuine authority. When she applied for a post in the important Orgburo, a unit in charge of personnel, she was turned down because she "lacked experience."

Stasova spent the years 1921–26 in Germany as a Comintern (Communist International) representative, attempting to create a unified revolutionary organization out of many hostile factions. Her conspiratorial experiences in Russia were useful in Germany, where because of her reputation for irreproachable honesty she was placed in charge of the party treasury. Her often abrasive personality sometimes brought on clashes with her German comrades, but all attested to her skills as a revolutionary organizer. In 1927, following her return to Moscow, she accepted a leadership post in the MOPR organization, which assisted imprisoned and exiled revolutionaries. Alert to the dangers of Fascism, in 1934 she was a founding member of the Women's Committee Against War and Fascism. After a decade of service with MOPR, in 1938 Stasova took on a new post, doing editorial work for *International Literature*—a journal in the forefront of anti-Fascist propaganda at that time—publishing the writings of, among others, *****Anna Seghers**, Alex Wedding, and Bertolt Brecht.

Remarkably, Elena Stasova, a woman universally known (and feared by some) for her Bolshevik integrity, survived the bloody Stalinist purges of the 1930s. Having been effectively pushed out the center of power in the early years of the revolution, she was no longer regarded as a

*Soviet postage stamp issued in honor of Elena Stasova, 1973.*

threat. Her honesty and idealism remained intact as she grew older and observed the massive perversions of her youthful ideals by the party when it achieved unchallenged power. Her retirement in 1946, once attributed to her declining health, is now believed to have been forced by Joseph Stalin, who despite Stasova's age had her imprisoned for eight months as a serious warning. After Stalin's death in 1953, she enjoyed immense prestige among a dwindling band of Old Bolsheviks fortunate enough to have survived the purges. Having been horrified by the terror of the 1930s, she now devoted her energies to rehabilitating the reputations of those killed by Stalin. Stasova was also active after 1953 in rendering assistance to those individuals who had survived the gulag system, so that they might begin to restore their lives. In 1961, she daringly signed a petition to the 22nd Congress of the Soviet Communist Party, asking it to rehabilitate the memory of Nikolai Bukharin, purged and murdered by Stalin in 1938. A Marxist idealist even in her last years, she feared that if young people were to learn the full extent of the crimes committed in the name of Communism, the next generation would lose faith in the system and its philosophical underpinnings. Refusing to consider that her belief may have been fatally flawed, she died in Moscow on December 31, 1966, still believing that the ideal of a Socialist society could one day be achieved.

**SOURCES:**

Clements, Barbara Evans. "Stasova, Elena Dmitrievna (1873–1966)," in Joseph L. Wieczynski, ed., *The Modern Encyclopedia of Russian and Soviet History*. Vol. 37. Sea Breeze, FL: Academic International Press, 1984, pp. 98–101.

Conquest, Robert. *The Great Terror: Stalin's Purge of the Thirties*. Harmondsworth, Middlesex, UK: Penguin Books, 1971.

Hornstein, David P. *Arthur Ewert: A Life for the Comintern*. Lanham, MD: University Press of America, 1993.

"Pioneers of the Revolution," in *Culture and Life* [Moscow]. No. 1, 1967, pp. 14–15.

**John Haag**, Associate Professor of History, University of Georgia, Athens, Georgia

# Stasova, Nadezhda (1822–1895)

*Leading 19th-century Russian philanthropist and feminist.* Pronunciation: Na-DEZH-da Stas-O-va. *Born Nadezhda Vasil'evna Stasova on June 12, 1822, in Tsarskoe Selo, Russia; died on September 27, 1895, in St. Petersburg; daughter of Vasilii P. Stasov (a court architect and academician); mother's name unknown; sister of Vladimir Vasilievich Stasov (an art critic) and Dmitri Vasilievich Stasov (a prominent lawyer); aunt of \*Elena Stasova (1873–1966); educated at home until age 16; never married; no children.*

*Ran Sunday School for working women (1860–62); helped establish Society to Provide Cheap Lodgings for women in St. Petersburg (1861); co-founded women's Publishing Workshop (1863); promoted the establishment of the Vladimir Courses (1870); was first director of the Bestuzhev Courses (1878); served as chair of the Society for Assistance to Graduate Science Courses; was president of the Russian Women's Mutual Philanthropic Society (1894); helped establish Children's Aid Society in St. Petersburg (1894).*

When Nadezhda Stasova was in her mid-20s, she experienced a personal crisis which was to change the course of her life. "My youth was extraordinarily light-hearted and without seriousness," she later recalled. "All my thoughts inclined to entertainment." Like most women of her privileged class, she had been brought up with only one purpose in mind—marriage, after which her life would be a pleasant if mindless one of child rearing and social functions. Nadezhda was duly engaged to a handsome guards officer but then, just before their scheduled marriage, he left her to marry a younger woman of better position and greater beauty. Stasova, embarrassed and devastated, suffered a nervous breakdown. With the help of hypnosis, she recovered but vowed never to marry. She devoted much of the next decade to caring for her invalid sister **Sofia Stasova** and then, after the latter's death in 1858, she turned her attention to less privileged women in Russian society. This took the form first of charitable activities in St. Petersburg and then of promoting the cause of higher education for all Russian women. For over 35 years, she was one of the leaders of the nascent women's movement in Russia.

Nadezhda Stasova was born on June 12, 1822 (o.s.) in Tsarskoe Selo, an aristocratic and genteel community surrounding one of the tsar's residences where her father Vasilii Stasov served as court architect. The family's standing was reflected in the fact that the tsar, Alexander I, agreed to be Nadezhda's godfather. Even privilege could not protect her mother who died of cholera in 1831. Her five brothers received an excellent gymnasium education during the 1830s; one of them, Vladimir Stasov, went on to become a progressive and renowned music and art critic later in the century. Nadezhda and her sister Sofia, however, were treated differently. "My father," she later wrote, "although he was an intelligent man, still thought (as they all did then), that we did not have the same needs as our brothers." As a result, she was given a home education which stressed the good manners and social graces needed by an aristocratic wife. Surreptitiously, however, she sampled the writings of the philosophes and of the men of the enlightenment found in her father's excellent library. It was perhaps this reading which motivated her to devote her life to improving the lot of less fortunate women after the collapse of their marriages.

Another formative influence in the development of Stasova's feminism was *Mariia Trubnikova whom she met in 1859, shortly after Sofia's death. Trubnikova, who had been in contact with feminist groups in Western Europe, was concerned about the plight of well-born but impoverished women in the Russian capital. Together with **Anna Filosofova**, Trubnikova and Stasova formed the "Society to Provide Cheap Lodgings and Other Assistance to the Needy Population of St. Petersburg"—one of Russia's earliest and most successful charitable organizations. In 1861, the Society opened a hostel which offered respectable, clean and inexpensive accommodation for widows, abandoned mothers, and other middle-class women. The key to helping these women stand on their feet was employment. Since few respectable professions were open to Russian women at this time, Trubnikova and Stasova established a co-operative Publishing Workshop in 1863 where women worked as translators, editors, binders and typesetters. Stasova also showed an interest in the fate of lower-class women. In 1860, she opened a Sunday School which gave a basic education in the evenings to a limited number of young shop girls and factory workers. When this venture was closed by the government in 1862, she sought to encourage vocational training and better medical treatment for St. Petersburg's increasing number of prostitutes.

After a decade of charitable work, "the Triumvirate"—Filosofova, Trubnikova and Stasova—came to the conclusion that only better education could provide the skills women needed to be self-sufficient. As Stasova remarked, new Russian women "desired not the moonlight, but rather the sunlight" which higher education could offer but which up to then was denied them. In 1868, she was instrumental in drafting a petition to the rector of the University of St. Petersburg requesting the establishment of a women's university or at least the holding of classes for women at the present university. The suspicious government responded that women were inadequately prepared for university-level instruction and that until such time as they were prepared they would have to be satisfied with less rigorous evening lectures in an off-campus setting with no governmental support. When the so-called Vladimir Courses opened in 1870, Stasova served as their patron, and she housed their library in her apartment. The Triumvirate continued to function as an aristocratic pressure group seeking through tact, patience and good contacts to win further educational concessions. In 1878, the government finally allowed professors to offer women separate university-level courses leading to formal degrees. Stasova was the first director of these Bestuzhev Courses, and she was instrumental in raising money to help women pay for their much-needed higher education.

After the reactionary government of Alexander III forced her out of these positions in 1889, and in recognition of over 30 years of service to the Russian women's movement, Stasova was chosen to be president of the new Russian Women's Mutual Philanthropic Society which functioned both as an upper-class women's club and as a provider of accommodation, meals and childcare for their less fortunate sisters. Nadezhda Stasova's role in this body, which Richard Stites has called "by far the most important feminist institution [in Russia] prior to 1905," was cut short by her sudden death in 1895 at the age of 73.

**SOURCES:**

Engel, Barbara Alpern. *Mothers and Daughters: Women of the Intelligentsia in Nineteenth-Century Russia.* Cambridge: Cambridge University Press, 1983.
Goldberg (Ruthchild), Rochelle Lois. "The Russian Women's Movement, 1859–1917." Unpublished Ph.D. dissertation, University of Rochester, 1976.
Stites, Richard. *The Women's Liberation Movement in Russia: Feminism, Nihilism, and Bolshevism, 1860–1930.* Princeton, NJ: Princeton University Press, 1977.

**SUGGESTED READING:**

Stasov, Vladimir. *Nadezhda Vasil'evna Stasova: Vospominaniia i ocherki* (Nadezhda Vasil'evna Stasova: Reminiscences and Sketches). St. Petersburg, 1899.

**R.C. Elwood**, Professor of History, Carleton University, Ottawa, Canada

# Statilia Messalina (fl. 66–68 CE).

*See Messalina, Statilia.*

# Statira I (c. 425–? BCE)

*Persian queen. Name variations: Stateira. Born around 425 BCE; death date unknown; daughter of Hydarnes (a Persian noble); mother's name unknown; half-sister of Teritouchones; married Arsaces, later known as Artaxerxes II Mnemon, king of Persia (d. 359); children: probably sons Darius, Ariaspes, and Ochus (who was later known as Artaxerxes III); possibly daughters Atossa and Amestris.*

Statira I, born around 425 BCE, was the daughter of Hydarnes, a Persian noble. She married Arsaces, the eldest son and heir of the reigning Achaemenid ruler Darius II and his wife *Parysatis I. (Darius II, like most Persian kings, had several wives and concubines.) Darius had arranged Statira's marriage to Arsaces as part of a policy to strengthen ties between the royal family and powerful aristocratic factions. One of the most influential of these was Statira's family, a fact made manifest by the fact that at about the time of her marriage, Statira's half-brother Teritouchones was also betrothed to **Amestris**, one of Darius' daughters. This second union, however, never occurred, for Teritouchones rejected Amestris (preferring instead to wed another of his own half-sisters). When this insult to the imperial dignity occurred, Parysatis exacted a terrible vengeance: she had all of Hydarnes' children executed except Statira, who escaped only because Arsaces intervened on her behalf.

After the death of his father Darius in 404 BCE, Arsaces assumed the throne under the name of Artaxerxes II. The reign of Artaxerxes II was a long one, for he did not die until 359 BCE. Nevertheless, his was not a peaceful rule either at home or abroad. Domestically, Artaxerxes faced a number of revolts across the far-flung Persian Empire, including insurrections led by a brother (Cyrus) and a son (Darius). To overcome these Artaxerxes came to rely heavily on the cunning of his mother Parysatis and his wife Statira, although when Cyrus was alive Parysatis favored him over Artaxerxes.

Statira was apparently Artaxerxes' only legitimate wife, a fact which pit her against Parysatis as both sought to be the dominant political influence in Artaxerxes' life. Statira was probably the mother of Artaxerxes' three attested legitimate sons: Darius, Ariaspes and Ochus. (Another of the king's sons, one Arsames, is said to have been "illegitimate." Whatever that meant in connection with the polygamous habits of the Achaemenids is not certain, but he cannot have been Statira's son.) The birth of so many children—she probably had daughters as well—suggests that Statira long remained in her husband's favor. In fact, perhaps at some time she became *too* influential, for Parysatis simply had Statira poisoned. For this heinous act, Parysatis was never sufficiently punished, and the whole affair indicates that Artaxerxes was easily manipulated by the women close to him, with his mother heading the list.

To prevent the rise of another strong rival, after Statira's death Parysatis is said to have urged Artaxerxes to marry his daughters (probably also the daughters of Statira) **Atossa** and **Amestris**. If he did so as attested, his incest (such unions were *not* common in Persia) clearly demonstrates Parysatis' power over her son. Parysatis' reason for so advising Artaxerxes undoubtedly was that she expected the newly acquired daughter-wives to be too inexperienced and too cowed by Parysatis to challenge her position at court.

After the death of Statira, Parysatis maintained her sway over Artaxerxes until she herself died. Statira's son Ochus ascended his father's throne, and thereupon ruled the Persian Empire from 359 to 338/7 BCE, under the name Artaxerxes III.

**William Greenwalt**,
Associate Professor of Classical History,
Santa Clara University, Santa Clara, California

# Statira II (c. 360–331 BCE)

*Persian queen and warrior. Name variations: Stateira. Born around 360 BCE; died in 331 BCE; probably the daughter of the Persian noble Arsanes but not the daughter of his wife Sisygambis; sister of a Persian noble named Pharnaces; married Darius III Codomannus (possibly her half-brother), king of Persia; children: two daughters, Statira III and Drypetis; and son, Ochus.*

Statira II was the wife and probably half-sister of Darius III, king of the Persian Empire, though many sources claim she was his sister. Like Darius, Statira was likely the daughter of the Persian noble Arsanes, but she was never named as the daughter of Darius' mother **Sisygambis**. Statira was also the sister of a Persian noble named Pharnaces, who would die during the Persians' defeat at the hands of Alexander III the Great at the Battle of Issus (333 BCE).

Statira in her prime was said to have been the most beautiful woman in Asia. She is also the only attested wife of Darius III, who fought his way to the Persian throne in 336. In Persian fashion, Statira II, probably with her two daughters *Statira III and **Drypetis** and young son Ochus, and certainly with her mother-in-law Sisygambis, accompanied Darius in his initial attempt to ward off Alexander the Great's invasion of the Persian Empire. Alexander routed Darius at the Battle of Issus, although the latter escaped. Alexander did, however, capture Darius' camp and entourage, including his mother, wife and children. Alexander treated Darius' family with the utmost respect and maintained them in a royal state just as if they were his own and not Darius' family. It is said that Alexander kept his distance from Statira lest her legendary beauty incite him to some undiplomatic indiscretion.

Statira (with the other members of Darius' family) remained in Alexander's custody until she died in 331. One source attests that she died in childbirth. If so, Alexander may have respected her status as the wife and queen of a rival, but someone did not, since she had remained in the custody of the Macedonians for about two years. Regardless of the cause of her death, Alexander grieved as if Statira were a member of his own family and provided for her such a magnificent funeral that Darius was both impressed and angry that his enemy honored Statira in a manner befitting a husband.

**William Greenwalt,**
Associate Professor of Classical History,
Santa Clara University, Santa Clara, California

## Statira III (fl. 324 BCE)

*Macedonian queen. Name variations: Stateira. Flourished around 324 BCE; daughter of Darius III Codomannus, king of Persia, and Statira II (c. 360–331 BCE); sister of Drypetis; married Alexander III the Great (356–323 BCE), in 324 BCE.*

Daughter of Darius III, king of Persia, and *Statira II, Statira III accompanied her father (and family) when he advanced against Alexander III the Great during the campaign which ended in the Persian defeat at the Battle of Issus (333 BCE). Thus, along with the rest of her family, except her father, Statira fell captive to the Macedonian conqueror. Although Darius attempted to ransom his family, Alexander refused to set any of his captives free, preferring to play the royal host to very valuable pawns. In 330, Darius was murdered by some of his own generals, although it still took Alexander several years before he was able to douse the last of Persia's resistance to his rule. During this time Statira III and her family (except her mother, who had died in captivity) remained in Alexander's hands.

By 324, Alexander had pacified most of his conquered empire. In an attempt to accommodate the Persian nobility, Alexander married Statira at a ceremony at Susa (amid sumptuous surroundings) which also saw some 90 Macedonian officers married to the daughters of Persian aristocrats. At this event, Alexander's bosom friend, Hephaestion, married Statira's sister **Drypetis**, in order that their anticipated offspring might be cousins. This was not Alexander's first marriage, for he had previously married a Bactrian (modern Afghani) princess named *Roxane, so Statira was introduced into a polygamous household. Nor was she the last wife

taken by Alexander, for shortly after her wedding, Alexander also wed *Parysatis II, the daughter of Artaxerxes III, a royal predecessor of Darius. Alexander's marriages to Statira and Parysatis were political, for by taking these women as wives, he laid claim to the pedigrees of Persia's last two Achaemenid kings.

A little more than a year after the Susa marriages, the future lay in tatters: Hephaestion had drunk himself to death, and so had Alexander (although in the latter case there were other contributing factors). Immediately after Alexander died, the ruthless and pregnant Roxane had Statira III and Parysatis II put to death, lest the Persians rally around either princess and threaten the legitimacy of the child (Alexander IV) gestating in her womb.

**William Greenwalt,**
Associate Professor of Classical History,
Santa Clara University, Santa Clara, California

## Stauffenberg, Litta von
### (c. 1905–1945)

*German aviator and test pilot who, although she was of Jewish origin, was exempted from the anti-Semitic Nuremberg Laws and persecution because of her extraordinary abilities as a test pilot. Name variations: Litta Schiller; Melitta Gräfin Schenk von Stauffenberg. Born Melitta Schiller in Krotoschin, Germany (later Poland), around 1905; shot down by an American fighter plane near Strasskirchen, Germany, on April 8, 1945; earned a degree in civil engineering from the Munich Institute of Technology, 1927; married Alexander Graf Schenk von Stauffenberg; sister-in-law of Claus von Stauffenberg.*

The story of Countess Litta von Stauffenberg, one of Nazi Germany's most talented military test pilots, is almost unbelievable, yet true. She was born Melitta Schiller around 1905 in Krotoschin, Germany. Her family, of Jewish origin, had converted to Lutheranism, and her father was a respected member of the Prussian civil service. In 1918, the Schiller home became part of newly independent Poland, but while her parents remained in Poland (they later moved to the Free City of Danzign), Litta moved to Germany to study, receiving a degree in civil engineering from the Munich Institute of Technology in 1927.

At the same time, she acquired several pilot's certificates. From 1927 on, Litta was involved in aerodynamics research, making test flights to check instruments that control dives. She worked at several facilities, including the German Aviation Testing Institute at Berlin-

Adlershof, the Askania Works at Berlin-Friedenau, and starting in October 1937, at the Air War Academy at Berlin-Gatow. The first two institutes were thinly disguised military test facilities, which worked virtually day and night, even before the Nazi takeover of Germany in 1933, to advance the nation's air combat capabilities. Both before and during World War II, Litta Schiller would fly well over 2,000 diving missions in Ju [Junkers] 87 and Ju 88 dive bombers, an accomplishment that would be surpassed by only one German test pilot, a man. Awarded an Air Captain's commission in 1937, she would also receive the Iron Cross class II in 1943 and the Pilot's Badge in Gold with Diamonds. In 1944, she would be nominated for the Iron Cross class I.

In August 1937, Litta Schiller married Alexander von Stauffenberg, a member of a distinguished noble family long established in the province of Baden-Württemberg. As Countess Stauffenberg, she now moved in extraordinary circles, meeting among others Alexander's brothers Berthold and Claus von Stauffenberg. By 1938, savage Nazi attacks on Germany's Jews seriously threatened Litta and her family, which included her parents, brother Otto and several sisters. In 1941, when German Jews began to be deported to the occupied territories of Eastern Europe to be murdered, the entire Schiller family was saved, because Litta von Stauffenberg had by this time become indispensable for her war work as a test pilot. A neighbor and friend who had known her parents when they lived in the Free City of Danzig used his influence to save them. In 1944, Litta's sisters and her brother Otto, who worked as an agricultural expert in the German Foreign Ministry, were all declared to be "equal to Aryans."

By 1942, the Stauffenberg brothers Berthold and Claus had become members of a plot to assassinate Adolf Hitler. Litta's husband Alexander was not informed of the conspiracy, but in late May or early June 1944, Claus von Stauffenberg asked his sister-in-law Litta if she would fly him to Hitler's headquarters and fly him out again after Hitler had been killed. She agreed to help. She warned him, however, that because of the lack of an adequate landing strip near Hitler's remote quarters in East Prussia, she would have to use a Fieseler "Stork"—a slow plane that required many fuelling stops. Since this would prohibit a fast escape, she was not involved in the actual assassination attempt, which took place on July 20, 1944, but failed to kill Hitler. In the evening of July 20, Claus von Stauffenberg was executed by troops loyal to Hitler. His brother

Berthold was arrested, cruelly tortured, found guilty of treason by a Nazi "court," and executed by strangulation on August 10, 1944.

Although he had not been involved in the plot to kill Hitler, Alexander von Stauffenberg was arrested a few days after July 20, and until the end of the war was held in several prisons and concentration camps, including the infamous Buchenwald camp near Weimar. Litta von Stauffenberg too was arrested only a few hours after her husband, as part of Reichsführer-SS Heinrich Himmler's enforcement of a policy of *Sippenhaft*—"blood guilt" and "blood liability"—which justified arresting all the relatives of a culprit accused of treason, his/her treachery being merely a manifestation of the diseased bloodline of their entire family. On September 2, 1944, however, Litta was released to enable her to immediately return to her duties as a test pilot, which were deemed of crucial importance to the Nazi war effort. Over the next months, Litta von Stauffenberg performed test dives with the Junkers 88 and night flights with the Arado 96, the Focke-Wulf 190 and the revolutionary new turbo-jet fighter, the Messerschmidt 262. She also worked on night-landing instruments, inventing a number of useful new devices.

Incredibly, Litta also was able to secure permission for flights at her own discretion, which enabled her to visit her imprisoned husband Alexander. Given the fact that there were no airfields near the camps and prisons where he was being held captive, the bombers she usually flew were of no use for these ventures. Only the very slow Fieseler "Stork" could easily land in any field, but this plane was at great risk of being shot down by the Allied (mostly American) planes that by this time held air supremacy over German skies. Litta flew at least twice to visit her husband at Buchenwald, even though she always stood a chance of being arrested, always standing "with one foot before a court martial." After a search, she discovered where the SS had taken the children of her two dead brothers-in-law. At Christmastime 1944, she visited them at Bad Sachsa in the Harz Mountains. Since no toys were available, she brought them the only presents she could find, a handful of bright, colorful war medals.

In January 1945, Claus von Stauffenberg's widow **Nina von Stauffenberg** gave birth to his posthumous daughter **Konstanze**. A few days later, after mother and infant had been transferred by the SS to a hospital in Potsdam, Litta visited them despite the great risks involved, arriving by bicycle and wearing the ribbon of the

Iron Cross class II and the Pilot Badge in Gold with Diamonds on her uniform jacket. The hospital's senior doctor, who had served in the Luftwaffe, recognized her and thereafter saw to it that Nina von Stauffenberg and her child received the best possible care.

On April 8, 1945, only a month before the end of the war in Europe, Litta von Stauffenberg was on her way to visit her husband in the Schönberg prison near Passau in Bavaria. Flying a slow and unarmed Bücker 181 trainer, she was shot down from behind by an American fighter near Strasskirchen. Although she was able to land her plane, Litta was severely wounded and died two hours later of her injuries. After Alexander's release from prison in May 1945, he searched desperately for Litta, only to learn that she had lost her life so close to the end of the war. In September 1945, he had her body exhumed from its temporary burial site and moved to the Stauffenberg family plot in Lautlingen, Württemberg. Shaken by his wife's death, Alexander withdrew from society for a couple of years, to meditate and write history and poetry. In 1948, he accepted a professorship in ancient history at Munich's Ludwig-Maximilian-Universität. He died in 1963.

**SOURCES:**

Baigent, Michael, and Richard Leigh. *Secret Germany: Stauffenberg and the Mystical Crusade Against Hitler.* London: Penguin, 1995.

Hoffmann, Peter. *Stauffenberg: A Family History, 1905–1944.* Cambridge: Cambridge University Press, 1995.

Letter from Prof. Dr. Graf A. Stauffenberg to Walter Hammer, Herrsching am Ammersee, September 24, 1952, Institut für Zeitgeschichte, Munich, Archiv Walter Hammer, ED 106/91.

Posner, Gerald L. *Hitler's Children.* NY: Random House, 1991.

Wunder, Gerd. *Die Schenken von Stauffenberg: Eine Familiengeschichte.* Stuttgart: Müller & Graff, 1972.

**John Haag**, Associate Professor of History, University of Georgia, Athens, Georgia

## Staupers, Mabel (1890–1989)

*African-American nurse and activist responsible for gaining black nurses admittance into the American military. Name variations: Mabel Keaton Staupers; Mabel Doyle Keaton Staupers. Born Mabel Doyle on February 27, 1890, in Barbados, West Indies; died on November 29, 1989; daughter of Thomas Doyle and Pauline Doyle; graduated from Freedmen's Hospital School of Nursing (now Howard University College of Nursing) in Washington, D.C., in 1917; married James Max Keaton, in 1917 (divorced); married Fritz C. Staupers, in 1931 (died 1949); no children.*

*Writings:* No Time for Prejudice: A Story of the Integration of Negroes in the United States *(1961).*

One of most significant figures in the history of African-Americans in the American nursing profession, Mabel Staupers was born Mabel Doyle in the West Indies in 1890, migrating to the United States with her parents Thomas and **Pauline Doyle** in 1903. The family settled in New York City's Harlem, where she completed her schooling, and in 1914 she moved to Washington, D.C., to attend the Freedmen's Hospital School of Nursing. She graduated with class honors three years later and began her career as a private-duty nurse.

Staupers' talents for leadership emerged in 1920 when she helped organize the Booker T. Washington Sanitarium, the first in-patient center in Harlem for black tuberculosis sufferers, and one of few city facilities at that time to employ black doctors. Instrumental in establishing the Harlem Committee of the New York Tuberculosis and Health Association, Staupers served as the committee's executive secretary for 12 years. Her experiences in Harlem, and also at the Jefferson Hospital Medical College in Philadelphia in the early 1920s, awakened Staupers to the discrimination and segregation within the medical community.

Elected executive secretary of the National Association of Colored Graduate Nurses (NACGN) in 1934, Staupers and president **Estelle Masse Riddle** formed a productive partnership that was to continue for 15 years. The NACGN had been founded in 1908 by *Martha Minerva Franklin** and *Adah Thoms** in order to advance the status of African-American nurses, most of whom were barred from nursing schools and professional associations and even from working as nurses in a number of states. Together they led the struggle of black nurses to win full integration into the American nursing profession.

A great organizer and astute political tactician, Staupers was a dynamic force for social change. She played a crucial role in the desegregation of the military's nursing corps during World War II. Staupers lobbied against the Army's strict quota and the Navy's total ban on black nurses, attacking the hypocrisy of Surgeon General Norman T. Kirk's plan to draft women into the understaffed Nurses' Corps. After an appeal for support to *Eleanor Roosevelt** in November 1944, Staupers' highly publicized campaign led both services to change their policies the following year.

Staupers welcomed this victory as another step in the black struggle for professional acceptance, saying, "The Negro nurse is not only fighting for integration in the war setup, she expects to walk along, step by step, with her white sisters in the postwar period." This goal was achieved in 1948 when the American Nurses Association (ANA) began admitting black members. Staupers dissolved the NACGN in 1949, and its members were integrated into the ANA. In 1951, she was honored by the National Association for the Advancement of Colored People (NAACP) with the Spingarn medal, presented to her by *Lillian Smith, activist and author of *Strange Fruit* (1944). In 1961, Staupers published an account of her battles on behalf of black nurses in *No Time for Prejudice: A Story of the Integration of Negroes in the United States.*

Staupers was married twice: at the age of 27 to James Max Keaton of Asheville, North Carolina, whom she later divorced, and from 1931 until his death in 1949 to Fritz C. Staupers of New York City. Mabel Staupers, who had no children, died at the age of 99.

**SOURCES:**

Bailey, Brooke. *The Remarkable Lives of 100 Women Healers and Scientists.* Holbrook, MA: Bob Adams, 1994.

Smith, Jessie Carney, ed. *Notable Black American Women.* Detroit, MI: Gale Research, 1992.

**Paula Morris**, D.Phil.,
Brooklyn, New York

# Stead, Christina (1902–1983)

*Australian novelist whose 1940 book* The Man Who Loved Children *is regarded by many critics as a forgotten 20th-century masterpiece. Name variations: always published as Christina Stead; lived with William Blake (Blech) from 1929 and often called herself "Mrs. Blech" or "Mrs. Blake," even though they did not marry until 1952. Born Christina Ellen Stead on July 17, 1902, in Sydney, Australia; died on March 31, 1983, in Balmain Hospital in Glebe, Australia; daughter of David Stead (an Australian scientist and politician) and Ellen (Butters) Stead (who died when Christina was two); attended Sydney Teachers' College; married William Blake (Blech), in 1952, after living with him since 1929; no children.*

*Was a student, then teacher (1921–25); was an office worker in Australia (1925–28), an office worker in London and Paris (1928–33), an independent writer and journalist (1933–83) in England, America, most of the Western European countries, and in Australia (1974 on).*

*Selected writings:* Seven Poor Men of Sydney *(1934); (short stories)* The Salzburg Tales *(1934);* The Beauties and the Furies *(1936);* The Man Who Loved Children *(1940);* For Love Alone *(1944);* Letty Fox: Her Luck *(1946);* Cotter's England *(1967, published in America as* Dark Places of the Heart*);* The People With the Dogs *(1952);* I'm Dying Laughing *(1986).*

The long trip abroad to earn one's fame and fortune is a common story in Australian history, and it was played out in Christina Stead's life. She left her hometown of Sydney in 1928 and stayed away from Australia for 41 years, moving restlessly between Britain, Europe, and America and establishing a reputation as a brilliant modern novelist. Her masterpiece, *The Man Who Loved Children* (1940), is one of the most harrowing yet persuasive 20th-century descriptions of life in a dysfunctional family, and biographers have shown that it is quite closely based on her own childhood.

She was born Christina Ellen Stead in 1902, in Sydney, Australia, the daughter of David Stead and **Ellen Butters Stead** who died in 1904 when Christina was only two. Her father lived with his sister for awhile then remarried and had six other children with his new wife **Ada Stead**. They lived in a series of big seaside houses. Christina, as the oldest, played a large role in bringing up her younger siblings but felt a jealous rivalry with her stepmother. David Stead was an idealistic socialist, atheist, and marine biologist who brought up his children to respect science and to be inquisitive. He also played an important role in Australia's early experiments with socialism. He was appointed head of a government scheme to run trawlers and bring fish to working-class people at cost, rather than at the inflated prices charged by retailers and middlemen in the profit system. Like many well-intentioned schemes of the kind, it backfired, partly because the onset of World War I in Europe made boats and fishing equipment difficult to procure from England, and partly because the private fishermen did what they could to obstruct the scheme. It lost money, and David Stead was investigated by the government for his incompetent management of the scheme. He served the Australian government in a series of minor posts during the 1920s, including work in Singapore and Malaya, but was unemployed when the Great Depression began.

Christina Stead, meanwhile, had a conventional young Australian girl's education but was stand-offish, unkempt, and often the odd one out. She did not excel in her studies but wrote a lot of ingenious poetry as a teenager and was able to win a scholarship to Sydney Teachers' College. She studied for a career in schoolteaching and was among the first Australians to apply psychological and I.Q. tests to children. She became restless as a teacher after a couple of years in the classroom, and was forced to withdraw periodically because of voice strain. She trained instead as a secretary in night school (1925), then went to work in the office of a hat factory. After three years of hard work, saving as much money as she could, she boarded a ship for England. The fact that Walter Duncan, a brilliant young man she had known at college, was also going abroad on a scholarship, contributed to her enthusiasm for the journey—an episode later fictionalized in her novel *For Love Alone*.

Arriving in London, she took a job as secretary for a grain importer. She soon forgot about Duncan and fell in love with her employer, an American Jew named William Blake. Before long they were living together. Blake (originally Blech), despite his work at the heart of world capitalism, in banking and international trade, was a learned and eloquent Marxist economic theorist, who contributed greatly to Stead's education in the Marxism she had learned in outline from her father. He was separated from his wife **Mollie Blake**, but she refused to give him a divorce until 1952, so he and Stead were unable to marry until they had lived together for 24 years. They had no children, and she apparently had a series of abortions. Blake gave Stead a feeling of social self-confidence she had never had before. She was self-conscious about her plain appearance but now began to adopt fashionable clothes, and was careful to lose her Australian accent.

With Blake, Stead moved to Paris in 1929 and continued to work in importing and banking. Blake entrusted her with numerous business missions abroad, enabling her to travel widely in Europe, even in the worsening conditions of the Great Depression. Among their friends was *Sylvia Beach**, owner of the famous bookstore Shakespeare and Co., who had also befriended James Joyce, Ernest Hemingway, *Janet Flanner**, *Djuna Barnes**, *Natalie Clifford Barney**, *Kay Boyle**, *Gertrude Stein**, *Mina Loy**, *Margaret Anderson**, and other English-speaking literary "exiles" of the 1920s. In Paris, Stead wrote her first novel, *Seven Poor Men of Sydney*, and the stories that were published as *The Salzburg Tales*. Beach liked them, passed them on to her English publisher-friend Peter Davies, and he gave Stead a contract for both books, which appeared to critical acclaim in 1934. Her future as a novelist seemed assured, but her third

book, *The Beauties and the Furies* (1936), had a more mixed reception—British reviewers thought it a decline from her first two. American critics, by contrast, notably Clifton Fadiman, gave it high praise and said that Stead was the equal of *Virginia Woolf**.

Like many left-wing intellectuals during the Great Depression of the 1930s, Stead became deeply involved in radical causes. She believed that the Depression had sounded the death-knell of capitalism and that revolutions comparable to that which had swept Russia in 1917 would transform the Western industrial nations. Nevertheless, as an independent-minded novelist, she was far too shrewd and observant to fall into the simple Marxist sloganeering characteristic of the era, and never hesitated to write devastating literary satires on the political left and its personalities. She attended, and reported on, the First International Congress of Writers for the Defense of Culture in Paris, and settled for a time in Republican Spain, just before Francisco Franco's

*Christina Stead*

right-wing coup overthrew the regime and launched the Spanish Civil War.

One of her Paris friends in the early 1930s was an English radical named Ralph Fox. He had helped found the Oxford University branch of the English Communist Party, had traveled widely in Russia, written a book about the revolution, a biography of Lenin, and a novel. Biographers speculate that she had a love affair with him, perhaps even with the connivance of Blake. However, Fox joined the International Brigade and was killed in Spain early in 1937.

*Standing in sympathies between eras, her novels keep the nineteenth-century's devotion to realism, its scope of social concern, texture of observed detail, interest in character. Yet her understanding of these is informed by Marx and Freud, by a material social critique and by depth analysis of individual fantasy life and family relations.*

—Joan Lidoff

Stead made her first visit to America in 1935 and then, as Franco, Hitler, and Mussolini gained power in Europe and Blake's businesses foundered in the Depression, returned in 1937. They stayed for the next nine years, through the Second World War, living amid a group of leftist writers and contributing articles and reviews to the Communist-run *New Masses*. Blake also published a well-written textbook, *An American Looks at Karl Marx* (1939), and two historical novels in quick succession, *The Painter and the Lady* (1940) and *The Copperheads* (1941). He became a Communist Party member and eventually drew the unwelcome attention of the FBI. His decision to abandon business made the couple far less prosperous than they had been hitherto.

After a year in Manhattan, made stressful by the presence of Blake's mother, with whom Stead feuded, they moved to Lambertville, New Jersey, where Stead gave all her attention to writing *The Man Who Loved Children*. The American-Soviet alliance (1942–45) during the Second World War made radicals popular for a time and Stead's literary reputation was sufficient to win her an invitation to write film scripts for Metro-Goldwyn-Mayer, and to teach a class on creative writing at New York University. She did not persist with either job, however, but devoted as much time as possible to her fiction. Among Blake's projects, as the Second World War drew to a close, was *An Intelligent American's Guide to the Peace* (1945), a masterful summary of the world situation in the wake of the conflict. He was paid a lump sum for it, and it appeared under the ostensible authorship of Sumner Welles, a prominent New Deal-era politician.

Most critics agree that Stead's best books were written during the New York years, especially *The Man Who Loved Children* (1940), *For Love Alone* (1944), and *Letty Fox: Her Luck* (1946). The first of these is an immense (500 page) fictional transfiguration of her childhood, moved to an American setting, full of convincing American detail, but replaying key scenes from her childhood. It shows in maddening detail the feuding of Sam and Henny Pollit, who have too little money to make ends meet and whose fights are complicated by the presence of their children, whose own perceptions are conveyed in amazingly convincing detail. Stead agreed with interviewers that she had an uncanny ability to recapture the feelings and impressions of childhood. Sales, unfortunately, did not match critical praise, and the couple remained unable to make a long-anticipated visit to Australia.

Her reputation remained stronger in America than Britain, and stronger in both than in Australia, where she was still virtually unknown, except among a small coterie of other writers. Australians who did mention her name sometimes noted, acidly, that she had abandoned her homeland for greener pastures, like many other talented Australians. To make matters worse, *Letty Fox* (1946), which dealt with a young woman's sexual promiscuity as she tried to make her way and find some security in modern New York, was banned in Australia by the censors; its sexual scenes were considered too graphic for their era. Stead condemned the ban, arguing in a letter to the censors that the book "deals with obscene material but is not obscene. It is very frank but written in an austere style." The fact that the Australian government was now keeping watch over Stead's work and knew her to be a Communist sympathizer (as were several of her siblings, still in Australia) also led to a denial of her application for a Commonwealth Literary Fund grant in 1952.

Leaving America soon after the war ended, in 1946, partly because they feared that as radicals they might become the targets of anti-Communist investigations, Stead and Blake traveled throughout Europe, living briefly in France, Italy, Belgium, Holland, Switzerland, and England. They were shocked to discover the privations of ordinary people in Western Europe in the aftermath of the war: rationing, malnutrition, shortages of everything, and services broken down or neglected. America was a land of abundance by comparison, whatever its political intolerance. They moved nearly every year to joyless flats and apartments in southern England, hard up and often depressed—Blake's eyesight deteriorated but he still wrote copiously and took extra work as a publisher's reader. The only time they lived more comfortably, ironically, was on a short visit to East Germany, where Blake's historical novels were honored by the Communist regime and earned him handsome royalties. Briefly Stead moved to the northeast English industrial city of Newcastle-on-Tyne to live with a working-class family, an experience that formed the basis of her later novel *Cotter's England* (1967, published as *Dark Places of the Heart* in America). She said that she found writing more difficult in England than anywhere else; that it was "depressing to the creative faculties and bad for the morals."

Publication of *The People With the Dogs* (1952), a satirical novel about America, led to bad reviews. *The New York Times* said that this time she "uses all too little of that vigor and imagination which Miss Stead put into at least two of her earlier books" and that it was "the work of a writer whose passion seems all spent." This and other hurtful reviews put a stop to Stead's work on novels for many years. She began to write a lot of journalism, reviews and translations, but felt discouraged from undertaking new fiction projects, though she still had many half-written novels.

Through most of her lifetime, Stead was not widely known or admired—hence her chronic poverty after the early 1930s—but she had a devoted following among some of the best living writers. The American novelist Randall Jarrell wrote an enthusiastic introduction to a reissue of *The Man Who Loved Children* in 1965, acclaiming it one of the great novels of the century. It included these words:

> Christina Stead's way of seeing and representing the world is so plainly different from anyone else's that after a while you take this for granted, and think cheerfully, "Oh, she can't help being original." The whole book is different from any book you have read before . . . the book has an astonishing sensory immediacy.

Stead was so pleased to receive this praise that when she read it aloud to Blake she burst into tears. This recognition gave her the courage to finish and publish several books she had worked on earlier, some dating back to the late 1940s and early 1950s, including *Cotter's England*.

She had often thought of returning to Australia but in the impoverished 1950s and early 1960s could not afford it. At that time she, as a woman, could not confer Australian citizenship on a husband who was an alien, and he would be allowed into the country only for a short visit, and on condition of already holding a return ticket. In the end, she returned only in 1969, after the trauma of Blake's death in 1968. Despite a sometimes stormy relationship, the two quirky writers had been compatible and had stayed together for 40 years.

Honored in her homeland, if belatedly, Stead, now almost 70, accepted a visiting fellowship at the Australian National University. She was well received and returned in 1974 to receive the Patrick White Prize for literature. She settled in Australia but continued to travel widely, earning more money now from speeches and writing, but becoming fragile in health. At one point, she had to be admitted to the hospital suffering from malnutrition.

Saul Bellow was another of Stead's admirers and, like Randall Jarrell, contributed to the revival of her reputation. He mentioned her work in his speech accepting the Nobel Prize for literature in 1976, saying that she too deserved the award. Feminists in the 1970s also acclaimed Stead. By 1980, her work was enjoying a revival, though still among intellectuals rather than the general reading public. It is harsh, often depressing, complicated writing that makes demands on the reader. Growing numbers found the high price worth paying, however, and by the time Stead died in 1983, at the age of 81, she had the consolation of knowing that her place in literary history was secure. Several more collections of her stories, another novel, *I'm Dying Laughing* (1986), and a two-volume collection of her letters have appeared in the years since her death.

**SOURCES:**

Brydon, Diana. *Christina Stead*. London: Macmillan, 1987.

Lidoff, Joan. *Christina Stead*. NY: Frederick Ungar, 1982.

Rowley, Hazel. *Christina Stead: A Biography*. NY: Henry Holt, 1993.

Stead, Christina. *I'm Dying Laughing*. London: Virago, 1986.

———. *The Man Who Loved Children*, 1940, NY: Henry Holt, 1968, with 1965 introduction by Randall Jarrell.

Williams, Chris. *Christina Stead: A Life of Letters*. London: Virago, 1989.

**SUGGESTED READING:**

Sheridan, Susan. *Christina Stead*. IN: Indiana University Press, 1988.

**COLLECTIONS:**

National Library of Australia, Christina Stead papers.

**Patrick Allitt**, Professor of History, Emory University, Atlanta, Georgia

## Stebbing, L. Susan (1885–1943)

*British philosopher. Name variations: Lizzie Susan Stebbing. Born on December 2, 1885, in Wimbledon, Surrey, England; died on September 11, 1943, in London, England; youngest of six children of Alfred Charles Stebbing (a barrister) and Elizabeth (Elstob) Stebbing; attended Girton College, Cambridge; University of London, M.A., 1912, D.Lit., 1931; never married; no children.*

L. Susan Stebbing was born in 1885, the youngest of six children of Alfred Charles Stebbing, a lawyer, and **Elizabeth Elstob Stebbing.** She developed her acute intellectual gifts at Girton College in Cambridge, eventually earning both a master's and a doctoral degree at the University of London, and started lecturing in philosophy at King's College in London in 1913. Her distinguished teaching career included service at Bedford College, the University of London, Columbia University in New York City, and the Kingsley Lodge School for Girls in Hampstead, the latter of which she served as principal from 1915 until her death in 1943.

Stebbing's keen interest in the sciences and mathematics caused her to align herself philosophically with the Cambridge analytic school, which married Hume's empiricism with developed mathematical logic. While she did not make any original contributions to the field of logic, Stebbing was recognized as an expert teacher in the subject, able to convey complicated ideas clearly and without bias. Her work *A Modern Introduction to Logic* (1930) was the first text to make the advancements in logic generally accessible. Stebbing firmly believed that the application of reason could eradicate evil, and expounded on this idea in her work *Ideals and Illusions* in 1941. She died in London on September 11, 1943.

**SOURCES:**
Legg, L.G. Wickham, and E.T. Williams, eds. *The Dictionary of National Biography, 1941–1950.* Oxford: Oxford University Press, 1960.

**Paula Morris,** D.Phil., Brooklyn, New York

## Stebbins, Alice.

*See Wells, Alice Stebbins.*

## Stebbins, Emma (1815–1882)

*American sculptor and painter. Born on September 1, 1815, in New York City; died on October 24, 1882, in New York City; daughter of John Stebbins (a New York banker) and Mary (Largin) Stebbins; sister of Henry George Stebbins, president of the New York Stock Exchange; studied painting in New York with portrait painter Henry Inman and sculpture in Rome under Benjamin Paul Akers; lifetime companion of Charlotte Cushman; never married; no children.*

*Created the fountain* The Angel of the Waters *installed in New York City's Central Park (1873); wrote* Charlotte Cushman: Her Letters and Memories of Her Life *(1878).*

Emma Stebbins was born in 1815 in New York City, the daughter of John Stebbins, a New York banker, and **Mary Largin Stebbins,** and enjoyed a privileged upbringing in a large family. Her parents, both of distinguished colonial pedigree, encouraged her artistic talent. Her early pictures drew the attention of portraitist Henry Inman, with whom she studied oil painting. From 1843, she was an exhibiting painter at the National Academy of Design in New York and the Pennsylvania Academy of the Fine Arts, best known for her crayon portraits. During a visit to Rome in 1857, at age 42, she decided to become a sculptor on the advice of English sculptor John Gibson. Stebbins took up studies with Maine-born sculptor, painter and author Benjamin Paul Akers.

In Rome, sculptor *Harriet Hosmer introduced Stebbins to the actress *Charlotte Cushman; Stebbins became her companion and eventual biographer. Through Cushman, Stebbins met such celebrated women artists as *Rosa Bonheur, *Elizabeth Barrett Browning and *George Sand. Cushman's influence helped Stebbins to win the commission for a bronze statue of Horace Mann (1864), erected outside the State House in Boston.

It is possible that the influence of her brother Henry George Stebbins, president of the New York Stock Exchange and head of the Central Park Commission, helped Stebbins win her most important commission. In 1873, her celebrated fountain *The Angel of the Waters*, also known as the Bethesda Fountain and now one of the city's best-known monuments, was installed in Central Park. Other works include *Columbus* (1867), originally erected in Central Park at 102nd Street, now in the Brooklyn Civic Center, and the innovative *Industry* (1859) and *Commerce* (1860) which depict a miner and a sailor, respectively, in modern dress.

In 1870, Stebbins and Cushman returned to the United States, living in New York City and Newport, Rhode Island, until Cushman's death in

1876. In 1878, Stebbins published *Charlotte Cushman: Her Letters and Memories of Her Life.* She died four years later at the age of 73 and was buried in Greenwood Cemetery in Brooklyn.

**SOURCES:**

James, Edward T., ed. *Notable American Women, 1607–1950.* Cambridge, MA: The Belknap Press of Harvard University, 1971.
Rubinstein, Charlotte Streifer. *American Women Artists.* Boston, MA: G.K. Hall, 1982.

**Paula Morris**, D.Phil.,
Brooklyn, New York

# Steber, Eleanor (1914–1990)

*American soprano. Born on July 17, 1914, in Wheeling, West Virginia; died on October 3, 1990, in Langhorne, Pennsylvania; daughter of William Charles Steber (a bank cashier) and Ida A. (Nolte) Steber (a singer); studied at the New England Conservatory and with Paul Althouse and William Whitney; married Edwin L. Bilby, in 1938.*

*Debuted in Boston (1936); won the Metropolitan Radio Auditions (1936); debuted at the Met (1936) and performed there (1936–62); debuted at Bayreuth (1953), Vienna (1953); sang in the first performance of Barber's* Knoxville: Summer of 1915 *(1948); sang Miss Wingrave in American premiere of Britten's* Owen Wingrave *(1973); taught at the Cleveland Institute of Music and the Juilliard School.*

Eleanor Steber, who had a fan club with chapters throughout the United States and its own newsletter, *The Silvertone,* was a singer of astonishing breadth and depth. Her career was particularly associated with the composer Samuel Barber. Steber premiered the title role of Barber's *Vanessa* in 1958; she had also appeared in the premiere of his *Knoxville: Summer of 1915* in 1948. During her lengthy career at the Metropolitan Opera, Steber became known for her performances of Mozart and Strauss. She was also known for her work in other modern operas, such as Berg's *Wozzeck* and Britten's *Owen Wingrave.* Steber was a champion of modern music and particularly of modern American music. After her retirement from the opera stage, she taught at the Juilliard School, Temple University, the New England Conservatory, and the Cleveland Institute of Music. Having worked her way through the New England Conservatory as a dormitory desk attendant and a piano accompanist when young, she founded the Eleanor Steber Music Foundation which provided assistance to aspiring singers.

**John Haag**,
Athens, Georgia

# Stecher, Renate (1950—)

*East German track-and-field champion. Born Renate Meissner in Suptitz, East Germany, on May 12, 1950; married Gerd Stecher (a hurdler); children: two daughters.*

*Was a top international sprinter who was undefeated in the 100 and 200 meters (1970–74); won the Olympic gold medal in both the 100 and 200 meters (1972); won Olympic silver in the 100 meters, bronze in the 200 meters, and silver in the 400-meter relay (1976); ran the first sub-11-second 100 meters ever (1973).*

An elite group of women sprinters have won Olympic gold in both the 100 and 200 meters, including *Fanny Blankers-Koen, *Marjorie Jackson, *Betty Cuthbert, *Wilma Rudolph, and Renate Stecher. In the early 1970s, Stecher was a dominant force in women's track and field. A product of the powerful East German sports machine, she was coached by Horst-Dieter Hille who produced some of the world's finest runners.

Carefully groomed, Stecher burst onto the scene in 1970 when she ran the 100 meters in 11 seconds, tying *Wyomia Tyus' 1968 world record. Just before the European Cup in Budapest, Stecher endured an attack of appendicitis and emergency surgery. Persuading her doctor to let her compete, she went from the hospital to the games where she came in second in the 100 meters, first in the 200 meters, and anchored the winning team in the 4x100-meter relay. In 1971, she defended her European Indoor title in the 60 meters. In the European Cup, Stecher won the 100 meters in 11.4 seconds, the 200 in 22.7, and finished second with her team in the 4x100-meter relay.

When the 1972 Olympics began in Munich, Renate Stecher was a clear favorite. In the 100 meters, the competition trailed Stecher who crossed the finish line in 11.07 seconds, while Australia's **Raelene Boyle** and Cuba's **Silvia Chibás** lagged behind at 11.23 and 11.24. In the 200 meters, the race was closer. Stecher arrived first with a time of 22.40 (an Olympic record), followed by Raelene Boyle at 22.45 and Poland's *Irena Szewinska with 22.74. Stecher also took a silver while anchoring the 400-meter relay team.

Renate Stecher continued to compete after the Olympics and on June 7, 1973, clocked a 10.9 world record, the first sub-11-second 100 meters ever. On July 20 in the East German championships in Dresden, she clocked 10.8 for another world record. From 1970 to 1974,

Stecher dominated the track, but as the Olympics approached, she was increasingly challenged by Poland's Szewinska whose performance continued to improve. In 1974, when Szewinska was named World Athlete of the Year, Stecher replied to an interviewer, "Irena had a great year and being named Athlete of the Year was a natural conclusion. . . . I really don't feel I 'lost' this past year; Irena just won and I finished second."

In the 1976 Montreal Olympics, Stecher won the silver in the 100 meters in 11.13, five seconds behind West Germany's **Annegret Richter** who took the gold. In the 200 meters, Stecher won the bronze with a time of 22.47, finishing behind East Germany's *Bärbel Wöckel-Eckert* (22.37) and Richter (22.39). With silver and bronze medals, however, Stecher remained one of the world's best sprinters. She retired after the 1976 Games. "The main thing for me always was that I simply loved the sport," she said. "I loved to run fast, and worked to get even faster. Most of all, I loved the sensation of speed."

**SOURCES:**

Hendershott, Jon. *Track's Greatest Women.* Los Altos, CA: Tafnews Press, 1987.

Wallechinsky, David. *The Complete Book of the Olympics.* NY: Viking, 1988.

**Karin Loewen Haag**,
Athens, Georgia

# Steel, Dawn (1946–1997)

*Film executive who was the first woman to head a major studio, Columbia Pictures. Born on August 19, 1946, in New York; died on December 20, 1997, in Los Angeles, California; only daughter and one of two children of Nat Steel (a zipper salesman and semipro weight lifter) and Lillian Steel (an electronics executive); briefly attended Boston University and New York University; married Ronald Rothstein (a financial investor), on December 31, 1975 (divorced 1977); married Chuck Roven (a producer), on May 30, 1985; children: one daughter, Rebecca Roven.*

Frequently referred to as "Steely Dawn" or "The Tank" because of her tough, abrasive style, Dawn Steel was president of Columbia Pictures from 1987 to 1991, and as such was the first woman in history to head a major studio, and the second woman after **Sherry Lansing** to hold such a powerful position in Hollywood. Steel's rise to power in the male-dominated film industry was something of a celluloid story in itself. A middle-class college dropout with no money or connections, she made her way to the top through sheer will, wit, and determination (plus a spark of creative genius). "Dawn saw life as: if you want something and try really, really hard, you should be able to get it," said her friend **Lucy Fisher**, vice-chair of Columbia-Tristar Pictures. Steel left Columbia in 1991, opting for a less demanding job as an independent producer. Four years later, she was diagnosed with a brain tumor, and died 20 months later, age 51.

The granddaughter of Russian Jews (her father changed the family name to Steel from Spielberg), Dawn Steel was born in 1946 and grew up on Long Island, where her father Nat was a zipper salesman and her mother **Lillian Steel** worked as an electronics executive. When Dawn was nine, Nat suffered a nervous breakdown, a defining moment in Steel's young life. "The man I adored had closed me out. I remember nothing that happened for the next two years. I climbed into a black hole that I didn't come out of for a very long time." Her father's illness also drained the family funds, leaving Steel's mother Lillian scurrying to keep the family solvent. Steel soon learned that if she wanted some of the things her friends had she would have to work for them. At 16, she took an after-school job selling shoes at Pappagallo's, not only earning money but, more important at the time, amassing her own wardrobe of the popular footwear. After high school, without any idea of what she wanted to do, she attended Boston University, majoring in marketing and supporting herself as a go-go dancing waitress. Running out of money, she transferred to New York University's School of Commerce, but lost interest after a year and left to join the workforce full time. After filling in as a receptionist in a clothing firm and serving as a statistician with a small sports book publisher, Steel took a job with *Penthouse* magazine, quickly working her way up from writer to director of merchandising. Four years later, she left the magazine to go into her own business, a mail-order enterprise from which she first sold phallic amaryllis plants ("Grow your own. . . . All it takes is $6.98 and a lot of love") and then designer toilet paper emblazoned with the Gucci logo. (Steel's business partner was then her first husband Ronald Rothstein whom she married in 1975 and divorced in 1977, around the time the angry Gucci family sued. The case was eventually settled out of court.)

Steel moved to Los Angeles in 1978, where she landed a job in the merchandising department at Paramount. Shortly after her arrival, she staged a brilliant party for toy manufacturers in conjunction with *Star Trek: The Motion Picture*, at which she "beamed" the movie characters onto the stage. A year later, having proven herself, she was promoted to vice-president of feature productions. Her first project, *Flashdance*, made her name in the industry. "She put it together at Paramount at a time when she was literally the only voice that wanted to make it," said James Wiatt, president of International Creative Management (ICM). "It put her on the map as someone who would fight for projects she believed in and someone who had instincts for material and concepts for movies."

As senior vice-president of Paramount from 1983, and president of production from 1985, Steel oversaw such hit movies as *Footloose*, *Top Gun*, *Beverly Hills Cop II*, *The Untouchables*, and *Fatal Attraction*. She also met and married producer Chuck Roven, the "perfect" man, after a checkered dating history that included Richard Gere and Martin Scorsese. While her personal life flourished, at work Steel was gaining a reputation for being difficult and demanding, and there were those among the ranks who began plotting to unseat her. In her straightforward book about her career, *They Can Kill You . . . But They Can't Eat You*, she attributed many of her escalating problems at work to the ups and downs of her pregnancy with daughter Rebecca, which she found difficult to deal with in the corporate setting. "I was being pressured from above and in my horrendous hormonal state I started pressuring below and became even more demanding of the people who worked for me than I had ever been." In 1987, about the time she was having her child, Steel was let go, learning of her termination from a headline in the trade paper *Variety*.

Undaunted, Steel quickly rebounded in a better job as head of Columbia Pictures, overseeing both marketing and production at the studio. During her tenure there, she oversaw the marketing campaigns for *When Harry Met Sally* and *Look Who's Talking*. She also initiated the release of **Carrie Fisher**'s *Postcards from the Edge* and *The Awakening*, and oversaw the restoration of *Lawrence of Arabia*. Although Steel mellowed somewhat after the birth of Rebecca, she was still an intimidating force, making it to the cover of *California* magazine's 1988 "Bosses from Hell" issue.

In 1991, shortly after Sony bought out Columbia, Steel left the studio to become an independent producer. "The higher I went up the ladder in corporate life, the less creative it was, the less fun it was, the less it was about movies and the more about budgets and board meetings and administration," she writes, explaining her departure. "For me it was hell." In her new job, Steel had come full circle. One of the first films she championed was *Cool Runnings*, the story of a Jamaican bobsled team that, like *Flashdance* back in 1983, no one thought stood a chance. The film turned out to be the surprise hit of 1993.

Steel approached her illness with her usual grit and bravado. "She worked harder on getting well than anybody I've ever seen," recalled **Amy Pascal**, who was president of Columbia Pictures in 1998. "At one point, President Clinton called and asked how she was doing, and she said, 'I'm fine, but what are you doing calling me? Don't you have a country to run?'" Following her death on December 20, 1997, Clinton, for whom Steel had hosted a fundraiser in her Hollywood home, praised her as "a pioneer in the film industry, blazing a trail for a new generation of young women." However, producer **Lynda Obst**, a longtime friend, notes that Steel never set out to be a feminist trailblazer. "She didn't even know the glass ceiling was there," she said. "That's why she was able to break it."

**SOURCES:**

Acker, Ally. *Reel Women*. NY: Continuum, 1991.

Katz, Ephraim. *The Film Encyclopedia*. NY: HarperCollins, 1994.

"Obituary," in *The Day* [New London, CT]. December 22, 1997.

Smith, Kyle, Lorenzo Benet, and Tom Cunneff. "Dawn of an Era," in *People Weekly*. January 12, 1998.

Steel, Dawn. *They Can Kill You . . . But They Can't Eat You: Lessons From the Front*. NY: Pocket Books, 1993.

*Dawn Steel*

## Steel, Flora Annie (1847–1929)

*English novelist. Born Flora Annie Webster at Sudbury Priory, Harrow-on-the-Hill, England, on April 2, 1847; died on April 12, 1929; sixth child and second daughter of George Webster (a sheriff clerk of Forfarshire) and Isabella (Macallum) Webster (heiress of a Jamaican sugar planter); married Henry William Steel (with the Indian civil service), in 1867; children: daughter (b. 1870).*

*Lived in India (1868–89); advocated education for Indian women; was first inspector of girls' schools; was a member of the Provincial Educational Board (1884); lived in North Wales (1900–13).*

Born in 1847 in Harrow, England, Flora Annie Steel grew up in Harrow and, following the onset of family financial difficulties, in Scotland. When she was 20, she married an officer with the Indian civil service, who had been a childhood friend, and accompanied him to India where they lived, chiefly in the Punjab, for the next 22 years. In many respects, her experiences exemplify the lifestyle of British women in India at the height of the British Raj. In their first three years of marriage, for example, Steel and her husband were posted to nine different locations. Like so many *memsahibs* (British women), Steel suffered the emotional trauma of sending her young daughter back to England to be educated in a supposedly healthier and more suitable climate.

Flora Annie Steel was not merely a typical *memsahib*. While in India, she became interested in Indian culture and history and began to write about those subjects for the British reading public. She published her first book, *Wide Awake Stories*, a collection of Indian folk tales, while still living in India. However, it was after her husband's retirement and their return to England in 1889 that Steel began to write in earnest the stories that would propel her to fame and popularity in Britain. Her bestselling novel about the Indian Mutiny of 1857, *On the Face of the Waters*, "sold like hot cakes," in Steel's own phrase. Her short stories, many of which were published in *Macmillan's Magazine*, and her series of historical romances of the Moghul Empire, were also quite popular. With her friend **Grace Gardiner**, Steel also authored *The Complete Indian Housekeeper and Cook*, a "how-to" housekeeping manual and cookbook intended as a guide for British women setting up household in India. The book proved enormously popular and was one of the most influential 19th-century texts in shaping the role of the colonial woman. Steel continued to write until the end of her long life. She died in 1929, shortly after completing her autobiography, *The Garden of Fidelity*. Some of her best work is contained in two collections of short stories: *From the Five Rivers* (1893) and *Tales from the Punjab* (1894). Later works are *In the Permanent Way* (1897), *Voices of the Night* (1900), *The Hosts of the Lord* (1900), *In the Guardianship of God* (1903), and *A Sovereign Remedy* (1906).

**Mary A. Procida**,
Visiting Assistant Professor of History,
Temple University, Philadelphia, Pennsylvania

## Steele, Alison (c. 1937–1995)

*American radio personality who was one of the first female rock 'n' roll disc jockeys in America. Name variations: the Nightbird. Born around 1937 in Brooklyn, New York; died in September 1995 in New York City; sister of Joyce Loman (who operated a feline boutique with her sister called Just Cats); married Ted Steele, a bandleader (divorced).*

Alison Steele, one of America's first female rock 'n' roll disc jockeys, began her broadcasting career as an errand girl at the age of 14 and worked her way up to associate producer at a New York radio station. In 1966, she was chosen from 800 applicants for an all-woman lineup of disc jockeys, a publicity stunt organized by New York station WNEW-FM. When the station abandoned the lineup 18 months later, Steele was the only woman asked to stay on.

Known to her loyal listeners as "the Nightbird" because of her specialty graveyard shifts, Steele was inducted into the Rock 'n' Roll Hall of Fame and was the first female winner of *Billboard* magazine's FM Personality of the Year (1976). She worked for several different New York stations and her distinctively sultry voice, inviting listeners to "Come fly with me," was much in demand for radio and television voice-overs. She died of cancer in New York City in 1995.

**SOURCES:**
*The Daily News* (obituary). September 28, 1995.
*Time*. October 9, 1995.

**Paula Morris**, D.Phil.,
Brooklyn, New York

## Steele, Anne (1717–1778)

*English hymn writer. Name variations: Theodosia. Born at Broughton, Hampshire, England, in 1717; died in 1778.*

Anne Steele was born in Broughton, Hampshire, England, in 1717. A few hours before her marriage, her fiancé drowned, deeply affecting her otherwise quiet life. Steele's hymns, noted one historian, "emphasize the less optimistic phases of Christian experience." In 1760, she published *Poems on Subjects chiefly devotional* under the name "Theodosia," and her complete works (144 hymns, 34 metrical psalms, and 50 moral poems) appeared in one volume in London in 1863, issued by Daniel Sedgwick. Steele was a Baptist, and her hymns were often used by members of that faith, though some of them, like "Father of mercies, in Thy word," found their way into the collections of other churches. Anne Steele has been called the *Frances Ridley Havergal of the 18th century.

# Steevens, Grissell (1653–1746)

*Co-founder, with her brother, of Dr. Steevens's Hospital, one of the first public hospitals in Ireland. Name variations: Grizell Steevens; Grizel Steevens; Grisilda Steevens; Madam Steevens. Born Grissell Steevens in 1653, probably in England; died at Dr. Steevens's Hospital, Dublin, on March 18, 1746; daughter of Rev. John Steevens and Constance Steevens; never married; no children.*

*Moved as a child with her family to Ireland, where her father became rector of Athlone (1660); inherited her brother's fortune on his death (1710); surrendered most of her share of the inheritance in order to permit the fulfillment of his desire for the erection of a hospital in Dublin for the care of the sick poor; helped fund and supervise the building of Dr. Steevens's Hospital, which opened 1733; involved in the management of the institution until her death, at age 93.*

In December 1710, Richard Steevens, an eminent and wealthy Dublin physician, knowing himself to be dying and wishing to set his affairs in order, consulted with his nearest living relative, his twin Grissell Steevens. According to an 18th-century account used by Cheyne Brady in his *History of Steevens's Hospital*:

> Before making his will he inquired of his sister whether she had any thoughts of entering the matrimonial state, informing her that if such were her intention he would bequeath her his fortune without reserve, but if not, he would leave it to her for life and devise it after her decease to found a hospital for sick poor, as he had observed in the course of his practice that many of them were lost for want of medical assistance. To his great gratification, he found that his sister entered fully into his benevolent designs and encouraged him in them, by voluntarily promising never to marry, but to devote her life to the forwarding of his charitable intention with all her might.

Thus, Grissell Steevens, at age 57, found herself not only a woman of property but also one with a mission which was to occupy her for the remainder of her long life, and which for 250 years was to keep her name and legend alive in her adopted city.

The voluntary hospital movement was one of the earliest and most dynamic manifestations of 18th-century philanthropic concern. Benevolent individuals, not least physicians such as Richard Steevens, noted the total lack of any provision for the sick poor, and advocated the introduction of some form of institutional relief. While the humanitarian impulse was an impor-

tant motivating factor in this development, other considerations included the self-interest of the middle and upper classes, concerned at the effect on the labor force and on society of a high death and disease rate among the poor, and the influence of the increasingly prestigious medical profession, which saw in hospitals a more efficient means of caring for the sick as well as a source of clinical material for research and teaching purposes. The process, once begun, was rapid. At the beginning of the century, Dublin had no public hospitals. In 1718, a house was opened in Cork Street "for the maimed and wounded poor"; Dr. Steevens's Hospital, opened 15 years later, was the second voluntary hospital in Dublin, and by 1750 the city had six such establishments. Women were involved in a number of these initiatives, although usually in a secondary and supportive capacity within male-run bodies. However, two of the first Dublin hospitals were founded by women, but while **Mary Mercer** did little more than finance the institution which bears her name, her contemporary, Steevens, played an exceptionally active part both in the establishment and in the subsequent management of her foundation.

Grissell Steevens was born in 1653, the daughter of Reverend John Steevens and **Constance Steevens**. John Steevens had been a cleric of the Church of England, but, having incurred the displeasure of the Cromwellian regime for his royalist views, had been forced in the early 1650s to leave his English parish and, with his wife and infant twins, Grissell and Richard, to flee to Ireland. Reverend Steevens' loyalty was rewarded after the Restoration of Charles II when in 1660 he was appointed rector of St. Mary's Church in Athlone. He was a conscientious incumbent who, unlike many other clerics of the period, lived in his parish, and his children grew up in Athlone, a prosperous and strongly Protestant town, built on the River Shannon, which served as a boundary between the fertile and largely Anglicized province of Leinster and the much poorer lands of Connacht, to which Irish opponents of Cromwell had been driven during the recent wars. Nothing is known of Grissell's childhood or early life. Whereas her brother was sent to the local grammar school and later to Trinity College, where he studied first divinity and then medicine, she was probably educated at home, perhaps by her father or mother. Constance is a shadowy figure, but she was certainly literate and was probably also a capable manager: in his will, John Steevens appointed her his "whole and sole executrix" and left to her such of his books as she wished "to reserve for her own use." In the same document, drawn up in 1682, shortly before his death, he bequeathed an equal inheritance to his two children, leaving to Richard £300 and the remainder of his books, and to Grissell £300 and a silver tankard presented to him by his parishioners.

Grissell and her mother would have had little reason to remain in Athlone after John Steevens' death. The outbreak in 1690 of the war between the forces of James II and William of Orange, in which Athlone was of major strategic importance, would surely have persuaded them to leave the town if they had not already done so. The fact that Constance, when she died some time after 1691, was buried in St. Peter's Church in Dublin suggests that she and Grissell had settled there to be near Richard, who was rapidly acquiring a considerable reputation in his profession.

Having completed his medical studies, Richard Steevens had opened a practice in Dublin in 1687. In 1692, he became one of the 14 Fellows of the College of Physicians in Ireland and in 1703 and again in 1710, the year of his death, he was elected president of the college. His practice was apparently a financially rewarding one, and in the course of his career he was able to invest in property to a value of £10,000, while accumulating over £1,700 in capital. This was the estate which in his will, dated December 14, 1710, the day before his death, he bequeathed to trustees for the use of his sister during her lifetime, and after her death "to provide one proper place or building within the City of Dublin for an hospital for maintaining and curing from time to time such sick and wounded persons whose distempers and wounds are curable."

Having assured her brother of her support for his scheme, Grissell now set about expediting it. In 1712, she submitted a petition to Queen *Anne, in which she set out plans for a hospital and requested a grant of land on which to begin building. When this proved unsuccessful, she determined to undertake the enterprise herself, financing the project out of her own inheritance, with the exception of £150 per year which she reserved for her own maintenance. On July 11, 1717, she executed a deed of trust, appointing 15 trustees, to whom she transferred £2,000 from her own private fortune, with which to purchase a site and to begin the building of a hospital. These trustees included those named by her brother as trustees in his will, as well as the aged but extremely able archbishop of Dublin, William King, who now, and until his death in 1729, became one of her most active supporters. Three years later, Grissell Steevens enlisted the aid of another notable churchman when she requested that Dr. Jonathan Swift, dean of St. Patrick's Cathedral, should be appointed to the board, of which he remained a member until his death.

At the first meeting on August 14, 1717, the board of trustees addressed the question of a site for the proposed hospital. A piece of ground of about three and a half acres, "lying between the end of St. James' Street and Bow Bridge," at the edge of the city and close to some of the poorest quarters, was suggested as a suitable location; Steevens' approval was sought and obtained, and the land was purchased by the trustees from its owner, Sir Samuel Cooke, for £600. Since there were neither quays nor a bridge over the River Liffey near the site, it was necessary to open a new road and arrange a ferry to carry materials for the building across the river. Meanwhile, Thomas Burgh, one of the trustees, who was the chief architectural and engineering authority in Ireland at that time, as well as architect of the Library in Trinity College, Dublin, and of the old Custom House on Essex Quay, was asked to draw up plans for the hospital.

According to a stone plaque above the entrance gate, construction began in 1720, and King, in a letter written in August of that year, reported that "they have proceeded so far in the building as to provide timber and agree for stones and are laying out the ground and intend to lay the foundation next spring." The scheme continued to be heavily dependent on Steevens' generosity. In 1722, King wrote that she "has so far gone into her brother's project, that she has advanced £400 every year towards building the hospital." Progress was reasonably rapid until 1724, when the building was reported ready for plastering, but then delays, possibly arising from lack of money, possibly from other factors, apparently set in. Another difficulty was posed by the fact that, in the decade since Richard Steevens' death, a number of his original trustees had themselves died: in 1730, the Irish Parliament constituted a new Board of Governors, which included prominent figures in church and state as well as all of Grissell Steevens' surviving trustees. In the same year, the committee established to oversee the erection of the hospital was asked "to consider of the number of curables to be received into the House," but a year later the institution was still not open. Steevens persisted, stressing her desire that patients be admitted without further delay and the committee was asked "to fit up the House for the reception of forty persons." In March 1733, the Church of Ireland Primate Hugh Boulter, one of the recently appointed governors, reported to the Board that she had deposited with him the sum of £500, "for the subsistence of the poor that shall be received into the Hospital and providing medicines," and the governors, in thanking her for this donation, informed her that they would "with the utmost expedition" have the house ready to receive patients. In July, its imminent opening was announced to the populace and to potential patients in handbills and in advertisements in the local newspapers. Meanwhile, the Board met to draw up rules for the management and running of the hospital: patients were to be admitted by a committee, which must include a physician or surgeon, on Monday and Friday of each week; sick and wounded persons of all religions were to be admitted, provided their disease was curable and was neither venereal or infectious, and, except in the case of those suffering from "sudden and violent accidents," a certificate of poverty, signed either by one of the governors or by an officer of the applicant's own parish, was to be submitted. The daily diet for the patients was drawn up, officers and staff were appointed and their duties prescribed, and on Monday, July 23, 1733, the hospital was at last officially declared open. Eight men and two women were accepted on that day, and by the end of the month there were 22 patients in the house. During the first year of its existence, 248 patients were admitted, of whom 164 were "dismissed cured," 26 were noted as "incurable," 19 died and 39 remained "in the House under cure." In fact, the hospital was still incomplete at the time of its opening, and further additions were made as funds became available for them. In 1737, Primate Boulter had a ward of ten beds fitted up at his expense, which he maintained until his death five years later, and in 1742, following the receipt of funds from a charitable lottery, a new ward, later known as Madam Steevens's Ward, was established.

Some time before the opening of the hospital, Steevens herself had moved into a ground-floor apartment which had been set aside for her. Although then about 80 years old, she almost certainly continued to take an active interest in its affairs, although, according to the hospital historian, T.P.C. Kirkpatrick, only one instance of direct intervention is recorded: in October 1735, Owen Lewis, the second surgeon, was "at the desire of Mrs. Steevens . . . dismissed from the service of the Hospital" for an unspecified reason. She also continued to act as an invaluable source of financial support. The hospital was maintained by voluntary subscriptions and occasional donations and legacies: in 1728, for in-

stance, *Esther Johnson, Swift's "Stella," possibly at the instigation of the dean, left £1,000 for the maintenance of a chaplain, while Dr. Edward Worth, one of the trustees, who died in 1732, left £1,000 and his valuable library of about 4,500 volumes to the institution. However, the hospital's principal benefactor continued to be Madam Steevens herself. From July 1717, when she signed the deed which provided for its building, to Christmas 1746, she donated in all £14,791 to the foundation. In her will, dated April 15, 1740, she left the residue of her estate, following the discharge of a number of bequests to friends and servants, "to the Governors of my brother Dr. Steevens's Hospital and their successors for the use of the said hospital," and a sum of £225 was subsequently paid to the Governors.

> 'Twould be a sin and a shame of us all, when the good woman has done so much and all that was in her power, . . . if we should be backward and obstruct so great and charitable a work for want of a little care and industry.
>
> —Archbishop William King

Although in 1740 Grissell Steevens described herself as "weak and infirm in body," she lived for another six years, dying on March 18, 1746, at the age of 93 in her apartment at the hospital. In her will, she had asked to be "buried late at night in St. Peter's Church, Dublin," where her mother and brother already lay, and that her funeral should be conducted "in as private a manner as possible." However, her request to be buried in St. Peter's was for some reason disregarded, and she was instead buried on March 20 in St. James's Church. Oddly, at a governors' meeting held on that day, no mention of her death and no appreciation of her work was recorded, and it was left to one of her former employees to arrange what might be regarded as a more suitable final resting place. When the former matron and steward of the hospital, Ann Challoner, died in 1756, she left instructions that a vault should be built in the hospital chapel, in which were to be placed the bodies of herself and her family and of Madam Steevens, and, in accordance with these directions, the body was transferred from St. James's to the newly built chapel of Dr. Steevens's Hospital.

In reporting Grissell Steevens' death, a contemporary newsheet, Faulkner's *Dublin Journal*, recorded the part which she had played in fulfilling her brother's dying wish:

[She] erected an Hospital at her own expense, and reserving only a small apartment therein for herself, gave yearly during her life not less than £500 for the maintenance and cure of such objects as went thither for relief. More need not be said. "Her works praise her" and "the righteous will be held in everlasting remembrance. Many daughters have done virtuously, but thou excellest them all."

Powerful and authoritarian, but respected in her own lifetime, Grissell Steevens was survived by her reputation, and long after her death she remained a legendary figure to her fellow citizens. During the 19th century, a widely circulated story insisted that Steevens' charity had been inspired by her own deformity, that she had, as the result of a beggarwoman's curse, been born with a pig's face, which she hid behind a thick veil. This rumor had absolutely no foundation in fact. Certainly the portrait painted in about 1740 by Michael Mitchel, and still hanging in the library of the hospital, depicts a face remarkable only for the confidence and steely will which it displays, and the tale as relating to Steevens does not appear in any 18th-century source, although different versions of a similar story were current in Europe and Britain over a century before she was born. A more appropriate memorial was provided by her institution, known to generations of Dubliners as "Madam Steevens's Hospital." Although the hospital itself closed in 1987, the newly restored building in which it was housed survives as one of the glories of Georgian Dublin and as a visible record of Grissell Steevens' benevolence and determination.

**SOURCES:**
Brady, Cheyne. *The History of Steevens's Hospital.* Dublin: Hodges, Smith, 1865.
Kirkpatrick, T.P.C. *History of Dr. Steevens's Hospital, Dublin 1720–1920.* Dublin: University Press, 1924.

**SUGGESTED READING:**
Fleetwood, John. *History of Medicine in Ireland.* Dublin: Browne & Nolan, 1951.
McCracken, J.L. "The social structure and social life, 1714–60," in *A New History of Ireland.* Edited by T.W. Moody and W.E. Vaughan. Vol. IV. Oxford: Clarendon Press, 1986, pp. 31–56.
Owen, David. *English Philanthropy 1660–1960.* London: Oxford University Press, 1965.

**COLLECTIONS:**
"A short history of the hospital founded by Dr. Richard Steevens, 1717–1785, by Samuel Croker King," Gilbert collection MS 108, Dublin City Library.

**Rosemary Raughter**,
freelance writer in women's history,
Dublin, Ireland

## Stefanska, Halina Czerny (1922—).

*See Czerny-Stefanska, Halina.*

## Steichen, Mary (1904–1998).

*See Calderone, Mary Steichen.*

## Steiff, Margarete (1847–1909)

*German entrepreneur who invented the teddy bear. Name variations: Gretel Steiff. Born Margarete Steiff in Giengen on the Brenz, Baden-Württemberg, Germany, in 1847; died in 1909; sister of Fritz Steiff.*

Born in Germany in 1847, Margarete Steiff, known as Gretel, contacted polio when she was 18 months old. The disease left her body paralyzed, except her left hand and arm. Steiff enrolled in a local sewing school and excelled at needlework. In 1872, she opened a dressmaking business; with its success, she opened a factory in 1877.

Throughout the years, Steiff had made toy cloth elephants and pin cushions for friends. In 1879, she added fluffy material to an elephant from a pattern she had seen in the fashion magazine *Modewelt*, and the Steiff toy animals were born. Within a year, her brother Fritz Steiff noticed that her crafts were in demand, and three years later her nephew Richard began to design other animals. In 1904, sister and brother founded their family toy business, Margarete Steiff GmbH, in Giengen. Steiff's most popular toy was the teddy bear, which started a craze that has not ceased. Teddy bears gained huge popularity at the turn of the 20th century, especially with the help of their namesake, Teddy Roosevelt. By 1907, Steiff shipped a million of them to America alone. When Margarete Steiff died two years later at age 62, she left the company to her nieces and nephews. Her nephew Hans-Otto Steiff ran the company as its president from 1951 to 1984 and remained on the board until his death on December 31, 1994. That same month, a Steiff bear—now a collectors' item—had been sold for a record $171,000 at a Christie's auction in London.

## Stein, Charlotte von (1742–1827)

*German playwright and lady-in-waiting who was the beloved of Johann Goethe. Name variations: Charlotte von Schardt; Baroness von Stein. Born Charlotte Albertine Ernestine von Schardt on December 25, 1742, in the duchy of Saxe-Weimar, Germany; died on January 6, 1827, near Weimar; eldest daughter of Johann Wilhelm von Schardt (hofmarschall or master of ceremonies) and Concordia (Irving) von Schardt; married Baron Josias von Stein, on May 8, 1764 (died 1793); children: Karl (b. 1765); Ernst (b. 1767); Fritz (b. 1772); and four daughters who did not survive infancy.*

Charlotte von Stein is remembered for her long friendship with the German poet and novelist Johann Wolfgang von Goethe, whose letters to her have made her almost mythical. Few people know that she was also a dramatist and intellectual figure at the Weimar court.

Born Charlotte von Schardt in 1742 into the minor nobility of Saxe-Weimar, part of the German Empire, she received a good education in philosophy and languages. At age 15, she was sent to the ducal household in Weimar to serve as lady-in-waiting to Duchess *Anna Amalia of Saxe-Weimar (1739–1807), a position commonly held by unmarried aristocratic women at the time. In 1764, the duchess arranged a marriage for Charlotte with Baron Josias von Stein, seven years her senior. He was the duke of Saxe-Weimar's chief equerry, an important administrative figure of considerable wealth.

The couple moved to the von Stein family castle at Kochberg, outside Weimar. Charlotte, now Baroness von Stein, spent most of the next ten years there in relative isolation from her friends and family, and from the cultural life of Weimar. She gave birth to seven children between 1765 and 1775; none of her four daughters survived infancy. She had three surviving sons, although the second, Ernst, was an invalid and would die of cancer at age 20. Seven pregnancies in a decade and the deaths of her daughters took a serious toll on von Stein's physical and mental health; her husband was unaffectionate and distant, and by her own account she suffered from constant loneliness and depression.

But in November 1775, she was introduced to a young though already celebrated poet, Johann Goethe, who seems to have fallen in love with her immediately. An emotional and sensitive intellectual, Goethe was attracted to the baroness' beauty as well as to her artistic sensibility and interest in the new Enlightenment learning. Thus began an intimate relationship which was to influence much of Goethe's later writing. He visited von Stein often at Kochberg, where they spent hours discussing poetry, literature, philosophy, art, and science. Goethe wrote many lyrical poems in her honor, and characters clearly based on von Stein—or on his idealized vision of her—appeared in his plays Iphigenia and Tasso, in the form of wise and benevolent women who have a healing effect on the male characters and help them overcome their conflicts.

As the friendship deepened, they also began a lengthy correspondence. Only Goethe's side of the epistolary relationship survives, however, as von Stein demanded the return of her letters at the end of their affiliation and destroyed them. Still, almost 1,800 notes and letters by Goethe to von Stein, full of intense emotion and worshipful praise of her virtues, testify to his devotion and ardor. One letter alone from von Stein to Goethe is known to exist, from the early months of the friendship, but it is quite revealing; in it, she expresses her renewed joy in life, her interest in the world around her due to Goethe's adoration. It is uncertain whether they were ever involved in a physical relationship; his letters show that von Stein was concerned with protecting her family's honor. Yet after 1781, the tone of Goethe's letters became overtly erotic and occasionally mention the possibility of marriage, which would seem to indicate that their relationship had become sexual, although historians still debate the question.

Physical or not, their friendship lasted until 1786 when Goethe left Weimar for Italy. He continued to write every day, but when he returned in 1788, they agreed to end the relationship. Goethe soon moved in with another woman, **Christiane von Vulpius**, whom he later married. However, von Stein and he remained acquaintances, still seeing one another often at court functions and sharing the same circle of friends among the Weimar elite, including the famed German writers Johann Herder and Friedrich Schiller and their families. Although some of von Stein's correspondence after 1788 indicate that she regretted the end of the affair, by 1793 they had reconciled.

In 1793, Josias von Stein died, though his widow had little reason to mourn him much. She continued to be an active figure in the intellectual life at the Weimar ducal court, and took up writing as well. Her first drama, Dido, features a poet clearly modeled on Goethe. Other plays followed, including Rino: A Play in Five Acts and Die Zwey Emilien. Although all of her works are tragedies and were previously interpreted as stemming from anger over the end of Goethe's love for her, they have lately been re-evaluated by feminist literary scholars who note the strong and fully developed female characters in von Stein's plays. The women are intellectually and politically active, and are shown as better leaders than the male politicians they come to replace. This re-evaluation has gained for von Stein a legitimate place among the female literary figures of what is now called the "Age of Goethe."

Charlotte von Stein did not remarry but remained a social figure at court until her death at her country home outside of Weimar in 1827, at age 85.

**SOURCES:**

Boyle, Nicholas. *Goethe: The Poet and the Age.* NY: Oxford University Press, 1992.

Cocalis, Susan L., and Rose Ferrel, eds. *Thalia's Daughters: German Women Dramatists from the Eighteenth Century to the Present.* Tübingen, Germany: Francke, 1996.

Goethe, Johann. *Selections from Goethe's Letters to Frau von Stein 1776–89.* Edited and translated by Robert M. Browning. Columbia, SC: Camden House, 1990.

**Laura York**, M.A. in History,
University of California, Riverside, California

# Stein, Edith (1891–1942)

*German philosopher, interpreter of the phenomenologist Edward Husserl and Jewish convert to Catholicism who became a nun and died at the Auschwitz concentration camp. Name variations: Sister Teresa Benedicta of the Cross; Sister Teresia Benedicata; Saint Teresa Benedicta. Born on October 12, 1891, in Breslau, Germany (now Wroclaw, Poland); died on August 9, 1942, in a gas chamber in Auschwitz; youngest of seven surviving children of Siegfried Stein (who had a lumber business) and Auguste Courant Stein (who continued the lumber business after her husband's death); attended Victoria School in Breslau, University of Breslau, and Göttingen University; awarded doctorate from University of Freiburg summa cum laude on August 3, 1916.*

*Served with the wartime Red Cross (February–October, 1916); worked as personal assistant to Edward Husserl (1916–18); baptized a Roman Catholic (January 1, 1922); taught at St. Magdalena in Speyer (1923–31); entered a Discalced Carmelite convent in Cologne, Germany (October 14, 1933); declared venerable, first step in the process of being canonized a Roman Catholic saint (January 26, 1987); second step, beatified (May 1, 1987); elevated to sainthood by Pope John Paul II (October 11, 1998).*

*Selected publications: (English translation)* Life in a Jewish Family, 1891–1916 *(Washington, DC: ICS Publications, 1986);* Finite and Eternal Being *(published posthumously, 1950).*

As a Jewish scholar of philosophy who converted to Roman Catholicism, then became a nun and died in the Nazi persecution of the Jews, Edith Stein is enigmatic and paradoxical. In her youth, she tried to live by intellect and reason; then, at age 30, she became captivated by spiritual matters. Having sought to live on an elevated, cerebral plane, she found herself persecuted for having Jewish blood. She then tried, unsuccessfully, to persuade Pope Pius XI to speak out against Nazi genocide against the Jews.

Some see her as the personification of interfaith unity. Others regard her as one who rejected her people at the darkest moment in their history. The controversy centers less around her right to make personal choices than the treatment of her life story after her death. Critics say the Roman Catholic Church is wrong to single out for sainthood one who rejected her Judaism at the pivotal time when the Nazis killed six million Jews.

Edith Stein was born in Breslau, Germany (now Wroclaw, Poland), on October 12, 1891; it was the Day of Atonement, Yom Kippur, the holiest day of the Jewish year. Her father Siegfried died on a business trip when Edith was 21 months old, leaving her mother **Auguste Courant Stein** to carry on the family lumber business, which she did with great success. Tiny and delicate, the youngest of seven siblings, Stein displayed great intellectual gifts and dedication from her earliest days as a student at the Victoria School in Breslau. When she began school, she took down a volume of Schiller and attempted to read it to her mother. "How far I got at the time, I cannot remember," she wrote. "But it is easy to surmise that such sudden outbursts alarmed my relatives. They called it 'nerves' and tried, as much as possible, to shield me from overexcitement."

As a girl, and throughout her life, she had a small sturdy frame, wavy dark hair and a serious, contemplative demeanor. She was shy and self-contained, and her closest friends were her sisters **Erna** and **Rosa Stein**, who were a few years older than herself. Seeking "truth," Stein distinguished herself in philosophy during her early studies at the University of Breslau. Her sister Erna, who also studied there in those years, wrote:

> We had a large circle of friends of both sexes with whom we spent our free time and our vacations in an atmosphere of freedom and lack of constraint which was unusual for that time. Because of her unassailable logic and her wide knowledge in matters of literature and philosophy, Edith set the pace for us in these discussions.

Stein enrolled at the University of Göttingen to study with Edmund Husserl, one of the 20th century's most prominent philosophers and an important influence on both Martin Heidegger and Jean-Paul Sartre. Husserl founded the school of phenomenology, which studied the nature of experience and held that consciousness exists only in relation to the objects it considers. His idea was that truth is objective, not relative, and that there is a knowable world of phenomena. In Stein's student days, phenomenology was a radical, controversial and exhilarating departure from the "idealism" of Emmanuel Kant. Philosophers like Stein defended it with religious fervor. Many of her professors, including Husserl, and some of her fellow students had converted from Judaism to Christianity, a few for career advancement. Stein herself was without faith. Although her mother was devoutly religious, she had provided little religious training for her children, and she tried, in vain, to persuade Edith to acknowledge God.

Like other philosophy students, Stein called Husserl "The Master." Girlfriends teased her that she thought of Husserl when other girls were dreaming of *busserl* (Austrian slang for kiss), but her favorite teacher was Adolf Reinach, Husserl's assistant. Edith became one of the favored students whom Adolf and his wife **Anna Reinach** invited into their home. Stein's unfinished autobiography, *Life in a Jewish Family*, makes clear her admiration for him as a person and a professor and her appreciation that Anna was so gracious in sharing their private hours.

What Stein called this "placid" student life ended on June 28, 1914, when a young Serbian assassinated Archduke Francis Ferdinand, heir to the thrones of Austria and Hungary, along with Countess *Sophie Chotek, in Sarajevo. Austria declared war on Serbia a month later. One by one, European nations joined in the war as each side called in its allies. Edith's lectures at Göttingen were suspended as she and her fellow Germans braced for invasion from Russia or France. Adolf Reinach volunteered for service and went to the front. In April 1915, Stein joined the Red Cross as a nurse's aide and went to work in the typhoid ward at a hospital for infectious diseases in Austria that accepted patients from all over the Austro-Hungarian Empire. On her first leave, she followed the practice of carrying letters her colleagues wanted mailed in Germany. A customs officer accused her of circumventing wartime censorship, and she was acquitted only after an appeal by the Red Cross. At home in Breslau, she taught Latin at her alma mater for a brief time and resumed work on her doctoral thesis.

In this work, "On the Problem of Empathy," she discussed the act of empathy as specific knowledge and then treated subjects that she described as "personally close to my heart and which continually occupied me anew in all later works: the constitution of the human person." In this, she included the self, the stream of consciousness, and aspects of individual personality and character. She submitted her thesis in three volumes to Husserl shortly after Easter 1916, and was awarded her doctorate summa cum laude on August 3. Husserl was then at the University of Freiburg, and she became his private assistant. She felt equal to the position only because other qualified male students were in military service. Husserl was coping with the loss of his 17-year-old son who had died at the front. As he expanded his theories, Stein asked him to read over his former work and evaluate his new thinking in light of it. Husserl's response was that his earlier writing was dated and might as well be burned. Frustrated, she resigned her post early in 1918. Husserl gave her a recommendation, but her applications for teaching posts were ignored, which she suspected was due to Husserl's spite. She returned to Breslau, tutored college and university students and wrote articles and essays.

> *What was not included in my plans lay in God's plan.*
>
> —Edith Stein

Reinach died in action in 1917, which was for Edith a devastating loss. A year later, Anna Reinach asked her to put his papers in order. Stein was impressed by the courage and strength Anna found in Christianity, to which both Reinachs had converted before his death. Then in the summer of 1921, when visiting a Lutheran friend, Edith found in her library the autobiography of the 19th-century French nun *Thérèse of Lisieux whose simple devotion to Christ elevated her to mysticism.

Stein studied the teachings of the Catholic Church so thoroughly that priests said she did not need to take formal instruction. Although the Stein family observed the religious holidays, Stein had never had instruction in her Jewish faith. Still, her mother was devout and regarded Edith's baptism on January 1, 1922, as a betrayal. Stein sought to join the Carmelite Order like St. Thérèse had, but the nuns urged her to wait in deference to the feelings of her mother and because she could do so much good in the world. Stein accepted a teaching position at St. Magdalena, a training institute for women teachers in Speyer. There she lived ascetically among Dominican nuns, rising early, wearing patched linen clothes and kneeling through three masses a day. When a nun commented that it was sometimes hard to stay awake during prayers, Stein rebuked her for her laziness. She lectured on the education and role of Catholic women, calling for more options in both religious and secular life. She said of priesthood for women, "Dogmatically, it seems to me that nothing could prevent the church from introducing such an unheard-of novelty."

Stein felt that she could win understanding for the Jews, and their history in Germany, by writing *Life in a Jewish Family*, the story of her life and family, which she thought would underscore the commonality of Jews and Christians as well as the German Jews' historic patriotism to their country.

She translated the letters of the Catholic convert and English cardinal John Henry Newman into German in 1928. The next year, she wrote a comparison of the philosophy of the 13th-century theologian St. Thomas Aquinas and phenomenology, the purpose of which was to introduce Thomist thought to modern philosophers. She then began *Finite and Eternal Being* on which she worked for seven years, but which, when it was finished, could not be published because she was Jewish. (It finally appeared posthumously in 1950.)

Her career as a lecturer before Catholic groups took her to France, Switzerland, and Austria, and she gave up her post at St. Magdalena in 1931. Stein insisted that her basic message was that one was completely dependent upon God. She borrowed a phrase from the Latin orator Cato and called it her *ceterum censeo*, a reiterated challenge. Increasingly, she felt that it was impossible for a person to exert a direct influence on life and that one was subject to God's plan. She renewed her efforts to obtain a professorship at Freiburg, but was unsuccessful. Martin Heidegger, another protégé of Husserl who knew her from Göttingen, taught there but declined to exert himself on her behalf. Heidegger, the renowned author of *Being and Time*, won fame for holding that anxiety is both a creative force and a basic characteristic of authenticity. He also supported the Nazis and helped to ban Jews from German academic life.

In 1932, the year Hitler came to power, Stein was appointed a lecturer at the German Institute for Scientific Pedagogy in Münster, which was run by Catholics. Her services were terminated on April 19, 1933, when Hitler and his Nazi Party banned Jews from teaching.

In the hope that her position as a Catholic, a Jew, and a respected academic would prove to be persuasive, Edith Stein wrote to Pope Pius XI, asking him write an encyclical publicly condemning the anti-Semitism of the Nazi Party. Critics feel that if the pope had spoken out at that early and pivotal time he could have persuaded German Catholics to stop Hitler, but her request was refused and the pope said nothing. He did, however, send her a papal blessing for herself and her family.

Since she had never established herself as a philosopher and her academic career had been ended because of her Jewish heritage, Stein felt the time was right to fulfill her dream of becoming a nun. Her niece, **Suzanne M. Batzdorff**, recalled running into Edith at the dentist's office when Suzanne was 12 and boldly telling Stein she was abandoning her people. Batzdorff wrote: "She remained gravely attentive throughout and then replied that she did not see the step she was about to take as a betrayal. Entering a convent could not, she said, guarantee her safety, nor could it shut out the reality of the world outside. As a Carmelite, she said, she would remain a part of her family and of the Jewish people. To her, that was entirely logical; to us, her Jewish relatives, it could never be a convincing argument. Despite our love for her, a gap had opened between us that could never be bridged."

Soon after Stein's 42nd birthday, she left for the Carmelite convent in Cologne. Her mother, who was 84, bade her a tearful, loving farewell, but never saw her again. Stein's older sister Rosa also decided to convert to Catholicism, although she waited until after their mother's death in 1934. Stein the intellectual became Sister Teresa Benedicta of the Cross, the humble nun. Growing up in a prosperous family, she had never done housework; now she mopped the convent floors and dusted its banisters and tables awkwardly, but happily. Her prioress commented that her joining the convent was "a descent from the height of a brilliant career into the depths of insignificance." Stein had found a more joyous approach to life. To entertain the other nuns, she acted in a Chaucerian skit in a red wig, and she became sufficiently tolerant of human frailty that she fell asleep during meditation.

Just before Kristallnacht (Night of Broken Glass), November 9, 1938, when the Nazis stepped up their persecution by rounding up Jews and destroying their property, Stein wrote to the mother superior of an Ursuline convent in Dorsten, Germany: "I cannot help thinking again and again of Queen *Esther, who was taken from her people for the express purpose of standing before the King for her people. I am a very poor and helpless little Esther, but the King who chose me is infinitely great and merciful."

Rosa Stein joined her sister in the convent, although she did not take vows. Edith tried to transfer to a Swiss convent for safety, but declined to go when nuns there refused to take

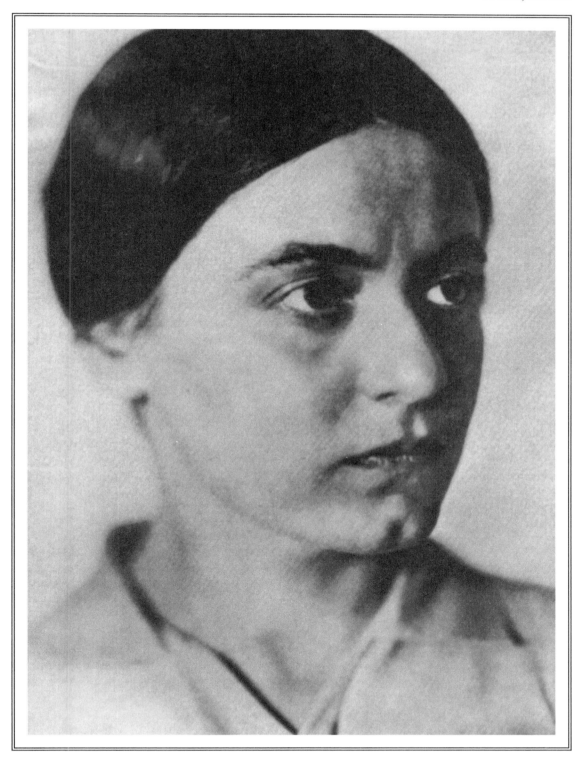

Edith
Stein

Rosa. For Stein's safety and that of her fellow nuns, her superiors transferred her, along with Rosa, to Echt in the Netherlands. Satisfied with convent life, she nonetheless remained involved with the world. Stein began writing a life of St. John of the Cross. When her sister nuns said they would not vote in the country's elections because they were rigged, Stein objected and said they must do their duty and vote. She, as a Jew, was disenfranchised. Edith and Rosa were summoned for questioning by the SS police in the spring of 1942; instead of greeting them with the official "Heil Hitler!," she saluted, "Praised be Jesus." The Netherlands were occupied by German forces, and when Dutch bishops protested against their attacks on Jews, the Nazis rounded up Catholics of Jewish origin. On the evening of August 2, immediately after the hour of meditation, they arrested the Stein sisters. Nuns who were present said Edith told Rosa, "Come. We are going for our people." She asked that the nuns send them clothes, showing that she was ignorant of what lay ahead.

While she was being held by the Nazis, Edith wrote to her mother superior urging her to fight on behalf of her and her sister. Early on August 7, 1942, Rosa and Edith Stein were deported from the Westerbork detention camp to Auschwitz. She dropped "heart-rending" notes from the train as they passed through towns where she had lived. Edith Stein and her sister Rosa died in the gas chamber, probably on August 9, 1942, soon after their arrival at Auschwitz. Their brother Paul, his wife, and their sister **Frida Stein** also died in the Holocaust.

Less than 50 years later, in 1987, Edith Stein was declared venerable by the Roman Catholic Church, the initial step towards canonization. That same year, two-year-old **Teresa Benedicta McCarthy** of Massachusetts, who had been named after Stein, recovered without ill effect after swallowing a massive overdose of Tylenol. Her parents had asked friends to pray to Sister Teresa Benedicta—Edith Stein—while their daughter lay suffering from severe liver damage in the hospital, and doctors could provide no scientific explanation for her complete recovery. This was judged by the Catholic Church the miracle performed through the intercession of Stein necessary for her canonization. On October 11, 1998, she was pronounced a saint and a martyr for Catholicism by Pope John Paul II, who spoke of her as "an eminent daughter of Israel and a faithful daughter of the church." Stein's canonization—perhaps, although not definitely, the first of a person born Jewish since the early years of the Church—came amidst bitter protests from many Jewish groups, which noted that she had been killed not because she was Catholic but because she was Jewish. (At Auschwitz, she is said to have answered a guard's question by declaring herself Catholic; the Nazi responded by calling her a "damn Jew.") Many also questioned the Vatican's reasons for canonizing a Jewish convert who, on becoming a nun, offered her life to God "for the sins of the unbelieving people" while the Church itself had still not responded fully to questions about its conduct during the Holocaust. While not replying to such criticisms directly, the pope

alluded to them during the canonization mass for Stein in St. Peter's Basilica. "In celebrating now and later the memory of the new saint," he said, "we will be unable not to also remember year after year the Shoah, that savage plan to eliminate a people, which cost millions of our Jewish brothers and sisters their lives."

**SOURCES:**
Batzdorff, Susanne M., ed. and trans. *Edith Stein Selected Writings*. Springfield, IL: Templegate, 1990.
*The Boston Globe*. October 10, 1998, p. A2; October 12, 1998, pp. A1, A8.
*The New York Times*. October 11, 1998, pp. 1, 14; October 12, 1998, p. A9.
*People*. May 19, 1997, pp. 161–162.
Stein, Edith. *Life in a Jewish Family, 1891–1916*. Washington, DC: ICS Publications, 1986.
*Time*. August 1, 1955; May 4, 1987.

**SUGGESTED READING:**
Herbstrith, Waltraud. *Edith Stein*. Trans. by Bernard Bonowitz. San Francisco, CA: Harper & Row, 1986.

**COLLECTIONS:**
Edith Stein archive, Carmelite Monastery, Cologne, Germany.

**Kathleen Brady,**
author of *Ida Tarbell: Portrait of a Muckraker*
(University of Pittsburgh Press)

# Stein, Gertrude (1874–1946)

*American novelist, poet, short-story writer, librettist, memoirist, and art collector whose house on the Left Bank of Paris became a salon for the "Lost Generation." Born in Allegheny, Pennsylvania, on February 3, 1874; died in Neuilly, France, on July 27, 1946; youngest child of Daniel Stein and Amelia (Keyser) Stein; entered Harvard Annex (Radcliffe), 1894; Harvard, B.A., 1898; attended Johns Hopkins Medical School, 1897–1901; lived with Alice B. Toklas for 39 years; never married; no children.*

*With brother Leo, settled in Paris, France (autumn 1903); met Pablo Picasso, Paris (1905); met Alice B. Toklas, Paris (September 8, 1907); published* The Making of Americans *(1925); went on lecture tour, Cambridge and Oxford universities (1926); established "Plain Edition" publishing company (1930); published* The Autobiography of Alice B. Toklas *(1933); premier of opera,* Four Saints in Three Acts, *New York (1934); went on lecture tour of U.S. (October 1934–May 1935); published* Everybody's Autobiography *(1937); published* Paris France *(1940); spent war years in Bilignin, France (1939–44); published* Wars I Have Seen *(1945); entered American Hospital, Neuilly, France (July 19, 1946); death of Alice B. Toklas (March 7, 1967).*

"It takes a lot of time to be a genius," Gertrude Stein declared, "you have to sit around so much doing nothing really doing nothing." And that is what she was and what she did. Catastrophic wars, economic depression, political upheavals, and rifts and quarrels with family and friends were not allowed to intrude on Stein's pursuit of "glory" as a self-proclaimed literary genius. She refused to remember things that might disturb her tranquillity and ignored events she could not bear to acknowledge.

Gertrude Stein was the youngest of five children, born in 1874 in Allegheny, Pennsylvania, into a middle-class Jewish family that doted on her. Being the youngest, she claimed, "saves you a lot of bother, everybody takes care of you." And everybody did, all her life. Her father and uncle were in the clothing business, providing a comfortable life for the Steins, albeit a rather itinerant lifestyle. By age five, Gertrude had lived in Vienna, Paris, and Baltimore, and in 1880, Daniel Stein moved his family to Oakland, California, where he was involved in the cable-car business. As a child, Gertrude and her brother Leo forged a bond that excluded the other members of the family. They had little respect for their parents; when Gertrude was 14, her mother **Amelia Stein** died but was not missed since "we had all already had the habit of doing without her," as Gertrude later wrote. Her father garnered no respect from Gertrude either. He simply became "more of a bother than he had been," according to his precocious daughter. The attitude of Leo and Gertrude towards their siblings was equally dismissive: Michael was much older than they, Simon was "fat and slow-witted," and **Bertha** was judged to be "simply annoying." Life became more pleasant, according to Gertrude, after her father died; Michael, age 26, became head of the family and moved everyone to San Francisco. For Gertrude, life revolved around books and food, and her brilliant ally and friend, Leo. Life was pleasant, and Michael successfully managed to provide for the future financial independence of his siblings because as Gertrude said, "none of us could earn . . . enough to live on and something had to be done."

Stein's adolescent years were difficult. Her large, bulky body (over 200 pounds) and confused sexual identity made her self-conscious. She and Leo "never said a word to each other about their inner life," and Stein was forced to confront her physical and emotional problems alone. In 1892, Leo entered Harvard University, and the following year Gertrude, who never finished high school, enrolled in Harvard Annex (which became Radcliffe College in 1894) and took up philosophy. She studied with William James whose teachings influenced her views on

how the human mind works and on the concept of time. The latter led to Stein's literary device, the "continuous present," the most marked and original feature of her writing style. Active in drama and philosophy clubs, and developing an interest in psychology, Stein found her environment intellectually stimulating. She published two articles in Harvard's *Psychological Review* and decided to pursue a career in medicine; admitted to Johns Hopkins School of Medicine in 1897, she received her B.A. degree from Harvard the next year. Leo was also a student at Johns Hopkins, and they shared a house in Baltimore.

Unable to sustain an interest in her medical studies, Gertrude failed her exams and left to join Leo in Europe. No doubt she was bored, as she claimed, but Stein also needed to escape from a love-triangle in which she felt trapped and vulnerable. She had fallen in love with **May Bookstaver** who continued her own affair with another woman. Gertrude was unable to handle the emotional turmoil and fled America to live with Leo, her source of security and guidance. After traveling in Italy and England, Leo decided to settle in Paris and become an artist. His decision would change Gertrude's life forever; in 1903, she took up residence with Leo at 27 rue de Fleurus in Paris. An expatriate and a writer, Gertrude Stein became solidly entrenched in the artistic and literary life of her adopted country. "Paris was where the twentieth century was," she stated, and it was here, as **Shari Benstock** wrote, that "she was to discover her sexual identity, her creative talents, and to establish . . . the most important artistic salon on the Left Bank." Having purged the hurtful vestiges of her love affair by writing a novel, *Q.E.D.* (*Things As They Are*, 1950), Stein set out "to avoid excitements and cultivate serenity" in new surroundings, in a new century.

Even among the cultural avant-garde of Paris, Gertrude and Leo Stein were regarded as eccentrics; the "odd-couple" smoked cigars, wore unmodish brown corduroy clothes, and filled their walls with modern art by obscure young artists such as Pablo Picasso, Matisse, Cézanne, Renoir, and Gauguin. By 1905, Picasso and Matisse had become friends with the Steins and brought their friends to visit; the Stein "salon" was inaugurated, attracting many of the artistic and literary luminaries of the 20th century. "Everybody brought somebody and they came at any time and it began to be a nuisance and it was in this way that Saturday evenings began," Gertrude recalled. Stein and Picasso were close friends, wrote one biographer, "similar in many ways. Both were direct . . . greedy, childish in their enthusiasms. . . . And both at that time, were beginning to be convinced they were geniuses." Picasso wanted to paint Stein's portrait; after about 90 sittings, he was dissatisfied with the face and painted it out. No one thought the mask-like visage looked like her. "It will," Picasso said. And it did. "It is the only reproduction of me which is always I, for me," Gertrude claimed. Leo was among the fiercest critics of Picasso's style and his sister's writing style; it was all "Godalmighty rubbish," he concluded. Having rejected Gertrude's literary efforts, he found himself rejected by her.

Stein devoted herself to her craft, writing late at night until dawn. She had completed a novel, *Fernhurst*, based on a lesbian sex scandal at Bryn Mawr in the 1890s, and began a long novel, *The Making of Americans*, in which her theory of human nature is elucidated: humans have certain characteristics which make them individuals but share "similar patterns of behavior and thought"; they are all "the same but different," she believed. Repetition is the distinguishing hallmark of her writing; repetition of action revealed people's "bottom nature," as she saw it, and repetition in speech "was the way in which it was expressed." This led to her idea of constancy, the "'continuous present,' a prolonging of the present moment or thought by the device of circling and retracing," a means of suspending "the passage of time inside a narrative form," without beginning, middle, or end. The works of Stein and Picasso incorporated the notion that "each part [of a composition] is as important as the whole." And in "Melanctha," a short story about a black woman and her lover, one finds all the elements of Stein's theories on language and the "continuous present." She laid no claim to having invented any style or device; as she wrote a friend, "If the communication is perfect the words have life, and that is all there is to good writing, putting down on the paper words which dance and weep and make love and fight and kiss and perform miracles."

As Stein developed her theories and honed her unique literary style, she slowly emerged from Leo's shadow. He had dominated their Saturday evenings and supervised their collection of art. But he was a man without direction, lacking perseverance in all his pursuits, and never became adept at creating or accomplishing anything. As he and Gertrude grew apart, Leo floundered, a sad, drifting figure compared to his vibrant, self-driven, androgynous sister who resembled a Roman emperor. With Gertrude able to live a comfortable, secure life, her dependence on her brother ended abruptly in 1907. Michael and his wife **Sarah Samuels Stein** had settled in Paris several years earlier, and Sarah invited Gertrude to meet two women from California who were visiting them.

#### ❧▶ Toklas, Alice B. (1877–1967)

*Longtime companion of Gertrude Stein. Born Alice Babette Toklas in San Francisco, California, on April 30, 1877; died on March 7, 1967; first child and only daughter of Ferdinand Toklas (a wholesaler in dry goods) and Emma (Levinsky) Toklas; attended Miss Lake's School for Girls; studied music at Washington University; lived with Gertrude Stein for 39 years.*

"I was the child who was raised by women, and influenced by women," said Alice B. Toklas, who grew up on San Francisco under the watchful eye of her mother, aunts, great-aunts, and grandmother, while her father marched off to make money, often commuting between Seattle and San Francisco. At 8, Toklas joined her parents on a grand tour of Europe; at 13, her beloved grandmother died, and she moved with her family to Seattle. When her mother **Emma Levinsky Toklas** was diagnosed with cancer, the family returned to San Francisco where Emma died on March 10, 1897. Alice, then about six weeks shy of her 20th birthday, became "the responsible grand-daughter," the cook and housekeeper in a house of men, who sat on her opinions while they talked politics. She hated it.

Toklas had a strong desire to see Paris, and, having experienced the San Francisco earthquake firsthand in 1906, an equally strong desire to leave the town of her birth. Then **Sarah Samuels (Stein)**, a friend of a close friend of Alice's, married Michael Stein. In 1907 in Paris, while visiting Sarah, Alice met *Gertrude Stein, the woman who held her "complete attention" from that first meeting on, "as she did for all the many years I knew her," said Toklas, "until her death, and all these empty ones since then."

Alice Toklas was under five feet tall and had a cyst between her eyebrows. To conceal it, she combed her hair forward and pulled hats down to her eyes. She put forth the image of a self-effacing handmaiden to Stein, but their true relationship was quite different. Alice had a strong nature and a great deal of sway over Stein, despite her unassuming presence.

*G*ertrude
*S*tein

On September 8, Gertrude met ◄⅜ **Alice B. Toklas** who would be her lifelong companion, her lover and wife. Soon Alice became indispensable to Gertrude's physical and mental well-being. While on holiday in Italy in the summer of 1908, Stein proposed to Toklas; they would remain a devoted couple until Gertrude's death in 1946. In 1909, Alice moved in with Gertrude and Leo, an awkward arrangement which led to a final rift between the Steins. Finally in 1913, Leo left, and ceased to exist for Gertrude. Toklas provided a quiet domestic environment (serving as secretary-typist, cook, and household manager) in which Stein's genius could concentrate on creating her "modernist" masterpieces.

The two women were convinced that it was essential to find a publisher for Gertrude's work, *Three Lives*. The editor of Grafton Press called it "a very peculiar book" and assumed Stein would be amenable to corrections of her punctuation and syntax—she was not. Question marks and exclamation points are "positively revolting," she noted, and commas "are servile," but she allowed that periods are acceptable, having "a life of their own." When the book was published in 1909, it drew praise and strengthened Stein's confidence in herself. This "eccentric of the Paris avant-garde" wrote every night, never revising, a slow, methodical process that was mirrored in the "slow heavy rhythm" of her daily life. To Stein, "what is known as work is something that I cannot do it makes me nervous, I can read and write and I can wander around and I can drive an automobile and I can talk and that is almost all, doing anything else makes me nervous." However, she was a prolific writer, and by 1912, she had completed her 1,000-page epic, *The Making of Americans*, as well as *Tender Buttons* and a collection called *Portraits*. The latter contained a portrait ("Ada") written with Toklas, "a joint declaration of their love." The contented, happy life they shared was evident to their many friends who visited them. Their social gatherings, however, were strictly segregated: Stein conversed only with her male visitors, while Toklas entertained their wives in the kitchen. Gertrude could be "chauvinistic," preferring the company of men, but Alice always occupied a special place in her life. "She is very necessary to me. . . . My Sweetie. She is all to me," Stein admitted. No one doubted it.

*I am an American and I have lived half my life in Paris, not the half that made me but the half in which I made what I made.*

—Gertrude Stein

Their quiescent, bourgeois life in Paris was enlivened by frequent, protracted holidays around Europe. But even then, Stein kept to her routine of writing every day. *Tender Buttons*, published in 1914, was described by a reviewer as "unreadable, impenetrable, hopelessly obscure." Hoping to have it also published in London, Gertrude and Alice went there, only to be detained when war broke out in August 1914. Back in Paris in October, Toklas was frightened by the bombings and blackouts, and they sought refuge in Majorca, having sold a Matisse paint-

ing to meet their expenses. Bored and cut off from friends, they decided to return to Paris and aid the French war effort. Gertrude had her cousin in New York send her a 1917 Ford, which she christened "Auntie"; after it was converted into a supply van, Stein and Toklas delivered hospital supplies to various depots in France. After the Armistice in November 1918, they were sent to Alsace to open a center for civilian relief. For their efforts, they were awarded Reconnaisance Français medals by the French government.

Stein and Toklas quickly resumed their familiar domestic routine in Paris, but the Stein salon changed dramatically. Before the war, artists had dominated the gatherings, but in the interwar years young writers, mostly Americans, flocked to the rue de Fleurus where many of the "lost generation" (Gertrude's term) found refuge and encouragement. Ernest Hemingway, Sherwood Anderson, and F. Scott Fitzgerald were among Stein's most ardent admirers. She read Hemingway's writings, advised him "to begin over again and concentrate," to avoid cleverness, and to remember that "remarks are not literature." Stein was fond of Hemingway, but Toklas was not. Known to be "fiercely possessive and jealous" of Gertrude's relations with both men and women, Alice was often able to convince her to break off friendships she considered a threat to their marriage. Afraid Hemingway might seduce Stein, Toklas created discord between them. These young writers were not seen as literary rivals by Gertrude, but James Joyce and T.S. Eliot were; her reaction to their successes was to ignore them, despite their presence in Paris. Flattered by attention from her American visitors, Stein still worried about her work that remained unpublished. But in the 1920s, the appearance of her *The Making of Americans* (1925) and other works, brought increased recognition of Stein's unique contribution to literature, although without financial rewards.

When invited to lecture in England in 1926, Stein agreed, hoping the lectures would generate interest in her work. Appearing before enthusiastic audiences at Cambridge and Oxford universities, she explained how she used words and her concept of rhythm and repetition; these same ideas are found in her *An Elucidation* (1927) in which she wrote, "Civilization began with a rose. A rose is a rose is a rose is a rose," which became her hallmark. The lectures were published and led to a reissue of *Three Lives* and a revival of interest in her work. Stein was finally accepted as a leading figure among "modernist" writers, but she never won the popular acclaim of Joyce or the poet Ezra Pound whom she said was "a village explainer, excellent if you were a village, but if you were not, not." Gertrude was an "explainer" too as she tried to answer her own question, "[W]hat do we mean by what we say and why do we say things the way we do?" She realized she would never attract many readers, and this depressed her. Rather than wait for commercial publishers to recognize the work of a "genius," Alice and Gertrude sold a Picasso painting to finance "Plain Edition," their own publishing house. At age 57, Stein was sought after more as a personality than as a writer, until she reluctantly agreed to write her memoirs. While at their summer home in Bilignin, in eastern France, Gertrude wrote *The Autobiography of Alice B. Toklas* in six weeks. Using Alice's voice, she chronicled her own life in Paris over a quarter of a century. Published in New York in 1933, it sold out nine days before publication, and was reprinted four times in two years. Stein was a celebrity, and received substantial royalties.

Not everyone was pleased with her recollection of people or events. Hemingway called it "a damned pitiful book"—Gertrude had said he

was "fragile and yellow." Matisse and others were also upset, no one more than Leo Stein. "She's basically stupid," he asserted, "and I am basically intelligent." Stein's reaction to her new celebrity status was curious; she began to question her own identity: "The moment you or anybody else knows what you are you are not it, you are what you or anybody else knows you are." She stopped writing.

Publicity from the autobiography generated great interest in another of Stein's projects, her collaboration with the young American composer Virgil Thomson, for whom she had written the libretto for *Four Saints in Three Acts*, an opera performed in New York in 1934 with an all-black cast. Her friends and her agent tried to persuade her to undertake a lecture tour in the United States. She finally consented and began writing lectures setting forth her theories and ideas on art and literature. In October 1934, Gertrude and Alice sailed for New York; Gertrude had been away for 30 years. Interviewed and photographed, Stein was delighted to be "a real lion, a real celebrity." Asked why she

*Alice B. Toklas (left) and Gertrude Stein.*

didn't write the way she talked, she responded, "Why don't you read the way I write?" For eight months, she traveled with Toklas across America, lecturing at some 30 universities. In California, when she visited Oakland, she felt uneasy: "What was the use of my having come from Oakland it was not natural to have come from there . . . there is no there, there." In May 1935, Gertrude and Alice sailed for France, for home.

But it was impossible to settle quietly into the old routine. Disturbing political events portended war which Stein had hoped "would go out of fashion, like duelling." If people would only stop saluting, war would disappear. Gertrude's old life was forever changed when Michael and Sarah left Paris for America, and former friends remained alienated because of the *Autobiography*. Even in remote Bilignin, the presence of French reservists and machine guns made Gertrude and Alice nervous. However, Stein remained productive; in *The Geographical History of America or the Relation of Human Nature to the Human Mind*, she focused on the nature of America, on fame, and the absence of any relation between human nature and the human mind. Secure in her literary niche, she wrote, "It is natural that again a woman should be the one to do the literary thinking of this epoch." A second series of lectures at Cambridge and Oxford in 1936, and the appearance of *Everybody's Autobiography* in 1937, led Stein to conclude that she was "the most important writer writing today," and "one of the masters of English prose." While in London, she and Alice attended the opening of a ballet based on Stein's *They Must. Be Wedded To Their Wife*. Gertrude could not ignore the civil war in Spain and the rise of fascist dictators in Europe, though she tried. Her view of the present state of the world was that "it was getting too crowded and it was getting too modern; people are losing their natural habits of living." And the tractable masses tended to follow dictators, the "fathers" who oppressed them—Gertrude had no love for fathers.

In 1937, Stein and Toklas were forced to move from their apartment on the rue de Fleurus, Gertrude's home for 35 years. They soon settled into a new apartment, along with their 131 paintings. Alice had for some time been typing and sending copies of Gertrude's manuscripts to Yale University Library for safekeeping. And Stein continued to write, refusing to permit preparations for war to distract her. But when France was attacked by Germany in 1940, she and Alice fled to Bilignin. She looked on their situation as an adventure, and she enjoyed the change. They contacted the American consul in Lyons who told them to leave France, but the people of Bilignin urged them to stay: "Everyone knows you here. . . . Why risk yourself among strangers?" Shortages of food and fuel were minor inconveniences, and they reluctantly sold a Cézanne painting to buy provisions. Moreover, they had a friend with close connections to the German-backed French government under Marshal Pétain. A local official was instructed to protect them. After the entry of the United States into the war in 1941, their situation became more dangerous. As Jews and enemy aliens, they were subject to arrest and deportation to a concentration camp. They lost the lease on their house and moved to the nearby village of Culoz where they were again protected by the mayor and the villagers. Curiously, Stein referred to this period as the happiest of her life; for the first time since arriving in France, she lived with and liked the French people who became "as real as she was herself to herself."

Stein paid tribute to her adopted home and to the French in her book *Paris France* (1940); in *Wars I Have Seen* (1945), she described her wartime experiences. In September 1944, the first American liberators arrived in Culoz, and Alice made a "victory" cake for them. Gertrude was asked to broadcast live to America: "thanks to the land of my birth and the land of my adoption we are free, long live France, long live America," she declared. In December 1944, the women returned to Paris. The Gestapo had searched their apartment, but the French authorities again protected Stein's valuable art collection. The Germans had absconded with the silver and other valuables and caused some damage, but to Gertrude it was still "the same, so much more beautiful, but it was the same." And she had had enough of looking at rural landscapes; she had missed her streets of Paris. Busy giving lectures at army camps and writing articles for American magazines, Stein renewed her attachment to Paris, walking "all day long and night too." She was noted for having "the grace and gift" for life, enjoying the simplest pleasures. "How many days are there in a week so nice?" she wrote at the end of *Wars I Have Seen*, "very many, happily, very many."

While on a lecture tour in Brussels for the U.S. Army in November 1945, Gertrude had an attack of intestinal pain. She was working on the libretto for Virgil Thomson's opera *The Mother of Us All*, loosely based on the life of the American suffragist *Susan B. Anthony, her last complete work. By April 1946, Stein was told she needed surgery; instead, she and Alice bought a new car and went on holiday, but she became ill and was taken to the American Hospital in Neuilly (a suburb of Paris). Gertrude had cancer and died on the operating table. Four days later, Alice wrote to a friend, "everything is empty and blurred." Later, she was persuaded to write a memoir, *What Is Remembered* (1963), "an act of service" to Gertrude. A reviewer for *Time* magazine remarked that it was a "book of a woman who all her life has looked in a mirror and seen someone else."

Gertrude Stein once wrote: "it was not what France gave you but what it did not take away from you that was important." And that is why she lived and died there, an American in Paris.

**SOURCES:**

Benstock, Shari. "Gertrude Stein and Alice B. Toklas: Rue de Fleurus," in *Women of the Left Bank: Paris, 1900–1940.* Austin, TX: University of Texas Press, 1986, pp. 143–193.

Hobhouse, Janet. *Everybody Who Was Anybody: A Biography of Gertrude Stein.* NY: Putnam, 1975.

Souhami, Diana. *Gertrude and Alice.* London: Pandora, 1991.

**SUGGESTED READING:**

Brinnin, John Malcolm. *The Third Rose: Gertrude Stein and Her World.* Reading, MA: Addison-Wesley, 1987.

Mellow, James R. *Charmed Circle: Gertrude Stein & Company.* NY: Praeger, 1974.

Stein, Gertrude. *The Autobiography of Alice B. Toklas.* NY: Random House, 1933.

Wagner-Martin, Linda. *Favored Strangers: Gertrude Stein and Her Family.* NJ: Rutgers University Press.

Wineapple, Brenda. *Sister Brother: Gertrude and Leo Stein.* Putnam, 1996.

**COLLECTIONS:**

Gertrude Stein's manuscripts, correspondence, and unpublished notebooks are located at the Beinecke Library, Yale University; other notable collections include those at the Bancroft Library, University of California, Berkeley, and the University of Texas, Austin.

**Jeanne A. Ojala**, Professor Emerita,
Department of History, University of Utah,
Salt Lake City, Utah

# Stein, Marion (1926—)

*Countess of Harewood. Name variations: Marion Thorpe. Born Mary Donata Nanetta Pauline Gustava Erwina Wilhelmina in Vienna, Austria, on October 18, 1926; married George Lascelles, 7th earl of Harewood, on September 29, 1949 (divorced 1967); married Jeremy Thorpe (an English Liberal politician), on March 14, 1973; children: (first marriage) David Lascelles, viscount Lascelles (b. 1950); James Lascelles (b. 1953); Robert Lascelles (b. 1955); Mark Lascelles (b. 1964).*

# Steinbach, Sabina von (fl. 13th c.)

*Austrian sculptor. Flourished in the 13th century in Strasbourg.*

Sabina von Steinbach was a popular, talented Austrian sculptor, but few facts are clear about her life. She was trained in the arts by her father, who was himself a sculptor, and eventually gained her own patrons; she continued to assist her father on his largest commissions. It is recorded that Sabina worked on the intricate stone carvings of the great cathedral of Strasbourg, her only known commissioned project.

**Laura York**, M.A. in History,
University of California, Riverside, California

# Steinem, Gloria (1934—)

*Best-known leader and speaker for the feminist movement during the 1970s who was a founder and editor of* Ms. *magazine, as well as a co-founder of the Ms. Foundation, Women's Action Alliance, and Women's Political Caucus. Pronunciation: STY-nem. Born Gloria Marie Steinem on March 25, 1934, at Clark Lake, Michigan; second daughter of Leo Steinem (an antique dealer during the winter and owner-manager of a resort entertainment hall during the summer) and Ruth (Nuneviller) Steinem (briefly a reporter for the* Toledo Blade*); attended Toledo High School, 1949–51, Western High School in Washington, D.C., 1951–52, and Smith College, 1952–56, granted a B.A.; member Phi Beta Kappa; married David Bale (an entrepreneur and political activist), on September 3, 2000; no children.*

*Spent earliest summers in Clark Lake, Michigan, and winters traveling with family; moved to Toledo, Ohio (1944); family broke up (1945); graduated high school (1952); graduated college (1956); spent a year in India (1956–57); obtained first job in publishing (1960); earned first byline,* Esquire *magazine (1962); briefly became an undercover Playboy bunny (1963); served as staff writer for* New York *magazine (1968–72); won Penney-Missouri Journalism Award (1969); served as editor of* Ms. *magazine (1972–88); operated on for breast cancer (1986); left* Ms. *to write several books (1988); worked as freelance writer and speaker (1988—).*

*Selected writings:* A Thousand Indias, *a guide book of India (1957);* The Beach Book *(1963); "After Black Power, Women's Liberation," award-winning article on the women's movement, for* New York *magazine (1969);* Outrageous Acts and Everyday Rebellions *(1983);* Marilyn *(1986);* Revolution from Within *(1992);* Moving Beyond Words *(1994).*

In the mid-1970s, the decade when the feminist movement was at the height of its power, Gloria Steinem was also at the height of her career. Always sensitive to issues of fairness and equality, Steinem had taken up the cause of women's liberation in 1969. By that time, she was already well known for her interviews with the elegant and chic personalities of New York and Washington, and had been described by *Newsday* as the "World's Most Beautiful By-line." Steinem's regular column, "The City Politic," which appeared weekly in *New York* magazine, made her name recognizable to thousands of readers. But feminism was the issue that became her natural element: the perfect realm for the young journalist.

The door to feminism was opened to Gloria Steinem in late March 1969, at a time when legislative hearings on abortion laws were being held in New York State. That night, armed with her press pass, she was allowed entry into a meeting in favor of legalizing elective abortion sponsored by a radical-left women's group called Redstockings. As she listened to women tell of their personal sufferings and difficulties obtaining abortions, Steinem was forced to remember her own experience. At age 22, alone in England, she was faced with the choice of giving up her dreams and plans or risking her life with a strange doctor. Steinem had chosen to have an abortion and never discussed her decision with anyone. Now, in this church basement, she began to identify with the problems these women had, and to see them differently than she ever had before. It was not only the inability to control their own bodies that created problems for women, Steinem realized, but society's refusal to value women equally with men. "I finally understood," she would later write, "why I identify with 'out' groups. I belong to one, too."

After the 1969 abortion hearings, Steinem would begin researching the women's movement. The result was an award-winning essay, "After Black Power, Women's Liberation," which appeared in *New York* magazine. It was one of the first articles on the new feminist movement to appear in a major publication and launched Steinem on her career as a feminist. A year later, in 1970, thousands of onlookers recognized Steinem's smiling face in the front row of marchers during the Women's Strike for Equality rally in New York City.

Gloria Marie Steinem was born on March 24, 1934, in a small resort town in Michigan called Clark Lake. She grew up wandering around Ocean Beach Pier, the entertainment center that her father Leo owned and managed every summer. During the winter, when the pier was closed, Leo filled a dome-topped trailer with their belongings, and he and **Ruth Steinem** and their two daughters—Gloria and **Suzanne Steinem**—headed west or south, where the weather was warmer. Leo would buy and sell antiques to make a living until the Michigan summer began and the entertainment pier reopened.

All this traveling prevented Steinem from attending school and making friends her own age. Instead, her earliest memories centered around the summers and the kindness of the entertainers who worked there. She remembered feeling protected by her father, but there were few memories of her mother. Her most vivid recollection from that period was in 1944 when the Ocean Beach Pier closed down and the family broke up.

Ruth Steinem had serious psychological problems and was not capable of running a household alone. She was often heavily medicated and sometimes completely non-functional. With Leo traveling and Suzanne away at college, Gloria, then only nine years old, would be alone with Ruth. The family understood the impossibility of such a situation. Their solution was for Gloria and her mother to move to Northampton, Massachusetts, near Smith College, where Suzanne was in her third year.

Ruth seemed better in the intimate, supportive atmosphere of a small town. When the school year ended and Suzanne left for New York City and a summer job, however, Ruth and Gloria followed; again, Ruth became severely depressed. At the end of the summer of 1945, with Suzanne back at Smith College, Ruth and Gloria returned to Toledo and moved into the house on Woodville Road that had once belonged to Ruth's parents. Gloria, now almost 11 years old, somehow managed to care for herself and her mother, attend school, and even have some good times. Dancing lessons, acting in plays, Saturday movies and trips to the library, combined with a rich fantasy life, kept her going during those difficult years. Sometimes, Ruth felt better and functioned normally.

Mother and daughter maintained themselves on rents received from Ruth's property at Clark Lake and from the other two apartments in the Toledo house where they lived. Occasionally, there were visits from Leo. Although his financial situation remained precarious and he was not in a position to change his daughter's life very much, Gloria always loved him and felt he loved her. When she was old enough, she took a part-time job, but it was not enough to lift them out of poverty. Eventually, the house fell into disrepair and became virtually unlivable; the tenants were gone and there was no

Gloria
Steinem

heat. This crisis precipitated another family decision and another move.

Steinem's first relief from the burden of caring for her mother in the deteriorating house came in 1951. That year, the church next door offered to buy the property. Suzanne saw this as an opportunity for her younger sister. Gloria would spend her senior year of high school living with Sue in Washington, D.C.; the money from the sale of the house would be put aside for Steinem's college tuition, and Leo would take care of Ruth. The only problem was convincing their father to agree.

Leo and Ruth had been divorced for several years, and at first he adamantly refused. Then, seeing Gloria's tears, Leo changed his mind and the plan was put into effect. It was Steinem's first and only carefree year in high school. When it ended, she was accepted at Smith College, from which Suzanne had graduated in 1946.

But Leo Steinem had agreed to take care of Ruth for only one year. With the end of the interval, Ruth, still suffering from severe depression, was sent to Washington, D.C., and placed in the care of Suzanne. During Gloria's first year at college, the sisters made the decision to hospitalize their mother in a private facility where she remained for several years. When Ruth was released, she was able to live independently.

Steinem loved college. Although she had not been a scholastic star in high school, by the time she was ready to graduate from Smith, she was in Phi Beta Kappa, had been selected for honors in government, her major, and was elected class historian. She had also accepted an engagement ring from her current beau but backed out when she received a fellowship to study in India for a year.

Before going to India, Steinem traveled to England where she stayed with a married friend in London and worked to save money for her trip. It was there that she realized she was pregnant with her ex-fiancé's child and faced the possibility of giving up her fellowship in India and returning to New York to marry. Then chance intervened. She overheard a conversation at a party and discovered that although they were technically illegal, abortions were possible in England with the consent of two physicians.

Steinem summoned her courage and shared her dilemma with the doctor who had first diagnosed her condition. He agreed to help, and when she boarded the plane for her flight to India, Steinem was no longer pregnant. No one but Steinem and her doctor ever knew of this incident in her life until the fight to legalize abortion began. In the early 1970s, she publicly announced that she was one of the thousands of women who had had illegal abortions.

Steinem's year in India was successful. She learned many things about herself and about this newly independent country and became a social activist. When she returned to the United States, she published her first book, *A Thousand Indias*. It was a travel guide to India, a project she had undertaken before she left.

Immediately after her return, Steinem enjoyed a brief time as a celebrity among those who knew her. She spoke at Smith College, wrote of her experiences, and was interviewed by the *Toledo Blade*, her hometown paper. Soon enough, however, the excitement passed, and Steinem began looking for work. Her goal was to find a job as a political writer, but this was not a realistic expectation for a woman in 1958. Instead, she worked for an association called Independent Service for Information, a Massachusetts-based group which educated and encouraged students to go abroad to Communist Youth Festivals to present the case for democracy. Although one of her tasks was to write educational material, it was not the kind of writing she sought. After two years, she broke into the publishing world with a job at a new magazine called *Help! For Tired Minds. Help!*'s editor was Harvey Kurtzman, previously a founder of the successful *Mad Magazine*. Although *Help!* was never a major publishing success, working for Kurtzman improved Steinem's journalism skills. One of her assignments was to contact well-known television and film actors and convince them to be on the magazine's cover. She generally got what she wanted.

Gloria Steinem's ability to deal with people had brought her continued success throughout her childhood, and it did not fail her now. The young assistant was well liked. She was invited to parties and offered a string of opportunities. In addition to becoming familiar with the world of show business, she was introduced by Kurtzman to the publishing world, and met many of the prominent people involved in it, including Bob Benton, art director at *Esquire* magazine, one of the men whom Steinem loved and almost married.

Through Benton, Steinem became acquainted with the staff at *Esquire* and began to write for the magazine. Her first byline appeared in Esquire's special college issue, an idea that she had proposed and sold to them. Her own article in that issue spoke about "the woman who does not feel forced to choose between a career and marriage, and is therefore free to find fulfillment in a combination of the two." Her article appeared in 1962, preceding by one year *Betty Friedan*'s book *The Feminine Mystique*. At just about the same time, she withdrew from a commitment to marry Benton. The two remained friends, but their romantic relationship ended.

Steinem's career advanced in the 1960s. Her freelance work initially augmented her job at *Help!*, then replaced it. She moved into a larger apartment in New York City and had more assignments than she could handle. One of the most outstanding of these was an undercover project from *Show* magazine. *Show* wanted her to get a job as a "Playboy bunny" at the famed Playboy Club in New York City, and report on what it was like to work there. Because she was young and attractive, Steinem was able to get a position and worked there for one week. Playboy bunnies, in actuality waitresses at the club's restaurant, had to wear scanty costumes, along with bunny ears and a fluffy tail, designed to show off their bodies and amuse and attract the male customers. Steinem found the work degrading and physically difficult. Her article for *Show*, "A Bunny's Tale: *Show*'s First Exposé for Intelligent People," appeared in the May and June issues of 1963.

Her experience with the Playboy Club sensitized Steinem to feminist issues, but there was as yet no movement to help her put them into perspective. During the 1960s, she took on many assignments that, with the benefit of hindsight, she might never have accepted. Among them was an agreement to pose as the *Glamour* girl for the February 1964 issue of *Glamour* magazine. Another was an arrangement to be photographed having her hair cut by the famous hairdresser Vidal Sassoon of London. Steinem had always enjoyed and profited from her good looks as well as her pleasant personality. After feminism helped change her perspective, she consistently refused to acknowledge her attractive appearance or discuss its advantages in her life. However, in the decade of the 1960s, she made good use of her appealing image, and it was an important factor in advancing her career.

Through journalism, Steinem made her way into the world of celebrities. She wrote for *The New York Times Magazine*, *McCall's*, and the *Ladies' Home Journal*. In 1963, she published a frothy book for Viking Press called *The Beach Book*, and gained a year's experience as a comedy writer for the popular television show "That Was the Week That Was." Gloria credited her father for her good sense of humor. Leo had died in a car accident in California a few years earlier, an event that considerably saddened Steinem, and in spite of his obvious parental failures, she always remembered him fondly.

By the mid-1960s, Steinem had become a celebrity. In addition to interviewing the rich and famous, she herself was being interviewed for newspapers and television shows. This development undoubtedly increased her confidence as well as her credibility and led her into a new area: politics and political writing. She first integrated her writing career with her political interests when she began to write about and actively support Senator George McGovern in his first bid for the presidency. Shortly afterward, she joined forces with Clay Felker, editor at *Esquire*, when he began publishing *New York* magazine. Steinem was an editor for the new weekly magazine and also wrote a political column, "The City Politic." From the appearance of *New York*'s first edition in July 1968, Steinem no longer wrote interviews of budding thespians or pieces on fashion. Instead, she wrote about Richard Nixon, Robert Kennedy, and Cesar Chavez, union leader and organizer of the California grape boycott. After the assassination of Martin Luther King, Jr., in 1968, she covered the Harlem riots and then the tumultuous Democratic National Convention in Chicago. Steinem was becoming more and more politically sensitized and aware, ready for her initiation into the newest revolution which was sweeping across the country: women's liberation.

The 1969 abortion hearings in New York were the catalyst. Steinem began to read about the new feminist philosophy and to view her own life—and her mother's—in light of what she was learning. Her award-winning article on the topic, and her participation in the Women's Strike for Equality March, catapulted her further into the thick of the movement. She began to understand and then to proselytize.

Steinem, naturally outgoing and friendly, was strangely shy addressing large crowds, and she was a nervous speaker when she first began appearing before audiences. Eventually, her positive experiences, coupled with the encouragement of the other women who shared the podium with her, helped her to overcome her dread of the speaker's platform. Ultimately, it became more important to her to convince people of her ideas than to worry about her own feelings. Steinem told biographers: "I saw a whole population of women who desperately wanted information."

Those speaking engagements taught Steinem a great deal about women and their problems. It was the questions directed to her from her audiences which first motivated Steinem to organize the Women's Action Alliance. The Alliance developed educational programs and services to assist women and women's organizations, and supported worthwhile projects that offered practical help to women. Among the ideas which surfaced from the women involved in the Action Alliance was a national magazine. That idea eventually became a reality when the premiere issue of *Ms.* appeared in 1972.

The first feminist women's magazine was an instant success, and Gloria Steinem left *New York* magazine and became editor of *Ms.* She remained at that job for 16 years. In addition to helping form the magazine's policies and contributing to each issue, Steinem also became heavily involved in all aspects of the new women's movement. As a co-founder of the Women's Political Caucus, organized in 1971, Steinem became politically active. Despite her long-term support for George McGovern, she was a delegate for *Shirley Chisholm who ran against McGovern for the presidential nomination of the Democratic Party in 1971. In an article for *Look* magazine, Steinem explained her support for Chisholm. A woman presidential candidate would help make voters aware of the needs of minority groups and women. If a woman ran and were elected, people would not "go on supposing the current social order reflects some natural order."

*We* now have words like "sexual harassment," "displaced homemaker," and "battered woman." Ten years ago, it was just called life.

—Gloria Steinem

Steinem knew Chisholm would lose the bid for the nomination, and she did, but through their work, Steinem and her colleagues in the Women's Political Caucus were introduced to politics and political action. After McGovern won the nomination, the women supported **Frances "Sissy" Farenthold** of Texas as a nominee for vice president. She came in second, losing to Thomas Eagleton. Most important, the Caucus worked for a women's platform at the convention and succeeded in getting almost all their planks accepted by the delegates as part of the party's policy. The one exception was the women's stand on reproductive rights.

A vital part of the feminist movement in the early 1970s was changing language, and Steinem was a major force behind such changes. It was she who coined the expression "reproductive rights" and pointed out that "battered woman" and "sexual harassment" were new terms for old ideas. "Ten years ago," she reminded her audiences, "it was just called life."

When the U.S. Congress voted to pass the Equal Rights Amendment (ERA) in 1972, the women's movement, with the National Organization for Women (NOW) in the forefront, launched a campaign to help ratify it in a majority of the states. Although Gloria Steinem never joined NOW, she was heavily involved in this struggle and was a visible presence in many cities where battles for the ERA were being waged. She became one of the most well-known speakers for the feminist movement and, during the decade of the 1970s, appeared on the covers of four major magazines. Her long blonde hair falling loose over her shoulders, her stylish aviator glasses, the blue jeans and leotard that she always wore, was a look that was emulated by other women, both feminists and non-feminists. Steinem became the recognized symbol of the women's movement.

Shortly after the establishment of *Ms.*, Steinem helped to establish the Ms. Foundation which granted money to support grassroots, self-help projects of women's groups and individual women. One of the foundation's most successful undertakings was the children's television show "Free To Be You and Me," directed by **Marlo Thomas**. An award-winning show, it was later adapted as both a book and a record, then converted into a video. The gist of "Free To Be You and Me" was that children should be allowed to develop more freely, without having gender stereotypes imposed on them.

Less than two years later, in 1974, Steinem added another organization to the list of groups she had helped to form. This one, the Coalition of Labor Union Women, was committed to helping working women whose unions were not supportive enough, or who wanted to organize new ones. She saw this group as having the potential to fight for an end to job discrimination against women.

The year 1974 was also the year Gloria Steinem turned 40. She proudly announced her age, saying: "This is what 40 looks like. We've been lying for so long, who would know?" Even at the height of her busy career as a journalist and feminist, and despite her oft-quoted "A woman needs a man like a fish needs a bicycle," she was rarely without a significant man in her life. In the early 1970s, it was Franklin Thomas, head of the Ford Foundation and a civil-rights activist. Because he was an African-American, Steinem found Frank especially sympathetic to women's problems. He understood what being treated like a stereotype was like, she believed. Despite their closeness and love, this relationship, too, ended without a commitment to marriage, and Steinem finally admitted to herself that she did not want to marry anyone. Frequently asked why she remained single and childless, her standard response was "I can't mate in captivity."

Gloria and Frank remained friends but Steinem moved on. Shortly before her 40th birthday, she met Stan Pottinger, a lawyer who headed the Civil Rights Division of the Justice Department and was also strongly committed to the feminist cause. Although he lived in Washington, D.C., and Steinem lived in New York, the two spent many weekends together. Stan and his children became an important part of her life for the next eight years, but marriage, at least then, was not contemplated.

Steinem's life was filled with commitments to causes, travel, and writing. Added to those activities was the need to fend off many attacks, both personal and political, which emanated from a variety of sources during the decade of the 1970s. The most serious of these was the accusation, leveled against her by the radical-feminist group Redstockings, that she had once been affiliated with the CIA. This charge stemmed from the fact that funding for the Independent Service organization, her first employer, was partially provided by CIA money. The charge quickly deteriorated into a personal attack. Other challenges, including ongoing disagreements with Betty Friedan, continued to haunt her well into the 1980s.

Steinem was not appointed an official delegate, but she did attend the international conference in Mexico City marking the opening of the United Nations' Decade of Women in 1975. She also worked hard to help organize the American Conference on Women which took place in Houston, Texas, in 1977. Although the Houston conference was not politically successful, Steinem was pleased with it. She felt that even though none of their resolutions had been adopted by the U.S. Congress, the women who attended had met new allies, learned new skills and gained a deeper commitment to continue the fight for the ERA.

Shortly after her return from Houston, Steinem left for Washington, D.C. As the recipient of a Woodrow Wilson fellowship, she planned to spend one year researching and writing her long-overdue book. Although this was her priority, she still devoted a good deal of time to *Ms.* and to speaking for the ERA, trying to ward off the growing opposition which threatened its chances for ratification. With the 1979 deadline for passage coming closer, and only three more states needed to make the Equal Rights Amendment a reality, women made one final effort and failed. The tide in the country was turning. The next step was convincing Congress to agree to an extension. A major march on Washington was organized for July 9, 1978. Steinem marched along with 100,000 others, and the ERA was granted a new deadline: June 30, 1982.

With a few more years of leeway, and her Woodrow Wilson fellowship at an end, Steinem returned to New York and continued her busy life, writing, speaking and raising funds for *Ms.* Together with **Harriet Lyons** and **Susanne Braun Levine**, editors and co-workers at *Ms.*, Steinem shared in compiling *The Decade of Women*. The book, partially the result of her year of research, was filled with photographs and information about women's accomplishments and setbacks over the last ten years; it won the Women in Communications Clarion Award for 1980.

The 1980s started auspiciously but quickly deteriorated for Steinem. In 1981, her mother died. Ruth Steinem had been living independently and had even managed to come to several of her daughter's speaking engagements before her final illness. Shortly after Ruth's death, Steinem wrote a moving essay about her mother, in which she noted, "I miss her; but no more in death than I did in life." The social changes which would have enabled Ruth Steinem to live a full life and achieve her potential had come 20 years too late.

The following year, 1982, saw the final blow to the Equal Rights Amendment. With Ronald Reagan, a conservative Republican, in the White House, the country had turned away from its commitment to equal rights for women. *Ms.* celebrated its tenth birthday in a somber mood, and Steinem, trying to make the best of this disappointment, said: "I am angry but not disheartened. . . . There is not a city or town without a women's center or a battered-wives hot line."

*Outrageous Acts and Everyday Rebellions*, Steinem's long-awaited book of essays on feminism, was finally published in 1983. Her friend **Letty Cottin Pogrebin** had helped her organize and edit it, and urged her to send it to a publisher. Although many considered the book itself to be outrageous, even revolutionary, it was an instant success. "Feminists are always thought of as radical," Steinem said. "The truth is we're sweetly reasonable. It's the system that is radically wrong."

Returning from a major publicity tour, Steinem and her friends prepared to celebrate her 50th birthday. The party was held in the Grand Ballroom of the Waldorf-Astoria Hotel in New York City, with guests including celebrities from the worlds of politics, show business, publishing, and the women's movement. Though a high point of Steinem's life, it marked the beginning of a decline for both the feminist movement and her spectacular career. It also marked the beginning of a new love affair with millionaire publisher and real-estate magnate Mort Zuckerman, who attended that 50th birthday party.

For too many years, Steinem had been struggling to keep *Ms.* afloat without ever reducing her other activities. Every week she was on a plane to fulfill another commitment to speak, to promote a book, or to negotiate with potential advertisers for *Ms.* Criticism from both outside and within the women's movement had also taken its toll. After repeated urging from her friends, Steinem began seeing a therapist. She also began a romance with Zuckerman that in later years she realized had been a big mistake.

Zuckerman and Steinem were as unlike as two people could be. He was part of the world of big business and high society, while she remained in the feminist world, concerned with the underprivileged, ready to take on what she saw as "rescue work" whenever someone needed it. They did have a few things in common, however, for neither had ever married and both saw themselves as neglected children. Zuckerman was attracted to Steinem and thought he could help the failing magazine she was working so hard to save. Steinem, on her part, enjoyed the pampering she received from Zuckerman, whose limousine and beautiful weekend retreat in Easthampton were always available to her. At that low point, she felt she needed this kind of nurturing and overlooked their disparate politics and conflicting ideals.

Then another blow struck. Steinem was diagnosed with breast cancer in 1986 and, for the first time, was forced to review her life and make major decisions about what she wanted. After surgery, she set to redecorating her apartment and making her life more comfortable. She curtailed her hectic schedule and in 1988, together with the other editors at *Ms.*, made the decision to sell the magazine to an Australian company.

In hindsight, she conceded that she should have done it earlier. The burden of fund raising for *Ms.* during the backlash of the 1980s had become so overwhelming that, as one biographer put it, she found herself taking responsibility for the magazine just as she had done for her mother during her childhood. Steinem admitted that she had written *Marilyn*, her picture essay about *Marilyn Monroe, to satisfy *Ms.*'s debt.

Once free of responsibility for the magazine, Steinem took a position at Random House Publishing and signed contracts for two books. She also continued supporting women's causes, especially her favorite, the Ms. Foundation, and speaking throughout the country, but her sched-

ule was considerably less taxing. Her therapy sessions, which continued throughout those years, ultimately gave her more insights into herself, and helped her to write *Revolution from Within*, which came out in 1992. Although some critics praised the book, many of the reviews, both from feminists and anti-feminists, were negative. The mainstream media concentrated mainly on the few pages that covered her love affair with Zuckerman, while the feminists accused her of abandoning the movement for selfish reasons.

Just two years later, in 1994, Steinem's *Moving Beyond Words* appeared in print to much less notice. A book of essays, like *Outrageous Acts*, but with no unifying theme or message, *Moving Beyond Words* provoked neither much criticism nor much praise.

In her 60s, Steinem continued to support liberal and humanistic causes and to be devoted to feminism in all its aspects. She remained a consulting editor for *Ms.* after it was taken over in 1989 by Lang Communications, an American company, with feminist **Robin Morgan** as editor-in-chief. Ten years later, with financing from a network of wealthy feminists ("What's different from the beginning of the women's movement is that now there *are* such women," she noted), Steinem bought back *Ms.* and rededicated it to its original mission. She occasionally reenters the limelight with an appearance at a major news event, such as her speech at the rally in support of **Anita Hill** after the Thomas-Hill Senate hearings, but in general her life is quieter. Her long, streaked blonde hair, once her hallmark, is now gray and tucked up in a bun, and she no longer wears her aviator glasses. She remains an important presence in American life, however, and her ideas, reflected in hundreds of articles and books, can be expected to command respect for many years to come. In September 2000, the media was delighted to learn that Steinem had gotten married. The ceremony, conducted in Oklahoma at the home of Steinem's longtime friend *Wilma Mankiller, did not contain the words "obey" or "man and wife." She and her new husband David Bale, a political activist and entrepreneur, took the public response and ribbing (much of it about fish riding bicycles) with good nature. "Though I've worked for many years to make marriage more equal," she said, "I never expected to take advantage of it myself. I'm happy, surprised and one day will write about it, but for now, I hope this proves what feminists have always said—that feminism is about the ability to choose what's right at each time of our lives."

**SOURCES:**
*The Boston Globe.* November 2, 2000, pp. D1, D5.

*The Day* [New London, CT]. November 6, 2000.

Henry, Sondra, and Emily Taitz. *One Woman's Power: A Biography of Gloria Steinem.* Afterword by Gloria Steinem. Minneapolis, MN: Dillon Press, 1987.

Steinem, Gloria. *Outrageous Acts and Everyday Rebellions.* NY: Holt, Rinehart & Winston, 1983.

**SUGGESTED READING:**

Davis, Flora. *Moving the Mountain: The Women's Movement in America Since 1960.* NY: Simon & Schuster, 1991.

Freeman, Jo. *The Politics of Women's Liberation.* NY: David McKay, 1975.

Friedan, Betty. *It Changed My Life: Writings on the Women's Movement.* NY: Random House, 1976.

Heilbrun, Carolyn G. *The Education of a Woman: The Life of Gloria Steinem.* NY: Dial Press, 1995.

Steinem, Gloria. *Ms.* Numerous articles from 1972 to 1986.

**RELATED MEDIA:**

"A Bunny's Tale" (television movie), starring **Kirstie Alley** as Steinem, first aired in 1985.

**COLLECTIONS:**

Correspondence, papers and writings located in the Smith College Archives, Northampton, Massachusetts.

**Emily Taitz**,
Adjunct Professor of Women's History at Adelphi University,
and co-author of *Written Out of History: Jewish Foremothers*
and *One Woman's Power: A Biography of Gloria Steinem*

# Stella.

*See Rich, Penelope (c. 1562–1607).*

*See Johnson, Esther (1681–1728).*

*See Lewis, Estelle Anna (1824–1880).*

# Steloff, Frances (1887–1989)

*American literary patron and bookseller who founded the Gotham Book Mart in New York City. Name variations: Fanny Steloff. Born Ida Frances Steloff on December 31, 1887, in Saratoga Springs, New York; died on April 15, 1989, in New York City; married David Moss (divorced around 1930); no children.*

Frances Steloff was born in 1887 into a poor family in the wealthy New York resort town of Saratoga Springs. Her mother died when she was three, and her father, a booklover and religious scholar, left his five children in the care of their stepmother while working as a traveling salesman to support them. At age 12, Steloff was informally adopted by a Boston couple vacationing in Saratoga. She moved to their home in Wakefield, near Boston, but was treated cruelly by the woman, an alcoholic who prevented Frances from attending school. Steloff performed household tasks for the couple before running away to New York when she was in her mid-teens, arriving with only the clothes on her back and the contents of her piggy bank. She worked at Loeser's department store in Brooklyn

and then in a number of bookstores, including Brentano's. Deprived of books as a child, she found her abiding passion in them. "Perhaps if I'd had a college education I might not have been so hungry for books," she once said.

The day after her 33rd birthday, Steloff opened her own store, the Gotham Book Mart. The shop began in the basement of a brownstone on 45th Street in New York City, funded by Steloff's meager savings—a $100 Liberty Bond and less than $100 in cash—and stocked with her own collection of out-of-print theater books. Her future husband David Moss, then head of stock at Brentano's, and her old friend Mr. Mischke from the Loeser's days helped her set up shop on New Year's Day, 1920. She later claimed that her first customer was the actor Glenn Hunter. In order to accommodate her earliest patrons, many of whom worked in the theaters on Broadway, Steloff kept her store open until midnight. As she poured her considerable energy and enthusiasm into her work, the Gotham Book Mart became a haven for literati between the wars.

An early supporter of authors like John Steinbeck and William Faulkner, Steloff helped launch the work of James Joyce, *Gertrude Stein, e.e. cummings, *Anais Nin and Ezra Pound. She was one of the founders of the James Joyce Society, which made the Gotham Book Mart its meeting place. Steloff championed new and controversial works, illegally importing and selling such banned books as D.H. Lawrence's *Lady Chatterley's Lover* and Henry Miller's *Tropic of Cancer.*

In 1938, Steloff and her staff produced their first catalog, with the emphasis on authors and all their works, not just newly released books. Called *The Book-Collector's Odyssey, or Travels in the Realms of Gold,* the catalog was a popular success. Two years later, to celebrate its 20th anniversary, Gotham Book Mart published *We Moderns,* a catalog of its experimental literature written by contributors like Carl Van Vechten and Conrad Aiken. *We Moderns* received enormous critical attention and established the store as a literary landmark.

"I felt that writers were very important and I wanted to do all I could for them," Steloff once said. Her practice of storing unsold books in the basement instead of returning them to publishers resulted in Gotham's unparalleled treasure chest of first editions by many of the great writers of the 20th century. Her passion for the written word, unstinting commitment to new authors, and respect for her customers made the Gotham Book Mart a mecca for booklovers. Gotham patrons have included among their number George and Ira Gershwin, Charlie Chaplin, *Katharine Hepburn, Woody Allen and Saul Bellow.

Frances Steloff received many honors during her lifetime, including the National Institute of Arts and Letters Distinguished Service to the Arts Award, an honorary doctorate from Skidmore College, and the Brandeis University Award for Notable Achievement in the Creative Arts. She sold her shop at the age of 80, continuing to live upstairs and remaining active in its operations until a few weeks before her death from pneumonia in 1989, age 101. Steloff's legacy, the Gotham Book Mart, still thrives. Now in larger premises, it has one of the most complete collections of 20th-century literature and poetry in the United States.

**SOURCES:**
Gilbert, Lynn, and Gaylen Moore. *Particular Passions.* NY: Clarkson Potter, 1981.
*The New York Times* (obituary). April 16, 1989.

Paula Morris, D.Phil.,
Brooklyn, New York

# Sten, Anna (1908–1993)

*Russian-born actress. Born Annel (Anjuschka) Stenskaja Sudakevich on December 3, 1908, in Kiev, Russia (now in Ukraine); died in New York City on November 12, 1993; married Fedor Ozep (a director), around 1930 (divorced); married Dr. Eugene Frenke (a director-producer, divorced).*

*Selected filmography:* The Girl With the Hat Box (When Moscow Laughs, *USSR, 1927*); Earth in Chains (The Yellow Ticket *or* The Yellow Pass, *USSR, 1928*); The House on Trubnaya Square *(USSR, 1928)*; The White Eagle (The Lash of the Czar, *USSR, 1928*); The Heir to Genghis Khan (Tempest Over Asia *or* Storm Over Asia, *USSR, 1928*); Der Mörder Dimitri Karamasoff (Karamazov *or* The Murderer Dimitri Karamazov *or* The Brothers Karamazov, *Ger., 1931*); Bomben auf Monte Carlo (Monte Carlo Madness, *Ger., 1931*); Salto Mortale (Trapeze, *Ger., 1931*); Stürme der Leidenschaft (Tempest, *Ger., 1932*); Nana *(US, 1934)*; We Live Again (Resurrection, *US, 1934*); The Wedding Night *(US, 1935)*; A Woman Alone (Two Who Dared, *U.K., 1936*); Exile Express *(US, 1939)*; The Man I Married *(US, 1940)*; So Ends Our Night *(US, 1941)*; Chetniks *(US, 1943)*; Three Russian Girls *(US, 1944)*; Let's Live a Little *(US, 1948)*; Soldier of Fortune *(US, 1955)*; Runaway Daughters *(US, 1956)*; The Nun and the Sergeant *(US, 1962)*.

The daughter of a Russian ballet master and a Swedish mother, actress Anna Sten was reportedly spotted by Constantin Stanislavski while appearing in an amateur play in Kiev; thus began her acting career with the famed Moscow Art Theater. Beginning in 1927, she acted in a number of Russian films, including the comedies *The Girl With the Hat Box* (1927) and *The Yellow Ticket* (1928), then made her way to Germany. Her performance as Grushenka in the film *The Brothers Karamazov* (1931) caught the attention of Samuel Goldwyn, who brought her to America with the hope of turning her into a second *Greta Garbo or *Marlene Dietrich. Goldwyn spent the better part of two years grooming Sten for stardom, teaching her English and subjecting her to one of the most lavish publicity campaigns ever undertaken in Hollywood. Her debut film, an adaptation of Émile Zola's *Nana* (1934), costarred Phillips Holmes and was directed by *Dorothy Arzner, one of the few women directors of the studio era. American audiences, however, never warmed to the Russian beauty, who became known in the industry as "Goldwyn's Folly." All of her American films were box-office disappointments, including her 1935 pairing with Gary Cooper in *The Wedding Night*.

Sten, who was married twice, to director Fedor Ozep and to director-producer Dr. Eugene Frenke, went on to perform in a few additional films, then devoted her time to a semiprofessional career as a painter. She held successful solo shows in Los Angeles and New York, and her works were part of an exhibition that toured Europe under the auspices of the Smithsonian Institution. The actress made her home in Manhattan, where she pursued her continuing interest in acting by occasionally attending classes at the Actors Studio. In 1960, she appeared briefly as Jenny in *The Threepenny Opera*, and later toured with the production. Sten died in Manhattan in November 1993.

**SOURCES:**

Katz, Ephraim. *The Film Encyclopedia.* NY: Harper-Collins, 1994.

Lamparski, Richard. *Whatever Became of . . . ?* 1st & 2nd series. NY: Crown, 1967.

"Obituary," in *The Day* [New London, CT]. November 15, 1993.

**Barbara Morgan**,
Melrose, Massachusetts

## Stepanova, Varvara (1894–1958)

*Innovative post-revolutionary Russian artist, graphic designer, textile designer, and theater designer. Name variations: (pseudonym) Varst. Born Varvara Feodorovna Stepanova in October 1894 in Kovno, Lithuania (Russia); died in Moscow on May 20, 1958; studied painting at the Kazan Art School, 1911; studied at the studios of Konstantin Yuon and Ivan Dudin, Moscow, 1912, and Stroganov School of Applied Art, Moscow, 1913; married Alexander Rodchenko (an artist); children: one daughter.*

Constructivist artist, teacher, and theorist Varvara Stepanova worked primarily in the areas of textiles, apparel, graphics, and theater set designs, frequently in concert with her husband, artist and designer Alexander Rodchenko. As members of the Soviet avant-garde in the years prior to 1930, they counted among their colleagues Vladimir Mayakovsky, Vladimir Tatlin, and *Liubov Popova.

Born in 1894 in Kovno, Lithuania (part of the Russian Soviet bloc), Varvara Feodorovna Stepanova was an accomplished student, earning a gold medal in high school. Her formal art education began at the Kazan Art School, where she started her studies in painting in 1911. She also met Rodchenko during this period, and the two formed a lifelong partnership. In addition to studying at the Stroganov School of Applied Art in Moscow, Stepanova furthered her understanding of art under the tutelage of Konstantin Yuon and Ivan Dudin at their Moscow studios. This extensive training was atypical among leading Russian avant-garde industrial designers, who usually had little or no formal education in the craft.

Early in Stepanova's career, she became interested in Cubo-Futurism, an increasingly important movement in the post-Revolution years because it criticized the previous political structure and confronted the traditions of representational art. During this time, Stepanova explored "zaum" poetry, which sought to coalesce abstractions of sight and sound. Using the technique of collage, she chose sounds rather than meanings to signify language, and the placement of words within the collages supplanted semantic foundation with a sense of texture. Her work in what is referred to as "graphic poetry," notes **M.N. Yablonskaya**, signaled her transition into a mature creative life.

Stepanova also painted a series of abstract human figures, focusing on the geometric or constructive elements of the human form in vari-

$\mathcal{V}$arvara

$\mathcal{S}$tepanova

ous poses and outlining these elements with bold lines. "Also noticeable in these works, and an important aspect of Stepanova's future development as a textile designer," according to Yablonskaya, "is her sense of texture and her love of the tactile qualities of the paint." *Figures* brought Stepanova considerable praise from critics, and increased her stature in the Russian art world. Moving progressively away from the idea of composition in art, Stepanova abandoned painting for Productivism.

Stepanova turned to the theater in 1922, working with director Vsevolod Meyerhold on a set design for his reinterpretation of the classic play *The Death of Tarelkin*. She created a dynamic set that not only facilitated the highly animated movements of the cast but also, through the simplicity of its design, could adapt to different mechanical needs of the play. She designed the costumes to integrate with the geometric forms of the set as well. Although her work was important artistically and celebrated critically, it did not appeal to audiences of the day. However, Stepanova's work in costume design soon expanded into designing for the clothing industry. She believed that clothing ought to derive out of its distinct need, e.g., for specific activities or specific professions. Stepanova's clothing designs, like her textile work, utilized simple geometric shapes in patterns and colors that were appropriate to their use. In 1923, she began working in a Moscow textile print factory in an attempt to convert these designs into clothing of a more utilitarian or every-day use. Many of Stepanova's designs were eventually put into production. "The Constructivist aesthetic really did join forces with industrial mass production," according to Yablonskaya, "and for once the products of Constructivism actually reached the market to which they were ideologically directed."

In addition to her work in textile and clothing design during the 1920s, Stepanova is especially noted for her innovative graphic designs of contemporary magazines such as *Cine-Photo*, *Soviet Cinema*, and *Red Student Life*, as well as various books. This was a time of intense collaboration between Stepanova and her husband. Working closely with the Futurist poet Mayakovsky, Stepanova designed posters for his poetry and Rodchenko illustrated his books. They also collaborated on a journal, published by a group of Futurist poets and Constructivist artists, that reflected their commitment to "Communist Futurism." Rodchenko provided the cover designs and Stepanova provided illustrations. Together, they also worked on many other publications at the time, including *Ten Years of Uzbekistan* (1934) and *USSR in Construction* (1936).

With the eventual decline of Constructivism, Stepanova and Rodchenko abandoned their artistic experimentation and worked on albums of photograph collections, including *15 Years of Soviet Cinema, Moscow Rebuilds*, and *Soviet Aviation*. Stepanova also returned to expressive figurative painting late in the 1930s, with landscapes such as the 1938 *View from a Window with a Dirigible*, and still-lifes. She died in Moscow on May 20, 1958.

**SOURCES:**

Chilvers, Ian. *A Dictionary of Twentieth-Century Art.* NY: Oxford University Press, 1998.

Hillstrom, Laurie Collier, and Kevin Hillstrom, eds. *Contemporary Women Artists.* Detroit, MI: St. James Press, 1999.

Yablonskaya, M.N. *Women Artists of Russia's New Age.* NY: Rizzoli, 1990.

**B. Kimberly Taylor**, freelance writer, New York, New York

## Stephanie (1837–1859)

*Queen of Portugal. Name variations: Stephanie Hohenzollern. Born on July 15, 1837; died on July 17, 1859; daughter of *Josephine of Baden (1813–1900) and Charles Anthony I of Hohenzollern-Sigmaringen (1811–1885), prince of Rumania; married Pedro V or Peter V (1837–1861), king of Portugal (r. 1853–1861), on May 18, 1858.*

## Stephanie de Beauharnais (1789–1860)

*Vicomtesse de Beauharnais and grand duchess of Baden. Born on August 28, 1789; died on January 29, 1860; daughter of Claude (1756–1819), count de Beauharnais; adopted as a daughter by Napoleon I Bonaparte (1769–1821), emperor of France; married Charles Ludwig, grand duke of Baden, on April 8, 1806; children: *Louise of Baden (1811–1854), princess of Baden; son (1812–1812); *Josephine of Baden (1813–1900); *Marie of Baden (1817–1888), princess of Zahringen; Alexander (1816–1817).*

## Stephanie of Belgium (1864–1945)

*Belgian princess. Name variations: Stephanie Saxe-Coburg. Born on May 21, 1864; died in 1945; daughter of Leopold II, king of the Belgians (r. 1865–1909), and Maria Henrietta of Austria (1836–1902); married Rudolf (1858–1889), crown prince of Austria and Hungary, on May 10, 1881; married Elemer, prince*

*Lonyai de Nagy, on March 22, 1900; children: (first marriage) *Elizabeth von Habsburg (1883–1963).*

Stephanie of Belgium was born in 1864, the daughter of Leopold II, king of the Belgians, and *Maria Henrietta of Austria. She married Rudolf, crown prince of Austria and Hungary, in 1881. In 1889, Rudolf died at Mayerling along with his mistress *Marie Vetsera as the result of a suicide pact. Stephanie's memoir, *I Was to Be an Empress*, was published in 1937.

## Stephen, Vanessa (1879–1961).

See Bell, Vanessa.

## Stephen, Virginia (1882–1941).

See Woolf, Virginia.

# Stephens, Alice Barber (1858–1932)

*American illustrator. Born on July 1, 1858, near Salem, New Jersey; died on July 13, 1932, in Rose Valley, Pennsylvania; daughter of Samuel Clayton Barber and Mary (Owen) Barber; educated at public schools; studied engraving at the Philadelphia School of Design for Women; studied life drawing and portraiture under Thomas Eakins at the Pennsylvania Academy of the Fine Arts; married Charles Hallowell Stephens, in June 1890; children: Daniel Owen Stephens (b. 1893).*

*Illustrated numerous books, including George Eliot's* Middlemarch; *illustrations appeared in a number of leading journals, including* Century, Cosmopolitan *and* Ladies' Home Journal.

Born Alice Barber in 1858 on a farm near Salem, New Jersey, Alice Stephens was the daughter of Samuel Clayton Barber, who was of English Quaker ancestry; her mother **Mary Owen Barber**'s family had emigrated from Wales before the American Revolution. The eighth of nine children, Stephens attended the Philadelphia School of Design for Women while still at elementary school after her family moved to that city. There she learned the art of wood engraving and at age 15 began supporting herself, making engravings for *Scribner's Monthly*, *Harper's Weekly* and the Philadelphia periodical *Woman's Words*.

In 1876, Stephens began attending life drawing and portrait classes given by Thomas Eakins at the Pennsylvania Academy of the Fine Arts, where she met her future husband Charles Hallowell Stephens, a fellow student and future instructor at the academy. Alice soon became a

sought-after book and magazine illustrator, working for such publications as *Century, Cosmopolitan* and *Frank Leslie's Weekly.* Her style was simple and striking, yet highly detailed, and she became accomplished in a wide variety of media, including oils, charcoal and watercolors. She traveled to Europe for the winter of 1886–87 and exhibited two works at the Paris Salon. While in Paris, she studied at the Académie Julian and Filippo Colarossi's school; she also made a sketching tour of Italy.

Stephanie of Belgium

Back in the United States, Stephens became a regular illustrator for the *Ladies' Home Journal* and for a number of publishers, including Houghton Mifflin and Thomas Y. Crowell. She illustrated books by *Louisa May Alcott, *Margaret Deland and Sir Arthur Conan Doyle, as well as special editions of Longfellow's *The Courtship of Miles Standish* and Nathaniel Hawthorne's *The Marble Faun.*

The decade following her marriage in 1890 was the peak of Stephens' career. One of the best-known illustrators of her day, Stephens worked from her studio on Chestnut Street in Philadelphia. She also painted in oil, winning prizes and medals for her work from the Pennsylvania Academy (for *Portrait of a Boy*, 1890), the Atlanta Exposition (1895), a women's exhibition at Earl's Court (for drawings for *Middlemarch* by George Eliot [*Mary Anne Evans] and *John Halifax, Gentleman* by *Dinah Maria Mulock Craik*, 1899), and the Paris Exposition (1900). Daniel Owen, her only child, was born in 1893.

After turning down an offer to teach life drawing at the Pennsylvania Academy—an unusual honor for a woman at that time—Stephens and her family spent 15 months abroad while she recovered from overwork and exhaustion. On their return in 1902, they moved to rural Rose Valley, Pennsylvania, into a converted stone barn named Thunderbird, where she spent her last 30 years. She continued painting landscapes and portraits for pleasure, illustrating with wash or charcoal, and teaching life drawing at the Philadelphia School of Design for Women.

In 1904, she served on the fine arts jury for the Louisiana Purchase Exposition in St. Louis. With *Emily Sartain, then director of the Philadelphia School, Stephens founded the Plastic Club and held a retrospective exhibition there in 1929.

Stephens was admired for her vigor as an artist and the way her dynamic and realistic drawings transcended the genre of commercial illustration. She died at Rose Valley at age 74, after a paralytic stroke, and was buried in West Laurel Hill Cemetery in Bala-Cynwyd, Pennsylvania.

**SOURCES:**

James, Edward T., ed. *Notable American Women, 1607–1950.* Cambridge, MA: The Belknap Press of Harvard University, 1971.

McHenry, Robert, ed. *Famous American Women.* NY: Dover, 1980.

Rubinstein, Charlotte Streifer. *American Women Artists.* Boston, MA: G.K. Hall, 1982.

**Paula Morris**, D.Phil.,
Brooklyn, New York

# Stephens, Ann S. (1810–1886)

*American writer. Name variations: Jonathan Slick. Born Ann Sophia Winterbotham on March 30, 1810, in Humphreysville (later Seymour), Connecticut; died of nephritis in Newport, Rhode Island, on August 20, 1886; third of ten children of John Winterbotham and Ann (Wrigley) Winterbotham (both immigrants from England); married Edward Stephens (a merchant), in 1831; children: Ann (b. 1841); Edward (b. 1845).*

*Ann S. Stephens*

Born in Connecticut in 1810, Ann S. Stephens married at an early age and moved with her husband Edward Stephens to Portland, Maine, where she founded and edited the *Portland Magazine* (1835–37). In 1836, she edited the *Portland Sketch Book*, a collection of miscellanies by Maine writers. The couple then moved to New York where she pursued a writing career. Her story "Mary Derwent," which won a $400 prize offered by a periodical, brought her prominence. Known for her humor, Stephens wrote many novels, including *Fashion and Famine* (1854), and edited the *Pictorial History of the War for the Union* (1865–66) in two volumes. She also wrote a goodly amount of frontier adventure tales. Her 1860 *Malaeska: The Indian Wife of the White Hunter*, the first dime novel, sold 500,000 copies and upped her visibility. Over the years, Stephens supported her family with the proceeds of her serialized books.

# Stephens, Catherine (1794–1882)

*English soprano and actress. Name variations: Catherine Capell-Coningsby, countess of Essex. Born in London, England, on September 18, 1794; died in London on February 22, 1882; married the earl of Essex, in 1838 (died 1839).*

Born in London in 1794, Catherine Stephens began studying singing in 1807 with Gesualdo Lanza. By 1812, she had begun singing small parts with an Italian company at the Pantheon in London. She made her debut as Mandane in Arne's *Artaxerxes* at Covent Garden on September 23, 1813. From 1813 until 1822, Stephens appeared at Covent Garden. She performed at Drury Lane from 1822 to 1828, when she returned to Covent Garden. Stephens fashioned herself as a singer with "English style based on Italian rudiments," and her technique made her one of the most popular artists of the period. Her frequent appearances would be considered extraordinary by modern standards, as Stephens sang in ballad operas, operas, and other entertainments. In 1819, she sang Susanna in the first performance of Mozart's *Le nozze di Figaro*, and she continued singing until 1835 when she retired. She married the aging earl of Essex three years later.

**John Haag**,
Athens, Georgia

# Stephens, Helen (1918–1994)

*American runner known as the "Missouri Express." Name variations: Helen Herring Stephens. Born in Fulton, Missouri, on February 3, 1918; died on January 17, 1994.*

*Won the gold medal in the 100 meters and another gold in the 4x100-meter relay in the Berlin Olympics (1936); ran races against Jesse Owens, the famed African-American track star.*

Helen Stephens was born in 1918 on a farm near Fulton, Missouri. One day in high school, she raced against potential members of the boys' track team, who were told they had 7 seconds to run the 50-yard dash. Stephens completed the dash in under 7 seconds, outrunning all the boys in the process. Nonplussed, coach W.B. Moore asked her to run again. After clocking her, he took his watch to be checked at the local jewelry store. The time of her first run was 5.8 seconds, the second 5.9; both times had broken world records. Moore leaked the story to the newspapers, and Stephens became a serious runner.

Competitions for women were nonexistent both in high school and college, so Moore entered her in the National AAU championships being held in St. Louis in 1935. In a blue gymsuit made by her mother and borrowed boys' running shoes and sweat pants, Stephens ran the 100 meters against *Stella Walsh, the 1932 Olympic champion, and tied with her. Stephens' showing caused a sensation, all the more so since Walsh had called her a "greenie from the sticks." Newspapers ran stories on the young runner, one dressing her up in overalls, with a shotgun and hunting dog, under the title "From farm to fame in 6.6 seconds."

Local business leaders formed the Fulton Athletic Club to sponsor Stephens, underwriting her expenses. A year before the 1936 Olympics, she trained with the boys, often running the 400 and 800 meters. At that time, women competed only in the 100-meter race, since longer distances were considered to be beyond their physical capacities. Stephens ran the longer distances with ease, however. At the Ozark District meet in St. Louis, an Olympic qualifying trial, she broke the world record before officials found that the track was a foot short, a fairly common occurrence in those days. Despite this, she went on to break many records.

The 1936 Olympics in Berlin were memorable for many reasons. Hitler's Nazi government worked hard to make a favorable world impression. Accommodations were spartan but comfortable, though athletes had complaints about the food. Breakfast, for example, consisted of apples and black bread until the Americans insisted on bacon and eggs. They suspected they were being underfed to give the Germans an advantage.

There were three heats in the 100-meter race in Berlin. Stephens ran 11.4 in the first heat and 11.5 in the semifinal heat, breaking the world record with both times. She won the gold medal in the 100 meters, beating Walsh by .02 of a second. Winning the 4x100-meter race was not a foregone conclusion, as the German relay team was favored. But America's *Betty Robinson, who had suffered terrible injuries in an earlier plane crash, performed surprisingly well, as did Stephens, and a German runner dropped the baton. Stephens had her second gold medal.

After her 100-meter win, Adolf Hitler had invited Stephens to his box, but her coach had tried to put Hitler's courier off, saying that Stephens was due to be interviewed for a radio broadcast. "I can't go back and tell the Führer that," said the messenger. "He'll shoot me." Nonetheless, Stephens did her broadcast while the messenger cooled his heels. But when Stephens was escorted to Hitler's stadium box, she noticed the 15 blackshirted guards waiting outside and began to realize that the messenger's fears might not be overblown. Even so, she refused to give a salute, preferring to offer Hitler "a good ol' Missouri handshake" instead. The Führer's greeting proved more intimate than Stephens expected. "You're a true Aryan type," he said as he pinched her behind. "You should be running for Germany." He then invited her to spend the weekend at Berchtesgaden, his mountain retreat, an invitation which was declined due to "being in training."

On her return to the States, Stephens endorsed Quaker Oats and played with the All-American Redheads, a women's basketball team. She toured the country with the team, playing local men's teams and generally beating them. She also ran five races against the African-American Olympic gold-medal-winner Jesse Owens, with whom she had become friendly during the Games. Stephens liked Owens, even though he had accidentally broken her finger in one race when he threw out his hand.

Helen Stephens continued to be physically active over the years. In 1986, at age 68, she entered 12 events in the regional Senior Olympics in St. Louis and won gold medals in 8 of them. While summing up her career, she quoted Dizzy Dean. "I wasn't the greatest," she said, "but I was amongst 'em."

**SOURCES:**
Carlson, Lewis H., and John J. Fogarty. *Tales of Gold.* Chicago, IL: Contemporary Books, 1987.
Condon, Robert J. *Great Women Athletes of the 20th Century.* Jefferson, NC: McFarland, 1991.

**Karin L. Haag**, freelance writer, Athens, Georgia

# Stephens, Kate (1853–1938)

*American feminist writer, editor and university professor. Born on February 27, 1853, in Moravia, New York; died on May 10, 1938, in Concordia, Kansas; daughter of Nelson Timothy Stephens (a lawyer) and Elizabeth (Rathbone) Stephens; University of Kansas, M.A. in Greek, 1878; engaged to Byron Caldwell*

*Smith (a professor), 1874 (died 1877); never married; no children.*

*Wrote polemical works, including* A Curious History in Book Editing *(1927) and* Lies and Libels of Frank Harris *(1929); wrote several books on Kansas, including* American Thumb-Prints: Mettle of Our Men and Women *(1905); wrote epistolary fiction in* A Woman's Heart *(1906), republished as* Pillar of Smoke, *and feminist essays in* Workfellows in Social Progression *(1916); her love letters from Byron Caldwell Smith were published as* The Professor's Love-Life: Letters of Ronsby Maldclewith *(1919), and republished (1930) as* The Love-Life of Byron Caldwell Smith.

Kate Stephens was born in 1853 in Moravia, New York, the third of five children born to lawyer (later Judge) Nelson Timothy Stephens and **Elizabeth Rathbone Stephens**. Encouraged in her reading and thinking by her father, Stephens entered the junior preparatory class of the University of Kansas at age 15. In 1875, she graduated from the regular college course as valedictorian and three years later received an M.A. in Greek.

In 1874, Stephens became engaged to the controversial young academic Byron Caldwell Smith. Stripped of his professorship because of his liberal religious views, Smith suffered from poor health and died in Colorado in 1877, aged only 27. Stephens published his love letters to her as *The Professor's Love-Life: Letters of Ronsby Maldclewith* in 1919; they were republished as *The Love-Life of Byron Caldwell Smith* in 1930.

Kate Stephens had a similarly rocky academic career teaching Greek language and literature at the University of Kansas. Despite the popularity of her classes, her pantheistic views and strong personality made her unpopular with other faculty members, and she was dismissed as professor in 1885. A year earlier, her father had died. Her mother became an invalid, and she herself suffered from nervous exhaustion and poor health. Her dismissal from the university, however, inspired Stephens to a life of active and outspoken feminism.

Kate and Elizabeth moved to Cambridge, Massachusetts, and in 1890, for financial reasons, Stephens became a junior editor at D.C. Heath and Company. There she had a spirited quarrel with the publishers and senior editor Charles Eliot Norton when he tried to claim sole credit for her series of children's readers, an episode she was to publicize in 1927 in her book *A Curious History in Book Editing*. She continued working in an editorial capacity for a variety of publishers after moving to New York City in 1894. Stephens became a member of the Pen and Brush club and an active committee member, receiving a War and Navy citation for her work at the New York War Camp Community Service during World War I.

In addition to articles, reviews and numerous letters to newspapers, Stephens wrote books on a variety of topics, including Kansas history, feminist issues and the nature of American democracy. Her attention-grabbing polemical writings, for which she is best known, were inspired by causes close to her heart. *Truths Back of the Jimmy Myth in a State University in the Middle West* (1924) argued her father's claim to founding the University of Kansas law school over that of her brother-in-law, Dr. James Green. In 1929, Stephens published *Lies and Libels of Frank Harris* (edited by Gerrit and **Mary Caldwell Smith**), a well-researched rebuttal of Irish-American Harris' portrait of Lawrence, Kansas, Byron Caldwell Smith, and Stephens herself in his notorious 1922 autobiography *My Life and Loves*.

After an adult life plagued by illness, Stephens returned to Lawrence in 1935, aged 82, where she spent her final years in better health. In 1938, she suffered a cerebral hemorrhage and died two months later at her niece's home in Concordia, Kansas. Stephens, who was buried in the family plot at Oak Hill Cemetery in Lawrence, left her entire estate of $30,000 to the University of Kansas, founding the Judge Stephens Lectureship of the School of Law.

SOURCES:
James, Edward T., ed. *Notable American Women, 1607–1950.* Cambridge, MA: The Belknap Press of Harvard University, 1971.

**Paula Morris**, D.Phil.,
Brooklyn, New York

# Stephenson, Jan (1951—)

*Australian golfer. Born in Sydney, New South Wales, Australia, on December 22, 1951; attended Hales Secretarial School in Sydney; lives in Fort Worth, Texas; married Eddie Vossler.*

*Five-time winner of the New South Wales Schoolgirl championships (1964–69); won the New South Wales Junior championships (1969–72); won the New South Wales Amateur twice, and was the New South Wales "Woman Athlete of the Year" (1971); turned professional (1972) and played the Australian LPGA tour before joining the U.S. tour full time; won the Australian LPGA title (1973); in U.S., won the Sarah Coventy-Naples Classic and the Birmingham Classic (1976), Women's International*

*(1978), Sun City Classic (1980), Peter Jackson Classic and Mary Kay Classic (1981), the LPGA championship and Lady Keystone (1982), Lady Keystone and U.S. Open (1983), Safeco Classic (1987), J.C. Penney LPGA Skins Game (1990).*

Born in Sydney, Australia, in 1951, Jan Stephenson looked more like a model than an athlete, a minus as well as a plus for any golfing professional. Some refused to take the stunning blonde's athletic abilities seriously, but Stephenson proved she was a contender. She was the New South Wales Schoolgirl champion from 1964 to 1969, the Junior champion from 1969 to 1972, and she won the Australian Junior championship three times and the New South Wales Amateur twice. When she turned professional in 1972, she won four titles and became a national champion as well. She came to the United States to play in the mid-1970s and was LPGA Rookie of the Year in 1974. In 1976, she won two tournaments, followed by another in 1978, and yet another in 1980. In 1981, she set the all-time LPGA low score of 198 for 54 holes to win the Mary Kay Classic.

Injury plagued Stephenson's career. During the first part of 1982, a foot injury had her sidelined. Nonetheless, she had three victories that year, including the LPGA championship for which she beat out *JoAnn Carner by two strokes. In 1983, Stephenson won the U.S. Open while sweltering under 100 degree temperatures, beating Carner by one stroke. She also won two other championships that year and finished in the top five in almost every category. In 1987, after an April auto accident caused her to miss six weeks of play, Stephenson returned to win the Safeco Classic. Stephenson's swing was precise rather than powerful, but her technical ability combined with hours of practice made her a professional golfer of the first rank.

**SOURCES:**
Markel, Robert, Nancy Brooks, and Susan Markel. *For the Record: Women in Sports.* NY: World Almanac, 1985.

**Karin Loewen Haag**,
Athens, Georgia

## Stephenson, Marjory (1885–1948)

*English biochemist. Born in 1885; died in 1948; attended Newnham College, 1903–06; studied under F.G. Hopkins; awarded a Beit Memorial fellowship for medical research.*

Marjory Stephenson was the foremost authority on bacterial metabolism during the 1930

*Jan Stephenson*

and 1940s. After a four-year career delay during World War I when she served with British Red Cross in France and Salonika, Stephenson continued her pursuits in biochemistry. She was appointed to the permanent staff of the Medical Research Council (1929); was a reader in chemical microbiology at the University of Cambridge; was one of the first two women (with *Kathleen Lonsdale) to be elected fellow of the Royal Society (1945); and was president of the Society of General Microbiology. Her volume on bacterial metabolism was part of the "Monographs on Biochemistry" series, while her 1930 book *Bacterial Metabolism* is considered a standard work.

**SOURCES:**
Kass-Simon, G., and Patricia Farnes, eds. *Women of Science: Righting the Record.* Bloomington, IN: Indiana University Press, 1990.

## Steptoe, Lydia (1892–1982).

*See Barnes, Djuna.*

# Stern, Catherine Brieger

## (1894–1973)

*German-born American educational innovator.
Name variations: Käthe Brieger. Born Käthe Brieger
on January 6, 1894, in Breslau, Germany; died on
January 8, 1973, in New York City; daughter of Oscar
Brieger (a physician) and Hedwig (Lyon) Brieger;
studied at home and at Mädchen Gymnasium in Breslau, 1904–12; University of Breslau, Ph.D. in mathematics and physics, 1918; studied Montessori teaching
method; married Rudolf Stern, in 1919 (died 1962);
children: daughter Toni Stern Gould (b. 1920); son
Fritz Stern (b. 1926).*

*Wrote on the theoretical framework of her teach-
ing experiences in* Methodik der täglichen Kinderhaupraxis *(1932) and on the practicalities of running a
kindergarten in* Wille, Phantasie und Werkgestaltung
*(1933); wrote on her theories and Gestalt principles in*
Children Discover Arithmetic *(1949); her materials published for classroom use as* Structural Arithmetic *(1951,
1965, 1966); with daughter Toni Stern Gould, wrote*
The Early Years of Childhood: Education Through Insight *(1955) and* Children Discover Reading *(1965).*

Catherine Brieger Stern, the only daughter of
Oscar and **Hedwig Brieger**, was born Käthe
Brieger in Breslau, Germany, in 1894. With three
prominent physicians in their immediate family,
she and her three brothers grew up in a close and
affluent circle of scholarly relatives. Stern inherited her lifelong interest in teaching children from
her close relationship with her mother, who
worked in an early volunteer kindergarten. Stern
began her education at home with a private tutor
and then attended the Mädchen Gymnasium in
Breslau from 1904 until 1912, returning there to
teach for a brief period after her father's death in
1914. At his earlier urging, she enrolled to study
physics at the University of Breslau and, despite
the disruption of World War I, during which she
served in a hospital, obtained her Ph.D. in mathematics and physics in 1918.

Attracted to the arts as well as to science,
Stern wrote poetry, produced plays and learned
French while studying in Breslau. There she also
met Rudolf Stern, a future physician and researcher, who, like her, came from a medical
family. They married on April 19, 1919, and had
two children in the next seven years. After
Rudolf's death in 1962, Stern would write: "we
were, almost every day, together" in the 43 years
of their marriage.

During her daughter's early childhood,
Stern studied the teaching methods of *Maria

Montessori and, after running her own
preschool at home, opened Breslau's first
Montessori kindergarten in 1924. Her school
grew in size and range of activities, including an
after-school club for older children and a
teacher-training institute. Stern obtained state
certification in order to teach at grade-school
level as well. In conjunction with her teaching
work, Stern read and wrote articles on educational theory and developed materials for teaching reading and arithmetic based on adapting
the learning process "to the natural development
of the child." She published two books, one on
the theory and the other on the practice of running her kindergarten: *Methodik der täglichen
Kinderhaupraxis* in 1932, written at the urging
of her close adviser, chemist Fritz Haber, and
*Wille, Phantasie und Werkgestaltung* in 1933.

Catherine's departure from the educational
drilling and repetition favored under Hitler's
regime and her Jewish heritage caused the Sterns
to flee Nazi Germany. They emigrated to North
America with Stern's mother in 1938, and settled in New York City. Stern became a U.S. citizen in 1944. In the United States, Stern continued the work she had begun in Germany,
teaching, researching, lecturing and writing. She
devised innovative teaching materials designed
to reduce dependence on rote learning methods—for example, creating blocks of different
lengths and colors to represent one to ten units
as tools for teaching the basic principles and relationships of mathematics. Renouncing the traditional approach to reading (spelling out single
letters or identifying words by their overall
shape), Stern stressed the correspondence of spoken sounds with letter clusters and taught children to see reading, spelling and writing as integral parts of the same constructive process.

In 1940, Stern met Max Wertheimer,
founder of the school of Gestalt psychology in
Berlin, who became an important supporter.
Wertheimer realized that Stern's materials were
the embodiment of his educational ideal of
learning by insight rather than rote. Stern
worked as Wertheimer's research assistant at the
New School for Social Research until his death
in 1943, giving demonstrations in his classes and
studying Gestalt theory, funded by grants from
the New York Foundation and the Oberländer
Trust. Their work together informed Wertheimer's *Productive Thinking* (1945, 1959) and
Stern's books *Children Discover Arithmetic*
(1949) and *Structural Arithmetic* (1951, 1965,
1966), the latter term coined by Wertheimer for
Stern's materials, which were known in England
as the Stern Apparatus.

From 1944 to 1951, Stern, her daughter **Toni Stern Gould** and her future daughter-in-law **Margaret J. Bassett** conducted the experimental Castle School in Manhattan, one of the first to teach numbers concepts and reading to preschool children. Stern and Gould wrote two books together, *The Early Years of Childhood: Education Through Insight* (1955), based on the Castle School years, and *Children Discover Reading* (1965). Aided by grants from the Carnegie Corporation (1958–62), Stern spent much of the 1950s and 1960s writing, researching and teaching. Having anticipated by a quarter of a century many of the ideas of the "modern mathematics" movement, Stern was consulted by the School Mathematics Study Group, proponents of the new math program.

Stern was a private woman uninterested in public honors, dedicated to her friends and family as well as her profession. She was also an avid reader with broad-ranging interests and a facility for languages. She remained professionally active until her death in January 1973, following a stroke. Stern's work was carried on by her daughter and daughter-in-law, and her educational materials continued to be used throughout the world, proving particularly useful in the field of special education.

**SOURCES:**

Sicherman, Barbara, and Carol Hurd Green, eds. *Notable American Women: The Modern Period.* Cambridge, MA: Belknap Press of Harvard University, 1980.

**Paula Morris**, D.Phil.,
Brooklyn, New York

## Stern, Daniel (1805–1876).

*See Wagner, Cosima for sidebar on Marie d'Agoult.*

## Stern, Edith Rosenwald

### (1895–1980)

*American philanthropist who was known especially for her charities and reforms in New Orleans. Name variations: Mrs. Edgar Rosenwald Stern; Effie Stern. Born Edith Rosenwald in Chicago, Illinois, in 1895; died in the summer of 1980; daughter of Julius (J.R.) Rosenwald and Augusta (Nusbaum) Rosenwald; sister of* **Marion Rosenwald Ascoli** *and* **Adele Rosenwald***; married Germon Sulzberger, in 1913 (divorced); married Edgar Bloom Stern (died 1959); children: Philip, Edgar, Jr., Audrey.*

Edith Rosenwald Stern was born in Chicago, Illinois, in 1895, the daughter of J.R. Rosenwald and **Augusta Nusbaum Rosenwald**. When Edith was a young girl, her father and her uncle Aaron Nusbaum purchased half interest in Sears, Roebuck, and set about reorganizing the growing company. By 1908, J.R. was in full control. It was said that Edith inherited her father's characteristics and that her nickname Effie stood for Efficiency. Though her father and mother were penurious when it came to personal spending, they gave freely to charities, establishing a school for blacks in the rural South. Since he was a Jew, explained J.R, he knew what discrimination felt like.

Edith inherited her parents' predilection for philanthropy. When she married Edgar Stern and moved to New Orleans, she was quick to notice the absence of any civic charity in that city, as well as the rampant discrimination toward blacks and Jews. In the 1920s, she built an estate in Metairie called Longue Vue, considered one of the most beautiful houses in the South. From there, she set out to win over the city of New Orleans and reform the public school system. First she built the Newcomb Nursery School, then the Metairie Country Day School. Frustrated by the political corruption that she encountered along the way, she gained permission to examine the city's rolls and unearthed 10,000 illegally registered voters. While suffering the cries of angry politicians, Stern systematically began to divest the voter rolls of the illegals while propping up black registration. "Soon," wrote Stephen Birmingham, "she had marshaled a small army of women for her Voters Service, and she organized a 'broom parade' of socially prominent women who, brooms in hand, marched on City Hall, the message, of course, being that it was time to sweep the rascals out."

Stern was made a trustee of Dillard University, a black college, and founded the New Orleans repertory theater, the Symphony Society, and the Isaac Delgado Museum of Art; she also caused more consternation when she gave a buffet supper in honor of *Marian Anderson. Edith and her husband founded the Stern Fund, which supported philanthropic activities for 20 years. She once commented to her sister Marion that upon her arrival in Metairie the streets had not been paved; her sister replied, "Good God, Edith, don't tell me you did that *too*!"

**SOURCES:**

Birmingham, Stephen. *Grandes Dames.* NY: Simon & Schuster, 1982.

## Stern, Frances (1873–1947)

*American social worker and dietitian. Born on July 3, 1873, in Boston, Massachusetts; died on December*

*23, 1947, in Newton, Massachusetts; daughter of Louis Stern (a dealer in boots and shoes) and Caroline (Oppenheimer) Stern; graduated from Garland Kindergarten Training School, 1897; studied food chemistry and sanitation at Massachusetts Institute of Technology, 1909, 1911, 1912; took economics and politics classes at London School of Economics, 1922; never married; no children.*

*Founded Boston Dispensary Food Clinic (1918), now known as the Frances Stern Nutrition Center; wrote a number of books and articles on diet and health, including* Food for the Worker *(with Gertrude T. Spitz, 1917),* Food and Your Body: Talks with Children *(with Mary Pfaffman, 1932, revised under the title* How to Teach Nutrition to Children, *1942), and* Applied Dietetics *(1936).*

Frances Stern was born in 1873, the youngest of seven children in an orthodox Jewish family of German immigrants. From her religious, community-minded family, Stern inherited a sense of social responsibility which informed her career in nutritional education, mostly based in her hometown of Boston. Her education took place in several staggered phases throughout her life, reflecting her developing sense of vocation. After completing grammar school, she taught Sunday school at Congregation Beth Israel at a young age, and in 1890 began teaching at the new Hebrew Industrial School in the North End. Stern's experiences there, witnessing the physical and emotional effects of poverty on children, set the course of her career. In 1895, with her friend **Isabel Hyams**, Stern opened the *Louisa Alcott Club in a tenement building in Boston's South End, teaching homemaking to young people living in the neighborhood's slums. At the same time she attended courses at the Garland Kindergarten Training School in Boston, graduating in 1897.

Isabel Hyams introduced Stern to her former teacher *Ellen Swallow Richards, a distinguished instructor in sanitary chemistry at the Massachusetts Institute of Technology (MIT) and founder of the home economics profession. Stern became her secretary and research assistant until Richards' death in 1911. Inspired by Richards' work and eager for a deeper understanding of the relationship between nutrition and social problems, Stern took courses in food chemistry and sanitation at MIT in 1909, 1911 and 1912.

In 1912, Stern developed a visiting housekeeping program for the Boston Association for the Relief and Control of Tuberculosis, later devising a similar program for the Boston Provi-

dent Association. Her work as an industrial health inspector for the State Board of Labor and Industries between 1912 and 1915 gave her important firsthand knowledge of the effects of diet on workers as well as children. Inspired by idealism yet informed by realism, Stern envisioned neighborhood centers that would provide practical nutritional education, expounding on her beliefs in *Food for the Worker*, written with **Gertrude T. Spitz** and published in 1917. The following year, at the request of Michael Davis, director of the Boston Dispensary, Stern established a food clinic, which was to become her major lifework.

World War I and its aftermath drew her away from Boston, first to Washington, D.C., to work in the Division of Home Conservation of the U.S. Food Administration and then as an industrial investigator for the Department of Agriculture, assessing the adequacy of workers' food. Stern spent the period between 1918 and 1922 in Europe, working for the American Red Cross and the Child and Family Welfare Association in France. While there, she studied economics and politics as a special student at the London School of Economics.

Returning to Boston, Stern threw herself into work at her clinic, creating an inviting atmosphere for her largely Russian, Italian, and Syrian clientele, and dispensing a variety of dietary advice to suit low budgets, medical needs and national tastes. In 1925, she set up a Nutrition Education Department to train doctors, dentists, social workers and nurses from all around the world in dietetics, undertaking further research into the impact of social environment on health. Stern's life also encompassed work on numerous committees and boards, writing and publishing, and caring for an invalid brother. Outgoing, attractive and vivacious, Stern made her comfortable home an open house for young people interested in educational, economic and welfare issues. One of the initial members of the American Dietetic Association, she was the first chair of its Social Services Section. She was an active member of the Welfare Committee of the Federated Jewish Charities, the American Public Health Association, and the American Home Economics Association. She also taught nutrition or dietetics at the Simmons College School of Social Work, Tufts College Medical School, MIT, and the State Teachers College at Framingham.

Although physically incapacitated by congestive heart disease in old age, Stern remained mentally alert and involved in the running of her clinic to the very end. After she died at home in Newton, Massachusetts, in 1947, a memorial service was held at Temple Israel in Boston and her ashes were placed in the Chapel of Peace at the Forest Hills Cemetery. The clinic, renamed the Frances Stern Food Clinic in her honor in 1943, is now known as the Frances Stern Nutrition Center.

**SOURCES:**

James, Edward T., ed. *Notable American Women, 1607–1950*. Cambridge, MA: The Belknap Press of Harvard University, 1971.

**Paula Morris**, D.Phil.,
Brooklyn, New York

## Stern, G.B. (1890–1973)

*English novelist, short-story writer, and playwright.*
*Name variations: Gladys Bronwyn Stern; Gladys Bertha Stern. Born Gladys Bertha Stern on June 17, 1890, in London, England; died on September 19, 1973; daughter of Albert Stern (a gem dealer) and Elizabeth (Schwabacher) Stern; educated in Germany and Switzerland; spent two years at the Academy of Dramatic Art; married Geoffrey Lisle Holdsworth (a journalist from New Zealand), in 1919 (divorced).*

*Author of over 40 novels; best known for a multi-volume saga of the Jewish family Rakonitz, based on her own family, collected as* The Rakonitz Chronicles *(1932) and* The Matriarch Chronicles *(1936).*

G.B. Stern was born in London in 1890, the second daughter of Albert and **Elizabeth Stern**. Her family was Jewish and involved in the gem business in London. However, when Stern was 14 years old, her family suffered financial ruin in an economic crash, and the remainder of her youth was spent in continuous relocation. She was 16 when she left high school to travel with her parents in Germany and in Switzerland, where she also studied, including two years at the Academy of Dramatic Art. In her autobiographical reminiscences, Stern recalled those years of moving frequently among apartments, boarding rooms, and hotels, and being unable to celebrate consecutive holidays in the same place. This pattern would continue into her adult life as she periodically resided in Cornwall, Italy, New York, and Hollywood.

As a child, Stern preferred the name Bronwyn to Bertha, and at the age of seven wrote her first play, which was produced in the family's billiard room. At 17, she penned her earliest published poem, which was accepted by the first magazine to which it was submitted, and, at 20, she wrote *Pantomime*, her first novel. However,

it was *Twos and Threes*, her second novel, that brought Stern to the attention of critics and readers in 1916. From then on, her novels appeared every two or three years in regular succession, with several reprinted in the United States. She was much appreciated by her contemporaries, among them W. Somerset Maugham.

Stern's five novels about the wealthy Jewish family Rakonitz brought her lasting literary recognition. Loosely based upon Stern's own family, it is a multi-generational saga that begins in the late 19th century and moves forward into the 1940s. *Children of No Man's Land*, the first book in the series, appeared in 1919. The second book, *Tents of Israel*, which Stern dedicated to John Galsworthy in recognition of the influence of his *Forsyte Saga* upon her own work, was published in 1924 and reissued in 1948 as *The Matriarch*. This was followed by *A Deputy Was King* in 1926, *Mosaic* in 1930, *Shining and Free* in 1935, and *The Young Matriarch* in 1942. The novels were collectively published as *The Rakonitz Chronicles* in 1932, and *The Matriarch Chronicles* in 1936. A 1929 stage version of the first two of the "matriarch" novels starred \***Mrs. Patrick Campbell**. The oppressive matriarch of the series was based on Stern's great-aunt, **Anastasia Schwabacher**, who lived to the age of 90 and who, according to **Joanne Shattock**, was upset with her portrayal and was "looking for Gladys with a gun" when the first novel was published. Stern herself was Toni, the young matriarch of the final volume in the series.

Stern also wrote several plays, a book about Robert Louis Stevenson, and co-wrote with \***Sheila Kaye-Smith** two books on \***Jane Austen**. Her autobiographical memoirs include *Monogram* (1936), *Another Part of the Forest* (1941), *Trumpet Voluntary* (1944), *Benefits Forgot* (1949), and *A Name to Conjure With* (1953). In 1954, Stern chronicled her conversion to Catholicism in 1947 in *All in Good Time*.

Stern met the man who would become her husband, Geoffrey Lisle Holdsworth, a New Zealand journalist, through their mutual friend Noel Coward who had provided him with some of Stern's writings. They were married in 1919 but were later divorced. She died in 1973.

**SOURCES:**

Buck, Claire, ed. *The Bloomsbury Guide to Women's Literature*. NY: Prentice Hall, 1992.

Kunitz, Stanley J., and Howard Haycraft, eds. *Twentieth Century Authors: A Biographical Dictionary of Modern Literature*. NY: H.W. Wilson, 1942.

Shattock, Joanne. *The Oxford Guide to British Women Writers*. NY: Oxford University Press, 1993.

**Martha Jones**, M.L.S.,
Natick, Massachusetts

# Stern, Irma (1894–1966)

*South African painter who introduced Expressionism to South Africa. Born in Schweizer-Reneke, Transvaal, South Africa, in 1894; died in Cape Town, South Africa, in 1966; studied at the Weimar Academy in Germany under Carl Fritjof Smith, 1913; studied at the Levin-Funcke Studio in Berlin with Gari Melchers and Martin Brandenburg, 1914; studied at the Bauhaus in Weimar; married Johannes Prinze, in 1926 (divorced 1935).*

Regarded as one of the most eminent 20th-century artists in South Africa, Irma Stern was born in 1894 in Transvaal, South Africa, to German-Jewish parents. In 1901, during the Boer War, the Sterns moved to Germany. Following a visit to Zanzibar in 1904 and a brief return to South Africa in 1909, the family settled in Berlin, where Stern received her formal education in art. She studied with Carl Fritjof Smith at the Weimar Academy beginning in 1913, and with Gari Melchers and Martin Brandenburg a year later at the Levin-Funcke Studio in Berlin. She was a founding member of Novembergruppe in 1916, exhibiting her work in Berlin, first at the Freie Sezession in 1918 and a year later at the Fritz Gurlitt Gallery. At age 26, Stern return to South Africa, where she would reside permanently.

Stern's extensive travels throughout Africa and Europe gave perspective to her art, which reflects an idealized merging of black and white cultural landscapes. "Unlike her contemporaries in the world of white South African art," notes Kevin Hillstrom, "Stern often chose the black inhabitants of her country as a subject." In Expressionist paintings characterized by vivid colors and lively brush strokes, Stern reveals an abiding awareness of, and respect for, the dignity of her subjects and their natural world.

Stern's artistic work was prodigious. During the 1930s and 1940s, her paintings increased substantially in number and included still-lifes, landscapes, and portraits. Although she was acclaimed by critics in Germany and France, where she exhibited her paintings, she attracted a number of critics in her homeland. According to Hillstrom, "Her sympathetic, idealized portraits of the black natives of South Africa occasionally drew the ire of the nation's apartheid government, while other observers charged that, while she created works that portrayed black people as dignified and tranquil in temperament, she never questioned the colonial underpinnings upon which apartheid rested." Stern overcame governmental objections to her work and, by the 1940s, she had secured her place in the history of South African art.

Stern exhibited her work worldwide throughout the 1950s and 1960s, and by this time her paintings were included in many important collections. Her many travels (to Zanzibar in 1939 and 1945, and to the Congo in 1942, 1946, and 1955) provided her with the visual experiences that informed her art. During the 1950s and 1960s, her travels to the French and Spanish Mediterranean areas contributed to the foundation for her later work. Following the artist's death in 1966, her Cape Town home was converted into the Irma Stern Museum, which houses a collection of own paintings and sculptures as well as the vast array of art and artifacts collected during her travels.

**SOURCES:**

*Harrap's Illustrated Dictionary of Art & Artists*. Kent, Great Britain: Harrap's Reference, 1990.

Hillstrom, Laurie Collier, and Kevin Hillstrom, eds. *Contemporary Women Artists*. Detroit, MI: St. James Press, 1999.

**Martha Jones**, M.L.S., Natick, Massachusetts

# Sterry, Mrs. A. (1871–1966).

*See Cooper, Charlotte.*

# Stetson, Augusta (1842–1928)

*Christian Science leader. Born Augusta Emma Simmons on October 12, 1842, in Waldoboro, Maine; daughter of Peabody Simmons (a carpenter and architect) and Salome (Sprague) Simmons; died of edema on October 12, 1928, in Rochester, New York; educated at Damariscotta High School and Lincoln Academy, New Castle, Maine; married Captain Frederick J. Stetson, in 1864 (died 1901); no children.*

Augusta Stetson was born in 1842 in Waldoboro, Maine, a descendant of *Mayflower* pilgrims who arrived in Plymouth in 1621. She grew up in nearby Damariscotta where her father was a carpenter and architect. Her family belonged to the local Methodist church, and Augusta was raised in a deeply religious household. Musically talented, she played the church organ at the age of 14.

In 1864, Augusta married Civil War veteran Captain Frederick J. Stetson who worked in his family's shipbuilding business, which took the couple to London, Bombay, and Burma (now Myanmar). The captain's imprisonment at Libby Prison during the Civil War had left him in poor health, however, which forced him to retire from the family business. The couple returned to the United States and resided with Augusta's parents in Boston, Massachusetts. Hoping to become a professional lecturer to support herself and her husband, Augusta enrolled in the Blish School of Oratory in 1882.

A pivotal experience in Stetson's life occurred when she attended an 1884 lecture by Christian Science founder *Mary Baker Eddy. Encouraged by Eddy to attend her Massachusetts Metaphysical College for a three-week course of instruction in the Christian Science religion, Stetson did so and then went to Maine to practice her new beliefs. She reported numerous healings during her stay, which impressed Eddy and prompted her to recall Stetson to Boston as one of the five preachers in her church there. Described as a tall, elegant woman with a stately appearance, a charismatic personality, and a resonant voice, Stetson impressed her audiences and attracted a number of personal devotees.

At Eddy's request, Stetson traveled to New York City in 1886, reluctantly leaving her family, to organize the church there; two years later, with Stetson as their preacher, a group of 17 people incorporated a Christian Science church. In 1890, she was formally ordained as a pastor, a title that later was changed to First Reader of the First Church of Christ, Scientist, New York City. The next year, she founded the New York City Christian Science Institute to train practitioners who treated patients and formed the core of support within the congregation. As membership in the church grew, they sought larger quarters and moved several times until it became clear that they required their own building. During this time Stetson brought her invalid husband to be with her in New York, where he died in 1901 of cerebral apoplexy. A new church was built at 96th Street and Central Park West, an imposing granite structure costing more than $1 million. Larger than the Mother Church in Boston, it was dedicated in 1903. The following year, a lavish residence for Stetson was constructed on an adjoining lot. Courting wealthy and fashionable New Yorkers, Stetson was unashamed of her luxurious residence, believing that it evinced the power and truth in Christian Science.

Stetson's success caused discomfort among the church leadership, however, and rumors circulated that her ultimate desire was to depose Eddy as leader of the church. Concerned about her personal following, Eddy quickly limited the term of a reader to three years. Stetson duly resigned her official position but continued to in-

fluence the First Church in New York. In 1908, Eddy managed to dissuade Stetson from her idea of building a branch of the First Church, which departed from the accepted practice of linking churches directly to the Mother Church. The following year, however, Eddy instructed the Christian Science board of directors to begin an investigation of the New York church and in particular of Stetson's inner circle of admirers. Evidence was presented that indicated Stetson had carried Christian Science teachings to extreme lengths, and in the fall of 1909, her license as a teacher and practitioner was revoked. Additionally, she and several of her followers were excommunicated and the trustees of the New York church who supported her were voted out of office.

Augusta Stetson

Despite her ejection from the Christian Science Church, Stetson remained in the home built with church funds and retained her position in the New York Christian Science Institute. With the support of her wealthy followers, she continued to teach her own version of Christian Science tenets; she also continued to express loyalty to Eddy, viewing her personal conflicts with church hierarchy as a test of allegiance, and believing that Eddy would rescue her from excommunication. Stetson gradually grew to interpret her experience as a victory and a higher calling to form a new, completely spiritual form of Christian Science, which she called the Church Triumphant. When Eddy died in 1910, many thought Stetson would come forward as her successor, but this did not occur. Supported by students and wealthy followers, Stetson promoted her own interpretation of Christian Science and lectured on the spiritual decline of the Mother Church. Large numbers came to hear her lectures, and she published a series of pamphlets outlining her views of the true church. Two collections were published at this time: *Reminiscences, Sermons, and Correspondence* (1913) and *Vital Issues in Christian Science* (1914), in which she chronicled the controversy of her experiences in the Church.

Under the assumption that religious music might combat the more brutish tendencies of human nature, Stetson formed the Choral Society of the New York City Christian Science Institute, which gave several successful concerts at the Metropolitan Opera House with Stetson herself seated prominently on stage. Also convinced that the national anthem was un-Christian, she penned a new patriotic anthem that was widely sung during World War I.

In the 1920s, sponsored once again by her wealthy followers, Stetson initiated a large newspaper advertising program to promote her religious views and published her major work, *Sermons Which Spiritually Interpret the Scriptures and Other Writings on Christian Science* (1924). The ideas presented by her students in their short-lived magazine, *American Standard*, coalesced with the purchase of a radio station for Stetson in 1925. She broadcast five times weekly, interspersing her own religious messages with Christian Science music and readings from the Bible and Eddy's works. Stetson used the forum to promulgate her own propaganda: the preservation of Nordic supremacy in America, traditional American virtues, and the belief that the founding documents of the United States were "divinely inspired" to protect the country from Catholicism. Claiming immortality, Stetson also predicted her own resurrection as well as that of Mary Baker Eddy.

For the remainder of her life, Stetson actively proselytized for her Church Triumphant. Residing with a nephew in Rochester, New York, she died from edema on October 12, 1928, at the age of 86. Her body was cremated and the remains interred at Damariscotta, Maine.

**SOURCES:**

James, Edward T., ed. *Notable American Women, 1607–1950*. Cambridge, MA: The Belknap Press of Harvard University, 1971.

McHenry, Robert, ed. *Famous American Women*. NY: Dover, 1980.

**Martha Jones**, M.L.S.,
Natick, Massachusetts

## Stetson, Charlotte Perkins (1860–1935).

*See Gilman, Charlotte Perkins.*

## Stettheimer, Florine (1871–1944)

*American artist whose lavish, satirical paintings were rediscovered to great acclaim 50 years after her death. Born in Rochester, New York, on August 19, 1871; died in New York City on May 11, 1944; fourth of five children and third daughter of Joseph Stettheimer (a banker) and Rosetta (Walter) Stettheimer; privately tutored; studied painting at the Art Students League, and in Munich, Berlin, and Stuttgart, Germany; never married; no children.*

*Selected works:* Flowers with Wallpaper/ Still Life No. 1 *(1915);* Bowl of Tulips *(1916);* Lake Placid *(1919);* Ashbury Park South *(1920);* Flowers *(1921);* Still Life with Flowers *(1921);* Portrait of Carl Van Vechten *(1922);* Spring Sale at Bendel's *(1922);* Portrait of Myself *(1923);* Beauty Contest *(1924);* Natatorium Undine *(1927);* Bouquet for Ettie *(1927);* Portrait of Stieglitz *(1928);* Three Flowers and a Dragonfly *(1928);* Cathedrals of Broadway *(1929);* Cathedrals of Fifth Avenue *(1931);* Birthday Bouquet/ Flowers with Snake *(1932);* Family Portrait No. 2 *(1933); costumes and set designed for opera* Four Saints in Three Acts *(1934);* Cathedrals of Wall Street *(1939);* Cathedrals of Art *(unfinished, 1942).*

Having faded into obscurity following her death in 1944, the work of artist Florine Stettheimer was rediscovered in 1995, when New York City's Whitney Museum of American Art mounted a glittering exhibit of her paintings entitled "Manhattan Fantastica." Robert Hughes called the exhibit "an evocation of a period in the history of the American art world between the wars that now, at the sour close of the 20th century, seems remote and glittering, like something enclosed in a bell jar." Stettheimer's paintings, sometimes described as "rococo subversive" because of the subtle social satire hidden within them, provide a whimsical, witty view of the Americana that comprised her rarefied world, from Wall Street to high fashion to the art establishment which she ultimately rejected. "Letting other people have your paintings is like letting them wear your clothes," she once remarked when discussing the sale of her work.

Stettheimer was born in 1871, the fourth of five children and third daughter, in a prominent German-Jewish banking family, and raised in Rochester, New York. Although her father left home when Florine was small, the family was left financially secure and able to carry on a genteel lifestyle, which included private tutors for the children. While Walter and **Stella**, the eldest Stettheimer siblings, married, the three younger sisters—**Carrie**, **Ettie**, and Florine, or as they came to be known, the "Stetties"— formed what Parker Tyler refers to as an "independent virgin cult." Devoted to one another and to their mother **Rosetta**, the three women pursued "a life of supreme leisure, half centered upon artistic pleasures, half upon artistic work." Ettie, who received a doctorate in philosophy from the University of Freiburg, became a novelist, writing two books under the pseudonym Henry Waste. Carrie spent 25 years creating an intricate doll house containing a small-scale art gallery, complete with miniature replicas of modern works, all painted by the artists themselves. Florine pursued painting, beginning her studies at New York's Art Students League in the 1890s. Between 1906 and 1914, while living abroad with her mother and sisters, she continued her art education in Berlin, Stuttgart, and Munich.

With the onset of World War I, the Stettheimers returned to New York, where they established a legendary salon which attracted the best and brightest of the avant-garde to their elegant city apartment at Alwyn Court on 58th Street and their summer home, André Brook. The select coterie included artists Marcel Duchamp, *Georgia O'Keeffe, and Gaston Lachaise, authors H.L. Mencken, Avery Hopwood, Sherwood Anderson, and Carl Van Vechten, and art critics Leo Stein, Paul Rosenfeld, and Henry McBride. Later, Marsden Hartley, Charles Demuth, Virgil

Florine
Stettheimer

Thomson, Cecil Beaton, and Pavel Tchelitchew joined them.

Stettheimer had her first and only one-woman show at Knoedler's in 1916, for which she had the walls of the gallery draped with white muslin and crowned with a copy of her white-and-gold bed canopy. The exhibition, however, attracted neither critics nor buyers, and so humiliated the artist that she thereafter never had another solo show, and only occasionally agreed to exhibit in groups.

Following this debacle, Stettheimer also abandoned the traditional modes of drawing and design she had been taught for a more personal style of expression, which is described by Tyler as "light, gay, gently satiric and streamlined, yet full of people and details drawn with a miniaturish, rather oriental delicacy." Her *Portrait of Myself*, painted in 1923, reveals her developing style. "The artist sits for this self-portrait in a graceful curve on a red chaise longue fancifully upholstered and seemingly suspended," writes art historian **Arlene Raven**. "Gravity-less, she floats free in midair. The stylish, supremely sophisticated Stettheimer wears spike-heeled pumps and a filmy dress whose transparent sleeves suggest gossamer wings. . . . Stettheimer holds an assortment of exotic blooms. . . . Florine's persona basks in the daylight streaming down from the sun she shines at the top right corner. This daylight energizes Stettheimer's flowers, held at pubic level, into full, wild blooms that make a striking diagonal spray into the left-hand bottom corner of the canvas."

Raven goes on to explain that flowers often appear in Stettheimer's works, providing a kind of symbolic link between art and everyday existence. Gigantic red, pink, and white blooms take center canvas in a later work, *Family Portrait No. 2* (1933). "Here Stettheimer paints herself as both participant and observer, behind a draped curtain at the left in a dark work suit and red high heels holding a palette of primary hues," writes Raven. "Stettheimer's sister Ettie . . . sits to the right of the artist. Sister Carrie . . . stands to the far right. Mother Rosetta Walter Stettheimer, resplendent in lace on a throne-like chair, occupies the gravitational hot spot of the picture; her body and clothing touch the three gigantic blossoms that create the core and apex of the triangular composition and literally stand for the women portrayed."

Following the death of her mother in 1937, Florine moved to her own large "bachelor quarters" at the Beaux Arts studios on Bryant Park. "Here she climaxed her gift for creative decor," writes Tyler, "with great cellophane curtains and cellophane flowers, glittering chandeliers, white furniture self-designed and bearing her initials, a fantastic boudoir all of lace, and a canopied bed somewhere between medieval orthodoxy and a Victorian dressing table." In this setting, she worked and oversaw her cultural dinner parties, at which she frequently held "unveilings" of her paintings. Her later works reflect the fantasy and theatricality of her mature style. Among them are four pseudo-baroque "Cathedrals" paintings in which she both glorified and satirized her beloved New York City: *Cathedrals of Broadway* (1929), *Cathedrals of Fifth Avenue* (1931), *Cathedrals of Wall Street* (1939), and *Cathedrals of Art* (unfinished, 1942).

In *Cathedrals of Fifth Avenue*, Stettheimer parodied the rituals surrounding a fashionable wedding; "flags are waving, mounted police keep back the crowds, and photographers snap pictures of the newly married couple exiting on a red carpet from St. Patrick's cathedral," writes art historian **Charlotte Streifer Rubinstein**. "Meanwhile, a Rolls-Royce with a dollar sign on its grille (simultaneously the F. Stettheimer initials) is pulled up to the entrance, containing the Stettheimer sisters, charmed witnesses to the scene. The word 'Tiffany's' is blazing in precious jewels in the sky, along with the eagle and the American flag. Fathers of the church reach down from heaven to give their blessing to this quasi-commercial marriage à la mode."

*Cathedrals of Wall Street* (1939) is equally busy with satiric comment. A portrait of Franklin Delano Roosevelt adorns the New York Stock Exchange center canvas, while *Eleanor Roosevelt and Fiorello La Guardia are accompanied by drum majorettes, marine musicians and a Salvation Army contingency. At the right of the canvas, overseeing the scene, is a statue of George Washington, flanked by two American flags. ("You couldn't get more American than this, unless you were Norman Rockwell," says Robert Hughes.)

Canvas was not Stettheimer's only creative outlet. In 1934, she designed the sets and costumes for the avant-garde opera *Four Saints in Three Acts*, written by Virgil Thomson and *Gertrude Stein for an all-black cast. Fashioned from cellophane, crystals, lace, feathers and seashells, and utilizing a shrill color palette, her designs won more praise from the critics than did the opera itself. Stettheimer also wrote poetry, privately publishing her collection *Crystal Flowers* in 1949.

Throughout her career, the artist continued to rebuff offers of exhibits from art dealers and museums, and periodically announced in dramatic fashion that she was going to have her 100 or so paintings buried beside her in a mausoleum after her death. Fortunately, however, they were willed instead to sister Ettie, who saw to it that they found their way into museum collections. In 1946, two years after the artist's death from cancer, her friend Marcel Duchamp arranged an exhibition of her work at the Museum of Modern Art. It had little impact, writes Hughes. "Nothing could have been less in synch with the industrial-strength seriousness of post-war American painting than the froufrou, gilt and needling little ironies of Stettheimer's style." Hughes maintains that what preserved her work was homosexual taste, and cites her influence in the works of Andy Warhol and Jasper Johns, and in the illustrations of Edward Gorey. Given the success of her 1995 exhibition, however, Stettheimer may have found a new generation of admirers among the mainstream as well.

**SOURCES:**

Bailey, Brooke. *The Remarkable Lives of 100 Women Artists.* Holbrook, MA: Bob Adams, 1994.

Harris, Ann Sutherland, and Linda Nochlin. *Women Artists: 1550–1950.* L.A. County Museum of Art: Knopf, 1976.

Hughes, Robert. "Camping Under Glass," in *Time.* September 18, 1995.

Raven, Arlene. "Manhattan Fantastica," in *On the Issues.* Fall 1885.

Rubinstein, Charlotte Streifer. *American Women Artists.* Boston, MA: G.K. Hall, 1982.

Tyler, Parker. "Florine Stettheimer," in *Notable American Women, 1607–1950.* Edited by Edward T. James. Cambridge, MA: The Belknap Press of Harvard University, 1971.

**Barbara Morgan**,
Melrose, Massachusetts

# Stevens, Alzina (1849–1900)

*American labor leader, journalist, and settlement worker. Born Alzina Ann Parsons on May 27, 1849, in Parsonsfield, Maine; died of diabetes in Chicago, Illinois, on June 3, 1900; daughter of Enoch Parsons (a farmer and manufacturer) and Louise (Page) Parsons; married a man named Stevens (divorced).*

*Organized and was first president of the Working Woman's Union No. 1 in Chicago; leader in the Knights of Labor in Toledo, Ohio; leader in lobbying for child labor laws; became first probation officer at Cook County Juvenile Court in Chicago.*

Alzina Stevens was born in 1849 in Parsonsfield, Maine, the seventh and last child of Enoch Parsons and **Louise Page Parsons**. Enoch, a veteran of the War of 1812, made a comfortable living as a farmer and small manufacturer on land granted to his father for Revolutionary War service. Following her father's death while Alzina was still a young girl, the family endured financial hardship and, at age 13, she took a job in a textile factory to ease the situation. The loss of her right index finger in an industrial accident became a visible lifelong reminder to her of the importance of improving child labor laws.

Stevens' lack of education was not a hindrance; she learned the printing trade at age 18, becoming a newspaper proofreader and typesetter. By 1872, she was working in Chicago, where she joined Typographical Union No. 16. Five years later, she established a labor group for women called the Working Woman's Union No. 1 and served as its president before moving to Toledo, Ohio, in 1882.

The *Toledo Bee* newspaper initially hired Stevens as a proofreader and compositor, but she advanced quickly to the positions of correspondent and editor. She soon became a driving force in the Knights of Labor in Toledo, and assisted in the formation of the \***Joan of Arc** Assembly, a woman's local assembly. As its "master workman," a title equivalent to "president," she was also a delegate to the city-wide District Assembly and attended the national conventions of the Knights of Labor from 1888 through 1890. Her popularity in the labor movement led to her nomination as director of woman's work in 1890, a position she refused, opting instead to apply herself to her duties as master workman at the district level. She was such an important figure in the Ohio labor movement that she was chosen to represent northwestern Ohio's labor organizations at the Populist Party's national convention in 1892.

Stevens returned to Chicago in late 1892 to ownership and editorship, with Lester C. Hubbard, of the short-lived *Vanguard*, a weekly publication devoted to economic and industrial reform. It was at this time that Alzina also became associated with the newly established Hull House. Founded by \***Jane Addams** and \***Ellen Gates Starr**, Hull House sought to achieve social and economic reform, and Stevens was a persuasive advocate on its behalf.

In 1893, the governor of Illinois appointed Stevens assistant factory inspector under \***Florence Kelley**, a position created as a result of the Workshop and Factories Act. In this role, she denounced wealthy department-store owner Marshall Field for his use of sweatshop labor in his business. During the governor's four-year administration, Stevens and Kelley prepared annual reports and published other writings. Their study of child labor conditions was printed in *Hull-House Maps and Papers* in 1895. The two women used their collected statistics to influence lawmakers to pass more protective child labor laws and stronger compulsory school attendance laws at the close of the 19th century.

With her well-known and abiding interest in child welfare, Stevens negotiated an informal arrangement with the police station nearest Hull House to give her temporary custody over many of its juvenile offenders. This experience resulted in her becoming the first Cook County (Chicago) Juvenile Court probation officer in 1899. At first she was supported financially by the privately organized Chicago Juvenile Court Committee, and worked alone, but within a few months she was supervising a staff of six, counseling offenders, and helping people on probation find jobs.

During the mid-1890s, when the Knights of Labor had begun to lose its influence, Stevens helped organize new unions for the American Federation of Labor. She walked the picket lines during strikes, becoming a close ally of Eugene V. Debs, whom she supported after the collapse of the Pullman strike in 1894. Critical of those opposed to unions, Stevens was equally critical of those who sentimentalized the labor movement. She held both the working class and the wealthy to the same standards.

Early in Stevens' life, she married unsuccessfully. Although she retained her husband's name, she never spoke about him or the marriage. Complications from diabetes resulted in Stevens' death in Chicago on June 3, 1900, at age 51. Her funeral was held at Hull House, and her cremated remains were interred at Chicago's Graceland Cemetery.

**SOURCES:**

James, Edward T., ed. *Notable American Women, 1607–1950.* Cambridge, MA: The Belknap Press of Harvard University, 1971.

Read, Phyllis J., and Bernard L. Witlieb. *The Book of Women's Firsts.* NY: Random House, 1992.

**Martha Jones**, M.L.S.,
Natick, Massachusetts

# Stevens, Lillian (1844–1914)

*American temperance reformer. Born Lillian Marion Norton Ames on March 1, 1844, in Dover, Maine; died of chronic nephritis on April 6, 1914, in Portland, Maine; daughter of Nathaniel Ames (a teacher) and Nancy Fowler (Parsons) Ames; educated at Foxcroft Academy and Westbrook Seminary in Portland; married Michael T. Stevens (a grain and salt dealer), in 1865; children: Gertrude Mary Stevens.*

One of four children, Lillian Stevens was born in Dover, Maine, in 1844, to Nathaniel and **Nancy Parsons Ames**. Her father was a teacher and a native of Maine, and her mother was of Scottish ancestry. After completing her education at the local Foxcroft Academy and Westbrook Seminary in Portland, Lillian worked as a teacher until her 1865 marriage to Michael T. Stevens, a grain and salt dealer. They settled on his family homestead in Stroudwater, Maine, and had one daughter, **Gertrude Mary Stevens**.

Like many women in the latter quarter of the 19th century, Stevens joined the temperance movement that was gaining popularity in the eastern United States. She helped found the Maine Woman's Christian Temperance Union in 1875, and advanced from her position as its first treasurer to the presidency in 1878. Active in state-wide campaigns, Stevens frequently spoke on behalf of Neal Dow, the celebrated prohibitionist of Portland, in his 1884 referendum efforts to include a ban on liquor in the state's constitution. She also pressed for legislation to enforce prohibition and to authorize the teaching of temperance in the state's schools.

Throughout her life, Stevens was committed to ameliorating the social conditions of women and children. In addition to supporting the cause of women's suffrage, she crusaded for a state reformatory for women, and helped local service organizations assist indigent women and children and reform those who were delinquent. She also opened her own home to neglected children until a more permanent residence could be found. A longtime representative of Maine at the National Conference of Charities and Correction, Stevens also served as treasurer of the National Council of Women from 1891 to 1895.

Toward the end of the 19th century, Stevens was an especially influential figure in the National Woman's Christian Temperance Union (WCTU). Through her close friendship with the union's president, *Frances Willard, who chose Stevens as her eventual successor, Stevens rose to the presidency upon Willard's death in 1898. Five years later, she was elected vice-president of the World's Women's Christian Temperance Union. Despite poor health, Stevens was a tireless director of the WCTU, attending conventions, engaging in lecture tours, and contributing to temperance publications. During her tenure, the WCTU's membership expanded by 50%.

Although Stevens and the WCTU supported other progressive legislation, such as the Pure Food and Drug Act of 1906, the Mann Act of 1910 (also called the White Slave Traffic Act), and the suffragist movement, they never lost sight of their primary focus—the elimination of alcohol. They experienced several important successes, including the removal of alcohol from military bases in 1901, and the adoption of prohibition by six southern states between 1907 and 1912. Believing that the movement was clearly gaining momentum, Stevens redoubled her efforts to secure federal legislation by devoting more of her time to Washington lobbying, joining prohibition demonstrations, and presenting petitions to Congress.

Stevens died of chronic nephritis in 1914, however, before the goal of national prohibition was (briefly) realized. Her assistant, *Anna Adams Gordon, carried on the work of the WCTU. Stevens was cremated and her ashes were interred at the Stroudwater Cemetery in Portland.

**SOURCES:**

James, Edward T., ed. Notable American Women, 1607–1950. Cambridge, MA: The Belknap Press of Harvard University, 1971.

Martha Jones, M.L.S.,
Natick, Massachusetts

# Stevens, Nettie Maria (1861–1912)

*First scientist to demonstrate that gender is determined by a particular chromosome. Born on July 7, 1861, in Cavendish, Vermont; died of breast cancer on May 4, 1912, in Baltimore, Maryland; daughter of Ephraim Stevens (a carpenter) and Julia (Adams) Stevens; graduated from Westford Academy, 1880, and Westford Normal School, 1883; Stanford University, B.A., 1899, M.A., 1900; Bryn Mawr College, Ph.D., 1903.*

Nettie Maria Stevens was born in 1861 to Ephraim and **Julia Adams Stevens**. One of four children, she and her sister **Emma Julia Stevens** were the only ones to live to adulthood. Little else is known about Stevens' background, except that she was an able and intelligent student. She received her early education at the Westford Academy in Westford, Massachusetts, where she graduated in 1880 with a concentration in the sciences; in 1883, she graduated at the top of her class from the Westford Normal School.

For the next 13 years, Stevens worked as a teacher and a librarian in Westford, Chelmsford, and Billerica, Massachusetts, before traveling across the country in 1892, at age 31, to enroll as a special status undergraduate student at Stanford University. Stevens' father and sister later followed her to California.

At Stanford, Stevens studied physiology with Oliver Peebles Jenkins and histology with Frank Mace MacFarland. She spent her summer months at the Seaside Laboratory in Pacific Grove, working first with MacFarland, and then in 1898 with Jacques Loeb, physician and associate professor of physiology at the University of Chicago. Her resultant study of *Boveria*, a protozoan parasite of sea cucumbers, was published in 1901 in the *Proceedings* of the California Academy of Sciences. She received her bachelor's degree in 1899, and her master's degree in 1900. Her master's thesis was published as *Studies on Ciliate Infusoria* a year later.

In 1900, Stevens return to the East to enroll in Bryn Mawr College as a graduate student in biology, a department dominated by two eminent faculty biologists, Edmund Beecher Wilson and Thomas Hunt Morgan, future Nobel laureate in genetics. Stevens' stellar research earned her an overseas study fellowship at the Naples Zoological Station for the 1901–02 term and later at the Zoological Institute of the University of Würzburg, Germany, where she worked with prominent German biologist Theodor Boveri. Stevens received her Ph.D. in 1903 and her dissertation, *Further Studies on the Ciliate Infusoria, Licnophora and Boveria*, was published later that year.

Stevens remained affiliated with Bryn Mawr as a Carnegie research fellow in biology from 1903 to 1905, and as an associate in experimental morphology from 1905 to 1912, during which time she returned to work with Boveri from 1908 to 1909. In 1905, Stevens received the *Ellen Richards Prize of $1,000—an award created to promote scientific research by women. As well, Bryn Mawr later endowed a research professorship for her.

Stevens published widely in the fields of cytology and experimental physiology. However, her most important contribution to science was the discovery that a particular chromosome was responsible for determining gender. At this time in scientific research, investigators were exploring the relationship between chromosomes and Gregor Mendel's laws of heredity, first described in 1866, but no direct relationship had been confirmed by experiments. Research up to this point had suggested only that a specific chromosome could be linked to a specific trait.

In 1903, Stevens first described, in an application for a Carnegie Institution grant, her research interest in this area. The same idea had been proposed, independent of her interests, by Edmund Beecher Wilson at Columbia University. Although the issue of priority in these two independent investigations has been questioned, it is accepted that the two came to the same conclusions separately from each other. Stevens' paper, *Studies in Spermatogenesis with Especial Reference to the Accessory Chromosome* (1905), published in the *Publications* of the Carnegie Institution, described her observation of the common mealworm. The nuclei of the egg always contained ten large chromosomes but the spermatocytes could have either ten large or have one of the large chromosomes replaced by a small chromosome, referred to as X and Y chromosomes. Stevens deduced that since a cell of the female contained 20 large chromosomes and the male had only 19 large chromosomes plus one small chromosome, this represented gender determination by a difference in the size of pairs of chromosomes. This theory was not universally accepted by other biologists. Stevens conducted additional research by observing other species of insects, and found further confirmation of her theory. The discovery had a profound effect upon the study of genetics and the theory of gender determination when it ended the long debate over whether sex was determined by heredity or by environmental influence of the embryo.

An esteemed research scientists, Stevens was also an inspiring and enthusiastic teacher. Before she could occupy the chair created for her by the trustees of Bryn Mawr, however, she died of breast cancer at Johns Hopkins Hospital in Baltimore in 1912. She was buried in Westfield, Massachusetts.

### SOURCES:

Bailey, Brooke. *The Remarkable Lives of 100 Women Healers and Scientists.* Holbrook, MA: Bob Adams, 1994.

James, Edward T., ed. *Notable American Women, 1607–1950.* Cambridge, MA: The Belknap Press of Harvard University, 1971.

McHenry, Robert, ed. *Famous American Women.* NY: Dover, 1980.

Ogilvie, Marilyn Bailey. *Women in Science: Antiquity through the Nineteenth Century.* London: Cambridge Press, 1993.

Read, Phyllis J., and Bernard L. Witlieb. *The Book of Women's Firsts.* NY: Random House, 1992.

**Martha Jones**, M.L.S.
Natick, Massachusetts

*Risë
Stevens*

# Stevens, Risë (1913—)

*American mezzo-soprano. Name variations: Rise Stevens. Born on June 11, 1913, in the Bronx, New York; daughter of Christian Steenbjorg also seen as Steenberg (a Norwegian) and an American mother; studied with **Anna Schoen-René** at the Juilliard School of Music and in Salzburg with \*Marie Gutheil-Schoder and Herbert Graf; married Walter G. Surovy, on January 6, 1939; children: Nicolas Vincent Surovy.*

*Debuted in Prague (1936), Metropolitan Opera (1938), Glyndebourne Festival (1939), Teatro alla Scala (1954); appeared in the films* The Chocolate Soldier *(1941), opposite Nelson Eddy, and* Going My Way, *starring Bing Crosby (1944); voted best female vocalist in radio (1947 and 1948); retired from singing (1964); served as co-director of the Metropolitan Opera National Company (1965–67); was president of Mannes College of Music (1975–78); was managing director of the Metropolitan Opera (from 1988).*

During the 1940s and 1950s, Risë Stevens had the good sense to drop heavier roles in Wagnerian opera and to appear in operas which best suited her voice and talents. She virtually owned the roles of Delilah and Carmen. Her interpretation of Carmen was initially conventional, but after Tyrone Guthrie directed a production of

*Carmen* at the Met, Stevens portrayed her as hard, calculating and tough. Although this interpretation might have left Carmen as little more than a prostitute, she probed deeper into her character with the result that Carmen's rejection of Don José became a great moment of theater on the opera stage. Stevens did not limit her talents to the opera. She appeared in movies, performed Broadway classics, sang popular songs such as Cole Porter's "Everything I Love," and traveled extensively with the Hollywood Victory Caravan during World War II. She also appeared frequently on television. After her retirement from the opera stage, Stevens was active as a teacher, a director, and president of Mannes College of Music. In 1988, she became managing director of the Met.

**John Haag**,
Athens, Georgia

# Stevenson, Fanny (1840–1914)

*Wife and caretaker of Robert Louis Stevenson who defied convention to marry him and is credited with a strong influence on his work. Name variations: Frances Vandegrift or Frances Van de Grift; Frances or Fanny Osbourne. Born Frances Vandegrift in 1840 in Indianapolis, Indiana; died of a stroke in February 1914 in Santa Barbara, California; daughter of Jacob Vandegrift or Van de Grift (a farmer and lumber merchant); mother's name unknown; educated in public schools in Indiana and the Grez School of Art in France; married Samuel Osbourne, in 1857 (divorced); married Robert Louis Stevenson (the writer), in 1880 (died 1894); children: (first marriage) Belle, Samuel Lloyd, Hervey.*

Born in Indiana in 1840, Frances Vandegrift was the eldest of six children of Jacob Vandegrift, a prosperous farmer and lumber merchant. Fanny was not a typical young Victorian woman. Dark, with curly hair and a propensity for dressing in bold and dramatic colors, she had many admirers until, at age 16, she married Samuel Osbourne, a native of Kentucky who was working as secretary to the governor of Indiana.

After two years of fighting for the Union in the Civil War, Sam left as a captain and went to the Sierra Nevada mountains in California to try his luck at silver mining. In 1864, Fanny liquidated the family assets and, with her young daughter **Belle Osbourne**, journeyed first to New York and then down the Atlantic coast to Panama, crossing the Isthmus and then sailing up the coast to San Francisco. Sam's fortunes were not as good as he had implied in his letters; the mines of the Comstock Lode had been exhausted and they lived in rough mining camps. At one point, it was believed Sam had been killed in an Indian attack. Fanny moved to San Francisco and supported herself as a seamstress. Their finances improved when Sam returned and became a court stenographer, and they joined the circle of intellectuals and adventurers in San Francisco.

Fanny had two more children, Samuel Lloyd and Hervey. She began to take art lessons in Oakland with Virgil Williams, who later established the San Francisco School of Design. Here, she met other artists and writers and transformed herself. She was becoming disillusioned with her marriage, as Sam not only kept mistresses on the side, he was also a chronic adventurer, unable to settle down in one place, and the family was always short of money. Fanny felt it necessary to support herself and her children. Money problems were constant throughout her life.

In 1875, accompanied by her three children, Fanny went to Paris to study art. Despite mone-

$\mathcal{F}$anny
$\mathcal{S}$tevenson

tary support from her husband, it was a troublesome time for the family. However, in her letters home she did not complain, and in the voluminous correspondence in which she chronicled her life, she usually glossed over whatever difficulties she was encountering, concentrating instead on positive goals and events. When, in the winter of 1876, her youngest son Hervey died after a long illness, she was broken physically and mentally. Her son had been diagnosed with "brain fever," an illness that also struck her later in life. Biographers question whether this mental instability was an inherited characteristic, as her father had also experienced a mental breakdown.

In 1876, Fanny was looking for inexpensive lodgings and found the Hotel Chevillon of Grez-sur-Loing in the French countryside. This was the home of a famous colony of English-speaking artists, writers, and musicians, and it was here that she experienced a spiritual rebirth. Fanny was 35 and Belle 16 when they first met 24-year-old writer Robert Louis Stevenson, scion of a wealthy Edinburgh family who was living at the colony. That winter, they all returned to Paris, and Fanny began studies at the Julian Academy, an art school established for women. Sam arrived in Paris to bring Fanny home, but she refused to relinquish her life in France.

By the following year, Fanny and Robert Louis Stevenson had become inseparable and lived openly together. Robert, like Sam, was a wanderer and adventurer. Although he had published his travel writings in journals and newspapers, he had not yet achieved literary fame. Robert suffered his entire life from chronic illnesses that confined him to bed, where he still managed to write daily. Fanny began her nearly 20-year quest to save him from his frequent bouts of consumption.

Fanny eventually returned to America out of concern for her daughter, because she did not want Belle to be a "fallen woman" like she herself had become; in 1879, Fanny settled in an artists' colony in Monterey, California. Despite overwhelming disapproval of their relationship from Fanny's family and Robert's parents and circle of literary friends, a quiet divorce was arranged. Robert came to America to retrieve Fanny and explore the countryside, resulting in two more books. Although sick and abandoned by his literary friends, Robert married Fanny in 1880.

In London after their marriage, Fanny eventually won over Robert's parents who agreed to an annual stipend to help support the family. His social circle, with the exception of Henry James, continued to hold mixed feelings about Fanny.

Some claimed she was an amateur who exerted too strong an influence on him, while others credited her with keeping him alive to produce his greatest works. In a 1994 *Library Journal* review of *Fanny Stevenson: A Romance of Destiny*, Elizabeth Devereaux presents biographer **Alexandra Lapierre**'s synopsis of the literary world's assessment of Fanny: "According to whoever was doing the foreword, Fanny was a muse, a saint, the woman behind the genius, or she was a virago, a castrating bitch. The only agreement was that she had a lot of influence on his writing."

The years from 1884 to 1887 were happy ones for Fanny, who made a home in Bournemouth, England. It was also a period in which Robert Louis Stevenson achieved international fame with the publication of *The Strange Case of Dr. Jekyll and Mr. Hyde*. In 1887, they returned to America, accompanied by Robert's widowed mother **Margaret Balfour Stevenson**. Soon after, Fanny separated briefly from her husband over a literary rift involving her publication of a story and accusations of plagiarism. She went to San Francisco in 1888 and then reunited with Belle who had married and was living in Honolulu.

Gathering her family back together again, Fanny suggested that they lease a ship, and for six months during 1888 and 1889, Fanny, her son Lloyd, Robert and his mother traveled the South Seas from the Marquesas Islands to Tahiti and Hawaii. Robert Stevenson's health improved remarkably during this trip. It was a time of political upheaval in the South Pacific. With native populations losing control of their own countries due to the influence of missionaries and white planters, Robert actively supported the islanders' rights to sovereignty. He also made a side trip, despite Fanny's protests, to visit Father Damien at the leper colony on Molokai, later publishing an impassioned essay supporting his work.

The Stevensons eventually settled on Samoa, where they purchased land and built a home they named Vailima. With the help of Samoan islanders, they carved a plantation out of the jungle, intending to raise coffee and cocoa. This work was largely due to Fanny's efforts. Together with Robert's mother and Fanny's children Lloyd and Belle, they lived a feudal life; Robert was in good health and writing every day. He also acted as a stepfather to Lloyd and to Belle's son. In 1894, Robert Louis Stevenson died of a stroke and, in accordance with his wish, was buried at the top of Mount Vaea on Samoa. Fanny remained on Vailima until 1897, when she was forced by lack of money and the political situation to sell the plantation.

Eventually she moved back to San Francisco and lived with Lloyd and his wife, working on her husband's literary estate. She published a new edition of his collected works, worked on his biography of Father Damien, and organized her journal of their South Seas travels. In 1914, she died of a stroke, and the following year her ashes were buried next to Robert's on Mount Vaea in Samoa. According to Devereaux, Lapierre regards Fanny as a modern thinker; Fanny "tries to have it all, but is not ahead of feminism, she is post-feminism—she takes her fight for freedom for granted. It's not that she always succeeds— she has many failures—but she dares."

**SOURCES:**

Lapierre, Alexandra. *Fanny Stevenson: A Romance of Destiny*. NY: Carroll & Graf, 1995.
*Parade Magazine*. April 30, 1995, p. 14.
*Publishers Weekly*. November 21, 1994, pp. 37–38; February 20, 1995, p. 185.

**SUGGESTED READING:**

Callow, Philip. *Louis: A Life of Robert Louis Stevenson*. Ivan R. Dee, 2001.

**Martha Jones**, M.L.S.,
Natick, Massachusetts

# Stevenson, Sara Yorke (1847–1921).

*See Fletcher, Alice Cunningham for sidebar.*

# Stevenson, Frances (1888–1972).

*See Lloyd George, Frances Stevenson.*

# Stevenson, Matilda (1849–1915)

*American anthropologist. Name variations: Matilda Coxe Stevenson; Tilly Stevenson. Born Matilda Coxe Evans on May 12, 1849, in San Augustine, Texas; died in Oxon Hill, Maryland, on June 24, 1915; daughter of Maria Matilda (Coxe) Evans and Alexander H. Evans; educated at Miss Anable's Academy in Philadelphia; married Colonel James Stevenson (an explorer and ethnologist), in 1872.*

Matilda Stevenson, or Tilly, as she was commonly known, was born in San Augustine, Texas, in 1849. She discovered her life's work through her husband James Stevenson, a government geologist who became an officer of the U.S. Geological Survey in 1879. That year, she accompanied him on an expedition to Mexico to study the Zuñi for the newly founded Bureau of American Ethnology. For several years, Stevenson continued to work alongside her husband with little recognition (her research paper "Zuñi

and the Zuñians," published privately in 1881, went unnoticed), until the famed British anthropologist Edwin B. Taylor brought her contributions to light in 1884. In an address before the Anthropological Society of Washington, Taylor noted the unique ability of women to obtain data on domestic and social life that was not readily disclosed to male researchers, and encouraged his colleagues to be more accepting of women in the field.

Stevenson continued her research on the Zuñi, with particular attention to the roles, duties, and rituals of Zuñi women. Her first major publication, "Religious Life of the Zuñi Child," published in the *Fifth Annual Report* of the Bureau of American Ethnology, 1883–84, was the earliest study of its kind to consider children. In 1885, she became the founder and first president of the Women's Anthropological Society of America. The organization was dissolved in 1899 after the establishment of the American Anthropological Association, which included women among its charter members.

Upon the death of her husband in 1888, Stevenson was appointed to the staff of the Bureau of American Ethnology. The following year, she undertook a study of the small tribe at the Sia pueblo in New Mexico (reported in the bureau's *Eleventh Annual Report*, 1889–90), after which she concentrated most of her work on the Zuñi, with whom she had established a trusting and affectionate relationship. Her later studies were broader in scope, encompassing every aspect of Zuñi life and examining the changes in the culture brought about by contact with outside influences. Her major work, *The Zuñi Indians: Their Mythology, Esoteric Fraternities, and Ceremonies*, a 600-page study with hundreds of illustrations, appeared in the *Twenty-third Annual Report* of the Bureau of American Ethnology, 1901–02. It was followed by "Ethnobotany of the Zuñi Indians" in the *Thirtieth Annual Report*, 1908–09.

Over her 25-year association with the Zuñi, Stevenson collected a herbarium of over 200 plants used by the tribe, as well as a number of sacred masks, which she donated to the Smithsonian Institution. In addition to her major publications, she also contributed articles on the Zuñis to *American Anthropologist* and other journals. In 1903, she prepared an exhibit of Zuñi artifacts for the Louisiana Purchase Exposition.

In her later years, Stevenson lived and worked near the San Ildefonso pueblo, concentrating much of her research on the Tewa Indians. Failing health forced her to return east to Oxon Hill, Maryland, where she died in the home of friends on June 24, 1915.

**SOURCES:**

James, Edward T., ed. *Notable American Women, 1607–1950.* Cambridge, MA: The Belknap Press of Harvard University, 1971.

McHenry, Robert, ed. *Famous American Women.* NY: Dover, 1980.

**Barbara Morgan,**
Melrose, Massachusetts

## Stevenson, Mrs. R.H.S. (1906–1944).

*See Menchik, Vera.*

## Stevenson, Sara Yorke (1847–1921).

*See Fletcher, Alice Cunningham for sidebar.*

# Stevenson, Sarah Hackett

## (1841–1909)

*American physician who was the first woman member of the American Medical Association. Born Sarah Ann Hackett Stevenson on February 2, 1841, in Buffalo Grove (now Polo), Ogle County, Illinois; died on August 14, 1909, in Chicago, Illinois; daughter of John Davis Stevenson (a merchant and farmer) and Sarah T. (Hackett) Stevenson; educated at Mount Carroll Seminary; graduated from State Normal University (now Illinois State University), 1863; Woman's Hospital Medical College of Chicago, M.D., 1874; attended South Kensington Science School, London; never married; no children.*

*Admitted to the American Medical Association (AMA) as its first female member; was the first female staff physician of Cook County Hospital (Illinois); was the first woman appointed to the Illinois State Board of Health.*

Sarah Hackett Stevenson was born in Illinois in 1841, the fourth of seven children of John Davis Stevenson of New York City and **Sarah T. Hackett Stevenson** of Philadelphia. Her paternal grandfather, Charles Stevenson, had emigrated from Ireland following the 1798 rebellion. In 1835, his wife's poor health compelled John to relocate to Illinois, where he established the first store in Buffalo Grove and later turned to farming.

Sarah the younger received her education at the Mount Carroll Seminary and the State Normal University (now Illinois State University), graduating in 1863. Interested in scientific subjects, she taught school for four years in Bloomington, Mount Morris, and Sterling, Illinois, where she also held the position of principal.

Stevenson then moved to Chicago to study anatomy and physiology at the Woman's Hospital Medical College, which had recently been established there by *Mary Harris Thompson. She also spent a year in London studying with Thomas Huxley at the South Kensington Science School. Stevenson returned to Chicago to complete her studies at the Woman's Hospital Medical College, where she received her M.D. degree in 1874, graduating as valedictorian of her class.

In 1875, after a brief period abroad, Stevenson opened her medical practice in Chicago. That year she also published a high school textbook, *Boys and Girls in Biology*, which was based on Huxley's lectures. In 1876, she was chosen as one of the delegates of the Illinois State Medical Society to the national convention of the American Medical Association (AMA) in Philadelphia. Five years earlier the AMA had refused even to discuss the admission of women, but this time, backed by William H. Byford, a prominent Chicago gynecologist, Stevenson became the first female member of the AMA. She also became the first woman to be appointed to the staff of Chicago's Cook County Hospital in 1881, and the first woman appointed to the Illinois State Board of Health in 1893.

Stevenson was professor of physiology and histology from 1875 to 1880, and of obstetrics from 1880 to 1894, at the Woman's Hospital Medical College, which became Northwestern University Woman's Medical School in 1891. While maintaining a large and successful private practice, she was also a consulting physician to the Woman's Hospital, the Provident Hospital, and an attending physician at the Mary Thompson Hospital. Together with *Lucy Flower and others, she founded the Illinois Training School for Nurses in 1880.

An advocate of women's rights, Stevenson became the best-known female physician in the Midwest and, by example, advanced the cause of medical education for women. In 1880, she published a popular work, *The Physiology of Woman*. Throughout her life and professional career, she backed various humanitarian and reform causes, including the temperance movement. She served as the first superintendent of the Department of Hygiene of the Woman's Christian Temperance Union (WCTU) from 1881 to 1882. In 1886, the Chicago WCTU organized the National Temperance Hospital (later renamed the *Frances Willard Hospital) as an institution using no medicines containing alcohol, and Stevenson served as president of its staff. She lent her support to many causes, including the American Medical Missionary College of Chicago. She also spoke in support of admission of a black member to the Chicago Woman's Club, of which she was a member and president during the 1893 Chicago World's Fair.

Stevenson suffered a cerebral hemorrhage in 1903 and retired from active practice. In 1906, she was honored by a reception attended by 1,500. Paralyzed thereafter, she spent the last three years of her life at St. Elizabeth's Hospital in Chicago, the final year in a coma. She died, age 68, in 1909, and was buried in St. Boniface Cemetery in Chicago.

**SOURCES:**

James, Edward T., ed. *Notable American Women, 1607–1950.* Cambridge, MA: The Belknap Press of Harvard University, 1971.

McHenry, Robert, ed. *Famous American Women.* NY: Dover, 1980.

Read, Phyllis J., and Bernard L. Witlieb. *The Book of Women's Firsts.* NY: Random House, 1992.

**Martha Jones**, M.L.S.,
Natick, Massachusetts

## Stevenson, Vera (1906–1944).

*See Menchik, Vera.*

## Stewart.

*See also Stuart (in Scotland, the spelling of the surname Stewart was changed to Stuart by brothers Matthew and John Stewart, who adopted the French spelling in 1537).*

## Stewart, Alice (1906—)

*British epidemiologist, condemned by government and the medical community for much of her career, who proved the link between prenatal X-rays and childhood cancers, contradicting the professed safety of low-dose radiation and challenging an establishment which wished time and again that she would just go away. Born on October 4, 1906, in Sheffield, England; daughter of Albert Ernest Naish (an internist) and Lucy Wellburn Naish (a physician); attended Cambridge and London Universities; married (divorced 1950); two children.*

*Qualified as a doctor (1931); began work at Oxford University's Department of Social Medicine (1945); was the first woman elected to both the Association of Physicians and the Royal College of Physicians (1947); published the Oxford Survey of Childhood Cancers (1958); officially retired from Oxford University and became research fellow at the University of Birmingham (1974); published results of Hanford study with Mancuso and Kneale in* Health Physics *(1977); ostracized by the medical and scientific community (1970s); received the Right Livelihood*

*Prize (1986); studied with Kneale the effects of radiation on Japanese atom-bomb survivors (1988); testified before the U.S. Senate and House committee hearings, warning of flaws in the Department of Energy's standards for assessing radiation hazards (1988 and 1989); resumed study of Hanford data (1990); received the Ramazzini Prize for epidemiology (1991).*

Although it was thanks to her research and perseverance that the dangerous practice of administering pelvic X-rays to pregnant women stopped in the late 1970s and early 1980s, Alice Stewart received little professional reward for her life's work at preventing leukemia and other cancers resulting from exposure to low levels of radiation. In lieu of promotion and funding, she was the subject of threat and ridicule. Those scientists who championed her findings—that international standards for "safe" radiation-exposure levels were responsible for increases in cancer victims—did so at risk to their own funding and reputations. According to Matt Henry in *Ecologist* (November 1999), their "cars [were] rammed off roads and evidence was stolen and suppressed." Decades later, the accuracy of her findings regarding childhood cancers and fetal X-ray would be common knowledge; yet it would remain not so widely known that Stewart had made the medical establishment aware of the link between prenatal pelvic X-rays and cancer about 20 years before the practice of X-raying pregnant women finally ceased.

Alice Stewart was born in Sheffield, England, on October 4, 1906, into a family with a strong commitment to the health of children. Both her mother **Lucy Naish**, one of the first female physicians to practice in Britain, and her father Albert Ernest Naish, also a physician, practiced in Sheffield where they became known for their devotion to the welfare of children. Both parents were also educators, with Lucy teaching anatomy and Albert serving as a professor of medicine. In a family of eight children, Alice was one of five who followed in their parents' footsteps as physicians. Stewart's biographer **Gayle Greene** notes that it was in her family that Stewart found the underpinnings for her medical philosophy: "She takes from both [parents] an idealism about medicine, a willingness to sacrifice financial gain to devote herself to the prevention rather than the cure of disease, and an ideal of medical science as committed to the betterment of society." In the coming years, these beliefs would help Stewart to stay a course riddled with pitfalls.

She received her training as a physician at Cambridge and London universities. After qualifying during 1931, she married a schoolmaster whom she had known in Cambridge, and they had two children (the couple would divorce in 1950 following a long separation). During World War II, Stewart instructed undergraduates in clinical medicine at Oxford, and she conducted three studies on the impact of wartime risks on workers—including exposure of munitions workers to TNT. By 1945, she had ended her clinical instruction and entered the realm of epidemiology, then a new field, in which practitioners utilize the dual attributes of diagnostic skill and knowledge of statistics to examine the incidence and prevalence of diseases. By entering a field that studied such characteristics as the socio-economic factors of disease, Stewart could help find preventative, rather than curative, treatments. In 1947, she became the first woman elected to both the Royal College of Physicians and the Association of Physicians.

While serving as head of the Oxford Institute for Social Medicine, she worked with biostatisticians to conduct a study of childhood cancers which would have major implications both for world public health and for her own career. Upon noticing a 50% increase in the number of children who were dying as a result of leukemia in England and Wales during the early 1950s, and that the percentage of increase was even higher in America, Stewart undertook the Oxford Survey of Childhood Cancers to determine the cause of the increase. Notes **Catherine Caufield**, "With her colleagues, Stewart interviewed mothers of 1,400 children who had died of cancer in England and Wales between 1953 and 1955. They also interviewed the same number of mothers with healthy children. Though not intentionally focused on radiation, the study turned out to be the first large-scale investigation of humans exposed to low doses of radiation." During the project, Stewart joined forces with George Kneale, a statistician with whom she would collaborate throughout her career.

In 1956, Stewart shared the survey's findings in a letter to the medical journal *Lancet*: mothers of children who had died of cancer before age ten had received twice the number of prenatal X-rays as the mothers of cancer-free children. Two years later, in June 1958, Stewart published a paper on the study in the *British Medical Journal*, noting that women who received pelvic X-rays while pregnant ran nearly twice the risk of having children who would develop cancer as mothers who did not. If Stewart expected the survey's findings to be received with concern from the medical establishment, her expectations went grossly unmet. Her paper contradicted the accepted notion that low doses

of radiation were perfectly safe (indeed, some would argue that low-dose radiation had positive health effects). Whereas, in a 1937 edition, a standard textbook entitled *Antenatal and Postnatal Care* had emphatically noted that prenatal X-rays were harmless—"It has been frequently asked whether there is any danger to the life of the child by the passage of X-rays through it; it can be said at once that there is none"—Stewart's Survey proved quite to the contrary.

Her discovery, in an age which pinned its hopes on the glories of nuclear medicine and nuclear power, brought ridicule and open hostility. Notes Gayle Greene:

> Radiography was the new toy of the medical profession and was being used for everything from examining the position of the fetus to treating acne and menstrual disorders, to measuring foot size in shoe stores. This was the fifties, the height of the arms race, when the governments of England and America were pouring vast resources into weapons testing and building a powerful nuclear industry dependent on public trust of the friendly atom. . . . Nuclear medicine was good publicity for nuclear power, nuclear power was a useful cover for the arms race, and there was little incentive to knowing that low-dose radiation could kill you.

"The antagonism was from the medical profession," Stewart later said. "Obstetricians and radiologists didn't like being told what they could do by me or by anyone else." To refute her findings, detractors claimed that results based on the memories of mothers about their own X-ray histories could not be considered reliable.

Not long thereafter, in the early 1960s, Stewart's findings were confirmed by an American study conducted by Brian MacMahon at Harvard University. By examining nearly three-quarters of a million births, the Harvard study found a 42% higher risk rate for leukemia and other cancers in the children of mothers who had received X-rays while pregnant. When MacMahon's findings supported Stewart's, no one could blame his results on any potential unreliability of women's memories; MacMahon's data regarding prenatal X-rays had come from hospital records.

So unpopular were such findings, however, that despite the public-health implications of Stewart's work it would be 20 years before the scientific community officially acknowledged the accuracy of her conclusion. Although Stewart's report sounded the warning cry as early as 1958, pregnant women would be X-rayed until the late 1970s and early 1980s.

In the years following the publication of her paper in the *British Medical Journal,* Stewart and Kneale continued their research into childhood cancers. She officially retired from Oxford University in 1974 because of conflicts with Sir Richard Doll, Britain's leading epidemiologist, and became a research fellow at the University of Birmingham.

Guidelines for low-dose radiation—the effects of which may impact workers at nuclear plants, "downwinders" and soldiers near test sites—were drawn up without regard to Stewart's alarming discovery. *Current Biography* (2000) notes: "Meanwhile, the International Commission on Radiological Protection (ICRP) ignored Stewart's finding and set a limit of radiation dosages based on a cost-benefit analysis, according to which a risk ratio of one to 5,000—or one death for every 5,000 workers exposed to radiation—was acceptable. Such an approach allowed for the expansion of atomic-energy programs." Stewart would later reflect on the reasons her findings were initially discounted: "When it came to my work on X-rays, nobody wanted to believe it. . . . [I]t was just the moment when the nuclear industry was taking off. If we were right, the industry couldn't develop properly." Her findings on prenatal X-ray and childhood cancers would not receive an official blessing from the medical community until 1976, when former chair of the ICRP Sir Edward Pochin asserted: "It now appears likely that absorbed doses of only a few rads in the foetus may induce malignancies of various types."

Another chapter in Stewart's investigation of low-level radiation effects opened in 1974 when she was contacted by Thomas Mancuso, a renowned American industrial hygienist. Mancuso had been hired ten years before by the Atomic Energy Commission (AEC) to conduct a mortality study of U.S. nuclear workers at Hanford Nuclear Reservation in Washington State (which had been constructed for plutonium production for the Manhattan Project during 1943). While he was conducting his study, the AEC received findings from an epidemiologist in Washington State who had evidence of a higher than average incidence of fatal cancers in former employees of Hanford who were living in Washington. The AEC wanted Mancuso to endorse a press release denying the accuracy of this claim. They also wanted him to publish his own preliminary findings which in fact did not support his colleague's.

Mancuso made no friends at the AEC by agreeing to do neither. Instead, believing that his preliminary findings might have been misleading, he contacted Alice Stewart with a request that she take a look at his data. With George Kneale, Stewart traveled to the United States where, writes Greene, "[t]heir investigations indicated that 'this industry is a good deal more dangerous than you are being told'—about twenty times more dangerous." Mancuso's preliminary findings had not indicated increases in cancer victims because he had begun his research years earlier, before the cancers had developed in some workers.

The assessments of the Hanford data made by Mancuso, Stewart, and Kneale appeared in a 1977 edition of *Health Physics.* More than a decade later, Tim Conner would note in the *Bulletin of the Atomic Scientists* (September 1990) that the "scientific controversy it ignited has not faded but, instead, has gained importance. The MSK analysis, as it is known, concluded that Hanford workers were dying of cancer from cumulative radiation exposures far below the standards established as safe." Their conclusions, that radiation-induced cancer would afflict 200 Hanford workers, had staggering implications for the nuclear industry as well as for potential workers' compensation claims.

> *I* speak out because I think there are not a lot of other people in such a good position. I have nothing to lose. . . . This area of research can be shut down. I've watched it happen.
>
> —**Alice Stewart**

Mancuso's funding was terminated by the Department of Energy (DOE), which had replaced the AEC, and it attempted to deny him access to the data he had spent more than a decade collecting. Stewart and Kneale headed home with a copy of the research, having in her words "put the cat among the pigeons." Direction of the mortality study was transferred to a DOE employee, **Ethel Gilbert**, who attacked the MSK analysis. The swift action of the DOE to shut down Mancuso's work led Congress to a 1978 investigation of a potential cover-up, but the DOE was cleared. Stewart, Mancuso, and Kneale wanted to continue their investigation, but they were denied additional access to the health records of the Hanford workers. It would be 13 years before they were finally granted access to the Hanford data again. As Stewart was ostracized throughout the 1970s by the scientific community for asserting that standards for acceptable radiation exposure—which are all based on A-bomb survivor studies from World

War II—were far from safe, those who championed her work did so at great risk. "Everyone in America who took our side in the years subsequent to Hanford lost their funding," she noted. "They don't burn you at the stake anymore, but they do the equivalent, in terms of cutting you off from your means to work, your livelihood." Indeed, had Stewart been unwilling to spend her life working for little or no money, the information she discovered might still remain unknown.

When an international conference was convened in 1985 by the Three Mile Island (TMI) Public Health Fund to determine the best data to study the health consequences of low-level radiation, it was decided that a study of the AEC-DOE nuclear weapons workers at all nuclear complexes would provide the best possible information. Stewart was selected as head of the study by the TMI Scientific Advisory Board. Under the Freedom of Information Act, TMI sought to obtain worker data from the DOE, including the Hanford data, but the DOE refused them access. Meanwhile, notes *Current Biography,* "data gathered after the 1986 Chernobyl disaster in Russia and other reports had also begun to show that low-level radiation was three to 10 times more dangerous than had been previously thought." In the year of Chernobyl, Stewart received an award known as the "Alternative Nobel," the prestigious Right Livelihood Prize, from the Swedish Parliament.

The incidence of radiation-related cancers revealed by Stewart's work led her to the conclusion that the standards for safe radiation levels set by the A-bomb studies are "patently false." Greene elucidates on the magnitude of such an assertion:

> The international regulatory committees and the national committees as well . . . all base their standards on the studies of the Hiroshima survivors. . . . Also at stake are the potential compensation claims of the million or more workers in U.S. and U.K. nuclear weapons facilities, of the hundreds of thousands of people living near nuclear installations or downwind from the Nevada test site, and the hundreds of U.S. and U.K. soldiers and veterans subjected to fallout from nuclear tests and operations.

During 1988, Stewart and Kneale examined 24,416 non-cancer deaths among A-bomb survivors who died between 1950 and 1982. From their investigations, Stewart again drew conclusions that no one particularly wanted to hear. She found that—because the young, the old, and the sick had died before the A-bomb survivor studies were initiated five years after the bomb-

ing—only the healthiest of the population had lived long enough to factor into the studies. In an abstract of a paper she delivered at the International Conference on Radiation and Health (1996), Stewart noted: "So it is possible that deaths before 1950 had left the LSS [Life Span Study] cohort permanently biased in favor of persons who had high levels of resistance to all (early and late) effects of radiation." In an interview with *New Scientist* magazine (August 5, 2000), Stewart discussed the additional findings of their research: "It shows that cancer was not the only effect of the A-bomb radiation. People died from immune system damage as well." Such damage would not have factored into the cancer studies and thus would not have been taken into account when the safety standards were originally set.

Stewart would spend the following years trying to convince government and the scientific establishment that the international standards for radiation-exposure limits were unsafe. Detractors pointed to the fact that some of the A-bomb survivors lived longer than average. From this information, it was suggested by some that the radiation had been "good" for them. In fact, however, such findings supported Stewart's conclusion that the only survivors who lived long enough to factor into the studies were the healthiest of the healthy—the top 10% of the physically fit.

A hero to the anti-nuclear movement, Stewart was sought out for hearings, inquiries, and conferences. In 1988 and 1989, she testified in U.S. Senate and House committee hearings. When others would not come forward to testify, she served as an expert witness on behalf of workers and veterans who had been exposed to radiation. If she harbored bitterness for having been sidelined by her colleagues, she did not let it show; in fact, Stewart sometimes attributed her determination to fight the good fight to having nothing to lose. A feminist, she took the obstacles in her path as challenges. "The world is designed by men for men," she told **Amy Raphael.** "Women do have a hard time, and unless they're constantly on the alert and trying to hold their own against the odds, the men will be ready to let everything slip back. There have been obvious difficulties for me—when I've wanted to spend more time with my children or vice versa—but I think it's possible to overcome them. The prize at the end for the child is, of course, that they will find an opening into a more interesting world."

In her later years, as she continued her research into her 80s and 90s, Stewart began to see some of the positive results of her fight. During 1989, still seeking access to the health records of AEC-DOE nuclear workers, the TMI fund used the Freedom of Information Act to take their case to the federal courts. The following year, the DOE had no choice but to begin providing data tapes to Stewart who resumed the Hanford study. Notes **Christine K. Cassel**, "Energy Secretary James Watkins, admitting past error, announced that worker health data would be released to the scientific community, and some of the DOE's health research functions were transferred to the Department of Health and Human Services." As Stewart and Kneale continued the Hanford work begun more than a decade before, their assessments supported the earlier findings. It seemed Stewart had been at least partially vindicated when a headline on the front page of *The New York Times* (January 29, 2000) read: "U.S. Acknowledges Radiation Killed Weapons Workers." The article went on to assert: "After decades of denials, the government is conceding that since the dawn of the nuclear age, workers have been exposed to radiation and chemicals that have produced cancer and death." The source for the government report: "[E]pidemiological studies performed from the mid-1960's onward, some disavowed by the government when they were published."

Stewart warned not only of the cancer effects of low-dose radiation, but also of the potential for permanent alteration of the gene pool due to radiation exposure: "Even more than the cancer is the threat to future generations . . . that's what you ought to be really afraid of. It's the genetic damage, the possibility of sowing bad seeds into the gene pool from which future generations are drawn. There will be a buildup of defective genes into the population. It won't be noticed until it's too late. Then we'll never root it out, never get rid of it. It will be totally irrevocable." While pursuing the Hanford study, Stewart began work on a follow-up study to a report published by Martin Gardner in 1990. In surveying children in communities neighboring the Sellafield, England, nuclear plant, Gardner found what Cassel has called "a correlation between a father's exposure to radiation and the incidence of childhood cancer in his offspring. This was the first study ever to demonstrate a correlation between paternal exposure and childhood cancer, and it suggests radiation damage at the level of the gene."

While it is impossible to know to what extent Stewart's conclusions about low-dose radiation will be accepted by government and the scientific community in the years to come, her place in history as a preventative force in childhood cancers is secure. Thanks to her perseverance, pregnant women no longer routinely receive pelvic X-rays, and her findings in regard to workers in nuclear facilities can no longer be ignored. At age 93, Stewart told *New Scientist*: "One of the reasons it's been so interesting for me is that no one has ever lost interest in what I've said about radiation. They may despise me, they may hate me, but the problem is there and will stay there if nobody's solved it." Still hard at work, she credited her tenacity to the controversy her efforts have typically inspired: "Perhaps the best thing that happened to me was that nobody believed me. . . . Each time, this pushed us to go on."

**SOURCES:**

"A-Bomb Data: Detection of Bias in the Life Span Study Cohort," in *Environmental Health Perspectives*. No. 105, supplement 6. December 1977.

Bequette, William C. "Government Hates to Hear 'I Told You So,'" in *Tri-City Herald*. February 13, 2000.

Cassel, Christine K. "Profiles in Responsibility," reprinted on familyreunion.org, 1989.

Caufield, Catherine. *Multiple Exposures: Chronicles of the Radiation Age*. NY: Perennial Library, 1989.

Conner, Tim. "Nuclear Workers at Risk," in *Bulletin of the Atomic Scientists*. Vol 46, no. 8. September 1990.

*Current Biography 2000*. NY: H.W. Wilson, 2000.

Greene, Gayle. *The Woman Who Knew Too Much: Alice Stewart and the Secrets of Radiation*. Ann Arbor, MI: University of Michigan Press, 1999.

Henry, Matt. "The Woman Who Knew Too Much," in *Ecologist*. November 1999.

Milliken, Robert. *No Conceivable Injury*. NY: Penguin, 1986.

*New Scientist*. August 5, 2000.

Wald, Matthew. "U.S. Acknowledges Radiation Killed Weapons Workers," in *The New York Times*. January 29, 2000.

Welsome, Eileen. *The Plutonium Files: America's Secret Medical Experiments in the Cold War*. NY: Dial Press, 1999.

## Stewart, Anastasia (1883–1923)

*Princess of Greece. Born on January 20, 1883, in Cleveland, Ohio; died on August 29, 1923; daughter of W.E. Stewart; married William Bateman Leeds; became first wife of Prince Christopher Oldenburg of Greece (1888–1940), on February 1, 1920. Christopher's second wife was \*Françoise of Guise (1902–1953).*

## Stewart, Anita (1895–1961)

*American silent film actress who headed her own production company, with Louis B. Mayer as her production executive. Name variations: Anna Stewart. Born Anna Stewart in Brooklyn, New York, on February 7,*

*1895; died in 1961; sister-in-law of director-actor Ralph Ince; sister of silent film actor George Stewart.*

*Selected filmography:* Her Choice *(1912);* The Godmother *(1912);* The Wood Violet *(1912);* The Song of the Shell *(1912);* The Moulding *(1913);* Two's Company Three's A Crowd *(1913);* The Song Bird of the North *(1913);* Sweet Deception *(1913);* The Swan Girl *(1913);* The Wreck *(1913);* A Million Bid *(1914);* Shadows of the Past *(1914);* Wife Wanted *(1914);* The Painted World *(1914);* Lincoln the Lover *(1914);* The Sins of the Mothers *(1915);* The Juggernaut *(1915);* The Goddess *(serial, 1915);* My Lady's Slipper *(1916);* The Suspect *(1916);* The Daring of Diana *(1916);* The Combat *(1916);* The Girl Philippa *(1917);* The Glory of Yolanda *(1917);* The Message of the Mouse *(1917);* Virtuous Wives *(1918);* A Midnight Romance *(1919);* Mary Regan *(1919);* Her Kingdom of Dreams *(1919);* The Mind-the-Paint Girl *(1919);* In Old Kentucky *(1919);* The Fighting Shepherdess *(1920);* The Yellow Typhoon *(1920);* Playthings of Destiny *(1921);* The Invisible Fear *(1921);* Sowing the Wind *(1921);* Her Mad Bargain *(1921);* A Question of Honor *(1922);* Rose o' the Sea *(1922);* The Woman He Married *(1922);* The Love Piker *(1923);* The Great White Way *(1924);* The Boomerang *(1925);* Never the Twain Shall Meet *(1925);* Rustling for Cupid *(1926);* The Prince of Pilsen *(1926);* Wild Geese *(1927);* Romance of a Rogue *(1928);* Name the Woman *(1928);* Sisters of Eve *(1928).*

Anita Stewart was born in Brooklyn in 1895 and began her acting career in 1911, when she joined Vitagraph films. She eventually became one of the company's major silent screen stars, appearing in dozens of films for Vitagraph. Often billed by her given name, Anna Stewart, early in her career, she was usually paired on screen with actor Earle Williams. Stewart became the focus of a landmark lawsuit in actor-studio relations when Vitagraph sued her for breach of contract. The studio had taken exception to Stewart signing with Louis B. Mayer in 1917 before the expiration of her Vitagraph contract, and the court ruled in Vitagraph's favor. Stewart retained her star status until the introduction of talking films, at which point she retired from acting to assume control of her own production company for a time, with Mayer as her production executive. In addition to her film performances, she wrote the novel *The Devil's Toy;* she died in 1961, age 66.

**SOURCES:**
Katz, Ephraim. *The Film Encyclopedia.* 3rd ed. NY: HarperCollins, 1998.
Slide, Anthony. *Silent Portraits: Stars of the Silent Screen in Historic Photographs.* Vestal, NY: Vestal Press, 1989.

**B. Kimberly Taylor,** freelance writer, New York, New York

## Stewart, Anna (1895–1961).

See Stewart, Anita.

## Stewart, Annabella (d. after 1471).

See Beaufort, Joan (c. 1410–1445) for sidebar.

## Stewart, Anne (fl. 1515)

*Countess of Lennox. Name variations: Anne Stuart; some sources show her as Lady Elizabeth Stuart. Flourished around 1515; daughter of John Stewart (c. 1440–1512), 1st earl of Atholl (John of Balveny), and \*Eleanor Sinclair (d. 1518, daughter of the earl of Orkney and Caithness); married John Stewart (d. 1526), 3rd earl of Lennox (r. 1473–1526, murdered by Sir James Hamilton of Finnart), on January 19, 1511; married Ninian, 3rd Lord Ross, on December 9, 1529; children: (first marriage) Matthew Stuart (1516–1571), 4th earl of Lennox (father of Lord Darnley); Robert Stewart (c. 1516–1586), 6th earl of Lennox; John Stuart (d. 1567), 5th Lord of Abigney;* **Helen Stewart** *(who married William Hay, 6th earl of Erroll); \*Elizabeth Stewart (mistress of James V [1512–1542], king of Scotland).*

## Stewart, Arabella (1575–1615).

See Stuart, Arabella.

## Stewart, Beatrice (d. around 1424)

*Countess of Douglas. Name variations: Beatrix Stuart; Beatrix Sinclair. Died around 1424; daughter of Robert Stewart of Fife (c. 1339–1420), 1st duke of Albany (and brother of Robert III, king of Scotland), and \*Margaret Graham (d. 1380), countess of Menteith; married James Douglas, 7th earl of Douglas.*

## Stewart, Cora Wilson (1875–1958)

*American educator who was a leader in the movement against adult illiteracy. Name variations: The Moonlight-School Lady. Born in Farmers, Kentucky, in 1875; died in 1958; attended Morehead Normal School (later Morehead State University) and the University of Kentucky.*

Born in Kentucky in 1875, Cora Wilson Stewart trained as a teacher at Morehead Normal School (now Morehead State University) and the University of Kentucky. She taught for a time in Rowan County, Kentucky, and at age 26 won election as school superintendent of the county. She was reelected eight years later, in 1909. Two years later, Stewart expanded her educational efforts by starting a campaign against adult illiteracy. On the night of September 5, 1911—which Stewart later called "the brightest moonlit night the world has ever seen"—50 schoolhouses in Rowan County welcomed some 1,200 adults to the first session of the Moonlight Schools. Volunteer teachers taught students from ages 18 to 86 how to read and write, initially only on nights when the moon shone bright enough to permit nighttime travel over dark roads. Soon, the Moonlight Schools became a movement that spread over a large part of the United States. As more and more adults began to learn how to read, Stewart wrote a textbook, *The Country Life Reader*, aimed specifically at adult students. In 1924, she was the recipient of *Pictorial Review*'s $5,000 Annual Achievement Award, unanimously chosen as the prizewinner by 20 judges who declared the Moonlight Schools to be the greatest contribution to America by any woman for that year. Two years later she became the director of the National Illiteracy Crusade. The first woman president of the Kentucky Education Association, Stewart also served as chair of the Commission on Illiteracy during the Hoover administration in the early years of the Great Depression (she herself had been nominated for president in 1920). The Cora Wilson Stewart Moonlight School, one of the original one-room schoolhouses in which adults learned to read and write, is now a historic landmark on the campus of Morehead State University in Kentucky. It stands as a testament to Stewart and to the struggle against illiteracy, what she called "a war without the loss of human blood, without the click of a gun or the firing of a cannon—a war fought with the book and the pen."

**SUGGESTED READING:**

Nelms, Willie. *Cora Wilson Stewart: Crusader against Illiteracy*. Jefferson, NC: McFarland, 1997.

**COLLECTIONS:**

Cora Wilson Stewart Papers, 1900–1940, University of Kentucky Libraries, Special Collections and Archives, Lexington.

## Stewart, Egidia (d. after 1388)

*Lady Nithsdale. Died after 1388; daughter of Robert II (1316–1390), king of Scotland (r. 1371–1390), and *Euphemia Ross (d. 1387, his second wife); married William Douglas of Nithsdale, in 1387; children: William, lord of Nithsdale; Egidia Douglas (who married Henry, earl of Orkney).*

## Stewart, Egidia

*Scottish princess. Name variations: Edgitha Stewart; Egidia Stuart. Daughter of Robert III (1337–1406),* king of Scotland (r. 1390–1406), and *Annabella Drummond (1350–1401).*

## Stewart, Eleanor (1427–1496).

*See Beaufort, Joan (c. 1410–1445) for sidebar.*

## Stewart, Eleanor (1868–1920).

*See Porter, Eleanor H.*

## Stewart, Eliza Daniel (1816–1908)

*American temperance leader who founded the first Woman's Temperance League, a precursor to the Woman's Christian Temperance Union. Name variations: Mother Stewart. Born Eliza Daniel on April 25, 1816, in Piketon, Ohio; died on August 6, 1908, in Hicksville, Ohio; daughter of James Daniel (a farmer) and Rebecca (Guthery) Daniel; educated in public school; attended Granville and Marietta, Ohio, seminaries; married Joseph Coover (died); married Hiram Stewart, in 1848; children: (second marriage) five who died in infancy; two stepsons.*

Eliza Daniel Stewart was born in Piketon, Ohio, in 1816. Her maternal grandfather, a Revolutionary War veteran, had settled in Piketon before the town was founded. Her parents, James, a farmer from Virginia, and **Rebecca Guthery Daniel**, were both of Scots-Irish descent and died when Eliza was a child. Her older brother, the Piketon postmaster, appointed Eliza in 1833 as the assistant postmaster, reportedly the first woman officially to hold this position. After a local education and studies at seminaries in Granville and Marietta, Ohio, she taught school. Her brief first marriage ended with her husband's death after a few months. She remarried in 1848 to Hiram Stewart, son of a prominent farmer in Athens County. In addition to mothering two stepsons, she had five children, all of whom died in infancy.

As a young woman raised in the Methodist Church, Stewart was interested in spiritual improvement and perceived alcohol to be a significant evil in society. Around 1858, she acted on her beliefs by organizing a lodge of the Good Templars, a temperance organization, in Athens, and gave her first temperance lecture in Pomeroy, Ohio. In addition to her temperance work, she earned the name "Mother Stewart" during the Civil War for organizing supplies to be sent to Union soldiers, and visiting sick and wounded soldiers in camps in the South.

Following the war, the family moved to Springfield, Ohio, where in 1867 Stewart founded and served as president of the city's first suffrage organization. On January 22, 1872, she stepped up her temperance activities by urging Springfield women to encourage the wives and mothers of drunks to prosecute liquor dealers under Ohio's Adair Act. The law, first passed in 1854, allowed the wife or mother of a drunkard to sue a liquor dealer for damages if they sold alcohol to her husband or son. Soon after this lecture, Stewart contributed to a court victory in just such a case. A similar success the next year inspired the women of Springfield, led by Stewart, to petition the city council to adopt a local ordinance against alcohol. Weekly meetings, and the publicity that accompanied them, resulted in invitations for Stewart to speak to women's groups elsewhere in the state. She established the first Woman's Temperance League, the predecessor of the Woman's Christian Temperance Union (WCTU), on December 2, 1873, in Osborn, Ohio.

Similar movements in Ohio and western New York were also gaining popularity that month, with groups of praying women overrunning saloons in Fredonia and Jamestown, New York. In Ohio, women were storming saloons in Hillsboro as well as the Washington Court House. Thus began a movement that rapidly swept through the Midwest and East in the early months of 1874. Stewart was one of the leaders of an invasion in Springfield. In January, she was elected president of a new temperance union in that city and later that year became leader of what is believed to be the first county union in the country. In November, she was a prominent participant in, and elected chair of, the resolutions committee of the Cleveland convention called by *Martha McClellan Brown and others, which formally organized the National Woman's Christian Temperance Union. Although Stewart was considered by some to represent the radical fringe element of the temperance movement, a speech by *Frances Willard convinced the group of Stewart's leadership abilities.

In 1876, Stewart took her message to Great Britain in support of the British Women's Temperance Association and the Scottish Christian Union. In 1879, she toured the South as chair of the WCTU's committee on Southern work and helped organize white and black temperance unions. She was a WCTU delegate to the World's Convention of Good Templars in Edinburgh in 1891, and in 1895 delivered the opening speech to the World's WCTU convention in London. Noted for being an effective speaker, Stewart also addressed temperance meetings in France, Germany, and Switzerland thereafter.

Stewart's two published works are a history of the early temperance movement. *Memories of the Crusade: A Thrilling Account of the Great Uprising of the Women of Ohio in 1873, against the Liquor Crime* (1888) and *The Crusader in Great Britain; or, The History of the Origin and Organization of the British Women's Temperance Association* (1893) recount her part in the history of the WCTU. Late in life, Stewart joined the Christian Catholic Church of Zion City, Illinois. Its founder, John Alexander Dowie, ordained her an elder, but she was soon disillusioned by its fanaticism and left the group. The last years of her life were spent as an invalid, cared for by her former private secretary in Hicksville, Ohio. She died there, age 92, on August 6, 1908, and was buried at Ferncliff Cemetery in Springfield, Ohio.

**SOURCES:**

James, Edward T., ed. *Notable American Women, 1607–1950*. Cambridge, MA: The Belknap Press of Harvard University, 1971.

McHenry, Robert, ed. *Famous American Women*. NY: Dover, 1980.

Read, Phyllis J., and Bernard L. Witlieb. *The Book of Women's Firsts*. NY: Random House, 1992.

**Martha Jones**, M.L.S.,
Natick, Massachusetts

# Stewart, Elizabeth (fl. 1300s)

*English noblewoman.* Name variations: Elizabeth Stuart; Elizabeth de la Haye. Flourished in the 1300s; daughter of *Elizabeth Muir (d. before 1355) and Robert II (1316–1390), earl of Atholl, earl of Strathearn (r. 1357–1390), king of Scots (r. 1371–1390); married Thomas Hay also known as Thomas de la Haye, great constable of Scot, before November 7, 1372; children: William; Gilbert of Dronlaw; Elizabeth de la Haye (who married George Leslie of Rothes); Alice de la Haye (who married Willam Hay of Locharret).

# Stewart, Elizabeth (c. 1390–?)

*Scottish noblewoman.* Born around 1390; daughter of Robert Stewart, 1st duke of Albany, and *Muriel Keith (d. 1449); married Malcolm Fleming.

# Stewart, Elizabeth (d. before 1411)

*Lady of Dalkeith.* Name variations: Elizabeth Douglas; Elizabeth Stuart; Lady Dalkeith. Died before 1411; daughter of Sir John Stewart of Kyle, later known as Robert III (1337–1406), king of Scotland (r. 1390–1406), and *Annabella Drummond (1350–1401); married James Douglas, lord of Dalkeith, *around 1387; children: William Douglas (b. 1390); James, 2nd lord of Dalkeith; Henry Douglas.*

# Stewart, Elizabeth

*Mistress of James V. Daughter of John Stewart, 3rd earl of Lennox, and Lady *Anne Stewart (fl. 1515); mistress of James V (1512–1542), king of Scotland (r. 1513–1542); children: Adam Stewart, prior of Charterhouse.*

# Stewart, Elizabeth (fl. 1578)

*Countess of Lennox and countess of Arran. Name variations: Lady Elizabeth Stewart; Elizabeth Stuart. Flourished around 1578; daughter of John Stewart, 4th earl of Atholl, and Elizabeth Gordon (daughter of George Gordon, 4th earl of Huntly, and Elizabeth Kieth); married Hugh Fraser, 6th Lord Lovat; married Robert Stewart (c. 1516–1586), 6th earl of Lennox (r. 1578–1586), on December 6, 1578 (divorced); married James Stewart, earl of Arran, on July 6, 1581.*

# Stewart, Ellen (c. 1920—)

*African-American theater producer, manager, and director who founded the pioneer La Mama Experimental Theater Company, spawning the "off-off-Broadway" renaissance and originating one of the most important experimental theaters in the world. Name variations: Mama Stewart. Born around 1920 in Alexandria, Louisiana; educated at Arkansas State University.*

Little is known of Ellen Stewart's early life other than that she was born in Alexandria, Louisiana, around 1920, and that she grew up in Chicago and was educated at Arkansas State University. According to **Gaylen Moore**, she wanted to attend fashion school and tossed a coin to decide whether it would be in San Francisco or New York City. After arriving in Manhattan in 1950, she worked at Saks Fifth Avenue as an elevator operator and lingerie finisher. Stewart told Moore that during lunchtime, she would remove the blue smock required by Saks for its "colored" help, revealing her own creations underneath, which drew the attention of women in the store who thought she was modeling Balenciaga. From that experience, she became an executive designer and ran the sportswear department at Saks. Stewart worked as a freelance designer until 1961 and was the only American designer to have two of her gowns worn at the coronation of Queen *Elizabeth II.

Despite her success, Stewart tired of the racism in the fashion industry and turned her attention to theater. After witnessing the frustration of her foster brother as he tried to build a theater career, Stewart rented a basement on Ninth Street and began renovations to start her own theater where her brother and his friends could write and produce their plays. Her new neighbors, less than thrilled by the prospect of a black woman in residence nearby, used the constant parade of male construction workers at the site to bring Stewart up on charges of prostitution.

Stewart had to clear another hurdle in getting a license to run her business. The difficulty in obtaining a theater license prompted her to seek a restaurant license instead, with the plan of putting on play productions within a coffeehouse setting. Although she knew nothing about theater, she learned as she went along and never gave up, which became a hallmark of her career. The pushcart wheel over the door of her theater became a symbol of her persevering spirit. In 1961, Stewart named the place La Mama because everyone called her Mama Stewart. As the theater evolved through various physical moves and ideological concepts, the name remained a constant.

The theater's first production was on July 27, 1962, with Tennessee Williams' *One Arm*. The first original play the group performed was by Michael Locascio. They also did Harold Pinter's *The Room*. Stewart had produced Pinter's play without permission, but her enthusiasm for his work won the playwright over, and he gave La Mama authorization to perform his plays. Years later, he proclaimed himself one of the La Mama playwrights.

Stewart was an untiring friend to aspiring playwrights, and her efforts to get their work published led to the international scope of La Mama. The lack of critical reviews for La Mama's productions caused publishers also to ignore the playwrights associated with the theater. However, when one of the plays was produced as a student production in Colombia, it won a prize and received international attention. The play was then produced at a festival in Germany, where it was seen by a Danish group, which contacted Stewart and requested more. Realizing that she could get reviews from international critics if her troupe toured other countries, Stewart took 22 plays and 16 actors to Europe in 1965. Mixed reviews from European critics prompted Stewart to seek out acting teachers to give her actors proper training in professional theater. Tom O'Horgan, later director of *Hair* on Broadway, started workshops to

Ellen
Stewart

teach acting and more directors and actors were added to the company.

Stewart's European experience also gave her an idea for an intensive exchange program, in which La Mama would travel abroad and foreign theater groups would perform at her theater in New York. As a result, American audiences had the opportunity to see dramatic troupes from all over the world, and La Mama's international influence exported American avant-garde theater to the world. Stewart told

Moore that her friend Bruce Howard, then an executive director of National Education Television (NET), produced "Three Plays from La Mama" in 1966. Although Howard eventually lost his job because of it, the telecast permitted the group, in 1969, to move to larger quarters and produce longer plays. By 1981, there were four La Mama theaters in the New York area. Branches of La Mama were also established in Boston, Amsterdam, Bogota, Israel, London, Melbourne, Morocco, Munich, Paris, Tokyo, Toronto, and Vienna. Stewart's international vision directly influenced her choice of plays to produce. While La Mama produced plays by established writers like Eugene O'Neill and Shakespeare, Stewart wanted works that transcended the borders of language and culture, plays that were comprehensible to any audience. As she told George W. Anderson, she believed in expressing the literal meaning of a play through visuals, music and dance "beyond the medium of language."

Although she received funding from the Rockefeller Foundation, the Ford Foundation, the National Arts Council, the Kaplan Fund, and the New York State Arts Council, this international scope often made financial support difficult to obtain. Some agencies faulted Stewart for not running a theater specifically focused on African-American culture, and others did not wish to support a theater that funneled American dollars to foreign dramatic troupes. In the early years, her actors, writers, and directors were not paid a salary, and international groups were paid with box-office receipts.

Stewart did not permit the hardships to deter her from her vision, and, as a result, La Mama boasted over 2,000 productions from an impressive corps of writers, including Andre Gide, George Bernard Shaw, William Saroyan, Jean Anouilh, *Gertrude Stein, Eugene Ionesco, Lanford Wilson, Jean Genet, Sam Shepard, Ross Alexander, Israel Horowitz, Peter Weiss, Eric Bentley, Andy Warhol, Harvey Fierstein, and Terrence McNally by the end of the 20th century. Some of the actors who started at La Mama include Billy Crystal, Danny DeVito, Robert De Niro, and **Bette Midler**. In 1985, Stewart received the MacArthur Foundation's "genius" grant, and in January 1993 she was inducted into the Theater Hall of Fame.

SOURCES:

Gilbert, Lynn, and Gaylen Moore. *Particular Passions: Talks with Women Who Have Shaped Our Times.* NY: Clarkston N. Potter, 1981, pp. 33–41.

Herbert, Ian. ed. *Who's Who in the Theatre.* 17th ed. Detroit, MI: Gale Research, 1981.

Moore, Gaylen. "Ellen Stewart: The Mama of La Mama," in *Ms.* April 1982, pp. 52–55.

Stewart, Ellen. "Interview with George W. Anderson," in *America.* Vol. 176, no. 4. February 8, 1997, pp. 28–32.

**Martha Jones**, M.L.S.,
Natick, Massachusetts

## Stewart, Euphemia (c. 1375–1415)

*Countess of Strathearn and countess of Caithness. Born around 1375; died in October 1415; daughter of David Stewart, earl of Strathearn; married Patrick Graham of Kilpont, before 1406; children: Malise Graham (d. before 1490), 1st earl of Strathearn; *Euphemia Graham (d. 1469); Elizabeth Graham (who married John Lyon of Glamis).*

## Stewart, Frances Teresa (1647–1702).

*See Stuart, Frances.*

## Stewart, Isabel (fl. 1390–1410)

*Countess of Ross. Flourished between 1390 and 1410; daughter of Robert Stewart of Fife (c. 1339–1420), 1st duke of Albany (and brother of Robert III, king of Scotland), and *Margaret Graham (d. 1380), countess of Menteith; married Alexander Leslie, 7th earl of Ross (some sources cite 9th earl of Ross), before 1398 (died 1402); married Walter of Dirleton, Lord Haliburton, around 1405; children: (first marriage) *Euphemia Leslie (d. after 1424), countess of Ross; (second marriage) Walter Haliburton; Christina Haliburton.*

## Stewart, Isabel (d. around 1410)

*Scottish princess and countess of Douglas. Name variations: Isabel Stewart; Isabella Stuart; Isabel Douglas; Isabel Edmondstone. Died around 1410; daughter of Robert II (1316–1390), king of Scots (r. 1371–1390), and *Elizabeth Muir (d. before 1355); married James Douglas, 2nd earl of Douglas, after September 24, 1371; married John Edmondstone, around 1389; children: (second marriage) one.*

## Stewart, Isabel (d. 1494).

*See Beaufort, Joan (c. 1410–1445) for sidebar.*

## Stewart, Isabel Maitland
(1878–1963)

*Canadian nurse and teacher. Born on January 14, 1878, in Raleigh, Ontario, Canada; died of a heart attack on October 5, 1963, in Chatham, New Jersey; daughter of Francis Beattie Stewart (a farmer and sawmill owner) and Elizabeth (Farquharson) Stewart;*

*educated in Canada and the United States; attended Winnipeg General Hospital School of Nursing, 1900–03; graduated from Teachers College, Columbia University, B.S., 1911, A.M., 1913.*

*Selected writings:* Opportunities in the Field of Nursing *(1912);* The Education of Nurses: Historical Foundations and Modern Trends; A Short History of Nursing *(5 vols., 1943).*

Isabel Maitland Stewart, the fourth of nine children, was born in 1878 in Raleigh, Ontario, the daughter of **Elizabeth Farquharson Stewart** and Francis Beattie Stewart, a farmer and sawmill owner. Upon the failure of his business when Stewart was a teenager, the family moved to Manitoba where Francis became a Presbyterian missionary. Stewart was encouraged by her family to pursue an education, and like her friends, envisioned a future that favored a career rather than marriage. Although she initially considered teaching, and taught school to pay for her education, Stewart instead decided to become a nurse.

She attended nursing school in Winnipeg from 1900 to 1903. While there, she helped to establish an alumnae association, an alumnae journal and the Manitoba Association of Graduate Nurses. Following her graduation, Stewart worked as a private nurse before returning to Winnipeg General Hospital as a supervisor of nursing. Stewart believed that nurses should learn the theory of nursing in the classroom while gaining practical knowledge on the wards. Interested in improving the standards of nursing education in Canada, Stewart learned about new nursing techniques being taught in the United States.

In 1908, she enrolled in Teachers College at Columbia University, where she trained under the guidance of *Mary Adelaide Nutting. Stewart had planned to return to Canada after graduation to establish a training program for Canadian nurses, but instead remained at the college as an instructor. In 1925, she became the director of the nursing department as the **Helen Hartley Jenkins** Foundation Professor of Nursing Education, succeeding Nutting. At the time she took the helm, the program was geared toward training nurse administrators, but Stewart used endowment money to create an expanded nursing education department. Under her direction, the program became the best of its kind in the nation, with some students even qualifying for doctoral degrees.

Stewart promoted her vision of nursing education through her participation in several pro-

fessional organizations, including the National League of Nursing Education, which she served as secretary and chair of the education committee. She was also influential in setting up the national curriculum guidelines published by the league. Believing that the nursing profession also ought to evaluate the social and emotional elements of illness, Stewart emphasized the necessity of more courses in science, psychology, sociology, and public health, and initiated the idea of standardized testing for nurses. In 1932, she helped to establish the Association of Collegiate Schools of Nursing, and also served on committees that helped to recruit and train nurses during both world wars.

Stewart presented her ideas about nursing education in her 1912 landmark work *Opportunities in the Field of Nursing*—one of the first publications to offer vocational guidance in the field. Although not published until much later, her other two texts, *The Education of Nurses: Historical Foundations and Modern Trends* and the five-volume set *A Short History of Nursing*, were no less influential. Acknowledging the value of other documents on the field of nursing, Stewart sought to preserve existing works on nursing through her support of the Adelaide Nutting Historical Nursing Collection housed at Teachers College.

Stewart was also interested in politics and the women's suffrage movement. At age 16, she wrote an essay on women's suffrage and later marched in parades on Fifth Avenue. She was also a member of the Foreign Policy Association for several years. She retired in 1947, and died of a heart attack at her nephew's home at the age of 85. Stewart's honors include the Mary Adelaide Nutting Award from the National League of Nursing Education (1947) and a medal from the government of Finland (1946). The Isabel Maitland Stewart Research Professorship in Nursing Education was established in 1961 at Teachers College.

**SOURCES:**

Sicherman, Barbara, and Carol Hurd Green, eds. *Notable American Women: The Modern Period.* Cambridge, MA: The Belknap Press of Harvard University, 1980.

**Karina L. Kerr**, M.A.,
Ypsilanti, Michigan

# Stewart, Jean (d. after 1404)

*Scottish princess. Name variations: Lady Jean Stuart. Died after 1404; interred at Scone Abbey, Perthshire; daughter of Robert II (1316–1390), king of Scots (r. 1371–1390), and *Elizabeth Muir; married Sir John Keith, on January 17, 1373; married Sir John Lyon of*

*essays and speeches published by William Lloyd Garrison in the* Liberator.

Not much is known about Maria Stewart's birth or early childhood except that she was born in Connecticut in 1803 to free black parents by the name of Miller. Orphaned at the age of five, she was indentured as a servant to a cleric until the age of 15 and lived with his family. She learned to read at Sabbath schools and had access to the family's library. At some point she moved to Boston and, at age 23, married 44-year-old James W. Stewart, a veteran of the War of 1812, who encouraged her to add his initial "W" to her name. They became part of Boston's black middle-class society until she was widowed three years later, at which point she was defrauded of the inheritance left by her husband.

Because of her husband's death and that of prominent antislavery activist David Walker, Stewart underwent a religious conversion, which resulted in a profound commitment to the cause of freedom. Although no longer aligned with any particular denomination, her religious beliefs converged with her politics. Stewart began to speak publicly, urging blacks to become educated and actively pursue their rights. She also submitted a manuscript to the editors of the *Liberator* who were recruiting black women to write for them. Founded by William Lloyd Garrison and Isaac Knapp, the *Liberator* was a weekly, Boston-based paper that became a major forum for the abolitionist movement. They published Stewart's *Religion and the Pure Principles of Morality, the Sure Foundation on Which We Must Build* as a 12-page pamphlet in 1831. Militant in tone and published only two months after Nat Turner's slave revolt in Virginia, the essay entreated the black community to press for their rights, while cautioning whites about the zealous devotion to freedom that blacks possessed.

Stewart continued to express her views through public speaking engagements and is remembered for four notable addresses. In 1832, she addressed the African-American Female Intelligence Society of America and presented a lecture to a mixed audience of women and men at Franklin Hall—the meeting place of the New England Anti-Slavery Society. In 1833, she spoke at the African Masonic Hall. Critical of the white community's failure to provide sufficient assistance to blacks, Stewart was equally critical of blacks for their failure to struggle harder for their rights. A strident opponent of sending blacks back to Africa, Stewart urged blacks to educate themselves and stand together to demand their entitlement. She also urged women, black and white, to involve themselves more actively in society. Criticized herself, however, by Boston's black community for speaking out too much, she delivered her farewell address on September 21, 1833, and moved to New York City. In 1835, Garrison published the text of her four speeches, together with other essays and poems, as *Productions of Mrs. Maria W. Stewart.*

In New York, Stewart joined a Female Literary Society and taught public school. She also worked for the North Star Association and attended the American Women's Anti-Slavery convention in 1837. In 1853, Stewart moved to Baltimore and privately taught black students. During the Civil War, she moved to Washington, where she became friends with *Elizabeth Keckley, *Mary Todd Lincoln's seamstress and confidante. Stewart also worked at the Freedman's Hospital as the head of housekeeping, a position formerly held by *Sojourner Truth. In 1871, she raised $200 and established a Sunday school near Howard University for the neighborhood's poor children, where university students frequently helped her as teachers. Finally, in 1879 she financed the publishing of a second edition of her speeches, *Meditations from the Pen of Mrs. Maria W. Stewart.* Stewart died that December, 50 years to the day after her husband's death, at the Freedman's Hospital.

**SOURCES:**

James, Edward T., ed. *Notable American Women, 1607–1950.* Cambridge, MA: The Belknap Press of Harvard University, 1971.

Richardson, Marilyn, ed. *Maria W. Stewart, America's First Black Woman Political Writer: Essays & Speeches.* IN: Indiana University Press, 1987.

Smith, Jessie Carney, ed. *Notable Black American Women.* Detroit, MI: Gale Research, 1992.

Weatherford, Doris. *American Women's History.* NY: Prentice Hall, 1994.

**Karina L. Kerr**, M.A.,
Ypsilanti, Michigan

# Stewart, Marjorie (d. after 1417)

*Countess of Moray. Name variations: Marjory Stuart. Died after May 6, 1417; daughter of Robert II (1316–1390), king of Scots (r. 1371–1390), and *Elizabeth Muir (d. before 1355); married John Dunbar, 1st earl of Moray, after July 11, 1370 or 1371; married Sir Alexander Keith of Grantown or Grandown, before April 24, 1403; children: (first marriage) Thomas, earl of Moray; Alexander; James; Euphemia Dunbar (who married Alexander Cumming); (second marriage) Christina Keith (who married Sir Patrick Ogilvy).*

## Stewart, Marjory (d. before 1432)

*Scottish royal. Name variations: Marjorie; sometimes referred to as Marcellina. Died before August 1432; daughter of Robert Stewart, 1st duke of Albany, and *Muriel Keith (d. 1449); married Duncan Campbell, 1st lord Campbell of Lochawe.*

## Stewart, Mary (d. 1458)

*Scottish princess. Name variations: Mary Stuart. Died in 1458; interred at Strathblane Church, Scotland; daughter of Sir John Stewart of Kyle, later known as Robert III (1337–1406), king of Scotland (r. 1390–1406), and *Annabella Drummond (1350–1401); married George Douglas, 13th (1st) earl of Angus, in 1387; married Sir James Kennedy of Dunure, in 1405; married Sir William Cunningham, in July 1409; married William of Kincardine, 1st Lord Graham, on November 13, 1413; married William Edmonstone or Edmondstone of Duntreath, in 1425; children: (first marriage) William (b. around 1398), 2nd earl of Angus; Elizabeth Douglas (who married Sir David Hay of Yester); (second marriage) James Kennedy (b. 1405), bishop of Dunkeld; Gilbert (b. around 1406), Lord Kennedy; Sir John Kennedy; (fourth marriage) Patrick Graham, archbishop of St. Andrews; Robert Graham.*

## Stewart, Mary (d. 1465).

*See Beaufort, Joan (c. 1410–1445) for sidebar.*

## Stewart, Mary (c. 1451–1488)

*Scottish princess. Name variations: Mary Stuart. Born around 1451; died in May 1488; daughter of *Mary of Guelders (1433–1463) and James II (1430–1460), king of Scotland (r. 1437–1460); sister of James III, king of Scotland (r. 1460–1488); married Thomas Boyd, 1st earl of Arran, on April 26, 1467 (divorced 1473); married James Hamilton, 1st Lord Hamilton, in April 1474; children: (first marriage) James, 2nd Lord Boyd; Margaret (Gizelda) Boyd (c. 1470–after 1516, who married Alexander, 4th Lord Forbes, and David Kennedy, 1st earl of Cassilis); (second marriage) James Hamilton; *Elizabeth Hamilton (who married Matthew Stewart, 2nd earl of Lennox); Patrick Hamilton of Kincavil; Robert Hamilton, seigneur d'Aubigny.*

## Stewart, Mary (1542–1587).

*See Mary Stuart.*

## Stewart, Mother (1816–1908).

*See Stewart, Eliza Daniel.*

## Stewart, Muriel (d. 1449).

*See Keith, Muriel.*

## Stewart, Nellie (1858–1931)

*Australian singer and actress. Name variations: Eleanor Stewart Towzey. Born Eleanor Stewart Towzey on November 22, 1858, in Wolloomooloo, Sydney, Australia; died on June 20, 1931, in Sydney; daughter of Richard Towzey (an actor who changed his last name to Stewart) and Theodosia Stewart (an actress); educated at a boarding school; married Richard Goldsborough Row in Sydney, in 1884 (divorced); lived with George Musgrove until his death in 1916; children: (with Musgrove) daughter Nancye.*

*Selected performances: Marguerite in* Faust *(1888); Nell Gwynn in* Sweet Nell of Old Drury *(1902); Paul Jones (1889); Blue-Eyed Susan (1892); Sweet Kitty Bellairs (1909); What Every Woman Knows (1910).*

Nellie Stewart was born Eleanor Stewart Towzey into a theatrical family in Sydney, Australia, on November 22, 1858, the daughter of actors Richard Towzey and **Theodosia Stewart**. She made her acting debut at age five with her father in *The Stranger* at the Haymarket in Melbourne. Stewart received some formal education in a boarding school, but also traveled extensively with her parents during her childhood, touring with *Rainbow Revels*, written for them by Garnet Walch. In 1881, she played the principal boy in George Coppin's *Sinbad the Sailor*, and was discovered by George Musgrove. After a successful run as the drummer boy in *La Fille du Tambour Major*, Stewart was cast in leading roles for the Royal Comic Opera Company, formed by J.C. Williamson, A. Garner, and Musgrove. Her talent for both dramatic and comic opera provided an international career for Stewart, who appeared on stage in Australia, New Zealand, England, and the United States.

She married Richard Goldsborough Row in 1884, but the marriage was short-lived and ended around the time Stewart left the Royal Comic Opera in 1887 to travel to England with Musgrove, with whom she lived until his death in 1916. After receiving training in acting and dancing, she returned to the Australian stage in productions directed by Musgrove. Australian audiences adored her in Gilbert and Sullivan roles, as well as her Marguerite in *Faust*. Her versatility as an actress led to an 80-show run in *Blue-Eyed Susan* at the Prince of Wales in London in 1891, but her biggest successes in England were the Drury Lane pantomimes of 1898 and 1899, where she played principal boy in *The Forty Thieves* and *Jack in the Beanstalk*.

By 1902, Stewart and Musgrove had returned to Australia, where her performance as *Nell Gwynn in *Sweet Nell of Old Drury* became the role for which she is most famous. Although her singing career had ended, Stewart continued doing comedy and drama in Australia, New Zealand, and America. In 1911, she appeared in the film *Sweet Nell*, and later released recordings. After Musgrove died in 1916, she performed less but opened the Nellie Stewart School of Acting, where she spent the remainder of her life teaching. In 1923, she published *My Life's Story*.

Throughout her life, Stewart gave many benefit performances, especially for the Women's Hospital and the Sydney Hospital, where the children's ward is named in her honor. Nellie Stewart died on June 20, 1931.

**SOURCES:**
Radi, Heather, ed. *200 Australian Women*. NSW, Australia: Women's Redress Press, 1988.
Wilde, William H., Joy Hooton, and Barry Andrews. *The Oxford Companion to Australian Literature*. Melbourne, Australia: Oxford University Press, 1985.

**Karina L. Kerr**, M.A.,
Ypsilanti, Michigan

## Stewart, Mrs. Thomas (b. 1926).

*See Lear, Evelyn.*

## Stewart-Mackenzie, Maria

### (1783–1862)

*Head of clan Mackenzie. Name variations: Lady Hood. Born Maria Elizabeth Frederica Mackenzie in 1783; died in 1862; married Sir Samuel Hood (1724–1816), an admiral, created Baron Hood of Catherington (an Irish peerage) in 1782, created 1st viscount Hood and governor of Greenwich in 1796; married James Alexander Stewart of Glasserton, in 1817.*

Born in 1783, Maria Stewart-Mackenzie, known as Lady Hood, married Sir Samuel Hood, an admiral, and accompanied him to the East Indies; she was also a friend of Sir Walter Scott. In 1815, Maria succeeded to the headship of clan Mackenzie. Two years later, following the death of Samuel, she married her second husband James Alexander Stewart of Glasserton.

## Stewart-Murray, Katharine

### (1874–1960)

*Duchess of Atholl and public servant. Name variations: Katharine Ramsay. Born in Edinburgh, Scotland,* in 1874; died in 1960; daughter of James Ramsay, 10th baronet of Bamff (East Perthshire), and Charlotte (Stewart) Fanning Ramsay; half-sister of Agnata Frances Ramsay; educated at Wimbledon High School and Royal College of Music; married John George Stewart-Murray, marquess of Tullibardine, later the duke of Atholl, in 1899 (died 1942); no children.

Katharine Stewart-Murray, duchess of Atholl, was born in 1874 into a scholarly aristocratic family, the daughter of Sir James Ramsay, 10th baronet of Bamff, and **Charlotte Stewart Ramsay**. Her father excelled in both classics and history at Oxford, and her half-sister, **Agnata Frances Ramsay**, followed in his footsteps as an honors student at Girton in classical studies (in the classics examination of 1887, she was the only first-class candidate). A scholar and musician herself, Katharine originally seemed more inclined toward her mother's musical interest and studied piano at the Royal College of Music, but her career path changed after her marriage in 1899 to John George Stewart-Murray, marquess of Tullibardine, who inherited the title of duke of Atholl upon his father's death.

Sharing her husband's interests in public service, the military, and politics, Stewart-Murray became involved in local government and Scottish social service, for which she was made Dame Commander of the Order of the British Empire in 1918. She became the first Scottish woman elected to the House of Commons in 1923, and quickly advanced to a ministerial position as parliamentary secretary for the Board of Education a year later. While her contemporaries considered her humorless and conventional, Stewart-Murray proved a passionate and uncompromising opponent of injustice wherever she found it. As a crusader against international cruelty and oppression, she ignored party loyalties and prejudices, thereby alienating her peers.

In 1929, together with leftist independent politician *Eleanor Rathbone, Stewart-Murray battled against the practice of genital mutilation of women in Africa, the same year she concluded her duties with the Board of Education. Two years later, she published the books *Women in Politics* and *The Conscription of a People*, the latter written in response to labor conditions in Soviet Russia. She temporarily surrendered the party whip when she spoke against the government's plan for a new constitution for India, and lost it permanently after she questioned Francisco Franco's role in the Spanish Civil War. Teaming with Rathbone again on this issue, she conducted her research in Spain, which resulted in her support of Spanish republican refugees, her criticism of the Conservative government's tolerance of fascism in Spain, and the book *Searchlight on Spain* in 1938. Her positions on these issues caused her to be termed the "Red Duchess."

Perpetually at odds with other members of the House, Stewart-Murray broke away from that political body completely as part of a passionate objection to Prime Minister Neville Chamberlain's policy of appeasing Adolf Hitler. She resigned her seat in Parliament in 1938, but sought re-election as a supporter of Winston Churchill's resistance to Nazi aggression. The loss of her seat and the death of her husband in 1942 did little to diminish her fervor. She became known as the "fascist beast" in the 1950s because of her alignment with right-wing forces against Stalinism and Communist oppression of refugees, as well as her apprehension over the plight of several Eastern European countries. From 1944 to 1960, she served as chair of the British League for European Freedom, and published her autobiography, *Working Partnership*, in 1958.

**SOURCES:**
*The Concise Dictionary of National Biography.* Oxford: Oxford University Press, 1992.
Williams, E.T., and Helen M. Palmer, eds. *The Dictionary of National Biography, 1951–1960.* Oxford University Press, 1971.

**Karina L. Kerr**, M.A.,
Ypsilanti, Michigan

## Stewart Streit, Marlene (b. 1934).

*See Streit, Marlene Stewart.*

## Stich-Randall, Teresa (1927—)

*American soprano. Born on December 24, 1927, in West Hartford, Connecticut; daughter of John Stich and Mary Teresa (Zils) Stich; studied at the Hartford School of Music, Columbia University, and the University of Perugia (Italy).*

*Sang with the NBC Symphony Orchestra under Arturo Toscanini; debuted with the Vienna State Opera (1952), Metropolitan Opera (1961); was the first American singer to be named an Austrian Kammersängerin (1962).*

In 1944, while a student at Columbia University, Teresa Stich-Randall created the role of *Gertrude Stein in Virgil Thomson's opera *The Mother of Us All*, a performance that attracted considerable attention. Within three years, Arturo Toscanini had recruited the young singer for his NBC broadcasts of *Aïda* and *Falstaff*. Many of her performances on radio were recorded, and

she continues to be known because of them to this day. Through her recordings, the radio, and the opera stage, Stich-Randall established herself as one of the great Mozart singers of the mid-20th century. Her range as a lyric soprano was also suited to Strauss and her EMI recording as Sophie in *Der Rosenkavalier* conducted by Herbert von Karajan remains a classic.

**John Haag**,
Athens, Georgia

## Stickney, Dorothy (1896–1998)

*American actress. Born Dorothy Hayes Stickney on June 21, 1896, in Dickinson, North Dakota; died at her home in Manhattan on June 2, 1998, age 101; daughter of Dr. Victor Hugo Stickney and Margaret (Hayes) Stickney; educated at La Salle Seminary, Auburndale, Massachusetts, and St. Catherine's College, St. Paul, Minnesota; studied drama at North Western Dramatic School, Minneapolis; married Howard Lindsay (an actor and playwright), in 1927.*

For four seasons, Dorothy Stickney and Howard Lindsay met nightly to star as husband and wife in the robust hit *Life with Father* at the old Empire Theater on Broadway. They then went home together to their aging brownstone at 50 West 11th Street. The play, based on Clarence Day's childhood reminiscences in which Stickney portrayed his mother **Vinnie Day**, opened in November 1939 and did not close until 1944—3,224 performances—the longest running non-musical show in Broadway history. "Little did we realize that the play would last through World War II," said Stickney.

Though Stickney was born in 1896 in North Dakota, her parents had originally come from Vermont, where her uncle William Stickney had been state governor. In her youth, Stickney suffered from corneal ulcers; since her eye impairment precluded college, she turned instead to the study of elocution and dancing. Her first stage appearance in New York was in *Toto*; her Broadway debut was in 1926 as the crazy charwoman Liz in *Chicago*. Stickney also appeared as Cherry in *The Beaux' Strategem* (1928), Mollie Molloy in *The Front Page* (1928), Mincing in *The Way of The World* (1931), and Granny in *On Borrowed Time* (1938). Her films include *The Little Minister* (1934), *The Remarkable Mr. Pennypacker* (1959), and *I Never Sang for My Father* (1970). Dorothy Stickney was also seen on television, as well as in her solo show, *A Lovely Light*, in which she presented the writings of *Edna St. Vincent Millay.

# Stignani, Ebe (1903–1975)

*Ebe Stignani*

*Italian mezzo-soprano. Name variations: Ebi Stignani. Born on July 11, 1903, in Naples, Italy; died on October 5, 1975, in Imola, a small community near Bologna where she lived with her family on a farm; daughter of a machinery salesman; studied with Agostino Roche, San Pietro di Maiella Conservatory, Naples; married Alfredo Sciti (an engineer), in 1940; children: son Dino.*

*Debuted in Naples (1925); was the leading mezzo at Teatro alla Scala (1926–53); retired (1958).*

As the leading mezzo-soprano at Teatro alla Scala from 1926 to 1953, Ebe Stignani was one of Italy's greatest singers. Her ability to maintain a dominant role in one of the world's most important opera houses was due to her talent and dedication. Her grandeur of tone, technique, and phrasing were outstanding. Stignani sang all the great Verdi roles, some Rossini, and the popular Bellini and Donizetti works. By her own admission, she was not a great figure on stage but her technical command of the music made her performances unforgettable; she also made recordings. "I was given a magnificent gift and in a way I am like a priestess," she once said, "for I feel that it is my responsibility to keep this flame lit in the best possible manner . . . . I am Stignani because of my voice."

**SUGGESTED READING:**

De Franceschi, B. *Ebe Stignani*. Imola, 1982.

> **John Haag,**
> Athens, Georgia

# Still, Caroline (1848–1919).

See Zakrzewska, Marie for sidebar on Caroline Still Anderson.

# Stimson, Julia (1881–1948)

*American nurse and the first woman in the U.S. Army to receive the rank of major. Born Julia Catherine Stimson on May 26, 1881, in Worcester, Massachusetts; died on September 29 or 30, 1948, in Poughkeepsie, New York; daughter of Henry A. Stimson (a*

*minister) and Alice Wheaton (Bartlett) Stimson; educated at public schools in St. Louis, and the Brearley School in New York City; Vassar College, B.A., 1901; attended Columbia University, 1901–03; graduated from New York Hospital Training School, 1908; Washington University, A.M., 1917.*

Julia Stimson was born in Worcester, Massachusetts, in 1881 and spent her early childhood years there. She was the second daughter born to Henry A. Stimson, a Congregationalist minister, and **Alice Bartlett Simpson**, whose father, the Reverend Samuel Colcord Bartlett, was president of Dartmouth College. Stimson came from an accomplished family: her cousin was Henry Lewis Stimson, secretary of war and later secretary of state; her brother Dr. Phillip Moen Stimson was a specialist in communicable diseases, and her sister Dr. **Barbara E. Stimson** was a specialist in orthopedic surgery. Another brother was a lawyer and another sister a dean and professor of history at Goucher College. When Julia was five years old, her father accepted a pastorate in St. Louis, Missouri, where she attended public schools. Julia went to the Brearley School after her father's profession took the family to New York City in 1892.

After receiving her B.A. in 1901 from Vassar, she pursued graduate studies in biology at Columbia University from 1901 to 1903. A year later, following a fortuitous meeting with **Annie Warburton Goodrich (1866–1954)**, the superintendent of the New York Hospital Training School for Nurses, Stimson began her studies there, graduating in 1908. She accepted her first professional assignment that same year as the superintendent of nurses and head of the department at Harlem Hospital, where she stayed until 1911. Along with another nurse, **Florence M. Johnson**, she developed a social service department at the hospital to better meet the needs of patients as well as the neighborhood's impoverished families. Stimson then returned to St. Louis where she served as acting social service administrator for Barnes and Children's Hospitals, associated with Washington University, where she became superintendent of nurses in 1913. During this time she obtained her master's degree in sociology, biology, and education from Washington University, graduating in 1917.

Stimson became involved with the Red Cross as a nurse in 1909 and became a member of the National Committee on Red Cross Nursing in 1914. Upon the United States' entry into World War I, Stimson joined the Army Nurse

Corps. Attached to the British Expeditionary Forces at Rouen, France, she went to Paris in 1918 and became chief of the Red Cross Nursing Service in France and coordinator of Red Cross and Army Nursing. Later that year, she was named director of nursing for the American Expeditionary Forces, placing her in charge of more than 10,000 nurses in the Army Nurse Corps. Her impressive service in the war merited her reception of the Distinguished Service Medal, awarded by General John J. Pershing, and a citation from the Allied Expeditionary Forces by Field Marshal Douglas Haig.

In 1919, Stimson returned to the United States and was named acting superintendent, and later permanent superintendent, of the Army Nurse Corps and dean of the Army School of Nursing. In 1920, she received the relative rank of major (fully commissioned rank was granted to nurses only in 1947)—the first woman in the U.S. Army to receive that rank. Stimson's accomplishments during her years as superintendent included raising the requirements for service in the Nursing Corps, adding postgraduate courses, and making service in the Nursing Corps an appealing career. She retired from the position in 1937.

Stimson was called back into active service during World War II to recruit nurses into the Army. On August 13, 1948, she was promoted to the full commissioned rank of colonel on the retired list. Julia Stimson was active in national nursing organizations throughout her life, even after retirement. She promoted nursing as a career and served on the board of directors of the National League of Nursing Education. She was also involved in the American Women's Association of New York (a founding member), the League of Women Voters, and the American Association of University Women. On September 30, 1948, she died after surgery in Poughkeepsie, New York, of acute circulatory collapse caused by generalized arteriosclerosis.

Stimson's works include *Nurses' Handbook of Drugs and Solutions* (a nursing text, 1910); *Finding Themselves* (a series of letters to her family, 1918); and articles in the *Military Surgeon*. Her awards and honors include the American Distinguished Service Medal; the British Royal Red Cross, 1st Class; the Medaille de la Reconnaissance Françaises; the Medaille d'Honneur de l'Hygiène Publique; the International *Florence Nightingale Medal; and an honorary degree from Mt. Holyoke College.

SOURCES:
*Current Biography, 1940.* NY: H.W. Wilson, 1940.

James, Edward T., ed. *Notable American Women, 1607–1950.* Cambridge, MA: The Belknap Press of Harvard University, 1971.
McHenry, Robert, ed. *Famous American Women.* NY: Dover, 1980.

**Karina L. Kerr**, M.A.,
Ypsilanti, Michigan

Julia Stimson

## Stine Ingstad, Anne (c. 1918–1997).

*See Ingstad, Anne-Stine.*

# Stinson, Katherine (1891–1977)

*American aviator.* Name variations: Katherine Stinson Otero; Kate Stinson. Born on February 14, 1891, in Ft. Payne, Alabama; died on July 8, 1977, in Santa Fe, New Mexico; daughter of Edward Anderson and Emma (Beaver) Stinson (with daughter, formed Stinson Aviation); sister of aviators Marjorie Stinson (c. 1895–1975) and Edward Anderson Stinson, Jr., and aeronautical engineer Jack Stinson; married Miguel A. Otero, Jr. (a judge and World War I pilot), in 1928 (died October 2, 1977); no children.

Was the first woman pilot in the world to perform a loop and the first to sky-write (1915); was the first woman pilot to fly at night (1915), the first *woman to fly a plane propelled by a jet engine, and the first woman pilot to tour China and Japan (1917).*

Katherine "Kate" Stinson was born in 1891 in Fort Payne, Dekalb County, Alabama, the first of four children of Edward and **Emma Beaver Stinson**. She hoped to travel to Europe to study music, but she lacked the necessary $1,000. Then she learned that the best barn-storming pilots could earn as much as that in a single day, so she persuaded aviation pioneer Max Lillie to teach her. Enthusiastically supported by her mother, Katherine sold her piano and eventually convinced her father to pay for the other half of her instruction at Max Lillie's Flying School at Cicero Field, Chicago. On July 24, 1912, flying a Wright biplane, she became the fourth American woman to earn a pilot's license. Professing to be 16 years old, rather than 21, Katherine became an exhibition pilot, promoting herself as the "Flying Schoolgirl." With her mother Emma, she formed the Stinson Aviation Company in Hot Springs, Arkansas, in 1914. A year later, she and her mother also leased 750

*Katherine Stinson*

acres in San Antonio, Texas, and turned it into Stinson Field, which is now Stinson Municipal Airport—the second oldest airport in the nation.

In the course of her career, Stinson set several aeronautical records; however, the year 1915 proved particularly significant. Not only was Stinson the first woman in the world to perform a loop, she became the first woman pilot to skywrite when she formed the letters "CAL," signifying California, for a celebration. Moreover, Stinson was the first woman to fly a plane propelled by a jet engine. Internationally famous as an exhibition pilot, Stinson was also the first woman pilot to fly at night. Attaching torches to the wingtips of her Laird biplane, she would land with only a burning tar barrel to guide her. Stinson added to her fame when, in 1917, she became the first woman pilot to tour China and Japan. After that, she barn-stormed the United States and Canada, performing thrilling aeronautical stunts in air shows. Because she was not allowed to join the air service during World War I, she joined the Red Cross as an ambulance driver instead and went to France, where occasionally she was able to fly as well. In 1918, fol-

lowing the war, Stinson was sworn in as a post office clerk in order to pilot a mail flight for the government from Chicago to New York. In July of that year, she flew the first air mail flight from Calgary to Edmonton, Alberta.

Her sister **Marjorie "Madge" Stinson** earned her pilot's license in 1914, and after performing aerial stunts across the nation she became a flight instructor at the Stinson School of Flying in San Antonio, Texas. An excellent instructor, she was called the "Flying Schoolmarm" and was responsible for training more than 80 American and Canadian pilots for World War I. In all probability, Katherine introduced her siblings to flying. Katherine's brother Edward "Eddie" Stinson, who was considered one of the best pilots of his day, joined forces with brother Jack, an aeronautical engineer, to form the Stinson Aeroplane Company in Dayton, Ohio; Eddie later relocated to Detroit, Michigan, where he designed his first airplane, the Stinson Detroiter.

In 1920, Stinson contracted tuberculosis and underwent a lengthy recovery. She gave up flying in 1928 to marry fellow pilot Miguel A. Otero. As part of a mutual pact, neither Stinson nor her husband ever piloted a plane again. They moved to New Mexico where she studied architecture and designed her own home, earning an architectural award in the process. On July 8, 1977, she died in Santa Fe, New Mexico. Her husband died three months later. They were interred at the New Mexico National Veteran Cemetery in Santa Fe. The Katherine Stinson Middle School in San Antonio, Texas, was named in her honor.

**SOURCES:**

Aero Space Museum Association of Calgary (web site).

"Genealogy of the Flying Stinsons," For Old Times Sake (web site).

Leinhard, John H. "Katherine Stinson," Engines of Our Ingenuity (web site).

Read, Phyllis J., and Bernard L. Witlieb. *The Book of Women's Firsts.* NY: Random House, 1992.

**Karina L. Kerr**, M.A.,
Ypsilanti, Michigan

# Stirling, Mary Anne (1815–1895)

*English actress. Name variations: Fanny Clifton; Mary Anne Kehl; Fanny Stirling; Lady Gregory. Born Mary Anne Kehl in 1815 in Mayfair, London; died on December 30, 1895, in London; daughter of Captain Kehl; married Edward Stirling (also known as Edward Lambert), around 1835 (died 1894); married Sir Charles Hutton Gregory, in 1894.*

Born in London in 1815 and educated in France, Mary Anne Stirling, called Fanny, re-

turned to London to become an actress. She performed in theaters outside London and then made her London debut in 1832 at the Coburg Theater under the name Fanny Clifton. She played tragic and comic parts equally well, and performed regularly until her retirement in 1870. Around 1835, she married actor, theater manager, and playwright Edward Stirling. In the 1830s and 1840s, he managed the Adelphi Royal Theater in London, where he and Mary Anne regularly performed together. She also played at the Theater Royal Drury Lane in the 1840s and 1850s, and was critically acclaimed for her Cordelia in *King Lear* at Princess's Theater in 1845. At the height of her fame, she performed and taught elocution at the Royal Academy of Music in London. Her greatest role was as *Peg Woffington in *Masks and Faces*, a role she created at the Haymarket (1852). In the 1860s, she appeared in the company of St. James's Theater playing mostly comedy roles. Edward Stirling retired in 1879, but Mary Anne continued performing throughout the 1880s. She was celebrated for her part as the Nurse in *Romeo and Juliet* at the Lyceum in 1882, and, in her final role, as Martha in *Faust* (1885). Widowed in 1894 at age 79, Mary Anne married again after a few months' bereavement. Her second husband was Sir Charles Hutton Gregory, a civil engineer in railroads, two years her junior. She died in 1895.

**SOURCES:**

Stirling, Edward. *Old Drury Lane; fifty years' recollections of author, actor, and manager.* London: Chatto & Windus, 1881.

**Laura York**, M.A. in History,
University of California, Riverside, California

# Stirling-Maxwell, Caroline (1808–1877).

*See Norton, Caroline.*

# Stirnemann, Gunda Niemann (b. 1966).

*See Niemann, Gunda.*

# Stives, Karen (1950—)

*American equestrian. Born on November 3, 1950.*

*Won Olympic individual silver and team gold in three-day event in Los Angeles (1984).*

In the Los Angeles Olympics in 1984, 33-year-old Karen Stives took the individual silver medal in the three-day event behind Mark Todd of New Zealand. *Virginia Leng won the bronze. In the same event, Stives also won team gold. Two years earlier, she had been near death, after a horse fell on her.

## Stöbe, Ilse (1911–1942)

*German anti-Nazi activist and spy. Name variations: Ilse Stobe; Ilse Stoebe. Born Ilse Müller in Berlin, Germany, on May 17, 1911; executed on December 22, 1942.*

*Worked in Warsaw as a correspondent for German and Swiss newspapers; while working at the German Foreign Ministry, supplied Moscow with valuable intelligence on Nazi political and military plans.*

Born in Berlin on May 17, 1911, Ilse Stöbe provided important intelligence information to the Soviet Union even before the Nazis came to power. She worked as a secretary for the influential Mosse publishing firm in Berlin, and was also employed for some years by the liberal editor and publicist Theodor Wolff. Since she respected her employers, who were Jewish, Nazi anti-Semitic propaganda was offensive to her. By her early 20s, Stöbe was convinced that Hitler's movement would bring misery to Germany and Europe, and she regarded Communism and the social changes taking place in the Soviet Union as the only hope. Determined to end fascist rule in Germany, she passed important information through the Soviet intelligence network. Starting in 1931, she carried out her assignment for more than a decade. The most important phase of her intelligence work was launched in 1939, when she began working in the information office of the German Foreign Ministry. Among the secrets she communicated to Moscow was the date for the Nazi invasion of the USSR. Her network at the German Foreign Office included the important official Rudolf von Scheliha. Arrested and tortured during their interrogations, both he and Stöbe were sentenced to death by the Reich War Tribunal. They were executed by decapitation on December 22, 1942, along with several other members of the "Red Orchestra" group, including *Libertas Schulze-Boysen. Stöbe's family paid dearly for her resistance; her mother died in the Ravensbrück concentration camp, while her brother Kurt, who continued his underground work after Ilse's execution, was eventually arrested and executed in June 1944. Until her death, Ilse's mother carried with her a letter from Ilse requesting her not to grieve over her death, since "in such cases there is no reason to mourn. And please do not wear a black dress."

**SOURCES:**

Biernat, Karl Heinz, and Luise Kraushaar. *Die Schulze-Boysen-Harnack-Organisation im antifaschistischen Kampf.* Berlin: Dietz, 1970.

Kraushaar, Luise. *Deutsche Widerstandskämpfer 1933–1945: Biographien und Briefe.* 2 vols. Berlin: Dietz, 1970.

Trepper, Leopold. *The Great Game: Memoirs of the Spy Hitler Couldn't Silence.* NY: McGraw-Hill, 1977.

**John Haag,**
Athens, Georgia

## Stöcker, Helene (1869–1943).

*See Stoecker, Helene (1869–1943).*

## Stocks, Mary Danvers (1891–1975)

*Baroness of Kensington and Chelsea, feminist, college administrator, social reformer, and writer. Born on July 25, 1891, in Kensington, London, England; died in London on July 6, 1975; daughter of Roland Danvers Brinton (a physician) and Helen Constance Rendel; educated at St. Paul's Girls' School and the London School of Economics, B.Sc. in economics; married John Leofric Stocks, in 1913 (died 1937); children: one son, two daughters.*

*Selected writings:* Eleanor Rathbone *(1949);* The Workers' Educational Association, the First Fifty Years *(1953);* A Hundred Years of District Nursing *(1960);* Ernest Simon of Manchester *(1963);* My Commonplace Book *(1970).*

Mary Danvers Stocks was born into a comfortably wealthy London family in 1891, and enjoyed a privileged childhood surrounded by loving family members with distinguished connections. Influenced by her maternal grandparents' commitment to philanthropic interests, she was an early volunteer in the meal program at St. Paul's Girls' School. She also acquired an interest in the suffrage movement from her mother's family and, while still a student at St. Paul's, participated in the Mud March of 1907. Despite her initial unhappiness with school, she enrolled at the newly opened London School of Economics in 1910, where she earned a degree and met her future husband, John Leofric Stocks. The couple married following completion of her studies in 1913 and Mary Stocks lectured at her alma mater and at King's College for Women while John served in the Army. Seriously wounded in the war, he returned home for a brief stay at Oxford. They eventually settled in Manchester, where John became a professor in the philosophy appointment at Manchester University in 1924. Stocks continued her lecturing and suffrage activities. She also became heavily involved with the Manchester University Settlement and the birth-control clinic she had opened in 1925—the first in the area.

Active in the National Union of Women's Suffrage Societies (NUWSS), which had become the National Union of Societies for Equal Citizenship (NUSEC), Stocks jointly edited its journal, the *Woman's Leader*, in the early 1920s. Although personally opposed to abortion, Stocks persuaded the organization to expand its policy to include the issue of birth control. Following the achievement of full women's suffrage in 1928 (women 30 and older had been granted the vote in 1918), Stocks urged leaders of the NUSEC to press for equal opportunities and equal pay for women; however, despite her influence, the group's focus became largely educational rather than political. In addition to serving on various committees studying crime and gambling during the early 1930s, Stocks also worked on government assignments, including the postal department, the BBC, and grants to universities.

The appointment of Stocks' husband as vice-chancellor of Liverpool University necessitated another move in 1936, and it also signaled a new direction for Stocks when John died suddenly of a heart attack in 1937. Returning to London, she worked briefly as the general secretary of the London Council of Social Service, and then accepted the position of principal of Westfield College in 1939. An effective and compassionate leader, Stocks saw the college through difficult times while also attracting public attention to the institution through her personal fame as a broadcaster on such radio programs as "The Brains Trust," "Petticoat Line," and "Any Questions." She retired in 1951.

Stocks' responsibilities to the college did not limit her activities in other spheres. Her service on such government committees as the Unemployment Insurance Statutory Committee and in organizations such as the Workers' Educational Association gave her the opportunity to contribute to noteworthy causes. And although she became a less vociferous advocate of feminism, it was because she believed that the major battles had been won. With her longtime friend *Eleanor Rathbone, she attempted to expand the concept of feminism to include the role of motherhood and the raising of families. She also found time to write on social and educational issues close to her heart with her biographies of Rathbone (1949) and Ernest Simon (1963). Stocks published a history of the Workers' Educational Association, of which she was deputy president for many years, titled *The Workers' Educational Association, the First Fifty Years* (1953). She also wrote another history text, *A Hundred Years of District Nursing*, in 1960, and ten years later saw publication of her autobiography, *My Commonplace Book*.

Stocks' service resulted in the bestowing of several honorary degrees and a peerage in 1966. She earned the respect of her peers in the House of Lords, assuming the Labor Party whip. Stocks died in London on July 6, 1975.

**SOURCES:**

Banks, Olive. *The Biographical Dictionary of British Feminists;* Vol. I: *1800–1930*. NY: New York University Press, 1985.

Blake, Lord, and C.S. Nicholls. *The Dictionary of National Biography, 1971–1980*. NY: Oxford University Press, 1986.

*The Concise Dictionary of National Biography*. NY: Oxford University Press, 1992.

Uglow, Jennifer, ed. *The International Dictionary of Women's Biography*. NY: Continuum, 1982.

**Karina L. Kerr**, M.A.,
Ypsilanti, Michigan

# Stockton, Betsey (c. 1798–1865)

*African-American educator. Born around 1798 into slavery; died on October 24, 1865, in Princeton, New Jersey; informally educated; never married; no children.*

Born into slavery around 1798, Betsey Stockton grew up in the home of the Reverend Ashbel Green, president of Princeton College, in Princeton, New Jersey. The family educated Stockton and eventually placed her in charge of the household. Stockton was baptized a Presbyterian around age 20 and was freed by the Greens at approximately the same time.

Stockton's advanced level of education and skills in teaching led her to travel with a Presbyterian missionary, the Reverend Charles S. Stewart, and his family to the Sandwich Islands (now Hawaii) in 1823 to open a missionary school in Lahaina, Maui. At this time, Hawaiian rulers forbade commoners to learn to read and write until all royalty had been educated. In 1824, instruction was extended to the entire population, and Stockton founded the missionary school at Lahaina, serving as both superintendent and teacher to about 30 students. Stockton is believed to have been the first black woman to arrive in the Sandwich Islands.

She remained in the islands with the Stewart family for another year, before moving to Cooperstown, New York. Stockton cared for the Stewart children following their mother's death. Later she taught at an infant school in Philadelphia, organized a school for Indians in Canada, and founded the Witherspoon Street Colored School in Princeton, New Jersey. She died on October 24, 1865, in Princeton.

**SOURCES:**

Peterson, Barbara Bennett. *Notable Women of Hawaii*. Honolulu, HI: University of Hawaii Press, 1984.

**Barbara Koch**, freelance writer,
Farmington Hills, Michigan

## Stockum, Hilda van (b. 1908).

*See van Stockum, Hilda.*

## Stoddard, Cora Frances

### (1872–1936)

*American temperance advocate who wrote educational materials on the physiological and social effects of alcohol. Born on September 17, 1872, in Irvington, Nebraska; died of cancer on May 13, 1936, in Oxford, Connecticut; daughter of Emerson Hathaway Stoddard (a farmer) and Julia Frances (Miller) Stoddard; Wellesley College, A.B., 1896.*

*Selected writings:* Alcohol's Ledger in Industry *(pamphlet, 1914);* Handbook of Modern Facts about Alcohol *(1914);* Wet and Dry Years in a Decade of Massachusetts Public Records *(1922);* History of Scientific Temperance Instruction *(n.d.).*

Shortly after her birth in Nebraska in 1872, where her father Emerson Hathaway Stoddard had been working as a farmer, Cora Stoddard's family moved to their native New England. They settled in East Brookline, Massachusetts, where her parents became active in the temperance movement. Her mother **Julia Miller Stoddard** was president of the local Women's Christian Temperance Union (WCTU).

After earning an A.B. degree from Wellesley College in 1896, Stoddard taught high school for a year, then worked in business for two years. She later moved to Boston, where she worked as secretary to **Mary Hanchett Hunt**, director of the Department of Scientific Temperance Instruction of the national WCTU. Stoddard helped Hunt write and review temperance teaching materials, which were required in public schools.

Stoddard left the WCTU in 1904 and took an administrative post in a normal school in Cortland, New York. Two years later, Hunt died and Stoddard returned to Boston where she cofounded the Scientific Temperance Federation to continue Hunt's work. She served as the organization's executive secretary for 30 years, compiling statistics, writing pamphlets and articles on the effects of alcohol, and editing the quarterly *Scientific Temperance Journal.* The journal was later published by the Anti-Saloon League, and Stoddard became active in that organization, which campaigned for Prohibition. In 1918, Stoddard returned to the WCTU as director of its Bureau of Scientific Temperance Investigation and later its Department of Scientific Temperance Instruction. After Prohibition was put in

force in 1920, she wrote about its effects and the correlation between Prohibition and drug addiction. Stoddard, who was crippled by arthritis, resigned all her positions in 1933 (the year Prohibition was repealed), except her post with the Scientific Temperance Federation, which she held until her death from cancer in 1936. She was 63.

**SOURCES:**

Edgerly, Lois Stiles, ed. and comp. *Give Her This Day: A Daybook of Women's Words.* Gardiner, ME: Tilbury House, 1990.

James, Edward T., ed. *Notable American Women, 1607–1950.* Cambridge, MA: The Belknap Press of Harvard University, 1971.

**Barbara Koch**, freelance writer,
Farmington Hills, Michigan

## Stoecker, Helene (1869–1943)

*German feminist and pacifist who was president and guiding spirit of the League for the Protection of Motherhood and Sexual Reform, and editor of the journal* Neue Generation *(The New Generation). Name variations: Helene Stöcker. Pronunciation: STIR-kir. Born on November 13(?), 1869, in Elberfeld, Germany; died on February 24, 1943, in New York City; daughter of Ludwig Stoecker (a textile merchant) and Hulda (Bergmann) Stoecker; attended middle-class schools; took four years of college preparatory work in feminist-sponsored courses in Berlin, and college work at Universities of Berlin and Bern; University of Bern, Ph.D., 1901; never married; no children.*

*At age 14, rejected her parents' Calvinism because of its obsession with "sin and damnation" (1883); at age 21, arrived in Berlin planning to prepare for a teaching career (1892) and became involved in women's causes; studied at the University of Berlin with the philosopher Wilhelm Dilthey (1896); left because one professor refused to accept female students (1899); earned Ph.D. at Bern (1901); returned to Berlin and became an officer in social reform organizations (1902); assumed the leadership of the League for the Protection of Motherhood and Sexual Reform (1905); founded the journal* The New Generation *(1908); attended conference of the Women's League for Peace and Freedom at the Hague (1915); founded War Resisters League (1921); founded War Resisters International and co-founded the Group of Revolutionary Pacifists (1926); refused to live in Germany after the Nazi accession to power, living in Switzerland and other countries before settling in New York City (1941).*

*Selected publications:* Die Liebe und die Frauen *(Minden in Westphalia: Bruns, 1909);* Die Frau und die Heiligkeit des Lebens *(Leipzig: Neuer Geist, 1921).*

When politically prominent German women of the first half of the 20th century are listed, Helene Stoecker is seldom included. Overshadowed by feminists whose organizations claimed larger numbers of followers, she nevertheless deserves prominence as one of the most politically involved women in Germany during the first 40 years of the 20th century. From 1905 through 1914, her organization, the League for the Protection of Motherhood and Sexual Reform, set an often controversial agenda for the German women's movement, raising issues that remain of interest within European and American women's movements.

There appear to be several reasons for Stoecker's modern obscurity. While her ideas on motherhood and the role of women in German society anticipated many controversies in modern women's movements, they also placed her at odds with both the mainstream of German middle-class feminism and the large and prominent women's movement of the Marxist Social Democratic Party in Germany. As a result, the membership of the League reached only some 4,600, an unimpressive figure in view of the estimate that more than 1 million Germans were involved in the German women's movement prior to 1933. Still another reason for Stoecker's recent obscurity has been the controversial and "radical" nature of her feminism, which led many of her contemporaries, when writing their memoirs, to ignore her or to belittle her significance. Unfortunately, many modern writers appear to have accepted this diminished view of her importance.

Born into a strict Calvinist family in 1869, Stoecker was the oldest daughter of eight children. She later recalled envying two sisters who died at a young age, because her parents told her they had escaped "original sin." As the oldest daughter, she bore a heavy responsibility during a long illness of her mother. Stoecker believed that the size of the household led her to hold strong opinions about love, marriage, and the family. But the experience of being responsible for younger siblings also convinced her that "motherhood" should not limit the "free development" of women.

Although she rejected the strict Calvinism of her parents by age 14, she seemed to gain from them a strong sense of idealism and self-reliance, and a determination to achieve her ideals. To these traits she would add an interest in scholarly work and "intellectual development." She benefited from changes in German universities during the 1890s which opened university admissions and classes to women (although individual professors were allowed to refuse to teach women students until 1908). She entered the University of Berlin in 1896, and served as an assistant to the philosopher Wilhelm Dilthey. When another professor refused to work with her, she chose to enroll in graduate study in Switzerland, at the University of Bern.

In 1901, she became one of the first German women to receive a Ph.D., writing her dissertation on 18th-century German literature. Although she would be very active in feminist and pacifist causes, her interest in "intellectual life" would remain with her. Her writings and speeches would often carry the tone of a scholar—a patient teacher who was explaining great ideas which would affect the everyday lives of her listeners and readers.

> Women should have the right to a free intellectual development and the right to love, without having to make a cruel choice between an intellectual and cultural life and happiness as a woman.
>
> —Helene Stoecker

German feminists before World War I included more conservative leaders such as *Gertrud Bäumer; middle-class (bourgeois) feminists such as *Minna Cauer; and Marxist-oriented women who joined the Social Democratic Party, such as *Lily Braun. Believing that Marxists were willing to wait for a future revolution to establish a new, gender-equal society, Stoecker chose to join the second group. She would be considered one of the most "radical" of the middle-class feminists in Germany.

During the 1890s, she was a frequent contributor to the *Freie Bühne*, a left-wing journal edited by Bruno Wille, a theatrical entrepreneur. In these articles, she frequently expressed the view that "the best characteristic of women," the "mother instinct," had been used against them, relegating women to the home in a "supposedly holy occupation." In reply to a speaker who complained that women who wanted to become dentists or lawyers really wanted "to make women into men," Stoecker insisted: "We want to relieve these gentlemen of their worry: we want to become something quite different from men."

As early as the 1890s, Stoecker declared that masculine domination of Germany's state and society had deprived German women of "an intellectual education, economic independence, a congenial life work and a respected social position." In 1898, she published a commentary on a debate in the Prussian lower house over the issue of establishing separate, state-supported secondary schools for women; Stoecker insisted that only a coeducational system would meet "women's deserved rights to free intellectual development." When the Prussian minister of education commented that women were weak "in drawing logical conclusions" but represented "a great and holy good for our people as mothers," Stoecker asked whether a "lack of education, lack of rights, and a second-class status for women are really a great good for our people."

During the period from 1892 through 1903, Stoecker became involved in the abolitionist movement in German feminism. The abolitionist movement, which also attracted some of Stoecker's friends such as the radical pacifist Minna Cauer, was directed against prostitution in Germany in general; it specifically sought to end the long tradition that each major German municipality contained one or more bordellos sponsored by the local government. Stoecker regarded the existence of prostitution as a symptom of larger problems in German society. The abolition of prostitution, she declared, was a prerequisite to ending the "social, legal, and economic manipulation of women" and to "restore to wives the proper respect for their work."

Abolitionist ideas became central to the League for the Protection of Motherhood and Sexual Reform, the organization which Stoecker came to control in 1905. The League had been founded in 1904 by the feminist *Ruth Bré and social reformer Walther Borgius. Bré, who hoped that the League would follow a vaguely Social Darwinistic program which was intended to improve conditions for mothers and infants, wanted to build agricultural living communities for unmarried mothers and their children. She was increasingly pushed into the background by Stoecker, who became general secretary of the League and its guiding spirit.

Under Stoecker's aegis the League campaigned for state-supported stipends for unmarried mothers; free medical care for mothers and mothers-to-be; increased education for the midwives who supervised a large proportion of Germany's births; paid pregnancy leave for pregnant women who also worked; and sex education in the schools as a means of combating prostitution, sexual disease, and pornography. The goal, for Stoecker, was to "unite the women's movement with motherhood" and to "make the best characteristic of women, the motherhood instinct," central to the German women's movement.

Despite the small size of its membership, the League by 1910 had attracted a number of well-known names, including the feminist *Ellen Key; the playwrights Frank Wedekind and Hermann Sudermann; the Marxist revisionist Eduard David; the zoologist Ernst Haeckel, one of the major popularizers of Darwinism in Germany; the physical chemist Wilhelm Ostwald; and the sexual researcher and homosexual-rights advocate Magnus Hirschfeld.

The most controversial and even notorious program of the League was Stoecker's own New Ethics, which sought greater economic, social, and political freedom for German women, particularly married women and especially in sexual matters. While some German feminists insisted that men should exhibit greater restraint regarding sex, Stoecker favored, instead, greater sexual freedom for women. Although Stoecker never married, she did not hide at least two affairs or "free marriages": one with Alexander Tille, who taught German at the University of Glasgow and whom she seriously considered marrying legally, and another with the lawyer Bruno Springer, with whom she lived from 1905 until his death in 1931.

She had rejected the idea of marrying Tille partly because she believed he had tried to dominate her. The New Ethics sought to avoid such a one-sided relationship between women and men. They sought to equalize the position of women and men in marriage, creating a "free union of independent and equal personalities." The goal, for both married and unmarried women, was "intellectual education, economic independence, a congenial life work, and a respected social standing."

The program of the League for the Protection of Motherhood and Sexual Reform reflected the spirit of the New Ethics: one meeting of the League passed a resolution favoring the full equality of husband and wife in marriage, including equality in the rights of both regarding the children; an easing of the requirements for divorce; and equal legal treatment for legitimate and illegitimate children. Stoecker's work to aid illegitimate children would be recognized, during the 1920s, when the German government removed the label "illegitimate" from birth records.

During the year 1908, Stoecker joined the German Monistic Alliance, led by Haeckel and Ostwald. Monism was a cultural movement, with Social Darwinistic overtones, which sought to apply the perceived "lessons" of natural science to German social and political life. Stoecker was a frequent contributor to the journal of the Alliance, writing a column which called for proof of health before marriages and genetic testing for

Helene
Stoecker

married couples. She was fascinated by eugenic ideas and insisted that contraception was "in the interests of the race." She believed, however, that premarital genetic counseling should be purely advisory; in no case were marriage licenses to be denied for "Darwinian" reasons.

Shortly after World War I began in 1914, Stoecker condemned the Social Democratic deputies in the Reichstag, the lower house of the German Parliament, who had voted in favor of emergency war appropriations for the German military. She accused them of failing to grasp the "shortcomings of power diplomacy." She also criticized the German army's invasion of neutral Belgium as an injustice and "the catastrophe of 1843." Stoecker's articles in 1915 suggested that the war was the direct result of masculine domination of society. War, although an atavism, was the "triumph of the state in the original form as a power organization."

The same year that these words appeared, Stoecker became a member of the Association for a New Fatherland, which was the first German "peace" organization to defy wartime military censorship. Its wartime activities centered on countering popular pressure in Germany to annex territories occupied by German troops, particularly Belgium and captured sections of Poland. Although the membership was small (a roster published in 1915 included less than 300 names), the list of members included several prominent German names, including Albert Einstein, the artist *Kathe Köllwitz, and the Prussian finance minister Hugo Simon. In 1916, military censors forbade the Bund to issue any further written statements or publications.

At war's end, Stoecker, in her first postwar book, described the conflict as being an antieugenic disaster, which women, particularly mothers, had been the first to condemn. "[N]umerous researchers, biologists and historians have demonstrated that cultural decline is the result of the loss of the best in wartime," she declared, "and not the result of loose living and luxury."

In 1921, Stoecker affiliated the League for the Protection of Motherhood and Sexual Reform with the German Peace Cartel, a coalition of both mainstream and left-liberal "reform" or "peace" organizations. Stoecker was a co-author of several major statements and letters to the Reichstag from the Cartel, including a 1923 Cartel statement proposing German and French negotiations on the Ruhr question, after French troops had occupied Germany's heavily industrialized Ruhr area.

German pacifists during the 1920s tended to divide into two basic groups. One group, centered around the German Society for the League of Nations, tended to believe that the League was the surest mechanism to prevent future European wars. Others, including Stoecker's associate, the so-called "radical pacifist" Kurt Hiller, argued that the only certain way to avoid future wars was for the European masses to refuse to participate in any way. Stoecker initially appeared to ally herself with the former faction of German pacifism, rejecting suggestions that the League might become a "potential launching point for an international system of police that might, through police action, lead to more frequent wars."

When the League of Nations proved ineffectual in efforts to convince the French to withdraw from the German Ruhr, Stoecker reported to Hiller that she had lost faith in the League as an agency to prevent future European wars. After 1924, she increasingly spoke of "war resistance" as the best war preventative. She had taken one step in that direction in 1921, when she had founded a German War Resisters' League; in 1926, Stoecker and Hiller jointly founded a War Resisters' International. The situation facing European pacifists, she wrote, included not only the "inability of the League of Nations to organize the peace," but also "the lack of restraints on any cabinet or parliament which wishes to impose itself on hundreds of free and blameless peoples." The masses lacked the "will" to "resist this monstrous slavery"; a "general strike or refusal of any participation in any war activity" was the "sole natural step" to deny governments the means to wage war.

Did war resistance require pacifists to attempt to change the political systems of their countries? Stoecker did not attempt to answer this question until 1925, when, as a member the German League for Human Rights, she increasingly became disenchanted with the Weimar Republic, the democratic government of Germany during the 1920s. The League, which had been founded in 1922 as a revised version of the Association for a New Fatherland, campaigned against anti-Semitism in Germany. It held rallies and forums which berated German judges and educators for discriminating against Jewish defendants or students. The League also worked to expose secret rearmament plans and preparations which were being made by the government of the Weimar Republic. Such military plans were in violation of the Treaty of Versailles, which Germany had signed at the end of World War I.

During the 1920s, Stoecker also sought to liberalize restrictions on abortion and secure state stipends and paid maternity leave for employed, pregnant women. She criticized the Catholic political party in Germany, the Center Party. The party's "strong fanaticism," she wrote, forced poor couples to "bring a child into the world without knowing how they will obtain the means to clothe that child." Stoecker published letters she had received from German women, detailing the hardships caused by German anti-abortion laws. She cited a case in which both a woman who had undergone an abortion and her lover were sentenced to two months in jail. Since the Center Party was an important part of the Weimar Republic, Stoecker found herself more willing to listen to parties on the German left, including the German Communist Party.

During the 1920s, Stoecker visited the Soviet Union three times. She came to hope that the USSR would become the sexually equal society that Germany was far from achieving. She wrote that in post-revolutionary Russia, "The revolution has changed everything. Women are fully equal, and the state provides protective care for women and their children. Mothers who work as factory workers or farmers have a four-month leave of absence; mothers who are office workers have a three-month leave. Mothers have a half hour recess, without deductions from their pay; they may not be required to work at night."

During the late 1920s, Stoecker did accept some programs of the German Communist Party, particularly the party's sponsorship of a League against Colonial Oppression. Stoecker was a German delegate to an international Conference against Colonial Oppression, held at Brussels in 1926. She also showed an interest in peace proposals advanced during 1927 by the Soviet Foreign Minister Maxim Litvinov. The proposals were sweeping in nature, encompassing the banning of all land, sea, and air weapons; abolition of all means of chemical warfare; banning of all forms of compulsory military service; and the dismantling of war industries and destruction of machines used to make weapons.

Ill when Adolf Hitler was appointed German chancellor in January 1933, Stoecker chose to leave Germany and live in Switzerland for several years. There, she participated in international efforts to aid friends who had remained behind. She was a prominent participant in successful campaigns by Germans in exile—such as Willy Brandt in Stockholm and Einstein in the United States—to secure a Nobel Peace Prize in 1936 for Carl von Ossietzky, an anti-Nazi publicist who was one of the first political prisoners of the Nazi government. With the approach of World War II, Stoecker left Switzerland, traveling to the United States via London, Stockholm, the Soviet Union, and Japan. She arrived in the United States just before it, too, entered the war. It was a war she had both predicted and feared.

**SOURCES:**
Frevert, Ute. *Women in German History: From Bourgeois Emancipation to Sexual Liberation.* Translated by Stuart McKinnon-Evans, with Terry Bond and Barbara Norden. NY: Berg, 1989.
Gerhard, Ute. *Unerhört: Die Geschichte der deutschen Frauenbewegung.* Reinbeck bei Hamburg: Rowohlt, 1990.
Greven-Aschoff, Barbara. *Die bürgerliche Frauenbewegung in Deutschland, 1894–1933.* Göttingen: Vandenhoeck and Ruprecht, 1981.
Hackett, Amy. "Helene Stoecker: Left-Wing Intellectual and Sex Reformer," in *When Biology became Destiny: Women in Weimar and Nazi Germany.* Edited by Renate Bridenthal, Atina Grossmann, and Marion Kaplan. NY: Monthly Review Press, 1984.

**SUGGESTED READING:**
Allen, Ann Taylor. *Feminism and Motherhood in Germany, 1800–1914.* New Brunswick, NJ: Rutgers University Press, 1991.
Evans, Richard J. *Comrades and Sisters: Feminism, Socialism, and Pacifism in Europe 1870–1945.* NY: St. Martin's Press, 1987.

**COLLECTIONS:**
Most of Stoecker's personal papers were burned by the Nazis. Some materials, including an autobiography, are housed in the Swarthmore Peace Collection, Swarthmore College, Swarthmore, Pennsylvania.

**Niles Holt**, Professor of History,
Illinois State University, Normal-Bloomington, Illinois

## Stokes, Caroline Phelps (1854–1909).

*See joint entry on Stokes, Olivia Phelps and Caroline Phelps Stokes.*

# Stokes, Olivia Phelps and Caroline Phelps Stokes

*American philanthropists who contributed substantial sums to various causes, particularly in the improvement of opportunities for African-Americans through the establishment of the Phelps-Stokes fund.*

*Stokes, Olivia Phelps (1847–1927). Name variations: Olivia Egleston Phelps. Born Olivia Egleston Phelps Stokes on January 11, 1847, in New York City; died of bronchial pneumonia on December 14, 1927, in Washington, D.C.; daughter of James Boulter Stokes and Caroline (Phelps) Stokes; sister of Caroline Phelps Stokes; educated at home; never married; no children.*

*Stokes, Caroline Phelps (1854–1909). Born Caroline Phelps Stokes on December 4, 1854, in New York City; died on April 26, 1909, in Redlands, California; daughter of James Boulter Stokes and Caroline (Phelps) Stokes; sister of Olivia Phelps Stokes; educated at home and at Miss Porter's School (founded by *Sarah Porter); never married; no children.*

Olivia and Caroline Stokes were two of ten children born to James and Caroline Stokes. The girls' parents were dedicated Christians who filled their home with inspirational literature and allowed their children to associate only with friends whose religious training they approved. The family was

STOKES, OLIVIA PHELPS AND CAROLINE PHELPS STOKES

wealthy from banking, real estate, and trade, and strongly believed in using their wealth to pursue Christian goals. They were active in the temperance movement, abolitionism, education of blacks, foreign missions, Bible and tract societies, the YMCA, and children's hospitals. The elder Caroline Stokes was a particularly strong influence on her daughters. She emphasized the importance of service to the poor, helped found the Colored Orphan Asylum of New York, and supported black students in the United States and Africa. She also taught a sewing class at the Phelps Chapel.

Unlike their siblings, Caroline and Olivia never married, but chose to live together in devoted companionship. Following their mother's example, they spent their energy and substantial wealth in philanthropic pursuits, in addition to extensive traveling. Among the institutions benefiting from the sisters' generosity were St. Paul's Chapel at Columbia University, Yale University, New York Zoological Society, New York Botanical Garden, Berea College, Peabody Home for Aged and Infirm Women in Ansonia, Connecticut, and many missionary causes.

However, the philanthropy for which they are best known did not occur until after the death in 1909 of Caroline, who had struggled for years with rheumatism. In her will, she bequeathed money to build chapels at such notable African-American educational institutions as Tuskegee Institute and Calhoun Colored School in Alabama. She also endowed a fund at Hampton Institute in Virginia to educate blacks and Native Americans. The balance of her estate established the Phelps-Stokes fund, which was dedicated to improving tenement housing in New York and educating Indians, "deserving" white students, and black students in the United States and Africa.

Olivia contributed generously to her sister's fund and, in 1915, had two model tenements built in New York. She wrote several books in her lifetime, including *Pine and Cedar: Bible Verses* (1885), *Forward in the Better Life* (1915), *Saturday Nights in Lent* (1922), and *Letters and Memories of ◄❧ Susan and Anna Bartlett Warner* (1925). Olivia died in 1927 at the age of 80.

SOURCES:

James, Edward T., ed. *Notable American Women, 1607–1950.* Cambridge, MA: The Belknap Press of Harvard University, 1971.

McHenry, Robert, ed. *Famous American Women.* NY: Dover, 1980.

Barbara Koch, freelance writer, Farmington Hills, Michigan

**Stokes, Olivia Phelps and Caroline Phelps Stokes.** *See joint entry under Stokes, Olivia Phelps.*

**Warner, Susan and Anna Bartlett Warner.** *See joint entry under Warner, Susan.*

# Stokes, Rose Pastor (1879–1933)

*Polish-born American Socialist and Communist leader. Name variations: Rose Pastor (took the name Pastor from stepfather). Born Rose Harriet Wieslander on July 18, 1879, in Augustów, Russian Poland; died of cancer on June 20, 1933, in Frankfurt-am-Main, Germany; daughter of Jacob Wieslander and Anna (Lewin) Wieslander; had little formal education; married James Graham Phelps Stokes, in 1905 (divorced 1925); married Isaac Romaine (also known as V.J. Jerome), in 1927; no children.*

Rose Pastor Stokes was born to Jewish parents in Russian-occupied Poland on July 18, 1879. Her father died shortly after her birth and when her mother remarried, Stokes took her stepfather's last name, Pastor. The family moved to London, where they lived in poverty. Rose worked from the age of four, helping her mother sew bows on shoes. Between ages seven and nine, she attended a free school, her only formal education.

When Stokes was 11, her family moved to the United States, settling in Cleveland, Ohio, where she worked in a cigar factory and attempted to educate herself. She wrote poems and in 1900 became a contributor to the *Jewish Daily News* in New York, joining the paper's staff when her family moved to the Bronx in 1903.

While working there, Stokes met James Graham Phelps Stokes, a wealthy Socialist sympathizer and nephew of the philanthropists ◄❧ **Olivia Phelps Stokes** and ◄❧ **Caroline Phelps Stokes**. The pair married on July 18, 1905, in what was termed by the press a "Cinderella" wedding given the differences in their economic backgrounds. Settling in New York's Russian quarter, the Stokeses surrounded themselves with radical and artistic friends, and became active in the Intercollegiate Socialist Society and the Socialist Party. Rose Stokes was a lecturer and labor organizer and was active in the New York hotel and restaurant workers' strike in 1912. She continued to write, contributing articles, reviews and poems to *Independent, Everybody's, Arena* and *Century*. In addition to her numerous articles, reviews and poems, Stokes translated Morris Rosenfeld's Yiddish *Songs of Labor and Other Poems* in 1914. In 1916, she wrote *The Woman Who Wouldn't*, a play about a female labor leader.

Because of their pacifist views, the Stokeses withdrew from the Socialist Party when the United States entered World War I; however, Rose Stokes had a change of heart and returned to the party after the Russian Revolution. In

March 1918, she was indicted under the Espionage Act for writing to the *Kansas City Star*: "I am for the people, while the Government is for the profiteers." A now-famous trial resulted in her conviction and a ten-year sentence for interfering with military recruitment. Her conviction was overturned on appeal and her case became a symbol of anti-radical harassment.

Stokes aligned herself with the more radical leftist elements and joined the Communist Party in 1919 where she worked on behalf of African-American workers. She often contributed to *Pravda* and the *Worker* (later the *Daily Worker*). Throughout the next decade, she continued to write, lecture and demonstrate, which led to frequent encounters with the law. Stokes' increasingly radical views led to her divorce in 1925. (*Anzia Yezierska's novel *Salome of the Tenements* [1923] is partially based on the Pastor-Stokes marriage.) Two years later, she married language teacher and Communist Isaac Romaine, although she retained her first husband's name.

In 1930, Stokes learned she had cancer and retired to Westport, Connecticut. Believing that her illness was the result of a police clubbing during a demonstration the year before, Communist friends raised money for medical treatment in Europe. She died in Frankfurt-am-Main, Germany, on June 20, 1933, age 53.

**SOURCES:**

James, Edward T., ed. *Notable American Women, 1607–1950*. Cambridge, MA: The Belknap Press of Harvard University, 1971.

McHenry, Robert, ed. *Famous American Women*. NY: Dover, 1980.

Stokes, Rose Pastor. *I Belong to the Working Class: The Unfinished Autobiography of Rose Pastor Stokes*. Herbert Shapiro and David L. Sterling, eds. Athens, GA: University of Georgia Press, 1992.

**SUGGESTED READING:**

Birmingham, Stephen. *"The Rest of Us": The Rise of America's Eastern European Jews*. NY: Berkley, 1985.

Howe, Irving, and Kenneth Libo. *How We Lived: A Documentary History of Immigrant Jews in America, 1880–1930*. NY: Richard Marek, 1979.

Scholten, Pat Creech. "Militant Women for Economic Justice: The Persuasion of *Mary Harris Jones, *Ella Reeve Bloor, Rose Pastor Stokes, *Rose Schneiderman and *Elizabeth Gurley Flynn," Ph.D. dissertation, Indiana University, 1978.

Shepard, Richard F., and Vicki Gold Levi. *Live & Be Well: A Celebration of Yiddish Culture in America from the First Immigrants to the First World War*. NY: Ballantine, 1982.

Tamarkin, Stanley Ray. "Rose Pastor Stokes: The Portrait of a Radical Woman, 1905–1919," Ph.D. dissertation, Yale University, 1983.

Yezierska, Anzia. *Salome of the Tenements*. IL: University of Illinois Press, 1996.

Zipser, Arthur, and Pearl Zipser. *Fire and Grace: The Life of Rose Pastor Stokes*. Athens, GA: University of Georgia Press, 1989.

**Barbara Koch**, freelance writer,
Farmington Hills, Michigan

## Stokowski, Olga (1882–1948).

*See Samaroff, Olga.*

## Stolz, Teresa (1834–1902)

*Bohemian soprano. Born Teresina (Terezie) Stolzová in Elbekoteletz (now Kostelec nad Labem), Bohemia, in 1834; died on August 23, 1902, in Milan; sister of twins Francesca (Fanny) Stolz and Ludmilla (Lidia) Stolz, both sopranos (b. 1827); studied at the Prague Conservatory, with Luigi Ricci in Trieste, and with Lamperti in Milan.*

*Debuted in Tbilisi (1857), Spoleto (1864), Teatro alla Scala (1865), and Milan (1874); retired (1879).*

Teresa Stolz's work is most closely associated with the work of Giuseppe Verdi. Between 1864 and 1872, she appeared throughout Italy singing numerous Verdi roles. When Verdi's *Don Carlo* was first given in its Italian version at La Scala in 1868, Stolz was chosen to sing Elisabetta. She was also Italy's first Aïda. Stolz's voice was powerful, both passionate and disciplined. In a review of Stolz's performance of Verdi's Requiem, **Blanche Roosevelt** wrote:

> Mme Stoltz's [sic] voice is a pure soprano, with immense compass and the most perfectly beautiful quality one ever listened to, from the lowest note to the highest. . . . The tones are as fine and clearly cut as diamonds, and as sweet as a silver bell, but the power she gives a high C is something amazing.

Stolz influenced Verdi both professionally and personally. He had her voice in mind when he wrote *Aïda*, so she played a major role in creating a voice type now known as a "Verdi soprano." The composer's attentions to Stolz strained his marriage to *Giuseppina Strepponi although the exact nature of this relationship is unknown. As a performer and friend, Teresa Stolz remained close to Verdi until his death in 1901. She died the following year. Her sisters, twins **Francesca** and **Ludmilla Stolz**, were both sopranos and both mistresses of Luigi Ricci, the composer. Ludmilla eventually married Ricci, and their daughter **Adelaide Ricci** (1850–1871) was also a singer in Paris.

**SUGGESTED READING:**

Walker, F. *The Man Verdi*. London, 1962.

**John Haag**,
Athens, Georgia

## Stone, Constance (1856–1902)

*Australian doctor and feminist who paved the way for women doctors in Melbourne and co-founded the Queen Victoria Memorial Hospital for women.* Name variations: Emma Constance Stone. Born Emma Constance Stone on December 4, 1856, in Hobart, Tasmania, Australia; died of tuberculosis on December 29, 1902; daughter of William Stone and Betsey (Haydon) Stone; educated at home before attending Woman's Medical College of Pennsylvania; University of Trinity College in Toronto, Canada, M.D.; studied at the Licentiate of the Society of Apothecaries in London; married David Egryn Jones (a minister); children: daughter Bronwen.

Constance Stone was born in 1856 in Tasmania, Australia, to English parents. Like many women of the time, Stone began her professional career as a teacher, in St. Kilda, Melbourne, but hoped to enter the field of medicine. Since the University of Melbourne barred women from medical studies, she had to leave her native Australia to study abroad. In 1884, she traveled to the United States to study medicine at the Woman's Medical College of Pennsylvania, and completed her M.D. at the University of Trinity College in Toronto, Canada. Stone rounded out her medical studies at the Licentiate of the Society of Apothecaries in London, where she also gained practical experience at the New Hospital for Women and Children. The hospital, administered entirely by women, was a precursor to the Queen Victoria Memorial Hospital which Stone would later establish in Australia.

Stone's intensive studies and extensive experience were rewarded when she became the first woman to be registered with the Medical Board of Victoria in 1890. Constance Stone pulled the fledgling medical community of Australian women together with the founding of the Victorian Medical Women's Society in 1895, and was active in suffrage work and social reform organizations. Working with her sister **Grace Clara Stone** and cousin **Emily Mary Page Stone**, who were also doctors, she conducted a clinic for women and children.

The genesis for the Queen Victoria Memorial Hospital was an outpatient dispensary which Stone ran three mornings a week in 1896, out of the church pastored by her husband. Most of the women doctors in Melbourne fell in line with Stone's vision for a hospital staffed entirely by women for the benefit of the poor of their gender. It operated out of temporary quarters until the facility could be built. Unfortunately, Stone became ill with tuberculosis shortly before the permanent hospital opened in 1899; she died on December 29, 1902.

**SOURCES:**

Radi, Heather, ed. *200 Australian Women.* NSW, Australia: Women's Redress Press, 1988.

Uglow, Jennifer S., comp. and ed. *The International Dictionary of Women's Biography.* NY: Continuum, 1982.

**Barbara Koch**, freelance writer,
Farmington Hills, Michigan

## Stone, Grace Zaring (1896–1991)

*American novelist.* Name variations: (pseudonym) Ethel Vance. Born on January 9, 1896, in New York City; died on September 29, 1991, in Mystic, Connecticut; daughter of Charles Wesley Zaring (a lawyer) and Grace (Owen) Zaring; great-granddaughter of Socialist reformer Robert Owen; educated at Catholic schools and the Isadora Duncan School of Dancing in Paris, France; married Ellis S. Stone (a naval officer), in 1917; children: daughter Eleanor Stone Perényi, later Baroness Perényi.

*Selected writings:* Letters to a Djinn *(1922);* The Heaven and Earth of Doña Elena *(1929);* The Bitter Tea of General Yen *(1930);* The Almond Tree *(1931);* The Cold Journey *(1934);* Escape *(1939);* Reprisal *(1942);* Winter Meeting *(1946);* The Secret Thread *(1949);* The Grotto *(1951);* Althea *(1962);* Dear Deadly Cara *(1968).*

Grace Zaring Stone was born in 1896 in New York City to Charles Wesley Zaring and **Grace Owen Zaring**, who died giving birth to her. Stone originally sought a career in music and was a student of dance at the *Isadora Duncan School of Dancing in Paris. However, her service with the British Red Cross during World War I and her 1917 marriage to a naval officer permanently halted those ambitions. Her husband's postings took them all over the world, including Europe, Asia, and the South Seas, and she began writing in the course of their travels.

Stone wrote her first book, *Letters to a Djinn,* in 1922, although later she rarely acknowledged this effort and credited *The Heaven and Earth of Doña Elena* (1929) as her first novel. This historical romance about a Spanish nun was written after two years in the West Indies. Her third novel, *The Bitter Tea of General Yen* (1930), was written following a trip to China. A bestseller about an American missionary who is captured by a seductive Chinese warlord in Shanghai, it was made into a movie starring *Barbara Stanwyck in 1932 and had the distinction of being the first film shown in the famed Radio City Music Hall in New York City.

Two of Stone's other novels also became movies, including a 1940 cinematic version of her most famous work, *Escape* (1939), starring *Norma Shearer and Robert Taylor, and *Winter Meeting* (1946), which became a star vehicle for *Bette Davis in 1948. The former was one of two anti-Nazi novels she wrote under the pseudonym "Ethel Vance" to protect both her husband, who was a military attaché in France during World War II, and her daughter, Eleanor (Perényi), who was living in occupied Czechoslovakia as Baroness Perényi. *Escape* was a mystery thriller about a German actress who receives a death sentence from the Nazis. Three years later Stone published her second anti-Nazi work, *Reprisal*, about a Nazi-occupied village in Brittany. Although Ethel Vance's true identity was revealed in 1942, Stone also used the pseudonym for two of her later novels, the aforementioned *Winter Meeting* and *The Secret Thread*.

After her husband's retirement, Stone continued traveling, hosting impressive literary salons in Rome and New York that boasted such notables as Robert Lowell, Gore Vidal, and *Mary McCarthy. She was named a fellow of the Royal Society of Literature in Great Britain and was elected to the Council of the Authors League in 1956. A longtime resident of Stonington, Connecticut, she died in a nursing home in nearby Mystic on September 29, 1991.

**SOURCES:**

Andrews, Deborah, ed. *The Annual Obituary, 1991.* Detroit, MI: St. James Press, 1991.

Kunitz, Stanley J., and Howard Haycraft, eds. *Twentieth Century Authors: A Biographical Dictionary of Modern Literature.* NY: H.W. Wilson, 1942.

Read, Phyllis J., and Bernard L. Witlieb. *The Book of Women's Firsts.* NY: Random House, 1992.

Seymour-Smith, Martin, and Andrew C. Kimmens, eds. *World Authors, 1900–1950.* NY: H.W. Wilson, 1996.

**Barbara Koch**, freelance writer,
Farmington Hills, Michigan

# Stone, Lucinda Hinsdale

## (1814–1900)

*American educator and champion of women's clubs. Born on September 30, 1814, in Hinesburg, Vermont; died on March 14, 1900, in Kalamazoo, Michigan; daughter of Aaron Hinsdale (a woolen mill owner) and Lucinda (Mitchell) Hinsdale; educated at a district school, Hinesburg Academy, and at female seminaries in Vermont; married James Andrus Blinn Stone (a Baptist minister), on June 10, 1840 (died 1888);*

*children: Clement Walker, Horatio Hackett, and James Helm.*

Lucinda Hinsdale Stone was born in 1814 in Hinesburg, Vermont, near Burlington. Her father died before her third birthday and she was raised by her mother, who strongly believed in women's education. Stone attended a district school before moving on to Hinesburg Academy. She then worked as a teacher while furthering her education at female seminaries in Middlebury and Burlington, Vermont. For three years, Stone also tutored the children of a plantation owner in Natchez, Mississippi. Witnessing slavery, she better comprehended its injustice, and the anti-slavery beliefs that would figure prominently in her educational philosophies were intensified.

She married the former principal of the Hinesburg Academy, James Andrus Blinn Stone, a Baptist minister, in 1840. The couple lived in Gloucester and Newton, Massachusetts, before settling in the frontier town of Kalamazoo, Michigan, where James Stone worked at a Baptist church and at Kalamazoo College. As principal of the college's "Female Department," Lucinda Stone believed education was an unending process and invited members of her staff to meetings in her home on weekends. To stimulate independent thinking, she secured speakers on such topics as abolitionism and women's rights, as well as such celebrities as Ralph Waldo Emerson. These gatherings became so popular that Stone expanded them to include other women in the community as the Kalamazoo Ladies' Library Association in 1852.

Although Kalamazoo College prospered under the Stones' direction, economic depression and conservative Baptist opposition to their liberal teaching methods resulted in a sharp decline in enrollment around 1857. The school's financial problems prompted James Stone to resign in 1863, and Lucinda Stone followed soon thereafter. She initiated a successful girls' school in their home, drawing students away from Kalamazoo College. As a result, the trustees offered to reinstate both Stones to their jobs; their refusal appears to have prompted unfounded charges of immorality against James by their church, which dropped them both from membership.

In 1866, after a fire destroyed their home, Stone inaugurated educational tours in which she would accompany girls to Europe and the Near East to study art and history. She conducted eight tours between 1867 and 1888; each lasted 12 to 18 months. She also organized women's travel clubs throughout Michigan, as well as the Michigan Women's Press Associa-tion. She became known as the "mother of clubs" and her weekly column, "Club Talks," was featured in many Michigan newspapers.

Stone was instrumental in convincing the University of Michigan to admit women begin-ning in 1870, and in 1896 to hire women faculty members. She received an honorary Ph.D. de-gree from the university in 1890. After Stone's husband died in 1888, she joined the Unitarian Church and remained active in it until her death on March 14, 1900, age 85.

**SOURCES:**

Edgerly, Lois Stiles, ed. and comp. *Give Her This Day.* Gardiner, ME: Tilbury House, 1990.

James, Edward T., ed. *Notable American Women, 1607–1950.* Cambridge, MA: The Belknap Press of Harvard University, 1971.

**Barbara Koch**, freelance writer, Farmington Hills, Michigan

# Stone, Lucy (1818–1893)

*American suffragist and abolitionist whose pioneer-ing lectures on suffrage and work to change the legal status of women regarding property, custody, and voting rights earned her the movement's title of "morning star." Name variations: Lucy Stone Black-well. Born Lucy Stone on August 13, 1818, in West Brookfield, Massachusetts; died of cancer on October 18, 1893, in Dorcester, Massachusetts; daughter of Francis Stone (a tanner and farmer) and Hannah (Matthews) Stone (a homemaker); attended Mt. Holyoke Seminary; Oberlin College, A.B., 1847; sis-ter-in-law of Elizabeth Blackwell (1821–1910), Emily Blackwell (1826–1910), and Antoinette Brown Black-well (1825–1921); married Henry Browne Blackwell, in May 1855; children: Alice Stone Blackwell (1857–1950).*

*Refused church voting rights as a teenager be-cause of gender; became first woman from Massachu-setts to obtain a college degree (1847); hired as a pub-lic lecturer by the Massachusetts Anti-Slavery Society (1847); expelled from her home church for her anti-slavery position (1851); wedding ceremony made no-torious for inclusion of protest against the legal domi-nance of husbands (1855); called attention to suffrage issue by protesting against taxation without represen-tation in New Jersey (1858); was a founding member of American Equal Rights Association (1866); was a founder of American Woman's Suffrage Association (1869); cofounded the weekly* Woman's Journal *news-paper (1870); was a member of New England Women's Press Association and Association of Colle-giate Alumnae.*

Lucy Stone was born on August 13, 1818, in West Brookfield, Massachusetts. The night be-fore, her mother had milked the cows, because the men in the family had to gather in the hay crop threatened by a rainstorm. The next day, on hearing that she had given birth to a daughter, **Hannah Matthews Stone** groaned, "Oh, dear. I am sorry it is a girl. A woman's life is so hard."

Toward the mid-19th century, at the time Lucy Stone was growing up, a woman's legal status had been much the same for generations. She was the legal ward of her father, husband, or brother, and treated in the same manner as a child; if she owned property in her own name, she had to have the permission of her male "pro-tector" in deciding its use. She could not make a contract or a will, could not sue or be sued, and if she had a husband, all her property and earn-ings belonged to him; it was also legal for him to beat her unless it was done "brutally"—a defini-tion left up to the community and the judge to define. Until the late 1800s, married women had no custody rights to their children, but if an unwed woman had a child, the father had no legal responsibility to the woman or the child. And since women could not vote or be elected to office, they had no voice in the election of those who made these laws.

In pre-Civil War America, public opinion and predominant religious doctrine strenuously reinforced these legalities. At a time when the public was bitterly divided about the issue of slavery, and largely unwilling even to consider the question of what was known then as woman's rights, Lucy Stone was one of the abo-litionists who recognized similarities between the positions of "free" women and of slaves. Thus, a career that began with espousing the cause of freedom and enfranchisement for African-Americans carried her quickly into the lifelong work she rendered "in vindication of the rights of women."

Lucy's childhood in the household of a stern father and a submissive mother cast the pattern for her campaign for women's rights. Born the eighth of nine children, she grew up seeing her mother forced to hide a few cents here and there to meet the family's needs. Francis Stone provid-ed only what he considered necessary without regard for his wife's judgment on household re-quirements. In this, he was like most people of his time, believing that women and men had dif-ferent "spheres" of activity which determined their correct and permanent relationships to each other. A woman's sphere was care of her family and home, and her proper relationship to

Lucy
Stone

a man was to be obedient and supportive in all things; when she married, she went from her father's household to that of her husband, where she performed domestic tasks while bearing and raising children; if the family farmed, she also helped with animals and crops. She was considered to need little formal education.

In the Stone family, life was hard for everyone, with farm work both early and late. Francis had given into Hannah, leaving behind the rough and smelly work at a tannery to take up farming in order to provide their children with a healthier and more wholesome atmosphere. In addition to their farm work and schooling, Lucy

and her sisters made extra money sewing rough shoes. Since Lucy was the fastest, she was required to make the most shoes per day.

On the other hand, the family had a strong tradition of individualism, public service, and education. The ancestors of Francis Stone had come from England in the 17th century for the sake of attaining religious liberty, and had been active in public life in Cambridge, Massachusetts. Hannah's family was also of English background, public-spirited, and accustomed to education. In Lucy's childhood, *Massachusetts Spy*, the *Advocate for Moral Reform*, and *Youth's Companion* were all household reading. Later, there were subscriptions to the *Liberator* and the *Anti-Slavery Standard*.

Early in life, Stone noticed the differences in the treatment of males and females, and felt the conflict between her strong individualism and the proper role for a young woman. There were no free public schools for girls, and when her father refused to buy her books, she collected nuts and berries to sell for book money. Raised in the Congregational Church, she saw that the women members had no voting rights, and upon reading the Biblical directive that a wife should be ruled by her husband, she asked her mother how she could do away with herself, because she could not accept being dominated by a man simply because of her gender. When Hannah replied, "It is a woman's lot, the curse of *Eve," Lucy began to suspect the source of this attitude. She decided to learn Hebrew and Greek in order to read the texts in the original to confirm the basis for so many unequal laws and customs.

*The cause has been like a daughter to me. . . . I have rejoiced in every helpful thing done for it, and I have felt the pain of any disadvantage.*

—Lucy Stone

Although Francis Stone expected to help his sons in attaining higher education, he was so surprised by Lucy's desire to go to college that he asked his wife if their daughter were insane. But Stone was qualified by then to teach in area schools, and she began saving on her own to continue her studies. After nine years, she entered Oberlin College in Ohio, the only institution of higher learning in the nation that had opened its doors to women. She was 25 years old.

Stone was a bright and earnest student, dividing her time between her classwork and duties as housekeeper for the Ladies Boarding Hall. During her first year, she also received special permission to teach in the classes set up for former slaves, where her manner and reasoning quieted the resistance of the men to having a female teacher. Two years later, her father had relented enough to loan her money, easing her workload, and her brothers helped out with small sums.

Although Oberlin supported the education of women and African-Americans, and took a centrist anti-slavery stance, there was no support on the campus for women's political rights. By 1845, Stone had been challenging this position for two years, when *Antoinette Brown (Blackwell) arrived. Brown, who was to become the first woman in America ordained as a minister, later wrote that she had been warned to avoid Lucy

Stone because of her radical views and behavior: "Of course, she became the one person whose acquaintance I most desired to make." The two became fast friends and, later, sisters-in-law.

At Oberlin, ironically, female students were allowed to study rhetoric, but not to practice what they learned by giving public addresses, even in class. Stone and Brown, seeking a means to debate, organized a small group which met in the woods, and later found a sympathetic black woman who allowed them to meet in her house. It was this connection, perhaps, that led to Stone's first public-speaking engagement, at a celebration of the freedom of West Indian slaves put on by the local African-American community. At school, she received a reprimand for appearing on a platform with men, as well as addressing an audience of both men and women.

Near the time of graduation, it was usual practice for the Oberlin senior class to choose several students to write and present essays at commencement. In her senior year, Stone received a strong nomination but declined to participate, because the women essayists were required to sit in silence while their papers were read by male professors. Many of Stone's colleagues also refused to participate, and there was even support from the school president for the women to be allowed to read, but there was opposition among the professors, and the Ladies' Board maintained the rule. Ironically, because Brown was in the Young Ladies' Course rather than the regular college program, she was allowed to present her essay. Nearly 40 years later, justice was served at the Oberlin Jubilee celebration when both Stone and Brown were invited to speak before a large audience of mixed races and sexes.

After college, Stone gave her first lecture at the church of her brother Bowman Stone, in Gardner, Massachusetts. The subject was women's rights, and the occasion was the first time an American woman ever spoke exclusively on this subject. Shortly afterward, she accepted a position as a lecturer with the Massachusetts Anti-Slavery Association, becoming one of a handful of women, including *Sarah and *Angelina Grimké and *Abby Kelley, willing to take a public stance in opposition to slavery, and thus to confront both racism and sexism. Traveling on the lecture circuit throughout the northeast, the western frontier, and border states, Stone faced the audiences who filled the lecture halls, often for no better reason than that they were curious to see a woman speaking in public. Despite the occasional verbal attack against her morality, and even physical ones against her person, Stone soon gained a reputation as a persuasive orator. Once, in midwinter, cold water was thrown on her through a window, but she never let such events discourage her from declaring her anti-slavery position. Several times, under the threat of a crowd, she was the only speaker who remained on the platform.

While still at Oberlin, Stone had become a Unitarian. In 1851, she was expelled from her home church for her anti-slavery position. At other times, the Anti-Slavery Society that employed her had to remind her that abolition was the subject she had been engaged to discuss, when her commitment to women's rights made it impossible for her to leave it out of her abolition speeches. When the issue came up, Stone would respond, "I was a woman before I was an abolitionist. I must speak for the women." And since the society did not want to lose such a convincing speaker, an agreement was eventually reached by which she spoke for the society on the weekends and arranged her women's rights lectures to occur during the week.

Audiences who came expecting a tall and aggressive woman with a strident voice were often quite surprised to find a small, genteel speaker with a musical voice. Stone's style and method were rational but not preachy, and earned her the title of "morning star" of the women's rights movement. *Elizabeth Cady Stanton noted, "She was the first speaker who really stirred the nation's heart on the subject of women's wrongs," and *Susan B. Anthony credited Stone with converting her to the cause.

At first, Stone charged nothing for her lectures on women's rights. Eventually, because "it kept out the stampers and the hoodlums, and in no wise prevented those who were interested in attending," she asked a small amount—"often but 12½ cents." In three years, she saved $7,000, to "put aside for old age. It represented my individual efforts." By this time, she was so well known that the Boston *Post* published a parody of a popular song, called "Lucy Long":

> I just come out before you
> To make a little moan;
> I'll put it in the Boston Post
> And call it Lucy Stone.

Succeeding verses described the sufferings of men due to Stone's speeches. The song ended:

> A name like Curtius' shall be his
> On fame's loud trumpet blown,
> Who with a wedding kiss shuts up
> The mouth of Lucy Stone!

When not traveling, Stone lived at her family's Massachusetts home. In 1850, returning from a trip west to care for a dying brother, she met Henry Browne Blackwell, the future brother-in-law of Antoinette (and brother of *Emily and *Elizabeth Blackwell). Henry at first tried to match Stone with his older brother Samuel, then found himself unable to forget her.

When they first met, Stone frequently wore the "bloomer" costume, invented by ❧▶ Elizabeth Smith Miller and popularized by *Amelia Bloomer. The outfit consisted of a jacket and a short skirt worn over trousers, and had been adopted by many advocates of women's rights for its liberating effects on physical movement compared to ordinary women's dress of the day. Henry Blackwell wrote that at first he found the costume unattractive, but he became accustomed to it and supported women who wore it. The unorthodox fashion was ridiculed by press and public alike, wearers were sometimes followed by crowds who could be both curious and antagonistic, and within a few years, most wearers decided that the harassment they received hindered their effectiveness by drawing attention away from the cause. Stone reluctantly gave up the comfort and practicality of the costume for one more publicly acceptable.

Henry Blackwell was an active abolitionist, which recommended him to Stone as a friend, but she had decided in her youth that she would never marry. Having been a firsthand witness to her mother's life, she preferred to keep her fate in her own hands. In 1853, after Blackwell began a concerted effort to change her mind, she made her position very clear in a letter:

> [B]elieve me Mr. Henry Blackwell when I say (and Heaven is my witness that I mean what I say) that, in the circumstances I have not the remotest desire of assuming any other relations than those I now sustain.

Blackwell persisted, arguing that a marriage did not have to be based on ownership and domination, and eventually they reached the understanding that led to their wedding on May 1, 1855. The wedding ceremony became notorious for the inclusion of a marriage protest they had written which denounced certain legal rights of a husband and specifically named laws that put a wife in the same legal category as "minors, lunatics, and idiots." The protest was later published and led to the change of some laws, but it also caused opponents of the couple to charge that their marriage was not legal. Meanwhile, the letters they exchanged over their two-year courtship had led to a convergence of philoso-

❧▶ *Miller, Elizabeth Smith. See Bloomer, Amelia for sidebar.*

phies that made their 38-year marriage one of the most egalitarian of its era.

Some years earlier, Stone had formed the opinion that a woman who takes her husband's name gives up some of her individuality. Consultations with several attorneys, including a future chief justice of the Supreme Court, led her to conclude that the practice was only custom, not law, and she chose to be called Mrs. Stone. Though Susan Anthony feared that the marriage would curtail Stone's activism, she was thrilled with the name decision. "Nothing has been done in the woman's rights movement for some time," she wrote, "that so rejoiced my heart."

The decision led Stone to experience many inconveniences, however, especially in signing legal papers and hotel registers. In 1879, she was denied her first legal opportunity to vote, in a Massachusetts school election, because she refused to register under her husband's name. In 1921, the Lucy Stone League was organized, in memory of her steadfastness, to promote women's keeping their own names, and for a period, women who did so were known as "Lucy Stoners."

In the first year of their marriage, Stone and Blackwell traveled a good deal. In 1857, her trips were halted for the birth of their only child, ❧▶ **Alice Stone Blackwell**, who was given both her parents' last names. Stone tried lecturing again when Alice was a baby but was also conflicted about her role as mother. After a few minor incidents while she was away, she decided to stay home with Alice, a decision that led Anthony to comment, "what marriage had not done to Lucy Stone, motherhood did."

As both a trendsetter and a product of Victorian times, Stone struggled to reconcile her calling with being "a good wife and mother," resulting in some depression and health problems over the next several years. She continued to correspond with other suffrage leaders and to speak at women's rights conventions, however. The family moved from Ohio to New Jersey, where their house was put in Stone's name, and in 1858, she called attention to the suffrage question by protesting taxation without representation, allowing some personal property to be sold for taxes. A friendly neighbor bought and returned the goods to her.

Henry Blackwell continued to travel on business and attend meetings on suffrage for both African-Americans and women. The couple's activism on various aspects of the issue involved them in fundamental differences with other leaders in both camps, and eventually led to a breach within the women's rights movement.

The first women's rights meeting, organized by Stanton, Anthony, and others, had been held at Seneca Falls, New York, in 1848, drawing a largely local and regional attendance. Stone was lecturing about women's rights by then, but did not attend; two years later, she was an organizer of the first national women's rights convention, held in October 1850 in Worcester, Massachusetts. After that, she was active in each subsequent yearly meeting until activism was halted by the outbreak of the Civil War.

After the war, abolitionists turned their attention to full rights for African-Americans through the guarantees of the 14th and 15th amendments to the Constitution, which addressed due process and voting rights. Women's rights advocates saw these changes as opportunities for women's suffrage, too. Stone lobbied in state legislatures, in Congress, and with the public for women to be included on all suffrage ballots. She went on the lecture circuit again. By early 1867, she was as active as ever.

In 1866, she was a founding member of the American Equal Rights Association, formed out of the 11th National Woman's Rights Convention. While the effort to link male African-American and women's suffrage was ultimately unsuccessful, more women's suffrage associations were organized. Stone and Blackwell moved their family back to Massachusetts to work with the associations there. Located at what was to be her base for the rest of her life, Stone became a founder of the *Woman's Journal*, a weekly newspaper, in 1870, and continued to work as a lecturer and editor.

Divisions in the women's rights movement were meanwhile evident by 1867. By the 1869 meeting of the American Equal Rights Association, a group led by Stanton and Anthony formed the National Woman's Suffrage Association. Shortly afterward, Lucy Stone, Henry Blackwell, and others formed the American Woman's Suffrage Association.

The split in the movement, which was to last 20 years, centered on philosophy and methods, and was complicated by personality conflicts. The Stanton-Anthony faction wanted all aspects of women's rights—including divorce, guardianship, and property laws—to be addressed along with the issue of suffrage. They believed that any allied legislation, persons, or actions advanced the cause, and thus stood against amendments that would give suffrage to blacks but not to women; they also accepted money and public association with advocates of radical social policies, including ***Victoria Woodhull**, the free-love and women's-rights advocate who campaigned as a candidate for the presidency in 1870. This group also believed the national Congress was the most important institution for bringing about changes in women's rights.

Stanton and Anthony also understood, as Stone did not, that the labor movement, which had begun to spread, grew out of the same philosophical roots that had produced the abolitionist and women's rights movements. In the labor movement, they saw allies who understood being powerless, and who could perhaps be persuaded that their cause might also be enhanced by women's suffrage.

Stone's position was more conservative. Ideally, both women and African-Americans should receive the vote together, but the first priority, in her view, should be given to blacks. She also favored temperance, which alienated many men who had to vote for women's suffrage in the statewide referenda, the voting level that the Stone-Blackwell faction believed held most promise. Regarding labor, Stone was ambivalent or even opposed to their protests, asserting that unions dominated workers, who, if educated, could be free of unions and make the desired changes in their lives.

Because she refused to discuss the conflicts publicly, Stone's factional disagreements appeared one-sided in published accounts of the split, and her role is incompletely represented. In private, however, as evidenced by her correspondence, she could be harsh in criticizing her rivals. Her fiery temper and acerbic tongue, so different from her public persona, were tormenting aspects of her character dating from childhood, but often hidden behind acceptable Victorian social forms.

The divisions did not stop the momentum of women's rights, however, and with the passing of older advocates, the two factions reunited, in 1890, as the National American Woman's Suffrage Association. Two years earlier, at the 1888 International Council of Women in Washington, D.C., Anthony, *Frances E. Willard and *Julia Ward Howe had praised Stone's efforts. Stone had stopped lecturing in 1887, after which the Woman's Journal remained her outlet. Her last editorial was published only days before her death, at age 75, on October 18, 1893. That same year, at the Chicago World's Fair, a bust of Stone by sculptor *Anne Whitney was displayed at the Women's Building. It was later placed in the Boston Public Library, while the Woman's Journal published continuously until 1917.

## Blackwell, Alice Stone (1857–1950)

*American feminist and reformer. Born on September 14, 1857, in Orange, New Jersey; died in Cambridge, Massachusetts, on March 15, 1950; daughter of Lucy Stone (1818–1893) and Henry Browne Blackwell (both reformers); niece of Elizabeth Blackwell, Emily Blackwell, and Antoinette Brown Blackwell; graduated Phi Beta Kappa from Boston University, 1881; never married; no children.*

Alice Stone Blackwell grew up surrounded by progressives. Her mother was *Lucy Stone; her father was Henry Browne Blackwell, brother of medical pioneers *Elizabeth and *Emily Blackwell and of Samuel Blackwell (husband of *Antoinette Brown Blackwell). After graduating from college (one of two women in a class of 26 males), Alice joined the editorial staff of her mother's Woman's Journal, an organ of her American Woman Suffrage Association, and soon became its primary force, a tenure that lasted for more than three decades. She also wrote a syndicated column that was printed in mainstream newspapers throughout the country.

It was Alice who encouraged her mother to reunite with the radical wing of the suffrage movement—*Susan B. Anthony's National Woman Suffrage Association. When the two groups consolidated in 1890 as the National American Woman Suffrage Association, Alice served as its corresponding secretary until 1918. She also founded Boston's League of Women Voters, stumped for the cause of Sacco and Vanzetti, and published and translated the work of oppressed minority groups, possibly because of a brief romance with an Armenian who died shortly after they met (it was her only known attachment). In 1930, she published a biography of her mother, Lucy Stone, which she had worked on for 40 years. After suffering severe financial reversals during the Great Depression, Alice Stone Blackwell spent her last years in a Cambridge apartment, blind but still aware; she died at age 92.

Lucy Stone had imagined that only a few people would attend her funeral; in fact, more than 1,100 crowded into the church. As progressive in death as she was in life, she had insisted on cremation, and became the first person so entombed in Massachusetts. Her husband and daughter continued to work for women's rights, remembering her last words: "Make the world better."

SOURCES:
Blackwell, Alice Stone. *Lucy Stone: Pioneer Woman Suffragist.* Boston, MA: Little, Brown, 1930.
Hays, Elinor Rice. *Morning Star: A Biography of Lucy Stone, 1818–1893.* NY: Harcourt, Brace & World, 1961.
Scott, Anne Firor, and Andrew M. Scott. *One Half the People: The Fight for Woman Suffrage.* American Alternatives Series. Harold M. Hyman, ed. NY: J.B. Lippincott, 1975.

Wheeler, Leslie, ed. *Loving Warriors: Selected Letters of Lucy Stone and Henry B. Blackwell, 1853 to 1893*. NY: Dial, 1981.

**SUGGESTED READING:**

Kerr, Andrea Moore. *Lucy Stone: Speaking Out for Equality*. New Brunswick, NJ: Rutgers University Press, 1992.

Lasser, Carol, and Marlene Merrill, eds. *Soul Mates: The Oberlin Correspondence of Lucy Stone and Antoinette Brown, 1846–1850*. Oberlin, OH: Oberlin College, 1983.

Stanton, Elizabeth Cady, Susan B. Anthony, and *Matilda Joslyn Gage*. eds. *History of Woman Suffrage*. Vols. I & II: NY: Fowler and Wells, 1881, 1882; Vols. II: Rochester, NY: Susan B. Anthony, 1886; Vol. IV: Rochester, NY: Susan B. Anthony and *Ida Husted Harper*, 1902; Vols. V & VI: NY: Ida Husted Harper, National American Woman's Suffrage Association, 1922.

**COLLECTIONS:**

Correspondence and papers collected under the title "The Blackwell Family Papers" in the Manuscript Division of the Library of Congress; and under the same title at the Arthur and Elizabeth Schlesinger Library on the History of Women in America, Radcliffe College.

**Margaret L. Meggs**,
Assistant to the Director, Women's Studies Program,
Vanderbilt University, Nashville, Tennessee,
and lecturer in Women's Studies,
Middle Tennessee State University, Murfreesboro

# Stone, Nikki (c. 1971—)

*American freestyle skier. Born around 1971 in Westboro, Massachusetts.*

A favorite in Lillehammer in 1994, aerial skier Nikki Stone, of Westboro, Massachusetts, failed to qualify for the final. In 1998 at Nagano, Stone won the gold medal in freestyle aerials with a clean high-degree of difficulty jump, a lay-tuck-full (also known as a triple twisting double somersault), amassing a total of 193 points. **Xu Nannan** of China won the silver with 186.97, while **Colette Brand** of Switzerland took the bronze with 171.83. Stone had been jumping despite a debilitating disc ailment that has given her chronic problems; doctors had advised her to stop competing. "A year and a half ago, I was the most miserable person you've ever met," she told reporters after her win. "Doctors were telling me I'd never jump again and I was believing them." Now "I'm walking on sunshine," she said.

# Stone, Toni (1921–1996)

*African-American baseball player who was the first woman to play as a regular on a big-league professional team. Name variations: Marcenia Lyle Alberga. Born Marcenia Lyle in 1921; died on November 2, 1996, in* Alameda, California; married Aurelious Alberga (an Army officer), in 1950 (died 1988); no children.

In 1953, when Toni Stone was recruited by Syd Pollack to play second base in the Negro American League, thus becoming the first woman to play on a big-league professional team, she was already a veteran player. At 32, the 5'7", 148-pounder was also accustomed to playing with men, having done so for years in the minor leagues, first with the barnstorming San Francisco Sea Lions and later with the New Orleans Creoles.

Characterizing herself as a roughneck and a "big sassy girl," Stone was one of four children of a barber and a beautician who moved from the South to St. Paul, Minnesota. She was attracted to baseball at an early age, although no one in her family could understand why; Stone was considered something of an outcast in her early days. As a child, she played hooky to hang around the St. Louis baseball school run by Gabby Street, a former big-league catcher. Ignoring her at first, Street finally gave in and let Stone play. He was so impressed with her natural ability that he bought her a pair of cleats and let her join the school.

During World War II, Stone went to live with her sister in San Francisco, where she played briefly with Al Love's championship American Legion team before winning a position on the semipro San Francisco Sea Lions, a team of black barnstormers. When she began to sense that she was not being used to her full potential, she jumped to the New Orleans Black Pelicans, then in 1949 to the New Orleans Creoles, who offered her $300 a month, her best deal to date. Stone played second base, distinguishing herself with "quite a few double plays unassisted." During her last year with the Creoles, she batted .265.

When Syd Pollack signed Stone in 1953, the Negro Leagues were already in decline. (After Jackie Robinson broke the color barrier with the Brooklyn Dodgers, other major league franchises began signing the best black players, signaling doom for the black leagues.) Although the Indianapolis Clowns (originally the Ethiopian Clowns of Miami) built their reputation on gimmicks, they were decidedly toned down by the time they moved to Indianapolis in 1939 and joined the Negro American League. Still, there were those who questioned Pollack's motives in signing Stone. (Early on, Pollack asked her to play in shorts, which she refused to do, telling him outright that she would quit baseball first.) Buster Howard, her manager on the Clowns, was one who believed that Stone was recruited mostly for show. "She did pretty good, but she couldn't compete with the men to save her life. Now, in women's baseball, she would be a top player. She knew the fundamentals." Stone remembered a good deal of sexism from her teammates. "They didn't mean any harm and in their way they liked me. Just that I wasn't supposed to be there. They'd tell me to go home and fix my husband some biscuits, or any damn thing. Just get the hell away from here."

One of Stone's fondest memories was playing against Satchel Paige in Omaha in 1953. He was so good that nobody could get a hit against him, she remembered. "I get up there and he says, 'Hey, T, how do you like it?' I said, 'It doesn't matter. Just don't hurt me.' When he wound up—he had these big old feet—all you could see was his shoe. I stood there shaking, but I got a hit. Right out over second base. Happiest moment in my life."

In 1954, Pollack sold Stone's contract to the Kansas City Monarchs, which had always been a serious team. After the first season, Stone felt she was once again being overlooked, and decided to leave baseball. She returned to Oakland where she worked as a nurse. Her husband Aurelious Alberga, whom she had married in 1953, was no doubt glad to have her quit the game, as he never approved of her playing baseball in the first place. "He would have stopped me if he could," said Stone.

Following Alberga's death in 1988, Stone remained in Oakland, living in the house the couple had bought when they were first married; she had continued to play recreational baseball until she was 60. In 1985, she was inducted into the Women's Sports Foundation's International Women's Sports Hall of Fame, and in 1991, the Baseball Hall of Fame honored her and other players of the Negro Leagues in a special ceremony. Stone died of heart failure on November 2, 1996, age 75.

**SOURCES:**

Gregorich, Barbara. *Women at Play: The Story of Women in Baseball*. NY: Harcourt Brace, 1993.
"Obituary," in *The Day* [New London, CT]. November 10, 1996.
Thomas, Robert McG., Jr. "Toni Stone, 75, First Woman to Play Big-League Baseball," in *The New York Times Biographical Service*. November 1996, p. 1637.

**Barbara Morgan**,
Melrose, Massachusetts

# Stonehouse, Ruth (1893–1941)

*American silent-film actress and director. Born in 1893; died in 1941.*

*Selected filmography (as an actress):* The Papered Door *(1911)*; Billy McGrath's Love Letters *(1912)*; Chains *(1912)*; From the Submerged *(1912)*; Neptune's Daughter *(1912)*; Sunshine *(1912)*; Twilight *(1912)*; Broken Threads United *(1913)*; Home Spun *(1913)*; In Convict's Garb *(1913)*; The Pathway of Years *(1913)*; The Spy's Defeat *(1913)*; Thy Will Be Done *(1913)*; A Woman's Way *(1913)*; An Angel Unaware *(1914)*; Ashes of Hope *(1914)*; The Battle of Love *(1914)*; Blood Will Tell *(1914)*; The Hand That Rocks the Cradle *(1914)*; Night Hawks *(1914)*; The Other Girl *(1914)*; Sparks of Fate *(1914)*; Splendid Dishonor *(1914)*; Trinkets of Tragedy *(1914)*; Above the Abyss *(1915)*; An Amateur Prodigal *(1915)*; The Fable of the Galumptious Girl *(1915)*; A Night in Kentucky *(1915)*; The Romance of an American Duchess *(1915)*; The Slim Princess *(1915)*; When My Lady Smiles *(1915)*; The Adventures of Peg o' the Ring *(serial, 1916)*; Dorothy Dares *(1916)*; The Heart of Mary Ann *(1916)*; Love Never Dies *(1916)*; Mary Ann in Society *(1916)*; Daredevil Dan *(1917)*; Follow the Girl *(1917)*; A Limb of Satan *(1917)*; Love Aflame *(1917)*; The Phantom Husband *(1917)*; The Stolen Actress *(1917)*; Tacky Sue's Romance *(1917)*; A Walloping Time *(1917)*; The Masked Rider *(serial, 1919)*; The Master Mystery *(serial, 1919)*; Puppy Love *(1919)*; Are All Men Alike? *(1920)*; Hope *(1920)*; The Land of Jazz *(1920)*; Parlor Bedroom and Bath *(1920)*; Don't Call Me Little Girl *(1921)*; I Am Guilty *(1921)*; Flames of Passion *(1923)*; The Flash *(1923)*; Lights Out *(1923)*; The Way of the Transgressor *(1923)*; Broken Barriers *(1924)*; A Girl of the Limberlost *(1924)*; Blood and Steel *(1925)*; Fifth Avenue Models *(1925)*; The Fugitive *(1925)*; A Two-Fisted Sheriff *(1925)*; Broken Homes *(1926)*; The Wives of the Prophet *(1926)*; Poor Girls *(1927)*; The Satin Woman *(1927)*; The Ape *(1928)*; The Devil's Cage *(1928)*.

Born in 1893, Ruth Stonehouse began her career as a dancer in vaudeville when she was eight years old. Also an aerialist, she later became an actress and formed a partnership with Bronco Billy Anderson at Essanay Studios of Chicago. As early as 1911, she had become one of the company's leading players, appearing opposite such silent-screen stars as Francis X. Bushman, Harry Houdini, and *Norma Shearer. As an actress, Stonehouse believed she was being typecast in submissive "little girl" roles; to combat this image, she began working behind the camera. In 1916, she joined other women directors hired by Universal Studios, such as *Lois Weber, *Ida May Park, *Cleo Madison, *Grace Cunard, Elsie Jane Wilson, and *Ruth Ann Bald-

**win**, to write, direct, and star in their own films. During the early 1920s, Stonehouse returned to acting in supporting roles for Universal and other studios, a career that ended in 1928. Although Stonehouse was proud of her work as a director, as noted in a *Women Film Directors* profile, her directorial film work has either been lost or is otherwise unavailable, thus impeding an accurate assessment. She died in 1941.

**SOURCES:**

Foster, Gwendolyn A., ed. *Women Film Directors: An International Bio-critical Dictionary.* Westport, CT: Greenwood Press, 1995.

Katz, Ephraim. *The Film Encyclopedia.* 3rd ed. rev. by Fred Klein and Ronald Dean Nolan. NY: Harper-Perennial, 1998.

Slide, Anthony. *Silent Portraits: Stars of the Silent Screen in Historic Photographs.* Vestal, NY: Vestal Press, 1989.

**Barbara Koch**, freelance writer,
Farmington Hills, Michigan

# Stopes, Marie (1880–1958)

*Founder of the first birth-control clinic in the British Empire who helped popularize the idea that women could and should enjoy sexually satisfying relationships, of which one component must be women's ability to control their own reproductive functions. Born Marie Carmichael Stopes on October 15, 1880, in Edinburgh, Scotland; died of cancer on October 2, 1958, in Surrey, England; daughter of Charlotte Carmichael Stopes (a Shakespearean scholar and suffragist) and Henry Stopes (an architect and noted amateur archaeologist); tutored by mother until age 12; attended St. George's High School, Edinburgh, and North London Collegiate School; University College of London University, B.Sc., 1902; University of Munich, Ph.D., 1903; London University, D.Sc., 1905; married Reginald Gates, on March 18, 1911 (divorced 1916); married Humphrey Verdon Roe, on May 16, 1918; children: (second marriage) Harry Verdon Stopes-Roe.*

*After earning undergraduate and graduate degrees in botany, became a lecturer at Manchester University; traveled to Japan on a grant from the Royal Society to study botany and to pursue a romantic relationship with a fellow botanist (1907); appointed lecturer in paleobotany at University College, London (1911); became one of the most eminent paleobotanists in Britain and a noted expert on coal formation; after failure of first marriage, wrote* Married Love, *describing the importance of women's sexuality, the first of several bestselling publications discussing questions of human sexuality and contraception; opened the Mothers' Clinic for Constructive Birth Control, the first birth control clinic in the British Em-*

*pire, and founded the Society for Constructive Birth Control to spread her ideas about birth control and eugenics (1921); brought a well-publicized defamation suit against the author of an anti-birth control book (1923); devoted the conclusion of her life to writing poetry and plays and assisting poets such as Alfred Douglas and Walter de la Mare.*

*Selected publications on birth control and sexuality:* Married Love *(1918);* Wise Parenthood *(1918);* The Truth About VD *(1920);* Radiant Motherhood *(1920).*

Shortly before World War I broke out, Marie Stopes began a desperate search for information at the British Museum Library. Although a noted paleobotanist, Stopes was researching neither plants nor fossils. Rather, she was hoping to shed some light on her own troubled marriage by delving into the library's materials on human sexuality. What Stopes discovered, to her shock, was that after three years of wedded life and at 33 years of age, she was still a virgin. Her marriage had never been consummated. Stopes realized that if she, a doctor of science, could have been so ignorant of the basic facts of human sexual relations, there must be millions of other women similarly suffering from the effects of Victorian morality. Stopes resolved to use her personal tragedy to help others find sexual fulfillment.

Born on October 15, 1880, in Edinburgh, Scotland, she was the elder of two daughters born to **Charlotte Carmichael Stopes** and Henry Stopes. Her mother was the first woman in Scotland to receive a university certificate (at a time when women were still barred from university degree programs), an ardent suffragist, a noted Shakespearean scholar, and a proponent of such "advanced" causes as the Rational Dress Movement. Despite these progressive tendencies, Charlotte Stopes was a religious woman and Marie and her sister Winifred Stopes were raised as members of the Free Church of Scotland. Stopes' father Henry was an engineer and architect who specialized in building breweries. However, he was also a passionate amateur archaeologist and, as he grew older, increasingly neglected his architectural practice in favor of fossil hunting.

Marie Stopes showed little academic promise in her early years. Educated at home by her mother until the age of 12, she was seriously behind her contemporaries when she enrolled at St. George's High School in Edinburgh, an educational institution for girls founded by some of her mother's suffragist friends. After two years, the Stopes family moved to London, and Marie entered North London Collegiate School, one of the best girls' schools in Britain. She continued to perform poorly, except in science.

At the urging of one of her science teachers, who saw signs of promise in the seemingly ungifted young woman, Stopes enrolled in University College at the University of London. She devoted herself to the study of botany. Perhaps hoping to prove herself academically, Stopes earned her degree with honors one year sooner than provided for in the normal curriculum, an almost unheard-of feat. In that same year, 1902, Stopes' beloved father died unexpectedly, leaving the family on the verge of poverty. Stopes realized that she would need to earn her own living, and perhaps contribute to the support of her mother and younger sister as well. However, her academic success had earned Stopes a fellowship for graduate studies. In 1903, she went to Munich where she studied plant fossils and received her doctoral degree. The following year, she accepted a position as a junior lecturer in botany at Manchester University in Britain, becoming the first woman appointed to the school's science faculty. Continuing her string of brilliant academic successes, Stopes earned her doctor of science degree in 1905, becoming the youngest person in Britain to attain that distinction. She authored numerous articles and books in her rather esoteric field of paleobotany and was soon recognized as the preeminent British authority on coal formation.

Although Stopes' professional life was enviably successful, her personal life seemed to careen from one catastrophe to another. She later claimed to have been a "late bloomer" in her own sexual development. Her father, furthermore, had instilled in her the quaint notion that no "nice girl" would even consider getting married before the age of 25—or, indeed, would kiss someone to whom she was not engaged. While studying in Munich, however, Stopes had met and fallen in love with a fellow botanist. Two hard facts stood in the way of their relationship: at a time when racially mixed marriages were virtually unheard of, her adored botanist, Kenjiro Fujii, was Japanese and, not less important, he was married. Never one to be deterred by reality, Stopes obtained a grant from the Royal Society in 1907 to finance her researches in paleobotany. Not coincidentally, the location of her field work would be Japan. Fujii, it is true, had divorced his wife, but when Stopes arrived with expectations of marrying him, he feigned illness and backed out of the affair. She later published their thinly disguised love letters in a book. Characteristically, Stopes made several impor-

tant botanical discoveries while in Japan, despite her personal troubles.

Back in England, Stopes experienced several other romantic disappointments. In 1911, however, while attending a scientific conference in the United States, Stopes met a fellow botanist, Dr. Reginald Gates. Within a week of their first encounter, Gates proposed; they were married just a few months later. Unusual for her day, Stopes insisted on maintaining certain rights even after becoming a wife. The couple decided to settle in London, where Stopes had a good position teaching at University College, even though it would prove difficult for Gates to obtain suitable employment in England. Stopes also insisted on retaining her maiden name, sending out announcements to her friends to that effect and explaining that her professional title of "Doctor" should alleviate any awkwardness about how to address her. It was also about this time that Stopes joined the Women's Social and Political Union, the militant women's suffrage organization.

*Jeanie, Jeanie, full of hopes*
*Read a book by Marie Stopes.*
*But to judge by her condition,*
*She must have read the wrong edition.*
**—Schoolyard jingle**

Despite Stopes' determination to make her marriage work on her own terms, much was amiss. In addition to his sexual problems (presumably he was impotent, although this has never been verified), Gates was often verbally abusive to Stopes. Stopes, not surprisingly, became increasingly estranged from her husband and turned to Aylmer Maude for comfort and advice. A noted translator and biographer of Tolstoy and 22 years her senior, Maude lived with Stopes and her husband as a paying boarder. Fortified by her researches on human sexuality at the British Library, and with Maude's encouragement, Stopes left her husband, obtaining a medical certification of her virginity and, in 1916, an annulment of her marriage.

Desperate for money after the expenses of her divorce case, Stopes wrote several plays, including a thinly disguised dramatization of her marriage to Gates and her relationship with Aylmer Maude, but failed to sell any of them. She was also working on a book that would explain in a simple, engaging manner her conclusions on the science and psychology of sex. Her motives in this endeavor were not purely pecuniary, however; as she later wrote, in "my own marriage I paid such a terrible price for sex-ignorance that I feel knowledge gained at such a cost should be placed at the service of humanity." She broadened the scope of her intended work when in 1915 she attended a lecture by *Margaret Sanger, the noted American birth-control activist. Stopes realized she must include information on contraception in her work on sexuality, and asked Sanger to share her information.

Even in the increasingly permissive atmosphere of World War I Britain, publications about sex were considered morally suspect. In the United States, Sanger had been indicted on obscenity charges for disseminating birth-control information through the mails. Stopes experienced great difficulty finding a publisher for her book, *Married Love*, although it included only a few pages on birth control and its descriptions of sexual intercourse were more mystical and romantic than explicitly descriptive. Stopes argued that men—and women—must acknowledge female sexuality to transform sex from a mere physical event into an act of mystical union. She wrote in *Married Love:*

> Man, through prudery, through the custom of ignoring the woman's side of marriage and considering his own whim as marriage law, has largely lost the art of stirring a chaste partner to physical love. He therefore deprives her of a glamour, the loss of which he deplores, for he feels a lack not only of romance and beauty, but of something higher which is mystically given as the result of the complete union. And she, knowing that the shrine has been desecrated, is filled with righteous indignation, though generally as blind as he is to the true cause of what has occurred.

However, as an acquaintance who reviewed the manuscript wrote to Stopes, her work also contained enough hard facts to shock British society: "You certainly put in a lot of important points—menstruation, positions, ejaculation without penetration, birth control, insemination, etc.—which will terrify Mrs. Grundy."

After incessant rejections, Stopes finally secured a publisher who would market her book— *if* she provided him with the necessary funds to launch the publication. Fortuitously, she was introduced shortly thereafter to Humphrey Verdon Roe, an aviator and successful businessman who also happened to be intensely committed to the cause of birth control. Roe not only agreed to put up the money to publish Stopes' book, he also fell deeply in love with her. They married on May 16, 1918.

Roe's investment proved to be a wise one in financial as well as personal terms. *Married Love* was an instant success. When it appeared in 1918, Stopes wrote that her book "crashed into English society like a bombshell. Its explosively contagious main theme—that woman like man has the same physiological reaction, a reciprocal need for enjoyment and benefit from union in marriage distinct from the exercise of maternal functions—made Victorian husbands gasp. A week or two after that book was published in 1918 all London was talking of it." By the end of the year, the book had gone into six editions. Its influence continued to be recognized many years after; in 1935, a group of American academics ranked *Married Love* 16th on a list of the 25 most influential publications of the past 50 years. Stopes quickly followed up the success of her book with *Wise Parenthood*, a short guide to birth control, a subject to which she had devoted only a few pages in *Married Love*.

With the widespread success of *Married Love*, Stopes herself became a famous figure. Letters from readers poured in, beseeching her help in saving their marriages, improving their sex lives, or preventing unwanted pregnancies. Stopes provided personal answers to many correspondents, although she adamantly refused to give sexual advice to the unmarried or to provide any information on abortion.

She realized that her publications would be of use only to the better educated, relatively well-off segment of the British population. She would need to use different, more radical, tactics to bring her message to working-class women in desperate need of reliable birth-control information. Humphrey Roe shared his wife's concern for providing advice on contraception to poor British women. Even before his introduction to Stopes, Roe had tried unsuccessfully to endow a birth-control clinic. The subject was considered so controversial that the hospital he approached refused his contribution rather than alienate other, more conservative, donors.

On March 17, 1921, Stopes and Roe opened the Mothers' Clinic for Constructive Birth Control in London, the first birth-control clinic in the British Empire. (Margaret Sanger had already opened a clinic in the U.S.) The clinic offered free consultations and provided contraceptives at cost, to avoid any allegations of profiting from poor women's birth control needs. The aims of the clinic were four: first, to help the poor; second, to test the true attitudes of the working class, previously assumed to be unremittingly hostile to contraception; third, to

Marie
Stopes

obtain scientific data about contraception; and finally, to collect data on women's sexuality, a much-understudied subject.

To publicize the work and goals of the clinic, Stopes and her husband founded the Society for Constructive Birth Control and Racial Progress in 1921. In May of that year, they held a large public meeting at Queen's Hall in London. Many well-known figures of the birth-control movement, including Stopes, spoke to the more than 2,000 in attendance. Stopes also pioneered several innovative methods of bringing birth-control information and services to a wider public. In 1923, a film based on Stopes' ideas about birth control and sexuality, *Maisie's Marriage*, was shown throughout Britain. Although quite tame by modern standards, the film outraged the censors, who tried to prevent its screening on the grounds of obscenity. At Stopes' clinic, women nurses, rather than male doctors, provided birth-control information. Stopes believed that female patients would be more at ease with other women and would thus speak more freely of their contraceptive needs and problems. To provide services to women living outside major urban areas, Stopes established traveling caravans staffed by nurses that moved around the villages of rural Britain dispensing birth-control advice and services.

As the reference to "Racial Progress" in the name of Stopes' birth-control society indicates, however, her goal in promoting contraception was not merely to guarantee women's reproductive freedom and autonomy. Stopes was also a firm advocate of eugenics and believed that selective use of birth control could enhance the quality of the British population. The Society for Constructive Birth Control promoted itself as a "pro-baby organisation." One of their official publications stated:

> We, therefore, as a Society, regret the relatively small families of those best fitted to care for children. In this connection our motto has been "Babies in the right place," and it is just as much the aim of Constructive Birth Control to secure conception to those married people who are healthy, childless, and desire children, as it is to furnish security from conception to those who are racially diseased, already overburdened with children, or in any specific way unfitted for parenthood.

Stopes undoubtedly saw herself and Roe as the type of people best suited to supply superior children for the improvement of the race. It was a great tragedy, therefore, both on the personal and the ideological level, when their first child was stillborn. In 1924, Stopes gave birth to a much-beloved son, Harry Verdon Stopes-Roe. He was to be their only child and, although Stopes tried to adopt several little boys to provide companionship for Harry, her single-minded devotion to her biological son prevented any of these adoption plans from succeeding on a long-term basis. Ironically, Stopes' obsession with racial improvement and eugenics eventually resulted in a lasting estrangement from her son. Stopes vociferously objected to her son's fiancée,

arguing that the woman was racially unsuitable. (Harry's future wife was mildly nearsighted.)

In 1923, Stopes brought a much-publicized libel suit against Halliday G. Sutherland, a doctor and the author of a book against contraception. In that book, Sutherland implied that Stopes (who was not mentioned by name in the work) was using the poor women patients at her clinic for experimentation and also that the methods of birth control prescribed at the clinic were harmful. The outcome of the trial was ambiguous. The jury found that the remarks, although true, were also defamatory and unfair, and awarded Stopes £100 damages. This verdict was reversed on appeal. The publicity attendant on the trial, however, benefited both Stopes and the birth-control cause. Sales of her books picked up and attendance at her clinic, which had initially been rather sluggish, increased dramatically, more than doubling from the previous year.

As a well-known pioneer in an extremely controversial area, Stopes often felt that the established institutions of Britain were united in opposition to her and to her work. The Sutherland case heightened Stopes' paranoia. Sutherland was a Catholic and the Catholic Church, which was opposed to contraception, had assisted in funding his defense of the lawsuit. As a result, Stopes developed a lifelong virulent antipathy to the Church and to most Catholics, insisting that there was a Catholic conspiracy against her and her work.

Stopes' rabid anti-Catholicism was merely one indicator of her growing irascibility. As she grew older, she adamantly refused to work with the burgeoning birth-control movement in Britain and around the world. She refused to assist in the development of new, more effective, methods of birth control, insisting that the cervical cap continue to be prescribed to virtually all patients at her clinic. By 1950, Stopes, working independently, had established five clinics in the United Kingdom; by contrast, the Family Planning Association, which represented the mainstream birth-control movement in Britain, had hundreds of clinics throughout the country. Her views on sexual morality did not change over the years either. Stopes remained steadfastly opposed to homosexuality, abortion, and birth-control advice for unmarried women.

By the 1930s, although still a name to be reckoned with, Marie Stopes had effectively withdrawn from the forefront of the fight for contraception. In 1938, she separated from her husband who had been her greatest ally in the birth-control struggle. For the remainder of her life, Stopes wrote poetry (some of which was published) and cultivated the friendship of well-known poets such as Lord Alfred Douglas (a surprising choice since he was a Catholic and the former lover of Oscar Wilde) and Walter de la Mare. Although Stopes had long averred that she would live to be 120, she developed cancer and died at her country home in Surrey, England, on October 2, 1958, just short of her 78th birthday.

**SOURCES:**

Box, Muriel, ed. *The Trial of Marie Stopes.* London: Femina, 1967.

Briant, Keith. *Passionate Paradox.* NY: W.W. Norton, 1962.

Eaton, Peter, and Marilyn Warnick. *Marie Stopes: A Checklist of Her Writings.* London: Croom Helm, 1977.

Hall, Ruth. *Passionate Crusader.* NY: Harcourt Brace Jovanovich, 1977.

Maude, Aylmer. *The Authorized Life of Marie C. Stopes.* London: Williams & Norgate, 1924.

Rose, June. *Marie Stopes and the Sexual Revolution.* London: Faber and Faber, 1992.

**COLLECTIONS:**

Papers at the British Library, London.

**Mary A. Procida**,
Visiting Assistant Professor of History,
Temple University, Philadelphia, Pennsylvania

# Stopford Green, Alice (1847–1929).

*See Green, Alice Stopford.*

# Storace, Nancy (1765–1817)

*English soprano. Name variations: Anna Storace; Ann Storace. Born Ann Selina Storace on October 27, 1765, in London; died on August 24, 1817, in London; sister of composer Stephen Storace (1762–1796); married John Abraham Fisher (a composer), in 1783; lived with John Braham (a tenor); children: (with Braham) one son (b. 1802).*

*Studied with Sacchini and Rauzzini in London; sang in Vienna (1783–87); premiered the role of Susanna in Mozart's* Le nozze di Figaro; *performed many operas by her brother (1787–1808); retired (1808).*

Nancy Storace was born Ann Selina Storace in 1765 in London, and began performing at age seven. Making her Florence debut at age ten, she outsang the castrato Marchesi and was asked to leave. She and her brother, composer Stephen Storace, were close friends with Mozart. At a chamber music concert at the Storaces' house, Mozart once played the viola, Haydn and Dittersdorf the first and second violins, and Vanhal the cello.

Storace was probably the first person to introduce Mozart's music to English audiences. She was the original Susanna in Mozart's *Le nozze di Figaro*, and it is for this role she is chiefly remembered. Since it was typical of composers to tailor roles to suit the talents of a specific singer, it is natural to assume the same was true in this case. Storace's gaiety, wit, strong personality, and sense of humor characterized Susanna as well. She sang only comic opera, as her voice and temperament were not suited to *opera seria*.

Her acting was criticized when she first appeared in Vienna's Burgtheater in 1783, but Storace quickly modified it to suit the audience. During her four years as prima donna there, she was Vienna's favorite soprano. When she left Vienna for London, Mozart wrote "Ch'io mi scordi di te" for a farewell performance in which he accompanied her on the piano. A thorough professional, she and Michael Kelly raised the standard of performance in London opera houses. Although she continued to perform, her voice deteriorated quickly, probably because she began singing professionally at such a young age.

**John Haag**,
Athens, Georgia

# Storchio, Rosina (1876–1945)

*Italian soprano. Born on May 19, 1876, in Venice; died on July 24, 1945, in Milan; studied under A. Giovannini and G. Fatuo at the Milan Conservatory.*

*Debuted at Teatro del Verme Milan and Teatro alla Scala (1895); created the role of Musetta in Leoncavallo's* Bohème *(1897); toured South America, North America, and Europe.*

The first performance of *Madame Butterfly* at Teatro alla Scala on February 17, 1904, was a disaster for the composer, Giacomo Puccini, and the leading soprano, Rosina Storchio. The audience's hisses, cat-calls, and laughter seem strange for what is now one of opera's most beloved works. Not long after, Toscanini conducted the work to better reviews, but Storchio refused to perform again in Italy until 1920, at the end of her career. Before she appeared in *Butterfly*, Storchio was a great favorite of Italian audiences. She performed in many premieres, including Leoncavallo's *Bohème* in Venice (1897) and *Zazà* at La Scala (1900), Giordano's *Siberia* at La Scala (1903), and Mascagni's *Lodoletta* in Rome (1917). Storchio made few recordings so one is forced to learn of her abilities through contemporary critics. "There will never be another Violetta to sing with such unutterable perfection," wrote Filippo Sacchi, "moving, laughing, loving, suffering as the slight and gentle Rosina Storchio [with] her enormous seductive eyes, her delightful coquetry, her gay tenderness, her fresh spontaneity." Unafraid to pioneer new works of opera, Storchio was a trailblazer and will certainly be remembered for her premiere performance of *Madame Butterfly*, a role she understood better than did her first audience.

**John Haag,**
Athens, Georgia

## Storer, Maria (1849–1932)

*American arts patron and ceramist. Name variations: Maria Nichols; Maria Longworth Nichols. Born Maria Longworth on March 20, 1849, in Cincinnati, Ohio; died on April 30, 1932, in Paris, France; daughter of Joseph Longworth (an arts patron) and Ann Maria (Rives) Longworth; educated privately; married George Ward Nichols (a journalist), in 1868 (died 1885); married Bellamy Storer (a lawyer), in 1889 (died 1922); children: (first marriage) Joseph Ward Nichols; Margaret Rives Nichols.*

*Selected writings: Probation (1910); Sir Christopher Leighton (1915); The Borodino Mystery (1916); In Memoriam Bellamy Storer (1923).*

Born in 1849, Maria Storer was the daughter of Joseph and **Ann Maria Longworth**, distinguished Cincinnatians. Her paternal grandfather Nicholas Longworth had become wealthy in real estate and moved from New Jersey to Cincinnati in 1803, and her father, in addition to administering the family's estate and serving in various civic capacities, was a generous financial supporter of the arts in that city. As well, Storer's maternal grandfather Landon Cabell Rives was a prominent physician who had moved to Cincinnati in 1829 from Virginia. Educated privately, Maria married writer George Ward Nichols on May 6, 1868, and the couple continued the family's patronage of the arts.

In 1873, Maria founded the May Music Festival, which became an annual event. That same year, she took up ceramic painting and over the years experimented with different techniques. During a visit to the Philadelphia Centennial Exposition of 1876, Storer viewed an exhibit of Japanese pottery and returned home to write a manual of pottery-making. In September 1880, she opened Ohio's first art pottery, calling it Rookwood after the family's estate. She assembled a staff of designers and artists, a Staffordshire potter and a chemist, who developed a number of notable glazes, colors, and designs that earned the pottery national acclaim. In 1889, Rookwood pottery was awarded a gold medal at the Paris Exposition. The following year, Maria sold her interest in the pottery ven-

ture and pursued other interests. In 1890, she earned another gold medal at the Paris Exhibition for her decorative bronze work.

George Nichols died in 1885 and Maria then married Cincinnati attorney Bellamy Storer, who served two terms in Congress between 1891 and 1895. When his friend William McKinley became president in 1897, Bellamy was appointed minister to Belgium. The Storers, who had joined the Catholic Church in 1896, were close friends of Archbishop John Ireland, a supporter of the Republican Party. They urged another friend, then-governor Theodore Roosevelt, to appeal to President McKinley to write a letter to Pope Leo XIII on Ireland's behalf, hoping to influence the Vatican to name Ireland a cardinal. McKinley cooperated and later sent the Storers to Rome to make a personal appeal; however, when Roosevelt became president, he gave his support instead to Archbishop John M. Farley. Storer continued to visit Rome frequently, actively campaigning for Ireland and repeating Roosevelt's earlier endorsement. Roosevelt, however, who had appointed Bellamy ambassador to Austria-Hungary, denied his previous endorsement and sternly reprimanded Storer, asking her to remove herself from Vatican politics while her husband was working as a diplomat. When the president received no reply, he removed Bellamy from his diplomatic post in 1906. The controversy was widely covered in the press, especially when Storer defended her actions and published some of Roosevelt's private letters. The rift between the Storers and President Roosevelt was permanent. When Storer's nephew Nicholas Longworth married *Alice Roosevelt (Longworth)*, the president's daughter, Storer refused to attend the wedding.

The Storers lived out their lives in Paris, Boston, and Cincinnati, where they continued to travel and support the arts. In her later years, Storer also wrote several books of popular fiction and a memorial to her late husband. She died at the home of her daughter **Margaret Rives Nichols**, the wife of the marquis de Chambrun, in Paris on April 30, 1932.

**SOURCES:**

James, Edward T., ed. *Notable American Women, 1607–1950.* Cambridge, MA: The Belknap Press of Harvard University, 1971.

McHenry, Robert, ed. *Famous American Women.* NY: Dover, 1980.

**Barbara Koch,** freelance writer,
Farmington Hills, Michigan

## Storni, Alfonsina (1892–1938)

*Argentine writer and social activist who was one of her nation's most celebrated poets. Name variations: (pseu-*

*donyms) Tao-Lao and Alfonsina. Pronunciation: Ahl-fon-SEE-na STOR-nee. Born Alfonsina Storni on May 29, 1892, in Sala Capriasca, Canton Ticino, Switzerland; died a suicide in Mar del Plata, Argentina, on October 25, 1938; daughter of Alfonso Storni (a small-time businessman) and Paulina Martignoni de Storni (a teacher); attended Escuela Normal of San Juan (San Juan Normal School); Escuela Normal Mixta de Maestros Rurales (Mixed Normal School for Rural Teachers) in Coronda, Santa Fe, teaching certificate, 1910; never married; children: one son, Alejandro.*

*Moved to Buenos Aires (1911), after becoming pregnant; worked several jobs while composing poetry and won a prize for her work (1917); became a poet and journalist of some note (1920s); composed some of her best work (1930s), but under the shadow of breast cancer.*

*Major works:* La inquietud del rosal *(The Restlessness of the Rose Bush, 1916);* El dulce daño *(Sweet Mischief, 1918);* Irremediablemente *(Irremediably, 1919);* Languidez *(Languor, 1920);* Ocre *(Ochre, 1925);* El mundo de siete pozos *(The World of Seven Wells, 1934);* Mascarilla y trébol *(Mask and Trefoil, 1938).*

The song "Alfonsina y el mar" (Alfonsina and the Sea), written by Argentine historian Félix Luna, relates the sad story of the death of Alfonsina Storni, one of Argentina's most celebrated poets. Suffering from a recurrence of breast cancer, she penned one last poem, "Voy a dormir" ("I Am Going to Sleep"), and under a cloudless sky walked into the ocean at the seaside resort of Mar del Plata. Her body washed up on the beach several hours later. The tragic death brought to termination a trying and tumultuous existence.

Alfonsina Storni's life had never been easy. Before her birth her father Alfonso Storni had gradually withdrawn from the family business, a small brewery; inclined to periods of moodiness, he vanished for weeks at a time. Alcoholism might have been part of his problem. On the advice of a doctor, the family traveled to Switzerland—homeland of the Storni clan—in the hopes that he would find a renewed purpose in life. It was here, in Sala Capriasca, Switzerland, on May 29, 1892, that **Paulina Martignoni de Storni** gave birth to Alfonsina. Four years later, in 1896, the family returned to the Province of San Juan, located in the western part of Argentina, cradled by the Andes. At age five, Alfonsina attended a local kindergarten in the Normal School of San Juan. Unable to make a living in San Juan, in 1900 the family traveled to Rosario, a large port city in the Province of Santa Fe. To

tide the family over, Paulina, certified as a teacher, opened a private school in her home. It was closed when the family found new lodgings across from the Sunchales Railway station and, on the first floor, opened the Café Suizo. The income generated by the café, which was never profitable, was supplemented by money earned by Paulina, Alfonsina, and her sister as seamstresses and dressmakers.

Alfonso, once again a failure at business, closed the café in 1904, the same year that Alfonsina wrote her first poem. Death claimed her father in 1906, and Alfonsina, to help the family, took employment in a hat factory. Despite, or perhaps because of, a difficult childhood, Storni in a speech delivered in 1938 remembered those years as ones in which fantasy colored and romanticized her life to an "exaggerated degree." Those fantasies led her to the theater, and in 1907 she acted in the play *La pasión* (The Passion) and shortly thereafter joined the company of José Tallaví and toured Argentina for nearly a year.

By 1908, her "career" in the theater was over, and she returned home. Paulina had remarried and lived in Bustinza, Santa Fe, where she had opened another private school in her house. Storni helped her mother and became a member of Comité Feminista de Santa Fe (Feminist Committee of Santa Fe), the first indication of the path the rest of her life would take. Intent on a career as a teacher, one of the few vocations open to women, Storni at age 17 enrolled in the Escuela Normal Mixta de Maestros Rurales in Coronda. She was described by her teachers as hard working and able, and graduated in 1910 with the title of rural teacher. Graduation ceremonies included a recitation by kindergarten children of one of Alfonsina's poems, "Un viaje a la luna" ("A Trip to the Moon").

Within the year, she had begun her teaching career at the Escuela Elemental No. 65 (Elementary School Number 65) in Rosario and published her first poems in the local literary press, *Mundo Rosarino* (The Rosario World) and *Monos y monadas* (Clowns and Monkeyshines). It was also in Rosario that she had an affair, an "outlaw" love she later called it, and became pregnant. At the end of the school year, she resigned her position and, like many young women, determined to move to Buenos Aires, Argentina's vibrant capital city, to seek her fortune.

Buenos Aires was not kind to Storni, and she barely made enough money to survive. In her words, written in 1938:

At 19 I am enclosed in an office: a song of keys taps out a lullaby, wood screens rise up like dikes above my head; blocks of ice chill the air at my back; the sun shines through the roof but I can't see it. . . . Rooted to my chair . . . I write my first book of verses, an awful book of verses. May God spare you, my friend, from *La inquietud del rosal* (The Restlessness of the Rose Bush)! . . . I wrote it to survive.

She gave birth to a son, Alejandro, on April 21, 1912, and, in addition to her office work, contributed items to the magazine *Caras y Caretas* (Faces and Masks). In 1913 and 1914, she moved from job to job—as a cashier in a pharmacy and a shop, and in the import firm of Freixas Brothers. In the words of biographer **Rachel Phillips**, Storni showed great courage and self-discipline in difficult times. "In Argentina there was a general work shortage, an absence of protective labor laws, and considerable prejudice against women who were forced to earn a living." That she had to work outside the home and was an unwed mother was not unusual, for about 22% of the children born in Argentina between 1914 and 1919, according to historian **Sandra McGee**, were illegitimate. What was important was that "it was not common in the circles in which Storni would eventually move."

*O*ur hypocrisy destroys us. . . . It is the falsity separating what we are and what we pretend to be. It is our feminine cowardice that has not learned to shout the truth from the rooftops.

—Alfonsina Storni

Despite the demands of the single mother and work, Storni made the time to participate in feminist activities and gave recitals of her poetry in Rosario and Buenos Aires at meetings sponsored by the Socialist Party, a party dedicated, among other things, to equal rights for women. **Gwen Kirkpatrick**, who has written the best account of Storni's journalism, noted that it was "during the period 1914–1930, when debates raged over the legal rights of women, that Storni established herself as a poet and wrote the journalistic pieces in favor of women's rights."

Alfonsina Storni established her reputation as a poet with the publication of *La inquietud del rosal* in 1916 and, within a year, found a new occupation as director of teachers in the Colegio Marcos Paz. The National Council of Women awarded Storni their annual prize for *Canto a los niños* (Song for Children) in 1917. In 1918, *El dulce daño* (Sweet Mischief) appeared; she also wrote for the magazine *Atlántida*, volunteered in the school for Niños Débiles (Impaired Children), and was a member of the Argentine

Committee to find homes for Belgian war orphans. Having experienced pay discrimination firsthand, Storni promoted equality in jobs and salaries through her work as one of the leaders of the Asociación pro Derechos de la Mujer (Association for the Rights of the Woman). Yet her growing image as a social activist and nonconformist contrasts sharply with her poetry, which was typical of a woman poet in the Argentina of the 1910s, i.e., the themes dealt with love and nature and were of the confessional variety. Storni herself was highly critical of her early work. Of the collection entitled *Irrediablemente* (Irremediably), published in 1919, she said that it was as bad as *Inquietud del rosal*. Both Phillips and Kirkpatrick agree that her early poems were dictated by the expectations of the market and Storni's need for money.

Alfonsina's real concerns were reflected in her public activities. While her poetry spoke of love and nature and the shortcomings of men in affairs of the heart, her journalism addressed the critical issues of women's suffrage and civil rights. World War I, she observed, was a watershed for women for it demonstrated the bankruptcy of patriarchy and opened the doors to radical changes in culture and society. A few of her poems were revealing as to her inner turmoil, however. In one, there is an identification with her mother, who had suffered mightily and silently, and stored up years of hurt in her heart. Storni wrote that "without wanting to, I think I've liberated it." And in *Hombre pequeño* (Little Man), she lashes out at those men who wanted to keep her in a cage.

The two Alfonsinas coexisted throughout the 1920s. *Languidez* (Languor) was published in 1920, for which she won several prizes. Later, she traveled across the Rio de la Plata to Montevideo to speak at the city's university and became a regular correspondent for the prestigious Buenos Aires daily newspaper *La Nación*. She wrote under the pen-names Tao-Lao and Alfonsina. Argentine citizenship was granted to her in 1920, and she continued a teaching career in public and private schools; in 1923, she was named professor at the Escuela Normal de Lenguas Vivas (Normal School of Living Languages). Kirkpatrick's review of Storni's journalistic activity demonstrates tremendous breadth. She wrote on the following themes: working women, the place of women in the national and cultural tradition, the role of the church, single mothers, marriage, good and bad models of motherhood, female poverty, migration to the city, and the "innate" characteristics of females. The dictates of high fashion were repeatedly attacked by Storni, and she equated the wearing of high heels with an urge to commit suicide. In one article on women's fashions, noted Kirkpatrick, she decried the excesses and "pathetic and ludicrous lengths to which women will go to serve this master."

It was with the publication of *Ocre* (Ochre) in 1925 that the two Alfonsinas began to move toward one another. Phillips sees a turning inward and a revealing self-exploration. "Here Storni is less the woman, loved or rejected, grieving or rejoicing, and more the human being concerned with the workings of her own psychic machine." In *Ocre*, Storni assesses the forces that limit people, male and female, and there is little of the hostility toward men that typified much of her earlier poetry. Chile's great poet, *Gabriela Mistral, in 1926 found in Storni's work an "active intelligence" more compelling than her emotional side. Storni herself recognized the change in focus of her poetry in a 1927 interview reported by Kirkpatrick. "I am not a totally unconstrained erotic," she said. "Passionate, yes, [but] I am a soul that governs a body, not a body that yanks around my soul." When queried about how she spent her time, she replied: "I work, I go back to work, I work again. What fun!" Kirkpatrick feels that she said this to remove the image of the poet from the ivory tower and to place her in the proper context of her links with working people.

Poetry was set aside by Storni in 1927, and she turned her attention to playwriting. Her first effort, *El amo del mundo* (The Master of the World), failed after only one performance, but its production spoke volumes about the constraints imposed on women artists. While the play was originally titled *Dos mujeres* (Two Women) "to reflect the competing courses and ideologies available to its heroines," writes **Francine Masiello**, the producers altered both title and text to remove the possibility of differences of opinion among women and stressed their identity within the context of masculine power. The producers argued that the changes were in anticipation of audience demand. Storni was furious, but the changes remained.

The poems, or anti-sonnets as she called them, collected by Storni in *El mundo de siete pozos* (The World of Seven Wells) and published in 1934, mark a critical breakthrough. Alejandro, her son, said that this was the happiest period in his mother's life. Her reputation and prestige were high, and she had a loyal following. Phillips notes that the new poetry showed a freedom of expression and affirmation of self that

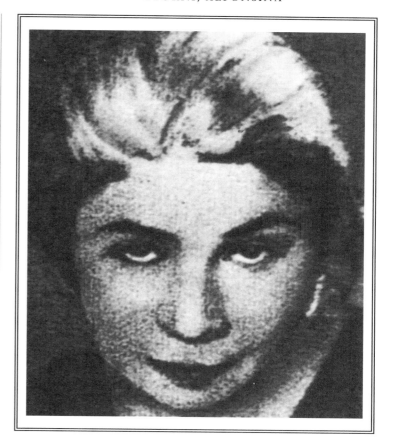

Alfonsina Storni

left the eroticism of earlier years behind. The critics were uniformly displeased, however. Granted, the poet broke with rhyme and metrical pattern, but the critics assailed her not for this, but for addressing themes not written about by women. In short, they attacked her as a rebel who had dared to transgress the "confessional" role reserved for women writers. It was with *El mundo de siete pozos* and her posthumously published *Mascarilla y trébol* (Mask and Trefoil) that the two Alfonsinas finally spoke with one voice. The liberated woman was joined by the liberated poet.

During a vacation on the marvelous beaches of Uruguay in 1935, Storni discovered a lump in her left breast. In May, she underwent surgery and the breast was removed. There followed a period of withdrawal from her friends and a renewed focus on her work, sharpened by worries that the cancer might recur. In January 1938, Alfonsina Storni, Gabriela Mistral and *Juana de Ibarbourou were brought together at the University of Montevideo to discuss their style and creativity. Storni also confessed to friends her fears that her cancer had recurred and that she wanted no further surgery. This fear was compounded by the suicide, a year earlier, of her dear friend and supporter, the Argentine writer Horacio Quiroga. He had been suffering from prostate cancer. Then, in February 1938, the writer and friend Leopoldo Lugones committed suicide, followed a few months later by the suicide of Horacio Quiroga's daughter, **Eglé**.

When Alfonsina Storni walked into the sea at Mar del Plata it was not because of the critics. Her cancer and the suicides of her friends, who showed her the way, were the compelling reasons that she did not resist the temptation of death as an escape.

**SOURCES:**

Anderson-Imbert, Enrique. *Spanish-American Literature: A History.* 2 vols. 2nd ed. Detroit, MI: Wayne State University Press, 1969.

Díaz-Diocaretz, Myriam. "'I will be a scandal in your boat': Women poets and the tradition," in Susan Bassnett, ed., *Knives and Angels: Women Writers in Latin America.* London: Zed, 1990.

Kirkpatrick, Gwen. "The Journalism of Alfonsina Storni: A New Approach to Women's History in Argentina," in *Women, Culture, and Politics in Latin America: Seminar on Feminism and Culture in Latin America.* Berkeley, CA: University of California Press, 1990.

Lindstrom, Naomi. "Argentina," in David William Foster, comp., *Handbook of Latin American Literature.* NY: Garland, 1987.

Masiello, Francine. *Between Civilization & Barbarism: Women, Nation, and Literary Culture in Modern Argentina.* Lincoln, NE: University of Nebraska Press, 1992.

Nalé Roxlo, Conrado. *Genio y figura de Alfonsina Storni.* Buenos Aires: Editorial Universitaria de Buenos Aires, 1964.

Phillips, Rachel. *Alfonsina Storni: From Poetess to Poet.* London: Tamesis, 1975.

**SUGGESTED READING:**

Storni, Alfonsina. *Selected Poems.* Trans. by Marion Freeman, Mary Crow, Jim Normington and Kay Short. Freedonia, NY: White Pine Press, 1987.

**Paul B. Goodwin, Jr.**, Professor of History, University of Connecticut, Storrs, Connecticut

## Stothard, Anna Eliza (1790–1883).

*See Bray, Anna Eliza.*

## Stouder, Sharon (1948—)

*American swimmer, among the first of the California "water babies" who would win so many international swimming events.* Name variations: Sharon Stouder Clark. *Born Sharon Marie Stouder in Altadena, California, on November 9, 1948; daughter of Ruby (Shiling) Souder and Galen Stouder; married Kenyon Clark, on September 8, 1979; children: Kerry and James.*

*Won three gold medals and a silver medal in the Tokyo Summer Olympics (1964).*

Many of America's greatest swimmers have come from California, where the sunny climate, beaches, and proliferation of pools make swimming a natural sport. Born in 1948 in Altadena, California, Sharon Stouder became one of California's first "water babies," the term applied to children who learned to swim as toddlers and went on to compete successfully. Stouder started swimming at three and began setting age-group records by eight. By 12, she was a veteran swimmer with 20 first-place wins in national age-group events. Although her specialty was the butterfly stroke, she won all national junior Olympic ratings for her age group.

In 1964, when the Olympic Games were held in Tokyo, 15-year-old Stouder won the 100-meter butterfly against Dutch recordholder **Ada Kok**, with a time of 1:4.7, breaking the previous 1:5.1 record. In the 4x100-meter freestyle, Souder and teammates *Donna de Varona, **Lillian Watson**, and **Kathleen Ellis** won the gold in world record time. Stouder won another gold medal in the 4x100-meter relay with Ellis, *Cathy Ferguson, and **Cynthia Goyette** with a world-record time of 4:33.9. She took silver in the 100-meter freestyle against *Dawn Fraser, the Australian who had broken the one-minute barrier for 100 meters in 1962. Stouder finished four-tenths of a second behind Fraser.

**SOURCES:**

Porter, David L., ed. *Biographical Dictionary of American Sports. Basketball and Other Indoor Sports.* NY: Greenwood, 1989.

**Karin L. Haag**, freelance writer, Athens, Georgia

## Stover, Mary Johnson (1832–1883).

*See Johnson, Eliza McCardle for sidebar.*

## Stowe, Emily Howard (1831–1903).

*See Denison, Flora MacDonald for sidebar.*

## Stowe, Harriet Beecher (1811–1896)

*American author whose best-known work,* Uncle Tom's Cabin, *helped to change the course of American history. Born Harriet Beecher on June 14, 1811, in Litchfield, Connecticut; died on July 1, 1896, in Hartford, Connecticut, of brain congestion complicated by partial paralysis; daughter of Lyman Beecher (d. 1863, a cleric) and Roxana (Foote) Beecher (d. 1816); attended Litchfield Female Academy, 1819–24, and then Hartford Female Seminary where she became a full-time instructor in 1829; married Calvin Ellis Stowe, on January 6, 1836 (died 1886); children: Eliza and Harriet Stowe (twins, b. September 1836); Henry Ellis Stowe (January 1838–1857); Frederick William Stowe (b. May 1840); Georgiana May Stowe (b. August 1843); Samuel Charles Stowe (1848–1849); Charles Edward Stowe (b. July 1850, author and his mother's biographer).*

*Death of mother (1816); moved to Cincinnati with her family (1832); published first writings in* Western Monthly Magazine *(1833); moved with husband and children to Brunswick, Maine (1850); published* Uncle Tom's Cabin *as a book (1852); moved with family to Andover, Massachusetts (1852); traveled to Europe for first time (1853); published second novel* Dred *(1856); oldest son Henry drowned (1857); published first New England novel,* The Minister's Wooing *(1859); published* The Pearl of Orr's Island *(1862); death of father (1863); moved with family to Hartford, Connecticut (1864); published* Lady Byron Vindicated *(1870); published last novel,* Poganuc People *(1878).*

It was an occurrence that 12-year-old Charles Stowe never forgot. On that special day in November 1862, he accompanied his mother to the White House where they visited President Abraham Lincoln. Charles recalled Lincoln sitting with his feet on the mantelpiece as they entered the small room, and the great man rising and saying as he warmed his hands by the fireplace, "I do love a fire in a room. I suppose it's because we always had one to home." (After the visit, the young lad wondered aloud why President Lincoln said "to home" rather than "at home.") Etched in his memory were Lincoln's words to his mother, "So this is the little woman who wrote the book that made this big war."

The big war which Lincoln alluded to was, of course, the Civil War which broke out in 1861. Many Americans had hoped the slavery question had been laid to rest after the successful negotiation of the Compromise of 1850, which among other provisions admitted California to the Union as a free state, abolished slavery in the District of Columbia, set up the territories of New Mexico and Utah without mention of slavery, and strengthened the Fugitive Slave Law. However, when some Northerners refused to comply with the Fugitive Slave Law, and when Harriet Beecher Stowe's *Uncle Tom's Cabin* appeared soon after the Compromise, the smoldering slave issue burst into flames again. With the coming of *Uncle Tom's Cabin*, there seemed to be no turning back.

Born in 1811, less than three years after Lincoln, Harriet Beecher Stowe joined a family which was deeply religious. Her father Lyman Beecher, a Congregational minister, possessed "the best theological brain in America" and came to be known as the "great gun of Calvinism." As a young girl, Harriet spent countless hours in her father's study. "Here," she later wrote, "I loved to retreat and niche myself down in a quiet corner with my favorite books around me." One of her father's tomes proved to be "a mine of wealth to me." Cotton Mather's *Magnalia* contained "wonderful stories. . . . Stories, too, about my own country. Stories that made me feel the very ground I trod on to be consecrated by some special dealing of God's providence."

Because her mother died when she was only five, Harriet had few memories of **Roxana Beecher**. She did recall "two incidents" which "twinkle like rays through the darkness." Young Harriet remembered one Sunday morning when the Beecher children seemed especially exuberant, her mother with "pleasant voice saying after us, 'Remember the Sabbath day to keep it holy.'" Stowe described another occasion when she and her brothers ate a bag of tulip bulbs, thinking they were onions despite their "odd, sweetish taste." When Roxana discovered the empty bag, wrote Stowe, she demonstrated "not even a momentary expression of impatience," but, instead, sat down patiently explaining, "My dear children, what you have done makes mamma very sorry; those were not onion-roots, but roots of beautiful flowers; and if you had let them alone, ma would have had next summer in the garden great beautiful red and yellow flowers such as you never saw."

Although Harriet became the most famous of the Beechers through the publication of *Uncle Tom's Cabin*, other members of the Beecher family also distinguished themselves. Harriet's brother Henry Ward Beecher became, like his father, a nationally known preacher. Prior to the Civil War, when Kansas became "bleeding Kansas" because of violence over the slavery issue, it was Henry Ward Beecher who urged communicants of Brooklyn's Plymouth church to send Sharpe's rifles, which came to be called "Beecher's Bibles," to those settlers opposed to slavery. At one church meeting, he exhorted, "There is more moral power in one Sharpe rifle, so far as the slaveholders of Kansas are concerned, than in a hundred Bibles." One might "just as well read the bible to buffalos," but "they have a supreme respect for the logic that is embodied in Sharpe's rifles."

Harriet's sister *Catharine Beecher "became one of the greatest figures in the development of higher education for women and in the establishment of professional home economics." Catharine was the driving force in the establishment of the Hartford Female Seminary. Later, she played a similar role in the founding and operation of the Western Female Institute in Cincinnati. In time, she became "a travelling missionary for the cause of women's higher education," publishing such works as *True Remedy for the Wrongs of Women*. Their half-sister ◄⧉ **Isabella Beecher Hooker** was also a leading suffragist.

## ⧉► Hooker, Isabella Beecher (1822–1907)

*American suffragist. Name variations: Isabella Beecher. Born Isabella Beecher in Litchfield, Connecticut, on February 22, 1822; died in Hartford, Connecticut, on January 25, 1907; daughter of Reverend Lyman Beecher and his second wife Harriet (Porter) Beecher; half-sister of Catharine Beecher and Harriet Beecher Stowe; educated mainly in schools founded by her half-sister Catharine; married John Hooker (a lawyer and real-estate entrepreneur), in August 1841.*

Born in Litchfield, Connecticut, in 1822, Isabella Beecher Hooker grew up in Boston, Cincinnati, and Hartford, with her half-sisters *Harriet Beecher (Stowe) and *Catharine Beecher. In 1841, Isabella married John Hooker, a young law student and descendant of Thomas Hooker, founder of Hartford. For ten years, the couple lived in Farmington, Connecticut, then moved to Hartford, where John and a brother-in-law bought a 100-acre lot, built houses for their families, and then sold off parcels to Harriet Beecher Stowe, Charles Dudley Warner, and Samuel Clemens (Mark Twain).

Influenced by her husband's studies and the essays of John Stuart Mill, Isabella Hooker became interested in the law as it related to women. Under the urging of *Caroline M. Severance, Hooker joined forces with *Susan B. Anthony, *Elizabeth Cady Stanton, and *Paulina Wright Davis, and helped found the New England Woman Suffrage Association in 1868. That same year, Hooker anonymously published "Mother's Letters to a Daughter on Woman's Suffrage" in *Putnam's Magazine*. In 1869, she organized the Connecticut Woman Suffrage Association, remaining president of that organization until 1905, and lobbied the state legislature for a married women's property act. Hooker was a main speaker at the 1870 convention of the National Woman Suffrage Association in Washington, D.C., and spent the next few years lobbying in Washington, along with her friend *Victoria Woodhull. She also accompanied Woodhull on her journey into Spiritualism.

Speaking before the Judiciary Committee of the U.S. Senate in 1872, Hooker began: "You sit here, gentlemen, in judgment on my rights as an American citizen, as though they were something different from your own; but they are not." In 1874, Hooker published *Womanhood: Its Sanctities and Fidelities*, and, in 1893, was on the Board of Lady Managers of the World's Columbian Exposition in Chicago.

After the death of her mother, Harriet spent about a year living in Nutplains, Connecticut, with her maternal aunt **Harriet Foote**. Her father then married **Harriet Porter (Beecher)** of Portland, Maine, which brought the young Harriet back to Litchfield, Connecticut. About Harriet and her brother Henry, the second Mrs. Lyman Beecher wrote in one letter, "They are lovely children as I ever saw; amiable, affectionate, and very bright."

When Harriet was about eight, she began attending Litchfield Female Academy. "Much of the training and inspiration of my early days consisted not in the things I was supposed to be studying," she wrote, "but in hearing, while seated unnoticed at my desk, the conversation of Mr. Brace with the older classes." Near the age of 12, she wrote a composition that was read aloud before "all the literati of Litchfield" including Lyman Beecher. The essay, "Can the Immortality of the Soul Be Proved by the Light of Nature," obviously impressed her father. He asked Brace, "Who wrote that composition?" "Your daughter, sir," replied the teacher. Harriet described that exchange as "the proudest moment of my life."

In 1886, Stowe would write that "somewhere between my twelfth and thirteenth year I was placed under the care of my sister Catharine, in the school she had just started in Hartford, Connecticut," called the Hartford Female Seminary. In the autumn of 1827, at age 16, Stowe began teaching a course on Virgil. In those years, too, she became more and more committed to Jesus Christ, once writing, "It was about this time that I first believed myself to be a Christian." She frankly admitted that "most of father's sermons were as unintelligible to me as if he had spoken in Choctaw," but that on one occasion he spoke "in direct, simple and tender language of the great love of Christ and his care for the soul." This caused her "as soon as father came home" to fall into his arms exclaiming, "Father, I have given myself to Jesus, and He has taken me."

In early October 1832, the Beechers moved to Cincinnati where Lyman had accepted the presidency of Lane Theological Seminary. One of Stowe's biographers wrote that "Harriet while living in New England had not given slavery much thought" but that "slavery was something one had to think about in Cincinnati." It was from Cincinnati that she crossed the Ohio River into Kentucky to visit a plantation which provided her with "her only first-hand impression of the patriarchal side of slavery and secured the scene of the Shelby's plantation in which she opened the story of *Uncle Tom's*

Harriet
Beecher
Stowe

*Cabin.*" It was also while living in Cincinnati, said Stowe, that "I learned incidently of the slave system in the history of various slaves who came into my family, and of the underground railroad which, I may say, ran through our house." It was in Cincinnati that she may have gained "her first harsh impression" of slave owners after reading an editorial by Thomas Brainerd, a respected Presbyterian cleric and a staunch supporter of her father. Brainerd had said that there could be "no apology" for a slaveholder "who raises *human beings to sell.*"

On January 6, 1836, Harriet married Calvin Ellis Stowe, a professor of Biblical literature at Lane Theological Seminary. Calvin, who was "nine years older, stoutish and a little bald," had lost his first wife **Eliza Stowe**, also a friend of Harriet's, through death. The following September, while her husband was in Europe, Harriet gave birth to twin daughters. She named one Eliza and the second Isabella. However, her husband upon his return home insisted that Isabella's name be changed to Harriet, so highly did he esteem his second wife. The Stowes would have one more daughter, **Georgiana May**, and four sons. One son, Frederick William, was named after the king of Prussia, one of Calvin's heroes. Samuel Charles, born in January 1848, lived but 18 months and died of cholera. On July 26, 1849, Stowe wrote, "My Charley—my beautiful, loving, gladsome baby . . . so full of life and hope and strength—now lies shrouded, pale and cold, in the room below."

> So this is the little woman who wrote the book that made this big war.
>
> —Abraham Lincoln

As the Stowe family grew, both her sister Catharine and her husband encouraged Harriet to write not merely to develop her skills, but to supplement the family income. About three years before her marriage, the *Western Monthly Magazine* had bought and published her first piece of fiction. Soon thereafter, she published with sister Catharine *Geography for Children* for which Harriet received $187 as her share. By 1842, Stowe had written enough short pieces to be collected and published by Harper's as *The Mayflower.* Calvin was so impressed that he wrote, "God has written it in his book that you must be a literary woman, and who are we that we should contend against God?" The *Boston Miscellany* now offered her not $2 a page but $20 for three pages, a princely sum indeed.

In the spring of 1850, the Stowes left Cincinnati for Brunswick, Maine, where Calvin

had agreed to become the Collins Professor of Natural and Revealed Religion at Bowdoin College. Harriet, who was pregnant, preceded her husband to their new home in a trip that was not easy. One story, possibly apocryphal, persists of how a certain Professor Smith, at the behest of the president of Bowdoin, went to meet the bedraggled Mrs. Stowe and her brood. He returned without her, reporting that he had found only an "old Irish woman with a lot of brats." Surely, Stowe must not have taken this too seriously, for in 1853, in what one writer calls "the most famous description of her herself," she wrote: "I am a little bit of woman, somewhat more than forty, about as thin and dry as a pinch of snuff; never very much to look at in my best days, and looking like a used-up article now."

In the same year the Stowes moved to Brunswick, the members of Congress spent several weeks discussing the slavery issue. Eventually out of all the debate came several proposals collectively called the Compromise of 1850. One of the concessions to the South included the enactment of the Fugitive Slave Act, designed to make the recapture of runaway slaves easier. This infuriated many opposed to slavery. From her sister-in-law **Isabella Jones Beecher**, Harriet received a letter which read, "Hattie, if I could use a pen as you can, I would write something to make this whole nation feel what an accursed thing slavery is." Harriet responded, "I will write something. I will if I live." And so *Uncle Tom's Cabin* was born.

*Uncle Tom's Cabin; or, Life among the Lowly,* as it was first titled, was initially published as a serial in the *National Era,* a Washington, D.C., publication edited by Dr. Gamaliel Bailey. For $300, Stowe wrote 40 installments, with the first appearing on June 5, 1851, and the last on April 1, 1852. Because *Uncle Tom's Cabin* was such an immediate hit, book publisher John P. Jewett soon agreed to publish Stowe's work in book form. Shortly before the *National Era* issued the last installment, *Uncle Tom's Cabin* appeared as a book of two volumes on March 20, 1852.

Stowe, who would receive a 10% royalty on all sales, remarked, "I hope it will make enough so I may have a silk dress." As it turned out, two days after publication the entire first edition of 5,000 copies was sold. In four months, the author had earned $10,000 in royalties. In the United States, some 300,000 copies were sold the first year, while at the same time 150,000 were purchased in England. In August 1852, the novel was dramatized, notwithstanding the disapproval of Stowe who refused assent on the grounds that "if the theaters began showing respectable, moral plays, the young people of Christian families would be allowed to go to see them and would develop the habit of promiscuous theater-going, as a result." As a dramatic production, *Uncle Tom's Cabin* was presented on the stage well into the 20th century.

Overnight *Uncle Tom's Cabin* made Harriet Beecher Stowe world famous. Henry W. Longfellow sent congratulations, characterizing *Uncle Tom's Cabin* as "one of the greatest triumphs recorded in literary history," while another literary giant, John Greenleaf Whittier, sent "ten thousand thanks for thy immortal work." *Jenny Lind, the famed "Swedish Nightingale" who was touring the United States at the time, sent Stowe "two choice tickets" for her final New York concert. When Harriet sent a thank-you note, Lind replied, "Certainly God's hand will remain with a blessing over your head." In England in 1856, Stowe and her husband met with Queen *Victoria; she also met such celebrities as Lord Palmerston, Charles Dickens, and George Eliot (*Mary Anne Evans). Oliver Wendell Holmes became a good friend.

Not everyone applauded Stowe's work. Many Southerners believed that the South had been portrayed unfairly. Others felt that Harriet had been too critical of the Christian church. In response, Stowe wrote *A Key to Uncle Tom's Cabin* in which she sought to refute those who thought her characters had been overdrawn and that the slave experience she described in *Uncle Tom's Cabin* was unrealistic. Out of this came another novel, *Dred, a Tale of the Great Dismal Swamp*.

Stowe proved to be a prolific writer, turning out numerous books and articles after the appearance of her most famous work. The publication in 1859 of her novel *The Minister's Wooing* drew this response from James Russell Lowell: "I am sure that *The Minister's Wooing* is going to be the best of your products hitherto, and I am sure of it because you show so thorough a mastery of your material, so true a perception of realities, without which the ideality is impossible." Other works that poured from her pen included *Agnes of Sorrento*, *The Pearl of Orr's Island: A Story of the Coast of Maine*, and *Oldtown Folks*. When in 1877 she published a collection of her religious writings, *Footsteps of the Master*, it was her 30th book. Her last novel, published in 1878, was a "fictional autobiography" titled *Poganuc People* which one of her biographers calls "invaluable as an authentic picture of New England village life in the early decades of the Nineteenth Century." Two short stories written in late 1878 for the *Atlantic Monthly*, "The Parson's Race Horse" and "A Student's Sea Story," were her last significant works in fiction.

Stowe's *Lady Byron Vindicated*, published in 1870, raised a furor much like that which had ensued after the appearance of *Uncle Tom's Cabin*. While visiting England, Stowe had become well acquainted with ☙▶ **Lady Byron**, the widow of Lord Byron. At the time of his death, Lord Byron was separated from his wife. He had left her because, he said, she was hard-hearted, cantankerous, and mercenary. To Harriet, Lady Byron confided that her husband had committed incest with his half-sister ☙▶ **Augusta Leigh**. When Lord Byron's last mistress ☙▶ **Countess Guiccioli** published a book vilifying Lady Byron, Harriet felt Lady Byron, now dead, deserved to have her honor defended. Thus, in the September 1869 issue of the *Atlantic Monthly*, she published "The True Story of Lady Byron's Life" in which she revealed Lady Byron's secret concerning her husband. The article provoked such a storm of criticism that Stowe felt compelled to write the volume *Lady Byron Vindicated*.

Although *Uncle Tom's Cabin* brought Harriet Beecher Stowe fame and some fortune, her life was not a bed of roses. In the same year *Uncle Tom's Cabin* was published, she had to move to Andover, Massachusetts, where her husband had accepted the chair of Sacred Literature at Andover Theological Seminary. She left Brunswick, Maine, with some reluctance: "I shall never find people whom I shall like better than those of Brunswick." In 1857, her oldest son Henry, who was a freshman at Dartmouth College, drowned in the Connecticut River. Her father Lyman Beecher died in 1863. Her son Frederick, who was wounded in the Battle of Gettysburg, "grew into a besotted drunkard," took a trip to San Francisco, and was never heard of again. In the fall of 1870, her daughter Georgiana fell victim to a nervous illness from which she never recovered. Her famous brother, Henry Ward Beecher, was publicly charged with committing adultery with *Elizabeth Tilton, wife of Theodore Tilton, a well-known editor.

In 1863, Harriet's husband retired, and the Stowes then moved to Hartford, Connecticut, where they had built a new home. It was in retirement that Harriet encouraged Calvin to write *Origin and History of the Books of the Bible*. About this venture, one biographer, Forrest Wilson, wrote, "Thus did a scheming and clearsighted wife manoeuvre the most indolent, pro-

◀☙
***Lady Byron.*** See *Lovelace, Ada Byron* for sidebar on Anne Milbanke.

◀☙
***Leigh, Augusta.*** See *Lamb, Caroline* for sidebar.

◀☙
***Guiccioli, Countess.*** See *Blessington, Marguerite* for sidebar.

crastinating, neurasthenic, temperamental, scholarly and likeable husband in the world into producing a masterpiece for the theological library."

Calvin Stowe lived until August 6, 1886, proving to be an amiable companion when not bothered by depression. In his retirement years, the Stowes spent most winters in Mandarin, Florida, and summers in Hartford. The death of her husband made Harriet more aware that life was fleeting, so in the winter following Calvin's death, she began collaborating with her son, Charles, in the writing of her life's story. When Charles completed the manuscript in September 1889, Harriet wrote the preface in which she stated, "I am going to my Father's."

Wilson describes her preface as her "valedictory to the world" for, he notes, "she wrote these sentences at the end of her lucid existence on earth." Harriet herself realized that mentally she was not what she had been. She wrote to an old friend, "My mind wanders like a running brook." More and more she thought about her own mortality, writing in one letter, "I am come to that stage of my pilgrimage that is within sight of the River of Death, and I must have all in readiness, day and night, for the messenger of the King." On July 1, 1896, less than three weeks after her 85th birthday, that long pilgrimage came to an end.

**Smith, Hannah Whitall.** *See Thomas, M. Carey for sidebar.*

**SOURCES:**

Fields, Anne. *Life and Letters of Harriet Beecher Stowe.* Boston, MA: Houghton, Mifflin, 1898.

Foster, Charles H. *The Rungless Ladder.* Durham, NC: Duke University Press, 1954.

Gilbertson, Catherine. *Harriet Beecher Stowe.* NY: D. Appleton-Century, 1937.

Stowe, Charles Edward. *Life of Harriet Beecher Stowe.* Boston, MA: Houghton, Mifflin, 1890.

Wilson, Forrest. *Crusader in Crinoline: The Life of Harriet Beecher Stowe.* Philadelphia, PA: J.B. Lippincott, 1941.

**Russell, Alys.** *See Berenson, Mary for sidebar.*

**SUGGESTED READING:**

Adams, John R. *Harriet Beecher Stowe.* NY: Twayne, 1963.

Ammons, Elizabeth, ed. *Critical Essays on Harriet Beecher Stowe.* Boston, MA: G.K. Hall, 1980.

Hedrick, Joan D. *Harriet Beecher Stowe: A Life.* NY: Oxford University Press, 1994.

Johnston, Johanna. *Runaway to Heaven: The Story of Harriet Beecher Stowe.* NY: Doubleday, 1963.

**COLLECTIONS:**

Collections of Stowe letters can be found in the Library of Congress, Boston Public Library, Harvard University Library, Yale University Library, and the Henry E. Huntington Library in San Marino, California; 16 volumes of Harriet Beecher Stowe writings were published in 1896 by Houghton, Mifflin under the title *The Writings of Harriet Beecher Stowe.*

**Robert Bolt,** Professor of History, Calvin College, Grand Rapids, Michigan

---

## Strachey, Philippa (1872–1968).

*See joint entry under Strachey, Pippa and Ray Strachey.*

# Strachey, Pippa and Ray Strachey
*British suffragists.*

*Strachey, Pippa (1872–1968). Name variations: Philippa Strachey. Born Philippa Strachey in 1872; died in 1968; fifth child and third daughter of Sir Richard Strachey (1817–1908) and Lady Jane Maria (Grant) Strachey (1840–1928); sister of Elinor Strachey (1860–1944), Dorothy Strachey (1865–1960, a writer who married Simon Bussy), Oliver Strachey (1874–1960), Marjorie Strachey (1882–1964), Joan Pernel Strachey (1876–1951), and Lytton Strachey (1880–1932); aunt of Julia Strachey (1901–1978, a writer, daughter of Oliver Strachey and Ruby Meyer Strachey); sister-in-law of Ray Strachey; never married.*

*Strachey, Ray (1887–1940). Name variations: Rachel Mary Costelloe; Rachel Strachey. Born Rachel Mary Costelloe on June 4, 1887; died following an operation in July 1940; daughter of Frank Costelloe and Mary Pearsall (Smith) Costelloe, also known as Mary Berenson (1864–1944); sister of Karin Costelloe Stephen (1889–1953, one of the first British psychoanalysts, who married Adrien Stephen, brother of Virginia Woolf); niece of ✥ Alys Russell (1866–1951); sister-in-law of Pippa Strachey; educated at a convent school, Lambeth boarding school, Kensington High School, Newnham College, and Bryn Mawr College; became second wife of Oliver Strachey (1874–1960), on May 31, 1911; children: Barbara Strachey (b. 1912); Christopher Strachey (1916–1975); stepchildren: Julia Strachey (1901–1978, a writer).*

Though 15 years apart in age, sisters-in-law Pippa and Ray Strachey formed a common bond in the pursuit of opportunities for British women during the early part of the 20th century. Their efforts within two of the major organizations for the advancement of women—the National Union of Women's Suffrage Societies and the Women's Service Bureau (later the London Society for Women's Service)—contributed to the winning of the right to vote for British women over the age of 30, in addition to labor gains. While Pippa worked largely behind the scenes in the suffrage movement, Ray played a more prominent role while chronicling the movement in her writings.

Pippa was born in 1872, the daughter of Sir Richard Strachey and Lady **Jane Strachey** (a disciple of John Stuart Mill). The large, wealthy English family also included her older sisters **Elinor Strachey** and **Dorothy Strachey**, who wrote *Olivia*, younger sisters **Marjorie Strachey** and **Joan Pernel Strachey**, an educator who became principal of Newnham College, and their famous brother Lytton Strachey, a member of the cultured Bloomsbury group of writers and artists in which *\*Virginia Woolf* was prominent. Pippa's mother was a passionate feminist who influenced her young daughter to join her in the National Union of Women's Suffrage Societies (NUWSS). Pippa's contribution to the union as secretary was pivotal but low-key as she worked mainly in the background to organize demonstrations.

Like Pippa, Ray Strachey also credited a female family member with her early development as an activist for women's rights. Born Rachel Mary Costelloe in 1887, Ray was raised mostly by her maternal grandmother ◀ **Hannah Whitall Smith**, after her mother Mary Pearsall Smith Costelloe abandoned the family and her father Frank Costelloe died in 1899. (Ray's mother married Bernard Berenson in 1900 and would be more commonly known as *\*Mary Berenson*.) A Philadelphian Quaker, Hannah Smith had been a temperance worker and suffragist in the United States prior to moving to London.

Ray met the Stracheys in 1909 while still in school, and her friendship with Pippa and Lady Jane Strachey fueled her own activism. Ray's attachment to the Strachey family was permanently fixed with her marriage to Pippa's brother Oliver in 1911. (Oliver previously had been married to **Ruby Meyer Strachey** and had a daughter **Julia Strachey**.) Although the marriage disintegrated over the years due to differences in temperament, the couple stayed together. The relationship between Ray and Pippa was more successful, despite the disparity in their backgrounds and demeanor. They enjoyed each other's company and shared an indifference to personal dress or comfort, writes Brian Harrison—Pippa would allow her stockings to fall in rolls around her ankles while the casually dressed Ray once went out to dinner wearing her dress inside out and backwards. Possessing an unerring political sense, Pippa could perceive the endless repercussions of an action. "Pippa therefore became the long-term strategist behind the scenes while Ray's vigorous, extrovert personality made her the executive arm," Harrison continues. "Whereas Ray was quick, positive, and rather impersonal, Pippa's decisions were wary and often painfully slow."

Pippa and Ray spent much time together and collaborated on feminist causes, particularly

*Pippa Strachey*

as they related to labor issues. Through the Women's Service Bureau, the pair worked for the interests of working women by pressing for the inclusion of women in job fields which previously were the exclusive domain of men. Pippa acted as secretary to the Women's Service Bureau when it became the London Society for Women's Service following the end of World War I, and devoted the rest of her life to the organization. Under her direction, the Women's Service Library came into being as a repository for documents on the women's suffrage movement. She also saw the founding of a club for the society, the Women's Service House, which was later renamed the Fawcett Society in honor of suffragist *\*Millicent Garrett Fawcett*. Pippa's service merited her the honor of Commander of the British Empire (CBE) in 1951. She did not retire from her post until she was into her 90s.

Ray took a more high-profile position both in the NUWSS and the Women's Service Bureau. She demanded that the War Office grant women war workers equal pay and suitable working conditions. Along with Pippa and Fawcett, Ray negotiated for the passage of the 1918 suffrage bill that granted the vote to women over 30. She also stood unsuccessfully for a seat in Parliament that same year, and again in 1922 and 1923, at which time she ended her hopes of becoming a politician. However, Ray brought her political influence to bear as the parliamentary secretary for *Nancy Astor, who had recently won election, by preparing briefs for Astor throughout her career.

In 1935, Ray assumed control of the Women's Employment Federation, a natural progression from her early days with the Women's Service Bureau. Ever the advocate for working women, she drew attention to the limitations imposed by society on women who were unfairly burdened with family concerns, and in 1937 published *Career Openings for Women*. Two years later, she worked to eradicate unemployment among professional women. Her vital work was cut short by her death in 1940, following surgery for a fibroid tumor. Her legacy, however, continued through her writings, which included biographies of American feminist and temperance worker *Frances Willard (1912), her grandmother (1914), and Millicent Garrett Fawcett (1931). In addition to editing the suffrage paper *The Common Cause* (later renamed the *Women's Leader*), Ray wrote her most famous work, *The Cause*. Published in 1928, it was a germinal work on the history of the British women's movement, and served as the only source of information on it until the 1970s. Pippa continued working on behalf of women for nearly 30 more years, dying at age 96 in 1968.

**SOURCES:**

Banks, Olive. *The Biographical Dictionary of British Feminists*, Vol. 1. NY: New York University Press, 1985.

Harrison, Brian. *Prudent Revolutionaries: Portraits of British Feminists between the Wars*. Oxford: Clarendon Press, 1987.

**SUGGESTED READING:**

Strachey, Barbara. *Remarkable Relations: The Story of the Pearsall Smith Women*. NY: Universe, 1982.

**Barbara Koch**, freelance writer,
Farmington Hills, Michigan

## Strachey, Ray (1887–1940).

*See joint entry under Strachey, Pippa and Ray Strachey.*

## Straight, Dorothy (1887–1968).

*See Whitney, Dorothy Payne.*

## Strang, Ruth (1895–1971)

*American educator and writer. Born Ruth May Strang on April 3, 1895, in Chatham, New Jersey; died from*

*the effects of arteriosclerosis on January 3, 1971, in Amityville, New York; daughter of Charles Garret Strang (a farmer) and Anna (Bergen) Strang; graduated from a two-year normal program in household science, Pratt Institute, Brooklyn, 1916; Teachers College of Columbia University, B.S., 1922, M.A., 1924, Ph.D., 1926; never married; no children.*

Born in 1895 in Chatham, New Jersey, the daughter of a none-too-successful farmer, Ruth Strang moved frequently during her childhood, accompanying her family to various towns in New Jersey, Long Island, and Arizona. After they finally settled in Brooklyn, New York, she attended Adelphi Academy there, but her father, who had provided financial assistance for her older brother's college studies, dashed her hopes of continuing her education at Wellesley College. Entering a two-year program in household science at Pratt Institute in Brooklyn, Strang graduated in 1916 and thereafter taught home economics in a lower-income neighborhood in New York City. Against the protests of her family, she then entered graduate school at Columbia University's Teachers College. Over the next six years, she would earn three degrees there—a B.A. (1922), an M.A. (1924), and finally a Ph.D. (1926)— while also taking a number of positions at the college, including supervisor of health education at the Horace Mann School in 1924 and research assistant in psychology the following year.

Doctoral degree in hand, Strang next studied national trends in student personnel administration on a research fellowship from the school. She began her three-decade career at Teachers College as an assistant professor of education in 1929, becoming an associate professor in 1936 and a full professor in 1940. In 1930, she published *An Introduction to Child Study* (later republished several times with updated revisions), the first of some 400 articles, monographs, books and pamphlets she would write. She also edited the influential *Journal* of the National Association for Women Deans, Administrators, and Counselors, of which she was a member, from 1938 to 1960. Strang's major contributions to Teachers College involved her twin interests in educational guidance and the teaching of reading. She was a key figure in the evolution of the department of guidance and student personnel administration into a major center for graduate studies, and her research at and direction of the High School and College Reading Center supported the development of reading and communication in many educational institutions across the country. Among her most important publications in these fields were *Educational Guidance: Its Principles and Practices* (1947), *The Role of the Teacher in Personnel Work* (1953), *Problems in the Improvement of Reading in Secondary Schools and High Schools* (1938), and *Explorations in Reading Patterns* (1942).

Strang's other interests revolved around the disciplines of health education, the teaching of gifted children, education in rural areas, and psychology and mental health (her 1957 book *The Adolescent Views Himself: A Psychology of Adolescence* is considered one of her best). She served for several years as a director of the American Association for Gifted Children, was a member of the board of directors of the International Council for the Improvement of Reading Instruction and of the National Society for the Study of Education (becoming chair of the board for the latter organization in 1960), and was a longtime member of the National Association of Remedial Teachers, for which she served as president in 1955. She also belonged to the Research Association and the National Education Association. In recognition of her achievements in the field of education, she was named a fellow of the American Association of Applied Psychology, the American Public Health Association, and the United Kingdom's Royal Society of Health.

Retiring from Teachers College as professor emerita at the mandatory age of 65, Strang immediately became a professor of education at the University of California during the summer of 1960. That fall, her previous experiences with the teaching of reading led her to the University of Arizona, where she served as a professor of education and head of the reading development center until 1968. After a yearlong visiting professorship at the Ontario Institute for Studies in Education, Strang finally retired, settling in Amityville, New York. There she struggled with arteriosclerosis until her death in 1971.

**SOURCES:**

Moritz, Charles, ed. *Current Biography 1960.* NY: H.W. Wilson, 1960.
Sicherman, Barbara, and Carol Hurd Green, eds. *Notable American Women: The Modern Period.* Cambridge, MA: The Belknap Press of Harvard University, 1980.

**Helga P. McCue**, freelance writer, Waterford, Connecticut

# Strange, Michael (1890–1950)

*American poet, playwright and actress. Name variations: Blanche Marie Louise Oelrichs; Blanche Oelrichs Thomas Barrymore Tweed. Born Blanche Marie Louise Oelrichs on October 1, 1890, in New York City; died of leukemia on November 5, 1950, in Boston, Massachusetts; daughter of Blanche (de Loosey) Oelrichs and Charles May Oelrichs (owner of a seat on the New York Stock Exchange); attended the Brearley School in New York, the Convent of the Sacred Heart in Manhattanville, and completed her education under private tutors; married Leonard Moorhead Thomas (a first secretary of the American legation to Madrid), in January 1910 (divorced 1919); married John Barrymore (the actor), in August 1920 (divorced 1928); married Harrison Tweed (a lawyer and yachtsman), in May 1929 (divorced 1942); children: (first marriage) sons Leonard Moorhead Thomas, Jr. (b. 1911) and Robin May Thomas (1915–1944); (second marriage) daughter Diana Barrymore (1921–1960).*

*Selected writings: Miscellaneous Poems (1916); Redemption (play, 1918); Poems (1919); Resurrecting Life (1921); Claire de Lune (play, 1921); Selected Poems (1928); Who Tells Me True (autobiography, 1940).*

Michael Strange was the stage name and literary pseudonym of Blanche Oelrichs, who was born into a prominent New York City family on October 1, 1890. The Oelrichs moved in the social circles of New York, Paris, and Newport, Rhode Island, and many years later she would note that while young she had been unaware of "how desperately at odds I had always been with my environment." Blanche's mischievous temperament was not well suited to a formal, Catholic-school education, and she was expelled from two schools before finally settling down with private tutors to complete her education. Her beauty and social rank made her one of the most sought-after debutantes in Newport prior to her marriage to Yale graduate and diplomat Leonard Moorhead Thomas in 1910. They would have two sons, Leonard, Jr., and Robin. They also traveled frequently, and on a trip to England in the first few years after her marriage Strange saw police mistreatment of women suffragists, some of whom were engaged in a campaign of civil disobedience in their fight for the vote. Converted to the cause, upon her return to America she bobbed her hair (long before most women did, and much to the consternation of her social peers) and worked actively for enfranchisement of women. In 1915, she marched in a women's suffrage parade up New York City's Fifth Avenue.

A more significant change had come with her literary awakening in 1914, when she began to write poetry. One of her efforts was printed in the *New York Sun*, and shortly thereafter her collection *Miscellaneous Poems* (1916) was published under the name Michael Strange. She would continue to use this pseudonym for the rest of her life, in both her literary and her stage careers. In 1918, she wrote the play *Redemption*, an adaptation of Tolstoy's *The Living Corpse*, which had a successful run on Broadway that year starring famed actor John Barrymore.

Strange's newfound creativity and her artistic circle of friends caused problems in her marriage, and she and her husband divorced in 1919. That year, she also published her second collection of poetry, *Poems*, and embarked on an affair with Barrymore. They were married the following year. Their daughter *Diana Barrymore** was born in March 1921; she would suffer an unhappy childhood and grow up to become an actress before committing suicide at age 38. The month after her birth, John and his sister *Ethel Barrymore** took the lead roles in Strange's play *Claire de Lune*, which received mixed reviews. *Resurrecting Life*, another volume of her poems, was published later that year. Increasingly intrigued with acting, in 1925 Strange performed in summer stock in Salem, Massachusetts, to gain practical experience. She received numerous offers from theater owners hoping to capitalize on the celebrity of the society woman who wrote poetry, dressed in men's shirts and ties, and was married to the hugely popular Barrymore. While Strange rejected most of these requests, over the course of the next two years she appeared in Strindberg's *Easter*, Wilde's *The Importance of Being Earnest*, Sophocles' *Electra*, and on Broadway in Rostand's *L'Aiglon*. Aside from scattered roles, however, little more came of her acting career after that. During these years, her marriage to Barrymore was falling apart, plagued as it was with jealousies, conflict, long separations and his heavy drinking. They divorced in 1928. A year later, she entered into her third and last marriage, to lawyer Harrison Tweed. This too would end in divorce, in 1942.

Though finished with both acting and her actor-husband, Strange was not yet done with the stage. With the encouragement and practical assistance of her friend ◄⚜ **Elisabeth Marbury,** she turned her attention to touring on the lecture circuit, presenting to audiences poetry readings set to music. Town Hall in New York City was the site of her first recital, given in 1935; she read her own poems and those of other prominent poets such as Edgar Allan Poe and *Dorothy Parker** to the music of a live harpist. Soon she expanded her program to radio, and by 1947 was using a full orchestra for her performances, which grew to include excerpts from such disparate writings as the Bible, the Declara-

⚜►
*Marbury,*
*Elisabeth.* See
*de Wolfe, Elsie for*
*sidebar.*

tion of Independence, the novels of Thomas Wolfe and *The Communist Manifesto*. Having published an autobiography, *Who Tells Me True*, in 1940, Strange died of leukemia in November 1950, in Boston, Massachusetts.

**SOURCES:**
James, Edward T., ed. *Notable American Women, 1607–1950*. Cambridge, MA: The Belknap Press of Harvard University, 1971.
McHenry, Robert, ed. *Famous American Women*. NY: Dover, 1980.

**Helga P. McCue,** freelance writer,
Waterford, Connecticut

## Strangford, Viscountess (c. 1845–1887).

*See Smythe, Emily Anne.*

## Strasberg, Susan (1938–1999)

*American actress. Born in New York City in 1938; died in New York City on January 21, 1999; daughter of Lee Strasberg (an acting teacher) and Paula Strasberg (an actress and co-founder of the Actors Studio); attended the Actors Studio; married actor Christopher Jones (divorced); children: one daughter, Jennifer.*

*Grew up around the Actors Studio; in 1955 starred in the Broadway hit* The Diary of Anne Frank *(1955); over the next 40 years appeared on stage, on television, and in films; wrote two autobiographies.*

Born in New York City in 1938, the daughter of **Paula Strasberg** and Lee Strasberg, co-founders of the Actors Studio, Susan Strasberg was considered an accomplished actress at an early age. She grew up among such luminaries of the New York stage as *Julie Harris**, *Maureen Stapleton**, Marlon Brando and Walter Matthau, who were members of the Actors Studio where her father taught Method acting and directed. She also had a special friendship and rivalry with *Marilyn Monroe**, which she describes in the autobiographical *Marilyn and Me: Sisters, Rivals, Friends* (1992). Strasberg was devastated when Monroe died in 1962.

In 1955, at age 17, Strasberg created the role of *Anne Frank** in *Frances Goodrich** and Albert Hackett's Broadway hit *The Diary of Anne Frank*. Her performance electrified audiences and established her as an exceptional talent in her own right. Strasberg recalled that when she auditioned for the role, she was so nervous that she clung to the script to keep from trembling and started to weep as she read the lines. When she finished her reading, everyone in the room was completely silent until Joseph Schildkraut, who was cast as Anne's father, said, "Hello, Anne."

That year Strasberg also appeared in two films, *The Cobweb*, directed by Vincente Minnelli, and *Picnic*, starring William Holden and *\*Kim Novak*. In 1957, she appeared in *Time Remembered* with \*Helen Hayes and Richard Burton. She had an ill-fated affair with Burton that she described in her memoir *Bittersweet* (1980). The autobiography also chronicled her destructive marriage to actor Christopher Jones, her drug abuse, and her daughter's birth defects (four holes in her heart and a cleft palate), which may have been the result of Susan's problems with drugs.

Strasberg's career spanned four decades; she acted in over 30 films, including *Stage Struck* and the 1957 remake of *Morning Glory*, made nearly two dozen television appearances, and appeared in many plays, including the touring company of *Agnes of God*. In the mid-1990s, she was diagnosed with breast cancer. Although it was thought to be in remission, Strasberg died unexpectedly on January 21, 1999. She was "a beautiful hothouse orchid that was slightly bruised," said her friend Leonard Finger.

**SOURCES:**
*The Boston Globe* (obituary). January 23, 1999.
"Frank Actress," in *People Weekly*. February 8, 1999.
Klemesrud, Judy. "Susan Strasberg Looks Back," in *The New York Times Biographical Service*. April 1980.

**Malinda Mayer**, writer and editor,
Falmouth, Massachusetts

# Stratas, Teresa (1938—)

*Canadian soprano and winner of three Grammy awards. Born Anastasia Strataki of Greek descent on May 26, 1938, in Toronto, Ontario, Canada; studied with Irene Jessner at Toronto, 1956–59; graduated from the University of Toronto, Faculty of Music, 1959.*

*Debuted with Canadian Opera in Toronto (1958); won Metropolitan Opera Auditions of the Air (1959); debuted at Metropolitan Opera (1959), Covent Garden (1961), Teatro alla Scala (1962); performed title role in first three-act production of Berg's Lulu in Paris (1979); made Broadway debut in musical Rags (1986); was made an Officer of the Order of Canada (1972).*

Teresa Stratas was born Anastasia Strataki of Greek descent in 1938 in Toronto, Ontario, and began her singing career in the clubs and cafes of the local Greek community there. Her ability was so great that she was admitted to the Opera School at the Royal Academy of Music at age 12; she then studied with **Irene Jessner** from 1956 to 1959. That year, she won the Metropol-

Susan
Strasberg

itan Opera Auditions of the Air and began a swift ascent in the opera world. Though small in stature, Stratas was a commanding figure on stage. Her 1974 performance of *Salome* for German television documents her singing and acting abilities. She also starred with Placido Domingo in Zeffirelli's acclaimed film version *La Traviata* in 1983. Her interest in other forms of entertainment led her to star in the 1986 Broadway show *Rags* for which she won a Tony Award for Best Actress in a musical. She has also won three Grammys and one Emmy.

**SUGGESTED READING:**
Rasky, Harry. *Stratas: An Affectionate Tribute*. London: Oxford University Press, 1989.

**John Haag**,
Athens, Georgia

# Stratemeyer, Harriet (c. 1893–1982).

*See Adams, Harriet Stratemeyer.*

# Strathearn, countess of.

*See Stewart, Euphemia (c. 1375–1415).*

## Strathearn, duchess of.

*See Horton, Ann (1743–1808).*

## Strathmore, Lady.

*See Elizabeth Bowes-Lyon for sidebar on Nina Cavendish-Bentinck.*

## Stratonice I (c. 319–254 BCE)

*Seleucid queen. Name variations: Stratoniki or Stratonike. Born around 319; died in 254 BCE; daughter of Demetrius Poliorcetes (a Macedonian general-king) and his first wife Phila I (daughter of Antipater); married Seleucus I Nicator (c. 360–280 BCE, a Macedonian general and founder of the Seleucid Empire, covering most of Asia Minor, Syria, Persia, and Bactria), around 298 BCE; married Antiochus I Soter (324–261 BCE), in 294; children: (first marriage) daughter, Phila II (b. around 300 BCE); (second marriage) Seleucus; Apama (born c. 290 BCE, mother of Berenice II of Cyrene); Antiochus II Theos (286–247 BCE); Stratonice II (c. 285–228 BCE).*

Stratonice I was the daughter of Demetrius Poliorcetes (a Macedonian general-king active in the generation following the death of Alexander III the Great) and his first wife ◄❧ **Phila I** (the well-respected daughter of Antipater). By the time Stratonice was a young woman, Alexander's short-lived empire, stretching from the Adriatic Sea to the Indian Ocean, had begun to disintegrate under the weight of political realities, not the least of which was the fact that Alexander had left no viable heir. As opportunity stoked the ambitions of Alexander's generals, the age of the Macedonian Successors began. This was an era of rapidly changing alliances that were embraced and abandoned as nearly every player sought political advantage against rivals attempting to carve independent realms

❧► **Phila I** (fl. c. 320 BCE)

*Macedonian noblewoman. Flourished around 320 BCE; daughter of Antipater; married Demetrius Poliorcetes (a Macedonian general-king); sister of Cassander, \*Eurydice (fl. 321 BCE) and \*Nicaea; children: Antigonus II Gonatus (who married his niece \*Phila II); \*Stratonice I (c. 319–254 BCE).*

Phila was the well-respected daughter of Antipater, Alexander's designated general for Europe when Alexander invaded Asia, and the most influential Macedonian between Alexander's death in 323 and his own in 319.

out of Alexander's conquests. Eventually, three more or less stable Macedonian kingdoms emerged (one each in Europe, Asia and Africa) to dominate the many lesser states which comprised the remnants of Alexander's empire. A rough balance of power among the Macedonians, however, did not develop until Stratonice I was about 40 years of age. Thus, she matured during interesting times.

Stratonice's first marriage in 298 was to Seleucus I Nicator, the founder of the Macedonian dynasty which at the time laid claim to all of Asia (with the exclusion of Anatolia), from the Mediterranean to modern Pakistan. This union was contracted to link the interests of Seleucus with those of Demetrius Poliorcetes, although the two had only recently waged open war. At the time of Stratonice's marriage, Demetrius was looking for any friends he could find. Engaged in (another) war with the dynast Lysimachus, Demetrius was a "king" without a kingdom because only a few years before, an alliance of Macedonian rivals (of which Seleucus had been a member), jealous of the extent of Demetrius' then substantial power in Asia (held jointly with his father Antigonus I), coalesced to destroy it. This war concluded in 301 with the death of Antigonus and the expulsion of Demetrius from Asia. Thus, in 298 Demetrius was a kind of freelance warlord, desperately hoping to create, or lay claim to, another realm. His reward for coming to terms with Seleucus was twofold: first, he regained diplomatic credibility; second, Seleucus ceded to Demetrius the region of Cilicia.

Seleucus' motivation for marrying Stratonice I was as Machiavellian as was that of Demetrius. In the aftermath of the war which drove Demetrius from Asia, Seleucus had laid claim to the lion's share of the kingdom once ruled jointly by Antigonus and Demetrius. As a result of the sudden and dramatic increase in his holdings, his one-time allies were in the process of turning covetous eyes upon his recently acquired possessions. When Seleucus learned that Ptolemy I Soter (in Egypt) was forging marital-political alliances with Lysimachus (in southeastern Europe and Anatolia) and Cassander (in Macedonia), Seleucus decided that true wisdom demanded a rapprochement with the militarily talented Demetrius. Hence, his marriage to Stratonice I. The marriage itself is interesting for several reasons. First, Seleucus (born c. 360) was much older than Stratonice and already had an heir Antiochus I Soter (born c. 324) with his first, Bactrian wife ❧► **Apama**; Antiochus I Soter was also older than Stratonice. Second, Seleucus remained married to at least Apama (and perhaps a second wife from India) when Stratonice came to his bed. Such polygamy was common among Seleucus' Macedonian contemporaries. And third, although Stratonice was to be her father's liaison with Seleucus, she also had close ties to her father's and husband's rivals: that is, Cassander was Phila's brother and thus Stratonice's uncle, while both Ptolemy and Lysimachus were themselves married to other daughters of Stratonice's grandfather Antipater (❧▶ **Eurydice** and ❧▶ **Nicaea**, respectively). Clearly, this was not a time when kinship ties outweighed political ambitions.

Stratonice I remained married to Seleucus for four years, during which time she gave birth to a daughter, ❧▶ **Phila II**. Then, in 294, something extraordinary happened which shocked even the sensibilities of Stratonice's worldly contemporaries. The episode began when Seleucus' son Antiochus began to waste away, the victim of a mysterious illness. Although all due care was taken to discover the origin of Antiochus' malady, Antiochus himself would not speak to the issue, and no one could discover its source until Erasistratus, one of the most famous physicians of the day, was given the case. Erasistratus quickly determined that Antiochus was suffering not from a physical ailment but from a psychological disorder he attributed to unrequited love. Nevertheless, the physical ramifications of the passion were extremely serious, for Antiochus was indeed deteriorating before everyone's eyes. However, when the doctor attempted to pry from Antiochus the identity of his affection, he met with complete and utter silence. As a result, Erasistratus could only observe Antiochus' behavior in the hope that some change would come upon the patient when he was in the presence of his beloved. Through such observation, Erasistratus came to determine that it was Stratonice I whom Antiochus loved.

Of course, the situation was delicate. How would Seleucus react when Erasistratus revealed the nature of Antiochus' problem? Antiochus himself recognized the perversity of his emotion for Stratonice; hence the noble silence while his body withered. Would an enlightened Seleucus strike out in anger against his son and heir? Would the king punish the messenger who disclosed the cause of his son's debilitation? Yet, Seleucus had asked Erasistratus to heal Antiochus, and the doctor took this charge seriously, both because of his vocation and because of the status of his patient. To deal with the dilemma, Erasistratus decided that discretion was called for. He reported to Seleucus that Antiochus had fallen in love with an unattainable woman. When Seleu-

cus pressed for the identity of the woman, Erasistratus dissembled by declaring that the woman Antiochus loved was Erasistratus' own wife. Hearing this, Seleucus implored Erasistratus to sacrifice his marriage for the good of the patient; in fact, he begged the physician to divorce his wife so that Antiochus could have her. Upon this suggestion Erasistratus feigned indignation, and charged that even though Seleucus loved Antiochus very much, *he* would never consider divorcing a beloved spouse just to save Antiochus' life. When Seleucus swore that he would do anything to save Antiochus—even render Stratonice to her stepson if that would effect a cure—Erasistratus revealed that it was not his own wife whom Antiochus loved, but Stratonice.

The stunned Seleucus verified the doctor's assertion and then acted upon his promise to give Stratonice to Antiochus. Realizing that it would be unusual (to say the least) for Stratonice to become the wife of her erstwhile stepson, even though she was much closer to Antiochus' age than to his own, Seleucus acted decisively and audaciously to forestall any moral indignation and/or political backlash. This was easier said than done, because Seleucus not only had to convince his subjects that a father and a son could be intimate with the same woman, he also had to convince the principals themselves that their marriage would not violate taboos of intimacy. In addition, he had to convince Stratonice's father that her transfer to Antiochus was not intended as an insult either to Stratonice or himself. Demetrius Poliorcetes was a special problem for Seleucus, for that ambitious adventurer had only recently secured for himself the throne of Macedonia—Cassander's dynasty hav-

*Eurydice (fl. 321 BCE).* See *Berenice I* for sidebar.

*Nicaea.* See *Arsinoe II Philadelphus* for sidebar.

---

❧▶ **Apama** (fl. 324 BCE)
*Bactrian mother of Antiochus I Soter. Name variations: Apame. Flourished around 324 BCE; born in Bactria; first wife of Seleucus I Nicator, Seleucid king (r. 301–281 BCE); children: Antiochus I Soter (born around 324). Seleucus I Nicator was also married to* **Stratonice I.**

❧▶ **Phila II** (c. 300 BCE–?)
*Seleucid princess and queen of Macedonia. Born around 300 BCE; daughter of* **Stratonice I** *(c. 319–254 BCE) and Seleucus I Nicator, Seleucid king; granddaughter of* **Phila I**; *married her uncle Antigonus II Gonatus (son of Demetrius Poliorcetes and Phila I, and brother of Stratonice), king of Macedonia; children: Demetrius II of Macedonia (who married* **Stratonice II**).

ing become extinct, with a little help from Demetrius himself. Who could tell what Demetrius might do to "avenge" a perceived wrong done to his daughter, especially if he could undermine Seleucus' hold over Asia by arguing that Seleucus was morally depraved for even suggesting that Antiochus and Stratonice should wed?

What Stratonice thought about all of this is unknown, but it seems that she was not terribly put out by the turn of events, in part because of Seleucus' insightful enhancement of her public status at the time of her second marriage. Seleucus carefully explained that his divorce of Stratonice so that she could marry Antiochus was in the long-term interest of all concerned, and then he presided over a very public event in the presence of an assembly of Macedonians under arms. There, Antiochus and Stratonice were married with no apologies given, and with Seleucus justifying the unusual situation by tersely pronouncing, "what the king ordains is *always* right." So much for those who might attack Stratonice's second marriage as incestuous. Then, in a stunning announcement, Seleucus proclaimed that Antiochus and Stratonice would henceforth assume the status of "king" and "queen" and rule jointly over Seleucus' territories to the east of the Euphrates River. Thus, far from intending his divorce from Stratonice to indicate disfavor, Seleucus actually promoted her status beyond what it had been, for although Stratonice had been one of Seleucus' wives, she had never before publicly borne the title of "queen." This was a rare honor for a woman at that time, and it clearly went far in winning over Stratonice and her father to her new domestic arrangement. Further enhancing the status of Stratonice was the fact that Antiochus always treated her as his beloved equal, and the fact that, unlike most of his Macedonian contemporaries, he never took another wife.

As queen, Stratonice maintained a very high profile, being especially zealous in her dedications at such religious sites as Delos, particularly important to the Seleucids since it was believed to be the birthplace of Apollo, whom they claimed as the ancestor of their line. At least one city foundation was named after Stratonice, and throughout the Seleucid Empire her subjects even came to worship her, usually in association with the goddess Aphrodite. Thus, few were allowed to forget the special honors which both of her husbands had showered upon Stratonice.

The fact that Stratonice retained her elevated position throughout her life is a testament to her personality and to the loyalty she displayed towards the dynasty of her husbands, for although she originally came to Seleucus as part of a political pact with Demetrius Poliorcetes, this alliance was of relatively short standing. Set up by Seleucus in Cilicia in 298 BCE, Demetrius used this base as a springboard for the conquest of Athens (295 BCE), and eventually for his return to Macedonia as that realm's king (294 BCE). There Demetrius ruled for seven years. However, he never held the interests of that land as his primary responsibility. Always remembering that he and his father had once ruled the majority of Macedonian Asia, and still angry at Lysimachus, Ptolemy and Seleucus for having deprived him of that realm (there was little room in Demetrius for any gratitude toward Seleucus), Demetrius spent his time as king of Macedon in creating a war machine with which he hoped to reunite Alexander's empire under his sole rule. Oblivious to the concerns of others, and putting Stratonice in an especially embarrassing position, Demetrius went about his business. By 288 BCE, he was in possession of a huge army and fleet.

Discovering Demetrius' intention and motivated by fear, Seleucus, Ptolemy, and Lysimachus renewed their disbanded alliance. Thereafter, in conjunction with Pyrrhus, king of Epirus, they launched a preemptive strike on Macedon from both east and west. Not eager to endure the ruin of their kingdom or to fight once again against expatriated Macedonians just to support maniacal ambitions, the majority of Demetrius' subjects then rebelled against his authority and toppled him from his second throne. Although most of Demetrius' supporters abandoned him, not all did. With a considerably smaller force than he had intended, Demetrius, in suicidal fashion, invaded the Seleucid Empire. There, he met with defeat, capture, and imprisonment (287 BCE), where he stayed until he drank himself to death two years later. During this period, despite Demetrius' selfish hope that Stratonice would somehow intervene and come to his rescue, she remained steadfast to the interests of Seleucus and Antiochus. Perhaps with a tinge of guilt, but certainly indicating where her loyalty then lay, when after Demetrius' death Stratonice inherited his jewelry, she dedicated that considerable legacy to the Delian Apollo—(again) the god claimed by the Seleucids as the founder of their line.

Upon Seleucus' death in 280, Antiochus and Stratonice assumed rule over the entire Seleucid realm, made all the larger by Seleucus' recent (281 BCE) victory over Lysimachus (in yet another conflict between rulers seemingly incapable of remaining content with but a part of what had briefly been a unified whole). Most of the rest of Antiochus' reign was spent in consolidating the Seleucid control of Asia, founding cities, and putting down those revolts which challenged his policy of centralization. Throughout these years, Stratonice remained at her husband's side, doing what she could to foster the development of Seleucid power.

As for children, in addition to the daughter Phila II that Stratonice had with Seleucus, she gave birth to four more with Antiochus: Seleucus, Antiochus II Theos, ❧➤ **Apama** and *****Stratonice II**. Their fates demonstrate the complexities of diplomacy and the perils of rule during the early Hellenistic period. In 276 BCE, Phila II married Antigonus II Gonatus, the son of Demetrius Poliorcetes and Phila I, and thus the full brother of Stratonice I. This union was contracted soon after Antigonus II defeated an army of Celts who were despoiling Macedon, for which service he was elevated to the throne of Macedonia. It took some time for Antigonus II to establish his control of Macedon, largely because of his father's earlier irresponsible reign as king there. Seleucus, the older of Antiochus' and Stratonice's two sons, never came to the throne because he was executed in 268 BCE on a conspiracy charge—it seems that he was loath to wait for his inheritance. Antiochus II Theos, therefore, succeeded to the Seleucid throne, reigning from 266 to 261 BCE as a co-regent with his father, and from 261 to 246 BCE as sole Seleucid monarch. Stratonice's daughter Apama married Magas of Cyrene and became the mother of *****Berenice II of Cyrene** of Egypt. Finally, the younger Stratonice (II) married her cousin-nephew, Demetrius II of Macedonia (the son of Antigonus II and her half-sister Phila II), before returning to meet her death in Asia.

Stratonice I outlived her second husband (who died in 261 BCE) by seven years. Although little is known of her activity during this period, she did maintain her rank as queen until her death in 254 BCE. Thus her son, Antiochus II, acknowledged her worth in the projection of his royal authority. A stalwart supporter of her husbands' interests and an embodiment of both feminine and royal virtues, she lived on long after her death both in cult and in the dedications erected to her memory by her descendants.

**William S. Greenwalt**, Associate Professor of Classical History, Santa Clara University, Santa Clara, California

# Stratonice II (c. 285–228 BCE)

*Seleucid princess. Name variations: Stratoniki or Stratonike. Born around 285; died in 228 BCE; daughter of the Seleucid king and queen, Antiochus I Soter and*

*Stratonice I (c. 319–254 BCE); married her cousin-nephew Demetrius II, king of Macedonia, in 255 BCE (marriage ended, 239); children: Apama.*

Stratonice II was the daughter of the Seleucid king and queen, Antiochus I Soter and *****Stratonice I**, and the sister of Antiochus II Theos. In order to secure better relations with the kingdom of Macedon, Antiochus II arranged with its king, Antigonus II Gonatus, for the marriage of his sister to Demetrius II (Antigonus II's son and heir) about 255 BCE. Stratonice's husband was about ten years her junior, and was both her cousin (Demetrius' father was the brother of Stratonice I) and her nephew (Demetrius' mother was ❧➤ **Phila II**, the daughter of Stratonice I and the half-sister of Stratonice II). We know nothing about Stratonice II's marriage except that it produced a daughter, ❧➤ **Apama** (who eventually married Prusias I of Bithynia), and that it ended in 239 after Demetrius succeeded his father on the Macedonian throne and thereupon married a second wife, **Phthia of Epirus**. Why Demetrius took a second wife so quickly after his accession can only be conjectured, but it seems that he had little affection for Stratonice II, and that he used her failure to produce a son as an excuse to acquire a new bride. Although polygamy was a well-established tradition among Macedonia's royalty, Stratonice had not grown up in such a household, since her mother (Stratonice I) had been the only spouse of her father. The younger Stratonice took offense at her husband's second marriage, and left him to return to the kingdom of her birth.

Back in Asia, Stratonice II made a beeline for Antioch, the capital of the Seleucid Empire, where she: 1) offered herself in marriage to the reigning king, her nephew Seleucus II; and 2) encouraged him to avenge her flight from Macedon by warring on Demetrius II. Seleucus declined to act upon either of Stratonice's suggestions, thereby turning her anger in his direction. Regardless, there was little that Stratonice could do to redress what she considered to be insults until Seleucus II mounted an expedition against the Parthians, and Antiochus Hierax was driven from Anatolia by Attalus I of Pergamon,

*Apama (c. 290 BCE–?)*. See Berenice II of Cyrene for sidebar.

*Phila II.* See Stratonice I for sidebar.

❧➤ **Apama** (fl. 245 BCE)
*Queen of Bithynia. Flourished around 245 BCE; daughter of *****Stratonice II** and Demetrius II, king of Macedonia; married Prusias I, king of Bithynia.*

probably in 229. A brief background: Antiochus Hierax was the brother of Seleucus II, both being sons of Stratonice's brother Antiochus II and his wife *Laodice I. When Antiochus II died in 246, Laodice angered her older son, Seleucus II, by encouraging him to share the Seleucid throne with the younger Antiochus Hierax (probably to allow her to play one off against the other for the perpetration of her own influence). Laodice's interference incited a civil war between the brothers (239–236) which was settled only after Seleucus ceded to Antiochus Hierax the Seleucid territories in Anatolia. There Antiochus Hierax (attempting to expand his realm) became the rival of Attalus I, who eventually drove Antiochus from his domain (probably in 229) back to the territory held by Seleucus II.

With Seleucus fighting the Parthians, and with a dispossessed younger brother once again at large within his realm, Stratonice appears to have hit upon a scheme to enhance her influence while avenging herself upon Seleucus II for spurning her matrimonial advances. Encouraging Antiochus Hierax to raise the standard of rebellion against his brother in Babylonia while she did everything she could to turn the city of Antioch against Seleucus, Stratonice hoped to topple Seleucus from his throne before he could react effectively. In this she failed: Seleucus quit his Parthian expedition to drive Antiochus Hierax from Babylonia (he fled to European Thrace, where he was murdered by some Celts in 227), thereafter to besiege Stratonice in Antioch. For a short period, Stratonice held the capital city, but without Antiochus Hierax to offer the Antiochenes in place of Seleucus II, her revolt quickly faded. Stratonice escaped capture in Antioch and fled to the port city of Seleucia. Instead of fleeing the Seleucid Empire for the safety of exile, however, she remained in Seleucia, apparently inspired to do so by a dream she interpreted as favorable to her ambitions. If sent by the gods, Stratonice's dream was a false one, for when Seleucus II caught up with her in Seleucia, he quickly put her to death (228 BCE).

**William S. Greenwalt**,
Associate Professor of Classical History,
Santa Clara University, Santa Clara, California

# Stratonice III (fl. 250 BCE)

*Seleucid princess. Name variations: Stratoniki or Stratonike. Born around 250 BCE; daughter of Antiochus II Theos and *Laodice I (c. 285–236 BCE); sister of Antiochus Hierax and Seleucus II; niece of *Stratonice I; married Ariarathes III, Persian ruler of Cappadocia.*

# Stratonike.

*Variant of Stratonice.*

# Stratonike.

*See Olympias (c. 371–316 BCE).*

# Stratoniki.

*Variant of Stratonice.*

# Stratton, Dorothy (b. 1899)

*American educator who was the first woman officer in the Coast Guard Reserve. Name variations: Dorothy Constance Stratton. Born on March 24, 1899 (some sources cite 1898), in Brookfield, Missouri; daughter of Richard Lee Stratton (a Baptist minister) and Anna (Troxler) Stratton; Ottawa University, Kansas, B.A., 1920; University of Chicago, M.A., 1924; Columbia University, Ph.D., 1932.*

*Became the first director of the Coast Guard Women's Reserve upon its creation (1942); served as director of personnel at the International Monetary Fund (1947–50); served as national executive director of the Girl Scouts of America (1950–60).*

Born in 1899 into a family that moved frequently to accommodate her father's Baptist ministry, Dorothy Stratton spent her youth in various small towns in Missouri and Kansas. She was a motivated and enthusiastic student with excellent grades, loving each school she attended and participating in many extracurricular activities. During her undergraduate years at Ottawa University in Kansas, she was an active member of the school paper, assistant editor of the school annual, a member of the student council, and a basketball and tennis player.

After graduating from college in 1920, Stratton began her career in an academic setting, taking a teaching position at a high school in Renton, Washington. She then took administrative posts in two California schools in the mid-1920s, and continued her own education at the University of Chicago, from which she received a master's degree in psychology in 1924. Stratton earned a doctorate in student personnel administration from Columbia University in 1932, with her thesis published the following year as *Problems of Students in a Graduate School*. That year she was appointed dean of women and associate professor of psychology at Purdue University. The university's reputation rested largely on the strength of its agricultural and engineering courses, so Stratton set about molding the science curriculum to make it more appealing to women students. Her experiment met with such success that women's enrollment doubled at Purdue. Stratton was also behind the construction of three residence halls for women and a center for employment placement for women at the school. Considering the "character, citizenship, and culture" of students nurtured by universities as being as important as the education received there, in 1940 she published, with **Helen B. Schleman**, *Your Best Foot Forward*, a social guide for women students based on extensive research. That same year she was promoted to a full professorship.

Though she was comfortably ensconced in the university setting, Stratton uprooted herself with the advent of World War II to lend her energies to the war effort. (She later credited *Lillian Moller Gilbreth**, then a professor of management at Purdue, with encouraging her to join the military.) In 1942, she left Purdue to serve on the selection board of the Women's Army Auxiliary Corps, and entered the Women Appointed for Volunteer Emergency Service (WAVES). After taking the first WAVES indoctrination class at Smith College in Massachusetts that year, Stratton became a lieutenant in this women's branch of the naval reserve.

In November 1942, she began serving in the office of the head of the Coast Guard, organizing a proposed women's reserve for that branch of the service. Towards the end of the month, the Coast Guard Women's Reserve was established by President Franklin D. Roosevelt, with the intention of allowing more male sailors to serve at sea by employing women in onshore jobs. By December, Stratton had become the reserve's director and first woman officer, with the rank of lieutenant commander. It was at her suggestion that the new women's reserve became known as SPARS, from the first letters of the Coast Guard motto "Semper Paratus, Always Ready." Although neither SPARS nor WAVES were combat units (SPARS were prohibited from serving outside the 48 contiguous states, and initially were forbidden to give direct orders to men), they were paid the same as were men in their ranks, and served vital supporting functions in the military. Some 10,000 enlisted women and 1,000 officers had joined the SPARS by the end of the war. Stratton, who had been promoted to commander and then to captain in quick succession in 1944, ended her service with the Coast Guard in 1946, at which time she was awarded the Legion of Merit.

Stratton served as director of personnel of the International Monetary Fund in Washington, D.C., from 1947 to 1950, following that position with ten years as executive director of the Girl Scouts of America. In 1962, she sat on the President's Commission on the Employment of the Handicapped and was consultant for vocational rehabilitation to the Department of Health, Education and Welfare. Still alert and active, and living in West Lafayette, Indiana, Stratton was honored for her pioneering efforts in the military on her 100th birthday in 1999.

**SOURCES:**

Block, Maxine, ed. *Current Biography 1943*. NY: H.W. Wilson, 1943.

McHenry, Robert, ed. *Famous American Women*. NY: Dover, 1980.

## Stratton, Helen (fl. 1891–1925)

*British children's book illustrator. Flourished between 1891 and 1925.*

Selected works as illustrator: Songs for the Little People *(1896)*; Beyond the Border *(1898)*; The Fairy Tales of Hans Christian Andersen *(1899)*; The Arabian Nights Entertainments *(1899)*; Grimm's Fairy Tales *(1903)*; Heroic Legends *(1908)*; The Princess and the Goblin *(1911)*; The Princess and Curdie *(1912)*; A Book of Myths *(1915)*.

A popular turn-of-the-century illustrator, Helen Stratton lent her art-nouveau style to numerous works of fairy tale and folklore. In 1898, she provided 167 illustrations for Walter Douglas Campbell's *Beyond the Border*, a folklore collection which was considered one of the best to appear after Jacobs and Batten's *Celtic Fairy Tales*. The following year, Stratton was at the height of her career with her illustrations for *The Fairy Tales of Hans Christian Andersen*. Notes Richard Dalby: "[Stratton's] bold and humorous style was perfectly suited to the phantasmagorical world of 'The Little Mermaid,' 'The Garden of Paradise,' 'The Star Queen,' 'The Emperor's New Clothes,' and thirty Andersen tales." Also in 1899, Stratton was among those illustrators, including W. Heath Robinson, whose work appeared on the pages of *The Arabian Nights Entertainments*. Her schedule at the time likely demanded the production of a minimum of two or three illustrations per day so as to meet the deadlines for such commissions.

Other Stratton-illustrated titles appeared in the following years, including *Grimm's Fairy Tales*, *Heroic Legends*, and *A Book of Myths*. In 1911 and 1912 respectively, her illustrations for the classics *The Princess and the Goblin* and *The Princess and Curdie* proved highly popular.

**SOURCES:**

Dalby, Richard. *The Golden Age of Children's Book Illustration*. NY: Gallery, 1991.

## Stratton, Mercy Lavinia (1841–1919).

*See Warren, Lavinia.*

## Stratton-Porter, Gene (1863–1924)

*American writer and naturalist who publicized her concern for the threatened wildlife habitats of North America through enormously successful magazine columns, novels, photograph collections, and films.* Name variations: *Gene Stratton Porter. Born Geneva Grace Stratton on August 17, 1863, in Wabash County, Indiana; died on December 6, 1924, in Los Angeles, California; daughter of Mark Stratton (a farmer and minister) and Mary (Schallenberger) Stratton; left Wabash high school without a degree, 1883; married Charles Darwin Porter (a chemist), on April 21, 1886; children: daughter Jeanette Porter-Meehan (b. 1888).*

*Began publishing photographs and nature essays in magazines (1900); published first book,* The Song of the Cardinal *(1903); was a bestselling fiction author and sought-after columnist (1905); began financing and producing films based on her work (1922).*

*Selected writings:* The Song of the Cardinal: A Love Story *(Bobbs-Merrill, 1903); (illustrated by E. Stetson Crawford)* Freckles *(Doubleday, Page, 1904 [other editions illustrated by Wladyslaw T. Benda, Doubleday, Page, 1912, Thomas Fogarty, Doubleday, Page, 1921, Ruth Ives, Junior Deluxe Editions, 1957, and Michael Lowenbein, Whitman, 1965]);* What I Have Done with Birds *(Bobbs-Merrill, 1907, also published as* Friends in Feathers, *Doubleday, Page, 1917); (illustrated by Oliver Kemp)* At the Foot of the Rainbow *(Outing Publishing, 1907);* Birds of the Bible *(Eaton & Mains, 1909); (illustrated by W.T. Benda)* A Girl of the Limberlost *(Doubleday, Page, 1909);* Music of the Wild *(Eaton & Mains, 1910); (illustrated by W.L. Jacobs)* The Harvester *(Doubleday, Page, 1911);* Moths of the Limberlost *(Doubleday, Page, 1912);* After the Flood *(Bobbs-Merrill, 1912); (illustrated by Herman Pfeifer)* Laddie: A True Blue Story *(Doubleday, Page, 1913);* Birds of the Limberlost *(Doubleday, Page, 1914); (illustrated by Frances Rogers)* Michael O'Halloran *(Doubleday, Page, 1915); (self-illustrated)* Morning Face *(Doubleday, Page, 1916);* A Daughter of the Land *(Doubleday, Page, 1918);* Homing with the Birds: The History of a Lifetime of Personal Experiences with the Birds *(Doubleday, Page, 1919);* Her Father's Daughter *(Doubleday, Page, 1921); (illustrated by Gordon Grant)* The Fire Bird *(Doubleday, Page, 1922); (poems, illustrated by Edward E. Winchell)* Jesus of the Emerald *(Doubleday, Page, 1923);* The White Flag *(Doubleday, Page, 1923); (illustrated by G.*

*Grant)* The Keeper of the Bees *(Doubleday, Page, 1925);* Tales You Won't Believe *(Doubleday, Page, 1925);* Let Us Highly Resolve *(Doubleday, Page, 1927); (illustrated by Lee Thayer)* The Magic Garden *(Doubleday, Page, 1927).*

*Adaptations—movies:* Michael O'Halloran *(produced by Gene Stratton-Porter, 1923, Republic Pictures, 1937, Windsor Pictures, 1948);* Girl of the Limberlost *(produced by Gene Stratton-Porter, 1924, Monogram Pictures, 1934, Columbia Pictures, 1945);* Keeper of the Bees *(produced by Gene Stratton-Porter, 1925, Monogram Pictures, 1935, Columbia Pictures, 1947);* Laddie *(produced by Gene Stratton-Porter, 1926, RKO Radio Pictures, 1935, RKO Pictures, 1940);* Any Man's Wife *(based on* Michael O'Halloran, *Republic Pictures, 1937);* Romance of the Limberlost *(based on* Girl of the Limberlost, *Monogram Pictures, 1938).*

During the first two decades of the 20th century, Gene Stratton-Porter was one of the most famous women in the United States. Her writing reached an audience of 50 million Americans and was translated into 14 languages abroad. Although her work is no longer popular with critics or the general public, its importance cannot be discounted. Stratton-Porter played a major role in the cultural life of the United States. She brought messages of hope to families struggling to better their situations and of support to women struggling with the arduous tasks expected of turn-of-the-century homemakers. Most important, through her novels and essays she helped all Americans rediscover the beauties of the natural world and gain an awareness of the need for cautious development and conservation practices.

Stratton-Porter grew up on a farm in the Wabash Valley of Indiana. Geneva (later shortened to Gene) was the youngest of 12 children, and by the time of her birth in 1863 her parents had already spent 25 years transforming their frontier territory into a beautiful, comfortable, and profitable home. Her father Mark Stratton was not only an energetic farmer but an active citizen. He encouraged the improvement of local roads, canals, and schools and served as minister for the nearby Methodist church. Her mother **Mary Schallenberger Stratton** served as the model for Gene's ideal of womanhood: she was "capable." She transformed the wild and domestic plants of her fields into food, medicine, and even perfume. Several older siblings remained at home, and Stratton-Porter benefited from hearing them recite their lessons, while their labor al-

*Opposite page*

𝒢ene 𝒮tratton-𝒫orter

lowed her to escape the household chores that usually would have fallen to a farm daughter.

Stratton-Porter always referred to the years of her farm life as an idyll, just as she portrayed them in her novel *Laddie*, a fictionalized account of her childhood. She drew on her memories to describe the traditions of country weddings and courtship, the round of chores and labor needed to run the farm, and the rules of rural social life. *Laddie* also offers a record of young Stratton-Porter's early love affair with nature. Gene enjoyed the run of the barns, woods and fields surrounding her home. She made friends with the birds and delighted in discovering their nests and their habits. She tended her own wildflower garden and nursed a steady stream of injured animals. As a child, Stratton-Porter explained to her parents that she could hear the rhythm of the earth, a pronouncement that led her father to call in the family doctor. The doctor confirmed what the family already suspected: there was absolutely nothing wrong with the child, but she was undeniably different from other girls.

Unfortunately, the image of the happy home portrayed in *Laddie* was not entirely accurate. Although her father was loving and always encouraged Gene's love of nature and her writing career, he was also imperious with his children and notoriously frugal with his cash. As an adolescent and young woman, Stratton-Porter chafed at his control. Nor is the portrait of the mother exact. Mary Porter had given birth to 12 children and built a homestead, but, a few years after Gene's birth, Mary contracted typhoid and never completely recovered her strength. Part of the reason Gene enjoyed such unusual freedom as a child was that her mother was increasingly confined to a chair or bed.

Most important, the real Laddie, Gene's older brother Leander, did not live to return from college and pursue his sweetheart as did the "Laddie" of Stratton-Porter's novel. Instead, Leander was drowned while swimming one hot summer day in 1872, at age 18. For Gene, it was a double tragedy. Not only did she lose a beloved older brother, but she soon lost her country home as well. Leander was the only brother who loved farming, and his parents had planned for him to take over their homestead. After his death, the father, now 60, had little heart for continuing the heavy work, and in 1874 he leased the farm and moved his family ten miles away into the town of Wabash, where they lived near an older daughter, **Anastasia**, her husband, and children. Leander's death also hastened his mother's decline. Mary Porter died early in 1875, only a few months

after the move to town. By age 12, Gene had lost her brother, her mother, and the magical world of her childhood.

The move to Wabash deprived Stratton-Porter of her plants and animals, but it gave her access to the public schools and to girls her own age. After recovering from the initial shock at the differences between country and town manners (an experience she described in her novel *Girl of the Limberlost*), she enjoyed her new social life. The schoolhouse, however, was another matter. "In the whole of my school life," she wrote later, "I never had one teacher who made the slightest effort to discover what I cared for personally, what I had been born to do, or who made any attempt to help me in any direction I evinced an inclination to develop." She had great difficulties with mathematics and withdrew from school without graduating in 1883. Stratton-Porter never regretted her lack of a high school diploma; she always insisted that her most profitable learning came from self-education and solitary reading.

*What* measure of success I have had comes through preserving my individual point of view.

—Gene Stratton-Porter

The year 1883 was also a time of family tension. With Gene's sister Anastasia dying at a cancer clinic, Mark Stratton had volunteered to move in with her husband and had committed his daughters to running the house and caring for Anastasia's young children. Gene resented her father's disposition of her and her sister's lives, and she was angry at his constant refusal to grant them the money they requested for clothes or entertainment. She knew her father was not poor; the battles they fought over money had less to do with finances than with a contest of wills between two strong individuals.

For several summers, Gene had accompanied her older sisters to Sylvan Lake, an Indiana resort that offered a "Chautauqua"—a series of educational and religious lectures held in a natural setting. In the summer of 1884, Stratton-Porter arrived home to find a letter from a young man who had also been vacationing at Sylvan Lake. Charles Darwin Porter wrote that he had seen Gene at the lectures and had hoped to arrange an introduction, but Gene had left before he had the chance. In his early 30s, Charles was a successful pharmacist from Decatur, Indiana. Even though he included the names of several mutual acquaintances as character references, Gene was hesitant to respond, writing in reply: "If you noted me sufficiently to remember me this long, then I am sure that you saw also that I behaved in a quiet and ladylike manner. But can I keep it if I correspond with an entire stranger?" The awkwardly begun courtship flourished, however, and in 1886 Gene Stratton married and moved to Decatur. Initially, she went by the married name of Gene Porter, although in later life she preferred Stratton-Porter. Her only child, **Jeanette Porter-Meehan**, was born in 1888.

Charles Porter was not only a pharmacist but an entrepreneur, and within a few years of their marriage he had expanded his drug store holdings, purchased a hotel, and opened a bank. Gene felt frustrated, however, by the similarities to her adolescence: she lived in a prosperous house but had no money of her own. She also chafed at the society of Decatur. Stratton-Porter had little interest in joining local clubs and was regarded as peculiar by the other women. Finally, in 1890, she persuaded Charles to move the family to the smaller town of Geneva, where Charles was closer to his new business ventures and she was closer to the countryside she loved.

Her new home lay less than a mile from the famous Limberlost Swamp of Indiana, a pocket of damp wilderness teeming with wildlife. Suddenly Gene seemed to rediscover the energy and passions of her youth as she explored the unfamiliar environment. During the next few years, neighbors grew accustomed to the sight of her khaki-clad figure in their fields, and she acquired a reputation as the "Birdwoman." Friends and strangers alike appeared at her door with unusual or injured animals.

Stratton-Porter experienced an intellectual renaissance as well. She embarked on a serious effort to broaden her education and improve her writing. She read avidly and joined discussion clubs that forced her to write and present papers before groups. She even founded her own literary society dedicated to the study of American and English literature. In 1893, she was inspired by the modern architecture on exhibit at the Chicago World's Fair and undertook the design and construction of a 14-room "cabin" at the edge of the Limberlost Swamp.

In 1895, her husband and daughter gave Gene a camera which she promptly turned upon her beloved swamp. Successful nature photography required unique skills at the turn of the century. There were no telephoto lenses, thus the photographer had to accustom animals to the sight of humans and their bulky equipment. The flash of the powder that marked the photo frightened the subjects, making retakes impossible. Despite the difficulties, Stratton-Porter found that she was uniquely qualified to photograph animals. "My first feeling on going afield," she wrote in *Homing with the Birds* in 1919, "was one of amazement at what my early days among the birds had taught me. . . . I knew what location each bird would choose for her nest, how she would build it, brood and care for her young. . . . The birds had not changed in the slightest; nor had I." Stratton-Porter was pleased with her work. Most Americans could study birds only through prints of the paintings by James Audubon. Stratton-Porter felt that Audubon's paintings looked like the stuffed corpses that had served as his models, while her own photos revealed the sparkling personalities of her feathered subjects.

By 1900, Gene Stratton-Porter had begun to see herself not as a nature lover but as a working naturalist. Tracking wildlife, recording observations, and capturing images in photographs combined her artistic and scientific interests. In 1900, she published her first magazine article on the habits of birds, and she was soon a regular contributor to several outdoor life publications.

Charles encouraged her work. Initially, he was concerned by her forays into the swamp (which possessed both human and natural dangers), and he began to plan weekends in the Wabash River valley to offer Gene a safer environment for her expeditions. Later, Charles grew confident that Gene (armed with a revolver) could protect herself. He also ordered and mixed the chemicals Gene required for her photography and paid an assistant to help cart the 40 pounds of plates and equipment into the woods. At home, both Charles and Jeanette grew accustomed to moving cocoons off chairs and injured birds off the table before sitting down to dinner.

Despite Charles' support, Gene was reluctant to let her husband know she was experimenting with new writing styles. At some time during the 1890s, she had showed samples of her poetry to a harsh critic (probably her father) whose response had devastated her self-confidence. When Gene began to submit fiction to magazines after 1901, she rented her own post-office box so that Charles would not find any rejection letters. She even hid her efforts to write her first novel from her husband until the final publishing stage, when she learned that married women could not sign legal documents without their husband's consent. Her fears of failure were unnecessary. The public loved her work, and Stratton-Porter quickly found wealth and respect as a writer. She published her first fiction

story in 1901, her first novel in 1903, and her second novel in 1904.

Between 1900 and her death in 1924, Stratton-Porter published 12 novels, 8 nonfiction books, and nearly 300 magazine articles. As her output suggests, she wrote effortlessly. Stratton-Porter was never able to understand how others struggled with "writer's block" and constant revisions. From 1900 on, she kept to an orderly schedule: during the warm weather, she completed fieldwork in the mornings and recorded her observations in the afternoons; winters were spent in the production of books and articles.

Although Stratton-Porter was proud of her writing, she was also honest about its limitations. She never considered her fiction writing as "literature"; rather, she saw it as merely a different vehicle for spreading her creed of nature appreciation. Nor did Stratton-Porter class her writing with that of the scientific community. She ignored census figures and migration statistics and concentrated instead on describing the breeding habits and social behavior of animals. Although many professional naturalists scorned her work, Stratton-Porter earned the praise of America's most famous conservationist, President Theodore Roosevelt, for her success in encouraging greater appreciation for the outdoors among the general public.

Stratton-Porter's works were popular in part because her themes dovetailed well with the concerns of a newly industrialized society. Americans were obsessed with the recent closing of the frontier and tormented with nostalgia for their rural past. Stratton-Porter was also popular because her stories embodied the Horatio Alger theme dear to aspiring Americans. Her wholesome characters struggled to better their situations and triumphed in love, money, and profession. Her novels differed from the normal format, however, in featuring strong female leads. Stratton-Porter had a special interest in providing models of intelligent and capable women. She worried that the Victorian ideal of the sheltered, fragile female was producing women far inferior to the pioneer women of the past. In later years, Stratton-Porter was equally impatient with the "flapper" movement, which she felt converted women into yet another kind of decorative object. Stratton-Porter could never be called a feminist (she always maintained that a woman's greatest contribution lay in providing a safe and welcoming home for her family), but she did see herself as a defender of all those women who worked hard to maintain a home, but who received little respect in either the Victorian or the "flapper" age. In Stratton-Porter's view, women and men were equal partners in constructing a family, a home, and a society.

After 1910, Stratton-Porter began to consider moving from the Limberlost Cabin. The discovery of oil in the region (Charles Porter himself operated 65 wells) and the search for hardwood for the booming Chicago furniture industry had devastated the environment and destroyed the potential for fieldwork. In 1912, she and Charles decided to build a new home at their old retreat of Sylvan Lake. Once again, Stratton-Porter designed and supervised construction of the house, which contained 20 rooms, including a professional darkroom. Increasingly conscious of the destruction of the natural environment, she embarked upon the creation of an extensive botanical garden dedicated to the preservation of native trees, shrubs and flowers. Over the years, she and her assistants transplanted thousands of varieties of plants to the grounds of "Wildflower Woods."

In 1918, Stratton-Porter admitted herself to a health clinic for a rest cure, an uncharacteristic act which hinted at her discouraged state. Her home at Sylvan Lake had fallen victim to the same development that earlier destroyed the Limberlost. Canals drained the water level and new roads replaced animals with people. Stratton-Porter's fame had also attracted a swarm of curiosity seekers who constantly invaded her privacy. In addition, her daughter Jeanette and her grandchildren had begun to pay extended visits that revealed what Stratton-Porter had long feared; her son-in-law was a hopeless alcoholic.

The 1918 rest cure helped Stratton-Porter bear up to another year in Indiana, but she was no longer enamored of her home. In 1919, she visited siblings in California, and in 1920 she committed herself to moving to Los Angeles. Charles remained in Indiana where he was still active in business. Jeanette wrote that her parents remained friendly and affectionate but were content to limit themselves to summertime visits in Indiana and occasional visits by Charles to California.

Jeanette finally obtained a divorce and followed her mother to California where she witnessed the final chapter in Stratton-Porter's varied career. In Los Angeles, Gene Stratton-Porter discovered a society that valued art and literature and considered her talented rather than eccentric. Stratton-Porter was also intrigued by the new medium of film. In 1917, her novel *Laddie* had been filmed, but Stratton-Porter had been unhappy with the liberties the producer took with the story. In 1921, she began supervising the production of her films, which were scripted by her daughter. Three years later, she founded her own film company, which gave her complete artistic and financial control over production.

Stratton-Porter maintained her older interests as well. She designed and supervised the construction of two new residences, a summer home on Catalina Island and a year-round residence in Bel Air. Stratton-Porter rediscovered her youthful enthusiasm for verse and wrote *Firebird* and *Euphorbia*, long narrative poems. She also explored the California countryside and the plants and animals it contained.

In California, Stratton-Porter continued to write fiction, although she realized that American taste had changed and her novels were no longer bestsellers. The American public, disillusioned with World War I and caught up in the materialism of the 1920s, no longer responded to her innocent rural characters. Nevertheless, Stratton-Porter felt her perspective was needed. In 1922, the editor of *McCall's* magazine asked if she had a message for the women of America. "Not one," she responded, "but one hundred." Her editorials helped *McCall's* rise to become one of the most popular American magazines of the '20s, reaching an audience of one million readers. In her columns, she offered advice on everything from how to attract wild birds to the garden to how to keep a sanitary kitchen and raise strong children. One frequent subject was the need for decency standards in the motion-picture industry. She was disgusted by Hollywood's tendency to add salacious material to every storyline, but she did not want to eliminate all adult content from films. She encouraged women to write to studios and demand that they separate adult and juvenile content so that families could take their children to the theaters.

In 1924, at age 61, Gene Stratton-Porter had recently completed a series of editorials for *McCall's*, two new novels, a narrative poem, and four films. Her husband Charles, who had his own apartment in the Bel Air house, had visited the previous winter, and her daughter Jeanette worked with her in the film industry. Her active life was ended abruptly, however, when her limousine was struck by a streetcar on December 6.

Stratton-Porter's influence on the American public could not be erased by her death. During her lifetime, her novels, films, and essays reached millions of Americans; for 17 years, her books sold at the rate of 1,700 copies a day. Her nature photographs are still praised for their artistry and their content, and her home, Limberlost Cabin, now a state historic site in Indiana, is dedicated to promoting conservation practices. Her greatest legacy, however, is evident in the grateful letters received by Stratton-Porter over the years from readers who learned to see the rich world surrounding them through her enthusiastic perspective.

**SOURCES:**

Long, Judith Reick. *Gene Stratton Porter: Novelist and Naturalist*. Indianapolis, IN: Indiana Historical Society, 1990.

Porter-Meehan, Jeanette. *The Lady of the Limberlost: The Life and Letters of Gene Stratton-Porter*. NY: Doubleday, Doran, 1928.

Richards, Bertrand. *Gene Stratton Porter*. Boston, MA: Twayne, 1980.

**SUGGESTED READING:**

Morrow, Barbara. *From Ben-Hur to Sister Carrie, Remembering the Lives of Lew Wallace, James Whitcomb Riley, Booth Tarkington, Gene Stratton-Porter and Theodore Dreiser*. Indianapolis, IN: Guild Press of Indiana, 1995.

Plum, Sydney Landon. *Coming Through the Swamp: The Nature Writings of Gene Stratton Porter*. Salt Lake City, UT: University of Utah Press, 1996.

**RELATED MEDIA:**

Reprints of Stratton Porter's writing, audio tapes and a video biography ("Gene Stratton-Porter, Voice of the Limberlost") are available from the Limberlost State Historic Site in Geneva, Indiana. The Indiana Historical Society also loans out visual material on Stratton-Porter for educational exhibits.

**Janice Lee Jayes**, historian, Washington, D.C.

# Straus, Ida (c. 1849–1912)

*American philanthropist. Born Ida Blun around 1849; died on April 15, 1912; married Isidor Straus; children: six, including Jesse Isidor Straus (b. 1872, an ambassador), Percy Selden Straus (b. 1876), and Nathan Straus.*

Ida and Isidor Straus were both well-known philanthropists who owned Macy's department store. They also shared a close marriage. "When they were apart, they wrote to each other every day," said **Joan Adler**, director of the Straus Historical Society. The Strauses were on the *Titanic* on the ill-fated night of April 15, 1912. As the ship foundered, Ida Straus, who refused to get into a lifeboat, urged her maid to take her place and handed the young woman her fur coat, saying, "I won't need this anymore." The Strauses were last seen in an embrace as the *Titanic* went down. Inscribed on their vault in a Bronx cemetery are the words: "Many waters cannot quench love, neither can the floods drown it."

**RELATED MEDIA:**

*Titanic* (film), starring **Kate Winslet** and Leonardo DiCaprio, directed by James Cameron, with Lew Palter and **Elsa Raven** portraying the Strauses, 1998.

# Strauss und Torney, Lulu von (1873–1956)

*German writer whose heroic ballads are considered among the best in the genre of the early 20th century. Born on September 20, 1873, in Bückeburg, Germany; died on June 19, 1956, in Jena, East Germany; daughter of a general major who served as adjunct to the duke of Schaumburg-Lippe; attended high school in Bückeburg; married Eugen Diederichs (a publisher), in 1916 (died 1930).*

*Selected works: (poetry)* Balladen und Lieder *(Ballads and Songs, 1902),* Neue Balladen und Lieder *(New Ballads and Songs, 1907),* Reif steht die Saat *(The Crop is Ripe, 1919, reissued with collected poems, 1926, 1929),* Erde der Väter *(Our Forefathers' Soil, 1936); (novels)* Aus Bauernstamm *(Made out of Peasant Wood, 1902),* Luzifer *(1907),* Judas *(1911),* Der jüngste Tag *(The Day of Judgement, 1922); (short stories)* Bauernstolz *(Peasant's Pride, 1901),* Das Erbe *(The Inheritance, 1905),* Das Meerminneke *(The Sea Maid, 1906),* Die Legende der Felsenstadt *(The Legend of the City of Rock, 1911),* Auge um Auge *(Eye for Eye, 1933); (nonfiction)* Die Dorfgeschichte in der modernen Literatur *(The Village Story in Modern Literature, 1901),* Das Leben der Heiligen Elisabeth *(The Life of Saint Elisabeth, 1926),* Deutsches Frauenleben zur Zeit der Sachsenkaiser und Hohenstaufer *(Life of Women at the Time of the Saxonian and Hohenstaufer Emperors, 1927),* Eugen Diederichs, Leben und Werk *(Eugen Diederichs, Life and Work, 1936),* Annette von Droste-Hülshoff *(1936); (memoirs)* Das verborgene Angesicht, Erinnerungen *(The Veiled Face, Memories, 1943).*

A prolific writer of poetry, prose, criticism and correspondence whose work is deeply linked to the northern region of Germany where she was born, Lulu von Strauss und Torney was popular and influential with the reading public of her day. In the later years of her life, the mythology, heroic human struggles, and romanticized "sons of the soil" which permeate her poetry and fiction also found much favor with members of the Nazi Party; their championing of her work is perhaps the largest reason why even her best writing is now little read.

Strauss und Torney was born in 1873, the daughter of a German officer who served as adjunct to the duke of Schaumburg-Lippe. She was raised in an intellectual atmosphere, traveling extensively while still young, and supplemented her high school education in Bückeburg with wide reading in the duke's library. In her 20s, she became associated with the literary circle of Börries von Münchhausen, a German revivalist of ballad poetry, and towards the end of the 19th century she, too, began writing ballads and stories. She also frequently visited Berlin, and there befriended poet *Agnes Miegel, whose work explored many of the same themes as her own, as well as Theodor Heuss, later the president of West Germany. (Her correspondence with Heuss would be published in 1965.) After publishing a collection of stories focusing on peasant life in 1901, Strauss und Torney saw the publication of her first collection of poetry, *Balladen und Lieder* (Ballads and Songs), in 1902.

Strauss und Torney steeped her ballads in myths, legends, and historical events, using dramatic structures that soon made her one of the leading ballad poets of the early 20th century. As a naturalistic poet, she frequently portrayed the conflict between man and nature, with the noble human mind emerging triumphant over weakness and failure. Although her stereotypical portrayal of peasants, traditions, and harvests has not aged well, and her lyric poetry in particular is considered weak, the recurrent theme of the unspoiled "people of the land" fit in well with the taste of the times. *Balladen und Lieder* was followed by several other popular poetry collections, including *Reif steht die Saat* (The Crop is Ripe, 1919), which was republished with the inclusion of her collected poems in 1926 and 1929. An enlarged collection, *Erde der Väter* (Our Forefathers' Soil), was published in 1936.

The themes of Strauss und Torney's poetry recur in her fiction, which consists mostly of historical novels set in rural Germany. *Auge um Auge* (Eye for an Eye), originally published in a collection in 1909 and republished as the title piece of another collection in 1933, is considered by some to be her most powerful novella. *Luzifer* (1907), set in the 13th century, was the first of her longer novels, followed by *Judas* (1911), which explores the result of news of the French Revolution reaching a rural area of Westphalia. Her 1921 novel *Der jüngste Tag* (Judgment Day), set in rural Westphalia during the turmoil of the Reformation, is regarded as her masterpiece.

Married in 1916 to publisher Eugen Diederichs, Strauss und Torney lived with him in Jena, Germany, where in addition to working on her own writing she served as a reader for his publishing company. She remained in Jena after her husband's death in 1930, and six years later published a biography of him. In 1938, she published another biography, *Annette von Droste-Hülshoff: Einsamkeit und Helle, Ihr Leben in Briefen* (*Annette von Droste-Hülshoff: Solitude and Clarity, Her Life in Letters), about the major 19th-century writer whose work, like her own, drew heavily upon rural German life. During World War II, while her popularity remained high, Strauss und Torney published her memoirs, *Das verborgene Angesicht, Erinnerungen* (The Veiled Face, Memories, 1943). She died in Jena, then a part of East Germany, in 1956.

**SOURCES:**

Bédé, Jean-Albert, and William B. Edgerton, eds. *Columbia Dictionary of Modern European Literature*. 2nd ed. NY: Columbia University Press, 1980.

Buck, Claire, ed. *The Bloomsbury Guide to Women's Literature*. NY: Prentice Hall, 1992.

Garland, Mary. *The Oxford Companion to German Literature*. 3rd ed. Oxford: Oxford University Press, 1997.

Wilson, Katharina M. *An Encyclopedia of Continental Women Writers*. NY: Garland, 1991.

# Streatfeild, Noel (1895–1986)

*British novelist and children's writer. Name variations: (pseudonyms) Noelle Sonning, Susan Scarlett. Born on December 24, 1895, in Amberley, near Arundel, Sussex, England; died on September 11, 1986, in London; daughter of William Champion Streatfeild (a vicar and later a bishop) and Janet Nancy (Venn) Streatfeild; attended St. Leonard's College and Laleham School in Eastbourne, Hastings; graduated from the Royal Academy of Dramatic Art in London; never married; no children.*

*Selected writings:* The Whicharts *(1931)*; Parson's Nine *(1932)*; Ballet Shoes: A Story of Three Children on the Stage *(1936)*; Caroline England *(1937)*; Tennis Shoes *(1937)*; The Circus is Coming *(1938, published in the U.S. as* Circus Shoes*)*; Clothes-Pegs *(1939)*; The House in Cornwall *(1940)*; The Children of Primrose Lane *(1941)*; I Ordered a Table for Six *(1942)*; Harlequinade *(1943)*; Curtain Up *(1944)*; Saplings *(1945)*; Party Frock *(1946)*; Grass in Piccadilly *(1947)*; Pirouette *(1948)*; The Painted Garden *(1949, published in the U.S. as* Movie Shoes*)*; Mothering Sunday *(1950)*; White Boots *(1951)*; Aunt Clara *(1952)*; The First Book of Ballet *(1953)*; The Bell Family *(1954)*; The Grey Family *(1956)*; Wintle's Wonders *(1957)*; The First Book of England *(1958)*; Ballet Annual *(1959)*; Look at the Circus *(1960)*; The Silent Speaker *(1961)*; Apple Bough *(1962)*; A Vicarage Family *(1963)*; The Children on the Top Floor *(1964)*; Away from the Vicarage *(1965)*; The Growing Summer *(1966)*; Caldicott Place *(1967)*; Gemma *(1968)*; Gemma and Sisters *(1968)*; Gemma Alone *(1969)*; Goodbye Gemma *(1969)*; Thursday's Child *(1970)*;

Beyond the Vicarage (1971); The Boy Pharaoh, Tutankhamen (1972); When the Siren Wailed (1974); A Young Person's Guide to Ballet (1975); Gran-Nannie (1976); Meet the Maitlands (1978); The Maitlands: All Change at Cuckly Place (1979).

The rebellious daughter of a country vicar, Noel Streatfeild was born in 1895 in Sussex, England, towards the end of the Victorian era. Her mother **Janet Venn Streatfeild**, a descendant of the prison reformer *Elizabeth Fry, and father William Champion Streatfeild, who would later become a bishop in the Church of England, were careful to observe all the proprieties inherent to their status as representatives of the Church, and raised their six children with love, strictness, and an inculcation of duty to their social and moral responsibilities. She later wrote of her home environment, "bound as it was within the walls of the vicarage . . . everything was clear-cut. God was in his Heaven; the King on his throne; you voted Conservative; the English were the finest people in the world; there was no grey about it—you were right or you were wrong." While the family was by no means wealthy, their social status demanded that they employ help, and Streatfeild grew up with a governess and several household servants; kindly nannies and women servants who offer love and guidance to higher-class youngsters would later appear in many of her children's books.

Streatfeild was expelled for insubordination from her first high school and, after the family moved to her father's new parish in Eastbourne, attended Laleham School there with her sisters. It was at Laleham that she first received recognition for her talents as a writer, although around that time, having frequently acted in parish plays, she was becoming more interested in the theater. This interest was stimulated when, as a teenager, she saw *Ninette de Valois** perform with a traveling troupe of child dancers, a possible early influence on her later highly successful stories about young dancers and actors. Streatfeild worked in a munitions factory during World War I and following the Armistice moved to London to study acting at the Royal Academy of Dramatic Art. Shortly after graduating, she signed a two-year contract with a Shakespearean repertory company. For the next ten years, she worked as an actress, including tours in South Africa and Australia, gaining detailed knowledge of the theater world that would later lend authenticity to such books as The Whicharts and Curtain Up. During that tour in Australia in 1929, however, Streatfeild found out through a newspaper article that her father unexpectedly

had died. Deeply shaken, she quit the stage soon after, moved back to London and began to write.

Her first published novel, The Whicharts (1931), was written for adults, but focuses on three young girls working in the theater. She published four more novels for adults over the next five years before **Mabel Carey**, a children's book editor at J.M. Dent publishers who had read The Whicharts, suggested she try writing a similar book for children. Streatfeild was markedly unenthusiastic, but at her publisher's urging finally agreed to try. The result was 1936's Ballet Shoes: A Story of Three Children on the Stage. The story of Pauline, Petrova and Posy and their hard work on stage and off proved hugely popular with children—it had sold 10 million copies by the 1990s—and remains perhaps her most famous book. (At one London bookstore, it was advertised with a window full of ballet shoes, among them a pair once worn by *Tamara Karsavina.) Again at Carey's suggestion, she next wrote the children's books Tennis Shoes (1937) and The Circus Is Coming (1938, published in the U.S. as Circus Shoes), having spent time with a traveling circus in America to research the book. The Circus Is Coming was awarded the Carnegie Medal as Best Children's Book of the Year. As **Nancy Huse** writes, Streatfeild is "credited with originating the widespread trend of 'career' and 'theater' novels for children, [but she] is more properly defined as a writer about vocation, especially about dedication to the arts. Her books include careful description of the work it takes to act Shakespearean roles, to dance in the chorus of a ballet, to sing in ways suited to a genre." Huse goes on to note how in many of Streatfeild's children's books, the child protagonists are working out of economic necessity, not sheer love of performing, and through their employment are supporting the family, biological or not, with whom they live.

Streatfeild lost her home and most of her possessions to bombs in the London Blitz during World War II. Working as a truck driver, an air-raid warden, and a full-time member of the Women's Voluntary Service organizing food distribution centers, she nonetheless wrote prolifically during the war. Among her children's books from these years were The House in Cornwall (1940) as well as The Children of Primrose Lane (1941) and Harlequinade (1943), the latter two set during wartime. Between 1939 and 1951, she also wrote a series of novels for adults under the pseudonym Susan Scarlett, many of them dealing with such issues as illegitimacy and homosexuality, including The Man in the Dark (1941) and Murder While You Work (1944). Using her own name, she also published the adult novel *I Ordered a Table for Six* (1942), concerning the after-effects of random, unexpected death. Streatfeild focused more deeply on writing for children after the war, although she would continue to write and publish adult novels through the beginning of the 1960s. *The Painted Garden* (1949, published in the U.S. as *Movie Shoes*), an unsentimental look at film acting, was inspired by a visit to Hollywood during which she watched child star *Margaret O'Brien making the movie version of *Frances Hodgson Burnett's *The Secret Garden*. *White Boots* (1951) focused on child ice skaters.

During the 1950s, Streatfeild also worked in radio, with a popular serial about the Bells, the family of a small-town vicar. The story was later made into a television series, and also spawned two of Streatfeild's children's books, *The Bell Family* (1954) and *New Town* (1960). In 1958, she published biographies of *Edith Nesbit, *Magic and the Magician: E. Nesbit and Her Children's Books*, and of Queen *Victoria. Now fully reconciled to and enjoying her role as a children's author, she also began compiling anthologies of children's literature, lecturing, writing book reviews for major magazines, and visiting libraries and schools. In the 1960s, she began writing an autobiographical trilogy, published as *The Vicarage Family* (1963), *Away from the Vicarage* (1965), and *Beyond the Vicarage* (1971). While some critics were beginning to feel that her work—particularly those stories that included such trappings as servants and nannies—was perhaps outdated, her popularity remained high, and her 1967 book *The Magic Summer* (originally published in England as *The Growing Summer*, 1966), in which four children spend a holiday in Ireland with their prickly great-aunt, is considered one of her best. Prominent and well respected throughout England, she also published numerous nonfiction books on history, opera, and ballet, as well as several advice books for children. About growing older, Streatfeild, who continued publishing until she was in her early 80s, once wrote: "Never willingly mention your health. People may ask how you are but they don't want to know. If you should be operated upon keep quiet about it." She died in London in 1986.

### SOURCES:

Commire, Anne, ed. *Something About the Author.* Vol. 20. Detroit, MI: Gale Research, 1980.

*Contemporary Authors, New Revision Series.* Vol. 31. Detroit, MI: Gale Research, 1990.

Huse, Nancy. "Noel Streatfeild," in *Dictionary of Literary Biography*, Vol. 160: *British Children's Writers, 1914–1960.* Edited by Donald R. Hettinga and Gary D. Schmidt. Detroit, MI: Gale Research, 1996.

Shattock, Joanne. *The Oxford Guide to British Women Writers.* Oxford: Oxford University Press, 1993.

# Street, Jessie (1889–1970)

*Australian women's rights advocate and United Nations official. Name variations: Jessie Lillingston; Jessie Mary Grey Street; Lady Street. Born Jessie Lillingston on April 18, 1889, in Chota Nagpur, India; died on July 2, 1970; daughter of Charles Lillingston (a British civil servant) and Mabel (Ogilvie) Lillingston; Women's College of Sydney University, B.A., 1910; married Kenneth Whistler Street (a lawyer and later a justice of the Supreme Court of New South Wales), in 1916; children: four.*

The daughter of Charles Lillingston and **Mabel Ogilvie Lillingston**, a descendant of one of the earliest white families to settle in Australia, Jessie Street was born in 1889 in India, where her father was posted with the British civil service. When she was seven years old, her mother inherited a station (ranch) near the Clarence River in New South Wales, Australia, and the family moved to the new property. Jessie was sent to England for her education, returning to attend college at the Women's College of Sydney University, from which she graduated in 1910. Bachelor's degree in hand, Street took ownership of a farm with the intention of proving the virtues of scientific dairy farming. She imported milking machines from Sweden and set up a milk test laboratory to great success. With her point made, she sold the farm and turned her attention to women's causes by becoming a member of the Conference on the International Council of Women. That conference in Rome was the first of many she would attend throughout Europe, America, India and Australia on behalf of both women's and social welfare causes.

Street traveled to the United States to train as a social worker in 1915, putting this experience to good use when she returned to Australia the following year and helped to establish the country's first Social Hygiene Association. She also married lawyer Kenneth Whistler Street that year and soon began a family that would grow to include four children. In 1918, she joined the League of Nations Union while maintaining her activities in various women's groups, including the National Council of Women, of which she served as secretary in 1920, and the Feminist Club. She would later serve as president of that group, which sought equal opportunities, social status and pay for women.

In 1929, feeling that current organizations were insufficient, Street set out to start a women's organization that would have real impact in bringing about equality. Aiming for greater parity in everything from social and moral standards to elected representation and employment and pay opportunities, as well as international harmony, her United Associations of Women (UAW) quickly found like-minded, primarily middle- and upper-class members throughout Australia. Street's social position as the wife of a Supreme Court Justice of New South Wales did not hurt her cause, and she spent most of the next 20 years as president of the organization. Advocating a campaign of gradual reform, she worked to unionize Australian nurses and fought legislation that forced women teachers who married to be dismissed from their jobs. Equal pay for women and wages for housewives were two other causes supported by the UAW.

Street's presidency of that organization led to her participation in the Australian Women's Charter, designed to address the needs of women during and after World War II, and in the Women for Canberra Movement. She also did assembly-line work in a shell factory for several years during the war, becoming a member of Australia's Amalgamated Iron and Munitions Workers Union. While her women's groups were not affiliated with any political parties, Street stood as the Labor Party candidate for a political seat in the Australian Parliament in 1943. Her campaign was unsuccessful (as would be a second run in 1946), but the political experience coupled with her extensive activist work made her the only woman selected to be part of Australia's delegation to the San Francisco conference on the foundation of the United Nations in 1945. Street focused her attention on the inclusion of equal rights for women in the charter of the United Nations and advocated the formation of the Commission on the Status of Women. After its creation, she served as vice-chair of the commission until 1949, when in the increasingly frosty atmosphere of the Cold War she was forced from the post on charges of being sympathetic to Communism. (The main evidence produced by her opponents was her relief work for Russian civilians, begun during the war, when the Soviet Union had been an ally.)

Back in Australia, Street became a constituent member of the Federal Council for Aboriginal Advancement, seeing significant parallels to the women's movement in the struggle of Aborigines for equal rights. "[T]he reasons given . . . for the discriminations practiced against coloured people were the same, and had the same basis," she noted, "as the discriminations practiced against women. . . . [T]he reason for these discriminations was to protect the status,

rights and privileges of the white man." She became Lady Street in 1956, when her husband was made a Knight Commander of the Order of St. Michael and St. George. Earlier a founder of and frequent contributor (1944–48) to *The Australian Women's Digest*, Street published her memoirs *Truth or Repose* in 1966, four years before her death.

**SOURCES:**

Radi, Heather, ed. *200 Australian Women: A Redress Anthology.* NSW, Australia: Women's Redress Press, 1988.

Rothe, Anna, ed. *Current Biography 1947.* NY: H.W. Wilson, 1947.

**Helga P. McCue,** freelance writer,
Waterford, Connecticut

# Street, Picabo (1971—)

*American Olympic downhill and slalom skier. Pronunciation: Peek-a-boo. Born in Triumph, Idaho, on April 3, 1971; daughter of Roland Street (a stonemason) and Dee Street (a music teacher).*

*Won a silver medal at the World Alpine Ski championships and a gold medal at the U.S. Alpine championships (1993); won a silver medal in the downhill event at the Olympic Games in Lillehammer, Norway (1994); became the first American woman to win a World Cup downhill title (1995), and repeated her performance the following year (1996); won the downhill title at the World championships (1996); won a gold medal at the Olympic Games in Nagano, Japan (1998).*

Picabo Street was born on April 3, 1971, in Triumph, Idaho, a town with only 50 residents. Her parents were archetypal "flower children," raising their own food and chopping wood for fuel. Intending to let their daughter choose her own name, Roland and **Dee Street** registered her as "Baby Girl" on her birth certificate. It was not until they discovered that Baby Girl needed a real name for a passport to Mexico that "Picabo," a Native American name meaning "shining waters," replaced Baby Girl.

Street's playmates in Triumph were all boys, and she fought to beat them in football, basketball, and soccer. These childhood games sharpened her zeal for winning, and she brought this competitive spirit to what became her sport of choice: skiing. Her first run on the slopes occurred when she was only five, and by the age of sixteen, Street had won the national junior titles in the downhill and super giant slalom (a combined slalom and downhill race commonly referred to as "Super-G") events. She had raw talent but was undisciplined by nature, leading to an expulsion from the U.S. ski team in July 1990 when she arrived at training camp out of shape and lackadaisical.

The expulsion was a wake-up call to the fun-loving athlete, who reevaluated her priorities and engaged in a rigorous training schedule to get back into shape. The discipline paid off as Street—ranked the best American woman skier and eighth in the world by 1992—pulled off a surprising silver-medal finish at the 1993 World Alpine Ski championships in Morioka, Japan. That year she also racked up significant victories in her homeland by winning both the U.S. Super-G title and the gold medal at the U.S. Alpine championships.

Despite these victories, Street had no expectations of taking a medal at the 1994 Olympic Games in Lillehammer, Norway. American skiers had been outperformed consistently by European competitors in past Olympics, and Street had not yet shed the "party-girl" reputation that kept many observers from taking her seriously. Thus, she surprised everyone, including herself, when she won the silver medal in the downhill event. The victory kicked off two seasons during which Street dominated the women's downhill events. During the 1995 season she won six of nine World Cup races, becoming the first American woman to take the World Cup downhill title. She repeated this victory the following year, while also winning a gold medal at the World championships in Sierra Nevada, Spain. Street's 1995 endorsement deal with Nike, to promote her own signature sneaker, was further proof of hergrowing stature in the world of sports; she was the company's only female winter athlete. Later endorsement deals included those with Pepsi and the U.S. Dairy Council (in a "Got Milk?" ad), and she also made a guest appearance on "Sesame Street."

With such impressive performances on the ski slopes, Street was positioned for a gold-medal run in the 1998 Winter Olympics in Nagano, Japan. However, a serious knee ligament injury in 1997 mandated a year of rehabilitation during which she was unable to enter any competitions. Even before she was back on skis, she demonstrated her characteristic competitive streak by riding piggyback while her coach skied the Nagano course so she could get a feel for what she would be facing. Her comeback trail included solid finishes in three World Cup downhill events, although she experienced a minor setback when she sustained a slight concussion in a fall just six days before the start of the Winter Games in February 1998. In the super giant slalom at Nagano, with Germany's

*Katja Seizinger the clear favorite to win, Street was second down the hill in 1:18.02, despite head and neck pain, and then watched astonished at the bottom as racer after racer failed to beat her time. She won by 100th of a second over Austria's Michaela Dorfmeister, who took the silver; Austria's Alexandra Meissnitzer won the bronze. (Seizinger came in 6th.) It was the closest race in the history of the Super G.

Street's injury problems were not yet over, however. Less than a month after her stunning Olympic victory, she fractured her femur in a devastating fall during the season's final World Cup downhill race in Switzerland, necessitating another long rehabilitation. The agonizing 21-month process might have ended the careers of other skiers, but Street conquered depression and pain for another comeback. She returned to the slopes in December 1999 with plans to ski competitively again in the 2002 Winter Olympics in Salt Lake City, Utah. Well aware of her status as a role model, she also makes public appearances to encourage girls and young women to pursue sports. "Girls get the message that they should be pretty objects instead of active beings," she told the *Christian Science Monitor.* "That doesn't mean a girl can't be feminine and enjoy her appearance, but she should also be able to hit 80 miles per hour on skis if she wants to."

SOURCES:
*The Christian Science Monitor.* December 15, 1995, p. 10.
*Current Biography Yearbook.* NY: H.W. Wilson, 1998.
*The Day* [New London, CT]. February 19, 1996, pp. C1–C2; December 18, 1997.
Johnson, Anne Janette. *Great Women in Sports.* Detroit, MI: Visible Ink, 1998.

Helga P. McCue, freelance writer,
Waterford, Connecticut

# Streeter, Ruth Cheney (1895–1990)

*First head of the Women's Reserve of the Marine Corps. Born on October 2, 1895, in Brookline, Massachusetts; died in September 1990 in Morristown, New Jersey; daughter of Charles Paine Cheney and Mary Ward (Lyon) Cheney Schofield; attended Bryn Mawr College, 1914–1916; married Thomas Winthrop Streeter (a lawyer, banker, and utility executive), in 1917; children: Frank Sherwin; Henry Schofield; Thomas Winthrop, Jr.; Lilian Carpenter.*

Born in Brookline, Massachusetts, in 1895, Ruth Cheney Streeter received her early education in Boston, and spent two years at Bryn Mawr College before leaving to marry Thomas Winthrop Streeter in 1917. The couple moved to Morristown, New Jersey, where she became active in community work while also raising four children. A member of some six women's clubs and the Junior League, Streeter volunteered as a health and welfare worker for several statewide relief commissions as well. Annually, she and her mother **Mary Cheney Schofield** (who had remarried after the death of Streeter's father) presented the Cheney Award to a member of the Army Air Corps for "acts of valor or extreme fortitude or sacrifice," in memory of her brother William Halsall Cheney, a pilot who had died in an air collision over Italy during World War I.

Streeter took this connection to aviation a step further in 1940, as World War II raged in Europe, when she began taking flying lessons. By the time she earned her commercial license two years later, the United States had joined the Allies in the war, and she used her flying skills in the service of the Civil Air Patrol. She also participated on national defense committees and in civilian assistance to the soldiers stationed at nearby Fort Dix.

In 1943, Congress approved the creation of a Women's Reserve (WR) of the Marine Corps in order to free up active male Marines for combat duty. Commissioned a major, Streeter was named the director of the WR, overseeing some 1,000 officers and 18,000 enlisted women by 1944. While members were not permitted to serve outside the United States, and married women who had children younger than 18 were not allowed to join, they were paid the same as male soldiers in their ranks, and enlisted women had the opportunity for promotion to commission as officers. WR members were chiefly called on to serve in the capacity of accountants, draftsmen, electricians, and office workers, performing clerical duties, communications, aviation support, cryptography, and machine assembly and repair. Although Streeter did not achieve her hope of serving "where there was the most action," remaining instead within the U.S. throughout the war, she reached the rank of colonel by the time it ended in 1945.

When Streeter retired at the end of that year, she returned to the home she shared with her husband in Morristown. There she renewed her civic activities, among them service as national president of the Society of Colonial Dames (1948–52) and membership in the New Jersey Historical Sites Council (1968–70). She died in 1990.

**SOURCES:**

Block, Maxine, ed. *Current Biography 1943*. NY: H.W. Wilson, 1943.

McHenry, Robert, ed. *Famous American Women*. NY: Dover, 1980.

**Helga P. McCue**, freelance writer,
Waterford, Connecticut

# Streich, Rita (1920–1987)

*German coloratura soprano. Born on December 18, 1920, in Barnaul, Russia; died on March 20, 1987, in Vienna, Austria; studied with Willi Domgraf-Fassbänder, Maria Ivogün, and Erna Berger.*

*Sang with the Berlin Staatsoper (1946–51), and the Berlin Städtische Oper (1951–53); debuted in London (1957); made American debut in San Francisco (1957); joined the Folkwang-Hochschule faculty in Essen (1974).*

Rita Streich, who studied with Willi Domgraf-Fassbänder, *Maria Ivogün, and *Erna Berger, was born in Barnaul, Russia, in 1920. With her small but pretty voice, she performed mostly German and Austrian operas during the 1950s and 1960s, because she was particularly suited to Mozart and Strauss. Streich was much more successful in comic opera than in more serious roles and was particularly admired for her portrayals of Sophie in Strauss' *Der Rosenkavalier* and Zerbinetta in *Ariadne auf Naxos*. Her delicate voice corresponds exactly to the text in recordings made with Herbert von Karajan in *Grossmächtige Prinzessin*. Streich, who did not perform widely in North America, was primarily known on the European opera stage.

**John Haag,**
Athens, Georgia

# Streit, Marlene Stewart (1934—)

*Canadian golfer. Name variations: Marlene Stewart. Born Marlene Stewart in Cereal, Alberta, Canada, on March 9, 1934; graduated from Rollins College in Florida, B.A., 1956; married J. Douglas Streit; children: Darlene Louise Streit; Lynn Elizabeth Streit.*

*Won the Canadian Women's Open (1951, 1954, 1955, 1956, 1958, 1959, and 1963); named Canadian Woman Athlete of the Year (1951, 1953, 1956, 1960, 1963); named Canadian Outstanding Athlete of the Year (1951, 1956); won the USGA Women's Amateur (1956); won the British Women's Amateur (1953); won the Australian Women's Amateur (1963); won the World Women's Amateur (1966).*

A top Canadian amateur golfer, Marlene Streit won the Canadian Women's Open seven times. In 1956, she took the USGA Women's Amateur and seven other tournaments, and was low amateur in the 1961 Women's Open. In 1966, in the longest final match in U.S. Women's Amateur history (41 holes), Streit lost to *JoAnne Carner by a squeaker. Streit almost won on the 36th hole, but her 13-foot putt went in, hit the back of the cup, and bounced back out. Marlene Streit was named Canadian Woman Athlete of the Year five times, Canadian Outstanding Athlete of the Year twice, and was elected to the Canadian Sports Hall of Fame in 1962. She was named an Officer of the Order of Canada in 1967.

## Strengell, Marianne (1909–1998)

*Finnish-born American textile designer.* Name variations: Marianne Hammarstrom. Born in Helsinki, Finland, in 1909; died on May 8, 1998, in Wellfleet, Massachusetts; trained in design at the Institute of Industrial Arts in Helsinki; married Olav Hammarstrom; children: son Chris Dusenbury.

An innovator in the development of American commercial-production textiles, Marianne Strengell was among the first to utilize synthetics in combination with natural fibers. She was born in Helsinki in 1909 and worked in Copenhagen as a rug, fabric, and furniture designer before immigrating to the United States in 1936. Her career in America began at Michigan's Cranbrook Academy where she became first an instructor in the weaving and textile design department and then department head. Strengell would remain at Cranbrook until her retirement in 1961. Around 1940, she designed custom fabrics for auto upholstery—with Ford Motor Company, General Motors Corporation, and Chrysler among her commissions—as well as fabrics for United Airlines. New York's Manhattan House and Owens Corning Fiberglass Building also received the benefit of her designs in their rugs and upholstery.

During the 1950s, the U.S. Foreign Operations Administration asked Strengell, who was by then a nationally recognized weaver and textile artist, to serve as an adviser to textile industry developments in Japan and the Philippines. After her retirement from Cranbrook, she played a similar role in Jamaica during the 1960s. At the time of her death in 1998, Strengell's work had appeared in more than 70 solo exhibitions and in such prestigious museums as the Metropolitan Museum of Art, the Art Institute of Chicago, and the National Museum of American Art.

**SOURCES:**

Bakri, Lama. "Marianne Hammarstrom, Know Worldwide for Weaving, Textile Art," in *The Detroit News.* May 14, 1998.
Pile, John. *Dictionary of 20th-Century Design.* NY: Facts on File, 1990.

**Helga P. McCue,** freelance writer, Waterford, Connecticut

## Streonaeshalch, abbess of.

*See Hilda of Whitby (614–680).*

## Strepponi, Giuseppina (1815–1897)

*Italian soprano.* Born Giuseppina Clelia Maria Josepha Strepponi on September 8, 1815, in Lodi; died at Sant'Agata on November 14, 1897; trained at the Milan Conservatory; became second wife of Giuseppe Verdi (the Italian composer), in 1859; children: (illegitimate) two.

Giuseppina Strepponi was trained at the Milan Conservatory and made her operatic debut in 1834. She was known for her smooth voice and spirited performances, a reputation which contributed to that of Italian composer Giuseppe Verdi when she promoted his first opera *Oberto.* Strepponi was Verdi's mistress from around 1847 until she married him in 1859. Her devotion to Verdi was such that her love for him endured through the troubled times of his relationship with *Teresa Stolz.

Among Strepponi's greatest successes were the roles of Amina in *La Sonnambula* and Lucia in *Lucia di Lammermoor.* After overwork led to an early decline, Strepponi retired in 1846 and turned to teaching. She died on November 14, 1897. Her last will and testament left instructions for a letter she had received from Verdi 51 years before to be rested on her heart and buried with her. By the time the envelope was discovered, however, her coffin had already been sealed.

**SOURCES:**

Morehead, Philip D. *The New International Dictionary of Music.* Meridian, 1991.
Warrack, John, and Ewan West. *The Oxford Dictionary of Opera.* NY: Oxford University Press, 1992.

**Helga P. McCue,** freelance writer, Waterford, Connecticut

## Streshnev, Eudoxia (1608–1645).

*See Eudoxia Streshnev.*

## Stretton, Hesba (1832–1911)

*English novelist and children's writer.* Name variations: Sarah Smith. Born Sarah Smith on July 27, 1832, in Wellington, Shropshire; died after a long illness on October 8, 1911, in Ham, Surrey; daughter of Benjamin Smith (a bookseller and publisher) and Anne (Bakewell) Smith; attended day school; never married; no children.

*Selected writings:* Fern's Hollow (1864); Enoch Roden's Training (1865); The Children of Cloverley (1865); The Clives of Burcot (1867); Jessica's First

Prayer *(1867); Pilgrim Street, a Story of Manchester Life (1867);* Paul's Courtship *(1867);* Little Meg's Children *(1868);* David Lloyd's Last Will *(1869);* Alone in London *(1869);* The Doctor's Dilemma *(1872);* Pilgrim Street *(1872);* Michel Lorio's Cross *(1873);* Hester Morley's Promise *(1873);* Through a Needle's Eye *(1879);* Under the Old Roof *(1882);* Jessica's Mother *(1904).*

Hesba Stretton, the pseudonym of Sarah Smith, was an ardent advocate for the welfare of impoverished children through both her writing and her volunteer work. Many of her some 50 novels, particularly those published by the Religious Tract Society in London, focus on the untaught, frequently abused street urchins who were a common feature of Victorian England. While these books are strongly moralistic and didactically Christian—Stretton was a fervent evangelical—they were also quite popular, several of them immensely so, and they skillfully drew readers' attention to a common problem which many well-bred people might have preferred to ignore.

Born in Wellington, Shropshire, in 1832, Stretton was the fourth of eight children of Benjamin and **Anna Bakewell Smith**. She came by her religion through her family, for her father was a printer who worked at a firm that dealt mostly in evangelical literature, and her mother was a deeply religious, strictly evangelical woman. Some critics have speculated that Anna's influence on her daughter was intensified by her death before Stretton was ten. After Benjamin switched careers, becoming a publisher and opening a bookstore, the young girl supplemented her education at a nearby day school by reading most of the books in his shop. This, plus exposure to the educated and literary-minded family friends who frequented her home, constituted her higher education. Her father also ran the local post office, and she would later use this setting in several of her novels and stories, including "A Provincial Post Office" and "The Postmaster's Daughter."

Stretton was in her 20s when she began writing, with her first story, "The Lucky Leg," appearing in 1859 in Charles Dickens' *Household Words.* In the following years, a number of her stories were published in his successor journal, *All the Year Round,* and in various evangelical magazines. She wrote more seriously after her father's retirement in 1862 precipitated a drop in the family income. In 1863, Stretton followed her sister Elizabeth Smith (who later changed her name to **Elizabeth Stretton**) to Manchester, where Elizabeth was working as a

governess. It was probably in Manchester, a large industrial city that was also the home of novelist *Elizabeth Gaskell, that her concern for neglected children was solidified, for Manchester's numerous factories had spawned a desperately impoverished underclass, many of them women and children. Stretton's first novel for children, however, 1864's *Fern's Hollow,* in which Christian values triumph over adversity, was set not in an urban slum but in the hills of the Welsh border. She published two more children's books the following year, *Enoch Roden's Training,* which incorporated her knowledge of the printing profession, and *The Children of Cloverley.* This latter book featured what would become her frequent theme of instinctually Christian children who, through their untaught virtues and innocent example, show their lost elders the true path.

In 1866, Stretton and her sister moved to London. That year the journal *Sunday at Home* published *Jessica's First Prayer,* which made Stretton's international reputation upon its republication in book form the following year. The story of Jessica, a destitute child of the slums whose drunken mother (an actress, which for Victorians was frequently synonymous with a prostitute) has so neglected her that she does not even know how to pray, the novel was hugely successful; it would be translated into numerous languages and sell nearly two million copies over the next 40-odd years. (Tsar Alexander II ordered a copy for every Russian classroom.) As was fairly common in publishing at the time, however, Stretton had sold her copyright to the Religious Tract Society, which alone reaped the enormous benefits of the book's popularity. She learned from this mistake, and later contracted to receive payment for each thousand of her books that sold. Her follow-up children's books, *Pilgrim Street, a Story of Manchester Life* (1867), *Little Meg's Children* (1868) and *Alone in London* (1869), all feature the same sort of innocent protagonists who inspire piety in the adults around them that had proved so popular with *Jessica's First Prayer.* The latter two books, which in addition to their moralizing contain a strong reformist message, together sold some 750,000 copies. Notes Leslie Howsam, "Stretton wrote with passion about the injustices children suffered in the urban slums of industrial England. She appealed to young readers by putting the Christian message into the mouths and personalities of her child characters, charging children with the responsibility of saving the adults around them and, by implication, the society in which they lived."

Buoyed by her growing success and financial stability, in the late 1860s Stretton also began writing for adults, a genre she found more to her taste than children's books. *Paul's Courtship* (1867), her first work for adults, was set in the world of printers and booksellers, while *David Lloyd's Last Will* (1869) took place in Manchester. Over the following 36 years, she would continue to publish both children's and adult novels, often with an underlying political as well as Christian theme. *Under the Old Roof* (1882), for example, explores one instance of the often devastating consequences to women of British property laws prior to that year's passage of the Married Women's Property Act, which finally allowed married women the right to own property. (Previously, everything they owned, earned, or inherited had been the legal property of their husbands.)

Financially secure, Stretton lived an unostentatious life with her sister Elizabeth, although they did take advantage of frequent travel to Europe. In her later years, she also became a more public advocate of the reforms she espoused in her writing. In 1884, she took part in the first meeting of the National Society for the Prevention of Cruelty to Children, of which she would remain an executive board member for ten years, and was among the founders (as was the immensely wealthy *Angela Burdett-Coutts) of a London chapter of the society. She also collected a relief fund for Russian peasants during the famine of 1892. That year Stretton and her sister moved outside London to a house in Richmond. She published her last novel in 1906, and within a year became too ill to leave her home. She died there in 1911, followed within months by her sister.

**SOURCES:**

Buck, Claire, ed. *The Bloomsbury Guide to Women's Literature.* NY: Prentice Hall General Reference, 1992.

Howsam, Leslie. "Hesba Stretton (Sarah Smith)," in *Dictionary of Literary Biography*, Vol. 163: *British Children's Writers, 1800–1880.* Edited by Meena Khorana. Detroit, MI: Gale Research, 1996.

Shattock, Joanne. *The Oxford Guide to British Women Writers.* Oxford: Oxford University Press, 1993.

**Helga P. McCue**, freelance writer,
Waterford, Connecticut

# Strickland, Agnes (1796–1874)

*English historian and writer. Born Agnes Strickland on August 19, 1796, in London, England; died on July 13, 1874, in Southwold, Suffolk; third daughter of Thomas Strickland of Reydon Hall, Suffolk (a shipper), and Elizabeth (Homer) Strickland; sister of Elizabeth Strickland (1794–1875), Jane Margaret Strickland (1800–1888), Catherine Parr Traill (1802–*

*1899), Susanna Moodie (1803–1885), and Samuel Strickland (1809–1867), all writers; tutored by her father in Greek, Latin, mathematics, and history; never married; no children.*

*Selected writings:* Worcester Field *(n.d.);* Demetrius and Other Poems *(1833);* Historical Tales of Illustrious British Children *(1833);* Tales and Stories from History *(1836);* The Lives of the Queens of England *(12 vols., 1840–48);* Alda, the British Captive *(1841); (ed.)* Letters of Mary, Queen of Scots *(1843);* Lives of the Queens of Scotland and English Princesses Connected with the Royal Succession of Great Britain *(1850–59);* Lives of the Bachelor Kings of England *(1861);* How Will It End? *(1865);* Lives of the Seven Bishops Committed to the Tower in 1688 *(1866);* Lives of the Tudor Princesses *(1868);* Lives of the Last Four Princesses of the Royal House of Stuart *(1872);* Guthred, the Widow's Slave *(1875);* The Royal Brothers *(1875).*

Born on August 19, 1796, in London, Agnes Strickland was one of Thomas Strickland and **Elizabeth Homer Strickland**'s nine children, six of whom went on to become writers. Her sister **Elizabeth Strickland** (1794–1875) would collaborate with Agnes on her major works (although Elizabeth chose to receive no credit in these endeavors). Another sister, **Jane Margaret Strickland** (1800–1888), would author a history of Rome as well as a biography entitled *Life of Agnes Strickland* (1887). Three other Strickland siblings emigrated to Canada and became prominent Canadian writers: *Catherine Parr Traill (1802–1899), who wrote juvenile fiction and published works about settler life; *Susanna Moodie (1803–1885), who authored a book on Canada as well as sentimental novels; and Samuel Strickland (1809–1867), who wrote *Twenty-Seven Years in Canada*, a work edited by Agnes.

Agnes and Elizabeth were educated by their father Thomas, a shipper, who promoted their historical interests while providing them with instruction in Greek, Latin, and mathematics. With his death in 1818, the family's financial difficulties necessitated new sources of income, and Agnes turned to publishing. Among her first efforts were original poetry and translations of Petrarch. She authored historical romances, including *Worcester Field* and *Demetrius and Other Poems* (1833), in verse, before writing prose histories, among them *Historical Tales of Illustrious British Children* (1833) and *Tales and Stories from History* (1836), for children. Agnes served as coeditor of *Fisher's Juvenile Scrapbook*, and Elizabeth also entered the arena of children's publishing, producing a number of books which met with success.

With Elizabeth's help, Agnes began work on an ambitious biographical series which was to prove the most successful work of her career. Although Elizabeth authored a number of the biographies in the 12-volume *Lives of the Queens of England* (1840–48), she preferred to be a silent contributor, and the series was published under Agnes' name only. Notes **Joanne Shattock**: "Agnes undertook exhaustive research for the books in official records and in private manuscript collections. When Lord John Russell refused her permission to consult state papers, as a woman, she circumvented him by lobbying Lord Normanby. The French historian Guizot was so impressed by her work that he arranged for her to have access to the French official archives." Indeed, Strickland was to be remembered as a successful historian for her tenacity at research rather than for her critical merit.

While still engaged with *Lives of the Queens of England*, in 1843 she edited a book on *Mary Stuart*, *Letters of Mary, Queen of Scots*. Elizabeth proved instrumental in much of Strickland's next works, including *Lives of the Queens of Scotland*, *Lives of the Bachelor Kings of England*, *Lives of the Seven Bishops Committed to the Tower in 1688*, and the 1868 work *Lives of the Tudor Princesses*. Meanwhile, *Lives of the Queens of England* continued to be a popular work (Agnes and Elizabeth secured the copyright in 1863 before the 1864–65 reprint). In addition to historical biography, Agnes wrote four novels. In 1871, she obtained an annual civil list pension of £100. In 1872, Strickland was partially paralyzed after a fall and died two years later, in 1874.

**SOURCES:**

*The Concise Dictionary of National Biography.* Vol. III: N–Z. NY: Oxford University Press, 1992.

Kunitz, Stanley J., ed. *British Authors of the Nineteenth Century.* NY: H.W. Wilson, 1936.

Shattock, Joanne. *The Oxford Guide to British Women Writers.* NY: Oxford University Press, 1993.

# Strickland, Catherine (1802–1899).

*See Traill, Catherine Parr.*

# Strickland, Mabel (1899–1988)

*Maltese newspaper publisher and political figure who was regarded as the most powerful woman in the Mediterranean region for a period after World War II. Name variations: Malta's Miss Mabel; "the Boadicca (\*Boudica) of Malta." Born Mabel Edeline Strick-* *land on Malta on January 8, 1899; died in Lija, Malta, on November 29, 1988; daughter of Baron Gerald Strickland of Sizergh Castle, Kendal (6th count della Catena of Malta), and Lady Edeline Sackville Strickland; had two sisters; never married.*

Mabel Strickland was born on the island of Malta into an aristocratic world of privilege when Queen *Victoria was in the 62nd year of her reign. At the time of Strickland's birth in 1899, her father served as chief secretary to the governor of Malta, and he would subsequently have a distinguished career in the colonial service, advancing to the governorships of several of the states that would later form the Commonwealth of Australia. Mabel's family could boast of impeccable bloodlines. Her father Gerald Strickland, Baron of Sizergh Castle, Kendal, in Cumbria, England, was a Royal Navy officer from one of England's best-established Roman Catholic families. From his Maltese mother, he inherited the title of count della Catena. Mabel's mother, who had been born Lady **Edeline Sackville**, was the daughter of the earl De La Warr. Leaving Malta for Australia as a child, Mabel was educated by a succession of governesses and to her eternal regret never learned the Maltese language. When the Stricklands returned to Malta in 1917, Mabel worked briefly at Royal Navy headquarters as a cipher officer on the staff of the R.N. commander in chief, Mediterranean.

By 1921, she had entered public life as an assistant secretary with her father's Constitutional Party. By the end of the 1920s, she was familiar with virtually every aspect of Maltese public life, including the growing pressure from Fascist Italy to lay claim to the island by involving itself in its often turbulent politics. During her father's tenure as Malta's prime minister (1927–32), Mabel played an important role as his advisor and as an interpreter of public opinion. As Italian demands grew more insistent in the 1930s, she informed the Italian consul general that he would be ill advised to display the Italian flag on his automobile, for a Fascist Italian on Malta stood a good chance of being "hunted down like a scabby dog." Fascists responded in kind by describing her as "Malta's She-Devil." Starting in 1935, Mabel Strickland was able to take on the Italians on a daily basis in the family-owned newspapers she edited, *The Times of Malta* and the Italian-language *Il-Berqa*. She took advantage of her editorial position not only to attack Mussolini's claims to Malta, but also to offer suggestions on social and economic development for the island that would increase its prosperity and make it less dependent on the naval base that made Malta so important a part of the British Empire.

The people of Malta were heroic during World War II. Their strategically located island, only 20 minutes' flying time south of Sicily, began to be bombed as soon as Mussolini entered the war on the side of Nazi Germany, on June 10, 1940. Massive air raids turned Malta into the most heavily bombed area in the world, but its people refused to surrender. Until more modern Hurricane and Spitfire planes arrived, Malta's air defense consisted of three Gladiator biplane fighters affectionately known as Faith, Hope, and Charity. The relentless air attacks soon resulted in the destruction of the offices of both of the Strickland newspapers. But Mabel, aware of how important the survival of her papers were to island morale, printed them in a rock cavern carved out beneath the capital city of Valletta. Although she never missed an issue, several did appear with fire-charred edges.

Malta's remaining out of Italian hands was essential for the survival of the British Empire. Since Mabel regarded the empire as the bulwark of Western civilization, she identified with the British as they withstood the Blitz in 1940–41. When *The Times* of London suffered bomb damage to its offices in October 1940, she wired the editor: "*Times of Malta* sends greetings and congratulations on your and your colleagues' escape and on your great achievement of uninterrupted publication regardless severe German bombing *Times* famous offices." The year 1940 was difficult for Strickland; it marked the start of her beloved Malta's fight for its very existence, and her father died as well. With Baron Strickland's passing, Mabel became de facto leader of his Constitutional Party, and also took on the responsibility of managing the family's business interests, particularly its two newspapers.

As the war dragged on with no apparent end in sight, Strickland never gave up hope. In February 1942, she cabled *The Times* to report to Britishers on the situation on her "indomitable island":

> For some 80 days in Malta there has been a period of almost continuous alert with few respites. Days and nights have been enlivened by the sound of air battles, anti-aircraft guns in action, and the whistling and crash of bombs. With this we have had to chronicle the wider happenings in the outside world, far-off Singapore and close-up Libya; but the spirit of Malta burns brightly. . . . Malta's chief consolation in her trial is that her defence is not static, that she is the target that hits back.

On April 15, 1942, King George VI made a gesture unique in British imperial history by awarding the entire Maltese nation the George Cross in recognition of its bravery under fire—an honor still proudly borne by the national flag in a post-colonial Malta.

Strickland was awarded the Order of the British Empire for her wartime devotion to duty in 1944. In the final months of World War II, she was a war correspondent for her newspapers, attached to the 21st Army Group of the British Army of the Rhine. As well, her keen interest in gardening (she was a member of the Royal Horticultural Society) took practical form in the large quantities of oranges, grapefruits, and tangerines she grew on her land which helped to feed the island's children.

The postwar era began for Malta in a world which saw the rapid decline and demise of the British Empire. These stresses were reflected in Strickland's Constitutional Party, which remained staunchly pro-British in orientation. On internal issues, the party was socially conservative, opposing direct taxes and any increase in inheritance taxes. By the end of 1945, the party was in crisis over many issues, and in February 1946 it was dissolved.

A new stage in Maltese political life began in 1947 when a nascent constitution established universal suffrage. A small but increasingly confident feminist movement had appeared on the scene on the eve of the war, one of its most vigorous leaders being **Inez Soler** (1910–1974). In 1945, in response to Malta's mood of rising expectations, the island's male political elite had appointed three women—**Mrs. J. Burns Debono, Helen Buhagiar**, and Mabel Strickland—to the National Assembly, but continued to deny suffrage to women. The conservative Roman Catholic Church objected strongly to giving women the right to vote, but in July 1945, by a poll of 145 to 137, they were given the ballot. In the general elections of October 1947, two women, **Agatha Barbara** (1923—) and Helen Buhagiar, ran for seats in the new Legislative Assembly. Of the two, only Agatha Barbara was successful. She went on to have a thriving career in politics, becoming the first Maltese woman to hold a Cabinet post (minister of education, 1955), and in 1982 capped her career by becoming the first woman president of Malta, a post she would hold until 1987.

In 1950, Strickland resigned her editorial positions to make a successful run for a seat in the Legislative Assembly as candidate of a revived Constitutional Party that was now her pliant personal instrument. During this period, she was often referred to both in Malta and the United Kingdom as being the most powerful woman in the Mediterranean region, something that seemed to be reconfirmed in 1951 when she was reelected to her assembly seat. Looking forward to the day when she might become Malta's first woman head of government, in 1953 she organized a new party, the Progressive Constitutional Party (PCP). But the tides of history moved strongly against the conservative ideals in which she so deeply believed. In the 1955 elections, PCP candidates performed pathetically, polling only 3,649 votes out of a total of 121,243 and failing to win a single seat in the Legislative Assembly.

The rise of militant nationalism linked to a desire for social reforms brought about a powerful labor movement and its political wing, the Malta Labour Party led by its fiery architect, Dom Mintoff. Although Strickland was able to win a seat in 1962 (which she held until 1966) as the candidate of her Progressive Constitutional Party, her colonial-rooted view of the world was in eclipse. In other ways, too, Strickland's political aspirations were doomed. Conservative Maltese values continued to argue against women moving into positions of high political leadership. Once, pointing to her ample breasts, Strickland exclaimed, "If it wasn't for *these* I would be Prime Minister of Malta." Her inability to speak the Maltese language also proved to be a significant handicap during political campaigns.

The elections of 1971 were bitterly contested, and Strickland braved stones and verbal attacks. In the elections, neither she nor any other Progressive Constitutional candidate won a legislative seat. Despite the risks, her newspapers continued to censure the Mintoff government, accusing it of being un-democratic and anti-Western. In response, Labour militants launched systematic attacks on her papers, which culminated in a fire-bombing in October 1979 that destroyed the editorial offices and computer room of *The Times of Malta*. Not only machinery, but irreplaceable records were destroyed. By now frail, Mabel Strickland was shaken by the destruction of her beloved newspaper, and her health never recovered.

At the time of the attack, she received a handwritten note from Mintoff, who expressed regret for the actions of "some hotheads," noting as well that in recent years he "had made it a point to protect [*The Times of Malta*] better than if it had been my own. . . . It is not in my style to crush opposition." Despite the massive

*Postage stamp issued in Malta in 1996 to honor Mabel Strickland.*

destruction, *The Times of Malta* was on the streets the following day, just as it had been during World War II. Mabel Strickland was a semi-invalid confined to her home during the last years of her life, dying in Lija, Malta, on November 29, 1988. With the cooling of the political passions of her era, most Maltese now remember "Miss Mabel" with nostalgic fondness, a clear indication of which was her being depicted on a commemorative postage stamp issued in her honor on April 24, 1996.

**SOURCES:**

Alexander, Joan. *Mabel Strickland.* Valletta, Malta: Progress, 1996.

———. *Voices and Echoes: Tales from Colonial Women.* London: Quartet, 1983.

Attard, Joseph. *The Battle of Malta.* London: Kimber, 1980.

Austin, Dennis. *Malta and the End of Empire.* London: Cass, 1971.

Berg, Warren G. *Historical Dictionary of Malta.* Lanham, MD: Scarecrow, 1995.

Boffa, Charles J. *The Second Great Siege: Malta 1940–1943.* Hamrun, Malta: St. Joseph's Institute, 1970.

Boswell, David Mark, and Brian W. Beeley. *Malta*. Santa Barbara, CA: ABC-Clio, 1998.

Bradford, Ernle Dusgate Selby. *Siege: Malta, 1940–1943*. NY: Morrow, 1986.

"Close-Down in Malta," in *The Times* [London]. March 26, 1979, p. 36.

D., C.P. "The Grand Old Lady of Malta," in *Manchester Guardian Weekly*. December 11, 1988, p. 10.

"Demonstrators Stone Malta Newspaper Office," in *The Times* [London]. February 2, 1972, p. 6.

Dobie, Edith. *Malta's Road to Independence*. Norman, OK: University of Oklahoma Press, 1967.

Frendo, Henry. "Britain's European Mediterranean: Language, Religion and Politics in Lord Strickland's Malta (1927–1930)," in *History of European Ideas*. Vol. 21, no. 1. January 1995, pp. 47–65.

———. "Italy and Britain in Maltese Colonial Nationalism," in *History of European Ideas*. Vol. 15, no. 4–6. August 1992, pp. 733–739.

———. *Party Politics in a Fortress Colony: The Maltese Experience*. 2nd ed. Valletta, Malta: Midsea, 1991.

"Hard Times for Mabel Strickland," in *The Times* [London]. February 2, 1972, p. 14.

Hornyold, Henry. *Genealogical Memoirs of the Family of Strickland of Sizergh*. Kendal, Eng.: Titus Wilson, 1928.

"Mabel Strickland," in *The Annual Obituary 1988*. Chicago, IL: St. James Press, 1990, pp. 590–592.

"Mabel Strickland," in *The Daily Telegraph* [London]. November 30, 1988, p. 21.

"Mabel Strickland: Fighter for Malta in War and Peace," in *The Times* [London]. November 30, 1988, p. 18.

*Malta Independence Conference, 1963*. London: Her Majesty's Stationery Office, 1963 [Cmnd. 2121].

"Mintoff Mob Burn Offices," in *The Daily Telegraph* [London]. October 16, 1979, p. 1.

Mizzi, John. "Mob Attack Fails to Stop 'Times of Malta,'" in *The Daily Telegraph* [London]. October 17, 1979, p. 5.

Pirotta, Joseph M. *Fortress Colony: The Final Act 1945–1964*. Vol. 1 (1945–1954). Valletta, Malta: Studia, 1987.

"Requiem Mass: The Hon. Mabel Strickland," in *The Times* [London]. January 21, 1989, p. 11.

Smith, Harrison. *Britain in Malta*. 2 vols. Valletta, Malta: Progress, 1953.

———. *Lord Strickland: Servant of the Crown*. Edited by Adrianus Koster. Amsterdam: Koster, 1983.

Strickland, Gerald, Baron. *Malta and the Phoenicians*. Edited by Mabel Strickland. Valletta, Malta: Progress, 1969.

Strickland, Mabel. *A Collection of Essays on Malta 1923–1954*. Valletta, Malta: Progress, 1955.

———. "Malta: The Indomitable Island," in *The Times* [London]. February 28, 1942, p.5.

———. *Maltese Constitutional and Economic Issues, 1955–1959*. Valletta, Malta: Progress, 1959.

———. "A Message from Malta," in *The Times* [London]. October 16, 1940, p. 5.

"The Times Diary," in *The Times* [London]. February 5, 1972, p. 14.

Woods, Oliver. "The Man of Malta Whom Time Did Not Mellow," in *The Times* [London]. January 1, 1972, p. 16.

**John Haag**, Associate Professor of History, University of Georgia, Athens, Georgia

# Strickland, Shirley (1925—)

*Australian track-and-field star. Name variations: Shirley de la Hunty; Shirley de la Hunty-Strickland. Born Shirley Strickland in Guildford, Western Australia, on July 18, 1925; attended Northam High School; graduated from the University of Western Australia; married; children: Phillip (b. 1953).*

*Won seven Olympic medals in track and field: bronze in 100 meters (1948, 1952), bronze in the 80-meter hurdles (1948) and gold (1952, 1956), silver in the 4x100-meter relay (1948, 1956), later discovered the winner of a bronze in the 200 meters (1948), but has not yet been entered into the official record; her record was equaled only by Poland's \*Irena Szewinska; awarded MBE (1951).*

Shirley Strickland grew up in a family of runners. Her brothers ran, and her father had been a professional sprinter in his youth, but Shirley was the star. In high school, she won 47 of her 49 races in sprints and hurdles. At the University of Western Australia, Strickland was a track-and-field as well as a field hockey star. Graduating with honors after majoring in science, she became a lecturer in physics and mathematics at Perth Technical College. Though Strickland was an obvious choice for the 1948 Olympic team, officials were not certain an Australian team could be sent; it was only two years after World War II, and the nation was still recovering. Since the Summer Olympics would be held in London, halfway round the world, it was an expensive trip. As the date approached, however, officials became increasingly determined to carry on a tradition. Australia was one of only four countries, including Greece, Great Britain, and the United States, to send athletes to every Summer Olympics since the modern games were revived in 1896. No one was surprised when Strickland was selected to make the trip to London.

The 1948 Summer Olympics were unusual in one respect; they were the first games dominated by a woman: track-and-field star \*Fanny Blankers-Koen. This 30-year-old Dutch athlete was given little chance of winning by the press, but Blankers-Koen won four gold medals and was Strickland's chief competitor throughout the games. In the 100-meter qualifying rounds, Blankers-Koen and Britain's ✍▶ Dorothy Manley finished ahead of Strickland, though the final proved exciting. While Blankers-Koen won her first gold, Manley and Strickland were in a photo finish, both clocking in at 12.2 seconds. The judges awarded the silver to Manley who had edged slightly ahead, while Strickland was given the bronze. In some ways, the 80-meter hurdles were a repeat of the 100 meters. Because the Dutch athlete got off to a slow start, Blankers-Koen and Britain's ✥➤ **Maureen Gardner** were in a photo finish, clocking the same time. Judges finally awarded first place to Blankers-Koen and second to Gardner; once again, Strickland took third place. In the 4x100-meter relay, Flying Fanny made the difference for the Dutch and the Australians had to settle for a silver.

In the 200 meters, there was another crunch of runners at the finish line, as the "Dutch housewife," as the press called Blankers-Koen, again took the gold. After studying the photos, judges awarded the silver to **Audrey Williamson** of Great Britain and the bronze to ✥➤ **Audrey Patterson** of the United States. Strickland, it was said, finished fourth. But photo-finish equipment was still experimental in 1948. Thirty-five years later, the photo of the finish of this 200-meter race was discovered, along with pictures of other races. On close look, there is no disputing that Strickland was third rather than fourth in the 1948 200 meters, though the race's new result has not yet been officially changed. Despite formidable competition from Fanny Blankers-Koen, Shirley Strickland had established her international reputation in the London games.

In the 1950 Commonwealth Games held in Auckland, New Zealand, Strickland captured the gold in the 80-meter hurdles and won two other gold medals on Australian relay teams. She finished second to teammate *Marjorie Jackson** in the 100 yards and the 220 yards. Continued victories prepared Strickland for the 1952 Helsinki Summer Games where the Australians were expected to give a fine showing. Now married and competing under the name of de la Hunty, Strickland was third in the 100 meters, and since Marjorie Jackson took first, the Aussies won two out of three of the top medals. The 80-meter hurdles pitted Strickland against Blankers-Koen once more. This year, the Dutch track star was suffering from an infection and reaction to medication. During the race, she hit several hurdles and failed to finish. Strickland blazed down the track with a 10.9 world record and an Olympic gold medal. Jackson took the gold in the 200 meters, so it was only natural that the Australians were expected to win the 4x100-meter relay. For three-quarters of the race, this proved to be the case until Marjorie Jackson fumbled the baton. The American team, anchored by *Mae Faggs**, took advantage of the fumble and surged to first place and the gold. Australia ended up in fifth place.

Most assumed Strickland would automatically qualify for the Australian team to compete in the 1954 Commonwealth Games. But her son, Phillip, was born in 1953, so she began training late that year and was not chosen to participate. When her appeal to be allowed on the team was turned down, she decided to compete as an independent. Unfortunately, her lack of training was telling, and she did not perform well. By 1955, Strickland was back in shape when she was invited to a major international competition in Warsaw, Poland. Australian officials had little enthusiasm for sending her, however, and tried to discourage her participation by decreeing that she had to be accompanied by a chaperon, despite the fact that she was 30 years old, a wife and mother, as well as a renowned international track-and-field star. Determined to run, Strickland prevailed and set a new world record of 11.3 seconds in the 100 meters, a record that would not be tied for three years and would not be bettered for six.

When the 1956 Melbourne Olympic Games arrived, Shirley de la Hunty-Strickland was determined to represent her country at its home games, though officials were still unenthused. First there was controversy when her photograph turned up on a cigarette carton label. Any Olympic athlete who attempted to make money from sports was immediately excluded from the Games. Fortunately for Australia, the matter was resolved. Although this was her third Olympics, the 31-year-old Strickland was determined. In the 80-meter hurdles, she streaked well ahead of the competition with a time of 10.7, another Olympic record. She was now the only woman to successfully defend an Olympic title. In the 4x100-meter relay, Strickland and her teammates finally captured the gold, defeating the United States and Great Britain. Though they counted for only 16% of their nation's contingent, the women of the Australian team in the 1956 games were extraordinary. Strickland, *Betty Cuthbert**, *Dawn Fraser**, **Marlene Matthews**, **Norma Thrower**, *Lorraine Crapp**, and others captured more than half of their teams' gold medals, ensuring Australia's third place finish overall.

Strickland's medals from three Olympic Games totaled three golds, one silver, three bronzes, and one disputed bronze, making Strickland one of the most prolific winners in Olympic history. She also set nine Olympic records, including six in the hurdles and three in the 4x100-meter relay. At that time, no woman or man in Olympic track-and-field history had ever set as many.

◄ஜ
*Gardner, Maureen.* See *Blankers-Koen, Fanny* for sidebar.

◄ஜ
*Patterson, Audrey.* See *Faggs, Mae* for sidebar.

◄ஜ
*Manley, Dorothy.* See *Blankers-Koen, Fanny* for sidebar.

SOURCES:

Hemery, David. *The Pursuit of Sporting Excellence.* Champaign, IL: Human Kinetics, 1986.

Hendershott, Jon. *Track's Greatest Women.* Los Altos, CA: Tafnews Press, 1987.

Matthews, Peter. *Track & Field Athletics. The Records.* Enfield, Middlesex: Guinness, 1986.

Vamplew, Wray, *et al. The Oxford Companion to Australian Sport.* Melbourne: Oxford University Press, 1992.

**Karin Loewen Haag**, freelance writer,
Athens, Georgia

## Strindberg, Mrs. August (1878–1961).

See Bosse, Harriet.

## Strindberg, Frida (1872–1943).

See Uhl, Frida.

## Stringer, C. Vivian (1948—)

*African-American coach, the third all-time winningest Division I coach in women's basketball. Name variations: Vivian Stringer. Born in Edenborn, Pennsylvania, on March 16, 1948; attended Slippery Rock State College, Pennsylvania; married gymnast Bill Stringer (died 1992); children: David, Janine, and Justin.*

*Became the first women's basketball coach in the U.S. to take two different college teams to the NCAA Final Four; named national coach of the year three times; became the third all-time winningest Division I coach in women's basketball.*

When Vivian Stringer was in high school, the closest she could get to sports was as the first African-American member of the cheerleading squad, because the school offered no basketball or track teams for women. However, during her undergraduate years at Slippery Rock State College, she was able to participate in the sports that she loved—basketball, field hockey, softball, and tennis. Her devotion was equally matched with athletic talent, and her performance merited her induction into the school's athletic Hall of Fame.

In 1971, she moved with her husband Bill Stringer to Cheyney State University where she volunteered as a basketball coach while he taught exercise physiology. During Stringer's 11 seasons at Cheyney, she developed a winning program for the school, taking the team to the finals of the first Final Four when the National Collegiate Athletics Association (NCAA) started a women's championship tournament in 1981. This success was overshadowed for Stringer, however, when her infant daughter **Janine** contracted meningitis, leaving her confined to a wheelchair.

Two years after her team's historic appearance in the NCAA tournament, in 1983 Stringer became head coach of the University of Iowa's women's basketball team, the Hawkeyes. Once again, she turned out a winning team, with ten straight 20-victory seasons. In addition to winning nine NCAA tournament berths, the Hawkeyes claimed six conference championships. During the team's highlight 1992–93 season, like Cheyney before them, they advanced to the NCAA Final Four. But for Stringer it was a time of grief. Her husband had died on Thanksgiving Day before the start of the season, and she contemplated giving up coaching. She remarked to the *Philadelphia Daily News:* "I very seriously thought of not working again. I just felt I couldn't get the energy or enthusiasm to do it. Athletics seems like such a contradiction between life and what happened to my husband. It all seemed like such play. But my sons helped me through that. Basketball kept some semblance of sanity. I wrapped myself up in it." At the end of the season, she was named Naismith National Coach of the Year and a notable black woman in sports by the Smithsonian Institution. Among the many other accolades Stringer received was the Carol Eckman Award in honor of the courage and integrity she brought to women's basketball. In 1994, she became one of only five active coaches with 500 career victories.

Although revered on the Iowa campus, Stringer decided she needed a change after 12 seasons with the Hawkeyes. In 1995, she accepted the richest deal ever extended to a women's basketball coach in the country when Rutgers University in New Jersey offered her a base salary of $150,000 a year (higher than any male coach at Rutgers) plus incentives which reportedly brought the package close to $300,000 a year. In return, Stringer promised to turn Rutgers' program into "the jewel of the East," using her combined strengths of recruiting, discipline, and intelligent strategy.

But her first two seasons at Rutgers proved to be rocky ones marred by losing records and a critical press that scrutinized her ample salary and failure to deliver the expected victories. In the face of such criticism, Stringer worked hard to acclimate her team to her style of playing and coaching while wondering if she had made a mistake in leaving what had been her number-one recruiting class at Iowa. "It was tough for me because I had been used to being embraced and I had enough success that I felt that everybody should know that, with a little bit of time, we would be pushing forward," she said. "I think maybe I was a little thin-skinned because I hadn't had that kind of push or expectations."

In the 1997–98 season, Stringer proved to her critics what she had known all along: that she could develop Rutgers' Scarlet Knights into one of the nation's top women's basketball teams. Through savvy recruiting, she stacked the team with such players as **Tasha Pointer, Tomora Young,** and **Shawnetta Stewart,** all of whom would garner Player of the Year accolades during 1998 and 1999. Training her players in a system of devastating defense, Stringer helped her team hold opponents to an average of just 55.8 points per game, while they racked up a 20-win season and an NCAA Tournament appearance. The following season was even more successful: another 20-win season which culminated with the team's ascension to the Elite Eight of the tournament and a rank of sixth in the nation. Stringer enjoyed the prestige of "Coach of the Year" titles in both seasons, and 1999 brought another promising batch of recruits which included two high-school All-Americans and the top junior-college player in the nation.

Stringer also used her administrative talents in the service of the sport through her participation in the Women's Basketball Coaches Association. She further influenced the sport through her election to the Women's Sports Foundation Advisory Board and by becoming a voting board member of the Amateur Basketball Association of the United States. Her expectations of team members remain high, and she is particularly noted for producing thinking players. "You can either give a person a fish or teach them to become a fisherman," she once noted. "I want [players] to be fishermen."

**SOURCES:**

Greenberg, Mel. "Stringer Highest Paid Women's Hoop Coach," in *The Day* [New London, CT]. July 15, 1995.

Johnson, Anne Janette. *Great Women in Sports.* Detroit, MI: Visible Ink, 1998.

**Helga P. McCue,** freelance writer,
Waterford, Connecticut

# Strong, Anna Louise (1885–1970)

*Radical American journalist and author who was an ardent defender of the Soviet Union (1920s–1940s) and of the People's Republic of China (1950s–1960s). Born Anna Louise Strong on November 24, 1885, in Friend, Kansas; died on March 29, 1970, in Beijing, China, of a heart attack; daughter of Sydney Dix Strong (a Congregationalist minister) and Ruth Maria (Tracy) Strong (a lay missionary leader); graduated from Oak Park (Ill.) high school, 1900; studied in Germany and Switzerland, 1902; attended Oberlin, 1902–03, and Bryn Mawr, 1903–04; Oberlin College, A.B., 1905; University of Chicago, Ph.D., 1908; common-law marriage to Joel Shubin, late 1931 (died 1942); no children.*

*Lived in Mt. Vernon, Ohio (1887), Cincinnati (1892), and Oak Park, Illinois (1897); organized "Know Your City" exhibits in Seattle, Walla Walla, Portland, and Spokane (1909–10); employed by Russell Sage Foundation, National Child Labor Committee (1910); named exhibit expert, U.S. Children's Bureau, Washington, D.C. (1912); elected to Seattle school board (1916–18); served as feature editor, Seattle Record (1918–21); became correspondent, American Friends Relief Mission in Russia (1921–22); served as correspondent, Hearst's International Magazine for Central and Eastern Europe (1922–25); worked as correspondent, North American Newspaper Alliance in Russia (1925), and for Federated Press (1925); worked as editor, Today (1951–56); wrote newsletter Letter from China (1962–70).*

*Selected publications: (poems) Storm Songs and Fables (Langston, 1904); (poem) The Song of the City (Howard Severence, 1906); (play) The King's Palace (Oak Leaves, 1908); Boys and Girls of the Bible (Howard Severence, 1908); The Psychology of Prayer (University of Chicago, 1908); Bible Hero Classics in the Words of the Scriptures (Howard Severence, 1909); Biographical Studies in the Bible (Howard Severence, 1911); The Seattle General Strike (Seattle Union-Record, 1919); Ragged Verse of "Anise" (Seattle Union-Record, 1921); The First Time in History: Two Years of Russia's New Life, September 1921 to December 1923 (Boni and Liveright, 1924); Children of the Revolution (Pigot, 1925); Red Star in Samarkand (Coward-McCann, 1929); The Road to the Grey Pamirs (Henry Holt, 1931); The Soviets Conquer Wheat: The Drama of Collective Farming (Henry Holt, 1931); From Stalingrad to the Kuzbas: Sketches of the Socialist Construction of the USSR (International Publishers, 1931); Dictatorship and Democracy in the Soviet Union (International Publishers, 1934); I Change Worlds: The Remaking of an American (Henry Holt, 1935); China's Millions (Coward-McCann, 1928, updated and revised, Knights, 1935); The New Soviet Constitution: A Study in Socialist Democracy (Henry Holt, 1936); This Soviet World (Henry Holt, 1936); Spain in Arms (Henry Holt, 1937); One-Fifth of Mankind (Modern Age, 1938); My Native Land (Viking, 1940); The New Lithuania (Workers' Library, 1941); The Soviets Expected It (Dial, 1941); Wild River (Little, Brown, 1943); Peoples of the USSR (Macmillan, 1944); I Saw the New Poland (Little,*

*Brown, 1946); The Stalin Era (Mainstream, 1956); The Rise of the Chinese People's Communes (New World Press, 1959); Tibetan Interviews (New World Press, 1960); When Serfs Stood Up in Tibet (New World Press, 1960); Cash and Violence in Laos and Vietnam (New World Press, 1962).*

On March 29, 1970, Xinhua (Hsinhua), the official press agency of the People's Republic of China, announced the death of Anna Louise Strong. She would, it was revealed, be buried with full honors in the Revolutionary Martyrs Cemetery. At age 84, she had succumbed to a heart attack. According to Beijing radio, leading officials such as Premier Zhou Enlai had recently visited her in the hospital.

For almost half a century, Strong had promoted Communist regimes with evangelical zeal. Moreover, she had also written a learned treatise on prayer, acted as a spearhead of the Seattle General Strike of 1919, been a friend of Leon Trotsky, dined in the White House with Franklin and *Eleanor Roosevelt, and founded the first English-language daily in the Soviet Union.

*Hers was a radicalism of the heart, not of the intellect.*

—Kenneth E. Shewmaker

In a front-page story reporting her death, *The New York Times* described Strong as a "large woman of powerful frame, with white hair and piercing blue eyes." Riding on rickety railroads and precarious airplanes, walking down dusty roads and even obliged at times to lie sick and weak on a stretcher, she traveled in the last five decades of her life all over the vast Communist world, from Manchuria to Tibet, from North Korea to Prague, from Moscow to Beijing (Peking), always returning to her adopted land.

Anna Louise Strong was born in a two-room parsonage in Friend, Kansas, on November 24, 1885, the eldest of three children of Congregational minister Sydney Dix Strong and **Ruth Tracy Strong**. Sydney's frequent change of pastorates—Mount Vernon, Ohio, in 1887 and Cincinnati in 1892—did not hinder the precociously bright Anna Louise from becoming literate at age four and writing verse at age six. In Cincinnati, she finished the 8th grade at age 11, frequently correcting her instructor in the process. When her father took a church in Oak Park, Illinois, she went to high school there, graduating when barely 15. In fact, by the time she was 12, she was already coordinating sewing lessons in settlement houses on Chicago's West Side. As a teen, Strong contributed to the youth magazine *American Weekly*. She spent a year and a half in Germany and Switzerland studying languages, entered Oberlin College in 1902, and transferred to Bryn Mawr a year later. Returning to Oberlin as a senior, she graduated with high honors.

For several months, Strong was associate editor of *Advance*, a Protestant weekly published in Chicago. Writing under four pseudonyms, each week she penned features for children, three women's columns, and half a dozen book reviews. Yet, as soon as circulation had increased, the obviously overworked Strong was fired.

In April 1906, she began graduate work at the University of Chicago, at the same time taking part-time work in a canning plant and ***Jane Addams**' Hull House. In 1908, she was awarded a Ph.D. magna cum laude. She defended her dissertation, published as *The Psychology of Prayer*, before the combined faculties of philosophy and theology. Drawing upon medieval mystics and contemporary authorities in social psychology, she argued that prayer could aid one in performing social duties. At age 23, she was the youngest person ever to have been awarded a doctorate from that university.

Once she completed her thesis, Strong went to Seattle, a progressive city with much municipal ownership. Here she joined her father in organizing "Know Your City" programs, which combined lectures, discussions, and walking tours. Together with Sydney, Anna also wrote a series of "Bible Hero Classics," whose purpose, she said, was "to make this generation acquainted with Abraham, David, Paul, and the others as they were with Alexander, Caesar, and King Arthur." By 1910, she had moved to New York, where she worked for the prestigious Russell Sage Foundation in the field of child hygiene and began exposés of urban life for *Survey* magazine. In September of that year, she took on a second task: showing stereoptic and cinema exhibits across the nation for the National Child Labor Committee. While preparing one particular exhibit in Kansas City, she joined the Socialist Party. During these years, Strong was pursued by a number of suitors, including reformers Judge Ben Lindsay and Roger Baldwin. She was briefly and informally engaged to Baldwin, but found him insufficiently pious.

In the fall of 1912, Strong took on a third assignment, directing exhibits for the U.S. Children's Bureau in Washington, D.C. On paper, at least, she was simultaneously affiliated with three major reform organizations. The spring of

1913 saw her in Dublin, where she arranged a child welfare display at the request of the wife of Ireland's lord lieutenant.

In October 1916, Strong moved back to Seattle, where she ran unsuccessfully for the state legislature but was elected to the city's school board. A strong Wilsonian, she was staunchly opposed to America's entry into World War I and was active in various peace groups. The U.S. declaration of war on Germany in April 1917 was a milestone for her, marking—in the words of biographers Tracy B. Strong and **Helene Keyssar**—"the beginning of Anna Louise's disaffection with the American political system." Anna Strong later wrote:

> Nothing in my whole life, not even my mother's death, so shook the foundations of my soul. . . . "Our America" was dead! The profiteers and the militarists had violated her and forced her to do their bidding. The people wanted peace; the profiteers wanted war—and got it.

Strong threw herself into radical activity, defending foes of conscription and anonymously writing or editing one-fourth of the copy for the *Seattle Daily Call*, a paper oriented towards the Industrial Workers of the World. In March 1918, such action led to her recall from the school board by 4,000 votes. When, in January 1918, "patriots" wrecked the *Call's* presses, Strong became feature editor and editorial writer of the *Seattle Union-Record*, an influential weekly that soon became a daily. The only general circulation paper operated by a trade union, it was run by the city's Central Labor Council. Under the pen name "Anise," she constantly accused the Wilson administration of moral bankruptcy and suppression of civil liberties. Pro-Soviet from the time the Bolshevik Revolution broke out, she was responsible for the *Union-Record's* printing of V.I. Lenin's speech to the 1918 Congress of Soviets, a daring journalistic feat. On February 4, 1919, she gained even greater fame, for she wrote an editorial, "No One Knows Where," which helped trigger the short-lived Seattle General Strike of 1919. In November 1919, the Department of Justice charged Strong with seeking to overthrow the government and encouraging sabotage. Yet, as the *Union-Record* had contained no pleas for violent revolution, a jury freed all defendants.

Disillusioned by the factionalism rampant among Seattle's left, Strong heeded the advice of muckraking journalist Lincoln Steffens and went to Russia. She was correspondent for Hearst's International News Service, publicist for the American Friends Service Committee, and envoy

Anna Louise Strong

of the Seattle Labor Council. Before entering Russia, she worked 10-to-12 hours a day aiding Belorussian refugees in Baranovice, Poland. In 1921, she traveled to the famine-ridden Volga town of Samara (later Kuibyshev), where she acted as a relief worker in daytime and a journalist at night. Contracting typhus there, she was delirious for a week and had to spend seven months in a Moscow hospital. In 1922, she was close enough to Leon Trotsky, the second most powerful figure in the land, to give him English lessons at least four times a week in return for political instruction. In 1923, she began her annual lecture tours in the United States, unaware that the Federal Bureau of Investigation had started establishing its file on her.

Already Strong was a pronounced enthusiast of the Soviet experiment, and her pro-Soviet articles started appearing in *Hearst's International Magazine, The Nation, Collier's, Survey,* and *Current History.* She was particularly impressed by those party members who sacrificed themselves in the mines of the Donbas, the deserts of Kazakhstan, and the woods of Karelia. She attacked the White Terror while rationalizing executions committed by the Red regime. Lenin, as her readers in the *Forum* discovered, was "The

Greatest Man of Our Time." She said, "No public man of our time has made such a gift to human life as Lenin. No man has been increasingly loved by so many millions of people."

In one sense, Strong had never abandoned her original vocation: social work. As she constantly maintained, "I wanted to fight the disorder of the world." In 1923, she fostered the John Reed Children's Colony, established in Khvalynsk as an agricultural commune for adolescents left homeless by the Volga famine. She raised money, pleaded its case in *Children of the Revolution* (1925), and personally worked in the Colony's apple orchard in her effort to create an American-style farm. Yet the experiment lasted only two years, for she could not counter corrupt management and careless bureaucrats. Three years later, she promoted a somewhat similar effort, a trade school called the American Industrial Workshops, located in a two-room shack some 15 miles from Moscow. Looted by two American experts, it also failed.

In the fall of 1925, Strong left Moscow for Beijing, where she interviewed major figures for the North American Newspaper Alliance. She found General Zhang Zuolin (Chang Tso-lin) "a gorgeous general backed by Japan," General Feng Youxiang (Feng Yu-hsiang) an engaging bandit, and ◄❧ **Song Qingling**, widow of the revered Dr. Sun Yat-sen, "the most gentle and exquisite creature I have known anywhere in the world." Early in 1927, Strong traveled to Mexico. There she found the people full of "grace and joy" but the politics chaotic.

Returning to China later that year, Strong renewed her friendship with Michael Borodin, Russian adviser to the Chinese Nationalists in Canton. When, early in June, Borodin made a 300-mile trip to Chengzhou, there to negotiate with Feng, Strong accompanied his delegation. Similarly, in mid-July, when Borodin was forced to flee Generalissimo Chiang Kai-shek, Strong was one of the five who made the uncharted trek through the Gobi desert. The trip began in 100 degree heat, covered 1,800 miles, and took six days just to reach Ulan Bator, the capital of Mongolia. Sometimes less than five miles a day were covered. Recounting these events in *China's Millions* (1928), Strong combined travelogue with eulogies of awakened worker and peasant masses.

Back in Moscow by October 1927, Strong publicly renounced the now discredited Trotsky. In 1928 and 1929, she took two trips to Central Asia, out of which came *Red Star in Samarkand* (1929) and *The Road to the Grey Pamirs*

❧► 
*Song Qingling.*
*See Song Sisters.*

(1931). Visiting the countryside three times between November 1929 and May 1930, she observed farm collectivization. In a private letter, she conceded that in the Ukraine there had been "much cruelty and terrible injustice," but reflected, "a hundred million people are being taken through three centuries in a decade." In print, in a book entitled *The Soviets Conquer Wheat* (1931), she wrote:

> How loyal is the Red Way! How [the collective farm] loves the Soviet government which gives it land and seed and bread and now sends tractors! How wonderful the clubwork, how fine the choruses and dramas. When someone starts the idea of a "socialist competition" with the next village, how work rushes along like a royal sport.

Describing forced labor camps in 1932, Strong wrote that workers were "free to leave if they like, but prefer to stay. For they found there in the camps a normal life which is better, more interesting than the abnormal one they lived outside." By the mid-1930s, she was telling *New Republic* readers that Soviet citizens played an active role in governing, that the OGPU secret police was a progressive force, that there had been no famine in the Ukraine, and that an unnamed Western power had assassinated Stalin's rival Sergei Kirov, an event that triggered the famous purge trials. Although frequently turned down in her bid to join the Russian Communist Party, in 1935 she took advantage of a trip to America to join the U.S. communists.

Late in 1931, Strong had entered into a common-law marriage with Joel Shubin, an agronomist, Menshevik-turned-Communist, and an editor of the Moscow *Peasant's Gazette*. Deputy minister of agriculture in the late '30s, Shubin died of overwork in 1942.

In the summer of 1930, Strong had founded the English-language *Moscow Daily News*, intended as a forum for Americans working in the Soviet Union and a source about developments both in Russia and back home. As associate editor, she personally typed most of the first issue and arranged the layout herself. Returning from a lecture tour in the U.S. early in 1931, she found her own reporting ignored and the paper poorly edited. Furthermore, the government was sponsoring a competing journal, the *Worker's News*, which was even more drab. In an effort to preserve the integrity of her journal, she met personally in 1932 with Joseph Stalin, Lazar Kaganovich, first secretary of the Moscow party committee, and Kliment Voroshilov, people's commissar of military and naval affairs. When Stalin merged the *Moscow Daily News* and

*Worker's News* and vested Strong with some formal authority, she said privately, "I'd like to take orders from those men anywhere in the world." Indeed, the conference was "the most important half-hour of my existence." Yet her dissatisfaction with the paper continued, and she resigned in 1936. The journal folded ten years later.

In 1935, Strong's autobiography, *I Change Worlds*, was published. Strong made sure that various sections were checked for "political reliability," having Stalin correct the chapter on himself in green pencil. In a letter that introduced the volume, Steffens expressed their common view: "The truth from now on is always dated, never absolute, never eternal." Strong uttered similar sentiments in *This Soviet World* (1936), in which she wrote: "I tell not the whole truth for truth is never 'whole'; there are always at least two truths in conflict, the truth that is dying and the truth that is coming into existence." Another Strong book, *The New Soviet Constitution* (1936), found preliminary nationwide "discussions" about that document "the most spectacularly widespread . . . in connection with any government in history." In 1936, she attended the purge trials, which she defended in *Soviet Russia Today*. Such old revolutionists as Trotsky, she commented, had sought to betray the Soviet Union into the hands of Fascist powers.

From December 1936 to early 1937, Strong covered the Spanish Civil War, visiting Valencia, Madrid, and Barcelona. Her book *Spain in Arms* (1937) portrayed the struggle in simplistic terms ("the fascists of the world were attacking the Spanish people") and predicted future war if the insurgents won. In late December 1937, she returned to China. Her account *One-Fifth of Mankind* (1938) predicted victory over Japan and stressed Communist-Guomindang unity. Earlier Strong had found Chiang Kai-shek a traitor to his people; now, he was a potential George Washington. Indeed, Mme Chiang (*\*Song Meiling*) wrote the introduction.

In 1940, while visiting the U.S., Strong defended the Nazi-Soviet Non-Aggression Pact, claiming it was in the interests of peace. To Strong, World War II was at first the "Second Imperialist War," although she was quick to defend the Soviet occupation of Poland. At the suggestion of Eleanor Roosevelt, Strong wrote a book on contemporary America, *My Native Land* (1940). Here she portrayed the New Deal as "a first-aid device," called Franklin Roosevelt the founder of a corporate state, and predicted the fall of American capitalism. She then briefly returned to the Soviet Union, during which she praised the Soviet occupation of Lithuania. By the end of the year, she went to China. This time she found the Guomindang undemocratic. Chiang's regime, she claimed, was using U.S. military aid to fight Communists, not the Japanese.

In 1941, Strong was back in America, where she spent most of the war years. Once Russia entered the war, she wrote a book whose title aptly conveyed its thesis: *The Soviets Expected It* (1941). She was showing the first signs of Paget's disease, a bone disorder that made walking painful. At one point, she lectured from a wheelchair. In 1943, she was technical adviser for the MGM film *Song of Russia*. A Strong novel, *Wild River* (1943), told of two Russian lovers dedicated to rebuilding their war-stricken land. Similarly her *Peoples of the USSR* (1944) was loaded with smiling heroes from every Russian republic portrayed in dreary Sovfoto shots.

In 1944, Strong returned to Russia as an accredited correspondent for the *Atlantic*, doing so despite FBI opposition. In 1946, in her book *I Saw the New Poland*, she not only accused Poland's anti-Communist Home Army of stupidity and cowardice; it had, she said, collaborated with the Germans while the liberating Red Army had acted heroically. For the first time, her lecture tour in the U.S. was a failure. With the advent of the Cold War, many Americans were unreceptive towards her oft-stated views.

By July 1946, Strong was back in China, where she lived in a 12-by-20-foot cave at Communist headquarters at Yenan. Again she conveyed her enthusiasm by books and pamphlets. In her most famous piece of reporting, she cited Mao Zedong's proclamation that "American reactionaries are merely a paper tiger." Returning to Russia by the fall of 1947, she sought to promote Mao's brand of revolution, only to find the Soviets discouraging her efforts. On the evening of February 13, 1949, she was arrested, then held in Moscow's Lubianka prison. Her quarters: a cell with a bunk, chair, and small table. After five days, she was deported, the interrogating commissar telling her:

> You are guilty of spying against the Soviet Union. We might have a trial, but this would take a long time and mean a long confinement for you. In view of your age, we think it better to expel you to Poland.

As Strong traveled to the U.S., she said to the press, "Do not use my arrest as material for the cold war. I do not know why I was arrested or why they unjustly call me a spy, but the police of any country can make mistakes." Never denouncing the Soviet regime per se, she always blamed her arrest on minor officials. When the American Communist Party refused to support her, she sold the story of her internment to the *New York Herald-Tribune*. Shunned by friends and allies of 30 years' standing, she confided in 1950 that she would rather be dead. She candidly wrote reformer Raymond Robins concerning her journalistic career, "The people I really cared for, on whose side I felt myself to be fighting—they winced if a single human weakness in the U.S.S.R. were noticed. So I let my audiences pressure me into giving what I knew was a partial picture. . . . I told no lies, but I didn't tell the truth. And I still think this may be the correct procedure." At one point, the 64-year-old Strong told an Oberlin student:

> You know, I am no longer young. At my age it is not easy to give up something to which one has devoted one's entire lifetime. . . . It is not a matter of age. It is a matter of dedication. . . . I have had doubts; of course, I have had doubts. But when one believes deeply in something, one must accept certain doubts. . . . If I were convinced that the Soviet Union did not justify my faith, the world would become a hopeless, dreadful place for me.

Living in Los Angeles, Strong was befriended by the Reverend Stephen Fritchman, the left-leaning minister of the First Unitarian Church, who found her a troubled spirit. When the Korean War broke out in 1950, she thought it a U.S. effort to entrap the Soviets into global conflict. From 1951 to 1956, she gave vent to her views in a mimeographed monthly, *Today*.

On March 4, 1955, the Soviets dropped all charges against Strong. A day later, *Pravda* blamed her arrest on secret police chief Lavrenti Beria. Ten days later, Strong claimed that Beria had been acting under orders from the U.S. Central Intelligence Agency. In her book *The Stalin Era* (1956), she conceded that "a great madness" had come down on the Soviet Union. However, she still praised Stalin, saying he was "a man who could bring diverse views into harmony with a speed that amounted to genius." Conceding that she had been silent when close friends were sent to Siberia, she asked:

> Why then could I protest when the same injustice came to me? Then I asked, "Why had I made no outcry?" And my answer was: "Because all those years I felt myself in the presence of something so vast, so important for all mankind's future, that it must not be halted or diverted, whatever the cost."

Indeed, she denounced party chair Nikita Khrushchev's 1956 speech to the 20th Party Congress: "It contains too much truth to be denied, but too much emotional exaggeration to be sanc-

tioned." Only Soviet suppression of the Hungarian Revolution caused her to protest publicly.

In 1958, Strong returned to Russia, staying there for less than two months before she took up permanent residence in Beijing, where she was much honored by Chinese officials. The government gave her a secretary and automobile, and she shared a cook and maid with residents of a well-preserved old house called the Peace Compound. In 1959, she defended the Chinese repression of a major rebellion in Tibet, even hailing showtrials of ex-landlords. From 1962 to 1970, she wrote a monthly four-page newsletter, *Letter from China*, which defended all aspects of Mao's regime and had some 40,000 readers. During her last ten years, she denounced Soviet "revisionism," called the Pathet Lao "very primitive democrats," compared John F. Kennedy to Genghis Khan, and found the Vietnam War an example of "American imperialism." A firm defender of China's Cultural Revolution, she became an honorary member of the Red Guard. On March 29, 1970, Anna Louise Strong died in Beijing, China.

**SOURCES:**

Pringle, Robert William, Jr. "Anna Louise Strong: Propagandist of Communism." Unpublished Ph.D. thesis, 1970.

Strong, Anna Louise. *I Change Worlds: The Remaking of an American*. NY: Henry Holt, 1935.

Strong, Tracy B., and Keyssar, Helene. *Right in Her Soul: The Life of Anna Louise Strong*. NY: Random House, 1983.

**SUGGESTED READING:**

Caute, David. *The Fellow Travellers: A Postscript to the Enlightenment*. NY: Macmillan, 1973.

Shewmaker, Kenneth E. *Americans and the Chinese Communists, 1927–1945: A Persuading Encounter*. Ithaca, NY: Cornell University Press, 1971.

Willen, Paul. "Anna Louise Strong Goes Home Again," in *The Reporter*. Vol. 12. April 7, 1955, pp. 28–31.

**COLLECTIONS:**

The papers of Anna Louise Strong until 1931, as well as some materials from the 1930s through 1950s, are located at the Suzzallo Library, University of Washington, Seattle. Valuable Strong letters to Sydney Dix Strong and Tracy Strong, Jr., her nephew, are also there. Her papers from 1958 until her death are at the Beijing Library, China. Other Strong materials are located at the Swarthmore College Peace Collection, Swarthmore, Pennsylvania, and the Hoover Institution on War, Revolution and Peace, Stanford, California.

**Justus D. Doenecke**,
Professor of History,
New College of the
University of South Florida,
Sarasota, Florida

# Strong, Harriet (1844–1929)

*American agriculturist and civic leader. Name variations: Hattie Russell. Born Harriet Russell on July 23,*

*1844, in Buffalo, New York; died on September 16, 1929, in an automobile accident near Whittier, California; daughter of Henry Pierpont Russell and Mary Guest (Musier) Russell; attended Young Ladies' seminary of Mary Atkins (Benicia, California), 1858–60; married Charles Lyman Strong (a mine superintendent), on February 26, 1863 (committed suicide in 1883); children: Harriet Russell, Mary Lyman, Georgina Pierpont, and Nelle de Luce.*

Harriet Strong was born on July 23, 1844, in Buffalo, New York, to a father who eventually took his large family across the country in a series of job-hunting moves. The family made it to the Pacific coast when Harriet, a self-described semi-invalid due to a spinal affliction, was around eight years old. While physically confined due to her condition, she studied music, literature, history, and art. From 1858 to 1860, she attended the Young Ladies' Seminary run by **Mary Atkins** in Benicia, California, where she continued her studies, particularly in music, English and French.

By 1861, Harriet's family had moved to Carson City after a discovery of silver in Nevada's Comstock Lode. From among her many admirers, she married Charles Lyman Strong, superintendent of the Gould and Curry mine, who was almost twice her age, on February 26, 1863. Although Charles was committed to Harriet and later to their four daughters, he was seldom at ease and overworked himself. Following his first breakdown not long after their marriage, he ended his employment with the mine, and the family moved to Oakland, California, where Charles alternately rested and continued to overwork. In 1883, despondent over a bad mining investment, he committed suicide.

Shortly before her husband's death, Harriet's health had assumed a new vitality under the care of a famed neurologist. Now faced with the prospect of supporting herself and her daughters, she is said to have undergone a fundamental change of personality which made possible her accomplishments in the years to come. Four years into untangling her husband's investment affairs in litigation (yet another four would be required), Strong turned to farming the 220 acres her husband had purchased in southern California. She undertook a study of irrigation, water storage, and flood control to successfully grow walnuts, citrus fruits, pomegranates, and pampas grass on her Rancho del Fuerte which would become more popularly known as the Strong Ranch. She later used her understanding of water control for the benefit of Los Angeles

County as an advocate of flood control and specific water-supply measures. Her 1887 and 1894 patents on sequential water storage dams were followed by patents for a number of household inventions. Known as both the "walnut queen" and the "pampas lady," Strong won national attention in Chicago at the World's Columbian Exposition of 1893.

Her achievements earned her distinction as the first woman member ever elected to the Los Angeles Chamber of Commerce. A staunch feminist, Strong instructed other women in the importance of business dealings and public affairs through her establishment of the Hamilton Club in 1920, and she was involved in many cultural organizations, including the Ebell Club of Los Angeles, which she founded to encourage women's cultural opportunities; the Ruskin Art Club; and the Los Angeles Symphony Association, of which she served as vice president. She also participated in the founding of a Christian Science church in Whittier after her conversion to that faith. An agriculturist and civic leader, Strong died near Whittier in a car accident, age 86, in 1929.

**SOURCES:**
James, Edward T., ed. *Notable American Women, 1607–1950.* Cambridge, MA: The Belknap Press of Harvard University, 1971.

**Helga P. McCue,** freelance writer, Waterford, Connecticut

# Strossen, Nadine (1950—)

*First woman president of the American Civil Liberties Union (ACLU), law professor, and writer. Born in Jersey City, New Jersey, on August 18, 1950; daughter of Woodrow John Strossen and Sylvia (Simicich) Strossen; graduated Phi Beta Kappa from Harvard-Radcliffe College, 1972; graduated magna cum laude from Harvard Law School, 1975; married Eli Michael Noam (a professor), in 1980.*

*Selected writings:* Defending Pornography: Free Speech, Sex, and the Fight for Women's Rights *(1995);* (contributor) Speaking of Race, Speaking of Sex: Hate Speech, Civil Rights, and Civil Liberties *(1996).*

Nadine Strossen, the only child of Woodrow and **Sylvia Strossen**, was born in 1950 in Jersey City, New Jersey, and grew up in Hopkins, Minnesota. She learned to value freedom of expression and to risk ostracism from the examples of relatives on both sides of her family. Her maternal grandfather endured public ridicule as a pacifist in Italy during World War I, and her German father's anti-Hitler activities landed him in the Buchenwald concentration camp during World War II. Although she considered the law an exciting profession and was a top debater in high school, Strossen did not think it possible for a woman to have a career in that field. However, she possessed an early sense of her own inalienable rights and was quick to defend them. And when she was given the honor of addressing the audience at her high school graduation, she abandoned the usual commencement remarks for an opportunity to speak out against the Vietnam War.

An accomplished student, Strossen graduated Phi Beta Kappa from Harvard-Radcliffe College in 1972. She was active in feminist and debating groups, which fostered her desire to become a lawyer. Upon entering Harvard Law School, Strossen assumed the much-coveted editorship of the *Law Review*. Graduating magna cum laude in 1975, she returned to Minnesota to become a law clerk in the Supreme Court there. Her work in general law and commercial litigation led in 1984 to a position at the New York University School of Law, where she eventually became associate professor of clinical law and supervising attorney of the Civil Rights Clinic. By 1988, she was a full professor of law at New York University Law School.

Even before her move to New York, Strossen had become involved with the American Civil Liberties Union (ACLU), as a member of the board of directors in 1983 and as national general counsel three years later. In 1991, she rose to the presidency, becoming the first woman and the youngest individual so elected. In her tenure as president, she has spoken to more than 200 groups each year and has visited more than 500 colleges worldwide. Concerned with the image of the ACLU as a radically leftist political group, Strossen has sought to change it, focusing upon the absolute commitment of the United States and the ACLU to the Bill of Rights and issues of free speech. According to *Current Biography*, although Strossen's convictions about the importance of free speech as "the bedrock of organizing and advocacy and activism on behalf of any other right" made her the ideal candidate for the high-profile job, it also made her the prime target of vocal opponents of ACLU activities. "You'd be surprised how many audiences are openly hostile to me," she once remarked in a magazine interview soon after accepting the post. "They think I'm the devil incarnate."

A professed feminist, Strossen endured heavy criticism from other prominent feminists, among them **Andrea Dworkin** and **Catharine MacKinnon**, for her opposition to the censorship of pornography. She rejected their labeling her an "apologist" for pornographers in her book *Defending Pornography*, which *The New York Times Book Review* named a Notable Book of 1995. In it, she argued that while the prosecution of violence against women is vital, the prosecution of pornography depicting violence against women is unconstitutional and dangerous to the right to free speech. Finding the claims linking pornography to violence against women unsubstantiated, Strossen suggests that even if a link could be identified, the risk of censorship would outweigh the evils attributed to pornography. In Strossen's opinion, the attempt to censor pornography might result in expanding the definition of what constitutes pornography to include less objectionable material. She bolsters her argument by citing examples in Canada, where antipornography legislation has been passed, in which nonviolent material with lesbian or feminist themes has been banned. Believing that her adversaries are looking for an easy solution to a complex social problem, she adds: "To solve a social problem, we need more speech." Strossen used a similar argument against making hate speech a crime in her contribution to the 1996 book *Speaking of Race, Speaking of Sex: Hate Speech, Civil Rights, and Civil Liberties.*

Strossen and the ACLU have continued their fight against censorship as it applies to the issue of the wide availability of information on the Internet. They have particularly argued against government regulatory proposals, the most prominent of which was the Communications Decency Act in 1996. The act was intended to limit minors' access to "indecent" or "patently offensive" material on the Internet by making the distribution of such illegal. The ACLU brought the case before a panel of federal judges, who agreed that it violated First Amendment rights, and the government's appeal became the Supreme Court case *Reno* v. *American Civil Liberties Union*. In a unanimous decision, the justices determined the act to be unconstitutional.

In 1986, the U.S. Jaycees honored Strossen with its "Ten Outstanding Young Americans" award, and she became the first American woman to win the Jaycees International's "Outstanding Young Persons of the World" award. The recipient of several honorary doctorates, Strossen was named to the *National Law Journal's* list of "100 most influential lawyers in America" in 1991 and 1994. She also earned the Media Institute's Freedom of Speech Award in 1994 and the "Women of Distinction" award from the Women's League for Conservative Judaism. The accolades continued when *Vanity Fair* magazine named her as one of "America's 200 Most Influential Women" in 1998 and *Ladies' Home Journal* included her in "The 100 Most Important Women in America" in 1999.

**SOURCES:**
*Current Biography Yearbook, 1997.* NY: H.W. Wilson, 1997.

Read, Phyllis J., and Bernard L. Witlieb. *The Book of Women's Firsts.* NY: Random House, 1992.

**B. Kimberly Taylor,** freelance writer, New York, New York

## Strozzi, Alessandra (1406–1469)

*Influential Florentine. Name variations: Alessandra Macinghi; Alessandra Macinghi Strozzi. Born Alessandra Macinghi in 1406 in Florence; died in 1469 in Florence; married Matteo di Simone Strozzi, in 1422 (died 1436); children: four surviving sons.*

Alessandra Strozzi was an Italian woman of the upper merchant class. Her family, the Macinghis of Florence, were wealthy merchants who had recently established themselves as one of Florence's most important families. At 15, Alessandra married Matteo di Simone Strozzi, and thus entered another influential family. Matteo held important city government posts and as such was deeply involved in local politics. He and his family had gained the enmity of the Medici family, and when Cosimo de Medici came to power in 1434, Matteo was banished from Florence. Alessandra and their seven children followed him into exile. Two years later, he died; a pregnant Alessandra and her four surviving children returned to Florence.

She never remarried, but dedicated herself to the onerous task of re-establishing the honor and good name of the Strozzis. All of her sons were subject to banishment when they came of age (13) and had to leave their mother, who sent them to relatives in other prosperous Italian cities. But she continued to work for their eventual return to Florence, and spent much of her time writing letters to each son, giving advice and counsel and sending them clothing and other supplies. Her letters have survived, and they give a picture of an intelligent, caring mother who thought almost single-mindedly of her sons' welfare, and who deprived herself of luxuries to save money for them. Alessandra was also an entrepreneur; she managed the family's holdings carefully and made investments which were usually profitable. She arranged her children's marriages with great concern for the economic benefit the Strozzis could reap from them.

With her hard work and business acumen, her family eventually regained the fortune it had lost when Matteo was banished. After the death of Cosimo de Medici in 1464, Alessandra petitioned for a lifting of the ban of exile on her sons; two years later, she succeeded. Her family name stood restored to its previous honor and her sons were allowed to return to Florence. Alessandra Strozzi died at age 63.

**SOURCES:**
Uitz, Erika. *The Legend of Good Women: The Liberation of Women in Medieval Cities.* Wakefield, RI: Moyer Bell, 1988.

**Laura York,** M.A. in History, University of California, Riverside, California

## Strozzi, Barbara (1619–1664)

*Italian composer. Born in Venice, Italy, in 1619; died in Venice in 1664; daughter of Isabella Briega (some sources cite Garzoni) and stepdaughter of Giulio Strozzi (a famous poet, librettist, and dramatist, who adopted Barbara at age nine as her parents were not married); studied with Francesco Cavalli.*

*Published her first volume of madrigals on texts by her stepfather (1644); published op. 2, Cantate, arietta, e duetti (1651) and op. 8 in Venice.*

Born in Venice in 1619, Barbara Strozzi grew up in the house of her mother **Isabella Briega** (some sources cite Garzoni) and her stepfather Giulio Strozzi, a famous poet, librettist, and dramatist. He adopted Barbara at age nine, as her biological father had not married her mother. It was a musical and literary family, and she was encouraged by her stepfather to make music her career. Strozzi's musical pursuits were limited, however, to the Accademia degli Unisoni, founded by her stepfather as a showcase for her talents. Most of her compositions, mainly vocal chamber music which was ideally suited for drawing rooms, were performed in homes rather than at court or on stage. Many of her texts came from lyrical poetry, often about some dramatic event or unrequited love. Strozzi was one of the era's most prolific composers. In the eight volumes she published between 1644 and 1664, there were over 100 works, mostly arias and secular cantatas.

**John Haag,** Athens, Georgia

## Strozzi, Clarice (1493–1528).

*See Medici, Clarice de.*

## Strozzi, Marietta Palla (fl. 1468)

*Florentine noblewoman. Flourished around 1468; daughter of Lorenzo Palla Strozzi.*

As a young heiress, with both parents dead, Marietta Palla Strozzi brought disfavor because she "lived where she liked and did what she would." Her features were immortalized by Desiderio.

## Struther, Jan (1901–1953).

*See Maxtone Graham, Joyce.*

## Stuart.

*See also Stewart (in Scotland, the spelling of the surname Stewart was changed to Stuart by brothers Matthew and John Stewart, who adopted the French spelling in 1537).*

## Stuart, Arabella (1575–1615)

*English princess whose unhappy life was dominated by the political exigencies of two wary monarchs, despite her disinterest in claiming the throne. Name variations: Lady Arabella Stuart; Arbella Stuart; Ara-*

*Arabella Stuart*

*bella or Arbella Seymour. Born in October 1575 in London, England; died on September 25, 1615, in the Tower of London; interred on September 28, 1615, in Westminster Abbey, London; daughter of Charles Stuart (1555–1576), 5th earl of Lennox, and Elizabeth Cavendish (d. 1582); married William Seymour (1587–1660), 2nd duke of Somerset (r. 1660–1660), on June 22, 1610; no children.*

In June 1611, King James I of England issued a warrant for the arrest of a royal princess who had contrived to escape from her confinement in England and flee to France. James considered the woman, who was his own cousin Arabella Stuart and his closest living relative, a potential threat to his power, and sent out search parties. The next day a small boat hurrying Arabella and her modest party across the English Channel was overtaken and all aboard were arrested. They were brought back to England and imprisoned in the Tower of London to await the king's justice.

As dramatic as it was, this escape attempt was only one of the many bids for freedom which dominated Arabella Stuart's life. Born in 1575, she was the only child of Charles Stuart, 5th earl of Lennox, and ❧➤ **Elizabeth Cavendish**. Her father was descended from *Margaret Tudor (1489–1541), daughter of Henry VII, and was third in the line of succession to the English throne. Arabella's mother was the daughter of the wealthy *Elizabeth Talbot and William Cavendish.

The secret marriage between Charles Stuart and Elizabeth Cavendish had displeased Queen *Elizabeth I, since everyone of royal blood was compelled by law to obtain the queen's permission to marry; no one doubted that she would have forbidden the dangerous union of her potential successor with the wealth of the Cavendish family. But Arabella's birth was even more threatening to the queen; the baby held a strong claim to the throne through her father—as strong a claim as Elizabeth's eventual successor, James I. In addition, Charles Stuart was the brother-in-law of Elizabeth's enemy and rival monarch, the Catholic *Mary Stuart, queen of Scots, who held the strongest claim to succeed Elizabeth. Queen Elizabeth was keenly aware that as a Protestant, she faced many enemies among her Catholic subjects who wanted to replace her with a Catholic monarch. The existence of a new claimant was especially dangerous since the child could become the center of conspiracies against the queen. This concern explains Queen Elizabeth's consistent efforts to keep Arabella as politically and financially weakened as possible.

When Charles Stuart died in April 1576, King James of Scotland seized the Stuart estates in Lennox, which should have become Arabella's inheritance. Then Arabella's grandmother *Margaret Douglas (1515–1578), countess of Lennox, died, and Queen Elizabeth seized the Lennox lands in England. This left the infant Arabella without any source of income; even the jewels left to her were stolen by the will's executor. In May 1578, King James revoked two-year-old Arabella's claim to the earldom of Lennox; she would never again be recognized as countess of Lennox.

Arabella did have one important supporter throughout the trials of her childhood: her maternal grandmother Elizabeth Talbot, countess of Shrewsbury, with whom she and her mother lived. The countess was untiring in her efforts to regain Arabella's estates and to persuade Queen Elizabeth to provide Arabella with an income such as many other royal relatives enjoyed, although Arabella would fail to appreciate Talbot's consistent advocacy for her financial and political well-being. Even after Queen Elizabeth finally agreed to an annual stipend, the countess would continue for years to press the queen to increase the sum and to regain Arabella's stolen inheritance from James of Scotland. The queen put the countess off with vague promises and never requested James to relinquish Lennox to Arabella.

Around 1580, the countess moved her daughter Elizabeth Cavendish and granddaughter Arabella to her country manor in Derbyshire, where Arabella would spend most of her childhood. Her tutors instructed her in reading, classical literature, and history; she was a gifted linguist, fluent in French, Italian, Spanish, and Latin, and reading Greek and Hebrew. She studied dancing, the lute, and embroidery as well. The countess also saw to it that Arabella was well taught in the tenets of Protestantism.

Arabella was six years old when her mother died after a sudden illness. In response, Queen Elizabeth cut off most of the annual allowance she and her mother had shared. Despite the countess' protests, Elizabeth refused to raise the sum. Talbot was forced to support her granddaughter herself, which, although she could easily afford it, she strongly resented as a matter of principle. Arabella was, after all, a royal princess and the queen's close relative, and thus was entitled to a large royal stipend. Elizabeth refused to relent.

In the same household in Derbyshire lived England's most famous political prisoner, Ara-

## Cavendish, Elizabeth (d. 1582)

*Countess of Lennox. Name variations: Bess of Hardwick. Birth date unknown; died in 1582; daughter of *Elizabeth Talbot (1518–1608), countess of Shrewsbury, and Sir William Cavendish, 1st earl of Devonshire; married Charles Stuart, 5th earl of Lennox, in 1574 (died April 1576); children: *Arabella Stuart (1575–1615).*

bella's aunt Mary Stuart, queen of Scots. Her grandparents were Mary's guardians during much of the unfortunate queen's confinement. It is not clear how much contact Arabella had with the captive queen. Their lives, however—as royal princesses orphaned young, denied their rightful titles, and confined in order to minimize their threat to reigning monarchs—would bear a striking resemblance in Arabella's later years.

The execution in 1587 of Mary Stuart had important consequences for Arabella. The removal of Queen Elizabeth's closest living relative left Arabella and her cousin James of Scotland with the strongest claims to succeed Elizabeth. For years, however, Elizabeth refused to name either James or Arabella as her heir, fearing the political factioning which would result.

Mary Stuart's death brought Elizabeth's attention to the 12-year-old girl growing up in Talbot's Hardwick House. Not long after, Arabella had her first face-to-face encounter with the monarch whose actions in many ways had determined the course of her life. The question of Arabella's marriage led Elizabeth to summon the girl to the court; with Arabella's parents dead and her claim to the throne so strong, Elizabeth was exercising royal prerogative in choosing a husband for her cousin. She was considering a betrothal to Duke Rainutio Farnese of Parma to seal a new treaty between England and the Italian city-state. Nothing came of this arrangement, and Arabella was soon sent home.

In 1588, she was recalled to court, Elizabeth still holding out the possibility of marriage to the duke. However, this trip to London was cut short when Arabella was banished from court for three years for, according to diplomatic reports, her "excessive familiarity" with the earl of Essex. It is not easy to believe that 13-year-old Arabella was actually guilty of inappropriate behavior with the earl, although she was certainly infatuated with him. The queen was more likely using the rumors as an expedient for removing Arabella from court. For Elizabeth, Arabella was becoming more and more of a problem with each passing year; she would have to be married, but her husband must be carefully chosen, since the wrong man might try to push Arabella's claim to the throne. Elizabeth resolved the issue, as she did many other difficult decisions, by simply putting off the question for as long as possible.

There was another reason for keeping Arabella away from court; she did not fit in to the court's hierarchical structure in any way. She was a royal princess by birth, yet held no title; court records refer to her only as "Lady Arabella." In a court setting strictly ordered by rank, Arabella had no clear place. Her quiet and lonely country upbringing further isolated her from her new companions and had not prepared her for the constant ritual and socializing of court life.

Recalled a second time to London in 1591, Arabella again found herself in trouble with the queen. Some of the queen's councilors secretly offered Arabella's hand to Rainutio Farnese again, assuring him that he and Arabella would succeed Elizabeth. The duke's death soon afterwards ended this plot. But then Arabella became the center of another unsuccessful plot, in which Catholic nobles planned to kidnap her, marry her to a Catholic and put her on the throne. There is no evidence that Arabella agreed to or even knew about these court intrigues against Elizabeth, although the fact that she was a compelling target for would-be conspirators was enough to cause the queen to send her home in 1592.

Arabella spent the next nine years in Derbyshire. She grew increasingly restless with her endless studies and quiet life dominated by her aging grandmother, who, she complained, monitored her behavior closely and treated her like a child. Arabella longed to establish her own independent household away from the countess, but she owned no estates and anyway had virtually no income to support her own staff. This desire for her own home became a recurring theme in Arabella's life. Despite the numerous plots regarding the queen and, later, James I, which involved Arabella, she harbored no desire to raise herself to the throne, and never displayed any ambition for royal power. Her goal throughout her life went no further than achieving her independence and making her own decisions.

Finally, in 1601 Talbot agreed to let Arabella, now 25 years old, have her own household and staff on the countess' lands. Not contented with this, Arabella became determined to make a complete break from her grandmother by finding herself a husband. In seeking her own mate, Arabella was not only disobeying the countess

but actually breaking the law which gave the queen the right to make royal marriage agreements. In 1602, she sent a secret messenger to propose marriage with the young noble Edward Seymour. It was an irrational choice, since Edward was the son of a disgraced family hostile to the queen; in proposing such a union, Arabella was ensuring the queen's anger if the marriage came to pass. But it did not; the Seymours were being closely watched by the crown, and Arabella's servant was arrested and forced to confess her plans. Arabella was questioned and apologized for causing trouble.

Yet her unpredictable behavior did not end; she wrote a series of rambling letters to various family members requesting their help in freeing her from her grandmother's care; she even threatened to go on a hunger strike until she could meet with the queen. In response, Queen Elizabeth sent a commissioner to meet with Arabella, and Arabella told him that she was the lover of King James. Various abortive plans to escape from Derbyshire followed. On hearing all this, the Queen's Privy Council wondered about Arabella's mental state but soon turned their attention to much more pressing matters: the queen's failing health and her death in March 1603, and the succession to the English throne by King James of Scotland.

James I would treat his cousin Arabella with the same caution Elizabeth had. One of his first acts as king was to order the earl of Kent to keep Arabella in his care, ending her brief period as mistress of her own household; this was a prudent move from James' point of view, since he needed to keep all potential rivals in check in order to consolidate his rule. Fortunately he enjoyed tremendous popular support in England, something Arabella never had nor sought. His party tried to ensure her lack of support by spreading rumors that Arabella was insane.

Arabella's irrational—and politically naive—behavior continued into James' reign, unintentionally reinforcing the rumors against her. She bluntly refused the royal summons to attend Queen Elizabeth's funeral as the only living royal princess, excusing herself by saying that the queen had never treated her with the respect she deserved. She did attend James' coronation in July, after which she remained at court in Queen *Anne of Denmark's retinue. The queen became a close friend, the first real friendship Arabella is known to have had, and she spent the next six years in relative happiness at court. Arabella's presence there served James' goals well: he could not forget that his claim to the throne was no stronger than hers, and that she had shown herself to be somewhat unstable and unpredictable (although she was never directly involved in a plot to overthrow him). Like Elizabeth, he sought to keep her under control, and never carried through on his promises to restore her father's property to her and to find her a husband.

Arabella was second in rank only to the queen, and because of her intimacy with the queen did not suffer from the isolation and awkward position she had experienced at Elizabeth's court. Arabella spent her days in idle games and pastimes—hunting, masques, dancing, music, and other diversions. In her letters to her family, she writes that although sometimes court life was tiresome, she was happier than she had ever been. Yet her happiness was always overshadowed by the same financial troubles she had experienced all her life. She received a moderate income from the king, but this was insufficient to support her in the style demanded by court society. Maintaining appearances was critically important in 16th-century court life; a high-ranking lady such as Arabella had to dress in the most expensive fashions, support numerous servants, give expensive gifts to her friends, and show charity to the poor. Because James would neither give her permission to leave the court nor increase her stipend so she could afford to stay, she was forced to borrow money from friends. This situation continued for years, until Arabella once again began to feel like a prisoner.

In 1606, with the aid of James and Anne, Arabella was reconciled with her grandmother, the steadfast advocate of her childhood whom she had grown to see as her jailer in her teenage years. She had had no contact with Elizabeth Talbot in years, but after their reunion she visited her regularly until Talbot's death in 1608. Talbot had reinstated Arabella into her will, leaving enough money for Arabella to finally purchase a house of her own in London. Still, she spent most of her time at court. The next year, Arabella made her first and only trip to the Midlands of England, where she had grown up. On her eight-week journey through the lands of her Cavendish family, she was reunited with distant relatives and old friends from her youth. The possibilities for independence inspired by this long trip intensified Arabella's lifelong desire to be her own mistress.

At age 34, Arabella was twice the age of most noblewomen when married. Yet there had been no serious betrothal negotiations on her behalf for 15 years, and it was obvious James had no intention of marrying off his rival. As she had done seven years before, Arabella decided to make her own agreement. In December 1609, James discovered that Arabella had communicated with the Seymour family about the possibility of a marriage. He ordered her confined to her suite but soon dropped the matter. In February, he was forced to call her before the Privy Council to answer to rumors that she had continued to discuss a marriage with William Seymour, the 22-year-old brother of Edward Seymour whom she had sought to marry in 1602. After swearing to her innocence, Arabella was forgiven and ordered to drop any plans for wedlock. She did not obey this order. Again she was behaving irrationally; by plotting to marry without James' permission, she was bound to alienate her strongest allies—James, Queen Anne, and their advisor Lord Cecil, all of whom had shown her friendship and respect despite her actions.

On June 22, 1610, Arabella and William Seymour married in a secret ceremony. On July 8, James was shocked to learn of the wedding, and had William imprisoned in the Tower of London; Arabella was arrested the next day. When questioned before the Privy Council, William denied the marriage, while Arabella confessed. The king ordered the couple kept apart, so that there could be no risk that a child would be born to threaten the succession. Confined in a noble's home, Arabella wrote letter after letter to James and court officials, begging to be restored to favor, but consistently defending her actions and refusing to admit that she had defied a royal command.

> [S]he is allowed to come to court . . . but so far a husband has not been found, and she remains without mate and without estate.
>
> —Venetian ambassador Nicholo Molin, 1607

Evidence suggests that despite the king's orders, William and Arabella managed to see one another occasionally, and in September Arabella wrongly believed herself pregnant. In consequence, the Council ordered that she be removed from London and put under the care of the bishop of Durham. Determined not to be taken from the court, and her short-lived marriage, Arabella managed to delay the trip until June 1611 by claiming to be ill. On June 3, with the help of several servants, Arabella disguised herself in men's clothing and, escaping her guards, rode to a prearranged site on the coast where she and her servants waited in vain for William Seymour. Then her party set out on their ill-fated voyage across the English Channel for France, from which they returned to London as prisoners. William Seymour had meanwhile managed to escape to the Netherlands, where James was content to let him remain; Arabella never saw him again.

There was no trial. Arabella remained a prisoner in the Tower, but was never charged with any crime. Her actions had consequences for her entire family, most notably her aunt ◀❧ **Mary Talbot**, who had helped plan her escape and suffered 12 years in the Tower for it, and her uncle Gilbert Talbot, who was forced to resign his position as privy councilor. Arabella's servants all served time in prison as well. Arabella's accommodations in the Tower were befitting a woman of her rank—she had a small retinue and elegant lodgings—yet she was a prisoner just the same. All her appeals to James and Anne for forgiveness went unanswered.

In 1614, she made a failed escape attempt, after which she fell into a deep depression. After years of struggling to control her own life, Arabella finally gave up all hope of such freedom, and her health began to decline rapidly. Her mental state deteriorated as well, and in September 1615 she began to refuse to eat. On September 25, she died of starvation at age 39. In a quiet ceremony, James had his cousin buried at Westminster Abbey, in the same vault holding the remains of her aunt, Mary Stuart, queen of Scots, whose unfortunate life had in so many ways mirrored her own.

William Seymour, her husband of a few weeks, was allowed to return to England in 1616, where he married ◀❧ **Frances Devereux** and eventually earned back royal favor. He served with distinction at James' court and at the courts of Charles I and Charles II, dying in 1660.

**SOURCES:**
Durant, David N. *Arbella Stuart: A Rival to the Queen.* London: Weidenfeld & Nicholson, 1978.
Handover, P.M. *Arbella Stuart.* London: Eyre & Spottiswoode, 1957.
McInnes, Ian. *Arabella: the Life and Times of Lady Arabella Seymour.* London: W.H. Allen, 1968.

**SUGGESTED READING:**
Hibbert, Christopher. *The Virgin Queen: Elizabeth I, Genius of the Golden Age.* NY: Dutton, 1976.
Stuart, Arbella. *The Letters of Lady Arbella Stuart.* Ed. by Sara Jayne Steen. NY: Oxford University Press, 1994.

**Laura York**, M.A. in History,
University of California, Riverside, California

## Stuart, Cora Wilson (1875–1958).

*See Stewart, Cora Wilson.*

## Stuart, Elizabeth (1596–1662).

*See Elizabeth of Bohemia.*

## Stuart, Elizabeth (d. 1673)

***Countess of Arundel.*** *Died on January 23, 1673; daughter of Esme or Esmé Stuart (b. 1579), 3rd duke of Lennox, and Baroness **Katherine Clifton**; married Henry Frederick Howard, earl of Arundel, in 1626; children: Thomas Howard (b. 1627), 5th duke of Norfolk; Henry Howard (b. 1628), 6th duke of Norfolk; Cardinal Philip Howard (b. 1629); Charles Howard of Greystoke (b. 1630), Lord of the Manor; Bernard Howard (b. 1641); Catherine Howard; Talbot Howard; Edward Howard (b. 1637); Francis Howard (b. 1639); Esmé Howard (b. 1645); **Elizabeth Howard** (1651–1705, who married Alex Macdonnel and Bartholomew Russell).*

## Stuart, Elizabeth (1635–1650).

*See Elizabeth Stuart.*

## Stuart, Frances (1647–1702)

***Duchess of Richmond and Lennox.*** *Name variations: Frances Blantyre; Frances Stewart; known as La Belle Stuart. Born Frances Teresa Stuart in 1647 (some sources cite 1648) in Scotland; died on October 15, 1702, in London; daughter of Walter Stuart (or Stew-*

---

❧▶ **Talbot, Mary** (d. 1632)

***Countess of Shrewsbury.*** *Name variations: Mary Cavendish. Interred on April 14, 1632, at St. Peter's, Sheffield, England; daughter of \*Elizabeth Talbot (1518–1608), countess of Shrewsbury, and Sir William Cavendish, 1st earl of Devonshire; married Gilbert Talbot (1552–1616), 7th earl of Shrewsbury, on February 9, 1567; children: **Mary Talbot** (d. 1649); **Elizabeth Talbot** (d. 1651); Lady **Alathea Talbot** (d. 1654, who married Thomas Howard, earl of Arundel).*

❧▶ **Devereux, Frances** (d. 1674)

***Duchess of Somerset.*** *Name variations: Frances Seymour. Died on April 24, 1674 (some sources cite 1679); daughter of Robert Devereux (b. 1566), 2nd earl of Essex, and **Frances Walsingham**; married William Seymour (1587–1660), 2nd duke of Somerset (r. 1660–1660), on March 3, 1616; children: William (b. 1621); Robert (b. 1624); Henry (b. 1626); Edward; John, 4th duke of Somerset; \*Frances Seymour (d. 1680); Lady \*Mary Seymour (d. 1673, who married Heneage Finch, 3rd earl of Winchelsea); Lady \*Jane Seymour (d. 1679).*

*art) and **Sophia Stuart**; married Charles Stuart, duke of Richmond and Lennox, in 1667; no children.*

Related to the Stuart royal family of England, Frances Stuart was for many years the center of life at the royal court. She was born in 1647 in Scotland but raised in France at the exiled court of the former English queen *Henrietta Maria. Her parents were royalists who fled England in 1649, when Frances was two years old, during the final years of the Civil War. They did not return until 1662, following the restoration of the Stuart monarchy under King Charles II. Frances, as an unmarried young woman of high rank and a relative of the king, was appointed a lady-in-waiting to the queen, *Catherine of Braganza.

Frances' beauty and kind, playful disposition quickly made her one of the most popular of the court women. She became a good friend of both the queen and the queen's rival, Charles II's mistress *Barbara Villiers, but she soon found herself the object of the king's attentions. Despite their age difference, Charles and Frances shared a preoccupation with frivolous pursuits, delighting in games, dancing, and fashion. Frances encouraged his attachment and those of her other admirers at court; soon she usurped Barbara Villiers' place, becoming the most important woman at court after the queen. But despite her youth and inexperience, Frances refused the king's attempts to make her his mistress, apparently recognizing the danger and instability of such a position. Charles believed he was in love with her and tried for months to seduce "La Belle Stuart," as she was called, even promising that he would marry her if Queen Catherine died. She clearly enjoyed his company, however, and by 1666 the two were spending so much time together that it was widely believed they were in fact lovers. This put Frances in a difficult situation; although she wanted to preserve her honor against court gossip, she was not going to marry the king, but as long as he loved her, he would not allow her to marry another.

This situation continued until 1667, when Charles Stuart, the twice-widowed young duke of Richmond and Lennox, fell in love with Frances. After the king discovered their plans to marry, he attempted to prevent the wedding, forcing Frances to elope with the duke. King Charles was furious, even dismissing the chancellor whom he thought had arranged the marriage. For a year he refused to receive the duke and duchess, and they lived far away at their

Frances
Stuart

estate in Kent. Frances was sorely missed at court; as the king's favorite, she had been a leader of its social life. Although Frances' letters to her husband are affectionate, Charles Stuart was an alcoholic and a gambler who was deeply in debt, and soon Frances wanted to return to her friends and the excitement of court life.

In 1668, she and her husband were staying briefly at their home in London when Frances contracted smallpox. This news frightened King Charles into reconciling with the Richmonds, even staying in their home while Frances recovered. After this reconciliation, Queen Catherine appointed Frances as a Lady of the Bed-Chamber, and the Richmonds returned at last to their lodgings in the royal palace of Whitehall. There the duke and duchess whiled away most of their time in dances, masquerades, suppers, and attending the theater. Frances' friendship with the king, who still retained an affection for her, rekindled rumors of an affair.

Frances' marriage ended in December 1672, when the duke, serving as ambassador for King Charles, died unexpectedly in Denmark. Frances' letters show that she mourned him, but her loss was only the beginning of her troubles. Since she had no children, all the duke's many titles and properties reverted to King Charles, except for Cobham Hall in Kent which she inherited. Charles Stuart had never been wealthy and, since they had spent lavishly on fashion, furnishings, and other luxuries, he left Frances deeply in debt. Facing this financial crisis she turned to the king, who, fortunately, treated her generously. He agreed to provide her with a substantial pension, allowing her to remain at the royal court where she once again lived at the center of court life. Even after her old friend the king died in 1685, Frances remained a fixture of London society until the Glorious Revolution of 1688 brought down the Stuart monarchy.

King William and Queen *Mary II would end Frances' pension, but by 1688 she was no longer dependent on it. Revealing a sense for business, as a widow Frances had, through careful planning and management of her small estates, expanded her properties considerably and created a personal fortune. With this wealth, she retired from court life in 1689, at age 41, and moved permanently to her home in London. Her retirement corresponds to the onset of chronic illness, which eventually made her an invalid. In her last few years the duchess left home only rarely. Her final public appearance was at the coronation of Queen *Anne in April 1702. Frances died a few months later at age 55 on October 15.

At her request, she was buried near her husband in the Richmond family vault in Westminster Abbey. The bulk of her fortune went to her Scottish nephew. For her legacy, Frances stipulated that her heir buy land and establish a new estate in Scotland to be called Lennoxlove. Many of Frances Stuart's personal possessions are still kept at Lennoxlove Manor, in East Lothian, Scotland.

**SOURCES:**

Fraser, Antonia. *King Charles II.* London: Weidenfeld & Nicholson, 1979.

Hartmann, Cyril H. *La Belle Stuart: Memoirs of court and society in the times of Frances Teresa Stuart, duchess of Richmond and Lennox.* NY: Dutton, 1924.

**Laura York**, M.A. in History,
University of California, Riverside, California

## Stuart, Helen Campbell (1839–1918).

*See Campbell, Helen Stuart.*

## Stuart, Jane (1812–1888)

*American artist who is best known for her copies of her father's famous paintings, one of which is hung in the Kennedy School of Government at Harvard University in Boston.* Born in 1812; died in 1888 in Newport, Rhode Island; youngest of the four daughters of Gilbert Stuart (1755–1828, famous portraitist of George Washington) and Charlotte (Coates) Stuart (b. around 1768); sister of **Anne Stuart**; self-trained by assisting her father in his painting studio; never married.

Born in 1812, Jane Stuart was one of ten children, and the fourth daughter, of Gilbert Stuart, the renowned portraitist of George Washington. Her mother **Charlotte Coates Stuart** was the daughter of a Berkshire, England, physician. Although she gained the desire to paint from her famous father, Jane learned her art by surreptitiously observing his formal training of other artists. Moody and abrasive, Gilbert felt that she had sufficient training as his assistant without further schooling, and relegated her to grinding his colors and filling in his backgrounds. Even with the absence of formal instruction, Jane Stuart demonstrated early talent that proved vital to the survival of her family when Gilbert died penniless in 1828. At just 16, Stuart supported her mother and three older sisters by painting portraits and miniatures in oils, in addition to numerous copies of her father's works, in her studio in Boston. She became one of the most skilled of the dozens of artists routinely commissioned to recreate Gilbert Stuart's classic paintings, such as his *Athenaeum*—so much so that dishonest art dealers often tried to pass off Stuart's work as that of her father's. One of her copies is on display at the Kennedy School of Government at Harvard University.

Stuart's ability to accurately copy her father's works belies the fact that she had her own distinctive style. Her original paintings *Scene from a Novel* (1834) and *Caroline Marsh* (1840) demonstrate the simple charm and romantic literary content of her work through the use of oval forms. Tragically, the destruction of her studio in a fire during the 1850s resulted in the loss of the body of her work along with most of the correspondence and mementos of her father's life. Stuart spent her later years among the wealthy residents of Newport, Rhode Island, where she was considered a colorful, eccentric character. Her love of fortune-telling and matchmaking combined with her prankish, creative humor contributed to her popularity in Newport society, although she herself did not have money. When the home in which she lived with her sister was sold by its owners, Stuart's wealthy friends came to their aid by buying them another dwelling. She lived there until her death in 1888.

**SOURCES:**
Rubinstein, Charlotte Streifer. *American Woman Artists.* Boston, MA: G.K. Hall, 1982.

**B. Kimberly Taylor**, freelance writer, New York, New York

## Stuart, Jessie Bonstelle (1871–1932).

*See Bonstelle, Jessie.*

## Stuart, Louisa (1752–1824).

*See Louise of Stolberg-Gedern.*

## Stuart, Maria Clementina (1702–1735).

*See Sobieski, Clementina.*

## Stuart, Mary (1542–1587).

*See Mary Stuart.*

## Stuart, Miranda (c. 1795–1865)

*British doctor who posed as a man throughout her career and served in the military in South Africa, the West Indies, Canada, and the Crimea. Name variations: James Barry; Miranda Stuart Barry. Born Miranda Stuart or Miranda Stuart Barry around 1795; died around the age of 70 of dysentery in London on July 25, 1865; Edinburgh College, M.D., 1812.*

Miranda Stuart's early life is shrouded in mystery, but it seems she was born in 1795 into an Irish Catholic family. She was apparently the granddaughter of Cork-based shipbuilder John Barry, and her father may have been his son James Barry, a painter. Born in an era when women were traditionally denied any profession outside the home, Stuart, posing as a man named James Barry, became the first female doctor in the United Kingdom and had a distinguished medical career in the British military. She passed herself off as a young orphaned boy to get into Edinburgh College in 1810. Diminutive in stature, she was a young woman of 15 at the time, but claimed to be only 10 in order to mask her feminine features under the cloak of pre-adolescent boyhood. Although 10 was considered an unusually young age for such studies, there were no age requirements for entrance. Stuart protected her identity during the course of her two-year college career by keeping to herself, and prepared her thesis on the hernia of the groin. After qualifying as a doctor in 1812, she studied surgery in London.

Stuart joined the army the following year, and took her first assignment as a military hospi-

tal assistant in Plymouth. No longer able to use extreme youth as an excuse for her less-than-masculine appearance, Stuart caused some comment with her beardless face, high-pitched voice and petite features, although her remarkable medical skills and the favor of British authorities deflected any criticism regarding her appearance. After achieving the level of assistant-surgeon, she was transferred to a garrison in Cape Town, South Africa, in 1816. She cut a colorful figure in Cape Town, wearing a plumed hat and carrying a sword, always accompanied by a servant and a dog named Psyche (all of her subsequent dogs were named Psyche). Stuart was considered to be the best physician in Cape Town, and although her manner was considered eccentric, she was respected and often lauded by her peers and patients.

Miranda Stuart

In 1822, Stuart was promoted to the civil post of medical inspector for Cape Colony and director of the Vaccine Board, although she retained some of her military responsibilities. She fought diligently on behalf of prisoners' health and improved prison conditions, and lobbied to have lepers perceived as "unfortunates" rather than as criminals. Perhaps to compensate for her effeminate appearance, Stuart also had a violent temper and frequent clashes with colleagues made her 13-year stay in Cape Town a volatile one. Even so, rumors circulated about Stuart possibly being a woman. One of her patients, Captain W.H. Dillon, wrote of Stuart in 1856, "Many surmises were in circulation relating to him. From the awkwardness of his gait and the shape of his person it was the prevailing opinion that he was a female." Another visitor to Cape Town, Lord Albemarle, commented on Stuart, "There was a certain effeminacy in his manner which he seemed to be always striving to overcome."

Stuart resigned from her civil post shortly before 1825 due to political changes and numerous political rows, but was urgently summoned in 1826 to attend to Mrs. Thomas Munnik, who was dying in childbirth. With characteristic decision, Stuart immediately performed a Caesarian section without the benefit of any sort of anaesthetic. Both the mother and child survived, and Stuart received credit for performing the first successful Caesarian in South Africa, and the second in the Western world. At her request, the baby boy became her godson, James Barry Munnik. Among the boy's descendants was South African Prime Minster James Barry Munnik Hertzog.

Her next post as assistant-surgeon in Mauritius, beginning in October 1829, proved to be no smoother than her tenure in Cape Town, and the rumors about her gender followed her. She found herself at odds with the governor, Sir Charles Colville, and took leave from Mauritius that same year to nurse a friend through a grave illness in London. She stayed there until the friend's death in 1831, and received a new post in Jamaica that same year. Jamaica had earned the nickname "White Man's Grave" because of the constant threat of yellow fever and other diseases, but Stuart's strict vegetarian diet and sanitary habits with regard to food preparation helped her escape illness. She stayed in Jamaica for four long, trying years, during which the constant presence of disease kept her busy. She next set out for St. Helena on April 18, 1836, and worked as principal medical officer on the island. In St. Helena, she introduced the concept of female nursing, as many of the women on the island were so impoverished that they turned to prostitution. In 1838, she was demoted for reasons that were repressed, sparking speculation that her gender may have been at issue, and was appointed staff-surgeon to the Windward and Leeward Islands in November of that year.

Stuart spent six years in the Windward and Leeward Islands, which also had a well-earned reputation for death. There, her hearty immune system finally broke down, and she contracted yellow fever in Trinidad in 1844. She survived and, in 1846, took up the position of principal medical officer in Malta, where efficiency and dedication earned her the highest regards possible. She was promoted to the rank of deputy inspector-general of hospitals, and soon relocated to Corfu. From April to June in 1855, she took a leave to Crimea, where she publicly berated *Florence Nightingale.

Stuart's next and last post as inspector-general was in Canada, where the climate and terrain were difficult for someone accustomed to the tropics. She campaigned for separate married quarters in the barracks, roasted meat instead of boiled, and feather or hair mattresses instead of hard straw mattresses. After relentless

attacks of bronchitis, she was sent home on sick leave in May 1859. Miranda Stuart lived for six more years, and died of dysentery on July 25, 1865. After her death, it was confirmed that she had been a woman, and that she had possibly given birth at least once as well.

**SOURCES:**

Griffin, Lynne, and Kelly McCann. *The Book of Women: 300 Notable Women History Passed By*. Holbrook, MA: Bob Adams, 1992.

Longford, Elizabeth. *Eminent Victorian Women*. London: Weidenfeld & Nicolson, 1981.

Uglow, Jennifer S., comp. and ed. *The International Dictionary of Women's Biography*. NY: Continuum, 1982.

**B. Kimberly Taylor**, freelance writer, New York, New York

# Stuart, Ruth McEnery

## (c. 1849–1917)

*American writer. Born Mary Routh McEnery in Marksville, Louisiana, on May 21, 1849 (some sources cite 1856); died in White Plains, New York, on May 6, 1917; eldest of eight children of James McEnery (a cotton merchant, planter, and slaveholder) and Mary Routh (Stirling) McEnery; married Alfred O. Stuart (a merchant and planter), on August 5, 1879 (died 1883); children: Stirling McEnery (1882–1905).*

*Selected writings:* A Golden Wedding and Other Tales *(1893);* Carlotta's Intended and Other Tales *(1894);* The Story of Babette, a Little Creole Girl *(1894);* Gobolinks, or Shadow-Pictures for Young and Old *(with Albert Bigelow Paine, 1896);* Sonny: A Story *(also published as* Sonny: A Christmas Guest *[1897], 1896);* Solomon Crow's Christmas Pockets and Other Tales *(1896);* In Simpkinsville: Character Tales *(1897);* The Snow-Cap Sisters: A Farce *(1897);* Moriah's Mourning and Other Half-Hour Sketches *(1898);* Holly and Pizen and Other Stories *(1899);* Napoleon Jackson: The Gentleman of the Plush Rocker *(1902);* George Washington Jones: A Christmas Gift That Went A-Begging *(1903);* The River's Children: An Idyll of the Mississippi *(1904);* The Second Wooing of Salina Sue and Other Stories *(1905);* Aunt Amity's Silver Wedding and Other Stories *(1909);* Sonny's Father in which the Father, now become Grandfather, a Kindly Observer of Life and a Genial Philosopher, in his Desultory Talks with the Family Doctor, Carries along the Story of Sonny *(1910);* The Haunted Photograph, Whence and Whither, A Case in Diplomacy *(1911);* Daddy Do-Funny's Wisdom Jingles *(1913);* The Cocoon: A Rest-Cure Comedy *(1915);* Plantation Songs and Other Verse *(1916).*

Ruth McEnery Stuart was born Mary Routh McEnery on May 21, 1849, although some sources indicate as late as 1856, in Marksville, Louisiana, to an Irish father and a Welsh-Scottish mother. Although her father emigrated from Ireland as a descendent of the landed gentry, he was not as prosperous as the rest of his family, and the Civil War aggravated the family's precarious finances. When Ruth was seven, her father moved the family to New Orleans, where he found work at the customhouse. This vibrant atmosphere exposed young Ruth to a number of cultural influences as she encountered Italians, Creoles, and African-Americans in the old French Market area of New Orleans, which is vividly reflected in her later stories. She attended both private and public schools, and evidence suggests that she may have taught at the Locquet-LeRoy Institute in New Orleans—a fashionable school for girls—for financial reasons. Little is known of her own formal education.

Ruth left New Orleans after her 1879 marriage to Alfred Oden Stuart, a merchant and planter nearly twice her age and three times previously married, but their life together in Washington, Arkansas, was cut short by her husband's death in 1883. He left little money to support Ruth and their infant son, so she returned to New Orleans to teach school. As so many women did during this era, Stuart turned to fiction writing as a means of earning a living, and drew on her impressive mastery of New Orleans dialects to create colorful characters in short stories. In January 1888, she published a story in African-American dialect, "Uncle Mingo's 'Speculations,'" in the *New Princeton Review*. She then wrote and published more stories in the same local-color style for various periodicals, including "Lamentations of Jeremiah Johnson" in *Harper's New Monthly Magazine*. The success of these stories led her into book publishing, and, with the exception of a period of depression following her son's death at the age of 13 in 1905, she consistently published at a pace averaging a volume a year. These stories were full of the dialects she had painstakingly mastered, including those of poor Southern whites, African-Americans, Latin-African Creoles, and the Italian and French immigrants to New Orleans. Her first book, *A Golden Wedding and Other Tales*, appeared in 1893, and her best-known work *In Simpkinsville: Character Tales* was published in 1897.

Stuart moved to New York City in 1891 to be closer to her publishers. In 1893, she began traveling successfully on the lecture circuit, where her writing talent, combined with a graceful manner, natural beauty, and ready repartee, endeared her to audiences. There was also a novelty factor, as few women writers took to the platform in the tradition of such literary wits as Mark Twain. She became a member of the "Harper Set," and for a brief period worked as the temporary editor of *Harper's Bazar* magazine. Numerous national magazines bid for her material and services, and her stories consistently sold well.

Stuart viewed her literary contributions as entertainment, and drew on humor, pathos, and dialect to buttress her tales. Her widespread reputation as a humorist and author of unique dialect stories seemed sufficient to ensure that her fame would last, but it soon faded after her death from bronchopneumonia, at age 67, on May 6, 1917. The historical value of her tales and character sketches is considerable, since they embody literary myths of the genteel South, and draw deeply from the well of universal humanity. **Kathryn B. McKee** notes that although later generations criticized Stuart for relying on "easily identifiable stereotypes," Stuart's literary significance "is in the sense that her work offers the modern reader valuable insight into the cultural concerns of the time in which she wrote, the uncertain transition between centuries that both intimidated and excited Americans."

**SOURCES:**

James, Edward T., ed. *Notable American Women, 1607–1950*. Cambridge, MA: The Belknap Press of Harvard University, 1971.

McHenry, Robert, ed. *Famous American Women*. NY: Dover, 1980.

McKee, Kathryn B. "Ruth McEnery Stuart," in *Dictionary of Literary Biography*, Vol. 202: *Nineteenth-Century American Fiction Writers*. Detroit, MI: Gale Group, 1999, pp. 242–250.

**B. Kimberly Taylor**, freelance writer, New York, New York

# Stuart-Wortley, Emmeline

## (1806–1855)

*English poet and travel writer. Born Emmeline Charlotte Elizabeth Manners on May 2, 1806; died in Beirut in November 1855; second daughter of John Henry Manners, 5th duke of Rutland, and Lady Elizabeth Howard (d. 1825, daughter of Frederick Howard, 5th earl of Carlisle, and **Margaret Leveson**); sister of Lord John Manners; married the Honourable Charles Stuart-Wortley, in 1831; children: three.*

*Selected writings:* Poems *(1833);* Travelling Sketches in Rhyme *(1835);* Impressions of Italy *(1837);* Sonnets *(1839).*

Born Emmeline Manners in 1806, Emmeline Stuart-Wortley inherited a prestigious family name as the second daughter of John Henry Manners, 5th duke of Rutland, and Lady **Elizabeth Howard**, daughter of the earl of Carlisle. Her brother, Lord John Manners (1818–1906), established a name for himself as a leader of the "Young England" movement surrounding the powerful English politician Benjamin Disraeli. Emmeline's chosen profession as a poet and travel writer followed her father's interest in writing, as he had published several volumes of his impressions of his journeys.

Emmeline did not begin writing poetry until after her marriage to the Honourable Charles Stuart-Wortley, in 1831. Much of her poetry first appeared in *Blackwood's Magazine*, and after her first collection, *Poems*, appeared in 1833, she published a book a year on average for the next decade. She drew on her travels in Europe for several of her volumes of poetry, including *Travelling Sketches in Rhyme* in 1835, *Impressions of Italy* in 1837, and *Sonnets* in 1839. She extended her travels to include such distant and exotic lands as the United States and the Middle East, which also served as material for her poetic imagination when she published a three-volume account titled *Travels in the United States*, followed by another edition in 1853. Stuart-Wortley's editing of two issues of the popular annual *Keepsake*, in 1837 and 1840, brought her into contact with such literary figures as *Mary Shelley, *Caroline Norton, and *Marguerite, Countess of Blessington.

Stuart-Wortley's travels took a tragic turn during a tour of the Middle East in 1855, when she sustained a broken leg after being kicked by a mule. Although she continued her journey from Beirut to Aleppo, she died upon her return to Beirut.

**SOURCES:**
*The Concise Dictionary of National Biography.* Oxford: Oxford University Press, 1992.
Shattock, Joanne. *The Oxford Guide to British Women Writers.* Oxford University Press, 1993.

**B. Kimberly Taylor**, freelance writer, New York, New York

# Stückelberger, Christine (1947—)

*Swiss equestrian in dressage. Name variations: Christine Stueckelberger or Stuckelberger. Born in Wallisellen, a village north of Zurich, Switzerland, on May 22, 1947; father was a doctor; mother was the daughter of the president of Switzerland.*

*Awards in dressage: On Merry Boy, European championships (1969, 1971, and 1973) and World championship (1972); on Granat, European championships (1975, 1977), Olympic gold medal in Montre-al (1976), Olympic team silver in Montreal (1976), World championship (1978); on Gauguin de Lully, Olympic team silver in Los Angeles (1984), silver medal in World championship (1986), and Olympic individual bronze in Seoul (1988).*

At age 11, Christine Stückelberger began formal training with Georg Wahl of the Berne Riding School who remained her coach throughout her career. Her doctor father had ridden occasionally while in the army; her mother, the daughter of the president of Switzerland, was a dog and horse lover and had taken riding lessons. Christine won her first major successes on Merry Boy: European championships in dressage in 1969, 1971, and 1973, and the World championship in 1972. She thought she had never had a better horse.

Meanwhile, she had purchased a four-year-old horse named Granat in southern Germany in 1969. Though he showed excellent movement, she soon discovered he was blind in the right eye; the former owner was so horrified that he refunded her money. Thus, Granat, a horse who was to become one of the greatest in equestrian history, was hers for free. Because of his handicap, Granat was difficult to train (sudden noises made him start), but this was countered by a gentle temperament. Stückelberger and Wahl used tricks to overcome his limitation. When he refused to turn on the forehand because of his inability to see in that direction, Wahl would stand on his right and speak to him, and when Granat turned he would give him a lump of sugar. Soon, whenever the horse heard Wahl, he would turn.

Mounted on Granat, Stückelberger took 15th place at the Munich Olympics in 1972 and 5th in the World championships at Copenhagen in 1974. In 1976, horse and rider arrived at the dressage training area in Bromont, site of the equestrian events for the Montreal summer Olympics. Wrote Guy Wathen: "A sizeable throng of spectators, mainly other riders of various teams, used to gather to watch the slim, elegant girl on the large and apparently unruly horse as they worked their way towards the dressage competitions of the Games. Sometimes the horse appeared totally to disregard the rider on his back, and sometimes it seemed nothing short of miraculous that she managed to stay there; at others he performed the movements of the Olympic test almost perfectly." In the individual Olympic competition, Stückelberger and Granat "produced a display of dressage that for sheer technical merit has seldom been bettered." She won the individual gold medal, 51 points ahead of silver medalist Harry Boldt and Woyceck, and 91 points ahead of bronze medalist Reiner Klimke and Mehmed. When Granat died in 1989, Stückelberger felt that she had lost a dear friend.

In 1975, she purchased Gauguin de Lully. Together, they won the Nashua World Cup Finals in Holland and Germany, the Olympic team silver medal in Los Angeles in 1984, the silver medal in the World championships in 1986, and the individual bronze medal at the Seoul Olympics in 1988. While she was training a young stallion in 1989, the horse bucked, and Stückelberger was thrown against a wall, breaking her back in two places. The two operations and convalescence that followed effectively cut short her career.

## Studer, Claire (1891–1977).

See Goll, Claire.

## Sture-Vasa, Mary Alsop (1885–1980).

See O'Hara, Mary.

## Sturgis, Caroline (1819–1888).

See Tappan, Caroline Sturgis.

## Sturgis, Ellen (1812–1848).

See Adams, Clover for sidebar on Ellen Sturgis Hooper.

## Styria, duchess of.

See Mary of Bavaria (d. 1608).

## Suavegotta (fl. 504)

*Queen of Reims and Metz (Austrasia). Flourished around 504; daughter of Sigismond, king of the Burgundians; married Thierry also known as Theuderic or Theodoric I (c. 490–534), king of Reims and Metz (r. 511–534); children: Thibert also known as Theodebert or Theudebert I (504–548), king of Metz (Austrasia, r. 534–548).*

## Subligny, Marie-Thérèse Perdou de (1666–1736)

*French ballerina. Name variations: Marie-Therese Perdou de Subligny. Born in 1666; died in 1736; daughter of an actor-playwright who is reputed by some to have edited* Letters of a Portuguese Nun *(\*Mariana Alcoforado), published in Paris in 1669.*

Marie-Thérèse Perdou de Subligny grew up in the house of a learned father, surrounded by his literary friends. He did not, however, pass this knowledge on to his daughter, who would go to her grave never having learned to read or write. For 17 years, Mlle de Subligny was the lead ballerina at the Opéra de France. Though lauded for her modesty, beauty and figure, she was criticized, says **Parmenia Migel**, for not having "her knees and feet sufficiently turned out." Replaced by \***Françoise Prévost** in 1705, Mlle de Subligny was the first French *danseuse* to have a career on both sides of the English Channel. In 1735, she emptied a chamber pot over the head of Francoeur, a violinist, and then brought suit against him. It was tossed out of court, however, because she could not sign the plea.

**SOURCES:**
Migel, Parmenia. *The Ballerinas: From the Court of Louis XIV to Pavlova.* NY: Macmillan, 1972.

## Sucher, Rosa (1847–1927)

*German operatic soprano. Born Rosa Hasselbeck (also seen as Haslbeck) in Germany in 1847 (some sources cite 1849); died in 1927; married Josef Sucher (a conductor-composer known for his interpretation of Wagnerian music), in 1876.*

Rosa Sucher was born Rosa Hasselbeck in Germany in 1847. Following her marriage to Josef Sucher, a conductor-composer renowned for his interpretation of Wagnerian music, she became famous for her performances in Wagner's operas, while two seasons in London (1882, 1892) showed off her talent both as a singer and an actress. She also sang in Hamburg (1879–88) and at Bayreuth (1886, 1888). In her later years, she appeared principally on the opera stages of Berlin, before retiring in 1903. Rosa Sucher is remembered especially for her portrayal of Isolde.

## Suchocka, Hanna (1946—)

*Polish politician who as prime minister of Poland was the first woman to lead the country since Queen Jadwiga in the 14th century. Pronunciation: HAHN-nah sue-HUT-ska. Born on April 3, 1946, in Pleszew, Poland; received a law and doctoral degree from Poznan University; also studied at the Institute of Public Law in Heidelberg, Germany, and participated in a course organized by Columbia University, in New York; never married; no children.*

*Was the fifth post-Communist prime minister of Poland (July 10, 1992–October 26, 1993).*

Born in 1946 and raised in Pleszew, a village in western Poland, where her parents owned the local pharmacy, Hanna Suchocka was a model child, achieving a perfect attendance record in school and regularly attending the local Catholic church. Although her parents had hoped she would pursue a career in pharmacy, she chose instead to study law at Poznan University. After graduating in 1968, she stayed on to accept a probational teaching position. A year later, she forfeited renewal of her contract when she refused to join the Communist Party, as all faculty members were expected to do. Objecting to the Communists' atheistic tenets, she joined the Democratic Party instead. "I decided I wanted to be an independent person," she said in an interview with Stephen Engelberg for *The New York Times Magazine* (September 12, 1993). "I wanted to have the freedom to go to church because I was authentically raised in this. It was not for show. It was real." After leaving the university faculty, she took a job at the Institute of Small Arts and Crafts and began working on her law degree, which she received in the early 1970s. In 1973, she was rehired by the university, where she later earned her doctoral degree, with a specialization in constitutional law.

*Hanna Suchocka*

Suchocka's political career began in 1980, with her election to the Sejm (lower house of Parliament) on the Democratic Party ticket.

After Solidarity, Suchocka joined the labor movement (founded by Lech Walesa) and soon became a legal adviser to the union. In 1984, after voting against the government's decision to outlaw Solidarity, Suchocka either left, or was asked to leave, the party.

Following the collapse of Communist rule in Poland in 1989, Suchocka returned to the Sejm, this time as a member of the Civic Committee. Conservative in her views, but gaining respect as a well-informed lawmaker, she was re-elected in 1991 as a member of the Democratic Union, a center-left party founded by Suchocka and a group of Solidarity leaders. The 1991 election was, however, the first full democratic polling held in post-Communist Poland, and it produced a Parliament with so many opposing factions that it became impossible to produce a coalition government that could endure. In the summer of 1992, the coalition of Waldemar Pawlak, leader of the Polish Peasants Party, collapsed after only five weeks in power. It was at this time that Suchocka, whose low-key style had earned her few enemies, was suggested as a candidate for the fifth post-Communist prime minister. After initially declining the offer, claiming that she was unprepared for such an undertaking, she eventually relented, and began assembling a working coalition. By July 1992, she had the backing of six parties, in addition to her own. Nominated by Lech Walesa on July 8, Suchocka was confirmed by Parliament two days later, by a vote of 233 to 61, with 113 abstentions. "My mission is to calm down disputes between political parties," she said in her inaugural address. "This is a government of social reconciliation." Suchocka was the first woman to lead the country since Queen *Jadwiga, of the Angevin dynasty, during the 14th century.

Suchocka succeeded in holding the diversified political parties together for 15 months, longer than any of her predecessors had been able to do. She also guided Poland further into capitalism, helping to strengthen the Polish economy in the process. "The Suchocka government seems to have literally snatched Poland's economy from the brink of failure," said Ian Hume, the director of the World Bank in Warsaw, in an interview for *The Christian Science Monitor* (May 7, 1993), "and created the conditions to see it emerge again as the leader among the post-Communist reforming countries."

However, with the free-market reforms came a rise in unemployment and the cost of consumer goods. In the end, Suchocka's restructuring attempt lost the support of her constituency, who clung to the security they had become accustomed to under Communist rule. The election of September 1993 saw her toppled from office in favor of a coalition of former Communists and other leftist leaders. On October 26, 1993, she relinquished the prime ministership to Pawlak, who had served briefly before her, although she continued to serve as a member of Parliament.

Suchocka, who never married, is known as a fiercely private woman, intelligent and hardworking, but lacking the hard-ball political instincts of *Margaret Thatcher, to whom she is frequently compared. However, it is also believed that Suchocka's easy-going political style may have helped her advance as far as she did. "Perhaps it is because I'm a woman that I have more patience and more of this willingness to compromise," she told **Francine Kiefer** of *The Christian Science Monitor*. "My closest staff frequently says, 'No! Enough! We just cannot go on like this,' [whereas] I still feel that there is some work that can be done and that a compromise can still be found."

**SOURCES:**
Graham, Judith, ed. *Current Biography*. NY: H.W. Wilson, 1994.

**Barbara Morgan**,
Melrose, Massachusetts

# Suckow, Ruth (1892–1960)

*American writer. Pronunciation: SOO-koh. Born on August 6, 1892, in Hawarden, Iowa; died in Claremont, California, in January 1960; second daughter of William John Suckow (a Congregational minister) and Anna Mary (Kluckhohn) Suckow; educated at Grinnell College in Iowa and the Curry School of Expression in Boston; University of Denver, A.B., 1917, A.M., 1918; married Ferner Nuhn (a writer and critic), in March 1929.*

*Selected writings:* Country People *(1924);* The Odyssey of a Nice Girl *(1925);* Iowa Interiors *(1926);* The Bonney Family *(1928);* Cora *(1929);* The Kramer Girls *(1930);* Children and Older People *(1931);* The Folks *(1934);* New Hope *(1942);* The John Wood Case *(1959).*

Ruth Suckow was born in 1892 in the small town of Hawarden, Iowa, the granddaughter of German immigrants who gave her an appreciation for family history during her visits with them. Another important childhood influence upon her writing was her father, a Congregational minister who held pastorates in several Iowa towns. Ruth was so moved by what she termed

the "purity and economy of style" of her father's sermons that she would baptize animals and hold funeral services for broken dolls. Her writing career essentially began in his study. She had a more troubled relationship with her mother, who put tremendous pressure on Ruth and her older sister **Emma Suckow**, perhaps hoping to realize her own unfulfilled dreams through them.

Ruth completed high school in the Iowa city of Grinnell, and pursued a degree at Grinnell College in 1910. Finding that the school's curriculum did not support her ambitions to become an actress, Suckow transferred at the end of her junior year to the Curry School of Expression in Boston where she studied for another two years. A brief attempt to run her own school of expression back in Iowa stalled, and she joined her ailing sister in Denver, Colorado. There she earned both bachelor's and master's degrees in English from the University of Denver and redirected her artistic course to writing. While studying beekeeping, she published her first poems. She returned to Iowa to live with her father after her mother's death in 1919, and spent the next six years raising bees and making honey, writing poems, and creating a series of short stories set in rural and small-town Iowa. These stories were the genesis of the literary career on which her reputation as a regional writer is based.

Suckow first achieved notice after the 1921 publication of her short story "Uprooted" brought her to the attention of journalist H.L. Mencken. Mencken promoted her with enthusiasm in *The Smart Set*, which led to the serialization of her novella *Country People* in *The Century Magazine* in 1924. Publishers Alfred and *Blanche Knopf turned it into a book later that year, and also collected her first stories under the title *Iowa Interiors* in 1926. Suckow became known for her ability to capture the plight of her characters in a swift, dramatic fashion, as well as for her acute, unsentimental vision of rural life.

The same year *Iowa Interiors* appeared, Suckow moved to New York City, where she capitalized on her growing reputation with three more novels in the space of four years. These works—*The Bonney Family* (1928), *Cora* (1929), and *The Kramer Girls* (1930)—featured young Midwestern women attempting to create identities for themselves separate from the expectations of family and friends. While lacking in consistency, the stories confronted real-life problems with an honesty that demonstrated the absence of easy solutions.

Suckow married fellow Iowa writer and critic Ferner Nuhn in 1929, and the pair spent most of the first five years of their marriage living in California, New Mexico, and Iowa. Throughout this nomadic existence, Suckow was at work on what would be her summary work, *The Folks*, published in 1934. This longest of her novels covered the time between the beginning of the 20th century to the Depression in the life of the Ferguson family, and was equally as sweeping in its portrayal of the emotional relationships of its characters. The exploration of such family ties was the bedrock of Suckow's fiction, and all her works vividly convey the complicated emotions those relationships engender. She demonstrated her greatest versatility in her ability to portray both the old and the young in her work.

Although Suckow produced novels and stories after 1935, her output thereafter was comparatively slender. Her husband took a post in the Department of Agriculture in Washington, D.C., and Suckow served on the Farm Tenancy Committee as an appointee of President Franklin D. Roosevelt in 1936. The next year found them again in Iowa, where they continued writing and promoting the arts. Suckow maintained contact with literary friends such as Robert Frost, *Dorothy Canfield Fisher, and

Norwegian novelist *Sigrid Undset. She also published a nostalgic novel about an Iowa community, *New Hope*, in 1942.

Suckow's suffering from arthritis in the 1940s necessitated a warmer climate, so she moved with her husband to Tucson, Arizona, in 1948. Their last home was in Claremont, California, to which they had relocated in 1952. She completed her last novel, *The John Wood Case*, in Claremont in 1959, and died at home eight years later.

**SOURCES:**

Kunitz, Stanley J., and Howard Haycraft, eds. *Twentieth Century Authors*. NY: H.W. Wilson, 1942.

Sicherman, Barbara, and Carol Hurd Green, eds. *Notable American Women: The Modern Period*. Cambridge, MA: Belknap Press of Harvard University, 1980.

**B. Kimberly Taylor**, freelance writer, New York, New York

## Südermannland, duchess of.

*See Ingeborg (c. 1300–c. 1360).*

## Suesse, Dana (1909–1987)

*American composer and pianist who wrote the song "You Oughta Be in Pictures."* Pronunciation: sweez. Name variations: Dana DeLinks. Born Nadine Dana Suesse on December 3, 1909, in Kansas City, Missouri; died on October 16, 1987, in New York City; daughter of Julius Suesse and Nina (Chilton) Suesse; married H. Courtney Burr, in 1940 (divorced 1954); married Edward DeLinks, in 1971 (died 1981); no children.

Dana Suesse enjoyed considerable celebrity as a composer in the 1930s and 1940s, but today her name is not well known, although much of her music is still performed. A musical prodigy, she was born in 1909 in Kansas City, Missouri, and given classical music training at a young age. She composed her first song and gave her first piano concert at age eight. At age ten, she won a prize for composition from the National Federation of Music. Suesse also studied voice and dancing, and wrote poetry. On graduation from high school in 1926, she refused a scholarship from the Chicago Conservatory and moved to New York City because of her interest in analyzing popular music styles. She studied piano and composition, and in the late 1920s worked as an arranger for music publishers. In an effort to succeed as a writer, she then turned from classical music and began composing popular tunes. Her first hit, "Syncopated Love Song," was written in 1930, followed in 1931 by "Ho Hum," recorded by Bing Crosby. The suc-

𝒟ana
𝒮uesse

cessful *Jazz Nocturne* was popularized with lyrics by Edward Heyman as "My Silent Love" in 1932.

By that time she had already been nicknamed "Sally of Tin Pan Alley" by a music reviewer commenting on her unique position as a popular female composer and the only professional American female symphony composer. Also in 1932, Suesse made her debut at Carnegie Hall performing her Concerto in Three Rhythms; the next year *The New Yorker* called her "the Girl Gershwin." Like George Gershwin, Suesse had proved that she could move easily from "serious" concert pieces to popular ballads and was an excellent pianist as well as composer. Her orchestral works *Symphonic Waltzes* and *Blue Moonlight* followed. Throughout the 1930s, Suesse composed numerous popular songs, including "The Night is Young and You're So Beautiful," "This Changing World," and "Yours for a Song," the latter written with lyricist and theater producer Billy Rose. In 1934, she wrote the music for what is still her most famous popular piece. In explaining how she came to compose it, Suesse said that she had boasted to a music publisher that she could write a hit song in 15 minutes. He dared her to prove it, and, collaborating with lyricist Edward Heyman, 20 minutes later she had produced "You Oughta Be in Pictures," which became an unofficial Hollywood theme song. She also scored several films, including *Sweet Surrender* (1935), *Young Man with a Horn* (1950), and *The Seven Year Itch* (1955), but did much more work for Broadway theater than for Hollywood, though she was never given the opportunity to compose her own Broadway musical.

Suesse, who married the Broadway producer Courtney Burr in 1940, contributed compositions to many of his plays. (They would divorce in 1954.) Although she had continued to produce orchestral works throughout the late 1930s and 1940s, in 1947 Suesse turned to classical work exclusively. She studied in Paris with *Nadia Boulanger from 1947 to 1950. Her work in Paris brought her back to jazz music, and on her return to the States she wrote Jazz Concerto in D Major, first performed in 1956. In 1971, at age 60, she married Edwin DeLinks, moving to Connecticut and then to the Virgin Islands. In 1974, she was honored with a concert of her works at Carnegie Hall, where she performed part of her *Concerto in Three Rhythms*. Suesse was widowed in 1981 and retired, at age 70, in New York. She was still composing at the time of her death at age 77 in 1988.

**SOURCES:**
"Suesse, Dana" in John A. Garraty and Mark C. Carnes, eds., *American National Biography*. NY: Oxford University Press, 1999.
"Suesse, Dana" in Edward Jablonski, ed., *The Encyclopedia of American Music*. NY: Doubleday, 1981.

**Laura York**, M.A. in History, University of California, Riverside, California

## Suffolk, countess of.

## Suffolk, duchess of.

## Suggia, Guilhermina (1888–1950)

*Portuguese cellist. Born on June 27, 1888, in Oporto, Portugal; died on July 31, 1950, in Oporto; daughter of Augusto Suggia and Eliza Suggia (both of Italian descent); married Dr. José Mena (an X-ray specialist); studied with Julius Klengel.*

*Debuted with the Gewandhaus concerts (1902); studied with Pablo Casals and later lived with him for several years before establishing herself as one of the world's finest cellists; immortalized in Augustus John's portrait of her.*

Modern-day visitors gape at the astonishing portrait in London's Tate Gallery. The woman wears a sumptuous geranium gown and sits erect, thrusting out her jaw as she holds her cello. She is slim, dark, olive-skinned, and graceful. This painting by artist Augustus John sums up the remarkable musician Guilhermina Suggia, who laid to rest the prejudice that a woman could not be a cello virtuoso. Born in Oporto, Portugal, in 1888 to parents of Italian descent, Suggia demonstrated musical abilities early. She and her sister **Virginia Suggia**, who played the piano, studied with their father who was also a fine cellist. Though Guilhermina hated authority and rigidity and often fought with her father, her progress was remarkable. At age seven, she gave her debut at the Palácio de Cristal. At age ten, she played before Pablo Casals. When she was

12, Suggia was the leader of the Porto City Symphony Orchestra's cello section. Before she left to study with Julius Klengel at the Leipzig Conservatory in Germany in 1902, the young musician had given 50 concerts.

No sooner had Suggia arrived in Germany than trouble erupted. She had won a royal scholarship to study in Leipzig, while at the same time she had accepted a fee for performing with the Gewandhaus orchestra on February 26, 1902. As punishment for abandoning her amateur status, her scholarship was withdrawn. But events went quite differently than might have been predicted: Suggia remained in Leipzig, studied with Klengel, joined the orchestra there, and kept her scholarship. Talented and tempestuous, Suggia was learning that rules were made to be broken.

In 1906, when she moved to Paris after her father's death, she found her financial situation precarious. She sought out Casals, who was performing and teaching there, and asked if she might study with him. He not only took her on as a student, but also offered to assist her financially. Casals was 11 years older than Suggia, whose dedication to the cello was as great as his own. It was not surprising, therefore, that their relationship soon developed into love.

For the next seven years, Casals and Suggia lived together. Though they sometimes posed as a married couple, no marriage appears to have taken place. But less than a year after she came to Paris, a program announced that a cello soloist named "Madame P. Casals-Suggia" would perform. Since she and Casals were well-known performers from a conservative Catholic country, their living together would not have been accepted, hence the possible use of a diversionary tactic.

These two musicians had very different personalities. Suggia was emotional, volcanic, and capricious, while Casals was organized, disciplined, and serious. Casals was well established as a concert artist while Suggia was only beginning her career. Though both continued their concert tours, these were happy times in Paris where they often met for long evenings with the "band of thieves" as they called their friends. This group included the violinists Fritz Kreisler, Georges Enesco, and Eugène Ysaÿe, the pianists Ferruccio Busoni and Raoul Pugno, and the violist Pierre Monteaux. They went on walks, played tennis, went fishing, and made music.

Guilhermina Suggia's entrance into Casals' life changed its pattern considerably. No longer did he tour for three-to-six months at a time. The two were seldom apart for more than a few days, never more than two weeks. Sometimes she accompanied him to concerts, and he did the same. With the passage of time, more and more differences began to surface between the two. Casals was an older, more established musician than Suggia. It was inevitable that she was cast in the role of a junior partner. Worse still, he did not want her to make a serious success of her career. He was uncomfortable with a woman who wanted professional independence. Suggia fought back, confronting his jealousy with tirades. But her mother **Eliza Suggia** sided with Casals, maintaining that for any woman with three fur coats, a little dog, and domestic security, giving up her career was a small price to pay. Suggia refused.

Living together was not simple for the two concert artists. Each had to practice for hours daily when not on tour. Casals' jealousy was further inflamed when his friend, composer Emanuel Moór, wrote pieces especially for Suggia. Despite their frequent arguments, she always admired Casals' abilities, a feeling which was mutual. When Julius Röntgen visited the couple in the summer of 1908, he found Casals "stretched out on the sofa in dressing-gown and Suggia playing the cello nearby. . . . After playing we went into the garden, Casals turned on the fountain, Suggia brought out the Spanish wine, and blackbirds were singing; [it was] the most beautiful summer afternoon." Such peaceful scenes alternated with fights over Suggia's career. The couple separated and reconciled many times, but eventually their tie was broken. It had been a pivotal relationship musically as well as emotionally for them both.

Increasingly, Suggia spent time in England, although she concertized internationally. In 1927, she married Dr. José Mena. Suggia never capitalized on Casals' name, though she always credited him with inspiring her. Her reputation both as an artist and a teacher continued to grow, and ultimately a prize was named in her honor. *Jacqueline du Pré, another famous cellist, would one day win the Suggia Prize as did many talented musicians. Flamboyant and determined, Suggia cut a wide swath in London society as well as on stage. She was an unforgettable presence. Devoted to her art no matter the price, she demonstrated that all women could achieve on stage. Her obituary in *The Times* of London summed up Suggia's remarkable career:

> Her playing impressed the listener by its indefinable style. Her technique and control were of a classical purity, but her interpretations were animated by a warmth of temperament and latent passion that belonged to her by

birth and nationality. Something of the beauty and power of her phrasing is conveyed in the well-known portrait of her by Augustus John, since they were derived not only from her bow arm, but from her total absorption, body and mind, in what she was playing.

**SOURCES:**

Baldock, Robert. *Pablo Casals*. Boston, MA: Northeastern University Press, 1993.

"Mme Suggia. One of the World's Leading Cellists," in *The Times* [London]. August 1, 1950, p. 6.

Suggia, Guilhermina. "The Violoncello," in *Music and Letters*. Vol. I, no. 2. April 1920.

**John Haag**, Associate Professor of History,
University of Georgia, Athens, Georgia

## Suggs, Louise (1923—)

*American golfer. Born in Atlanta, Georgia, on September 7, 1923.*

*Was the first member of the LPGA Hall of Fame (1951) and first woman elected to the Georgia Hall of Fame (1966); was also a member of the World Golf Hall of Fame; won the USGA Women's Amateur (1947); won the British Women's Amateur, three North and South Amateurs and three Western Amateurs, as well as being a member of the U.S. Curtis Cup team (1948); won 50 LPGA events, including the Titleholders championship (1946, 1954, 1956, 1959), the USGA Women's Open (1949, 1952), the LPGA championship (1957); won the Vare trophy (1957).*

Although Louise Suggs was not an all-around athlete like the legendary *Babe Didrikson Zaharias, she was formidable on the golf course. As an amateur, she won the Southern, Western, Georgia, and North and South titles, and was U.S. amateur in 1947 following Zaharias. In 1948, Suggs was British Amateur champion and a member of the Curtis Cup team. A founding member of the LPGA, Suggs wanted opportunities for women to play professionally with the ability to earn money to support themselves.

In 1949, her first year as a pro, she won three events—the U.S. Women's Open (beating runner-up Zaharias by 14 strokes), the Western Open, and the All-American Open. Her tour debut was "so momentous," wrote **Jolee Edmondson**, "and her subsequent performance so impressive that she was the first woman elected to the LPGA Hall of Fame—and only three years after she turned pro." In 1952, she took the U.S. Women's Open a second time with a record 284 (69–70–75) total that stood for years.

For the next decade, contests between Suggs and *Patty Berg electrified the galleries. In 1954, 1956, and 1959, Suggs had Titleholders victories

(she had also won the Titleholders in 1946; though it was a pro event, she had entered as an amateur). In 1957, by now nicknamed Sweet Swinger and Miss Sluggs, she won the Vare trophy with an average score of 74.64, the lowest in the LPGA for that year. She was LPGA champion again that year. At the Royal Poinciana Invitational at Palm Beach in 1961, in a field of men and women pros, including Sam Snead and Dow Finsterwald, who played off the same tee in a Par-3, Suggs took first. In 1979, Louise Suggs was inducted into the World Golf Hall of Fame.

**SOURCES:**

Edmondson, Jolee. *The Woman Golfer's Catalogue*. NY: Stein & Day, 1980.

Markel, Robert, Nancy Brooks, and Susan Markel. *For the Record. Women in Sports*. NY: World Almanac, 1985.

**Karin Loewen Haag**,
Athens, Georgia

## Suharto, Siti (1923–1996)

*First lady of Indonesia. Name variations: Ibu Tien. Born Siti Hartinah in Solo, Central Java, on August 23, 1923; died of a heart attack at the military hospital in Jakarta on April 28, 1996; marriage arranged by family to General Thojib N.J. Suharto (later president of Indonesia), in 1947; children: three daughters and three sons, including daughter Siti Hardiyanti Rukmana, known as Tutut (b. 1948); daughter Siti Hadiati Harijadi, known as Titik (b. 1958); and sons Sigit (b. 1951); Hutomo Mandala Putra, known as Tommy (b. 1961); Bambang Trihatmodjo (b. 1952).*

Siti Suharto worked side-by-side with her husband Major General Thojib N.J. Suharto during Indonesia's fight for independence from Dutch rule in 1945. When the Republic of Indonesia was established in 1950, Sukarno was its first president. In 1968, with the country in chaos, General Suharto became president, some say "benevolent despot," and remained so for 32 years.

Throughout her tenure as first lady of Indonesia, Siti Suharto stayed out of politics, except on one issue. Despite being a traditional Muslim wife, she adamantly opposed polygamy, the practice of allowing men to have more than one wife. Siti led a women's organization that pushed through a law making it illegal for a Muslim man in Indonesia to add a second wife without permission from his first wife.

President Suharto became very rich during his reign. Siti, known as Ibu Tien, was sometimes derided by Indonesians as "Madame Tien Percent" for taking a cut, "but at least she tried to curb the greed of her rapacious brood," wrote **Melinda Liu** in *Newsweek*. After her death in 1996, Suharto lost the will to rule and the will to control his children. They enriched themselves on a grand scale.

**SOURCES:**

Liu, Melinda, with Ron Moreau. "Always the Best Revenge," in *Newsweek*. June 1, 1998.

## Sühbaataryn Yanjmaa (1893–1962).

*See Yanjmaa, Sühbaataryn.*

## Suiko (554–628)

*Japanese empress, the first woman sovereign of Japan, who established Buddhism as the religion of Japanese rulers and initiated steps to centralize the state under imperial rule.* Name variations: Suiko-tenno. Pronunciation: Sue-e-koe. Reigned from 592 to 628; born in Asuka Village, Japan, in 554; died in Nara, Japan, in 628; daughter of Emperor Kimmei and a woman from the politically powerful Soga family; sister of Emperor Yomei; empress-consort to her half-brother Emperor Bidatsu.

Suiko ascended to the throne of Japan following a period of political and religious conflicts in which her predecessor had been killed. Conservatives continued to champion the Shintō religion, while progressives, including her mother's family, the prominent Soga, promoted Buddhism. Because of her lineage (daughter of Emperor Kommei, widow of her own half-brother, Emperor Bidatsu, and full-blooded sister of Emperor Yomei), it was hoped that Suiko could reconcile the opposing factions. Initially, she declined, but counselors persuaded her to accept the role of *sumer amikoto* (the one who controls soothsaying). Suiko appeased both religious groups by simultaneously serving Shintō and Buddhist deities. The historical chronicle, the *Nihongi*, describes her as beautiful, as well as progressive in her thinking, commanding the respect and affection of the government counselors.

Suiko's reign was marked by a number of historically significant developments. She was a devout Buddhist, and her reign was a golden period for the establishment of Buddhist temples and the creation of Buddhist-inspired art. While the more secular aspects of imperial rule were entrusted to her nephew, Prince Shōtoku Taishi, Suiko nevertheless mustered troops, dispatched emissaries to foreign countries, and conducted diplomatic relations with neighboring sovereigns. Suiko was known to have been capable of overruling male government officials and demonstrated a capacity for discerning judgment.

Two of the most significant steps in centralizing the state under imperial rule were initiated during Suiko's reign. The first was the establishment of a system for recruiting and promoting government officials. Called the cap-ranking system, it enabled capable men of any social rank to enter government service. Also, the first written "constitution" in Japanese history was promulgated during the reign of Suiko. The Seventeen Article Constitution, a set of moral injunctions to be observed by government officials, established a government bureaucracy in the service of the sovereign. In 628, Suiko fell ill, and the chronicles assert that during a solar eclipse, she lost her sight and died shortly thereafter.

**SOURCES:**

Aoki, Michiko Y. "*Jitō Tennō: The Female Sovereign," in *Heroic With Grace: Legendary Women of Japan*. Chieko Mulhern, ed. Armonk, NY: M.E. Sharpe, 1991, pp. 40–76.

Tsurumi, E. Patricia. "The Male Present Versus the Female Past: Historians and Japan's Ancient Female Emperors," in *Bulletin of Concerned Asian Scholars*. Vol. 14, no. 4, 1983, pp. 71–75.

**Linda L. Johnson**, Professor of History, Concordia College, Moorhead, Minnesota

# $\mathcal{A}$CKNOWLEDGMENTS

Photographs and illustrations appearing in *Women in World History, Volume 14,* were received from the following sources:

© Beaver-Allied, **p. 704**; Painting by Oswald Birley, **p. 254**; Courtesy of the Chinese Information Service, **p. 567**; Photo by Jerry Cooke, courtesy of Robyn Smith, **p. 495**; Photo by Howard Coster, **p. 501**; © EMI Records, photo by Maurice Rinaldi, **p. 99**; Courtesy of the Federation of Football Associations, **pp. 523, 531**; Painting by Thomas Gainsborough, **p. 301**; Courtesy of the Historical Society of Glastonbury, **p. 439**; Courtesy of Harry Langdon Photography, **p. 871**; Photos by George Hurrell, **p. 225** (for MGM), **p. 784**; Courtesy of the John F. Kennedy Library, **p. 288**; Photo by James J. Kriegsman, **p. 419**; Courtesy of Elisabeth Legge-Schwarzkopf, **p. 27**; Courtesy of the Library of Congress, **pp. 132, 513, 818, 828**; Courtesy of Marie Stopes International, London, **p. 853**; Photo by Rollie McKenna, **p. 161**; Courtesy of the National Portrait Gallery, **p. 389**, photo by Cecil Beaton, **p. 867**; Courtesy of National Screen Service Corp., **p. 305**; © National Broadcasting Company, **p. 723**; © Nelson Entertainment, 1989, **p. 333**; Courtesy of the Royal Norwegian Embassy, photo by Eirik Bergesen, **p. 577**; Photo by Don Perdue, **p. 337**; Photo by Frank Powolny, **p. 350**; Photo by Man Ray, **p. 773**; Painting by Pierre-Auguste Renoir, **p. 121**; Painting by Dante Gabriel Rossetti, **p. 297**; Painting by Richard Rothwell, **p. 243**; Courtesy of the Sisters of Charity, photo by Joseph Dawley, **p. 127**; Courtesy of Eleanor Smeal, **p. 429**, Courtesy of Sophia Smith Collection, Smith College, Northampton, Massachusetts, **p. 211**; Courtesy of Dusty Springfield, **p. 661**; Courtesy of Gloria Steinem, **p. 777**; Courtesy of the Swarthmore College Peace Collection, **pp. 35, 37, 835**; Photo by Hans Hammarskiold. Kungl. Husgeradskammaren, Stockholm, **p. 344**; © Tigon British Film Productions, Ltd., 1971, **p. 155**; © Twentieth Century-Fox, **p. 457**, 1945, **p. 668**, 1937; Courtesy of the U.S. House of Representatives. **pp. 359, 504, 633, 707**; © United Artists, **p. 48**, 1940, **p. 717**, 1937; © Walt Disney Productions, 1961, **p. 461**; © Warner Bros., 1941, **p. 721**; Photo by Laszlo Willinger, **p. 613**.